ATHLETI 4

THE INTERNATIONAL TRACK AND FIELD ANNUAL

ASSOCIATION OF
TRACK & FIELD STATISTICIANS

EDITED BY PETER MATTHEWS

A member of the Harmsworth Group of Companies

Published by Harmsworth Active
for Harmsworth Magazines Ltd.

Harmsworth Active
Astley House
33 Notting hill Gate
London W11 3JQ
Tel: 071-243-5000
Fax: 071-727-4222

This publication incorporates the ATFS Annual.

Photographs supplied by Mark Shearman, 22 Grovelands Road, Purley, Surrey, CR8 4LA.
Tel: 081-660-0156 Fax: 081-660-3437

British Library Cataloguing in Publication Data

Athletics: the international track and
field annual – 1994
1. Athletics. Track & Field events –
Serials
1. International athletics annual (London)
796.4'2'05

IBSN 1-873-05721-0

Printed and bound in England by Clays Ltd, St Ives plc

CONTENTS

Special Features

INTRODUCTION

The peak of athletics activity and enthusiasm was surely reached in Stuttgart in August 1993, with the staging of the 4th IAAF World Championships in Athletics. The deeds of the athletes who starred on those marvellous days feature prominently in ATHLETICS 1994.

This is the tenth edition of the International Athletics Annual that I have edited from introducing the first of the series in this greatly expanded style in 1985, although of course the ATFS have been publishing their detailed statistical review of the year continually from 1951.

I have made no major changes this year, although minor additions include responding to requests for the inclusion of a full list of World and Continental records to have been broken during the year and to indicating with an asterisk in the men's and men's indexes those athletes who have also been featured in the biographical profiles earlier in the book. The key sections remain the review of the past year, with results from major events, national champions and biographies of over 660 top athletes, records, all-time lists, and deep year lists for 1993 of all men's and women's events with indexes of athletes in the top 100 of their event.

We have also greatly increased the depth of the lists that were introduced a few years ago for the half marathon, as this distance has now become such an important one. It is important that road racing achievements should not be forgotten, but I should remind the reader that care must be taken when assessing road race times in particular due to the variations in severity of the courses. Much work has been done by AIMS and other bodies in ensuring that courses are accurately measured, but we are uncertain about various courses and that is another reason for caution in assessing the lists.

As always I am grateful to all ATFS members and others who have helped with the data collection process for this Annual, whether in a big way or with just a few snippets of detail. We are also indebted to various national federations and to the IAAF, with whom we maintain a close relationship.

Accuracy of information is vitally important to me and to all who contribute to this Annual. Nonetheless the gathering of statistical information from a sport that is practised all over the world is highly demanding. Thus we have no doubt missed a few performances and corrections and additions are always most welcome, so that we can maintain the meticulous documentation of the sport by the ATFS. Our lists are as complete as we can make them but still results elude us from some parts of the world. Once again I urge readers to let us have the information that we need for our annual tasks, and to let us have such data in good time.

To the surprise of some the ordering of athletics statistics is not simply a black and white, cut and dried matter. Rather there are all too often shades of grey! The compilers, taking advice from experts, often have to make judgements. Should a certain time be shown as doubtful, or with a rolling start, and, if no gauge was used, was it wind assisted? What should we use as the date of birth of an athlete who has been entered at major championships by his or her national federation with three different dates of birth? Some statistics, which we include here, that should not be taken too seriously, are heights and weights of athletes. The weights of course vary, and while the heights are less likely too, they certainly do in information presented to us!

I once again look forward with you all to an enthralling year of athletics during 1994.

Peter Matthews

ABBREVIATIONS

Championships and Organisations

AAA	Amateur Athletic Association (GBR)
AfCh	African Championships
AfG	African Games
AsCh	Asian Championships
AsG	Asian Games
CAC	Central American and Caribbean Championships
CAmG	Central American and Caribbean Games
CG	Commonwealth Games
EC	European Championships
ECp	European Cup
EI	European Indoor Championships
EJ	European Junior Championships
GWG	Goodwill Games
IAAF	International Amateur Athletic Federation
NCAA	National Collegiate Athletic Association (USA)
OG	Olympic Games
PAm	Pan American Games
SACh	South American Championships
TAC	The Athletics Congress (USA)
WCh	World Championships
WCp	World Cup
WI	World Indoor Championships
WJ	World Junior Championships
WSG	World Student Games (Universiade)

Miscellaneous

b	date of birth
dnf	did not finish
dnq	did not qualify
dns	did not start
exh	exhibition
h	heat
hr	hour
i	indoor
kg	kilograms
km	kilometres
m	metres
m/s	metres per second
M	mile
pb	personal best
qf	quarter final
sf	semi final
w	wind assisted
y	yards

Events

C-C	cross-country
Dec	decathlon
DT	discus
h	hurdles
Hep	heptathlon
HJ	high jump
HT	hammer
JT	javelin
LJ	long jump
Mar	marathon
Pen	pentathlon
PV	pole vault
R	relay
SP	shot
St	steeplechase
TJ	triple jump
W	walk
Wt	weight

Countries

ALB	Albania
ALG	Algeria
ANG	Anguilla
ANO	Angola (ANG)
ANT	Antigua
ARG	Argentina
ARM	Armenia
AUS	Australia
AUT	Austria
AZE	Azerbaijan
BAH	Bahamas
BAR	Barbados
BEL	Belgium
BER	Bermuda
BHR	Bahrain (BHN)
BLS	Belarus
BOS	Bosnia Herzegovina
BRA	Brazil
BUL	Bulgaria
BUR	Burundi
CAF	Central African Republic
CAN	Canada
CAY	Cayman Islands
CGO	Congo (CON)
CHI	Chile (CHL)
CHN	People's Republic of China
CIV	Ivory Coast (IVC)
CMR	Cameroon (CAM)
COL	Colombia
CRC	Costa Rica
CRO	Croatia
CUB	Cuba
CYP	Cyprus
DEN	Denmark
DJI	Djibouti
DMN	Dominica
DOM	Dominican Republic
ECU	Ecuador
EGY	Egypt
Eng	England
ESA	El Salvador
ESP	Spain (SPA)
EST	Estonia
ETH	Ethiopia
FIJ	Fiji
FIN	Finland

FRA	France
FRG	Federal Republic of Germany (1948-90)
GAB	Gabon
GAM	The Gambia
GBR	United Kingdom of Great Britain & Northern Ireland (UK)
GDR	German Democratic Republic (1948-90)
GEO	Georgia
GER	Germany (pre 1948 and from 1991)
GHA	Ghana
GRE	Greece
GRN	Grenada
GUA	Guatemala
GUY	Guyana
HAI	Haiti
HKG	Hong Kong
HOL	Holland (Netherlands)
HON	Honduras
HUN	Hungary
INA	Indonesia
IND	India
IRL	Ireland (IRE)
IRN	Iran
IRQ	Iraq
ISL	Iceland (ICE)
ISR	Israel
ISV	US Virgin Islands (UVI)
ITA	Italy
JAM	Jamaica
JOR	Jordan
JPN	Japan (JAP)
KEN	Kenya
KGZ	Kyrgyzstan
KOR	Korea (SKO)
KUW	Kuwait
KZK	Kazakhstan
LAT	Latvia
LES	Lesotho
LIE	Liechtenstein
LIT	Lithuania
LUX	Luxembourg
MAD	Madagascar
MAR	Morocco (MOR)
MAS	Malaysia
MEX	Mexico
MNT	Montserrat
MOL	Moldova
MON	Monaco
MOZ	Mozambique
MRI	Mauritius (MAU)
MYA	Myanmar (formerly BIR Burma)
NAM	Namibia
NCA	Nicaragua (NIC)
NGR	Nigeria (NIG)
NGU	Papua New Guinea (PNG)
NI	Northern Ireland
NOR	Norway
NZL	New Zealand (NZ)
OMA	Oman
PAK	Pakistan
PAN	Panama
PAR	Paraguay
PER	Peru
PHI	Philippines
POL	Poland
POR	Portugal
PRK	North Korea (Korean PDR) (NKO)
PUR	Puerto Rico (PR)
QAT	Qatar
ROM	Romania
RSA	South Africa
RUS	Russia
RWA	Rwanda
SAU	Saudi Arabia
Sco	Scotland
SEN	Sénégal
SEY	Seychelles
SIN	Singapore
SLE	Sierra Leone
SLO	Slovenia
SOM	Somalia
SRI	Sri Lanka
STL	St Lucia
SUD	Sudan
SUI	Switzerland (SWZ)
SUR	Surinam
SVK	Slovakia
SWE	Sweden
SYR	Syria
TAN	Tanzania
TCH	Czech Republic (Czechoslovakia to 1991)
THA	Thailand
TJK	Tadjikistan
TKM	Turkmenistan
TPE	Taiwan (Chinese Taipeh) (TAI)
TRI	Trinidad & Tobago
TUN	Tunisia
TUR	Turkey
UAE	United Arab Emirates
UGA	Uganda
UKR	Ukraine
URS	Soviet Union (SU) (to 1991)
URU	Uruguay
USA	United States
UZB	Uzbekistan
VEN	Venezuela
Wal	Wales
YUG	Yugoslavia
ZAM	Zambia
ZIM	Zimbabwe

Notes

1 *These are mostly IAAF (and usually IOC) abbreviations. In Annuals prior to 1992 ATFS abbreviations were used. Where these differ from those formerly used the ATFS ones are shown in brackets. There are also some additional ones.*

2 *Other IAAF members not shown, as athletes not included in lists in this book.*

3 *See also list of abbreviations in the Introduction to the World Lists section.*

ACKNOWLEDGMENTS

I am most grateful for the help of many people, most of them ATFS members in the compilation of this Annual. On behalf of the ATFS I would like to thank all those who contributed to a greater or lesser extent. The main compilers collect information from a wide range of sources, of which the most important are the major magazines and newsletters devoted to the sport, and the end of year national lists produced by dedicated individuals and by national federations.

As well as many excellent national publications devoted to athletics, we can single out for particular value as sources of international results two great long-lasting magazines Track *& Field News* (USA) with its results spin-off Track *Newsletter,* which has been expanded in 1994, and *Leichtathletik* (Germany). To those we added the British weekly *Athletics Today*, which became a prime source for results. However, that magazine ceased publication in July 1993. It is greatly missed by enthusiasts of our sport all over the world. I am delighted that its editor Randall Northam has worked on the lay-out for this Annual and will be helping the publishers with the marketing.

Continuity of results publication is also being maintained as the other AT co-editor Mel Watman is, with my assistance, producing *Athletics International*. Our aim in this newsletter (26 issues per year) is to publish all results to the ATFS standards to which we list in this Annual. Many of the national contributors to AI are included in the acknowledgments list below. In order to ensure that the record of 1994 is as complete as possible I urge results contribution worldwide to AI and then in turn our lists in *Athletics 1995* will be as comprehensive as we can make them.

These 1993 lists are as detailed as I can make them, although there are still some disappointments - at the time of writing no information had been received from Korea or the ex-Soviet republics in Asia, and all too little from such important African countries as Kenya and Nigeria. No US lists have been received this year, although *Track Newsletter* details should ensure that not too much of major importance is missing. Germany is another country for which many ancillary details (such as wind speeds) are missing. Nonetheless I am confident that our annual lists are the most comprehensive that we have ever published.

As I write these notes with seven days to go before my final deadline, and with some 250 pages of lists still to layout and much still to check, I am all too well aware that even more hours and even more faxes sent around the world could fill in a few gaps. But one has to finish in time for the new track season!

The lists this year started with those produced in late 1993 by Richard Hymans, who as usual compiled the men's index. I then expanded these with national lists and with the lists produced by the principal compilers Alfons Juck and Jiri Havlín, with the latter compiling the women's index. Alfons Juck, in Bratislava, was assisted by Robert Blaho and Peter Horváth with special help from Vaclav Klvana (decathlon) and Dr Zdenek Jebavy (walks).

Marco Buccellato produced deep world lists, which were a most useful check, and other major help in general came from Winfried Kramer, Roberto Quercetani, Silvio Garavaglia, Pino Mappa and Nejat Kök.

Further information on specific areas was provided by:

Records Bob Sparks, *Juniors* Milan Skocovsky, *Marathon* Dr. David Martin, *Ultrarunning* Andy Milroy, *Indoor marks* Ed Gordon, *Men's middle and long distance events* Ian Smith, *Long jump* Francisco Ascorbe, *Heptathlon* Milan Urban, *Men's pentathlon* Dr Hans-Peter Car.

The following specialists supplied information for their respective areas and countries:

Africa: Yves Pinaud; *Asia*: Heinrich Hubbeling; *Australia*: Paul Jenes; *Austria*: Erich Kamper and Karl Graf; *Belgium*: André de Hooghe and Jan Scheers; *Brazil:* José C Gonçalves; *Bulgaria*: Grigor Khristov and Alexander Vangelov; *CAC & Trinidad & Tobago*: Bernard Linley; *Canada*: Cecil Smith; *China*: Gao Dianmin;*Cuba*: Basilio Fuentes; *Czech Republic* Milan Skocovsky; *Denmark*: Erik Laursen; *Estonia*: Erlend Teemägi and Eugen Piisang; *Finland*: Juhani Jalava, Mirko Jalava and Matti Hannus; *France*: Yves Pinaud; *Germany*: Klaus Amrhein, Heinrich Hubbeling, Heinz Vogel, Sven Kuus; *Greece*: Karolos Sargologos; *Hungary*: Gabriel Szabó and Zoltán Suberts; *Iceland*: Gunnar Páll Joakimsson; *India*: Ranjit Bhatia; *Ireland*: Liam Hennessy; *Israel*: David Eiger; *Italy*: Ottavio Castellini and Raul Leoni; *Jamaica*: Richard Ashenheim; *Japan*: Yoshimasa Noguchi, Naoshi Ito and Isao Sugawara; *Latvia*: Andris Stagis; *Liechtenstein:* Robert Schumacher; *Lithuania*: Danute Svitojuté; *Netherlands*: Louis Weisscher; *New Zealand*: Barry Hunt and Peter Heidenstrom; *Norway*: Tore Johansen, Stein Fossen, Hans T Halvorsen, Jan Jørgen Moe, Jo Nesse, Ole Petter Sandvig; *Poland*: Tadeusz Wolejko, Wojciech Gaczkowski, Janusz Rozum and Henryk Paskal; *Portugal*: Luis Lopes; *Russia*: Sergey Tikhonov; *South Africa*: Gert le Roux, Hans Prinsloo and Riël Hauman; *South America*: Luis Vinker; *Spain*: José Maria Garcia, José Luis Hernández, Manuel Villuendas, Francisco Ascorbe and Josep Corominas; *Sweden*: A.Lennart Julin and Owe Fröberg; *Switzerland*: Fulvio Regli and Alberto Bordoli; *Syria and Arab world*: Fouad Habbash;*UK*: Peter Matthews and Ian Hodge; *USA*: *Track Newsletter*,, Roger Cass and Hal Bateman; *Yugoslavia*: Ozren Karamata and Olga Acic.

Also national federation lists from Belarus, Cyprus, Luxembourg, Romania, Slovenia, Ukraine.

General assistance: Luigi Mengoni, Lionel Peters, *Walks*: Palle Lassen and Egon Rasmussen. Computer expertise: Rob Whittingham. My apologies to anybody whose name I may have missed.

Finally I would like to thank the IAAF for its continuing cooperation and assistance. The move of their office from London to Monte Carlo, will, however, mean that I can no longer make my periodic visits to check through their results and magazines, so I must urge contributors to ensure that all parts of the world are fully researched to cover any gaps

MEMBERS OF THE ATFS
(ASSOCIATION OF TRACK & FIELD STATISTICIANS)

<u>**Executive Committee**</u>
President
Bob Sparks GBR
Secretary General
Scott Davis US)
Treasurer
Palle Lassen DEN *
Past Presidents
Rooney Magnusson SWE
Dr Don Potts USA
Dr Roberto Quercetani ITA *
Committee
Jírí Havlín TCH
Paul Jenes AUS
A.Lennart Julin SWE
Nejat Kök TUR
Peter J Matthews GBR *
Yves Pinaud FRA *
Luis R Vinker ARG-SAm
Area representatives
Gert le Roux RSA-Afr
Bernard Linley TRN-CAC
Tatsumi Senda JPN-Asi
* *Liaison group with IAAF*

<u>**Members**</u> *At 31 December 1993*

Argentina
Gerardo Bönnhoff
Luis R.Vinker

Australia
Ron Casey
Paul Jenes
Fletcher McEwen
Ray McFadden
Michael J McLaughlin
David Tarbotton

Austria
Karl Graf
Erich Kamper (HM)
Dr Georg Werthner

Belgium
André de Hooghe
Alain Monet

Bermuda
Robert Oliver

Brazil
José C Gonçalves
Ulf Lagerström

British Virgin Islands
Reynold O'Neal

Bulgaria
Georgi Kabarov
Grigor Khristov
Alexander Vangelov

Canada
Paul F Houde
Bill McNulty
Tom MacWilliam
Ted Radcliffe
Cecil Smith

Chile
J Francisco Baraona

China
Gao Dianmin

Croatia
Mladen Delic

Cuba
Prof. Jesús Argüelles
Basilio Fuentes
Severo Nieto

Cyprus
Antonios Dracos

Czech Republic
Milos Alter
Vladimir Braun
Svatopluk Dubsky
Ludek Follprecht
Pavel Formánek
Premysl Hartman
Jírí Havlín
Jírí Hetfleis
Milan Hlavácek
Stanislav Hrncir
Dr Zdenek Jebavy
Dr Vladimír Jorda
Jírí Kánsky;
Zdenek Kaslík
Vaclav Klvana
Otto Kudelka
Karel Mísek
Miroslav Ondruska
Josef Potucek
Josef Ríha
Milan Skocovsky
Dr Lubomír Slavícek
Jírí Stavjar
Jírí Stola
Milan Sy;kora
Milan Urban
Vladimír Visek
Josef Zdychynec

Denmark
Hans A Larsen
Palle Lassen
Valborg Lassen
Erik Laursen
Egon Rasmussen
Emanuel Rose

Ecuador
Ramiro Almeida
Fausto Mendoza

Estonia
Leo Heinla
Jaan Otsason
Eugen Piisang
Ants Teder
Erlend Teemägi

Finland
Matti Hannus
Juhani Jalava
Erkki Kiilonen
Asko Koski
Esa Laitinen
Esko Saarinen
Arvo Siltanen
Björn-Johan Weckman (HM)

France
André Alberty
Luc Beucher
Alain Bouillé
Jacques Carmelli

Jean-Louis Absin de Cassière
Jean Creuzé
Jean Gilbert-Touzeau
Vincenzo Guglielmelli
André Halphen
Guy Kerfant
Gérard Leconte
Robert Pariente
Jean-Claude Patinaud
Yves Pinaud
Daniel Urien

Georgia
Yevgeniy Gagua

Germany
Walter Abmayr
Klaus Amrhein
Dr Hans-Peter Car
Werner Gessner
Emmerich Götze
Max Heilrath
Raymund Herdt
Heinrich Hubbeling
Dieter Huhn
Heinz Klatt
Winfried Kramer
Rolf von der Laage
Dr Karl Lennartz
Jürgen Martin
Ekkehard zur Megede
Reinhard Müller
Axel Schäfer
Fritz Steinmetz (HM)
Otto Verhoeven
Heinz Vogel (HM)

Greece
Akis Andrikopoulos
Angelos Cocconis
John A Kyriacos
Karolos Sargologos
Leandros J Slavis

Hungary
Endre Jahlich
György Lévai
Zoltán Subert
Gabriel Szabó
Dr István Zahumenszky

India
Ranjit Bhatia
Rameshchandra G Kharkar
R Murali Krishnan
P K Mahanand
Jal D Pardivala
Norris Pritam

Iran
Fred Sahebjam

Ireland
Fionnbar Callanan
Liam Hennessy
Tony O'Donoghue

Israel
Elchanan Bar-Lev
David Eiger
Moshe Genuth
Prof. Uri Goldbourt

Italy
Marco Buccellato
Ottavio Castellini
Gastone Dannecker
Gianni Galeotti
Tiziano Gambalonga
Silvio Garavaglia
Michelangelo Granata
Raul Leoni
Fabio Majocchi
Giorgio Malisani
Gabriele Manfredini
Giuseppe Mappa
Salvatore Massara
Luigi Mengoni (HM)
Gianni Menicatti
Pino Montagna
Matteo Piombo
Dr Roberto Quercetani (HM)
Dr Giorgio Rizzoli
Mauro Rossi
Carlo Santi
Pier Paulo Temeroli
Raffaelo Tummolo

Jamaica
Richard G Ashenheim

Japan
Atsushi Hoshino
Naoshi Ito
Wakaki Maeda
Yoshimasa Noguchi
Tatsumi Senda
Isao Sugawara
Seiichi Tanabe

Latvia
Andris Stagis

Liechtenstein
Robert Schumacher

Malaysia
Balwant Singh Kler
Datuk Gurbaksh Singh Kler

Mexico
Prof. Jorge Molina Celis

Netherlands
Anton de Groot
Nic Lemmens
Louis Weisscher

New Zealand
Barry Hunt

Norway
Hans T Halvorsen
Tore Johansen
Jan Jørgen Moe
Ingmund Ofstad
Einar Otto Øren
Ole Petter Sandvig
Bernt A Solaas
Magne Teigen

Papua New Guinea
Bob Snow

Philippines
Col Romulo A Constantino
Sy Yinchow

Poland
Zbigniew Dobrowolny
Marek Drzewowski
Wojciech Gaczkowski
Zygmunt Gluszek
Daniel Grinberg
Henryk Kurzynski
Zbigniew Lojewski
Adam Parczewski
Henryk Paskal
Maciej Petruczenko
Stefan J K Pietkiewicz
Jozef Pliszkiewicz
Janusz Rozum
Maciej Rychwalski
Leslaw Skinder
Tadeusz Smolarski
Wlodzmierz Szymanski
Janusz Wasko
Edward Wiecek
Tadeusz Wolejko

Portugal
Luis O Lopes

Romania
Adrian Ionescu
Nicolae Marasescu
Romeo Vilara
Tudor Vornicu

Russia
Vladimir Andreyev
Nikolay Ivanov
Rostislav V Orlov
Vladimir A Otkalenko
Vladimir Spychkov
Sergey Tikhonov

Singapore
Ong Teong Cheng

Slovakia
Róbert Blaho
Peter Horváth
Alfon Juck
Ladislav Krnac
Marián Malek

South Africa
Naomi Beinart
Hennie A J Ferreira
Riël Haumann
De Villiers Lamprecht
Gert J J le Roux
Harry Lombaard
Allister Matthews
Hans Prinsloo
John van Wyk
Fritz Vermaak

Spain
Andres de Acuña
Juan-Manuel Alonso
Francisco Ascorbe
Felix Capilla
Josep Corominas
Pedro Escamilla
José María García
Ignacio Romo
Alberto Sánchez
Manuel Villuendas

Sweden
Mats Åkesson
Owe Fröberg
Jöran Hedberg
A.Lennart Julin
Ove Karlsson
Rooney Magnusson (HM)
Stig L Nilsson (HM)
Ture Widlund

Switzerland
Alberto Bordoli
Antonin Heyda
Fulvio Regli (HM)

Syria
Fouad Habbash

Trinidad & Tobago
Bernard A Linley

Turkey
Turhan Göker
Nejat Kök
Cüneyt E Koryürek
I Süreyya Yigit

Ukraine
Leonid Epshtayn
Anatoliy K Kashcheyev

UK
Ian Buchanan
Mark Butler
Mark Cawte
Justin Clouder
Eric L Cowe
Leslie J Crouch
Dr David P Dallman
Stan Greenberg
Roger W H Gynn
Ian M M Hodge
Andrew Huxtable (HM)
Richard Hymans
Tony Isaacs
Alan Lindop
Peter H Lovesey
Tim Lynch-Staunton
Norris D McWhirter (HM)
David Martin
Peter V Martin
Peter J Matthews
Ted O'Neill
Lionel Peters
Martin Rix
Ian R Smith
Bob Sparks
M David Terry
Melvyn F Watman
Rob Whittingham

USA
Jon W Alquist
David A Batchelor
Hal Bateman
Jed Brickner
Dave Carey
Tom Casaky
Roger Cass
Pete Cava
Scott S Davis
Wally Donovan
James O Dunaway
Tom Feuer
Edward C Gordon
Robert Hersh
Dr István Hidvegi
Jeff Hollobaugh
Mike Hubbard
David Johnson
Michael Kennedy
Dr Clifford E Larrabee
Frank Litsky
Steven McPeek
Dr Bill Mallon
Dr David E Martin
Alan Mazursky
Cordner B Nelson
Rich Perelman
Jack Pfeifer
Martin A Post
Dr Donald H Potts (HM)
Mike Renfro
Stan Saplin
Alan Sigmon
James I Spier
J Larry Story
Carol R Swenson
Michael Takaha
Howard Willman
Robert Womack
Frank Zarnowski

Yugoslavia
Olga Acic
Ozren Karamata

Zambia
Matthew Mulwanda

In Memoriam
- died in 1993
Joe Stutzen RSA
- died in 1994
Albert D Nelson USA

METRIC - IMPERIAL CONVERSION TABLES

Throughout this book measurements are given in the metric system. For those readers who are more familiar with imperial units we give a basic conversion table which specifically covers those distances achieved by top class athletes in the field events.

1.70m	5ft 7in	5.60	18ft 4½in	17.50	57ft 5in	66.00	216ft 6in
1.75	5ft 8¾in	5.80	18ft 0¼in	18.00	59ft 0¾in	68.00	223ft 1in
1.80	5ft 10¾in	6.00	19ft 8¼in	18.50	60ft 8½in	70.00	229ft 8in
1.85	6ft 0¾in	6.25	20ft 6¼in	19.00	62ft 4in	72.00	236ft 3in
1.90	6ft 2¾in	6.50	21ft 4in	19.50	63ft 11¾in	74.00	242ft 9in
1.95	6ft 4¾in	6.75	22ft 1¾in	20.00	65ft 7½in	76.00	249ft 4in
2.00	6ft 6¾in	7.00	22ft 11¾in	20.50	67ft 3¼in	78.00	255ft 11in
2.05	6ft 8¾in	7.25	23ft 9½in	21.00	68ft 10¾in	80.00	262ft 5in
2.10	6ft 10¾in	7.50	24ft 7¼in	21.50	70ft 6½in	82.00	269ft 0in
2.15	7ft 0½in	7.75	25ft 5¼in	22.00	72ft 2¼in	84.00	275ft 7in
2.20	7ft 2½in	8.00	26ft 3in	22.50	73ft 10in	86.00	282ft 2in
2.25	7ft 4½in	8.25	27ft 0¾in	23.00	75ft 5½in	88.00	288ft 8in
2.30	7ft 6½in	8.50	27ft 10¾in	50.00	164ft 0in	90.00	295ft 3in
2.35	7ft 8½in	8.75	28ft 8½in	52.00	170ft 7in	92.00	301ft 10in
2.40	7ft 10½in	9.00	29ft 6½in	54.00	177ft 2in	94.00	308ft 5in
4.60	15ft 1in	15.00	49ft 2½in	56.00	183ft 9in	96.00	314ft 11in
4.80	15ft 9in	15.50	50ft 10¼in	58.00	190ft 3in	98.00	321ft 6in
5.00	16ft 4¾in	16.00	52ft 6in	60.00	196ft 10in	100.00	328ft 1in
5.20	17ft 0¾in	16.50	54ft 1¾in	62.00	203ft 5in	102.00	334ft 8in
5.40	17ft 8½in	17.00	55ft 9¼in	64.00	210ft 0in	104.00	341ft 2in

Yards	Metres
50	45.72
54.68	50
60	54.86
65.62	60
100	91.44
109.36	100
218.72	200
220	201.17
437.44	400
440	402.34
874.89	800
880	804.67
1000	914.40
1093.61	1000

Miles/Yards		Metres
1m		1609.34
1m	427.23	2000
1m	1520.84	3000
2m		3218.69
3m		4828.03
3m	188.07	5000
6m		9656.06
6m	376.13	10000
10m		16093.44
12m	752.27	20000
18m	1128.40	30000
26m	385	42194.99 (marathon)
31m	120.66	50000

In the biographies section weights of athletes are given in kilograms, the following guide will help those who are more familiar with weights in pounds:

50kg	110lb	100kg	220lb
60	132	110	243
70	154	120	265
80	176	130	287
90	198	140	309

DIARY OF 1993

BY MEL WATMAN AND PETER MATTHEWS

JANUARY

6 **Miyazaki**, Japan. Appropriately, the first record breaking performance of 1993 came from a Chinese woman as Wang Xiuting ran 20km on the road in 65:11 for a world best.

17 **Moscow**, Russia. Irina Privalova claimed the first world indoor mark of the year with 35.45 for 300m (unofficial times of 11.8 at 100m and 23.4 at 200m en route) to better Merlene Ottey's 1981 best.

17 **Hobart**, Australia. 18 year-old Debbie Sosimenko added over five metres to the Commonwealth women's hammer best with a throw of 58.90.

17 **Montreal**, Canada. Ben Johnson failed a drugs test and this second failure meant a ban for life from the sport. Whearas it had been steroids in 1987, this time it was for excess testerone levels, Before the test result was confirmed he ran at several indoor meetings, with bests of 5.56 for 50m and 6.60 for 60m in February.

24 **Jakarta**, Indonesia. Addis Abebe scooped the biggest cash prize in athletics history for a 27:40 10k in the Bob Hasan race. That clipped a second off the world road best of Arturo Barrios and so in addition to his $25,000 first prize the diminutive Ethiopian won a bonus of $500,000.

24 **Tokyo Half Marathon**, Japan. Steve Moneghetti won in 60:08, with Todd Williams 60:11 and Dionicio Cerón 60:17 also inside the world road best for the distance, but the drop of 33 metres in the 21.1k course was over the acceptable 1 in 1000 limit for record purposes. Women's winner was ElanaMeyer 67:22.

29 **Zweibrücken**, Germany. Chinese pole vaulter Sun Caiyun (19) cleared a world indoor best of 4.06. Two days later she went a centimetre higher at Landau.

31 **Osaka Marathon**, Japan. Junko Asari equalled the Asian record with 2:26:26. Second placed Tomie Abe ran 2:26:27, the fastest ever for a marathon début.

FEBRUARY

2 **Moscow**, Russia. Zhanna Tarnopolskaya, with 6.09, and Irina Privalova 6.05 set ratified world indoor 50m records in their heats in Moscow, but Privalova's time of 6.00 in the final was ruled out by the IAAF as the photo finish print indicated the camera was not on the finishing line. A time of 6.04 by Privalova in Grenoble five days later was also disallowed because, in the belief that the 6.00 would be ratified, no special doping test for record purposes was carried out. Rodion Gataullin cleared 6m for the first time since 1989.

5 **Millrose Games** (86th), New York. Greg Foster began his farewell season with a 60mh win over Tony Dees, but the crowd was most enthused by the return of Eamonn Coghlan, who improved the 40 plus world indoor best for the mile to 4:05.95 (with a 1500m record of 3:49.81 en route). Lance Deal added 28cm to his own world indoor best with 24.82 for the 35 pound weight, throwing at the Bronx.

Addis Abebe: took the richest prize in athletics history

9 **DN Galen**, Stockholm, Sweden. Moses Kiptanui took 1.15 off hisworld indoor 3000m record, running virtually solo.

11 **Madrid**, Spain. Irina Privalova ran a world indoor record 6.92 for 60mand Gail Devers was second with a US record 7.05. Helped by the 640m altitude Bruny Surin ran a Canadian 60m record 6.51 and Lyudmila Narozohilenko missed the 60mh world mark by just 0.01 with 7.70.

13 **Liévin**, France. Merlene Ottey made up for the loss of her 60m record with a world indoor 200m mark of 21.87. In the same lane (five) of this fast track Frank Fredericks ran 20.37, to miss the men's mark by just 0.01. Sergey Bubka set his 17th world indoor pole vault record at 6.14, clearing on his second attempt, having won with his earlier 6.05 as Rodion Gataullin was second at 6.00 – the first time two men have cleared 6m in the same competition. Lyudmila Narozhilenko tied her world 60m hurdles figures of 7.69, but that – along with a 7.68 in San Sebastián on March 2 and her times in Seville on March 4 – was rescinded by the IAAF after the athlete yielded a positive doping test in Liévin and was banned for four years. Not ratified but worthy of world record status was a 2:34.84 1000m by Lyubov Kremlyova, compared to Brigitte Kraus's hand-timed 2:34.8 of 15 years ago.

13 **Birmingham**, GBR. Britain easily beat weak USA teams, 162 - 121 men and 150 - 120 women. Mike Stulce's 21.77 was the world's best indoor shot mark for four years.

20 **Azusa**, California, USA. Lance Deal improved the outdoor world best with the 35 pound weight with distances of 25.28 and 25.41.

20 **Birmingham**, GBR. Yvonne Murray set a European indoor 2000m best of 5:40.90 and Noureddine Morceli won the mile in 3:50.70, a time beaten only by Eamonn Coghlan indoors.

20 **Sunkist Invitational**, Los Angeles, USA. Gail Devers, 6.10 for 50m, and Jackie Joyner-Kersee, 6.84 for 50mh, set American records.

21 **Donyestk**, Ukraine. At his annual competition in his home town, Sergey Bubka came up with his 18th world indoor record (and 34th world record in all!) with a third time clearance at 6.15 *20ft 2in*.

26 **US Indoor Championships**, New York. Lance Deal improved his indoor weight record slightly to 24.84 at Princeton, his sixth title at this event and fifth in succession, while in Madison Square Garden Ireland's Eamonn Coghlan (40) set a world veterans mile best (indoors or out) of 4:01.39 and Gail Devers improved the US 60m record to 6.99. Deal and women's 3000m walk champion Debbi Lawrence were the overall indoor Grand Prix winners.

27-28 **Russian Championships,** Moscow. The daughter of a world ranking triple jumper of the 1950s, Yolanda Chen surpassed her father's achievements by leaping to a world indoor record of 14.46.

MARCH

4 **San Sebastián**, Spain. Lyudmila Narozhilenko ran yet faster for 60m hurdles, 7.66 heat and 7.63 final after a super-fast start, but these were not ratified as world records when news came through of her drugs ban.

6 **Karlsruhe**, Germany. Jens-Peter Herold ran a European record 4:56.22 for 2000m.

12-13 **NCAA Indoor Championships**, Indianapolis. Arkansas won their tenth consecutive men's title, with Erick Walder winning both long and triple jumps (8.33 and 16.86), and Louisiana State the women's for the fourth time in seven years. Holli Hyche won both 55mm and 200m for Indiana State.

12-14 **World Indoor Championships**, Toronto, Canada. On the final day at the massive Sky Dome there were two world records: Inessa Kravets triple jumped 14.47 and Dan O'Brien scored 6476 for heptathlon with 60m 6.67, LJ 7.84, SP 16.02, HJ 2.13, 60mh 7.85, PV 5.20 and 1000m 2:57.96. Irina Privalova established a European 200m record of 22.15. Mikhail Shchennikov completed wins at 5000m walk at each of these championships since 1987, while Stefka Kostadinova also won a fourth title, including the World Indoor Games of 1985, having missed out in 1991. She had a great duel with Heike Henkel, and both cleared 2.02. At 1500m Yekaterina Podkopayeva, became at 40 the oldest ever world indoor champion and Marcus O'Sullivan won his third title. Butch Reynolds won the 400m title on his return to international competiton after his IAAF ban. Mark McKoy got away with a flier to win the 60mh in 7.41, but his reaction time was an 'impossible' 0.063; Colin Jackson and Tony Dees followed, both in 7.43. 537 competitors from 93 nations participated. *For first eight at each event see page 606-7 of Athletics 1993.*

13 **Lisbon**, Portugal. Sammy Lelei ran a sensational half marathon time of 59:24, but it won't count as a world best as the course was found to be 97m short.

14 **Beijing. China**. A sign of things to come: a Chinese women's team set a world best of 2:14:16 for a six-stage Ekiden Relay over the marathon distance. Qu Yunxia ran 15:13 for 5k, Zhong Huandi 32:08 for 10k, Wang Junxia 14:52, Wang Yanfang 32:58, Zhang Linli 15:23 and Wang Huabi 23:42 for 7.195k.

28 **World Cross Country Championships**, Amorebieta, Spain. Kenya won all four team titles, with a clean sweep of the individual medals in three of the races. Only in the women's event, won by Albertina Dias of Portugal, did anyone else have a look in. The other races went to William Sigei, Phillip Mosima and Gladys Ondeyo. Ismael Kirui and Catherina McKiernan were the overall winners of the winter-long IAAF World Cross Challenge which culminated at the championships. 656 runners from 55 nations participated. *For leading results see page 608 of Athletics 1993.*

APRIL

3 **Stramilano**, Milan, Italy. The 1991 world 10,000m champion Moses Tanui became the first to run a road half marathon in under an hour on a seemingly legitimate course when he clocked 59:47 in the four-lap race. Teammates Andrew Masai 60:42 and Paul Tergat 60:45 followed.

3 **The Hague**, Netherlands. Benson Masya, ran 60:24 on an out and back half marathon course.

4 **Berlin**, Germany. Carsten Eich set a European half marathon best of 60:34.

4 **Tianjing**, China. In a sensational women's marathon, eight Chinese broke 2:27 with the ubiquitous Wang Junxia running out the winner in 2:24:07, an Asian record and the fastest ever début. Even more astonishing were the world junior 10,000m champion's splits of 74:58 for the first half and an unheard of 69:09 for the second. Qu Yunxia, the Olympic 1500m bronze medallist, followed in 2:24:32 with yet another marathon débutante, world junior 3000m champion Zhang Linli, third in 2:24:42.

Inessa Kravets: a world triple jump record at the World Indoor Championships

6 **Pietersburg**, South Africa. Jan Zelezny opened his season, hoping for a javelin throw in the region of 88-90m. Instead, with his first (and only) attempt, he smashed Steve Backley's world record with 95.54. He had a slight brezze at his back and the track is at 1230m altitude. He threw 90.60m a week later at sea-level in Stellenbosch.

10 **El Paso**, USA. Kareem Streete-Thompson, from the Cayman Islands (but in the process of taking on US nationality), long jumped 8.36 (+0.6) at high altitude for a Commonwealth record.

11 **Seoul**, Korea. A week after her marathon exploit Wang Junxia covered her 7k stage in 21:20 as China set a world best of 2:13:14 for a seven-leg Ekiden Relay.

18 **London Marathon**, GBR. In his first attempt at the distance, Britain's Eamonn Martin won in 2:10:50. Katrin Dörre overtook fast-starting Lisa Ondeiki and Liz McColgan to take the women's race in 2:27:09.

19 **Boston Marathon**, USA. Cosmos N'Deti triumphed in 2:09:33, with Kim Jae-ryong and Luchetz Swartbooi also under 2:10. Olga Markova (2:25:27) was women's winner for the second successive year.

24 **European Champion Clubs' Women's Road Race**, Pomigliano D'Arco. Won by the Sporting Club de Braga, Portugal.

24/25 **IAAF Race Walking World Cup**, Monterrey, Mexico. Walking at home in very hot conditions Carlos Mercenario – the only man to have won both at 20km and 50km in this event – scored a second 50km victory and, with 20km winner Daniel Garcia, helped Mexico take the team title. China's Wang Yan, who at 14 (in 1986) had become the youngest ever world record breaker in athletics, won the women's 10km by eight seconds from Sari Essayah; Italy were team champions. 304 walkers from 36 nations participated. *See Championships section for results.*

Eamonn Martin takes the London Marathon

MAY

2 **Berlin**, Germany. Tendai Chimusasa, a German-based Zimbabwean, set a world 25k road best of 1:14:25.

8 **S&W Modesto Invitational**, USA. Andre Cason returned for his first race for nearly a year to run 10.01w for 100m, although beaten by Jon Drummond and Olapade Adeniken, who each ran 10.00w. Mark Crear beat a classy field 110mh field in 12.9w.

13-16 **East Asian Games**, Shanghai, China. The host nation took 29 of the 41 gold medals, the others going to Japan (6), South Korea and Taipei (3 each).

16 **San Francisco**, USA. 18 year-old Ismael Kirui won the Bay to Breakers 12k road race in a world best time of 33:42.

16 **São Paulo**, Brazil. Maria Mutola ran an African record 1:57.38 at the first IAAF/ Mobil Grand Prix meeting of the year.

22 **New York** Grand Prix, USA. Maria Mutola improved her African record to 1:56.56, but had to work hard to hold off her distant cousin Tina Paulino 1:56.62. There were world leading times at 400mh for Kevin Young 48.71 and Sandra Farmer-Patrick 54.69, and for Mark Crear, 13.31 for 110mh.

22-23 **Barrientos Memorial**, Havana, Cuba. Jumpers starred with winners including Javier Sotomayor HJ 2.40, Ivan Pedroso LJ 8.49, Yoelvis Quesada TJ 17.68 and Niurka Montalvo TJ 14.51 (CAC record).

29 **Bruce Jenner Classic**, San Jose, USA. Sergey Bubka achieved a US all-comers pole vault record of 6.00 and Kevin Young improved theworld leading mark for 400mh to 48.17.

29-30 **European Men's Club Cup**, Budapest, Hungary. Winners were Fiamme d'Oro of Italy. *See Championships section for details.*

29-30 **Götzis**, Austria. Eduard Hamalainen won the decathlon with 8604 (adding 121 points to his best) from Paul Meier 8460 (a 268 point improvement) and Mike Smith 8362. In the heptathlon Svetla Dimitrova came from behind to beat Tatyana Blokhina, 6594 to 6569.

JUNE

1 **Slovnaft, Bratislava**, Slovakia. Merlene Ottey started her outdoor campaign with a 11.10/22.27 double, Mike Powell won the long jump with 8.43 and Ana Biryukova produced the second longest

ever women's triple jump, 14.74w, with Inna Lasovskaya second at 14.70.

2-5 **NCAA Championships**, New Orleans, USA. The University of Arkansas retained their men's title with 69 points, from Louisiana State and Ohio State, who tied on 45. Louisiana State won a record 7th successive women's title with 93 from Wisconsin 44 and UCLA 38. The classiest event was the long jump, won by Erick Walder of Arkansas, who won the long jump with a meeting record and 1993 world leading 8.53, from Dion Bentley 8.39 and Kareem Streete-Thompson 8.31. Chris Nelloms returned from his near-fatal shooting the previous May to win the 200m in 20.27. The women's star was Holli Hyche with a 100m/200m double in 11.14/22.34 and Juliet Campbell ran a 1993 world leading 400m time of 50.58. Tanya Hughes won the high jump for the third successive year. *See USA section for winners.*

2-6 **Chinese Women's Championships**, Jinan. Wang Junxia won the 3000m in an Asian record of 8:27.68, the world's fastest for five years, with Qu Yunxia second in 8:29.30. Ma Ningning, in 4th place, set a world junior record of 8:36.45 – at the age of 16! Wang had earlier run 3:58.00 in the heats of the 1500m and also won the 10.000m in an Asian record 31:08.42.*See China section for winners.*

5 **Sevilla**, Spain. Four women beat 7 metres in the long jump; Heike Drechsler won at 7.08w. Igor Astapkovich produced a 1993 world leading 82.28 to win the hammer, with Andrey Abduvaliyev and Sergey Alay also over 80m.

5 **European Women's Club Cup**, Limassol, Cyprus. Winners were Sisport Fiat of Italy. *See Championships section.*
European Challenge Relays, Portsmouth, GBR. *See Championships section for winners*

9 **Golden Gala**, Rome, Italy. Frank Fredericks beat Michael Johnson for the second successive year at this meeting, 20.18 to 20.33. There were six early season world leading marks: Alessandro Lambruschini 3000mSt 8:17.54, Ezequiel Bitok 5000m 13:10.66, Colin Jackson 110mh 13.11 as he beat Mark McKoy 13.20, Lars Riedel DT 67.80, Viorica Beclea 1M 4:21.69 and Sally Gunnell 400mh 54.64. After winning the pole vault at 5.90, Sergey Bubka had three good tries at a world record 6.14.

11 **St Denis**, France. In appalling conditions Noureddine Morceli opened his outdoor campaign with a 1500m win in 3:36.04; Olympic medallists Mohamed Suleiman and Rashid El Basir were 2nd and 3rd in 3:42.84 and 3:43.64 respectively.

12-13 **European Cup - First and Second groups**. Competing at Brussels, Patrick Sjöberg maintained his unbeaten record in the competition by winning the high jump for the fifth time. *See Championships section for details.*

15-19 **US Championships**, Eugene. Andre Casonran the fastest ever series of 100m marks, clocking a 9.79w heat and 9.79w semi, and 9.85w to win the final next day from Dennis Mitchell 9.85 and Carl Lewis 9.90. Jon Drummond's 9.99w was thus not enough to gain him a World Championships place, and similarly missing out were Andrew Valmon 44.28, Antonio Pettigrew 44.45 and Derek Mills 44.62 at 400m, the fastest ever 5th and 6th places. Out ahead were Michael

Patrick Sjöberg: still unbeaten in the European Cup high jump

Jackie Joyner Kersee: dissuaded by husband Bob from long jumping in Stuttgart

Johnson 43.74 (third on world all-time list), Butch Reynolds 44.12 and Quincy Watts 44.24. There were world leading performances from Mark Everett, who beat Johnny Gray 1:44.43 to 1:44.67 at 800m, Kevin Young 400mh 47.69, Jearl Miles, 50.43 for 400m, Sandra Farmer-Patrick, 53.96 for 400mh, and Jackie Joyner-Kersee, 6770 heptathlon, JJK also won the long jump with 7.02, but was later dissuaded by husband Bob Kersee from attempting this event in Stuttgart. Other winners whose marks were helped by excess wind assistance included Michael Marsh 200m in 19.97w from Carl Lewis, whose 20.07 was his fastest since the 1988 Olympics, Mike Powell 8.53w long jump, Mike Conley 17.69w triple jump, and Gail Devers 10.82w 100m. Devers, however, lost her first competition of 1993 at 100mh, 12.73w behind Lynda Tolbert 12.72w. *See USA section for winners.*

17 **Bahamas Championships, Nassau.** Craig Hepburn long jumped a Commonwealth record of 8.41 (+1.5). His previous best was 8.17 and he never jumped farther than 7.95 again in 1993.

17-20 **Mediterranean Games**, Narbonne, France. A 53.9 last lap carried Noureddine Morceli to the second fastest ever 1500m time of 3:29.20. The Olympic 1-2 Fermin Cacho and Rashid El Basir followed in 3:32.43 and 3:37.30. *See Championships section for winners.*

18-20 **Russian Championships**, Moscow. Only third until then with 14.25, Yolanda Chen produced a world record triple jump of 14.97 (+0.9) in the final round. Marina Azyabina ran a 1993 best of 12.47 for 100m hurdles in the semis, before winning the final with 12.69. *See Russia section for winners.*

19 **Belfast**, GBR. Former world 5000m record holder Dave Moorcroft (40) set a world veterans outdoor mile record of 4:02.53.

20 **Hengelo**, Netherlands. Somia O'Sullivan took 4.52 off her Irish 3000mrecord, with 8:33.40 from Yelena Romanova 8:35.43.

23-27 **African Championships,** Durban, South Africa. Athletes from the host nation dominated, but the finest performances came from Maria Mutola, winner of the women's 800m in an African record of 1:56.36, William Sigei, who took the 10,000m in 27:25.23, followed by Fita Bayissa and Hail Gebresilasie, and Simon Chemwoiyo, who won a top-class 5000m. Hakim Toumi won his eighth African hammer title, a record for any event; he had previously won in 1984-5, 1987-9, 1991-2. *See Championships section for medallists.*

25 **Mazda Indy Games**, Indianapolis, USA. Gwen Torrence tried the 400m, and won in a world leading 50.37 from Natasha Kaiser-Brown 50.52.

26/27 **European Cup Super League**, Rome, Italy. Russia won the men's match with 128 points to Britain's 124. There were meeting records for three Britons: David Grindley 400m 44.75 400m, Colin Jackson 110mh 13.10 and the 4x400m team 3:00.25; Jan Zelezny 89.84 javelin and for Russia's Rodion Gataullin, who not only cleared 6.00 in the pole vault, but achieved the rare feat of outjumping Sergey Bubka, 5.80. France was a close 3rd with 123. Linford Christie won his fourth European Cup 100m, and, with his 200m in 1987, tied Harald Schmid's record for most individual victories. Giovanni Evangelisti, who won the long jump for the first time, competed for the seventh time to tie Schmid's record. Russia also triumphed in the women's Cup, with Irina Privalova beating Marie Josée-Pérec at 100m and 200m and anchoring the 4x100m team to 42.39. Russia'a 141 points took them well clear of Romania and Ukraine. The only women's meeting best was Sally Gunnell's 53.73 for 400mh. *See Championships section for first threes.*

29 **Lucerne**, Switzerland. Werner Günthör produced a season's best shot of 21.94 and beat the top four Americans,

JULY

1-3 **Jamaican Championships**, Kingston. Juliet Campbell ran a world leading 50.11 for 400m and Merlene Ottey won the 100m/200m double. *See Jamaica section for winners.*

2 **Britain v USA**, Edinburgh. Britain's men scored their first ever victory outdoors against an American team lacking most of the big stars, 199-190. Britons won all the individual track events.

2 **BNP Meeting**, Villeneuve d'Ascq, France. Mark McKoy produced the finest ever one-day 100m/110mh double with 10.08 and 13.08 within an hour. He was 4th at 100m behind Andre Cason 10.03, Frank Fredericks 10.04 and Carl Lewis 10.07. Noureddine Morceli moved to 3rd on the world all-time 1000m list with 2:13.73 after 1:45.71 at 800m. Khalid Skah ran a pb 13:06.82 to win the 5000m, a race in which there were the best ever marks for places 3-4 and 8-16, with 4 men under 13:10 and 12 under 13:20. There was also great depth in the women's 1000m, won by Ella Kovacs in 2:32.40. Gail Devers beat Irina Privalova 10.96 to 11.00 at 100m.

2-4 **South American Championships**, Lima, Peru. Robson da Silva won the 100m/200m double to take his gold medal collection at these biennial championships to a record 13. *See Championships section for medallists.*

5 **DN Galan**, Stockholm, Sweden. An astonishing 27:55.7 10,000m in high altitude (1667m) Nairobi three weeks earlier was a portent for Richard Chelimo's world 10,000m record of 27:07.91 in the stadium which has witnessed more world records than any other. The Kenyan led at 5000m in 13:33.76 and won by 150m from the former record

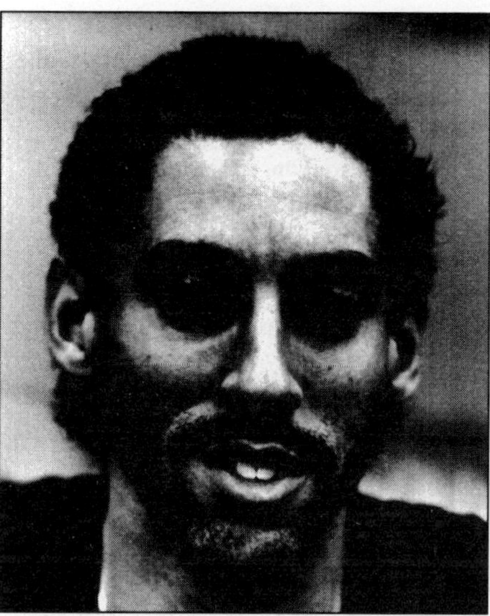

Mark McKoy: produced the finest ever one-day 100m/110mh double in the BNP meeting

holder Arturo Barrios 27:34.27. World bests for 1993 were run by Elana Meyer, 14:50.29 for 5000m and by Moses Kiptanui, 8:12.52 for 3000m steeplechase.

7 **Athletissima '93**, Lausanne, Switzerland. Chelimo's brother, Ismael Kirui, led a Kenyan 1-2-3-4 at 5000m in 13:06.71, but was denied a world junior record as officials failed to arrange a doping test. Gail Devers, 10.82 for 100m, and Kevin Young, 47.37 for 400mh, improved their world leading marks for the season, and other bests came from Johnny Gray, 1:44.27 for 800, and from Carl Lewis, 19.99 for 200m as he beat Michael Johnson 20.06 and ran his best time for fivr years.

10 **Bislett Games**, Oslo, Norway. Chelimo's world 10,000m record lasted only five days as fellow Kenyan Yobes Ondieki, despite poor conditions, ran a barrier-breaking 26:58.38, for the biggest improvement on the record since Ron Clarke ushered in the sub-28 era in 1965. Ondieki (32) had only once before raced 10,000m on the track ... 28:25.44 10 years ago. Reaching halfway in 13:28.05, he won by over 100m from William Sigei (27:16.81). The kilometre splits were 2:41.12, 2:39.64, 2:41.84, 2:43.82, 2:41.63, 2:42.80, 2:42.70, 2:41.67, 2:45.00, 2:38.16.

Paul Bitok outkicked Khalid Skah at 5000m and Trine Hattestad thrilled the crowd with her Norwegian javelin record of 72.12, the best women's mark for two years. The Dream Mile was won by Noureddine Morceli in a personal best of 3:47.78, well clear of Abdi Bile 3:51.66 and Steve Cram 3:52.17 as all 14 finishers broke four minutes. Sonia O'Sullivan further improved her Irish record to 8:28.74, the fastest time run by a woman for the distance since the 1988 Olympics; Yvonne Murray and Elana Meyer followed in 8:30.30 and 8:32.81. Martin Steele surprised with a world leading 1:43.84, 1.44 off his best for 800m.

10 **Livorno**, Italy. Ileana Salvador of Italy equalled Kerry Saxby's women's world 10k road walking record of 41:30 in Livorno, her actual time being 41:29.4, and Mikhail Shchennikov won the men's 20k in 1:18:33. However the walkers themselves were reported to have considered the courses to be short.

10/11 **European Cups for Combined Events**. At Oulu, Finland, France (decathlon) and Russia (heptathlon) were the premier group winners. The individual winners were Paul Meier 8366 and Tatyana Zhuravlyova 6330. The best heptathlon score was by Svetlana Buraga for Belarus with 6477 in Group C2 at Tallinn. *See Championships section.*

14-18 **World Student Games**, Buffalo, USA. Held in the USA for the first time, the host nation's athletes easily headed the medals table with 28 (way ahead of Cuba 8), with 12 winners. Three men retained their titles: Derrick Adkins 400mh, István Bagyula PV and Robert Korzeniowski 20kmW. Korzeniowski and Kennedy Manyisa (marathon) were the only two athletes to set championship bests. *See Championships section for medallists.*

15-17 **Pan-American Junior Championships**, Winnipeg, Canada. *See Championships section for winners.*

15 **Nikaïa**, Nice, France. Sergey Bubka was back to winning ways at 5.93 in the vault, but failed his three tries at a world record 6.14.

23 **TSB Games**, Crystal Palace, London, GBR. Samuel Matete just beat Kevin Young at 400mh, 48.85 to 48.86, so the latter's win streak ended at 25.

24 **Stara Zagora**, Bulgaria. The 100th high jump competition at 2 metres or above for Stefka Kostadinova.

27 **Salamanca**, Spain. Javier Sotomayor of Cuba cleared 2.23, 2.32 and 2.38 first time, and then a world record 2.45m *8ft 0.5in* at the second attempt. Benefitting from 806m altitude Mike Powell recorded a season's best 8.70 long jump

28 **Sestriere**, Italy. Benefitting from the 2037m altitude at this Alpine resort, but hampered by a headwind of 1.6m, Colin Jackson set a European 110m hurdles record of 12.97. Susen Tiedtke scored an upset long jump win as her last round 7.19w passed Heike Drechsler's 7.12w.

29- 1 Aug **European Junior Championships**, San Sebastián, Spain. Britain was the most successful nation with eight gold medals. Russia topped Britain's medal tally of 14 with 18 but only two were gold, one from Yelena Lysak who set a world junior triple jump record of 13.86. Adam Dobrzynski 3000mSt, Susana Feitor 5000m walk and Gabriela Szabo 3000m also set Championship records. *See Championships section for medallists.*

30 **Kuts Memorial**, Moscow, Russia. Irina Privalova ran a fast time of 49.89 at her début at 400m.

Irina Privalova ran 49.89 at her début at 400m.

30 **Vauxhall Invitational**, Gateshead, GBR. A hugely hyped match-up at 100m over 100m between Linford Christie and Carl Lewis attracted a sell-out crowd and a huge viewing audience on ITV. Christie easily handled Lewis, 10.08 to 10.22, but Jon Drummond almost spoilt the script as he was second in 10.12.

30 - Aug 1 **Central American & Caribbean Championships**, Cali, Colombia. Rather overshadowed by the CAC Games held later in the year. *See Championships section for winners.*

31 **Hechtel**, Belgium. Khalid Skah ran the fsatest ever time for 2 miles 8:12.17, and Elana Meyer improved her year's best for 5000m to 14:46.41.

AUGUST

1 **Weltklasse in Köln**, Germany. Moses Kiptanui, not in quite the same form as when he set the world record here in 1992, was second at 3000m with 7:35.79, as Paul Bitok (2nd in 1992) won with 7:34.98. Jim Spivey, 3rd in 7:37.04, smashed his best and ran the fastest time by an American for ten years. A record six men bettered 7:40 and ten 7:40.

Samuel Matete: ended Kevin Young's winning streak in London

4 **Weltklasse, Zürich**, Switzerland. Ismael Kirui set a world junior 5000m record of 13:06.50, but such was the stunning quality of the field (seven men broke 13:09!) that he placed fifth behind Khalid Skah's yearly leading time of 13:04.67, Yobes Ondieki, Richard Chelimo and Haile Gebresilassie. There was also unprecedented depth in the 1500m won by Noureddine Morceli in 3:30.06, with 8 men under 3:34 and 11 under 3:36. Leroy Burrell, who failed to make the US team for Stuttgart, edged Linford Christie in the 100m, 10.02 - 10.03, with most of the rest of the world's best following, while Merlene Ottey won the women's event in 10.93 from Gwen Torrence and Gail Devers. More world leading times in a meeting, once again, of extraordinary depth, came from Moses Kiptanui, 8:10.29 steeplechase, Maria Mutola, another African record 1:55.62 for 800m, Sally Gunnell, 400mh 53.52, and Heike Drechsler, LJ 7.21.

7 **Gatorade Herculis Grand Prix**, Monte Carlo. Noureddine Morceli was just a couple of strides short of Moses Kiptanui's world 3000m record with 7:29.24. He was well ahead of Kiptanui's pace at 1000m 2:27.4 and 2000m 5:00.09. Merlene Ottey won the 100m and 200m in 10.90 and 21.77, the latter a 1993 best, as was Gwen Torrence's 400m of 49.83.

7 **Torhout**, Belgium. Winners of world 100km road running titles were Konstantin Santalov and Carolyn Hunter-Rowe. *See Championships section for medallists.*

14-22 **4th IAAF World Championships**, Stuttgart, Germany. There were world records by Sally Gunnell with 52.74 for 400m hurdles (the first women's track world record since the 1988 Olympics), Colin Jackson, 12.91 for 110m hurdles, Ana Biryukova with a 15.09 triple jump (5.57 hop, 4.47 step and 5.05 jump), the USA team of Jon Drummond, Andre Cason, Dennis Mitchell and Leroy Burrell with a record equalling 37.40 4x100m semi-final, and the USA 4x400m's 2:54.29: Andre Valmon 44.5, Quincy Watts 43.6, Butch Reynolds 43.23, Michael Johnson 42.94 (the fastest ever split). Continental records included a European 100m mark of 9.87 by Linford Christie (33), second fastest ever to Carl Lewis's 9.86/+1.2 in the 1991 World Champs, and a 37.77 sprint relay by Britain's all-medallist team of Jackson, Tony Jarrett, John Regis and Christie. Two Kenyans accounted for world junior records: Ismael Kirui won the 5000m in 13:02.75 and Sally Barsosio, merely 15, took third place in the 10,000m in 31:15.38.

The USA with 25 medals (13 gold, 7 silver, 5 bronze) dominated the proceedings, ahead of Russia's 16 (3-8-5), but China claimed the second highest number of golds with four – all in women's events. Huang Zhihong won the shot with 20.57 and the finishing prowess of their distance runners became the biggest talking point of the championships as Liu Dong took the 1500m in 4:00.50 (57.48 last lap), Qu Yunxia led a clean sweep of the medals in the 3000m in 8:28.71 (59.22 last lap) and Wang Junxia moved to second on the world all-time 10,000m list with 30:49.30, covering the second half in 15:05.89.

Other highlights included Michael Johnson's 43.65 400m, the third fastest time ever, Sergey Bubka's 6.00 pole vault which enabled him to become the only athlete to win a fourth consecutive world title, and Merlene Ottey's 200m victory, her first individual outdoor title at world/Olympic level after numerous silvers and bronzes since 1980.

Four finalists were disqualified following positive doping tests: Mike Stulce (3rd shot), Romas Ubartas (4th discus), Dmitriy Polyunin (3rd javelin) and Liliya Nurutdinova (7th 800m). *See Championships section for report and results.*

25 **Linz**, Austria. Werner Günthör improved his year's shot best to 21.98, a centimetre more than in Stuttgart.

27 **ISTAF, Berlin**, Germany. Ismael Kirui collected another world junior record, 7:39.82 for 3000m, but Noureddine Morceli again fell just short of a world record, clocking 3:46.78 for the mile in a race where a record equalling number of 14 men broke 4 minutes. Morceli took 55.6 for the final 440y, passing 1500m in 3:31.66. Jackie Joyner-Kersee beat Heiek Drechsler by 1 cm, 7.08 to 7.07, in the long jump. Sonia O'Sullivan ran an Irish record 14:45.92 for 5000m.

The USA quartet that shattered the world 4x400m record in Stuttgart

28 **Ingelheim**, Germany. Sabine Braun scored a world best of 6214 for a 45 minute heptathlon with marks of 13.43, 1.83, 14.44, 24.82, 6.43, 44.96 and 2:32.35.

29 **McDonald's Games, Sheffield**, GBR. Jan Zelezny achieved his second world javelin record of the year. After opening with 87.06, he reached 95.34 in the second round and a new mark of 95.66 in the third. A no throw and 89.02 compleed the series before he passed his final try.

29 **Padua**, Italy. Ileana Salvador walked 3000m in 11:48.24 for a world best.

SEPTEMBER

3 **Van Damme Memorial**, Brussels, Belgium. Noureddine Morceli ran another fast mile, 3:47.30, on a cool evening in the last of the Golden Four meetings (Oslo, Zürich and Berlin). He and four others (Michael Johnson, Maria Mutola, Sonia O'Sullivan and Trine Hattestad) who won at all four meetings literally struck gold as four kilogram bars, worth about $52,000, were presented to each of them. Colin Jackson's 12.99 was his record third sub-13 second time of the year and Sandra Farmer-Patrick beat Sally Gunnell over 400mh, 53.70 to 54.08. The 10,000, won by Khalid Skah in a Moroccan record 27:17.7, had the greatest depth of the year, with five others, four Kenyans and Vincent Rousseau, inside 27:25.

5 **Rieti**, Italy. Perseverance paid off for Morceli as he finally smashed Steve Cram's 1985 world mile record of 3:46.32 with a stunning 3:44.39 – the biggest improvement since Jim Ryun's 3:51.3 in 1966. In perfect conditions he was paced through 400m in 54.39, 800m in 1:51.80 and 1000m in 2:20.76 before moving ahead just before 1200m (2:48.75), reaching 1500m in 3:29.57, the fourth fastest ever.

5 **ICMR Mountain Racing World Cup**, Gap, France. *See Championships section for medallists.*

8-13 **Chinese National Games**, Beijing. The women's 10,000m result on the opening day reverberated around the world as Ingrid Kristiansen's hitherto unapproached world record of 30:13.74 was destroyed by Wang Junxia with 29:31.78. Wang, who began racing at the distance only in 1992 (best of 32:29.90 to winthe world junior title), covered the first half of the race in 15:05.69 and the second in 14:26.09, way inside Kristiansen's world 5000m record of 14:37.33. Her split for the last 3000m was an incredible 8:17.47, itself much faster than the listed world record! Zhong Huandi, who led for 7000m, was just inside the old record with 30:13.37. Three days later Wang ran 1500m in 3:51.92, the second fastest ever as Qu Yunxia won in 3:50.46. Both women broke Tatyana Kazankina's 1980 world record of 3:52.47. World champion Liu Dong, who had earlier won the 800m in an Asian record of 1:55.54 with Qu second in 1:56.24, led at 400m in 57.13 and 800m in 2:00.71 before dropping out. Qu reached 1200m in 3:05.20. The world record spree continued on day 5 with Kazankina's 3000m figures of 8:22.62 being broken by no fewer than five runners in the heats! In the first Zhang Linli ran 8:22.06 ahead of Zhang Lirong, 8:22.44, and in the second Wang Junxia ran 8:12.19 from Qu Yunxia 8:12.27 and Ma Lijuan 8:19.78. Next day the indefatigable Wang continued to astound as she sped to 3000m victory in 8:06.11 with Qu also inside the day-old record with 8:12.18 and Zhang Linli third in 8:16.50. Wang's kilometre splits were 2:41.98, 2:47.67 and 2:36.46.
Asian records were set in every women's track event, including both relays, surely an unprecedented feat. World junior records were set by Wang Yuan in the 800m, 1:57.18 in a heat, Gao Hongmiao, 2nd in the 10km walk in 41:57, Wang Yuan, 7th in the 1500m in 3:59.81 and 4:01.79 in a heat the previous day, and Ren Ruiping 14.29 triple jump. The men were also hot, with five national records.

10 **IAAF Mobil Grand Prix Final**, Crystal Palace, London. With its structure changed (so that the winner of each event on the night was declared Grand Prix champion) and much more prize money on offer this year, this was by far the best GP Final yet. As overall champions Sergey Bubka and Sandra Farmer-Patrick amassed $130,000 apiece. The early pace for the men's title was set by Noureddine Morceli, who won the 1500m in 3:31.60, but although he had the maximum points, so too did others, and his individual event score on the Hungarian tables was passed by Jan

Zelezny, at 87.58 and then 88.28 in the javelin, before Bubka secured the prize at 6.05. He later tried the world record height of 6.14, his third try very close indeed. Sonia O'Sullivan's 3000m score (for 8:38.12) stood the pace until the final event, when it was exceeded by both Farmer-Patrick and Sally Gunnel, with the former scoring the decisive victory, 53.69 to 53.82.*See Championships section for results.*

18 **Fukuoka**, Japan. Stefka Kostadinova achieved a season's best 2.05 in the high jump and Sergey Bubka won the pole vault at 5.90, before both tried unsuccessfully at world records.

19 **Amagasaki,** Japan. Izumi Maki set a world record for the very infrequently run 20,000m on the track with 66:48.8.

19 **Amsterdam**, Netherlands. Josephat Machuka of Kenya ran 45:22 for 10 miles on an uncertified road course

19 **Great North Run** half marathon from Newcastle to South Shields, GBR. Moses Tanui won in 60:15 in blustery conditions.

24-27 **Pan-Arab Championships**, Latakia, Syria. *See Championships section for winners.*

26 **Amiens**, France. Ann Trason ran 100km in a world best 7:09:44

OCTOBER

3 **World Half Marathon Championships**, Brussels, Belgium. Running on home ground, Vincent Rousseau won in 61:06, followed by Steve Moneghetti and Carl Thackery, with Kenya taking the team title. Meck Mothuli (17), 62:11, led South Africa to junior team honours. Conceição Ferreira won the women's race in 70:07 ahead of Mari Tanigawa and Tecla Lorupe, with Romania taking the team award. 254 competitors from 49 nations participated. *See Championships section for leading results.*

7-17 **World Veterans Championships**, Miyazaki, Japan. A total of 57 world age-group records were set by a record-breaking entry. *See Championships section for leading results.*

17 **Reims Marathon**, France. A memorable month for Vincent Rousseau, Europe's fastest at 10,000m in 1993 with 27:23.18, continued with victory in 2:09:13. His only previously completed marathon was 2:13:09 when placing fifth in Rotterdam in April.

24 **World Marathon Cup**, San Sebastián, Spain. Wang Junxia was content to run at a modest pace for much of the race. A 72:41 second half carried her to victory in 2:28:16 well clear of her Chinese team-mates Zhang Linli, Zhang Lirong and Ma Liyan. Britain's Richard Nerurkar, like Wang also running his second marathon after winning the first earlier in the year, took the men's race in 2:10:03 ahead of Severino Bernardini, with Kebede Gemechu in third place leading Ethiopia to the team prize. *See Championships section for leading results.*

NOVEMBER

14 **New York Marathon**, USA. Winners were Andres Espinosa (second in 1991 and 1992) in 2:10:04 and Uta Pippig in 2:26:24, with the race run in unseasonaly hot weather.

23-28 **Central American & Caribbean Games**, Ponce, Puerto Rico. The return of Ana Quirot, who suffered very severe burns in Jnauray 1993, to take silver in the 800m was a highlight. This added to the eight gold mdals that she had won at these Games from 1978. Javier Sotomayor closed his brilliant year by adding a centimetre to his Games record for the high jump, his 2.35 being his 14th competition at that height or more in 1993. Cuba was easily the dominant nation with 25 gold among 56 medals, with Mexico next at 9 in 22.

30 - 4 Dec **Asian Championships**, Manila, Philippines. Wang Junxia brought her season to a close with a 10,000m win, remarkable for its slowness - 34:19.32! There were, however championship records at 12 men's and 8 women's events. The Qataris Talal Mansoor 100m and Ibrahim Ismail 400m won their events for the third time, as did Chinese hammer thrower Bi Zhong. Competing for the first time were the Asian nations of the ex-USSR, with Grigoriy Yegorov, who won the pole vault, becoming the first athlete to win both European and Asian medals. Another Kazakh medallist, Oleg Sakirkin has also won European Indoor medals. *See Championships section for medallists.*

DECEMBER

5 **Fukuoka**, Japan. Dionicio Cerón of Mexico ran the fastest marathon of the year, 2:08:51.

REVIEW OF 1993
By Peter Matthews

IT WAS a very close as to who deserved the vote of world athlete of the year in 1993. While Linford Christie won many sportsman of the year awards in Britain, his compatriot Colin Jackson had perhaps the edge in support from athletics enthusiasts and won the IAAF poll. The margin between them was perhaps as slight as the margins by which they beat or did not beat world records in winning gold in Stuttgart. Very close examination of the photo was needed to see that Christie's 100m time was but marginally over 9.86, the world mark

THE IAAF conducted their usual world-wide poll, inviting people in the world of athletics to select their top tens of 1993. The result for men is shown, followed in the second column by my own selections and in the final column those of the international experts polled by *Track & Field News*:

IAAF position, name	*points*	*PJM*	*T&FN*
1. Colin Jackson	2295.5	3	2
2. Noureddine Morceli	2238	1	1
3. Linford Christie	2176	5	7
4, Javier Sotomayor	1799.5	6	4
5. Sergey Bubka	1674	7	6
6. Michael Johnson	1511	4	5
7. Jan Zelezny	1494	2	3
8. Yobes Ondieki	1175	10	10
9. Frankie Fredericks	648		12
10. Dan O'Brien	601	8	11
11. Mike Powell	580.5	9	8
12. Ismael Kirui	546		16
13. Kevin Young	425		14
14. Haile Gebresilasie	168		
15. Moses Kiptanui	167		
Mike Conley			9

EAA European Athletes of the Year

1. Linford Christie	224
2. Colin Jackson	201
3. Sergey Bubka	163
4. Jan Zelezny	161
5= Werner Günthör	27
5= Lars Riedel	27

Colin Jackson: IAAF athlete of the Year

that Carl Lewis had set in 1991. Colin Jackson however surprised many, including himself, by taking a hundredth of a second off Roger Kingdom's mark for 110m hurdles, His victory was however, no surprise, for he had been clearly the world's number one high hurdler for a couple of years.

The only doubters it seemed were various writers who illogically doubted his big meeting temperament. True, he had not taken a world title, but he had amassed a stack of medals in his career, and would have won the World Indoor 60m hurdles at Toronto in March, but for his great friend Mark McKoy's blatant false start.

Despite what might be thought my natural support for the two great British sprinters, my own nomination of the top male athlete of 1993 is Noureddine Morceli. The determining factor was his overwhelming superiority over his rivals, and that criteria made, in my opinion, Jan Zelezny his main rival for the title. Zelezny's javelin throwing was magnificent, with two huge world records and usually a

Noureddine Morceli in 1993

Event	Date	Venue - meeting	Time
All wins			
Indoors			
1M	5 Feb	New York - Mill	3:55.06
1M	7 Feb	Fairfax	3:55.61
1M	20 Feb	Birmingham - TSB	3:50.70
		1500m 3:34.73	
1M	27 Feb	New York - US Ch	3:54.59
Outdoors			
1500m	11 Jun	St Denis	3:36.04
1500m	20 Jun	Narbonne - Med G	3:29.20
1000m	2 Jul	Villeneuve d'Ascq	2:13.74
		800m 1:45.71	
1500m	5 Jul	Stockholm - DNG	3:31.83
1M	10 Jul	Oslo - Bisl	3:47.78
		1500m 3:32.48	
1500m	4 Aug	Zürich - WK	3:30.06
3000m	7 Aug	Monte Carlo	7:29.24
		2000m 5:00.09	
1500m	19 Aug	Stuttgart - ht	3:37.84
	20 Aug	Stuttgart - sf	3:40.07
	22 Aug	Stuttgart	3:34.24
1M	27 Aug	Berlin - ISTAF	3:46.78
		1500m 3:31.67	
1M	3 Sep	Brussels - VD	3:47.30
		1500m 3:32.19	
1M	5 Sep	Rieti	3:44.39
		1500m 3:29.57	
1500m	10 Sep	London - GPF	3:31.60

vast margin over his rivals. However his season was not quite perfect, with a loss to Seppo Räty and less than devastating from in Stuttgart, even though he showed his character by winning despite being below his best.

Morceli is the King of middle distance running. That is, admittedly easier than a few years back when the British trio of Steve Ovett, Seb Coe and Steve Cram swept all before them, or indeed when Saïd Aouita and Abdi Bile succeeded them as the four-lap kings. Nonetheless Morceli overcame his severe disappointment at failing in the 1992 Olympics, to become the double world champion in 1993. After a series of narrow misses at world records from 1000m to 3000m, he eventually succeeded at gaining his first outdoor world mark, taking nearly two seconds off Steve Cram's eight year-old mile record.

Event by event survey

100 METRES

LINFORD CHRISTIE followed his 1992 Olympic triumph with an even better year in 1993 at the age of 33. His 9.87 in Stuttgart was ever so close to being a 9.86, which would have tied the world record, and he lost only three of his 16 finals at 100m. Leroy Burrell edged ahead in Zürich, with Christie, Jon Drummond, Carl Lewis, Andre Cason, Daniel Effiong, Olapade Adeniken and Frankie Fredericks following to make up a stellar field as always at that meeting.

Christie was also beaten by Burrell and Drummond in Berlin and by Drummond in Rieti. Both Drummond and Burrell, 4th and 5th in the US Trials behind Cason, Dennis Mitchell and Lewis, made up for their disappointment with a great series of runs in Europe, Burrell beat Drummond 6-2 overall and was even 3-1 up on Cason, but the latter's US Trial win and World silver was more than enough for second ranking. Cason ran 9.79w, 9.79w and 9.85w in Eugene and three successive sub-10 second pbs in Stuttgart. It was thought at first that Mitchell might have to miss the Worlds through injury, but he was back to his best to get the bronze medal.

Lewis, who is ranked in the world top ten for a record 14th successive year at the event, did not win a 100m final all year, and was 3-1 down to Drummond. but he had a 3-1 advantage over Fredericks, who was 3-2 up on Bruny Surin. Michael Green did not run the Worlds but beat 8th placer Ray Stewart 3-0 and Adeniken 2-1.

1. Christie; 2. Cason; 3. Mitchell; 4. Burrell; 5. Drummond; 6. Lewis; 7. Fredericks; 8. Surin; 9. Effiong; 10. Green

200 METRES

FRANK FREDERICKS achieved his first top ranking (after second place in 1991 and 1992) with 11 wins in his 14 finals at 200m outdoors. His smooth finishing took him to a series of great wins, including over John Regis and Carl Lewis in Stuttgart, where all three broke 20 seconds.

Fredericks also broke 20 secs in Rieti, and Lewis in Lausanne, when he beat Michael Johnson. Johnson was third behind Fredericks and Regis in the Grand Prix final, but otherwise lost only to Fredericks, over whom he gained a late season victory in Fukuoka to give Fredericks a 3-1 seasonal advantage.

Marsh beat Lewis at the US Trials, but was no better than third in European races.

There follows quite a gap to the best newcomer to the rankings, Dean Capobianco, 5th in Stuttgart with four second places in top European meetings. He was ahead of Effiong in Nice and both beat Robson da Silva 3-0. Chris Nelloms was only 6th at the US Trials but had a much better record than 3rd placer Jason Hendrix. Brian Bridgewater was 7th in Eugene and fared poorly in other invitationals, but won the World Student Games title, when he beat Nelloms.

1. Fredericks; 2. Regis; 3. Lewis; 4. Johnson; 5. Marsh; 6. Capobianco; 7. Effiong; 8. da Silva; 9. Nelloms; 10. Trouabal

400 METRES

MICHAEL JOHNSON won four indoor and eight outdoor finals at 400m to take his win streak to 32 since 1989. He ran three sub-44 second times and the fastest ever relay leg, that majestic solo 42.94 in Stuttgart to bring the great US team home to the world record. Butch Reynolds shook off the trauma of his suspension to win the World Indoor title and to improve one place on the World bronze that he had won in 1987.

In 1993 he beat both Quincy Watts and Samson Kitur 6-1. Watts lost a shoe in Stuttgart, but beat bronze medallist Kitur 5-1. David Grindley was unfortune to be injured and

Dean Capobianco: the best newcomer at 200

unable to run in Stuttgart for he had a 4-2 advantage over Kitur and was 2-2 against both Watts and Reynolds, beating all these men to take the Grand Prix title.

Steve Lewis was injured while Andrew Valmon and Antonio Pettigrew were 4th and 5th in the US Trials (in 44.28 and 44.45!), but these three all compiled impressive season's records, with Lewis beating Kitur 4-1, Valmon 3-1 and Bada 4-0. Kitur however gets a higher ranking through his faster times, including his Stuttgart runs, and as he beat Lewis in the Grand Prix final. Valmon beat Bada 5-2 and Bada was 4-2 up on Pettigrew.

1. Johnson; 2. Reynolds; 3. Watts; 4. Grindley; 5. Kitur; 6. Lewis; 7. Valmon; 8. Bada; 9. Pettigrew; 10. Ochieng

800 METRES

NO ONE athlete was dominant at 800m in 1993, and top ranking goes to Nixon Kiprotich who did not run in Stuttgart, but who beat the World champion Paul Ruto 4-1 and Billy Konchellah 3-1. The latter was highly favoured to win in Stuttgart but left his formidable kick too late and had to yield to Ruto and to Giuseppe D'Urso.

The under-rated Ruto, however beat Konchellah 4-1, including at the Kenyan Trials.

Generally form was muddled during the year, making a ranking very difficult.

African champion Sammy Langat and William Tanui make it five Kenyans in the top seven. Johnny Gray was inconsistent, as ever, and was behind Langat (2nd) when fifth in Brussels, but he had five times in the 1:44s, and big wins in Lausanne (ahead of Ruto) and Zürich, and was 4-1 up on Ruto, 2-1 v Konchellah and 3-2 v Tanui. Langat beat Tanui 2-1 and Tanui beat Ruto 4-3. Both Gray and José Luiz Barbosa, each in the top ten for the ninth time, went out in the World semi-finals. D'Urso had little to back his World Champs form, with 5th in Rieti in 1:44.89 his only other sub 1;45.5 time.

1. Kiprotich; 2, Ruto; 3. Konchellah; 4. Gray;
5. Langat; 6. Tanui; 7. D'Urso; 8. Barbosa;
9. Robb; 10. Steele

1500 METRES

NOUREDDINE MORCELI and Fermin Cacho are first and second just as they were in 1992, but this year Morceli had a huge lead, going through the year undefeated to complete four successive years at the top. He ran the six fastest 1500m times of the year and after several near misses at world records took 1.93 secs off Steve Cram's 8 year-old world mile record in Rieti; in all he won 14 finals at 1500m or 1 mile in 1993.

Abdi Bile followed the top two to take the bronze medal in Stuttgart, a fine return to form for the 1987 World champion, with Mohamed Suleiman fourth. The order of the first four in Stuttgart was exactly the same as in Zürich, which race produced times that filled seven of the top eight rankings for the year. Only, Morceli, the winner in 3:30.06, ran faster elsewhere, with his 3:29.20 to win the Mediterranean Games title.

Fifth to 8th in Zürich were Simon Doyle, Johan Landsman, Jonah Birir and David Kibet. Jim Spivey was ninth, in his year's best of 3:34.67, but he was fifth in Stuttgart, and beat Doyle 3-2. Spivey and Matthew Yates, 6th in Stuttgart, were closely matched, 2-2 overall. Yates won three important races, while Spivey won but once, in a slow time in Lucerne, and was 6th in the Grand Prix Final, in which Yates was third to Morceli and Bile. Spivey was 4th and Yates 5th in the Oslo Dream Mile, behind Morceli, Bile and Steve Cram.

Doyle and El Basir were 2-2, 9th and 7th respectively in Stuttgart, but the former had much the faster times. Marcus O'Sullivan, who missed Stuttgart, and Birir were 4-4.

1. Morceli; 2. Cacho; 3. Bile; 4. Suleiman;
5. Spivey; 6. Yates; 7. Doyle; 8. El Basir;
9. Birir; 10. O'Sullivan

3000 METRES

NOUREDDINE MORCELI missed the world record by just 0.28 secs in Monte Carlo. His time of 7:29.24 was more than 5 seconds faster than the year's second best time, 7:34.98 run by Paul Bitok as he led six men under 7:40 in Köln. Brahim Jabbour was second to Mohammed Issangar in Nice and to Morceli in Monte Carlo, and there also six men beat 7:40.

In the rarely run 2 miles Khalid Skah ran a world best time of 8:12.17at Hechtel.

5000 METRES

AN all-African top ten, for the first time ever. Ismael Kirui ran away from the field to a brilliant victory in Stuttgart, with his third improvement of the world junior record in 1993. His first had been in a win in Lausanne over William Sigei and Paul Bitok. After a loss to Richard Chelimo in Copenhagem Kirui improved his record when fifth in Zürich, in the race which had the best depth of times for the year.

Taking the first four places were Khalid Skah, Yobes Ondieki, Chelimo and Haile Gebresilassie, with Francesco Pannetta running the year's best by a European in sixth place (13:06.76).

Ondieki did not run the Worlds but was beaten by Kirui in Brussels, and the teenager ended his year with a Grand Prix final victory over Chelimo.

Skah had three big wins: St Denis, Lille (when Aïssa Belaout and Brahim Jabbour also broke 13:10) and Zürich, and was second at Oslo to Paul Bitok, but slipped to fifth in Stuttgart.

Simon Chemwoiyo won the African title from Gebresilassie, Worku Bikila and Bitok, but whereas the two Ethiopians ran consistently well thereafter, and were 2nd and 4th in Stuttgart, the form of both Chemwoyo and Bitok (after Oslo) fell away in Europe.

Fita Bayissa ran the event just twice: second in London to Sigei, with Gebresilassie 3rd and Bikila 4th, and third in Stuttgart.

Brahim Jabbour was sixth in Stuttgart but was just beaten by Aïssa Belaout when he ran his fastest time, in Lille.

Europe's best was Rob Denmark, winner in Seville and at the European Cup, and 9th in Stuttgart.

1. I Kirui; 2. Gebresilasie; 3. Skah; 4. Bayissa; 5. Ondieki; 6. Chelimo; 7. Bikila; 8. Sigei; 9. Bitok; 10. Belaout

10,000 METRES

THE world record fell twice within a week in July. First Richard Chelimo ran 27:07.91 in Stockholm and then Yobes Ondieki broke through the 27-minute barrier in Oslo. Although that was Ondieki's one run of the year at the event, his marvellous run, well ahead of William Sigei, is enough to give him top ranking against the World Championships medallists, all of whom lost other races.

In Stuttgart Gebresilassie won from Moses Tanui and Chelimo, while Sigei faded to tenth. The latter had however won a top-class African Championships race from Fita Bayissa and Gebresilassie.

The best depth of times came in Brussels, with six men under 27:25. Khalid Skah, whose other 10,000m of the year as a win at the Mediterranean Games, won from Tanui, Paul Tergat, Chelimo, Vincent Rousseau and Ondoro Osoro.

Ismael Kirui did not beat 28 minutes but at high altitude he won both the Kenyan Championships and Trials races, beating Sigei and Tanui in these races, after third in the Inter-Services, won by Chelimo in an extraordinary 27:55.7 altitude time.

Rousseau's Brussels time enables him to be considered the top European ahead of World fourth and sixth placers Stephan Franke and Francesco Panetta.

1. Ondieki; 2. Gebresilasie; 3. Tanui; 4. Chelimo; 5. Skah; 6. Sigei; 7. Bayissa; 8. I Kirui; 9. Tergat; 10. Rousseau

MARATHON

WITHOUT detracting from a splendid run by Mark Plaatjes to win the World title from Luchetz Swartbooi, it has to be said that most of the world's best marathoners gave the Championships a miss. I have commented before on the fact that this is a trend that is likely to continue. Despite the glory of an Olympic title who would want to run a marathon in Atlanta in July in 90°F and 90% humidity? Plaatjes was earlier third in Houston and sixth in Boston.

The year's fastest time came in December at Fukuoka when Dionicio Cerón won in 2:08:51.

Yobes Ondieki, world 10,000 metres record at Oslo

As he had previously won major marathons at Rotterdam and Mexico City he has the best claim to top ranking at the event, but any list has to be very subjective as the best men did not meet or swapped victories. I have given priority to those who had two good races rather than to those with just one. Richard Nerurkar did not better 2:10, but he won two good races in controlled fashion in 2:10s, Hamburg and the World Cup, which with Fukuoka had the greatest depth of quality times in 1993. Nerurkar thus ranks second as all those who did beat 2:10 also had some poorer results.

Three other marathons were won in under 2:10: Cosmas N'Deti, who did not finish in Stuttgart and who was second in Honolulu, won in Boston from Kim Jae-ryong, later 4th in Stuttgart, and Swartbooi was third; Vincent Rousseau won in Reims, after 5th in Rotterdam on his début, and Kim Wan-ki won in Gyeongju, with second in the World Student Games his other run at the distance. Like Nerurkar, Eamonn Martin won on his marathon début - in London.

Although only 13th in Boston, Andrés Espinosa won a tough New York race, in which Swartbooi was a non-finisher. Gert Thys broke 2:10 for second in Fukuoka, and had been third in Otsu in March, a race won by Mike O'Reilly,

4th in Fukuoka. Second in the World Cup was Severiano Bernardini, who had been 5th in Boston.

1. Cerón; 2. Nerurkar; 3. Plaatjes; 4. Swartbooi; 5. N'Deti; 6. Kim Jae-ryong; 7. Kim Wan-ki; 8. Rousseau; 9. Espinosa; 10. Thys

3000 METRES STEEPLECHASE

A KENYAN clean sweep of the medals in Stuttgart was prevented by Alessandro Lambruschini, but the African nation's dominance of the event is maintained with five of the top seven men.

Kiptanui did not quite match his 1992 form, but with four wins, including theWorld title, and three second places, he was clearly the best for his third successive year ranked first. Philip Sang is the perennial runner-up, but had some consolation with a win over Kiptanui in the Grand Prix final.

Olympic champion Matthew Birir had an indifferent season, with several poor races, but ran well when it mattered, with second to Kiptanui and ahead of Sang in the Kenyan Trials, and fourth in Stuttgart. There he ran 8:09.42, but his next best time for the year was 8:23.11. He was beaten 4-1 by up-and-coming American Mark Croghan, who finished a place behind him in the Worlds.

Moses Kiptanui, not as sharp as in 1992 but still the world champion

Not running Stuttgart, but third in the Grand Prix and with a 7-0 record over Birir and 2-3 against Croghan was former Olympic champion Julius Kariuki. He was, however, beaten 3-1 by another Kenyan Richard Kosgei, who also had clear win-loss advantage over Birir.

Steffen Brand showed fine big race form, with a European Cup win and sixth in Stuttgart, although only tenth in Zürich, where Marc Davis ran 8:14.26 for fourth. The latter's fall in the heats in Stuttgart left him drained in the final, and he just misses a ranking to Larbi El Khattabi and Angelo Carosi who finished ahead of him there.

1. Kiptanui; 2. Sang; 3. Lambruschini; 4. Croghan; 5. Kosgei; 6. Kariuki; 7. Birir; 8. Brand; 9. El Khattabi; 10. Carosi

110 METRES HURDLES

COLIN JACKSON retains his top ranking, and this time was unchallenged as he swept to victory in a world record time in Stuttgart. His only loss of the year came inconsequentially in his first race afterwards when he finished laughing in third place in Berlin behind Jack Pierce and Mark McKoy. Jackson had the greatest ever year at the event with three sub-13 second times and 13 under 13.20.

Olympic champion Mark McKoy declined to contest the Canadian Championships and was thus not selected for Stuttgart. He lost 1-4 to Jackson, but was 2-1 up on Tony Jarrett and 5-3 over Jack Pierce, the silver and bronze medallists in Stuttgart, and 7-1 over Tony Dees. Pierce beat Jarrett 5-3, but the latter was ahead of him not only in Stuttgart but also in the Grand Prix final, when the order was Jackson, Jarrett, McKoy, Mark Crear, Dees, Tony Li, Pierce and Emilio Valle.

After the top five there is quite a gap to Crear, the best newcomer to the rankings, who was third in the US Trials, one place ahead of NCAA champion Glenn Terry. Crear beat Valle 5-1. Courtney Hawkins failed to finish that race, but was 3-3 v Crear and 3-0 ahead of Valle, the World fourth placer. Florian Schwarthoff and Igor Kazanov were 5th and 6th in Stuttgart, but Tony Li, who like Crear went out in the semis, beat Kazanov 2-0.

1. Jackson; 2. McKoy; 3. Jarrett; 4. Pierce; 5. Dees; 6. Crear; 7. Hawkins; 8. Valle; 9. Schwarthoff; 10. Li

Kevin Young: took world title by four metres

400 METRES HURDLES

KEVIN YOUNG lost his 25-race unbeaten record to Samuel Matete in London, and lost twice more, but won the world title to retain his top ranking after going into that race 3-3 for the year against Matete, who finished some four metres behind.

The World Championships form holds up well in this event, with Kriss Akabusi, retired from Championships, still getting a ranking at the age of 35.

1. Young; 2. Matete; 3. Graham;
4. Diagana; 5. Keter; 6. Tverdokhleb;
7. Adkins; 8. Hense; 9. Akabusi; 10. Kinyor

HIGH JUMP

SURPRINGLY in such an event there is just one change in the personnel making up the world top ten in 1993, compared to the previous year, with Dalton Grant just regaining a place.

Javier Sotomayor was a class apart at the top, with five meetings (including one indoors) at 2.40 or better, 15 over 2.35 and 22 of his 23 competitions at 2.30 or higher. Artur Partyka took the World silver and won the European Cup, but his record apart from that was thin and he had some poor results, whereas Hollis Conway, 6th in Stuttgart, beat him 3-1 and was also 3-2 up on Troy Kemp and 2-1 over Ralf Sonn, although losing 1-3 to Steve Smith. Partyka did, however, beat Kemp 3-2 outdoors.

Patrik Sjöberg had a good competitive record until his season was terminated by injury, although his best outdoors was only 2.32, compared to the 2.39, with which he had taken the World Indoor silver behind Sotomayor's 2.41. Smith was third in both World competitions at 2.37.

1. Sotomayor; 2. Smith; 3. Conway;
4. Partyka; 5. Kemp; 6. Sonn; 7. Sjöberg;
8. Forsyth; 9. Grant; 10. Topic

POLE VAULT

SERGEY BUBKA is again supreme, although he did not manage to add an outdoor world record to the two he had set indoors in 1993. Rodion Gataullin had a great win over Bubka at the European Cup, but missed Stuttgart selection as he was only 4th in the Russian Championships, behind Denis Petuschinsky, Maksim Tarasov and Igor Trandenkov. Gataullin went on, however, to compile a fine season's record, beating World silver medallist Grigoriy Yegorov 6-4. Tarasov, however beat Gataullin 4-0 and Yegorov 3-2.

Places 5, 6 and 7 could well be shared. Trandenkov was 5-4 v Huffmann and 4-4 with Petuschinsky, Huffman beat Petuschinsky 6-5. All had a clear margin over Jean Galfione, who set French records at 5.92 and 5.93. Huffman and Galfione are the only men in the lists other than ex-Soviets.

1. S.Bubka; 2. Tarasov; 3. Gataullin;
4. Yegorov; 5. Trandenkov; 6. Huffman;
7. Petuschinsky; 8. Bukreyev; 9. Galfione;
10. Potapovich

LONG JUMP

WITH Carl Lewis passing the event this year, Mike Powell was in a different class to the rest of the world and won all his 25 competitions in 1993 easily.

Before injury Ivan Pedroso looked the only threat to Powell, as in Madrid where he jumped 8.41w to Powell's 8.50w.

Five men are ranked for the first time this year, but Larry Myricks makes a final appearance, 17 years after his first top ten ranking. He beat inconsistent Joe Greene, 3rd in the US Trials when Myricks was only 11th, 5-1.

Erick Walder lost form somewhat after the US season, but found that a modest 8.05 was enough for third in Stuttgart, behind Stanislav Tarasenko and Vitaliy Kirilenko. Ivailo Mladenov was a surprise fifth there, but confirmed his breakthrough with 8.20 for second in the Grand Prix Final behind Powell.

Kareem Streete-Thompson won the World Student Games title, representing the USA, although the Cayman Islander will not be able to take part in other major championships for his new country until he gets full citizenship in 1995. He was third in the NCAAs behind Walder and Dion Bentley, as all three exceeded 8.30.

1. Powell; 2. Pedroso; 3. Walder;
4. Tarasenko; 5. Kirilenko; 6. Mladenov;
7. Streete-Thompson; 8. Eregbu; 9. Myricks;
10. Greene

TRIPLE JUMP

MIKE CONLEY had just three big competitions, winning the US and World titles and beating many of the world's best in Bad Cannstatt. His season was completed by three low-key victories and a third place in Sheffield.

Leonid Voloshin had five competitions at 17.20 or more, although he won only one of them, in Seville. He was narrowly defeated at the Russian Championships by Vasiliy Sokov, was third in Bad Cannstatt, when Denis Kapustin, third in the Russian Champs, took second and second in Stuttgart and Sheffield. On the latter occasion the winner was Jonathan Edwards, the World bronze medallist.

Larry Myricks: still ranked in the long jump 17 years after his first appearance

Overall form confirms the world top seven order, with Yoelvis Quesada deserving a ranking from his early season form and Sokov and Maris Bruziks, who both narrowly failed to qualify in the very high standard event at Stuttgart, also having better series of marks than other finalists.

If indoor form is added, Camara and Bruziks, 1st and 2nd at the World Indoors, would move up one and three places respectively.

1. Conley; 2. Voloshin; 3. Edwards;
4. Jaros; 5. Camara; 6. Kapustin;
7. Souza Silva; 8. Quesada; 9. Sokov;
10. Bruziks

SHOT

WERNER GÜNTHÖR ended his career on a high note by winning his third successive world title and winning 18/20 in 1993. The world record holder Randy Barnes returned from drugs suspension to take the World silver and beat Günthör twice afterwards, although the Swiss had a 5-2 advantage overall.

Not ranked due to his drugs ban is Mike Stulce, originally third in Stuttgart, who was second to Barnes in the US Champs.

Jim Doehring was only fifth in the US Trials, but is ranked third with a 6-3 advantage over Kevin Toth, US third, and 3-0 over Aleksandr Bagach.

1. Günthör; 2. Barnes; 3. Doehring;
4. Bagach; 5. Palchikov; 6. Peric; 7. Toth;
8. Klimenko; 9. Hunter; 10. Weil

DISCUS

LARS RIEDEL retained his world title, and is a clear number one losing only three of his 18 competitions in 1993. Tony Washington was the only man to beat him twice, but the US champion disappointed with tenth place in Stuttgart, before taking second place behind Riedel and ahead of the World bronze and silver medallists Jürgen Schult and Dmitriy Shevchenko in the Grand Prix final.

Washington beat Costel Grasu, 4th in Stuttgart, 3-1 and Adewale Olukoju 4-2.

Olukoju missed the World Champion-ships and did not quite reproduce his long throws from US meetings in Europe, but was second in

Lars Riedel: lost only three of 18 competitions

the World Student Games, just 2cm behind Alexis Elijarde, and had a victory over World 5th placer Vladimir Zinchenko and a 3-1 record over Vaclavas Kidykas.

Sergey Lyakhov lost 3-2 to Vaclavas Kidykas but beat Adewale Olukoju 3-0 and Mike Buncic 2-0. Buncic was 2-2 v Kidykas and gets the final ranking on 8th to 11th in Stuttgart. Attila Horváth, who started slowly through injury also just misses a ranking.

Romas Ubartas lost a ranking, which his form otherwise sustained, due to a positive drug test.

1. Riedel; 2. Shevchenko; 3. de Bruin;
4. Schult; 5. Washington; 6. Grasu;
7. Zinchenko; 8. Lyakhov; 9. Olukoju;
10. Kaptyukh

HAMMER

JUST AS in 1992 Andrey Abduvaliyev won the major championship, but lost on the other occasions that they met to Igor Astapkovich; this year the score was 1-4. Abduvaliyev, however, was easily dominant in Stuttgart and went on to achieve the year's longest throw at Nitra, while Astapkovich also lost in Reims to Sergey Litvinov.

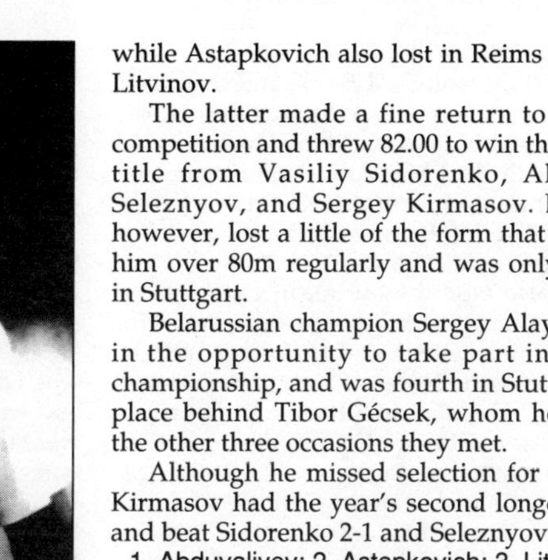

The latter made a fine return to big-time competition and threw 82.00 to win the Russian title from Vasiliy Sidorenko, Aleksandr Seleznyov, and Sergey Kirmasov. Litvinov, however, lost a little of the form that had seen him over 80m regularly and was only seventh in Stuttgart.

Belarussian champion Sergey Alay revelled in the opportunity to take part in a major championship, and was fourth in Stuttgart, one place behind Tibor Gécsek, whom he beat on the other three occasions they met.

Although he missed selection for Stuttgart. Kirmasov had the year's second longest throw and beat Sidorenko 2-1 and Seleznyov 3-2.

1. Abduvaliyev; 2. Astapkovich; 3. Litvinov;
4. Alay; 5. Gécsek; 6. Kirmassov;
7. Sidorenko; 8. Seleznyov; 9. Deal;
10. Alisevich

JAVELIN

JAN ZELEZNY added 4.08m to the world record in his first competition of the year in April, and went on to win 14 of his 15 competitions in 1993, improving his world record in Sheffield at the end of August.

He won the World title, despite being below his best that day, and exceeded 90m in five competitions; his one loss was to Seppo Räty at Lahti in June. The world silver medallist Kimmo Kinnunen had a 4-3 season's advantage over the bronze medallist Mick Hill and was 1-1 against 4th placer Steve Backley, who was held back by injury to just two competitions.

Most difficult to rank is Räty, who beat Kinnunen 7-1, but who threw only 74.30 in qualifying in Stuttgart and who was behind Zelezny, Backley and Tom Pukstys in the London GP, at which Kinnunen was 7th.

Räty was beaten 4-1 by Pukstys and 2-1 by Vladimir Sasimovich, who was another who had a clear lead over Kinnunen, 7-2, and who also beat Pukstys 3-2. 5th to 9th in Stuttgart read: Ari Pakarinen, Dag Wennlund, Sasimovich, Patrik Bodén and Pukstys. Wennlund was, however, behind on overall record, losing 6-1 to Bodén.

Raymond Hecht was the year's second longest thrower, but managed only 75.00 in Stuttgart. However he beat Gavin Lovegrove 4-1 and Pakarinen also beat Lovegrove 2-1.

1. Zelezny; 2. Kinnunen; 3. Hill; 4. Backley;
5. Sasimovich; 6. Pukstys; 7. Räty;
8. Bodén; 9. Hecht; 10. Pakarinen

DECATHLON

DAN O'BRIEN won the US title and then took the World gold medal with the year's top score. He was chased hard by Eduard Hämäläinen in Stuttgart with Paul Meier third, and these two had been first and second at Götzis earlier in the year. Mike Smith was third at Götzis, but did not finish in Stuttgart.

Meier also won the European Cup A from Christian Plaziat and Alain Blondel. The Frenchmen finished 6th and 5th respectively in Stuttgart, while at Talence Plaziat was 2nd and Blondel 4th. There Steve Fritz, 7th in Stuttgart, won, with Vitaliy Kolpakov 3rd, as Hämäläinen failed to finish.

Christian Schenk won the German Trial and was fourth in Stuttgart

1. O'Brien; 2. Hämäläinen; 3. Meier; 4. Schenk; 5. Plaziat; 6. Blondel; 7. Fritz; 8. Smith; 9. Kolpakov; 10. Muzzio

20 KILOMETRES WALK

VALENTIN MASSANA was second to Daniel Garcia in the World Cup and won his four other 20km races, including the World title, unusual consistency at an event all too often plagued by disqualifications.

Mikhail Shchennikov produced the year's fastest time (1:18:33) at the night meeting in Livorno (but that course may have been short) and also won in Sesto SG, when he beat World silver medallist Giovanni Di Benedictis, but was 5th in the World Cup and at L'Hospitalet and was ruled out by the judges in Stuttgart, as were the Mexicans Bernardo Segura and Daniel Garcia, who broke 1:20 in that order at Eschborn. Garcia and Segura took silver and bronze at the World Student Games behind Robert Korzeniowski, who was 4th in the World Cup and 3rd and 2nd respectively at the Spanish classics of L'Hospitalet and La Coruña, both won by Massana. Daniel Plaza was 2nd and 4th in those race and added 6th in the World Cup and 3rd in the Worlds.

1. Massana; 2. Korzeniowski; 3. Plaza; 4. Shchennikov; 5. Garcia; 6. De Benedictis; 7. Segura; 8. Misyulya; 9. Ihly; 10. Kollár

50 KILOMETRES WALK

JESUS GARCIA won the world title in the year's fastest time, and backed that up with second places at the Spanish Championships (to Valentin Massana, who did not contest other 50km races) and at the Word Cup behind Carlos Mercenario, who won at Podebrady but who was 8th in Stuttgart.

Valentin Kononen and Valeriy Spitsyn were second and third in Stuttgart, having been 8th and 23rd in the World Cup. Robert Korzeniowski, who was disqualified in third place near the end of the World Championships race, won the Polish title in 3:44:24.

1. Garcia; 2. Kononen; 3. Mercenario; 4. Spitsyn; 5. Noack; 6. Korzeniowski; 7. Massana; 8. Labrador; 9. Berrett; 10. Piller

Eduard Hamäläïnen: chased hard in Stuttgart after world decathlon champion Dan O'Brien

WOMEN ATHLETES OF 1993

NEWS OF the achievements in 1993 by the Chinese women, particularly the group coached by Ma Junren was received with shock, disbelief and even anger by many people in the Western world. 'There must be something wrong' was the initial, often instinctive, attitude when confronted with Wang Junxia's 29:31.78 for 10,000 metres. The split times did not seem to make sense - had she perhaps run a lap short?

Then came the world records at 1500m and 3000m and marks set long ago by athletes from Eastern Europe, themselves perhaps discredited in the minds of many due to allegations of state-controlled drug taking, were annihilated.

In some early Athlete of the Year polls such as those conducted by the IAAF or by *Athletics International* many people simply ignored the Chinese, but calmer, more rational assessments, particularly by experts, meant that the brilliance, dedication and hard work of the Chinese group came to be appreciated as the months rolled by.

Not that the doubts had dispersed but rather that there was no *evidence* to suggest that the Chinese women were using drugs, and indeed no more likely to have done so than some of their Western rivals.

When Sally Gunnell ran a world record to win the 400m hurdles in Stuttgart after one of the great duels of all-time against Sandra Farmer-Patrick I thought that she would be my choice as athlete of the year.

Even then, however, Wang Junxia had done enough to warrant very serious consideration for the top ranking.

Her deeds at the Chinese National Games, backed as if needed by easy wins in the World Cup Marathon and at the Asian Games, leave absolutely no doubt that she was the Athlete of 1993. And Qu Yunxia was a worthy choice for second spot - for all but those of course who continued to choose to ignore the Chinese.

I said above 'as if it mattered' when referring to Wang's end of season gold medals. Perhaps, however, they mattered a lot, because they showed that the Chinese group were not just producing the goods in China, but quite prepared to contest the major events - and to be drug tested.

Sally Gunnell (above) was voted Athlete of the Year in the IAAF's poll but Wang Junxia (below) was my athlete of 1993

Tested they were too back in China by the IAAF testing group, and while several Chinese sportsmen and women were caught and disqualified at their National Games, these did not include any from Ma's extraordinary group of women distance runners.

Amazing hard work, with the Eastern mind-set and regard for authority, dedication and discipline, and the benefits of such work at high altitude , have reaped their rewards.

We saw the potential of Qu some years back, she went on to Olympic bronze, and the might of the Chinese squad was clearly shown at the World Juniors in 1992. In 1993 came the deluge, as can be seen by reading through the event rankings that follow.

Event by event survey

100 METRES

THE TOP four were the same as in 1992, except that I have ranked them in exactly the opposite order!

Despite being Olympic champion Gail Devers had an inferior overall record to her rivals in 1992; in 1993, however, she not only won the world title, but lost only one of her eight finals at 100m. That was her third place in Zürich, behind Merlene Ottey and Gwen Torrence.

She beat then both in Stuttgart and had also handed Ottey her only other loss of the year, 10.82 to 10.96 in Lausanne, with Torrence third in 10.97 and Irina Privalova fourth in 11.06. That order was identical in Stutttgart, although there Ottey lost by a mere 0.002 sec.

Privalova was an isolated fourth, beaten 7-0 by Torrence, but losing only to the top three. Mary Onyali and Natalya Voronova were 5h and 6th in Stuttgart, with the former having a 3-2 lead over the season.

Marie-José Pérec ran the event just four times, but was second to Privalova and ahead of Zhanna Tarnopolskaya in the European Cup and won her other races in good times.

Juliet Cuthbert started the year late and missed selection for Stuttgart, but ended well with third place in the Grand Prix behind Torrence and Privalova, and ahead of Voronova, Michelle Finn and Onyali.

1. Devers; 2. Ottey; 3. Torrence;
4. Privalova; 5. Onyali; 6. Voronova;
7. Mitchell; 8. Pérec; 9. Cuthbert; 10. Finn

200 METRES

MERLENE OTTEY'S long-awaited triumph to win the World title made her top ranking a formality. She raced much more sparingly than in the past, and contested just two indoor and six outdoor events at 200m, losing just once when third at St Denis in June running into a gale behind Marie-José Pérec and Galina Malchugina.

The US champion Gwen Torrence similarly raced little at 200m, and her only loss was her second place, beaten by just 0.02 secs by Ottey in Stuttgart. Privalova followed then home to take the bronze medal ahead of Pérec, to whom she just lost when both ran 21.99 in Lille after winning when both ran 22.30 in the European Cup.

As in the 100m Mary Onyali followed the top four at a distance, but she beat Galina Malchugina 3-0. Natalya Voronova and Malchugina both ran 22.50 for 6th and 7th in

THE IAAF conducted their usual world-wide poll, inviting people in the world of athletics to select their top tens of 1993. The result for women is shown, followed in the second column by my own selections and in the final column by those of the international experts polled by *Track & Field News*:

IAAF position, name,	*points*	*PJM*	*TFN*
1. Sally Gunnell	2274	3	3
2. Wang Junxia	2256	1	1
3. Gail Devers	2208	4	2
4. Merlene Ottey	2064	7	7
5. Maria Mutola	1519	5	5
6. Qu Yunxia	1435	2	4
7. Heike Drechsler	1051	6	6
8. Jackie Joyner-Kersee	769	10	8
9. Sandra Farmer-Patrick	699	8	9
10. Sonia O'Sullivan	538		15
11. Gwen Torrence	534		13
12. Ana Biryukova	439		11
13. Trine Hattestad	398		10
14. Liu Dong	278	9	16=
15. Junko Asari	277		12

EAA European Athletes of the Year

1. Sally Gunnell	245
2. Heike Drechsler	193
3. Ana Biryukova	87
4. Sonia O'Sullivan	79
5. Trine Hattestad	77

Stuttgart and were 3-3 in 1993, but the latter had a better set of times and was well ahead in her three.

Cathy Freeman had a 5-2 advantage over her Australian rival Melinda Gainsford. Holli Hyche, NCAA champion at 100m and 200m was undefeated at the event, but pulled up in her heat at the US Trials through injury, and was thus untested by leading runners and narrowly misses a ranking

1. Ottey; 2. Torrence; 3. Privalova; 4. Pérec; 5. Onyali; 6. Malchugina; 7. Voronova; 8. Young; 9. Freeman; 10. Gainsford

400 METRES

JEARL MILES ran the year's fastest time to win the World title and won eight of her ten finals outdoors. She is an easy choice for top ranking, but may not have been the world's best, for Gwen Torrence ran 49.83 to win in Monte Carlo from Ximena Restrepo 50.46 and Miles 50.46. Torrence also ran a lead-off 49.1 in the World Championships relay, but that does not count in this ranking and she ran 400m otherwise just one indoors and twice outdoors. She did, however, beat Natasha Kaiser-Brown, the World silver medallist twice.

The World Championships form is confirmed overall, with Sandie Richards beating Tatyana Alekseyeva 3-0 and Restrepo 2-1, with those two 1-1. The rankings are then completed by slotting in not only Torrrence but also Asian champion Ma Yuqin, who ran an Asian record 49.81 at the Chinese National Games, and, with a somewhat token tenth ranking, Irina Privalova, who ran 49.89 on her début at the event. Next best is Maicel Malone, but her best was 51.10.

1. Miles; 2. Torrence; 3. Kaiser-Brown; 4. Richards; 5. Alekseyeva; 6. Restrepo; 7. Ma Yuqin; 8. Myers; 9. Campbell; 10. Privalova

800 METRES

MARIA MUTOLA was unbeaten both indoors (five finals) and outdoors (11 finals) and won both World titles. She improved her African record four times. She was challenged hard by distant cousin Tina Paulino, who ran 1:56.62 behind Mutola's 1:56.56 in New York, but Paulino was fourth in Zürich behind Mutola, Svetlana Masterkova, who did not run in Stuttgart after failing to finish at the Russian Championships and Ella Kovacs, the European Cup winner.

Paulino and Liu Li of China fell in the

Jearl Miles: won eight of ten 400 metres finals including the World Championships

Stuttgart final, and that put paid to their chances of medals, as Lyubov Gurina and Kovacs took silver and bronze. Liu was later third in the Chinese National Games, when the winner Liu Dong ran the year's second fastest time and Qu Yunxia came second, and won the Asian title.

Gurina ran consistently well and beat Masterkova 2-1, while Masterkova beat Kovacs 4-0. Although she went out in a heat in Stuttgart, the US champion Joetta Clark beat the World fourth and fifth placers Diane Modahl and Meredith Rainey 5-1 and 7-1 respectively.

Liu Dong and Qu Yunxia ran the event only in China, but they beat Liu Li into third place at the Chinese National Games in super-fast times.

1. Mutola; 2. Gurina; 3. Masterkova; 4. Kovacs; 5. Paulino; 6. Liu Dong; 7. Qu Yunxia; 8. Liu Li; 9. Rogachova; 10. Clark

1500 METRES

THE SENSATION of this event came at the Chinese National Games as the 13 year-old world record of Tatyana Kazankina was beaten by both Qu Yunxia and Wang Junxia. These two had won longer distances in Stuttgart, but Qu had beaten the World champion Liu Dong, who set the pace for them in Beijing, in the East Asian Games 1500m.

The depth in standard in the Chinese National Games, and in the heats of the Chinese Championships in June is such that Chinese women dominate the rankings. A guide to their form is provided by Lu Yi, 8th at the Chinese Games in 4:00.05 after placing 4th in Stuttgart.

Sonia O'Sullivan, World silver medallist, was the top European although she was beaten 2-1 by Lyubov Kremlyova, who won the Grand Prix but who was only third in the Russian Championships.

Viorica Beclea and O'Sullivan broke 4 minutes in Monte Carlo, but Beclea was only 9th in Stuttgart, although she returned to place third in the Grand Prix final, in which the World bronze medallist Hassiba Boulmerka was only fifth.

Qu Yunxia: did not run the 1500 metres in Stuttgart but later ran a world record at that distance to go with her 3000m gold

1. Qu Yunxia; 2. Wang Junxia; 3. Liu Dong; 4. O'Sullivan; 5. Zhang Linli; 6. Kremlyova; 7. Beclea; 8. Boulmerka; 9. Wang Renmei; 10. Lu Li

3000 METRES

THE GREATEST of all the amazing distance running achievements at the Chinese National Games came in the 3000m. First Zhang Linli broke the world record with 8:22.06 in her heat, then Wang Junxia and Qu Yunxia ran 8:12.19 and 8:12.27 in theirs.

In the final Wang improved to a staggering 8:06.11 from Qu 8:12.18, Zhang Linli 8:16.50, Ma Liyan 8:21.26 and Zhang Lirong 8:21.84, all under the pre-meeting world record.

Earlier Qu and the Zhangs had swept the medals in Stuttgart, while Wang had won the Chinese title from Qu and Zhang Lirong.

Sonia O'Sullivan was supreme in Europe, her fourth place in Stuttgart coming in addition to five wins, all in the 8:28 to 8:38 range in Grand Prix races. Although her 9th place in Stuttgart made her only the third British athlete in the final (Alison Wyeth 5th and Paula Radcliffe 7th) Yvonne Murray was the next best Western athlete, beating Elana Meyer 2-0 and Wyeth 3-1.

1. Wang Junxia; 2. Qu Yunxia; 3. Zhang Linli; 4. Zhang Lirong; 5. O'Sullivan; 6. Ma Liyan; 7. Murray; 8. Meyer; 9. Wyeth; 10. Romanova

10,000 METRES

RAN FOUR, won four is Wang Junxia's record at 10,000m, the Chinese, World and Asian titles, and the sensational 29:31.78 at the Chinese National Games, when she sped away from a very fast field opening up a gap of over 40 seconds in the second half of the race. Zhong Huandi won the Esat Asian Games, and after 4th at the Chinese Championships, followed Wang with second in both Stuttgart and Beijing.

Sally Barsosio was immensely lucky to be reinstated after disqualification in Stuttgart, but her running ability was there for all to see, and she had earlier won both Kenyan Championships and Trials.

The World Championships order is followed exactly in these rankings for the first seven places, with Uta Pippig moving ahead of Anne-Marie Letko due to her fast time in Hengelo and Zhang Lirong, third in Beijing completing the list. Although 4th to 6th in Beijing all ran faster times than those ranked, they also ran much poorer times in their only other races, at the Chinese Championships.

1. Wang Junxia; 2. Zhong Huandi;
3. Barsosio; 4. Lorupe; 5. Jennings;
6. Ferreira; 7. Dias; 8. Pippig; 9. Letko;
10. Zhang Lirong

MARATHON

IN THE first major race of the year Junko Asari tied the Asian record to win the Osaka marathon by one second from Tomoe Abe, with Yoshiko Yamamoto. Asari and Abe later placed first and third in the World Championships, with Manuela Machado second, and Yamamoto was again under 2:30 to win in Amsterdam.

In April the big race winners were Olga Markova at Boston and Katrin Dörre at London, where she came from behind to beat Lisa Ondieki and Liz McColgan. Two weeks earlier the world was amazed by the performances of the Chinese squad in Tianjing. There the middle and long distance runners of Ma Junren's squad produced the four sub 2:25 times of the year - 1. Wang Junxia, 2. Qu Yunxia, 3, Zhang Linli, 4. Zhang Lirong. Fifth placed Zhong Huandi and sixth Ma Liyan ran times that were otherwise bettered in 1993 only by Markova. All were to produce sensational track times later in the year at much shorter distances. Five of them returned to run in the World Cup marathon, won with ease by Wang in 2:28:16 with Zhang Linli, Zhang Lirong and Ma Liyan filling places 2-4. Qu failed to finish.

Big race winners in the last part of the year, were Renata Kokowska, who had been 4th in London, in Berlin, Uta Pippig in New York and Valentina Yegorova in Tokyo, from Mari Tanigawa and Dörre. Dörre had also placed 6th in the Worlds and Machado won the Lisbon Marathon, having earlier run 4th at Boston.

1. Asari; 2. Wang Junxia; 3. Machado;
4. Abe; 5. Qu Yunxia; 6. Zhang Linli;
7. Zhang Lirong; 8. Markova; 9. Dörre;
10. Pippig

100 METRES HURDLES

GAIL DEVERS was beaten by Lynda Tolbert by 0.01 at the US Trials, her first competition of the year at the event, but thereafter was undefeated in five major competitions. She had a big margin (12.46 to 12.60) over Maya Azyabina in Stuttgart and also beat Azyabina when they met later at Sheffield. Those two defeats were the only two suffered by Azyabina, who ran a most impressive series of fast times. Tolbert, Stuttgart bronze medallist, was possibly the best bet for third, although she lost 2-3 to Michelle Freeman, who was only 7th in the Worlds, and 1-4 to Aliuska López. Freeman beat López, Worlds 4th, 4-1.

Yordanka Donkova and LaVonna Martin ended their seasons prior to Stuttgart, with the former having a 3-1 advantage. Martin failed to finish her semi at the US Trials, but beat 3rd placer there, Dawn Bowles, who went on to 6th in Stuttgart, 4-0.

Chinese and Asian champion Zhang Yu was undefeated, but did not meet Western athletes.

1. Devers; 2. Azyabina; 3. Tolbert;
4. Freeman; 5. López; 6. Sokolova;
7. Donkova; 8. Martin; 9. Bowles;
10. Zhang Yu

400 METRES HURDLES

SALLY GUNNELL'S world record in Stuttgart was the first in a women's track event since 1980. Her form had been such that it was felt the record could well go in one of the big summer races, but it was more of a surprise that Sandra Farmer-Patrick ran so brilliantly as to also better the old mark.

Prior to the World Champs Gunnell had won all her six races at the distance, four under 54 seconds, with 53.52 at Zürich in her last race, while Farmer-Patrick had a best of 53.96 to win the US Trials before 2nd at Lausanne in 54.52 to Gunnell's 53.86 and third in Oslo in 54.89 behind Kim Batten and Tonya Buford.

After Stuttgart, Farmer-Patrick beat Gunnell twice, 53.70 to 54.08 in Brussels and 53.69 to 53.82 at the Grand Prix Final.

The form of 3rd to 6th in Stuttgart, Margarita Ponomaryova, Kim Batten, Tonya Buford and Deon Hemmings was confirmed by their overall campaigns. Batten beat Buford 10-2 as the two Americans were regularly matched, but was 3-4 down to Ponomaryova. Buford beat Hemmings 8-3.

Rosey Edeh was 7th in Stuttgart, but was then beaten 2-0 by Tatyana Ledovskaya, who made a late start to the season and narrowly missed a place in the World final, and was 2-3 down to Ana Knoroz and 1-2 to World Student Games champion Heike Meissner.

Han Qing was the fifth fastest, with her 53.96 at the Chinese National Games, but did not appear elsewhere, so is hard to slot in.

1. Gunnell; 2. Farmer-Patrick;
3. Ponomaryova; 4. Batten; 5. Buford;
6. Hemmings; 7. Ledovskaya; 8. Knoroz;
9. Han Qing; 10. Meissner

HIGH JUMP

THERE WAS a major shock in Stuttgart, as the two women who have dominated world high jumping in recent years,

Stefka Kostadinova and Heike Henkel failed to qualify for the final. That left the way clear for Ioamnet Quintero to win from her compatriot Silvia Costa, with Sigrid Kirchmann taking a surprise bronze medal. Another favourite Galina Astafei was fourth equal with Yelena Rodina, who returned to competition in 1993 after a two-year drug ban.

Nonetheless Kostadinova was a clear choice for top ranking, with ten competitions at 2 metres or over outdoors and another three indoors to take her career total to 105. Her best of 2.05 came in September in Fukuoka. She won 19 of her 24 competitions outdoors and 5 of 7 indoors, including her fourth World Indoor title.

Henkel challenged her indoors, with the score 2-2 between them and both cleared 2.02 in Toronto. Henkel cleared 2m five times indoors and twice outdoors, but then lost form through injury and was beaten 3-1 by Quintero and 5-1 by Astafei. Astafei won the European Cup at 2.00 from Henkel's 1.96.

There was little between those ranked in the second half of the top ten, with Kirchman particularly difficult to place, as her best, apart from her 1.97 in Stuttgart, was only 1.93.

If I had included indoor form then Inga Babakova, 3rd inthe World Indoors at 2.00, would have ranked 6th, but outdoors her best was 1.96. She beat Costa 5-0, but then lost form, while Costa overcame her poor early season form to jump well in the major meetings.

1. Kostadinova; 2. Quintero; 3. Astafei;
4. Henkel; 5. Costa; 6. Topchina;
7. Shevchik; 8. Kirchmann; 9. Rodina;
10. Bevilacqua

LONG JUMP

HEIKE DRECHSLER was over 7 metres in 20 of her 28 competitions in 1993. She was beaten only twice, by Susen Tiedtke at Sestriere and by Jackie Joyner-Kersee by just 1 cm in Berlin. Drechsler gained immediate revenge for the latter defeat by beating JJK by 1 cm in Innsbruck the following day.

JJK decided to concentrate on the heptathlon in 1993, so she had only six long jump competitions, including two in heptathlons, but was over 7m each time.

World silver medallist Larisa Berezhnaya was consistently just under 7m, but lost 3-1 to Irina Mushailova, whose fourth place in the Russian Championships cost her a Stuttgart place. There are three Russians and three Ukrainians ranked from 3 to 10, split by two former Eastern European athletes, Renata Nielsen, who moved from Poland to Denmark and Ludmila Ninova, Bulgaria to Austria. Nielsen had inferior marks, but won the World bronze and beat Yelena Khlopotnova 4-2 and Ninova 3-1; the latter two were 3-3.

Inessa Kravets was over 7m, when third in in Seville to Drechsler and Ninova, but was banned for three months for use of stimulants, and loses a rankings place.

1. Drechsler; 2. Joyner-Kersee;
3. Mushailova; 4. Berezhnaya; 5. Nielsen;
6. Khlopotnova; 7. Ninova; 8. Sinchukova;
9. Galkina; 10. Tiedtke

TRIPLE JUMP

AFTER WORLD indoor records at 14.46 by Yolanda Chen and 14.47 by Inessa Kravets, the world outdoor record was improved twice.

Chen jumped 14.97 at the Russian Championships, with Inna Lasovskaya, who had earlier set a national record at 14.70, second at 14.68. Ana Biryukova was third on that occasion at 14.60, but she was the one to produce the first 15m jump ever, winning the World title with 15.09, with Chen 39 cm behind in second place.

The former world record holder Inessa Kravets missed Stuttgart through serving a 3-months ban for the use of stimulants, but had good wins in her last two competitions, beating most of the world's best at Lausane and Nice. She had 3-2 advantages over the third and fourth best Russians Lasovskaya and Irina Mushailova and would have ranked fourth but for her ban.

Galina Chistyakova, 2-4 down to Mushailova, then made it five Russians in the top six, with the final ranking places going to those placed 3-6 in Stuttgart. Niurka Montalvo's better overall record, which included winning the World Student Games and CAC titles elevating her above World third placer Iva Prandzheva.

Ren Ruiping smashed the world junior record at the Chinese National Games and later won the Asian title.

1. Biryukova; 2. Chen; 3. Lasovskaya;
4. Mushailova; 5. Chistyakova; 6. Montalvo;
7. Prandzheva; 8. Radtke; 9. Ren Ruiping;
10. Capriotti

SHOT

HUANG ZHIHONG lost two early season clashes with Cong Yuzhen, but won the World title by a margin of 60cm over silver medallist Svetlana Krivelyova, and also beat many of the world's best in Brussels. Krivelyova won the World Indoor title, and after a series of meetings at just over 19m in May - June, returned to her best with 20.84, the world best of 1993, in August. She also won the Grand Prix Final from Astrid Kumbernuss, Viktoria Pavlysh, Stephanie Storp, Kathrin Neimke and Valentina Fedyushina.

The top seven in the World Champ-ionships are ranked in that order, followed by Storp, only 11th in Stuttgart but who beat Neimke 4-3 and Russian champion and European Cup winner Anna Romanova 2-1.

Several Chinese figure prominently in the event: Sui Xinmei and Cong were 4th and 5th in the Worlds, but also finished in the same positions in the Chinese National Games, where the first three were Zhou Tianhua, who also won the Chinese and World Student Games titles, Zhang Liuhong, who also won East Asian and Asian titles, and Zhang Zhiying. However Zhou was later revealed to have failed a drugs test at the Chinese National Games and, originally ranked third, she is excluded.

Anna Biryukova: the first 15m triple jump by a woman

There is little to choose between any of those ranked 3 to 10, and indeed Romanova, who lost form at year's end had a 1993 best better than all but Sui.

1. Huang; 2. Krivelyova; 3. Zhang Liuhong;
4. Neimke; 5. Sui; 6. Cong; 7. Kumbernuss;
8. Fedyushina; 9. Storp; 10. Romanova

DISCUS

OLGA BUROVA, Daniela Costian and Min Chunfeng won the World medals ahead of Maritza Martén. The yearly leader at 68.14, Larisa Korotkevich, failed to qualify for the final in Stuttgart, but had the best series of marks, with three meetings over 67m, a performance matched otherwise only by Burova, and won the European Cup from Larisa Mikhalchenko and Reneta Katewicz.

Ilke Wyludda made a late return to competition after injury and led the qualifiers in Stuttgart in only her second competition of the year, but managed only 11th in the final.

Apart from Stuttgart the meeting to bring together the most top competitors was the ISTAF meeting, where the order was Burova, Costian, Wyludda, Korotkevich, Grasu and Anja Gündler, who had excelled to take World fifth place, but whose year best was 62.92, much less than her rivals. Gündler was also third in the World Student Games, won by Katewicz.

Ellina Zvereva threw over 65m four times and was unbeaten, except for a non-qualifying 59.84 in Stuttgart.

1. Burova; 2. Costian; 3. Min; 4. Martén;
5. Korotkevich; 6. Zvereva; 7. Grasu;
8. Mikhalchenko; 9. Wyludda; 10. Katewicz

JAVELIN

AFTER several years of long throws but disappointing competitive results in championshps, Trine Hattestad at last came into her own with the World title as well as the year lead at 72.12 and the only other 70m plus performance. Her only two losses in 1993 were at the hands of the Shikolenko sisters, Tatyana in the European Cup B and Natalya in Köln.

Although Karen Forkel won the silver and Natalya Shikolenko the bronze in Stuttgart the latter had a 4-2 win-loss advantage. Yekaterina Ivakina was 6 cm behind Tatyana Shikolenko for 5th in Stuttgart, but beat her on the other two occasions that they met.

Ha Xiaolan won at both the East Asian Games and Chinese National Games. Zhang Li was second at the latter, and won the Chinese and Asian titles.

1. Hattestad; 2. N Shikolenko; 3. Forkel;
4. Ivakina; 5. T Shikolenko; 6. Renk;
7. Tilea; 8. Ha Xiaoyan; 9. Zhang Li;
10. Nerius

HEPTATHLON

JACKIE JOYNER-KERSEE was down on her 7000 plus scores of the past, but was still good enough to win the World title as well as her other heptathlon of the year, the US Trials. The first two at the other big heptathlons of the year were Svetla Dimitrova and Tatyana Blokhina, in that order at Götzis and the reverse at Talence. Blokhina also won the Russian title, but failed to finish in the European Cup and Worlds.

Sabine Braun, on the other hand, did not finish either Götzis or Talence, but was World silver medallist, with Svetlana Buraga third and Dimitrova fourth. Dimitrova, however, won at Brescia and Buraga failed to finish there and in Talence.

The top competitors were split in the European Cup, with Tatyana Zhuravlyova winning the A event and Buraga the C.

Ma Miaolan recorded a score beaten only by Joyner-Kersee and Braun in 1993 to win the Chinese National Games and also won the Chinese title, but did not meet other top competitors.

1. Joyner-Kersee; 2. Braun; 3. Dimitrova;
4. Blokhina; 5. Buraga; 6. Ma Miaolan;
7. Clarius; 8. Wlodarczyk; 9. Flemming;
10. Carter

10 KILOMETRES WALK

THERE IS so much conflicting evidence at this event that a ranking is exceedingly tricky. There were disqualifications suffered by many of the leading walkers at main events, there were fast times at Livorno (short course?) or in China, and there were the World Cup and World Championships held in very hot weather.

Sari Essayah was World champion and second in the World Cup, so there is little doubt about her eminence, but Wang Yan, who won the World Cup was disqualified in Stuttgart. She had however won both Chinese races in Shenzheng in February and was third at the National Games behind Li Chunxiu, who also won the East Asian Games title, and Gao Hongmiao, second in both Shenzheng races. Gao won the Asian title from Li.

Ileana Salvador won the World silver medal, having been 6th in the World Cup which she followed by a series of fast races, winning in Sesto from AnnaRita Sidoti and Sayko and matching the world best with 41:30 in Livorno, when world fourth placer Elisabeta Perrone was second.

Yelena Nikolayeva was third in the World Cup and the winner in La Coruña before 7th place in Stuttgart. Kerry Saxby-Junna had fast times in Australia, was fifth in the World Cup and beat Salvador and Essayah in Fana, but did not finish in Stuttgart. Madelein Svensson failed the judges' test in Stuttgart, but otherwise had a fine set of performances. She was third in Eschborn behind Sidoti and Tatyana Ragozina.

1. Essayah; 2. Salvador; 3. Li Chunxiu;
4. Wang Yan; 5. Nikolayeva;
6. Saxby-Junna; 7. Gao Hongmiao;
8. Sidoti; 9. Svensson; 10. Perrone

Trine Hattestad: gold at last

Cross-Country - National Champions 1993

	MEN	WOMEN
Australia	Andrew Lloyd	Susie Power
Austria	Dietmar Millonig	Susanne Fischer
Belgium	Vincent Rousseau	Véronique Collard
Canada (Nov)	Joseph Kibur	Paula Schnurr
Czech Republic	Michel Kucera	
Denmark	Kåre Sørensen	Gitte Karlshøj
England	Richard Nerurkar	Gillian Stacey
Finland	Harri Hänninen	Päivi Tikkanen
France	Brahim Lahlafi MAR	Odile Ohier
Germany	Stephan Freigang	Claudia Dreher
Hungary	Imre Berkovics	Judit Földing/Nagy
India	Kailash Mane	Celinamma
Ireland	Noel Curtis	Catherina McKiernan
Israel	Dev Kremer	Edna Lankri
Italy	Vicente Modica	Rosanna Munerotto
Kenya	William Sigei	Helen Kimaiyo
Luxembourg	Justin Gloden	Danièle Kaber
Netherlands	Henk Gommer	Irma Heeren
New Zealand	Richard Potts	Sharon Clode
Northern Ireland	Dermot Donnelly	Vikki McConnell
Norway	Terje Næss	Christin Sørum
Portugal	Domingos Castro	M Albertina Dias
Romania	Augustin Barbu	Iulia Negura
Russia	Oleg Strizhakov	Olga Churbanova
Scotland	Richard Quinn	Vikki McPherson
Slovakia	Róbert Stefko	Ravilya Kryulina RUS
South Africa	Meshack Megotsi	Elana Meyer
Spain	Francisco Guerra	Julia Vaquero
Sweden	Jonny Danielson	Malin Ewerlöf
Switzerland	Arnold Mächler	Daria Nauer
UK Trials	Steve Tunstall	Suzanne Rigg
US Trials	Todd Williams	Annette Peters
USA (Nov)	Todd Williams	Lynn Jennings
Wales	Justin Hobbs	Wendy Ore
Asian	Hamid Sadjadi IRN	Minori Hayakiri JPN
NCAA (Nov)	Josephat Kapkory KEN	Carole Zajac
South America	Valdenor dos Santos BRA	Silvana Pereira BRA

Where countries have national championships over more than one distance the winners of the event over c.10-12 km for men, or 5-8km for women are listed.

Classic races - 1993

Durham 2/1	Fita Bayissa ETH	Derartu Tulu ETH
Mallusk 9/1	Simon Chemwoiyo KEN	Catherina McKiernan IRL
Fuensalida 10/1	Domingos Castro POR	Iulia Negura ROM
Sevilla 17/1	Fita Bayissa ETH	Catherina McKiernan IRL
Hannut 31/1	Vincent Rousseau BEL	Natalya Sorokivskaya KZK
San Sebastián 31/1	Fita Bayissa ETH	Luchia Yisak ETH
Akgarve 7/2	Ondoro Osoro KEN	Tecla Lorupe KEN
Diekeirch 14/2	James Kariuki KEN	Suzanne Rigg GBR
Chiba 21/2	Mathias Ntawalikura RWA	Viktoriya Nenasheva RUS
Nairobi 27/2	William Sigei KEN	Helen Kimaiyo KEN
San Vittore Olona 6/3	Fita Bayissa ETH	Esther Kiplagat KEN
Lidingöloppet	30k Josephat Ndeti KEN	15k Annemari Sandell FIN
Bolbec 28/11	Khalid Boulami MAR	Catherina McKiernan IRL
Brussels 19/12	Ismail Kirui KEN	Albertina Dias POR

IAAF Cross-country Challenge

See *Athletics 1993* page 608 for the top 12 men and women in the 1992/3 series

1993 MARATHON DIARY
BY DR. DAVID E. MARTIN

FROM A few viewpoints, 1993 was an ordinary year for the marathon. First, no one came close to challenging the accepted world best marathon performances of 2:21:06 for women (by Ingrid Kristiansen in '85) and 2:06:50 for men (by Belayneh Dinsamo in '88). Nevertheless, fine performances were achieved - 34 performances by men faster than 2:11:00, 35 by women faster than 2:30:00.

Second, approximately 1050 marathon performances faster than 2:20:00 were run by men world-wide; for women, the equivalent time to achieve that depth is 2:55:00. This level of achievement has been remarkably constant since 1983. Third, the world-wide fascination among serious fitness devotees to challenge the 42,195 meter distance kept the big marathons, such as New York and London, approaching their capacity with around 25,000 participants, and as well ensured lively participation around the world at more than a thousand smaller races.

But from a few other viewpoints, 1993 was an incredibly exciting and stimulating year, with never a dull moment. For one, there was the addition of many new nations into the IAAF family, particularly South Africa and the nations emerging from the former Soviet Union, Czechoslovakia, and Yugoslavia challenged statisticians to sort out the identity of many athletes who now were free to roam the globe. The South African men performed the best among these nations, with victories at Stockholm (Daniel Mbuli), Melbourne (Jerry Modiga), Enschede (Jan Tau), and Berlin (Xolile Yawa - whose superb 2:10:57 over Driss Dacha (MAR), countryman David Tsebe, and Alfredo Shahanga (TAN) provided an African sweep). By year's end, fully 58 nations had men run faster than 2:20:00, 53 with women faster than 2:55:00. Asia, Europe, and North America dominated in terms of numbers, but Africa and South America had increased activity as well.

Some outstanding personal bests were achieved by athletes already near the top of their game. Among the women, Japan's Junko Asari won the January Osaka International Ladies marathon (2:26:26), which equalled the national record (already being shared by Yoshiko Yamamoto and Yumi Kokamo). Asari went on to represent Japan well at the Stuttgart World Championships as a gold medallist (2:30:03). Second place at Osaka was diminutive (1.49 m, 38 kg) Tomoe Abe, who débuted in 2:26:27 and later accompanied Asari to Stuttgart, where she captured the bronze medal. Uta Pippig (GER) and Olga Appell (MEX) both capped excellent seasons of road racing by setting new national bests with their one-two (2:26:24, 2:28:56) placings on a warm November day in New York. Renata Kokowska's 2:26:20 at Berlin was not a national best, but her 29 second victory over Spain's Maria Albertina Dias not only gave both personal bests but also provided Kokowska with her third victory and second course record over

Junko Asari: won in Osaka as well as Stuttgart

this beautiful circuit through the city. Several outstanding performances were not personal bests, but easily as noteworthy. A few good examples include: 1) the splendid 2:25:27 win by Olga Markova over Kim Jones at Boston, 2) the top three at London, all under 2:30:00 (Katrin Dörre, Lisa Ondieki, and Liz McColgan), and 3) the top two at the November Tokyo women's race (Barcelona gold medallist Valentina Yegorova and Mari Tanigawa, who with Dörre again all bettered 2:30:00).

Some outstanding personal bests by the men were also notable. On Patriot's Day (Monday) at Boston in mid-April, Kenya's Cosmas Ndeti scored his first victory in only his second marathon, improving from 2:14:28 (at Honolulu in '92) to 2:09:33 over an outstanding field that chased him right to the finish tape. Korea's Kim Jae-ryong was only 10 seconds behind, in turn trailed (by 14 seconds) by Namibia's Lucketz Swartbooi. A favourable tailwind was partially negated by warm temperatures, with nine runners breaking 2:13:00 - among them the '91 Tokyo gold medallist Hiromi Taniguchi (2:11:02), ex-South-African-about-to-become-USA-citizen Mark Plaatjes (2:12:39) and rising Italian star Severino Bernardini (2:12:56). It was a world-class marathon weekend, with very fast performances having been scored at London and Rotterdam the day previous. Britain's Eamonn Martin débuted before a home-town crowd with a three-second sprint finish (2:10:50) over Mexico's Isidro Rico, while on the Continent, another Mexican, Dionicio Ceron, ran wonderfully (2:11:06) to defeat Simon Naali (TAN) and Harri Hänninen (FIN) with less than a minute separating the three.

Some of these above-mentioned men figured importantly as the year developed. The two major IAAF marathons were at Stuttgart (World Championships) in August and at San Sebastián (World Marathon Cup) at the end of October. While the latter saw perfect racing conditions, as well as a large prize purse, the Stuttgart races had warm, humid conditions with earnings limited to a Mercedes for the victor. At Stuttgart, Mark Plaatjes stole the show. A USA citizen for scarcely three weeks, it was his first international championship competition, and he was not a pre-meet favourite. Typically a front-runner, for reasons even he couldn't explain he ran conservatively in the early stages. Every single runner in front of him fell back, one by one. Swartbooi was the most resilient, but couldn't challenge as Plaatjes passed him in the final 2 km to become the first American man to win a major marathon championship (2:13:57) since Frank Shorter in '72.

In contrast to the slow times at Stuttgart, the San Sebastián race was a runner's dream. Good weather, a flat fast three-loop course that was also good for spectating, excellent support by federations world-wide for this event, and emphasis placed on team as well as individual performance provided a unique experience for everyone. Ten men broke 2:11:00, a record. While Bernardini's Boston experience gave him the confidence to score a personal best 2:10:12, it wasn't enough for the victory. That went to Britain's Richard Nerurkar, a scant nine seconds faster. It was only Nerurkar's second outing at the distance, but his début 2:10:57 victory at Hamburg in May let the world know he had found his event. The team trophy went to Ethiopia (3, 4, 7) with Italy less than 90 seconds behind in total time.

Cosmas Ndeti: won Boston

As usual, selecting the best male marathoner of the year again became a challenge. Plaatjes' Stuttgart gold medal, his Boston sixth, and an additional third at Houston are impressive indeed. Some might argue in favour of Ceron, however, whose victory at Rotterdam gave him an invitation to the December Fukuoka marathon, where his 2:08:51 win was also the year's fastest time.

He did not compete at the IAAF Championships, but during that period his 2:14:47 performance over a good Mexican field at the 2,300 m altitude of Mexico City was most impressive. It is probably the highest, fastest effort ever delivered, and raised considerable attention in view of the recent decision to hold the '97 IAAF World Championships in that city.

In terms of selecting the top world woman in the event for '93, the decision was far less difficult. The Chinese women simply were out of this world, with Wang Junxia perhaps even a cut above the best of them. This story began in Tianjin early in April, while the rest of the world was focusing on the European/Boston scene. The Tianjin marathon course has typically produced fast times, and is an out/back course from Minyuan Stadium. It has not been certified by an IAAF/AIMS-approved measurer, but has been generally presumed correct. Initial reports informing the world that an unprecedented 8 runners from the same nation had gone under 2:27:00 caused many to simply toss the results into their 'short course file' without another look. But the men's edition was won by Zhang Fukui in a perfectly reasonable 2:11:10.

Either the women were superbly fit, running the races of their lives, or else the men ran a different course. Well, both sexes ran the same route, and later in the year it became clear that 'Coach Ma's army' indeed had some superb athletes that had achieved new heights in performance. Wang's 2:24:07 at Tianjin was a Chinese record, and in depth of talent at the top level, no nation could match them. Interestingly, at Stuttgart, Chinese athletes focused on track events, but when the story broke that China would field a strong team to San Sebastián, rumours of a world record attempt ran rampant.

To the world coaching community, the excellent track performances by Chinese women from June through September made such thoughts seem silly, but nonetheless, China's women brought back the team title most handily, with Wang (2:28:16) and her team-mates taking the four top places. Spanish women placed 5, 6, and 7 for a very impressive second place team effort (the men hadn't fared badly, either, placing fourth).

The year ended with a race that typified the world marathon running scene. At Honolulu, close to 23,000 runners - as many from Asia as from the West - braved wind and rain, and mild temperatures to go the distance in sporting camaraderie. And at the front the battle among the elite was furious indeed. Korea's Lee Bong-ju, seventh in '92 and barely breaking 2:20:00, fought valiantly to keep pace with, and then in the final stages, edge ahead of a stellar group of seven Africans to win in a quick 2:13:16. Boston winner Cosmas Ndeti was only 24 seconds behind, with '92 winner Benson Masya winner relegated to eighth. Among the women, the perennial Dutch star Carla Beurskens notched her seventh victory; at age(less) 41, her 2:32:20 gave her the four fastest performances at this event. As the marathon ages gracefully, so do its participants!

Dionicio Ceron: propably the top man of 1993

Important World Marathons - Results Diary 1993

Date	*Venue*	*Men's Winner*	*Time*	*Women's Winner*	*Time*
3 Jan	Hanoi	Douglas Kurtis USA	2:39:14	Thi Teo Dong VIE	3:25:51
5 Jan	Tiberias	Leme Chengere ETH	2:17:30	Frith Van der Merwe RSA	2:39:11
10 Jan	Marrakech	El Maati Chaham Mar	2:11:55	Tammy Slusser USA	2:38:01
24 Jan	Houston	Frank Bjørkli NOR	2:13:21	Kristy Johnston USA	2:29:05
30 Jan	Kathmandu	Ieuan Ellis GBR	2:24:10	Carlene Wickham GBR	3:25:20
31 Jan	Hong Kong	Peter Handcock NZL	2:18:34	Zina Marchant GBR	2:41:20
31 Jan	Osaka	*Women only*		Junko Asari JPN	2:26:26
6 Feb	Las Vegas	Douglas Kurtis USA	2:18:55	Kathleen Smith USA	2:41:19
7 Feb	Long Beach	Brad Hawthorne USA	2:18:34	Linda Somers USA	2:38:42
7 Feb	Oita	Maurilio Castillo MEX	2:13:04	*Men only*	
7 Feb	Valencia	Leonid Shvetsov RUS	2:15:04	Mónica Pont ESP	2:35:30
14 Feb	Tokyo	Abebe Mekonnen ETH	2:12:00	*Men only*	
21 Feb	Sevilla	Vicente Antón ESP	2:14:37	Karen Macleod GBR	2:34:30
7 Mar	Los Angeles	Joseildo da Silva BRA	2:14:29	Lyubov Klochko UKR	2:39:49
7 Mar	Nagoya	*Women only*		Kamila Gradus POL	2:27:38
14 Mar	Barcelona	Volmir Herbstrith BRA	2:13:25	Emma Scaunich ITA	2:36:16
14 Mar	Hong Kong	Cheung Yankwei HKG	2:43:56	Susan Detleefs RSA	3:16:08
14 Mar	Otsu	Michael O'Reilly GBR	2:11:01	*Men only*	
14 Mar	Puteaux	Chouki Achour ALG	2:13:43	Adriana Andreescu ROM	2:34:38
20 Mar	Cape Town	Josiah Thugwane RSA	2:14:25	Sonja Laxton RSA	2:43:01
21 Mar	Gyeongju	Kim Wan-ki KOR	2:09:25	Chung Young-im KOR	2:45:52
21 Mar	Vigarano	Marcello Curioni ITA	2:15:37	Maura Bulzoni ITA	3:00:41
27 Mar	Naaldwijk	Marnix Goegebeur BEL	2:13:27	Ágota Farkas HUN	2:37:11
4 Apr	Tianjin	Zhang Fukui CHN	2:11:10	Wang Junxia CHN	2:24:07
18 Apr	Brasilia	Clair Wathier BRA	2:21:40	Cleusa Irineu BRA	2:47:31
18 Apr	Canberra	Gerard Barrett AUS	2:22:20	Joanne Cowan AUS	2:42:00
18 Apr	Hannover	Kurt Stenzel GER	2:13:25	Birgit Jerschabek GER	2:30:34
18 Apr	London	Eamonn Martin GBR	2:10:50	Katrin Dörre GER	2:27:09
18 Apr	Rotterdam	Dionicio Ceron MEX	2:11:06	Anne van Schuppen HOL	2:34:15
18 Apr	Santa Rosa	José Villagra ARG	2:23:53	Nelida Olivet ARG	2:48:12
18 Apr	Wien	Carlos Patricio POR	2:11:00	Bente Moe NOR	2:38:21
19 Apr	Boston	Cosmas Ndeti KEN	2:09:33	Olga Markova RUS	2:25:27
24 Apr	Beograd	Jacob Ngunzu KEN	2:16:09	Suzana Ciric YUG	2:40:27
24 Apr	Kaliningrad	Andrey Tarasov RUS	2:12:57	Firiya Sultanova RUS	2:32:11
25 Apr	Madrid	Martin Vrábel SVK	2:16:13	Alzira Lario ESP	2:43:28
25 Apr	Paris	Leszek Beblo POL	2:10:46	Mitsuyo Yoshida JPN	2:29:16
25 Apr	Santiago	Antonio Aros CHI	2:15:04	Galina Gurianova RUS	2:51:41
25 Apr	Torino	Walter Durbano ITA	2:11:13	Emma Scaunich ITA	2:34:17
25 Apr	Worben	Thierry Constantin SUI	2:14:07	Elisabeth Krieg SUI	2:41:53
1 May	Rotorua	David Rush NZL	2:21:30	Maree Turner NZL	2:39:48
2 May	Pittsburgh	Abel Gisemba KEN	2:16:55	Lizanne Bussières CAN	2:35:39
2 May	Vancouver	Hayashi Murozumi JPN	2:18:37	Enikö Fehér HUN	2:47:27
9 May	Budapest	Tibor Bárdos HUN	2:25:27	Sofia Sotiriadou GRE	2:54:57
9 May	Munchen	Gidamis Shahanga TAN	2:14:28	Fatima Neves POR	2:39:34
16 May	Cleveland	Donald Janicki USA	2:11:39	Lyubov Klochko UKR	2:34:47
23 May	Hamburg	Richard Nerurkar GBR	2:10:57	Gabriela Wolf GER	2:34:36
23 May	København	Stanis Cembrzynski POL	2:22:58	Tatyana Forminych RUS	2:54:12
26 May	Bucuresti			Cristina Pomacu ROM	2:37:47
26 May	Sofia			Rumyana Panowska BUL	2:38:25
30 May	Bilbao	Francisco Villamiriel ESP	2:18:00	Josefa Cruz ESP	2:40:34
30 May	Vladimir	Ivan Selichev RUS	2:17:52	Tatyana Goncharova RUS	2:50:12
5 Jun	Stockholm	Daniel Mbuli RSA	2:16:30	Grete Kirkeberg NOR	2:37:58
6 Jun	Melbourne	Jerry Modiga RSA	2:15:07	Dominique Rembert FRA	2:44:22
13 Jun	Caen	Allaoua Khellil ALG	2:13:35	Irina Sklyarenko UKR	2:41:59
13 Jun	Enschede	Jan Tau RSA	2:12:19	Weronika Troxler POL	2:44:33
17 Jun	Narbonne	*Women only*		Elena Javornik SLO	2:42:58

20 Jun	Narbonne	Davide Milesi ITA	2:18:42	*Men only*	
19 Jun	Duluth	Douglas Kurtis USA	2:16:38	Lorraine Hochella USA	2:34:46
26 Jun	Lausanne	Nikolay Tabak UKR	2:19:51	Franziska Moser SUI	2:42:06
26 Jun	Praha	Petr Klimes TCH	2:19:38	Nursiya Bagmanova RUS	2:55:43
27 Jun	Rio de Janeiro	João Batista Pacau BRA	2:20:01	Nerce Freitas Da Costa BRA	2:54:04
11 Jul	Brugge	Marnix Goegebeur BEL	2:13:26	Yelena Sipatova RUS	2:41:01
17 Jul	Buffalo	Kennedy Manyisa KEN	2:12:19	Noriko Kawaguchi JPN	2:37:47
18 Jul	Gold Coast	Sean Quilty AUS	2:15:31	Eriko Asai JPN	2:29:29
25 Jul	Blumenau	Luis Dos Santos BRA	2:12:15	Arlete Soares Adao BRA	2:43:58
25 Jul	Noumea	Hassan Sebtaoui FRA	2:23:21	Sylviane Geffray FRA	2:51:30
1 Aug	Arusha	Benedict Ako TAN	2:13:46	Blanka James TAN	2:49:59
7 Aug	Helsinki	Martin Fíz ESP	2:12:47	Anne Jääskeläinen FIN	2:43:32
7 Aug	Omsk	Eduard Tukhbatulin RUS	2:13:02	Yelena Razdrogina RUS	2:38:20
14/15 Aug	Stuttgart	Mark Plaatjes USA	2:13:57	Junko Asari JPN	2:30:03
22 Aug	Reykjavik	Ceslovas Kundrotis LIT	2:17:06	Elisabet Singer AUT	2:55:07
29 Aug	Mexico City	Dionicio Ceron MEX	2:14:47	Maricarmen Diaz MEX	2:43:16
29 Aug	Sapporo	Tadesse Gebre ETH	2:15:34	Nobuko Fujimura JPN	2:33:10
4 Sep	Lille	Csaba Szücs HUN	2:14:24	Alevtina Naumova RUS	2:36:50
4 Sep	Moskva	Yuriy Kazmin RUS	2:20:09	Tatyana Forminych RUS	2:44:50
11 Sep	Vilnius	Alek Rimashevsky LIT	2:25:25	Gailute Keliuotiene LIT	3:01:25
12 Sep	Bruxelles	Ronny Ligneel BEL	2:16:14	Véronique Collard BEL	2:44:29
19 Sep	Heraklion	Ben Khalifa TUN	2:24:53	Sirye Eichelmann EST	2:49:49
19 Sep	Montreal	Marek Adamski POL	2:15:19	Alla Dudayeva RUS	2:43:26
26 Sep	Amsterdam	Kenichi Suzuki JPN	2:11:56	Yoshiko Yamamoto JPN	2:29:12
26 Sep	Berlin	Xolile Yawa RSA	2:10:57	Renata Kokowska POL	2:26:20
26 Sep	Warszawa	Julius Mtibani TAN	2:20:26	Praskovya Grigorenko BLS	2:55:25
2 Oct	Tyumen	Vyach Endyuskin RUS	2:18:30	Garifa Kuku KZK	2:47:50
3 Oct	Denver	Juan Salvador MEX	2:19:32	Emma Cabrera MEX	2:41:12
3 Oct	Kosice	Wieslaw Palcynski POL	2:14:11	Yelena Plastinina UKR	2:42:11
3 Oct	Lyon	Mohamed Salmi ALG	2:13:09	Christel Rogiers BEL	2:34:04
3 Oct	St. Paul	Ed Eyestone USA	2:14:34	Lisa Weidenbach USA	2:33:38
10 Oct	Appleton	Sean Wade NZL	2:19:45	Tamara Karlyukova RUS	2:39:03
10 Oct	Eindhoven	Mohamed Salmi ALG	2:12:47	Liesbeth van Ast HOL	2:40:57
10 Oct	Venezia	Artur Castro BRA	2:10:06	Elena Javornik SLO	2:37:27
17 Oct	Beijing	Hu Gangjun CHN	2:10:57	Li Yemei CHN	2:30:36
17 Oct	Detroit	Peter Maher CAN	2:19:53	Amy Legacki USA	2:43:07
17 Oct	Frankfurt	Stephan Freigang GER	2:11:53	Sissel Grottenberg NOR	2:36:50
17 Oct	Reims	Vincent Rousseau BEL	2:09:13	Judit Nagy HUN	2:32:07
24 Oct	Auckland	Kerry Rodger NZL	2:19:58	Raewyn Rodger NZL	2:46:17
24 Oct	Carpi	Graziano Calvaresi ITA	2:11:49	Marian Freriks HOL	2:39:53
24 Oct	Columbus	Brad Hudson USA	2:16:31	Jennifer Martin USA	2:39:17
24 Oct	Echternach	Ceslovas Kundrotas LIT	2:13:28	Zinaida Semyonova RUS	2:37:15
24 Oct	Essen	Salvatore Di Dio GER	2:17:27	Czeslawa Mentlewicz POL	2:43:38
24 Oct	Washington	Dominique Bariod FRA	2:23:56	Kelly Ebert USA	2:48:41
25 Oct	Dublin	John Treacy IRL	2:14:40	Cathy Shurn IRL	2:38:14
31 Oct	Chicago	Luis Dos Santos BRA	2:13:14	Ritva Lemettinen FIN	2:33:18
31 Oct	San Sebastián	Richard Nerurkar GBR	2:10:03	Wang Junxia CHN	2:28:16
7 Nov	Cesano Boscone	Igor Sidorenko RUS	2:18:28	Ornella Cadamuro ITA	2:41:11
9 Nov	Jerusalem	Hassan Sebtaoui Mar	2:25:53	Dominique Rembert FRA	3:03:52
14 Nov	New York	Andrés Espinosa MEX	2:10:04	Uta Pippig GER	2:26:24
21 Nov	St. Louis	Jo Leuchtmann USA	2:20:46	Karlene Herrell USA	2:50:34
21 Nov	Tokyo	*Women only*		Valentina Yegorova RUS	2:26:40
28 Nov	Lisboa	Saïd Ermili Mar	2:12:29	M Manuela Machado POR	2:31:31
5 Dec	Fukuoka	Dionicio Ceron MEX	2:08:51	*Men only*	
5 Dec	Sacramento	Jerry Lawson USA	2:10:27	Linda Somers USA	2:34:11
6 Dec	Calvia	Ian Bloomfield GBR	2:17:44	Yelena Sipatova RUS	2:42:09
9 Dec	Palermo	Boay Akonay TAN	2:13:52	Valeria Colpo ITA	2:48:30
12 Dec	Honolulu	Lee Bong-ju KOR	2:13:16	Carla Beurskens HOL	2:32:20

1993 ROAD RACE REVIEW

by David E. Martin

THE COMPLEX world of road racing had more than its usual share of incredible performances during 1993, and its increasingly global nature made it ever more difficult to document. It used to be that road racing - with its variety of trappings such as prize money, open and veterans divisions, wheelchair sections, and accompanying commercial expositions held in a prominent hotel - was virtually non-existent in the former Communist bloc nations, relatively rare outside Europe and North America, and even then limited to the very largest races.

Not so any more, as road races - from road miles to marathons - from New York to Moscow and Hanoi - brought together both an invited field of the world's best athletes with the local community of runners of all ages and abilities. While the runners at the top of their game aspired to achieve world bests, the many thousands running behind them had a good time of another sort. Races such as the Peachtree 10K in Atlanta with a large portion of its 45,000 runners filling area hotels for a weekend of fun and fitness is but one example of how huge the economic impact of such athleticism can be on a local community economy.

The incredible depth of excellence at the more established road races continued unabated as more athletes from more nations were vying for financial rewards which, while similar to previous years, now seemed more difficult to obtain. Those athletes with the wisest strategy found it preferable to train very hard for a few months peak, and then back off to regroup and regain supreme fitness for another racing period. Thus, there tended to be brief winning streaks, followed by a relative disappearance, either due to rest, injury, burnout, or altered focus.

Occasionally, however, some of the truly talented athletes managed to alternate a focus on track or cross country during one period with a focus on road racing during a subsequent period. One good example is the American Lynn Jennings. She placed third at the World Cross Country Championships in March, won the Bay To Breakers race in May as well as the Freihofer's Women's Race in early June, and then switched to a mid-year track emphasis. She won her national 10K track championships in Eugene and eventually placed fifth in Stuttgart. From August through October she then focused entirely on road racing, remaining undefeated, with impressive wins at Flint (10M) in August, Alexandria (8K) in September, Providence (5K), New Orleans (10K), and Tulsa (15K) in October.

Her arch rival, Anne-Marie Letko, nearly nine years younger, followed the same strategy with good success. Although not as successful at the World Cross Country, she lowered her personal 10K track best by 49 seconds (second to Lynn at Eugene and eighth at Stuttgart). Earlier, during the spring road race season, her wins at Bermuda (10K and half marathon) and Spokane (an American record), gave a good hint that she was on the way to an excellent year.

During the summer, Letko duelled the German star Uta Pippig on both road and track. It was Pippig/Letko 1/2 at Peachtree in July, but Letko/Pippig 8/9 in the 10K Stuttgart track final. Then, in her fall road racing schedule, she was runner-up to Jennings at Flint and Alexandria, third at Boston and Tulsa. Pippig, however, remained a notch above her at year's end, with her impressive victories at Boulder, Davenport, Atlanta, Pittsburgh and Chula Vista culminating in her New York City marathon personal best. Unfortunately, Pippig and Jennings never met on the roads.

Brazil's Carmen de Oliveira put the South American continent on the map with her Gasparilla victory early in the year, runner-up at the Boston and Tulsa races, and third at Davenport. She also placed an impressive third and seventh at the Boston and Tokyo Women's marathons. And Colleen de Reuck represented South Africa extremely well with her victories at Den Haag in April, Falmouth in August, Philadelphia in September, and other fine performances at San Francisco and Providence (2nd), Boulder (4th), and Davenport, Boston, and Tulsa (5th).

From the start of the year, at least for the men, it was clear that the African dimension would be prominent, as particularly Ethiopians, Kenyans, and South Africans dominated in both numbers and quality. The richest prize ever offered in all of athletics went to Ethiopia's Abebe Mekonnen, who focused for the better part of a year on trying to beat the heat, humidity, and travel challenge posed by competing in the Bob Hasan 10K race in Jakarta.

He ran a new world road best of 27:40, lowering Arturo Barrios' existing record by one second as he watched helpless from the vantage point of second place (28:01). Mekonnen took the US $25,000 first prize plus US$ 500,000 bonus put up by the organizers. While Derartu Tulu posted a fine 32:10 to win the women's division, her effort went scarcely noticed.

Philemon Hanneck of Zimbabwe was a star whose brilliance was perhaps a bit brighter than the rest. Based in Texas and thus closer to the lucrative USA road racing scene, he started the year out superbly with a warm-up 13:26 at the Los Angeles Rogaine 5K - a 13 second margin over an excellent international field. Three weeks later he journeyed 150km further south, to Carlsbad, challenged many of the same athletes over the same distance, and this time extended his margin of victory to 24 seconds with an even faster 13:22. That remained the year's fastest time.

However, one week before Carlsbad, he flew to New Orleans for the Crescent City Classic, challenging a field particularly loaded with superb Kenyan talent. His convincing 21 second victory (27:45) over William Koech would remain the fastest point-to-point 10K mark for the year. Later, he won again, this time in September at the downhill 10K Pittsburgh Great Race - again with a huge margin (28:14 compared to Eddy Hellebuyck's 28:35). He raced elsewhere as well, but this gives a flavour for his fitness during an incredible year.

To be sure, other athletes stood out with brilliant performances. There was Namibia's Lucketz Swartbooi, who established himself as a world-class marathoner with his third place 2:09:57 at Boston and his Stuttgart silver medal. However, on the roads he was also deadly serious, with victories at the Philadelphia and Sapporo half marathons, and at Tulsa.

There also was Arturo Barrios, winner at the altitude race in Boulder and also at Spokane. Belgium's Vincent Rousseau won the IAAF World Half Marathon Championships in Bruxelles and this prepared him for his wonderful new Belgian marathon national record for the marathon at Reims (2:09:13) a few weeks later. Second in that IAAF race was Australia's Steve Moneghetti, who had earlier tied with Ethiopia's Tadesse Gebre in the Gold Coast half marathon in a literal photo-finish 61:49. Moneghetti had been at the top level since January, with his Tokyo City (half) marathon victory.

The Association of International Marathons and Road Races (AIMS) topped 100 members as it clearly established itself after ten years as the most influential non-IAAF group uniting the sport of road racing together. Virtually all of the major marathons, and a few road races, have linked together organisationally for the betterment of race conditions and management.

Through close co-operation with the IAAF to follow federation guidelines, and particularly through their global wealth of expertise in everything from course measurement/certification to medical care of participants, athletes participating in AIMS events have had better racing conditions than ever before. Other road race circuits of a more regional nature have also contributed greatly to encouraging a high standard of event administration, safety for participants, and in many instances a lucrative prize structure (cash, cars, and more) for those elite who capture the top awards.

One of the better known of these circuits is the North American Association of Road Racing Athletes ARRA), which finished its 13th year of linking the top dozen or so road races in that region together.

Other smaller series, linked together by a single sponsor, such as the BUPA Series of road races in Britain during the second half of the year, contributed substantially to an increased vitality of road racing. If nothing else, the huge participation of serious fitness athletes, often numbering in the tens of thousands at the larger road races, has provided a huge base of spectator support for other aspects of athletics such as the major track meetings.

The additional impact of increased physical fitness among all these participating citizens of their respective nations is also noteworthy.

1993 ROAD RACE DIARY

By Dr. David E. Martin

Date	Venue	Race	Men's winner	Women's winner
24 Jan	Tokyo	1/2 Mar	Steve Moneghetti AUS 60:08	Elana Meyer RSA 67:22
24 Jan	Jakarta	Bob Hasan 10K	Addis Abebe ETH 27:40 WB	Derartu Tulu ETH 32:10
27 Feb	Tampa	Gasparilla 15K	Val Dos Santos BRA 42:41	Carmen de Oliveira BRA 49:03
14 Mar	Lisboa	1/2 Mar (short)	Sammy Lelei KEN 59:24	Nadezhda Ilyina RUS 69:47
14 Mar	Jacksonville	River Run 15K	Benson Masya KEN 44:00	Gwyn Coogan USA 51:26
20 Mar	New Orleans	Crescent City 10K	Philemon Hanneck ZIM	Judi St. Hilaire USA 31:56
27 Mar	Mobile	Azalea 10K	William Koech KEN 28:06	Wilma van Onna HOL 32:07
28 Mar	Carlsbad	Carlsbad 5K	Philemon Hanneck ZIM 13:22	Shelly Steely USA 15:36
3 Apr	Den Haag	City-City 1/2 Mar	Benson Masya KEN 60:24 CR	Colleen de Reuck RSA 70:50
3 Apr	Milano	Stramilano1/2 Mar	Moses Tanui KEN 59:47 WB	Rosanna Munerotto ITA 71:07
4 Apr	Berlin	1/2 Mar	Carsten Eich GER 60:34 CR	Päivi Tikkanen FIN 72:30
4 Apr	Washington	Cherry Blossom 10M	William Sigei KEN 46:29	Judi St. Hilaire USA 52:27
10 Apr	Paderborn	Österlauf 10K	Carsten Eich GER 27:47	Yelena Vyazova UKR 32:10
18 Apr	Washington	Sallie Mae 10K	Simon Chemwoiyo KEN 28:10	Gladys Ondeyo KEN 32:05
24 Apr	New York	Trevira 10M	Simon Chemwoiyo KEN 46:27	Inna Pushkaryova RUS 55:18
2 May	Spokane	Bloomsday 12K	Arturo Barrios MEX 33:55	Anne-Marie Letko USA 39:19
16 May	Cleveland	Revco 10K	German Silva MEX 28:04 CR	Lisa Ondieki AUS 31:53 CR
16 May	San Francisco	Bay/Breakers 12K	Ismael Kirui KEN 33:42 WB	Lynn Jennings USA 39:14
31 May	Boulder	Bolder 10K	Arturo Barrios MEX 29:04	Uta Pippig GER 33:39
5 Jun	Albany	Freihofer's 5K	Women only	Lynn Jennings USA 15:35
19 Jun	Peoria	Steamboat 4M	Martin Pitayo MEX 17:53	Carolyn Schuwalow AUS 20:21
27 Jun	Portland	Cascade 15K	Sammy Lelei KEN 43:17	Carolyn Schuwalow AUS 49:16
4 Jul	Atlanta	Peachtree 10K	Thomas Osano KEN 28:06	Uta Pippig GER 32:15
11 Jul	Utica	Boilermaker 15K	Thomas Osano 43:39 =CR	Gitte Karlshøj DEN 51:07
18 Jul	Gold Coast	1/2 Mar	Steve Moneghetti AUS 61:48 & Tadesse Gebre ETH 61:48	Kaori Kumura JPN 70:40
24 Jul	Davenport	Bix 7M	Thomas Osano KEN 32:10	Uta Pippig GER 36:27
14 Aug	Asbury Park	10K Classic	Simon Karori KEN 28:22	Wilma van Onna HOL 32:52
22 Aug	Falmouth	7.1M Road Race	Simon Karori KEN 32:30	Colleen de Reuck RSA 36:42
28 Aug	Flint	Bobby Crim 10M	Alejandro Cruz MEX 47:05	Lynn JenningsUSA 52:53
28 Aug	Durban	South Run 1/2 Mar	Michael Kidane ETH 61:06	Zola Pieterse RSA 71:49
22 Aug	Glasgow	1/2 Mar	Mark Flint GBR 61:56	Tatyana Pozdnyakova UKR 73:14
6 Sep	New Haven	Labor Day 20K	Simon Karori KEN 59:12	Gordon Bakoulis USA 70:37
12 Sep	Alexandria	Women's 8K		Lynn Jennings USA 25:24
19 Sep	Philadelphia	1/2 Mar	Lucketz Swartbooi NAM 61:26	Colleen de Reuck RSA 70:26
19 Sep	South Shields	GN Run 1/2 Mar	Moses Tanui KEN 60:15	Tecla Lorupe KEN 72:55
25 Sep	Birmingham	Midland Run 10K	Paul Davies-Hale GBR 28:37	Tecla Lorupe KEN 32:38
26 Sep	Pittsburgh	Great Race 10K	Philemon Hanneck ZIM 28:14	Uta Pippig GER 31:52
3 Oct	Bruxelles	IAAF 1/2 Mar	Vincent Rousseau BEL 61:06	Conceição Ferreira POR 70:07
11 Oct	Boston	Tufts Women's 10K		Lynn Jennings USA 32:02
17 Oct	Chula Vista	Barrios 10K	Philemon Hanneck ZIM 28:23	Uta Pippig GER 32:17 CR
17 Oct	Providence	Downtown 5K	Michal Bartoszak POL 13:42	Lynn Jennings USA 15:19
30 Oct	Tulsa	Tulsa Run 15K	Lucketz Swartbooi NAM 44:38	Lynn Jennings USA 49:47
21 Nov	Melbourne	Olympic Dream 10K	Gary Staines GBR 28:29	Carolyn Schuwalow AUS 32:48
31 Dec	São Paulo	São Silvestre 15K	Simon Chemwoiyo KEN 43:20	Helen Kimaiyo KEN 50:26

CR = Course Record, WB = World Best

Ultramarathon summary 1993

By Andy Milroy

NINETEEN NINETY-TWO had been a watershed year for ultra running in many ways and the trends continued in 1993. The 100km, as the sport's flagship, developed further, with increasing strength in depth, particularly among the women. The other major strand, the 24 hours, is progressively emulating the 100km's development in terms of high profile events and status.

Each year the IAU World Challenge 100km grows in stature. There had been 12 national federation teams in Palamos in 1992; at Torhout there were 22 men's and 10 women's teams! The strength in depth was the greatest yet seen – 21 men under seven hours and five women under eight hours. The winner, Konstantin Santalov (RUS) retained his title with a fine 6:26:26 and after a long tussle, Carolyn Hunter-Rowe (GBR) held off Valentina Shatyayeva (RUS) by 20 seconds to win the women's race in 7:27:19.

The first major event after the World Challenge was the European 100km Championships at Winschoten, Holland. Crowds of 40,000 watched Santalov retain his crown in 6:25.52 and Marta Vass (HUN) at last claim an international title with 7:43:06. The following weekend at Amiens, Santalov lined up for another 100km and again proved too strong for the opposition producing a phenomenal 6:23:15 to win.

The top 100km runners seldom met head-to-head when fully fit. Valmir Nunes (BRA) won the first IAU North American 100km championship and finished ahead of Santalov in two of his four 100km outings, and Jean-Paul Praet (BEL) also beat his Russian rival once.

Another Russian, Aleksandr Masarygin dominated the early part of the season, running 6:20:59 in January and 6:22:19 in April. Santalov dropped out of both races and there seemed to be a question mark over his fitness. He answered these questions in Moscow in May when he ran 6:15:17. (the course, a short loop, seems to have been measured by steel tape) However in May he finished second to Nunes in Madrid and the following month dropped out of the Night of Flanders 100km with chest pains. Praet won in 6:28:12.

Santalov had a mixed season until it came to the major championships so my rankings would be: 1, Santalov, 2, Masarygin, 3, Praet, 4, Nunes. (A record five men ran under 6:30 9n 1993).

In 1993 there were at least 112 male performances under seven hours by some 72 runners, a further increase on the year before, itself a record. Nineteen were from Russia so their strength in depth shows no signs of weakening.

However, it was perhaps the women's performances that were to make the greatest impact on 100km running in 1993. Valentina Lyakhova (RUS) ran 7:44:43 in April, then in May, Carolyn Hunter-Rowe ran &:34:54 to establish herself as the leading contender for the world title. Previously in March she had set world track bests for 30 miles, 50km and 40 miles. At Torhout she confirmed her status with a very controlled win.

The leading American, Ann Trason, was absent from that, but made one of her rare forays into European 100km running at Amiens in September, apparently hoping to break 7:30. She did so with a vengence – 7:09:44, a new world road best. Lyakhova ran 7:31:25 behind her.

Ranking the top women is also difficult. Trason ran some 17 minutes faster than anyone else. Lyakhova and Shatyayeva were consistent, both having performances under 7:45, and Vass won the European title as well as beating Shatyayeva at the Night of Flanders. Hunter-Rowe's two fine performances and success in the competitive heat of Torhout clinches her no. 1 status just ahead of Trason, with Shatyayeva third and Lyakhova and Vass fourth and fifth respectively.

Comparatively the women's improvement in terms of strength in depth was again greater than the men's, although it must be remembered that they were starting form a much lower base level. Thirteen women ran under 8 hours, 35 under 8:30 (10 and 29 in '92).

At 24 hours Nikolay Safin (RUS) produced the best performance yet seen indoors with 275.576km in February with Valeriy Goubar second with 260.323km. The IAU European Challenge at Basel in Switzerland had the greatest ever strength in depth with 39 runners over 200km. Safin won with 264.718km from Helmut Dreyer (GER) 259.265km and Milan Tohovcak (CZE) 257.728km. Unfortunately the men's race was marred by a first in Ultrarunning. The winner was subsequently disqualified for failing the doping controls, apparently for using steroids.

The women's race promised to be the greatest ever and despite the fact that a number of notable runners were not their best there were some excellent performances. Sigrid Lomsky the 51 year-old German set an absolute world best of 243.657km (the first woman over 150 miles) and behind her were fellow Germans, Helga Backhaus (223.647km) and Anna Dyck (214.980km). Three weeks later Backhaus and Dyck produced even better marks at Apeldoorn in Holland – 226.330km and 215.888km respectively.

Jean-Pierre Guyomarch continued to dominate the event in France with 260.024km at the French 24 Hour Championships at Fleurbaix in August and Kevin Setnes produced a US 24 Hour road best of 258.181 at the US Championships, with Tom Possert close behind on 254.793km. Another US 100km team member, Sue Ellen Trapp, won the women's event, setting a US road best of 233.816.

The US event offered prize money, as did a number of 24 Hour races for the first time. The Madrid 24 Hours in October was one and attracted Konstantin Santalov. Running a very controlled race, he won easily with a personal best of 260.750km. A month later in the oldest of the road 24 Hour races, Niort, Seigi Arita won in a Japanese record of 255.775km to become the first man from his country to set a world class 24 Hour performance.

Without a World Challenge 24 Hour event choosing a world no. 1 for 1993 is difficult. A shadow must be cast over Safin's 275km by his subsequent disqualification. Arguably the best performer, simply in terms of distance is Santalov. His performance in Madrid indicates there is more to come. Undoubtedly he is the best ultrarunner in the world at the moment. There can be no dispute that Sigrid Lomsky is the world's top female performer for 1993.

Surgères in France was once again the venue for the top men's 48 Hour mark. Gilbert Mainix surpassed Jean-Gilles Boussiquet's French mark with 423.426km for third place on the all-time list. The top women's mark came at the end of the year in California, USA. Sue Ellen Trapp, going from strength to strength, produced a world 48 Hour best of 360.109km. Only Hilary Walker, on the track, has ever run further.

Boussiquet set the best 6 Day mark at the La Rochelle indoor race with 964.2km. Interestingly Santalov was at the race and expressed an interest in taking part this year. He won a 400km road race last year.

For those seeking a still longer race, there were 1000 mile and 13000 mile races at Ward's Island, New York, USA, from September 15 onwards. István Sipos (HUN) won, setting a world best for 2000km en route, and covering the 1000 miles in 12:22:52:37. The only other finishers were women – Antana Locs (CAN) and Suprabha Beckjord (USA). But for those keen on 'serious' distance running there was the Trans-America race, over 4700km long. The winner was Ray Bell (USA) 486h41:08, some 16 hours ahead of Pat Farmer (USA) and Lorna Michael (USA), the first woman, in third.

The London to Brighton was a repeat of the year before when Stephen Moore (GBR) and Russell Crawford (RSA) battled it out for much of the race. Again Moore proved the stronger, winning in 6:07:22, some four minutes ahead, with another South African, Stewart Peacock, in third. Carolyn Hunter-Rowe totally dominated the women's event, producing the best ever time of 6:34:10 – despite the fact that the current course is the longest ever used, some 88.514km.

The Comrades was awaited with considerable interest since it was the first time it had been open to foreign runners for some time. The IAU entered an International team and one of its members, Charly Doll (GER), confounded the South African pundits by winning from the front in 5:39:41, ahead of Theopolous Rafiri and Mahlala Mahololi. The first woman was Tilda Tearle in 6:54:34.

The longest of the classics, the Spartathlon, was won by Rune Larsson (SWE) who saves his best performances for the event. His time of 26:57:12 placed him 45 minutes ahead of Marcel Foucat (FRA) with Milan Furin (SLO) third. Sigrid Lomsky (GER) was the first woman in 32:34:32 with Marie Bertrand (FRA) second.

Perhaps the most fascinating result of the year occurred in the Leadville 100 mile trail race held in August in the USA. It was won by a Tarahumara Indian, Victoriano Churro, with another, Cerrildo Chacarito, second. The winner was 55 years-old and had apparently done no specific training. However an American group had spent some time getting them used to the course. The Leadville race was part of an ongoing programme of introducing the Tarahumaras to conventional distance racing.

The Far East continues to be a growth area. The Japanese 100km community is, of course, getting geared up for the World Challenge event to be held at Lake Saroma in June when they expect at least 2000 competitors. New Chinese and Japanese 24 Hour track marks were set in the Hong Kong 24 Hours and a major 24 Hour track event is planned for Guangzhou, the capital of Guangdong Province, China, in April 1994. Tomoya Takaishi (JPN) took on the longest event of the year, the Trans-Am, and finished fifth.

OBITUARIES 1993

Evelyne ADAMS (USA) (b. 10 Sep 1909) on 20 April in Oceanside, California. née Hall, she was the 1932 Olympic silver medallist at 80mh, sharing the world record at 11.7 with winner Babe Didriksen. She won the AAU 80mh title in 1930, had a 100m pb of 12.0 '32. and ran on the Illinois Women's AA team that set a world record of 49.4 for 4x110y in 1932. She was the women's coach-manager at the 1951 Pan American Games.

Weems A. BASKIN Jr (USA) on May 10 in Columbia, South Carolina, at the age of 88. He won the 1927 NCAA title at 110mh for Auburn University in 14.9 and was head coach at Georgia for 7 years, Mississippi for 9 years and South Carolina for 21 years.

Uwe BEYER (Germany) (b. 14 Apr 1945) on 15 April of a heart attack while on holiday in Turkey. Ranked in the world top ten hammer throwers each year 1964-73, he was also prominent in recent year as a veteran, winning the world M45 title in 1991. 1971 European champion, having taken bronze medals at the 1964 Olympics and at the 1966 Europeans. He failed to qualify for the 1968 Olympic final, was 4th at the 1972 Olympics and 5th at the 1974 Europeans. At the European Cup he was 2nd in 1965 and 1970 and 3rd in 1967. He was FRG champion for eight successive years 1964-71, set 12 national records, from 64.48 in 1964 to 74.90 in 1971 and made 32 international appearances 1964-74.
Progression (position on world lists) at HT: 1963- 59.93, 1964- 68.09 (9), 1965- 67.84 (8), 1966- 68.48 (5), 1967- 69.08 (5), 1968- 72.46 (3), 1969- 71.46 (6), 1970- 72.36 (4), 1971- 74.90 3), 1972- 73.88 (7), 1973- 73.10 (7), 1974- 71.04 (24), 1976- 74.90 (17), 1977- 68.25 (92), 1979- 64.26, 1981- 61.42, 1982- 58.10, 1983- 66.18, 1984- 63.52, 1985- 63.76, 1986- 58.54, 1990- 59.20, 1991- 58.44, 1992- 57.10.

Árpád BODÓ (Hungary) (b. 13 Mar 1933) on 30 June in Budapest. The first Hungarian to high jump 2 metres officially, in all he set seven national records with a best of 2.04 (1958). He was Hungarian champion 1957 and competed in 16 internationals 1955-60.

Ulrich BREMBACH (Germany) (b. 4 Feb 1936) on 2 August. Third in the GDR discus championships 1971, with a pb of 60.94m in 1968.

Edera CORDIALE (Italy) (b. 30 Jan 1920) later Gentile. Won the Olympic discus silver medal in 1948 and the European bronze in 1950. 14th at the 1952 Olympics, won nine Italian titles, 1943 and 1946-53, and set three Italian records, 43.56 '47, 45.02 '48 and 46.19 '50.

Gérard CÔTÉ (Canada) (b. 26 Jul 1913 St Barnabé, Québec) in St Hyacinthe, Québec. Four times winner of the Boston Marathon, 1940, 1943-4 and 1948, he would have been a prime contender for Olympic honours but for World War II; he was 17th in 1948. He was also AAU champion by winning the Yonkers marathon in 1940, 1943 and 1946; Canadian champion in 1942-3, 1948 and 1954 and 11th in the 1950 Empire Games.
Annual progression at marathon (position on world list): 1936- 2:42:23, 1937- 2:43:40, 1938- 2:37:16 (9), 1939- 2:35:33 (15), 1940- 2:28:29 (3), 1941- 2:33:42 (6), 1942- 2:39:59 (12), 1943- 2:28:26 (1), 1944- 2:31:51 (1), 1945- 2:54:06, 1946- 2:36:34 (6), 1947- 2:32:11 (4), 1948- 2:31:02 (1=), 1949- 2:42:39, 1950- 2:51:59, 1951- 2:51:15.

Hans DEUTSCHLÄNDER (Germany) (b. 14 Feb 1926) on 29 September in Berlin. Three internationals 1951-4 and a German 2000m record of 5:19.2 (1952). Other bests: 1000m 2:26.0 (1953), 1500m 3:49.8 (1954), 3000m 8:23.6 (1952), 5000m 14:58.0 (1952).

John EDGINGTON (GB) (b. 5 Apr 1936). British international walker, 8th at 20km in the 1964 Olympics in his best ever time of 1:32:46.

Mihály ESZTERGOMI (Hungary) (b. 13 Jun 1912) on 25 November in Budapest. Competed 11 times for Hungary between 1933 and 1958, and was 21st in the 1952 Olympic marathon.. He was Hungarian champion 1949-50 and his personal bests were: 5000m 14:50.8 (1943), 10,000m 31:00.2 (1943), Mar 2:33:11 (1955).

Detlef GERSTENBERG (Germany) (b.5 Mar 1957 Eisenhüttenstadt) in January of cancer of the pancreas and hepatitis, allegedly brought on by the use of steroids and testosterone. He represented the GDR at the hammer, winning the 1975 European Juniors and placing 4th in

1978 and 6th in 1982 at the Europeans and 5th in 1980 Olympics. He set three GDR records: 78.94 in 1980 and 80.26 and 80.50 in 1984.
Progression (position on world lists) at HT: 1974- 61.58, 1975- 70.58 (45), 1976- 71.52 (48), 1977- 75.28 (13), 1978- 76.94 (6), 1979- 77.82 (5), 1980- 78.94 (7), 1982- 77.02 (15=), 1983- 76.50 (40), 1984- 80.50 (10).

Miguel Angel GÓMEZ (Spain) (b. 24 Apr 1968) on 6 April in a motorcycle accident. Spanish 200m champion 1989 and 1992, with a best of 20.76 when he won the silver medal at the 1991 Mediterranean Games. He set a Spanish junior record for 200m at 21.19 in 1987 and also ran 20.69w in 1991 with bests at 100m 10.54 '89, 10.43w '91 and 110mh 14.24 '87. He was 5th in the World Indoor 200m in 1991.

Ludmila HAVLICKOVÁ (Czech) (b. 10 Jul 1902). A pioneer of Czech athletics, she was the first Czechoslovak high jump champion in 1923, winning again in 1925, setting national records for HJ 1.37 (1925), LJ 4.56 (1922) and DT 28.31 (1925).

Peter HIGGINS (GB) (b.16 Nov 1928) on 8 September. At the 1956 Olympics he won a bronze medal at 4x400m, running a 46.3 third leg (Britain's fastest of the race), and was a semi-finalist at 400m, having run a pb 47.42 in his quarter-final. He was placed in the first three in the AAA 440y each year 1954-9, winning in 1957, and won a gold medal at 4x440y relay at the 1954 Commonwealth Games, when he was a semi-finalist at 440y.

Heikki HOLLMÉN (Finland) (b. 4 Jul 1966) committed suicide in Oulu on February 15. The Finnish discus champion 1991-2, his pb was 63.98 in April 1992. He had studied at Brigham Young University in the USA in 1987-8.

Maria JEIBMANN (Germany) (b. 9 Dec 1927) at Düsseldorf on 15 May. née Arenz. FRG champion at 400m 1959-61, she set national records at 56.3 in 1958 and 55.9 in a heat of the 1958 Europeans, with a pb of 55.6 (19162). She competed in 23 internationals 1951-63.

Prof. Dr. August KIRSCH (Germany) on 23 December at age 68. President of the DLV 1970-85, member of the IAAF Council from 1981, and president of the Organising Committee of the 1986 European Championships and 1993 World Championships in Stuttgart. A national 4x400m relay champion in 1948, he was a distinguished sports scientist.

Ferenc KLICS (Hungary) (b. 20 Jan 1924) on 25 April. A top ranked discus thrower for many years - 5th at the Olympics in 1948 and 1952, 7th in 1956 and 10th in 1960 and at the Europeans 4th in 1954 and 5th in 1958. He won nine Hungarian, two AAA (1949 and 1954) and three World Student titles, competed in 59 internationals for Hungary and set a European record with 55.79 at Budapest in 1954.
Progression (position on world lists) at DT: 1946- 45.53, 1947- 49.07 (12), 1948- 49.64 (14), 1949- 50.60 (12), 1950- 51.76 (10), 1951- 51.55 (6), 1952- 53.44 (2), 1953- 53.35 (5), 1954- 55.79 (3), 1956- 53.66 (17), 1957- 54.13 (14), 1958- 55.66 (14), 1959- 55.02 (16), 1960- 55.67 (21), 1961- 54.79 (33), 1962- 55.49 (29), 1963- 55.29 (32), 1964- 53.33 (98).

Erich KRUZYCKI (Germany) (b. 18 Feb 1911 Danzig) on 28 August. He had his best year in 1951 at the age of 40 when he was German champion at 10000m, won the São Paulo midnight race, and ran his pbs of 5000m 14:37.0 and 10000m 30:36.0. He won four World veterans titles (M65) in both 1977 and 1979.

Henri LABORDE (USA) (b. 11 Sep 1909 San Francisco) on September 16 in Portland, Oregon. Olympic discus silver medallist 1932 and went on to win NCAA and IC4A titles for Stanford University in 1933, when he was the year's top thrower.
Progression (position on world lists) at DT: 1931- 46.30 (19), 1932- 48.47 (7), 1933- 50.38 (1), 1934- 49.47 (6), 1935- 49.27 (8). pb SP 15.08 '32.

Lars LARSSON (Sweden) (b. 17 Jun 1911). At the 3000m steeplechase he was European champion in 1938 and 6th at the 1936 Olympics, when with 9:16.6 he set the first of three Swedish records for the event, improving to 9:10.8 in 1938 and 9:09.0 in 1939. He was Swedish champion each year 1936-40 and had a pb of 9:07.0 in 1940.
Progression (position on world lists) at 3000mSt: 1935- 9:25.4* (4), 1936- 9:14.6*/9:16.6 (7), 1937- 9:21.6 (6), 1938- 9:10.8 (2), 1939- 9:09.0 (4), 1940- 9:07.0 (2), 1941- 9:39.6 (16), 1942- 9:32.4 (13), 1943- 9:36.4 (11). * no water-jump. pb 5000m 14:58.0 '36.

Jimmy LuVALLE (USA) (b. 10 Nov 1912 Los Angeles) on 30 January in Te Anau, New Zealand. Having won the NCAA title at 440y in 1935 he was 2nd in the AAU, third in the US Olympic Trials and took the Olympic bronze at 400m in 1936 in a time of 46.84. Along with the other men who had run the individual 400m for the USA he was left out of the relay team.
Progression (position on world lists) at 400m (*

440y less 0.3 sec): 1931- 48.5* (26=), 1933- 46.9 (2), 1934- 47.1* (2), 1935- 47.1* (4), 1936-46.3 (2), 1937- 9:21.6 (6). Best 220y straight 20.8 (1934).

Séraphin MARTIN (France) (b. 2 Jul 1906) on April 22 aged 86. One of the top middle distance runners of his era, he ran a world record for 1000m 2:26.8 (1926) and for 800m in the French Championships of 1928, when his time of 1:50.6 compared to the previous best of 1:51.6 for 880y by Otto Peltzer (Ger). This was his third French 800m record, following 1:53.4 in 1926 and 1:52.8 in 1927. He also set French records twice at 1000m and 1500m, with bests of 2:26.0 (1927) and 3:54.6 (1926). He was 6th in 1928 and 7th in 1932 in the Olympic 800m, and was French champion at 800m 1927-9 and 1500m 1927.
Progression (position on world lists) at 800m: 1925- 1:57.6, 1926- 1:53.4 (5=), 1927- 1:52.8 (1), 1928- 1:50.6 (1), 1929- 1:54.0 (12=), 1930- 1:53.7 (11=), 1931- 1:56.3* (50=), 1932- 1:53.2 (13=).

John MORRISS (USA) (b. 23 Jul 1908) on 12 May in Houston. After placing 4th in the US trials for the 1932 Olympics he set two officially ratified world records for 110m hurdles at 14.4 in 1933, the first in Budapest on 12 August and the second when winning the World Student Games title in Torino on 8 September. He had earlier won the AAU title in 14.6, having won his heat in 14.3; although that was ratified as an American record it was not accepted by the IAAF due to 'incomplete information'. He was a graduate of Southwestern Louisiana and coached for 48 years.
Progression (position on world lists) at 110mh: 1929- 15.2y (35=), 1930- 14.7y (7=), 1931- 14.8y (15=), 1932- 14.4 (4=), 1933- 14.3 (4), 1934- 14.6 (11=), 1935- 14.3w (8=), 1936- 14.5 (20=).

Fritz MÜLLER (Germany) (b. 24 Dec 1914 Celle) on 10 August in Aachen. At pentathlon he won the World Student Games title in 1937 and 1939, was German champion in 1939 and 1941, and set German records and world bests with 3824 points in 1937 and 3667 in 1939 (3841 and 3843 on the 1985 tables). At the decathlon he was German champion in 1937, 1939 and 1941 and his best of 7267 points equates to 6793 on the 1985 tables. Other bests: 100m 10.8 (1937), 200m 21.7 (1939), LJ 7.22 (1937), JT 62.74 (1937).
Progression (position on world lists) at Dec: (1920 tables): 1934- 5975.065, (1934 tables): 1935- 6485 (12), 1936- 6232 non-consecutive days, 1937- 6991 (2), 1939- 7267 (1), 1941- 6920 (1).

Ursula NOCTOR (Ireland) (b. 21 Jan 1965) of cancer on April 4. pbs 10000m 34:16.4 '90, Marathon 2:39:25 '90.

Josef ODLOZIL (Czech) (b. 11 Nov 1938 Otrokovice) died on 10 September from injuries caused by head injuries suffered when he was attacked on 7 August in a discotheque in Domasov, near his weekend house in Moravia. He won a silver medal for 1500m at the 1964 Olympics, and after that married the great gymnast Vera Caslavská. He was 8th at 1500m in the 1968 Olympics and 2nd in the 1967 European Indoor 1500m, but at 800m in 1962 and 1500m in 1966 did not make European finals outdoors. Czechoslovakian champion at 800m 1960, 1962-3; 1500m 1964-7. He set a world record with 5:01.2 for 2000m in 1965 and set CS records: 1000m 2:18.6 (1965), 1500m 3:37.6 (1965), 1M 3:56.4 (1964, behind Peter Snell's WR 3:54.1) and 3:55.55 (1965).
Progression (position on world lists) at 1500m: 1958- 4:05.2, 1959- 4:05.4, 1960- 3:53.4, 1961- 3:47.4 (84=), 1962- 3:46.3 (74=), 1963- 3:43.6 (26=), 1964- 3:39.3 (8), 1965- 3:39.7 (6), 1966- 3:37.6 (4), 1967- 3:41.9 (25), 1968- 3:41.0 (32), 1969- 3:49.6. Other pbs: 400m 49.0 '60, 800m 1:48.2 '61.

Francis O'SULLIVAN (GB) (b. 9 May 1905) on 1 June. He was 13th in the 1938 European Championships at the marathon. In the AAA championships he was 3rd in 1936 and 2nd in 1938 and had a best time of 2:38:18 (1936).

Hubert PÄRNAKIVI (Estonia) (b.16 Oct 1932) on 28 October. He won two silver and one bronze medal in USSR championships and 28 Estonian national titles at five distances. Between 1952 and 1962 he set 10 Estonian records with pbs: 1500m 3:50.2 (1961), 3000m 8:12.2 (1959), 5000m 13:59.8 (1958), 10,000m 29:17.4 (1958), 3000mSt 8:54.4 (1958). In the first USSR v USA match in 1958 he won the last event, the 5000m, with a finishing burst to ensure victory for his team by two points.

John PENNEL (USA) (b. 25 Jul 1940 Memphis) died on 26 September at Santa Monica from cancer of the stomach. Set nine world records at the pole vault from 4.95m at Memphis on 23 Mar 1963 via the first 17ft clearance (17ft 0 3/4 in *5.20m*) at Coral Gables, Florida on 24 Aug 1963, to 5.44m at Sacramento on 21 Jun 1969, although only four of these were officially accepted. Such was the rate of progress of the world standard in the early days of the fibreglass pole, especially in 1963 when the record was broken or equalled ten times in all, that

recognition of several of his efforts was not applied for. He also set two world indoor bests in 1966. The Sullivan Award winner of 1963, he won both AAU and World Student Games titles in 1965. He disappointed at the Olympics, placing 11th in 1964 and 5th in 1968.
Progression (position on world lists) at pole vault: 1956- 3.42, 1957- 3.80, 1958- 4.14, 1959- 4.32, 1960- 4.58 (14=), 1961- 4.44 (61=), 1962- 4.67i/4.58 (25=), 1963- 5.20 (1), 1964- 5.09 (5), 1965- 5.18 (1), 1966- 5.35 (1), 1968- 5.35 (5=), 1969- 5.44 (1), 1970- 5.33 (7), 1971- 5.03i.

Negusse ROBA (Ethiopia) on 14 April at the age of 54. Celebrated coach of many of Ethiopia's top distance runners and head coach of the national team for 20 years.

Roger ROCHARD (France) (b. 20 Apr 1913) on 25 February. The European 5000m champion of 1934 in a French record time of 14:36.8, he made 19 international appearances for France 1931-8. He also set French records for 3000m with 8:36.2 in 1933, 8:28.6 in 1938 and 8:25.7 in 1941, the latter behind Raphaël Puzajon, with the same time. Rochard was French 5000m champion four times, 1931-2 and 1934-5.

Colin RIDGEWAY (Australia) (b. 19 Feb 1939) was shot dead by an intruder at his home in Dallas, Texas, USA on May 13. He had a high jump best of 2.14 in 1962, and was Australia's first 7 ft jumper. At the age of 17 he was 7th equal at the 1956 Olympics. Played both Australian Rules football for Carlton and was a kicker for the Dallas Cowboys at American Football in the 1960s. He had previously survived shooting by Mexican bandits several years ago. He had lived in the USA from 1960.

Henri SCHUBERT (Aus) on 10 July at the age of 80. Hugely respected coach of hundreds of leading athletes, such as Pam Ryan, Judy Pollock and Debbie Flintoff.

Dr **George SHEEHAN** (USA) on 1 November, aged 74, of prostate cancer at his home in Ocean Grove, New Jersey. A good miler at Manhattan College, he began running again in 1962 and at 50 set a world age best of 4:47 for the mile. He ran in 21 consecutive Boston Marathons and became one of running's most respected and widely read philosophers. A cardiologist, he gave up his medical practice in 1984 to concentrate on running, and his inspirational speaking and writing.

Janusz SIDLO (Pol) (b. 19 Jun 1933 Szopienice) on 2 August in Warsaw. Ranked in the world's top ten javelin throwers each year 1953-70, he competed in five Olympic Games though with only one medal: '52- dnq, '56- 2, '60- 8, '64- 4, '68- 7. He fared better in European Championships, winning in 1954 and 1958, third in 1969 and 7th in 1962 and 1966. He won 14 Polish titles, 1951-61, 1963, 1966 and 1969, and appeared in a record 61 internationals for Poland. He made a sensational improvement in 1953 in adding 6.88m to the Polish javelin record, throwing 80.15m, also a European record. He improved that with a world record 83.66 in 1956, and set three more national records with a best 14 years later at 86.22. He also set a record with five wins between 1951 and 1959 at the World Student Games.
Progression (position on world lists) at javelin: 1949- 53.09, 1950- 59.10, 1951- 67.88 (25), 1952- 68.42 (24), 1953- 80.15 (2), 1954- 79.03 (3), 1955- 80.07 (2), 1956- 83.66 (2), 1957- 82.98 (5), 1958- 81.97 (3), 1959- 85.56 (2), 1960- 85.14 (1), 1961- 82.12 (8), 1962- 80.98 (6), 1963- 82.27 (5), 1964- 85.09 (2), 1965- 85.50 (3), 1966- 84.86 (4), 1967- 82.96 (11), 1968- 84.40 (10), 1969- 83.80 (7), 1970- 86.22 (8), 1971- 79.26 (56=), 1972- 73.54, 1973- 74.48, 1983- 53.68, 1984- 56.68.

Anne SMITH (UK) (b. 31 Aug 1941 Amersham) on 9 November of a brain haemorrhage. After a British women's mile record of 4:44.2 in 1966, Smith set two world records for the 1

Anne Smith

mile in 1967: 4:39.2 to win the Surrey Championship at Wimbledon Park on 13 May (British record 4:21.0 for 1500m en route) and, the first mark officially ratified by the IAAF for the event, 4:37.0 to win the Southern title at Chiswick on 3 June, passing 1500m in a world record 4:17.3. In each of these races she won by a huge margin. Unfortunate that 1500m was not a championship distance when she was at her peak, at 800m she was 8th at the 1964 Olympics, having set a British record 2:04.8 in her semi-final. WAAA champion at 880y 1964-7, setting a British record in this race at 2:04.2 in 1966, in which year she also won the Commonwealth Games bronze medal. She competed in 12 internationals for Britain 1963-6. A PE teacher, she was coached by Gordon Pirie.
Progression (position on world lists) at 800m (y 880y), 1500m/1M: 1959- 2:15.9y, 1960- 2:12.7y, 1961- 2:13.8y, 5:30.3M; 1962- 2:24.9y, 1963- 2:07.0 (11=), 1964- 2:04.8 (12=), 1965- 2:05.3 (6), 4:46.3M (1); 1966- 2:03.2 (3), 4:30.7 (4)/4:44.2M (1); 1967- 2:04.4y (5=), 4:17.3 (2)/4:37.0M (1); 1968- 2:03.4 (11). pb 4540y 56.0 (1967).

Bernard Joseph **'Joe'_ SMITH** (USA) on 25 January. A 1.88m 6' 2" milkman, in 1942 he won the Boston marathon in 2:26:51.2, then the fastest ever time by a US marathoner. Five months earlier, in November 1941, he had won the 1941 Yonkers marathon in 2:36:06.3, He was also fifth in Boston in 1941 and 1949 in the AAU marathon in 1949,

Archie WILLIAMS (USA) (b. 1 May 1915 Oakland, California) on 24 June at Fairfax, California. He burst through in 1936 from a 49-second runner the previous year to 47.4 for 440y in April, 46.8 in May and a world record of 46.1 for 400m, running on to 440y in 46.5, in a heat at the NCAAs at Chicago on 19 June. He won the final in 47.0 and then won the Olympic Trials in 46.6 and the Olympic title in Berlin in 46.5 (46.66 on auto-timing). He was then a sophomore at the University of California at Berkeley and in this, his one great year, he ran 8 of the world's 12 fastest times at 400m (46.7 or better). At AAU Championships he was 3rd in 1936 and 6th in 1939. Having qualified as an engineer, he found it difficult to gain suitable employment due to the colour bar in the USA, but became a pilot, and spent 22 years in the US Air Force 1942-64, retiring as a lieutenant colonel. He then taught mathematics and computer science.
Progression (position on world lists) at 400m: 1935- 49+; 1936- 46.1 (1), 1937- 48.0* (24=), 1938- 47.0 (10), 1939- 47.3 (16=). pb 200m 21.4 '36.

Lorenz ZEILHOFER (Germany) (b. 8 Jul 1899) on 14 February. He was 2nd in the 1933 German marathon championship in 2:37:45, after 3rd in 1932.

OBITUARIES 1994

Robert BOBIN (France) (b. 2 Aug 1920) on 10 February. As a triple jumper he competed at the 1948 Olympics, was French champion in 1949 and 1950, and set three national record 1947-8, with a best of 14.65. He was the Technical Director of French athletics from 1958 to 1973, President of the French Federation 1987-93, and was elected a member of the IAAF Council in 1993.

Patrick EL MABROUK (France) (b. 10 Oct 1928 Talga, Algeria) on 3 February. Starting running in 1948, he won the first of five successive French 1500m titles in 1949, adding four at 800m: 1951, 1953-5. He set French records for 1500m in 1949 and 1952. From 1948 to 1955 he competed in 26 internationals for France, with the highlights 2nd in the 1950 Europeans and 5th in the 1952 Olympics at 1500m.
Progression (position on world lists) at 1500m: 1948- 3:51.1 (13=), 1949- 3:47.2 (5), 1950- 3:47.8 (5), 1951- 3:48.2 (5), 1952- 3:46.0 (6=), 1953- 3:48.2 (16=), 1954- 3:55.8. Other bests: 800m 1:50.1 (1951), 1000m 2:22.7 (1952), 1M 4:08.6 (1951), 2000m 5:24.6 (1951).

Jack (John Patrick) **METCALFE** (Australia) (b. 3 Feb 1912) in January. A great all-rounder, he set a world record for the triple jump with 15.78 in Sydney on 14 Dec 1935. At the 1936 Olympics he won the bronze medal in that event and was also 12th equal at high jump. At the Commonwealth Games of 1934 and 1938 he won the triple jump on each occasion, and was 3rd and 5th at long jump and 4th and 7th at high jump, adding the javelin bronze in 1938. He only once competed at the Australian Championships, winning triple jump and decathlon in 1937. A solicitor by profession, he managed the athletics team at the 1948 Olympics and was a track referee at the 1956 Games.
Progression (position on world lists) at TJ: 1930- 14.55 (16), 1932- 15.08 (9), 1933- 15.30 (1), 1934- 15.63 (3), 1935- 15.78 (1), 1936- 15.50 (3), 1937 - 15.16 (6), 1938- 15.49 (2). pbs: HJ 1.99 (1934), LJ 7.42 (1938), Dec 6773 (old tables) (1933).

Albert D **'Bert' NELSON** (USA) (b. 21 Nov 1921) on 9 January. Co-founder in 1948 of *Track & Field News*, the bible of the sport in the USA and long-time member of the ATFS. He had been a half miler in high school and graduated from the University of California.

Dr. Arthur Espie **(Lord) PORRITT** (New Zealand) (b. 10 Aug 1900) on 1 January at his home in St John's Wood, London. The Olympic bronze medallist at 100m (and semi-finalist at 200m) in 1924 went on to a hugely distinguished career. He lived most of his life in Britain, where he was president of the Royal College of Surgeons 1960-3 and sergeant-surgeon 1952-67, first to King George VII and then to Queen Elizabeth II. He was chairman of the Commonwealth Games Federation 1945-66 and a member of the International Olympic Committee 1934-67, until he was appointed Governor-General of New Zealand, which office he held 1967-72. He was awarded the KCMG in 1950, advanced to GCMG 1967 and GCVO 1970, and a baronetcy in 1963, and was created a Life Peer as Lord Porritt of Hampstead and Wanganui in 1973. After Otago University he won a Rhodes scholarship to Oxford University, becoming FRCS in 1928. At the first International Universities Games in 1924 he won the 100m and 200m and was second at 110m hurdles. He captained the New Zealand Olympic teams of 1924 and 1928 and was team manager in 1936, although knee trouble in 1928 forced him to give up competitive athletics.
Best times: 100y 9.8 (1913), 100m 10.9 (1924), 220y 21.8 (1924), 110mh 15.8 (1924), 220yh 25.4 (1925). LJ 6.73 (1925).

Helen STEPHENS (USA) (b. 3 Feb 1918 Fulton, Missouri) on 17 January at St Louis, Missouri.
Stephens had a phenomenal two and a half year career as a teenager, setting many world records, although none were officially ratified. In her first race, just a few days after her 17th birthday in 1935, she equalled the world indoor best of 6.6 for 50m and beat the great Stella Walsh. She improved to 6.4 twice in 1936. Outdoors in 1935 she set world marks at 100 yards, running 10.8 three times. At 100m she started with two 11.9s, then an 11.8 and twice 11.6, the second to win the AAU title, and at 200m recorded a 24.4 with 23.9 for 220 yards on a straight track. Finally at Toronto in September she ran times that could scarcely be believed, 10.4 for 100y and 23.2 for 220y. Still only 18, in 1936 she improved at 100m, running 11.5 twice, and won Olympic gold medals at 100m and sprint relay. In the three years 1935-7 she won 14 AAU titles: outdoors at 100m 1935-6, 200m 1935 and at shot and discus in 1936; and indoors at 50m and shot 1935-7, 200m 1937 and standing long jump 1935-6.
With an impressive 1.83m *6 ft*, 75kg *165 lb* physique, she dwarfed her rivals and also set US records with 13.61m and 13.70 indoors at the 8lb shot, and had a discus best of 40.70m. She turned professional as a runner and basketball player, and after a career at the Defense Mapping Agency Aerospace centre in St Louis, coached at her old school in Missouri. Her physical abilities remained strong and she took seven gold medals at the 1981 Senior Olympics.
Biography as printed in the Guinness International Who's Who of Sport.

Cliff TEMPLE (b.29 Jan 1947) committed suicide on January 8. Athletics correspondent of the *Sunday Times* for 24 years from 1969, author and coach to many international athletes. A member of the NUTS from 1966 he edited the magazine *Women's Athletics* that was published in 1968-9. At that time he was the compiler of the UK women's ranking lists. A witty, friendly man, devoted to athletics and sorely missed.

Bert Nelson

We were very saddened to learn of Bert Nelson's death early in 1994. Bert's last few years were blighted by the cruel ravages of Parkinson's Disease, which must have been a cause of great distress to his family and many friends. The illness was eventually to prevent him from attending the great California track meets which had been his life-long joy.
Bert's contribution, with his brother Cordner, to the recording and documentation of athletics history will always be remembered with gratitude and pleasure by those who were raised on regular doses of *Track & Field News*. My own fascination with the sport, which first laid its hold on me during the summer of 1951, was nurtured by the magazine from the beginning of 1952 onwards, and I often browse through my somewhat dog-eared copies to relive the memories of those exciting and formative years.
Thank you, Bert, on behalf of the ATFS for all that you achieved in a lifetim's devoted service to our sport.

Bob Sparks, ATFS President

OLYMPIC GAMES

THE FIRST Olympic Games of the modern era were staged in Athens, Greece from the 6th to 15th April 1896. Those in Atlanta 1996, the Games of the XXVI Olympiad, will be the 23nd to be staged, including the intercalated Games of 1906.

Just 59 athletes from ten nations contested the athletics events in 1896. In 1992 there was a record participation for a summer Games, at all sports, with 9369 competitors from 169 nations, with 157 contesting track and field.

Most gold medals - Men

10 Raymond Ewry USA StHJ and StLJ 1900-04-06-08, StTJ 1900-04
9 Paavo Nurmi FIN 9G: 1500m 1924, 5000m 1924, 10000m 1920-28, 3000mSt 1924, CC 1920-24, CC team 1920-24;
8 Carl Lewis USA 100m, 200m, LJ & 4x100mR 1984; 100m, LJ 1988; LJ, 4x100mR 1992

Most medals: 12 Paavo Nurmi FIN 9G as above; 3S 5000m 1920-28, 3000mSt 1928

Most gold medals - Women

4 Fanny Blankers-Koen HOL 100m, 200m, 80mh & 4x100mR 1948
4 Betty Cuthbert AUS 100m, 200m, 4x100mR 1956, 400m 1964
4 Bärbel Wöckel GDR 200m & 4x100mR 1976-80
4 Evelyn Ashford USA 100m 1984, 4x100mR 1984-88-92

Most medals: 7 Shirley de la Hunty AUS 3G 80mh 1952-56, 4x100mR 1956; 1S 4x100mR 1948; 3B 100m 1948-52, 80mh 1948
7 Irena Szewinska POL 3G 200m 1968, 400m 1976, 4x100mR 1964; 2S 200m & LJ 1964, 2B 100m 1968, 200m 1972

***Most gold medals at one Games*:** 5 Paavo Nurmi FIN 1924

***Most medals at one Games*:** 6 - 4 gold, 2 silver Ville Ritola FIN 1924

Olympic Games Records

after Barcelona 1992

Men

100m	9.92	Carl Lewis USA 1988
200m	19.73	Michael Marsh USA *1992
400m	43.50	Quincy Watts USA 1992
800m	1:43.00	Joaquim Cruz BRA 1984
1500m	3:32.53	Sebastian Coe GBR 1984
5000m	13:05.59	Saïd Aouita MAR 1984
10000m	27:21.46	Brahim Boutayeb MAR 1988
Marathon	2hr 09:21	Carlos Lopes POR 1984
3000mSt	8:05.51	Julius Kariuki KEN 1988
110mh	12.98	Roger Kingdom USA 1988
400mh	46.78	Kevin Young USA 1992
4x100mR	37.40	USA 1992
4x400mR	2:55.74	USA 1992
20km walk	1hr 19:57	Jozef Pribilinec TCH 1988
50km walk	3hr 38:29	Vyacheslav Ivanenko URS 1988
High jump	2.38	Gennadiy Avdeyenko URS 1988
Pole vault	5.90	Sergey Bubka URS 1988
Long jump	8.90A	Bob Beamon USA 1968
Triple jump	18.17w	Mike Conley USA 1992
	17.63	Mike Conley USA 1992
Shot	22.47	Ulf Timmermann GDR 1988
Discus	68.82	Jürgen Schult GDR 1988
Hammer	84.80	Sergey Litvinov URS 1988
Javelin	89.66	Jan Zelezny TCH 1992
old	94.58	Miklós Németh HUN 1976
Decathlon	8847	Daley Thompson GBR 1984

Women

100m	10.62	Florence Griffith-Joyner USA 1988
	10.54w	Florence Griffith-Joyner USA 1988
200m	21.34	Florence Griffith-Joyner USA 1988
400m	48.65	Olga Bryzgina URS 1988
800m	1:53.43	Nadezhda Olizarenko URS 1980
1500m	3:53.96	Paula Ivan ROM 1988
3000m	8:26.53	Tatyana Samolenko URS 1988
10000m	31:05.21	Olga Bondarenko URS 1988
Marathon	2hr 24:52	Joan Benoit USA 1984
100mh	12.38	Yordanka Donkova BUL 1988
400mh	53.17	Debbie Flintoff-King AUS 1988
4x100mR	41.60	GDR 1980
4x400mR	3:15.17	USSR 1988
10 km walk	44:32	Chen Yueling (Chn) 1992
High jump	2.03	Louise Ritter USA 1988
Long jump	7.40	Jackie Joyner-Kersee USA 1988
Triple jump		*to be contested for the first time in 1996*
Shot	22.41	Ilona Slupianek GDR 1980
Discus	72.30	Martina Hellmann GDR 1988
Javelin	74.68	Petra Felke GDR 1988
Heptathlon	7291	Jackie Joyner-Kersee USA 1988

* performance made in qualifying round, A at high altitude, Mexico City 2240m

OLYMPIC GAMES MEDALLISTS 1992

Men

	Gold	Silver	Bronze
100m	Linford Christie GBR 9.96	Frank Fredericks NAM 10.02	Dennis Mitchell USA 10.04
200 m	Michael Marsh USA 20.01	Frank Fredericks NAM 20.13	Michael Bates USA 20.38
400m	Quincy Watts USA 43.50	Steve Lewis USA 44.21	Samson Kitur KEN 44.24
800m	William Tanui KEN 1:43.66	Nixon Kiprotich KEN 1:43.70	Johnny Gray USA 1:43.97
1500m	Fermin Cacho ESP 3:40.12	Rachid ElBasir MAR 3:40.62	Mohamed Suleiman QAT 3:40.69
5000m	Dieter Baumann GER 13:12.52	Paul Bitok KEN 13:12.71	Fita Bayissa ETH 13:13.03
10000m	Khalid Skah MAR 27:46.70	Richard Chelimo KEN 27:47.72	Addis Abebe ETH 28:00.07
Mar	Hwang Young-jo KOR 2:13:23	Koichi Morishita JPN 2:13:45	Stephan Freigang GER 2:14:00
3000mSt	Matthew Birir KEN 8:08.44	Patrick Sang KEN 8:09.55	William Mutwol KEN 8:10.74
110mh	Mark McKoy CAN 13.12	Tony Dees USA 13.24	Jack Pierce USA 13.26
400mh	Kevin Young USA 46.78	Winthrop Graham JAM 47.66	Kriss Akabusi GBR 47.82
HJ	Javier Sotomayor CUB 2.34	Patrik Sjöberg SWE 2.34	= Artur Partyka POL 2.34 = Hollis Conway USA 2.34 = Tim Forsyth AUS 2.34
PV	Maksim Tarasov EUN 5.80	Igor Trandenkov EUN 5.80	Javier Garcia ESP 5.75
LJ	Carl Lewis USA 8.67	Mike Powell USA 8.64	Joe Greene USA 8.34
TJ	Mike Conley USA 18.17w	Charlie Simpkins USA 17.60	Frank Rutherford BAH 17.36
SP	Mike Stulce USA 21.70	Jim Doehring USA 20.96	Vyacheslav Lykho EUN 20.94
DT	Romas Ubartas LIT 65.12	Jürgen Schult GDR 64.94	Roberto Moya CUB 64.12
HT	Andrey Abduvaliyev EUN 82.54	Igor Astapkovich EUN 81.96	Igor Nikulin EUN 81.38
JT	Jan Zelezny TCH 89.66	Seppo Räty FIN 86.60	Steve Backley GBR 83.38
Dec	Robert Zmelík TCH 8611	Antonio Peñalver ESP 8412	David Johnson USA 8309
20 KmW	Daniel Plaza ESP 1:21:45	Guillaume LeBlanc CAN 1:22:25	Gio De Benedictis ITA 1:23:11
50 Km W	Andrey Perlov EUN 3:50:13	Carlos Mercenario MEX 3:52:09	Ronald Weigel GER 3:53:45
4 x 100 mR	USA 37.40	NGR 37.98	CUB 38.00
4 x 400 mR	USA 2:55.74	CUB 2:59.51	GBR 2:59.73

Women

	Gold	Silver	Bronze
100 m	Gail Devers USA 10.82	Juliet Cuthbert JAM 10.83	Irina Privalova EUN 10.84
200m	Gwen Torrence USA 21.81	Juliet Cuthbert JAM 22.02	Merlene Ottey JAM 22.09
400m	Marie-José Perec FRA 48.83	Olga Bryzgina EUN 49.05	Ximena Restrepo COL 49.64
800m	Ellen van Langen HOL 1:55.54	Lilia Nurutdinova EUN 1:55.99	Ana Quirot CUB 1:56.80
1500m	Hassiba Boulmerka ALG 3:55.30	Lyudmila Rogachova EUN 3:56.91	Qu Yunxia CHN 3:57.08
3000m	Yelena Romanova EUN 8:46.04	Tatyana Dorovskikh EUN 8:46.85	Angela Chalmers CAN 8:47.22
10000m	Derartu Tulu ETH 31:06.02	Elana Meyer RSA 31:11.75	Lynn Jennings USA 31:19.89
Mar	Val. Yegorova EUN 2:32:41	Yuko Arimori JPN 2:32:49	Lorraine Moller NZL 2:33:59
100mh	Paraskevi Patoulidou GRE 12.64	LaVonna Martin USA 12.69	Yordanka Donkova BUL 12.70
400mh	Sally Gunnell GBR 53.23	Sandra Farmer-Patrick USA 53.69	Janeene Vickers USA 54.31
HJ	Heike Henkel GER 2.02	Galina Astafei ROM 2.00	Ioamnet Quintero CUB 1.97
LJ	Heike Drechsler GER 7.14	Inessa Kravets EUN 7.12	Jackie Joyner-Kersee USA 7.07
SP	Svetlana Krivelyova EUN 21.06	Huang Zhihong CHN 20.47	Kathrin Neimke GER 19.78
DT	Maritsa Martén CUB 70;06	Tsvetanka Khristova BUL 67.78	Daniela Costian AUS 66.24
JT	Silke Renk GER 68.34	Natalya Shikolenko EUN 68.26	Karen Forkel GER 66.86
Hep	Jackie Joyner-Kersee USA 7044	Irina Belova EUN 6845	Sabine Braun GER 6649
4 x 100mR	USA 42.11	EUN 42.16	NGR 42.81
4 x 400 mR	EUN 3:20.20	USA 3:20.92	GBR 3:24.23
10 kmW	Chen Yueling CHN 44:32	Yelena Nikolayeva EUN 44:33	Li Chunxiu CHN 44:41

WORLD CHAMPIONSHIPS 1993

THE FOURTH in the series of IAAF World Championships in Athletics, held in beautiful weather in Stuttgart, Germany from 14-22 August provided a feast of athletics, a meeting fit to rival even its most distinguished precursors.

After speculation about possible boycotts for lack of prize money, none such transpired and Mercedes cars were awarded to every winner. An unprecedented 187 nations took part, with 1624 competitors.

There was a total of 585,000 spectators for all sessions of the Championships with an estimated 180,000 also estimated to have lined the marathon course. There were peak figures of over 52.000 for each of the last four days, with an amazing 51,500 on the morning of the Thursday, when the evening figure reached a peak 52,700.

Many tributes were paid to the enormously enthusiastic and friendly crowds. They were, however, not always very knowledgeable, and there were many occasions when all too many spectators seemed keener on the awful Mexican waves than on the athletics, so that some events were disturbed. That is, however, but a small criticism against the magnificence of this great track and field meeting.

MEN

100 METRES (15 +0.3)

CHRISTIE became, at 32, the oldest ever world sprint champion, and missed tying the world record of 9.86 by no more than 1/1000th second. Cason was quickest in each of the preliminary rounds, running successively 10.09 and pbs of 9.96 and 9.94 (+0.3), while Christie also won each of his races in 10.24, 10.00 and 9.97 (+0.9). Effiong was second to Cason in the first semi in 9.98. In the final Mitchell was quickest into his stride and reached 30m in 3.82 from Cason 3.83. Christie reacted well and by 30m was third and into full stride. Having held Cason's slim lead from 30m to 60m, Christie caught him at 80m and went away to a majestic win. His 9.87 against a wind of 0.3 could be regarded as even better than the world record, which was with a wind of 1.2. Lewis started well, but was clearly last at 60m, so that although his last 20m (1.72) was equal to that of Christie and compared to 1.77 for Cason and Mitchell he finished outside the medals for the first time at a championships.

1	Linford Christie	GBR	9.87 *
2	Andre Cason	USA	9.92
3	Dennis Mitchell	USA	9.99
4	Carl Lewis	USA	10.02
5	Bruny Surin	CAN	10.02
6	Frank Fredericks	NAM	10.03
7	Daniel Effiong	NGR	10.04
8	Raymond Stewart	JAM	10.18

Intermediate times

	30m	60m	80m	100m
Christie	3.85	6.45	8.15	9.87
Cason	3.83	6.43	8.15	9.92
Mitchell	3.82	6.46	8.22	9.99
Lewis	3.95	6.59	8.30	10.02
Surin	3.86	6.49	8.24	10.02
Fredericks	3.87	6.50	8.25	10.03
Effiong	3.89	6.50	8.25	10.04
Stewart	3.80	6.51	8.34	10.18

Linford Christie: a majestic win

200 METRES (20, +0.3)

LEWIS was fastest in the first two rounds, with 20.45 and 20.21. Then the first four in the first semi-final, Marsh 20.10, Fredericks 20.11, Regis 20.16 and Capobianco 20.21, all ran faster than Lewis, who won the second in 20.26. Robson da Silva was third in that race in 20.34 but then disqualified for stepping outside his lane.

In the final Regis, who ran a great bend, led at 100m in 10.28 from Lewis 10.31 and Capobianco 10.36. Fredericks, 4th in 10.39, narrowed the gap over the next 50m and then finished much the fastest to win by a metre, his well-earned gold in an African record time coming after silvers in Tokyo and Barcelona and for the World Indoor 60m. It was thef irst ever won for Namibia. Regis broke 20 secs for the first time (a European low altitude best) and Lewis won his first World bronze to take his medal tally from four Championships to a record ten.

1	Frank Fredericks	NAM	19.85
2	John Regis	GBR	19.94
3	Carl Lewis	USA	19.99
4	Michael Marsh	USA	20.18
5	Dean Capobianco	AUS	20.18
6	Jean-Charles Trouabal	FRA	20.20
7	Emmanuel Tuffour	GHA	20.49
8	Damien Marsh	AUS	20.56

Michael Johnson: remarkably even-paced

Multiple World Championships medallists

Winners of the most medals
10 Carl Lewis 1983-93
10 Merlene Ottey 1983-93
6 Heike Daute/Drechsler 1983-93
6 Gwen Torrence 1991-3
5 Calvin Smith 1983-93
5 John Regis 1987-93

Most individual event golds
5 Carl Lewis 1983-91
4 Jackie Joyner-Kersee 1987-93
4 Sergey Bubka 1983-93

400 METRES (17)

JOHNSON, in lane 3, ran one of the most even paced races ever to win a major 400m title -the first 200m in 21.65 and the second in a remarkable 22.00. At 200m Bada 21.02 and Reynolds 21.39 were ahead of him, with Kitur 21.83 and Watts 21.85 in 4th and 5th. Watts suffered the misfortune of his shoe falling apart, while Bada took 24.09 for the second half of the race. Leaders at 300m were Johnson 32.12, Reynolds 32.22, Bada 32.26 and Kitur 32.69. Watts had won the first semi in 44.63 and Kitur the second in 44.34 from Johnson 44.39.

1	Michael Johnson	USA	43.65 *
2	Butch Reynolds	USA	44.13
3	Samson Kitur	KEN	44.54
4	Quincy Watts	USA	45.05
5	Sunday Bada	NGR	45.11
6	Gregory Haughton	JAM	45.63
7	Simon Kemboi	KEN	45.65
8	Kennedy Ochieng	KEN	45.68

800 METRES (17)

LOOKING most impressive as he won the first semi in 1:45.04, Konchellah was highly favoured to complete yet another comeback and win his third world title. In the final, however, he was overconfident and left his devastating kick far too late. He was thus unable to catch his front-running compatriot Ruto, who led through 200m 24.80, 400m 51.16 and 600m 1:17.96, at which point Konchellah still lagged in last place at 1:19.16, but D'Urso had moved up from 6th at 400m to 2nd (1:18.56). D'Urso won the second semi in 1:44.83 and Robb

1:44.92, pbs both, and Ruto was third in 1:45.05 to advance to the final as a fastest loser, but José Luiz Barbosa and Johnny Gray, 6th and 8th, were well out of contention. McKean won the third semi in 1:45.64.

1	Paul Ruto	KEN	1:44.71
2	Giuseppe D'Urso	ITA	1:44.86
3	Billy Konchellah	KEN	1:44.89
4	Curtis Robb	GBR	1:45.54
5	Hezekiel Sepeng	RSA	1:45.64
6	Freddie Williams	CAN	1:45.79
7	William Tanui	KEN	1:45.80
8	Tom McKean	GBR	1:46.17

1500 METRES (22)

THE THREE previous world champions all lined up in the second semi final, but the 1983 winner Steve Cram was last. In the final the 1987 winner Bile came third, but 1991 winner Morceli was a class apart. In the final he kicked decisively at the bell and ran the last lap in 50.64. Olympic champion Cacho was second. 400m splits were 60.85, 1:59.32 and 2:56.41.

1	Noureddine Morceli	ALG	3:34.24
2	Fermin Cacho	ESP	3:35.56
3	Abdi Bile	SOM	3:35.96
4	Mohamed Suleiman	QAT	3:36.87
5	Jim Spivey	USA	3:37.42
6	Matthew Yates	GBR	3:37.61
7	Rashid El Basir	NAR	3:37.68
8	Mohamed Taki	MAR	3:37.76

5000 METRES (16)

KIRUI gave a wondrous display of front running and thoroughly deserved not only the gold medal but also a world junior record time. His compatriot Mike Chesire set a stunning pace, 61.3 for the first lap followed by a 59.0 to reach 800m in 2:00.24 and 1000m in 2:31.76. He eased up slightly so that he was caught by some at 1600m in 4:08.4. Kirui took the lead and after 2000m in 5:11.27 kicked away with a 60.21 lap.

From then he was on his own, through 3000m in 7:45.62 and 4000m 10:26.85. The three Ethiopians and Skah were some 40m behind, and gradually gained ground on Kirui, who slowed to 64 second laps. Bayissa and Gebresilasie cut Kirui's lead from 25m to 10m on the penultimate lap, but despite Gebresilasie's last 400m in 56.5 Kirui held on by increasing his tempo to a 59.59 last lap. The first four all set personal bests, and at 18 years 177 days Kirui was the youngest ever world champion.

1	Ismael Kirui	KEN	13:02.75*
2	Haile Gebresilassie	ETH	13:03.17
3	Fita Bayissa	ETH	13:05.40
4	Worku Bikila	ETH	13:06.64
5	Khalid Skah	MAR	13:07.18
6	Brahim Jabbour	MAR	13:18.87
7	Alois Nizigama	BUR	13:20.59
8	Paul Bitok	KEN	13:23.41

10,000 METRES (22)

AFTER a slow early pace in warm weather, the race was won on a dramatic last lap. Fita Bayissa led at 5000m in 13:59.38, but dropped out soon afterwards, to leave Chelimo in front. By 8000m (22:18.20) Tanui and Gebresilasie were on their own. Tanui slowed the pace from the front but the Ethiopian waited. At the bell Tanui kicked hard but was stepped on by Gebresilasie so that his left shoe was flipped off. Although Tanui led into the last bend, he was unable to match the Ethiopian's finish, with Gebresilasie's last 400m 54.98 to Tanui's 55.66.

1	Haile Gebresilassie	ETH	27:46.02
2	Moses Tanui	KEN	27:46.54
3	Richard Chelimo	KEN	28:06.02
4	Stephane Franke	GER	28:10.69
5	Alois Nizigama	BUR	28:13.43
6	Francesco Panetta	ITA	28:27.05
7	Todd Williams	USA	28:30.49
8	Antonio Silio	ARG	28:36.88

Paul Ruto: unexpected win at 800 metres

MARATHON (14)

THE win by Plaatjes, denied until now his chance of major championships by his South African birth and the need to qualify for his new country of the USA, was the stuff of fairy tales. He ran a cautious race as another man from the south of Africa, Swartbooi, led for over half the race, having broken away at 25km (1:18:23). Plaatjes caught and passed the group behind Swartbooi - Simon Robert Naali (eventually 11th 2:19:30), Merande and Kim - the last at 35km, but at that point was 89 seconds behind the leader. Plaatjes was still 37 seconds behind at 40km, but could see the lead van, and steadily narrowed the gap to sweep past with some 1000m to go. van Vlaanderen came from even further back to take the bronze.

1	Mark Plaatjes	USA	2:13:57
2	Lucketz Swartbooi	NAM	2:14:11
3	Bert van Vlaanderen	HOL	2:15:12
4	Kim Jae-ryong	KOR	2:17:14
5	Tadao Uchikoshi	JPN	2:17:54
6	Konrad Dobler	GER	2:18:28
7	Boniface Merande	KEN	2:18:52
8	Aleksey Zhelonkin	RUS	2:18:52

3000 METRES STEEPLECHASE (21)

FOR the first time ever five men broke 8:10, but, although pressed hard by Sang, Kiptanui won comfortably, with kilometre splits of 2:42.3, 2:44.4 and 2:39.7. Thus the first two were identical to 1991, and as then a Kenyan was 4th with Birir showing much his best form of the year, but held back by Lambruschini from a Kenyan sweep of the medals.

1	Moses Kiptanui	KEN	8:06.36 *
2	Patrick Sang	KEN	8:07.53
3	Aless Lambruschini	ITA	8:08.78
4	Matthew Birir	KEN	8:09.42
5	Mark Croghan	USA	8:09.76
6	Steffen Brand	GER	8:15.33
7	Larbi Khattabi	MAR	8:17.96
8	Angelo Carosi	ITA	8:23.42

110 METRES HURDLES (20, +0.5)

RUNNING in lane three Jackson displayed nearly immaculate form, just brushing the final hurdle to take 0.01 off the world record with his 12.91. Jarrett (in an English record) made it a British 1-2, Pierce matched his pb for 3rd and Valle ran 13.20 for the fastest ever times for each of places 1-4. Dees knocked down the 6th hurdle and lost his balance. Super-fast semis were won by Jackson 13.13, Pierce 13.11 and Jarrett 13.14 (from Dees 13.19 and Valle 13.19).

Mark Plaatjes: a cautious marathon win

1	Colin Jackson	GBR	12.91 *
2	Tony Jarrett	GBR	13.00
3	Jack Pierce	USA	13.06
4	Emilio Valle	CUB	13.20
5	Florian Schwarthoff	GER	13.27
6	Igor Kazanov	LAT	13.38
7	Dietmar Koszewski	GER	13.60
8	Anthony Dees	USA	14.13

400 METRES HURDLES (19)

ALTHOUGH he had lost his last two races prior to Stuttgart, Young was back in top form to win by a big margin. Diagana led for the first half of the final, but Young drew away from the 7th hurdle, as there was a fine battle for the other medals, Diagana just missing out but running the fastest ever fourth place time as well as a French record. Matete's great finish took him past Graham to grab the silver. Young's 47.99 was the fastest of the semis, as Graham 48.09 and Matete 48.18 were the other winners. Keter set a Kenyan record 48.24 behind Matete.

1	Kevin Young	USA	47.18 *
2	Samuel Matete	ZIM	47.60
3	Winthrop Graham	JAM	47.62
4	Stéphane Diagana	FRA	47.64
5	Erick Keter	KEN	48.40
6	Oleg Tverdokhleb	UKR	48.71
7	Derrick Adkins	USA	49.07
8	Barnabas Kinyor	KEN	49.23

HIGH JUMP (22)

SOTOMAYOR had first time clearances at 2.25, 2.34 and 2.37, before winning the gold with 2.40 on his second attempt and failing twice at a world record height of 2.46. Partyka and Smith both cleared 2.37 on their first attempt, but the former had just two previous failures to Smith's three.

1	Javier Sotomayor	CUB	2.40 *
2	Artur Partyka	POL	2.37
3	Steve Smith	GBR	2.37
4	Ralf Sonn	GER	2.34
5	Troy Kemp	BAH	2.34
6	Hollis Conway	USA	2.34
7	Arturo Ortiz	ESP	2.31
8	Tony Barton	USA	2.31

POLE VAULT (19)

BUBKA became the only athlete to win world titles at each of the four celebrations. He entered, as usual, at 5.70 and cleared both that and his next height of 5.90 on his first attempts. The only other man to clear that height was Yegorov, who jumped 5.60, 5.75, 5.85 and 5.90 without failure. Bubka sailed over 6.00 first time, but that was beyond Yegorov. Bubka's attempts at 6.14 were delayed through judging errors over how long he was allowed for his first vault. That upset the great man and may have cost him the chance of yet another world record, although his last try was close.

The qualifying standard was the highest ever at 5.65, with four men eliminated on count back even at that height and in the final there were the best marks ever for places 6-11.

1	Sergey Bubka	UKR	6.00 *
2	Grigoriy Yegorov	KZK	5.90
3=	Maksim Tarasov	RUS	5.80
3=	Igor Trandenkov	RUS	5.80
5	Scott Huffman	USA	5.80
6	Denis Petuschinsky	RUS	5.80
7	Valeriy Bukreyev	EST	5.75
8	Jean Galfione	FRA	5.70

LONG JUMP (20)

POWELL was in a class of his own, even though he struggled to find his normal form at first in the final as Walder and Ivan Pedroso (injured on a first round jump) were unable to match their qualifying marks of 8.30 and 8.23 respectively. Powell's series: x, 8.16, 8.28, 8.22, 8.43, 8.59. After three rounds Tarasenko was 2nd with 8.01 and Mladenov 3rd 8.00, and although the jumps improved the event was still well below usual championship standards. In the 4th round Tarasenko hit 8.16 and in the 5th Kirilenko 8.15 and Walder 8.05.

1	Mike Powell	USA	8.59
2	Stanislav Tarasenko	RUS	8.16
3	Vitaliy Kirilenko	UKR	8.15
4	Erick Walder	USA	8.05
5	Ivaylo Mladenov	BUL	8.00
6	Nikolay Antonov	BUL	7.97
7	Aleksandr Glovatskiy	BLS	7.95
8	Francois Fouche	RSA	7.93

TRIPLE JUMP (16)

CONLEY (4th, 2nd and 3rd in previous World Championships) is a master of coming through at the end of a competition, but here he took the lead with a 3rd round 17.70 after a no jump and 17.21, and improved to 17.86 (5.75, 5.47, 6.64) in the 5th before ending with 17.77, thus producing three jumps better than the final round 17.65 which earned Voloshin the silver medal. Voloshin had led in the 1st round with 17.48, but then had four no jumps, and Edwards improved from 17.24 in the 2nd to 17.31 in the 4th and to 17.44 in the 5th. Jaros was temporarily in 3rd place when he ended the 3rd round with 17.34.

The qualifying round had been of the high-

Javier Sotomayor: five jumps to win world title

est ever standard, with Conley 17.39 and Voloshin 17,34 leading the way and eight men finding jumps of between 16.81 and 16.86 not good enough. In the final defending champion Kenny Harrison was 10th with 17.06 as there were the best ever performances for places 7 to 11.

1	Mike Conley	USA	17.86
2	Leonid Voloshin	RUS	17.65
3	Jonathan Edwards	GBR	17.44
4	Ralf Jaros	GER	17.34
5	Pierre Camara	FRA	17.28
6	Denis Kapustin	RUS	17.19
7	Anisio Silva	BRA	17.19
8	Brian Wellman	BER	17.12

SHOT (21)

GÜNTHÖR repeated his 1987 and 1991 wins with a series of 21.97, 21.55, 21.59, 20.94, 20.67 and 20.51. Thus although he declined steadily, Barnes, who threw 21.80 in both 3rd and 6th rounds, could not catch him. Stulce's best came in the third round, but much later he lost the bronze on a positive drugs test

1	Werner Günthör	SUI	21.97
2	Randy Barnes	USA	21.80
3	Aleksandr Bagach	UKR	20.40
4	Yevgeniy Palchikov	RUS	20.05
5	Dragan Peric	YUG	19.95
6	Gert Weil	CHI	19.95
7	Sven Buder	GER	19.74
8	Jonny Reinhardt	GER	19.53

Mike Stulce USA(3rd 20.94) drugs dq

DISCUS (17)

OLYMPIC champion Ubartas and defending champion Riedel led the qualifiers with 65.92 and 65.88 respectively. In the final Schult took a first round lead with 64.32, but three men went over 65m in the 2nd, first Grasu 65.24, then Riedel with 67.72 to which Schult responded with 66.12.

Shevchenko moved into 2nd with 66.14 in the 5th, and after Riedel had closed with 67.34, Shevchenko challenged but unavailingly with 66.90. Ubartas matched Grasu's 65.24 in the 5th round and his 63.98 next best moved him to 4th, a place he lost four days later due to a positive drugs test.

1	Lars Riedel	GER	67.72
2	Dmitriy Shevchenko	RUS	66.90
3	Jürgen Schult	GER	66.12
4	Costel Grasu	ROM	65.24
5	Vladimir Zinchenko	UKR	62.02
6	Nick Sweeney	IRL	61.66
7	Vasiliy Kaptyukh	BLS	61.64
8	Mike Buncic	USA	61.06

Romas Ubartas LIT (4th 65.24) drugs dq

HAMMER (15)

WITH marvellous TV close-ups of his exhortations displayed on the giant scoreboard,

Andrey Abduvaliyev : a TV star!

Jan Zelezny: below parr but still a winner

Abduvaliyev added the world title to his Olympic one of 1992. He became the first Asian men's world champion. Litvinov took a first round lead at 78.56, but thereafter the 1983 and 1987 champion slipped back in the placings. The lead passed to Seleznyov, 78.58 in the 2nd, and then the three medal winning throws came in succession in the 4th round: first Abduvaliyev (who started with 78.08, x, 78.02) and then Astapkovich and Gécsek, so that the 1992 Olympic medal order was repeated. The winner added 80.56 in the 6th.

1	Andrey Abduvaliyev	TJK	81.64
2	Igor Astapkovich	BLS	79.88
3	Tibor Gécsek	HUN	79.54
4	Sergey Alay	BLS	79.02
5	Vasiliy Sidorenko	RUS	78.86
6	Aleksandr Seleznyov	RUS	78.58
7	Sergey Litvinov	RUS	78.56
8	Christophe Epalle	FRA	76.22

JAVELIN (16)

DESPITE being well below his best form Zelezny still won. Mick Hill opened the final with 82.80 and that remained the lead until Kinnunen threw 84.78 in the 3rd. Zelezny opened with 81.86 and two bad fouls, before moving up to second with 83.82 in the 4th round and into the lead in the 5th with 85.98, ending with 84.62. Polyunin's 83.38 was in the 3rd round, and although Hill improved in the last round to 82.96 he was out of the medals, until he received the news some days later at home that Polyunin had failed the drugs test.

The qualifiers were led by Zelezny 83.22 and Pakarinen 83.06, as former world record holders, Seppo Räty 74.30 and Tom Petranoff 75.26, failed to make the final.

1	Jan Zelezny	TCH	85.98 *
2	Kimmo Kinnunen	FIN	84.78
3	Mick Hill	GBR	82.96
4	Steve Backley	GBR	81.80
5	Ari Pakarinen	FIN	81.08
6	Dag Wennlund	SWE	80.52
7	Vladimir Sasimovich	BLS	78.70
8	Patrik Bodén	SWE	78.00

Dmitriy Polyunin UZB (3rd 83.38) drugs dq

DECATHLON (19/20)

O'BRIEN retained his title, but not without a struggle, firstly with his own form on the first day and then from a magnificent challenge by Hämäläinen, who set four pbs in a row on the second day. At the end of the first day O'Brien led by just four points from the inspired German Meier, 4598 to 4594, with Schenk third 4429 and Hämäläinen 5th 4384. O'Brien had long jumped 7.99, but was well below par at shot and high jump.

On day two Hämäläinen opened with the fastest 110m hurdles ever in a decathlon, 13.57, to narrow the gap on O'Brien to 147 points and followed with 49.26 DT and 5.30 PV to 47.92 and 5.20 for O'Brien so the gap was down to 87. O'Brien, however had the better javelin 62.56 to 61.88 and concentrated on beating his rival in the 1500m to secure the gold. He did that with 4:40.08 as Hämäläinen was just 0.74 ahead. Meier held off his compatriot Schenk to take the bronze amid hugely enthusiastic support.

1	Dan O'Brien	USA	8817 *
2	Eduard Hämäläinen	BLS	8724
3	Paul Meier	GER	8548
4	Christian Schenk	GER	8500
5	Alain Blondel	FRA	8444
6	Christian Plaziat	FRA	8398
7	Steve Fritz	USA	8324
8	Rob Muzzio	USA	8237

4 X 100 METRES RELAY (22)

AFTER Calvin Smith had had a run out in the heats when Mitchell was rested, the US squad of Jon Drummond, Andre Cason, Dennis Mitchell and Leroy Burrell equalled the world record set by the US at the Olympics, running 37.40 in the first semi-final, despite no better than good passes.

They went on to win the final in 37.48, with Burrell slowing to take the batôn from Mitchell, from national records by Britain and Canada. After hurdles medallists Colin Jackson and Tony Jarrett, John Regis ran a brilliant third leg (9.29) for Britain, but a fumbled exchange to Linford Christie cost the British any chance of making a challenge to the USA.

This was a turning point in the history of the event for it was the first time that Carl Lewis had not anchored the winning US team at a major championship for more than a decade.

All but Drummond of the winning team had taken part in on the 37.50 record run in Tokyo 1991. Splits for the US team: (semi/final): Drummond 10.44/10.58, Cason 8.96/8.86, Mitchell 9.43/9.45, Burrell 8.92/8.98.

1	USA	37.48
2	Great Britain	37.77
3	Canada	37.83
4	Cuba	38.39
5	Australia	38.69
6	Germany	38.78
7	Ivory Coast	38.82
8	Sweden	39.22

4 X 400 METRES RELAY (22)

ANDREW VALMON'S opening 400m of 44.5 gave the US a clear lead. From then it was three great athletes against the clock, and succeeding superbly: Quincy Watts 43.6, Butch Reynolds 43.23 and Michael Johnson 42.94.

The latter's solo effort was the fastest 400m leg ever run, and the team took 1.45 secs off the world record that the same team, with Steve Lewis instead of Reynolds, had run in Barcelona.

Despite a poor opening 46.2 from Kennedy Ochieng, Kenya came back to take the silver medals from Germany, with Samson Kitur running 43.75 to close.

Britain, defending champions, were struck by injury, and their virtually B team did not advance from the heats, in which the US team of Valmon, Andrew Pettigrew, Derek Mills and Johnson had run 2:58.72, the fastest time ever run in a preliminary round.

1	USA	2:54.29 *
2	Kenya	2:59.82
3	Germany	2:59.99
4	France	3:00.09
5	Russia	3:00.44
6	Cuba	3:00.46
7	Jamaica	3:01.44
8	Bulgaria	3:05.35

20 KILOMETRES WALK (15)

THE finish was played out in conditions of farce, as a walking judge caught up with decisions made earlier by his colleagues out on the course and disqualified several of the leaders.

How discouraging it must be to enter the stadium after an hour and 20 minutes hard endeavour, with a medal in sight, to have ones hopes dashed in such a manner.

Massana, clearly shown on the TV screens (a benefit the judges lack) to be lifting just as much as the others, was first in and went on to win, but the two following him, Mikhail Shchennikov and Daniel Garcia were both pulled. After a steady first half, reached by 24 men between 42:26 and 42:35, the pace exploded over the last 5km, with Massana's second 10k taking him 40:01.

1	Valentin Massana	ESP	1:22:31
2	Giovanni Di Benedictis	ITA	1:23:06
3	Daniel Plaza	ESP	1:23:18
4	Jaime Barroso	ESP	1:23:41
5	Yevgeniy Misyula	BLS	1:23:45
6	Sergio Galdino	BRA	1:23:52
7	Robert Ihly	GER	1:24:21
8	Igor Kollár	SVK	1:24:23

50 KILOMETRES WALK (21)

GARCIA was always prominent, with a group of six at 20km 1:29:36, five seconds behind Mercenario's 2:13:39 at 30km, and taking the lead before 40km 2:57:09. At that point Noack was 2nd in 2:57:24, followed by Noack, Robert Korzeniowski (later disqualified), Kononen and Mercenario, who was beginning to struggle. Kononen finished well to take silver and Spitsyn moved through to third.

1	Jesús Angel Garcia	ESP	3:41:41
2	Valentin Kononen	FIN	3:42:02
3	Valeriy Spitsyn	RUS	3:42:50
4	Axel Noack	GER	3:43:50
5	Basilio Labrador	ESP	3:46:46
6	René Piller	FRA	3:48:57
7	Tim Berrett	CAN	3:50:23
8	Carlos Mercenario	MEX	3:50:53

WOMEN

100 METRES (16, -0.3)

PRIVALOVA was off fastest in the final, but was passed first by Devers and then by Torrence and Ottey. Ottey caught Devers by 80m, but the latter came back as it needed very careful examination of the photos from both sides to separate them at the finish. Devers was originally credited with victory in 10.81 to Ottey's 10.82. The Jamaicans protested and although the winner's time was adjusted to 10.82, the verdict remained the same (10.816 to 10.820). Ottey was rewarded with a two-minute standing ovation from the sympathetic crowd at the victory ceremony

Onyali set an African record with 10.97 in the 2nd round before the meeting record was improved to 10.87 (-0.3) by Ottey and Torrence in the first semi. Devers won the second semi in 11.03.

1	Gail Devers	USA	10.82
2	Merlene Ottey	JAM	10.82
3	Gwen Torrence	USA	10.89
4	Irina Privalova	RUS	10.96
5	Mary Onyali	NGR	11.05
6	Natalya Voronova	RUS	11.20
7	Nicole Mitchell	JAM	11.20
8	Liliana Allen	CUB	11.23

Intermediate times

	30m	60m	80m	100m
Devers	4.09	6.95	8.88	10.82
Ottey	4.13	6.98	8.87	10.82
Torrence	4.14	7.00	8.92	10.89
Privalova	4.09	7.00	8.96	10.96
Onyali	4.13	7.06	9.03	11.05

200 METRES (19, 0.0)

AT LAST Ottey captured a world outdoor title, after four silver and two bronze medals at individual World Championships events with a further four Olympic bronzes. She was, however, very nearly caught by Torrence after leading 11.15 to 11.28 at 100m and 16.33 to 16.44 at 150m. Privalova and Pérec battled for the bronze, the Russian ahead at 100m 11.30 to 11.33, but level at 150m in 16.54 before holding on best to the line.

1	Merlene Ottey	JAM	21.98
2	Gwen Torrence	USA	22.00
3	Irina Privalova	RUS	22.13
4	Marie-José Pérec	FRA	22.20
5	Mary Onyali	NGR	22.32
6	Natalya Voronova	RUS	22.50
7	Galina Malchugina	RUS	22.50
8	Dannette Young	USA	23.04

400 METRES (17)

FROM a pb of 50.19 Miles improved to 49.82 to win the final, when she hauled back the fast-starting Alekseyeva. Kaiser-Brown made it a US 1-2 with a pb 50.17 to add to the one she had set at 50.41 to win the first semi, Miles taking the second in 50.45.

1	Jearl Miles	USA	49.82
2	Natasha Kaiser-Brown	USA	50.17
3	Sandie Richards	JAM	50.44
4	Tatyana Alekseyeva	RUS	50.52
5	Ximena Restrepo	COL	50.91
6	Sandra Myers	ESP	51.22
7	Juliet Campbell	JAM	51.40
dq	Norfalia Carabali (8th)	COL	

Intermediate times

	100m	200m	300m	400m
Miles	12.43	23.95	36.33	49.82
Kaiser-Brown	12.41	23.78	36.47	50.17
Richards	12.23	23.77	36.51	50.44
Alekseyeva	12.07	23.48	36.10	50.52
Restrepo	12.18	23.71	36.24	50.91
Myers	12.09	23.63	36.45	51.22

Merlene Ottey: a major title at last

800 METRES (17)

MUTOLA'S fifth African record of the season was too good for the rest of the field and she became Mozambique's first gold medallist. Rainey set the pace in the final with a very fast 55.49 at 400m, at which point Mutola was 7th in 56.36.

Still 7th at 500m, Mutola moved up to join Gurina at 600m in 1:25.96 and drove well clear. Gurina, at 36 years 11 days, became the second oldest women's medallist ever at World Championships. Kovacs was third, and behind them was chaos as Paulino fell with about 200m to go and brought down Liu and Nurutdinova.

1	Maria Mutola	MOZ	1:55.43
2	Lyubov Gurina	RUS	1:57.10
3	Ella Kovacs	ROM	1:57.92
4	Diane Modahl	GBR	1:59.42
5	Meredith Rainey	USA	1:59.57
6	Liu Li	CHN	2:04.45
7	Tina Paulino	MOZ	3:19.89

Liliya Nurutdinova RUS (7th 3:19.18) drugs dq

A fifth African record of the season for Maria Mutola

1500 METRES (22)

THE Chinese controlled the pace from the start, Lu leading at 400m in 68.20 and Liu at 800m 2:17.58. Then Liu looked at Lu and was off, taking just 60.15 for the 400m from 800m to 1200m and finishing with a 57.48 last 400m. O'Sullivan came back from only 4th in the 3000m, a race she had been highly favoured to win, to take a highly acclaimed silver medal from defending champion Boulmerka.

1	Liu Dong	CHN	4:00.50
2	Sonia O'Sullivan	IRL	4:03.48
3	Hassiba Boulmerka	ALG	4:04.29
4	Lu Yi	CHN	4:06.06
5	Angela Chalmers	CHN	4:07.95
6	Teresa Kiesl	AUT	4:08.04
7	Anna Brzezinska	POL	4:08.11
8	Fabia Trabaldo	ITA	4:08.23

3000 METRES (16)

THE first kilometre of the final was slow as Annette Peters (10th 8:45.56) led at 2:59.06. Then Yvonne Murray (9th 8:43.46) increased the pace with a 66-second lap, but she did not sustain the pace, so that 2000m was reached in 5:49.45.

With 700m to go the three Chinese zipped away from the field with an awe-inspiring display. O'Sullivan fought as best she could but nobody could catch them as Qu covered the last kilometre in 2:39.26, the last 600m in 1:30.07, the last 400 in 59.22.

1	Qu Yunxia	CHN	8:28.71 *
2	Zhang Linli	CHN	8:29.25
3	Zhang Lirong	CHN	8:31.95
4	Sonia O'Sullivan	IRL	8:33.38
5	Alison Wyeth	GBR	8:38.42
6	Yelena Romanova	RUS	8:39.69
7	Paula Radcliffe	GBR	8:40.40
8	Lyudmila Borisova	RUS	8:40.78

10000 METRES (21)

WANG and Zhong took the lead from the start, sharing the lead for most of the race. Zhong led at 1000m 3:04.00, 3000m 9:20.16 and 5000m 15:43.48, and Wang at 2000m 6:11.84. Sally Barsosio meanwhile was causing havoc. The 15 year-old (or 18 perhaps?) Kenyan, with no experience in such company, caused Elana Meyer so much anguish that the South African gave up and dropped out soon after 3000m.

The problem was that on every lap Meyer came up and tried to get past Barsosio, but each time the Kenyan girl sped up and cut across her. Barsosio was warned and should have been pulled out. She later cut up Jennings and Dias in even worse fashion than she had impeded Meyer, but those two vigorously pushed her away. Barsosio took over from the Chinese to lead at 4000m 12:28.72 and 6000m 18:54.53. After Zhong led at 7000m 22:06.80,

Wang took off and that was that. She ran the last 3000m in an amazing 8:42.42 with a last 400m of 61.07.

Barsosio was originally disqualified but was later, most luckily despite her brilliant world junior record, reinstated due to the fact that no official second warning had been issued.

1	Wang Junxia	CHN	30:49.30 *
2	Zhong Huandi	CHN	31:12.55
3	Selina Barsosio	KEN	31:15.38
4	Tecla Lorupe	KEN	31:29.91
5	Lynn Jennings	USA	31:30.53
6	Conceição Ferreira	POR	31:30.60
7	Albertina Dias	POR	31:33.03
8	Anne Marie Letko	USA	31:37.26

MARATHON (15)

IN 23°C and 68% humidity there was a 1-3-11 (Akemi Matsuno 2:38:04) finish for Japan. Jones set the pace to 30km, where she tripped at a water station. Then Machado opened up a 15m gap on Asari and Abe. Asari stayed close and moved ahead at 36km, extending her lead all the way to the finish. Her 10km splits: 35:26, 1:10:41, 1:47:14, 2:22:17.

1	Junko Asari	JPN	2:30:03
2	Manuela Machado	POR	2:30:54
3	Tomoe Abe	JPN	2:31:01
4	Ramilya Burangulova	RUS	2:33:03
5	Madina Biktagirova	BLS	2:34:36
6	Katrin Dörre	GER	2:35:20
7	Frith van der Merwe	RSA	2:35:56
8	Kim Jones	USA	2:36:33

100 METRES HURDLES (20, +0.2)

DEVERS achieved the first big championships sprint and hurdles double since Fanny Blankers-Koen at the 1948 Olympics. Her emphatic victory was rewarded with an American record time of 12.46. That was also the world best for 1993, previously 12.47 by Azyabina, who was second here, starting cautiously after committing a false start. Tolbert had been quickest away, but was passed by the top two and also caught by López, before surging again to take the bronze. López equalled her Cuban record in 4th place. Devers had been fastest in heats and semis at 12.74 and 12.67.

1	Gail Devers	USA	12.46
2	Marina Azyabina	RUS	12.60
3	Lynda Tolbert	USA	12.67
4	Aliuska López	CUB	12.73
5	Eva Sokolova	RUS	12.78
6	Dawn Bowles	USA	12.90
7	Michelle Freeman	JAM	12.90
8	Cécile Cinelu	FRA	12.95

400 METRES HURDLES (19)

ONE of the greatest women's races ever resulted in both gold and silver medallists breaking the world record of 52.94 set by Marian Stepanova in 1986.

Gunnell was the clear favourite, but Farmer-Patrick, who had left the European circuit to concentrate on honing her preparation with Bobby Kersee, started fast in lane 6 and maintained her form with a lead of 0.28 by the 4th hurdle.

Gunnell, two lanes inside her, was hurdling beautifully and took the lead by 0.10 at the 7th hurdle. The American retook the lead and edged away 0.02 at the 8th, 0.04 at the 9th and 0.08 at the 10th. Then Gunnell's driving finish enabled her to gain a classic victory. Ponomaryova ran a personal best time to take the bronze, her previous best had been the world record 53.58 way back in 1984.

1	Sally Gunnell	GBR	52.74 *
2	Sandra Farmer-Patrick	USA	52.79
3	Margarita Ponomaryova	RUS	53.48
4	Kim Batten	USA	53.84
5	Tonja Buford	USA	54.55
6	Deon Hemmings	JAM	54.99
7	Rosie Edeh	CAN	55.19
8	Natalya Torshina	UKR	55.78

Gail Devers: the first sprint and hurdles double winner at a major event since 1948

HIGH JUMP (21)

WORLD record holder Stefka Kostadinova had one of those days in failing to qualify. She had plenty of height but kept coming down on the bar, thus failing to clear the requisite 1.93. Heike Henkel also failed that height but was advanced to the final on count back.

However, her injured Achilles meant that she did not take part. Without the big two the Cubans took the top places, Quintero won the gold with a second attempt clearance at 1.99. Costa was clear up to and including 1.97, a height cleared for an Austrian record by Kirchmann on her second attempt.

1	Ioamnet Quintero	CUB	1.99
2	Silvia Costa	CUB	1.97
3	Sigrid Kirchmann	AUT	1.97
4=	Yelena Rodina	RUS	1.94
4=	Galina Astafei	ROM	1.94
6	Antonella Bevilacqua	ITA	1.94
7	Tanya Hughes	USA	1.91
8	Valentina Gotovska	LAT	1.91

LONG JUMP (15)

TEN years after Heike Daute had become the youngest ever world champion at 18 in 1983, Heike (now Drechsler) regained her title, helped by the fact that Jackie Joyner-Kersee, the 1987 and 1991 champion, was persuaded to miss the event to concentrate on the heptathlon.

Drechsler took the lead half way through the first round at 6.79, but lost that to Berezhnaya's 6.98.

Then Drechsler settled proceedings with a 7.09 in the second, following with 6.83, 7.11, 7.10 and 7.09 as nobody else exceeded 7m. Nielsen jumped 6.76 in each of the first two rounds for the bronze, the first ever World Championships medal for Denmark.

1	Heike Drechsler	GER	7.11
2	Larisa Berezhnaya	UKR	6.98
3	Renata Nielsen	DEN	6.76
4	Yelena Khlopotnova	UKR	6.75
5	Lyudmila Galkina	RUS	6.74
6	Ludmila Ninova	AUT	6.73
7	Nicole Boegman	AUS	6.70
8	Agata Karczmarek	POL	6.57

TRIPLE JUMP (21)

THE first 15 metre triple jump ever by a woman came in the fifth round when Biryukova leapt to 15.09 (5.57 hop, 4.47 step, 5.05 jump). She had taken a 1st round lead with 14.62, improving to 14.77 in the 2nd, before x, 14.54, 15.09 and x. Chen, the previous record holder, was fortunate to make the final eight as her 13.78 and three no jumps meant she was 8th after three and four rounds.

In the 5th, however she jumped 14.48 and ended with 14.70. Montalvo jumped into medal contention with a 5th round 14.22, but Prandzheva improved from 14.07 to 14.23 in the 6th to take a surprise medal.

1	Ana Biryukova	RUS	15.09
2	Yolanda Chen	RUS	14.70
3	Iva Prandzheva	BUL	14.23
4	Niurka Montalvo	CUB	14.22
5	Helga Radtke	GER	14.19
6	Antonella Capriotti	ITA	14.18
7	Sarka Kaspárková	TCH	14.16
8	Urszula Wlodarczyk	POL	13.80

SHOT (15)

HUANG defended her title and won easily with a series of 19.75, 20.31, 20.19, 20.57, x, 20.46. Krivelyova led the qualifiers with 19.96 from Kumbernuss 19.92, and took a first round lead in the final at 19.97, but thereafter strove in vain to catch Huang. No could Neimke exceed her opening 19.71.

1	Huang Zhihong	CHN	20.57
2	Svetlana Krivelyova	RUS	19.97
3	Kathrin Neimke	GER	19.71
4	Sui Xinmei	CHN	19.61
5	Cong Yuzhen	CHN	19.58
6	Astrid Kumbernuss	GER	19.42
7	Valentina Fedyushina	UKR	19.27
8	Belsis Laza	CUB	19.27

DISCUS (19)

ONLY just back from injury Ilke Wyludda led the qualifiers at 64.06, but could manage only 11th with 60.42 in the final. Costian took a first round lead with 63.90 and increased that to 64.78 in the 2nd, but later that round Burova threw 67.40 and that was not surpassed.

Her series was a fine one: 63.28, 67.40, 65.80, 67.06, 65.00, x. Min moved to second with a 3rd round 65.26, and Costian responded with 65.36 in the 4th. Svetla Mitkova's 61.18 was the best ever non-qualifying throw.

1	Olga Burova	RUS	67.40
2	Daniela Costian	AUS	65.36
3	Min Chunfeng	CHN	65.26
4	Maritza Martén	CUB	64.62
5	Anja Gündler	GER	62.92
6	Barbara Echevarría	CUB	62.52
7	Nicoleta Grasu	ROM	62.10
8	Franka Dietzsch	GER	62.06

Placings in the first eight by nation

Nation	*1st*	*2nd*	*3rd*	*4th*	*5th*	*6th*	*7th*	*8th*	*Medals*	*Places*	*Points*
USA	13	7	5	5	6	3	4	7	25	50	256
Russia	3	8	5	5	5	6	3	3	16	38	182
Germany	2	2	4	5	6	6	3	4	8	32	131
GB & NI	3	3	4	3	1	1	1	2	10	18	95
Kenya	3	3	4	2	1	-	3	3	10	19	92
China	4	2	2	2	1	1	-	-	8	12	75
Cuba	2	1	-	5	-	3	-	2	3	13	59
Jamaica	1	1	3	1	-	2	4	1	5	13	53
Belarus	-	2	2	2	2	-	3	-	4	11	50
Spain	2	1	2	1	1	1	1	-	5	9	49
Ukraine	1	1	2	2	1	1	1	-	4	9	46
France	-	-	-	4	2	4	-	3	-	13	43
Italy	-	3	1	1	-	3	-	2	4	10	43
Finland	1	2	-	-	1	-	1	-	3	5	28
Ethiopia	1	1	1	1	-	-	-	-	3	4	26
Canada	-	-	1	-	2	1	2	-	1	6	21
Romania	-	-	1	2	-	-	2	1	1	6	21
Australia	-	1	-	-	2	-	2	1	1	6	20
Bulgaria	-	-	1	1	1	1	-	1	1	5	19
Japan	1	-	1	-	1	-	-	-	2	3	18
Namibia	1	1	-	-	-	1	-	-	2	3	18
Poland	-	1	-	-	1	1	1	2	1	6	18
Ireland	-	1	-	1	-	1	-	-	1	3	15
Algeria	1	-	1	-	-	-	-	-	3	3	14
Nigeria	-	-	-	-	3	-	1	-	-	4	14
Austria	-	-	1	-	-	2	-	-	1	3	12
Czech Rep	1	-	-	-	-	-	2	-	1	3	12
Morocco	-	-	-	-	1	1	2	1	-	5	12
Portugal	-	1	-	-	-	1	1	-	1	3	12
Mozambique	1	-	-	-	-	-	1	-	1	2	10
Switzerland	1	-	-	-	-	-	-	1	1	2	9
Norway	1	-	-	-	-	-	-	-	1	1	8
Tajikistan	1	-	-	-	-	-	-	-	1	1	8
Kazakhstan	-	1	-	-	-	-	-	1	1	2	8
South Africa	-	-	-	-	1	-	1	1	-	3	7
Zambia	-	1	-	-	-	-	-	-	1	1	7

Four other nations gained one bronze medal: Denmark, Hungary, Netherlands and Somalia A further 17 nations had at least one placer in the first eight, making in all 57 nations, of whom 36 had medallists.

JAVELIN (22)

HATTESTAD had disappointed in many previous major championships, with a best of only fifth, but came good here to lead the qualifiers with 66.52 and with the final throw of the first round of the final threw 69.18, more than four metres better than any other throw until she ended the competition with 66.18.

Natalya Shikolenko had opened the final with 65.64, but that was passed by Forkel in the third round and unable to improve herself Shikolenko was challenged by her younger sister Tatyana, who threw a final round 65.18.

1	Trine Hattestad	NOR	69.18
2	Karen Forkel	GER	65.80
3	Natalya Shikolenko	BLS	65.64
4	Tatyana Shikolenko	BLS	65.18
5	Yekaterina Ivakina	RUS	65.12
6	Silke Renk	GER	64.00
7	Claudia Isaila	ROM	61.54
8	Felicia Tilea	ROM	61.24

HEPTATHLON (16/17)

DIMITROVA beat Joyner-Kersee at 100mh 12.85 to 12.89 and JJK lost ground when she could manage only 1.81 in the high jump, as Braun's 1.90 added to her 13.25 hurdles was enough for the lead.

Braun increased her lead with a 14.62 shot to 41 points over Buraga and 77 over JJK (14.38), but JJK's 23.19 behind Dimitrova's 23.10 took her into a slender first day lead with 4011 to Buraga 4003 and Braun (who ran only 24.12) 3997.

On the second day Joyner-Kersee showed the qualities of a great champion, as despite being below her supreme best she fought hard to regain her title by a margin of 50 points from Braun, who had won in 1991 when JJK withdrew injured.

JJK increased her lead to 161 points with a splendid third round 7.04 long jump, but although Braun came from 190 points down to take a 7-point lead with a 53.44 javelin to JJK's 43.76, JJK was able to hold off her rival in the 800m, 2:14.49 to 2:17.82.

1	Jackie Joyner-Kersee	USA	6837
2	Sabine Braun	GER	6787
3	Svetlana Buraga	BLS	6635
4	Svetla Dimitrova	BUL	6508
5	Urszula Wlodarczyk	POL	6394
6	Kym Carter	USA	6357
7	Jane Flemming	AUS	6343
8	Birgit Clarius	GER	6341

4 X 100 METRES RELAY (22)

GAIL DEVERS was again involved in a very tight photo-finish, but this time just lost the verdict to Irina Privalova, as both Russia and the USA shared the winning time of 41.49. Jamaica, anchored by Merlene Ottey (who matched Carl Lewis with a record ten World Championships medals), were third. All these teams and Cuba and Finland set national records, as place times 2-6 were the best ever.

The Russians started with Olga Bogoslovskaya and Galina Malchugina, while after a poor exchange from Michelle Finn, Gwen Torrence ran hard for the USA. Wanda Vereen lost a couple of metres on the third leg to Natalya Voronova, who handed over just ahead. Times for the last 100m were Devers 9.86 and Privalova 9.89.

1	Russia	41.49 *
2	USA	41.49
3	Jamaica	41.94
4	France	42.67
5	Germany	42.79
6	Cuba	42.89
7	Finland	43.37
8	Great Britain	43.86

4 X 400 METRES RELAY (22)

POSSIBLY the two best 400m runners in the world had not contested the individual event, but certainly made their presence felt here. Irina Privalova ran the fastest split of the race to anchor the Russian team with 48.47, but by then the Americans were far way, for Gwen Torrence had sent them on their way with 49.0 from the start, the fastest ever opening leg.

She was followed by Maicel Malone 49.4, Natasha Kaiser-Brown 49.48 and Jearl Miles 48.78, while the Russian first three were Yelena Ruzina 50.8, Tatyana Alekseyeva 49.3 and Ponomaryova 49.78. Sally Gunnell's 49.90 anchor against the individual bronze medallist Sandie Richards 50.16 took Britain to the bronze medals.

1	USA	3:16.71 *
2	Russia	3:18.38
3	Great Britain	3:23.41
4	Jamaica	3:23.83
5	Germany	3:25.49
6	France	3:27.08
7	Czech Republic	3:27.94
8	Switzerland	3:28.52

10 KILOMETRES WALK (14)

ESSAYAH took the first gold medal of the Championships. Madelein Svensson, who led at 5km in 21:52 made a break soon after that, but was disqualified with Essayah in second place, struggling to stay with the Swede, just before 7km.

The World Cup winner Wang Yan was ruled out a kilometre later and Essayah, who clocked 21:05 for the second 5km, was left in full control. Kerry Saxby-Junna, holder of the world best time, failed to finish.

1	Sari Essayah	FIN	42:59
2	Ileana Salvador	ITA	43:08
3	Encarnación Granados	ESP	43:21
4	Elisabetta Perrone	ITA	43:26
5	Beate Anders	GER	43:28
6	Katarzyna Radtke	POL	43:33
7	Yelena Nikolayeva	RUS	43:47
8	Yelena Sayko	RUS	43:56

* Championships record

World Junior Championships

THE Fifth World Junior Champ-ionships will be held at Lisbon, Portugal in 1994.
Medals were won by athletes from a record 31 countries in 1988 and 1990.

Previous championships have been held:

Venue	Dates	Athletes	Nations
Athens, Greece	16-20 July 1986	1188	143
Sudbury, Canada	27-31 July 1988	1052	122
Plovdiv, Bulgaria	8-12 Aug 1990	1033	86
Seoul, Korea	16-20 Sep 1992	988	90

Most gold medals 1986-92
Men - 4 Chris Nelloms USA 4x400mR 1988, 400m, 4x100mR & 4x400mR 1990
Women - 4 Gillian Russell JAM 100mh & 4x100mR 1990 & 1992
3 Grit Breuer GDR 400m, 4x100mR & 4x400mR 1988
3 Nicole Mitchell JAM 4x100mR 1990, 100m & 4x100mR 1992
Most medals - 5 Katrin Krabbe GDR 3rd 200m, 2nd 4x100mR 1986; 1st 200m & 4x100mR, 2nd 100m 1988
Youngest champions
Men: 16yr 215d Jonah Birir KEN 800m 1988
Women: 15yr 102d Wang Yan CHN 5000m walk 1986
Youngest medallists:
Men: 15yr 169d Ismael Kirui KEN 2nd 10,000m 1990
Women: 14yr 182d Selina Barsosio KEN 3rd 10,000m 1992

Medal table for leading nations 1986-92

Nation	1st	2nd	3rd
GDR 1986-90	22	10	18
USSR/CIS	22	18	27
USA	18	15	9
Kenya	17	12	6
China	12	6	6
Romania	9	6	4
Cuba	8	13	5
Ethiopia	8	5	6
GBR	7	11	8
FRG/GER	5	8	8
Jamaica	5	5	6
Bulgaria	5	3	6

Championship bests after 1992

Men

Event	Mark	Athlete	Year
100m	10.17	Derrick Florence USA	1986
	10.17	Andre Cason USA	qf 1988
	10.17	Davidson Ezinwa NGR	1990
200m	20.47	Aleksandr Goremykin URS	1990
400m	45.43	Chris Nelloms USA	1990
800m	1:44.77	Benson Koech KEN	1992
1500m	3:37.94	Atoi Boru KEN	1992
5000m	13:36.06	Haile Gebresilasie ETH	1992
10000m	28:03.99	Haile Gebresilasie ETH	1992
20km Rd	59:27	Metaferia Zeleke ETH	1988
2000mSt	5:28.56	Juan Azkueta ESP	1986
3000mSt	8:31.02	Matthew Birir KEN	1990
110mh	13.44	Colin Jackson GBR	1986
400mh	49.50	Kelly Carter USA	1988
HJ	2.37	Dragutin Topic YUG	1990
	2.37	Steve Smith GBR	1992
PV	5.65	István Bagyula HUN	1988
LJ	8.20	James Stallworth USA	q 1990
TJ	17.04	Yoelvis Quesada CUB	1992
SP	19.21	Viktor Bulat URS	1990
DT	60.60	Vasil Baklarov BUL	1986
HT	72.00	Vitaliy Alisevich URS	1986
JT	78.84	Vladimir Zasimovich URS	1986
Dec	7729	Michael Kohnle FRG	1988
10kmW	39:55.52	Ilya Markov URS	1990
4x100mR	39.13	USA	1990
4x400mR	3:01.90	USA	1986

Women

Event	Mark	Athlete	Year
100m	11.18	Diana Dietz GDR	1988
200m	23.10	Diane Smith GBR	1990
400m	50.62	Fatima Yusuf NGR	1990
800m	2:00.67	Birte Bruhns GDR	1988
1500m	4:05.14	Liu Dong CHN	1992
3000m	8:46.86	Zhang Linli CHN	1992
10000m	32:22.90	Wang Junxia CHN	1992
100mh	12.96	Aliuska López CUB	sf 1988
400mh	55.84	Nella Voronkova URS	1990
HJ	2.00	Galina Astafei ROM	1988
LJ	6.82	Fiona May GBR	1988
	6.88w	Fiona May	1988
TJ	13.47	Anja Vokuhl GER	1992
SP	18.54	Ines Wittich GDR	1988
DT	6824	Ilke Wyludda GDR	1988
JT	63.04	Claudia Isaila ROM	1992
Hep	6289	Svetla Dimitrova BUL	1988
5kmW	21:20.03	Gao Hongmiao CHN	1992
4x100mR	43.48	GDR	1988
4x400mR	3:28.39	GDR	1988

The 5000m will replace the 10000m on the women's programme from 1996.

I.A.A.F. WORLD CUP

THE seventh edition of the IAAF World Cup meeting will be staged at the Crystal Palace Stadium in London, GBR in 1994. The idea of having a competition between teams representing the continents and top athletics nations was conceived in 1975 and the first World Cup was staged in Düsseldorf FRG on 2-4 Sep 1977. Subsequent World Cups have been held: 1979 Montreal, 1981 Rome, 1985 Canberra, 1989 Barcelona, 1992 Havana.

The competing teams represent each of the five continents, with national teams from the USA and the top two men's and women's teams from the European Cup. In 1989 the host nation Spain competed as a ninth team, as did Italy in 1981.

From 1994 the intention is that the event will be staged every four years.

Best Performances

Men

100m	10.00	Ben Johnson CAN	1985
200m	20.00	Robson da Silva BRA	1989
400m	44.47	Mike Franks USA	1985
800m	1:44.04	Alberto Juantorena CUB	1977
1500m	3:34.45	Steve Ovett GBR	1977
5000m	13:13.82	Miruts Yifter ETH	1977
10000m	27:38.43	Werner Schildhauer GDR	1981
3000mSt	8:19.89	Boguslaw Maminski POL	1981
110mh	13.07	Colin Jackson GBR	1992
	12.87w	Roger Kingdom USA	1989
400mh	47.31	Edwin Moses USA	1981
HJ	2.34	Patrik Sjöberg SWE	1989
PV	5.85	Sergey Bubka URS	1985
LJ	8.52	Larry Myricks USA	1979
TJ	17.58	Willie Banks USA	1985
SP	22.00	Ulf Timmermann GDR	1985
DT	69.08	Gennadiy Kolnootchenko URS	1985
HT	82.12	Jüri Tamm URS	1985
JT	88.26	Jan Zelezny TCH	1992
(old)	96.96	Uwe Hohn GDR	1985
4x100mR	38.03	USA	1977
4x400mR	2:59.12	USA	1981

Women

100m	11.02	Evelyn Ashford USA	1981
200m	21.83	Evelyn Ashford USA	1979
400m	47.60	Marita Koch GDR	1985
800m	1:54.44	Ana Quirot CUB	1989
1500m	4:03.33	Tamara Sorokina URS	1981
3000m	8:36.32	Svyetlana Ulmasova URS	1979
10000m	31:33.92	Kathrin Ullrich GDR	1989
100mh	12.60	Cornelia Oschkenat GDR	1989
400mh	53.84	Sandra Farmer-Patrick USA	1989
HJ	2.04	Silvia Costa CUB	1989
LJ	7.27	Heike Drechsler GDR	1985
TJ	13.88	Li Huirong CHN	1992
SP	20.98	Ilona Slupianek GDR	1979
DT	71.54	Ilke Wyludda GDR	1989
JT	70.32	Petra Felke GDR	1989
4x100mR	41.37	GDR	1985
4x400mR	3:19.50	GDR	1985

Most individual event wins

Men: 4 Miruts Yifter AFR/ETH 5000m & 10000m 1977-79

Women: 4 Evelyn Ashford USA 100m & 200m 1981-83

Triple winner at one meeting: Ana Quirot CUB won 400m, 800m and 4x400m relay for the Americas in 1989.

Team Positions

	Men						Women					
Team	1977	1979	1981	1985	1989	1992	1977	1979	1981	1985	1989	1992
Africa	6	6	7	5	5	1	7	7	9	8	7	6
Americas	5	5	5	6	6	4	5	5	5	4	3	3
Asia	8	8	9	8	7	7	8	8	8	7	6	7
Europe	4	2	1	4	2	3	1	3	2	3	4	2
GBR	-	-	-	-	3	2	-	-	-	-	-	-
GDR	1	3	2	3	4	-	2	1	1	1	1	-
FRG/GER	3	-	-	-	-	-	-	-	-	-	-	5
Italy	-	-	6	-	-	-	-	-	6	-	-	-
Oceania	7	7	8	7	9	8	6	6	7	6	9	8
Spain	-	-	-	-	8	-	-	-	-	-	8	-
USA	2	1	3	1	1	5	4	4	4	5	5	4
USSR/CIS	-	4	4	2	-	6	3	2	3	2	2	1

WORLD HALF MARATHON CHAMPIONSHIPS

At Brussels, Belgium 3 October.
Leading results
Men
1. Vincent Rousseau BEL 61:06
2. Steve Moneghetti AUS 61:10
3. Carl Thackery GBR 61:13
4. Lameck Aguta KEN 61:15
5. Valdenor dos Santos BRA 61:17
6. Antonio Silio ARG 61:35
7. John Andrews AUS 61:37
8. Adam Motlagale RSA 61:42
9. Rainer Wachenbrunner GER 62:00
10. Jan Ikov DEN 62:02
11. Kozo Akutsu JPN 62:07
12. Kidane Gebremichael ETH 62:10
13. Thomas Osano KEN 62:10
14. Haruo Urata JPN 62:12
15. Mark Flint GBR 62:13
16. Joseph Cheromei KEN 62:15

129 finishers
Teams: 1. KEN 3:05:40, 2. AUS 3:05:43, 3. GBR 3:06:10, 4. JPN 3:06:40, 5. RSA 3:07:15, 6. BEL 3:07:33, 7. ETH 3:07:38, 8. POR 3:07:46, 9. ITA 3:07:50, 10. BRA 3:08:01, 11. GER 3:08:18, 12. FRA 3:10:24, 13. USA 3:10:46, 14. ESP 3:10:56. 26 nations placed.

Junior Men
1. Meck Mothuli RSA 62:11
2. Biruk Bekele ETH 63:32
3. Isaac Radebe RSA 63:35
4. Frank Pooe RSA 64:00
5. Tegenu Abebe ETH 64:19
6. Aleksey Sobolev RUS 65:12

33 finishers
Teams: 1. RSA 3:09:46, 2. ETH 3:13:34, 3. ITA 3:17:12, 4. RUS 3:18:26. 7 nations placed.

Women
1. M Conceição Ferreira POR 70:07
2. Mari Tanigawa JPN 70:09
3. Tecla Lorupe KEN 70:12
4. Miyoko Asahina JPN 70:15
5. Elena Murgoci ROM 70:17
6. Anuta Catuna ROM 70:39
7. Iulia Negura ROM 71:22
8. Albertina Machado POR 71:39
9. Adriana Barbu Andreescu ROM 71:52
10. Akari Takemoto JPN 71:58
11. Maria Muñoz ESP 72:04
12. Suzanne Rigg GBR 72:07
13. Natalya Galushko BLS 72:08
14. Annick Clouvel FRA 72:12
15. Rosa Oliveira POR 72:26
16. Julia Sakala ZIM 72:28

80 finishers.
Teams: 1, ROM 3:32:18, 2, JPN 3:32:22, 3, POR 3:34:12, 4, GBR 3:38:54, 5, ESP 3:39:04, 6, RUS 3:40:12, 7. FRA 3:41:18, 8. USA 3:42:54, 9. GER 3:43:13, 10. BEL 3:44:18, 11. UKR 3:44:50, 12. IRL 3:45:14, 13. RSA 3:45:43, 14. HOL 3:47:58. 17 nations placed..

THE event was first held in 1992 when the winners were
Men: Benson Masya KEN 60:24
Men Team: Kenya
Women: Liz McColgan GBR 68:53
Women Team: Japan
Junior Men: Kasse Tadesse ETH 64:51
Junior Men Team: Italy

Previous winners of the Women's World Road Race Championships (10km 1983-4, 15km 1984-91)

Team
1983 USA
1984 GBR
1985 GBR
1986 USSR
1987 Portugal
1988 USSR
1989 China
1990 Portugal
1991 Germany

Individual
1983 Wendy Sly GBR 32:23
1984 Aurora Cunha POR 33:04
1985 Aurora Cunha POR 49:17
1986 Aurora Cunha POR 48:31
1987 Ingrid Kristiansen NOR 47:17
1988 Ingrid Kristiansen NOR 48:24
1989 Wang Xiuting CHN 49:34
1990 Iulia Negura ROM 50:12
1991 Iulia Negura ROM 48:42

The 1994 World Half Marathon Championships will be held in Oslo, Norway on 24 September

WORLD CUP MARATHON

The fifth edition of this event was run at San Sebastián, Spain 31 Oct 1993. Leading results:

Men

1. Richard Nerurkar GBR 2:10:03
2. Severino Bernardini ITA 2:10:12
3. Kebede Gemechu ETH 2:10:16
4. Becho Tadesse ETH 2:10:27
5. Rodrigo Gavela ESP 2:10:27
6. Tumo Turbo ETH 2:10:31
7. Turbe Bedaso ETH 2:10:34
8. Luca Barzaghi ITA 2:10:53
9. Koichi Takahashi JPN 2:10:55
10. Diego Garcia ESP 2:10:58
11. Dave Buzza GBR 2:11:06
12. Fenando Couto POR 2:11:18
13. Walter Durbano ITA 2:11:36
14. Tafa Tesfaye ETH 2:11:57.
15. Raffaello Alliegro ITA 2:12:37

Teams: 1. ETH 6:31:17; 2. ITA 6:32:41; 3. GBR 6:34:06; 4. ESP 6:37:13; 5. POR 6:38:28; 6. UKR 6:41:13; 7. JPN 6:42:18; 8. RUS 6:44:47; 9. FRA 6:45:13; 10. USA 6:50:54

Women

1. Wang Junxia CHN 2:28:16
2. Zhang Linli CHN 2:29:42
3. Zhang Lirong CHN 2:29:45
4. Ma Liyan CHN 2:30:44
5. Maria Muñoz ESP 2:31:01
6. Monica Pont ESP 2:31:21
7. Rocio Rios ESP 2:31:33
8. Firaya Sultanova RUS 2:33:46
9. Olga Michurina RUS 2:34:31
10. Lynn Harding GBR 2:35:04
11. Ornella Ferrara ITA 2:35:08
12. Maria Rebello FRA 2:35:37
13. Lorraine Hochella USA 2:35:38
14. Tatyana Pentukova RUS 2:35:50
15. Fatima Neves POR 2:36:15

Teams: 1. CHN 7:27:43; 2. ESP 7:33:55; 3. RUS 7:44:07; 4. FRA 7:50:40; 5. USA 7:51:12; 6. ITA 7:54:11; 7. BLS 7:56:05; 8. GBR 7:56:15; 9. ROM 7:59:31; 10. GER 8:14:41.

IAAF WORLD RACE WALKING CUP 1993

At Monterrey, Mexico 24/25 April

Men's 20 Kilometres

1. Daniel Garcia MEX	1:24:26
2. Valentin Massana ESP	1:24:32
3. Alberto Cruz MEX	1:24:37
4. Robert Korzeniowski POL	1:24:47
5. Mikhail Shchennikov RUS	1:24:49
6. Daniel Plaza ESP	1:24:52
7. Giovanni De Benedictis ITA	1:25:09
8. Robert Ihly GER	1:25:32
9. Igor Kollár SVK	1:26:00
10. Giovanni Perricelli ITA	1:26:17
11. Vladimir Andreyev RUS	1:26:26
12. Li Mingcai CHN	1:26:26
13. Nicholas A'Hern AUS	1:27:11
14. Ignacio Zamudio MEX	1:27:24
15. Clodomiro Moreno COL	1:27:33
16. Magnus Morenius SWE	1:27:42
17. Orlando Diaz COL	1:28:05
18. Jacek Muller POL	1:28:09
19. Denis Langlois FRA	1:28:11
20. Chen Shaoguo CHN	1:28:31

Teams: 1. MEX 265, 2. ITA 244, 3. ESP 240

Men's 50 Kilometres

1. Carlos Mercenario MEX	3:50:28
2. Jesús Garcia ESP	3:52:44
3. German Sánchex MEX	3:54:15
4. Miguel Rodriguez MEX	3:54:22
5. Tim Berrett CAN	3:55:12
6. Valentin Kononen FIN	3:57:28
7. Simon Baker AUS	3:58:36

Previous World Cup Marathon winnerss

	Team		Individual	
	Men	*Women*	*Men*	*Women*
1985	Djibouti	Italy	Ahmed Salah DJI 2:08:09	Katrin Dörre GDR 2:33:30
1987	Italy	USSR	Ahmed Salah DJI 2:10:55	Zoya Ivanova URS 2:30:39
1989	Ethiopia	USSR	Metaferia Zeleke ETH 2:10:28	Sue Marchiano USA 2:30:48
1991	GBR	USSR	Yakov Tolstikov URS 2:09:17	Rosa Mota POR 2:26:14

8. Hartwig Gauder GER 3:59:10
9. Giuseppe De Gaetano ITA 4:00:19
10. Jean-Claude Corre FRA 4:01:12
11. Martin Bermudez MEX 4:01:37
12. René Piller FRA 4:02:33
13. Tomasz Lipiec POL 4:03:09
14. Massimo Quiriconi ITA 4:04:11
15. Basilio Labrador ESP 4:04:35
16. José Marin ESP 4:04:37
17. Andres Marin ESP 4:04:52
18. Thierry Toutain FRA 4:05:18
19. Paulo Bianchi ITA 4:05:29
20. Jaime Barroso ESP 4:06:28

Teams: 1. MEX 275, 2. ESP 251, 3. FRA 245

Overall men's team: 1. MEX 540, 2. ESP 491, 3. ITA 487, 4. FRA 453, 5. POL 452, 6. RUS 424, 7. AUS 405, 8. SVK 375, 9. GER 353, 10. FIN 330, 11. USA 322, 12. HUN 295, 13. GBR 286, 14. SWE 258, 15. RSA 242, 16. COL 225, 17. BLS 222, 18. CHN 221, 19. DEN 217, 20. CAN 211, 30 nations scored.

Women's 10 Kilometres

1. Wang Yan CHN 45:10
2. Sari Essayah FIN 45:18
3. Yelena Nikolayeva RUS 45:22
4. Madelein Svensson SWE 45:43
5. Kerry Saxby/Junna AUS 45:55
6. Ileana Salvador ITA 46:02
7. Annarita Sidoti ITA 46:14
8. Susana Feitor POR 46:28
9. Long Yuwen CHN 46:34
10. Elisabetta Perrone ITA 46:49
11. Yelena Gruzinova RUS 46:56
12. Olimpiada Ivanova RUS 47:02
13. Beate Anders GER 47:06
14. Cristina Pellino ITA 47:23
15. Allison Baker CAN 47:34
16. Maria Rosza HUN 47:37
17. Beata Kaczmarska POL 47:54
18. Liu Hongyu CHN 47:56
19. Andrea Alföldi HUN 47:59
20. Natalya Misyulya BLS 47:59

Overall women's teamı:
1, ITA 196, 2. CHN 193, 3. RUS 193, 4. AUS 170, 5. HUN 160, 6. ESP 144, 7. MEX 135, 8, GER 127, 9. JPN 123, 10. BLS 121, 11. POR 113, 12. SWE 108, 13. USA 97, 14. FRA 88, 15. CAN 86, 16. FIN 83, 17. KZK 83, 18.UKR 82. 24 nations scored.

Previous team winners

Men

5 GDR 1965, 1967, 1970, 1973, 1985
4 USSR 1975, 1983, 1987, 1989
3 Mexico 1977, 1979, 1993
2 United Kingdom 1961, 1963
2 Italy 1981, 1991

Women

4 USSR 1981, 1987, 1989, 1991
2 China 1983, 1985
1 United Kingdom 1979
1 Italy 1993

WORLD UNIVERSITY GAMES 1993

At Buffalo, USA July 14-18

Men

100m	1. Daniel Effiong NGR 10.07w
(+2.6)	2. Sam Jefferson USA 10.13w
	3. Glenroy Gilbert CAN 10.14w
200m	1. Brian Bridgewater USA 20.14w
(+2.4)	2. Chris Nelloms USA 20.17w
	3. Ivan Garcia CUB 20.55w
400m	1. Ibrahim Hassan GHA 45.87
	2. Evan Clarke JAM 46.27
	3. Danny McFarlane JAM 46.60
800m	1. Marko Koers HOL 1:48.57
	2. Oleg Stepanov RUS 1:49.50
	3. Nico Motchebon GER 1:49.52
1500m	1. Abdel. Chekhemani FRA 3:46.32
	2. Bill Burke USA 3:46.33
	3. Gary Lough GBR 3:46.77
5000m	1. Khalid Khannouchi MAR 14:05.33
	2. Sergey Fedotov RUS 14:06.15
	3. Toshinari Takaoka JPN 14:06.21
10000m	1. Antonio Serrano ESP 28:16.16
	2. Yasuyuki Watanabe JPN 28:17.26
	3. Vincenzo Modica ITA 28:17.73
Mar	1. Kennedy Manyisa KEN 2:12:19 *
	2. Kim Wan-ki KOR 2:15:35
	3. Hyung Jea-young KOR 2:15:53
3000mSt	1. Michael Buchleitner AUT 8:30.82
	2. Vladimir Pronin RUS 8:32.03
	3. Bizuneh Yae Tura ETH 8:32.07
110mh	1. Dietmar Koszewski GER 13.48
	2. Glenn Terry USA 13.58
	3. Stellios Bisbas GRE 13.72
400mh	1. Derrick Adkins USA 49.35
	2. Yoshihiko Saito JPN 49.61
	3. Dusan Kovács HUN 50.12

HJ 1. Tony Barton USA 2.30
2. Stevan Zoric YUG 2.30
3= Arturo Ortiz ESP 2.27
3= Ruslan Stipanov UKR 2.27

PV 1. István Bagyula HUN 5.70
2. Alberto Giacchetto ITA 5.60
3. Jean Galfione FRA 5.60

LJ 1. Kar. Streete-Thompson USA 8.22w
2. Obina Eregbu NGR 8.18
3. Vitaliy Kirilenko UKR 8.04

TJ 1. Tosi Fasinro GBR 16.91w
2. Oleg Sakirkin KZK 16.89
3. Julian Golley GBR 16.88

SP 1. Aleksandr Klimenko UKR 19.72
2. Paulo Dal Saglio ITA 19.64
3. Chris Volgenau USA 19.54

DT 1. Alexis Elizalde CUB 62.98
2. Adewale Olukoju NGR 62.96
3. Nick Sweeney IRL 62.52

HT 1. Vadim Kolesnik UKR 77.00
2. Balazs Kiss HUN 76.88
3. Christophe Epalle FRA 76.80

JT 1. Louis Fouche RSA 79.64
2. Ed Kaminski USA 77.52
3. Mika Parviainen FIN 77.14

20kW 1. Robert Korzeniowski POL 1:22:01 *
2. Daniel Garcia MEX 1:22:58
3. Bernardo Segura MEX 1:24:11

4x100m 1. USA 38.65
Bridgewater, Oaks, Miller, Jefferson
2. Japan 38.97
3. Cuba 39.20

4x400m 1. USA 3:02.34
Jones, Payne, Lyles, Turner
2. Japan 3:03.21
3. Hungary 3:04.27

Women

100m (-2.1) 1. Dahlia Duhaney JAM 11.56
2. Liliana Allen CUB 11.57
3. Beatrice Utondu NGR 11.59

200m (+3.2) 1. Flirtisha Harris USA 22.56w
2. Dahlia Duhaney JAM 22.79w
3. Wang Huei-Chen TAI 22.80w

400m 1. Michelle Collins USA 52.01
2. Youlanda Warren USA 52.18
3. Nancy McLean CUB 52.84

800m 1. Amy Wickus USA 2:03.72
2. Inez Turner JAM 2:04.14
3. Daniele Antipov ROM 2:04.75

1500m 1. Lynne Robinson GBR 4:12.03
2. Juli Speights USA 4:12.43
3. Sarah Howell CAN 4:13.30

3000m 1. Clare Eichner USA 9:04.32
2. Iulia Ionescu ROM 9:05.10
3. Rosalind Taylor USA 9:06.25

10,000m 1. Iulia Negura ROM 32:22.99
2. Suzana Ciric YUG 32:22.99
3. Camelia Tecuta ROM 32:26.68

Mar 1. Noriko Kawaguchi JPN 2:37:47
2. Franca Fiacconi ITA 2:38:44
3. Nao Otani JPN 2:40:17

100mh (-1.2) 1. Dawn Bowles USA 13.16
2. Marsha Guialdo USA 13.24
3. Nicole Ramalalanirna MAD 13.28

Original winner Ime Akpan NGR 13.11 was later disqualified due to a positive drugs test

400mh 1. Heike Meissner GER 56.10
2. Debbie Parris JAM 56.11
3. Trevaia Williams USA 56.57

HJ 1. Tanya Hughes USA 1.95
2. Neli Zilinskiene LIT 1.95
3. Polina Grigorenko UKR 1.95

LJ 1. Mirela Dulgheru ROM 6.69w
2. Vanessa Monar-Enweani CAN 6.57w
3. Daphne Saunders BAH 6.53

TJ 1. Niurka Montalvo CUB 14.16w
2. Sarka Kaspárková TCH 14.00w
3. Monika Toth ROM 13.96w

SP 1. Zhou Tianhua CHN 19.17
2. Belsis Laza CUB 18.48
3. Katrin Koch GER 16.70

DT 1. Renata Katewicz POL 62.40
2. Jacqui McKernan GBR 60.72
3. Anja Gündler GER 60.56

JT 1. Lee Young-sun KOR 58.62
2. Tanje Damaske GER 57.68
3. Valerie Tulloch CAN 56.52

Hep 1. Ulla Wlodarczyk POL 6127
2. Birgit Gautzsch GER 5934
3. Kelly Blair USA 5926

10kW 1. Long Yuwen CHN 46:16.75
2. Olga Leonenko UKR 46:18.40
3. Larisa Ramazanova RUS 46:18.58

4x100m 1. USA 43.37
Braddock, Taplin, Harris, Gaines
2. Nigeria 44.25
3. Canada 45.20

4x400m 1. USA 3:26.18
Irving, Malone, Warren, Collins
2. Cuba 3:28.95
3. Nigeria 3:34.97

* Games record

WORLD VETERANS CHAMPIONSHIPS

THE FIRST major veterans championships were the US Masters in 1968, although the Veterans AC had been formed in London back in 1931. In Germany there was a major veteran's meeting in Berlin in 1937 and the "I Internationales Altersklassen-Sportfest" at Köln in 1972.

In recent years veterans athletics has flourished,and World Veterans Championships have been held biennially since the then entitled World Masters in Toronto in 1975. The other venues have been: 1977 Göteborg, 1979 Hannover, 1981 Christchurch, 1983 Puerto Rico, 1985 Rome, 1987 Melbourne, 1989 Eugene, 1991 Turku, 1993 Miyazaki.

Veterans compete in five-year age bands, from the minimum ages of 40 (men) and 35 (women). Thus M40 is the age-range for men aged 40 to 44, M45 for those aged 45 to 49 etc..

The 10th World Veterans Athletics Championships were held at Miyazaki, Japan on 7-17 October 1993. A total of 57 world age-group records were set, 15 by men and 42 by women, and 21 of these (18 women) were set by Germans. USA athletes collected a total of 152 individual medals - 60 gold, 54 silver and 38 bronze; adding 9-5-4 at relays.

The most successful individual was Philippa Raschker, who in the W45 age-group won seven gold and two silver medals at individual events, including a world record 3.14 at pole vault, and a relay bronze. Nine medals were also won by Johnnye Valien at W65 (2G, 3S, 4B) and the oldest competitior Paul Spangler, 94, was unopposed to win seven golds.

A world record number of 9328 men and 1492 women competed (7862 and 1247 respectively from Japan).

Men - best performances by winners (M40 unless stated): 100m/200m: José Luiz Zogaib BRA 11.29/22.60, 400m: Tom Thompson USA 51.47, 800m/1500m: Carlos Cabral POR 1:57.25/4:00.60, 5000m: Ichio Sato JPN 14:59.77, 10000m M45: Omer Van Noten BEL 32:12.15, Mar: Takeshi Soh JPN 2:22:39, 3000mSt: Bruce Meder NZL 9:37.20, 110mh: Bruce Martin USA 15.42, 400mh: Bill Cheadle USA 56.68, HJ: Steve Harkins USA 1.95, PV: Itsuo Takanezawa JPN 4.40, LJ: Katsumi Fukura JPN 6.56, TJ: Crescenzo Chetti ITA 13.97, SP M45: Reinhart Krone GER 15.36, DT M45: Luciano Baraldo ITA47.34, HT M45: Shigenobu Murofushi JPN 63.46, JT: Jorma Markus FIN 75.08*, Dec: Steve Kemp CAN 6388, 5000mW/20kmW: Fabio Ruzzier ITA 21:45.69/1:35:18

Women - best performances by winners (W35 unless stated): 100m: Angela Mullinger GBR 12.35, 200m: Evelyn Ashford USA 24.14 (23.67h), 400m/400mh: Alison Brown GBR 57.12/64.83, 800m W45: Judy Bandiera 2:17.06*, 1500m/5000m W40: Carol McLatchie USA 4:38.73/17:13.49, 10000m/2000mSt: Mariet Ceronio RSA 37:10.14/7:45.56, Mar: Shinobu Kurosaki JPN 2:58:24, 100mh: Jocelyn Kirby GBR 14.29, HJ W40: Stanka Prezelj SLO 1.60, PV W45: Phil Raschker USA 3.14, LJ/TJ/Hep: Conceição Geremias BRA 5.85/12.40*/5646, SP/DT W40: Christine Schultz AUS 13.61/44.32, HT W45: Inge Faldager DEN 44.56*, JT: Maret Kalviste EST 50.30, 5000mW/10kmW W40: Heather McDonald 25:03.39/51:38.

* world age-group records

There were many fewer big names than at previous championships, but amongst the medallists were the following 'greats':

Frank Shorter USA	M45 2nd 10,000m & CC
Phil Mulkey USA	M60 1st 100mh, HJ, PV, Dec (8546*), 2nd LJ
Takeshi Soh JPN	1st M40 Mar
Evelyn Ashford USA	W35 1st 200m
Karin Illgen GER	W50 1st DT, 2nd SP
Rosemary Chrimes GBR	W60 1st HJ, SP, DT (37.56*)
Nina Ponomaryova UKR	W60 3rd DT

Two men have won world titles at each of the ten Championships from 1975: Reg Austin who won the M55 100m and 200m, and Jim Vernon who won the M75 PV.

AFRICAN CHAMPIONSHIPS 1993

At Durban, South Africa 23-27 June.
First three at each event:

Men

100m (-0.3) 1. Daniel Effiong NGR 10.39
2. Jean-Olivier Zirignon CIV 10.53
3. Nelson Boateng GHA 10.55

200m (+1.7) 1. Johan Rossouw RSA 20.65
2. Oluyemi Kayode NGR 20.79
3. Nelson Boateng GHA 21.01

400m 1. Kennedy Ochieng KEN 45.29
2. Ibrahim Hassan GHA 45.90
3. Sinom Kemboi KEN 46.06

800m 1. Samuel Kibet Langat KEN 1:45.43
2. Paul Ruto KEN 1:45.99
3. Arthémon Hatungimana BUR 1:46.42

1500m 1. David Kibet KEN 3:45.67
2. Johan Landsman RSA 3:46.03
3. Johan Fourie RSA 3:46.22

5000m 1. Simon Chemoiywo KEN 13:09.68
2. Haile Gebresilasie ETH 13:10.41
3. Worku Bikila ETH 13:12.53

10,000m 1. William Sigei KEN 27:25.23
2. Fita Bayissa ETH 27:26.90
3. Haile Gebresilasie ETH 27:30.17

3000mSt 1. Joseph Keter KEN 8:22.34
2. Chris Koskei KEN 8:24.58
3. Semretu Alemanyehu ETH 8:31.51

110mh (+0.4) 1. Kobus Schoeman RSA 13.93
2. Moses Oyiki Orode NGR 14.21
3. Winpie Nel RSA 14.22

400mh 1. Erick Keter KEN 49.38
2. Dries Vorster RSA49.59
3. Hamadou Mbaye SEN 50.22

HJ 1. Flippie van Vuuren RSA 2.22
2. Kemraj Naiko MRI 2.19
3. Pierre Vorster RSA 2.13

PV 1. Okkert Brits RSA 5.40
2. Rian Botha RSA 5.20
3. Bryan Mardaymooto MRI 4.60

LJ 1. Obinna Eregbu NGR 8.32w
2. Ayodele Aladefa NGR 8.05w
3. James Sabulei KEN 7.99

TJ 1. Toussaint Rabenala MAD 16.72
2. Wikus Olivier RSA 16.35
3. Paul Nioze SEN 16.11

SP 1. Carel le Roux RSA 18.29
2. Chima Ugwu NGR 18.07
3. Jaco Snyman RSA 17.38

DT 1. Mickael Conjungo CAF 59.92
2. Christo Kruger RSA 54.42
3. Dawie Kok RSA 54.08

HT 1. Hakim Toumi ALG 69.82
2. Samir Haouam ALG 63.76
3. Charlie Koen RSA 60.46

JT 1. Tom Petranoff RSA 82.40
2. Philip Spies RSA 77.68
3. Louis Fouché RSA 77.10

Dec 1. Pierre Faber RSA 7164
2. Danie van Wyk RSA 7108
3. Hassan Farouk Sayed EGY 6770

4x100m 1. GHA 39.53
2. NGR 39.97
3. RSA 40.25

4x400m 1. KEN 3:03.10
2. NGR 3:06.03
3. SEN 3:06.38

20kW 1. Getachew Demissie ETH 1:28:56
2. Chris Britz RSA 1:29:28
3. Riecus Blignouat RSA 1:30:55

Women

100m (-1.2) 1. Beatrice Utondu NGR 11.39
2. Elinda Vorster 11.45
3. Christy Opara-Thompson NGR 11.60

200m (+1.9) 1. Mary Onyali NGR 22.71
2. Yolanda Steyn RSA 23.22
3. Evette de Klerk RSA 23.29

400m 1. Argentina Paulino MOZ 51.82
2. Emily Odoemenam NGR 52.26
3. Aïssatou Tandian SEN 53.00

800m 1. Maria Mutola MOZ 1:56.36
2. Gladys Wamuyu KEN 2:01.24
3. Ilse Wicksell RSA 2:03.75

1500m 1. Elana Meyer RSA 4:12.56
2. Gwen Griffiths RSA 4:13.17
3. Getenesh Urge ETH 4:13.68

3000m 1. Gwen Griffiths RSA 9:13.92
2. Merina Denboba ETH 9:14.48
3. Helen Chepngeno KEN 9:14.49

10,000m 1. Birhane Adere ETH 32:48.52
2. Lydia Cheromei KEN 32:54.55
3. Fatuma Roba ETH 32:55.32

100mh (+0.3) 1. Nicole Ramalalanirina MAD 13.32
2. Taiwo Aladefa NGR 13.50
3. Annemarie le Roux RSA 13.74

400mh 1. Omotayo Akinremi NGR 57.59
2. Lana Uys RSA 57.60
3. Karen Swanepoel RSA 58.23

HJ 1. Charmaine Weavers RSA 1.90
2. Lucienne N'Da CIV 1.86
3. Desiré du Plessis RSA 1.80

LJ 1. Christy Opara-Thompson NGR 6.57
2. Beatrice Utondu NGR 6.44
3. Hiwot Sisay ETH 6.23

TJ	1. Petrusa Swart RSA 12.95w
	2. Béryl Laramé SEN 12.20w
	3. Sonya Agbéssi BEN 12.02w
SP	1. Louise Meintjies RSA 14.66
	2. Elizabeth Olaba KEN 14.42
	3. Luzanda Swanepoel RSA 14.23
DT	1. Lizette Etsebeth RSA 54.16
	2. Nanette van der Walt RSA 51.58
	3. Sandra Willms RSA 50.56
JT	1. Liezel Roux RSA 48.24
	2. Rhona Dwinger RSA 47.60
	3. Michelle Bradbury RSA 43.92
Hep	1. Chrisna Oosthuizen RSA 5339
	2. Maralize Visser RSA 5159
	3. Caroline Kola KEN 4925
4x100m	1. NGR 43.49
	2. MAD 44.93
	3. RSA 45.15
4x400m	1. NGR 3:33.21
	2. RSA 3:37.24
	3. GHA 3:39.66
5000mW	1. Dounia Kara ALG 24:33.56
	2. Amsale Yakobe ETH 24:39.04
	3. Felicity Falconer RSA 25:32.68

ASIAN GAMES

THE FIRST Asian Games were held at New Delhi, India on 8-11 Mar 1951, when ten nations took part. These multi-sport Games have since 1954 been held at four-yearly intervals, and the 12th Games will be staged at Hiroshima, Japan in 1994.

Asian Games records prior to 1994

Men

100m	10.30	Talal Mansoor QAT 1986 & 1990 (twice)
200m	20.71	Jang Jae-keun KOR 1986
400m	45.00	Susumu Takano JPN 1986
800m	1:46.81	Charles Boromeo IND 1982
1500m	3:43.49	Faleh Naji Jarallah IRQ1982
5000m	13:50.22	Mohamed Suleiman QAT 1990
10000m	28:26.74	Masanari Shintaku JPN 1986
Mar	2hr 08:21	Takeyuki Nakayama JPN 1986
3000mSt	8:34.64	Kazuhiro Yamada JPN 1990
110mh	13.82	Yu Zhicheng CHN 1990 (twice)
400mh	49.31	Ahmed Hamada BHR 1986
4x100mR	38.99	China 1990
4x400mR	3:02.33	Japan 1986
20kmW	1hr 23:16	Mao Xinyuan CHN 1990
50kmW	4hr 08:33	Zhou Zhaowen CHN 1990
HJ	2.33	Zhu Jianhua CHN 1982
PV	5.62	Liang Xuereng CHN 1990
LJ	8.07	T.C.Yohanan IND 1974
TJ	17.51w	Chen Yanping CHN 1990
	17.31	Zou Sixin CHN 1990
SP	18.89	Cheng Shaobo CHN 1990
DT	61.18	Zhang Jinglong CHN 1990
HT	71.30	Bi Zhong CHN 1990
JT	77.26	Masami Yoshida JPN 1990
(old)	79.24	Shen Mao Mao CHN 1978
Dec	7799	Munehiro Kaneko JPN 1990

Women

100m	11.50	Tian Yumei CHN 1990 ht
200m	23.42	Han Qing CHN 1990
400m	52.13	Li Guilian CHN 1990
800m	2:01.04	Li Wenhong CHN 1990
1500m	4:18.40	Chang Jong-ae PRK 1982
3000m	8:57.12	Zhong Huandi CHN 1990
10000m	31:50.98	Zhong Huandi CHN 1990
Mar	2hr 35:19	Zhao Youfeng CHN 1990
100mh	12.73	Liu Huajin CHN 1990
400mh	56.05	Chen Juying CHN 1990
4x100mR	44.36	China 1990
4x400mR	3:33.57	China 1990
10km walk	44:47	Chen Yueling CHN 1990
HJ	1.94	Megumi Sato JPN 1990
LJ	6.69	Xiong Qiying CHN 1990
SP	20.55	Sui Xinmei CHN 1990
DT	63.56	Hou Xuemei CHN 1990
JT	66.00	Zhang Li CHN 1990
Hep	6231	Ma Miaolan CHN 1990

Susumu Takano

ASIAN CHAMPIONSHIPS

THESE ATHLETICS (as oppose to the multi-sport Asian Games) championships are now staged biennially.

1993 Championships at Manila, Philippines, November 30 - December 4

Men

100m (+0.7)
1. Talal Mansoor QAT 10.22 *
2. Li Tao CHN 10.38
3. Lin Wei CHN 10.46

200m (+1.8)
1. Huang Danwei CHN 20.83
2. Koichi Konakatomi JPN 20.98
3. Zhao Cunlin CHN 21.07

400m
1. Ibrahim Ismail QAT 45.55 *
2. Shon Ju-il KOR 46.47
3. Koji Itoh JPN 46.63

800m
1. Lee Jin-il KOR 1:48.24
2. Kim Yong-hwan KOR 1:49.03
3. Malek Shirmoradifar IRN 1:49.40

1500m
1. Kim Soon-hyung KOR 3:38.60 *
2. Bahadur Prasad IND 3:38.95
3. Ahmed Ibrahim QAT 3:43.02

5000m
1. Bahadur Prasad IND 13:41.70 *
2. Alyan Sultan Al-Kahtani SAU 13:48.03
3. Mohammed Amer Ahmed UAE 13:49.74

10,000m
1. Alyan Sultan Al-Kahtani SAU 29:48.05
2. M Ramachandran MAS 30:16.08
3. Baek Seung-da KOR 30:24.02

3000mSt
1. Sa'ad Shaddad Mouazze SAU 8:32.08*
2. Mohammed Amer Ahmed UAE 8:39.02
3. Sajadi Hezave IRN 8:43.29

110mh (+1.0)
1. Li Tong CHN 13.49 *
2. Chen Yanhao JPN 13.66
3. Yoshiaki Hoki JPN 13.93

400mh
1. Zaïd Abou Hamed SYR 49.10 *
2. Chanont Keanchan THA 50.46
3. Ali Ismail Doka QAT 50.89

HJ
1. Lee Jin-taek KOR 2.24
2. Xu Yang CHN 2.21
3. Stanilov Mingosan KGZ 2.18

PV
1. Grigoriy Yegorov KZK 5.70
2. Igor Potapovich KZK 5.50
3. Kim Chul-kyun KOR 5.20

LJ
1. Nobuharu Asahara JPN 8.13 *
2. Chao Chih-Kuo TAI 8.09
3. Nai Huei-Fang TPE 8.08

TJ
1. Aleksey Fatyanov AZE 16.89
2. Oleg Sakirkin KZK 16.82
3. Sergey Arzamasov KZK 16.78

SP
1. Liu Hao CHN 19.04 *
2. Bilal Saad Mubarak QAT 18.28
3. Sergey Kot UZB 17.85

DT
1. Ajit Bhadoria IND 55.52
2. Sergey Kot UZB 54.90
3. Ma Wei CHN 54.32

HT
1. Bi Zhong CHN 70.54
2. Koji Murofushi JPN 65.54
3. Naser Jaralla KUW 60.42

JT
1. Zhang Lianbao CHN 78.92
2. Vladimir Parfenov UZB 77.32
3. Kota Suzuki JPN 74.78

Dec
1. Oleg Veretelnikov UZB 7601
2. Ramil Ganiyev UZB 7558
3. Kim Tae-keun KOR 7397

20kmW
1. Chen Shaoguo CHN 1:26:29.69*
2. Hirofumi Sakai JPN 1:28:31.26
3. Sergey Korepanov KZK 1:29:06.36

4x100m
1. CHN 39.47
2. JPN 39.65
3. THA 40.02

4x400m
1. JPN 3:09.03
2. SAU 3:10.25
3. SRI 3:10.49

Women

100m (+0.8)
1. Tian Yumei CHN 11.36
2. Liu Xiaomei CHN 11.49
3. Wang Huei-chen TPE 11.60

200m (-0.6)
1. Chen Zhaojing CHN 23.24 *
2. Damayanthi Darsha SRI 23.29
3. Wang Huei-chen TPE 23.42

400m
1. Ma Yuqin CHN 51.23 *
2. Rabia Abdul Salam MAL 52.56
3. Kalawati Saramma IND 52.83

800m
1. Liu Li CHN 2:04.18
2. Liu Huirong CHN 2:04.32
3. Sriyani Menikee SRI 2:04.90

1500m
1. Yan Wei CHN 4:17.78 *
2. Ichikawa Yosuika JPN 4:19.66
3. Molly Chacko IND 4:20.989

3000m
1. Qu Yunxia CHN 9:15.74
2. Zhang Linli CHN 9:16.19
3. Molly Chacko IND 9:24.57

10,000m
1. Wang Junxia CHN 34:19.32
2. Zhang Lirong CHN 35:28.99
3. Palaniappan Jayanthi MAS 36:14.84

100mh (+0.4)
1. Zhang Yu CHN 13.07 *
2. Sriyani Kulawansa SRI 13.38
3. Olga Shishiginna KZK 13.57

400mh
1. Natalya Torshina KZK 56.70
2. Leng Xueyan CHN 57.02
3. Reawadee Watanasin THA 58.90

HJ
1. Svetlana Zalevskaya KZK 1.92
2. Svetlana Ruban UZB 1.92
3. Chinami Sadahiro JPN 1.89

LJ
1. Yao Weili CHN 6.73
2. Yelina Selina KZK 6.49
3. Elma Muros PHI 6.29

TJ
1. Ren Ruiping CHN 14.05 *
2. Kim Hyu-in KOR 12.69
3. Noraishi Ismail MAL 12.45

SP
1. Zhang Liuhong CHN 18.68
2. Lee Myong-sun KOR 16.08
3. Aya Suzuki JPN 15.13

DT
1. Cao Qi CHN 61.58
2. Zhao Yonghua CHN 57.78
3. Ikuko Kitamori JPN 50.40

JT
1. Zhang Li CHN 62.14 *
2. Oksana Yarygina UZB 59.84
3. Xiao Yanha CHN 57.44

Hep
1. Ghada Shouaa SYR 6259*
2. Wu Shuling CHN 5479
3. Ma Chun-ping TPE 5376

10kmW
1. Gao Hongmiao CHN 47:08.98 *
2. Li Chunxiu CHN 48:01.14
3. Yuka Mitsumori JPN 48:03.02

4x100m
1. CHN 43.84
2. TPE 45.12
3. IND 45.34

4x400m
1. CHN 3:33.76
2. IND 3:36.06
3. MAS 3:41.66

Medal Table Leaders

Nation	G	S	B
CHN	23	11	4
KOR	3	4	3
KZK	3	3	3
JPN	2	5	7
IND	2	2	5
SAU	2	2	-
QAT	2	1	2
SYR	2	-	-
UZB	1	5	1
AZE	1	-	-
TPE	-	2	4
MAS	-	2	3
SRI	-	2	2
THA	-	1	2

Five other nations won 1 or 2 medals

CENTRAL AMERICAN & CARIBBEAN GAMES

THESE Games were first held in Mexico City in 1926, and have been held every four years since except for 1942, with the Games being held a year early in 1993.

Central American & Caribbean Games 1993
Ponce, Puerto Rico, November 23-28,

100m (-1.6)
1. Joel Isasi CUB 10.38
2. Andrés Simon CUB 10.49
3. Patrick Delice TRI 10.62

200m (+1.3)
1. Andrew Tynes BAH 20.64
2. Ivan Garcia CUB 20.71
3. Jorge Aguilera CUB 20.91

400m
1. Norberto Tellez CUB 45.80
2. Neil De Silva TRI 46.07
3. Omar Mena CUB 46.32

800m
1. Javier Soto PUR 1:49.40
2. Héctor Herrera CUB 1:49.99
3. Dale Jones ANT 1:50.05

1500m
1. José López Martinez VEN 3:43.89
2. Desmond Hector GUY 3:46.08
3. Arturo Espejel MEX 3:46.74

5000m
1. Isaac Garcia MEX 13:57.84
2. Gabino Apolonio MEX 14:06.43
3. Juan Ceballos PUR 14:31.08

10,000m
1. Dionicio Cerón MEX 28:58.11*
2. Isaac Garcia MEX 29:33.74
3. Juan Ceballos PUR 30:11.60

Mar
1. Benjamin Paredes MEX 2:14:23*
2. Julio Hernández COL 2:17:21
3. Samuel López MEX 2:17:38

3000mSt
1. Ruben Garcia MEX 8:38.43*
2. Héctor Arias MEX 8:40.19
3. Juan Ramon Conde CUB 8:45.62

110mh (-1.6)
1. Emilio Valle CUB 13.87
2. Wagber Marseille HAI 14.10
3. Alexis Sánchez CUB 14.14

400mh
1. Domingo Cordero PUR 49.60*
2. Pedro Piñera 50.12
3. Juan Gutierrez MEX 50.47

HJ
1. Javier Sotomayor CUB 2.35*
2. Marino Drake CUB 2.20
3. Antonio Burgos PUR 2.14

PV
1. Edgardo Diaz PUR 5.30
2. Alberto Manzano CUB 5.30
no 3rd

LJ
1. Wendell Williams TRI 7.95
2. Michael Francis PUR 7.92
3. Jaime Jefferson CUB 7.85

TJ 1. Yoelvis Quesada CUB 17.06*
2. Daniel Osorio CUB 16.52
3. Sergio Saavedra VEN 16.30
SP 1. Jorge Montenegro CUB 18.88
2. Carlos Fandino CUB 18.68
3. Yoger Medina VEN 17.96
DT 1. Alexis Elizalde CUB 61.24
2. Luis M Delis CUB 59.32
3. Yoger Medina VEN 54.94
HT 1. Alberto Sánchez CUB 72.20*
2. Eladio Hernández CUB 69.58
3. Guillermo Guzman MEX 65.52
JT 1. Luis Lucumi COL 74.58
2. Ovidio Trimino CUB 73.08
3. Emeterio González CUB 71.24
Dec 1. Eugenio Balanque CUB 7889*
2. Raúl Duany CUB 7715
3. José Roman PUR 7262
20kmW 1. Daniel Garcia MEX 1:26:22
2. Héctor Moreno COL 1:26:32
3. Julio René Martinez GUA 1:29:43
50kmW 1. Edel Oliva CUB 3:55:21*
2. German Sánchez MEX 3:56:18
3. Julio César Urias GUA 4:03:24
4x100m 1. CUB 39.24
2. PUR 40.01
3. COL 40.09
4x400m 1. CUB 3:05.62
2. TRI 3:06.96
3. JAM 3:07.23

Women
100m (-1.3?) 1. Liliana Allen CUB 11.52
2. Miriam Ferrer CUB 11.81
3. Chandra Sturrup BAH 11.89
200m (+1.6) 1. Liliana Allen CUB 23.14
2. Idalmis Bonne CUB 23.53
3. Ximena Restrepo COL 23.88
400m 1. Julia Duporty CUB 51.81
2. Zoila Stewart Lee CRC 52.57
3. Nancy McLeon CUB 52.59
800m 1. Letitia Vriesde SUR 2:04.28
2. Ana Quirot CUB 2:05.22
3. Daisy Ocasio PUR 2:06.52
1500m 1. Letitia Vriesde SUR 4:18.45*
2. Isabel Juárez MEX 4:20.20
3. Susana Diaz MEX 4:21.45
3000m 1. Isabel Juárez MEX 9:16.27*
2. Adraina Fernández MEX 9:18.93
3. Milagros Rodriguez CUB 9:22.36
10,000m 1. Maria del Carmen Diaz MEX 34:49.67*
2. Luicia del Rendon MEX 35:13.30
3. Carmen Serrano PUR 36:19.66
Mar 1. Emma Cabrera MEX 2:42:29*
2. Maria Reyna MEX 2:43:39
3. Emperatriz Wilson CUB 2:54:41
100mh (-2.1) 1. Aliuska López CUB 13.46
2. Oraidis Ramirez CUB 13.49
3. Joyce Melendez PUR 14.22
400mh 1. Lency Montelier CUB 57.61
2. Maribelcy Peña COL 58.68
3. Winsome Cole JAM 60.23
HJ cancelled (too few entries)
LJ 1. Niurka Montalvo CUB 6.37
2. Eloina Echevarria CUB 5.91w
3. Suzette Lee JAM 5.53
TJ 1. Niurka Montalvo CUB 13.57*
2. Eloina Echevarria CUB 13.02
3. Suzette Lee JAM 12.40
SP 1. Herminia Fernández CUB 18.00
2. Yumileidi Cumba CUB 17.67
3. Laverne Eve BAH 15.35
DT 1. Barbara Echevarria CUB 61.02
2. Maritza Marten CUB 59.44
3. Maria I Urrutia COL 53.12
JT 1. Isel López CUB 61.48
2. Xiomara Rivera CUB 57.02
3. Patricia Alonzo VEN 50.38
Hep 1. Magalys Garcia CUB 5903*
2. Regla Cardenas CUB 5838
3. Zorababelia Cordoba COL 5326
10kW 1. Maria Colin MEX 47:58*
2. Marialiliana Bermeo COL 49:22
3. Maria Guzman ESA 53:17
4x100m 1. CUB 44.59
2. COL 44.62
3. JAM 45.75
4x400m 1. CUB 3:31.27*
2. COL 3:36.82
3. JAM 3:37.72
* Games record

Medal table of leading nations

Nation	*1st*	*2nd*	*3rd*
Cuba	25	22	9
Mexico	9	8	5
Puerto Rico	3	2	7
Surinam	2	-	-
Colombia	1	6	4
Trinidad & Tobago	1	2	1
Venezuela	1	-	4
Bahamas	1	-	2
Jamaica	-	-	6

EUROPEAN JUNIOR CHAMPIONSHIPS

THE BIENNIAL European Junior Championships were held at San Sebastián, Spain from 29 July to 1 August 1993 with 623 athletes from 30 nations competing. Medallists:

100m (+0.6)
1. Danny Joyce GBR 10.63
2. Rafael Gruszecki GER 10.64
3. Ejike Wodu GBR 10.77

200m (+2.2)
1. Andrea Colombo ITA 21.14
2. Joakim Ohman SWE 21.14
3. Maurizio Checcucci ITA 21.24

400m
1. Guy Bullock GBR 46.13
2. Rikard Rasmusson SWE 46.84
3. Valentin Koulbatskiy UKR 46.88

800m
1. Andrzej Zahorski POL 1:53.49
2. Vladimir Gorelov RUS 1:53.81
3. David Matthews IRL 1:54.00

1500m
1. Reyes Estévez ESP 3:45.00
2. Javier Rodriguez ESP 3:46.33
3. Massimo Pegoretti ITA 3:47.07

5000m
1. Vener Kashayev RUS 13:54.32
2. Mounir Khélil FRA 14:08.47
3. Arnaud Crépieux FRA 14:10.71

10,000m
1. Ricardo Fernández ESP 29:37.75
2. Valeriy Kuzmin RUS 29:40.00
3. Aleksey Sobolev RUS 29:41.68

3000mSt
1. Adam Dobrzynski POL 8:44.71*
2. Stefano Ciallella ITA 8:51.46
3. Pascal Garin FRA 8:52.68

110mh (+0.9)
1. Robin Korving HOL 13.85
2. Tibor Bédi HUN 14.06
3. Frank Busemann GER 14.21

400mh
1. Carlos Silva POR 50.27
2. Francesco Ricci ITA 51.04
3. Noel Levy GBR 51.47

HJ
1. Aleksandr Zhuravlyov UKR 2.21
2. Vyacheslav Voronin RUS 2.18
3. Tomás Janku TCH 2.18

PV
1. Khalid Lachheb FRA 5.40
2. Taoufik Lachheb FRA 5.35
3. Viktor Chistyakov RUS 5.35

LJ
1. Carl Howard GBR 7.76
2. Kenneth Kastrén FIN 7.61
3. Yassin Guellet BEL 7.59

TJ
1. Paolo Camossi ITA 16.41
2. Rostislav Dimitrov BUL 16.35
3. Larry Achike GBR 16.31

SP
1. Manuel Martinez ESP 19.02
2. Elia Louca CYP 18.48
3. Arsi Harju FIN 17.82

** Championships record*

DT
1. Leonid Cherevko BLS 54.98
2. Timo Sinervo FIN 54.30
3. Mika Loikkanen FIN 54.26

HT
1. Vadim Burakov BLS 67.16
2. Sergey Kotchetkov UKR 66.04
3. Viktor Khersontsev RUS 65.44

JT
1. Dimitris Polymerou GRE 72.80
2. Matti Narhi FIN 71.74
3. Jörg Tobisch GER 70.24

Dec
1. Christer Holger SWE 7534
2. Jan Podebradsky TCH 7396
3. Stefan Vogt GER 7338

10,000mW
1. Michele Didoni ITA 40:05.62
2. Dmitriy Yesipchuk RUS 40:26.08
3. Heiko Valentin GER 40:37.78

4x100m
1. GBR (Allyn Condon, Joyce, Paul Bolton, Ejike Wodu) 40.01
2. FRA 40.03
3. UKR 40.21

4x400
1. GBR (Nick Budden, Condon, Paul Slythe, Bullock) 3:07.39
2. GER 3:08.39
3. POL 3:08.75

Women

100m (+0.5)
1. Hana Benésová TCH 11.56
2. Katharine Merry GBR 11.58
3. Oksana Dyachenko RUS 11.66

200m (+0.8)
1. Katharine Merry GBR 23.35
2. Hana Benésová TCH 23.53
3. Sophia Smith GBR 23.63

400m
dq. Mariana Florea ROM 52.14 ¶
1. Maria Nedelcu ROM 52.24
2. Lucie Rangassamy FRA 53.16
3. Sandra Kuschmann GER 53.17

¶ later revealed tohave failed a drugs test prior to the Championships

800m
1. Ludmilla Formánová TCH 2:06.88
2. Tytti Reho FIN 2:08.11
3. Emilie Neveu FRA 2:08.13

1500m
1. Marta Dominguez ESP 4:17.26
2. Elena Cosoveanu ROM 4:17.53
3. Anne Bruns GER 4:20.02

3000m
1. Gabriela Szabo ROM 8:50.97*
2. Anne-Mari Sandell FIN 8:51.22
3. Denisa Costescu ROM 9:13.03

10,000m
1. Patrizia Ritondo ITA 34:26.06
2. Silvia Shimeyeva RUS 34:27.13
3. Lyudmila Biktasheva RUS 34:28.04

100mh (+0.5)
1. Diane Allahgreen GBR 13.42
2. K atjaFust GER 13.55
3. Sophie Marrot FRA 13.69

400mh 1. Ionela Tirlea ROM 56.43
2. Anita Oppong GER 57.90
3. Lana Jekabsone LAT 58.07

HJ 1. Sabrina de Leeuw BEL 1.89
2. Desislava Alexandrova BUL 1.89
3. Natalya Shimon UKR 1.86

LJ 1. Erica Johansson SWE 6.56
2. Olga Rubleva RUS 6.44
3. Christina Nicolau ROM 6.44

TJ 1. Yelena Lysak RUS 13.86*
2. Natalya Klimovets BLS 13.65
3. Irina Melnikova RUS 13.53

SP 1. Marika Tuliniemi FIN 17.93
2. Nadine Kleinert GER 17.07
3. Corrie de Bruin HOL 16.76

DT 1. Corrie de Bruin HOL 55.30
2. Viktoria Boyko UKR 53.14
3. Lyudmila Starovoitova BLS 52.02

JT 1. Mikaela Ingberg FIN 56.64
2. Kirsty Morrison GBR 55.92
3. Ewe Rybak POL 54.80

Hep 1. Kathleen Gutjahr GER 5650
2. Karin Specht GER 5548
3. Lyudmila Maschenko RUS 5432

5000mW 1. Susana Feitor POR 21:21.80*
2. Natalya Trofimova RUS 21:39.75
3. Irina Stankina RUS 21:49.65

4x100m 1. GBR (Allahgreen, Merry, Sophia Smith, Debbie Mant) 44.31
2. FRA 44.38
3. GER 44.60

4x400m 1. ROM (S Tuta, Florea, Tirlea, Nedelcu) 3:31.13
2. GER 3:33.91
3. RUS 3:39.76

Medal table

Nation	1st	2nd	3rd	Points	
GBR	8	2	4	138	3rd
ITA	4	2	2	106	5
ROM	4	2	2	85	7
SPA	4	1	-	80	8
RUS	2	7	9	195	1
FIN	2	5	2	98	6
TCH	2	2	1	66	9
SWE	2	2	-	43	12
BLS	2	1	1	38	13
POL	2	-	2	57	11
HOL	2	-	1	27	16
POR	2	-	-	35	14
GER	1	7	6	184	2
FRA	1	4	5	109	4
UKR	1	2	3	63	10
BEL	1	-	1	19	17
GRE	1	-	-	18	18
BUL	-	2	-	15	19
HUN	-	1	-	29	15
CYP	-	1	-	8	23
IRL	-	-	1	6	24=
LAT	-	-	1	6	24=

6 other nations had top eight placers
Points - 8 for 1st down to 1 for 8th

EUROPEAN CUP 1993

THE European Cup has been contested biennially by European nations, with each team entering one athlete per event and one team in each relay. From 1994 the event is to be staged annually. The Cup is dedicated to the memory of Dr Bruno Zauli, the former President of the European Committee of the IAAF, who died suddenly in 1963 soon after the decision had been made to start this competition.

The groupings of nations for 1993 were rearranged to take account of the ex-Soviet and Yugoslav republics. The top group was renamed as the Super League, with a First League and three groups in the Second League.

Super League at Rome, Italy, June 26/27
Men: 1, RUS 128, 2. GBR 124, 3. FRA 123, 4. GER 119, 5. ITA 112, 6. UKR 97, 7. ESP 76, 8. POL 65, 9. TCH 54

First three per event

100m (+1.3) 1. Linford Christie GBR 10.22
2. Alek. Porkhomovskiy RUS 10.28
3. Daniel Sangouma FRA 10.42

200m (-0.9) 1. John Regis GBR 20.38
2. Andrey Fedoriv RUS 20.54
3. Robert Kurnicki GER 20.59

400m 1. David Grindley GBR 44.75*
2. Dmitriy Golovastov RUS 45.65
3. Jean-Louis Rapnouil FRA 45.91

800m 1. Andrey Bulkovskiy UKR 1:47.32
2. Andrea Benvenuti ITA 1:47.63
3. Tom McKean GBR 1:47.67

1500m 1. Andrey Bulkovskiy UKR 3:37.51
2. Fermin Cacho ESP 3:38.09
3. Pascal Thiebaut FRA 3:38.12

5000m 1. Rob Denmark GBR 13:30.02
2. Aless. Lambruschini ITA 13:30.96
3. Abel Antón ESP 13:31.35

10,000m 1. Thierry Pantel FRA 28:02.71
2. Francesco Panetta ITA 28:13.99
3. Carlos Adan ESP 28:16.19
3000mSt 1. Steffen Brand GER 8:17.77
2. Francesco Panetta ITA 8:22.95
3. Thierry Brusseau FRA 8:24.60
110mh 1. Colin Jackson GBR 13.10*
(-0.2) 2. Florian Schwarthoff GER 13.50
3. Dan Philibert FRA 13.62
400mh 1. Stéphane Diagana FRA 48.08
2. Olaf Hense GER 48.48
3. Oleg Tverdokhleb UKR 48.70
HJ 1. Artur Partyka POL 2.30
2. Jean-Charles Gicquel FRA 2.30
3. Roberto Ferrari ITA 2.30
PV 1. Rodion Gataullin RUS 6.00 *
2. Sergey Bubka UKR 5.80
3. Javier Garcia ESP 5.70
LJ 1. Giovanni Evangelisti ITA 8.04w
2. Angel Hernández ESP 8.04w
3. Stanislav Tarasenko RUS 7.93
TJ 1. Pierre Camara FRA 17.46w
2. Jonathan Edwards GBR 17.27
3. Ralf Jaros GER 17.18
SP 1. Aleksandr Bagach UKR 20.15
2. Paolo Dal Soglio ITA 19.79
3. Yevgeniy Palchikov RUS 19.64
DT 1. Lars Riedel GER 66.30
2. Dmitriy Shevchenko RUS 63.96
3. Vladimir Zinchenko UKR 62.42
HT 1. Sergey Litvinov RUS 80.78
2. Cristophe Epalle FRA 76.08
3. Andrey Skvaryuk UKR 76.00
JT 1. Jan Zelezny TCH 89.84*
2. Mick Hill GBR 80.76
3. Andrey Shevchuk RUS 79.16
4x100m 1. GBR 38.53
2. FRA 38.72
3. RUS 38.89
4x400m 1. GBR 3:00.25*
2. RUS 3:00.75
3. FRA 3:00.94

Women: 1. RUS 141, 2. ROM 102, 3. UKR 97.5, 4. GER 96; 5. GBR 96, 6. FRA 75, 7. POL 62. 8. ITA 55.5, 9. FIN 44

100m 1. Irina Privalova RUS 11.08
(-0.3) 2. Marie-Josée Pérec FRA 11.27
3. Zhanna Tarnopolskaya UKR 11.29
200m 1. Irina Privalova RUS 22.30
(+0.8) 2. Marie-José Pérec FRA 22.30
3. Silke Knoll GER 22.89
400m 1. Yelena Ruzina RUS 51.54
2. Elsa Devassoigne FRA 51.92
3. Linda Keough GBR 52.14
800m 1. Ella Kovacs ROM 1:57.5
2. Lyubov Kremlyova RUS 1:59.8
3. Yelena Storchevaya UKR 2:00.1
1500m 1. Vera Chuvashova RUS 4:16.03
2. Violeta Beclea ROM 4:16.36
3. Yvonne Murray GBR 4:17.51
3000m 1. Margereta Keszeg ROM 8:51.88
2. Yelena Kopytova RUS 8:52.27
3. Alison Wyeth GBR 8:52.98
10,000m 1. Viktoria Nenasheva RUS 32:33.46
2. Iulia Negura ROM 32:36.05
3. Tamara Koba UKR 32:39.50
100mh 1, Marina Azyabina RUS 12.63
(+0.3) 2. Jackie Agyepong GBR 13.17
3. Liliana Nastase ROM 13.22
400mh 1. Sally Gunnell GBR 53.73*
2. Anna Knoroz RUS 54.42
3. Nicoleta Carutasu ROM 54.94
HJ 1. Galina Astafei ROM 2.00
2. Heike Henkel GER 1.96
3. Katarzyna Majchrzak POL 1.92
LJ 1. Heike Drechsler GER 7.02
2. Yelena Sinchukova RUS 6.94w
3. Fiona May GBR 6.73
TJ 1. Yolanda Chen RUS 14.34w
2. Helga Radtke GER 14.05
3. Innessa Kravets UKR 13.99
SP 1. Anna Romanova RUS 19.43
2. Valentina Fedyushina UKR 18.91
3. Stephanie Storp GER 18.85
DT 1. Larisa Korotkevich RUS 64.58
2. Larissa Mikhalchenko UKR 63.04
3. Renata Katewicz POL 61.68
JT 1. Felicia Tirlea ROM 62.68
2. Karen Forkel GER 61.92
3. Yekaterina Ivakina RUS 61.74
4x100m 1. RUS 42.79
2. FRA 43.01
3. GER 43.46
4x400m 1. RUS 3:24.23
2. UKR 3:27.37
3. GER 3:27.80

** European Cup record*
The bottom three teams were relegated

First League at Brussels, Belgium, Jun 12/13
Men: 1. SWE 112, 2. ROM 99.5, 3. HUN 97, 4. BUL 94.5, 5. SWZ 87.5, 6. FIN 86, 7. NOR 72, 8. BEL 71.5
Winners:
100m Patrick Stevens BEL 10.52
200m Patrick Stevens BEL 20.72
400m Anton Ivanov BUL 46.32
800m Atle Douglas NOR 1:49.78
1500m Ovidiu Olteanu ROM 3:51.70
5000m Ovidiu Olteanu ROM 13:50.08

Sandra Myers: won the 200 and 400m in Brussels

10000m	Jonny Danielson SWE 28:45.57
3000mSt	William van Dijck BEL 8:37.17
110mh	Georghe Boroi ROM 13.49
400mh	Marc Dollendorf BEL 49.82
HJ	Patrik Sjöberg 2.29
PV	István Bagyula HUN 5.50
LJ	Bogdan Tudor ROM 7.78
TJ	Tord Henriksson SWE 17.16w
SP	Werner Günthör SUI 21.63
DT	Costel Grasu ROM 63.24
HT	Tibor Gécsek HUN 74.78
JT	Seppo Räty FIN 84.22
4x100m	SWE 39.85
4x400m	SWE 3:08.31

Women: 1. BLS 91.5, 2. ESP 81, 3. SWZ 79, 4. TCH 78, 5. BUL 77.5, 6. NOR 70. HUN 67, 8. BEL 67

100m	Petya Pendareva BUL 11.46
200m	Sandra Myers ESP 23.28
400m	Sandra Myers ESP 52.23
800m	Natalya Dukhnova BLS 2:01.94
1500m	Sandra Gasser SUI 4:16.02
3000m	Daria Nauer SUI 9:13.81
10000m	Helena Barócsi HUN 33:33.92
100mh	Sylvia Dethier BEL 13.34
400mh	Ann Maenhout BEL 56.51
HJ	Tatyana Shevchik BLS 1.90
LJ	Rita Ináncsi HUN 6.62
TJ	Sarka Kaspárková TCH 13.69
SP	Svetla Mitkova BUL 18.36
DT	Ellina Zvereva BLS 66.32
JT	Tatyana Shikolenko BLS 61.06
4x100m	BUL 44.83
4x400m	TCH 3:32.73

The top two teams were promoted and the bottom four relegated

Second League Group C1 at Villach, Austria
Men: 1. GRE 125, 2. AUT 107.5, 3. ISR 78, 4. CRO 69.5, 5. SLO 69.5, 6. CYP 57.5, 7. TUR 52
Women: 1. AUT 82, 2. SLO 78.5, 3. GRE 75, 4. TUR 49.5, 5. CYP 37, 6. CRO 34
Group 2 at Copenhagen, Denmark
Men: 1. DEN 72, 2. LAT 65, 3. EST 62, 4. LIT 58, 5. ISL 41
Women: 1. LIT 70, 2. DEN 64, 3. LAT 53, 4. ISL 36, 5. EST 30
Group 3 at Rotterdam, Netherlands
Men: BLS 98, 2. POR 84, 3. HOL 78, 4. SVK 75, 5. IRL 48, 6. MOL 38
Women: 1. POR 75, 2. SWE 70.5, 3. HOL 69, 4. IRL 52, 5. SVK 51.5, 6. MOL 38
Winners of each group were promoted.

1994 Matches
Super League Birmingham, GBR 25/26 Jun
Men: RUS, GBR, FRA, GER, ITA, UKR, SWE, ROM
Women: RUS, ROM, UKR, GER, GBR, FRA, BLS, ESP
First League Santiago de Compostella, Spain 11/12 Jun
Men: ESP, POL, TCH, HUN, BUL, GRE, DEN, BLS
Women: POL, ITA, FIN, SUI, TCH, AUT, LIT, POR
Second League 1 Dublin, Ireland 11/12 Jun
Men: BEL, HOL, IRL, ISL, POR, LIT
Women: BEL, DEN, HOL, GRE, IRL, ISL
Second League 2 Istanbul, Turkey 11/12 Jun
Men: NOR, CRO, CYP, ISR, SUI, SVK, TUR
Women: BUL, CRO, CYP, NOR, ISR, SVK, TUR
Second League 2 Ljubljana, Slovenia 11/12 Jun
Men: ALB, EST, FIN, AUT, LAT, MOL, SLO
Women: ALB, EST, LAT, MOL, HUN, SLO, SWE
From 1995 there will be a Super League, then two groups in the First League and two groups in the Second League.

Previous Winners

Men

USSR	1965, 1967, 1973, 1985, 1987, 1991
GDR	1970, 1975, 1977, 1979, 1981, 1983
GBR	1989

Women

USSR	1965, 1967, 1985
GDR	1970, 1973, 1975, 1977, 1979, 1981 1983, 1987, 1989
Germany	1991

EUROPEAN COMBINED EVENTS CUP

THIS competition has been held biennially since 1973, and now annually. Nations are now divided into A, B, C1 and C2 groups.

1993 Results all on July 10/11
Group A Oulu, Finland
Men Dec: 1. FRA 24,163, 2. GER 24,025, 3. FIN 23,087, 4. ESP 22,898; 5, SWE 22,431; 6, HOL 22,301; 7, SUI 21,764; 8, UKR 20,874.
1. Paul Meier GER 8366
2. Christian Plaziat FRA 8277
3. Alain Blondel FRA 8204
Women Hep: 1. RUS 18,595. 2. GER 17,708. 3. POL 17,287. 4. FIN 17,268, 5. FRA 17,093, 6. ROM 16,657, 7. HOL 16,655, 8. SWE 15,697.
1. Tatyana Zhuravlyova RUS 6330
2. Larisa Nikitina RUS 6256
3. Ulla Wlodarczyk POL 6121
The bottom two teams were relegated

Group B: Valladolid, Spain
Men Dec: 1. HUN 23,349, 2. TCH 22,446, 3. RUS 22,242, 4. GBR 21,812, 5. POL 21,732, 6. ITA 21,678, 7. AUT 20,222, DEN & NOR incomplete. *Individual:* Alex Kruger GBR 7985.
Women Hep: 1. UKR 17,214, 2. GBR 17,193, 3. SUI 17,043, 4. ITA 16,981, 5. ESP 16,290, 6. TCH 15,516, 7. DEN 15,475, 8. HUN 15,286, BUL scratched. *Individual:* Clova Court GBR 5901
The top two teams were promoted and the bottom three relegated

Group C1 at Hechtel, Belgium
Men Dec: 1. BEL 20,063, 2. POR 20,017, 3. ISL 19,473, 4. IRL 18,103
Women Hep: 1. BEL 14,678, 2. IRL 14,450.
Group C2 at Tallinn, Estonia
Men Dec: 1. BLS 22,640, 2. EST 21,494, 3. LAT 20,929, 4. ROM 20,054. *I ndividual*: Igor Matsanov BLS 7738
Women Hep: 1. BLS 19,001, 2. NOR 15,644, 3. EST 15,449.
Individual: Svetlana Buraga BLS 6477
Winners of both C groups were promoted

1994 Matches on 2/3 July
Super League Lyon, FRA
Men: FRA, GER, FIN, ESP, SWE, HOL, HUN, TCH
Women: RUS, GER, POL, FIN, FRA, ROM, UKR, GBR
First League Bressanone, ITA
Men: SUI, UKR, RUS, GBR, POL, ITA, BLS, BEL
Women: HOL, SWE, SUI, ITA, ESP, TCH, BLS, BEL
Second League 1 Copenhagen, DEN
Men: AUT, DEN, IRI, ISL, NOR, POR plus individual entries from SLO, SVK
Women: DEN, HUN, IRL, ISL, NOR, POR plus individual entries from AUT, SLO, SVK
Second League 2 Tallinn, EST
Men: EST, GRE, LAT, ROM, TUR, BUL plus individual entries from CYP, ISR, LIT, MAC, MOL
Women: BUL, EST, GRE, LAT, LIT, TUR plus individual entries from ISR, MAC, MOL

Previous winners
Men's decathlon 1973 Poland, 1975 USSR, 1977 USSR, 1979 GDR, 1981 FRG, 1983 FRG, 1985 USSR, 1987 GDR, 1989 GDR, 1991 GER
Women's pentathlon 1973 GDR, 1975 GDR, 1977 USSR, 1979 GDR
Women's heptathlon 1981 GDR, 1983 GDR, 1985 GDR, 1987 USSR, 1989 USSR, 1991 GER

EUROPEAN UNDER 23 CUP

THIS competition was held for the first time in 1992, when Britain won the men's match and Germany the women's.

The composition of teams to contest the competition in 1994 on July 30/31 has been determined by performances in the 1991 European Junior Championships.

Group A at Ostrava, Czech Republic
Men: ESP, FRA, GBR, GER, GRE, ITA, RUS, TCH
Women: BUL, FIN, GBR, GER, ITA, ROM, RUS, TCH
Group B at Lillehammer, Norway
Men: AUT, BUL, CYP, FIN, HUN, NOR, POL, UKR
Women: ESP, FRA, GRE, HOL, HUN, NOR, POL, UKR

EUROPEAN CUP FOR CHAMPION CLUBS

CONTESTED annually since 1975 by the champion clubs of European nations. In the first year 12 clubs took part in Liège, Belgium, but the number increased to a peak of 21 clubs in 1987, and the teams were divided into two divisions from 1988, and then into three.

Men's winners (of Group A from 1988)

Year	*Winners*
1975	TV Wattenscheid, FRG
1976	Alco Rieti, ITA
1977	TV Wattenscheid, FRG
1978	TV Wattenscheid, FRG
1979	Fiat Iveco Torino, ITA
1980	Fiat Iveco Torino, ITA
1981	Dukla Praha, TCH
1982	Fiamme Oro Padova, ITA
1983	Fiamme Oro Padova, ITA
1984	Pro Patria Milano, ITA
1985	Pro Patria Milano, ITA
1986	Racing Club de France, FRA
1987	Racing Club de France, FRA
1988	Racing Club de France, FRA
1989	Crvena Zvezda Beograd, YUG
1990	Larios, ESP
1991	Larios, ESP
1992	Larios, ESP
1993	Fiamme Oro Padova, ITA

1993 first four (May 29-30)
1. Fiamme Oro ITA 127.5, 2. Larios ESP 110, 3. CSKA Sofia BUL 99, 4. Racing Club de France 97.

Most individual wins
9 Fernando Mamede (Sporting Club de Portugal) 1500m 1975, 1977-8; 5000m 1978-9; 10000m 1979-80, 1982, 1986
8 Amadou Dia Bâ (Racing Club de France/Sen) 400mh 1984-90, 1992

Women's Winners
The women's competion has been staged

European Champion Clubs Cup best performances

Men

Event	Mark	Athlete	Year
100m	10.12	Ozmond Ezinwa NGR (Larios, ESP)	1993
hand timed	10.0	Pietro Mennea (Atletica Rieti, ITA)	1979
200m	20.58	Ralf Lübke (Bayer Leverkusen, FRG)	1985
	20.1m	Pietro Mennea (Atletica Rieti, ITA)	1979
400m	45.46	Cayetano Cornet (Larios, ESP)	1990
800m	1:46.60	Sebastian Coe (Haringey, GBR)	1989
1500m	3:38.44	Manuel Pancorbo (Larios, ESP)	1992
5000m	13:27.87	Gennaro Di Napoli (Fiamme Oro Padova, ITA)	1990
10000m	27:33.37	Fernando Mamede (Sporting Lisboa, POR)	1982
3000mSt	8:15.56	Francesco Panetta (Pro Patria Milano, ITA)	1987
110mh	13.60	Tony Jarrett (Haringey, GBR)	1992
400mh	49.24	Amadou Dia Bâ SEN (Racing Club de France, FRA)	1989
High jump	2.27	Novica Canovic (Crvena Zvejda, YUG)	1986
	2.27	Arturo Ortiz (Larios, ESP)	1991
Pole vault	5.80	Pierre Quinon (Racing Club de France, FRA)	1985
Long jump	8.22	Giovanni Evangelisti (Pro Patria Osma, ITA)	1985
	8.33w	Jacques Rousseau (Racing Club de France)	1977
Triple	16.89	Milan Mikulás (Olympia Praha, TCH)	1993
Shot	21.13	Alessandro Andrei (Fiamme Oro Padova, ITA)	1984
Discus	66.60	Marco Bucci (Pro Patria Milano, ITA)	1984
Hammer	80.22	Heinz Weis (Bayer Leverkusen, FRG)	1989
Javelin	82.06	Radoman Scekic (Crvena Zvezda, YUG)	1991
(old)	86.10	Klaus Tafelmeier (Bayer Leverkusen, FRG)	1985
4x100mR	38.88	Pro Patria Milano, ITA	1991
4x400mR	3:04.21	Larios, ESP	1990

European Champion Clubs Cup best performances

Women

100m	11.22	Katrin Krabbe (SC Neubrandenburg, GDR)	1990
200m	22.78	Marie-José Pérec (Stade Français, FRA)	1993
400m	50.53	Marie-José Pérec (Stade Français, FRA)	1991
800m	2:02.64	Vesna Bajer (Crvena Zvezda, YUG)	1988
1500m	4:12.51	Wendy Sly (Borough of Hounslow, GBR)	1983
3000m	8:57.93	Yvonne Mai (SC Neubrandenburg, GDR)	1990
100mh	12.90	Laurence Elloy (Stade Française, FRA)	1985
	12.86w	Sally Gunnell (Essex Ladies, GBR)	1988
400mh	57.39	Hélène Huart (Racing Club de France, FRA)	1987
High Jump	1.97	Ulrike Meyfarth (Beyer Leverkusen, FRG)	1982
Long jump	6.90	Ludmila Ninova (SV Schwechat, AUT)	1992
Shot	19.95	Astrid Kumbernuss (SC Neubrandenburg, GDR)	1990
Discus	65.42	Astrid Kumbernuss (SC Neubrandenburg, GDR)	1990
Javelin	63.88	Ingrid Thyssen (Beyer Leverkusen, FRG)	1984
4x100mR	43.93	Trudovye Reservye Moskva, URS	1990
4x400mR	3:31.62	Essex Ladies, GBR	1992

annually from 1981. A record 22 clubs contested the 1990 meeting, with 20 taking part in 1993.

Year	*Winners*
1981	Bayer Leverkusen, FRG
1982	Bayer Leverkusen, FRG
1983	Bayer Leverkusen, FRG
1984	Bayer Leverkusen, FRG
1985	Bayer Leverkusen, FRG
1986	Bayer Leverkusen, FRG
1987	Bayer Leverkusen, FRG
1988	Bayer Leverkusen, FRG
1989	Bayer Leverkusen, FRG
1990	SC Neubrandenburg, GDR
1991	Stade Français, FRA
1992	Levski Spartak, BUL
1993	Sisport Fiat, ITA

1993 first four (Jun 5)
1. Sisport Fiat ITA 257.5, 2. Levski Sofia, BUL 247, 3. Ibl Olympija SLO 239, 4. Stade Français FRA 239.

SOUTH AMERICAN CHAMPIONSHIPS

THE FIRST official South American Championships were held at Montevideo, Uruguay in 1919. Since then they have been held regularly, every two or three years. Of the 36 championships Santiago, Chile has staged the most, seven, as well as three unofficial ones (of which there were eight 1918-57). Women's events have been held at the last 26 championships, first in Lima, Peru in 1939.

SOUTH AMERICAN CHAMPIONSHIPS 1993 *Lima, Peru, July 2-4*

Men

100m 1. Robson da Silva BRA 10.58
2. Arnaldo de Oliveira BRA 10.69
3. Oscar Fernández PER 10.73

200m 1. Robson da Silva BRA 20.9
2. Andre Domingos da Silva BRA 21.1
3. Wilson Cañizales COL 21.3

400m 1. Wilson Cañizales COL 46.5
2. Inaldo Justino Sena BRA 47.5
3. Alejandro Krauss CHI 47.6

800m 1. Pablo Squella CHI 1:51.98
2. Luis Migueles ARG 1:52.12
3. Peter Gross CHI 1:52.24

1500m 1. Adauto Domingues BRA 3:46.4
2. Pablo Squella CHI 3:51.0
3. Marcelo Cascabelo ARG 3:51.5

5000m 1. Ronaldo da Costa BRA 13:58.7
2. Valdenor Pereira dos Santos BRA 13:59.6
3. Juan José Castillo PER 13:59.9

10000m 1. Antonio Silio ARG 28:37.5 *
2. Juan José Castillo PER 28:56.8
3. Valdenor Pereira dos Santos BRA 29:20.4

3000mSt 1. Adauto Domingues BRA 8:36.9
2. Marcelo Cascabelo ARG 8:38.8
3. Oscar Amaya ARG 8:48.9

110mh 1. Pedro Paulo Chiamulera BRA 14.30
2. Joilto Santos Bonfim BRA 14.38
3. Ricardo D'Andrilli ARG 14.75

400mh 1. Eronildes Nunes de Araujo BRA 49.8
2. Pedro Paulo Chiamulera BRA 50.1

400mh 3. Llimy Rivas COL 50.7
HJ 1. Hugo Muñoz PER 2.22 *
2. Fernando Moreno ARG 2.16
3. José Luis Mendes BRA 2.16
PV 1. Oscar Armando Veit ARG 4.95
2. Fernando Pastoriza ARG 4.80
3. Cristian Aspillaga CHI 4.70
LJ 1. Paulo Sergio de Oliveira BRA 7.99
2. Abraham Abreu VEN 7.60
3. Ricardo Valiente PER 7.38
TJ 1. Anisio Souza Silva BRA 17.21
2. Ricardo Valiente PER 16.45
3. Aveliono Jose de Souza BRA 16.31
SP 1. Adilson Ramos de Souza Oliveira BRA 17.88
2. Yoger Medina VEN 17.52
3. João Joaquim dos Santos BRA 16.66
DT 1. Ramón Jiménez Gaona PAR 59.46 *
2. João Joaquim dos Santos BRA 55.28
3. Yoger Medina VEN 52.90
HT 1. Andrés Charadia ARG 71.14 *
2. Marcelo Pugliese ARG 67.36
3. José Manuel Llano CHI 57.44
JT 1. Rodrigo Zelaya CHI 72.86
2. Luiz Fernando da Silva BRA 70.56
3. Ivan Roberto da Costa BRA 68.08
Dec 1. José Ricardo de Assis Nunes BRA 6861
2. Aldemar Alves BRA 6598
3. Antonio Rodriguez CHI 6381
20kmW 1. Jefferson Pérez ECU 1:24:03
2. Querubin Moreno CHI 1:24:50
3. Orlando Diaz COL 1:26:37
4x100m 1. Chile 40.2
2. Peru 41.2
3. Venezuela 41.8
4x400m 1. Brazil 3:09.0
2. Colombia 3:09.1
3. Chile 3:09.5

Women

100m 1. Cleide Amaral BRA 11.92
2. Patricia Rodriguez COL 12.10
3. Katia Regina de Jesus BRA 12.22
200m (-3.4) 1. Patricia Rodriguez COL 24.2
2. Katia Regina de Jesus BRA 24.6
3. Olga Conte ARG 24.7
400m 1. Maria M Figueiredo BRA 52.67
2. Lucia de Paula Mendes BRA 53.06
3. Sara Montecinos CHI 53.73
800m 1. Maria M Figueiredo BRA 2:04.2
2. Lucia de Paula Mendes BRA 2:04.5
3. Sara Montecinos CHI 2:06.4
1500m 1. Soraya Vieira Telles BRA 4:23.1
2. Alejandra Ramos CHI 4:31.4
3. Miriam Achote ECU 4:31.9
3000m 1. Marilú Salazar PER 9:44.9
2. Griselda Gonzalez ARG 9:45.5
3. Alejandra Ramos CHI 9:52.1
10000m 1. Carmen Souza Oliveira BRA 33:49.4
2. Marilú Salazar PER 33:57.8
3. Martha Tenorio ECU 34:04.4
100mh 1. Vania Regina dos Santos BRA 14.28
2. Vania Maria da Silva BRA 14.28
3. Anabella von Kesselstat ARG 14.30
400mh 1. Anabella von Kesselstat ARG 57.2
2. Jupira Maurina da Graca BRA 57.4
3. Tatiana Espinosa PER 65.8
HJ 1. Orlane Lima dos Santos BRA 1.87
2. Alejandra Garcia ARG 1.84
3. Alejandra Chomali CHI 1.75
LJ 1. Andrea Avila ARG 6.45 *
2. Maria Aparecida Barbosa BRA 6.26
3. Gilda Massa PER 6.00
TJ 1. Andrea Avila ARG 13.91 *
2. Maria Aparecida Barbosa BRA 12.77
3. Conceição Geremias BRA 12.71
SP 1. Elisangela Maria Adriano BRA 15.67
2. Maria Isabel Urrutia COL 15.09
3. Carmen Chalá ECU 14.83
DT 1. Maria Isabel Urrutia COL 55.14 *
2. Elisangela Maria Adriano BRA 53.16
3. Liliana Martinelli ARG 52.80
JT 1. Carla Souza Bispo BRA 49.20
2. Zorobabelia Cordoba COL 48.74
3. Isabel Ordoñez ECU 42.66
Hep 1. Zorobabelia Cordoba COL 5410
2. Conceição Geremias BRA 5105
3. Elizabeth Arteaga BOL 4282
10000W 1. Miriam Ramon ECU 48:18.0 *
2. Giovanna Irusta BOL 53:06.5
3. Giovanna Morejon BOL 57:45.6
4x100m 1. Brazil 45.1
2. Argentina 45.9
3. Chile 46.5
4x400m 1. Brazil 3:36.49
2. Argentina 3:43.42
3. Chile 3:43.43

** Championships record*

Leading national scores

Nation	*Points*	*1st*	*2nd*	*3rd*
1. Brazil	426	22	17	6
2. Argentina	183	6	10	6
3. Chile	161	2	2	12
4. Peru	152	2	4	6
5. Colombia	103	5	4	3
6. Ecuador	87	1	-	4
7. Venezuela	33	-	2	2
8. Bolivia	28	-	1	3

GOODWILL GAMES

THE THIRD Goodwill Games will be staged at St Petersburg, Russia from 23 July to 7 August 1994, with the athletics events held between 24 and 29 July. The Games were founded as a result of the belief of Ted Turner, Chairman and President of Turner Broadcasting System Inc., that the world's top athletes should be able to compete in an environment free of political pressures. Previous Games were staged in Moscow in 1986 and Seattle in 1990.

In 1994 a total of 24 sports will be contested, with about 2000 sports men and women expected to take part. The athletics events at previous Games featured principally competitors from the USA and USSR. In 1994 each event will feature at least one US and one Russian or team, but invitations are being issued to many of the world's top athletes.

The 1998 Games will be held in New York.

Previous winners

Men	**1986**	**1990**
100m	Ben Johnson CAN 9.95	Leroy Burrell USA 10.05
200m	Floyd Heard USA 20.12	Michael Johnson USA 20.54
400m	Antonio McKay USA 44.98	Roberto Hernández CUB 44.79
800m	Johnny Gray USA 1:46.52	George Kersh USA 1:45.10
1500m	Igor Lotarev URS 3:40.18	Joe Falcon USA 3:39.97
5000m	Doug Padilla USA 13:46.65	Paul Williams CAN 13:33.52
10000m	Domingos Castro POR 28:11.21	Hammou Boutayeb MAR 27:26.43
Mar	Belayneh Dinsamo ETH 2:14:42	Dave Mora USA 2:14:50
3000mSt	Hagen Melzer GDR 8:23.06	Brian Diemer USA 8:32.24
110mh	Greg Foster USA 13.25	Roger Kingdom USA 13.47
400mh	Edwin Moses USA 47.94	Winthrop Graham JAM 48.78
HJ	Doug Nordquist USA 2.34	Hollis Conway USA 2.33
PV	Sergey Bubka URS 6.01	Rodion Gataullin URS 5.92
LJ	Robert Emmiyan URS 8.61	Carl Lewis USA 8.38
TJ	Mike Conley USA 17.69	Kenny Harrison USA 17.72
SP	Sergey Smirnov URS 21.79	Randy Barnes USA 21.44
DT	Romas Ubartas URS 67.12	Romas Ubartas URS 67.14
HT	Yuriy Sedykh URS 84.72	Igor Astapkovich URS 84.12
JT	Tom Petranoff USA 83.46	Viktor Zaitsev URS 84.16
Dec	Grigoriy Degtyarov URS 8322	Dave Johnson USA 8403
20kmW	Aleksey Pershin URS 1:23:39	Ernesto Canto MEX 1:23:13.12
4x100mR	USA 37.98	USA 38.45
4x400mR	USSR 3:01.25	USA 2:59.42
Women		
100m	Evelyn Ashford USA 10.91 Heike Drechsler GDR (2nd) 10.91	Carlette Guidry USA 11.03
200m	Pam Marshall USA 22.12	Dannette Young USA 22.64
400m	Olga Vladykina URS 49.96	Ana F Quirot CUB 50.34
800m	Lyubov Gurina URS 1:57.52	Ana F Quirot CUB 1:57.42
1500m	Tatyana Samolenko URS 4:05.50	Natalya Artyomova URS 4:09.48
3000m	Mariana Stanescu ROM 8:38.83	PattiSue Plumer USA 8:51.59
5000m	Olga Bondarenko URS 15:03.51	Yelena Romanova URS 15:02.23
10000m		Wanda Panfil POL 32:01.17
Mar	Nadezhda Gumerova URS 2:33:35	Zoya Ivanova URS 2:34:38
100mh	Yordanka Donkova BUL 12.40	Natalya Grigoryeva URS 12.70
400mh	Marina Styepanova URS 53.81	Sandra Farmer-Patrick USA 55.16
HJ	Stefka Kostadinova BUL 2.03	Yelena Yelesina URS 2.02
LJ	Galina Chistyakova URS 7.27	Inessa Kravets URS 6.93
SP	Natalya Lisovskaya URS 21.37	Natalya Lisovskaya URS 20.60
DT	Tsvetanka Khristova BUL 69.54	Ilke Wyludda GDR 68.08
JT	Petra Felke GDR 70.78	Natalya Shikolenko URS 61.62
Hep	Jackie Joyner USA 7148	Jackie Joyner-Kersee USA 6783
10kmW	Karry Saxby AUS 45:08.13	Nadezhda Ryashkina URS 41:56.23
4x100mR	USA 42.12	USA 42.46
4x400mR	USA 3:21.22	USSR 3:23.70

OTHER INTERNATIONAL CHAMPIONSHIPS 1993

1st EAST ASIAN GAMES

May 13-16, Shanghai, China

Men: 100m: Chin Sun-kok KOR 10.23, 200m: Zhao Cunlin CHN 20.99, 400m: Yu Baoyi CHN 46.77, 800m: Lee Jin-il KOR 1:47.13, 1500m: Kim Sun-hyoung KOR 3:56.17, 5000m: Yosuke Osawa JPN 13:47.61, 10,000m: Nozomi Saho JPN 29:03.55, 3000mSt: Akira Nakamura JPN 8:51.72, 110mh: Zheng Jinsu CHN 13.77w, 400mh: Shunji Karube 49.93, HJ: Takahisa Yoshida JPN 2.26, PV: Ge Yun CHN 5.20, LJ: Nai Huifong TPE 8.34, TJ: Zou Sixin CHN 16.77w/SP: Ma Yongfeng CHN 19.50, DT: Ma Wei CHN 57.18, HT: Bi Zhong CHN 74.60, JT: Zhang Lianbiao CHN 77.56, Dec: Munehiro Kaneko JPN 7995, 20kmW: Chen Shaoguo CHN 1:21:29.1, 4x100m/4x400m: CHN 39.36/ 3:04.35

Women: 100m/200m: Wang Huichen TPE 11.38/23.47, 400m: Len Xuiyan CHN 53.75, 800m: Zhang Yumei CHN 2:01.68, 1500m: Qu Yunxia CHN 4:04.42, 3000m: Zhang Lirong CHN 8:40.30, 10,000m: Zhong Huandi CHN 32:32.37, 100mh: Zhang Yu CHN 13.23, 400mh: Zhang Weimin CHN 56.21, HJ: Wang Wei CHN 1.89, LJ: Yang Juan CHN 6.45, TJ: Zhang Jing CHN 13.64, SP: Zhang Liuhong CHN 19.88, DT: Min Chunfeng CHN 63.12, JT: Ha Xiaoyan CHN 64.52, Hep: Zhu Yuqing CHN 6064, 10kW: Li Chunxiu CHN 45:00.32, 4x100m/4x400m: CHN 44.23/3:33.41.

EUROPEAN CHALLENGE RELAYS

June 5, Portsmouth GBR

Men: 4x100/4x200: UKR 38.85/1:21.32, 4x400: RUS 3:01.87, 4x800: BLS 7:11.42, MedR: RUS 1:49.68, 4x110mh: GBR 54.67.

Women: 4x100: UKR 43.55, 4x200: RUS 1:31.49, 4x400: GBR 3:24.36, 4x800: RUS 7:57.08, MedR: RUS 2:01.10, 4x100mh: RUS 52.00.

5th GAMES of the SMALL STATES OF EUROPE

May 25-29, Malta

Men: 100m/200m: Ioannis Marcoullides CYP 10.66/21.28, 400m: Evripedes Demosthenous CYP 48.48, 800m: Yiannakis Kleanthous CYP 1:51.83, 1500m: Andreas Christodoulou CYP 3:48.18, 5000m: Georgios Louciades CYP 14:28.11, 10000m: Lahcen Essoussi MON 31:18.20, 110mh: Prodromos Katsantoms CYP 14.41, HJ: Neophytos Kalagerou CYP 2.16, PV: Fotis Stephani CYP 5.00, LJ: Christaris Kleanthous CYP 7.05, TJ: Marios Hadjiandreou CYP 15.65, SP: Petur Gudmundsson ISL 19.60, DT: Eggert Bogason ISL 53.54, HT: Gudmundur Karlsson ISL 63.80, JT: Sigundur Einarsson ISL 74.74, 4x100m/4x400m: CYP 41.28/3:16.62

Women: 100m/100mh: Manuela Marxer LIE 12.21/13.94, 200m/400m: Dora Kyriacou CYP 24.47/54.55, 800m/1500m/3000m: Frida Run Thornadóttir ISL 2:12.21/4:30.81/9:31.00, HJ: Thordis Gisladóttir ISL 1.80, LJ: Sonia Delprete MON 6.11, SP: Elli Evangelidou CYP 15.13, JT: Vigdis Gudjonsdóttir ISL 48.02, 4x100m/ 4x400m: CYP 47.55/3:52.62.

MEDITERRANEAN GAMES

Jun e 17-20, Narbonne:, France

Men: 100m: Alexandros Terzian GRE 10.20, 200m: Daniel Sangouma FRA 20.76, 400m: Konstantinos Kederis GRE 45.70, 800m: Mahjoub Haïda MAR 1:48.70, 1500m: Noureddine Morceli MAR 3:29.20*, 5000m: Thierry Pantel FRA 13:39.04, 10000m: Khalid Skah MAR 28:46.38, Mar: Davide Milesi ITA 2:18:42*, 3000mSt: Abdelaziz Sahere MAR 8:25.24, 110mh: Dan Philibert FRA 13.62, 400mh: Zaïd Abou Hamed SYR 49.09*, HJ: Jean Charles Gicquel FRA 2.26, PV: Stavros Tsitouras GRE 5.55, LJ: Spyros Vasdekis GRE 8.03, TJ: Pierre Camara FRA 17.03, SP: Paulo Dal Soglio ITA 20.22, DT: Luciano Zerbini ITA

60.90, JT: Ivan Mustapic CRO 79.46*, 4x100m/4x400m: FRA 38.96/3:02.99*.

Women. 100m: Magalie Simioneck FRA 11.39, 200m: Maguy Nestoret FRA 23.42, 400m: Elsa Devassoigne FRA 52.44, 800m: Hassiba Boulmerka ALG 2:03.86, 1500m: Fréderique Quentin FRA 4:11.09, 3000m: Valentina Tauceri ITA 9:00.10, Mar: Helena Javornik SLO 2:42:58*, 100mh: Brigita Bukovec SLO 13.10, 400mh: Nezha Bidouane MAR 56.09, HJ: Britta Bilac SLO 1.92, LJ: Corinne Hérigault FRA 6.54w, SP/DT: Agnese Maffeis ITA 17.04/ 57.16, JT/Hep: Nathalie Teppe FRA 60.90 /6256, 4x100m: FRA 43.55. ** Games records.*

PAN-AMERICAN JUNIOR CHAMPIONSHIPS

Winnipeg, Canada July 15-17

Men: 100m: Jonathan Burrell USA 10.38, 200m: Jermaine Stafford USA 20.94, 400m: Calvin Harrison USA 45.79, 800m: Kevin Sullivan CAN 1:48.95, 1500m: Eric O'Brien USA 3:51.51, 5000m: F Santos Biscola BRA 14:35.85, 10,000m: E Rodrigues Bastos BRA 30:21.12, 3000mSt: Jean-Nicolas Duval CAN 9:04.49, 110mh: Jeff Jackson USA 14.09, 400mh: Alejandro Argudin CUB 51.08, HJ: Dillon Phelps USA 2.21, PV: Lawrence Johnson USA 5.50, LJ: J Carlos Garzón CUB 7.74, TJ: Eliecer Urrutia CUB 16.32w, SP:Adam Nelson USA 16.56, DT: Manuel Pequeño CUB 51.60, HT: Lester St Rose CUB 61.44, JT: Delyle Woods USA 71.88, Dec: Raúl Duany CUB 7482, 10kmW: Jefferson Perez ECU 39:51, 4x100m/4x400m: USA 39.72/ 3:04.38

Women: 100m: Nicole Mitchell JAM 11.67, 200m: Jennifer Wilson USA 23.63, 400m: Claudine Williams JAM 52.01, 800m: Jawauna McMullen USA 2:06.99, 1500m: Janeth Colizalitin ECU 4:30.61, 3000m: Shelley Taylor USA 9:44.45, 10,000m: A Mejia MEX 36:10.68, 100mh: Damaris Anderson CUB 13.65, 400mh: Tonya Williams USA 58.18, HJ: Amy Acuff USA 1.83, LJ: Lacena Golding JAM 6.27, TJ: Olga Cepero CUB 13.01, SP: Yumileidi Cumba CUB 17.55, DT: Mindy Wirtz USA 49.96, JT: M Caridad Alvárez CUB 57.00, Hep: Regla Cardenas CUB 5600, 5kmW: R Maribel MEX 24:38, 4x100m: USA 45.10, 4x400m: Jamaica 3:32.70.

8th PAN-ARAB CHAMPIONSHIPS

Latakia, Syria Sep 24-27

Men: 100m: Saad Mouftah QAT 10.52, 200m/400m: Ibraham Ismaïl QAT 20.93/45.84, 800m/5000m: Mohamed Suleiman QAT 1:47.9/14:23.74, 1500m: Ahmad Ibrahim QAT 3:52.07, 10,000m: Sakhri Azrime ALG 30:15.3, Half Mar: Mokhtar Hizaoui TUN 1:08:34, 3000mSt: Saad Shadad SAU 8:51.22, 110mh: M Sami Mohamad EGY 14.33, 400mh: Zaïd Abou Hamed SYR 49.23, HJ: Abdallah Al Sheib QAT 2.19, PV: Walid Zaïd QAT 4.80, LJ: Mousbeh Saïd UAE 7.74w, TJ: Karim Sassi TUN 15.88, SP: Bilal Saad QAT 18.57, DT: Khalid Soleiman SAU 50.94, HT: Walid Al Bikhit KUW 67.22, JT: Maher Redame TUN 70.54, Dec: Hajou Abdulrahman ALG 6918, 20kW: Oamouk Moussa ALG 1:39:00, 4x100mR/4x400mR: Qatar 40.7/3:08.3.

Women: 100m/200m/400m: Karima Miskim EGY 12.23/24.68/56.0, 800m/100mh/HJ/LJ/JT: Ghada Shouaa SYR 2:14.7/14.44/1.75/6.07/ 50.54, 1500m: Alya Al Matani JOR 4:49.0, 3000m: Amal Al Matari JOR 10:25.2, TJ: Maïma Barakat ALG 12.04, SP: Wafaa I Baghdadi EGY 15.16, DT: Monia Kari TUN 49.16, Hep: Sheirein Khaïry EGY 3564, 10kmW: Doumia Kara ALG 55:32.4, 4x100mR/ 4x400mR: EGY 49.10/4:01.1.

XIV CENTRAL AMERICAN & CARIBBEAN CHAMPIONSHIPS

Cali, Colombia, July 30 - August 1 (Altitude: 1046m)

Men: 100m: (+2.1) Obadele Thompson BAR 10.30w, 200m: (+4.1) Andrew Tynes BAH 20.50w*, 400m: Gregory Haughton JAM 45.35, 800m: Alaín Miranda CUB 1:47.29, 1500m: Ricardo Herrera MEX 3:47.6, 5000m/10000m: Herder Vásquez COL 14:09.3/29:10.8*, Half Mar: Marcelino Cristano MEX 62:11, 3000mSt: Gustavo Castillo MEX 8:46.96, 110mh: (+2.7) Erik Batle CUB 13.84w, 400mh: José Pérez CUB 50.00 (49.28h), HJ: Gilmar Mayo COL 2.15, PV: Angel García CUB 5.60*, LJ: Elmer Williams PUR 7.96, TJ: Sergio Saavedra VEN

16.89, SP: Carlos Fandiño CUB 19.04, DT: Frank Bicet CUB 55.26, HT: Alberto Sánchez CUB 74.98*, JT: Luis Lucumi COL 73.54, Dec: Raúl Duany CUB 7749, 20kmW: Héctor Moreno COL 1:24:31, 4x100m: BAH 39.33, 4x400m: JAM 3:02.57*

Women: 100m: (+2.3) Miriam Ferrer CUB 11.42w, 200m: (+6.2) Inalmis Bonne CUB 23.22w, 400m: Norfalia Carabali COL 51.33, 800m: InezTurner JAM 2:07.48, 1500m/3000m: Isabel Juárez MEX 4:23.94/9:29.82*, 10,000m/Half Mar: Stella Castro COL 34:20.6/72:07*, 100mh: (+1.7) Joyce Meléndez PUR 13.24, 400mh: Dellili A Parris JAM 57.10*, HJ: Gloria Lagoyyette COL 1.71, LJ/TJ: Niurka Montalvo CUB 6.58/14.09, SP: Herminia Hernández CUB 17.33, DT: Marlene Sánchez CUB 54.58, JT: Isel López CUB 58.68, Hep: Magalys Garcia CUB 5884, 10,000mW: Eloisa Pérez MEX 47:29.6*, 4x100m/4x400m:JAM 44.25*/3:27.36*.
Most successful nations (G-S-B medals): CUB 16-17-11, COL 9-3-7, MEX 6-7-8, JAM 6-6-6, PUR 2-5-32, BAH 2-2-0.

XVII SOUTH EAST ASIA GAMES

Singapore, June 13-17
Men: 100m: Mardi Lestari INA 10.46, 200m: Niti Piyapan THA 20.93, 400m: Elieser Wettebosy INA 46.37, 400mh: Chanont Keanchan THA 50.54, HJ: Lou Cwee Peng MAS 2.21, LJ/TJ: Mohd Zaki Sadri MAS 7.77/16.27, 4x100m/4x400m: Thailand 39.61/3:07.30

Women - 100m/200m: Lydia De Vega PHI 11.60/23.37, 400m: Noodang Pimphoo THA 52.60, 400mh/LJ: Elma Muros 58.65/6.44, 4x100m: THA 44.65, 4x400m: MAS 3:35.83.

2ND EAST ASIAN JUNIOR CHAMPIONSHIPS

Hong Kong, 13/14 November
Men: 100m: Atsuo Narita JPN 10.60, 200m: Han Chaoming CHN 21.42; 400m: Yuji Yasui JPN 47.39, 800m: Motoyuki Kohara JPN 1:55.45, 1500m: Song Minyou CHN 3:53.09, 5000m: Gu Chung-won KOR 14:34.19, 110mh: Yasunori Yoshioka JPN 14.37, 400mh: Nobuyuki Suzuki JPN 52.21, HJ: Gao Yuanming CHN 2.11, LJ: Takanori Sugibayashi JPN 7.24, SP: Li Shaojie CHN 15.26, DT: Li Shaojie CHN 57.86, JT: Kiyoshi Ishiba JPN 67.42, 4x100m:/4x400m: JPN 40.77/3:10.78;
Women: 100m/200m: Huang Mei 11.78/24.46, 400m: Yukino Fujita JPN 56.35, 800m: Wang Yuan CHN 2:03.03, 1500m: Ma Ningning CHN 4:14.74, 3000m: Wang Xiaoxia CHN 9:15.42, 100mh: Akiko Morimoto JPN 13.81, 400mh: Kyoko Nishioka JPN 59.83, HJ: Yoko Ota JPN 1.81, LJ: Wang Kuo-hui TPE 5.90, SP: Cheng Xiaoyan CHN 17.46, DT: Yu Qingmei CHN 54.50, JT: Liang Chunlian CHN 55.14, 4x100m: TPE 46.29, 4x400m: CHN 3:43.85.

IAU 100KM CHALLENGE

Torhout, Belgium , August 7
Men: 1. Konstantin Santalov RUS 6:26:26; 2. Jean-Paul Praet BEL 6:28:59; 3. Peter Hermanns BEL 6:36:26. Team: 1. BEL 19:51:42; 2. RUS 19:59:48; 3. RSA 20:09:59.
Women: 1. Carolyn Hunter-Rowe GBR 7:27:19; 2. Valentina Shatyayeva RUS 7:27:39; 3. Valentina Lyakhova RUS 7:38:01. Team: 1. RUS 22:54:00; 2. GBR 23:37:35; 3. USA 24:35:25.

9th ICMR MOUNTAIN RACING WORLD CUP

Gap, France 5 September
Men: 10,942m/790m height change: 1. Martin Jones ENG 51:43, 2. Dave Dunham USA 51:48, 3. Michel Humbert FRA 51:54; team: 1. ITA, 2. FRA, 3. ENG.
Women: 7,094m/395m height change: 1. Isabelle Guillot FRA 36:11. 2. Gudrun Pflüger AUT 36:45, 3. Carol Greenwood ENG 37:27; team: 1. ITA, 2, ENG, 3, FRA.
Junior men: 7,094m/395m height change: 1. Gabriele de Nard ITA 32:26, 2. Maurizio Gemetto ITA 33:03, 3. R Skalsky TCH 33:14; team: 1. ITA, 2. TCH, 3. WAL.

IAAF/MOBIL GRAND PRIX

INTRODUCED in 1985, the Grand Prix links the world's leading invitational meetings, so that athletes earn points over the season, with a final contested by the leaders in the points tables. Half the standard events are held each year.

There is an Individual Event Grand Prix for each event and an Overall Grand Prix for men and women. The number of meetings constituting the Grand Prix circuit was increased by three to 20 in 1990, but (including the final) decreased to 19 in 1991, 18 in 1992 and 17 in 1993.

Qualified athletes for the Grand Prix are those who, in the current or preceding year have achieved a performance equal to or better than the 50th best in the world in the past year.

Scoring

For events prior to the Grand Prix Final: 9 points for 1st, then 7-6-5-4-3-2-1 for 2nd to 8th. Although an athlete may compete at any of the meetings, only his or her best five points scores count. Up to 1992 double points were then added in the final for the overall totals for each eventand when athletes finished level on points at the end of the season, places were determined by their individual performances in the final.

In 1993 athletes qualified for the final as before, but their points earned during the year (up to 45) were then only included in the overall classification, to which treble points were awarded from the final itself. Individual events prize money was determined on the final only.

Award structure

From 1993 payments were substantially increased to:

For each event: first $30,000, second $20,000, third $14,000, fourth $10,000, fifth $8000, sixth $7000, seventh $6000, eight $5000.

Men's and women's overall Grand Prix awards (all events): first $100,000, second $50,000, third $30,000, fourth $20,000, fifth $15,000, sixth $13,000, seventh $12,000, eight $10,000.

Grand Prix meetings for 1993 and 1994

1993		*1994*
16 May	Mobil Banespa Meeting, São Paulo (BRA)	15 May
22 May	New York Games (USA)	22 May
29 May	Bruce Jenner's Symantec Classic, San Jose (USA)	28 May
9 June	Golden Gala, Roma (ITA)	8 June
2 July	BNP Meeting, Villeneuve d'Ascq (FRA)	8 July
5 July	DN Galan, Stockholm (SWE)	12 July
7 July	Athletissima, Lausanne (SUI)	6 July
10 July	Mobil Bislett Games, Oslo (NOR)	22 July
23 July	TSB Games, London (GBR)	15 July
21 July	Nikaia Mobil Meeting, Nice (FRA)	19 July
1 Aug	ASV Sportfest der Weltklasse, Köln (FRG)	21 Aug
4 Aug	Weltklasse, Zürich (Swi)	17 Aug
7 Aug	Gatorade Herculis, Monte Carlo	2 Aug
27 Aug	ISTAF, Berlin (GER)	30 Aug
3 Sep	Memorial Ivo van Damme, Bruxelles (BEL)	19 Aug
10 Sep	Grand Prix Final, London (1993), Paris (1994)	3 Sep

not a Grand Prix meeting in 1993.

Grand Prix II meetings 1994

staging up to six Grand Prix events with points 5-4-3-2-1 adding to the main GP points: Bratislava 1/6, Hengelo 4/6, Sevilla 5/6, St Denis 10/6, Indianapolis 25/6, Helsinki 29/6, Gateshead 1/7, Linz 29/7, Rieti 28/8.

IAAF International Invitation meetings at outdoor venues:

1993: Melbourne 25/2, Vancouver 31/5, Bratislava 1/6, St Denis 11/6, Moscow 13/6, Budapest 15/6, Hengelo 20/6, Barcelona 19/7, Sestriere 28/7, Gateshead 30/7, Linz 25/8, Sheffield 29/8, Koblenz 1/9, Rieti 7/9, Tokyo 19/9.

1994: Melbourne 24/2, Tokyo 3/5, Vancouver 29/5, Bratislava 1/6, Budapest 3/6, Hengelo 4/6, Sevilla 5/6, Moscow 5/6, St Denis 10/6, Indianapolis 25/6, Helsinki 29/6, Gateshead 1/7, Barcelona 25/7, Linz 29/7, Sestriere 31/7, Rieti 28/8, Sheffield 4/9, Tokyo 17/9.

Grand Prix Final 1993

At London (Crystal Palace) September 10

MEN

200 metres (0.0)

1. Frank Fredericks NAM 20.34
2. John Regis GBR 20.34
3. Michael Johnson USA 20.41
4. Robson da Silva BRA 20.55
5. Jeff Williams USA 20.76
6. Dennis Mitchell USA 20.89
7. Patrick Stevens BEL 21.18
8. Sidney Telles BRA 21.72

400 metres

1. David Grindley GBR 44.81
2. Butch Reynolds USA 44.96
3. Quincy Watts USA 45.06
4. Samson Kitur KEN 45.13
5. Steve Lewis USA 45.21
6. Andrew Valmon USA 45.25
7. Sunday Bada NGR 45.28
8. Ian Morris TRI 47.64

1500 metres

1. Noureddine Morceli ALG 3:31.60
2. Abdi Bile SOM 3:34.65
3. Matthew Yates GBR 3:35.04
4. Jonah Birir KEN 3:35.13
5. Marcus O'Sullivan IRL 3:35.48
6. Jim Spivey USA 3:36.28
7. Simon Doyle AUS 3:37.12
8. Jens-Peter Herold GER 3:37.21

5000 metres

1. Ismael Kirui KEN 13:23.26
2. Richard Chelimo KEN 13:24.30
3. Stephane Franke GER 13:25.36
4. Mohamed Issangar MAR 13:28.66
5. Aïssa Belaout ALG 13:29.56
6. Ondoro Osoro KEN 13:31.95
7. Bob Kennedy USA 13:32.06
8. Gary Staines GBR 13:42.65

3000m steeplechase

1. Patrick Sang KEN 8:15.53
2. Moses Kiptanui KEN 8:15.66
3. Julius Kariuki KEN 8:16.26
4. Mark Croghan USA 8:17.31
5. Larbi Khattabi MAR 8:18.81
6. Angelo Carosi ITA 8:19.77
7. Matthew Birir KEN 8:27.65
8. Shaun Creighton AUS 8:35.18

110 metres hurdles(-0.1)

1. Colin Jackson GBR 13.14
2. Tony Jarrett GBR 13.35
3. Mark McKoy CAN 13.36
4. Mark Crear USA 13.42
5. Tony Dees USA 13.45
6. Li Tong CHN 13.46
7. Jack Pierce USA 13.47
8. Emilio Valle CUB 13.71

Pole vault

1. Sergey Bubka UKR 6.05
2. Grigoriy Yegorov KZK 5.90
3. Maksim Tarasov RUS 5.80
4. Rodion Gataullin RUS 5.80
5. Scott Huffman USA 5.70
6. Igor Trandenkov RUS 5.60
7. Igor Potapovich KZK 5.50

nh Denis Petushinskiy RUS

Long jump

1. Mike Powell USA 8.54
2. Ivaylo Mladenov BUL 8.20
3. Tony Barton USA 8.12
4. Larry Myricks USA 7.96
5. Vitaliy Kirilenko UKR 7.92
6. Obinna Eregbu NGR 7.86
7. Mike Conley USA 7.79
8. Vernon George USA 7.74

Discus

1. Lars Riedel GER 64.90
2. Anthony Washington USA 64.62
3. Jürgen Schult GER 64.12
4. Dmitriy Shevchenko RUS 63.24
5. Sergey Lyakhov RUS 61.80

6. Ade Olukoju NGR 61.54
7. Costel Grasu ROM 60.08
8. Vaclavas Kidykas LIT 57.72

Javelin
1. Jan Zelezny TCH 88.28
2. Raymond Hecht GER 84.84
3. Mick Hill GBR 83.52
4. Gavin Lovegrove NZL 83.40
5. Tom Pukstys USA 78.26
6. Kimmo Kinnunen FIN 77.04
7. Juha Laukkanen FIN 76.50
8. Vladimir Sasimovich BLS 70.74

Overall standings:
1. Bubka 72pts (1253pts on scoring tables)
2. Zelezny 72 (1250)
3. Jackson 72 (1232)
4. Powell 72 (1227)
5. Morceli 72 (1221)
6. Fredericks 72 (1176)
7. Riedel 67 (1120)
8. Sang 62 (1197)

WOMEN
100 metres (-0.4)
1. Gwen Torrence USA 11.03
2. Irina Privalova RUS 11.09
3. Juliet Cuthbert JAM 11.22
4. Natalya Voronova RUS 11.33
5. Michelle Finn USA 11.37
6. Mary Onyali NGR 11.38
7. Wendy Vereen USA 11.51
8. Pauline Davis BAH 11.56

800 metres
1. Maria Mutola MOZ 1:57.35
2. Lyubov Gurina RUS 1:59.07
3. Svetlana Masterkova RUS 1:59.28
4. Joetta Clark USA 2:00.28
5. Meredith Rainey USA 2:00.34
6. Ella Kovacs ROM 2:01.29
7. Diane Modahl GBR 2:01.74
8. Alissa Hill USA 2:02.41

1 Mile
1. Lyubov Kremlyova RUS 4:24.40
2. Sonia O'Sullivan IRL 4:24.97
3. Violeta Beclea ROM 4:27.64
4. Lyudmila Rogachova RUS 4:28.02
5. Hassiba Boulmerka ALG 4:28.06
6. Yekaterina Podkopayeva RUS 4:28.75
7. Anna Brzezinska POL 4:29.15
8. Alison Wyeth GBR 4:31.81

3000 metres
1. Sonia O'Sullivan IRL 8:38.12
2. Yvonne Murray GBR 8:41.99
3. Alison Wyeth GBR 8:47.96
4. Lyudmila Borisova RUS 8:48.74
5. Margareta Keszeg ROM 8:51.20
6. Elena Fidatov ROM 8:52.28
7. Helen Chepngeno KEN 8:58.27
8. Esther Kiplagat KEN 8:59.86

400 metres hurdles
1. Sandra Farmer-Patrick USA 53.69
2. Sally Gunnell GBR 53.82
3. Kim Batten USA 53.86
4. Margarita Ponomaryova RUS 55.09
5. Tonja Buford USA 55.35
6. Deon Hemmings JAM 55.63
7. Rosie Edeh CAN 56.53
8. Anna Knoroz RUS 57.19

High jump
1. Stefka Kostadinova BUL 1.98
2. Galina Astafei ROM 1.91
3. Hanne Haugland NOR 1.91
4. Silvia Costa CUB 1.88
5. Yelena Gribanova RUS 1.85
6. Angie Bradburn USA 1.85
7. Tisha Waller USA 1.80
8. Antonella Bevilacqua ITA 1.80

Triple jump
1. Yolanda Chen RUS 14.39
2. Galina Chistyakova RUS 14.12
3. Irina Mushailova RUS 13.83
4. Inna Lasovskaya RUS 13.78
5. Sarka Kasparkova TCH 13.60
6. Michelle Griffith GBR 13.59
7. Yelena Semiraz UKR 13.08

Shot
1. Svetlana Krivelyova RUS 19.61
2. Astrid Kumbernuss GER 19.37
3. Viktoriya Pavlysh UKR 19.22
4. Stephanie Storp GER 19.20
5. Kathrin Neimke GER 19.05
6. Valentina Fedyushina UKR 18.72
7. Connie Price-Smith USA 18.56
8. Ramona Pagel USA 17.59

Overall standings:
1. Farmer-Patrick 72pts (1217pts)
2. O'Sullivan 72 (1206)
3. Kostadinova 72 (1195)
4. Mutola 72 (1190)
5. Gunnell 66 (1214)
6. Torrence 66 (1192)
7. Chen 65 (1195)
8. Krivelyova 62 (1118)

IAAF/MOBIL Overall Grand Prix winners

Year	*Men*	*Women*
1985	Doug Padilla USA	Mary Slaney USA
1986	Saïd Aouita MAR	Yordanka Donkova BUL
1987	Tonie Campbell USA	Merlene Ottey JAM
1988	Saïd Aouita MAR	Paula Ivan ROM
1989	Saïd Aouita MAR	Paula Ivan ROM
1990	Leroy Burrell USA	Merlene Ottey JAM
1991	Sergey Bubka URS	Heike Henkel GER
1992	Kevin Young USA	Heike Drechsler GER
1993	Sergey Bubka UKR	Sandra Farmer-Patrick USA

IAAF/MOBIL Individual Grand Prix event winners

MEN

100 metres
1986 Chidi Imoh NGR
1988 Chidi Imoh NGR
1990 Leroy Burrell USA
1992 Dennis Mitchell USA

200 metres
1985 Calvin Smith USA
1987 Thomas Jefferson USA
1989 Robson da Silva BRA
1991 Michael Johnson (USA)
1993 Frank Fredericks NAM

400 metres
1985 Mike Franks USA
1987 Innocent Egbunike NGR
1989 Danny Everett USA
1991 Roger Black GBR
1993 David Grindley GBR

800 metres
1986 José Luiz Barbosa BRA
1988 Tom McKean GBR
1990 Nixon Kiprotich KEN
1992 Nixon Kiprotich BRA

1500 metres
1985 Steve Scott USA
1987 Abdi Bile SOM
1989 Abdi Bile SOM
1991 Noureddine Morceli ALG
1993 Noureddine Morceli ALG

1 mile
1986 Steve Scott USA
1988 Saïd Aouita MAR
1990 Noureddine Morceli MAR
1992 Wilfred Kirochi KEN

5000 metres
1985 Doug Padilla USA
1986 Saïd Aouita MAR
1987 Arturo Barrios MEX
1988 Eamonn Martin GBR
1989 Arturo Barrios MEX
1990 Khalid Skah MAR
1991 M Brahim Boutayeb MAR
1992 Paul Bitok KEN
1993 Ismael Kirui KEN

3000 metres steeplechase
1986 William van Dijck BEL
1988 Julius Kariuki KEN
1990 Julius Kariuki KEN
1991 Moses Kiptanui KEN
1993 Patrick Sang KEN

110 metres hurdles
1985 Mark McKoy CAN
1987 Tonie Campbell USA
1989 Roger Kingdom USA
1991 Tony Dees USA
1993 Colin Jackson GBR

400 metres hurdles
1986 Andre Phillips USA
1988 Danny Harris USA
1990 Danny Harris USA
1992 Kevin Young USA

High Jump
1986 Jim Howard USA
1988 Javier Sotomayor CUB
1990 Hollis Conway USA
1992 Patrik Sjöberg SWE

Pole Vault
1985 Sergey Bubka URS
1987 Sergey Bubka URS
1989 Rodion Gataullin URS
1991 Sergey Bubka URS
1993 Sergey Bubka UKR

Long Jump
1985 Mike Conley USA
1987 Larry Myricks USA
1989 Larry Myricks USA
1991 Llewellyn Starks USA
1993 Mike Powell USA

Triple Jump
1986 Mike Conley USA
1988 Mike Conley USA
1990 Mike Conley USA
1992 Mike Conley USA

Shot
1986 Werner Günthör SUI
1988 Remigius Machura TCH

1990 Ulf Timmermann GDR
1992 Werner Günthör SUI

Discus
1985 Imrich Bugár TCH
1987 Romas Ubartas URS
1989 Wolfgang Schmidt FRG
1991 Romas Ubartas LIT
1993 Lars Riedel GER

Hammer
1986 Yuriy Sedykh URS
1988 Tibor Gécsek HUN
1990 Yuriy Sedykh URS
1992 Igor Astapkovich BLS

Javelin
1985 Tom Petranoff USA
1987 Tom Petranoff USA
1989 Steve Backley GBR
1991 Jan Zelezny TCH
1993 Jan Zelezny TCH

WOMEN

100 metres
1985 Alice Brown USA
1987 Merlene Ottey JAM
1989 Merlene Ottey JAM
1991 Merlene Ottey JAM
1993 Gwen Torrence USA

200 metres
1986 Evelyn Ashford USA
1988 Grace Jackson JAM
1990 Merlene Ottey JAM
1992 Merlene Ottey JAM

400 metres
1986 Diane Dixon USA
1988 Ana Quirot CUB
1990 Ana Quirot CUB
1992 Sandie Richards JAM

800 metres
1985 Jarmila Kratochvílová TCH
1987 Ana Quirot CUB
1989 Ana Quirot CUB
1991 Ana Quirot CUB
1993 Maria Mutola MOZ

1500 metres
1986 Maricica Puica ROM
1988 Paula Ivan ROM
1990 Doina Melinte ROM
1992 Lyudmila Rogachova RUS

1 mile
1987 Elly Van Hulst HOL
1989 Paula Ivan ROM
1991 Natalya Artyomova URS
1993 Lyubov Kremlyova RUS

3000 metres
1985 Mary Slaney USA
1987 Maricica Puica ROM
1989 PattiSue Plumer USA
1991 Susan Sirma KEN
1993 Sonia O'Sullivan IRL

5000 metres
1986 Svetlana Guskova URS
1988 Liz McColgan GBR
1990 PattiSue Plumer USA
1992 Sonia O'Sullivan IRL

100 metres hurdles
1986 Yordanka Donkova BUL
1988 Claudia Zaczkiewicz FRG
1990 Monique Ewanje-Epée FRA
1992 Lynda Tolbert USA

400 metres hurdles
1985 Judi Brown King USA
1987 Debbie Flintoff-King AUS
1989 Sandra Farmer-Patrick USA
1991 Sandra Farmer-Patrick USA
1993 Sandra Farmer-Patrick USA

High Jump
1985 Stefka Kostadinova BUL
1987 Stefka Kostadinova BUL
1989 Jan Wohlschlag USA
1991 Heike Henkel GER
1993 Stefka Kostadinova BUL

Long Jump
1985 Galina Chistyakova URS
1987 Vali Ionescu ROM
1989 Galina Chistyakova URS
1990 Heike Drechsler GDR
1992 Heike Drechsler GER

Shot
1985 Helena Fibingerová TCH
1987 Helena Fibingerová TCH
1989 Natalya Lisovskaya URS
1991 Huang Zhihong CHN
1993 Svetlana Krivelyova RUS

Discus
1986 Tsvetanka Khristova BUL
1988 Hilda Ramos CUB
1990 Ilke Wyludda GDR
1992 Ilke Wyludda GER

Javelin
1986 Petra Felke GDR
1988 Manuela Alizadeh FRG
1990 Petra Felke GDR
1992 Trine Hattestad NOR

EUROPEAN CHAMPIONSHIPS

THE FIRST European Championships were staged at the Stadio Comunale, Torino, Italy in 1934 for men only. Women's championships were held separately in 1938, but men's and women's events were combined at one venue from 1946. The championships are held at four-yearly intervals, although there was a break in that pattern when they were held in 1969 and 1971. The 1990 Championships were held at Split in Yugoslavia and those of 1994 will be in Helsinki, Finland.

Championship bests

Men

100m	10.00w/10.09	Linford Christie GBR	1990
200m	20.11	John Regis GBR	1990
400m	44.59	Roger Black GBR	1986
800m	1:43.84	Olaf Beyer GDR	1978
1500m	3:35.59	Steve Ovett GBR	1978
5000m	13:10.15	Jack Buckner GBR	1986
10000m	27:30.99	Martti Vainio FIN	1978
Mar	2:10:54	Gelindo Bordin ITA	1986
3000m St	812.66	Francesco Panetta ITA	1990
110mh	13.18	Colin Jackson GBR	1990
400mh	47.48	Harald Schmid FRG	1982
4x100mR	37.79	France	1990
4x400mR	2:58.22	United Kingdom	1990
20 kmW	1:21:15	Jozef Pribilinec TCH	1986
50 kmW	3:40:55	Hartwig Gauder GDR	1986
HJ	2.34	Igor Paklin URS	1986
	2.34	Dragutin Topic YUG	1990
	2.34	Aleksey Yemelin URS	1990
	2.34	Georgi Dakov BUL	1990
PV	5.85	Sergey Bubka URS	1986
	5.85	Rodion Gataullin URS	1990
LJ	8.41	Robert Emmiyan URS	1986
	8.41w	Lutz Dombrowski GDR	1982
TJ	17.74	Leonid Voloshin URS	1990
SP	22.22	Werner Günthör SUI	1986
DT	67.20	Wolfgang Schmidt GDR (q)	1978
HT	86.74	Yuriy Sedykh URS	1986
JT	87.30	Steve Backley GBR	1990
Dec	8811	Daley Thompson GBR	1986

Women

100m	10.89	Katrin Krabbe GDR	1990
200m	21.71	Heike Drechsler GDR	1986
400m	48.15	Marita Koch GDR	1982
800m	1:55.41	Olga Minayeva URS	1982
1500m	3:57.80	Olga Dvirna URS	1982
3000m	8:30.28	Svetlana Ulmasova URS	1982
10000m	30:23.25	Ingrid Kristiansen NOR	1986
Mar	2:28:38	Rosa Mota POR	1986
100mh	12.38	Yordanka Donkova BUL	1986
400mh	53.32	Marina Styepanova URS	1986
4x100mR	41.68	GDR	1990
4x400mR	3:16.87	GDR	1986
10kmW	44:00	Anna Rita Sidoti ITA	1986
HJ	2.02	Ulrike Meyfarth FRG	1982
LJ	7.30	Heike Drechsler GDR	1990
SP	21.59	Ilona Slupianek GDR	1982
DT	71.36	Diane Sachse GDR	1986
JT	77.44	Fatima Whitbread GBR (q)	1986
Hept	6717	Anke Behmer GDR	1986

Most gold medals at all events:

Men

5 Harald Schmid FRG 1978-86
4 Janis Lusis URS 1962-71
4 Valeriy Borzov URS 1969-74
4 Roger Black GBR 1986-90

Women

6 Marita Koch GDR 1978-86
5 Fanny Blankers-Koen HOL 1946-50
5 Irena Szewinska POL 1966-74
5 Marlies Göhr GDR 1978-86
4 Maria Itkina URS 1954-62
4 Nadezhda Chizhova URS 1966-74
4 Renate Stecher GDR 1969-74

Most medals (gold/silver/bronze)

Men

6 Harald Schmid FRG 5/1/0 1978-86
6 Pietro Mennea ITA 3/2/1 1971-74

Women

10 Irena Szewinska POL 5/1/4 1966-78
8 Fanny Blankers-Koen HOL 5/1/2 1938-50
8 Renate Stecher GDR 4/4/0 1969-74
7 Marlies Göhr GDR 5/1/1 1978-86
6 Yevgeniya Sechenova URS 2/2/2 1946-50
6 Marita Koch GDR 6/0/0 1978-86

Medals by Nation European Championships 1934-90

Nation	*Men*			*Women*			*Total*
	G	*S*	*B*	*G*	*S*	*B*	*Medals*
USSR	65	69	60	54	41	43	332
GDR	39	37	32	51	45	33	237
United Kingdom	53	33	37	10	16	20	168
FR Germany	27	24	36	9	20	18	134
Poland	17	21	18	14	5	17	92
France	24	26	18	4	6	11	89
Finland	25	22	30	3	1	3	84
Sweden	19	28	30	1	2	2	84
Italy	24	27	17	3	2	10	83
Czechoslovakia	11	9	21	5	7	6	59
Hungary	9	10	15	4	4	2	44
Germany *	14	7	7	5	6	4	43
Netherlands	7	5	5	7	7	6	37
Romania	-	4	1	3	12	2	22
Bulgaria	3	2	2	4	8	2	21
Norway	2	8	5	1	-	4	20
Switzerland	3	4	5	-	3	1	16
Yugoslavia	3	4	1	3	2	2	15
Belgium	2	7	5	-	-	-	14
Spain	2	4	4	1	-	-	11
Denmark	2	3	2	-	1	1	9

Other medal winning nations: 5 Iceland, Greece, Austria; 4 Portugal, 3 Estonia, Ireland; 1 Latvia, Turkey
* Germany - 1934 and 1938 Championships. After the war the Federal Republic took part from 1954 and the GDR from 1958.

Helsinki Timetable 1994

The 1994 European Athletics Championships, which return to Helsinki after an interval of 23 years, will be spread over eight consecutive days with the timetable especially geared for the athletes' needs.

Sunday, Aug 7

09.30 400mh (M) heats (5)
09.40 SP (W) qual A
10.15 800m (W) heats (5)
10.20 TJ (W) qual A
10.30 HJ (M) qual A & B
11.00 Marathon (W) start
11.15 100m (W) heats (6)
11.20 SP (W) qual B
12.00 TJ (W) qual B
12.15 100m (M) heats (6)
13.25 Marathon (W) finish
16.00 Opening Ceremony
17.00 100m (W) 2nd round (4)
17.00 SP (W) final
17.40 100m (M) 2nd round (4)
18.20 JT (M) qual A
18.25 1500m (M) heats (3)
19.00 10,000m (M) final
19.45 JT (M) qual B
19.55 3000m (W) heats (3)

Monday, Aug 8

09.30 Heptathlon 100mh (W; 4)
10.10 100mh (W) heats (5)
10.40 Heptathlon HJ (W)
10.55 400m (W) heats (5)
11.35 400m (M) heats (5)
17.20 Heptathlon SP (W)
18.00 20km Walk (M) start
18.10 100m (W) semis (2)
18.10 TJ (W) final
18.30 100m (M) semis (2)
18.50 JT (M) final
18.55 400mh (M) semis (2)
19.20 20km Walk (M) finish
19.40 Heptathlon 200m (W; 4)
20.10 800m (W) semis (2)
20.35 100m (W) final
20.55 100m (M) final

Tuesday, Aug 9
09.30 DT (W) qual A
10.00 400mh (W) heats (5)
10.20 PV (M) qual A & B
10.30 Heptathlon LJ (W)
11.00 DT (W) qual B
16.00 Heptathlon JT A (W)
17.20 Heptathlon JT B (W)
18.15 HJ (M) final
18.20 100mh (W) semis (2)
18.40 400m (M) semis (2)
19.00 10km Walk (W) start
19.10 Heptathlon 800m (W; 3)
19.20 LJ (M) qual A
19.40 10km Walk (W) finish
19.50 LJ (M) qual B
20.00 400m (W) semis (2)
20.25 100mh (W) final
20.40 1500m (M) final
21.05 3000mSt (M) heats (3)

Wednesday, Aug 10
09.30 HT (M) qual A
09.30 200m (W) heats (6)
10.30 200m (M) heats (6)
10.50 HT (M) qual B
12.10 HT (M) qual C
18.15 200m (W) 2nd round (4)
18.15 DT (W) final
18.50 200m (M) 2nd round (4)
19.00 LJ (M) final
19.25 Wheelchair 800m (W)
19.40 Wheelchair 1500m (M)
19.55 800m (W) final
20.10 400mh (W) semis (2)
20.35 400mh (M) final
20.50 3000m (W) final

Thursday, Aug 11
09.30 110mh (M) heats (5)
09.30 TJ (M) qual A
09.40 JT (W) qual A
11.00 TJ (M) qual B
11.10 JT (W) qual B
16.40 HT (M) final
17.00 PV (M) final
18.20 200m (W) semis (2)
18.30 LJ (W) qual A
18.40 200m (M) semis (2)
19.00 800m (M) heats (5)
19.15 LJ (W) qual B
19.50 400m (W) final
20.05 400m (M) final
20.20 200m (W) final
20.35 200m (M) final
20.55 5000m (M) heats (2)

Friday, Aug 12
09.30 Decathlon 100m (M; 4)
09.30 DT (M) qual A
10.00 HJ (W) qual A & B
10.40 Decathlon LJ (M)
11.00 DT (M) qual B
12.30 Decathlon SP (M)
16.40 Decathlon HJ (M)
16.50 SP (M) qual A & B
18.15 LJ (W) final
18.20 110mh (M) semis (2)
18.45 800m (M) semis (2)
18.50 JT (W) final
19.10 400mh (W) final
19.25 3000mSt (M) final
19.50 Decathlon 400m (M; 4)
20.30 110mh (M) final
20.50 1500m (W) heats (3)

Saturday, Aug 13
09.00 50km Walk (M) start
09.30 Decathlon 110mh (M; 4)
10.20 4x100m (W) heats (2)
10.30 Decathlon DT A (M)
10.50 4x100m (M) heats (2)
12.00 Decathlon DT B (M)
12.50 50km Walk (M) finish
13.30 Decathlon PV (M)
16.00 Decathlon JT A (M)
17.30 Decathlon JT B (M)
18.10 TJ (M) final
18.20 4x400m (W) heats (2)
18.45 4x400m (M) heats (2)
18.50 SP (M) final
19.15 4x100m (W) final
19.30 4x100m (M) final
19.50 Decathlon 1500m (M; 2)
20.25 10,000m (W) final

Sunday, Aug 14
09.30 Marathon (M) start
11.40 Marathon (M) finish
14.30 HJ (W) final
15.20 800m (M) final
15.40 DT (M) final
15.45 1500m (W) final
16.10 4x400m (W) final
16.35 4x400m (M) final
17.00 5000m (M) final
18.00 Closing ceremony

Most medals at one event:

5 Igor Ter-Ovanesyan URS long jump 3/2/0 1966-71

Most medals at one Championships:
Men
4 John Regis GBR 2/1/1 1990
Women
4 Fanny Blankers-Koen HOL 3/1/0 1950
4 Irena Kirszenstein/Szewinska POL 3/1/0 1966
4 Stanislawa Walasiewicz POL 2/2/0 1938

Most championships contested
6 Ludvik Danek TCH 1962-78
6 Abdon Pamich ITA 1954-71
6 Nenad Stekic YUG 1971-90

Qualifying Standards

To be achieved between 1 March 1993 and 27 July 1994

Event	*Men*	*Women*
100	10.60	11.65
200	21.30	23.80
400	46.90	53.40
800	1:47.50	2:03.00
1500	3:40.00	4:14.00
3000	9:05.00	
5000	13:35.00	
10,000	28:30.00	33:00.00
3000mSt	8:35.00	
100mh	13.60	
110mh	14.00	
400mh	50.80	58.00
HJ	2.25	1.86
PV	5.50	
LJ	7.90	6.45
TJ	16.60	13.00
SP	19.00	16.50
DT	61.00	57.00
HT	72.00	
JT	78.00	58.00
Dec	7750	
Hep	5850	

No standards apply for the marathons, walks and relays.

Commonwealth Games

THE 15th Commonwealth Games will be staged in Victoria, Canada in 1994 from 22 to 28 August. These multi-sport competitions are held every four years, and contested by athletes representing the nations of the British Commonwealth.

They were first staged as the British Empire Games at Hamilton, Canada in 1930. The Games became the British Empire and Commonwealth Games in 1954, and simply the British Commonwealth Games in 1970, in which year the Games went metric, rather than the yards and miles Imperial distances raced hitherto.

Championship bests (prior to 1994)

Men

100m	9.93w	Linford Christie ENG	1990
	10.02	Linford Christie ENG	1990
200m	20.10w	Marcus Adam ENG	1990
	20.43	Allan Wells SCO	1982
	20.43	Mike McFarlane ENG	1982
400m	44.60	Darren Clark AUS	1990
800m	1:43.22	Steve Cram ENG	1986
1500m	3:32.16	Filbert Bayi TAN	1974
5000m	13:14.4	Ben Jipcho KEN	1974
10000m	27:46.4	Richard Tayler NZL	1974
Mar	2:09:12	Ian Thompson ENG	1974
3000mSt	8:20.64	Julius Kariuki KEN	1990
110mh	13.08	Colin Jackson WAL	1990
400mh	48.83	Alan Pascoe ENG	1974
HJ	2.36	Nick Saunders BAH	1990
PV	5.35	Simon Arkell AUS	1990
LJ	8.39w	Yusuf Alli NGR	1990
	8.13	Gary Honey AUS	1982
TJ	17.81w	Keith Connor ENG	1982
	16.95	Marios Hadjiandreou CYP	1990
SP	20.74	Geoff Capes ENG	1978
DT	64.04	Brad Cooper BAH	1982
HT	75.66	Sean Carlin AUS	1990
JT	86.02	Steve Backley ENG	1990
(old)	89.48	Michael O'Rourke NZL	1982
Dec	8663	Daley Thompson ENG	1986
4x100mR	38.67	England	1990
4x400mR	3:02.40	Kenya	1990
	3:02.8y	Trinidad & Tobago (at 4 x 440 yards)	1966
30kmW	2:07:47	Simon Baker AUS	1986

Women

100m	10.92w	Angella Taylor CAN	1982
	11.00	Angella Taylor CAN in sf	1982
200m	22.19w	Merlene Ottey JAM	1982
	22.50	Raelene Boyle AUS	1974
400m	51.02	Marilyn Neufville JAM	1970
800m	2:00.25	Diane Edwards ENG	1990
1500m	4:06.34	Mary Stewart ENG	1978
3000m	8:38.38	Angela Chalmers CAN	1990
10000m	31:41.42	Liz McColgan SCO	1986
Mar	2:25:28	Lisa Martin AUS	1990
100mh	12.78w	Shirley Strong ENG	1982
	12.91	Kay Morley WAL	1990
400mh	54.94	Debbie Flintoff AUS	1986
HJ	1.93	Katrina Gibbs AUS	1978
LJ	6.91w	Shonel Ferguson BAH	1982
	6.78	Jane Flemming AUS	1990
SP	19.00	Gael Martin AUS	1986
DT	62.98	Margaret Ritchie SCO	1982
JT	69.80	Tessa Sanderson ENG	1986
Hep	6695	Jane Flemming AUS	1990
4x100mR	43.15	England	1982
4x400mR	3:27.19	England	1978
10kmW	45:03	Kerry Saxby AUS	1990

Commonwealth Games Oldests
(y years, d days)

Men

Winner	42y 335d	Jack Holden ENG marathon 1950
Medallist	42y 335d	Jack Holden

Women

Winner	37y 60d	Rosemary Payne SCO DT 1970
Medallist	40y 252d	Rosemary Payne SCO 2nd DT 1974

Commonwealth Games Youngests

Men

Winner	16y 263d	Sam Richardson CAN LJ 1934
Medallist	16y 260d	Sam Richardson CAN 2nd TJ 1934

Women

Winner	17y 137d	Debbie Brill CAN HJ 1970
Medallist	c15y	Sabine Chebichi KEN 3rd 800m 1974

Most gold medals - all events

Men

6 Don Quarrie JAM 100m 1970-74, 200m 1970-74-78, 4x100mR 1970
4 Harry Hart RSA SP and DT 1930-34
4 Charles Asati KEN 400m and 4x400mR 1970-74
4 Allan Wells SCO 100m 1982, 200m 1978-82, 4x100mR 1978

Women

7 Marjorie Jackson AUS 100y 1950-54, 220y 1950-54, 4x110yR 1954, 440yR and 660yR 1950
7 Raelene Boyle AUS 100m 1970-74, 200m 1970-74, 400m 1982, 4x100mR 1970-74
6 Pam Kilborn/Ryan AUS 80mh 1962-66-70, LJ 1962, 4x100mR 1966-70
5 Decima Norman AUS 100y, 220y, LJ, 440yR, 660yR 1938
5 Valerie Sloper/Young NZL SP 1962-66-70, DT 1962-66
4 Yvette Williams NZL LJ 1950-54, SP and DT 1954

Most medals - all events

Men

6 Don Quarrie 1970-78
6 Harry Hart 1930-34
6 Allan Wells 1978-82

Women

9 Raelene Boyle 1970-82
8 Denise Robertson/Boyd AUS 1974-82
7 Marjorie Jackson 1950-54
7 Valerie Young 1958-72
7 Kathy Cook ENG 1978-86
7 Angella Issajenko CAN 1982-86
6 Pam Ryan 1962-70
6 Gael Martin AUS 1978-86
6 Merlene Ottey JAM 1982-90

Most medals at one Games

Men 4 Keith Gardner 1958 2G, 1S, 1B
Women 5 Decima Norman 1938 5G; 5 Shirley Strickland 1950 3G, 2S

Most Games contested: 6 Robin Tait NZL 1962-82, successively 4-3-6-1-4-8 at discus

MAJOR INTERNATIONAL EVENTS 1994-98

1994

European Indoor Championships - Paris (Bercy) (11-13 Mar)
World Cross-Country Championships - Budapest, Hungary (26 Mar)
World Road Relay Championships - Litohoro-Pieria, Greece (16-17 Apr)
European Veterans Championships - Athens, Greece (3-12 Jun)
Ibero-American Championships - San Juan, Puerto Rico
European Cup - First and Second Leagues (11-12 Jun)
European Cup - Super League - Birmingham, GBR (25-26 Jun)
European Cup Combined Events (2-3 Jul) - various venues
World Junior Championships - Lisbon, Portugal (20-24 Jul)
Goodwill Games - St Petersburg, Russia (24-30 Jul)
European Under 23 Cup - A at Ostrava, B at Lillehammer (30-31 July)
European Championships - Helsinki, Finland (7-14 Aug)
Commonwealth Games - Victoria, Canada (22-28 Aug)
IAAF/Mobil Grand Prix Final - Paris, France (3 Sep)
World Cup - London (Crystal Palace) (8-10 Sep)
World Half Marathon Championships - Oslo, Norway (24 Sep)
Asian Games - Hiroshima, Japan (9-16 Oct)
European Cross-country Championships - Alnwick, GBR (Dec)

1995

World Indoor Championships - Barcelona, Spain (10-12 Mar)
World Cross-Country Championships - Durham, GBR (25 Mar)
Pan American Games - Mar del Plata, Argentina (3-18 Mar)
World Marathon Cup - Athens, Greece (9 Apr)
World Race Walking Cup - Beijing, China (29-30 Apr)
European Cup -First and Second Leagues (18-19 Jun)
European Cup - Super League - Villeneuve d'Ascq, France (24-25 Jun)
European Cup Combined Events (1-2 Jul)
European Junior Championships - Nyiregyháza, Hungary (27-30 Jul)
All-Africa Games - Zimbabwe
World Student Games - Fukuoka, Japan
World Championships - Göteborg, Sweden (4-13 Aug)
IAAF Grand Prix Final - Monte Carlo, Monaco (9 Sep)
World Half Marathon Championships - Montbéliard, France (1 Oct)
World Veterans Games - Buffalo, USA

1996

European Indoor Championships - Stockholm, Sweden
Olympic Games - Atlanta, Georgia, USA (20 Jul - 4 Aug)

1997

World Championships - Mexico City, Mexico

1998

European Championships - Budapest, Hungary

Don't judge a book by its cover

A. Lennart Julin

GLANCING THROUGH a book like this would quite easily give you the impression that everything in the sport of athletics could be objectively quantified, and then organised and preserved in statistical compilations. But, however essential, the absolute results are not everything in our favourite sport.

In fact, quite often the road travelled is much more interesting than the destination reached. We have all been fascinated by stories about how the legends – Nurmi, Zátopek et al – went about making their historical achievements.But how true are all those stories? This question comes inevitably to mind after looking more carefully into a very recent and much discussed episode in our sport – the men's 10,000 metres final in Barcelona. Because the discrepancies are startling when comparing what has been written and said about the race with the evidence of the video tape.

The plain result - 1, Khalid Skah 27:46.70, 2, Richard Chelimo 27:47.72 – in no way reflects the full drama. You could of course envision an exciting two man last lap battle for the gold medal. However, as we all remember, the decisive stages of this race were much more extraordinary than just your 'average' sprint finish.

Boutayeb, Chelimo and Skah (l to r) in that notorious Olympic 10,000 metres final.

This was due to a 'Third Man' – Skah's countryman Hammou Boutayeb – who, after he was lapped on lap 22, interfered in what should have been a 'pure' duel between two runners. Boutayeb's actions caused an increasing uproar among the spectators, made an official run out to caution him on lap 24 and finally made the referee to disqualify – the winner Skah!

The rationale for the disqualification was that Skah had received 'assistance' from Boutayeb. However, following a protest from Morocco, the Jury of Appeal reviewed the situation and reinstated Skah as the gold medallist. The spectators, however, did not share this view; instead they whistled and booed at Skah during the victory ceremony the next day.

Of course they followed their emotions, and they were far from alone in condemning Skah and viewing him as an unworthy winner. Studying what has been written and said – both instantaneously and with more hindsight – about this incident, there seems to be a consensus view (even among experts renowned for expertise and impartiality) about the incident which could be summarised thus:

"Richard Chelimo, well aware of his inferior sprint finish, was pushing the pace hard up front to try and get away from Skah before the last lap. When Skah took over the lead with five laps to go he drastically slowed down the pace to suit his needs. When the duo caught up with Boutayeb, the latter, according to a cunning secret plan made before the race, took over Skah's 'braking'. Boutayeb, in the process, actively impeded Chelimo, stopping him from increasing the pace in order to drop Skah."

Right? No – wrong! And very much so!

A careful study of the tape of the live TV transmission shows that the picture painted is invented by our minds (unintentionally) to fit our prejudices and sympathies. Things have to 'make sense' to us and our brain is never recording images objectively like a video. We see rather what ought to happen to fit our frames of reference.

But what did actually happen on those last crucial laps in Barcelona? This is what the video tape tells us:

On lap 19 Chelimo and Skah were alone up front with the Kenyan leading. However, he showed a slight tendency to slow down and early on lap 20 he was passed by the Moroccan. Skah did not at all slow down! Instead he injected more speed (a 33.0 half lap following a strong 33.4, 33.6, 33.9), perhaps trying to take advantage of Chelimo's apparent labouring.

The Kenyan, however, managed to stay in contact. Skah did now slow down (33.7, 35.4) – but only to once again attempt to drop Chelimo by a distinct increase in pace (32.8). This attempt, however, was no more successful than the first. Therefore Skah seemingly decided to revert to his traditional tactic of just relying on his great last lap speed.

At the same time as Skah let Chelimo resume the lead – with 1300 metres remaining – the pair caught and then lapped Boutayeb. The latter moved out to let them pass only to find that they were coming by on the outside. So Boutayeb moved inwards again. After being passed he tucked in behind Skah, who was now tailing Chelimo.

But simultaneously the pace was reduced drastically (to 34.8, 35.2) by Chelimo. That 70 second pace obviously felt slow even for Boutayeb, who got uneasy and left his last place, moving past the other two with 995 metres to go. He held the lead through the bend for about 15 seconds but then readily relinquished it to Chelimo. Boutayeb moved out to the line between lanes one and two and let the leading pair go through on the inside.

But to do that he had to almost slow to a stop as Chelimo continued his 'pedestrian' pace (34.6). In fact the Kenyan de-accelarated even more (17.6 first 100 metres of the penultimate lap) and this made the impatient Boutayeb return, in the middle of the back straight, to the front. Chelimo was seemingly not interested in this 'pacing'. Instead he continued his slowish 17.6 rhythm. At this stage with 600 metres to go there was a distinct gap between Boutayeb and Chelimo.

Entering the finishing straight leading to the bell, Boutayeb finally gave up trying to speed things up for the leaders. He slowed markedly, moved very wide and let Chelimo and Skah through on the inside after having led for 25 seconds. When the official cautioned Boutayeb he was already running third – and in the middle of lane two!

Up front Chelimo had increased the pace slightly, but it was still slower (34.2, 33.9) than the average of the race – and much slower than when Skah was leading on laps 20-22. The outcome then was inevitable: Skah burst the final two 100 metres sections in 13.6, 12.0 and won by approximately a second.

Now that is what REALLY happened. So it was Chelimo, not either of the Moroccans, who decreased the pace in the final stages. And at no point was Chelimo hindered by Boutayeb from moving more quickly. On the contrary, the Kenyan clearly ignored Boutayeb's 'suggestions' to increase the pace. The logical conclusion is that Chelimo, certainly aware of Skah's superior finishing speed, was too tired to attempt breaking the Moroccan by forcing a stiff pace.

Please also note that Skah was totally passive during the whole period of Boutayeb's 'interference'. To disqualify him was an outrage with no support whatsoever in wording or the meaning of the rules. He didn't do anything improper – in fact he didn't do anything at all, only concentrating on covering every move (or lack of move) by Chelimo. The runner receiving 'help' (pacing) by Boutayeb was Chelimo.

Of course Boutayeb should be condemned for behaving in an unacceptable way. By interfering with runners 400 metres ahead of him he showed a deplorable lack of understanding for the principles governing our sport. It is very sad that through his actions the fight for the 1992 Olympic 10,000 metres gold medal will be forever tainted as questionable.

That is the case even if things – as shown above – were not as bad as portrayed by the media. It was bad enough that 'unauthorised personnel interfered'. It is also quite likely that the manoeuvres by Boutayeb psychologically affected Chelimo, disturbing his concentration at a very crucial moment of the race.

However, the most interesting point proved by this case is that even today myths are born. It obviously does not help either that it concerns a heavily publicised event like the Olympics or that everybody around the world can see through TV the actual happenings with their own eyes (both live and over and over again with the help of the video recorder).

Obviously it is not only beauty that is in the eye of the beholder!

Africa rules the waves

by R L Quercetani

EUROPE WAS for many years the dominant force in the middle and long distance track events, i.e. 800 through 10,000 metres and 3000 metres steeplechase. Other areas of the world, notably North America and Oceania, had their share of honours and glory at times, but the overall power of the 'Old Continent' could never be matched.

It took a challenge from an entirely new athletic area, Africa, to finally turn the tide. Prior to World War Two the 'Dark Continent' had shown only glimpses of its potential, mainly through athletes from the Maghreb who at that time used to compete under French colours. The undisputed 'chef-de-file' of that group was Boughera El Ouafi, an Algerian who won the Olympic marathon at Amsterdam in 1928. The feat of this ill-fated athlete (who was to die in 1959 from wounds suffered during a brawl in the northern 'banlieu' of Paris) is of historical significance, even it happens to fall outside our present sphere of research, (So of course, does the better known Abebe Bikila of Ethiopia who triumphed in the 1960 and 1964 Olympic marathons).

Alain Mimoun and Patrick El Mabrouk, who starred for France in the early post-war years, were also of Algerian extraction.

The first fully African distance runner to distinguish himself in world class competition was Nyandika Maiyoro of Kenya, seventh in the 5000 metres at the Melbourne Olympics in 1956 and sixth in the same event four years later in Rome. One had to wait until 1964 for the first medal winners from Africa in this department: Mohamed Gammoudi of Tunisia, second in the 10,000 metres at the Tokyo Games while two days later Wilson Kiprugut of Kenya earned a bronze in the 800 metres. That was the beginning of a wondrous tale, statistically summarised in Table I (Olympic medals by Areas, 1960 through 1992).

The real breakthrough occurred in 1968, when Africans took 10 (out of a possible 15) medals in middle and long distances at the Mexico Games. The rich harvest was said by some to be partly the result of rarefied atmosphere, a condition most Africans were familiar with, much in contrast to their rivals from Europe, America and Oceania. In fact the likes of Ron Clarke, Jürgen Haase, Gaston Roelants and partly even Jim Ryun, performed well below their best at Mexico City. This theory was confirmed, but only to some extent, at the 1972 Games in Munich where Africa's medal tally was down to six – still imposing if compared to seven for Europe.

Politically inspired boycotts blurred the picture in the next three editions of the Games, with Africa virtually absent in 1976, and only partly present in 1980 and 1984. They made a fine come-back in Seoul in 1988, winning eight of the 15 medals at stake. Europe was by then outshone in number of top-notchers but still had the edge in terms of good performers. As late as in 1990, runners from Europe took 52 entries in the 20-deep world year lists for the five events as against 33 for Africa.

Mohamed Gammoudi: the first Olympic track distance medallist from Africa takes the silver in Tokyo

Kip Keino: the younger generation want to emulate his success

The early nineties provided the turning point. What has happened in the last three years is indeed stupendous. As shown in Table 2 (World Championships – medals by Areas, 1983 through 1993), both at Tokyo in 1991 and Stuttgart in 1993 African distance men won 12 out of the 15 medals at stake – a stunning 80 per cent. And they had exactly the same tally at the Barcelona Olympics in 1992. The rest of the world had to be content with less than a quarter, although of course Europe took gold at 1500 and 5000 metres!

No less impressive is the impact of African runners in current World Year Lists, as shown in Table 3 (World Year Lists – Entries by Areas 1960 through 1993). It was up to 47% of the world's élite in 1991, remained virtually the same in 1992 (46%) and rose to a new height, 56%, in 1993. An extreme case is offered by the 5000 metres list of 1993, where Africans take no less than 17 of the top 20 positions! This state of affairs was aptly reflected in the finishing order of the 5000m in Stuttgart where Rob Denmark of Britain in ninth place was the only non-African in the top ten!

Kenya, the new Finland

Kenya is the pilot nation in this African advance. The 47 African medals in the Olympic Games, 1960 through 1992, are broken down as follows:

27 Kenya, 7 Ethiopia, 5 Morocco, 4 Tunisia, 2 Tanzania and Algeria.

The 29 African medals in the World Championships, 1983 through 1993, are broken down thus:

16 Kenya, 4 Morocco and Ethiopia, 3 Algeria, 2 Somalia

In the 1993 world lists, 20-deep, Kenya appears with eight entries in the 800m, four in the 1500m, 10 in the 5000m, six in the 10,000m and seven in the steeplechase. That stunning figure for the 5000m obviously amounts to 50% of the world's élite!

To find a similar dominance by one nation in the distance department one has to go back to Finland and her golden Thirties when the Scandinavian country ruled the roost in the 5000m, 10,000m and steeplechase.

Observers from many parts of the world – coaches, physiologists and journalists – have visited Kenya to understand how can a poor farming country of 24 million people with only two synthetic tracks, relatively few coaches and virtually no medicine programme produce so many outstanding athletes in one of the sport's noblest departments.

To quote from 'Kenya Track & Field 1993' (a media guide released in connection with the World Championships in Stuttgart) ... "Far from the laboratory and microscope, the origins of Kenyan success are found on the bare feet of the Kenyan children who walk or fun through the bush to school, with a second trip for lunch, totalling 10 to 15 kilometres a day, all this at an altitude of 550 to 9000 feet in the lush mountain region of western Kenya known as the Great Rift Valley."

To the advantage of early conditioning one should add another factor: the great resonance throughout Kenya of the successes achieved by Kip Keino and others in the sixties and seventies.

Nowadays many Kenyans are driven towards athletics by a not-so-secret hope of emulating their great elders, thereby achieving a new social and economic status. Incentives for top-class athletes have never been so great as in the present day and age. This obviously applies to other African countries too. But then the Kenyans may be right when they say: "Mambu Baddu" – the best is yet to come.

Table 1

Olympic medals by Areas

	Africa	Europe	N Amer	CAC	S Amer	Asia	Oceania
1960	-	10	-	1	-	-	4
1964	2	5	4	-	-	-	4
1968	10	1	3	-	-	-	1
1972	6	7	1	-	-	-	1
1976*	-	11	1	1	-	-	2
1980*	6	9	-	-	-	-	-
1984*	3	9	2	-	1	-	-
1988	8	6	-	-	1	-	-
1992	12	1	1	-	-	1	-

Table 2

World Championship medals by Areas

	Africa	Europe	N Amer	CAC	S Amer	Asia	Oceania
1983	1	12	1	-	1	-	-
1987	4	9	1	-	1	-	-
1991	12	1	1	-	1	-	1
1993	12	3	-	-	-	-	-

Table 3

World Year Lists (Top 20) - Entries by Areas

	Africa	Europe	N Amer	CAC	S Amer	Asia	Oceania
1960	3	72	13	1	-	-	11
1970	10	71	13	-	-	-	6
1980	20	55	16	-	-	4	5
1990	33	52	12	-	1	-	2
1991	47	37	10		4	1	1
1992	46	32	19	-	1	1	1
1993	56	38	11	-	2	1	2

Note these tables are construed on results obtained in the following track events: 800, 1500, 5000, 10,000 metres, 3000 metres steeplechase

The Italian Connection

By Bernard Linley

AT THE Tokyo Olympics in 1964, Italy had no less than five finalists in the men's hurdles events – more than the USA (4) and the Soviet Union (2), the only other countries with more than one. This was an outward sign of the quality of Italy's hurdling 'school', guided by coach Sandro Calvesi from his base in Brescia, even though only one of the five (Salvatore Morale, 50.1 for third in the 400m hurdles) actually won a medal. Among the Italians were high hurdler Eddy Ottoz (fourth in 13.84) and intermediate hurdler Roberto Frinolli (sixth in 50.7), the lone Italian finalists at Mexico City four years later, where Ottoz took the bronze (13.46) and Frinolli was eighth (50.13) after winning his semi-final in a national record 49.14.

These two dominated their Italian and European counterparts in the mid-Sixties. Ottoz was European champion in 1966 and 1969, Frinolli in 1969; Ottoz represented his country 27 times (1963-69), Frinolli 36 times (1961-72); Ottoz won five national titles, Frinolli six; Ottoz was extrovert in temperament, Frinolli more closed and serious of mien.

Eddy Ottoz, born in Mandelieu (France) on June 3 1944, grew up and still lives in the French speaking Val d'Aosta region in north west Italy close to the French frontier where his family produces the liqueur marketed under their surname. Well known is his reputation for practical jokes and one-liners like that about Italian men and Russian women not shaving before their events, when asked about his five o'clock shadow.

His time in the Mexico Olympic final was his career best and still a national record.

Roberto Frinolli, born in Rome on November 13 1940, had a much different personality. In a way each race was an ordeal for him, and he was badly betrayed by nerves in both Olympic finals after running excellent semi-finals. Frinolli was a perfectionist and had a textbook smooth hurdling style, developed during innumerable training sessions working on his technique.

Roberto's career best was at the Mexico City Olympics and this remained the Italian record until the 1991 World Championships when Frabrizio Mori ran 48.92).

Both champions were married in the sixties and in 1970 Laurent Ottoz was born to Eddy and Liana (the daughter of coach Calvesi and Gabre Gabric, who was 10th in the 1936 Olympic discus) and Giorgio Frinolli was born to Roberto and Daniela Beneck (a member of the Italian swimming team at the Tokyo Olympics, along with her sister Anna, married to hurdler Morale).

Although neither father pushed their son into athletics, today both sons are very successful in their parental specialities, having gained selection on the Italian team and won national titles. Each has earned a semi-final place on the world scene (Laurent at the Barcelona Olympics, Giorgio at the Stuttgart World Championships).

They both compete for non-civilian clubs (Laurent for the customs police, Fiamme Gialle, and Giorgio for the prison officers, Fiamme Azzurre) and are coached by their fathers. Italian writers and others are still eagerly awaiting the moment when each breaks their respective 'family' records, and these must be psychological barriers for both youngsters.

While Laurent and Giorgio are microseconds away from overtaking Eddy and Roberto on the Italian and family all-time lists for 110m hurdles (13.51 to 13.46) and 400m hurdles (49.22 to 49.14), they are nevertheless paid-up members of two hurdling dynasties and on the way to finals places and perhaps medals at world events.

Yet we cannot conclude without a reference to two brothers presently overshadowed by the major protagonists: Patrick Ottoz (born 1971) has run the hurdles in 14.55 and 52.24, while Bruce Frinolli (born 1968) has long jumped 7.88. Either or both may yet emerge into the spotlight shining on their brothers.

Laurent Ottoz		Giorgio Frinolli	
born Brescia April 10 1970		born Rome July 12 1970	
180 cm 64kg		184cm 73kg	
110mh progression		400mh progression	
1985	15.3	1988	54.4
1986	15.0	1989	52.40
1987	14.55	1990	51.68
1988	14.3	1991	50.20
1989	14.09	1992	50.19
1990	13.76	1993	49.22
1991	13.56	Other pb 400 46.80 - 93	
1992	13.51		
1993	13.55		
Other pb 400mh 50.28 - 92			

Helsinki Olympic stadium log book by Matti Hannus

The European Championships are being held in Helsinki in 1994 – a fitting time, therefore, to look back at the great events which have happened in the Helsinki Olympic Stadium

THE IDEA of a grand-scale sports arena in Helsinki at first developed in the brilliant mind of Lauri Pihkala, a man of many hats: an active athlete – the first Finn to break the two minute barrier at the 800 metres, coach, writer, philosopher and professor, in the 1910's.

During the following Big Decade of Finnish athletics, Pihkala's ambitious plan slowly evolved. Many different options were examined by the Finnish government, until the first shovels finally hit the ground in Töölö, not far from the Helsinki city centre, on a cold morning of February 12 1934.

On June 8 1936 the work had progressed well enough for the cornerstone of the Stadium to be laid, accompanied by Count Henri de Baillet-Latour, the Belgian President of the International Olympic Committee at the time.

The names of the two architects behind the beautiful building are certainly worth remembering: Yrjö Lindegren and Toivo Jäntti, the first destined to win the architecture gold medal at the 1948 Olympic Games in London.

On a beautiful Sunday, June 12 1938, they were happy to attend the inauguration ceremony of their brand-new stadium. In addition to the opening festivities, a few athletic events were held with the great Matti Järvinen winning the javelin with an excellent 73.39 from Kalvero Toivonen (70.68) and Tapio Rautavaara (fifth 63.74), another Olympic champion ten years later.

Those days Helsinki had just 250,000 inhabitants – half of the present number. They all had reason to be proud of the most prominent landmark of their city – the noble Olympic stadium tower, 72 metres in height. Contrary to a common misunderstanding, this figure has absolutely nothing to do with Matti Järvinen's winning distance at the 1932 Olympics (72.71) or with javelin throwing generally

Guarded by Paavo Nurmi's famous statue (a work of art by professor Wäinö Aaltonen), Helsinki Olympic Stadium has during its 56 year existence offered competition at World Championship level – besides track and field – in bandy, boxing and speed skating. But that is not all by any means: in addition to several political and religious meetings and pop concerts, the stadium has seen football, archery, equestrianism, hockey, ice hockey, American football, wrestling, gymnastics, Finnish baseball, ice speedway, basketball (including the Harlem Globetrotters) and – believe it or not – orienteering, biathlon and cross country skiing (but not ski jumping!).

Not far from the stadium, the nostalgic Eläintarha (Zoological Gardens) track, built in the early 1910s, still serves well for training and competition. Among its greatest moments we may mention Paavo Nurmi's fantastic pair of world records within one hour on June 19, 1500 metres in 3:52.6 and 5000 metres in 14:28.2, Matti Järvinen's final javelin mark of 77.23 on June 18 1936 and its last world record, the magnificent 13.5 by Dick Attlesey of the USA in the 110 metres hurdles on July 10 1950.

After 23 years, the athletics fraternity of the Old Continent will again gather in Helsinki for the continental title meeting.

In honour of the complete rejuvenation of the stadium for the 1994 European Championships, here is a log book of one of the best-known sports arenas in the world – the Helsinki Olympic Stadium.

July 10-11 1938: in the stadium's first international match, Finland's men defeat Hungary 87.5 - 73.5

August 6-8 1938: stadium hosts the Finnish Championships for the first time (later 1939, 1942, 1943, 1944, 1946, 1951, 1959, 1969, 1979 and 1991).

June 16 1939: the first world record: 14:08.8 for the 5000 metres by Taisto Mäki. The time will remain a Finnish record for 16 years.

September 17 1939: a milestone in athletics history is achieved, 'Flying Shepherd' Mäki circling the cinder track 25 times for a 10,000 metres world record of 29:52.6 – the first man under 30 minutes.

November 30 1939: Soviet Union attacks Finland, starting the Winter War which lasts until March 13 1940. Weakened by the war, Finland abandons the XII Olympic Games awarded to Helsinki in 1940.

July 20-22 1940: Winter War Memorial Games in the stadium.

September 7-8 1940: International match between Germany, Sweden and Finland is highlighted by such luminaries as Rudolf Harbig and Gunder Hägg. On the second day of the meet the stadium is filled with 50,076 spectators. Three of the competitors will take part in the Helsinki Olympic Games 12 years later: Väinö Suvivuo (110mh), Veikko Nyqvist (DT) and Germany's Karl Storch (silver in the hammer).

June 1941: Another war between the Soviet Union and Finland starts, this time lasting more than three years.

February 26-27 1944: During the most severe bombing of Helsinki, the stadium is hit by several missiles, but luckily is not destroyed beyond repair.

August 25 1944: Viljo Heino breaks Mäki's 10,000 metres world record with a time of 29:35.4. Martti Jukola, the legendary sportswriter: "No man ever strode forward more beautifully than Heino."

September 23-24 1944: a couple of weeks after the Armistice, the final War Championships are held. Most of the 200 athletes arrive straight from the front without preparation. Among the winning performances were 23.7 for 200 metres, 110m hurdles in 16.2 (18.3 for a medal) and a 48.78 hammer throw.

July 17-18 1945: in the inaugural post-war international match Finland defeats Denmark (111-92). The average age of the host team is well over 30 years.

June 30 1947: In the Finnish Sports Festival 5000 metres, Viljo Heino is narrowly beaten by a new star from Czechoslovakia, Emil Zátopek (14:15.2 and 14:15.4).

September 11-12 1948: In the traditional dual match Finland is beaten by Sweden 138-76, the biggest ever losing margin. In the 20 events the only host winners are Pekka Simola (LJ) and Veikko Nyqvist (DT).

July 23-24 1951: A new era starts, Finland beating Sweden 216-194 (the first match with six athletes per event). Voitto Hellsten, the greatest fighter of Finnish athletics in the 1950's, starts his unforgettable career.

July 19 1952: The most memorable day of Finnish sports. Witnessed by a record number of 70,435 spectators, the torch from Greece is carried to the rain-swept Opening Ceremony of the XV Olympic Games by 55-year-old Paavo Nurmi. During the next two weeks 11 world records are established. Among the greatest Helsinki Olympians we still remember Adhemar Ferreira da Silva of Brazil, Bob Mathias and Horace Ashenfelter of the USA, Joseph Barthel of Luxembourg, Marjorie Jackson of Australia, Jamaica's 4x400 metres relay team and of course Emil Zátopek, King of the Games, the winner of the 5000 metres, 10,000 metres and marathon. Several of the winning performances will remain stadium records until the European Championships 19 years later.

July 1 1955: 3000 metres steeplechase world record of 8:47.8 by Pentti Karvonen (in 1953 Olavi Rinteenpää had run a then unofficial 8:44.4). From now on a miniature silver stadium will be awarded for every new stadium record.

July 28 1955: A new 1500 metres world mark of 3:40.8 by Sandor Iharos of Hungary – still today the only world record in Helsinki achieved in an international dual match.

September 6-7 1958: The successful 1950's are climaxed by the Finns' 55 point victory over Sweden. For the first time the match is televised.

June 29-30 1959: Gerhardius Potgeieter of South Africa is awarded the eternal Challenge Prize at the inaugural World Games thanks to his 400 metres hurdles victory in 50.8.

May 28 1961: Finnish cross country championships are held in the wooded cliff area behind the Olympic stadium.

July 30-31 1962: The World Socialist Youth Festival in Helsinki is highlighted by Valeriy Brumel's high jump of 2.22 and eight other stadium records.

August 21 1962: the first sub-4 minute mile in Helsinki. Jim Beatty of the USA runs 3:56.3, improving the stadium record by seven seconds.

July 4 1963: In the World Games, Tampere policeman Pentti Eskola long jumps 8.04, which will stay unbeaten for ten years.

July 16 1963: Pauli Nevala's javelin soars to 86.33 in the match between Scandanavia and the Balkans – just 41 cms from Carlo Lievore's world record.

June 30 1965: the greatest ever 5000 metres mass finish in the World Games: Michel Jazy 13:27.6 (ER); Kip Keino 13:28.2; Ron Clarke 13:29.4; Mike Wiggs 13:33.0; Thor Helland

13:37.4; Bengt Nojde 13:37.8; Bill Baillie 13:41.8; Billy Mills 13:42.2.

August 16 1965: In the Nordic Championships 800 metres Juha Väätäinen's 1:50.7 narrowly beats 19 year-old Anders Gärderud's 1:50.8 – both athletes became better known in the 1970's in other contexts!

June 28 1967: Australian Judy Pollock's great solo run in the World Games 800 metres with a world record 2:01.0.

August 1-2 1970: Men's European Cup semi-final is won by the GDR from Poland and upcoming Finland.

September 6 1970: Pauli Nevala again. In the match v Sweden (the last held on the old Helsinki cinders) his javelin hits another near-miss – 92.64, just six cm from team-mate Jorma Kinnunen's world record.

August 10-15 1971: The star of the European Championships is 30-year-old ex-sprinter Juha Väätäinen, who kicks madly to two continental titles at 10,000 and 5000 metres. Eleven years earlier Väätäinen had won the Finnish Junior 400 metres hurdles! Other great champions included Valeriy Borzov, Karel Lismont, Janis Lusis and Renate Stecher. Three world records – Karin Burneleit 1500 metres 4:09.6; Faina Melnik DT 64.22; GDR 4x400 women 3:29.3.

August 20 1972: Pekka Vasala speeds to an 800 metres European record 1:44.5 in the match against Sweden.

September 14 1972: A night of two world records witnessed by 40,000 people. Lasse Viren 5000 metres in 13:16.4 and Anders Gärderud 3000 metres steeplechase 8:20.8.

June 19 and 27 1973: A pair of steeplechase world records by smiling Kenyan Ben Jipcho – 8:19.8 and 8:14.0.

August 30-31 1975: Unbelievable but true – Finnish men beat their Soviet rivals (109-103).

June 30 1977: High-stepping Kenyan Samson Kimobwa gallops to a 10,000 metres world record of 27:30.47 – the last individual world record by a male athlete in the Helsinki Stadium.

August 13-14 1977: The GDR wins men's and women's European Cup finals, highlighted by two world records: Karin Rossley's 55.63 in the 400 metres hurdles and Rosemarie Ackermann's 1.97 in the high jump.

August 12-13 1978: Finland's men beat Sweden 240-168, the largest winning margin.

July 9 1980: Mac Wilkins' amazing discus throw in the windless air – 70.98, just 18 cm from Wolfgang Schmidt's world record.

July 29 1982: Tiina Lillak's world record throw of 72.40 in the World Games is surprisingly the first ever javelin world record in the Helsinki Stadium.

August 7-14 1983: Inaugural IAAF World Championships – according to most experts the best-ever athletics meeting up to that time. Two world records – 47.99 in the 400 metres by Jarmila Kratochvílová of Czechoslovakia and 37.86 by the USA relay men – and a crop of new stars, including Carl Lewis, Steve Cram, Sergey Bubka, Daley Thompson and Heike Daute. Mary Decker's middle distance double and Tiina Lillak's final throw will never be forgotten.

July 7 1986: American Tom Petranoff's 85.38 is the best ever with the newly-approved javelin, however not officially recognised.

July 2 1987: Saïd Aouita of Morocco attacks Steve Cram's mile world record, his splendid 3:46.76 missing the target by 44/100ths of a second.

June 19 1989: Great 10,000 metres running by Salvatore Antibo (27:16.50) and Addis Abebe (27:17.82).

An illustrious story – but as a footnote such athletics pioneers as Jesse Owens, Herb Elliott, Wilma Rudolph, Jim Ryun and Bob Beamon strangely never bothered to compete in Finland.

Tiina lillak: the only thrower to set a javelin world record in the Helsinki stadium

DRUGS BANS

AUTOMATIC disqualification for athletes found to have used anabolic steroids was introduced by the IAAF from 1 January 1975. The first athlete to be disqualified from a major competition had been Eduard de Noorlander (Hol), sixth in the 1969 European decathlon, and drugs testing had been introduced at the Olympic Games in 1972. In addition to testing at competitions, random testing out of competition has been introduced by several national federations in recent years.

In 1990 the IAAF Doping Commission produced procedural guidelines for doping controls. Copies of their booklet are available from the IAAF. At the IAAF Congress held in Tokyo in August 1991 it was determined that for serious doping offences athletes would henceforth receive a minimum four year suspension.

The following cases were reported of athletes failing drug tests in 1993

Suspension: Life - life ban, 4y = 4 years, 3m = 3 months, P = pending hearing

Name	*Date*	*Suspension*
Men		
Hassan Akanani KUW	25 Sep	P
Dion Bentley USA	19 Jun	3m
Andreas Berger AUT	6 Jul	4y
Vivian Chukwuemaka NGR	17 Jun	P
Erik de Bruin HOL	1 Aug	P*
Mohamed El Zinkawi KUW	25 Sep	P
Mohamed Esmail EGY	24 Sep	P
Igor Flegontov RUS	11 Jun	P
Alberto Giacchetto		4y
Peter Gordon GBR	12 Jun	4y
Denis Gulin RUS	17 Apr	4y
Daniel Ivanov BUL	13 Mar	4y
Vadim Ivanov RUS	17 Apr	4y
Ben Johnson CAN	17 Jan	Life
Roshman Jones USA		4y
Gernot Kellermayr AUT	7 Jul	4y
Dimitris Koutsoukis GRE	12 Jun	P
Dennis Lewis USA		4y
Tomasz Lipiec POL	Jul	
Juan Martinez CUB	22 May	P
John Ngugi KEN	13 Feb	4y
Oral Ogilvie CAN	26 Jan	4y
Godfrey Okugbe NGR	17 Jun	P
Dmitriy Polyunin UZB	16 Aug	4y
Nikolai Raev BUL	13 Mar	4y
Franz Ratzenberger AUT	7 Jul	4y
Thomas Renner AUT	6 Jul	4y
Michele Russo ITA	22 May	4y
Shelley Ryder CAN	25 May	4y
Nikolay Safin RUS	2 May	4y
Ronnie Skold SWE	26 Mar	P
Mike Stulce USA	21 Aug	P
Dragutin Topic YUG	5 Mar	3m
Romas Ubartas LIT	17 Aug	P
Anatoliy Vanyushkin RUS	17 Apr	4y
Spyros Vasdekis GRE	7 Mar	3m
Anatoliy Vasilyev RUS	27 Mar	4y
Keith Witthauer USA	5 Jun	3m
Yang Hongtao CHN	11 Sep	4y
Yu Wenge CHN	6 Apr	P
Luciano Zerbini ITA	8 Aug	4y
Women		
Ime Akpan NGR	17 Jun	P
Irina Belova RUS	12 Mar	P
Tatyana Dorovskikh UKR	15 Jun	P
Lyudmila Dzhigalova UKR	30 Jul	4y
Zulfia Filyova RUS	26 Jun	4y
Dulce Garcia CUB	22 May	P
Guo Yan CHN	13 Sep	4y
Tsvetanka Khristova BUL	28 Mar	4y
Inessa Kravets UKR	7 Jul	3m
Yulia Klikushina RUS	17 Apr	4y
Minna Lainio FIN	15 Mar	4y
Milena Megli ITA	25 Sep	3m
Lyudmila Narozhilenko RUS	13 Feb	4y
Liliya Nurutdinova RUS	17 Aug	4y
Giannina Re ITA	29 Nov	4y?
Marina Shmonina RUS	13 Mar	4y
Stefania Simova BUL	28 Mar	4y
Agnieszka Stanczyk POL	Jul	
Olga Voloshina RUS	16 Feb	4y
Wang Yawen CHN	15 May	P
Zhou Tianhua CHN	Sep	P

To add to 1992 suspensions

Men		
Sándor Barczo HUN	18 Oct	

* reinstated by the Dutch federation after their Disciplinary Committee considered that "reasonable doubt has been established".

ATHLETICS REFERENCE BOOKS 1993/4

Reviewed by Peter Matthews

The Golden Book of the Olympic Games by Erich Kamper and Bill Mallon. 672 pages $55 in the USA. Published in English by Vallardi & Associati, Milan, Italy. A great statistical compilation that follows the definitive works previously produced by the authors. Their aim was to produce a single reference volume on the Games that would contain all information desired by any Olympic enthusiast. Full details are given for the first three in every event, with dates of birth and death of all medallists included in a country by country survey - and so much else, with analyses of medals and mosts, youngest and oldest. Available from Sportsbooks, PO Box 171C, Esher, Surrey, UK, KT10 OYP £41 (UK) £43 (Europe) £50 rest of world (including postage and packing)

CIS Athletics Statistics by Richard Hymans. A5 390 pages. £15 or 40 Swiss Francs inc. postage from the author, 39 Kenyon St, Fulham, London SW6 6JZ. The third edition of this most comprehensive handbook of statistics of the former USSR. Contents include national records for each republic, at least 100 deep performance and performer lists for all events, detailed results of all USSR Championships, and statistical profiles of leading athletes - 430 men and 323 women.

Stuttgart '93 by Matti Hannus and Tapio Pekola. 208 pages, lavishly illustrated with colour photos by Mark Shearman. Complete results and text (in Finnish) - a beautiful souvenir of a great World Championships. 290 Finnmarks from Juoksiya magazine, PL 50, 00441 Helsinki. This is the eighth book that Juoksiya have published on major meetings - Montreal 1976, Prague 1978, Moscow 1980, Helsinki 1983, Los Angeles 1984, Rome 1987, Tokyo 1991, Stuttgart 1993. All except the Helsinki one written by ATFS member Matti Hannus.

Suomen Yleisurheilu 1900-50 series. Adding to his previous booklets on Finnish athletics for 1933-37, Esa Laitinen has compiled five more: 1900-04 (138p), 1905-06 (138p), 1907 (116p), 1908 (136p), 1909 (146p), each A5 size. These give detailed summaries of the Finnish sesaons, with results and deep rankings lists for each year. There are also world best performances, detailed results from the Olympic Games and notes on leading athletes born in each year of this decades. Including postage each booklet is FIM 70 in Europe or FIM 80 elsewhere from Esa Laitinen, Haapalammentie 20 A 3 40800 Vaajakoski, Finland.

Junior World Rankings 1991

Junior world lists, 50 deep for 1991, compiled by Milan Skocovsky and Lionel Peters are included in this booklet, available from Palle Lassen, price including postage £5 or US $8.00 in Europe, US $11.00 outside Europe. Further yearbooks are expected.

Coppa Europa Bruno Zauli by Raul Leoni. A4 156pp. Complete results of all European Cup competitions 1965-91. From Raul Leoni, Via Paulo Maria Martinez, 11, 00151 Roma, Italy.

Strength and Speed Ratings by Del Harder. 185 pages, $13.47 plus £2.00 postage from Education Plus, 18584 Carlwyn Drive, Castro Valley, CA 94546. A review of all men's athletics events - and also weightlifting and powerlifting - with records and comparative standards for each age group and a summary of the evolution of records. Amongst many fascinating details are such items as the fastest times by big men or the best throws by light men.

IAAF Handbooks. From the IAAF, 3 Hans Crescent, Knightsbridge, London SW1X 0LN, England.

IAAF/ATFS Stuttgart Statistics Handbook 1993 for the World Championships A5 608pp. £15. This most comprehensive book, edited by Mark Butler, includes full results of the previous World Championships with analyses of medallists etc., winners of area championships, all-time lists, world record progressions, national records, complete results of the 1993 World Indoor Championships, World Cross-country Championships and World Race Walking Cup, and an extensive who's who in world athletics.

IAAF/ATFS Toronto Statistics Handbook for the 4th World Indoor Championships. A5 396pp. £6. Contents of this superb production include complete results of previous World Indoor Championships, medallists from European and US indoor championships, world indoor lists for 1991/2 and all-time, national indoor records, evolution ofworld indoor bests and a world who's who.

IAAF Directory and Calendar 1993. Ring-bound, pocket-sized, compendium of 365 pages.

ANNUALS

Annuals in varying sizes are produced for most major athletics nations. The following, containing year lists, records and in some cases results for the previous season for their respective countries. Most should be obtainable from their national federations, whose addresses are given elsewhere. Some of those noted cover 1993, but at the time of writing most cover 1992.

Annuario dell'Atletica 1993. A5 595p. The Italian annual was delayed at the printers this year, so that copies were not received until 1994.

Asian athletics 1992. A5 60 pages. DM 20 in Europe or US $15 for overseas airmail from the author, Heinrich Hubbeling, Haydnstrasse 8, 48691 Vreden, Germany. Top 30s for 1992 for athletes from Asian nations, together with continuation lists for countries other than China and Japan.

El Atletismo Subamericano 1993 by Luis Vinker for the South American area of the IAAF. A5 156 pages. Results of international meetings, records and South American ranking lists for 1992.

L'Athlétisme Africain/African Athletics 1993 by Yves Pinaud and Walter Abmayr A5, 152p. The 12th edition of this invaluable work. 100 deep men's and women's lists for Africa for 1992, with all-time lists, and national championships results. FF 90 from Editions Polymédias, 121 Avenue d'Italie, 75013 Paris, France.

Athlerama 92-93. The 31st edition of the French Annual is edited by Yves Pinaud. A5, 428pp. This splendid yearbook is packed with information on French athletics. 100 FF inc. postage from Fédération Française d'Athlétisme, 10 rue du Faubourg Poissonnière, 75480 Paris Cedex 10. As well as detailed ranking lists for French athletes in 1992, there are all-time lists, championship results and profiles of all French record-breakers of the year, with a special feature giving year lists for 1932.

Athletics Australia Handbook of Records and Results 1992-93 A5 148p. Covering the Australian season to the end of April 1993, with lists records, results and ranking lists compiled by Paul Jenes. The book has been extended by 24 pages this year.

British Athletics 1993 Compiled by the NUTS, general editor Rob Whittingham. A5, 400p. Detailed results and statistics on 1992 for the UK, with colour photos included for the first time to make this the most attractive British annual yet published. A new feature is the inclusion of Peter Matthews's detailed Merit Rankings for 1992; with those of the first (1968) and a review of the 25 years 1968-92. £9.95 plus postage from Umbra Software Ltd, Unit 1, Bredbury Business Park, Bredbury Park Way, Stockport SK6 2SN, England.

1993 Canadian Athletics Annual 174pp. $11 plus $2 postage from its chief compiler Cecil Smith, 17 Drury Crescent, Brampton, Ontario, Canada L6T 1L1. Published by Athletics Magazine. Detailed Canadian lists (now 50 deep for each event), records and results for 1992, as well as 25-deep all-time lists.

Caribbean Athletics Annual 1992 A5, 144pp. £10 or US $15 including postage from the compiler, Bernard Linley, Via Cassia 987, 00189 Roma, Italy. Extended by 36 pages this year, results are given of major meetings and championships in the Caribbean in 1992, with 20-deep lists for 1992 and 35-deep all-time lists. There is also a compilation of all finalists at the CAC Games from 1926 to 1990.

Laursen's Lille Lommebog 1992 by Erik Laursen. A5 116pp, includes Danish ranking lists for 1992 and all-time lists for all events. 44 Danish kroner including postage in Europe or 56 kroner outside Europe from the author, Sandbakken 95, 8270 Høbjerg, Denmark.

Deutsche Bestenliste 1992 A5 164 pp. 20 DM. Edited by Klaus Amrhein for the Deutschen Gesellschaft für Leichtathletik-Dokumentation e.V. Detailed year lists for Germany for 1992. See DGLD details at the end of this review.

DLV-Jahrbuch 1992/93. A5 504pp. Edited by Lutz Nebenthal. 25 DM from the DLV, Julius-Reiber-Strasse 19, 6100 Darmstadt, Germany.Articles and review, with detailed results of 1992 meetings, records and top ten lists as well as illustrations, some in colour.

Eesti Kergejoustik 1993. 128pp. Estonian ranking lists for 1992 are contained in this handbook published by the national federation: Eesti Kergejôustikuliit, Regati pst. 1, Tallinn EE0103. Also available is a 160 page booklet containing deep all-time lists to 1 Jan 1992; this also includes lists of national champions from 1988 and statistical profiles of leading athletes.

Israeli Amateur Athletic Association 1993 Annual compiled by David Eiger and Arik Cooks. 28 pages. From David Eiger, 10 Ezra Hozsofer Str, Herzliya 46371, Israel. Top ten1993 and all-time lists etc..

Jaarboek Atletiekleven 1992. A4, 316 pp. 650 Belgian Francs rom the Vlaamse Atletiekliga vzw, Sint Laurenstraat 14, 26, bus 3, 1000 Brussels, Belgium. 1992 Belgian rankings and all-time lists for all age groups, with comprehensive championship and international results, and lots of photographs.

Japan Athletics Annual '93. A5 126pp. Compiled for the Japan AAF. 30 deep lists for senior and 10 deep for juniors for 1992, all-time top 30s, records, profiles and results. Available from Yoshimasa Noguchi, Track & Field Magazine Sha Co, Ltd, 3-10-10 Misaki-cho, Chiyoda-ku, Tokyo 101, Japan.

KNAU Statistisch Jaarboek 1992, from the KNAU, Postbus 567, 3430 An Nieuwegein, Netherlands. A5, 316pp - price 45 Dutch florins (or Dfl. 35 if cash sent by registered letter). Edited by Louis Weisscher, this yearbook has again grown. There are comprehensive ranking lists for 1992 for the Netherlands, all-time top tens, an extensive chronology of 1992, championships and international match results and records, and a special article on the history of Dutch women's 800m running, e topic particularly pertinent with Ellen van Langen winning the Olympic title.

Latvijas Vieglatletikas Gadagramata. 152 pp. Comprehensive coverage of Latvian athletics in 1993, compiled by ATFS member Andris Stagis with Irma Jaunzeme. From the Latvia Track and Field Athletics Federation, Tërbatas iela 4, Riga LV-1723.

Legkaya Atletika '92-93. A5 318pp. In Cyrillic script, world and CIS lists for 1992 and detailed results affecting the CIS nations. Compiled by Sergey Tikhonov, Aleksey Shedchenko, Yevgeniy Chen and Nikolay Ivanov.

Norges Beste - Friidrettskalenderen 1993. A5 288pp. The Norwegian annual includes not only national lists for 1992, but also Nordic top 20s, all-time lists and results of leading meetings. From Jo Nesse, Gjønnesskogen 2, 1340 Bekkestua, Norway.

Pacific Statistics. Issue no.8 (A5 size), including 1992 review and lists, is available for £2.50 (£3.50 for air-mail outside Europe) from Tony Isaacs, 11 Manton Close, Trowbridge, Wilts BA14 0RZ, England.

SA Athletics 1993. A5, 216p. Rand 15 (R20 including postage or R35 air mail) postage from SA Athletics Annual, Postbus 35209, Menlo Park, 0102 South Africa. The usual excellent assemblage of all-time lists, records, championship results and detailed 1992 lists for South Africa.

Schweizer Leichtathletik Jahrbuch 1993, the Swiss Athletics Annual. A5 280pp. As usual, attractively produced with detailed championship results and comprehensive lists for all age groups for 1993, with records for all Swiss Cantons. A special feature details Swiss top tens and results for 1933.

Scottish Athletics Yearbook 1994. A5 175p. Scottish lists compiled by Arnold Black and championship results for 1993. £3 plus postage (50p in UK, £1 elsewhere) from Colin Shields, 21 Bogton Avenue, Glasgow G44 3JJ, Scotland.

Sverige Bästa 1992, edited by A.Lennart Julin. A5 288pp. 150 Swedish crowns inc. postage from Svenska Fri-Idrottsförbundet, Förlaget, Sofiatornet, Stadion,S-114 33, Stockholm, Sweden. As ever a model of precision, with deep 1992 lists for Sweden. Well illustrated including a colour cover of Niklas Wallenlind.

TAFWA All-Time Indoor List 1994 by Ed Gordon. A5 130pp. The annual compilation which includes deep all-time indoor lists of performers and performances for all events, men and women. From Ed Gordon, 180 Ardmore Road, Berkeley, CA 94707, USA.

Tutto Atletica '92 by Carlo Santi. A5 360pp. 20,000 lira, Editoriale Sport ItalChronological list of important World and Italian results for 1992, records and 20-deep world and Italian lists, with 10-deep all-time lists and 1992 Italian Championship results.

FAST United States Track and Field Annual 1993, A5 498 pp. General editors Scott Davis, Dave Johnson and Howard Willman. 50 deep US year lists for 1992 and 60 plus deep US all-time lists, with 10-deep junior and collegiate lists. The extensive index of nearly 300 pages includes all athletes ranked in the year lists, showing yearly progressions and championships records for each. From Scott Davis, 4432 Snowbird Circle, Cerritos, CA 90701, USA, $18 USA, $27 overseas air mail, $20 sea mail.

Welsh Athletics Annual 1993 A5 240pp. Edited by Alan and Brenda Currie. Very comprehensive coverage of Welsh athletics, with lists, results and features. £6 including postage with cheques payable to 'Welsh Athletics' from the Athletics Association of Wales, Morfa Stadium, Landore, Swansea SA1 7DF.

Yleisurheilu 1993. A5 608p. The Finnish annual, edited by Jouko Nousiainen and Juhani Jalava for the Finnish Federation, includes very deep lists for all age groups for Finland 1993, with index of athletes and results of championships and international matches. This was the fastest production of any annual, as I received my copy on December 24! It also contains indoor and outdoor world lists for 1993 - not quite to the year's end!

Who Is Who 1992 der Deutschen Leichtathletik. A5 256 p. The second edition of this most useful book by Klaus Amrhein contains detailed biographical details of leading German athletes, together with championships and international match results for Germany in 1992. From the author at Lindenweg 3, 6112 Klein Zimmern, Germany for DM 25 or US$ 20 (banknotes only).

Yugoslav Athletics Annual 1992. A pocket sized book of 238 pages with results and year lists for 1992 in Cyrillic script, edited by ATFS member Ozren Karamata, from whom the book can be purchased for 15 Deutsche Mark, cash only, at Matije Gupca 17, 11080 Zemun, Yugoslavia.

Statistical bulletins

The **German** statistical group, the DGLD, produces annual national ranking lists for Germany and most impressive quarterly bulletins of up to 200 pages, with articles and statistial compilations. Details of membership (DM 80 per year) from Klaus Amrhein, Lindenweg 3, 64846 Klein Zimmern, Germany.

The **Spanish** group, the AEEA, produce 4 bulletins each year packed with statistical items, including deep Spanish and world all-time and year lists. Contact Manuel Villuendas, Sagusta 7, 28914 Leganes-Madrid, Spain.

Track Stats is published quarterly by the NUTS in Britain. Subscription £8 UK, £11 Europe, £14 USA and elsewhere from Tim Lynch-Staunton, 17 St. Martins Drive, Walton-on-Thames, Surrey, KT12 3BW, England. Contents include articles, deep all-time lists, career profiles etc. - on British and world athletics.

General

Idrottsboken 1993. 608 pp, A4. 689 Swedish kroner from Strömbergs/Brunnhages, Box 65, S-162 11 Vällingby, Sweden. The 49th edition of this magnificent book is as ever beautifully illustrated and packed with features and results for 1992 on a very large number of sports. Coverage is both international as well as Swedish. The editorial team headed by Ulf Pettersson includes ATFS member Ove Karlsson.

Guinness Encyclopedia of Sports Records and Result by Peter Matthews. Third Edition of the authoritative reference source for the records, results and statistics of all important international sports and sports events. 416 pages. Price £14.99.

Guinness International Who's Who in Sport by Peter Matthews with Ian Buchanan and Bill Mallon. Biographies for nearly 3000 of the top sports men and women of all-time (and leading horses and greyhounds). Athletics is very well represented with more than 450 entries. 730 pages, price £14.99.
These books can be obtained, postage extra (£1.50 per book), from Guinness Publishing, 33 London Road, Enfield, Middlesex EN2 6DJ, England.

Previous editions of the ATFS Annual

Editions for 1991-3 from Harmsworth Active, 3rd Floor, Astley House, 33 Notting Hill Gate, London W21 3JQ, England. Bob Sparks, 94 Reigate Road, Ewell, Epsom, Surrey KT17 3DZ, England has ATFS Annuals for 1982-4 for sale at £10 each, including postage. Bob may be able to help with other editions and also has copies of the ATFS Natonal Statistics books on the USSR and Poland for sale.

Books for review would be welcomed by the editor: Peter Matthews, 10 Madgeways Close, Great Amwell, Ware, Herts SG12 9RU, England.

NATIONAL CHAMPIONS 1993 AND BIOGRAPHIES OF LEADING ATHLETES

By Peter Matthews

THIS SECTION incorporates biographies of 663 of the world's top athletes, 387 men and 275 women, listed by nation, with national champions at standard events in 1993 for the leading countries prominent in athletics.

The selection of athletes profiled has changed quite considerably from last year's Annual, not only that all entries have been updated, but also that more newcomers than usual have been introduced to replace those who have retired or faded a little from the spotlight.

The choice of who to include is always invidous, but I have concentrated on those who are currently in the world's top 10-12 per event, those who have the best championship records and those who I consider may make notable impact during the coming year.

Since this section was introduced in the 1985 Annual, biographies have been given for a total of 1792 athletes (1069 men and 723 women). This year there are 146 newcomers (77 men, 69 women), with 37 (25 men, 12 women) reinstated from previous Annuals. There are now just 40 athletes (28 men, 12 women) who have been featured in all ten editions of this Annual 1985-94.

These figures give a good idea of the rate of change in the élite in our sport. The most notable change is that this year there are 32 athletes (29 women) from China compared to 18 last year and 7 in 1985, while the numbers included from Eastern Europe continue to drop sharply. There were 13 Kenyans profiled in the 1985 Annual (all men); this year there are 47 (including 5 women).

Once again no doubt some of those dropped from this compilation will also again make their presence felt; the keen reader can look up their credentials in previous Annuals, and, of course, basic details may be in the athletes' index at the end of this book.

The biographical information includes:

a) Name; date and place of birth; height (in metres); weight (in kilograms).
b) Previous name(s) for married women; club or university; occupation.
c) Major championships record - all placings in such events as the Olympic Games, World Championships, European Championships, Commonwealth Games, World Cup and European Cup Final; leading placings in the World Indoor Championships, European or World Junior Championships, and other Continental Championships; and first three in European Indoors or World Student Games.
d) National titles won or successes in other major events.
e) Records set: world, continental and national; indoor world bests (WIB).
f) Progression of best marks over the years at major event(s).
g) Personal best performances at other events.
h) Other comments.

See Introduction to this Annual for lists of abbreviations used for events and championships. Note that for comparison purposes decathlons and heptathlons made before the introduction of the current tables have been rescored using the 1984 IAAF Tables, except those marked *, for which event breakdowns were unavailable. Women's pentathlons (p) have not been rescored.

I am most grateful to various ATFS members who have helped check these details. Additional information or corrections would be welcomed for next year's Annual.

Peter Matthews

ALGERIA

Governing body: Fédération Algerienne d'Athlétisme, BP 88, El Biar, Alger. Founded 1963. **National Champions 1993**: **Men:** 100m/200m: Amar Hacini 10.4/20.8, 400m: Sadek Boumendil 45.9, 800m: Kada Mouhaouch 1:51.6, 1500m: Abdelhamid Slimani 3:53.4, 5000m: Mohamed Belabbès 14:12.9, 10000m: Mahieddine Belhadj 29:30.0, 3000mSt: Mourad Belhadj 8:38.9, 110mh: Noureddine Tadjine 14.2, 400mh: Nabil Selmi 52.7 (Fadhel Khayatti TUN 51.0), HJ: Othmane Belfaa 2.24, PV: Belgacem Touami 5.15, LJ: Abderrahmane Hadjou 7.30, TJ: Lotfi Khaida 16.22, SP: Tahar Chachoua 14.47, DT/JT: Mourad Mahour Bacha 47.52/60.70, HT: Hakim Toumi 71.42, 10000mW: Abdelwahab Ferguène 40:56.0. **Women**: 100m: Saliha Hamadi 12.2, 200m: Mokhtaria Safi 24.8, 400m: Hassiba Halilou 56.4, 800m: Anissa Khali 2:14.2, 1500m/3000m: Leïla Bendahmane 4:29.1/9:32.7, 100mh: Nouria Mérah 14.4, 400mh: Amel Baraket 63.2, HJ/SP: Nacèra Zaaboub -/12.12, LJ/TJ: Naïma Baraket 5.49/12.10, DT: Aïcha Dahmous 44.54, HT: Samia Dahmani 31.84, JT: Malika Hamou 35.12, 5000mW: Dounia Kara 25:00.9.

Réda ABDENOUZ b.25 Sep 1968 Hussein Dey 1.70m 63kg. ERC Alger. Student.
At 800m: OG: '88- sf, '92- 7; WCh: '87- qf, '91- h. 2nd GP 1990. Algerian champion 1988-90.
Four Algerian 800m records 1988-90.
Progression at 800m: 1984- 1:57.2, 1985- 1:55.9, 1986- 1:50.0, 1987- 1:47.35, 1988- 1:45.65, 1989- 1:46.7, 1990- 1:44.98, 1991- 1:45.40, 1992- 1:45.19, 1993- 1:45.40. pbs: 400m 47.7 '88, 1000m 2:17.98 '93, 1500m 3:47.15 '91.

Aïssa BELAOUT b. 12 Aug 1968 1.70m 63kg.
At 5000m: WCh: '93- dnf.
Algerian 5000m record 1993.
Progression at 5000m: 1991- 13:45.5, 1992- 13:23.11, 1993- 13:08.03. pbs: 1500m: 3:38.45 '92, 3000m 7:38.70 '93.

Azzedine BRAHMI b.13 Sep 1966 Sétif 1.78m 64kg. M.C.Alger.
At 3000mSt: OG: '88- 13, '92- 8; WCh: '91- 3, '93- dnf; Won AfCh 1988-9, Arab 1989, Algerian 1986, 1988-9 (1500m 1991).
Algerian 3000m steeple records 1988 & 1991.
Progression at 3000mSt: 1985- 9:01.3, 1986- 8:40.80, 1987- 8:36.52, 1988- 8:16.54, 1989- 8:26.94, 1990- 8:22.36, 1991- 8:13.29, 1992- 8:11.27, 1993- 8:20.86. pbs: 1500m 3:46.1 '91, 3000m 7:51.70 '91, 5000m 13:56.9 '88, 2000mSt 5:18.38 '92.

Noureddine MORCELI b.28 Feb 1970 Ténès 1.72m 62kg. Was a student at Riverside CC, USA 1989-90.
At 1500m: OG: '92- 7; WCh: '91- 1, '93- 1; WJ: '88- 2; WI: '91- 1; AfCh: '89- 4. Algerian champion 1989. Won GP 1500m and second overall 1990. 9th World Jnr CC 1988.
World records 1500m 1992, mile 1993. WIR 1500m 3:34.16 '91. Algerian records 1990-3: 1500m (6), 1M (5), 3000m (2), 800m, 1000m, and 5000m. African indoor 1M records 3:53.50 and 3:50.81 '91.
Progression at 1500m, 1 mile: 1986- 3:50.7, 1987- 3:53.1, 1988- 3:40.41, 1989- 3:37.87, 3:59.79; 1990- 3:32.60, 3:53.06; 1991- 3:31.00, 3:49.12; 1992- 3:28.82, 3:49.79; 1993- 3:29.20, 3:44.39 pbs: 800m 1:44.79 '91, 1000m: 2:13.73 '93, 3000m 7:29.24 '92, 5000m 13:25.20 '90.
Unbeaten in 15 1500m/1M races in 1991, but lost four in 1992 including a poor run at the Olympics prior to getting the world record. Unbeaten again in 1993. Coached by elder brother Abderahmane, 1500m: 3 WSG, 4 WCp and pb 3:36.26 in 1977.

Women

Yasmina AZZIZI b.25 Feb 1966 1.76m 76kg. RC Kouba.
At Hep: OG: '92- dnf; WCh: '91- 5; AfG: '87- 1 (4 100mh), AfCh: '85- 3; '88- 1 (1 JT, 3 100mh, 5 HJ), '89- 1 (3 HJ, 3 JT). At 100mh: WCp: '89- 8. Won Pan-Arab LJ & Hep 1987, 100m, 100mh, HJ, JT 1989; Algerian 100m 1986, 100mh 1986, 1989; 200m 1989, 100mh 1989, LJ 1986, 1989, JT 1989.

Hassiba Boulmerka

Seven African heptathlon records 1986-91. Algerian records for 100m, 200m, 100mh, HJ, LJ, SP, Hep.
Progression at Hep: 1982- 3056*, 1984- 4201, 1985- 4909, 1986- 5483, 1987- 5663, 1988- 5824, 1989- 5957h, 1990- 6056, 1991- 6392. pbs: 100m 11.69 '91, 200m 23.38 '92, 800m 2:17.17 '91, 100mh 13.02 '92, HJ 1.79 '91, LJ 6.15 '91, SP 16.09 '92, JT 51.08 '89.
Six pbs for fifth in 1991 World Champs, adding 278 points to her African heptathlon record.

Hassiba BOULMERKA b.10 Jul 1968 Constantine 1.65m 57kg. CM Belcourt.
At (800m)/1500m: OG: '88- h/h; '92- 1; WCh: '91- 1, '93- 3; AfCh: '88- 1/1, '89- 1/1; WJ: '86- sf/h. At 800m: WCp: '89- 7; AfG: '87- 4. Won Algerian 800m 1987-9, 1500m 1987-90, Arab 800m 1987, 1989; 1500m 1992. 3rd GP 1M 1991.
African records: 1500m (4), 1M (3) 1990-2; Algerian records at 800m & 1500m 1988-92, 3000m 1993.
Progression at 800m, 1500m: 1984- 2:25.4, 4:55.9; 1985- 2:18.6, 4:53.3; 1986- 2:06.86, 4:26.96; 1987- 2:04.33, 4:23.96; 1988- 2:02.09, 4:08.33; 1989- 2:00.21, 4:13.85; 1990- 2:00.44, 4:05.02; 1991- 1:58.72, 4:00.00; 1992- 2:01.51, 3:55.30; 1993- 4:04.29. pbs: 400m 56.7 '90, 1M 4:20.79 '91, 3000m 8:56.16 '93.
In 1991 she became the first African woman to win a world title and in 1992 the first athlete to win an Olympic gold medal for Algeria with the fastest 1500m by a woman for four years.

ARGENTINA

Governing body: Confederación Argentina de Atletismo, 21 de Septimebre no. 207, 3260 Concepción del Uruguay, Entre Rios.

National Championships first held in 1920 (men), 1939 (women). **1993 Champions: Men**: 100m/200m: Carlos Gats 10.61/21.57, 400m: Christian Diaz 48.73, 800m: Luis Migueles 1:50.87, 1500m: Manuel Balmaceda CHI 3:46.3, 5000m: Antonio Ibánez 14:16.9; 10000m: Oscar Amaya 29:10.8, 3000mSt: Mariano Tarilo 9:00.5, 110mh: Ricardo D'Andrilli 14.2, 400mh: Miguel Pérez 52.81, HJ: Fernando Moreno 2.11, PV/LJ: Oscar Veit 5.10/7.28, TJ: Fernando Pecchenino 14.48, SP: Adrián Marzo 16.60, DT: Marcelo Pugliese 54.40, HT: Andrés Charadia 70.44, JT: Juan Garmendia 59.70, Dec: Gustavo Occhiuzzo 5922, 20kmW: Benjamin Lorefice 1:25:56. **Women**: 100m/200m: Danielle Lebreo 11.90/ 25.05, 400m: Ana Comaschi 54.6, 800m: Alejandra Cepeda 2:14.20, 1500m: Marta Orellana 4:28.0, 3000m: Mirian Rios 9:41.6, 10000m: Vilma Paillos 35:24.6, , 100mh/400mh: Veronica de Paoli 13.7/59.75, HJ: Solange Witteven 1.70, LJ/TJ: Andrea Avila 6.18/13.73, SP: Silvana Filippi 14.87, DT: Liliana Martinelli 55.04, HT: Zulma Lambert 47.44, JT: Mariela Arch 44.08, Hep: Mariela Andrade 4756, 10000mW: Linda Carriego 52:16.3.

AUSTRALIA

Governing body: Athletics Australia, 21 O'Shanassy St, N.Melbourne, Victoria 3051. Founded 1897.
National Championships first held in 1893 (men) (Australasian until 1927), 1930 (women). **1993 Champions**: **Men**: 100m: Dean Capobianco 10.17, 200m: Damien Marsh 20.29w, 400m: Darren Clark 45.65, 800m: Simon Lewin 1:47.06, 1500m: Simon Doyle 3:46.03, 1M: Glenn Stojanovic 4:00.80, 5000m: Peter O'Donoghue 13:55.1, 10,000m: Rod Higgins 29:02.7, Half Mar: Malcolm Norwood 63:13, Mar: Sean Quilty 2:15:31, 3000mSt: Shaun Creighton 8:29.31, 110mh: Kyle Vander-Kuyp 13.57, 400mh: Shunji Karube JPN 50.21, HJ: Tim Forsyth 2.28, PV: James Miller 5.45, LJ: Mike Powell USA 8.43, TJ: Peter Burge 15.87w, SP: John Minns 18.22, DT: Werner Reiterer 60.16, HT: Sean Carlin 74.74, JT: Andrew Currey 78.40, Dec: Peter Winter 7600, 5000mW: Nick A'Hern 18:58.7, 20kmW: Paul Copeland 1:29:42, 50kmW: Michael Harvey 3:57:20*. **Women**: 100m/200m: Melinda Gainsford 11.26w/22.49, 400m/400mh: Renee Poetschka 51.00/57.04, 800m: Narelle Parr 2:03.92, 1500m/1M: Susie Power 4:14.89/4:35.28, 3000m: Krishna Stanton 8:58.6, 10,000m: Susan Hobson 33:53.6, Half Mar/Mar: Kerryn McCann 76:37/2:40:09, 100mh/Hep: Jane Flemming 12.98/6278, HJ: Alison Inverarity 1.86, LJ/TJ: Nicole Boegman 6.72w/13.27, SP/DT: Daniela Costian 16.30/62.82, HT: Debbie Sosimenko 57.58, JT: Louise McPaul 59.14, 5000mW: Kerry Junna-Saxby 20:30.0, 10kmW: Jenny Billington 46:06, 20kmW: Anne Manning 1:34:27*. * courses not measured according to AA guidelines.

Simon BAKER b.6 Feb 1958 Oakleigh, Vic. 1.86m 70kg. Club: Oakleigh. Qualified mechanical engineer, now coaching at the Institute of Sport, Canberra.
At 50kmW: OG: '88- 6, '92- 19; WCh: '91- dnf, '93- 14; WCp: '89- 1, '91- 2, '93- 7. At 30kmW: CG: '86- 1, '90- 7. At 20kmW: OG: '84- 14, '88- 11; WCh: '83- 29, '87- 24; WCp: '83- 14, '85- 12, '87- 11, '91- 2. Won AUS 5000mW 1988-9, 20kmW 1985, 1988; 50kmW 1989.
Two Commonwealth 50km road walk bests 1988-9 and track record 1990.

Progression at 20kmW, 50kmW: 1983- 1:24:43; 1984- 1:24:29; 1985- 1:25:22; 1986- 1:23:13; 1987- 1:21:57, 3:58:51; 1988- 1:21:19, 3:44:07; 1989- 1:23:25, 3:43:13; 1990- 1:21:52.4t, 3:43:50.0t; 1991- 3:46:36; 1992- 1:22:16, 4:05:08; 1993- 1:24:32, 3:57:11. Track pbs: 3000mW 11:26.0 '89, 5000mW 19:24.12i '89, 19:32.15 '88, 10kmW 40:35.0 '89, 1HrW 14609m '86. Road 30kmW 2:06:39 '89.

Dean CAPOBIANCO b.11 May 1970 1.80m 70kg. Student.
At 200m: OG: '92- qf; WCh: '91- qf, '93- 5; WJ: '88- sf/2 4x400mR. Won AUS 100m 1991, 1993, 200m 1991-2.
Progression at 200m: 1987- 21.5, 1988- 21.46/21.0w, 1989- 21.28/20.6w, 1990- 20.60, 1991- 20.39, 1992- 20.57/20.53w, 1993- 20.18. pbs: 100y 9.2 '93, 100m 10.25/10.17w/9.9w '93, 400m 45.47 '94, 110mh 14.15 '89.
Australian junior 110m hurdles record 1989.

Darren CLARK b.6 Sep 1965 Sydney 1.78m 76kg. Randwick Botany (NSW).
At 400m: OG: '84- 4, '88- 4; WCh: '83 & '87- sf; WI: '93- 3; CG: '86- 2 (2 4x400mR), '90- 1 (sf 200m); WCp: '85- 4 (3 at 200m). Won AUS 200m 1989, 400m 1986, 1989-90, 1993; AAA 400m 1983-6.
Four Australian 400m records 1984-8. Two Commonwealth 300m bests 1985-6.
Progression at 400m: 1982- 46.62, 1983- 45.05, 1984- 44.75, 1985- 44.80, 1986- 44.72, 1987- 44.97, 1988- 44.38, 1989- 45.35, 1990- 44.60, 1993- 45.53. pbs: 100m 10.47/10.3 '83, 10.36w '87, 200m 20.49 '83, 300m 31.88 '86, 600m 1:16.91 '88.

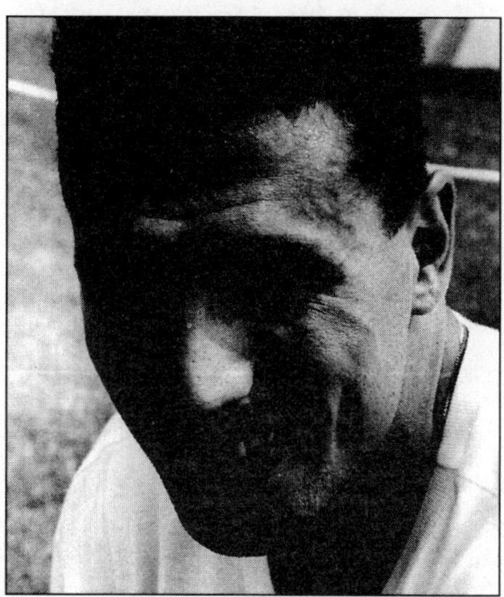

World age-17 best to win AAA 1983. Ran a 43.86 relay leg in 1984 Olympics. Much affected by injuries, after missing the 1990 European season with a virus complaint he decided to take up rugby league with Balmain Tigers, stating that he could not compete against drug takers. Returned to athletics in 1993.

Shaun CREIGHTON b.14 May 1967 1.80m 65kg. Ballarat H. Sport and recreation officer.
At 3000mSt: WCh: '91- h, '93- 9; CG: '90- 5; WSG: '91- 1; WCp: '92- 3. Won AUS 3000mSt 1991-3.
Two Australian 3000m steeple records 1992-3.
Progression at 3000mSt: 1988- 9:04.8, 1989- 8:39.8, 1990- 8:33.59, 1991- 8:27.20, 1992- 8:20.37, 1993- 8:16.22. pbs: 1000m 2:23.1 '90, 1500m 3:38.59 '93, 1M 3:59.8 '90, 2000m 5:03.00 '92, 3000m 7:46.10 '93, 5000m 13:37.61 '91, 2000mSt 5:30.7 '92.
Broke Kerry O'Brien's 22 year-old Australian record in December 1992.

Simon DOYLE b.9 Nov 1966 Queensland 1.85m 74kg. Degree in agriculture from University of Queensland.
At 1500m: WCh: '91- 12, '93- 9; CG: '90- 4 (8 800m). At 800m: WCp: '89- 5. Won AUS 800m 1989, 1991; 1500m 1991, 1993; 5000m 1990.
Australian records 1500m (2), 1M (2) 1991; 2000m 1992.
Progression at 1500m: 1987- 3:44.3, 1988- 3:41.6, 1989- 3:38.32, 1990- 3:34.27, 1991- 3:31.96, 1993- 3:33.39. pbs: 400m 48.1 '91, 800m 1:45.38 '91, 1000m 2:18.22 '89, 1M 3:49.91 '91, 2000m 5:00.84 '92, 3000m 7:46.62 '92, 5000m 13:28.71 '92.
Made a great impression in 1990 with wins at 1500m in three Grand Prix meetings. Ill at 1991 World Championships and injured 1992.

Tim FORSYTH b.17 Aug 1973 1.96m 73kg. Yallourn/Newborough.
At HJ: OG: '92- 3=; WCh: '91- dnq 21, '93- 9; WI: '91- 8=; WJ: '90- 2. Won AUS HJ 1991-3.
Eight Australian high jump records 1990-3.
Progression at HJ: 1989- 2.16, 1990- 2.29, 1991- 2.31, 1992- 2.34, 1993- 2.35.

Damien MARSH b.28 Mar 1971 1.88m 81kg.
At 200m: WCh: '93- 8; WI: '93- 2. At 100m: WJ: '90- 6. Won AUS 200m 1993.
Australian 100m record 1993.
Progression at 200m: 1988- 21.35, 1989- , 1990- 21.61, 1991- 20.89/20.6, 1992- 20.70, 1993- 20.49/20.29w, 1994- 20.43. pb 100m 10.19 '93.

Darren Clark: returned to athletics in 1993 after a spell in Rugby League

Stephen MONEGHETTI b.26 Sep 1962 Ballarat 1.76m 60kg. Ballarat YCW Harriers. Maths teacher.
At Mar: OG: '88- 5, '92- 48; WCh: '87- 4, '91- 11; CG: '86- 3 (5 at 10000m), '90- 2. At 10000m: WCh: '93- h; WCp: '89- 6. World CC: '87- 11, '89- 4, '92- 6. Won World Students CC 1986, AUS 10000m 1988. 2nd World Half Mar 1993.
World half marathon bests on certified courses: 60:34 to win Great North Run 1990 and in Tokyo (but 33m overall drop) 60:27 in 1992 and 60:06 in 1993.
Progression at 10000m, Mar: 1982- 30:41.7; 1983- 29:00.0; 1984- 28:56.50; 1985- 28:49.37; 1986- 28:20.95, 2:11:18; 1987- 28:07.37, 2:12:49; 1988- 28:18.98, 2:11:49; 1989- 27:55.05, 2:09:06; 1990- 28:01.76, 2:08:16; 1991- 27:57.45, 2:19:18; 1992- 27:47.69, 2:23:42; 1993- 28:03.65, 2:12:36; 1994- 2:08:55. pbs: 3000m 8:01.53 '86, 5000m 13:30.84 '89.
Top class marathon runner, but just two wins in eleven races, when he set his pb in Berlin 1990, and in Tokyo 1994; 2nd London 1989.

Kyle VANDER-KUYP b.30 May 1971 Paddington, NSW 1.92m 76kg.
At 110mh: WCh: '93-sf; CG: '90- 6; WJ: '90- 3; WCp: '92- 5. Won AUS 110mh 1992-3.
Three Australian 110mh records 1993.
Progression at 110mh: 1989- 14.23/14.04w, 1990- 13.85, 1991- 13.88, 1992- 13.74, 1993- 13.48, 1994- 13.52/13.2. pbs: 100m 10.5 '91, 200m 21.57 '93, 400m 46.9 '91, 400mh 52.3 91.
First aboriginal to set an Australian record.

Women

Nicole BOEGMAN b.5 Mar 1967 Sydney 1.74m 62kg. née Boegman. Revesby, NSW and Hounslow, UK. Receptionist/typist.
At LJ: OG: '88- 5, '92- dnq; WCh: '87- 8, '91- dnq 14, '93- 7; CG: '86- 8; WCp: '89- 3; WI: '85- 5, "91- 5. Won AUS LJ 1987-8, 1992-3; TJ 1993; WAAA LJ 1988-9.
Australian long jump record 1988, TJ 1993.
Progression at LJ: 1981- 5.72w, 1982- 6.45, 1983- 6.55/6.71w, 1984- 6.43, 1985- 6.50/6.67w, 1986- 6.55/6.63w, 1987- 6.67, 1988- 6.87, 1989- 6.74/ 6.82w, 1990- 6.60, 1991- 6.72, 1992- 6.63/6.73w, 1993- 6.75/6.81w. pbs: 100m 11.86 '88, 11.7w '93; 200m 24.27 '90, 400m 58.5 '90, 100mh 15.15 '81, TJ 13.27 '93.
Missed 1990 Commonwealth Games due to fractured left leg. Married Gary Staines, UK 5000m Olympian, in 1990.

Daniela COSTIAN b.30 Apr 1965 Braila, Romania 1.82m 84kg. Univ. of Queensland.
At DT: OG: '92- 3; WCh: '91- 5, '93- 2; ECh: '86- 7dq; EJ: '83- 5; WSG: '85- 3. Balkan champion 1988. 3rd GP 1992. Won AUS SP 1991, DT 1989-93. Five Australian discus records 1991-4.
Progression at DT: 1979- 32.30, 1980- 40.16, 1981- 40.60, 1982- 55.08, 1983- 60.50, 1984- 65.22, 1985- 67.54, 1986- 69.66, 1988- 73.84, 1989- 66.78, 1990- 68.96, 1991- 66.06, 1992- 66.24, 1993- 66.02, 1994- 68.72. pb SP 16.30 '93.
Suspended for contravening IAAF doping rules at the 1986 European Championships. Left Romania and sought political asylum in Turkey after winning 1988 Balkan title; then went to Australia, gaining citizenship in 1990.

Jane FLEMMING b.14 Apr 1965 Melbourne 1.68m 56kg. Knox-Sherbrooke. Student at Australian Institute of Sport.
At Hep: OG: '88- 7; WCh: '87- 10, '93- 7, CG: '86- 2 (6 at 100mh), '90- 1 (1 LJ, 4 100mh); WSG: '89- 3. Won AUS 100m 1988, 1990; 100mh 1988, 1993; Hep 1985-8, 1993.
Four Australian heptathlon records 1987-90, Commonwealth record 1990.
Progression at Hep: 1982- 5232, 1983- 5472*, 1985- 5901, 1986- 6278w, 1987- 6390, 1988- 6492, 1989- 6286, 1990- 6695, 1992- 6046, 1993- 6343. pbs: 100m 11.50 '88, 11.4w '93; 200m 23.32 '93, 23.37w '88; 800m 2:11.75 '88, 100mh 12.98 '93, 400mh 57.88 '93, HJ 1.87 '87, LJ 6.78 '90, SP 14.03 '93, DT 45.04 '89, JT 49.28 '90.
Double gold medallist at 1990 Commonwealth Games, when originally selected only for the long jump due to injury doubts.

Cathy FREEMAN b.16 Feb 1973 1.64m 52kg. Ringwood. Student.
At 200m: WCh: '93- sf; CG: '90- 1 4x100mR; WJ: '90- 5, '92- 2. At 400m: OG: '92- qf. Won AUS 200m 1990-1, AAA 200m 1993, 400m 1992.
Progression at 200m, 400m: 1988- 24.50, 55.53; 1989- 23.86, 1990- 23.36; 1991- 23.50, 54.24; 1992- 23.09, 51.14; 1993- 22.37, 51.34. pbs: 100y 10.62 '93, 100m 11.43 '93, 11.42w '89.
Coached by Raelene Boyle.

Melinda GAINSFORD b.1 Oct 1971 1.75m 65kg.
At 200m (100m): OG: '92- sf (qf); WCh: '93- (sf); WI: '93- 2; WCp '92- 4 (4). Won AUS 100m and 200m 1992-3, AAA 100m & 200m 1992.
Progression at 200m: 1989- 24.02/23.89w, 1990- 23.89/23.50dq, 1991- 23.62, 1992- 22.68/22.26w, 1993- 22.49. pbs: 100m 11.22/11.15w '93, 400m 52.81 '92.

Alison INVERARITY b.12 Aug 1970 1.81m 60kg. Architecture student.
At HJ: OG: '92- 8; WCh: '91- 11; WI: '93- 5; WSG: '91- 1. Australian champion 1991, 1993.
Progression at HJ: 1985- 1.72, 1986- 1.77, 1987-

Lisa Ondieki:

1.83, 1989- 1.80, 1990- 1.90, 1991- 1.94, 1992- 1.96, 1993- 1.95. pb TJ 12.37 '91.
Daughter of Australian Test cricketer John Inverarity.

Kerry JUNNA-SAXBY b.2 Jun 1961 Ballina, NSW 1.66m 59kg. née Saxby. Ballina. Tour guide, Australian Institute of Sport.
At 10kmW: OG: '92- 15; WCh: '87- 2, '91- 5, '93- dnf; CG: '90- 1; WCp: '85- 10, '87- 4, '89- 2, '91- 5, '93- 5. Won GWG 1986. At 3000mW: WI: '89- 1, '91- 2, '93- 2. Won AUS 5000mW & 10kmW 1986-90, (5kW 1991-3), 3000mW 1987, 20kmW 1986-9.
World walking bests 1985-91 (no.): road: 5km (4) 20:34 '87, 10km (2) 1987-8, 15km 1:09:33 '85, 20km (3) 1:29:40 '88; track: 1500m(2) 5:50.51 '91; 3000m (5) 11:51.26 '91; 5000m (5) 20:17.19 '90; 10,000m (3) 42:14.2 '88 (mx) '89 & 42:25.2 '90. WIB 3000mW 12:01.65 '89.
Four Commonwealth 10000mW track records.
Progression at 10kmW: 1983- 50:52, 1984- 48:22, 1985- 46:13, 1986- 44:53, 1987- 42:52, 1988- 41:30/ 42:14.2t, 1989- 42:46.45t, 1990- 41:57.22t, 1991- 42:30/43:53.41t, 1992- 42:23.9t, 1993- 42:22.6t.
Her sister Sharon won the Australian schools under-17 800m in 2:10.1 in 1978.

Lisa ONDIEKI b.12 May 1960 Gawler, SA 1.66m 47kg. née O'Dea, formerly married to Kenny Martin (US steeplechaser/marathoner), married Yobes Ondieki on 10 Feb 1990. Nike TC, USA; was at University of Oregon.
At Mar: OG: '84- 7, '88- 2, '92- dnf; WCh: '87- dnf; CG: '86- 1, '90- 1. TAC champion 1985. At 10000m: WCp: '85- dnf.
Commonwealth marathon bests 1986, 1988, Australian records: 10000m (5) 1983-92, Mar (4) 1983-6. World 10 miles road best 52:23 '87.
Progression at 10,000m, Mar: 1983- 33:12.1, 2:32:22; 1984- 32:50.6, 2:27:40; 1985- 32:17.86, 2:29:48; 1986- 2:26:07, 1987- 32:22.56, 2:30:59; 1988- 2:23:51, 1990- 2:25:28, 1991- 2:29:02, 1992- 31:11.72, 2:24:40; 1993- 2:27:27. pbs: 1500m 4:21.2 '83, 3000m 9:07.38 '90, 5000m 15:34.7 '85, 400mh 60.5 '79, Half Mar 1:08:33 '92.
Started as a 400m hurdler, switching to distance running in 1981. Has won 8 out of 18 marathons. Won at Osaka 1988, when she ran the world's fastest for a loop course, and at New York 1992 after 2nd 1985-6, 3rd 1991. Commonwealth half marathon best 1:09:39 to win Great North Run 1986, and had further wins in 1987 and 1989. Daughter Emma born 22 Oct 1990.

AUSTRIA

Governing body: Österreichischer Leichtathletik Verband, A - 1040 Vienna, Prinz Eugenstrasse 12. Founded 1900.
National Championships first held in 1911 (men), 1918 (women). **1993 Champions**: **Men**: 100m: Martin Schützenauer 10.52, 200m: Thomas Griesser 21.32, 400m: Klaus Angerer 47.27, 800m: Michael Wildner 1:49.74, 1500m: Bernhard Richter 3:51.87, 5000m: Michael Buchleitner 14:26.15, 10000m: Dietmar Millonig 29:49.68, Half Mar: Helmut Schmuck 66:08, Mar: Peter Pfeifenberger 2:27:04, 3000mSt: Hans Funder 8:50.91, 110mh: Christian Maislinger 14.53, 400mh: Andresa Rapek 51.04, HJ: Niki Grundner 2.16, PV: Martin Tischler 5.40, LJ: Teddy Steinmayr 7.57, TJ: Alfred Stummer 15.40, SP: Klaus Bodenmüller 19.26, DT: Erwin Pirklbauer 54.56, HT: Johann Lindner 73.78, JT: Gregor Högler 72.24, Dec: Leonhard Hudec 7374, 20kmW/50kmW: Stefan Wögerbauer 1:36:47/4:18:52. **Women**: 100m/200m: Sabine Tröger 11.28/23.12, 400m/400mh: Andrea Pospischek 55.37/60.79, 800m: Therese Kiesl 2:02.03, 1500m: Stephanie Graf 4:23.46, 3000m: Erika König-Zenz 9:28.64, 10000m: Susanne Fischer 35:10.15, Mar: Carina Lilge-Leutner 2:54:24, 100mh: Gabriele Miklautsch 14.13, HJ: Sigrid Kirchmann 1.93, LJ: Ludmila Ninova 6.35, TJ: Gudrun Fischbacher 12.32, SP: Sabine Bieber 14.63, DT: Ursula Weber 58.80, JT: Monika Brodschneider 55.22, Hep: Christina Öppinger 5144, 10kmW: Viera Toporek 51:19.

Klaus BODENMÜLLER b.6 Sep 1962 Feldkirch 1.94m 110kg. LG Montfort. Soldier.
At SP: OG: '88- dnq 16, '92- 6; W Ch: '87- 7, '93- dnq; EC: '86- dnq 14, '90- 10; WI: '91- 2; EI: '90- 1, '92- 3. Austrian champion 1987, 1989, 1991-3.
Two Austrian shot records 1987, indoors 1990.
Progression at SP: 1980- 16.20, 1981- 16.09, 1982- 17.31, 1983- 17.89, 1984- 18.17, 1985- 18.24, 1986- 19.97, 1987- 20.79, 1988- 20.25i/19.92, 1989- 20.00, 1990- 21.03i/20.44, 1991- 20.44i/19.83, 1992- 20.57i/20.48, 1993- 20.14. pb DT 55.62 '87.
Added 24cm to his all-time best when he scored an upset win at the 1990 European Indoors.

Women

Theresia KIESL b.26 Oct 1963 Sarleinsbach 1.72m 59kg. née Stöbich. ULC-Linz-Oberbank.
At 1500m: OG: '92- sf; WCh: '93- 6; EI: '91- 5. Won Austrian 800m 1989-93, 1500m 1989, 1991-2. Austrian records 1000m 1991, 1500m (4) 1991-3.
Progression at 1500m: 1980- 4:52.0, 1981- 4:51.05, 1982- 4:39.27, 1983- 4:27.57, 1984- 4:29.03, 1985- 4:26.54, 1986- 4:28.22, 1988- 4:25.87, 1989- 4:19.63, 1990- 4:32.56, 1991- 4:10.99, 1992- 4:07.46, 1993- 4:06.89. pbs: 400m 56.20 '91, 800m 2:00.75 '93, 1000m 2:41.55 '91, 3000m 8:55.56 '93, 5000m 17:49.34 '84, 10000m 37:51.78 '86.
Daughter born 1987.

Sigrid KIRCHMANN b.29 Mar 1966 Bad Ischl 1.81m 63kg. Union Ebensee. Teacher. PE graduate of University of Salzburg.
At HJ: OG: '92- 5; WCh: '87 & '91- dnq, '93- 3; EC: '86- 11, '90- 4; EJ: '83- 7. Won Austrian HJ 1982-4, 1986-8, 1990-1, 1993; Hep 1986.
Austrian records HJ 1987 (2) and 1993, heptathlon 1987.
Progression at HJ: 1980- 1.67, 1981- 1.72, 1982- 1.85, 1983- 1.86, 1984- 1.87, 1985- 1.91, 1986- 1.90, 1987- 1.95, 1988- 1.90i/1.87, 1989- 1.88i/1.87, 1990- 1.93, 1991- 1.91, 1992- 1.94, 1993- 1.97. pbs: 100mh 13.87 '85, LJ 6.03 '85, SP 12.40 '85, JT 52.68 '86, Hep 5944 '85.

Ludmila NINOVA b.25 Jun 1960 Kula, Bulgaria 1.75m 61kg. SV Schwechat. Instructor. Former married name Rudoll.
At LJ: OG: '92- dnq 13; WCh: '87- 9, '91- 7, '93- 6 (11 TJ); WI: '93- 7; ECh: '86- 5; WSG: '87- 2; EI: '92- 3; WCp: '92- 3. Won Balkan LJ 1986, BUL 1987-8, AUT 1991-3. 2nd GP 1987.
Three Bulgarian long jump records 1984-6. Austrian records LJ and TJ 1991 & 1993
Progression at LJ: 1979- 5.89, 1980- 5.80, 1982- 5.93, 1983- 6.23, 1984- 6.80, 1985- 6.64, 1986- 6.88, 1987- 6.87, 1988- 6.85, 1991- 6.95, 1992- 6.92/7.00w, 1993- 7.06. pbs: HJ 1.72 '84, TJ 13.67i '92, 13.60 '93; Hep 5124 '84.
Left Bulgaria for Austria and returned to competition in 1991.

BAHAMAS

Governing body: Bahamas Amateur Athletic Association, P.O.Box SS 5517, Nassau.
National Champions 1993: Men: 100m: Andrew Tynes 10.31w, 200m: Sylvanus Hepburn 20.88, 400m: Theron Cooper 47.69, 800m: Clinton Johnson 1:57.07, 1500m: Ashland Murray 4:08.3, 5000m: David Bell 16:12.68, 3000mSt: David Ferguson 10:26.65, 110mh: Andrew Smith 14.13w, 400mh: Jason Hanna 54.31, HJ: Troy Kemp 2.30, PV: Kenny Moxey 305, LJ: Craig Hepburn 8.41, TJ: Steve Hanna 16.44, SP:Antonio Green 13.71, DT: Marvin Whylly 52.30, JT: Jermaine Curry 61.98; **Women**: 100m: Pauline Davis 11.16, 200m: Chandra Sturrup 23.61, 400m/800m: Vernetta Rolle 55.02/2:13.05, 1500m/3000m: Lucille Guerrier 5:07.60/11:36.63, 100mh/HJ: Neketa Sears 15.19/1.42, 400mh: Shermaine McKenzie 63.30, LJ: Dedra Davis 6.76w, TJ: Abigail Ferguson 12.29, SP/DT: Marcia Taylor 11.69/40.56, JT: Laverne Eve 56.90.

Troy KEMP b.18 Jun 1966 1.87m 69kg. Was at Boise State University, USA.
At HJ: OG: '88- dnq 21=, '92- 7; WCh: '87- dnq 20=, '91- 5=, '93- 5; WI: '93- 4=; PAm: '87- 2, '91- 2; won TAC indoors 1989. 2nd GP 1992.
Commonwealth high jump record 1993.
Progression at HJ: 1984- 2.10, 1985- 2.13, 1986- 2.22, 1987- 2.28, 1988- 2.30i/2.27, 1989- 2.32, 1990- 2.31, 1991- 2.35, 1992- 2.34, 1993- 2.37.

Frank RUTHERFORD b.23 Nov 1964 1.85m 79kg. Was at University of Houston, USA.
At TJ: OG: '88- dnq 26, '92- 3; WCh: '87- dnq 24, '91- dnq 15, '93- dnq; PAm: '87- 3; WI: '87- 3, '91- 8; CAmG: '86- 2; WCp: '92- 2. Won NCAA 1987 (and indoors 1986-7).
Progression at TJ: 1984- 16.37, 1985- 16.49, 1986- 17.05, 1987- 17.24, 1988- 17.12, 1989- 17.19, 1990- 17.22, 1991- 17.09, 1992- 17.41, 1993- 16.59i/16.46. pb LJ 7.76i '87.
Won the first ever Olympic medal in athletics for the Bahamas.

Women

Pauline DAVIS b.9 Jul 1966 1.68m 57kg. University of Alabama, USA.
At 100m/200m/4x100mR: OG: '84, '88 & '92- sf/sf; WCh: '83- qf/qf, '87- qf/sf, '91- sf/7, '93- sf/sf; CG: '90- 3/3; PAm: '87- 3/3; WCp: '89- 4R/1 4x400mR; CAmG: '86- 1/1/2R. At 60m: WI: '91- 5. Won CAC 100m and NCAA 400m

1989. 3rd GP 100m 1989, 2nd 400m 1990.
National records 100m, 200m, 400m.
Progression at 100m, 200m/400m: 1983- 11.56/11.3, 23.57, 1984- 11.51/11.1, 22.97, 1985- 11.47, 23.37/23.22w, 1986- 11.27/11.11w, 22.83, 1987- 11.19/11.16w, 22.49/22.1w; 1988- 11.17/ 11.12w, 22.67/51.11, 1989- 11.14/10.9, 22.50/ 50.18, 1990- 11.16, 22.55/50.05; 1991- 11.18/ 11.08w, 22.73; 1992- 11.31/11.30w, 22.44, 51.30; 1993- 11.16, 22.89. pbs: 60m 7.16i '91, 300m 36.50 '93.

BELARUS

Governing body: Track & Field Athletics Federation of the Republic of Belarus, Scorina av. 49, Minsk 220005. Founded 1991.
National Champions 1993: **Men**: 100m/200: Leonid Safronnikov 10.64/21.53, 400m: Sergey Molchan 46.84, 800m: Ivan Komar 1:45.73, 1500m: Andrey Gorbatsevich 3:45.43, 5000m: Oleg Savelyev 14:04.2, 10000m: Y Brandes 29:49.7, 3000mSt: Aleksey Tarasyuk 8:36.95, 110mh: Sergey Usov 13.87, 400mh: Igor Kurochkin 50.81, HJ: Oleg Zhukovskiy 2.25, PV: Konstantin Semyonov 5.50, LJ: Viktor Rudenik 7.97, TJ: Oleg Denischik 17.70, SP: Aleksandr Klimov 19.73, DT: Vladimir Dubrovchik 63.26, HT: Sergey Alay 80.30, JT: Nikolay Kosyanok 71.58, Dec: Aleksandr Zhdanovich 7912, 20kmW: Yevgeniy Misulya 1:19:56, 50kmW: Viktor Ginko 4:02:31. **Women**: 100m/200m: Yelena Denischik 11.56/24,06, 400m: Irina Skvarchevskaya 54.64, 800m: Natalya Dukhnova 1:59.68, 1500m: Oksana Mernikova 4:05.71, 3000m: Galina Baruk 9:16.48, 10000m: Yelena Vinitskaya 34:23.6, 100mh: Svetlana Buraga 13.19, 400mh: Tatyana Kurochkina 57.14, HJ: Galina Isachenko 1.86, LJ: Anzhella Atroschenko 6.72, TJ: Yelena Stakhova 13.41, SP: Natalya Gurskaya 16.31, DT: Ellina Zvereva 65.04, HT: Svetlana Sudak 56.32, JT: Tatyana Shikolenko 61.82, Hep: Taisia Dobrovitskaya 6337, 10kmW: Valentina Tsybulskaya 45:26.

Sergey ALAY b.11 Jun 1965 1.84m 98kg. Minsk TR.
At HT: '93- 4. BLS champion 1993.
Progression at HT: 1984- 71.26, 1985- 75.02, 1986- 79.64, 1987- 80.52, 1988- 81.52, 1989- 78.78, 1990- 79.92, 1991- 81.16, 1992- 82.00, 1993- 81.44.

Vitaliy ALISEVICH b.15 Jun 1967 1.86m 112kg. Minsk SA.
At HT: WJ: '86- 1.
Progression at HT: 1983- 61.46, 1984- 62.94, 1985- 70.20, 1986- 73.22, 1987- 78.60, 1988- 82.16, 1989- 77.70, 1990- 77.52, 1991- 79.16, 1992- 80.00, 1993- 81.32.

Igor ASTAPKOVICH b.4 Jan 1963 Minsk 1.91m 118kg. Grodno Sp. Sports student.
At HT: OG: '92- 2; WCh: '91- 2, '93- 2; EC: '90- 1; WSG: '87- 1, '89- 1; ECp: '89- 2, '91- 1. Won GWG 1990. USSR champion 1989-90, CIS 1992. Won GP 1992 (2nd 1988).
Progression at HT: 1981- 66.56, 1982- 68.08, 1983- 75.02, 1984- 79.98, 1985- 80.16, 1986- 80.68, 1987- 82.96, 1988- 83.44, 1989- 82.52, 1990- 84.14, 1991- 84.26, 1992- 84.62, 1993- 82.28.
World number one in 1990, when he lost just once, and won the Goodwill Games (84.12) and European titles with pbs. Since then he has won three major silver medals.

Eduard HÄMÄLÄINEN b.21 Jan 1969 Grodno 1.92m 88kg. Grodno SA.
At Dec: OG: '92- dnf; WCh: '91- 7, '93- 2; WJ: '88- 3. CIS champion 1992. At Hep: WI inv: '93- 3.
Progression at Dec: 1987- 7369, 1988- 7596, 1989- 7891, 1990- 7845, 1991- 8233, 1992- 8483w, 1993- 8724. pbs: 100m 10.74 '93, 400m 47.41 '93, 1500m 4:22.5 '87, 60mh 7.93i '93, 110mh 13.57 '93, HJ 2.10 '92, PV 5.30 '93, LJ 7.49/7.67w '93; SP 15.99 '93, DT 49.26 '93, JT 61.88 '93, Hep 6075i '93.
Won Götzis decathlon 1993, when he ran 13.65 for 110mh, the fastest ever run in a decathlon, a record he improved to 13.57 in the World Championships.

Vasiliy KAPTYUKH b.27 Jun 1967 2.01m 110kg. Minsk TR.
At DT: WCh: '91- dns, '93- 7; EC: '90- 4; WJ: '86- 3; EJ: '85- 3. Won ECp B3 1993
Progression at DT: 1985- 57.18, 1986- 60.24, 1988- 61.60, 1989- 62.92, 1990- 63.72, 1991- 62.88, 1992- 63.34, 1993- 66.18.

Yevgeniy MISYULYA b.9 Mar 1964 1.77m 68kg. Minsk TR.
At 20kmW: OG: '88- 27; WCh: '91- 3, '93- 5; WCp: '89- 3. USSR champion 1991, BLS 1993.
World road 20km walk best 1989.
Progression at 20kmW: 1985- 1:22:25, 1986- 1:20:41.6t, 1988- 1:19:16, 1989- 1:18:54, 1990- 1:20:15, 1991- 1:19:13, 1992- 1:19:03, 1993- 1:19:56. Track pbs: 5000mW 18:39.2i '88, 10000mW 40:01.0 '85. Road 30kmW 2:02:45 '91.

Aleksandr POTASHOV b.12 Mar 1962 1.87m 80kg. Vitebsk Sp.
At 50kmW: OG: '88- 4, "92- dq; WCh: '91- 1; EC: '90- dq; WCp: '87- 7, '89- 5. USSR champion 1990. At 10000mW: EJ: '81- 2.
Progression at 50kmW: 1982- 4:10:44, 1983- 3:56:54, 1984- 4:00:46, 1985- 3:54:40, 1986- 3:51:17, 1987- 3:46:28, 1988- 3:41:00, 1989- 3:48:02, 1990- 3:40:02, 1991- 3:53:09, 1993-

4:03:20. pbs: 10000mW 40:02.0 '85, 20kmW 1:21:21 '80, 30kmW 2:04:00 '93.
Disqualified after finishing second in the World Cup 50km 1991.

Vladimir SASIMOVICH b.14 Sep 1968 Minsk 1.78m 86kg. Minsk TR.
At JT: WCh: '91- 2, '93- 8; WJ: '86- 1; EJ: '87- 2; WCp: '92- 3; ECp: '93- 1B3. USSR champion 1991, BLS 1993. 3rd GP 1991.
World junior javelin record 1986.
Progression at JT: 1984- 65.42, 1985- 77.60, new: 1986- 78.84, 1987- 77.12, 1988- 79.28, 1989- 81.06, 1990- 81.28, 1991- 87.08, 1992- 86.16, 1993- 86.48.

Sergey USOV b.16 Jan 1964 Tashkent 1.88m 87kg. Tashkent Dyn.
At 110mh: OG: '92- sf; WCh: '93- h; EC: '90- 7; EJ: '83- 2; WCp: '85- 2, '92- 2; ECp: '85- 1. USSR champion 1985, CIS 1992, BLS 1993. At 60mh: WI: '91- 5, '93- 8.
Progression at 110mh: 1980- 15.38, 1981- 14.62, 1982- 14.29/13.8i, 1983- 13.96, 1984- 13.74, 1985- 13.56, 1987- 13.39, 1988- 13.27, 1989- 13.56, 1990- 13.54, 1991- 13.55, 1992- 13.34, 1993- 13.55. pbs: 50mh 6.64i '86, 60mh 7.58i '91.

Women

Svetlana BURAGA b.4 Sep 1965 1.68m 56kg. née Besprozvannaya. Minsk Sp. Instructor.
At Hep: OG: '88- 10; WCh: '87- 14, '93- 3; ECp: '87- 1, '93- 1C. Won BLS 100mh 1993.
Progression at Hep: 1983- 5352, 1985- 5743, 1986- 6073, 1987- 6585, 1988- 6597, 1990- 6174, 1991- 6104, 1992- 6075, 1993- 6635. pbs: 200m 23.18 '87, 800m 2:08.45 '88, 100mh 12.83/12.8 '88, HJ 1.84 '93, LJ 6.79i/6.63 '87, SP 14.55 '93, JT 42.80 '87.

Tatyana LEDOVSKAYA b.21 May 1965 Shchekino, Tulsk region 1.71m 60kg. Minsk Sp.
At 400mh/R- 4x400m relay: OG: '88- 2/1R, '92- 4; WCh: '91- 1/1R, '93- sf; EC: '90- 1/2R; WI: '91- 3; WCp: '89- 2; ECp: '89- 3. USSR champion 1988-9. World record 4x400m relay 1988.
Progression at 400mh: 1987- 56.92, 1988- 53.18, 1989- 54.68, 1990- 53.62, 1991- 53.11, 1992- 53.55, 1993- 54.60. pbs: 200m 23.32/22.7 '88, 400m 50.4/50.93 '88.
Made exceptionally rapid progress in 1988, taking 1.3 off her best in Seoul. Again showed her ability to peak for the big events by winning gold medals in Split and Tokyo, with indifferent form otherwise. Again with no form behind her ran well for fourth in Barcelona.

Tatyana SHEVCHIK b.11 Jun 1969 1.78m 59kg. Minsk Sp.
At HJ: OG: '92- 16; WCh: '93- ; ECp: '93- 1B. Won USSR indoor HJ 1990.
BLS high jump record 1993.
Progression at HJ: 1985- 1.86, 1986- 1.83, 1987- 1.83, 1988- 1.86, 1989- 1.86, 1990- 1.92, 1991- 1.95, 1992- 1.96, 1993- 2.00.

Natalya SHIKOLENKO b.1 Aug 1964 Andizhan, Uzbekistan 1.82m 79kg. Minsk Dyn. Student.
At JT: OG: '92- 2; WCh: '91- 11, '93- 3; EC: '90- nt; ECp: '89- 4. Won USSR title 1990-1, CIS 1992, BLS 1993; GWG 1990. 2nd GP 1992.
Progression at JT: 1980- 49.94, 1981- 51.14, 1982- 55.06, 1983- 60.48, 1984- 63.64, 1985- 64.60, 1986- 63.56, 1987- 66.18, 1988- 66.48, 1989- 69.38, 1990- 65.76, 1991- 67.32, 1992- 70.36, 1993- 68.96.

Tatyana SHIKOLENKO b.10 May 1968 Krasnodar, Russia 1.75m 79kg.
At JT: WCh: '93- 4; WJ: '86- 4; EJ: '85- 5; WSG: '91- 1.
Progression at JT: 1984- 59.40, 1985- 59.90, 1986- 55.70, 1987- 59.74, 1988- 64.70, 1989- 60.74, 1990- 64.98, 1991- 63.56, 1992- 62.20, 1993- 65.18.
Younger sister of Natalya.

Irina YATCHENKO b.31 Oct 1965 Gomel 1.85m 94kg. Grodno TR.
At DT: OG: '92- 7; WCh: '91- 7; EC: '90- 5. 2nd GP 1992
Progression at DT: 1982- 50.72, 1983- 57.04, 1984- 59.54, 1985- 60.56, 1986- 57.58, 1987- 63.00, 1988- 67.44, 1989- 62.38, 1990- 68.60, 1991- 64.92, 1992- 68.94, 1993- 58.74.

Lidia YURKOVA b.15 Jan 1967 1.75m 63kg. Mogilev U. née Okolo-Kulak.
At 100mh: EC: '90- 3; WSG: '89- 2; EJ: '85- 3. At 60mh: WI: '91- 4. Won USSR 100mh 1989. 3rd GP 1990.
Progression at 100mh: 1983- 13.84, 1984- 13.73/13.2, 1985- 13.30, 1986- 13.17/12.9, 1987- 13.02/13.0, 1988- 12.99/12.5/12.83w, 1989- 12.70, 1990- 12.66, 1992- 12.86. pbs: 60m 7.1i '90, 60mh 7.86/7.6i '90.

Ellina ZVEREVA b.16 Nov 1960 Dolgoprudny 1.82m 90kg. formerly Kisheyeva. Minsk Dyn. Student.
At DT: OG: '88- 5; WCh: '91- 9; EC: '90- 6; ECp: '93- 1B. USSR champion 1986, BLS 1993.
Progression at DT: 1979- 44.06, 1980- 51.38, 1981- 59.88, 1982- 62.52, 1983- 65.18, 1984- 68.56, 1985- 66.64, 1986- 68.96, 1987- 60.84, 1988- 71.58, 1990- 66.20, 1991- 63.80, 1992- 66.26/68.82dq, 1993- 66.32.
Four year ban reported after positive steroids test when first at CIS Trials 1992, but back in 1993.

Vincent Rousseau: a great year in 1993

BELGIUM

Governing bodies: Ligue Royale Belge d'Athlétisme, Rue St.Laurent 14-26 (Bte 6), 1000 Bruxelles (KBAB). Vlaamse Atletiek Liga (VAL); Ligue Belge Francophone d'Athlétisme (LBFA). Original governing body founded 1889.

National Championships first held in 1889 (men), 1921 (women) **1993 Champions**: **Men**: 100m/200m: Patrick Stevens 10.49/20.81, 400m: Marc Dollendorf 47.29, 800m: Nathan Kahan 1:47.22, 1500m: Christophe Impens 3:48.22, 5000m: Ruddy Walem 13:53.14, 3000mSt: Graeme Croll GBR 8:54.26, 110mh: Hubert Grossard 13.47, 400mh: Jean-Pol Bruwier 51.10, HJ: Geoff Parsons GBR 2.17, PV: Alan Denaeyer 5.00, LJ: Tom Hofmans 7.63, TJ: Mambo Kedjeloba 15.51, SP: Ioav Sherf ISR 17.05, DT: Jo Vandaele 53.40, HT: Alex Malachenko 67.64, JT: Jean-Paul Schlatter 70.38. **Women** - 100/200: Aileen McGillivary GBR 11.65/23.29, 400m: Katrien Maenhout 54.36, 800m: Anneke Matthijs 2:03.85, 1500m/3000m: Anja Smolders 4:22.16/9:21.79, 100mh: Caroline Delplancke 13.61, 400mh: Francoise Dethier 58.02, HJ: Sabine De Leeuw 1.89, LJ: Sandrine Hennart 6.61, TJ: Karen Hambrook GBR 12.36, SP: Greet Meulemeester 15.63, DT: Brigitte De Leeuw 45.66, JT: Ingrid Didden 45.02.

Hubert GROSSARD b. 28 Mar 1968 Genk 1.83m 70kg. AV Toekomst.
At 110mh: WCh: '93- sf. Belgian champion 1988-9, 1991-3.
Three Belgian 110mh records 1992-3.
Progression at 110mh: 1987- 14.78, 1988- 14.07, 1989- 13.95, 1990- 14.11, 1991- 13.89, 1992- 13.56, 1993- 13.47.

Vincent ROUSSEAU b.29 Jul 1962 Mons 1.76m 60kg. MOHA. Soldier.
At 5000m: OG: '88- sf; WCh: '87- 5; EC: '86- 13, '90- h. 2nd GP 1986. At 10000m: OG: '92- h; WCh: '91- h, '93- 7; WCp: '85- 5. Won World Half Mar 1993, Belgian 5000m 1984, 1989; 1500m 1985-6, 1988; CC 1984, 1987-8, 1990-3.
Belgian 5000m and 10000m records 1993, marathon 1993 and 1994.
Progression at 5000m, 10000m, Mar: 1980- 14:30.5, 1981- 14:08.32, 1982- 13:40.21, 1983- 13:33.2, 1984- 13:24.81, 1985- 13:18.94, 28:40.63; 1986- 13:15.01, 1987- 13:28.56, 1988- 13:19.16, 28:47.78; 1989- 13:28.30, 1990- 13:25.61, 28:27.1; 1991- 13:38.95, 27:50.17; 1992- 13:17.28, 1993- 13:10.99, 27:23.18, 2:09:13; 1994- 2:09:08. pbs: 1500m 3:36.38 '85, 1M 3:54.69 '85, 2000m 4:58.97 '87, 3000m 7:39.41 '89, 2M 8:32.01 '93, Half Mar 61:06 '93, 60:23 (33m dh) '94.
Had a great year in 1993 when on the track he set Belgian records and achieved his best big race placing with fifth in the World 5000m. He then won his first major championship, the World Half Marathon, fittingly through the streets of Brussels. He had run 2:13:09 for fifth on his marathon début In Rotterdam in April, and he ran 2:09:13 to win at Reims in October, followed by 2:09:08 for 2nd Tokyo 1994. Until 1993 his talent was shown by many wins at cross-country and on the track, but had not been seen to true effect in major races.

William VAN DIJCK b.24 Jan 1961 Leuven 1.85m 65kg. Looise AV.
At 3km St: OG: '84- sf, '88- 5, '92- 9; WCh: '83- sf, '87- 3, '91- 9; EC: '86- 5, '90- 5; WCp: '92- 2. Belgian champion 1983, 1985-8, 1990-2. Won GP 1986.
Eight Belgian 3000m steeplechase records 1983-6.
Progression at 3kmSt: 1981- 8:44.92, 1982- 8:36.40, 1983- 8:21.73, 1984- 8:18.75, 1985- 8:13.77, 1986- 8:10.01, 1987- 8:12.18, 1988- 8:13.99, 1989- 8:22.5, 1990- 8:16.94, 1991- 8:19.29, 1992- 8:14.58, 1993- 8:24.03. pbs: 800m 1:51.8 '83, 1500m 3:41.2 '85, 1M 3:57.59 '85, 2000m 5:06.84 '89, 3000m 7:45.40 '88, 5000m 13:23.40 '85, 10000m 28:58.75 '93, 2000mSt 5:22.24 '87.

BERMUDA

Governing body: Bermuda Track and Field Association, P.O.Box DV 397, Devonshire. Founded 1946.

Brian WELLMAN b.2 Aug 1967 1.75m 72kg. University of Arkansas, USA.
At TJ: OG: '88- dnq, '92- 5; WCh: '91- 6, '93- 8; WJ: '86- 9; WI: '93- 3; CG: '90- 11; PAm: '91- 5; WSG: '91- 1. 2nd PAm Jnr 1986; Won NCAA 1991. 3rd GP 1992.
Progression at TJ: 1986- 16.18, 1988- 16.38, 1989- 16.44w, 1990- 16.23, 1991- 17.07/17.41w, 1992- 17.24/17.30w, 1993- 17.27i/17.14.
Advanced to third in 1993 World Indoors after drugs disqualification of Nikolay Raev.

BRAZIL

Governing body: Confederação Brasileira de Atletismo (CBAT), Palacio dos Esportes, Avenida Brasil 2540, Bloco A-3, Andar-Salas 311/7, Rio de Janeiro. Founded 1914 (Confederação 1977).

1993 National Champions: **Men**: 100m/200m: Robson C da Silva 10.32/20.39, 400m/400mh: Eronildes Nuñes Araújo 46.72/49.15, 800m: José Luiz Barbosa 1:46.20, 1500m: Edgar Martins de Oliveira 3:38.45, 5000m: Ronaldo da Costa 13:37.37, 10000m: Valdenor Pereira dos Santos 28:34.60, 3000mSt: Wander do Prado Moura 8:36.07, 110mh: Joilto Santos Bonfim 13.78, HJ: José Luis Mendes 2.13, PV: Pedro F Da Silva Filho 4.95, LJ: Paulo Sergio de Oliveira 7.91, TJ: Anisio Souza Silva 17.29, SP: Adilson Souza Oliveira 18.07, DT: João Joaquim dos Santos 57.60, HT: Pedro Rivail Attilio 59.96, JT: Luiz Fernando Silva 72.24, JT: Iran Roberto da Costa 66.22, Dec: José Ricardo de Assis 7265, 20kmW: Sergio Vieira Galdino 1:23:09.1. **Women**: 100m/200m: Cleide Amaral 11.60/ 23.4, 400m/800m: Maria M Figueiredo 52.15/ 2:01.08, 1500m: Soraya Vieira Telles 4:11.80, 3000m: Viviany Anderson de Oliveira 9:20.91, 10000m: Carmen de Oliveira 33:42.28, 100mh: Vânia María Ferreira da Silva 13.72, 400mh: Jupira Maurina da Graça 57.59, HJ: Orlane M dos Santos 1.88, LJ/TJ: Maria Aparecida de Souza 6.17/12.97, SP/DT: Elisângela Maria Adriano 17.11/53.52, JT: Sueli Pereira Dos Santos 54.68, Hep: Concepción A Geremias 5549, 10kmW: Nailse Pereira de Azevedo 50:24.75.

José Luiz BARBOSA b.27 May 1961 Tres Lagoas 1.84m 68kg. Electropaulo.
At 800m: OG: '84- sf, '88- 6 (h 1500m), '92- 4; WCh: '83- sf, '87- 3, '91- 2, '93- sf; WI: '87- 1, '89- 2, '93- dnf; PAm: '83- 2 (2 4x400mR), '87- 2; SACh: '83- 1; WCp: '92- 4. Won AAA 1985.
Progression at 800m: 1978- 2:10, 1979- 1:53.20, 1980- 1:50.35, 1981- 1:48.3, 1982- 1:47.4, 1983- 1:44.3, 1984- 1:44.98, 1985- 1:44.79, 1986- 1:44.10, 1987- 1:43.76, 1988- 1:43.20, 1989- 1:44.20, 1990- 1:44.84, 1991- 1:43.08, 1992- 1:45.06, 1993- 1:44.18. pbs: 400m 45.9 '83, 1000m 2:17.36 '85, 1500m 3:37.04 '91.
He had his best year at 800m in 1991, when he allied better tactics to his usual front-running style. He has run 37 sub-1:45 times to end 1993.

Robson Caetano DA SILVA b.4 Sep 1964 Rio de Janeiro 1.87m 74kg. Electropaulo.
At 200m (100m, R- 4x100m relay): OG: '84- sf, '88- 3 (5), '92- 4 (sf); WCh: '83- (qf), '87- 4 (qf), '91- 4 (7), '93- dq sf; WI: '87- 3, '89- dq; WSG: '89- 1; WCp: '85- 1/2R, '89- 1, '92- 1/4R (4); PAm: '83- sf/3R, '87- 2; SACh: '85- 1 (2/1R), '87- 1 (1/1R), '89- 1/1R, '91- 1 (1/1R), '93- 1 (1). Won GP 1989, 3rd 1987. Won PAm-J 100m 1982, SAm-J LJ 1981, 100m & 200m 1983.
S.American records: two 100m, five 200m 1985-9, 400m 1991. WIB 300m: 32.19 '89.
Progression at 100m, 200m: 1979- 11.4, 1980- 11.2, 1981- 11.0, 22.3; 1982- 10.34w/10.54/10.2; 21.46/21.4; 1983- 10.40/10.3, 20.95/20.8; 1984- 10.50/10.3, 20.71; 1985- 10.22/10.1, 20.44; 1986- 10.02, 20.28; 1987- 10.20/10.0, 20.20; 1988- 10.00, 20.04; 1989- 10.17, 19.96/19.7A; 1990- 10.12, 20.23; 1991- 10.08, 20.15; 1992- 10.17, 20.15; 1993- 10.20/10.19w, 20.16. pbs: 60m 6.63i '87, 400m 45.06 '91, 45.0 '90; LJ 7.40 '81.
After several years of world class form reached world number one status at 200m in 1989. In 1992 equalled record with three successive wins at one event in the World Cup.

Anisio Souza SILVA b.18 Jun 1969 1.85m 79kg.
At TJ: WCh: '93- 7; WJ: '88- 8; PAm: '91- 2; SAm: '91- 1, '93- 1.
Progression at TJ: 1988- 16.21, 1989- 16.42, 1990- 17.00, 1991- 16.72, 1992- 16.97, 1993- 17.32. pb LJ 7.36 '90.

Women

M.Magnólia de Souza FIGUEIREDO b.11 Nov 1963 Natal 1.70m 60kg.
At 400m (800m): OG: '88- qf; WCh: '87- sf, '93- (sf); PAm: '87- 5; SAm: '91- 1 (1/1R), '93- 1 (1). At 800m: WCh: '91- sf; At 200m: WI: '89- 5.
Seven S.American 400m records 1988-90. Brazilian records 200m 1988, 800m (2) 1991-3.
Progression at 400m, 800m: 1983- 55.4, 1986- 53.05, 1987- 51.74, 1988- 51.32, 1989- 51.57, 1990- 50.62; 1991- 51.56, 1:59.53; 1992- 52.31, 1:59.59; 1993- 52.15, 1:59.51. pbs: 100m: 11.6 '83, 200m: 22.99 '88.

BULGARIA

Governing body: Bulgarian Athletics Federation, 75 bl. Vassil Levski, Sofia 1000. Founded 1924.

National Championships first held in 1926 (men), 1938 (women). **1993 Champions: Men**: 100m: Radoslav Paskalev 10.65, 200m: Tzvetoslav Stankoulov 20.80, 400m: Anton Ivanov 45.61, 800m: Dian Petkov 1:48.71, 1500m/5000m: Khristo Stefanov 3:47.90/ 14:23.85, 10000m: Ivan Chotov 30:12.10, Mar: Georgi Georgiev 2:28:11, 3000mSt: Bourgaz Yordanov 9:04.47, 110mh: Georgi Georgiev 13.95, 400mh: Plamen Nyagin 50.34, HJ: Robert Marinov 2.30, PV: Delko Lesev 5.30, LJ: Ivaylo Mladenov 8.35w, TJ: Kotzo Kotov 16.46, SP: Radoslav Despotov 18.35, DT: Kamen Dimitrov 60.54, HT: Petar Tzvetanov 49.36, JT: Emil Tzvetanov 72.88, Dec: Krassimir Petlichki 7427, 10kmW: Avni Khassan 46:08.30, 20kmW: Avni Hassan Bekir 1:34:02. **Women**: 100m/200m: Petya Pendareva 11.23/22.78, 400m: Yuliana Marinova 54.46, 800m/1500m: Petya Strashilova 2:11.18/4:21.09, 3000m: Galina Goranova 9:10.80, 10000m: Roumyana Panovska 34:36.48, Mar: Gergana Voynova 2:46:46, 100mh: Svetla Dimitrova 12.71, 400mh: Valya Demireva 59.90, HJ: Eleonora Milousheva 1.83, LJ: Yurka Khristova 6.24, TJ: Iva Prandzheva 14.15, SP/DT: Svetla Mitkova 18.90/60.66, JT: Antoaneta Selenska 60.70, Hep: Yurka Khristova 6028, 5000mW: Nevena Minova 22:33.00, 10kmW: Ginka Radeva 46:54.

Nikolai ANTONOV b.17 Aug 1968 Razgrad 1.94m 86kg. CSKA.
At 200m: OG: '92- sf; WCh: '91- 7, '93- qf (6 LJ); EC: '90- 5; WJ: '86- 4 (7 100m); WI: '91- 1, '93- 5; EI: '88- 2, '90- 2, '92- 1; ECp: '91- 6. Won Bulgarian 100m 1989-90, 200m 1987, 1989-91.
Five Bulgarian 200m records 1989-91.
Progression at 200m, LJ: 1985- 21.43, 1986- 20.88/20.5, 1987- 21.17, 1988- 20.65i/20.98, 1989- 20.66, 1990- 20.67/20.64w, 7.53; 1991- 20.20, 7.59/7.69i; 1992- 20.41i/20.50, 1993- 20.84i/20.88, 8.15. pb 100m 10.39 '88.
Improved Bulgarian 200m record from 20.52 to 20.28 and 20.20 at the 1991 World Champs.

Georgi DAKOV b.21 Oct 1967 Pleven 1.96m 80kg. Slavia Sofia.
At HJ: OG: '92- 14; WCh: '87- dnq 24, '91- dnq 23=; EC: '86- 11=, '90- 3; EJ: '85- 3; ECp: '91- 4. Won BUL HJ 1986-8, 1990-1. 2nd GP 1990.
Six Bulgarian high jump records 1986-90.
Progression at HJ: 1980- 1.85, 1981- 1.85, 1982- 1.90, 1983- 2.03, 1984- 2.20, 1985- 2.24, 1986- 2.29, 1987- 2.28, 1988- 2.30, 1989- 2.32, 1990- 2.36, 1991- 2.31i/2.30, 1992- 2.30, 1993- 2.28. pb LJ 7.32 '86.
On 8 Aug 1993 he married Yulia Baycheva, European champion in 1990 at rhythmic gymnastics, and world team gold medallist in 1993.

Ivaylo MLADENOV b.6 Oct 1973 Vratza 1.83m 68kg. Vratza.
At LJ: WCh: '93- 5; WI: '93- 6; WJ: '92- 3; EJ: '91- 5. 2nd GP 1993. Bulgarian champion 1993.
Progression at LJ: 1990- 7.18, 1991- 7.94, 1992- 7.89, 1993- 8.27/8.35w. pb TJ 15.10 '91.

Women

Svetla DIMITROVA b.27 Jan 1970 Botevgrad 1.72m 59kg. Spirala.
At Hep: OG: '88- 12, '92- 5; WCh: '93- 4; WJ: '86- 1, '88- 1; E.Cup: '89- 3dq. Won Bulgarian Hep 1989, 100mh 1993.
Progression at Hep: 1986- 6041, 1988- 6343, 1989- 6534 dq/6428, 1992- 6658. pbs: 200m 23.06w '92, 23.10 '93; 800m 2:07.90 '92, 100mh 12.71 '93, HJ 1.88 '86, LJ 6.64 '92, SP 15.50 '93, JT 48.18 '93.
Suspended following a positive drugs test when third in the 1989 European Cup heptathlon in what would have been a world junior record. Won Götzis heptathlon 1993.

Yordanka DONKOVA b.28 Sep 1961 Gorni Bogrov, Sofia 1.77m 67kg. Levski Spartak, Sofia. PE student.
At 100mh: OG: '80- sf, '88- 1, '92- 3; WCh: '87- 4; EC: '82- 2, '86- 1/2R; EJ: '79- 8; ECp: '81- 5, '87- 2/2R. At Hep: ECp: '83- 7. At 60mh: WI: '87- 2; EI: '82- 3, '84- 3, '87- 2, '89- 1. Won Balkan 100mh 1980, 1984, 1986; BUL 1984, 1986. Won GP 100mh and overall 1986, 2nd 1988.
Eleven Bulgarian 100mh records 1982-8, including five world records: four 1986, one 1988. WIB 60mh 7.74 '86.
Progression at 100mh: 1977- 14.84, 1978- 13.91, 1979- 13.57, 1980- 13.24, 1981- 13.39/12.9, 1982- 12.44, 1983- 12.65, 1984- 12.50, 1985- 13.24, 1986- 12.26/12.0w, 1987- 12.33, 1988- 12.21, 1992- 12.67, 1993- 12.81. pbs: 100m 11.27 '82, 200m 22.95 '82, 50mh 6.77i '93, 55mh 7.44i '87, HJ 1.78 '82, LJ 6.39 '82, Hep 6187 '83.
Displayed the finest ever sprint hurdling by a woman in 1986, with very sharp speed and technique, running ten sub-12.50 times. She ran a further four such times in 1987, and a record 12 in 1988 when she was unbeaten. She lost three fingers on her right hand in an accident on her fifth birthday. Son born February 1991.

Stefka KOSTADINOVA b.25 Mar 1965 Plovdiv 1.80m 60kg. Trakia Plovdiv. PE student. Married her coach Nikolai Petrov on 6 Nov 1989.
At HJ: OG: '88- 2, '92- 4; WCh: '87- 1, '91- 6, '93- dnq 15=; WI: '85- 1, '87- 1, '89- 1, '93- 1; EC: '86- 1; EJ: '81- 10; EI: '85- 1, '87- 1, '88- 1, '92- 2; WCp: '85- 1; ECp: '85- 1, '87- 1. Won GWG 1986, Balkan 1985-6, 1988; Bulgarian 1985-6,

1988, 1991. Won GP 1985, 1987 (3rd overall), 1993; 2nd 1991.
Three world records 1986-7. WIB: 2.04 & 2.05 '87, 2.06 '88.
Progression at HJ: 1977- 1.45, 1978- 1.66, 1979- 1.75, 1980- 1.84, 1981- 1.86, 1982- 1.90, 1983- 1.83i, 1984- 2.00, 1985- 2.06, 1986- 2.08, 1987- 2.09, 1988- 2.07, 1989- 2.04i/1.93, 1991- 2.03, 1992- 2.05, 1993- 2.05.
World number one high jumper 1985-8. After 34 successive wins 1984-6, lost once to Heike Redetzky before 19 further wins 1986-7. Had her 100th competition at 2 metres or more on 24 Jul 1993, with 105 in all and 20 of the 24 all-time performances at 2.05m or more to end 1993. A knee injury affected her form in 1989 and she broke a bone in her left foot when trying to return in 1990. Won a record four World Indoor titles.

Svetlana LESEVA b.18 Mar 1967 Mikhaylovgrad 1.78m 63kg. née Isaeva. Trakia Plovdiv. PE student.
At HJ: OG: '92- dnq; WCh: '87- 7, '91- dnq 14=; EC: '86- 2, '90- 9; WSG: '87- 1; EJ: '83- 4=, '85- 3; WI: '91- 8=; ECp: '91- 1. 3rd GP 1987. Bulgarian champion 1990.
Progression at HJ: 1981- 1.80, 1982- 1.79, 1983- 1.87, 1984- 1.84, 1985- 1.93, 1986- 1.97, 1987- 2.00, 1988- 1.93, 1989- 1.75i, 1990- 1.90, 1991- 1.98, 1992- 1.95, 1993- 1.80.
Married to Delko Lesev, pole vault 5.75i '92, 5.70 '91, 7th Worlds 1987, 2nd WJ 1986. Son, also named Delko, born 1989.

Svetla MITKOVA b.17 Jun 1964 Medovo 1.78m 96kg. Rozova Dolina, Kazanluk.
At SP(/DT): OG: '88- 10/4, '92- 6; WCh: '83- -/10, '87- 9/5, '91- 10/-, '93- 10/dnq 13; EC: '86- 12/5; EJ: '81: 3/2; ECp: '83- 5, '85- 5, '87- 4, '89- 6; EI: '92- 2. Bulgarian champion shot 1984-7, 1990-3; discus 1983, 1990, 1993; Balkan shot 1988. 2nd GP DT 1986.
Progression at SP, DT: 1979- 13.80, 44.30; 1980- 14.10, 50.70; 1981- 17.16, 59.84; 1982- 18.03, 60.58; 1983- 18.83, 66.80; 1984- 19.11, 64.84; 1985- 18.87, 54.34; 1986- 20.05, 68.90; 1987- 20.91, 69.72; 1988- 20.58, 69.14; 1989- 18.08, 58.80; 1990- 18.58, 61.88; 1991- 19.74, 62.52; 1992- 20.41, 64.10; 1993- 20.00, 61.18.

Anelia NUNEVA b.30 Jun 1962 Byala, Ruse 1.69m 62kg. Levski Spartak, Sofia. PE student. Married name Vechernikova.
At 100m/R- 4x100m relay (200m): OG: '88- 8, '92- 6 (dns sf); WCh: '83- sf (6), '87- 6/4R; EC: '82- 4 (6), '86- 2/2R; WCp: '85- 4; ECp: '83- 2 (4), '85- 3, '87- 2/2R; WSG: '85- 2/3R. At 60m: WI: '87- 2; EI: '84- 2, '87- 2, '92- 2. Won Balkan 100m 1984-6, 200m 1986. 2nd GP 100m 1987.
Bulgarian records 1982-8: six 100m, two 200m.
Progression at 100m, 200m: 1978- 12.23, 25.60; 1979- 12.10, 25.90; 1980- 12.50; 1981- 11.34/11.31w, 23.58; 1982- 11.14, 22.93; 1983- 11.07, 22.58; 1984- 11.10, 22.67; 1985- 11.14, 22.73; 1986- 11.04/10.9, 22.58; 1987- 10.86, 22.01; 1988- 10.85, 22.88; 1991- 11.43; 1992- 11.10, 22.62; 1993- 11.32, 23.18. pbs: 55m 6.64i '87, 60m 7.03i '87
Ran seven sub-11.00 100m races in 1987 and five in 1988. She was heading for a medal in the Olympic final when she pulled a hamstring. Gave birth to a son in October 1989. After illness returned to racing in summer 1991.

Iva PRANDZHEVA b.15 Feb 1972 Plovdiv 1,74m 57kg. Trakia Plovdiv.
At TJ: WCh: '93- 3. At LJ: EJ: '91- 3, WJ: '90- 1. Won Bulgarian LJ 1992, TJ 1993.
Two Bulgarian triple jump records 1993.
Progression at LJ, TJ: 1987- 6.17, 1988- 6.27, 1989- 6.27, 1990- 6.53, 1991- 6.54, 1992- 6.62, 1993- 6.58, 14.23/14.32w. pb 100m 11.5/12.04 '93.

BURUNDI

Venuste NIYONGABO b.9 Dec 1973 1.70m 55kg.
At 1500m (800m): WCh: '93- sf; WJ: '93- 2 (4).
Burundi records at 1500m, 1M, 2000m 1993.
Progression at 1500m: 1991- 3:45.71 1992- 3:38.59, 1993- 3:36.30. pbs: 800m 1:46.15 '93, 1M 3:54.71 '93, 2000m 4:58.15 '93.
World's fastest of 1993 at 2000m.

Aloÿs NIZIGAMA b.1966. 1.68m 55kg.
At 10000m (5000m): WCh: '91- 6, '93- 5 (7). At 5000m: AfG: '91- 4; AfCh: '92-4.
Burundi record holder at 5000m and 10000m from 1990.
Progression at 5000m, 10000m: 1990- 13:59.9, 29:27.7, 1991- 13:41.21, 28:03.03; 1992- 13:29.08, 27:54.69; 1993- 13:20.59/27:47.77. pbs: 3000m 7:42.42 '92.

CANADA

Governing body: Athletics Canada, 1600 James Naismith Drive, Gloucester, Ontario K1B 5NA. Formed as the Canadian AAU in 1884.
National Championships first held in 1884 (men), 1925 (women). **1993 champions: Men**: 100m: Atlee Mahorn 10.25, 200m: Glenroy Gilbert 20.63, 400m: Troy Jackson 46.69, 800m: Freddie Williams 1:47.13, 1500m: Kevin Sullivan 3:41.58, 5000m/10000m: David Reid 13:54.64/29:00.04, 3000mSt: Graeme Fell 8:28.90; 110mh: Tim Kroeker 13.73, 400mh: Mark Jackson 50.82, HJ: Alex Zaliauskas 2.24,

PV: Doug Wood 5.30, LJ: Edrick Floreal 7.89w, TJ: Karl Dyer 15.46, SP: Scott Cappos 17.77, DT: Ray Lazdins 54.52, HT: Boris Stoikos 67.82, JT: Steve Feraday 74.46, Dec: David Cook 7352, 20kmW: Tim Berrett 1:26:45.3. **Women**: 100m: Karen Clarke 11.66, 200m: Stacey Bowen 23.83, 400m: Camille Noel 52.98, 800m: Nicola Knapp 2:04.23, 1500m: Angela Chalmers 4:15.31, 3000m: Leah Pells 9:03.13, 10000m: Lisa Harvey 33:40.31, 100mh: Sonia Paquette 13.43, 400mh: Rosey Edeh 55.28, HJ: Wanita Dykstra 1.83, LJ: Vannessa Monar-Enweani 6.42w, TJ: Kelly Dinsmore 12.99, SP: Georgette Reed 15.07, DT/HT: Theresa Brick 51.70/51.80, JT: Eileen Volpatti 53.24, Hep: Catherine Bond-Mills 6058, 10kmW: Alison Baker 46:46.39.

Tim BERRETT b.23 Jan 1965 Tunbridge Wells, England 1.78m 65kg. Brainsport Athletics Saskatoon. Graduate student, University of Alberta.
At 50kmW (20kmW): OG: '92- dq; WCh: '91- 15 (22), '93- 7 (20); WCp: '93- 5. Won Canadian 20kmW 1992-3.
Canadian track record 50,000m walk 1991.
Progression at 20kmW, 50kmW: 1984- 1:26:13, 1985- 1:34:55t, 1988- 1:25:09, 1989- 1:25:08, 1990- 1:24:25, 1991- 1:23:10, 3:56:14t; 1992- 1:22:38.1t, 3:50:55; 1993- 1:22:47, 3:50:23. pbs: 3000mW , 5000mW 18:47.56i '93, 10000mW 40:21.17 '91.
A British junior international for four years 1981-4, he moved to Canada in 1987 to study at Queen's University, Kingston.

Mark McKOY b.10 Dec 1961 Georgetown, Guyana 1.81m 70kg. North York TC. PE graduate of Louisiana State University, USA.
At 110mh/R- 4x100m relay: OG: '84- 4, '88- 7, '92- 1; WCh: '83- 4, '87- 7, '91- 4; CG: '82- 1/2R, '86- 1/1R; WSG: '83- 3; PAm: '83- 6. Won GP 1985, 3rd 1987, 1993. On 1980 Olympic team. At 60mh: WI: '87- fell, '91- 3, '93- 1. Won Canadian 110mh 1981-8, 1990-1.
Eleven Canadian and six Commonwealth 110mh records 1982-92. WIB: 50mh 6.25 '86, 60mh 7.47 '86. Commonwealth indoor record 50yh 5.95 '85.
Progression at 110mh: 1979- 14.19, 1980- 14.02, 1981- 13.97, 1982- 13.37, 1983- 13.53/13.51w, 1984- 13.27/13.16w, 1985- 13.27, 1986- 13.35/ 13.31w, 1987- 13.23, 1988- 13.17, 1990- 13.45, 1991- 13.27, 1992- 13.11/13.06w, 1993- 13.08. pbs: 60m 6.49i '93, 100m 10.08 '93, 200m 20.96 '85, 60yh 6.89i '86, 60mh 7.44i '91, 7.41r '93; 400mh 53.75 '79.
Lived in England 1962-74. Suspended for two years from representing Canada after leaving Seoul prior to the sprint relay following the Johnson disqualification; admitted drug use to the Dubin enquiry, and as a result he was suspended from funding. Brought down by Greg Foster when leading 1987 World Indoor 60mh. Married Yvette Grabner, twin sister of Yvonne Mai, in 1991. After training with Colin Jackson in Wales made first improvement for four years with a Canadian record and then the Olympic title in 1992. In 1993 he won the World Indoor title, although lucky to get away with a second 'false' start., but lost his outdoor Worlds place when he refused to return for Canadian Championships. Now lives in Austria and may take up Austrian citizenship.

Michael SMITH b.16 Sep 1967 Kenora, Ontario 1.95m 98kg. Student at University of Toronto.
At Dec: OG: '88- 14, '92- dnf; WCh: '87- dnf, '91- 2, '93- dnf; CG: '86- 7, '90- 1; WJ: '86- 2. Won CAN Dec 1989-90. At Hep: WI inv: '93- 2.
Canadian decathlon records 1990 and 1991.
Progression at Dec: 1986- 7523, 1987- 8126, 1988- 8039, 1989- 8317, 1990- 8525, 1991- 8549, 1992- 8409, 1993- 8362. pbs: 100m 10.43 '85, 400m 47.05 '92, 1500m 4:20.04 '87, 110mh 14.34 '90, 14.24w '91; HJ 2.14 '89, PV 5.15i/5.00 '93, LJ 7.76 '93, SP 15.97i '92, 15.69 '91; DT 49.84 '91, JT 69.38 '91, Hep 6279i '93.
Won the Commonwealth gold in 1990, when he added over 200 points to his best decathlon score and opened the second day with three personal bests. Won at Götzis 1991. Three no jumps in long jump at 1993 Worlds.

Bruny SURIN b.12 Jul 1967 Cap-Haïtien, Haiti 1.80m 81kg. Vidéotron, Montreal. Student.
At 100m/4x100m relay: OG: '92- 4; WCh: '91- 8, '93- 5/3R; CG: '90- 3 (7 LJ). At LJ: OG: '88- dnq 15; PAm: '87- dnq 15. At TJ: WJ: '86- 11. At 60m: WI: '91- 8, '93- 1. Won Canadian 100m 1989-92.
Four Canadian 100m records 1989-92.
Progression at 100m, LJ: 1986- 10.95, 7.66, 1987- 10.62, 8.03; 1988- 10.71, 8.02/8.19w; 1989- 10.14/10.1, 8.00; 1990- 10.24/10.12w, 7.85w; 1991- 10.07/10.01w, 1992- 10.05/9.9, 1993- 10.02. pbs: 50m 5.67i '93, 55m 6.17i '93, 60m 6.45i '93, 200m 20.48 '93, TJ 15.96 '86.
Moved to Canada in 1975.

Women

Angela CHALMERS b.6 Sep 1963 Brandon, Manitoba 1.72m 55kg. Winnipeg Raiders. Studied dietetics at Northern Arizona University, USA. Married Ed Espinoza in March 1989 and lives in Arizona.
At 3000m (1500m): OG: '88- 14 (h), '92- 3 (sf); WCh: '93- (5); CG: '90- 1 (1); PAm: '87- 2; WSG: '85- 3. Won Canadian 1500m 1989-90, 1993; NCAA CC 1986.

Progression at 1500m, 3000m: 1978- 4:27.3; 1979- 4:23.7; 1981- 4:21.37; 1983- 4:22.0i; 1984- 4:15.36, 9:33.58; 1985- 4:12.13, 9:00.02; 1986- 4:19.5i, 9:31.3; 1987- 4:06.43, 8:56.45; 1988- 4:05.78, 8:48.60; 1989- 4:03.18, 8:46.64; 1990- 4:06.91, 8:38.38; 1991- 4:07.02, 9:00.43; 1992- 4:02.11, 8:42.85; 1993- 4:07.95, 9:01.23. pbs: 800m 2:02.34 '88, 1M 4:24.91 '91, 2000m 5:47.38 '91.
In 1990 became the first to win the Commonwealth Games 1500m/3000m double.

Rosey EDEH b.13 Aug 1966 London, GBR 1.78m 54kg. Québec. Degree in art history from Rice University, USA.
At 400mh/4x400mR: OG: '88- h, '92- sf; WCh: '91- h, '93- 7; CG: '90- 7/3R; WSG: '89- 2; WCp: 1R. Canadian champion 1988-9, 1991, 1993.
Four Canadian 400mh records 1989-93.
Progression at 400mh: 1988- 56.26, 1989- 56.10, 1990- 56.25, 1991- 56.53, 1992- 55.26, 1993- 54.53. pbs: 200m 23.98w '84, 400m 52.38 '92, 100mh 13.83 '89.
Her family moved to Canada when she was two.

CHILE

Governing body: Federación Atlética de Chile, Calle Santo Toribio No 660, Nuñoa, Santiago de Chile. Founded 1917.

Bruny Surin: World Indoor 60 metres champion

Gert WEIL b.3 Jan 1960 Puerto Montt 1.97m 124kg. Administrator. Larios, Spain.
At SP: OG: '84- 10, '88- 6, '92- dnq 13; WCh: '87- 10, '91- 9, '93- 6; WI: '89- 6, '91- 6; PAm: '83- 2, '87- 1, "91- 1; WCp: '85- 5, '89- 4, '92- 4. Won SACh 1979-81-83-85-87-89-91 and Jnr 1978.
Nine South American shot records 1984-6.
Progression at SP: 1978- 14.88, 1979- 16.42, 1980- 16.77, 1981- 17.48, 1982- 17.54, 1983- 18.29, 1984- 19.94, 1985- 20.47, 1986- 20.90, 1987- 20.68, 1988- 20.74, 1989- 20.73, 1990- 20.11, 1991- 19.68, 1992- 19.56, 1993- 19.95. pb DT 55.98 '87.
Married Ximena Restrepo on 31 Jan 1992.

CHINA

Governing body: Athletic Association of the People's Republic of China, 9 Tiyuguan Road, Beijing 100061.
National Championships first held in 1910 (men), 1959 (women). **1993 Champions**. **Men**: 100m: Chen Wenzhong 10.45; 200m: Huang Janwei 21.02, 400m: Zhao Cunlin 46.44, 800m/ 1500m: Lin Jun 1:52.33/3:46.29, 5000m: Ning Limin 13:51.09, 10000m: Han Zongmin 29:40.30, Mar: Zhang Fukui 2:11:10, 3000mSt: Gao Shuhai 8:57.28, 110mh: Zheng Jinsuo 13.74, 400mh: Du Yuechun 50.43, HJ: Xu Yang 2.20, PV: Ge Yun 5.25, LJ: Xu Bin 8.07, TJ: Zou Sixin 16.69, SP: Xie Shengying 18.34, DT: Zhang Cunbiao 61.22, HT: Bi Zhong 72.02, JT: Zhang Lianbiao 77.50, Dec: Zhao Bingchun 7573, 20kmW: Li Mingcai 1:21:36, 50kmW: Chen Shaoguo 3:59:36. **Women**: 100m: Wang Lei 11.33, 200m: Chen Zhaojing 22.60, 400m: Ma Yuqin 50.86, 800m: Chen Xuehui 2:01.17, 1500m: Wei Li 4:28.50, 3000m/10000m/Mar: Wang Junxia 8:27.68/31:08.42/2:24:07,100mh: Zhang Yu 13.05, 400mh: Guo Yue 55.88, HJ: Ge Ping 1.88, PV: Sun Caiyun 3.90, LJ: Yao Weili 7.01, TJ: Zhang Yan 13.92, SP: Zhou Tianhua 19.16, DT: Zhang Cuilan 62.00, JT: Zhang Li 63.10, Hep: Ma Miaolan 6242, 10000mW/ 10kmW: Wang Yan 43:01.0/42:26.

HUANG Geng b.10 Jul 1970 Henan Province 1.79m 71kg.
At LJ: OG: '92- 8; WCh: '91- dnq 28; AsiC: '91- 1; AsiG: '90- 2. Chinese champion 1990, 1992.
Progression at LJ: 1989- 7.88, 1990- 8.18, 1991- 8.17, 1992- 8.22, 1993- 8.30.

LI Tong b.6 May 1967 Hangzhou, Zhejiang 1.90m 80kg. Computer science student at Washington State University.
At 110mh: OG: '92- sf; WCh: '91- 8, '93- sf; AsiC: '93- 1. Won NCAA indoor 55mh 1990-1.
At LJ: WJ: '86- 7.
Eight Asian 110mh records 1989-93, Asian records at 50mh, 55mh, 60mh.

Progression at 110mh: 1988- 14.21, 1989- 13.68/13.49w, 1990- 13.62, 1991- 13.37/13.31w, 1992- 13.59/13.3, 1993- 13.26. pbs: 100m 10.42 '92, 10.4 '87; 200m 21.01 '92, 50mh 6.54i '92, 55mh 7.08i '91, 60mh 7.69i '93, HJ: 2.10 '85, LJ 7.70 '86.
Started career at 400m and decathlon, then long jump, before high hurdles. Known in the USA as Tony Li. Fell when leading in 1990 Asian Games, 1991 NCAA and World Student Games.

ZOU SIXIN b.8 May 1967 Hunan 1.75m 67kg.
At TJ: OG: '92- 8; WCh: '91- dnq 24, '93- dnq; WI: '91- 4; AsiG: '90- 2; AsiC: '91- 2. Chinese champion 1991, 1993; EAG 1993.
Progression at TJ: 1986- 16.08, 1987- 16.03, 1988- 16.50, 1989- 16.77, 1990- 17.31, 1991- 16.95, 1992- 17.07, 1993- 17.26. pb LJ 7.74 '92.

Women

CAO Qi b. Jan 1974.
At DT: OG: '92- 5; AsiC: '93-1.
Progression at DT: 1992- 61.56, 1993-66.08.

CONG Yuzhen b. 22 Jan 1963 1.71m 90kg.
At SP: OG: '88- 9; WCh: '93- 5; AsiC: '87- 1.
Progression at SP: 1981- 16.51, 1982- 16.56, 1983- 17.25, 1984- 17.80, 1985- 18.93, 1986- 18.69, 1987- 19.86, 1988- 20.47, 1989- 19.39, 1990- 19.89, 1993- 19.58.

CUI Yingzi b.26 Oct 1971 Liaoning 1.63m 51kg.
At 10kmW: OG: '92- 5; WCp: '91- 20. At 5000mW: 2nd Asi J 1990.
Two Asian 10000m walk records 1991-2.
Progression at 10kmW: 1989- 44:36.8t, 1991- 42:55.28, 1992- 42:46.7t, 1993- 43:50. pb 5000mW 21:13.2 '88.

GAO Hongmiao b.8 Jul 1974 1.62m 51kg.
At 10kmW: AsiC: '93- 1. At 5000mW: WJ: '92- 1.
World junior 10,000m walk records track 1992, road 1993.
Progression at 10kmW: 1991- 42:56.09, 1992- 42:49.7, 1993- 41:57. pb 5000mW 21:20.03 '92.

HAN Qing b.4 Mar 1970 1.70m 55kg.
At 200m: 3rd EAG 1993.
Chinese 400mh record 1993.
Progression at 200m, 400mh: 1989- 58.74, 1990- 23.03, 56.53; 1991- 23.31, 1992- 22.79, 1993- 22.87, 53.96. pbs: 400m 52.49 '92.

HUANG Zhihong b.7 May 1965 Lanxi county, Zhejiang 1.74m 100kg. Student at Loughborough University, GBR.
At SP: OG: '88- 8, '92- 2; WCh: '87- 11, '91- 1, '93- 1; WSG: '89- 1; WCp: '89- 1; WI: '89- 2, '91- 2; AsiG: '86- 1, '90- 2; AsiC: '89- 1, '91- 1. Won GP 1991. Chinese champion 1988-92.
Progression at SP: 1983- 16.12, 1984- 17.04, 1985- 18.01, 1986- 18.89, 1987- 20.22, 1988- 21.28, 1989- 20.73, 1990- 21.52, 1991- 20.85, 1992- 20.47, 1993- 20.57.
The first Asian athlete to have won a World Cup event (1989) and the first to have won a Grand Prix series (1991).

LI Chunxiu b.13 Aug 1969 Qinghai Province. 1.70m 60kg.
At 10kmW: OG: '92- 3; WCp: '89- 14; won Asi-J 1986, EAG 1993.
Asian 10km road walk best 1993.
Progression at 10kmW: 1986- 46:45.0t, 1987- 46:41.5t, 1989- 46:00, 1990- 44:06, 1991- 44:41, 1992- 42:47.6t, 1993- 41:48. pb 5000mW 21:54.9 '88, 21:03R '89.

LI Huirong b.14 Apr 1965 Tianjin 1.73m 67kg. Student at Beijing Institute of PE.
At TJ: WSG: '91- 1; WCp: '92- 1; WI Inv '91- 2. Chinese champion 1990-2.
World triple jump bests 1987 and 1990, seven Asian bests 1987-92 and indoor best 1990.
Progression at TJ: 1987- 14.04, 1988- 14.16, 1989- 14.34, 1990- 14.54, 1991- 14.42, 1992- 14.55, 1993- 13.22. pb LJ 6.55/6.59w '88.

LIU Dong b.27 Dec 1973 Liaoning 1.73m 55kg.
At 1500m: WCh: '93- 1; WJ: '92- 1, EAG: '93- 2.
Two Asian 800m records 1993.
Progression at 800m, 1500m: 1991- 2:02.4, 1992- 2:02.96, 4:05.14; 1993- 1:55.54, 4:00.50.

LIU Li b.12 Mar 1971 Liaoning 1.67m 47kg.
At 800m: WCh: '93- 6; WJ: '90- 5; AsiC: '93- 1. At 1500m: OG: '92- 5, WJ: '90- 5; won Asi J 800m 1990.
Progression at 800m, 1500m: 1989- 2:04.81, 1990- 2:02.38, 4:16.38; 1991- 2:01.6, 4:09.58; 1992- 4:00.20, 1993- 1:56.96, 3:59.34.

LU Yi b.10 Apr 1974 Liaoning 1.78m 59kg.
At 1500m: WCh: '93- 4; WJ: '92- 1. At 800m: EAG: '93- 2.
Unratified world junior 1500m record 1993.
Progression at 800m, 1500m: 1992- 2:02.91, 4:15.05; 1993- 1:57.77, 4:00.05.

MA Liyan b.3 Nov 1968
At Mar: WCp: '93- 4.
Progression at 3000m, 10000m, Mar: 1993- 8:19.78, 31:10.46, 2:25:46.

MA Miaolan b.18 Jan 1970 Zhejiang 1.76m 63kg.
At Hep: AsiG: '90- 1; AsiC: '87- 2, '89- 2. Won Chinese Hep 1990, 1993.
Asian heptathlon records 1990 and 1993.
Progression at Hep, LJ: 1986- 6.09, 1987- 6.51,

6034; 1988- 5509, 1989- 6.31, 6021; 1990- 6.62, 6306; 1993- 6.97/7.06w, 6750. pbs: 100mh 13.28 '93, HJ 1.89 '93, TJ 14.12 '93.

MA Yuqin b.11 Sep 1972 Zunhua, Hebei Prov.
At 400m: AsiC: '93- 1; won Asi J 1990.
Three Asian 400m records 1993.
Progression at 400m: 1989- 53.8, 1990- 52.97, 1991- 52.04, 1992- 52.95, 1993- 49.81. pb 200m 22.95 '93.

MIN Chunfeng b.17 Mar 1969 Jiangxi Prov. 1.75m 79kg.
At DT (SP): OG: '92- 11; WCh: '91- 6, '93- 3; AsiC: '91- 1 (2); WJ: '86- 3, '88- 4; WCp: '92- 3 (6). Chinese champion 1991, EAG 1993.
Progression at DT: 1984- 53.14, 1985- 54.70, 1986- 55.10, 1987- 62.50, 1988- 60.60, 1990- 63.50, 1991- 66.76, 1992- 63.92, 1993- 65.26. pb SP 16.93 '88.

QU Yunxia b.25 Dec 1972 Liaoning 1.70m 58kg.
At 1500m (800m): OG: '92- 3; WSG: '91- 3; WJ: '90- 1 (6 800m); AsiC: '91- 1 (1); won Asi J 1990. At 3000m: Asi C: '93- 1. World CC: '92- 6. Chinese champion 1500m and 3000m 1992, EAG 1500m 1993.
World 1500m record 1993, Four Asian 1500m records 1991-3.
Progression at 1500m, 3000m: 1989- 4:11.36, 1990- 4:11.89, 1991- 4:07.71, 8:55.1; 1992- 3:57.08, 8:58.58; 1993- 3:50.46, 8:12.18. pbs: 800m 1:56.24 '93, 5000m 15:28.91 '91, Mar: 2:24:32 '93.
Second in 2:24:32 on marathon début at Tianjin April 1993.Took 2.01 sec off the 13-year old world record for 1500m and was also ten seconds inside the previous world record for 3000m when second to Wang Junxia at the Chinese National Games 1993, a month after winning the World title at 3000m.

REN Ruiping b.1 Jan 1975.
At TJ: AsiC: '93- 1.
Two World junior triple jump records 1993.
Progression at TJ: 1991- 13.10, 1993- 14.29.

SUI Xinmei b.29 Jan 1965 Shandong 1.72m 90kg. Student at Shanghai Institute of PE.
At SP: WCh: '93- 4; WI: '91- 1; AsiG: '90- 1; AsiC: '89- 2; WSG: '91- dq 1.
Progression at SP: 1985- 16.24, 1986- 18.87, 1987- 18.87, 1988- 20.08, 1989- 19.81, 1990- 21.66, 1991- 20.54i/19.94 dq, 1993- 20.32.
Disqualified on a positive drugs test, having won the 1991 World Student Games shot title, and was banned for two years.

WANG Junxia b.9 Jan 1973 Jiahoe City, Jilin Province 1.60m 45kg.
At 10000m: WCh: '93- 1; WJ: '92- 1, AsiC: '93- 1. At Mar: WCp: '93- 1. World CC: '92- 2 Jnr. Won Chinese 3000m, 10,000m and marathon 1993.
World records: 3000m (2), 10000m 1993. Asian records 3000m (3), 10000m (3), marathon 1993.
Progression at 1500m, 3000m, 10,000m, Mar: 1991- 4:17.18, 1992- 8:55.50, 32:29.90; 1993- 3:51.92, 8:06.11, 29:31.78, Mar 2:24:07 '93.
Ran 2:24:07 on marathon début in Tianjin in April 1993 two weeks after running a world best Ekiden relay 5k split of 14:52. Went on to double success at the Chinese Championships and to win the World 10000m title with a last 3k in 8:42.49. That was all put into the shade however by her feats at the Chinese National Games in September, when she took 41.96 sec off the world record for 10,000m on the 8th, ran second to Qu Yunxia at 15000m in 3:51.92, inside the 13 year-old world record, on the 11th, and then set 3000m world records of 8:12.29 on the 12th and 8:06.11 on the 13th, compared to the 8:22.62 which had remained the world record since 1984. Moved to Liaoning province in 1986.

WANG Xiuting b.15 Jan 1965 Shandong Prov. 1.58m 48kg. PE student.
At 10000m (3000m): OG: '88- 7 (h), '92- 6; WCh: '87- 8 (h), '91- 3; AsiG: '86- 1, '90- 2. World 15km Rd: '88- 2, '89- 1. Won CHN 3000m 1989.
Three Asian 10000m records, one at 3000m & 5000m 1987, 5000m 1991.

Dong Liu: won thw world 1500 metres in Stuttgart

Progression at 10000m: 1986- 32:47.77, 1987- 31:27.00, 1988- 31:40.23, 1990- 31:52.18, 1991- 31:35.99, 1992- 31:28.06, 1993- 31:32.23. pbs: 3000m 8:50.68 '87, 5000m 15:23.58 '91. Road: 15km 49:34 '89, Half Mar 1:10:14 '91, Mar 2:28:56 '92.
Fifth on marathon début Jan 1992 in Osaka, then second Beijing 1993.

WANG Yan b.9 Apr 1971 Liaoning 1.61m 46kg. Student.
At 10kmW: WCh: '93- dq; WCp: '93- 1. Chinese champion 1993.
World walk records 1986: 3km: 12:39.1, 5km: 21:33.8, the latter at age 14 years 334 days, the youngest ever to set a world record. World junior record at 10km walk 1986.
Progression at 10kmW: 1984- 49:01, 1985- 46:09, 1986- 44:59.3t, 1987- 45:22.24t, 1992- 42:50, 1993- 42:26.

WANG Yuan b.8 Apr 1976 1.65m 53kg.
At 800m: WCh: '93- h.
World junior records 800m and 1500m (2) 1993.
Progression at 800m, 1500m: 1993- 1:57.18, 3:59.81.

ZHANG Li b.26 Jun 1961 Tianjin 1.70m 82kg. Employee of Hikari Camera in Japan.
At JT: WCp: '89- 2; AsiG: '90- 1; AsiC: '93- 1. Chinese champion 1988, 1993.
Asian javelin record 1990.
Progression at JT: 1981- 56.30, 1982- 56.04, 1983- 57.86, 1987- 64.14, 1988- 62.84, 1989- 63.44, 1990- 70.42, 1993- 64.06.
Had a baby in 1991.

ZHANG Linli b.6 Mar 1973 Liaoning 1.64m 48kg.
At 3000m: WCh: '93- 2; WJ: '92- 1; AsiC: '93- 2; EAG: '93- 2. At Mar: WCp: '93- 2.
At 3000m: Asian record 1992 andWorld 1993.
Progressicn at 1500m, 3000m, 10000m: 1991- 4:15.96, 9:01.7; 1992- 8:46.86, 1993- 3:57.46, 8:16.50, 31:16.28. pbs: 5000m 15:35.70 '91, Mar 2:24:42 '93.
Set a world 3000m record of 8:22.06 in first heat of Chinese National Games 1993, before third in the final in 8:16.50.

ZHANG Lirong b.3 Mar 1973 Liaoning 1.56m 48kg.
At 3000m: WCh: '93- 3; WJ: '92- 3; won EAG 1993. At 10000n: AsiC: '93- 2; At Mar: WCp: '93- 3.
World Junior 3000m record 1993.
Progression at 1500m, 3000m, 10000m, Mar: 1991- 4:19.17, 9:10.2, 2:33:59; 1992- 8:48.45, 33:37.1; 1993- 3:59.70, 8:21.84, 31:09.25, 2:24:52.

ZHANG Liuhong b.16 Jan 1969 1.81m 86kg.
At SP: WI: '93- 3; AsiC: '93- 1. Won EAG 1993.
Progression at SP: 1987- 16.74, 1988- 17.73, 1989- 17.93, 1990- 19.60, 1991- 19.74, 1993- 19.90

ZHANG Yu b.8 Apr 1971 Tianjin 1.76m 64kg.
At 100mh: OG: '92- sf; WCh: '91- sf; WCp: '92- 4; AsiC: '91- 1, '93- 1. Chinese champion 1991-3, AsiJ 1990, EAG 1993.
Asian 100mh record 1993.
Progression at 100mh: 1989- 13.75, 1990- 13.38, 1991- 13.03/13.0, 1992- 12.92, 1993- 12.64. pbs: 100m 11.5 '91, 200m 23.4 '92, 60mh 8.26i '93.

ZHONG Huandi b.28 Jun 1967 Yunnan Prov. 1.55m 43kg.
At 10000m (3000m): OG: '92- 4; WCh: '91- 2, '93- 2; WSG: '87- 2; AsiG: '90- 1 (1); AsiC: '89- 1 (1), '91- 1 (1); WCp: '92- 3 (6). At Mar: OG: '88- 30. World 15kmRd: ''88-4, '89- 2, '90- 3. Won Chinese 3000m 1989-90; 10000m 1989-92.
Asian 10000m record 1992.
Progression at 10000m, Mar: 1986- 33:31.58, 1987- 32:53.68, 2:32:13; 1989- 32:25.27, 1990- 31:50.98, 1991- 31:35.08, 1992- 31:21.08; 1993- 30:13.37, 2:25:36. pbs: 3000m 8:41.67 '93, 5000m 15:30.15 '89, 15kmRd 49:44 '89.

ZHU YUQING b.22 Apr 1963 1.80m 68kg.
At Hep: OG: '92- 16; WCh: '87- 8, '91- 12; AsiG: '86- 1; AsiC: '91- 1. At 100mh: OG: '92- qf. Won Chinese Hep 1991-2, EAG Hep 1993.
Three Asian heptathlon records 1986-92.
Progression at Hep: 1985- 5375, 1986- 5611, 1987- 6211, 1990- 5985, 1991- 6231, 1992- 6384, 1993- 6394. pbs: 200m 23.45 '92, 800m 2:22.65 '93, 100mh 13.05 '93, HJ 1.83 '93, LJ 6.10 '87, SP 15.12 '87, JT 46.52 '93.

COLOMBIA

Governing body: Federación Colombiana de Atletismo, Calle 28 No. 25-18, Bogotá. Founded 1937.
National Champions 1993: **Men**: 200m: Luis Vega 21.2, 400m: Wilson Canizales 48.9, 800m: Victor Cano 1:56.2, 1500m/5000m: Herder Vásquez 3:56.6/14:58.3, 10000m: Jacinto López 31:37.1, 3000mSt: Leonardo Garcia 9:39.4, 110mh: Julian González 15.4, 400mh: Llimi Rivas 53.3, HJ/TJ: Gilmar Mayo 1.90/15.38, PV: William Amador 3.60, LJ: Oscar Acosta 7.14, SP: Celso Aragon 15.60, DT: Rogilio Ospino 51.86, HT: Fredy Mendoza 47.46, JT: Luis Lucumí 62.24, 20kW: Orlando Diaz 1:26:29, 30kmW: Querubin Moreno 2:30:58. **Women**: 100m/200m: Patricia Rodriguez 11.9/24.3, 400m: Janeth Lucumi 57.8, 800m: Martha Gomez 2:24.2, 1500m: Rocio Estrada 5:01.8,

3000m/10000m: Stella Castro 10:18.5/36:17.5, 100mh: Martha Dinas 14.7, HJ: Janeth Lagoyette 1.60, LJ: Zorobabelia Cordoba 5.75, SP/DT: M Isabel Urrutia 14.69/55.00, HT: Maria Villamizar 47.18, JT: Bertha Gómez 46.28, 10kmW: Liliana Bermeo 51:24.

Ximena RESTREPO b.10 Mar 1969 Medellin 1.75m 58kg. Studied broadcasting at University of Nebraska. Married Gert Weil (nine SAm shot records to 20.90 '86, PAm champion 1987 & 1991) on 31 Jan 1992.
At 400m: OG: '92- 3; WCh: '91- 6, '93- 5; PAm: '91- 2 (2 200m); WJ: '88- sf (sf 100m, 200m); WCp: '92- 1R; won NCAA 1991. 2nd GP 1992. At 200m: OG: '88- h; SAm: '87- 1 (2 100m, 4x100m), '91- 1/2R/2R; CAmG: '93- 3 (2 4x100m). South American records 200m 1991, 400m (3) 1991-2, Colombian 400m (8), 200m 1990-2.
Progression at 400m: 1988- 53.48, 1989- 55.55i, 1990- 51.64, 1991- 50.14, 1992- 49.64, 1993- 50.38. pbs: 100m 11.54/11.3 '91, 11.30w '89; 200m 22.92/22.4A '91, 400mh 59.1 '89.
First Colombian to win an Olympic athletics medal.

CROATIA

Governing body: Hrvatski Atletski Savez, Tg Sportova 11, 41000 Zagreb. Founded 1912.
National Champions 1993: **Men**: 100m/200m: Djulijano Koludra 10.68/21.63, 400m: Igor Marjanovic 48.30, 800m/1500m: Slobodan Mijolovic 1:53.34/3:51.94, 5000m: Romeo Zivko 14:28.2, 10000m: Mladen Krsek 31:28.65, 3000mSt: Sasa Ljubojevic, 110mh/Dec: Nedeljko Visnjic 14.76/618?, 400mh: Franjo Pavlovic 53.31, HJ: Ivan Penavic 2.06, PV: Edvard Josipovic 4.40, LJ: Sinisa Ergotic 7.44, TJ: Miljenko Vukovic 14.96, SP: Stevimir Ercegovic 14.82, DT: Miroslav Virijevic 50.50, HT: Ivica Jakelic 56.80, JT: Jose Ugrina 69.56. **Women**: 100m/200m: Mateja Zepcevic 12.26/25.40, 400m: Mijena Sola 56.99, 800m/1500m: Mara Zuzul 2:11.28/4:28.14, 3000m: Slavica Brcic 10:20.78, 10000m: Ljubica Bekavac 37:59.92, 100mh: Margita Papic 14.22, 400mh: Milena Zatezalo 63.04, LJ/TJ: Silvija Babic 5.99/12.01, SP: Paola Delton 11.22, DT: Aleksandra Kuzet 42.50, JT: Valentina Belaic 52.56, Hep: Anita Horvat 3668.

CUBA

Governing body: Federación Cubana de Atletismo, 13 y C Vedado 601, Zone Postal 4, Habana 10400. Founded 1922. **National Champions 1993**. **Men**: 100m: Joel Isasi 10.32, 200m: Ivan Garcia 20.65, 400m: Robelis Darroman 46.49, 800m: Osiris Mora 1:49.07, 1500m: Silvio Garcia 3:53.01, 5000m/3000mSt: Juan Ramon Conde 14:25.52/8:57.70, 10,000m: Angel Rodriguez 29:54.86, 110mh: Emilio Valle 13.65w, 400mh: Pedro Piñera 50.61, HJ: Javier Sotomayor 2.34, PV: Alberto Monzano 5.55, LJ: Ivan Pedroso 8.47, TJ: Yoelvis Quesada 17.60w, SP: Jorge Montenegro 17.85, DT: Roberto Moya 62.80, HT: Alberto Sánchez 75.86, JT: Ovidio Trimino 74.86, 20kmW: Daniel Vargas 1:28:40.47. **Women**: 100m/200m: Liliana Allen 11.34/ 23.12, 400m/800m: Nancy McLean 52.66/2:08.68; 1500m: Maura Contrera 4:37.85, 3000m/ 10000m: Milagros Rodriguez 9:41.25/ 34:43.0, 100mh: Aliuska López 13.04, 400mh: Elsa Jiménez 56.78, HJ: Ioamnet Quintero 1.92, LJ/TJ: Niurka Montalvo 6.75w/14.02, SP: Belsis Laza 18,72, DT: Maritza Martén 61.56, JT: Dulce Garcia 63.44, 10kmW: Maribel Calderin 52:11.04.

Marino Rafael **DRAKE** b.13 Jun 1967 Limonar, Matanzas 1.93m 73kg.
At HJ: OG: '92- 8=; WCh: '91- 5=, '93- dnq; CAmG: '90- 2, '93- 2.
Progression at HJ: 1984- 2.05, 1985- 2.20, 1986- 2.20, 1987- 2.21, 1989- 2.15, 1990- 2.32, 1991- 2.34, 1992- 2.30, 1993- 2.25.

Roberto HERNANDEZ b.6 Mar 1967 Limonar, Matanzas 1.79m 74kg. Student.
At 400m/R- 4x400m relay: OG: '92- 8/2R; WCh: '87- 4/3R, '91- 4, '93- qf; PAm: '87- 3/2R, '91- 1; CAmG: '90- 1 (1 200m); WJ: '86- 2/2R; WSG: '85- 2/1R, 89- 1; WCp: '89- 1/1R; WI: '87- 2. Won GWG 1990, CAC 1985, 1989; Cuban 1985, 1988, 1990-2 (200m 1988). Won PAm-J 200m & 400m 1986.
Cuban 400m records 1988 and 1990. Two world 300m bests 1990.
Progression at 400m: 1983- 48.0, 1984- 46.44, 1985- 45.14, 1986- 45.05, 1987- 44.61, 1988- 44.22, 1989- 44.58/44.3A, 1990- 44.14, 1991- 44.40, 1992- 44.52, 1993- 46.01. pbs: 200m 20.24 '88, 20.2 '85; 300m 31.48 '90.
Has run 53 times sub 45 secs, including a then season's record 17 in 1990 and 12 in 1991.

Jaime JEFFERSON b.17 Jan 1962 Guantanamo 1.89m 78kg.
At LJ: OG: '92- 5; WCh: '87- 6, '91- 9, '93- dnq 15; WI: '89- 5, '91- 2, '93- 3; PAm: '83- 1, '87- 3, '91- 1; CAmG: '86- 1, '90- 2, '93- 3; WSG: '85- 1, '89- 1; WCp: '89- 8. CAC champion 1985, 1989; Cuban 1984-6, 1988-91.
Seven Cuban long jump records 1984-90.
Progression at LJ: 1981- 7.25, 1982- 7.50, 1983- 8.05, 1984- 8.37, 1985- 8.24/8.28w, 1986- 8.47, 1987- 8.51, 1988- 8.37, 1989- 8.29, 1990- 8.53,

1991- 8.26, 1992- 8.21/8.41w, 1993- 8.06. pbs: 100m 10.2/10.35/10.33w '85, 200m 21.22 '92, TJ 16.28 '85.

Roberto MOYA b.11 Feb 1965 Ciudad Habana 1.93m 110kg.
At DT: OG: '92- 3; WCh: '91- 8, '93- dnq 17; PAm: '91- 2; CAmG: '90- 1; WSG: '89- 3; WCp: '92- 2. Won CAC 1987 & 1989, Cuban 1989, 1992-3.
Progression at DT: 1984- 49.10, 1985- 56.48, 1986- 59.04, 1987- 62.92, 1988- 61.20, 1989- 63.78, 1990- 65.68, 1991- 63.92, 1992- 64.64, 1993- 64.08. pb SP 15.79 '87.

Ivan PEDROSO b.17 Dec 1972 1.77m 65kg. Larios, Spain.
At LJ: OG: '92- 4; WCh: '93- nj; WI: '93- 1; WJ: '90- 4; PAm: '91- 3; WCp: '92- 1. Won PAm J 1991, Cuban 1992-3.
Equalled Cuban long jump record 1992.
Progression at LJ: 1988- 7.43, 1989- 7.43, 1990- 8.06, 1991- 8.22, 1992- 8.53/8.79w, 1993- 8.49. pb TJ 16.05 '91.
Injured at 1993 World Championships.

Yoelvis Luis **QUESADA** b.4 Aug 1973 Sancti Spiritus 1.80m 73kg.
At TJ: OG: '92- 6; WCh: '91- 7, '93- 12; WI: '93- 5; WJ: '90- 2, '92- 1; PAm: '91- 1; CamG: '93- 1. Won CACJ 1990, PAmJ 1991, Cuban 1991-3.
Progression at TJ: 1989- 16.11, 1990- 16.68, 1991- 17.13, 1992- 17.23, 1993- 17.68. pb LJ 7.76 '93.
World age-16 best 1990.

Javier SOTOMAYOR b.13 Oct 1967 Limonar, Matanzas 1.95m 82kg. PE teacher, graduate of Habana Institute of PE. Larios, Spain.
At HJ: OG: '92- 1; WCh: '87- 9, '91- 2, '93- 1; PAm: '87- 1, '91- 1; CAmG: '90- 1, '93- 1; WJ: '86- 1; WCp: '85- 3, '89- 3, '92- 2; WSG: '89- 1; WI: '85- 2, '87- 4, '89- 1, '91- 3=, '93- 1. Cuban champion 1984, 1986-9, 1991-3; CAC 1985, 1989; PAm-J 1986. Won GP 1988 (third overall).
World high jump records 1988, 1989 the first 8-foot jump, and 1993. WIB 2.43m 1989. World junior record 1986, seven Cuban records 1984-9.
Progression at HJ: 1980- 1.65, 1981- 1.84, 1982- 2.00, 1983- 2.17, 1984- 2.33, 1985- 2.34, 1986- 2.36, 1987- 2.37, 1988- 2.43, 1989- 2.44, 1990- 2.36, 1991- 2.40, 1992- 2.36, 1993- 2.45.
Master technician, with very fast, head-on approach. Set world age bests each year from 15 to 19 in 1983-7. Married high jumper (1.90 '90) Maria del Carmen Garcia in Sept. 1989.
Has cleared 2.30m or better in 137 meetings (47 at 2.35 or more), 1984-93.

Emilio VALLE b.21 Apr 1967 Sancti Spiritus 1.82m 70kg. Larios, Spain.
At 110mh: OG: '92- 6; WCh: '93- 4; WJ: '86- 3 (1 400mh); PAm: '91- 4; CAmG: '90- 1 (1 4x400mR), '93- 1; WSG: '89- 2; WCp: '89- 3, '92- 3. Won CAC 110mh 1989, Cuban 110mh 1988-9, 1992-3; 400mh 1987. At 60mh: WI: '89- 5, '91- 4, '93- 7.
Cuban 110mh record 1993.
Progression at 110mh: 1984- 14.4, 1985- 14.46, 1986- 13.97, 1987- 13.76, 1988- 13.60, 1989- 13.30/13.21w, 1990- 13.64, 1991- 13.74, 1992- 13.39, 1993- 13.19. pbs: 100m 10.82 '93, 200m 21.70 '93, 60mh 7.59i '89, 400mh 50.02 '86.

Women

Liliana ALLEN b.24 May 1970 Holguín 1.70m 62kg.
At 100m/4x100mR (200m): OG: '92- 8; WCh: '91- sf/6R, '93- 8; WJ: '88- 3/2R (3); PAm: '87- 4, '91- 1/2R (1); CAmG: '90 & '93- 1/1R (1); WCp: '89- 5/4R, '92- 2; WSG: '89- 1 (2), '93- 2 (5). At 60m: WI: '89- 4, '91- 3, '93- 4. Won CACJ 100m 1986, PAmJ 100m/200m 1989, Cuban 100m 1988-93, 200m 1988, 1990-3.
Cuban 100m records 1989 and 1992.
Progression at 100m, 200m: 1985- 12.20; 1986- 11.83, 24.81; 1987- 11.42/11.19w, 23.83; 1988- 11.18, 23.13/22.97w; 1989- 11.14/10.9, 23.00/22.7; 1990- 11.22/11.19w, 23.22; 1991- 11.21, 23.11; 1992- 11.10, 22.98; 1993- 11.19, 23.12/22.90w. pb 60m 7.12i '91.

Silvia COSTA b.4 May 1964 Pinar del Rio 1.79m 60kg. Larios, Spain.
At HJ: OG: '92- 6; WCh: '83- 10=, '87- 4, '93- 2; WI: '85- 3=, '93- 7=; PAm: '79- 8, '83- 2, '87- 2; WSG: '83- 2, '85- 1, '89- 2; WCp: '85- 4, '89- 1; CAmG: '82- 1, '86- 1, '90- 2. Won CAC 1985, 1989, Cuban 1981-8. 2nd GP 1989.
Two world junior high jump records 1982. 15 Cuban records 1980-9.
Progression at HJ: 1977- 1.57, 1978- 1.64, 1979- 1.82, 1980- 1.90, 1981- 1.88, 1982- 1.95, 1983- 1.98, 1984- 1.99, 1985- 2.01, 1986- 1.99, 1987- 1.96, 1988- 2.02, 1989- 2.04, 1990- 1.82, 1991- 1.96i, 1992- 1.97, 1993- 1.98. pb 100mh 13.73 '88.
Married to Lázaro Martinez (1992 Olympic 4x400m silver medallist, pb 45.37 '83, 45.1 '89). Daughter born 1990. She returned to competition but then suffered a ruptured Achilles.

Bárbara ECHEVARRIA b.6 Aug 1966 Holguin 1.70m 94kg.
At DT: OG: '92- dnq 15; WCh: '91- 12, '93- 6; PAm: '91- 1; CAmG: '90- 1, '93- 1. Won CAC 1987, Cuban 1991.
Progression at DT: 1983- 45.90, 1984- 49.52, 1985- 50.42, 1986- 54.70, 1987- 57.64, 1988- 60.26, 1989- 68.18, 1990- 64.14, 1991- 67.42, 1992- 64.66, 1993- 62.52.

Belsy LAZA b.5 Jun 1967 1.74m 96kg.
At SP: OG: '92- 4; WCh: '91- 9, '93- 8; WI: '89- 6, '91- 5, '93- 7; WSG: '89- 2; PAm: '87- 3, '91- 1; WCp: '89- 6, '92- 1; CAmG: '90- 1 Cuban champion 1987-93.
Cuban & CAC shot record 1992.
Progression at SP: 1982- 12.66, 1983- 13.82, 1984- 16.09, 1985- 16.90, 1986- 17.85, 1987- 18.49, 1988- 19.34, 1989- 19.98, 1990- 19.16, 1991- 19.54, 1992- 20.96, 1993- 19.33.

Aliuska LOPEZ b.29 Aug 1969 Ciudad Habana 1.69m 53kg. Larios, Spain.
At 100mh: OG: '92- 6; WCh: '87- sf, '91- 7/6R, '93- 4; PAm: '87- 3 (2R), '91- 1; CAmG: '90 & '93- 1/1R; WJ: '86- 2, '88- 1; WSG: '87- 2; WCp: '92- 1. At 60mh: WI: '91- 3, '93- 5. Won Cuban 100mh 1986-9, 1993.
Two world junior 100mh records 1987; six Cuban records 1986-93.
Progression at 100mh: 1984- 14.4, 1985- 13.5/13.97, 1986- 13.14, 1987- 12.84, 1988- 12.96, 1989- 12.87, 1990- 12.73, 1991- 12.91, 1992- 12.87, 1993- 12.73. pbs: 100m 11.53 '87, 200m 24.22 '87, 60mh 8.02i '90, 400mh 64.32 '86.

Isel LOPEZ b.11 Jul 1970 Santiago de Cuba 1.74m 74kg.
At JT: OG: '92- dnq 13; WCh: '91- nt; WJ: '86- 7, '88- 2; WSG: '91- 2; CAmG: '93- 1. Cuban champion 1990, 1992, CAC 1993.
Progression at JT: 1985- 45.50, 1986- 57.44, 1987- 58.78, 1988- 60.52, 1989- 63.54, 1990- 66.16, 1991- 62.32, 1992- 65.62, 1993- 61.48.

Maritza MARTEN b.17 Aug 1963 Ciudad Habana 1.77m 83kg.
At DT: OG: '92- 1; WCh: '87- 9, '91- 10, '93- 4; PAm: '83- 2, '87- 1; CAmG: '86- 2; WCp: '85- 3, '89- 3, '92- 1; WSG: '85- 1, '89- 3. Won PAm-J 1982, CAC 1985, Cuban champion 1982-7, 1989-90, 1993. 2nd GP 1988.
Cuban discus record 1985.
Progression at DT: 1977- 41.34, 1978- 47.46, 1979- 53.30, 1980- 54.94, 1981- 53.70, 1982- 59.54, 1983- 63.94, 1984- 67.76, 1985- 70.50, 1986- 66.86, 1987- 66.98, 1988- 67.02, 1989- 70.50, 1990- 65.48, 1991- 66.26, 1992- 70.68, 1993- 65.96. pb SP 16.04 '89.

Niurka MONTALVO b.4 Jun 1968 1.70m 53kg.
At TJ (LJ): WCh: '93- 4; WI: '91- 5; WSG: '93- 1; CAmG: '93- 1 (1). Won CAC LJ 1987, 1990, 1993; TJ 1993, Cuban LJ 1988, 1990, 1993, TJ 1993.
Cuban records: long jump 1990 & 1992, five triple jump 1992-3.
Progression at LJ, TJ: 1984- 5.83, 1985- 6.18, 1986- 6.29, 1987- 6.32/6.52w, 1988- 6.62, 1989- 6.53, 1990- 6.87. 1991- 6.69, 12.51; 1992- 6.88, 13.92; 1993- 6.64/6.75w, 14.51.

Ioamnet QUINTERO b.18 Sep 1972 1.89m 70kg. Larios, Spain.
At HJ: OG: '92- 3; WCh: '93- 1; WI: '93- 6; PAm: '91- 1; WJ: '90- 4; WCp: '92- 1. Won PAmJ 1987, Cuban 1990-3.
Progression at HJ: 1987- 1.72, 1988- 1.80, 1989- 1.89, 1990- 1.95, 1991- 1.93, 1992- 1.98, 1993- 2.01i/2.00.
Snapped Achilles tendon at Brussels 1993, just two weeks after winning the world title.

Ana Fidelia QUIROT b.23 Mar 1963 Palma Soriano, Santiago de Cuba 1.65m 59kg. Graduate of Habana Institute of PE.
At 400m/800m/R- 4x400m relay: OG: '92- -/3; WCh: '87- -/4, '91- -/2; PAm: '79- 2R, '83- 2/3R, '87- 1/1, '91-1/1/2R; WSG: '85- 2/3, '89- 1/1; WCp: '85- 4/4, '89- 1/1/1R; CAmG: '78- 1R, '82- 4/-/1R, '86- 1/1/1R, '90- 1/1/1R, '93- 2 800m. Won GWG 400m & 800m 1990, CAC 400m 1983, 400m & 800m 1985, 1989; Cuban 400m 1985, 1988-9, 1991; 800m 1985, 1989, 1991-2. Won GP 800m 1987, 1989, 1991; 400m 1988 & 1990, 3rd overall 1988.
Cuban records: six 400m, seven 800m, one 1000m 1985-91.
Progression at 400m, 800m: 1977- 57.0; 1978- 53.74; 1979- 55.24; 1980- 55.0; 1981- 54.2; 1982- 52.61; 1983- 51.83; 1984- 50.87; 1985- 50.86, 1:59.45; 1986- 50.41, 1:58.80; 1987- 50.12, 1:55.84; 1988- 49.62, 1:56.36; 1989- 50.01/49.2A, 1:54.44; 1990- 50.03, 1:57.42; 1991- 49.61, 1:57.34; 1992- 51.05, 1:56.80; 1993- 2:05.22. pbs: 200m 23.07 '88, 22.9 '84; 1000m 2:33.12 '89.
Following an accident in January 1993, when she suffered severe burns, she gave birth to a daughter, who died from complications due to the premature birth. She made a very brave comback at the end of 1993 to win the ninth Central American and Caribbean Games medal of her career. Won 39 succesive 800m finals from the Grand Prix final in 1987 to third in Zürich 1990. After two early season losses won 15 successive races at 400m 1990. Formerly married to Raúl Cascaret, world freestyle wrestling champion at 74kg 1985-6. Elder sister was Cuban basketball international.

CZECH REPUBLIC

Governing body : Cesky atléticky svaz, Mezi stadiony PS 40, 16017 Praha 6 Strahov. AAU of Bohemia founded in 1897.
National Championships first held in 1907 (Bohemia), 1919 (Czechoslovakia). **1993 Champions**: **Men**: 100m/200m: Jirí Valík 10.40/20.96, 400m: Petr Puncochár 47.59, 800m: Václav Hrich 1:49.01, 1500m: Milan Drahonovky 3:49.82, 5000m: Jan Pesava 13:45.63,

10000m: Miroslav Sajler 29:44.31, 3000mSt: Jirí Soptenko 8:50.25, 110mh: Jirí Hudec 13.98, 400mh: Petr Holubec 51.93, HJ: Tomás Janku 2.19, PV: Zdenek Lubensky 5.30, LJ: Milan Gombala 7.83, TJ: Jaroslav Mrstík 16.07, SP: Miroslav Menc 18.46, DT: Imrich Bugár 58.20, HT: Pavel Sedlácek 71.40, JT: Milos Steigauf 72.04, Dec: Kamil Damasek 7507, 20kmW: Jirí Malysa 1:25:25, 50kmW: Milos Holusa 3:59:48. **Women**: 100m/200m: Hana Benesová 11.45/ 23.66, 400m: Nada Kostovalová 52.91, 800m: Eva Kasalová 2:06.79, 1500m: Ivana Kubesová 4:20.15, 3000m: Vera Kuncická 9:43.66, 10000m: Radka Pátková 36:00.18, 100mh: Iveta Rudová 13.91, 400mh: Zuzana Machotková 58.20, HJ: Sarka Nováková 1.91, LJ: Kohoutová 6.12, TJ: Sárka Kaspárková 13.72, SP: Sona Vasicková 16.53, DT: Vladimíra Malátová 62.92, JT: Nikola Tomecková 52.26, Hep: Dagmar Urbankova 5508, 10kmW: Kamila Holpuchová 44:20.

Jan ZELEZNY b.16 Jun 1966 Mlada Boleslav 1.86m 77kg. Dukla Praha.
At JT: OG: '88- 2, '92- 1; WCh: '87- 3, '91- dnq 18, '93- 1; EC: '86- dnq 18, '90- dnq 13; EJ: '83- 6, '85- 4; WCp: '92- 1; ECp: '87- 3, '89- 2, '91- 1. Won GP JT and 2nd overall 1991 and 1993. CS champion 1986, 1990.
Four world javelin records 1987-93, eight CS records 1986-93.
Progression at JT: 1979- 44.44, 1982- 57.22, 1983- 74.34, 1984- 80.32, 1985- 84.68, new: 1986- 82.48, 1987- 87.66, 1988- 86.88, 1989- 84.74, 1990- 89.66, 1991- 90.72, 1992- 94.74, 1993- 95.66.
Lost just once to Seppo Räty in both 1992 and 1993. His 94.74 throw in 1992 was made with a new 'Németh' javelin, later ruled illegal by the IAAF. In 1993 he added 4.08m to Backley's world record when he threw 95.44 at Pietersburg, South Africa in April, and he added a further 12 cm at Sheffield in August. Entered hospital at the end of the 1989 season due to a fractured vertebra, but recovered to regain the world record in 1990. In 1991 he was most unlucky not to qualify for the World final, when he fell, perhaps over the line, on a long throw; otherwise lost only once, to Steve Backley. His father, Jaroslav, threw the javelin 68.46m in 1969.

Robert ZMELIK b.18 Apr 1969 Prostejov 1.85m 81kg. Dukla Praha. Soldier.
At Dec: WCh: '91- 4; EC: '90- 4; WJ: '86- 10, '88- 2; EJ: '87- dnf. At Hep: EI: '92- 2. At LJ: WI: '91- 6.
Five CS decathlon records 1990-2. World best for 1 hour decathlon 7897 '92.
Progression at Dec: 1986- 7108, 1987- 7329, 1988- 7659, 1989- 7847, 1990- 8249, 1991- 8379, 1992- 8627, 1993- 8188. pbs: 100m 10.75 '93, 10.55w '92; 200m 21.71 '91, 21.4 '88; 400m 48.20 '91, 1500m 4:21.24 '91, 50mh 6.54i '91, 110mh 13.75 '90, 13.4dt '92; HJ 2.11 '91, PV 5.20ex/5.15 '92, LJ 8.09i/8.06 '92, TJ 14.73 '85, SP 14.65i/ 14.53 '92, DT 45.40 '92, JT 62.84 '91, Hep 6118i '92.
Added 260 points to CS decathlon record when fourth in Split, and a further 130 points when fourth in Tokyo.

Women

Sárka KASPARKOVA b.20 May 1971 Karviná 1.85m 66kg. AAC Brno. Teacher.
At TJ: WCh: '93- 7; WI: '93- 7; EI: '92- 4. At HJ: OG: '92- dnq; WJ: '88- 6; EJ: '89- 3. Won CS HJ 1988, CZE TJ 1993, Eur U23Cp TJ 1992.
Four Czech triple jump records 1992-3.
Progression at HJ, TJ: 1983- 1.42, 1984- 1.59, 1985- 1.71, 1986- 1.77, 1987- 1.80, 1988- 1.89, 1989- 1.91, 1990- 1.81, 1991- 1.78, 1992- 1.92, 14.00; 1993- 1.95i, 14.16. pb LJ 6.27/6.29w '93.

DENMARK

Governing body: Dansk Athletik Forbund, Idraettens Hus, Brøndby Stadion 20, DK-2605 Brøndby.
National Championships first held in 1894.
1993 Champions: **Men**: 100m: Claus Hirsbro 10.51, 200m: Lars Pedersen 21.24, 400m: Niels-

Sarka Kasparkova: switched from the high jump to the triple

Ole Lindberg 49.68, 800m: Wilson Kipketer 1:48.15, 1500m: Robert Kiplagat 3:48.10, 5000m/10000m: Klaus Hansen 13:57.60/ 29:28.18, Mar: Niels Kristian Vejen 2:28:42, 3000mSt: Kåre Sørensen 8:51.73, 110mh/ 400mh: Bogdan Deoniziak 14.40/52.19, HJ: Lars Werge Andersen 2.12, PV: Martin Voss 5.40, LJ: Michael Skifter Andersen 7.28, TJ: Karsten Nielsen 14.97w, SP: Jan A Sørensen 16.91, DT: Allan Laursen 51.38, HT: Jan Bielecki 66.12, JT: Kenneth Petersen 73.12, Dec: Poul Gundersen 6736, 10kmW/20kmW: Claus Jørgensen 43:03.1/1:31:16.5, 50kmW: Torben Christiansen 4:32:35. **Women**: 100m/200m: Christina Schnohr 12.08/24.76, 400m/800m/ 400mh: Ane Skak 57.80/2:08.39/59.31, 1500m/ 3000m: Bettina Romer Andersen 4:26.43/9:32.72, 10000m: Gitte Karlshøj 33:46.88, Mar: Anni Lønstad 2:58:35, 100mh: Christina Holm 14.13, HJ: Pia Zinck 1.80, LJ: Renata P Nielsen 6.84, TJ: Dorthe Jensen 12.00, SP: Bettina Høst Poulsen 13.44, DT: Vivian Krafft 49.10, HT: Malene Kjærsgaard 46.50, JT: Jette Ø.Jeppesen 62.20, Hep: Lone Nielsen 5269, 5kmW/10kmW: Dorte Krogsgaard 27:45.2/56:42.9.

Women

Renata NIELSEN b.18 May 1966 1.75m 62kg. née Pytelewska POL, married to Lars Nielsen.
At LJ: OG: '92- 11; WCh: '93- 3 (dnq 20 TJ); WI: '91- 10, '93- 9. Polish champion 1990, Danish 1990, 1992-3.
Danish records 1993: 4 LJ, 3 TJ.
Progression at LJ: 1982- 6.12/6.13w, 1983- 6.23 /6.37w, 1984- 5.89, 1985- 6.24/6.27w, 1986- 6.14/6.34w, 1987- 6.23i/6.11, 1989- 6.05, 1990- 6.53, 1991- 6.86, 1992- 6.65, 1993- 6.84. pbs: 100m 12.02 '93, 200m 25.42 '90, TJ 13.71 '93.

ESTONIA

Governing body: Eesti Kergejôustikuliit, Regati pst. 1, Tallinn EE0103. Founded 1920.
National Championships first held in 1917.
1993 Champions: **Men**: 100m/200m: Andrei Morozov 10.66/21.44, 400m: Raines Jaansoo 47.57, 800m: Raivo Raspel 1:53.62, 1500m: Arvi Uba 3:55.83, 5000m: Henno Haava 14:38.60, 10000m: Meelis Veilberg 30:23.60, Mar: Rein Valdmaa 2:28:42, 3000mSt: Pavel Loskutov 9:04.29, 110mh: Hendrik Leetmäe 14.76, 400mh: Marek Helinurm 51.99, HJ: Ain Evard 2.16, PV: Valeriy Bukreyev 5.60, LJ: Urmas Treiel 7.45, TJ: Sergei Tanaga 15.87, SP: Margus Tammaru 17.14, DT: Aleksander Tammert 53.30, HT: Jüri Tamm 73.84, JT: Donald Sild 76.66, Dec: Indrek Kaseorg 7966, 20000mW: Mart Järviste 1:46:21.05. **Women**: 100m: Rutti Luksepp 12.36, 200m/400m: Killu Ratas 25.58/56.61, 800m: Agneta Land 2:13.99, 1500m/3000m: Sirje Eichelmann 4:24.44/9:28.06, Mar: Siiri Kangur 2:56:10, 100mh/LJ/TJ/Hep: Virge Naeris 14.20/6.25/12.56/5878, HJ: Liina Pôldots 1.71, SP/DT: Eha Rünne 16.05/52.10, JT: Maret Kalviste 50.82.

Valeriy BUKREYEV b.15 Jun 1964 Tallinn 1.86m 82kg.
At PV: OG: '92- dnq; WCh: '93- 7. Estonian champion 1991-3.
Six Estonian pole vault records 1986-93.
Progression at PV: 1977- 3.00, 1978- 3.40, 1979- 4.00, 1980- 4.40, 1981- 4.70, 1982- 5.02, 1983- 5.25, 1984- 5.39, 1985- 5.20, 1986- 5.45, 1987- 5.61, 1988- 5.66, 1989- 5.60, 1990- 5.60, 1991- 5.65, 1992- 5.70, 1993- 5.81/5.86ex. pb HJ 2.05 '84.

Jüri TAMM b.5 Feb 1957 Pärnu 1.93m 120kg. Tallinn. Teacher.
At HT: OG: '80- 3, '88- 3, "92- 5; WCh: '87- 2; WCp: '85- 1; ECp: '85- 1; WSG: '81- 2, '83- 1. USSR champion 1987-8, Estonian 1991, 1993. 3rd GP 1990.
World hammer record in 1980, only to be overtaken by Yuriy Sedykh in same competition. World bests 35lb weight 1991 (24.33) and 1992.
Progression at HT: 1973- 36.52, 1974- 49.16, 1975- 54.76, 1976- 66.86, 1977- 72.44, 1978- 74.58, 1979- 75.18, 1980- 80.46, 1981- 77.26, 1982- 74.82, 1983- 79.18, 1984- 84.40, 1985- 84.08, 1986- 80.88, 1987- 82.02, 1988- 84.16, 1989- 78.58, 1990- 79.94, 1991- 80.56, 1992- 81.86, 1993- 76.94. pb 35lbWt 25.17 '92.

ETHIOPIA

Governing body: Ethiopian Athletic Federation, Addis Ababa Stadium, PO Box 3241, Addis Ababa.

ADDIS Abebe b.1970 or 14 Sep 1972? 1.60m 50kg. Soldier.
At 10000m (5000m): OG: '92- 3 (h); WCh: '91- 13; WJ: '88- 1 (3); WCp: '89- 2, '92- 1; AfCh: '89- 1 (2), '90- 3. World CC: '89- 1 Jnr, '91- 9, '93- 8.
World junior records in 1988 and 1989 at both 5000m and 10000m.
Progression at 5000m, 10000m: 1988- 13:23.27, 27:50.24; 1989- 13:23.17, 27:17.82; 1990- 13:35.67, 27:42.65; 1991- 13:21.27, 27:47.70; 1992- 13:17.61, 27:38.37. pb 3000m 8:00.4 '89.
Collected the biggest ever prize in athletics history, $500,000, for his world road record 27:40 for 10k in Jakarta 24 Jan 1993. Was surely older than his official age of 15 when he ran world junior records in 1988.

FITA Bayissa b.15 Dec 1972 1.75m 52kg. Policeman.

At 5000m (10000m): OG: '92- 3 (9); WCh: '91- 2, '93-3 (dnf); WJ: '90- 1; AfG: '91- 1, '93- (2); WCp: '92- 1. World CC: '90- 3 Jnr, '91- 3 Jnr, '92- 3. World junior 5000m record 1991.
Progression at 5000m, 10000m: 1990- 13:42.59, 1991- 13:16.64; 1992- 13:13.03, 27:14.26; 1993- 13:05.40, 27:26.90. pb 3000m 7:55.50 '92.
Won IAAF World Cross Challenge 1991/2. Won at Bislett Games in 10,000m début in 27:14,26 in 1992.

HAILE Guebre Selassie b.18 Apr 1973 1.60m 64kg. Policeman.
At 5000m/10000m: WCh: '93- 2/1; WJ: '92- 1/1; AfG: '93 - 2/3. World CC: '91- 8J, '92- 2J, '93- 7. Ethiopian 5000m record 1993.
Progression at 5000m, 10000m: 1992- 13:36.06, 28:31.62; 1993- 13:03.17, 27:30.17. pb 3000m 7:47.8 '93.
After finishing a place behind Ismael Kirui at two successive World Junior cross-country championships, he outkicked his rival to complete a brilliant double at the 1992 World Juniors.

WORKU Bikila b.1970. Policeman.
At 5000m: WCh: '93- 6; OG: '92- 6; AfrG: '93- 3. World CC: '93- 9.
Progression at 5000m: 1992- 13:23.52, 1993- 13:06.64. pb 3000m 7:47.6 '93.

Haile Guebre Silassie: A controversial 10,000 metres win at Stuttgart

Women

DERARTU Tulu b. 21 Mar 1972 Arusi province 1.55m 44kg. Prison administrator in Addis Ababa.
At 10000m (3000m): OG: '92- 1; WCh: '91- 8; WJ: '90- 1; AfG: '91- 1; AfCh: '90- 1 (1), '92 - 1 (1); WCp: '92- 1 (1). World CC: '89- 23, '90- 15, '91- 2.
Two African 10000m records 1992. World junior 10000m record 1984 (32:08.74), Ethiopian records 1500m, 5000m (2), 10000m (4) 1991-2.
Progression at 3000m, 10000m: 1990- 9:11.21, 32:56.26; 1991- 9:01.04, 31:45.95; 1992- 9:01.12, 31:06.02. pbs: 1500m 4:12.08 '92, 5000m 15:21.29 '91. Undefeated on the track in 1992, but missed most of 1993 season through injury.

FINLAND

Governing body: Suomen Urheiluliitto, Radiokatu 20, SF-00240 Helsinki. Founded 1906.
National Championships first held in 1907 (men), 1913 (women). **1993 Champions**: **Men**: 100m: Janne Haapasalo 10.59, 200m: Ari Pakarinen 21.10, 400m: Janne Pajunen 48.13, 800m/1500m: Ari Suhonen 1:48.02/3:42.51, 5000m/10,000m: Santtu Mäkinen 14:07.48/ 28:50.39, Mar: Yrjö Pesonen 2:19:43, 3000mSt: Ville Hautala 8:39.10, 110mh: Antti Haapakoski 13.81, 400mh: Vesa-Pekka Pihlavisto 50.19, HJ: Juha Isolehto 2.24, PV: Jani Lehtonen 5.70, LJ: Juha Kivi 7.99, TJ: Heikki Herva 16.25, SP: Markus Koistinen 18.91, DT: Martti Halmesmäki 56.72, HT: Marko Wahlman 72.60, JT: Seppo Räty 85.68, Dec: Mikko Valle 7764, 20kmW: Kari Ahonen 1:28:33, 50kmW: Antero Lindman 3:59:57. **Women**: 100m/200m: Sanna Hernesniemi 11.41/23.31, 400m: Satu Jääskeläinen 53.28, 800m: Marjo Piiponen 2:06.19, 1500m: Monika Rönnholm 4:20.26, 3000m: Päivi Tikkanen 9:11.64, 10000m: Ritva Lemettinen 33:20.41, Mar: Anne Jääskeläinen 2:43:32, 100mh: Jutta Kemilä 13.72, 400mh: Marjut Töyli 58.23, HJ: Johanna Manninen 1.84, LJ: Nina Saarman 6.28, TJ: Marikka Salminen 13.44, SP: Asta Ovaska 16.56, DT: Kati Siltovuori 52.28, JT: Päivi Alafrantti 61.66, Hep: Helle Aro 6106, 5000mW/10kmW: Sari Essayah 20:38.65/44:38. Women's 800m/1500m originally won by Minna Lainio 2:01.99/4:10.70, but lost when she received a four-year drugs ban.

Petri KESKITALO b.10 Mar 1967 Kokkola 1.87m 87kg. Oulun Pyrintö. PR consultant.
At Dec: OG: '88- 11, '92- dnf; WCh: '87- dnf, '91- 5, '93- 11; EC: '86- 16, '90- dnf; WJ: '86- 1; EJ: '83- 5, '85- dnf. Won Finnish LJ 1986, Dec 1987; ECp B Dec 1989.

Three Finnish decathlon records 1988-91.
Progression at Dec: 1983- 7300, 1984- 7491, 1986- 7623, 1987- 8016, 1988- 8143, 1989- 8170, 1990- 8012, 1991- 8318, 1993- 8076. pbs: 100m 10.73/10.67w '86, 200m 21.85 '84, 400m 48.9 '84, 49.77 '88, 1500m 4:46.03 '91, 110mh 14.03/ 13.94w '88, HJ 2.03 '91, PV 5.03 '93, LJ 7.82 '88, TJ 14.09 '81, SP 15.44 '91, DT 46.78 '88, JT 69.22 '91.
He was Finland's top 14-year-old in eight events in 1981, and in the top three in three more. Made a fine comeback in 1991 after operations on both Achilles tendons.

Kimmo KINNUNEN b.31 Mar 1968 Äänekoski 1.87m 98kg. Forest foreman. Äänekosken Urheilijat.
At JT: OG: '88- 10, '92- 4; WCh: '91- 1, '93- 2; EC: '90- 8; WJ: '86- 5; EJ: '85- 9, '87- 5. 2nd GP 1991.
Progression at JT: 1984- 60.74, 1985- 78.40, new: 1986- 71.72, 1987- 72.94, 1988- 80.24, 1989- 83.10, 1990- 81.46, 1991- 90.82, 1992- 83.42, 1993- 84.78.
Improved his pb from 85.46 to 88.48 in qualifying, and to 90.82 with his first throw in the final to take the gold medal in Tokyo 1991. Threw a 16-year-old world best with 600g javelin, 82.36 in 1984. Coached by his father Jorma, who set a world record of 92.70m in 1969 and competed at three Olympic Games, with the silver medal in 1968. His brother Jarkko (b.21 Apr 1970) was second in 1989 European Juniors, pb 79.70 '90.

Valentin KONONEN b.7 Mar 1969 Helsinki 1.81m 68kg. Korson Kaiku. Marketing student.
At 50kmW: OG: '92- 7; WCh: '91- 5, '93- 2; EC: '90- 6; WCp: '93- 6. Won Finnish 20kmW 1991-2.
Finnish walks records: track 10,000m (2) 1992-3, 20,000m 1993, road 50km 1993.
Progression at 50kmW: 1989- 4:02:34, 1990- 3:56:40, 1991- 3:48:54, 1992- 3:52:27, 1993- 3:42:02. pbs: 5000mW 20:09.2 '92, 10000mW 39:30.95 '93, 20kmW:1:22:22.6t '93.
Brother and sisters are performers with the Finnish National Ballet.

Juha LAUKKANEN b.6 Jan 1969 Pielavesi 1.86m 95kg. Laukkalan Luja. Student.
At JT: OG: '92- 6; WJ: '88- 10. Finnish champion 1992. World junior javelin record 1987.
Progression at JT: 1986- 74.40, 1987- 79.46, 1988- 77.08, 1989- 78.68, 1990- 83.36, 1991- 87.06, 1992- 88.22, 1993- 84.58.

Jani LEHTONEN b.11 Aug 1968 Helsinki 1.79m 72kg. Keski-Uusimaan Urh., Tuusula.
At PV: OG: '92- dnq 14=; WCh: '91- dnq 15=, '93- dnq 19; EC: '90- nh; WI: '93- 5; WJ: '87- 8; EJ: '86- 7. Finnish champion 1989, 1993.
Four Finnish pole vault records 1990-3.
Progression at PV: 1982- 3.81, 1983- 4.10, 1984- 4.51, 1985- 4.90, 1986- 5.15, 1987- 5.31, 1988- 5.30, 1989- 5.60, 1990- 5.71, 1991- 5.73, 1992- 5.60, 1993- 5.82. pb 100m 10.63 '91.

Ari PAKARINEN b.14 May 1969 1.82m 90kg, Pyhäselän Urheilljat.
At JT: WCh: '91- dnq 19, '93- 5
Progression at JT: 1987- 64.04, 1988- 71.46, 1989- 79.30, 1990- 80.76, 1991- 82.52, 1992- 84.00, 1993- 83.06.

Seppo RÄTY b.27 Apr 1962 Helsinki 1.89m 110kg. Tohmajärven Urheilijat. Former factory worker.
At JT: OG: '88- 3, '92- 2; WCh: '87- 1, '91- 2, '93- dnq 28; EC: '86- dnq 17, '90- 5. Won ECp B 1993. Finnish champion 1985-6, 1989-91, 1993.
Two world javelin records 1991 and six Finnish records 1986-92. WIB 81.48 in 1990.
Progression at JT: 1978- 59.04, 1979- 63.20, 1980- 71.14, 1981- 75.44, 1982- 72.74, 1983- 74.38, 1984- 82.60, 1985- 85.72, new: 1986- 81.72, 1987- 83.54, 1988- 83.26, 1989- 83.92, 1990- 86.92, 1991- 96.96R, 1992- 90.60, 1993- 85.68.
One of the most surprising world champions of 1987, when he twice improved his national record in Rome. In 1991 he sensationally twice improved his best by five metres with world records at 91.98 and 96.96.

Women

Päivi ALAFRANTTI b.8 May 1964 Tervola, Lappland 1.78m 80kg. Viipurin Urheilijat. Sports instructor.
At JT: OG: '88- 10, '92- dnq; WCh: '91- 8, '93- dnq 13; EC: '90- 1; WSG: 89- 3; ECp: '93- 5. Finnish champion 1989, 1993.
Progression at JT: 1977- 38.58, 1978- 42.68, 1979- 43.44, 1980- 43.56, 1981- 39.26, 1982- 51.24, 1983- 45.74, 1984- 58.66, 1985- 60.60, 1986- 57.04, 1987- 57.66, 1988- 63.18, 1989- 64.92, 1990- 67.68, 1991- 66.14, 1992- 66.06, 1993- 64.98. pbs: SP 15.28 '84, DT 44.92 '89.
Improved her pb by over 2 metres to take gold in Split, and the first ever European medal by a Finnish woman at the javelin; but only after a judging error that gave her three no throws in qualifying was corrected. World indoor javelin record 59.12m in 1990. At weightlifting has set Finnish records and was ninth in the 1987 world championships.

Sari ESSAYAH b.21 Feb 1967 Haukivuori 1.62m 50kg. Lapinlahden Veto. Economics student.
At 10kmW: OG: '92-4; WCh: '87- 19, '91- 3, '93- 1; EC: '90- 5; WSG: '91- 1; WCp: '89- 37, '91- 2. At 5000mW: EJ: '85- 11; WSG: '89- 3. At

3000mW: WI: '93- 7. Finnish champion 5000mW 1987-93, 10kmW 1989-91, 1993.
Finnish records 1987-93: track 3000m (7), 5000m (6), 10,000m; 10km road (3).
Progression at 10kmW: 1983- 53:54, 1984- 52.08, 1985- 48:51.3t, 1987- 47:30, 1988- 44:26, 1989- 45:22, 1990- 43:47, 1991- 43:13, 1992- 43:37/ 44:15.8t, 1993- 42:37.0t. pbs: 3000m 11:59.60 '93, 5000m 20:38.65 '93, 20kmW 1:39:59 '89, Mar (running) 3:02:37 '88.
Married to triathlete Robert Knapp.

Heli RANTANEN b.26 Feb 1970 1.74m 72kg. Lammin Säkiä.
At JT: OG: '92-6; WCh: '91- 9, '93- 11; EC: '90- 13; EJ: '89- 5. Finnish champion 1991-2.
Progression at JT: 1984- 39.46, 1985- 48.68, 1986- 51.34, 1987- 50.04, 1988- 47.94, 1989- 54.74, 1990- 60.88, 1991- 64.66, 1992- 63.98, 1993- 61.38. pb SP: 12.85 '90.

Ringa ROPO b.16 Feb 1966 Kangasniemi 1.77m 63kg. Helsingin Kisa-Veikot. Marketing student.
At LJ: OG: '92- dnq 14; WCh: '87- dnq 13, '91- 9; EC: '90- 8; WI: '89- 4; EI: '89- 3. At HJ: EJ: '83- 10=. Won FIN HJ 1987, LJ 1986-92; ECp B 1989.
Five Finnish long jump records 1988-90.
Progression at LJ: 1980- 5.75, 1981- 5.70, 1982- 5.74, 1983- 5.98, 1986- 6.29, 1987- 6.55, 1988- 6.67, 1989- 6.82/6.84w, 1990- 6.85, 1991- 6.79, 1992- 6.75/6.93w, 1993- 6.63. pbs: 60m 7.49i '92, 100m 11.73 '89, 200m 24.42 '88, 24.28w, 100mh 14.28 '86, HJ 1.88i/1.86 '87, DT 36.90 '86.
Had a serious back injury in 1984, after which she changed from HJ to LJ. Ankle operation July 1993. Her husband Juha Junnila (LJ 7.44 '87), was elected Finland's Male Model of the year in 1989. Ringa had been voted 'Miss World Championships' at Budapest 1989.

Satu RUOTSALAINEN b.21 Oct 1966 Oulu 1.75m 63kg. Oulun Pyrintö. Physiotherapist
At Hep: OG: '88- 15, '92- dnf; WCh: '91- 4; EC: '90- dnf. Won Finnish 100mh 1988-91, Hep 1987, 1990.
Four Finnish heptathlon records 1987-91.
Progression at Hep: 1982- 4530, 1983- 5165, 1984- 5199, 1985- 5580, 1987- 5948, 1988- 6101, 1989- 6224, 1990- 6040, 1991- 6404, 1992- 6362. pbs: 100m 12.12 '91, 200m 24.07 '92, 23.80w '92; 800m 2:13.06 '88, 100mh 13.35 '92, HJ 1.88 '91, LJ 6.63 '92, SP 13.41i '91, 13.25 '92; JT 47.38 '88.
Achilles tendon operation in May 1993.

FRANCE

Governing body: Fédération Française d'Athlétisme, 10 rue du Faubourg Poissonnière, 75480 Paris Cedex 10. Founded 1920.

National Championships first held in 1888 (men), 1918 (women). **1993 Champions**: **Men**: 100m/200m: Jean-Charles Trouabal 10.19/ 20.74, 400m: Stéphane Diagana 45.26, 800m: Jean-Christophe Vialettes 1:47.91, 1500m: Éric Dubus 3:42.91, 5000m: Atiq Naaji 13:41.52 (M'Hamed Choumassi MAR 13:40.92), 10000m: Mustapha Essaïd 28:25.70, Half Mar: Bruno Léger 62:27, Mar: Dominique Chauvelier 2:12:11, 3000mSt: Thierry Brusseau 8:36.94, 110mh: Dan Philibert 13.52w, 400mh: David Niaré 50.30 (Hubert Rakotombélontsoa MAD 49.94), HJ: Xavier Robilliard 2.24, PV: Jean Galfione 5.93, LJ: Kader Klouchi 7.82 (Cheikh Tidiane Touré SEN 7.88), TJ: Pierre Camara 17.30, SP: Luc Viudes 18.29, DT: Jean-Claude Retel 60.32, HT: Raphaël Piolanti 78.72, JT: Pascal Lefèvre 80.00, 20kmW: Denis Langlois 1:23:01, 50kmW: Thierry Toutain 3:47:38. **Women**: 100m: Valérie Jean-Charles 11.38, 200m: Maguy Nestoret 23.62, 400m: Francine Landre 51.92, 800m: Barbara Gourdet 2:02.55, 1500m: Blandine Bitzner 4:14.05, 3000m: Annette Sergent-Palluy 9:04.75, 10000m: Rosario Murcia 33:00.96, Half Mar: Annick Clouvel 72:31, Mar: Maria Rebelo 2:30:26, 100mh: Patricia Girard 12.91, 400mh: Carole Nelson 57.35, HJ: Maryse Maury 1.86, LJ: Corinne Hérigault 6.33, TJ: Caroline Honoré 13.65, SP: Fabienne Locuty 15.73, DT: Isabelle Devaluez 52.62, JT: Martine Bégue 64.46, 10kmW: Valérie Lévêque 49:27.

Alain BLONDEL b.7 Dec 1962 Petit-Quevilly 1.86m 80kg. Stade Sotteville. Computer scientist.
At Dec: OG: '88- 6, '92- 15; WCh: '87- 7, '91- 13, '93- 5; EC: '86- 8, '90- 5; ECp: '91- 3, '93- 3. French champion 1986, 1992.
Progression at Dec: 1981- 5873, 1982- 6494*, 1983- 6959, 1984- 7668, 1985- 7763, 1986- 8185, 1987- 8228, 1988- 8387, 1989- 8182, 1990- 8216, 1991- 8211, 1992- 8285, 1993- 8444. pbs: 100m 10.74w '86, 10.89 '90; 200m 21.78 '88, 21.73w '89; 400m 47.44 '88, 1500m 4:09.90 '90, 110mh 14.07 '86, 14.0w '90; 400mh 51.16 '87, HJ 2.04 '84, PV 5.40 '93, LJ 7.50/7.56i '87, 7.59w '86; SP 14.06 '93, DT 47.28 '90, JT 64.46 '92, 1Hr Dec: 7715 '90, Hep 6087i '91.

Pierre CAMARA b.10 Sep 1965 Castres 1.81m 74kg. Neuilly-Plaisance.
At TJ: OG: '92- 11; WCh: '91- dnq 22, '93- 5; WI: '93- 1; EC: '90- dnq 15; ECp: '89- 5, '93- 1. French champion 1988, 1990, 1992-3.
Progression at TJ: 1983- 15.35, 1984- 16.40, 1986- 16.52i/16.29, 1986- 16.28i/16.02, 1987- 16.82, 1988- 16.79, 1989- 16.87, 1990- 16.87, 1991- 17.08, 1992- 17.34, 1993- 17.30/17.46w/17.59i. pb LJ 7.54 '84.

Lives with Laurence Bily (French 100m rec 11.04 '90, 2nd EI 60m 1989 and 1990); their son Nathy born 28 Nov 1993. Pierre's father came from Guinea.

Philippe COLLET b.13 Dec 1963 Nancy 1.77m 76kg. ASPTT Grenoble. Company manager.
At PV: OG: '88- 5=, '92- 7; WCh: '87- dnq, '91- nh; EC: '86- 3, '90- 4; EI: '86- 3; WCp: '85- 2, '89- 1, '92- 2; EJ: '81- 11; ECp: '85- 2, '89- 4, '91- 4=; WSG: '85- 2.Won FRA PV 1985, 1988-9, 1991-2.
French indoor pole vault records 1989 (2nd) & 1990 in Masters at Grenoble.
Progression at PV: 1978- 3.30, 1979- 4.10, 1980- 4.90, 1981- 5.10, 1982- 5.20, 1983- 5.60, 1984- 5.60, 1985- 5.80, 1986- 5.85, 1987- 5.80i/5.75, 1988- 5.80, 1989- 5.92i/5.75, 1990- 5.94i/5.80, 1991- 5.80, 1992- 5.80, 1993- 5.20. pbs: 100m 10.81w '85, Dec 7011 '86.

Stéphane DIAGANA b.23 Jul 1969 Saint-Affrique 1.86m 75kg. EA Franconville. Biology student.
At 400mh: OG: '92- 4; WCh: '93- 4; EC: '90- 5; WCp: '92- 3; ECp: '93- 1. Won French 400m 1992-3, 400mh 1990.
Seven French 400mh records 1990-3.
Progression at 400mh: 1987- 54.1, 1989- 51.60, 1990- 48.92, 1991- 51.90, 1992- 48.13, 1993- 47.64. pbs: 200m 20.81i '92, 20.95 '93, 400m 45.18 '92, 60mh 8.10i '88, 110mh 14.56 '87.

Stephane Diagana: a French record when finishing fourth in Stuttgartt

His father came from the Congo, of Sénégalese origin. From a best of 51.60 pre 1990, he ran 50.11 to win the French title, then 49.26 and 48.92 in Split. In 1992 he ran 48.55 prior to the Olympics where he ran French records in each round.

Christophe EPALLE b.23 Jan 1969 St Etienne 1.94m 109kg. Stade Bordeaux. Student.
At HT: OG: '92- 10; WCh: '93- 8; WJ: '88- 8; WSG: '91- 5, '93- 3; ECp: '93- 2. Won NCAA HT & 35lbWt indoors1991.
French hammer record 1993.
Progression at HT: 1985- 49.76, 1986- 56.76, 1987- 60.54, 1988- 63.52, 1989- 67.00, 1990- 68.90, 1991- 73.52, 1992- 76.86, 1993- 79.98. pbs: SP 17.48 '91, DT 54.98 '92, 35lbWt 22.73i '91.

Jean GALFIONE b.9 Jun 1971 Paris 1.84m 82kg. Stade Français. Student.
At PV: OG: '92- dnq 13; WCh: '91- 10, '93- 8; WI: '93- 3; WJ: '90- 1; EJ: 89- 9; EI: '92- 4; WSG: '93- 3; ECp: '93- 4. French champion 1993.
Two French pole vault records 1993.
Progression at PV: 1987- 4.15, 1988- 5.16, 1989- 5.50, 1990- 5.60i/5.45, 1991- 5.80, 1992- 5.90, 1993- 5.93. pbs: 100m 10.7 '92, 110mh 15.2 '92, HJ 2.01 '92, Dec 7068 '92.

Serge HÉLAN b.24 Feb 1964 Pointe-à-Pitre, Guadeloupe 1.76m 70kg. CA Montreuil
At TJ: OG: '84- 8, '92- dnq 20; WCh: '87- dnq 17, '91- dnq 21, '93- 9; EC: '86- 9, '90- dnq; EJ: '83- 6; WI: '89- 6; EI: '87- 1, '92- 2. French champion 1986-7, 1989, 1991. At LJ: WI: '85- 6.
French triple jump records 1986 and 1991.
Progression at TJ: 1981- 13.98, 1982- 15.83, 1983- 16.12, 1984- 16.66, 1985- 16.69, 1986- 17.13, 1987- 17.15i/16.84, 1988- 17.01, 1989- 17.12i/16.78, 1990- 17.10, 1991- 17.45, 1992- 17.18, 1993- 17.25. pb LJ 8.12 '92.

Antonio 'Tony' MARTINS Bordelo b.23 Aug 1963 Vimioso, Portugal 1.69m 58kg. J A Marignane SA. French citizen from 1989. Navy fireman.
At 10000m: OG: '92- 15; World CC: '92- 12. Won French 5000m 1992.
French records 5000m and 10000m 1992 (first since Alain Mimoun 1952 to hold both).
Progression at 5000m, 10000m: 1986- 14:26.0, 30:10.6; 1987- 14:08.46, 1988- 13:46.80, 1989- 13:34.48, 1990- 13:45.17, 1991- 13:31.25, 1992- 13:14.47, 27:22.78; 1993- 13:21.23, 27:42.35. pbs: 1500m 3:44.5 '89, 3000m 7:47.22 '91.

Dan PHILIBERT b.6 Aug 1970 Paris 1.83m 77kg. US Créteil. Student.
At 110mh: OG: '92- sf; WCh: '91- 5, '93- sf; WJ:

'88- 7; EJ: 89- h. French champion 1991-3.
Progression at 110mh: 1987- 14.08/13.92w, 1989- 13.84/13.65w/13.6, 1990- 13.66, 1991- 13.33, 1992- 13.35, 1993- 13.42. pbs: 50mh 6.66i '91, 60mh 7.67i '91.
Martiniquean father. Won the Mediterranean Games 110mh 1991 and 1993.

René PILLER b.23 Apr 1965 Héricourt 1.68m 56kg. GA Haut-Saônois. Railways employee.
At 50kmW: OG: '92- 15; WCh: '91- 8, '93- 6; EC: '90- 15; WCp: '93- 12. Won French 50km 1989, 1990, 1992; 100kmW 1988, 1991.
Progression at 50kmW: 1986- 4:18:01, 1987- 4:06:52, 1988- 3:54:06.5t, 1989- 3:51.17, 1990- 3;56:36.1t, 1991- 3:55:48, 1992- 4:02:12, 1993- 3:48:57. pbs: 5000mW 20:09.03 '93, 10kmW , 20kmW 1:22:16 '92, 1HrW 14715m '92, 100kmW 9:14:12 '88.

Christian PLAZIAT b.28 Oct 1963 Lyon 1.91m 87kg. Ind. Lyonnais.
At Dec: OG: '88- 5, '92- dnf; WCh: '87- 4, '91- 9, '93- 6; EC: '86- 7, '90- 1; ECp: '89- 1, '91- 1, '93- 2. French champion 1987-90. At Hep: EI: '92- 1. At HJ: EJ: '81- 12.
Six French decathlon records 1987-90. WIB octathlon 7084 '89, heptathlon 6273 '90, 6277 '91, 6289 & 6418 '92.
Progression at Dec: 1981- 6489, 1982- 7221, 1983- 7770, 1985- 8211w/8018, 1986- 8196, 1987- 8315, 1988- 8512, 1989- 8485, 1990- 8574, 1991- 8518, 1992- dnf, 1993- 8398. pbs: 60m 6.83i '92, 100m 10.55/10.44w '90, 10.3w '88, 10.4 '86; 200m 21.52/21.5 '90, 400m 47.10 '90, 1500m 4:23.49 '88, 50mh 6.69i '92, 60mh 7.91i '92, 110mh 13.92/13.86w '92, 13.9 '91, 400mh 51.03 '91, HJ 2.20 '83, PV 5.20i '92, 5.10 '88, LJ 7.90 '90, TJ 14.94i '90, 14.93 '89, SP 15.86 '86, DT 49.08 '86, JT 63.02 '85, new 58.22 '87.
Won all four decathlons contested in 1989, including Götzis, and in 1990 won both in French records, at Talence and in Split.

Pascal THIÉBAUT b.6 Jun 1959 Nancy 1.75m 60kg. ASPTT Nancy.
At 5000m: OG: '88- 11, '92- 13; WCh: '87- h; EC: '90- h; ECp: '91- 3. At 3000m: WI: '87- 7, '91- 6; EI: '87- 3. At 1500m: OG: '84- sf; WCh: '83- h, '91- sf; EC: '86- h; ECp: '83- 4, '85- 7, '89- 1, '93- 3. Won French 1500m 1984-6, 1992.
French 5000m record 1987.
Progression at 1500m, 5000m: 1976- 3:58.3; 1977- 3:53.6; 1978- 3:50.3; 1979- 3:45.4; 1980- 3:42.3; 1981- 3:40.62; 1982- 3:40.27; 1983- 3:36.07; 1984- 3:35.8; 1985- 3:35.50; 1986- 3:35.54, 13:37.05; 1987- 3:34.91, 13:14.60; 1988- 3:35.61, 13:17.48; 1989- 3:34.68, 13:26.32; 1990- 3:41.41, 13:31.45; 1991- 3:36.73, 13:19.72; 1992- 3:34.08, 13:19.24; 1993- 3:36.11, 13:40.11. pbs: 800m 1:47.1 '84, 1000m 2:17.71 '85, 1M 3:52.02 '84, 2000m 4:56.70 '87, 3000m 7:42.64 '89.

Thierry TOUTAIN b.14 Feb 1962 Fourmies 1.82m 75kg. GA Haut-Saônois. Policeman.
At 20kmW: OG: '88- 18, '92- dq WCh: '91- 9; EC: '90- 3; WCp: '89- 10, '91- 3. At 50kmW: WCh: '87- 14; WCp: '87- 15, '93- 18. Won French 20kmW 1989-91, 50kmW 1988, 1993.
At 30km and 2 hours track walk: French records 2:09:15.3 and 27,894m 1989, World 1991. French road and track walk records 20km 1990, 1 hour track and 50km 1993.
Progression at 20kmW: 1982- 1:33:25.5, 1983- 1:40:18.41t, 1984- 1:29:50.4, 1985- 1:33:05.0t, 1986- 1:30:25.3, 1987- 1:28:58.97t, 1988- 1:22:55, 1989- 1:22:06, 1990- 1:21:25, 1991- 1:20:56, 1992- 1:21:14.9t. pbs: 50kmW 3:47:38 '93; track 3000mW 19:53.11i '88, 5000mW 19:49.1 '93, 20kmW 1:21:14.9 '92, 30kmW 2:03:56.5 '91, 1HrW 15167m '93, 2HrW 29,090m '91.

Jean-Charles TROUABAL b.20 May 1965 Paris 1.87m 77kg. CO Ulis. PE teacher.
At 200m/R- 4x100m relay: OG: '92- h; WCh: '91- 6/2R, '93- 6; EC: '90- 2/1R; ECp: '91- 1/1R, '93- 2R. At 100m: OG: '88- qf. Won French 100m 1992-3, 200m 1988, 1990-3.
World 4x100m record 1990.
Progression at 200m: 1984- 21.7, 1985- 21.38, 1986- 21.54, 1987- 20.94/20.88w, 1988- 20.55, 1989- 20.71/20.68w, 1990- 20.31, 1991- 20.30, 1992- 20.40, 1993- 20.20. pbs: 60m 6.65i '92, 100m 10.19 '93, 400m 46.92 '90.
Martiniquean origin.

Women

Monique EWANJÉ-ÉPÉE b.11 Jul 1967 Poitiers 1.73m 62kg. US Créteil.
At 100mh: OG: '88- 7, '92- h; WCh: '91- 4; EC: '86- sf, '90- 1; EJ: '85- 1 (6 Hep); WSG: '89- 1; ECp: '89- 1B, '91- 2. French champion 1989-91. At 60mh: WI: '91- 2; EI: '90- 2, '92- 2. Won GP 100mh 1990.
European junior record 1985, two French 100mh records 1989-90.
Progression at 100mh: 1983- 14.6, 1984- 13.78, 1985- 13.10, 1986- 13.07, 1987- 12.98, 1988- 12.87/12.86w, 1989- 12.65, 1990- 12.56, 1991- 12.67, 1992- 13.01. pbs: 100m 11.86/11.6 '86, 200m 24.83 '85, 50mh 6.81 '91, 60mh 7.82i '91, HJ 1.74 '85, LJ 6.23 '85, SP 12.32 '85, Hep 5493 '85.
Married Christophe Tourret (5.20 PV '90) on 13 Dec 1991; daughter Mary-Lou born on 23 Sep 1993. Her father was from Cameroun; her sister Maryse (b.4 Sep 1964), now Maury, set four French high jump records 1983-5, best 1.96 '85, was fourth at the 1984 Olympics, and at the European Indoors: '83- 3, '84- 2, '89- 3.

Marie-José Pérec: switched to the 200 metres for 1993

Patricia GIRARD b.8 Apr 1968 Pointe-à-Pitre, Guadeloupe 1.62m 48kg. Neuilly Plaisance Sports.
At 100mh/4x100mR: OG: '88- 7R, '92- 4R (sf 100m); WCh: '93- sf/R; ECp: '93- 2R. French champion 1993. At 60mh: WI: '93- 3; EI: '90- 4.
Progression at 100mh: 1985- 14.4, 1986- 13.82w, 1987- 13.45, 1988- 13.42, 1989- 13.53, 1992- 12.91, 1993- 12.91. pbs: 50m 6.28i '93, 60m 7.17i '90, 100m 11.20 '93, 200m 23.49 '92, 60mh 8.01i '93.
Two year drugs ban after positive test 17 Mar 1990.

Marie-José PÉREC b.9 May 1968 Basse Terre, Guadeloupe 1.80m 60kg. Stade Français.
At 400m/4x100mR: OG: '92- 1; WCh: '91- 1/5R; EC: '90- 3; WCp: '89- dq; won E.Cup B 1989. At 200m: OG: '88- qf; WCh: '93- 4/4R; EI: '89- 1; WI: '89- 6; WCp: '92- 1/2R; ECp: '93- 2/2R (2 100m). Won French 100m 1991, 200m 1992, 400m 1988, 400mh 1989.
French records: 100m 1991, three 200m 1991-3, seven 400m 1988-92.
Progression at 200m/400m: 1984- 25.44/25.0; 1985- 24.14; 1986- 24.33/24.00w; 1987- 24.52; 1988- 22.72, 51.35; 1989- 22.36, 51.05; 1990- 22.92, 50.84; 1991- 22.26, 49.13; 1992- 22.20, 48.83; 1993- 21.99. pbs: 60m 7.29i '92, 100m 10.96 '91, 300m 36.81 '88, 400mh 55.76 '89.
Disqualified for breaking lane after winning the 1989 World Cup 400m in 50.30. Ran French records of 50.53 and 49.32 in her first two races at 400m in 1991, then 49.76 to win in Nice and then improved to 49.13 to win the world title.

GERMANY

Governing body: Deutscher Leichtathletik Verband (DLV), Julius-Reiber-Strasse 19, PO Box 110463, D-6100 Darmstadt. Founded 1898.
National Championships first held in 1891.
1993 Champions: **Men**: 100m: Marc Blume 10.30, 200m: Robert Kurnicki 20.46, 400m: Thomas Schönlebe 46.28, 800m: Nico Motchebon 1:49.69, 1500m: Jens-Peter Herold 3:49.86, 5000m: Rainer Wachenbrunner 13:51.96, 10000m: Stephane Franke 27:57.98, Half Mar: Stephan Freigang 65:34, Mar: Kurt Stenzel 2:13:25, 3000mSt: Steffen Brand 8:26.81, 110mh: Dietmar Koszewski 13.56, 400mh: Michael Kaul 50.39, HJ: Hendrik Beyer 2.33, PV: Tom Lobinger 5.50, LJ: Georg Ackermann 8.00w, TJ: Ralf Jaros 17.13, SP: Sven Buder 20.15, DT: Lars Riedel 65.48, HT: Jörn Hubner 72.62, JT: Raymund Hecht 81.88, Dec: Christian Schenk 8109, 20kmW: Robert Ihly 1:23:15, 50kmW: Hartwig Gauder 3:52:46. Women: 100m: Melanie Paschke 11.23, 200m: Silke Knoll 22.74, 400m: Anja Rücker 52.43, 800m: Birte Bruhns 2:01.73, 1500m: Simone Weidner 4:15.62, 3000m: Claudia Lokar 9:02.66, 10000m: Kathrin Wessel 32:09.52, Half Mar/Mar: Birgit Jerschabek 74:08/2:30:34, 100mh: Kristin Patzwahl 12.98, 400mh: Silvia Rieger 55.42, HJ: Heike Henkel 2.00, PV: Carmen Haage 3.85, LJ: Susen Tiedtke 6.77, TJ: Helga Radtke 14.05, SP: Kathrin Neimke 19.56, DT: Anja Gündler 61.84, HT: Simone Mathes 53.36, JT: Silke Renk 65.46, Hep: Birgit Clarius 6500, 5000mW/10kmW: Beate Anders 22:55.75/43:12.
In championships won below, note FRG and GDR to 1990, GER from 1991.

Dieter BAUMANN b.9 Feb 1965 Blaustein 1.78m 64kg. LG Bayer Leverkusen. Photographic worker.
At 5000m: OG: '88- 2, '92- 1; WCh: '91- 4; EC: '86- h. At 1500m: WCh: '87- sf; ECp: '87- 5. At 3000m: WI: '89- 3; EI: '87- 2, '89- 1. At 1500m: WI: '87- 7; ECp: '87- 5, '89- dq. Won FRG 1500m 1987-9, 5000m 1986, 1988, 1991-2.
German records 3000m 1991, 5000m 1992.
Progression at 1500m, 5000m: 1982- 4:03.75, 15:42.96; 1983- 3:52.99, 14:40.4; 1984- 3:50.37, 14:21.59; 1985- 3:40.48, 13:48.0; 1986- 3:36.40, 13:35.04; 1987- 3:33.54, 13:30.85; 1988- 3:34.82, 13:15.52; 1989- 3:34.25, 13:18.58; 1990- 3:40.38; 1991- 3:34.93, 13:24.58; 1992- 3:33.91, 13:09.03. pbs: 800m: 1:48.40 '90, 1000m 2:18.79i '89, 2:22.4

'86, 1M 3:51.12 '92, 2000m 4:59.88 '87, 3000m 7:33.91 '91, 10000m 29:03.33 '89.
Missed most of 1990 season through injury. Undefeated in 5000m finals in 1992, when he added Olympic gold to the silver he had won in 1988. Missed 1993 season through injury. Married to his coach Isabell (née Hozang) who ran at 1500m in the 1981 European Juniors.

Wolf-Hendrik BEYER b.14 Feb 1972 Düsseldorf 2.00m 82kg. LG Bayer Leverkusen.
At HJ: OG: '92- dnq; WCh: '93- dnq 18; WI: '93- 7; WJ: '90- 4; ECp: '93- 4. GER champion 1993.
Progression at HJ: 1988- 2.00, 1989- 2.17, 1990- 2.23, 1991- 2.25i/2.20, 1992- 2.32, 1993- 2.36i/2.33.

Steffen BRAND b.10 Mar 1965 Recklinghausen 1.76m 66kg. Bayer Leverkusen. Medical student.
At 3000mSt: OG: '92- 5; WCh: '93- 6; ECp: '93- 1. At 5000m: ECp: '87- 5, '89- 6. At 1500m: EI: '90- 4. Won FRG 5000m 1990, GER 3000mSt 1992-3.
Progression at 5000m, 3000mSt: 1983- 14:47.30, 1984- 14:19.17, 1985- 14:04.37, 1986- 14:17.90, 1987- 13:41.37, 1988- 13:38.99, 1989- 13:48.0, 1990- 13:29.25, 1992- 13:37.38, 8:16.60; 1993- 13:37.92, 8:15.33. pbs: 800m 1:50.0 '88, 1000m 2:21.22 '90, 1500m 3:37.85 '87, 3000m 7:52.83 '90.
Started at steeplechase as a junior (2000m 5:56.22 in 1983), and after missing 1991 through injury, returned with great success in 1992.

Oliver-**Sven BUDER** b.23 Jun 1966 Erlabrunn 2.00m 130kg. TV Wattenscheid. Student.
At SP: WCh: '91- 4, '93- 7; EC: '90- 2; EJ: '85- 1; ECp: '93- 4; WI: '91- 7, '93- 8; EI: '90- 3. Won GER 1991, 1993.
Progression at SP: 1984- 16.58, 1985- 19.34, 1986- 19.29, 1987- 20.14, 1988- 19.05, 1989- 20.22, 1990- 21.06, 1991- 20.20, 1992- 19.76i/19.70, 1993- 20.15. pb DT 54.14 '91.

Stéphane FRANKE b.12 Feb 1964 Versailles, France 1.76m 60kg. Salamander Kornwestheim.
At 10000m: OG: '92- h; WCh: '91- 12, '93- 4; ECp: '91- 3. Won GER 10000m 1993. 3rd GP 5000m 1993
Progression at 5000m, 10,000m: 1988- 14:14.43, 1989- 14:04.3, 1990- 13:50.90, 1991- 28:04.41, 1992- 13:48.12, 28:11.99; 1993- 13:13.17, 27:57.98. pbs: 800m 1:50.81 '88, 1000m 2:24.03 '85, 1500m 3:42.69 '85, 3000m 7:40.11 '93, Mar 2:19:18 '93.
Studied at George Mason and Cal State Pomona Universities, USA. In 1993 he made a great breakthrough. with World 4th at 10k; he reduced his 5000m best by 15 secs with 13:33.03 on 1 June and then another 20 secs to 13:13.17 fo 3rd in Brussels.

Stephan FREIGANG b.27 Sep 1967 Löbau 1.77m 64kg. SC Cottbus. Sports student.
At Mar: OG: '92- 3; WCh: '91- 18. At 10000m: WJ: '86- 4 (4 at 20km Rd); WSG: '91- 1; ECp: '89- 5. At 5000m: ECp: '93- 7. Won GDR 5000m 1989, GER Half Mar 1993.
Progression at 10,000m, Mar: 1986- 29:02.43, 1987- 29:32.70, 2:14:34; 1988- 29:14.36, 2:12:28; 1989- 28:51.01, 1990- 28:05.22, 2:09:45; 1991- 28:05.47, 2:12:00; 1992- 28:33.45, 2:14:00; 1993- 27:59.72, 2:11:53. pbs: 1500m 3:48.88 '93, 5000m 13:30.40 '93, Half Mar 61:14 '92.
At the marathon broke 2:10 when fourth in Berlin 1990; won at Budapest 1987, Palermo 1991, Frankfurt 1993.

Hartwig GAUDER b.10 Nov 1954 Vaihingen 1.86m 72kg. TSV Erfurt. Studied Architecture.
At 50kmW: OG: '80- 1, '88- 3, '92- 6; WCh: '87- 1, '91- 3, '93- dnf; EC: '82- 4, '86- 1, '90- 3; WCp: '81- 2, '85- 1, '87- 2, '91- 6, '93- 8. At 20kmW: EC: '78- 7; WCp: '79- 7. At 10000mW: EJ: '73- 1. Won GDR 20kmW 1975-6, 1985-6; 50kmW 1979, 1982, 1986; GER 1993.
WIB 1 hour walk 14906m 1986. GDR records: track 20kmW 1978; road 20kmW 1979, 30kmW (4) 1979-84 to 2:12:11 '84.
Progression at 20kmW, 50kmW: 1972- 1:34:19; 1973- 1:32:55; 1974- 1:28:47; 1975- 1:26:29; 1976- 1:26:25; 1977- 1:27:07; 1978- 1:24:22.7t; 1979- 1:21:39, 4:01:20; 1980- 1:23:36.6i, 3:48:15; 1981- 1:23:27, 3:46:57; 1982- 1:29:29, 3:49:44; 1983- 1:21:33, 3:43:23; 1984- 1:22:53, 3:41:24; 1985- 1:23:03, 3:43:33; 1986- 1:21:15, 3:40:55; 1987- 1:20.51, 3:40:53; 1988- 1:23:15, 3:39:45; 1990- 1:21:30, 3:47:08; 1991- 1:24:00, 3:49:10; 1992- 1:25:49, 3:56:47; 1993- 1:23:31, 3:52:46. Track pbs: 3000mW 11:20.0 '84, 5000mW 18:59.67i '88, 10000mW 39:13.15i '88, 20000mW 1:22:47.47 '90.
Family moved from West Germany to GDR when he was aged five. His feat of winning European junior and senior, Olympic and World titles is matched only by Daley Thompson and Khristo Markov. Returned in 1990 after a year's retirement.

Dietmar HAAF b.6 Mar 1967 Bad Cannstatt 1.73m 64kg. Salamander Kornwestheim. Electronics student at Stuttgart University, formerly USC, USA.
At LJ: OG: '92- dnq 14; WCh: '87- dnq, '91- 4; EC: '86- 10, '90- 1; WI: '89- 2, '91- 1; EI: '90- 1; WJ: '86- 1; EJ: '85- 5; ECp: '91- 1. FRG champion 1986-92.
Progression at LJ: 1981- 5.83, 1982- 6.48, 1983- 7.07, 1984- 7.54/7.66w, 1985- 7.78, 1986- 7.97, 1987- 8.05/8.10w, 1988- 8.04, 1989- 8.25i/7.99/ 8.22w, 1990- 8.25, 1991- 8.23/8.30w, 1992- 8.16,

1993- 8.09. pbs: 100m 10.5 '87, 10.82 '85; 200m 21.62 '86.
The smallest world class long jumper, he has a fine major meeting record. FRG indoor LJ record 1989.

Raymond HECHT b.11 Nov 68 Gardelegen 1.91m 93kg. TV Wattenscheid. Mechanical engineer.
At JT: WCh: '91- 12, '93- dnq 23; EC: '90- 10; ECp: '93- 4; EJ: '87- 3. GER champion 1993. 2nd GP 1993.
Three German javelin records 1991-3.
Progression at JT: 1984- 66.20, 1985- 69.32; new: 1986- 71.08 (71.14 old), 1987- 75.90, 1990- 83.24, 1991- 90.84, 1992- 79.58, 1993- 88.90.
As a junior was ranked fourth in the world in 1987. Missed 1988-9 and re-emerged in 1990.

Olaf HENSE b.19 Nov 1967 Dortmund. 1.87m 74kg. LG Olympia Dortmund.
At 400mh/4x400m relay: OG: '92- sf; WCh: '91- h, '93- sf/3R; EC: '90- sf; ECp: '93-2. German champion 1991-2.
Progression at 400mh: 1983- 56.29, 1984- 56.24, 1985- 55.15, 1986- 53.0, 1987- 52.28, 1988- 50.60, 1989- 50.21, 1990- 49.65, 1991- 49.73, 1992- 49.01, 1993- 48.48. pbs: 200m 21.72 '92, 400m 45.96 '93, 800m 1:49.60 '93.

Jens-Peter HEROLD b.2 Jun 1965 Neuruppin 1.76m 66kg. SCC Berlin. Mechanic.
At 1500m: OG: '88- 3, '92- 6; WCh: '87- 6, '91- 4, '93- h; EC: '90- 1; EI: '87- 2, '90- 1; WCp: '89- 3 (2 800m); ECp: '87- 3, '89- 4, '91- 2, '93- 6 (4 800m). Won GDR 800m 1987, 1989; 1500m 1987-90, GER 1500m 1991-3. 2nd GP 1M 1990, 2nd= 1500m 1991.
GDR records 1500m 1987, 1M (now GER) 1988.
Progression at 1500m: 1979- 4:23.5, 1981- 4:12.8, 1983- 3:48.87, 1984- 3:49.67, 1985- 3:43.9, 1986- 3:37.92, 1987- 3:33.28, 1988- 3:33.33, 1989- 3:34.00, 1990- 3:33.2, 1991- 3:34.3, 1992- 3:32.77, 1993- 3:34.42. pbs: 400m 49.5 '85, 800m 1:44.88 '90, 1000m 2:16.52 '93, 1M 3:49.22 '88, 2000m 4:56.23i '93, 3000m 8:00.60i '91, 5000m 14:14.5 '86.
Employed his finishing kick to best effect when he won gold in Split to complete the European double, indoors and out; his first major titles.

Robert IHLY b.5 May 1963 Asbest, USSR 1.74m 64kg. LG Offenburg. Engineer
At 20kmW: OG: '92- 11; WCh: '91- 6, '93- 7; EC: '90- 9; WCp: '93- 8. Won FRG/GER 20kmW 1990-3, 50kmW 1989-90.
Three FRG 20km walk records 1990, two road, one track.
Progression at 20kmW/50kmW: 1983- 1:30:00, 1984- 1:27:30, 1985- 1:25:47, 1986- 1:25:40?, 1987- 1:27:40, 4:02:08; 1988- 1:26:46/4:01:44, 1989- 1:23:45/4:05:45, 1990- 1:20:28/4:00:23, 1991- 1:20:52, 1992- 1:19:59, 1993- 1:21:26. pbs: 3000mW 19:04.52i '92, 1HrW 14605m '90; road 10kmW 39:31 '90.

Ralf JAROS b.13 Dec 1965 Düsseldorf 1.93m 85kg. Bayer Leverkusen. Businessman.
At TJ: OG: '84- dnq 17, '92- dnq 13; WCh: '91- 9, '93- 4; EC: '90- 12; WI: '85- 6; EJ: '83- 7; ECp: '85- 6, '91- 1, '93- 3. FRG/GER champion 1984-5, 1990-3. German TJ record 1991.
Progression at TJ: 1980- 13.86, 1981- 14.91, 1982- 15.92/16.27w, 1983- 16.51i/16.14, 1984- 16.81, 1985- 17.29, 1986- 16.94, 1987- 16.68, 1989- 16.65, 1990- 17.08, 1991- 17.66, 1992- 17.28, 1993- 17.34. pb LJ 7.93i '88, 7.78 '92.
After five years of having problems with his knees, has been world ranked 1991-3.

Michael KOHNLE b.3 May 1970 Göppingen 1.94m 90kg. TS Göppingen. Bankkaufmann.
At Dec: WCh: '91- 12, '93- 9; EC: '90- 11; WJ: '88- 1; EJ: '87- 4, '89- 1; ECp: '91- 8, '93- 11. Won FRG 1990.
Progression at Dec: 1987- 7279, 1988- 7790, 1989- 8114, 1990- 8289, 1991- 8062, 1992- 7994, 1993- 8075. pbs: 100m 10.69 '88, 10.58w '90, 10.3 '89; 200m 21.69 '88, 400m 48.31 '91, 1500m 4:38.65 '88, 60mh 8.16i '91, 110mh 14.27 '89, HJ 2.06 '90, PV 5.10 '89, LJ 7.70 '92, SP 15.52 '89, DT 45.82 '89 (45.86?), JT 63.36 '92.
Won the 1989 European junior title with the second best junior decathlon mark of all-time.

Dietmar KOSZEWSKI b.26 Jul 1967 Berlin 1.93m 89kg. LAC Halensee Berlin. Student.
At 110mh: OG: '92- sf; WCh: '91- h, '93- 7; EC: '90- 3; WSG: '89- 5, '93- 1. FRG champion 1989, GER 1993. At 60mh: EI: '90- 5. At Dec: WJ: '86- dnf.
Progression at 110mh: 1985- 14.56, 1986- 14.23, 1987- 14.03, 1988- 13.74/13.69w, 1989- 13.57, 1990- 13.41/13.39w, 1991- 13.47, 1992- 13.43, 1993- 13.44. pbs: 100m 10.88 '89, 200m 21.09 '89, 400m 48.43 '92, 50mh 6.51i '94, 60mh 7.55i '93, 400mh 53.28 '87, HJ 1.98 '84, PV 4.40 '85, LJ 7.47 '86, TJ 15.20 '85, Dec 7278 '86.
FRG junior champion at pentathlon, decathlon and TJ in 1985 before switching to hurdles.

Paul MEIER b.27 Jul 1971 Velbert 1.96m 90kg. Bayer Leverkusen. Mechanical engineering student.
At Dec: OG: '92- 6; WCh: '93- 3; WJ: '90- 8; ECp: '93- 1. EI Pen: '92- 5.
Progression at Dec: 1990- 7233, 1991- 7797, 1992- 8192, 1993- 8548. pbs: 100m 10.53 '93,

200m 21.46 '93, 400m 47.36 '93, 1500m 4:32.05 '93, 110mh 14.39 '93, HJ 2.15 '92, PV 4.90 '92, LJ 7.86/7.95w '93; SP 16.02 '92, DT 49.00 '92, JT 62.74 '92, Hep: 6067i '93.
Made great progress to thetop in 1992-3.

Dietmar MÖGENBURG b.15 Aug 1961 Leverkusen 2.01m 78kg. TV Wattenscheid. Studied architecture.
At HJ: OG: '84- 1, '88- 6, '92- dnq; WCh: '83- 4, '87- 4; WI: '89- 2; EC: '82- 1, '86- 4, '90- 4=; EI: '80- 1, '81- 2=, '82- 1, '84- 1, '86- 1, '88- 2, '89- 1, '90- 3=; EJ: '79- 1; ECp: '79- 1, '83- 3. FRG champion 1980-5, 1987-90.
Five FRG high jump records 1979-84, including world and world junior record 2.35m 1980 and a European record 2.36m 1984. WIB 2.39 '85.
Progression at HJ: 1972- 1.41, 1973- 1.67, 1974- 1.74, 1975- 1.90, 1976- 2.05, 1977- 2.10, 1978- 2.23, 1979- 2.32, 1980- 2.35, 1981- 2.30, 1982- 2.34i/2.30, 1983- 2.32, 1984- 2.36, 1985- 2.39i/2.31, 1986- 2.34i/2.30, 1987- 2.35, 1988- 2.37i/2.34, 1989- 2.35i/2.31, 1990- 2.33, 1991- 2.23, 1992- 2.30, 1993- 2.24i. pb LJ 7.76 '80.
A fine competitor, who won many important competitions from the 1979 European Cup Final high jump at age 17. 83 competitions at 2.30m or over to end 1992.

Axel NOACK b.23 Sep 1961 Görlitz 1.81m 68kg. Berliner TSC. Building worker.
At 20kmW: OG: '88- 8, '92- 20; WCh: '87- dnf, '91- 11; EC: '86- dq, '90- dnf; WCp: '87- 6, '91- 9. At 50kmW: WCh: '93- 4; WCp: '85- 3. At 5kmW: EI: '90- 3. GDR champion 20kmW 1987, 50kmW 1984.
World 20km road walk best 1987.
Progression at 20kmW, 50kmW: 1981- 1:35:23; 1982- 1:33:23; 1983- 1:24:19, 4:22:41; 1984- 1:26:20, 4:00.41; 1985- 1:26:54, 3:56.22; 1986- 1:21:55; 1987- 1:19:12; 1988- 1:20:39; 1989- 1:33:16, 4:10:51; 1990- 1:21:12, 4:13:42; 1991- 1:21:24, 1992- 1:21:25, 1993- 1:26:41, 3:43:50. track pbs: 3000mW 11:06.3i '90, 11:36.11 '87; 5000mW 18:38.8i '90, 19:28.09 '87; 10000mW 39:07.38 '88, 20000mW 1:22:26.10 '90.

Lars RIEDEL b.28 Jun 1967 Zwickau 1.99m 110kg. USC Mainz. Computer salesman.
At DT: OG: '92- dnq 14; WCh: '91- 1, '93- 1; EC: '90- dnq 15; WJ: '86- 4; ECp: '91- 2, '93- 1. GER champion 1992-3. Won GP 1993, 2nd 1991.
Progression at DT: 1985- 52.02, 1986- 58.66, 1988- 62.26, 1989- 60.84, 1990- 64.86, 1991- 67.78, 1992- 68.66, 1993- 68.42. pbs: SP 15.93 '91, JT 61.14 '93, Dec 6087 '93.
In 1990 he exceeded his previous best by over 2m for second at the GDR Championships. Then threw consistently far in 1991, when he was world champion. In 1992 improved to 67.90, but failed at the Olympics before making a fine comeback with four throws over 68m at the ISTAF meeting. Was clearly world number one in 1993.

Christian SCHENK b.9 Feb 1965 Rostock 2.00m 93kg. USC Mainz. Medical student.
At Dec: OG: '88- 1; WCh: '87- 5, '91- 3, '93- 4; EC: ' 90- 3; EJ: '83- 2; ECp: '85- 4, '89- 2, '91- 2. GER champion 1991, 1993.
Progression at Dec: 1983- 7558, 1984- 8036, 1985- 8163, 1987- 8304, 1988- 8488, 1989- 8351, 1990- 8481, 1991- 8402, 1992- 7925, 1993- 8500. pbs: 100m 11.10 '88, 400m 48.88 '89, 1500m 4:13.77 '90, 110mh 14.89 '89, HJ 2.27 '88, PV 5.00 '91, LJ 7.73 '90, SP 15.80 '90, DT 50.66 '93, JT 67.14 '85, new 65.32 '93, Hep 6021i '93.
A rare straddle high jumper, who excelled at the 1988 Olympics with pbs at five of the ten events. That was his first win in 16 decathlons! Won at Götzis 1990. His father Eberhard was GDR 110mh champion 1955, with pb 14.8 '54.

Jürgen SCHULT b.11 May 1960 Neuhaus/Kreis Hagenow 1.93m 110kg. Schweriner SC. Trainee journalist.
At DT: OG: '88- 1, '92- 2; WCh: '83- 5, '87- 1, '91- 6, '93- 3; EC: '86- 7, '90- 1; EJ: '79- 1; WCp: '85- 2, '89- 1; ECp: '83- 1, '85- 4, '87- 2, '89- 1, '91- 2. GDR champion 1983-90. 3rd GP 1993.
World discus record 1986.
Progression at DT: 1978- 51.82, 1979- 57.22, 1980- 61.26, 1981- 61.56, 1982- 63.18, 1983- 66.78, 1984- 68.82, 1985- 69.74, 1986- 74.08, 1987- 69.52, 1988- 70.46, 1989- 68.12, 1990- 67.08, 1991- 67.20, 1992- 69.04, 1993- 66.12. pb SP 17.45 '82.
Although he has not got near his world record distance he has been most consistent, winning World, Olympic and European titles, and being undefeated in 1988 and 1989.

Florian SCHWARTHOFF b.7 May 1968 Dortmund 2.01m 76kg. TV Heppenheim. Architectural student.
At 110mh: OG: '88- qf, '92- 5; WCh: '87- sf, '91- 7, '93- 5; EC: '90- sf; ECp: '89- 3, '91- 2 (5 200m), '93- 2; EJ: '87- 2; WSG: '89- 3. FRG champion 1987-8, 1990-2. At 60mh: WI: '93- 4; EI: '90- 3.
Four FRG 110mh records 1988-92 and three at 60mh indoors in 1990.
Progression at 110mh: 1986- 14.13, 1987- 13.69, 1988- 13.50, 1989- 13.37, 1990- 13.37, 1991- 13.38, 1992- 13.13, 1993- 13.27. pbs: 100m 10.68 '92, 10.46w '90; 200m 20.86 '91, 60mh 7.52i '90, LJ 7.69 '86.
Perhaps the tallest ever top-class high hurdler.

Ralf SONN b.17 Jan 1967 Weinheim 1.97m 85kg. MTG Mannheim. Medical student.
At HJ OG: '92- 6; WCh: '93- 4; EC: '90- 7; EI: '89- 4, '92- 3=; ECp: '89- 6, '91- 7. Won GER title 1992.

Progression at HJ: 1980- 1.65, 1981- 1.76, 1982- 1.75, 1983- 2.00, 1984- 2.06, 1985- 2.11, 1986- 2.16, 1987- 2.23, 1988- 2.25, 1989- 2.32, 1990- 2.36i/2.31, 1991- 2.39i/2.20, 1992- 2.36i/2.32, 1993- 2.36i/2.34. pb LJ 7.15 '87.

Torsten VOSS b.24 Mar 1963 Güstrow 1.86m 88kg. LASV Bayer Uerdingen/Dormagen. Car mechanic.
At Dec: OG: '88- 2; WCh: '83- 7, '87- 1; EC: '82- dnf, '86- 4; EJ: '81- 2, ECp: '85- 1. GDR champion 1982-3, 1987, 1990.
World junior decathlon record 1982.
Progression at Dec: 1977- 5083*, 1978- 6325*, 1979- 7160, 1980- 7518, 1981- 8003, 1982- 8397, 1983- 8335, 1984- 8543, 1985- 8559, 1986- 8450, 1987- 8680, 1988- 8399, 1990- 8275, 1993- 8074. pbs: 100m 10.54 '84, 10.53w '86; 200m 21.45 '87, 400m 47.51 '87, 1500m 4:17.00 '81, 110mh 13.94 '85, HJ 2.11 '81, PV 5.15i '86, LJ 8.02 '84, SP 15.92 '93, DT 46.52 '88, JT 62.90 '82, new 61.76 '88.
Added 121 points to his pb to win the 1987 world title, when he set no individual event pbs, but performed consistently close to them. Seriously ill after having an injection with an infected needle in 1990.

Ronald WEIGEL b.8 Aug 1959 Hildburghausen 1.77m 62kg. LAC Halensee Berlin. Trainee journalist, former soldier.
At 50kmW (20kmW): OG: '88- 2 (2), '92- 3; WCh: '83- 1, '87- 2, '91- dnf (16), '93- dnf; EC: '86- dq, '90- 9; WCp: '87- 1, '91- 3. At 10kmW: EJ: '77- 2. At 5000mW: WI: '91- 9, '93- 5; EI: '87- 2. Won GDR 20kmW 1984, 1988-9; 50kmW 1983, 1985, 1988. GER 50kmW 1991-2.
At 20km walk: European track records 1:20:54.9 1983 and 1:19:18.3 1990. WIB: 5000mW: 18:44.97 '87 & 18:11.41 '88, 20kmW: 1:20:40 '80. World fastest 50km road walk 1984 and 1986; GDR record 10000mW 1980, road bests at 20kmW (2) 1984; 30kmW (4) 1983-8, best 2:11:44 '88; 50kmW (4) 1982-6.
Progression at 20kmW, 50kmW: 1975- 1:40:56; 1976- 1:30:49; 1977- 1:27:51; 1978- 1:27:00; 1979- 1:25:00; 1980- 1:20:40i, 1:22:50; 1981- 1:22:40, 3:49:53; 1982- 1:25:12t, 3:44:20; 1983- 1:20:54.9t, 3:41:31; 1984- 1:19:56, 3:38:31; 1985- 1:22:12, 3:47.15; 1986- 1:20:39, 3:38:17; 1987- 1:20:40, 3:41:30; 1988- 1:20:00, 3:38:56; 1989- 1:21:36; 1990- 1:19:18.3t, 3:44:50; 1991- 1:21:04, 3:45:57; 1992- 1:22:51, 3:51:37; 1993- 1:23:51. Track pbs: 3000mW 11:18.0 '84, 5000mW 18:53.38 '84, 18:11.41i '88; 10000mW 38:12.13 '80, 1hrW 14750mi '84.

Heinz WEIS b.14 Jul 1963 Trier 1.93m 110kg. LG Bayer Leverkusen. Businessman.
At HT OG: '88- 5, '92- 6; WCh: '87- 6, '91- 3; EC: '90- 8; WSG: '85- 1, '87- 2, '89- 2, "91- 3; WCp: '89- 1; ECp: '89- 1, '91- 4. FRG champion 1988-92. 3rd GP 1990.
Three FRG hammer records 1988-9.
Progression at HT: 1980- 53.34, 1981- 60.86, 1982- 61.56, 1983- 65.30, 1984- 68.98, 1985- 78.18, 1986- 76.08, 1987- 80.18, 1988- 82.52, 1989- 82.84, 1990- 81.36, 1991- 80.44, 1992- 80.46, 1993- 75.56. pb SP 14.30 '87.
World number one in 1989.

Women

Beate ANDERS b.4 Feb 1968 Leipzig 1.69m 54kg. LAC Halensee Berlin. Student teacher. Married Bernd Gummelt (2nd 1990 EC 50km walk) in 1993.
At 10kmW: OG: '92- 16; WCh: '87- 16, '91- 10, '93- 5; EC: '90- 6; WCp: '89- 1, '91- 7, '93- 13. At 3000mW: WI: '89- 2, '91- 1, '93- 4; EI: '89- 1, '90- 1, '92- 3. GDR champion 5000mW 1988, 1990; 10kmW: 1987-90. GER 5000mW and 10kmW 1991-3.
World record 3000m and 5000m walks 1990. WIR 3000mW 12:02.2 '89, 11:59.36 '90. 11:56.0 '91. European records 10,000mW 1990, 3000mW 1993. GDR records: track 5000mW (2) 1988-90, road 10kmW (5) 1987-90; GER 10,000m 1993.
Progression at 10kmW: 1987- 46:08, 1988- 44:33, 1989- 43:08, 1990- 42:29.4t, 1991- 43:53, 1992- 42:11.5t, 1993- 43:09. pbs: 3000mW 11:52.01 '93, 5000mW 20:07.52 '90, 20kmW 1:36:55 '89.

Heike BALCK b.19 Aug 1970 Schwerin 1.80m 54kg. Schweriner SC. Social worker.
At HJ: WCh: '91- 12, '93- dnq 20; EC: '90- 5=; WCp: '89- 4; ECp: '89- 3; WJ: '88- 7; EJ: '87- 3; WI: '91- 3. GDR champion 1989-90.
World junior high jump record 1989.
Progression at HJ: 1983- 1.50, 1984- 1.63, 1985- 1.75, 1986- 1.85, 1987- 1.93, 1988- 1.94, 1989- 2.01, 1990- 1.97, 1991- 1.96i/1.95, 1992- 1.92, 1993- 1.95.

Peggy BEER b.15 Sep 1969 Berlin 1.76m 66kg. LAC Halensee Berlin. Student.
At Hep: OG: '92- 6; WCh: '91- 7; EC: '90- 3; WJ: '86- 4, '88- 3; EJ: '87- 1; ECp: '91- 1. GER champion 1991.
Progression at Hep: 1984- 5479, 1985- 5459, 1986- 5900, 1987- 6068, 1988- 6067w, 1989- 6241, 1990- 6531, 1991- 6494, 1992- 6460. 1993- dnf. pbs: 200m 23.59 '91, 800m 2:05.79 '90, 60mh 8.14i '91, 100mh 13.25 '92, HJ 1.88 '86, LJ 6.41/6.48w '91, SP 13.94 '92, JT 48.10 '92, Pen 4627i '93.
Her father Klaus won seven GDR title and did his pb of 8.19 to win the 1968 Olympic long jump silver. Her brother Ron had a LJ best of 8.23 '88, was the 1983 European Junior champion and GDR champion 1986 and 1988.

Katrin Dorre: successfully defended London Marathon title in 1993

Sabine BRAUN b.19 Jun 1965 Essen 1.74m 62kg. TV Wattenscheid. Student of sport and biology.
At Hep: OG: '84- 6, '88- 14, '92- 3; WCh: '87- 18, '91- 1, '93- 2; EC: '90- 1; EJ: '83- 2; WSG: '89- 2; ECp: '85- 4, '89- 5. At LJ: EJ: '83- 8; WCp: '85- 5; ECp: '85- 3, '89- 6. Won FRG LJ 1985, Hep 1989, GER 100mh 1992.
3 FRG heptathlon records 1989-90, GER 1992.
Progression at Hep: 1982- 5477, 1983- 6254, 1984- 6436, 1985- 6323, 1986- 6418, 1987- 5621, 1988- 6432, 1989- 6575, 1990- 6688, 1991- 6672, 1992- 6985, 1993- 6797. pbs: 100m 11.59 '85, 200m 23.60 '85, 400m 55.03 '83, 800m 2:09.41 '84, 100mh 13.05 '92, HJ 1.94 '92, LJ 6.73 '85, SP 14.84 '92, JT 54.10 '86.
Missed major events in 1986-7 through injury. Won at Götzis each year 1990-2. World best 6214 for 45-minute heptathlon 1993.

Birte BRUHNS b.4 Nov 1970 Rostock 1.69m 54kg. ASV Köln. Student.
At 800m/4x400m relay: WCh: '91- sf, '93- sf; EC: '90- sf; WJ: '88- 1/1R; EJ: '87- 1/1R, '89- 1/1R. GER champion 1993.
World age 17 record 1988.
Progression at 800m: 1984- 2:17.43, 1985- 2:11.0, 1986- 2:06.7, 1987- 1:59.96, 1988- 1:59.17, 1989- 2:00.52, 1990- 2:00.52, 1991- 1:59.55, 1992- 2:01.84, 1993- 1:59.66. pb 400m 52.97 '89.
Her four European Junior gold medals is the most ever won by a woman.

Birgit CLARIUS b.18 Mar 1965 Giessen 1.76m 65kg, LAC Quelle Fürth/München 1860. Student of dietetics.
At Hep: OG: '92- 7; WCh: '93- 8; EC: '86- dnf, '90- 7; WSG: '89- 4, '91- 1; ECp: '89- 8. At Pen: WI inv: '93- 3; EI: '92- 4. Won FRG Hep 1990, GER 1992-3.
Progression at Hep: 1982- 5535, 1983- 5347, 1984- 5961, 1986- 6179, 1988- 6204, 1989- 6247w, 1990- 6359, 1991- 6419, 1992- 6478, 1993- 6500. pbs: 200m 24.69 '93, 800m 2:08.33 '93, 100mh 13.61 '93; 400mh 58.65 '91, HJ 1.84 '92, LJ 6.28 '92, 6.34w '91; SP 15.60 '92, JT 51.60 '90, Pen: 4641i '93.
No competition through illness in 1985 and 1987.

Franka DIETZSCH b.22 Jan 1968 Wolgast 1.83m 95kg. SC Neubrandenburg. Student.
At DT: OG: '92- 12; WCh: '91- dnq 13, '93- 8; WJ: '86- 2; WSG: '89- 4.
Progression at DT: 1982- 43.80, 1983- 50.04, 1984- 51.16, 1985- 56.94, 1986- 64.34, 1987- 66.34, 1988- 65.56, 1989- 68.26, 1990- 67.42, 1991- 61.22, 1992- 64.64, 1993- 62.06. pb SP 15.02 '85.

Katrin DÖRRE b.6 Oct 1961 Leipzig 1.70m 56kg. LG Odenwald. Studied medicine at University of Leipzig. Married to her coach Wolfgang Heinig.
At Mar: OG: '88- 3, '92- 5; WCh: '91- 3, '93- 6; EC: '86- dnf; WCp: '85- 1, '87- 3, '91- 4; ECp: '85- 1, '88- 1. World 15km Rd: '90- 6. Won GDR 3000m 1980.
Six GDR marathon records 1982-7.
Progression at Mar: 1982- 2:43:19, 1983- 2:37:41, 1984- 2:26:52, 1985- 2:30:11, 1986- 2:29:33, 1987- 2:25:24, 1988- 2:26:21, 1990- 2:33:21, 1991- 2:27:43, 1992- 2:27:34, 1993- 2:27:09. pbs: 800m 2:05.4 '80, 1000m 2:44.8 '80, 1500m 4:18.7 '79, 3000m 9:04.01 '84, 10000m 33:00.0 '84, 1Hr 17709m '88 (GDR rec). Road: 10km 32:14 '92, Half Mar 70:04 '93.
Has won 16 of her 28 marathons, including her first 11 1982-6, with major wins Osaka 1984 and 1991, Tokyo 1984-5, 1987, Nagoya 1986, London 1992-3. Second Tokyo 1992, third New York 1990, Tokyo 1991 & 1993, Osaka 1992. Daughter Katharina born August 1989.

Heike DRECHSLER b.16 Dec 1964 Gera 1.81m 68kg. née Daute. TuS Jena. Trained as optical instrument maker.
At LJ/R - 4x100m relay: OG: '88- 2 (3 100m & 200m), '92- 1; WCh: '83- 1, '87- 3 (2 100m), '91- 2/3R, '93- 1; WI: '87- 1 (1 200m), '91- 2; EC: '82- 4, '86- 1 (1 200m), '90- 1 (2 200m); EI: '83- 3, '85- 3, '86- 1, '87- 1, '88- 1; EJ: '81- 1; WCp: '85- 1, '92- 1; ECp: '83- 1, '85- 2, '87- 1/1R (2 4x400mR), '91- 1/2R, '93- 1. Won GDR LJ 1981, 1983-8, 1990; 200m 1986, 1988; GER LJ 1992, 100m 1992. Won GP LJ and second overall 1990, won both 1992.

World records: three LJ 1985-6, two 200m 1986. WIB: LJ (6): 6.88 '83, 6.99 '84 & '85, 7.25 & 7.29 '86, 7.37 '88; 100y: 10.24 '86, 10.24 & 10.15 '87; 200m: 22.27 '87. World junior LJ records 1981 and 1982, heptathlon 1981. Eight GDR LJ records 1983-8, GER record 1992.
Progression at 100m, 200m, LJ: 1977- 4.40, 1978- 5.69, 1979- 12.3, 6.07; 1980- 6.64/6.70w, 1981- 11.75, 24.16, 6.91/7.01w; 1982- 6.98, 1983- 7.14/7.27w, 1984- 7.40, 1985- 23.19, 7.44; 1986- 10.91/10.80w, 21.71, 7.45; 1987-10.95, 22.18, 7.40; 1988- 10.91/10.85w, 21.84, 7.48; 1990- 11.14, 22.19, 7.30; 1991- 11.09, 22.58/22.4, 7.37/7.39w; 1992- 11.24, 7.48/7.63w; 1993- 11.36, 23.16, 7.21. pbs: 800m 2:17.07 '81, 100mh 14.12 '80, HJ 1.88i '92, TJ 13.35 '93, SP 13.31 '81, Hep 5812 '81.
The youngest gold medallist of the 1983 world championships, she has jumped consistently over 7 metres ever since. Her 7.63w at the high altitude of Sestriere in 1992 was the first 25 ft long jump by a woman; the wind just over the legal limit at +2.1. Made a sensational breakthrough in 1986 into a great sprinter, winning the GDR indoor 100y title in 10.24, and equalling Marita Koch's world 200m record. Showed further versatility with 50.0 400m relay leg in the 1987 European Cup. Had 27 successive LJ wins until injured at the 1987 World Champs; where she had to withdraw from the relay. Coached by husband father-in-law Erich; son, Toni, born 1 Nov 1989.

Karen FORKEL b.24 Sep 1970 Wolfen 1.72m 63kg. SV Halle. Student of computer technology at Halle University.
At JT: OG: '92- 3; WCh: '91- 12, '93- 2; EC: '90- 2, WJ: '88- 1; EJ: '87- 3; '89- 1; ECp: '93- 2. Won GDR JT 1990, GER 1991. 3rd GP 1990.
Progression at JT: 1983- 34.20, 1984- 40.96, 1985- 44.64, 1986- 51.42, 1987- 59.78, 1988- 64.68, 1989- 70.12, 1990- 69.38, 1991- 70.20, 1992- 69.58, 1993- 67.94.
Threw 68.14 in qualifying but only 57.90 for last place in final of 1991 World Champs when she was the favourite for gold.

Anja GÜNDLER b.18 Mar 1972 Frankenberg 1.84m 85kg. OSC Berlin.
At DT: WCh: '93- 5; WJ: '90- 3; EJ: '91- 1; WSG: '93- 3. German champion 1993.
Progression at DT: 1986- 40.04, 1987- 48.68, 1988- 53.96, 1989- 55.42, 1990- 59.52, 1991- 60.66, 1992- 60.34, 1993- 62.92. pb SP 17.44 '90.

Heike HENKEL b.5 May 1964 Kiel 1.82m 63kg. née Redetzky. LG Bayer Leverkusen.
At HJ: OG: '84- 11=, '88- dnq 13, '92- 1; WCh: '87- 6, '91- 1, '93- ns; EC: '86- 6, '90- 1; EJ: '81- 5; ECp: '85- 6, '87- 3, '89- 4=, '91- 3, '93- 2; WI: '87- 6, '89- 3, '91- 1, '93- 2; EI: '88- 2=, '90- 1, '92- 1. Won overall & HJ GP 1991, FRG/GER HJ 1984-8, 1990-3.
Two German HJ records 1991. WIR 2.07 '92.
Progression at HJ: 1978- 1.58, 1979- 1.68, 1980- 1.85, 1981- 1.87i/1.85, 1982- 1.89, 1983- 1.87i/1.80, 1984- 1.91, 1985- 1.92, 1986- 1.93, 1987- 1.96, 1988- 1.98, 1989- 2.00, 1990- 2.01i/2.00, 1991- 2.05, 1992- 2.04/2.07i, 1993- 2.02i/2.01. pbs: 100m 12.3 '80, 100mh 14.04/14.0 '81, LJ 6.13 '81.
Married Rainer Henkel, world swimming champion in 1986 at 400m and 1500m freestyle, in May 1989. In 1990 she twice improved the FRG indoor high jump record, previously set in 1982 by Ulrike Meyfarth, and in 1991 she took Meyfarth's outdoor record. World's best 1991-2. In all she has won 26 national titles. Had to withdraw from the World final in 1993 due to injury. Expecting a baby in February 1994.

Silke-Beate KNOLL b.21 Feb 1967 Rottweil 1.63m 52kg. LG Olympia Dortmund. Student of Slavic languages.
At 200m/R- 4x100m relay: OG: '88- qf, '92- sf/5R; WCh: '87- h/5R, '91- sf, '93- sf; EC: '90- 5/2R (4 4x400mR); EJ: '85- 1 4x400mR; WI: '89- 4; EI: '88- 3; WSG: '89- 3R; ECp: '87- 3R, '93- 3/3R. Won FRG 200m 1990. GER 1992-3.
WIR 4x200mR 1988.
Progression at 200m: 1982- 25.8, 1983- 26.1, 1984- 25.7, 1985- 23.8, 1986- 23.67, 1987- 23.07, 1988- 22.97i/23.06, 1989- 22.96i/23.34, 1990- 22.40, 1991- 22.81, 1992- 22.29, 1993- 22.75/22.74w. pbs: 100m 11.17 '92, 300m 35.81 '90 (FRG record), 400m 52.06 '90, LJ 5.76 '85.

Astrid KUMBERNUSS b.5 Feb 1970 Grevesmühlen 1.86m 90kg. SC Neubrandenburg. Sports student.
At SP: WCh: '93- 6; EC: '90- 1; EI: '92- 3; EJ: '89- 1; ECp: '91- 2. 3rd GP 1991, 2nd 1993. At DT: WJ: '88- 2; EJ: '87- 2, '89- 1.
World junior shot record 1989.
Progression at SP, DT: 1983- 11.16, 33.48; 1984- 13.44, 44.00; 1985- 14.23, 46.96; 1986- 15.39, 53.92; 1987- 18.20, 63.88; 1988- 18.73, 66.60; 1989- 20.54, 64.74; 1990- 20.77, 65.42; 1991- 19.67, 60.88; 1992- 20.03i/19.69, 1993- 19.92, 59.64.

Heike MEISSNER b.29 Jan 1970 Dresden 1.72m 56kg. Dresdner SC. Student.
At 400mh: OG: '92- sf/6R; WCh: '91- 7, '93- sf; WSG: '93- 1; EJ: '89- 3; ECp: '91- 3. GDR champion 1990, GER 1991-2.
Progression at 400mh: 1986- 59.61, 1987- 60.99, 1989- 56.77, 1990- 56.78, 1991- 54.77, 1992- 55.09, 1993- 54.64. pbs: 100m 12.0 '91, 200m 24.28 '93, 400m 52.46 '92, 800m 2:12.1 '90.

Kathrin NEIMKE b.18 Jul 1966 Magdeburg 1.80m 91kg. SC Magdeburg. Repro photographer.
At SP: OG: '88- 2, '92- 3; WCh: '87- 2, '91- 8, '93- 3; EC: '90- 3; WI: '91- 6, '93- 8; EI: '88- 3; WSG: '87- 2; WCp: '92- 3. GDR champion 1988, GER 1992-3.
Progression at SP: 1981- 11.92, 1982- 12.98, 1983- 15.76, 1984- 16.09, 1985- 18.09, 1986- 19.68, 1987- 21.21, 1988- 21.11, 1990- 20.51, 1991- 19.57i/18.92, 1992- 19.78, 1993- 19.78. pb DT 58.82 '86.

Uta PIPPIG b.7 Sep 1965 Leipzig 1.67m 55kg. SC Charlottenburg Berlin. Medical student.
At 10000m: OG: '92- 7; WCh: '91- 6, '93- 9. At Mar: WCh: '87- 14; WCp: '87- 8, '89- 3. At 3000m: ECp: '91- 2. World 15k road: '91- 3. Won GDR Mar 1986-7, FRG CC 1990.
FRG records 5000m and 10000m 1990, marathon 1990 and 1991. WIB 5000m 1991.
Progression at 10000m, Mar: 1984- 36:54.8, 2:47:42; 1985- 34:42.62, 2:36:45; 1986- 34:04.63, 2:37:56; 1987- 2:30:50; 1988- 2:32:20; 1989- 32:42.55, 2:35:17; 1990- 31:40.92, 2:28:03; 1991- 31:51.36, 2:26:52; 1992- 31:21.36, 2:27:12; 1993- 31:29.70, 2:26:24. pbs: 1500m 4:11.39i '91, 4:14.80 '92; 3000m 8:40.99 '93, 5000m 15:15.04 '93, 15:13.72i '91; 15k road 48:44 '91 (GER rec).
Left Potsdam, GDR for the FRG in January 1990. Won Berlin Marathon 1990, 1992. Boston 2nd 1990, 3rd 1991-2. After a series of track pbs in 1993 she won the New York marathon.

Helga RADTKE b.16 May 1962 Sassnitz 1.71m 64kg. SC Empor Rostock.
At LJ (TJ): OG: '92- dnq 20; WCh: '83- 12, '87- 4, '91- dnq 13, '93- dnq 13 (5); WI: '85- 1, '87- 2; EC: '86- 3, '90- 3; EI: '83- 2, '86- 2, '90- 3; EJ: '79- 1; WCp: '89- 4; ECp: '89- 2. At TJ: WI: '93- 5; EI: '92- 3; WCp: '92- 6; ECp: '93- 2. Won GDR LJ 1989, GER TJ 1993.
Eight German triple jump records 1991-2.
Progression at LJ, TJ: 1976- 5.32, 1977- 5.68, 1978- 5.74, 1979- 6.63, 1980- 6.71, 1982- 6.83, 1983- 6.83, 1984- 7.21, 1985- 7.19, 1986- 7.17, 1987- 7.16/7.17w, 1988- 6.76i/6.73, 1989- 7.15, 1990- 6.97, 13.63i; 1991- 6.74, 13.83; 1992- 6.79, 6.83w, 14.30/14.44w; 1993- 6.66, 14.19. pbs: 100m 11.6 '85, 100mh 14.67 '79, HJ 1.75 '82.

Silke RENK b.30 Jun 1967 Querfurt 1.73m 75kg. SV Halle. Sports science student at Leipzig University.
At JT: OG: '88- 5, '92- 1; WCh: '91- 3, '93- 6; EC: '90- 4; WSG: '89- 1. GER champion 1992-3. 3rd GP 1992.
Progression at JT: 1981- 42.62, 1982- 45.28, 1983- 51.16, 1984- 51.36, 1985- 59.08, 1986- 62.06, 1987- 64.74, 1988- 71.00, 1989- 66.16, 1990- 66.50, 1991- 68.34, 1992- 68.34, 1993- 65.80.
Successively 5-4-3 at major championships 1988-91, and then won Olympic title.

Silvia RIEGER b.14 Nov 1970 Emden 1.75m 55kg. TuS Eintracht Hinte. Bank clerk.
At 400mh/4x400mR: OG: '92- h; WCh: '93- sf; EC: '90- sf; WJ: '88- 3; EJ: '87- 1/2R, '89- 1/3R; ECp: '93- 4. FRG champion 1990, GER 1993.
Progression at 400mh: 1985- 64.7, 1986- 60.9, 1987- 57.44, 1988- 57.88, 1989- 56.33, 1990- 55.18, 1991- 55.15, 1992- 55.10, 1993- 54.90. pbs: 100m 11.8 '87, 12.02 '92; 200m 24.0 '90, 24.16 '91; 400m 53.3 '92, 800m 2:07.21 '92, 100mh 13.7 '93, 13.90 '92; LJ 5.92 '87.
Improved pb from 56.33 to 55.18 to win 1990 FRG 400mh.

Stephanie STORP b.28 Nov 1968 Braunschweig 1.94m 95kg. VfL Wolfsburg. Works for Volkswagen.
At SP: OG: '92- 7; WCh: '87- 10, '91- 6, '93- 11; WI: '89- 4; EC: '86- 11 (10 DT), '90- 7; WI: '91- 4, '93- 2; EI: '89- 1; WJ: '86- 2 (4 DT); EJ: '85- 3 (6 DT); ECp: '93- 3. 3rd GP 1989.
Progression at SP: 1983- 12.88, 1984- 15.18, 1985- 17.72, 1986- 19.11, 1987- 19.90, 1988- 19.73, 1989- 20.30i/20.08, 1990- 20.34, 1991- 19.80, 1992- 19.59, 1993- 19.71. pb DT 58.88 '89, JT 47.92 '89.

Susen TIEDTKE b.23 Jan 1969 Berlin 1.74m 56kg. SC Charlottenburg Berlin. Clerk. Married US long jumper Joe Greene 4 Dec 1993.
At LJ: OG: '92- 8; WCh: '91- 5, '93- 9; WI: '93- 2; EJ: '87- 3. GER champion 1993.
Progression at LJ: 1986- 6.22, 1987- 6.44, 1988- 6.08, 1989- 6.53, 1990- 6.58, 1991- 7.00, 1992- 6.74/7.02w, 1993- 6.85/7.19w.
Was GDR youth champion gymnast at 13, and a candidate for the 1984 Olympics, which the GDR boycotted. Jumped 6.03 in her first ever LJ in May 1986. Coached by her father Jürgen Tiedtke (PV 4.50 in 1964). In 1966 her mother Ingrid was 5th in the European 200m and ran a pb of 23.5. Her uncle Manfred Tiedtke was 10th in 1968 OG decathlon.

Christine WACHTEL b.6 Jan 1965 Altentreptow 1.66m 56kg. SC Empor Rostock. Economist.
At 800m/R- 4x400m relay: OG: '88- 2, '92- h; WCh: '87- 2, '91- 6/3R, '93- sf; EC: '86- 8, '90- 2; WI: '87- 1, '89- 1, '91- 1; EI: '87- 1; EJ: '83- 2/1R; WCp: '85- 1, '89- 2R; ECp: '85- 3, '87- 3, '89- 1R, '91- 2, '93- 8. Won GDR 800m 1983, 1985, 1987-8, GER 1991-2. 3rd GP 1989.
World junior 800m record 1983. World 1000m record 1990. WIB 800m 1:57.64 & 1:56.40 '88.
1:56.40 '88.
Progression at 800m: 1976- 2:29.5, 1977- 2:19.8,

1978- 2:16.4, 1979- 2:09.1, 1980- 2:04.7, 1981- 2:03.35, 1982- 2:01.16, 1983- 1:59.40, 1984- 1:58.24, 1985- 1:56.71, 1986- 1:58:59, 1987- 1:55.32, 1988- 1:56.40i/1:56.64, 1989- 1:58.21, 1990- 1:56.11, 1991- 1:58.84, 1992- 1:59.35, 1993- 1:59.86. pbs: 400m 51.62 '89, 1000m 2:30.67 '90, 1500m 4:18.03 '82, 400mh 58.08 '82.
Three successive World Indoor titles.

Kathrin WESSEL b.14 Aug 1967 Annaberg 1.72m 52kg. SC Berlin. Student teacher. née Ullrich, married Andre Weßel (5000m 13:51.61 '89, 10000m 28:32.47 '88) in 1992.
At 10000m: OG: '88- 4, '92- h; WCh: '87- 3, '91- 4, '93- 13; EC: '90- 2; WCp: '89- 1; ECp: '87- 1, '89- 1, '91- 1. At 3000m: EJ: '85- 8. Won GDR 3000m & 10000m 1987-90, CC 1987, 1989-90; GER 10000m 1991-3.
GDR records 1987-9: 10000m and 5000m (2); GER records 5000m and 10000m 1991.
Progression at 3000m, 10000m: 1982- 9:36.37, 1983- 9:23.78. 1984- 9:17.04, 1985- 9:14.47, 1986- 9:09.92, 1987- 8:50.51, 31:11.34; 1988- 8:41.79i/ 8:44.81, 31:26.79; 1989- 8:45.43, 31:33.92; 1990- 9:00.37, 31:47.70; 1991- 8:47.11, 31:03.62; 1992- 8:49.08i/8:51.14, 31:20.62; 1993- 8:53.45, 32:00.52. pbs: 800m 2:09.54 '83, 1000m 2:44.1 '86, 1500m 4:06.91i '88, 2000m 5:49.38 '91, 5000m 14:58.71 '91.
Has compiled a good record in major races, with a fine finishing kick.

Ilke WYLUDDA b.28 Mar 1969 Leipzig 1.85m 97kg. SV Halle. PE student.
At DT: OG: '92- 9; WCh: '87- 4, '91- 2, '93- 11; EC: '90- 1; WJ: '86- 1, '88- 1; EJ: '85- 1 (2 SP), '87- 1 (1 SP); WCp: '89- 1, '92- 2; ECp: '89- 1, '91- 1. Won GDR DT 1989-90, GER 1991-2. Won GWG 1990, GP 1990, 1992.
Eleven world junior records at discus 1986-8 and two at shot 1987-8.
Progression at SP, DT: 1982- 13.72, 46.54; 1983- 15.18, 51.12; 1984- 16.42, 57.74; 1985- 18.27, 62.36; 1986- 19.08, 65.86; 1987- 20.11, 71.64; 1988- 20.23, 74.40; 1989- 19.18, 74.56; 1990- 18.42, 71.10; 1991- 18.96, 69.12; 1992- 70.96, 1993- 64.06.
Holds GDR age records for DT age 13-15, SP 14-15 as well as world bests at junior level, where she was dominant 1986-8. Unbeaten in her senior career, 1989 to World championships 1991, where she was beaten by Tsvetanka Khristova after 41 successive discus victories. Operation on right knee March 1993 and left knee September 1993.

GREECE

Governing body: Hellenic Amateur Athletic Association (SEGAS), 137 Syngrou Avenue, Athens 171 21. Founded 1896.
National Championships first held in 1896 (men), 1930 (women). **1993 Champions**: **Men**: 100m/200m: Alexandros Terzian 10.45/20.92, 400m: Kostas Kederis 46.27, 800m: Michalis Anagnostou 1:50.07, 1500m: Spiros Christopoulos 3:45.19, 5000m: Panasotis Papoulias 14:21.34, 10000m: Manolis Chanzos 29:22.43, 3000mSt: Adonis Vouzis 8:44.10, 110mh: Stelios Bisbas 13.82, 400mh: Thanasis Kalogiannis 49.93, HJ: Labros Papakostas 2.26, PV: Christos Palakis 5.35, LJ: Spiros Vasdekis 8.09w, TJ: Theodoros Tadanozis 16.44, SP: Ilias Louka CYP 17.76, DT: Christos Papadopoulos 56.90, HT: Savas Saritzoglou 71.90, JT: Kostas Gatziudis 76.46, Dec: Savas Stafilidis 7462, 20kmW: Theodoros Stamatopoulos 1:29:43.3. **Women**: 100m/200m: Katerina Kofa 11.86/24.09, 400m: Dora Kiriakou 53.99, 800m: Vasiliki Vraka 2:09.90, 1500m: Theoni Kostopoulou 4:31.94, 3000m: Marina Polizou 9:50.51, 10000m: Chrisostomia Iakovou 36:17.55, 100mh: Christina Tabaki 14.01, 400mh: Anna Pabori 61.94, HJ: Niki Bakogianni 1.90, LJ: Eleni Karabesini 6.13w, TJ: Olga Vasdekis 13.32, SP: Kaliopi Ouzouni 15.65, DT: Anastasia Kelesidou 55.52, JT: Anna Vourdoli 55.34, Hep: Alessandra Kourli 5249, 10kmW: Alexandra Kourli 6251.

Konstantinos KOUKODIMOS b.14 Sep 1969 Melbourne, Australia 1.86m 80kg. GAS Archelaos, Katerini.
At JT: OG: '92- 6; WCh: '91- 12, '93- dnq 13; WI: '91- 4; EC: '90- 10; WJ: '86- 8, '88- 8; EJ: '87- 6; WCp: '92- 5. Won Greek LJ 1990-2, Balkan 1988, 1991-2. Won Med Games 1991.
Three Greek long jump records 1990-1.
Progression at LJ: 1985- 7.26, 1986- 7.69, 1987- 7.78, 1988- 7.91i/7.87, 1989- 7.74, 1990- 7.97i/ 7.96, 1991- 8.26, 1992- 8.22, 1993- 7.94?. pb 100m 10.5 '88.

HUNGARY

Governing body: Magyar Atlétikai Szövetség, 1143 Budapest, Dózsa György utca 1-3. Founded 1897.
National Championships first held in 1896 (men), 1932 (women). **1993 Champions**. **Men**: 100m/200m: Pál Rezák 10.63/20.97w, 400m: Gusztáv Menczer 47.35, 800m: Miklós Árpási 1:50.17, 1500m: Róbert Banai 3:52.02, 5000m/ 10000m: Zoltán Káldy 14:06.57/29:06.24, Half Mar: Péter Jáger 64:24, Mar: Zoltán Holba 2:20:32, 3000mSt: Gábor Markó 8:51.53, 110mh: Levente Csillag 14.01, 400mh: Dusán Kovács 50.51, HJ: Péter Deutsch 2.14, PV: Pál Rohánszky 5.30, LJ: Tibor Ordina 8.04, TJ: Gyula Pálóczi 16.79w, SP: József Kóczián 18.72, DT:

Attila Horváth 62.20, HT: Tibor Gécsek 81.00, JT: József Belák 69.80, Dec: Sándor Munkácsi 7528, 20kmW: Sándor Urbanik 1:23:31, 50kmW: Gyula Dudás 4:08:26. **Women**: 100m/200m: Éva Barati 11.62/23.84, 400m Mónika Mádai 53.81, 800m: Szilvia Csoszánszky 2:08.77, 1500m/3000m: Éva Dóczi 4:25.75/9:18.41, 10000m/Half Mar: Helén Barocsi 33:46.35/73:09, Mar: Márta Vass 2:56:47, 100mh: Zita Bálint 13.80, 400mh: Szilvia Ray 60.89, HJ: Krisztina Solti 1.92, LJ/Hep: Rita Ináncsi 6.50/5980, TJ: Ildikó Fekete 13.71, SP: Hajnal Herth-Vörös 14.68, DT: Katalin Csöke-Tóth 53.12, JT: Kinga Zsigmond 59.24, 10kmW: Maria Rosza-Urbanik 45:25.

István BAGYULA b.2 Jan 1969 Budapest 1.85m 76kg. Csepel SC. Former student at George Mason University, USA.
At PV: OG: '88- 7, '92- 9; WCh: '87- dnq, '91- 2, '93- 10; EC: '90- 10; WI: '89- 6; EI: '92- 2; WJ: '86- dnq, '88- 1; EJ: '87- 3; WSG: '91- 1, '93- 1; ECp: '91- 3. Won Hungarian PV 1988-9, NCAA 1990-2 (and 1990-1 indoors).
World junior pole vault record 1988; seven Hungarian records 1988-91.
Progression at PV: 1982- 4.30, 1983- 4.63, 1984- 4.90, 1985- 5.10, 1986- 5.50, 1987- 5.50, 1988- 5.65, 1989- 5.60i/5.51, 1990- 5.70i/5.60, 1991- 5.92, 1992- 5.82i/5.80, 1993- 5.70.
Excellent season in 1991, when it took Bubka's last chance clearance at 5.95 to beat him at the World Championships.

Tibor GÉCSEK b.22 Sep 1964 Szentgotthard 1.84m 100kg. Szombathelyi. Diesel engine mechanic.
At HT: OG: '88- 6, '92- 4; WCh: '87- 7, '91- 4, '93- 3; EC: '90- 2; EJ: '83- 6; ECp: '91- 2. Hungarian champion 1986-93. Won GP 1988, 2nd 1990.
Four Hungarian hammer records 1987-8.
Progression at HT: 1980- 34.26, 1981- 50.62, 1982- 60.60, 1983- 67.90, 1984- 73.66, 1985- 77.62, 1986- 77.66, 1987- 79.14, 1988- 81.68, 1989- 77.30, 1990- 80.92, 1991- 80.72, 1992- 81.02, 1993- 81.00. pbs: SP 14.65 '85, DT 48.72 '85.

Attila HORVATH b.28 Jul 1967 Köszeg 1.94m 117kg. Haladás VSE.
At DT: OG: '92- 5; WCh: '91- 3; EC: '90- 8; WJ: '86- 5; EJ: '85- 1; ECp: '91- 1. 3rd GP 1991. Hungarian champion 1987, 1990-3.
Progression at DT: 1982- 44.06, 1983- 52.44, 1984- 56.28, 1985- 61.84, 1986- 60.76, 1987-62.94, 1988- 64.18, 1989- 63.44, 1990- 65.46, 1991- 67.06, 1992- 65.24, 1993- 64.52. pbs: SP 17.55 '92, HT 65.64 '85.
World age 17 best discus 1985.

Dezsö SZABO b.4 Sep 1967 Budapest 1.84m 82kg. Újpestt Tornaegylet.
At Dec: OG: '88- 13, '92- 4; WCh: '91 & '93- dnf; EC: '90- 2; WSG: '89- 3. At Hep: WI: '93- 5. Won Hungarian Dec 1987-91, PV 1987, 1990, 1992.
Four Hungarian decathlon records 1988-90.
Progression at Dec: 1984- 6529, 1985- 6981, 1986- 7330, 1987- 7918, 1988- 8209, 1989- 8080, 1990- 8436, 1991- 8141, 1992- 8199, 1993- 8101. pbs: 100m 10.88 '90, 10.86w '88; 200m 22.17 '91, 21.83w '90; 400m 47.17 '90, 1500m 4:11.07 '90, 110mh 14.52 '90, HJ 2.06 '88, PV 5.40 '90, LJ 7.58 '89, 7.65w '88, SP 13.73 '92, DT 43.74 '91, JT 62.48 '91, Hep 6130i '90.
Five pbs when he won European silver medal.

Sándor URBANIK b.15 Dec 1964 Esztergom 1.72m 56kg. Tatabányai Bányász SC. Electrician.
At 20kmW: OG: '88- 21, '92- 8; WCh: '91- 14, '93- 10; EC: '86- 15, '90- 15. At 5000mW: WI: '87- 6, '89- 4, '91- 6; EI: '88- 3. Won Hungarian 20kmW 1986-93.
Six Hungarian records 20kmW 1985-92.
Progression at 20kW: 1985- 1:23:47, 1986- 1:22:11, 1987- 1:23:37, 1988- 1:21:34, 1989- 1:24:47, 1990- 1:22:12, 1991- 1:21:05, 1992- 1:20:55, 1993- 1:23:31. pbs: 3000mW 11:11.4?i '89, 5000mW 18:34.77i '89, 19:09.83 '93; 10000mW 40:00.43 '85.
His wife Maria Rosza (b.12 Feb 1967) is Hungarian record holder at 10km walk, 43:21 '93, and was 12th in the 1992 Olympics and 10th in the 1993 World Champs at this event.

Tibor Gécsek: world bronze in hammer

ICELAND

Governing body: Frjálsíþróttasamband Islands, P.O.Box 1099, Iþróttamidstödinni Laugardal, 121 Reykjavik. Founded in 1947.
National Championships first held in 1927.
1993 Champions: **Men**: 100m: Haukur Sigurdsson 10.7w, 200m/400m: Gunnar Gudmundsson 21.48w/48.62, 800m/1500m: Finnbogi Gylfason 1:55.75/4:02.62, 5000m/10000m/Mar: Jóhann Ingibergsson 15:18.14/32:05.03/2:32:44, 3000mSt: Svein Ernstsson 9:34.57, 110mh: Olafur Gudmundsson 15.11w, 400mh: Eigill Eidsson 54.41, HJ: Einar Kristjánsson 2.01, PV/Dec: Audunn Gudjónsson 4.10/6819, LJ/TJ: Jón Oddsson 7.19/14.15, SP: Pétur Gudmundsson 18.92, DT: Vésteinn Hafsteinsson 58.90, HT: Jón A Sigurjónsson 57.22, JT: Unnar Gardarsson 69.62. **Women**: 100m/200m/100mh: Gudrún Arnardóttir 11.84w/24.11w/13.55w, 400m: Svanhildur Kristjónsdóttir 56.14, 800m/1500m: Frida Rún Tórdardóttir 2:16.8/4:40.98, 3000m: Martha Ernstdóttir 9:40.63, Mar: Anna Cosser 3:02:07, 400mh: Törhalla Magnúsdóttir 67.2, HJ: Tórdis Gísladóttir 1.75. LJ: Snjólaug Vilhelmsdóttir 5.74, TJ: Sigrídúr Anna Gudjónsdóttir 11.80, SP: Gudbjörg Gylafadóttir 13.39, DT: Halla Heimisdóttir 37.66, JT: Birgitta Gudjónsdóttir 46.00, Hep: Sunna Gestsdóttir 4458.

INDIA

Governing body: Amateur Athletic Federation of India, Room No.1148A, Gate No 28, East Block, Jawaharlal Nehru Stadium, Lodi Complex, New Delhi 110003. Founded 1946.
National Championships first held as Indian Games in 1924. **1993 All India Open Meet** winners: **Men**: 100m: M S Sreadharan 10.7, 200m: Anand Natarajan 21.1, 400m: 400m/800m: Avtar Singh 47.7/1:49.2, 1500m/5000m: Bahadur Prasad 3:43.5/14:25.1, 10000m: Narendra Singh 31:05.1, 3000mSt: Balkar Singh 8:54.3, 110mh: Dharmendra Singh, 400mh: Rajinder Singh 52.5, HJ: Chandar Pal 2.17, PV: M C Eldo 4.75, LJ: Shyam Kumar 7.72, TJ: Rajinder Singh 15.45, SP: Satkaran Singh 17.34, DT: Shakti Singh 52.34, HT: Rajesh Bharadwaj 65.46, JT: Yusuf Khan 67.66, Dec: Anil Kumar Singh 6676. **Women**: 100m: Zenia Ayrton 11.7, 200m/400m: K Saramma 23.4/53.3, 800m: Shiny Wilson 2:06.0, 1500m: Jyotirmoy Sikdar 4:26.6, 3000m: Aparna Bhoyar 9:55.4, 10000m: L Leelamma 36:53.6, 100mh: K K Geetha 14.4, 400mh: Sylvina Pais 58.9, HJ: Angela Lincy 1.77, LJ: Mujitha Begum 5.91, SP: Amandeep Kaur 14.35, DT: Neelam J Singh 42.50, JT: Gurmeet Kaur 47.58, Hep: K.K.Geetha 5054.

1993 All-India Inter-State Meet winners: **Men**: 100m: R Bharadwaj 10.7, 200m: Harjinder Singh 21.7, 400m: Jata Shankar 47.7, 800m: Jossey Mathew 1:49.6, 1500m/5000m: Bahadur Prasad 3:46.9/14:20.6, 10000m: Madan Singh 29:26.0, 3000mSt: Amrit Pal 9:04.0, 110mh: Manjit Singh Randhawa 14.9, 400mh: Majinder Singh 53.4, HJ: Nelluswami Annavi 2.05, PV: Vijay Pal Singh 4.80, LJ: Shyam Kumar 7.68, TJ: Manpreet Singh 15.32, SP: Avtar Singh 17.33, DT: Ajit Bhadoria 54.20, HT: Jasdev Singh Waraich 61.56, JT: Satbir Singh 71.12, Dec: A D Ganpati 6445. **Women**: 100m: E B Shyla 11.9, 200m: K Saramma 24.2, 400m: Shiny Wilson 54.4, 800m: K S Bijimol 2:12.8, 1500m: Jyotirmoy Sikdar 4:31.9, 3000m: Aparna Bhoyar 9:43.9, 10000m: L Leelamma 36:05.7, 100mh: K K Geetha 14.3, 400mh: Sylvina Pais 59.2, HJ: P S Bindu 1.66, LJ: Tapani Daur 5.94, SP: Amandeep Kaur 14.09, DT: Neelam J Singh 41.22, JT: Gurmeet Kaur 47.14, Hep: Ranjita Deori 3775, 10kW: Kabita Garari 58:46.3.

IRELAND

Governing Body: Bórd Lúthchleas na h'Eireann (BLE), 11 Prospect Road, Glasnevin, Dublin 9. Founded in 1967. Original Irish AAA founded in 1885.
National Championships first held in 1873.
1993 BLE champions: **Men**: 100m/200m: Kieran Finn 10.48w/21.42w, 400m: Sean McAteer 48.07, 800m: P J O'Rourke 1:53.61, 1500m: Niall Bruton 3:50.93, 5000m: Paul Donovan 14:36.95, 10000m: Noel Berkeley 29:23.20, Mar: Seamus O'Donnell 2:23:38, 3000mSt: Enda Fitzpatrick 8:57.30, 110mh: T J Kearns 13.62w, 400mh: Nigel Keough 53.94, HJ: Mark Mandy 2.10, PV: Neill Young GBR 4.40, LJ: Jonathan Kron 7.40, TJ: Michael McDonald GBR 15.26, SP: Paul Quirke 17.54, DT: Nick Sweeney 57.30, HT: Pat McGrath 65.46, JT: Terry McHugh 72.28, Dec: JohnHallissey 5971, 10kmW/20kmW: Pat Murphy 44:21.56/1:33:32. **Women**: 100m/200m: Michelle Carroll 11.74w/24.25, 400m/400mh: Stephanie McCann GBR 55.68/60.21, 800m: Geraldine Nolan 2:08.12, 1500m: Anita Philpott 4:24.36, 3000m: Catherina McKiernan 9:13.4, Mar: Brid Murphy 2:51:33, 100mh: Patricia Naughton 14.31w, HJ: Sharon Foley 1.75, LJ: Terri Horgan 6.29, TJ: Siobhan Hoey 12.02w, SP: Kelly Kane 13.01, DT: Mary Mahon 42.60, HT: Brenda Thompson 35.20, JT: Mary Real 47.48, Hep: Brid Hallissey 5071, 5000mW: Elizabeth Paolini 23:05.1, 10kmW: Perri Williams 51:44.

Frank O'MARA b.17 Jul 1960 Limerick City 1.76m 61kg. Limerick and Reebok TC, USA. Post graduate law student at University of Arkansas, with a degree in civil engineering and a Masters degree in business administration.

At 5000m: OG: '88 & 92- h; WCh: '87- 9, '91- h; EC: '90- h. At 3000m: WI: '87- 1, '89- 5, '91- 1. At 1500m: OG: '84- ht; EC: '86- 8. Won Irish 1500m 1983, 1986, 1988, 1991; NCAA 1500m 1983.
Irish 5000m record 1987. Ran on Ireland's 4x1M world best 1985.
Progression at 1500m/1M, 5000m: 1979- 3:45.0; 1980- 3:40.36/3:59.19; 1981- 3:39.85/3:58.86; 1983- 3:37.7/3:52.50; 1984- 3:37.91; 1985- 3:34.02/3:55.92, 14:04.02; 1986- 3:35.04/3:51.06, 13:24.70; 1987- 3:36.23/3:53.58, 13:13.02; 1988- 3:38.44, 13:26.75; 1989- 3:36.92/3:56.23i; 1990- 3:37.88, 13:24.55; 1991- 3:41.21/3:58.00i, 13:18.82; 1992- 13:16.66, 1993- 13:17.72. pbs: 800m 1:47.72 '84, 2000m 4:59.00 '87, 3000m 7:40.41 '89, 2M 8:17.78 '88, 10000m 27:58.01 '91.

Marcus O'SULLIVAN b.22 Dec 1961 Cork City 1.75m 60kg. Leevale and New Balance TC, USA. Degree in accountancy from Villanova University.
At 1500m: OG: '84- sf, '88- 8, '92- sf; WCh: '87- sf; WI: '87- 1, '89- 1, '91- 4, '93- 1; EC: '86- 6; EI: '85- 2. At 5000m: 1990- dnf. Won AAA 1500m 1985, Irish 1500m 1984, 800m 1986, 1989, 1992.
WIB 1500m 3:35.6 1989, and 3:35.4 unofficial 1988. Ran on Ireland's 4x1M world best 1985. Three Irish 800m records 1984-5.
Progression at 1500m, 1M: 1980- 3:47.7; 1981- 3:48.5, 4:03.0i; 1982- 3:42.7, 4:00.1; 1983- 3:43.2, 3:56.65; 1984- 3:37.40, 3:55.82; 1985- 3:37.20, 3:52.64; 1986- 3:35.76, 3:53.55; 1987- 3:36.7, 3:52.76; 1988- 3:35.4i/3:36.04, 3:50.94i; 1989- 3:35.36, 3:51.64; 1990- 3:35.23, 3:55.51; 1991- 3:36.44, 3:55.17i/3:56.23; 1992- 3:34.57, 3:57.38i/3:57.68; 1993- 3:34.69, 3:52.76. pbs: 800m 1:45.87 '85, 1000m 2:19.15 '87, 2000m 4:58.08 '88, 3000m 7:42.53 '89, 5000m 13:27.32 '90.

Women

Catherina McKIERNAN b. 30 Nov 1969 1.65m 48kg. Cavan. Receptionist.
At 3000m: OG: '92- h. At 10000m: WCh: '93- dnf. World CC: '92- 2, '93- 2. Won Irish 3000m & CC 1990-2.
Irish 10000m record 1993
Progression at 3000m, 10000m: 1988- 9:52.0, 1990- 9:16.60, 1991- 8:54.61, 1992- 8:51.33, 1993- 8:58.04, 32:14.74. pbs: 1500m 4:21.30 '90, 1M 4:37.74 '92.
Won IAAF cross-country challenge 1991/2 and 1992/3 after 5th place 1990/1.

Sonia O'SULLIVAN b.28 Nov 1969 Cobh 1.73m 53kg. Ballymore-Cobh and New Balance TC, USA. Accountancy student at Villanova University.
At 3000m (1500m): OG: '92- 4 (sf); WCh: '93- 4 (2); EC: '90- 11; WJ: '88- h; WSG: '91- 2 (1). World CC: '92- 7. Won overall and 3000m GP 1993, 5000m 1992, NCAA 3000m 1990-1, CC 1990; Irish CC 1987, 800m 1992, 1500m 1987, 1990; 5000m 1990.
WIB 5000m 15:17.28 '91, Irish records 1990-3: 1500m (4), 1M, 2000m (2), 3000m (5), 5000m (3).
Progression at 1500m, 3000m: 1986- 10:02.7, 1987- 9:01.52, 1988- 9:13.6, 1989- 9:10.62, 1990- 4:08.49, 8:52.65; 1991- 4:05.81, 8:54.16; 1992- 4:01.23, 8:39.67; 1993- 3:59.60, 8:28.74. pbs: 800m 2:03.39 '92, 1000m 2:34.66 '93, 1500m 4:01.23 '92, 1M 4:22.94 '93, 2000m 5:40.77 '93, 5000m 14:45.92 '93.
Brilliant form in 1992, when she set six Irish records from 1500m to 5000m, including five in eleven days inAugust, and improved further in 1993.

ISRAEL

Governing body: Israeli Athletic Association, 4 Marmorek Street, PO Box 4575, Tel Aviv 61044. Founded as Federation for Amateur Sport in Palestine 1931.
National Championships first held in 1935.
1993 Champions: **Men**: 100m/200m: Adi Paz 10.64/21.35, 400m: Doron Shitruk 48.52, 800m:

Sonia O'Sullivan: won overall GP title as well as setting six Irish records

Willem Luycks 1:53.93, 1500m/5000m/10000m/Mar: Dov Kremer 3:52.04/14:31.98/30:09.8/2:19:57, 3000mSt: Avi Ma'ayan 9:21.49, 110mh: Tzafrir Minzer 15.31w, 400mh: Aleksey Bazarov 50.53, HJ: Itai Margalit 2.18, PV: Yevgeniy Krasnov 5.50, LJ: Mark Malisov 7.38, TJ: Freddy Naim 14.98, SP: Yoav Sharf 17.07, DT: Sergey Lukashok 59.30, HT: Igor Giller 63.30, JT: Vadim Bavikin 76.20, Dec: Erez Meltzer 6610, 20kW: Vladimir Ostrovskiy 1:39:31, 50kmW: Ben-Ami Shahar 5:43:20. **Women**: 100m: Galit Maretzki 12.44, 200m/400m: Sharon Lev 25.40/55.42, 800m/1500m/10000m: Edna Lankri 2:05.19/4:16.20/36:26.8, 3000m: Nili Avramski 10:12.94, Mar: Idit Ganot 3:03:26, 100mh: Keren Sari 15.65, 400mh: Puah Neiger 60.05, HJ: Ada Nwadike 1.66, LJ/TJ: Sarah Rosenberg 5.87/12.21, SP: Tzila Asher 13.92, DT: Ilana Goldberg 37.96, JT: Dorit Ashkenazi 43.02, 10kmW: Yulia Kotler 51:00.

ITALY

Governing Body: Federazione Italiana di Atletica Leggera (FIDAL), Via della Camilluccia n.701-703, 00135 Roma. Constituted 1926. First governing body formed 1896.

National Championships first held in 1906 (men), 1927 (women). **1993 champions**: **Men**: 100m: Enzo Madonia 10.53, 200m: Giorgio Marras 20.83, 400m: Andrea Nuti 45.56, 800m: Giuseppe D'Urso 1:45.68, 1500m: Alessandro Lambruschini 3:38.24, 5000m: Giuliano Baccani 13:46.33, 10000m: Stefano Baldini 28:25.98, Mar: Walter Durbano 2:11:13, 3000mSt: Gianni Crepaldi 8:29.25, 110mh: Fausto Frigerio 13.89, 400mh: Georgio Frinolli 49.33, HJ: Ettore Ceresoli 2.25, PV: Massimo Allevi 5.50, LJ: Simone Bianchi 7.98, TJ: Andrea Matarazzo 16.45, SP/DT: Luciano Zerbini 19.72/64.26, HT: Enrico Sgrulletti 72.62, JT: Fabio De Gaspari 79.02, Dec: Ubaldo Ranzi 7871w, 10000mW/20km: Giovanni Di Benedictis 41:13.20/1:26:39, 50kmW: Giuseppe De Gaetano 3:51:54. **Women**: 100m/200m: Giada Gallina 11.85/23.93, 400m: Francesca Carbone 53.99, 800m: Nicoletta Tozzi 2:05.07, 1500m: Fabia Trabaldo 4:12.13, 3000m: Valentina Tauceri 9:08.49, 10000m: Maria Guida 33:43.06, Mar: Emma Scaunich 2:34:17, 100mh: Carla Tuzzi 13.32, 400mh: Elena Zamperioli 57.96, HJ: Antonella Bevilacqua 1.92, LJ/TJ: Antonella Capriotti 6.70/13.91, SP/DT: Agnese Maffeis 17.04/57.20, JT: Claudia Coslovich 53.88, Hep: Giuliana Spada 5962, 5000mW/20kmW: Ileana Salvador 20:48.55/1:31:53; 10kmW: Rossella Giordano 46:31.

Alessandro ANDREI b.3 Jan 1959 Firenze 1.91m 118kg. Fiamme Oro Padova. Policeman.
At SP: OG: '84- 1, '88- 7, '92- 11; WCh: '83- 7, '87- 2, '91- 11; EC: '82- 10, '86- 4; EI: '84- 3; EJ: '77- 9; WSG: '85- 1; WCp: '81- 7, '85- 3; ECp: '83- 4, '85- 2, '87- 2, '89- 3, '91- 3. Italian champion 1983-6, 1989-92.
21 Italian shot records 1982-7, inc. three world records on 12 Aug 1987.
Progression: 1976- 15.32, 1977- 17.46, 1978- 17.38i, 1979- 18.41, 1980- 19.58, 1981- 19.92, 1982- 20.35, 1983- 20.19, 1984- 21.50, 1985- 21.95, 1986- 22.06, 1987- 22.91, 1988- 20.61, 1989- 20.60i/20.03, 1990- 19.60i/19.48, 1991- 19.84, 1992- 20.79, 1993- 19.87/20.01i. pb DT 47.54 '79.
At Viareggio in 1987 all his six puts were over 22m, inc. records at 22.72, 22.84 and 22.91 although a raised circle may have been used.

Salvatore ANTIBO b.7 Feb 1962 Altofonte, Palermo 1.70m 52kg. CUS Palermo. Accountany student.
At 5000m/10000m: OG: '84- sf/4, '88- sf/2, '92- 16/4; EC: '82- h/6, '86- 10/3, '90- 1/1; ECp: '87- 3/2. At 5000m: WCh: '83- 13; EJ: '81- 2; ECp: '89- 1, '91- 1. At 10000m: WCh: '87- 16, '91- 20, '93- 12; WCp: '89- 1.
Italian records: 5000m 1990, three 10000m 1988-9, 2M 1988.
Progression at 5000m, 10000m: 1979- 15:06.9; 1980- 14:04.62; 1981- 13:48.55, 30:16.4; 1982- 13:31.84, 28:16.25; 1983- 13:32.44, 29:32.47; 1984- 13:33.65, 27:48.02; 1985- 13:21.26, 28:27.49; 1986- 13:21.41, 27:39.52; 1987- 13:27.39, 28:33.77; 1988- 13:16.1, 27:23.55; 1989- 13:14.30, 27:16.50; 1990- 13:05.59, 27:25.16; 1991- 13:10.10, 27:24.55; 1992- 13:10.08, 27:48.6; 1993- 13:45.96, 28:27.48. pbs: 1500m 3:42.2 '87, 2000m 5:05.92 '86, 3000m 7:43.57 '91, 2M 8:20.79 '87, Half Mar 62:39 '88.
His Italian 10000m records were when second at Bislett and Olympics in 1988 and winning at Helsinki 1989. In 1990 he was undefeated, with a superb European double, including his eighth successive win at 10000m and recovering from a fall at the start in the 5000m. Had a black-out in World final 1991.

Walter ARENA b.30 May 1964 Catania 1.73m 67kg. Fiamme Azzurre Roma. Warder.
At 20kmW: OG: '92- 18; WCh: '87- dq, '91- 7, '93- dq; EC: '86- 5, '90- 6; WCp: '85- 34, '87- 15, '89- 7, '91- 6; WSG: '89- 1. At 10000mW: EJ: '81- 5, '83- 1. At 5000mW: WI: '87- 7.
Italian track walk records 10000m 1987 & 1990, 20000m 1990.
Progression at 20kmW: 1984- 1:24:36, 1985- 1:24:51.4t, 1986- 1:22:42, 1987- 1:22:49, 1988- 1:22:10, 1989- 1:21:45, 1990- 1:19:24.1t, 1991- 1:21:01, 1992- 1:23:34.5t, 1993- 1:22:15.7. Track pbs: 1MW 5:51.5 '84, 3000mW 11:29.86 '89, 5000mW 18:44.99 '91, 10000mW 38:38.0 '90, 1HrW 14727 '90.

Andrea BENVENUTI b.13.12.69 Negrar, Venezia 1.85m 75kg. Fiamme Azzure Roma.
At 800m: OG: '92- 5; WCh: '93- h; WJ: '88- sf; WCp: '92- 3; ECp: '93- 2. Italian champion 1992. 2nd GP 1992.
Italian 1000m record 1992.
Progression at 800m: 1985- 1:56.5, 1986- 1:52.1, 1987- 1:51.77i/1:52.1, 1988- 1:49.6, 1989- 1:48.83, 1990- 1:48.33, 1991- 1:46.76, 1992- 1:43.92, 1993- 1:44.55. pbs: 400m 47.32 '92, 600m 1:15.13 '93, 1000m 2:15.76 '92, 1500m 3:41.60 '92.

Salvatore BETTIOL b.28 Nov 1961 Volpago del Montello 1.70m 57kg. Paf Verona.
At Mar: OG: '92- 5; WCh: '87- 13, '91- 6, '93- dnf; EC: '90- 4; WCp: '87- 3, '89- 7, '91- 10. Italian champion 1987, 1991. World CC best: '89- 17.
Progression at Mar: 1984- 2:17:16, 1985- 2:14:17, 1986- 2:13:27, 1987- 2:11:28/2:10:01 sh; 1988- 2:11:41; 1989- 2:10:08, 1990- 2:10:40, 1991- 2:11:48, 1992- 2:14:15, 1993- 2:11:44. pbs: 1500m 3:57.5 '86, 3000m 8:03.31 '89, 5000m 13:56.21 '89, 10000m 29:04.4 '88, Half Mar 62:21 '92.
Consistent marathon runner, but only two wins in 17 races: Venice 1986-7; at New York: 6th 1986, 2nd 1988, 4th 1989. Second London 1990.

Angelo CAROSI b.20 Jan 1964 Priverno 1.82m 66kg. Forestale. Forest warden.
At 3000mSt: WCh: '91- 7, '93- 8; EC: '90- 4. Italian champion 1989, 1991.
Progression at 3000mSt: 1984- 8:56.46, 1985- 8:51.62, 1986- 8:37.23, 1987- 8:27.38, 1989- 8:23.83, 1990- 8:17.48, 1991- 8:20.28, 1992- 8:39.81, 1993- 8:19.66. pbs: 1500m 3:42.43 '87, 3000m 7:49.91 '93, 2M 8:35.41 '90, 5000m 13:25.38 '93, 10000m 28:59.4 '90, 2000mSt 5:21.23 '90.

Paulo DAL SOGLIO b.29 Jul 1970 Schio, Vicenza 1.89m 110kg. Carabinieri Bologna.
At SP: WCh: '93- dnq; WI: '93- 5; WJ: '88- dnq; EJ: '89- 6; WSG: '93- 2; ECp: '93- 2.
Progression at SP: 1988- 17.69, 1989- 18.23, 1990- 18.48, 1991- 18.60, 1992- 19.76, 1993- 20.43/20.65i.

Giovanni DE BENEDICTIS b.8 Jan 1968 Pescara 1.80m 55kg. Carabinieri Bologna. Soldier.
At 20kmW: OG: '88- 9, '92- 3; WCh: '91- 4, '93- 2; EC: '90- 8; WCp: '89- 14, '91- 5, '93- 7. At 10000mW: WJ: '86- 4; EJ: '85- 3, '87- 1. Won Italian 10000mW 1988-91, 20kmW 1989-91. At 5000mW: WI: '89- 5, '91- 2; EI: '89- 3, '90- 2, '92- 1.
World best 2 miles walk 11:47.02 in 1989 and at 3000m 1990.
Progression at 20kmW: 1986- 1:30:41, 1987- 1:26:47. 1988- 1:21:18, 1989- 1:22:01, 1990- 1:22:14, 1991- 1:20:29, 1992- 1:22:17.0t, 1993- 1:21:16. pbs: 3000mW 10:47.11 '90, 5000mW 18:19.97i '92, 18:42.50 '91; 10000mW 39:10.35 '90, 1HrW 14680 '90.
Inside world record for 5000m walk but pipped by Shchennikov for world indoor title in 1991.

Giuseppe D'urso: unexpected world silver medal

Gennaro DI NAPOLI b.5 Mar 1968 Napoli 1.85m 61kg. Snam Gas Metano.
At 1500m: OG: '88- sf, '92- sf; WCh: '91- 8, '93- 12; EC: '90- 2; EJ: '87- 1; WCp: '89- 4; ECp: '89- 3, '91- 3. At 3000m: WI: '93- 1; EI: '92-1; Won Italian 1500m 1990-2.
Italian records: 1500m 1989 & 1990, 2000m 1991.
Progression at 1500m: 1985- 3:57.09, 1986- 3:49.4, 1987- 3:41.2, 1988- 3:34.72, 1989- 3:32.98, 1990- 3:32.78, 1991- 3:33.74, 1992- 3:33.80, 1993- 3:36.01. pbs: 800m 1:45.84 '90, 1000m 2:17.28 '91, 1M 3:53.48 '92, 2000m 4:55.0 '91, 3000m 7:42.68 '93, 5000m 13:27.87 '90.

Giuseppe D'URSO b.15 Sep 1969 Catania 1.78m 56kg. Fiamme Azzurre.

At 800m: WCh: '91- h; '93- 2; EC: '90- 7; WJ: '88- 5; WSG: '91- 1. Italian champion 1993.
Progression at 800m: 1985- 1:56.1, 1986- 1:51.97, 1988- 1:47.61, 1989- 1:46.9, 1990- 1:46.41, 1991- 1:45.94, 1992- 1:45.31, 1993- 1:44.83. pbs: 400m 48.9 '88, 1000m 2:16.19 '93, 1500m 3:43.15 '92, 1M 4:00.01 '93.

Giovanni EVANGELISTI b.11 Sep 1961 Rimini 1.79m 70kg. Assindustria Padova. Architect.
At LJ: OG: '84- 3, '88- 4, '92- dnq; WCh: '83- dnq, '87- 4, '91- 7; WI: '85- 3, '87- 3, '91- 3; EC: '82- 6, '86- 3, '90- 7; EI: '82- 3, '87- 2, '88- 3; WCp: '81- 6; ECp: '81- 8, '83- 6, '85- 8, '87- 4, '89- 4, '91- 3, '93- 1. Italian champion 1981-2, 1986, 1992.
Eight Italian long jump records 1982-7.
Progression at LJ: 1976- 5.40, 1977- 6.10, 1978- 6.68, 1979- 7.30, 1980- 7.84, 1981- 7.94, 1982- 8.10i/8.07/8.21w, 1983- 8.09/8.11w, 1984- 8.24, 1985- 8.14i/8.01, 1986- 8.24, 1987- 8.43, 1988- 8.07/8.37w, 1989- 8.15, 1990- 8.19, 1991- 8.13/8.35w, 1992- 8.07/8.29w, 1993- 7.94/8.04w. pbs: 100m 10.4 '81, 10.73 '84; TJ 16.30 '80.
Has won several major championship bronze medals, but that originally awarded at the 1987 World Championships was due to a judging conspiracy (eventually accepted by IAAF). His 8.38m was probably some 50cm less, and his earlier 8.19m placed him fourth.

Alessandro LAMBRUSCHINI b.7 Jan 1965 Fucecchio, Firenze 1.78m 63kg. Fiamme Oro Padova.
At 3000mSt: OG: '88- 4, '92- 4; WCh: '87- 9, '93- 3; EC: '86- h, '90- 3; WCp: '89- 2; ECp: '89- 1, '91- 1. At 2000mSt: EJ: '83- 4. At 5000m: ECp: '93- 2 (4 1500m). Won Italian 1500m 1986, 1993; 3000mSt 1986-7, 1990, 1992.
World best 2000m steeplechase 1989.
Progression at 3000mSt: 1983- 9:06.0, 1984- 8:55.43, 1985- 8:36.09, 1986- 8:18.39, 1987- 8:19.17, 1988- 8:12.17, 1989- 8:21.21, 1990- 8:15.82, 1991- 8:19.33, 1992- 8:13.38, 1993- 8:08.78. pbs: 800m: 1:47.81 '86, 1000m 2:18.12 '88, 1500m 3:35.27 '87, 1M 3:59.46 '92, 2000m 5:03.83 '92, 3000m 7:48.59 '93, 5000m 13:30.96 '93, 10,000m: 29:56.5, 2000mSt 5:18.36 '89, 400mh 55.7.

Francesco PANETTA b.10 Jan 1963 Siderno 1.75m 64kg. Paf Verona. Student.
At 3000mSt (10000m): OG: '84- sf (h), '88- 9; WCh: '87- 1 (2), '91- 8, '93- (6); EC: '86- 2, '90- 1; ECp: '85- 7, '87- 1, '89- (1), '91- (2), '93- 2 (2). At 2000mSt: EJ: '81- 7. World CC: '81- 9 Jnr, '84- 10, '89- 12. Won Italian 3000mSt 1985, 1988; 5000m 1988, 10000m 1986, CC 1987-90.
Italian 3000m, 10000m and 3000mSt records 1987.
Progression at 3000mSt, 10000m: 1981- 9:09.3; 1982- 8:33.24, 29:31.6; 1983- 8:35.39, 28:41.2; 1984- 8:26.90, 28:03.99; 1985- 8:21.60, 27:44.65; 1986- 8:16.85, 27:51.05; 1987- 8:08.57, 27:26.95; 1988- 8:16.04, 27:33.14; 1989- 8:21.19, 27:24.16; 1990- 8:12.66, 28:10.73; 1991- 8:14.41, 28:03.10; 1992- 27:45.46; 1993- 8:22.95, 28:13.99. pbs: 1500m 3:39.88 '87, 2000m 5:04.1 '88, 3000m 7:42.73 '87, 2M 8:30.7 '86, 5000m 13:06.76 '93, Half Mar 61:48 '87.
Followed his valiant silver (when he had led by some 40m at 2000m) in the 1986 European steeplechase with gold and silver in Rome 1987, and outkicked Mark Rowland for the gold in Split 1990.

Giovanni PERRICELLI b.25 Aug 1967 Milano 1.70m 57kg. Fiamme Azzurre. Customs officer.
At 50kmW: OG: '88- 11, '92- dnf; WCh: '91- dnf, '93- 13; EC: '90- 7; WCp: '91- 5. At 20kmW: WCp: '93- 10. Won Italian 50kmW 1987, 1989, 1991-2.
Progression at 50kmW: 1987- 3:47:50 (49.3km), 1988- 3:47:14, 1989- 3:58:10, 1990- 4:03:36, 1991- 3:49:40, 1992- 3:55:01, 1993- 3:54:30. pbs: 5000mW 19:17.88i/19:43.83 '93, 10000mW 40:15.49 '90, 20kmW 1:21:37 '91.

Women

Antonella BEVILACQUA b.15 Oct 1971 Foggia 1.71m 56kg. Snam Gas Metano.
At HJ: OG: '92- dnq 22; WCh: '93- 6; WJ: '90- 8; EJ: '89- 5=; ECp: '93- 4=. Won EU23 Cp 1992, Italian champion 1991-3.
Progression at HJ: 1985- 1.67, 1986- 1.79, 1987- 1.82, 1988- 1.82, 1989- 1.83, 1990- 1.89, 1991- 1.89i/1.86, 1992- 1.95, 1993- 1.94/1.95i.

Roberta BRUNET b.20 May 1965 Aosta 1.68m 55kg. Sisport Fiat.
At 3000m: OG: '88- h, '92- 10; WCh: '91- 6, '93- h; EC: '90- 3; ECp: '93- 4. At 1500m: EC: '86- h; EJ: '83- 7. At 800m: ECp: '85- 7. Won Italian 1500m 1985-6, 1988-90; 3000m 1986, 1988-90, 1992.
Italian 5000m record 1990.
Progression at 3000m: 1980- 10:19.1, 1981- 9:46.58, 1982- 9:38.78, 1983- 9:28.17, 1984- 9:14.61, 1985- 9:08.21, 1986- 9:01.55, 1988- 8:47.66, 1989- 8:55.12, 1990- 8:46.19, 1991- 8:42.64, 1992- 8:44.21, 1993- 8:47.92. pbs: 800m 2:07.24 '93, 1500m 4:08.92 '88, 1M: 4:41.02 '85, 2000m 5:50.32 '86, 5000m 15:51.20 '90.

Antonella CAPRIOTTI b.4 Feb 1962 Roma 1.65m 55kg. Sisport Fiat.
At LJ(/TJ): OG: '88 & '92- dnq; WCh: '87- dnq, '93- dnq/6; WI: '87- 8, '89- 5; '93- (4); EI: '89- 4;

ECp: '85- 7. Won Italian LJ 1984-90, 1993, TJ 1992-3.
Italian records: LJ (6) 1985-8, TJ (6) 1990-3.
Progression at LJ, TJ: 1977- 5.05, 1978- 5.38, 1980- 6.07, 1983- 6.38, 1984- 6.31, 1985- 6.56, 1986- 6.47, 1987- 6.51, 1988- 6.72i/6.70, 1989- 6.67i/6.57, 1990- 6.58, 13.14; 1991- 6.58/6.60w, 13.28/13.29w; 1992- 6.60/6.79w, 13.66; 1993- 6.72i/6.70, 14.18. pbs: 100m 11.88 '81, 11.8 '79; 200m 24.55 '80, 100mh 14.09 '82.

Elisabeta PERRONE b.9 Jul 1968 Camburzano, Vercelli. Snam Gas Metano.
At 10kmW: OG: '92- 19; WCh: '93- 4; WCp: '93- 11.
Progression at 10kmW: 1988- 53:08, 1989- 51:18, 1990- 48:23, 1991- 46:19, 1992- 44:19, 1993- 41:56/44:01.6t. pbs: 3000mW 11:56.40 '93, 5000mW 20:53.71 '93, 20kmW: 1:33:37 '93.

Ileana SALVADOR b.16 Jan 1962 Noale 1.63m 52kg. Sisport Fiat. Teacher. Married to Maurizio Facchin.
At 10kmW: OG: '92- dq; WCh: '91- 7, '93- 2; EC: '90- 3; WCp: '87- 45, '89- 3, '91- 6., '93- 6 At 5kmW: WSG: '89- 1. At 3000mW: WI: '89- 3, '91- 3, '93- 3; EI: '89- 2, '90- 2, '92- 2. Won Italian 5000mW 1989-93, 10kmW 1987, 1989-90, 1992.
World bests 3000m track and 10km road walk 1993. Unratified world records at 5000m and 10000m track walks and a further European 5000m walk record 1989. Five Italian 10000m track records 1988-93, three road 1989-93.
Progression at 10kmW: 1987- 49:36, 1988- 45:58.1t, 1989- 42:39.2t, 1990- 43:27/42:40Sh, 1991- 43:36, 1992- 42:07, 1993- 41:30/42:23.7t. Track pbs: 1MW 6:19.39 '91, 3000mW 11:48.24 '93; 2MW 13:11.00i '90 & 13:23.04 '89 (world bests), 5000mW 20:25.2 '92; road 20kmW 1:31:53 '93.
Disqualified at the 1992 Olympics having originally been listed as bronze medallist.

Annarita SIDOTI b.25 Jul 1969 Gioiosa Marea, Sicily 1.50m 42kg. Tyndaris Caleca Patti. Natural sciences student.
At 10kmW OG: '92- 7; WCh: '91- 9, '93- 9; EC: '90- 1; WCp: '89- 8, '91- 9, '93- 7; WSG: '91- 3. At 5000mW: WJ: '88- 4; EJ: '87- 7. At 3000mW: WI: '93- 6; EI: '90- 3, '92- 4. Won Italian 10kmW 1991, 20kmW 1992.
Progression at 10kmW: 1987- 49:37, 1988- 47:57.9t, 1989- 44:59, 1990- 44:00, 1991- 43:37, 1992- 43:03, 1993- 42:41. Track pbs: 1MW 6:46.53 '90, 3000mW 12:04.51i '92, 12:34.52 '93; 5000mW 21:19.2 '92, 10000mW 43:33.7 '93; road 20kmW 1:36:54 '92.
Perhaps the smallest ever major champion when she won the 1990 European title.

JAMAICA

Governing body: Jamaica Amateur Athletic Association, PO Box 272, Kingston 5. Founded 1932. **1993 Champions Men**: 100m: Michael Green 10.09, 200m: Ray Stewart 20.80, 400m: Dennis Blake 45.72, 800m: Clive Terrelonge 1:46.94, 1500m: LintonMcKenzie 3:46.1, 5000m: Norval Jones 15:51.09, 10000m: Oral Anderson 35:41.3, 3000mSt: Preston Campbell 10:00.8, 110mh: Andrew Parker 13.62, 400mh: Winthrop Graham 49.42, HJ: Dennis Fearon 2.08, PV: Shawn Cousins 3.55, LJ: Neil Gardener 7.64, TJ: Jerome Douglas 15.76, SP/DT: Howard Brown 14.90/50.18, JT: Raymond Passley 42.47. **Women**: 100m: Merlene Ottey 11.00/22.29, 400m: Juliet Campbell 50.11, 800m: Michelle Ballentine 2:09.53, 1500m: Janice Turner 4:24.44, 100mh: Michelle Freeman 12.77, 400mh: Deon Hemmings 55.46, HJ: Karen Beautle 1.73, LJ: Dionne Rose 6.63, TJ: Suzette Lee 13.02, SP/DT: Cecilia Clarke 11.11/37.28, JT: Olivia McKoy 38.66.

Winthrop GRAHAM b.17 Nov 1965 St.Elizabeth 1.78m 72kg. Was at University of Texas. Married Yvonne Mai GER 18 Jan 1992.
At 400mh/R- 4x400m relay: OG: '88- 5/2R, '92- 2; WCh: '87- sf, '91- 2/3R, '93- 3; PAm: '87- 1/3R. Won CAC 1987, NCAA 1989, GWG 1990. 3rd GP 1990, 1992.
Seven Jamaican 400mh records 1987-93.
Progression at 400mh: 1984- 53.1, 1985- 51.64, 1986- 50.03, 1987- 48.49, 1988- 48.04, 1989- 48.20, 1990- 48.03, 1991- 47.74, 1992- 47.62, 1993- 47.60. pb 400m 45.59 '88, 45.5 '89.
Steady improvement to silver medals in both Tokyo and Barcelona.

Michael GREEN b.7 Nov 1970 1.76m 73kg. Was at Clemson University.
At 100m: WCh: '91- sf; PAm: '91- 6; NCAA and Jamaican champion 1993. Won NCAA indoor 55m 1992-3.
Progression at 100m: 1990- 10.34w, 1991- 10.21/10.02w, 1992- 10.14/10.08w, 1993- 10.09/10.03w. pbs: 55m 6.08i '92, 60m 6.55i '93, 200m 20.72i '92, 20.86 '91, 20.73w '93.

Gregory HAUGHTON b. 10 Nov 1973 1.85m 79kg. Student at Central Arizona University.
At 400m/4x400mR: WCh: '93- 6; WJ: '92- sf/2R. Won CAC 1993.
Progression at 400m: 1991- 47.30, 1992- 46.88, 1993- 44.78. pbs: 200m 20.99 '93, 300m 33.00 '93.

Ray STEWART b.18 Mar 1965 Kingston 1.78m 73kg. Degree in radio and television from Texas Christian University, USA.
At 100m/R- 4x100m relay: OG: '84- 6/2R, '88-

7, '92- 7; WCh: '83- sf, '87- 2/3R, '91- 6, '93- 8 (qf 200m); CG: '90- sf/3R; PAm: '83- 5, '87- 2/3R; CAmG: '86- 3/2R. Won Jamaican 100m 1984, 1986, 1988-9, 1991; NCAA 1987, 1989.
Jamaican 100m records 1989 and 1991.
Progression at 100m: 1982- 10.73, 1983- 10.22, 1984- 10.19, 1986- 10.29/10.21w, 1987- 10.08 /9.89w/9.8w, 1988- 10.08/10.01w, 1989- 9.97, 1990- 10.17, 1991- 9.96, 1992- 10.06, 1993- 10.11. pbs: 55m 6.07i '89, 60m 6.41 '91, 200m 20.41 '88, 20.31w '87.
Youngest man in the 1984 Olympic 100m final. After World silver and bronze medals in 1987 he was the world's best 100m man in 1989.

Women

Juliet CAMPBELL b.17 Mar 1970 1.75m 62kg. Student at Auburn University, USA.
At 400mh: OG: '92- qf; WCh: '93- 7/4R. Won Jamaican and NCAA 400m 1993.
Jamaican 400mh record 1993.
Progression at 400m: 1989- 53.1, 1990- 53.01, 1991- 53.59, 1992- 51.11, 1993- 50.11. pbs: 100m 11.15w '93, 11.49 '90; 200m 22.80/22.66w '93.

Juliet CUTHBERT b.4 Sep 1964 1.60m 52kg. Was at University of Texas.
At 100m (200m): OG: '84- sf; '88- 7, '92- 2 (2); WCh: '83- qf/3R, '91- 6/1R. Won NCAA 100m 1986, 200m 1985-6; Jamaican 100m 1992. 3rd GP 100m 1993.
Progression at 100m, 200m: 1979- 11.6w, 1980- 12.25/12.0, 24.3/24.66; 1983- 11.39w/11.63, 23.29; 1984- 11.42, 24.26; 1985- 11.18, 22.78/ 22.39w; 1986- 11.24/10.97w, 22.71/22.35w; 1987- 11.07/10.95w, 22.59/22.25w/21.8w; 1988- 11.03/10.96w, 22.59; 1990- 11.16, 22.90; 1991- 11.12, 22.71; 1992- 10.83/10.7, 21.75; 1993- 11.16, 22.93. pbs: 50m 6.75i '91, 60m 7.23i '88, 400m 53.1 '86. Member of 1980 Jamaican Olympic relay squad.

Michelle FREEMAN b.5 May 1969 1.70m 61kg. Student at University of Florida.
At 100mh/R- 4x100m relay: OG: '92- qf; WCh: '91- sf, '93- 7/3R; WJ: '88- h (sf 100m); PAm: '91- 5. At 100m: CG: '90- h. At 60mh: WI: '93- dnf. Won Jamaican 100mh 1991-3, NCAA 1992. 3rd GP 1992. WIR 55mh 1992. Four Jamaican records 100mh 1990-2.
Progression at 100mh: 1988- 13.70, 1989- 13.61/13.4, 1990- 13.18/13.09w, 1991- 12.98, 1992- 12.75, 1993- 12.77. pbs: 55m 6.67i '92, 100m 11.16 '93, 11.13w '92; 200m 22.87 '92, 55mh 7.34i '92, 60mh 7.90i '93.
Had to withdraw from 1988 Olympic team through injury.

Deon HEMMINGS b.9 Oct 1968 1.76m 61kg. Student at Central State University, Ohio.
At 400mh: OG: '92- 7; WCh: '91- h, '93- 6; PAm: '91- 2. WI '93- 1 4x400m.
Jamaican 400mh record 1993.
Progression at 400mh: 1990- 61.72, 1991- 56.5, 1992- 54.70, 1993- 54.12. pbs: 100m 11.74 '91, 300m 37.71 '93, 400m 51.77 '93.

Nicole MITCHELL b.5 Jun 1974 1.68m 60kg.
At 100m/4x100mR: OG: '92- 7; WCh: '93- 8/3R; PAm: '91- 2; WJ: '90- 2/1R, '92- 1/1R. Won PAmJ 100m 1993.
Progression at 100m: 1990- 11.37, 1991- 11.4/ 11.2, 1992- 11.30/11.1/11.26w, 1993- 11.18/ 11.02w/11.0w. pb 200m 23.25 '93.

Merlene OTTEY b.10 May 1960 Cold Spring 1.74m 57kg. Larios, Spain. Graduate of Nebraska University. Now lives in Italy. Formerly married to Nat Page (USA).
At 100m/200m/R- 4x100m relay: OG: '80- -/3, '84- 3/3, '88- sf/4, '92- 5/3; WCh: '83- 4/2/3R, '87- 3/3, '91- 3/3/1R, '93- 2/1/3R; WI 200m (60m): '87- 2 (4), '89- 1 (3), '91- 1 (2); CG: '82: 2/1/3R, '90- 1/1/3R; PAm: '79- -/3. Won NCAA 100m 1982-3, 200m 1983; TAC 100m 1984-5, 200m 1982 and 1984-5; CAC 100m & 200m 1985. Won overall GP 1987 & 1990 (2nd 1991-2); 100m 1987, 1989, 1991; 200m 1990, 1992.
Commonwealth records: 200m (7), 100m (5) 1980-91. WIR: 50m 6.00 '94, 60m 6.96 '92, 200m (3) 22.24 twice '91, 21.87 '93; 300y (8) 1980-2 best 32.63 '82, 300m (3), best 35.83 '81.
Progression at 100m, 200m: 1975- 25.9; 1976- 12.0, 24.7; 1977- 12.2, 25.1; 1978- 12.6, 24.5; 1979- 11.59/11.4, 23.10/22.79w; 1980- 11.36/11.0, 22.20; 1981- 11.07/10.97w, 22.35; 1982- 11.03/ 10.97w, 22.17; 1983- 11.07/10.98w, 22.19/ 22.11w/21.9w; 1984- 11.01, 22.09; 1985- 10.92, 21.93; 1986- 11.06/10.7w, 22.43; 1987- 10.87/ 10.8, 22.06; 1988- 11.00/10.7, 21.99; 1989- 10.95, 22.21; 1990- 10.78, 21.66; 1991- 10.79/10.78w, 21.64; 1992- 10.80, 21.94; 1993- 10.93, 21.87i/ 22.27. pbs: 150m 16.46 (world best) '89, 400m 51.12 '83.
In 1993 she at last won the World title outdoors at 200m, having lost the 100m by a mere 1/1000th of a second - on both occasions she received overwhelming receptions fromthe crowd on the victory rostrum. Previously she had won four Olympic and five World bronze medals and the 1983 World 200m silver, but also anchored the Jamaican team to World gold in the sprint relay in 1991. Ranked in the world's top ten each year 1980-93. Won 73 successive finals (and 15 heats) 21 May 1989 to 8 Mar 1991, when beaten by Irina Privalova in World Indoor 60m. Her unbeaten runs at 100m:

57 finals from 3rd in 1987 World Champs, and 36 finals at 200m from 6 May 1989, were ended in Tokyo 1991. In 1990 she won all 36 finals, with a one-day 10.93 and 21.66 double at Zürich, both into the wind, and a one year record of seven sub-22.00 200m times. Has a record 37 legal times sub 11.00 for 100m (previous best 33 by Marlies Göhr). Appointed a roving ambassador for Jamaica in 1993.

Sandie RICHARDS b.6 Nov 1968 1.70m 61kg. Was at University of Texas.
At 400m/R- 4x400m relay: OG: '88- qf/5R, '92- 7/5R; WCh: '87- sf/6R, '93- 3/4R; WI: '93- 1/2R; WJ: '86- 3; WSG: '87- 3; PAm: '87- 8/3R, '91- 6/3R. Won JAM 400m 1991-3, PAm Jnr 1986, GP 1992.
Jamaican 400m record 1987.
Progression at 400m: 1986- 52.18, 1987- 50.92, 1988- 51.62, 1989- 51.46, 1990- 51.94, 1991- 51.06, 1992- 50.19, 1993- 50.44. pbs: 200m 23.66 '86, 23.15w '87; 800m 2:04.79 '93.

Gillian RUSSELL b.28 Sep 1973 1.66m 48kg. Student at University of Miami.
At 100mh/R- 4x100m relay: OG: '92- sf; WCh: '93- sf; WJ: '88- sf, '90- 1/1R, '92- 1/1R. NCAA champion 1993.
Progression at 100mh: 1988- 13.79, 1989- 13.90, 1990- 13.31, 1991- 13.73, 1992- 13.07, 1993- 13.00. pbs: 100m 11.41 '93, 11.3/11.53w '92; 55mh 7.58i '92.
Has a record four World Junior gold medals.

JAPAN

Governing body: Nippon Rikujo-Kyogi Renmei, 1-1-1 Jinnan, Shibuya-Ku, Tokyo 150. Founded 1911.
National Championships first held in 1914 (men), 1925 (women). **1993 Champions**: **Men**: 100m: Satoru Inoue 10.57, 200m: Michihiko Komura 21.30, 400m: Shunji Karube 46.32, 800m: José Luiz Barbosa BRA 1:46.21, 1500m: Yasunori Uchitomi 3:46.46, 5000m: Alois Nizigama BUR 13:29.99, 10000m: Stephen Mayaka KEN 28:25.24, Mar: Dionicio Ceron MEX 2:08:51, 3kmSt: Bizuneh Yae Tura ETH 8:29.71, 110mh: Yusuke Tsuge 14.08, 400mh: Yoshihiko Saito 48.68, HJ: Satoru Nonaka 2.28, PV: Toshiyuki Hashioka 5.50, LJ: Tetsuya Shida 7.98w, TJ: Edrick Floreal CAN 16.81, SP/DT: Adewale Olukoju NGR 17.47/61.72, HT: Akiyoshi Ikeda 66.28, JT: Takahiro Yamada 70.96, Dec: Munehiro Kaneko 7874, 20kmW: Satoshi Yanagisawa 1:29:50, 50kmW: Fumio Imamura 3:57:30. **Women**: 100m: Ayako Nomura 11.91, 200m: Chiaki Takagi 24.84, 400m: Ai Ota 54.50, 800m: Mariko Ikeda 2:10.84, 1500m: Yoshiko Ichikawa 4:22.86, 3000m: Iulia Ionescu ROM 8:58.86, 10000m: Midori Fumoto 33:26.36, Mar: Valentina Yegorova RUS 2:26:40, 100mh: Chan Sauying HKG 13.63, 400mh: Ikiko Yamagata 58.96, HJ: Megumi Sato 1.84, LJ: Liliane Nastase ROM 6.45w, TJ: Naomi Hashioka 13.02, SP: Aya Suzuki 15.59, DT: Ikuko Kitamori 53.12, JT: Akiko Miyajima 57.26, Hep: Yukiko Ueno 5185, 10kmW: Yuko Mitsumori 45:05.

Koichi MORISHITA b.5 Sep 1967 Yazu Town, Tottori Pref. 1.65m 53kg. Asahi Kasei Chemical employee.
At Mar: OG: '92- 2. At 10000m: WCh: '91- 10; AsG: '90- 1 (2 5000m).
Progression at 10000m, Mar: 1985- 30:42.7, 1986- 29:29.8, 1989- 28:17.0, 1990- 28:26.77, 1991- 28:03.13, 2:08:53; 1992- 28:01.98, 2:10:19. pbs: 1500m 3:52.07 '85, 5000m 13:37.64 '91, 3000mSt 8:57.43 '86.
Has won both his marathons, the world's fastest of 1991 when he won at Beppu on his début and Tokyo 1992. Coached by Shigeru and Takeshi So.

Takeyuki NAKAYAMA b.20 Dec 1959 Ikeda Town, Nagano Pref. 1.80m 58kg. Employee, Daiei Store.
At Mar: OG: '88- 4, '92- 4; WCh: '91- dnf; AsG: '86- 1; WCp: '85- 2. Japan champion 1987.
Asian records: marathon 1985, 10000m 1987.
Progression at 10000m/Mar: 1983- 2:14:15, 1984- 29:10.00/2:10:00, 1985- 28:26.9/2:08:15, 1986- 28:07.0/2:08:21, 1987- 27:35.33/2:08:18, 1988- 28:01.74/2:11:05, 1990- 2:10:57, 1991- 2:09:12, 1992- 2:10:25. pbs: 1500m 3:54.5 '81, 5000m 13:43.80 '85, 30km 1:31:50 '83.
Has won five of his 16 marathons: Fukuoka 1984 & 1987, Seoul 1985, Tokyo 1990, Asian Games 1986. 2nd Tokyo 1987 & 1992, Beppu 1991.

Yoshihiko SAITO b.12 Feb 1972 Tomioka City, Gunma Pref. 1.77m 63kg. Student at Hosei University.
At 400mh: OG: '92- h; WCh: '91- h, '93- sf; WJ: '90- 2; WSG: '91- 2, '93- 2; AsCh: '91- 1. Won Asian Jnr 1990, Japan champion 1992-3. At 4x400mR: WI: '93- 3R.
Four Asian (and two Asian junior) 400mh records 1991-3.
Progression at 400mh: 1987- 57.65, 1988- 53.37, 1989- 51.44, 1990- 49.87, 1991- 49.10, 1992- 49.01, 1993- 48.68. pbs: 400m 46.43/46.3 '93, 110mh 14.59 '89, 14.4 '90.

Hiromi TANIGUCHI b.4 Apr 1960 Nango Town, Miyazaki Pref. 1.76m 56kg. Graduate of

Nihon College of PE, employee of Asahi Kasei Chemical.
At Mar: OG: '92- 8; WCh: '91- 1; AsG: '86- 2.
Progression at Mar: 1985- 2:10:01, 1986- 2:10:08, 1987- 2:09:50, 1988- 2:07:40, 1989- 2:09:34, 1990- 2:10:56, 1991- 2:11:55, 1992- 2:14:42, 1993- 2:11:02. pbs: 1500m 3:54.0 '82, 5000m 13:49.17 '89, 10000m 28:34.18 '89.
Has won 7 of 17 marathons including Beppu 1985, Tokyo and London 1987, Tokyo and Sapporo 1989, Rotterdam 1990. Fastest time when second in Beijing 1988.

Women

Tomoe ABE b.13 Aug 1971 1.50m 38kg. Employee.
At Mar: WCh: '93- 3.
Progression at Mar: 1993- 2:26:27, 1994- 2:26:09. pbs: 3000m 9:22.15 '89, 5000m 15;53.46 '93, 10000m 32:55.78 '93, 20km Rd 1:07:39 '93.
In 1993 was 2nd in Osaka on marathon début in 2:26:27 and 3rd in Stockholm. Won Osaka 1994.

Yuko ARIMORI b.17 Dec 1966 Okayama City 1.66m 47kg. Graduate of Nihon College of PE. Employee of Recruit.
At Mar: OG: '92- 2; WCh: '91- 4.
Japanese marathon record 1991.
Progression at Mar: 1990- 2:32:51, 1991- 2:28:01, 1992- 2:32:49. pbs: 800m 2:20.2 '84, 1500m 4:35.2 '88, 3000m 9:51.2 '88.
Four marathons; second Osaka 1991.

Junko ASARI b.22 Sep 1969 1.64m 42kg. Daihatsu employee.
At Mar: WCh: '93- 1.
Progression at Mar: 1991- 2:37:01, 1992- 2:28:57, 1993- 2:26:26, 1994- 2:26:10. pbs: 3000m 9:22.1 '89, 5000m 16:06.04 '93, 10000m 32:25.45 '92, 20km 1:08:51.9/1:07:54Rd '92.
Wins at Osaka and Stockholm in 1993 came in her fourth and fifth marathons. 3rd Osaka 1994.

Akemi MATSUNO b.27 Apr 1968 Ueki Town, Kukamoto Pref. 1.48m 35kg. Nikonikodo Store employee.
At 10000m: OG: '88- h; WCh: '91- h; AsG: '90- 3. At Mar: WCh: '93- 11. Won Japanese 10000m 1988, 1990.
Two Japanese 10000m records 1988-9.
Progression at 10000m/Mar: 1987- 35:15.6, 1988- 32:19.57, 1989- 31:54.0, 1990- 31:56.93, 1991- 32:31.18, 1992- 2:27:02. pbs: 3000m 9:29.86 '88, 5000m 15:45.9 '89.
Second in 1992 Osaka Marathon in world's second fastest ever début marathon by a woman. Second Nagoya 1993.

Mari TANIGAWA b.27 Oct 1962 Fukuoka 1.60m 44kg. Shiseido employee.
World Half Mar: '93- 2. At Mar: WCp: '91- 14; Japanese champion 1991.
Progression at Mar: 1988- 3:00:58, 1989- 2:43:04, 1990- 2:34:10, 1991- 2:31:27, 1992- 2:31:09, 1993- 2:28:22. pbs: Half Mar 70:09 '93.
Second in marathons at Nagoya 1992 and Tokyo 1993.

Yoshiko YAMAMOTO b.6 Jun 1970 Kobe City 1.59m 44kg. Daiei Store employee.
Progression at Mar: 1989- 2:38:10, 1990- 2:35:11, 1991- 2:36:22, 1992- 2:26:26, 1993- 2:29:12. pbs: 5000m 15:53.2 '91, 10000m 32:51.78 '91, 20k Rd 1:06:30 '93, Half Mar 1:11:50 '93.
Won Paris marathon 1990. Great improvement in 1992 to run 2:27:58 for 4th in Osaka, second in Boston Marathon, when she equalled the Asian record, and third in New York. Fourth and fifth successive sub-2:30 runs when 3rd Osaka and 1st Amsterdam 1993.

Sachiko YAMASHITA b.20 Aug 1964 Osaka 1.56m 40kg. Graduate of Tettori University. Kyocera Corporation employee.
At Mar: OG: '92- 4; WCh: '91- 2.
Progression at Mar: 1989- 2:34:59, 1990- 2:33:17, 1991- 2:29:57, 1992- 2:36:26. pbs: 800m 2:14.3 '82, 1500m 4:32.1 '88, 3000m 9:33.79 '90, 5000m 16:09.84 '91, 10000m 33:10.28 '89.
Has run seven marathons, with her first win in Nagoya 1991 in 2:31:02. Then won silver medal in Tokyo, the first at a World Championships by a Japanese woman.

KAZAKHSTAN

Governing body: Athletic Federation of the Republic of Kazakhstan, Abai Street 48, 480072 Alma-Ata. Founded 1959.

Igor POTAPOVICH b.6 Sep 1967 Alma-Ata 1.85m 75kg. Alma-Ata Dyn.
At PV: WCh: '93- dnq 14=; EI: '89- 2; WJ: '86- 1; WCp: '92- 1; AsiC: '93- 2.
Progression at PV: 1981- 3.10, 1982- 4.20, 1983- 4.80, 1984- 5.10, 1985- 5.20, 1986- 5.50, 1987- 5.60, 1988- 5.65, 1989- 5.75i/5.70, 1990- 5.85, 1991- 5.90, 1992- 5.92, 1993- 5.80.

Oleg SAKIRKIN b.23 Jan 1966 Chimkent 1.82m 72kg. Chimkent TR, Kazakh SSR.
At TJ: WCh: '87- 3, '93- dnq; WSG: '89- 3, '93- 2; ECp: '89- 1, '91- 7; EI: '88- 1, '90- 2; AsiC: '93- 2.
Progression at TJ: 1978- 12.20, 1979- 13.30, 1980- 13.87, 1981- 14.12, 1982- 14.80, 1983- 15.50, 1984- 15.93, 1985- 16.39, 1986- 17.12, 1987- 17.43, 1988- 17.50, 1989- 17.58, 1990- 17.36i/16.92, 1991- 17.43, 1992- 17.20, 1993- 17.17. pbs: 100m 10.7, LJ 7.76 '87.

Grigoriy YEGOROV b.12 Jan 1967 Chimkent 1.85m 75kg. Alma-Ata Dyn. Sports student.
At PV: OG: '88- 3; WCh: '93- 2; EC: '90- 2; WI: '89- 2, '93- 2; ECp: '87- 1, '91- 1; EI: '89- 1, '90- 2; WJ: '86- 5; EJ: '85- 2; AsiC: '93- 1. 2nd GP 1993.
Asian pole vault record holder.
Progression at PV: 1981- 3.00, 1982- 4.10, 1983- 5.00, 1984- 5.45, 1985- 5.55, 1986- 5.61i/5.50, 1987- 5.70, 1988- 5.85, 1989- 5.81, 1990- 5.90i/5.87, 1991- 5.85, 1992- 5.85, 1993- 5.90. pb 100m 10.7.
Has a great record with medals at each of the major events that he has contested as a senior.

Women

Natalya TORSHINA b.4 Oct 1968. 1.72m 57kg.
At 400mh: WCh: '93- 8; AsiC: '93-1.
KZK 400mh records 1992 and 1993.
Progression at 400mh: 1990- 59.53, 1991- 55.77, 1992- 55.43, 1993- 54.53.

KENYA

Governing body: Kenya Amateur Athletic Association, Nyayo National Stadium, PO Box 46722, Uhuru-High-Way, Nairobi. Founded 1951.
1993 National Champions: **Men**:
100m/200m: Kennedy Ondiek 10.2/20.7, 400m: Kennedy Ochieng 44.5, 800m: William Tanui 1:45.5, 1500m: David Kibet 3:41.3, 5000m: Joseph Kibor 13:40.6, 10000m: Ismael Kirui 28:07.1, Mar: Nicholas Kioko 2:13:16, 3000mSt: Joseph Keter 8:36.0; 110mh/400mh: Barnabas Kinyor 14.2/48.7, HJ: Abdul Wako 2.10, PV: Gilbert Sanga 4.20, LJ: James Sabulei 7.94, TJ: Jacob Katonen 16.47, SP/DT: James Nyambureti 17.38/54.59, HT: Patrick Njorege 59.90, JT: Edward Ndiwa 69.22, 20kmW: Justus Kavulanya 1:24:40. **Women**: 100m: Jane Nyamogo 11.5, 200m: Hellen Chemtai 24.4, 400m/800m: Gladys Wamuyu 54.3/2:02.5, 1500m: Lenah Chesire 4:12.5, 3000m/10000m: Selina Barsosio 9:10.6/32:43.4, 100mh/400mh: Caroline Kola 14.6/59.7, HJ: Frida Mirichia 1.63, LJ: Eunice Basweti 5.87, TJ: Helen Jemtai 12.23, SP/DT: Elizabeth Olaba 14.23/42.56, JT: Milka Johnson 44.65, 10kmW: Grace Karimi 52.46.

Lameck AGUTA b.10 Oct 1971.
World Half Mar: '92- 4, '93- 4.
Progression at 10000m: 1991- 28:14.77, 1992- 27:56.21, 1993- 28:34.22. pbs: 5000m 13:31.61 '92, Road: 15km 43:41 '92, Half Mar 60:55dh '92, Mar 2:17:36 '93.

Philip BARKUTWO b.6 Oct 1966 1.71m 60kg. Nandi. Soldier.
At 3000mSt: WCp: '92- 1; won AAA 1990.
Progression at 3000mSt: 1988- 8:38.8, 1989- 8:38.1, 1990- 8:14.93, 1991- 8:08.39, 1992- 8:05.37, 1993- 8:23.44. pbs: 1500m 3:40.15 '90, 3000m 7:44.33 '92, 5000m 13:26.19 '92, 2000mSt 5:23.91 '92.

Jonah Kipchirchir **BIRIR** b.27 Dec 1971 Eldama Ravine, Baringo 1.68m 61kg. Tugen. K-Way Club, Italy,
At 800m: WJ: '88- 1, '90- 2. At 1500m: OG: '92- 5; WCh: '93- sf; WCp: '92- 2. World CC: '89- 13 Jnr.
African junior 800m record 1990.
Progression at 1500m: 1989- 3:41.1, 1990- 3:43.4, 1991- 3:39.10, 1992- 3:33.36, 1993- 3:33.86. pbs: 800m 1:45.95 '91, 1000m 2:18.06 '92, 1M 3:52.54 '92, 3000m 7:49.33i '92.
Elder brother of Matthew Birir, although reportedly born only six months earlier!

Matthew Kiprotich **BIRIR** b.5 Jul 1972 Eldama Ravine, Baringo 1.72m 62kg. Tugen.
At 3000mSt: OG: '92- 1; WCh: '93- 4; WJ: '88- 2, '90- 1. World Jnr CC: '90- 6.
World junior 3000m steeplechase records 1990 and 1991.
Progression at 3000mSt: 1987- 8:56.8, 1988- 8:43.4, 1989- 8:56.77, 1990- 8:28.43, 1991- 8:24.47, 1992- 8:08.84, 1993- 8:09.42. pbs: 5000m 13:49.61 '90, 2000mSt 5:23.49 '92.

Paul BITOK b.26 Jun 1970 Kilibwoni 1.73m 58kg. Nandi. Airman (SPTE).
At 5000m: OG: '92- 2; WCh: '93- 8; WJ: '88- 9; AfrG: '93- 4. Won GP 1992.
Progression at 5000m: 1988- 14:08.8, 1992- 13:08.89, 1993- 13:08.68. pbs: 2000m 5:05.6 '92, 3000m 7:33.28 '92.
Member of the winning World Road Relay team 1992. No relation to the other notable Bitoks.

Richard CHELIMO b.21 Apr 1972 Chesubet 1.65m 55kg. Elgeyo Marakwet. Civil servant with Kenyan Army (private).
At 10000m: OG: '92- 2; WCh: '91- 2, '93- 3; WJ: '90- 1. World CC: '90- 2 Jnr, '91- 4, '92- 5. 2nd GP 5000m 1991-3. Won Kenyan 10000m 1992.
World 10000m record 1993. World junior records: 5000m (3) and 10000m 1991. African and Commonwealth 10000m record 1991.
Progression at 5000m, 10000m: 1989- 14:16.2, 1990- 13:59.49, 28:18.57; 1991- 13:11.76, 27:11.18; 1992- 13:10.46, 27:15.53; 1993- 13:05.14, 27:07.91. pbs: 3000m 7:41.63 '93, 2M 8:26.29 '91.
He won the 1990 World Juniors by 22 seconds from his brother Ismael Kirui. Since then has run many fast times, with two silvers and a bronze in major 10000m races.

Simon CHEMOIYWO b.2 May 1969 1.70m 60kg. Elgeiyo. (Or Chemwoyo).

At 5000m: Afr G: '93- 1.
Progression at 5000m: 1992- 13:18.95, 1993- 13:09.68. pbs: 3000m 7:49.51 '92, 10000m: 28:11.0 '93. Road 10km 28:10 '93, 10M: 46:27 '93.

Mike CHESIRE b.1 Dec 1969 1.67m 57kg. K-Way Club, Italy. Elgeiyo.
At 5000m: WCh: '93- 14.
Progression at 5000m: 1991- 13:29.13, 1992- 13:53.51, 1993- 13:16.15. pbs: 3000m 7:47.40i/ 7:51.78 '93, 2M 8:27.57 '93.

Paul ERENG b.22 Aug 1967 Trans-Nzoia, near Kitale 1.86m 72kg. University of Virginia, USA. Turkana.
At 800m: OG: '88- 1, '92- sf; WCh: '91- 4; WI: '89- 1, '91- 1. Won NCAA 1988-9, Kenyan 800m 1991.
WIB 800m 1:44.84 '89.
Progression at 400m/800m: 1984- 49.6, 1985- 47.6, 1986- 47.0, 1987- 45.6, 1988- 46.3/1:43.45, 1989- 1:43.16, 1990- 1:43.78, 1991- 1:44.06, 1992- 1:46.1, 1993- 1:44.96. pb 1000m 2:17.37 '89.
Made amazing progress in 1988, his first year of 800m running, to end the year with a brilliant victory at the Olympics.

Ibrahim Kipkemboi HUSSEIN b.3 Jun 1958 Kapsabet, Nandi 1.78m 57kg. Economics student. Was at University of New Mexico.
At Mar: OG: '88- dnf, '92- 37; CG: '90- 5.
Kenyan marathon records 1988 and 1992.
Progression at Mar: 1984- c.2:20, 1985- 2:12:08, 1986- 2:11:44, 1987- 2:11:01, 1988- 2:08:43, 1989- 2:12:41, 1990- 2:13:20, 1991- 2:11:06, 1992- 2:08:14. pbs: 1500m 3:42.9 '83, 1M 4:00.2 '83, 3000m 7:51.19 '84, 5000m 13:50.65 '84, 3000mSt 8:35.4 '84.
Has won seven of his 16 marathons: Honolulu 1985-7, New York 1987, Boston 1988, 1991-2. Third New York 1991. His brother Mbarak Hussein has bests of 800m: 1:46.68 and 1500m: 3:37.61 in 1990.

Julius KARIUKI b.12 Jun 1961 Nyahururu 1.81m 62kg. Mission Viejo club, formerly biochemistry student at Riverside CC, California. Kikuyu.
At 3000mSt: OG: '84- 7, '88- 1; WCh: '91- 4; CG: '90- 1; AfCh: '85- 1; WCp: '85- 1, '89- 1. Won GP 1988 & 1990, 3rd 1993. At 3000m: WI: '87- 6. At 10000m: WSG: '89- 1.
World best 2000m steeplechase 1990.
Progression at 3000mSt: 1981- 9:34.5, 1984- 8:17.47, 1985- 8:20.74, 1986- 8:15.92, 1988- 8:05.51, 1989- 8:12.18, 1990- 8:13.28, 1991- 8:11.28, 1992- 8:16.77, 1993- 8:13.38. pbs: 1000m 2:20.98 '90, 1500m 3:37.79 '86, 1M 4:00.43 '86, 2000m 5:04.71 '86, 3000m 7:47.35 '86, 5000m 13:35.72 '89, 10000m 28:35.46 '89, 2000mSt 5:14.43 '90.
Ran the second fastest time ever, and the fastest on auto timing to win at 1988 Olympics.

Joseph KEINO b. 1963 178m 60kg. General Service Unit (GSU). Marakwet.
World Half Mar: '92- 6.
Progression at 10000m: 1987- 30:37.0, 1988- 28:59.4, 1989- 28:12.6, 1991- 27:36.88, 1992- 27:35.77, 1993- 27:55.9. pbs: 5000m 13:30.54 '91; road: 10M 46:05 '91, Half Mar 60:33 '91.

Simon KEMBOI b.3 Jan 1967Moiben, near Eldoret 1.78m 74kg. Nandi.
At 400m/4x40m relay: OG: '92- sf; WCh: '93- 7/2R; WCp: '92- 1R; AfCh: '93- 3. Won Kenyan 400m 1992.
Progression at 400m: 1991- 45.6, 1992- 44.8/45.40, 1993- 44.94/44.7. pb 200m 21.3 '92.

William KEMEI b.22 Feb 1969 Kapsabet 1.83m 64kg. Nandi.
At 1500m: AfG: '91- 1. 2nd GP 1M 1992.
Kenyan records for 1500m and 1 mile 1992.
Progression at 1500m: 1988- 3:49.2, 1991- 3:34.77, 1992- 3:32.41, 1993- 3:36.80. pb 1M 3:48.80 '92.

Erick KETER b.22 Ju 1966 Kabaruso, Kericho 1.70m 60kg. Kenya Ports Authority. Kipsigis.
At 400mh/4x400mR: OG: '92- sf; WCh: '91- 7, '93- 5; AfG: '91- 1/1R, '93- 1/1R?.
Four Kenyan 400mh records 1991-3.
Progression at 400mh: 1989- 53.9, 1990- 53.2, 1991- 48.47, 1992- 48.28, 1993- 48.24. pbs: 400m 46.78 '91, 110mh 14.7 '86.
Made a startling breakthrough in 1991, improving from 53.2 in 1990 to 49.6 in May and to Kenyan records of 48.62 and 48.47 in the preliminary rounds in the World Championships.

Joseph KETER b. 1968. Nandi.
At 3000mSt: AfG: '93- 1. Kenyan champion 1993.
Progression at 3000mSt: 1991- 8:44.0, 1992- 8:21.74, 1993- 8:21.04. pb 3000m 7:52.78 '93.

David Ruto **KIBET** b. 24 Nov 1963 Burnt Forest, Uasin Gishu 1.89m 68kg. Parachutist in Kenyan Air Force (lance corporal). Nandi.
At 1500m: OG: '92- 10; WCh: '91- 7, '93- sf; AfCh: '90-3; AfrG: '93- 1. Kenyan champion 1990-1, 1993. Kenyan 1500m record 1992.
Progression at 1500m: 1988- 3:41.6, 1989- 3:39.9, 1990- 3:34.96, 1991- 3:33.51, 1992- 3:32.13, 1993- 3:33.88. pbs: 1000m 2:18.47 '91, 1M 3:51.80 '91, 2000m 3:55.31 '92, 3000m 7:49.9i '91, 2M 8:22.34i '92.

Originally a high jumper. Winner of Dream Mile 1992.

Robert Langat **KIBET** b.15 Dec 1965 (4 May 1964?) Litein, Kericho. Air Force technician (corporal). Kipsigis.
At 800m: WCh: '91- sf; CG: '90- 9; AfG: '91- 2; AfCh: '90- 2. At 1500m: AfCh: '89- 2. Won Kenyan 800m 1989.
Progression at 800m: 1986- 1:49.9, 1988- 1:46.7, 1989- 1:43.70, 1990- 1:44.29, 1991- 1:44.06, 1992- 1:44.20, 1993- 1:44.26. pbs: 400m 46.3 '89, 600m 1:15.6 '91, 1000m 2:21.29 '90, 1500m 3:37.4 '91, 1M 3:56.34 '89, 400mh: 51.0 '88.
Forced to give up 400m hurdling through a knee injury, he made a dramatic debut on the world scene at 800m in 1989.

Nixon KIPROTICH b.4 Dec 1962 Baringo 1.85m 68kg. Tugen.
At 800m: OG: '88- 8, '92- 2; CG: '90- 2; WCp: '89- 3; AfCh: '89- 1 (3 1500m). East African champion 1988. Won GP 1990 & 1992.
Progression at 800m: 1986- 1:47.58, 1987- 1:46.8, 1988- 1:44.5, 1989- 1:43.38, 1990- 1:44.43, 1991- 1:47.98, 1992- 1:43.31, 1993- 1:43.54. pbs: 400m 45.8 '89, 1000m 2:16.45 '89, 1500m 3:38.76 '89, 1M 4:01.79 '89, TJ 14.78 '85.

Moses KIPTANUI b.1 Oct 1971 (but age 22 in 1992 he said!) Elgeyo Marakwet area 1.79m 69kg. Marakwet. Soldier (corporal).
At 3000mSt: WCh: '91- 1, '93- 1; AfG: '91- 1; won GP 1991, 2nd 1993. At 1500m: WJ: '90- 1; AfCh: '90- 1. Won Kenyan 3000mSt 1991, 1500m 1992.
World records at 3000m and 3000m steeplechase, Kenyan records 2000m and 5000m and WIR 3000m (7:37.31) in 1992.
Progression at 1500m, 3000mSt, 5000m: 1989- 8:46.6, 1990- 3:36.73; 1991- 3:35.40, 8:06.46; 1992- 3:34.00, 8:02.08, 13:00.93; 1993- 3:35.44, 8:06.36, 13:14.62. pbs: 1M 3:52.06 '91, 2000m 4:52.53 '92, 3000m 7:28.96 '92, 2M 8:16.18i '92.
Made an astonishing (even by Kenyan standards) breakthrough into top-class. In 1990, with no known form the previous year he won the World Junior and African senior titles at 1500m. In 1991 he turned to the steeplechase, running 8:31.0 to win the Kenyan services title in June, and then a month later threatening the world record with 8:07.89 in Stockholm. He went on to win the world title easily and to run 8:06.46. In 1992 he did not make the Kenyan Olympic team as he was 4th at 3000mSt in the Kenyan Trials, slowed by injury. However he showed sensational form in August when he set world records for 3000m in Köln and three days later for the steeplechase in Zürich, followed by close attempts at world records for 2000m and on his début at 5000m.

Wilfred Oanda KIROCHI b.12 Dec 1969 Kisii 1.67m 62kg. Mosocho Railway Club, Nairobi. Kisii. Hotel management student in Italy.
At 1500m: WCh: '91- 2; CG: '90- 2; WJ: '86- 1, '88- 1; AfG: '87- 2. Won GP 1M 1992 (2nd 1500m 1989). Won East & Central African 1500m 1987. World CC: '87- 1J, '88- 1J, '89- 3. Kenyan 1500m record 1989.
Progression at 1500m: 1983- 3:52.0, 1984- 3:49.0, 1985- 3:55.2, 1986- 3:40.8, 1987- 3:39.01, 1988- 3:36.07, 1989- 3:32.57, 1990- 3:32.90, 1991- 3:33.8, 1992- 3:32.49, 1993- 3:39.44. pbs: 800m 1:45.05 '89, 1000m 2:17.64 '91, 1M 3:49.77 '91, 2000m 5:15.86 '88, 3000m 7:46.76 '89, 5000m 14:00.4 '90.
Had unparalleled success as a junior, with four world titles, although he may well have been too old (b.1966?). Now based in Verona, Italy.

Dominic KIRUI b.12 Apr 1967 1.77m 62kg. Kipsigis.
At 5000m: OG: '92- 14. World CC: '92- 7, '93- 2.
Progression at 5000m: 1991- 13:36.26, 1992- 13:17.26. pbs: 3000m 7:45.68 '91, 10000m: 28:11.92 '91. Road 10km: 27:46 '92.
Third IAAF Cross Challenge 1992/3.

Ismael Kirui: only 18 when he won in Stuttgart?

Ismael KIRUI b.20 Feb 1975 Marakwet 1.60m 54kg. Marakwet.
At 5000m: WCh: '93- 1; WJ: '92- 2. Won GP 1993. At 10000m: WJ: '90- 2. World CC: Jnr '90- 4, '91- 7, '92- 1; Snr: '93- 3. Won Kenyan 10000m 1993.
World junior records 3000m, 5000m (3) 1993.
Progression at 5000m: 1990- 13:59.6, 28:40.77; 1992- 13:15.67, 29:35.0; 1993- 13:02.75, 28:07.1. pbs: 3000m 7:39.82 '93.
Won IAAF Cross Challenge 1992/3. Younger brother of Richard Chelimo to whom he was runner-up at the 1990 World Juniors.

Samson KITUR b.25 Feb 1966 Moiben, Eldoret 1.82m 75kg. Nandi. K-Way club, Italy.
At 400m/4x400mR: OG: '92- 3; WCh: '91- sf/5R, '93- 3/2R; CG: '90- 2/1R; AfG: '91- 1/1R; AfCh: '90- 1; WI: '91- 2. Kenyan champion 1989, 1991.
Progression at 400m: 1989- 45.2, 1990- 44.88, 1991- 45.23, 1992- 44.18, 1993- 44.34. pbs: 100m 10.3 '89, 200m 21.14/20.7 '90, 800m 1:47.53 '90.
Younger brother of Simeon (49.70 for 400mh 1984) and David (Kenyan record 44.73 for 400m 1987, 6th WCh).

Benson KOECH b.10 Nov 1974 1.73m 65kg. Student. Elgeiyo.
At 800m: WJ: '92- 1.
Progression at 800m, 1500m: 1991- 3:43.4, 1992- 1:44.77, 3:42.7; 1993- 1:46.00, 3:36.47.
A student from the renowned St Patrick's School in Iten, he made an astonishing break-through at the 1992 World Juniors when, with a pre Games best of 1:49.6 he ran successively 1:48.46, 1:47.57 and 1:44.77, the third best of all-time by a junior. Ran 3:58.3 road mile in Denmark in 1991.

Billy KONCHELLAH b.20 Oct 1961 Kilgoris 1.88m 74kg. Maccabi Union TC, USA. Masai.
At 800m: OG: '84- 4; WCh: '87- 1, '91- 1, '93- 3; AfG: '87- 1.
African junior 800m record 1979.
Progression at 800m: 1980- 1:46.79, 1981- 1:49.79, 1982- 1:51.3, 1984- 1:44.03, 1985- 1:43.72, 1986- 1:50.6i, 1987- 1:43.06, 1989- 1:46.34, 1990- 1:46.72i, 1991- 1:43.96, 1993- 1:44.22. pbs: 200m 21.2/21.20w '80, 400m 45.38 '79, 600m 1:17.4 '82, 1000m 2:16.71 '85, 1500m 3:44.5 '85.
A man of five brilliant comebacks! He made a great impact as a junior in 1979-80, then little until his Olympic fourth place in 1984.He has suffered from severe asthma attacks, but came back as the world's top 800m runner in 1987. Ill again in 1988, and little of note until back he came to retain his world title in 1991 after moving to the clean air of Albuquerque. Back again in 1993 he looked likely to retain his world title but left his usual late charge far too late and had to settle for bronze.

Kibiego KORORIA b.25 Dec 1971 1.80m 64kg. Sabaot.
World Junior CC: '89- 2, '90- 1.
Progression at 5000m/10000m: 1989- 13:53.7/ 29:48.5, 1990- 13:29.91/28:03.79, 1993- 13:11.89, 28:10.20. pb 3000m 7:44.98 '93.

Richard (John) KOSGEI b.29 Dec 1970 1.70m 52kg. Student at Barton County CC, USA.
Progression at 3000mSt: 1989- 8:51.67, 1990- 9:12.0, 1991- 8:33.84, 1992- 8:28.64, 1993- 8:12.68. pbs: 1500m 3:39.55 '93, 3000m 7:57.3 '92, 5000m 13:41.34 '92, 2000mSt 5:25.17 '92.

Sammy LANGAT Kibet b.1970. 1.68m 57kg. Kipsigis.
At 800m: AfCh: '92- 4, '93- 1.
Progression at 800m: 1992- 1:46.84, 1993- 1:44.06.

Sammy LELEI b.14 Aug 1964 Eldoret 1.60m 52kg. Farmer. Nandi.
Progression at Mar: 1993- 2:12:12. pbs: 10000m 28:44.0 '92. Road: 10km 27:56 '92, 15km 42:42 '92, Half Mar 60:42 '93.
Won the Lisbon half marathon in 59:24 in 1993, but the course was found to be 97m short. Fifth in Boston and eighth in New York marathons 1993.

Benson MASYA b.14 May 1970 Kitui region. Kamba tribe.
Won World Half Mar 1992.
Progression at Mar: 1991- 2:18:24, 1992- 2:14:19. pbs: 10,000m 28:45.5 '91, 3000mSt 9:13.0 '91. Road: 10km 28:08 '92, Half Mar 60:24 '92.
Won Great North Run in 61:28 in 1991, and repeated on the course to win the first World half marathon title 1992 in a world best time on a certified course. Won Honolulu Marathon 1991 and 1992. Formerly a bantamweight boxer.

William MUTWOL b.10 Oct 1967 Kapsowar, Elgeyo Marakwet 1.67m 56kg. Civil servant working for Kenyan Army (private). Marakwet.
At 3000mSt: OG: '92- 3; AfG: '91- 2; AfCh: '90- 2. Won Kenyan 3000mSt 1992. World CC: '86- 9 Jnr, '90- 5, '91- 12, '92- 2.
Progression at 3000mSt: 1984- 9:00.7, 1985- 8:46.4, 1986- 8:49.4, 1987- 8:39.1, 1988- 8:34.6, 1989- 8:39.0, 1990- 8:12.75, 1991- 8:11.85, 1992- 8:10.74. pbs: 1500m 3:46.0 '90, 3000m 7:49.71 '92, 5000m 13:22.15 '92, 2000mSt 5:24.11 '90.
Member of the winning World Road Relay team 1992. Ran world road best for 5km of 13:12 in 1992.

Kennedy OCHIENG b.30 Dec 1971 Kogutu 1.68m 64kg. Luo. Works for Kenyan Ports Authority.
At 400m/4x400mR: WCh: '93- 8/2R; AfCh: '92- 2/3R, '93- 1; WJ: '90- sf. Won Kenyan and AAA 400m 1993.
Progression at 400m: 1990- 46.6, 1991- 46.85, 1992- 45.2, 1993- 44.6/44.82.

Yobes ONDIEKI b.21 Feb 1961 Kisii 1.70m 55kg. Kisii. Business administration student in Albuquerque, formerly at Iowa State University.
At 5000m: OG: '88- 12, '92- 5; WCh: '91- 1; CG: '90- 9. 3rd GP 1990.
World 10000m record 1993, Kenyan 5000m records 1989 and 1991.
Progression at 5000m, 10000m: 1980- 15:01.0, 1981- 14:36.51, 1982- 13:49.5, 1983- 13:35.5, 28:25.44; 1984- 13:51.95, 1985- 14:14.26, 1988- 13:17.06, 1989- 13:04.24, 1990- 13:05.60, 1991- 13:01.82, 1992- 13:03.58, 1993- 13:05.09, 26:58.38. pbs: 1500m 3:34.36 '90, 1M 3:55.32 '91, 2000m 5:01.6 '89, 3000m 7:34.18 '92.
On 10 July 1993 in Oslo he became the first man to run 10,000m in under 27 minutes, taking nearly ten seconds off the five-day-old world record set by compatriot Richard Chelimo. This was only the second track 10km of his career.
His best result while at Iowa State was second in 1985 NCAA cross-country. Emerged into world class in 1988, and then had a magnificent season in 1989, when he became the first man to beat Saïd Aouita at 5000m for ten years. Fell in Commonwealth Games final 1990, but overcame his bad luck in major events by a decisive win in Tokyo 1991, after running away from the field on the second lap. Married Australian marathon runner Lisa Martin in February 1990.

Thomas OSANO b. 4 Jun 1970 Kisii 1.64m 54kg. Oki Electric Co, Japan.
At 10000m: WCh: '91- 4; AfG: '91- 1; Won Japanese 10000m 1991. World CC: '87- 10 Jnr, '89- 4 Jnr.
Progression at 10,000m: 1990- 28:02.28, 1991- 27:28.87, 1992- 27:55.34. pb 5000m 13:28.8 '91.
Training in mechanics in Japan.

Ondoro OSORO b.3 Dec 1967 Kisii 1.68m 63kg. Civil servant working for Kenyan Armed Forces (private). Kisii.
At 5000m: WCh: '91- h; AfG: '91- 3. World CC: '91- 5.
Progression at 5000m, 10000m: 1985- 14:05.4, 29:10.3; 1986- 30:03.2, 1987- 29:56.2, 1989- 13:36.2, 28:44.4; 1990- 14:02.1, 29:08.6; 1991- 13:11.77, 1992- 13:49.3, 1993- 13:15.21, 27:24.24. pbs: 3000m 7:45.03 '91, 2M 8:29.67 '91, Half Mar 62:10 '93.
Won IAAF World Cross Challenge 1991 (2nd 1992).

Paul RUTO b. 3 Nov 1960 1.84m 68kg. Nandi.
At 800m: WCh: '93- 1; AfG: '93- 2.
Progression at 800m: 1985- 1:51.9, 1987- 1:48.2, 1988- 1:47.4, 1990- 1:47.0, 1991- 1:44.92, 1992- 1:44.33, 1993- 1:44.65. pb 1M 4:05.19 '93.

Patrick Kiprop **SANG** b.11 Apr 1964 Kapsisiywa, Nandi 1.80m 65kg. Was at the University of Texas 1983-6. LC Zürich.
At 3000mSt: OG: '88- 7, '92- 2; WCh: '87- 8, '91- 2, '93- 2; WSG: '89- 1; AfG: '87- 1. Won GP 1993, 2nd 1990-1, 3rd 1988.
Progression at 3000mSt: 1982- 9:13.2, 1983- 8:41.00, 1984- 8:22.45, 1985- 8:23.68, 1986- 8:31.1, 1987- 8:14.75, 1988- 8:12.00, 1989- 8:06.03, 1990- 8:15.50, 1991- 8:13.44, 1992- 8:09.55, 1993- 8:07.53. pbs: 1500m 3:44.17 '86, 2000m 5:03.46 '88, 3000m 7:49.05 '89, 5000m 13:34.95 '92.
Won the silver medal in each major steeplechase 1991-3.

William SIGEI b.11 Oct 1969 Kericho 1.78m 57kg. Kipsigis. Civil servant in Armed Forces.
At 10000m: WCh: '93- 10; Afr G: '93- 1. Won Kenyan 5000m 1992, CC 1993. World CC: '92- 8, '93- 1.
Progression at 5000m, 10000m: 1987- 28:53.1, 1988- 27:40.59, 1989- 13:44.6, 1991- 13:56.3, 1992- 13:15.01, 28:35.0/27:45Rd; 1993- 13:07.35, 27:16.81. pbs: 1500m 3:49.0 '87, 3000m 7:39.51 '92.
Member of the winning World Road Relay team 1992. Older brother Paul Sigei has been a leading 10,000m runner.

Moses TANUI b.20 Aug 1965 Nandi district 1.65m 65kg. K-Way Club, Italy.
At 10000m (5000m): OG: '88- 8, '92- 8; WCh: '91- 1, '93- 2; CG: '90- 2 (5); AfCh: '89- 2 (3). Won Kenyan 10000m 1988-91. World CC: '88- 6, '89- 9, '90- 2, '91- 2, '93- 4.
Progression at 10000m: 1987- 28:53.1, 1988- 27:40.59, 1989- 28:14.67, 1990- 27:43.62, 1991- 27:35.89, 1992- 28:12.71, 1993- 27:18.32. pbs: 1500m 3:41.8 '89, 3000m 7:41.87 '93, 2M 8:33.47 '88, 5000m 13:21.75 '91, Mar 2:15:36 '93.
Won the Stramilano half marathon each year 1990-3, setting a world best 59:47 in 1993, and Great North Run 1993. Ninth in New York on his marathon début 1993.

William Kiptarus **TANUI** b.22 Feb 1964 Kemeloi, Nandi 1.83m 70kg. Clerk in Kenyan Air Force (corporal).
At 800m: OG: '92- 1; WCh: '93- 7; AfG: '91- 1;

William Sigei: won world cross country in 1993

AfCh: '90- 1; WCp: '92- 2. At 1500m: CG: '90- 6. Won Kenyan 800m 1990, 1992-3; AAA 1990. 3rd GP 800m 1990, 1992.
Progression at 800m, 1500m: 1986- 1:48.2; 1987- 1:47.6; 1988- 1:47.3; 1989- 1:47.5, 3:36.6; 1990- 1:43.39, 3:34.25; 1991- 1:43.30, 3:36.53; 1992- 1:43.37, 3:36.2; 1993- 1:44.30, 3:37.8. pbs: 1000m 2:15.83 '90, 1M 3:53.80 '93.
Emerged in 1989 to win Commonwealth Games trial 1500m, and was world number one at 800m in 1990. Finished first in the 1991 World Indoor 800m, but disqualified for breaking early from his lane. A vegetarian.

Paul TERGAT b.17 Jun 1969 Baringo 1.82m 62kg. Civil servant working for Kenyan Armed Forces. Turgen.
World Half Mar: '92- 5. World CC: '93- 10.
Progression at 5000m, 10000m: 1991- 28:50, 1992- 13:48.64, 1993- 13:20.16, 27:18.43. pbs: 1500m 3:45 '91, Half Mar 60:45 '93.
A former basketball player, he made a sensational impact when he emerged for third in the Kenyan Armed Forces CC, followed closely by wins in the Kenyan CC Championships and the Nairobi CC in 1992; he had however to miss his first run outside Kenya at the World CC Championships through injury.

Women

Delilah ASIAGO b.24 Feb 1972 1.64m 50kg. Oki Electronics, Japan. Kisii.
At 10000m: WCh: '91- 12. At 3000m: AfG: '91- 3.
World junior 10000m record 1991.
Progression at 10000m: 1987- 34:50.6, 1988- 36:08.3, 1989- 36:01.4, 1990- 32:49.48, 1991- 31:40.56, 1992- 31:57.24. pbs: 3000m 8:55.53 '91, 5000m 15:32.4 '91, Half Mar 1:09:05 '91.
Trained in Japan from 1989.

Selina (Sally) BARSOSIO b.21 Mar 1978 1.65m 43kg. Elgeyo Marakwet.
At 10000m: WCh: '93- 3; WJ: '92- 3; AfCh: '92- 5 (5 3000m). Won Kenyan 10000m 1993. World CC: '93- 3J.
World Junior (not ratified as no drugs test) and Kenyan 10000m record 1993.
Progression at 10000m: 1992- 32:41.76, 1993- 31:15.38. pb 3000m 8:59.70 '93.
A prodigious talent at 15 (18 according to some sources), but remarkably fortunate to be reinstated after disqualification in the 1993 World 10,000m. She had caused havoc during the race by continually baulking Elana Meyer and running across several other runners.

Helen Chepchirchir**KIMAIYO** b.8 Sep 1968 Moiben 1.63m 50kg. Uasin Gishu. Clerk with Kenyan Post & Telecoms. Married to Charles Kipkorir.
At 10000m: OG: '92- 9. At 3000m (1500m): OG: '84- h; WCp: '89- 5; Af Ch: '85- 1 (3), '87- 2, '89- 1 (2). World CC: '92- 11, '93- 12. Won Kenyan 1500m 1989, 3000m 1984-5, 1989, 1992; CC 1992.
Kenyan records3000m 1984, 10000m 1992.
Progression at 10000m: 1985- 34:18.23, 1992- 31:38.91, 1993- 32:43.4. pbs: 800m 2:07.83 '84, 1500m 4:15.2 '91, 3000m 8:55.05 '92, 5000m 15:19.20 '92; Road 10M 52:10 '92.
Has two children.

Esther KIPLAGAT b.8 Dec 1966 1.68m 50kg. Accountancy student at Jackson State University, USA.
At 1500m: AfrG: '87- 4. At 3000m: OG: '92- h; WCh: '93- 15. 2nd GP 5000m 1992. Won Kenyan 5000m 1985, 3000m 1993.
Progression at 3000m: 1982- 10:28.3, 1983- 9:32.0, 1984- 9:23.11, 1986- 9:41.4, 1988- 9:53.4, 1989- 9:13.95, 1990- 9:08.84i/9:09.64, 1991- 8:51.2, 1992- 8:44.45, 1993- 8:43.76. pbs: 800m 2:04.64 '90, 1500m 4:10.38 '91, 1M 4:34.36 '92, 5000m 15:07.87 '92, 10000m 32:50.25 '84, road 10km 31:57 '93.

Tecla LORUPE Chepkite b.9 May 1973 Kapsoit, West Pokot 1.53m 40kg. Works for

Kenyan Post & Telecommunication Corporation. At 10000m: OG: '92- 17; WCh: '93- 4. World Half Mar: '93- 3.
Kenyan 10000m record 1993.
Progression at 10000m: 1992- 31:34.30mx/ 32:34.07, 1993- 31:21.20. pbs: 5000m 15:08.03 '93, Half Mar 1:10:12 '93.

KOREA

Governing body: Korea Amateur Athletic Federation, 10 Chamshil Dong, Songpa-Gu, Seoul. Founded 1945.

HWANG Young-cho b.22 Mar 1970 Samchok 1.68m 57kg. Kyugju University.
At Mar: OG: '92- 1; WSG: '91- 1. Won Asian 10000m 1991.
Korean marathon record 1992.
Progression at Mar: 1991- 2:12:35, 1992- 2:08:47. pbs: 5000m 13:59.70 '90, 10000m 29:32.01 '91.
Won Seoul marathon 1991 and 1992. The first athlete to win an Olympic medal while representing Korea, although Sohn Kee-chung had won the 1936 marathon in Japanese colours.

KIM Jae-ryong b.25 Apr 1966 1.72m 60kg.
At Mar: OG: '92- 10; WCh: '93- 4. At 5000m/10000m: AsG: '90- 5/2, AsCh: '91- 4/3.
Progression at Mar: 1987- 2:13:25, 1988- 2:20:11, 1989- 2:19:01, 1991- 2:11:51, 1992- 2:09:30, 1993- 2:09:43. pbs: 5000m 13:51.89 '87, 10000m 28:49.61 '90.
Won Seoul marathon 1992 a nd Boston 1993

KIM Woan-ki b.8 Jul 1968 1.70m 57kg.
At Mar: OG: '92- 28; WCh: '91- dnf; AsG: '90- 5; WSG: '93- 2.
Korean marathon record 1990.
Progression at Mar: 1990- 2:11:34, 1991- 2:11:02, 1992- 2:09:31, 1993- 2:09:25. pbs: 5000m 14:03.70 '91, 10000m 29:43.7 '92.
Won Seoul marathon 1990 and second in 1992. Third in New York in 1992.

LATVIA

Governing body: Latvia Track and Field Athletics Federation, Terbatas Str. 4, Riga LV-1723. Founded 1921. Athletes competed for USSR prior to 1992.
National Championships first held in 1920 (men), 1922 (women) **1993 Champions**: **Men**: 100m: Guntis Zalitis 10.3, 200m: Sergey Inshakov 21.0, 400m: Vyacheslav Kocheryagin 47.1, 800m: Einars Tupuritis 1:51.5, 1500m: Ainars Keris 3:56.5, 5000m: Uldis Pastars 14:45.9, 10000m/Half Mar/Mar: Aleksandr Prokopchuk 30:55.9/68:11/2:26:41, 3000mSt: Girts Fogels 9:02.7, 110mh: Igor Kazanov 13.6, 400mh: Egils Tebelis 51.8, HJ: Gints Klepeckis 2.13, PV: Aleksandr Matusevich 5.20, LJ: Helmuts Rodke 7.64, TJ: Maris Bruzhiks 16.57, SP: Aleksej Lukashenko 18.59, DT: Andris Smochs 47.80, HT: Ernests Vingris 53.62, JT: Marcis Shtrobinders 81.78, Dec: Rojs Piziks 7699, 20kmW: Modris Liepinsh 1:27:05.5, 50kmW: Evalds Lavrentjevs 4:22:50. **Women**: 100m/100mh: Ludmila Olijare 11.8/13.5, 200m: Linda Spulge 24.3, 400m: Lana Yekabsone 54.4, 800m/1500m: Kristina Graudina 2:16.0/4:45.5, 3000m: Yelena Chelnova 10:10.1, 10000m: Tatjana Ribakova 39:51.6, Half Mar: Marija Gavrilova 80:39, Mar: Anita Klapote 3:03:04, 400mh: Inga Feldmane 63.3, HJ: Valentina Gotovska 1.85, LJ/TJ: Yelena Blazhevica 6.44/13.46, SP/DT: Iveta Garancha 13.95/50.56, JT: Iveta Lochmele 50.42, Hep: Anta Holste 4903, 10kmW: Ilza Pavlovska 56:13.6, 20kmW: Anita Liepina 1:45:28.
Maris BRUZHIKS b.25 Aug 1962 Plavinas 1.87m 73kg.
At TJ: OG: '92- 10; WCh: '93 dnq 16; EC: '86- 2; EI: '86- 1, '92- 4; WI: '87- 7, '93- 2; WSG: '87- 3; WCp: '92- 4. Latvian champion 1983-4, 1988-9, 1992-3. WIB triple jump 17.54 '86.
Progression at TJ: 1977- 11.60, 1978- 13.57, 1979- 14.60, 1980- 15.43, 1981- 15.48i, 1982- 15.55, 1983- 16.47, 1984- 17.15, 1985- 17.38, 1986- 17.54i/17.33, 1987- 16.97i/16.90, 1988- 17.56, 1989- 17.19/17.42w, 1990- 16.98, 1991- 17.38, 1992- 17.29i/17.01, 1993- 17.36i/17.28. pbs: HJ 2.15i '85, LJ 7.91 '84.

Igor KAZANOV b.24 Sep 1963 Daugavpils 1.86m 81kg. Daugavpils.
At 110mh: OG: '92- sf; WCh: '87- 5, '91- sf, '93- 6; EC: '86- sf, '90- dnf; ECp: '87- 1, '91- 4. Won USSR 110mh 1984, 1987, 1990, Latvian 1983, 1988, 1993. At 60mh: WI: '89- 3, '91- 2, '93- 5; EI: '90- 1, '92- 1.
Held European 60mh indoor record for one day in 1989.
Progression at 110mh: 1980- 14.2, 1981- 14.38, 1982- 14.1/14.53, 1983- 14.08/13.7, 1984- 13.59, 1985- 13.3/13.62, 1986- 13.42/13.14w, 1987- 13.38/13.3, 1988- 13.38/13.1, 1989- 13.68/ 13.43w, 1990- 13.41, 1991- 13.47, 1992- 13.34, 1993- 13.26. pbs: 50mh 6.48i '92, 60mh 7.42i '89.
Son of Russian emigrants to Latvia.

Women

Valentina GOTOVSKA b.3 Sep 1965 Kraslava 1.76m 59kg. née Tolstik. Kraslava.
At HJ: OG: '92- 13=; WCh: '93- 8; EC: '90- 7. Won Latvian HJ 1982, 1989-93, ECp B2 1993.
Progression at HJ: 1981- 1.65, 1982- 1.78, 1988- 1.90, 1989- 1.95, 1990- 1.97, 1991- 1.92, 1992- 1.92, 1993- 1.95.

LITHUANIA

Governing body: Athletic Federation of Lithuania, Zemaitas 6, Vilnius 232675. Founded 1921. Athletes competed for USSR prior to 1992.

Vaclavas KIDYKAS b.17 Oct 1961 Vytenai, Klaipeda 1.97m 118kg. Kaunas. Veterinary student.
At DT: OG: '88- dnq 13, '92- dnq 15; WCh: '87- 8, '93- 11; EC: '86- 3; WSG: '85- 2, '87- 2; ECp: '87- 1. Lithuanian champion 1989-90, 1993.
Lithuanian discus record 1985.
Progression at DT: 1978- 33.24, 1979- 41.42, 1980- 47.86, 1981- 55.42, 1982- 59.80, 1983- 61.42, 1984- 62.60, 1985- 67.34, 1986- 67.00, 1987- 66.80, 1988- 68.44, 1989- 64.32, 1990- 67.04, 1991- 65.98, 1992- 66.12, 1993- 65.26. pb SP 18.33 '91.

LUXEMBOURG

Governing body: Fédération Luxembourgeoise d'Athlétisme, BP 1055, L-1010 Luxembourg. Founded 1928.
1993 National Champions: **Men**: 100m/200m: Laurent Kemp 10.74/21.96, 400m: Cédric Flamini 49.85, 800m: Carlos Calvo 1:58.90, 1500m/5000m: Claude Assel 3:52.46/15:05.77, 10000m: Nico Steffen 31:54.64, Mar: Luc Dhamen 2:29:00, 3000mSt: Marc Urwald 10:03.97, 110mh: Raymond Conzemius 15.70, 400mh: Romain Bartringer 59.14, HJ: Jean-Claude Husting 2.08, PV/LJ: Bernard Felten 4.60/6.82, TJ: Richard Czerwonka 13.87, SP: Marcel Weber 14.06, DT: Carlo Bartolucci 52.04, HT: Charles De Ridder 59.74, JT: Marc Goedert 59.84, Dec: Frank Krier 5950, 20kmW: Marco Sowa 1:30:45. **Women**: 100m/200m/100mh/LJ: Véronique Linster 11.87/24.98/13.92/5.50, 400m/SP: Sandra Felten 57.86/11.12, 800m/400mh/Hep: Claudia Czerwonka 2:19.81/64.86/4578, 1500m/3000m/10000m/Mar: Danièle Kaber 4:38.55/9:51.67/35:33.71/2:43:08, HJ: Sonny Leches 1.68, DT: Edith Jeblick-Grün 39.42, JT: Katia Brunelli 32.42.

MEXICO

Governing body: Federación Mexicana de Atletismo, Anillo Periférico y Av. del Conscripto, 11200 M.Hidalgo D.F. Founded 1933.

Arturo BARRIOS b.12 Dec 1963 Mexico City 1.74m 60kg. Reebok RT, USA. Mechanical engineering graduate of Texas A&M University, USA.
At 10000m: OG: '88- 5 (h 5000m), '92- 5; WCh: '87- 4. At 5000m: PAm: '87- 1, '91- 1; CAmG: '90- 1 (1 1500m); WCp: '92- 2. Won PAm-J 1980 (3 at 3000mSt), GP 1987 & 1989.
World records: 10000m 1989, 20000m and 1 hour 1991; also CAC records: 2000m 1989, 3000m 1987, 5000m 1987 & 1989, Mexican 1500m record 1989.
Progression at 5000m, 10000m: 1980- 14:26.4, 31:20.4; 1982- 14:49.6, 31:50.6; 1983- 14:14.9; 1984- 14:03.46, 29:23.9; 1985- 13:46.37, 28:42.77; 1986- 13.25.83, 27:50.28; 1987- 13:13.52, 27:56.1; 1988- 13:17.82, 27:25.07; 1989- 13:07.79, 27:08.23; 1990- 13:08.52, 27:18.22; 1991- 13:24.17, 27:37.36; 1992- 13:10.52, 27:34.60; 1993- 13:09.58, 27:34.27. pbs: 1500m: 3:37.61 '89, 2000m 5:03.4 '89, 3000m 7:35.71 '89, 2M 8:24.99 '86, 20000m 56:54.03 '91, 1Hr 21101m '91, Half Mar 60:42 '92, Mar 2:12:21 '93, 2000mSt 5:46.0 '80, 3000mSt 8:46.9 '83.
First came to the fore as a road runner; in 1986 he set a world 10km best for a loop course of 27:41 at Phoenix. Concentrated on track racing with much success from 1987, but completed four successive wins in the San Francisco Bay to Breakers 12km 1987-90. Third New York marathon 1993.

Dionicio CERON b.8 Oct 1965 1.70m 58kg. Civil engineering student at Mexico City University.
At Mar: OG: '92- dnf. At 10000m: won CAmG 1990 & 1993, CAC 1991.
CAC marathon record to win Beppu 1992.
Progression at Mar: 1990- 2:12:18, 1991- 2:10:02, 1992- 2:08:36, 1993- 2:08:51. pbs: 10000m 28:14.48 '91. Road: 15km 42:42 '90, Half Mar 60:46 '90, 60:17 dh '93.
Emerged on US road running circuit in 1990, when he set a world half marathon best on a loop course. Second Rotterdam marathon 1991. Won Beppu marathon in 1992, and Rotterdam, Mexico City and Fukuoka in 1993.

Alberto CRUZ b. 6 Jun 1972.
At 20kmW: WCp: '93- 3. At 10,000mW: WJ: '88- 1, '90- 2; won CAC 1991. At 10,000mW: won CAC Jnr 1988 & 1990, PAm Jnr 1989 & 1991.
Progression at 20kmW: 1989- 1:25:48, 1990- 1:22:52, 1991- 1:22:44, 1992- 1:24:42, 1993- 1:24:26. pbs: 10000mW: 39:56.49 '90.

Andrés ESPINOSA b.4 Feb 1963. Soldier.
At Mar: WCp: '91- 57.
Progression at Mar: 1990- 2:14:10, 1991- 2:10:00, 1992- 2:10:44, 1993- 2:10:04. pbs: 10000m 27:59.86 '92, road 15km 43:41 '92.
Has compiled a most consistent record in US marathons: 2nd in San Francisco 1990, and New York 1991 and 1992, 3rd Boston 1992 before winning in New York 1993.

Daniel GARCIA b.28 Oct 1971.

At 20kmW: OG: '92-7; WCh: '93- dq; WCp: '93- 1; WSG: '93- 2; CAmG: '93- 1.
Progression at 20kmW, 50kmW: 1991- 4:04:51, 1992- 1:22:16.1t, 3:57:38; 1993- 1:19:42, 3:52:23.

Salvador GARCIA b.1 Dec 1962 or 29 Oct 1960 Nichoucán State 1.73m 63kg. Soldier
At Mar: OG: '92- dnf.
Progression at Mar: 1988- 2:11:50, 1989- 2:10:47, 1990- 2:13:19, 1991- 2:09:28, 1992- 2:09:16, 1993- 2:22:25. pb 10000m 28:19.6 '91.
Won 8 of his 19 marathons, including New Jersey 1989, Long Beach 1990, New York 1991 (after second 1990), Rotterdam 1992. Ran slightly downhill road 10k in 27:54 in 1989. Started running in 1985. After failing to finish in Barcelona he was demoted from lieutenant to sergeant.

Carlos MERCENARIO b.3 May 1967 1.75m 63kg.
At 20kmW: OG: '88- 7; WCh: '87- dq, '91- 12; WCp: '87- 1; PAm: '87- 1; CAmG: '90- 2. At 50kmW: OG: '92- 2; WCH: '93- 8; WCp: '91- 1, '93- 1; PAm: "91- 1. Won PAm-J 10kmW 1984 & 1986.
At 20km road walk: world junior best when second America's Cup 1986, world best 1987.
Progression at 20kmW, 50kmW: 1985- 1:24:07, 1986- 1:21:33, 1987- 1:19:24, 1988- 1:20:53, 1989- 1:21:53, 1990- 1:19:30, 3:50:10; 1991- 1:21:37, 3:42:03; 1992- 1:25:52, 3:48:05.9t; 1993- 1:21:39, 3:50:28.
In 1993 he became the first man to win World Cup races at both 20km and 50km, and tied the record with three individual wins.

German SÁNCHEZ b.15 Sep 1966.
At 50kmW: OG: '92- dq; WCh: '93- 12, WCp: '93- 3; CAmG: '93- 2. Won America's Cup 1992.
Progression at 50kmW: 1991- 4:03:40, 1992- 3:51:02, 1993- 3:54:07. Pb 20kmW ?.

German SILVA b.9 Jan 1968 1.60m 50kg.
At 10000m: OG: '92- 6; WCh: '93- 9. At 3000mSt: PAm: '91- 6; won CAmG 1990.
Progression at 10000m: 1990- 28:02.03, 1991- 28:19.48, 1992- 27:46.52, 1993- 28:03.64. pbs: 5000m 13:26.11 '93, 3000mSt 8:33.52 '89.

Women

Olga APPELL b.2 Aug 1963 Durango 1.75m 59kg. née Avalos.
At Mar: OG: '92- dnf; PAm: '91- 1.
Mexican records: 10000m and Marathon (3).
Progression at Mar: 1990- 2:40:04, 1991- 2:33:18, 1992- 2:30:22, 1993- 2:28:56. pbs: 10000m 32:09.6 '92, Half Mar 68:34 '93 (33m dh).
Won Long Beach and Sapporo marathons in 1992, second New York 1993. Applied for US citizenship 1993.

MOROCCO

Governing Body: Fédération Royale Marocaine d'Athlétisme, Complex Sportif Prince Moulay Abdellah, PO Box 1778 R/P, Rabat. Founded 1957.

Moulay Brahim BOUTAYEB b.15 Aug 1967 Khémisset 1.78m 61kg. Larios, Spain.
At 10000m: OG: '88- 1, AfCh: '88- 1. At 5000m: OG: '92- 4; WCh: '87- h, '91- 3, '93- h; WJ: '86- 4; AfCh: '88- 1. Won GP 1991, 2nd 1988 & 1990, 3rd 1992. Won Arab 5000m and 10000m 1989.
African 10000m record 1988.
Progression at 5000m, 10000m: 1985- 14:22.4; 1986- 13:52.49, 29:29.43; 1987- 13:17.47, 28:40.34; 1988- 13:18.68, 27:21.46; 1989- 13:12.10, 27:42.25; 1990- 13:12.26, 27:59.45; 1991- 13:10.44, 27:53.11; 1992- 13:13.27, 28:58.55; 1993- 13:42.30, 28:24.61. pbs: 1000m 2:24.57 '87, 1500m 3:36.35 '92, 1M 3:54.86 '87, 2000m 5:07.74 '87, 3000m 7:38.39 '91, 2M 8:21.00 '89.
Ran fastest ever 5000m by a teenager in 1987, a year before winning the Olympic 10000m title. Now a rally driver.

Rashid EL BASIR (or **LABSIR**) b.4 Oct 1968 1.80m 61kg.
At 1500m: OG: '92- 2; WCh: '91- sf, '93- 7; WI: '93- 9.
Progression at 1500m: 1989- 3:41.23, 1990- 3:37.52, 1991- 3:36.57, 1992- 3:34.40, 1993- 3:35.51. pbs: 800m: 1:46.53 '92, 1000m: 2:20.8 '91, 1M: 3:54.84 '92, 3000m: 7:51.89 '91.

Larbi EL KHATTABI b.16 May 1967 1.74m 68kg.
At 3000mSt: OG: '92- 10; WCh: '93- 7.
Progression at 3000mSt: 1986- 9:28.1, 1987- 9:00.2, 1988- 8:52.55, 1989- 8:30.87, 1990- 8:40.0, 1991- 8:42.39, 1992- 8:23.82, 1993- 8:16.60. pbs: 3000m 8:04.05 '89, 5000m 13:47.49 '89.

Mohamed ISSANGAR b.12 Dec 1964 1.80m 62kg.
At 5000m: OG: '92- 9; WCh: '91- h; AfCh: '88- 3, '90- 3.
Progression at 5000m: 1988- 13:40.9, 1989- 13:19.54, 1990- 13:08.51, 1991- 13:18.03, 1992- 13:18.94, 1993- 13:14.23. pbs: 1500m 3:39.51 '91, 1M 3:57.03 '90, 3000m 7:39.30 '93.
Burst onto the Grand Prix scene in 1989 and in 1990 showed further improvement by winning at Lausanne, Oslo and London.

Brahim JABBOUR b.1 Jan 1970 1.78m 56kg.
At 5000m: WCh: '93- 6.
Progession at 5000m: 1992- 13:36.44, 1993- 13:08.86. pbs: 3000m 7:36.54 '93. pbs: 1500m 3:40.44 '92, 2000m 5:17.03 '92, 3000m 7:36.54 '93.
Enormous improvement in 1993.

Abdelaziz SAHERE b.18 Sep 1967 1.83m 63kg. Olympique Marocain, Rabat.
At 3000mSt: OG: '88- h; WCh: '91- 6, '93- 13; AfCh: '88- 2, '90- 1 (2 1500m); 3rd GP 1991. At 1500m: WI: '90- 8.
Four Moroccan 3000m steeple records 1991.
Progression at 3000mSt: 1986- 9:03.6, 1987- 8:39.0, 1988- 8:22.45, 1990- 8:28.53, 1991- 8:12.21, 1992- 8:19.65, 1993- 8:15.25. pbs: 800m 1:49.9 dq '90, 1000m 2:23.59 '89, 1500m 3:36.13 '90, 1M 3:56.14 '90, 3000m 7:53.21 '88.
Married to Nezha Bidouane (400mh pb 55.08 '92, African champion 1990).

Khalid SKAH b.29 Jan 1967 Midelt 1.72m 60kg. Based in the summer in Norway. IL i BUL, Oslo.
At 10000m (5000m): OG: '92- 1; WCh: '91- 3 (6), '93- (5); AfCh: '89- (5). Won GP 5000m 1990. World CC '90- 1, '91- 1, '92- 4, '93- 6.
World 2 miles best 1993. Moroccan 10000m record 1993.
Progression at 5000m, 10000m: 1986- 14:28.4, 1987- 14:26.11, 1988- 13:56.1, 1989- 13:17.30, 1990- 13:09.55, 27:29.27; 1991- 13:17.72, 27:23.29; 1992- 13:09.10, 27:46.70; 1993- 13:06.82, 27:17.74. pbs: 1000m 2:26.0 '90, 1500m 3:42.06 '90, 2000m 5:03.9 '90, 3000m 7:37.09 '90, 2M 8:12.17 '93, 3000mSt 8:44.17 '90.
Second in the Arab junior and 68th in the World Junior CC in 1986. After winning the World CC he ran 27:29.27 in his track début at 10000m in Brussels 1990. At first disqualified after Olympic 10000m in 1992 due to the alleged help rendered by lapped teammate Hammou Boutayeb, he was reinstated and awarded gold medal.

MOZAMBIQUE

Governing body: Federaçao Mocambicana de Atletismo, CP 1094, Maputo. Founded 1978.

Maria Lurdes **MUTOLA** b. 27 Oct 1972 Maputo 1.62m 61kg. Student at Springfield (Oregon) High School, USA.
At 800m (1500m): OG: '88- h, '92- 5 (9); WCh: '91- 4, '93- 1; WI: '93- 1; AfCh: '88- 2, '90- 1 (1); AfG: '91- 1, '93- 1; WCp: '92- 1/3R. Won GP 1993.
African records: seven 800m 1991-3, 1000m 1993. African junior records 800m (3) and 1500m 1991.
Progression at 800m, 1500m: 1988- 2:04.36, 1989- 2:05.7, 4:31.5; 1990- 2:13.54, 4:25.27; 1991- 1:57.63, 4:12.72; 1992- 1:57.49, 4:02.60; 1993- 1:55.43, 4:04.97. pbs: 400m 53.10 '91, 1000m: 2:32.57 '93, 1M 4:36.09 '91, 3000m 10:04.4 '90.
Star soccer player at school in Maputo; enabled to attend school in the USA by a grant from the Olympic Solidarity Committee.

Frank Fredericks: won gold at last after three major silver medals

Argentina da Gloria **PAULINO** b.7 Jul 1973 1.66m 59kg.
At 800m: WCh: '93- 7. At 400m: AfG: '93- 1.
Progression at 400m, 800m: 1992- 52.34, 2:03.81; 1993- 51.82, 1:56.62.
Distant relative of Maria Mutola, only started running in 1992, when she ran 2:03.82 for 800m in her first ever track race. Fell in World Championships final 1993.

NAMIBIA

Governing body: Namibia AAU, PO Box 11086, Windhoek.
Frank FREDERICKS b.2 Oct 1967 Windhoek 1.80m 70kg. Doing a masters course in business administration at Brigham Young University, USA.
At 100m/200m: OG: '92- 2/2; WCh: '91- 5/2, '93- 6/1; AfG: '91- 1/1. At 60m: WI: '93- 2. Won NCAA 100m & 200m 1991, South African 200m 1987. Won GP 200m 1993 (2nd 1991).
African records: 100m 1991, 200m (7) 1989-93.
Progression at 100m, 200m: 1985- 10.73, 21.68; 1986- 10.1, 20.6; 1987- 10.36, 20.58/20.41w; 1988- 10.32, 20.57; 1989- 10.02, 20.31/20.09w;

1990- 10.16/10.14w, 20.32/20.20w; 1991- 9.95/9.89w; 20.08/20.0/19.90w; 1992- 10.02/ 9.91w, 19.97; 1993- 10.03, 19.85. pbs: 55m 6.13i '93, 60m 6.47 '91, 400m 46.28 '89, LJ 7.57i '91.
After three major silver medals, including the first Olympic medal ever won by a Namibian, he became their first world champion with his very strong finish in the 200m in 1993. A former soccer player, Fredreicks was sent to the USA by the Rossing Uranium Mine to study computer science and became the first non US sprinter to win the NCAA double. Able to compete internationally once Namibia gained independence in 1990 and IAAF affiliation 1991.

Luchetz SWARTBOOI b.7 Feb 1966. Librarian's assistant.
At Mar: OG: '92- dnf; WCh: '93- 2.
Progression at Mar: 1992- 2:10:01, 1993- 2:09:57. road pbs; 10k 28:24 '93, Half Mar 61:26 '93.
Won two fast marathons in Namibia in 1992 and led early on in the Olympics. Third Boston Marathon 1993.

NETHERLANDS

Governing body: Koninklijke Nederlandse Atletiek-Unie (KNAU), PO Box 567, 3430 AN Nieuwegein. Founded 1901.
National Championships first held in 1910 (men), 1921 (women). **1993 Champions**: **Men**: Half 100m: Frenk Perri 10.65, 200m: Regillio v d Vloot 21.37, 400m: Arjan Achterkamp 47.26, 800m: Tom Baltus 1:47.46, 1500m: Gerbn IJpelaar 3:51.68, 5000m: Henk Gommer 14:10.12, 10000m: Tonnie Dirks 28:33.54, Half Mar: John Vermeule 63:53, Mar: Bert van Vlaanderen 2:13:17, 3000mSt: MarcelLaros 8:47.73, 110mh: Robin Korving 13.99, 400mh: Marco Beukenkamp 50.40, HJ: Björn Groen 2.17, PV: Richel Keysers 5.00, LJ: Frans Maas 7.95, TJ: Arthur Lynch 15.74, SP/DT: Erik de Bruin 19.16/63.06, HT: Shaun Pickering GBR 59.40, JT: Johan van Lieshout 74.40, Dec: Ruben van Balen 7800, 20kmW/50kmW: Harold van Beek 1:35:28/4:27:40. **Women**: 100m/200m: Jacqueline Poelman 11.48/23.50, 400m: Ester Goossens 52.73, 800m/1500m: Stella Jongmans 2:06.65/4:19.79, 3000m: Elly van Hulst 9:10.23, 10000m: Christine Toonstra 33:27.20, Half Mar: Marjan Freriks 75:47, Mar: Anne van Schuppen 2:34:15, 100mh: Ine Langenhuizen 13.79, 400mh: Mirian Knijn 58.54, HJ: Blanca Gelauf 1.79, LJ: Mieke van der Kolk 6.17w, TJ: Ingrid v Lingen 12.39, SP/DT: Jacqueline Goormachtigh 17.15/57.98, JT: Ingrid Lammertsma 53.90, Hep: Anoeschka Daans 5715.

Erik DE BRUIN b.25 May 1963 Hardinxveld 1.86m 110kg. Haag Atletiek.
At DT (SP): OG: '84- 9 (8), '88- 9; WCh: '91- 2; EC: '86- 6, '90- 2; EJ: '81- 3 (8); WSG: '89- 2. 3rd GP 1989. Won Dutch SP 1981-8, 1990-3; DT 1981-93, indoor SP 1981-93.
Dutch records: 16 shot, 10 discus 1982-91.
Progression at SP, DT: 1979- 14.71, 48.04; 1980- 16.22, 55.76; 1981- 17.36, 55.94; 1982- 17.99, 57.88; 1983- 19.49i/18.95, 56.70; 1984- 20.58i/ 20.20, 63.66; 1985- 20.60i/20.24, 66.38; 1986- 20.95, 66.78; 1987- 20.49i, 65.84; 1988- 20.30i/ 20.16, 66.08; 1989- 20.54i/20.30, 67.58; 1990- 19.73, 65.64; 1991- 19.51, 68.12; 1992- 19.81i, 64.50; 1993- 1.58i/19.16, 67.06. pb HT 60.24 '87.
Received four year drugs ban after positive test for Human Growth Hormone at Köln 1 Aug 1993; however the Dutch courts later cleared him of all blame. His sister Corrie (b. 26 Oct 1976) won the European Junior discus and was third at shot in 1993; at age 14 she threw the discus 54.68 and at 15 the shot 16.60 and the discus 56.48 for Dutch junior records.

Women

Ellen VAN LANGEN b.9 Feb 1966 Oldenzaal 1.72m 56kg. ADA. Economics graduate of Amsterdam University.
At 800m: OG: '92- 1; WCh: '91- h; EC: '90- 4; WSG: '89- 2. Won Dutch 800m 1989-90, 1992; 1500m 1990; ECp B3 800m 1993.
Three Dutch 800m records 1990-2.
Progression at 800m: 1986- 2:14.2, 1987- 2:09.89, 1988- 2:06.30, 1989- 1:59.82, 1990- 1:57.57, 1991- 1:58.86, 1992- 1:55.54, 1993- 1:59.23. pbs: 400m 53.66 '89, 1500m 4:06.92 '92, 1M 4:31.88 '92.
Played soccer until 1986. Achilles injury in 1991 but came back with a brilliant season at 800m in 1992. Injuries cost her most of the 1993 season.

NEW ZEALAND

Governing body: Athletics New Zealand, PO Box 741, Wellington.
National Championships first held in 1887 (men), 1926 (women). **1993 Champions**: **Men**: 100m: Gus Nketia 10.43, 200m: Mark Keddell 20.95, 400m: Callum Taylor 47.71, 800m: Michael Calver 1:49.10, 1500m/3000m: Robbie Johnston 3:42.26/7:53,21, 5000m/10000m: Paul Smith 13:54.40/28:43.63, Mar: Paul Herlihy 2:15:50, 3000mSt: Kyle Dransfield 8:50.83, 110mh: Kahl Schlierling 15.05, 400mh: Johnathan Schmidt 51.77, HJ: Roger Te Puni 2.12, PV: Paul Gibbons 4.75, LJ/TJ: Nigel Park 7.47/15.49. SP/DT: Henry Smith 16.07/51.68, HT: Patrick Hellier 60.06, JT: Gavin Lovegrove 76.82, Dec: Doug Pirini 7645, 5000mW/20kmW: Scott Nelson 20:22.90/1:25:56, 50kmW: Gary Little

4:45:09. **Women:** 100m/200m/400m: Michelle Seymour 11.58/23.90/53.66, 800m/1500m: Geraldine MacDonald 2:08.65/4:19.60, 3000m /5000m: Linden Wilde 9:23.54/15:44.65, 10000m: Helen Moros 32:32.24, Mar: Gabrielle O'Rourke 2:38:20, 100mh: Vanessa Jack 14.04, 400mh: Lynnette Massey 58.93, HJ: Tracy Phillips 1.80, PV: Melina Hamilton 2.90, LJ: Frith Maunder 5.87, TJ: Leanne Stapylton-Smith 12.40, SP: Christine King 14.85, DT: Beatrice Faumuina 54.84, HT: Teresa Came 49.84, JT: Kirsten Hellier 58.94, Hep: Cassandra Kelly 5152, 3000mW/10kmW: Lin Murphy 14:38.90/50:43.0.

Gavin LOVEGROVE b.21 Oct 1967 Hamilton 1.87m 90kg.
At JT: OG: '92- 9; WCh: '87- dnq 23, '91- 4, '93- dnq 15; CG: '86- 3, '90- 3; WJ: '86- 3. Won NZ title 1987, 1990-3; Australian 1987, 1989.
Eight NZ javelin records 1986-92, world junior record 1986.
Progression at JT: 1984- 74.70, 1985- 79.12, new: 1986- 79.58, 1987- 80.20, 1988- 80.70, 1989- 83.90, 1990- 82.64, 1991- 85.18, 1992- 86.14, 1993- 84.54. pb SP 14.52 '86.

Women

Lorraine MOLLER b.1 Jun 1955 Putaruru 1.74m 58kg. Former school teacher. PE diploma from University of Otago. Lives in Boulder, USA.
At Mar: OG: '84- 5, '88- 33, '92- 3; CG: '86- 2. At 10000m: WCh: '87- 21. At 3000m: WCh: '83- 14; CG: '82- 3 (3 at 1500m), '86- 5. At 800m: CG: '74- 5. World CC: '75- 5.
Two Commonwealth marathon bests 1979-80, & NZ best 1986. World best 10 miles track 1993.
Progression at Mar: 1979- 2:37:37, 1980- 2:31:42, 1981- 2:29:36, 1982- 2:36:13, 1983- 2:43:59, 1984- 2:28:34, 1985- 2:34:55, 1986- 2:28:17, 1987- 2:30:40, 1988- 2:37:52, 1989- 2:30:21, 1991- 2:33:20, 1992- 2:33:59, 1993- 2:30:31. pbs: 800m 2:03.63 '74, 1500m 4:10.35 '85, 1M 4:32.97 '85, 2000m 5:47.97 '85, 3000m 8:51.78 '83, 5000m 15:32.90 '86, 10000m 32:40.17 '88, 10M 54:21.8 '93.
Won her first eight marathons, before second to Joyce Smith at London in 1982. Of 28 marathons she has won 15, including Avon 1980, 1982 and 1984; Boston 1984; Osaka 1986-7, 1989; Sapporo 1991. Her Olympic bronze medal in 1992 came just four days after the death of her former husband marathoner Ron Daws, whom she had married in 1981.

NIGERIA

Governing body: The Athletic Federation of Nigeria, P.O.Box 211, Lagos. Founded 1944.
1993 National Champions: **Men**: 100m: Daniel Effiong 10.14, 200m: Oluyemi Kayode 21.00, 400m: Sunday Bada 45.03, 800m: Michael Egbeasor 1:49.92, 1500m: Abiodun Salami 3:49.26, 5000m: Timon Gunem 14:15.50, 10000m: Umoru Mohammed 30:02.71, 3000mSt: Zakaria Fwangfur 9:09.09, 110mh: Moses Oyiki Orode 14.22, 400mh: Ambrose Monye 50.99, HJ: Anthony Idiata 2.12, PV: Hassan Sambo 4.10, LJ: Obinnah Eregbu 8.11, TJ: Festus Igbinoghene 15.69, SP: Chima Ugwu 18.04, DT: Vincent Oghene 56.74, HT: Gabriel Opuana 44.44, JT: Pius Bazighe 71.48, Dec: Tommy Ozono 6228. **Women**: 100m: Mary Onyali 11.24, 200m: Calista Uba 24.01, 400m: Emily Odoemenam 52.69, 800m/1500m: Fidelia Victor 2:08.93/4:25.93, 3000m: Mercy Emmanuel 10:09.58, 10000m: Angela Amajuobi 37:17.35, 100mh: Taiye Aladefa 13.77 (Ime Akpan 13.29 drugs dq), 400mh: Saidat Onanuga 60.60, TJ: Salamatu Alimi 11.91, SP: Vivian Chukwuemeka 13.34, DT/JT: Felicia Ojiego Nkiru 45.10/44.22.

Olapade ADENIKEN b.19 Aug 1969 1.86m 78kg. Was at University of Texas at El Paso, USA.
At 100m/200m/R- 4x100m relay: OG: '88- sf/sf, '92- 6/5/2R; WCh: '91- sf/5/4R; WJ: '88- 4/2/2R; WSG: '89- 2 100m; AfCh: '88- 4/-/1R, '89- 1/1R; WCp: '89- 4/3/4R. '92- 2/3R. Won NCAA 100m/200m 1992. 2nd GP 100m 1992.
African junior records 100m and 200m 1988. Nigerian records 100m 1992, 200m (2) 1991-2.
Progression at 100m, 200m: 1986- 10.65/10.5, 21.86; 1987- 10.3, 21.1; 1988- 10.29/9.9, 20.67; 1989- 10.16/10.05w, 20.38/20.22w; 1990- 10.10, 20.37/20.18w; 1991- 10.10/10.00w, 20.30/ 20.09w; 1992- 9.97, 20.11/20.00w; 1993- 10.15/ 10.00w, 20.12. pbs: 55m 6.17i '90, 400m 46.34 '90.

Sunday BADA b.22 Jun 1969. 1.88m 79kg.
At 400m/4x400mR: OG: '92- sf/5R; WCh: '93- 5; WI: '93- 2; AfCh: '90- 3/1R (3 200m); '91- 2/2R; WCp: '92- 1/1R. Nigerian champion 1990-3.
Progression at 400m: 1990- 46.19, 1991- 45.81, 1992- 44.99, 1993- 44.63. pbs: 200m 20.80 '92, 300m 32.66 '92.

Daniel Philip EFFIONG b. 17 Jun 1972. 1.87m 79kg. Student at Azusa Pacific Universty, USA.
At 100m/4x100mR: WCh: '93- 7 (qf 200m); WSG: '93- 1; AfCh: '90- 4; '93- 1/2R. At 200m: WSG: '91- 2; AfG: '91- 3. Won Nigerian 100m 1993, 200m 1992.
Progression at 100m, 200m: 1990- 10.29/10.1, 21.4; 1991- 10.18, 20.56/20.5; 1992- 10.11, 20.45/20.38w; 1993- 9.98/9.97w, 20.15.
Formerly known as Daniel Phillips (or Phillip), but now as Effiong.

Obinna EREGBU b.9 Nov 1969. 1.83m 75kg. Student at Central Arizona University, USA, formerly at Iowa State.
At LJ: WCh: '93- dnq 18; WSG: '93- 2; AfG: '93- 1; Nigerian champion 1993. At 100m: WJ: '86- 6.
Progression at LJ: 1986- 7.54, 1988- 7.88, 1989- 7.83, 1990- 7.82i/7.95w, 1991- 8.04/8.06w, 1992- 8.09/8.18w, 1993- 8.18/8.32w. pbs: 55m 5.9/6.13i '93, 60m 6.63i '93, 100m 10.37 '91, 10.25w '92, 10.3 '90.

Davidson EZINWA b.22 Nov 1971 1.82m 80kg. Student at Azusa Pacific College, California.
At 100m/4x100m relay: OG: 92- 8/2R; CG: '90- 2/2R (5 200m); WJ: '88- 2R, '90- 1/3R (2 200m); WCp: '89- 4R; AfG: '91- 2/1R; At 200m: AfCh: '89- 2/1R. Won Nigerian 100m 1992, 200m 1989.
African 200m record 1990. Nigerian records: 100m 1992, 200m (2) 1991-2.
Progression at 100m, 200m: 1988- 10.44/10.3, 20.92; 1989- 10.33/10.1, 19.9/20.82, 1990- 10.05, 20.30/20.0w; 1991- 10.04, 20.55/20.51w; 1992- 9.96/9.91w, 20.25; 1993- 10.14. pbs: 50m 5.64i '92, 60y 6.12i '92.
World age bests at 17 200m 1989 and 18 , 10.05 for 100m in January 1990 at the Nigerian trials, followed by two silver medals in Auckland. His twin brother Osmond also ran on the Nigerian 4x100m silver medal teams at the 1988 World Juniors and in Auckland, where he was 8th equal at 100m.

Adewale OLUKOJU b.27 Jul 1968 Zaria 1.88m 110kg. Student at Azusa Pacific University, USA.
At (SP/)DT: OG: '88- dnq 23; WCh: '91- 11; CG: '90- 2/1; WJ: '86- 6/7; WSG: '91- 1, '93- 2; AfG: '91- 2/1; AfCh: '87- 1/1, '88- 3/1 '92- 3/1; WCp: '92- 5.
Three African discus records 1989-91. African junior records for shot (18.13) and discus 1987.
Progression at DT: 1984- 56.88?, 1985- 50.88, 1986- 54.00, 1987- 56.92, 1988- 63.60/64.12u, 1989- 65.54, 1990- 64.56, 1991- 67.80, 1992- 64.40, 1993- 66.48. pbs: SP 19.44i '90, 18.75 '89; HT 58.40 '90.

Women

Mary ONYALI b.3 Feb 1968 1.65m 52kg. Graduated in telecommunications from Texas Southern University, USA,
At 200m/R- 4x100m relay (100m): OG: '88- sf, '92- sf/3R (7); WCh: '87- 6, '91- 7/4R (5 4x400mR), '93- 5/5; AfG: '87- 1/1R (3, 1 4x400mR), '91- (1)/1R, '93- 1/1R; AfCh: '85- 2, '89- 1 (1); WSG: '87- 2/3R; WI: '87- 5; WJ: '86- 2/3R (dq); WCp: '89- 2 (2). Won NCAA 1988. 3rd GP 1988. At 100m: AfCh: '88- 1; 3rd GP 1991. Won Nigerian 100m 1985-8, 1991-3; 200m

Mary Onyali: African Games winner

1985-8, 1990, 1992.
African records: seven 100m 1986-93, seven 200m 1986-90; junior 100m 1986, 200m 1986-7.
Progression at 100m, 200m: 1984- 12.2, 25.3; 1985- 11.91/11.8, 23.85, 1986- 11.28, 22.90/ 22.77w, 1987- 11.31/11.24w/11.2, 22.52; 1988- 11.09, 22.43; 1989- 11.14, 22.45; 1990- 11.09/ 10.9w, 22.31; 1991- 11.04, 22.72; 1992- 11.15/ 11.08w, 22.60/22.45w; 1993- 10.97, 22.32. pbs: 60m 7.24i '93, 400m 52.50 '87.
Concentrating on 100m in 1991 she ran African records of 11.07 and 11.04 before a sensational 10.81 in semi-final of Nigerian Championships, which was later declared faulty.

Fatima YUSUF b.2 May 1971 Owo, Ondo State 1.80m 64kg. Student at Azusa Pacific University.
At 400m/4x400mR: WCh: '91- sf/5R; CG: '90- 1 (3 4x100mR); WJ: '88- h, '90- 1 (dq sf 200m); AfG: '91- 1/1R (2 200m); AfCh: '89- 2/1R. 90- 1/1R (1 200m, 4x100mR); WCp: '89- 5R. 3rd GP 400m 1990.
Three African 400m records 1990-1.
Progression at 400m: 1987- 54.23, 1988- 54.23, 1989- 51.99, 1990- 50.59/50.5, 1991- 50.41, 1992- 51.83, 1993- 52.59. pbs: 100m 11.76 '90, 200m 22.84 '91, 300m 36.25 '90, 800m 2:14.56 '91.
In 1990 she broke the African record to win the Commonwealth title while still a junior, and went on to win the World Junior title and four gold medals at the African Championships.

NORWAY

Governing body: Norges Fri-Idrettsforbund, Karl Johansgaten 2, 0154 Oslo 1. Founded 1896.
National Championships first held in 1897 (men), 1947 (women). **1993 Champions**: **Men**: 100m/200m: Geir Moen 10.50/20.80, 400m/800m: Atle Douglas 47.61/1:44.74, 1500m: Tommy Gjølga 3:42.53, 5000m/10000m: John Halvorsen 13:52.4/29:10.94, Half Mar: Frank Bjørkli 63:06, Mar: Helge Dolsvåg 2:19:33, 3000mSt: Jim Svenøy 8:41.27, 110mh: Gaute M Gundersen 14.04, 400mh: Jan Erik Brudvik 51.76, HJ: Steinar Hoen 2.27, PV: Trond Barthel 5.45, LJ: Morten Næss 7.47, TJ: Ketill Hanstveit 16.38, SP: Kjell Ove Hauge 17.98, DT: Svein Inge Valvik 58.72, HT: Anders Halvorsen 62.64, JT: Arne Indrebø 74.72, Dec: Sean Clancy 7092, 10kmW: Sverre K Jensen 43:01; 20kmW: Martin Engelsviken 1:27:13. **Women**: 100m/200m/400m: Sølvi Meinseth 11.77/23.54w/53.83, 800m: Toril Lauritsen 2:05.48, 1500m/3000m: Hilde Stavik 4:12.93/8:58.92, 5000m: Torhild Dybwad 16:25.67, Half Mar: Grete Kirkeberg 72:21, Mar: Marianne Fløymo 2:48:15, 100mh: Monica Grefstad 13.26, 400mh: Mari Bjone 58.40, HJ: Hanne Haugland 1.86, LJ: Anne Brit Sandberg 6.28, TJ: Lene Espegren 13.54, SP: Grete Gjermshus 13.86, DT: Mette Bergmann 59.28, JT: Trine Hattestad 64.66, Hep: Monica Penne 5170, 5000mW/10kmW: Hilde Gustavsen 22:44.20/48:25.6.

Georg ANDERSEN b.7 Jan 1963 Arendal 1.90m 110kg. IF Urædd, Porsgrunn. Policeman.
At SP: OG: '88- 10; WCh: '91- dq (2); EC: '90- 3; WI: '89- 3; EI: '89- 3. Norwegian champion 1987-8, 1990. 3rd GP 1988, 2nd 1990.
Progression at SP: 1979- 12.76, 1980- 13.57, 1981- 15.85, 1982- 16.17, 1983- 17.32, 1984- 17.95, 1985- 18.60, 1986- 19.64, 1987- 20.13, 1988- 20.63, 1989- 20.98i/20.48, 1990- 20.86, 1991- 20.81 dq. pb DT 62.10 '86.
Lost his 1991 World Championships silver medal due to failing a drugs test on July 4 and served two year ban. In contrast he had gained the 1990 European bronze; originally fourth but Lykho disqualified.

Women

Else Katrine **Trine HATTESTAD** b.18 Apr 1966 Lørenskog 1.72m 65kg. née Solberg. IF Minerva. Fitness instructor.
At JT: OG: '84- 5, '88- dnq 18, '92- 5; WCh: '87- dnq 24, '91- 5;, '93- 1; EC: '82- dnq, '86- 9; EJ: '81- 5, '83- 2. Won Norwegian JT 1983-6, 1988-9, 1991-3. Won GP 1992 (3rd 1986).
Eleven Norwegian javelin records 1981-93.
Progression at JT: 1978- 31.04, 1979- 44.08, 1980- 49.54, 1981- 56.06, 1982- 58.02, 1983- 61.58, 1984- 65.02, 1985- 68.94, 1986- 67.80, 1987- 68.20, 1988- 67.50, 1989- 71.12, 1991- 71.44, 1992- 69.50, 1993- 72.12.
After disappointing in previous major events, came through in 1993 to win the World title. Banned for two years after a drugs test when she won the European Cup C1 javelin in Brussels in 1989. However, after discoveries of variances in the results of tests, she was reinstated and successfully sued her federation for $50,000 loss of earnings. Son born in 1991. She was the top goalscorer at handball in Norwegian second division in 1984, and but for her interest in the javelin would have been a candidate for the national team.

Hanne HAUGLAND b.14 Dec 1967 1.78m 60kg. SK Vidar.
At HJ: WCh: '87- dnq 20=, '93- 9=; EC: '90- 8; EI: '89- 2. Won Norwegian HJ 1986-7, 1989-90, 1992-3; LJ 1989-90. 3rd GP 1993.
Norwegian HJ records 1987 and 1989.
Progression at HJ: 1981- 1.61, 1982- 1.70, 1983- 1.80, 1984- 1.84, 1985- 1.87, 1986- 1.89, 1987- 1.93, 1988- 1.91, 1989- 1.96i/1.94, 1990- 1.92, 1991- 1.96i/1.86, 1992- 1.92i/1.90, 1993- 1.93. pbs: 100m 12.25 '89, 100mh 14.07 '91, LJ: 6.34 '91, TJ 12.94/13.21w '93, Hep 4756 '88.
Her grandfather Eugen Haugland won seven Norwegian TJ titles between 1931 and 1948 and was fourth in European TJ 1946, and her father Terje had a long jump pb of 7.87 '70 (EC: '69- 11, '71- 13). Three generations as European finalists were completed by Hanne in Split.

POLAND

Governing body: Polski Zwiazek Lekkiej Atletyki (PZLA), 02 034 Warszawa, ul.Wawelska 5. Founded 1919.
National Championships first held in 1920 (men), 1922 (women). **1993 Champions**: **Men**: 100m/200m: Marek Zalewski 10.12w/20.84, 400m: Tomasz Czubak 46.97, 800m: Piotr Piekarski 1:50.10, 1500: Andrzej Jakubiec 3:47.36, 5000m: Michal Bartoszak 14:21.93, 10000m: Zbigniew Nadolski 29:39.19, Half Mar: Marek Sukiennik 65:42, Mar: Tadeusz Lawicki 2:19:56, 3kmSt: Boguslaw Maminski 8:38.74, 110mh: Piotr Wojcik 13.58, 400mh: Piotr Kotlarski 50.24, HJ: Artur Partyka 2.28, PV: Boguslaw Kopkowski 5.20, LJ: Roman Golanowski 7.80, TJ: Jacek Butkiewicz 16.34, SP: Helmut Krieger 19.05, DT: Marek Stolarczyk 59.12, HT: Lech Kowalski 72.16, JT: Tomasz Damszel 77.60, Dec: Grzegorz Strominski 7686, 20kmW/50kmW: Robert Korzeniowski 1:23:47/3:44:24. **Women**: 100m: Dorota Krawczak 11.43w, 200m: Izabela Czajko 23.64, 400m: Elzbieta Kilinska 53.14, 800m/

Artur Partyka: silver in Stuttgart

1500m: Malgorzata Rydz 2:02.65/4:08.98, 3000m: Anna Brzezinska 9:07.20, 10000m: Anna Rybicka 33:20.38, Half Mar: Czeslawa Mentlewicz 81:14, Mar: Violetta Uryga 2:45:16, 100mh: Maria Kamrowska 13.25, 400mh: Sylwia Pachut 56.18, HJ: Beata Holub 1.90, LJ: Agata Karczmarek 6.87, TJ: Agnieszka Stanczyk 14.05, SP: Krystyna Danilczyk 17.96, DT: Marzena Wysocka 60.48, JT: Genowefa Patla 55.90, Hep: Urszula Wlodarczyk 5793, 5000mW/10kmW: Katarzyna Radtke 22:30.53/45:32.

Jan HURUK b.27 Jan 1960 Orsk 1.78m 65kg. GRYF Slupsk.
At Mar: OG: '92- 7; WCh: '91- 4; EC: '90- dnf; WCp; '91- 3. Won Polish 10000m 1987.
Polish marathon record 1990.
Progression at Mar: 1988- 2:17:11, 1989- 2:13:12, 1990- 2:10:16, 1991- 2:10:21, 1992- 2:10:07, 1993- 2:11:57. pbs: 3000m 7:55.05 '89, 5000m 13:34.63 '88, 10000m 28:18.42 '89, 3000mSt 8:38.63 '85.
Won Marrakech marathon 1990, second London 1992.

Robert KORZENIOWSKI b.30 Jul 68 Lubaczów 1.70m 63kg. AZS AWF Katowice.
At 20kmW: OG: '92- dnf (dq 50kmW); WCh: '91- 10; EC: '90- 4; WCp: '89- 40, '91- 7, '93- 4; WSG: '91- 1, '93- 1. At 10kmW: EJ: '87- dq. At 5000mW: WI: '93- 2. Won Polish 20kmW 1990-3, 50kmW 1993.
World best 5km road walk: 18:21 '90. Polish records 1990-3: 3000mW (5), 10kmW (2), 20kmW (2), 50km W (2).
Progression at 20kmW, 50kmW: 1987- 1:29:40, 1988- 1:26:04, 1989- 1:23:19, 1990- 1:19.32, 1991- 1:21:19, 1992- 1:19:14, 3:46:42; 1993- 1:20:55, 3:44:24. pbs: 3000mW 12:22.0 '88, 5000mW 18:17.22 '92, 10000mW 40:17.43 '90, 1 Hr 14,794m '92; road 10kmW 39:19 '92, 35kmW 2:28:30 (world best) '93.
Disqualified in 2nd place in the stadium just before finish of the 1992 Olympic 50km walk.

Artur PARTYKA b.25 Jul 1969 Stalowa Wola 1.92m 69kg. LKS Lódz. Student.
At HJ: OG: '88- dnq 20, '92- 3=; WCh: '91- 12, '93- 2; EC: '90- 11; WJ: '88- 1; EJ: '87- 1; WI: '91- 2; EI: '90- 1; ECp: '93- 1. Won POL HJ 1989-93.
Two Polish high jump records 1993.
Progression at HJ: 1984- 1.94, 1985- 2.04, 1986- 2.18, 1987- 2.23, 1988- 2.28, 1989- 2.32, 1990- 2.34i/2.33, 1991- 2.37i/2.32, 1992- 2.34, 1993- 2.37.
Has an excellent record in major events.

Women

Kamila GRADUS b.19 Mar 1967 Warszawa 1.58m 46kg. Legia Warszawa.
At Mar: WCh: '91- 6, '93- 9.
Progression at Mar: 1986- 2:42:54, 1988- 2:39:23, 1989- 2:37:37, 1990- 2:28:56, 1991- 2:26:55, 1992- 2:30:09, 1993- 2:27:38. pbs: 5000m 16:35.66 '92, 10000m 33:34.38 '92.
Ran sub 2:30 at Boston when 4th 1990 and 5th 1991. Won Nagoya Marathon 1993.

Renata KATEWICZ b.2 May 1965 1.80m 90kg. Zaglebie Lubin. Cook.
At DT: OG: '88- dnq 13; WCh: '87- 11, '93- dnq 15; EC: '86- 8; EJ: '83- 6;WSG: '93- 1; ECp: '85- 4, '87- 6, '93- 3. Polish champion 1985-7, 1992.
Four Polish discus records 1985-8.
Progression at DT: 1982- 50.38, 1983- 58.52, 1984- 60.60, 1985- 63.26, 1986- 64.34, 1987- 64.56; 1988- 66.18, 1989- 63.80, 1990- 2:28:50, 1991- 60.42, 1992- 63.80, 1993- 65.94. pb SP 17.27 '87.

Renata KOKOWSKA b.4 Dec 1958 Glubczyn 1.70m 57kg. née Pyrr. Bukowina Walcz. Agricultural technician.
At Mar: WCh: '87- dnf; WCp: '91- 6. At 10000m: ECp: '85-7, '87- 8. At 1500m: ECp: '83- 7. Won Polish 3000m 1985-6, 5000m 1984, 1986; 10000m 1984-8.
Four Polish 10000m records 1984-7.
Progression at 10000m, Mar: 1984- 34:04.66, 1985- 34:03.28, 1986- 33:27.95, 2:36.11; 1987-

33:00.60, 2:33:07; 1988- 33:07.08, 2:29:16; 1989- 2:31:19, 1990- 2:28:50, 1991- 2:27:36, 1992- 2:29:59, 1993- 2:26:20. pbs: 800m 2:06.5 '78, 1500m 4:13.91 '84, 3000m 9:00.24 '86, 5000m 15:56.19 '86, 10000m 33:14.87 '91.
Won Amsterdam marathon 1990, Berlin 1988, 1991, 1993; 2nd 1990, 1992. 2nd London 1992.

Wanda PANFIL b.26 Jan 1959 Ropoczno 1.67m 54kg. Lechia Tomaszów. Married to Mauricio Gonzalez (Mex, 10000m pb 27:43.64 '88) and now lives in Mexico.
At Mar: WCh: '91- 1; OG: '88- 22, '92- 22. At 10000m: EC: '90- 7; ECp: '89- 5; won GWG 1990. At 3000m: ECp: '83- 6, '85- 4, '87- 8. Won Polish 3000m 1984, 1987; 5000m 1985, 1987-8; marathon 1988.
Polish records: four marathon 1987-91, six 5000m 1984-9, 2000m & 3000m 1990.
Progression at 10000m, Mar: 1987- 33:06.31, 2:32:01; 1988- 2:32:23; 1989- 33:18.57, 2:27:05; 1990- 32:01.17, 2:26:31; 1991- 31:53.83, 2:24:18; 1992- 2:29:29. pbs: 800m 2:04.62 '82, 1500m 4:13.94 '85, 2000m 5:45.36 '90, 3000m 8:52.07 '90, 5000m 15:41.29 '89.
Has won six of her 12 marathons: Debno 1988, Nagoya, London and New York 1990; Boston 1991; including five in succession to her world title in 1991. 2nd Berlin 1987, London 1989.

Malgorzata RYDZ b.18 Jan 1967 Klobuck 1.62m 52kg. née Kapkowska. Budowlani Czestochowa.
At 1500m (800m): OG: '92- 7; WCh: '91- 8, '93- h; WI: '89- 8; WCp: '92- 2; ECp: '89- 4, '91- 5 (5), '93- 4 (7). Won Polish 800m 1988, 1991-3, 1500m 1988-93.
Progression at 1500m: 1985- 4:28.8, 1988- 4:14.00, 1989- 4:08.40, 1990- 4:12.45, 1991- 4:05.52, 1992- 4:01.91, 1993- 4:02.29. pbs: 400m 54.87 '93, 800m 2:00.68 '91, 2000m 5:48.39 '90, 3000m 8:58.64 '93.

Urszula WLODARCZYK b.22 Dec 1965 Walbrzych 1.80m 66kg. AZS-AWF Wroclaw.
At Hep: OG: '92- 8; WCh: '91- 6, '93- 5; WSG: 91- 2 (4 TJ), '93- 1; ECp: '91- 4, '93- 3. At Pen: WI inv: '93- 2; EI: '92- 3. Won Polish 100mh 1991, TJ and Hep 1990-2.
Two Polish triple jump records 1991.
Progression at Hep: 1982- 4779*, 1983- 4914, 1984- 5173, 1985- 5504, 1986- 5721, 1987- 5831, 1988- 5825, 1989- 5898, 1990- 6021, 1991- 6425, 1992- 6407, 1993- 6394. pbs: 100m 11.94 '91, 200m 24.03/23.89w '92; 800m 2:10.92 '91, 100mh 13.31 '92, HJ 1.84 '91, LJ 6.59/6.67w '93, TJ 13.98 '93, SP 14.62 '91, JT 46.22 '91, Pen 4667i '93.

PORTUGAL

Governing body: Federação Portuguesa de Atletismo, Av.Infante Santo, 68-7°, E/F 1, 1300 Lisboa. Founded 1921.
National Championships first held in 1910 (men), 1937 (women). **1993 Champions**: **Men**: 100m: Pedro Agostinho 10.51, 200m: Luís Cunha 21.36, 400m: José Mendes 47.67, 800m: António Abrantes 1:50.93, 1500m: Mário Silva 3:40.09, 5000m: Luís Jesus 13:50.60, 10000m: Domingos Castro 28:01.40; Mar: Domingos Neves 2:15:16, 3000mSt: João Junqueira 8:25.81, 110mh: João Lima 14.31, 400mh: Pedro Rodrigues 50.52, HJ: F Esteves Costa 2.04, PV: Nuno Fernandes 5.40, LJ: Rui Barros 7.32, TJ: José Leitão 15.99w, SP/DT: Fernando Alves 17.09/52.70, HT: António Peixoto 63.50, JT: Carlos Cunha 68.04, Dec: Mário Anibal Ramos 7570, 20kmW: José Urbano 1:29:13, 50kmW: José Pinto 4:02:13. Women: 100m/200m: Lucrécia Jardim 11.46/23.26, 400m: Elsa Amaral 54.28, 800m: Carla Sacramento 2:02.95, 1500m: Marina Bastos 4:17.79, 3000m: Fernanda Ribeiro 9:02.92, 10000m: M Albertina Dias 31:44.57, Mar: Manuela Machado 2:31:31, 100mh: Sandra Barreiro 13.95, 400mh: Marta Moreira 57.23, HJ: Isabel Branco 1.78, LJ: Cristina Morujão 6.09, TJ: Ana Oliveira 13.27, SP/DT: Teresa Machado 15.56/57.52, JT: Helena Gouveia 49.18, Hep: Mónica Sousa 4905, 10kmW: Isilda Gonçalves 47:57.

Domingos CASTRO b.22 Nov 1963 Guimarães 1.67m 56kg. Sporting Club de Portugal.
At 5000m: OG: '88- 4, '92- 11 (h 10k); WCh: '87- 2; '91- 5. At 10000m: WCh: '93- h; EC: '86- 5; won GWG 1986. World CC: '90- 7, '92- 11, '93- 12. Won Portugese 5000m 1986-7, 1989; 10000m 1986-7, 1992-3; CC 1990, 1993.
Progression at 5000m, 10000m: 1982- 14:59.3; 1983- 13:48.52, 30:29.1; 1984- 13:52.54, 30:39.6; 1985- 13:38.60; 1986- 13:19.03, 28:01.62; 1987- 13:18.59, 28:09.54; 1988- 13:16.09, 27:43.30; 1989- 13:14.41, 27:36.00; 1991- 13:24.71; 1992- 13:19.98, 27:39.03; 1993- 13:14.65, 27:34.53. pbs: 1500m 3:39.2 '86, 3000m 7:43.32 '89.
In 1987 he was a surprise silver medallist at 5000m in Rome. Desperately unlucky to miss a medal at 5000m in Seoul.
Twin brother of **Dionisio**, who at 5000m was 4th at EC 1990 and 8th WCh 1987 and 1991, pbs: 5000m13:13.59 '90, 10000m 27:42.84 '88, 20000m 57:18.4 '90; world record 20,000m 57:18.4 '90.

Women

Maria Albertina DIAS b.26 Apr 1965 Porto 1.63m 48kg. Maratona Cube da Maia.
At 10000m: OG: '88- 10, '92- 13; WCh: '91- dnf,

'93- 7. At 3000m: WI: '91- 4. World CC: '89- 18, '90- 2, '91- 6, '92- 3, '93- 1. World road 15km: '89- 8, '91- 12. Won Portugese 1500m 1992, 3000m 1986, 1989, 1991; 10000m 1993, CC 1992-3.
Portugese records 1M 1991, 3000m 1991 & 1992, 5000m 1993.
Progression at 3000m, 10000m: 1984- 9:41.33, 1985- 9:18.2, 1986- 9:17.96, 34:12.81; 1987- 9:08.17, 32:41.5; 1988- 9:00.40, 32:07.13; 1989- 8:48.87, 32:07.95; 1990- 8:57.17, 32:27.84; 1991- 8:43.50, 32:03.76; 1992- 8:43.08, 31:42.70; 1993- 8:43.76, 31:33.03. pbs: 800m 2:07.9 '88, 1500m 4:09.60 '91, 1M 4:29.97 '91, 5000m 15:05.12 '93, Half Mar 70:06 '92, Mar 2:26:49 '93.
Second IAAF World Cross Challenge 1992. Brilliant marathon début for 2nd in Berlin 1993.

Maria Conceição FERREIRA b.13 Mar 1962 Aveleda 1.48m 40kg. SC Braga.
At 10000m: OG: '92- dnf; WCh: '87- h, '91- 11, '93- 6; EC: '86- 26. At Mar: OG: '84- 39, '88- 20; EC: '90- dnf. World road 15km: '88- 8, '90- 9, '91- 9; Half Mar: '93- 1. Won Portugese 3000m 1990, 10000m 1986, 1988; CC 1989-91.
Portugese 10000m record 1992.
Progression at 10000m/Mar: 1984- 34:13.89/ 2:43:58, 1985- 33:17.41, 1986- 33:21.25, 1987- 32:25.7, 1988- 32:28.8/2:34:23; 1989- 32:06.51/ 2:32:50; 1990- 31:45.75/2:30:34; 1991- 31:51.47/ 2:30:18; 1992- 31:16.42; 1993- 31:30.60. pbs: 1500m 4:19.8 '93, 3000m 8:53.27 '91, 5000m 15:54.01 '86, Half Mar 70:07 '93.
Ran on winning World Road Relay team 1992.

M Manuela MACHADO b.9 Aug 1963 Viana do Castelo 1.61m 52kg. Sporting Club de Braga.
At Mar: OG: '92- 7; WCh: '91- 7, '93- 2; EC: '90- 10. Won POR Mar 1993.
Progression at Mar: 1988- 2:45:37, 1989- 2:38:45, 1990- 2:33:46, 1991- 2:32:33, 1992- 2:27:42, 1993- 2:30:54. pbs: 800m 2:14.8i '87, 1500m 4:24.0 '91, 3000m 9:09.28 '92, 10000m 32:25.6 '93.
Her World silver in 1993 was her best placing in eight marathons, but in December 1993 she won at Lisbon.

Carla SACRAMENTO b.10 Dec 1971 Lisboa 1.68m 53kg. Maratona Clube de Maia.
At 800m (1500m): OG: '92- sf (sf 1500m); WCh: '93- h (11); WI: '93- (7); EI: '92- 4. Won Portugese 800m 1986-7, 1993; 1500m 1991.
Portugese records 1989-93: 800m (5), 1500m (3), 1000m (2).
Progression at 800m, 1500m: 1985- 2:15.15/ 2:13.56dq, 1986- 2:10.48, 1987- 2:09.3, 4:35.96; 1988- 2::04.27, 4:29.41; 1989- 2:03.89, 4:21.92; 1990- 2:04.83, 4:15.06; 1991- 2:04.94, 4:20.43; 1992- 2:00.57, 4:04.10; 1993- 1:59.42, 4:06.33. pbs: 200m 25.49 '92, 400m 55.21 '89, 1000m 2:39.2 '93, 1M 4:31.05 '92, 3000m 9:32.7 '90.

QATAR

Governing body: Qatar Amateur Athletic Federation, PO Box 8139, Doha. Founded 1963.

Ibrahim ISMAIL Muftah b.10 May 1972 1.85m 75kg.
At 400m: OG: '92- 7; WCh: '91- sf, '93- sf; WJ: '90- 6; AsG: 90- 2; AsCh: '89- 1; '91- 1 (2 200m), '93- 1; WCp: '92- 4. Won Asian J 1988, 1990 (2nd 200m).
Asian junior records 400m 1989-91. Qatar 400m records 1986-93.
Progression at 400m: 1988- 46.59, 1989- 45.60, 1990- 45.57, 1991- 45.37, 1992- 44.89, 1993- 44.85. pbs: 100m 10.66 '91, 10.3 '88; 200m 20.85 '92.

Talal MANSOOR Al-Rahim b. 8 May 1964 1.80m 73kg.
At 100m (200m): OG: '84- hR, '88- qf, '92- sf; AsG: '86- 1, '90- 1; AsCh: '87- 1 (1), '91- 1, '93- 1; WCp: '92- 5. At 60m: WI: '93- 3.
Asian 100m records 1990 and 1992.
Progression at 100m: 1985- 10.36, 1986- 10.30, 1987- 10.29, 1988- 10.33, 1990- 10.18, 1991- 10.24, 1992- 10.14, 1993- 10.22/10.20w. pbs: 60m 6.51i '93, 200m 20.62 '92, 400m 48.80 '87.

Mohamed SULEIMAN b. 23 Nov 1969 Somalia 1.69m 66kg.
At 1500m (5000m): OG: '88- h, '92- 3; WCh: '91- 9, '93- 4; WJ: '88- 7; AsG: '86- 3, 90- 1 (1); AsCh: '87- 5, '89- 3, '91- 1 (1); WCp: '92- 1; Asi J: '86- 2 (3 2000mSt), '88- 1.
Asian records: 1500m (6), 1M (3), 3000m 1991-3.
Progression at 1500m: 1986- 3:44.68, 1987- 3:44.51, 1988- 3:41.95, 1989- 3:41.38, 1990- 3:40.57, 1991- 3:34.57, 1992- 3:34.12, 1993- 3:33.29. pbs: 800m 1:47.31 '93, 1M 3:55.15 '92, 2000m 5:06.08 '92, 3000m 7:38.20 '93, 5000m 13:25.15 '92, 2000mSt 5:47.25 '88, 3000mSt 8:43.8 '89.
The first ever Olympic medallist from Qatar. He ran the fastest ever 1500m in qualifying, 3:34.77 in Barcelona. All Qatar records from 1500m to 5000m.

ROMANIA

Governing body: Federatia Romana de Atletism, Str. Vasile Conta 16, 70139 Bucuresti. Founded 1912.
National Championships first held in 1921 (men), 1925 (women). **1993 Champions**: **Men**: 100m/200m: Daniel Cojocaru 10.45/20.97, 400m: Valentin Chiriac 47.54, 800m: Ion Bogde 1:50.73, 1500m/5000m: Ovidiu Olteanu

3:42.00/14:15.08, 10000m: Mircea Latis 30:01.00, Half Mar: Nicolae Negru 64:47, Mar: Gheorghe Sandu 2:25:54, 3000mSt: Florin Ionescu 8:34.93, 110mh: George Boroi 13.83, 400mh: Gabriel Masinistru 51.38, HJ: Eugen Popescu 2.20, PV: Razvan Enescu 5.00, LJ: Daniel Barbulescu 7.34, TJ: Ionut Eftenie 16.54, SP: Gheorghe Guset 19.54, DT: Costel Grasu 63.54, HT: Zoltán Szabó 65.22, JT: Constantin Miclea 70.94, Dec: Romeo Hurduc 6727, 20kmW/50kmW: Constantin Balan 1:30:56/4:17:22. Women: 100m: Lia Murgu 11.70, 200m: Teodora Luca 24.20, 400m: Mariana Florea 53.78, 800m/1500m: Violeta Beclea 2:03.26/4:08.29, 3000m: Gabriela Szabo 8:59.00, 10000m: Alina Tecuta 33:19.00, Half Mar: Anuta Catuna 69:22, Mar: Cristina Pomacu 2:37:47, 2000mSt: Lelia Deselnicu 7:00.67, 100mh: Erica Niculae 13.58, 400mh: Nicoleta Carutasu 57.60, HJ: Oana Musunoi 1.84, PV: Gabriela Mihalcea 3.70, LJ: Marieta Ilcu 6.50, TJ: Ionela Gogoase 13.70, SP: Mihaela Oana 18.87, DT: Nicoleta Grasu 61.62, HT: Mihaela Melinte 60.02, JT: Carla Dumitru 57.30, Hep: Florina Martin 5313, 10kmW: Norica Campean 46:09.

George BOROI b. 26 Aug 1964 Berislavesti 1.82m 71kg. Steaua Bucuresti.
At 110mh: OG: '92- qf; WCh: '93- sf; EC: '90- h. WI 60mh: '91- 7, '93- 6. Won ROM 100m 1989, 110mh 1989-90, 1993. ROM 110mh record 1993.
Progression at 110mh: 1983- 14.67, 1984- 14.50, 1985- 14.57, 1986- 14.03, 1987- 13.94, 1988- 13.74, 1989- 13.67, 1990- 13.73, 1991- 13.61, 1992- 13.53, 1993- 13.34. pbs: 100m 10.54 '93, 200m 21.55 '90, 60mh 7.50i '94.

Costel GRASU b.5 Jul 1967 Fetesti 1.93m 114kg. Mining worker. Dinamo Bucuresti.
At DT: OG: '92- 4; WCh: '91- dnq 21, '93- 4; Won ECp DT C1 '91, B '93; Balkan DT 1992, ROM SP 1989, 1991, DT 1989, 1991-3.
Progression at DT: 1983- 45.76, 1984- 54.52, 1985- 55.22, 1986- 55.54, 1987- 54.86, 1988- 60.82, 1989- 60.72, 1990- 59.46, 1991- 64.18, 1992- 67.08, 1993- 66.90. pb SP 19.42 '89.
Married to Nicoleta (née Gradinaru) (qv).

Sorin MATEI b.6 Jul 1963 Bucuresti 1.84m 71kg. Teacher. Universitatea Craieva.
At HJ: OG: '80- 13, '88- dnq 20=, '92- 13; WCh: '83- 17, '87- 6, '91- dnq 17=; EC: '82- dnq, '86- 14; WI: '87- 5=, '91- 6=; EI: '88- 3, '92- 2; EJ: '81- 5; WSG: '87- 3. 3rd GP 1988.
Ten Romanian high jump records 1980-90.
Progression at HJ: 1977- 1.88, 1978- 2.03, 1979- 2.12i, 1980- 2.27, 1981- 2.22, 1982- 2.28, 1983- 2.30, 1984- 2.34, 1985- 2.35, 1986- 2.32, 1987- 2.32, 1988- 2.37, 1989- 2.30, 1990- 2.40, 1991- 2.35, 1992- 2.36i/2.30, 1993- 2.35i/2.30.
One of the smallest top-class high jumpers, his 2.40m record in 1990 gives him a differential of 56cm over his own height, equal third best ever.

Women

Galina ASTAFEI b.7 Jun 1969 Bucuresti 1.81m 60kg. Student. USC Mainz. Married to volleyball international Alin Stavariu.
At HJ: OG: '88- 5, '92- 2; WCh: '87- dnq 17=, '93- 4=; WI: '93- 4; EC: '90- dnq 17; EI: '89- 1, '90- 3; WJ: '86- 2, '88- 1; EJ: '87- 2; WSG: '89- 1; WCp: '89- 3, '92- 2; ECp: '89- 1, '93- 1. 2nd GP 1993. Romanian champion 1986, 1988-9, 1992.
Three world junior and three Romanian high jump records 1988.
Progression at HJ: 1984- 1.80, 1985- 1.89, 1986- 1.93, 1987- 1.93i/1.88, 1988- 2.00, 1989- 2.00, 1990- 1.98, 1992- 2.00, 1993- 2.00.

Violeta BECLEA b.26 Mar 1965 Dolhesti Mari 1.66m 50kg. Technician. Rapid Bucuresti.
At 800m: WI: '89- 4, '91- 2; EI: '90- 3. At 1500m: OG: '92- sf; WCh: '91- 10, '93- 9; WI: '93- 2; ECp: '93- 2. Won Romanian 800m 1993, 1500m 1990-1, 1993. 3rd GP 1M 1993.
Progression at 800m, 1500m: 1982- 2:05.07, 4:23.85, 1983- 2:03.63, 1985- 2:00.75, 4:11.01; 1986- 1:58.7, 4:04.56; 1987- 1:59.53, 4:07.56; 1988- 1:59.35, 4:07.94; 1989- 1:58.94, 4:07.24; 1990- 2:01.05, 4:03.14; 1991- 2:00.19, 4:02.21; 1992- 4:03.29; 1993- 1:59.13, 3:59.35. pbs: 1000m 2:36.74 '89, 1M 4:21.69 '93, 3000m 8:57.00 '91.

Mirela DULGHERU b.5 Oct 1966 Ploiesti 1.70m 65kg. Teacher. Prahova Ploiesti
At 1500m: OG: '92- 4; WCh: '93- 11; WSG: '93- 1; WI: '91- 9, '93- 8; EI: '90- 4. Balkan champion 1989, 1992, Romanian 1992.
Progression at LJ: 1984- 6.34, 1985- 6.31, 1986- 6.60, 1987- 6.74, 1988- 6.51, 1989- 6.76i/6.67, 1990- 6.84, 1991- 6.88i/6.61, 1992- 7.14, 1993- 6.99i/6.77/6.83w. pbs: 60m 7.21i '92, 100m 11.39 '89.

Elena FIDATOV b.24 Jul 1960 Tulcea 1.68m 52kg. Coach. CSU Bacau.
At 1500m: OG: '92- 11; WCh: '91- 14, '93- h (h 3000m); EC: '90- 5. Won Balkan 1500m 1992, ROM 1500m 1988, 3000m 1986-7, 1990.
Progression at 1500m, 3000m: 1978- 9:42.4, 1980- 9:31.2, 1981- 4:18.97, 9:28.10; 1982- 9:29.29, 1984- 4:11.6, 8:54.32; 1985- 4:10.05, 8:47.60; 1986- 4:03.92, 8:50.26; 1987- 4:05.88, 8:42.16; 1988- 4:07.72, 8:50.24; 1989- 4:10.26, 8:59.43; 1990- 4:05.8, 9:02.62; 1991- 4:06.99, 9:09.88; 1992- 4:04.55, 8:50.25; 1993- 4:05.61, 8:44.93. pbs: 1M 4:31.69 '91, 5000m 15:41.83 '86, 10000m 33:49.99 '85.

Nicoleta GRASU b.11 Sep 1971 Secuieni 1.76m 88kg. Administration officer. Dinamo Bucuresti.
At DT: OG: '92- dnq 13; WCh: '93- 7; WJ: '90- 6. Won Balkan 1992, ROM 1993.
Progression at DT: 1987- 50.82, 1988- 51.06, 1989- 52.54, 1990- 56.02, 1991- 59.90, 1992- 65.66, 1993- 65.16. pb SP 15.00 '92.
Married to Costel Grasu (qv).

Marieta ILCU b.16 Oct 1962 Darabani, Botosani 1.72m 64kg. Student. Metalul Hunedoara.
At LJ: OG: '92- dnq 16; WCh: '87- dnq 14, '91- 6; EC: '90- 2; WI: '89- 2, '91- 3, '93- 1; EI: '92- 2; WSG: '85- 3, '87- 1, '89- 2; WCp: '89- 2; ECp: '89- 4, '93- 6. 2nd GP 1989, 3rd 1990. Won ROM LJ 1985, 1990-1, 1993; 100m 1988-90.
Progression at LJ: 1979- 6.09, 1980- 6.34, 1981- 6.32, 1982- 6.34, 1983- 6.30, 1984- 6.69, 1985- 6.87, 1986- 6.80, 1987- 6.93, 1988- 6.98, 1989- 7.08, 1990- 7.06, 1991- 6.77/6.89i, 1992- 6.98, 1993- 6.94i/6.50. pbs: 60m 7.1i '91, 100m 11.36/11.3 '88, 200m 23.40 '88.

Margareta KESZEG b.31 Aug 1965 Medias 1.65m 51kg. Married name Elena. Universitatea Craieva.
At 3000m: OG: '92- 11; WCh: '91- 5; EC: '90- 5; WI: '89- 3; WI: '91- 2, '93- 2; EI: '90- 2, '92- 1; WCp: '92- 3; ECp: '91- 1, '93- 1. Won ROM 3000m 1989, 1992. At 1500m: EJ: '83- 1; WI: '85- 5; WSG: '85- 2. 3rd 1500m GP 1990, 2nd 3000m 1991.
Progression at 3000m: 1985- 8:46.44, 1986- 8:51.54, 1987- 8:52.81, 1988- 8:51.96, 1989- 8:44.33, 1990- 8:47.81, 1991- 8:42.02, 1992- 8:39.94, 1993- 8:45.86. pbs: 800m 2:03.37 '83, 1500m 4:04.49 '86, 1M 4:24.02 '91.

Ella KOVACS b.11 Dec 1964 Ludus, Mures 1.70m 55kg. Student. Steaua Bucuresti.
At 800m: OG: '92- 6; WCh: '91- 3, '93- 3; EC: '90- 5; WI: '91- 3, '93- 5; EI: '85- 1, '92- 1; WCp: '92- 4; ECp: '91- 1, '93- 1. Won Balkan 1989, ROM 1991-2.
Progression at 800m: 1982- 2:04.55, 1984- 1:58.42, 1985- 1:55.68, 1986- 1:59.91, 1987- 1:56.76, 1988- 1:58.10, 1989- 1:58.60, 1990- 1:58.33, 1991- 1:57.58, 1992- 1:57.19, 1993- 1:56.58. pbs: 400m 53.22 '90, 1000m 2:32.40 '93, 1500m 4:06.38 '84.

Liliana NASTASE b.1 Aug 1962 Vinju Mare, Mehedinti 1.69m 67kg. née Alexandru. Teacher. Steaua Bucuresti.
At Hep: OG: '92- 4 (qf 100mh); WCh: '87- 5, '91- 2; EC: '90- dnf; WSG: '85- 2, '87- 1; ECp: '91- 1B. At Pen: WI inv: '93- 1; EI: '92- 1. At 100m: ECp: '89- 8. Won Balkan Hep 1985, 100mh 1983; ROM 100mh 1984, 1991-2; Hep 1984-8, 1991.
Eight Romanian heptathlon records 1984-9. WIB pentathlon 4705u '90, 4655 '91, 4726 '92.
Progression at Hep: 1980- 4652*, 1982- 5378*, 1983- 5753, 1984- 6086, 1985- 6313, 1986- 6172, 1987- 6364, 1988- 6352. 1989- 6602, 1990- 6435, 1991- 6493, 1992- 6619, 1993- 6260. pbs: 100m 11.85 '89, 200m 23.35 '92, 800m 2:07.6 '91, 60mh 8.08i '91, 100mh 12.81 '91, 12.8w '84, 400mh 59.41 '83, HJ 1.82 '92, LJ 6.78 '89, SP 14.44i/14.36 '92, JT 47.72 '89, Hep: 4737i '93.

Iulia NEGURA b.26 Jan 1967 Vacu 1.65m 57kg. PE student. CSU Bacau.
At 10000m: WCh: '91- 17, '93- 16; WSG: '93- 1; ECp: '91- 3, '93- 3. World road 15km: 90- 1, '91- 1, Half Mar: '92- 10, '93- 7. World CC: '90- 12. Won Romanian 10000m 1990-1.
Progression at 10000m: 1987- 34:43.10, 1988- 33:25.2, 1989- 32:58.04, 1990- 33:14.74, 1991- 31:52.58, 1993- 32:11.58. pbs: 1500m 4:13.25 '89, 3000m 8:53.19 '91, 5000m 15:34.30 '89. Road 15km 48:42 '91, Half Mar 70:59 '92.
Retained her World 15km road title in 1991, when she ran 1:30 faster than she had in 1990.

Felicea TILEA b.29 Sep 1967 Nagura Ilvei 1.67m 74kg. CSM Zalau.
At JT: WCh: '93- 8; EC: '90- dq (9); ECp: '93- 1. ROM champion 1990.
Progression at JT: 1986- 51.42, 1987- 51.44, 1989- 59.54, 1990- 64.02, 1993- 65.62.
Two-year drugs ban after positive test for steroids when 9th at 1990 European Championships.

RUSSIA

Governing body: All-Russia Athletic Federation, Luzhnetskaya Naberezhnaya 8, Moscow 119871. Founded 1911.
National Championships First held in 1911, USSR women's from 1922. **1993 Russian Champions**: **Men**: 100m: Aleksandr Porkhomovskiy 10.28, 200m: Oleg Fatun 20.98, 400m: Dmitriy Kosov 45.80, 800m: Aleksey Oleynikov 1:47.09, 1500m: Sergey Melnyikov 3:42.15, 5000m: Andrey Tikhonov 13:47.67, 10000m: Gennadiy Temnikov 28:40.27, Half Mar: Yuriy Chizhov 63:33, Mar: Andrey Tarasov 2:12:56, 3000mSt: Vladimir Pronin 8:33.73, 110mh: Igor Kazanov LAT 13.40, 400mh: Aleksandr Belikov 50.27, HJ: Aleksey Yemelin 2.28, PV: Denis Petushinsky 5.80, LJ: Stanislav Tarasenko 8.08, TJ: Vasiliy Sokov 17.59, SP: Yevgeniy Palchikov 20.16, DT: Dmitriy Shevchenko 65.20, HT: Sergey Litvinov 82.00, JT: Yuriy Rybin 81.30, Dec: Andrey Kotsyubenko 7886, 20kmW: Vladimir Andreyev 1:20:44, 50kmW: Daniel Garcia MEX 3:53:23. **Women**: 100m: Natalya

Voronova 11.21, 200m: Irina Privalova 22.50, 400m: Yelena Ruzina 51.35, 800m: Lyubov Gurina 1:58.89, 1500m: Lyudmila Rogachova 4:05.77, 3000m: Yelena Romanova 8:58.75, 5000m: Tatyana Pentukova 15:48.15, 10000m: Olga Bondarenko 32:02,44, Half Mar: Klara Kashapova 1:13:34, Mar: Fariya Sultanova 2:32:11, 2000mSt: Svetlana Rogova 6:17.42, 100mh: Marina Azyabina 12.69, 400mh: Anna Knoroz 54,67, HJ: Yelena Topchina 1.94, PV: Svetlana Abramova 3.80, LJ: Yelena Sinchukova 6.79, TJ: Yolanda Chen 14.97, SP: Anna Romanova 20.19, DT: Larisa Korotkevich 67.52, HT: Olga Kuzenkova 60.34, JT: Yekaterina Ivakina 65.36, Hep: Tatyana Blokhina 6605, 10kmW: Yelena Arshintseva 43:11.

Note: Clubs are shown in the biographies after height and weight. Based on the major cities, they have affiliations, abbreviated as follows: Dyn - Dynamo, Sp - Spartak, TR - Trudovye Reservye, VS - Army.

Dmitriy BAGRYANOV b.18 Dec 1967 Moskva 1.88m 81kg. Moskva Sp
At LJ: OG: '92- 7; WCh: '91- dnq; WI: '91- 7; EI: '92- 1. Won USSR LJ 1991, CIS 1992.
Progression at LJ: 1990- 7.61, 1991- 8.20, 1992- 8.35, 1993- 8.07, 1994- 8.23i. pb 400mh 50.19 '89.
Switched from 400m hurdles to long jump.
Pyotr BOCHKARYOV b.13 Nov 1967 Moskva 1.86m 82kg. Moskva Sp
At PV: WSG: '91- 3; EI: '92- 1.
Progression at PV: 1982- 3.80, 1983- 4.50, 1984- 4.90, 1985- 5.20, 1986- 5.30, 1987- 5.30i, 1988- 5.60, 1989- 5.50, 1990- 5.70, 1991- 5.75, 1992- 5.85, 1993- 5.80.

Rodion GATAULLIN b.23 Nov 1965 Tashkent 1.89m 78kg. St Petersburg Sp. Doctor.
At PV: OG: '88- 2; WCh: '87- 3, '91- 4; WI: '89- 1, '93- 1; EC: '86- nh, '90- 1; EI: '88- 1, '90- 1; EJ: '83- 1; WSG: '85- 1, '87- 2; ECp: '89- 1, '93- 1. USSR champion 1985, 1989, 1991. Won GWG 1990, GP 1989.
World junior pole vault record 1984. WIB 6.00 and 6.02 '89, Russian records 1992 and 1993.
Progression at PV: 1977- 2.80, 1978 - 3.10, 1979- 3.80, 1980- 4.20, 1981- 4.80, 1982- 5.20, 1983- 5.55, 1984- 5.65, 1985- 5.75, 1986- 5.85, 1987- 5.90, 1988- 5.95, 1989- 6.02i/6.00, 1990- 5.92, 1991- 5.90, 1992- 5.95, 1993- 6.00. pbs: 110mh 14.4, LJ 7.27 '90.
The world's second six-metre vaulter. Moved from Tashkent in Uzbekistan to St Petersburg in order to compete for Russia. Married to Tatyana Reshetnikova (12.73 for 100mh '92).

Denis KAPUSTIN b.5 Oct 1970 1.89m 86kg. Kazan Sp. Student.
At TJ: WCh: '93- 6; EJ: '89- 1; WSG: '91- 4.
Progression at TJ: 1989- 16.37/16.63w, 1990- 16.68, 1991- 17.34, 1992- 17.48, 1993- 17.54. pb TJ: 7.68i '91.

Sergey KIRMASOV b.25 Mar 1970. Mogilets Sp.
At HT: EJ: '89-1. Russian champion 1992.
Progression at HT: 1988- 71.20, 1989- 75.52, 1990- 77.66, 1991- 81.14, 1992- 79.92, 1993- 82.54.

Sergey LITVINOV b.23 Jan 1958 Tsukarov, Krasnodar 1.80m 100kg. Rostov-on-Don VS. Teacher.
At HT: OG: '80- 2, '88- 1; WCh: '83- 1, '87- 1, '93- 7; EC: '82- 3, '86- 2; EJ: '75- 3, '77- 2; WCp: '79- 1; ECp: '79- 2, '83- 1, '87- 1, '93- 1. USSR champion 1979 and 1983, Russian 1993. 2nd GP 1986.
Three world hammer records, in 1980, 1982 and 1983; two world junior records 1976-7.
Progression at HT: 1974- 60.68, 1975- 65.32, 1976- 72.38, 1977- 74.32, 1978- 76.22, 1979- 79.82, 1980- 81.66, 1981- 79.60, 1982- 83.98, 1983- 84.14, 1984- 85.20, 1985- 76.94, 1986- 86.04, 1987- 83.48, 1988- 84.80, 1990- 81.74, 1991- 79.42, 1992- 80.26, 1993- 82.16.
Only two men have thrown the hammer more than 85m, yet Litvinov twice threw over this distance and lost to Yuriy Sedykh - at Cork in 1984 and at the 1986 European Championships, when he opened with 85.74. Litvinov his great rival to win the 1988 Olympic title. After a couple of quiet years he returned to top form in 1993.

Sergey LYAKHOV b.1 May 1968 1.95m 105kg. Moskva Dyn.
At DT: WCh: '91- 9. USSR champion 1990.
Progression at DT: 1986- 52.54, 1987- 60.06, 1988- 62.64, 1989- 63.64, 1990- 64.36, 1991- 63.88, 1992- 66.64, 1993- 66.12.

Vyacheslav LYKHO b.16 Jan 1967 1.96m 120kg. Moskva Dyn.
At SP: OG: '92- 3; WCh: '87- 9; EC: '90- 3 dq; WJ: '86- 2. USSR champion 1990.
Progression at SP: 1985- 16.40i/15.83, 1986- 19.53i/19.34, 1987- 21.20, 1988- 20.96, 1989- 20.88, 1990- 21.16i/21.00, 1991- 20.77, 1992- 20.94, 1993- 20.31i. pb DT 53.54 '86.
Lost 1990 European bronze when test for stimulants proved positive; three month ban.

Vladimir MELIKHOV b.30 Mar 1969 Volgograd 1.86m 76kg. Volgograd VS.
At TJ: WJ: '88-1; WI: '93- 4.
Progression at TJ: 1988- 16.76, 1989- 16.56, 1990- 17.03, 1991- 17.13, 1993- 17.28.

Sergey NIKOLAYEV b.12 Nov 1966 1.90m 122kg. St Petersburg Sp.
At SP: WCh: '91- 5; EC: '90- 7; WCp: '92- 2. European junior LJ record 1987.
Progression at SP: 1985- 17.12, 1987- 19.21, 1988- 19.97, 1989- 21.35, 1990- 20.41, 1991- 20.40i/20.34, 1992- 20.93, 1993- 19.74/20.44i.

Igor NIKULIN b.14 Aug 1960 Moscow 1.91m 106kg. St Petersburg VS. Teacher.
At HT: OG: '92- 3; WCh: '83- 4, '87- 5; EC: '82- 2, '86- 3, '90- 3; EJ: '79- 1; WSG: '81- 3, '85- 3; WCp: '92- 1. USSR champion 1981 and 1984. 3rd GP 1988, 2nd 1992.
Progression at HT: 1975- 48.50, 1976- 58.14, 1977- 63.40, 1978- 71.60, 1979- 75.20, 1980- 80.34, 1981- 77.50, 1982- 83.54, 1983- 82.92, 1984- 82.56, 1985- 78.88, 1986- 82.34, 1987- 82.00, 1988- 83.78, 1989- 78.40, 1990- 84.48, 1991- 80.62, 1992- 83.44, 1993- 78.98.
One of the world's most consistent throwers since he became the youngest ever 80m hammer thrower in 1980. His father Yuriy was fourth in the 1964 Olympic hammer.

Yevgeniy PALCHIKOV b.12 Oct 1968 Irkutsk 1.98m 118kg. Irkutsk Sp. Student.
At SP: WCh: '93- 4; EJ: '87- 2; ECp: '93- 3. Russian champion 1993.
Progression at SP: 1986- 16.40, 1987- 18.63, 1988- 19.09, 1989- 19.56, 1990- 18.57i, 1991- 19.64, 1992- 19.75, 1993- 20.86.

Andrey PERLOV b.12 Dec 1961 1.78m 65kg. Novosibirsk Dyn.
At 50kmW: OG: '92- 1; WCh: '91- 2; EC: '90- 1; WCp: '85- 2, '87- 5, '89- 2. At 20 kmW: WSG: '85- 2. At 10kmW: EJ: '79- dq. Won USSR 50kmW 1984-5, 20kmW 1990.
World junior record 20km track walk 1:22:42.8 in 1980. World road bests 30kmW 2:02:41 and 50kmW in 1989, 20kmW 1990.
Progression at 20kmW, 50kmW: 1979- 1:25:45; 1980- 1:21:16; 1981- 1:25:18.3t, 4:05:29; 1982- 1:22:42, 4:08:45; 1983- 1:23:10.6t, 3:45:49; 1984- 1:23:12, 3:43:06; 1985- 1:25:52, 3:39:47; 1987- 3:45:09; 1988- 3:49:14; 1989- 1:21:29, 3:37:41; 1990- 1:18:20, 3:51:48; 1991- 1:19:58, 3:52.20; 1992- 1:26:46, 3:50:13. Track pbs: 10000mW 39:40.8 '83, 20000mW 1:22:42.8 '82.
In 1991 he was disqualified on last lap when leading the World Cup 50km, and given second place when coming in together with Aleksandr Potashov in World Championships.

Denis PETUSHINSKY b.28 Jun 1967 Irkutsk 1.88m 81kg. Novosibirsk Dyn. Student.
At PV: WCh: '93- 6; RUS champion 1993.
Progression at PV: 1985- 5.10, 1986- 5.40, 1987- 5.50, 1988- 5.65, 1989- 5.65i/5.60, 1990- 5.71, 1991- 5.72, 1992- 5.72i/5.70, 1993- 5.90.

Oleg PROTSENKO b.11 Aug 1963 Soltsy, Novgorod 1.91m 82kg. Moskva Dyn. Sports student.
At TJ: OG: '88- 4; WCh: '87- 8; WI: '85- 4, '87- 2; EC: '86- 3, '90- 8; WCp: '85- 2; ECp: '85- 3, '87- 1. 2nd GP 1988, 3rd 1990. USSR champion 1985-6. European TJ record 1985, WIB 17.67m 1987.
Progression at TJ: 1979- 15.05i, 1980- 15.94, 1981- 16.68, 1982- 16.59, 1983- 17.27, 1984- 17.52, 1985- 17.69, 1986- 17.59, 1987- 17.67i/17.61, 1988- 17.68, 1989- 17.04, 1990- 17.75, 1991- 17.27, 1992- 17.25, 1993- 17.03i/16.58. pb LJ 8.00i '86, 8.18w '87.
World age-17 best triple jump 1981.

Yuriy SEDYKH b.11 Jun 1955 Novocherkassk 1.85m 110kg. Moskva VS. Graduate of the Kiev Institute of Physical Culture.
At HT: OG: '76- 1, '80- 1, '88- 2; WCh: '83- 2, '91- 1; EC: '78- 1, '82- 1, '86- 1; EJ: '73- 1; WSG: '75- 3, '77- 2, '79- 3; WCp: '77- 4, '81- 1; ECp: '77- 3, '81- 1. USSR champion 1976, 1978, 1980. Won GWG 1986. GP 1986 & 1990 (3rd 1992).
World junior records 1973 and 1974, and eight Soviet records, including six world records: 80.38, 80.64 and 81.80 in 1980, 86.34 in 1984, 86.66 and 86.74 in 1986.
Progression at HT: 1971- 57.02, 1972- 62.96, 1973- 69.04, 1974- 70.86, 1975- 75.00, 1976- 78.86, 1977- 76.60, 1978- 79.76, 1979- 77.58, 1980- 81.80, 1981- 80.18, 1982- 81.66, 1983- 80.94, 1984- 86.34, 1985- 82.70, 1986- 86.74, 1987- 80.34, 1988- 85.14, 1989- 81.92, 1990- 82.80, 1991- 82.62, 1992- 82.18, 1993- 76.92. pb 35lb Wt 23.46 '79 (three WIB).
The greatest ever hammer thrower reached his peak at the 1986 Europeans when he responded to Litvinov's opening 85.74 with five throws averaging 86.16 including his 6th world record. Coached by his predecessor as Olympic champion, Anatoliy Bondarchuk. In 1991 he became, at 36, the oldest ever world champion.

Aleksandr SELEZNYOV b.25 Jan 1963 Smolensk 1.82m 100kg. Smolensk Sp. Teacher.
At HT: WCh: '93- 6; WSG: '91-4; EJ: '83- 2.
Progression at DT: 1981- 64.70, 1982- 68.08, 1983- 74.28, 1984- 75.80, 1985- 76.96, 1986- 75.90, 1987- 76.50, 1988- 78.80, 1989- 79.02, 1990- 80.50, 1991- 80.62, 1992- 77.58, 1993- 81.70.

Mikhail SHCHENNIKOV b.24 Dec 1967 Sverdlovsk 1.82m 70kg. Moskva VS. Serviceman.
At 20kmW: OG: '88- 6, '92- 12; WCh: '91- 2, '93- dq; EC: '90- dnf; WCp: '89- 2, '91- 1, '93- 5. USSR champion 1988. At 10000mW: WJ: '85- 1;

EJ: '86- 1. At 5000mW: WI: 1st '87, '89, '91, '93; EI: '89- 1, '90- 1.
World road best 20km walk 1988. At 5000mW WJR 19:19.3 '86, WIR 18:27.79 '87, 18:27.10 '89, 18:23.55 '91 (all when winning WI titles).
Progression at 20kmW: 1986- 1:33:56, 1987- 1:23:08, 1988- 1:19:08, 1989- 1:20:34, 1990- 1:19:07, 1991- 1:19:46, 1992- 1:19:53, 1993- 1:18:33. pbs: 3000mW 11:05.14i '87, 5000mW 18:15.91i '89, 18:52.01 '91; 10000mW 39:27.59 '88.
Won a record four World Indoor titles. Disqualified outside stadium at finish of 20km walk in 1993 World Champs when in third place.

Dmitriy SHEVCHENKO b.13 May 1968 Taganrog, Rostov-na-Donu 1.98m 120kg. Krasnodar Dyn. Serviceman.
At DT: OG: '92- 8; WCh: '91- 7, '93- 2; ECp '93- 2. USSR champion 1991, Russian 1993.
Progression at DT: 1986- 57.30, 1987- 60.34, 1988- 59.68, 1989- 59.38/61.62?, 1990- 64.10, 1991- 63.70, 1992- 67.30, 1993- 66.90.

Vladimir SHISHKIN b.12 Jan 1964 Gorkiy 1.90m 76kg. Nizhniy Novgorod Dyn. Serviceman.
At 110mh: OG: '88- 4, '92- qf; WCh: '91- 6, '93- h; EC: '90- 5; ECp: '89- 2, '93- 4. USSR champion 1988-9, 1991, Russian 1993.
Progression at 110mh: 1981- 14.7, 1982- 14.0, 1983- 14.15/13.7, 1984- 13.94, 1985- 13.6, 1986- 13.50/13.36w, 1987- 13.55/13.4, 1988- 13.21/ 13.0, 1989- 13.51/13.27w, 1990- 13.55/13.3, 1991- 13.39, 1992- 13.46, 1993- 13.54. pb 60mh 7.64i '88.

Vasiliy SIDORENKO b.1 May 1961 Volgograd 1.87m 106kg. Volgograd Dyn. Welder
At HT: WCh: '93- 5. Russian champion 1992.
Progression at HT: 1979- 59.98, 1980- 68.78, 1981- 69.30, 1983- 74.10, 1984- 76.80, 1985- 80.40, 1986- 80.70, 1987- 80.02, 1988- 80.52, 1989- 82.30, 1990- 80.98, 1991- 79.76, 1992- 82.54, 1993- 80.04.

Sergey SMIRNOV b.17 Sep 1960 Leningrad 1.92m 126kg. St Petersburg VS. Engineer.
At SP: OG: '88- 8; WCh: '83- dnq; EC: '86- dnc, '90- 4; WI: '87- 3, '93- 7; EI: '86- 2, '87- 3; WSG: '83- 3; WCp: '85- 2; ECp: '85- 1, '87- 5, '91- 2. Won GWG 1986. USSR champion 1985-7.
Two USSR shot records 1985-6.
Progression at SP: 1980- 16.31, 1981- 18.86, 1982- 20.42, 1983- 21.00, 1984- 21.63, 1985- 22.05, 1986- 22.24, 1987- 21.74, 1988- 21.88, 1989- 20.80, 1990- 21.34i/21.01, 1991- 20.55i/20.33, 1992- 21.01i/20.87, 1993- 20.94i/19.66.

Vasiliy SOKOV b.7 Apr 1968 Dushanbe 1.86m 73kg. Moskva VS. Serviceman.
At TJ: OG: '92- 9; WCh: '91- 4, '93- dnq 15 (dnq LJ); EI: '92- 3; ECp: '93- 4. At LJ: EJ: '87- 9. Won RUS TJ 1993.
Progression at LJ, TJ: 1985- 15.75, 1986- 7,34, 16.35; 1987- 7.77, 16.61; 1988- 8.18; 1989- 8.06, 17.37/17.73w; 1990- 17.47; 1991- 7,87, 17.52, 1992- 7.67, 17.30i/17.06, 1993- 8.00i, 17.59.
Concentrated on triple jumping rather than long jumping with immediate success in 1989.

Valeriy SPITSYN b.5 Dec 1965 Magnitogorsk 1.78m 67kg. Chelyabinsk Dyn.
At 50kmW: OG: '92- 4; WCh: '93- 3; WCp: '91- 8. CIS champion 1992, RUS 1988.
Progression at 50kmW: 1988- 4:06:02, 1989- 3:48:38, 1990- 3:54:26, 1991- 3:50:18, 1992- 3:54:39/3:33:32 short, 1993- 3:42:50. pbs: 20kmW 1:22:15 '91, 30kmW 2:04:24 '92.

Stanislav TARASENKO b.23 Jul 1966 Zhukovka, Rostov/Don region 1.88m 82kg. Tugavog. Sp. Soldier.
At LJ: WCh: '93- 2; ECp: '93- 3. Russian champion 1991-3.

Leonid Voloshin: silver again!

Progression at LJ: 1989- 7.96, 1990- 7.94, 1991- 8.01, 1992- 8.08, 1993- 8.23/8.28w, 1994- 8.43i.

Maksim TARASOV b.2 Dec 1970 Yaroslavl 1.94m 80kg. Yaroslavl VS. Soldier.
At PV: OG: '92- 1; WCh: '91- 3, '93- 3=; WJ: '88- 2; EJ: '89- 1. Won CIS PV 1992. 3rd GP 1993.
Three world junior records 1989.
Progression at PV: 1982- 2.90, 1983- 3.30, 1984- 3.80, 1985- 4.50, 1986- 5.00, 1987- 5.40, 1988- 5.60, 1989- 5.80, 1990- 5.85, 1991- 5.85/5.90ex, 1992- 5.90, 1993- 5.90. pbs: 100m 10.8 '89, HJ 1.95, LJ 7.40.
All world age bests from 16 to 19, 1987-90.

Igor TRANDENKOV b.17 Aug 1966 Leningrad 1.91m 80kg. St Petersburg Dyn. Teacher.
At PV: OG: '92- 2; WCh: '93- 3=; WI: '93- 4; EJ: '85- 1.
Progression at PV: 1979- 2.80, 1980- 3.30, 1981- 3.60, 1982- 3.90, 1983- 5.10, 1984- 5.30, 1985- 5.45, 1986- 5.50i/5.40, 1987- 5.60, 1988- 5.60, 1989- 5.70, 1990- 5.75, 1991- 5.60, 1992- 5.90, 1993- 5.90i/5.80.
Married to Marina Trandenkova (b. 7 Jan 1967) OG 92: qf 200m/2R; ECp '93 1R; pbs: 100m 11.08 '92, 200m 22.50 '92.

Leonid VOLOSHIN b.30 Mar 1966 Ordzhonikidze 1.80m 72kg. Krasnodar Dyn. Serviceman.
At TJ: OG: '92- 4; WCh: '91- 2, '93- 2; EC: '90- 1; WI: '91- 2; EI: '92- 1. At LJ: OG: '88- 8; EJ: '85- 4. Won USSR LJ 1988, TJ 1991. 2nd GP 1992.
WIR triple jump 1994 - 17.74i.
Progression at LJ, TJ: 1982- 6.92; 1983- 7.22, 14.90; 1984- 7.59i, 15.72i; 1985- 7.79; 1986- 8.06; 1987- 8.09; 1988- 8.46, 15.72; 1989- 8.15, 16.68; 1990- 8.09, 17.74; 1991- 7.93/7.94i/8.09w, 17.75; 1992- 17.53i/17.36/17.64w, 1993- 7.85, 17.65.
Made a spectacular conversion from long jump to triple jump in 1990, when he jumped 17.40 in Bryansk, followed by two pbs in Split and a further win at the Grand Prix final. Improved his pb again when second in Tokyo 1991.

Aleksey YEMELIN b.16 Oct 1968 Moskva 2.03m 94kg. Moskva Dyn. Serviceman
At HJ: WCh: '93- dnq 14=; EC: '90- 2; WI: '91- 3=; EI: '89- 3; ECp: '93- 5. USSR champion 1990, Russian 1993.
Progression at HJ: 1986- 2.10, 1987- 2.20, 1988- 2.29i/2.28, 1989- 2.32i/2.30, 1990- 2.34, 1991- 2.31i/2.29/2.30ex, 1992- 2.29i/2.25, 1993- 2.30.

Women

Tatyana ALEKSEYEVA b.7 Oct 1963 Novosibirsk 1.70m 60kg. Novosibirsk Dyn. Teacher.
At 400m/4x400mR: WCh: '91- gold ran ht, '93- 4/2R; WI: '93- 2; WSG: '85- 1/1R; ECp: '93- 1R.
Progression at 400m: 1982- 52.81, 1983- 52.6, 1984- 51.39, 1985- 51.39, 1987- 52.72, 1988- 52.08, 1989- 50.74, 1990- 51.50, 1991- 50.83, 1992- 51.04, 1993- 50.49. pbs: 100m 11.16 '84, 200m 22.77 '84, 22.71w '91, 300m 36.10+ '93.

Tatyana Alekseyeva: just missed a medal in Stuttgart

Marina AZYABINA b.15 Jun 1963 Izhevsk 1.74m 62kg. Izhevsk Sp. Biologist.
At 100mh: OG: '92- sf; WCh: '93- 2; WSG: '91- 1; ECp: '93- 1. CIS Champion 1992, Russian 1993.
Progression at 100mh: 1983- 13.6, 1984- 13.5, 1985- 13.4, 1987- 13.34/13.1, 1988- 13.00, 1989- 12.98, 1990- 12.86, 1991- 12.89, 1992- 12.76, 1993- 12.47. pbs: 100m 11.78 '93, 60mh 8.02i '93.

Anna BIRYUKOVA b. 27 Sep 1967 Sverdlovsk 1.74m 58kg. née Derevyankina. Moskva Sp. Teacher.
At TJ: WCh: '93- 1.
World triple jump record 1993.

Yolanda Chen: briefly held the world triple jump record last year

Progression at LJ, TJ: 1984- 6.47, 1988- 6.55, 1989- 6.86i/6.87, 13.30i; 1990- 6.89, 1991- 6.54i, 1993- 6.73, 15.09.
3rd 1989 and 2nd 1990 in USSR long jump. She retired in 1991 though injury, but after her son Aleksandr was born in March 1992 she returned to competition in 1993, and at the triple jump made rapid progress to 14.74w in Bratislava on 1 June and a world record to win the first world title at the event in August.

Tatyana BLOKHINA b. 12 Mar 1970 Kuybyshev 1.86m 70kg. St Petersburg Sp.
At Hep: WCh: '93- dnf; EJ: '87- 4, '89- 1. Russian champion 1993.
Progression at Hep: 1987- 5833, 1988- 5864, 1989- 6032, 1991- 5990, 1992- 6484, 1993- 6703.
pbs: 200m 23.71 '92, 800m 2:09.27 '92, 60mh 8.36i '93, 100mh 13.40 '93, HJ: 1.95 '92, LJ 6.21w '93, 5.99 '93; SP 14.94 '93, JT 52.16 '93, Pen 4669i '93.
Won Talence heptathlon 1993.

Lyudmila BORISOVA b.3 Aug 1966 Leningrad 1.72m 57kg. St Petersburg Sp. Student.
At 3000m: WCh: '91- 13, '93- 8; WI: '89- 6; WSG: '91- 4. USSR champion 1991.
Progression at 1500m, 3000m: 1986- 4:14.88, 9:12.0; 1987- 4:09.42, 9:05.91; 1988- 4:06.94, 1989- 4:13.65, 9:04.75i/9:08.31; 1990- 4:04.56, 9:04.39; 1991- 4:08.75, 8:51.49; 1992- 4:03.66, 8:49.87; 1993- 8:40.78. pb 800m: 2:01.30 '88.

Ramilya BURANGULOVA b.11 Jul 1961 Kutuy Bashkotatarstan 1.54m 48kg. née Gareyeva. Ufa Sp. Teacher.
At Mar: OG: '92- 8; WCh: '91- 8, '93- 4; WCp: '91- 7. USSR champion 1990.
Progression at Mar: 1983- 2:42:21, 1984- 2:38:21, 1988- 2:39:58, 1989- 2:38:13, 1990-2:32:22, 1991- 2:30:41, 1992- 2:28:12, 1993- 2:28:03. pb road 15km 50:12 '89.
Second in Los Angeles and third Tokyo marathons 1992.

Olga BUROVA b.17 Sep 1963 Irbit Severdlovsk region 1.80m 80kg. née Davydova. Volgograd Sp. Servicewoman.
At DT: OG: '92- 5; WCh: '93- 1; EC: '90- 2; WCp: '89- 5; ECp: '89- 4. USSR champion 1989-90.
Progression at DT: 1981- 54.72, 1982- 47.90, 1983- 58.30, 1984- 56.88, 1985- 59.20, 1986- 58.28, 1987- 60.20, 1988- 65.34, 1989- 68.10, 1990- 68.32, 1991- 63.68, 1992- 68.38, 1993- 67.40.

Yolanda CHEN b.26 Jul 61 Moskva 1.69m 55kg. Moskva Sp.
At LJ: EC: '90- 5; WSG: '89- 1; EI: '89- 2. At TJ: WCh: '93- 2; WI: '93- 2; ECp: '93- 1. Won RUS TJ 1993, GP TJ 1993.
World triple jump record and WIR 14.46 1993.
Progression at LJ, TJ: 1974- 4.97, 1975- 5.30, 1976- 5.55, 1977- 5.74, 1978- 6.16, 1979- 6.14, 1980- 6.44, 1981- 6.60, 1982- 6.75, 1983- 6.77, 1984- 6.83, 1985- 6.51i, 1986- 6.80, 1987- 6.50, 1988- 7.16, 1989- 7.05i/6.74/6.87w, 1990- 7.03i/6.97/7.11w, 1991- 6.82i/6.67, 12.82; 1992- 6.68, 13.72; 1993- 6.90i/6.65, 14.97. pbs: 100m 11.8, HJ 1.71.
Father, Yevgeniy Chen, was world ranked triple jumper 1954-8, pb 16.00 '58.

Galina CHISTYAKOVA b.26 Jul 1962 Izmail,

Ukraine 1.69m 54kg. Moskva Sp. Teacher. Married to Aleksandr Beskrovniy (TJ: 17.53m '84, 1 EJ '79, 5 EC '82).
At LJ: OG: '88- 3; WCh: '87- 5; WI: '87- 4, '89- 1; EC: '86- 2; EI: '85- 1, '87- 2, '88- 2, '89- 1, '90- 1; WCp: '85- 2, '89- 1; ECp: '85- 1, '87- 2, '89- 1. Won GWG 1986, GP 1985 & 1989 (2nd overall). At TJ: WCp: '92- 2; won CIS 1992, 2nd GP 1993. World LJ record 1988, four USSR records 1984-8. World TJ record 1989. WIB: LJ 7.25 '85, five TJ 13.58 '86; 13.86, 13.96, 13.98 '87, 14.45 '89.
Progression at LJ, TJ: 1973- 3.75, 1974- 4.20, 1975- 4.96, 1976- 5.25, 1977- 5.80, 1978- 6.04, 1979- 6.43, 1980- 6.43, 1981- 6.36/6.54w, 1982- 6.43, 1984- 7.29, 1985- 7.28, 1986- 7.34, 13.58i; 1987- 7.27, 13.98i; 1988- 7.52, 1989- 7.30i/7.24/ 7.36w, 14.52; 1990- 7.35, 14.15i; 1991- 6.69, 14.04; 1992- 6.60/6.66w, 14.62; 1993- 6.33, 14.40. pb 100m 11.6 '84.
Gave birth to a daughter in 1983. Injured her knee after jumping 7.35 in Bratislava 1990.

Lyudmila GALKINA b. 20 Jan 1972 Saratov 1.72m 57kg. Saratov Sp. Student.
AT LJ (TJ): WCh: '93- 5; EJ: '89- 3, '91- 2 (1).
Progression at LJ: 1988- 6.34, 1989- 6.52/6,62w, 1990- 6.63, 1991- 6.62, 1992- 6.60, 1993- 6.75. pb TJ 13.67 '91.

Yuliya GRAUDYN b.13 Nov 1970 Moscow 1.71m 60kg. née Filippova. Moskva Sp.
At 60mh: WI: '93- 4.
Progression at 100mh: 1988- 13.21, 1989- 13.36, 1991- 13.18, 1992- 12.82, 1993- 12.85. pb 60mh 7.93i '94, 7.6i '93.
Won original 60m final at World Indoors, but only 4th in the re-run.

Yelena GRIBANOVA b.2 Mar 1972. Moskva Sp.
At HJ: WCp: '92- 5. Russian champion 1992.
Progression at HJ: 1988- 1.85, 1989- 1.89i, 1991- 1.92, 1992- 1.96, 1993- 1.97i/1.96.

Lyubov GURINA b.6 Aug 1957 Matushkino, Kirov region 1.67m 57kg. Kirov Sp. Decorator.
At 800m: OG: '92- 8; WCh: '83- 2, '87- 3, '93- 2; EC: '86- 3, '90- 7; WI: '91- 4; EI: '90- 1. Won GWG 1986. USSR champion 1987, Russian 1993. 2nd GP 1991, 1993. At 1500m: OG: '88- h. World record 4x800m relay 1984.
Progression at 800m, 1500m: 1976- 2:15.7, 1977- 2:08.0, 1978- 2:04.6, 1979- 2:00.2, 1980- 1:59.9, 1981- 1:58.72, 1982- 1:57.3, 1983- 1:56.11, 1984- 1:56.26, 1986- 1:57.52, 4:06.34; 1987- 1:55.56, 1988- 1:56.56, 1989- 1:59.74, 1990- 1:58.56, 1991- 1:58.50, 1992- 1:57.39, 4:03.32; 1993- 1:57.10, 4:03.32. pbs: 400m 51.38 '83, 1000m 2:32.97 '93, 1M 4:34.07i '92.

Yekaterina IVAKINA b.4 Dec 1964 Stavropol 1.68m 67kg. née Slyadneva. St Petersburg Sp. Servicewoman.
At JT: WCh: '93- 5; ECp: '93- 3. Russian champion 1993.
Progression at DT: 1985- 53.02, 1986- 57.92, 1987- 60.42, 1988- 64.04, 1989- 63.08, 1990- 61.90, 1992- 64.10, 1993- 65.36.

Anna KNOROZ b.30 Jul 1970 Moskva 1.62m 50kg. née Chuprina. St Petersburg VS. Student
At 400mh/4x400mR: WCh: '93- sf; WSG: '91- 3/2R; EJ: '89- 2R; ECp: '93- 2. USSR champion 1991, RUS 1992-3.
Progression at 400mh: 1987- 59.6, 1988- 57.66, 1989- 56.70, 1991- 55.12, 1992- 55.15, 1993- 54.42. pb 400m 52.78 '93.

Larisa KOROTKEVICH b.3 Jan 1967 Krivye Vitebsk region 1.80m 86kg. Krasnodar Dyn. Teacher.
At DT: OG: '92- 4; WCh: '87- 10, '93- dnq 14; EJ: '85- 3; WCp: '92- 4; ECp: '93- 1. Russian champion 1993.
Progression at DT: 1983- 52.74, 1984- 56.70, 1985- 59.02, 1986- 64.42, 1987- 64.94, 1988- 66.08, 1989- 60.74, 1990- 67.50, 1991- 63.44, 1992- 71.30, 1993- 68.14.

Lyubov KREMLYOVA b.21 Dec 1962 Maykop 1.66m 52kg. Moskva VS. Teacher
At 3000m: EC: '90- 4; ECp: '91- 3; WI: 91- 3. At 1500m: EI: '92- 2. At 800m: ECp: '93- 2. Won GP 1M 1993, 2nd 1500m 1992.
Progression at 800m, 1500m, 3000m: 1981- 4:21.2; 1983- 2:00.05, 4:05.67; 1984- 1:58.95, 4:02.04; 1985- 4:12.3; 1986- 1:59.1, 4:01.57; 1987- 2:00.9, 4:07.1; 1988- 1:59.7, 4:02.41, 8:52.09; 1989- 2:01.70, 4:05.53, 8:52.99; 1990- 4:03.20, 8:46.94; 1991- 2:00.08, 4:05.54, 8:49.72; 1992- 1:59.71, 3:58.71, 8:46.99; 1993- 1:59.8, 4:04.88. pbs: 1000m 2:33.55 '93, 1M 4:22.46 '93, 2000m 5:41.26 '92.

Svetlana KRIVELYOVA b.13 Jun 1969 Bryansk 1.84m 91kg. Moskva Dyn. Teacher.
At SP: OG: '92- 1; WCh: '91- 3, '93- 2; WJ: '88- 4; WI: '91- 8, '93- 1; WSG: '91- 1. USSR champion 1991, Russian 1992. Won GP 1993.
Progression at SP: 1985- 15.18, 1986- 16.76, 1987- 17.51, 1988- 18.35, 1989- 18.36, 1990- 19.70, 1991- 20.36, 1992- 21.06, 1993- 20.84.
Took World Student Games gold medal in 1991 after Sui Xinmei disqualified.

Inna LASOVSKAYA b.17 Dec 1969 Moskva 1.77m 68kg. Moskva Sp. Servicewoman.
At TJ: WCh: '93- nj; WI: '93- 3.
Russian triple jump record 1993. Four WIR 14.16 '89, 14.61, 14.78 and 14.90 '94.
Progression at TJ: 1989- 14.40i, 1990-

14.09i/13.65, 1991- 14.05, 1992- 14.13i/14.07, 1993- 14.70, 1994- 14.90i. pb LJ 6.68 '88.

Galina MALCHUGINA b.17 Dec 1962 Bryansk 1.68m 65kg. née Mikheyeva. Bryansk Sp. Teacher.
At 200m/4x100mR: OG: '88- 8/3R, '92- 8/2R; WCh: '91- 5/2R, '93- 7/1R; EC: '90- 3; EJ: '79- 7/2R; WSG: '89- 1/2R; WCp: '89- 5/2R; ECp: '91- 1R: WI: '91- 5; EI: '90- 3. 3rd GP 200m 1990, 1992. Won USSR 100m 1991.
Progression at 100m, 200m: 1978- 24.76, 1979- 11.72, 23.70; 1980- 24.21/24.0; 1981- 11.58, 23.16; 1982- 11.62, 23.28/23.2; 1984- 11.51, 22.74; 1985- 11.42, 23.06; 1987- 11.56, 23.15/22.2w; 1988- 11.07/10.8, 22.42; 1989- 11.47/10.99w, 22.68; 1990- 11.10, 22.23; 1991- 11.20, 22.49; 1992- 10.96, 22.22; 1993- 11.25, 22.22. pb 60m 7.16i '90.

Olga MARKOVA b.6 Aug 1968 St Petersburg 1.63m 47kg. St Petersburg VS.
Progression at Mar: 1988- 2:42:12, 1989- 2:40:00, 1990- 2:37:06, 1991- 2:28:27, 1992- 2:23:43, 1993- 2:25:27, 1994- 2:32:22. pbs: 1500m 4:24.0 '88, 3000m 9:15.0 '90, 10000m 33:51.83 '91. Road: 15km 49:30 '92, Half Mar 1:11:42 '90.
Lives in Gainesville, Florida. At the marathon has three wins in 11 races. In 1991 she was 3rd in Los Angeles and 2nd in New York, and in 1992 won Boston to go to 4th on the world all-time list and was 2nd in New York.

Svetlana MASTERKOVA b.17 Jan 1968 Moskva 1.72m 59kg. Moskva TR. Student.
At 800m: WCh: '91- 8; WI: '93- 2; EJ: '85- 6; ECp: '91- 3. Won USSR 800m 1991. 3rd GP 1993.
Progression at 800m: 1982- 2:11.7, 1983- 2:04.3, 1984- 2:04.59, 1985- 2:02.69, 1986- 2:03.34, 1989- 2:02.70, 1990- 1:59.83, 1991- 1:57.23, 1992- 1:57.63, 1993- 1:57.48. pb 400m 53.12 '92, 1000m 2:41.86i '92.

Irina MUSHAILOVA b.6 Jan 1967 Krasnodar 1.69m 64kg. Krasnodar Dyn. Student.
At LJ: OG: '92- 5; WI: '93- 4; EJ: '85- 6; ECp: '91- 3. Won USSR 800m 1991. 3rd GP 1993.
Progression at LJ, TJ: 1988- 6.39w, 1989- 6.61, 1990- 6.75, 1991- 6.76, 13.81; 1992- 6.89, 13.47i; 1993- 7.02, 14.79.

Larisa NIKITINA b.29 Apr 1965 Kostroma 1.77m 70kg. Married name Turchinskaya. Moskva Sp. Teacher.
At Hep: WCh: '87- 2, '93- dnf; EJ: '83- 7; WSG: '89- 1; ECp: '89- 1. USSR champion 1987, 1989. European heptathlon record 1989.
Progression at Hep: 1981- 5263, 1982- 5520*, 1983- 5674, 1984- 6276, 1985- 6171, 1986- 6316, 1987- 6564, 1988- 6506, 1989- 7007, 1990- 6320, 1993- 6415. pbs: 200m 23.97 '89, 800m 2:15.31 '89, 100mh 13.40 '89, HJ 1.89 '89, LJ 6.75 '89, SP 16.45 '89, JT 59.28 '89, Hep 4547i '93.
Drugs ban 1990-2.

Yelena NIKOLAYEVA b.1 Feb 1966 Akshiki Chuvashskaya 1.68m 58kg. née Kuznyetsova. Cheboksary Dyn. Student.
At 10kmW: OG: '92- 2; WCh: '87- 5, '93- 7; WCp: '87- 5, '93- 3. USSR champion 1987-8, CIS 1992. At 3000mW: WI: '91- 5, '93- 1.
Three world 10km track walk records 1986-8, European records 3000m 1992, 5000m: 21:32.4 '87, 21:08.65 '88.
Progression at 10kmW: 1984- 48:29.1, 1985- 46:37, 1986- 44:32.50t, 1987- 43:57, 1988- 43:36.41t, 1991- 43:25, 1992- 42:40, 1993- 43:11. pbs: 3000mW 11:49.73i '93, 11:54.8 '92; 5000mW 21:00.80 '91.

Vera ORDINA b.4 Jun 1968 1.72m 56kg. St Petersburg VS.
At 400mh: OG: '92- 5.
Progression at 400mh: 1985- 59.28, 1986- 59.30, 1987- 56.2/56.77, 1988- 57.50, 1989- 55.42, 1990- 55.86, 1991- 55.31, 1992- 54.37, 1993- 55.33. pb 100mh 13.35/13.0 '88.

Larisa PELESHENKO b.29 Feb 1964 Slantsy Leningrad region 1.87m 95kg. née Agapova. St Petersburg Sp. Teacher.
At SP: WCh: '93- 9; EI: '88- 2; WSG: '87- 3, '89- 4; ECp: '89- 3.
Progression at SP: 1981- 14.60, 1982- 15.95, 1983- 18.23, 1984- 19.30, 1985- 18.78i, 1986- 19.26, 1987- 20.99, 1988- 20.89, 1989- 19.68, 1990- 19.56, 1992- 19.65, 1993- 19.90i/19.23.

Yekaterina PODKOPAYEVA b.11 Jun 1952 Ulyanovsk, nr Kaluga 1.64m 54kg. née Poryvkina. Moskva VS. Teacher.
At 800m/1500m: WCh: '83- 3/3; At 1500m: OG: '92- 8; WI: '93- 1; WCp: '89- 2, '92- 1; EI: '92- 1. At 800m: ECp: '79- 2. Won USSR 800m 1979, 1984; 1500m 1989.
WIB 2000m 5:43.30 '83.
Progression at 800m/1500m: 1970- 2:20.2, 1971- 2:15.3, 1972- 2:08.6, 1973- 2:06.8, 1974- 2:09.0, 1975- 2:05.6, 1976- 2:05.2/4:15.7, 1977- 2:06.6/ 4:13.7, 1978- 2:00.6/4:11.7, 1979- 1:57.2, 1980- 1:58.9/ 3:57.4, 1982- 4:10.07, 1983- 1:55.96/ 4:00.3, 1984- 1:57.07/3:56.65, 1985- 1:56.65/ 4:01.96, 1988- 2:01.37/4:04.57, 1989- 2:00.16/ 4:05.26 1990- 1:59.7/4:03.62, 1991- 4:08.59, 1992- 4:02.03, 1993- 4:02.48. pbs: 400m 52.74 '85, 1000m 2:36.08i/2:37.27 '93, 1M 4:23.78 '93, 2000m 5:40.96 '92, 3000m 8:56.02 '89.
Drugs suspension 1990. The oldest ever European Indoor champion at 39 and World Cup winner at 40 in 1992, and World Indoor champion at 40 in 1993.

Margarita PONOMARYEVA b.19 Jun 1963 Balkhash, Kazakhstan 1.78m 58kg. Married name was Khromova. St Petersburg Sp. Economist.
At 400mh/4x400mR: OG: '92- 6; WCh: '87- sf, '91- 8, '93- 3/2R; EC: '86- 8, '90- 5; EJ: '81- 3/2R; WSG: '89- 1/3R; WCp: '85- 6, '92- 3/2R; ECp: '91- 1/1R. 3rd GP 1991. At 4x400mR: WI: '91- 2. Won CIS 400mh 1992.
World 400mh record 1984. WIR 4x400mR 1991.
Progression at 400mh: 1981- 57.45, 1983- 56.9, 1984- 53.58, 1985- 55.48, 1986- 54.57, 1987- 54.58, 1988- 54.95, 1989- 54.98, 1990- 55.22, 1991- 54.08, 1992- 53.66, 1993- 53.48. pb 400m 51.10 '91.

Irina PRIVALOVA b.22 Nov 1968 Malakhovka, near Moskva 1.74m 63kg. Married name was Sergeyeva. Moskva Sp. Student of journalism.
At 100m (/200m, R- 4x100m relay): OG: '92- 3/4/2R; WCh: '91- 4/4/2R, '93- 4/3/1R (2 4x400mR); EC: '90- 6; WJ: '86- sf/5R; EJ: '85- h; ECp: '89- 3/5; '91- 1/1/1R, '93- 1/1/1R. At 60m/200m: WI: '91- 1/2, '93- 2/1. Won USSR 100m 1989-90, CIS 100m/200m 1992, RUS 200m 1993. 2nd GP 100m 1993.
Two USSR/CIS 100m records 1991-2, three 200m 1992, Russian 200m 1993; WIR: 50m 6.05 and 6.00 (not ratified - inaccurate camera alignment) '93, 6.03 '94; 60m 6.92 '93, 300m 1993. European IR 60m 6.97, 200m 22.26 in 1992.
Progression at 100m, 200m, 400m: 1982- 11.9, 1983- 11.7, 1984- 11.79; 1985- 11.59, 24.54; 1986- 11.3i/11.52/11.37w, 24.10; 1987- 11.44/11.2, 23.3; 1989- 11.26, 23.00; 1990- 11.21, 23.01; 1991- 10.98, 22.21; 1992- 10.82/10.81w, 21.93; 1993- 10.94, 21.88, 49.89. pbs 300m 35.45i '93, 100mh 13.4 '87, HJ 1.72 '82, LJ 6.48i '85, 6.45 '84, TJ 13.72i '89.
Son born 1988. Formerly a skater, she long jumped 6.45 at age 15 in 1984. Won CIS title in 1992 with 10.81 for 100m to equal European record, but time later adjusted to 10.82. Ran 49.89 on 400m début July 1993.

Yelena RODINA b.14 Aug 1967 1.82m 61kg. Moskva VS. Teacher. Married name Gulyayeva.
At HJ: WCh: '93- 4=; ECp: '91- 1dq; WI: '91- 6=. USSR champion 1988, 1991.
Progression at HJ: 1981- 1.70, 1982- 1.70, 1983- 1.80, 1984- 1.84, 1985- 1.80, 1987- 1.80, 1988- 1.94, 1989- 1.89i/1.88, 1990- 1.92i/1.91, 1991- 1.99, 1993- 1.98.
Two years suspension after being disqualified on positive drugs test when winning the 1991 European Cup high jump.

Lyudmila ROGACHOVA b.30 Oct 1966 Lad Balka Stavropol region 1.66m 57kg. Stavropol Sp. Teacher.
At 1500m: OG: '92- 2; WCh: '91- 3, '93- 13; WI: '91- 1; EC: '90- 4; WSG: '89- 3. Won USSR 1500m 1990, CIS 800m 1992, RUS 1500m 1993, GP 1500m 1992.
Progression at 800m, 1500m: 1980- 2:14.4, 4:44.6; 1981- 2:10.2, 4:32.4; 1982- 2:09.2, 4:30.6; 1983- 2:06.46, 4:26.6; 1984- 2:03.7, 4:15.8; 1985- 2:05.84, 4:19.2; 1986- 2:05.6, 4:17.6; 1987- 2:00.54, 4:08.10; 1988- 1:56.82, 4:04.29; 1989- 1:59.08, 4:07.5; 1990- 1:57.1, 4:02.3i/4:03.07; 1991- 1:58.67, 4:02.72; 1992- 1:57.93, 3:56.91; 1993- 1:58.13, 4:05.77. pbs: 1000m 2:33.96 '93, 1M 4:21.30 '92.
Front ran Olympic 1500m 1992, and held on to smash through 4 minutes for the first time, but run down by Hassiba Boulmerka.

Anna ROMANOVA b.9 Mar 1968 Bryansk 1.81m 88kg. Bryansk Sp. Teacher.
At SP: WCh: '93- dnq 13; WI: '93- 5; WJ: '86- 4; EI: '92- 5; ECp: '93- 1. Russian champion 1993.
Progression at SP: 1984- 15.67, 1985- 17.32, 1986- 17.50i/17.43, 1987- 18.23, 1988- 19.06, 1989- 19.02i/17.89, 1990- 19.06, 1991- 18.95i/ 18.69, 1992- 20.01i/19.58, 1993- 20.24.

Yelena ROMANOVA b.20 Mar 63 1.60m 51kg. née Malykhina. Volgograd VS. Student.
At 3000m (10000m): OG: '88- 4, '92- 1; WCh: '87- 5 (h), '91- 2 (dnf), '93- 6; EC: '90- 2 (1); WSG: '83- 2. At 1500m: EJ: '81- 2. Won GWG 5000m 1990. World CC: '88- 6, '89- 9, '90- 2, '91- 8. Won RUS 3000m 1993.
Progression at 1500m, 3000m, 10000m: 1976- 5:13.2, 1977- 4:46.7, 1978- 4:32.2, 1979- 4:25.9, 1980- 4:22.5, 1981- 4:16.09, 8:56.03; 1982- 4:10.72, 8:59.18; 1983- 4:09.0, 8:59.79; 1985- 4:18.0, 9:11.03; 1986- 4:04.60, 8:47.79i/8:56.34; 1987- 4:07.4, 8:41.15; 1988- 4:04.96, 8:30.45; 1989- 8:55.80, 1990- 8:43.68, 31:46.83; 1991- 8:36.06, 32:06.73; 1992- 4:00.91, 8:33.72; 1993- 8:35.48. pbs: 800m 2:04.0, 5000m 14:59.70 '91.
Son born 1984. In 1990 after gaining silver at 3000m was an unexpected entrant in the European 10000m, at which she won the gold medal and took her pb from 32:25.08 to 31:46.83.

Yelena RUZINA b.3 Apr 1964 Voronezh 1.73m 59kg. née Rykunova. Voronezh Dyn. Teacher.
At 400m (R- 4x400m relay): OG: '92- sf/1R; WCh: '93- 2R; EC: '90- sf/2R; WCp: '89- 5/3R, '92- 2R; ECp: '89- 2R, '91- 1R, '93- 1R. Won RUS 400m 1993.
Progression at 400m: 1989- 51.37, 1990- 50.65, 1991- 51.09, 1992- 50.78, 1993- 51.14. pbs: 100m 11.2 '84, 11.75 '91, 200m 22.73 '88, 22.7/22.6w '86, 300m 36.22i '92.

Yelena SAYKO b. 15 May 1966 Chelyabinsk 1.64m 50kg. Chelyabinsk Dyn.
At 10kmW: OG: '92- 8; WCh: '91- dq, '93- 8; WCp: '91- 3.
Progression at 10kmW: 1988- 45:19, 1989- 44:45, 1990- 44:04, 1991- 42:22, 1992- 43:13, 1993- 42:04. track pbs: 3000mW 12:34.61i '89, 5000mW 21:19.81 '92. road 5kmW 21:13 '89.

Yelena SINCHUKOVA b.23 Jan 1961 Kemerovo 1.74m 66kg. née Ivanova. Moskva VS. Servicewoman.
At LJ: WCh: '91- 4, '93- 10; EC: '82- 3; WCp: '92- 2; ECp: '93- 2. At Pen: EJ: '79- 6. Won USSR LJ 1991, Russian 1993.
Progression at LJ: 1978- 6.19, 1979- 6.36, 1981- 6.17, 1982- 6.81, 1983- 6.53i, 1984- 7.01, 1985- 6.84i/6.81, 1986- 6.88, 1987- 7.05, 1991- 7.20, 1992- 7.04, 1993- 6.85/6.94w. pbs: TJ 14.09 '92, Pen 4144* '79.

Eva SOKOLOVA b.25 Mar 1962 Leningrad 1.70m 60kg. née Nikolayeva. St Petersburg Sp. Teacher.
At 100mh: WCh: '93- 5; USSR champion 1987.
Progression at 100mh: 1980- 13.92, 1981- 13.3, 1982- 13.53/13.1, 1983- 13.34/13.1, 1986- 13.07, 1987- 12.82, 1988- 13.18, 1989- 12.70, 1990- 13.04, 1991- 13.24, 1992- 13.05, 1993- 12.75/12.63w. pbs: 60mh 7.91i '94.
Son born in 1984.

Yelena TOPCHINA b.28 Oct 1966 Leningrad 1.79m 58kg. St Petersburg VS. Student.
At HJ: WCh: '93- 11=; EJ: '83- 1; EI: '90- 5; Russian champion 1993.
Progression at HJ: 1981- 1.80, 1982- 1.88, 1983- 1.94, 1984- 1.88, 1985- 1.90, 1986- 1.92, 1987- 1.86i, 1989- 1.91, 1990- 1.96i/1.95, 1991- 1.93i/ 1.89, 1993- 1.99.
Served two year drugs disqualification 1991-3.

Irina TYUKHAY b.14 Jan 1967 Krasnoyarsk 1.71m 64kg. Krasnoyarsk Sp.
At Pen: WI Inv: '93- 4.
Progression at Hep: 1984- 5226*, 1985- 5863, 1986- 5922, 1987- 5844, 1988- 6129, 1989- 6230, 1990- 5947, 1991- 6063, 1992- 6478, 1993- 6406. pbs: 200m 24.29 '92, 800m 2:15.92 '92, 60mh 8.20i '93, 100mh 13.32/13.0 '88, HJ 1.89 '92, LJ 6.73 '92, SP 14.61 '89, JT 43.20 '89, Pen 4686i '93.

Natalya VORONOVA b.9 Jul 1965 Moskva 1.69m 61kg. née Pomoshnikova. Moskva Sp. Student of journalism.
At 100m (200m)/4x100mR: OG: '88- 6/3R; WCh: '87- sf/3R, '93- 6/6/1R; WI: '93- (3); EJ: '83- 1 (4, 2R); WSG: '89- 3/2R; WCp: '89- 7/2R, '92- 2 (1); ECp: '85- 2R, '93- 1R. Won USSR 100m 1984 (tie), Russian 100m 1992-3, 200m 1992.
Progression at 100m, 200m: 1980- 12.5, 25.9; 1981- 11.9, 25.1; 1982- 11.8, 24.8; 1983- 11.48, 23.34; 1984- 11.42/11.2, 23.1; 1985- 11.27, 23.25/22.6; 1986- 11.20/11.0, 23.02; 1987- 11.07, 23.0; 1988- 10.98, 23.1; 1989- 11.36/11.05w, 1992- 11.11, 22.98; 1993- 11.17/11.16w, 22.35. pb 60m 7.06i '93.

Valentina YEGOROVA b.16 Feb 1964 Chuvash ASSR 1.56m 52kg. Cheboksary Sp. née Vasilyeva.
At Mar: OG: '92- 1; EC: '90- 2; WCp: '91- 3.
Progression at Mar: 1988- 2:30:59, 1989- 2:40:14, 1990- 2:29:47, 1991- 2:28:18, 1992- 2:29:41, 1993- 2:26:40. pbs: 3000m 9:11.2 '85, 5000m 15:40.49 '86, 10000m 32:56.13 '89.
Fourth in Los Angeles and Tokyo marathons in 1992 on either side of Olympic triumph, that was the second marathon win of her career (now 15 races); previously at Ufa 1988., and she won theTokyo marathon in 1993.

Yelena YELESINA b.4 Apr 1970 Chelyabinsk 1.84m 57kg. Chelyabinsk Sp.
At HJ: WCh: '91- 2; EC: '90- 3; WJ: '88- 2; EJ: '87- 3=, '89- 1; WSG: '91- 4; EI: '92- 3. Won GWG 1990. USSR champion 1990.
Progression at HJ: 1983- 1.55, 1984- 1.65, 1985- 1.70, 1986- 1.83, 1987- 1.89, 1988- 1.98, 1989- 1.95, 1990- 2.02, 1991- 1.98, 1992- 1.94i/1.93, 1993- 1.91.

Tatyana ZHURAVLYOVA b.19 Dec 1967 Saratov 1.83m 74kg. Stavropol Dyn. Student.
At Hep: WCh: '91- 8, '93- 10; WSG: '91- 4; ECp: '93- 1. Russian champion 1993.
Progression at Hep: 1987- 5670, 1988- 6156, 1989- 6158, 1990- 6292, 1991- 6370, 1993- 6369. pbs: 200m 24.18 '91, 800m 2:08.21 '93, 100mh 13.70 ', HJ 1.83 ', LJ 6.60 '93, SP 16.45 ', JT 44.80 '93.

RWANDA

Governing body: Fédération Rwandaise d'Athlétisme, BP 1044, Kigali. Founded 1973.

NTAWULIKURA, Mathias b. 14 Jul 1964 1.71m 66kg. Pro Patria Milano, Italy.
At 5000m: WCh: '93- 10. At 10000m: OG: '92- h; WCh: '91- 7; AfG: '91- 5/5; AfCh: '88- 5/5. World CC: '91- 18, '92- 13.
Progression at 5000m, 10000m: 1988- 13:48.2, 29:51.79; 1989- 13:52.37, 1990- 13:34.76, 28:41.10; 1991- 13:19.88, 27:49.32; 1992- 13:11.29, 27:52.51; 1993- 13:14.82, 27:47.59. pbs: 3000m 7:41.64 '92, Half Mar 61:48 '91.
First came to world notice with in 1991 with 12th in World CC challenge and with many national records, from two at 3000m in the World Indoor championships (8th).

SLOVAKIA

Governing body: Slovak Athletic Federation, Junacka 6, 83280 Bratislava. Founded 1939.
National Championships first held in 1939.
1993 Champions: Men: 100m/110mh: Igor Kovác 10.69/13.83, 200m: Lubos Balosák 21.11, 400m: Stefan Balosák 46.99, 800m: Rastislav Misko 1:55.59, 1500m: Robert Stefko 3:46.17, 5000m/10000m: Robert Petro 14:26.95/31:38.20, 3000mSt: Milos Kovacech 8:44.48, 400mh: Jozef Kucej 50.98, HJ: Robert Ruffini 2.28, PV: Michal Senkovic 4.91, LJ: Andrej Benda 7.57, TJ: Marek Samsely 15.62, SP: Karel Sula 17.68, DT: Jaroslav Zitnansky 53.26, HT: Martin Kliment 61.10, JT: Michal Huncík 71.64, 20kmW: Igor Kollár 1:21:10. **Women**: 100m/200m: Jarmila Zifcáková 12.18/24.79, 400m: Andrea Zsideková 55.35, 800m: Miriam Maseková 2:11.42, 1500m: Andrea Sollárová 4:24.00, 3000m: Lenka Stancelová 10:10.33, 10,000m: Anna Baloghová 38:04.56 (Silvia Vivod CRO 33:54.53), 100mh: Ludmila Cörgöová 14.77, 400mh: Pavla Jelínková 61.14 (Irena Dominc SLO 57.83), HJ: Lenka Riháková 1.81, LJ: Katarina Svachová 5.92, TJ: Anna Kubosová 12.46, SP: Radka Charfreitagová 13.42, DT: Ivona Holubová 49.36, JT: Elena Revayová 53.50, 10kmW: Zuzana Zemsková 47:25.9.

Pavol BLAZEK b.9 Jul 1958 Trnava 1.68m 58kg. Dukla B.Bystrica. Soldier.
At 20kmW (50kmW): OG: '80- 14 (10), '88- 15 (12), '92- 17; WCh: '83- 6 (17), '87- 11 (18), '91- 17, '93- 15; EC: '78- 14, '82- 3 (dnf), '86- 6, '90- 1; WCp: '79- 18, '81- 11, '83- 9, '85- 10, '87- 21, '89- 8. At 5000mW: WI: '89- 6. Won CS 20kmW 1981, 1990-1.
World best 20km road walk 1990.
Progression at 20kmW: 1977- 1:33:34, 1978- 1:27:50, 1979- 1:25:14, 1980- 1:25:00t, 1981- 1:24:07, 1982- 1:23:59, 1983- 1:21:37, 1984- 1:21:24t, 1985- 1:22:30, 1986- 1:21:21, 1987- 1:21:36, 1988- 1:20:17, 1989- 1:21:53, 1990- 1:18:13, 1991- 1:21:43, 1992- 1:21:55.6t, 1993- 1:21:15.4t. Track pbs: 3000mW: 11:12.1i '88, 5000mW 18:41.34i '89, 19:09.73 '90, 10000mW 39:31.83i '86, 20000mW 1:19:54.0 '90, Road 50kmW 3:47:31 '88.
At his fourth European Championships took the gold medal, although after he had finished was first listed as disqualified.

Roman MRAZEK b.21 Jan 62 Sokolov 1.68m 55kg. Dukla B.Bystrica. Soldier.
At 20kmW (50kmW): OG: '88- 5 (17), '92- (5); WCh: '83- 27, '87- 6, '91- 15; EC: '86- dq (20), '90- dq; WCp: '83- 20, '85- 13, '87- 14, '89- 4, '91- 23. CS champion 1987. At 5000mW: WI: '85- 4, '87- 4, '89- 2; EI: '87- 3, '88- 2, '89- 2.
World best 3000m walk 1989
Progression at 20kmW, 50kmW: 1980- 1:40:19, 1981- 1:36:56, 1982- 1:29:08, 1983- 1:24:30, 1984- 1:24:19, 4:09:34; 1985- 1:22:18, 4:05:29; 1986- 1:21:41, 4:19:06; 1987- 1:21:27, 4:12:12; 1988- 1:20:43, 3:50:46; 1989- 1:20:56, 1990- 1:20:21, 1991- 1:22:02, 1992- 1:20:57, 3:55:02; 1993- 1:23:47. Track pbs: 3000mW 10:56.34 '89, 5000mW 18:28.80 '89, 10000mW 38:47.84 '87, 20000mW 1:20:47.6 '90.

SLOVENIA

Governing body: Atletska zveza Slovenije, 61000 Ljubljana, Milcinskega 2. Current organisation founded 1945. Athletes competed for Yugoslavia prior to 1991.
National Championships first held in 1920 (men), 1922 (women). **1993 Champions**: **Men**: 100m: Damjan Spur 10.863, 200m: Tomazz Bozic 22.37, 400m/400mh: Miro Kocuvan 47.37/50.20, 800m: Rafko Marinic 1:50.06, 1500m/5000m: Izudin Hrapic 3:55.00/14:22.67, 3000mSt: Janko Podgorsek 8:59.60, 110mh: RokKop 14.74, HJ: Robert Herga 2.14, PV: Milan Krajnc 4.90, LJ: Gregor Cankar 7.36, TJ: Oliver Batagelj 15.31, SP: Dejan Dokl 15.85, DT: Igor Primc 52.12, HT: Branko Grubic 55.90, JT: Milan Stjepovic 73.52, Dec: Matjaz Polak 6707. **Women**: 100m/200m: Jerneja Perc 11.95/25.07, 400m/400mh: Irina Dominc 55.40/59.40, 800m: Marija Stevanec 2:15.43, 1500m: Jolanda Steblovnik 4:31.97, 3000mUdovc 10:12.72, 5000m: Marijana Vidovic 18:01.77, 100mh: Brigita Bukovec 12.89w, 400mh: Irena Dominc 57.40, HJ: Britta Bilac 1.91, LJ: Mateja Bezjak 5.71, TJ: Andreja Ribac 12.59, SP: Natasa Erjavec 16.79, DT: Lidija Kocs 39.50, JT: Kristina Jazbinsek 54.56, Hep: Hedvika Korosak 5097.

Britta BILAC b.4 Dec 1968 1.81m 61kg. née Vörös. Ex GDR.
At HJ: OG: '92- 15; WCh: '93- 11=; EI: '90- 2. SLO champion 1992-3.
Three Slovenian high jump records 1992.
Progression at HJ: 1983- 1.72, 1984- 1.77, 1985- 1.79, 1986- 1.85, 1987- 1.84, 1988- 1.88, 1989- 1.91, 1990- 1.94i, 1991- 1.92, 1992- 1.94, 1993- 1.97i/1.94, 1994- 2.00.
Married to Borut Bilac (b. 14 Apr 1965) 3rd 1990 European LJ, pb. 8.24 '90.

SOMALIA

Governing body: Somali Amateur Athletic Association, PO Box 3792, Mogadishu. Founded 1959.

Abdi BILE Abdi b. 28 Dec 1962 Las Anod 1.85m 75kg. Studied marketing at George Mason University, USA.

At 1500m: OG: '84- sf (qf 800m); WCh: '87- 1, '93- 3; AfCh: '82- 8, '85- 2; WCp: '89- 1. NCAA champion 1985, 1987. 1st GP 1987 & 1989, 2nd 1993.
Two African 1000m records 1989.
Progression at 800m, 1500m: 1981- 1:50.0; 1982- 1:52.8, 3:51.6; 1984- 1:46.1, 3:35.89dq; 1985- 1:47.24, 3:34.24; 1986- 1:51.2, 3:34.01; 1987- 1:44.47, 3:31.71; 1988- 1:44.42, 3:33.6; 1989- 1:43.60, 3:30.55; 1990- 1:46.64, 3:34.28; 1991- 1:46.39, 3:34.6; 1993- 1:45.17, 3:32.83. pbs: 1000m 2:14.50 '89, 1M 3:49.40 '88, 2000m 4:59.77 '87, 3000m 7:52.23 '89.
The first Somali world champion at any sport. Missed the 1988 Olympics due to a stress fracture in his left foot, but in 1989 he won the Oslo Dream Mile and World Cup 1500m, with national records at 800m, 1000m, 1500m and 3000m. Made a fine comeback in 1993 to win the World bronze medal.

SOUTH AFRICA

Governing body: Athletics South Africa, P.O. Box 1261, Pretoria 0001. Original body founded 1894. IAAF Membership terminated in 1976 and provisionally reinstated in 1992.
National Championships first held in 1894 (men), 1929 (women). **1993 Champions**: **Men**: 100m: Johan Venter 10.42, 200m: Johan Rossouw 20.61, 400m: Bobang Phiri 46.49, 800m: Ezekiel Sepeng 1:46.00, 1500m: Johan Landsman 3:46.44, 5000m: Shadrack Hoff 13:36.30, 10000m: Abel Lekgari 28:53.73, Half Mar: Michael Kidane ETH 61:06, Mar: Josiah Thugwane 2:14:25, 3000mSt: Shadrack Mogotsi 8:26.52, 110mh: Wimpie Nel 14.14, 400mh: Dries Vorster 50.07, HJ: Flippie van Vuuren 2.20, PV: Okkert Brits 5.35, LJ: François Fouché 7.77, TJ: Wikus Olivier 16.35, SP: Burger Lambrechts 18.43, DT: Christo Kruger 55.60, HT: Roumen Koprivchin BUL 67.50, JT: Tom Petranoff 82.38, Dec: Danie van Wyk 7293, 50kmW: Johan Moerdyk 4:09:37. **Women**: 100m/200m: Elinda Vorster 11.59/ 23.02, 400m: Evette de Klerk 53.89, 800m: Ilse Wicksell 2:04.31, 1500m: Gwen Griffiths 4:17.54, 3000m: Elana Meyer 8:41.64, 10000m: Nicole Whiteford 34:20.13, Half Mar: Zola Pieterse 71:49, Mar: Sonja Laxton 2:43:01, 100mh: Annemarie le Roux 13.54, 400mh: Lana Uys 56.66, HJ: Desire du Plessis 1.87, LJ: Luzaan du Preez 6.26, TJ: Petrusa Swart 12.23, SP: Luzanda Swanepoel 14.74, DT: Lizette Etsebeth 54.80, JT: Liezel Roux 52.92, Hep: Chrisna Oosthuizen 5103, 5000mW/10kmW: Felicita Falconer 25:49.70/54:38.

Johan LANDSMAN b. 12 May 1964 Cape Town 1.78m 62kg.
At 1500m: WCh: '93- h; AfCh: '92- 2, '93- 2. SA champion 1991-3.
Progression at 1500m: 1988- 3:43.40, 1989- 3:42.02, 1991- 3:36.30, 1992- 3:37.32, 1993- 3:33.56. pbs: 800m 1:45.63 '91, 1000m 2:20.89 '92, 1M 3:56.61 '91, 2000m 5:09.16 '92, 3000m 7:48.75 '92, 5000m 13:32.09 '92.

Tom PETRANOFF b.8 Apr 1958 Aurora, Illinois 1.86m 105kg. Shoe consultant. Ex-USA, gained South African citizenship in September 1991.
At JT: OG: '84- 10, '88- dnq 18; WCh: '83- 2, '87- 4, '93- dnq 22; WCp: '85- 3, '92- 2; AfCh: '92- 1; AfG: '93- 1. Won TAC 1985-6, GWG 1986. Won GP 1985, 1987. SA champion 1990-3.
World javelin record 1983. Three US bests, the last also a world best with new javelin 1986. African record 1992.
Progression at JT: 1977- 77.48, 1978- 79.74, 1979- 78.18, 1980- 85.44, 1981- 76.04, 1982- 88.40, 1983- 99.72, 1984- 89.50, 1985- 91.56, 1986- 92.38, new: 1986- 85.38, 1987- 83.24, 1988- 79.46, 1989- 85.34, 1990- 86.46, 1991- 89.16, 1992- 87.26, 1993- 84.58.
Attended Palomar College, California, where he went to play baseball. Banned by TAC at the end of 1988 after competing in South Africa. There he improved his best to 86.32 and 86.46 in 1990 and 87.32 and 89.16 in 1991, although these were ineligible for US records. Selected, but eventually not allowed to compete at the 1992 Olympics for South Africa; however he represented Africa in the World Cup.

Gert THYS b. 12 Nov 1971 Prieska.
At Mar: WCh: '93- dnf.
Progression at Mar: 1992- 2:17:16, 1993- 2:09:31. pbs: 5000m 13:55.30 '91, Road: 10km 28:38 '90, 15km 43:04 '92, Half Mar 61:39 '93.
2nd Fukuoka Marathon 1993.

David TSEBE b.9 Nov 1966 Mafeking 1.72m 56kg. Welfare officer.
SA champion marathon 1990, half marathon 1990, 1992,.
Progression at Mar: 1988- 2:12:14, 1989- 2:10:47, 1990- 2:09:50, 1991- 2:10:32, 1992- 2:08:07, 1993- 2:12:07. pbs: 5000m: 13:52.19 '89, 10000m: 28:32.2 '89; road 10km 28:26 '90, 15km 43:16 '90, Half Mar 61:03 '90.
Won Berlin marathon 1992. Second in 1988 Honolulu marathon under an assumed name.
His brother Rami (b.7 Oct 1964) has pbs: 5000m 13:40.43 '89, 10000m 27:59.8 '89, Half Mar 61:03 '90; Mar 2:13:29 '89.

Women

Elana MEYER b.10 Oct 1966 Albertina 1.58m 45kg. née van Zyl.

At 10000m: OG: '92- 2; WCh: '93- dnf. At 1500m: AfCh: '92- 1, '93- 1. Won SA 1500m 1992; 3000m 1987-9, 1992-3; 10000m 1991.
World road bests half marathon & 15km 1991.
SA records 2000m 1987, 3000m 1991, 5000m (2) 1991-2, 10000m (4) 1989-92.
Progression at 3000m, 10000m: 1981- 10:00.2, 1982- 9:24.9, 1983- 9:09.32, 1984- 9:12.20, 1985- 8:58.73; 1986- 9:17.16, 1987-8:52.39, 1988- 8:54.84, 1989- 8:55.78, 32:28.9; 1990- 8:54.83, 1991- 8:32.00, 31:33.46; 1992- 8:38.45, 31:11.75; 1993- 8:32.81, 32:28.02. pbs: 800m 2:06.23 '85, 1000m 2:43.63 '87, 1500m 4:02.15 '92, 1M 4:30.21 '89, 2000m 5:40.7 '92, 5000m 14:44.15 '92. Road (all SA records): 10km 31:33 '91, 15km 46:57 '91, Half Mar 67:59 '91, 67:22 (33m dh) '93.
Gave up in World 10000m final in 1993 after being repeatedly baulked by Sally Barsosio.

Zola PIETERSE b.Bloemfontein 26 May 1966 1.61m 43kg. née Budd. British citizenship by parentage obtained 6 April 1984. Returned to South Africa April 1988, and married Mike Pieterse on 15 Apr 1989.
At 3000m: OG: '84- 7, '92- h; EC: '86- 4 (9 at 1500m); ECp: '85- 1; AfCh: '92- 4. World CC: '85- 1, '86- 1. Won SA 1500m 1982-3, 1991; 3000m 1982-3, 1990-1; Half Mar 1993; UK 1500m 1984, WAAA 3000m 1985, 1500m 1986.
World 5000m best 15:01.83 '84; world junior bests 1500m (2), 1M, 2000m (2), 3000m (3), 5000m (4). As British citizen: 1984 world best 2000m, world junior best 1M, European junior records 1500m (4:04.39) and 3000m (8:40.22), 1985 WR 5000m, 1986WIB 3000m 8:39.79. Commonwealth indoor records: 3000m 1985-6; 1500m 1986. UK & Commonwealth records 1500m, 1M, 3000m (2) and 5000m 1985.
Progression at 1500m, 3000m/5000m: 1980- 4:24.3; 10:06.5; 1981- 4:19.0; 1982- 4:09.1, 8:59.2; 1983- 4:06.87, 8:39.00/15:10.65; 1984- 4:01.81, 8:37.5/15:01.83; 1985- 3:59.96, 8:28.83/14:48.07; 1986- 4:01.93, 8:34.43; 1989- 4:20.5; 1990- 4:12.91, 9:17.22; 1991- 4:06.4, 8:35.72; 1992- 4:09.72, 8:53.15; 1993- 4:18.72, 8:52.85. pbs: 800m 2:00.9 '84, 1000m 2:37.9 '83, 1M 4:17.57 '85, 2000m 5:30.19 '86, road 10km 32:20 '83, Half Mar 71:49 '93.
Not permitted to run for England in the 1986 Commonwealth Games.

SPAIN

Governing body: Real Federación Española de Atletismo, Calle Miguel Angel 16, Madrid 28010. Founded 1920.
National Championships first held in 1917 (men), 1931 (women). **1993 Champions**: 100m: Enrique Talavera 10.39, 200m: Jordi Mayoral 21.10, 400m: Cayetano Cornet 46.36, 800m: Luis Javier González 1:51.59, 1500m: Fermin Cacho 3:46.24, 5000m: Abel Antón 13:44.16, 10,000m: Alejandro Gómez 28:25.53, Half Mar: Alberto Juzdado 63:40, Mar: Ricardo Castano 2:15:27, 3000mSt: Antonio Peula 8:34.44, 110mh: Carlos Sala 13.91w, 400mh: Santiago Fraga 50.42, HJ: Arturo Ortiz 2.26, PV: Daniel Martí 5.60, LJ: Angel Hernández 8.10, TJ: Raul Chapado 16.09, SP: Manuel Martínez 18.82, DT: José L Valencia 52.56, HT: Francisco Fuentes 65.34, JT: Raimundo Fernández 74.02, Dec: Xavier Brunet 7497, 20kW/50kW: Valentín Massana 1:25:36/ 3:46:11; Women: 100m: Patricia Morales 11.76w, 200m: Bárbara Lovaco 24.25, 400m: Sandra Myers 52.28, 800m: Amaya Andrés 2:06.85, 1500m: M Teresa Zuñiga 4:26.57, 3000m: Estela Estévez 9:03.87, 5000m: Julia Vaquero 15:50.43, 10000m: Rocio Rios 33:55.18, Half Mar: Maria Muñoz 72:19, Mar: Mónica Pont 2:35:30, 100mh: M José Mardomingo 13.36, 400mh: Miriam Alonso 58.20, HJ: Bélen Sáenz 1.78, LJ: Luisa López 6.28w, TJ: Concepción Paredes 13.40, SP: Margarita Ramos 16.92, DT: Sonia Godall 54.08, JT: Cristina Larrea 56.10, Hep: Patricia Guevara 5424, 10000mW: Encarna Granados 45:59.18, 10kW: Reyes Sobrino 47:32.

Abel ANTON b.24 Oct 1962 Ojoel, Soria 1.79m 63kg. Kelme.
At 5000m: OG: '88- sf, '92- 8; WCh: '87- 14, '91- 11, '93- 11; EC: '86- h, '90- 11; EJ: '81- 5; WCp: '92- 4; ECp: '93- 3. At 10000m: ECp: '87- 1. At 3000m: EI: '89- 2. Won Spanish 5000m 1992-3.
Progression at 5000m: 1981- 14:18.29, 1982- 14:13.94, 1983- 14:06.04, 1984- 13:27.95, 1985- 13:25.81, 1986- 13:32.61, 1987- 13:21.44, 1988- 13:20.67, 1990- 13:29.81, 1991- 13:26.52, 1992- 13:21.86, 1993- 13:17.48. pbs: 1000m 2:20.44 '86, 1500m 3:37.5 '85, 2000m 5:01.35 '87, 3000m 7:46.08 '87, 10000m 28:09.04 '93.

Jaime BARROSO b.15 May 1968 Barcelona 1.65m 55kg. Fútbol Club, Barcelona.
At 20kmW: WCh: '93- 4; WSG: '91- 2. At 50kmW: OG: '92- 14; WCp: '93- 20. Won Spanish 50kmW 1992.
Progress at 20kmW, 50kmW: 1987- 1:32:26.6t, 1988- 1:28:42, 1989- 1:23:37, 1990- 1:30:33, 1991- 1:25:01, 3:56:22; 1992- 1:28:20, 3:48:08; 1993- 1:23:02, 4:06:28. pbs: 10000mW 42:39.18 '88; road 10kmW 40:24 '89.

Fermin CACHO b.16 Feb 1969 Agreda, Soria 1.75m 63kg. Joma-Sport.
At 1500m: OG: '92- 1; WCh: '91- 5, '93- 2; EC: '90- 11; WJ: '88- 3; EJ: '87- 12; WCp: '89- 6, '92- 4; ECp: '93- 2; WI: '91- 2; EI: '90- 2. Won Spanish 1500m 1989-93.
Spanish 1000m record 1993.

Progression at 1500m: 1986- 3:58.17, 1987- 3:45.9, 1988- 3:42.56, 1989- 3:36.23, 1990- 3:37.04, 1991- 3:32.03, 1992- 3:32.69, 1993- 3:32.01. pbs: 800m 1:45.37 '91, 1000m 2:16.13 '93, 1M 3:50.74 '91, 3000m 7:46.11i '92.
Good footballer at school, concentrated on athletics from age 17.

Javier GARCIA b.22 Jul 1966 Barcelona 1.77m 71kg. Kelme. Quantity surveying student.
At PV: OG: '88- dnq, '92- 3; WCh: '91 & '93- dnq; EC: '90- 5; EJ: '85- 6; WI: '89- 8, '91- 7; WCp: '89- 4; ECp: '89- 6, '93- 3; WSG: '89- 3. Spanish champion 1989-90, 1992.
Five Spanish pole vault records 1989-92.
Progression at PV: 1982- 3.51, 1983- 4.70, 1984- 5.15, 1985- 5.30, 1986- 5.43, 1987- 5.50i/5.40, 1988- 5.55, 1989- 5.71, 1990- 5.75, 1991- 5.72i/ 5.60, 1992- 5.77i/5.75, 1993- 5.70.

Jesús Angel GARCIA b.17 Oct 1969 Madrid 1.70m 55kg.
At 50kmW: OG: '92- 10; WCh: '93- 1; WCp: '92- 2.
Progression at 50kmW: 1991- 4:05:10, 1992- 3:48:24, 1993- 3:41:41. pbs: 10000mW 42:27.52 '90, 20kmW 1:24:11 '91; road 10kmW 40:38 '91.

Basilio LABRADOR b.29 Mar 1967 1.65m 62kg. Ceat.
At 50kmW: WCh: '91- dnf, '93- 5; EC: '90- 4; WCp: '89- 19, '91- 23, '93- 15.
Progression at 50kmW: 1989- 3:59:51, 1990- 3:54:45, 1991- 4:03:42, 1992- 4:04:14, 1993- 3:46:46. pbs: 10000mW 42:24.2 '90, 20kmW 1:23:44 '93; road 10kmW 41:27 '90.

Valentin MASSANA b.5 Jul 1970 Barcelona 1.62m 50kg. CN Barcelona.
At 20kmW: OG: '92- dq; WCh: '91- 5, '93- 1; EC: '90- 5; WCp: '91- 10, '93- 2. At 10kmW: WJ: '88- 2: EJ: '87- 2, '89- 1. At 5000mW: WI:.'91- 5. Won Spanish 20kmW 1991-3, 50kmW 1993.
Spanish record 20km walk 1992.
Progression at 20kmW: 1987- 1:31:50, 1990- 1:22:33, 1991- 1:20:29, 1992- 1:19:25, 1993- 1:20:50. pbs: 5000mW 18:59.60i '91, 19:36.5 '89; 10000mW 40:14.17 '89, 1HrW 14,367m '90, 50kmW: 3:46:11 '93; road 10kmW 39:27 '92.

Arturo ORTIZ b.18 Sep 1966 Geneva, Switzerland 1.90m 73kg. Larios. Student.
At HJ: OG: '88- 14, '92- dnq; WCh: '87- 12=, '91- 10=, '93- 7; EC: '90- 8=; WSG: '91- 2, '93- 3=; WI: '91- 9; EI: '90- 2; ECp: '87- 6, '89- 5, '93- 7. Spanish champion 1987-8, 1989-93.
Six Spanish high jump records 1987-91.
Progression at HJ: 1984- 2.01, 1985- 2.13, 1986- 2.19, 1987- 2.27, 1988- 2.28, 1989- 2.25, 1990- 2.32, 1991- 2.34, 1992- 2.32, 1993- 2.31.

Antonio PEÑALVER b.1 Dec 1968 Alhama, Murcia 1.91m 77kg. Alfil. Student.
At Dec: OG: '88- 23, '92- 2; WCh: '91- 8; EC: '90- 6; WJ: '86- 7; EJ: '87- 8; ECp: '91- 1B, '93- 9. Spanish champion 1989. At Hep: EI: '92- 3.
Nine Spanish decathlon records 1988-92.
Progression at Dec: 1986- 7229, 1987- 7044, 1988- 7891, 1989- 8050, 1990- 8214, 1991- 8306, 1992- 8534w/8478, 1993- 7715. pbs: 100m 11.01 '90, 10.76w '92; 200m 22.0 '90, 400m 48.88 '88, 1500m 4:25.49 '88, 110mh 14.09/13.92w '92; HJ 2.12 '92, PV 5.00 '90, LJ 7.55 '90, SP 17.32 '91, DT 50.66 '91, JT 63.08 '91, Hep 6062i '92.
Missed 1993 World Championships due to a broken finger.

Daniel PLAZA b.3 Jul 1966 Barcelona 1.81m 63kg. Sideco.
At 20kmW: OG: '88- 12, '92- 1; WCh: '91- dq, '93- 3; EC: '90- 2; WCp: '87- 22, '89- 11, '91- 4, '93- 6. At 10kmW: EJ: '85- 2. Won Spanish 20kmW 1986, 1989.
Progression at 20kmW: 1984- 1:29:27t, 1985- 1:28:30, 1986- 1:26:50.5t, 1987- 1:24:01, 1988- 1:21:53, 1989- 1:22:09, 1990- 1:21:56, 1991- 1:20:47, 1992- 1:20:42, 1993- 1:21:11. Track pbs: 5000mW 19:07.24 '90, 10000mW 40:34.3 '90, 20000mW 1:26:50.5 '86, 1HrW 14,842m '90; road: 10kmW 39:38 '90, 50kmW 3:49:31 '92.
In 1992 he became Spain's first ever Olympic champion in athletics. Disqualified in Tokyo 1991 after finishing third.

Valentin Massana: gained some consolation for Olympic disqualification with gold in Stuttgart

Women

Encarnación GRANADOS b.30 Jan 1972 Gerona 1.68m 50kg. GEiEG.
At 10kmW: WCh: '93- 3. Spanish champion 1992 (road), 1993 (track).
Progression at 10kmW: 1991- 48:38, 1992- 44:51, 1993- 43:21. pbs: track 5000mW 22:12.7 '93, road 5kmW 21:38 '93.

Sandra MYERS b. 9 Jan 1961 Little River, Kansas 1.68m 58kg. Kelme. Music graduate of UCLA. Piano teacher.
At 400m: WCh: '91- 3, '93- 6; WI: '91- 2, '93- 4; EI: '92- 1. At 400mh: WCp: '81- 7. At 100m: OG: '88- h; WCp: '89- 6. At 200m: EC: '90- 4; EI: '90- 4. Won TAC 400mh 1981, ECup B 100m & 200m 1991, 200m 1993; Spanish 100m 1988, 200m 1988-9, 400m 1990, 1993; LJ 1989.
Spanish records 1988-91: 100m (4), 200m (3), 400m (4), LJ. US 400mh record 1980.
Progression at 400mh: 1980- 56.40, 1981- 56.38, 1983- 58.40, 1984- 61.53, 1987- 58.0; at 200m, 400m: 1987- 23.4, 52.7; 1988- 23.34, 53.76; 1989- 23.54i, 23.77; 1990- 22.38, 51.01; 1991- 22.62, 49.67, 1992- 23.00i, 51.21i/51.91; 1993- 23.28, 50.83. pbs: 60m 7.23i '90, 100m 11.06 '91, 600m 1:26.99 '93, 800m 2:10.18 '93, 100mh 13.48 '89, LJ 6.68i/6.60 '88.
As a teenager was principally a long jumper, taking up the 400mh with immediate success in 1980 winning AIAW titles at that event and LJ when at Cal State Northridge. Moved to Spain and took up Spanish citizenship, married to coach Javier Echarri. Breakthrough at 400m in May 1990 with Spanish records 51.22 and 51.18, and improved massively at 200m to place fourth in Split. In 1991 became the first Spanish women to win a World Championships medal. Missed 1992 Olympics through injury.

Maria Teresa ZUÑIGA b.28 Dec 1964 Eibar, Guipuzcoa 1.67m 56kg. Club Deportivo Aurrerá. Police officer.
At 800m: OG: '88- 7; WCh: '91- h, '93- 12; EC: '90- sf; WCp: '89- 5. At 1500m: OG: '92- 6; WI: '93- 5. Won Spanish 400m 1988, 800m 1982-3, 1990, 1992; 1500m 1989, 1993.
Spanish records: 800m (2) 1988, 1500m (2) 1988-92, 1000m 1989.
Progression at 800m, 1500m: 1979- 2:18.8i/2:19.02, 1980- 2:11.5, 1981- 2:10.4, 1982- 2:07.38, 4:21.8; 1983- 2:05.36, 1984- 2:06.59, 1985- 2:05.50i/2:08.54, 1986- 2:06.83, 1987- 2:02.61, 4:12.99; 1988- 1:57.45, 4:06.44; 1989- 1:58.49, 4:14.45; 1990- 2:00.11, 4:13.17i/4:22.67; 1991- 2:02.16, 1992- 2:01.28, 4:00.59; 1993- 4:07.46. pbs: 200m 24.3 '88, 400m 52.71 '88, 1000m 2:34.66 '89, 1M 4:28.56 '92.

SURINAM

Governing body: De Surinaamse Athletiek Bond, PO Box 1758, Panamaraibo. Founded 1955.

VRIESDE, Letitia b. 5 Oct 1964 1.59m 55kg. AVR, HOL.
At 800m/1500m: OG: '88- sf/h, '92- sf/sf; WCh: '91- 5/9; PAG: '91- 4/2; CAmG '90- 2/1, '93- 1/1.
South American records: five 800m 1990-2, two 1000m & two 1500m 1991. Surinam 3000m records 1990-1.
Progression at 800m, 1500m: 1986- 2:14.6, 4:34.01; 1987- 2:08.37, 4:36.86; 1988- 2:01.83, 4:16.29; 1989- 2:03.44, 4:24.64; 1990- 1:59.79, 4:11.88; 1991- 1:58.25, 4:05.67; 1992- 1:57.96, 4:08.82; 1993- 2:00.30. pbs: 400m 53.09 '90, 1000m 2:32.25 '91, 1M 4:30.45 '92, 3000m 9:15.64 '91.

SWEDEN

Governing body: Svenska Friidrottsförbundet, Box 5628, S-114 86 Stockholm. Founded 1895.
National Championships first held in 1896 (men), 1927 (women). **1993 Champions**: **Men**: 100m: Peter Karlsson 10.48, 200m: Torbjörn Eriksson 20.66, 400m: Marko Granat 46.74, 800m: Martin Enholm 1:47.92, 1500m: Joakim Hennings 3:45.08, 5000m/10000m/Half Mar: Jonny Danielson 13:48.99/28:42.00/65:22, Mar: Jörgen Mårtensson 2:19:01, 3000mSt: Andreas Ahl 8:45.91, 110mh: Niklas Eriksson 14.25, 400mh: Niklas Wallenlind 49.79, HJ: Patrick Thavelin 2.20, PV: Patrik Stenlund 5.40, LJ: Mattias Sunneborn 7.89, TJ: Tord Henriksson 16.52, SP: Kent Larsson 20.03, DT: Dag Solhaug 59.78, HT: Tore Gustafsson 70.50, JT: Patrik Bodén 81.84, Dec: Glenn Håkansson 7415, 20kmW: Stefan Johansson 1:27:05, 50kmW: Bo Gustafsson 4:13:46. **Women**: 100m/200m: Marika Johansson 11.86/23.39, 400m/400mh: Monica Westén 54.42/55.92, 800m/1500m/3000m: Maria Akraka 2:02.44/4:19.32/9:11.81, 10000m: Marie Granberg 34:12.54, Half Mar: Magdalena Thorsell 78:28, Mar: Liz Hjalmarsson 2:46:2, 100mh: Helena Fernström 13.80, HJ: Ingela Sandqvist 1.81, LJ: Erica Johansson 6.22, TJ: Karin Grelsson 12.80, SP: Linda-Marie Mårtensson 16.20, DT: Anna Söderberg 52.18, JT: Karin Colberg 54.00, Hep: Karin Funke 5259, 5000mW: Madelein Svensson 21:34.1, 10000kmW: Monica Gunnarsson 48:07.4.

Patrik BODÉN b.30 Jun 1967 Fryksände 1.87m 106kg. IF Göta. Studied engineering at University of Texas.
At JT: OG: '92- dnq 16; WCh: '91- 8, '93- 9; EC:

'90- 3; WJ: '86- 8. Swedish champion 1992-3, won NCAA 1989-91.
World javelin record 1990.
Progression at JT: 1983- 58.14, 1984- 63.58, 1985- 74.26; new: 1986- 74.66, 1987- 78.10, 1988- 76.52, 1989- 82.28, 1990- 89.10, 1991- 85.58R, 1992- 84.20, 1993- 88.26. pbs: SP 15.76 '93, DT 49.28 '89, HT 53.44 '92.
Was fourth at LJ in National age 12 championships in 1979. Operations on right shoulder in 1990 and October 1991, on knees in 1990 and June 1991.

Sven NYLANDER b.1 Jan 1962 Varberg 1.94m 85kg. Malmö AI. Was at Southern Methodist University, USA.
At 400mh: OG: '84- 4, '92- sf; WCh: '83- 4, '87- 4, '91- sf, '93- sf; EC: '82- 7, '86- 3, '90- 2; Won NCAA 1983. At 110mh: EJ: 79- 6. Won Swedish 400mh 1982, 1987, 1990, 1992; 110mh 1979, 1983.
Five Swedish 400mh records 1982-7.
Progression at 400mh: 1978- 54.8, 1979- 52.62, 1981- 51.58, 1982- 49.64, 1983- 48.88, 1984- 48.97, 1985- 50.39, 1986- 48.83, 1987- 48.37, 1988- 49.35, 1990- 48.43, 1991- 49.39, 1992- 48.75, 1993- 49.21. pbs: 100m 10.63 '87, 200m 21.18 '86, 400m 47.8i '81, 48.10 '82; 110mh 13.98/13.73w/13.7 '86, LJ 6.82i '79.
Had a remarkable record of making all major championships finals 1982-7, setting national records three times in these races. Returned in 1990 and again ran brilliantly for the European silver, but in 1991 went out in the semis in Tokyo; the first time that he did not make a major final.

Patrik SJÖBERG b.5 Jan 1965 Göteborg 2.00m 82kg. Örgryte IS.
At HJ: OG: '84- 2, '88- 3=, '92- 2; WCh: '83- 11, '87- 1, '91- 7; EC: '82- 10=, '86- 6; EI: 1st 1985, 1987-8, 1992; EJ: '81- 8, '83- 3; WCp: '85- 1, '89- 1; WI: '85- 1, '87- dnq, '89- 3, '91- 13, '92- 2. Won GP 1992 (2nd 1988). Won SWE HJ 1981-7, 1989.
Twelve Swedish high jump records 1982-7, European record 1985, World record 1987. WIB: 2.38 '85, 2.41 '87.
Progression at HJ: 1975- 1.30, 1976- 1.40, 1977- 1.59, 1978- 1.80, 1979- 1.91, 1980- 2.07, 1981- 2.21, 1982- 2.26, 1983- 2.33, 1984- 2.33, 1985- 2.38, 1986- 2.34, 1987- 2.42, 1988- 2.39i/2.37, 1989- 2.40, 1990- 2.34, 1991- 2.34, 1992- 2.34/2.38i. pbs: LJ 7.72 '87, TJ 15.87 '83.
Extraordinary record for the Swedish team since his début at the age of 16, having never lost in 21 appearances, including five European Cup (C/B) wins. Missed 1993 World Championships through injury. By the end of the 1993 season he had jumped 2.30 or higher in 110 competitiopns.

Niklas WALLENLIND b.21 Nov 1968 Göteborg 1.85m 75kg. Mölndals AIK.
At 400mh: OG: '92- 5; WCh: '91- 8, '93- sf; EC: '90- 3; EJ: 87- 1. Swedish champion 400mh 1989, 1993; 400m 1989-92.
Swedish 400mh record 1992.
Progression at 400mh: 1985- 55.3, 1986- 54.26, 1987- 50.65, 1988- 50.95, 1989- 50.28, 1990- 48.52, 1991- 49.77, 1992- 48.35, 1993- 49.45. pbs: 100m 11.06 '90, 200m 21.44 '92, 400m 46.37 '92, 800m 1:53.41 '87, TJ 12.10 '92.
Won the European Junior gold in 1987 in 50.65, having entered the meeting with a pb of 52.28. In 1990 he made similar improvement to take the European bronze in 48.52, after 48.80 in the semis and a pre-meet best of 49.74.

Dag WENNLUND b.9 Oct 1963 Mariestad 1.88m 97kg. Mariestads AIF. Was at University of Texas, USA.
At JT: OG: '88- 8, '92- dnq 15; WCh: '87- 8, '91- 7, '93- 7; EC: '86- dnq 15, '90- dnq 16; EJ: '81- 12. Swedish champion 1985-6, 1991. Won NCAA 1986-7.
Three Swedish javelin records 1985-7.
Progression at JT: 1980- 65.06, 1981- 70.50, 1982- 78.20, 1983- 81.06, 1984- 82.34, 1985- 92.20. new: 1986- 81.86, 1987- 82.64, 1988- 81.30, 1989- 82.52, 1990- 79.62, 1991- 85.52R, 1992- 80.80, 1993- 82.58. pbs: SP 13.09 '82, DT 40.74 '84, HT 41.70 '84.

Women

Erica JOHANSSON b.5 Feb 1974 Mölndal 1.76m 69kg. Mölndals AIK.
At LJ: WI: '93- 6; WJ: '90-2; '92- 1; EJ: '89- 2, '91- 4, '93- 1. Swedish champion 1990-3.
Six Swedish records 1989-92.
Progression at LJ: 1988- 5.71, 1989- 6.50, 1990- 6.56i/6.53, 1991- 6.55i/6.52, 1992- 6.72, 1993- 6.78i/6.56. pbs: 100m 12.40 '89, 200m 25.02i '90, 25.12 '89; HJ 1.78 '89.
Foot injury caused her to miss much of the 1993 season, yet she still won the European Junior title after eight weeks out of competition. At the 1989 European Juniors, aged 15, she improved from 6.25 to 6.50 to take the silver medal and equal the Swedish senior record.

Madelein SVENSSON b.20 Jul 1969 Sollefteå 1.68m 48kg. Forsmo IF.
At 10kW: OG: '92- 6; WCh: '91- 2, '93- dq; EC: '90- 17; WCp: '93- 4. At 3000mW: WI: '93- 8. Swedish champion 5000mW/10000mW 1991-2. Swedish records 10k & 20k walks 1991, 5000m & 10000m track walks 1992, 3000mW 1993.
Progression at 10kW: 1989- 47:35, 1990- 45:49, 1991- 43:13, 1992- 42:13.7t, 1993- 42:52. pbs: 3000mW 12:14.01i '92, 12:25.05 '93; 5000mW

21:09.26 '92, 20,000mW 1:35:29.5 '91.
Breakthrough in 1991, when she won the eight nations meeting in June in 43:27, and improved further to gain a surprise silver medal in Tokyo. At the end of the 1993 season she announced that she was giving up walking and would pursue a running career in future.

Monica WESTÉN b.15 Mar 1966 Huddinge 1.75m 62kg. IF Göta.
At 400mh: OG: '92- h; WCh: '91- sf, '93- sf; EC: '90- 3; WCp: '92- 6 4x400mR. Won Swedish 400m 1991, 1993; 100mh 1988, 400mh 1989-93, HJ 1987-8, 1990, Hep 1987-90.
Swedish heptathlon record 1990.
Progression at 400mh: 1979- 78.4, 1980- 73.1, 1981- 64.53, 1982- 60.74, 1983- 61.69, 1984- 60.04, 1985- 58.70, 1986- 58.35, 1987- 57.57, 1988- 57.60, 1989- 56.04, 1990- 54.69, 1991- 55.51, 1992- 55.48, 1993- 55.53. pbs: 100m 12.44 '89, 200m 24.32 '90, 400m 53.43 '89, 800m 2:01.86 '93, 100mh 13.56 '89, HJ 1.89 '90, LJ 6.21 '90, SP 11.64i '92, 11.57 '89; JT 35.96 '91, Hep 6085 '90.
After previously concentrating on the heptathlon, she broke through to world class in 1990 at 400mh. Sisters Kristina, Ulla and Agneta had HJ bests of 1.70, 1.50 and 1.81i respectively.

SWITZERLAND

Governing body: Schweizerischer Leichtathletikverband (SLV), Postfach 8222, CH 3001, Bern. Formed 1905 as Athletischer Ausschuss des Schweizerischen Fussball-Verbandes.
National Championships first held in 1906 (men), 1934 (women). **1993 Champions**: **Men**: 100m: David Dollé 10.29w, 200m: Kevin Widmer 20.90, 400m: Matthias Rusterholz 46.68, 800m: Enrico Cariboni 1:51.66, 1500m: Markus Hacksteiner 3:52.19, 5000m/Half Mar: Pierre Délèze 13:59.40/64:48, 10000m: Arnold Mächler 28:43.77, Mar: Thierry Constantin 2:14:07, 3kmSt: Kasimir Kunz 8.55.41, 110mh: Gunnar Schrör 14.14, 400mh: Daniel Ritter 50.38, HJ: Thomas Friedli 2.12, PV: Raynald Mury 5.45, LJ: NicolasToffel 7.65, TJ: Beat Bollinger 15.19, SP: Werner Günthör 21.28, DT: Christian Erb 59.92, HT: Oliver Sack 68.26, JT: Gregory Wiesner 71.90, Dec: Mirko Spada 7813, 10000mW: Urbain Girod 45:41.32, 20kmW: Aldo Bertoldi 1:28:30, 50kmW: Pascal Charrière 4:07:36. **Women**: 100m/200m: Sara Wüest 11.68/23.54, 400m: Regula Zürcher-Scalabrin 52.19, 800m: Anita Brägger 2:06.11, 1500m: Sandra Gasser 4:13.35, 3000m: Mirjam Schmocker 9:39.03, 10000m/Half Mar: Isabella Moretti 34:25.49/74:58, Mar: Elisabeth Krieg 2:41:53, 100mh: Julia Baumann 13.04, 400mh: Nicole Schumann 58.44, HJ: Claudia Ellinger 1.84, LJ/Hep: Manuela Marxer LIE 5.93/5662, TJ: Doris Stelzmüller 13.03, SP/DT: Nathalie Ganguillet 15.72/49.16, JT: Claudia Bögli 50.06, 5000mW/10kmW: Heidi Mäder 25:48.15/52:21.

David DOLLÉ b. 30 May 1969 1.91m 87kg. LC Zürich. Mechanic.
At 200m: WCh: '93- sf.
Swiss records 1992-3: 100m (3), 200m (1).
Progression at 100m, 200m: 1987- 10.90, 22.03; 1988- 10.61, 21.58; 1989- 10.54, 21.46; 1990- 10.77, 21.34; 1991- 10.64, 21.26; 1992- 10.30, 20.75; 1993- 10.25, 20.43.
Parents were Swiss and black American.

Werner GÜNTHÖR b.1 Jun 1961 2.00m 130kg. LC Zürich. Sports student.
At SP: OG: '84- 5, '88- 3, '92- 4; WCh: '83- dnq 15, '87- 1, '91- 1; WI: '87- 2, '91- 1; EC: '86- 1; WCp: '89- 2, '92- 3; EI: '84- 2, '85- 3, '86- 1, '87- 2. Swiss champion 1981-9, 1991-3. Won GP 1986, 1992 (2nd overall).
13 Swiss shot records 1984-8. WIB 22.26 '87.
Progression at SP: 1977- 12.12, 1978- 13.60, 1979- 15.08, 1980- 16.42, 1981- 16.65, 1982- 17.51i, 1983- 20.01, 1984- 20.80, 1985- 21.55i/ 21.26, 1986- 22.22, 1987- 22.47, 1988- 22.75, 1989- 22.18, 1991- 22.03, 1992- 21.91, 1993- 21.94. pbs: HJ 2.00 '85; DT 54.48 '85, JT 74.88 '81.
Bobsledding with the Swiss team in 1989/90. Back operation in March 1990. Won six successive European Cup B SP 1983-93. Unbeaten in 1991, when he retained his world title and was far superior to anyone else in the world. Announced his retirement at the end of 1993.

Women

Julie BAUMANN b.17 June 1964 St.Jerome, Québec, Canada 1.64m 54kg. Psychology graduate of Concordia University, Canada. née Rocheleau.
At 100mh: OG: '88- 6 (qf 100m); WCh: '91- 5, '93- sf; CG: '86- 4. At 60mh: WI: '93- 1. Won Swiss 100mh 1991, 1993.
Commonwealth 100mh record 1988.
Progression at 100mh: 1981- 14.32, 1982- 14.19, 1983- 13.93, 1984- 13.81, 1985- 13.8, 1986- 13.46/13.32w, 1987- 13.38, 1988- 12.78, 1991- 12.76, 1992- 12.93/12.87w, 1993- 12.99. pbs: 50m 6.30i '89, 60m 7.34i '88, 50mh 6.84i '89, 60mh 7.95i '92, 100m 11.13 '88, 200m 24.00 '91.
Won the Mobil Grand Prix series at sprint hurdles, and was third overall, in 1988 when she set seven Canadian indoor records. Banned for two year following a positive drugs test in 1989. Swiss citizenship following her marriage.

Sandra GASSER b.27 Jul 1962 Bern 1.69m 51kg. STV Bern.

At 1500m: WCh: '87- dq (3rd), '91- h, '93- h; EC: '90- 3; WI: '87- 6, '93- 3; EI: '84- 3, '87- 1, '90- 2. At 3000m: EC: '86- h. Won Swiss 800m 1985-7, 1992; 1500m 1991-3.
Swiss records at 800m (3), 1000m, 1500m (2), 1M 1987; 1000m 1989.
Progression at 1500m: 1981- 4:26.09, 1983- 4:19.92, 1984- 4:10.04, 1985- 4:13.64, 1986- 4:12.07, 1987- 3:59.06dq/4:01.10, 1990- 4:06.11, 1991- 4:05.94, 1992- 4:12.47, 1993- 4:07.86. pbs: 800m 1:58.90 '87, 1:58.65mx '90; 1000m 2:31.51 '89, 1M 4:23.84 dq '87, 4:24.94 '90; 3000m 8:54.13 '90, 400mh 60.87 '81.
Suspended following a positive drugs test in Rome 1987, losing her World bronze and the Grand Prix mile win and third place overall. She protested her innocence but lost her appeal against the IAAF, so served a two-year ban.

TAJIKISTAN

Governing body: Light Athletic Federation of Republic of Tajikistan, Firdavsi Street 63, app. 54, Dushanbe 734061. Founded 1932.

Andrey ABDUVALIYEV b.30 Jun 1966 Leningrad 1.86m 112kg. Dushanbe Dyn.
At HT: OG: '92- 1; WCh: '91- 5, '93- 1; EJ: '85- 1. Won USSR HT 1991.
Two Asian hammer records 1993.
Progression at HT: 1981- 52.40, 1982- 59.70, 1983- 65.20, 1984- 71.54, 1985- 73.20, 1986- 74.76, 1987- 74.06, 1988- 80.38, 1989- 81.00, 1990- 83.46, 1991- 82.80, 1992- 82.54, 1993- 82.78.
Trains under Anatoliy Bondarchuk at the Kiev Hammer School. In 1990 he withdrew from the Europeans at the warm-up, and in 1991 disappointed by failing to complete the USSR clean sweep in the hammer in the Worlds. He won the Olympic gold, although that was one of only two wins in ten competitions during 1992. After Tajikistan became a member of the Asian AA in May 1993, he won the World title with his second Asian record of the year.

TRINIDAD & TOBAGO

Governing body: National Amateur Athletic Association of Trinidad & Tobago, 1Second Street, St Joseph, Trinidad. Founded 1945, reformed 1971.

Ian MORRIS b.30 Nov 1961 Siparia 1.75m 65kg. Was at Abilene Christian University, USA.
At 400m: OG: '88- 7, '92- 4; WCh: '87- h (h 200m), '91- 6, '93- sf; WI: '87- 4, '89- 2, '93- 2R; PAm: '87- 4; WCp: '85- 6R, '92- 1R; CAmG: '86- 2/2R, '93- 4/2R.
Three national 400m records 1988-92.
Progression at 400m: 1985- 45.38/45.1, 1986- 45.02, 1987- 45.03, 1988- 44.60, 1989- 45.33, 1990- 46.59i/46.5, 1991- 45.00/44.9, 1992- 44.21, 1993- 44.89. pbs: 200m 20.71 '88, 20.4/20.45w '87; 300m 32.27 '92.
Started athletics in 1985, having previously played soccer.

TURKEY

Governing body: Türkiye Amator Atletizm Federasyonu, Ulus Ishani A Blok Kat 3, Ankara. Founded 1922.
National Champions 1993: **Men**: 100m/200m: Benhur Özden 10.7/21.89, 400m: Alper Basyigit 49.36, 800m: Burhan Varol 1:52.79; 1500m/5000m: Zeki Öztürk 3:45.73/13:54.9, 10000m: Kenal Dal 30:27.45, 3000mSt: Nihat Bagci 8:53.49, 110mh: Toros Akti 14.6, 400mh: Serdar Uçan 54.42, HJ: Kemal Güner 2.12, PV: Murat Dündar 4.50, LJ: Murat Ayaydin 7.33, TJ: Bayram Demir 14.74, SP: Ekrem Ay 18.27, DT: Hüseyin Yilmaz 48.66, HT: Ferit Ünal 56.52, JT: Çetin Goçmenoglu 63.88, Dec: Alper Kasapoglu 6434. **Women**: 100m/200m: Aksel Gürcan 11.87/24.38, 400m: Gülcan Özkan 58.71, 800m/1500m: Melahat Kokalp 2:10.79/4:26.42, 3000m: Fatmagül Bosnak 10:03.13, 100mh/LJ/TJ: Figen Ugras 15.12/5.80/12.04, 400mh: Nazan Kuzlu 61.64, HJ: Billur Dulkadir 1.65, SP: Meliha Sarikoca 13.48, DT: Hüsniye Keskin 49.94, HT: Birsen Elma 45.98, JT: Aysel Tas 50.94.

UKRAINE

Governing body: Ukrainian Athletic Federation, Kuibishev Str., 42252023 Kiev 23. Founded 1991.
National Champions 1993: **Men**: 100m: Aleksandr Shlychkov 10.31, 200m: Aleksey Chikhachev 20.84, 400m: Vasiliy Lozinskiy 46.87, 800m: Andrey Mitin 1:51.91, 1500m: Leonid Lyashenko 3:46.17, 5000m: Yevgeniy Sirotin 14:01.38, 10000m: Viktor Karpenko 28:55.38, 3000mSt: Aleksey Patserin 8:49.98, 110mh Vladimir Belokon 13.48, 400mh: Vyacheslav Orinchuk 50.80, HJ: Vyacheslav Tyrtyshnik 2.23, PV: Aleksandr Chernyayev 5.50, LJ: Vitaliy Kirilenko 8.15, TJ: Vladimir Inozemtsev 16.98, SP: Andrey Nemchaninov 20.21, DT: Vladimir Zinchenko 64.78, HT: Vadim Kolesnik 78.76, JT: Andrey Novikov 76.36, Dec: Vitaliy Kolpakov 8297, 20kmW: Vladimir Soyka 1:25:14.9t, 50kmW: Vitaliy Popovich 3:51:44. **Women**: 100m/200m: Irina Slyusar 11.55/23.43, 400m: Yelena Nasonkina 52.43, 800m: Yelena Zavadskaya 2:02.06, 1500m: ?, 3000m: Zoya Kaznovskaya 8:58.36, 10000m: Yelena Vyasova 32:56.90, 100mh: Nadezhda Bodrova 12.92, 400mh: Yelena

Pavlova 58.10, HJ: Larisa Serebryanskaya 1.88, LJ: Larisa Berezhnaya 6.93, TJ: Olga Boyko 13.40, SP: Viktoria Pavlysh 18.05, DT: Olga Nikishina 62.32, JT: Irina Kostyuchenko 58.74, Hep: Marina Shcherbina 5993, 5kmW: Tatyana Ragozina 21:22.6.

Aleksandr BAGACH b.21 Nov 1966 1.94m 125kg. Brovary TR.
At SP: WCh: '93- 3; WI: '93- 3; EI: '92- 1; ECp: '89- dq3, '93- 1. USSR champion 1989.
Progression at SP: 1984- 18.44, 1985- 18.79, 1986- 19.36, 1987- 20.01, 1988- 20.65i/20.21, 1989- 21.42dq, 1991- 20.41, 1992- 21.19, 1993- 21.32i/20.85.
Disqualified for a positive drugs test after placing third at the 1989 European Cup, but stepped up to third after Mike Stulce caught for drugs use at 1993 World Championships.

Sergey BUBKA b.4 Dec 1963 Voroshilovgrad (now Lugansk) 1.83m 80kg. OSC Berlin and Donetsk U.
At PV: OG: '88- 1, '92- nh; WCh: '83- 1, '87- 1, '91- 1, '93- 1; WI: '85- 1, '87- 1, '91- 1; EC: '86- 1, '90- 6; EJ: '81- 7=; EI: '85- 1; WCp: '85- 1; ECp: '85- 1, '93- 2. USSR champion 1984. Won GWG 1986. Won overall GP 1991, 1993, 3rd 1987; won PV 1985, 1987, 1991, 1993; 2nd 1989.
16 world pole vault records 1984-92, including the world's first six-metre jump. 18 WIB from 5.81 '84 to 6.15 '93.
Progression at PV: 1975- 2.70, 1976- 3.50, 1977- 3.60, 1978- 4.40, 1979- 4.80, 1980- 5.10, 1981- 5.40, 1982- 5.55, 1983- 5.72, 1984- 5.94, 1985- 6.00, 1986- 6.01, 1987- 6.03, 1988- 6.06, 1989- 6.03i/6.00, 1990- 6.05i/5.90, 1991- 6.10/6.12i, 1992- 6.13, 1993- 6.15i/6.05.
The surprise world champion in 1983 has gone on to dominate the world of pole vaulting, and was not beaten in a championship from then until sixth in Split after injury earlier in 1990. Won his fourth successive World title in 1993 and by the end of 1993 had jumped 6.000m or higher in 31 competitions, and 5.90m plus in 73. On 15 Mar 1991 he became the first vaulter to clear 20 feet when he set his 13th world indoor record at 6.10m.

Vasiliy BUBKA b.26 Nov 1960 Voroshilovgrad 1.84m 76kg. Donetsk U. Teacher. Elder brother of Sergey.
At PV: WCh: '93- 9; EC: '86- 2; WI: '85- 3. USSR champion 1985.
Progression at PV: 1975- 3.25, 1976- 4.20, 1977- 4.90, 1978- 5.05, 1979- 5.20i, 1980- 5.20, 1981- 5.30, 1982- 5.50, 1983- 5.60i, 1984- 5.70i, 1985- 5.85, 1986- 5.80, 1987- 5.75, 1988- 5.86, 1989- 5.80, 1990- 5.81, 1991- 5.82, 1992- 5.80, 1993- 5.70.

Andrey Bulkovskiy: middle distance double at European Cup final

Andrey BULKOVSKIY b.22 Jul 1972 Lvov 1.77m 60kg.
At 1500m (800m): WCh: '93- h; EJ: '91- 2; ECp: '93- 1 (1).
Progression at 1500m: 1986- 4:09.0, 1987- 4:02.0, 1988- 3:56.98, 1989- 3:51.8, 1990- 3:49.40, 1991- 3:45.52, 1992- 3:44.52, 1993- 3:37.51. pbs: 800m 1:47.32 '93, 3000m 8:30.68 '93.
Ethnically Polish. He caused a sensation with sprint finishes to win the European Cup Superleague double in 1993.

Vladimir INOZEMTSEV b.25 May 1964 Krasniy Luch, nr Voroshilovgrad 1.85m 75kg. Lugansk Dyn.
At TJ: WCh: '93- dnq 19; WI: '89- 4; EJ: '83- 9; WCp: '89- 2. USSR champion 1989-90, UKR 1993. USSR triple jump record 1990.
Progression at TJ: 1981- 16.02, 1982- 16.12, 1983- 16.40, 1984- 16.68, 1985- 16.93i/16.86, 1986- 17.43i/17.16, 1987- 17.29i/17.16, 1988- 17.29i/17.04, 1989- 17.62, 1990- 17.90, 1991- 17.11/17.53i, 1992- 16.99i/16.77, 1993- 16.98.

Vitaliy KIRILENKO b.25 Apr 1968 1.92m 80kg.
At LJ: WCh: '93- 3; WSG: '93- 3. UKR champion 1993.
Progression at LJ: 1989- 7.88, 1991- 7.90, 1992- 8.05, 1993- 8.21.

Aleksandr KLIMENKO b.27 Mar 1970 Kiev 1.94m 115kg. Kiev U.
At SP: OG: '92- 8; WCh: '91- 3, '93- dnq 13; WI: '93- 4; WSG: '91- 1, '93- 1; WJ: '88- 1; EJ: '89- 1;

EI: '92- 2. USSR champion 1991, UKR 1992. 2nd GP 1992.
Progression at SP: 1987- 16.69, 1988- 19.18, 1989- 19.38, 1990- 19.63i/19.54, 1991- 20.37, 1992- 20.84, 1993- 20.84i/20.78.

Vitaliy KOLPAKOV b.2 Feb 1972 1.95m 92kg.
At Dec: WJ: '90- 4; EJ: '91- 1; ECp: '93- 5. UKR champion 1992-3.
Progression at Dec: 1989- 6927, 1990- 7384, 1991- 7813, 1992- 7902, 1993- 8297. pbs: 100m 10.97 '93, 400m 47.83 '93, 1500m 4:32.20 '93, 110mh 14.33 '93, HJ 2.14 '91, PV 4.80 '93, LJ 7.80 '93, SP 15.32 '93, DT 46.88 '93, JT 60.02 '93, 1 Hr Dec 7652 '93.

Dmitriy KOVTSUN b.29 Sep 1955 Mukhivka, nr Ternopol 1.91m 116kg. Kiev TR.
At DT: OG: '92- 7; EC: '78- 7, '82- 9; WCp: '81- 4, '92- 6; ECp: '81- 2; WSG: '81- 4.
Progression at DT: 1971- 33.00, 1972- 40.20, 1973- 47.80, 1974- 54.16, 1975- 53.50, 1976- 60.16, 1977- 60.42, 1978- 62.24, 1979- 63.90, 1980- 67.84, 1981- 64.10, 1982- 66.04, 1983- 65.28, 1984- 68.64, 1985- 65.86, 1986- 66.94, 1987- 67.38, 1988- 67.06, 1991- 65.90, 1992- 67.22, 1993- 63.70. pb SP 19.28 '82. Drugs ban 1988.

Vitaliy POPOVICH b.22 Oct 1962 1.72m 66kg. Kiev U.
At 50kmW: WCh: '91- 4, '93- dq; WCp: '89- 6. USSR champion 1991.
Progression at 50kmW: 1984- 4:09:09, 1986- 3:55.50.8t, 1988- 3:46:30, 1989- 3:43:57, 1990- 3:47:12, 1991- 3:44:01, 1992- 3:36:12 sh, 1993- 3:51:44. pbs: 20kmW 1:22:06 '88, 30kmW 2:05:17 '89.

Oleg TVERDOKHLEB b.3 Nov 1969 Dnepropetrovsk 1.84m 70kg. Dnepropetrovsk U.
At TJ: OG: '92- 6; WCh: '93- 6; WSG: '91- 3; WCp: '92- 5; ECp: '93- 3.
Progression at 400mh: 1986- 53.31, 1987- 51.68, 1988- 50.90; 1989- 50.07, 1990- 50.32, 1991- 49.80, 1992- 48.63, 1993- 48.62. pb 400m 46.38 '93.

Vladimir ZINCHENKO b.25 Jul 1959 1.92m 115kg. Zaporozhye SA.
At DT: OG: '92- dnq; WCh: '87- 5, '93- 5; ECp: '93- 3. USSR champion 1987, CIS 1992, UKR 1992-3.
Progression at DT: 1977- 60.60, 1978- 59.96, 1979- 62.02, 1980- 66.14, 1981- 60.74, 1983- 66.70, 1984- 66.16, 1985- 66.46, 1986- 63.26, 1987- 67.58, 1988- 68.88, 1989- 63.20, 1990- 61.14, 1991- 64.64, 1992- 65.90, 1993- 65.28. pb SP 19.37i '83.

Women

Inga BABAKOVA b.27 Jun 1967 Ashkabad 1.81m 55kg. née Butkus. Nikopol U.
At HJ: WCh: '91- 3; WI: '93- 3; ECp: '93- 4=. 3rd GP 1991. UKR champion 1991-2.
Progression at HJ: 1987- 1.89, 1988- 1.92, 1989- 1.89i, 1991- 2.02, 1992- 2.00, 1993- 2.00i/1.96.
Improved ten centimetres in 1991, having had no previous international experience.

Larisa BEREZHNAYA b.28 Feb 1961 Kiev 1.78m 66kg. Kiev SA. PE student.
At LJ: WCh: '91- 3, '93- 2; EC: '90- 4; ECp: '91- 2, '93- 5; WI: '89- 3, '91- 1, '93- 5; EI: '92- 1. Won USSR LJ 1989, UKR 1993.
Progression at LJ: 1980- 6.24, 1983- 6.68, 1984- 6.63, 1985- 6.65i, 1986- 7.19, 1987- 6.90, 1988- 7.07, 1989- 7.20i/7.18w/7.12, 1990- 7.10/7.13w, 1991- 7.24, 1992- 7.08i/7.01/7.15w, 1993- 6.99. pb 100mh 13.6 '79.

Valentina FEDYUSHINA b.18 Feb 1965 Feodosiya 1.90m 92kg. Simferopol SA.
At SP: OG: '88- dnq 13; WCh: '93- 7; WI: '93- 4; EI: '92- 4; ECp: '93- 2.
Progression at SP: 1982- 15.69, 1983- 17.31, 1984- 18.15, 1985- 19.01, 1986- 19.19/18.88, 1987- 20.28, 1988- 21.08, 1989- 17.56i, 1990- 19.90, 1991- 21.60i/19.04, 1992- 20.51i/20.30, 1993- 20.16.

Yelena KHLOPOTNOVA b.4 Aug 1963 Ust-Kamenogorsk 1.72m 64kg. formerly Kokonova, née Stetsura. Kharkov U. Student.
At LJ: WCh: '93- 4; EI: '86- 3, '90- 2; WSG: '91- 3.

Larisa Berezhnaya: second in Stuttgart after taking bronze in Tokyo

USSR champion 1984-5. UKR 1992.
USSR long jump record 1985.
Progression at LJ: 1981- 6.20, 1982- 6.50, 1983- 6.83, 1984- 7.09, 1985- 7.31, 1986- 7.00i, 1987- 6.95, 1988- 7.29, 1989- 6.89i, 1990- 7.06i, 1991- 6.94, 1992- 6.95, 1993- 6.83/7.01w.

Irina KOSTYUCHENKOVA b.11 May 1961 Chelyabinsk 1.71m 78kg. Kharkov U. Teacher.
At JT: OG: '88- 4, '92- dnq 20; WCh: '87- 12, '91- dnq 17; EC: '86- 8; WSG: '87- 1; WCp: '92- 2; ECp: '91- 2, '93- 6. USSR champion 1986, 1988, UKR 1993.
Progression at JT: 1979- 51.96, 1980- 49.72, 1982- 57.68, 1983- 57.80, 1984- 55.22, 1985- 63.24, 1986- 65.56, 1987- 66.72, 1988- 67.00, 1990- 61.72, 1991- 64.80, 1992- 63.88, 1993- 63.68.

Inessa KRAVETS b.5 Oct 1966 Dnepropetrovsk 1.78m 58kg. née Shulyak. Kiev U.
At LJ: OG: '88- 10. '92- 2; EC: '90- 6; WSG: '91- 1. At TJ: WI: '93- 1; EI: '92- 1; ECp: '93- 3. Won GWG 1990. Won USSR LJ 1988, 1990; TJ 1991; CIS LJ 1992. 2nd GP 1990, 1992.
World triple jump record 1991, three WIR 1991-3.
Progression at LJ, TJ: 1982- 6.19, 1983- 6.27, 1984- 6.44, 1985- 6.45i/6.39, 1986- 6.61, 1987- 6.72, 1988- 7.27, 1989- 6.88i/6.86, 1990- 7.10, 14.08; 1991- 6.95, 14.95; 1992- 7.37, 14.41; 1993- 6.87/7.02w, 14.70. pbs: 200m 24.0 '90, HJ 1.75 '83.
Three month drugs ban for stimulants 1993.

Larisa MIKHALCHENKO b.16 May 1963 Lvov 1.80m 93kg. Kharkov Dyn. Teacher.
At DT: OG: '88- 10; WCh: '87- 7, '91- 3, '93- 10; EJ: '81- 3; ECp: '91- 2, '93- 2. Won USSR DT 1991.
Progression at DT: 1979- 47.96, 1980- 52.14, 1981- 54.74, 1982- 56.28, 1983- 62.00, 1984- 58.22, 1985- 64.92, 1986- 64.48, 1987- 64.88, 1988- 70.80, 1989- 63.22, 1990- 65.02, 1991- 69.20, 1982- 67.08, 1993- 63.90.

Viktoria PAVLYSH b.15 Jan 1969 1.74m 80kg.
At SP: OG: '92- 8. 3rd GP 1993. Ukrainian champion 1993.
Progression at SP: 1986- 15.73, 1987- 16.48, 1988- 16.28, 1989- 17.28, 1990- 17.86, 1991- 18.76, 1992- 19.66, 1993- 19.22.

Zhanna TARNOPOLSKAYA b.6 Jul 1972 Nezhina, nr Chernigov 1.66m 52kg. Kiev Sp.
At 100m/200m: WCh: '93- sf/-; EJ: '91- 1/1/4R; ECp: '93- 3/4. At 60m: WI: '93- 3; EI: '92- 1.
WIR 50m at 6.09 for a few minutes in 1993.
Progression at 100m: 1988- 11.5, 1989- 11.64/11.5, 1990- 11.99, 1991- 11.29/11.0, 1992- 11.17, 1993- 11.08. pbs: 50m 6.09i '93, 60m 7.07i '93, 200m 22.79 '93.

Olga TURCHAK b.5 Mar 1967 Alma-Ata 1.90m 60kg. Odessa VS. Student.
At HJ: OG: '88- 4, '92- 13=; EC: '86- 3, '90- 10; WI: '87- 8; EJ: '85- 2. USSR champion 1986.
World junior high jump record 1984.
Progression at HJ: 1983- 1.84, 1984- 1.96, 1985- 1.95, 1986- 2.01, 1987- 1.94i/1.92, 1988- 2.00, 1989- 1.94, 1990- 1.96, 1992- 1.95, 1993- 1.95.

Inna YEVSEYEVA b.14 Aug 1964 1.82m 62kg. Zhitomir U. Student.
At 800m: OG: '88- 6, '92- 4; WCh: '91- h; WSG: '89- 3, '91- 1; EI: '92- 2.
WIR 1000m 1992.
Progression at 800m: 1983- 2:02.7, 1985- 2:02.7, 1986- 2:00.6, 1988- 1:56.0, 1989- 1:59.75, 1990- 2:01.49, 1991- 1:58.30, 1992- 1:57.20, 1993- 1:59.03. pbs: 400m 50.80/50.6 '86, 600m 1:25.87i '88, 1000m 2:33.93i '92, 1500m 4:12.6 '88, 400mh 55.85 '86.

UNITED KINGDOM

Governing body: British Athletics Federation, 225a Bristol Road, Edgbaston, Birmingham, B5 7UB. Founded 1991 (replacing BAAB, founded 1932). The Amateur Athletic Association was founded in 1880 and the Women's Amateur Athletic Association in 1922.

National Championships (first were English Championships 1863-79): UK Nationals first held in 1977. **1993 UK Champions**: **Men**: 100m: Linford Christie 10.26, 200m: John Regis 20.21w, 400m: Du'aine Ladejo 46.14, 800m: Martin Steele 1:46.34, 1500m: Curtis Robb 3:39.58, 3000m: Spencer Barden 8:01.86, 5000m: Jon Brown 13:39.68, Half Mar: Paul Evans 61:45, 3000mSt: Spencer Duval 8:32.77, 110mh: Andy Tulloch 13.70, 400mh: Gary Cadogan 49.80, HJ: Dalton Grant 2.28, PV: Neil Winter 5.35, LJ: Ian Simpson 7.55, TJ: Tosi Fasinro 17.30w, SP: Paul Edwards 19.06, DT: Darrin Morris 57.70, HT: Paul Head 71.48, JT: Mick Hill 86.94. **Women**: 100m: Bev Kinch 11.37, 200m: Katharine Merry 23.20, 400m: Phylis Smith 51.70, 800m: Kelly Holmes 2:00.86, 1500m: Jayne Spark 4:14.66, Half Mar: Katherine Bailey 76:41, 100mh: Jackie Agyepong 13.22, 400mh: Gowry Retchakan 56.62, HJ: Debbie Marti 1.90, LJ: Fiona May 6.67w, TJ: Michelle Griffith 13.72, SP: Myrtle Augee 17.12, DT: Jacqueline McKernan 56.72, HT: Lorraine Shaw 55.14, JT: Sharon Gibson 56.90.

National Road Walk Champions: **Men**: 20kmW: Andrew Penn 1:25:57, 50kmW: Les Morton 4:03:55. **Women**: 5kmW: Joanne Pope 25:13, 10kmW: Victoria Larby 47:51.

AAA Championships first held in 1880

(women 1922). **1993 Champions: Men**: 100m: Linford Christie 10.13, 200m: Jeff Williams USA 20.47, 400m: Kennedy Ochieng KEN 45.32, 800m: Martin Steele 1:47.83, 1500m: Matthew Yates 3:38.75, 3000m: Joseph Keter KEN 7:56.39, 5000m: Jon Brown 13:35.67, 10000m: Paul Evans 28:17.49; Half Mar: Steve Brace 65:00, Mar: Eamonn Martin 2:10:50, 3000mSt: Colin Walker 8:33.45, 110mh: Colin Jackson 13.15, 400mh: Gary Cadogan 50.60, HJ: Tim Forsyth AUS 2.32, PV: SimonArkell AUS 5.60, LJ: Fred Salle 7.72, TJ: Francis Agyepong 16.05, SP: Matt Simson 18.79, DT: Rob Weir 57.44, HT: Paul Head 72.32, JT: Colin Mackenzie 81.44, Dec: Barry Walsh IRL 7275, 10000mW: Martin Bell 42:29.63. **Women**: 100m: Bev Kinch 11.44, 200m: Cathy Freeman AUS 22.71, 400m: Phylis Smith 52.15, 800m: Kelly Holmes 2:02.69, 1500m: Alison Wyeth 4:11.03, 3000m: Yvonne Murray 8:52.28, 5000m: Suzanne Rigg 15:57.67, 10000m: Vikki McPherson 33:49.29, Mar: Katrin Dörre GER 2:27:09, 100mh: Sally Gunnell 13.08, 400mh: Jacqui Parker 58.14, HJ: Debbie Marti 1.86, PV: Kate Staples 3.20, LJ: National e Espegren NOR 13.43, SP: Myrtle Augee 17.24, DT: Daniela Costian AUS 61.58, HT: Debbie Sosimenko AUS 56.86, JT: Shelley Holroyd 60.10, Hep: Clova Court 5957, 5000mW: Vicky Lupton 22:34.50.

Stephen BACKLEY b.12 Feb 1969 Sidcup 1.96m 95kg. Cambridge H. Postponed sports science studies at Loughborough University.
At JT: OG: '92- 3; WCh: '91- dnq 15, '93- 4; EC: '90- 1; CG: '90- 1; WJ: '88- 2; EJ: '87- 1; WCp: '89- 1; ECp: '89- 1; WSG: '89- 1, '91- 1. Won GP 1989 (3rd overall), UK 1988-90; AAA 1989, 1992.
Three world javelin records 1990-2, world junior record 1988. Eight UK and Commonwealth records 1989-92.
Progression at JT (old): 1985- 64.34, 1986- 64.98 (69.74), 1987- 78.16, 1988- 79.50, 1989- 85.90, 1990- 90.98, 1991- 91.36, 1992- 91.46, 1993- 85.10.
The first British male thrower to set a world record: 89.58 in Stockholm with a Sandvik javelin, and 90.98 at Crystal Palace on his second throw with a Németh model, both 1990. When these were banned at the end of 1991 his 89.58 was reinstated as the world record and in New Zealand in1992 he achieved the first 90m throw with the revised javelin specification.

Steve Backley: short season nearly ended with medal

Roger BLACK b.31 Mar 1966 Portsmouth 1.90m 79kg. Team Solent.
At 400m/R- 4x400m relay: OG: '92- sf/3R; WCh: '87- 2R, '91- 2/1R; EC: '86- 1/1R, '90- 1/1R; CG: '86- 1/1R; EJ: '85- 1/1R; ECp: '87- 2/2R, '91- 1/1R. Won UK 200m 1987, 400m 1990, 1992. Won 400m GP 1991.
UK 400m record and European 300m best 1986, Three European & Commonwealth 4x400mR records 1987-91.
Progression at 400m: 1984- 47.7, 1985- 45.36, 1986- 44.59, 1987- 44.99, 1989- 46.2, 1990- 44.91, 1991- 44.62, 1992- 44.72, 1993- 45.86. pbs: 100m 10.57 '91, 10.4 '87; 200m 20.60 '90, 300m 32.08 '86, 600m 1:16.2 '91, 800m 1:52.1 '90.
Started his international career with six gold medals in three international championships in 1985-6. Missed the 1987 World 400m (though he ran in the relay), 1988 and most of 1989 through injury, but returned to another European double; his four European gold medals equalling the men's record.

Linford CHRISTIE b.2 Apr 1960 St.Andrews, Jamaica 1.89m 77kg. Thames Valley Harriers.
At 100m/R- 4x100m relay (200m): OG: '88- 2/2R (4), '92- 1/4R (sf); WCh: '87- 3, '91- 4/3R, '93- 1/2R; EC: '86- 1/3R (sf), '90- 1/2R (3); CG: '86- 2, '90- 1/1R; WCp: '89- 1/2R, '92- 1 (2); ECp: '87- 1 (1), '89- 1/1R, '91- 1/1R, '93- 1/1R. At 200m: WI: '91- 2; EI: '86- 1, '88- 3. At 60m: WI: '91- 2; EI: '88- 1, '90- 1. Won UK 100m 1985, 1987, 1990-3; 200m 1985 (tie), 1988; AAA 100m 1986, 1988-9, 1991-3; 200m 1988. 3rd GP 100m 1992.
European records: 100m (3) 1988-93, 4x100m 1993, indoor 60m 1990. Commonwealth

records: 100m (2) 1991-3, 4x100m (4) 1989-93. UK records: five 100m 1986-93, one 200m 1988. WIR 4x200mR 1991.
Progression at 100m, 200m: 1977- 10.9, 23.2; 1978- 22.5; 1979- 10.7/10.6w, 21.89/21.8; 1980- 10.73/10.6/10.5w, 22.0/21.4w; 1981- 10.85/10.7, 21.6/21.70i; 1982- 10.50, 21.38/21.2; 1983- 10.46/10.4, 21.71i/21.31w; 1984- 10.44/10.31w, 21.0/21.44; 1985- 10.42/10.20w, 21.37i; 1986- 10.04, 20.51; 1987- 10.03, 20.48; 1988- 9.97, 20.09; 1989- 10.10/10.08w, 20.51; 1990- 10.02/9.93w, 20.33; 1991- 9.92/9.90w, 20.43; 1992- 9.96, 20.25; 1993- 9.87, 20.39/20.19w. pbs: 60m 6.43+ '91, 6.51i '90; 300m 33.80 '88, 400m 47.75 '91.
After a late start to an international sprinting career, become established as Europe's fastest man and reached the pinnacle of sprinting fame with gold medals at the 1992 Olympics and 1993 World Championships, where he missed tying the world record for 100m by a tiny margin. His 21 major championships medals (eight gold) is a British male record; elevated a place at 1987 Worlds and 1988 Olympics following the disqualification of Ben Johnson. In October 1993 his home track, the West London Stadium was renamed as the Linford Christie Stadium.

Steve CRAM b.14 Oct 1960 Gateshead 1.86m 69kg. Jarrow & Hebburn.
At 1500m (800m): OG: '80- 8, '84- 2, '88- 4 (qf); WCh: '83- 1, '87- 8, '91- sf, '93- sf; CG: '78- h, '82- 1, '86- 1 (1); EC: '82- 1, '86- 1 (3), '90- 5; ECp: '81- 3, '83- 1, '85- 1, '87- 2. At 3000m: EJ: '79- 1. Won AAA 1500m 1981-3; 800m 1984, 1986, 1988; UK 5000m 1989.
World records at 1500m, 1M and 2000m 1985, and on 4 x 800m relay team 1982.
Progression at 1500m/1M: 1973- 4:31.5, 1974- 4:22.3, 1975- 4:13.9, 1976- 4:07.1, 1977- 3:47.7, 1978- 3:40.09/3:57.43, 1979- 3:42.5/3:57.03, 1980- 3:34.74/3:53.8, 1981- 3:34.81/3:49.95, 1982- 3:33.66/3:49.90, 1983- 3:31.66/3:52.56, 1984- 3:33.13/3:49.65, 1985- 3:29.67/3:46.32, 1986- 3:30.15/3:48.31, 1987- 3:31.43/3:50.08, 1988- 3:30.95/3:48.85, 1989- 3:35.3/3:51.58, 1990- 3:33.03/3:53.99, 1991- 3:34.18/3:52.11, 1992- 3:42.24/3:58.7, 1993- 3:35.63/3:52.17. pbs: 400m 49.1 '82, 600m 1:16.79 '83, 800m 1:42.88 '85, 1000m 2:12.88 '85, 2000m 4:51.39 '85, 3000m 7:43.1 '83, 2M 8:14.93 '83, 5000m 13:28.58 '89, 10km Rd 28:46 '92, Half Mar 65:33 '92.
World age 17 mile best in 1978. In 1986 became third man to win Commonwealth 800m/1500m double. Has increasingly suffered from calf and other leg injuries.

Robert DENMARK b.23 Nov 1968 Billericay 1.74m 60kg. Basildon. Sports sciences graduate of Newcastle Polytechnic.
At 5000m: OG: '92- 7; WCh: '91- 9, '93- 9; ECp: '93- 1. At 3000m: WI: '91- 3. Won AAA Indoor 3000m 1990-91, rd 10km 1992.
Progression at 1500m: 1990- 14:08.02, 1991- 13:13.01, 1992- 13:10.24, 1993- 13:16.48. pbs: 800m 1:48.84 '90, 1500m 3:38.34 '92, 1M 3:55.38 '90, 3000m 7:39.55 '93, 2M 8:21.97 '91, road 10km 28:36 '92.
At the 1991 world indoors he improved his 3000m best from 7:54.41 (23rd on the UK indoor all-time list) to 6th place with 7:48.92 in his heat, and then he took 2.2 seconds off Jack Buckner's British record in the final.

Jonathan EDWARDS b.10 May 1966 London 1.81m 70kg. Gateshead. Physics graduate from Durham University.
At TJ: OG: '88- dnq 23, '92- dnq; WCh: '93- 3; CG: '90- 2; WI: '93- 6; WCp: '89- 3, '92- 1; ECp: '93- 2. Won UK 1989, 1992; AAA 1989.
Progression at TJ: 1983- 13.84, 1984- 14.87/15.01w, 1985- 15.09, 1986- 16.05, 1987- 16.35, 1988- 16.74, 1989- 17.28, 1990- 16.51/16.93w, 1991- 17.43, 1992- 17.34, 1993- 17.44/17.70w. pbs: 60m 6.77i '93, 100m 10.7/10.80 '92, 10.63w '90, 10.6w '89; LJ 7.41/7.45w '92.
A committed Christian previously refused to compete on Sundays, thus passing the 1991 World Championships, but did so in 1993.

Peter ELLIOTT b.9 Oct 1962 Rawmarsh, Rotherham 1.81m 67kg. Rotherham.
At 1500m: OG: '88- 2; EC: '90- 4; CG: '90- 1; ECp: '91- 1. At 800m: OG: '84- sf, '88- 4; WCh: '83- 4, '87- 2; CG: '86- 3; EI: '83- 2; EJ: '81- 4; ECp: '83- 3. Won UK 800m 1983-4, 1986; 3000m 1991; AAA 800m 1982, 1987; 1500m 1984, 1988.
Ran on world record 4 x 800m team 1982. WIB 1500m 3:34.20 '90.
Progression at 800m, 1500m: 1975- 2:20.8; 1976- 2:05.9; 1977- 2:01.9; 1978- 1:52.05; 1979- 1:50.7; 1980- 1:51.3; 1981- 1:47.35, 3:53.3; 1982- 1:45.61, 3:49.1; 1983- 1:43.98; 1984- 1:45.49, 3:36.97; 1985- 1:49.4, 3:39.79; 1986- 1:44.06, 3:35.62; 1987- 1:43.41, 3:33.23; 1988- 1:44.12, 3:32.94; 1989- 1:47.10, 3:37.6, 3:52.93M; 1990- 1:42.97, 3:32.69; 1991- 1:44.27, 3:32.94; 1992- 1:46.52, 3:54.65M. pbs: 400m 48.2 '84, 600m 1:16.6 '83, 1000m 2:16.30 '90, 1M 3:49.20 '88, 2000m 4:52.82 '87, 3000m 8:07.51 '91.
In 1984 became the first British runner to beat Seb Coe at 1500m since 1976. Missed most of 1985, 1989 and 1991-2 seasons and all of 1993 through injury. Had a magnificent Olympics in 1988 despite a groin injury. After Commonwealth gold he was brought down in a heat of the 1990 European 1500m, but allowed to run in the final, although the ensuing controversy undoubtedly affected him. Won the 5th Avenue Mile in 1989 and 1990, the latter in 3:47.83.

Dalton GRANT b.8 Apr 1966 London 1.86m 73kg. Haringey. Part-time social worker.
At HJ: OG: '88- 7=, '92- dnq; WCh: '91- 4, '93- dnq 14=; EC: '90- 4=; WI: '87- 8=, '89- 4, '93- 4=; EI: '89- 2; CG: '86- 7, '90- 2; EJ: '85- 6; WCp: '89- 2; ECp: '89- 1, '91- 1. Won AAA 1989-90, UK 1990-1, 1993.
Nine UK high jump records 1988-91, three Commonwealth records 1989-91. Four UK indoor records 1989 to 2.35, equalling the Commonwealth record.
Progression at HJ: 1981- 1.90, 1982- 2.10, 1983- 2.10, 1984- 2.16, 1985- 2.22, 1986- 2.20, 1987- 2.28i/2.25, 1988- 2.31, 1989- 2.35i/2.34, 1990- 2.34, 1991- 2.36, 1992- 2.28, 1993- 2.34. pbs: 60mh 8.4i '92, 110mh 15.38 '91, LJ 7.00/7.14w '93, TJ 14.93 '86.
In 1991 from a season's best of 2.20 he won the European Cup with 2.30. Then further moderate form until Tokyo, where he entered at 2.31, 1 cm above his year's best, cleared that, passed 2.34 and then cleared 2.36!

David GRINDLEY b.29 Oct 1972 1.88m 79kg. Wigan H. Engineering student at Manchester Metropolitan University.
At 400m/4x400mR: OG: '92- 6/3R; WJ: '90- 2R; EJ: '91- 1/1R; EI: '92- 3; ECp: '93- 1/1R. Won GP 1993.
UK 400m record 1992.
Progression at 400m: 1988- 49.6, 1989- 50.1, 1990- 46.39, 1991- 45.41, 1992- 44.47, 1993- 44.53. pbs: 200m 21.50 '92, 20.89w '93; 300m 32.45 '93, 600m 1:17.1 '91, 800m 1:52.7 '91.

David Grindley: missed worlds but won GP

Dramatic improvement in 1990, starting with nearly two seconds off his 400m pb with 48.0 and further with international wins in 47.52, 47.26 and 46.39. In 1991 he won double European Junior gold and in 1992 broke the British record to make the Olympic final. Had to miss 1993 Worlds through injury.

Tom HANLON b.20 May 1967 Iserlohn, FR Germany 1.83m 69kg. Racing Club, Edinburgh. Graphic artist.
At 3kmSt: OG: '92- 6; WCh: '91- 11, '93- 15; EC: '90- CG: '86- 10, '90- 12; WCp: '89- 5; ECp: '89- 4, '91- 6. At 2kmSt: WJ: '86- 4; EJ: '85- 4. Won AAA 3000m 1991.
Progression at 3000mSt: 1985- 8:52.98, 1986- 8:47.49, 1987- 8:27.60, 1988- 8:20.73, 1989- 8:16.52, 1990- 8:16.31, 1991- 8:12.58 1992- 8:13.65, 1993- 8:19.99. pbs: 1500m 3:38.08 '92, 1M 4:00.1 '87, 3000m 7:51.31 '92, 2M 8:37.67 '87, 5000m 13:39.95 '89, 2kmSt 5:21.77 '92.

Michael HILL b.22 Oct 1964 Leeds 1.90m 95kg. Leeds City. Student.
At JT: OG: '88- dnq 20, '92- 11; WCh: '87- 7, '91- 5, '93- 3; EC: '86- 8, '90- 4; CG: '86- 2, '90- 2; EJ: '83- 11; WCp: '92- 5; ECp: '87- 4, '91- 6, '93- 2. Won UK 1985-7, 1992-3; AAA 1987, 1990-1. 2nd GP 1987, 3rd 1993.
UK and Commonwealth javelin record 1987.
Progression at JT: 1980- 56.32, 1981- 59.14, 1982- 64.72, 1983- 74.36, 1984- 71.08, 1985- 82.30, 1986- 82.04; new: 1986- 78.56, 1987- 85.24, 1988- 81.30, 1989- 82.56, 1990- 85.88, 1991- 86.32, 1992- 85.32, 1993- 86.94.
Earned World bronze 1993 after disqualification of Dmitriy Polyunin. Operations on left knee in 1989 and March 1990. A seven handicap golfer.

Colin JACKSON b.18 Feb 1967 Cardiff 1.82m 73kg. Brecon.
At 110mh: OG: '88- 2, '92- 7; WCh: '87- 3, '91- sf, '93- 1/2 4x100mR; EC: '90- 1; CG: '86- 2, '90- 1; WJ: '86- 1; EJ: '85- 2; WCp: '89- 2, '92- 1; ECp: '87- 2, '89- 1, '91- 1, '93- 1. Won UK 1986, 1989-90, 1992; AAA 1986, 1988-90, 1992-3. Won GP 1993, 3rd 1989. At 60mh: WI: '87- 4, '89- 2, '93- 2; EI: '87- 2, '89- 1.
World 110mh record 1993, 7 European 8 Commonwealth and 9 UK records at 110mh 1988-93; 8 UK, 3 Commonwealth & European records at 60mh toW IR 7.36 '94. European junior 110mh record 1986. World best 200mh 1991.
Progression at 110mh: 1984- 13.92, 1985- 13.69, 1986- 13.44/13.42w, 1987- 13.37, 1988- 13.11, 1989- 13.11/12.95w, 1990- 13.08/12.8w, 1991- 13.09, 1992- 13.04, 1993- 12.91. pbs: 60m 6.55i '94, 100m 10.29 '90, 200m 21.19/21.0 '88, 21.18w '89; 60mh 7.36i '94, 200mh 22.63 '91, HJ 1.81 '82, LJ 7.96w '86, 7.56 '85; JT 52.86 '84.

World number one in 1992 with record 15 sub-13.20 times although a second round injury held him back to 7th in the Olympic final. Had a majestic season in 1993 with 13 times under 13.20 and the world record to win his first World title. Injury cost him the chance of medal at the 1986 European Championships, and he had operations on right knee 1990 and on left in 1991, after he had to withdraw from World Champs semis following a warm-up accident.

Anthony JARRETT b.13 Aug 1968 Enfield, London 1.88m 80kg. Haringey. Part-time community worker.
At 110mh/R - 4x100m relay: OG: '88- 6, '92- 4/4R; WCh: '91- 3/3R, '93- 2/2R; EC: '90- 2; CG: '90- 2 (resR); EJ: '87- 1/1R; ECp: '89- 1R, '93- 1R. UK champion 1987-8. 2nd GP 1993. At 60mh: EI: '90- 2.
Progression at 110mh: 1985- 15.1, 1986- 14.14/14.06w, 1987- 13.72, 1988- 13.45/13.35w, 1989- 13.31, 1990- 13.21, 1991- 13.13, 1992- 13.17/13.04w, 1993- 13.00. pbs: 100m 10.55 '93, 10.42w '87, 200m 20.67 '90, 60mh 7.50i '90, 200mh 22.77w '91, 23.8 '88.

Tom McKEAN b.27 Oct 1963 1.83m 71kg. Motherwell AC.
At 800m: OG: '88- qf, '92- sf; WCh: '87- 8, '91 -h, '93- 8; WI: '93- 1; EC: '86- 2, '90- 1; CG: '86- 2, '90- 7 (2 4x400mR); EI: '90- 1; WCp: '89- 1; ECp: '85- 1, '87- 1, '89- 1, '91- 1, '93- 3. Won UK 1985, AAA 1991. Won GP 1988.
Progression at 800m: 1977- 2:05.0, 1978- 1:58.6, 1979- 1:55.3, 1980- 1:56.15, 1981- 1:53.2, 1982- 1:49.01, 1983- 1:49.48, 1984- 1:48.40, 1985- 1:46.05, 1986- 1:44.61, 1987- 1:44.45, 1988- 1:45.05, 1989- 1:43.88, 1990- 1:44.44, 1991- 1:44.20, 1992- 1:44.75, 1993- 1:45.66. pbs: 200m 22.3 '82, 400m 47.60 '86, 1000m 2:18.91 '85, 1500m 3:45.39 '91.
Has a splendid European record with indoor and outdoor titles, and a men's record four successive European Cup victories. His first in 1985 came after 34 successive wins at 800m, mostly in minor races. He has met with disaster elsewhere. In the Worlds his eighth place in the 1987 was his only loss that year. and in 1991 he coasted in his heat, was pipped on the post and did not even qualify for the semis. He was disqualified in the 1988 Olympic qf for pushing,

Eamonn MARTIN b. 9 Oct 1958 Basildon 1.82m 68kg. Basildon. Components testing engineer at Ford Motors.
At 10000m: OG: '88- dnf, '92- h; WCh: '91- 15; CG: '90- 1; ECp: '91- 1, '93- dnf. At 5000m: OG: '84- 13, '88- sf; WCh: '83- sf; EC: '90- 13. Won GP 1988. Won English CC 1984 & 1992, AAA 5000m 1988, 1990-1; 10000m 1989, 1992.
Progression at 5000m, 10000m: 1979- 14:47.8; 1983- 13:20.94; 1984- 13:23.33; 1985- 13:44.07; 1987- 13:39.12; 1988- 13:22.88, 27:23.06; 1989- 13:17.84, 28:13.69; 1990- 13:29.62, 28:08.57; 1991- 13:32.99, 28:00.53 1992- 13:28.18, 28:02.56; 1993- 13:50.90. pbs: 800m 1:52.00 '84, 1500m 3:40.54 '83, 1M 3:59.30 '83, 2000m 5:01.09 '84, 3000m 7:40.94 '83, 2M 8:18.98 '88, Mar 2:10:50 '93.
Won English Schools junior cross-country 1973, and intermediate 1500m 1975. Had operations on both Achilles and missed most of 1985 and 1986 seasons. After good road race results made the fastest ever track début at 10000m to smash the ten-year-old British record in Oslo 1988. Took his first major medal with the 1990 Commonwealth 10000m gold. Won the London Marathon on his début at the distance in 1993.

Richard NERURKAR b.6 Jan 1964 Wolverhampton 1.77m 61kg. Bingley H. Masters degree at Harvard University, USA, formerly at Oxford University. Formerly a language teacher.
At 10000m: OG: '92- 17; WCh: '91- 5; EC: '90- 5. At Mar: WCp: '93- 1. Won AAA 10000m 1990, English CC 1990-1.
Progression at 5000m, 10000m: 1987- 13:45.45, 28:57.40; 1988- 13:37.3i, 28:29.0; 1989- 13:27.86i/13:29.11, 28:37.14; 1990- 13:23.36, 28:05.16; 1991- 13:31.88, 27:57.14; 1992- 13:28.94, 28:07.44; 1993- 13:30.06, 27:40.03. pbs: 1500m 3:48.7 '90, 1M 4:05.1 '90, 3000m 7:48.00 '92, 2M 8:32.1 '90, Half Mar 61:33 '92, Mar: 2:10:03 '93.
He was a useful runner while at school (won Northern Schools at age 14) but did not make a major impression until after graduation. Excelled for fifth places in European and World Championships. In 1993 he won his first two marathons, at Hamburg (2:10:57 on his début) and the World Cup.

John REGIS b.13 Oct 1966 Lewisham, London 1.81m 88kg. Belgrave H.
At 200m/R- 4x100mR (/4x400mR) (100m): OG: '88- sf/2R (h), '92: 6/4R/3R; WCh: '87- 3, '91- sf/3R/1R, '93- 2/2R; EC: '90- 1/2R/1R (3); CG: '86- 8, 90- 2/1R (7); WCp: '89- 2R; ECp: '89- 1/1R, '91- 2/1R, '93- 1/1R/1R; WI: '89- 1; EI: '87- 3, '89- 2. Won UK 200m 1985 (=), 1986, 1991, 1993; 100m 1988; AAA 200m 1986-7, 1990, 1992. 3rd GP 200m 1991, 2nd 1993. At 100m: EJ: '85- 3/1R.
Three UK 200m records 1987-93. European & Commonwealth 4x400m record 1990, Commonwealth 4x100m records 1989 and 1990. WIR 4x200m 1991. European 300m bests 1991, 1992.
Progression at 100m, 200m: 1982- 11.3, 22.6; 1983- 11.1, 22.0; 1984- 10.8, 21.31; 1985- 10.51/10.45w, 20.78; 1986- 10.43, 20.41; 1987- 10.37,

Steve Smith: world indoor and outdoor bronzes

20.18; 1988- 10.31, 20.32; 1989- 10.39, 20.35; 1990- 10.20/10.07w, 20.11; 1991- 10.22, 20.12; 1992- 10.32, 20.09; 1993- 10.15, 19.94. pbs: 60m 6.71i '91, 300m 31.67 '92, 400m 45.48 '93, 200mh 22.79 '91, TJ 14.28 '82.
In 1987 he very nearly won the World title, as he led at 195m. He ran a 43.93 third leg to ensure Britain's 4x400 gold at the 1990 Europeans, when he won four medals, the most ever by a man at one Championships. Cousin of soccer international Cyrille Regis.

Jonathan RIDGEON b.14 Feb 1967 Bury St Edmunds 1.83m 75kg. Belgrave H. Graduate of Cambridge University.
At 110mh: OG: '88- 5; WCh: '87- 2; EC: '86- 6; CG: '86- 5; WSG: '87- 1; WJ: '86- 2 (1 at 4x100mR); EJ: '85- 1. Won AAA 1987. At 60mh: WI: '85- 2; EI: '88- 2. At 400mh/4x400m: WCp: '92- 2/3R.
Three UK 110mh records 1987. European junior record 1985.
Progression at 110mh, 400mh: 1984- 13.92, 1985- 13.46, 1986- 13.66, 1987- 13.29, 1988- 13.52/13.45w, 1991- 13.90, 1992- 13.62, 48.73; 1993- 50.42. pbs: 100m 10.49 '86, 10.3w '85; 200m 21.08 '87, 20.9 '92; 400m 46.75 '92, 60mh 7.56i '88, 200mh 22.9w '87, 23.00w/23.2 '87, LJ 7.35 '87.
Following his European Junior title and world age-18 best in 1985, was overtaken by arch-rival Colin Jackson in 1986, but was the UK male athlete of the year in 1987. Olympic finalist despite virus infection 1988. Missed the 1989 outdoor and 1990 seasons when he had operations on both Achilles tendons. Switched successfully to 400m hurdling in 1992, improving from 51.30 on his début on 11 July to 48.73 on 6 September. Injured in second race in 1993.

Curtis ROBB b.7 Jun 1972 Liverpool 1.86m 66kg. Liverpool H. Medical student at Sheffield University.
At 800m: OG: '92- 6; WCh: '93- 4; WSG: '91- 2=; EJ: '91- 1. At 1500m: ECp: '93- 5. Won UK and AAA 800m 1992, UK 1500m 1993.
Progression at 800m, 1500m: 1988- 4:00.3, 1989- 3:50.4; 1990- 1:48.36, 3:46.9; 1991- 1:46.63, 3:49.69; 1992- 1:45.16, 1993- 1:44.92, 3:38.56. pbs: 400m 48.9 '93, 1000m 2:18.99 '92
AAA junior champion at 1500m 1990-1.

David SHARPE b.8 Jul 1967 Jarrow 1.81m 66kg. Jarrow & Hebburn AC.
At 800m: EC: '90- 2; EJ: '85- 8; WJ: '86- 1 (5 at 1500m); EI: '88- 1; WCp: '92- 1. Won UK 1990-1.
Progression at 800m: 1984- 1:51.02, 1985- 1:48.47, 1986- 1:45.64, 1987- 1:46.09, 1988- 1:45.70, 1989- 1:47.20, 1990- 1:45.12, 1991- 1:46.63, 1992- 1:43.98, 1993- 1:46.09. pbs: 400m 48.04 '90, 1000m 2:17.79 '92, 1500m 3:42.7 '85, 1M 3:59.02 '90.
UK junior records at 800m and 1000m in 1986. Has a devastating finishing kick.

Steve SMITH b.29 Mar 1973 Liverpool 1.86m 70kg. Liverpool H.
At HJ: OG: '92- 12; WCh: '91- dnq 29, '93- 3; WI: '93- 3; WJ: '90- dnq, '92- 1; EJ: '91- 1; ECp: '93- 6. Won AAA 1992.
World junior record 1992, two British & Commonwealth records 1992-3.
Progression at HJ: 1987- 1.84, 1988- 1.99, 1989- 2.09, 1990- 2.25, 1991- 2.29, 1992- 2.37, 1993- 2.37, 1994- 2.38i. pbs: 100m 11.2 '93, LJ 7.51 '92, 7.65w '93; TJ 13.61 '90.
Improved UK junior record from 2.31 to 2.33, 2.35 and 2.37 in taking the 1992 World Junior ttitle. Cleared 2.37 again for bronze at World indoors and out 1993. Gambled at Olympics, when he very nearly won a medal, narrowly failing at 2.34, but actually clearing only 2.24.

Martin STEELE b.30 Sep 1962 Huddersfield 1.70m 66kg. Longwood H. Residential care officer.
At 800m: WCh: '93- sf; EI: '92- 4; Won AAA and UK 1993.
Progression at 800m: 1985- 1:51.8, 1986- 1:49.0, 1987- 1:46.66, 1988- 1:46.95, 1989- 1:47.1, 1990- 1:46.65, 1991- 1:46.63, 1992- 1:46.26, 1993- 1:43.84. pbs: 200m 22.3 '88, 400m 47.4 '90, 600m 1:16.0 '93, 1000m 2:19.50i '91, 1500m 3:42.8 '92.
Took up athletics at the age of 21. A tough competitor he has found it hard to break into the British team outdoors, although he won the

AAA indoor 800m in 1991-2. Made a great breakthrough in 1993, taking a second off his pb with 1:45.8 in Belfast then winning in Oslo in 1:43.84 and taking both national titles.

Matthew YATES b.4 Feb 1969 Rochford 1.90m 76kg. Newham & Essex Beagles.
At 1500m: OG: '92- sf; WCh: '91- 10, '93- 6; EI: '92- 1. At 800m: EC: '90-8; CG: '90- 3. Won AAA 1500m 1991, 1993. 3rd GP 1993.
Progression at 800m, 1500m: 1985- 4:01.73; 1986- 1:53.1; 1987- 1:51.2, 3:51.3; 1988- 1:50.69, 3:51.2; 1989- 1:47.58, 3:44.17; 1990- 1:46.25, 3:35.15; 1991- 1:47.18, 3:34.00; 1992- 1:45.05, 3:38.55; 1993- 1:46.00, 3:35.04. pbs: 1000m 2:16.34 '90, 1M 3:52.75 '93, 3000m 7:50.82i '93.
Won the 5th Avenue Mile 1991.

Women

Sally GUNNELL b.29 Jul 1966 Chigwell 1.67m 56kg. Essex Ladies. Solicitor's clerk. Married Jon Bigg (800m: 1:48.40 '85) 19 Oct 1992.
At 400mh (R- 4x400m relay): OG: '88- 5, '92- 1/3R; WCh: '91- 2/4R, '93- 1/3R; EC: '90- 6/3R; CG: '90- 1/1R; WCp: '89- 3; ECp: '89- 2/3R, '91- 2/3R, '93- 1/5R. 2nd GP 1989 & 1991. At 100mh: OG: '88- sf; WCh: '87- sf; EC: '86- ht; CG: '86- 1, '90- 2; EJ: '83- sf (13 Hep). At 400m: WI: '89- 6; EI: '88- 4, '89- 1, '90- 4. Won UK 100mh 1986, AAA 100mh 1986-9, 1991-3; 400mh 1988.
World 400mh record 1993, Commonwealth 1991. UK records: eight at 400mh 1988-93, one 100mh 1988, four 4x400mR 1990-1.
Progression at 100mh, 400mh: 1982- 15.0; 1983- 13.71; 1984- 13.30; 1985- 13.48/13.46w; 1986- 13.11; 1987- 13.01, 59.9; 1988- 12.82/12.80w, 54.03; 1989- 13.26, 54.64; 1990- 13.12, 55.38; 1991- 13.02, 53.16; 1992- 13.13, 53.23; 1993- 13.08, 52.74. pbs: 100m 11.83 '90, 11.8 '87, 11.79w '86; 200m 23.30 '93; 300m 36.44 '93, 400m 51.11 '91, 800m 2:08.36i '91, 2:13.22 '84; 60mh 8.27i '90, HJ 1.67 '83, LJ 6.08 '83, SP 11.18 '84, Hep 5493 '84.
First national title was 1980 WAAA junior LJ. Switched to 400mh from 100mh in 1988, and from her début of 59.9 in 1987 improved rapidly to 54.03 in Seoul.

Elizabeth McCOLGAN b.24 May 1964 Dundee 1.68m 45kg. née Lynch. Dundee Hawkhill H. Married steeplechaser Peter McColgan (pb 8:29.35 and 7 CG 1986 for 3000mSt) in 1987.
At 10000m (3000m): OG: '88- 2, '92- 5; WCh: '87- 5, '91- 1; CG: '86- 1, '90- 1 (3); EC: '86- 7 (12); WSG: '86- 3. At 3000m: WI: '89- 2 (6 1500m). Won World Half Mar 1992. Won UK 3000m 1989, 1991-2; 5000m 1988, 10000m 1986. World CC: '87- 2, '91- 3. GP: 3rd 3000m 1987, won 5000m 1988.
Four Commonwealth 10000m records 1986-91. UK half marathon best 1991. WIR 5000m 15:03.17 '92. Fastest ever half marathon on a certified course at Tokyo in January 1992.
Progression at 3000m, 10000m, Mar: 1979- 11:15.1; 1980- 10:41.8; 1982- 9:42.3; 1983- 9:34.5; 1984- 9:49.2; 1985- 9:03.80, 33:19.14; 1986- 8:46.53, 31:41.42; 1987- 8:39.85, 31:19.82; 1988- 8:42.50, 31:06.99; 1989- 8:34.80i, 8:44.93; 1990- 8:43.14, 32:23.56; 1991- 8:38.23, 30:57.07, 2:27:32; 1992- 8:41.07, 31:26.11, 2:27:38; 1993- 2:29:37. pbs: 800m 2:05.9 '87, 1000m 2:41.8 '87, 1500m 4:01.38 '87, 1M 4:26.11 '87, 2000m 5:40.24 '87, 5000m 15:01.08 '87, Half Mar 67:11 '92.
NCAA indoor mile champion 1986, while at University of Alabama. World road 10km bests on a loop course 31:07 '87, 30:59 '88 and 30:38 '89 a week after her World indoor silver at 3000m (and 6th at 1500m just 13 minutes later). Made an very fast return after daughter Eilish born 25 Nov 1990 to place third in World CC in March 1991, prior to her gold medal in Tokyo. Won her first two marathon races, the then fastest ever début marathon 2:27:32 at New York 1991 and Tokyo 1992, then third in London 1993.

Fiona MAY b.12 Dec 1969 Slough 1.81m 60kg. Derby. Married to Gianni Iapichino (5.60 PV). Now lives in Italy.
At LJ: OG: '88- 6, '92- dnq; WCh: '91- dnq 19, '93- dnq 14; EC: '90- 7; CG: '90- 3; WJ: '86- 8, '88- 1; EJ: '87- 1; WSG: '91- 2; ECp: '89- 3, '91- 3, '93- 3. Won UK 1989, 1991, 1993; AAA 1989-92.
Progression at LJ: 1982- 5.34, 1983- 5.91, 1984- 6.30, 1985- 6.22/6.23w, 1986- 6.27/6.47w, 1987- 6.53/6.64w, 1988- 6.82/6.88w, 1989- 6.98w/6.80, 1990- 6.88, 1991- 6.77/6.91w, 1992- 6.73/6.76w, 1993- 6.86. pbs: 60m 7.7i '92, 100m 12.16 '88, 11.88w/12.1 '89; 200m 25.4 '89, HJ 1.72 '83.

Diane MODAHL b.17 Jun 1966 Manchester 1.70m 56kg. née Edwards. Sale H. Secretary. Married Vicente Modahl (Nor) in September 1992.
At 800m: OG: '88- 8, '92- sf; WCh: '87- sf, '93- 4; EC: '86- sf, '90- 8; CG: '86- 2, '90- 1; ECp: '89- 5, '93- 5/5R. Won UK 1987, AAA 1986-7, 1989, 1992.
Progression at 800m: 1979- 2:18.9, 1980- 2:16.4, 1981- 2:12.4, 1982- 2:09.5, 1983- 2:07.5, 1984- 2:02.75, 1985- 2:02.00, 1986- 2:00.60, 1987- 1:59.30, 1988- 1:59.66, 1989- 1:59.71, 1990- 1:58.65, 1991- 2:00.61, 1992- 1:59.96, 1993- 1:59.00. pbs: 400m 53.28A '92, 53.38 '93, 600m 1:26.18 '87, 1000m 2:35.86 '93, 1500m 4:12.3 '89, 1M 4:35.32 '92.
Cousin of world super-middleweight boxing champion Chris Eubank.

Yvonne MURRAY b.4 Oct 1964 Musselburgh. 1.70m 50kg. Edinburgh SPC. Clerk.
At 3000m (1500m): OG: '88- 3, '92- 8; WCh: '87- 7 (h), '93- 9; EC: '86- 3, '90- 1; CG: '82- 10 (10), '86- 3 (5), '90- 2 (4); EJ: '81- 6; WCp: '89- 1; ECp: '87- 2, '89- 2, '91- 5, '93- (3); WI: '87- 5, '93- 1; EI: '85- 3, '86- 2, '87- 1. Won UK 3000m 1985, 1987, 1993; 5000m 1983; AAA 1500m 1992, 3000m 1988, 1990-1. 2nd GP 1993.
Commonwealth 2000m record 1986. UK junior 3000m record 1982.
Progression at 1500m, 3000m: 1979- 4:49.6; 1980- 4:30.0, 10:11.8; 1981- 4:29.23, 9:30.0; 1982- 4:15.1, 9:07.77; 1983- 4:15.94, 9:04.14; 1984- 4:11.5, 8:58.54; 1985- 4:08.9, 9:00.97, 9:00.94i; 1986- 4:05.76, 8:37.15; 1987- 4:01.20, 8:42.07; 1988- 4:06.34, 8:29.02; 1989- 4:03.13, 8:38.51; 1990- 4:07.68, 8:39.46; 1991- 4:14.0, 8:36.05; 1992- 4:05.87, 8:36.63; 1993- 4:08.63, 8:30.30. pbs: 800m 2:00.80 '87, 1000m 2:37.29 '89, 1M 4:23.08 '86, 2000m 5:29.58 '86, 5000m 15:50.54 '84, 10000m 33:43.80 '85, road 5km 15:20 '93.
At the 1986 Europeans she improved her 3000m pb by 5.76 sec. in the heat and a further 12.41 sec. in the final. Improved by 8.13 in the 1988 Olympics. In 1989 she became the first British woman to win a World Cup event and in 1990 won the European title with a devastating kick from 600m to go.

Paula RADCLIFFE b.17 Dec 1973 Northwich 1.72m 51kg. Bedford & County. Student at Loughborough University.
At 3000m: WCh: '93- 7; WJ: '92- 4; EJ: '91- 4. World CC: '91- 15J, '92- 1J, '93- 18.
Progression at 1500m, 3000m: 1988- 4:41.0, 1989- 4:34.9, 1990- 4:31.3, 9:41.4; 1991- 4:23.68, 9:23.29; 1992- 4:16.82, 8:51.78; 1993- 4:11.6, 8:40.40. pbs: 400m 58.9 '92, 800m 2:05.97 '93, 1000m 2:47.17 '93, 1M 4:36.4 est '93, 2000m 5:39.20 '93, 5000m 16:16.77i '92.
Her great aunt won an Olympic swimming silver medal in 1924.

Gowry RETCHAKAN b.21 Jun 1960 Paddington, London 1.59m 45kg. Thurrock H. Married ITV statistician Ian Hodge in September 1990; former married name Varadakumar. Worked for the IAAF development department.
At 400mh: OG: '92- sf; WCh: '91- sf, '93- sf; EC: '90- h; WCp: '92- 2; won WAAA 1990-2, UK 1992-3. At 100mh: AsiG (for Sri Lanka): '82- 6.
Progression at 400mh: 1984- 64.7, 1985- 59.9, 1988- 61.04, 1989- 57.17, 1990- 56.73, 1991- 54.88, 1992- 54.63, 1993- 55.84. pbs: 100m 12.3 '91, 200m 24.9/24.7w '92, 400m 55.1 '91!, 800m 2:07.37i '93, 2:11.8 '91; 60mh 8.7i '92, 100mh 14.0 '92, 14.52w '89, 14.65 '82; 200mh 28.1 '89, TJ 10.75 '89.
First national title as a junior in Sri Lanka in 1977. Son Sunni born 1987.

Alison WYETH b.26 May 1964 Southampton 1.78m 58kg. Parkside. Formerly IAAF Development officer.
At 3000m: OG: '92- 9; WCh: '91- 11, '93- 5; EC: '90- 10; CG: '90- 11; ECp: '93- 3; 3rd GP 1993. At 1500m: WSG: '87- h. Won UK 1500m 1990-1; AAA 1500m 1993, 3000m 1989.
Progression at 1500m, 3000m: 1984- 4:28.7, 9:59.5; 1985- 4:27.3, 1986- 4:33.0, 9:51.65; 1987- 4:12.02, 9:31.11; 1988- 4:11.16, 9:23.17 (9:11.3 mx), 1989- 4:10.83, 8:48.96; 1990- 4:10.77, 8:52.26; 1991- 4:07.5, 8:44.73; 1992- 4:05.52, 8:43.93; 1993- 4:03.17, 8:38.42. pbs: 800m 2:04.8 '89, 1M 4:24.87 '91, 2000m 5:38.50 '93. 5000m 15:47.97 '89.

USA

Governing body: USA Track and Field (formerly TAC - The Athletics Congress of the USA), P.O.Box 120, Indianapolis, Indiana 46206. Founded 1979, when it replaced the AAU (founded 1888) as the governing body.
National Championships first held in 1876 (men), 1923 (women). **1993 Champions**: **Men**: 100m: Andre Cason 9.85w, 200m: Michael Marsh 19.97w, 400m: Michael Johnson 43.74, 800m: Mark Everett 1:44.43, 1500m: William

Paula Radcliffe: world junior cc title and 7th in world 3000 metres

Burke 3:42.74, 5000m: Matt Giusto 13:23.60, 10000m: Todd Williams 28:02.05, Half Mar/ Mar: Ed Eyestone 63:19/2:14:34, 3000mSt: Marc Davis 8:20.93, 110mh: Jack Pierce 13.19, 400mh: Kevin Young 47.69, HJ: Hollis Conway 2.31, PV: Scott Huffman 5.70, LJ: Mike Powell 8.53, TJ: Mike Conley 17.69, SP: Randy Barnes 21.28, DT: Anthony Washington 63.24, HT: Lance Deal 78.10, JT: Tom Pukstys 83.06, Dec: Dan O'Brien 8331, 20kmW: Allen James 1:29:09, 50kmW: Jonathan Matthews 4:01:36. **Women**: 100m: Gail Devers 10.82w, 200m: Gwen Torrence 22.57w, 400m: Jearl Miles 50.43, 800m: Joetta Clark 2:01.47, 1500m/3000m: Annette Peters 4:11.53/8:48.59, 5000m: Christine McNamara 16:11.85, 10000m: Lynn Jennings 31:57.83, Half Mar: Elaine Van Blunk 72:11, Mar: Linda Somers 2:34:11, 2000mSt: Marisa Sutera 7:27.30, 100mh: Lynda Tolbert 12.72w, 400mh: Sandra Farmer-Patrick 53.96, HJ: Tanya Hughes 1.90, LJ/Hep: Jackie Joyner-Kersee 7.02/6770, TJ: Claudia Haywood 13.86w, SP/DT: Connie Price-Smith 19.02/63.52, HT (Exh): Sonja Fitts 54.92, JT: Donna Mayhew 62.98, 10kmW: Debbi Lawrence 45:55.

NCAA Championships first held in 1921 (men), 1982 (women). **1993 champions**: **Men**: 100m: Michael Green JAM 10.09, 200m: Chris Nelloms 20.27, 400m: Calvin Davis 45.04, 800m: Jose Parrilla 1:46.51, 1500m: Marko Koers HOL 3:38.05, 5000m: Jon Dennis GBR 13:59.00, 10000m: Jonah Koech KEN 28:28.67, 3000mSt: Donovan Bergstrom 8:29.08, 110mh: Glenn Terry 13.43, 400mh: Bryan Bronson 49.07, HJ: Randy Jenkins 2.28, PV: Mark Buse 5.60, LJ: Erick Walder 8.53, TJ: Tyrell Taitt 16.91w, SP: Brent Noon 20.41, DT: Brian Milne 61.08, HT: Balasz Kiss HUN 75.24, JT: Eric Smith 79.20, Dec: Chris Huffins 8007. **Women**: 100m/200m: Holli Hyche 11.14/22.34, 400m: Juliet Campbell JAM 50.58, 800m: Kim Sherman 2:02.99, 1500m/3000m: Clare Eichner 4:20.12/9:03.06, 5000m: Kay Gooch 16:31.02, 10000m: Carole Zajac 34:18.14, 100mh: Gillian Russell JAM 13.02w, 400mh: Debbie Ann Parris 56.37, HJ: Tanya Hughes 1.92, LJ: Daphne Saunders 6.77, TJ: Claudia Haywood 13.54, SP: Dawn Dumble 17.17, DT: Danyel Mitchell 56.86, JT: Ashley Selman 57.44, Hep: Kelly Blair 6038.

Derrick ADKINS b.2 Jul 1970 Brooklyn, New York 1.88m 80kg. Reebok. Studied engineering at Georgia Tech.
At 400mh: WCh: '91- 6, '93- 7; WSG: '91- 1, '93- 1. Won PAm-J 1989.
Progression at 400mh: 1987- 52.65, 1988- 50.71, 1989- 50.25, 1990- 49.53, 1991- 48.60, 1992- 48.64, 1993- 48.39. pbs: 400m 46.87i '93, 110mh 13.69 '92.

Charles AUSTIN b.19 Jun 1967 Bay City, Texas 1.84m 77kg. Mazda TC. Was at Southwest Texas State University.
At HJ: OG: '92- 8=; WCh: '91- 1; WI: '91- 6=. Won NCAA 1990, 2= TAC 1991.
US high jump record 1991.
Progression at HJ: 1986- 2.11, 1987- 2.16, 1988- 2.19, 1989- 2.27, 1990- 2.35, 1991- 2.40, 1992- 2.33i/2.32, 1993- 2.35i. pb TJ 14.91i '90.

Randy BARNES b.16 Jun 1966 Charleston, W.Virginia 1.94m 137kg. Goldwin TC. Was at Texas A&M University.
At SP: OG: '88- 2; WCh: '93- 2; WCp: '89- 3; WI: '89- 2. Won US Oly Trials 1988, US 1989, 1993; GWG 1990.
World shot record 1990. WIB 22.66 '89.
Progression at SP: 1984- 15.77, 1985- 18.56, 1986- 21.88, 1987- 20.94, 1988- 22.42, 1989- 22.66i/22.18, 1990- 23.12, 1993- 21.80. pb DT 61.18 '86.
A spinner, from a 1985 best of 20.36m with the 12lb shot, he made a sensational start to his senior career, from 19.83 indoors to 21.08 and 21.88 in April 1986, the latter improving Randy Matson's university record (WR 21.78 '67). Returned to competition February 1993 after two years ban for positive drugs test for methyltestosterone at Malmö August 1990.

Tony BARTON b.17 Oct 1969 Washington DC 1.90m 74kg. Nike. Was at George Mason University.
At HJ: WCh: '93- 8; WCp: '92- 5; WJ: '88- dnq; WSG: '93- 1=. At LJ: 3rd GP 1993.
Progression at HJ: 1987- 2.10, 1988- 2.18, 1989- 2.22i/2.21, 1990- 2.31, 1991- 2.30i/2.27, 1992- 2.32, 1993- 2.31. pbs: LJ 8.12 '93, TJ 15.96 '90.

Dion BENTLEY b.26 Aug 1971 Pittsburgh 1.93m 86kg. Was at University of Florida.
At HJ: WJ: '90- 2. Won PAm-J 1989.
Progression at LJ: 1988- 7.80, 1989- 8.16, 1990- 8.05/8.07w, 1991- 7.98i, 1992- 7.98i/7.96, 1993- 8.39.
Three month drugs ban from June 1993.

Arthur BLAKE b.19 Aug 1966 Bartow, Florida 1.80m 68kg. Was at Florida State University.
At 110mh: OG: '88- 8, '92- sf; WSG: '87- 2. Won TAC jnr and PAm-J 1984.
Progression at 110mh: 1984- 13.84, 1985- 13.87/13.86w, 1986- 13.57/13.39w, 1987- 13.29, 1988- 13.24, 1989- 13.25, 1990- 13.25, 1991- 13.43, 1992- 13.26, 1993- 13.41. pbs: 100m 10.38 '90, 200m 20.63 '87, 50mh 6.49i '90, 55mh 6.99i '90, 60mh 7.51i '90, 400mh 50.66 '84.
World age-17 best for 110mh 1984.

Bryan BRIDGEWATER b,7 Sep 1970 Los Angeles 1.78m 75kg. Was at Cal State, LA.

At 200m/4x100mR: WSG: '93- 1/1R. Won PAm-J 100m & 200m 1989.
Progression at 100m, 200m: 1987- 10.63/10.3, 21.11/20.8; 1988- 10.55/10.28w, 20.53; 1989- 10.32, 20.44w; 1990- 10.35w, 20.56/20.2w; 1992- 10.15, 20.15; 1993- 10.08, 20.11.

Tim BRIGHT b.28 Jul 1960 Taft, California 1.88m 79kg. Mizuno TC. Was at Abilene Christian University.
At Dec: OG: '84- 12, '88- 7; WCh: '87- dnf; At PV: OG: '92- nh; WCh: '91- 6; WCp: '85- 3, '89- 2; won TAC 1991-2.
Progression at PV, Dec: 1978- 4.37; 1979- 4.90; 1980- 5.03; 1981- 5.33; 1982- 5.51, 7445w; 1983- 5.35i, 7737; 1984- 5.50i/5.40, 8106; 1985- 5.52, 8221; 1986- 5.70, 8302; 1987- 5.75, 8340; 1988- 5.75, 8287; 1989- 5.81, 7087; 1990- 5.82, 1991- 5.75, 1992- 5.80, 1993- 5.73. pbs: 100m: 10.90 '87, 10.73w/10.7 '85, 400m 48.72 '86, 1500m 4:39.35 '86, 110mh 14.16 '87, 14.09w '85, 13.9 '83, 13.8w '90; HJ 2.11 '86, LJ 7.38 '88, 7.49w '85, SP 14.38 '86 (14.41?), DT 44.80 '84, JT 61.60 '88.
Has concentrated on the pole vault since 1988, when his 5.70 at the 1988 Olympics was the best ever in a decathlon. Was fourth in the 1988 US Trials at pole vault on the same day that he was second in the decathlon. Married Julie Goodrich (LJ 6.40 '88, 3rd PanAm '91 in 6.53w) in 1989.

Mike BUNCIC b.25 Jul 1962 Fair Lawn, New Jersey 1.93m 111kg. Degree in education from University of Kentucky.
At DT: OG: '88- 10, '92- dnq 18; WCh: '91- 5, '93- 9; WSG: '85- 6, '87- 5.

Progression at DT: 1981- 53.04, 1982- 58.78, 1983- 59.68, 1984- 64.74, 1985- 66.42, 1986- 65.10, 1987- 68.98, 1988- 68.92, 1989- 68.88, 1990- 67.72, 1991- 69.36, 1992- 64.60, 1993- 67.12. pb SP 19.53 '89.
Yugoslav parents. US junior discus champion 1981, USA Champs second 1989-91 and 1993, third 1986, 1988.

Leroy BURRELL b.21 Feb 1967 Philadelphia 1.83m 82kg. Santa Monica TC. Studied communications at University of Houston.
At 100m/4x100m relay: OG: '92- 5/1R; WCh: '91- 2/1R (qf 200m), '93- 1R; WCp: '89- 2. Won overall and 100m GP 1990, GWG 1990. Won TAC 100m 1989, 1991, NCAA: 55m indoors and 100m 1990, indoor LJ 1989-90.
World records: 100m 1991, 4x100mR (4) 1991-3, 4x200mR 1989 & 1992. WIR 60m 6.48 in 1991.
Progression at 100m, 200m: 1985- 10.43, 21.51; 1986- 10.46/10.32w/10.1w, 20.94/20.71w; 1988- 10.31/10.09w, 1989- 9.94, 20.40; 1990- 9.96/ 9.94w, 20.14/19.61w; 1991- 9.88, 20.31/20.02w; 1992- 9.97/9.96w, 20.12; 1993- 10.02/9.85w, 20.35. pbs: 55m 6.09i '89, 60m 6.41 '92, LJ: 8.37 '89, TJ 15.04 '85.
World's fastest man of 1990, when he won 19 of 22 finals at 100m; and the fastest ever 200m, with wind assistance. In 1991 he went into the World Championships unbeaten at 100m, having won all eight finals, with a world record 9.90 at TAC, but despite improving to 9.88 he lost to Carl Lewis. Younger sister Dawn was top US high school long jumper at 6.16i in 1991.

Andre CASON b.20 Jan 1969 Virginia Beach 1.70m 70kg. Goldwin TC. Student at Texas A&M University.
At 100m/4x100mR: WCh: '91- 1R, '93- 2/1R; WJ: '88- 1/1R; WSG: '89- 1/1R; PAm: '91- 2; WCp: '89- 1R. 3rd TAC 1989. At 60m: WI: '91- 1. Two world records 4x100m relay 1991-3, world indoor records 60m 6.45 and 6.41 in 1992.
Progression at 100m: 1985- 10.83, 1986- 10.38, 1987- 10.49/10.2, 1988- 10.08, 1989- 10.04, 1990- 10.12/10.08w, 1991- 9.99, 1992- 10.08/9.88w, 1993- 9.79w/9.92. pbs: 50m 5.62i '92, 55m 6.04i '90, 60m 6.41i '92, 200m 20.70 '89, 20.11w '90; LJ 7.58i '87.
Fourth in the TAC 100m in 1991, he followed his relay gold in Tokyo by becoming the 12th sub 10.00 runner in history. His 1992 season ended with a torn left Achilles in the US Trials 100m heats. In a marvellous season in 1993 he twice ran 9.79w at the US Trials before 9.85w in the final and then improved his pb three times at the World Champs, although second to Linford Christie.

Andre Cason: improved pb three times before taking silver in Stuttgart

Mike CONLEY b.5 Oct 1962 Chicago 1.85m 77kg. Foot Locker AC. Was at University of Arkansas. Coach, dog trainer and deputy sherriff.
At TJ OG: '84- 2, '92- 1; WCh: '83- 4, '87- 2, '91- 3, '93- 1; PAm: '87- 1; WI: '87- 1, '89- 1; WCp: '89- 1; WSG: '83- 2. At LJ: WCh: '83- 3, '87- 8; WI: '89- 3; WCp: '85- 1. Won US Trials TJ 1984, NCAA LJ/TJ 1984-5 (2nd 200m 1985). Won US LJ 1985, TJ 1984, 1987-9, 1993; GWG TJ 1986, AAA TJ 1983. Won GP LJ 1985 (3rd 1989), TJ 1986, 1988, 1990 & 1992.
WIB triple jump 17.76 '87.
Progression at LJ, TJ: 1978- 5.84, 13.00; 1979- 7.14, 13.99; 1980- 6.84, 15.13; 1981- 7.46/7.56w, 15.80/15.83w; 1982- 8.19, 17.01; 1983- 8.38w/8.28, 17.23i/17.37w; 1984- 8.21/8.23w, 17.50; 1985- 8.43/8.53w, 17.71/17.72w; 1986- 8.33/8.63w, 17.69/17.84w; 1987- 8.32/8.55w, 17.87; 1988- 8.23, 17.59/17.62w; 1989- 8.15, 17.65i/17.57; 1990- 17.56; 1991- 7.98, 17.62; 1992- 8.34, 17.72/18.17w; 1993- 8.16, 17.86. pbs: 100m 10.36 '86, 200m 20.21/20.12w '85, 20.0 '84.
The greatest ever LJ/TJ combined exponent. Won the NCAA double indoors and out 1984-5. In 1988 only fourth at the US Trials but won the Grand Prix TJ and was second overall. First or second in TAC triple jump each year 1983-92. Unbeaten at triple jump in 1989. After the Olympic title in 1992, he took gold at his fourth World Championships in 1993. Had been an outstanding high school basketball player and is a black belt at taekwondo.

Mike Conley: finally won world title

Hollis CONWAY b.8 Jan 1967 Chicago, Illinois 1.83m 68kg. Reebok. Business graduate of Southwestern Louisiana University.
At HJ: OG: '88- 2, '92- 3=; WCh: '91- 3, '93- 6; WJ: '86- 2; WSG: '89- 2, '91- 1; PAm: '91- 3; WI: '91- 1, '93- 8. Won NCAA 1989, US 1990-3, GWG 1990. Won GP 1990 (3rd 1992).
Two US HJ records 1989, also indoors 2.37 for 1989 NCAA and 2.40 for 1991 World Indoors.
Progression at HJ: 1981- 1.72, 1982- 1.88, 1983- 2.03, 1984- 2.08, 1985- 2.18, 1986- 2.29, 1987- 2.34, 1988- 2.36, 1989- 2.39, 1990- 2.38, 1991- 2.40i/2.37, 1992- 2.35, 1993- 2.38. pbs: LJ 7.64 '88, TJ 16.17 '87.
Has jumped 56cm over his own height, close to the record of 59cm by Franklin Jacobs.

Mark CREAR b. 2 Oct 1968 San Francisco 1.86m 82kg. Nike International. Was at the University of Southern California.
At 110mh: WCh: '93- sf. NCAA champion 1992.
Progression at 110mh: 1990- 13.65/13.51w, 1992- 13.33, 1993- 13.26/13.22w/12.9w. pbs: 50mh 6.43i '93, 55mh 7.18i '94, 60mh 7.60i '93.

Mark CROGHAN b.8 Jan 1968 Akron, Ohio 1.75m 60kg. Nike. Was at Ohio State University.
At 3000mSt: OG: '92- sf; WCh: '91- h, '93- 5; Won TAC 1991, NCAA 1990-1.
Progression at 3000mSt: 1989- 8:46.07, 1990- 8:25.99, 1991- 8:10.69, 1992- 8:14.11, 1993- 8:09.76. pbs: 1500m 3:43.6 '91, 1M 4:08.81i '91, 3000m 7:52.19 '91, 2M 8:33.70 '92, 5000m 13:44.22 '92.
Took up steeplechase as a college junior.

Marc DAVIS b. 17 Dec 1969 Oceanside, San Diego 1.83m 65kg. Nike International. Was at University of Arizona.
At 3000mSt: WCh: '93- 11. US champion 1993. Won NCAA 5000m 1989, 3000mSt 1992.
Progression at 3000mSt: 1986- 9:24.5, 1987- 9:31.26, 1988- 9:12.6, 1991- 8:43.79, 1992- 8:33.93, 1993- 8:14.26. pbs: 1500m 3:37.12 '93, 3000m 7:38.03 '93, 2M 8:28.3 '93, 5000m 13:32.58 '89.

Lance DEAL b.21 Aug 1961 Riverton, Wyoming 1.83m 116kg. New York AC. Was at Montana State University. Wood and metal worker.
At HT: OG: '88- dnq 17, '92- 7; WCh: '91- dnq 13, '93- 9; WCp: '89- 2, '92- 3. US champion 1989, 1993. Won PAm-J discus 1980.
World bests 35lb weight: outdoors 24.05 '90, 25.41 '93; indoors: 24.17 '91, 24.54, 24.65, 24.67 '92, 24.82 '93.
Progression at HT: 1984- 62.52, 1985- 68.48, 1986- 74.66, 1987- 75.94, 1988- 75.64, 1989- 78.34, 1990- 77.66, 1991- 78.44, 1992- 81.08, 1993- 80.80. pbs: SP 18.35i '81, 18.22 '84, DT 61.62 '84.

An all-American linebaacker at American football in high school, he switched from discus to hammer in 1984. US indoor Grand Prix overall champion 1993.

Tony DEES 6 Aug 1963 Pascagoula, Mississippi 1.93m 95kg. Nike International. Was at University of Mississippi, now finishing degree at University of Tampa.
At 110mh: OG: '92- 2; WCh: '93- 8. Won GP 1991. At 60mh: WI: '93- 3.
Progression at 110mh: 1982- 13.98, 1983- 13.68/13.6, 1984- 13.65, 1985- 13.86, 1986- 13.65, 1987- 13.86, 1988- 13.54/13.51w, 1989- 13.61, 1990- 13.24/13.09w, 1991- 13.05, 1992- 13.08, 1993- 13.12. pbs: 55m 6.12i '90, 100m 10.15/10.03w '91, 200m 20.54 '84, 20.37w/20.2w '83; 50mh 6.43i '91, 55mh 6.98i '90, 60mh 7.43i '93.
After several years as a useful sprinter/hurdler, broke through to top class in 1990, when he won the TAC indoor 55mh. Previous championships bests were fourth places NCAA 60yh 1983, TAC 55mh 1988. In 1991 he ran the year's fastest time and took the Grand Prix title but was only sixth at TAC and missed Tokyo.

Brian DIEMER b.10 Oct 1961 Grand Rapids, Michigan 1.76m 64kg. Nike International. Graduate of University of Michigan. Landscape designer.
At 3000mSt: OG: '84- 3, '88- sf, '92- 7; WCh: '83- sf, '87- 4, '91- 5, '93- h; WCp: '89- 4. Won NCAA 1983, US 1988-90, 1992-3; GWG 1990.
Progression at 3000mSt: 1981- 8:45.48, 1982- 8:37.96, 1983- 8:22.13, 1984- 8:13.16, 1985- 8:20.64, 1986- 9:09.4, 1987- 8:14.46, 1988- 8:20.44, 1989- 8:16.92, 1990- 8:20.61, 1991- 8:16.57, 1992- 8:16.51, 1993- 8:22.41. pbs: 1500m 3:42.48 '89, 1M 3:59.93i '83, 2000m 5:07.89i '87, 3000m 7:47.31 '92, 2M 8:30.49i '83, 3M 13:14.60i '84, 5000m 13:47.15 '82, 10000m 30:08.8 '80.
Splendidly consistent record at major meetings from his Olympic bronze in 1984 to his first failure in 1993.

Jim DOEHRING b.27 Jan 1962 Santa Barbara, California 1.83m 118kg. Reebok RT. Was at San Jose State University.
At SP: OG: '88- 11, '92- 2; WI: '93- 2. Won TAC 1990.
Progression at SP: 1981- 18.34, 1983- 18.31, 1984- 19.97, 1985- 20.62, 1986- 21.29, 1987- 20.45i/19.67, 1988- 21.04, 1989- 21.57, 1990- 21.20, 1991- 20.75idq, 1992- 21.60, 1993- 21.56i/21.15.
Two year drugs ban from random test December 1990 was lifted in 1992.

Jon DRUMMOND b.9 Sep 1968 Philadelphia 1.75m 72kg. Nike International. Was at Texas Christian University.
At 200m/4x100m relay: WCh: '93- 1R; WSG: '91- 1/1R. At 60m: WI: '93- 4. Won AAA 200m 1991. World record 4x100m relay 1993.
Progression at 100m, 200m: 1986- 10.5; 1987- 10.28/10.23w, 20.64; 1988- 10.25/10.0w, 20.79i; 1989- 10.21, 20.82; 1990- 10.10, 1991- 10.19/10.03w, 20.58; 1992- 10.12, 20.37; 1993- 10.03/9.92w, 21.05i. pbs: 50m 5.67i '92, 60m 6.54i '93.

Danny EVERETT b.1 Nov 1966 Van Alystine, Texas 1.88m 72kg. Santa Monica TC. Studied economics when at UCLA.
At 400m/R- 4x400m relay: OG: '88- 3/1R, '92- sf; WCh: '87- 1R, '91- 3/2R. Won TAC 1992, NCAA 1988. GP: 2nd 1987, won 1989.
World records 4x400m relay 1988, 4x200m 1989; world best 300m 1990. WIR 400m 45.02 '92; 45.05 in 1990 disallowed as run in lanes. .
Progression at 200m, 400m: 1984- 48.65; 1985- 20.97, 45.76; 1986- 20.65, 45.10; 1987- 20.42, 44.47; 1988- 20.23, 43.98; 1989- 20.17, 44.36; 1990- 20.08, 44.06; 1991- 20.13, 44.42; 1992- 20.47/20.14w, 43.81. pbs: 300m 31.48 '90, 800m 1:49.55 '88.
Became fourth sub-44 sec. 400m runner when second at the 1988 US Olympic Trials. Although only fourth at TAC 1991 gained his chance in the individual 400m at the World Championhips when Quincy Watts withdrew. Ran second fastest ever 400m to win US Trials in 1992, but suffered an Achilles injury which meant that he went out in Olympic semis. Had operations on both Achilles in November 1992 and on right Achilles in December 1993.

Mark EVERETT b.2 Sep 1968 Milton, Florida 1.77m 64kg. Nike International. Finishing sports administration degree at University of Florida.
At 800m: OG: '88- h, '92- dnf; WCh: '91- 3/res R, '93- sf; WI: '93- 1R. US champion 1988, 1990-1, 1993; NCAA 1990.
WIB 600y 1:07.53 in 1992, beating the 22-year-old mark by Martin McGrady.
Progression at 400m, 800m: 1986- 47.55y, 1987- 46.37, 1:47.36; 1988- 45.91, 1:44.46; 1989- 46.09i, 1:47.86; 1990- 45.46, 1:44.70; 1991- 44.59, 1:43.93; 1992- 45.47, 1:43.40; 1993- 1:44.43. pbs: 100m 10.9 '86, 200m 21.9 '86, 500m 1:00.19i '92, 600y 1:07.53i '92.
An ungainly looking but effective runner. Silver medal as he ran in the heats of the 4x400m relay at the 1991 World Championships.

Steve FRITZ b. 1 Nov 1967 Salina, Kansas 1.90m 89kg. Accusplit. Was at Kansas State University.

At Dec: WCh: '93- 7; WSG: '91- 1.
Progression at Dec: 1988- 7015, 1989- 7707, 1990- 7924, 1991- 8079, 1992- 8073, 1993- 8324. pbs: 100m 10.80 '93, 400m 48.40 '93, 1500m 4:28.11 '92, 110mh 13.99 '93, HJ 2.15 '91, PV 5.10 '91, LJ 7.82 '92, SP 14.41 '92, DT 46.80 '90, JT 62.62 '93.

Johnny GRAY b.19 Jun 1960 Los Angeles 1.90m 75kg. Santa Monica TC. Studied civil engineering at Cal State, Los Angeles.
At 800m: OG: '84- 7, '88- 5, '92- 3; WCh: '87- qf, '91- 6, '93- sf; PAm: '87- 1. Won US Olympic Trials 1988, TAC 1985-7, 1989, 1992; GWG 1986. Five US 800m records 1984-5. Two 600m world bests 1984-6. WIB 1000y 2:04.39 '86.
Progression at 800m: 1977- 2:06.0y, 1978- 1:51.1, 1979- 1:49.39, 1980- 1:47.06, 1982- 1:45.41, 1983- 1:45.50, 1984- 1:42.96, 1985- 1:42.60, 1986- 1:43.46, 1987- 1:44.09, 1988- 1:42.65, 1989- 1:43.39, 1990- 1:43.72, 1991- 1:43.84, 1992- 1:42.80, 1993- 1:44.03. pbs: 400m 46.3 '83, 600m 1:12.81 '86, 1000m 2:17.27 '84, 1500m 3:42.43 '90, 1M 4:07.64 '84.
His Olympics progression: 7th, 5th, 3rd! Ran fastest ever 800m relay leg, 1:43.3, on 6 Apr 1985 at Tempe. Has 14 sub 1:44 times for 800m. His many fast runs and big wins in invitational meetings have been regularly interspersed with very bad runs.

Joe GREENE b.17 Feb 1967 Wright-Patterson AF Base, Dayton, Ohio. 1.83m 68kg. Mazda TC. Was at Ohio State University.
At LJ: OG: '92- 3; WCh: '93- dnq 17; WI: '93- 2; won NCAA 1989.
Progression at LJ: 1986- 7.34w, 1987- 7.80/7,81w, 1988- 7.88, 1989- 8.10/8.41w, 1990- 8.11i/8.02/8.28w, 1991- 8.24/8.34w, 1992- 8.38/8.66w, 1993- 8.33/8.35w. pb TJ 16.88 '89, 16.93w '90.
Married German long jumper Susen Tiedtke on 4 Dec 1993.

Calvin HARRISON b.20 Jan 1974 1.86m 75kg. Student at Hartnell Junior College, Salinas..
Progression at 400m: 1993- 45.07. Won PAm-J 1993 (1R). pb 200m 20.57 '93.
Twin brother Alvin ran with Calvin on the winning Pan-American junior relay team, was third fastest US high school athlete at 46.25 and also third when Calvin won the US Junior title in 45.07 in 1993.

Kerry **'Kenny' HARRISON** b.13 Feb 1965 Milwaukee 1.78m 75kg. Mizuno TC. Was at Kansas State University.
At TJ: WCh: '91- 1, '93- 10; WSG: '87- 2. Won NCAA 1986, TAC 1990-1, GWG 1990. 2nd PAm-J 1984.
Progression at TJ: 1982- 14.84, 1983- 15.96, 1984- 16.50, 1985- 16.29i, 1986- 17.07/17.41w, 1987- 17.07/17.42w, 1988- 17.15/17.56w, 1989- 17.47/17.74w, 1990- 17.93, 1991- 17.78, 1992- 17.06/17.58w, 1993- 17.27. pb LJ 8.17i '86, 8.14 '87, 8.23w '88.
Second on the all-time list with 17.93 at Helsinki, and lost only once in 1990. Won all eight competions in 1991, culminating in the world title.

Courtney HAWKINS b.11 Jul 1967 West Palm Beach, Florida 1.87m 75kg. Santa Monica TC. Was at University of Kansas.
At 110mh: 3rd TAC 1989.
Progression at 110mh: 1986- 13.95, 1987- 13.80, 1989- 13.41/13.3, 1990- 13.28, 1991- 13.30, 1992- 13.66, 1993- 13.25. pbs: 55mh 7.10i '91, 60mh 7.47i '92.

Floyd HEARD b.24 Mar 1966 West Point, Mississippi 1.78m 71kg. Santa Monica TC. Was at Texas A&M University.
At 200m/R- 4x100m relay: WCh: '87- 6, '91- sf; PAm: '87- 1; WCp: '89- 2; WSG: '87- 2/1R. Won TAC 1986 & 1989, NCAA 1986-7, GWG 1986.
World records: 4x200mR 1989, 1992; 4x100mR 1991.
Progression at 200m: 1983- 21.43, 1984- 21.00/20.7w, 1985- 20.61, 1986- 20.12/20.03w, 1987- 19.95, 1988- 20.50, 1989- 20.09, 1990- 20.27, 1991- 20.36, 1992- 20.22/20.17w, 1993- 20.40. pbs: 55m 6.10i '89, 100m 10.10/10.04w '91, 400m 47.5 '85.

Steve HOLMAN b.2 Mar 1970 Indianapolis 1.86m 66kg. Nike. Graduated from Georgetown University.
At 1500m: OG: '92- sf; WI: '93- 4. Won NCAA 1992.
Progression at 1500m: 1988- 3:52.8, 1989- 3:45.41, 1990- 3:39.60, 1991- 3:38.37, 1992- 3:34.95, 1993- 3:35.29. pbs: 800m 1:47.54 '92, 1000m 2:19.96i '93, 1M 3:52.73 '93, 2000m 5:07.72 '92, 3000m 7:46.27i '93, 5000m 13:47.63i '92.
Actual Christian names are Clyfton Orlando.

Scott HUFFMAN b.30 Nov 1964 Quinter, Kansas 1.75m 75kg. Mizuno TC. Was at University of Kansas.
At PV: WCh: '93- 5; WI: '91- 9. 3rd GP 1991. US champion 1993.
Progression at PV: 1983- 5.00, 1984- 5.03, 1985- 5.62, 1986- 5.60, 1987- 5.59, 1988- 5.65, 1989- 5.56, 1990- 5.80/5.85ex, 1991- 5.80, 1992- 5.85, 1993- 5.85.
Has developed an interesting straddle technique in clearing the PV bar.

Sam JEFFERSON b.19 Apr 1971 Waco, Texas 1.68m 69kg. Student at University of Houston.
At 100m/4x100m: WSG: '93- 2/1R.
Progression at 100m, 200m: 1988- 10.3w, 1989- 10.53/10.31w, 1990- 10.53.10.50w, 1991- 10.31/10.22w, 21.42; 1992- 10.27/10.24w, 20.74w; 1993- 10.13/10.05w, 20.32.

Dave JOHNSON b.7 Apr 1963 Missoula, Montana 1.90m 91kg. Reebok. Was at Azusa Pacific University.
At Dec: OG: '88- 9, '92- 3; WCh: '91- dnf; WSG: '89- 1. Won TAC 1986, 1989-90, 1992; GWG 1990.
Progression at Dec: 1982- 6297*, 1983- 7225*, 1984- 7933, 1985- 7948, 1986- 8203w, 1987- 8045, 1988- 8245, 1989- 8549, 1990- 8600w, 1991- 8467, 1992- 8727w/8705. pbs: 100m 10.79 '89, 10.77w '85; 400m 48.19 '91, 1500m 4:23.00 '91, 110mh 14.17 '91, HJ 2.10 '90, PV 5.28 '91, LJ 7.59 '89, SP 15.05 '92, DT 49.88 '91, JT 74.58 '92.
Started in college as a footballer. Topped decathlon world lists in 1989 and 1990. After failing to finish three times he came back in April 1992 with 8727w for sixth all-time, including the best ever second day score of 4411. He improved that record to 4455 later that year at the US Trials.

Michael JOHNSON b.13 Sep 1967 Dallas 1.85m 78kg. Nike International. Degree in marketing from Baylor University.
At 400m/4x400mR: WCh: '93- 1/1R; WSG: '89- 2R. At 200m: OG: '92- sf/1R; WCh: '91- 1; Won NCAA and GWG 200m 1990; US 200m 1990-2, 400m 1993. Won GP 1991 (third overall), 3rd 1993.
World records 4x400m relay 1992 and 1993. US indoor 200m records 20.59 to win 1989 NCAA and 20.55 in Jan 1991.
Progression at 200m, 400m: 1986- 21.30, 1987- 20.41, 46.29; 1988- 20.07, 45.23; 1989- 20.47/20.06w, 46.49; 1990- 19.85, 44.21; 1991- 19.88, 44.17; 1992- 19.79, 43.98; 1993- 20.06, 43.65. pbs: 100m 10.12 '93; 300m 31.72 '93.
His upright style, with little knee lift and rapid, short strides made a considerable impact when he burst onto the international scene and was the best in the world at both 200m and 400m in 1990. He ran a 43.5 400m relay split in April 1988 before a broken leg curtailed his season. Has a record 11 sub-20 sec. times. His run of 32 successive wins at 200m from May 1990 was ended by Frank Fredericks in Rome on 9 Jun 1992 and he was ill at the 1992 Olympics, but at 400m he has won 32 successive finals 1990-3. His 42.93 anchor on the 1993 US gold medal team is the fastest 400m relay leg ever run.

Bob KENNEDY b.18 Aug 1970 Bloomington, Indiana 1.83m 66kg. Santa Monica TC. Student at University of Mississippi.
At 5000m: OG: '92- 12; WCh: '91- 12, '93- h. At 3000m: WI: '93- 4. Won US CC 1992, PAm-J 1500m 1989, NCAA 1500m 1990.
Progression at 5000m: 1989- 14:21.40, 1990- 13:42.80, 1991- 13:22.17, 1992- 13:28.18, 1993- 13:14.91. pbs: 400m 47.04 '91, 1000m 2:17.20 '93, 1500m 3:38.32 '91, 1M 3:56.71 '93, 3000m 7:38.45 '93.

George KERSH b.3 Jul 1968 Pearl, Mississippi 1.85m 72kg. Santa Monica TC. Student at University of Mississippi.
At 800m: WCh: '91- sf; WJ: '86- 8. Won NCAA 1991, GWG 1990.
Progression at 800m: 1985- 1:53.74y, 1986- 1:48.86, 1987- 1:46.58, 1988- 1:45.35, 1989- 1:45.59, 1990- 1:44.84, 1991- 1:44.07, 1992- 1:44.00, 1993- 1:45.54. pbs: 400m 47.04 '91, 1000m 2:17.20 '93, 1500m 3:43.44 '92, 1M 4:08.17 '87.
Fastest world junior at 800m '87. Fourth in 1992 US Trials, missing Olympic place by 0.03 sec.

Roger KINGDOM b.26 Aug 1962 Vienna, Georgia 1.85m 91kg. Foot Locker AC. Was at University of Pittsburgh.
At 110mh: OG: '84- 1, '88- 1; PAm: '83- 1; WSG: '89- 1; WCp: '89- 1. Won NCAA 1983, US Olympic Trials 1988, TAC 1985, 1988-90; GWG 1990. At 60mh: WI: '89- 1. Won GP 110mh and second overall 1989.
World 110m hurdles record 1989.
Progression at 110mh: 1982- 14.07, 1983- 13.44, 1984- 13.16/13.1/13.00w, 1985- 13.14, 1986- 13.40/13.39w, 1987- 13.51/13.3/13.44w, 1988- 12.97, 1989- 12.92/12.87w, 1990- 13.21/13.11w, 1992- 13.29, 1993- 13.40/13.38w. pbs: 200m 21.08w '84, 50mh 6.47i '89, 55mh 6.98i '89, 60mh 7.37i '89, HJ 2.14i '84.
Became the second man to run 110m hurdles in sub-13.00, at high altitude in 1988, when he won all 25 races at 110mh. Ran the third fastest ever time, 12.98, to take the Olympic title. Improved further in 1989 with the world record in Zürich and the fastest ever wind-aided time at the World Cup. Has run 44 (and 9 wa) sub 13.30 times, including a record 18 (and 3w) in 1989. He ran 60m hurdles indoors in 1989 in a time of 7.37, corrected from the originally announced 7.36, which equalled the world record. Missed 1991 outdoor season following two operations on his right knee. Now a keen golfer.

Carl LEWIS b.1 Jul 1961 Birmingham, Alabama 1.88m 80kg. Santa Monica TC. Was at University of Houston.

At 100m/LJ/R- 4 x100m relay: OG: '84- 1/1/1R (1 200m), '88- 1/1 (2 200m); '92- 1 LJ/1R; WCh: '83- 1/1/1R, '87- 1/1/1R; '91- 1/2/1R, '93- 4/- (3 200m); PAm: LJ '79- 3, '87- 1/1R; WCp: '81- 9/1. Won TAC 100m 1981-3, 1986, 1990; 200m 1983, 1987; LJ 1981-3, 1986-7, 1991. Won PAm-J 100m & 200m 1980; NCAA 100m, LJ 1981; 100m/200m/LJ at US Olympic Trials 1984, 100m/LJ (2nd 200m) 1988; GWG LJ 1990.
World records: 4x100mR (5) 1983-92, 4x200mR 1989, 1992; 100m 1988 (with the disallowance of Ben Johnson's 9.83) and 1991. Low altitude world bests at 100m (3), 200m, LJ (4). WIB: 60y: 6.02 '83, LJ: 8.49 '81, 8.56 '82, 8.79 '84. US records 100m 1987 and 1988, 200m 1983.
Progression at LJ, 100m, 200m: 1974- 5.51, 1975- 6.07; 1976- 6.93, 11.1y; 1977- 7.26, 10.6y; 1978- 7.85, 10.5/9.3y; 1979- 8.13, 10.3/10.67, 20.9; 1980- 8.11/8.35w, 10.21/ 10.16w, 20.66; 1981- 8.62/8.73w, 10.00/9.99w, 20.73; 1982- 8.76, 10.00, 20.27; 1983- 8.79, 9.97/9.93w, 19.75; 1984- 8.79i/8.71, 9.99, 19.80; 1985- 8.62/8.77w, 9.98/9.90w, 20.69/20.3w; 1986- 8.67w/8.37i/ 8.35, 10.06/9.91w, 20.41/20.23w/20.1; 1987- 8.75/8.77w, 9.93, 19.92; 1988- 8.76, 9.92/9.78w, 19.79; 1989- 8.54, 10.05, 20.47; 1990- 8.51, 10.05; 1991- 8.87/8.91w, 9.86/9.80w, 20.46; 1992- 8.68/8.72w, 10.07/9.95w, 20.15; 1993- 10.02/ 9.90w, 19.99. pbs: 50m 5.72i '87, 60m 6.46 '92, 300m 32.18 '84, 400m 47.01 '93.
Won 65 successive long jumps from a defeat by Larry Myricks at the US Indoors on 28 Feb 1981 until his epic clash with Mike Powell on 31 Aug 1991. He has 67 long jumps over 28ft (8.53m), and the most legal times: 15 sub-10.00 100m and 9 sub-20.00 200m. Anchored 11 of the 15 sub-38 sec times run at 4x100m relay pre 1993. Emulated Jesse Owens in winning four Olympic gold medals and has added four more. He has a record eight World Champion-ships gold medals and nine medals in all. Sullivan Award winner 1981. Sister Carol was World long jump bronze medallist in 1983 and made the US Olympic teams of 1980, 1984 and 1988.

Steve LEWIS b.16 May 1969 Los Angeles 1.88m 84kg. Santa Monica TC. Was at UCLA.
At 400m/R- 4x400m relay: OG: '88- 1/1R, '92- 2/1R. Won NCAA & TAC 1990.
Five world junior 400m records 1988. World 4x400m relay records 1988 and 1992.
Progression at 400m: 1982- 54.2, 1983- 51.9, 1984- 50.8, 1985- 47.93, 1986- 46.50, 1987- 45.76, 1988- 43.87, 1989- 44.47, 1990- 44.75, 1991- 44.52, 1992- 44.08, 1993- 44.54. pbs: 100m 10.41 '92, 200m 20.58 '92, 300m 31.82 '92.
Had a sensational 1988 season when he ran the nine fastest ever 400m times by a junior, and won two Olympic gold medals.

A 200 metres bronze was Carl Lewis's only medal in 1993

Michael MARSH b.4 Aug 1967 Los Angeles 1.78m 68kg. Santa Monica TC. Was at UCLA.
At 200m/4x100mR: OG: '92- 1/1R; WCh: '91- resR, '93- 4; WJ: '86- dq R; WSG: '89- 1R. US champion 1993.
World records three 4x100mR 1991-2, 4x200mR 1992. US and world low-altitude 200m record 1992.
Progression at 100m, 200m: 1985- 10.6, 20.82; 1986- 10.22, 20.69; 1987- 10.26/10.16w, 20.59/ 20.52w/20.5; 1988- 10.12/9.94w, 20.35; 1989- 10.07, 20.42; 1990- 10.08/10.07w, 20.47/20.44w; 1991- 10.15/10.00w, 20.44; 1992- 9.93, 19.73; 1993- 10.20/9.97w, 20.04/19.97w. pbs: 50m 5.73i '90, 60m 6.57i '92, 300m 32.10 '93, 400m 45.53 '93.
Gold medal as he ran in the heats of the 4x100m relay. at the 1991 Worlds. After three major championships appearances at the sprint relay, made individual event début with the Olympic gold at 200m in 1992, running a world low-altitude best for 200m in the semi-final.

Anthuan MAYBANK b. 30 Dec 1969 Georgetown, South Carolina 1.85m 75kg. Was at University of Iowa.
Progression at 400m, LJ: 1988- 46.82, 1989- 46.39, 7.83; 1990- 47.25, 1991- 45.76, 7.81i; 1992- 45.04, 8.06i/7.81; 1993- 44.99, 8.25/8.40w. pb 200m 20.70 '93.

Dennis MITCHELL b.20 Feb 1966 Cherry Point, North Carolina 1.74m 69kg. Mazda TC. Was at University of Florida.

At 100m/4x100mR OG: '88- 4, '92- 3/1R; WCh: '91- 3/1R, '93- 3/1R. At 200m: WI: '85- 6. At 60m: WI: '93- 6. Won US 100m 1992, NCAA 200m 1989, PAm Jnr 400m 1984, GP 100m 1992. At 4x100m relay: four world records 1991-3, world junior record 1983.
Progression at 100m, 200m: 1982- 10.50w, 1983- 10.47/10.2, 20.7/21.09/20.73w; 1984- 10.56/10.3, 21.06; 1985- 10.21, 20.49/20.47w; 1986- 10.33/10.23w, 20.52; 1987- 10.12/10.11w, 20.36/20.21w; 1988- 10.03/9.86w, 20.29; 1989- 10.03/10.00w, 20.09; 1990- 10.16/10.05w, 20.33; 1991- 9.91, 20.63; 1992- 10.04/9.94w/9.92rw, 20.20/20.18w; 1993- 9.99/9.85w, 20.25. pbs: 60m 6.42 '91, 300m 32.22 '88, 400m 45.26 '86.
Twin sister Denise was 3rd NCAA and 6th TAC in pb 51.72 at 400m in 1987.

Rob MUZZIO b 25 Jun 1964 Wurzburg, GER 1.88m 91kg. VISA TC. Was at George Mason University.
At Dec: OG: '92- 5; WCh: '87- 13, '91- 20, '93- 8; won NCAA 1984-5, PAm Jnr 1982.
Progression at Dec: 1982- 7097*, 1983- 7511, 1984- 8205, 1985- 7968, 1986- 7746w, 1987- 8134, 1990- 8098, 1991- 8119, 1992- 8195, 1993- 8237. pbs: 100m 10.88/10.8 '87, 400m 48.68 '84, 1500m 4:23.64 '85, 110mh 14.51 '93 (14.15?); HJ 2.04 '91, PV 5.10 '90, LJ 7.22 '87, SP 17.00 '87, DT 51.04 '90, JT 64.50 '93.

Chris NELLOMS b.14 Aug 71 Dayton, Ohio 1.75m 74kg. Accusplit SC. Student at Ohio State University.

At 400m/4x400mR: WJ: '88- 1R, '90- 1/1R (1 4x100mR). Won PAm-J 400m 1989. At 200m: WSG: '93- 2.
Progression at 200m, 400m: 1987- 21.55, 47.53; 1988- 21.04, 45.80; 1989- 20.4/20.90/20.73w, 46.19; 1990- 20.47/20.36w, 45.36; 1991- 20.62/ 20.55w, 46.24; 1992- 20.27/19.94w, 45.84; 1993- 20.23/20.17w. pbs: 100m 10.33/10.03w '92, 300m 32.38 '93.
He has a record four World Junior gold medals, with a unique triple in 1990 and a relay gold from 1988. Set US high school record of 13.30 for the junior 110mh in 1990. US high school athlete of the year 1990, unbeaten at 400m from 1980 until 18 Jan 1991 when he lost indoors to Antonio Mackay. His second at 1989 TAC juniors was his only 200m loss in 1989-90. He was shot and almost killed in August 1992, but has since made a determined recovery and returned to top-class form.

Brent NOON b.29 Aug 1971 1.88m 123kg. Student at University of Georgia.
Progression at SP: 1992- 20.26, 1993- 20.48. NCAA champio 1992-3.
With 23.21 with the 6.25kg shot Noon became the second best ever ever in US high school history, but took a year out in 1991.

Dan O'BRIEN b.18 Jul 1966 Portland 1.89m 84kg. Reebok TC. Was at University of Idaho.
At Dec: WCh: '91- 1, '93- 1; won TAC 1991 (2nd 1990). At Hep: WI inv '93- 1.
World decathlon record 1992. US decathlon record in Tokyo and best at TAC (not a record due to wind assistance) in 1991. WIR Pentathlon 4497 '92, Heptathlon 6476 '93.
Progression at Dec: 1982-5583*, 1983- 6438*, 1984- 6873*, 1988- 7891, 1989- 7987, 1990- 8483w, 1991- 8844w/8812, 1992- 8891, 1993- 8817. pbs: 50m 5.84i '93, 60m 6.67i '93, 100m 10.41/10.23w '91; 400m 46.53 '91, 1500m 4:33.19 '89, 50mh 6.65i '93, 55mh 7.18i '91, 60mh 7.85i '93, 110mh 13.93 '93, 13.81w '89, HJ 2.16i '92, 2.13 '90; PV 5.25 '91, LJ 8.08 '92, 8.11w '91; SP 16.69 '92, DT 52.86 '90, JT 62.58 '92.
His first day 4656 at the 1990 TAC was the second best ever; a year later in the second best decathlon of all-time, 8844, he scored 4747 (70 more than Daley Thompson's best ever), but there was no wind gauge for the 100m at which he ran 10.23, the fastest ever run in a decathlon, and the wind was over the limit for the 110mh. He excelled in Tokyo, where he would surely have smashed the world record but for a near disaster in the high jump, clearing only his

Dan O'Brien: set world indoor heptathlon best and had no problems defending world decathlon title

opening height 1.91m and losing up to 200 points; he improved at 400m from 47.70 to 46.53. After a legal wind first day record 4698 at the 1992 US Olympic Trials, failed his opening height of 4.90 in the vault, and thus missed the Olympics. Came back in September with 4720 first day and a total of 8896 in Talence.
Finnish mother, black father, adopted at the age of two by an Oregon couple.

David PATRICK b.12 Jun 1960 Centralia, Illinois 1.83m 72kg. Reebok TC. Graduate of University of Tennessee.
At 800m: WCh: '83- 8. At 400mh: OG: '92- 8; WCh: '87-sf, '93- h; WCp: '89- 1; PAm: '87- 3; WSG: '81- 5 (2R), '87- 1/1R. Won TAC 400mh 1982, 1984, 1989-90; 800m 1983; NCAA 400mh 1982.
Progression at 400mh: 1979- 52.97, 1980- 50.90, 1981- 49.25, 1982- 48.44, 1983- 48.05, 1984- 48.80, 1985- 49.01, 1986- 48.59, 1987- 48.56, 1988- 47.75, 1989- 48.33, 1990- 48.22, 1991- 48.65, 1992- 48.01, 1993- 48.95. pbs: 400m 45.81 '89, 800m 1:44.70 '83.
Despite running 47.75 was fourth in 1988 US Olympic Trials. Married Sandra Farmer 2 Jan 1988; they achieved a unique husband and wife World Cup double in 1989. Twin brother Mark had pb 49.88 for 400mh and bronze medal at the World Student Games in 1983.

Antonio PETTIGREW b.3 Nov 1967 Macon, Georgia 1.83m 77kg. Reebok TC. Was at St Augustine's College.
At 400m/4x400m relay: WCh: '91- 1/2R, '93- res (1)R; WCp: '89- 5/2R, '92- 4R. Won TAC 1989, 1991.
Progression at 400m: 1986- 47.19, 1987- 46.31, 1988- 45.36, 1989- 44.27, 1990- 45.26, 1991- 44.36, 1992- 44.71, 1993- 44.45. pbs: 200m 20.70/ 20.62w '89, 300m 32.33 '89.

Jack PIERCE b.23 Sep 1962 Cherry Hill, New Jersey 1.85m 84kg. Mizuno TC. Was at Morgan State University.
At 110mh: OG: '92- 3; WCh: '87- 4, '91- 2, '93- 3. US champion 1992-3. At 60mh: WI: '91- 8.
Progression at 110mh: 1981- 14.18/14.09w, 1982- 13.77/13.7w, 1983- 13.61/13.6/13.44w, 1984- 13.60, 1985- 13.36, 1986- 13.55/13.4/ 13.53w, 1987- 13.41, 1988- 13.41, 1989- 13.24/ 13.16w, 1990- 13.43, 1991- 13.06, 1992- 13.13, 1993- 13.06. pbs: 200m 20.90 '84, 55mh 7.04i '89, 60mh 7.54i '89.
In 1991 he very nearly won the gold in Tokyo, when he took 0.17 off his pb and lost by just a millimetre or two to Greg Foster.

Mark PLAATJES b.2 Jun 1962 Johannesburg, South Africa 1.73m 64kg. Physical therapist in Illinois. Was at Witwatersrand University. US resident status granted 1989, became US citizenship in December 1992.
At Mar: WCh: '93- 1. SA champion 1981 and 1985. SA marathon record 1985.
Progression at Mar: 1980- 2:19:55, 1981- 2:16:17, 1982- 2:17:09, 1983- 2:17:19, 1984- 2:14:03, 1985- 2:08:58, 1986- 2:16:55, 1988- 2:10:41, 1989- 2:16:51, 1990- 2:13:44, 1991- 2:10:29, 1992- 2:14:23, 1993- 2:12:39. pbs: 3000m 8:10.02 '86, 5000m 14:03.65 '85, 10000m 28:31.67 '85, Half Mar 62:38 '85.
Other major marathon wins Columbus 1988, Los Angeles 1991. 2nd Berlin 1991.

Mike POWELL b.10 Nov 1963 Philadelphia 1.88m 77kg. Foot Locker AC. Sociology degree from UCLA, formerly at UC/Irvine.
At LJ: OG: '88- 2, '92- 2; WCh: '91- 1, '93- 1; WSG: '87- 1. Won GP 1991, 2nd 1989, 3rd 1987 & 1991. US champion 1990, 1992-3.
World long jump record 1991.
Progression at LJ: 1982- 7.48, 1983- 8.06, 1984- 7.98/8.14w, 1985- 8.17/8.28w, 1986- 8.04/ 8.22w, 1987- 8.27, 1988- 8.49, 1989- 8.49/8.55w, 1990- 8.66, 1991- 8.95, 1992- 8.64/8.99w, 1993- 8.70. pbs: 100m 10.45 '85, 200m 21.21/20.99w '85, HJ 2.16 '84, TJ 15.75 '84.
Played point guard at basketball on his high school team. Topped the world long jump rankings in 1990, and after losing 15 times to Carl Lewis from 1983 to 1991 won that epic

Mike Powell: a second world title in Stuttgart

contest in Tokyo to end the latter's winning streak and to take the world record that Bob Beamon had set back in 1968. 1991 Sullivan Award winner. 25 successive long jump wins to 29 Aug 1993.

Tom PUKSTYS b.28 May 1968 Glen Ellyn, Illinois 1.88m 91kg. Mizuno, NYAC. Was at University of Florida.
At JT: OG: '92- 10; WCh: '91- dnq 26, '93- 10; WCp: '92- 4. US champion 1992-3.
US javelin record 1993.
Progression at JT: 1987- 71.34, 1988- 75.72, 1989- 74.82, 1990- 83.30, 1991- 81.68, 1992- 83.20, 1993- 85.70.

Harry 'Butch' REYNOLDS Jr b.8 Jun 1964 Akron, Ohio 1.90m 80kg. Foot Locker AC. Ohio State University.
At 400m/R- 4x400m relay: OG: '88- 2/1R; WCh: '87- 3/1R, '93- 2/1R; WI: '93- 1. Won NCAA and TAC 1987, Olympic Trials 1988. 2nd GP 1993.
World records 400m 1988, 4x400mR 1988 and 1993. WIB 500m 1:00.86 '86, 600y 1:06.87 '87 (oversized track).
Progression at 400m: 1983- 48.1, 1984- 45.47, 1986- 45.36, 1987- 44.10, 1988- 43.29, 1989- 44.30, 1990- 44.22, 1991- 47.40, 1992- 44.14, 1993- 44.12. pbs: 200m 20.46 '87, 300m 32.05 '87.
In 1987 ran 12 sub 45.00 times and the three fastest ever low-altitude times, 44.10, 44.13 and 44.15. In 1988 ran a low-altitude record of 43.93 to win the US Trials, smashed Lee Evans's 20-year-old world record in Zürich, but was surprisingly defeated at the Olympics. Two year ban after positive drugs test in 1990 for Nandrolene at Monaco; reinstated by TAC in 1991 due to alleged irregularities in testing procedure, but the IAAF resisted his vigorous claims to run again internationally. Court rulings in the USA allowed him to run inthe 1992 US Trials, at which he was 5th in the 400m, but the IAAF extended his ban to the end of 1992 for bringing the sport into disrepute. On 14 Dec 1992 the US District Court in Columbus, Ohio awarded for him against the IAAF: $6,839,902 for loss of earnings during his two-year suspension, and $20,356,008 punitive damages. Brother Jeff has 400m pb 44.98 '88.

Calvin SMITH b.8 Jan 1961 Bolton, Mississippi 1.78m 69kg. Mazda TC. Graduate of University of Alabama.
At 200m/R- 4x100m relay: WCh: '83- 1/1R (2 at 100m), '87- 1, '93- resR (1). At 100m: OG: '84- 1R, '88- 3; WSG: '81: 2/1R; WCp: '85- 1R, '92- 3/1R. Won TAC 200m 1982, AAA 100m 1990. Won GP 200m 1985, 2nd 1987 3rd 100m 1988 & 1990. 2nd PAm-J 100m & 200m 1980.

Butch Reynolds: silver in worlds but gold in courts

World records: 100m 1983 and twice at 4x100mR 1983-4; low-altitude 100m best 1983.
Progression at 100m, 200m: (y 100y/220y): 1978- 9.6y, 21.5y; 1979- 10.36/10.30w, 20.7/21.22; 1980- 10.17/10.12w, 20.64; 1981- 10.21, 21.00; 1982- 10.05/9.91w, 20.31/20.20w; 1983- 9.93, 19.99; 1984- 10.11/9.94w, 20.33; 1985- 10.10, 20.14; 1986- 10.14, 20.29; 1987- 10.07, 20.10; 1988- 9.97/9.87w, 20.08, 1989- 10.05, 20.30; 1990- 10.04, 20.54; 1991- 10.38, 21.13; 1992- 10.14, 20.70/20.6; 1993- 10.06, 20.50. pb 50m 5.70i '84, 60y 6.12i '83, 60m 6.61i '93, 400m 46.43 '82.
Thrives off hard racing, his repeat world championships gold in 1987 was his 22nd sub 20.70 race of the year (14th sub 20.50).

Jim SPIVEY b.7 Mar 1960 Schiller Park, Illinois 1.80m 63kg. Asics TC. Graduate of Indiana University.
At 1500m: OG: '84- 5, '92- 8; WCh: '87- 3, '93- 5; PAm: '87- 2; WI: '87- 4; WSG: '81- 4. Won NCAA 1982, TAC 1984-5, 1987, 1992. GP 1M/1500m: 3rd 1986, 2nd 1987-8. At 5000m: WCh: '83- sf.
US 2000m record 1987.
Progression at 1500m, 1M: 1976- 4:35.5M; 1977- 4:18.3M; 1978- 4:06.2 (1600m); 1979- 3:44.66; 1980- 3:38.56, 3:58.9i; 1981- 3:37.24, 3:57.0; 1982- 3:37.34, 3:55.56; 1983- 3:36.4, 3:50.59; 1984- 3:34.19, 3:53.88; 1985- 3:35.15, 3:52.95; 1986- 3:34.4, 3:49.80; 1987- 3:34.37, 3:51.91; 1988- 3:31.01, 3:50.57; 1989- 3:36.85, 3:57.17; 1990- 3:34.47, 3:56.44; 1991- 3:33.81, 3:49.83; 1992-

3:32.94, 3:52.69; 1993- 3:34.67, 3:52.37. pbs: 800m 1:46.5 '82, 1000m 2:16.54 '84, 2000m 4:52.44 '87, 3000m 7:37.04 '93, 2M 8:24.14 '86, 5000m 13:19.24 '83.
Has a renowned finishing kick. Missed Olympic selection in 1988 as he was fourth in the US Trials, but showed that he would have been a prime contender with his 3:31.01 in Koblenz.

Lee STARKS b.10 Feb 1967 Jonesboro, Louisiana 1.85m 68kg. Sports TC. Was at Northwestern (LA) State and Louisiana State University.
At LJ: WSG: '89- 3; PAm: '91- 2. Won NCAA 1990, 3rd TAC 1989-90. Won GP 1991.
Progression at LJ: 1985- 7.16, 1986- 7.71w, 1987- 8.04, 1988- 8.03/8.12w, 1989- 8.19/8.48w, 1990- 8.24, 1991- 8.50, 1992- 8.40. pb 100m 10.45 '90.
Broke right leg at New York Games 1992.

Kareem STREETE-THOMPSON b.30 Mar 1973 Ithaca, New York 1.83m 82kg. Student at Rice University.
At LJ: OG: '92- dnq (h 100m); WCh: '91- dnq; CG: '90- 11 (qf 100m); WJ: '88- dnq; '90- 3; WSG: '93- 1. Won CAC Jnr 1992.
Progression at LJ: 1988- 6.84, 1989- 7.83, 1990- 7.95, 1991- 8.09/8.40w, 1992- 8.12/8.39w, 1993- 8.36. pbs: 55m 6.21i, 100m 10.30/10.19w '93, 200m 21.68 '92.
Fromthe Cayman Islands, he has determined to become a US citizen.

Gregg TAFRALIS b.9 Apr 1958 San Francisco 1.83m 129kg. Health instructor.
At SP: OG: '88- 9; WCh: '87- dnq 13; PAm: '87- 2; WI: '87- 4. 3rd GP 1992.
Progression at SP: 1979- 17.63, 1980- 17.91, 1981- 18.24, 1982- 20.12, 1983- 20.20, 1984- 21.25, 1985- 21.32, 1986- 21.45, 1987- 21.32, 1988- 21.36, 1989- 21.32, 1990- 19.57i, 1991- 19.43, 1992- 21.98, 1993- 19.93i/19.77. pb DT 62.38 '86.

Kory TARPENNING b.27 Feb 1962 Portland 1.80m 75kg. Nike International. PE graduate of University of Oregon.
At PV: OG: '88- 10, '92- 4; WI: '91- 4; WCp: '92- nh. Won Olympic Trials 1988, TAC 1988-9. 2nd GP 1991.
Progression at PV: 1980- 4.52, 1981- 5.03, 1982- 5.10i, 1983- 5.28, 1984- 5.50, 1985- 5.65, 1986- 5.70, 1987- 5.80, 1988- 5.89, 1989- 5.80, 1990- 5.83, 1991- 5.75, 1992- 5.86, 1993- 5.75. pb LJ 7.69w/7.68 '91.
Currently living in Paris, training with Jean-Claude Perrin.

Glenn TERRY b.10 Feb 1971 Cleveland 1.93m 82kg. Student at University of Indiana.
At 110mh: WSG: '93- 2; WJ: '90- sf. Won PAm-J 1989, NCAA 110mh and indoor 55mh 1993.
Progression at 110mh: 1989- 13.83, 1990- 13.64/13.4w, 1991- 13.75, 1992- 13.64, 1993- 13.35/13.24w. pb 55mh 7.09i '93.

Kevin TOTH b.27 Feb 1962 Cleveland 1.93m 141kg. Nike. Was at McNeese State University.
At SP: WCh: '93- 9.
Progression at SP: 1990- 18.06, 1991- 18.78, 1992- 20.99, 1993- 21.29.

Andrew VALMON b.1 Jan 1965 Brooklyn, New York 1.86m 78kg. Mazda TC. Was at Seton Hall University. Eastman Kodak sales rep.
At 400m/4x400mR: OG: '88- resR, '92- 1R; WCh: '91- 5/2R, '93- 1R; WI: '91- 2. 2nd PAm Jnr 1984, 2nd GP 1991.
World records 4x400m relay 1992 and 1993.
Progression at 400m: 1983- 46.81, 1984- 45.92, 1985- 45.13, 1986- 45.61, 1987- 44.89, 1988- 44.55, 1989- 45.21, 1990- 44.35, 1991- 44.65, 1992- 44.51, 1993- 44.28. pbs: 200m 21.14 '91, 21.0 '86, 300m 32.04 '90, 800m 1:50.58 '93.
Gold medal as he ran in preliminary rounds for the US 4x400mR team at the 1988 Olympics. Ran pb 44.28 in US Trials 1993 yet only 4th.

Erick WALDER b.5 Nov 1971 Mobile, Alabama 1.86m 77kg. Student atUniversity of Arkansas.
At LJ: WCh: '93- 4. At TJ: WJ: '90- 15. Won NCAA LJ 1993 indoors and out, indoor LJ & TJ 1992.
Progression at LJ, TJ: 1989- 7.36, 15.56; 1990- 16.25/16.31w, 1991- 7.79/7.84w, 16.05i; 1992- 8.47/8.58w, 16.88i/16.58/16.66w; 1993- 8.53, 16.86i/16.67/16.87w. pb HJ 2.11 '90.

Anthony WASHINGTON b.16 Jan 1966 Glasgow, Montana 1.86m 107kg. Stars & Stripes TC. Graphic artist. Graduate of Syracuse University.
At DT: OG: '92- 12; WCh: '91- dnq 28, '93- 11; PAm: '91- 1; WSG: '91- 2; WCp: '92- 1. US champion 1991, 1993. 2nd GP 1993.
Progression at DT: 1985- 52.88, 1986- 56.46, 1987- 60.16, 1988- 61.86, 1989- 64.18, 1990- 61.34, 1991- 65.04, 1992- 67.88, 1993- 66.86. pb HT 59.58 '89.
Set pbs when fourth at 1989 TAC and when winning TAC and Pan-Am Games in 1991.

Quincy WATTS b.19 Jun 1970 Detroit 1.90m 88kg. Nike International. Student at University of Southern California.
At 400m/4x400m relay: OG: '92- 1/1R; WCh: '91- 2R, '93- 4/1R; PAm: '91- 4/2R. Won NCAA 1992, 3rd GP 1993. At 4x100mR: WJ: '88- 1.

World records 4x400m relay 1992 and 1993.
Progression at 400m: 1987- 47.56, 1988- 46.67, 1990- 47.02, 1991- 44.98, 1992- 43.50, 1993- 44.13. pbs 100m 10.30/10.17w '87, 200m 20.50 '87, 300m 32.07 '93.
A surprise third in TAC 400m 1991, but gave up his World place to Danny Everett, before producing the fastest legs, 43.6 and 43.4 (third best of all-time), in the relay. Double gold in 1992 Olympics, including fastest ever, 43.1 on second leg of 4x400m relay. A fine basketball player in high school, he also played as a wide receiver at football for USC.

Todd WILLIAMS b.7 Mar 1969 Detroit 1.78m 66kg. Team Adidas. Was at University of Tennessee.
At 10000m: OG: '92- 10; WCh: '93- 7. Won US 10000m 1993, CC 1991, 1993.
Progression at 5000m, 10000m: 1988- 14:24.29i, 29:46.5; 1989- 14:14.08, 28:57.7; 1990- 13:48.16i/13:55.26, 28:41.97; 1991- 13:41.50i/13:49.27, 28:18.4; 1992- 13:36.99, 28:05.9; 1993- 13:20.13, 27:40.37. pbs: 3000m 7:47.69 '93, 2M 8:24.54 '92, Half Mar 61:52 '91, 60:11 (33m dh) '93.

Kevin YOUNG b.16 Sep 1966 Los Angeles 1.93m 82kg. Nike International. Sociology graduate of UCLA.
At 400mh: OG: '88- 4, '92- 1; WCh: '91- 4, '93- 1; PAm: '87- 2. US champion 1992-3, NCAA 1987-8. Won 400mh and overall GP 1992.
World 400mh record 1992.
Progression at 400mh: 1985- 51.09, 1986- 48.77, 1987- 48.15, 1988- 47.72, 1989- 47.86, 1990- 48.45, 1991- 47.83, 1992- 46.78, 1993- 47.18. pbs: 400m 45.11 '92, 800m 1:51.42 '88, 110mh 13.65 '92, 200mh 22.74 '92, LJ 7.73 '86, TJ 14.91 '85.
Reached world no. one ranking in 1989, after 10-5-3 in 1986-8. From 1989 has run 13 strides all the way. as opposed to previous practice of 12 strides between the first 4-5 hurdles of 400mh. World athlete of the year in 1992, when he ran a record ten times sub-48 seconds, won all his 17 finals at 400mh and took 0.24 off the world record set by Ed Moses in 1983 to win the Olympic title. He stretched his win streak to 25 finals until his loss 48.85 to 48.86 to Samuel Matete at London on 23 Jul 1993.

Women

Kim BATTEN b.29 Mar 1969 McRae, Georgia 1.70m 57kg. Reebok RC. Was at Florida State University.
At 400mh: WCh: '91- 5, '93- 4; 3rd GP 1993. At 400m: WI: '93 -6.
Progression at 400mh: 1986- 61.1, 1987- 60.94, 1988- 58.31, 1989- 58.60, 1990- 55.45, 1991- 53.98, 1992- 54.35, 1993- 53.84. pbs: 200m 23.54 '90, 400m 52.20 '92, 50mh 7.01i '92, 55mh 7.55i '92, 100mh 13.14/13.06w '91, 13.0 '90; LJ 6.21i '91, 6.15/6.34w '90, TJ 12.95i '91, 12.92 '90.
Collegiate 400m hurdles record 1991.

Dawn BOWLES b.12 Nov 1968 Neptune, New Jersey. 1.63m 48kg. Foot Locker AC. Sociology student at Louisiana State University.
At 100mh: WCh: '93- 6; PAm: '91- 4; WSG: '93-2. Won NCAA 1991.
Progession at 100mh: 1985- 14.51/14.2, 1986-14.04, 1987- 13.63/13.48w, 1988- 13.30/13.10w, 1990- 13.17, 1991- 12.82/12.70w, 1992- 12.84/12.70w, 1993- 12.84/12.74w. pbs: 100m 11.56 '92, 200m 23.96/23.80w '92, 55mh 7.51i '92, 60mh 8.11i '93.

Tonja BUFORD b.13 Nov 1970 Dayton, Ohio 1.76m 62kg. Mizuno TC. Student at University of Illinois.
At 400mh: OG: '92- sf; WCh: '93- 5; PAmG: '91-3. Won NCAA 1992.
Progression at 400mh: 1987- 62.5, 1988- 61.86, 1989- 60.93, 1990- 59.46, 1991- 56.45, 1992-54.75,. 1993- 54.38. pbs: 100m 11.50 '92, 200m 23.42 '92, 400m 53.17 '93, 55mh 7.60i '93, 100mh 13.07/12.94w '92.

Kym CARTER b.12 Mar 1964 Inglewood, California 1.88m 80kg. Was at Louisiana State University.
At Hep: OG: '92- 11; WCh: '91- 20, '93- 7. At Pen: WI inv: '93- 5.
Progression at Hep: 1987- 5549, 1990- 6003w, 1991- 6183, 1992- 6256, 1993- 6357. pbs: 200m 24.00 '93, 800m 2:06.80 '92, 100mh 13.53 '93, HJ 1.89 '82, LJ 6.10 '92, 6.25w '93; SP 15.49 '90, JT 40.68 '92, Pen 4566i '93.
Fifth ranked US high jumper in 1982.

Joetta CLARK b.1 Aug 1962 East Orange, New Jersey 1.72m 52kg. Foot Locker AC. Graduate of University of Tennessee. Legal investigator.
At 800m: OG: '88- sf, '92- 7; WCh: '87- sf, '91- sf, '93- h; WCp: '85- 5, '89- 9, '92- 2; WSG: '85- 6 (3 4x400mR), '87- 3; WI: '87- 6, '93- 3. US champion 1988-9, 1992-3; NCAA 1983-4.
Progression at 800m: 1976- 2:20.0, 1977- 2:11.3y, 1978- 2:05.29, 1979- 2:03.54, 1980- 2:03.83, 1981-2:03.45, 1982- 2:01.32, 1983- 2:01.34, 1984-2:00.15, 1985- 1:58.98, 1986- 2:00.2, 1987- 1:59.45, 1988- 1:59.79, 1989- 1:59.83, 1990- 1:59.69, 1991-1:58.95, 1992- 1:58.06, 1993- 1:58.17. pbs: 400m 52.20 '92, 1000m 2:37.9i '86, 2:39.13 '91; 1500m 4:17.2 '88, 1M 4:35.17 '92, 400mh 57.11 '85.
Daughter of the celebrated school principal, Joe Clark. Her brother (and coach) J.J.Clark has a 1500m pb of 3:41.5.

Gail DEVERS b.19 Nov 1966 Seattle 1.62m 52kg. Nike International. Studying sociology

and assistant coach at UCLA. Married Ron Roberts in June 1988.
At 100m/R- 4x100m relay (100mh): OG: '88- (sf); '92- 1/1R (5); WCh: '93- 1/2R (1); PAm: '87- 1/1R. At 60m: WI: '93- 1. Won NCAA 100m 1988, US 100m 1993, 100mh 1991-2. 2nd GP 100mh 1992.
US records 100mh (4) 1988-93, indoor 60m 1993.
Progression at 100m, 100mh: 1983- 11.69; 1984- 11.51/11.34w, 14.32; 1985- 11.19, 13.16/13.15w; 1986- 11.12/10.96w, 13.08; 1987- 10.98/10.85w, 13.28/13.1w; 1988- 10.97/10.86w, 12.61; 1991- 11.29, 12.48; 1992- 10.82, 12.55; 1993- 10.82, 12.46. pbs: 50m 6.10i '93, 60m 6.95i '93, 200m 22.71/22.55w '87, 400m 52.66 '87, 800m 2:11.07 '82, 55mh 7.58i '92, 60mh 7.93i '92, 400mh 59.26 '85, LJ 6.77 '88, TJ 12.97/13.31w '86.
The fastest ever woman sprinter-hurdler. A serious thyroid disorder (Graves's Disease) caused her to miss competition in 1989-90, but after being close to having to have a foot amputated she made an astonishingly speedy return to the top to win the TAC 100mh in 1991, and on to world silver and the US record in Berlin. In 1992 she was a surprise winner of the Olympic 100m but tripped over the last hurdle when well clear of the field in the 100mh.

Sandra FARMER-PATRICK b.18 Aug 1962 Kingston, Jamaica 1.73m 63kg. Flo-Jo International. Degree in industrial psychology from Cal.State University, Los Angeles.
At 400mh: OG: '84- 8, '92- 2; WCh: '83- h, '87- 4, '91- 4, '93- 2; CG: '82- 9; PAm: '83- 4, '87- 2; WCp: '89- 1, '92- 1; CAmG: '82- 1/3R. US champion 1989, 1992-3. Won overall GP 1993 (3rd 1989), individual 1989, 1991 & 1993; 2nd 1987.
Jamaican 400mh record holder from 1977, three US records 1989-93.
Progression at 400mh: 1977- 58.90, 1978- 59.8, 1979- 58.31, 1980- 58.62, 1981- 57.54, 1982- 57.4, 1983- 56.43, 1984- 56.05, 1985- 55.75, 1986- 55.89, 1987- 54.38, 1988- 54.49, 1989- 53.37, 1990- 54.46, 1991- 53.54, 1992- 53.59, 1993- 52.79. pbs: 200m 23.32 '89, 400m 51.35 '92, 800m 2:10.94 '84, 100mh 13.58/13.0w '89.
Born Sandra Miller, she took her grandmother's name of Farmer, when she moved from Kingston, Jamaica to Brooklyn, NY at the age of nine. She competed for the US as a junior, but then internationally for Jamaica. Married Dave Patrick (400mh) 2 Jan 1988 and changed nationality to US, but disqualified after winning semi at US Olympic Trials 1988. Unbeaten in 15 finals at 400mh in 1989, but second in TAC 1990. She ran the race of her life to take 0.58 off her 4-year old US record and run under the old world record, but second to Sally Gunnell at the 1993 Worlds.

Michelle FINN b.8 May 1965 Orlando 1.65m 52kg. Mazda TC. Graduate of Florida State University.
At 200m: OG: '92- 7/res R; WCh: '93- sf/2R (sf 100m). At both indoor 55m and outdoor 100m won NCAA 1985 and TAC 1990. At 60m: WI: '91- 5.
Progression at 100m, 200m: 1978- 11.3y, 1982- 11.79, 1983- 11.56, 24.44; 1984- 11.43, 23.61/23.47w; 1985- 11.26/11.04w, 23.32/22.9/ 22.77w/ 22.6w; 1986- 11.20, 22.97; 1987- 11.21/11.11w, 23.19/23.04w; 1988- 11.32/11.22w, 23.33; 1989- 11.24/11.22w, 22.88; 1990- 11.05/10.96w, 22.76; 1991- 11.22/11.16w, 23.29; 1992- 11.17/10.97w, 22.39; 1993- 11.16/11.06w, 23.01/22.81w. pbs: 50m 6.13i '92, 55m 6.61i '90, 60m 7.07i '92, LJ 6.17 '86.
Gold medal as ran in heats for winning US relay team at 1992 Olympics.

Carlette GUIDRY b.4 Sep 1968 Houston 1.68m 50kg. Nike International. Studied speech communication at Texas University. Married Mon White (400m 46.37 '90) in November 1991.
At 100m: WCh: '91- 8; At 200m/4x100mR: OG: '92- 5/1R; WJ: '86- 4/1R (7 LJ). Won TAC 100m 1991, PAm-J 200m & LJ 1986, GWG 100m 1990, NCAA 60m & 200m indoors 1990. 2nd TAC 100m & NCAA 200m 1990.
Progression at 100m, 200m: 1983- 11.6; 1984- 24.45/24.28w; 1985- 11.61, 23.84; 1986- 11.59/11.48w, 23.46/22.9; 1987- 11.56/11.52w, 23.35; 1988- 11.11, 22.99/22.96w/22.7; 1989-

Sandra Farmer-Patrick: second in Stuttgart but won the overall GP

Lynn Jennings: a record 7 US CC titles

11.30/11.29w, 22.90; 1990- 11.03, 22.62; 1991- 10.94/10.91w, 22.78/22.44w; 1992- 11.09/ 11.07w, 22.24; 1993- 11.35/11.24w, 22.98/ 22.76w. pbs: 55m 6.66i '90, 60m 7.12i '93, 400m 52.46 '90, LJ 6.42 '86, 6.47w '87; TJ 12.99 '86.
Including four at relays has won eight NCAA titles indoors and out.

Yolanda HENRY b.2 Dec 1964 Houston 1.68m 52kg. Mazda TC. Graduate of Abilene Christian University. Supervisor, juvenile detention centre.
At HJ: WCh: '91- dnq 17=; WI: '91- 4; WSG: '89- 4. Won TAC 1990-1.
Progression at HJ: 1982- 1.75, 1984- 1.78, 1985- 1.83, 1986- 1.89, 1987- 1.91, 1988- 1.89, 1989- 1.94, 1990- 2.00, 1991- 1.95/1.96i, 1992- 1.92, 1993- 1.94. pbs: 100mh 14.22/14.06w '86, 400mh 57.45 '87, Hep 4995 '85.
She set a women's record with a high jump of 32 cm above her own head in 1990.

Tanya HUGHES b.25 Jan 1972 1.85m.
At HJ: OG: '92- 11=; WCh: '93- 7; PAm: '91- 4; WJ: '90- 11; WSG: '93- 1. Won US HJ 1992-3, NCAA 1993.
Progression at HJ: 1985- 1.65, 1986- 1.70, 1987- 1.75, 1988- 1.81, 1989- 1.87, 1990- 1.85, 1991- 1.94, 1992- 1.97, 1993- 1.95.

Lynn JENNINGS b.1 Jul 1960 Princeton, New Jersey 1.65m 52kg. Nike International. History graduate of Princeton University. Freelance writer.
At 10000m: OG: '88- 6, '92- 3; WCh: '87- 6, '91- 5, '93- 5. At 3000m: '93- 3. World CC: '86- 2, '87- 4, '88- 4, '89- 6, '90- 1, '91- 1, '92- 1, '93- 3. Won US 3000m 1988, 1990; 10000m 1987, 1991-3, record seven CC titles, 1985, 1987-91, 1993.
WIB: 2 miles 9:28.15 TAC '86, 5000m 15:22.64 '90. US 10000m record 1992. US road 10km record 31:06 '90.
Progression at 3000m, 10000m: 1979- 9:51.2, 1982- 9:35.6, 1983- 9:01.44, 1984- 9:45.4, 1985- 8:49.86, 32:03.37; 1986- 8:53.19i, 1987- 8:49.23, 31:45.43;, 1988- 8:48.19, 31:39.93; 1989- 9:15.74, 1990- 8:40.45i/8:46.08, 1991- 8:53.0, 31:54.44; 1992- 8:44.60, 31:19.89; 1993- 8:52.55, 31:30.53. pbs: 800m 2:06.26i '92, 2:06.54 '86; 1500m 4:06.4 '90, 1M 4:24.14 '90, 2000m 5:49.8i '90, 5:52.62 '86; 2M 9:28.15i '86, 5000m 15:07.92 '90.
TAC junior 1500m and CC champion 1977. As an unofficial entrant ran 2:46+ for third woman at age 17 in 1978 Boston marathon. After reuniting with her high school coach John Babington, she won three succeanya 1990 she become the first runner to win TAC titles in outdoor and indoor track, road racing and cross-country in one year.

Esther JONES b.7 Apr 1969 Chicago 1.78m 61kg. Nike. Student at Louisiana State University.
At 200m/4x100m relay (100m): OG: '92- 1R; WCh: '91- sf; WJ: '88- 4 (4); WSG: '89- 3/1R; WCp: '89- 3R. Won NCAA 100m and 200m 1990. 2nd TAC 100m 1988-9, TAC 200m 1989, NCAA 100m 1989.
Progression at 100m, 200m: 1986- 11.70, 23.81; 1987- 11.41, 23.49; 1988- 11.22/11.18w, 23.05/23.00w; 1989-11.12/11.07w, 22.53/22.37w; 1990- 11.62, 23.70; 1991- 11.17/11.12w, 22.76; 1992- 11.15, 22.47; 1993- 11.45/11.31w, 23.12. pb 55m 6.69i '89, 60m 7.28i '92.

Kim JONES b.2 May 1958 Sonoma, California 1.70m 52kg. née Seelye, formerly Rosenquist. Nike International. Was at Eastern Washington University.
At Mar: WCh: '87- dnf, '93- 8.
Progression at Mar: 1984- 2:48:48, 1985- 2:35:59, 1986- 2:32:31, 1987- 2:35:41, 1988- 2:32:03; 1989- 2:27:54, 1990- 2:30:50, 1991- 2:26:40, 1992- 2:35:46, 1993- 2:30:00. pb 10000m 33:08.1 '88.
Mother of two, she was a 440y/880y runner at school, but did not run seriously until 1982, two years after birth of her daughter Jamie. Marathon début 5th at Honolulu 1984. In 1989 was second in Houston and won the Twin Cities marathon (as she had in 1986) with pbs when third at Boston 2:29:34 and second in New York. More seconds at New York 1990, Boston and Berlin 1991, Boston 1993. Suffers from asthma.

Marion JONES b.12 Oct 1975 Los Angeles 1.78m 61kg. Studying journalism at North Carolina State University.

At 100m/200m: WJ: '92- 5/7/2R. Won TAC junior 100m & 200m 1991-2.
Progression at 100m, 200m: 1989- 12.01, 24.46/24.06w/23.8w; 1990- 11.62, 23.70; 1991- 11.17, 22.76; 1992- 11.14, 22.58; 1993- 11.28/11.2, 23.01/22.79w. pbs: 400m 52.91 '92, LJ 6.71 '93.
5th at 100m and 4th at 200m in 1992 US Olympic Trials, but declined Olympic relay reserve place. Plays basketball.

Jackie JOYNER-KERSEE b.3 Mar 1962 East St.Louis, Illinois 1.78m 70kg. McDonald's TC. Was at UCLA, where she is now assistant basketball coach. Sister of triple jumper Al Joyner. Married coach Bobby Kersee on 11 Jan 1986.
At Hep/LJ: OG: '84- 2/5, '88- 1/1, '92- 1/3; WCh: '83- dnf/-, '87- 1/1, '91- dnf/1, '93- 1/-. Won US Hep 1982, 1987, 1991-3; LJ 1987, 1990-3; NCAA Hep 1982-3, GWG Hep 1986, 1990, PAm-J LJ 1980; 3rd GP LJ 1985, 1992. Won Mobil Indoor GP 1987 & 1989.
World records: four heptathlon1986-8,long jump 1987. US records: 100mh (2) 1988, LJ (3) 1985-7, heptathlon (6) 1984-8. Two WIB 55mh 7.37 '89.
Progression at LJ, Hep: 1974- 5.10, 1975- 5.22, 1976- 5.31, 1977- 5.69, 1978- 5.55/6.06w; 1979- 6.28/6.30w; 1980- 6.34/6.42w; 1981- 6.39/ 6.47w, 5754w; 1982- 6.44/6.61w, 6066; 1983- 6.74/6.77w, 6390; 1984- 6.81, 6579; 1985- 7.24, 6718; 1986- 7.12/7.15w, 7158; 1987- 7.45, 7128; 1988- 7.40/7.45w, 7291; 1990- 7.12, 6783; 1991- 7.32, 6878; 1992- 7.17, 7044; 1993- 7.08/7.09w, 6837. pbs: 100m 11.71 '86, 200m 22.30 '87, 400m 53.64 '90, 800m 2:08.51 '88, 50mh 6.84i '93, 60mh 7.81i '89, 100mh 12.61 '88, 400mh 55.05 '85, HJ 1.93 '88, TJ 13.20 '85, SP 16.84 '88, JT 50.12 '86.
Sullivan Award winner 1986. Won both long jump and heptathlon by huge margins at the 1987 World Championships and went on to the Olympic double in 1988. Won 12 successive heptathlons 1985-91, before she pulled up with a hamstring injury at the 1991 Worlds. The previous day she had retained her long jump title, but had suffered a severe ankle injury. In her career has won 22/32 heptathlons and has the five highest ever scores, the first five over 7000. Won at Götzis 1986.

Natasha KAISER-BROWN. b.14 May 1967 Des Moines, Iowa 1.75m 59kg. née Kaiser. Mizuno. Was at University of Missouri. Married to Brian Brown (HJ 2.34i '90, US champion 1989).
At 400m/4x400mR: OG: '92- silver R; WCh: '93- 2/1R; PAm: '91- 4/1R.
Progression at 400m: 1984- 54.09, 1985- 55.0, 1986- 51.48, 1987- 52,57, 1988- 51.73, 1989- 50.86, 1990- 51.55, 1991- 51.20, 1992- 50.42, 1993- 50.17. pbs: 100m 11.83 '93, 11.60w '89; 200m 23.36 '92

Anne Marie LETKO b.7 Mar 1969 Rochester, NY 1.70m 52kg. Nike. Was at Wake Forest University. At 10000m: WCh: '91- dnf; '93- 8; WSG: '91- 1; WCp: '92- 5.
Progression at 10000m: 1988- 35:51.75, 1990- 33:06.21, 1991- 32:26.65, 1992- 33:47.20, 1993- 31:37.26. pb 3000m 9:15.03i '90.
Prominent for much of the 1993 New York Marathon (her début), but dropped out at 23 miles.

Maicel MALONE b.12 Jun 1969 Indianapolis 1.78m 62kg. Was at Arizona State University. Married James Trapp (100m 10.16/10.04w '91, 200m: 20.49 '91) 16 Aug 1991.
At 400m/R- 4x100m relay: WCh: '93- 1R; WSG: '91- 1/1R, '93- 1R; WJ: '86- 3/1R (sf 200m), '88- 2/2R; PAm: '91- 1R; Won NCAA 1988, 1990, indoors 1990. 2nd Pan-American Junior 100m and 200m 1986.
Progression at 400m: 1984- 55.22, 1985- 53.7, 1986- 52.42, 1987- 52.7, 1988- 50.96, 1989- 52.09, 1990- 51.13, 1991- 50.33, 1992- 52.16i, 1993- 51.37. pbs: 100m 11.47 '91, 11.18w '86, 200m 22.91 '91, 300m 36.9i '91.
Olympic relay reserve 1988. Won NCAA indoor 400m 1990-2 (US indoor record 51.05 '91). Son born 3 Nov 1992.

LaVonna MARTIN b.18 Nov 1966 Dayton, Ohio 1.70m 66kg. Reebok RC. Graduate of University of Tennessee. Married to Edrick Floreal CAN LJ 8.20 '91, 8.39w '89; TJ 17.29 '89.
At 100mh: OG: '88- sf, '92- 2; WCh: '87- 8; PAm: '87- 1. At 60mh: '93- 2. Won PAm-J 1984, NCAA 1987, TAC 1987, 1990. Won Mobil Indoor GP 1990.
Progression at 100mh: 1983- 13.63, 1984- 13.55, 1985- 13.10/13.02w, 1986- 12.95, 1987- 12.80, 1988- 12.85, 1989- 13.01, 1990- 12.74, 1992- 12.69, 1993- 12.78. pbs: 100m 11.46 '86, 11.44w '88; 200m 23.24 '87, 22.94w '85; 400m 52.6 '85, 55mh 7.41i '90, 60mh 7.93i '93, 400mh 57.84 '85.
Received two-year ban after positive steroids test 1990; claimed she was given furosenide unknowingly by her coach Tatyana Zelentsova.

Jearl MILES b.4 Sep 1966 Gainesville 1.70m 60kg. Reebok RC. Was at Alabama A&M University .
At 400m: OG: '92- sf/2R; WCh: '91- 5/2R, '93- 1/1R; WI: '93- 3; PAm: '91- 3; WSG: '89- 2/1R; WCp: '92- 1. US champion 1993.
Progression at 400m: 1986- 52.41, 1987- 52.36, 1988- 51.28, 1989- 51.52, 1990- 51.76, 1991- 50.19, 1992- 50.30, 1993- 49.82. pbs: 200m 23.29 '93, 800m 2:04.78 '92, LJ 6.36/6.47w '88.

Annette PETERS b. 31 May 1965 Reno, Nevada 1.65m 49kg. née Hand. Nike West. Was at the

University of Oregon. Elementary school teacher
At 3000m: OG: '92- h; WCh: '91- 8, '93- 10; WSG: '87- 4. US champion 1500m & 3000m 1993, NCAA 5000m 1988.
US 5000m record 1993.
Progression at 3000m: 1985- 9:19.23, 1986- 9:04.45, 1987- 8:59.90, 1988- 8:59.15, 1989- 9:00.61, 1990- 8:54.64, 1991- 8:44.02, 1992- 8:42.09, 1993- 8:43.59. pbs: 800m 2:13.2 '86, 1500m 4:08.87 '93, 1M 4:38.19 '88, 2000m 5:38.08 '92, 5000m 14:56.07 '93, 10000m 32:15.8 '91.

PattiSue PLUMER b.27 Apr 1962 Covina, California 1.63m 51kg. Nike International. Graduate of Stanford University. Lawyer. Married Steve Levere 30 Dec 1989.
At 3000m (1500m): OG: '88- 13, '92- 5 (10); WCp: '89- 3; WI: '85- 3. Won TAC 1989, 1992; GWG 1990. At 1500m: WCh: '91- 12. At 5000m: Won NCAA 1984, TAC 1990-1. Won GP 3000m 1989, 5000m 1990, 2nd 5000m 1986, 3rd 3000m 1991.
US 5000m record 1989.
Progression at 1500m, 3000m: 1981- 9:42.02, 1982- 8:55.98, 1983- 4:18/71, 8:53.54i/8:53.81; 1984- 4:11.36, 8:54.91; 1985- 9:01.85i, 1986- 4:19.75, 8:46.24; 1988- 4:13.64, 8:45.21; 1989- 4:06.57, 8:42.12; 1990- 4:06.58, 8:41.45i/8:44.07; 1991- 4:05.04, 8:45.89; 1992- 4:03.42, 8:40.98. pbs: 800m 2:00.3 '90, 1M 4:24.90 '91, 2000m 5:42.82 '89, 5000m 15:00.00 '89.
A splendidly consistent top-class runner. Won the 1990 Fifth Avenue Mile in course record 4:16.68. Gave birth to daughter May 1993.

Meredith RAINEY b.15 Oct 1968 New York 1.67m 54kg. Nike Boston. Social studies graduate of Harvard University.
At 800m: OG: '92- h; WCh: '91- h, '93- 5. US champion 1990, NCAA 1989.
Progression at 800m: 1989- 2:02.67, 1990- 1:59.73, 1991- 1:59.30, 1992- 1:59.18, 1993- 1:57.63. pbs: 400m 51.56 '90, 1000m 2:40.80 '90.

Judi St. HILAIRE b.5 Sep 1959 Lindonville, Vermont 1.73m 48kg. Nike International. Graduate of University of Vermont. Trained as a dental hygienist.
At 3000m: WCh: '91- 7. At 10000m: OG: '92- 8. 2nd World 15km road 1985. Won TAC 5000m 1983, 10000m 1980.
Progression at 3000m, 10000m: 1979- 9:33.5, 1980- 9:22.4, 33:31.02; 1981- 9:52.53Mi, 33:17.8; 1982- 9:37.2, 1983- 9:20.21, 1985- 9:11.4, 1987- 32:59.99, 1991- 8:44.02, 32:21.0; 1992- 9:05.72, 31:38.04. pbs: 1500m 4:14.80 '92, 1M 4:39.3i '90, 2000m 5:51.3 '91, 5000m 15:36.40 '91. Road 15km 49:00 '89, half marathon 1:11:13 '85, Mar 2:37:49 '84.

Meredith Rainey: fifth in Stuttgart 800 metres

Outstanding record at road running, with very little track experience until 1991, when she took 27 seconds off her pre-season 3000m best; Similar improvement when took over 40 secs off her 10000m best at the Olympics.

Shelly STEELY b.23 Oct 1962 Reading, Pennsylvania 1.68m 52kg. Mizuno TC. Degree in health science from University of Florida. Married Aaron Ramirez (At 10000m: 17 WCh '91) 28 Sep 1991.
At 3000m: OG: '92- 7. Won TAC 1991 (2nd 1984). 3rd GP 5000m 1992.
Progression at 3000m: 1984- 9:03.86, 1985- 9:09.02i, 1986- 9:03.95, 1987- 9:44.30, 1988- 9:11.42i, 1989- 9:18.60, 1990- 9:01.86, 1991- 8:47.68, 1992- 8:41.28, 1993- 8:52.99. pbs: 800m 2:05.12 '91, 1500m 4:05.07 '92, 1M 4:25.49 '92, 2000m 5:45.56 '92, 5000m 15:08.67 '92, 10000m 32:41.14 '90.

Rochelle STEVENS b.8 Sep 1966 Memphis 1.70m 55kg. Maybelline TC. Graduate of Morgan State University. Teacher.
At 400m/4x400mR: OG: '92- 6/2R; WCh: '91- 2R; PAm: '87- 1R; WSG: '87- 1R; WCp: '89- 4/4R. Won NCAA 1988, TAC 1989, 1992.
Progression at 400m: 1985- 53.31, 1986- 51.90, 1987- 51.23, 1988- 51.23, 1989- 50.75, 1990- 50.39, 1991- 50.71, 1992- 50.06, 1993- 52.39. pbs: 100m 11.37 '88, 11.1 '87, 200m 22.84 '87, 300m 37.25 '93, 800m 2:11.01 '83.
Olympic relay reserve 1988.

Lynda TOLBERT b.3 Oct 1967 Washington, DC 1.63m 52kg. Nike Central. Was at Arizona State University

At 100mh OG: '92- 7; WCh: '93- 3; WCp: '89- 3=. Won NCAA 1988, 1990; US 1989, 1993; GP 1992.
Progression at 100mh: 1984- 14.12, 1985- 13.72, 1986- 13.61/13.50w, 1987- 13.06, 1988- 12.76/ 12.75w, 1989- 12.75, 1990- 12.82, 1991- 13.40/ 13.00w, 1992- 12.71/12.66w, 1993- 12.67. pbs: 100m 11.49/11.41w '88, 55mh 7.44i '90, 60mh 8.06i '88, LJ 6.10 '87.

Gwen TORRENCE b.12 Jun 1965 Atlanta 1.70m 57kg. Mazda TC. Was at University of Georgia, studying family and child development.
At 100m/200m/R- 4x100m relay (4x400mR): OG: '88- 5/6, '92- 4/1/1R (2R); WCh: '87- 5, '91- 2/2, '93- 3/2/2R (1R); PAm: '87- 1/1R; WSG: '85- 1R, '87- 1/1/1R. Won US 100m 1992, 200m 1988, 1991-3; NCAA 100m and 200m 1987. Won GP 100m 1993, 2nd 100m 1991, 200m 1992. At 60m: WI: '89- 2, '91- 4. Won NCAA indoor 55m 1986-7 (6.56 WIB '87), TAC 1988 (tie), 1989.
Progression at 100m, 200m, 400m: 1982- 24.2; 1983- 11.92, 24.34/23.9y; 1984- 11.41/11.37w, 23.54; 1985- 11.40/11.11w, 22.96; 1986- 11.30/ 11.01w, 22.53; 1987- 11.09/11.08w, 22.40/ 22.33w/22.2w; 1988- 10.91/10.78w, 22.02; 1989- 11.12, 1990- 11.28, 22.82; 1991- 10.96/10.85w, 22.07; 1992- 10.86/10.82w, 21.72, 49.64; 1993- 10.87, 22.00, 49.83. pbs: 60m 7.07i '89.
Won 49 successive races at indoor short sprints from 31 Jan 1986 to defeat by Dawn Sowell on 17 Feb 1989, including tie with Evelyn Ashford in 1988. Married to Manley Waller (100m 10.26 '86); son born 1989. Ran 49.1 lead-off 400m relay leg at 1993 World Championships, at which she won four medals.

Janeene VICKERS b.3 Dec 1968 Torrance, California 1.70m 62kg. World Class AC. Was at UCLA.
At 400m/4x400mR: OG: '92- 3; WCh: '91- 3; WJ: '86- 4/1R. 2nd PAm-J 400m 1986. Won NCAA 1989-90, TAC 1990.
Progression at 400mh: 1987- 57.80, 1988- 56.10, 1989- 55.27, 1990- 54.80, 1991- 53.47, 1992- 54.31, 1993- 56.21. pbs: 100m 11.56/11.41w '91, 200m 23.20 '91, 400m 51.57 '91, 100mh 13.16 '91, 13.05w '90.
US high school athlete of the year 1987, when she first tried the 400m hurdles. The previous year she had a 400m best of 52.25.

Dannette YOUNG b.6 Oct 1964 Jacksonville 1.70m 55kg. Reebok RC. Was at Alabama A&M. Sales clerk.
At 200m/R- 4x100m relay: OG: '88- resR; WCh: '91- 6, '93- 8; WCp: '89- 4; WSG: '87- 3/1R. 2nd GP 1988. Won TAC 1989, GWG 1990.
Progression at 200m, 400m: 1982- 24.0y, 1983- 23.76, 1984- 23.38/23.32w, 1985- 22.92/22.85w, 1986- 23.12/22.84w, 1987- 22.72, 1988- 22.23/ 22.21w, 52.46; 1989- 22.29, 1990- 22.40/22.19w, 1991- 22.24, 53.07; 1992- 22.55, 50.46; 1993- 22.51/22.44w, 51.59. pb 100m 11.10 '88.
Has won two Olympic relay medals after running in heats only: gold at 4x100m 1988, silver 4x400m 1992. Son born 1980.

VENEZUELA

Governing body: Federación Venezolana de Atletismo, Apartado Postal 29059, Caracas.
National Champions 1993: **Men**: 100m: Jorge Cañizales 10.5; 200m: Douglas Figuera 21.8, 400m: Henry Aguiar 47.79, 800m: Mark Olivo 1:51.41, 1500m: José López 3:44.4, 5000m: Félix Ladera 14:29.1, 10000m: Luis Lugo 31:21.6, 3000mSt: Amada Rivas 9:14.5, 110mh: Federico Ifill 14.60, 400mh: Wilfredo Ferrer 51.8, HJ: Anardo Smith 2.07, PV: Konstantin Zagustin 4.80, LJ: Miguel Padron 7.40, TJ: Sergio Saavedra 16.69, SP/DT: Yoger Medina 17.93/53.96, HT: Aldo Bello 55.18, JT: Clemente Flores 61.26, Dec: Diogenes Estéves 6769, 20kmW: Carlos Ramones 1:24:50. **Women**: 100m/200m/HJ/LJ: Carmen Rodriguez 11.90/24.6/1.70/5.67, 400m: Xiomara Diaz 53.3, 800m: Shamira Valero 2:18.6, 1500m: Uvilma Ruiz 4:44.3, 3000m: Monica López 11:12.4, 10000m: Monica Sarmiento 39:20.4, 100mh: Teresa Rodriguez 15.58, 400mh: Josahen Romero 65.0, TJ:

Gwen Torrence: four medals but only one gold in Stuttgart

Mariana Prazuela 11.89, SP: Lila Morales 13.18, DT: Neolanis Suarez 44.40, JT: Patricia Alonzo 45.40; Hep: Libia Riego 4005, 10kmW: Alba Villafranca 56:00.1.

YUGOSLAVIA

Governing body: Atletski Savez Jugoslavije, Strahinjica Bana 73a, 11000 Beograd. Founded in 1921.

National Championships first held in 1920 (men) and 1923 (women). **1993 champions**: **Men**: 100m/200m: Slobodan Brankovic 10.33/ 20.98, 400m: Nenad Djurovic 47.53, 800m: Dejan Pajkic 1:49.8, 1500m/5000m: Ljubisa Djokic 3:48.78/14:08.1, 10000m: Borislav Devic 30:24.6, Mar: Goran Raicevic 2:23:29, 3000mSt: Predrag Mladenovic 9:04.9, 110mh: Mirko Marjanovic 14.59, 400mh: Zoran Budisa 54.27, HJ: Dragutin Topic 2.34, PV: Fedja Kamasi 4.90, LJ: Stevan Grujic 7.64, TJ: Zeljko Obradovic 16.12, SP/DT: Dragan Peric 21.26/57.78, HT: Dragan Majstorovic 56.00, JT: Radoman Scekic 75.24, Dec: Slavoljub Nikolic 6728h, 10000mW: Aleksandar Rakovic 43:07.0. **Women**: 100m/200m: Marina Filipovic 11.71/23.79, 400m/800m: Livija Abraham 55.12/2:13.5, 1500m/3000m/Mar: Suzana Ciric 4:21.95/9:20.2/2:40:27, 100mh: Svetlana Stetic 14.65, 400mh: Aleksandra Gligic 61.64, HJ: Jasna Antonijevic 1.71, LJ: Radojka Kurcubic 5.95, TJ/Hep: Dejana Rakita 12.22/ 4074, SP/DT: Danijela Curovic 17.89/54.04, JT: Ivana Kojic 49.94.

Dragan PERIC b.8 May 1964 Zivinice 1.86m 107kg. AK Partizan.

At SP: OG: '92- 7; WCh: '91- 7, '93- 5; EC: '90- 13. Yugoslav champion SP 1990-3, DT 1992-3. Yugoslav shot record 1993.

Progression at SP: 1980- 11.35, 1981- 12.23, 1982- 14.88, 1983- 17.24, 1985- 16.89, 1986- 17.70, 1987- 18.86, 1988- 19.92, 1989- 20.42, 1990- 20.06, 1991- 20.47, 1992- 20.91, 1993- 21.26. pb DT 61.94 '91.

Dragutin TOPIC b.12 Mar 1971 Belgrade 1.97m 77kg. Crvena Zvezda. Student at Belgrade University of PE.

At HJ: OG: '92- 8=; WCh: '91- 9, '93- dnq; EC: '90- 1; WJ: '90- 1; EJ: '89- 4; EI: '92- 3=. Yugoslav champion 1993.

World junior high jump record 1990, five Yugoslav records 1990-3.

Progression at HJ: 1985- 1.85, 1986- 1.95, 1987- 1.95, 1988- 2.06, 1989- 2.23, 1990- 2.37, 1991- 2.32/2.34i, 1992- 2.35, 1993- 2.38. pbs: LJ 7.48i '93, TJ 15.66 '92, Dec 6155h '93.

Completed a marvellous major championships double in Split. Was at high school in Illinois, USA for a year in 1987/8, but played basketball while there and did not compete as a high jumper. Now plays basketball very occasionally for Spartak Subotica in the Yugoslav League Division One.

ZAMBIA

Governing body: Zambia Amateur Athletic Association, PO Box 23036, Kitwe.

Samuel MATETE b.7 Jul 1968 Chingola 1.83m 77kg. Student at Auburn University, formerly at Blinn CC, USA 1988-90.

At 400mh: OG: '88- h, '92- dq sf; WCh: '91- 1. '93- 2; CG: '90- 5; AfG: '87- sf; AfCh: '88- 5 (4.400m); WJ: '88- 5; WCp: '92- 1/1R. 2nd GP 1990, 1992. Won NCAA 1991.

African 400mh record 1991. Zambian records 1989-91: 11 at 400mh, 2 at 400m.

Progression at 400mh: 1987- 51.48, 1988- 50.5, 1989- 48.67, 1990- 47.91, 1991- 47.10, 1992- 47.91, 1993- 47.60. pbs: 100m 10.77 '89, 200m 21.04 '89, 400m 44.88 '91.

Five national records in a month in 1989 from 49.94 to 48.67. He moved up to world number two in 1990. In 1991 he was unbeaten in 23 races at 400mh, improving to 47.80 and then to 47.10 (the second fastest ever run) in Zürich prior to becoming the first Zambian world champion. In 1992 he was disqualified after finishing third in his Olympic semi for trailing leg knocking down hurdle in another lane. Apparently over age when he competed in the 1988 World Junior Championships.

Samuel Matete: world silver but ended Kevin Young's winning streak

INTRODUCTION TO WORLD LISTS AND INDEX

Records

World, World Junior, Olympic, Continental and Area records are listed. In running events up to and including 400 metres, only fully automatic times are shown. Marks listed are those which are considered statistically acceptable by the ATFS, and thus may differ from official records where, for instance the performance was set indoors.

World All-time and Year Lists

These lists are presented in the following format: Mark, Wind reading (where appropriate), Name, Nationality (abbreviated), Date of birth, Position in competition, Meeting name (if significant), Venue, Date of performance.

In standard events the best 30 or so performances are listed followed by the best marks for other athletes. Position, meet and venue details have been omitted for reasons of space beyond 100th in year lists.

Indexes

These lists contain the names of all athletes ranked with full details in the world year lists. The format of the index is as follows:

Family name, First name, Nationality, Birthdate, Height (cm) and Weight (kg), 1993 best mark, Lifetime best as at the end of 1992 and the relevant year.

An asterisk before the name indicates an athlete who is profiled in the Biographies section.

Meeting Abbreviations

The following abbreviations have been used for meetings with, in parentheses, the first year that they were held.

AAA (GBR) Amateur Athletic Association Championships (1880)
AAU (USA) Amateur Athletic Union Championships (1888) (now TAC)
AfrC African Championships (1979)
AfG African Games (1965) (or AfrG)
AmCp America's Cup (World Cup Trial)
APM Adriaan Paulen Memorial, Hengelo
Arena Arena International, Bern, Switzerland
AsiC Asian Championships (1973)
AsiG Asian Games (1951)
ASV Weltklasse in Köln, ASV club meeting (1934)
Athl Athletissima, Lausanne (1976)
Balk Balkan Games (1929)
Barr (Cuba) Barrientos Memorial (1950)
BGP Budapest Grand Prix (1978) (now HGP)
Bisl Bislett Games, Oslo
BNP BNP meeting, Paris, Lille or Villeneuve d'Ascq
CAC Central American and Caribbean Championships (1967)
CAG Central American and Caribbean Games (1926)
CalR California Relays (1942)
CISM International Military Championships (1946)
CG Commonwealth Games (1930)
DNG DN Galan, Stockholm (1966)
Drake Drake Relays (1910)
Drz Druzhba/Friendship Games
EC European Championships (1934)
ECP European Clubs Cup (1975)
EI European Indoor Championships (1970, Games 1966-9)
EJ European Junior Championships (1970)
EP European Cup - track & field (1965), multi-events (1973)
EsC Eschborn Cup - Women's World Race Walking Cup (1979)
EU23P European Under 23 Cup (1992)
Expo Expo 92 meeting, Sevilla
FBK Fanny Blankers-Koen meeting, Hengelo (now APM)
FlaR Florida Relays (1939)
FOT (USA) Final Olympic Trials (1920)
GGala Golden Gala, Roma (from 1980), Verona (1988), Pescara (1989), Bologna (1990)
GO Golden Oval, Dresden
GPB Bratislva Grand Prix (formerly PTS) (1990)
GPF IAAF Grand Prix final (1985)
GS Golden Spike, Ostrava (1969)
Gugl Gugl Internationales, Linz (1988)
GWG Goodwill Games (1986)

HB	Hanns Braun Memorial, München (1930)
Herc	Herculis, Monte Carlo, Monaco (1987)
HGP	Hungalu Budapest Grand Prix
IAAFg	IAAF Golden events (1978)
IAC	IAC meeting (1968), formerly Coke meeting
IbAmC	Ibero-American Championships (1983)
Int	International meeting
ISTAF	Internationales Stadionfest, Berlin (1921)
Izv	(SU) Izvestia Cup
Jen	Bruce Jenner Classic, San Jose (1979)
Jer	Harry Jerome Track Classic (1984)
JO	Jesse Owens Memorial (1981)
JP	Jan Popper Memorial (1987), formerly *Journalists' Lath*, Praha
-j	Junior, championships or international match
KansR	Kansas Relays, Lawrence (1923)
King	Martin Luther King Games (1969)
Kuso	Janusz Kusocinski Memorial (1954)
Kuts	Vladimir Kuts Memorial
LAT	Los Angeles Times indoors (1960, from 1968 at Inglewood)
LB	Liberty Bell, Philadelphia
LT	Lugano Trophy, IAAF World Race Walking Cup (1961)
MAI	Malmö AI Galan, Sweden (formerly Idag) (1958)
McV	McVitie's Challenge, Crystal Palace, London (1985-9), Sheffield (1990-1)
Mast	Masters pole vault, Grenoble (1987)
McD	McDonald's Games, Sheffield (1992)
MedG	Mediterranean Games (1951)
Mill	Millrose Games, New York indoors (1908)
MSR	Mt. San Antonio College Relays (1959)
NC	National Championships
NC-j	National Junior Championships
NC-y	National Youth Championships
NCAA	National Collegiate Athletic Association Championships (1921)
Nik	Nikaïa, Nice (1976)
ND	Nina Dumbadze Memorial
NM	Narodna Mladezhe, Sofia (1955)
NP	National Cup
Nurmi	Paavo Nurmi Games (1957)
NYG	New York Games (1989)
OD	(GDR) Olympischer Tag (Olympic Day)
OG	Olympic Games (1896)
OT	Olympic Trials
PAG	Pan American Games (1951)
PennR	Pennsylvania Relays (1895)
Pepsi	Pepsi Cola Invitational
PG	Parcelforce Games, formerly Peugeot (Talbot) Games (1980), Royal Mail Parcels Games 1989-90, Parcelforce Games 1991
PO	Pre Olympic Meet
Prav	(SU) Pravda Cup
PTS	Pravda Televízia Slovnaft, Bratislava (1957) (now GPB)
Pre	Steve Prefontaine Memorial (1976)
RomIC	Romanian International Championships (1948)
Ros	Evzen Rosicky Memorial, Praha (1947)
R-W	Rot-Weiss meeting, Koblenz
SACh	South American Championships (1919) (or SoAmC)
SEAG	South East Asia Games
SGP	Softeland Grand Prix (walking)
Slovn	Slovnaft '92, Bratislava (formerly PTS)
Spart	(SU) Spartakiad (1956)
S&W	S & W Invitational, Modesto (previously CalR)
TAC	(USA) The Athletics Congress Championships (1980-91)
TexR	Texas Relays (1925)
Toto	Toto International Super Meet, Tokyo
TSB	TSB International, Crystal Palace, London (Formerly PG)
USOF	US Olympic Festival
VD	Ivo Van Damme Memorial, Brussels (1977)
Veniz	Venizelia, Khania, Crete
WA	West Athletic Meet (AUT/BEL/DEN/HOL/IRL/POR/SPA/SWZ)
WAAA	(GBR) Women's Amateur Athletic Association Championships (1922-91)
WC	World Championships (1983)
WP	World Cup - track & field (1977), marathon (1985)
WG	World Games, Helsinki (1961)
WI	World Indoor Championships (1987), World Indoor Games (1985)
WJ	World Junior Championships (1986)
WK	Weltklasse, Zürich (1962)
WPT	World Cup Trials (1977)
WUG	World University Games (1923)
Znam	Znamenskiy Brothers Memorial (1958)

Dual and triangular matches are indicated by "v" (versus) followed by the name(s) of the opposition. Quadrangular and larger inter-nation matches are denoted by the number of nations and -N; viz 8-N designates an 8-nation meeting.

Miscellaneous abbreviations

A	Made at an altitude of 1000m or higher
D	Made in decathlon competition
H	Made in heptathlon competition
h	Made in heat
i	Indoor mark
mx	Made in mixed men's and women's race
O	Made in octathlon
P	Made in pentathlon
Q	Made in qualifying round
q	Made in quarter-final
r	Race number in a series of races
s	Semi-final
w	Wind-assisted
=	Tie (ex-aequo)
+	Intermediate time in longer race
*	Converted time from yards to metres: For 200m: 220 yards less 0.11 second For 400m: 440 yards less 0.26 second For 110mh: 120yh plus 0.03 second

General Notes

Altitude aid

Marks set at an altitude of 1000m or higher have been suffixed by the letter "A". Although there are not separate world records for altitude assisted events, it is understood by experts that in all events up to 400m in length (with the possible exclusion of the 110m hurdles), and in the horizontal jumps, altitude gives a material benefit to performances. For events beyond 800m, however, the thinner air of high altitude has a detrimental effect. Supplementary lists are included in relevant events for athletes with seasonal bests at altitude who have low altitude marks qualifying for the main list.

Some leading venues over 1000m

Addis Ababa ETH	2365m
Air Force Academy USA	2194
Albuquerque USA	1555
Bloemfontein RSA	1392
Bogotá COL	2600
Boulder USA	1655
Calgary CAN	1045
Cali COL	1046
Ciudad México MEX	2247
Colorado Springs USA	1823
Denver USA	1609
Echo Summit USA	2250
El Paso USA	1126
Flagstaff USA	2105
Font-Romeu FRA	1850
Fort Collins USA	1521
Germiston RSA	1661
Guadalajara MEX	1567
Harare ZIM	1473
Johannesburg RSA	1748
Leninaken ARM	1556
Nairobi KEN	1675
Nakuru KEN	1650
Pietersberg RSA	1230
Pocatello USA	1361
Potchefstroom RSA	1351
Pretoria RSA	1400
Provo USA	1380
Reno USA	1369
Rustenburg RSA	1157
Secunda RSA	1628
Sestriere ITA	2050
Soria ESP	1056
South Lake Tahoe USA	1909
Tsakhkadzor GEO	1980
Windhoek NAM	1725

Some others over 500m

Alma-Ata KZK	847
Bern SUI	555
Boise USA	831
Canberra AUS	581
Caracas VEN	922
Edmonton CAN	667
Lubbock USA	988
Madrid ESP	640
München GER	520
Salamanca ESP	806
São Paulo BRA	725
Sofia BUL	564
Spokane USA	576
Tucson USA	728

Automatic timing

In the main lists for sprints and hurdles, only times recorded by fully automatic timing devices are included.

Hand timing

In the sprints and hurdles supplementary lists are included for races which are hand timed. Any athlete with a hand timed best 0.01 seconds or more better than his or her automatically timed best has been included, but hand timed lists have been terminated close to the differential levels considered by the

IAAF to be equivalent to automatic times, i.e. 0.24 sec. for 100m, 200m, 100mh, 110mh, and 0.14 sec. for 400m and 400mh.
This effectively recognises bad hand timekeeping, for there should be no material difference between hand and auto times, but what often happens is that badly trained timekeepers anticipate the finish, as opposed to reacting to the flash at the start.
In events beyond 400m, automatically timed marks are integrated with hand timed marks, the latter identifiable by times being shown to tenths. All-time lists also include some auto times in tenths of a second, where the 1/100th time is not known, but the reader can differentiate these from hand timed marks as they are identified with the symbol '.

Indoor marks
Indoor marks are included in the main lists for field events and straightway track events, but not for other track events. This is because track sizes vary in circumference (200m is the international standard) and banking, while outdoor tracks are standardized at 400m. Athletes whose seasonal bests were set indoors are shown in a supplemental list if they also have outdoor marks qualifying for the world list.

Mixed races
For record purposes athletes may not, except in road races, compete in mixed sex races. Statistically there would not appear to be any particular logic in this, and women's marks set in such races, permitted and fairly common in a few nations such as Australia and Canada, are shown in our lists - annotated with mx. In such cases the athlete's best mark in single sex competition is appended.

Supplementary marks
Non-winning marks in a field event series which, had they been winning marks, would have qualified for the top 30 performances list are included in a supplement at the end of the relevant events. Not included this year due to lack of information on series in 1993.

Tracks
As with climatic conditions it should be borne in mind that the type and composition of tracks and runways will effect standards of performance.

Wind assistance
In the lists for 100m, 200m, 100mh, 110mh, long jump and triple jump, anemometer readings have been shown where available. The readings are given in metres per second to one decimal place. Where the figure was given originally to two decimal places, it has been rounded to the next tenth upwards, e.g. a wind reading of +2.01 m/s, beyond the IAAF legal limit of 2.0, is rounded to +2.1; or -1.22 m/s is rounded up to -1.2.
For multi-events a wind-assisted mark in one in which any of these events is aided by a wind over 4.0 m/s; such assisted marks are shown with a capital W.

Drugs bans
The IAAF have determined that the IAAF Executive Council may decertify an athlete's records, titles and results if he or she later admits to having used a banned substance before those performances. We have not removed any such athletes from all-time lists, but for information have shown ¶ after the name of any athlete who has at any stage in his or her career undergone a drugs suspension of a year or more (thus not including the 3 month bans for ephedrine etc.). This should not be taken as implying that the athlete was using drugs at that time. Nor have those athletes who have subsequently unofficially admitted to using banned substances been indicated; the ¶ is used only for those who have been caught.

Venues
From time to time place names are changed. Our policy is to use names in force at the time that the performance was set. Thus Leningrad prior to 1991, St Petersburg from its re-naming.

Amendments
Keen observers may spot errors in the lists. They are invited to send corrections to the editor.

Peter Matthews, 10 Madgeways Close, Great Amwell, Ware, Herts SG12 9RU, England

Event Record Name Nat Venue Date

WORLD & CONTINENTAL RECORDS

(as at 31 Dec 1993)

Key W = World, Afr = Africa, Asi = Asia, CAC = C.America & Caribbean, E = Europe, NAm = N.America, Oce = Oceania, SAm = S.America, WJ = World Junior

A = altitude over 1000m
* = awaiting ratification
+ = timing by photo-electric-cell
§ = not officially ratified

100 METRES

Event	Record	Name	Nat	Venue	Date
W,NAm	9.86¶	Carl LEWIS	USA	Tokyo	25 Aug 91
E	9.87	Linford CHRISTIE	GBR	Stuttgart	15 Aug 93
Afr	9.95	Frank FREDERICKS	NAM	Tokyo	25 Aug 91
CAC	9.96	Ray STEWART	JAM	Tokyo	25 Aug 91
SAm	10.00A	Róbson da SILVA	BRA	Ciudad de México	22 Jul 88
Asi	10.14	Talal MANSOOR	QAT	Budapest	18 Jun 92
Oce	10.19	Damien MARSH	AUS	Melbourne	25 Feb 93
WJ	10.05 §	Davidson EZINWA	NGR	Bauchi	3 Jan 90
	10.09A	Mel LATTANY	USA	Air Force Academy	31 Jul 78

¶ Performances of 9.79 & 9.83 by Ben Johnson (CAN) have been disallowed following disqualification for drug abuse

200 METRES

Event	Record	Name	Nat	Venue	Date
W,E	19.72A	Pietro MENNEA	ITA	Ciudad de México	12 Sep 79
NAm	19.73	Michael MARSH	USA	Barcelona	5 Aug 92
Afr	19.85	Frank FREDERICKS	NAM	Stuttgart	20 Aug 93
CAC	19.86A	Donald QUARRIE	JAM	Cali	3 Aug 71
SAm	19.96	Róbson da SILVA	BRA	Bruxelles	25 Aug 89
Oce	20.06A	Peter NORMAN	AUS	Ciudad de México	16 Oct 68
Asi	20.41	CHANG Jae-keun	KOR	Jakarta	27 Sep 85
WJ	20.07 §	Lorenzo DANIEL	USA	Starkville	18 May 85
	20.13	Roy MARTIN	USA	Indianapolis	16 Jun 85

400 METRES

Event	Record	Name	Nat	Venue	Date
W,NAm	43.29	Butch REYNOLDS	USA	Zürich	17 Aug 88
CAC	44.14	Roberto HERNANDEZ	CUB	Sevilla	30 May 90
Afr	44.17	Innocent EGBUNIKE	NGR	Zürich	19 Aug 87
E	44.33	Thomas SCHÖNLEBE	GER	Roma	3 Sep 87
Oce	44.38	Darren CLARK	AUS	Seoul	26 Sep 88
Asi	44.56	Mohamed AL MALKY	OMN	Budapest	12 Aug 88
SAm	45.06	Róbson da SILVA	BRA	São Paulo	19 May 91
	45.0 m	Róbson da SILVA	BRA	Rio de Janeiro	31 Aug 90
UJ	43.87	Steve LEWIS	USA	Seoul	28 Sep 88

800 METRES

Event	Record	Name	Nat	Venue	Date
W,E,C	1:41.73+	Sebastian COE	GBR	Firenze	10 Jun 81
SAm	1:41.77	Joaquim CRUZ	BRA	Koln	26 Aug 84
Afr	1:42.28	Sammy KOSKEI	KEN	Koln	26 Aug 84
NAm	1:42.60	Johnny GRAY	USA	Koblenz	28 Aug 85
CAC	1:43.44	Alberto JUANTORENA	CUB	Sofia	21 Aug 77
Oce	1:44.3 m	Peter SNELL	NZL	Christchurch	3 Feb 62
Asi	1:45.77	Sri Ram SINGH	IND	Montréal	25 Jul 76
WJ	1:44.9 my§	Jim RYUN	USA	Terre Haute	10 Jun 66
	1:44.3 m	Joaquim CRUZ	BRA	Rio de Janeiro	27 Jun 81

World Records at other events recognised by the IAAF

Event	Record	Name	Nat	Venue	Date
1000m	2:12.18	Sebastian COE	GBR	Oslo	11 Jul 81
2000m	4:50.81	Saïd AOUITA	MAR	Paris	16 Jul 87

MARATHON

W,Afr	2:06:50	Belayneh DINSAMO	ETH	Rotterdam	17 Apr 88
E	2:07:12	Carlos LOPES	POR	Rotterdam	20 Apr 85
Asi	2:07:35	Taisuke KODAMA	JPN	Beijing	19 Oct 86
Oce	2:07:51	Rob DE CASTELLA	AUS	Boston	21 Apr 86
CAC	2:08:36	Dionisio CERON	MEX	Beppu	2 Feb 92
NAm	2:08:52	Alberto SALAZAR	USA	Boston	19 Apr 82
SAm	2:09:55	Osmiro SILVA	BRA	Marrakesh	13 Jan 91
WJ	2:12:49	Negash DUBE	ETH	Beijing	18 Oct 87
	2:12:49	Tesfaye DADI	ETH	Berlin	9 Oct 8

8

110 METRES HURDLES

W, E	12.91	Colin JACKSON	GBR	Stuttgart	20 Aug 93
NAm	12.92	Roger KINGDOM	USA	Zürich	16 Aug 89
CAC	13.19	Emilio VALLE	CUB	Stuttgart	19 Aug 93
Asi	13.26	LI Tong	CHN	Verona	16 Jun 93
Oce	13.48	Kyle VANDER-KUYP	AUS	Stuttgart	19 Aug 93
SAm	13.62 A	Elvis CEDEÑO	VEN	Ciudad de México	22 Jul 88
Afr	13.63 A§	Wessel BOSMAN	RSA	Johannesburg	23 Apr 88
	13.64A	Kobus SCHOEMAN	RSA	Pretoria	15 May 93
WJ	13.23	Renaldo NEHEMIAH	USA	Zürich	16 Aug 78

400 METRES HURDLES

W,NAm	46.78	Kevin YOUNG	USA	Barcelona	6 Aug 92
Afr	47.10	Samuel MATETE	ZAM	Zürich	7 Aug 91
E	47.48	Harald SCHMID	GER	Athinai	1 Sep 82
	47.48 §	Harald SCHMID	GER	Roma	1 Sep 87
CAC	47.60	Winthrop GRAHAM	JAM	Zürich	4 Aug 93
Asi	48.68	Yoshihiko SAITO	JPN	Tokyo	12 Jun 93
SAm	49.10	Eronildo NUNES de Araujo	BRA	Barcelona	3 Aug 92
Oce	49.32	Bruce FIELD	AUS	Christchurch	29 Jan 74
WJ	48.02	Danny HARRIS	USA	Los Angeles	17 Jun 84

3000 METRES STEEPLECHASE

W,Afr	8:02.08	Moses KIPTANUI	KEN	Zürich	19 Aug 92
E	8:07.62	Joseph MAHMOUD	FRA	Bruxelles	24 Aug 84
NAm	8:09.17	Henry MARSH	USA	Koblenz	28 Aug 85
Oce	8:14.05	Peter RENNER	NZL	Koblenz	29 Aug 84
Asi	8:19.52	Masanari SHINTAKU	JPN	Stockholm	8 Jul 80
SAm	8:19.80	Clodoaldo DO CARMO	BRA	Bruxelles	28 Aug 92
CAC	8:27.55	Juan Ramón CONDE	CUB	Habana	5 Jul 91
WJ	8:24.47	Matthew BIRIR	KEN	Getxo	29 Jun 91

HIGH JUMP

W,CAC	2.45	Javier SOTOMAYOR	CUB	Salamanca	27 Jul 93
E	2.42	Patrik SJÖBERG	SWE	Stockholm	30 Jun 87
	2.42 i§	Carlos THRÄNHARDT	GER	Berlin	26 Feb 88
NAm	2.40 i§	Hollis CONWAY	USA	Sevilla	10 Mar 91
		Charles AUSTIN	USA	Zürich	7 Aug 91
Asi	2.39	ZHU Jianhua	CHN	Eberstadt	10 Jun 84
Oce	2.35	Tim FORSYTH	AUS	Canberra	25 Jan 93
Afr	2.28	Othmane BELFAA	ALG	Amman	20 Aug 83
		Othmane BELFAA	ALG	Athinai	11 Jul 91
SAm	2.25	Claudio FREIRE	BRA	Rio de Janeiro	10 Oct 82
	2.25 A	Fernando PASTORIZA	ARG	Ciudad de México	23 Jul 88
WJ	2.37	Dragutin TOPIC	YUG	Plovdiv	12 Aug 90
		Steve SMITH	GBR	Seoul	20 Sep 92

1500 METRES

W,Afr	3:28.82	Noureddine MORCELI	ALG	Rieti	6 Sep 92
E	3:29.67	Steve CRAM	GBR	Nice	16 Jul 85
NAm	3:29.77	Sydney MAREE	USA	Koln	25 Aug 85
Oce	3:31.96	Simon DOYLE	AUS	Stockholm	3 Jul 91
Asi	3:33.29	Mohamed SULEIMAN	QAT	Zürich	4 Aug 93
SAm	3:34.63	Joaquim CRUZ	BRA	Hengelo	14 Aug 88
CAC	3:37.61	Arturo BARRIOS	MEX	Hengelo	13 Aug 89
WJ	3:34.92	Kipkoech CHERUIYOT	KEN	München	26 Jul 83

1 MILE

W, Afr	3:44.39	Noureddine MORCELI	ALG	Rieti	5 Sep 93
E	3:46.32	Steve CRAM	GBR	Oslo	27 Jul 85
NAm	3:47.69	Steve SCOTT	USA	Oslo	7 Jul 82
Oce	3:49.08	John WALKER	NZL	Oslo	7 Jul 82
SAm	3:53.00	Joaquim CRUZ	BRA	Los Angeles	13 May 84
Asi	3:55.15	Mohamed SULEIMAN	QAT	København	25 Aug 92
CAC	3:57.34	Byron DYCE	JAM	Stockholm	1 Jul 74
WJ	3:51.3 m§	Jim RYUN	USA	Berkeley	17 Jul 66

3000 METRES

W,Afr	7:28.96	Moses KIPTANUI	KEN	Koln	16 Aug 92
E	7:32.79	Dave MOORCROFT	GBR	London	17 Jul 82
NAm	7:33.37 §	Sydney MAREE	USA	London	17 Jul 82
	7:36.79	Steve SCOTT	USA	Ingelheim	1 Sep 81
CAC	7:35.71	Arturo BARRIOS	MEX	Nice	IO Jul 89
Oce	7:37.49	John WALKER	NZL	London	17 Jul 82
Asi	7:38.20	Mohamed SULEIMAN	QAT	Berlin	27 Aug 93
SAm	7:45.34	Clodoaldo DO CARMO	BRA	Koblenz	26 Aug 92
WJ	7:39.82	Ismael KIRUI	KEN	Berlin	27 Aug 93

5000 METRES

W,Afr	12:58.39	Said AOUITA	MAR	Roma	22 Jul 87
E	13:00.41	Dave MOORCROFT	GBR	Oslo	7 Jul 82
NAm	13:01.15	Sydney MAREE	USA	Oslo	27 Jul 85
CAC	13:07.79	Arturo BARRIOS	MEX	London	14 Jul 89
Oce	13:12.87	Dick QUAX	NZL	Stockholm	5 Jul 77
SAm	13:19.64	Antonio SILIO	ARG	Roma	17 Jul 91
Asi	13:20.43	Toshinari TAKAOKA	JPN	Stockholm	2 Jul 92
WJ	13:02.75	Ismael KIRUIi	KEN	Stuttgart	16 Aug 93

10,000 METRES

W, Afr	26:58.38	Yobes ONDIEKI	KEN	Oslo	10 Jul 93
CAC	27:08.23	Arturo BARRIOS	MEX	Berlin	18 Aug 89
E	27:13.81	Fernando MAMEDE	POR	Stockholm	2 Jul 84
NAm	27:20.56	Mark NENOW	USA	Bruxelles	5 Sep 86
Asi	27:35.33	Takeyuki NAKAYAMA	JPN	Helsinki	2 Jul 87
SAm	27:38.72	Antonio SILIO	ARG	Bruxelles	3 Sep 93
Oce	27:39.89	Ron CLARKE	AUS	Oslo	14 Jul 65
WJ	27:11.18	Richard CHELIMO	KEN	Hengelo	25 Jun 91

World Records at other events recognised by the IAAF

20km	56:55.6	Arturo BARRIOS	MEX	La Flèche	30 Mar 91
1 Hour	21,101 m	Arturo BARRIOS	MEX	La Flèche	30 Mar 91
25km	1:13:55.8	Toshihiko SEKO	JPN	Christchurch	22 Mar 81
30km	1:29:18.8	Toshihiko SEKO	JPN	Christchurch	22 Mar 81

POLE VAULT

W,E	6.15 i§	Sergiy BUBKA	UKR	Donetsk	21 Feb 93
	6.13	Sergiy BUBKA	UKR	Tokyo	19 Sep 92
NAm	5.96	Joe DIAL	USA	Norman	18 Jun 87
Asi	5.90	Grigoriy YEGOROV	KZK	London	10 Sep 93
	5.90i	Grigoriy YEGOROV	KZK	Moskva	2 Feb 93
	5.90	Grigoriy YEGOROV	KZK	London	10 Sep 93
SAm	5.76	Tom HINTNAUS	BRA	Zürich	21 Aug 85
Oce	5.72	Simon ARKELL	AUS	Adelaide	14 Feb 93
Afr	5.71	Okkert BRITS	RSA	Potchefstrooml	8 May 93
CAC	5.65	Angel GARCIA	CUB	Habana	12 Jun 92
WJ	5.80	Maksim TARASOV	RUS	Bryansk	14 Jul 89

LONG JUMP

W,NAm	8.95	Mike POWELL	USA	Tokyo	30 Aug 91
E	8.86 A	Robert EMMIYAN	ARM	Tsakhkadzor	22 May 87
CAC	8.53	Jaime JEFFERSON	CUB	Habana	12 May 90
		Ivan PEDROSO	CUB	Sevilla	17 Jul 92
SAm	8.36	João Carlos de OLIVEIRA	BRA	Rieti	21 Jul 79
Asi	8.36	CHEN Zunrong	CHN	Shizuoka	5 May 92
Oce	8.27	Gary HONEY	AUS	Budapest	20 Aug 84
Afr	8.27	Yusuf ALLI	NGR	Lagos	8 Aug 89
UJ	8.34	Randy WILLIAMS	USA	München	8 Sep 72

TRIPLE JUMP

W,NAm	17.97	Willie BANKS	USA	Indianapolis	16 Jun 85
E	17.92	Khristo MARKOV	BUL	Roma	31 Aug 87
SAm	17.89 A	João Carlos de OLIVEIRA	BRA	Ciudad de México	15 Oct 75
CAC	17.78	Lazaro BETANCOURT	CUB	Habana	15 Jun 86
Oce	17.46	Ken LORRAUAY	AUS	London	7 Aug 82
Asi	17.34	ZOU Zhenxian	CHN	Roma	5 Sep 81
Afr	17.26	Ajayi AGBEBAKU	NGR	Edmonton	8 Jul 83
WJ	17.50	Volker MAI	GER	Erfurt	23 Jun 85

SHOT

W,NAm	23.12	Randy BARNES	USA	Westwood	20 May 90
E	23.06	Ulf TIMMERMANN	GER	Khania	22 May 88
SAm	20.90	Gert WEIL	CHL	Wirges	17 Aug 86
Afr	20.76	Ahmed Kamel SHATTA	EGY	Al Qâhira	24 Mar 88
CAC	20.28	Paúl RUIZ	CUB	Rostock	29 May 88
Oce	19.80	Les MILLS	NZL	Honolulu	3 Jul 67
Asi	19.78	MA Yongfeng	CHN	Beijing	9 Jun 90
WJ	21.05 i§	Terry ALBRITTON	USA	New York	22 Feb 74
	20.65 §	Mike CARTER	USA	Boston	4 Jul 79
	20.38	Terry ALBRITTON	USA	Walnut	27 Apr 74

DISCUS

W,E	74.08	Jürgen SCHULT	GER	Neubrandenburg	6 Jun 86
NAm	72.34 ¶	Ben PLUCKNETT	USA	Stockholm	7 Jul 81
	71.32 §	Ben PLUCKNETT	USA	Eugene	4 Jun 83
CAC	71.06	Luis DELIS	CUB	Habana	21 May 83
Afr	68.48 §	John VAN REENEN	RSA	Stellenbosch	14 Mar 75
	67.80	Adewale OLUKOJU	NGR	Modesto	11 May 91
Oce	65.62 §	Werner REITERER	AUS	Melbourne	15 Dec 87
	65.08	Wayne MARTIN	AUS	Newcastle	3 Jan 79
Asi	65.02	YU Wenge	CHN	Nanjing	20 May 92
SAm	64.30	Ramón JIMÉNEZ	PAR	Eugene	23 May 92
WJ	65.62 §	Werner REITERER	AUS	Melbourne	15 Dec 87
	63.64	Werner HARTMANN	GER	Strasbourg	25 Jun 78

¶ Disallowed by the IAAF following retrospective disqualification for drug abuse, but ratified by the AAU/TAC

HAMMER

W,E	86.74	Yuriy SEDYKH	UKR/RUS	Stuttgart	30 Aug 86
Asi	82.78	Andrey ABDUVALIYEV	TJK	Nitra	28 Aug 93
NAm	81.88	Jud LOGAN	USA	University Park	22 Apr 88
Oce	77.12	Sean CARLIN	AUS	Haringey	5 Jul 92
CAC	75.86	Alberto SANCHEZ	CUB	Habana	13 May 93
SAm	74.38	Andrés CHARADIA	ARG	Santa Fé	6 Jun 92
Afr	74.02	Hakim TOUMI	ALG	El Djezair	25 May 93
WJ	78.14	Roland STEUK	GER	Leipzig	30 Jun 78

JAVELIN (1986 Model)

W,E	95.66	Jan ZELEZNY	TCH	Sheffield	29 Aug 93
NAm	89.16 §	Tom PETRANOFF	USA	Potchefstroom	1 Mar 91
	85.70	Tom PUKSTYS	USA	Kuortane	26 Jun 93
Asi	87.60	Kazuhiro MIZOGUCHI	JPN	San Jose	27 May 89
Afr	87.26 @	Tom PETRANOFF	RSA	Belle Vue Mauricia	28 Jun 92
Oce	86.14	Gavin LOVEGROVE	NZL	Wellington	18 Jan 92
CAC	79.24	Ramón GONZALEZ	CUB	Athínai	20 Jun 87
SAm	77.80	Luís LUCUMI	COL	Medellin	7 Aug 89
WJ	80.94	Aki PARVIAINEN	FIN	Jyväskylä	5 Jul 92
Invalid implement - no longer accepted					
W,E	96.96	Seppo RÄTY	FIN	Punkalaidun	2 Jun 91
CAC	84.86	Ramón GONZALEZ	CUB	Potsdam	3 Jul 90

@ Tom Petranoff a South African citizen from September 1991

DECATHLON (1984 Tables)

W,NAm	8891	Dan O'BRIEN	USA	Talence	5 Sep 92
E	8847	Daley THOMPSON	GBR	Los Angeles	9 Aug 84
Oce	8366 m	Simon POELMAN	NZL	Christchurch	22 Mar 87
	8207	Simon POELMAN	NZL	Auckland	29 Jan 90
SAm	8291 m	Tito STEINER	ARG	Provo	23 Jun 83
	8266	Pedro da SILVA	BRA	Walnut	24 Apr 87
Asi	8009 m	YANG Chuan-Kuang	TPE	Ualnut	28 Apr 63
	7995	Munehiro KANEKO	JPN	Shanghai	14 May 93
Afr	7934 m	Ahmed MAHOUR BACHA	ALG	Alger	9 Jul 85
	7577	Ahmed MAHOUR BACHA	ALG	Alger	8 May 85
CAC	7908	Enrique BALANQUE	CUB	Habana	24 Apr 92
WJ	8397	Torsten VOSS	GER	Erfurt	7 Jul 82

20 000M WALK (Track)

W,E	1:18:35.2	Stefan JOHANSSON	SUE	Fana	15 May 92
CAC	1:18:40.0	Ernesto CANTO	MEX	Fana	5 May 84
Oce	1:20:12.3	Nick A'HERN	AUS	Fana	8 May 93
Asi	1:20:24.4	LI Mingcai	CHN	Jinan	15 Mar 92
SAm	1:21:30.8	Marcelo PALMA	BRA	São Paulo	15 Jun 91
NAm	1:22:38.1	Tim BERRETT	CAN	Fana	15 May 92
Afr	1:24:56.6	Abdelwahab FERGUÈNE	ALG	Neuilly-Plaisance	3 May 92
WJ	1:22:42	Andrey PERLOV	RUS	Donetsk	6 Sep 80

20 KM WALK (ROAD)

W,E	1:18:13	Pavol BLAZEK	TCH	Hildesheim	16 Sep 90
Oce	1:19:22	Dave SMITH	AUS	Hobart	19 Jul 87
CAC	1:19:24	Carlos MERCENARI~O	MEX	New York	3 May 87
Asi	1:19:43	CHEN Shaoguo	CHN	Beijing	8 Sep 93
SAm	1:20:19	Querubín MORENO	COL	New York	3 May 87
NAm	1:21:13	Guillaume LEBLANC	CAN	St. Léonard	5 Oct 86
Afr	1:22:51	Abdelwahab FERGUENE	ALG	Hildesheim	23 Aug 92
UJ	1:21:33	Carlos MERCENARIO	MEX	St. Léonard	5 Oct 86

50,000M WALK (Track)

W,CAC	3:41:38.4	Raúl GONZALEZ	MEX	Fana	25 May 79
Oce,C	3:43:50.0	Simon BAKER	AUS	Melbourne	9 Sep 90
E	3:46:11 §	Mykola UDOVENKO	UKR	Uzhgorod	3 Oct 80
	3:48:59	Vladimir REZAYEV	RUS	Fana	2 May 80
NAm	3:56:13.0	Tim BERRETT	CAN	Saskatoon	21 Jul 91
Asi	4:07:24.7	Fumio IMAMURA	JPN	Otsu	10 Mar 91
SAm	4:17:11.0	Mauricio CORTEZ	COL	Caracas	16 Nov 86
Afr	4:21:44.5	Abdelwahab FERGUÈNE	ALG	Toulouse	25 Mar 84

50 KM WALK (Road)

W,E	3:37:41	Andrey PERLOV	RUS	Sankt Peterburg	5 Aug 89
CAC	3:41:20	Raúl GONZALEZ	MEX	Praha-Podebrady	11 Jun 78
Oce,C	3:43:13	Simon BAKER	AUS	L'Hospitalet	28 May 89
Asi	3:46:41	SUN Xiaoguang	CHN	Zhenzou	5 Mar 91
NAm	3:47:48	Marcel JOBIN	CAN	Québec	20 Jun 81
SAm	4:01:31	Héctor MORENO	COL	Seoul	30 Sep 88
Afr	4:09:37	Johan MOERDYK	RSA	Cape Town	30 Oct 93

4 x 100 METRES RELAY

W, NAm	37.40	USA (Marsh, Burrell, Mitchell, C.Lewis)	Barcelona	8 Aug 92
	37.40	USA (Drummond, Cason, Mitchell, Burrell)	Stuttgart	21 Aug 93
E	37.77	GBR (Jackson, Jarrett, Regis, Christie)	Stuttgart	21 Aug 93
Afr	37.98	NGR (Kayode, Imoh, Adeniken, D.Ezinwa)	Barcelona	8 Aug 92
CAC	38.00	CUB (Simon, Lamela, Isasi, Aguilera)	Barcelona	8 Aug 92
Oce	38.46	AUS (Henderson, Marsh, Capobianco, Jackson)	Stuttgart	20 Aug 93
Asi	38.77	JPN (Aoto, Susuki, Inoue, Sugimoto)	Barcelona	8 Aug 92
SAm	38.8 m	BRA (Oliveira, da Silva, Nakaya, Correia)	São Paulo	1 May 84
	39.02A	BRA (de Castro, dos Santos, Pegado,Filho)	Ciudad de México	4 Sep 79
WJ	39.00A	USA (Jessie, Franklin, Blalock, Mitchell)	Air Force Academy	18 Jul 83

4 X 400 METRES RELAY

W,NAm	2:54.29	USA (Valmon, Watts, Reynolds, Johnson)	Stuttgart	21 Aug 93
E	2:57.53	GBR (Black, Redmond, Regis, Akabusi)	Tokyo	1 Sep 91
CAC	2:59.13	CUB (Martínez, Herrera, N Tellez, Hernández)	Barcelona	7 Aug 92
Afr	2:59.32	NGR (Uti, Ugbisie, Peters, Egbunike)	Los Angeles	11 Aug 84
Oce	2:59.70	AUS (Frayne, Clark, Minihan, Mitchell)	Los Angeles	11 Aug 84
Asi	3:01.26	JPN (Konakatomi, Takano, Uatanabe, Ito)	Tokyo	1 Sep 91
SAm	3:01.38	BRA (E Araujo, Tenorio, De Menezes, De Souza)	Barcelona	7 Aug 92
WJ	3:01.90	USA (Campbell, Rish, Waddle, Reed)	Athinai	20 Jul 86

WORLD RECORDS AT OTHER EVENTS RECOGNISED BY THE I.A.A.F.

4 x 200m	1:19.11	Santa Monica Track Club (Marsh, Burrell, Hearr\d, C Lewis)	USA	Philadelphia	25 Apr 92
4 x 800m	7:03.89	United Kingdom Team (Elliott, Cook, Cram, Coe)	GBR	London	30 Aug 82
4 x l500m	14:38.8 m	F.R.Germany Team (Wessinghage, Hudak, Lederer, Fleschen)	GER	Koln	17 Aug 77
Track Walking					
2 Hours	29,572m	Maurizio DAMILANO	ITA	Cuneo	4 Oct 92
30km	2:01:44.1*	Maurizio DAMILANO	ITA	Cuneo	4 Oct 92

WOMEN

100 METRES

W,NAm	10.49	Florence GRIFFITH JOYNER	USA	Indianapolis	16 Jul 88
CAC	10.78	Merlene OTTEY	JAM	Sevilla	30 May 90
E	10.81	Marlies GÖHR	GER	Berlin	8 Jun 83
Afr	10.97	Mary ONYALI	NGR	Stuttgart	15 Aug 93
Asi	11.02	LIU Xiaomei	CHN	Beijing	8 Sep 93
Oce	11.19	Kerry JOHNSON	AUS	Auckland	28 Jan 90
SAm	11.26 §	Jennifer INNIS	GUY	Walnut	15 Jul 84
	11.31	Esmeralda GARCIA	BRA	Caracas	24 Aug 83
WJ	10.88 §	Marlies OELSNER/GÖHR	GER	Dresden	1 Jul 77
	10.89	Kathrin KRABBE	GER	Berlin	20 Jul 88

200 METRES

W,NAm	21.34	Florence GRIFFITH JOYNER	USA	Seoul	29 Sep 88
CAC	21.64	Merlene OTTEY	JAM	Bruxelles	13 Sep 91
E	21.71	Marita KOCH	GER	Chemnitz	10 Jun 79
	21.71 §	Mari ta KOCH	GER	Potsdam	21 Jul 84
	21.71	Heike DRECHSLER	GER	Jena	29 Jun 86
	21.71 §	Heike DRECHSLER	GER	Stuttgart	29 Aug 86
Afr	22.06 A§	Evette DE KLERK	RSA	Pietersburg	8 Apr 89
	22.31	Mary ONYALI	NGR	Villeneuve d'Ascq	29 Jun 90
Oce	22.35	Denise BOYD	AUS	Sydney	23 Mar 80
Asi	22.56	WANG Huei-Chen	TPE	Yilian	30 Oct 92
	22.56	CHEN Zhaojing	CHN	Beijing	13 Sep 93
SAm	22.92	Ximena RESTREPO	COL	Lincoln	20 May 91
WJ	22.19	Natalya BOCHINA	RUS	Moskva	30 Jul 80

400 METRES

W,E	47.60	Marita KOCH	GER	Canberra	6 Oct 85
NAm	48.83	Valerie BRISCO	USA	Los Angeles	6 Aug 84
C	49.43	Kathy COOK	Eng	Los Angeles	6 Aug 84
CAC	49.57	Grace JACKSON	JAM	Nice	10 Jul 88
	49.2 mA	Ana QUIROT	CUB	Bogotá	13 Aug 89
SAm	49.64	Ximena RESTREPO	COL	Barcelona	5 Aug 92
Asi	49.81	MA Yuqin	CHN	Beijing	11 Sep 93
Afr	50.12 A§	Myrtle BOTHMA	RSA	Germiston	11 Apr 86
	50.41	Fatima YUSUF	NGR	Lausanne	10 Jul 91
Oce	50.24	Maree HOLLAND	AUS	Seoul	25 Sep 88
WJ	49.42	Grit BREUER	GER	Tokyo	27 Aug 91

800 METRES

W,E	1:53.28	Jarmila KRATOCHVÍLOVÁ	TCH	München	26 Jul 83
CAC	1:54.44	Ana QUIROT	CUB	Barcelona	9 Sep 89
Afr	1:55.43	Maria Lurdes MUTOLA	MOZ	Stuttgart	17 Aug 93
Asi	1:55.94	LIU Dong	CHN	Beijing	9 Sep 93
NAm	1:56.90	Mary SLANEY	USA	Bern	16 Aug 85
SAm	1:57.96	Letitia VRIESDE	SUR	Hengelo	28 Jun 92
Oce	1:59.0 m	Charlene RENDINA	AUS	Melbourne	28 Feb 76
WJ	1:57.18	WANG Yuan	CHN	Beijing	8 Sep 93

World Records at other events recognised by the IAAF

l000m	2:30.6 m§	Tatyana PROVIDOKHINA	RUS	Podolsk	20 Aug 78
	2:30.67	Christine WACHTEL	GER	Berlin	17 Aug 90
2000m	5:28.69	Maricica PUICA	ROM	London	11 Jul 86

1500 METRES

W, Asi	3:50.46	QU Yunxia	CHN	Beijing	11 Sep 93
E	3:52.47	Tatyana KAZANKINA	RUS	Zürich	13 Aug 80
Afr	3:55.30	Hassiba BOULMERKA	ALG	Barcelona	8 Aug 92
NAm	3:57.12	Mary DECKER/SLANEY	USA	Stockholm	26 Jul 83
SAm	4:05.67	Letitia VRIESDE	SUR	Tokyo	31 Aug 91
Oce	4:06.47	Christine PFITZINGER	NZL	San Jose	27 Jun 87
CAC	4:14.7 @	Charlotte BRADLEY	MEX	Sofia	23 Aug 77
WJ	3:59.81	WANG Yuan	CHN	Beijing	1 Sep 93

1 MILE

W,E	4:15.61	Paula IVAN	ROM	Nice	10 Jul 89
NAm	4:16.71	Mary SLANEY	USA	Zürich	21 Aug 85
Afr	4:20.79	Hassiba BOULMERKA	ALG	Oslo	6 Jul 91
Oce	4:29.28	Penny JUST	AUS	Oslo	27 Jul 85
SAm	4:30.05	Soraya TELLES	BRA	Praha	9 Jun 88
WJ	4:17.57§	Zola BUDD	GBR	Zürich	21 Aug 85

3000 METRES

W, Asi	8:06.11	WANG Junxia	CHN	Beijing	13 Sep 93
E	8:22.62	Tatyana KAZANKINA	RUS	Sankt Peterburg	26 Aug 84
NAm	8:25.83	Mary SLANEY	USA	Roma	7 Sep 85
Afr	8:32.00 §	Elana MEYER	RSA	Durban	29 Apr 91
	8:32.81	Elana MEYER	RSA	Oslo	10 Jul 93
Oce	8:44.1 m	Donna GOULD (in mixed race)	AUS	Eugene	13 Jul 84
	8:45.53	Anne AUDAIN	NZL	Brisbane	4 Oct 82
SAm	9:08.83	Carmen de OLIVEIRA	BRA	Lisboa	29 Jun 90
CAC	9:09.2 m	Luisa SERVIN	MEX	Victoria, BC	3 Jun 92
WJ	8:28.83 §	Zola BUDD	GBR	Roma	7 Sep 85
	8:36.45	MA Ningning	CHN	Jinan	6 Jun 93

5000 METRES

W,E	14:37.33	Ingrid KRISTIANSEN	NOR	Stockholm	5 Aug 86
Afr	14:44.15 §	Elana MEYER	RSA	Bellville	6 Feb 92
	14:46.41	Elana MEYER	RSA	Hechtel	31 Jul 93
NAm	14:56.07	Annette PETERS	USA	Berlin	27 Aug 93
Asi	15:05.69+	ZHONG Huandi	CHN	Beijing	8 Sep 93
Oce	15:13.23	Anne AUDAIN	NZL	Auckland	17 Mar 82
SAm	15:22.01	Carmen de OLIVEIRA	BRA	Hechtel	31 Jul 93
CAC	15:51.79	Santa VELAZQUEZ	MEX	Grudziadz	20 Jun 89
WJ	14:48.07 §	Zola BUDD	GBR	London	26 Aug 85

10,000 METRES

W, Asi	29:31.78	WANG Junxia	CHN	Beijing	8 Sep 93
E	30:13.74	Ingrid KRISTIANSEN	NOR	Oslo	5 Jul 86
Af r	31:06.02	DERARTU Tulu	ETH	Barcelona	7 Aug 92
Oce	31:11.72	Lisa ONDIEKI	AUS	Helsinki	30 Jun 92
NAm	31:19.89	Lynn JENNINGS	USA	Barcelona	7 Aug 92
SAm	31:47.76	Carmen de OLIVEIRA	BRA	Stuttgart	21 Aug 93
CAC	32:09.6 m	Olga APPELL	MEX	Walnut	17 Apr 92
WJ	31:15.38 §	Selina BARSOSIO	KEN	Stuttgart	21 Aug 93
	31:40.56	Delilah ASIAGO	KEN	Tokyo	16 Jun 91

World Records at other events recognised by the IAAF

1 Hour	18,084 m	Silvana CRUCIATA	ITA	Roma	4 May 81
20km	1:06:48.8	Izumi MAKI	JPN	Amagasaki	20 Sep 93
25km	1:29:29.2	Karolina SZABÓ	HUN	Budapest	22 Apr 88
30km	1:47:05.6	Karolina SZABÓ	HUN	Budapest	22 Apr 88

MARATHON

W,E	2:21:06	Ingrid KRISTIANSEN	NOR	London	21 Apr 85
NAm	2:21:21	Joan BENOIT/SAMUELSON	USA	Chicago	20 Oct 85
Oce	2:23:51	Lisa MARTIN/ONDIEKI	AUS	Osaka	31 Jan 88
Asi	2:24:07	WANG Junxia	CHN	Tianjin	4 Apr 93
Afr	2:27:36 §	Frith VAN DER MERWE	RSA	Port Elizabeth	24 Feb 90
	2:35:04	Addis GEZAHEGN	ETH	Rotterdam	21 Apr 91
CAC	2:28:56	Olga APPELL	MEX	New York	14 Nov 93
SAm	2:31:18	Carmen de OLIVEIRA	BRA	Boston	19 Apr 93
WJ	2:30:15	GU Dongmei	CHN	Tianjin	4 Apr 93

100 METRES HURDLES

W,E	12.21	Yordanka DONKOVA	BUL	Stara Zagora	20 Aug 88
NAm	12.46	Gail DEVERS	USA	Stuttgart	20 Aug 93
Asi	12.64	ZHANG Yu	CHN	Beijing	9 Sep 93
CAC	12.73	Aliuska LOPEZ	CUB	Dijon	24 Jun 90
	12.73	Aliuska LOPEZ	CUB	Stuttgart	20 Aug 93
Oce	12.93	Pam RYAN	AUS	München	4 Sep 72
Afr	13.02	Yasmina AZZIZI	ALG	Brescia	16 May 92
SAm	13.16	Nancy VALLECILLA	ECU	Indianapolis	13 Aug 87
WJ	12.84	Aliuska LOPEZ	CUB	Zagreb	16 Jul 87

400 METRES HURDLES

W, E	52.74	Sally GUNNELL	GBR	Stuttgart	19 Aug 93
NAm	52.79	Sandra FARMER-PATRICK	USA	Stuttgart	19 Aug 93
Oce	53.17	Debbie FLINTOFF-KING	AUS	Seoul	28 Sep 88
Afr	53.74 A	Myrtle BOTHMA	RSA	Johannesburg	18 Apr 86
	54.53	Myrtle BOTHMA	RSA	Barcelona	3 Aug 92
Asi	53.96	CHEN Juying	CHN	Beijing	9 Sep 93
CAC	54.12	Deon HEMMINGS	JAM	Stuttgart	17 Aug 93
SAm	57.12 A	Liliana CHALA	ECU	Ciudad de México	24 Jul 88
WJ	55.20	Leslie MAXIE	USA	San Jose	9 Jun 84

HIGH JUMP

W,E	2.09	Stefka KOSTADINOVA	BUL	Roma	30 Aug 87
CAC	2.04	Silvia COSTA	CUB	Barcelona	9 Sep 89
NAm	2.03	Louise RITTER	USA	Austin	8 Jul 88
		Louise RITTER	USA	Seoul	30 Sep 88
Afr	2.01 §	Desiré DU PLESSIS	RSA	Johannesburg	16 Sep 86
	1 95	Lucienne N'DA	CIV	Belle Vue Mauricia	28 Jun 92
Oce	1 98	Vanessa WARD	AUS	Perth	12 Feb 89
Asi	1.97	JIN Ling	CHN	Hamamatsu	7 May 89
SAm	1.92	Orlane DOS SANTOS	BRA	Bogotá	11 Aug 89
WJ	2.01 §	Olga TURCHAK	KAZ	Moskva	7 Jul 86
	2.01	Heike BALCK	GER	Chemni tz	18 Jun 89

LONG JUMP

W,E	7.52	Galina CHISTYAKOVA	RUS	Sankt Peterburg	11 Jun 88
NAm	7.45	Jackie JOYNER-KERSEE	USA	Indianapolis	13 Aug 87
Asi	7.01	YAO Weili	CHN	Jinan	6 Jun 93
CAC	6.96 A	Madeline de JESUS	PUR	Ciudad de México	24 Jul 88
Oce	6.87	Nicole BOEGMAN	AUS	Gateshead	14 Aug 88
Af r	6.85 A§	Karen KRUGER/BOTHA	RSA	Johannesburg	23 Mar 90
	6.78	Karen BOTHA	RSA	Belle Vue Mauricia	25 Jun 92
SAm	6.82	Jennifer INNIS (now USA)	GUY	Nice	14 Aug 82
WJ	7.14 §	Heike DAUTE/DRECHSLER	GER	Bratislava	4 Jun 83
	6.98	Heike DAUTE/DRECHSLER	GER	Potsdam	18 Aug 82

TRIPLE JUMP

W,E	15.09	Ana BIRYUKOVA	RUS	Stuttgart	21 Aug 93
Asi	14.55	LI Huirong	CHN	Sapporo	19 Jul 92
CAC	14.51	Niurka MONTALVO	CUB	Habana	22 May 93
NAm	14.23	Sheila HUDSON	USA	New Orleans	20 Jun 92
SAm	13.91A	Andrea AVILA	ARG	Lima	4 Jul 93
Afr	13.46A §	Charmaine BARNARD	RSA	Bloemfontein	12 Apr 92
	12.97	Juliana YENDORK (now USA)	GHA	Norwalk	3 Jun 89
Oce	13.27	Nicole BOAGMAN	AUS	Brisbane	6 Mar 93
WJ	14.29 §	REN Ruiping	CHN	Beijing	13 Sep 93

SHOT

W,E	22.63	Natalya LISOVSKAYA	RUS	Moskva	7 Jun 87
Asi	21.76	LI Meisu	CHN	Shijiazhuang	23 Apr 88
CAC	20.96	Belsy LAZA	CUB	Ciudad de México	2 May 92
NAm	20.18	Ramona PAGEL	USA	San Diego	25 Jun 88
C,Oce	19.74	Gael MARTIN	AUS	Berkeley	14 Jul 84
SAm	17.36	Elisangela ADRIANO	BRA	Austin	9 May 92
Afr	17.32 §	Mariette VAN HEERDEN	RSA	Germiston	29 Nov 80
	16.86	Grace APIAFI	NGR	Santa Barbara	19 May 90
WJ	20.54	Astrid KUMBERNUSS	GER	Orimattila	1 Jul 89

DISCUS

W, E	76.80	Gabriele REINSCH	GER	Neubrandenburg	9 Jul 88
Asi	71.68	XIAO Yanling	CHN	Beijing	14 Mar 92
CAC	70.88	Hilda RAMOS	CUB	Habana	8 May 92
Oce	66.24	Daniela COSTIAN	AUS	Barcelona	3 Aug 92
NAm	66.10	Carol CADY	USA	San Jose	31 May 86
Afr	58.80 §	Nanette VAN DER WALT	RSA	Port Elizabeth	15 Feb 86
	57.58	Nanette VAN DER WALT	RSA	Germiston	25 Apr 92
SAm	58.50	Maria URRUTIA	COL	Valencia	26 Jun 92
WJ	74.40	Ilke WYLUDDA	GER	Berlin	13 Sep 88

JAVELIN

W,E	80.00	Petra FELKE/MEIER	GER	Potsdam	9 Sep 88
CAC	71.82	Ivonne LEAL	CUB	Kobe	30 Aug 85
Asi	70.42	ZHANG Li	CHN	Tianjin	6 Aug 90
Oce	69.80	Sue HOWLAND	AUS	Belfast	30 Jun 86
NAm	69.32	Kate SCHMIDT	USA	Fürth	11 Sep 77
SAm	63.74	Sueli PEREIRA dos SANTOS	BRA	La Chaux-de-Fonds	8 Aug 93
Afr	62.34 §	Susan LION-CACHET	RSA	Pretoria	7 Nov 87
	62.16	Samia DJEMAA	ALG	Alger	19 Jun 87
WJ	71.88	Antoaneta TODOROVA	BUL	Zagreb	15 Aug 81

HEPTATHLON (1984 Tables)

W,NAm	7291	Jackie JOYNER-KERSEE	USA	Seoul	24 Sep 88
E	7007	Larisa NIKITINA	RUS	Bryansk	24 Jun 89
Asi	6750	MA Miaolan	CHN	Beijing	12 Sep 93
Oce	6695	Jane FLEMMING	AUS	Auckland	28 Jan 90
Afr	6392	Yasmina AZZIZI	ALG	Tokyo	27 Aug 91
CAC	6040	Diane GUTHRIE	JAM	Philadelphia	22 Apr 92
SAm	6017	Conceição GEREMIAS	BRA	Caracas	25 Aug 83
WJ	6465	Sybille THIELE	GER	Schwechat	28 Aug 83

Other Relay World Records recognised by the IAAF

4x200m	1:28.15	GDR (Göhr,R Müller, Wöckel, Koch)	Jena	9 Aug 80
4x800m	7:50.17	USSR (Olizarenko, Gurina, Borisova, Podya;lovskaya)	Moskva	5 Aug 84

5000 METRES WALK (Track)

W	20:07.52 §	Beate ANDERS	GER	Rostock	23 Jun 90
	20:17.19	Kerry JUNNA-SAXBY	AUS	Sydney	14 Jan 90
E	20:07.52 §	Beate ANDERS	GER	Rostock	23 Jun 90
	20:38.65 *	Sari ESSAYAH	FIN	Mikkeli	31 Jul 93
	20:50.03	Ileana SALVADOR	ITA	Macerata	6 Sep 89
Oce	20:17.19	Kerry SAXBY/JUNNA	AUS	Sydney	14 Jan 90
Asi	20:37.7 m	JIN Bingjie	CHN	Hefei	3 Mar 90
NAm	21:28.17	Teresa VAILL	USA	Philadelphia	24 Apr 93
SAm	22:30.45	Bertha VERA	ECU	Seoul	20 Sep 92
CAC	23:38.25	Maria COLIN	MEX	Monterrey	9 Apr 86
Afr	23:10.88	Amsale YAKOBE	ETH	Seoul	20 Sep 92
WJ	20:37.7 m	JIN Bingjie	CHN	Hefei	3 Mar 90

10,000 METRES WALK (Track)

W,E	41:56.23	Nadyezhda RYASHKINA	RUS	Seattle	24 Jul 90
Oce	41:57.22	Kerry JUNNA-SAXBY	AUS	Seattle	24 Jul 90
Asi	42:46.7 m	CUI Yingzi	CHN	Jinan	15 Mar 92
		CHEN Yueling	CHN	Jinan	15 Mar 92
NAm	44:30.1 m	Alison BAKER	CAN	Fana	15 May 92
CAC	47:17.15	Maíia COLIN	MEX	Indianapolis	12 Aug 87
SAm	47:41.1 Am	Liliana BERMEO	COL	Cali	31 Jul 91
Afr	51:24.6 m	Sabeha MANSOURI	ALG	Boumerdes	6 Apr 89
WJ	42:55.38	CUI Yingzi	CHN	Tangshan	27 Sep 91

10 KM WALK (Road)

W,Oce	41:30	Kerry JUNNA-SAXBY	AUS	Canberra	27 Aug 88
Asi	41:48	LI Chunxiu	CHN	Beijing	8 Sep 93
E	42:03	Yelena ARSHINTSEVA	RUS	Adler	14 Feb 93
CAC	43:27	Graciella MENDOZA	MEX	Hull	8 Oct 89
NAm	45:06	Ann PEEL	CAN	New York	3 May 87
		Janice McCAFFREY	CAN	Washington	29 Mar 92
SAm	46:13	Miriam RAMON	ECU	Stutthgart	14 Aug 93
Afr	51:00	Agnetha CHELIMO	KEN	Nairobi	26 Jul 91
WJ	41:57	GAO Hongmiao	CHN	Beijing	8 Sep 93

4x100 METRES RELAY

W,E	41.37	GDR (Gladisch, Rieger, Auerswald, Göhr)	Canberra	6 Oct 85
NAm	41.49	USA (Finn, Torrence, Vereen, Devers)	Stuttgart	22 Aug 93
CAC,C	41.94	JAM (Duhaney, Cuthbert, McDonald, Ottey)	Tokyo	1 Sep 91
	41.94	JAM (Freeman, Campbell, Mitchell, Ottey)	Stuttgart	22 Aug 93
Afr	42.39	NGR (Utondu, Idehen, Opara-Thompson, Onyali)	Barcelona	7 Aug 92
Asi	43.16	CHN/Guangxi (Xiao, Tian, Huang, Qu)	Beijing	11 Sep 93
Oce	43.18	AUS (Wilson, Wells, Boyd, Boyle)	Montréal	31 Jul 76
SAm	44.60	BRA (Amaral, Gomes, C.Santos, V.Santos)	Manaus	15 Sep 90
WJ	43.33 §	GDR (Breuer, Krabbe, Dietz, Henke)	Berlin	20 Jul 88
	43.48	GDR (Breuer, Krabbe, Dietz, Henke)	Sudbury	31 Jul 88

4x400 METRES RELAY

W,E	3:15.17	URS (Ledovskaya, Nazarova, Pinigina, Bryzgina)	Seoul	1 Oct 88
NAm	3:15.51	USA (D.Howard, Dixon, Brisco, Griffith Joyner)	Seoul	1 Oct 88
CAC	3:23.13	JAM (Richards, Thomas, Rattray, Powell)	Seoul	1 Oct 88
Asi	3:24.28	CHN / Hebei (An, Bai, Cao, Ma)	Beijing	11 Sep 93
Afr	3:24.45	NGR (Yusuf, Onyali, Bakare, Opara)	Tokyo	1 Sep 91
Oce	3:25.56	AUS (Canty, Burnard, Rendina, Nail)	Montréal	31 Jul 76
SAm	3:29.22A	BRA (Oliveira, García, Telles, Souza)	Ciudad de México	24 Jul 88
WJ	3:28.39	GDR (Derr, Fabert, Wöhlk, Breuer)	Sudbury	31 Jul 88

WORLD BESTS - NON-STANDARD EVENTS

Men

Event	Mark	Name	Nat	Venue	Date
60m	6.38	Ben Johnson ¶	CAN	Rome (in 100m)	30 Aug 87
drugs dq	6.37	Ben Johnson		Seoul (in 100m)	24 Sep 88
150m	14.8	Pietro Mennea	ITA	Cassino	22 May 83
300m	31.48	Danny Everett	USA	Jerez de la Frontera	3 Sep 90
	31.48	Roberto Hernández	CUB	Jerez de la Frontera	3 Sep 90
500m	1:00.08	Donato Sabia	ITA	Busto Arsizio	26 May 84
600m	1:12.81	Johnny Gray	USA	Santa Monica	24 May 86
2000m Steeple	5:14.43	Julius Kariuki	KEN	Rovereto	21 Aug 90
200mh	22.63	Colin Jackson	GBR	Cardiff	1 Jun 91
(hand time)	22.5	Martin Lauer	FRG	Zürich	7 Jul 59
220yh straight	21.9	Don Styron	USA	Baton Rouge	2 Apr 60
300mh	34.6	David Hemery	GBR	London (CP)	15 Sep 72
35lb weight	25.41	Lance Deal	USA	Azusa	20 Feb 93
Pentathlon	4282	Bill Toomey	USA	London (CP)	16 Aug 69
(1985 tables)		(7.58, 66.18, 21.3, 44.52, 4:20.3)			
Double decathlon	14274	Indrek Kaseorg	EST	Punkalaidun	12/13 Sep 92

11.75, 7.00, 200mh 25.01, 12.13, 5k 17:36.07, 2:04.84, 1.99, 400m 50.72, HT 32.26, 3kSt 10:50.14
15.11, DT 37.04, 200m 23.30, 4.30, 10:18.50, 400mh 54.00, 57.78, 4:47.36, TJ 14.05, 10k 45:35.95

Women

Event	Mark	Name	Nat	Venue	Date
60m	6.9	Alice Annum	GHA	Mainz	17 Jun 75
150m	16.10	Florence Griffith-Joyner	USA	Seoul (in 200m)	29 Sep 88
300m	34.1	Marita Koch	GDR	Canberra (in 400m)	6 Oct 85
500m	1:05.9	Tatana Kocembová	TCH	Ostrava	2 Aug 84
600m	1:23.5	Doina Melinte	ROM	Poiana Brasov	27 Jul 86
2000m Steeple	6:14.52	Svetlana Rogova	RUS	Moscow	11 Jun 92
200mh	25.7	Pamela Ryan	AUS	Melbourne	25 Nov 71
Pole vault	4.11	Sun Caiyun	CHN	Guangzhou	21 Mar 93
Hammer (4kg)	65.40	Olga Kuzenkova	RUS	Bryansk	4 Jun 92
Double heptathlon	10824	Irina Stasenko	RUS	Punkalaidun	12/13 Sep 92

100mh 14.95, HJ 1.57, 1500m 4:44.41, 400mh 61.82, SP 12.71, 200m 25.58, 100m 12.86
LJ 5.56, 400m 59.09, JT 37.52, 800m 2:17.88, 200mh 28.98, DT 30.32, 3000m 10:46.93

LONG DISTANCE WORLD BESTS - MEN TRACK

	hr:min:sec	*Name*	*Nat*	*Venue*	*Date*
15 km	0:42:34.0	Arturo Barrios	MEX	La Flèche	30 Mar 91
10 miles	0:45:57.6	Jos Hermens	HOL	Papendal	14 Sep 75
15 miles	1:11:43.1	Bill Rodgers	USA	Saratoga, Cal.	21 Feb 79
20 miles	1:39:14.4	Jack Foster	NZL	Hamilton, NZ	15 Aug 71
30 miles	2:42:00	Jeff Norman	GBR	Timperley, Cheshire	7 Jun 80
50 km	2:48:06	Jeff Norman	GBR	Timperley, Cheshire	7 Jun 80
40 miles	3:48:35	Don Ritchie	GBR	Hendon, London	16 Oct 82
50 miles	4:51:49	Don Ritchie	GBR	Hendon, London	12 Mar 83
100 km	6:10:20	Don Ritchie	GBR	Crystal Palace	28 Oct 78
150 km	10:36:42	Don Ritchie	GBR	Crystal Palace	15 Oct 77
100 miles	11:30:51	Don Ritchie	GBR	Crystal Palace	15 Oct 77
200 km	15:11:10#	Yiannis Kouros	GRE	Montauban, Fra	15-16 Mar 85
200 miles	27:48:35	Yiannis Kouros	GRE	Montauban, Fra	15-16 Mar 85
500 km	60:23.00	Yiannis Kouros	GRE	Colac, Aus	26-29 Nov 84
500 miles	105:42:09	Yiannis Kouros	GRE	Colac, Aus	26-30 Nov 84
1000 km	136:17:00	Yiannis Kouros	GRE	Colac, Aus	26-31 Nov 84
1000 mile	13d 23:25:18u	Georg Yermolayev	LAT	Odessa	Nov 92
	14d 11:59:04	Tony Rafferty	AUS	Granville,NSW	13-25 Aug 89
	kilometres				
2 hrs	37.994	Jim Alder	GBR	Walton-on-Thames	17 Oct 64
12 hrs	162.400	Yiannis Kouros	GRE	Montauban, Fra	15 Mar 85
24 hrs	283.600	Yiannis Kouros	GRE	Montauban, Fra	15-16 Mar 85
48 hrs	452.270	Yiannis Kouros	GRE	Montauban, Fra	15-17 Mar 85
6 days	1030.000 indoors	Jean-Gilles Bousiquet	FRA	La Rochelle	16-23 Nov 92
Outdoors	1023.200	Yiannis Kouros	GRE	Colac, Aus	26 Nov-1 Dec 84

 # Running watch time, no stopped times known.

LONG DISTANCE ROAD BESTS

Where superior to track bests and run on properly measured road courses.

	hr:min:sec	Name	Nat	Venue	Date
15 km	0:42:28	Mike Musyoki	KEN	Portland, Oregon	26 Jun 83
Half mar	0:59:47	Moses Tanui	KEN	Milan	3 Apr 93
30 km	1:28:40	Steve Jones	GBR	Chicago	10 Oct 85
20 miles	1:35:22	Steve Jones	GBR	Chicago	10 Oct 85
30 miles	2:37:31	Thompson Magawana	RSA	Claremont-Kirstenbosch	12 Apr 88
50 km	2:43:38	Thompson Magawana	RSA	Claremont-Kirstenbosch	12 Apr 88
40 miles	3:45:39	Andy Jones	CAN	Houston	23 Feb 91
50 miles	4:50:21	Bruce Fordyce	RSA	London-Brighton	25 Sep 83
1000 miles	10d:10:30:35	Yiannis Kouros	GRE	New York	21-30 May 88
	kilometres				
12 hrs	162.543	Yiannis Kouros	GRE	Queen's, New York	7 Nov 84
24 hours	286.463	Yiannis Kouros	GRE	New York	28-29 Sep 85
6 days	1028.370	Yiannis Kouros	GRE	New York	21-26 May 88
Uncertain measurement					
10 miles	0:45:13	Ian Stewart	GBR	Stoke-on-Trent	8 May 77

LONG DISTANCE TRACK EVENTS - WOMEN

	hr:min:sec	Name	Nat	Venue	Date
15 km	0:49:44.0	Silvana Cruciata	ITA	Rome	4 May 81
10 miles	0:54:21.8	Lorraine Moller	NZL	Auckland	9 Jan 93
20 miles	1:59:09 !	Chantal Langlacé	FRA	Amiens	3 Sep 83
30 miles	3:19:41	Carolyn Hunter-Rowe	GBR	Barry, Wales	7 Mar 93
50 km	3:26:45	Carolyn Hunter-Rowe	GBR	Barry, Wales	7 Mar 93
40 miles	4:26:43	Carolyn Hunter-Rowe	GBR	Barry, Wales	7 Mar 93
50 miles	6:12:11	Hilary Walker	GBR	London (Tooting Bec)	16 Oct 93
100 km	7:50:09 *	Ann Trason	USA	Hayward, Cal.	3-4 Aug 91
100 miles	14:29:44	Ann Trason	USA	Santa Rosa, USA	18-19 Mar 89
200 km	19:28:48	Eleanor Adams	GBR	Melbourne	19-20 Aug 89
200 miles	39:09:03	Hilary Walker	GBR	Blackpool	5-7 Nov 88
500 km	77:53:46	Eleanor Adams	GBR	Colac, Aus.	13-15 Nov 89
500 miles	130:59:58	Sandra Barwick	NZL	Campbelltown, Aus	18-23 Nov 90
	kilometres				
2 hrs	32.652	Chantal Langlacé	FRA	Amiens	3 Sep 83
12 hrs	147.600	Ann Trason	USA	Hayward, Cal	3-4 Aug 91
24 hrs	240.169	Eleanor Adams	GBR	Melbourne	19-20 Aug 89
48 hrs	366.512	Hilary Walker	GBR	Blackpool	5-7 Nov 88
6 days	883.631	Sandra Barwick	NZL	Campbelltown, NSW	18-24 Nov 90
Indoors where superior to track best					
200 km	19:00:31	Eleanor Adams	GBR	Milton Keynes	3/4 Feb 90

*Timed on one running watch only, * lap recirded by computer*

LONG DISTANCE ROAD BESTS - WOMEN

Run on properly measured road courses.

	hr:min:sec	Name	Nat	Venue	Date
15 km	0:46:57	Elana Meyer	RSA	Cape Town	2 Nov 91
10 miles	0:51:41	Jill Hunter	GBR	New York	20 Apr 91
	0:50:31 u	Ingrid Kristiansen	NOR	Amsterdam	11 Oct 89
Half mar	1:06:40 ?	Ingrid Kristiansen	NOR	Sandnes	5 Apr 87
	1:07:11	Liz McColgan	GBR	Tokyo - 33m drop	26 Jan 92
25 km	1:21:21	Ingrid Kristiansen	NOR	London	10 May 87
30 km	1:38:27	Ingrid Kristiansen	NOR	London	10 May 87
20 miles	1:46:04	Ingrid Kristiansen	NOR	London	10 May 87
30 miles	3:01:16	Frith van der Merwe	RSA	Claremont - Kirstenbosch	25 Mar 89
50 km	3:08:13	Frith van der Merwe	RSA	Claremont - Kirstenbosch	25 Mar 89
40 miles	4:26:13	Ann Trason	USA	Houston	23 Feb 91
50 miles	5:40:18	Ann Trason	USA	Houston	23 Feb 91
100 km	7:09:44	Ann Trason	USA	Amiens	27 Sep 93
100 miles	13:47:41	Ann Trason	USA	Queen's New York	4 May 91
200 km	19:08:21 +	Sigrid Lomsky	GER	Basel	1-2 May 93
1000 km	7d 01:11:00	Sandra Barwick	NZL	New York	16-23Sep 91
1000 miles	12d 14:38:40	Sandra Barwick	NZL	New York	16-29 Sep 91
	kilometres				
24 hours	243.657	Sigrid Lomsky	GER	Basel	1-2 May 93

+ time at 201 km on one running watch

WORLD & CONTINENTAL RECORDS SET IN 1993

100 metres					
Oce	10.19	Damien MARSH	AUS	Melbourne	25 Feb 93
Eur	9.87	Linford CHRISTIE	GBR	Stuttgart	15 Aug 93
200 metres					
Afr	19.85	Frank FREDERICKS	NAM	Stuttgart	20 Aug 93
1500 metres					
Asi	3:33.29	Mohamed SULEIMAN	QAT	Zurich	4 Aug 93
1 mile					
W,Afr	3:44.39	Noureddine MORCELI	ALG	Rieti	5 Sep 93
3000 metres					
Asi	7:38.20	Mohamed SULEIMAN	QAT	Berlin	27 Aug 93
WJ	7:39.82	Ismael KIRUI	KEN	Berlin	27 Aug 93
5000 metres					
WJ	13:06.71 #	Ismael KIRUI	KEN	Lausanne	7 Jul 93
	13:06.50	Ismael KIRUI	KEN	Zurich	4 Aug 93
	13:02.75	Ismael KIRUI	KEN	Stuttgart	16 Aug 93
10,000 metres					
W,Afr	27:07.91	Richard CHELIMO	KEN	Stockholm	5 Jul 93
	26:58.38	Yobes ONDIEKI	KEN	Oslo	10 Jul 93
SAm	27:38.72	Antonio SILIO	ARG	Bruxelles	3 Sep 93
110 metres Hurdles					
Oce	13.57	Kyle VANDER-KUYP	AUS	Brisbane	6 Mar 93
Afr	13.64A	Kobus SCHOEMAN	RSA	Pretoria	15 May 93
Asi	13.26	LI Tong	CHN	Verona	16 Jun 93
Oce	13.52	Kyle VANDER-KUYP	AUS	Jansankoski	9 Jul 93
Eur	12.97A	Colin JACKSON	GBR	Sestriere	27 Jul 93
CAC	13.19	Emilio VALLE	CUB	Stuttgart	19 Aug 93
Oce	13.48	Kyle VANDER-KUYP	AUS	Stuttgart	19 Aug 93
W,Eur	12.91	Colin JACKSON	GBR	Stuttgart	20 Aug 93
400 metres Hurdles					
Asi	48.68	Yoshihiko SAITO	JAP	Tokyo	12 Jun 93
CAC	47.60	Winthrop GRAHAM	JAM	Zurich	4 Aug 93
High Jump					
Oce	2.35	Tim FORSYTH	AUS	Canberra	25 Jan 93
W,CAC	2.45	Javier SOTOMAYOR	CUB	Salamanca	27 Jul 93
Pole Vault					
Afr	5.50	Okkert BRITS	RSA	Pretoria	1 Feb 93
Asi	5.90i	Grigoriy YEGOROV	KZK	Moskva	2 Feb 93
W,Eur	6.14i	Sergey BUBKA	UKR	Lievin	13 Feb 93
Oce	5.72	Simon ARKELL	AUS	Adelaide	14 Feb 93
W,Eur	6.15i	Sergey BUBKA	UKR	Donetsk	15 Feb 93
Afr	5.51	Okkert BRITS	RSA	Germiston	1 Mar 93
	5.55	Okkert BRITS	RSA	Bloemfontein	8 Mar 93
	5.60	Okkert BRITS	RSA	Pietersburg	6 Apr 93
	5.70	Okkert BRITS	RSA	Pietersburg	6 Apr 93
	5.71	Okkert BRITS	RSA	Potchefstroom	8 May 93
Asi	5.65	Igor POTAPOVICH	KZK	San Jose	29 May 93
	5.75	Igor POTAPOVICH	KZK	San Jose	29 May 93
	5.83	Grigoriy YEGOROV	KZK	Villeneuve d'Ascq	2 Jul 93
	5.90	Grigoriy YEGOROV	KZK	Stuttgart	19 Aug 93
	5.90 *	Grigoriy YEGOROV	KZK	London	10 Sep 93
Hammer					
CAC	75.86	Alberto SANCHEZ	CUB	Habana	13 May 93
Afr	74.02	Hakim TOUMI	ALG	El Djezair	25 May 93
Asi	81.20	Andrey ABD W ALIYEV	TJK	Rehlingen	31 May 93
	81.64	Andrey ABD W ALIYEV	TJK	Stuttgart	15 Aug 93
	82.78	Andrey ABD W ALIYEV	TJK	Nitra	28 Aug 93

Javelin					
W, Eur	95.54	Ján ZELEZNY	TCH	Pietersburg	6 Apr 93
NAm	85.70	Tom PUKSTYS	USA	Kuortane	26 Jun 93
W,Eur	95.66	Ján ZELEZNY	TCH	Sheffield	29 Aug 93
20000m Walk (Track)					
Oce	1:20:12.3	Nick A'HERN	Aus	Fana	8 May 93
20km Walk (Road)					
Asi	1:19:43	CHEN Shaoguo	CHN	Beijing	8 Sep 93
50km walk (road)					
Afr	4:09:37	Johan Moerdyk	RSA	Cape Town	30 Oct 93
4x100 metres					
W,NAm	37.40	USA (Drummond, Cason, Mitchell, Burrell)		Stuttgart	21 Aug 93
Oce	38.46	AUS (Henderson,Marsh,Capobianco,Jackson)		Stuttgart	21 Aug 93
Eur	37.77	GBR (Jackson, Jarrett, Regis, Christie)		Stuttgart	22 Aug 93
4x400 metres					
W,NAm	2:54.29	USA (Valmon, Watts, H.Reynolds, Johnson)		Stuttgart	22 Aug 93

WOMEN

100 metres					
Afr	10.97	Mary ONYALI	NGR	Stuttgart	15 Aug 93
Asi	11.19	LIU Xiaomei	CHN	Beijing	8 Sep 93
	11.02	LIU Xiaomei	CHN	Beijing	8 Sep 93
200 metres					
Asi	22.56	CHEN Zhaojing	CHN	Beijing	13 Sep 93
400 metres					
Asi	50.94	MA Yuqin	CHN	Shijiazhuang	29 Apr 93
	50.86	MA Yuqin	CHN	Jinan	4 Jun 93
	49.81	MA Yuqin	CHN	Beijing	11 Sep 93
800 metres					
Afr	1:57.38	Maria MUTOLA	MOZ	Sao Paulo	16 May 93
	1:56.56	Maria MUTOLA	MOZ	New York	22 May 93
	1:56.36	Maria MUTOLA	MOZ	Durban	26 Jun 93
	1:55.62	Maria MUTOLA	MOZ	Zurich	4 Aug 93
	1:55.43	Maria MUTOLA	MOZ	Stuttgart	17 Aug 93
Asi	1:56.96	LIU Li	CHN	Bei;ing	8 Sep 93
WJ	1:57.18	WANG Yuan	CHN	Bei;ing	8 Sep 93
Asi	1:56.25	LIU Dong	CHN	Beijing	8 Sep 93
	1:55.54	LIU Dong	CHN	Beijing	9 Sep 93
1500 metres					
WJ	4:04.24 #	LU Yi	CHN	Beijing	3 Jun 93
	4:01.79	WANG Yuan	CHN	Beijing	10 Sep 93
	4:01.71 *	LI Ying	CHN	Beijing	10 Sep 93
W,Asi	3:50.46	QU Yunxia	CHN	Beijing	11 Sep 93
WJ	3:59.81	WANG Yuan	CHN	Beijing	11 Sep 93
3000 metres					
Asi	8:40.30	ZHANG Lirong	CHN	Shanghai	16 May 93
Afr	8s32.81	Elana MEYER	RSA	Oslo	10 Jul 93
Asi	8:27.68	WANG Junxia	CHN	Jinan	6 Jun 93
WJ	8:36.45	MA Ningning	CHN	Jinan	6 Jun 93
W,Asi	8:22.06	ZHANG Linli	CHN	Beijing	12 Jun 93
	8:12.19	WANG Junxia	CHN	Beijing	12 Jun 93
	8:06.11	WANG Junxia	CHN	Beijing	12 Jun 93
5000 metres					
Afr	14:50.29	Elana MEYER	RSA	Stockholm	5 Jul 93
	14:46.41	Elana MEYER	RSA	Hechtel	31 Jul 93
SAm	15:22.01	Carmen de OLIVEIRA	BRA	Hechtel	31 Jul 93
NAm	14:56.07	Annette PETERS	USA	Berlin	27 Aug 93
Asi	15:05.69+	ZHONG Huandi	CHN	Beijing	8 Sep 93
10000 metres					
SAm	32:24.37	Carmen de OLIVEIRA	BRA	Coquitlam	30 May 93
Asi	31:08.42	WANG Junxia	CHN	Jinan	2 Jun 93

SAm	32:08.72	Carmen de OLIVEIRA	BRA	Hengelo	20 Jun 93
Asi	30:49.30	WANG Junxia	CHN	Stuttgart	21 Aug 93
WJ	31:15.38 #	Selina BARSOSIO	KEN	Stuttgart	21 Aug 93
SAm	31:47.76	Carmen de OLIVEIRA	BRA	Stuttgart	21 Aug 93
W,Asi	29:31.78	WANG Junxia	CHN	Beijing	27 Aug 93
20000 metres					
W,Asi	1:06:48.8	Izumi MAKI	JAP	Amagasaki	19 Sep 93
Marathon					
Asi	2:26:26	Junko ASARI	JAP	Osaka	31 Jan 93
	2:24:07	WANG Junxia	CHN	Tianjin	4 Apr 93
WJ	2:30:15	GU Dongmei	CHN	Tianjin	4 Apr 93
SAm	2:31:18	Carmen de OLIVEIRA	BRA	Boston	19 Apr 93
CAC	2:28:56	Olga APPELL	MEX	New York	14 Nov 93
100 metres Hurdles					
NAm	12.46	Gail DEVERS	USA	Stuttgart	20 Aug 93
CAC	12.73	Aliuska LOPEZ	CUB	Stuttgart	20 Aug 93
Asi	12.64	ZHANG Yu	CHN	Beijing	9 Sep 93
400 metres Hurdles					
CAC	54.12	Deon HEMMINGS	JAM	Stuttgart	17 Aug 93
W,Eur	52.74	Sally GUNNELL	GBR	Stuttgart	19 Aug 93
NAm	52.79	Sandra FARMER-PATRICK	USA	Stuttgart	19 Aug 93
Asi	53.96	HAN Qing	CHN	Beijing	9 Sep 93
Long Jump					
Asi	7.0i	YAO Weili	CHN	Jinan	6 Jun 93
Triple Jump					
Oce	13.27	Nicole BOEGMAN	AUS	Brisbane	6 Mar 93
CAC	13.74	Niurka MONTALVO	CUB	Habana	12 Feb 93
	13.99A	Niurka MONTALVO	CUB	Ciudad de Mexico	9 May 93
	14.31	Niurka MONTALVO	CUB	Habana	22 May 93
	14.46	Niurka MONTALVO	CUB	Habana	22 May 93
	14.51	Niurka MONTALVO	CUB	Habana	22 May 93
WJ	13.91 #	REN Ruiping	CHN	Jinan	3 Jun 93
W,Eur	14.97	Yolanda CHEN	RUS	Moskva	18 Jun 93
SAm	}3.91	Andrea AVILA	Arg	Lima	4 Jul 93
WJ	13.78	Yelena LYSAK	RUS	San Sebastian	1 Aug 93
	13.83	Yelena LYSAK	RUS	San Sebastian	1 Aug 93
	13.86	Yelena LYSAK	RUS	San Sebastian	1 Aug 93
W,Eur	15.09	Ana BIRYUKOVA	RUS	Stuttgart	21 Aug 93
WJ	14.29	REN Ruiping	CHN	Beijing	13 Sep 93
Javelin					
SAm	63.74	Sueli dos SANTOS	BRA	La Chaux-de-Fonds	8 Aug 93
Heptathlon					
Asi	6750	MA Miaolan	CHN	Beijing	12 Sep 93
5000 metres Walk (Track)					
NAm	21:28.17	Theresa VAILL	USA	Philadelphia	24 Apr 93
Eur	20:38.65 ?	Sari ESSAYAH	FIN	Mikkeli	31 Jul 93
10000 metres Walk (Track)					
SAm	47:41.1	Liliana BERMEO	COL	Cali	31 Jul 93
10km Walk (Road)					
Eur	42:03	Yelena ARSHINTSEVA	RUS	Adler	14 Feb 93
Asi	42:26	WANG Yan	CHN	Shenzhong	18 Feb 93
WJ	42:32	GAO Hongmiao	CHN	Shenzhong	18 Feb 93
SAm	46:13	Miriam RAMON	ECU	Stuttgart	14 Aug 93
Asi	41:48	LI Chunxiu	CHN	Beijing	8 Sep 93
WJ	41:57	GAO Hongmiao	CHN	Beijing	8 Sep 93
4x100 metres					
NAm	41.49	USA (Finn, Torrence, Vereen, Devers)		Stuttgart	22 Aug 93
CAC	41.94	JAM (Freeman, Campbell, Mitchell, Ottey)		Stuttgart	22 Aug 93
Asi	43.16	CHN/Guangxi (Xiao, Tian, Huang, Qu)		Beijing	11 Sep 93
4x400 metres					
Asi	3:29.59	CHN/Hebei Province		Jinan	6 Jun 93
	3:24.28	CHN/Hebei (An, Bai, Cao, Ma)		Beijing	13 Sep 93

WORLD INDOOR RECORDS

Event	Record	Name	Nat	Venue	Date
Men	as at 1 April 1994				
50 metres	5.61	Manfred Kokot	GDR	E.Berlin	4 Feb 73
	5.61	James Sanford	USA	San Diego	20 Feb 81
	5.55 #	Ben Johnson ¶	CAN	Ottawa	31 Jan 87
60 metres	6.41	Andre Cason	USA	Madrid	14 Feb 92
	6.41 #	Ben Johnson	CAN	Indianapolis	7 Mar 87
200 metres	20.36	Bruno Marie-Rose	FRA	Liévin	22 Feb 87
400 metres	45.02	Danny Everett	USA	Stuttgart	2 Feb 92
800 metres	1:44.84	Paul Ereng	KEN	Budapest	4 Mar 89
1000 metres	2:15.26	Noureddine Morceli	ALG	Birmingham	22 Feb 92
1500 metres	3:34.16	Noureddine Morceli	ALG	Sevilla	28 Feb 91
1 mile	3:49.78	Eamonn Coghlan	IRL	East Rutherford	27 Feb 83
3000 metres	7:37.31	Moses Kiptanui	KEN	Sevilla	21 Feb 92
5000 metres	13:20.4	Suleiman Nyambui	TAN	New York	6 Feb 81
50 m hurdles	6.25	Mark McKoy	CAN	Kobe	5 Mar 86
60 m hurdles	7.30	Colin Jackson	GBR	Sindelfingen	6 Mar 94
High jump	2.43	Javier Sotomayor	CUB	Budapest	4 Mar 89
Pole vault	6.15	Sergey Bubka	UKR	Donyetsk	21 Feb 93
Long jump	8.79	Carl Lewis	USA	New York	27 Jan 84
Triple jump	17.77	Leonid Voloshin	RUS	Grenoble	6 Feb 94
Shot	22.66	Randy Barnes	USA	Los Angeles	20 Jan 89
5000m walk	18:15.25	Grigoriy Kornev	RUS	Moskva	7 Feb 92
	18:11.41 mx	Ronald Weigel	GDR	Wien (in mixed sex race)	13 Feb 88
4 x 200m	1:22.11	United Kingdom	GBR	Glasgow	3 Mar 91
		(Linford Christie, Darren Braithwaite, Ade Mafe, John Regis)			
4 x 400m	3:03.05	Germany	GER	Sevilla	10 Mar 91
		(Rico Lieder, Jens Carlowitz, Karsten Just, Thomas Schönlebe)			
4 x 800m	7:17.8	USSR	URS	Sofia	14 Mar 71
		(Valentin Taratynov, Stanislav Meshcherskikh, Aleksey Taranov, Viktor Semyashkin)			
Heptathlon	6476	Dan O'Brien	USA	Toronto	13/14 Mar 93
	(6.67 60m, 7.84 LJ, 16.02 SP, 2.13 HJ, 7.85 60mh, 5.20 PV, 2:57.96 1000m)				
Women					
50 metres	6.00	Merlene Ottey	JAM	Moskva	4 Feb 94
60 metres	6.92	Irina Privalova	RUS	Madrid	11 Feb 93
200 metres	21.87	Merlene Ottey	JAM	Liévin	13 Feb 93
400 metres	49.59	Jarmila Kratochvílová	TCH	Milano	7 Mar 82
800 metres	1:56.40	Christine Wachtel	GDR	Wien	13 Feb 88
1000 metres	2:33.93	Inna Yevseyeva	UKR	Moskva	7 Feb 92
1500 metres	4:00.27 +	Doina Melinte	ROM	East Rutherford	9 Feb 90
1 mile	4:17.14	Doina Melinte	ROM	East Rutherford	9 Feb 90
3000 metres	8:33.82	Elly van Hulst	HOL	Budapest	4 Mar 89
5000 metres	15:03.17	Elizabeth McColgan	GBR	Birmingham	22 Feb 92
50 m hurdles	6.58	Cornelia Oschkenat	GDR	Berlin	20 Feb 88
60 m hurdles	7.69	Lyudmila Narozhilenko	URS	Chelyabinsk	4 Feb 90
High jump	2.07	Heike Henkel	GER	Karlsruhe	9 Feb 92
Long jump	7.37	Heike Drechsler	GDR	Wien	13 Feb 88
Triple jump	14.90	Inna Lasovskaya	RUS	Liévin	13 Feb 94
Shot	22.50	Helena Fibingerová	TCH	Jablonec	19 Feb 77
3000m walk	11:44.00	Alina Ivanova	UKR	Moskva	7 Feb 92
4 x 200m	1:32.55	SC Eintracht Hamm	FRG	Dortmund	20 Feb 88
		(Helga Arendt, Silke-Beate Knoll, Mechthild Kluth, Gisela Kinzel)			
4 x 400m	3:27.22	Germany	GER	Sevilla	10 Mar 91
		(Sandra Seuser, Annett Hesselbarth, Katrin Schreiter, Grit Breuer)			
4 x 800m	8:25.5	Villanova	USA	Gainesville	7 Feb 87
		(Gina Procaccio, Debbie Grant, Michelle DiMuro, Celeste Halliday)			
Pentathlon	4991	Irina Belova	RUS	Berlin	14/15 Feb 92
		(8.22 60mh, 1.93 HJ, 13.25 SP, 6.67 LJ, 2:10.26 800m)			

¶ The IAAF stripped Johnson of his records in January 1990, after he had admitted long-term steroid use.

AMENDMENTS TO ATHLETICS 1993

Men 1992

100m: 10.39 Hodge ISV not BVI, 10.40 0.8 Guido Kluth GER 71 12 Sep. wa: 10.15A 6.3 Donovan Bailey 1 and 10.29A 6.3 Peter Ogilvie 3 Provo 26 May (from 10.23w/ 10.33w), 10.31 2.6 Everton Anderson 10 May (from 10.37w), 10.40 2.8 Bennie Buys RSA 66 10 Apr
200m: 19.91 Johnson 13 Jul, 20.94 0.1 Glenroy Gilbert CAN 68 9 May, move 20.98 Osagiobare to best low altitude (20.89A); wa: 20.78w Lawson TRI, 20.84w +2.1 Donovan Bailey CAN 67 10 May, 20.95w Seibert Straughn BAR 67 4 Apr
400m: 45.71 Chukwu drugs dq in this competition, best before then 45.79 on 14 Mar, 46.26 Chuck Wilson, 46.30 Devon Edwards, 46.44 Lamont Leach JAM, 46.48 Orr JAM, add 46.34 Troy McIntosh BAH 22 May. Delete 46.11A Bekele
800m: 1:47.34 Joseph Kiptanui KEN 71 11 Apr, 1:47.46 Johns 69, 1:47.78 Toledo
1000m: 2:19.92 Christoph Meyer GER 66 18 Jul
3000m: 7:41.53 Aouita repeated
5000m: Richard Chelimo b.21.4.72 (also 10000m), 13:33.77 Fíz (not 13:35.06), 13:35.06 Paul (not 13:34.25), 13:38.83A Salvador, delete 13:39.85 Korir (13:31.28)
15km Rd: 43:39 Alejandro Gómez ESP 11.4.67 1 Bilbao 29 Nov
Marathon: 2:08:07 Tsebe and 2:08:38 Matias on 27 Sep, add 2:10:54 Kim Woan-ki 3 New York 1 Nov, delete 2:13:39 Kim Chung-yong (see 2:13:06) and 2:14:05 Sato (see 2:13:12)
3000mSt: 8:23.82 El Khattabi 16.5.67
100km: 6:30:37 Catalan 4.8.48, 6:49:24 Schneider
110mh: 13.95 + 1.5 Jai Taurima AUS 72 14 Nov
400mh: delete 50.23A Rivera (was Piñera)
PV: 5.60 Holl and 5.56 Atzbacher on 22 Jul
LJ: 8.25 1.6 Masaki Morinaga JPN 27.3.72 2 Shizuoka 5 May, 8.07 -0.5 Nai 30 Oct, 7.95 Exh Ergotic - 7.90 27 May, 7.86 Jacob Katonen KEN 26 Aug, 7.85 Romain DMN, 7.81 1.8 Marti Digno CUB 65 21 May, 8.11w 5.4 Romain, 7.81w 2.6 Mangold, 7.98w 4.6 Khaida
SP: 18.36 Erbach - questionable circumstances
DT: 65.66 Kokhanovksiy repeated, 65.36 Martinez, 64.40 Gravelle 3, 63.98un Hollmén, delete 60.82 Vykpysh (63.24)
Dec: 7630 Görz - 11.22/0.3, 7.36/1.1; 7567 Neumaier 10.95/2.5, 7.17/1.2
4x100m: 39.32A MEX Rojas, Nava, Adam, Cardenas
4x400m: 3:05.13A MEX Escalante, Nava, Karin, Vallin; 3:05.49 JAM Fagan, H Davis, Burnett, T Graham
20kmW: add CHN: 1:22:52.1 Wang Qing .8.70 (11), 1:23:09.4 Zhai Wanbo .4.67 (12), 1:24:02.5 Gao Yunbing .10.75 (13), Ye Liansheng 30.1.71 (14), 1:24:17.4 —bo (15) all NC Jinan 15 Mar; 1:23:36.82 Li Zewen .10.73 (1) and 1:23:39.41 Wang Jun (2) Dalian 28 Sep
50kmW: add CHN: 4:00:56 Fu - - (11), 4:02:22 Zhou - (12), 4:05:20 Liu Han 1.6.72 (13), 4:07:10 Zhang - - (14), 4:07:33 Xu - - (15), 4:08:25 - - - (16), 4:08:32 Xu Yu - (17) all NC Jinan 18 Mar; 4:02:23 Zhao Yongsheng .3.71 (1), 4:02:45 Zhai Wanbo .4.67 (2), 4:05:38 - - - (30 all Dalian 1 Oct; add 4:03:02 Rodrigo Serrano and 4:04:24 Miguel Solis Roque MEX both Ciudad México 5 Apr (note this venue not Ciudad Victoria for other marks in Mexico on this date)

Junior men 1992

100m: Carrigan 10.24 & 10.27 on 19 Jun, 10.43w Evans 1h; delete unconfirmed 10.39 Shelton, 10.40 Thomas
200m: 20.99w Dade, 20.4 Boldon; delete 21.07u Silah (21.7)
800m: delete unconfirmed marks for Ethiopians (all phony)
5000m, 10000m: Delete Richard Chelimo b.21.4.72, Machuka may have been b.12.2.75
110mh: 14.32 Andrea Alterio ITA 11.6.73 1 Parma 19 Sep, 14.27w 5.0 Maresuke Minowa JPN 9.8.73 1 and 14.29w Tatsuya Shimotori JPN 27.3.73 2 Niigata 30 Aug,14.30w +2.9 de los Santos; hand: 14.1 Ilya Chernykh RUS 73 1 Moskva 26 Jun
400mh: 51.02 Kawamura 15.9.74, 51.51 Yasuda 10.12.74
HJ: 2.21 Ledet 20.7.73, 2.21 Broxterman 28.11.73, 2.20 Isayev 27.7.73
PV: 5.33i Kühnke 15 Feb, 5.30 Andrey Podkorytov .73, 5.25 K Lachheb 16.1.75, 5.23 Guidry 1st
LJ: 7.71 Vitaliy Makarevich, 7.71 da Cruz 6.2.74, 7.70 Zhukov, 7.69 Watanabe at Tendo, 7.68 Oshima not Oashi, 7.68 0.4 Vladimir Malyavin 2 Bryansk 17 Aug, 7.74w Howard 14 Jun, 7.73w Dilworth 14.2.74
TJ: 16.57 0.9 Mhdlongwa, 16.06 -0.1 Peshcherov, 16.21w Nagama, 16.20w 4.0 Clyne
SP: Belonog 18.95 2 Kiev, 17.18 Lukovkin 1st, 17.01i Valeriy Karpovich BLS 73 3 Minsk 11 Feb
DT: 54.84 Tokarev 1st, 52.96 Klajic 26.8.73, delete 53.82u Medina
HT: Yevgenyev 72.56 1 Rybinsk 14 Jun, 69.32 Vizzoni 4.11.73, 69.12 Metla 4th, 68.90 Pakhomov not in CIS lists, 68.58 Khersontsev 8.7.74, 67.00 Kalinin 3rd
Dec: 7440 Huber LJ 6.96w, 7325 Razbeyko, 7169 Aleksandr Dimov RUS 73 7 Blagach 26 Jul (11.10, 7.19, 13.43, 1.92, 51.16, 16.30, 40.28, 4.50, 42.94, 4:41.28), 7142 lopez 13.2.73
10000mW: Jacek and Grzegorz Muller both b. 3.11.73, 41:42.75 Didoni on 16 Sep, 41:56.00 Breznai at Budapest, 42:04.6 Dmitriy Pevchev RUS 73 2 St Petersburg 14 May, 42:07.85 Feodosiy Chumachenko
4x100m: 39.88 NGR Aliu

Women 1992

100m: 11.41 -0.2 Andrea Philipp GER 29.7.71 3h2 OD Jena 28 May, 11.44A Angella Issajenko CAN 28.9.58 1 Provo 26 May, 11.49 1.6 Haggenmüller, 11.55 0.6 Michelle Williams JAM 67 5 Jun, 11.58 0.9 Schnupfer, 11.58 1.7 Hanitriniana Rakotondrabe MAD 26 Jun; add CHN: 11.49 Li Shuxiang and Huang Peilan 62 both 17 May, 11.49 You Yanyun 72 18 May, 11.50 Tang Haiyun 73 18 Oct, 11.54 Hu Ling 73 24 Oct, 11.55 Chen Yan 18 Oct, 11.59 Huang Xaoyan 69 17 Apr, 11.60 Chen Chaoyi 17 Oct; hand: 11.3 Yelena Bobrovskaya KGZ 24 Apr, 11.4 Merlene Dawkins JAM 73 28 Mar, 11.4 Twilet Malcolm JAM 69 2 Jul; wind: 11.03 3.3 Ajunwa ¶ 1 Villeneuve d'Ascq 6 Jul, 11.43w Twiggs 4.10.72, 11.46 Malcolm, 11.55w ?? Tara Perry CAN 74 17 Apr
200m: 22.06 0.2 Privalova 2 GPF Torino 4 Sep, 23.42 Feagin and 23.53 Wilson both +0.3, 23.52 0.8 Twilet Malcolm JAM 69 4 Jul, 23.61 0.7 Haggenmüller, 23.67 2.0 Michelle Williams 2 May (delete at 23.48); delete unconfirmed 22.61 Maybery; hand: delete 23.5 Pei Fang
400m: 50.22 Bryzgina 1 GPF Torino 4 Sep, 51.43

Carabali 1 Palma 13 May (delete 51.06A mark), 52.75 Julia Duporty CUB 71 18 Jul and 53.30 Odalis Limonta CUB 72 18 Jul, 52.99 Catherine Scott JAM 12 Jul (from 53.22), 53.32 Karen Gydesen, 53.35 Julie Harrison JAM 3 Jul, 53.37 Suzie Tanefo CAM 69 1 Aug, 53.43 Nezha Bidouane MAR 69 20 Jun; add CHN: 53.31 Zhao Juanling 1 Oct, 53.38 Bai Xiaoyun 73 8 May, 53.41 Zheng Jianqing 71 18 Oct, 53.45 Liu Weiwei 71 17 May

800m: 2:03.7 Paula Schnurr CAN 64 15 Jul

1500m: 4:02.16 Qu on 16 May, 4:09.04 Li Ying 24.5.73 (and 3000m 8:57.20), 4:12.08 Derartu Tulu ETH 72 13 Sep, 4:13.84 Li Haiyan CHN 8 May. 4:14.86 Susan Sirma KEN 66 6 Jul

1M: 4:21.80 Melinte 1 Bisl Oslo 4 Jul

3000m: 8:46.86 Zhang Linli 6.3.73, 8:59.83 Luminita Zaituc ROM 9.10.68 3 Bad Homburg 24 May, 9:00.96 Jane Ngotho KEN 29.11.69 8h1 OG Barcelona 31 Jul, 9:01.12 Derartu Tulu ETH 21.3.72 1 AfC Belle Vue Mauricia 28 Jun, 9:03.32 Getenesh Urge ETH 72 28 Jun, 9:08.9 Lucy Harvey CAN 70 3 Jun

3000m/10000m: Wang Junxia b.9.1.73

5000m: 15:46.19 Claudia Borgschulze GER 64 20 Aug

10000m: 31:32.25 Tulu 27 Jun, 31:45.58 Meyer at Cape Town, 33:20.30 Kiplagat 23 May (from 33:43.10); add CHN 33:09.50 Dong Li 73 17 May, 33:23.53 Hong Tuo 72 17 May, 33:26.89 Feng Wenhui 74 29 Sep (from 33:41.8), 33:28.05 Hu Xiaolan 67 17 May, 33:43.87 Wang Ruiping 73 29 Sep

15km: 50:00 Claudia Metzner GER 5.5.66 1 Schortens 22 Aug

Mar: 2:36:35 Wilson confirmed, 2:38:49 Webb 64, delete 2:37:00 Jing Li

100km: 8:14:14 Benöhr 8.10.57

100mh: 13.29 Ludmila Olijare LAT 5.2.58 1 RigaCp Riga 31 May, 13.40 0.0 Schneeweis, 13.42 -1.8 Bolm, 13.51 Connie Graham CAN 63 4 May (from 13.56A), 13.54A Leslie Estwick CAN 60 26 May (from 13.55A), 13.61 Zhang Jing CHN 71 17 Oct; wa: 13.35A 2.2 Seema Kamal CAN 69 2 Provo 26 May

400mh: 57.35 Julie Harrison JAM 3 NC Kingston 3 Jul, 57.54A McDermid (not 57.34), 57.62 Kareth Smith JAM 67 3 Jul (from 58.03), 58.36 Omatoyo Akinremi 30 My (from 58.64); add CHN: 57.50 Zhu Mingming 68 6 NC Nanjing 20 May, 57.84 Liu Jingfen 71 19 May, 58.44 Gue Yue 69 19 May, 58.57 Lai Lomgmei 73 19 Oct

HJ: 2.00 Henkel 21 Aug (not 16 Aug), 1.89 Zalevskaya 14.6.73

PV: 3.90 Sun Caiyun at Wuhan repeated, 3.86 Rieger 1 Bietigheim8 Jul, 3.85 Rieger 1 Schelklingen 13 Jun, 3.85 Rieger 1 Wiesloch 2 Sep, 3.80 Shao 2

LJ: add CHN: 6.49 1.4 Zhou Xiu - .11.70 Fuzhou 27 Oct, 6.42 1.5 Lu Junhun CHN 73 16 Jun, 6.40 1.2 Huang Jiping 68 27 Oct, 6.37 1.8 Yang Zhan xiang 72 24 Apr, 6.37 0.4 Zhang Yan 72 20 May; delete 6.68 Elechi (was 6.08); delete 6.68 Elechi (was 6.08)

TJ: 13.42i Kotova UKR 1 Feb, 13.19 -0.3 Madobuko; add CHN: 13.12 Fu Xianhong 70 18 Apr, 13.09 Wang Lin 3 Oct, 13.05 Li Zhixia 3 Apr, 13.04 Wang Yijing 11 Apr, 13.03 Yan Xueqin 15 Sep, 13.02 Guo Qian 71 25 Apr, 13.01 Chen Huoqiang 15 Sep, 13.00 Xiang Xiuli 18 Oct

SP: 19.98 Krivelyova Q OG Barcelona 5 Aug, 15.82 Fouzia Fatihi MAR 70 26 Jun; add CHN: 18.57 Zhen Wenhua 1 Wuhan 3 Oct (from 18.24), 18.33 He Xiuqin 67 4 Shijiazhuang 25 Apr, 18.23 Dong Bo .3.71 Beijing 3 May 3 May (from 17.97) , 18.16 Zhou Hongzhen 71 2 Shanghai 19 Apr, 18.08 Wang Wenge 1 Dalian 9 Aug, 17.73 Liu Ying 21.1.74 5 Shijiazhuang 25 Apr (from 17.59), 17.70 Wang Hong 6 Dalian 28 Sep, 16.40 Min Chunfeng 26 Sep, 16.36 Tian Xue 21 May. 50th best 17.84, 100th 16.40

DT: 67.90 Wyludda 1 GPF Torino 4 Sep, 61.56 Cao Qi .1.64, add CHN: 58.50 Luan Zhili 1 Jinan 28 Aug (from 56.56), 57.38 Fu - li 15.2.70 9 Apr, 56.94 Qiu Ying 6 NC Nanjing 18 May, 56.78 Wang Yanhai 1 Beijing 28 Mar, 56.68 Wang Enfang - Dalian 29 Sep, 56.26 Wang Jinling 69 7 NC Nanjing 18 May, 56.04 Li Yuan 71 9 Aug, 56.00 Huang Jianlan 17 May, 55.72 Zhang Yanhua 31 Mar, 55.64 Zhang Yujin 70 25 Apr, 55.24 Zhao Yonghua 69 15 Aug, 55.08 Li Shimei 17 Apr, 54.86 Li Qiumei 74 29 Aug, 54.72 Li Feng 18 May; delete 55.20 Allam. 100th best 56.20.

HT: 62.70 Sudak 17.11.71 (and 59.64 1 Staiki 12 May), 55.90 Gubkina 28.5.72, 55.42 Simone Mathes, 54.86 Kozhemyakina 15.3.75, 54.62 Lishchun 2, 54.20 Baydak 3, 53.80 Bychkova 4, 53.76 Meyer 1, 53.04 Potsovich 5

JT: **60.12 Tolkkinen**, 57.56 Völker; add CHN: 59.86 Han Jingli Jinan 11 Apr, 59.76 Zhang Min 1 Wuhan 30 Sep, 59.70 Tang Lishuang 25.2.66 Beijing 22 Mar, 59.66 Zhang Guihua .3.70 2 Wuhan 30 Sep, 59.46 Liu Cui Wuhan 4 Oct, 58.74 Wang Jinling .10.65 1 Guangzhou 17 Aug, 58.38 Chen Mei 1 Wuhan 11 Apr, 57.16 Golovizina, 56.82 Gao Ping .3.70 1 Jinan 3 Apr, 54.80 Li Lei 29 Aug, 54.76 Liu Cui 71 31 Mar, 54.32 Sun Fei 73 8 May, 54.26 Wu Haihong 19 Apr. 100th best 56.36.

Heptathlon: 6845 Belova 2

4x100mR: 44.04 UKR 1 Schwechat 1 Jul, 45.20 CAN 1 North York 5 Jun, 45.25 Guadeloupe 3 Fort-de-France 25 Apr, 45.35 KZK 3 Vladimir 23 Aug, 45.38 MAD 26 Jun, 45.5 KEN 1 Naurobi 13 Jun, delete 46.09 POR (45.27)

4x400mR: 3:25.20 GBR, 3:29.38 POR, 3:31.26 SUI all h2; 3:31.41 CHN, 3:33.81 HUN 5h1; 3:39.2 BAR Eli, Phillips, Sandiford, Hinkson 1 Bridgetown 21 Jun

5000mW: 21:19.2 Sidoti 1 Messina 25 Apr was OK, 21:55.33 Shimarayeva, 21:55.40A Janice McCaffrey1 Calgary 19 Jul, 21:56.91 Trofimova 17.1.75, 22:07.21 Aleftina Gerasimova, 22:09.84 Martynova .75, 22:56.18 Raquel del Caz ESP 73 31 May

10kmW: add CHN track at Jinan 15 Mar (result known to 44:41.7 only): 43:22.2 Sun Yan 11 (from 44:24), 43:39.1 Xu Lijuan 72 12, 43:42.8 Su Juan 13, 43:52.7 Zhu Ping 15, 43:56.8 Chen Yan 16 (from 44:29), 44:02.2 Yuan Yufang 17, 44:11.7 Ni Fenglian 71, 44:22.6 Long Yuwen, 44:41.7 Fu Liqin; road Dalian 1 Oct: 45:00 Xu Chunjuan 72 5, 45:16 Liu Hongyu 7, 45:18 Wang Jinli 8, 46:48 Yu Lili; 45:40 Wang Ruiping Jinan 18 Mar, 46:10 Feng Haixia 73 18 Mar.

20kmW: 1:36:54 AnnaRita Sidoti ITA 25.7.69 1 Gradisca 4 Oct

Junior Women 1992

100m: M Jones 11.28 -0.7, 11.50 Tang Haiyun CHN 73 2 Wuhan 18 Oct, 11.54 Hu Ling CHN 73 1 Changsha 24 Oct; wa: 11.50 2.3 Kathy Travis USA 12.3.73 3 Norman 18 May, 11.53 Russell 6h, 11.55 ?? Tara Perry CAN .74 1h MSR Walnut 17 Apr. Hand: 11.3 Pukha 10.1.73

200m: M Jones 22.91 -0.9; 23.42 Feagin and 23.53 Wilson both +0.3, 23.44 0.1 Robinson, 23.49w Fynes 17.10.74, 23.59w 2.1 Noel 3 NC Montreal 21 Jun (not 23.53w), delete 23.51w Idehen

400m: 52.99 Catherine Scott 4 WelshG Cwmbran 12 Jul (from 53.22)

800m: 2:05.4 Tang Xueqing CHN 74 2 Dalian 28Sep, 2:05.7 Vitryak UKR, delete 2:05.6 Genet

1500m/3000m: 4:09.04/8:57.20 Li Ying 24.5.73, 4:11.33/ 9:06.02 Cosoveanu
1500m: 4:16.82 Radcliffe 4 Jul, 4:18.12 Anderson 25 Feb
3000m: 8:46.86 Zhang Linli 6.3.73,
3000m/10000m: Wang Junxia b.9.1.73
5000m: 16:07.96 Zhan Jiangying CHN .6.74 5 Dalian 5 Oct
10000m: Cheromei 33:02.3A on 1 Jul, 33:26.89 Feng Wenhui 6 Dalian 29 Sep (from 33:41.8), 33:38.64 Kato 22 May, 33:43.87 Wang Ruiping CHN 73 29 Sep, 33:55.18 Nanu 1 Aug, 33:59.30 Zheng Guixia CHN 26.4.73 11 NC Nanjing 17 May
100mh: 13.42 Bolm 11 Jul, 13.42 Anderson 2s1, 13.45 Niculae 15 Aug, 13.65 Zhou Jing 3 Changsha 24 Oct (from 13.79), 13.80 Zhang Yanren h Hangzhu 7 May (from 13.81), 13.81 1.2 Kuriya Toyomori JPN 26.6.73 4 Tendo 6 Oct, . hand: 13.5 Zhou Jing - Beijing 29 Aug
400mh: 58.02 Rhodes 28 Jun, 58.57 Lai Longmei CHN 73 h Wuhan 19 Oct, 58.65 Jekabsone 16.10.74, 58.85 Silje Rasmussen
HJ: 1.89 Zalevskaya 14.6.73
PV: 3.70 Zhang Caiying? CHN 731 Changsha 24 Oct
LJ: 6.42 1.5 Lu Junhun CHN 3.10.73 16 Jun, 6.34 Zhao Tianyi CHN .2.73 1 Wuhan 30 Sep, 6.31 Oppinger 1, 6.30 Dedra Davis
TJ: 13.68 Matyashova 7.8.73? - 13.56 0.9, 13.25 Rodovich .76, 13.09i Nikolayeva - & 13.00 Brovary 1 Jul, 12.98 Godinez 5 May, 12.95 Twylana Harrison
SP: 17.73 Liu Ying 21.1.74 5 Shijiazhuang 25 Apr (from 17.59)
DT: 61.56 Cao Qi .1.74 Q Dalian 29 Sep (from 54.82), 58.50 Luan Zhili 1 Jinan 28 Aug (from 56.56), 54.86 Li Qiumei CHN 74 Beijing 29 Aug (from 52.46)
HT: 55.42 Simone Mathes, 54.86 Kozhemyakina 15.3.75, 54.62 Lishchun, delete 55.90 Gubkina (b.72)
JT: 57.16 Golovizina,
Hep: 5667 Kovalyova 28.2.73, 5535 Specht 2 Dresden 20 Sep, 5508 Shouaa SP 16.05, 200m 25.78; 5482 Mashchenko at Balgach, 5469 Van Diessen SP 11.90; 5421 Bianca Hoeben, 5418 Wang - 14.48, 1.73, 11.68, 25.52, 5.94, 32.86, 2:28.80; 5408 Retzke,
5000mW: 21:55.33 Shimarayeva, 21:56.91 Trofimova 17.1.75, 22:07.21 Aleftina Gerasimova, 22:09.84 Martynova .75
4x400m: 3:31.57 ROM Petrea, 3:41.72 TPE Tsu, 3:43.40 GBR 9 Aug

1991 World Lists

Men 200m: 20.82 -0.6 Lovelace; **1 Mile**: 3:59.77 Francois van Rensburg RSA 70; **Mar**: 2:14:19 Maurizio Lorenzetti ITA 63 27 Oct, 2:14:22 Marco Milani ITA 60 1 Apr, 2:14:24 Csaba Szücs HUN 65 20 Oct; **LJ**: 8.44 -1.0 Powell, 8.35 0.8 Myricks, 8.35 0.0 Starks, 8.34 2.0 Starks, 8.32 0.5 Starks, 8.30 1.7 Powell, 8.26 0.4 Starks; **30kmW**: 2:05:12 (not 2:05:17) Potashov; **TJ**: 16.99w Olivier
Women 100m: 11.36 2.0 Anzhelika Shevchuk URS 23.2.69 3s1 NC Kiev 10 Jul, 11.41w 3.2 Malcolm, 11.44w 2.2 Idehen, 11.52Aw McDuffie 2B El Paso, 11.52w 6.2 Bayless 1h3 SWAC Houston, 11.53w 6.2 Cole; **200m**: 23.48 Stacey Bowen CAN 17.12.69 Atlanta 23 May (but not in CAN lists?); **800m**: delete 2:01.92 Groenendaal (2:04.05 in Roma); **100mh**: delete 12.44 Grigoryeva and 12.55 Narozhilenko in Caorle; 13.35 .4 Frazier; **HJ**: 1.87 Alcorn 2 Logan; best out 1.93 Bradburn 2 Athl Lausanne 10 Jul; **LJ**: 7.25 1.7 and 7.19 0.2 Drechsler; 7.21w 3.6 Byelevskaya; **TJ**: 14.42 -1.4 Li, 14.35 -0.4 Kravets, 13.41i Kontsevaya 2, 13.40 -1.0 Fan, 13.23 0.6 Hudson, 13.48w 2.8 Natalya Telepnyeva URS 66 4 Krasnodar 23 Jun; **SP:** 21.60i Fedysuhina 1 Simferopol 28 Dec

1990 World Lists

Men 100m: 10.23 Williams and 10.25 Thomas 1.3; **200m**: 20.60 Williams 3, 20.67 Warren & 20.70 Brockenburr 0.6; **400m**: 45.44dt Roach from St Kitts; **3000m**: delete 7:53.05 Jonah Koech (now at 7:51.30); **2000mSt**: 5:31.44 Gianni Lacerenza ITA 19.10.67 6 Rovereto 21 Aug; **110mh**: 13.80 1.2 Knight; **Lj**: 7.81i Yuriy Naumkin URS 69 24 Jan, 8.32w 2.5 Powell 1 NYG New York 29 Jul (8.11w, 8.32w, x, 8.07w, 8.08w, 8.23w); 7.93w 3.3 Wörner; **4x400m**: 3:04.13 AUS 2nd runner Stone
Women 100mh: delete 13.03 Kuznyetsova (was 13.73)

1985 World Lists

Men 200m: hand timed 20.5 Besik Gotsiridze GEO 61 1 Liman 8 May

1984 World Lists

Women DT: 65.30 Dmitriyeva on 8 Sep doubtful as she did 63.54 for 6th in USSR Champs that day - next 64.04 1 Potltava 30 Sep

1983 World Lists

Men TJ: 16.72 Mai Guoqiang CHN 62

With acknowledgements to Winfried Kramer, Francisco Ascorbe, José Maria García, Luigi Mengoni, Richard Hymans, Keith Morbey, Einar Otto Øren, P Bertignon and others

World Indoor Championships 1993

Correction to results published on pages 606-7 of Athletics 1993 due to drugs disqualifications:.
Men LJ and TJ: 3rd placed Daniel Ivanov and Nikolai Raev were disqualified, so move up those originally 4-8, and add LJ 8. Nai Hui-fang TPE 7.70, TJ 8. Parkev Grigoryan ARM 16.20.
Women Pen: winner Belova disqualified so move up 2-8 to 1-7 and add 8. DeDe Nathan USA 4128, 4x400m: Marina Shmonina dq so RUS team lost the gold medal, move up JAM and USA to 1-2.

AMENDMENTS TO THIS ANNUAL

CROSS-COUNTRY 1993: Polish champions - men: Leszek Beblo, women: Irena Czuta.

OBITUARIES

Dr Friedrich-Wilhelm TARNOGRICKI (Germany) (b. 4 Sep 1904 Dresden) in December in Berlin. With a 800m pb of 1:54.4 when 2nd in the 1928 German Championships, he made three international appearances, being eliminated in the heats of the 1928 Olympics.

Dr George Sheehan - add (b. 5 Nov 1918 New York) pbs: 1M 4:19 (1939), Mar 3:01 at Boston.

Vera TREZOITKO (Brazil) (b. 18 Dec 1929) on 23 December. Four times Brazilian champion at shot and once at javelin, she set national records with shot 13.12 (1961) and discus 41.26 (1955) with a javelin best of 39.82. At the shot she was South American champion in 1953 and Ibero-American champion in 1962.

LATE AMENDMENTS

Men 1993

100m: 10.34 +1.2 Telles,10.39 +0.9 Ribeiro; hand: 10.1 +0.3 Arnaldo de Oliveira Silva, 10.2 +03 Domingos da Silva
200m: 20.81 Francis 70, 20.93 Patterson 72, 20.96 Thomas 71, 20.92w Dibble 72
400m: 46.32 Sinclair 71 (and 400mh 50.78)
800m: 1:47.0 Victor Silvio 25.8.64
3000m: 7:49.80 Barngetuny 20.5.73 (& 2kmSt 5:25.31, 3kmSt 8:28.85)
LJ: 8.03 +0.4 Ferreira Junior, 7.91 +0.8 de Oliveira, delete 7.82 as this was by Ferreira Junior not Ferreira Rocha
TJ: 16.47 +0.3 de Souza, 16.32 -0.8 Baptista
Dec: 7531 Petlicki delete as just above 7425
4x400mR: 3:01.44 JAM *Correct team to:* Blake 46.0, Haughton 45.5, Ev Clarke 45.32, Graham 44.55, WC Stuttgart 22 Aug

Junior Men 1993

110mh 14.23 & LJ 7.71 Neal Gardener 8.12.74

Women 1993

100m: delete 11.49 Amaral (see 11.39) and adjust numbering thereafter
200m: 23.60 Carnegie 65, 23.66 Katia de Jesus Santos
400m: 52.02 Grant 25.9.70, 52.36 Mendes OK
2000m: 5:41.23 O'Sullivan - delete date of birth that follows
LJ: 6.41 (?w) Terri Horgan IRL 67 3 Jul
SP: 15.99 Alexandra Borges Amaro BRA 72 6 Jun

Junior Women

400m: delete 52.02 Beverley Grant (b1970), add 53.63 Suziann Reid USA 14.1.77 1 Baton Rouge 1 Aug

Men's Index 1993

Add + to Gicquel (new biography), Sepeng, Hezekiel; Yawa, Xolile b. 29 Sep 63; delete Mogotsi, Meshack 3KmSt 8:36.55 (this was Shadrack)
add ht/wt for ITA athletes *(from Raul Leoni):*
Alliegro 168/53, Barazaghi 178/57, Bernardini 177/61, Bianchi 178/62, Calvaresi 170/60, Cimarrusti 177/68, De Gaetano 186/72, Di Lello 180/69, Durbano 163/50, Fiorini 177/66, Fizialetti 170/58, Lizio 176/64, Penocchio 180/64, Rota 180/62, Trentin 178/62

Women's Index 1993

Hafner 176/67
Add + to Bozhanova, Goncharenko, Ribeiro

1994 World Indoor Lists

Men: 60m: 6.60 Jason John GBR 2r2 Wein 6 Feb
800m: 1:47.51 Valeriy Starodubtsev
50mh: 6.58 Mark Crear
35lb Wt: 21.92 Ron Willis USA 1 Indianapolis 12 Mar (21.98 was outdoors)
Women: 60m: 7.21 Holli Hyche USA 1 Glasgow 12 Feb
60mh: 7.59 Dionne Rose 1 Murfreesboro 26 Feb

Biographies

BULGARIA: Donkova - El: 87- 1, and add 92- 3

World Cross-country 1994: Feyisa Melese ETH shows as born in 1963. Interesting to note that when he won the 1986 World Junior CC title, he was given as born in 1967!

These are simply the amendments that I received or came across in the three days 5 to 7 April 1994. Now all the pages are printed, and further amendments must wait until next year.

Peter Matthews

An African challenge to the Chinese

by Ladislav Krnac

MARIA MUTOLA, the world 800 metres champion, could be the biggest talking point of women's track at the Atlanta Olympic Games in 1986 despite the Chinese invasion of Stuttgart last year.

If so she will no doubt state that a major part of her success was due to the IOC's Solidarity programme which sent her from Mozambique to the Springfield High School in Eugene, Oregon, on a renewable four-month scholarship in March 1991. By that time she had run in the Seoul Olympics as a 15 year-old and won the African Championships 800 and 1500 metres aged 17.

Springfield took the chance with Maria Lurdes Mutola because of a Portuguese speaker on the staff. Her assistant coach Jeff Fund remembers that at first communication was hard – without pictures – as Maria (27.10.1972), the youngest of six children, was one of only five black students at Springfield High.

"It looked like she could be more at ease with somebody else from Mozambique. I am sure she prefers a much warmer environment. In Eugene it often rains and the temperatures are around ten degrees in winter. She hates rain," added Fund.

"But we are satisfied with her great dedication to accomplish the given goal. She trains mostly outside the stadium, likes to practice and is easy to coach."

Fund was left looking after her on the final lap of the IAAF Mobil Grand Prix series after his wife Margo, Mutola's coach, left right after Stuttgart. What is she like? "I would say she has two personalities – a Mozambique one and a non-Portuguese, non-African one. She is a typical teenager, liking rock and roll and off course Mozambique music. She has many skills and is good at working with glass."

On the track Mutola is formidable. The milestones of her career so far are:

1986 (13 years-old) – Poet Jose Craveirinha stripped the Mozambique women's soccer world of a promising player but enriched the world of track and field with a unique running talent.

1988 (15) Mutola finished seventh in the second heat of the Seoul Olympics over 800 (2:04.36)

1990 (17) African champion at 800 and 1500.

1991 (18) She won her first official competition in the USA on April 24 – 1500 in 4:17.42, ran her first under two minute 800 on June 28 (1:59.4) and under dramatic circumstances was fourth in the 800 final of the Tokyo World Championships (1:57.63).

1992 (19) Fifth at Barcelona Olympics in 1:57.49.

1993 (20) World Indoor Champion (1:57.55) in Toronto, world outdoor champion (1:55.43) in Stuttgart, by the greatest winning margin in the history of Olympic Games or World Championships – almost two seconds.

Her exploits last year provided more proof that it is possible to peak twice a year, especially if you are young, healthy (no injury since autumn 1991) and winning all the time.

Let us take a more analytical look at her three most important races so far:

1991. August 26, Tokyo (WCh final): Mutola ran the slowest first 400 metres of all (57.0) but the fastest (60.6) second half. Gap between the two laps – 3.6 seconds.

1992. August 3, Barcelona (OG final): this time she produced the fastest first 400 (55.7) and the slowest second half (62.8). Gap – 7.1.

1993, August 17, Stuttgart (WCh final): fifth fastest first lap (56.3), fastest second half (59.1). This time the gap was only 2.8.

In Toronto (WI final) she won with 58.85 and 58.70 splits.

After her 1993 world season's best in Zürich I asked if she should think about the world record. The answer showed her maturity. "First of all I would have to come close to something like 1:54 ..."

Jeff Fund says her most important aim is Olympic gold in Atlanta in 1996.

Like most successful people – not just those on the track – Mutola received her share of criticism, beginning with complaints about her very physical running style. Double Olympic 800 metres champion Mal Whitfield, who knows the African scene, told the New York Times: "These women are very hungry and they mean business. They're going to be cruel to our women runners in Atlanta."

Jeff Fund has said they do not know how Jarmila Kratochvílová trained before her 1983 world record (1:53.28) but for the 1994 season they plan to do more 400s and 1500s. Kratochvílová's route to the world record went hand in hand with a 48 second 400 metres.

The big question is - what are the limits of Maria Mutola over 800 metres, presuming her rise is not interrupted by injury, sickness or over-confidence (the worst sickness ...)?

Jeff Fund, not very pleased to be asked, paused for a while before answering. "Around 1:51."

And he said it before the Chinese bomb exploded in Bejing.

WORLD MEN'S ALL-TIME LISTS

100 METRES

Mark	Wind	Name		Nat	Born	Pos	Meet	Venue	Date
9.83	1.0	Ben	Johnson ¶	CAN	30.12.61	1	WC	Roma	30 Aug 87
9.86	1.2	Carl	Lewis	USA	1.7.61	1	WC	Tokyo	25 Aug 91
9.87	0.3	Linford	Christie	GBR	2.4.60	1	WC	Stuttgart	15 Aug 93
9.88	1.2	Leroy	Burrell	USA	21.2.67	2	WC	Tokyo	25 Aug 91
9.90	1.9		Burrell			1	TAC	New York	14 Jun 91
9.91	1.2	Dennis	Mitchell	USA	20.2.66	3	WC	Tokyo	25 Aug 91
9.92	1.1		Lewis			1	OG	Seoul	24 Sep 88
9.92	1.2		Christie			4	WC	Tokyo	25 Aug 91
9.92	0.3	Andre	Cason	USA	20.1.69	2	WC	Stuttgart	15 Aug 93
9.93A	1.4	Calvin	Smith	USA	8.1.61	1	USOF	Air Force Academy	3 Jul 83
9.93	1.0		Lewis			2	WC	Roma	30 Aug 87
9.93	1.1		Lewis			1	WK	Zürich	17 Aug 88
9.93	1.9		Lewis			2	TAC	New York	14 Jun 91
9.93	1.3		Lewis			1s1	WC	Tokyo	25 Aug 91
9.93	-0.6	Michael	Marsh	USA	4.8.67	1	MSR	Walnut	18 Apr 92
9.94	0.8		Burrell			1	TAC	Houston	16 Jun 89
9.94	1.1		Burrell			1s2	WC	Tokyo	25 Aug 91
9.94	0.3		Cason			1s1	WCh	Stuttgart	15 Aug 93
9.95A	0.3	Jim	Hines	USA	10.9.46	1	OG	Ciudad México	14 Oct 68
9.95	0.8		Johnson			1r1	GWG	Moskva	9 Jul 86
9.95	0.0		Johnson			1	ASV	Köln	16 Aug 87
9.95	1.2	Frank	Fredericks (10)	NAM	2.10.67	5	WC	Tokyo	25 Aug 91
9.96	0.1	Mel	Lattany	USA	10.8.59	1r1		Athens, Ga.	5 May 84
9.96	1.9		Lewis			1h4	OT	Indianapolis	15 Jul 88
9.96	0.4		Lewis			1q1	OT	Indianapolis	15 Jul 88
9.96	0.7		Burrell			1	BNP	Villeneuve d'Ascq	29 Jun 90
9.96A	1.2		Burrell			1rA		Sestriere	8 Aug 90
9.96	0.0		Burrell			1r1	Athl	Lausanne	10 Jul 91
9.96	1.2	Ray	Stewart	JAM	18.3.65	6	WC	Tokyo	25 Aug 91
9.96	-0.6	Davidson	Ezinwa	NGR	22.11.71	2r1	MSR	Walnut	18 Apr 92
9.96	0.5		Christie			1	OG	Barcelona	1 Aug 92
9.96	-0.1		Cason			1q4	WCh	Stuttgart	14 Aug 93
		(32 performances by 13 athletes)							
9.97	1.2	Olapade	Adeniken	NGR	19.8.69	1	Tex R	Austin	4 Apr 92
9.98A	0.6	Silvio	Leonard	CUB	20.9.55	1	WPT	Guadalajara	11 Aug 77
9.98	0.3	Daniel	Effiong	NGR	17.6.72	2s1	WC	Stuttgart	15 Aug 93
10.00	2.0	Marian	Woronin	POL	13.8.56	1	Kuso	Warszawa	9 Jun 84
10.00	1.0	Chidi	Imo	NGR	27.8.63	1	ISTAF	Berlin	15 Aug 86
10.00#A	1.6	Robson	da Silva	BRA	4.9.64	1	IbAm	Ciudad México	22 Jul 88
		10.02 1.8				1	IbAmC	Habana	27 Sep 86
10.01A	0.9	Pietro	Mennea	ITA	28.6.52	1		Ciudad México	4 Sep 79
		(20)							
10.02A	2.0	Charles	Greene	USA	21.7.44	1q4	OG	Ciudad México	13 Oct 68
10.02	1.0	James	Sanford	USA	27.12.57	1	Pepsi	Westwood	11 May 80
10.02	0.7	Daniel	Sangouma	FRA	7.2.65	2	BNP	Villeneuve d'Ascq	29 Jun 90
		Some observers felt that this was run with the benefit of a flying start, but it was artified as a French record							
10.02	0.3	Bruny	Surin	CAN	12.7.67	5	WC	Stuttgart	15 Aug 93
10.03A	1.9	Stanley	Floyd	USA	23.6.61	1r1	NCAA	Provo	5 Jun 82
10.03	-2.5&	Viktor	Bryzgin	UKR	22.8.62	1rA	Znam	Leningrad	7 Jun 86
10.03	0.4	Joe	DeLoach	USA	5.6.67	1	NCAA	Eugene	4 Jun 88
10.03	1.7	Jon	Drummond	USA	9.9.68	1rA		Rieti	5 Sep 93
10.04A	0.3	Lennox	Miller	JAM	8.10.46	2	OG	Ciudad México	14 Oct 68
10.04	1.8	Mark	Witherspoon	USA	3.9.63	1	TAC	San José	27 Jun 87
		(30)							
10.04	0.5	Emmit	King	USA	24.3.59	1	TAC	Tampa	17 Jun 88
10.05	-1.1	Steve	Riddick	USA	18.9.51	1	WK	Zürich	20 Aug 75
10.05	1.8	Harvey	Glance	USA	28.3.57	1r1	FlaR	Tampa	30 Mar 85
10.06	1.1	Bob	Hayes	USA	20.12.42	1	OG	Tokyo	15 Oct 64
10.06	0.0	Hasely	Crawford	TRI	16.8.50	1	OG	Montreal	24 Jul 76
10.06	1.6	Ron	Brown	USA	31.3.61	3	WK	Zürich	24 Aug 83
10.06	2.0	Leandro	Peñalver	CUB	23.5.61	1	PAG	Caracas	24 Aug 83
10.06	1.9	Frank	Emmelmann	GDR	15.9.61	1		Berlin	22 Sep 85
10.06	0.3	Andrés	Simon	CUB	15.9.61	1		Habana	1 Aug 87

MEN All-time

Mark	Wind	Name		Nat	Born	Pos	Meet	Venue	Date
10.06A	2.0	Johan	Rossouw	RSA	20.10.65	1		Johannesburg	23 Apr 88
		(40)							
10.06	1.3	Patrick	Williams	JAM	11.11.65	1	S&W	Modesto	5 May 90
10.07	0.0	Valeriy	Borzov	UKR	20.10.49	1q3	OG	München	31 Aug 72
10.07	0.0	Don	Quarrie	JAM	25.2.51	2	OG	Montreal	24 Jul 76
10.07	1.7	Clancy	Edwards	USA	9.8.55	1	NCAA	Eugene	2 Jun 78
10.07A	1.8	Eddie	Hart	USA	24.4.49	1	USOF	Air Force Academy	30 Jul 78
10.07	-0.1	Steve	Williams	USA	13.11.53	1	WK	Zürich	16 Aug 78
10.07A	0.6	Mike	Roberson	USA	25.3.56	1s1	WUG	Ciudad México	8 Sep 79
10.07	0.5	Lee	McRae	USA	23.1.66	1	WUG	Zagreb	14 Jul 87
10.07	0.5	Brian	Cooper	USA	21.8.65	2	TAC	Tampa	17 Jun 88
10.08		six men	100th best 10.14						

& wind reading of -2.5 almost certainly incorrect, but mark accepted as a national record.
# Times recorded in the 1988 Ibero-American Championships may not have been automatically recorded.

Disqualified for drug abuse

Mark	Wind	Name		Nat	Born	Pos	Meet	Venue	Date
9.79	1.1	Ben	Johnson	CAN	30.12.61	-	OG	Seoul	24 Sep 88

Doubtful wind readings

Mark	Wind	Name		Nat	Born	Pos	Meet	Venue	Date
9.91	-2.3	Davidson	Ezinwa	NGR	22.11.71	1		Azusa	11 Apr 92
10.02	1.2	Ronald	Desruelles ¶	BEL	14.2.55	1		Naimette	11 May 85

Low altitude marks for athletes with lifetime bests at high altitude

Mark	Wind	Name	Pos Meet	Venue	Date	Mark	Wind	Name	Pos	Venue	Date
10.03	0.8	Hines	1s1 AAU	Sacramento	20 Jun 68	10.07	2.0	Floyd	1	Austin	24 May 80
10.03	1.7	Leonard	1	Habana	13 Sep 77						

Wind-assisted marks

Mark	Wind	Name		Nat	Born	Pos	Meet	Venue	Date
9.78	5.2	Carl	Lewis	USA	1.7.61	1	OT	Indianapolis	16 Jul 88
9.79	5.3	Andre	Cason	USA	20.1.69	1h4	NC	Eugene	16 Jun 93
9.79	4.5		Cason			1s1	NC	Eugene	16 Jun 93
9.80	4.3		Lewis			1q2	WC	Tokyo	24 Aug 91
9.85	5.3	Leroy	Burrell	USA	21.2.67	2h4	NC	Eugene	16 Jun 93
9.85	4.8		Cason			1	NC	Eugene	17 Jun 93
9.85	4.8	Dennis	Mitchell	USA	20.2.66	2	NC	Eugene	17 Jun 93
9.86	5.2		Mitchell			2	OT	Indianapolis	16 Jul 88
9.87	11.2	William	Snoddy	USA	6.12.57	1		Dallas	1 Apr 78
9.87	4.9	Calvin	Smith	USA	8.1.61	1s2	OT	Indianapolis	16 Jul 88
9.87	5.2		C.Smith			3	OT	Indianapolis	16 Jul 88
9.88	2.3	James	Sanford	USA	27.12.57	1		Westwood	3 May 80
9.88	5.2	Albert	Robinson	USA	28.11.64	4	OT	Indianapolis	16 Jul 88
9.88	3.1		Cason			1rA	S&W	Modesto	16 May 92
9.89	4.2	Ray	Stewart	JAM	18.3.65	1s1	PAG	Indianapolis	9 Aug 87
9.89	4.1	Frank	Fredericks	NAM	2.10.67	1q4	WC	Tokyo	24 Aug 91
9.90	2.5		Lewis			1	MSR	Walnut	28 Apr 85
9.90	5.2	Joe	DeLoach	USA	5.6.67	5	OT	Indianapolis	16 Jul 88
9.90	3.7		Johnson			1	NC	Ottawa	6 Aug 88
9.90	3.0		Stewart			1		Vigo	30 Jun 89
9.90	4.3		Christie			2q2	WC	Tokyo	24 Aug 91
9.90	4.8		Lewis			3	NC	Eugene	17 Jun 93
9.91	5.3	Bob	Hayes	USA	20.12.42	1s1	OG	Tokyo	15 Oct 64
9.91	2.1		C.Smith			1	vGDR	Karl-Marx-Stadt	9 Jul 82
9.91	4.5		Lewis			1	TAC	Eugene	20 Jun 86
9.91	4.2	Mark	Witherspoon	USA	3.9.63	2s1	PAG	Indianapolis	9 Aug 87
9.91	5.9		Stewart			1	MSR	Walnut	22 Apr 89
9.91	5.1		Fredericks			1	BNP	Villeneuve d'Ascq	6 Jul 92
		28 wind assisted marks to 9.91							
9.92A	4.4	Chidi	Imo	NGR	27.8.63	1s1	AfrG	Nairobi	8 Aug 87
9.92	5.3	Jon	Drummond	USA	9.9.68	3h4	NC	Eugene	16 Jun 93
9.93	7.5	Pablo	Montes	CUB	23.11.45	1s	CAC	Panama City	1 Mar 70
9.94	2.7	Vitaliy	Savin	KZK	23.1.66	1	CIS Ch	Moskva	22 Jun 92
9.95	8.9	Willie	Gault	USA	5.9.60	1		Knoxville	2 Apr 83
9.95	2.4	Mel	Lattany	USA	10.8.59	1		Athens, Ga	7 May 83
9.97	7.7	Andrés	Simon	CUB	15.9.61	1s1	WUG	Kobe	30 Aug 85
9.97	3.4	Roy	Martin	USA	25.12.66	1	SWC	Houston	18 May 86
9.97	4.4	Daniel	Effiong	NGR	17.6.72	1=rA		Austin	8 May 93
9.98	11.2	Cole	Doty	CAN	6.6.55	2		Dallas	1 Apr 78
9.98	5.2	Emmit	King	USA	24.3.59	7	OT	Indianapolis	16 Jul 88
9.98	5.2	Daron	Council	USA	26.12.64	1h4	TAC	Houston	15 Jun 89
9.99	7.2	Pietro	Mennea	ITA	28.6.52	1	vGRE	Bari	13 Sep 78

Mark	Wind	Name		Nat	Born	Pos	Meet	Venue	Date
9.99#A	2.7	Leandro	Peñalver	CUB	23.5.61	1h2	IbAmC	Ciudad México	22 Jul 88
		10.00 6.0				1s2	PAG	Indianapolis	9 Aug 87
10.00	2.6	Jeff	Phillips	USA	16.5.57	2	NCAA	Baton Rouge	5 Jun 81
10.00	2.6	Lorenzo	Daniel	USA	23.3.66	1	SEC	Knoxville	18 May 86
10.00	3.7	Desai	Williams	CAN	12.6.59	2	NC	Ottawa	6 Aug 88
10.00	4.3	Tim	Jackson	AUS	4.7.69	1	CGT	Sydney	2 Dec 89
10.01	2.3	Ron	Brown	USA	31.3.61	2	MSR	Walnut	24 Apr 83
10.01#A	2.7	José	Arqués	ESP	16.5.60	2h2	IbAmC	Ciudad México	22 Jul 88
10.01	4.3	Bruny	Surin	CAN	12.7.67	3q2	WC	Tokyo	24 Aug 91
10.01	4.1	Atlee	Mahorn	CAN	27.10.65	3q4	WC	Tokyo	24 Aug 91
10.01	2.8	Glenroy	Gilbert	CAN	31.8.68	1h1	SEC	Knoxville	15 May 93
10.01	2.8	Michael	Green	JAM	7.11.70	1		Clemson	16 May 93
10.02	5.9	Allan	Wells	GBR	3.5.52	1	CG	Brisbane	4 Oct 82
10.02	2.9	Terry	Scott	USA	23.6.64	1	NCAA	Austin	1 Jun 85
10.02A	6.2	Aaron	Thigpen	USA	18.9.64	1	WAC	Provo	10 May 86
10.02	4.5	Lee	McRae	USA	23.1.66	2	TAC	Eugene	20 Jun 86
10.03	3.5	Harvey	Glance	USA	28.3.57	1rA	CalR	Modesto	9 May 87
10.03	2.6	Tony	Dees	USA	6.8.63	2		Luzern	6 Jul 91
10.03	2.4	James	Trapp	USA	28.12.70	1rA		Austin	9 May 92
10.03	5.1	Chris	Nelloms	USA	14.8.71	1	Big 10	Minneapolis	23 May 92
10.04	11.2	Ray	Brooks	USA	24.1.56	3		Dallas	1 Apr 78
10.04	2.2	Floyd	Heard	USA	24.3.66	1s2	TAC	New York	13 Jun 91
10.04	2.8	Devlon	Dunn	USA	1.4.67	1		Pieksamäki	3 Jul 91
10.04		Anthony	Phillips	USA	5.10.70	1		Abilene	8 May 93
Hand timing									
9.8		Harvey	Glance	USA	28.3.57	1		Auburn	9 Apr 77
9.8	-0.8		Glance			1	FlaR	Gainesville	28 Mar 81
9.8	0.4	Jeff	Phillips	USA	16.5.57	1		Knoxville	22 May 82
Wind-assisted									
9.7	3.8	Osvaldo	Lara	CUB	13.7.55	1		Santiago de Cuba	24 Feb 82
9.7	3.5	Ben	Johnson ¶	CAN	30.12.61	1		Perth	24 Jan 87

200 METRES

Mark	Wind	Name		Nat	Born	Pos	Meet	Venue	Date
19.72A	1.8	Pietro	Mennea	ITA	28.6.52	1	WUG	Ciudad México	12 Sep 79
19.73	-0.2	Michael	Marsh	USA	4.8.67	1s1	OG	Barcelona	5 Aug 92
19.75	1.5	Carl	Lewis	USA	1.7.61	1	TAC	Indianapolis	19 Jun 83
19.75	1.7	Joe	DeLoach	USA	5.6.67	1	OG	Seoul	28 Sep 88
19.79	1.7		Lewis			2	OG	Seoul	28 Sep 88
19.79	1.0	Michael	Johnson	USA	13.9.67	1	OT	New Orleans	28 Jun 92
19.80	-0.9		Lewis			1	OG	Los Angeles	8 Aug 84
19.82A	2.0		Lewis			1		Sestriere	11 Aug 88
19.83A	0.9	Tommie	Smith	USA	12.6.44	1	OG	Ciudad México	16 Oct 68
19.84	0.2		Lewis			1q3	OT	Los Angeles	19 Jun 84
19.85	0.4		Johnson			1	IAC	Edinburgh	6 Jul 90
19.85	0.3	Frank	Fredericks	NAM	2.10.67	1	WC	Stuttgart	20 Aug 93
19.86A	1.0	Don	Quarrie	JAM	25.2.51	1	PAG	Cali	3 Aug 71
19.86	-0.2		Lewis			1	OT	Los Angeles	21 Jun 84
19.86	1.0		Marsh			2	OT	New Orleans	28 Jun 92
19.87	0.8	Lorenzo	Daniel	USA	23.3.66	1	NCAA	Eugene	3 Jun 88
19.88A	1.5		Johnson			1		Sestriere	8 Aug 90
19.88	-0.9		Johnson			1	GPF	Barcelona	20 Sep 91
19.89	1.0		Johnson			1	VD	Bruxelles	13 Sep 91
19.90	0.3		Johnson			1	TAC	Norwalk	16 Jun 90
19.91	1.9		Johnson			1		Salamanca	13 Jul 92
19.92A	1.9	John	Carlos (10)	USA	5.6.45	1	FOT	Echo Summit	12 Sep 68
19.92	1.3		Lewis			1		Madrid	4 Jun 87
19.93	-1.5		Daniel			1	SEC	Auburn	15 May 88
19.94	1.4		Johnson			1	McV	Sheffield	15 Sep 91
19.94	1.1		Marsh			1rA		Austin	9 May 92
19.94	0.3	John	Regis	GBR	13.10.66	2	WC	Stuttgart	20 Aug 93
19.95	1.9	Floyd	Heard	USA	24.3.66	1	SWC	Lubbock	17 May 87
19.95	-1.0		Marsh			1rA	WK	Zürich	19 Aug 92
19.96A	0.2		Mennea			1h9	WUG	Ciudad México	10 Sep 79
19.96	0.0		Mennea			1		Barletta	17 Aug 80
19.96	-0.9	Kirk	Baptiste	USA	20.6.63	2	OG	Los Angeles	8 Aug 84

Mark	Wind	Name		Nat	Born	Pos	Meet	Venue	Date
19.96	1.0		DeLoach			1	OT	Indianapolis	20 Jul 88
19.96	0.4	Robson Caetano	da Silva	BRA	4.9.64	1	VD	Bruxelles	25 Aug 89
19.96	0.8		Fredericks			1rA		Rieti	5 Sep 93
		(35/14)							
19.99	0.6	Calvin	Smith	USA	8.1.61	1	WK	Zürich	24 Aug 83
20.00	0.0	Valeriy	Borzov	UKR	20.10.49	1	OG	München	4 Sep 72
20.01	-1.0	Michael	Bates	USA	19.12.69	3rA	WK	Zürich	19 Aug 92
20.03	1.6	Clancy	Edwards	USA	9.8.55	1		Westwood	29 Apr 78
20.03	1.5	Larry	Myricks	USA	10.3.56	2	TAC	Indianapolis	19 Jun 83
20.05	1.0	Roy	Martin	USA	25.12.66	3	OT	Indianapolis	20 Jul 88
		(20)							
20.05	1.0	Albert	Robinson	USA	28.11.64	4	OT	Indianapolis	20 Jul 88
20.06A	0.9	Peter	Norman	AUS	15.6.42	2	OG	Ciudad México	16 Oct 68
20.06	1.7	Silvio	Leonard	CUB	20.9.55	1	Kuso	Warszawa	19 Jun 78
20.07		James	Mallard	USA	29.11.57	1		Tuscaloosa	20 Apr 79
20.08	0.9	LaMonte	King	USA	18.12.59	1	TAC	Walnut	15 Jun 80
20.08A	1.6	Dwayne	Evans	USA	13.10.58	1		Albuquerque	13 Jun 87
20.08	0.3	Danny	Everett	USA	1.11.66	2	TAC	Norwalk	16 Jun 90
20.09	1.7	Linford	Christie	GBR	2.4.60	4	OG	Seoul	28 Sep 88
20.09A	1.9	Dennis	Mitchell	USA	20.2.66	1	NCAA	Provo	2 Jun 89
20.10	1.7	Millard	Hampton	USA	8.7.56	1	OT	Eugene	22 Jun 76
		(30)							
20.11	0.7	Attila	Kovács	HUN	2.9.60	1	NC	Miskolc	21 Aug 87
20.11	0.2	Olapade	Adeniken	NGR	19.8.69	1	NCAA	Austin	6 Jun 92
20.11	1.2	Bryan	Bridgewater	USA	7.9.70	1	NCAA II	Abilene	29 May 93
20.12	1.0	Mark	Witherspoon	USA	3.9.63	2	TAC	Houston	17 Jun 89
20.12	-0.8	Leroy	Burrell	USA	21.2.67	1s1	OT	New Orleans	27 Jun 92
20.14	1.8	James	Gilkes	GUY	21.9.52	1		Ingelheim	12 Sep 78
20.15A	0.3	Mike	Miller	USA	29.12.59	1h2	NCAA	Provo	2 Jun 82
20.15	0.0	Daniel	Effiong	NGR	17.6.72	1rA	WK	Zürich	4 Aug 93
20.16	-0.1	Steve	Williams	USA	13.11.53	1		Stuttgart	26 Aug 75
20.16	1.5	Elliott	Quow	USA	3.3.62	3	TAC	Indianapolis	19 Jun 83
		(40)							
20.16	-0.4	Gilles	Quénéhervé	FRA	17.5.66	2	WC	Roma	3 Sep 87
20.17	0.4	Atlee	Mahorn	CAN	27.10.65	1q1	WC	Tokyo	26 Aug 91
20.17	1.0	James	Trapp	USA	28.12.70	6	OT	New Orleans	28 Jun 92
20.18	0.2	Henry	Thomas	USA	10.7.67	1		Eagle Rock	14 May 88
20.18	0.3	Dean	Capobianco	AUS	11.5.70	5	WC	Stuttgart	20 Aug 93
20.19	0.0	Larry	Black	USA	20.7.51	2	OG	München	4 Sep 72
20.19	0.7	James	Sanford	USA	27.12.57	1		Westwood	28 Apr 79
20.19	1.9	Phil	Epps	USA	11.11.59	1		College Station	20 Mar 82
20.19	0.6	John	Dinan	AUS	18.11.59	1		Canberra	6 Mar 86
20.20	0.7	Greg	Foster	USA	4.8.58	2		Westwood	28 Apr 79
		(50)							
20.20	1.1	Daniel	Sangouma	FRA	7.2.65	1	FrancG	Casablanca	18 Jul 89
20.20		Jimmy	French	USA	2.4.70	1h2		Fayetteville	11 May 91
20.20	0.8	Nikolay	Antonov	BUL	17.8.68	2q3	WC	Tokyo	26 Aug 91
20.20	0.3	Jean-Charles	Trouabal	FRA	20.5.65	6	WC	Stuttgart	20 Aug 93
		(54)	100th best 20.32						

 # Some statisticians question whether times recorded in the 1988 Ibero-American Championships were automatic.

Low altitude marks for athletes with lifetime bests at high altitude

20.06 0.4 Quarrie 1 WK Zürich 16 Aug 74 — 20.20 -0.8 Mitchell 3s1 OT New Orleans 27 Jun 92

Wind-assisted marks

Mark	Wind	Name		Nat	Born	Pos	Meet	Venue	Date
19.61	>4.0	Leroy	Burrell	USA	21.2.67	1	SWC	College Station	19 May 90
19.79A	4.0		Marsh			1		Sestriere	21 Jul 92
19.86	4.6	Roy	Martin	USA	25.12.66	1	SWC	Houston	18 May 86
19.88	3.4	Lorenzo	Daniel	USA	23.3.66	1	SEC	Tuscaloosa	17 May 87
19.90	3.6	Frank	Fredericks	NAM	2.10.67	1	NCAA	Eugene	1 Jun 91
19.91	>4.0		Johnson			2	SWC	College Station	19 May 90
19.91		James	Jett	USA	28.12.70	1		Morgantown	18 Apr 92
19.94	4.0	James	Sanford	USA	27.12.57	1s1	NCAA	Austin	7 Jun 80
19.94	3.7	Chris	Nelloms	USA	14.8.71	1	Big 10	Minneapolis	23 May 92
19.95	3.4	Mike	Roberson	USA	25.3.56	1h3	NCAA	Austin	5 Jun 80
20.00A	3.4	Olapade	Adeniken	NGR	19.8.69	1		Air Force Academy	23 May 92
20.01	2.5	Derald	Harris	USA	5.4.58	1		San José	9 Apr 77
20.05A	3.8	Cyprean	Enweani	CAN	19.3.64	1		Calgary	3 Jul 88

Mark	Wind	Name		Nat	Born	Pos	Meet	Venue	Date
20.07A	2.1	James	Butler	USA	21.6.60	1r1	NCAA	Provo	4 Jun 82
20.09	3.7	Brady	Crain	USA	8.8.56	1	TAC	San José	9 Jun 80
20.09	2.2	Dwayne	Evans	USA	13.10.58	1		Walnut	1 Jun 86
20.10	4.6	Stanley	Kerr	USA	19.6.67	2	SWC	Houston	18 May 86
20.10	2.4	Marcus	Adam	GBR	28.2.68	1	CG	Auckland	1 Feb 90
20.11	3.7	Allan	Wells	GBR	3.5.52	1		Edinburgh	20 Jun 80
20.11	>4.0	Andre	Cason	USA	20.1.69	3	SWC	College Station	19 May 90
20.12	3.6	Mike	Conley	USA	5.10.62	1h3	NCAA	Austin	30 May 85
20.14	3.4	Daron	Council	USA	26.12.64	2	SEC	Tuscaloosa	17 May 87
20.14A	2.5	Tshakile	Nzimande	RSA	19.11.61	1		Pietersburg	15 Feb 92
20.15	3.6	Jimmy	French	USA	2.4.70	3	NCAA	Eugene	1 Jun 91
20.15	2.4	Sidney	Telles	BRA	26.7.66	1		Americana	13 Feb 93
20.16	3.9?	Danny	Peebles	USA	30.5.66	2	NCAA	Baton Rouge	5 Jun 87
20.17	2.4	Chris	Nelloms	USA	14.8.71	2	WUG	Buffalo	17 Jul 93

Best low altitude

Mark	Wind	Name		Nat	Born	Pos	Meet	Venue	Date
20.09	3.6	Olapade	Adeniken	NGR	19.8.69	2	NCAA	Eugene	1 Jun 91

Hand timing

Mark	Wind	Name		Nat	Born	Pos	Meet	Venue	Date
19.7A		James	Sanford	USA	27.12.57	1		El Paso	19 Apr 80
19.7A	0.2	Robson C.	da Silva	BRA	4.9.64	1	AmCp	Bogotá	13 Aug 89
19.8"	1.3	Don	Quarrie	JAM	25.2.51	1	Pre	Eugene	7 Jun 75
19.8*	1.3	Steve	Williams	USA	13.11.53	2	Pre	Eugene	7 Jun 75
19.8		James	Mallard	USA	29.11.57	1	SEC	Tuscaloosa	13 May 79
19.9		Mel	Lattany	USA	10.8.59	2		Tuscaloosa	13 May 79
19.9		Davidson	Ezinwa	NGR	22.11.71	1		Bauchi	18 Mar 89

Wind-assisted

Mark	Wind	Name		Nat	Born	Pos	Meet	Venue	Date
19.8*		Carl	Lawson	JAM	27.10.47	1		Moscow	19 May 73
19.8*	3.4	James	Gilkes	GUY	21.9.52	1	NCAA	Austin	8 Jun 74
19.8	4.4	Desmond	Ross	USA	30.12.61	1	Big8	Manhattan	11 May 85
19.9*		Gerald	Tinker	USA	19.1.51	1		Kent	5 May 73
19.9*	3.4	Reggie	Jones	USA	30.12.53	2	NCAA	Austin	8 Jun 74
19.9		Silvio	Leonard	CUB	20.9.55	1		Habana	22 May 77
19.9	4.4	Chidi	Imo	NGR	27.8.63	2	Big8	Manhattan	11 May 85

" during 220 yards race, * 220 yards less 0.1 seconds

300 METRES

In 300m races only, not including intermediate times in 400m races

Mark	Name		Nat	Born	Pos	Meet	Venue	Date
31.48	Danny	Everett	USA	1.11.66	1		Jerez de la Frontera	3 Sep 90
31.48	Roberto	Hernández	CUB	6.3.67	2		Jerez de la Frontera	3 Sep 90
31.67	John	Regis	GBR	13.10.66	1	Vaux	Gateshead	17 Jul 92
31.69		Hernández			1	PTS	Bratislava	20 Jun 90
31.70	Kirk	Baptiste	USA	20.6.63	1	Nike	London	18 Aug 84
31.72	Michael	Johnson	USA	13.9.67	1	Vaux	Gateshead	30 Jul 93
31.73	Thomas	Jefferson	USA	8.6.62	1	DCG	London	22 Aug 87
31.74	Gabriel	Tiacoh	CIV	10.9.63	1		La Coruña	6 Aug 86
31.82	Steve	Lewis	USA	16.5.69	2	Vaux	Gateshead	17 Jul 92
31.88	Darren	Clark	AUS	6.9.65	1	UlstG	Belfast	30 Jun 86
	(10/9)							
31.97	Innocent	Egbunike	NGR	30.11.61	1	IAC	London	8 Aug 86
32.04	Andrew	Valmon	USA	1.1.65	3		Jerez de la Frontera	3 Sep 90
32.05	Butch	Reynolds ¶	USA	8.6.64	1	Giro	Belfast	20 Jul 87
32.05	Robson Caetano	da Silva	BRA	4.9.64	1		Jerez de la Frontera	17 Sep 91
32.07	Quincy	Watts	USA	19.6.70	2	Vaux	Gateshead	30 Jul 93
32.08	Roger	Black	GBR	31.3.66	4	IAC	London	8 Aug 86
32.10	Michael	Marsh	USA	4.8.67	3	Vaux	Gateshead	30 Jul 93
32.14	Todd	Bennett	GBR	6.7.62	2	Nike	London	18 Aug 84
32.16	Mel	Lattany	USA	10.8.59	1		Gateshead	31 Jul 83
32.16	Walter	McCoy	USA	15.11.58	3	Nike	London	18 Aug 84
32.17	Darrell	Robinson	USA	23.12.63	1	DCG	Birmingham	19 Aug 86
	(20)							
32.18	Carl	Lewis	USA	1.7.61	4	Nike	London	18 Aug 84
32.19	Atlee	Mahorn	CAN	27.10.65	5	IAC	London	8 Aug 86
32.22	Dennis	Mitchell	USA	20.2.66	1		Jerez	28 Jun 88
32.22	Dean	Capobianco	AUS	11.5.70	3	Vaux	Gateshead	17 Jul 92
32.23	Pietro	Mennea	ITA	28.6.52	1		Rieti	21 Jul 79
32.26	Mike	Franks	USA	23.9.63	1		Bern	16 Aug 85

Indoors

Mark	Name		Nat	Born	Pos	Meet	Venue	Date
32.19	Robson C.	da Silva	BRA	4.9.64	1		Karlsruhe	24 Feb 89

400 METRES

Mark	Wind	Name		Nat	Born	Pos	Meet	Venue	Date
43.29		Butch	Reynolds ¶	USA	8.6.64	1	WK	Zürich	17 Aug 88
43.50		Quincy	Watts	USA	19.6.70	1	OG	Barcelona	5 Aug 92
43.65		Michael	Johnson	USA	13.9.67	1	WC	Stuttgart	17 Aug 93
43.71			Watts			1s2	OG	Barcelona	3 Aug 92
43.74			Johnson			1	NC	Eugene	19 Jun 93
43.81		Danny	Everett	USA	1.11.66	1	OT	New Orleans	26 Jun 92
43.83			Watts			1	WK	Zürich	19 Aug 92
43.86A		Lee	Evans	USA	25.2.47	1	OG	Ciudad México	18 Oct 68
43.87		Steve	Lewis	USA	16.5.69	1	OG	Seoul	28 Sep 88
43.93			Reynolds			1	OT	Indianapolis	20 Jul 88
43.93			Reynolds			2	OG	Seoul	28 Sep 88
43.94			Johnson			1	ISTAF	Berlin	27 Aug 93
43.97A		Larry	James	USA	6.11.47	2	OG	Ciudad México	18 Oct 68
43.97			Watts			1s1	OT	New Orleans	24 Jun 92
43.98			Everett			2	OT	Indianapolis	20 Jul 88
43.98			Johnson			1rA	TSB	London	10 Jul 92
44.00			Watts			1	NCAA	Austin	6 Jun 92
44.06A			Evans			1	FOT	Echo Summit	14 Sep 68
44.06			Everett			1		Sevilla	30 May 90
44.08			Lewis			2	OT	New Orleans	26 Jun 92
44.09			Everett			3	OG	Seoul	28 Sep 88
44.10			Reynolds			1	JO	Columbus	3 May 87
44.11			Lewis			1s2	OT	Indianapolis	18 Jul 88
44.12			Reynolds			2	NC	Eugene	19 Jun 93
44.13			Reynolds			1	NCAA	Baton Rouge	6 Jun 87
44.13A			Watts			1		Sestriere	28 Jul 93
44.13			Reynolds			2	WC	Stuttgart	17 Aug 93
44.14		Roberto	Hernández	CUB	6.3.67	2		Sevilla	30 May 90
44.14			Reynolds ¶			2s1	OT	New Orleans	24 Jun 92
44.15			Reynolds			1	PTG	London	10 Jul 87
		(30/8)							
44.17		Innocent	Egbunike	NGR	30.11.61	1rA	WK	Zürich	19 Aug 87
44.18		Samson	Kitur (10)	KEN	25.2.66	2s2	OG	Barcelona	3 Aug 92
44.21		Ian	Morris	TRI	30.11.61	3s2	OG	Barcelona	3 Aug 92
44.26		Alberto	Juantorena	CUB	21.11.50	1	OG	Montreal	29 Jul 76
44.27		Alonzo	Babers	USA	31.10.61	1	OG	Los Angeles	8 Aug 84
44.27		Antonio	Pettigrew	USA	7.11.67	1	TAC	Houston	17 Jun 89
44.28		Andrew	Valmon	USA	1.1.65	4	NC	Eugene	19 Jun 93
44.30		Gabriel	Tiacoh	CIV	10.9.63	1	NCAA	Indianapolis	7 Jun 86
44.33		Thomas	Schönlebe	GDR	6.8.65	1	WC	Roma	3 Sep 87
44.38		Darren	Clark	AUS	6.9.65	3s1	OG	Seoul	26 Sep 88
44.40		Fred	Newhouse	USA	8.11.48	2	OG	Montreal	29 Jul 76
44.41A		Ron	Freeman	USA	12.6.47	3	OG	Ciudad México	18 Oct 68
		(20)							
44.45A		Ronnie	Ray	USA	2.1.54	1	PAG	Ciudad México	18 Oct 75
44.45		Darrell	Robinson	USA	23.12.63	2	Pepsi	Westwood	17 May 86
44.47		Michael	Franks	USA	23.9.63	1	WP	Canberra	5 Oct 85
44.47		David	Grindley	GBR	29.10.72	4s2	OG	Barcelona	3 Aug 92
44.48		Roddie	Haley	USA	6.12.65	1	SWC	Houston	18 May 86
44.50		Erwin	Skamrahl	FRG	8.3.58	1r1		München	26 Jul 83
44.50		Derek	Redmond	GBR	3.9.65	1s2	WC	Roma	1 Sep 87
44.50		Bert	Cameron	JAM	16.11.59	4s1	OG	Seoul	26 Sep 88
44.56		Mohamed	Al Malky	OMA	1.12.62	1	HGP	Budapest	12 Aug 88
44.58		Patrick	Delice	TRI	12.11.67	1	NCAA II	Abilene	29 May 93
		(30)							
44.59		Roger	Black	GBR	31.3.66	1	EC	Stuttgart	29 Aug 86
44.59A		Raymond	Pierre	USA	19.9.67	1	NCAA	Provo	3 Jun 89
44.59		Mark	Everett	USA	2.9.68	1	WG	Helsinki	27 Jun 91
44.60A		John	Smith	USA	5.8.50	1	PAG	Cali	1 Aug 71
44.60		Viktor	Markin	URS	23.2.57	1	OG	Moskva	30 Jul 80
44.61		Kevin	Robinzine	USA	12.4.66	4	OT	Indianapolis	20 Jul 88
44.62		Derek	Mills	USA	9.7.72	6	NC	Eugene	19 Jun 93
44.63		Sunday	Bada	NGR	22.6.69	3s2	WC	Stuttgart	16 Aug 93
44.66		Vince	Matthews	USA	16.12.47	1	OG	München	7 Sep 72

Mark	Wind	Name		Nat	Born	Pos	Meet	Venue	Date
44.66		Tyrone	Kemp	USA	4.4.69	1	Gator	Gainesville	8 Apr 89
		(40)							
44.67*		Curtis	Mills *(440y -0.26)*	USA	6.10.48	1	NCAA	Knoxville	21 Jun 69
44.68		Sunder	Nix	USA	2.12.61	1	USOF	Indianapolis	24 Jul 82
44.69		Antonio	McKay	USA	9.2.64	4=	WK	Zürich	13 Aug 86
44.70		Karl	Honz	FRG	28.1.51	1	NC	München	21 Jul 72
44.70		Cliff	Wiley	USA	21.5.55	1	TAC	Sacramento	21 Jun 81
44.70		Tim	Simon	USA	11.9.66	1h2	TAC	Norwalk	15 Jun 90
44.71		Andre	Phillips	USA	5.9.59	3	Pepsi	Westwood	17 May 86
44.71		Miles	Murphy	AUS	19.5.67	1	NC	Perth	26 Mar 88
44.72		Hartmut	Weber	FRG	17.10.60	1	EC	Athinai	9 Sep 82
44.73		Willie	Smith	USA	28.2.56	1		Tuscaloosa	15 Apr 78
		(50)							
44.73A		James	Rolle	USA	2.2.64	1	USOF	Air Force Academy	2 Jul 83
44.73		David	Kitur	KEN	12.10.62	3s2	WC	Roma	1 Sep 87
		(52)	100th best 44.98						
Performance made after positive drugs test and subsequent disqualification									
44.71		Mark	Rowe	USA	28.7.60	2	TAC	Houston	17 Jun 89
Low altitude best: 44.60			Pierre			1	PAG	Indianapolis	13 Aug 87
Hand timing									
44.1		Wayne	Collett	USA	20.10.49	1	OT	Eugene	9 Jul 72
44.2*		John	Smith	USA	5.8.50	1	AAU	Eugene	26 Jun 71
44.2		Fred	Newhouse	USA	8.11.48	1s1	OT	Eugene	7 Jul 72
44.4A		Vince	Matthews	USA	16.12.47	1		Echo Summit	31 Aug 68
44.5"		Tommie	Smith	USA	12.6.44	1		San José	20 May 67
44.5A		Kennedy	Ochieng	KEN	30.12.71	1	NC	Nairobi	3 Jul 93
44.6		Adolph	Plummer	USA	3.1.38	1	WAC	Tempe	25 May 63

** 440 yards less 0.3 seconds, " during 440 yards race*

600 METRES

Mark	Name		Nat	Born	Pos	Meet	Venue	Date
1:12.81	Johnny	Gray	USA	19.6.60	1		Santa Monica	24 May 86
1:13.2+	John	Kipkurgat	KEN	16.3.44	1		Pointe-à-Pierre	23 Mar 74
1:13.80	Earl	Jones	USA	17.7.64	2		Santa Monica	24 May 86
1:14.15	David	Mack	USA	30.5.61	3		Santa Monica	24 May 86
1:14.3 A	Lee	Evans	USA	25.2.47	1		Echo Summit	31 Aug 68
1:14.6 A	Larry	James	USA	6.11.47	2		Echo Summit	31 Aug 68
1:14.8 A	Mark	Winzenried	USA	13.10.49	3		Echo Summit	31 Aug 68
1:14.84	James	Robinson	USA	27.8.54	2		Sacramento	21 Jul 84
1:14.9	Martin	McGrady	USA	20.4.46	1		Melbourne	17 Mar 70
1:14.95	Steve	Heard	GBR	29.4.62	1		London	14 Jul 91

800 METRES

Mark	Name		Nat	Born	Pos	Meet	Venue	Date
1:41.73!	Sebastian	Coe	GBR	29.9.56	1		Firenze	10 Jun 81
1:41.77	Joaquim	Cruz	BRA	12.3.63	1	ASV	Köln	26 Aug 84
1:42.28	Sammy	Koskei	KEN	14.5.61	2	ASV	Köln	26 Aug 84
1:42.33		Coe			1	Bisl	Oslo	5 Jul 79
1:42.34		Cruz			1r1	WK	Zürich	22 Aug 84
1:42.41		Cruz			1	VD	Bruxelles	24 Aug 84
1:42.49		Cruz			1		Koblenz	28 Aug 85
1:42.54		Cruz			1	ASV	Köln	25 Aug 85
1:42.60	Johnny	Gray	USA	19.6.60	2r1		Koblenz	28 Aug 85
1:42.65		Gray			1	WK	Zürich	17 Aug 88
1:42.80		Gray			1	OT	New Orleans	24 Jun 92
1:42.88	Steve	Cram	GBR	14.10.60	1rA	WK	Zürich	21 Aug 85
1:42.96		Gray			1		Koblenz	29 Aug 84
1:42.97	Peter	Elliott	GBR	9.10.62	1		Sevilla	30 May 90
1:42.98		Cruz			1r1	ISTAF	Berlin	23 Aug 85
1:43.00		Cruz			1	OG	Los Angeles	6 Aug 84
1:43.06	Billy	Konchellah	KEN	20.10.61	1	WC	Roma	1 Sep 87
1:43.07		Coe			2	ASV	Köln	25 Aug 85
1:43.08	José Luiz	Barbosa	BRA	27.5.61	1		Rieti	6 Sep 91
1:43.10		Gray			1	APM	Hengelo	14 Aug 88
1:43.16	Paul	Ereng	KEN	22.8.67	1	WK	Zürich	16 Aug 89
1:43.19		Cram			1		Rieti	7 Sep 86
1:43.20		Barbosa			2	WK	Zürich	17 Aug 88

Mark	Wind	Name		Nat	Born	Pos	Meet	Venue	Date
1:43.22			Cram			1	CG	Edinburgh	31 Jul 86
1:43.22			Ereng			1	Nik	Nice	10 Jul 89
1:43.23			Cruz			2r1	WK	Zürich	21 Aug 85
1:43.28			Gray			2	VD	Bruxelles	24 Aug 84
1:43.28			Gray			3	ASV	Köln	26 Aug 84
1:43.28			Koskei			2		Koblenz	29 Aug 84
1:43.30		William	Tanui	KEN	22.2.64	2		Rieti	6 Sep 91
		(30/10)							
1:43.31		Nixon	Kiprotich	KEN	4.12.62	1		Rieti	6 Sep 92
1:43.35		David	Mack	USA	30.5.61	3r1		Koblenz	28 Aug 85
1:43.40		Mark	Everett	USA	2.9.68	1	Bisl	Oslo	4 Jul 92
1:43.44		Alberto	Juantorena	CUB	21.11.50	1	WUG	Sofia	21 Aug 77
1:43.5*		Rick	Wohlhuter	USA	23.12.48	1		Eugene	8 Jun 74
1:43.54		William	Wuycke	VEN	21.5.58	2		Rieti	7 Sep 86
1:43.56		Rob	Druppers	HOL	29.4.62	4	ASV	Köln	25 Aug 85
1:43.57		Mike	Boit	KEN	6.1.49	1	ISTAF	Berlin	20 Aug 76
1:43.60		Abdi	Bile	SOM	28.12.62	3	WK	Zürich	16 Aug 89
1:43.62		Earl	Jones	USA	17.7.64	2r1	WK	Zürich	13 Aug 86
		(20)							
1:43.63		Agberto	Guimarães	BRA	18.8.57	3		Koblenz	29 Aug 84
1:43.65		Willi	Wülbeck	FRG	18.12.54	1	WC	Helsinki	9 Aug 83
1:43.70		Robert	Kibet	KEN	15.12.65	2	Bisl	Oslo	1 Jul 89
1:43.7		Marcello	Fiasconaro	ITA	19.7.49	1	vCS	Milano	27 Jun 73
1:43.84		Olaf	Beyer	GDR	4.8.57	1	EC	Praha	31 Aug 78
1:43.84		Martin	Steele	GBR	20.9.62	1rA	Bisl	Oslo	10 Jul 93
1:43.86		Ivo	Van Damme	BEL	21.2.54	2	OG	Montreal	25 Jul 76
1:43.86		Saïd	Aouita	MAR	2.11.59	1	ASV	Köln	21 Aug 88
1:43.88		Donato	Sabia	ITA	11.9.63	1		Firenze	13 Jun 84
1:43.88		Tom	McKean	GBR	27.10.63	1	vKEN	London	28 Jul 89
		(30)							
1:43.9		José	Marajo	FRA	10.8.54	1		Saint Maur	12 Sep 79
1:43.91		John	Kipkurgat	KEN	16.3.44	1	CG	Christchurch	29 Jan 74
1:43.92		John	Marshall	USA	5.11.63	3	OT	Los Angeles	19 Jun 84
1:43.92		James	Robinson	USA	27.8.54	4	OT	Los Angeles	19 Jun 84
1:43.92		Andrea	Benvenuti	ITA	13.12.69	1	Herc	Monaco	11 Aug 92
1:43.92		Paul	Ruto	KEN	3.11.60	2rA		Rieti	5 Sep 93
1:43.95		Philippe	Collard	FRA	26.2.60	1	Nik	Nice	13 Jul 87
1:43.97		José	Parrilla	USA	31.3.72	3	OT	New Orleans	24 Jun 92
1:43.98		David	Sharpe	GBR	8.7.67	1rB	WK	Zürich	19 Aug 92
1:44.00		George	Kersh	USA	3.7.68	4	OT	New Orleans	24 Jun 92
		(40)							
1:44.03		Peter	Braun	FRG	1.8.62	1r1		Koblenz	6 Aug 86
1:44.06		Moussa	Fall	SEN	28.8.63	4	WK	Zürich	17 Aug 88
1:44.06		Sammy	Langat (Kibet)	KEN	70	3rA		Rieti	5 Sep 93
1:44.07		Luciano	Susanj	YUG	10.11.48	1	EC	Roma	4 Sep 74
1:44.09		Steve	Ovett	GBR	9.10.55	2	EC	Praha	31 Aug 78
1:44.10		Vladimir	Graudyn	RUS	26.8.63	1	Bisl	Oslo	2 Jul 88
1:44.10		Ari	Suhonen	FIN	19.12.65	4	WK	Zürich	16 Aug 89
1:44.12		Edwin	Koech	KEN	23.7.61	2s1	OG	Los Angeles	5 Aug 84
1:44.20		Juma	N'diwa	KEN	28.11.60	1		München	26 Jul 83
1:44.24		James	Maina Boi	KEN	4.4.54	1	WK	Zürich	15 Aug 79
1:44.24		Charles	Nkazamyampi	BUR	1.11.64	2		Salamanca	27 Jul 93
		(51)	100th best 1:44.92						

*! photo-electric cell time, * 880 yards less 0.6 seconds*

1000 METRES

Mark	Wind	Name		Nat	Born	Pos	Meet	Venue	Date
2:12.18		Sebastian	Coe	GBR	29.9.56	1	OsloG	Oslo	11 Jul 81
2:12.88		Steve	Cram	GBR	14.10.60	1		Gateshead	9 Aug 85
2:13.40			Coe			1	Bisl	Oslo	1 Jul 80
2:13.73		Noureddine	Morceli	ALG	28.2.70	1	BNP	Villeneuve d'Ascq	2 Jul 93
2:13.9		Rick	Wohlhuter	USA	23.12.48	1	King	Oslo	30 Jul 74
2:14.09		Joaquim	Cruz	BRA	12.3.63	1	Nik	Nice	20 Aug 84
2:14.50		Abdi	Bile	SOM	28.12.62	1		Jerez de la Frontera	13 Sep 89
2:14.51			Bile			1	RMPG	London	14 Jul 89
2:14.53		Willi	Wülbeck	FRG	18.12.54	2	Bisl	Oslo	1 Jul 80
2:14.54			Cruz			1	Pre	Eugene	21 Jul 84

Mark Wind	Name		Nat	Born	Pos	Meet	Venue	Date
2:14.90		Coe			1		London (Har.)	16 Jul 86
2:14.95	Sammy	Koskei	KEN	14.5.61	1	VD	Bruxelles	30 Aug 85
2:15.09		Cram			1		Edinburgh	23 Jul 85
2:15.11		Cruz			1		Bern	16 Aug 85
2:15.12		Cram			1	Coke	London	17 Sep 82
2:15.16	Said	Aouita	MAR	2.11.59	1	McV	London	28 Aug 88
2:15.23	Rob	Druppers (10)	HOL	29.4.62	1		Utrecht	17 Aug 85
2:15.25	Andreas	Busse	GDR	6.5.59	1		Berlin	31 Jul 83
2:15.28		Cruz			1		Bern	29 Jul 83
2:15.3 '	Mike	Boit	KEN	6.1.49	1		Wattenscheid	23 Sep 77
	(20/12)							
2:15.5	Ivo	Van Damme	BEL	21.2.54	1		Namur	14 Jul 76
2:15.76	Andrea	Benvenuti	ITA	13.12.69	1		Nuoro	12 Sep 92
2:15.81	Agberto	Guimarães	BRA	18.8.57	2		Bern	29 Jul 83
2:15.83	William	Tanui	KEN	22.2.64	1		Auckland	20 Jan 90
2:15.89	Juma	N'diwa	KEN	28.11.60	3	VD	Bruxelles	30 Aug 85
2:15.91	Steve	Ovett	GBR	9.10.55	1		Koblenz	6 Sep 79
2:16.0 '	Danie	Malan	RSA	26.6.49	1	HB	München	24 Jun 73
2:16.0	Vladimir	Malozemlin	RUS	26.1.56	1		Kiev	11 Jun 81
2:16.1	Tom	Byers	USA	12.5.55	1		København	6 Aug 81
	(20)							
2:16.13	Fermin	Cacho	ESP	16.2.69	1		Andújar	6 Sep 93
2:16.19	Giuseppe	D'Urso	ITA	15.9.69	1		Parma	15 Sep 93
2:16.2	Jürgen	May	GDR	18.6.42	1		Erfurt	20 Jul 65
2:16.2	Franz-Josef	Kemper	FRG	30.9.45	1		Hannover	21 Sep 66
2:16.25	James	Maina Boi	KEN	4.4.54	3	R-W	Koblenz	6 Sep 79
2:16.30	Peter	Elliott	GBR	9.10.62	1		Hamilton	17 Jan 90
2:16.3	James	Robinson	USA	27.8.54	2		København	6 Aug 81
2:16.3	Andreas	Hauck	GDR	19.6.60	1		Potsdam	12 Jul 84
2:16.32	Samuel	Tirop	KEN	13.1.59	2		Auckland	20 Jan 90
2:16.34	Matthew	Yates	GBR	4.2.69	2	IAC	Edinburgh	6 Jul 90
	(30)							
2:16.40	Steve	Scott	USA	5.5.56	2	Nik	Nice	23 Aug 81
2:16.4	Thomas	Wessinghage	FRG	22.2.52	3		Wattenscheid	23 Sep 77
2:16.4	Nikolay	Shirokov	RUS	.55	2		Kiev	11 Jun 81
2:16.45	Nixon	Kiprotich	KEN	4.12.62	2	RMPG	London	14 Jul 89
2:16.5	Bodo	Tümmler	FRG	8.12.43	2		Hannover	21 Sep 66
2:16.52	Jens-Peter	Herold	GER	2.6.65	2	BNP	Villeneuve d'Ascq	2 Jul 93
2:16.54	Jim	Spivey	USA	7.3.60	2	Pre	Eugene	21 Jul 84
2:16.56	William	Wuyke	VEN	21.5.58	3		Bern	29 Jul 83
2:16.57	John	Walker	NZL	12.1.52	3	Bisl	Oslo	1 Jul 80
2:16.58	Omer	Khalifa	SUD	18.12.56	2		Padova	13 Sep 87
	(40)	50th best 2:16.82, 100th 2:17.67						
Indoors: 2:15.26		Morceli			1		Birmingham	22 Feb 92

1500 METRES

Mark	Name		Nat	Born	Pos	Meet	Venue	Date
3:28.82	Noureddine	Morceli	ALG	28.2.70	1		Rieti	6 Sep 92
3:29.20		Morceli			1	MedG	Narbonne	20 Jun 93
3:29.46	Saïd	Aouita	MAR	2.11.59	1	ISTAF	Berlin	23 Aug 85
3:29.57+		Morceli			1M		Rieti	5 Sep 93
3:29.67	Steve	Cram	GBR	14.10.60	1	Nik	Nice	16 Jul 85
3:29.71		Aouita			2	Nik	Nice	16 Jul 85
3:29.77	Sebastian	Coe	GBR	29.9.56	1		Rieti	7 Sep 86
3:29.77	Sydney	Maree	USA	9.9.56	1	ASV	Köln	25 Aug 85
3:30.06		Morceli			1A	WK	Zürich	4 Aug 93
3:30.15		Cram			1	VD	Bruxelles	5 Sep 86
3:30.55	Abdi	Bile	SOM	28.12.62	1		Rieti	3 Sep 89
3:30.63		Aouita			1	APM	Hengelo	13 Aug 89
3:30.69		Aouita			1	Bisl	Oslo	4 Jul 87
3:30.75		Morceli			1rA	WK	Zürich	19 Aug 92
3:30.77	Steve	Ovett	GBR	9.10.55	1		Rieti	4 Sep 83
3:30.92	José Luis	González	ESP	8.12.57	3	Nik	Nice	16 Jul 85
3:30.95		Cram			1	VD	Bruxelles	19 Aug 88
3:31.00		Morceli			1	WG	Helsinki	27 Jun 91
3:31.00		Morceli			1rA	WK	Zürich	7 Aug 91
3:31.01	Jim	Spivey	USA	7.3.60	1	R-W	Koblenz	28 Aug 88

Mark	Wind	Name		Nat	Born	Pos	Meet	Venue	Date
3:31.01			Morceli			1	DNG	Stockholm	3 Jul 91
3:31.13		José Manuel	Abascal (10)	ESP	17.3.58	1		Barcelona	16 Aug 86
3:31.20			Bile			1	GG	Pescara	19 Jul 89
3:31.24			Maree			1	ASV	Köln	28 Aug 83
3:31.34			Cram			1	OsloG	Oslo	27 Jun 85
3:31.36			Ovett			1		Koblenz	27 Aug 80
3:31.43			Cram			1rA	WK	Zürich	19 Aug 87
3:31.54			Aouita			1	FBK	Hengelo	6 Jul 84
3:31.57			Ovett			1	BGP	Budapest	29 Jul 81
3:31.58		Thomas	Wessinghage	FRG	22.2.52	2		Koblenz	27 Aug 80
		(30/11)							
3:31.75		Pierre	Délèze	SUI	25.9.58	1	WK	Zürich	21 Aug 85
3:31.76		Steve	Scott	USA	5.5.56	4	Nik	Nice	16 Jul 85
3:31.96		Harald	Hudak	FRG	28.1.57	3		Koblenz	27 Aug 80
3:31.96		Simon	Doyle	AUS	9.11.66	2	DNG	Stockholm	3 Jul 91
3:32.01		Fermin	Cacho	ESP	16.2.69	2	WK	Zürich	4 Aug 93
3:32.13		David	Kibet	KEN	24.11.63	2		Rieti	6 Sep 92
3:32.16		Filbert	Bayi	TAN	23.6.53	1	CG	Christchurch	2 Feb 74
3:32.4		John	Walker	NZL	12.1.52	1	OsloG	Oslo	30 Jul 75
3:32.41		William	Kemei	KEN	22.2.69	2rA	WK	Zürich	19 Aug 92
		(20)							
3:32.49		Wilfred	Kirochi	KEN	12.12.66	1	VD	Bruxelles	28 Aug 92
3:32.69		Peter	Elliott	GBR	9.10.62	1	McV	Sheffield	16 Sep 90
3:32.77		Jens-Peter	Herold	GER	2.6.65	4		Rieti	6 Sep 92
3:32.78		Gennaro	Di Napoli	ITA	5.3.68	1		Rieti	9 Sep 90
3:33.07		Kipkoech	Cheruiyot	KEN	2.12.64	1		Grosseto	10 Aug 86
3:33.1		Jim	Ryun	USA	29.4.47	1	vComm	Los Angeles	8 Jul 67
3:33.12		Joseph	Chesire	KEN	12.11.57	2	Nik	Nice	15 Jul 92
3:33.16		Ben	Jipcho	KEN	1.3.43	3	CG	Christchurch	2 Feb 74
3:33.28		Omer	Khalifa	SUD	18.12.56	2		Grosseto	10 Aug 86
3:33.29		Mohamed	Suleiman	QAT	23.11.69	4	WK	Zürich	4 Aug 93
		(30)							
3:33.34		Steve	Crabb	GBR	30.11.63	3	Bisl	Oslo	4 Jul 87
3:33.36		Jonah	Birir	KEN	12.12.71	5	VD	Bruxelles	28 Aug 92
3:33.39		Mike	Hillardt	AUS	22.1.61	4	ISTAF	Berlin	23 Aug 85
3:33.5+		Ray	Flynn	IRL	22.1.57	2	OsloG	Oslo	7 Jul 82
3:33.54		Dieter	Baumann	FRG	9.2.65	2rA	R-W	Koblenz	13 Aug 87
3:33.54		Hervé	Phélippeau	FRA	16.9.62	2	GG	Bologna	18 Jul 90
3:33.56		Johan	Landsman	RSA	12.5.64	6	WK	Zürich	4 Aug 93
3:33.6+		Joe	Falcon	USA	23.6.66	3	Bisl	Oslo	14 Jul 90
3:33.67+		Mike	Boit	KEN	6.1.49	2	VD	Bruxelles	28 Aug 81
3:33.68		Jürgen	Straub	GDR	3.11.53	1		Potsdam	31 Aug 79
		(40)							
3:33.74		Willi	Wülbeck	FRG	18.12.54	4		Koblenz	27 Aug 80
3:33.79		David	Moorcroft	GBR	10.4.53	1	FBK	Hengelo	27 Jul 82
3:33.83		John	Robson	GBR	31.1.57	2	VD	Bruxelles	4 Sep 79
3:33.87		Johan	Fourie	RSA	2.12.59	1	NC	Stellenbosch	10 Apr 87
3:33.89		Rod	Dixon	NZL	13.7.50	4	CG	Christchurch	2 Feb 74
3:33.99		Steve	Lacy	USA	17.1.56	4	OsloG	Oslo	15 Jul 80
3:33.99		Todd	Harbour	USA	24.3.59	2	WK	Zürich	18 Aug 82
3:34.0		Jean	Wadoux	FRA	29.1.42	1		Colombes	23 Jul 70
3:34.00		Matthew	Yates	GBR	4.2.69	3r1	VD	Bruxelles	13 Sep 91
3:34.0A		Moses	Kiptanui	KEN	1.10.71	1	NC	Nairobi	13 Jun 92
		(50)	100th best 3:35.27 + *during mile race*						

1 MILE

3:44.39	Noureddine	Morceli	ALG	28.2.70	1		Rieti	5 Sep 93
3:46.32	Steve	Cram	GBR	14.10.60	1	Bisl	Oslo	27 Jul 85
3:46.76	Saïd	Aouita	MAR	2.11.59	1	WG	Helsinki	2 Jul 87
3:46.78		Morceli			1	ISTAF	Berlin	27 Aug 93
3:46.92		Aouita			1	WK	Zürich	21 Aug 85
3:47.30		Morceli			1	VD	Bruxelles	3 Sep 93
3:47.33	Sebastian	Coe	GBR	29.9.56	1	VD	Bruxelles	28 Aug 81
3:47.69	Steve	Scott	USA	5.5.56	1	OsloG	Oslo	7 Jul 82
3:47.78		Morceli			1	Bisl	Oslo	10 Jul 93
3:47.79	José Luis	González	ESP	8.12.57	2	Bisl	Oslo	27 Jul 85

Mark	Wind	Name		Nat	Born	Pos	Meet	Venue	Date
3:48.31			Cram			1	Bisl	Oslo	5 Jul 86
3:48.40		Steve	Ovett	GBR	9.10.55	1	R-W	Koblenz	26 Aug 81
3:48.53			Coe			1	WK	Zürich	19 Aug 81
3:48.53			Scott			1	Bisl	Oslo	26 Jun 82
3:48.73			Scott			2	Bisl	Oslo	5 Jul 86
3:48.8			Ovett			1	Bisl	Oslo	1 Jul 80
3:48.80		William	Kemei	KEN	22.2.69	1	ISTAF	Berlin	21 Aug 92
3:48.83		Sydney	Maree	USA	9.9.56	1		Rieti	9 Sep 81
3:48.85			Maree			2	Bisl	Oslo	26 Jun 82
3:48.85			Cram			1	Bisl	Oslo	2 Jul 88
3:48.95			Coe			1	OsloG	Oslo	17 Jul 79
3:49.08		John	Walker (10)	NZL	12.1.52	2	OsloG	Oslo	7 Jul 82
3:49.12			Aouita			1	Nik	Nice	13 Jul 87
3:49.12			Morceli			1	Athl	Lausanne	10 Jul 91
3:49.20		Peter	Elliott	GBR	9.10.62	2	Bisl	Oslo	2 Jul 88
3:49.21			Scott			1	ISTAF	Berlin	17 Aug 83
3:49.22			Coe			3	Bisl	Oslo	27 Jul 85
3:49.22		Jens-Peter	Herold	GDR	2.6.65	3	Bisl	Oslo	2 Jul 88
3:49.25			Ovett			1	OsloG	Oslo	11 Jul 81
3:49.31		Joe	Falcon	USA	23.6.66	1	Bisl	Oslo	14 Jul 90
		(30/13)							
3:49.34		David	Moorcroft	GBR	10.4.53	3	Bisl	Oslo	26 Jun 82
3:49.40		Abdi	Bile	SOM	28.12.62	4	Bisl	Oslo	2 Jul 88
3:49.45		Mike	Boit	KEN	6.1.49	2	VD	Bruxelles	28 Aug 81
3:49.77		Ray	Flynn	IRL	22.1.57	3	OsloG	Oslo	7 Jul 82
3:49.77		Wilfred	Kirochi	KEN	12.12.69	2	Bisl	Oslo	6 Jul 91
3:49.80		Jim	Spivey	USA	7.3.60	3	Bisl	Oslo	5 Jul 86
3:49.91		Simon	Doyle	AUS	9.11.66	4	Bisl	Oslo	6 Jul 91
		(20)							
3:49.98		Thomas	Wessinghage	FRG	22.2.52	3	ISTAF	Berlin	17 Aug 83
3:50.34		Todd	Harbour	USA	24.3.59	5	OsloG	Oslo	11 Jul 81
3:50.38		Pierre	Délèze	SUI	25.9.58	4	R-W	Koblenz	25 Aug 82
3:50.52		Hauke	Fuhlbrügge	GER	21.3.66	6	Bisl	Oslo	6 Jul 91
3:50.54		José Manuel	Abascal	ESP	17.3.58	2	GP-GG	Roma	10 Sep 86
3:50.64		Graham	Williamson	GBR	15.6.60	4		Cork	13 Jul 82
3:50.73		Wilson	Waigwa	KEN	15.2.49	2	R-W	Koblenz	31 Aug 83
3:50.74		Fermin	Cacho	ESP	16.2.69	7	Bisl	Oslo	6 Jul 91
3:50.82		Johan	Fourie	RSA	2.12.59	1		Port Elizabeth	11 Mar 87
3:50.84		Tom	Byers	USA	12.5.55	6	R-W	Koblenz	25 Aug 82
		(30)							
3:50.98		José	Marajo	FRA	10.8.54	4	OsloG	Oslo	9 Jul 83
3:51.0		Filbert	Bayi	TAN	23.6.53	1	King	Kingston	17 May 75
3:51.02		John	Gladwin	GBR	7.5.63	2	WK	Zürich	19 Aug 87
3:51.06		Frank	O'Mara	IRL	17.7.60	4	GP-GG	Roma	10 Sep 86
3:51.1		Jim	Ryun	USA	29.4.47	1	AAU	Bakersfield	23 Jun 67
3:51.12		Dieter	Baumann	GER	9.2.65	3	ISTAF	Berlin	21 Aug 92
3:51.31		Tony	Morrell	GBR	3.5.62	4	Bisl	Oslo	14 Jul 90
3:51.34		John	Gregorek	USA	15.4.60	6	Bisl	Oslo	26 Jun 82
3:51.39		Rich	Harris	USA	4.3.59	3	R-W	Koblenz	29 Aug 84
3:51.41		Peter	Rono	KEN	31.7.67	4	Athl	Lausanne	10 Jul 91
		(40)							
3:51.57		Jack	Buckner	GBR	22.9.61	4	R-W	Koblenz	29 Aug 84
3:51.59		Eamonn	Coghlan	IRL	24.11.52	5	OsloG	Oslo	9 Jul 83
3:51.62		Chuck	Aragon	USA	29.3.59	3	OsloG	Oslo	21 Jul 84
3:51.64		Marcus	O'Sullivan	IRL	22.12.61	5	Bisl	Oslo	1 Jul 89
3:51.76		Steve	Crabb	GBR	30.11.63	1hc	IAC	London	14 Aug 87
3:51.80		David	Kibet	KEN	24.11.63	1		Jerez de la Frontera	17 Sep 91
3:51.82		Mike	Hillardt	AUS	22.1.61	1	R-W	Koblenz	28 Aug 85
3:51.94		Suleiman	Nyambui	TAN	13.2.53	4	Athl	Lausanne	14 Jul 81
3:51.96		Gennaro	Di Napoli	ITA	5.3.68	1		S Donato Milanese	30 May 92
3:52.02		Craig	Masback	USA	31.3.55	3	OsloG	Oslo	17 Jul 79
3:52.02		Pascal	Thiébaut	FRA	6.6.59	4	OsloG	Oslo	21 Jul 84
		(51)	100th best 3:54.45						
Indoor marks									
3:49.78		Eamonn	Coghlan	IRL	24.11.52	1		East Rutherford	27 Feb 83
3:50.94		Marcus	O'Sullivan	IRL	22.12.61	1		East Rutherford	13 Feb 88

MEN All-time

2000 METRES

Mark	Wind	Name		Nat	Born	Pos	Meet	Venue	Date
4:50.81		Saïd	Aouita	MAR	2.11.59	1	BNP	Paris	16 Jul 87
4:51.39		Steve	Cram	GBR	14.10.60	1	BGP	Budapest	4 Aug 85
4:51.52		John	Walker	NZL	12.1.52	1	Bisl	Oslo	30 Jun 76
4:51.98			Aouita			1	VD	Bruxelles	5 Sep 86
4:52.20		Thomas	Wessinghage	FRG	22.2.52	1		Ingelheim	31 Aug 82
4:52.40		José Manuel	Abascal	ESP	17.3.58	1		Santander	7 Sep 86
4:52.44		Jim	Spivey	USA	7.3.60	1	Athl	Lausanne	15 Sep 87
4:52.53		Moses	Kiptanui	KEN	1.10.71	1	ISTAF	Berlin	21 Aug 92
4:52.82		Peter	Elliott	GBR	9.10.62	2	Athl	Lausanne	15 Sep 87
4:53.06		Jack	Buckner	GBR	22.9.61	3	Athl	Lausanne	15 Sep 87
4:53.69		Gary	Staines (10)	GBR	3.7.63	4	Athl	Lausanne	15 Sep 87
4:54.02			Aouita			1		Rieti	4 Sep 85
4:54.20		Sydney	Maree	USA	9.9.56	2		Rieti	4 Sep 85
4:54.46		Pierre	Délèze	SUI	25.9.58	5	Athl	Lausanne	15 Sep 87
4:54.71		Steve	Scott	USA	5.5.56	2		Ingelheim	31 Aug 82
4:54.88			Abascal			1		Santander	3 Sep 85
4:54.98			Aouita			1		Madrid	4 Jun 85
4:55.0		Gennaro	Di Napoli	ITA	5.3.68			Torino	26 May 91
4:55.20			Cram			1	McV	London	28 Aug 88
4:55.31		David	Kibet	KEN	24.11.63	2	ISTAF	Berlin	21 Aug 92
		(20/15)							
4:56.1		Michel	Jazy	FRA	13.6.36	1		Saint Maur	12 Oct 66
4:56.41		Johan	Fourie	RSA	2.12.59	1		Stellenbosch	22 Apr 85
4:56.70		Pascal	Thiébaut	FRA	6.6.59	2	BNP	Paris	16 Jul 87
4:57.1		Willy	Polleunis	BEL	27.12.47	1		Louvain	21 Sep 78
4:57.53		José Luis	Carreira	ESP	30.3.62	2		Santander	7 Sep 86
		(20)							
4:57.66		Eamonn	Coghlan	IRL	24.11.52	1		London	29 Aug 83
4:57.71		Steve	Ovett	GBR	9.10.55	1	OsloG	Oslo	7 Jul 82
4:57.8		Harald	Norpoth	FRG	22.8.42	1		Hagen	10 Sep 66
4:57.83		Jens-Peter	Herold	GER	2.6.65	3	ISTAF	Berlin	21 Aug 92
4:58.08		Marcus	O'Sullivan	IRL	22.12.61	3	McV	London	28 Aug 88
4:58.1		Francis	González	FRA	6.2.52	1		Rennes	22 Jun 79
4:58.15		Venuste	Niyongabo	BUR	9.12.73	1		Noisy le Grand	3 Jul 93
4:58.21		Noureddine	Morceli	ALG	28.2.70	1		St Denis	4 Jun 92
4:58.29		Peter	Wirz	SUI	29.7.60	2		Langenthal	27 Jul 84
4:58.38		Graham	Williamson	GBR	15.6.60	2		London	29 Aug 83
		(30)							
4:58.51		Peter	Koech	KEN	18.2.58	4	BNP	Paris	16 Jul 87
4:58.51		Cyrille	Laventure	FRA	29.3.64	1		Chartres	8 Sep 90
4:58.56		Rémy	Geoffroy	FRA	22.3.63	5	BNP	Paris	16 Jul 87
4:58.65		Stefano	Mei	ITA	3.2.63	1		Viareggio	15 Aug 84
4:58.84		Sebastian	Coe	GBR	29.9.56	1		Bordeaux	5 Jun 82
4:58.97		Vincent	Rousseau	BEL	29.7.62	1		Hechtel	8 Aug 87
4:59.00		Frank	O'Mara	IRL	17.7.60	6	Athl	Lausanne	15 Sep 87
4:59.02		Evgeni	Ignatov	BUL	25.6.59	4		Rieti	4 Sep 85
4:59.04		Rich	Harris	USA	4.3.59	2		Viareggio	15 Aug 84
4:59.1		Peter	Daenens	BEL	23.11.60	1		Neerpelt	19 Aug 83
		(40)							
4:59.21		Filbert	Bayi	TAN	23.6.53	1		Schaan	17 Sep 78
4:59.28		Todd	Harbour	USA	24.3.59	3	Nik	Nice	14 Aug 82
4:59.40		Ray	Flynn	IRL	22.1.57	1		Stuttgart	29 Aug 82
4:59.43		Mike	Boit	KEN	6.1.49	5		Rieti	4 Sep 85
4:59.54		Markus	Ryffel	SUI	5.2.55	2		Schaan	17 Sep 78
4:59.56		Robert	Nemeth	AUT	5.6.58	1		Klagenfurt	8 Aug 84
4:59.56		Mogens	Guldberg	DEN	2.8.63	7	Athl	Lausanne	15 Sep 87
4:59.57		Nick	Rose	GBR	30.12.51	2		London	3 Jun 78
4:59.59		Alex	González	FRA	16.3.51	2		Bordeaux	5 Jun 82
4:59.6		Jürgen	Straub	GDR	3.11.53	1		Potsdam	5 Jul 80
		(50)	100th best 5:02.60						
Indoor marks									
4:54.07		Eamonn	Coghlan	IRL	24.11.52	1		Inglewood	20 Feb 87
4:56.23		Jens-Peter	Herold	GER	2.6.65	1		Karlsruhe	6 Mar 93

3000 METRES

Mark	Wind	Name		Nat	Born	Pos	Meet	Venue	Date
7:28.96		Moses	Kiptanui	KEN	1.10.71	1	ASV	Köln	16 Aug 92
7:29.24		Noureddine	Morceli	ALG	28.2.70	1	Herc	Monaco	7 Aug 93
7:29.45		Saïd	Aouita	MAR	2.11.59	1	ASV	Köln	20 Aug 89
7:32.1		Henry	Rono	KEN	12.2.52	1	Bisl	Oslo	27 Jun 78
7:32.23			Aouita			1	ASV	Köln	17 Aug 86
7:32.54			Aouita			1	WK	Zürich	13 Aug 86
7:32.79		David	Moorcroft	GBR	10.4.53	1		London	17 Jul 82
7:32.94			Aouita			1	VD	Bruxelles	30 Aug 85
7:33.28		Paul	Bitok	KEN	26.6.70	2	ASV	Köln	16 Aug 92
7:33.3			Aouita			1	VD	Bruxelles	24 Aug 84
7:33.37		Sydney	Maree	USA	9.9.56	2		London	17 Jul 82
7:33.91		Dieter	Baumann	GER	9.2.65	1	ASV	Köln	8 Sep 91
7:34.18		Yobes	Ondieki	KEN	21.2.61	3	ASV	Köln	16 Aug 92
7:34.74			Ondieki			2	ASV	Köln	8 Sep 91
7:34.79			Aouita			1	Bisl	Oslo	1 Jul 89
7:34.98			Bitok			1	ASV	Köln	1 Aug 93
7:35.00			Bitok			1	Nik	Nice	15 Jul 92
7:35.01			Ondieki			1	Nik	Nice	10 Jul 89
7:35.1		Brendan	Foster (10)	GBR	12.1.48	1		Gateshead	3 Aug 74
7:35.43			Ondieki			1	BNP	Villeneuve d'Ascq	25 Jun 89
7:35.47			Kiptanui			2	Nik	Nice	15 Jul 92
7:35.71		Arturo	Barrios	MEX	12.12.63	2	Nik	Nice	10 Jul 89
7:35.79			Kiptanui			2	ASV	Köln	1 Aug 93
7:35.84		Doug	Padilla	USA	4.10.56	1	OsloG	Oslo	9 Jul 83
7:36.54		Brahim	Jabbour	MAR	1.1.70	2	Herc	Monaco	7 Aug 93
7:36.69		Steve	Scott	USA	5.5.56	1		Ingelheim	1 Sep 81
7:36.72			Ondieki			1	vUK	London	28 Jul 89
7:36.75		Thomas	Wessinghage	FRG	22.2.52	2		Ingelheim	1 Sep 81
7:37.04		Jim	Spivey	USA	7.3.60	3	ASV	Köln	1 Aug 93
7:37.09		Khalid	Skah	MAR	29.1.67	1	ASV	Köln	19 Aug 90
		(30/17)							
7:37.49		John	Walker	NZL	12.1.52	3		London	17 Jul 82
7:37.6		Emiel	Puttemans	BEL	8.10.47	1		Århus	14 Sep 72
7:37.60		Eamonn	Coghlan	IRL	24.11.52	1	Bisl	Oslo	1 Jul 80
		(20)							
7:37.70		Rudy	Chapa	USA	7.11.57	1		Eugene	10 May 79
7:37.73		William	Sigei	KEN	14.10.69	3	Herc	Monaco	7 Aug 93
7:37.74		Cyrille	Laventure	FRA	29.3.64	2	ASV	Köln	19 Aug 90
7:38.03		Marc	Davis	USA	17.12.69	4	Herc	Monaco	7 Aug 93
7:38.20		Mohamed	Suleiman	QAT	23.11.69	1	ISTAF	Berlin	27 Aug 93
7:38.39		M. Brahim	Boutayeb	MAR	15.8.67	2	Nik	Nice	15 Jul 91
7:38.45		Bob	Kennedy	USA	18.8.70	4	ASV	Köln	1 Aug 93
7:38.70		Aïssa	Belaout	ALG	12.8.68	5	Herc	Monaco	7 Aug 93
7:39.09		Peter	Koech	KEN	18.2.58	4		London	17 Jul 82
7:39.27		Filbert	Bayi	TAN	23.6.53	3	Bisl	Oslo	1 Jul 80
		(30)							
7:39.30		Mohamed	Issangar	MAR	12.12.64	5	ASV	Köln	1 Aug 93
7:39.38		Paul	Kipkoech	KEN	6.1.63	2	ASV	Köln	17 Aug 86
7:39.41		Vincent	Rousseau	BEL	29.7.62	4	Nik	Nice	10 Jul 89
7:39.5		Kipchoge	Keino	KEN	17.1.40	1		Hälsingborg	27 Aug 65
7:39.55		Robert	Denmark	GBR	23.11.68	6	ASV	Köln	1 Aug 93
7:39.69		António	Leitão	POR	22.7.60	2	VD	Bruxelles	26 Aug 83
7:39.82		Ismael	Kirui	KEN	20.2.75	4	ISTAF	Berlin	27 Aug 93
7:40.11		Stephane	Franke	GER	12.2.64	5	ISTAF	Berlin	27 Aug 93
7:40.19		Bill	McChesney	USA	8.1.59	2	ASV	Köln	22 Aug 82
7:40.3		Suleiman	Nyambui	TAN	13.2.53	2	Bisl	Oslo	27 Jun 78
		(40)							
7:40.4		Nick	Rose	GBR	30.12.51	3	Bisl	Oslo	27 Jun 78
7:40.41		Frank	O'Mara	IRL	17.7.60	5	Nik	Nice	10 Jul 89
7:40.43		Jack	Buckner	GBR	22.9.61	1	Bisl	Oslo	5 Jul 86
7:40.49		Dragan	Zdravkovic	YUG	16.12.59	2	OsloG	Oslo	9 Jul 83
7:40.52		Wilson	Waigwa	KEN	15.2.49	4	VD	Bruxelles	26 Aug 83
7:40.64		Wodajo	Bulti	ETH	11.3.57	5	VD	Bruxelles	26 Aug 83
7:40.94		Eamonn	Martin	GBR	9.10.58	3	OsloG	Oslo	9 Jul 83

Mark Wind		Name	Nat	Born	Pos	Meet	Venue	Date
7:41.00	Francis	González	FRA	6.2.52	2		Lausanne	18 Jul 79
7:41.00	Markus	Ryffel	SUI	5.2.55	3		Lausanne	18 Jul 79
7:41.0	Rod	Dixon	NZL	13.7.50	1		Milano	2 Jul 74
	(50)	100th best 7:43.20						
Indoors:	7:36.66	Aouita but ran inside measuring lines			1		Athinai	11 Mar 92
	7:38.46	Kiptanui			1		Stockholm	9 Feb 93

2 MILES

Mark		Name	Nat	Born	Pos	Meet	Venue	Date
8:12.17	Khalid	Skah	MAR	29.1.67	1		Hechtel	31 Jul 93
8:13.45	Saïd	Aouita	MAR	2.11.59	1		Torino	28 May 87
8:13.51	Steve	Ovett	GBR	9.10.55	1	IAC	London	15 Sep 78
8:13.68	Brendan	Foster	GBR	12.1.48	1	Kraft	London	27 Aug 73
8:14.0	Lasse	Viren	FIN	22.7.49	1		Stockholm	14 Aug 72
8:14.32	Rod	Dixon	NZL	13.7.50	1		Stockholm	18 Jul 74
8:14.66	Henry	Rono	KEN	12.2.52	2	IAC	London	15 Sep 78
8:14.93	Steve	Cram	GBR	14.10.60	1	Nike	London	29 Aug 83
8:15.53	Tim	Hutchings	GBR	4.12.58	2	McV	London	12 Sep 86
8:15.98	Geoff	Turnbull	GBR	15.4.61	3	McV	London	12 Sep 86
	(10)							
Indoor marks								
8:13.2	Emiel	Puttemans	BEL	8.10.47	1		Berlin	18 Feb 73
8:15.02	Doug	Padilla	USA	4.10.56	1	LAT	Inglewood	16 Feb 90

5000 METRES

Mark		Name	Nat	Born	Pos	Meet	Venue	Date
12:58.39	Saïd	Aouita	MAR	2.11.59	1	GG	Roma	22 Jul 87
13:00.40		Aouita			1	Bisl	Oslo	27 Jul 85
13:00.41	David	Moorcroft	GBR	10.4.53	1	OsloG	Oslo	7 Jul 82
13:00.86		Aouita			1		La Coruña	6 Aug 86
13:00.93	Moses	Kiptanui	KEN	1.10.71	1	VD	Bruxelles	28 Aug 92
13:01.15	Sydney	Maree	USA	9.9.56	2	Bisl	Oslo	27 Jul 85
13:01.82	Yobes	Ondieki	KEN	21.2.61	1	WK	Zürich	7 Aug 91
13:02.75	Ismael	Kirui	KEN	20.2.75	1	WC	Stuttgart	16 Aug 93
13:03.17	Haile	Gebresilasie	ETH	18.4.73	2	WC	Stuttgart	16 Aug 93
13:03.58		Ondieki			1	Athl	Lausanne	8 Jul 92
13:04.24		Ondieki			1	Bisl	Oslo	1 Jul 89
13:04.52		Aouita			1	OsloG	Oslo	27 Jun 85
13:04.67	Khalid	Skah	MAR	29.1.67	1	WK	Zürich	4 Aug 93
13:04.78		Aouita			1		Firenze	13 Jun 84
13:05.09		Ondieki			2	WK	Zürich	4 Aug 93
13:05.14	Richard	Chelimo	KEN	21.4.72	3	WK	Zürich	4 Aug 93
13:05.39		Guebre Silassie			4	WK	Zürich	4 Aug 93
13:05.40	Fita	Bayissa (10)	ETH	15.12.72	3	WC	Stuttgart	16 Aug 93
13:05.59		Aouita			1	OG	Los Angeles	11 Aug 84
13:05.59	Salvatore	Antibo	ITA	7.2.62	1	GG	Bologna	18 Jul 90
13:05.60		Ondieki			1	VD	Bruxelles	10 Aug 90
13:06.20	Henry	Rono	KEN	12.2.52	1		Knarvik	13 Sep 81
13:06.36		Aouita			1	GPF	Monaco	1 Sep 89
13:06.50		Kirui			5	WK	Zürich	4 Aug 93
13:06.64	Worku	Bikila	ETH	70	4	WC	Stuttgart	16 Aug 93
13:06.71		Kirui			1	Athl	Lausanne	7 Jul 93
13:06.76	Francesco	Panetta	ITA	10.1.63	6	WK	Zürich	4 Aug 93
13:06.82		Skah			1	BNP	Villeneuve d'Ascq	2 Jul 93
13:07.18		Skah			5	WC	Stuttgart	16 Aug 93
13:07.29	Wodajo	Bulti	ETH	11.3.57	1		Rieti	16 Sep 82
	(30/15)							
13:07.35	William	Sigei	KEN	14.10.69	2	Athl	Lausanne	7 Jul 93
13:07.54	Markus	Ryffel	SUI	5.2.55	2	OG	Los Angeles	11 Aug 84
13:07.70	António	Leitão	POR	22.7.60	2		Rieti	16 Sep 82
13:07.79	Arturo	Barrios	MEX	12.12.63	1	RMPG	London	14 Jul 89
13:08.03	Aïssa	Belaout	ALG	12.8.68	2	BNP	Villeneuve d'Ascq	2 Jul 93
	(20)							
13:08.51	Mohamed	Issangar	MAR	12.12.64	1	PG	London	20 Jul 90
13:08.54	Fernando	Mamede	POR	1.11.51	1		Tokyo	17 Sep 83
13:08.68	Paul	Bitok	KEN	26.6.70	1	Bisl	Oslo	10 Jul 93

Mark Wind	Name		Nat	Born	Pos	Meet	Venue	Date
13:08.86	Brahim	Jabbour	MAR	1.1.70	3	BNP	Villeneuve d'Ascq	2 Jul 93
13:09.03	Dieter	Baumann	GER	9.2.65	1	Expo	Sevilla	6 Jun 92
13:09.50	Peter	Koech	KEN	18.2.58	2	DNG	Stockholm	6 Jul 82
13:09.68	Simon	Chemwoyo	KEN	2.5.69	1	AfrC	Durban	27 Jun 93
13:09.76	Ibrahim	Kinuthia	KEN	22.5.63	1	GGala	Roma	17 Jul 91
13:09.80	Ian	Hamer	GBR	18.4.65	1	GGala	Roma	9 Jun 92
13:10.06	Alberto	Cova	ITA	1.12.58	3	Bisl	Oslo	27 Jul 85
	(30)							
13:10.15	Jack	Buckner	GBR	22.9.61	1	EC	Stuttgart	31 Aug 86
13:10.24	Robert	Denmark	GBR	23.11.68	3	GGala	Roma	9 Jun 92
13:10.40	Hansjörg	Kunze	GDR	28.12.59	1		Rieti	9 Sep 81
13:10.44	M Brahim	Boutayeb	MAR	15.8.67	3	GGala	Roma	17 Jul 91
13:10.66	Ezekiel	Bitok	KEN	15.2.66	1	GGala	Roma	9 Jun 93
13:10.88	Jonah	Koech	KEN	2.2.68	6	GGala	Roma	9 Jun 92
13:10.99	Vincent	Rousseau	BEL	29.7.62	3	Bisl	Oslo	10 Jul 93
13:11.14	John	Ngugi	KEN	10.5.62	2	VD	Bruxelles	10 Aug 90
13:11.29	Mathias	Ntawulikura	RWA	14.7.64	7	GGala	Roma	9 Jun 92
13:11.50	Tim	Hutchings	GBR	4.12.58	4	OG	Los Angeles	11 Aug 84
	(40)							
13:11.57	Stefano	Mei	ITA	3.2.63	2	EC	Stuttgart	31 Aug 86
13:11.69	Hammou	Boutayeb	MAR	.56	2	DNG	Stockholm	2 Jul 90
13:11.77	Ondoro	Osoro	KEN	3.12.67	5	GGala	Roma	17 Jul 91
13:11.89	Kibiego	Kororia	KEN	25.12.71	3	GGala	Roma	9 Jun 93
13:11.93	Alberto	Salazar	USA	7.8.58	3	DNG	Stockholm	6 Jul 82
13:11.99	Valeriy	Abramov	RUS	22.8.56	2		Rieti	9 Sep 81
13:12.14	Aloÿs	Nizigama	BUR	66	5	BNP	Villeneuve d'Ascq	2 Jul 93
13:12.29	Suleiman	Nyambui	TAN	13.2.53	1		Stockholm	18 Jun 79
13:12.29	Wilson	Omwoyo	KEN	15.4.65	6	BNP	Villeneuve d'Ascq	2 Jul 93
13:12.34	José Luis	González	ESP	8.12.57	1	Bisl	Oslo	4 Jul 87
	(50)	100th best 13:17.48						

10 000 METRES

Mark	Name		Nat	Born	Pos	Meet	Venue	Date
26:58.38	Yobes	Ondieki	KEN	21.2.61	1	Bisl	Oslo	10 Jul 93
27:07.91	Richard	Chelimo	KEN	21.4.72	1	DNG	Stockholm	5 Jul 93
27:08.23	Arturo	Barrios	MEX	12.12.63	1	ISTAF	Berlin	18 Aug 89
27:11.18		Chelimo			1	APM	Hengelo	25 Jun 91
27:11.62	John	Ngugi	KEN	10.5.62	1	VD	Bruxelles	13 Sep 91
27:13.81	Fernando	Mamede	POR	1.11.51	1	DNG	Stockholm	2 Jul 84
27:14.26	Fita	Bayissa	ETH	15.12.72	1	Bisl	Oslo	4 Jul 92
27:15.53		Chelimo			2	Bisl	Oslo	4 Jul 92
27:16.50	Salvatore	Antibo	ITA	7.2.62	1	WG	Helsinki	29 Jun 89
27:16.81	William	Sigei	KEN	14.10.69	2	Bisl	Oslo	10 Jul 93
27:17.48	Carlos	Lopes	POR	18.2.47	2	DNG	Stockholm	2 Jul 84
27:17.74	Khalid	Skah (10)	MAR	29.1.67	1	VD	Bruxelles	3 Sep 93
27:17.82	Addis	Abebe	ETH	.70	2	WG	Helsinki	29 Jun 89
27:18.22		Barrios			1	ISTAF	Berlin	17 Aug 90
27:18.32	Moses	Tanui	KEN	20.8.65	2	VD	Bruxelles	3 Sep 93
27:18.43	Paul	Tergat	KEN	17.6.69	3	VD	Bruxelles	3 Sep 93
27:18.45		Barrios			1	DNG	Stockholm	3 Jul 89
27:19.15		Ngugi			1		Koblenz	4 Sep 90
27:20.56	Mark	Nenow	USA	16.11.57	1	VD	Bruxelles	5 Sep 86
27:21.22		Chelimo			4	VD	Bruxelles	3 Sep 93
27:21.46	M.Brahim	Boutayeb	MAR	15.8.67	1	OG	Seoul	26 Sep 88
27:22.47#	Henry	Rono	KEN	12.2.52	1		Wien	11 Jun 78
27:22.78	Antonio	Martins	FRA	23.8.63	3	Bisl	Oslo	4 Jul 92
27:22.95		Mamede			1		Paris	9 Jul 82
27:23.06	Eamonn	Martin	GBR	9.10.58	1	Bisl	Oslo	2 Jul 88
27:23.18	Vincent	Rousseau	BEL	29.7.62	5	VD	Bruxelles	3 Sep 93
27:23.29		Skah			1	Bisl	Oslo	6 Jul 91
27:23.44		Lopes			1	OsloG	Oslo	9 Jul 83
27:23.55		Antibo			2	OG	Seoul	26 Sep 88
27:24.16	Francesco	Panetta	ITA	10.1.63	3	WG	Helsinki	29 Jun 89
	(30/20)							
27:24.24	Ondoro	Osoro	KEN	3.12.67	6	VD	Bruxelles	3 Sep 93
27:24.95	Werner	Schildhauer	GDR	5.6.59	1	NC	Jena	28 May 83
27:25.16	Kipkemboi	Kimeli	KEN	30.11.66	3	OG	Seoul	26 Sep 88

Mark	Wind	Name		Nat	Born	Pos	Meet	Venue	Date
27:25.48		Hammou	Boutayeb	MAR	.56	2	Bisl	Oslo	14 Jul 90
27:25.61		Alberto	Salazar	USA	7.8.58	2	Bisl	Oslo	26 Jun 82
27:26.00		Hansjörg	Kunze	GDR	28.12.59	4	Bisl	Oslo	2 Jul 88
27:26.11		Saïd	Aouita	MAR	2.11.59	1	Bisl	Oslo	5 Jul 86
27:26.95		Alex	Hagelsteens	BEL	15.7.56	3	Bisl	Oslo	26 Jun 82
27:28.87		Thomas	Osano	KEN	4.6.70	3	Bisl	Oslo	6 Jul 91
27:29.16		Craig	Virgin	USA	2.8.55	1		Paris	17 Jul 80
		(30)							
27:29.41		Wodajo	Bulti	ETH	11.3.57	1	WG	Helsinki	2 Jul 87
27:30.17		Haile	Guebre Silassie	ETH	18.4.73	3	AfrC	Durban	25 Jun 93
27:30.3 '		Brendan	Foster	GBR	12.1.48	1	AAA	London	23 Jun 78
27:30.47		Samson	Kimobwa	KEN	15.9.55	1	WG	Helsinki	30 Jun 77
27:30.80		David	Bedford	GBR	30.12.49	1	AAA	London	13 Jul 73
27:30.99		Martti	Vainio ¶	FIN	30.12.50	1	EC	Praha	29 Aug 78
27:31.16		Thierry	Pantel	FRA	6.7.64	3	Bisl	Oslo	14 Jul 90
27:31.19		Nick	Rose	GBR	30.12.51	3	OsloG	Oslo	9 Jul 83
27:31.48		Venanzio	Ortis	ITA	29.1.55	2	EC	Praha	29 Aug 78
27:31.52		Aleksandr	Antipov	LIT	9.3.55	3	EC	Praha	29 Aug 78
		(40)							
27:32.52		Are	Nakkim	NOR	13.2.64	4	Bisl	Oslo	14 Jul 90
27:34.38		Jean-Louis	Prianon	FRA	22.2.60	2	WG	Helsinki	2 Jul 87
27:34.53		Domingos	Castro	POR	22.11.63	3	DNG	Stockholm	5 Jul 93
27:34.58		Julian	Goater	GBR	12.1.53	5	Bisl	Oslo	26 Jun 82
27:34.96		Julius	Korir -2	KEN	12.5.58	1	ISTAF	Berlin	10 Sep 91
27:35.33		Takeyuki	Nakayama	JPN	20.12.59	3	WG	Helsinki	2 Jul 87
27:35.77		Joseph	Keino	KEN	63	2	ISTAF	Berlin	21 Aug 92
27:36.2		Gabriel	Kamau	KEN	20.3.57	1	MSR	Walnut	24 Apr 82
27:36.27		David	Black	GBR	2.10.52	5	EC	Praha	29 Aug 78
27:36.64		Gerard	Tebroke	HOL	9.11.49	6	EC	Praha	29 Aug 78
		(50)	100th best 27:43.89						

disqualified as an unsanctioned competitor

20 000m and 1 hour: No changes to lists shown in ATHLETICS1993

HALF MARATHON

Included in these lists are the slightly downhill courses: Newcastle to South Shields 30.5m, Tokyo 33m. Lisboa 40m

Mark	Name		Nat	Born	Pos	Meet	Venue	Date
59:47	Moses	Tanui	KEN	20.8.65	1		Milano	3 Apr 93
60:06	Steve	Moneghetti	AUS	26.9.62	1		Tokyo	24 Jan 93
60:11	Matthews	Temane	RSA	14.12.60	1	NC	East London	25 Jul 87
60:11	Zithulele	Sinqe	RSA	9.6.63	2	NC	East London	25 Jul 87
60:11	Todd	Williams	USA	7.3.69	2		Tokyo	24 Jan 93
60:15		Tanui			1		Newcastle	19 Sep 93
60:17	Dionicio	Ceron	MEX	9.10.65	3		Tokyo	24 Jan 93
60:23	Vincent	Rousseau	BEL	29.7.62	1		Tokyo	23 Jan 94
60:24	Benson	Masya	KEN	14.5.70	1	WC	South Shields	20 Sep 92
60:24		Masya			1		Den Haag	3 Apr 93
60:27		Moneghetti			1		Tokyo	26 Jan 92
60:28		Ceron			2		Tokyo	23 Jan 94
60:31*	Julius	Korir	KEN	12.5.58	1		Remich	22 Sep 91
60:33*	Joseph	Keino (10)	KEN	.63	2		Remich	22 Sep 91
60:34		Moneghetti			1	GNR	Newcastle	16 Sep 90
60:34	Carsten	Eich	GER	9.1.70	1		Berlin	4 Apr 93
60:40	Antonio	Silio	ARG	9.5.66	2	WC	South Shields	20 Sep 92
60:42	Arturo	Barrios	MEX	12.12.62	2		Tokyo	26 Jan 92
60:42	Andrew	Masai	KEN	13.12.60	2		Milano	3 Apr 93
60:42	Sammy	Lelei	KEN	14.8.64	2		Berlin	4 Apr 93
60:43	Mike	Musyoki	KEN	28.5.56	1	GNR	Newcastle	8 Jun 86
60:45	Boay	Akonay	TAN	3.1.70	3	WC	South Shields	20 Sep 92
60:45	Paul	Tergat	KEN	17.6.69	3		Milano	3 Apr 93
60:46		Ceron			1		Philadelphia	16 Sep 90
60:47*	Carlos	Monteiro	POR	14.12.65	1		Setúbal	4 Apr 93
60:50	Zablon	Miano (20)	KEN		2		Den Haag	3 Apr 93
60:51*		Tanui			1	Stra	Milano	13 Apr 91
60:51*	Domingos	Castro	POR	22.11.63	2		Setúbal	4 Apr 93
60:54*	Carlos	Patricio	POR	9.1.64	3		Setúbal	4 Apr 93

Mark	Wind	Name		Nat	Born	Pos	Meet	Venue	Date
60:55		Mark	Curp	USA	5.1.59	1		Philadelphia	18 Sep 85
60:55		Lameck	Aguta	KEN	10.10.71	4	WC	South Shields	20 Sep 92
		(30/24)							
60:56		Xolile	Yawa	RSA	29.9.62	3	NC	East London	25 Jul 87
60:58		Lawrence	Peu	RSA	13.2.66	1	NC	East London	18 May 91
60:59		Steve	Jones	GBR	4.8.55	2	GNR	Newcastle	8 Jun 86
61:00		John	Treacy	IRE	4.6.57	1	GNR	Newcastle	24 Jul 88
61:02*#		Mohamed	Kedir	ETH	18.9.54	1	Stra	Milano	4 Apr 82
61:03		Nick	Rose	GBR	30.12.53	3		Philadelphia	15 Sep 85
		(30)							
61:03		David	Tsebe	RSA	9.11.66	1	NC	Durban	22 Jul 90
61:03		Rammy	Tsebe	RSA	7.10.64	2	NC	Durban	22 Jul 90
61:03		Vicenzo	Modica	ITA	2.3.71	4		Milano	3 Apr 93
61:04		Carl	Thackery	GBR	14.10.62	1		Barnsley	12 Apr 87
61:04		Cosmas	N'Deti	KEN	24.11.71	3		Tokyo 33m dh	26 Jan 92
61:04		Lee Bong-ju		KOR		4		Tokyo 33m dh	26 Jan 92
61:06*		Thomas	Robert Naali	TAN	69	3		Remich	22 Sep 91
61:06		Michael	Kidane	ETH	57	1		Durban	28 Aug 93
61:10		Joseph	Kibor	KEN	72	2		Durban	28 Aug 93
61:11		Adam	Motlagale	RSA	6.3.61	3	NC	Durban	28 Aug 93
		(40)							
61:14		Solomon	Namanyane	RSA	25.12.63	4	NC	Durban	23 Jul 89
61:14		Stephan	Freigang	GER	27.9.67	1		Berlin	5 Apr 92
61:17		Jon	Tau	RSA	18.1.60	4	NC	East London	25 Jul 87
61:17		Hamid	Essabani	MAR	.63	1		Aïn Seba	1 Mar 92
61:17		Tendai	Chimusa	ZIM	28.1.71	1		Lisboa 40m dh	15 Mar 92
61:17		David	Lewis	GBR	15.10.61	7	WC	South Shields	20 Sep 92
61:17		Valdenor	Pereira Santos	BRA	21.12.69	5	WC	Bruxelles	3 Oct 93
61:18*#		Rod	de Castella	AUS	27.2.57	2	Stra	Milano	4 Apr 82
61:18		Artur	de Freitas Castro	BRA	12.11.67	8	WC	South Shields	20 Sep 92
61:19		Saïd	Ermili	MAR	.63	2		Lisboa 40m dh	15 Mar 92
		(50)							
61:19*		Fernando	Couto	POR	4.12.59	4		Setúbal	4 Apr 93

* courses not known to have been certified as the correct distance. # Rolling start used at Milan
Note that the East London course had an overall drop of 46.5m prio to 1991

MARATHON

Mark	Name		Nat	Born	Pos	Meet	Venue	Date
2:06:50	Belayneh	Dinsamo	ETH	28.6.65	1		Rotterdam	17 Apr 88
2:07:07	Ahmed	Salah	DJI	.56	2		Rotterdam	17 Apr 88
2:07:12	Carlos	Lopes	POR	18.2.47	1		Rotterdam	20 Apr 85
2:07:13	Steve	Jones	GBR	4.8.55	1		Chicago	20 Oct 85
2:07:35	Taisuke	Kodama	JPN	26.7.58	1		Beijing	19 Oct 86
2:07:35	Abebe	Mekonnen	ETH	9.1.64	1		Beijing	16 Oct 88
2:07:40	Hiromi	Taniguchi	JPN	4.4.60	2		Beijing	16 Oct 88
2:07:51	Robert	de Castella	AUS	27.2.57	1		Boston	21 Apr 86
2:07:57	Kunimitsu	Itoh	JPN	6.1.55	2		Beijing	19 Oct 86
2:08:01	Juma	Ikangaa	TAN	19.7.60	1		New York	5 Nov 89
	(10)							
2:08:04	Zithulele	Sinqe	RSA	9.6.63	1	NC	Port Elizabeth	3 May 86
2:08:05		Jones			1		Chicago	21 Oct 84
2:08:07	David	Tsebe	RSA	9.11.66	1		Berlin	27 Sep 92
2:08:08	Djama	Robleh	DJI	.58	2		Chicago	20 Oct 85
2:08:09		Salah			1	WP	Hiroshima	14 Apr 85
2:08:10		Ikangaa			1		Tokyo	9 Feb 86
2:08:14	Ibrahim	Hussein	KEN	3.6.58	1		Boston	20 Apr 92
2:08:15	Takeyuki	Nakayama	JPN	20.12.59	2	WP	Hiroshima	14 Apr 85
2:08:15	Willie	Mtolo	RSA	5.5.64	2	NC	Port Elizabeth	3 May 86
2:08:16		Jones			1		London	21 Apr 85
2:08:16	Steve	Moneghetti	AUS	26.9.62	1		Berlin	30 Sep 90
2:08:18		de Castella			1		Fukuoka	6 Dec 81
2:08:18		Nakayama			1	NC	Fukuoka	6 Dec 87
2:08:19	Gelindo	Bordin	ITA	2.4.59	1		Boston	16 Apr 90
2:08:20		Jones			1		New York	6 Nov 88
2:08:21		Nakayama			1	AsG	Seoul	5 Oct 86
2:08:26		Robleh			3	WP	Hiroshima	14 Apr 85
2:08:27	Toshihiko	Seko	JPN	15.7.56	1		Chicago	26 Oct 86
2:08:29		Dinsamo			2		Tokyo	9 Feb 86

Mark Wind	Name		Nat	Born	Pos	Meet	Venue	Date
2:08:32	Gidamis	Shahanga	TAN	4.9.57	2		Berlin	30 Sep 90
	(30/20)							
2:08:33	Charles	Spedding	GBR	9.5.52	2		London	21 Apr 85
2:08:33	Manuel	Matias	POR	30.3.62	1		Seoul	20 Mar 94
2:08:34	Derek	Clayton	AUS	17.11.42	1		Antwerpen	30 May 69
2:08:33	Kim Wan-ki		KOR	8.7.68	2		Seoul	20 Mar 94
2:08:36	Dionisio	Ceron	MEX	9.10.65	1	Beppu	Oita	2 Feb 92
2:08:44	Wodajo	Bulti	ETH	11.3.57	3		Rotterdam	17 Apr 88
2:08:47	Jörg	Peter	GDR	23.10.55	3		Tokyo	14 Feb 88
2:08:47	Hwang Young-cho		KOR	22.3.70	2	Beppu	Oita	2 Feb 92
2:08:52	Alberto	Salazar	USA	7.8.58	1		Boston	19 Apr 82
2:08:53	Koichi	Morishita	JPN	5.9.67	1	Beppu	Oita	3 Feb 91
	(30)							
2:08:54	Dick	Beardsley	USA	21.3.56	2		Boston	19 Apr 82
2:08:55	Takeshi	Soh	JPN	9.1.53	2		Tokyo	13 Feb 83
2:08:57	Alejandro	Cruz	MEX	10.2.68	1		Chicago	30 Oct 88
2:08:58	Mark	Plaatjes	RSA	2.6.62	1	NC	Port Elizabeth	4 May 85
2:08:59	Rod	Dixon	NZL	13.7.50	1		New York	23 Oct 83
2:09:00	Greg	Meyer	USA	18.9.55	1		Boston	18 Apr 83
2:09:01	Gerard	Nijboer	HOL	18.8.55	1		Amsterdam	26 Apr 80
2:09:03	Michael	Heilmann	GDR	26.10.61	4	WP	Hiroshima	14 Apr 85
2:09:03	Douglas	Wakiihuri	KEN	26.9.63	1		London	23 Apr 89
2:09:04	Tena	Negere	ETH	72	1		Fukuoka	6 Dec 92
	(40)							
2:09:06	Shigeru	Soh	JPN	9.1.53	1	Beppu	Oita	5 Feb 78
2:09:08	Geoff	Smith	GBR	24.10.53	2		New York	23 Oct 83
2:09:08	Vincent	Rousseau	BEL	29.7.62	2		Tokyo	13 Feb 94
2:09:12	Ian	Thompson	GBR	16.10.49	1	CG	Christchurch	31 Jan 74
2:09:12	Rodolfo	Gómez	MEX	30.10.50	3		Tokyo	13 Feb 83
2:09:14	Isidro	Rico	MEX	15.5.61	3		Seoul	20 Mar 94
2:09:15	John	Treacy	IRL	4.6.57	3		Boston	18 Apr 88
2:09:16	Allister	Hutton	GBR	18.7.54	3		London	21 Apr 85
2:09:16	Salvador	Garcia	MEX	1.11.62	1		Rotterdam	5 Apr 92
2:09:17	Yakov	Tolstikov	RUS	20.5.59	1	WCp	London	21 Apr 91
	(50)	100th best 2:10:10						
148m short: 2:08:13		Alberto Salazar	USA	7.8.58	1		New York	25 Oct 81

Note: Downhill point-to-point courses - Port Elizabeth (RSA) had a net drop of 149m between start (203m) and finish (54m). Boston (USA) has a net drop of 139m between start (143m) and finish (4m).

100 KILOMETRES

Mark	Name		Nat	Born	Pos	Meet	Venue	Date
Track								
6:10:20	Don	Ritchie	GBR	6.7.44	1		London (CP)	28 Oct 78
6:25:28	Cavin	Woodward	GBR	1.8.47	1		Tipton	25 Oct 75
Road - certified courses								
6:15:17 *	Konstantin	Santalov	RUS	3.1.66	1	IAU	Moskva	8 May 93
6:15:30	Jean-Paul	Praet *	BEL	8.11.55	1		Torhout	24 Jun 89
6:16:41		Praet			1	IAU EC	Winschoten	12 Sep 92
6:20:59	Aleksandr	Masarygin	RUS	18.10.60	1		Rognonas	31 Jan 93
6:22:19		Masarygin			1	IAU	Rodenbach	24 Apr 93
6:22:28		Santalov			1		Barcelona	3 May 92
6:23:15		Santalov			1	IAU	Amiens	25 Sep 93
6:23:25		Santalov			1	IAU WC	Palamos	16 Feb 92
6:24:24		Santalov			1		Amiens	19 Oct 91
6:24:46		Praet			1	IAU NC	Torhout	19 Jun 92
6:24:55		Santalov			1	IAU	Amiens	24 Oct 92
6:25:07	Bruce	Fordyce	RSA	3.12.55	1		Stellenbsoch	4 Feb 89
6:25:52		Santalov			1	IAU EC	Winschoten	18 Sep 93
6:26:13	Jean-Marc	Bellocq	FRA	8.2.57	1		Amiens	13 Oct 90
6:26:20		Santalov			1	IAU	Winschoten	7 Sep 91
6:26:24		Masarygin			1	IAU	Rodenbach	25 Apr 92
6:26:26		Santalov			1	IAU WC	Torhout	8 Aug 93
6:27:20	Valmir	Nuñes	BRA	16.1.64	1	IAU	Torrelavega	3 Oct 92
6:27:29	Andrzej	Magier	POL	23.1.62	2	IAU	Rodenbach	24 Apr 93
6:28:11	Don	Ritchie	GBR	6.7.44	1		Santander	25 Sep 82
	(20/8)							

Mark	Wind	Name	Nat	Born	Pos	Meet	Venue	Date
6:29:34		Karl-Heinz Doll	FRG	9.1.54	1	IAU NC	Hanau	28 Apr 90
6:30:35		Roland Vuillemenot	FRA	21.8.46	1	IAU NC	Chavagnes	22 May 93
6:30:37		Domingo Catalan	ESP	4.8.48	2	IAU WC	Palamos	16 Feb 92
6:31:14		Deon Holtzhausen	RSA	27.7.52	2		Stellenbosch	4 Feb 89
6:31:41		Valeriy Mikhailovskiy	RUS	2.1.59	2		Rognonas	31 Jan 93
6:33:03		Erik Seedhouse	GBR	19.6.64	3	IAU WC	Palamos	16 Feb 92
6:33:11		Jerzy Wroblewicz	POL	.61	1	IAU	Kalisz	10 Oct 92
6:33:38		Lucien Tselman	BEL	9.7.57	3	IAU	Amiens	25 Sep 93
6:33:40		Jan Szumiec	POL	.54	1		Rodenbach	23 Apr 88
6:33:42		Roland Vuillemenot	FRA	21.8.46	4	IAU NC	Amiens	24 Oct 92
		(20)						
6:33:47		Bernard Curton	FRA	13.11.52	4	IAU WC	Palamos	16 Feb 92
6:33:53		Jaroslav Janicki	POL	6.7.66	1	IAU	Kalisz	9 Oct 93
6:33:57		Andy Jones	CAN	9.11.61	1		New Orleans	14 Dec 91
6:33:57		Peter Hermanns	BEL	26.8.60	2	IAU EC	Winschoten	18 Sep 93
6:34:21		Farid Zharipov	RUS	22.3.57	5	IAU WC	Palamos	16 Feb 92
6:34:39		Przemyslaw Jamont	POL	.60	1		Kalisz	14 Oct 89
6:34:45		Werner Dörrenbacher	FRG	.54	1		Rodenbach	31 Oct 87
6:35:22		Philemon Mogashane	RSA		3		Stellenbosch	4 Feb 89
6:36:02		Andrzej Lisowski	POL	.61	1		Kalisz	15 Oct 88
6:36:34		Narihisa Kojima	JPN	16.8.64	1	IAU	Lake Saroma	5 Jul 92
		(30)						

Note that at the time of his 6:15:30 Praet was under suspension by the Belgian Federation.

Mark	Wind	Name	Nat	Born	Pos	Meet	Venue	Date
6:28:59 disqualified		Praet				IAU WC	Torhout	8 Aug

* Moskva course was a small loop measured by steel tape

Performances on courses not known to be measured by calibrated bicycle

Mark	Wind	Name	Nat	Born	Pos	Meet	Venue	Date
6:17:56		Václav Kameník	TCH	17.2.51	1		Grünheide	3 Apr 82
6:17:57		Jan Szumiec	POL	54	1		Winschoten	13 Sep 86
6:18:00		Don Ritchie	GBR	6.7.44	1		Hartola	1 Jul 78
6:19:35		Domingo Catalan	ESP	4.8.48	1		Torhout	20 Jun 87
6:23:51		Kameník			1		Genève	3 Nov 85
6:24:38		Erno Kis-Kiraly	HUN	58	1		Budapest	19 Nov 89
6:25:06		Yiannis Kouros	GRE	13.2.56	1		Torhout	22 Jun 85
6:26:05		Cavin Woodward	GBR	1.8.47	1		Migennes	10 Jun 78
6:26:26		Vitaliy Kovel	URS	.47	1		Odessa	10 Apr 83
6:27:08		Bruno Scelsi	FRA	3.10.54	1		Vogelgrun	13 Sep 86
6:27:55		Peter Rupp	SWZ	46	2		Genève	3 Nov 85

Questionable distances/courses

Mark	Wind	Name	Nat	Born	Pos	Meet	Venue	Date
6:03:51		Jean-Paul Praet	BEL	8.11.55	1		Torhout	20/21 Jun 86
6:14:12		Vitaliy Kovel	URS		1		Odessa	7/8 Apr 84
6:15:17 dh		Domingo Catalan	ESP	4.8.48	1		Auron-Nice	16 Nov 86

24 HOURS

Track

Mark	Wind	Name	Nat	Born	Pos	Meet	Venue	Date
283.600km		Yiannis Kouros	GRE	13.2.56	1		Montauban	15/16 Mar 85
280.469		Kouros			1		Melbourne	4/5 Aug 90
274.480		Dave Dowdle	GBR	7.11.54	1		Gloucester	22/23 May 82
272.624		Jean-Gilles Boussiquet	FRA	26.7.44	1		Lausanne	2/3 May 81
268.251		Don Ritchie	GBR	6.7.44	1		London (He)	26/27 Oct 91
265.932		Rae Clark	USA	7.2.52	1	TAC	Portland	29 Sep 90
264.108		Boussiquet			1		Blackburn	11/12 Oct 80
263.466		Mark Pickard	GBR	8.3.60	1		London (He)	10/11 Oct 81
262.790		Valeriy Goubar	RUS	.49	1		Odessa	Oct 88
262.668		Kouros			1		New York	2/3 Jul 84
		(10/7)						
262.640		Rune Larsson	SWE	11.5.56	1		Honefoss	12/13 Jul 86
261.204		Park Barner	USA	13.1.44	1		Huntington Beach	1/2 Jun 79
260.099		Mike March	AUS	18.6.43	1		Coburg	25/26 Feb 89
259.603		Ron Bentley	GBR	10.11.30	1		Walton	3/4 Nov 73
258.845		Viktor Suborin	URS		1		Jurmala	Jul 84

Road races (where superior to track bests)

Mark	Wind	Name	Nat	Born	Pos	Meet	Venue	Date
286.463km		Yiannis Kouros	GRE	13.2.56	1		New York	28/29 Sep 85
284.853		Kouros			1		New York	7/8 Nov 84
276.209		Wolfgang Schwerk	FRG	55	1		Köln	8/9 May 87
274.715		Bernard Gaudin	FRA	.49	1		Niort	13/14 Nov 82
274.119		Hans-Martin Erdmann	FRG	39	2		Köln	8/9 May 87

Mark	Wind	Name		Nat	Born	Pos	Meet	Venue	Date
268.000		A	Komissarenko	URS		1		Tula	Sep 82
264.246		Paul	Beckers	BEL	22.8.62	1	IAU	Torhout	1/2 Aug 92
263.172		Janos	Bogár	HUN	23.6.64	1		Szeged	3/4 Jul 93
262.419		Jean-Gilles	Boussiquet	FRA	26.7.44	1		Le Mans	30/31 Jan 82
262.112		Anatoliy	Kruglikov	RUS	.57	1	IAU	Niort	7/8 Nov 92
		(10/9)							
261.475		Ron	Teunisse	HOL	12.6.52	1	ECp	Apeldoorn	25/26 May 90
261.292		Jean-Pierre	Guyomarc'h	FRA	.54	1		Courçon	19/20 Sep 92
261.128		James	Zarei	IRN/GBR	13.1.44	1		Chorley	23/24 Aug 86
261.028		Peter	Samulski	FRG	14.12.38	1	ECp	Elze	17/18 Aug 90
260.895		Helmut	Schieke	FRG	28.6.39	2	ECp	Apeldoorn	25/26 May 90
260.750		Konstantin	Santalov	RUS	3.1.66	1		Madrid	16/17 Oct 93
260.180		Valeriy	Christenok	RUS	62	1	ECp	Niort	2/3 Nov 91
259.265		Helmut	Dreyer	GER	2.10.57	1	IAU EC	Basel	1/2 May 93
258.181		Kevin	Setnes	USA	27.1.54	1	NC	Sylvania	18/19 Sep 93
258.108		Peter	Mann	FRG	39	1		Apeldoorn	9/10 May 86
258.003		Marcel	Foucat	FRA	.50	2	ECp	Niort	2/3 Nov 91
Disqualified for positive drugs test									
264.718		Nikolay	Safin	RUS	.58	dq	IAU EC	Basel	1/2 May 93
Indoors									
275.576		Nikolay	Safin ¶	RUS	.58	1		Moskva	27/28 Feb 93
268.590		Anatoliy	Kruglikov	RUS	.57	1		Podolsk	22/23 Feb 92
267.543		Don	Ritchie	GBR	6.7.44	1	IAU	Milton Keynes	3/4 Feb 90
262.585		Dick	Tout	NZL	1.5.48	1		Milton Keynes	18/19 Feb 89
260.323		Valeriy	Goubar	RUS	.49	2		Moskva	27/28 Feb 93

2000 METRES STEEPLECHASE

Mark	Wind	Name		Nat	Born	Pos	Meet	Venue	Date
5:14.43		Julius	Kariuki	KEN	12.6.61	1		Rovereto	21 Aug 90
5:16.22		Phillip	Barkutwo	KEN	6.10.66	2		Rovereto	21 Aug 90
5:18.36		Alessandro	Lambruschini	ITA	7.1.65	1		Verona	12 Sep 89
5:18.38		Azzedine	Brahmi	ALG	13.9.66	1		Verona	17 Jun 92
5:19.68		Samson	Obwocha	KEN	.54	1		Birmingham	19 Jul 86
5:19.86		Mark	Rowland	GBR	7.3.63	1	McV	London	28 Aug 88
5:20.00		Krzysztof	Wesolowski	POL	9.12.56	1	Bisl	Oslo	28 Jun 84
5:20.25		Julius	Korir	KEN	21.4.60	2		Birmingham	19 Jul 86
5:20.81		Boguslaw	Maminski	POL	18.12.55	2	Bisl	Oslo	28 Jun 84
5:21.2		Eshetu	Tura	ETH	19.1.50	1		Montreal	14 Jul 76
		(10)							

3000 METRES STEEPLECHASE

Mark	Wind	Name		Nat	Born	Pos	Meet	Venue	Date
8:02.08		Moses	Kiptanui	KEN	1.10.71	1	WK	Zürich	19 Aug 92
8:05.25			Kiptanui			1		Rieti	6 Sep 92
8:05.35		Peter	Koech	KEN	18.2.58	1	DNG	Stockholm	3 Jul 89
8:05.37		Philip	Barkutwo	KEN	6.10.66	2		Rieti	6 Sep 92
8:05.4		Henry	Rono	KEN	12.2.52	1		Seattle	13 May 78
8:05.51		Julius	Kariuki	KEN	12.6.61	1	OG	Seoul	30 Sep 88
8:06.03		Patrick	Sang	KEN	11.4.64	2	DNG	Stockholm	3 Jul 89
8:06.36			Kiptanui			1	WC	Stuttgart	21 Aug 93
8:06.46			Kiptanui			1	VD	Bruxelles	13 Sep 91
8:06.79			Koech			2	OG	Seoul	30 Sep 88
8:07.53			Sang			2	WC	Stuttgart	21 Aug 93
8:07.62		Joseph	Mahmoud	FRA	13.12.55	1	VD	Bruxelles	24 Aug 84
8:07.89			Kiptanui			1	DNG	Stockholm	3 Jul 91
8:07.96		Mark	Rowland	GBR	7.3.63	3	OG	Seoul	30 Sep 88
8:08.02		Anders	Gärderud	SWE	28.8.46	1	OG	Montreal	28 Jul 76
8:08.39			Barkutwo			1	GGala	Roma	17 Jul 91
8:08.53			Kiptanui			2	GGala	Roma	17 Jul 91
8:08.57		Francesco	Panetta (10)	ITA	10.1.63	1	WC	Roma	5 Sep 87
8:08.78		Alessandro	Lambruschini	ITA	7.1.65	3	WC	Stuttgart	21 Aug 93
8:08.84		Matthew	Birir	KEN	25.11.69	1	OG	Barcelona	7 Aug 92
8:09.11		Bronislaw	Malinowski	POL	4.6.51	2	OG	Montreal	28 Jul 76
8:09.17		Henry	Marsh	USA	15.3.54	1	R-W	Koblenz	28 Aug 85
8:09.18		Boguslaw	Maminski	POL	18.12.55	2	VD	Bruxelles	24 Aug 84
8:09.42			Birir			4	WC	Stuttgart	21 Aug 93

Mark	Wind	Name		Nat	Born	Pos	Meet	Venue	Date
8:09.55			Sang			2	OG	Barcelona	7 Aug 92
8:09.70			Gärderud			1	DNG	Stockholm	1 Jul 75
8:09.70			Malinowski			1	OG	Moskva	31 Jul 80
8:09.76		Mark	Croghan	USA	8.1.68	5	WC	Stuttgart	21 Aug 93
8:10.01		William	van Dijck	BEL	24.1.61	1	VD	Bruxelles	5 Sep 86
8:10.29			Kiptanui			1	WK	Zürich	4 Aug 93
		(30/17)							
8:10.32		Hagen	Melzer	GDR	16.6.59	2	WC	Roma	5 Sep 87
8:10.36		Frank	Baumgartl	GDR	29.5.55	3	OG	Montreal	28 Jul 76
8:10.74		William	Mutwol	KEN	10.10.67	3	OG	Barcelona	7 Aug 92
		(20)							
8:11.04		Krzysztof	Wesolowski	POL	9.12.56	1	VD	Bruxelles	30 Aug 85
8:11.27		Azzedine	Brahmi	ALG	13.9.66	1	Bisl	Oslo	4 Jul 92
8:11.80		Julius	Korir	KEN	21.4.60	1	OG	Los Angeles	10 Aug 84
8:11.93		Rainer	Schwarz	FRG	5.6.59	2	R-W	Koblenz	28 Aug 85
8:12.0 '		George Kip	Rono	KEN	4.1.58	1	GGala	Roma	5 Aug 80
8:12.11		Colin	Reitz	GBR	6.4.60	2	VD	Bruxelles	5 Sep 86
8:12.21		Abdelaziz	Sahere	MAR	18.9.67	2	VD	Bruxelles	13 Sep 91
8:12.48		Filbert	Bayi	TAN	23.6.53	2	OG	Moskva	31 Jul 80
8:12.5 '		Mariano	Scartezzini	ITA	7.11.54	2	GGala	Roma	5 Aug 80
8:12.58		Graeme	Fell	CAN	19.3.59	3	R-W	Koblenz	28 Aug 85
		(30)							
8:12.58		Tom	Hanlon	GBR	20.5.67	3	Herc	Monaco	3 Aug 91
8:12.60		Tapio	Kantanen	FIN	31.5.49	4	OG	Montreal	28 Jul 76
8:12.68		Richard	Kosgei	KEN	29.12.70	1	Bisl	Oslo	10 Jul 93
8:12.69		Micah	Boinett	KEN	19.12.65	1	Nik	Nice	15 Jul 92
8:13.16		Brian	Diemer	USA	10.10.61	2	R-W	Koblenz	29 Aug 84
8:13.57		Eshetu	Tura	ETH	19.1.50	3	OG	Moskva	31 Jul 80
8:13.75		Uwe	Pflügner	GDR	24.11.66	2	APM	Hengelo	12 Aug 90
8:13.88		Raymond	Pannier	FRA	12.2.61	1	Nik	Nice	13 Jul 87
8:13.91		Ben	Jipcho	KEN	1.3.43	1	WG	Helsinki	27 Jun 73
8:14.05		Michael	Karst	FRG	28.1.52	1	DNG	Stockholm	5 Jul 77
		(40)							
8:14.05		Peter	Renner	NZL	27.10.59	3	R-W	Koblenz	29 Aug 84
8:14.13		Joshua	Kipkemboi	KEN	22.2.59	1	R-W	Koblenz	6 Aug 86
8:14.17		Samson	Obwocha	KEN	.54	2	R-W	Koblenz	6 Aug 86
8:14.26		Marc	Davis	USA	17.12.69	4	WK	Zürich	4 Aug 93
8:15.06		Patriz	Ilg	FRG	5.12.57	1	WC	Helsinki	12 Aug 83
8:15.07		Féthi	Baccouche	TUN	16.11.60	1	WG	Helsinki	2 Jul 87
8:15.28		Bruno	Le Stum	FRA	25.12.59	3	Nik	Nice	15 Jul 91
8:15.32		Dan	Glans	SWE	2.5.47	3	DNG	Stockholm	10 Aug 76
8:15.33		Steffen	Brand	GER	10.3.65	6	WC	Stuttgart	21 Aug 93
8:15.74		Domingo	Ramón	ESP	10.3.58	4	OG	Moskva	31 Jul 80
		(50)	100th best 8:21.08						

110 METRES HURDLES

Mark	Wind	Name		Nat	Born	Pos	Meet	Venue	Date
12.91	0.5	Colin	Jackson	GBR	18.2.67	1	WC	Stuttgart	20 Aug 93
12.92	-0.1	Roger	Kingdom	USA	26.8.62	1	WK	Zürich	16 Aug 89
12.93	-0.2	Renaldo	Nehemiah	USA	24.3.59	1	WK	Zürich	19 Aug 81
12.97A	2.0		Kingdom			1		Sestriere	11 Aug 88
12.97A	-1.6		Jackson			1A		Sestriere	28 Jul 93
12.98	1.5		Kingdom			1	OG	Seoul	26 Sep 88
12.99	1.2		Jackson			1	VD	Bruxelles	3 Sep 93
13.00	0.9		Nehemiah			1	Pepsi	Westwood	6 May 79
13.00	0.5	Tony	Jarrett	GBR	13.8.68	2	WC	Stuttgart	20 Aug 93
13.02	0.6		Kingdom			1	ISTAF	Berlin	18 Aug 89
13.03	-0.2	Greg	Foster	USA	4.8.58	2	WK	Zürich	19 Aug 81
13.03	0.3		Kingdom			1		Athinai	3 Sep 88
13.04	0.0		Nehemiah			1		Koblenz	26 Aug 81
13.04	1.6		Kingdom			1	ISTAF	Berlin	26 Aug 88
13.04	-0.5		Jackson			1	ASV	Köln	16 Aug 92
13.05	1.4	Tony	Dees	USA	6.8.63	1		Vigo	23 Jul 91
13.05	1.8		Jackson			1	ISTAF	Berlin	21 Aug 92
13.06	1.4		Foster			2		Vigo	23 Jul 91
13.06	0.7		Foster			1	WC	Tokyo	29 Aug 91
13.06	0.7	Jack	Pierce	USA	23.9.62	2	WC	Tokyo	29 Aug 91

Mark	Wind	Name		Nat	Born	Pos	Meet	Venue	Date
13.06	-0.6		Jackson			1	TSB	London	10 Jul 92
13.06	-0.5		Jackson			1rA	WK	Zürich	19 Aug 92
13.06	0.5		Pierce			3	WC	Stuttgart	20 Aug 93
13.07	-0.1		Nehemiah			1	ASV	Köln	23 Aug 81
13.07	0.3		Nehemiah			1	VD	Bruxelles	28 Aug 81
13.07	0.4		Jackson			1	Lucoz	Sheffield	14 Aug 92
13.07	0.3		Jackson			1	WP	Habana	27 Sep 92
13.08	0.5		Jackson			1	CG	Auckland	28 Jan 90
13.08	0.4		Dees			1rA	S&W	Modesto	16 May 92
13.08	-0.6		Dees			2	TSB	London	10 Jul 92
13.08	1.2	Mark	McKoy	CAN	10.12.61	1	BNP	Villeneuve d'Ascq	2 Jul 93
		(31/8)							
13.13	1.4	Florian	Schwarthoff	GER	7.5.68	2		Bad Homburg	24 May 92
13.17	-0.4	Sam	Turner	USA	17.6.57	2	Pepsi	Westwood	15 May 83
		(10)							
13.17	0.0	Tonie	Campbell	USA	14.6.60	3	WK	Zürich	17 Aug 88
13.19	-0.3	Emilio	Valle	CUB	21.4.67	3s3	WC	Stuttgart	19 Aug 93
13.20	2.0	Stéphane	Caristan	FRA	31.5.64	1	EC	Stuttgart	30 Aug 86
13.20	1.8	Aleksandr	Markin	RUS	8.9.62	1	Znam	Leningrad	11 Jun 88
13.21	0.6	Alejandro	Casañas	CUB	29.1.54	1	WUG	Sofia	21 Aug 77
13.21	1.8	Vladimir	Shishkin	RUS	12.1.64	2	Znam	Leningrad	11 Jun 88
13.24	0.3	Rod	Milburn	USA	18.5.50	1	OG	München	7 Sep 72
13.24	2.0	Arthur	Blake	USA	19.8.66	2	Athl	Lausanne	24 Jun 88
13.25	0.1	Andre	Phillips	USA	5.9.59	1	USOF	Baton Rouge	28 Jul 85
13.25	1.3	Courtney	Hawkins	USA	11.7.67	1	Indy	Indianapolis	25 Jun 93
		(20)							
13.26	1.6	Willie	Gault	USA	5.9.60	1	USOF	Indianapolis	25 Jul 82
13.26	-0.3		Li Tong	CHN	6.5.67	1		Verona	16 Jun 93
13.26	1.2	Mark	Crear	USA	2.10.68	3	BNP	Villeneuve d'Ascq	2 Jul 93
13.26	0.0	Igor	Kazanov	LAT	24.9.63	2s1	WC	Stuttgart	19 Aug 93
13.27	1.8	Sergey	Usov	BLS	16.1.64	3	Znam	Leningrad	11 Jun 88
13.28	1.1	Guy	Drut	FRA	6.12.50	1	NC	St. Etienne	29 Jun 75
13.28	1.0	Andrey	Prokofyev	RUS	6.6.59	1r2	GWG	Moskva	6 Jul 86
13.28	-1.0	Philippe	Tourret	FRA	8.7.67	1	Herc	Monaco	12 Aug 90
13.29	1.9	Rod	Woodson	USA	10.3.65	1		Irvine	14 Jun 87
13.29	-0.1	Jonathan	Ridgeon	GBR	14.2.67	1	WUG	Zagreb	15 Jul 87
		(30)							
13.30	2.0	Cletus	Clark	USA	20.1.62	3	Athl	Lausanne	24 Jun 88
13.31		Keith	Talley	USA	28.1.64	2r1	GWG	Moskva	6 Jul 86
13.33A	0.0	Willie	Davenport	USA	8.6.43	1	OG	Ciudad México	17 Oct 68
13.33	0.7	Dan	Philibert	FRA	6.8.70	5	WC	Tokyo	29 Aug 91
13.34	1.8	Dedy	Cooper	USA	22.5.56	2		Houston	3 May 80
13.34	1.0	George	Boroi	ROM	26.8.64	1	RomIC	Bucuresti	18 Jun 93
13.35	2.0	Arto	Bryggare	FIN	26.5.58	1h1	OG	Los Angeles	5 Aug 84
13.35	0.1	Tomasz	Nagorka	POL	2.10.67	1	NC	Pila	15 Jul 90
13.35	1.9	Glenn	Terry	USA	10.2.71	1h1	WUG	Buffalo	16 Jul 93
13.37	2.0	Thomas	Munkelt	GDR	3.8.52	1	EP	Helsinki	14 Aug 77
		(40)							
13.37	0.2	Milan	Stewart	USA	31.10.60	2		Paris	22 Jul 86
13.38A	1.8	Ervin	Hall	USA	5.3.47	1s1	OG	Ciudad México	17 Oct 68
13.38	1.6	Jerry	Wilson	USA	4.11.50	1	AAU	Eugene	20 Jun 75
13.39	1.9	Larry	Cowling	USA	6.7.60	1	vGDR	Karl-Marx-Stadt	10 Jul 82
13.40	2.0	Holger	Pohland	GDR	5.4.63	1	vURS	Tallinn	21 Jun 86
13.41	0.0	Charles	Foster	USA	2.7.53	4	OG	Montreal	28 Jul 76
13.41	0.5	Al	Joyner	USA	19.1.60	1h6	OT	Indianapolis	22 Jul 88
13.41	-0.8	Dietmar	Koszewski	FRG	26.7.67	1		Hamburg	28 Jul 90
13.41	1.4	Herwig	Röttl	AUT	30.1.68	3		Bad Homburg	24 May 92
13.42*	0.0	Tom	Hill	USA	17.11.49	1	AAU	Bakersfield	26 Jun 70
		(50)							
13.42	0.8	Javier	Moracho	ESP	18.8.57	1	NC	Barcelona	16 Aug 87
13.42A	0.9	Robert	Reading	USA	9.6.67	1h1	NCAA	Provo	1 Jun 89
13.42	1.8	David	Nelson	GBR	11.3.67	3h4	WC	Tokyo	27 Aug 91
		(53)	100th best 13.51						
Low altitude best: 13.38	0.0		Davenport			3	OG	Montreal	28 Jul 76
Wind-assisted									
12.87	2.6	Roger	Kingdom	USA	26.8.62	1	WP	Barcelona	10 Sep 89
12.91	3.5	Renaldo	Nehemiah	USA	24.3.59	1	NCAA	Champaign	1 Jun 79

Mark	Wind	Name		Nat	Born	Pos	Meet	Venue	Date
12.95	2.6		Jackson			2	WP	Barcelona	10 Sep 89
12.99	2.7		Jackson			1	v3N	Birmingham	23 Jun 89
13.00	3.5		Nehemiah			1	USOF	Syracuse	26 Jul 81
13.00	2.7		Kingdom			1		Sacramento	21 Jul 84
13.01	3.6		Jackson			1	v USA	Edinburgh	2 Jul 93
13.04	4.0		Jarrett			1	BNP	Villeneuve d'Ascq	6 Jul 92
13.06	2.1	Mark	McKoy	CAN	10.12.61	1	Gugl	Linz	13 Aug 92
13.14	2.9	Igor	Kazanov	LAT	24.9.63	1r1	Znam	Leningrad	8 Jun 86
13.19A	2.5	Robert	Reading	USA	9.6.67	1	NCAA	Provo	3 Jun 89
13.20	2.4	Arthur	Blake	USA	19.8.66	2	IAC	Edinburgh	6 Jul 90
13.21A	2.5	Eric	Cannon	USA	2.3.67	2	NCAA	Provo	3 Jun 89
13.22	2.7	Mark	Crear	USA	2.10.68	1h4	NC	Eugene	17 Jun 93
13.24	2.4	Glenn	Terry	USA	10.2.71	1s2	WUG	Buffalo	18 Jul 93
13.28	2.7	Henry	Andrade	USA	17.4.62	3		Sacramento	21 Jul 84
13.33	2.9	Gennadiy	Chugunov	AZE	26.11.63	3r1	Znam	Leningrad	8 Jun 86
13.34	3.6	Allen	Johnson	USA	1.3.71	3	vUSA	Edinburgh	2 Jul 93
13.36*	3.5	Ricky	Stubbs	USA	18.12.51	1	TexR	Austin	13 Apr 74
13.38*	2.3	Charles	Foster	USA	2.7.53	1	NCAA	Austin	7 Jun 74
13.38	3.4	Al	Lane	USA	27.4.62	1h3	NCAA	Eugene	31 May 84
13.38	4.0	Eric	Reid	USA	17.2.65	2	SEC	Tuscaloosa	17 May 87
13.39		Colin	Williams	USA		1		Dallas	1 Apr 78
13.39		Dietmar	Koszewski	FRG	26.7.67	1		Berlin	14 Jul 90
13.40	3.4	Liviu	Giurgian	ROM	22.7.62	1		Beograd	27 Jun 86
*120 yards time plus 0.03 seconds									
Hand timing									
12.8	1.0	Renaldo	Nehemiah	USA	24.3.59	1		Kingston	11 May 79
13.0	1.8	Guy	Drut	FRA	6.12.50	1	ISTAF	Berlin	22 Aug 75
13.0	1.0	Greg	Foster	USA	4.8.58	2		Kingston	11 May 79
13.0*	2.0	Rod	Milburn	USA	18.5.50	1s1	AAU	Eugene	25 Jun 71
13.0	0.8	Mark	McKoy	CAN	10.12.61	1	Nik	Nice	16 Jul 85
13.0		Stéphane	Caristan	FRA	25.1.64	1		Creteil	3 May 86
13.0		Vladimir	Shishkin	RUS	12.1.64	1		Staiki	7 May 88
13.1		Tonie	Campbell	USA	14.6.60	1		Nassau	7 May 83
13.1A*	0.9	Lance	Babb	USA	8.11.50	2	ITA	El Paso	10 May 75
13.1		Igor	Kazanov	LAT	24.9.63	2		Staiki	7 May 88
13.1	1.9	Philippe	Tourret	FRA	8.7.67	1		Pau	10 Jun 89
Wind-assisted									
12.8	2.4	Colin	Jackson	GBR	18.2.67	1		Sydney	10 Jan 90
12.9	4.1	Mark	Crear	USA	2.10.68	1rA	S&W	Modesto	8 May 93
13.0		Alejandro	Casañas	CUB	29.1.54	1	Barr	Habana	22 May 77
13.0		Tonie	Campbell	USA	14.6.60	1		Los Angeles	16 Jul 86
13.0		Keith	Talley	USA	28.1.64	1		Tuscaloosa	26 Mar 88
13.0	4.1		Li Tong	CHN	6.5.67	2rA	S&W	Modesto	8 May 93
13.1*	3.2	Tom	Hill	USA	17.11.49	1s1	USTFF	Wichita	13 Jun 70
13.1*	4.5	Larry	Shipp	USA	15.5.54	1	KansR	Lawrence	20 Apr 74
13.1		Ronnie	McCoy	USA	20.5.63	1		Naperville	10 May 85
* 120 yards time									

200 METRES HURDLES

Mark	Wind	Name		Nat	Born	Pos	Meet	Venue	Date
22.63	-0.3	Colin	Jackson	GBR	18.2.67	1		Cardiff	1 Jun 91
22.69		Glenn	Davis	USA	12.9.34	1		Bern	20 Aug 60
22.74	-0.8	Kevin	Young	USA	16.9.66	1		Belfast	31 Aug 92
22.77	-0.3	Nigel	Walker	GBR	15.6.63	2		Cardiff	1 Jun 91
22.79	-0.7	Axel	Schaumann	FRG	4.7.61	1		Stuttgart	29 Aug 82
22.79	-0.3	John	Regis	GBR	13.10.66	3		Cardiff	1 Jun 91
22.77w	3.1	Anthony	Jarrett	GBR	13.8.68	1		London (Ha)	14 Jul 91
Hand timed									
22.5		Martin	Lauer	FRG	2.1.37	1		Zürich	7 Jul 59

400 METRES HURDLES

Mark	Wind	Name		Nat	Born	Pos	Meet	Venue	Date
46.78		Kevin	Young	USA	16.9.66	1	OG	Barcelona	6 Aug 92
47.02		Edwin	Moses	USA	31.8.55	1		Koblenz	31 Aug 83
47.10		Samuel	Matete	ZAM	27.7.68	1rA	WK	Zürich	7 Aug 91
47.13			Moses			1		Milano	3 Jul 80
47.14			Moses			1	Athl	Lausanne	14 Jul 81
47.17			Moses			1	ISTAF	Berlin	8 Aug 80

Mark	Wind	Name		Nat	Born	Pos	Meet	Venue	Date
47.18			Young			1	WC	Stuttgart	19 Aug 93
47.19		Andre	Phillips	USA	5.9.59	1	OG	Seoul	25 Sep 88
47.23		Amadou	Dia Bâ	SEN	22.9.58	2	OG	Seoul	25 Sep 88
47.27			Moses			1	ISTAF	Berlin	21 Aug 81
47.32			Moses			1		Koblenz	29 Aug 84
47.37			Moses			1	WP	Roma	4 Sep 81
47.37			Moses			1	WK	Zürich	24 Aug 83
47.37			Moses			1	OT	Indianapolis	17 Jul 88
47.37			Young			1	Athl	Lausanne	7 Jul 93
47.38			Moses			1	Athl	Lausanne	2 Sep 86
47.38		Danny	Harris	USA	7.9.65	1	Athl	Lausanne	10 Jul 91
47.40			Young			1	WK	Zürich	19 Aug 92
47.42			Young			1	ASV	Köln	16 Aug 92
47.43			Moses			1	ASV	Köln	28 Aug 83
47.45			Moses			1	AAU	Westwood	11 Jun 77
47.46			Moses			1	WC	Roma	1 Sep 87
47.48		Harald	Schmid	FRG	29.9.57	1	EC	Athinai	8 Sep 82
47.48			Harris			2	WC	Roma	1 Sep 87
47.48			Schmid			3	WC	Roma	1 Sep 87
47.49			Harris			1	Athl	Lausanne	12 Jul 90
47.50			Moses			1	WC	Helsinki	9 Aug 83
47.51			Phillips			1	VD	Bruxelles	5 Sep 86
47.53			Moses			1	WP	Montreal	24 Aug 79
47.53			Moses			1	ISTAF	Berlin	15 Aug 86
		(30/7)							
47.60		Winthrop	Graham	JAM	17.11.65	1	WK	Zürich	4 Aug 93
47.64		Stéphane	Diagana	FRA	23.7.69	4	WC	Stuttgart	19 Aug 93
47.75		David	Patrick	USA	12.6.60	4	OT	Indianapolis	17 Jul 88
		(10)							
47.82		John	Akii-Bua	UGA	3.12.49	1	OG	München	2 Sep 72
47.82		Kriss	Akabusi	GBR	28.11.58	3	OG	Barcelona	6 Aug 92
47.92		Aleksandr	Vasilyev	BLS	26.7.61	2	EP	Moskva	17 Aug 85
48.12A		David	Hemery	GBR	18.7.44	1	OG	Ciudad México	15 Oct 68
48.16		Tony	Rambo	USA	30.5.60	3s1	OT	Los Angeles	17 Jun 84
48.24		Eric	Keter	KEN	22.7.66	2s2	WC	Stuttgart	17 Aug 93
48.28		Tranel	Hawkins	USA	17.9.62	3	OT	Los Angeles	18 Jun 84
48.34		Vasiliy	Arkhipenko	UKR	28.1.57	2	EP	Torino	4 Aug 79
48.34		McClinton	Neal	USA	11.7.68	4rA	Athl	Lausanne	8 Jul 92
48.35		Niklas	Wallenlind	SWE	21.11.68	3s1	OG	Barcelona	5 Aug 92
		(20)							
48.37		Sven	Nylander	SWE	1.1.62	4	WC	Roma	1 Sep 87
48.39		Quentin	Wheeler	USA	27.4.55	2	AAU	Walnut	17 Jun 79
48.39		Derrick	Adkins	USA	2.7.70	3	ASV	Köln	1 Aug 93
48.42		David	Lee	USA	23.4.59	4	WK	Zürich	24 Aug 83
48.44A		Harry	Schulting	HOL	11.2.56	1	WUG	Ciudad México	12 Sep 79
48.46A		Larry	Cowling	USA	6.7.60	2	NCAA	Provo	4 Jun 82
48.46A		Dries	Vorster	RSA	25.10.62	1		Pretoria	11 Apr 89
48.48		James	Walker	USA	25.10.57	1	SEC	Tuscaloosa	13 May 79
48.48		Toma	Tomov	BUL	6.5.58	2	BGP	Budapest	11 Aug 86
48.48		Olaf	Hense	GER	19.11.67	2	EP	Roma	26 Jun 93
		(30)							
48.50		Uwe	Ackermann	GDR	12.9.60	1	vUSA	Karl-Marx-Stadt	9 Jul 82
48.50		Henry	Amike	NGR	4.10.61	4s1	WC	Roma	31 Aug 87
48.51		Ralph	Mann	USA	16.6.49	2	OG	München	2 Sep 72
48.52		Reggie	Davis	USA	17.1.64	2	Gator	Knoxville	23 May 87
48.55		Jim	Bolding	USA	24.3.49	1		Paris	8 Jul 75
48.55		Tom	Andrews	USA	15.6.54	1	AAU	Westwood	12 Jun 76
48.58		Volker	Beck	GDR	30.6.56	3	EP	Torino	4 Aug 79
48.59		Alan	Pascoe	GBR	1.10.47	1	DNG	Stockholm	30 Jun 75
48.60		Aleksandr	Yatsevich	RUS	8.9.56	2	EC	Athinai	8 Sep 82
48.61		Vadim	Zadoinov	MOL	24.5.69	4	EC	Split	29 Aug 90
		(40)							
48.62		Oleg	Tverdokhleb	UKR	3.11.69	3s1	WC	Stuttgart	17 Aug 93
48.63		Bart	Williams	USA	20.9.56	2	Athl	Lausanne	10 Jul 84
48.64		Jim	Seymour	USA	27.7.49	4	OG	München	2 Sep 72

Mark	Wind	Name		Nat	Born	Pos	Meet	Venue	Date
48.65		Edgar	Itt	FRG	8.6.67	2	HGP	Budapest	12 Aug 88
48.68		Kevin	Henderson	USA	4.2.65	1	TAC	Tampa	18 Jun 88
48.68		Yoshihiko	Saito	JPN	12.2.72	1	NC	Tokyo	12 Jun 93
48.69		Mike	Shine	USA	19.9.53	2	OG	Montreal	25 Jul 76
48.71		Vladimir	Budko	BLS	4.2.65	1	Spart	Tashkent	18 Sep 86
48.72A		Dale	Laverty	USA	30.4.65	2		El Paso	20 Apr 86
48.73A		Paul	Montgomery	USA	20.4.61	3	NCAA	Provo	4 Jun 82
48.73		Jonathan	Ridgeon	GBR	14.2.67	2		Rieti	6 Sep 92
		(51)	100th best 49.18						

Low altitude bests

48.52 Hemery 3 OG München 2 Sep 72 48.71 Schulting 2 WK Zürich 15 Aug 79

48.59 Vorster 1 Durban 29 Apr 91

Hand timing

Mark	Wind	Name		Nat	Born	Pos	Meet	Venue	Date
48.1		Jim	Bolding	USA	24.3.49	1		Milano	2 Jul 74
48.4		Ralph	Mann	USA	16.6.49	1	OT	Eugene	2 Jul 72
48.5		Aleksandr	Yatsevich	RUS	8.9.56	1		Kiev	9 Aug 82
48.6		Jean-Claude	Nallet	FRA	15.3.47	1	vUSA	Colombes	8 Jul 70
48.6		Dick	Bruggeman	USA	13.6.47	2	OT	Eugene	2 Jul 72

HIGH JUMP

Mark	Wind	Name		Nat	Born	Pos	Meet	Venue	Date
2.45		Javier	Sotomayor	CUB	13.10.67	1		Salamanca	27 Jul 93
2.44			Sotomayor			1	CAC	San Juan	29 Jul 89
2.43			Sotomayor			1		Salamanca	8 Sep 88
2.43i			Sotomayor			1	WI	Budapest	4 Mar 89
2.42		Patrik	Sjöberg	SWE	5.1.65	1	DNG	Stockholm	30 Jun 87
2.42i		Carlo	Thränhardt	FRG	5.7.57	1		Berlin	26 Feb 88
2.41		Igor	Paklin	KGZ	15.7.63	1	WUG	Kobe	4 Sep 85
2.41i			Sjöberg			1		Piraeus	1 Feb 87
2.41i			Sotomayor			1	WI	Toronto	14 Mar 93
2.40		Rudolf	Povarnitsyn	UKR	13.6.62	1		Donyetsk	11 Aug 85
2.40i			Thränhardt			1		Simmerath	16 Jan 87
2.40i			Sjöberg			1		Berlin	27 Feb 87
2.40			Sotomayor			1	NC	Habana	12 Mar 89
2.40			Sjöberg			1	EP-B	Bruxelles	5 Aug 89
2.40			Sotomayor			1	AmCp	Bogota	13 Aug 89
2.40		Sorin	Matei	ROM	6.7.63	1	PTS	Bratislava	20 Jun 90
2.40i		Hollis	Conway	USA	8.1.67	1	WI	Sevilla	10 Mar 91
2.40			Sotomayor			1		Saint Denis	19 Jul 91
2.40		Charles	Austin	USA	19.12.67	1	WK	Zürich	7 Aug 91
2.40			Sotomayor			1	Barr	Habana	22 May 93
2.40			Sotomayor			1	TSB	London	23 Jul 93
2.40			Sotomayor			1	WC	Stuttgart	22 Aug 93
2.40i			Sotomayor			1		Wuppertal	4 Feb 94
2.40i			Sotomayor			1	TSB	Birmingham	26 Feb 94
2.39		Zhu Jianhua		CHN	29.5.63	1		Eberstadt	10 Jun 84
2.39i		Dietmar	Mögenburg (10)	FRG	15.8.61	1		Köln	24 Feb 85
2.39			Sjöberg			1	EP-B	Göteborg	27 Jun 87
2.39i			Sjöberg			1	EI	Budapest	5 Mar 88
2.39			Conway			1	USOF	Norman	30Jul 89
2.39i		Ralf	Sonn	GER	17.1.67	1		Berlin	1 Mar 91
2.39i			Sjoberg			2	WI	Toronto	14 Mar 93
2.39			Sotomayor			1		Pau	26 Jun 93
2.39i			Sotomayor			1		Madrid	11 feb 94
		(33/11)							
2.38i		Gennadiy	Avdeyenko	UKR	4.11.63	2	WI	Indianapolis	7 Mar 87
2.38		Sergey	Malchenko	RUS	2.11.63	1		Banská Bystrica	4 Sep 88
2.38		Dragutin	Topic	YUG	12.3.71	1		Beograd	1 Aug 93
2.38i		Steve	Smith	GBR	29.3.73	2		Wuppertal	4 Feb 94
2.37		Valeriy	Sereda	RUS	30.6.59	1		Rieti	2 Sep 84
2.37		Tom	McCants	USA	27.11.62	1	JO	Columbus	8 May 88
2.37		Jerome	Carter	USA	25.3.63	2	JO	Columbus	8 May 88
2.37		Sergey	Dymchenko	UKR	23.8.67	1		Kiev	16 Sep 90
2.37i		Artur	Partyka	POL	25.7.69	1		Sulingen	3 Feb 91
		(20)							

Mark	Wind	Name		Nat	Born	Pos	Meet	Venue	Date
2.37		Troy	Kemp	BAH	18.6.66	1		Pau	26 Jun 93
2.37i		Dalton	Grant	GBR	8.4.66	1	EI	Paris	13 Mar 94
2.36		Gerd	Wessig	GDR	16.7.59	1	OG	Moskva	1 Aug 80
2.36		Sergey	Zasimovich	KGZ	6.9.62	1		Tashkent	5 May 84
2.36		Eddy	Annys	BEL	15.12.58	1		Ghent	26 May 85
2.36i		Jim	Howard	USA	11.9.59	1		Albuquerque	25 Jan 86
2.36i		Jan	Zvara	TCH	12.2.63	1	vGDR	Jablonec	14 Feb 87
2.36i		Gerd	Nagel	FRG	22.10.57	1		Sulingen	17 Mar 89
2.36		Nick	Saunders	BER	14.9.63	1	CG	Auckland	1 Feb 90
2.36		Doug	Nordquist	USA	20.12.58	2	TAC	Norwalk	15 Jun 90
		(30)							
2.36		Georgi	Dakov	BUL	21.10.67	2	VD	Bruxelles	10 Aug 90
2.36		Lambros	Papakostas	GRE	20.10.69	1	NC	Athinai	21 Jun 92
2.36i		Hendrik	Beyer	GER	14.2.72	1		Berlin	5 Mar 93
2.36i		Steinar	Hoen	NOR	8.2.71	1		Balingen	12 Feb 94
2.35i		Vladimir	Yashchenko	UKR	12.1.59	1	EI	Milano	12 Mar 78
2.35		Jacek	Wszola	POL	30.12.56	1		Eberstadt	25 May 80
2.35i		Aleksandr	Kotovich	UKR	6.11.61	1		Vilnius	13 Jan 85
2.35i		Brent	Harken	USA	1.12.61	1		Moscow	15 Feb 91
2.35		Darrin	Plab	USA	26.9.70	2	OT/NC	New Orleans	28 Jun 92
2.35		Tim	Forsyth	AUS	17.8.73	1		Canberra	25 Jan 93
		(40)							
2.35i		Jean-Charles	Gicquel	FRA	24.2.67	2	EI	Paris	13 Feb 94
2.34		Paul	Frommeyer	FRG	28.6.57	1		Recke	17 Jun 83
2.34		Dwight	Stones	USA	6.12.53	1	OT	Los Angeles	24 Jun 84
2.34i		Yuriy	Sergiyenko	UKR	19.3.65	1	UkrCh	Kiev	2 Feb 85
2.34		Dennis	Lewis	USA	20.3.59	1		Los Angeles	30 Mar 85
2.34		Róbert	Ruffíni	TCH	26.1.67	1	v2-N	Praha	3 Jul 88
2.34i		Aleksey	Yemelin	RUS	16.10.68	1	NC	Chelyabinsk	4 Feb 90
2.34i		Brian	Brown	USA	6.6.67	1	NCAA	Indianapolis	9 Mar 90
2.34		Rolandas	Verkys	LIT	17.3.67	1	Kuso	Warszawa	16 Jun 91
2.34		Arturo	Ortiz	ESP	18.9.66	2	EP/B	Barcelona	22 Jun 91
		(50)							
2.34		Marino	Drake	CUB	13.6.67	2		Saint Denis	19 Jul 91
2.34		Andrey	Sankovich	BLS	15.7.65	1		Gomel	15 May 93
		(52)	100th best 2.31						

Best outdoor marks for athletes with indoor bests

Mark	Name	Pos	Meet	Venue	Date
2.37	Thranhärdt	2		Rieti	2 Sep 84
2.37	Smith	1	WJ	Seoul	20 Sep 92
2.37	Partyka	2	WC	Stuttgart	22 Aug 93
2.36	Mögenburg	3		Eberstadt	10 Jun 84
2.36	Zvara	1		Praha	23 Aug 87
2.36	Howard	1		Rehlingen	8 Jun 87
2.36	Grant	4	WC	Tokyo	1 Sep 91
2.35	Nagel	1		Forbach	7 Aug 88
2.34	Yashchenko	1	Prav	Tbilisi	16 Jun 78
2.34	Yemelin	2	EC	Split	1 Sep 90
2.34	Sonn	4	WC	Stuttgart	22 Aug 93

Ancillary jumps

Sotomayor 2.40 on 8 Sep 88 and 29 Jul 89

POLE VAULT

Mark	Wind	Name		Nat	Born	Pos	Meet	Venue	Date
6.15i		Sergey	Bubka	UKR	4.12.63	1		Donyetsk	21 Feb 93
6.14i			S Bubka			1		Liévin	13 Feb 93
6.13i			S Bubka			1		Berlin	21 Feb 92
6.13			S Bubka			1	TOTO	Tokyo	19 Sep 92
6.12i			S Bubka			1	Mast	Grenoble	23 Mar 91
6.12			S Bubka			1		Padova	30 Aug 92
6.11i			S.Bubka			1		Donyetsk	19 Mar 91
6.11			S Bubka			1		Dijon	13 Jun 92
6.10i			S.Bubka			1		San Sebastian	15 Mar 91
6.10			S Bubka			1	MAI	Malmö	5 Aug 91
6.09			S Bubka			1		Formia	8 Jul 91
6.08i			S.Bubka			1	NC	Volgograd	9 Feb 91
6.08			S Bubka			1	Znam	Moskva	9 Jun 91
6.07			S.Bubka			1	Super	Shizuoka	6 May 91
6.06			S.Bubka			1	Nik	Nice	10 Jul 88
6.05			S.Bubka			1	PTS	Bratislava	9 Jun 88
6.05i			S.Bubka			1		Donyetsk	17 Mar 90
6.05i			S Bubka			1		Berlin	5 Mar 93
6.05			S Bubka			1	GPF	London	10 Sep 93
6.05i			S Bubka			1		Grenoble	6 Feb 94

Mark	Wind	Name		Nat	Born	Pos	Meet	Venue	Date
6.03			S.Bubka			1	Ros	Praha	23 Jun 87
6.03i			S.Bubka			1		Osaka	11 Feb 89
6.02i		Rodion	Gataullin	RUS	23.11.65	1	NC	Gomel	4 Feb 89
6.01			S.Bubka			1	GWG	Moskva	8 Jul 86
6.01i			S Bubka			1		Grenoble	7 Feb 93
6.00			S.Bubka			1		Paris	13 Jul 85
6.00i			Gataullin			1		Leningrad	22 Jan 89
6.00	ex?		S.Bubka			1		Donyetsk	11 Sep 89
6.00			Gataullin			1		Tokyo	16 Sep 89
6.00i			S.Bubka			1	WI	Sevilla	9 Mar 91
6.00			S Bubka			1	GPB	Bratislava	4 Jun 91
6.00i			S Bubka			1	Sunk	Los Angeles	15 Feb 92
6.00			S Bubka			1		St Denis	4 Jun 92
6.00			S Bubka			1	ISTAF	Berlin	21 Aug 92
6.00i			Gataullin			1		Moskva	2 Feb 93
6.00i			Gataullin			2		Liévin	13 Feb 93
6.00			S Bubka			1	Jen	San José	29 May 93
6.00			Gataullin			1	EP	Roma	27 Jun 93
6.00			S Bubka			1	WC	Stuttgart	19 Aug 93
6.00i			S Bubka			1		Clermont-Ferrand	28 Jan 94
		(40/2)							
5.96		Joe	Dial	USA	26.10.62	1		Norman	18 Jun 87
5.94i		Philippe	Collet	FRA	13.12.63	1	Mast	Grenoble	10 Mar 90
5.93i		Billy	Olson	USA	19.7.58	1		East Rutherford	8 Feb 86
5.93		Jean	Galfione	FRA	20.6.71	1	NC	Annecy	25 Jul 93
5.92		István	Bagyula	HUN	2.1.69	1	Gugl	Linz	5 Jul 91
5.92		Igor	Potapovich	KZK	6.9.67	2		Dijon	13 Jun 92
5.91		Thierry	Vigneron	FRA	9.3.60	2	GGala	Roma	31 Aug 84
5.91i		Viktor	Ryzhenkov	UZB	25.8.66	2		San Sebastian	15 Mar 91
		(10)							
5.91		Dean	Starkey	USA	27.3.67	1	S&W	Modesto	16 May 92
5.90		Pierre	Quinon	FRA	20.2.62	2	Nik	Nice	16 Jul 85
5.90i		Ferenc	Salbert	FRA	5.8.60	1	Mast	Grenoble	14 Mar 87
5.90		Miroslaw	Chmara	POL	9.5.64	1	BNP	Villeneuve d'Ascq	27 Jun 88
5.90i		Grigoriy	Yegorov	KZK	12.1.67	1		Yokohama	11 Mar 90
5.90		Maksim	Tarasov	RUS	2.12.70	2		St Denis	4 Jun 92
5.90		Igor	Trandenkov	RUS	17.8.66	2	ASV	Köln	16 Aug 92
5.90		Denis	Petushinskiy	RUS	29.1.67	1	Znam	Moskva	13 Jun 93
5.90i		Pyotr	Bochkaryov	RUS	3.11.67	1	EI	Paris	12 Mar 94
5.89		Kory	Tarpenning	USA	27.2.62	1	OT	Indianopolis	21 Jul 88
		(20)							
5.87		Earl	Bell	USA	25.8.55	1		Jonesboro	14 May 88
5.86		Vasiliy	Bubka	UKR	26.11.60	1		Chelyabinsk	16 Jul 88
5.86		Bill	Payne	USA	21.12.67	1	SWC	Houston	19 May 91
5.85		Konstantin	Volkov	RUS	28.2.60	1	Izv	Kiev	22 Jun 84
5.85		Scott	Huffman	USA	30.11.64	1		Austin	9 May 92
5.84		Mike	Tully	USA	21.10.56	1		Irvine	1 May 88
5.83i		Jani	Lehtonen	FIN	11.8.68	1	DNG	Stockholm	8 Mar 94
5.82		Aleksandr	Krupskiy	RUS	4.1.60	1	BGP	Budapest	20 Aug 84
5.82		Aleksandr	Parnov	UZB	10.5.59	1		Sumgait	21 Aug 85
5.82		Tim	Bright	USA	28.7.60	1	Nik	Nice	10 Jul 90
		(30)							
5.81		Vladimir	Polyakov	RUS	17.4.60	1	vGDR	Tbilisi	26 Jun 81
5.81i		Marian	Kolasa	POL	12.8.59	1		Praha	13 Feb 86
5.81		Valeriy	Bukreyev	EST	15.6.64	1		Riga	29 May 93
5.80		Pavel	Bogatyryov	RUS	19.3.61	1		Schwechat	19 Jun 85
5.80i		Dave	Volz	USA	2.5.62	2		New York	14 Feb 86
5.80		Atanas	Tarev	BUL	31.1.58	2	Athl	Lausanne	2 Sep 86
5.80		Aleksandr	Obizhayev	LAT	16.9.59	2	SU Ch	Bryansk	17 Jul 87
5.80A		Doug	Fraley	USA	7.3.65	2		Sestriere	21 Jul 92
5.80i		Werner	Holl	GER	28.1.70	1		Nordlingen	7 Mar 93
5.80		Greg	Duplantis	USA	22.1.62	2		Århus	1 Jul 93
		(40)							
5.80i		Lawrence	Johnson	USA	7.5.74	1		Knoxville	18 Feb 94
5.78		Wladyslaw	Kozakiewicz	POL	8.12.53	1	OG	Moskva	30 Jul 80

MEN All-time

Mark	Wind	Name		Nat	Born	Pos	Meet	Venue	Date
5.77		Philippe	Houvion	FRA	5.1.57	1		Paris	17 Jul 80
5.77i		Hermann	Fehringer	AUT	8.12.62	1	NC	Wien	24 Feb 91
5.77i		Javier	Garcia	ESP	22.7.66	3	Mast	Grenoble	14 Mar 92
5.76		Jeff	Buckingham	USA	14.6.60	1		Lawrence	16 Jul 83
5.76		Tom	Hintnaus	BRA	15.2.58	1	WK	Zürich	21 Aug 85
5.75		Jean-Michel	Bellot	FRA	16.12.53	1		Colombes	25 Sep 82
5.75		Brad	Pursley	USA	24.5.60	1		Abilene	29 Mar 83
5.75i		Sergey	Kulibaba	KZK	24.7.59	1		Klaipeda	18 Mar 87
		(50)							
5.75i		Valeriy	Ishutin	UZB	5.9.65	2		Leningrad	22 Jan 89
5.75		Dave	Watson	USA	27.1.64	3	PTS	Bratislava	20 Jun 90
5.75		Peter	Widén	SWE	2.7.67	5	WC	Tokyo	29 Aug 91
5.75i		Delko	Lesev	BUL	6.1.67	1		Sofia	9 Feb 92
5.75i		Philippe	D'Encausse	FRA	24.3.67	1	Mast	Grenoble	20 Mar 93
5.75		Pat	Manson	USA	29.11.67	4	Jen	San José	29 May 93
		(56)	100th best 5.67						

Best outdoor marks for athletes with lifetime bests indoors

Mark	Name	Pos	Meet	Venue	Date	Mark	Name	Pos	Meet	Venue	Date
5.90	Yegorov	2	WC	Stuttgart	19 Aug 93	5.80	Ryzhenkov	1	vGDR	Rostock	24 Jun 90
5.85	Collet	2		Paris	22 Jul 86	5.80	Volz	2	OT	New Orleans	21 Jun 92
5.82	Lehtonen	1		Kuortane	26 Jun 93	5.77	Fehringer	2	Gugl	Linz	5 Jul 91
5.80	Kolasa	1		Kamp-Lintfort	1 Sep 86	5.75	Garcia	1		San Cugat	3 Aug 90
5.80	Olson	1		Dallas	11 Apr 87	5.75	D'Encausse	2		Pau	26 Jun 88
5.80	Salbert	1		Dreux	4 Jun 87						

Unsanctiond meeting: 5.84 Konstantin Volkov 1 Irkutsk 2 Aug 81

Exhibition

Mark	Name		Nat	Born	Pos	Venue	Date
5.86	Valeriy	Bukreyev	EST	15.6.64	1	Chiari	5 Sep 93
5.86i	Larry	Jessee	USA	31.3.52	1	Newcastle	16 Oct 85

Ancillary jumps: S Bubka: 6.05i 13 Feb 93, 6.00i 9 Feb 91, 6.00i 19 Mar 91

LONG JUMP

Mark	Wind	Name		Nat	Born	Pos	Meet	Venue	Date
8.95	0.3	Mike	Powell	USA	10.11.63	1	WC	Tokyo	30 Aug 91
8.90A	2.0	Bob	Beamon	USA	29.8.45	1	OG	Ciudad México	18 Oct 68
8.87	-0.2	Carl	Lewis	USA	1.7.61	*	WC	Tokyo	30 Aug 91
8.86A	1.9	Robert	Emmiyan	ARM	16.2.65	1		Tsakhkadzor	22 May 87
8.79	1.9		Lewis			1	TAC	Indianapolis	19 Jun 83
8.79i	-		Lewis			1		New York	27 Jan 84
8.76	1.0		Lewis			1	USOF	Indianapolis	24 Jul 82
8.76	0.8		Lewis			1	OT	Indianapolis	18 Jul 88
8.75	1.7		Lewis			1	PAG	Indianapolis	16 Aug 87
8.74	1.4	Larry	Myricks	USA	10.3.56	2	OT	Indianapolis	18 Jul 88
8.72	-0.2		Lewis			1	OG	Seoul	26 Sep 88
8.71	-0.4		Lewis			1	Pepsi	Westwood	13 May 84
8.71	0.1		Lewis			1	OT	Los Angeles	19 Jun 84
8.70	0.8		Myricks			1	TAC	Houston	17 Jun 89
8.70	0.7		Powell			1		Salamanca	27 Jul 93
8.68	1.0		Lewis			Q	OG	Barcelona	5 Aug 92
8.67	0.4		Lewis			1	WC	Roma	5 Sep 87
8.67	-0.7		Lewis			1	OG	Barcelona	6 Aug 92
8.66	0.8		Lewis			-	MSR	Walnut	26 Apr 87
8.66	1.0		Myricks			1		Tokyo	23 Sep 87
8.66	0.9		Powell			1	BNP	Villeneuve d'Ascq	29 Jun 90
8.65	0.2		Lewis			1	VD	Bruxelles	24 Aug 84
8.65	0.7		Lewis			1	TAC	San José	26 Jun 87
8.64	1.7		Lewis			1	TAC	New York	15 Jun 91
8.64	-0.5		Powell			2	OG	Barcelona	6 Aug 92
8.63	2.0		Myricks			2	TAC	San José	26 Jun 87
8.63	0.6		Powell			2	TAC	New York	15 Jun 91
8.62	0.8		Lewis			1	TAC	Sacramento	20 Jun 81
8.62	-0.1		Lewis			1	VD	Bruxelles	30 Aug 85
8.62	0.0		Powell			1	OT	New Orleans	24 Jun 92
		(30/5)							
8.54	0.9	Lutz	Dombrowski	GDR	25.6.59	1	OG	Moskva	28 Jul 80
8.53	1.2	Jaime	Jefferson	CUB	17.1.62	1	Barr	Habana	12 May 90
8.53	1.6	Ivan	Pedroso	CUB	17.12.72	1	Ib Am	Sevilla	17 Jul 92
8.53	0.9	Erick	Walder	USA	5.11.71	1	NCAA	New Orleans	3 Jun 93
8.50	0.2	Llewellyn	Starks	USA	10.2.67	2		Rhede	7 Jul 91
		(10)							

Mark	Wind	Name		Nat	Born	Pos	Meet	Venue	Date
8.46	1.2	Leonid	Voloshin	RUS	30.3.66	1	NC	Tallinn	5 Jul 88
8.45	2.0	Nenad	Stekic	YUG	7.3.51	1	PO	Montreal	25 Jul 75
8.44	1.7	Eric	Metcalf	USA	23.1.68	1	TAC	Tampa	17 Jun 88
8.43	0.8	Jason	Grimes	USA	10.9.59	-	TAC	Indianapolis	16 Jun 85
8.43	1.6	Mike	Conley	USA	5.10.62	1		Lausanne	10 Jul 85
8.43	1.8	Giovanni	Evangelisti	ITA	11.9.61	1		San Giovanni Vald.	16 May 87
8.43i	-	Stanislav	Tarasenko	RUS	23.7.66	1		Moskva	26 Jan 94
8.41	1.5	Craig	Hepburn	BAH	10.12.69	1	NC	Nassau	17 Jun 93
8.39	0.8	Dion	Bentley	USA	26.8.71	2	NCAA	New Orleans	3 Jun 93
8.38	0.4	Konstantin	Semykin	RUS	26.5.60	1	Drz	Moskva	17 Aug 84
		(20)							
8.38	-0.1	Joe	Greene	USA	17.2.67	1	Pre	Eugene	6 Jun 92
8.38	0.1	Roland	McGhee	USA	15.10.71	1	JO	Columbus	9 May 93
8.37A	0.4	Leroy	Burrell	USA	21.2.67	2	NCAA	Provo	2 Jun 89
8.36	1.0	João Carlos	de Oliveira	BRA	28.5.54	1		Rieti	21 Jul 79
8.36	1.6	Frank	Pashchek	GDR	25.6.56	1	OD	Berlin	28 May 80
8.36	1.5	Chen Zunrong		CHN	20.10.62	*		Shizuoka	5 May 92
8.36A	0.6	Kareem	Streete-Thompson	USA	30.3.73	1		El Paso	10 Apr 93
8.35	0.0	Ralph	Boston	USA	9.5.39	1	CalR	Modesto	29 May 65
8.35A	0.0	Igor	Ter-Ovanesyan	RUS	19.5.38	1	PO	Ciudad México	19 Oct 67
8.35	0.8	Josef	Schwarz	FRG	20.5.41	1	vUSA	Stuttgart	15 Jul 70
		(30)							
8.35	-0.6	Arnie	Robinson	USA	7.4.48	1	OG	Montreal	29 Jul 76
8.35	2.0	Henry	Lauterbach	GDR	22.10.57	1		Erfurt	2 Aug 81
8.35	2.0	Sergey	Layevskiy	UKR	3.3.59	1		Dnepropetrovsk	16 Jul 88
8.35	1.4	Dmitriy	Bagryanov	RUS	18.12.67	1		Granada	30 May 92
8.34	0.0	Randy	Williams	USA	23.8.53	Q	OG	München	8 Sep 72
8.34	0.0	Vladimir	Ochkan ¶	UKR	13.1.68	1	RigC	Riga	5 Jun 88
8.34	1.1	Nai Hui-Fang		TPE	26.2.69	1	EAsiG	Shanghai	15 May 93
8.33	1.0	Sergey	Rodin	RUS	28.5.63	1		Leningrad	27 Jul 83
8.33i	-	Reggie	Kelly	USA	30.9.62	1		Jackson	3 Dec 83
8.33	2.0	Vladimir	Ratushkov	RUS	1.1.65	1	Znam	Volgograd	11 Jun 89
		(40)							
8.32		Ubaldo	Duany	CUB	16.5.60	2	NC	Santiago de Cuba	22 Feb 86
8.32A		Ralph	Spry	USA	16.6.60	1		Albuquerque	9 Jun 88
8.31	0.7	Atanas	Atanasov	BUL	7.10.56	1		Sofia	4 Jul 84
8.31	1.2	Igor	Streltsov	UKR	1.5.65	2		Dnepropetrovsk	16 Jul 88
8.30	1.8	László	Szálma	HUN	21.10.57	1		Budapest	7 Jul 85
8.30	2.0	Andreas	Steiner	AUT	21.2.64	1		Innsbruck	5 Jun 88
8.30	0.0		Huang Geng	CHN	10.7.70	1	NG	Beijing	9 Sep 93
8.29A		Grigoriy	Petrosyan	ARM	21.2.58	1		Yerevan	20 Oct 86
		(50)	100th best 8.21						
Low altitude marks for athletes with high altitude bests									
8.33	1.3		Beamon			1	AAU	Sacramento	20 Jun 68
8.31	-0.1		Ter-Ovanesyan			1		Yerevan	10 Jun 62
8.31	1.2		Streete-Thompson			3	NCAA	New Orleans	3 Jun 93
Wind-assisted marks									
8.99A	4.4	Mike	Powell	USA	10.11.63	1		Sestriere	21 Jul 92
8.91	2.9	Carl	Lewis	USA	1.7.61	2	WC	Tokyo	30 Aug 91
8.90	3.7		Powell			1	S&W	Modesto	16 May 92
8.79	3.0	Ivan	Pedroso	CUB	17.12.72	1	Barr	Habana	21 May 92
8.77	3.9		Lewis			1	Pepsi	Westwood	18 May 85
8.77	3.4		Lewis			1	MSR	Walnut	26 Apr 87
8.73	4.6		Lewis			Q	TAC	Sacramento	19 Jun 81
8.73	3.2		Lewis			Q	TAC	Indianapolis	17 Jun 83
8.73A	2.6		Powell			1		Sestriere	31 Jul 91
8.72	2.2		Lewis			1	NYG	New York	24 May 92
8.67	3.3		Lewis			1	TAC	Eugene	20 Jun 86
8.66	2.4		Myricks			1	MSR	Walnut	22 Apr 89
8.66A	4.0	Joe	Greene	USA	17.2.67	2		Sestriere	21 Jul 92
8.64A	3.1		Myricks			1	USOF	Air Force Academy	2 Jul 83
8.63	2.1		Lewis			1	Pepsi	Westwood	10 May 81
8.63	3.9	Mike	Conley	USA	5.10.62	2	TAC	Eugene	20 Jun 86
8.58	3.7	Erick	Walder	USA	5.11.71	1	SEC	Starkville	16 May 92
8.57	5.2	Jason	Grimes	USA	10.9.59	1	vFRG,AFR	Durham	27 Jun 82
8.49	2.6	Ralph	Boston	USA	9.5.39	1	FOT	Los Angeles	12 Sep 64

Mark	Wind	Name		Nat	Born	Pos	Meet	Venue	Date
8.46	3.4	Randy	Williams	USA	23.8.53	1		Eugene	18 May 73
8.46		Vernon	George	USA	6.10.64	1		Houston	21 May 89
8.44		Keith	Talley	USA	28.1.64	Q		Odessa	16 May 85
8.42		Anthony	Bailous	USA	6.4.65	Q		Odessa	16 May 85
8.42A	4.5	Milan	Gombala	TCH	29.1.68	3		Sestriere	21 Jul 92
8.41	4.3	Shamil	Abbyasov	KGZ	16.4.57	2	vUSA	Indianapolis	3 Jul 82
8.41	3.3	Andre	Ester	USA	27.4.65	1	TexR	Austin	4 Apr 87
8.40	4.3	Henry	Hines	USA	12.2.49	1	CalR	Modesto	27 May 72
8.40	3.2	Kareem	Streete-Thompson	CAY	30.3.73	1		Houston	5 May 91
8.40	2.1	Anthuan	Maybank	USA	30.12.69	1	DrakeR	Des Moines	24 Apr 93
8.39	6.2	Gary	Honey	AUS	26.7.59	2		Sacramento	21 Jul 84
8.39	3.5	Edrick	Floreal	CAN	5.10.66	1		Fayetteville	22 Apr 89
8.39	5.7	Yusuf	Alli	NGR	28.7.60	1	CG	Auckland	1 Feb 90
8.39	2.4	Chen Zunrong		CHN	20.10.62	1		Shizuoka	5 May 92
8.37	3.5	Arnie	Robinson	USA	7.4.48	1	OT	Eugene	25 Jun 76
8.37	2.8	Jacques	Rousseau	FRA	10.3.51	1	NC	Lille	26 Jun 76
8.37		Sergey	Rodin	RUS	28.5.63	1		Moskva	6 Jul 84
8.36	5.2	Ralph	Spry	USA	16.6.60	1	NCAA	Houston	3 Jun 83
8.35A	5.5	Reggie	Jones	USA	8.5.71	2		Sestriere	28 Jul 93
8.35	2.2	Ivaylo	Mladenov	BUL	6.10.73	1	NC	Sofia	1 Aug 93
8.34		Mike	McRae	USA	9.7.55	1	SW	Modesto	12 May 84
8.34	2.7	Jarmo	Kärnä	FIN	4.8.58	1		Riga	4 Jun 89
8.33		Phil	Shinnick	USA	21.4.43	1	CalR	Modesto	25 May 63
8.33	2.1	Charlton	Ehizuelen	NGR	30.11.53	1	KansR	Lawrence	19 Apr 75
8.33	3.7	Andrzej	Klimaszewski	POL	14.5.60	1	Kuso	Warszawa	13 Jun 80
8.33	3.6	Sergey	Vasilenko	KZK	27.9.65	1B	Znam	Leningrad	11 Jun 88
8.33	5.6	David	Culbert	AUS	17.3.67	1		Melbourne	11 Nov 89
8.32	3.8	David	Giralt	CUB	28.6.59	1	WPT	Québec City	11 Aug 79
8.32A	3.1	Francois	Fouché	RSA	5.6.63	1		Johannesburg	13 May 89
8.32	2.7	Obinna	Eregbu	NGR	9.11.69	1	AfrC	Durban	27 Jun 93
8.31		Mike	Davis	USA	5.1.64	1		Houston	18 May 86
8.31	3.1	Gordon	Laine	USA	24.2.58	4	OT	Indianapolis	18 Jul 88
8.31	5.9	Gordon	McKee	USA	12.10.66	1		San Angelo	12 Apr 90

Supplementary (non-winning) marks

Mark	Wind	Name	Date
8.84	1.7	Lewis	30 Aug 91
8.71	0.6	Lewis	19 Jun 83
8.68	0.3	Lewis	18 Jul 88
8.68	0.0	Lewis	30 Aug 91
8.67	-0.2	Lewis	5 Sep 87
8.66		Lewis	26 Apr 87

Wind-assisted:

Mark	Wind	Name	Date
8.84A38		Powell	21 Jul 92
8.83	2.3	Lewis	30 Aug 91
8.80A	4.0	Powell	21 Jul 92
8.78A		Powell	21 Jul 92
8.75	2.1	Lewis	16 Aug 87
8.75A	3.4	Powell	21 Jul 92
8.73	2.4	Lewis	18 May 85
8.73		Powell	16 May 92
8.71		Powell	31 Jul 91
8.68	3.7	Lewis	16 Aug 87
8.68	4.1	Lewis	16 Aug 87
8.67	2.6	Myricks	17 Jun 89
8.66		Lewis	26 Apr 87

TRIPLE JUMP

Mark	Wind	Name		Nat	Born	Pos	Meet	Venue	Date
17.97	1.5	Willie	Banks	USA	11.3.56	1	TAC	Indianapolis	16 Jun 85
17.93	1.6	Kenny	Harrison	USA	13.2.65	1	DNG	Stockholm	2 Jul 90
17.92	1.6	Khristo	Markov	BUL	27.1.65	1	WC	Roma	31 Aug 87
17.90	1.0	Vladimir	Inozemtsev	UKR	25.5.64	1	GPB	Bratislava	20 Jun 90
17.89A	0.0	João Carlos	de Oliveira	BRA	28.5.54	1	PAG	Ciudad México	15 Oct 75
17.87	1.7	Mike	Conley	USA	5.10.62	1	TAC	San José	27 Jun 87
17.86	1.3	Charles	Simpkins	USA	19.10.63	1	WUG	Kobe	2 Sep 85
17.86	0.3		Conley			1	WC	Stuttgart	16 Aug 93
17.84	0.7		Conley			1		Bad Cannstatt	4 Jul 93
17.81	2.0		Markov			1	Nar	Sofia	31 May 87
17.80	0.6		Markov			1	BGP	Budapest	11 Aug 86
17.79	-0.8		Harrison			1	OD	Berlin	4 Jul 90
17.78	1.0	Nikolay	Musiyenko	UKR	16.12.59	1	Znam	Leningrad	7 Jun 86
17.78	0.6	Lázaro	Betancourt ¶	CUB	18.3.63	1	Barr	Habana	15 Jun 86
17.78	-0.8		Harrison			1	WC	Tokyo	26 Aug 91
17.77	1.9		Markov			1	EP-B	Budapest	11 Aug 85
17.77	1.0	Aleksandr	Kovalenko (10)	RUS	8.5.63	1	NC	Bryansk	18 Jul 87
17.77	1.4		Markov			1	NC	Sofia	3 Sep 88
17.77i	-	Leonid	Voloshin	RUS	30.3.66	1		Grenoble	6 Feb 94
17.76i	-		Conley			1	TAC	New York	27 Feb 87
17.75	0.3	Oleg	Protsenko	RUS	11.8.63	1	Znam	Moskva	10 Jun 90
17.75	1.0		Voloshin			2	WC	Tokyo	26 Aug 91

Mark	Wind	Name		Nat	Born	Pos	Meet	Venue	Date
17.74	0.0		Harrison			1		Grossetto	13 Aug 90
17.74	0.8		Voloshin			1	EC	Split	31 Aug 90
17.72	0.9		Harrison			1	GWG	Seattle	26 Jul 90
17.72	0.1		Conley			1	WK	Zürich	19 Aug 92
17.71	1.9		Conley			2	TAC	Indianapolis	16 Jun 85
17.71	2.0		Banks			1		Barcelona	8 Jul 85
17.69	1.0		Protsenko			1	NC	Leningrad	4 Aug 85
17.69	0.2		Conley			1	GWG	Moskva	9 Jul 86
17.69	1.5	Igor	Lapshin	BLS	8.8.63	1		Minsk	31 Jul 88
		(31/13)							
17.68	-0.5	Yoelvis	Quesada	CUB	4.8.73	1	Barr	Habana	23 May 93
17.66	1.7	Ralf	Jaros	GER	13.12.65	1	EP	Frankfurt-am-Main	30 Jun 91
17.65	1.0	Aleksandr	Yakovlev	UKR	8.9.57	1	Znam	Moskva	6 Jun 87
17.60	0.6	Vladimir	Plekhanov	RUS	11.4.58	2	NC	Leningrad	4 Aug 85
17.59i	-	Pierre	Camara	FRA	10.9.65	1	WI	Toronto	13 Mar 93
17.59	0.3	Vasiliy	Sokov	RUS	7.4.68	1	NC	Moskva	19 Jun 93
17.58	1.5	Oleg	Sakirkin	KZK	23.1.66	2	NC	Gorkiy	23 Jul 89
		(20)							
17.57A	0.0	Keith	Connor	GBR	16.9.57	1	NCAA	Provo	5 Jun 82
17.56	1.9	Maris	Bruziks	LAT	25.8.62	1		Riga	3 Sep 88
17.55	0.3	Vasiliy	Grishchenkov	RUS	23.1.58	1	Spa	Moskva	19 Jun 83
17.54	0.5	Denis	Kapustin	RUS	5.10.70	2		Bad Cannstatt	4 Jul 93
17.53	1.0	Aleksandr	Beskrovniy	RUS	5.4.60	2	Spa	Moskva	19 Jun 83
17.53	1.6	Zdzislaw	Hoffmann	POL	27.8.59	1		Madrid	4 Jun 85
17.53	1.0	Gennadiy	Valyukevich	BLS	1.6.58	1		Erfurt	1 Jun 86
17.53	1.6	Al	Joyner	USA	19.1.60	Q	TAC	San José	26 Jun 87
17.53	0.9	Milán	Mikulás	TCH	1.4.63	1	NC	Praha	17 Jul 88
17.53	1.9	Oleg	Denishchik	BLS	10.11.69	2	NC	Kiev	12 Jul 91
		(30)							
17.50	0.4	Volker	Mai	GDR	3.5.66	1	vURS	Erfurt	23 Jun 85
17.48	1.9	Jorge	Reyna	CUB	10.1.63	1		Santiago de Cuba	27 Feb 87
17.46	1.7	Ken	Lorraway	AUS	6.2.56	1		London	7 Aug 82
17.45	1.9	Aleksandr	Leonov ¶	BLS	7.2.62	1		Sochi	24 May 87
17.45	1.0	Serge	Hélan	FRA	24.2.64	1	NC	Dijon	27 Jul 91
17.44	-0.?	Viktor	Saneyev	GEO	3.10.45	1		Sukhumi	17 Oct 72
17.44	2.0	Dirk	Gamlin	GDR	26.10.63	1		Dresden	7 Jul 85
17.44	0.1	Jonathan	Edwards	GBR	10.5.66	3	WC	Stuttgart	16 Aug 93
17.43	0.0	Peter	Bouschen	FRG	16.5.60	1		Düsseldorf	2 Jun 88
17.41	0.0	John	Herbert	GBR	20.4.62	3	WUG	Kobe	2 Sep 85
		(40)							
17.41	-0.8	Frank	Rutherford	BAH	23.11.64	2	GP	São Paulo	17 May 92
17.40A	0.4	Pedro	Pérez Dueñas	CUB	23.2.52	1	PAG	Cali	5 Aug 71
17.40	1.9	Oleg	Grokhovskiy	KZK	3.5.68	2	NP	Alma-Ata	8 Sep 91
17.37	0.7	Vyacheslav	Bordukov	RUS	1.1.59	2	Nar	Sofia	19 May 84
17.37i	-	Vasif	Asadov	AZE	27.8.65	2	NC	Volgograd	12 Feb 88
17.36	1.3	Ray	Kimble	USA	19.4.53	1	S&W	Modesto	9 May 87
17.36	1.8	Vladimir	Chernikov	UZB	3.8.59	1		Odessa	21 Aug 88
17.35	-0.3	Jaak	Uudmäe	EST	3.9.54	1	OG	Moskva	25 Jul 80
17.35	1.7	Jacek	Pastusinski	POL	8.9.64	5	WC	Roma	31 Aug 87
17.34	0.3	Zou Zhenxian		CHN	10.11.55	2	WP	Roma	5 Sep 81
17.34	0.1	Ján	Cado	TCH	7.5.63	1	PTS	Bratislava	26 May 84
		(51)	100th best 17.17						

Best outdoor marks for athlete with lifetime bests indoors

Camara: 17.34 1.5 (Q) OG Barcelona 1 Aug 92 and 17.46w 2.4 (1) EP Roma 27 Jun 93

Wind-assisted marks

Mark	Wind	Name		Nat	Born	Pos	Meet	Venue	Date
18.20	5.2	Willie	Banks	USA	11.3.56	1	OT	Indianapolis	16 Jul 88
18.17	2.1	Mike	Conley	USA	5.10.62	1	OG	Barcelona	3 Aug 92
17.93	5.2	Charles	Simpkins	USA	19.10.63	2	OT	Indianapolis	16 Jul 88
17.91	3.2		Simpkins			1	TAC	Eugene	21 Jun 86
17.86	3.9		Simpkins			1	OT	New Orleans	21 Jun 92
17.84	2.3		Conley			2	TAC	Eugene	21 Jun 86
17.82	3.6		Banks			1	Jen	San José	31 May 86
17.81	4.6	Keith	Connor	GBR	16.9.57	1	CG	Brisbane	9 Oct 82
17.75		Gennadiy	Valyukevich	BLS	1.6.58	1		Uzhgorod	27 Apr 86
17.74	3.5		Harrison			1	Oda	Hiroshima	3 May 89
17.73	4.1	Vasiliy	Sokov	RUS	7.4.68	1		Riga	3 Jun 89
17.72	3.2		Conley			1	NCAA	Austin	1 Jun 85

Mark	Wind	Name		Nat	Born	Pos	Meet	Venue	Date
17.70	2.9	Jonathan	Edwards	GBR	10.5.66	1	v USA	Edinburgh	2 Jul 93
17.63	4.3	Robert	Cannon	USA	9.7.58	3	OT	Indianapolis	16 Jul 88
17.58	5.2	Al	Joyner	USA	19.1.60	5	OT	Indianapolis	16 Jul 88
17.56	3.7	Ron	Livers	USA	20.7.55	1	AAU	Walnut	17 Jun 79
17.55	3.6	Zdzislaw	Hoffmann	POL	27.8.59	1	Kuso	Warszawa	9 Jun 84
17.54	3.2	Ken	Lorraway	AUS	6.2.56	2	CG	Brisbane	9 Oct 82
17.53	4.8	Ray	Kimble	USA	19.4.53	7	OT	Indianapolis	16 Jul 88
17.51	3.0	Chen Yanping		CHN	17.1.66	1	AsG	Beijing	3 Oct 90
17.48	2.9	Georges	Sainte-Rose	FRA	3.9.69	1		Montgeron	23 Jun 91
17.47	3.7	Joseph	Taiwo	NGR	24.8.59	1	GP	São Paulo	17 May 92
17.41	4.7	Brian	Wellman	BER	8.9.67	1	SWC	Houston	19 May 91
17.38	4.2	Milan	Tiff	USA	5.7.49	1	AAU	Westwood	11 Jun 77
17.38	2.8	Vyacheslav	Bordukov	RUS	1.1.59	1		Moskva	16 Aug 87

Ancillary marks

Mark	Wind	Name	Date
17.77		Inozemtsev	20 Jun 90
17.77	-0.3	Conley	16 Aug 93
17.76	1.1	Conley	4 Jul 93
17.74	1.2	Markov	11 Aug 86
17.73	1.9	Markov	31 Aug 87
17.73	1.6	Markov	3 Sep 88

Wind-assisted

Mark	Wind	Name	Date
18.06	4.9	Banks	16 Jul 88
17.75	2.3	Markov	3 Sep 88
17.72	3.8	Connor	9 Oct 82

SHOT

Mark		Name		Nat	Born	Pos	Meet	Venue	Date
23.12		Randy	Barnes ¶	USA	16.6.66	1		Westwood	20 May 90
23.10			Barnes			1	Jen	San José	26 May 90
23.06		Ulf	Timmermann	GDR	1.11.62	1		Khania	22 May 88
22.91		Alessandro	Andrei	ITA	3.1.59	1		Viareggio	12 Aug 87
22.86		Brian	Oldfield	USA	1.6.45	1	ITA	El Paso	10 May 75
22.75		Werner	Günthör	SUI	1.6.61	1		Bern	23 Aug 88
22.66i			Barnes			1	Sunkist	Los Angeles	20 Jan 89
22.64		Udo	Beyer	GDR	9.8.55	1		Berlin	20 Aug 86
22.62			Timmermann			1		Berlin	22 Sep 85
22.61			Timmermann			1		Potsdam	8 Sep 88
22.60			Timmermann			1	vURS	Tallinn	21 Jun 86
22.56			Timmermann			1		Berlin	13 Sep 88
22.55i			Timmermann			1	NC	Senftenberg	11 Feb 89
22.52		John	Brenner	USA	4.1.61	1	MSR	Walnut	26 Apr 87
22.51			Timmermann			1		Erfurt	1 Jun 86
22.47			Timmermann			1		Dresden	17 Aug 86
22.47			Günthör			1	WG	Helsinki	2 Jul 87
22.47			Timmermann			1	OG	Seoul	23 Sep 88
22.45			Oldfield			1	ITA	El Paso	22 May 76
22.43			Günthör			1	v3-N	Lüdenscheid	18 Jun 87
22.42			Barnes			1	WK	Zürich	17 Aug 88
22.39			Barnes			2	OG	Seoul	23 Sep 88
22.36+			Timmermann			1		Athinai	16 May 88
22.31			Beyer			1	NC	Potsdam	20 Aug 87
22.28			Oldfield			1	ITA	Edinburgh	18 Jun 75
22.28			Barnes			1	MSR	Walnut	22 Apr 90
22.26i			Günthör			1	NC	Magglingen	8 Feb 87
22.26			Brenner			1		Westwood	18 Apr 87
22.25			Günthör			1	WK	Zürich	19 Aug 87
22.24		Sergey	Smirnov	RUS	17.9.60	2	vGDR	Tallinn	21 Jun 86
22.24i			Timmermann			1	WC	Indianapolis	7 Mar 87
		(31/8)							
22.10		Sergey	Gavryushin	RUS	27.6.59	1		Tbilisi	31 Aug 86
22.09		Sergey	Kasnauskas	BLS	20.4.61	1		Staiki	23 Aug 84
		(10)							
22.02i		George	Woods	USA	11.2.43	1	LAT	Inglewood	8 Feb 74
22.02		Dave	Laut	USA	21.12.56	1		Koblenz	25 Aug 82
22.00		Aleksandr	Baryshnikov	RUS	11.11.48	1	vFRA	Colombes	10 Jul 76
21.98		Gregg	Tafralis	USA	9.4.58	1		Los Gatos	13 Jun 92
21.96		Mikhail	Kostin	RUS	10.5.59	1		Vitebsk	20 Jul 86
21.93		Remigius	Machura ¶	TCH	3.7.60	1		Praha	23 Aug 87
21.85		Terry	Albritton	USA	14.1.55	1		Honolulu	21 Feb 76
21.82		Al	Feuerbach	USA	14.1.48	1		San José	5 May 73
21.78		Randy	Matson	USA	5.3.45	1		College Station	22 Apr 67
21.77i		Mike	Stulce ¶	USA	21.7.69	1	v GBR	Birmingham	13 Feb 93
		(20)							

Mark	Wind	Name		Nat	Born	Pos	Meet	Venue	Date
21.76		Mike	Carter	USA	29.10.60	2	NCAA	Eugene	2 Jun 84
21.74		Janis	Bojars	LAT	12.5.56	1		Riga	14 Jul 84
21.73		Augie	Wolf ¶	USA	3.9.61	1		Leverkusen	12 Apr 84
21.69		Reijo	Ståhlberg	FIN	21.9.52	1	WCR	Fresno	5 May 79
21.68		Geoff	Capes	GBR	23.8.49	1	4-N	Cwmbran	18 May 80
21.68		Edward	Sarul	POL	16.11.58	1		Sopot	31 Jul 83
21.67		Hartmut	Briesenick	GDR	17.3.49	1		Potsdam	1 Sep 73
21.61		Kevin	Akins	USA	27.1.60	1	S&W	Modesto	14 May 83
21.60		Jim	Doehring	USA	27.1.62	2		Los Gatos	13 Jun 92
21.58		Vladimir	Kiselyov	UKR	1.1.57	3	Drz	Moskva	17 Aug 84
		(30)							
21.53		Yevgeniy	Mironov ¶	RUS	1.11.49	1	NC	Kiev	24 Jun 76
21.51		Ralf	Reichenbach	FRG	31.7.50	1	ISTAF	Berlin	8 Aug 80
21.44		Mikhail	Domorosov	BLS	5.3.55	2		Staiki	23 Aug 84
21.43		Mike	Lehmann	USA	11.3.60	2	Jen	San José	28 May 83
21.42i		Fred	DeBernardi	USA	2.3.49	1	ITA	Portland	20 Apr 74
21.42		Aleksandr	Bagach ¶	UKR	21.11.66	1	NC	Gorkiy	22 Jul 89
21.35		Ron	Semkiw	USA	28.3.54	1		Mesa	5 Mar 74
21.35		Sergey	Nikolayev	RUS	12.11.66	1		Voronezh	5 Aug 89
21.33		Hans	Höglund	SWE	23.7.52	1	NCAA	Provo	6 Jun 75
21.32		Heinz-Joachim	Rothenburg	GDR	9.4.44	1		Potsdam	3 Jun 72
		(40)							
21.31		Hans-Peter	Gies	GDR	9.5.47	2		Potsdam	25 Aug 72
21.30		Helmut	Krieger	POL	17.7.58	1	NC	Grudziadz	27 Jun 86
21.29		Kevin	Toth	USA	29.12.67	1		Hechtel	31 Jul 93
21.26		Pétur	Gudmundsson	ISL	9.3.62	1		Mosfellsbaer	10 Nov 90
21.26		Dragan	Peric	YUG	8.5.64	1	NC	Beograd	24 Jul 93
21.25		Hans-Jürgen	Jacobi	GDR	26.7.50	2	NC	Cottbus	16 Jul 80
21.25i		Maris	Petrashko	LAT	6.3.61	1		Vilnius	7 Jan 89
21.24i		Sören	Tallhem	SWE	16.2.64	1	NCAA	Syracuse	9 Mar 85
21.22		Lars Arvid	Nilsen ¶	NOR	15.4.65	1	NCAA	Indianapolis	6 Jun 86
21.22		Klaus	Görmer	GDR	5.7.63	3	NC	Potsdam	20 Aug 87
		(50)	100th best 20.78						

Not recognised by GDR authorities

Mark	Wind	Name		Nat	Born	Pos	Meet	Venue	Date
22.11		Rolf	Oesterreich	GDR	24.8.49	1		Zschopau	12 Sep 76

Subsequent to drugs disqualification

Mark	Wind	Name		Nat	Born	Pos	Meet	Venue	Date
22.84			Barnes			1		Malmö	7 Aug 90
21.82		Mike	Stulce	USA	14.7.69	1		Brenham	9 May 90

Best outdoor marks for athletes with lifetime bests indoors

Mark	Name	Pos	Meet	Venue	Date
21.70	Stulce ¶	1	OG	Barcelona	31 Jul 92
21.63	Woods	2	CalR	Modesto	22 May 76
21.41	DeBernardi	1	ITA	El Paso	27 Apr 74

Ancillary marks at 22.01 or better

Mark	Name	Date	Mark	Name	Date	Mark	Name	Date
22.84	Andrei	12 Aug 87	22.72	Andrei	12 Aug 87	22.55	Barnes	20 May 90
22.76	Barnes	20 May 90	22.70	Günthör	23 Aug 88	22.45	Timmermann	22 May 88
22.74	Andrei	12 Aug 87	22.58	Beyer	20 Aug 86	22.44	Barnes	20 May 90

DISCUS

Mark	Wind	Name		Nat	Born	Pos	Meet	Venue	Date
74.08		Jürgen	Schult	GDR	11.5.60	1		Neubrandenburg	6 Jun 86
71.86		Yuriy	Dumchev	RUS	5.8.58	1		Moskva	29 May 83
71.32		Ben	Plucknett ¶	USA	13.4.54	1	Pre	Eugene	4 Jun 83
71.26		John	Powell	USA	25.6.47	1	TAC	San José	9 Jun 84
71.26		Rickard	Bruch	SWE	2.7.46	1		Malmö	15 Nov 84
71.26		Imrich	Bugár	TCH	14.4.55	1	Jen	San José	25 May 85
71.18		Art	Burns	USA	19.7.54	1		San José	19 Jul 83
71.16		Wolfgang	Schmidt	GDR	16.1.54	1		Berlin	9 Aug 78
71.14			Plucknett			1		Berkeley	12 Jun 83
71.06		Luis M.	Delís ¶	CUB	6.12.57	1	Barr	Habana	21 May 83
71.00			Bruch			1		Malmö	14 Oct 84
70.98		Mac	Wilkins (10)	USA	15.11.50	1	WG	Helsinki	9 Jul 80
70.98			Burns			1	Pre	Eugene	21 Jul 84
70.92			Schmidt	FRG		1		Norden	9 Sep 89
70.86			Wilkins			1		San José	1 May 76
70.82			Plucknett			1		Salinas	1 Jun 83
70.72			Bugár			1	vHUN,AUT	Schwechat	18 Jun 83
70.66			Wilkins			1	AAU	Walnut	16 Jun 79
70.58			Delís			1		Salinas	19 May 82

Mark	Wind	Name	Nat	Born	Pos	Meet	Venue	Date
70.48		Wilkins			1		San José	29 Apr 78
70.48		Wilkins			1	Pre	Eugene	31 May 78
70.48		Bruch			1		Malmö	12 Sep 84
70.46		Schult			1		Berlin	13 Sep 88
70.44		Wilkins			2	TAC	San José	9 Jun 84
70.38		Jay Silvester	USA	27.8.37	1		Lancaster	16 May 71
70.36		Wilkins			1	SW	Modesto	14 May 83
70.30		Dumchev			1		Bryansk	31 Jul 88
70.26		Bugár			1	vITA	Cagliari	8 Sep 84
70.24		Schmidt			1		Potsdam	18 Aug 78
70.24		Bugár			1		Nitra	26 Aug 84
		(30/11)						
70.06		Romas Ubartas ¶	LIT	26.5.60	1		Smolininkay	8 May 88
70.00		Juan Martínez ¶	CUB	17.5.58	2	Barr	Habana	21 May 83
69.70		Gejza Valent	TCH	3.10.53	2		Nitra	26 Aug 84
69.62		Knut Hjeltnes ¶	NOR	8.12.51	2	Jen	San José	25 May 85
69.46		Al Oerter	USA	19.9.36	1	TFA	Wichita	31 May 80
69.44		Georgiy Kolnootchenko	BLS	7.5.59	1	vUSA	Indianapolis	3 Jul 82
69.40		Art Swarts ¶	USA	14.2.45	1		Scotch Plains	8 Dec 79
69.36		Mike Buncic	USA	25.7.62	1		Fresno	6 Apr 91
69.26		Ken Stadel	USA	19.2.52	2	AAU	Walnut	16 Jun 79
		(20)						
68.88		Vladimir Zinchenko	UKR	25.7.59	1		Dnepropetrovsk	16 Jul 88
68.66		Lars Riedel	GER	28.6.67	1	ISTAF	Berlin	21 Aug 92
68.64		Dmitriy Kovtsun ¶	UKR	29.9.55	1		Riga	6 Jul 84
68.52		Igor Duginyets	UKR	20.5.56	1	NC	Kiev	21 Aug 82
68.50		Armin Lemme	GDR	28.10.55	1	vUSA	Karl-Marx-Stadt	10 Jul 82
68.48		John van Reenen	RSA	26.3.47	1		Stellenbosch	14 Mar 75
68.44		Vaclavas Kidikas	LIT	17.10.61	1		Sochi	1 Jun 88
68.30		Stefan Fernholm	SWE	2.7.59	1		Västerås	15 Jul 87
68.12		Markku Tuokko ¶	FIN	24.6.51	1	WCR	Fresno	5 May 79
68.12		Iosif Nagy	ROM	20.11.46	2		Zaragoza	22 May 83
		(30)						
68.12		Erik de Bruin	HOL	25.5.63	1		Sneek	1 Apr 91
68.08		Hein-Direck Neu ¶	FRG	13.2.44	1		Bremerhaven	27 May 77
68.00		Svein Inge Valvik	NOR	20.9.56	1		Juarez	31 May 82
67.88		Tony Washington	USA	16.1.66	1	S&W	Modesto	16 May 92
67.82		Velko Velev ¶	BUL	4.1.48	1		Riga	13 Aug 78
67.80		Alwin Wagner	FRG	11.8.50	1		Melsungen	1 Jul 87
67.80		Adewale Olukoju	NGR	27.7.68	1	S&W	Modesto	11 May 91
67.76		Vitaliy Pishchalnikov	RUS	1.4.58	1		Stavropol	9 May 84
67.64		Vésteinn Hafsteinsson ¶	ISL	12.12.60	1		Selfoss	31 May 89
67.62		Randy Heisler	USA	7.8.61	1		Bloomington	29 Jun 87
		(40)						
67.62		Marco Martino	ITA	21.2.60	1	v4N	Spoleto	28 May 89
67.60		Rolf Danneberg	FRG	1.3.53	1		Berlin	30 May 87
67.56		Wolfgang Warnemünde	GDR	8.5.53	1		Rostock	2 Jun 80
67.54		Siegfried Pachale	GDR	24.10.49	1		Karl-Marx-Stadt	29 May 76
67.54		Hilmar Hossfeld	GDR	18.1.54	2	OT	Jena	17 May 80
67.54		Werner Hartmann	FRG	20.4.59	1		Georgsheil	29 Apr 82
67.38		Tim Vollmer	USA	13.9.46	2		Lancaster	16 May 71
67.38		Ferenc Tégla	HUN	15.7.47	1		Szentes	12 Oct 77
67.32		Rob Gray ¶	CAN	5.10.56	1		Etobicoke	30 Apr 84
67.30		Ion Zamfirache	ROM	23.8.53	1		Bucuresti	19 May 85
67.30		Dmitriy Shevchenko	RUS	13.5.68	1		Sochi	29 May 92
		(51) 100th best 65.68						

not a single change to the world top 50 and only one to the top 100 in 1993!

Subsequent to drugs disqualification ! recognised as US record

Mark	Wind	Name	Nat	Born	Pos	Meet	Venue	Date
72.34!		Ben Plucknett	USA	13.4.54	1	DNG	Stockholm	7 Jul 81
71.20		Plucknett			1	CalR	Modesto	16 May 81
70.84		Kamy Keshmiri ¶	USA	23.1.69	1		Salinas	27 May 92

Sloping ground

Mark	Wind	Name	Nat	Born	Pos	Meet	Venue	Date
72.08		John Powell	USA	25.6.47	1		Klagshamn	11 Sep 87
69.80		Stefan Fernholm	SWE	2.7.59	1		Klagshamn	13 Aug 87

Ancillary marks

71.08 Plucknett 4 Jun 83 70.40 Wilkins 31 May 78

HAMMER

Mark	Wind	Name		Nat	Born	Pos	Meet	Venue	Date
86.74		Yuriy	Sedykh	RUS	11.6.55	1	EC	Stuttgart	30 Aug 86
86.66			Sedykh			1	vGDR	Tallinn	22 Jun 86
86.34			Sedykh			1		Cork	3 Jul 84
86.04		Sergey	Litvinov	RUS	23.1.58	1	OD	Dresden	3 Jul 86
85.74			Litvinov			2	EC	Stuttgart	30 Aug 86
85.68			Sedykh			1	BGP	Budapest	11 Aug 86
85.60			Sedykh			1	PTG	London	13 Jul 84
85.60			Sedykh			1	Drz	Moskva	17 Aug 84
85.20			Litvinov			2		Cork	3 Jul 84
85.14			Litvinov			1	PTG	London	11 Jul 86
85.14			Sedykh			1	Kuts	Moskva	4 Sep 88
85.02			Sedykh			1	BGP	Budapest	20 Aug 84
84.92			Sedykh			2	OD	Dresden	3 Jul 86
84.88			Litvinov			1	GP-GG	Roma	10 Sep 86
84.80			Litvinov			1	OG	Seoul	26 Sep 88
84.72			Sedykh			1	GWG	Moskva	9 Jul 86
84.64			Litvinov			2	GWG	Moskva	9 Jul 86
84.62		Igor	Astapkovich	BLS	4.1.63	1	Expo	Sevilla	6 Jun 92
84.60			Sedykh			1	8-N	Tokyo	14 Sep 84
84.58			Sedykh			1	Znam	Leningrad	8 Jun 86
84.48		Igor	Nikulin	RUS	14.8.60	1	Athl	Lausanne	12 Jul 90
84.46			Sedykh			1		Vladivostok	14 Sep 88
84.40		Jüri	Tamm	EST	5.2.57	1		Banská Bystrica	9 Sep 84
84.36			Litvinov			2	vGDR	Tallinn	22 Jun 86
84.26			Sedykh			1	Nik	Nice	15 Jul 86
84.26			Astapkovich			1		Reims	3 Jul 91
84.16			Tamm			1		Kharkov	19 Jun 88
84.14			Litvinov			1	Spart	Moskva	21 Jun 83
84.14			Sedykh			1	WG	Helsinki	7 Jul 86
84.14			Astapkovich			1	EC	Split	31 Aug 90
		(30/5)							
83.46		Andrey	Abduvaliyev	TJK	30.6.66	1		Adler	26 May 90
83.40@		Ralf	Haber	GDR	18.8.62	1		Athinai	16 May 88
		82.54				1		Potsdam	9 Sep 88
82.84		Heinz	Weis	FRG	14.7.63	1	ISTAF	Berlin	18 Aug 89
82.64		Günther	Rodehau	GDR	6.7.59	1		Dresden	3 Aug 85
82.54		Vasiliy	Sidorenko	RUS	1.5.61	1		Krasnodar	24 May 92
		(10)							
82.54		Sergey	Kirmasov	RUS	25.3.70	1		Sochi	22 May 93
82.40		Plamen	Minev	BUL	28.4.65	1	NM	Plovdiv	1 Jun 91
82.24		Benjaminas	Viluckis	LIT	20.3.61	1		Klaipeda	24 Aug 86
82.24		Vyacheslav	Korovin	RUS	8.9.62	1		Chelyabinsk	20 Jun 87
82.16		Vitaliy	Alisevich	BLS	15.6.67	1		Parnu	13 Jul 88
82.08		Ivan	Tanev	BUL	1.5.57	1	NC	Sofia	3 Sep 88
82.00		Sergey	Alay	BLS	11.6.65	1		Staiki	12 May 92
81.88		Jud	Logan ¶	USA	19.7.59	1		University Park	22 Apr 88
81.78		Christoph	Sahner	FRG	23.9.63	1		Wemmetsweiler	11 Sep 88
81.70		Aleksandr	Seleznyov	RUS	25.1.63	2		Sochi	22 May 93
		(20)							
81.68		Tibor	Gécsek	HUN	22.9.64	1		Szombathely	13 Sep 88
81.52		Juha	Tiainen	FIN	5.12.55	1		Tampere	11 Jun 84
81.44		Yuriy	Tarasyuk	BLS	11.4.57	1		Minsk	10 Aug 84
81.32		Klaus	Ploghaus	FRG	31.1.56	1		Paderborn	25 May 86
81.20		Igor	Grigorash	RUS	18.8.59	1		Kiev	23 Aug 84
81.18		Albert	Sinka	HUN	22.11.62	1		Székesfehérvár	7 Aug 88
81.10		Sergey	Ivanov	RUS	3.1.62	1		Chelyabinsk	27 Jun 87
81.08		Lance	Deal	USA	21.8.61	1		Eugene	16 May 92
80.92		Matthias	Moder	GDR	17.6.63	1		Halle	11 Jun 85
80.90		Yaroslav	Chmyr	UKR	29.11.67	1		Chernigov	2 Jun 90
		(30)							
80.80		Karl-Hans	Riehm	FRG	31.5.51	1		Rhede	30 Jul 80
80.80		Andrey	Skvaryuk	UKR	9.3.67	1		Kiev	3 May 93
80.78		Donatas	Plunge	LIT	11.11.60	1		Volgograd	22 Sep 89

Mark	Wind	Name		Nat	Born	Pos	Meet	Venue	Date
80.68		Viktor	Litvinenko	UKR	22.12.57	2		Kiev	23 Aug 84
80.64		Emanuil	Dyulgherov	BUL	7.2.55	1		Sofia	25 Aug 84
80.62		Viktor	Apostolov ¶	BUL	1.10.62	1		Sofia	28 Jul 90
80.60		Imre	Szitás	HUN	4.9.61	1		Szombathely	11 Jul 88
80.50		Detlef	Gerstenberg	GDR	5.3.57	1		Berlin	15 Jul 84
80.48		Boris	Zaychuk	RUS	28.8.47	2		Sochi	24 May 80
80.38		Frantisek	Vrbka	TCH	23.7.58	2	EP	Moskva	18 Aug 85
		(40)							
80.36		Aleksey	Krykun	UKR	12.12.68	1		Donetsk	29 May 93
80.32		Nikolay	Lysenko	RUS	14.7.66	1		Ordzhonikidze	24 Sep 88
80.24		Grigoriy	Shevtsov	RUS	16.8.58	1		Volgograd	9 May 83
80.20		Igor	Shchegolev	RIS	26.10.60	1		Volgograd	6 Sep 86
80.18		Zdzislaw	Kwasny	POL	6.11.60	2	EP	London	21 Aug 83
80.16		Anatoliy	Chyuzhas	BLS	18.4.56	2		Klaipeda	27 May 84
80.14		Tore	Gustafsson	SWE	11.2.62	1		Lappeenranta	4 Jul 89
80.02		Ken	Flax	USA	20.4.63	1	S&W	Modesto	7 May 88
79.98		Christophe	Epalle	FRA	23.1.69	1		Clermont-Ferrand	20 May 93
79.92		Jörg	Schaefer	FRG	17.7.59	1	ISTAF	Berlin	15 Aug 86
		(50)	100th best 77.80						

@ Meeting held under normal competitive conditions, but unsanctioned by GDR federation

Extra trial 81.04 Mariusz Tomaszewski POL 23.4.56 - Zabrze 1 Jul 84

Chain exceeding maximum legal length: 81.12 Grigoriy Shevtsov 1 Sochi 12 May 83

Questionable measurement: 82.40 Plamen Minev 1 Sofia 8 Aug 87

Ancillary marks

86.68	Sedykh	30 Aug 86	85.52	Sedykh	13 Jul 84	85.26	Sedykh	11 Aug 86
86.62	Sedykh	30 Aug 86	85.46	Sedykh	30 Aug 86	85.24	Sedykh	11 Aug 86
86.00	Sedykh	3 Jul 84	85.42	Sedykh	11 Aug 86	85.20	Sedykh	3 Jul 84
86.00	Sedykh	22 Jun 86	85.42	Litvinov	3 Jul 86	85.04	Sedykh	13 Jul 84
85.82	Sedykh	22 Jun 86	85.28	Sedykh	30 Aug 86			

JAVELIN

For the first time this year, performances known to have been made made with the now-banned roughnehed tail javelins (mostly used in 1991) have been placed in a separate list at the end of this section.

Mark	Wind	Name		Nat	Born	Pos	Meet	Venue	Date
95.66		Jan	Zelezny	TCH	16.6.66	1	McD	Sheffield	29 Aug 93
95.54A			Zelezny			1		Pietersburg	6 Apr 93
94.74	Irreg		Zelezny			1	Bisl	Oslo	4 Jul 92
91.46		Steve	Backley	GBR	12.2.69	1		North Shore City	25 Jan 92
91.40			Zelezny			1	BNP	Villeneuve d'Ascq	2 Jul 93
90.68			Zelezny			1	Nik	Nice	21 Jul 93
90.60			Zelezny			1		Stellenbosch	13 Apr 93
90.60		Seppo	Räty	FIN	27.4.62	1		Nurmijärvi	20 Jul 92
90.18			Zelezny			1	TOTO	Tokyo	19 Sep 92
90.06		Raymond	Hecht	GER	11.11.68	1		Eichenbach	12 Feb 94
90.02			Zelezny			1	GS	Ostrava	24 Jun 92
89.66			Zelezny			1	OG	Barcelona	8 Aug 92
89.64			Zelezny			1	EP	Roma	27 Jun 93
89.58			Backley			1	DNG	Stockholm	2 Jul 90
89.16A		Tom	Petranoff	USA	8.4.58	1		Potchefstroom	1 Mar 91
89.10		Patrik	Bodén	SWE	30.6.67	1		Austin	24 Mar 90
89.00			Räty			1	vSWE	Heslinki	29 Aug 92
88.90			Hecht			2	BNP	Villeneuve d'Ascq	2 Jul 93
88.46			Backley			1	NC	Cardiff	3 Jun90
88.36			Räty			2	TOTO	Tokyo	19 Sep 92
88.36			Zelezny			1	Athl	Lausanne	7 Jul 93
88.34			Zelezny			1		Lahti	25 Aug 92
88.28			Zelezny			1	GPF	London	10 Sep 93
88.26			Zelezny			1	WP	Habana	27 Sep 92
88.26			Bodén			1		Reykjavik	17 Jun 93
88.22		Juha	Laukkanen	FIN	6.1.69	1		Kuortane	20 Jun 92
88.14			Backley			1	AAA	Birmingham	28 Jun 92
87.94			Backley			2	Bisl	Oslo	14 Jul 90
87.72			Backley			1	TSB	London	10 Jul 92
87.66			Zelezny			1		Nitra	31 May 87
		(30/7)							
87.60		Kazuhiro	Mizoguchi	JPN	18.3.62	1	Jen	San José	27 May 89

Mark	Wind	Name		Nat	Born	Pos	Meet	Venue	Date
87.20		Viktor	Zaitsev	UZB	6.6.66	1	OT	Moskva	23 Jun 92
87.08		Vladimir	Sasimovich	BLS	14.9.68	3	WC	Tokyo	26 Aug 91
		(10)							
86.94		Mike	Hill	GBR	22.10.64	1	NC	London	13 Jun 93
86.80		Einar	Vihljálmsson	ISL	1.6.60	1		Reykjavik	29 Aug 92
86.64		Klaus	Tafelmeier	FRG	12.4.58	1	NC	Gelsenkirchen	12 Jul 87
86.50		Tapio	Korjus	FIN	10.2.61	1		Lahti	25 Aug 88
86.20		Andrey	Moruyev	RUS	8.5.70	1	CISM	Tours	28 Oct 93
86.14		Gavin	Lovegrove	NZL	21.10.67	1		Wellington	18 Jan 92
85.74		Dmitriy	Polyunin ¶	UZB	6.4.69	2	OT	Moskva	23 Jun 92
85.70		Andrey	Shevchuk	RUS	8.3.70	2	Slovn	Bratislava	1 Jun 93
85.70		Tom	Pukstys	USA	28.5.68	2		Kuortane	26 Jun 93
85.16		Viktor	Yevsyukov	KZK	6.10.56	1	vGDR	Karl-Marx-Stadt	21 Jun 87
		(20)							
84.86		Ramón	González	CUB	24.8.65	1		Potsdam	3 Jul 90
84.84		Volker	Hadwich	GDR	23.9.64	1	vITA,TCH	Macerata	5 Sep 89
84.80		Pascal	Lefévre	FRA	25.1.65	2	Nik	Nice	10 Jul 90
84.78		Kimmo	Kinnunen	FIN	31.3.68	2	WC	Stuttgart	16 Aug 93
84.56		Klaus-Peter	Schneider	FRG	7.4.58	1	NC	Hamburg	13 Aug 89
84.54		Yuriy	Rybin	RUS	5.3.63	1	NC-w	Adler	24 Feb 91
84.36		Harri	Hakkarainen	FIN	16.10.69	1	v2N	Bondoufle	18 Sep 93
84.30		Lev	Shatilo	RUS	21.10.62	1	Znam	Moskva	7 Jun 87
84.16		Peter	Borglund	SWE	29.1.64	1		Gävle	7 Jul 93
84.14		Silvio	Warsönke	GDR	2.8.67	1		Rostock	29 May 88
		(30)							
84.12		Boris	Henry	GER	14.12.73	1		Gengenbach	29 Aug 93
84.06		Detlef	Michel	GDR	13.10.55	1		Berlin	13 Sep 88
84.00		Ari	Pakarinen	FIN	14.5.69	2		Pyhäselkä	5 Sep 92
83.88		Dave	Stephens	USA	8.2.62	1		Knoxville	3 May 91
83.84		Roald	Bradstock	GBR	24.4.62	1		Tucson	2 May 87
83.44		Oleg	Pakhol	RUS	12.5.64	1		Nizhniy Novgorod	18 Jul 90
83.40		Marko	Hyytiäinen	FIN	27.11.66	1		Heinola	11 Jun 90
83.34		Sejad	Krdzalic	YUG	5.1.60	1		Beograd	30 May 87
83.32		Sigurdur	Einarsson	ISL	28.9.62	1		Mosfellsbær	5 Jul 92
83.30		Gerald	Weiss	GDR	8.1.60	1		Jena	3 Jun 88
		(40)							
83.30		Marek	Kaleta	EST	17.12.61	1		Pieksämäki	12 Aug 90
83.28		Peter	Schreiber	FRG	9.8.64	1		Wattenscheid	6 Jul 90
83.20		Heino	Puuste	EST	7.9.55	2	vGDR	Tallinn	22 Jun 86
83.00		Brian	Crouser ¶	USA	9.7.62	1		Corvallis	16 May 87
82.76		Zhang Lianbiao		CHN	25.1.69	Q	NC	Beijing	10 Jun 93
82.74		Duncan	Atwood ¶	USA	11.10.55	1	TAC	San José	26 Jun 87
82.70		Ivan	Mustapic	CRO	9.7.66	1		Zagreb	25 Jul 92
82.64		Dag	Wennlund	SWE	9.10.63	1	TexR	Austin	4 Apr 87
82.62		Jorma	Markus	FIN	28.11.52	1		Pihtipudas	1 Jul 90
82.38		Colin	Mackenzie	GBR	30.6.63	1		Edinburgh	7 Aug 93
		(50)	100th best (inc. roughened javelins)						
Javelins with roughened tails, now banned by the IAAF									
96.96		Seppo	Räty	FIN	27.4.62	1		Punkalaidun	2 Jun 91
91.98			Räty			1	Super	Shizuoka	6 May 91
91.36			Backley			1	McV	Sheffield	15 Sep 91
90.98			Backley			1	PG	London	20 Jul 90
90.84		Raymond	Hecht	GER	11.11.68	1		Gengenbach	8 Sep 91
90.82		Kimmo	Kinnunen	FIN	31.3.68	1	WC	Tokyo	26 Aug 91
90.72			Zelezny			1	Athl	Lausanne	10 Jul 91
90.40			Zelezny			1	GPB	Bratislava	4 Jun 91
89.86			Zelezny			1	PG	London	12 Jul 91
89.66			Zelezny			1	Bisl	Oslo	14 Jul 90
89.64			Räty			1		Elimäki	9 Jun 91
89.62			Räty			1	WG	Helsinki	27 Jun 91
89.58			Zelezny			2	McV	Sheffield	15 Sep 91
89.36			Räty			1	vSWE	Stockholm	3 Aug 91
		(14 performances over 89m)							
87.00		Peter	Borglund	SWE	29.1.64	1		Stockholm	13 Aug 91
85.52		Dag	Wennlund	SWE	9.10.63	1	NC	Helsingborg	27 Jul 91
85.08		Radoman	Scekic	YUG	1.10.67	1		Zagreb	12 Jun 91

Mark	Wind	Name		Nat	Born	Pos	Meet	Venue	Date
84.94		Sigurdur	Einarsson	ISL	28.9.62	2	Super	Shizuoka	6 May 91
84.54		Terry	McHugh	IRL	22.8.63	1	vE,RUS	Limerick	14 Jun 91
84.46	R?	Andreas	Linden	GER	20.2.65	1		Gersthofen	9 Jun 91
84.20		Mike	Barnett	USA	21.5.61	1		Santa Barbara	11 Jul 91
83.92		Andrey	Maznichenko	UKR	29.9.66	3	NC-w	Adler	24 Feb 91
82.82		Peter	Blank	FRG	10.4.62	1	NC	Düsseldorf	12 Aug 90
82.60		Colin	Mackenzie	GBR	30.6.63	1	v3N	Oristano	1 Jun 91
82.42		Peter	Esenwein	GER	7.12.67	Q	NC	Hannover	27 Jul 91

Ancillary marks

95.34	Zelezny	29 Aug 93	90.10x	Zelezny	4 Jul 92	89.20 Backley	20 Jul 90
91.24x	Zelezny	4 Jul 92	89.88	Zelezny	21 Jul 93	89.02 Zelezny	29 Aug 93
90.78x	Zelezny	4 Jul 92	89.74	Zelezny	27 Jun 93	89.00 Backley	25 Jan 92
90.48R	Backley	2 Jun 91	89.54	Zelezny	27 Jun 93	*x irregular javelin*	

PENTATHLON Long jump, Javelin, 200m, Discus, 1500m

Mark	Name		Nat	Born	Pos	Venue	Date
4282	Bill	Toomey	USA	10.1.39	1	London	16 Aug 69
	7.58 66.18 21.3 44.52 4:20.3						
4273	Rein	Aun	EST	5.10.40	1	Tartu	18 Jul 68
	7.33 72.26 21.9 50.06 4:34.5						
4230	Kurt	Bendlin	FRG	22.5.43	1	Bonn	31 Oct 70
	7.31 72.10 21.3w 45.16 4:33.4						
4223		Bendlin			1	Krefeld	31 Jul 65
	7.47 77.42 21.8 44.53 4:43.7						
4222	Guido	Kratschmer	FRG	10.1.53	1	Salzburg	5 May 84
	7.48 65.86 21.58 48.72 4:37.29						
4172	Raimo	Pihl	SWE	28.10.49	1	Göteborg	13 Jul 74
	7.18 76.50 22.1 44.86 4:34.9						
4169		Bendlin			1	Bonn	10 Oct 70
	7.46 69.20 21.6 44.40 4:34.7						
4146		Kratschmer			1	Bensheim	10 May 86
	7.38w 64.34 21.3 48.70 4:42.3						
4144	Hans-Joachim	Haberle	FRG	7.4.59	1	Leverkusen	6 Jul 84
	7.16 65.74 21.6 47.08 4:28.0						
4108	Lennart	Hedmark	SWE	18.5.44	1	Karlskrona	7 Jun 75
	7.18 73.34 22.2 44.76 4:35.4						
	(10/7)						
4083	Heinz-Dieter	Antretter	FRG	8.9.55	1	Voerde	29 Sep 79
	7.56 62.04 22.0 42.94 4:24.6						
4079	Herbert	Peter	FRG	24.6.57	1	Lahr	11 Jul 82
	7.13w 62.36 22.26 42.00 4:07.50						
4051	Vasiliy	Kuznyetsov	RUS	7.2.32	1	Torino	3 Sep 59
	7.18 72.79 22.2 49.51 4:59.5						
	(10)						
4049	Siegfried	Wentz	FRG	7.3.60	2	Salzburg	15 Jun 85
	7.24 62.00 22.02 48.22 4:37.54						
4031	Frank	Müller	FRG	18.6.68	1	Attendorn	21 May 89
	7.41 58.40 21.50 41.90 4:26.45						
4028	Bruce	Jenner	USA	28.12.49	1	San José	3 May 75
	7.00 63.78 22.3 46.32 4:22.3						
4024	Georg	Werthner	AUT	7.4.56	1	Krems	18 May 83
	7.09 71.58 22.84 41.10 4:23.53						
4018	Fred	Samara	USA	6.4.50	2	San José	3 May 75
	7.43 63.30 21.7 41.60 4:32.8						
4017	Fred	Dixon	USA	5.11.49	1	Santa Barbara	13 Jul 74
	7.20 64.22 21.6 45.86 4:41.8						
4007	Kenneth	Riggberger	SWE	15.12.49	2	Karlskrona	7 Jun 75
	6.72 62.92 21.8 44.88 4:16.7						
3985	Rainer	Sonnenburg	FRG	2.10.60	1	Hamburg	5 May 84
	7.54 60.50 21.7 42.52 4:38.4						
3976	Karl-Heinz	Fichtner	FRG	16.8.62	1	Unterhaching	25 Apr 87
	7.44 57.46 22.37 45.80 4:32.70						
3975	Fritz	Mehl	FRG	18.9.55	4	Salzburg	5 May 84
	7.11 61.62 22.07 44.04 4:29.20						
	(20)						

Mark Wind	Name		Nat	Born	Pos	Meet	Venue	Date

DECATHLON

Mark Wind	Name		Nat	Born	Pos	Meet	Venue	Date
8891	Dan	O'Brien	USA	18.7.66	1		Talence	5 Sep 92
		10.43w 8.08 16.69 2.07 48.51			13.98 48.56 5.00 62.58 4:42.10			
8847	Daley	Thompson	GBR	30.7.58	1	OG	Los Angeles	9 Aug 84
		10.44 8.01 15.72 2.03 46.97			14.33 46.56 5.00 65.24 4:35.00			
8844w		O'Brien			1	TAC	New York	13 Jun 91
		10.23 7.96 16.06 2.08 47.70			13.95W 48.08 5.10 57.40 4:45.54			
8832	Jürgen	Hingsen	FRG	25.1.58	1	OT	Mannheim	9 Jun 84
		10.70w 7.76 16.42 2.07 48.05			14.07 49.36 4.90 59.86 4:19.75			
8825		Hingsen			1		Filderstadt	5 Jun 83
		10.92 7.74 15.94 2.15 47.89			14.10 46.80 4.70 67.26 4:19.74			
8817		O'Brien			1	WC	Stuttgart	20 Aug 93
		10.57 7.99 15.41 2.03 47.46			14.08 47.92 5.20 62.56 4:40.08			
8812		O'Brien			1	WC	Tokyo	30 Aug 91
		10.41 7.90 16.24 1.91 46.53			13.94 47.20 5.20 60.66 4:37.50			
8811		Thompson			1	EC	Stuttgart	28 Aug 86
		10.26 7.72 15.73 2.00 47.02			14.04 43.38 5.10 62.78 4:26.16			
8792	Uwe	Freimuth	GDR	10.9.61	1	OD	Potsdam	21 Jul 84
		11.06 7.79 16.30 2.03 48.43			14.66 46.58 5.15 72.42 4:25.19			
8774		Thompson			1	EC	Athinai	8 Sep 82
		10.51 7.80 15.44 2.03 47.11			14.39 45.48 5.00 63.56 4:23.71			
8762	Siegfried	Wentz	FRG	7.3.60	2		Filderstadt	5 Jun 83
		10.89 7.49 15.35 2.09 47.38			14.00 46.90 4.80 70.68 4:24.90			
8741		Hingsen			1	NC	Ulm	15 Aug 82
		10.74w 7.85 16.00 2.15 47.65			14.64 44.92 4.60 63.10 4:15.13			
8730		Thompson			1		Götzis	23 May 82
		10.50w 7.95 15.31 2.08 46.86			14.31 44.34 4.90 60.52 4:30.55			
8730		Hingsen			2	EC	Stuttgart	28 Aug 86
		10.87w 7.89w 16.46 2.12 48.79			14.52 48.42 4.60 64.38 4:21.61			
8727w/8705	Dave	Johnson	USA	7.4.63	1		Azusa	24 Apr 92
		10.96 7.52w/7.43 14.61 2.04 48.19			14.17 49.88 5.28 66.96 4:29.38			
8724	Eduard	Hämäläinen	BLS	21.1.69	2	WC	Stuttgart	20 Aug 93
		10.72 7.05 15.49 2.09 47.64			13.57 49.26 5.30 61.88 4:39.34			
8714		Thompson			1	WC	Helsinki	13 Aug 83
		10.60 7.88 15.35 2.03 48.12			14.37w 44.46 5.10 65.24 4:29.72			
8709	Aleksandr	Apaychev	UKR	6.5.61	1	vGDR	Neubrandenburg	3 Jun 84
		10.96 7.57 16.00 1.97 48.72			13.93 48.00 4.90 72.24 4:26.51			
8698	Grigoriy	Degtyarov	RUS	16.8.58	1	NC	Kiev	22 Jun 84
		10.87 7.42 16.03 2.10 49.75			14.53 51.20 4.90 67.08 4:23.09			
8695		Hingsen			2	OG	Los Angeles	9 Aug 84
		10.91 7.80 15.87 2.12 47.69			14.29 50.82 4.50 60.44 4:22.60			
8680	Torsten	Voss (10)	GDR	24.3.63	1	WC	Roma	4 Sep 87
		10.69 7.88 14.98 2.10 47.96			14.13 43.96 5.10 58.02 4:25.93			
8676		Wentz			3	EC	Stuttgart	28 Aug 86
		10.83 7.60 15.45 2.12 47.57			14.07 45.66 4.90 65.34 4:35.00			
8667	Guido	Kratschmer	FRG	10.1.53	1		Filderstadt	14 Jun 80
		10.58w 7.80 15.47 2.00 48.04			13.92 45.52 4.60 66.50 4:24.15			
8667		Thompson			1	vFRA	Arles	18 May 86
		10.56 7.81 15.39 1.98 47.52			14.35 47.62 4.90 63.28 4:30.04			
8663		Thompson			1	CG	Edinburgh	28 Jul 86
		10.37 7.70w 15.01 2.08 47.30			14.22 43.72 5.10 60.82 4:39.63			
8649		Johnson			1	OT	New Orleans	27 Jun 92
		11.18 7.27 15.05 2.00 48.21			14.44 48.70 5.20 74.58 4:27.17			
8648		Thompson			1		Götzis	18 May 80
		10.55 7.72 14.46 2.11 48.04			14.37 42.98 4.90 65.38 4:25.49			
8645		Wentz			1		Götzis	24 May 87
		10.85w 7.49w 15.82 2.05 47.55			13.96 48.20 4.80 65.50 4:34.58			
8634	Bruce	Jenner	USA	28.12.49	1	OG	Montreal	30 Jul 76
		10.94 7.22w 15.35 2.03 47.51			14.84 50.04 4.80 68.52 4:12.61			
	(30/12)							
8627	Robert	Zmelík	TCH	18.4.69	1		Götzis	31 May 92
		10.62w 8.02 13.93 2.05 48.73			13.84 44.44 4.90 61.26 4:24.83			
8574	Christian	Plaziat	FRA	28.10.63	1	EC	Split	29 Aug 90
		10.72 7.77 14.19 2.10 47.10			13.98 44.36 5.00 54.72 4:27.83			
8549	Michael	Smith	CAN	16.9.67	2	WC	Tokyo	30 Aug 91
		10.81 7.68 15.69 2.09 47.53			14.78 48.42 4.40 65.46 4:29.14			

Mark Wind	Name		Nat	Born	Pos	Meet	Venue	Date
8548	Paul	Meier	GER	27.7.71	3	WC	Stuttgart	20 Aug 93
		10.57 7.57 15.45 2.15 47.73 14.63 45.72 4.60 61.22 4:32.05						
8547	Igor	Sobolevskiy	UKR	4.5.62	2	NC	Kiev	22 Jun 84
		10.64 7.71 15.93 2.01 48.24 14.82 50.54 4.40 67.40 4:32.84						
8534	Siegfried	Stark	GDR	12.6.55	1		Halle	4 May 80
		11.10w 7.64 15.81 2.03 49.53 14.86w 47.20 5.00 68.70 4:27.70						
8534w/8478	Antonio	Peñalver	ESP	1.12.68	1		Alhama	24 May 92
		10.76w 7.42w/7.19 16.50 2.12 49.50 14.32 47.38 5.00 59.32 4:39.94						
8519	Yuriy	Kutsenko	RUS	5.3.52	3	NC	Kiev	22 Jun 84
		11.07 7.54 15.11 2.13 49.07 14.94 50.38 4.60 61.70 4:12.68						
	(20)							
8506	Valter	Külvet	EST	19.2.64	1		Staiki	3 Jul 88
		11.05 7.35 15.78 2.00 48.08 14.55 52.04 4.60 61.72 4:15.93						
8500	Christian	Schenk	GER	9.2.65	4	WC	Stuttgart	20 Aug 93
		11.22 7.63 15.72 2.15 48.78 15.29 46.94 4.80 65.32 4:24.44						
8491	Aleksandr	Nevskiy	UKR	21.2.58	2		Götzis	20 May 84
		10.97 7.24 15.04 2.08 48.44 14.67 46.06 4.70 69.56 4:19.62						
8485	Konstantin	Akhapkin	RUS	19.1.56	1	NC	Moskva	2 Aug 82
		11.10 7.72 15.25 2.02 49.14 14.38 45.68 4.90 62.42 4:19.60						
8466	Nikolay	Avilov	UKR	6.8.48	1	OG	München	8 Sep 72
		11.00 7.68 14.36 2.12 48.45 14.31 46.98 4.55 61.66 4:22.82						
8447	Robert	De Wit	HOL	7.8.62	1	NC	Eindhoven	22 May 88
		11.07 6.98 15.88 2.04 48.80 14.32 46.20 5.00 63.94 4:20.98						
8444	Alain	Blondel	FRA	7.12.62	5	WC	Stuttgart	20 Aug 93
		10.94 7.20 14.06 1.94 48.12 14.40 45.74 5.40 62.22 4:19.89						
8437	Richardas	Malakhovskis	LIT	28.4.65	2		Staiki	3 Jul 88
		10.93 7.04 14.94 2.09 47.77 14.34 44.04 4.90 59.58 4:13.67						
8436	Deszö	Szabó	HUN	4.9.67	2	EC	Split	29 Aug 90
		11.06 7.49 13.65 1.98 47.17 14.67 40.78 5.30 61.94 4:11.07						
8417	Sergey	Zhelanov	RUS	14.6.57	4	NC	Kiev	22 Jun 84
		11.04 7.50 14.31 2.13 48.94 14.40 43.44 5.00 65.90 4:37.24						
	(30)							
8415	Dave	Steen	CAN	14.11.59	3		Talence	17 Jul 88
		11.02 7.56 13.99 1.98 48.22 14.95 44.08 5.20 65.36 4:21.46						
8400h	Aleksandr	Grebenyuk	RUS	22.5.51	1	NC	Riga	3 Jul 77
		10.7 7.12 15.50 2.02 48.8 14.3 45.52 4.70 71.52 4:27.3						
8397	Fred	Dixon	USA	5.11.49	1	vURS	Bloomington	14 Aug 77
		10.85 7.44 15.20 2.04 48.54 14.94 47.14 4.60 67.88 4:30.21						
8381w	John	Sayre	USA	25.3.61	1	TAC	Indianapolis	18 Jun 85
		10.86W 7.41w 14.22 2.00 49.98 14.84W 46.08 5.30 67.68 4:37.07						
8375	Pavel	Tarnavetskiy	UKR	22.2.61	3	WC	Roma	4 Sep 87
		11.01 7.43 15.32 2.07 49.22 14.86 47.66 4.90 58.60 4:23.96						
8366	Vadim	Podmaryov	UZB	4.9.58	1		Tashkent	26 May 85
		11.09 7.56 15.28 2.08 50.00 14.89 48.58 4.60 67.46 4:32.31						
8366h	Simon	Poelman	NZL	27.5.63	1	NC	Christchurch	22 Mar 87
		10.6 7.34 15.11 2.06 49.4 14.1 46.66 4.95 56.94 4:27.2						
8364	Igor	Maryin	RUS	28.4.65	2	NC	Kiev	31 Jul 88
		10.91 7.79 15.10 2.04 49.22 15.71 43.16 5.00 67.70 4:32.19						
8362	Thomas	Fahner	GDR	18.7.66	3		Götzis	19 Jun 88
		11.04 7.55w 15.01 1.93 47.94 14.54 46.66 4.60 68.40 4:27.77						
8356	Viktor	Gruzenkin	RUS	19.12.51	5	NC	Kiev	22 Jun 84
		10.92 7.67 15.98 2.07 50.06 14.65 46.70 4.60 65.74 4:43.00						
	(40)							
8340	Tim	Bright	USA	28.7.60	1	TAC	San José	24 Jun 87
		10.90w 7.31 14.35 2.11 49.24 14.16 41.12 5.50 57.68 4:44.49						
8334	Rainer	Pottel	GDR	29.8.53	1	EP	Birmingham	30 Aug 81
		11.06 7.68 14.38 2.01 48.35 14.57 39.52 4.80 67.46 4:22.67						
8334	Stefan	Niklaus	SUI	17.4.58	1	NC	Lausanne	3 Jul 83
		10.82 7.32 15.44 2.01 47.47 14.79 48.68 4.40 67.84 4:41.29						
8330	Mikhail	Medved	UKR	30.1.64	3	NC	Kiev	31 Jul 88
		11.24 7.46 15.73 2.07 50.13 14.40 45.32 5.00 64.50 4:41.26						
8327w	William	Motti ¶	FRA	25.7.64	1	EP-B	Arles	5 Jul 87
		10.98W 7.39 15.13 2.13 48.83 14.57w 47.66 4.40 61.82 4:30.39						
8326	Andreas	Rizzi	FRG	6.5.59	4		Filderstadt	5 Jun 83
		10.52 7.71 14.78 2.00 46.82 14.91 43.62 4.70 50.92 4:21.04						
8324	Steve	Fritz	USA	1.11.67	7	WC	Stuttgart	20 Aug 93
		10.83 7.52 13.87 2.03 48.40 13.99 41.62 4.90 57.68 4:23.56						

Mark	Wind	Name		Nat	Born	Pos	Meet	Venue	Date
8320		Gernot	Kellermayr ¶	AUT	5.4.66	4		Götzis	30 May 93
			10.47 7.66 14.83 1.96 47.56			14.12 42.50 5.00 58.24 4:54.78			
		(50)	100th best 8163						

w wind-aided between 2.0 and 4.0 metres per second; W wind-aided in excess of 4 metres per second

ONE-HOUR DECATHLON

Mark	Name		Nat	Born	Pos	Venue	Date
7897	Robert	Zmelík	TCH	18.4.69	1	Ostrava	24 Sep 92
		10.89 7.64 14.52 2.08 55.53			14.25 41.92 4.80 60.34 4:55.16		
7774	Simon	Poelman	NZL	27.5.63	1	Auckland	24 Feb 90
		11.10 7.07 15.75 2.05 55.51			15.19 44.64 4.80 58.38 4:40.55		
7715	Alain	Blondel	FRA	7.12.62	1	Zürich	23 Sep 90
		11.10 7.00 12.07 1.95 52.47			14.60 43.24 5.00 60.02 4:43.62		
7652	Vitaliy	Kolpakov	UKR	2.2.72	1	Ostrava	24 Sep 93
		11.00 7.42 15.32 2.08 55.64			14.97 42.06 4.70 60.02 5:07.95		
7647		Poelman			1	Auckland	24 Feb 88
7634	William	Motti	FRA	25.7.64	2	Ostrava	24 Sep 93
		11.59 7.18 15.40 2.10 58.60			16.28 50.40 4.70 71.46 5:13.35		
7591	Steve	Fritz	USA	1.11.67	3	Ostrava	24 Sep 93
		11.15 7.12 13.89 1.95 54.88			14.88 45.46 4.90 62.60 5:03.37		
7587	Christian	Schenk	GDR	9.2.65	1	Saarbrücken	15 Sep 90
7572	Christian	Plaziat	FRA	28.10.63	2	Saarbrücken	15 Sep 90
7561w	Beat	Gähwiler	SUI	26.1.65	1	St.Moritz	24 Jul 90

4 x 100 METRES RELAY

Mark	Team	Runners	Pos	Meet	Venue	Date
37.40	USA	Marsh, Burrell, Mitchell, Lewis	1	OG	Barcelona	8 Aug 92
37.40	USA	Drummond, Cason, D.Mitchell, L.Burrell	1s1	WC	Stuttgart	21 Aug 93
37.48	USA	Drummond, Cason, D.Mitchell, L.Burrell	1	WC	Stuttgart	22 Aug 93
37.50	USA	Cason, Burrell, Mitchell, Lewis	1	WC	Tokyo	1 Sep 91
37.67	USA	Marsh, Burrell, Mitchell, Lewis	1	WK	Zürich	7 Aug 91
37.75	USA	Cason, Burrell, Mitchell, Marsh	1h2	WC	Tokyo	31 Aug 91
37.77	GBR	C.Jackson, Jarrett, Regis, L.Christie	2	WC	Stuttgart	22 Aug 93
37.79	FRA	Morinière, Sangouma, Trouabal, Marie-Rose	1	EC	Split	1 Sep 90
37.79	Santa Monica TC/USA	Marsh, Burrell, Heard, Lewis	1	Herc	Monte Carlo	3 Aug 91
37.83	USA	Graddy, R.Brown, C.Smith, Lewis	1	OG	Los Angeles	11 Aug 84
37.83	CAN	Esmie, Gilbert, Surin, Mahorn	3	WC	Stuttgart	22 Aug 93
37.86	USA	E.King, Gault, C.Smith, Lewis	1	WC	Helsinki	10 Aug 83
37.87	FRA	Morinière, Sangouma, Trouabal, Marie-Rose	2	WC	Tokyo	1 Sep 91
37.90	USA	McRae, L.McNeill, Glance, Lewis	1	WC	Roma	6 Sep 87
37.93	Santa Monica TC/USA	Witherspoon, Burrell, Heard, Lewis	1		Barcelona	16 Jul 90
37.97	Santa Monica TC/USA	Marsh, Burrell, Heard, Lewis	1	MSR	Walnut	18 Apr 92
37.98	USA	McRae, Heard, Glance, Lewis	1	GWG	Moskva	9 Jul 86
37.98	GBR	Braithwaite, Regis, Adam, Christie	2	EC	Split	1 Sep 90
37.98	NGR	Kayode, Imoh, Adeniken, D.Ezinwa	2	OG	Barcelona	8 Aug 92
37.99	USA	Drummond, Cason, C.Smith, Dees	1	WK	Zürich	4 Oct 93
37.99	CAN	Esmie, Gilbert, Surin, Mahorn	2s1	WC	Stuttgart	21 Aug 93
38.00	CUB	Simon, Lamela, Isasi, Aguilera	3	OG	Barcelona	8 Aug 92
38.00	Santa Monica TC (USA)	Heard, Burrell, Marsh, C.Lewis	1	MSR	Walnut	17 Apr 93
38.02	URS	Yevgenyev, Bryzgin, Muravyov, Krylov	2	WC	Roma	6 Sep 87
38.03	USA	Collins, Riddick, Wiley, S.Williams	1	WP	Düsseldorf	3 Sep 77
38.05	GBR	John, Jarrett, Braithwaite, L.Christie	3s1	WC	Stuttgart	21 Aug 93
38.08	GBR	Adam, Jarrett, Regis, Christie	4	OG	Barcelona	8 Aug 92
38.09	GBR	Jarrett, Regis, Braithwaite, Christie	3	WC	Tokyo	1 Sep 91
38.10	USA	Glance, Baptiste, C.Smith, Evans	1	WP	Canberra	5 Oct 85
38.12	Santa Monica TC/USA	Witherspoon, L.Burrell, C.Lewis, M.Marsh	1		Ingolstadt	19 Jul 92
38.12	USA	Drummond, Cason, C.Smith, L.Burrell	1h3	WC	Stuttgart	21 Aug 93
	(31/7 nations, inc USSR)					
38.29	GDR	Schröder, Kübeck, Prenzler, Emmelmann	2	vUSA	Karl-Marx-Stadt	9 Jul 82
38.33	POL	Zwolinski, Licznerski, Dunecki, Woronin	2	OG	Moskva	1 Aug 80
38.37	ITA	Tilli, Simionato, Pavoni, Mennea	2	WC	Helsinki	10 Aug 83
	(10)					
38.39A	JAM	Stewart, Fray, Forbes, L.Miller	1s1	OG	Ciudad México	19 Oct 68
38.46	U/RUS	Zharov, Krylov, Fatun, Goremykin	4	EC	Split	1 Sep 90
38.46	AUS	Henderson, Marsh, Capobianco, Jackson	4s1	WC	Stuttgart	21 Aug 93
38.54	FRG	Heer, Haas, Klein, Schweisfurth	1	R-W	Koblenz	28 Aug 88

Mark	Wind	Name	Nat	Born	Pos	Meet	Venue	Date
38.61	GHA	Gariba, Boateng, Amegatcher, Tuffour			5s1	WC	Stuttgart	21 Aug 93
38.67	HUN	Karaffa, Nagy, Tatár, Kovács			1	BGP	Budapest	16 Jun 86
38.73A	CIV	Ouré, Meité, Nogboum, Kablan			2	WUG	Ciudad México	13 Sep 79
38.77	JPN	Aoto, Suzuki, Inoue, Sugimoto			6	OG	Barcelona	8 Aug 92
38.82	TCH	Matousek, Demec, Kynos, Bohman			4	OG	München	10 Sep 72
38.85	UKR	Streltsov, Vanyaikin, Shlychkov, Dologodin			1	EurR	Portsmouth	5 Jun 93
38.96	SWE	Mårtensson, T.Eriksson, Hedner, Leandersson			3s2	WC	Stuttgart	21 Aug 93
	(20)							
38.97A	TRI	Fabien, Short, Archer, Roberts			3h1	OG	Ciudad México	19 Oct 68
38.99	BUL	Pavlov, Ivanov, Karaniotov, Petrov			5	OG	Moskva	1 Aug 80
38.99	CHN	Wu Jianhui, Cai Jianmin, Zhao Cuilin, Zheng Chen			1	AsiG	Beijing	3 Oct 90
39.00	GRE	Genovelis, Panagiotopoulos, Nafpliotis, Terzian			6s1	WC	Stuttgart	21 Aug 93
39.02A	BRA	de Castro, dos Santos, Pegado, Araujo			1		Ciudad México	4 Sep 79
39.10	ESP	Gascon, Talavera, Arques, Rodriguez			6	EC	Split	1 Sep 90
39.19	SUI	Fähndrich, U.Gisler, Muster, Ziegler			1		Bern	5 Aug 78
39.20	QAT	Suliman, Marzouk, Muftah, Mansour			1	AsCh	Singapore	26 Jul 87
39.26	BV Quatro Vîcklabruck/AUT 92							
		Kellermayr, Renner, Berger, Ratzenberger			1		Bad Homburg	24 May 92
39.27	TPE	Lai, Lin, Cheng, Hsieh			2	AsiG	Beijing	3 Oct 90
	(30)							
Best low altitude marks								
38.41	JAM	Mair, Smith, Wright, Stewart			3	WC	Roma	6 Sep 87
38.77	CIV	Lagazane, Zirignon, Waota, Meité			1h1	WC	Stuttgart	21 Aug 93
Hand timing								
38.8	BRA	Oliveira, R da Silva, Nakaia, Correia			1		São Paulo	1 May 84

4 x 200 METRES RELAY

Mark	Team / Name	Pos	Meet	Venue	Date
1:19.11	Santa Monica TC/USA M.Marsh, L.Burrell, F.Heard, C.Lewis	1	PennR	Philadelphia	25 Apr 92
1:19.38	Santa Monica TC/USA Everett, Burrell, Heard, C.Lewis	1	R-W	Koblenz	23 Aug 89
1:19.45	Santa Monica TC/USA DeLoach, Burrell, C.Lewis, Heard	1	PennR	Philadelphia	27 Apr 91
1:20.20	Texas Christian University/USA/Jamaica	1	PennR	Philadelphia	26 Apr 86
	Tatum, A.Smith JAM, Reid, Sholars				
1:20.23	Tobias Striders/PAN/USA/JAM/GUY)	1		Tempe	27 May 78
	Abrahams PAN, Simmons USA, Quarrie JAM, Gilkes GUY				
1:20.26	University of Southern California/USA)	2		Tempe	27 May 78
	J.Andrews, Sanford, Mullins, C.Edwards				
1:20.3*	University of Southern California/USA/JAM)	1		Fresno	13 May 72
	Garrison, L.Brown, Deckard, Quarrie JAM				
1:20.33	Santa Monica TC/USA DeLoach, Burrell, Heard, C.Lewis	1		St.Denis	23 Jun 89
1:20.37	Arizona State University/USA Moore, Evans, Jones, King	1	MSR	Walnut	26 Apr 81
Best non-US nations					
1:20.79	Central Arizona DC/Jamaica	1		Walnut	24 Apr 88
	Bucknor, Campbell, O'Conner, Davis)				
1:21.29	GBR Adam, Mafe, Christie, Regis	1		Birmingham	23 Jun 89
1:21.32	UKR Vanyaykin, Tverdokhleb, Streltsov, Dolgodin	1	EurR	Portsmouth	5 Jun 93

** 4 x 220 yards time less 0.4 sec.*

4 x 400 METRES RELAY

Mark	Nat	Name	Pos	Meet	Venue	Date
2:54.29	USA	Valmon 44.5, Watts 43.6, Reynolds 43.23, Johnson 42.94	1	WC	Stuttgart	22 Aug 93
2:55.74	USA	Valmon 44.6, Watts 43.00, M.Johnson 44.73, S.Lewis 43.41	1	OG	Barcelona	8 Aug 92
2:56.16A	USA	Matthews 45.0, Freeman 43.2, James 43.9, Evans 44.1	1	OG	Ciu. México	20 Oct 68
2:56.16	USA	Everett 44.0, S.Lewis 43.6, Robinzine 44.7, Reynolds 43.9	1	OG	Seoul	1 Oct 88
2:57.29	USA	Everett 45.1, Haley 44.0, McKay 44.20, Reynolds 44.00	1	WC	Roma	6 Sep 87
2:57.53	GBR	Black 44.7, Redmond 44.0, Regis 44.22, Akabusi 44.59	1	WC	Tokyo	1 Sep 91
2:57.57	USA	Valmon 44.9, Watts 43.4, D.Everett 44.31, Pettigrew 44.93	2	WC	Tokyo	1 Sep 91
2:57.91	USA	Nix 45.59, Armstead 43.97, Babers 43.75, McKay 44.60	1	OG	Los Angeles	11 Aug 84
2:58.22	GBR	Sanders 45.85, Akabusi 44.48, Regis 43.93, Black 43.96	1	EC	Split	1 Sep 90
2:58.65	USA	Frazier 45.3, B.Brown 44.62, Newhouse 43.8, Parks 45.00	1	OG	Montreal	31 Jul 76
2:58.72	USA	Valmon 45.1, Pettigrew 44.0, Mills 44.65, Johnson 44.96	1h2	WC	Stuttgart	21 Aug 93
2:58.86	GBR	Redmond 45.2, Akabusi 44.5, Black 44.81, Brown 44.34	2	WC	Roma	6 Sep 87
2:59.06	USA	Everett 45.3, Franks 44.6, Pierre 44.7, McKay 44.5	1s2	WC	Roma	5 Sep 87
2:59.12	USA	McCoy 45.20, Wiley 44.41, W.Smith 44.58, Darden 44.93	1	WP	Roma	6 Sep 81
2:59.13	GBR	Akabusi 45.87, Cook 44.74, T.Bennett 44.17, P.Brown 44.35	2	OG	Los Angeles	11 Aug 84
2:59.13	CUB	Martínez 45.6, Herrera 44.38, Tellez 44.81, Hernández 44.34	1h2	OG	Barcelona	7 Aug 92
2:59.14	USA	Hall 45.6, M.Johnson 44.46, C.Jenkins 44.59, Watts 44.49	2h2	OG	Barcelona	7 Aug 92

Mark Wind		Name	Nat	Born	Pos	Meet	Venue	Date
2:59.16	CUB	Peñalver 45.2, Pavó 45.2, Martínez 44.90, Hernández 43.88			3	WC	Roma	6 Sep 87
2:59.32	NGR	Uti 45.34, Ugbisie 44.48, Peters 44.94, Egbunike 44.56			3	OG	Los Angeles	11 Aug 84
2:59.49	GBR	Mafe 46.0, Redmond 44.5, Richardson 44.8, Akabusi 44.2			1h3	WC	Tokyo	31 Aug 91
2:59.51	CUB	Martínez 45.5, Herrera 44.45, Tellez 45.04, Hernández 44.52			2	OG	Barcelona	8 Aug 92
2:59:52	USA	Frazier 45.5, B.Brown 45.3, Newhouse 43.63, Parks 45.1			1h1	OG	Montreal	30 Jul 76
2:59.54	USA	Rowe 45.8, Robinzine 45.0, Pierre 43.67, Haley 45.04			1	PAG	Indianapolis	16 Aug 87
2:59.54	USA	C.Daniel 46.2, Valmon 44.5, Pettigrew 44.6, Simon 44.3			1	GWG	Seattle	26 Jul 90
2:59.55	USA	J.Reynolds 45.4, Watts 43.9, M.Everett 44.5, D.Everett 45.8			1h1	WC	Tokyo	31 Aug 91
2:59.6	USA	Frey 46.3, Evans 44.5, T.Smith 43.8, T.Lewis 45.0			1		Los Angeles	24 Jul 66
2:59.63	KEN	D.Kitur 45.4, S.Kitur 45.13, Kipkemboi 44.76, Kemboi 44.34			3h2	OG	Barcelona	7 Aug 92
2:59.64A	KEN	Asati 44.6, Nyamau 45.5, Bon 45.1, Rudisha 44.4			2	OG	Ciu. México	20 Oct 68
2:59.70	AUS	Frayne 45.38, Clark 43.86, Minihan 45.07, Mitchell 45.39			4	OG	Los Angeles	11 Aug 84
2:59.71A	CUB	Martínez, Valentín, Stevens, Hernández			1	IbAmC	Ciu. México	24 Jul 88
	(30/6 nations)							
2:59.86	GDR	Möller 45.8, Schersing 44.8, Carlowitz 45.3, Schönlebe 44.1			1	vSU	Erfurt	23 Jun 85
2:59.95	YUG	Jovkovic, Djurovic, Macev, Brankovic 44.3			2h3	WC	Tokyo	31 Aug 91
2:59.96	FRG	Dobeleit 45.7, Henrich 44.3, Itt 45.12, Schmid 44.93			4	WC	Roma	6 Sep 87
3:00.09	FRA	Rapnouil 45.5, Hilaire 45.5, Farraudière 44.86, Diagana 44.19			4	WC	Stuttgart	22 Aug 93
	(10)							
3:00.10	JAM	O'Connor 45.9, Morris 44.8, Graham 44.81, Fagan 44.77			3	WC	Tokyo	1 Sep 91
3:00.16	URS	Lovachov, Lomtyev, Kurochkin, Markin 43.9			1	Drz	Moskva	18 Aug 84
3:00.44	RUS	Kliger 45.72, Kosov 45.09, Vdovin 44.73, Golovastov 44.90			5	WC	Stuttgart	22 Aug 93
3:00.58A	POL	Gredzinski 46.8, Balachowski 44.7, Werner 44.5, Badenski 44.5			4	OG	Ciu. México	20 Oct 68
3:01.12	FIN	Lönnqvist 46.7, Salin 45.1, Karttunen 44.8, Kukkoaho 44.5			6	OG	München	10 Sep 72
3:01.26	JPN	Konakatomi, Takano 44.0, Watanabe, Ito			4h1	WC	Tokyo	31 Aug 91
3:01.37	ITA	Bongiorni 46.2, Zuliani 45.0, Petrella 45.3, Ribaud 44.9			4	EC	Stuttgart	31 Aug 86
3:01.38	BRA	Nunes 46.5, Rocha 45.30, Menezes 44.81, S.Telles 44.76			1h3	OG	Barcelona	7 Aug 92
3:01.60	BAR	Louis 46.67, Peltier 44.97, Edwards 45.04, Forde 44.92			6	OG	Los Angeles	11 Aug 84
3:01.61	BUL	Georgiev 45.9, Stankulov 46.0, Raykov 45.07, Ivanov 44.66			2h1	WC	Stuttgart	21 Aug 93
3:01.7	TRI	Skinner 46.0, Bernard 45.3, Roberts 45.4, Mottley 45.0			3	OG	Tokyo	21 Oct 64
	(20)							
3:02.09	UGA	Govile 46.72, Kyeswa 44.60, Rwamu 46.40, Okot 44.37			7	OG	Los Angeles	11 Aug 84
3:02.11	MAR	Kasbane, Dahane, Belcaid, Lahlou 44.5			1h2	WC	Tokyo	31 Aug 91
3:02.57	SWE	Carlgren 46.0, Faager 45.5, Öhman 45.3, Rönner 45.8			7	OG	München	10 Sep 72
3:02.64	CAN	Seale 47.0, Domansky 45.3, Hope 45.5, Saunders 44.8			4	OG	Montreal	31 Jul 76
3:02.74	ESP	Sánchez, Cornet, Fernández, Palacios			6	EC	Split	1 Sep 90
3:02.82	TCH	Brecka 46.9, Malovec 44.9, Zahorak 45.4, Sajdok 45.6			5	EC	Athinai	11 Sep 82
3:03.18A	HOL	Pont, Gijsbers, Klarenbeek, Schulting			2	WUG	Ciu. México	13 Sep 79
3:03.36	RSA	Reinach, Myburgh, Kotze, J.Oosthuizen			1		Stellenbosch	25 Apr 83
3:03.50	CIV	Kablam 46.5, Nogboum 46.3, Melejde 46.3, Tiacoh 44.4			3h3	OG	Los Angeles	10 Aug 84
3:03.63	ALG	Hacini 45.8, Mariche 46.2, Talhaodi 46.51, Boumendil 45.08			4h2	WC	Stuttgart	21 Aug 93
	(30)							

4 x 800 METRES RELAY

Mark		Name	Pos	Meet	Venue	Date
7:03.89	GBR	Elliott 1:49.14, Cook 1:46.20, Cram 1:44.54, Coe 1:44.01	1		London	30 Aug 82
7:06.5	Santa Monica TC/USA)		1	MSR	Walnut	26 Apr 86
		J Robinson 1:49.8, Mack 1:46.7, E Jones 1:45.2, Gray 1:44.8				
7:07.40	URS	Masunov, Kostetskiy, Matvetev, Kalinkin	1		Moskva	5 Aug 84
7:08.0*	University of Chicago Track Club/USA 7:10.4 - 4x880y		1	King	Durham	12 May 73
		Bach, Sparks, Paul, Wohlhuter				
7:08.1	URS	Podolyakov, Kirov, Laozemlin, Reshetnyak	1		Podolsk	12 Aug 78
7:08.5	FRG	Kinder, Adams, Bogatzki, Kemper	1		Wiesbaden	13 Aug 66
7:08.96	Arizona State Univ/USA	Richardson, Davis, Sctt, Stahr	1		Tempe	7 Apr 84
7:09.1*	KEN	Bon, Nyamau, Saisi, Ouko)/7:11.6 - 4 x 880y)	1	IAC	London	5 Sep 70
	(8 performances)					
7:11.1	BLS		1		Moskva?	25 Jul 79
7:11.3	ITA	Giocondi, Barsotti, D'Urso, Benvenuti	1	EurR	Sheffield	5 Jun 92
7:11.96	RUS	Melnikov, Samoylov, Loginov, Oleynikov	2	EurR	Portsmouth	5 Jun 93

4 x 1500 METRES RELAY

Mark		Name	Pos	Meet	Venue	Date
14:38.8	FRG		1		Köln	16 Aug 77
		Wessinghage 3:38.8, Hudak 3:40.2, Lederer 3:42.6, Fleschen 3:37.3				
14:40.4	NZL	Polhill 3:42.9, Walker 3:40.4, Dixon 3:41.2, Quax 3:35.9	1		Oslo	22 Aug 73
14:45.63	URS	Kalutskiy, Yakovlev, Legeda, Lotarev	1		Leningrad	4 Aug 85
14:46.3	USA	Aldridge, Clifford, Harbour, Duits	1	Int	Bourges	23 Jun 79

Mark	Wind	Name		Nat	Born	Pos	Meet	Venue	Date
14:48.2	FRA	Begouin, Lequement, Philippe, Dien				2	Int	Bourges	23 Jun 79
14:49.0	FRA	Vervoort, Nicolas, Jazy, Wadoux				1		St Maur	25 Jun 65
14:50.2	NZL	Melville, Dixon, Quax, Walker				1		Auckland	17 May 75
14:50.2	Univ. of Arkansas/USA/GBR/IRL)					1	PennR	Philadelphia	27 Apr 85
		Iovine, G Taylor/GBR, Swain/GBR, Donovan/IRL							
14:50.82	RSA	Temane, Brunner, Gericke, Fourie				1		Port Elizabeth	15 Oct 84
	(9 performances)								
14:56.8	GBR	Mottershead, Cooper, Emson, Wood				3	Int	Bourges	23 Jun 79

4 x 1 MILE RELAY

Mark	Nat	Name	Pos	Venue	Date
15:49.08	IRL	Coghlan 4:00.2, O'Sullivan 3:55.3, O'Mara 3:56.6, Flynn 3:56.98	1	Dublin	17 Aug 85
16:02.4	NZL	Ross, Polhill, Tayler, Quax	1	Auckland	3 Feb 72

3000 METRES TRACK WALK

Mark	Name		Nat	Born	Pos	Meet	Venue	Date
10:47.11	Giovanni	De Benedictis	ITA	8.1.68	1		S.Giovanni Valdarno	19 May 90
10:56.22	Andrew	Jachno	AUS	13.4.62	1		Melbourne	7 Feb 91
10:56.34+	Roman	Mrázek	TCH	21.1.62	1k	PTS	Bratislava	14 Jun 89
11:00.2+	Jozef	Pribilinec	TCH	6.7.60	1k		Banská Bystrica	30 Aug 85
11:00.56	David	Smith	AUS	24.7.55	1		Perth	24 Jan 87
11:07.75	Maurizio	Damilano	ITA	6.4.57	1		Formia	29 Jul 81
11:08.5	Frants	Kostyukevich	BLS	4.4.63	2		Banská Bystrica	30 Aug 85
11:11.2	Erling	Andersen	NOR	22.9.60	1		Fana	23 Sep 81
11:11.45	Nick	A'Hern	AUS	6.1.69	2		Melbourne	7 Feb 91
11:13.8	Stefan	Johansson	SWE	11.4.67	1		Canberra	12 Jan 93
Indoors								
10:54.61	Carlo	Mattioli	ITA	23.10.54	1		Milano	6 Feb 80
10:56.88	Reima	Salonen	FIN	23.12.55	1		Turku	5 Feb 84
11:00.86+	Frants	Kostyukevich	BLS	4.4.63	1k	EI	Genova	28 Feb 92
11:05.14+	Mikhail	Shchennikov	RUS	24.12.67	1k	WI	Indianapolis	7 Mar 87
11:06.3	Axel	Noack	GDR	23.9.61	1		Berlin	6 Jan 90
11:08.2	Ilya	Markov	URS	19.6.72	2		Hlohevec	4 Dec 92
11:12.0	Martin	Toporek	AUT	15.2.61	1		Wien	10 Feb 83
11:12.1+	Pavol	Blazek	TCH	9.7.58	1		Jablonec	20 Feb 88
11:12.3	Torsten	Hafemeister	GDR	28.3.65	2		Berlin	6 Jan 90

k during 5000m walk

5000 METRES TRACK WALK

Mark	Name		Nat	Born	Pos	Meet	Venue	Date
18:17.22	Robert	Korzeniowski	POL	30.7.68	1		Reims	3 Jul 92
18:28.80	Roman	Mrázek	TCH	21.1.62	1	PTS	Bratislava	14 Jun 89
18:30.43	Maurizio	Damilano	ITA	6.4.57	1		Caserta	11 Jun 92
18:31.76	Frants	Kostyukevich	BLS	4.4.63	1	BNP	Villeneuve d'Ascq	2 Jul 93
18:35.87	Robert	Korzeniowski	POL	30.7.68	2	BNP	Villeneuve d'Ascq	2 Jul 93
18:36.84	Jozef	Pribilinec	SVK	6.7.60	3	BNP	Villeneuve d'Ascq	2 Jul 93
18:42.50	Giovanni	de Benedictis	ITA	8.1.68	1		Formia	8 Jul 91
18:42.66	Ralf	Kowalsky	GDR	22.3.62	1		Berlin	9 Jun 84
18:44.99	Walter	Arena	ITA	30.5.64	2		Formia	8 Jul 91
	(10)							
Indoors - where superior to outdoor best								
18:11.41	Ronald	Weigel	GDR	8.8.59	1mx		Wien	13 Feb 88
18:15.25	Grigoriy	Kornev	RUS	14.3.61	1		Moskva	7 Feb 92
18:15.91 ?	Mikhail	Shchennikov	RUS	24.12.67	1	NC	Gomel	4 Feb 89
18:16.54 ?	Frants	Kostyukevich	BLS	4.4.63	2	NC	Gomel	4 Feb 89
18:19.97	Giovanni	Di Benedictis	ITA	8.1.68	1	EI	Genova	28 Feb 92
18:23.10		Kornev			1	CISCh	Moskva	2 Feb 92
18:23.55		Shchennikov			1	WI	Sevilla	10 Mar 91
18:23.60		de Benedictis			2	WI	Sevilla	10 Mar 91
18:23.88		Kostyukevich			1	NC	Volgograd	9 Feb 91
18:25.40		Kostyukevich			2	EI	Genova	28 Feb 92
	(10/5)							
18:27.80	Jozef	Pribilinec	TCH	6.7.60	2	WI	Indianapolis	7 Mar 87
18:27.95	Stefan	Johansson	SWE	11.4.67	3	EI	Genova	28 Feb 92
18:31.63	Vladimir	Andreyev	RUS	7.9.66	2		Moskva	7 Feb 92
18:32.32	Mikhail	Orlov	RUS	25.6.67	3	CISCh	Moskva	2 Feb 92
18:34.77	Sándor	Urbanik	HUN	15.12.64	4	WI	Budapest	5 Mar 89
	(10)							

Mark Wind	Name		Nat	Born	Pos	Meet	Venue	Date
18:38.71	Ernesto	Canto	MEX	18.10.59	3	WI	Indianapolis	7 Mar 87
18:38.8	Axel	Noack	GDR	23.9.61	1		Potsdam *	10 Feb 90
18:39.2	Yevgeniy	Misyulya	BLS	13.3.64	2		Minsk	30 Jan 88
18:40.32	Ronald	Weigel	GDR	8.8.59	2	EI	Paris	13 Mar 94
18:41.34	Pavol	Blazek	TCH	9.7.58	6	WI	Budapest	5 Mar 89
18:41.37	Igor	Plotnikov	RUS	12.7.64	4	CISCh	Moskva	2 Feb 92
18:43.20	Denis	Langlois	FRA	10.10.68	3	EI	Paris	13 Mar 94

Unknown irregularity prevented ratification of record for Gomel race 4 Feb 89

10,000 METRES TRACK WALK

Mark	Name		Nat	Born	Pos	Meet	Venue	Date
38:02.60	Jozef	Pribilinec	TCH	6.7.60	1		Banská Bystrica	30 Aug 85
38:06.6	David	Smith	AUS	24.7.55	1		Sydney	25 Sep 86
38:12.13	Ronald	Weigel	GDR	8.8.59	1		Potsdam	11 May 86
38:18.0	Valdas	Kazlauskas	LIT	7.8.58	1		Moskva	18 Sep 83
38:38.0	Walter	Arena	ITA	30.5.64	1		Catania	13 Apr 90
38:47.54	Roman	Mrázek	TCH	21.1.62	1	PTS	Bratislava	12 Jun 87
38:54.3	Roland	Wieser	GDR	6.5.56	1		Potsdam	13 Jul 80
38:54.75	Ralf	Kowalsky	GDR	22.3.62	1		Cottbus	24 Jun 81
38:59.9	Werner	Heyer	GDR	14.11.56	2		Potsdam	13 Jul 80
39:05.8	Maurizio (10)	Damilano	ITA	6.4.57	1		Limbiate	25 Oct 88
39:07.38	Axel	Noack	GDR	23.9.61	1	vIta	Neubrandenburg	10 Jul 88
39:08.5	Nikolay	Polozov	URS	10.10.51	1		Leningrad	23 Feb 86
39:10.10	Nick	A'Hern	AUS	6.1.69	1		Sydney	13 Jan 91
39:10.35	Giovanni	de Benedictis	ITA	8.1.68	1	NC	Pescara	12 Sep 90
39:11.2	Salvatore	Cacia	ITA	15.6.67	2		Catania	13 Apr 90
39:19.32	Anatoliy	Solomin	RUS	2.7.52	1		Roma	23 May 81
Indoors								
38:31.4	Werner	Heyer	GDR	14.11.56	1		Berlin	12 Jan 80
38:46.0	Reima	Salonen	FIN	23.12.55	1		Turku	9 Mar 88
39:13.15	Hartwig	Gauder	GDR	10.11.54	2	NC	Senftenberg	26 Feb 88
39:14.0	Pyotr	Pochenchuk	BLS	26.7.54	1		Moskva	6 Feb 83
39:20.8	Viktor	Semyonov	URS	28.6.49	1		Moskva	17 Feb 80

15,000 METRES TRACK WALK

Mark	Name		Nat	Born	Pos	Meet	Venue	Date
58:22.4	Jozef	Pribilinec	TCH	6.7.60	1		Hildesheim	6 Sep 86
58:50.4	David	Smith	AUS	24.7.55	2		Hildesheim	6 Sep 86
58:52.9+	Stefan	Johansson	SWE	11.4.67	1	SGP	Fana	15 May 92
59:00.5+	Ernesto	Canto	MEX	18.10.59	1	SGP	Fana	5 May 84

t = track walk

20 KILOMETRES WALK

Mark	Name		Nat	Born	Pos	Meet	Venue	Date
1:18:13	Pavol	Blazek	TCH	9.7.58	1		Hildesheim	16 Sep 90
1:18:20	Andrey	Perlov	RUS	12.12.61	1	NC	Moskva	26 May 90
1:18:33	Mikhail	Shchennikov	RUS	24.12.67	1		Livorno	10 Jul 93
1:18:35.2t	Stefan	Johansson	SWE	11.4.67	1	SGP	Fana	15 May 92
1:18:37	Aleksandr	Pershin	RUS	4.9.68	2	NC	Moskva	26 May 90
1:18:40.0t	Ernesto	Canto	MEX	18.10.59	1	SGP	Fana	5 May 84
1:18:51	Frants	Kostyukevich	BLS	4.4.63	3	NC	Moskva	26 May 90
1:18:54	Yevgeniy	Misyulya	BLS	13.3.64	1	NC-w	Sochi	19 Feb 89
1:18:54	Maurizio	Damilano	ITA	6.4.57	1	7N	La Coruña	6 Jun 92
1:18:56	Grigoriy (10)	Kornev	RUS	14.3.61	4	NC	Moskva	26 May 90
1:18:58		Ar Pershin			1	NC-w	Sochi	17 Feb 91
1:19:03		Misyulya			1	NC-w	Sochi	22 Feb 92
1:19:05		Kostyukevich			2	NC-w	Sochi	17 Feb 91
1:19:07		Shchennikov			5	NC	Moskva	26 May 90
1:19:08		Shchennikov			1	NC	Kiev	30 Jul 88
1:19:08	Yuriy	Kuko	BLS	23.1.68	2		Livorno	10 Jul 93
1:19:12	Axel	Noack	GDR	23.9.61	1	vSU	Karl-Marx-Stadt	21 Jun 87
1:19:13		Misyulya			1	NC	Kiev	11 Jul 91
1:19:14	Robert	Korzeniowski	POL	30.7.68	1	NC	Warszawa	20 Jun 92
1:19:17	Vladimir	Andreyev	RUS	7.9.66	3	NC-w	Sochi	17 Feb 91
1:19:18.3t	Ronald	Weigel	GDR	8.8.59	1	SGP	Fana	26 May 90

Mark	Wind	Name		Nat	Born	Pos	Meet	Venue	Date
1:19:21			Andreyev			6	NC	Moskva	26 May 90
1:19:22		David	Smith	AUS	24.7.55	1		Hobart	19 Jul 87
1:19:22.5t		Aleksey	Pershin	RUS	23.9.62	1	SGP	Fana	7 May 88
1:19:24		Carlos	Mercenário	MEX	23.5.67	1	LT	New York	3 May 87
1:19:24.1t		Walter	Arena	ITA	30.5.64	2	SGP	Fana	26 May 90
1:19:25		Valentin	Massana (20)	ESP	5.7.70	2	7N	La Coruña	6 Jun 92
1:19:29		Valdas	Kazlauskas	LIT	7.8.58	2	NC-w	Sochi	19 Feb 89
1:19:30		Jozef	Pribilinec	TCH	6.7.60	1	LT	Bergen	24 Sep 83
1:19:32		Viktor	Mostovik	MOL	7.1.63	2	LT	New York	3 May 87
1:19:32			Korzeniowski			2		Hildesheim	16 Sep 90
		(31/23)							
1:19:33		Nick	A'Hern	AUS	6.1.69	1		Melbourne	15 Dec 90
1:19:35		Domingo	Colin	MEX	4.8.52	1		Cherkassy	27 Apr 80
1:19:39		Bernardo	Segura	MEX	11.2.70	1		Eschborn	12 Jun 93
1:19:41		Igor	Plotnikov	RUS	12.7.64	4	NC-w	Sochi	17 Feb 91
1:19:41		Dmitriy	Dolnikov	RUS	19.11.72	1		Adler	14 Feb 93
1:19:42		Daniel	Garcia	MEX	28.10.71	2		Eschborn	12 Jun 93
1:19:43		Anatoliy	Solomin	UKR	2.7.52	3	LT	Bergen	24 Sep 83
		(30)							
1:19:43		Nikolay	Matyukhin	RUS	13.12.68	2		Adler	14 Feb 93
1:19:48		Yevgeniy	Zaikin	RUS	19.6.57	5	NC-w	Sochi	17 Feb 91
1:19:52		Reima	Salonen	FIN	23.12.55	1	IM	Pihtipudas	21 Jun 86
1:19:52		Vyacheslav	Cherepanov	RUS	2.11.64	4		Adler	14 Feb 93
1:19:53		Yevgeniy	Yevsyukov	RUS	2.1.50	2		Cherkassy	27 Apr 80
1:19:53		Yuriy	Gordeyev	RUS	64	3		Livorno	10 Jul 93
1:19:58		Oleg	Troshin	RUS	1.8.64	1		Moskva	22 Apr 90
1:19:59		Robert	Ihly	GER	5.5.63	3	7N	La Coruña	6 Jun 92
1:20:00		José	Marin	ESP	20.1.50	2		Barcelona	17 Apr 83
1:20:03		Viktor	Ginko	BLS	7.12.65	5		Livorno	10 Jul 93
		(40)							
1:20:04		Anatoliy	Gorshkov	UKR	4.8.58	3	LT	New York	3 May 87
1:20:06		Sergey	Protsyshin	UKR	26.2.59	4	NC	Kiev	30 Jul 88
1:20:06.8t		Daniel	Bautista	MEX	4.8.52	1		Montreal	17 Oct 79
1:20:07		Mikhail	Orlov	RUS	25.6.67	2		Moskva	22 Apr 90
1:20:09		Jacek	Muller	POL	3.11.73	4		Eschborn	12 Jun 93
1:20:10		Igor	Lyubomirov	RUS	9.11.61	2	Znam	Leningrad	11 Jun 88
1:20:10		Artur	Shumak	BLS	19.10.63	2	SPA	Kiev	11 Jul 91
1:20:18		Alessandro	Pezzatini	ITA	25.8.57	2		Piacenza	13 May 84
1:20:19		Querubin	Moreno	COL	29.12.59	4	LT	New York	3 May 87
1:20:19		Vyacheslav	Smirnov	RUS	1.1.59	3	Znam	Leningrad	11 Jun 88
1:20:19		Ilya	Markov	RUS	19.6.72	5		Adler	14 Feb 93
		(51)							
Other 20,000 metres track bests									
1:19:54.0		Pavol	Blazek	TCH	9.7.58	3	SGP	Fana	26 May 90
1:20:12.3		Nick	A'Hern	AUS	6.1.69	1	SGP	Fana	8 May 93
1:20:24.4		Li Mingcai		CHN	22.8.71	1	NC	Jinan	15 Mar 92

30 000m 2 hours TRACK

2:01:44.1	29572m	Maurizio	Damilano	ITA	6.4.57	1	Cuneo	4 Oct 92
2:03:56.5	29090	Thierry	Toutain	FRA	14.2.62	1	Héricourt	24 Mar 91
2:04:55.5	28800	Guillaume	Leblanc	CAN	14.4.62	1	Sept-Iles	16 Jun 90
2:06:07.3	28565		Damilano			1	San Donato Milano	5 May 85
2:06:54.0	28358	Ralf	Kowalsky	GDR	22.3.62	1	Berlin	28 Mar 82
2:07:59.9	28165	José	Marin	ESP	21.1.50	1	Barcelona	8 Apr 79

30 KILOMETRES WALK (ROAD)

Where superior to track times shown above

2:02:41	Andrey	Perlov	RUS	12.12.61	1	NC-w	Sochi	19 Feb 89
2:02:45	Yevgeniy	Misyulya	BLS	13.3.64	1		Mogilyov	28 Apr 91
2:03:06	Daniel	Bautista	MEX	4.8.52	1		Cherkassy	27 Apr 80
2:04:00	Aleksandr	Potashov	BLS	12.3.62	1		Adler	14 Feb 93
2:04:24	Valeriy	Spitsyn	RUS	5.12.65	1	NC-w	Sochi	22 Feb 92
2:04:30	Vitaliy	Matsko	RUS	8.6.60	2	NC-w	Sochi	19 Feb 89
2:04:50		Potashov			3	NC-w	Sochi	19 Feb 89
2:05:01	Sergey	Katureyev	RUS	67	2	NC-w	Sochi	22 Feb 92

Mark Wind	Name		Nat	Born	Pos	Meet	Venue	Date
2:05:05	Pyotr	Pochenchuk	UKR	26.7.54	2		Cherkassy	27 Apr 80
2:05:12	Valeriy	Suntsov	RUS	10.7.55	3		Cherkassy	27 Apr 80
2:05:12		Potashov			1	NC-w	Sochi	17 Feb 91
2:05:17	Vitaliy	Popovich	UKR	22.10.62	4	NC-w	Sochi	19 Feb 89
2:05:17		Spitsyn			2	NC-w	Sochi	17 Feb 91
	(13/10)							
2:05:36	Viktor	Ginko	BLS	7.12.65	2		Adler	14 Feb 93
2:05:53	Andrey	Plotnikov	RUS	12.8.67	3		Adler	14 Feb 93
2:05:58	Vyacheslav	Smirnov	RUS	1.1.59	5	NC-w	Sochi	19 Feb 89
2:05:59	David	Smith	AUS	24.7.55	1		Canberra	10 May 86
2:06:01	Giovanni	Perricelli	ITA	25.8.67	1		Sesto S Giovanni	1 May 92
2:06:25	Anatoliy	Grigoryev	RUS	.60	3	NC-w	Sochi	17 Feb 91
2:06:31	Artur	Shumak	BLS	19.10.63	6	NC-w	Sochi	19 Feb 89
2:06:39	Simon	Baker	AUS	6.2.58	1		Melbourne	7 May 89
2:07:01	Viktor	Mostovik	MOL	7.1.63	1			20 Feb 86
2:07:04	Vyacheslav	Ivanenko	URS	1.3.61	2			20 Feb 86
	(20)							
2:07:04	Modris	Liepins	LAT	3.8.66	1	NC	Riga	21 Sep 91
2:07:08	Yevgeniy	Zaikin	RUS	20.7.57	1		Kiev	3 Oct 81
2:07:13	Ivan	Tikhonov	RUS	1.5.50	4		Cherkassy	27 Apr 80
2:07:20	Stanislav	Vezhel	BLS	11.10.58	7	NC-w	Sochi	19 Feb 89
2:07:29	Raúl	González	MEX	29.2.52	1		Eschborn	30 Sep 79
2:07:33	Valdimir	Gerus	TJK	10.2.49	2		Kiev	3 Oct 81
2:07:43	Pavol	Blazek	TCH	9.7.58	3		Sesto San Giovanni	1 May 91
2:07:45	Martín	Bermúdez	MEX	19.7.58	2		Hull	8 Oct 89
2:07:56	Ian	McCombie	GBR	11.1.61	1	CGT	Edinburgh	27 Apr 86
2:07:56	Vladimir	Soyka	UKR	29.10.65	8	NC-w	Sochi	19 Feb 89
	(30)							
2:07:58	Valentin	Massana	ESP	5.7.70	1		El Prat de Llobregat	28 Mar 93

t = track walk

50 KILOMETRES WALK

Mark Wind	Name		Nat	Born	Pos	Meet	Venue	Date
3:37:41	Andrey	Perlov	RUS	12.12.61	1	NC	Leningrad	5 Aug 89
3:38:17	Ronald	Weigel	GDR	8.8.59	1	IM	Potsdam	25 May 86
3:38:29	Vyacheslav	Ivanenko	RUS	1.3.61	1	OG	Seoul	30 Sep 88
3:38:31		Weigel			1		E.Berlin	20 Jul 84
3:38:56		Weigel			2	OG	Seoul	30 Sep 88
3:39:45	Hartwig	Gauder	GDR	10.11.54	3	OG	Seoul	30 Sep 88
3:39:47		Perlov			1		Leningrad	3 Aug 85
3:40:02	Aleksandr	Potashov	RUS	12.3.62	1	NC	Moskva	27 May 90
3:40:07		Perlov			1		Kharkov	5 Sep 87
3:40:07	Andrey	Plotnikov	RUS	12.8.67	2	NC	Moskva	27 May 90
3:40:46	José	Marin	ESP	21.1.50	1		Valencia	13 Mar 83
3:40:53		Gauder			1	WC	Roma	5 Sep 87
3:40:55		Gauder			1	EC	Stuttgart	31 Aug 86
3:41:00		Potashov			4	OG	Seoul	30 Sep 88
3:41:20	Raul	González	MEX	29.2.52	1		Podebrady	11 Jun 78
3:41:24		Gauder			2		E.Berlin	20 Jul 84
3:41:30		Weigel			2	WC	Roma	5 Sep 87
3:41:38.4t		González			1	SGP	Fana	25 May 79
3:41:31		Weigel			1		Naumberg	1 May 83
3:41:41	Jesús	Garcia	ESP	17.10.69	1	WC	Stuttgart	21 Aug 93
3:41:51	Venyamin	Nikolayev (10)	RUS	7.10.58	2		Leningrad	3 Aug 85
3:41:54		Ivanenko			2	EC	Stuttgart	31 Aug 86
3:42:00	Stanislav	Vezhel	BLS	11.10.58	3	NC	Moskva	27 May 90
3:42:02	Valentin	Kononen	FIN	7.3.69	2	WC	Stuttgart	21 Aug 93
3:42:03	Carlos	Mercenario	MEX	23.5.67	1	WP	San José	2 Jun 91
3:42:04	Yevgeniy	Yevsyukov	RUS	2.1.50	3		Leningrad	3 Aug 85
3:42:20	Pavel	Szikora	TCH	26.3.52	1		Dudince	4 Apr 87
3:42:26		Weigel			1	LT	New York	2 May 87
3:42:33		Weigel			1		Naumburg	1 May 88
3:42:36	Reima	Salonen	FIN	19.10.55	1	NC	Vantaa	24 May 86
	(30/16)							
3:42:37	Valeriy	Suntsov	RUS	10.7.55	4		Leningrad	3 Aug 85
3:42:50	Valeriy	Spitsyn	RUS	5.12.65	3	WC	Stuttgart	21 Aug 93

Mark	Wind	Name		Nat	Born	Pos	Meet	Venue	Date
3:43:13		Simon	Baker	AUS	6.2.58	1	LT	L'Hospitalet	28 May 89
3:43:14		Dietmar	Meisch	GDR	10.2.59	3	LT	New York	2 May 87
		(20)							
3:43:36		Martín	Bermúdez	MEX	19.7.58	1	LT	Eschborn	30 Sep 79
3:43:50		Axel	Noack	GER	23.9.61	4	WC	Stuttgart	21 Aug 93
3:43:57		Vitaliy	Matsko	RUS	8.6.60	2	NC	Leningrad	5 Aug 89
3:43:57		Vitaliy	Popovich	UKR	22.10.62	3	NC	Leningrad	5 Aug 89
3:43:59		Enrique	Vera-Ybánez	MEX	31.5.54	2	LT	Eschborn	30 Sep 79
3:44:08		Viktor	Dorovskikh	RUS	19.10.50	5		Leningrad	3 Aug 85
3:44.12		Anatoliy	Grigoryev	RUS	.61	1		Yevpatoriya	1 Oct 89
3:44:24		Erling	Andersen	NOR	22.9.60	2	WCp-s	Borås	15 Jun 85
3:44:24		Robert	Korzeniowski	POL	30.7.68	1	NC	Zamosc	26 Sep 93
3:44:33		Jorge	Llopart	ESP	5.5.52	1		Reus	26 Aug 79
		(30)							
3:44:45		Aleksey	Volgin	RUS	.68	1		Novopolotsk	16 Sep 90
3:44:49		Bo	Gustafsson	SWE	29.9.54	7	OG	Seoul	30 Sep 88
3:45:43		Raffaello	Ducceschi	ITA	25.2.62	8	OG	Seoul	30 Sep 88
3:45:51		Uwe	Dünkel	GDR	3.11.60	1		E.Berlin	18 Jul 81
3:45:51		Sergey	Protsyshin	UKR	17.4.59	4	EC	Stuttgart	31 Aug 86
3:46:08		Vyacheslav	Smirnov	RUS	.57	4	NC	Leningrad	5 Aug 89
3:46:11.0t		Nikolay	Udovenko	URS	6.10.56	1		Uzhgorod	3 Oct 80
3:46:11		Valentin	Massana	ESP	5.7.70	1	NC	Reus	14 Feb 93
3:46:28		Valeriy	Yarets	RUS	.56	6		Leningrad	3 Aug 85
3:46:34		Willi	Sawall	AUS	7.11.41	1		Adelaide	6 Apr 80
		(40)							
3:46:41		Sun Xiaoguang		CHN	15.1.65	1		Zhengzhou	5 Mar 91
3:46:43		Bernd	Gummelt	GDR	21.12.63	2		Berlin	20 May 90
3:46:46		Basilio	Labrador	ESP	29.3.67	5	WC	Stuttgart	21 Aug 93
3:46:51		Maurizio	Damilano	ITA	6.4.57	1	NC	Pomigliano	25 Mar 90
3:46:55		Vyacheslav	Fursov	RUS	19.7.54	5	LT	Eschborn	30 Sep 79
3:46:57		Vladimir	Rezayev	RUS	4.1.50	2		Moskva	27 Jul 79
3:47:13		Pyotr	Gaus	URS	.52	3		Moskva	3 Jul 82
3:47:14		Giovanni	Perricelli	ITA	25.8.67	11	OG	Seoul	30 Sep 88
3:47:16		Sergey	Yung	RUS	10.8.55	4		Moskva	3 Jul 82
3:47:17		Zhou Yongshen		CHN	.71	2		Zhengzhou	5 Mar 91
		(50)							
50,000 metres track best									
3:43:50.0		Simon	Baker	AUS	6.2.58	1		Melbourne	9 Sep 90

JUNIOR MEN'S ALL-TIME LISTS

100 METRES

Mark	Wind	Name		Nat	Born	Pos	Meet	Venue	Date
10.05		Davidson	Ezinwa	NGR	22.11.71	1		Bauchi	4 Jan 90
10.07	2.0	Stanley	Floyd	USA	23.6.61	1		Austin	24 May 80
10.08	0.0	Andre	Cason	USA	13.1.69	1	TAC-j	Tallahassee	24 Jun 88
10.09A	1.8	Mel	Lattany	USA	10.8.59	2r2	USOF	Colorado Springs	30 Jul 78
10.10	1.9	Stanley	Kerr	USA	19.6.67	1	TAC-j	Towson	28 Jun 86
10.11	1.9	Harvey	Glance	USA	28.3.57	1	FOT	Eugene	20 Jun 76
10.13	1.9	Derrick	Florence	USA	19.6.68	2	TAC-j	Towson	28 Jun 86
10.14	0.8	Ronnie Ray	Smith	USA	28.3.49	2s1	AAU	Sacramento	20 Jun 68
10.14	2.0	Sven	Matthes	GDR	23.8.69	1		Berlin	13 Sep 88
10.16i	-	Eugen	Ray	GDR	26.7.57	1		Berlin	25 Jan 76
10.16	1.9	Houston	McTear	USA	12.2.57	2	FOT	Eugene	20 Jun 76
Wind-assisted									
10.07	2.9	Lee	McRae	USA	23.1.66	2h5	NCAA	Austin	30 May 85
10.08	4.0	Johnny	Jones	USA	4.4.58	1		Austin	20 May 77
10.09	4.1	Stanley	Blalock	USA	18.3.64	1		Athens	19 Mar 83
10.09	3.1	Innocent	Asunze	NGR	30.12.72	1r1		Lagos	10 Jun 90
10.10		Rodney	Bridges	USA	31.5.71	1s1	JUCO	Odessa	18 May 90
10.11	4.0	Rod	Richardson	USA	17.9.62	1		Austin	22 May 81
10.12	3.7	Calvin	Smith	USA	8.1.61	1h5	NCAA	Austin	5 Jun 80
10.12A		Jerome	Harrison	USA	17.2.62	1		Colorado Springs	25 Jul 81
10.12		Héctor	Fuentes	CUB	27.7.74	1		Artemisa	22 Apr 93
Hand timing									
9.9	1.8	Johnny	Jones	USA	4.4.58	1	TexR	Austin	2 Apr 77
9.9		Oladape	Adeniken	NGR	19.8.69	2	NC	Bauchi	2 Jul 88
9.8w		Michael	Taylor	USA	4.8.65	1		Shreveport	11 Apr 83
Doubful timing: 9.8		Osmond	Ezinwa	NGR	22.11.71	1h2		Bauchi	3 Jan 90

200 METRES

Mark	Wind	Name		Nat	Born	Pos	Meet	Venue	Date
20.07	1.5	Lorenzo	Daniel	USA	23.3.66	1	SEC	Starkville	18 May 85
20.13	1.7	Roy	Martin	USA	25.12.66	1		Austin	11 May 85
20.22	1.7	Dwayne	Evans	USA	13.10.58	2	FOT	Eugene	22 Jun 76
20.23	0.5	Michael	Timpson	USA	6.6.67	1		University Park	16 May 86
20.24	0.2	Joe	DeLoach	USA	5.6.67	3		Los Angeles	8 Jun 85
20.29	1.5	Clinton	Davis	USA	17.8.65	1	TAC-j	University Park	26 Jun 83
20.30		Davidson	Ezinwa	NGR	22.11.71	1h1		Bauchi	3 Jan 90
20.37	1.0	Jürgen	Evers	FRG	29.4.65	1	EJ	Schwechat	28 Aug 83
20.37	0.2	Roberto	Hernández	CUB	6.3.67	1		Sevilla	24 May 86
20.39A	1.0	Marshall	Dill	USA	9.8.52	2	PAG	Cali	3 Aug 71
20.39	0.9	Stanley	Kerr	USA	19.6.67	1	TAC-j	Towson	29 Jun 86
20.42	1.8	Silvio	Leonard	CUB	20.9.55	2		Potsdam	13 Jun 74
Wind-assisted									
20.01	2.5	Derald	Harris	USA	5.4.58	1		San José	9 Apr 77
20.10	4.6	Stanley	Kerr	USA	19.6.67	2r2	SWC	Houston	18 May 86
20.34A	2.2	Marshall	Dill	USA	9.8.52	1s2	PAG	Cali	3 Aug 71
20.36	4.8	Chris	Nelloms	USA	14.8.71	1		Indianapolis	9 Jun 90
20.39	3.3	Stanley	Floyd	USA	23.6.61	1h4	NCAA	Austin	5 Jun 80
Hand timing			** 220 yards less 0.1 secs*						
19.9		Davidson	Ezinwa	NGR	22.11.71	1		Bauchi	18 Mar 89
20.1		Marshall	Dill	USA	9.8.52	1		Windsor	1 Jul 71
20.1		Harvey	Glance	USA	28.3.57	1		Auburn	17 Apr 76
20.1*	1.8	Willie	Turner	USA	14.10.68	2		Sacramento	10 Jun 67

400 METRES

Mark	Wind	Name		Nat	Born	Pos	Meet	Venue	Date
43.87		Steve	Lewis	USA	16.5.69	1	OG	Seoul	28 Sep 88
44.69		Darrell	Robinson	USA	23.12.63	2	USOF	Indianapolis	24 Jul 82
44.73A		James	Rolle	USA	2.2.64	1	USOF	Colorado Springs	2 Jul 83
44.75		Darren	Clark	AUS	6.9.65	4	OG	Los Angeles	8 Aug 84
44.75		Deon	Minor	USA	22.1.73	1s1	NCAA	Austin	5 Jun 92
45.01		Thomas	Schönlebe	GDR	6.8.65	1		Berlin	15 Jul 84
45.05A		Wayne	Collett	USA	20.10.49	1q2	FOT	Echo Summit	13 Sep 68
45.05		Roberto	Hernández	CUB	6.3.67	2		Santiago de Cuba	21 Feb86
45.07		Calvin	Harrison	USA	20.1.74	1	NC-j	Spokane	27 Jun 93
45.09		Kevin	Robinzine	USA	12.4.66	4	TAC	Indianapolis	16 Jun 85

Mark	Wind	Name		Nat	Born	Pos	Meet	Venue	Date
45.09		Henry	Thomas	USA	10.7.67	2r2	ISTAF	W.Berlin	23 Aug 85
45.17		William	Reed	USA	1.4.70	1	TAC-j	Tucson	20 Jul 87
44.9'A hand		Steve	Williams	USA	13.11.53	1	WAC	El Paso	13 May 72

800 METRES

* 880 yards less 0.6 seconds

Mark	Name		Nat	Born	Pos	Meet	Venue	Date
1:44.3*	Jim	Ryun	USA	29.4.47	1	USTFF	Terre Haute	10 Jun 66
1:44.3	Joaquim	Cruz	BRA	12.3.63	1		Rio de Janeiro	27 Jun 81
1:44.77	Benson	Koech	KEN	10.11.74	1	WJ	Seoul	19 Sep 92
1:45.34	José	Parrilla	USA	31.3.72	1	SEC	Baton Rouge	19 May 91
1:45.45	Andreas	Busse	GDR	6.5.59	1	GS	Ostrava	7 Jun 78
1:45.46	Hezekiel	Sepeng	RSA	30.6.74	3s1	WC	Stuttgart	15 Aug 93
1:45.64	David	Sharpe	GBR	8.7.67	5	VD	Bruxelles	5 Sep 86
1:45.77	Steve	Ovett	GBR	9.10.55	2	EC	Roma	4 Sep 74
1:45.84	Detlef	Wagenknecht	GDR	3.1.59	1	NC	Leipzig	2 Jul 78
1:45.96A	Jozef	Plachy	TCH	28.2.49	3s2	OG	Ciudad México	14 Oct 68
1:46.06	Vincent	Malakwen	KEN	19.7.74	2B		Rieti	5 Sep 93
1:46.16	Jonah	Birir	KEN	12.12.71	3		Rovereto	21 Aug 90

1000 METRES

Mark	Name		Nat	Born	Pos	Meet	Venue	Date
2:18.31	Andreas	Busse	GDR	6.5.59	1		Dresden	7 Aug 77
2:18.37	Vincent	Malakwen	KEN	19.7.74	1	ISTAF	Berlin	27 Aug 93
2:18.46	Benson	Koech	KEN	10.11.74	4	Pre	Eugene	5 Jun 93
2:18.70	Steffan	Oehme	GDR	30.8.63	5		Cottbus	30 May 81

1500 METRES

Mark	Name		Nat	Born	Pos	Meet	Venue	Date
3:34.92	Kipkoech	Cheruiyot	KEN	2.12.64	1		München	26 Jul 83
3:36.07	Wilfred Oanda	Kirochi	KEN	12.12.69	4		Rieti	31 Aug 88
3:36.1+	Jim	Ryun	USA	29.4.47	1		Berkeley	17 Jul 66
3:36.4A	Atoi	Boru	KEN	25.10.73	1	NC	Nairobi	13 Jun 92
3:36.47	Benson	Koech	KEN	10.11.74	4	Herc	Monte Carlo	7 Aug 93
3:36.73	Moses	Kiptanui	KEN	1.9.71	6		Rovereto	21 Aug 90
3:36.6+	Graham	Williamson	GBR	15.6.60	3	OsloG	Oslo	17 Jul 79
3:37.5	Tom	Byers	USA	12.4.55	3		Torino	24 Jul 74
3:37.95	William	Koila	KEN	4.8.74	1		New Delhi	4 Sep 91
3:38.07	Ari	Paunonen	FIN	10.3.58	1	NC	Tampere	31 Jul 77
3:38.2	José	M.Abascal	ESP	17.3.58	1		Barcelona	10 Sep 77
3:38.3	Igor	Lotarev	RUS	30.8.64	1		Krasnodar	7 Aug 83

1 MILE

Mark	Name		Nat	Born	Pos	Meet	Venue	Date
3:51.3	Jim	Ryun	USA	29.4.47	1		Berkeley	17 Jul 66
3:53.15	Graham	Williamson	GBR	15.6.60	3	OsloG	Oslo	17 Jul 79
3:53.92	Kipkoech	Cheruiyot	KEN	2.12.64	8	ISTAF	W.Berlin	17 Aug 83
3:55.63	Ari	Paunonen	FIN	10.3.58	3		London	26 Jun 77
3:56.87	Mike	Hillardt	AUS	22.1.61	5	ISTAF	W.Berlin	8 Aug 80

3000 METRES

Mark	Name		Nat	Born	Pos	Meet	Venue	Date
7:39.82	Ismael	Kirui	KEN	20.2.75	3	ISTAF	Berlin	27 Aug 93
7:42.93	Andrew	Sambu	TAN	5.10.72	1		Grossetto	11 Aug 91
7:43.20	Ari	Paunonen	FIN	10.3.58	3		Köln	22 Jun 77
7:47.47	Charles	Cheruiyot	KEN	2.12.64	3	ISTAF	W.Berlin	17 Aug 83
7:48.28	Jon	Richards	GBR	19.5.64	9	OsloG	Oslo	9 Jul 83
7:49.74	Eliud	Barngenuty	KEN	.73	1		Nuoro	12 Sep 92
7:50.22+	Richard	Chelimo	KEN	21.4.72	1	GG	Roma	17 Jul 91
7:51.53	Christian	Leuprecht	ITA	28.5.71	5		Padova	16 Sep 90
7:51.84	Steve	Binns	GBR	25.8.60	2		Gateshead	8 Sep 79
7:53.4	Eddy	De Pauw	BEL	8.6.60	2		Bornem	3 Aug 79
7:54.2	Raf	Wijns	BEL	7.1.64	4		Bosvoorde	4 Aug 83
7:54.7	Mohamed	Choumassi	MAR	2.12.69	1		Västerås	30 Jun 88

5000 METRES

Mark	Name		Nat	Born	Pos	Meet	Venue	Date
13:02.75	Ismael	Kirui	KEN	20.2.75	1	WC	Stuttgart	16 Aug 93
13:11.76	Richard	Chelimo	KEN	21.4.72	4	GG	Roma	17 Jul 91
13:16.64	Fita	Bayissa	ETH	15.12.72	2	WC	Tokyo	1 Sep 91
13:20.12	Andrew	Sambu	TAN	5.10.72	3	MAI	Malmö	5 Aug 91
13:23.17	Addis	Abebe	ETH	5.9.70	1	Znam	Volgograd	11 Jun 89

Mark	Wind	Name		Nat	Born	Pos	Meet	Venue	Date
13:25.33		Charles	Cheruiyot	KEN	2.12.64	1		München	26 Jul 83
13:26.88		Terry	Thornton	RSA	23.9.67	1		Stellenbosch	8 Nov 86
13:27.04		Steve	Binns	GBR	25.8.60	3	IAC	London	14 Sep 79
13:28.85		Josphat	Machuka	KEN	12.12.73	3	AfrCh	Belle Vue Mauricia	27 Jun 92
13:29.91		Kibiego	Kororia	KEN	25.12.71	2		Vigo	5 Jul 90
13:33.6 '		Berhanu	Girma	ETH	.60	2r1		Sochi	8 Jun 79
13:33.9		Christian	Leuprecht	ITA	28.5.71	1		Lana	28 Sep 90
3 miles time: 13:04.0		Gerry	Lindgren	USA	9.3.46	2	AAA	London	10 Jul 65

10000 METRES

Mark	Wind	Name		Nat	Born	Pos	Meet	Venue	Date
27:11.18		Richard	Chelimo	KEN	21.4.72	1	APM	Hengelo	25 Jun 91
27:17.82		Addis	Abebe	ETH	5.9.70	2	WG	Helsinki	29 Jun 89
27:57.68		Josphat	Machuka	KEN	12.12.73	3	VD	Bruxelles	25 Aug 92
28:03.79		Kibiego	Kororia	KEN	25.12.71	2		Kobe	29 Apr 90
28:03.99		Haile	Guebre Silassie	ETH	18.4.73	1	WJ	Seoul	18 Sep 92
28:07.1A		Ismael	Kirui	KEN	20.2.75	1	NC	Nairobi	3 Jul 93
28:07.70		Petro	Metta	TAN	18.12.73	1		Formia	8 Jul 91
28:12.78		Bidelu	Kibret	ETH	.69	11	VD	Bruxelles	19 Aug 88
28:18.57		Richard	Chelimo	KEN	21.4.73	1	WJ	Plovdiv	8 Aug 90
28:22.48		Christian	Leuprecht	ITA	28.5.71	3		Koblenz	4 Sep 90
28:25.77		Mohamed	Choumassi	MAR	2.12..69	21	Bis	Oslo	2 Jul 88
28:27.56		Joseph	Kibor	KEN	.22.12.72	5	CG	Auckland	27 Jan 90
Notable 6 miles times									
27:11.6		Gerry	Lindgren	USA	9.3.46	2	AAU	San Diego	27 Jun 65
27:30.8		Garry	Bjorklund	USA	22.4.51	3	AAU	Bakersfield	27 Jun 70

MARATHON

Mark	Wind	Name		Nat	Born	Pos	Meet	Venue	Date
2:12:49		Negash	Dube	ETH	20.5.68	2		Beijing	18 Oct 87
2:12:49		Tesfayi	Dadi	ETH	19.5.69	5		W.Berlin	9 Oct 88

3000 METRES STEEPLECHASE

Mark	Wind	Name		Nat	Born	Pos	Meet	Venue	Date
8:24.47		Matthew	Birir	KEN	5.7.72*	3		Getxo	29 Jun 91
8:24.58		Christopher	Koskei	KEN	14.8.74	2	AfrC	Durban	25 Jun 93
8:24.87			Sun Ripeng	CHN	25.1.74	1	NG	Beijing	11 Sep 93
8:29.50		Ralf	Pönitzsch	GDR	20.10.57	4	vPOL,URS	Warszawa	19 Aug 76
8:29.85		Paul	Davies-Hale	GBR	21.6.62	3	vPOL,SUI	London	31 Aug 81
8:30.29		Anton	Nicolaisen	RSA	25.1.68	1		Durban	7 Dec 87
8:31.27		Shigeyuki	Aikyo	JPN	29.1.64	9h1	WC	Helsinki	9 Aug 83
8:31.32		Eliud	Barngenuty	KEN	.73	2		Bologna	9 Sep 92
8:31.62		Mwangangi	Muindi	KEN	14.8.73	1	WJ	Seoul	20 Sep 92
8:31.85		Arsenios	Tsiminos	GRE	19.1.61	3	vSPA,BEL-j	Barcelona	31 Aug 80
8:32.43		Ayele	Mezegebu	ETH	6.1.73	2	WJ	Seoul	20 Sep 92
8:32.48		Stephen	Chepseba	KEN	24.4.74	3	WJ	Seoul	20 Sep 92

* Birir's birthdate previously reported as 25.11.69

110 METRES HURDLES

Mark	Wind	Name		Nat	Born	Pos	Meet	Venue	Date
13.23	0.0	Renaldo	Nehemiah	USA	24.3.59	1r2	WK	Zürich	16 Aug 78
13.44	-0.8	Colin	Jackson	GBR	18.2.67	1	WJ	Athinai	19 Jul 86
13.46	1.8	Jon	Ridgeon	GBR	14.2.67	1	EJ	Cottbus	23 Aug 85
13.47	1.9	Holger	Pohland	GDR	5.4.63	2	vUSA	Karl-Marx-Stadt	10 Jul 82
13.52	2.0	Alejandro	Casañas	CUB	29.1.54	1		Warszawa	28 Jun 72
13.52	0.6	Ubeja	Anderson	USA	30.3.74	1		Knoxville	16 May 93
13.57	1.4	Robert	Gaines	USA	14.4.57	2s1	FOT	Eugene	24 Jun 76
13.57*	0.5	Greg	Foster	USA	4.8.58	1	WCR	Fresno	7 May 77
13.64	2.0	Glenn	Terry	USA	10.2.71	1		Indianapolis	23 May 90
13.65	0.9	Antti	Haapakoski	FIN	6.2.71	1		Jamsankoski	26 Jul 90
13.66	2.0	Arto	Bryggare	FIN	26.5.58	4	EP	Helsinki	14 Aug 77
13.67	1.7	James	Walker	USA	25.10.57	1	vFRG-j	Lüdenscheid	8 Jul 76
Wind-assisted				** 120 yards hurdles time plus 0.03 sec.*					
13.42	4.5	Colin	Jackson	GBR	18.2.67	2	CG	Edinburgh	27 Jul 86
13.54	4.1	Rod	Wilson	USA	24.9.61	1h2	NCAA	Austin	6 Jun 80
13.55	3.1	Arto	Bryggare	FIN	26.5.58	1	vUK	Oulu	10 Jul 77
13.65	3.2	Dan	Philibert	FRA	6.8.70	1		Créteil	9 Jul 89

400 METRES HURDLES

Mark	Wind	Name		Nat	Born	Pos	Meet	Venue	Date
48.02		Danny	Harris	USA	7.9.65	2s1	FOT	Los Angeles	17 Jun 84
48.74		Vladimir	Budko	BLS	4.2.65	2	DRZ	Moskva	18 Aug 84

Mark	Wind	Name		Nat	Born	Pos	Meet	Venue	Date
49.10		Yoshihiko	Saito	JPN	12.2.72	1		Kanazawa	17 Oct 91
49.33A		Joseph	Maritim	KEN	22.10.68	4	AfrG	Nairobi	9 Aug 87
49.45		Belfred	Clark	USA	19.8.65	1	TAC-j	Los Angeles	24 Jun 84
49.50		Kelly	Carter	USA	15.2.69	1	WJ	Sudbury	29 Jul 88
49.61		Harald	Schmid	FRG	29.9.57	1	vUSA-j	Lüdenscheid	7 Jul 76
49.62		Dennis	Otono	NGR	16.4.58	2	NCAA	Champaign	4 Jun 77
49.64		Jószef	Szalai	HUN	8.3.61	3	BGP	Budapest	11 Aug 80
49.66		Edgar	Itt	FRG	8.6.67	1	NC-j	Wetzlar	7 Sep 86
49.71		Ruslan	Mishchenko	UKR	24.4.64	1	EJ	Schwechat	28 Aug 83
49.73		Rohan	Robinson	AUS	15.11.71	1	WJ	Plovdiv	10 Aug 90

HIGH JUMP

Mark	Wind	Name		Nat	Born	Pos	Meet	Venue	Date
2.37		Dragutin	Topic	YUG	12.3.71	1	WJ	Plovdiv	12 Aug 90
2.37		Steve	Smith	GBR	29.3.73	1	WJ	Seoul	20 Sep 92
2.36		Javier	Sotomayor	CUB	13.10.67	1		Santiago de Cuba	23 Feb 86
2.35i		Vladimir	Yashchenko	UKR	12.1.59	1	EI	Milano	12 Mar 78
		2.34				1	Prv	Tbilisi	16 Jun 78
2.35		Dietmar	Mögenburg	FRG	15.8.61	1		Rehlingen	26 May 80
2.34		Tim	Forsyth	AUS	17.8.73	1	Bisl	Oslo	4 Jul 92
2.33		Zhu Jianhua		CHN	29.5.63	1	AsiG	New Delhi	1 Dec 82
2.33		Patrik	Sjöberg	SWE	5.1.65	1	OsloG	Oslo	9 Jul 83
2.31		Jörg	Freimuth	GDR	10.9.61	3	OG	Moskva	1 Aug 80
2.31		Lochsley	Thomson	AUS	20.8.73	3	NC	Adelaide	8 Mar 92
2.30		Dothel	Edwards	USA	9.9.66	1	v3-N	Pullman	21 Jul 85
2.30		Jagan	Hames	AUS	31.10.75	2	NC	Sydney	13 Mar 94

POLE VAULT

Mark	Wind	Name		Nat	Born	Pos	Meet	Venue	Date
5.80		Maksim	Tarasov	RUS	2.12.70	1	vGDR-j	Bryansk	14 Jul 89
5.71		Lawrence	Johnson	USA	7.5.74	1		Knoxville	12 Jun 93
5.65		Rodion	Gataullin	UZB	23.11.65	2	NC	Donyetsk	8 Sep 84
5.65		István	Bagyula	HUN	2.1.69	1	WJ	Sudbury	28 Jul 88
5.62		Gérald	Baudouin	FRA	15.11.72	1	NC-j	Dreux	7 Jul 91
5.61		Thierry	Vigneron	FRA	9.3.60	1		Longwy	30 Sep 79
5.61i		Grigoriy	Yegorov	KZK	12.1.67	1	vGDR-j	Moskva	16 Feb 86
		5.55				1	vGDR-j	Minsk	22 Jun 85
5.60		Konstantin	Volkov	RUS	28.2.60	1	EP	Torino	5 Aug 79
5.60		Andrey	Grudinin	RUS	3.5.69	1		Simferopol	27 May 88
5.60i		Jean	Galfione	FRA	20.6.71	1		Miremas	24 Mar 90
5.57		Dave	Volz	USA	2.5.62	1		Bloomington	18 Apr 81

5.55: five men - Sergey Bubka UKR 82, Delko Lesev BUL 86, Roman Barabashov UKR 87, Daniel Marti ESP 92
James Miller AUS 93

LONG JUMP

Mark	Wind	Name		Nat	Born	Pos	Meet	Venue	Date
8.34	0.0	Randy	Williams	USA	23.8.53	Q	OG	München	8 Sep 72
8.28	0.8	Luis	A.Bueno	CUB	22.5.69	1		Habana	16 Jul 88
8.24	0.2	Eric	Metcalf	USA	23.1.68	1	NCAA	Indianapolis	6 Jun 86
8.24	1.8	Vladimir	Ochkan	UKR	13.1.68	1	vGDR-j	Leningrad	21 Jun 87
8.22		Larry	Doubley	USA	15.3.58	1	NCAA	Champaign	3 Jun 77
8.22		Ivan	Pedroso	CUB	17.12.72	1		Santiago de Cuba	3 May 91
8.21A	2.0	Vance	Johnson	USA	13.3.63	1	NCAA	Provo	4 Jun 82
8.20	1.5	James	Stallworth	USA	29.4.71	Q	WJ	Plovdiv	9 Aug 90
8.18		LaMonte	King	USA	18.12.59	2	CalR	Modesto	20 May 78
8.16	1.1	Dion	Bentley	USA	26.8.71	1	PAm-j	Santa Fé	23 Jun 89
8.15	1.2	Leroy	Burrell	USA	21.2.67	1		Los Angeles	19 Apr 86
8.14	1.5	Sheddric	Fields	USA	13.4.73	1	WelshG	Cwmbran	14 Jul 91
Wind assisted									
8.40	3.2	Kareem	Streete-Thompson	CAY	30.3.73	1		Houston	5 May 91
8.35	2.2	Carl	Lewis	USA	1.7.61	1	NCAA	Austin	6 Jun 80
8.23	4.4	Peller	Phillips	USA	23.6.70	1		Sacramento	11 Jun 88
8.21	2.8	Masaki	Morinaga	JPN	27.3.72	1		Hamamatsu	7 Sep 91

TRIPLE JUMP

Mark	Wind	Name		Nat	Born	Pos	Meet	Venue	Date
17.50	0.3	Volker	Mai	GDR	3.5.66	1	vSU	Erfurt	23 Jun 85
17.42	1.3	Khristo	Markov	BUL	27.1.65	1	Nar	Sofia	19 May 84
17.40A	0.4	Pedro	Perez Duenas	CUB	23.2.52	1	PAG	Cali	5 Aug 71
17.27		Aliacer	Urrutia	CUB	22.9.74	1		Artemisa	23 Apr 93

Mark	Wind	Name		Nat	Born	Pos	Meet	Venue	Date
17.23	0.2	Yoelvis	Quesada	CUB	4.8.73	1	NC	Habana	13 May 92
17.03	0.6	Osiris	Mora	CUB	3.10.73	2	WJ	Seoul	19 Sep 92
17.00		Gustavo	Platt	CUB	29.7.54	1		Habana	5 May 73
17.00		Yevgeniy	Timofeyev	RUS	22.2.74	1		Krasnodar	26 May 93
16.98	-0.2	Sergey	Bykov	UKR	11.5.71	1	WJ	Plovdiv	12 Aug 90
16.97	0.2	Igor	Parygin	RUS	3.2.67	1	WJ	Athinai	20 Jul 86
16.91		Héctor	Marquetti	CUB	7.4.68	1	CAC	Caracas	26 Jul 87
16.86	1.5	Yuriy	Gorbachenko	UKR	19.7.66	1		Odessa	15 Sep 85
Drugs disqualification: 16.94	2.2	Juan M Lopez		CUB	7.4.67	2	WJ	Athinai	20 Jul 86

SHOT

Mark	Name		Nat	Born	Pos	Meet	Venue	Date
21.05i	Terry	Albritton	USA	14.1.55	1	AAU	New York	22 Feb 74
	20.38				2	MSR	Walnut	27 Apr 74
20.65	Mike	Carter	USA	29.10.60	1	vSU-j	Boston	4 Jul 79
20.20	Randy	Matson	USA	5.3.45	2	OG	Tokyo	17 Oct 64
20.20	Udo	Beyer	GDR	9.8.55	2	NC	Leipzig	6 Jul 74
19.99	Karl	Salb	USA	19.5.49	4	FOT	Echo Summit	10 Sep 68
19.74	Andreas	Horn	GDR	31.1.62	2	vSU-j	Cottbus	24 Jun 81
19.71	Vladimir	Kiselyov -1	UKR	1.1.57	1		Yalta	15 May 76
19.68	Ron	Semkiw	USA	28.3.54	1	vAFR	Dakar	4 Aug 73
19.53i	Vyacheslav	Lykho	RUS	16.1.67	1		Moskva	28 Dec 86
19.53	Manuel	Martinez	ESP	7.12.74	Q	WC	Stuttgart	20 Aug 93
19.51	Viktor	Belyi	RUS	.64	6		Leningrad	26 Jul 83
19.48	Viktor	Bulat	RUS	1.4.71	1		Minsk	19 May 90

DISCUS

Mark	Name		Nat	Born	Pos	Meet	Venue	Date
65.62	Werner	Reiterer	AUS	27.1.68	1		Melbourne	15 Dec 87
63.64	Werner	Hartmann	FRG	20.4.59	1	vFRA	Strasbourg	25 Jun 78
63.26	Sergey	Pachin	UKR	24.5.68	2		Moskva	25 Jul 87
63.22	Brian	Milne	USA	7.1.73	1		University Park	28 Mar 92
62.52	John	Nichols	USA	23.8.69	1		Baton Rouge	23 Apr 88
62.04	Kenth	Gardenkrans	SWE	2.10.55	2		Helsingborg	11 Aug 74
61.84	Attila	Horváth	HUN	28.7.67	2		Budapest	18 May 85
61.84	Andreas	Seelig	GDR	6.7.70	1		Halle	15 May 88
61.54	Pedro	Acosta	CUB	15.1.70	1		Habana	15 Jul 89
61.40	Vladimir	Dubrovchik	URS	7.1.72	1		Staiki	25 Jun 91
61.34		Li Shaojie	CHN	1.1.75	1		Jinan	1 Apr 93
61.30	Wolfgang	Schmidt	GDR	16.1.54	4	NC	Dresden	22 Jul 73

HAMMER

Mark	Name		Nat	Born	Pos	Meet	Venue	Date
78.14	Roland	Steuk	GDR	5.3.59	1	NC	Leipzig	30 Jun 78
78.00	Sergey	Dorozhon	UKR	17.2.64	1		Moskva	7 Aug 83
76.54	Valeriy	Gubkin	BLS	11.1.67	2		Minsk	27 Jun 86
76.42	Ruslan	Dikiy	TJK	18.1.72	1		Togliatti	7 Sep 91
75.52	Sergey	Kirmasov	RUS	25.3.70	1		Kharkov	4 Jun 89
75.24	Christoph	Sahner	FRG	23.9.63	1	vPOL-j	Göttingen	26 Jun 82
75.22	Jaroslav	Chmyr	UKR	29.11.66	1		Kiev	9 Sep 85
75.20	Igor	Nikulin	RUS	14.8.60	2		Leselidze	1 Jun 79
75.10	Eduard	Piskunov	UKR	26.9.67	1		Grodno	5 Jul 86
74.78	Matthias	Moder	GDR	17.6.63	1	NC-j	Cottbus	24 Jul 82
74.66	Ilya	Konovalov	RUS	14.3.71			Minsk	18 Jan 90
74.32	Sergey	Litvinov	RUS	23.1.58	1		Simferopol	7 Apr 77

JAVELIN

Mark	Name		Nat	Born	Pos	Meet	Venue	Date
80.94	Aki	Parviainen	FIN	26.10.74	4	NC	Jyväskylä	5 Jul 92
80.30	Kostas	Gatsioudis	GRE	17.12.73	1	NC	Athens	20 Jun 92
80.26	Vladimir	Ovchinnikov	RUS	2.8.70	Q	OG	Seoul	24 Sep 88
79.58	Gavin	Lovegrove	NZL	21.10.67	2		Noumea	26 Oct 86
79.50	Stephen	Backley	GBR	12.12.69	1	NC	Derby	5 Jun 88
79.46	Juha	Laukkanen	FIN	6.1.69	1		Joutsa	19 Jul 87
79.30	Li Rongxiang		CHN	.2.72			Beijing	25 Apr 91
78.84	Vladimir	Sasimovich	BLS	14.9.68	1	WJ	Athinai	18 Jul 86
78.62	Aleksey	Shchepin	RUS	3.4.72	1	v3N-j	Espoo	15 Jun 91
78.38	Jarkko	Kinnunen	FIN	21.4.70	2	vGDR-j	Orimattila	1 Jul 89
77.96	Andrey	Shevchuk	RUS	8.3.70	1		Adler	24 Feb 89
77.40	Jarkko	Heimonen	FIN	6.3.72	1		Espoo	19 Aug 90

DECATHLON

Mark	Name		Nat	Born	Pos	Meet	Venue	Date
8397	Torsten	Voss	GDR	24.3.63	1	NC	Erfurt	7 Jul 82
	10.76 7.66 14.41 2.09 48.37 14.37 41.76 4.80 62.90 4:34.04							
8114	Michael	Kohnle	FRG	3.5.70	1	EJ	Varazdin	26 Aug 89
	10.95 7.09 15.27 2.02 49.91 14.40 45.82 4.90 60.82 4:49.43							
8104	Valter	Külvet	EST	19.2.64	1		Viimsi	23 Aug 81
	10.7w 7.26w 13.86 2.09 48.5 14.8 47.92 4.50 60.34 4:37.8							
8082	Daley	Thompson	GBR	30.7.58	1	EP/s	Sittard	31 Jul 77
	10.70 7.54 13.84 2.01 47.31 15.26 41.70 4.70 54.48 4:30.4							
8036	Christian	Schenk	GDR	9.2.65	5		Potsdam	21 Jul 84
	11.54 7.18 14.26 2.16 49.23 15.06 44.74 4.20 65.98 4:24.11							
7906	Mikhail	Romanyuk	UKR	6.2.62	1	EJ	Utrecht	21 Aug 81
	11.26 7.11 13.50 1.98 49.98 14.72 42.94 4.90 59.74 4:30.63							
7827	Igor	Maryin	RUS	28.4.65	1		Frunze	9 Sep 84
	11.30 7.25 13.55 2.04 50.65 15.21 43.70 4.70 62.92 4:42.05							
7815	Thomas	Fahner	GDR	18.7.66	1	EJ	Cottbus	23 Aug 85
	11.13 7.17 13.33 2.00 49.31 15.18 42.02 4.90 62.02 4:51.46							
7813	Vitaliy	Kolpakov	UKR	2.2.72	1	EJ	Thesaloniki	9 Aug 91
	11.28 7.19 14.65 2.14 49.05 14.93 41.90 4.60 51.92 4:48.73							
7776	Sepp	Zeilbauer	AUT	24.9.52	5	EC	Helsinki	12 Aug 71
	10.96 7.38 13.49 2.04 48.8 15.06 39.70 4.00 48.96 4:27.5							
7775	Siegfried	Wentz	FRG	7.3.60	1	EJ	Bydgoszcz	17 Aug 79
	11.29 7.15 14.75 2.01 49.95 15.08 42.74 4.00 64.52 4:30.6							
7762	Eric	Kaiser	FRG	7.3.71	1	WJ	Plovdiv	9 Aug 90
	11.02 7.50 12.82 2.03 49.30 14.30 40.28 4.10 58.12 4:40.66							

10000 METRES WALK

Mark	Name		Nat	Born	Pos	Meet	Venue	Date
38:54.75	Ralf	Kowalsky	GDR	22.3.62	1		Cottbus	24 Jun 81
39:44.71	Giovanni	De Benedictis	ITA	8.12.68	1	EJ	Birmingham	7 Aug 87
39:50.73	Jefferson	Pérez	ECU	1.1.74	1	PAJ	Winnipeg	16 Jul 93
39:55.52	Ilya	Markov	RUS	19.6.72	1	WJ	Plovdiv	10 Aug 90
39:56.49	Alberto	Cruz	MEX	6.6.72	2	WJ	Plovdiv	10 Aug 90
39:59.58	Sergey	Tyulenyev	RUS	14.3.71	1		Kharkov	4 Jun 90
40:05.62	Michele	Didoni	ITA	7.3.74	1	EJ	San Sebastián	30 Jul 93
40:14.17	Valentin	Massana	ESP	5.7.70	1	EJ	Varazdin	25 Aug 89
40:26.08	Dmitriy	Yesipchuk	RUS	17.11.74	2	EJ	San Sebastián	30 Jul 93
40:26.72	Dmitriy	Dolnikov	RUS	19.11.72	1		Krasnodar	1 Jun 91
40:27.2	Andrey	Perlov	RUS	12.12.61	1		Ryazan	1 Jul 80
40:35.20	Vladimir	Stankin	RUS	2.1.74	1		Krasnodar	16 May 92

4 x 100 METRES RELAY

Mark	Nat	Team	Pos	Meet	Venue	Date
39.00A	USA	Jessie, Franklin, Blalock, Mitchell	1		Colorado Springs	18 Jul 83
39.13	USA	Nelloms, Bridges, Harris, Stallworth	1	WJ	Plovdiv	12 Aug 90
39.21	GBR	Condon, Campbell, Baulch, Fergus	1	WJ	Seoul	20 Sep 92
39.25	FRG	Dobeleit, Klameth, Evers, Lübke	1	EJ	Schwechat	28 Aug 83
39.53	URS	Inschakov, Gromadskiy, Semenov, Goremykin	1h3	WJ	Plovdiv	11 Aug 90
39.54	NGR	Tetengi, Ezinwa, Nwankwo, Adeniken	1h2	WJ	Sudbury	30 Jul 88
39.69	GDR	Malke, Hoff, Thiele, Prenzler	1		Potsdam	10 Aug 77
39.69	FRA	Thessard, Patrick Barré, Panzo, Pascal Barré	1		Dôle	6 Aug 77
39.89	POL	Cywinski, Kusiowski, Zalewski, Mackowiak	1h1	EJ	Varazdin	26 Aug 89
39.92	ITA	Amici, Orlandi, Carniel, Marras	6	WJ	Plovdiv	12 Aug 90
39.99	JPN	Okuyama, Sugimoto, Kato, Nakamichi	1	AsiC-j	Singapore	11 Sep 88

4 x 400 METRES RELAY

Mark	Nat	Team	Pos	Meet	Venue	Date
3:01.90	USA	Campbell, Rish, Waddle, Reed	1	WJ	Athinai	20 Jul 86
3:03.80	GBR	Grindley, Patrick, Winrow, Richardson	2	WJ	Plovdiv	12 Aug 90
3:04.22	CUB	Cadogan, Mordoche, González, Hernández	2	WJ	Athinai	20 Jul 86
3:04.58	GDR	Preusche, Löper, Trylus, Carlowitz	1	EJ	Utrecht	23 Aug 81
3:05.16	JAM	Christie, Mason, Davis, Patterson	3	WJ	Athinai	20 Jul 86
3:05.51	AUS	Burmeister. Robinson, Hollingsworth, Greene	3	WJ	Plovdiv	12 Aug 90
3:05.60	URS	Angelov, Oleynikov, Belikov, Golovastov	4	WJ	Plovdiv	12 Aug 90
3:05.77	FRG	Gruber, Seybold, Mikisch, Just	2	EJ	Schwechat	28 Aug 83
3:06.66	JPN	Hayashi, Nishihata, Ono, Sudo	3	WJ	Seoul	20 Sep 92
3:06.95	ITA	Campana, Petrella, Milocco, D'Amico	5	EJ	Schwechat	28 Aug 83

Note that care should be taken with junior lists as some athletes may be over age.

WOMEN'S ALL-TIME WORLD LISTS

100 METRES

Mark	Wind	Name		Nat	Born	Pos	Meet	Venue	Date
10.49	0.0	Florence	Griffith-Joyner	USA	21.12.59	1q1	OT	Indianapolis	16 Jul 88
10.61	1.2		Griffith-Joyner			1	OT	Indianapolis	17 Jul 88
10.62	1.0		Griffith-Joyner			1q3	OG	Seoul	24 Sep 88
10.70	1.6		Griffith-Joyner			1s1	OT	Indianapolis	17 Jul 88
10.76	1.7	Evelyn	Ashford	USA	15.4.57	1	WK	Zürich	22 Aug 84
10.78A	1.0	Dawn	Sowell	USA	27.3.66	1	NCAA	Provo	3 Jun 89
10.78	1.7	Merlene	Ottey	JAM	10.5.60	1	Expo	Sevilla	30 May 90
10.79A	0.6		Ashford			1	USOF	A.Force Academy	3 Jul 83
10.79	1.7		Ottey			1		Vigo	23 Jul 91
10.80	1.6		Ottey			1		Salamanca	13 Jul 92
10.81	1.7	Marlies	Göhr'	GDR	21.3.58	1	OD	Berlin	8 Jun 83
10.81	1.2		Ashford			2	OT	Indianapolis	17 Jul 88
10.82	1.4		Ottey			1	ISTAF	Berlin	17 Aug 90
10.82	2.0	Irina	Privalova	RUS	12.11.68	1	CIS Ch	Moskva	22 Jun 92
10.82	-1.0	Gail	Devers	USA	19.11.66	1	OG	Barcelona	1 Aug 92
10.82	1.5		Devers			1	Athl	Lausanne	7 Jul 93
10.82	-0.3		Devers			1	WC	Stuttgart	16 Aug 93
10.82	-0.3		Ottey			2	WC	Stuttgart	16 Aug 93
10.83	1.7	Marita	Koch	GDR	18.2.57	2	OD	Berlin	8 Jun 83
10.83	0.0	Sheila	Echols	USA	2.10.64	1q2	OT	Indianapolis	16 Jul 88
10.83	-1.0	Juliet	Cuthbert (10)	JAM	9.4.64	2	OG	Barcelona	1 Aug 92
10.84	1.7		Göhr			2	WK	Zürich	22 Aug 84
10.84	0.0		Ottey			1	Athl	Lausanne	10 Jul 91
10.84	0.2		Ottey			1	ISTAF	Berlin	10 Sep 91
10.84	1.3	Chioma	Ajunwa ¶	NGR	25.12.70	1		Lagos	11 Apr 92
10.84	-1.0		Privalova			3	OG	Barcelona	1 Aug 92
10.85	1.6		Ashford			2s1	OT	Indianapolis	17 Jul 88
10.85	2.0	Anelia	Nuneva	BUL	30.6.62	1h1	NC	Sofia	2 Sep 88
10.85	1.5		Ottey			1		Rieti	9 Sep 90
		(30 performances by 12 athletes)							
10.86	0.6	Silke	Gladisch'	GDR	20.6.64	1	NC	Potsdam	20 Aug 87
10.86	0.0	Diane	Williams	USA	14.12.60	2q1	OT	Indianapolis	16 Jul 88
10.86	-1.0	Gwen	Torrence	USA	12.6.65	4	OG	Barcelona	1 Aug 92
10.89	1.8	Katrin	Krabbe	GDR	22.11.69	1		Berlin	20 Jul 88
10.91	0.2	Heike	Drechsler'	GDR	16.12.64	2	GWG	Moskva	6 Jul 86
10.92	0.0	Alice	Brown	USA	20.9.60	2q2	OT	Indianapolis	16 Jul 88
10.93	1.8	Ewa	Kasprzyk	POL	7.9.57	1	NC	Grudziadz	27 Jun 86
10.94	1.0	Carlette	Guidry	USA	4.9.68	1	TAC	New York	14 Jun 91
		(20)							
10.95	1.0	Bärbel	Wöckel'	GDR	21.3.55	2	NC	Dresden	1 Jul 82
10.96	1.2	Marie-José	Pérec	FRA	9.5.68	1	NC	Dijon	27 Jul 91
10.96	2.0	Galina	Malchugina	RUS	17.12.62	2	CIS Ch	Moskva	22 Jun 92
10.97	0.0	Angella	Issajenko'	CAN	28.9.58	3	ASV	Köln	16 Aug 87
10.97	0.2	Mary	Onyali	NGR	3.2.68	1q2	WC	Stuttgart	15 Aug 93
10.98	0.1	Marina	Zhirova	RUS	6.6.63	2	EP	Moskva	17 Aug 85
10.98	0.8	Angela	Bailey	CAN	28.2.62	2	BGP	Budapest	6 Jul 87
10.98	1.6	Natalya	Pomoshchnikova'	RUS	9.7.65	2q2	OG	Seoul	24 Sep 88
10.99	1.3	Valerie	Brisco-Hooks	USA	6.7.60	1	Pepsi	Westwood	17 May 86
11.01	0.6	Annegret	Richter	FRG	13.10.50	1s1	OG	Montreal	25 Jul 76
		(30)							
11.01	0.8	Pam	Marshall	USA	16.8.60	2	Athl	Lausanne	15 Sep 87
11.02	2.0	Romy	Müller'	GDR	26.7.58	3	OT	Dresden	24 May 80
11.02	-0.2	Lyudmila	Kondratyeva	RUS	11.4.58	2	Drz	Praha	16 Aug 84
11.02	0.0		Liu Xiaomei	CHN	11.1.72	1	NG	Beijing	8 Sep 93
11.03	2.0	Monika	Hamann'	GDR	8.6.54	2	NC	Dresden	1 Jul 77
11.04	0.6	Inge	Helten	FRG	21.12.50	1h1		Fürth	13 Jun 76
11.04	1.7	Ingrid	Auerswald'	GDR	2.9.57	4	WK	Zürich	22 Aug 84
11.04	0.6	Laurence	Bily	FRA	5.5.63	1	NC	Tours	13 Aug 89
11.04	1.3	Lyudmila	Narozhilenko	RUS	21.4.64	1		Khania	31 May 92
11.05	1.0	Kerstin	Behrendt	GDR	2.9.67	3	OT	Potsdam	8 Sep 88
		(40)							

Mark	Wind	Name		Nat	Born	Pos	Meet	Venue	Date
11.05	0.0	Michelle	Finn	USA	8.5.65	3	GWG	Seattle	24 Jul 90
11.05	0.2	Irina	Slyusar	UKR	19.3.63	1		Kiev	15 Jul 92
11.06A	1.0	Evette	de Klerk'	RSA	21.8.65	1	NC	Germiston	20 Apr 90
11.06	1.7	Sandra	Myers	ESP	9.1.61	2		Vigo	23 Jul 91
11.07	-0.2	Renate	Stecher'	GDR	12.5.50	1	OG	München	2 Sep 72
11.07	2.0	Olga	Bogoslovskaya'	RUS	20.5.64	3	CIS Ch	Moskva	22 Jun 92
11.08A	1.2	Wyomia	Tyus	USA	29.8.45	1	OG	Ciudad México	15 Oct 68
11.08	2.0	Brenda	Morehead	USA	5.10.57	1	OT	Eugene	21 Jun 76
11.08	-0.1	Jeanette	Bolden	USA	26.1.60	2	WK	Zürich	13 Aug 86
11.08	0.8	Nelli	Cooman	HOL	6.6.64	3	EC	Stuttgart	27 Aug 86
		(50)							
11.08		Marina	Molokova	RUS	24.8.62	1		Sochi	16 May 87
11.08		Grace	Jackson	JAM	14.6.61	2s1	NC	Kingston	15 Jul 88
11.08	0.0	Maya	Azarashvili	GEO	6.4.64	1		Kiev	14 Aug 88
11.08	0.3	Beatrice	Utondu	NGR	23.11.69	1s1	NC	Lagos	2 Aug 91
11.08	2.0	Marina	Trandenkova	RUS	7.1.67	4	CIS Ch	Moskva	22 Jun 92
11.08	0.1	Zhanna	Tarnopolskaya	UKR	6.7.72	1		Odessa	21 May 93
		(56)	100th best 11.18						
Probably semi-automatic timing									
10.87	1.9	Lyudmila	Kondratyeva	RUS	11.4.58	1		Leningrad	3 Jun 80
10.99	1.9	Natalya	Bochina	RUS	4.1.62	2		Leningrad	3 Jun 80
Low altitude best: 10.91	1.6		Sowell			1	TAC	Houston	16 Jun 89
Wind-assisted marks									
10.54	3.0		Griffith-Joyner			1	OG	Seoul	25 Sep 88
10.60	3.2		Griffith-Joyner			1h1	OT	Indianapolis	16 Jul 88
10.70	2.6		Griffith-Joyner			1s2	OG	Seoul	25 Sep 88
10.78	3.1		Ashford			1		Modesto	12 May 84
10.78	5.0	Gwen	Torrence	USA	12.6.65	1q3	OT	Indianapolis	16 Jul 88
10.78	2.3		Ottey			1s2	WC	Tokyo	27 Aug 91
10.79	3.3	Marlies	Göhr'	GDR	21.3.58	1	NC	Cottbus	16 Jul 80
10.80	2.9	Pam	Marshall	USA	16.8.60	1	TAC	Eugene	20 Jun 86
10.80	2.8	Heike	Drechsler'	GDR	16.12.64	1	Bisl	Oslo	5 Jul 86
10.81	2.4	Irina	Privalova	RUS	12.11.68	1		Rieti	26 Sep 92
10.81	3.8		Privalova			1		Rieti	5 Sep 93
10.82	2.2	Silke	Gladisch'	GDR	20.6.64	1s1	WC	Roma	30 Aug 87
10.82A	2.8		Torrence			1		Sestriere	21 Jul 92
10.82	2.2		Devers			1	NC	Eugene	17 Jun 93
10.83	3.9		Echols			1h2	OT	Indianapolis	16 Jul 88
10.83	3.0		Ashford			2	OG	Seoul	25 Sep 88
10.84	2.9	Alice	Brown	USA	20.9.60	2	TAC	Eugene	20 Jun 86
10.84	2.4		Torrence			2		Rieti	26 Sep 92
		(17 performances)							
10.89	3.1	Kerstin	Behrendt	GDR	2.9.67	2		Berlin	13 Sep 88
10.90	2.7	Chryste	Gaines	USA	14.9.70	2		Austin	9 May 92
10.91	4.6	Carlette	Guidry	USA	4.9.68	1s1	NCAA	Eugene	31 May 91
10.92	3.3	Bärbel	Wöckel'	GDR	21.3.55	2	NC	Cottbus	16 Jul 80
10.92	3.4	Angella	Taylor'	CAN	28.9.58	1s2	CG	Brisbane	4 Oct 82
10.93	3.8	Sonia	Lannaman	GBR	24.3.56	1	EP/sf	Dublin	17 Jul 77
10.93	3.3	Ingrid	Auerswald'	GDR	2.9.57	3	NC	Cottbus	16 Jul 80
10.93	4.2	Holli	Hyche	USA	6.9.71	2h2	NC	Eugene	16 Jun 93
10.94	3.9	Jackie	Washington	USA	17.7.62	1		Houston	18 May 86
10.94A	3.0	Evette	de Klerk'	RSA	21.8.65	1h	NC	Germiston	20 Apr 90
10.96	2.9	Brenda	Morehead	USA	5.10.57	1s2	AAU	Walnut	16 Jun 79
10.96	4.2	Olga	Naumkina'	RUS	20.5.64	1	Znam	Volgograd	11 Jun 89
10.96A	2.5	Michelle	Finn	USA	8.5.65	1		Sestriere	8 Aug 90
10.97	3.3	Gesine	Walther	GDR	6.10.62	4	NC	Cottbus	16 Jul 80
10.97	3.0	Grace	Jackson	JAM	14.6.61	4	OG	Seoul	25 Sep 88
10.99	2.4	Chandra	Cheeseborough	USA	10.1.59	2		Modesto	14 May 83
10.99	5.1	Esther	Jones	USA	7.4.69	2	NCAA	Eugene	1 Jun 91
11.00	2.1	Laurence	Bily	FRA	5.6.63	1		Dijon	24 Jun 90
11.01	4.0	Heather	Hunte'	GBR	14.8.59	1		London	21 May 80
11.01	2.8	Kerry	Johnson	AUS	23.10.63	1h3	CGT	Sydney	2 Dec 89
11.01		Beatrice	Utondu	NGR	23.11.69	1		Springfield	1 May 93
11.02	5.0	Jennifer	Inniss	USA	21.11.59	3q3	OT	Indianapolis	16 Jul 88
11.02	2.1	Nicole	Mitchell	JAM	5.6.74	1	Mutual	Kingston	1 May 93
11.05A	2.2	Silvia	Chivás	CUB	10.9.54	1	WPT	Guadalajara	12 Aug 77

Mark	Wind	Name		Nat	Born	Pos	Meet	Venue	Date
11.05	2.5	Ulrike	Sarvari	FRG	27.6.64	2rB	WK	Zürich	17 Aug 88
11.05A	4.1	Tina	Iheagwam	NGR	3.4.68	1		El Paso	16 Apr 89
11.05	6.1	Beverly	McDonald	JAM	15.2.70	1		Arlington	10 Apr 93
11.06	2.8	Linda	Haglund ¶	SWE	15.6.56	1	ISTAF	Berlin	21 Aug 81
11.06	3.7	Randy	Givens	USA	27.3.62	1	NCAA	Eugene	1 Jun 84
11.06		Teresa	Foster	USA	11.4.72	1		Abilene	14 May 92
Low altitude best: 11.04	3.0		Finn			1	NCAA	Austin	1 Jun 85
Hand timing									
10.7		Merlene	Ottey	JAM	10.5.60	1h		Kingston	15 Jul 88
10.7	1.1	Juliet	Cuthbert	JAM	9.4.64	1	NC	Kingston	4 Jul 92
10.8	1.8	Renate	Stecher'	GDR	12.5.50	1	NC	Dresden	20 Jul 83
10.8	-0.1	Annegret	Richter	FRG	13.10.50	1		Gelsenkirchen	27 Jun76
10.8	0.5	Irina	Slyussar	UKR	19.3.63	1		Ordzhonik	13 Jul 85
10.8	0.6	Galina	Malchugina	RUS	17.12.62	1h	NP	Vladivostok	13 Sep 88
10.8	1.0	Marina	Molokova	RUS	24.8.62	1h	NP	Vladivostok	13 Sep 88
Wind assisted									
10.7	3.4	Merlene	Ottey	JAM	10.5.60	1h2		Shizuoka	27 Apr 86
10.8A		Margaret	Bailes	USA	23.1.51	1		Flagstaff	29 Sep 68
10.8	3.6	Sonia	Lannaman	GBR	24.3.56	1	vSU	Kiev	22 May 76

200 METRES

Mark	Wind	Name		Nat	Born	Pos	Meet	Venue	Date
21.34	1.3	Florence	Griffith-Joyner	USA	21.12.59	1	OG	Seoul	29 Sep 88
21.56	1.7		Griffith-Joyner			1s1	OG	Seoul	29 Sep 88
21.64	0.8	Merlene	Ottey	JAM	10.5.60	1	VD	Bruxelles	13 Sep 91
21.66	-1.0		Ottey			1	WK	Zürich	15 Aug 90
21.71	0.7	Marita	Koch	GDR	18.2.57	1	v Can	Karl-Marx-Stadt	10 Jun 79
21.71	0.3		Koch			1	OD	Potsdam	21 Jul 84
21.71	1.2	Heike	Drechsler'	GDR	16.12.64	1	NC	Jena	29 Jun 86
21.71	-0.8		Drechsler			1	EC	Stuttgart	29 Aug 86
21.72	1.3	Grace	Jackson	JAM	14.6.61	2	OG	Seoul	29 Sep 88
21.72	-0.1	Gwen	Torrence	USA	12.6.65	1s2	OG	Barcelona	5 Aug 92
21.74	0.4	Marlies	Göhr'	GDR	21.3.58	1	NC	Erfurt	3 Jun 84
21.74	1.2	Silke	Gladisch'	GDR	20.6.64	1	WC	Roma	3 Sep 87
21.75	-0.1	Juliet	Cuthbert	JAM	9.4.64	2s2	OG	Barcelona	5 Aug 92
21.76	0.3		Koch			1	NC	Dresden	3 Jul 82
21.76	0.7		Griffith-Joyner			1q1	OG	Seoul	28 Sep 88
21.77	-0.1		Griffith-Joyner			1q2	OT	Indianapolis	22 Jul 88
21.78	-1.3		Koch			1	NC	Leipzig	11 Aug 85
21.77	1.0		Ottey			1	Herc	Monaco	7 Aug 93
21.79	1.7		Gladisch			1	NC	Potsdam	22 Aug 87
21.80	-1.1		Ottey			1	Nik	Nice	10 Jul 90
21.81	-0.1	Valerie	Brisco (10)	USA	6.7.60	1	OG	Los Angeles	9 Aug 84
21.81	0.4		Ottey			1	ASV	Köln	19 Aug 90
21.81	-0.6		Torrence			1	OG	Barcelona	6 Aug 92
21.82	1.3		Koch			1	NC	Karl-Marx-Stadt	18 Jun 83
21.83	-0.2	Evelyn	Ashford	USA	15.4.57	1	WP	Montreal	24 Aug 79
21.83	0.5		Ottey			1	ASV	Köln	8 Sep 91
21.84	-1.1		Ashford			1	VD	Bruxelles	28 Aug 81
21.84	1.0		Drechsler			1	NC	Rostock	26 Jun 88
21.85	0.3	Bärbel	Wöckel'	GDR	21.3.55	2	OD	Potsdam	21 Jul 84
21.85	1.3		Griffith-Joyner			1	OT	Indianapolis	23 Jul 88
		(30/12)							
21.88	2.0	Irina	Privalova	RUS	22.11.68	1		Rieti	5 Sep 93
21.93	1.3	Pam	Marshall	USA	16.8.60	2	OT	Indianapolis	23 Jul 88
21.95	0.3	Katrin	Krabbe	GDR	22.11.69	1	EC	Split	30 Aug 90
21.97	1.9	Jarmila	Kratochvílová	TCH	26.1.51	1	PTS	Bratislava	6 Jun 81
21.99	0.9	Chandra	Cheeseborough	USA	10.1.59	2	TAC	Indianapolis	19 Jun 83
21.99	1.1	Marie-José	Pérec	FRA	9.5.68	1	BNP	Villeneuve d'Ascq	2 Jul 93
22.01	-0.5	Anelia	Nuneva'	BUL	30.6.62	1	NC	Sofia	16 Aug 87
22.04A	0.7	Dawn	Sowell	USA	27.3.66	1	NCAA	Provo	2 Jun 89
		(20)							
22.06A	0.7	Evette	de Klerk'	RSA	21.8.65	1		Pietersburg	8 Apr 89
22.10	-0.1	Kathy	Cook'	GBR	3.5.60	4	OG	Los Angeles	9 Aug 84
22.13	1.2	Ewa	Kasprzyk	POL	7.9.57	2	GWG	Moskva	8 Jul 86
22.19	1.5	Natalya	Bochina	RUS	4.1.62	2	OG	Moskva	30 Jul 80
22.21	1.9	Irena	Szewinska'	POL	24.5.46	1		Potsdam	13 Jun 74

Mark	Wind	Name		Nat	Born	Pos	Meet	Venue	Date
22.22	1.2	Galina	Malchugina	RUS	17.12.62	1q3	OG	Barcelona	3 Aug 92
22.23	-0.2	Dannette	Young	USA	6.10.64	1	Herc	Monaco	2 Aug 88
22.24	0.3	Gesine	Walther	GDR	6.10.62	2	NC	Dresden	3 Jul 82
22.24	0.1	Maya	Azarashvili	GEO	6.4.64	1		Kiev	16 Aug 88
22.24	0.8	Carlette	Guidry	USA	4.9.68	2	OT	New Orleans	28 Jun 92
		(30)							
22.25A	0.8	Angella	Taylor'	CAN	28.9.58	1		Colorado Springs	20 Jul 82
22.27	1.2	Elvira	Barbashina'	UZB	25.2.63	3	GWG	Moskva	8 Jul 86
22.29	0.7	Silke-Beate	Knoll	GER	21.2.67	1		Ingolstadt	19 Jul 92
22.30	0.0	Jackie	Joyner-Kersee	USA	3.3.62	1H	OT	Indianapolis	15 Jul 88
22.31	0.1	Lyudmila	Kondratyeva	RUS	11.4.58	1		Moskva	12 Jun 80
22.31	0.9	Randy	Givens	USA	27.3.62	4	TAC	Indianapolis	19 Jun 83
22.31	1.1	Mary	Onyali	NGR	3.2.68	2	BNP	Villeneuve d'Ascq	29 Jun 90
22.32	-0.8	Marie-Christine	Cazier	FRA	23.8.63	2	EC	Stuttgart	29 Aug 86
22.32	-0.5	Melinda	Gainsford	AUS	1.10.71	1		Hobart	26 Feb 94
22.33	1.4	Inger	Miller	USA	12.12.72	1	MSR	Walnut	17 Apr 93
		(40)							
22.34	1.6	Holli	Hyche	USA	6.9.71	1	NCAA	New Orleans	5 Jun 93
22.35	1.8	Denise	Boyd'	AUS	15.12.52	1	NC	Sydney	23 Mar 80
22.35	-0.5	Natalya	Voronova	RUS	9.7.65	3s1	WC	Stuttgart	19 Aug 93
22.36	1.7	Kerstin	Behrendt	GDR	2.9.67	3		Karl-Marx-Stadt	12 Jun 88
22.37	1.3	Sabine	Rieger/Günther	GDR	6.11.63	2	v URS	Cottbus	26 Jun 82
22.37	2.0	Cathy	Freeman	AUS	16.2.73	3		Rieti	5 Sep 93
22.38	1.6	Renate	Stecher'	GDR	12.5.50	1	NC	Dresden	21 Jul 73
22.38	1.7	Brenda	Morehead	USA	5.10.57	1		Nashville	12 Apr 80
22.38	2.0	Lillie	Leatherwood	USA	6.7.64	1	SEC	Tuscaloosa	17 May 87
22.38	0.3	Sandra	Myers	ESP	9.1.61	4	EC	Split	30 Aug 90
		(50)	100th best 22.68						
Low altitudebest: 22.37	1.4		Taylor'			1	NC	Ottawa	1 Aug 82
Wind-assisted marks									
21.84	2.3		Torrence			1		Austin	9 May 92
21.85	2.6		Koch			1		Karl-Marx-Stadt	27 May 79
21.85	2.6	Bärbel	Wöckel'	GDR	21.3.55	1	v USA	Karl-Marx-Stadt	10 Jul 82
22.19A	3.1	Angella	Taylor'	CAN	28.9.58	1		Colorado Springs	21 Jul 82
22.19	3.4	Dannette	Young	USA	6.10.64	1	USOF	Minneapolis	15 Jul 90
22.26	4.2	Melinda	Gainsford	AUS	1.10.71	1		Sydney	22 Feb 92
22.33	3.7	Alice	Brown	USA	20.9.60	3s1	OT	Indianapolis	23 Jul 88
22.37	2.5	Esther	Jones	USA	7.4.69	1	NYG	New York	22 Jul 89
Hand timing									
21.9	0.0	Bärbel	Wöckel'	GDR	21.3.55	1		Tbilisi	27 Jun 81
22.0	-0.6	Marina	Molokova	RUS	24.8.62	1	Ros	Praha	23 Jun 87
22.1		Natalya	Bochina	RUS	4.1.62	1		Moskva	7 Jul 84
22.2	-0.3	Irena	Szewinska'	POL	24.5.46	1		Warszawa	20 Jul 74
Wind assisted									
21.6	2.5	Pam	Marshall	USA	16.8.60	1	TAC	San José	26 Jun 87
22.1	2.5	Pauline	Davis	BAH	9.7.66	6	TAC	San José	26 Jun 87

300 METRES

Mark		Name		Nat	Born	Pos	Meet	Venue	Date
35.46		Kathy	Cook'	GBR	3.5.60	1	Nike	London	18 Aug 84
35.46		Chandra	Cheeseborough	USA	10.1.59	2	Nike	London	18 Aug 84
35.83i		Merlene	Ottey	JAM	10.5.60	1	AIAW	Pocatello	14 Mar 81
		35.99				3	Nike	London	18 Aug 84
Indoors									
35.45i		Irina	Privalova	RUS	12.11.68	1		Moskva	17 Jan 93

400 METRES

Mark		Name		Nat	Born	Pos	Meet	Venue	Date
47.60		Marita	Koch	GDR	18.2.57	1	WP	Canberra	6 Oct 85
47.99		Jarmila	Kratochvílová	TCH	26.1.51	1	WC	Helsinki	10 Aug 83
48.16			Koch			1	EC	Athinai	8 Sep 82
48.16			Koch			1	Drz	Praha	16 Aug 84
48.22			Koch			1	EC	Stuttgart	28 Aug 86
48.26			Koch			1		Dresden	27 Jul 84
48.27		Olga	Vladykina'	UKR	30.6.63	2	WP	Canberra	6 Oct 85
48.45			Kratochvílová			1	NC	Praha	23 Jul 83
48.59		Tatána	Kocembová'	TCH	2.5.62	2	WC	Helsinki	10 Aug 83
48.60			Koch			1	EP	Torino	4 Aug 79

Mark	Wind	Name		Nat	Born	Pos	Meet	Venue	Date
48.60			Vladykina			1	EP	Moskva	17 Aug 85
48.61			Kratochvílová			1	WP	Roma	6 Sep 81
48.65			Bryzgina'			1	OG	Seoul	26 Sep 88
48.73			Kocembová			2	Drz	Praha	16 Aug 84
48.77			Koch			1	v USA	Karl-Marx-Stadt	9 Jul 82
48.82			Kratochvílová			1	Ros	Praha	23 Jun 83
48.83		Valerie	Brisco	USA	6.7.60	1	OG	Los Angeles	6 Aug 84
48.83		Marie-José	Pérec	FRA	9.5.68	1	OG	Barcelona	5 Aug 92
48.85			Kratochvílová			2	EC	Athinai	8 Sep 82
48.86			Kratochvílová			1	WK	Zürich	18 Aug 82
48.86			Koch			1	NC	Erfurt	2 Jun 84
48.87			Koch			1	VD	Bruxelles	27 Aug 82
48.88			Koch			1	OG	Moskva	28 Jul 80
48.89			Koch			1		Potsdam	29 Jul 79
48.89			Koch			1		Berlin	15 Jul 84
48.94			Koch			1	EC	Praha	31 Aug 78
48.96			Vladykina			1	NC	Leningrad	3 Aug 85
48.97			Koch			1	WP	Montreal	26 Aug 79
48.97			Koch			1		Berlin	22 Sep 85
48.98			Vladykina			1	Izv	Kiev	22 Jun 84
		(30/6)							
49.05		Chandra	Cheeseborough	USA	10.1.59	2	OG	Los Angeles	6 Aug 84
49.11		Olga	Nazarova	RUS	1.6.65	1s1	OG	Seoul	25 Sep 88
49.19		Mariya	Pinigina'	UKR	9.2.58	3	WC	Helsinki	10 Aug 83
49.24		Sabine	Busch	GDR	21.11.62	2	NC	Erfurt	2 Jun 84
		(10)							
49.28		Irena	Szewinska'	POL	24.5.46	1	OG	Montreal	29 Jul 76
49.30		Petra	Müller'	GDR	18.7.65	1		Jena	3 Jun 88
49.42		Grit	Breuer	GER	16.2.72	2	WC	Tokyo	27 Aug 91
49.43		Kathy	Cook'	GBR	3.5.60	3	OG	Los Angeles	6 Aug 84
49.47		Aelita	Yurchenko	UKR	1.1.65	2	Kuts	Moskva	4 Sep 88
49.56		Bärbel	Wöckel'	GDR	21.3.55	1		Erfurt	30 May 82
49.57		Grace	Jackson	JAM	14.6.61	1	Nik	Nice	10 Jul 88
49.58		Dagmar	Rübsam'	GDR	3.6.62	3	NC	Erfurt	2 Jun 84
49.61		Ana Fidelia	Quirot	CUB	23.3.63	1	PAG	Habana	5 Aug 91
49.64		Gwen	Torrence	USA	12.6.65	2	Nik	Nice	15 Jul 92
		(20)							
49.64		Ximena	Restrepo	COL	10.3.69	3	OG	Barcelona	5 Aug 92
49.66		Christina	Lathan'	GDR	28.2.58	3	OG	Moskva	28 Jul 80
49.66		Lillie	Leatherwood	USA	6.7.64	1	TAC	New York	15 Jun 91
49.67		Sandra	Myers	ESP	9.1.61	1	Bisl	Oslo	6 Jul 91
49.75		Gaby	Bussmann	FRG	8.10.59	4	WC	Helsinki	10 Aug 83
49.81			Ma Yuqin	CHN	11.9.72	1	NG	Beijing	11 Sep 93
49.82		Jearl	Miles	USA	4.9.66	1	WC	Stuttgart	17 Aug 93
49.84		Diane	Dixon	USA	23.9.64	3s1	OG	Seoul	25 Sep 88
49.86		Charity	Opara ¶	NGR	20.5.72	1	Slov	Bratislava	1 Jun 92
49.87		Denean	Howard/Hill	USA	5.10.64	4s1	OG	Seoul	25 Sep 88
		(30)							
49.89		Irina	Privalova	RUS	12.11.68	1	Kuts	Moskva	30 Jul 93
49.91		Marita	Payne'	CAN	7.10.60	4	OG	Los Angeles	6 Aug 84
49.91		Jillian	Richardson	CAN	10.3.65	5s1	OG	Seoul	25 Sep 88
49.99		Pam	Marshall	USA	16.8.60	1	Pepsi	Westwood	17 May 86
50.03		Gesine	Walther	GDR	6.10.62	2		Jena	13 May 84
50.05		Pauline	Davis	BAH	9.7.66	2	ASV	Köln	19 Aug 90
50.06		Rochelle	Stevens	USA	8.9.66	1s2	OT	New Orleans	22 Jun 92
50.07		Irina	Nazarova'	RUS	31.7.57	4	OG	Moskva	28 Jul 80
50.07		Kirsten	Emmelmann'	GDR	19.4.61	2	ISTAF	Berlin	23 Aug 85
50.11		Juliet	Campbell	JAM	17.3.70	1		Kingston	3 Jul 93
		(40)							
50.12A		Myrtle	Bothma'	RSA	18.2.64	1	NC	Germiston	11 Apr 86
50.14		Riita	Salin	FIN	16.10.50	1	EC	Roma	4 Sep 74
50.15		Ellen	Streidt'	GDR	27.7.52	2	OD	Berlin	10 Jul 76
50.17		Nina	Zyuskova	UKR	15.5.52	5	OG	Moskva	28 Jul 80
50.17		Natasha	Kaiser-Brown	USA	14.5.67	2	WC	Stuttgart	17 Aug 93
50.19		Irina	Baskakova	RUS	25.8.56	2	Spa	Moskva	21 Jun 83

Mark	Wind	Name		Nat	Born	Pos	Meet	Venue	Date
50.19		Sandie	Richards	JAM	6.11.68	7	OG	Barcelona	5 Aug 92
50.19		Renee	Poetschka	AUS	1.5.71	1	NC	Sydney	12 Mar 94
50.24		Maree	Holland	AUS	25.7.63	3s2	OG	Seoul	25 Sep 88
50.26		Brigitte	Rohde'	GDR	8.10.54	1rB	v GBR,Yug	Split	1 May 76
		(50)	100th best 50.93						
Hand timing									
48.9		Olga	Nazarova	RUS	1.6.65	1	NP	Vladivostok	13 Sep 88
49.2A		Ana Fidelia	Quirot	CUB	23.3.63	1	AmCp	Bogotá	13 Aug 89
49.9		Lyudmila	Dzhigalova	UKR	22.10.62	1		Kiev	24 Jun 88

600 METRES

Mark	Wind	Name		Nat	Born	Pos	Meet	Venue	Date
1:23.5		Doina	Melinte	ROM	27.12.56	1		Poiana Brasov	27 Jul 86
1:24.48+		Sigrun	Wodars	GDR	7.11.65	1	WP	Barcelona	7 Sep 89
1:24.56		Martina	Steuk'	GDR	11.11.59	1		Erfurt	1 Aug 81
1:24.7+		Ana Fidelia	Quirot	CUB	23.3.63	2	WP	Barcelona	7 Sep 89
1:24.85		Ines	Vogelgesang	GDR	27.11.63	1		Berlin	31 Jul 83
1:25.0+		Anita	Weiss'	GDR	16.7.55	1	OG	Montreal	26 Jul 76
1:25.08+		Christine	Wachtel	GDR	6.1.65	1	WC	Roma	31 Aug 87

800 METRES

Mark	Wind	Name		Nat	Born	Pos	Meet	Venue	Date
1:53.28		Jarmila	Kratochvílová	TCH	26.1.51	1		München	26 Jul 83
1:53.43		Nadezhda	Olizarenko'	R/UKR	28.11.53	1	OG	Moskva	27 Jul 80
1:54.44		Ana Fidelia	Quirot	CUB	23.3.63	1	WP	Barcelona	9 Sep 89
1:54.68			Kratochvílová			1	WC	Helsinki	9 Aug 83
1:54.81		Olga	Mineyeva	RUS	1.9.52	2	OG	Moskva	27 Jul 80
1:54.85			Olizarenko			1	Prav	Moskva	12 Jun 80
1:54.94		Tatyana	Kazankina ¶	RUS	17.12.51	1	OG	Montreal	26 Jul 76
1:55.04			Kratochvílová			1		Oslo	23 Aug 83
1:55.05		Doina	Melinte	ROM	27.12.56	1	NC	Bucuresti	1 Aug 82
1:55.1 '			Mineyeva			1	Znam	Moskva	6 Jul 80
1:55.26		Sigrun	Wodars/Grau	GDR	7.11.65	1	WC	Roma	31 Aug 87
1:55.32		Christine	Wachtel	GDR	6.1.65	2	WC	Roma	31 Aug 87
1:55.41			Mineyeva			1	EC	Athinai	8 Sep 82
1:55.42		Nikolina	Shtereva	BUL	25.1.55	2	OG	Montreal	26 Jul 76
1:55.43		Maria	Mutola (10)	MOZ	27.10.72	1	WC	Stuttgart	17 Aug 93
1:55.46		Tatyana	Providokhina	RUS	26.3.53	3	OG	Moskva	27 Jul 80
1:55.5			Mineyeva			1	Kuts	Podolsk	21 Aug 82
1:55.54		Ellen	van Langen	HOL	9.2.66	1	OG	Barcelona	3 Aug 92
1:55.54			Liu Dong	CHN	27.12.73	1	NG	Beijing	9 Sep 93
1:55.56		Lyubov	Gurina	RUS	6.8.57	3	WC	Roma	31 Aug 87
1:55.60		Elfi	Zinn	GDR	24.8.53	3	OG	Montreal	26 Jul 76
1:55.62			Mutola			1A	WK	Zürich	4 Aug 93
1:55.68		Ella	Kovacs	ROM	11.12.64	1	RomIC	Bucuresti	2 Jun 85
1:55.69		Irina	Podyalovskaya	BLS	19.10.59	1	Izv	Kiev	22 Jun 84
1:55.70			Wodars			2	WP	Barcelona	9 Sep 89
1:55.74		Anita	Weiss'	GDR	16.7.55	4	OG	Montreal	26 Jul 76
1:55.80			Providokhina			1	EC	Praha	31 Aug 78
1:55.82			Mushta'			2	EC	Praha	31 Aug 78
1:55.84			Quirot			4	WC	Roma	31 Aug 87
1:55.86			Wachtel			1	NC	Potsdam	21 Aug 87
		(30/18)							
1:55.96		Lyudmila	Veselkova	RUS	25.10.50	2	EC	Athinai	8 Sep 82
1:55.96		Yekaterina	Podkopayeva' ¶	RUS	11.6.52	1		Leningrad	27 Jul 83
		(20)							
1:55.99		Lilia	Nurutdinova ¶	RUS	15.12.63	2	OG	Barcelona	3 Aug 92
1:56.0		Valentina	Gerasimova	KZK	15.5.48	1	NC	Kiev	12 Jun 76
1:56.0		Inna	Yevseyeva	UKR	14.8.64	1		Kiev	25 Jun 88
1:56.1		Ravilya	Agletdinova'	BLS	10.2.60	2	Kuts	Podolsk	21 Aug 82
1:56.2 '		Totka	Petrova ¶	BUL	17.12.56	1		Paris	6 Jul 79
1:56.2		Tatyana	Mishkel	UKR	10.6.52	3	Kuts	Podolsk	21 Aug 82
1:56.21		Martina	Kämpfert'	GDR	11.11.59	4	OG	Moskva	27 Jul 80
1:56.21		Zamira	Zaytseva	UZB	16.2.53	2		Leningrad	27 Jul 83
1:56.24			Qu Yunxia	CHN	25.12.72	2	NG	Beijing	9 Sep 93
1:56.42		Paula	Ivan	ROM	20.7.63	1	Balk	Ankara	16 Jul 88
		(30)							

Mark	Wind	Name		Nat	Born	Pos	Meet	Venue	Date
1:56.44		Svetlana	Styrkina	RUS	1.1.49	5	OG	Montreal	26 Jul 76
1:56.51		Slobodanka	Colovic	YUG	10.1.65	1		Beograd	17 Jun 87
1:56.57		Zoya	Rigel	RUS	15.10.52	3	EC	Praha	31 Aug 78
1:56.6		Tamara	Sorokina'	RUS	15.8.50	5	Kuts	Podolsk	21 Aug 82
1:56.62		Tina	Paulino	MOZ	7.7.73	2	NYG	New York	22 May 93
1:56.64		Nadezhda	Loboyko	KZK	30.6.61	1	NC	Kiev	7 Jul 90
1:56.67		Fita	Lovin'	ROM	14.1.51	2	Prav	Moskva	12 Jun 80
1:56.7		Dalia	Matuseviciene	LIT	12.11.62	2		Kiev	25 Jun 88
1:56.76		Svetlana	Masterkova	RUS	17.1.68	2rA		Zürich	4 Aug 93
1:56.78		Lyudmila	Borisova	RUS	30.7.59	3	Izv	Kiev	22 Jun 84
		(40)							
1:56.82		Lyudmila	Rogachova	RUS	10.10.66	1		Parnu	13 Jul 88
1:56.84		Nina	Ruchayeva	RUS	17.4.56	2		Moskva	19 Jul 84
1:56.90		Mary	Slaney	USA	4.8.58	1		Bern	16 Aug 85
1:56.9		Olga	Dvirna	RUS	11.2.53	6	Kuts	Podolsk	21 Aug 82
1:56.91		Kim	Gallagher	USA	11.6.64	3	OG	Seoul	26 Sep 88
1:56.95		Jolanta	Januchta	POL	16.1.55	1	BGP	Budapest	11 Aug 80
1:56.96		Zuzana	Moravcíková	TCH	30.12.56	1		Leipzig	27 Jul 83
1:56.96			Liu Li	CHN	12.3.71	1h2	NG	Beijing	8 Sep 93
1:56.97		Valentina	Zhukova'	BLS	26.10.59	5	Izv	Kiev	22 Jun 84
1:57.0 '		Olga	Vakhrusheva	UKR	26.11.47	3	Prav	Moskva	12 Jun 80
		(50)	100th best 1:58.3						

1000 METRES

Mark	Wind	Name		Nat	Born	Pos	Meet	Venue	Date
2:30.6		Tatyana	Providokhina	RUS	26.3.53	1		Podolsk	20 Aug 78
2:30.67		Christine	Wachtel	GDR	6.1.65	1	ISTAF	Berlin	17 Aug 90
2:30.85		Martina	Kämpfert'	GDR	11.11.59	1		Berlin	9 Jul 80
2:31.50		Natalya	Artyomova ¶	RUS	5.1.63	1	ISTAF	Berlin	10 Sep 91
2:31.5		Maricica	Puica	ROM	29.7.50	1		Poiana Brasov	1 Jun 86
2:31.51		Sandra	Gasser ¶	SUI	27.7.62	1		Jerez de la Frontera	13 Sep 89
2:31.6 '		Beate	Liebich	GDR	21.2.58	2		Berlin	9 Jul 80
2:31.65		Olga	Dvirna	RUS	11.2.53	1		Athinai	1 Sep 82
2:31.74		Anita	Weiss'	GDR	16.7.55	1		Potsdam	13 Jul 80
2:31.77		Sigrun	Wodars/Grau	GDR	7.11.65	2	ISTAF	Berlin	17 Aug 90
		(10)							
2:31.85		Doina	Melinte	ROM	27.12.56	3	ISTAF	Berlin	17 Aug 90
2:31.95		Ulrike	Bruns'	GDR	17.11.53	1	ISTAF	Berlin	18 Aug 78
2:32.25		Letitia	Vriesde	SUR	5.10.64	2	ISTAF	Berlin	10 Sep 91
2:32.29		Christiane	Wartenberg'	GDR	27.10.56	2		Potsdam	13 Jul 80
2:32.40		Ella	Kovacs	ROM	11.12.64	1	BNP	Villeneuve d'Ascq	2 Jul 93
2:32.57		Maria	Mutola	MOZ	27.10.72	1	Pre	Eugene	5 Jun 93
2:32.6		Raisa	Belousova	RUS	29.2.52	2	Kuts	Podolsk	5 Aug 79
2:32.70		Jolanta	Januchta	POL	16.1.55	1	WK	Zürich	19 Aug 81
2:32.77		Yvonne	Mai	GDR	22.8.65	5	ISTAF	Berlin	17 Aug 90
2:32.8		Tamara	Sorokina'	RUS	15.8.50	1		Podolsk	24 Jul 76
		(20)							

1500 METRES

Mark	Wind	Name		Nat	Born	Pos	Meet	Venue	Date
3:50.46			Qu Yunxia	CHN	25.12.72	1	NG	Beijing	11 Sep 93
3:51.92			Wang Junxia	CHN	9.1.73	2	NG	Beijing	11 Sep 93
3:52.47		Tatyana	Kazankina ¶	RUS	17.12.51	1	WK	Zürich	13 Aug 80
3:53.96		Paula	Ivan'	ROM	20.7.63	1	OG	Seoul	1 Oct 88
3:54.23		Olga	Dvirna	RUS	11.2.53	1	NC	Kiev	27 Jul 82
3:55.0 '			Kazankina ¶			1	Znam	Moskva	6 Jul 80
3:55.30		Hassiba	Boulmerka	ALG	10.7.68	1	OG	Barcelona	8 Aug 92
3:56.0			Kazankina ¶			1		Podolsk	28 Jun 76
3:56.14		Zamira	Zaytseva	UZB	16.2.53	2	NC	Kiev	27 Jul 82
3:56.22			Ivan			1	WK	Zürich	17 Aug 88
3:56.50		Tatyana	Pozdnyakova	RUS	4.3.56	3	NC	Kiev	27 Jul 82
3:56.56			Kazankina ¶			1	OG	Moskva	1 Aug 80
3:56.63		Nadezhda	Ralldugina	RUS	15.11.57	1	Drz	Praha	18 Aug 84
3:56.65		Yekaterina	Podkopayeva' ¶	RUS	11.6.52	1		Rieti	2 Sep 84
		(10)							
3:56.7 '		Lyubov	Smolka	UKR	29.11.52	2	Znam	Moskva	6 Jul 80
3:56.7		Doina	Melinte	ROM	27.12.56	1		Bucuresti	12 Jul 86
3:56.8 '		Nadezhda	Olizarenko'	R/UKR	28.11.53	3	Znam	Moskva	6 Jul 80

Mark	Wind	Name		Nat	Born	Pos	Meet	Venue	Date
3:56.9 '			Zaytseva			4	Znam	Moskva	6 Jul 80
3:56.91		Lyudmila	Rogachova	RUS	10.10.66	2	OG	Barcelona	8 Aug 92
3:57.05		Svetlana	Guskova	MOL	19.8.59	4	NC	Kiev	27 Jul 82
3:57.08			Qu Yunxia			3	OG	Barcelona	8 Aug 92
3:57.12		Mary	Slaney	USA	4.8.58	1	vNord	Stockholm	26 Jul 83
3:57.22		Maricica	Puica	ROM	29.7.50	1		Bucuresti	1 Jul 84
3:57.24			Decker			1	VD	Bruxelles	30 Aug 85
3:57.4 '		Totka	Petrova ¶	BUL	17.12.56	1	Balk	Athinai	11 Aug 79
3:57.4 '			Podkopayeva			5	Znam	Moskva	6 Jul 80
3:57.46			Zhang Linli	CHN	6.3.73	3	NG	Beijing	11 Sep 93
3:57.48			Puica			1	NC	Bucuresti	31 Jul 82
3:57.70			Pozdnyakova			2		Rieti	2 Sep 84
3:57.71		Christiane	Wartenberg'	GDR	27.10.56	2	OG	Moskva	1 Aug 80
		(30/20)							
3:57.72		Galina	Zakharova	RUS	7.9.56	1	NP	Baku	14 Sep 84
3:57.92		Tatyana	Dorovskikh ¶	UKR	12.8.61	4	OG	Barcelona	8 Aug 92
3:58.2 '		Natalia	Marasescu' ¶	ROM	3.10.52	1	NC	Bucuresti	13 Jul 79
3:58.37		Tatyana	Providokhina	RUS	26.3.53	1	Kuts	Podolsk	22 Aug 82
3:58.40		Ravilya	Agletdinova '	BLS	10.2.60	1	EP	Moskva	18 Aug 85
3:58.5 '		Ileana	Silai ¶	ROM	14.10.41	2	NC	Bucuresti	13 Jul 79
3:58.64			Wang Renmei	CHN	5.7.70	4	NG	Beijing	11 Sep 93
3:58.65		Gabriella	Dorio	ITA	26.6.57	2		Tirrenia	25 Aug 82
3:58.67		Hildegard	Körner'	GDR	20.12.59	2	WC	Roma	5 Sep 87
3:58.71		Lyubov	Kremlyova	RUS	21.12.62	1	WK	Zürich	19 Aug 92
		(30)							
3:58.76		Svetlana	Ulmasova	UZB	4.2.53	2	Kuts	Podolsk	22 Aug 82
3:58.89		Tamara	Sorokina'	RUS	15.8.50	1	Znam	Leningrad	26 Jul 81
3:59.01		Giana	Romanova	RUS	10.3.55	1	EC	Praha	3 Sep 78
3:59.06		Sandra	Gasser ¶	SUI	27.7.62	3	WC	Roma	5 Sep 87
3:59.16		Natalya	Artyomova ¶	RUS	5.1.63	1	WK	Zürich	7 Aug 91
3:59.34			Liu Li	CHN	12.3.71	5	NG	Beijing	11 Sep 93
3:59.35		Violeta	Beclea	ROM	26.3.65	1	Herc	Monaco	7 Aug 93
3:59.48		Yelena	Sipatova	RUS	7.6.55	4	Kuts	Podolsk	22 Aug 82
3:59.60		Sonia	O'Sullivan	IRL	28.11.69	2	Herc	Monaco	7 Aug 93
3:59.67		Anna	Bukis	POL	8.9.53	3	BGP	Budapest	29 Jul 81
		(40)							
3:59.70			Zhang Lirong	CHN	3.3.73	6	NG	Beijing	11 Sep 93
3:59.8		Raisa	Katyukova'	BLS	16.9.50	2		Podolsk	28 Jun 76
3:59.81			Wang Yuan	CHN	8.4.76	7	NG	Beijing	11 Sep 93
3:59.90		Angelika	Zauber	GDR	5.11.58	1	NC	Jena	9 Aug 81
3:59.90		Cornelia	Bürki	SUI	3.10.53	5	WC	Roma	5 Sep 87
3:59.9		Ulrike	Klapezynski'	GDR	17.11.53	1		Potsdam	14 Jul 76
3:59.9		Beate	Liebich	GDR	21.2.58	1	OT	Potsdam	5 Jul 80
3:59.96		Zola	Budd'	GBR	26.5.66	3	VD	Bruxelles	30 Aug 85
4:00.05			Lu Yi	CHN	10.4.74	8	NG	Beijing	11 Sep 93
4:00.07		Andrea	Lange'	GDR	3.6.66	2	NC	Potsdam	22 Aug 87
		(50)	100th best 4:02.9						

1 MILE

Mark		Name		Nat	Born	Pos	Meet	Venue	Date
4:15.61		Paula	Ivan'	ROM	20.7.63	1	Nik	Nice	10 Jul 89
4:15.8		Natalya	Artyomova ¶	RUS	5.1.63	1		Leningrad	5 Aug 84
4:16.71		Mary	Slaney	USA	4.8.58	1	WK	Zürich	21 Aug 85
4:17.00			Artyomova			1	GPF	Barcelona	20 Sep 91
4:17.33		Maricica	Puica	ROM	29.7.50	2	WK	Zürich	21 Aug 85
4:17.44			Puica			1		Rieti	16 Sep 82
4:17.57		Zola	Budd'	GBR	26.5.66	3	WK	Zürich	21 Aug 85
4:18.08			Decker			1		Paris	9 Jul 82
4:18.13		Doina	Melinte	ROM	27.12.56	1	Bisl	Oslo	14 Jul 90
4:18.25			Puica			1	Nik	Nice	15 Jul 86
		(10/6)							
4:19.41		Kirsty	McDermott/Wade	GBR	6.8.62	2	Bisl	Oslo	27 Jul 85
4:20.79		Hassiba	Boulmerka	ALG	10.7.68	1	Bisl	Oslo	6 Jul 91
4:20.89		Lyudmila	Veselkova	RUS	25.10.50	1		Bologna	12 Sep 81
4:21.30		Lyudmila	Rogachova	RUS	10.10.66	1	Athl	Lausanne	8 Jul 92
		(10)	50th best 4:25.52						

Mark	Wind	Name		Nat	Born	Pos	Meet	Venue	Date
Indoors									
4:17.14		Doina	Melinte	ROM	27.12.56	1		East Rutherford	9 Feb 90
4:17.55 os			Decker-Slaney			1		Houston	16 Feb 80

2000 METRES

Mark	Wind	Name		Nat	Born	Pos	Meet	Venue	Date
5:28.69		Maricica	Puica	ROM	29.7.50	1	PTG	London	11 Jul 86
5:28.72		Tatyana	Kazankina ¶	RUS	17.12.51	1		Moskva	4 Aug 84
5:29.41+			Wang Junxia	CHN	9.1.73	1h2	NG	Beijing	12 Sep 93
5:29.58		Yvonne	Murray	GBR	4.10.64	2	PTG	London	11 Jul 86
5:29.64		Tatyana	Pozdnyakova	UKR	4.3.56	2		Moskva	4 Aug 84
5:29.65			Wang Junxia			1+	NG	Beijing	13 Sep 93
5:30.19		Zola	Budd'	GBR	26.5.66	3	PTG	London	11 Jul 86
5:30.92		Galina	Zakharova	RUS	7.9.56	3		Moskva	4 Aug 84
5:32.7 '		Mary	Slaney	USA	4.8.58	1		Eugene	3 Aug 84
5:33.85		Christina	Boxer'	GBR	25.3.57	2	PTG	London	13 Jul 84
5:35.16+			Zhang Linli	CHN	6.3.73	1h1	NG	Beijing	12 Sep 93
		(11/10)							
5:35.2+			Zhang Lirong	CHN	4.6.73	2h1	NG	Beijing	12 Sep 93
5:35.59		Cornelia	Burki	SUI	3.10.53	4	PTG	London	11 Jul 86

3000 METRES

Mark	Wind	Name		Nat	Born	Pos	Meet	Venue	Date
8:06.11			Wang Junxia	CHN	9.1.73	1	NG	Beijing	13 Sep 93
8:12.18			Qu Yunxia	CHN	25.12.72	2	NG	Beijing	13 Sep 93
8:12.19			Wang Junxia			1h2	NG	Beijing	12 Sep 93
8:12.27			Qu Yunxia			2h2	NG	Beijing	12 Sep 93
8:16.50			Zhang Linli	CHN	6.3.73	3	NG	Beijing	13 Sep 93
8:19.78			Ma Liyan	CHN	3.11.68	3h2	NG	Beijing	12 Sep 93
8:21.26			Ma Liyan			4	NG	Beijing	13 Sep 93
8:21.84			Zhang Lirong	CHN	3.3.73	5	NG	Beijing	13 Sep 93
8:22.06			Zhang Linli			1h1	NG	Beijing	12 Sep 93
8:22.44			Zhang Lirong			2h1	NG	Beijing	12 Sep 93
8:22.62		Tatyana	Kazankina ¶	RUS	17.12.51	1		Leningrad	26 Aug 84
8:25.83		Mary	Slaney	USA	4.8.58	1	GG-GP	Roma	7 Sep 85
8:26.53		Tatyana	Samolenko' ¶	UKR	12.8.61	1	OG	Seoul	25 Sep 88
8:26.78		Svetlana	Ulmasova	UZB	4.2.53	1	NC	Kiev	25 Jul 82
8:27.12		Lyudmila	Bragina (10)	RUS	24.7.43	1	v USA	College Park	7 Aug 76
8:27.15		Paula	Ivan'	ROM	20.7.63	2	OG	Seoul	25 Sep 88
8:27.68			Wang Junxia			1	NC	Jinan	6 Jun 93
8:27.83		Maricica	Puica	ROM	29.7.50	2	GG-GP	Roma	7 Sep 85
8:28.71			Qu Yunxia			1	WC	Stuttgart	16 Aug 93
8:28.74		Sonia	O'Sullivan	IRL	28.11.69	1	Bisl	Oslo	10 Jul 93
8:28.83		Zola	Budd'	GBR	26.5.66	3	GG-GP	Roma	7 Sep 85
8:29.02		Yvonne	Murray	GBR	4.10.64	3	OG	Seoul	25 Sep 88
8:29.25			Zhang Linli			2	WC	Stuttgart	16 Aug 93
8:29.30			Qu Yunxia			2	NC	Jinan	6 Jun 93
8:29.36		Svetlana	Guskova	MOL	19.8.59	2	NC	Kiev	25 Jul 82
8:29.59			Guskova			1		Moskva	6 Aug 84
8:29.69			Decker			1	ASV	Köln	25 Aug 85
8:29.71			Decker			1		Oslo	7 Jul 82
8:30.12			O'Sullivan			1	WK	Zürich	4 Aug 93
8:30.28			Ulmasova			1	EC	Athinai	9 Sep 82
		(30/16)							
8:30.45		Yelena	Romanova	RUS	20.3.63	4	OG	Seoul	25 Sep 88
8:31.67		Natalya	Artyomova ¶	RUS	5.1.63	5	OG	Seoul	25 Sep 88
8:31.75		Grete	Waitz'	NOR	1.10.53	1		Oslo	17 Jul 79
8:32.00		Elana	Meyer'	RSA	10.10.66	1		Durban	29 Apr 91
		(20)							
8:32.0		Tatyana	Pozdnyakova	UKR	4.3.56	1		Ryazan	11 Aug 84
8:33.40		Galina	Zakharova	RUS	7.9.56	3	NC	Kiev	25 Jul 82
8:33.53		Natalia	Marasescu' ¶	ROM	3.10.52	2	EC	Praha	29 Aug 78
8:33.53		Yelena	Sipatova	RUS	7.6.55	1		Moskva	12 Jul 80
8:33.9 '		Tatyana	Sychova	RUS	29.11.57	2		Moskva	12 Jul 80
8:33.97		Elly	van Hulst	HOL	9.6.59	1	WK	Zürich	17 Aug 88
8:33.99		Olga	Bondarenko'	RUS	2.6.60	1	EC	Stuttgart	28 Aug 86

Mark	Wind	Name		Nat	Born	Pos	Meet	Venue	Date
8:34.0 '		Faina	Krasnova'	RUS	7.12.57	3		Moskva	12 Jul 80
8:34.02		Alla	Yushina	RUS	20.8.58	2		Leningrad	27 Jul 83
8:34.10		Ingrid	Kristiansen'	NOR	21.3.56	1	WK	Zürich	13 Aug 86
		(30)							
8:35.11		Brigitte	Kraus	FRG	12.8.56	2	WC	Helsinki	10 Aug 83
8:35.74		Alla	Libutina	TJK	2.1.53	6	NC	Kiev	25 Jul 82
8:35.74		Zamira	Zaytseva	UZB	16.2.53	2	EP	Moskva	17 Aug 85
8:36.0 '		Lyubov	Smolka	UKR	29.11.52	4		Moskva	12 Jul 80
8:36.38		Ulrike	Bruns'	GDR	17.11.53	1	OD	Berlin	20 Jul 84
8:36.40		Olga	Dvirna	RUS	11.2.53	1		Sochi	30 May 82
8:36.45			Ma Ningning	CHN	1.6.76	4	NC	Jinan	6 Jun 93
8:37.06		Wendy	Sly'	GBR	5.11.59	5	WC	Helsinki	10 Aug 83
8:37.11		Doina	Melinte	ROM	27.12.56	1	v Eng,Rus	Bucuresti	15 Jun 86
8:37.25		Vicki	Huber	USA	29.5.67	6	OG	Seoul	25 Sep 88
		(40)							
8:37.30		Lynn	Williams	CAN	11.7.60	3	WK	Zürich	17 Aug 88
8:37.96		Agnese	Possamai	ITA	17.1.53	6	WC	Helsinki	10 Aug 83
8:38.1		Yelena	Zhupiyova'	UKR	18.4.60	1		Kharkov	11 Aug 85
8:38.22		Olga	Kuzyukova	RUS	17.5.53	8		Leningrad	27 Jul 83
8:38.23		Liz	McColgan'	GBR	24.4.64	1	Nik	Nice	15 Jul 91
8:38.38		Angela	Chalmers	CAN	6.9.63	1	CG	Auckland	28 Jan 90
8:38.42		Alison	Wyeth	GBR	26.5.64	5	WC	Stuttgart	16 Aug 93
8:38.60		Cindy	Bremser	USA	5.5.53	2	WK	Zürich	22 Aug 84
8:38.71		Cornelia	Bürki	SUI	3.10.53	2	PTG	London	20 Jul 85
8:38.83		Mariana	Stanescu	ROM	7.9.64	1	GWG	Moskva	6 Jul 86
		(50)	100th best 8:45.69						

Indoor marks

Mark	Wind	Name		Nat	Born	Pos	Meet	Venue	Date
8:33.82		Elly	van Hulst	HOL	9.6.59	1	WI	Budapest	4 Mar 89
8:34.80		Liz	McColgan'	GBR	24.5.64	2	WI	Budapest	4 Mar 89

5000 METRES

Mark	Wind	Name		Nat	Born	Pos	Meet	Venue	Date
14:37.33		Ingrid	Kristiansen'	NOR	21.3.56	1		Stockholm	5 Aug 86
14:44.15		Elana	Meyer	RSA	10.10.66	1		Bellville	6 Mar 92
14:45.92		Sonia	O'Sullivan	IRL	28.11.69	1	ISTAF	Berlin	27 Aug 93
14:46.41			Meyer			1		Hechtel	31 Jul 93
14:48.07		Zola	Budd'	GBR	26.5.66	1	McV	London	26 Aug 85
14:49.35			Meyer'			1		Cape Town	8 Apr 91
14:50.29			Meyer	RSA		1	DNG	Stockholm	5 Jul 93
14:50.43			Meyer			1		Port Elizabeth	19 Dec 91
14:51.42			Meyer			1	DNG	Stockholm	2 Jul 92
14:51.45			Meyer			1	ISTAF	Berlin	21 Aug 92
14:54.08		Natalya	Artyomova ¶	RUS	5.1.63	1		Podolsk	9 Sep 85
14:55.76		Olga	Bondarenko'	RUS	2.6.60	2		Podolsk	9 Sep 85
14:56.07		Annette	Peters	USA	31.5.65	2	ISTAF	Berlin	27 Aug 93
14:57.43			Kristiansen			2	McV	London	26 Aug 85
14:58.70			Kristiansen			1	FBK	Hengelo	27 Jun 86
14:58.71		Kathrin	Ullrich	GER	14.8.67	1	ISTAF	Berlin	10 Sep 91
14:58.89			Kristiansen			1	Bisl	Oslo	28 Jun 84
14:59.01			Ullrich			1	DNG	Stockholm	3 Jul 89
14:59.11			O'Sullivan			2	ISTAF	Berlin	21 Aug 92
14:59.49			O'Sullivan			1	Toto	Fukuoka	18 Sep 93
14:59.70		Yelena	Romanova	RUS	20.3.63	2	ISTAF	Berlin	10 Sep 91
		(21/10)							
15:00.00		PattiSue	Plumer	USA	27.4.62	2	DNG	Stockholm	3 Jul 89
15:01.08		Elizabeth	Lynch/McColgan	GBR	24.5.64	1		Oslo	5 Aug 87
15:01.30		Lynn	Williams	CAN	11.7.60	3	DNG	Stockholm	3 Jul 89
15:02.12		Svetlana	Guskova	MOL	19.8.59	1	v GDR	Tallinn	21 Jun 86
15:03.52		Susan	Sirma	KEN	26.5.66	3	ISTAF	Berlin	10 Sep 91
15:04.87		Uta	Pippig	GER	7.9.65	4	ISTAF	Berlin	10 Sep 91
15:05.12		Albertina	Dias	POR	26.4.65	2		Hechtel	31 Jul 93
15:05.50		Svetlana	Ulmasova	UZB	4.2.53	2	GWG	Moskva	8 Jul 86
15:05.69+			Zhong Huandi	CHN	28.6.67	1	NG	Beijing	8 Sep 93
15:05.8e+			Wang Junxia	CHN	9.1.73	2	NG	Beijing	8 Sep 93
		(20)							
15:05.91		Jane	Ngotho	KEN	29.11.69	5	ISTAF	Berlin	10 Sep 91

Mark	Wind	Name		Nat	Born	Pos	Meet	Venue	Date
15:06.04		Maricica	Puica	ROM	29.7.50	1	WG	Helsinki	4 Jul 85
15:06.53		Mary	Slaney	USA	4.8.58	1	Pre	Eugene	1 Jun 85
15:06.96		Aurora	Cunha	POR	31.5.59	2	WG	Helsinki	4 Jul 85
15:07.56		Cathy	Branta-Easker	USA	6.1.63	3	WG	Helsinki	4 Jul 85
15:07.68		Christine	Toonstra	HOL	22.6.66	1		Hechtel	18 Jul 92
15:07.87		Esther	Kiplagat	KEN	8.12.66	3	ISTAF	Berlin	21 Aug 92
15:07.92		Lynn	Jennings	USA	1.7.60	1	DNG	Stockholm	2 Jul 90
15:08.03		Tecla	Lorupe	KEN	5.5.71	3	ISTAF	Berlin	27 Aug 93
15:08.67		Shelly	Steely	USA	23.10.62	4	ISTAF	Berlin	21 Aug 92
		(30)	50th best 15:16.93, 100th 15:28.63						

10 000 METRES

Mark	Wind	Name		Nat	Born	Pos	Meet	Venue	Date
29:31.78			Wang Junxia	CHN	9.1.73	1	NG	Beijing	8 Sep 93
30:13.37			Zhong Huandi	CHN	28.6.67	2	NG	Beijing	8 Sep 93
30:13.74		Ingrid	Kristiansen'	NOR	21.3.56	1	Bisl	Oslo	5 Jul 86
30:23.25			Kristiansen			1	EC	Stuttgart	30 Aug 86
30:48.51			Kristiansen			1	Bisl	Oslo	1 Jul 89
30:49.30			Wang Junxia			1	WC	Stuttgart	21 Aug 93
30:57.07		Liz	McColgan	GBR	24.5.64	1	APM	Hengelo	25 Jun 91
30:57.21		Olga	Bondarenko'	RUS	2.6.60	2	EC	Stuttgart	30 Aug 86
30:59.42			Kristiansen			1	Bisl	Oslo	27 Jul 85
31:03.62		Kathrin	Ullrich	GER	14.8.67	1	EP	Frankfurt-am-Main	30 Jun 91
31:05.21			Bondarenko			1	OG	Seoul	30 Sep 88
31:05.85			Kristiansen			1	WC	Roma	4 Sep 87
31:06.02		Derartu	Tulu	ETH	21.3.72	1	OG	Barcelona	7 Aug 92
31:06.99			McColgan			1	Bisl	Oslo	2 Jul 88
31:07.88		Jill	Hunter	GBR	14.10.66	2	EP	Frankfurt-am-Main	30 Jun 91
31:08.42			Wang Junxia			1	NC	Jinan	2 Jun 93
31:08.44			McColgan			2	OG	Seoul	30 Sep 88
31:09.25			Zhang Lirong	CHN	3.3.73	3	NG	Beijing	8 Sep 93
31:09.40		Yelena	Zhupiyova' (10)	UKR	18.4.60	2	WC	Roma	4 Sep 87
31:10.46			Ma Liyan	CHN	6.9.68	4	NG	Beijing	8 Sep 93
31:11.34			Ullrich			3	WC	Roma	4 Sep 87
31:11.72		Lisa	Ondieki'	AUS	12.5.60	1	WG	Helsinki	30 Jun 92
31:11.75		Elana	Meyer	RSA	10.10.66	2	OG	Barcelona	7 Aug 92
31:12.55			Zhong Huandi			2	WC	Stuttgart	21 Aug 93
31:13.78			Bondarenko			1	Izv	Kiev	24 Jun 84
31:14.31			McColgan			1	WC	Tokyo	30 Aug 91
31:15.00		Galina	Zakharova	RUS	7.9.56	2	Izv	Kiev	24 Jun 84
31:15.38		Sally	Barsosio	KEN	21.3.78	3	WC	Stuttgart	21 Aug 93
31:15.66			Kristiansen			1	Bisl	Oslo	4 Jul 87
31:16.28			Zhang Linli	CHN	6.3.73	5	NG	Beijing	8 Sep 93
		(30/16)							
31:16.42		M Conceição	Ferreira	POR	13.3.62	2	WG	Helsinki	30 Jun 92
31:18.18		Viorica	Ghican	ROM	9.6.65	1	WG	Helsinki	27 Jun 90
31:19.76		Ulrike	Bruns'	GDR	17.11.53	3	EC	Stuttgart	30 Aug 86
31:19.89		Lynn	Jennings	USA	10.7.60	3	OG	Barcelona	7 Aug 92
		(20)							
31:21.20		Tecla	Lorupe	KEN	5.5.71	1		Warstein	6 Jul 93
31:21.36		Uta	Pippig	GER	7.9.65	2	OD	Jena	28 May 92
31:23.92			Liu Jianying	CHN	19.11.71	6	NG	Beijing	8 Sep 93
31:27.00			Wang Xiuting	CHN	11.5.65	1	NC	Guangzhou	29 Nov 87
31:27.58		Raisa	Sadreydinova	RUS	9.5.52	1	NC	Odessa	7 Sep 83
31:27.99			Hou Juhua	CHN	.67	2	NC	Guangzhou	29 Nov 87
31:28.83			Wei Li	CHN	.1.72	7	NG	Beijing	8 Sep 93
31:28.92		Francie	Larrieu Smith	USA	23.11.52	1	TexR	Austin	4 Apr 91
31:29.41		Aurora	Cunha	POR	31.5.59	2	Bisl	Oslo	5 Jul 86
31:31.54			Wang Yongmei	CHN	3.10.68	8	NG	Beijing	8 Sep 93
		(30)							
31:32.15			Feng Wenhui	CHN	21.1.74	9	NG	Beijing	8 Sep 93
31:32.50			Wang Yanfang	CHN	10.7.71	11	NG	Beijing	8 Sep 93
31:33.03		M Albertina	Dias	POR	26.4.65	7	WC	Stuttgart	21 Aug 93
31:35.01		Lyudmila	Baranova	RUS	.50	1		Krasnodar	29 May 83
31:35.3		Mary	Slaney	USA	4.8.58	1		Eugene	16 Jul 82
31:37.26		Anne Marie	Letko	USA	7.3.69	8	WC	Stuttgart	21 Aug 93

Mark	Wind	Name		Nat	Born	Pos	Meet	Venue	Date
31:38.02		Lyudmila	Matveyeva	RUS	1.2.57	1	NC	Kiev	2 Aug 88
31:38.04		Judy	St Hilaire	USA	5.9.59	8	OG	Barcelona	7 Aug 92
31:38.91		Helen	Kimaiyo	KEN	8.9.68	9	OG	Barcelona	7 Aug 92
31:40.38		Izumi	Maki	JPN	10.12.68	1		Kobe	3 May 92
		(40)							
31:40.51		Fernanda	Ribeiro	POR	23.6.69	10	WC	Stuttgart	21 Aug 93
31:40.56		Delilah	Asiago	KEN	24.2.72	1	JapC	Tokyo	16 Jun 91
31:41.09		Lydia	Cheromei	KEN	11.5.77	2	Afr Ch	Belle Vue Mauricia	27 Jun 92
31:42.02		Yekaterina	Khramenkova	BLS	16.6.56	4	NC	Kiev	2 Aug 88
31:42.43		Svetlana	Guskova	MOL	19.8.59	5	EC	Stuttgart	30 Aug 86
31:42.53		Véronique	Collard	BEL	9.6.63	1	NC	Lommel	25 Apr 92
31:42.8		Lesley	Welch/Lehane	USA	12.3.63	1		Dedham	11 Jun 88
31:42.83		Rosario	Murcia	FRA	23.9.64	2	Bel Ch	Lommel	25 Apr 92
31:43.36		Lieve	Slegers	BEL	6.4.65	3	NC	Lommel	25 Apr 92
31:43.55		Christine	Toonstra	HOL	22.6.66	4	Bel Ch	Lommel	25 Apr 92
		(50)	100th best 32:05.47						

3000 METRES STEEPLECHASE

Mark	Wind	Name		Nat	Born	Pos	Meet	Venue	Date
6:14.52		Svetlana	Rogova	RUS	4.8.67	1	Znam	Moskva	11 Jun 92
6:16.41		Marina	Pluzhnikova	RUS	25.2.63	1	NC	Kiev	2 Aug 88
6:17.42			Rogova			1	NC	Moskva	19 Jun 93
6:17.80		Irina	Mozharova	RUS	19.7.58	1	NC	Gorkiy	23 Jul 89
6:18.67			Rogova			2	NC	Gorkiy	23 Jul 89
6:18.87			Rogova			1		Sochi	30 May 92
6:19.10			Rogova			1	NC	Kiev	6 Jul 90
6:19.26			Rogova			1	Znam	Moskva	11 Jun 91
6:19.46			Rogova			1	CISCh	Moskva	24 Jun 92
6:19.88			Pluzhnikova			1	Rus		12 Jul 88
		(10/3)							
6:21.16		Lyudmila	Pushkina	UKR	2.10.65	2	CISCh	Moskva	24 Jun 92
6:21.42		Antonina	Grishayeva	MOL	59	2	Znam	Moskva	11 Jun 91
6:22.03		Stefania	Statkuviene	LIT	6.3.63	3	URSCh	Gorkiy	23 Jul 89
6:22.36		Svetlana	Lyegkodukh	UKR	24.11.69	1		Kiev	30 May 92
6:23.12		Anzhelika	Averkova	UKR	13.3.69	4	Znam	Moskva	11 Jun 91
6:24.18		Yelena	Krasnova	RUS		2	NC	Kiev	2 Aug 88
6:24.26		Irina	Matrosova	RUS	5.4.62	4	NC	Gorkiy	23 Jul 89
6:24.32		Olga	Stefanishina	UKR	21.11.61	1		Lugansk	10 May 91
6:24.71		Lyudmila	Kuropatkina	RUS	.66	3	CISCh	Moskva	24 Jun 92

HALF MARATHON

Included in these lists are the slightly downhill courses: Newcasrtle to South Shields 30.5m, Tokyo 33m. Lisboa 40m

Mark	Wind	Name		Nat	Born	Pos	Meet	Venue	Date
66:40*		Ingrid	Kristiansen	NOR	21.3.56	1	NC	Sandnes	5 Apr 87
67:11		Liz	McColgan	GBR	24.5.64	1		Tokyo	26 Jan 92
67:22		Elana	Meyer	RSA	10.10.66	1		Tokyo	24 Jan 93
67:59			Meyer			1	NC	East London	18 May 91
68:32			Kristiansen			1		New Bedford	19 Mar 89
68:33		Lisa	Ondieki	AUS	12.5.60	2		Tokyo	26 Jan 92
68:34		Joan	Benoit	USA	16.5.57	1		Philadelphia	16 Sep 84
68:34		Olga	Appell	MEX	2.8.63	2		Tokyo	24 Jan 93
68:38		Colleen	de Reuck	RSA	13.4.64	1	NC	Durban	23 Jul 89
68:41		Junko	Kataoka	JPN	13.6.70	1		Tokyo	23 Jan 94
68:42			McColgan			1		Dundee	11 Oct 92
68:49		Grete	Waitz	NOR	1.10.53	1	GNR	Newcastle	24 Jul 88
68:53			McColgan			1	WC	South Shields	20 Sep 92
69:03*			Kristiansen			1		Drammen	5 Oct 86
69:03*?			Martin (Ondieki)			1		Surfers Paradise	24 Jul 88
69:04			Meyer			2		Tokyo	23 Jan 94
69:05*			Kristiansen			1		Den Haag	23 Mar 91
69:05		Delilah	Asiago (10)	KEN	24.2.72	1	GWR	Exeter	5 May 91
69:05		Nadia	Prasad/Bernard	FRA	6.10.67	1		Las Vegas	5 Feb 94
69:14			Benoit			1		Philadelphia	18 Sep 83
69:14			Appell			3		Tokyo	23 Jan 94
69:15			McColgan			2	GWR	Exeter	5 May 91
69:19*#			Waitz			1	Stra	Milan	4 Apr 82
69:21		Megumi	Fujiwara	JPN	19.6.69	2	WC	South Shields	20 Sep 92

Mark	Wind	Name		Nat	Born	Pos	Meet	Venue	Date
69:22		Anuta	Catuna	ROM	1.10.68	1	NC	Bucuresti	21 Aug 93
69:26			van Zyl - Meyer			2	NC	Durban	23 Jul 89
69:29			Asiago			1		Yamaguchi	22 Mar 92
69:33		Rosa	Mota	POR	29.6.58	1	GNR	Newcastle	16 Sep 90
69:35		Valentina	Yegorova	RUS	16.2.64	1		Sankt Peterburg	12 Jun 93
69:37		Aurora	Cunha	POR	31.5.59	2		New Bedford	19 Mar 89
69:37		Midori	Fumoto	JPN	18.12.71	1		Gold Coast	12 Jul 92
		(31/17)							
69:38		Rosanna	Munerotto	ITA	3.12.62	3	WC	South Shields	20 Sep 92
69:39		Cathy	O'Brien	USA	19.7.64	1		Philadelphia	16 Sep 90
69:39		Andrea	Wallace	GBR	22.11.66	1		Bath	21 Mar 93
		(20)							
69:48*		Dorthe	Rasmussen	DEN	27.1.60	2		Den Haag	23 Mar 91
69:56		Susan	Tooby	GBR	24.10.60	2	GNR	Newcastle	24 Jul 88
70:00		Angelina	Kanana	KEN	65	1		Remich	26 Sep 93
70:01		Heléna	Barócsi	HUN	9.7.66	1		Lisboa 40m dh	15 Mar 92
70:04*		Carla	Beurskens	HOL	10.2.52	1		Amsterdam	31 Mar 90
70:04		Katrin	Dörre	GER	6.10.61	3		Tokyo	24 Jan 93
70:04		Kaori	Kumura	JPN	22.8.70	1	AusC	Gold Coast	18 Jul 93
70:07		Conceição	Ferreira	POR	13.3.62	1	WC	Bruxelles	3 Oct 93
70:09		Mari	Tanigawa	JPN	27.10.62	2	WC	Bruxelles	3 Oct 93
70:12		Tecla	Lorupe	KEN	9.5.71	3	WC	Bruxelles	3 Oct 93
		(30)							
70:13		Elena	Murgoci	ROM	20.5.60	2	NC	Bucuresti	21 Aug 93
70:15		Miyoko	Asahina	JPN	24.9.69	4	WC	Bruxelles	3 Oct 93
70:26		Colleen	De Reuck	RSA	13.4.64	1		Philadelphia	19 Sep 93
70:28		Mariko	Hara	JPN	27.12.70	2		Gold Coast	12 Jul 92
70:28		Fatuma	Roba	ETH		6	WC	South Shields	20 Sep 92
70:35*		Uta	Pippig	GER	7.9.65	3		Den Haag	23 Mar 91
70:37			Wang Yongmei	CHN	3.10.68	1		Okayama	6 Dec 92
70:38		Naomi	Yoshida	JPN	14.4.69	1		Yamaguchi	20 Mar 93
70:40		M Albertina	Dias	POR	26.4.65	2		Lisboa 40m dh	15 Mar 92
		(40)							
70:41		Janis	Klecker	USA	18.7.60	1		New Bedford	18 Mar 90
70:46		Janete	Mayal	BRA	19.7.63	3		Lisboa 40m dh	15 Mar 92
70:47		Silvia	Mosqueda	USA	8.9.66	1		Philadelphia	20 Sep 87
70:47		Lesley	Lehane	USA	12.3.63	1		Philadelphia	18 Sep 88
70:51		Eriko	Asai	JPN	20.10.59	7	WC	South Shields	20 Sep 92
70:53		Birgit	Jerschabek	GER	17.5.69	8	WC	South Shields	20 Sep 92
70:54*		Iris	Biba	FRG	27.5.64	2		Amsterdam	31 Mar 90
70:55		Judi	St.Hilaire	USA	5.9.59	2		Philadelphia	16 Sep 84
70:57		Miki	Igarashi	JPN	22.8.71	4		Yamaguchi	22 Mar 92
70:58		Nadezhda	Ilyina	RUS	2.4.64	9	WC	South Shields	20 Sep 92
		(50)							

 # Rolling start used at Milan

Uncertain distance

Mark	Wind	Name		Nat	Born	Pos	Meet	Venue	Date
68:37		Rosa	Mota	POR	29.6.58	1		Québec	11 Jun 89
68:56		Carla	Beurskens	HOL	10.2.52	1		Luxembourg	21 Sep 86
69:28			Beurskens			1		Den Haag	5 Apr 86
69:03		Carole	Rouillard	CAN	15.3.60	1		Québec	10 Jun 90
70:06		M Albertina	Dias	POR	26.4.65	1		Ovar	5 Oct 92
70:53		Danièle	Kaber	LUX	20.4.60	2		Luxembourg	21 Sep 86
70:58		Karolina	Szabó	HUN	17.11.61	1		Den Haag	28 Mar 87

Short courses

Mark	Wind	Name		Nat	Born	Pos	Meet	Venue	Date
67:59			Kristiansen			1		Oslo (220m)	13 Sep 86
69:47		Nadezhda	Ilyina	RUS	2.4.64	1		Lisboa (97m)	13 Mar 93
70:02		Manuela	Dias	POR	19.6.63	2		Lisboa (97m)	13 Mar 93
70:04		Tatyana	Pozdnyakova	UKR	4.3.56	3		Lisboa 97m)	13 Mar 93
70:06		Maria	Rebelo	FRA	29.1.56	4		Lisboa (97m)	13 Mar 93

MARATHON

Mark	Wind	Name		Nat	Born	Pos	Meet	Venue	Date
2:21:06		Ingrid	Kristiansen	NOR	21.3.56	1		London	21 Apr 85
2:21:21		Joan	Benoit'	USA	16.5.57	1		Chicago	20 Oct 85
2:22:43			Benoit			1		Boston	18 Apr 83
2:22:48			Kristiansen			1		London	10 May 87
2:23:05			Kristiansen			2		Chicago	20 Oct 85
2:23:29		Rosa	Mota	POR	29.6.58	3		Chicago	20 Oct 85

Mark	Wind	Name		Nat	Born	Pos	Meet	Venue	Date
2:23:43		Olga	Markova	RUS	6.8.68	1		Boston	20 Apr 92
2:23:51		Lisa	Martin/Ondieki	AUS	12.5.60	1		Osaka	31 Jan 88
2:24:07			Wang Junxia	CHN	9.1.73	1		Tianjin	4 Apr 93
2:24:18		Wanda	Panfil	POL	26.1.59	1		Boston	15 Apr 91
2:24:26			Kristiansen			1		London	13 May 84
2:24:30			Mota			1		Boston	18 Apr 88
2:24:32			Qu Yunxia	CHN	25.12.72	2		Tianjin	4 Apr 93
2:24:33			Kristiansen			1		Boston	17 Apr 89
2:24:40			Ondieki			1		New York	1 Nov 92
2:24:42			Zhang Linli	CHN	6.3.73	3		Tianjin	4 Apr 93
2:24:52			Benoit			1	OG	Los Angeles	5 Aug 84
2:24:52			Zhang Lirong (10)	CHN	3.3.73	4		Tianjin	4 Apr 93
2:24:54		Grete	Waitz	NOR	1.10.53	1		London	20 Apr 86
2:24:55			Kristiansen			1		Boston	21 Apr 86
2:25:17			Mota			1	WC	Roma	29 Aug 87
2:25:21			Mota			1		Boston	20 Apr 87
2:25:24		Katrin	Dörre	GDR	6.10.61	1		Tokyo	15 Nov 87
2:25:24			Mota			1		Boston	16 Apr 90
2:25:27			Markova			1		Boston	19 Apr 93
2:25:28			Martin			1	CG	Auckland	31 Jan 90
2:25:29			Waitz			1		London	17 Apr 83
2:25:30			Kristiansen			1		New York	5 Nov 89
2:25:36			Zhong Huandi	CHN	28.6.67	5		Tianjin	4 Apr 93
2:25:40			Mota			1	OG	Seoul	23 Sep 88
		(30/13)							
2:25:46			Ma Liyan	CHN	3.11.68	6		Tianjin	4 Apr 93
2:25:56		Véronique	Marot	GBR	16.9.55	1		London	23 Apr 89
2:26:09		Tomoe	Abe	JPN	13.8.71	1		Osaka	30 Jan 94
2:26:09		Nobuko	Fujimura	JPN	18.12.65	2		Osaka	30 Jan 94
2:26:10		Junko	Asari	JPN	22.9.69	3		Osaka	30 Jan 94
2:26:20		Renata	Kokowska	POL	4.12.58	1		Berlin	26 Sep 93
2:26:23		Madina	Biktagirova ¶	BLS	20.9.64	1	OT	Los Angeles	1 Mar 92
		(20)							
2:26:24		Uta	Pippig	GER	7.9.65	2		New York	14 Nov 93
2:26:26		Julie	Brown	USA	4.2.55	1		Los Angeles	5 Jun 83
2:26:26		Yumi	Kokamo	JPN	26.12.71	1		Osaka	26 Jan 92
2:26:26		Yoshiko	Yamamoto	JPN	6.6.70	2		Boston	20 Apr 92
2:26:26		Mitsuyo	Yoshida	JPN	29.10.66	4		Osaka	30 Jan 94
2:26:34		Carla	Beurskens	HOL	10.2.52	2		Tokyo	15 Nov 87
2:26:36			Wang Yanfang	CHN	10.7.71	7		Tianjin	4 Apr 93
2:26:38			Xie Lihua	CHN	19.7.65	8		Tianjin	4 Apr 93
2:26:40		Kim	Jones	USA	2.5.58	2		Boston	15 Apr 91
2:26:40		Valentina	Yegorova	RUS	16.2.64	1		Tokyo	21 Nov 93
		(30)							
2:26:46		Allison	Roe	NZL	30.5.56	1		Boston	20 Apr 81
2:26:49		M Albertina	Dias	POR	26.4.65	2		Berlin	26 Sep 93
2:26:51		Priscilla	Welch	GBR	22.11.44	2		London	10 May 87
2:26:55		Kamila	Gradus	POL	19.3.67	5		Boston	15 Apr 91
2:27:02		Akemi	Matsuno	JPN	27.4.68	2		Osaka	26 Jan 92
2:27:05		Tatyana	Polovinskaya	UKR	14.3.65	4	OG	Seoul	23 Sep 88
2:27:06		Zhao Youfeng		CHN	5.5.65	5	OG	Seoul	23 Sep 88
2:27:16		Mun Gyong-ae		PRK	8.4.69	1		Beijing	15 Oct 89
2:27:32		Liz	McColgan	GBR	24.5.64	1		New York	3 Nov 91
2:27:35		Francie	Larrieu-Smith	USA	23.11.52	2	WCp	London	21 Apr 91
		(40)							
2:27:36		Frith	van der Merwe	RSA	26.5.64	1		Port Elizabeth	24 Feb 90
2:27:42		M Manuela	Machado	POR	9.8.63	4		Boston	20 Apr 92
2:27:49		Laura	Fogli	ITA	5.10.59	6	OG	Seoul	23 Sep 88
2:27:51		Patti	Catalano	USA	6.4.53	2		Boston	20 Apr 81
2:27:51		Miyoko	Asahina	JPN	24.9.69	5		Osaka	30 Jan 94
2:27:57		Zoya	Ivanova	KZK	14.3.52	3		Tokyo	15 Nov 87
2:28:01		Yuko	Arimori	JPN	17.12.66	2		Osaka	27 Jan 91
2:28:03		Ramila	Burangulova	RUS	11.7.61	3		Nagoya	7 Mar 93
2:28:06		Sarah	Rowell	GBR	19.11.62	2		London	21 Apr 85
2:28:07		Carey	May/Edge	IRL/CAN	19.7.59	1		Osaka	27 Jan 85
		(50)	100th best 2:29:49						

Mark	Wind	Name		Nat	Born	Pos	Meet	Venue	Date

Note: Slightly downhill point-to-point courses: Port Elizabeth (RSA) had a net drop of 149m between start (203m) and finish (54m). Boston (USA) has a net drop of 139m between start (143m) and finish (4m).

Short courses

Mark	Wind	Name		Nat	Born	Pos	Meet	Venue	Date
2:25:25		Lyubov	Klochko	UKR	26.9.62	1		Belaya Cerkov	6 Sep 87
2:25:29		Allison	Roe	NZL	30.5.56	1		New York	25 Oct 81

Certified road courses — 100 KILOMETRES

Mark	Wind	Name		Nat	Born	Pos	Meet	Venue	Date
7:09:44		Ann	Trason	USA	30.8.60	1	IAU	Amiens	25 Sep 93
7:18:57		Birgit	Lennartz	GER	22.11.65	1	NC	Hanau	28 Apr 90
7:26:52			Lennartz			1		Unna	30 Sep 89
7:27:19		Carolyn	Hunter-Rowe	GBR	25.1.64	1	IAU WC	Torhout	8 Aug 93
7:27:20			Lennartz			1	IAU NC	Rheine-Elte	5 Sep 92
7:27:39		Valentina	Shatyayeva	RUS	.63	2	IAU WC	Torhout	8 Aug 93
7:30:49		Ann	Trason	USA	30.8.60	1	WCh	Santander	1 Oct 88
7:31:25		Valentina	Lyakhova	RUS	24.6.58	2	IAU	Amiens	25 Sep 93
7:33:12			Trason			1		Duluth	28 Oct 89
7:33:24			Trason			1		Queens, New York	4 May 91
7:34:05		Irina	Petrova	RUS	13.2.74	1	IAU	Torrelavega	3 Oct 92
7:34:54			Hunter-Rowe			1	IAU NC	Nottingham	23 May 93
7:35:21			Lennartz			1	NC	Scheesel	12 Oct 91
7:37:05		Marta	Vass	HUN	6.7.62	1	IAU	Torhout	19 Jun 92
7:38:01			Lyakhova			3	IAU WC	Torhout	8 Aug 93
7:38:52			Lyakhova			2	IAU	Torrelavega	3 Oct 92
7:39:59			Hunter-Rowe			1	IAU NC	Nottingham	31 May 92
7:40:55			Vass			1	IAU	Torhout	18 Jun 93
7:41:42			Vass			1		Torhout	23 Jun 90
7:42:00			Lennartz			1		Hamm	8 Oct 88
		(20/7)							
7:44:29 *		Yelena	Maskina	RUS	.62	1	IAU	Moskva	8 Aug 93
7:44:37		Nurzhia	Bagmanov	RUS	8.6.63	1	IAU WC	Palamos	16 Feb 92
7:46:44		Nadezhda	Gumerova	KGZ	1.1.49	2	IAU	Torhout	19 Jun 92
7:47:29		Marcy	Schwam	USA	11.2.53	1		Santander	19 Sep 81
7:48:33		Eleanor	Adams/Robinson	GBR	20.11.47	1	IAU	Santander	7 Oct 89
7:49:16		Sandra	Kiddy	USA	27.11.36			Duluth	27 Oct 84
7:50:09		Hilary	Walker	GBR	9.11.53	2	IAU EC	Winschoten	18 Sep 93
7:50:40		Sybille	Möllensiep	GER	7.6.62	2	IAU	Rodenbach	24 Apr 93
7:50:57		Iris	Reuter	GER	27.6.61	2	IAU NC	Rheine-Elte	4 Sep 93
7:56:40		Agnes	Eberle	SUI	.50	1		Rodenbach	25 Apr 87
7:56:55		Jutta	Philippin	GER	14.4.60	3	IAU NC	Rheine-Elte	4 Sep 93
7:58:54		Hanni	Zehender	FRG	24.5.46	2	NC	Hanau	28 Apr 90
		(20)							
7:59:19		Viviane	Vanderhaeghan	BEL	.63	2	IAU EC	Winschoten	12 Sep 92

Performances on courses not known to be measured by calibrated bicycle

Mark	Wind	Name		Nat	Born	Pos	Meet	Venue	Date
7:26:01		Chantal	Langlacé	FRA	6.1.55	1		Migennes	17 Jun 84
7:50:37		Christa	Vahlensieck	FRG	27.5.49	1		Unna	5 Sep 76

t = track race — 24 HOURS

Mark	Wind	Name		Nat	Born	Pos	Meet	Venue	Date
243.657		Sigrid	Lomsky	GER	16.1.42	1	IAU EC	Basel	1/2 May 93
240.169t		Eleanor	Adams	GBR	20.11.47	1		Melbourne	19/20 Aug 89
236.453		Hilary	Walker	GBR	9.11.53	1		Preston	27/28 Aug 88
233.816		Sue Ellen	Trapp	USA	4.3.46	1	NC	Sylvania	18/19 Sep 93
232.107		Angela	Mertens	BEL	11.11.41	1		Heusden	15/16 Oct 88
231.008			Lomsky			1	IAU EC	Apeldoorn	29/30 May 92
230.618			Walker			1		Feltham	23/24 May 87
230.275		Ann	Trason	USA	30.8.60	1	TAC	Queen's, NY	16/17 Sep 89
230.013t		Marianne	Savage	GBR	26.1.49	1		Solihull	2/3 Jul 88
227.038		Monika	Kuno	FRG	13.11.43	1	ECp	Mittersill	15/16 Jun 90
		(10/8)							
226.330		Helga	Backhaus	GER	19.1.53	1	IAU	Apeldoorn	21/22 May 93
222.556		Randi	Bromka	USA	6.5.52	1	IAU NC	Sacramento	30/31 Dec 92
222.020		Tamara	Merslikina	URS	43	1		Mittersill	26/27 May 89
220.500t		Sandra	Barwick	NZL	27.2.49	1		Hong Kong	Feb 89
219.735t		Sue Ellen	Trapp	USA	3.3.46	1	NC	Portland	28/29 Oct 91
217.201t		Susan	Olsen	USA		2	NC	Portland	28/29 Oct 91
216.648t		Ros	Paul	GBR	27.5.59	1		Nottingham	22/23 Aug 82
215.888		Anna	Dyck	GER	28.8.44	2	IAU	Apeldoorn	21/22 May 93

Mark	Wind	Name		Nat	Born	Pos	Meet	Venue	Date
215.461t		Wu Wing-yee		HKG	31.8.62	1		Hong Kong	9/10 Feb 91
215.402		Waltraud	Reisert	FRG	39	1		Apeldoorn	9/10 May 86
215.068t		Sandra	Brown	GBR	1.4.49	1		London (TB)	16/17 Oct 93
Other track bests									
226.237		Angela	Mertens	BEL	11.11.41	1		Izgem	2/3 Jul 88
225.307		Hilary	Walker	GBR	9.11.53	1		Blackpool	5-6 Nov 88
218.150		Monika	Kuno	FRG	13.11.43	1		Frechen	25/26 Jun 88
Indoors									
237.861		Eleanor	Adams	GBR	20.11.47	1	IAU	Milton Keynes	3/4 Feb 90
229.992			Adams			1		Milton Keynes	18/19 Feb 89
228.112		Marianne	Savage	GBR	26.1.49	2	IAU	Milton Keynes	3/4 Feb 90

100 METRES HURDLES

Mark	Wind	Name		Nat	Born	Pos	Meet	Venue	Date
12.21	0.7	Yordanka	Donkova	BUL	28.9.61	1		Stara Zagora	20 Aug 88
12.24	0.9		Donkova			1h		Stara Zagora	28 Aug 88
12.25	1.4	Ginka	Zagorcheva	BUL	12.4.58	1	v TCH,GRE	Drama	8 Aug 87
12.26	1.5		Donkova			1	Balk	Ljubljana	7 Sep 86
12.26	1.7	Lyudmila	Narozhilenko ¶	RUS	21.4.64	1rB		Sevilla	6 Jun 92
12.27	-1.2		Donkova			1		Stara Zagora	28 Aug 88
12.28	1.8		Narozhilenko			1	NC	Kiev	11 Jul 91
12.28	0.9		Narozhilenko			1rA		Sevilla	6 Jun 92
12.29	-0.4		Donkova			1	ASV	Köln	17 Aug 86
12.32	1.6		Narozhilenko			1		St Denis	4 Jun 92
12.33	1.4		Donkova			1		Fürth	14 Jun 87
12.34	-0.5		Zagorcheva			1	WC	Roma	4 Sep 87
12.35	0.1		Donkova			1h2	ASV	Köln	17 Aug 86
12.36	1.9	Grazyna	Rabsztyn	POL	20.9.52	1	Kuso	Warszawa	13 Jun 80
12.36	-0.6		Donkova			1	NC	Sofia	13 Aug 86
12.36	1.1		Donkova			1		Schwechat	15 Jun 88
12.37	1.4		Donkova			1	ISTAF	Berlin	15 Aug 86
12.38	0.0		Donkova			1	BGP	Budapest	11 Aug 86
12.38	-0.7		Donkova			1	EC	Stuttgart	29 Aug 86
12.38	0.2		Donkova			1	OG	Seoul	30 Sep 88
12.39	1.5	Vera	Komisova'	RUS	11.6.53	1	GG	Roma	5 Aug 80
12.39	1.5		Zagorcheva			2	Balk	Ljubljana	7 Sep 86
12.39	1.8	Natalya	Grigoryeva ¶	UKR	3.12.62	2	NC	Kiev	11 Jul 91
12.40	0.4		Donkova			1	GWG	Moskva	8 Jul 86
12.42	1.8	Bettine	Jahn	GDR	3.8.58	1	OD	Berlin	8 Jun 83
12.42	1.0		Zagorcheva			1		Sofia	14 Aug 85
12.42	-0.2		Donkova			1	VD	Bruxelles	5 Sep 86
12.42	0.2		Narozhilenko			1	GGala	Roma	9 Jun 92
12.43	-0.9	Lucyna	Kalek (Langer)	POL	9.1.56	1		Hannover	19 Aug 84
12.43	0.7		Zagorcheva			1	BGP	Budapest	6 Jul 87
		(30/8)							
12.44	-0.5	Gloria	Siebert'	GDR	13.1.64	2	WC	Roma	4 Sep 87
12.45	1.3	Cornelia	Oschkenat'	GDR	29.10.61	1		Neubrandenburg	11 Jun 87
		(10)							
12.46	0.2	Gail	Devers	USA	19.11.66	1	WC	Stuttgart	20 Aug 93
12.47	1.1	Marina	Azyabina	RUS	15.6.63	1s2	NC	Moskva	19 Jun 93
12.50	0.0	Vera	Akimova'	RUS	5.6.59	1		Sochi	19 May 84
12.54	0.4	Kerstin	Knabe	GDR	7.7.59	3	EC	Athinai	9 Sep 82
12.54	0.9	Sabine	Paetz/John'	GDR	16.10.57	1		Berlin	15 Jul 84
12.56	1.2	Johanna	Klier'	GDR	13.9.52	1	NC	Cottbus	17 Jul 80
12.56	1.2	Monique	Ewanje-Epée	FRA	11.7.67	1	BNP	Villeneuve d'Ascq	29 Jun 90
12.59	-0.6	Anneliese	Ehrhardt	GDR	18.6.50	1	OG	München	8 Sep 72
12.61	0.3	Svetlana	Gusarova	KZK	29.5.59	2	NC	Leningrad	3 Aug 85
12.61	0.2	Jackie	Joyner-Kersee	USA	3.3.62	1	Jenn	San José	28 May 88
		(20)							
12.62	1.2	Mihaela	Pogacian'	ROM	27.1.58	2	BNP	Villeneuve d'Ascq	29 Jun 90
12.63	1.8	Zofia	Bielczyk	POL	22.9.58	1h1	Kuso	Warszawa	18 Jun 79
12.63	1.4	Heike	Theele'	GDR	4.10.64	2	NC	Jena	27 Jun 86
12.64	0.4	Paraskevi	Patoulidou	GRE	29.3.65	1	OG	Barcelona	6 Aug 92
12.64	0.1		Zhang Yu	CHN	8.4.71	1	NG	Beijing	9 Sep 93
12.65A	0.0	Danuta	Perka	POL	22.6.56	1h3	WUG	Ciudad México	9 Sep 79
12.65	0.0	Nadezhda	Korshunova	UKR	18.5.61	2		Sochi	19 May 84

Mark	Wind	Name		Nat	Born	Pos	Meet	Venue	Date
12.66	0.0	Yelena	Biserova	RUS	24.3.62	3		Sochi	19 May 84
12.66	0.7	Lidiya	Yurkova '	BLS	15.1.67	1s2	NC	Kiev	5 Jul 90
12.67	0.6	Tatyana	Anisimova	RUS	19.10.49	2	EC	Praha	2 Sep 78
		(30)							
12.67	0.2	Lynda	Tolbert	USA	3.10.67	3	WC	Stuttgart	20 Aug 93
12.68	1.1	Yelizaveta	Chernyshova	RUS	26.1.58	1h1	Znam	Volgograd	10 Jun 89
12.69	0.2	Laurence	Elloy	FRA	3.12.59	2h1	GWG	Moskva	8 Jul 86
12.69	0.4	LaVonna	Martin	USA	18.11.66	2	OG	Barcelona	6 Aug 92
12.70A	1.5	Tananjalyn	Stanley	USA	11.1.67	1	NCAA	Provo	3 Jun 89
12.70	0.0	Eva	Sokolova	RUS	25.3.62	1		Sevilla	20 Jun 89
12.71	-0.7	Yelena	Politika	UKR	24.8.64	2	NC	Kiev	15 Jul 86
12.71	-0.5	Svetla	Dimitrova	BUL	27.1.70	1		Sofia	31 Jul 93
12.73	0.6	Gudrun	Berend'	GDR	27.4.55	3	EC	Praha	2 Sep 78
12.73	1.9	Aliuska	López	CUB	29.8.69	2		Dijon	24 Jun 90
		(40)							
12.73	-0.8		Liu Huajin	CHN	7.2.60	1	AsiG	Beijing	2 Oct 90
12.73	-0.3	Florence	Colle	FRA	4.12.65	2	WK	Zürich	7 Aug 91
12.73	1.7	Tatyana	Reshetnikova	RUS	14.10.66	2rB		Sevilla	6 Jun 92
12.74	1.5	Anne	Piquereau	FRA	15.6.64	3		Saint Denis	19 Jul 91
12.75	0.4	Claudia	Zaczkiewicz'	FRG	4.7.62	2s2	OG	Seoul	30 Sep 88
12.75	-0.2	Michelle	Freeman	JAM	5.5.69	2	VD	Bruxelles	28 Aug 92
12.75	0.1		Xie Liuying	CHN	1.67	2	NG	Beijing	9 Sep 93
12.76		Nina	Derbina'	RUS	5.7.56	1		Leningrad	22 Jun 80
12.76	1.7	Xenia	Siska	HUN	3.11.57	3	BGP	Budapest	20 Aug 84
12.76	1.3	Julie	Baumann' ¶	SUI	17.6.64	1		Wintherthur	7 Sep 91
		(50)	100th best 12.93						
Low altitude best: 12.69	1.9		Perka			4	Kuso	Warszawa	13 Jun 80
Wind assisted									
12.28	2.7	Cornelia	Oschkenat'	GDR	29.10.61	1		Berlin	25 Aug 87
12.29	3.5		Donkova			1	Athl	Lausanne	24 Jun 88
12.35	2.4	Bettine	Jahn	GDR	3.8.58	1	WC	Helsinki	13 Aug 83
12.37	2.7	Gloria	Uibel/Siebert'	GDR	13.1.64	2		Berlin	25 Aug 87
12.39	2.8		Rabsztyn			1	4-N	Bremen	24 Jun 79
12.42	2.4	Kerstin	Knabe	GDR	7.7.59	2	WC	Helsinki	13 Aug 83
12.51	3.2	Johanna	Klier'	GDR	13.9.52	1	NC	Cottbus	17 Jul 80
12.51	3.6	Sabine	Paetz/John'	GDR	16.10.57	1		Dresden	27 Jul 84
12.53	2.2	Mihaela	Pogacian	ROM	27.1.58	1	IAC	Edinburgh	6 Jul 90
12.63	2.8	Eva	Sokolova	RUS	25.3.62	1s1	NC	Moskva	19 Jun 93
12.66	2.6	Yelena	Politika	UKR	24.8.64	3	NC	Tallinn	5 Jul 88
12.66	4.7	Lynda	Tolbert	USA	3.10.67	1	BNP	Villeneuve d'Ascq	6 Jul 92
12.67	2.4	Natalya	Petrova	RUS	16.11.57	4	WC	Helsinki	13 Aug 83
12.70	4.1	Rhonda	Blanford	USA	15.12.63	1	NCAA	Austin	1 Jun 85
12.70	5.0	Dawn	Bowles	USA	12.11.68	1	NCAA	Eugene	1 Jun 91
12.70	4.7	Anne	Piquereau	FRA	15.6.64	2	BNP	Villeneuve d'Ascq	6 Jul 92
Unconfrmed timing									
12.66	3.0	Tatyana	Anisimova	RUS	19.10.49	2		Leningrad	4 Jun 80
12.71	3.0	Irina	Litovchenko	RUS	29.5.50	3		Leningrad	4 Jun 80
Hand timed									
12.3	1.5	Anneliese	Ehrhardt	GDR	18.6.50	1	NC	Dresden	22 Jul 73
12.3		Marina	Azyabina	RUS	15.6.63	1		Yekaterinburg	30 May 93
12.5	0.9	Pamela	Ryan'	AUS	12.8.39	1		Warszawa	28 Jun 72
12.5	0.0	Teresa	Nowak	POL	29.4.42	1		Warszawa	22 Jun 74
12.5	1.7	Lidia	Okolo-Kulak'	BLS	15.1.67	1		Staiki	28 May 88
12.5		Liu Huajin		CHN	7.2.60	1		Beijing	17 Sep 88
Wind assisted									
12.0	2.1	Yordanka	Donkova	BUL	28.9.61	1		Sofia	3 Aug 86
12.1	2.1	Ginka	Zagorcheva	BUL	12.4.58	2		Sofia	3Aug 86
12.5	3.4	Maria	Merchuk'	MOL	28.12.59	1		Volgograd	25 Sep 81

400 METRES HURDLES

Mark	Name		Nat	Born	Pos	Meet	Venue	Date
52.74	Sally	Gunnell	GBR	29.7.66	1	WC	Stuttgart	19 Aug 93
52.79	Sandra	Farmer-Patrick	USA	18.8.62	2	WC	Stuttgart	19 Aug 93
52.94	Marina	Styepanova'	RUS	1.5.50	1s	Spart	Tashkent	17 Sep 86
53.11	Tatyana	Ledovskaya	BLS	21.5.66	1	WC	Tokyo	29 Aug 91
53.16		Gunnell			2	WC	Tokyo	29 Aug 91
53.17	Debbie	Flintoff-King	AUS	20.4.60	1	OG	Seoul	28 Sep 88

Mark	Wind	Name		Nat	Born	Pos	Meet	Venue	Date
53.18			Ledovskaya			2	OG	Seoul	28 Sep 88
53.23			Gunnell			1	OG	Barcelona	5 Aug 92
53.24		Sabine	Busch	GDR	21.11.62	1	NC	Potsdam	21 Aug 87
53.32			Styepanova			1	EC	Stuttgart	30 Aug 86
53.37			Farmer-Patrick			1	NYG	New York	22 Jul 89
53.47		Janeene	Vickers	USA	3.10.68	3	WC	Tokyo	29 Aug 91
53.48		Margarita	Ponomaryova'	RUS	19.6.63	3	WC	Stuttgart	19 Aug 93
53.52			Gunnell			1	WK	Zürich	4 Aug 93
53.54			Farmer-Patrick			1	Nik	Nice	15 Jul 91
53.55			Busch			1		Berlin	22 Sep 85
53.55			Ledovskaya			1	Herc	Monaco	11 Aug 92
53.58			Ponomaryova			1	Izv	Kiev	22 Jun 84
53.58		Cornelia	Ullrich'	GDR	26.4.63	2	NC	Potsdam	21 Aug 87
53.59			Farmer-Patrick			1	ISTAF	Berlin	21 Aug 92
53.60			Busch			2	EC	Stuttgart	30 Aug 86
53.60			Farmer-Patrick			2	Herc	Monaco	11 Aug 92
53.61			Farmer-Patrick			1	Athl	Lausanne	10 Jul 91
53.62			Busch			1h2	NC	Jena	27 Jun 86
53.62			Busch			1	WC	Roma	3 Sep 87
53.62			Ledovskaya			1	EC	Split	31 Aug 90
53.62			Farmer-Patrick			1	OT	New Orleans	21 Jun 92
53.62			Gunnell			1	WK	Zürich	7 Aug 91
53.63		Ellen	Fiedler'	GDR	26.11.58	3	OG	Seoul	28 Sep 88
53.64			Busch			1	VD	Bruxelles	5 Sep 86
		(30/10)							
53.65A		Myrtle	Bothma'	RSA	18.2.64	mx		Pretoria	12 Mar 90
53.84		Kim	Batten	USA	29.3.69	4	WC	Stuttgart	19 Aug 93
53.96			Han Qing	CHN	4.3.70	1	NG	Beijing	9 Sep 93
54.02		Anna	Ambraziené'	LIT	14.4.55	1	Znam	Moskva	11 Jun 83
54.04		Gudrun	Abt	FRG	3.8.62	6	OG	Seoul	28 Sep 88
54.12		Deon	Hemmings	JAM	9.10.68	2s3	WC	Stuttgart	17 Aug 93
54.14		Yekaterina	Fesenko/Grun	RUS	10.8.58	1	WC	Helsinki	10 Aug 83
54.15		Ann-Louise	Skoglund	SWE	28.6.62	4	EC	Stuttgart	30 Aug 86
54.23		Judi	Brown King	USA	14.7.61	1	PAG	Indianapolis	12 Aug 87
54.24		Susanne	Losch	GDR	12.2.66	1	v FRG	Düsseldorf	19 Jun 88
		(20)							
54.25		Anita	Protti	SUI	4.8.64	6	WC	Tokyo	29 Aug 91
54.27		Genowefa	Blaszak'	POL	22.8.57	1	DNG	Stockholm	2 Jul 85
54.28		Karin	Rossley	GDR	5.4.57	1		Jena	17 May 80
54.34		Tatyana	Pavlova'	UZB	12.12.58	1h1	NC	Leningrad	2 Aug 85
54.35		Petra	Krug	GDR	9.11.63	1	vSU	Bryansk	14 Jul 89
54.36		LaTanya	Sheffield	USA	11.10.63	3s1	OG	Seoul	26 Sep 88
54.37		Vera	Ordina	RUS	4.6.68	2s1	OG	Barcelona	3 Aug 92
54.38		Tonja	Buford	USA	13.12.70	2s1	WC	Stuttgart	17 Aug 93
54.39		Tatyana	Kurochkina'	BLS	15.9.67	7	OG	Seoul	28 Sep 88
54.42		Anna	Knoroz	RUS	30.7.70	2	EP	Roma	26 Jun 93
		(30)							
54.52			Ling Xueyan	CHN	14.2.72	3	NG	Beijing	9 Sep 93
54.53		Natalya	Torshina	KZK	4.10.68	3s2	WC	Stuttgart	17 Aug 93
54.53		Rosey	Edeh	CAN	13.8.66	4s2	WC	Stuttgart	17 Aug 93
54.55		Bärbel	Broschat	GDR	2.11.57	1	WC	Sittard	16 Aug 80
54.55		Cristieana	Matei'	ROM	2.1.62	2	GWG	Moskva	7 Jul 86
54.56		Yelena	Filipishina	RUS	18.6.62	2		Moskva	20 Jul 84
54.61		Nawal	El Moutawakil	MAR	15.4.62	1	OG	Los Angeles	8 Aug 84
54.62		Tuija	Helander-Kuusisto	FIN	23.5.61	5	WC	Roma	3 Sep 87
54.63		Gowry	Retchakan	GBR	21.6.60	5s2	OG	Barcelona	3 Aug 92
54.64		Petra	Pfaff	GDR	16.10.60	4	WC	Helsinki	10 Aug 83
		(40)							
54.64		Heike	Meissner	GER	29.1.70	3s1	WC	Stuttgart	17 Aug 93
54.68		Birgit	Uibel'	GDR	30.10.61	1		Dresden	19 May 84
54.69		Monica	Westén	SWE	15.3.66	1		Stockholm	13 Aug 90
54.78		Marina	Sereda'	UKR	12.4.64	2	Spart	Tashkent	18 Sep 86
54.80		Tatyana	Storozheva	RUS	22.3.54	1		Moskva	12 Jun 80
54.82		Schowonda	Williams	USA	3.12.66	4s1	WC	Roma	1 Sep 87
54.86		Tonja	Brown	USA	5.9.60	3	GG-GP	Roma	7 Sep 85

Mark	Wind	Name		Nat	Born	Pos	Meet	Venue	Date
54.89		Tatyana	Zelentsova	UZB	5.8.48	1	EC	Praha	2 Sep 78
54.90		Sharrieffa	Barksdale	USA	16.2.61	1		Knoxville	24 May 86
54.90		Silvia	Rieger	GER	14.11.70	5s2	WC	Stuttgart	17 Aug 93
		(50)	100th best 55.76						
Low altitude bests: 54.44			Bothma			1	NC	Durban	22 Apr 89
Drugs disqualification									
54.47			Guo Yue	CHN	23.1.69	2	NG	Beijing	9 Sep 93
54.6 hand		Chantal	Beaugeant	FRA	16.2.61	1		Tours	28 May 89

HIGH JUMP

Mark	Name		Nat	Born	Pos	Meet	Venue	Date
2.09	Stefka	Kostadinova	BUL	25.3.65	1	WC	Roma	30 Aug 87
2.08		Kostadinova			1	NM	Sofia	31 May 86
2.07	Lyudmila	Andonova ¶	BUL	6.5.60	1	OD	Berlin	20 Jul 84
2.07		Kostadinova			1		Sofia	25 May 86
2.07		Kostadinova			1		Cagliari	16 Sep 87
2.07		Kostadinova			1	NC	Sofia	3 Sep 88
2.07i	Heike	Henkel'	GER	5.5.64	1	NC	Karlsruhe	8 Feb 92
2.06		Kostadinova			1	EP	Moskva	18 Aug 85
2.06		Kostadinova			1		Fürth	15 Jun 86
2.06		Kostadinova			1		Cagliari	14 Sep 86
2.06		Kostadinova			1		Wörrstadt	6 Jun 87
2.06		Kostadinova			1		Rieti	8 Sep 87
2.06i		Kostadinova			1		Piraeus	20 Feb 88
2.05	Tamara	Bykova	RUS	21.12.58	1	Izv	Kiev	22 Jun 84
2.05		Kostadinova			1		Wörrstadt	14 Jun 86
2.05		Kostadinova			1		Rieti	7 Sep 86
2.05i		Kostadinova			1	WI	Indianapolis	8 Mar 87
2.05		Kostadinova			1	Bisl	Oslo	4 Jul 87
2.05		Kostadinova			1		Padova	13 Sep 87
2.05		Kostadinova			1	BGP	Budapest	12 Aug 88
2.05		Henkel			1	WCh	Tokyo	31 Aug 91
2.05i		Kostadinova			1	NC	Sofia	1 Feb 92
2.05		Kostadinova			1		San Marino	4 Jul 92
2.05		Kostadinova			1	Toto	Fukuoka	18 Sep 93
2.04		Bykova			1		Pisa	25 Aug 83
2.04		Kostadinova			1	VD	Bruxelles	30 Aug 85
2.04		Kostadinova			1		Rieti	4 Sep 85
2.04		Kostadinova			1		Bern	20 Aug 86
2.04i		Kostadinova			1	v Ita,Spa	Genova	31 Jan 87
2.04		Kostadinova			1	v TCH,Gre	Drama	8 Aug 87
2.04		Bykova			2	WC	Roma	30 Aug 87
2.04i		Kostadinova			1	4-N	Piraeus	6 Feb 88
2.04i		Kostadinova			1	EI	Budapest	6 Mar 88
2.04		Kostadinova			1		Formia	19 Jun 88
2.04i		Kostadinova			1		Piraeus	8 Mar 89
2.04	Silvia	Costa	CUB	4.5.64	1	WP	Barcelona	9 Sep 89
2.04		Henkel			1	Herc	Monaco	3 Aug 91
2.04i		Henkel			1		Karlsruhe	31 Jan 92
2.04i		Henkel			1		Berlin	21 Feb 92
2.04i		Henkel			1		Sindelfingen	8 Mar 92
2.04		Henkel			1		Wörrstadt	30 May 92
2.04		Kostadinova			1		Stara Zagora	27 Jun 92
2.04		Kostadinova			1		Worrstadt	29 May 93
	(43/5)							
2.03	Ulrike	Meyfarth	FRG	4.5.56	1	EP	London	21 Aug 83
2.03	Louise	Ritter	USA	18.2.58	1		Austin	8 Jul 88
2.02i	Susanne	Beyer'	GDR	24.6.61	2	WI	Indianapolis	8 Mar 87
2.02	Yelena	Yelesina	RUS	4.4.70	1	GWG	Seattle	23 Jul 90
2.02	Inga	Babakova'	UKR	27.6.67	2	ISTAF	Berlin	10 Sep 91
	(10)							
2.01	Sara	Simeoni	ITA	19.4.53	1	v Pol	Brescia	4 Aug 78
2.01	Olga	Turchak	UKR	5.3.67	2	GWG	Moskva	7 Jul 86
2.01	Desiré	du Plessis	RSA	20.5.65	1		Johannesburg	16 Sep 86
2.01i	Gabriele	Günz	GDR	8.9.61	2		Stuttgart	31 Jan 88
2.01	Heike	Balck	GDR	19.8.70	1	vSU-j	Karl-Marx-Stadt	18 Jun 89

Mark	Wind	Name		Nat	Born	Pos	Meet	Venue	Date
2.01i		Ioamnet	Quintero	CUB	8.9.72	1		Berlin	5 Mar 93
2.01i		Alina	Astafei	ROM	7.6.69	1		Otterburg	19 Feb 94
2.00		Rosemarie	Ackermann'	GDR	4.4.52	1	ISTAF	Berlin	26 Aug 77
2.00i		Coleen	Sommer'	USA	61.6.60	1		Ottawa	14 Feb 82
2.00		Charmaine	Gale/Weavers	RSA	27.2.64	1		Pretoria	25 Mar 85
		(20)							
2.00i		Emilia	Dragieva'	BUL	11.1.65	3	WI	Indianapolis	8 Mar 87
2.00		Lyudmila	Avdyeyenko'	UKR	14.12.63	1	NC	Bryansk	17 Jul 87
2.00		Svetlana	Isaeva'	BUL	18.3.67	2	v TCH,Gre	Drama	8 Aug 87
2.00i		Larisa	Kositsyna	RUS	14.12.63	2	NC	Volgograd	11 Feb 88
2.00		Jan	Wohlschlag'	USA	14.7.58	1	Bisl	Oslo	1 Jul 89
2.00		Yolanda	Henry	USA	2.12.64	1	Expo	Sevilla	30 May 90
2.00		Biljana	Petrovic	YUG	28.2.61	1		St. Denis	22 Jun 90
2.00		Tatyana	Shevchik	BLS	11.6.69	1		Gomel	14 May 93
2.00i		Yelena	Rodina/Gulyayeva ¶	RUS	14.8.67	1		Moskva	27 Jan 94
2.00i		Britta	Bilac'	SLO	4.12.68	1		Frankfurt	9 Feb 94
		(30)							
1.99i		Debbie	Brill	CAN	10.3.53	1		Edmonton	23 Jan 82
1.99i		Andrea	Bienias'	GDR	11.11.59	2	EI	Milano	7 Mar 82
1.99i		Katalin	Sterk	HUN	30.9.61	3	EI	Milano	7 Mar 82
1.99		Kerstin	Brandt'	GDR	9.12.61	3	EP	London	21 Aug 83
1.99		Yelena	Topchina ¶	RUS	21.10.66	1		Rieti	5 Sep 93
1.98i		Andrea	Mátay	HUN	27.9.55	1	NC	Budapest	17 Feb 79
1.98		Valentina	Poluyko	BLS	15.7.55	1		Leningrad	26 Jul 83
1.98		Lyudmila	Butuzova	KZK	28.2.57	2	Znam	Sochi	10 Jun 84
1.98		Niculina	Vasile	ROM	13.2.58	1	RomIC	Bucuresti	2 Jun 85
1.98		Vanessa	Ward'	AUS	5.1.63	1		Perth	12 Feb 89
		(40)							
1.98		Andrea	Arens/Baumert	FRG	5.5.67	1	NC	Hamburg	12 Aug 89
1.98i		Yelena	Panikarovskikh'	RUS	4.12.59	1	NP	Moskva	25 Feb 90
1.97		Pam	Spencer	USA	8.10.57	1	VD	Bruxelles	28 Aug 81
1.97i		Zhanna	Nyekrasova	RUS	12.5.57	1	NP	Moskva	13 Feb 82
1.97		Jutta	Kirst	GDR	10.11.54	1	v USA	Karl-Marx-Stadt	10 Jul 82
1.97		Yelena	Popkova	RUS	13.10.55	2	NC	Kiev	21 Aug 82
1.97		Olga	Juha	HUN	22.3.62	4	EP	London	21 Aug 83
1.97i		Marina	Doronina	RUS	29.1.61	1		Vilnius	14 Jan 84
1.97		Danuta	Bulkowska	POL	31.1.59	2		Wörrstadt	9 Jun 84
1.97		Olga	Byelkova	UZB	21.2.55	2	Izv	Kiev	22 Jun 84
		(50)							
1.97		Joni	Huntley	USA	4.8.56	3	OG	Los Angeles	10 Aug 84
1.97i		Lisa	Bernhagen	USA	22.1.66	1		Flagstaff	21 Feb 87
1.97		Jin Ling		CHN	25.1.67	1	Shiz	Hamamatsu	7 May 89
1.97		Valentina	Gotovska	LAT	3.9.65	1		Vilnius	4 Aug 90
1.97		Tanya	Hughes	USA	25.1.72	1	Pac-10	Eugene	22 May 92
1.97i		Yelena	Gribanova	RUS	2.3.72	3		München	12 Feb 93
1.97i		Alison	Inverarity	AUS	12.8.70	5	WI	Toronto	13 Mar 93
1.97		Sigrid	Kirchmann	AUT	29.3.66	3	WC	Stuttgart	21 Aug 93
1.97		Olga	Bolshova	MOL	16.6.68	3		Rieti	5 Sep 93
1.97i		Antonella	Bevilacqua	ITA	15.10.71	1	NC	Genova	12 Feb 94
		(60)	100th best 1.04						

Best outdoor marks

2.00	Quintero	1	Herc	Monaco	7 Aug 93
2.00	Astafei	1	WJ	Sudbury	29 Jul 88
1.99	Beyer'	3	WC	Roma	30 Aug 87
1.99	Gulyayeva	1	Znam	Moskva	9 Jun 91
1.98	Sommer	1	v FRG,Afr	Durham	26 Jun 82
1.98	Kositsyna	2	NM	Sofia	21 May 83
1.98	Brill	2		Rieti	2 Sep 84
1.98	Sterk	1	NC	Budapest	17 Aug 86
1.97	Bienias	1		Leipzig	27 Jul 83
1.97	Günz	1		Halle	26 Jun 87

Ancillary jumps: Kostadinova 2.06 and 2.04 on 30 Aug 87, 2.04 on 18 Aug 85 and 3 Sep 88

POLE VAULT

Mark	Wind	Name		Nat	Born	Pos	Meet	Venue	Date
4.11			Sun Caiyun	CHN	21.7.73	1		Guangzhou	21 Mar 93
4.08i		Nicole	Rieger	GER	5.2.72	1		Karlsruhe	1 Mar 94
4.08i			Sun Caiyun			2		Karlsruhe	1 Mar 94
4.07i			Sun Caiyun			1		Landau	31 Jan 93
4.06i			Sun Caiyun			1		Zweibrücken	29 Jan 93
4.05			Zhang Chunzhen	CHN	.9.70	1		Guangzhou	10 Aug 91
4.05			Sun Caiyun			1	NC	Nanjing	21 May 92

Mark	Wind	Name		Nat	Born	Pos	Meet	Venue	Date
4.03			Sun Caiyun			1		Guangzhou	11 Apr 92
4.02			Zhang Chunzhen			1	NC	Beijing	5 Jun 91
4.02i			Rieger			1	NC	Dortmund	26 Feb 94
4.01i			Rieger			1		Landau	20 Feb 94
4.00			Zhang Chunzhen			1		Guangzhou	24 Mar 91
4.00			Cai Weiyan	CHN	25.10.73	1		Wuhan	19 Oct 92
4.00i			Rieger			1		Clermont-Ferrand	28 Jan 94
4.00i		Andrea	Müller	GER	29.6.74	1		Sindelfingen	6 Mar 94
4.00i			Rieger			2		Sindelfingen	6 Mar 94
3.96i		Gabriela	Mihalcea	ROM	27.1.64	1		Bucuresti	6 Feb 94
3.95i			Shao Jingwen	CHN	8.3.71	2		Landau	31 Jan 93
3.95i			Rieger			1		Zweibrücken	29 Jan 94
3.93		Tanja	Cors	GER	22.4.71	1		Bad Gendersheim	23 May 93
3.92			Rieger			1		Landau	22 Jul 92
		(21/8)							
3.90		Carmen	Haage	GER	10.9.71	1		Spaichingen	15 Aug 92
3.90		Svetlana	Abramova	RUS	27.10.70	1		Schwechat	30 May 93
		(10)							
3.80		Wu Weili		CHN	20.4.70	2	NC	Beijing	26 Jun 90
3.80		Daniela	Köpernick	GER	25.7.73	1	NC	München	21 Jun 92
3.80		Zhu Rong		CHN	5.4.72			Beijing	15 Aug 92
3.80		Galina	Yenvarenko	RUS	70	2	NC	Moskva	18 Jun 93
3.80		Christine	Adams	GER	28.2.74	1		Gladbeck	18 Jul 93
3.80i		Marina	Andreyeva	RUS	.73	2	vGER	Ludwigshafen	19 Feb 94
3.76		Zhou Minxin		CHN				Fuzhou	22 Apr 89
3.75i		Daniela	Bártová	TCH	.74	1		Praha	22 Feb 94
		(18)							

LONG JUMP

Mark	Wind	Name		Nat	Born	Pos	Meet	Venue	Date
7.52	1.4	Galina	Chistyakova	RUS	26.7.62	1	Znam	Leningrad	11 Jun 88
7.48	1.2	Heike	Drechsler	GER	16.12.64	1	v Ita	Neubrandenburg	9 Jul 88
7.48	0.4		Drechsler			1	Athl	Lausanne	8 Jul 92
7.45	0.9		Drechsler'			1	v URS	Tallinn	21 Jun 86
7.45	1.1		Drechsler			1	OD	Dresden	3 Jul 86
7.45	0.6	Jackie	Joyner-Kersee	USA	3.3.62	1	PAG	Indianapolis	13 Aug 87
7.45	1.6		Chistyakova			1	BGP	Budapest	12 Aug 88
7.44	2.0		Drechsler			1		Berlin	22 Sep 85
7.43	1.4	Anisoara	Cusmir'	ROM	28.6.62	1	RomIC	Bucuresti	4 Jun 83
7.40	1.8		Daute' (Drechsler)			1		Dresden	26 Jul 84
7.40	0.7		Drechsler			1	NC	Potsdam	21 Aug 87
7.40	0.9		Joyner-Kersee			1	OG	Seoul	29 Sep 88
7.39	0.3		Drechsler			1	WK	Zürich	21 Aug 85
7.39	0.5	Yelena	Byelevskaya'	BLS	11.10.63	1	NC	Bryansk	18 Jul 87
7.39			Joyner-Kersee			1		San Diego	25 Jun 88
7.37i	-		Drechsler			1	v Aut,Yug	Wien	13 Feb 88
7.37A	1.8		Drechsler			1		Sestriere	31 Jul 91
7.37		Inessa	Kravets	UKR	5.10.66	1		Kiev	13 Jun 92
7.36	0.4		Joyner			1	WC	Roma	4 Sep 87
7.36	1.8		Byelevskaya			2	Znam	Leningrad	11 Jun 88
7.36	1.8		Drechsler			1		Jena	28 May 92
7.35	1.9		Chistyakova			1	GPB	Bratislava	20 Jun 90
7.34	1.6		Daute'			1		Dresden	19 May 84
7.34	1.4		Chistyakova			2	v GDR	Tallinn	21 Jun 86
7.34			Byelevskaya			1		Sukhumi	17 May 87
7.34	0.7		Drechsler			1	v URS	Karl-Marx-Stadt	20 Jun 87
7.33	0.4		Drechsler			1	v URS	Erfurt	22 Jun 85
7.33	2.0		Drechsler			1		Dresden	2 Aug 85
7.33	-0.3		Drechsler			1	Herc	Monaco	11 Aug 92
7.32	-0.2		Daute'			1	OD	Berlin	20 Jul 84
7.32i	-		Drechsler			1	TAC	New York	27 Feb 87
7.32	0.0		Joyner-Kersee			1	WCh	Tokyo	25 Aug 91
7.32			Drechsler			*		Padova	15 Sep 91
		(33/6)							
7.31	1.5	Yelena	Kokonova'	UKR	4.8.63	1	NP	Alma-Ata	12 Sep 85

Mark	Wind	Name		Nat	Born	Pos	Meet	Venue	Date
7.24	1.0	Larisa	Berezhnaya	UKR	28.2.61	1	Blanc	Granada	25 May 91
7.21	1.6	Helga	Radtke	GDR	16.5.62	2		Dresden	26 Jul 84
7.20	-0.5	Valy	Ionescu	ROM	31.8.60	1	NC	Bucuresti	1 Aug 82
		(10)							
7.20	2.0	Irena	Ozhenko'	LIT	13.11.62	1		Budapest	12 Sep 86
7.20	0.8	Yelena	Sinchukova'	RUS	23.1.61	1	HGP	Budapest	20 Jun 91
7.17	1.8	Irina	Valyukevich	BLS	19.11.59	2	NC	Bryansk	18 Jul 87
7.16		Yolanda	Chen	RUS	26.7.61	1		Moskva	30 Jul 88
7.14	1.8	Niole	Medvedyeva	LIT	20.10.60	1		Riga	4 Jun 88
7.14	1.2	Mirela	Dulgheru	ROM	5.10.66	1	Balk G	Sofia	5 Jul 92
7.12	1.6	Sabine	Paetz/John'	GDR	16.10.57	2		Dresden	19 May 84
7.09	0.0	Vilma	Bardauskiene	LIT	15.6.53	Q	EC	Praha	29 Aug 78
7.08	0.5	Marieta	Ilcu	ROM	16.10.62	1	RumIC	Pitesti	25 Jun 89
7.07	0.0	Svetlana	Zorina	RUS	2.2.60	1		Krasnodar	15 Aug 87
		(20)							
7.06	0.4	Tatyana	Kolpakova	KGZ	18.10.59	1	OG	Moskva	31 Jul 80
7.06	-1.3	Chioma	Ajunwa ¶	NGR	25.12.70	1		Lagos	12 Jun 92
7.06	2.0	Ljudmila	Ninova	AUT	25.6.60	2		Sevilla	5 Jun 93
7.04	0.5	Brigitte	Wujak'	GDR	6.3.55	2	OG	Moskva	31 Jul 80
7.04	0.9	Tatyana	Proskuryakova'	RUS	13.1.56	1		Kiev	25 Aug 83
7.04	2.0	Yelena	Yatsuk	UKR	16.3.61	1	Znam	Moskva	8 Jun 85
7.04	0.3	Carol	Lewis	USA	8.8.63	5	WK	Zürich	21 Aug 85
7.02	2.0	Irina	Mushailova	RUS	6.1.67	2	Athl	Lausanne	7 Jul 93
7.01	-0.4	Tatyana	Skachko	UKR	18.8.54	3	OG	Moskva	31 Jul 80
7.01	-0.3	Eva	Murková	TCH	29.5.62	1	PTS	Bratislava	26 May 84
		(30)							
7.01	-1.0	Marina	Kibakina'	RUS	2.8.60	1		Krasnoyarsk	10 Aug 85
7.01	1.4		Yao Weili	CHN	6.5.68	1	NC	Jinan	3 Jun 93
7.00	2.0	Jodi	Anderson	USA	10.11.57	1	OT	Eugene	28 Jun 80
7.00		Margarita	Butkiene	LIT	19.8.49	1		Vilnius	25 May 83
7.00	-0.2	Birgit	Grosshennig	GDR	21.2.65	2		Berlin	9 Jun 84
7.00	0.6	Silvia	Khristova'	BUL	22.8.65	1		Sofia	3 Aug 86
7.00		Susen	Tiedtke	GER	23.1.69	2		Seoul	18 Aug 91
6.99	2.0	Siegrun	Siegl'	GDR	29.10.54	1	OD	Dresden	19 May 76
6.97	2.0	Agata	Karczmarek	POL	29.11.63	1		Lublin	6 Aug 88
		(40)							
6.97	1.3		Ma Miaolan	CHN	18.1.70	*	NG	Beijing	10 Sep 93
6.96	2.0	Anna	Wlodarczyk ¶	POL	24.3.51	1	NC	Lublin	22 Jun 84
6.96	1.8	Christine	Schima	GDR	6.9.62	3		Dresden	26 Jul 84
6.96A	0.0	Madeline	de Jesus	PUR	4.11.57	1	IbAC	Ciudad México	24 Jul 88
6.94	1.3	Yelena	Chicherova	RUS	9.8.58	2	Izv	Kiev	21 Jun 84
6.94	-1.0	Sheila	Echols	USA	2.10.64	1	NCAA	Baton Rouge	5 Jun 87
6.92	1.6	Angela	Voigt'	GDR	18.5.51	1		Dresden	9 May 76
6.92	0.8	Vera	Olenchenko	UZB	21.3.59	1		Baku	22 Sep 85
6.92	1.6	Heike	Grabe	GDR	11.3.62	2	PTS	Bratislava	13 Jun 87
6.92	1.7	Liu Shuzhen		CHN	7.5.66	1	NC	Beijing	24 Jun 90
		(50)	100th best 6.81						
Wind assisted									
7.63A	2.1	Heike	Drechsler	GER	16.12.64	1		Sestriere	21 Jul 92
7.45	2.6	Jackie	Joyner-Kersee	USA	3.3.62	1	OT	Indianapolis	23 Jul 88
7.39	2.6		Drechsler			1		Padova	15 Sep 91
7.39	2.9		Drechsler			1	Expo	Sevilla	6 Jun 92
7.36	2.2		Chistyakova			1	Znam	Volgograd	11 Jun 89
7.35	3.4		Drechsler			1	NC	Jena	29 Jun 86
		(6 performances)							
7.19A	3.7	Susen	Tiedtke	GER	23.1.69	1		Sestriere	28 Jul 93
7.17	3.6	Eva	Murková	TCH	29.5.62	1		Nitra	26 Aug 84
7.06	3.4		Ma Miaolan	CHN	18.1.70	1	NG	Beijing	10 Sep 93
7.00	3.8	Ramona	Neubert'	GDR	26.7.58	1	v GBR	Dresden	14 Jun 81
7.00	4.2	Sue	Hearnshaw'	GBR	26.5.61	1	NC	Cwmbran	27 May 84
7.00	2.2	Lyudmila	Ninova	AUT	25.6.60	1		São Paulo	17 May 92
6.98	3.4	Ines	Schmidt	GDR	7.7.60	2		Nitra	26 Aug 84
6.98	3.3	Fiona	May	GBR	12.12.69	1	NC	Jarrow	4 Jun 89
6.97	2.7	Anna	Wlodarczyk ¶	POL	24.3.51	1	4-N	Warszawa	15 Jul 84
6.96		Tatyana	Shchelkanova	RUS	18.4.37	P	NC	Dnepropetrovsk	14 Aug 66
6.93	4.6	Beverly	Kinch	GBR	14.1.64	5	WC	Helsinki	14 Aug 83
6.93A	4.4	Ringa	Ropo	FIN	16.2.66	3		Sestriere	21 Jul 92

TRIPLE JUMP

Mark	Wind	Name		Nat	Born	Pos	Meet	Venue	Date
15.09	0.5	Ana	Biryukova	RUS	27.9.67	1	WC	Stuttgart	21 Aug 93
14.97	0.9	Yolanda	Chen	RUS	26.7.61	1	NC	Moskva	18 Jun 93
14.95	-0.2	Inessa	Kravets	UKR	5.10.66	1	Znam	Moskva	10 Jun 91
14.90i	-	Inna	Lasovskaya	RUS	17.12.69	1		Liévin	13 Feb 94
14.88i	-		Lasovskaya			1	EI	Paris	13 Feb 94
14.79	1.7	Irina	Mushailova	RUS	6.1.67	1	DNG	Stockholm	5 Jul 93
14.78i	-		Lasovskaya			1		Moskva	27 Jan 94
14.74	0.4		Biryukova			1	Gugl	Linz	25 Aug 93
14.72i	-		Biryukova			2	EI	Paris	13 Feb 94
14.71	1.6		Chen			1	BNP	Villeneuve d'Ascq	2 Jul 93
14.70	0.6		Lasovskaya			2	Slovn	Bratislava	1 Jun 93
14.70	0.1		Chen			2	WC	Stuttgart	21 Aug 93
14.68	1.0		Biryukova			*	Slovn	Bratislava	1 Jun 93
14.68	0.2		Lasovskaya			2	NC	Moskva	18 Jun 93
14.67i	-		Lasovskaya			1		Grenoble	6 Feb 94
14.65	1.8		Chen			2	DNG	Stockholm	5 Jul 93
14.65i	-		Lasovskaya			1		Madrid	11 Feb 94
14.64	-1.0		Lasovskaya			1	GGala	Roma	9 Jun 93
14.62	1.4	Galina	Chistyakova	RUS	26.7.62	1	vFra	Villeneuve d'Ascq	13 Sep 92
14.61i	-		Lasovskaya			1		Moskva	14 Jan 94
14.60	0.4		Biryukova			3	NC	Moskva	18 Jun 93
14.59	0.2		Kravets			1	Gugl	Linz	5 Jul 91
14.55	0.9		Li Huirong	CHN	14.4.65	1	Nanbu	Sapporo	19 Jul 92
14.54	1.1		Li Huirong			1	Nanbu	Sapporo	25 Aug 90
14.54	1.2		Chen			1	TSB	London	23 Jul 93
14.52	0.4		Chistyakova			1	DNG	Stockholm	3 Jul 89
14.52	0.5		Lasovskaya			1		Luzern	29 Jun 93
14.52	-0.7		Lasovskaya			2	Athl	Lausanne	7 Jul 93
14.52i	-	Sofia	Bozhanova	BUL	4.10.67	3	EI	Paris	13 Feb 94
14.51	1.8	Niurka	Montalvo	CUB	4.6.68	1	Barr	Habana	22 May 93
14.51i	-		Biryukova			2		Grenoble	6 Feb 94
		(31/9)							
14.46i	-	Sarka	Kaspárková	TCH	20.5.71	4	EI	Paris	12 Mar 94
14.38i	-	Iva	Prandzheva	BUL	15.2.72	5	EI	Paris	12 Mar 94
14.35	0.5	Yelena	Semiraz	UKR	21.11.65	2	NC	Kiev	13 Jul 91
14.30	1.2	Helga	Radtke	GER	16.5.62	1		Rostock	20 May 92
14.29	1.4		Ren Ruiping	CHN	1.1.75	1	NG	Beijing	13 Sep 93
14.28	0.9		Zhang Yan	CHN	.6.72	2	NG	Beijing	13 Sep 93
14.23	1.8	Sheila	Hudson	USA	30.6.67	1	TAC	New Orleans	20 Jun 92
14.21i	-	Natalya	Kayukova	RUS	12.12.66	1		Moskva	28 Feb 92
14.18	-0.1	Antonella	Capriotti	ITA	4.2.62	6	WC	Stuttgart	21 Aug 93
14.17	-0.5	Zhanna	Gureyeva	BLS	10.6.70	3	GGala	Roma	9 Jun 93
14.12	0.8		Ma Miaolan	CHN	18.1.70	3	NG	Beijing	13 Sep 93
		(20)							
14.09	0.7	Yelena	Sinchukova	RUS	23.1.61	2	vFra	Villeneuve d'Ascq	13 Sep 92
14.07	2.0	Eloina	Echevarría	CUB	23.8.61	1	NC	Habana	14 May 92
14.05	1.9	Concepcion	Paredes	ESP	19.7.70	*		Madrid	29 May 93
14.03	0.8		Liu Jingming	CHN	1.2.72	5	NG	Beijing	13 Sep 93
14.00	-1.8	Lyudmila	Dubkova	RUS	27.2.68	1		Rostov na Donu	17 Jul 93
13.98	1.0	Urszula	Wlodarczyk	POL	22.12.65	2	NC	Kielce	25 Jul 93
13.97	2.0	Li Jing		CHN	21.10.69	2	NC	Beijing	26 Jun 90
13.95	1.8	Olga Lidia	Cepero	CUB	4.2.75	1		Habana	11 Feb 94
13.93i	-	Valy	Ionescu	ROM	31.8.60	1	LAT	Inglewood	21 Feb 87
13.93i	-	Iolanda	Oanta	ROM	11.10.65	1		Bacau	23 Jan 93
		(30)							
13.93		Monica	Toth	ROM	7.3.70	1		Bucuresti	29 May 93
13.92	-	Irina	Babakova	UKR	5.11.65	1		Moskva	3 Jun 90
13.92i	-	Anja	Vokuhl	GER	17.8.73	2	NC	Sindelfingen	28 Feb 93
13.92	0.1		Zhang JIng	CHN	10.3.70	1		Guangzhou	21 Mar 93
13.91	0.3	Zhou Xiulian		CHN	.11.70	1		Fuzhou	30 Oct 92
13.91	0.1	Agnieszka	Stanczyk ¶	POL	20.1.71	1		Poznan	30 May 93
13.91A	1.3	Andrea	Avila	ARG	4.4.70	1	SAmC	Lima	4 Jul 93
13.91i	-	Yelena	Lysak	RUS	19.10.75	1		Moskva	4 Feb 94
13.90i	-	Natalya	Telepnyova	RUS	66	2		Moskva	28 Feb 92

Mark	Wind	Name		Nat	Born	Pos	Meet	Venue	Date
13.88	1.5	Inara	Curko	LAT	11.11.66	1		Bryansk	10 Sep 89
		(40)							
13.88		Tanja	Bormann	GER	11.4.70	2		Bad Homburg	10 Jun 93
13.85	0.2	Tatyana	Matyashova	RUS	2.8.73	1	Prav	Sochi	25 May 91
13.84	1.0	Svetlana	Davydova	RUS	71	1		Samara	2 Jun 91
13.84		Liu Jinming		CHN	1.2.72	1		Jinan	25 Apr 92
13.84	1.7	Yelena	Chicherova	RUS	9.8.58	1	NC	Moskva	19 Jul 92
13.83i	-	Tatyana	Fyodorova	RUS	.67	3		Moskva	25 Feb 90
13.82	1.8	Wendy	Brown	USA	28.1.66	1	TAC	Tampa	17 Jun 88
13.82	2.0	Isabel	Aldecoa	CUB	21.6.71	2	NC	Habana	14 May 92
13.80	1.3	Olga	Kontsevaya	RUS	.72	1		Sochi	13 May 90
13.80		Viktoriya	Vershinina	UKR	11.6.71	1		Donetsk	30 Jun 93
13.80	1.6	Laiza	Carrillo	CUB	27.11.68	2		Habana	12 Feb 94
		(51)							

Best outdoor mark for athlete with all-time best indoors

Mark	Wind	Name	Pos	Meet	Venue	Date
14.23	-0.2	Prandzheva	3	WC	Stuttgart	21 Aug 93
14.16	0.1	Kaspárková	7	WC	Stuttgart	21 Aug 93
14.08	0.0	Bozhanova	1	NarM	Plovdiv	2 Jun 91
13.87		Vokuhl	3		Bad Homburg	10 Jun 93
13.86	1.8	Lysak	1	EJ	San Sebastián	1 Aug 93

Previously disqualified for drugs use

Mark	Wind	Name		Nat	Born	Pos	Meet	Venue	Date
14.70	0.5	Inessa	Kravets			1	Nik	Nice	21 Jul 93
14.61	0.2		Kravets			1	Athl	Lausanne	7 Jul 93
14.05	0.3	Agnieszka	Stanczyk	POL	20.1.71	1	NC	Kielce	25 Jul 93

Wind assisted

Mark	Wind	Name		Nat	Born	Pos	Meet	Venue	Date
14.74	2.7		Biryukova			1	Slovn	Bratislava	1 Jun 93
14.44		Helga	Radtke	GER	16.5.62	1		Rostock	1 May 92
14.32	4.9	Iva	Prandzheva	BUL	15.2.72	1		Sofia	3 Jul 93
14.16	3.2	Concepcion	Paredes	ESP	19.7.70	1		Madrid	29 May 93
14.07	2.8		Wang Xiangrong	CHN	.2.76	4	NG	Beijing	13 Sep 93
13.96	3.7	Monica	Toth	ROM	7.3.70	3	WUG	Buffalo	17 Jul 93
13.93	5.3	Michelle	Griffith	GBR	6.10.71	1	vUSA	Edinburgh	2 Jul 93
13.86	2.9	Claudia	Haywood	USA	25.9.69	1	NC	Eugene	17 Jun 93

SHOT

Mark	Name		Nat	Born	Pos	Meet	Venue	Date
22.63	Natalya	Lisovskaya	RUS	16.7.62	1	Znam	Moskva	7 Jun 87
22.55		Lisovskaya			1	NC	Tallinn	5 Jul 88
22.53		Lisovskaya			1		Sochi	27 May 84
22.53		Lisovskaya			1		Kiev	14 Aug 88
22.50i	Helena	Fibingerová	TCH	13.7.49	1		Jablonec	19 Feb 77
22.45	Ilona	Slupianek' ¶	GDR	24.9.56	1		Potsdam	11 May 80
22.41		Slupianek			1	OG	Moskva	24 Jul 80
22.40		Slupianek			1		Berlin	3 Jun 83
22.38		Slupianek			1		Karl-Marx-Stadt	25 May 80
22.36		Slupianek			1		Celje	2 May 80
22.34		Slupianek			1		Berlin	7 May 80
22.34		Slupianek			1	NC	Cottbus	18 Jul 80
22.32		Fibingerová			1		Nitra	20 Aug 77
22.24		Lisovskaya			1	OG	Seoul	1 Oct 88
22.22		Slupianek			1		Potsdam	13 Jul 80
22.19	Claudia	Losch	FRG	10.1.60	1		Hainfeld	23 Aug 87
22.14i		Lisovskaya			1	NC	Penza	7 Feb 87
22.13		Slupianek			1		Split	29 Apr 80
22.06		Slupianek			1		Berlin	15 Aug 78
22.06		Lisovskaya			1		Moskva	6 Aug 88
22.05		Slupianek			1	OD	Berlin	28 May 80
22.05		Slupianek			1		Potsdam	31 May 80
22.04		Slupianek			1		Potsdam	4 Jul 79
22.04		Slupianek			1		Potsdam	29 Jul 79
21.99		Fibingerová			1		Opava	26 Sep 76
21.98		Slupianek			1		Berlin	17 Jul 79
21.96		Fibingerová			1	GS	Ostrava	8 Jun 77
21.96		Lisovskaya			1	Drz	Praha	16 Aug 84
21.96		Lisovskaya			1		Vilnius	28 Aug 88
21.95		Lisovskaya			1	IAC	Edinburgh	29 Jul 88
	(30/4)							
21.89	Ivanka	Khristova	BUL	19.11.41	1		Belmeken	4 Jul 76
21.86	Marianne	Adam	GDR	19.9.51	1	v URS	Leipzig	23 Jun 79

Mark	Wind	Name		Nat	Born	Pos	Meet	Venue	Date
21.76			Li Meisu	CHN	17.4.59	1		Shijiazhuang	23 Apr 88
21.73		Natalya	Akhrimenko	RUS	12.5.55	1		Leselidze	21 May 88
21.66			Sui Xinmei ¶	CHN	29.1.65	1		Beijing	9 Jun 90
21.61		Verzhinia	Veselinova	BUL	18.11.57	1		Sofia	21 Aug 82
		(10)							
21.60i		Valentina	Fedyushina	UKR	18.2.65	1		Simferopol	28 Dec 91
21.58		Margitta	Droese'	GDR	10.9.52	1		Erfurt	28 May 78
21.57 @		Ines	Müller'	GDR	2.1.59	1		Athinai	16 May 88
		21.45				1		Schwerin	4 Jun 86
21.53		Nunu	Abashidze ¶	UKR	27.3.55	2	Izv	Kiev	20 Jun 84
21.52			Huang Zhihong	CHN	7.5.65	1	NC	Beijing	27 Jun 90
21.45		Nadezhda	Chizhova	RUS	29.9.45	1		Varna	29 Sep 73
21.43		Eva	Wilms	FRG	28.7.52	2	HB	München	17 Jun 77
21.42		Svetlana	Krachevskaya'	RUS	23.11.44	2	OG	Moskva	24 Jul 80
21.31 @		Heike	Hartwig'	GDR	30.12.62	2		Athinai	16 May 88
		21.27				1		Khania	22 May 88
21.27		Liane	Schmuhl	GDR	29.6.61	1		Cottbus	26 Jun 82
21.21		Kathrin	Neimke	GDR	18.7.66	2	WC	Roma	5 Sep 87
		(20)							
21.19		Helma	Knorscheidt	GDR	31.12.56	1		Berlin	24 May 84
21.10		Heidi	Krieger	GDR	20.7.65	1	EC	Stuttgart	26 Aug 86
21.06		Svetlana	Krivelyova	RUS	13.6.69	1	OG	Barcelona	7 Aug 92
21.05		Zdenka	Silhavá' ¶	TCH	15.6.54	2	NC	Praha	23 Jul 83
21.01		Ivanka	Petrova-Stoycheva	BUL	3.2.51	1	NC	Sofia	28 Jul 79
21.00		Mihaela	Loghin	ROM	1.6.52	1		Formia	30 Jun 84
21.00		Cordula	Schulze	GDR	11.9.59	4	OD	Potsdam	21 Jul 84
20.99		Larisa	Peleshenko'	RUS	29.2.64	1		Leselidze	13 May 87
20.96		Belsy	Laza	CUB	5.6.67	1		Ciudad México	2 May 92
		(30)							
20.95		Elena	Stoyanova ¶	BUL	23.1.52	2	Balk	Sofia	14 Jun 80
20.91		Svetla	Mitkova	BUL	17.6.64	1		Sofia	24 May 87
20.80		Sona	Vasícková	TCH	14.3.62	1		Praha	2 Jun 88
20.77		Astrid	Kumbernuss	GDR	5.2.70	1	vSU	Rostock	24 Jun 90
20.72		Grit	Haupt/Hammer	GDR	4.6.66	3		Neubrandenburg	11 Jun 87
20.61		María Elena	Sarría	CUB	14.9.54	1		Habana	22 Jul 82
20.60		Marina	Antonyuk	RUS	12.5.62	1		Chelyabinsk	10 Aug 86
20.53		Iris	Plotzitzka	FRG	7.1.66	1	ASV	Köln	21 Aug 88
20.50i		Christa	Wiese	GDR	25.12.67	2	NC	Senftenberg	12 Feb 89
20.47		Nina	Isayeva	RUS	6.7.50	1		Bryansk	28 Aug 82
		(40)							
20.47			Cong Yuzhen	CHN	22.1.63	2	IntC	Tianjin	3 Sep 88
20.44		Tatyana	Orlova	BLS	19.7.55	1		Staiki	28 May 83
20.40			Zhou Tianhua ¶	CHN	10.4.66	1		Beijing	5 Sep 91
20.34		Stephanie	Storp	FRG	28.11.68	1		Wolfsburg	1 Jul 90
20.27		Danguole	Bimbaite'	LIT	10.12.62	2		Leselidze	13 May 87
20.27		Lyudmila	Voyevudskaya	UKR	22.6.59	1		Nikolayev	7 Aug 87
20.24		Anna	Romanova	RUS	9.3.68	1		Bryansk	29 May 93
20.23		Ilke	Wyludda	GDR	28.3.69	1	NC-j	Karl-Marx-Stadt	16 Jul 88
20.22		Margitta	Gummel'	GDR	29.6.41	2	OG	München	7 Sep 72
20.21		Svetlana	Melnikova	RUS	29.1.51	1	RigC	Riga	5 Jun 82
		(50)	100th best 19.35						

Just one change - addition of Romanova at 20.24 - to the top 50 this year

Best outdoors: 21.08 Fedyushina 1 Leselidze 15 May 88

@ meeting held under competitive conditions, but unsanctioned by GDR federation.

DISCUS

Mark	Wind	Name		Nat	Born	Pos	Meet	Venue	Date
76.80		Gabriele	Reinsch	GDR	23.9.63	1	v Ita	Neubrandenburg	9 Jul 88
74.56		Zdenka	Silhavá' ¶	TCH	15.6.54	1		Nitra	26 Aug 84
74.56		Ilke	Wyludda	GDR	28.3.69	1	NC	Neubrandenburg	23 Jul 89
74.44			Reinsch			1		Berlin	13 Sep 88
74.40			Wyludda			2		Berlin	13 Sep 88
74.08		Diana	Gansky'	GDR	14.12.63	1	v URS	Karl-Marx-Stadt	20 Jun 87
73.90			Gansky			1	EP	Praha	27 Jun 87
73.84		Daniela	Costian ¶	ROM	30.4.65	1		Bucuresti	30 Apr 88
73.78			Costian			1		Bucuresti	24 Apr 88
73.42			Reinsch			1		Karl-Marx-Stadt	12 Jun 88

Mark	Wind	Name		Nat	Born	Pos	Meet	Venue	Date
73.36		Irina	Meszynski	GDR	24.3.62	1	Drz	Praha	17 Aug 84
73.32			Gansky			1		Neubrandenburg	11 Jun 87
73.28		Galina	Savinkova'	RUS	15.7.53	1	NC	Donyetsk	8 Sep 84
73.26			Savinkova			1		Leselidze	21 May 83
73.26			Sachse'			1		Neubrandenburg	6 Jun 86
73.24			Gansky			1		Leipzig	29 May 87
73.22		Tsvetanka	Khristova ¶	BUL	14.3.62	1		Kazanlak	19 Apr 87
73.10		Gisela	Beyer	GDR	16.7.60	1	OD	Berlin	20 Jul 84
73.04			Gansky			1		Potsdam	6 Jun 87
73.04			Wyludda			1	EP	Gateshead	5 Aug 89
72.96			Savinkova			1	v GDR	Erfurt	23 Jun 85
72.94			Gansky			2	v Ita	Neubrandenburg	9 Jul 88
72.92		Martina	Hellmann'	GDR	12.12.60	1	NC	Potsdam	20 Aug 87
72.90			Costian			1		Bucuresti	14 May 88
72.78			Hellmann			2		Neubrandenburg	11 Jun 87
72.78			Reinsch			1	OD	Berlin	29 Jun 88
72.72			Wyludda			1		Neubrandenburg	23 Jun 89
72.70			Wyludda			1	NC-j	Karl-Marx-Stadt	15 Jul 88
72.54			Gansky			1	NC	Rostock	25 Jun 88
72.52			Hellmann			1		Frohburg	15 Jun 86
72.52			Khristova			1	BGP	Budapest	11 Aug 86
		(31/10)							
72.14		Galina	Murashova	LIT	22.12.55	2	Drz	Praha	17 Aug 84
71.80		Maria	Vergova-Petkova	BUL	3.11.50	1	NC	Sofia	13 Jul 80
71.68		Xiao Yanling ¶		CHN	27.3.68	1		Beijing	14 Mar 92
71.58		Ellina	Zveryova' ¶	BLS	16.11.60	1	Znam	Leningrad	12 Jun 88
71.50		Evelin	Jahl'	GDR	28.3.56	1		Potsdam	10 May 80
71.30		Larisa	Korotkevich	RUS	3.1.67	1	RusCp	Sochi	29 May 92
71.22		Ria	Stalman	HOL	11.12.51	1		Walnut	15 Jul 84
70.88		Hilda	Ramos	CUB	1.9.64	1		Habana	8 May 92
70.80		Larisa	Mikhalchenko	UKR	16.5.63	1		Kharkov	18 Jun 88
70.68		Maritza	Martén	CUB	16.8.63	1	Ib Am	Sevilla	18 Jul 92
		(20)							
70.50		Faina	Melnik	RUS	9.6.45	1	Znam	Sochi	24 Apr 76
70.34 @		Silvia	Madetzky	GDR	24.6.62	3		Athinai	16 May 88
		69.34				1		Halle	26 Jun 87
69.86		Valentina	Kharchenko	RUS	.49	1		Feodosiya	16 May 81
69.72		Svetla	Mitkova	BUL	17.6.64	2	NC	Sofia	15 Aug 87
69.50		Florenta	Craciunescu'	ROM	7.5.55	1	Balk	Stara Zagora	2 Aug 85
69.08		Carmen	Romero	CUB	6.10.50	1	NC	Habana	17 Apr 76
69.08		Mariana	Lengyel'	ROM	14.4.53	1		Constanta	19 Apr 86
68.94		Irina	Yatchenko	BLS	31.10.65	1	Nik	Nice	15 Jul 92
68.92		Sabine	Engel	GDR	21.4.54	1	v URS,Pol	Karl-Marx-Stadt	25 Jun 77
68.64		Margitta	Pufe'	GDR	10.9.52	1	ISTAF	Berlin	17 Aug 79
		(30)							
68.62		Yu Hourun		CHN	9.7.64	1		Beijing	6 May 88
68.62		Hou Xuemei		CHN	27.2.62	1	IntC	Tianjin	4 Sep 88
68.60		Nadezhda	Kugayevskikh	RUS	19.4.60	1		Oryol	30 Aug 83
68.58		Lyubov	Zverkova	RUS	14.6.55	1	Izv	Kiev	22 Jun 84
68.38		Olga	Burova '	RUS	17.9.63	2	RusCp	Sochi	29 May 92
68.26		Franka	Dietzsch	GDR	22.1.68	3		Neubrandenburg	23 Jun 89
68.18		Tatyana	Lesovaya	KZK	24.4.56	1		Alma-Ata	23 Sep 82
68.18		Irina	Khval	RUS	17.5.62	1		Moskva	8 Jul 88
68.18		Barbara	Echevarría	CUB	6.8.66	2		Habana	17 Feb 89
67.96		Argentina	Menis	ROM	19.7.48	1	RomIC	Bucuresti	15 May 76
		(40)							
67.90		Petra	Sziegaud	GDR	17.10.58	1		Berlin	19 May 82
67.82		Tatyana	Belova	RUS	12.2.62	1		Irkutsk	10 Aug 87
67.80		Stefenia	Simova ¶	BUL	5.6.63	1		Stara Zagora	27 Jun 92
67.54		Svetlana	Petrova	BLS	19.12.51	1		Brest-Litovsk	20 Sep 78
67.48		Meg	Ritchie	GBR	6.7.52	1	MSR	Walnut	26 Apr 81
67.40		Brigitte	Michel	GDR	19.8.56	2		Halle	14 Jun 79
67.34		Irina	Shabanova	RUS	2.8.64	1		Krasnodar	15 Aug 87
67.32		Natalya	Gorbachova	RUS	24.7.47	1		Leningrad	4 Jun 83
67.26		Svetla	Bozhkova	BUL	13.3.51	2		Sofia	5 Jul 80
		(50)	100th best 64.68	Only change in top 100 this year Cao Qi 66.08 at 70th					

Mark	Wind	Name		Nat	Born	Pos	Meet	Venue	Date
Unofficial meeting									
78.14		Martina	Hellmann	GDR	12.12.60	1		Berlin	6 Sep 88
75.36		Ilke	Wyludda	GDR	28.3.69	2		Berlin	6 Sep 88

HAMMER

Mark	Wind	Name		Nat	Born	Pos	Meet	Venue	Date
66.84		Olga	Kuzenkova	RUS	4.10.70	1		Sochi	27 Feb 94
65.40			Kuzenkova			1		Bryansk	4 Jun 92
64.64			Kuzenkova			1		Krasnodar	20 Feb 93
64.44		Alla	Fyodorova	KGK	66	1	NCw	Adler	24 Feb 91
64.44			Kuzenkova			1		Rostov na Donu	17 May 92
64.12			Kuzenkova			1		Rostov na Donu	17 Jul 93
63.86			Kuzenkova			1	CIS Ch	Moskva	22 Jun 92
63.70		Svetlana	Sudak	BLS	17.11.71	1		Grodno	4 May 93
63.28			Kuzenkova			1		Moskva	26 Jan 94
63.08		Larisa	Shtyrogrizhnaya	TJK	61	2	NCw	Adler	24 Feb 91
63.00			Kuzenkova			1	NC-w	Sochi	18 Feb 94
62.98			Kuzenkova			1	NC	Moskva	19 Jul 92
62.70			Fyodorova			1		Adler	9 Feb 91
62.70			Sudak			1		Moskva	28 Feb 92
62.60			Kuzenkova			1		Cork	9 Jul 93
62.56			Fyodorova			1		Alma-Ata	11 May 91
62.52		Mihaela	Melinte	ROM	27.3.75	1	NC-j	Bucuresti	8 Aug 93
62.38			Fyodorova			1		Adler	26 May 91
62.38		Debbie	Sosimenko	AUS	5.4.74	1		Sydney	19 Feb 94
62.34			Kuzenkova			1		Moskva	27 Jan 93
		(20/6)							
61.96		Larisa	Baranova	RUS	29.6.61	1		Adler	11 Feb 90
61.80		Lyubov	Vasilyeva '	RUS	14.8.57	1		Moskva	18 Jun 91
61.66		Yulia	Styepanova	UKR	8.5.70	1		Kiev	1 Jun 91
61.50		Yelena	Pichugina	RUS	.64	1		Frunze	30 Sep 89
		(10)							
61.20		Aya	Suzuki	JAP	18.11.67	1		Wakayama	30 Apr 89
60.36		Yelena	Rogachevskaya	UKR	12.12.63	2		Bryansk	19 Jun 90
59.86		Yelena	Lanina	RUS	.69	1	Kuts	Moskva	20 Aug 89
59.80		Natalya	Vasilenko	UKR	15.8.74	1		Chernigov	26 Jun 93
59.62		Lyudmila	Gubkina	BLS	28.5.72	1		Pinsk	6 Jul 93
59.50		Tatyana	Konstantinova	RUS	.70	2		Moskva	26 Jan 94
59.06		Natalya	Panarina	RUS	6.5.75	1		Chelyabinsk	6 Jun 93
58.60		Yelena	Khrulyova	RUS	73	3		Adler	26 May 91
58.52		Carol	Cady	USA	6.6.62	1		Los Gatos	11 Jun 88
58.36		Oksana	Zatsepilova	RUS	20.4.74	2		Moskva	6 Aug 93
		(20)							
58.24		Marina	Pirog	UKR	74	2		Chernigov	26 Jun 93
58.20		Olga	Sokolova	RUS	.72	1		Adler	24 Feb 90
58.20		Lyudmila	Novikova	RUS	29.1.64	1		Leningrad	27 May 90
58.16		Viktoriya	Polyanskaya	RUS	71	1		Krasnodar	25 Apr 93
58.10		Natalya	Ignatova	RUS	3.1.74	2		Chelyabinsk	6 Jun 93
58.10		Oksana	Silchenko	BLS	10.8.70	1		Grodno	25 Jul 93
57.96		Livia	Mehes	ROM	6.3.65	2	NC	Bucuresti	5 Sep 93
57.24		Diana	Bireva	URS	.63	4		Adler	25 Feb 90
57.16		Sonja	Fitts	USA	4.10.70	1	NYG	New York	24 May 92
56.76		Esther	Augee	GBR	1.1.64	1		Bromley	15 May 93
		(30)							
Unconfirmed:		58.94	Carol Cady	USA	6.6.62	1		Stanford	10 Jul 88

JAVELIN

Mark	Wind	Name		Nat	Born	Pos	Meet	Venue	Date
80.00		Petra	Felke	GDR	30.7.59	1		Potsdam	9 Sep 88
78.90			Felke			1		Leipzig	29 Jul 87
78.14			Felke			1	OT	Jena	3 Jun 88
77.52			Felke			1	Super	Tokyo	8 Oct 88
77.44		Fatima	Whitbread	GBR	3.3.61	Q	EC	Stuttgart	28 Aug 86
76.88			Felke			1	vIta,Cs	Macerata	5 Sep 89
76.82			Felke			1	v FRG	Düsseldorf	19 Jun 88
76.80			Felke			1		Khania	22 May 88
76.76			Felke			1		Berlin	27 Aug 88
76.64			Whitbread			1	WC	Roma	6 Sep 87

WOMEN All-time

Mark	Wind	Name		Nat	Born	Pos	Meet	Venue	Date
76.50			Felke			1		Rostock	29 May 88
76.34			Whitbread			1	Bisl	Oslo	4 Jul 87
76.32			Whitbread			1	EC	Stuttgart	29 Aug 86
75.72			Felke			1		Granada	17 Jun 89
75.62			Whitbread			1	NC	Derby	25 May 87
75.40			Felke			1		Schwerin	4 Jun 85
75.16			Felke			1	Bisl	Oslo	2 Jul 88
75.04			Felke			1	GO	Dresden	17 Aug 86
74.94			Felke			1	v URS	Erfurt	22 Jun 85
74.92			Felke			1	OD	Berlin	29 Jun 88
74.90			Felke			1	OD	Berlin	27 Jun 85
74.76		Tiina	Lillak	FIN	15.4.61	1		Tampere	13 Jun 83
74.74			Whitbread			1		Crawley	26 Aug 87
74.72			Felke			1		Celje	5 May 84
74.70			Felke			1		Berlin	22 Sep 85
74.68			Felke			1	OG	Seoul	26 Sep 88
74.62			Felke			1		Berlin	13 Sep 88
74.56			Felke			1	ISTAF	Berlin	23 Aug 85
74.32			Felke			1		Neubrandenburg	11 Jun 87
74.24			Lillak			1		Fresno	7 Apr 84
74.24			Felke			1	OD	Potsdam	21 Jul 84
		(31/3)							
74.20		Sofia	Sakorafa	GRE	29.4.57	1	NC	Khania	26 Sep 82
73.58		Tessa	Sanderson	GBR	14.3.56	1		Edinburgh	26 Jun 83
72.70		Anna	Verouli ¶	GRE	13.11.56	1		Khania	20 May 84
72.16		Antje	Kempe-Zöllkau	GDR	23.6.63	2		Celje	5 May 84
72.12		Trine	Hattestad'	NOR	18.4.66	1	Bisl	Oslo	10 Jul 93
71.88		Antoaneta	Todorova'	BUL	8.6.63	1	EP	Zagreb	15 Aug 81
71.82		Ivonne	Leal	CUB	27.2.66	1	WUG	Kobe	30 Aug 85
		(10)							
71.00		Silke	Renk	GDR	30.6.67	2	NC	Rostock	25 Jun 88
70.76		Beate	Koch	GDR	18.8.67	1		Rostock	22 Jun 89
70.42		Zhang Li		CHN	26.6.61	1		Tianjin	6 Aug 90
70.36		Natalya	Shikolenko	BLS	1.8.64	1	CIS Ch	Moskva	22 Jun 92
70.20		Karen	Forkel	GER	24.9.70	1		Halle	9 May 91
70.14		Mayra	Vila ¶	CUB	5.6.60	2		Madrid	14 Jun 85
70.14		María	Caridad Colón	CUB	25.3.58	1	Barr	Habana	15 Jun 86
70.08		Tatyana	Biryulina	UZB	16.7.55	1		Podolsk	12 Jul 80
69.96		Ruth	Fuchs	GDR	14.12.46	1		Split	29 Apr 80
69.86		Natalya	Kolenchuková' ¶	BLS	29.4.64	1	NC	Leningrad	3 Aug 85
		(20)							
69.80		Sue	Howland ¶	AUS	4.9.60	2		Belfast	30 Jun 86
69.68		Ingrid	Thyssen	FRG	9.1.56	1	ISTAF	Berlin	21 Aug 87
69.60		Susanne	Jung	GDR	17.5.63	2	NC	Potsdam	22 Aug 87
69.56		Beate	Peters	FRG	12.10.59	1	NC	Berlin	12 Jul 86
69.32		Kate	Schmidt	USA	29.12.53	1		Fürth	11 Sep 77
69.28		Petra	Rivers	AUS	11.12.52	1	NC	Brisbane	20 Mar 82
68.80		Eva	Raduly-Zörgö	ROM	23.10.54	1	Znam	Moskva	5 Jul 80
68.78		Xu Demei		CHN	23.5.67	1	WC	Tokyo	1 Sep 91
68.28		Saida	Gunba	GEO	30.8.59	2	Znam	Moskva	5 Jul 80
67.90		Dulce M.	García ¶	CUB	2.7.65	3	Barr	Habana	15 Jun 86
		(30)							
67.88		Natalya	Cherniyenko	UKR	1.10.65	1		Sochi	26 May 90
67.84		Jadviga	Putiniene	LIT	30.12.45	3	Znam	Moskva	5 Jul 80
67.68		Päivi	Alafrantti	FIN	8.5.64	1	EC	Split	30 Aug 90
67.64		Teresé	Nekrosaité	LIT	19.10.61	2		Duisburg	7 Jun 92
67.40		Tuula	Laaksalo	FIN	21.4.53	2		Pihtipudas	24 Jul 83
67.32		Regine	Kempter	GDR	4.4.67	2	NC	Jena	27 Jun 86
67.24		Ute	Hommola	GDR	20.1.52	1	v GBR	Dresden	13 Jun 81
67.24		Svetlana	Pestretsova	KZK	6.3.61	1	Kuts	Moskva	5 Sep 88
67.20		Fausta	Quintavalla	ITA	4.5.59	1		Milano	22 Jun 83
67.18		Zsuzsa	Malovecz	HUN	21.5.62	1	5-N	Forli	22 May 88
		(40)							
67.00		Corina	Girbea'	ROM	26.5.59	1	v Hun	Debrecen	13 Jun 82
67.00		Zinaida	Gavrilina	UKR	22.9.61	1	NC	Donyetsk	9 Sep 84
67.00		Irina	Kostyuchenkova	UKR	11.5.61	2	Znam	Leningrad	12 Jun 88

Mark	Wind	Name		Nat	Born	Pos	Meet	Venue	Date
66.96		Ute	Richter	GDR	14.7.58	1		Neubrandenburg	21 May 83
66.80		Olga	Gavrilova	RUS	8.2.57	1	WP	Canberra	4 Oct 85
66.80		Jana	Köpping	GDR	12.4.66	3	NC	Jena	27 Jun 86
66.56		Elena	Burgárová	TCH	13.11.52	2		Nitra	26 Aug 84
66.52		Alexandra	Beck	GDR	13.6.68	1		Khania	24 May 86
66.48		Eva	Helmschmidt	FRG	20.4.57	1	v Hol,Pol	Bielefeld	4 Jun 83
66.18		Isel	López	CUB	11.7.70	1	Barr	Habana	12 May 90
		(50)	100th best 63.92	Hattestad only change in top 50					

HEPTATHLON

Mark	Wind	Name		Nat	Born	Pos	Meet	Venue	Date
7291		Jackie	Joyner-Kersee	USA	3.3.62	1	OG	Seoul	24 Sep 88
		12.69/+0.5	1.86 15.80	22.56/+1.6		7.27/+0.7		45.66 2:08.51	
7215			Joyner-Kersee			1	OT	Indianapolis	16 Jul 88
		12.71/-0.9	1.93 15.65	22.30/ 0.0		7.00/-1.3		50.08 2:20.70	
7158			Joyner-Kersee			1	USOF	Houston	2 Aug 86
		13.18/-0.5	1.88 15.20	22.85/+1.2		7.03/+2.9		50.12 2:09.69	
7148			Joyner			1	GWG	Moskva	7 Jul 86
		12.85/+0.2	1.88 14.76	23.00		7.01/-0.5		49.86 2:10.02	
7128			Joyner-Kersee			1	WC	Roma	1 Sep 87
		12.91/+0.2	1.90 16.00	22.95/+1.2		7.14/+0.9		45.68 2:16.29	
7044			Joyner-Kersee			1	OG	Barcelona	2 Aug 92
		12.85/-0.9	1.91 14.13	23.12/+0.7		7.10/+1.3		44.98 2:11.78	
7007		Larisa	Nikitina ¶	RUS	29.4.65	1	NC	Bryansk	11 Jun 89
		13.40/+1.4	1.89 16.45	23.97/+1.1		6.73/+4.0		53.94 2:15.31	
6985		Sabine	Braun	GER	19.6.65	1		Götzis	31 May 92
		13.11/-0.4	1.93 14.84	23.65/+2.0		6.63/+2.9		51.62 2:12.67	
6979			Joyner-Kersee			1	TAC	San José	24 Jun 87
		12.90/+2.0	1.85 15.17	23.02/+0.4		7.25/+2.3		40.24 2:13.07	
6946		Sabine	Paetz'	GDR	16.10.57	1	NC	Potsdam	6 May 84
		12.64/+0.3	1.80 15.37	23.37/+0.7		6.86/-0.2		44.62 2:08.93	
6935		Ramona	Neubert	GDR	26.7.58	1	v URS	Moskva	19 Jun 83
		13.42	1.82 15.25	23.49		6.79/+0.7		49.94 2:07.51	
6910			Joyner			1	MSR	Walnut	25 Apr 86
		12.9	1.86 14.75	23.24/+2.8		6.85/+2.1		48.30 2:14.11	
6897			John'			2	OG	Seoul	24 Sep 88
		12.85/+0.5	1.80 16.23	23.65/+1.6		6.71/ 0.0		42.56 2:06.14	
6878			Joyner-Kersee			1	TAC	New York	13 Jun 91
		12.77	1.89 15.62	23.42		6.97		43.28 2:22.12	
6875			Nikitina			1	EP-A	Helmond	16 Jul 89
		13.55/-2.1	1.84 15.99	24.29/-2.1		6.75/-2.5		56.78 2:18.67	
6859		Natalya	Shubenkova	RUS	25.9.57	1	NC	Kiev	21 Jun 84
		12.93/+1.0	1.83 13.66	23.57/-0.3		6.73/+0.4		46.26 2:04.60	
6858		Anke	Behmer'	GDR	5.6.61	3	OG	Seoul	24 Sep 88
		13.20/+0.5	1.83 14.20	23.10/+1.6		6.68/+0.1		44.54 2:04.20	
6847			Nikitina			1	WUG	Duisburg	29 Aug 89
		13.47	1.81 16.12	24.12		6.66		59.28 2:22.07	
6845			Neubert			1	v URS	Halle	20 Jun 82
		13.58	1.83 15.10	23.14		6.84w		42.54 2:06.16	
6845		Irina	Belova ¶	RUS	17.2.68	2	OG	Barcelona	2 Aug 92
		13.25/-0.1	1.88 13.77	23.34/+0.2		6.82/0.0		41.90 2:05.08	
6841			Joyner			1	Int	Götzis	25 May 86
		13.09/-1.3	1.87 14.34	23.63/-0.8		6.76/-0.3		48.88 2:14.58	
6837			Joyner-Kersee			1	WC	Stuttgart	17 Aug 93
		12.89/0.1	1.81 14.38	23.19/		7.04/1.4		43.76 2:14.49	
6813			Paetz			1	OD	Potsdam	21 Jul 84
		12.71/+0.4	1.74 16.16	23.23w		6.58		41.94 2:07.03	
6805			Behmer			1	Int	Götzis	19 Jun 88
		13.28/+1.6	1.84 14.38	22.73/+4.0		6.62/+1.1		40.48 2:04.64	
6803		Jane	Frederick	USA	7.4.52	1	Int	Talence	16 Sep 84
		13.27/+1.2	1.87 15.49	24.15/+1.6		6.43/+0.2		51.74 2:13.55	
6797			Braun			2	WC	Stuttgart	17 Aug 93
		13.25/0.1	1.90 14.62	24.12/		6.54/1.0		53.44 2:17.82	
6789			Neubert			2	OD	Potsdam	21 Jul 84
		13.48/+0.4	1.74 15.03	23.47w		6.71		47.88 2:04.73	

Mark	Wind	Name	Nat	Born	Pos	Meet	Venue	Date
6788		Neubert			1	v URS	Kiev	28 Jun 81
	13.70	1.86 15.41	23.58		6.82/+0.2		40.62 2:06.72	
6783		Joyner-Kersee			1	GWG	Seattle	23 Jul 90
	12.79	1.87 13.93	24.26/		6.91/ 47.64 2:17.41			
6775		Vater'			3	OD	Potsdam	21 Jul 84
	13.30/+0.4	1.86 14.86	23.20w		6.84/+0.5		34.04 2:03.76	
	(30/9)							
6750		Ma Miaolan (10)	CHN	18.1.70	1	NG	Beijing	12 Sep 93
	13.28/1.5	1.89 14.98	23.86/		6.64/ 45.82 2:15.33			
6703	Tatyana	Blokhina	RUS	12.3.70	1	Decast	Talence	11 Sep 93
	13.69/-0.6	1.91 14.94	23.95/-0.4		5.99/-0.3		52.16 2:09.65	
6702	Chantal	Beaugeant ¶	FRA	16.2.61	2	Int	Götzis	19 Jun 88
	13.10/+1.6	1.78 13.74	23.96/+3.5		6.45/+0.2		50.96 2:07.09	
6695	Jane	Flemming	AUS	14.4.65	1	CG	Auckland	28 Jan 90
	13.21/+1.4	1.82 13.76	23.62/+2.4		6.57/+1.6		49.28 2:12.53	
6660	Ines	Schulz	GDR	10.7.65	3	Int	Götzis	19 Jun 88
	13.56/+0.4	1.84 13.95	23.93/+2.8		6.70/+0.7		42.82 2:06.31	
6658	Svetla	Dimitrova ¶	BUL	27.1.70	2		Götzis	31 May 92
	13.41/-0.7	1.75 14.72	23.06/+2.4		6.64/+1.9		43.84 2:09.60	
6646	Natalya	Grachova	UKR	21.2.52	1	NC	Moskva	2 Aug 82
	13.80	1.80 16.18	23.86		6.65/+3.5		39.42 2:06.59	
6635	Sibylle	Thiele	GDR	6.3.65	2	GWG	Moskva	7 Jul 86
	13.14/+0.6	1.76 16.00	24.18		6.62		45.74 2:15.30	
6635	Svetlana	Buraga	BLS	4.9.65	3	WC	Stuttgart	17 Aug 93
	12.95/0.1	1.84 14.55	23.69/		6.58/-0.2		41.04 2:13.65	
6623	Judy	Simpson'	GBR	14.11.60	3	EC	Stuttgart	30 Aug 86
	13.05/+0.8	1.92 14.73	25.09/+0.0		6.56/+2.5		40.92 2:11.70	
6619	Liliana	Nastase	ROM	1.8.62	4	OG	Barcelona	2 Aug 92
	12.86/-0.9	1.82 14.34	23.70/+0.2		6.49/-0.3		41.30 2:11.22	
	(20)							
6616	Malgorzata	Nowak'	POL	9.2.59	1	WUG	Kobe	31 Aug 85
	13.27/+4.0	1.95 15.35	24.20/+0.0		6.37/+3.9		43.36 2:20.39	
6604	Remigia	Nazaroviene'	LIT	2.6.67	2	URSCh	Bryansk	11 Jun 89
	13.26/+1.4	1.86 14.27	24.12/+0.7		6.58/+0.9		40.94 2:09.98	
6572	Heike	Tischler	GDR	4.2.64	2	EC	Split	31 Aug 90
	14.08/-0.9	1.82 13.73	24.29/+0.9		6.22/-0.7		53.24 2:05.50	
6552	Nadezhda	Vinogradova'	RUS	1.5.58	2	NC	Kiev	21 Jun 84
	13.92/+1.0	1.80 15.19	23.84/+0.2		6.67/+0.1		38.60 2:06.80	
6551	Yelena	Martsenyuk	RUS	21.2.61	2		Staiki	2 Jul 88
	13.54/-0.4	1.82 15.32	24.25/+0.3		6.25/+0.7		47.56 2:12.72	
6541	Mila	Kolyadina	RUS	31.12.60	4	v GDR	Moskva	19 Jun 83
	14.05	1.82 16.28	24.81		6.48/+0.8		48.26 2:15.26	
6539	Tatyana	Shpak	UKR	17.11.60	3		Staiki	2 Jul 88
	13.57/-0.4	1.76 15.30	23.61/+0.5		6.52/-0.6		39.28 2:07.25	
6536	Yekaterina	Smirnova	RUS	22.10.56	3	v GDR	Moskva	19 Jun 83
	13.41	1.82 14.82	24.84		6.56/+1.1		45.66 2:13.38	
6531	Peggy	Beer	GDR	15.9.69	3	EC	Split	31 Aug 90
	13.27/-0.2	1.82 13.46	23.99/+0.4		6.38/+0.9		42.10 2:05.79	
6523	Sabine	Everts	FRG	4.3.61	1	v URS	Mannheim	10 Jun 82
	13.45	1.89 12.39	23.73		6.75		36.02 2:07.73	
	(30)							
6510	Svetlana	Moskalets	RUS	1.11.69	1		Moskva	7 Aug 93
	13.40/	1.82 13.54	23.55/		6.70/ 41.82 2:15.87			
6500	Birgit	Clarius	GER	18.3.65	1	NC	Vaterstetten	20 Jun 93
	13.61/1.3	1.81 15.22	24.69w/2.1		6.08/-0.6		50.20 2:11.29	
6493	Svetlana	Filatyeva '	RUS	3.4.64	1		Kiev	14 Aug 88
	13.77	1.89 13.89	24.94		6.30		48.44 2:11.89	
6487	Birgit	Dressel	FRG	4.5.60	4	EC	Stuttgart	30 Aug 86
	13.56/-1.6	1.92 14.12	24.68/+0.0		6.28/+1.1		45.70 2:15.78	
6478	Irina	Tyukhay	RUS	14.1.67	1		Yekaterinburg	3 Aug 92
	13.33/	1.89 14.60	24.53/		6.73/ 36.44 2:17.00			
6474	Marianna	Maslennikova	RUS	17.5.61	2	NC	Kiev	2 Aug 88
	13.37/+0.4	1.83 13.68	24.07/-0.0		6.28/+0.2		40.42 2:05.60	
6461	Valentina	Kurochkina	RUS	13.12.59	1		Tallinn	11 Aug 83
	13.89	1.85 14.40	24.51		6.63/+1.2		43.98 2:15.94	
6453	Valentina	Dimitrova	BUL	4.5.56	2	Int	Götzis	29 May 83
	14.31/+0.8	1.86 16.07	24.78/+1.0		6.26/+1.4		42.26 2:08.74	

Mark	Wind	Name		Nat	Born	Pos	Meet	Venue	Date
6453		Cornelia	Heinrich'	FRG	2.6.60	2	Int	Götzis	18 Jun 89
		13.66/+1.9	1.90 15.33	24.58/+3.1		6.49/+2.2		41.26 2:20.56	
6442		Marion	Reichelt'	GDR	23.12.62	2	EP	Arles	5 Jul 87
		13.47/+3.2	1.87 12.91	23.62/+1.9		6.68/+0.2		37.80 2:15.15	
		(40)							
6427m		Antonina	Sukhova	RUS	1.1.59	1		Tula	26 Aug 84
		13.0	1.82 13.79	24.8		6.41		45.88 2:13.5	
6425		Birgit	Gautzsch	GDR	14.12.67	2	vSU	Cottbus	20 Aug 89
		13.37/-1.2	1.80 13.78	23.84/-1.5		6.47/-0.1		43.92 2:17.13	
6425		Urszula	Wlodarczyk	POL	22.12.65	1		Talence	21 Sep 91
		13.62/-0.4	1.84 13.24	24.12/+0.2		6.29/+0.6		46.22 2:12.82	
6424		Jodi	Anderson	USA	11.10.57	2	OT	Los Angeles	17 Jun 84
		13.52	1.80 13.40	24.49		6.36		48.52 2:13.20	
6424		Irina	Matyusheva'	UKR	5.9.65	3	NC	Kiev	2 Aug 88
		13.40/+0.4	1.86 13.54	24.40/-0.0		6.28/+0.3		40.20 2:08.24	
6423m		Lyubov	Ratsu	MOL	6.2.61	1		Kisinau	28 Aug 83
		13.6	1.80 14.75	24.2		6.53		41.86 2:11.6	
6404		Satu	Ruotsalainen	FIN	21.10.66	4	WC	Tokyo	27 Aug 91
		13.54/+1.1	1.88 12.46	24.20/+0.2		6.18/0.0		47.04 2:13.24	
6403		Emilia	Dimitrova ¶	BUL	13.11.67	6	GWG	Moskva	7 Jul 86
		13.73	1.76 13.46	23.17		6.29		43.30 2:09.85	
6399		Olga	Yakovleva	RUS	22.11.57	1	NP	Tashkent	27 Sep 82
		13.53	1.79 15.14	24.26		6.13		41.42 2:09.20	
6394			Zhu Yuqing	CHN	22.4.63	2	NG	Beijing	12 Sep 93
		13.05/1.5	1.83 15.07	24.15/		6.06/ 45.50 2:22.65			
		(50)	100th best 6196						

45-MINUTE HEPTATHLON

Mark	Name		Nat	Born	Pos	Venue	Date
6214	Sabine	Braun	GER	19.6.65	1	Ingelheim	28 Aug 93
	13.43	1.83 14.44	24.82		6.43	44.96 2:32.35	
6154	Petra	Vaideanu'	ROM	24.8.65	2	Ingelheim	28 Aug 93
	13.62	1.77 14.56	25.71		5.92	47.90 2:15.73	
6043	Kym	Carter	USA	12.3.64	3	Ingelheim	28 Aug 93
	13.53	1.74 14.78	24.18		5.91	36.84 2:17.61	
6038	Urszula	Wlodarczyk	POL	22.12.65	4	Ingelheim	28 Aug 93
	13.55	1.80 14.52	26.27		6.34	34.60 2:21.26	
5915	Peggy	Beer	GER	15.9.69	1	St Moritz	12 Jul 92
	13.25	1.77 13.24	24.64		6.16	41.56 2:35.28	
5886	Tatyana	Zhuravlyova	RUS	19.12.67	5	Ingelheim	28 Aug 93
		1.80 13.57	24.80		6.32	30.34 2:18.55	

4 x 100 METRES RELAY

Mark	Nat	Team	Pos	Meet	Venue	Date
41.37	GDR	Gladisch, Rieger, Auerswald, Göhr	1	WP	Canberra	6 Oct 85
41.49	RUS	Bogoslovskaya, Malchugina, Voronova, Privalova	1	WC	Stuttgart	22 Aug 93
41.49	USA	Finn, Torrence, Vereen, Devers	2	WC	Stuttgart	22 Aug 93
41.53	GDR	Gladisch, Koch, Auerswald, Göhr	1		Berlin	31 Jul 83
41.55	USA	Brown, Williams, Griffith, Marshall	1	ISTAF	Berlin	21 Aug 87
41.58	USA	Brown, Williams, Griffith, Marshall	1	WC	Roma	6 Sep 87
41.60	GDR	Müller, Wöckel, Auerswald, Göhr	1	OG	Moskva	1 Aug 80
41.61A	USA	Brown, Williams, Cheeseborough, Ashford	1	USOF	Air Force Academy	3 Jul 83
41.63	USA	Brown, Williams, Cheeseborough, Ashford	1	v GDR	Los Angeles	25 Jun 83
41.65	USA	Brown, Bolden, Cheeseborough, Ashford	1	OG	Los Angeles	11 Aug 84
41.65	GDR	Gladisch, Koch, Auerswald, Göhr	1	EP	Moskva	17 Aug 85
41.68	GDR	Möller, Krabbe, Behrendt, Günther	1	EC	Split	1 Sep 90
41.69	GDR	Gladisch, Koch, Auerswald, Göhr	1	OD	Potsdam	21 Jul 84
41.73	GDR	Möller, Behrendt, Lange, Göhr	1		Berlin	13 Sep 88
41.76	GDR	Gladisch, Koch, Auerswald, Göhr	1	WC	Helsinki	10 Aug 83
41.79	GDR	Gladisch, Drechsler, Auerswald, Göhr	1	v URS	Karl-Marx-Stadt	20 Jun 87
41.84	GDR	Gladisch, Gunther, Auerswald, Göhr	1	EC	Stuttgart	31 Aug 86
41.85	GDR	Müller, Wöckel, Auerswald, Göhr	1	OT	Potsdam	13 Jul 80
41.85	GDR	Gladisch, Koch, Auerswald, Göhr	1	WK	Zurich	22 Aug 84
41.87	GDR	Möller, Krabbe, Behrendt, Günther	1	EP	Gateshead	5 Aug 89
41.91	GER	Breuer, Krabbe, Richter, Drechsler	1h2	WC	Tokyo	31 Aug 91
41.94	GDR	Müller, Wöckel, Auerswald, Göhr	1	NC	Cottbus	17 Jul 80
41.94	GDR	Gladisch, Drechsler, Auerswald, Göhr	1	EP	Praha	27 Jun 87
41.94	JAM	Duhaney, Cuthbert, McDonald, Ottey	1	WC	Tokyo	1 Sep 91

Mark	Wind	Name	Nat	Born	Pos	Meet	Venue	Date
41.94	JAM	Freeman, Campbell, Mitchell, Ottey			3	WC	Stuttgart	22 Aug 93
41.95	GDR	Gladisch, Oschkenat, Behrendt, Göhr			2	WC	Roma	6 Sep 87
41.96	USA	Brown, Williams, Griffith, Marshall			1h2	WC	Roma	5 Sep 87
41.97	GDR	G.Walther, Wöckel, Schölzel, Göhr			1		Potsdam	28 Aug 82
41.97	GDR	Gladisch, Koch, Auerswald, Göhr			1		Leipzig	27 Jul 83
41.98	GDR	Gladisch, Günther, Auerswald, Göhr			1	GO	Dresden	17 Aug 86
41.98	USA	Brown, Echols, Griffith-Joyner, Ashford			1	OG	Seoul	1 Oct 88
		(31 performances by 4 nations)						
42.08mx	BUL	Pavlova, Nuneva, Georgieva, Ivanova			mx		Sofia	8 Aug 84
	42.31	Zagorcheva, Nuneva, Georgieva, Donkova			2	EP	Praha	27 Jun 87
42.39	NGR	Utondu, Idehen, Opara-Thompson, Onyali			2h2	OG	Barcelona	7 Aug 92
42.43	GBR	Hunte, Smallwood, Goddard, Lannaman			3	OG	Moskva	1 Aug 80
42.58	FRA	Girard, Sidibe, Bily, Pérec			3h2	OG	Barcelona	7 Aug 92
42.59	FRG	Possekel, Helten, Richter, Kroniger			2	OG	Montreal	31 Jul 76
42.71	POL	Tomczak, Pakula, Pisiewicz, Kasprzyk			3	EP	Moskva	17 Aug 85
	(10)							
42.77	CAN	Bailey, Payne, Taylor, Gareau			2	OG	Los Angeles	11 Aug 84
42.89	CUB	Ferrer, López, Duporty, Allen			6	WC	Stuttgart	22 Aug 93
42.97	UKR	Khristosenko, Kot, I Slyusar, German			1	SPA	Taskent	16 Sep 86
42.98	TCH	Sokolová, Soborová, Kocembová, Kratochvilová			1	WK	Zürich	18 Aug 82
43.16	Guangxi (CHN)	Xiao Y, Tian Y, Huang M, Ou Y			1	NG	Beijing	11 Sep 93
43.18	AUS	Wilson, Wells, Robertson, Boyle			5	OG	Montreal	31 Jul 76
43.35	KZK	Aleksandrova, Kvast, Miljauskiene, Sevalnikova			2	SPA	Taskent	16 Sep 86
43.37	FIN	Pirtimaa, Hanhijoki, Hernesniemi, Salmela			7	WC	Stuttgart	22 Aug 93
43.44A	HOL	van den Berg, Sterk, Hennipman, Bakker			4	OG	Ciudad México	20 Oct 68
43.67	ITA	Masullo, Dal Bianco, Ferrian, Tarolo			2	MedG	Athinai	11 Jul 91
	(20)							
43.82	UZB	Shmonina, Olenchenko, Barabashina, Vilisova			3	SPA	Moskva	20 Jun 93
44.05A	RSA	(Springboks) de Klerk, Vorster, Basson, Winkler			1		Pretoria	29 Apr 89
44.08	ESP	Morales, Castro, Garcia, Myers			5h2	WC	Tokyo	31 Aug 91
44.12	GHA	Bawuah, Yankey, Addy, Appiah			5h3	OG	Seoul	30 Sep 88
44.15	BAH	Clarke, Davis, Greene, Fowler			4h1	OG	Los Angeles	11 Aug 84
44.18	ROM	Voinea, Militaru, Pogacian, Ilcu			2	Balk	Stara Zagora	2 Aug 85
44.23	SWE	Sköglund, Haglund, Möller, Pihl			2	vFra,Sui	Thonon-l-Bains	21 Jun 80
44.23	TRI	Bernard, Forde, Hope, Williams			7	OG	Los, Angeles	11 Aug 84
44.31	SUI	Werthmüller, Wehrli, Keller, Lusti			3	4-N	Bremen	23 Jun 79
44.34	HUN	Siska, Ecseki, Nemeth, Orosz			2	vBul,Pol,	Budapest	27 Jun 82
	(30)							

Best at low altitude

43.54	HOL	Cooman, Poelman, de Lange, Huybrechtse	3	Duisburg	7 Jun 92
44.10	RSA	(Orange Free State) du Toit, Rademeyer, Basson, Naude	1 NC	Stellenbosch	11 Apr 87

4 x 200 METRES RELAY

1:28.15	GDR	Göhr, R.Müller, Wöckel, Koch	1		Jena	9 Aug 80
1:30.8	UKR	Makhova, Zyuskova, Prorochenko, Kulchunova	1		Moskva	29 Jul 79
1:31.49	RUS	Sotnikova, Zhirova, Mizera, Sokolova	1	EurR	Portsmouth	5 Jun 93
1:31.57	GBR	Elder, Hartley, Colyear, Lannaman	1		London	20 Aug 77
1:31.96	Texas	Southern University (Nigeria/USA)	1	DrakeR	Des Moines	28 Apr 89
		Eseimokumoh, Utondu, Webber USA, Onyali				
1:31.98	UKR	A Slyussar, I Slyussar, Fomenko, Tarnopolskaya	2	EurR	Portsmouth	5 Jun 93
1:32.17	FRA	Bily, Gaschet, Rega, Naigre	1		Paris	9 Jul 82

4 x 400 METRES RELAY

3:15.17	URS	Ledovskaya 50.12, Nazarova 47.82, Pinigina 49.43, Bryzgina 47.80	1	OG	Seoul	1 Oct 88
3:15.51	USA	D.Howard 49.82, Dixon 49.17, Brisco 48.44, Griffith-Joyner 48.08	2	OG	Seoul	1 Oct 88
3:15.92	GDR	G.Walther 49.8, Busch 48.9, Rübsam 49.4, Koch 47.8	1	NC	Erfurt	3 Jun 84
3:16.71	USA	Torrence 49.0, Malone 49.4, Kaiser-Brown 49.48, Miles 48.78	1	WC	Stuttgart	22 Aug 93
3:16.87	GDR	Emmelmann 50.9, Busch 48.8, Müller 48.9, Koch 48.3	1	EC	Stuttgart	31 Aug 86
3:18.29	USA		1	OG	Los Angeles	11 Aug 84
		Leatherwood 50.50, S.Howard 48.83, Brisco-Hooks 49.23, Cheeseborough 49.73				
3:18.29	GDR	Neubauer 50.58, Emmelmann 49.89, Busch 48.81, Müller 48.99	3	OG	Seoul	1 Oct 88
3:18.38	RUS	Ruzina 50.8, Alekseyeva 49.3, Ponomaryova 49.78, Privalova 48.47	2	WC	Stuttgart	22 Aug 9
3:18.43	URS	Ledovskaya 51.7, Dzhigalova 49.2, Nazarova 48.87, Bryzgina 48.67	1	WC	Tokyo	1 Sep 91
3:18.58	URS	I.Nazarova, Olizarenko, Pinigina, Vladykina	1	EP	Moskva	18 Aug 85
3:18.63	GDR	Neubauer 51.4, Emmelmann 49.1, Müller 48.64, Busch 49.48	1	WC	Roma	6 Sep 87
3:19.04	GDR	Siemon' 51.0, Busch 50.0, Rübsam 50.2, Koch 47.9	1	EC	Athinai	11 Sep 82

Mark	Wind	Name	Nat	Born	Pos	Meet	Venue	Date
3:19.12	URS	Baskakova, I.Nazarova, Pinigina, Vladykina			1	Drz	Praha	18 Aug 84
3:19.23	GDR	Maletzki, Rohde, Streidt, Brehmer			1	OG	Montreal	31 Jul 76
3:19.49	GDR	Emmelmann, Busch, Neubauer, Koch			1	WP	Canberra	4 Oct 85
3:19.50	URS	Yurchenko, O.Nazarova, Pinigina, Bryzgina			2	WC	Roma	6 Sep 87
3:19.60	USA	Leatherwood, S.Howard, Brisco-Hooks, Cheeseborough			1		Walnut	25 Jul 84
3:19.62	GDR	Kotte, Brehmer, Köhn, Koch			1	EP	Torino	5 Aug 79
3:19.66	GDR	Busch, Emmelmann, Neubauer, Müller			1	v FRG	Düsseldorf	20 Jun 88
3:19.73	GDR	K.Walther, Busch, Koch, Rübsam			1	WC	Helsinki	14 Aug 83
3:19.83	GDR	Rübsam, Steuk, Wöckel, Koch			1	EP	Zagreb	16 Aug 81
3:20.10	GDR	Emmelmann, Busch, Neubauer, Müller			2	EP	Moskva	18 Aug 85
3:20.12	URS	Prorochenko, Goyshchik, Zyuskova, I.Nazarova			1	OG	Moskva	1 Aug 80
3:20.15	USA	Stevens,.Dixon, Miles, Leatherwood			2	WC	Tokyo	1 Sep 91
3:20.20	CIS	Ruzina, Dzhigalova, Nazarova, Bryzgina			1	OG	Barcelona	8 Aug 92
3:20.21	GDR	Emmelmann, Busch, Müller, Neubauer			1	v URS	Erfurt	23 Jun 85
3:20.23	GDR	Siemon, Busch, Rübsam, Koch			1	v USA	Karl-Marx-Stadt	10 Jul 82
3:20.32	TCH	Kocembová, Moravcíková, Matejkovicová, Kratochvílová			2	WC	Helsinki	14 Aug 83
3:20.35	GDR	Löwe, Krug, Lathan, Koch			2	OG	Moskva	1 Aug 80
3:20.37	GDR	Kotte, Brehmer, Köhn, Koch			1	WP	Montreal	24 Aug 79
	(30 performances by 4 nations)							
3:21.21	CAN	Crooks, Richardson, Killingbeck, Payne			2	OG	Los Angeles	11 Aug 84
3:21.94	UKR	Dzhigalova, Olizarenko, Pinigina, Vladykina			1	URSCh	Kiev	17 Jul 86
3:22.01	GBR	Hanson, Smith, Gunnell, Keough			4	WC	Tokyo	1 Sep 91
3:22.49	FRG	Thimm, Arendt, Thomas, Abt			4	OG	Seoul	1 Oct 88
3:23.13	JAM	Richards, Thomas, Rattray-Williams, Powell			5	OG	Seoul	1 Oct 88
3:24.28	Hebei (CHN)	An X, Bai X, Cao C, Ma Y			1	NG	Beijing	13 Sep 93
	(10)							
3:24.45	NGR	Yusuf, Onyali, Bakare, Opara			5	WC	Tokyo	1 Sep 91
3:24.65	POL	Kasprzyk, Wojdecka, Kapusta, Blaszak			3	EC	Stuttgart	31 Aug 86
3:24.91	CUB	Duporte, Limonta, McLeon, Quirot			2	PAG	Habana	11 Aug 91
3:25.16	FRA	Ficher, Dorsile, Elien, Pérec			5	EC	Split	1 Sep 90
3:25.56	AUS	Canty, Burnard, Rendina, Nail			4	OG	Montreal	31 Jul 76
3:25.7a	FIN	Eklund, Pursiainen, Wilmi, Salin			2	EC	Roma	8 Sep 74
3:25.81	BUL	Ilieva, Stamenova, Penkova, Damyanova			1	v Hun,Pol	Sofia	24 Jul 83
3:27.54	LIT	Navickaite, Valiuliene, Mendzoryte, Ambraziene			3	SPA	Moskva	22 Jun 83
3:27.57	ESP	Merino, Lacambra, Myers, Ferrer			7	WC	Tokyo	1 Sep 91
3:27.74	ROM	Korodi, Lazarciuc, Samungi, Tarita			4	OG	Moskva	1 Aug 80
	(20)							
3:27.86	HUN	Orosz, Forgács, Tóth, Pál			5	OG	Moskva	1 Aug 80
3:28.52	SUI	Burkart, Zürcher/Scalabrin, Brillante, Lüthi			8	WC	Stuttgart	22 Aug 93
3:28.56	BLS	Kupriyanovich, Ledovskaya, Kurochkina, Kalinnikova			4	URSCh	Tallinn	7 Jul 88
3:28.94A	KEN	Shitandayi, Wanjiru, Kavaya, Chepkurui			2	AfrG	Nairobi	12 Aug 87
3:29.22A	BRA	Montalvão, Oliveira, Telles, Figueiredo			1	IbAmC	Ciudad México	24 Jul 88
3:29.38	POR	Moreira, Coelho, Amaral, Jardim			4h2	OG	Barcelona	7 Aug 92
3:30.2	LAT	Dundare, Shtula, Barkane, Klimovich			1		Moskva	30 Jul 75
3:30.22A	RSA	Botes, Naude, Bothma, Armstrong			1		Johannesburg	18 Apr 86
3:30.7'	BEL	Alaerts, Berg, Michel, Wallez			5h2	OG	Moskva	31 Jul 80
3:30.82	ITA	Lombardo, Campana, Masullo, Rossi			6	OG	Los Angeles	11 Aug 84
	(30)							

4 x 800 METRES RELAY

Mark	Team	Name	Pos	Meet	Venue	Date
7:50.17	USSR	Olizarenko, Gurina, Borisova, Podyalovskaya	1		Moskva	5 Aug 84
7:51.62	USSR II	Ruchayeva, Agletdinova, Zvagintseva, Zhukova	2		Moskva	5 Aug 84
7:52.4	USSR	Providovhina, Gerasimova, Styrkina, Kazankina	1		Podolsk	16 Aug 76
7:54.10	GDR	Zinn, Hoffmeister, Weiss, Klapezynski	1	NC	Karl-Marx-Stadt	6 Aug 76
7:56.6	RSFSR (URS)		1	NC	Donyetsk	8 Sep 80
7:56.6	Ukraine (URS)		2	NC	Donyetsk	8 Sep 80
7:56.9	Leningrad (URS)		3	NC	Donyetsk	8 Sep 80
7:57.08	RUS	Kuznetsova, Betekhtiina, Burkanova, Masterkova	1	EurR	Portsmouth	5 Jun 93
7:57.21	ROM	Slageanu, Constantin, Beclea, Itcou	2	EurR	Portsmouth	5 Jun 93
7:58.5	LIT	Kastetskaya, Bislyte, Simonaviciute, Baikauskaite		URSCh	Donyetsk	8 Sep 80

3000 METRES TRACK WALK

Mark		Name	Nat	Born	Pos	Venue	Date
11:48.24	Ileana	Salvador	ITA	16.1.62	1	Padova	29 Aug 93
11:51.26	Kerry	Junna-Saxby	AUS	2.6.61	1	Melbourne	7 Feb 91
11:52.01	Beate	Anders	GER	4.2.68	1	Lapinlahti	27 Jun 93
11:52.71		Junna-Saxby			1	Melbourne	25 Feb 93
11:54.8	Yelena	Nikolayeva	RUS	17.3.66	1	Alitus	16 May 92

Mark Wind	Name		Nat	Born	Pos	Meet	Venue	Date
11:56.40	Elisabetta	Perrone	ITA	9.7.68	2		Padova	29 Aug 93
11:57.08		Junna-Saxby			1		Christchurch	16 Jan 93
11:59.41		Salvador			1		Caserta	11 Jun 92
11:59.60	Sari	Essayah	FIN	21.2.67	2		Lapinlahti	27 Jun 93
12:01.0+		Anders			1	vURS	Rostock	23 Jun 90
	(10/6)							
12:09.91	Sada	Eidikite/Buksniene	LIT	22.6.67	1mx		Lapinlahti	25 Jun 89
12:16.00	Katarzyna	Radtke	POL	31.8.69	1		Sopot	1 May 93
12:22.09	Gabrielle	Blythe	AUS	9.3.69	2	NEC	Melbourne	24 Feb 94
12:25.05	Madelein	Svensson	SWE	20.7.69	1		Stockholm	8 Jul 93
12:25.4	Anne-Marie	Judkins	NZL	1.3.64	1		Östersund	1 Jun 92
	(10)							
12:26.17	Natalya	Serbinenko	UKR	27.1.59	2		Udine	28 Jun 92
12:26.87	Anne	Manning	AUS	13.11.59	3	NEC	Melbourne	24 Feb 94
12:27.0+	Alina	Ivanova	RUS	25.6.69	1	vGDR	Bryansk	15 Jul 89
12:27.74	Jane	Saville	AUS	5.11.74	2		Melbourne	25 Feb 93
Indoor marks								
11:44.00	Alina	Ivanova	RUS	25.6.69	1		Moskva	7 Feb 92
11:49.73	Yelena	Nikolayeva	RUS	1.2.66	1	WI	Toronto	13 Mar 93
11:49.99		A Ivanova			1	EI	Genova	29 Feb 92
11:50.90	Beate	Anders/Gummelt	GER	4.2.68	1	WI	Sevilla	9 Mar 91
11:53.23		Salvador			2	EI	Genova	29 Feb 92
11:53.82		Junna-Saxby			3	WI	Toronto	13 Mar 93
11:54.32	Anna Rita	Sidoti	ITA	25.7.69	1	EI	Paris	12 Feb 94
11:55.35		Salvador			4	WI	Toronto	13 Mar 93
11:55.41		Anders			3	EI	Genova	29 Feb 92
11:56.0		Anders			1	NC	Dortmund	17 Feb 91
11:56.01		Gummelt			2	EI	Paris	12 Feb 94
11:57.11		A Ivanova			1	CIS Ch	Moskva	2 Feb 92
11:57.14		Anders			4	WI	Toronto	13 Mar 93
11:57.48	Yelena	Arshintseva	RUS	5.4.71	3	EI	Paris	12 Feb 94
11:57.49		Nikolayeva			4	EI	Paris	12 Feb 94
11:58.36		Salvador			1		Genova	13 Feb 93
11:59.36		Anders			1	EI	Glasgow	4 Mar 90
	(17 performances)							
12:04.46	Leonarda	Yukhnevich	BLS	1.5.63	5	EI	Paris	12 Feb 94
12:05.49	Olga	Krishtop	RUS	8.10.57	1	WI	Indianapolis	6 Mar 87
12:07.70	Olga	Kardopoltseva	BLS	11.9.66	4	WI	Sevilla	9 Mar 91
12:08.06	Yelena	Sayko	RUS	24.12.67	3	NC	Moskva	27 Feb 93
12:10.43	Victoria	Lina	ROM	8.3.65	5	EI	Genova	29 Feb 92
12:11.48	Vera	Makolova	RUS	17.2.66	1	NC	Chelyabinsk	3 Feb 90
12:12.51	Leonarda	Yuknevich	BLS	1.5.63	2		Moskva	7 Feb 92
12:12.98	Nadezhda	Ryashkina	RUS	22.1.67	4	WI	Budapest	4 Mar 89
12:13.67	Sada	Buksnienė	LIT	22.6.67	6	EI	Genova	29 Feb 92
12:14.01	Madelein	Svensson	SWE	20.7.69	1		Liévin	25 Jan 92
12:14.28	Natalya	Serbinenko'	UKR	27.1.59	3	NC	Chelyabinsk	3 Feb 90
12:14.74	Pier-Carola	Pagani	ITA	10.11.63	8	EI	Genova	29 Feb 92
12:15.39	Lidiya	Fesenko	RUS	5.10.62	1		Budapest	26 Feb 91
12:15.48	Olga	Leonenko	UKR	13.2.70	1	NC	Kiev	13 Feb 94
12:15.81	Tatyana	Ragozina	UKR	3.9.64	1	NC	Kiev	14 Feb 93
12:16.83	Olimpiada	Ivanova	RUS	5.5.70	3		Moskva	4 Feb 94
12:18.83	Tamara	Surovtseva	BLS	12.6.60	4	NC	Chelyabinsk	3 Feb 90
12:19.08	Ildikó	Ilyés	HUN	3.7.62	2		Budapest	16 Feb 91
12:19.57	Yelena	Gruzinova	RUS	67	1		Moskva	2 Feb 93
12:20.79	Debbie	Lawrence	USA	15.10.61	3h1	WI	Toronto	12 Mar 93
12:20.86	Yulia	Korolyova	RUS	25.7.73	2		Moskva	2 Feb 93
12:21.07	Larisa	Ramazanova	RUS	71	4		Moskva	4 Feb 94
12:21.63	Rimma	Makarova	RUS	18.7.63	3	CIS Ch	Moskva	2 Feb 92
12:23.7	Tamara	Kovalenko	RUS	5.6.64	1		Moskva	28 Jan 93
12:24.04	Niorica	Cimpan	ROM	22.3.72	9	EI	Paris	12 Feb 94
12:26.25	Mária	Rosza	HUN	12.2.67	2	vAUT	Wien	14 Feb 91
12:26.37	Yekaterina	Samoylenko	UKR	23.1.63	1		Budapest	5 Feb 93
12:26.69	Natalya	Spiridonova	RUS	24.4.63	1	NC	Volgograd	10 Feb 88
12:27.0	Kathrin	Born	GDR	4.12.70	2		Potsdam	28 Jan 89
12:27.20	Anikó	Szebenszky	HUN	12.8.65	5	WI	Budapest	4 Mar 89

5000 METRES TRACK WALK

Mark Wind		Name	Nat	Born	Pos	Meet	Venue	Date
20:07.52	Beate	Anders	GDR	4.2.68	1	vSU	Rostock	23 Jun 90
20:17.19	Kerry	Junna-Saxby	AUS	2.6.61	1		Sydney	14 Jan 90
20:22.9 mx		Junna-Saxby			mx		Canberra	28 Feb 92
20:27.59	Ileana	Salvador	ITA	16.1.62	1		Trento	3 Jun 89
20:30.0		Junna-Saxby			1	NC	Brisbane	6 Mar 93
20:32.75		Saxby			1	NC	Brisbane	19 Mar 89
20:36.96		Saxby			1	CGT	Sydney	3 Dec 89
20:37.7		Jin Bingjie	CHN	1.4.71	1	NC	Hefei	3 Mar 90
20:38.0		Chen Yueling	CHN	1.4.68	2	NC	Hefei	3 Mar 90
20:38.14		Junna-Saxby			1		Sydney	20 Feb 93
20:38.65	Sari	Essayah	FIN	21.2.67	1	NC	Mikkeli	31 Jul 93
20:40.06		Junna-Saxby			1		Sydney	20 Feb 94
20:40.6	Olga	Kardopoltseva	BLS	11.9.66	1		Alushta	5 May 90
20:42.31		Salvador			1	NC	Bologna	23 Jun 92
20:44.02		Essayah			1	NC	Helsinki	28 Jul 91
20:45.03		Junna-Saxby			1	NC	Sydney	11 Mar 93
20:45.32		Saxby			1	NC	Perth	27 Mar 88
20:45.6		Salvador			1		Torino	23 May 92
20:46.91		Anders			1	NC	Dresden	19 Aug 90
20:48.55		Salvador			1	NC	Bologna	2 Aug 93
	(20/7)							
20:49.4+	Nadezhda	Ryashkina	RUS	22.1.67	1=	GWG	Seattle	24 Jul 90
20:50.3		Fan Xiaoling	CHN	29.3.71	2	NC	Zhengzhou	3 Mar 91
20:50.60	Alina	Ivanova	RUS	25.6.69	1	vGDR	Bryansk	15 Jul 89
	(10)							
20:51.96	Katarzyna	Radtke	POL	31.8.69	1		Sopot	20 Jun 93
20:52.24	Tamara	Surovtseva	BLS	12.6.60	2	vGDR	Rostock	23 Jun 90
20:53.71	Elisabetta	Perrone	ITA	9.7.68	2	NC	Bologna	2 Aug 93
20:56.7		Zuo Xiaohui	CHN	.71	4	NC	Zhengzhou	3 Mar 91
20:59.7	Anne-Marie	Judkins	NZL	1.3.64	2		Brunflo	28 Jun 92
21:00.80	Yelena	Nikolayeva	RUS	17.3.66	1		Schwechat	12 Jun 91
21:01.8	Susana	Feitor	POR	28.1.75	1	SGP	Fana	8 May 93
21:02.6		Li Jingxue	CHN	12.4.71	2		Anshan	2 Sep 89
21:03.8		Xiong Yan	CHN	1.4.67	3	NC	Hefei	3 Mar 90
21:06.7		Sun Yan	CHN	4.5.73	5	NC	Zhengzhou	3 Mar 91
	(20)							
21:09.26	Madelein	Svensson	SWE	20.7.69	2		København	25 Aug 92
21:13.16		Cui Yingzi	CHN	26.3.71	1		Jinan	30 Oct 88
21:15.4	Maria Grazia	Orsani	ITA	11.6.69	1		Avellino	8 May 93
21:18.1		Wang Yili	CHN	4.4.71	3		Anshan	2 Sep 89
21:18.39	Yelena	Arshintseva	RUS	71	1		Schwechat	1 Jul 92
21:19.2	Anna Rita	Sidoti	ITA	25.7.69	1		Messina	25 Apr 92
21:19.81	Yelena	Sayko	RUS	15.5.66	1		København	25 Aug 92
21:20.03		Gao Hongmiao	CHN	17.3.74	1	WJ	Seoul	20 Sep 92
21:20.2		Yan Hong	CHN	23.10.66	1		Xinglong	29 Mar 87
21:20.42	Natalya	Spiridonova	RUS	6.4.63	3	vGDR	Rostock	23 Jun 90
	(30)							
21:20.63	Kathrin	Born	GER	4.12.70	2	NC	Hannover	27 Jul 91
21:22.6	Tatyana	Ragozina	UKR	3.9.64	1		Alushta	21 Feb 93
21:24.71		Guan Ping	CHN	1.2.66	1		Beijing	8 Oct 89
21:24.76	Mária	Rosza	HUN	12.2.67	1		Budapest	18 Aug 90
21:26.1		Kong Yan	CHN	5.4.71	5	NC	Hefei	3 Mar 90
21:26.6mx	Anne	Manning	AUS	13.11.59	mx		Sydney	12 Feb 94
	21:46.43				2	NC	Sydney	11 Mar 94
21:27.9		Liu Caimei	CHN	.71	7	NC	Hefei	3 Mar 90
21:28.17	Theresa	Vaill	USA	20.11.62	1	PennR	Philadelphia	24 Apr 93
21:29.8		Ni Fenglian	CHN	18.11.70			Anshan	2 Sep 89
21:30.92	Oksana	Shchastnaya	URS	24.4.71	1	EJ	Birmingham	7 Aug 87
21:31.15	Natalya	Serbinenko	UKR	27.1.59	1		Kiev	15 Jul 92
21:32.00	Debbi	Lawrence	USA	15.10.61	1	PennR	Philadelphia	25 Apr 92
	(40)							
Unconfirmed								
21:21.9	Kristin	Andreassen	NOR	15.2.68	1		Västerås	19 Jul 90
21:25.0	Tan Lihong		CHN	13.2.73				92

WOMEN All-time

Mark	Wind	Name		Nat	Born	Pos	Meet	Venue	Date
Indoor marks									
21:22.6		Tamara	Kovalenko	RUS	5.6.64	1		Moskva	26 Feb 92
21:23.8		Zinaida	Sviridenko	RUS	24.12.68	2		Moskva	26 Feb 92
21:25.8		Rimma	Makarova	RUS	18.7.63	3		Moskva	26 Feb 92
21:27.8		Maria	Kozneva	RUS	18.5.68	4		Moskva	26 Feb 92

5 KILOMETRES ROAD WALK *Leading performances*

Mark	Name		Nat	Born	Pos	Meet	Venue	Date
20:25	Kerry	Junna-Saxby	AUS	2.6.61	1		Hildesheim	10 Jun 89
20:26	Ileana	Salvador	ITA	16.1.62	1		Barcelona	5 Apr 92
20:34		Saxby			1		Hildesheim	24 Sep 87
20:36	Alina	Ivanova	RUS	25.6.69	1		L'Hospitalet	21 Apr 91
20:37	Olga	Kardopoltseva	BLS	11.9.66	2		L'Hospitalet	21 Apr 91
20:38	Vera	Makolova	RUS	17.2.66	1	NC	Leningrad	5 Aug 89
20:40		Saxby			1		L'Hospitalet	6 May 90
20:43		Saxby			1		L'Hospitalet	10 May 92
20:43		Junna-Saxby			1		L'Hospitalet	12 May 92
20:44		Salvador			1	WSG	Duisburg	29 Aug 89
Athletes with marks superior to 5000m track bests								
20:53	Sada	Eidikite'	LIT	22.6.67	2		Hildesheim	10 Jun 89
21:04	Tamara	Kovalenko	RUS	25.4.64	1		Odessa	20 Aug 88
21:04	Yelena	Bronyukova	RUS	.67	2	NC	Leningrad	5Aug 89
21:13	Yelena	Sayko	RUS	24.12.67	4	NC	Leningrad	5 Aug 89
21:22	Pier-Carola	Pagani	ITA	10.11.63	2		L'Hospitalet	6 May 90
21:25	Maria	Reyes Sobrino	ESP	6.1.67	1		La Coruña	16 May 87
21:26	Irina	Shumak/Tolstik	BLS	4.12.65	2		Odessa	20 Aug 88
21:26	Yekaterina	Samoylenko	UKR	23.1.63	1		Gross-Gerau	15 Aug 92
21:30+	Natalya	Serbinenko'	UKR	27.1.59	1k		Sochi	19 Feb 89
21:31	Lidiya	Fesenko	RUS	5.10.62	2		Gross-Gerau	15 Aug 92
21:32	Leonarda	Yukhnevich	BLS	1.5.63	5	NC	Leningrad	5 Aug 89

10 KILOMETRES WALK t = track

Mark	Name		Nat	Born	Pos	Meet	Venue	Date
41:30	Ileana	Salvador	ITA	16.1.62	1	4-N	Livorno	10 Jul 93
41:30	Kerry	Junna-Saxby	AUS	2.6.61	1	NC	Canberra	27 Aug 88
41:48		Li Chunxiu	CHN	.8.69	1	NG	Beijing	8 Sep 93
41:56	Elisabeta	Perrone	ITA	9.7.68	2	4-N	Livorno	10 Jul 93
41:56.23t	Nadezhda	Ryashkina	RUS	22.1.67	1	GWG	Seattle	24 Jul 90
41:57		Gao Hongmiao	CHN	8.7.74	2	NG	Beijing	8 Sep 93
41:57.22t		Junna-Saxby			2	GWG	Seattle	24 Jul 90
42:03	Yelena	Arshintseva	RUS	5.4.71	1		Adler	14 Feb 93
42:04	Yelena	Sayko	RUS	24.12.67	2		Adler	14 Feb 93
42:07		Salvador			1		Sesto San Giovanni	1 May 92
42:11.5t	Beate	Anders	GER	4.2.68	1	SGP	Fana	15 May 92
42:13.7t	Madelein	Svensson (10)	SWE	20.7.69	2	SGP	Fana	15 May 92
42:14.2t		Saxby			1mx		Canberra	26 Jan 88
42:16	Alina	Ivanova	RUS	25.6.69	1		Novopolotsk	27 May 89
42:17		A Ivanova			1		Sochi	17 Feb 91
42:22		Sayko			1		Alitus	5 May 91
42:22.6t		Junna-Saxby			1	SGP	Fana	8 May 93
42:23.7t		Salvador			2	SGP	Fana	8 May 93
42:23.9t		Junna-Saxby			3	SGP	Fana	15 May 92
42:24	Olympiada	Ivanova	RUS	5.5.70	3	4-N	Livorno	10 Jul 93
42:25.2t		Saxby			1	SGP	Fana	26 May 90
42:26		Wang Yan	CHN	3.5.71	1		Shenzhen	18 Feb 93
42:26.29t		Junna-Saxby			1		Sydney	10 Jan 93
42:29		Sayko			2	NC-w	Sochi	16 Feb 91
42:29.4t		Anders			2	SGP	Fana	26 May 90
42:30 mx		Saxby			1 mx		Melbourne	4 May 91
42:32		Gao Hongmiao			2		Shenzhen	18 Feb 93
42:34		Ryashkina			1		Moskva	26 May 90
42:34	Yelena	Gruzinova	RUS	67	3		Adler	14 Feb 93
42:37		Junna-Saxby			2		Sesto San Giovanni	1 May 92
42:37		O Ivanova			4		Adler	14 Feb 93
42:37.0t	Sari	Essayah	FIN	21.2.67	3	SGP	Fana	8 May 93
	(32/15)							
42:40	Yelena	Nikolayeva	RUS	17.3.66	1		Moskva	26 Apr 92

Mark Wind	Name		Nat	Born	Pos	Meet	Venue	Date
42:41	Anna Rita	Sidoti	ITA	25.7.69	1		Eschborn	13 Jun 93
42:44	Irina	Strakhova	RUS	4.3.59	3		Sochi	17 Feb 91
42:44		Long Yuwen	CHN	.8.75	3		Shenzhen	18 Feb 93
42:44	Olga	Kardopoltseva	BLS	11.9.66	2		Alitus	5 May 91
	(20)							
42:45	??	Li Yuxin	CHN	73	4		Shenzhen	18 Feb 93
42:45.45t		Saxby			1mx		Sydney	14 Jan 89
42:46	Tamara	Kovalenko	RUS	25.4.64	1		Moskva	29 Jul 90
42:46		Wang Yan			3	NG	Beijing	8 Sep 93
42:46.7t		Chen Yueling	CHN	1.4.68	2	NC	Jinan	15 Mar 92
42:46.7t		Cui Yingzi	CHN	26.1.71	1	NC	Jinan	15 Mar 92
42:47	Larisa	Ramazanova	RUS	71	2		Eschborn	13 Jun 93
42:47		Liu Hongyu	CHN	1.12.75	5		Shenzhen	18 Feb 93
42:47.4t	Katarzyna	Radtke	POL	31.8.69	4	SGP	Fana	8 May 93
42:50		Gu Yan	CHN	17.3.74	4	NG	Beijing	8 Sep 93
42:50.0t		Guan Ping	CHN	1.2.66	5	NC	Jinan	15 Mar 92
42:52	Lidiya	Fesenko	RUS	5.10.62	4	NC-w	Sochi	16 Feb 91
	(30)							
42:53.9t		Tan Lihong	CHN	13.2.73	6	NC	Jinan	15 Mar 92
42:57		Zhang Qinghua	CHN	6.2.73	6		Shenzhen	18 Feb 93
42:58	Nina	Alyushenko	RUS	.68	5	NC-w	Sochi	16 Feb 91
43:01.6t	Anne-Marie	Judkins	NZL	1.3.64	2		Örnsköldsvik	4 Jul 92
43:04	Vera	Makolova	RUS	17.2.66	1	NC	Leningrad	4 Aug 89
43:07		Song Lijuan	CHN	.2.76	6	NG	Beijing	8 Sep 93
43:09.4t		Fan Xiaoling	CHN	14.5.71	7	NC	Jinan	15 Mar 92
43:11	Olga	Krishtop'	RUS	8.10.57	3	NC	Moskva	26 May 90
43:11.4t		Zhu Xiaolan	CHN	1.7.72	9	NC	Jinan	15 Mar 92
43:13	Natalya	Spiridonova	RUS	24.4.63	2		Moskva	29 Jul 90
	(40)							
43:15	Natalya	Misyulya	BLS	14.4.66	4	4-N	Livorno	10 Jul 93
43:15.6t		Jin Bingjie	CHN	1.4.71	1		Anshan	4 Sep 89
43:21	Encarnacion	Granados	ESP	30.1.72	3	WC	Stuttgart	14 Aug 93
43:21	Mária	Rosza	HUN	12.2.67	1		Békéscsaba	28 Aug 93
43:22	Yevgeniya	Guryeva	RUS	12.6.69	4		Moskva	26 Apr 92
43:26	Svetlana	Kaburkina	RUS	3.5.67	1		Bucaresti	19 Jun 88
43:27	Graciella	Mendoza	MEX	23.3.63	1		Hull	8 Oct 89
43:28		Kong Yan	CHN	.4.71	8	NG	Beijing	8 Sep 93
43:28+	Gabrielle	Blythe	AUS	9.3.68	2k		Hawkesbury	10 Jul 93
43:30		Sun Yan	CHN	.9.73	8		Shenzhen	18 Feb 93
	(50)							
Other track bests								
42:47.6		Li Chunxiu	CHN	13.8.69	3	NC	Jinan	15 Mar 92
42:49.7		Gao Hongmao	CHN	17.3.74	4	NC	Jinan	15 Mar 92
43:01.0		Wang Yan	CHN	3.5.71	1		Shenzhen	21 Feb 93
43:10.4		Zhang Qinghua	CHN	6.2.73	8	NC	Jinan	15 Mar 92
43:13.5	Tamara	Kovalenko	RUS	25.4.64	1		Bryansk	9 Sep 89
43:15.1		Gu Yan	CHN	.11.73	10	NC	Jinan	15 Mar 92
43:33.7	Anna Rita	Sidoti	ITA	25.7.69	2		Torino	4 Apr 93

20 KILOMETRES WALK

Mark Wind	Name		Nat	Born	Pos	Meet	Venue	Date
1:29:40	Kerry	Junna-Saxby	AUS	2.6.61	1		Värnamo	13 May 88
1:30:42	Olga	Kardopoltseva	BLS	11.9.66	1		Kaliningrad	29 Apr 90
1:31:53	Ileana	Salvador	ITA	16.1.62	1	NC	Baia Domizia	25 Sep 93
1:31:58	Tamara	Romanova	RUS	2.7.67	1	CIS Ch	Moskva	25 Apr 92
1:31:59		Kardopoltseva			1		Yevpatoriya	30 Sep 89
1:31:59	Tamara	Surovtseva	BLS	12.6.60	2		Kaliningrad	29 Apr 90
1:32:05	Olga	Volkova	RUS	11.11.64	2	CIS Ch	Moskva	25 Apr 92
1:32:21	Lyudmila	Lyubomirova	RUS	62	3	CIS Ch	Moskva	25 Apr 92
1:32:33	Nadezhda	Ryashkina	RUS	22.1.67	1	NC	Mogilyov	4 Sep 88
1:32:38	Marina	Smyslova	RUS	5.6.66	1		Novosibirsk	14 Sep 91
1:32:44		Saxby			1	NC	Melbourne	20 Aug 89
1:32:51		Saxby			1	NC	Canberra	14 Jun 87
1:32:51	Zinaida	Sviridenko	RUS	24.12.68	4	CIS Ch	Moskva	26 Apr 92
	(13/10)							
1:33:03	Olympiada	Ivanova	RUS	5.5.70	1		Yaroslavl	6 Aug 93
1:33:25	Tatyana	Ragozina	UKR	3.9.64	3		Novosibirsk	14 Sep 91

Mark	Wind	Name		Nat	Born	Pos	Meet	Venue	Date
1:33:37		Elisabetta	Perrone	ITA	9.7.68	2	NC	Baia Domizia	25 Sep 93
1:33:39		Marina	Smyslova	RUS	5.6.66	1		Novopolotsk	16 Sep 90
1:34:03		Vera	Makolova	RUS	17.2.66	2	NC	Mogilyov	4 Sep 88
1:34:03		Yelena	Fyodorova	RUS	64	5	CIS Ch	Moskva	26 Apr 92
1:34:16		Inna	Galyanina	RUS	.66	2		Yevpatoriya	30 Sep 89
1:34:27		Anne	Manning	AUS	13.11.59	1	NC	Hawkesbury	10 Jul 93
1:34:31		Irina	Strakhova	RUS	4.3.59	1		Värnamo	29 May 87
1:34:31		Tatyana (20)	Titova	RUS	25.8.69	1		Alushta	4 Oct 87

WOMEN'S NAME CHANGES

A list of women, appearing in the all-time lists, who have competed with distinction at two or more names. Mostly indicated by ' in the lists.Original name shown in the left-hand column, married name in the right.

Agapova	Peleshenko	Kemenchendzhi	Merchuk	Reichenbach	Müller I.
Agletdinova	Kotovich	Khamitova	Samolyenko	Reichstein	Bienias
Anders	Gummelt		- Dorovskikh	Reidick	Zaczkiewicz
Andersen	Waitz	Khristova S.	Moneva	Riefstahl	Oschkenat
Andrei	Marasescu	Kirszenstein	Szewinska	Rieger S.	Günther S.
Armstrong E.	de Klerk	Kiryukhina	Tsyoma	Rienstra	Sommer
Auerswald	Lange I.	Klapezynski	Bruns	Robertson	Boyd
Barkusky	Weiss	Kocembová	Slaninová	Rodina	Gulyayeva
Bartonová	Silhavá	Kokonova	Khlopotnova	Ropo	Junnila
Benoit	Samuelson	Kolenchukova	Yermolovich	Röhde	Köhn
Berend	Wakan	Kovarik	Uibel - Siebert	Rübsam	Neubauer
Besprozvannaya	Buraga	Krentser	Bondarenko O.	Sablovskaite	Nazaroviene
Bimbaite	Urbikiene	Kulchunova	Pinigina	Sachse	Gansky
Boxer	Cahill	Künzel	Wujak	Saunders	Nunn
Brehmer	Lathan	Kushenko	Matyusheva	Savinkova	Yermakova
Browne	Ward	Kuznyetsova Y	Nikolayeva	Saxby	Junna
Chesbro	Wohlschlag	Lange A.	Hahmann	Schaller	Klier
Christensen	Kristiansen	Langer	Kalek	Schlaak	Jahl
Chuprina	Knoroz	Livermore	Simpson J.	Schmalfeld	Voigt
Cojocaru	Matei	Ludwigs	Wodars - Grau	Schneider	Müller R.
Cusmir	Stanciu	Lynch E.	McColgan	Schoknecht	Slupianek
Daute	Drechsler	Makeyeva	Styepanova M.	- Briesenick	
Davydova	Burova	Martin L	Ondieki	Sharipova	Serbinenko
Decker	Slaney	Matekovicová	Strnadová	Shulyak	Kravets
Dedner	Brandt	Matsuta	Kurochkina	Siemon	Emmelmann
Derevinskaya	Grigoryeva	McDermott	Wade	Simpson M.	Bothma
Dolzhenko	Krachevskaya	Meissner	Stecher	Smallwood	Cook K.
Droese	Pufe	Meyer M	Hamann	Smith W.	Sly
Duginyets	Panikarovskikh	Mihalache	Vaideanu	Sonntag	Uibel
Eckert	Wöckel	Mityayeva	Byelevskaya	Stetsura	Kokonova
Farmer S.	Patrick	Möbius	Paetz - John	Khlopotnova	
Feuerbach	Ullrich C.	Müller P.	Schersing	Stoica	Pogacean
Gale	Weavers	Mushta	Olizarenko	Stoll	Wartenberg
Garrett	Audain	Naumkina	Bogoslovskaya	Strandvall	Pursiainen
Gîrbea	Ivan C.	Nasonova O.	Antonova	Stropahl	Streidt
Gladisch	Möller	Navickaité	Jeseviciené	Tacu	Craciunescu
Göhler	Neubert	Neumann E.	Fiedler	Taylor A.	Issajenko
Grabner	Mai	Nikitina V.	Komisova	Terpe	Theele
Guzowska	Nowak M.	Nikitina I.	Lebedinskaya	Tiedtke	Greene
Haupt	Hammer	Nowaczyk	Blaszak	Todorova A.	Selenska
Hearnshaw	Telfer	Nygrynová	Strejcková	Tolstykh	Shumak
Helander	Kuusisto	Oelsner	Göhr	Uibel G	Siebert
Helm	Beyer S.	Okolo-Kulak	Yurkova	Ullrich H.	Körner
Helmbold	Gummel	Opitz	Hellmann	Vasilyeva L	Karpova
Hunte	Oakes H.	Payne M.	Wiggins	Vater	Behmer
Ilie	Ivan P.	Petrus	Avdyeyenko	Vinogradova N.	Miromanova
Ionescu	Lengyel M.	Ponomaryova M.	Khromova	Vladykina	Bryzgina
Isaeva	Leseva	Pomoshchnikova	Voronova	Witschas	Ackermann
Joyner	Kersee	Poryvkina	Podkopayeva	Yarets	Krishtop
Kämpfert	Steuk	Privalova	Sergeyeva	Zhupiyeva	Vyasova
Kastetskaya	Ambraziene	Proskuryakova	Rodionova	Zubova	Pavlova T.
Katyukova	Smekhnova	Rafira	Lovin	Zveryova	Kisheyeva
Kazachkova	Sorokina	Redetzky	Henkel		

WORLD JUNIOR WOMEN'S ALL-TIME LISTS

Based on the age regulations introduced for 1988, that is under 20 in year of competition.

100 METRES

Mark	Wind	Name		Nat	Born	Pos	Meet	Venue	Date
10.88	2.0	Marlies	Oelsner	GDR	21.3.58	1	NC	Dresden	1 Jul 77
10.89	1.8	Katrin	Krabbe	GDR	22.11.69	1rB		Berlin	20 Jul 88
11.03	1.7	Silke	Gladisch	GDR	20.6.64	3	OD	Berlin	8 Jun 83
11.08	2.0	Brenda	Morehead	USA	5.10.57	1	FOT	Eugene	21 Jun 76
11.13	2.0	Chandra	Cheeseborough	USA	16.1.59	2	FOT	Eugene	21 Jun 76
11.13	-1.0	Grit	Breuer	GDR	16.2.72	1		Jena	6 Jun 90
11.14		Liliana	Allen	CUB	24.5.70	1		Habana	1 Jun 89
11.14	1.7	Marion	Jones	USA	12.10.75	1		Norwalk	6 Jun 92
11.17A	0.6	Wenda	Vereen	USA	24.4.66	4	USOF	Air.Force Academy	3 Jul 83
11.18	-0.8	Silvia	Chivas	CUB	10.9.54	1h1	OG	München	1 Sep 72
11.18	-0.4	Diana	Dietz	GDR	30.8.69	1	WJ	Sudbury	28 Jul 88
11.18	1.1	Nicole	Mitchell	JAM	5.6.74	3	NC	Kingston	2 Jul 93
Uncertain timing									
10.99	1.9	Natalya	Bochina	RUS	4.1.62	2		Leningrad	3 Jun 80
Wind assisted									
10.97	3.3	Gesine	Walther	GDR	6.10.62	4	NC	Cottbus	16 Jul 80
11.02	2.1	Nicole	Mitchell	JAM	5.6.74	1	Mutual	Kingston	1 May 93
11.06	2.2	Brenda	Morehead	USA	5.10.57	1s	FOT	Eugene	21 Jun 76
11.09		Angela	Williams	TRI	15.5.65	1		Nashville	11 Apr 84
11.12		Marion	Jones	USA	12.10.75	1h		Cerritos	31 May 91
11.13	2.2	Beverly	Kinch	GBR	14.1.64	1	WUG	Edmonton	6 Jul 83
Hand timed									
10.9A	-0.8	Liliana	Allen	CUB	24.5.70	1	AmCp	Bogota	12 Aug 89
10.8wA		Margaret	Bailes	USA	23.1.51	1		Flagstaff	29 Sep 68

200 METRES

Mark	Wind	Name		Nat	Born	Pos	Meet	Venue	Date
22.19	1.5	Natalya	Bochina	RUS	4.1.62	2	OG	Moskva	30 Jul 80
22.37	1.3	Sabine	Rieger	GDR	6.11.63	2	vURS	Cottbus	26 Jun 82
22.42	0.4	Gesine	Walther	GDR	6.10.62	1		Potsdam	29 Aug 81
22.45	0.5	Grit	Breuer	GDR	16.2.72	2	ASV	Köln	8 Sep 91
22.51	2.0	Katrin	Krabbe	GDR	22.11.69	3		Berlin	13 Sep 88
22.52	1.2	Mary	Onyali	NGR	3.2.68	6	WC	Roma	3 Sep 87
22.58	0.8	Marion	Jones	USA	12.10.75	4	TAC	New Orleans	28 Jun 92
22.70		Marita	Koch	GDR	18.2.57	1		Halle	15 May 76
22.70A	1.9	Kathy	Smallwood	GBR	3.5.60	2	WUG	Ciudad México	12 Sep 79
22.72	1.3	Silke	Gladisch	GDR	20.6.64	3	NC	Karl-Marx-Stadt	18 Jun 83
22.74A	2.0	Raelene	Boyle	AUS	24.6.51	2	OG	Ciudad México	18 Oct 68
22.76A		Evette	de Klerk	RSA	21.8.65	1		Sasolburg	21 Apr 84
Wind assisted									
22.34	2.3	Kathrin	Krabbe	GDR	22.11.69	1	WJ	Sudbury	30 Jul 88
22.49	2.3	Brenda	Morehead	USA	5.10.57	1	FOT	Eugene	24 Jun 76
22.53	2.5	Valerie	Brisco	USA	6.7.60	2	AAU	Walnut	17 Jun 79
22.64	2.3	Chandra	Cheeseborough	USA	16.1.59	2	FOT	Eugene	24 Jun 76
22.75	2.5	Wendy	Vereen	USA	24.4.66	1		Los Angeles	14 Apr 84

400 METRES

Mark	Wind	Name		Nat	Born	Pos	Meet	Venue	Date
49.42		Grit	Breuer	GDR	16.2.72	2	WC	Tokyo	27 Aug 91
49.77		Christina	Brehmer	GDR	28.2.58	1		Dresden	9 May 76
50.19		Marita	Koch	GDR	18.2.57	3	OD	Berlin	10 Jul 76
50.59		Fatima	Yusuf	NGR	2.5.71	1	HGP	Budapest	5 Aug 90
50.86		Charity	Opara	NGR	20.5.72	2		Bologna	7 Sep 91
50.87		Denean	Howard	USA	5.10.64	1	TAC	Knoxville	20 Jun 82
50.87		Magdalena	Nedelcu	ROM	12.5.74	1	NC-j	Bucuresti	31 Jul 92
50.90		Sheila	Ingram	USA	23.3.57	3s1	OG	Montreal	28 Jul 76
50.92		Margit	Sinzel	GDR	17.6.58	5	OD	Berlin	10 Jul 76
50.92		Sandie	Richards	JAM	6.11.68	1		Odessa	16 May 87
50.96		Maicel	Malone	USA	12.6.69	1s1	FOT	Indianapolis	17 Jul 88
50.98		Dagmar	Rübsam	GDR	3.6.62	2	NC	Jena	8 Aug 81
Hand-timed									
50.1			Brehmer			1	Znam	Sochi	25 Apr 76
50.5		Fatima	Yusuf	NGR	2.5.71	1	NC	Lagos	25 Aug 90

800 METRES

Mark	Wind	Name	Nat	Born	Pos	Meet	Venue	Date
1:57.18		Wang Yuan		CHN	8.4.76		2h2	NG
Beijing	8 Sep 93							
1:57.45	Hildegard	Ullrich	GDR	20.12.59	5	EC	Praha	31 Aug 78
1:57.63	Maria	Mutola	MOZ	27.10.72	4	WC	Tokyo	26 Aug 91
1:57.77		Lu Yi	CHN	10.4.74	4	NG	Beijing	9 Sep 93
1:57.86	Katrin	Wühn	GDR	19.11.65	1		Celje	5 May 84
1:58.18	Marion	Hübner	GDR	29.9.62	2		Erfurt	2 Aug 81
1:58.24	Christine	Wachtel	GDR	6.1.65	3		Potsdam	25 May 84
1:58.37	Gabriela	Sedláková	TCH	2.3.68	4	ISTAF	Berlin	21 Aug 87
1:59.13	Maria	Pîntea	ROM	10.8.67	1		Bucuresti	15 Jun 86
1:59.17	Birte	Bruhns	GDR	4.11.70	1		Berlin	20 Jul 88
1:59.32	Martina	Kämpfert	GDR	11.11.59	2	NC	Leipzig	1 Jul 78
1:59.42	Rommy	Schmidt	GDR	20.6.59	3		Potsdam	19 Aug 78

1000 METRES

Mark	Wind	Name	Nat	Born	Pos	Meet	Venue	Date
2:35.4	Irina	Nikitina	RUS	16.1.61	5	Kuts	Podolsk	5 Aug 79
2:35.4	Katrin	Wühn	GDR	19.11.65	3		Potsdam	12 Jul 84
2:36.36	Margrit	Klinger	FRG	22.6.60	2	ISTAF	Berlin	17 Aug 79
2:37.2	Véronique	Renties	FRA	3.7.60	2		Nice	19 Aug 79

1500 METRES

Mark	Wind	Name	Nat	Born	Pos	Meet	Venue	Date
3:59.81		Wang Yuan	CHN	8.4.76	7	NG	Beijing	11 Sep 93
3:59.96	Zola	Budd	GBR	26.5.66	3	VD	Bruxelles	30 Aug 85
4:00.05		Lu Yi	CHN	10.4.74	8	NG	Beijing	11 Sep 93
4:01.71		Li Ying	CHN	24.6.75	4h2	NG	Beijing	10 Sep 93
4:03.5	Svetlana	Guskova	MOL	19.8.59	3	Kuts	Podolsk	13 Aug 78
4:04.42	Astrid	Pfeiffer	GDR	6.12.64	3	vUSA	Los Angeles	25 Jun 83
4:04.97	Ana	Padurean	ROM	5.9.69	1		Bucuresti	13 Jun 87
4:05.14	Liu Dong		CHN	27.12.73	1	WJ	Seoul	20 Sep 92
4:05.35	Dorina	Calenic	ROM	4.4.69	2		Bucuresti	13 Jun 87
4:05.96	Lynne	MacDougall	GBR	18.2.65	6	BGP	Budapest	20 Aug 84
4:06.02	Birgit	Friedmann	FRG	8.4.60	7		Dortmund	1 Jul 78
4:06.19	Maria	Pîntea	ROM	10.8.67	8		Pitesti	28 Jun 86

1 MILE

Mark	Wind	Name	Nat	Born	Pos	Meet	Venue	Date
4:17.57	Zola	Budd	GBR	26.5.66	3	WK	Zürich	21 Aug 85
4:30.08	Lynne	MacDougall	GBR	18.2.65	4	IAC	London	7 Sep 84

2000 METRES

Mark	Wind	Name	Nat	Born	Pos	Meet	Venue	Date
5:33.15	Zola	Budd	GBR	26.5.66	1		London	13 Jul 84

3000 METRES

Mark	Wind	Name	Nat	Born	Pos	Meet	Venue	Date
8:28.83	Zola	Budd	GBR	26.5.66	3	GG	Roma	7 Sep 85
8:36.45		Ma Ningning	CHN	20.9.76	4	NC	Jinan	6 Jun 93
8:42.39		Li Ying	CHN	24.6.75	8	NG	Beijing	13 Sep 93
8:44.1mx	Donna	Gould	AUS	10.6.66	-		Eugene	13 Jul 84
8:46.86	Zhang Linli		CHN	6.3.73	1	WJ	Seoul	20 Sep 92
8:47.6	Svetlana	Guskova	MOL	19.8.59	4	Znam	Vilnius	18 Jul 78
8:48.28	Gabriela	Szabo	ROM	14.11.75	2	WJ	Seoul	20 Sep 92
8:48.45	Zhang Lirong		CHN	3.3.73	3	WJ	Seoul	20 Sep 92
8:50.26	Rodica	Prescura	ROM	.70	2		Bucuresti	12 Jun 88
8:51.22	Annemari	Sandell	FIN	2.1.77	2	EJ	San Sebastián	1 Aug 93
8:51.59	Lydia	Cheromei	KEN	11.5.77	10	VD	Brussels	28 Aug 92
8:51.78	Paula	Radcliffe	GBR	17.12.73	4	WJ	Seoul	20 Sep 92

5000 METRES

Mark	Wind	Name	Nat	Born	Pos	Meet	Venue	Date
14:48.07	Zola	Budd	GBR	26.5.66	1	McV	London	26 Aug 85
15:17.31	Lydia	Cheromei	KEN	11.5.77	7	ISTAF	Berlin	12 Aug 92
15:21.29	Derartu	Tulu	ETH	21.3.72	1	Super	Shizuoka	6 May 91
15:26.33	Annemari	Sandell	FIN	2.1.77	4	DNG	Stockholm	5 Jul 93
15:27.3 mx	Donna	Gould	AUS	10.6.66	-		Adelaide	6 Jun 84
	15:40.6				1		Adelaide	15 Feb 84
15:28.91	Qu Yunxia		CHN	25.12.72	2		Tangshan	26 Sep 91

Mark	Wind	Name		Nat	Born	Pos	Meet	Venue	Date
15:32.4+e		Delilah	Asiago	KEN	24.2.72	1'	Bisl	Oslo	6 Jul 91
15:35.70		Zhang Linli		CHN	6.3.73			Tangshan	26 Sep 91
15:37.17		Hou Juhua		CHN	.67	1		Guangzhou	24 Oct 86
15:38.29		Akemi	Masuda	JPN	1.1.64	11	Bisl	Oslo	26 Jun 82
15:38.33		Wang Hongxia		CHN	.68	3	NC	Zhengzhou	7 Jun 87
15:40.1		Marlene	Renders	BEL	24.12.68	1		Hechtel	8 Aug 87

10000 METRES

Mark	Wind	Name		Nat	Born	Pos	Meet	Venue	Date
31:15.38		Sally	Barsosio	KEN	21.3.78	3	WC	Stuttgart	21 Aug 93
31:32.15			Feng Wenhui	CHN	21.1.74	9	NG	Beijing	8 Sep 93
31:40.56		Delilah	Asiago	KEN	24.2.72	1	JPN Ch	Tokyo	15 Jun 91
31:41.09		Lydia	Cheromei	KEN	11.5.77	2	AfrCh	Belle Vue Mauricia	27 Jun 92
31:45.95		Derartu	Tulu	ETH	21.3.72	1h2	WC	Tokyo	27 Aug 91
32:09.94			Ma Ningning	CHN	20.9.76	3	NC	Jinan	2 Jun 93
32:12.51		Marleen	Renders	BUL	24.12.68	12	WC	Roma	4 Sep 87
32:16.24		Masami	Ishizaka	JPN	27.3.71	2	WUG	Duisburg	29 Aug 89
32:25.74		Olga	Nazarkina	RUS	11.6.70	1	EJ	Varazdin	25 Aug 89
32:26.41		Mónica	Gama	POR	8.3.70	2	EJ	Varazdin	25 Aug 89
32:29.90		Wang Junxia		CHN	9.1.73	1	WJ	Seoul	19 Sep 92
32:30.5		Rika	Ota	JPN	2.4.71	1		Amagasaki	22 Sep 90

MARATHON

Mark	Wind	Name		Nat	Born	Pos	Meet	Venue	Date
2:30:15			Gu Dongmei	CHN	5.1.74	9		Tianjin	4 Apr 93
2:30:30		Akemi	Masuda	JPN	1.1.64	1		Eugene	11 Sep 83
2:31:03			Feng Wenhui	CHN	21.1.74	10		Tianjin	4 Apr 93
2:32:04		Zhen Guixia		CHN	26.4.73	2	NC	Tianjin	12 Apr 92
2:33:59		Zhang Lirong		CHN	3.3.73			Dalian	27 Oct 91
2:37:35		Wu Mei		CHN	9.11.73	3	NC	Tianjin	12 Apr 92
2:38:10		Yoshiko	Yamamoto	JPN	6.6.70	9		Osaka	29 Jan 89
2:38:41		Yu Song-hui		NKO	.68	2		Pyongyang	5 Oct 87

100 METRES HURDLES

Mark	Wind	Name		Nat	Born	Pos	Meet	Venue	Date
12.84	1.5	Aliuska	López	CUB	29.8.69	2	WSG	Zagreb	16 Jul 87
12.95	1.5	Candy	Young	USA	21.5.62	2	AAU	Walnut	16 Jun 79
12.95A	1.5	Cinnamon	Sheffield	USA	8.3.70	2	NCAA	Provo	3 Jun 89
13.00	0.7	Gloria	Kovarik	GDR	13.1.64	3h2	NC	Karl-Marx-Stadt	16 Jun 83
13.00	2.0	Lyudmila	Khristosenko	UKR	14.10.66	1	NC-j	Krasnodar	16 Jul 85
13.05	1.8	Heike	Terpe	GDR	4.10.64	4	OD	Berlin	8 Jun 83
13.07	0.2	Monique	Ewanje-Epée	FRA	11.7.67	2		Paris	22 Jul 86
13.07	1.1	Gillian	Russell	JAM	28.9.73	3	NC	Kingston	3 Jul 92
13.09	1.3	Ulrike	Denk	FRG	10.5.64	1		Rhede	29 Jul 83
13.10	0.7	LaVonna	Martin	USA	18.11.66	1	PennR	Philadelphia	27 Apr 85
13.10	-0.7	Heike	Tillack	GDR	6.1.68	1	WJ	Athinai	18 Jul 86
13.11	-0.1	Benita	Fitzgerald	USA	6.7.61	2	FOT	Eugene	25 Jun 80
13.12	0.2	Cornelia	Feuerbach	GDR	26.4.63	4r2		Cottbus	22 Aug 82
Wind assisted									
13.02	4.1	LaVonna	Martin	USA	18.11.66	5	NCAA	Austin	1 Jun 85
13.10	4.5	Karen	Nelson	CAN	3.12.63	4	CG	Brisbane	8 Oct 82
Hand timed									
12.8		Lyudmila	Khristosenko	UKR	14.10.66	1		Krasnodar	29 Jun 85
12.9		Lidia	Okolo-Kulak	BLS	15.1.67	1h		Minsk	1 Aug 86
12.9w		Gudrun	Berend	GDR	27.4.55	2h		Potsdam	13 Jun 74
12.9w	2.8	Svetla	Dimitrova ¶	BUL	27.1.70	1H		Sofia	18 Jun 88
12.9w	2.8	Ime	Akpan	NGR	27.4.72	1		Las Vegas	14 Apr 90

400 METRES HURDLES

Mark	Wind	Name		Nat	Born	Pos	Meet	Venue	Date
55.20		Lesley	Maxie	USA	4.1.67	2	TAC	San José	9 Jun 84
55.53		Radostina	Dimitrova	BUL	1.6.66	3	OD	Potsdam	21 Jul 84
55.65		Schowonda	Williams	USA	3.12.66	3	NCAA	Austin	31 May 85
55.72			Zheng Liyuan	CHN	1.4.74	5	NG	Beijing	9 Sep 93
55.74A		Myrtle	Simpson	RSA	18.2.64	2	NC	Bloemfontein	16 Apr 83
55.84		Nelli	Voronkova	BLS	6.6.72	1	WJ	Plovdiv	10 Aug 90
55.93		Sofia	Sabeva	BUL	11.1.69	1	NC-j	Sofia	3 Jul 88
56.00		Ann-Louise	Skoglund	SWE	28.6.62	1		Göteborg	11 Aug 81
56.16		Esther	Mahr	USA	4.1.61	2s2	WC	Sittard	15 Aug 80

Mark	Wind	Name		Nat	Born	Pos	Meet	Venue	Date
56.22		Claudia	Bartl	GDR	2.5.68	1	EJ	Cottbus	25 Aug 85
56.28		Nadezhda	Asenova	BUL	28.3.62	1		Sofia	12 Jul 81
56.33		Sylvia	Rieger	FRG	14.11.70	8	WK	Zürich	16 Aug 89
Hand timed									
56.2		Vera	Ordina	RUS	4.6.68	1		Leningrad	27 Jun 87

HIGH JUMP

Mark	Wind	Name		Nat	Born	Pos	Meet	Venue	Date
2.01		Olga	Turchak	KZK	5.3.67	2	GWG	Moskva	7 Jul 86
2.01		Heike	Balck	GDR	19.8.70	1	vSU-j	Karl-Marx-Stadt	18 Jun 89
2.00		Stefka	Kostadinova	BUL	25.3.65	1		Sofia	25 Aug 84
2.00		Alina	Astafei	ROM	7.6.69	1	WJ	Sudbury	29 Jul 88
1.98		Silvia	Costa	CUB	4.5.64	2	WUG	Edmonton	11 Jul 83
1.98		Yelena	Yelesina	RUS	4.4.70	1	Druzh	Nyiregyháza	13 Aug 88
1.97		Svetlana	Isaeva	BUL	18.3.67	2		Sofia	25 May 86
1.96A		Charmaine	Gale	RSA	27.2.64	1	NC-j	Bloemfontein	4 Apr 81
1.96i		Desislava	Aleksandrova	BUL	27.10.75	2	EI	Paris	12 Mar 94
1.95		Larisa	Kositsyna	RUS	14.12.63	4	NC	Kiev	21 Aug 82
1.95		Maryse	Ewanje-Epée	FRA	4.9.64	3		Rieti	4 Sep 83
1.95		Ionat	Quintero	CUB	18.9.72	1		Columbus	28 Jul 90

POLE VAULT

Mark	Wind	Name		Nat	Born	Pos	Meet	Venue	Date
4.05		Sun Caiyun		CHN	21.7.73	1	NC	Nanjing	21 May 92
4.00		Cai Weiyan		CHN	25.10.73	1		Wuhan	19 Oct 92
3.90		Nicole	Rieger	GER	5.2.72	1	NC-j	Berlin	21 Jul 91
3.80		Zhang Chunzhen	CHN	.70	1		Guangzhou		9 Sep 89
3.80		Daniela	Köpernick	GER	25.7.73	1	NC	München	21 Jun 92
3.80		Christine	Adams	GER	28.2.74	1		Gladbeck	18 Jul 93
3.75		Shao Jingwen		CHN	8.3.71	3	NC	Beijing	26 Jun 90
3.70		nine juniors							

LONG JUMP

Mark	Wind	Name		Nat	Born	Pos	Meet	Venue	Date
7.14	1.1	Heike	Daute	GDR	16.12.64	1	PTS	Bratislava	4 Jun 83
7.00	-0.2	Birgit	Grosshennig	GDR	21.2.65	2		Berlin	9 Jun 84
6.91	0.0	Anisoara	Cusmir	ROM	29.6.62	1		Bucuresti	23 May 81
6.90	1.4	Beverly	Kinch	GBR	14.1.64	*	WC	Helsinki	14 Aug 83
6.88	0.6	Natalya	Shevchenko	RUS	28.12.66	2		Sochi	26 May 84
6.84		Larisa	Baluta	UKR	13.8.65	2		Krasnodar	6 Aug 83
6.82	1.8	Fiona	May	GBR	12.12.69	*	WJ	Sudbury	30 Jul 88
6.81	1.6	Carol	Lewis	USA	8.8.63	1	TAC	Knoxville	20 Jun 82
6.81	1.4	Yelena	Davydova	KZK	16.11.67	1	NC-j	Krasnodar	17 Jul 85
6.79		Carmen	Sirbu	ROM	17.2.67	3	RomIC	Bucuresti	2 Jun 85
6.78		Kathy	McMillan	USA	7.11.57	1	AAU	Los Angeles	12 Jun 76
6.78i	-	Erica	Johansson	SWE	5.2.74	2	NC	Malmö	21 Feb 93
Wind assisted									
7.27	2.2	Heike	Daute	GDR	16.12.64	1	WC	Helsinki	14 Aug 83
6.93	4.6	Beverly	Kinch	GBR	14.1.64	5	WC	Helsinki	14 Aug 83
6.88	2.1	Fiona	May	GBR	12.12.69	1	WJ	Sudbury	30 Jul 88
6.84	2.8	Anu	Kaljurand	EST	16.4.69	2		Riga	4 Jun 88

TRIPLE JUMP

Mark	Wind	Name		Nat	Born	Pos	Meet	Venue	Date
14.29	1.4		Ren Ruiping	CHN	1.1.75	1	NG	Beijing	13 Sep 93
13.95	1.8	Olga Lidia	Cepero	CUB	4.2.75	1		Habana	11 Feb 94
13.91i	-	Yelena	Lysak	RUS	19.10.75	1		Moskva	4 Feb 94
		13.86	1.8			1	EJ	San Sebastián	1 Aug 93
13.85	0.2	Tatyana	Matyashova	RUS	2.8.73	1	Prav	Sochi	25 May 91
13.80	1.3	Olga	Kontsevaya	RUS	.71	1		Sochi	13 May 90
13.79	0.0	Zhang Yan		CHN	.6.72			Hangzhou	12 Oct 91
13.73		Liu Jinming		CHN	1.2.72			Dalian	7 May 91
13.73	1.6		Wang Xiangrong	CHN	1.2.76	*	NG	Beijing	13 Sep 93
13.68		Irina	Melnikova	RUS	9.1.74	1		Sverdlovsk	31 Jul 90
13.67	1.0	Lyudmila	Galkina	RUS	20.5.72	1	EJ	Thessaloniki	10 Aug 91
13.65	1.1	Natalya	Klimovets	BLS	11.4.74	2	EJ	San Sebastián	1 Aug 93
13.58		Wendy	Brown	USA	28.1.66	Q	NCAA	Austin	30 May 85
Wind assisted									
14.07	2.8		Wang Xiangrong	CHN	1.2.76	4	NG	Beijing	13 Sep 93

SHOT

Mark	Wind	Name		Nat	Born	Pos	Meet	Venue	Date
20.54		Astrid	Kumbernuss	GDR	5.2.70	1	vFin-j	Orimattila	1 Jul 89
20.51i		Heidi	Krieger	GDR	20.7.65	2		Budapest	8 Feb 84
		20.24				5		Spilt	30 Apr 84
20.23		Ilke	Wyludda	GDR	28.3.69	1	NC-j	Karl-Marx-Stadt	16 Jul 88
20.12		Ilona	Schoknecht	GDR	24.9.56	2	NC	Erfurt	23 Aug 75
19.90		Stephanie	Storp	FRG	28.11.68	1		Hamburg	16 Aug 87
19.63		Wang Yawen		CHN	23.8.73	1		Shijiazhuang	25 Apr 92
19.57		Grit	Haupt	GDR	4.6.66	1		Gera	7 Jul 84
19.48		Ines	Wittich	GDR	14.11.69	5		Leipzig	29 Jul 87
19.42		Simone	Michel	GDR	18.12.60	3	vSU	Leipzig	23 Jun 79
19.23		Zhang Zhiying		CHN	19.7.73	1	NC-j	Hangzhou	8 May 92
19.05		Cordula	Schulze	GDR	11.9.59	3		Potsdam	6 Aug 78
19.00		Wang Hui		CHN	6.7.73			Beijing	11 Apr 92

DISCUS

Mark	Wind	Name		Nat	Born	Pos	Meet	Venue	Date
74.40		Ilke	Wyludda	GDR	28.3.69	2		Berlin	13 Sep 88
67.38		Irina	Meszynski	GDR	24.3.62	1		Berlin	14 Aug 81
67.00		Jana	Günther	GDR	7.1.68	6	NC	Potsdam	20 Aug 87
66.80		Svetla	Mitkova	BUL	17.6.64	1		Sofia	2 Aug 83
66.60		Astrid	Kumbernuss	GDR	5.2.70	1		Berlin	20 Jul 88
66.34		Franka	Dietzsch	GDR	22.1.68	2		St Denis	11 Jun 87
66.30		Jana	Lauren	GDR	28.6.70	1	vSU-j	Karl-Marx-Stadt	18 Jun 89
66.08			Cao Qi	CHN	1.1.74	1	NG	Beijing	12 Sep 93
65.96		Grit	Haupt	GDR	4.6.66	3		Leipzig	13 Jul 84
65.22		Daniela	Costian	ROM	30.4.65	3		Nitra	26 Aug 84
64.52		Martina	Opitz	GDR	12.12.60	3	NC	Karl-Marx-Stadt	12 Aug 79
64.42		Larisa	Korotkovich	BLS	23.1.67	1		Minsk	28 Apr 86

HAMMER

Mark	Wind	Name		Nat	Born	Pos	Meet	Venue	Date
62.52		Mihaela	Melinte	ROM	27.3.75	1	NC-j	Bucuresti	7 Aug 93
59.80		Natalya	Vasilenko	UKR	30.10.74	1		Chernigov	27 Jun 93
59.06		Natalya	Panarina	RUS	6.5.75	1		Chelyabinsk	6 Jun 93
58.90		Debbie	Sosimenko	AUS	5.4.74	1		Hobart	17 Jan 93
58.60		Yelena	Khrulyova	RUS	.73	3		Adler	26 May 91
58.36		Oksana	Zatsepilova	RUS	20.4.74	2		Moskva	6 Aug 93
58.24		Marina	Pirog	UKR	28.8.74	2		Chernigov	27 Jun 93
58.20		Olga	Sokolova	RUS	.72	1	NC-wj	Adler	24 Feb 90
58.10		Natalya	Ignatova	RUS	3.1.74	2		Chelyabinsk	6 Jun 93
56.52		Oksana	Lukyanyts	URS	.71	1		Bryansk	8 Sep 89
56.48		Alice	Meyer	FRA	18.5.72	1		Antony	3 Jul 91
56.44		Yelena	Grankina	UKR	30.6.74	2		Kiev	2 May 93

JAVELIN

Mark	Wind	Name		Nat	Born	Pos	Meet	Venue	Date
71.88		Antoaneta	Todorova	BUL	8.6.63	1	EP	Zagreb	15 Aug 81
71.82		Ivonne	Leal	CUB	27.2.66	1	WUG	Kobe	30 Aug 85
70.12		Karen	Forkel	GDR	24.9.70	1	EJ	Varazdin	26 Aug 89
68.94		Trine	Solberg	NOR	18.4.66	1	vSU	Oslo	16 Jul 85
68.38		Antje	Kempe	GDR	23.6.63	Q	EC	Athinai	8 Sep 82
67.32		Regina	Kempter	GDR	4.4.67	2	NC	Jena	27 Jun 86
66.52		Alexandra	Beck	GDR	13.6.68	1		Khania	24 May 86
64.88		Anja	Reiter	GDR	15.7.69	1	EJ	Birmingham	8 Aug 87
64.66		Sun Fei		CHN	16.3.73	1		Nanjing	21 May 91
64.56		Jana	Köpping	GDR	12.4.66	2	OD	Berlin	27 Jun 85
64.56		Xiomara	Rivera	CUB	24.12.68	1	CAC-j	Ciudad México	26 Jun 86
64.40		Heike	Galle	GDR	20.3.67	1	Znam	Leningrad	8 Jun 86

HEPTATHLON

Mark	Wind	Name		Nat	Born	Pos	Meet	Venue	Date
6465		Sibylle	Thiele	GDR	6.3.65	1	EJ	Schwechat	28 Aug 83
		13.49 1.90	14.63 24.07	6.65	36.22 2:18.36				
6436		Sabine	Braun	FRG	19.6.65	1	vBul	Mannheim	9 Jun 84
		13.68 1.78	13.09 23.88	6.03	52.14 2:09.41				
6428		Svetla	Dimitrova ¶	BUL	27.1.70	1	NC	Sofia	18 Jun 89
		13.49 1.77	13.98 23.59	6.49	40.10 2:11.10				

Mark	Wind	Name		Nat	Born	Pos	Meet	Venue	Date
6403		Emilia	Dimitrova	BUL	13.11.67	6	GWG	Moskva	7 Jul 86
		13.73 1.76 13.46 23.17		6.29 43.30 2:09.85					
6276		Larisa	Nikitina	RUS	29.4.65	8	NC	Kiev	21 Jun 84
		13.87 1.86 14.04 25.26		6.31 48.62 2:22.76					
6218		Jana	Sobotka	GDR	3.10.65	6	OD	Potsdam	21 Jul 84
		14.40 1.74 13.28 24.19		6.27 43.64 2:06.83					
6198		Anke	Schmidt	GDR	5.2.68	7		Götzis	24 May 87
		13.80 1.72 13.32 23.82		6.63 25.78 2:12.44					
6194		Camelia	Cornateanu	ROM	23.1.67	2	NC	Pitesti	8 Aug 86
		14.35 1.86 14.70 24.97		6.15 38.94 2:11.93					
6187		Ionica	Domniteanu	ROM	8.1.69	1	Bal-j	Pitesti	26 Jul 87
		13.51 1.77 14.56 24.66		6.00 43.86 2:17.60					
6179		Valentina	Savchenko	UKR	13.5.68	1	Drz	Plovdiv	5 Aug 84
		13.88 1.59 15.10 24.15		6.07 48.16 2:12.42					
6166		Beatrice	Mau	GDR	20.2.71	1	WJ	Plovdiv	11 Aug 90
		13.73 1.69 12.87 24.30		6.32 50.14 2:19.94					
6112		Nathalie	Teppe	FRA	22.5.72	1		Talence	1 Jul 90
		13.78 1.75 12.59 25.29		5.89 55.44 2:18.34					
Disqualified for positive drugs test									
6534		Svetla	Dimitrova	BUL	27.1.70	H	EP	Helmond	16 Jul 89
		13.30 1.84 14.35 23.33		6.47 39.20 2:13.56					

5000 METRES WALK

Mark	Name		Nat	Born	Pos	Meet	Venue	Date
20:37.7	Jin Bingjie		CHN	1.4.71	1	NC	Hefei	3 Mar 90
21:01.8	Susana	Feitor	POR	28.1.75	1	SGP	Fana	8 May 93
21:02.6	Li Jingxue		CHN	10.2.70	2		Anshan	2 Sep 89
21:06.7	Sun Yan		CHN	4.5.73	5	NC	Zhengzhou	3 Mar 91
21:13.16	Cui Yingxi		CHN	26.1.71	1		Jinan	30 Oct 88
21:18.1	Wang Yili		CHN	4.4.71	3		Anshan	2 Sep 89
21:20.03	Gao Hongmiao		CHN	17.3.74	1	WJ	Seoul	20 Sep 92
21:26.1	Kong Yan		CHN	5.4.71	5	NC	Hefei	3 Mar 90
21:27.9	Liu Caimei		CHN	.71	7	NC	Hefei	3 Mar 90
21:29.8	Ni Fenglian		CHN	13.11.70			Anshan	2 Sep 89
21:30.92	Oksana	Shchastnaya	URS	24.4.71	1	EJ	Birmingham	7 Aug 87
21:31.7	Chen Yueling		CHN	1.4.68	1	NC	Guangzhou	23 Oct 87

4 x 100 METRES RELAY

Mark	Nat	Team	Pos	Meet	Venue	Date
43.48	GDR	Breuer, Krabbe, Dietz, Henke	1	WJ	Sudbury	31 Jul 88
	Unsanctioned race 43.33	Breuer, Krabbe, Dietz, Henke	1		Berlin	20 Jul 88
43.73A	USA	Gilmore, Finn, Simmons, Vereen	2		Colorado.Springs	19 Jul 83
	43.78	Guidry, Smith, Liles, Malone	1	WJ	Athinai	20 Jul 86
43.82	JAM	Russell, R.Campbell, Frazer, Mitchell	1	WJ	Plovdiv	12 Aug 90
43.87	URS	Lapshina, Doronina, Bulatova, Kovalyova	1	vGDR-j	Leningrad	20 Jun 87
44.04	CUB	Riquelme, Allen, Lopez, Valdivia	2	WJ	Sudbury	31 Jul 88
44.13	NGR	Iheagwam, Nwajei, Ogunkoya, Onyali	3	WJ	Athinai	20 Jul 86
44.16	GBR	Soper, DSmith, FGraser, Merry	2	WJ	Plovdiv	12 Aug 90
44.23	FRA	Ropars, Simioneck, Declerk, Sidibé	1	EJ	Varazdin	27 Aug 89
44.63	FRG	Eichler, Rasch, Steger, Sommer	2	EJ	Donyetsk	21 Aug 77
44.90	JPN	Ito, Kakinuma, Shoji, Kaneko	6	WJ	Seoul	20 Sep 92
44.93	POL	Stachurska, Nania, Filip, Witkowska	2	EJ	Athinai	24 Aug 75
Hand timed						
43.9	FRA	Ropars, Simioneck, Declerk, Sidibé	1		Thaon	12 Aug 89

4 x 400 METRES RELAY

Mark	Nat	Team	Pos	Meet	Venue	Date
3:28.39	GDR	Deer, Fabert, Wöhlk, Breuer	1	WJ	Sudbury	31 Jul 88
3:30.38	AUS	Scamps, Poetschka, Hanigan, Andrews	1	WJ	Plovdiv	12 Aug 90
3:30.45	USA	Harris, Pritchett, Downing, Vickers	1	WJ	Athinai	20 Jul 86
3:30.72	BUL	Kireva, Angelova, Rashova, Dimitrova	3	v2N	Sofia	24 Jul 83
3:31.09	JAM	Williams, Cole, Turner, Scott	2	WJ	Plovdiv	12 Aug 90
3:31.13	ROM	Tuta, Florea, Tîrlea, Nedelcu	1	EJ	San Sebastián	1 Aug 93
3:31.41	URS	Zakharova, Kiryukhina, Ponomaryova, Zhdanova	2	EJ	Utrecht	23 Aug 81
3:31.81	CUB	Casanova, Duporti, Limonta, MacLean	3	WJ	Plovdiv	12 Aug 90
3:31.94	FRG	Wahl, Lix, Ley, Leistenschneider	3	EJ	Schwechat	28 Aug 83
3:33.56	NGR	Opara, Akinremi, Onyebuchi, Yusuf	1h2	WJ	Plovdiv	11 Aug 90
3:34.83	JPN	Amano, Kasajima, Yamagata, Kakinuma	5	WJ	Seoul	20 Sep 92
3:35.10	GBR	Honley, Robinson, Flockhart, Hall	3	EJ	Cottbus	25 Aug 85

MEN'S WORLD LISTS 1993

100 METRES

Mark	Wind	Name		Nat	Born	Pos	Meet	Venue	Date
9.87	0.3	Linford	Christie	GBR	2.4.60	1	WC	Stuttgart	15 Aug
9.92	0.3	Andre	Cason	USA	20.1.69	2	WC	Stuttgart	15 Aug
9.94	0.3		Cason			1s1	WCh	Stuttgart	15 Aug
9.96	-0.1		Cason			1q4	WCh	Stuttgart	14 Aug
9.97	0.9		Christie			1s2	WCh	Stuttgart	15 Aug
9.98	0.3	Daniel	Effiong	NGR	17.6.72	2s1	WC	Stuttgart	15 Aug
9.99	1.0		Effiong			1s1	JUCO	Odessa	21 May
9.99	0.3	Dennis	Mitchell	USA	20.2.66	3	WC	Stuttgart	15 Aug
10.00	0.1		Christie			1q3	WCh	Stuttgart	14 Aug
10.02	0.0	Leroy	Burrell	USA	21.2.67	1rA	WK	Zürich	4 Aug
10.02	0.3	Carl	Lewis	USA	1.7.61	3s1	WC	Stuttgart	15 Aug
10.02	0.3		Lewis			4	WCh	Stuttgart	15 Aug
10.02	0.3	Bruny	Surin	CAN	12.7.67	5	WC	Stuttgart	15 Aug
10.03	1.5		Cason			1	BNP	Villeneuve d'Ascq	2 Jul
10.03	0.0		Christie			2A	WK	Zürich	4 Aug
10.03	0.3	Frank	Fredericks	NAM	2.10.67	6	WC	Stuttgart	15 Aug
10.03	1.7	Jon	Drummond	USA	9.9.68	1rA		Rieti	5 Sep
10.03	1.7		Christie			2A		Rieti	5 Sep
10.04	1.5		Fredericks			2	BNP	Villeneuve d'Ascq	2 Jul
10.04	0.8		Cason			1A	Athl	Lausanne	7 Jul
10.04	0.3		Effiong			7	WCh	Stuttgart	15 Aug
10.05	0.5		Effiong			1	JUCO	Odessa	22 May
10.05	0.0		Drummond			3A	WK	Zürich	4 Aug
10.05	0.0		Drummond			1	Herc	Monaco	7 Aug
10.05	0.3		Fredericks			4s1	WCh	Stuttgart	15 Aug
10.06	1.7		Christie			1	vUSA	Edinburgh	2 Jul
10.06	1.7	Calvin	Smith	USA	8.1.61	2	vGBR	Edinburgh	2 Jul
10.06	-0.1		Fredericks			2q4	WCh	Stuttgart	14 Aug
10.06	0.9		Mitchell			2s2	WCh	Stuttgart	15 Aug
10.06	1.0		Christie			1	VD	Bruxelles	3 Sep
10.06	0.0		Christie			1A	Toto	Fukuoka	18 Sep
		(31/10)							
10.08	1.2	Bryan	Bridgewater	USA	7.9.70	1		Abilene	29 May
10.08	1.5	Mark	McKoy	CAN	10.12.61	4	BNP	Villeneuve d'Ascq	2 Jul
10.09	1.7	Michael	Green	JAM	7.11.70	1	NCAA	New Orleans	5 Jun
10.11	1.7	Vincent	Henderson	USA	20.10.72	3	vGBR	Edinburgh	2 Jul
10.11	-0.1	Raymond	Stewart	JAM	18.3.65	2q2	WC	Stuttgart	14 Aug
10.12	1.1	Michael	Johnson	USA	13.9.67	1		Arlington	1 May
10.12	1.8	Osmond	Ezinwa	NGR	22.11.71	1rA	ECP	Budapest	29 May
10.13	2.0	Sam	Jefferson	USA	19.4.71	1		Houston	17 Apr
10.14A	1.0	David	Oaks	USA	12.5.72	1		Boulder	18 May
10.14	0.4	Davidson	Ezinwa	NGR	22.11.71	1		Salamanca	27 Jul
		(20)							
10.15	1.2	Gerry	Woodberry	USA	23.10.69	1		College Station	1 May
10.15	0.2	Fabian	Muyaba	ZIM	30.9.70	1h4	SEC	Knoxville	15 May
10.15	1.9	John	Regis	GBR	13.10.66	1rB	ECP	Budapest	29 May
10.15	-0.2	Olapade	Adeniken	NGR	19.8.69	2	Slovn	Bratislava	1 Jun
10.15	1.3	Andreas	Berger ¶	AUT	9.6.61	1		Kapfenberg	5 Jun
10.16		Glenroy	Gilbert	CAN	31.8.68	1	Gator	Knoxville	1 May
10.16	1.6	Aleksandr	Porkhomovskiy	RUS	12.8.72	1		Southampton	6 Jun
10.17	0.9	Jeff	Laynes	USA	3.10.70	1		Fresno	3 Apr
10.18		Vitaliy	Savin	KZK	23.1.66	1		Alma-Ata	15 Jun
10.19	1.7	Damien	Marsh	AUS	28.3.71	1		Melbourne	25 Feb
		(30)							
10.19	-0.9	Jean-Charles	Trouabal	FRA	20.5.65	1	NC	Annecy	24 Jul
10.19	2.0	Nobuharu	Asahara	JPN	21.6.72	1s1		Naruto	26 Oct
10.20	0.0	Michael	Marsh	USA	4.8.67	2	NYG	New York	22 May
10.20	1.2	Randall	Evans	USA	26.10.70	2		Abilene	29 May
10.20	1.4	Alexandros	Terzian	GRE	24.6.68	1	MedG	Narbonne	17 Jun
10.20	0.0	Chidi	Imo	NGR	27.8.63	2rB	WK	Zürich	4 Aug
10.20	0.0	Robson	da Silva	BRA	4.9.64	1rA		Massa Marittima	6 Aug
10.20	-0.1	Atlee	Mahorn	CAN	27.10.65	4q2	WC	Stuttgart	14 Aug

Mark	Wind	Name		Nat	Born	Pos	Meet	Venue	Date
10.21	0.5	Wendell	Gaskin	USA	7.1.73	2	JUCO	Odessa	21 May
10.21	1.9	Satoru	Inoue	JPN	21.7.71	1h1		Tokyo	21 May
		(40)							
10.21	1.2	Anthony	Phillips	USA	5.10.70	3	NCAA II	Abilene	29 May
10.22		Patrick	Delice	TRI	12.11.67	1		Prairie View	27 Mar
10.22	0.7	Talal	Mansour	QAT	8.5.64	1	AsiC	Manila	2 Dec
10.23	0.7	Ato	Boldon	TRI	30.12.73	1		Fresno	5 May
10.23	-0.9	Daniel	Sangouma	FRA	7.2.65	2	NC	Annecy	24 Jul
10.23	1.4	Jeff	Williams	USA	31.12.64	2		København	25 Jul
10.23	0.8	Andrey	Fedoriv	RUS	11.8.63	1h2		Moskva	6 Aug
10.23	0.9	Emmanuel	Tuffour	GHA	2.12.66	6s2	WC	Stuttgart	15 Aug
10.23	0.9	Robert	Esmie	CAN	5.7.72	7s2	WC	Stuttgart	15 Aug
10.24	1.5	Daniel	Cojocaru	ROM	27.5.69	1	RomIC	Bucuresti	18 Jun
		(50)							
10.24	1.6	Jean-Olivier	Zirignon	CIV	27.4.71	2s1	WUG	Buffalo	15 Jul
10.24	2.0		Li Tao	CHN	15.1.68	1	NG	Beijing	8 Sep
10.25	0.9	Anthony	Barnes	USA	23.12.65	3r1		Fresno	3 Apr
10.25	0.2	Reggie	Jones	USA	8.5.71	2h4	SEC	Knoxville	15 May
10.25	1.0	Michael	Barron	USA	21.2.73	2s1	JUCO	Odessa	20 May
10.25	1.0	Dean	Capobianco	AUS	11.5.70	2	AAA	Birmingham	16 Jul
10.25	0.6	David	Dollé	SUI	30.5.69	1		Meilen	12 Sep
10.26	1.7	Tim	Jackson	AUS	4.7.69	2		Melbourne	25 Feb
10.26	1.0	James	Jett	USA	28.12.70	1		Tuscaloosa	28 Mar
10.26	0.6	Henry	Neal	USA	28.10.70	2	SunA	Tempe	3 Apr
		(60)							
10.26	1.2	Peter	Hargraves	USA	30.8.72	4	NCAA II	Abilene	29 May
10.26	1.8	Arnaldo Oliveira	Silva	BRA	26.3.64	1		Genève	5 Jun
10.26	2.0		Lin Wei	CHN	16.10.74	2	NG	Beijing	8 Sep
10.26	2.0		Xia Xianghai	CHN	17.8.70	3	NG	Beijing	8 Sep
10.28	1.9	Paul	Henderson	AUS	13.3.71	1h4		Sydney	19 Feb
10.28		Larry	King	USA	27.8.68	1		San Luis Obispo	20 Mar
10.28		Kirk	Cummins	BAR	8.1.72	2		Prairie View	27 Mar
10.28	1.2	Bernard	Young	BAH	29.8.66	5	NCAA II	Abilene	29 May
10.28	1.8	Attila	Kovács	HUN	2.9.60	2rA	ECP	Budapest	29 May
10.28	1.6	Oluyemi	Kayode	NGR	7.7.68	2s2	NCAA	New Orleans	4 Jun
		(70)							
10.28	0.6	Wayne	Watson	JAM	26.3.65	3	NC	Kingston	2 Jul
10.28	0.8	Steffen	Görmer	GER	28.7.68	1rB		Rhede	6 Aug
10.28	0.4	Joel	Isasi	CUB	31.7.67	3r1		Rovereto	1 Sep
10.29	0.6	Salaam	Gariba	GHA	23.1.69	3	SunA	Tempe	3 Apr
10.29		Marcel	Carter	USA	26.3.71	1		Gainesville	17 Apr
10.29	1.0	Mike	Sulcer	USA	14.9.71	3s1	JUCO	Odessa	21 May
10.29		Eric	Akogyiram	GHA	25.6.69	1		Fairfax	26 May
10.29	1.8	Carlo	Occhiena	ITA	24.9.72	3rA	ECP	Budapest	29 May
10.29	0.6	Dennis	Mowatt	JAM	28.10.69	4	NC	Kingston	2 Jul
10.29	2.0		Cui Hui	CHN	18.6.73	4	NG	Beijing	8 Sep
		(80)							
10.29	2.0		Ye Hu	CHN	15.4.73	5	NG	Beijing	8 Sep
10.30	0.9	Kareem	Streete-Thompson	CAY/USA	30.3.73	1	Drake R	Des Moines	24 Apr
10.30	0.2	Aki	Bradley	USA	7.2.71	3h4	SEC	Knoxville	15 May
10.30	0.6	Jonathon	Carter	USA	5.5.72	1		Tallahassee	26 May
10.30	1.6	Jason	John	GBR	17.10.71	2		Southampton	6 Jun
10.30	0.1	James	Trapp	USA	28.12.70	1		Reims	30 Jun
10.30	-0.8	Marc	Blume	GER	28.12.73	1	NC	Duisburg	11 Jul
10.31A	0.7	Johann	Venter	RSA	30.12.71	1		Boksburg	6 Feb
10.31	1.3	Donovan	Powell	JAM	13.6.71	1		Abilene	13 May
10.31	1.4	Tony	McCall	USA	16.6.74	1		Los Angeles (Ww)	12 Jun
		(90)							
10.31	0.5	Pavel	Galkin	RUS	9.10.68	2	NC	Moskva	18 Jun
10.31	1.7	Aaron	Thigpen	USA	18.9.64	6		Edinburgh	2 Jul
10.31	-0.1	Ezio	Madonia	ITA	7.8.66	1	CISM	Tours	28 Aug
10.32	1.7	Steve	Brimacombe	AUS	7.5.71	4		Melbourne	25 Feb
10.32	1.3	Tony	Miller	USA	15.3.69	4r1	MSR	Walnut	17 Apr
10.32	-0.2	Vladislav	Dologodin	UKR	23.2.72	1		Kiev	15 May
10.32		Neville	Hodge	ISV	8.12.55	2		Fairfax	26 May
10.32	1.8	Lenny	Paul	GBR	25.5.58	4rA	ECP	Budapest	29 May
10.32	1.3	Tim	Harden	USA	27.1.74	2h3	NCAA	New Orleans	3 Jun

Mark	Wind	Name		Nat	Born	Pos	Meet	Venue	Date
10.32	0.6	Ibrahim (100)	Meité	CIV	18.11.76	1s1	NC	Annecy	24 Jul
10.32	1.8	Max	Morinière	FRA	16.2.64	5s2	NC	Annecy	24 Jul
10.32		Giorgio	Marras	ITA	15.10.71	1		Nuoro	27 Jul

Mark	Wind	Name		Nat	Born	Date
10.33	1.3	Bode	Osagiobare	NGR	70	17 Apr
10.33	1.0	Aham	Okeke	NOR	69	21 May
10.33	1.8	Plamen	Stoyanov	BUL	72	29 May
10.33	1.8	Jirí	Valík	TCH	66	29 May
10.33	-0.7	Oumar	Loum	SEN	73	29 May
10.33	1.8	Pál	Rezák	HUN	66	23 Jun
10.33	-1.7	Yiannis	Zisimedes	CYP	67	30 Jun
10.33	1.0	Tatsuo (110)	Sugimoto	JPN	70	1 Aug
10.34		Sidnei	Telles	BRA	66	21 Mar
10.34	1.4	Sheddric	Fields	USA	73	10 Apr
10.34		John	Myles-Mills	GHA	66	1 May
10.34	1.3	Lamar	Chisley	USA	72	13 May
10.34	0.1	Riley	Washington	USA	73	26 May
10.34	1.1	Toby	Box	GBR	72	12 Jun
10.34	0.3	Aleksandr	Slychkov	UKR	70	2 Jul
10.34	1.3	Wolfgang	Haupt	GER	63	18 Jul
10.34	1.8	Pascal	Théophile	FRA	70	24 Jul
10.34		Nigel (120)	Stoddart	JAM	66	24 Jul
10.34	1.8	Nelson	Boateng	GHA	68	30 Jul
10.35		Jorge	Aguilera	CUB	66	5 Mar
10.35		Clinton	Bufuku	ZAM	72	20 Mar
10.35		Keevan	Mills	USA	70	27 Mar
10.35	0.2	Marlon	Thomas	USA	71	16 May
10.35A	1.8	Andrew	Tynes	BAH	72	22 May
10.35	1.4	Brian	Taylor	GBR	70	29 May
10.35	1.0	Colin	Jackson	GBR	67	12 Jun
10.35	0.5	Kevin	Braunskill	USA	69	25 Jun
10.35	0.0	Ron (130)	Clark	USA	69	25 Jun
10.35	0.6	Aleksey	Chikhachev	UKR	71	2 Jul
10.35	1.8	Pablo	Nolet	ESP	70	20 Jul
10.35	1.7	Victor	Omagbemi	NGR	67	27 Jul
10.35	1.7	Hideki	Onohara	JPN	68	26 Oct
10.36		Stefan	Burkart	SUI	57	17 Apr
10.36A	-0.8	Johan	Rossouw	RSA	65	15 May
10.36	1.1	Jimmy	Oliver	USA		19 May
10.36A	1.8	Donovan	Bailey	CAN	67	22 May
10.36		Andres	Simón	CUB	61	22 May
10.36	-1.4	Marek (140)	Zalewski	POL	70	12 Jun
10.36	0.6	Gregory	Meghoo	JAM	65	2 Jul
10.36	-0.1	Darren	Braithwaite	GBR	69	16 Jul
10.36	0.4	Robert	Kurnicki	GER	65	6 Aug
10.36	-0.3	Edvin	Ivanov	RUS	70	6 Aug
10.36	2.0	Chen Wenzhong		CHN	70	8 Sep
10.37		Joel	Lamela	CUB	71	5 Mar
10.37	1.0	Greg	Saddler	USA	74	28 Mar
10.37A	1.9	Alejandro	Cardenas	MEX	74	8 May
10.37	1.8	Barry	Smith	USA	71	10 Jun
10.37	1.4	Driss (150)	Bensaddou	MAR	67	2 Jul
10.37	0.0	Christian	Konieczny	GER	72	9 Jul
10.37		Leonardo	Prevot	CUB	71	23 Jul
10.37	-0.9	Eric	Perrot	FRA	69	24 Jul
10.37			Zhang Hong	CHN	67	8 Sep
10.38	0.0	Curtis	Johnson	USA	73	8 May
10.38	1.3	Travis	Hannah	USA	70	17 Apr
10.38A	1.8	O'Brian	Gibbons	CAN	70	22 May
10.38	-3.0	Jonathan	Burrell	USA	74	27 Jun
10.38	0.3	Michael	Rosswess	GBR	65	16 Jul
10.38	0.4	Michael (160)	Huke	GER	69	6 Aug
10.38	1.1	Patrick	Stevens	BEL	68	28 Aug
10.39		Ivan	García	CUB	72	5 Mar
10.39		Renward	Wells	BAH	70	3 Apr
10.39	1.1	Franklin	Nwankpa	NGR	73	1 May
10.39		Jason	Shelton	JAM	74	1 May
10.39	1.3	Godfrey	Hewlett	USA	72	13 May
10.39		Edson	L Ribeiro	BRA	72	30 May
10.39	1.0	Darren	Campbell	GBR	73	12 Jun
10.39	1.4	Franck	Amegnigan	TOG	71	2 Jul
10.39	1.0	Enrique (170)	Talavera	ESP	67	3 Jul
10.39	-0.9	Gaetan	Desmangle	FRA	68	24 Jul
10.40	1.9	Will	Glover	USA	71	3 Apr
10.40	1.1	Marcus	Adam	GBR	68	10 Apr
10.40	0.1	Boris	Goins	USA	67	30 Apr
10.40A	1.8	Peter	Ogilvie	CAN	72	22 May
10.40	0.3	Kevin	Little	USA	68	29 May
10.40	1.2	Brian	Amos	USA	71	29 May
10.40	0.6	Olivier	Théophile	FRA	68	24 Jul
10.40	0.0	Peter	Karlsson	SWE	70	9 Aug
10.40	1.3	Yoshitaka (180)	Ito	JPN	70	17 Oct

Unconfirmed: 10.34 Ray Nelson JAM 8 May

Rolling start

Mark	Wind	Name		Nat	Born	Pos	Meet	Venue	Date
10.09	1.8	Daniel	Sangouma	FRA	7.2.65	1s2	NC	Annecy	24 Jul
10.29	1.8	Gaetan	Desmangles	FRA	15.12.68	3s2	NC	Annecy	24 Jul
10.31	1.8	Bruno	Marie-Rose	FRA	20.5.65	4s2	NC	Annecy	24 Jul

Mark	Wind	Name		Nat	Born	Date
10.33	0.0	Slobodan	Brankovic	YUG	67	24 Jul
10.34	1.0	Szabolcs	Alexa	HUN	69	15 May

Note - Sangouma (10.23) with reaction time of 0.062 seconds - faster than generally accepted level of 0.100

Doubtful timing

Mark	Wind	Name		Nat	Born	Pos	Meet	Venue	Date
10.19	0.9	Takayuki	Nakamichi	JPN	17.4.69	1		Houston	21 May
10.22	0.9	David	Texada	USA	23.5.71	2		Houston	21 May

Wind-assisted marks

Mark	Wind	Name		Nat	Born	Pos	Meet	Venue	Date
9.79	5.3	Andre	Cason	USA	20.1.69	1h4	NC	Eugene	16 Jun
9.79	4.5		Cason			1s1	NC	Eugene	16 Jun
9.85	5.3	Leroy	Burrell	USA	21.2.67	2h4	NC	Eugene	16 Jun
9.85	4.8		Cason			1	NC	Eugene	17 Jun
9.85	4.8	Dennis	Mitchell	USA	20.2.66	2	NC	Eugene	17 Jun
9.90	4.8	Carl	Lewis	USA	1.7.61	3	NC	Eugene	17 Jun
9.92	5.3	Jon	Drummond	USA	9.9.68	3h4	NC	Eugene	16 Jun
9.93	4.5		Burrell			2s1	NC	Eugene	16 Jun
9.96	4.0		Mitchell			1h3	NC	Eugene	16 Jun
9.96	2.3		Mitchell			1s2	NC	Eugene	16 Jun
9.97	4.4	Michael	Marsh	USA	4.8.67	1=rA		Austin	8 May
9.97	4.4	Daniel	Effiong	NGR	17.6.72	1=rA		Austin	8 May
9.99	4.8		Drummond			4	NC	Eugene	17 Jun
9.99	2.5		Christie			1	McD	Sheffield	29 Aug

Mark	Wind	Name		Nat	Born	Pos	Meet	Venue	Date
10.00	3.6		Drummond			1rA	S&W	Modesto	8 May
10.00	3.6	Olapade	Adeniken	NGR	19.8.69	2rA	S&W	Modesto	8 May
10.01	3.6		Cason			3rA	S&W	Modesto	8 May
10.01	2.8	Glenroy	Gilbert	CAN	31.8.68	1h1	SEC	Knoxville	15 May
10.01	2.8	Michael	Green	JAM	7.11.70	1		Clemson	16 May
10.02	3.5		Lewis			1h2	NC	Eugene	16 Jun
10.02	4.0		Marsh			2h3	NC	Eugene	16 Jun
10.03	4.1		Green			1		Chapel Hill	17 Apr
10.03	2.5		Green			1h1	NCAA	New Orleans	3 Jun
10.04		Anthony	Phillips	USA	5.10.70	1		Abilene	8 May
10.05	4.4	Sam	Jefferson	USA	19.4.71	3rA		Austin	8 May
10.05	2.3		Lewis			2s2	NC	Eugene	16 Jun
10.06	2.3		Marsh			3s2	NC	Eugene	16 Jun
		(27 performances)							
10.11	6.3	Kevin	Braunskill	USA	31.3.69	1rC	S&W	Modesto	8 May
10.12		Héctor	Fuentes	CUB	27.7.74	1		Artemisa	22 Apr
10.12	2.4	Chris	Nelloms	USA	14.8.71	1	Big10	East Lansing	23 May
10.12	3.7	Marek	Zalewski	POL	27.7.70	1	NC	Kielce	23 Jul
10.12	2.5	Jason	John	GBR	17.10.71	2	McD	Sheffield	29 Aug
10.13	3.5	Floyd	Heard	USA	24.3.66	2h2	NC	Eugene	16 Jun
10.14	2.2	John	Mair	JAM	20.11.63	1		Kingston	1 May
10.14	2.2	Yiannis	Zisimedes	CYP	17.8.67	1		Larnaka	30 Jun
10.15	4.8	Tim	Jackson	AUS	4.7.69	1s1		Sydney	20 Feb
10.15	4+	Ron	Clark	USA	1.11.69	1r1		College Station	10 Apr
10.16		Brian	Amos	USA	26.12.71	2		Abilene	8 May
10.16		Gregory	Meghoo	JAM	11.8.65	1		Ann Arbor	15 May
10.17	4.7	Dean	Capobianco	AUS	11.5.70	1	NC	Brisbane	6 Mar
10.17	2.6	Joel	Isasi	CUB	31.7.67	4	WUG	Buffalo	15 Jul
10.18	4.0	Aaron	Thigpen	USA	18.9.64	3h3	NC	Eugene	16 Jun
10.19		Anthony	Phillips	USA	5.10.70	1r2		Prairie View	27 Mar
10.19	3.6	Kareem	Streete-Thompson	USA	30.3.73	1		El Paso	10 Apr
10.19	4.4	Jonathan	Carter	USA	5.5.72	4		Austin	8 May
10.19	4.5	Randall	Evans	USA	26.10.70	5s1	NC	Eugene	16 Jun
10.19	3.2	Andrey	Fedoriv	RUS	11.8.63	1		Cork	9 Jul
10.19	2.7	Andre Domingos	da Silva	BRA	26.11.72	1		La Chaux de Fonds	8 Aug
10.20	4.4	Talal	Mansour	QAT	8.5.64	1		Doha	3 Feb
10.20	6.3	Larry	King	USA	27.8.68	2rC	S&W	Modesto	8 May
10.21	2.2	Donovan	Powell	JAM	13.6.71	2		Kingston	1 May
10.21	3.5	Anthony	Barnes	USA	23.12.65	4h2	NC	Eugene	16 Jun
10.22		Orlando	Parker	USA	7.3.72	1		Athens	17 Apr
10.22	3.8	Jorge Luis	Aguilera	CUB	16.1.66	1rB		Rieti	5 Sep
10.22	3.4	Ezio	Madonia	ITA	7.8.66	1h3	CISM	Tours	28 Aug
10.23	3.4		Jin Suk-kuk	KOR	25.10.70	1	EAsiG	Shanghai	13 May
10.23	3.2	Michael	Rosswess	GBR	11.6.65	2		Cork	9 Jul
10.24		Wayne	Watson	JAM	26.3.65	2		Kingston	20 Mar
10.24A	3.6	Andrew	Tynes	BAH	13.2.72	2		El Paso	10 Apr
10.24	6.3	Kevin	Little	USA	3.4.68	3rC	S&W	Modesto	8 May
10.24	3.4		Lin Wei	CHN	16.10.74	2	EAsiG	Shanghai	13 May
10.24	2.8	Nelson	Boateng	GHA	14.5.68	2h1	SEC	Knoxville	15 May
10.25	3.4		Chen Wenzhong	CHN	29.8.70	3	EAsiG	Shanghai	13 May
10.25	2.8	Greg	Saddler	USA	29.6.74	3h1	SEC	Knoxville	15 May
10.25	2.5	Toby	Box	GBR	9.9.72	5	McD	Sheffield	29 Aug
10.26	2.6	Victor	Omagbemi	NGR	22.5.67	6	WUG	Buffalo	15 Jul
10.26	3.4	Patrick	Stevens	BEL	31.1.68	2h3	CISM	Tours	28 Aug
10.27	2.7	Paul	Henderson	AUS	13.5.71	2		Sydney	20 Feb
10.27A	3.6	Godfrey	Hewlett	USA	25.8.72	4		El Paso	10 Apr
10.27	4.5	Tony	Miller	USA	15.3.69	3h1	NC	Eugene	16 Jun
10.27	3.8	Aham	Okeke	NOR	19.8.69	1		Tønsberg	30 Jun
10.27	2.7	Ibrahim	Meité	CIV	18.11.76	2		La Chaux de Fonds	8 Aug
10.28	3.2	Hideki	Onohara	JPN	16.10.68	1s		Fukuoka	2 Oct
10.29	2.8	Clyde	Rudolph	USA	15.2.72	4h1	SEC	Knoxville	15 May
10.29	2.2	Marlon	Thomas	USA	5.2.71	1h3	SEC	Knoxville	15 May
10.29	2.3	Max	Morinière	FRA	16.2.64	2		Noisy le Grand	3 Jul
10.29	3.6	Thomas	Leandersson	SWE	8.2.66	1		Halmstad	17 Jul
10.29	2.1	David	Dollé	SUI	30.5.69	1	NC	St Gallen	31 Jul

Mark	Wind	Name		Nat	Born	Pos	Meet	Venue	Date
10.29	2.5	Darren	Campbell	GBR	12.9.73	6	McD	Sheffield	29 Aug
10.30	3.8	Geir	Moen	NOR	26.6.69	2		Tønsberg	30 Jun
10.30	3.4	Peter	Ogilvie	CAN	2.5.72	4s2	WUG	Buffalo	15 Jul
10.30A	2.1	Obadele	Thompson	BAR	75	1	CAC	Cali	30 Jul
10.31		Alfredo	García	CUB	5.2.74	2		Artemisa	22 Apr
10.31		Evon	Clarke	JAM	2.3.65	1		New York	8 May
10.31	4.0	Rodney	Lewis	USA	17.7.66	6h3	NC	Eugene	16 Jun
10.31	3.8	Andrés	Simón	CUB	15.9.61	2rB		Rieti	5 Sep

Mark	Wind	Name		Nat	Born	Date
10.32	4.4	Driss	Bensaddou	MAR	67	26 Jun
10.32	3.8	Domenico	Nettis	ITA	72	5 Sep
10.33		Keevan	Mills	USA	72	23 Apr
10.33		Tony	Tate	USA	73	16 May
10.33	3.6	Sylvanus	Hepburn	BAH	72	17 Jun
10.34		Jason	Shelton	JAM	74	20 Mar
10.34	6.7	Glen	Elferink	RSA	73	10 Apr
10.34		Reyner	Padron	CUB	75	22 Apr
10.34	3.5	Kevin	Doss	USA	71	7 May
10.34		Rod	Washington	USA	73	8 May
10.34	2.1	Sanusi	Turay	SLE	68	15 May
10.34		Brandon	Jones	USA	72	15 May
10.34	4.1	Stefan	Burkart	SUI	57	20 May
10.34	2.8	Bryan	Howard	USA	76	4 Jun
10.34	4.0	Rod	Tolbert	USA	67	16 Jun
10.34	3.3	László	Karaffa	HUN	64	22 Jul
10.34	2.1	Leonardo	Prevot	CUB	71	30 Jul
10.35	6.7	Hosia	Abdallah	USA	74	10 Apr
10.35	2.1	Obadiah	Cooper	USA	70	14 May
10.35A	1.8	Donovan	Bailey	CAN	67	22 May
10.35	2.4	Charles Louis	Seck	SEN	65	3 Jul
10.35	2.9	Christian	Konieczny	GER	72	10 Jul
10.36A	2.2	Miguel	Miranda	MEX	69	13 Mar
10.36		Taw	McLeroy	USA		8 May
10.36	3.6	Marcus	Adam	GBR	68	8 May
10.36	2.4	Olivier	Théophile	FRA	68	3 Jul
10.36	3.6	Lars	Hedner	SWE	67	17 Jul
10.37		Gaspar	Lopez	CUB	74	22 Apr
10.37	4.0	Brian	Lewis	USA	74	8 May
10.37	4.1	Atsuo	Narita	JPN	75	29 May
10.37	2.6	Paulo	Neves	POR	74	10 Jun
10.37	5.3	Dino	Napier	USA	69	16 Jun
10.37	4.9	Allyn	Condon	GBR	74	3 Jul
10.37	3.3	Juan	Trapero	ESP	69	10 Aug
10.38	2.1	Anthony	Jones	USA	71	14 May
10.38	6.0	Marco	Raso	ITA	71	6 Jun
10.38		Enrique	Talavera	ESP	67	12 Jun
10.38	4.9	Ejike	Wodu	GBR	74	3 Jul
10.38	4.9	Kevin	Mark	GBR	76	3 Jul
10.38	3.9	Eiichi	Matsunobu	JPN	67	2 Oct
10.38	2.7	Tetsuya	Nakamura	JPN	73	26 Oct
10.39	4.7	Shane	Naylor	AUS	67	6 Mar
10.39		Hosia	Abdallah	USA	74	27 Mar
10.39A		Walter	Reed	USA	74	4 Apr
10.39	2.9	Derrick	Sutherland	CAN	68	12 Jun
10.39	5.3	Darryl	Hudson	USA	64	16 Jun
10.39	2.6	Franck	Waota	CIV	71	8 Aug
10.40		six men				

Best at low altitude

Mark	Wind	Name		Nat	Born	Pos	Meet	Venue	Date
10.21	5.3	Kareem	Streete-Thompson	USA	30.3.73	4h4	NC	Eugene	16 Jun

Hand timing

Mark	Wind	Name		Nat	Born	Pos	Meet	Venue	Date
9.9	1.1	Kestytis	Klimas	LIT	26.4.69	1		Kaunas	22 May
9.9A		Kennedy	Ondiek	KEN	12.12.66	1		Nairobi	28 Jul
10.1		Clyde	Rudolph	USA	15.2.72	1		Richmond	27 Mar
10.1		Tim	Harden	USA	27.1.74	2		S Richmond	27 Mar
10.1		Andrey	Grigoryev	RUS	.70	h		Sochi	24 Apr
10.1		Joel	Isasi	CUB	31.7.67	1		Habana	7 May
10.1A	1.9	Ivan	Garcia	CUB	29.2.72	1		Ciudad México	8 May
10.1		Arnaldo	De Oliveira	BRA	26.3.64	1		São Paulo	12 May
10.1		Igor	Levitov	RUS	66	1		Abakan	29 May
10.1A		Donald	Onchiri	KEN		1		Nairobi	12 Jun
10.1A		Joseph	Gikonyo	KEN	7.2.65	2		Nairobi	28 Jul
10.1	1.6	Nobuharu	Asahara	JPN	21.6.72	1		Amagasaki	25 Sep
10.1		Bryan	Skinner	AUS	4.3.73	1		Brisbane	8 Oct

Mark	Wind	Name		Nat	Born	Date
10.2		Tim	Jackson	AUS	69	2 Jan
10.2	1.8	Hosia	Abdallah	USA	74	20 Mar
10.2	0.8	Andrey	Cherkashin	BLS	70	4 May
10.2	0.9	Leonid	Safronnikov	BLS	71	4 May
10.2		Jorge	Aguilera	CUB	66	7 May
10.2		Andre	Domingos	BRA	72	12 May
10.2	2.0	Sergey	Kornelyuk	BLS	69	15 May
10.2		Guntis	Zalitis	LAT	67	20 May
10.2		Wenceslao	Ferrin	COL	69	23 May
10.2	-1.2	Pál	Rezák	HUN	66	17 Jul
10.2		Ezio	Madonia	ITA	66	9 Jul
10.2		Andreas	Koch	GER	69	5 Sep
10.2		Rocco	Ceselin	ITA	69	14 Sep
10.2		Haruyasu	Kato	JPN	71	2 Oct
10.2	1.1	Shane	Naylor	AUS	67	9 Dec

Doubtful timing Auburn 1 May (0.5): 9.7 Orlando Parker USA 7.3.72 (1), 9.8 Marlon Thomas USA 5.2.71 (2), 10.0 RobertScott USA 1.1.72 (3)

Wind-assisted

Mark	Wind	Name		Nat	Born	Pos	Meet	Venue	Date
9.9	3.4	Derrick	Thompson	USA	24.2.73	1		Fayetteville	8 May
9.9	3.5	Dean	Capobianco	AUS	11.5.70	1		Perth	20 Nov
10.0		Jermaine	Stafford	USA	25.12.74	1		Conondauga	1 May
10.0	3.5	Paul	Henderson	AUS	13.3.71	2		Perth	20 Nov
10.1		Ben	Singleton	USA	26.5.75				16 Apr
10.1		Andrew	Berry	USA	.74				16 Apr
10.1	3.4	J J	Meadors	USA		2		Fayetteville	8 May
10.1	3.4	Lawrence	Forbes	USA	26.1.73	3		Fayetteville	8 May
10.1	2.2	Marco	Menchini	ITA	20.11.68	1r1		Donnas	24 Jul
10.1	3.5	Shaun	Mayne	AUS	27.5.70	3		Perth	20 Nov

10.2 others

200 METRES

Mark	Wind	Name		Nat	Born	Pos	Meet	Venue	Date
19.85	0.3	Frank	Fredericks	NAM	2.10.67	1	WC	Stuttgart	20 Aug
19.94	0.3	John	Regis	GBR	13.10.66	2	WC	Stuttgart	20 Aug
19.96	0.8		Fredericks			1rA		Rieti	5 Sep
19.99	1.1	Carl	Lewis	USA	1.7.61	1r1	Athl	Lausanne	7 Jul
19.99	0.3		Lewis			3	WC	Stuttgart	20 Aug
20.02?	1.4	Sidnei	Telles	BRA	26.7.66	1		São Paulo	21 Mar
20.04	0.6	Michael	Marsh	USA	4.8.67	1s1	NC	Eugene	18 Jun
20.06	1.1	Michael	Johnson	USA	13.9.67	2r1	Athl	Lausanne	7 Jul
20.08A	-1.7		Fredericks			1A		Sestriere	28 Jul
20.10	0.6		Marsh			1s1	WC	Stuttgart	19 Aug
20.11	1.2	Bryan	Bridgewater	USA	7.9.70	1	NCAA II	Abilene	29 May
20.11	0.6		Fredericks			2s1	WC	Stuttgart	19 Aug
20.12	0.7	Olapade	Adeniken	NGR	19.8.69	1	Slovn	Bratislava	1 Jun
20.15	0.7		Johnson			1h1		Arlington	1 May
20.15	2.0	Joe	DeLoach	USA	5.6.67	1h4	NC	Eugene	17 Jun
20.15	0.6		Lewis			2s1	NC	Eugene	18 Jun
20.15	0.0	Daniel	Effiong (10)	NGR	17.6.72	1rA	WK	Zürich	4 Aug
20.16	1.5		Lewis			1B		Austin	8 May
20.16	0.5		Johnson			1	Indy	Indianapolis	25 Jun
20.16	1.1	Robson	Da Silva	BRA	4.9.64	3r1	Athl	Lausanne	7 Jul
20.16	0.0		Da Silva			2rA	WK	Zürich	4 Aug
20.16	-0.3		Effiong			1	Herc	Monaco	7 Aug
20.16	0.6		Regis			3s1	WC	Stuttgart	19 Aug
20.17	-0.3		Fredericks			2	Herc	Monaco	7 Aug
20.18	0.4		Fredericks			1	GG	Roma	9 Jun
20.18	0.3		Marsh			4	WC	Stuttgart	20 Aug
20.18	0.3	Dean	Capobianco	AUS	11.5.70	5	WC	Stuttgart	20 Aug
20.19	0.5		Johnson			1	Toto	Fukuoka	18 Sep
20.20	1.7		Lewis			1h2	NC	Eugene	17 Jun
20.20	0.3	Jean-Charles	Trouabal	FRA	20.5.65	6	WC	Stuttgart	20 Aug
		(30/13)							
20.22A	1.4	Andrew	Tynes	BAH	13.2.72	1rA		El Paso	10 Apr
20.23	0.0	Chris	Nelloms	USA	14.8.71	3rA	WK	Zürich	4 Aug
20.25	0.0	Jason	Hendrix	USA	24.10.72	2	JUCO	Odessa	22 May
20.25	0.7	Dennis	Mitchell	USA	20.2.66	2	Slovn	Bratislava	1 Jun
20.32		Patrick	Delice	TRI	12.11.67	1		Prairie View	27 Mar
20.32	1.8	Sam	Jefferson	USA	19.4.71	1	SWC	Austin	21 May
20.34	1.7	Marcel	Carter	USA	26.3.71	1s2	NCAA	New Orleans	4 Jun
		(20)							
20.34	1.7	David	Oaks	USA	12.5.72	2h2	NC	Eugene	17 Jun
20.35	0.7	Oluyemi	Kayode	NGR	7.7.68	2	NCAA	New Orleans	5 Jun
20.35	0.6	Leroy	Burrell	USA	21.2.67	3s1	NC	Eugene	18 Jun
20.37	0.7	Glenroy	Gilbert	CAN	31.8.68	3	NCAA	New Orleans	5 Jun
20.38	0.4	Vladislav	Dologodin	UKR	23.2.72	1		Kiev	16 May
20.39	-0.1	Linford	Christie	GBR	2.4.60	1	ASV	Köln	1 Aug
20.40	0.6	Floyd	Heard	USA	24.3.66	4s1	NC	Eugene	18 Jun
20.41	2.0	Tim	Williams	USA	27.5.63	3h4	NC	Eugene	17 Jun
20.42	1.1	Atlee	Mahorn	CAN	27.10.65	2	Gugl	Linz	25 Aug
20.43	0.0	David	Dollé	SUI	30.5.69	1		Meilen	12 Sep
		(30)							
20.44	1.6	Emmanuel	Tuffour	GHA	2.12.66	1rA		Lindau	8 Aug
20.46	2.0	Robert	Kurnicki	GER	27.3.65	1	NC	Duisburg	11 Jul
20.47	1.1	Jeff	Williams	USA	31.12.64	1	McD	Sheffield	29 Aug
20.48	1.1	Bruny	Surin	CAN	12.7.67	3	Gugl	Linz	25 Aug
20.49	0.9	Damien	Marsh	AUS	28.3.71	1		Sydney	21 Feb
20.49	1.3	Ron	Clark	USA	1.11.69	3rB		Austin	8 May
20.49	1.7	Kevin	Braunskill	USA	31.3.69	5h2	NC	Eugene	17 Jun
20.50	1.2	Randall	Evans	USA	26.10.70	3	NCAA II	Abilene	29 May
20.50	1.1	Calvin	Smith	USA	8.1.61	3	McD	Sheffield	29 Aug
20.51		Brian	Irvin	USA	30.7.70	1		Fairfax	26 May
		(40)							
20.52	2.0	Charles	Mitchell	USA	29.1.75	1		Sacramento	12 Jun
20.52	0.6	Nelson	Boateng	GHA	14.5.68	5s1	WC	Stuttgart	19 Aug
20.54	-0.9	Andrey	Fedoriv	RUS	11.8.63	2	EP	Rome	27 Jun

Mark	Wind	Name		Nat	Born	Pos	Meet	Venue	Date
20.54	1.3	James	Trapp	USA	28.12.70	4	BNP	Villeneuve d'Ascq	2 Jul
20.55A	1.3	Johan	Rossouw	RSA	20.10.65	1		Pretoria	15 May
20.55A	0.7	Tony	Miller	USA	15.3.69	1		Provo	26 May
20.56	1.8	Kevin	Little	USA	3.4.68	2	Drake R	Des Moines	24 Apr
20.56	0.4	Dmitriy	Vanyaikin	UKR	14.1.66	2		Kiev	16 May
20.57	2.0	Calvin	Harrison	USA	20.1.74	2		Sacramento	12 Jun
20.58	-0.2	Andre Domingos	Da Silva	BRA	26.11.72	2		Americana	27 Feb
		(50)							
20.58	0.0	Oumar	Loum	SEN	31.12.73	1r4		Weinstadt	7 Aug
20.59	0.1	Ato	Boldon	TRI	30.12.73	1		Redding	22 May
20.59		Derrick	Thompson	USA	24.2.73	1		Fayetteville	26 May
20.59	1.5	Clyde	Rudolph	USA	15.2.72	4s1	NCAA	New Orleans	4 Jun
20.60	0.8	Carlo	Occhiena	ITA	24.9.72	5rA		Rieti	5 Sep
20.61	0.5	Daryl	Frazier	USA	23.1.71	2		Gainesville	30 Apr
20.61	0	Ibrahim	Hassan	GHA	71	2r4		Weinstadt	7 Aug
20.62	2.0	Michael	Huke	GER	30.3.69	2	NC	Duisburg	11 Jul
20.63	1.0	Paul	Henderson	AUS	13.3.71	1s1	NC	Brisbane	6 Mar
20.63	0.1	Barry	Smith	USA	22.2.71	2		Redding	22 May
		(60)							
20.63	1.8	Daniel	Sangouma	FRA	7.2.65	3		Noisy le Grand	3 Jul
20.64		Sylvanus	Hepburn	BAH	2.3.71	1s	NC	Nassau	17 Jun
20.64	1.8	Bryan	Bronson	USA	9.9.72	4		Noisy le Grand	3 Jul
20.65		Edward	Hervey	USA	14.3.74	1		Walnut	1 May
20.65	0.4	Ivan	Garcia	CUB	29.2.72	1	NC	Habana	13 May
20.66	0.8	Torbjörn	Eriksson	SWE	17.4.71	1	NC	Kvarnsveden	25 Jul
20.66	1.1	Giorgio	Marras	ITA	15.10.71	1h3	NC	Bologna	3 Aug
20.67	1.7	Rod	Tolbert	USA	11.6.67	6h2	NC	Eugene	17 Jun
20.67	-0.8	Thomas	Renner ¶	AUT	24.12.67	1		Salzburg	18 Jun
20.67	-0.3	Stanislav	Georgiev	BUL	6.2.71	1		Sofia	19 Jun
		(70)							
20.68	2.0	Björn	Sinnhuber	GER	1.8.68	3	NC	Duisburg	11 Jul
20.69		John	Myles-Mills	GHA	19.4.66	1		Fairfax	1 May
20.69	2.0	Aki	Bradley	USA	7.2.71	2h1	SEC	Knoxville	15 May
20.69	1.8	Gerry	Woodberry	USA	23.10.69	2	SWC	Austin	21 May
20.69	1.1	Troy	Douglas	BER	30.11.62	4	Gugl	Linz	25 Aug
20.70	0.0	Danny	McCray	USA	11.3.74	1		Waco	17 Apr
20.70	-3.0	Jermaine	Stafford	USA	25.12.74	1	NC-j	Spokane	27 Jun
20.71	1.2	Evon	Clarke	JAM	2.3.65	4	NCAA II	Abilene	29 May
20.71	1.6	Oleg	Fatun	RUS	23.3.59	2h3	WC	Stuttgart	17 Aug
20.72	1.5	Roshaan	Griffith	USA	21.2.74	3rA		Austin	8 May
		(80)							
20.72	0.4	Joel	Isasi	CUB	31.7.67	2	NC	Habana	13 May
20.72	0.4	Satoru	Inoue	JPN	21.7.71	1		Tokyo	23 May
20.72	1.2	Bernard	Young	BAH	29.8.66	5	NCAA II	Abilene	29 May
20.72	1.9	Patrick	Stevens	BEL	31.1.68	1	EP/B	Bruxelles	13 Jun
20.72	0.0	Kevin	Widmer	SUI	23.9.70	2		Meilen	12 Sep
20.75	1.0	James	Jett	USA	28.12.70	1		Tuscaloosa	28 Mar
20.75	1.7	Fabian	Muyaba	ZIM	30.9.70	5s2	NCAA	New Orleans	4 Jun
20.76A	1.4	John	Lawson	RSA	24.4.66	1		Boksburg	6 Feb
20.76	0.4	Jeff	Laynes	USA	3.10.70	1		Los Angeles (Ww)	24 Apr
20.76	-1.2	Nate	Langlois	USA	9.7.71	1		Notre Dame	1 May
		(90)							
20.76	0.3	Konstadinos	Kederis	GRE	11.6.73	1	EP/C1	Villach	12 Jun
20.78A	-1.7	Tony	Walton	USA	3.6.69	2		Ciudad México	9 May
20.78	1.8	Ethridge	Green	USA	10.11.69	3	SWC	Austin	21 May
20.78	1.2	Sean	Adams	USA	24.5.71	6	NCAA II	Abilene	29 May
20.78	0.1	James	Brown	USA	72	1		Ponce	12 Jun
20.78	0.1	Ian	Morris	TRI	30.11.61	2	IDag	Malmö	9 Aug
20.79	1.3	Anthuan	Maybank	USA	30.12.69	2		Tempe	20 Mar
20.79		Daniel	Cojocaru	ROM	27.5.69	1	RomIC	Bucuresti	19 Jun
20.80	1.0	Tony	Tate	USA	31.12.73	2		Indianapolis	26 May
20.80	1.7	Dino	Napier	USA	24.11.69	6s2	NC	Eugene	18 Jun
		(100)							
20.80	0.0	Raymond	Stewart	JAM	8.3.65	1	NC	Kingston	3 Jul
20.80	0.8	Geir	Moen	NOR	26.6.69	1	NC	Tønsberg	31 Jul
20.80	-1.1	Tzvetoslav	Stankulov	BUL	1.2.69	1	NC	Sofia	1 Aug
20.80	-1.4	Aleksandr	Porkhomovskiy	RUS	12.8.72	1		Moskva	7 Aug

Mark	Wind	Name		Nat	Born	Pos	Meet	Venue	Date
20.81	1.8	Derry	Pemberton	ISV	71				17 Apr
20.81	-0.9	Kirk	Francis	USA					17 Apr
20.81	1.8	Tod	Long	USA	70				24 Apr
20.81		Vincent	Henderson	USA	72				26 May
20.81	-0.2	Mikhail	Vdovin	RUS	67				16 Jul
20.81	0.1	Nobuharu	Asahara	JPN	72				12 Sep
		(110)							
20.83	1.8	Tunji	Bello	NGR	72				1 May
20.83A	-0.1	Jannie	Viljoen	RSA	71				8 Mar
20.83	-1.1	Tshakile	Nzimande	RSA	61				24 Apr
20.83	0.1	Tim	Harden	USA	74				15 May
20.83	-0.5	Alexandros	Terzian	GRE	68				17 Aug
20.83	1.8	Huang Danwei		CHN	72				4 Dec
20.84	1.0	Greg	Saddler	USA	74				28 Mar
20.84	1.0	Lamar	Chisley	USA	72				13 May
20.84A	-1.3	Travis	Grant	USA	72				18 May
20.84	0.2	Aleksey	Chikhachev	UKR	71				2 Jul
		(120)							
20.84	0.9	Marek	Zalewski	POL	70				25 Jul
20.84	1.4	Victor	Omagbemi	NGR	67				27 Jul
20.85		Antonio	Pettigrew	USA	67				27 Mar
20.85	2.0	Jason	Rouser	USA	70				8 May
20.85		Dwight	Ferguson	BAH					17 Jun
20.85	0.2	Igor	Streltsov	UKR	65				2 Jul
20.86	1.3	Lorenzo	Daniel	USA	66				1 May
20.86	1.2	Darren	Campbell	GBR	73				4 Aug
20.87	0.0	Koji	Ito	JPN	70				17 Apr
20.87	0.4	Jorge	Aguilera	CUB	66				13 May
		(130)							
20.88		Michael	Green	JAM	70				3 Apr
20.88	1.0	Obadiah	Cooper	USA	70				26 May
20.88	1.8	Andreas	Berger ¶	AUT	61				3 Jul
20.88	1.0	Donovan	Bailey	CAN	67				1 Aug
20.88		Jamil	Cherry	USA	76				7 Aug
20.88	-0.2	Nikolay	Antonov	BUL	68				17 Aug
20.89	2.0	Bode	Osagiobare	NGR	70				8 May
20.89	2.0	Slobodan	Brankovic	YUG	67				4 Jul
20.89	2.0	Hansjörg	Metzger	GER	69				11 Jul
20.89A	-1.7	Toby	Box	GBR	72				28 Jul
		(140)							
20.90A	0.7	Francois	du Toit	RSA	70				27 Mar
20.90		Jonathan	Burrell	USA	74				1 May
20.90	2.0	Chris	King	USA	69				15 May
20.90	1.7	Gilles	Quénéhervé	FRA	66				30 May
20.91	0.4	Zhao Cunlin		CHN	65				26 Apr
20.91	2.0	Henry	Neal	USA	70				8 May
20.91	1.5	Aaron	Thigpen	USA	64				8 May
20.91	0.4	Oleg	Kramarenko	UKR	70				16 May
20.91		Charles	Miles	USA	70				23 May
20.91	0.1	Karim	Saunders	USA	69				12 Jun
		(150)							
20.91		Antonious	Dotson	USA	70				3 Jul
20.91	1.0	Pablo	Nolet	ESP	70				27 Jul
20.92	-1.5	Wendell	Gaskin	USA	73				3 Apr
20.92	0.2	Alain	Reimann	SUI	67				19 Jun
20.92		Salaam	Gariba	GHA	69				25 Jul
20.92A	0.9	Ezio	Madonia	ITA	66				28 Jul
20.93		Kerchavel	Patterson	USA					1 May
20.93	0.0	Darius	Brewington	USA	75				22 May
20.93	-1.5	Michael	Barron	USA	73				3 Apr
20.93		George	Page	USA	74				10 Apr
		(160)							
20.93A	-1.3	David	Knight	USA	70				18 May
20.93	0.1	Chris	Jones	USA	73				12 Jun
20.93	0.5	Niti	Piyapan	THA	72				16 Jun
20.93		Daniel	Barbulescu	ROM	71				3 Jul
20.93	0.6	Ricardo	Greenidge	CAN	71				3 Jul
20.93	0.0	Ibrahim	Ismail	QAT	72				27 Sep
20.94		Joel	Lamela	CUB	71				6 Mar
20.94	-0.4	Keevan	Mills	USA	72				17 May
20.94	2.0	Brashant	Carter	USA					18 May
20.94		Delavantie	Brown	JAM					26 May
		(170)							
20.94	1.3	Edgardo	Guilbe	PUR	66				27 Nov
20.95	-0.5	Mark	Keddell	NZL	75				6 Mar
20.95	0.6	Stephane	Diagana	FRA	69				24 Apr
20.95	0.1	Stephen	Lewis	MTN	68				12 Jun
20.95	1.0	Allyn	Condon	GBR	74				26 Jun
20.95	1.1	Hermann	Lomba	FRA	60				25 Jul
20.95		Florian	Gamper	GER	72				31 Jul

Maybank (20.79) also 20.79 -0.1 5 Köln 1 Aug

Best low altitude marks

Mark	Wind	Name		Nat	Born	Pos	Meet	Venue	Date
20.48	1.7		Tynes			3s2	NCAA	New Orleans	4 Jun
20.55	0.6		Rossouw			3q2	WC	Stuttgart	19 Aug

Indoors

Mark	Wind	Name		Nat	Born	Pos	Meet	Venue	Date
20.58	-	Michael	Bates	USA	19.12.69	2		Liévin	13 Feb
20.84	-	Nikolay	Antonov	BUL	68				20 Feb
20.87	-	Christoph	Postinger	AUT	72				2 Mar
20.89	-	Marcus	Adam	GBR	68				20 Feb
20.95	-	Stéphane	Diagana	FRA	69				13 Feb

Wind-assisted marks

Mark	Wind	Name		Nat	Born	Pos	Meet	Venue	Date
19.97	2.5	Michael	Marsh	USA	4.8.67	1	NC	Eugene	19 Jun
20.07	2.5		Lewis			2	NC	Eugene	19 Jun
20.08	2.1		Regis			1	v USA	Edinburgh	2 Jul
20.14	2.4		Bridgewater			1	WUG	Buffalo	17 Jul
20.15	2.4		Telles			1		Americana	13 Feb
20.17	2.4	Chris	Nelloms	USA	14.8.71	2	WUG	Buffalo	17 Jul
20.18A	2.6	Oluyemi	Kayode	NGR	7.7.68	1		El Paso	22 May
20.19	2.1	Linford	Christie	GBR	2.4.60	2	vUSA	Edinburgh	2 Jul
20.21	2.5		Regis			1	NC	London	13 Jun
20.29	3.4	Damien	Marsh	AUS	28.3.71	1	NC	Brisbane	7 Mar
20.35	3.0	Derrick	Thompson	USA	24.2.73	1		Fayetteville	8 May
20.36	3.4	Paul	Henderson	AUS	13.3.71	2	NC	Brisbane	7 Mar
20.40	2.3	Fabian	Muyaba	ZIM	30.9.70	2h2	SEC	Knoxville	15 May
20.51	2.1	Jason	John	GBR	17.10.71	5	vUSA	Edinburgh	2 Jul
20.53	3.9	Ivan	Garcia	CUB	29.2.72	1rB		Rieti	5 Sep
20.55	2.6	Danny	McCray	USA	11.3.74	1rA		College Station	10 Apr
20.55	2.1	Darren	Campbell	GBR	12.9.73	6	vUSA	Edinburgh	2 Jul
20.59		Jeff	Laynes	USA	3.10.70	1		Northridge	6 Mar
20.59	3.6	Sylvanus	Hepburn	BAH	2.3.71	1h5	NC	Nassau	16 Jun
20.60	2.6	Daniel	Sangouma	FRA	7.2.65	2rA		Limoges	10 Jul
20.61		Sean	Adams	USA	24.5.71	1		Stephenville	24 Apr
20.62		James	Brown	USA	72	1		Houston	1 May
20.62	3.4	Lamar	Chisley	USA	15.3.72	1		Austin	7 May

Mark	Wind	Name		Nat	Born	Pos	Meet	Venue	Date
20.64	2.6	Gerry	Woodberry	USA	23.10.69	2rA		College Station	10 Apr
20.65	7.8	Aaron	Payne	USA	16.5.71	2	Big10	East Lansing	23 May
20.66	3.4	Mark	Ladbrook	AUS	6.2.72	3	NC	Brisbane	7 Mar
20.66	6.5?	Glen	Elferink	RSA	21.5.73	1		Arlington	10 Apr
20.67		Windell	Dobson	JAM	5.1.70	1		New Orleans	15 May
20.67	4.0	Aleksandr	Porkhomovskiy	RUS	12.8.72	2		Cork	9 Jul
20.70		Marlon	Thomas	USA	5.2.71	1		Athens	17 Apr
20.70	5.2	Obadiah	Cooper	USA	8.3.70	1		Champaign	14 May
20.70	2.7	Patrick	Stevens	BEL	31.1.68	1	CISM	Tours	30 Aug
20.73	2.4	Michael	Green	JAM	7.11.70	1h1		Chapel Hill	16 Apr
20.74		Von	Brown	USA	8.1.73	1		New Orleans	10 Apr
20.74A		Tyler	Anderson	USA	27.4.70	1		Provo	24 Apr
20.74		Jeff	Roberts	USA	21.6.74	2		Abilene	8 May
20.74	2.3	Van	Smith	USA	27.5.73	3h2	SEC	Knoxville	15 May
20.74	2.3	Aham	Okeke	NOR	19.8.69	1		Drammen	31 May
20.77	5.2	Scott	Turner	USA	26.2.72	2		Champaign	14 May
20.80	2.5	Owusu	Dako	GBR	23.5.73	4	NC	London	13 Jun

Mark	Wind	Name		Nat	Born	Date
20.81A	3.0	Peter	Ogilvie	CAN	72	22 May
20.81			Zhang Qing	CHN	68	12 Sep
20.82A	3.0	Brad	McCuaig	CAN	70	22 May
20.82A	2.6	Terry	Bowen	USA	71	22 May
20.82	2.8	Toby	Box	GBR	72	17 Jul
20.84		Tony	Gaiter	USA	74	5 Mar
20.84	4.0	Nigel	Stickings	GBR	71	9 Jul
20.85A	2.6		Castle	USA		22 May
20.86		Gregory	Haughton	JAM	73	5 May
20.86	4.1	Edgardo	Guilbe	PUR	66	31 Jul
20.87	2.3	Michael	Rosswess	GBR	65	17 Jul
20.87	2.7	Ibrahim	Ismail	QAT	72	30 Aug
20.89	2.1	Karim	Saunders	USA	69	15 May
20.89	2.5	David	Grindley	GBR	72	13 Jun
20.90	3.4	Stuart	Uhlman	AUS	71	7 Mar
20.90A	4.1	Neil	De Silva	TRI	69	31 Jul
20.90	2.7	Florian	Gamper	GER	72	30 Aug
20.91	3.5	Osmond	Ezinwa	NGR	71	24 Apr
20.91	2.2	Joel	Lamela	CUB	71	23 May
20.91	2.8	Sergej	Inzakov	LAT	71	17 Jul
20.92		James	Dibble	USA		
20.93	5.2	Earl	Jenkins	USA	70	14 May
20.93		Andre	De Saussure	USA	75	27 May
20.93	2.7	Georgios	Panagiotopoulos	GRE	69	30 Aug
20.94		Godfrey	Hewlett	USA	72	
20.94	3.4	Glenn	McCarthy	AUS	70	7 Mar
20.94	2.6	Hermann	Lomba	FRA	60	10 Jul
20.94	3.9	Giovanni	Puggioni	ITA	66	5 Sep
20.95	3.5	Nick	Rennie	AUS	74	6 Mar

Doubtful

Mark	Wind	Name		Nat	Born	Pos	Meet	Venue	Date
20.49w		David	Shepherd	USA	2.6.70	1		Lubbock	17 Apr

Hand timing

Mark	Wind	Name		Nat	Born	Pos	Meet	Venue	Date
20.3		Aaron	Payne	USA	16.5.71	1		Oxford, Ohio	17 Apr
20.6		Charles	Miles	USA	12.10.70	1rC		Wilmington	10 Apr
20.6	-0.8	Mikhail	Vdovin	RUS	15.1.67	1		Bryansk	30 May

Mark	Wind	Name		Nat	Born	Date
20.7A		Kennedy	Ondiek	KEN	66	19 May
20.7		Igor	Levitov	RUS	66	30 May
20.7		Seliano	More	CUB	70	10 Jun
20.7A		Simeon	Kipkemboi	KEN	60	12 Jun
20.7		Alexander	Lack	GER	72	20 Jun

Wind assisted

Mark	Wind	Name		Nat	Born	Pos	Meet	Venue	Date
20.4	2.6	Sean	Adams	USA	24.5.71	1		College Station	20 Mar
20.4		Travis	Hannah	USA	31.1.70	2r2		Los Angeles	10 Apr
20.5		Carlos	Gats	ARG	11.12.69	1		Buenos Aires	20 Nov
20.6		Marcus	Adam	GBR	28.2.68	3rA		Los Angeles	10 Apr
20.6A	2.9	Manuel	Cardeñas	MEX	4.9.74	1		Ciudad México	2 May

Mark	Wind	Name		Nat	Born	Date
20.7	2.3	Aki	Bradley	USA	71	10 Apr
20.7	2.3	Sheddric	Fields	USA	73	10 Apr
20.7		Andrew	Berry	USA	74	24 Apr
20.7A	2.9	Raymundo	Escalante	MEX	64	2 May

300 METRES

Mark	Name		Nat	Born	Pos	Meet	Venue	Date
31.72	Michael	Johnson	USA	13.9.67	1	Vaux	Gateshead	30 Jul
31.98	John	Regis	GBR	13.10.66	1	Pearl	Belfast	19 Jun
32.07	Quincy	Watts	USA	19.6.70	2	Vaux	Gateshead	30 Jul
32.10	Michael	Marsh	USA	4.8.67	3	Vaux	Gateshead	30 Jul
32.12		Regis			4	Vaux	Gateshead	30 Jul
32.38	Chris	Nelloms	USA	14.8.71	5	Vaux	Gateshead	30 Jul
32.45	David	Grindley	GBR	29.10.72	2	Pearl	Belfast	19 Jun
32.48	Kevin	Braunskill	USA	31.3.69	6	Vaux	Gateshead	30 Jul
32.77	Giorgio	Marras	ITA	15.10.71	1		Oristano	2 May
32.86	Kevin	Widmer	SUI	23.9.70	1		Bulle	15 Sep
32.92	Ade	Mafe	GBR	12.11.66	7	Vaux	Gateshead	30 Jul
32.92	Patrick	Delice	TRI	12.11.67	8	Vaux	Gateshead	30 Jul
33.00	Du'aine	Ladejo	GBR	14.2.71	3	Pearl	Belfast	19 Jun

During 400m races

Mark	Name		Nat	Born	Pos	Meet	Venue	Date
32.22+	Butch	Reynolds	USA	8.6.64	2	WC	Stuttgart	17 Aug
32.26+	Sunday	Bada	NGR	22.6.69	3	WC	Stuttgart	16 Aug
32.35+	David	Grindley	GBR	29.10.72	1		Roma	26 Jun
33.00+	Gregory	Haughton	JAM	10.11.73	4+	WC	Stuttgart	17 Aug

Mark	Name		Nat	Born	Pos	Meet	Venue	Date

400 METRES

Mark	Name		Nat	Born	Pos	Meet	Venue	Date
43.65	Michael	Johnson	USA	13.9.67	1	WC	Stuttgart	17 Aug
43.74		Johnson			1	NC	Eugene	19 Jun
43.94		Johnson			1	ISTAF	Berlin	27 Aug
44.12	Butch	Reynolds	USA	8.6.64	2	NC	Eugene	19 Jun
44.13A	Quincy	Watts	USA	19.6.70	1		Sestriere	28 Jul
44.13		Reynolds			2	WC	Stuttgart	17 Aug
44.22		Johnson			1rA	WK	Zürich	4 Aug
44.24		Watts			3	NC	Eugene	19 Jun
44.28	Andrew	Valmon	USA	1.1.65	4	NC	Eugene	19 Jun
44.34	Samson	Kitur	KEN	25.2.66	1s2	WC	Stuttgart	16 Aug
44.37		Reynolds			1	Indy	Indianapolis	25 Jun
44.38		Johnson			1		Houston	21 May
44.39		Johnson			2s2	WC	Stuttgart	16 Aug
44.45	Antonio	Pettigrew	USA	3.11.67	5	NC	Eugene	19 Jun
44.45		Johnson			1	VD	Bruxelles	3 Sep
44.50	David	Grindley	GBR	29.10.72	2rA	WK	Zürich	4 Aug
44.53		Grindley			1	Athl	Lausanne	7 Jul
44.54		Kitur			1rA	ASV	Köln	1 Aug
44.54	Steve	Lewis	USA	16.5.69	3rA	WK	Zürich	4 Aug
44.54		Kitur			3	WC	Stuttgart	17 Aug
44.58	Patrick	Delice	TRI	12.11.67	1	NCAA II	Abilene	29 May
44.59		Kitur			1		Rieti	5 Sep
44.60		Watts			1		Los Angeles (Ww)	1 May
44.60A		Valmon			2		Sestriere	28 Jul
44.62	Derek	Mills (10)	USA	9.7.72	6	NC	Eugene	19 Jun
44.62		Reynolds			4rA	WK	Zürich	4 Aug
44.63		Watts			1s1	WC	Stuttgart	16 Aug
44.63	Sunday	Bada	NGR	22.6.69	3s2	WC	Stuttgart	16 Aug
44.65		Watts			5A	WK	Zürich	4 Aug
44.67		Watts			1	Herc	Monaco	7 Aug
44.68		Reynolds			1	Banes	São Paulo	16 May
44.68		Reynolds			2	ISTAF	Berlin	27 Aug
	(32/11)							
44.78	Greg	Haughton	JAM	10.11.73	4s2	WC	Stuttgart	16 Aug
44.79	Evon	Clarke	JAM	2.3.65	2	NCAA II	Abilene	29 May
44.82	Kennedy	Ochieng	KEN	30.12.71	1rB	WK	Zürich	4 Aug
44.85	Ibrahim	Ismail	QAT	10.5.72	5s2	WC	Stuttgart	16 Aug
44.89	Ian	Morris	TRI	30.11.61	2rB	WK	Zürich	4 Aug
44.94	Simon	Kemboi	KEN	1.3.67	3s1	WC	Stuttgart	16 Aug
44.99	Anthuan	Maybank	USA	30.12.69	1	Drake R	Des Moines	24 Apr
45.04	Calvin	Davis	USA	2.4.72	1	NCAA	New Orleans	5 Jun
45.07	Calvin	Harrison	USA	20.1.74	1	NC-j	Spokane	27 Jun
	(20)							
45.22	Wesley	Russell	USA	3.3.71	2		Columbus	9 May
45.22	Darnell	Hall	USA	26.9.71	3s2	NC	Eugene	18 Jun
45.23	Chris	Jones	USA	8.10.73	2h2	NCAA	New Orleans	3 Jun
45.26	Stéphane	Diagana	FRA	23.7.69	1	NC	Annecy	25 Jul
45.30	Lamont	Smith	USA	11.12.72	1	JUCO	Odessa	22 May
45.30	Ade	Mafe	GBR	12.11.66	5	TSB	London	23 Jul
45.35A	Andrea	Nuti	ITA	4.8.67	3		Sestriere	28 Jul
45.36	David	Oaks	USA	12.5.72	2	Drake R	Des Moines	24 Apr
45.36	Jason	Rouser	USA	22.3.70	1	USOF	San Antonio	31 Jul
45.40	Neil	De Silva	TRI	15.11.69	1		Wilberforce	8 May
	(30)							
45.42	Solomon	Amagatcher	GHA	20.12.70	1	SEC	Knoxville	16 May
45.45	Aaron	Payne	USA	16.5.71	3	JO	Columbus	9 May
45.45A	Tod	Long	USA	18.12.70	1		Boulder	18 May
45.48	Dawda	Jallow	GAM	22.12.69	2		Atlanta	3 Apr
45.48	John	Regis	GBR	13.10.66	1	MSR	Walnut	17 Apr
45.51	Norberto	Tellez	CUB	23.12.72	4q3	WC	Stuttgart	15 Aug
45.53	Darren	Clark	AUS	6.9.65	1r1		Sydney	23 Jan
45.53	Michael	Marsh	USA	4.8.67	1		Houston	2 May
45.54	Benyounès	Lahlou	MAR	3.11.64	1		Cannes	26 Jun
45.55	Jean-Louis	Rapnouil	FRA	24.1.66	2	NC	Annecy	25 Jul
	(40)							

Mark	Name		Nat	Born	Pos	Meet	Venue	Date
45.56	Devon	Edwards	USA	17.2.73	2h1		Abilene	28 May
45.57	Troy	Douglas	BER	30.11.62	5q3	WC	Stuttgart	15 Aug
45.59	Abedenigo	Matilu	KEN	21.11.68	1r2		Weinstadt	7 Aug
45.60	Ibrahim	Hassan	GHA	71	1		Rhede	6 Aug
45.61	Anton	Ivanov	BUL	18.7.71	1	NC	Sofia	31 Jul
45.63	Brian	Irvin	USA	30.7.70	1		Chapel Hill	8 May
45.65A	David	Knight	USA	2.4.70	2		Boulder	18 May
45.65	Dmitriy	Golovastov	RUS	14.7.71	2	EP	Rome	26 Jun
45.66	Bryan	Bronson	USA	9.9.72	3	Drake R	Des Moines	24 Apr
45.66	Rico	Lieder	GER	25.3.71	4q1	WC	Stuttgart	15 Aug
	(50)							
45.68	Forest	Johnson	USA	19.2.72	3		Atlanta	3 Apr
45.69	Scott	Turner	USA	26.2.72	1h3		East Lansing	22 May
45.70	Gabriel	Luke	USA	26.11.69	2	SWC	Austin	21 May
45.70A	Hayden	Stephen	TRI	9.1.72	1		El Paso	22 May
45.70	Konstadinos	Kederis	GRE	11.6.73	1	MedG	Narbonne	18 Jun
45.72	Dennis	Blake	JAM	6.9.70	1	NC	Kingston	3 Jul
45.73	Kevin	Lyles	USA	23.7.73	1		Fairfax	26 May
45.74	Tony	Miller -2	USA	12.2.71	1		Abilene	13 May
45.74	Deon	Minor	USA	22.1.73	3		Austin	22 May
45.75	David	McKenzie	GBR	3.9.70	3	AAA	Birmingham	17 Jul
	(60)							
45.76A	Alessandro	Aimar	ITA	5.6.67	4		Sestriere	28 Jul
45.77	Marcus	Brooks	USA	21.12.70	1h1	SEC	Knoxville	15 May
45.79	Atlee	Mahorn	CAN	27.10.65	1	OD	Jena	13 Jun
45.80	Omokaro	Alohan	NGR	18.9.71	2	SEC	Knoxville	16 May
45.80	Bryan	Jones	USA	13.2.72	2h3		East Lansing	22 May
45.80	Dmitriy	Kosov	RUS	28.9.68	1	NC	Moskva	20 Jun
45.81	Ferdana	Johnson	USA	6.10.72	1		Houston	1 May
45.82	Danny	McFarlane	JAM	14.2.72	2	NC	Kingston	3 Jul
45.83	Ivan	Jean-Marie	STL	28.9.72	1s1	JUCO	Odessa	21 May
45.85		Zhao Cunlin	CHN	20.5.65	1	NG	Beijing	11 Sep
	(70)							
45.86A	Bobang	Phiri	RSA	5.5.68	2		Pretoria	15 May
45.86	Roger	Black	GBR	31.3.66	6	NYG	New York	22 May
45.88	Michael	Joubert	AUS	11.5.70	2	Pre	Eugene	5 Jun
45.88	Innokentiy	Zharov	RUS	23.11.68	2	NC	Moskva	20 Jun
45.89	Mikhail	Vdovin	RUS	15.1.67	3	NC	Moskva	20 Jun
45.90	Pierre-Marie	Hilaire	FRA	19.11.65	2s1	NC	Annecy	24 Jul
45.91	Raoul	Howard	USA	11.3.74	3		Abilene	13 May
45.91	Otis	Scott	USA	19.4.71	1h3	JUCO	Odessa	20 May
45.91	Sadek	Boumendil	ALG	19.8.72	6q1	WC	Stuttgart	15 Aug
45.92	Sidnei	Telles	BRA	26.7.66	1		Americana	27 Feb
	(80)							
45.92A	Du'aine	Ladejo	GBR	14.2.71	5		Sestriere	28 Jul
45.93	Wade	Payne	BAR	3.10.71	3s2	JUCO	Odessa	21 May
45.95	Hachim	Ndiaye	SEN	28.10.63	1		Yamoussoko	10 Apr
45.95	Robert	Smith	USA	4.3.72	3h3		East Lansing	22 May
45.96	Samuel	Matete	ZAM	27.7.68	1		San Marcos	23 Apr
45.96	Olaf	Hense	GER	19.11.67	1r1		Bad Homburg	10 Jun
45.97	Winthrop	Graham	JAM	17.11.65	4	Indy	Indianapolis	25 Jun
45.98A	Sean	Maye	USA	24.6.69	2		El Paso	22 May
45.98	Marco	Vaccari	ITA	17.7.66	1	NC	Bologna	2 Aug
45.99	Thomas	Schönlebe	GER	6.8.65	2rA		Lindau	8 Aug
	(90)							
46.01	Jacques	Farraudière	FRA	27.1.66	4	NC	Annecy	25 Jul
46.01	Roberto	Hernández	CUB	6.3.67	3h2	WC	Stuttgart	14 Aug
46.03	Kevin	Young	USA	16.9.66	4	MSR	Walnut	17 Apr
46.04	Masayoshi	Kan	JPN	25.2.72	1		Naruto	28 Oct
46.05	Joshua	Coull	AUS	11.8.69	1r1		Canberra	25 Jan
46.05	Ben	Beyers	USA	19.5.74	1h2		East Lansing	22 May
46.05	Clarence	Daniel	USA	11.6.61	1		Tallahassee	26 May
46.06	Hassan	Bosso	NGR	.62	2	NC	Lagos	18 Jun
46.07	Francis	Ogola	UGA	1.7.73	1		Istanbul	4 Sep
46.08	Derrick	Baker	USA	28.12.70	1	Pac-10	Berkeley	22 May
	(100)							

Mark	Name		Nat	Born	Date
46.09	Jose	Parrilla	USA	72	30 Jun
46.10	Derek	Shepard	USA	73	7 May
46.11	Cayetano	Cornet	ESP	63	22 May
46.12	Amar	Hacini	ALG	71	31 May
46.12	Patrick	O'Connor	JAM	66	3 Jul
46.13	André	Jaffory	FRA	68	6 Jun
46.13	Guy	Bullock	GBR	75	31 Jul
46.15	Rich	Jones	USA	73	22 May
46.15	Wayne	McDonald	GBR	70	16 Jul
46.15A	Herman	de Jager	RSA	71	30 Oct
	(110)				
46.16	Dean	Capobianco	AUS	70	25 Feb
46.16	Danny	McCray	USA	74	20 May
46.16	Eric	Keter	KEN	66	10 Jun
46.16	Andrea	Montanari	ITA	65	2 Aug
46.17	Jason	Kougellis	AUS	70	6 Mar
46.18	Omar	Mena	CUB	66	24 Nov
46.19	Nilton Cesar	Messias	BRA	71	24 Apr
46.19	Ethridge	Green	USA	69	26 May
46.20	Alvin	Daniel	TRI	68	1 May
46.20	Desmond	Johnson	USA	77	8 May
	(120)				
46.20	Matthias	Rusterholz	SUI	71	29 Jun
46.20	Bouchaib	Belkaid	MAR	67	5 Jul
46.21	Jeff	Laynes	USA	70	20 Mar
46.21	Inaldo Justino	Sena	BRA	71	24 Apr
46.21A	Arnaud	Malherbe	RSA	72	15 May
46.21	Chris	Abrahams	JAM	71	21 May
46.21	Kevin	Widmer	SUI	70	18 Sep
46.24A	Michael	McLean	CAN	70	26 May
46.24	Tzvetoslav	Stankulov	BUL	69	31 Jul
46.25	Curtis	McIntire	USA	73	14 May
	(130)				
46.25	Robert	Guy	TRI	64	28 May
46.25	Lutz	Becker	GER	69	6 Jun
46.25	Alvin	Harrison	USA	74	26 Jun
46.26	Ed	Odom	USA	73	16 May
46.28	Mark	Graham	CAN	73	3 Jul
46.29	Simon	Hollingsworth	AUS	72	25 Jan
46.29	Eric	Crichlow	USA	69	17 Apr
46.29	Anthony	Pryce	JAM		2 Jul
46.30	Wilson	Cañizales	COL	64	29 Apr
46.30A	Alfred	Visagie	RSA	72	15 May
	(140)				
46.30	Udime	Ekpeyong	NGR	75	22 May
46.31	Will	Glover	USA	71	22 May
46.31	Antonious	Dotson	USA	70	29 May
46.32	Eronildes	Nunes De Araujo	BRA	70	27 Feb
46.32	Chip	Jenkins	USA	64	3 Apr
46.32	Shunji	Karube	JPN	69	13 Jun
46.32	Winston	Sinclair	JAM		2 Jul
46.33	Carl	McPherson	JAM	73	5 May
46.33	Bruno	Konczylo	FRA	68	8 Aug
46.34	Danny	Fredericks	USA	70	26 May
	(150)				
46.34	Fabio	Grossi	ITA	67	3 Jul
46.34	Rodrigue	Nordin	FRA	71	29 Aug
46.34	Koji	Ito	JPN	70	18 Sep
46.35	Henry	Hagan	GHA	71	1 May
46.35	Marlon	Ramsey	USA	75	15 May
46.35	Kriss	Akabusi	GBR	58	13 Jun
46.35?	Edsel	Chase	BAR	68	1 May
46.36A	John	Lawson	RSA	66	6 Apr
46.37	Kieran	Finn	IRL	61	23 Jan
46.37	Elieser	Wattebosi	INA	64	14 Jun
	(160)				
46.37	Dmitriy	Kliger	RUS	68	20 Jun
46.38	Mark	Keddell	NZL	75	30 Jan
46.38	Troy	Johnson	USA	70	8 May
46.38	Oleg	Tverdokhleb	UKR	69	15 May
46.38A	Keteng	Baloseng	BOT	67	15 May
46.39	Gerald	McCladdie	USA	71	22 May
46.40	Anthony	Ryan	AUS	69	25 Jan
46.40		Powell			22 May
46.40	Paul	Greene	AUS	72	14 Jul
46.40	Olivier	Noirot	FRA	69	25 Jul
	(170)				
46.42	Edielson	Rocha Tenorio	BRA	67	21 Mar
46.42	Shigekazu	Omori	JPN	72	21 May
46.42	Seiji	Inagaki	JPN	73	13 Jun
46.43	Daniel	Bittner	GER	71	6 Jun
46.43	Yoshihiko	Saito	JPN	72	27 Jun
46.44A	Henry	Mohoanyane	LES	63	8 Mar
46.44	Alan	Turner	USA	69	3 Apr
46.44	Devon	Morris	JAM	61	24 Apr
46.44A	Terrence	Warren	USA	69	18 May
46.45	Larry	Gardner	USA	68	15 May
	(180)				
46.45A	Juan G	Vallin	MEX	69	11 Jul
46.45	Ralph	Pfersich	GER	66	10 Jul
46.45		Si Yandong	CHN	73	10 Sep
46.45	Tomonari	Ono	JPN	74	28 Oct
46.46	Rene	Rodriguez	USA	74	9 May
46.46	Mark	Richardson	GBR	72	17 Jul
46.46	Kenji	Tabata	JPN	74	25 Jul
46.47	Victor	Omagbemi	NGR	67	8 May
46.47	Kiril	Raykov	BUL	69	31 Jul
46.47		Son Ju-Il	KOR	69	4 Dec
	(190)				
46.47	Hezron	Maina	KEN	74	12 Dec
46.48	Sean	Adams	USA	71	13 May
46.48	Riaan	Sullivan	RSA	71	15 May
46.48	Marlin	Cannon	USA	70	17 Jun
46.48	Hector	Herrera	CUB	59	8 Aug
46.49	Robelis	Darroman	CUB	74	12 May
46.49	Jean-Claude	Yékpé	BEN	68	24 Jul

Best low altitude marks

44.24	Watts	3	NC	Eugene	19 Jun
45.56	Nuti	1	NC	Bologna	2 Aug
45.98	Ladejo	6	NCAA	New Orleans	5 Jun

46.16	Knight	
46.21	Long	4 Jun
46.31	Stephen	4 Jun
46.48	Aimar	2 Aug
46.49	Phiri	23 Apr

Indoors

45.94	Mark	Richardson	GBR	26.7.72	3	Birmingham	20 Feb
46.27	Devon	Morris	JAM	61			7 Feb

Unconfirmed

46.00	Antonious	Dotson	USA	70	7 Jun
46.11	Wendell	Gaskin	USA	73	

Hand timing

44.5A	Kennedy	Ochieng	KEN	30.12.71	1	NC	Nairobi	3 Jul
44.6A		Ochieng	KEN		1		Nairobi	19 May
44.7A	Simon	Kemboi	KEN	1.3.67	2	NC	Nairobi	3 Jul
45.0A	Abedenigo	Matilu	KEN	21.11.68	3	NC	Nairobi	3 Jul

Mark	Name		Nat	Born	Pos	Meet	Venue	Date
45.1A	Charles	Gitonga	KEN	5.10.71	2		Nairobi	19 May
45.2	Du'aine	Ladejo	GBR	14.2.71	1		College Station	1 May
45.2A	Fred	Onyancha	KEN		5		Nairobii	29 Jul
45.4	Danny	McCray	USA	11.3.74	2		College Station	1 May
45.5A	Simeon	Kipkemboi	KEN	15.4.60	2		Nairobi	15 May
45.6A	Joseph	Magut	KEN	62	5	NC	Nairobi	3 Jul
45.9	Sadek	Boumendil	ALG	72	1		Alger	21 Jul
46.1A	Julius	Chepkwony	KEN					12 Jun
46.2	Kennedy	Oyunge	KEN					3 Jul
46.2	Wilson	Cañizales	COL	64				23 May
46.3	Yoshihiko	Saito	JPN	72				2 Oct

600 METRES

Mark	Name		Nat	Born	Pos	Meet	Venue	Date
1:15.13A	Andrea	Benvenuti	ITA	13.12.69	1		Sestriere	28 Jul
1:16.0+	Martin	Steele	GBR	20.9.62	1r1	Bisl	Oslo	10 Jul
1:16.06A	Marco	Chiavarini	ITA	25.5.72	2		Sestriere	28 Jul
1:16.95A	Maximilian	Irange	TAN	71	3		Sestriere	28 Jul
1:17.07A	Davide	Cadoni	ITA	4.5.73	4		Sestriere	28 Jul

800 METRES

Mark	Name		Nat	Born	Pos	Meet	Venue	Date
1:43.54	Nixon	Kiprotich	KEN	4.12.62	1rA		Rieti	5 Sep
1:43.84	Martin	Steele	GBR	20.9.62	1rA	Bisl	Oslo	10 Jul
1:43.92	Paul	Ruto	KEN	3.11.60	2rA		Rieti	5 Sep
1:44.03	Johnny	Gray	USA	19.6.60	1rA	WK	Zürich	4 Aug
1:44.06	Sammy	Langat Kibet	KEN	70	3rA		Rieti	5 Sep
1:44.09		Kiprotich			1	Herc	Monaco	7 Aug
1:44.18	José Luiz	Barbosa	BRA	27.5.61	1		Salamanca	27 Jul
1:44.22	Billy	Konchellah	KEN	20.10.61	1	ISTAF	Berlin	27 Aug
1:44.24	Charles	Nkazamyampi	BUR	1.11.64	2		Salamanca	27 Jul
1:44.26	Robert	Kibet	KEN	4.5.64	4rA		Rieti	5 Sep
1:44.27		Gray			1rA	Athl	Lausanne	7 Jul
1:44.30	William	Tanui (10)	KEN	22.2.64	2	Herc	Monaco	7 Aug
1:44.42		Kiprotich			2	ISTAF	Berlin	27 Aug
1:44.43	Mark	Everett	USA	2.9.68	1	NC	Eugene	19 Jun
1:44.48	Joseph	Tengelei	KEN	8.12.70	1		Saarijärvi	26 Jun
1:44.55	Andrea	Benvenuti	ITA	13.12.69	2rA	WK	Zürich	4 Aug
1:44.57		Gray			3	Herc	Monaco	7 Aug
1:44.65		Ruto			4	Herc	Monaco	7 Aug
1:44.67		Gray			2	NC	Eugene	19 Jun
1:44.69		Tanui			3A	WK	Zürich	4 Aug
1:44.71		Ruto			1	WC	Stuttgart	17 Aug
1:44.72		Langat			2B	Bisl	Oslo	10 Jul
1:44.73		Barbosa			4A	WK	Zürich	4 Aug
1:44.74	Atle	Douglas	NOR	9.6.68	1	NC	Tønsberg	31 Jul
1:44.74		Gray			3	ISTAF	Berlin	27 Aug
1:44.77		Kiprotich			5A	WK	Zürich	4 Aug
1:44.83	Giuseppe	D'Urso	ITA	15.9.69	1s2	WC	Stuttgart	15 Aug
1:44.84	Marko	Koers	HOL	3.11.72	3rA	Bisl	Oslo	10 Jul
1:44.84	Luis Javier	González	ESP	17.6.69	3		Salamanca	27 Jul
1:44.86		D'Urso			2	WC	Stuttgart	17 Aug
1:44.88		Douglas		9.6.68	1		Drammen	31 May
1:44.89		Konchellah		20.10.61	3	WC	Stuttgart	17 Aug
1:44.89		D'Urso		15.9.69	5r1		Rieti	5 Sep
	(33/17)							
1:44.92	Curtis	Robb	GBR	7.6.72	2s2	WC	Stuttgart	15 Aug
1:44.96	Paul	Ereng	KEN	22.8.67	2rB	WK	Zürich	4 Aug
1:44.97	Mahjoub	Haida	MAR	1.7.70	5	ISTAF	Berlin	27 Aug
	(20)							
1:45.13	Jose	Parrilla	USA	31.3.72	3	NC	Eugene	19 Jun
1:45.13	Freddie	Williams	CAN	24.2.62	2s1	WC	Stuttgart	15 Aug
1:45.17	Abdi	Bile	SOM	28.12.62	1		Kristiinankaupunki	13 Jul
1:45.40	Réda	Abdenouz	ALG	25.9.68	9rA	WK	Zürich	4 Aug
1:45.46	Wilson	Kipketer	DEN	12.12.70	1		Lappeenranta	27 Jul
1:45.46	Fermin	Cacho	ESP	16.2.69	8	Herc	Monaco	7 Aug
1:45.46	Hezekiel	Sepeng	RSA	30.6.74	3s1	WC	Stuttgart	15 Aug
1:45.54	George	Kersh	USA	3.7.68	4	NC	Eugene	19 Jun

Mark	Name		Nat	Born	Pos	Meet	Venue	Date
1:45.61	Clive	Terrelonge	JAM	30.6.69	8	ISTAF	Berlin	27 Aug
1:45.62	Kennedy	Osei	GHA	21.10.66	2		Ingolstadt	21 Jul
	(30)							
1:45.64	David	Singoei Kiptoo	KEN	26.6.65	2		Kristiinankaupunki	13 Jul
1:45.64	Tom	McKean	GBR	27.10.63	1s3	WC	Stuttgart	15 Aug
1:45.67	Nico	Motchebon	GER	13.11.69	9	ISTAF	Berlin	27 Aug
1:45.71+	Noureddine	Morceli	ALG	28.2.70	1	BNP	Villeneuve d'Ascq	2 Jul
1:45.71	Patrick	Konchellah	KEN	63	2		Lappeenranta	27 Jul
1:45.73	Ivan	Komar	BLS	18.3.70	1	NC	Gomel	24 Jun
1:45.75	Nathan	Kahan	BEL	12.2.71	4s2	WC	Stuttgart	15 Aug
1:45.8A	William (Sammy?)	Serem	KEN	68	3	NC	Nairobi	3 Jul
1:45.82	Stanley	Redwine	USA	10.4.61	3rB	WK	Zürich	4 Aug
1:45.83	Vebjørn	Rodal	NOR	16.9.72	1	APM	Hengelo	20 Jun
	(40)							
1:45.84	Stephen	Ole Marai	KEN	11.11.62	1		Cottbus	23 Jun
1:45.85	Ari	Suhonen	FIN	19.12.65	4rB	WK	Zürich	4 Aug
1:45.87	Simon	Kemboi	KEN	1.3.67	1rB		Rieti	5 Sep
1:45.88	Gilmar	Santos	BRA	16.12.70	1		São Paulo	16 May
1:45.96A	Johan	Landsman	RSA	12.5.64	1		Pretoria	3 May
1:45.97	Jens-Peter	Herold	GER	2.6.65	2r1		Cottbus	23 Jun
1:46.00	Benson	Koech	KEN	10.11.74	4	APM	Hengelo	20 Jun
1:46.00	Matthew	Yates	GBR	4.2.69	3	Vaux	Gateshead	30 Jul
1:46.06	Vincent	Malakwen	KEN	19.7.74	2rB		Rieti	5 Sep
1:46.09	David	Sharpe	GBR	8.7.67	4	Vaux	Gateshead	30 Jul
	(50)							
1:46.15	Venuste	Niyongabo	BUR	9.12.73	1		Cagliari	11 Sep
1:46.22	Mikael	Söderman	FIN	5.11.65	4		Kristiinankaupunki	13 Jul
1:46.23	Tomás	de Teresa	ESP	5.9.68	7rB	WK	Zürich	4 Aug
1:46.24	Terril	Davis	USA	21.4.68	5	NC	Eugene	19 Jun
1:46.30	Marco	Runge	GER	13.12.71	1rA		Kassel	26 May
1:46.31	Cliffie	Miller	RSA	1.2.64	1		Yamoussouko	10 Apr
1:46.31	Johannes	Makoena	RSA	25.9.69	2		Yamoussouko	10 Apr
1:46.33	Brad	Sumner	USA	4.8.70	6	NC	Eugene	19 Jun
1:46.34	Jean-Christophe	Vialettes	FRA	19.12.67	1rA		Noisy-le-Grand	3 Jul
1:46.35	Scott	Peters	USA	14.7.71	1		Gainesville	17 Apr
	(60)							
1:46.36	Jussi	Udelhoven	NOR	25.2.66	6	ASV	Köln	1 Aug
1:46.37	Joaquim	Cruz	BRA	12.3.63	3rB		Rieti	5 Sep
1:46.38A	Marius	van Heerden	RSA	8.9.74	2		Pretoria	3 May
1:46.38	Simon	Bowen	JAM	23.11.70	2		Fairfax	8 May
1:46.42	Arthémon	Hatungimana	BUR	21.1.74	3	AfrC	Durban	27 Jun
1:46.52	William	Best	CAN	3.9.70	1h		North York	24 Jul
1:46.55	Benvenuto Silva	Filho	BRA	16.7.72	3		São Paulo	16 May
1:46.57	Tonny	Baltus	HOL	28.12.65	7	APM	Hengelo	20 Jun
1:46.61	Andrey	Sudnik	BLS	20.8.67	2rA		Noisy le Grand	3 Jul
1:46.62	Andrew	Lill	GBR	9.8.71	1rB	Vaux	Gateshead	30 Jul
	(70)							
1:46.63	Davide	Cadoni	ITA	4.5.73	2rA		Verona	16 Jun
1:46.65	Edgar	de Oliveira	BRA	11.11.67	2		Rio de Janeiro	26 Jun
1:46.65	Mark	Dailey	USA	11.12.68	3		Lappeenranta	27 Jul
1:46.67	Viktor	Zemlyanskiy	RUS	10.2.63	1		Leppävirta	17 Jun
1:46.67	Tor Øyvind	Ødegård	NOR	28.2.69	1		Stockholm	3 Aug
1:46.69	Conrad	Nichols	USA	23.6.73	2		Luzern	29 Jun
1:46.75	Anatoliy	Makarevich	BLS	19.5.70	3rA		Noisy le Grand	3 Jul
1:46.75	José	Arconada	ESP	18.1.64	5		Salamanca	27 Jul
1:46.76	Terrance	Herrington	USA	31.7.66	1		Chapel Hill	8 May
1:46.78A	David	Hlabahlaba	RSA	9.10.61	3		Pretoria	15 May
	(80)							
1:46.79A	Johan	Botha	RSA	10.1.74	4		Pretoria	15 May
1:46.82	Babacar	Niang	SEN	9.9.58	1rA		Hechtel	31 Jul
1:46.87	Mário	Silva	POR	23.7.61	2		Lisboa	19 Jun
1:46.87	Oliver	Münzer	AUT	16.2.70	2		Århus	1 Jul
1:46.95	Barry	Acres	AUS	19.7.65	1		Canberra	25 Jan
1:46.95	Valeriy	Starodubtsev	RUS	14.2.62	4rA		Hechtel	31 Jul
1:46.99	Simon	Doyle	AUS	9.11.66	3		Luzern	29 Jun
1:47.0	Silvio	Victor	BRA	64	1		São Paulo	17 Apr
1:47.03	Tommy	Asinga	SUR	20.11.68	2		Indianapolis	8 May

Mark	Name		Nat	Born	Pos	Meet	Venue	Date
1:47.04	Alexander	Adam	GER	10.5.68	1		Köln	15 Jul
	(90)							
1:47.05	Alain	Miranda	CUB	19.10.75	1		Habana	26 Jun
1:47.05	Chris	Caldwell	USA	29.1.71	3		Gävle	7 Jul
1:47.06	Simon	Lewin	AUS	3.1.72	1	NC	Brisbane	6 Mar
1:47.07	Carsten	Otte	GER	29.4.71	3rA		Kassel	26 May
1:47.09	Aleksey	Oleynikov	RUS	10.8.72	1	NC	Moskva	20 Jun
1:47.09	Jimmy	Jean-Joseph	FRA	15.10.72	1		Bron	26 Jun
1:47.10	Luc	Bernaert	BEL	24.6.66	8	APM	Hengelo	20 Jun
1:47.12	Barnabas	Kinyor	KEN	3.8.61	2rB	Pearl	Belfast	19 Jun
1:47.12	Angel	Carnesolta	CUB	11.9.69	1		Habana	24 Jul
1:47.13		Lee Jin-il	KOR	2.11.73	1	EAsiG	Shanghai	15 May
		1:46.11	unconfirmed					

Mark	Name		Nat	Born	Date
	(100)				
1:47.14	Davide	Tirelli	ITA	66	11 Sep
1:47.15	Gareth	Brown	GBR	67	30 Jul
1:47.16	Piotr	Piekarski	POL	64	5 Jun
1:47.17	Savieri	Ngidhi	ZIM	68	10 Apr
1:47.2A	Bekele	Banbere	ETH		27 May
1:47.2A	Henry	Ongeta	KEN	68	3 Jul
1:47.21	Tommy	Gjølga	NOR	69	24 Aug
1:47.22	Dedric	Jones	USA	71	17 Apr
1:47.22	Mateo	Cañellas	ESP	72	24 Jun
1:47.23	Ousmane	Diarra	FRA	64	6 Jun
	(110)				
1:47.24	Simon	Still	AUS	69	25 Jan
1:47.24	Martin	Enholm	SWE	65	5 Jul
1:47.24	Ahmed	Belkessam	ALG	62	4 Aug
1:47.24	Paul	Byrne	AUS	76	11 Dec
1:47.25	Mbarak	Hussein	KEN	65	26 Jun
1:47.26	Andrea	Giocondi	ITA	69	3 Aug
1:47.27	Todd	Black	USA	69	7 Jul
1:47.28	Tomonari	Ono	JPN	74	29 Apr
1:47.29	Jarmo	Kokkola	FIN	68	27 Jul
1:47.30	John-Henry	May	GER	67	23 Jun
	(120)				
1:47.31	Marco	Reinert	GER	71	26 May
1:47.31	Mohamed	Suleiman	QAT	69	8 Aug
1:47.32	Saïd	Ouboudou	MAR		29 May
1:47.32	Andrey	Bulkovskiy	UKR	72	27 Jun
1:47.36	Mitiku	Megersa	ETH	73	27 Jun
1:47.36	Andrea	Abelli	ITA	71	3 Jul
1:47.39	Maximilian	Irange	TAN	71	16 Jun
1:47.39	Patrick	Grammens	BEL	71	31 Jul
1:47.43	Sasha	Smiljanic	CUB	73	5 Jul
1:47.43	Lee	Cadwallader	GBR	69	30 Jul
	(130)				
1:47.44	Sean	Abrahams	RSA	70	24 Apr
1:47.44	Joe	Tamblyn	USA	66	21 May
1:47.44	Ryszard	Ostrowski	POL	61	30 Jun
1:47.49	Brad	Horton	USA	65	8 May
1:47.49	Yoshito	Konno	JPN	71	12 Jun
1:47.50	Andrés M	Diaz	ESP	69	27 Jul
1:47.5A	Hailu	Zewde	ETH	74	27 May
1:47.52	Oleg	Styepanov	RUS	70	19 Jun
1:47.53	Paul	WALKer	GBR	73	13 Jun
1:47.54	Andrey	Loginov	RUS	72	13 Jun
	(140)				
1:47.54	Michael	Wildner	AUT	70	14 Aug
1:47.55	Lucas	Sang	KEN	61	19 Jun
1:47.56	Carlos	Ward	USA	63	26 May
1:47.56	Ranjit	Subasinghe	SRI	66	25 Dec
1:47.57	Barnabas	Korir	KEN	65	1 Sep
1:47.58	Vladimir	Graudyn	RUS	63	13 Jun
1:47.59	Ibrahim	Aden	SOM		10 Jul
1:47.59	Peter	Hackley	GBR	71	30 Jul
1:47.61	Brad	Carter	USA	72	8 May
1:47.62	Lewis	Lacy	USA	71	2 Jun
	(150)				
1:47.62	Vincent	Terrier	FRA	68	14 Jul
1:47.63	Dieudonné	Kwizéra	BUR	67	10 Jul
1:47.63	Kenneth	Tholén	SWE	69	13 Jul
1:47.64A	Jurgens	Kotze	RSA	73	2 May
1:47.67	Kevin	McKay	GBR	69	30 Jul
1:47.67	Joachim	Dehmel	GER	69	1 Aug
1:47.67	Kim Yong-hwan		KOR		
1:47.68	Lars	Jucken	GER	72	1 Aug
1:47.68	Mbiganyi	Thee	BOT	62	26 Aug
1:47.69	Orlando	Castro	ESP	70	29 May
	(160)				
1:47.70	Greg	Rhymer	USA		8 May
1:47.70	Bjørn Arild	Bøhleng	NOR	72	31 May
1:47.70	Wieslaw	Paradowski	POL	73	28 Aug
1:47.72	Mohamed	Taki	MAR	71	29 May
1:47.72	Hauke	Fuhlbrügge	GER	66	23 Jun
1:47.74	Steve	Heard	GBR	62	19 Jun
1:47.77	Joseph	Chepsiror	KEN	71	10 Apr
1:47.77	Louie	Quintana	USA	73	15 May
1:47.78	Farah	Ibrahim Ali	QAT	74	23 Jun
1:47.79	Mario	Vernon-Watson	JAM	71	1 Aug
	(170)				
1:47.80	Bill	Burke	USA	69	26 May
1:47.81	Khaled	Azerkan	SWE	73	3 Aug
1:47.83	Jack	Armour	USA	62	30 Jul
1:47.84	Thorsten	Kallweit	GER	68	1 Aug
1:47.85	Sergey	Kozhevnikov	RUS	70	20 Jun
1:47.85	Joakim	Nilsson	SWE	70	7 Jul
1:47.85	Moisés	Fernández	ESP	67	10 Jul
1:47.86	Patrick	Robinson	USA		21 May
1:47.86	Reuben	Chesang	KEN	66	22 May
1:47.86	John	Little	USA	71	24 May
	(180)				
1:47.87A	Karel	Mouton	RSA	67	2 May
1:47.87	Matt	Holthaus	USA	71	8 May
1:47.88	Rüdiger	Stenzel	GER	68	29 May
1:47.9	Pavel	Dolguzhev	RUS	68	14 Aug
1:47.9	Mahmoud	Kheirat	SYR	71	25 Sep

Indoor marks

Mark	Name		Nat	Born	Pos	Venue	Date
1:46.62	Mark	Eplinius	GER	17.9.70	2	Stuttgart	7 Feb
1:46.87	Amos	Rota	ITA	16.2.70	2	Genova	17 Feb

Mark	Name		Nat	Born	Date
1:47.39	Rob	van Helden	HOL	65	6 Mar
1:47.83	Ray	Brown	USA	61	5 Feb

1000 METRES

Mark	Name		Nat	Born	Pos	Meet	Venue	Date
2:13.73	Noureddine	Morceli	ALG	28.2.70	1	BNP	Villeneuve d'Ascq	2 Jul
2:16.13	Fermin	Cacho	ESP	16.2.69	1		Andújar	6 Sep
2:16.19	Giuseppe	D'Urso	ITA	15.9.69	1		Parma	15 Sep
2:16.52	Jens-Peter	Herold	GER	2.6.65	2	BNP	Villeneuve d'Ascq	2 Jul
2:17.05	Charles	Nkazamyampi	BUR	1.11.64	3	BNP	Villeneuve d'Ascq	2 Jul
2:17.20	George	Kersh	USA	3.7.68	4	BNP	Villeneuve d'Ascq	2 Jul
2:17.60	José Luiz	Barbosa	BRA	27.5.61	1	Pre	Eugene	5 Jun
2:17.98	Réda	Abdenouz	ALG	25.9.68	5	BNP	Villeneuve d'Ascq	2 Jul
2:18.07	Abdi	Bile	SOM	28.12.62	2	Pre	Eugene	5 Jun
2:18.07	Davide	Tirelli	ITA	12.8.66	2		Parma	15 Sep
	(10)							
2:18.25	Ahmed	Belkessam	ALG	27.3.62	6	BNP	Villeneuve d'Ascq	2 Jul
2:18.37	Vincent	Malakwen	KEN	19.7.74	1	ISTAF	Berlin	27 Aug
2:18.46	Benson	Koech	KEN	10.11.74	4	Pre	Eugene	5 Jun
2:18.63	Nixon	Kiprotich	KEN	4.12.62	7	BNP	Villeneuve d'Ascq	2 Jul

Mark	Name		Nat	Born	Date	Mark	Name		Nat	Born	Date
2:19.06	Atoi	Boru	KEN	73	27 Aug	2:19.83	Gareth	Brown	GBR	67	22 Aug
2:19.30	Reuben	Chesang	KEN	66	9 May	2:19.84	Marco	Runge	GER	71	9 May
2:19.58	Sammy	Langat Kibet	KEN	70	22 Aug	2:19.88	Gilmar	Santos	BRA	70	5 Jun
2:19.66	Ousmane	Diarra	FRA	64	2 Jul	2:20.0	Michael	Busch	GER	66	5 Aug

Indoors

Mark	Name		Nat	Born	Pos	Meet	Venue	Date
2:18.16	Mark	Eplinius	GER	17.9.70	2		Berlin	5 Feb
2:18.31	David	Strang	GBR	13.12.68	1		Boston	13 Jan
2:18.57	Wilson	Kipketer	DEN	12.12.70	3		Berlin	5 Feb

Mark	Name		Nat	Born	Date	Mark	Name		Nat	Born	Date
2:19.96	Steve	Holman	USA	70	20 Feb	2:19.98	Andrey	Loginov	RUS	72	13 Feb

1500 METRES

Mark	Name		Nat	Born	Pos	Meet	Venue	Date
3:29.20	Noureddine	Morceli	ALG	28.2.70	1	MedG	Narbonne	20 Jun
3:29.57+		Morceli			1M		Rieti	5 Sep
3:30.06		Morceli			1A	WK	Zürich	4 Aug
3:31.60		Morceli			1	GPF	London	10 Sep
3:31.67+		Morceli			1M	ISTAF	Berlin	27 Aug
3:31.83		Morceli			1	DNG	Stockholm	5 Jul
3:32.01	Fermin	Cacho	ESP	16.2.69	2	WK	Zürich	4 Aug
3:32.19+		Morceli			1M	VD	Bruxelles	3 Sep
3:32.43		Cacho			2	MedG	Narbonne	20 Jun
3:32.48+		Morceli			1M	Bisl	Oslo	10 Jul
3:32.83	Abdi	Bile	SOM	28.12.62	3	WK	Zürich	4 Aug
3:33.29	Mohamed	Suleiman	QAT	23.11.69	4	WK	Zürich	4 Aug
3:33.36		Cacho			1		Barcelona	19 Jul
3:33.39	Simon	Doyle	AUS	9.11.66	5	WK	Zürich	4 Aug
3:33.56	Johan	Landsman	RSA	12.5.64	6	WK	Zürich	4 Aug
3:33.86	Jonah	Birir	KEN	12.12.71	7	WK	Zürich	4 Aug
3:33.88	David	Kibet	KEN	24.11.63	8	WK	Zürich	4 Aug
3:34.13		Suleiman			1A	ASV	Köln	1 Aug
3:34.16		Bile			2A	ASV	Köln	1 Aug
3:34.24		Morceli			1	WC	Stuttgart	22 Aug
3:34.39		Doyle			1	Nik	Nice	21 Jul
3:34.42	Jens-Peter	Herold	GER	2.6.65	1		Rieti	5 Sep
3:34.61	Atoi	Boru (10)	KEN	25.10.73	2		Rieti	5 Sep
3:34.65		Bile			2	GPF	London	10 Sep
3:34.67	Jim	Spivey	USA	7.3.60	9	WK	Zürich	4 Aug
3:34.69	Marcus	O'Sullivan	IRL	22.12.61	3	ASV	Köln	1 Aug
3:34.75	Isaac	Viciosa	ESP	26.12.69	3		Rieti	5 Sep
3:34.82		Suleiman			1	CISM	Tours	30 Aug
3:34.91		Spivey			4		Rieti	5 Sep
3:35.04	Matthew	Yates	GBR	4.2.69	3	GPF	London	10 Sep
	(30/14)							
3:35.09	Branko	Zorko	CRO	1.7.67	10	WK	Zürich	4 Aug
3:35.29	Steve	Holman	USA	2.3.70	5		Rieti	5 Sep
3:35.42	Davide	Tirelli	ITA	12.8.66	6		Rieti	5 Sep
3:35.44	Moses	Kiptanui	KEN	1.10.71	3	Nik	Nice	21 Jul
3:35.51	Rachid	El Basir	MAR	4.10.68	11	WK	Zürich	4 Aug
3:35.63	Steve	Cram	GBR	14.10.60	5	ASV	Köln	1 Aug
	(20)							

Mark	Name		Nat	Born	Pos	Meet	Venue	Date
3:35.65	Whaddon	Niewoudt	RSA	6.1.70	1		Port Elizabeth	17 May
3:35.74	Bill	Burke	USA	15.10.69	6	ASV	Köln	1 Aug
3:35.74	William	Tanui	KEN	22.2.64	7		Rieti	5 Sep
3:35.84	François	van Rensburg	RSA	2.8.70	3		Port Elizabeth	17 May
3:36.01	Gennaro	Di Napoli	ITA	5.3.68	1		Bologna	3 Sep
3:36.03	Hauke	Fuhlbrügge	GER	21.3.66	3	OD	Jena	13 Jun
3:36.08	Rüdiger	Stenzel	GER	16.4.68	4	OD	Jena	13 Jun
3:36.11	Pascal	Thiébaut	FRA	6.6.59	5	Nik	Nice	21 Jul
3:36.19	Mohamed	Taki	MAR	71	7	ASV	Köln	1 Aug
3:36.20	Manuel	Pancorbo	ESP	7.7.66	8	ASV	Köln	1 Aug
	(30)							
3:36.21	Terrance	Herrington	USA	31.7.66	4	Athl	Lausanne	7 Jul
3:36.30	Michael	Busch	GER	20.11.66	5	OD	Jena	13 Jun
3:36.30	Venuste	Niyongabo	BUR	9.12.73	6	Nik	Nice	21 Jul
3:36.45	John	Mayock	GBR	26.10.70	8		Rieti	5 Sep
3:36.47	Benson	Koech	KEN	10.11.74	4	Herc	Monaco	7 Aug
3:36.59	Vyacheslav	Shabunin	RUS	27.9.69	1		Moskva	6 Aug
3:36.63	Christoph	Impens	BEL	9.12.69	4		Barcelona	19 Jul
3:36.80	William	Kemei	KEN	22.2.69	7	Athl	Lausanne	7 Jul
3:37.00	Luc	Bernaert	BEL	24.6.66	5		Barcelona	19 Jul
3:37.03	Eric	Dubus	FRA	28.2.66	2		Reims	30 Jun
	(40)							
3:37.03	Victor	Rojas	ESP	9.12.68	6		Barcelona	19 Jul
3:37.12	Marc	Davis	USA	17.12.69	1	Vaux	Gateshead	30 Jul
3:37.16	Niall	Bruton	IRL	27.10.71	10	ASV	Köln	1 Aug
3:37.30	Noureddine	Béhar	MAR	8.4.66	3		Reims	30 Jun
3:37.31	Johan	Fourie	RSA	2.12.59	4		Port Elizabeth	17 May
3:37.31	Mark	Dailey	USA	11.12.68	2	Vaux	Gateshead	30 Jul
3:37.46	Philemon	Harineki	ZIM	12.5.71	9	Athl	Lausanne	7 Jul
3:37.47	Samir	Benfarès	FRA	6.6.68	3		Hechtel	31 Jul
3:37.51	Andrey	Bulkovskiy	UKR	22.7.72	1	EP	Roma	26 Jun
3:37.60	Saïd	Aouita	MAR	2.11.59	1	APM	Hengelo	20 Jun
	(50)							
3:37.70	Andrey	Loginov	RUS	27.11.72	5		Port Elizabeth	17 May
3:37.73	Marc	Corstjens	BEL	31.8.65	2	APM	Hengelo	20 Jun
3:37.94	Tonino	Viali	ITA	16.9.60	3	GGala	Roma	9 Jun
3:37.94	Christian	Cushing-murray	USA	18.10.67	5	BNP	Villeneuve d'Ascq	2 Jul
3:37.97	Rodney	Finch	GBR	5.8.67	5	Vaux	Gateshead	30 Jul
3:38.05	Marko	Koers	HOL	3.11.72	1	NCAA	New Orleans	5 Jun
3:38.08	M'Hamed	Choumassi	MAR	2.12.69	2		St Maur	28 Jul
3:38.24	Alessandro	Lambruschini	ITA	7.1.65	1	NC	Bologna	2 Aug
3:38.27	Herve	Phélippeau	FRA	16.9.62	6		Hechtel	31 Jul
3:38.31	Matthew	Barnes	GBR	12.1.68	6	TSB	London	23 Jul
	(60)							
3:38.35	Robert	Kiplagat	DEN	12.12.70	4		København	25 Jul
3:38.39	Michal	Bartoszak	POL	21.6.70	1		Sopot	9 Jun
3:38.45	Edgar	de Oliveira	BRA	11.11.67	1		Rio de Janeiro	27 Jun
3:38.56	Curtis	Robb	GBR	7.6.72	5	EP	Roma	26 Jun
3:38.59	Shaun	Creighton	AUS	14.5.67	2		Luzern	29 Jun
3:38.60		Kim Soon-hyung	KOR	15.7.73	1	AsiC	Manila	3 Dec
3:38.6	Mickaël	Damian	FRA	9.11.69	2		Mérignac	23 Jun
3:38.61	Waldemar	Glinka	POL	9.1.68	2		Sopot	9 Jun
3:38.62	Antonio	Herrador	ESP	29.11.66	7		Barcelona	19 Jul
3:38.63	Mahmoud	Kalboussi	TUN	9.2.65	8	BNP	Villeneuve d'Ascq	2 Jul
	(70)							
3:38.65	Abdelhak	Abdellah	MAR	13.8.68	8		Barcelona	19 Jul
3:38.65	Joseph	Chesire	KEN	12.11.57	9	Herc	Monaco	7 Aug
3:38.66	Simon	Fairbrother	GBR	28.3.68	7	TSB	London	23 Jul
3:38.83	Mirko	Döring	GER	21.7.71	2		Bad Homburg	10 Jun
3:38.85	Vincent	Terrier	FRA	22.12.68	1		St Maur	7 Jul
3:38.94	Réda	Abdenouz	ALG	25.9.68	5	GGala	Roma	9 Jun
3:38.95	Bahadur	Prasad	IND	1.9.65	2	AsiC	Manila	3 Dec
3:38.99	Naude	Jordaan	RSA	7.7.67	8	TSB	London	23 Jul
3:39.06	Andy	Keith	GBR	25.12.71	2	NCAA	New Orleans	5 Jun
3:39.08	Peter	Rono	KEN	31.7.67	2	Slovn	Bratislava	1 Jun
	(80)							

Mark	Name		Nat	Born	Pos	Meet	Venue	Date
3:39.13	Kevin	McKay	GBR	9.2.69	3		Luzern	29 Jun
3:39.16	Angel	Fariña	ESP	21.5.67	9		Barcelona	19 Jul
3:39.17	Fabio	Olivo	ITA	5.2.66	6	GGala	Roma	9 Jun
3:39.38	Werner	Edler-Muhr	AUT	4.2.69	2rB	Athl	Lausanne	7 Jul
3:39.39	Allen	Klassen	CAN	17.3.68	1		Montreal	5 Jul
3:39.43	Kevin	Sullivan	CAN	20.3.74	1		North York	23 Jul
3:39.44	Wilfred	Kirochi	KEN	12.12.66	10	Nik	Nice	21 Jul
3:39.46	Karol	Dudij	POL	24.8.70	3		Sopot	9 Jun
3:39.46	Jerry	Schumacher	USA	6.8.70	4		Luzern	29 Jun
3:39.48	Lahoussine	Siba	MAR	67	2		Montreal	5 Jul
	(90)							
3:39.50	Azat	Rakipov	BLS	29.11.68	5		Luzern	29 Jun
3:39.5	Atiq	Naaji	FRA	21.11.66	1		St Maur	22 Sep
3:39.51	Abdelkader	Chékhémani	FRA	18.7.71	3		St Maur	28 Jul
3:39.51	Paul	Vandergrift	USA	16.5.69	7	Vaux	Gateshead	30 Jul
3:39.55	John ??	Kosgei	KEN	72	3		Bad Homburg	10 Jun
3:39.61	Ahmed	Ibrahim Warsama	QAT	66	3	CISM	Tours	30 Aug
3:39.62	Dominique	Löser	GER	21.1.73	6	OD	Jena	13 Jun
3:39.62	Marcel	Laros	HOL	10.10.71	10	APM	Hengelo	20 Jun
3:39.62	Robert	Denmark	GBR	23.11.68	2	AAA	Birmingham	17 Jul
3:39.66	Matt	de Freitas	GBR	19.9.68	8	Vaux	Gateshead	30 Jul
	(100)							

Mark	Name		Nat	Born	Date
3:39.67	Mark	Carroll	IRL	72	5 Jun
3:39.70	Sergey	Melnikov	RUS	68	26 Jun
3:39.71	Bernhard	Richter	AUT	70	20 Jun
3:39.72+	David	Strang	GBR	68	10 Jul
3:39.80	Stephen	Ole Marai	KEN	62	29 Jun
3:39.81	Joe	Falcon	USA	66	26 May
3:39.82	Rudy	Vlasselaer	BEL	65	30 Aug
3:39.88	Reuben	Chesang	KEN	66	23 Jun
3:39.94	Joseph	Kiprobon	KEN	65	29 Jun
3:39.85	Mário	Silva	POR	61	30 Jul
	(110)				
3:40.23	Carlos	Cuenca	ESP	72	29 Jun
3:40.34	Vladimir	Kolpakov	RUS	65	1 Jun
3:40.37	Louie	Quintana	USA	73	23 May
3:40.44	Abdellah	Béhar	FRA	63	13 Jun
3:40.45	Cyrille	Laventure	FRA	64	30 Jul
3:40.45	Francesco	Panetta	ITA	63	2 Aug
3:40.48	Gareth	Lough	GBR	70	19 May
3:40.5	Simon	Lewin	AUS	72	19 Jan
3:40.53	José Luiz	Barbosa	BRA	61	6 Aug
3:40.54	Dieudonné	Kwizéra	BUR	67	29 Aug
	(120)				
3:40.60	Peter	O'Donoghue	AUS	61	25 Jan
3:40.60	Bob	Kennedy	USA	70	8 May
3:40.60	Tendai	Chimusasa	TAN	71	23 Jun
3:40.62	Cliffie	Miller	RSA	64	29 Mar
3:40.69	Adauto	Domingues	BRA	61	27 Jun
3:40.70	Nacer	Brahmia	ALG	63	7 Aug
3:40.71	Jean	Verster	RSA	65	30 Jul
3:40.72	Ian	Gillespie	GBR	70	29 Aug
3:40.74	Jan	Sokal	POL	67	9 Jun
3:40.74	Michael	Buchleitner	AUT	69	1 Jul
	(130)				
3:40.75	Ronnie	Harris	USA	65	5 Jul
3:40.78	Keith	Yuen	USA	70	26 May
3:40.79	Ovidiu	Olteanu	ROM	70	29 May
3:40.85	Spyros	Christopoulos	GRE	64	30 Aug
3:40.91	Patrik	Johansson	SWE	72	28 Jul
3:40.91	Mogens	Guldberg	DEN	63	29 Aug
3:40.95	Darryl	Frerker	USA	63	16 Jan
3:40.96	João Carlos	Leite	BRA	68	17 Apr
3:40.96	Paul	McMullen	USA	72	8 May
3:41.00	Claus	Wittekind	GER	72	13 Jun
	(140)				
3:41.0A	Jonah	Kiptarus	KEN	71	29 Jul
3:41.04	Alexandre	Billaudaz	FRA	72	28 Jul
3:41.05	Christophe	Lemonnier	FRA	67	13 Jun
3:41.06	Gino	Van Geyte	BEL	67	29 May
3:41.07	John	Schiefer	USA	71	26 May
3:41.14	Francois	Peyroux	FRA	67	7 Jul
3:41.15	Pierre	Morath	SUI	70	4 Aug
3:41.22	Abdoulkader	Soumah	FRA	66	9 May
3:41.23	Krzysztof	Baldyga	POL	72	9 Jun
3:41.24	Tim	Pitcher	USA	70	17 Apr
	(150)				
3:41.24	Thierry	Pantel	FRA	64	31 May
3:41.30	Donovan	Bergstrom	USA	68	7 Jul
3:41.31	Pavel	Dolgushev	RUS	68	7 Aug
3:41.32	Marcel	Versteeg	HOL	65	29 May
3:41.4	Shannon	Lemora	USA	70	22 May
3:41.40	Enrique	Molina	ESP	68	29 May
3:41.41	Jan	Jonsson	SWE	68	5 Jul
3:41.42	Bart	Meganck	BEL	68	30 Jul
3:41.44	Ari	Suhonen	FIN	65	28 Aug
3:41.45	Phil	Clode	NZL	65	16 Jan
	(160)				

Indoors

Mark	Name		Nat	Born	Pos	Meet	Venue	Date
3:34.73+		Morceli			1+		Birmingham	20 Feb
3:38.08	Gino	van Geyte	BEL	16.3.67	1		Gent	27 Feb
3:38.97	Azat	Rakipov	BLS	29.11.68	4		Stuttgart	7 Feb

1 MILE

Mark	Name		Nat	Born	Pos	Meet	Venue	Date
3:44.39	Noureddine	Morceli	ALG	28.2.70	1		Rieti	5 Sep
3:46.78		Morceli			1	ISTAF	Berlin	27 Aug
3:47.30		Morceli			1	VD	Bruxelles	3 Sep
3:47.78		Morceli			1	Bisl	Oslo	10 Jul
3:51.66	Abdi	Bile	SOM	28.12.62	2	Bisl	Oslo	10 Jul
3:52.17	Steve	Cram	GBR	14.10.60	3	Bisl	Oslo	10 Jul

Mark	Name		Nat	Born	Pos	Meet	Venue	Date
3:52.37	Jim	Spivey	USA	7.3.60	4	Bisl	Oslo	10 Jul
3:52.37		Bile			2	ISTAF	Berlin	27 Aug
3:52.56	Simon	Doyle	AUS	9.11.66	3	ISTAF	Berlin	27 Aug
3:52.73	Steve	Holman	USA	2.3.70	4	ISTAF	Berlin	27 Aug
3:52.75	Matthew	Yates	GBR	4.2.69	5	Bisl	Oslo	10 Jul
3:52.76	Marcus	O'Sullivan	IRL	22.12.61	5	ISTAF	Berlin	27 Aug
3:52.93	Jens-Peter	Herold	GER	2.6.65	6	ISTAF	Berlin	27 Aug
3:52.96	Manuel	Pancorbo (10)	ESP	7.7.66	6	Bisl	Oslo	10 Jul
3:53.29		Yates			7	ISTAF	Berlin	27 Aug
3:53.68	Fermin	Cacho	ESP	16.2.69	7	Bisl	Oslo	10 Jul
3:53.80	William	Tanui	KEN	22.2.64	8	ISTAF	Berlin	27 Aug
3:54.16		Bile			2	VD	Bruxelles	3 Sep
3:54.48		O'Sullivan			1	Indy	Indianapolis	25 Jun
3:54.53	David	Kibet	KEN	24.11.63	8	Bisl	Oslo	10 Jul
3:54.57	Marc	Corstjens	BEL	31.8.65	9	Bisl	Oslo	10 Jul
	(21/14)							
3:54.71	Vénuste	Niyongabo	BUR	9.12.73	3	VD	Bruxelles	3 Sep
3:55.25	Rachid	El Basir	MAR	4.10.68	10	Bisl	Oslo	10 Jul
3:55.63	Matt	Giusto	USA	25.10.66	1		San Francisco	15 May
3:55.75	Christoph	Impens	BEL	9.12.69	7	VD	Bruxelles	3 Sep
3:56.71	Bob	Kennedy	USA	18.8.70	1	Pre	Eugene	5 Jun
3:56.75	Terrance	Herrington	USA	31.7.66	3	Indy	Indianapolis	25 Jun
	(20)							
3:56.83	Bill	Burke	USA	15.10.69	2	Pre	Eugene	5 Jun
3:56.86	David	Strang	GBR	13.12.68	3	Pre	Eugene	5 Jun
3:56.89	Rüdiger	Stenzel	GER	16.4.68	11	ISTAF	Berlin	27 Aug
3:56.89	Luc	Bernaert	BEL	24.6.66	9	VD	Bruxelles	3 Sep
3:57.01	Branko	Zorko	CRO	1.7.67	12	ISTAF	Berlin	27 Aug
3:57.06	Philemon	Harineki	ZIM	12.5.71	1	ECarr	Portsmouth	5 Jun
3:57.16	Mark	Dailey	USA	11.12.68	12	Bisl	Oslo	10 Jul
3:57.26	Kevin	McKay	GBR	9.2.69	2	ECarr	Portsmouth	5 Jun
3:57.30	John	Mayock	GBR	26.10.70	3	ECarr	Portsmouth	5 Jun
3:57.31	Allen	Klassen	CAN	17.3.68	4	Pre	Eugene	5 Jun
	(30)							
3:57.38	Jonah	Birir	KEN	12.12.71	10	VD	Bruxelles	3 Sep
3:57.58	Ahmed	Ibrahim Warsama	QAT	66	3		Rieti	5 Sep
3:57.75	Greg	Whiteley	USA	6.1.67	2		San Francisco	15 May

Mark	Name		Nat	Born	Date
3:58.03	Ronnie	Harris	USA	65	5 Jun
3:58.11	Paul	Larkins	GBR	63	5 Jun
3:58.2	Darryl	Frerker	USA	63	27 Jan
3:58.23	Bob	Lesko	USA	69	5 Jun
3:58.24	Whaddon	Niewoudt	RSA	70	6 Mar
3:58.27	Paul	Vandegrift	USA	69	23 Jan
3:58.29	Niall	Bruton	IRL	71	9 Jul
	(30)				
3:58.48	Matthew	De Freitas	GBR	68	5 Jun
3:58.6	Peter	O'Donoghue	AUS	61	27 Jan
3:58.64	Ian	Gillespie	GBR	70	5 Jun
3:58.64	Mark	Carroll	IRL	72	9 Jul
3:58.76	Johan	Fourie	RSA	59	5 Jun
3:58.76	Andrea	Cori	ITA	66	5 Sep
3:58.83	Dan	Maas	USA	69	5 Jun
3:58.86	Edgar	de Oliveira	BRA	67	24 Apr
3:58.87	Tom	Buckner	GBR	63	5 Jun
3:58.89	Bachir	Bouahra	QAT	73	25 Aug
	(40)				
3:58.96	Michal	Bartoszak	POL	70	10 Sep
3:58.97	Stan	Roberts	RSA	67	6 Mar
3:59.08	Ernie	Freer	USA	65	5 Jun
3:59.14	Chris Cushing-murray		USA	67	5 Jun
3:59.24	Robert	Kiplagat	KEN	72	19 Jun
3:59.29	Kevin	Sullivan	CAN	74	19 Jun
3:59.33	Lahoussine	Siba	MAR	67	24 Jul
3:59.5	Phil	Clode	NZL	65	27 Jan
3:59.57	Aaron	Ramirez	USA	64	15 May
3:59.57	Wilson	Kipketer	KEN	72	5 Jul
	(50)				
3:59.60	Robert	Denmark	GBR	68	19 Jun
3:59.66	Johan	Landsman	RSA	64	6 Mar
3:59.70	Jim	Sorensen	USA	67	15 May
3:59.70	Tony	Morrell	GBR	62	5 Jul
3:59.80	Richard	Potts	NZL	71	15 Dec
3:59.96	Joe	Falcon	USA	66	22 May
3:59.98	Tommy	Gjølga	NOR	69	8 Aug

Indoors

Mark	Name		Nat	Born	Pos	Meet	Venue	Date
3:50.70		Morceli			1		Birmingham	20 Feb
3:54.59		Morceli			1	USC	New York	26 Feb
3:56.89	John	Mayock	GBR	26.10.70	3		Birmingham	20 Feb
3:57.05	Mohamed	Suleiman	QAT	23.11.69	4		Birmingham	20 Feb
3:57.44	Joe	Falcon	USA	23.6.66	2		Fairfax	7 Feb
3:57.7	Andrew	Keith	GBR	25.12.71	1		Allston	21 Dec

Mark	Name		Nat	Born	Date
3:59.58	Joseph	Chesire	KEN	57	20 Feb
3:59.68	Erik	Nedeau	USA	71	27 Feb
3:59.88	Steve	Scott	USA	56	20 Feb
3:59.95	Brad	Schlapak	USA	66	16 Jan

2000 METRES

Mark	Name		Nat	Born	Pos	Meet	Venue	Date
4:58.15	Venuste	Niyongabo	BUR	9.12.73	1		Noisy le Grand	3 Jul
5:00.02	Cyrille	Laventure	FRA	29.3.64	2		Noisy le Grand	3 Jul
5:00.09+	Noureddine	Morceli	ALG	28.2.70	1	Herc	Monaco	7 Aug
5:04.09+	Moses	Kiptanui	KEN	1.10.71	1=	ISTAF	Berlin	27 Aug
5:04.09+	David	Kibet	KEN	24.11.63	1=	ISTAF	Berlin	27 Aug
5:04.4+	Ismael	Kirui	KEN	20.2.75	3	ISTAF	Berlin	27 Aug

Mark	Name		Nat	Born	Date	Mark	Name		Nat	Born	Date
5:05.0+	Rachid	El Basir	MAR	68	1 Jul	5:05.86	Mário	Silva	POR	61	3 Jul
5:05.18+	Stephan	Plätzer	GER	66	1 Aug	5:06.03	Isaac	Viciosa	ESP	69	6 Sep
5:05.2+	Paul	Bitok	KEN	70	1 Aug	5:06.41	Enrique	Molina	ESP	68	6 Sep

+ = During 3000 metres or 2 miles races

Indoors

Mark	Name		Nat	Born	Pos	Meet	Venue	Date
4:56.23	Jens-Peter	Herold	GER	2.6.65	1		Karlsruhe	6 Mar
5:01.09	Mirko	Döring	GER	21.7.71	2		Karlsruhe	6 Mar
5:02.43	Reuben	Chesang	KEN	66	3		Karlsruhe	6 Mar
5:02.49	Dieter	Baumann	GER	9.2.65	1		Sindelfingen	14 Feb
5:04.15	Carsten	Eich	GER	9.1.70	2		Sindelfingen	14 Feb
5:04.89	Bernhard	Richter	AUT	11.12.70	4		Karlsruhe	6 Mar

Mark	Name		Nat	Born	Date	Mark	Name		Nat	Born	Date
5:05.79	Hauke	Fuhlbrügge	GER	6	6 Mar	5:06.0+	Khalid	Skah	MAR	7	10 Feb

3000 METRES

Mark	Name		Nat	Born	Pos	Meet	Venue	Date
7:29.24	Noureddine	Morceli	ALG	28.2.70	1	Herc	Monaco	7 Aug
7:34.98	Paul	Bitok	KEN	26.6.70	1	ASV	Köln	1 Aug
7:35.79	Moses	Kiptanui	KEN	1.10.71	2	ASV	Köln	1 Aug
7:36.54	Brahim	Jabbour	MAR	1.1.70	2	Herc	Monaco	7 Aug
7:37.04	Jim	Spivey	USA	7.3.60	3	ASV	Köln	1 Aug
7:37.73	William	Sigei	KEN	11.10.69	3	Herc	Monaco	7 Aug
7:38.03	Marc	Davis	USA	17.12.69	4	Herc	Monaco	7 Aug
7:38.20	Mohamed	Suleiman	QAT	23.11.69	1	ISTAF	Berlin	27 Aug
7:38.45	Bob	Kennedy	USA	18.8.70	4	ASV	Köln	1 Aug
7:38.70	Aïssa	Belaout	ALG	12.8.68	5	Herc	Monaco	7 Aug
	(10)							
7:38.77		Kennedy			2	ISTAF	Berlin	27 Aug
7:39.05		Kiptanui			3	ISTAF	Berlin	27 Aug
7:39.30	Mohamed	Issangar	MAR	12.12.64	5	ASV	Köln	1 Aug
7:39.43	Yobes	Ondieki	KEN	21.2.61	6	Herc	Monaco	7 Aug
7:39.55	Robert	Denmark	GBR	23.11.68	6	ASV	Köln	1 Aug
7:39.82	Ismael	Kirui	KEN	20.2.75	4	ISTAF	Berlin	27 Aug
7:40.0+	Khalid	Skah	MAR	29.1.67	1M		Hechtel	31 Jul
7:40.11	Stephane	Franke	GER	12.2.64	5	ISTAF	Berlin	27 Aug
7:41.06		Issangar			1	Nik	Nice	21 Jul
7:41.17		Bitok			7	Herc	Monaco	7 Aug
7:41.41		Jabbour			2	Nik	Nice	21 Jul
7:41.49		Issangar			8	Herc	Monaco	7 Aug
7:41.60	Matt	Giusto	USA	25.10.66	7	ASV	Köln	1 Aug
7:41.63	Richard	Chelimo	KEN	21.4.72	9	Herc	Monaco	7 Aug
7:41.87	Moses	Tanui	KEN	20.8.65	6	ISTAF	Berlin	27 Aug
7:41.95		Bitok			3	Nik	Nice	21 Jul
7:42.12		Belaout			7	ISTAF	Berlin	27 Aug
7:42.17		Ondieki			4	Nik	Nice	21 Jul
7:42.38	Enrique	Molina	ESP	25.2.68	8	ISTAF	Berlin	27 Aug
7:42.45		Sigei			5	Nik	Nice	21 Jul
	(30/20)							
7:42.58	Frank	O'Mara	IRL	17.7.60	8	ASV	Köln	1 Aug
7:42.68	Gennaro	Di Napoli	ITA	5.3.68	10	Herc	Monaco	7 Aug
7:43.20	Ondoro	Osoro	KEN	3.12.67	9	ISTAF	Berlin	27 Aug
7:43.24	Aloÿs	Nizigama	BUR	66	13	Herc	Monaco	7 Aug
7:43.4	Thierry	Pantel	FRA	6.7.64	1		Montpellier	4 Jun
7:43.51	Arturo	Barrios	MEX	12.12.63	10	ISTAF	Berlin	27 Aug
7:43.57	Philemon	Harineki	ZIM	12.5.71	9	ASV	Köln	1 Aug
7:43.79	Mathias	Ntawulikura	RWA	14.7.64	10	ASV	Köln	1 Aug
7:43.92	M'Hamed	Choumassi	MAR	2.12.69	1	Slovn	Bratislava	1 Jun
7:44.08	Carlos	Monteiro	POR	14.12.65	6	Nik	Nice	21 Jul
	(30)							
7:44.82	Mike	Chesire	KEN	1.12.69	11	ISTAF	Berlin	27 Aug

Mark	Name		Nat	Born	Pos	Meet	Venue	Date
7:44.98	Kibiego	Kororia	KEN	25.12.71	12	ISTAF	Berlin	27 Aug
7:45.57	Peter	O'Donoghue	AUS	1.10.61	1		Adelaide	14 Feb
7:45.78	Francesco	Panetta	ITA	10.1.63	1		Massa Marittima	6 Aug
7:46.10	Shaun	Creighton	AUS	14.5.67	11	ASV	Köln	1 Aug
7:46.60	Jean	Verster	RSA	23.4.65	9	Nik	Nice	21 Jul
7:46.64	Ralf	Dahmen	GER	9.2.68	12	ASV	Köln	1 Aug
7:46.66	Abdellah	Béhar	FRA	5.7.63	2	Slovn	Bratislava	1 Jun
7:47.16	Wilson	Omwoyo	KEN	25.11.65	10	Nik	Nice	21 Jul
7:47.21	Jacky	Carlier	FRA	8.11.61	1		Reims	30 Jun
	(40)							
7:47.55	Cyrille	Laventure	FRA	29.3.64	2		Reims	30 Jun
7:47.6+	Worku	Bikila	ETH	70	m	WK	Zürich	4 Aug
7:47.68	Michal	Bartoszak	POL	21.6.70	1		Rovereto	1 Sep
7:47.69	Todd	Williams	USA	7.3.69	3		Reims	30 Jun
7:47.8+	Haile	Guebre Silassie	ETH	18.4.73	m	WK	Zürich	4 Aug
7:48.13	Vincent	Rousseau	BEL	29.7.62	1		Watermael	24 Jun
7:48.53	Abel	Antón	ESP	24.10.62	16	ISTAF	Berlin	27 Aug
7:48.59	Alessandro	Lambruschini	ITA	7.1.65	1		Milano	2 Jun
7:48.94	Andrey	Tikhonov	RUS	11.12.66	4		Reims	30 Jun
7:48.97	Gary	Staines	GBR	3.7.63	3		Rovereto	1 Sep
	(50)							
7:49.27	Jean-Pierre	Lautredoux	FRA	5.5.66	5		Reims	30 Jun
7:49.32	Domingos	Castro	POR	22.11.63	1		Funchal	17 Jul
7:49.57	Johan	Landsman	RSA	12.5.64	1		Stellenbosch	15 Feb
7:49.80	Eliud	Barngetuny	KEN	73	2		Milano	2 Jun
7:49.91	Angelo	Carosi	ITA	20.1.64	4		Rovereto	1 Sep
7:50.01	Brahim	Lahlafi	MAR	15.4.68	6		Reims	30 Jun
7:50.05	Vénuste	Niyongabo	BUR	9.12.73	1		Parma	15 Sep
7:50.36	Claes	Nyberg	SWE	3.3.71	7		Reims	30 Jun
7:50.63	Reuben	Reina	USA	16.11.67	19	ISTAF	Berlin	27 Aug
7:50.70	Aaron	Ramirez	USA	29.7.64	4	Jen	San José	29 May
	(60)							
7:50.70	John	Mayock	GBR	26.10.70	3	Pearl	Belfast	19 Jun
7:50.94	Fabio	Olivo	ITA	5.2.66	4		Milano	2 Jun
7:51.00	Eduardo	Henriques	POR	24.3.68	4	Pearl	Belfast	19 Jun
7:51.07	Ruddy	Walem	BEL	30.6.67	8		Reims	30 Jun
7:51.44	José	Regalo	POR	22.11.63	2		Funchal	17 Jul
7:51.58	John	Nuttall	GBR	11.1.67	1	Vaux	Gateshead	30 Jul
7:51.70	Julian	Paynter	AUS	15.7.70	3		Adelaide	14 Feb
7:51.72	Jon	Brown	GBR	27.2.71	13	ASV	Köln	1 Aug
7:51.73	Josephat	Kapkory	KEN	2.1.67	2		Caorle	24 Jul
7:51.76	Henk	Gommer	HOL	17.11.62	2		Rhede	6 Aug
	(70)							

Mark	Name		Nat	Born	Date
7:52.02	Meshack	Dandane	RSA	68	15 Feb
7:52.08	Phil	Clode	NZL	65	6 Aug
7:52.09	Paul	Patrick	AUS	71	14 Feb
7:52.20	Billy	Dee	GBR	61	19 Jun
7:52.26	Risto	Ulmala	FIN	63	9 Aug
7:52.27	Shaddrack	Hoff	RSA	73	30 Jul
7:52.34	Naude	Jordaan	RSA	67	30 Jul
7:52.45	Andrew	Sambu	TAN	72	3 Jul
7:52.53	Jonny	Danielson	SWE	64	9 Aug
7:52.58	Joseph	Keter	KEN	68	3 Jul
	(80)				
7:52.67	Clodoaldo	Lopes do Carmo	BRA	68	6 Aug
7:52.69	Johan	Fourie	RSA	59	16 Jun
7:52.74	Paul	Vandegrift	USA	69	16 Jan
7:52.88	Jonah	Koech	KEN	68	1 Sep
7:53.00	Reuben	Chesang	KEN	66	26 May
7:53.07	Renato	Gotti	ITA	64	1 Sep
7:53.2+	Charles	Cheruiyot	KEN	64	2 Jul
7:53.21	Robbie	Johnston	NZL	67	7 Feb
7:53.27	Johnstone	Kipkoech	KEN	68	26 May
7:53.33	Victor	Rojas	ESP	68	6 Sep
	(90)				
7:53.38	Paul	Taylor	GBR	66	30 Jul
7:53.5	Marcel	Versteeg	HOL	65	4 Jun
7:53.73	Mikhail	Dasko	RUS	61	30 Jun
7:54.10	Mogens	Guldberg	DEN	63	1 Sep
7:54.22	Steve	Cram	GBR	60	5 Jun
7:54.49	Anacleto	Jiménez	ESP	67	25 May
7:54.60	Julius	Kariuki	KEN	61	15 Feb
7:54.62	Niall	Bruton	IRL	71	19 Jun
7:54.70	Tom	Hanlon	GBR	67	30 Jul
7:54.76	Gianni	Crepaldi	ITA	68	2 Jun
	(100)				
7:54.86	Julius	Korir	KEN	63	26 May
7:54.90	Vyacheslav	Shabunin	RUS	69	1 Jun
7:54.96	John	Doherty	IRL	61	12 Jun

Indoors

Mark	Name		Nat	Born	Pos	Meet	Venue	Date
7:38.46		Kiptanui			1		Stockholm	9 Feb
7:39.67	Khalid	Skah	MAR	29.1.67	1		Gent	10 Feb
7:43.60	Dieter	Baumann	GER	9.2.65	1		Stuttgart	7 Feb
7:46.27	Steve	Holman	USA	2.3.70	2		Boston	23 Jan

Mark	Name		Nat	Born	Pos	Meet	Venue	Date
7:47.78	Philip	Barkutwo	KEN	6.10.66	3		Genova	17 Feb
7:48.98	Eric	Dubus	FRA	28.2.66	2		Stuttgart	7 Feb
7:49.20	Joe	Falcon	USA	23.6.66	1	NC	New York	26 Feb
7:49.84	Reuben	Reina	USA	16.11.67	3	NC	New York	26 Feb
7:50.48	Hauke	Fuhlbrügge	GER	21.3.66	2		Berlin	5 Feb
7:50.82	Matthew	Yates	GBR	4.2.69	2		Sevilla	4 Mar
7:50.90	Brendan	Matthias	CAN	12.8.69	2h2	WI	Toronto	12 Mar
7:51.16	Mogens	Guldberg	DEN	2.8.63	3		Stockholm	9 Feb

Mark	Name		Nat	Born	Date	Mark	Name		Nat	Born	Date
7:52.52	Christophe	Impens	BEL	69	10 Feb	7:53.72	João	N'Tyamba	ANO	68	7 Feb
7:52.55	Victor	Rojas	ESP	68	4 Mar	7:53.76	Yves	Brenier	FRA	66	10 Feb
7:52.56	Mirko	Döring	GER	71	12 Mar	7:54.11	Cândido	Maia	POR	69	12 Mar
7:52.73	Brian	Abshire	USA	63	26 Feb	7:54.19	Barnabas	Korir	KEN	65	17 Feb
7:53.17	Ovidiu	Olteanu	ROM	70	12 Mar	7:54.57	Manuel	Pancorbo	ESP	66	4 Mar
7:53.50	Gino	Van Geyte	BEL	67	10 Feb	**Unconfirmed**: 7:53.96	Joseph	Chesire	KEN	57	

2 MILES

Mark	Name		Nat	Born	Pos	Meet	Venue	Date
8:12.17	Khalid	Skah	MAR	29.1.67	1		Hechtel	31 Jul

Mark	Name		Nat	Born	Date	Mark	Name		Nat	Born	Date
8:27.57	Mike	Chesire	KEN	69	11 Sep	8:30.16	Jean	Verster	RSA	65	31 Jul
8:28.3	Marc	Davis	USA	69	22 Jul	8:32.01	Vincent	Rousseau	BEL	62	31 Jul

5000 METRES

Mark	Name		Nat	Born	Pos	Meet	Venue	Date
13:02.75	Ismael	Kirui	KEN	20.2.75	1	WC	Stuttgart	16 Aug
13:03.17	Haile	Guebre Silassie	ETH	18.4.73	2	WC	Stuttgart	16 Aug
13:04.67	Khalid	Skah	MAR	29.1.67	1	WK	Zürich	4 Aug
13:05.09	Yobes	Ondieki	KEN	21.2.61	2	WK	Zürich	4 Aug
13:05.14	Richard	Chelimo	KEN	21.4.72	3	WK	Zürich	4 Aug
13:05.39		Guebre Silassie			4	WK	Zürich	4 Aug
13:05.40	Fita	Bayissa	ETH	15.12.72	3	WC	Stuttgart	16 Aug
13:06.50		Kirui			5	WK	Zürich	4 Aug
13:06.64	Worku	Bikila	ETH	70	4	WC	Stuttgart	16 Aug
13:06.71		Kirui			1	Athl	Lausanne	7 Jul
13:06.76	Francesco	Panetta	ITA	10.1.63	6	WK	Zürich	4 Aug
13:06.82		Skah			1	BNP	Villeneuve d'Ascq	2 Jul
13:07.18		Skah			5	WC	Stuttgart	16 Aug
13:07.35	William	Sigei	KEN	11.10.69	2	Athl	Lausanne	7 Jul
13:08.02		Worku Bikila			7	WK	Zürich	4 Aug
13:08.03	Aïssa	Belaout (10)	ALG	12.8.68	2	BNP	Villeneuve d'Ascq	2 Jul
13:08.68	Paul	Bitok	KEN	26.6.70	1	Bisl	Oslo	10 Jul
13:08.86	Brahim	Jabbour	MAR	1.1.70	3	BNP	Villeneuve d'Ascq	2 Jul
13:09.35		Skah			2	Bisl	Oslo	10 Jul
13:09.58	Arturo	Barrios	MEX	12.12.63	4	BNP	Villeneuve d'Ascq	2 Jul
13:09.68	Simon	Chemoiywo	KEN	2.5.69	1	AfrC	Durban	27 Jun
13:10.18		Bitok			3	Athl	Lausanne	7 Jul
13:10.41		Guebre Silassie			2	AfrC	Durban	27 Jun
13:10.66	Ezekiel	Bitok	KEN	15.2.66	1	GGala	Roma	9 Jun
13:10.95	Jonah	Koech	KEN	2.2.68	2	GGala	Roma	9 Jun
13:10.99	Vincent	Rousseau	BEL	29.7.62	3	Bisl	Oslo	10 Jul
13:11.82		Kirui			1	VD	Bruxelles	3 Sep
13:11.89	Kibiego	Kororia	KEN	25.12.71	3	GGala	Roma	9 Jun
13:12.14	Aloÿs	Nizigama	BUR	66	5	BNP	Villeneuve d'Ascq	2 Jul
13:12.29	Wilson	Omwoyo	KEN	25.11.65	6	BNP	Villeneuve d'Ascq	2 Jul
13:12.42		Ondieki			2	VD	Bruxelles	3 Sep
	(31/20)							
13:13.17	Stephane	Franke	GER	12.2.64	3	VD	Bruxelles	3 Sep
13:14.23	Mohamed	Issangar	MAR	12.12.64	7	BNP	Villeneuve d'Ascq	2 Jul
13:14.62	Moses	Kiptanui	KEN	1.10.71	4	VD	Bruxelles	3 Sep
13:14.65	Domingos	Castro	POR	22.11.63	3		København	25 Jul
13:14.76	Philemon	Harineki	ZIM	12.5.71	4	GGala	Roma	9 Jun
13:14.82	Mathias	Ntawulikura	RWA	14.7.64	8	BNP	Villeneuve d'Ascq	2 Jul
13:14.91	Bob	Kennedy	USA	18.8.70	4	Bisl	Oslo	10 Jul
13:15.21	Ondoro	Osoro	KEN	3.12.67	4		København	25 Jul
13:15.85	Brahim	Lahlafi	MAR	15.4.68	6	Bisl	Oslo	10 Jul
13:16.15	Mike	Chesire	KEN	1.12.69	5	VD	Bruxelles	3 Sep
	(30)							

Mark	Name		Nat	Born	Pos	Meet	Venue	Date
13:16.48	Robert	Denmark	GBR	23.11.68	1		Sevilla	5 Jun
13:17.48	Abel	Antón	ESP	24.10.62	3		Sevilla	5 Jun
13:17.65	Ibrahim	Kinuthia	KEN	22.5.63	6	GGala	Roma	9 Jun
13:17.71	Thierry	Pantel	FRA	6.7.64	3		St Denis	11 Jun
13:17.72	Frank	O'Mara	IRL	17.7.60	11	BNP	Villeneuve d'Ascq	2 Jul
13:19.71	José Carlos	Adán	ESP	22.7.67	5		Sevilla	5 Jun
13:19.78	Jon	Brown	GBR	27.2.71	12	BNP	Villeneuve d'Ascq	2 Jul
13:20.13	Todd	Williams	USA	7.3.69	1	Pre	Eugene	5 Jun
13:20.16	Paul	Tergat	KEN	17.6.69	2		Rieti	5 Sep
13:21.23	Antonio	Martins	FRA	23.8.63	8	WK	Zürich	4 Aug
	(40)							
13:22.79	Carlos	Monteiro	POR	14.12.65	7	Bisl	Oslo	10 Jul
13:22.82	Moses	Tanui	KEN	20.8.65	9	GGala	Roma	9 Jun
13:23.31	Peter	O'Donoghue	AUS	1.10.61	1		Melbourne	25 Feb
13:23.60	Matt	Giusto	USA	25.10.66	1	NC	Eugene	19 Jun
13:23.94	Mustapha	Essaïd	FRA	20.1.70	13	BNP	Villeneuve d'Ascq	2 Jul
13:23.98	Toshinari	Takaoka	JPN	24.9.70	14	BNP	Villeneuve d'Ascq	2 Jul
13:24.55	Greg	Whiteley	USA	6.1.67	2	Pre	Eugene	5 Jun
13:24.96	Antonio	Serrano	ESP	8.3.65	9	Bisl	Oslo	10 Jul
13:25.38	Angelo	Carosi	ITA	20.1.64	4		Rieti	5 Sep
13:25.92	Jim	Spivey	USA	7.3.60	3	Pre	Eugene	5 Jun
	(50)							
13:26.03	Steve	Plasencia	USA	28.10.56	4	Pre	Eugene	5 Jun
13:26.11	German	Silva	MEX	9.1.68	11	Bisl	Oslo	10 Jul
13:26.46	Martin	Pitayo	MEX	10.1.60	15	BNP	Villeneuve d'Ascq	2 Jul
13:27.07	Mikhail	Dasko	RUS	26.1.61	8		Sevilla	5 Jun
13:27.12	Jean-Pierre	Lautredoux	FRA	5.5.66	16	BNP	Villeneuve d'Ascq	2 Jul
13:27.2	John	Gregorek	USA	15.4.60	1		Dedham	5 Jun
13:27.83	M'Hamed	Choumassi	MAR	2.12.69	1		Maia	10 Jul
13:27.89	Gennaro	Di Napoli	ITA	5.3.68	2		Hechtel	31 Jul
13:28.27	Jacky	Carlier	FRA	8.11.61	3		Hechtel	31 Jul
13:28.39	Abdellah	Béhar	FRA	5.7.63	1		Antony	1 May
	(60)							
13:28.41	Dan	Nelson	USA	15.5.64	5	Pre	Eugene	5 Jun
13:28.73	Katsuhiko	Hanada	JPN	12.6.71	4		Hechtel	31 Jul
13:29.08	Oleg	Strizhakov	RUS	18.7.63	5		Hechtel	31 Jul
13:29.12	Andrey	Tikhonov	RUS	11.12.66	2		Maia	10 Jul
13:29.46	Tendai	Chimusasa	ZIM	28.1.71	1		Arnsberg	9 Jun
13:29.47	Jonny	Danielson	SWE	4.9.64	12	Bisl	Oslo	10 Jul
13:29.67	Alyan Sultan	Al-Qahtani	SAU	23.8.71	6		Hechtel	31 Jul
13:29.85	John	Nuttall	GBR	11.1.67	9		Sevilla	5 Jun
13:30.06	Richard	Nerurkar	GBR	6.1.64	2		Århus	1 Jul
13:30.08	Gideon	Chirchir	KEN	66	2		Arnsberg	9 Jun
	(70)							
13:30.25	Henk	Gommer	HOL	17.11.62	7		Hechtel	31 Jul
13:30.36	Robbie	Johnston	NZL	21.8.67	2		Melbourne	25 Feb
13:30.40	Thomas	Osano	KEN	4.6.70	3	NYG	New York	22 May
13:30.40	Stephen	Freigang	GER	27.9.67	3		Arnsberg	9 Jun
13:30.44	Peter	Sherry	USA	22.8.68	6	Pre	Eugene	5 Jun
13:30.47	José	Regalo	POR	22.11.63	3		Maia	10 Jul
13:30.96	Alessandro	Lambruschini	ITA	7.1.65	2	EP	Roma	27 Jun
13:30.97	Carsten	Eich	GER	9.1.70	1		Kerkrade	29 May
13:31.17	Teodoro	Cuñado	ESP	13.2.70	10		Sevilla	5 Jun
13:31.18	Enrique	Molina	ESP	25.2.68	1		Pontevedra	3 Aug
	(80)							
13:31.23	Réda	Benzine	ALG	71	13	Bisl	Oslo	10 Jul
13:31.26	Antonio	Silio	ARG	9.5.66	11		Sevilla	5 Jun
13:31.29	Zoltán	Káldy	HUN	7.1.69	9		Hechtel	31 Jul
13:31.42	Antonio	Prieto	ESP	11.1.58	12		Sevilla	5 Jun
13:31.52	Rainer	Wachenbrunner	GER	11.1.62	4		Arnsberg	9 Jun
13:31.63	Risto	Ulmala	FIN	7.5.63	7		København	25 Jul
13:31.78	Michal	Bartoszak	POL	21.6.70	4	EP	Roma	27 Jun
13:31.80	Reuben	Chesang	KEN	66	5		Arnsberg	9 Jun
13:32.15	Julius	Ondieki	KEN		2		Kerkrade	29 May
13:32.46		Hong Bo	CHN	.10.73	1	NG	Beijing	9 Sep
	(90)							

Mark	Name		Nat	Born	Pos	Meet	Venue	Date
13:32.47	John	Doherty	IRL	22.7.61	3		Århus	1 Jul
13:32.51	Kasuhiro	Kawauchi	JPN	9.3.73	10		Hechtel	31 Jul
13:32.63	Fernando	Couto	POR	4.12.59	1		Pontevedra	3 Aug
13:32.70	Phil	Clode	NZL	11.3.65	3		Melbourne	25 Feb
13:32.89		Han Zongmin	CHN	1.1.70	2	NG	Beijing	9 Sep
13:33.05	Martin	Fíz	ESP	3.3.63	13		Sevilla	5 Jun
13:33.21	Paul	Patrick	AUS	15.9.71	4		Melbourne	25 Feb
13:33.24	Julius	Korir	KEN	5.12.63	6		Arnsberg	9 Jun
13:33.31	Luís	Jesus	POR	19.11.68	4		Maia	10 Jul
13:33.40	Reuben	Reina	USA	16.11.67	7	Pre	Eugene	5 Jun
	(100)							

Mark	Name		Nat	Born	Date
13:33.42	Gary	Staines	GBR	63	7 Jul
13:33.48	Carlos	de la Torre	ESP	66	25 Jul
13:33.49	Hauke	Fuhlbrügge	GER	66	29 May
13:33.60	Anacleto	Jiménez	ESP	67	3 Aug
13:33.77	Khalid	Boulami	MAR	69	7 Jul
13:33.87	Alberto	Juzdado	ESP	66	5 Jun
13:33.87	Manuel	Pancorbo	ESP	66	3 Sep
13:34.01	Ruddy	Walem	BEL	67	3 Sep
13:34.41		Zhang Fukui	CHN	70	9 Sep
13:34.55	William	Van Dijck	BEL	61	29 May
	(110)				
13:34.60	Marcel	Versteeg	HOL	65	31 Jul
13:35.25	El Miloudi	Badine	MAR	70	5 Jun
13:35.28	Jan	Pesava	TCH	72	27 Jun
13:35.28	Andrew	Sambu	TAN	72	31 Jul
13:35.35	Vicenzo	Modica	ITA	71	9 Jun
13:35.38	Hans	Ulin	BEL	70	31 Jul
13:35.43	Alberto	Maravilha	POR	65	10 Jul
13:35.50	Jun	Hiratsuka	JPN	69	10 Jul
13:35.71	William	Koech	KEN	61	19 Jun
13:36.09	Julian	Paynter	AUS	70	25 Feb
	(120)				
13:36.14	Francesco	Bennici	ITA	71	17 Apr
13:36.30	Shaddrack	Hoff	RSA	73	24 Apr
13:36.39	Markus	Neukirch	GER	68	29 May
13:36.57	Samwel	Otieno	KEN	73	3 Aug
13:36.70	Brahim	El Ghazali	MAR	68	11 Jul
13:36.98	James	Kariuki	KEN	72	19 Jun
13:37.29		Hu Gangjun	CHN	70	9 Sep
13:37.34	Eliud	Barngetuny	KEN	73	9 Jun
13:37.37	Ronaldo	da Costa	BRA	70	25 Jun
13:37.39	Valdenor Pereira Santos		BRA	69	25 Jun
	(130)				
13:37.44	Atiq	Naaji	FRA	66	23 Jun
13:37.45	Joseph	Kiprobon	KEN	65	2 May
13:37.59	Kamel	Kohil	ALG	71	2 Jun
13:37.89	Boay	Akonay	TAN	70	23 Jun
13:37.92	Steffen	Brand	GER	65	29 May
13:38.08	Dionísio	Castro	POR	63	10 Jul
13:38.25	Anton	Nicolaisen	RSA	68	24 Apr
13:38.45	Pat	Porter	USA	59	8 Jun
13:38.47	Akira	Nakamura	JPN	67	15 Jul
13:39.04	Shannon	Butler	USA	67	5 Jun
	(140)				
13:39.05	João	Junqueira	POR	65	1 Jun
13:39.12	Piotr	Gladki	POL	72	9 Jun
13:39.15	Jim	Farmer	USA	65	5 Jun
13:39.2	Jon	Solly	GBR	63	8 Jun
13:39.32	Rafael	Illán	ESP	70	1 Jun
13:39.48	Shaun	Creighton	AUS	67	25 Jan
13:39.75	Saïd	Aouita	MAR	59	5 May
13:39.83	Azzedine	Sakhri	ALG	68	31 Jul
13:39.87	Brian	Abshire	USA	63	16 Apr
13:39.87	Yasuyuki	Watanabe	JPN	73	1 Jul
	(150)				
13:40.04	Rod	De Highden	AUS	69	25 Feb
13:40.11	Pascal	Thiébaut	FRA	59	11 Jun
13:40.30	Robert	Stefko	SVK	68	13 Jun
13:40.4	Mohamed	Belabbés	ALG	66	5 Jul
13:40.47	John	Mayock	GBR	70	23 Jul
13:40.5	Joseph	Keter	KEN	68	12 Jun
13:40.6	Joseph	Kibor	KEN	72	3 Jul
13:40.63	Paul	Evans	GBR	61	16 Jul
13:40.7	Josephat	Machuka	KEN	73	29 Jul
13:40.88	Artur de Freitas Castro		BRA	67	9 Jun
	(160)				
13:40.88	Charles	Cheruiyot	KEN	64	15 Jul
13:41.01	Michal	Kucera	TCH	72	23 Jun
13:41.24	Alejandro	Gómez	ESP	67	5 Jun
13:41.40	Hendrik	Thukwane	RSA	69	24 Apr
13:41.46	Marc	Olesen	CAN	64	2 Jun
13:41.47	Eduardo	Henriques	POR	68	5 Jun
13:41.49		Yang Guocai	CHN	75	9 Sep
13:41.53	Harri	Hänninen	FIN	63	15 Jul
13:41.6	Diomède	Cishahayo	BUR	62	30 Jul
13:41.70	Bahadur	Prasad	IND	65	4 Dec
	(170)				
13:41.74	Michael	Fietz	GER	67	9 Jun
13:41.77	Josephat	Kapkory	KEN	67	6 Aug
13:41.81	Julius	Randich	KEN		22 May
13:42.0	Mickael	Dufermont	FRA	69	5 Jul
13:42.22	Stephenson	Nyamu	KEN	71	17 Apr
13:42.25	Toshiyuki	Hayata	JPN	68	15 Jul
13:42.30	Brahim	Boutayeb	MAR	67	14 Aug
13:42.35	Cyrille	Laventure	FRA	64	2 May
13:42.35	Paulo	Guerra	POR	70	19 Jun
13:42.56	Leopold	Sirabahenda	BUR	68	30 Aug
	(180)				

10 000 METRES

Mark	Name		Nat	Born	Pos	Meet	Venue	Date
26:58.38	Yobes	Ondieki	KEN	21.2.61	1	Bisl	Oslo	10 Jul
27:07.91	Richard	Chelimo	KEN	21.4.72	1	DNG	Stockholm	5 Jul
27:16.81	William	Sigei	KEN	11.10.69	2	Bisl	Oslo	10 Jul
27:17.74	Khalid	Skah	MAR	29.1.67	1	VD	Bruxelles	3 Sep
27:18.32	Moses	Tanui	KEN	20.8.65	2	VD	Bruxelles	3 Sep
27:18.43	Paul	Tergat	KEN	17.6.69	3	VD	Bruxelles	3 Sep
27:21.22		Chelimo			4	VD	Bruxelles	3 Sep
27:23.18	Vincent	Rousseau	BEL	29.7.62	5	VD	Bruxelles	3 Sep
27:24.24	Ondoro	Osoro	KEN	3.12.67	6	VD	Bruxelles	3 Sep
27:25.23		Sigei			1	AfrC	Durban	25 Jun

Mark	Name		Nat	Born	Pos	Meet	Venue	Date
27:26.90	Fita	Bayissa	ETH	15.12.72	2	AfrC	Durban	25 Jun
27:30.17	Haile	Guebre Silassie	ETH	18.4.73	3	AfrC	Durban	25 Jun
27:34.27	Arturo	Barrios	MEX	12.12.63	2	DNG	Stockholm	5 Jul
27:34.53	Domingos	Castro	POR	22.11.63	3	DNG	Stockholm	5 Jul
27:38.72	Antonio	Silio	ARG	9.5.66	7	VD	Bruxelles	3 Sep
27:39.38	Alejandro	Gómez	ESP	11.4.67	3	Bisl	Oslo	10 Jul
27:40.03	Richard	Nerurkar	GBR	6.1.64	4	Bisl	Oslo	10 Jul
27:40.37	Todd	Williams	USA	7.3.69	5	Bisl	Oslo	10 Jul
27:42.3		Tanui			1		Trento	5 Aug
27:42.35	Antonio	Martins	FRA	23.8.63	8	VD	Bruxelles	3 Sep
27:46.02		Guebre Silassie			1	WC	Stuttgart	22 Aug
27:46.54		Tanui			2	WC	Stuttgart	22 Aug
27:47.33	Antonio	Serrano	ESP	8.3.65	1	APM	Hengelo	20 Jun
27:47.59	Mathias	Ntawulikura	RWA	14.7.64	6	Bisl	Oslo	10 Jul
27:47.77	Aloÿs	Nizigama (20)	BUR	66	1	CISM	Tours	28 Aug
27:47.79	Paul	Evans	GBR	13.4.61	4	DNG	Stockholm	5 Jul
27:50.32		Silio			2	APM	Hengelo	20 Jun
27:51.37		Nizigama			1		Fukuoka	2 Oct
27:51.41	Armando	Quintanilla	MEX	19.4.68	7	Bisl	Oslo	10 Jul
27:54.75		Nizigama			9	VD	Bruxelles	3 Sep
	(30/21)							
27:55.9	Joseph	Keino	KEN	63	1		Kasarani	10 Jun
27:57.84	Tendai	Chimusasa	ZIM	28.1.71	3	APM	Hengelo	20 Jun
27:57.98	Stephane	Franke	GER	12.2.64	1	NC	Trier	16 May
27:58.47	Nozomi	Saho	JPN	6.3.73	1		Kumamoto	4 Apr
27:58.59	Mahieddine	Belhadj	ALG	20.1.63	11	VD	Bruxelles	3 Sep
27:59.49	José Carlos	Adán	ESP	22.7.67	1		Getxo	2 May
27:59.64	Paul	Patrick	AUS	15.9.71	1	Zat	Melbourne	16 Dec
27:59.72	Stephan	Freigang	GER	27.9.67	4	APM	Hengelo	20 Jun
	(30)							
27:59.91	Jun	Hiratsuka	JPN	8.1.69	2		Kobe	25 Apr
28:00.72	Josephat	Machuka	KEN	12.12.73	4	AfrC	Durban	24 Jun
28:00.97	Martin	Fíz	ESP	3.3.63	2		Getxo	2 May
28:02.24	Gary	Staines	GBR	3.7.63	2	Zat	Melbourne	16 Dec
28:02.41	Steve	Plasencia	USA	28.10.56	2	NC	Eugene	18 Jun
28:02.44	Dan	Nelson	USA	15.5.64	3	NC	Eugene	18 Jun
28:02.54	Tadashi	Fukushima	JPN	29.9.64	2		Kumamoto	4 Apr
28:02.71	Thierry	Pantel	FRA	6.7.64	1	EP	Rome	26 Jun
28:03.64	German	Silva	MEX	9.1.68	5	DNG	Stockholm	5 Jul
28:03.65	Steve	Moneghetti	AUS	26.9.62	3	Zat	Melbourne	16 Dec
	(40)							
28:03.89	Pedro	Arco	ESP	7.7.64	5		Getxo	2 May
28:06.70	Luís	Jesus	POR	19.11.68	6		Getxo	2 May
28:06.91	José	Regalo	POR	22.11.63	7		Getxo	2 May
28:07.1A	Ismael	Kirui	KEN	20.2.75	1	NC	Nairobi	3 Jul
28:09.04	Abel	Antón	ESP	24.10.62	8		Getxo	2 May
28:09.19	Carlos	Monteiro	POR	14.12.65	6	DNG	Stockholm	5 Jul
28:10.20	Kibiego	Kororia	KEN	25.12.71	6	APM	Hengelo	20 Jun
28:11.0A	Simon	Chemoiywo	KEN	2.5.69	2		Nairobi	11 Jun
28:11.14	Paulo	Guerra	POR	21.8.70	7	DNG	Stockholm	5 Jul
28:11.60	Katsuhiko	Hanada	JPN	12.6.71	8	Bisl	Oslo	10 Jul
	(50)							
28:12.76	Rolando	Vera	ECU	27.4.65	8	DNG	Stockholm	5 Jul
28:13.99	Francesco	Panetta	ITA	10.1.63	2	EP	Rome	26 Jun
28:14.31	Samwel	Otieno	KEN	10.4.73	1		Maia	30 Jun
28:15.25	Juvenal	Ribeiro	POR	9.3.64	2		Maia	30 Jun
28:15.48	Robbie	Johnston	NZL	21.8.67	4	Zat	Melbourne	16 Dec
28:15.94	João	Junqueira	POR	24.6.65	9		Getxo	2 May
28:16.1	Vincenzo	Modica	ITA	2.3.71	1		Palermo	15 Jun
28:16.27	Yuichiro	Fukushima	JPN	23.4.70	2		Fukuoka	2 Oct
28:16.95	Julius	Randich	KEN		1	NAIA	Abbotsford	22 May
28:17.26	Yasuyuki	Watanabe	JPN	8.6.73	2	WUG	Buffalo	16 Jul
	(60)							
28:17.36	Haruo	Urata	JPN	9.3.62	3		Kobe	25 Apr
28:17.69	Alberto	Maravilha	POR	17.12.65	12		Getxo	2 May
28:18.13	Henrique	Crisóstomo	POR	10.3.62	13		Getxo	2 May

Mark	Name		Nat	Born	Pos	Meet	Venue	Date
28:18.21	Risto	Ulmala	FIN	7.5.63	13	VD	Bruxelles	3 Sep
28:18.29	Stephen	Mayaka	KEN	16.11.72	4	WUG	Buffalo	16 Jul
28:18.58	Toshiyuki	Hayata	JPN	2.5.68	3		Fukuoka	2 Oct
28:18.62	James ??	Kariuki	KEN	.72	3		Maia	30 Jun
28:18.97	Boay	Akonay	TAN	3.1.70	5h1	WC	Stuttgart	20 Aug
28:21.24	Joe	Falcon	USA	23.6.66	1	MSR	Walnut	16 Apr
28:21.33	Phil	Clode	NZL	11.3.65	5	Zat	Melbourne	16 Dec
	(70)							
28:22.48	Paul	Dugdale	GBR	13.5.65	9	Bisl	Oslo	10 Jul
28:22.68	Joseph	Otwori	KEN	20.1.69	5	WUG	Buffalo	16 Jul
28:23.39	Junji	Haraguchi	JPN	22.6.67	5		Fukuoka	2 Oct
28:23.80	Bob	Kempainen	USA	18.6.66	3	MSR	Walnut	16 Apr
28:23.96	Gerard	Donakowski	USA	20.2.60	4	NC	Eugene	18 Jun
28:24.50	Rainer	Wachenbrunner	GER	11.1.62	2	NC	Trier	16 May
28:24.59	Oleg	Strizhakov	RUS	18.7.63	4	EP	Roma	26 Jun
28:24.61	Brahim	Boutayeb	MAR	15.8.67	9	DNG	Stockholm	5 Jul
28:25.43	Ibrahim	Seid	ETH		5	AfrC	Durban	24 Jun
28:25.70	Mustapha	Essaïd	FRA	20.1.70	1	NC	Annecy	23 Jul
	(80)							
28:25.70	Diomède	Cishahayo	BUR	62	14	VD	Bruxelles	3 Sep
28:25.98	Stefano	Baldini	ITA	25.5.71	1	NC	Bologna	2 Aug
28:26.48	Xolile	Yawa	RSA	29.9.62	1		Port Elizabeth	6 Mar
28:26.53	Antonio	Prieto	ESP	11.1.58	14		Getxo	2 May
28:26.63	Thomas	Doyi	BUR		6	AfrC	Durban	24 Jun
28:26.87	Alberto	Juzdado	ESP	20.8.66	7	APM	Hengelo	20 Jun
28:27.25	Charles	Omwoyo	KEN	62	8	APM	Hengelo	20 Jun
28:27.48	Salvatore	Antibo	ITA	7.2.62	1h2	WC	Stuttgart	20 Aug
28:27.59	José Andrés	Pérez	ESP	27.11.69	15		Getxo	2 May
28:27.63	Pat	Porter	USA	31.5.59	1	Jer	Coquitlam	30 May
	(90)							
28:28.1	Toshinari	Takaoka	JPN	24.9.70			Hofu	27 Nov
28:28.67	Jonah	Koech	KEN	2.2.68	1	NCAA	New Orleans	2 Jun
28:29.8A	Julius	Ondieki	KEN		3	NC	Nairobi	3 Jul
28:30.01	Sid-Ali	Sakhri	ALG	20.12.61	3	Jer	Coquitlam	30 May
28:30.60	Ed	Eyestone	USA	15.6.61	5	NC	Eugene	18 Jun
28:31.93	Shinichi	Akiyoshi	JPN	10.2.71	2		Mito	9 May
28:31.93	Andrew	Lloyd	AUS	14.2.59	6	Zat	Melbourne	16 Dec
28:32.00	Dave	Lewis	GBR	15.10.61	2	AAA	London	12 Jun
28:32.03	Josephat	Kapkory	KEN	2.1.67	4	MSR	Walnut	16 Apr
28:32.19	Jon	Solly	GBR	28.6.63	4	Jer	Coquitlam	30 May
	(100)							

Mark	Name		Nat	Born	Date
28:32.26	Francesco	Bennici	ITA	71	2 Aug
28:32.31	Yoshuke	Osawa	JPN	67	9 May
28:32.62	Jonny	Danielson	SWE	64	5 Jul
28:32.89	Pat	Carroll	AUS	61	16 Dec
28:33.11	Yuichi	Tajiri	JPN	71	2 Oct
28:33.12	Masatoshi	Ibata	JPN	72	30 May
28:33.54	Tonnie	Dirks	HOL	61	23 Jul
28:33.75	Billy	Dee	GBR	61	12 Jun
28:34.0A	Musyoki	Nguku	KEN	74	29 Jul
28:34.01	Eiji	Tajima	JPN	70	25 Apr
	(110)				
28:34.08	Róbert	Stefko	SVK	68	10 Jul
28:34.22	Lameck	Aguta	KEN	71	5 Jul
28:34.31	Azzedine	Sakhri	ALG	68	30 May
28:34.6	Valdenor Pereira Santos		BRA	69	27 Jun
28:35.17	Martin	Pitayo	MEX	60	3 Sep
28:35.60	Rod	Higgins	AUS	67	16 Dec
28:35.69	Naoki	Yamagashira	JPN	69	25 Apr
28:35.8	Ronaldo	Da Costa	BRA	70	27 Jun
28:36.16	Mark	Coogan	USA	66	5 Jul
28:36.66	Peter	Sherry	USA	68	16 Jul
	(120)				
28:37.13	Sakae	Osaki	JPN	64	12 Jun
28:37.29	Ashley	Johnson	USA	61	22 Apr
28:38.01	John	Vermeule	HOL	61	23 Jul
28:38.58	Danilo	Goffi	ITA	72	2 Aug
28:38.8A	Dominic	Kirui	KEN	67	12 Jun
28:38.93	Harri	Hänninen	FIN	63	10 Jul
28:39.6	Delmir Alves	dos Santos	BRA	66	27 Jun
28:40.16	Akira	Nakamura	JPN	67	25 Apr
28:40.27	Gennadiy	Temnikov	RUS	61	12 Jun
28:40.32	Akira	Sakemi	JPN	70	15 May
	(130)				
28:40.49	Andrew	Pearson	GBR	71	12 Jun
28:40.49	Arnold	Mächler	SUI	64	5 Jul
28:40.74	Carsten	Eich	GER	70	15 May
28:40.81	Jiu Shangxuan		CHN	62	13 Sep
28:41.72	Sun Ripeng		CHN	74	13 Sep
28:41.80	Keith	Dowling	USA	69	22 Apr
28:42.33	Han Zongmin		CHN	70	13 Sep
28:42.76	Smaïl	Shgir	MAR	72	23 Jul
28:42.92	Axel	Krippschock	GER	62	15 May
28:43.2	Artur d eFreitas Castro		BRA	67	27 Jun
	(140)				
28:43.30	Masafumi	Yorita	JPN	68	2 Oct
28:43.47	Battista	Domenighini	ITA	69	2 Aug
28:43.60	Eddy	Hellebuyck	BEL	61	8 Aug
28:43.63	Paul	Smith	NZL		7 Mar
28:43.78	Santtu	Mäkinen	FIN	70	5 Jul
28:43.91	Seiichi	Miyajima	JPN	69	25 Apr
28:44.25	Ezekiel	Bitok	KEN	66	5 Jul
28:44.59	Katsuhiro	Kawauchi	JPN	73	25 Apr

Mark	Name		Nat	Born	Date
28:44.60	Masayuki	Nishi	JPN	64	15 May
28:44.77	John	Halvorsen	NOR	66	10 Jul
	(150)				
28:45.09	Carlos	de la Torre	ESP	66	2 May
28:45.35	Miroslaw	Zerkowski	POL	56	28 Aug
28:45.5	Yoshinori	Yokota	JPN	68	28 Nov
28:45.51	Dan	Middleman	USA	69	22 Apr
28:45.52	Kennedy	Manyisa	KEN	69	31 May
28:45.61		Hong Bo	CHN	73	13 Sep
28:45.91	Luciano	Brito	POR	68	2 May
28:45.95	Andy	Bristow	GBR	61	3 Sep
28:46.1	Hisayuki	Okawa	JPN	71	28 Nov
28:46.12	Ezael	Thlobo	RSA	64	6 Mar
	(160)				
28:46.45	Francesco	Ingargiola	ITA	73	2 Aug
28:46.7	Masaaki	Iijima	JPN	71	28 Nov
28:46.82	Zbigniew	Nadolski	POL	67	28 Aug
28:47.20	Kozo	Akutsu	JPN	60	12 Jun
28:47.20	Petro	Metta	TAN	73	20 Jun
28:47.9	Thomas	Cherusei	KEN		10 Jun
28:47.9	Teruo	Oga	JPN		28 Nov
28:47.92	Javier	Cortés	ESP	71	2 May
28:47.97	Dong Jiangmin		CHN	73	13 Sep
28:48.18	Andrew	Sambu	TAN	72	28 Oct

ROAD RUNNING LISTS

10 KILOMETRES

Best performances

Mark	Name		Nat	Born	Pos	Meet	Venue	Date
27:40	Addis	Abebe	ETH	5.9.70	1	Hasan	Jakarta	24 Jan
27:45	Philemon	Harineki	ZIM	12.5.71	1	Cres C	New Orleans	20 Mar
27:47	Carsten	Eich	GER	9.1.70	1		Paderborn	10 Apr
28:01	Arturo	Barrios	MEX	12.12.63	2	Hasan	Jakarta	24 Jan
28:04	German	Silva	MEX	9.1.68	1	Revco	Cleveland	16 May
28:05	Joseph	Keino	KEN	63	2	Revco	Cleveland	16 May
28:05	Thomas	Osano	KEN	4.6.70	1	Peach	Atlanta	4 Jul
28:05	Jon	Brown	GBR	27.2.71	1		Barnsley	17 Oct
	(8/8)							

Others with performances superior to track 10,000m bests

Mark	Name		Nat	Born	Pos	Meet	Venue	Date
28:06	William	Koech	KEN	2.12.61	2	Cres C	New Orleans	20 Mar
28:10	Simon	Chemoiywo	KEN	2.5.69	1		Washington	18 Apr
28:10	Philip	Mosima	KEN	75	2		Washington	18 Apr
28:10	Sammy	Lelei	KEN	14.8.64	2	Peach	Atlanta	4 Jul
28:14	Wilson	Omwoyo	KEN	25.11.65	2		Barnsley	17 Oct
28:16	Isaac	Garcia	MEX	20.2.67	3	Revco	Cleveland	16 May
28:17	Benson	Masya	KEN	14.5.70	3	Cres C	New Orleans	20 Mar
28:20	Delmir	dos Santos	BRA	12.1.66	4	Revco	Cleveland	16 May
28:21	Benjamin	Simatei	KEN		2		Dresden	20 Mar
28:21	Anthony	Kiprono	KEN	2.6.73				30 May
28:21	Kipkempoi	Kimeli	KEN	30.11.66	3	Peach	Atlanta	4 Jul
28:22	Leszek	Beblo	POL	8.7.66	3		Dresden	20 Mar
28:22	Julius	Korir	KEN	63	1		Essen	1 May
28:22	Anthony	Mwingereza	TAN		2		Essen	1 May
28:22	Simon	Karori	KEN	25.8.59	1		Asbury Park	14 Aug
28:24	Lucketz	Swartbooi	NAM	6.2.66	4	Peach	Atlanta	4 Jul
28:26	Andrés	Espinosa	MEX	4.2.63	3		Mobile	27 Mar
28:27	Alejandro	Cruz	MEX	10.2.68	5	Peach	Atlanta	4 Jul
28:28	Zablon	Miano	KEN		2		Belfast	17 Apr
28:29	Simon	Robert Naali	TAN	9.3.66	3		Paderborn	10 Apr
28:30	Ibrahim	Kinuthia	KEN	22.5.63	4	Cres C	New Orleans	20 Mar
28:30	Michal	Bartoszak	POL	21.6.70	3		Washington	18 Apr
28:30	Rod	DeHaven	USA	21.9.66	6	Revco	Cleveland	16 May
28:30	Nada	Saktay	TAN	59	4		Paderborn	10 Apr
28:31	Paul	Bitok	KEN	26.6.70				3 Apr
28:32	Jackson	Kipngok	KEN		4		Washington	18 Apr
28:32	Khalid	Kairouni	MAR		1		West Chester	5 Dec
28:34	Tonnie	Dirks	HOL	12.2.61				2 Jun
28:35	Ivan	Uvizl	TCH	16.8.58	4		Dresden	20 Mar
28:35	Eddy	Hellebuyck	BEL	22.1.61			Pittsburgh	26 Sep

Downhill

Mark	Name		Nat	Born	Pos	Meet	Venue	Date
27:44	Ed	Eyestone	USA	15.6.61	24	Jul		

Uncertain distance

Apr 25, Würzburg: 1. Tendai Chimusasa 27:37, 2. Charles Omwoyo KEN 28:20, 3. Ikaji Salum TAN 28:20
Aug 21, Goor: 1. Martin ten Kate 28:13
Sep 5, Magdeburg: 1. Mwingerza 28:11, 2. Rainer Wachenbrunner 28:14, 3. Salum 28:17
Dec 18, Santiago: 1. Diomède Cishahayo BUR 27:57; 2, Valenzuela CHL 27:59; 3, Silio ARG 28:02

15 KILOMETRES ROAD

Mark	Name		Nat	Born	Pos	Meet	Venue	Date
42:41	Valdenor	dos Santos	BRA	21.12.69	1	Gasp	Tampa	27 Feb
42:51	Delmir	dos Santos	BRA	12.1.66	2	Gasp	Tampa	27 Feb
42:53	Arturo	Barrios	MEX	12.12.63	3	Gasp	Tampa	27 Feb
42:58	José	Castillo	PER		4	Gasp	Tampa	27 Feb
43:12	Alejandro	Cruz	MEX	10.2.68	5	Gasp	Tampa	27 Feb
43:13	Yobes	Ondieki	KEN	21.2.61	6	Gasp	Tampa	27 Feb
43:17	Sammy	Lelei	KEN	14.8.64	1	Casc	Portland	27 Jun
43:17	Xolile	Yawa	RSA	29.9.62	2	Casc	Portland	27 Jun
43:18		Cruz			3	Casc	Portland	27 Jun
43:20	Godfrey	Kiprotich	KEN	23.11.64	4	Casc	Portland	27 Jun
43:20	Simon	Chemoiywo	KEN	2.5.69	1		São Paulo	31 Dec
43:21	Fita	Bayissa	ETH	15.12.72	2		São Paulo	31 Dec
43:22	Andrew	Masai	KEN	13.12.60	1		La Courneuve	30 May
43:28	Antonio	Silio	ARG	9.5.66	7	Gasp	Tampa	27 Feb
43:31	William	Sigei	KEN	11.10.69	3		São Paulo	31 Dec
	(16/15)							
43:35	Khalid	Skah	MAR	29.1.67	1		Nijmegan	21 Nov
43:39	Thomas	Osano	KEN	4.6.70	1		Utica	11 Jul
43:45	Vanderlei	Cordeiro	BRA	69	8	Gasp	Tampa	27 Feb
43:45	Gideon	Mutisya	KEN		6	Casc	Portland	27 Jun
43:47	Martin	Fíz	ESP	3.3.63	1		Bilbao	28 Nov
	(20)							
43:48	Andrés	Espinosa	MEX	4.2.63	10	Gasp	Tampa	27 Feb

Mark	Name		Nat	Born	Date
43:54	Kipkempoi	Kimeli	KEN	66	27 Jun
43:54	Tonnie	Dirks	HOL	61	21 Nov
43:56	Samwel	Maritim	KEN	65	21 Nov
43:59	Mohamed	El Massoudi	MAR	69	30 May
44:00	Benson	Masya	KEN	70	7 Mar
44:00	Lazarus	Nyakeraka	KEN		27 Jun
44:02	Silvio	Guerra	ECU	68	31 Dec
44:03	Saïd	Ermili	MAR	63	30 May
44:03	Gilbert	Ruto	KEN		30 May
44:03	Bert	van Vlaanderen	HOL	64	21 Nov
44:04	Samuel	Nyangincha	KEN	62	27 Jun
44:04	Francisco	Guerra	ESP	57	28 Nov
44:05	Marnix	Goegebeur	BEL	62	21 Nov
44:06	Helder	Vasquez	COL	67	27 Feb

10 MILES ROAD

Mark	Name		Nat	Born	Pos	Meet	Venue	Date
46:02	Richard	Nerurkar	GBR	6.1.64	1		London	17 Oct
46:11	Gary	Staines	GBR	3.7.63	1		Portsmouth	10 Oct
46:21	Zablon	Miano	KEN		1		Erewash	5 Sep
46:25	John	Treacy	IRL	4.6.57	2		Portsmouth	10 Oct
46:27	Silvio	Guerra	ECU	18.9.68	1		New York	24 Apr
46:29	William	Sigei	KEN	11.10.69	1		Washington	4 Apr
46:32	William	Mutwol	KEN	10.10.67	2		New York	24 Apr
46:33	Anthony	Kiprono	KEN	2.6.73	2		Washington	4 Apr
46:41	Takeo	Nakahara	JPN	17.9.68	1		Karatsu	7 Feb
46:43	Delmir	dos Santos	BRA	12.1.66	4		New Yprk	24 Feb
46:46	Tetsuya	Kumagaya	JPN		2		Karatsu	7 Feb
46:47	Stephen	Mayaka	KEN	16.11.72	3		Karatsu	7 Feb
46:50	Wilson	Omwoyo	KEN	25.11.65	1		Antwerp	28 Sep
46:51	Masatoshi	Ibata	JPN	20.8.72	4		Karatsu	7 Feb
46:53	Carl	Thackery	GBR	14.10.62	2		Antwerp	28 Sep
46:59	Valdenor	dos Santos	BRA	21.12.69	4		New York	24 Apr

Downhill 400ft: Feb 14, Austin: 1. Simon Peter TAN 46:39, 2. Gideon Mutisya TAN 46:43

Course not officially measured: Sep 19, Amsterdam: 1. Josephat Machuka KEN 45:22, 2. Paul Tergat KEN 46:07, 3. Charles Omwoyo KEN 46:18, 4. Sammy Maritim KEN 46:20, 5. Ijaki Salum TAN 46:40

HALF MARATHON

Note: courses slightly over the permissable downhill extent of 1/1000: Newcastle 30.5m, Tokyo 33m, Bruxelles 44m.

Mark	Name		Nat	Born	Pos	Meet	Venue	Date
59:47	Moses	Tanui	KEN	20.8.65	1		Milano	3 Apr
60:06	Steve	Moneghetti	AUS	26.9.62	1		Tokyo	24 Jan
60:11	Todd	Williams	USA	7.3.69	2		Tokyo	24 Jan
60:15		Tanui			1		Newcastle	19 Sep
60:17	Dionicio	Ceron	MEX	9.10.65	3		Tokyo	24 Jan
60:24	Benson	Masya	KEN	14.5.70	1		Den Haag	3 Apr
60:34	Carsten	Eich	GER	9.1.70	1		Berlin	4 Apr
60:42	Andrew	Masai	KEN	13.12.60	2		Milano	3 Apr
60:42	Sammy	Lelei	KEN	14.8.64	2		Berlin	4 Apr
60:45	Paul	Tergat	KEN	17.6.69	3		Milano	3 Apr

Mark	Name		Nat	Born	Pos	Meet	Venue	Date
60:50	Zablon	Miano (10)	KEN		2		Den Haag	3 Apr
61:03	Vicenzo	Modica	ITA	2.3.71	4		Milano	3 Apr
61:06	Guebre Michael	Kidane	ETH	63	1		Durban	28 Aug
61:06	Vincent	Rousseau	BEL	29.7.62	1	WC	Bruxelles	3 Oct
61:10	Joseph	Kibor	KEN	72	2		Durban	28 Aug
61:10		Moneghetti			2	WC	Bruxelles	3 Oct
61:11	Adam	Motlagale	RSA	6.3.61	3	NC	Durban	28 Aug
61:12	Boay	Akonay	TAN	3.1.70	1		Remich	26 Sep
61:13	Carl	Thackery	GBR	14.10.62	3	WC	Bruxelles	3 Oct
61:15	Lameck	Aguta	KEN	10.10.71	4	WC	Bruxelles	3 Oct
61:17	Hamid	Essebani	MAR				Ain Seba	1 Mar
61:17	Valdenor	dos Santos (20)	BRA	21.12.69	5	WC	Bruxelles	3 Oct
61:23	Julius	Ondieki	KEN		3		Berlin	4 Apr
61:25	Xolile	Yawa	RSA	29.9.62	4	NC	Durban	28 Aug
61:26	Alejandro	Gómez	ESP	11.4.67	1		Vigo	18 Apr
61:26	Lucketz	Swartbooi	NAM	6.2.66	1		Philadelphia	19 Sep
61:28	William	Koech	KEN	2.12.61	1		Gualtieri	12 Apr
61:29	Joaquim	Silva	POR	13.1.61	1		Valadares	30 May
61:30	Anthony	Kiprono	KEN	2.6.73	2		Gualtieri	12 Apr
61:30	Keith	Brantly	USA	23.5.62	2		Philadelphia	19 Sep
	(30/28)							
61:31	John	Mabitle	RSA	62	5	NC	Durban	28 Aug
61:31	Andrés	Espinosa	MEX	4.2.63	3		Philadelphia	19 Sep
	(30)							
61:33	Joseph	Keino	KEN	63	3		Gualtieri	12 Apr
61:35	Jan	Tau	RSA	18.11.60	6	NC	Durban	28 Aug
61:35	Antonio	Silio	ARG	9.5.66	6	WC	Bruxelles	3 Oct
61:37	Eddy	Hellebuyck	BEL	22.1.61	4		Tokyo	24 Jan
61:37	John	Andrews	AUS	9.3.58	7	WC	Bruxelles	3 Oct
61:38	Paul	Evans	GBR	13.4.61	1		Reading	28 Mar
61:39	Gert	Thys	RSA	12.11.71	7	NC	Durban	28 Aug
61:40	Masaki	Oya	JPN	11.7.66	5		Tokyo	24 Jan
61:40	Lawrence	Peu	RSA	13.2.66	8	NC	Durban	28 Aug
61:43	Bigboy	Goromonzi	ZIM	67	9		Durban	28 Aug
	(40)							
61:48	Ezekiel	Bitok	KEN	15.2.66	1		Granollers	17 Jan
61:49	Tadesse	Guebre	ETH		1=		Gold Coast	18 Jul
61:51	Simon	Mphulanyane	RSA	10.9.70	10	NC	Durban	28 Aug
61:51	António	Pinto	POR	22.3.66	1		Maia	14 Nov
61:53	Richard	Nerurkar	GBR	6.1.64	3		Newcastle	19 Sep
61:54	Tadashi	Fukushima	JPN	29.9.64	1		Yamaguchi	20 Mar
61:54	John	Vermeule	HOL	4.12.61	3		Den Haag	3 Apr
61:55	Getaneh	Tessema	ETH	68	4		Den Haag	3 Apr
61:56	Sid Ali	Sakhri	ALG	20.11.65	1		Ivry-sur-Seine	4 Apr
61:56	Mark	Flint	GBR	19.2.63	1		Glasgow	22 Aug
	(50)							
61:56	Gideon	Mutisya	KEN	67	4		Philadelphia	19 Sep
61:58	Samwel	Maritim	KEN	65	5		Den Haag	3 Apr
61:59	Francesco	Panetta	ITA	10.1.63	6		Milano	3 Apr
61:59	Henrique	Crisóstomo	POR	10.3.62	2		Valadares	30 May
62.00	Oleg	Strizhakov	RUS	18.7.63	2		Lyon	16 May
62:00	Rainer	Wachenbrunner	GER	11.1.62	9	WC	Bruxelles	3 Oct
62:02	Jan	Ikov	DEN	26.5.61	10	WC	Bruxelles	3 Oct
62:03	Ryo	Watanabe	JPN	.71	2		Yamaguchi	20 Mar
62:03	Haruo	Urata	JPN	9.3.62	3		Yamaguchi	20 Mar
62:03	Koji	Shimizu	JPN	17.10.69	4		Yamaguchi	20 Mar
	(60)							
62:03	Abdellah	Béhar	FRA	5.7.63	2		Ivry-sur-Seine	4 Apr
62:04	Shinichi	Akiyoshi	JPN	10.2.71	5		Yamaguchi	20 Mar
62:05	Arturo	Barrios	MEX	12.12.63	7		Milano	3 Apr
62:06	Luis	Dos Santos	BRA	30.4.71	6		Tokyo	24 Jan
62:07	Kozo	Akutsu	JPN	11.11.60	11	WC	Bruxelles	3 Oct
62:08	Joaquim	Pinheiro	POR	20.12.60	8		Milano	3 Apr
62:08	João	Lopes	POR	67	1		Esposende	18 Apr
62:09	Takeharu	Honda	JPN	24.4.67	7		Tokyo	24 Jan
62:09	Kenjiro	Jitsui	JPN	16.12.68	8		Tokyo	24 Jan

Mark	Name		Nat	Born	Pos	Meet	Venue	Date
62:10	Takahiro	Hattori	JPN	27.11.71	6		Yamaguchi	20 Mar
	(70)							
62:10	Thomas	Osano	KEN	4.6.70	13	WC	Bruxelles	3 Oct
62:11	Hiroaki	Takeda	JPN	19.10.65	9		Tokyo	24 Jan
62:11A	Marcelino	Crisanto	MEX	1.9.65	1	CAC	Cali	1 Aug
62:11	Meck	Mothuli	RSA	12.4.76	1	WJ	Bruxelles	3 Oct
62:12	Stephenson	Nyamu	KEN	20.11.71	4		Gualtieri	12 Apr
62:13	Francis	Nade	TAN	24.11.74	5		Gualtieri	12 Apr
62:14	Hiroshi	Yamada	JPN	26.8.68	7		Yamaguchi	20 Mar
62:15	Godfrey	Kiprotich	KEN	23.11.64	3		Ivry-sur-Seine	4 Apr
62:15	Joseph	Cheromei	KEN		16	WC	Bruxelles	3 Oct
62:16	Akira	Nakamura	JPN	26.6.67	10		Tokyo	24 Jan
	(80)							
62:16	Wilson	Omwoyo	KEN	25.11.65	1		Luxeuil-les-Bains	5 Sep
62:16	Simon	Karori	KEN	25.8.59	5		Philadelphia	19 Sep
62:17A	Feyissa	Abebe	ETH	70	1		Addis Ababa	24 Apr
62:17	Petro	Metta	TAN	18.12.73	6		Philadelphia	19 Sep
62:18	Bo	Reed	USA	15.3.66	1		Las Vegas	6 Feb
62:19	Graziano	Calvaresi	ITA	18.10.66	17	WC	Bruxelles	3 Oct
62:21	Gebre	Tadesse	ETH		11		Tokyo	24 Jan
62:21	José	Iniquez	MEX		1		Ontario	21 Mar
62:22	Seiichi	Miyajima	JPN	27.9.69	8		Yamaguchi	20 Mar
62:25	Vladimir	Afanasyev	RUS	68	1		Beograd	24 Apr
	(90)							
62:27	Bruno	Léger	FRA	8.1.67	1	NC	Nuaille	12 Sep
62:30	Sam	Ngatia	KEN		2		Ontario	21 Mar
62:30	Dave	Lewis	GBR	15.10.61	3		Glasgow	22 Aug
62:30	Paul	Aufdemberge	USA	30.12.64	20	WC	Bruxelles	3 Oct
62:31	Leykun	Gebre Medhin	ETH		21	WC	Bruxelles	3 Oct
62:32	Rolando	Vera	ECU	27.4.65	1		Onderdijk	17 Jul
62:32	Larbi	Zeroual	MAR	71	2		Luxeuil-les-Bains	5 Sep
62:32	Artur	DeFreitas Castro	BRA	12.11.67	1		Gargnano	29 Sep
62:32	Alberto	Maravilha	POR	17.12.65	22	WC	Bruxelles	3 Oct
62:33	Billy	Dee	GBR	18.12.61	7		Berlin	4 Apr
	(100)							
62:33	António	Costa	POR	60	2		Ovar	5 Oct

Mark	Name		Nat	Born	Date
62:34	Peter	Whitehead	GBR	64	22 Aug
62:36	Leszek	Beblo	POL	66	3 Apr
62:37	Yutaka	Nakatsubo	JPN		20 Mar
62:37	Delmir Alves	dos Santos	BRA	66	21 Aug
62:38	Ezael	Thlobo	RSA	64	3 Oct
62:40	Jacob	Ngunzu	KEN		3 Apr
62:40	Heinz-Bernd	Bürger	GER	66	3 Oct
62:41	Abdelaziz	Bougraa	MAR	66	12 Sep
62:42	Robert	Stefko	SVK	68	4 Apr
	(110)				
62:42	Raffaello	Alliegro	ITA	64	26 Sep
62:42	Davide	Milesi	ITA	64	3 Oct
62:43	Yasuhiro	Shimizu	JPN	64	20 Mar
62:43	Zdenek	Mezulianik	TCH	65	21 Mar
62:43	Nzaeli	Kioko	KEN		29 Sep
62:43	Ronny	Ligneel	BEL	64	3 Oct
62:45	Antony	Mwingereza	TAN	74	7 Mar
62:45	Barnabas	Qamunga	TAN	67	3 Apr
62:45	Ahmed	Salah	DJI	56	4 Apr
62:45	Marnix	Goegebeur	BEL	62	26 Sep
	(120)				
62:45	Julius	Sumawe	TAN	65	3 Oct
62:45	Mohamed	Ezzher	FRA	60	3 Oct
62:46	Daisuke	Tokunaga	JPN	65	20 Mar
62:46	Vyacheslav	Shabunin	RUS	69	4 Apr
62:46	Carlos	Patricio	POR	64	25 Jul
62:47	Juma	Mnyampanda	TAN	67	12 Apr
62:48	Andy	Green	GBR	62	3 Apr
62:48	Zbigniew	Nadolski	POL	67	26 Sep
62:49	António	Salvador	POR	67	3 Oct
62:49	Luigi	Di Lello	ITA	68	3 Oct
	(130)				

Uncertain distances:

Setúbal 4 Apr - all POR: 60:47 Carlos Monteiro 14.12.65 (2), 60:51 Domingos Castro 22.11.63 (2), 60:54 Carlos Patricio 9.1.64 (3), 61:19 Fernando Couto 4.12.59 (4), 61:22 Juvenal Ribeiro 9.3.64 (5), 62:36 Paulo Catarino 30.9.63 (6), 62:37 António Rodrigues 14.6.63 (7)

Morogoro (NC) 30 Jun - all TAN: 61:19 John Lory (1), 61:28 Severin Hayuma (2), 61:54 Ikaji Salum (3), 62:03 Basha Surumu (4), 62:31 Emanuel Sarwatt (5)

Short course - Lisboa 13 Mar (97m short)

Mark	Name		Nat	Born	Pos
59:24	Sammy	Lelei	KEN	14.8.64	1
60:35	Tendai	Chimusasa	ZIM	28.1.71	2
60:36	Stephan	Freigang	GER	27.9.67	3
60:40	Cosmus	Ndeti	KEN	21.11.71	4
60:47	Boniface	Merande	KEN	13.2.62	5
61:30	Luca	Barzaghi	ITA	1.6.68	6
61:57	Said	Ermili	MAR	63	9
61:57	Akira	Nakamura	JPN	26.6.67	10
61:58	Katsuhiko	Hanada	JPN	12.6.71	11
61:59	Nobuyuki	SatoJPN	8.8.72		12
62:00	Harri	Hänninen	FIN	18.10.63	14
62:01	António	Rodrigues	POR	14.6.63	15
62:03	Steve	Brace	GBR	7.7.61	17
62:06	Gelindo	Bordin	ITA	2.4.59	19
62:06	Colin	Moore	GBR	25.11.60	20
62:07	Vladimir	Kotov	BLS	24.2.58	21

MARATHON

Mark	Name		Nat	Born	Pos	Meet	Venue	Date
2:08:51	Dionicio	Cerón	MEX	9.10.65	1		Fukuoka	5 Dec
2:09:13	Vincent	Rousseau	BEL	29.7.62	1		Reims	17 Oct
2:09:25		Kim Wan-ki	KOR	8.7.68	1		Gyeongju	21 Mar
2:09:31	Gert	Thys	RSA	12.11.71	2		Fukuoka	5 Dec
2:09:33	Cosmas	N'Deti	KEN	24.11.71	1		Boston	19 Apr
2:09:43		Kim Jae-ryong	KOR	25.4.66	2		Boston	19 Apr
2:09:57	Lucketz	Swartbooi	NAM	6.2.66	3		Boston	19 Apr
2:10:03	Richard	Nerurkar	GBR	6.1.64	1	WCp	San Sebastián	31 Oct
2:10:04	Andrés	Espinosa	MEX	4.2.63	1		New York	14 Nov
2:10:06	Artur de Freitas	Castro	BRA	12.11.67	1		Venezia	10 Oct
	(10)							
2:10:12	Severino	Bernardini	ITA	31.3.66	2	WCp	San Sebastián	31 Oct
2:10:16	Kebede	Gemechu	ETH	73	3	WCp	San Sebastián	31 Oct
2:10:20	Valdenor	Dos Santos	BRA	21.12.69	3		Fukuoka	5 Dec
2:10:24	Leszek	Beblo	POL	8.7.66	2		Reims	17 Oct
2:10:27		Lee Bong-ju	KOR		1		Kwangju	16 Oct
2:10:27	Becho	Tadesse	ETH	68	4	WCp	San Sebastián	31 Oct
2:10:27	Rodrigo	Gavela	ESP	5.1.66	5	WCp	San Sebastián	31 Oct
2:10:29	Jerry	Lawson	USA	2.7.66	1		Sacramento	5 Dec
2:10:31	Slawomir	Gurny	POL	2.9.64	3		Reims	17 Oct
2:10:31	Tumo	Turbo	ETH	.70	6	WCp	San Sebastián	31 Oct
	(20)							
2:10:34	Turbe	Bedaso	ETH	19.3.69	7	WCp	San Sebastián	31 Oct
2:10:39	Mike	O'Reilly	GBR	23.4.58	4		Fukuoka	5 Dec
2:10:41	Shinji	Kawashima	JPN	4.6.66	5		Fukuoka	5 Dec
2:10:44	Aleksey	Zhelonkin	RUS	1.1.66	6		Fukuoka	5 Dec
2:10:45	Isidro	Rico	MEX	15.5.61	7		Fukuoka	5 Dec
2:10:46		Beblo			1		Paris	25 Apr
2:10:50	Eamonn	Martin	GBR	9.10.58	1		London	18 Apr
2:10:53		Rico	MEX		2		London	18 Apr
2:10:53	Luca	Barzaghi	ITA	1.6.68	8	WCp	San Sebastián	31 Oct
2:10:55	Koichi	Takahashi	JPN	7.6.62	9	WCp	San Sebastián	31 Oct
2:10:57	Belaye	Wolashe	ETH	3.5.69	2		Paris	25 Apr
2:10:57	Xolile	Yawa	RSA	29.9.62	1		Berlin	26 Sep
2:10:57		Hu Gangjun	CHN	4.12.70	1		Beijing	17 Oct
2:10:58	Diego	García	ESP	12.10.61	10	WCp	San Sebastián	31 Oct
	(34/32)							
2:11:00	Carlos	Patricio	POR	9.1.64	1		Wien	18 Apr
2:11:02	Hiromi	Taniguchi	JPN	4.4.60	4		Boston	19 Apr
2:11:03	Robert	Kempainen	USA	18.6.66	2		New York	14 Nov
2:11:04	Toshiyuki	Hayata	JPN	2.5.68	8		Fukuoka	5 Dec
2:11:06	Dave	Buzza	GBR	6.12.62	11	WCp	San Sebastián	31 Oct
2:11:07	Grzegorz	Gajdus	POL	16.1.67	3		London	18 Apr
2:11:09	Sid-Ali	Sakhri	ALG	20.12.61	3		Paris	25 Apr
2:11:09	Daisuke	Tokunaga	JPN	28.11.65	2		Beijing	17 Oct
	(40)							
2:11:10		Zhang Fukui	CHN	27.1.70	1		Tianjin	4 Apr
2:11:13	Walter	Durbano	ITA	31.3.63	1		Torino	25 Apr
2:11:15	Wieslaw	Perszke	POL	18.2.60	2		Otsu	14 Mar
2:11:18	António M	Rodrigues	POR	14.6.63	4		Paris	25 Apr
2:11:18	Fernando	Couto	POR	4.12.59	12	WCp	San Sebastián	31 Oct
2:11:38	Thomas	Robert Naali	TAN	69	2		Hamburg	23 May
2:11:39	Don	Janicki	USA	23.4.60	1		Cleveland	16 May
2:11:43	Driss	Dacha	MAR	29.12.62	2		Berlin	26 Sep
2:11:44	Simon	Robert Naali	TAN	9.3.66	2		Rotterdam	18 Apr
2:11:44	Salvatore	Bettiol	ITA	28.11.61	2		Venezia	10 Oct
	(50)							
2:11:47	Samwel	Okemwa	KEN	68	4		Otsu	14 Mar
2:11:49	Graziano	Calvaresi	ITA	18.10.66	1		Carpi	24 Oct
2:11:53	Stephan	Freigang	GER	27.9.67	1		Frankfurt	17 Oct
2:11:53	Shin	Nakashima	JPN	16.12.63	9		Fukuoka	5 Dec
2:11:55	Chaham	El Maati	MAR	15.3.66	1		Marrakesh	10 Jan
2:11:56	Viktor	Chumakov	BLS	31.5.57	6		Paris	25 Apr
2:11:56	Kenichi	Suzuki	JPN	6.4.67	1		Amsterdam	26 Sep

Mark	Name		Nat	Born	Pos	Meet	Venue	Date
2:11:57	Jan	Huruk	POL	27.1.60	5		Otsu	14 Mar
2:11:57	Karel	David	TCH	8.2.64	3		Hamburg	23 May
2:11:57	Tafa	Tesfaye	ETH	15.11.62	14	WCp	San Sebastián	31 Oct
	(60)							
2:11:58	Harri	Hänninen	FIN	18.10.63	3		Rotterdam	18 Apr
2:11:58	Julius	Sumawe	TAN	12.9.65	4		Hamburg	23 May
2:12:00	Abebe	Mekonnen	ETH	9.1.64	1		Tokyo	14 Feb
2:12:07	David	Tsebe	RSA	9.11.66	3		Berlin	26 Sep
2:12:08	Luigi	Di Lello	ITA	31.5.68	2		Carpi	24 Oct
2:12:10	Csaba	Szücs	HUN	29.1.65	8		Paris	25 Apr
2:12:11	Raffaello	Alliegro	ITA	30.5.64	2		Torino	25 Apr
2:12:11	Dominique	Chauvelier	FRA	3.8.56	9		Paris	25 Apr
2:12:11	Belayneh	Dinsamo	ETH	28.6.66	3		Beijing	17 Oct
2:12:12	Sammy	Lelei	KEN	14.8.64	5		Boston	19 Apr
	(70)							
2:12:12	Andy	Green	GBR	14.12.62	10		Paris	25 Apr
2:12:15	Mukhamet	Nazhipov	RUS	10.9.64	2		Cleveland	16 May
2:12:15	Luiz Antonio	Dos Santos	BRA	6.4.64	1		Blumenau	25 Jul
2:12:19	Jan	Tau	RSA	18.11.60	1		Enschede	13 Jun
2:12:19	Kennedy	Manyisa	KEN	69	1	WUG	Buffalo	18 Jul
2:12:21	Arturo	Barrios	MEX	12.12.62	3		New York	14 Nov
2:12:22	Diamantino	Dos Santos	BRA	3.2.61	3		Carpi	24 Oct
2:12:23	Frank	Bjørkli	NOR	30.1.65	5		London	18 Apr
2:12:23	Bertranrd	Itsweire	FRA	30.5.65	11		Paris	25 Apr
2:12:24	Alfredo	Shahanga	TAN	14.4.65	4		Berlin	26 Sep
	(80)							
2:12:24	Marco	Gozzano	ITA	26.9.63	4		Carpi	24 Oct
2:12:27	Tonnie	Dirks	HOL	12.2.61	2		Amsterdam	26 Sep
2:12:27	Eddy	Hellebuyck	BEL	22.1.61	10		Fukuoka	5 Dec
2:12:29	Saïd	Ermili	MAR	63	1		Lisbon	28 Nov
2:12:30	Jon	Solly	GBR	28.6.63	2		Sacrmento	5 Dec
2:12:33	Willie	Mtolo	RSA	5.5.64	4		Rotterdam	18 Apr
2:12:34		Baek Seung-do	KOR	16.6.68	7		London	18 Apr
2:12:36	Steve	Moneghetti	AUS	26.9.62	2		Tokyo	14 Feb
2:12:39	Mark	Plaatjes	USA	1.6.61	6		Boston	19 Apr
2:12:39	Marti	ten Kate	HOL	16.12.58	3		Amsterdam	26 Sep
	(90)							
2:12:40	Ahmed	Salah	DJI	31.12.56	8		London	18 Apr
2:12:40	Joaquim	Pinheiro	POR	20.12.60	4		New York	14 Nov
2:12:41	Viktor	Mozgovoy	BLS	6.8.61	2		Marrakech	10 Jan
2:12:47	Martin	Fíz	ESP	3.3.63	1		Helsinki	7 Aug
2:12:47	Mohamed	Salmi	ALG	11.11.63	1		Eindhoven	10 Oct
2:12:49	Keith	Brantly	USA	23.5.62	5		New York	14 Nov
2:12:50	Hyoung Jae-young		KOR	24.2.71	2		Gyeongju	21 Mar
2:12:50	Boniface	Merande	KEN	13.2.62	7		Boston	19 Apr
2:12:50	Pete	Maher	CAN	30.3.60	3		Cleveland	16 May
2:12:50	Vladimir	Kotov	BLS	21.2.58	2		Eindhoven	10 Oct
	(100)							

Mark	Name		Nat	Born	Date	Mark	Name		Nat	Born	Date
2:12:52	Inocencio	Miranda	MEX	61	14 Nov	2:13:11	Terje	Næss	NOR	61	17 Oct
2:12:53	Tena	Negere	ETH	72	5 Dec	2:13:12	Juan	Torres	ESP	59	24 Oct
2:12:54	Martin	Pitayo	MEX	60	25 Apr		(120)				
2:12:55	Brian	Sherriff	ZIM	61	14 Feb	2:13:14	Andrzej	Krzyscin	POL	67	26 Sep
2:12:56	Aleksey	Tarasov	RUS	69	25 Apr	2:13:16	Nzaeli	Kioko	KEN		11 Jul
2:12:59	Karel	Dolega	POL	63	17 Oct	2:13:17	Bert	van Vlaanderen	HOL	64	18 Apr
2:13:02	Eduard	Tukhbatullin	RUS	71	7 Aug	2:13:17	Raf	Wijns	BEL	64	25 Apr
2:13:03	Simon	Qamunga	TAN	67	10 Oct	2:13:17	Vladimir	Bukhanov	UKR	61	31 Oct
2:13:03	Juvenal	Ribeiro	POR	64	31 Oct	2:13:22	Mário	Sousa	POR	61	25 Apr
2:13:04	Mauricio	Castillo	MEX	62	7 Feb	2:13:25	Volmir	Herbstrith	BRA	65	14 Mar
	(110)					2:13:25	Kurt	Stenzel	GER	62	18 Apr
2:13:04	Takeharu	Honda	JPN	67	14 Feb	2:13:26	Marnix	Goegebeur	BEL	62	11 Aug
2:13:05	Andrew	Masai	KEN	60	25 Apr	2:13:26	Lemma	Chengere	ETH	73	31 Oct
2:13:05	Chouki	Achour	ALG	65	25 Apr		(130)				
2:13:06	Antonio	Peña	ESP	70	31 Oct	2:13:27		Wu Yihao	CHN	69	4 Apr
2:13:07	György	Markó	HUN	60	17 Oct	2:13:28	Bruno	Léger	FRA	67	25 Apr
2:13:08	John	Vermeule	HOL	61	10 Oct	2:13:28	Ceslovas	Kundrotas	LIT	61	24 Oct
2:13:09	Alberto	Juzdado	ESP	66	31 Oct	2:13:28	Peter	Fonseca	CAN	66	24 Oct
2:13:10		Huh Ei-guh	KOR	64	21 Mar	2:13:31	Antoni	Niemczak	POL	55	14 Feb

Mark	Name		Nat	Born	Date
2:13:32	Yakov	Tolstikov	RUS	59	7 Aug
2:13:33	Peter	Fleming	GBR	61	31 Oct
2:13:34	Nivaldo	Filho	BRA	60	5 Dec
2:13:35	Allaoua	Khéllil	ALG	64	13 Jun
2:13:36	Paul	Evans	GBR	61	14 Nov
2:13:37	Carlos	Tarazona	VEN	65	19 Apr
	(140)				
2:13:37	Zbigniew	Nadolski	POL	67	5 Dec
2:13:37	Rainer	Wachenbrunner	GER	62	5 Dec
2:13:40	David	Mungai	KEN	68	16 May
2:13:41	João	Batista Pacau	BRA	63	28 Nov
2:13:45	Tadao	Uchikoshi	JPN	65	14 Feb
2:13:46	Benedict	Ako	TAN		1 Aug
2:13:46	Juan Carlos	Monteiro	ESP	61	31 Oct
2:13:47	Miroslaw	Plawgo	POL	70	26 Sep
2:13:48	Marcelino	Crisanto	MEX	65	14 Mar
2:13:48	Josphat	N'Deti	KEN	73	12 Dec
	(150)				
2:13:49	Ivan	Uvizl	TCH	58	23 May
2:13:50	Jean-Baptiste	Protais	FRA	60	25 Apr
2:13:51	Andrzej	Witczak	POL	59	14 Mar
2:13:51	Roberto	Crosio	ITA	66	24 Oct
2:13:52	Tekeye	Selasie	ETH	57	13 Jun
2:13:52	Boay	Akonay	TAN	70	8 Dec
2:13:54	Abel	Mokibe	RSA	62	25 Apr
2:13:56	Gianluigi	Curreli	ITA	66	14 Mar
2:13:57	Tesfaye	Bekele	ETH	71	10 Jan
2:13:57	Nikolay	Tabak	UKR	56	31 Oct
	(160)				
2:13:59	Viktor	Vykhristenko	UKR	66	31 Oct
2:14:00	Steve	Brace	GBR	61	18 Apr
2:14:00	Luiz Amarilha	Ibarra	BRA	65	25 Apr
2:14:01	Futoshi	Shinohara	JPN	62	14 Mar
2:14:02	Toru	Mimura	JPN	62	7 Feb
2:14:03	Yoshito	Hashiguchi	JPN	62	19 Dec
2:14:07	Thierry	Constantin	SUI	68	25 Apr
2:14:07	Leonid	Shvetsov	RUS	69	17 Oct
2:14:11	Wieslaw	Palczynski	POL	63	3 Oct
2:14:12	Sergey	Romanchuk	RUS	69	14 Mar
	(170)				
2:14:14	Kenjiro	Jitsui	JPN	68	14 Feb
2:14:16	Abdelilah	Zéroual	MAR	67	8 Dec
2:14:17	Tadesse	Belayneh	ETH	66	31 Oct
2:14:22		Chang Ki-shik	KOR	70	21 Mar
2:14:23	Samuel	Nyangincha	KEN	62	19 Apr
2:14:23	Tendai	Chimusasa	TAN	71	26 Sep
2:14:23	Gerard	Kappert	HOL	61	17 Oct
2:14:23	Benjamin	Paredes	MEX	62	28 Nov
2:14:25	Josiah	Thugwane	RSA	71	20 Mar
2:14:27	Hidemitsu	Asato	JPN	66	14 Mar
	(180)				
2:14:27	Mbarak	Hussein	KEN	66	12 Dec
2:14:28	Gidamis	Shahanga	TAN	57	9 May
2:14:28	Paulo	Catarino	POR	63	10 Oct
2:14:28	Dariusz	Nawrocki	POL	64	24 Oct
2:14:29	Joseildo	Rocha Da Silva	BRA	65	7 Mar
2:14:29		Ning Limin	CHN	73	4 Apr
2:14:30	Derek	Froude	NZL	59	14 Mar
2:14:33	Barnabas	Qamunga	TAN	67	23 May
2:14:33	Aleksandr	Khlynin	UKR	56	24 Oct
2:14:33	Martin	Grüning	GER	62	31 Oct
	(190)				
2:14:34	Tomio	Sueyoshi	JPN	61	14 Feb
2:14:34		Kim Won-tak	KOR	64	21 Mar
2:14:34	Ed	Eyestone	USA	61	3 Oct
2:14:34	Isamu	Sennai	JPN	60	5 Dec
2:14:36	Osmiro	de Souza Silva	BRA	61	16 May
2:14:36	Andrew	Symonds	GBR	65	11 Aug
2:14:37	Vicente	Antón	ESP	59	21 Feb
2:14:37	Hideyuki	Oe	JPN		14 Mar
2:14:40	Thabiso	Moqhali	LES	67	18 Apr
2:14:40	John	Treacy	IRL	57	25 Oct
	(200)				

Boston (USA) has a net drop of 139 m between start (143 m) and finish (4 m)

100 KILOMETRES

Mark	Name		Nat	Born	Pos	Meet	Venue	Date
6:15:17 *	Konstantin	Santalov	RUS	3.1.66	1	IAU	Moskva	8 May
6:20:59	Aleksandr	Masarygin	RUS	18.10.60	1		Rognonas	31 Jan
6:22:19		Masarygin			1	IAU	Rodenbach	24 Apr
6:23:15		Santalov			1	IAU	Amiens	25 Sep
6:25:52		Santalov			1	IAU EC	Winschoten	18 Sep
6:26:26		Santalov			1	IAU WC	Torhout	8 Aug
6:27:29	Andrzej	Magier	POL	23.1.62	2	IAU	Rodenbach	24 Apr
6:28:12	Jean-Paul	Praet	BEL	8.11.55	1	IAU	Torhout	18 Jun
6:28:58	Valmir	Nuñes	BRA	16.1.64	1		Madrid	23 May
6:30:35	Roland	Vuillemenot	FRA	21.8.46	1	IAU NC	Chavagnes	22 May
6:30:35		Masarygin			2	IAU	Amiens	25 Sep
6:31:41	Valeriy	Mikhaylovskiy	RUS	2.1.59	2		Rognonas	31 Jan
6:33:38	Lucien	Tselman	BEL	9.7.57	3	IAU	Amiens	25 Sep
6:33:53	Jaroslav	Janicki	POL	6.7.66	1	IAU	Kalisz	9 Oct
6:33:57	Peter	Hermanns (10)	BEL	26.8.60	2	IAU EC	Winschoten	18 Sep
6:34:26		Santalov			2		Madrid	23 May
6:36:26		Hermanns			2	IAU WC	Torhout	8 Aug
6:36:38	Mikhail	Kokorev	RUS	.65	3	IAU EC	Winschoten	18 Sep
6:37:45	Mike	Hartley	GBR	6.8.55	4	IAU EC	Winschoten	18 Sep
6:38:08	Stanislav	Korablin	RUS	14.10.57	4	IAU	Amiens	25 Sep
6:38:54	Cornet	Matonane	RSA	26.12.52	3	IAU WC	Torhout	8 Aug
6:39:07		Vuillemenot			5	IAU EC	Winschoten	18 Sep
6:39:19		Praet			5	IAU	Amiens	25 Sep
6:39:21	Yuriy	Starikov	RUS	7.11.57	2	IAU	Torhout	18 Jun
6:39:41 *	Igor	Ryabov	RUS	.67	2	IAU	Moskva	8 May
	(25/16)							

Mark	Name		Nat	Born	Pos	Meet	Venue	Date
6:40:05	Thierry	Blot	FRA	11.10.60	2	IAU NC	Chavagnes	22 May
6:41:16	Denis	Gack	FRA	24.2.59	6	IAU EC	Winschoten	18 Sep
	6:40:10						Kiel	16 Oct
6:41:25	Sergey	Soldatov	RUS	.60	3	IAU	Rodenbach	24 Apr
6:41:56	Nick	Bester	RSA	10.6.50	5	IAU WC	Torhout	8 Aug
	(20)							
6:42:04	Damien	Bregula	POL	18.6.63	6	IAU	Amiens	25 Sep
6:42:38 *	Yevgeniy	Karnaukov	RUS	.61	3	IAU	Moskva	8 May
6:42:41	Erik	Seedhouse	GBR	19.6.64	1		Palamos	7 Mar
6:43:12	Heinz	Hüglin	GER	25.12.50	3	IAU	Torhout	18 Jun
6:43:14	Toshio	Kashihara	JPN	28.12.54	1	IAU	Lake Saroma	27 Jun
6:43:17 *	Leonid	Krupskiy	RUS	.52	4	IAU	Moskva	8 May
6:44:14	Don	Wallace	AUS	19.7.61	1	IAU	North Otago	31 Dec
6:45:12	Aleksey	Kononov	RUS	6.6.60	4	IAU	Torhout	18 Jun
6:45:17	Nikolay	Gromov	RUS	.59	7	IAU	Amiens	25 Sep
6:46:23 *	Sergey	Ishmulkin	RUS		5	IAU	Moskva	8 May
	(30)							
6:46:28	Volker	Becker-Wirbel	GER	20.5.62	1	IAU NC	Rheine-Elte	4 Sep
6:46:42	Farid	Zharipov	RUS	22.3.57	5	IAU	Torhout	18 Jun
6:47:57	Ryszard	Plochocki	POL	11.3.61	7	IAU EC	Winschoten	18 Sep
6:48:24 *	Aleksandr	Yepifinov	RUS		6	IAU	Moskva	8 May
6:48:31	Narihisa	Kojima	JPN	16.8.64	2	IAU	Lake Saroma	27 Jun
6:48:47	Dr Lutz	Aderhold	GER	31.7.52	4	IAU	Rodenbach	24 Apr
6:49:09	Lucas	Matlala	RSA	20.3.68	6	IAU WC	Torhout	8 Aug
6:49:30	Dietmar	Knies	GER	5.9.51	5	IAU	Rodenbach	24 Apr
6:49:53	Jetman	Msutu	RSA	18.7.57	7	IAU WC	Torhout	8 Aug
6:49:59	Patrick	Macke	GBR	18.6.55	3	IAU	Lake Saroma	27 Jun
	(40)							
6:28:59 disqualified		Praet				IAU WC	Torhout	8 Aug

* Moskva course was a small loop measured by steel tape

24 HOURS

Mark	Name		Nat	Born	Pos	Meet	Venue	Date
Track races								
246.800km	Valeriy	Moskalenko	UKR		1		Odessa	23/24 Oct
246.170	Anatoliy	Kruglikov	RUS	.57	1		Surgères	7/8 May
246.119	Patrick	Ligerot	FRA		1	IAU	Arcueil	9/10 Oct
243.200	M	Vorobyev	UKR		2		Odessa	23/24 Oct
241.063	Marc	Schmitt	FRA		2	IAU	Arcueil	9/10 Oct
Road races								
263.172	Janos	Bogár	HUN	23.6.64	1		Szeged	3/4 Jul
260.750	Konstantin	Santalov	RUS	3.1.66	1		Madrid	16/17 Oct
260.024	Jean-Pierre	Guyomarc'h	FRA	.54	1	NC	Fleurbaix	28/29 Aug
259.265	Helmut	Dreyer	GER	2.10.57	1	IAU EC	Basel	1/2 May
258.181	Kevin	Setnes	USA	27.1.54	1	NC	Sylvania	18/19 Sep
257.965	Milan	Tuhovcak	TCH	.53	2	IAU EC	Basel	1/2 May
255.775	Seigi	Arita	JPN	.56	1	IAU	Niort	6/7 Nov
254.793	Tom	Possert	USA	22.11.62	2	NC	Sylvania	18/19 Sep
253.701	Patrick	Macke	GBR	18.6.55	1	IAU	Plzen	7/8 Aug
252.420	René	de Sousa	FRA		2	NC	Fleurbaix	28/29 Aug
248.713	Roland	Teunisse	HOL	12.6.52	2		Madrid	16/17 Oct
247.900	Gennadiy	Grishev	RUS	.58	3	IAU EC	Basel	1/2 May
247.736	Jean-Pierre	Delhotel	FRA	.46	3	NC	Fleurbaix	28/29 Aug
244.743	Mick	Francis	GBR	18.9.58	4	IAU EC	Basel	1/2 May
244.742	Valery	Klement	GER	.57	5	IAU EC	Basel	1/2 May
242.058	Max	Granier	FRA	.51	4	NC	Fleurbaix	28/29 Aug
Disqualified for positive drugs test								
264.718	Nikolay	Safin ¶	RUS	.58	dq	IAU EC	Basel	1/2 May
Indoor								
275.576	Nikolay	Safin ¶	RUS	.58	1		Moskva	27/28 Feb
260.323	Valeriy	Goubar	RUS	.49	2		Moskva	27/28 Feb
242.641	Valeriy	Christenok	RUS	.62	3		Moskva	27/28 Feb

2000 METRES STEEPLECHASE

Mark	Name		Nat	Born	Pos	Venue	Date
5:25.31	Eliud	Barngetuny	KEN	73	1	Caserta	6 Jun
5:25.65	Richard	Kosgei	KEN	29.12.70	2	Caserta	6 Jun
5:27.27	Julius	Kariuki	KEN	12.6.61	1	Padova	29 Aug

5:30.9 Abdelaziz Sahere MAR 67 17 Apr 5:31.45 Azzedine Brahmi ALG 66 29 Aug

3000 METRES STEEPLECHASE

Mark	Name		Nat	Born	Pos	Meet	Venue	Date
8:06.36	Moses	Kiptanui	KEN	1.10.71	1	WC	Stuttgart	21 Aug
8:07.53	Patrick	Sang	KEN	11.4.64	2	WC	Stuttgart	21 Aug
8:08.78	Alessandro	Lambruschini	ITA	7.1.65	3	WC	Stuttgart	21 Aug
8:09.42	Matthew	Birir	KEN	5.7.72	4	WC	Stuttgart	21 Aug
8:09.76	Mark	Croghan	USA	8.1.68	5	WC	Stuttgart	21 Aug
8:10.29		Kiptanui			1	WK	Zürich	4 Aug
8:11.08		Sang			1	ISTAF	Berlin	27 Aug
8:11.09		Sang			2	WK	Zürich	4 Aug
8:12.52		Kiptanui			1	DNG	Stockholm	5 Jul
8:12.59		Lambruschini			2	ISTAF	Berlin	27 Aug
8:12.68	Richard	Kosgei	KEN	29.12.70	1	Bisl	Oslo	10 Jul
8:12.70		Kiptanui			2	Bisl	Oslo	10 Jul
8:13.18		Croghan			3	ISTAF	Berlin	27 Aug
8:13.38	Julius	Kariuki	KEN	12.6.61	3	WK	Zürich	4 Aug
8:13.44		Croghan			3	Bisl	Oslo	10 Jul
8:14.26	Marc	Davis	USA	17.12.69	4	WK	Zürich	4 Aug
8:14.98		Kosgei			1	Herc	Monaco	7 Aug
8:15.25	Abdelaziz	Sahere	MAR	18.9.67	1	BNP	Villeneuve d'Ascq	2 Jul
8:15.33	Steffen	Brand (10)	GER	10.3.65	6	WC	Stuttgart	21 Aug
8:15.37		Croghan			5	WK	Zürich	4 Aug
8:15.53		Sang			1	GPF	London	10 Sep
8:15.63		Sang			2	Herc	Monaco	7 Aug
8:15.66		Kiptanui			2	GPF	London	10 Sep
8:15.94		Sang			2	BNP	Villeneuve d'Ascq	2 Jul
8:16.22	Shaun	Creighton	AUS	14.5.67	3	BNP	Villeneuve d'Ascq	2 Jul
8:16.26		Kariuki			3	GPF	London	10 Sep
8:16.60	Larbi	El Khattabi	MAR	16.5.67	4	ISTAF	Berlin	27 Aug
8:17.30	Graeme	Fell	CAN	19.3.59	4	BNP	Villeneuve d'Ascq	2 Jul
8:17.31		Croghan			4	GPF	London	10 Sep
8:17.54		Lambruschini			1	GGala	Roma	9 Jun
	(30/13)							
8:19.34	Gideon	Chirchir	KEN	66	1	OD	Jena	13 Jun
8:19.66	Angelo	Carosi	ITA	20.1.64	3h3	WC	Stuttgart	19 Aug
8:19.99	Tom	Hanlon	GBR	20.5.67	4	Herc	Monaco	7 Aug
8:20.86	Azzedine	Brahmi	ALG	13.9.66	2	GGala	Roma	9 Jun
8:21.04	Joseph	Keter	KEN	68	1	Nik	Nice	21 Jul
8:21.24	Martin	Strege	GER	21.2.66	4h3	WC	Stuttgart	19 Aug
8:22.41	Brian	Diemer	USA	10.10.61	3	NC	Eugene	18 Jun
	(20)							
8:22.95	Francesco	Panetta	ITA	10.1.63	2	EP	Roma	27 Jun
8:23.44	Philip	Barkutwo	KEN	6.10.66	7	Herc	Monaco	7 Aug
8:23.48	Johnstone	Kipkoech	KEN	20.12.68	6	GGala	Roma	9 Jun
8:23.52	Kurt	Black	USA	4.10.68	4	NC	Eugene	18 Jun
8:23.56	Jens	Volkmann	GER	31.5.67	3	OD	Jena	13 Jun
8:23.65	Ricardo	Vera	URU	16.9.62	6h3	WC	Stuttgart	19 Aug
8:24.03	William	van Dijck	BEL	24.1.61	8	GGala	Roma	9 Jun
8:24.58	Christopher	Koskei	KEN	14.8.74	2	AfrC	Durban	25 Jun
8:24.60	Thierry	Brusseau	FRA	22.7.64	3	EP	Roma	27 Jun
8:24.80	Saad Shaddad	Al-Asmari	SAU	24.1.68	2		Rabat	6 Jun
	(30)							
8:24.87		Sun Ripeng	CHN	25.1.74	1	NG	Beijing	11 Sep
8:24.92	Michael	Buchleitner	AUT	14.10.69	4h1	WC	Stuttgart	19 Aug
8:25.81	João	Junqueira	POR	24.6.65	1	NC	Lisboa	24 Jul
8:26.31	Whaddon	Niewoudt	RSA	6.1.70	6	BNP	Villeneuve d'Ascq	2 Jul
8:26.52	Shadrack	Mogotsi	RSA	12.12.62	1	NC	Bellville	23 Apr
8:26.63	Tom	Nohilly	USA	27.4.66	5	NC	Eugene	18 Jun
8:26.65	Wender	do Prado Moura	BRA	22.2.69	1		Eagle Rock	8 May
8:27.10	Matt	McGuirk	USA	15.8.64	5	Pre	Eugene	5 Jun
8:27.26	Tom	Buckner	GBR	16.4.63	6h1	WC	Stuttgart	19 Aug
8:27.35	Gianni	Crepaldi	ITA	19.10.68	9	GGala	Roma	9 Jun
	(40)							
8:27.60	Karl	Van Calcar	USA	11.1.65	6	NC	Eugene	18 Jun
8:27.96	Kim-Lars	Bauermeister	GER	20.11.70	5	OD	Jena	13 Jun

Mark	Name		Nat	Born	Pos	Meet	Venue	Date
8:28.01	Torsten	Herwig	GER	19.10.68	1		Berlin	30 May
8:28.20	Antonio	Peula	ESP	21.3.66	5	Nik	Nice	21 Jul
8:28.51	Jim	Svenøy	NOR	22.4.72	10	Bisl	Oslo	10 Jul
8:28.69	Dan	Reese	USA	15.10.63	7	Pre	Eugene	5 Jun
8:28.85	Eliud	Barngetuny	KEN	73	1		Århus	1 Jul
8:28.91	Gustavo	Castillo	MEX	26.4.70	8	Pre	Eugene	5 Jun
8:28.93	Anton	Nicolaisen	RSA	25.1.68	3	NC	Bellville	23 Apr
8:28.96	Fabien	Lacan	FRA	24.9.68	1		Dôle	13 Jul
	(50)							
8:29.00	Ville	Hautala	FIN	19.11.68	11	Bisl	Oslo	10 Jul
8:29.04	Vítor	Almeida	POR	6.3.70	2	NC	Lisboa	24 Jul
8:29.08	Donovan	Bergstrom	USA	3.3.70	1	NCAA	New Orleans	4 Jun
8:29.56	Inocencio	López	ESP	30.10.66	1		Pontevedra	1 Jun
8:29.64	Francis	O'Neill	USA	25.2.70	4	NCAA	New Orleans	4 Jun
8:29.71	Bizuneh Yai	Tura	ETH	15.2.70	1	JPN Ch	Tokyo	13 Jun
8:30.71	Francisco J	Munuera	ESP	7.7.72	2		Pontevedra	1 Jun
8:30.77	Joël	Bourgeois	CAN	25.4.71	2	NC	Coquitlam	30 Jul
8:31.28	Reuben	Chesang	KEN	66	2		Pau	26 Jun
8:31.29	Fernando	Sinovas	ESP	8.7.68	1		Valencia	12 Jun
	(60)							
8:31.51	Alemayehu	Simretu	ETH	66	3	AfrC	Durban	25 Jun
8:31.57	Markus	Hacksteiner	SUI	18.11.64	3		Luzern	29 Jun
8:32.03	Vladimir	Pronin	RUS	27.5.69	2	WUG	Buffalo	17 Jul
8:32.07	Joseph	Sainah	KEN	3.1.66	2		Lisboa	19 Jun
8:32.67	Elisardo	de la Torre	ESP	10.10.71	1		Gijon	15 May
8:32.67	Justin	Chaston	GBR	4.11.68	12	Bisl	Oslo	10 Jul
8:32.77	Spencer	Duval	GBR	5.1.70	1	NC	London	12 Jun
8:32.98	Ali	Belghazi	ALG	22.9.62	4		Pau	26 Jun
8:33.45	Colin	WALKer	GBR	29.10.62	1	AAA	Birmingham	17 Jul
8:33.60		Gao Shuhai	CHN	18.10.68	2	NG	Beijing	11 Sep
	(70)							
8:33.66	Akira	Nakamura	JPN	26.6.67	2	NC	Tokyo	13 Jun
8:33.67		Qin Gang	CHN	10.4.72	3	NG	Beijing	11 Sep
8:33.70		Meng Xianxin	CHN	4.1.69	4	NG	Beijing	11 Sep
8:33.76	David	Kemei	KEN	70	3		Lisboa	19 Jun
8:33.86	Ramiro	Morán	ESP	17.5.69	3		Sevilla	5 Jun
8:33.96	Vladimir	Golyas	RUS	25.1.71	2	NC	Moskva	19 Jun
8:34.0	Dan	Nelson	USA	15.5.64	1		Eugene	15 May
8:34.01	Andrea	Bello	ITA	5.11.65	2	NC	Bologna	3 Aug
8:34.09	Danny	Lopez	USA	25.9.68	11	Pre	Eugene	5 Jun
8:34.12	Eduardo	Henriques	POR	24.3.68	3		Maia	10 Jul
	(80)							
8:34.38	Marcelo	Cascabelo	ARG	6.2.64	5		Cottbus	23 Jun
8:34.4	Vasiliy	Omelyusik	BLS	17.3.65	1		Grodno	4 May
8:34.55	Héctor	Arias	MEX	12.10.71	3	Jer	Coquitlam	31 May
8:34.64	Henryk	Jankowski	POL	15.10.61	6		Cottbus	23 Jun
8:34.65	Pablo	Bundo	ESP	13.10.70	2h2	NC	Gandia	2 Jul
8:34.66	Marcel	Laros	HOL	10.10.71	1		Amersfoort	27 Aug
8:34.89	Zeba	Crook	CAN	28.12.66	3	NC	Coquitlam	30 Jul
8:34.93	Florin	Ionescu	ROM	3.2.71	1	NC	Bucuresti	5 Sep
8:35.10	Jon	Azkueta	ESP	2.7.67	3h2	NC	Gandia	2 Jul
8:35.32	Aleksey	Patserin	UKR	16.5.67	7	EP	Roma	27 Jun
	(90)							
8:35.40	Bruno	Coutant	FRA	27.4.63	5		Pau	26 Jun
8:35.50	Clodoaldo	Lopes do Carmo	BRA	27.4.68	1		Hamburg	4 Aug
8:35.52	Adauto	Domingues	BRA	20.5.61			São Paulo	28 Jul
8:35.57	Jorge	Bello	ESP	28.3.63	5h2	NC	Gandia	2 Jul
8:35.64	Mohamed	Ahmed Amer	UAE	23.4.67	2		Hamburg	4 Aug
8:35.71	Michael	Heist	GER	2.5.65	7	OD	Jena	13 Jun
8:35.88	Béla	Vágó	HUN	3.10.63	4		Lisboa	19 Jun
	8:35.38 ??						Budapest	29 May
8:36.20	Steve	Hefferman	USA	27.5.68	6	Jer	Coquitlam	31 May
8:36.20	Benito	Nogales	ESP	1.8.65	3	NC	Gandia	4 Jul
8:36.57	Artur	Osman	POL	1.3.70	1	Mal	Grudziadz	18 Jun
	(100)							
8:36.61	Mohamed	Al Dossary	SAU	12.8.61	8	Nik	Nice	21 Jul

Mark	Name		Nat	Born	Date
8:36.95	Aleksey	Tarasyuk	BLS	67	24 Jun
8:37.21	Milos	Kovacech	SVK	70	15 Jun
8:37.22	Dominique	Sirieix	FRA	68	26 Jun
8:37.25	Eugenio	Frangi	ITA	71	19 Sep
8:37.28	Gábor	Markó	HUN	60	13 Jun
8:37.4A	Laban	Chege	KEN		19 May
8:37.4A	Simeon	Rono	KEN	71	3 Jul
8:37.46	Christian	Stang	GER	69	13 Jun
8:37.47	Ralph	Sagasser	GER	69	11 Jul
	(110)				
8:37.68	Darren	Mead	GBR	68	26 Jun
8:37.75	Daniel	das Neves	BRA	72	26 Jun
8:37.80	Albert	Casals	ESP	70	2 Jul
8:38.0A	Barnabas	Barmao	KEN		19 May
8:38.23	Angelo	Giardiello	ITA	70	3 Aug
8:38.37	Pascal	Drewitz	FRA	70	6 Jun
8:38.43	Ruben	Garcia	MEX	70	28 Nov
8:38.44	Gennadiy	Panin	RUS	67	12 Jun
8:38.47	Hamadi	Chabouh	TUN	62	30 Aug
8:38.54	Mauro	Pregnolato	ITA	64	13 Jun
	(120)				
8:38.74	Boguslaw	Maminski	POL	55	24 Jul
8:38.83	Cesar	Sánchez	ESP	63	2 Jul
8:38.88	Steffen	Brandis	GER	73	23 Jun
8:38.90	Ion	Avramescu	ROM	71	31 Jul
8:38.9	Mourad	Bouldjadj	ALG	68	27 Jul
8:39.0	Juan Antonio	Conde	CUB	65	9 Oct
8:39.0	Juan Ramon	Conde	CUB	65	9 Oct
8:39.04	Jean-Pierre	Poulin	CAN	70	30 Jul
8:39.07	Samuel	Kibiri	KEN	66	8 Jun
8:39.11	Nikolay	Karpovich	BLS	67	24 Jun
	(130)				
8:39.14	Henri	Belkacem	FRA	64	28 May
8:39.14	Martin	Keino	KEN	72	4 Jun
8:39.20	Fabio	Olivo	ITA	66	3 Jul
8:39.27	Philippe	Bolzer	FRA	65	9 May
8:39.48	Peder	Troldborg	DEN	63	1 Jul
8:39.61	Harald	Graham	USA	66	16 Jun
8:39.95	Giuliano	Baccani	ITA	68	13 Jun

110 METRES HURDLES

Mark	Wind	Name		Nat	Born	Pos	Meet	Venue	Date
12.91	0.5	Colin	Jackson	GBR	18.2.67	1	WC	Stuttgart	20 Aug
12.97A	-1.6		Jackson			1A		Sestriere	28 Jul
12.99	1.2		Jackson			1	VD	Bruxelles	3 Sep
13.00	0.5	Tony	Jarrett	GBR	13.8.68	2	WC	Stuttgart	20 Aug
13.06	0.5	Jack	Pierce	USA	23.9.62	3	WC	Stuttgart	20 Aug
13.08	1.2	Mark	McKoy	CAN	10.12.61	1	BNP	Villeneuve d'Ascq	2 Jul
13.10	-0.2		Jackson			1	EP	Roma	27 Jun
13.11	0.4		Jackson			1	GGala	Roma	9 Jun
13.11	-0.1		Pierce			1s2	WC	Stuttgart	19 Aug
13.12	0.8		Jackson			1	Nik	Nice	21 Jul
13.12	0.0	Tony	Dees	USA	6.8.63	1	Herc	Monaco	7 Aug
13.13	0.4		Jackson			1A	Vaux	Gateshead	30 Jul
13.13	0.0		Jackson			1s1	WC	Stuttgart	19 Aug
13.14	1.2		Pierce			2	BNP	Villeneuve d'Ascq	2 Jul
13.14	-0.3		Jarrett			1s3	WC	Stuttgart	19 Aug
13.14	-0.1		Jackson			1	GPF	London	10 Sep
13.14	0.5		Jackson			1	Toto	Fukuoka	18 Sep
13.15	1.1		Jackson			1	AAA	Birmingham	16 Jul
13.19	1.5		Pierce			1	NC	Eugene	18 Jun
13.19	0.0		Dees			1A	WK	Zürich	4 Aug
13.19	-0.3		Dees			2s3	WC	Stuttgart	19 Aug
13.19	-0.3	Emilio	Valle	CUB	21.4.67	3s3	WC	Stuttgart	19 Aug
13.20	0.4		McKoy			2	GGala	Roma	9 Jun
13.20	-1.0		Jackson			1	TSB	London	23 Jul
13.20	0.5		Valle			4	WC	Stuttgart	20 Aug
13.21	1.5		Dees			2	NC	Eugene	18 Jun
13.21	0.0		Jackson			1=	Bisl	Oslo	10 Jul
13.21	0.0		Pierce			1=	Bisl	Oslo	10 Jul
13.21	-0.4		Pierce			1h2	WC	Stuttgart	19 Aug
13.22	0.0		Pierce			2	Herc	Monaco	7 Aug
13.23	-0.8		Jackson			1h1	AAA	Birmingham	16 Jul
13.23	-0.7		Jackson			1h1	WC	Stuttgart	19 Aug
		(32/6)							
13.25	1.3	Courtney	Hawkins	USA	11.7.67	1	Indy	Indianapolis	25 Jun
13.26	-0.3		Li Tong	CHN	6.5.67	1		Verona	16 Jun
13.26	1.2	Mark	Crear	USA	2.10.68	3	BNP	Villeneuve d'Ascq	2 Jul
13.26	0.0	Igor	Kazanov	LAT	24.9.63	2s1	WC	Stuttgart	19 Aug
		(10)							
13.27	1.3	Greg	Foster	USA	4.8.58	2	Indy	Indianapolis	25 Jun
13.27	0.5	Florian	Schwarthoff	GER	7.5.68	5	WC	Stuttgart	20 Aug
13.34	1.0	George	Boroi	ROM	26.8.64	1	RomIC	Bucuresti	18 Jun
13.35	1.9	Glenn	Terry	USA	10.2.71	1h1	WUG	Buffalo	16 Jul

Mark	Wind	Name		Nat	Born	Pos	Meet	Venue	Date
13.40	1.9	Roger	Kingdom	USA	26.8.62	2s2	NC	Eugene	17 Jun
13.41	-0.1	Arthur	Blake	USA	19.8.66	1rB	NYG	New York	22 May
13.42	0.0	Dan	Philibert	FRA	6.8.70	5s1	WC	Stuttgart	19 Aug
13.43	1.9	Brian	Amos	USA	26.12.71	1	NCAA II	Abilene	29 May
13.44	1.9	Dietmar	Koszewski	GER	26.7.67	1s1	WUG	Buffalo	16 Jul
13.47	1.6	Allen	Johnson	USA	1.3.71	2	NCAA	New Orleans	5 Jun
		(20)							
13.47	-0.5	Hubert	Grossard	BEL	28.3.68	1	NC	Bruxelles	25 Jul
13.48	0.0	Vladimir	Belokon	UKR	13.2.69	1	NC	Kiev	3 Jul
13.48	1.0	Eric	Kaiser	GER	7.3.71	1s2	NC	Duisburg	10 Jul
13.48	-0.3	Kyle	Vander-Kuyp	AUS	30.5.71	4s3	WC	Stuttgart	19 Aug
13.52	0.6	Ubeja	Anderson	USA	30.3.74	1	SEC	Knoxville	16 May
13.52	0.7	Igor	Kovác	SVK	12.5.69	1	EP/C3	Rotterdam	13 Jun
13.54		Rod	Jett	USA	28.10.66	1		Berkeley	20 Mar
13.54	0.3	Vladimir	Shishkin	RUS	12.1.64	2	NC	Moskva	20 Jun
13.55	0.7	Sergey	Usov	BLS	16.1.64	2	EP/C3	Rotterdam	13 Jun
13.55	0.0	Gennadiy	Dakshevich	UKR	15.3.66	2	NC	Kiev	3 Jul
		(30)							
13.55A	-1.6	Laurent	Ottoz	ITA	10.4.70	2		Sestriere	28 Jul
13.56	1.9	Eugene	Swift	USA	14.9.64	6s2	NC	Eugene	17 Jun
13.57	1.9	Jerry	Roney	USA	5.1.70	7s2	NC	Eugene	17 Jun
13.57	0.0	Eduard	Hämäläinen	BLS	21.1.69	D	WC	Stuttgart	20 Aug
13.58	0.6	Chris	Phillips	USA	24.7.72	2	SEC	Knoxville	16 May
13.58	1.0	Pawel	Grzegorzewski	POL	20.7.66	1		Krakow	1 Jul
13.59	1.4	Sebastien	Thibault	FRA	25.7.70	1		La Chaux de Fonds	8 Aug
13.59	0.4	Andrew	Tulloch	GBR	1.4.67	3h4	WC	Stuttgart	19 Aug
13.59	-0.5		Chen Yanhao	CHN	2.1.72	1	NG	Beijing	13 Sep
13.60	-0.9	Yevgeniy	Pechyonkin	RUS	9.10.73	3		Pau	26 Jun
		(40)							
13.62	0.1	Ronald	Mehlich	POL	26.9.69	2	Kuso	Kielce	16 Jun
13.62	1.5	Larry	Harrington	USA	24.11.70	6	NC	Eugene	18 Jun
13.62	0.2	Andrew	Parker	JAM	11.1.65	1	NC	Kingston	3 Jul
13.62	0.6	Andrey	Dydalin	RUS	7.6.66	1h1		Moskva	6 Aug
13.64A	-0.9	Kobus	Schoeman	RSA	16.11.65	2		Pretoria	15 May
13.64	1.0	Anthony	Knight	JAM	17.11.70	1		Clemson	16 May
13.64	1.2	Mike	Fenner	GER	24.4.71	2		Zeven	29 May
13.64	0.1	Piotr	Wojcik	POL	7.2.65	2	v2N	Praha	17 Jun
13.64A	-1.6	Fausto	Frigerio	ITA	13.2.66	5		Sestriere	28 Jul
13.65	-0.3	Pat	Duffy	USA	4.5.65	4	Jen	San José	29 May
		(50)							
13.66	0.3	Stelios	Bisbas	GRE	9.11.68	1	EP/C1	Villach	13 Jun
13.66	0.1	Dmitriy	Kolesnichenko	UKR	28.2.72	4	Kuso	Kielce	16 Jun
13.66A	-1.6	T J (Thomas)	Kearns	IRL	2.6.66	6		Sestriere	28 Jul
13.66A	-1.6	Sean	Cahill	IRL	26.4.67	7		Sestriere	28 Jul
13.67	1.3	Antti	Haapakoski	FIN	6.2.71	1		Kuortane	26 Jun
13.68	-0.5	Vincent	Clarico	FRA	8.1.66	1		Praha	11 Sep
13.69	1.0	Robert	Reading	USA	9.6.67	2r1		Fresno	3 Apr
13.69	1.3	Kai	Kyllönen	FIN	30.1.65	2		Jämsänkoski	9 Jul
13.69	-0.4	Hugh	Teape	GBR	26.12.63	2h3	AAA	Birmingham	16 Jul
13.70	1.0	Viktor	Bolkun	UKR	2.7.70	2h1	NC	Kiev	3 Jul
		(60)							
13.70	0.0	Andrey	Karatayev	UKR	6.3.66	4	NC	Kiev	3 Jul
13.71A	1.0	Tim	Kroeker	CAN	25.5.71	1rB		Provo	26 May
13.71	0.1	Jirí	Hudec	TCH	15.8.64	5	Kuso	Kielce	16 Jun
13.71	1.0	Vladislav	Guba	UKR	17.12.71	3h1	NC	Kiev	3 Jul
13.72	1.2	David	Nelson	GBR	11.3.67	2	NC	London	12 Jun
13.72	0.0	David	Ashford	USA	24.1.64	1		Bugeat	4 Jul
13.73	1.3	Renaldo	Nehemiah	USA	24.3.59	8	Indy	Indianapolis	25 Jun
13.73		Claude	Edorh	GER	27.2.72	2		Gladbeck	26 Jun
13.74	1.7	Rodney	Thompson	USA	21.11.70	1h3	SEC	Knoxville	15 May
13.74	0.9	Duane	Ross	USA	5.12.72	2s2	NCAA	New Orleans	4 Jun
		(70)							

Mark	Wind	Name		Nat	Born	Pos	Meet	Venue	Date
13.74	-0.1		Zheng Jinsu	CHN	30.6.70	1	NC	Beijing	11 Jun
13.75A	-0.1	Omar	Portuondo	CUB	1.5.70	1		Ciudad México	9 May
13.75	1.1	Pekka	Vesterinen	FIN	13.4.66	3		Keuruu	25 Jun
13.75	1.3	Sergey	Kurach	RUS	28.3.70	3		Kuortane	26 Jun
13.75	0.8	Mathieu	Jouÿs	FRA	13.2.72	2h		La Chaux de Fonds	8 Aug
13.76A	-0.1	Keith	Talley	USA	28.1.64	2		Ciudad México	9 May
13.76		Jonathan	N'senga	BEL	21.4.73	1		Bruxelles	15 Jun
13.77A		Robert	Foster	JAM	12.7.70	1		Albuquerque	1 May
13.78		Brandon	Gantt	USA	28.8.72	1h2	JUCO	Odessa	20 May
13.78		Terry	Winston	USA	11.1.72	4		Atlanta	22 May
		(80)							
13.78	1.2	Jailto	Bonfim	BRA	11.2.65	1		Rio de Janeiro	27 Jun
13.79	1.0	Malcolm	Dixon	USA	11.10.59	5r1		Fresno	3 Apr
13.79		Dmitriy	Buldov	RUS	2.7.68	1		Sochi	22 May
13.79		Mustapha	Sdad	MAR	11.4.70	1		Rabat	29 May
13.79	1.2	Pedro	Chiamulera	BRA	29.6.64	2		Rio de Janeiro	27 Jun
13.80	1.3		Liu Tao	CHN	.1.70	2		Shiajiazhuang	25 Apr
13.80		Rory	Norris	USA	3.3.72	2		Arlington	1 May
13.80		Marcus	Dixon	USA	6.7.70	2		Tallahassee	26 May
13.81	1.6	Jeff	Jackson	USA	14.3.74	1		San Marcos	27 Mar
13.81		Kevin	White	USA	16.8.74	1		Houston	30 Mar
13.81	1.6	Aleksandr	Markin	RUS	8.9.62	4s1	NC	Moskva	20 Jun
		(90)							
13.82		Derek	Spears	USA	21.3.73	1s1	JUCO	Odessa	21 May
13.82	-0.3	Herwig	Röttl	AUT	30.1.68	1		Kapfenberg	5 Jun
13.82	1.3	Timur	Yudakov	RUS	12.7.66	1h2	Znam	Moskva	13 Jun
13.83	0.2	Matthew	Love	JAM	1.8.70	2	NC	Kingston	3 Jul
13.84	1.5	Mikhail	Edel	RUS	7.9.69	2		Indianapolis	15 May
13.84	0.6	Ross	Flowers	USA	10.8.71	1	Pac-10	Berkeley	22 May
13.84		Wagner	Marseille	HAI	13.9.70	2		Williamsburg	23 May
13.84A	-0.2	Luigi	Bertocchi	ITA	10.6.65	1rB		Sestriere	28 Jul
13.85	0	Chad	Black	USA	3.10.72	3		Chapel Hill	15 May
13.85	1.9	Marco	Morgan	USA	14.4.71	2	NCAA II	Abilene	29 May
		(100)							
13.85	0.9	Robin	Korving	HOL	29.7.74	1	EJ	San Sebastián	31 Jul
13.85	-0.2	Sergey	Vetrov	RUS	8.5.68	3		Moskva	6 Aug

Mark	Wind	Name		Nat	Born	Date
13.86		James	Armstrong	USA	67	10 May
13.86		Kevin	McQueen	USA	70	26 May
13.86		Shannon	Flowers	USA	71	27 May
13.87A	-0.5	Wimpie	Nel	RSA	66	6 Apr
13.87	0.7	Kendell	Mabry	USA	71	17 Apr
13.87	1.5	John	Owens	USA	66	15 May
13.88		Sherman	Morris	USA	70	20 Mar
13.88	0.6	James	Rainey	USA	71	16 May
		(110)				
13.88	0.8	Niklas	Eriksson	SWE	69	3 Jun
13.88	1.3	Igor	Borisov	BLS	67	13 Jun
13.88		Stefan	Mattern	GER	65	24 Jul
13.89	0.0	Charles	Johnson	USA	68	15 May
13.89	1.9	Robert	Zmelík	TCH	69	15 Jun
13.90		Chris	Roney	USA	70	24 Apr
13.90		Micah	Otis	USA	72	9 May
13.90		Matt	Fuller	USA	73	22 May
13.90	-0.1	Cletus	Clark	USA	62	22 May
13.90	0.8	Georgi	Georgiev	BUL	68	13 Jun
		(120)				
13.90	0.1	Artur	Kohutek	POL	71	16 Jun
13.91	-1.9	Tiberia	Patterson	USA	71	24 Apr
13.91	0.7	Tomasz	Nagorka	POL	67	1 Jun
13.91		Reinaldo	Quintero	CUB	70	25 Jun
13.91	0.0	Vladimir	Dobrydneyv	UKR	70	3 Jul
13.91	-0.3	Carlos	Sala	ESP	60	27 Jul
13.91	0.9	Andrea	Bergna	ITA	68	2 Aug
13.92	1.7	David	Cooper	AUS	72	6 Mar
13.92	0.0	Brett	Shields	USA	70	24 Apr
13.92	1.4	Richard	Murphy	USA	72	1 May
		(130)				
13.92	-0.3	Mauro	Re	ITA	67	16 Jun
13.92		Mircea	Oaida	ROM	69	31 Jul
13.92	0.4	Miguel	Soto	PUR		19 Aug
13.93	1.7	John	Caliguri	AUS	62	6 Mar
13.93	1.1	Zhang Feng		CHN	72	11 Apr
13.93	2.0	Curt	Young	USA	74	13 May
13.93	0.3	Dan	O'Brien	USA	66	29 May
13.93	0.0	Thierry	Richard	FRA	61	4 Jul
13.93	1.0	Yoshiaki	Hoki	JPN	70	2 Dec
13.94	-1.6	Willie	Hibler	USA	74	3 Apr
		(140)				
13.94	1.3	Wan Wenyaun		CHN	72	25 Apr
13.94	0.6	Leo	Simmons	USA	68	22 May
13.94	1.5	Marcelin	Dally	CIV	62	5 Jun
13.94	-0.3	Gianni	Tozzi	ITA	62	16 Jun
13.95	0.8	Gunnar	Schrör	SUI	67	13 Jun
13.95		Erick	Batle	CUB	74	18 Jun
13.96		Earl	Diamond	USA	66	27 Mar
13.96	1.3	Bob	Gray	USA	70	15 Apr
13.96	0.4	Stéphane	Rémion	FRA	70	15 May
13.96	0.6	Mark	Anderson	USA	58	22 May
		(150)				
13.96		Tim	McCrate	USA	71	26 May
13.96	0.6	Keevan	Mills	USA	72	3 Jun
13.96	0.8	Diego	Puppo	ITA	69	12 Jun

Mark	Wind	Name		Nat	Born	Date	
13.96	0.2	Gaute M	Gundersen	NOR	72	19	Jun
13.96	1.0	Falk	Balzer	GER	73	10	Jul
13.96	1.4	Franck	Ledoux	FRA	67	8	Aug
13.96	-0.5	Zhou Zhong		CHN	66	13	Sep
13.97		Johnny	Westbrook	USA	71	1	May
13.97		Eric	Honroth	USA	71	26	May
13.97		Luc	Anceaux	FRA	67	5	Jun
		(160)					
13.97	0.6	Dimitris	Siatounis	GRE	69	17	Jul
13.97		Moses	Oyiki	NGR	65	6	Nov
13.98	1.6	Olivier	Vallaeys	FRA	66	18	Jul
13.98	1.4	Guntis	Peders	LAT	73	31	Jul
13.98	1.4	Franck	Ledoux	FRA	67	8	Aug
13.98		Judex	Lefou	MRI	66	14	Sep
13.99		Thierry	Herbe	FRA	71	1	May
13.99		Prodomos	Katsantonis	CYP	75	15	May
13.99		Darren	Nutt	USA	71	26	May
13.99	1.3	Igor	Pintusevich	UKR	73	13	Jun
		(170)					
13.99	0.0	Steve	Fritz	USA	67	20	Aug

Unconfirmed

Mark	Wind	Name		Nat	Born	Date	
13.74		Delavantie	Brown	JAM		8	May
13.85		Andrew	Smith	BAH			

Low altitude bests

Mark	Wind	Name	Pos	Meet	Venue	Date	
13.57	0.4	Ottoz	5	GGala	Roma	9	Jun
13.68	-0.1	Kearns	5s2	WC	Stuttgart	19	Aug
13.70	-0.1	Cahill	4h2	WC	Stuttgart	19	Aug
13.71	-0.6	Kroeker	3h6	WC	Stuttgart	19	Aug
13.72	0.2	Frigerio	1		Bellinzona	10	Jul
13.74	1.1	Schoeman	3		Rhede	6	Aug
13.77	2.0	Foster	2h1	NCAA	New Orleans	3	Jun
13.95	0.8	Bertoccho	2r3		Southampton	6	Jun

Wind-assisted marks

Mark	Wind	Name		Nat	Born	Pos	Meet	Venue	Date	
13.01	3.6		Jackson			1	v USA	Edinburgh	2	Jul
13.09	2.1		Jackson			1	McD	Sheffield	29	Aug
13.22	2.7	Mark	Crear	USA	2.10.68	1h4	NC	Eugene	17	Jun
13.24	2.4	Glenn	Terry	USA	10.2.71	1s2	WUG	Buffalo	18	Jul
13.34	3.6	Allen	Johnson	USA	1.3.71	3	vUSA	Edinburgh	2	Jul
13.38	4.6	Roger	Kingdom	USA	26.8.62	1h1	NC	Eugene	17	Jun
13.42		Brian	Amos	USA	26.12.71	1		Abilene	8	May
13.46		Rod	Jett	USA	28.10.66	1		Chico	1	May
13.49	2.3	Larry	Harrington	USA	24.11.70	3s1	NC	Eugene	17	Jun
13.51	3.5	Pat	Duffy	USA	4.5.65	1rB	S&W	Modesto	8	May
13.51		Tim	Kroeker	CAN	25.5.71	1rC	S&W	Modesto	8	May
13.52	3.5	Eugene	Swift	USA	14.9.64	2rB	S&W	Modesto	8	May
13.54	2.5	Renaldo	Nehemiah	USA	24.3.59	3h2	NC	Eugene	17	Jun
13.60	3.0	Stelios	Bisbas	GRE	9.11.68	1	Veniz	Khania	5	Jun
13.60	3.6	Hugh	Teape	GBR	26.12.63	6	vUSA	Edinburgh	2	Jul
13.62	2.8	T J (Thomas)	Kearns	IRL	2.6.66	1	NC	Dublin	25	Jul
13.63	5.5	Malcolm	Dixon	USA	11.10.59	2		Austin	8	May
13.63	3.8	Kai	Kyllönen	FIN	30.1.65	1		Punkalaidun	30	May
13.64	2.1	Vincent	Clarico	FRA	8.1.66	2	NC	Annecy	25	Jul
13.65	6.6	Marcus	Dixon	USA	6.7.70	3		Austin	8	May
13.65	3.5	Robert	Foster	JAM	12.7.70	3rB	S&W	Modesto	8	May
13.67	2.1	Mathieu	Jouÿs	FRA	13.2.72	3	NC	Annecy	25	Jul
13.69		Darian	Jones	USA	15.10.69	1		Lafayette, La.	20	Mar
13.69	2.2	Claude	Edorh	GER	27.2.72	2	NC	Duisburg	10	Jul
13.71		Richard	Murphy	USA	28.4.72	2		Waco	17	Apr
13.71	3.1	Wagner	Marseille	HAI	13.9.70	3s1	NCAA	New Orleans	4	Jun
13.72	5.3	Keith	Talley	USA	28.1.64	1		Tuscaloosa	28	Mar
13.72	2.2	Keevan	Mills	USA	10.7.72	1		Monroe	17	May
13.72	2.4	Guntis	Peders	LAT	15.8.73	3s2	WUG	Buffalo	18	Jul
13.73		Cletus	Clark	USA	20.1.62	1		Houston	17	Apr
13.73	2.7	Shannon	Flowers	USA	17.9.71	5h4	NC	Eugene	17	Jun
13.75	4.3	Kevin	White	USA	16.8.74	1		Houston	20	Mar
13.77	3.1	Kehinde	Aladefa	NGR	19.12.74	1h1		Abilene	28	May
13.78	3.1	Marco	Morgan	USA	14.4.71	2h1		Abilene	28	May
13.79	4.8	John	Owens	USA	29.10.66	6h3	NC	Eugene	17	Jun
13.80		Ross	Flowers	USA	10.8.71	2	S&W	Modesto	8	May
13.81	3.3	Kendall	Mabry	USA	71	1		San Angelo	10	Apr
13.84	4.0	Tibor	Bédi	HUN	22.3.74	1		Veszprém	22	Jul
13.84A	2.7	Erik	Batle	CUB	10.12.74	1	CAC	Cali	1	Aug

Mark	Wind	Name		Nat	Born	Date	
13.85	5.5	Gregory	Williams	JAM	66	8	May
13.85	2.3	Hubert	Rochard	FRA	68	17	Jul
13.86		Phillip	Lewis	USA		20	Mar
13.86		Larry	Moore	USA	70	10	Apr
13.87		Derrick	Fobb	USA		27	Mar
13.87	2.2	Kevin	Ellis	USA		17	May
13.88	2.4	Yoshiaki	Hoki	JPN	70	14	May
13.90			LeBlanc	USA		27	Mar

Mark	Wind	Name		Nat	Born	Date
13.90	5.0	Darren	Nutt	USA	71	7 Apr
13.90		Kris	Roney	USA	70	24 Apr
13.91		Mark	Whitsett	USA	69	15 May
13.91	2.1	Stéphane	Rémion	FRA	70	25 Jul
13.92		Henry	Andrade	CVD	62	8 May
13.92	3.6	Tim	McCrate	USA	71	23 May
13.92	2.1	Thierry	Richard	FRA	61	25 Jul
13.99	3.0	Neil	Owen	GBR	73	3 Jul
13.94	2.2	Hans-Peter	Lott	GER	69	10 Jul
13.94	2.1	Franck	Ledoux	FRA	67	25 Jul
13.96	2.2	Falk	Balzer	GER	73	10 Jul
13.97	2.2	Willie	Gault	USA	60	24 Apr
13.97	3.3	Olivier	Coche	FRA	72	10 Jul
13.99	2.1	Drew	Fucci	USA	67	7 Apr
13.99A	2.6	Braam	Steynberg	RSA	72	8 May

Rolling start: 13.81w 4.0 Levente Csillag HUN 22.3.73 1 Veszprém 22 Jul

Best wind-assisted low altitude mark: 13.72 3.3 Schoeman 3 Lappeenranta 27 Jul

Hand timing

Mark	Wind	Name		Nat	Born	Pos	Meet	Venue	Date
13.4	0.6	Pawel	Grzegorzewski	POL	20.7.66	1		Sopot	10 Jul
13.4	0.6	Piotr	Wojcik	POL	7.2.65	2		Sopot	10 Jul
13.5		Jerry	Roney	USA	5.1.70	1		Wilmington	10 Apr
13.5		Timur	Yudakov	RUS	12.7.66	1h		Moskva	13 May
13.5	0.2	Robert	Reading	USA	9.6.67	1		Cerritos	30 May
13.6	0.5	Tiberia	Patterson	USA	26.1.71	1		Bowling Green	15 May
13.6	0.5	Eric	Honroth	USA	7.5.71	2		Bowling Green	15 May

Mark	Wind	Name		Nat	Born	Date
13.7A	0.2	Francois	du Toit	RSA	70	13 Feb
13.7		Brian	Taylor	GBR	70	1 Apr
13.7		Eugene	Harris	USA	72	17 Apr
13.7	1.7	Rodney	Thompson	USA	70	17 Apr
13.7	-0.2	Pekka	Vesterinen	FIN	66	13 Jun
13.8	1.8	Takahiro	Matsuhisa	JPN	68	3 Apr
13.8	2.0	Yusuke	Tsuge	JPN	71	11 Apr
13.8	-2.5	Georgi	Georgiev	BUL	68	19 May
13.8		Sergey	Manakov	RUS	72	29 May
13.8		Valeriy	Pankov	RUS	72	29 May
13.8	0.2	Tony	House	USA	66	30 May
13.8		Vladimir	Dobrydneyv	UKR	70	8 Jun
13.8		Mikhail	Edel	RUS	69	12 Jun
13.8	-0.2	John	Caliguri	AUS	62	13 Jun
13.8	1.3	David	Cooper	AUS	72	8 Oct
13.8 ?		Abdul	Razzaq	PAK		

Wind assisted

Mark	Wind	Name		Nat	Born	Pos	Meet	Venue	Date
12.9	4.1	Mark	Crear	USA	2.10.68	1rA	S&W	Modesto	8 May
13.0	4.1		Li Tong	CHN	6.5.67	2rA	S&W	Modesto	8 May
13.3	4.1	Larry	Harrington	USA	24.11.70	3rA	S&W	Modesto	8 May

Mark	Wind	Name		Nat	Born	Date
13.7	2.7	Juan	Jackson	USA	68	20 Mar
13.7	2.7	Keevan	Mills	USA	72	20 Mar
13.7	4.1	Henry	Andrade	CVD	62	8 May

Questionable timing

Mark	Name		Nat	Born	Pos	Date
13.45	Sherman	Morris	USA	22.7.70	1	13 Jun
13.88	Mike	Kearse	USA		2	13 Jun

200 METRES HURDLES

Mark	Wind	Name		Nat	Born	Pos	Meet	Venue	Date
22.81	-3.1	Colin	Jackson	GBR	18.2.67	1		Thurrock	12 Sep
23.50		Marco	Beukenkamp	HOL	13.3.63	1		Hilversum	19 Sep

400 METRES HURDLES

Mark	Name		Nat	Born	Pos	Meet	Venue	Date
47.18	Kevin	Young	USA	16.9.66	1	WC	Stuttgart	19 Aug
47.37		Young			1	Athl	Lausanne	7 Jul
47.60	Winthrop	Graham	JAM	17.11.65	1	WK	Zürich	4 Aug
47.60	Samuel	Matete	ZAM	27.7.68	2	WC	Stuttgart	19 Aug
47.62		Graham			3	WC	Stuttgart	19 Aug
47.64	Stéphane	Diagana	FRA	23.7.69	4	WC	Stuttgart	19 Aug
47.69		Young			1	NC	Eugene	18 Jun
47.73		Young			1	BNP	Villeneuve d'Ascq	2 Jul
47.75		Young			1	ASV	Köln	1 Aug
47.82		Matete			2	WK	Zürich	4 Aug
47.94		Matete			1	Herc	Monaco	7 Aug
47.99		Young			1s3	WC	Stuttgart	17 Aug
48.08		Diagana			1	EP	Roma	26 Jun
48.08		Young			3	WK	Zürich	4 Aug
48.09		Graham			1s1	WC	Stuttgart	17 Aug
48.10		Young			2	Herc	Monaco	7 Aug
48.15		Matete			1		Rieti	5 Sep
48.17		Young			1	Jen	San José	29 May
48.17		Graham			3	Herc	Monaco	7 Aug
48.18		Matete			1s2	WC	Stuttgart	17 Aug
48.20A		Young			1		Sestriere	28 Jul
48.24	Eric	Keter	KEN	22.7.66	2s2	WC	Stuttgart	17 Aug

Mark	Name		Nat	Born	Pos	Meet	Venue	Date
48.28		Young			1s2	NC	Eugene	17 Jun
48.28		Matete			2	ASV	Köln	1 Aug
48.39	Derrick	Adkins	USA	2.7.70	3	ASV	Köln	1 Aug
48.40		Keter			5	WC	Stuttgart	19 Aug
48.46		Matete			1	Slovn	Bratislava	1 Jun
48.48	Olaf	Hense	GER	19.11.67	2	EP	Roma	26 Jun
48.49		Matete			1h1	WC	Stuttgart	16 Aug
48.50		Diagana			2s3	WC	Stuttgart	17 Aug
	(30/7)							
48.62	Oleg	Tverdokhleb	UKR	3.11.69	3s1	WC	Stuttgart	17 Aug
48.68	Yoshihiko	Saito	JPN	12.2.72	1	NC	Tokyo	12 Jun
48.73	Kriss	Akabusi	GBR	28.11.58	4	EP	Rome	26 Jun
	(10)							
48.75	Shunji	Karube	JPN	8.5.69	2	NC	Tokyo	12 Jun
48.95	David	Patrick	USA	12.6.60	3	NC	Eugene	18 Jun
48.97	Torrance	Zellner	USA	6.1.70	4	NC	Eugene	18 Jun
49.06	Barnabas	Kinyor	KEN	3.8.61	4s1	WC	Stuttgart	17 Aug
49.07	Bryan	Bronson	USA	9.9.72	1	NCAA	New Orleans	4 Jun
49.08	Kazuhiro	Yamazaki	JPN	10.5.71	1		Tokyo	17 Oct
49.09	Zaid Abou	Hamed	SYR	22.4.70	1	MedG	Narbonne	19 Jun
49.10	Jordan	Gray	USA	9.2.71	2	NCAA	New Orleans	4 Jun
49.15	Eronildo	Nunes	BRA	31.12.70	1		Rio de Janeiro	25 Jun
49.21	Hidekazu	Katsuki	JPN	18.4.69	3	NC	Tokyo	12 Jun
	(20)							
49.21A	Kevin	Henderson	USA	4.2.65	3		Sestriere	28 Jul
49.21	Sven	Nylander	SWE	1.1.62	5s1	WC	Stuttgart	17 Aug
49.22	Giorgio	Frinolli	ITA	12.7.70	5	EP	Rome	26 Jun
49.23	Fabrizio	Mori	ITA	28.6.69	3s2	WC	Stuttgart	17 Aug
49.24	Larry	Sanders	USA	26.4.70	1	NCAA II	Abilene	29 May
49.25	Gary	Cadogan	GBR	8.10.66	2h3	WC	Stuttgart	16 Aug
49.27	Gideon	Biwott	KEN	16.6.64	2h4	WC	Stuttgart	16 Aug
49.28A	José	Pérez	CUB	19.3.71	1h1	CAC	Cali	30 Jul
49.36	Rohan	Robinson	AUS	15.11.71	5s3	WC	Stuttgart	17 Aug
49.38	Richard	Murphy	USA	28.4.72	2	SWC	Austin	21 May
	(30)							
49.45	Niklas	Wallenlind	SWE	21.11.68	7	WK	Zürich	4 Aug
49.52	Dries	Vorster	RSA	25.10.62	6s1	WC	Stuttgart	17 Aug
49.54	Vadim	Zadoinov	MOL	24.5.69	3		Bologna	3 Sep
49.55	Domingo	Cordero	PUR	17.10.65	2h1	WC	Stuttgart	16 Aug
49.59		Yang Xianjun	CHN	2.11.72	1	NG	Beijing	9 Sep
49.66A	Maurice	Mitchell	USA	14.5.71	1		Boulder	18 May
49.71	Miro	Kocuvan	SLO	15.6.71	8s3	WC	Stuttgart	17 Aug
49.71	Ashraf	Saber	ITA	2.4.73	2	v2N	Bondoufle	18 Sep
49.74	Amadou	Dia Bâ	SEN	22.9.58	2		Weinstadt	7 Aug
49.75	Edgar	Itt	GER	8.6.67	2		Konstanz	29 Aug
	(40)							
49.77	Marty	Beck	USA	2.3.70	5s1	NC	Eugene	17 Jun
49.77	Paolo	Bellino	ITA	19.8.69	6		Rieti	5 Sep
49.80	Igor	Kurochkin	BLS	2.5.66	1	UKR Ch	Kiev	2 Jul
49.82	Marc	Dollendorf	BEL	7.2.66	1	EP/B	Bruxelles	12 Jun
49.83	Eric	Thomas	USA	7.12.73	4s2	NC	Eugene	17 Jun
49.83	Jean-Paul	Bruwier	BEL	18.2.71	3s1	WUG	Buffalo	15 Jul
49.86A	Ferrins	Pieterse	RSA	22.3.67	1		Pretoria	15 May
49.87	Fadhel	Khayatti	TUN	18.1.65	2		Tarare	13 Jul
49.89	Mitchell	Francis	JAM	13.6.72	2		Kingston	1 May
49.89	Mark	Thompson	JAM	2.8.67	2	NC	Kingston	2 Jul
	(50)							
49.92	Dusán	Kovács	HUN	31.7.71	2	EP/B	Bruxelles	12 Jun
49.93	Athanassios	Kalogiannis	GRE	10.9.65	1	NC	Athinai	23 Jul
49.93		Gao Yonghong	CHN	4.5.70	2	NG	Beijing	9 Sep
49.94	Marco	Morgan	USA	14.4.71	2	NCAA II	Abilene	29 May
49.94	Bob	Gray	USA	31.1.70	6s1	NC	Eugene	17 Jun
49.94	Hubert	Rakotombélontsoa	MAD	8.12.68	1	FRA Ch	Annecy	25 Jul
50.00	Alejandro	Argudin	CUB	10.3.74	1	NC	Habana	14 May
50.00A	Juan G	Vallin	MEX	7.9.69	1		Ciudad México	11 Jul
50.04A	Charles	Johnson	USA	3.1.72	2		Boulder	18 May

Mark	Name		Nat	Born	Pos	Meet	Venue	Date
50.04	Abdelhak	Lahlali	MAR	71	2h2	MedG	Narbonne	18 Jun
	(60)							
50.04A	Pedro	Piñera	CUB	20.12.71	2	CAC	Cali	31 Jul
50.05	Hamadou	Mbaye	SEN	21.4.60	4h6	WC	Stuttgart	16 Aug
50.07	Pedro	Rodrigues	POR	8.7.71	4h3	WC	Stuttgart	16 Aug
50.08	Mugur	Mateescu	ROM	13.6.69	1		Bucuresti	29 May
50.08	Aleksey	Bazarov	ISR	14.10.63	5h4	WC	Stuttgart	16 Aug
50.08		Du Yuechun	CHN	5.1.72	3	NG	Beijing	9 Sep
50.12	Noriaki	Matsue	JPN	17.7.71	2h2	NC	Tokyo	11 Jun
50.13		Guo Chaohui	CHN	.8.73	4	NG	Beijing	9 Sep
50.14	David	Niaré	FRA	27.9.69	1		Dôle	1 Jun
50.17	Regan	Nichols	USA	26.7.73	1		Abilene	13 May
	(70)							
50.17	Michael	Kaul	GER	25.7.67	4	OD	Jena	13 Jun
50.18A	Grant	Roberts	RSA	22.5.71	2		Bloemfontein	8 Mar
50.18	Jozef	Kucej	SVK	23.3.65	6h1	WC	Stuttgart	16 Aug
50.19	Vesa-Pekka	Pihlavisto	FIN	15.4.65	1		Mikkeli	1 Aug
50.23	Tony	McKennie	USA	26.10.67	6s2	NC	Eugene	17 Jun
50.23	Sammy	Biwott	KEN	23.7.74	3		Lisboa	19 Jun
50.24	Marek	Helinurm	EST	6.5.63	2		Kuortane	26 Jun
50.24	Piotr	Kotlarski	POL	5.6.69	1	NC	Kielce	25 Jul
50.27	Aleksandr	Belikhov	RUS	27.12.72	1	NC	Moskva	19 Jun
50.27	Carlos	Silva	POR	8.6.74	1	EJ	San Sebastián	1 Aug
	(80)							
50.33	Mark	Jackson	CAN	15.5.69	1		Luzern	29 Jun
50.34	Peter	Crampton	GBR	4.6.69	4	Vaux	Gateshead	30 Jul
50.34	Plamen	Nyagin	BUL	12.3.71	1	NC	Sofia	1 Aug
50.35	Laurent	Ottoz	ITA	10.4.70	2		Pesaro	16 May
50.35	Donovan	Bassett	USA	25.10.72	5	NCAA	New Orleans	4 Jun
50.36	Tony	McCullough	USA	71	3	NCAA II	Abilene	29 May
50.37	Hideki	Kobayashi	JPN	23.6.71	7	NC	Tokyo	13 Jun
50.38	Daniel	Ritter	SUI	28.12.65	1	NC	St Gallen	31 Jul
50.40	Andrew	Dean-Neil	USA	28.6.65	1		Clemson	16 May
50.40	Oscar	Pitillas	ESP	16.10.71	4		Granada	29 May
	(90)							
50.40	Stéphane	Caristan	FRA	31.5.64	7		St Denis	11 Jun
50.40	Marco	Beukenkamp	HOL	15.5.63	1		Amsterdam	25 Jul
50.42	Jonathan	Ridgeon	GBR	14.2.67	1	ECP	Budapest	30 May
50.42	Santiago	Fraga	ESP	12.12.68	1	NC	Gandia	4 Jul
50.43	El Habni	Abdelmaksoud	EGY		3	PanAr	Latakia	27 Sep
50.44A	Eugene	van der Westhuizen	RSA	30.8.74	1		Cape Town	20 Mar
50.44	Ali	Ismail Doka	QAT	73	4		Latakia	27 Sep
0.45	John	Rothell	USA	29.3.72	2		Austin	8 May
50.45	William	Porter	USA	15.4.73	2		Abilene	13 May
50.45	Fredrik	Wållgren	SWE	1.10.70	3		Kuortane	26 Jun
	(100)							

Mark	Name		Nat	Born	Date
50.46A	Amado	Amador Torres	MEX	71	20 Jun
50.46	Chanond	Keachan	THA	70	1 Dec
50.48A	Llimi	Rivas	COL	68	31 Jul
50.49	Derek	Spears	USA	73	8 May
50.49	Lawrence	Lynch	GBR	67	17 May
50.51A	Johan	Steynberg	RSA	72	15 May
50.51	Andreas	Rapek	AUT	65	16 Jun
50.52	Nabil	Oakaf	MAR	72	29 May
50.54	Keith	Blake	USA		26 May
50.55	Marcus	Carter	USA	72	22 May
	(110)				
50.55	Kehinde	Aladefa	NGR	74	29 May
50.56	Shigeyuki	Eda	JPN	70	12 Jun
50.56	Niklas	Eriksson	SWE	69	25 Jul
50.58	Massimo	Redaelli	ITA	71	3 Aug
50.63	Mauro	Maurizi	ITA	68	6 Jun
50.64	Mauro	Valdinei Mendes	BRA	65	24 Apr
50.67	Andrey	Borovikov	RUS	68	19 Jun
50.67	Akira	Michishita	JPN	65	29 Oct
50.69A	Cornelius	Du Rand	RSA	72	15 May
50.70	Pat	Mann	USA	66	8 May

Mark	Name		Nat	Born	Date
	(120)				
50.70	Gianluca	Magagna	ITA	71	3 Jul
50.71	Eric	Davisson	USA	71	8 May
50.71	Franck	Grondin	FRA	69	10 Jul
50.72	Rüdiger	Klingeler	GER	69	13 Jun
50.72	Judex	Lefou	MRI	66	26 Aug
50.74	Greg	Evans	GBR	72	12 Jun
50.74	Atsushi	Yamamoto	JPN	70	3 Oct
50.75	Stafan	Flenoy	USA		22 May
50.75	Michael	Grün	GER	68	8 Aug
50.76	Brian	Kelley	USA	71	10 Apr
	(130)				
50.76	Joey	Woody	USA		26 May
50.77	Kostas	Pochanis	CYP	73	16 Aug
50.78	Winston	Sinclair	JAM		2 Jul
50.79A	Jaco	Jonker	RSA	75	3 Apr
50.79	Derek	Knight	USA	67	10 Jun
50.80	Tom	McGuirk	USA	72	22 May
50.80	Vyacheslav	Orinchuk	UKR	70	3 Jul
50.81	Sylvain	Moreau	FRA	66	24 Jul
50.82	Claes	Sandgren	SWE	66	25 Jul

Mark	Name		Nat	Born	Date
50.84	Kevin (140)	Cripanuk	USA	70	2 Jun
50.86	Steffen	Kolb	GER	73	20 Jun
50.87	Juan	Hernández	CUB	68	19 Jun
50.87	Udo	Schiller	GER	67	10 Jul
50.87	Jan Erik	Brudvik	NOR	69	18 Aug
50.87		Shen Yi	CHN	67	9 Sep
50.90	Brent	Schott	USA		13 May
50.90	Massimo	Balestra	SUI	65	1 Aug
50.91	Gordon	Bugg	USA	66	29 May
50.91	Brian	Whittle	GBR	64	5 Jun
50.92	Mohamed (150)	Debbab	MAR	68	6 Jun
50.93	Norge	Bell	CUB	71	14 May
50.93	Javier	Paumier	CUB	69	2 Jul
50.93	Henri Kleine	Koerkamp	HOL	65	24 Jul
50.93	Takahiro	Inoue	JPN	74	12 Sep
50.96	Pascal	Maran	FRA	67	30 Jun
50.98	Brian	Wright	USA	69	5 Jun
50.99	Deng Jianzhou		CHN	69	21 Mar
50.99A	Johan	Jonker	RSA	70	2 Apr
50.99	Ambrose	Monye	NGR	59	16 Jun

Best low altitude marks

Mark	Name	Pos	Meet	Venue	Date
49.30	Henderson	2s1	NC	Eugene	17 Jun
49.34	Pérez	4s2	WC	Stuttgart	17 Aug
49.75	Mitchell	3		New Orleans	4 Jun
50.12	Piñera	2	CAG	Ponce	28 Nov
50.28	Roberts	5	AfrC	Durban	27 Jun
50.36	Pieterse	1rB	TSB	London	23 Jul
50.47	Vallin				28 Nov
50.54	Steynberg				24 Apr

Hand timing

Mark	Name		Nat	Born	Pos	Meet	Venue	Date
48.7A	Barnabas	Kinyor	KEN	3.8.61	1	NC	Nairobi	3 Jul
49.2A	Gideon	Biwott	KEN	16.6.64	1		Nairobi	12 Jun
49.5A	Gideon	Yego	KEN	6.5.60	2		Nairobi	12 Jun
50.1A	Pedro	Chiamulera	BRA	29.6.64	2	SACh	Lima	3 Jul
50.3	Sergey	Podrez	RUS	71	1		Voronezh	14 Aug
50.4	William	Porter	USA	73				20 Mar
50.4	Andrey	Borovikov	RUS	68				30 May
50.7	Leigh	Miller	AUS	63				14 Mar
50.8	Bill	Mobley	USA	72				26 May

HIGH JUMP

Mark	Name		Nat	Born	Pos	Meet	Venue	Date
2.45	Javier	Sotomayor	CUB	13.10.67	1		Salamanca	27 Jul
2.41i		Sotomayor			1	WI	Toronto	14 Mar
2.40		Sotomayor			1	Barr	Habana	22 May
2.40		Sotomayor			1	TSB	London	23 Jul
2.40		Sotomayor			1	WC	Stuttgart	22 Aug
2.39i	Patrik	Sjoberg	SWE	5.1.65	2	WI	Toronto	14 Mar
2.39		Sotomayor			1		Pau	26 Jun
2.38	Hollis	Conway	USA	8.1.67	1		Eberstadt	3 Jul
2.38	Dragutin	Topic	YUG	12.3.71	1		Beograd	1 Aug
2.38		Sotomayor			1		Rhede	6 Aug
2.37i		Conway			1	NC	New York	26 Feb
2.37i		Sotomayor			1		Chicago	5 Mar
2.37i	Steve	Smith	GBR	29.3.73	3	WI	Toronto	14 Mar
2.37	Troy	Kemp	BAH	18.6.66	1		Pau	26 Jun
2.37	Artur	Partyka	POL	25.7.69	2	WC	Stuttgart	22 Aug
2.37		Smith			3	WC	Stuttgart	22 Aug
2.36i	Ralf	Sonn	GER	17.1.67	1		Wuppertal	5 Feb
2.36i		Smith			2		Wuppertal	5 Feb
2.36i	Hendrik	Beyer	GER	14.2.72	1		Berlin	5 Mar
2.36i		Sonn			2		Berlin	5 Mar
2.36		Sotomayor			2		Eberstadt	3 Jul
2.36		Partyka			3		Eberstadt	3 Jul
2.36		Kemp			4		Eberstadt	3 Jul
2.36		Topic			1	SerbCh	Beograd	4 Jul
2.36		Sotomayor			1	McD	Sheffield	29 Aug
2.35i	Charles	Austin (10)	USA	19.12.67	1		Arnstadt	23 Jan
2.35	Tim	Forsyth	AUS	17.8.73	1		Canberra	25 Jan
2.35i	Sorin	Matei	ROM	8.7.63	1		Balingen	6 Feb
2.35		Sotomayor			1		Habana	12 Feb
2.35i		Smith			1	v USA	Birmingham	13 Feb
2.35		Sotomayor			1		Verona	16 Jun
2.35		Sotomayor			1		La Coruña	16 Jul
2.35		Sotomayor			1	Toto	Fukuoka	18 Sep
2.35		Sotomayor			1	CAG	Ponce	24 Nov
	(34/12)							
2.34i	Yuriy	Sergiyenko	UKR	19.3.65	3		Wuppertal	5 Feb
2.34i	Dalton	Grant	GBR	8.4.66	4=	WI	Toronto	14 Mar

Mark	Name		Nat	Born	Pos	Meet	Venue	Date
2.34	Andrey	Sankovich	BLS	15.7.65	1		Gomel	15 May
2.32	Steinar	Hoen	NOR	8.2.71	1		Fana	26 May
2.32	Takahiro	Kimino	JPN	19.2.73	2	Toto	Fukuoka	18 Sep
2.31i	Tom	McCants	USA	27.11.62	1		Fairfax	7 Feb
2.31i	Arturo	Ortiz	ESP	18.9.66	3		Gundelsheim	12 Feb
2.31	Takahisa	Yoshida	JPN	17.2.70	1		Mito	9 May
	(20)							
2.31	Oleg	Zhukovskiy	BLS	15.2.70	2		Gomel	15 May
2.31	Tony	Barton	USA	17.10.69	8	WC	Stuttgart	22 Aug
2.31		Xu Yang	CHN	27.6.70	1	NG	Beijing	11 Sep
2.30i	Gennadiy	Avdeyenko	BLS	4.11.63	6		München	12 Feb
2.30	Alex	Zaliauskas	CAN	20.4.71	1	FlaR	Gainesville	27 Mar
2.30	Vladimir	Sokolov	RUS	5.10.63	1		Bryansk	29 May
2.30	Jean-Charles	Gicquel	FRA	24.2.67	2	EP	Roma	26 Jun
2.30	Roberto	Ferrari	ITA	24.3.67	3	EP	Roma	26 Jun
2.30	Robert	Marinov	BUL	1.2.67	1		Sofia	3 Jul
2.30	Stevan	Zoric	YUG	25.5.71	2	WUG	Buffalo	17 Jul
	(30)							
2.30	Aleksey	Yemelin	RUS	16.10.68	1		Moskva	7 Aug
2.30		Lee Jin-taek	KOR	13.4.72	1		Seoul	14 Oct
2.29i	Lambros	Papakostas	GRE	20.10.69	1		Piraeus	30 Jan
2.28i	Aleksandr	Buglakov	BLS	11.8.72	1		Gomel	27 Jan
2.28	Ray	Doakes	USA	12.8.73	1		Fayetteville	8 May
2.28	Vladimir	Zaboronok	BLS	11.11.68	3		Gomel	14 May
2.28	Kevin	Crist	USA	16.7.70	1		Tallahassee	26 May
2.28	Aleksey	Denisov	RUS	30.3.67	1		Abakan	29 May
2.28	Randy	Jenkins	USA	18.9.70	1	NCAA	New Orleans	3 Jun
2.28	Przemyslaw	Radkiewicz	POL	25.8.70	1		Lublin	4 Jun
	(40)							
2.28	Satoru	Nonaka	JPN	5.9.63	1	NC	Tokyo	13 Jun
2.28	Konstantin	Galkin	RUS	25.3.65	1		Vaasa	15 Jun
2.28	Robert	Ruffini	SVK	26.1.67	1	NC	Banská Bystrica	3 Jul
2.28	Xavier	Robilliard	FRA	13.6.67	1		Vénissieux	2 Jul
2.28	Georgi	Dakov	BUL	21.10.67	2	NC	Sofia	1 Aug
2.28	Masaaki	Uno	JPN	13.12.72	1		Fukuoka	8 Aug
2.28	Cristian	Popescu	ROM	12.8.62	1	CISM	Tours	28 Aug
2.28		Bi Hongyong	CHN	16.11.74	2	NG	Beijing	9 Sep
2.28		Zhou Zhongge	CHN	15.2.67	3	NG	Beijing	9 Sep
2.28i	Sergey	Malchenko	RUS	2.11.63	1		Moskva	26 Dec
	(50)							
2.27i	Rolandas	Verkys	LIT	17.3.67	1		Panevézys	6 Feb
2.27i	Juha	Isolehto	FIN	6.6.68	1		Tampere	7 Mar
2.27i	Percell	Gaskins	USA	25.4.72	1	NCAA	Indianapolis	12 Mar
2.27	Monterrio	Holder	USA	17.10.70	1	DogwR	Knoxville	10 Apr
2.27	Cameron	Wright	USA	7.11.72	1		Terre Haute	15 May
2.27	Ruslam	Stipanov	UKR	19.9.71	3=	WUG	Buffalo	17 Jul
2.26i	Itai	Margalit	ISR	25.1.70	1		Lincoln	12 Feb
2.26i	Carlo	Thränhardt	GER	5.7.57	1		Otterberg	13 Feb
2.26i	Sergey	Klyugin	RUS	24.3.74	1		Pesaro	20 Feb
2.26	Chris	Anderson	AUS	6.4.68	1		Perth	27 Feb
	(60)							
2.26i	Gustavo	Becker	ESP	17.6.66	1	NC	San Sebastián	27 Feb
2.26i	Oleg	Muravyov	RUS	6.5.68	1		Moskva	28 Feb
2.26i	Tom	Lange	USA	21.2.70	1		Baton Rouge	4 Mar
2.26	Anton	Riepl	GER	28.2.69	1		Vilsbiburg	1 May
2.26		Xu Xiaodong	CHN	12.12.73	1		Beijing	4 May
2.26	Jeff	Wylie	USA	28.12.68	1		Indianapolis	15 May
2.26	Torsten	Marschner	GER	17.11.68			Frankfurt	16 May
2.26	Joël	Vincent	FRA	19.1.69	1		Sotteville	23 May
2.26	Konstantin	Isayev	RUS	7.7.73	2		Bryansk	29 May
2.26	Brent	Harken	USA	1.12.61	1	Jer	Coquitlam	31 May
	(70)							
2.26	Grigoriy	Fyodorkov	RUS	9.11.64	2		Moskva	7 Aug
2.26	Uwe	Bellmann	GER	8.6.68	1		Mals	14 Aug
2.25i	Vladimir	Pchelintsev	KZK	70	1		Karaganda	22 Jan
2.25i	Pierre	Bernhard	FRA	15.2.68	7		Wuppertal	5 Feb

Mark	Name		Nat	Born	Pos	Meet	Venue	Date
2.25i	Rick	Noji	USA	22.10.67	2=	Mill	New York	5 Feb
2.25i	Dimitrios	Kokotis	GRE	12.4.72	1		Piraeus	15 Feb
2.25	Gabe	Beechum	USA	28.8.71	1		Tempe	26 Mar
2.25	Brian	Brown	USA	9.1.67	1	SunA	Tempe	3 Apr
2.25	Matt	Hemingway	USA	24.10.72	1		Hot Springs	10 Apr
2.25	Christopher	Gayre	USA	73	1		Tallahassee	17 Apr
	(80)							
2.25	Doug	Nordquist	USA	20.12.58	1		Azusa	24 Apr
2.25	Steve	Smith	USA	11.1.71	1		Terre Haute	1 May
2.25	Dan	Raatjes	USA	9.2.68	1		Flagstaff	8 May
2.25A	Ian	Thompson	BAH	8.12.68	1		Ciudad México	8 May
2.25	Otis	Winston	USA	7.11.72	1	JO	Columbus	9 May
2.25	Oleg	Vorobey	BLS	24.11.70	5		Gomel	14 May
2.25	Marino	Drake	CUB	13.6.67	2	NC	Habana	14 May
2.25	Sergey	Kolesnik	UKR	31.5.69	1		Odessa	21 May
2.25	Brendan	Reilly	GBR	23.12.72	2	NC	London	13 Jun
2.25	Sergey	Dymchenko	UKR	23.8.67	4		Reims	30 Jun
	(90)							
2.25	Jaroslaw	Kotewicz	POL	16.3.69	2		Praha	17 Jul
2.25	Leonid	Pumalaynen	RUS	13.4.70	1		Moskva	25 Jul
2.25	Ettore	Ceresoli	ITA	11.4.70	1	NC	Bologna	3 Aug
2.25	Wolfgang	Kreissig	GER	29.8.70	2		Lindau	8 Aug
2.25		Tao Xu	CHN	.1.72	4	NG	Beijing	11 Sep
2.25	Koji	Fujishima	JPN	2.7.70	1		Katsuura	25 Sep
2.25	Jagan	Hames	AUS	31.10.75	1		Adelaide	27 Nov
2.25	Lochsley	Thomson	AUS	20.8.73	1		Sydney	4 Dec

Mark	Name		Nat	Born	Date
2.24i	Zdenek	Kubista	TCH	66	27 Jan
2.24i	Jake	Jacoby	USA	61	29 Jan
	(100)				
2.24i	Dietmar	Mögenburg	GER	61	29 Jan
2.24i	Alexander	Farr	GER	70	6 Feb
2.24i	Matti	Viitala	FIN	66	6 Feb
2.24i	Kenny	Banks	USA	66	5 Mar
2.24i	Chris	Murrell	USA	71	12 Mar
2.24	Brian	Stanton	USA	61	13 Mar
2.24	Fernando	Moreno	ARG	67	15 May
2.24	Alex	Rosen	USA	73	23 May
2.24	Aleksandr	Zhuravlyov	UKR	74	25 May
2.24	Valentin	Budovskiy	UKR	70	25 May
	(110)				
2.24	Robert	Kolodziejczyk	POL	70	4 Jun
2.24	Federico	Rodeghiero	ITA	71	16 Jun
2.24	Andrea	Liverani	ITA	64	29 Jun
2.24	Péter	Deutsch	HUN	68	1 Jul
2.24	Miha	Prijon	SLO	71	1 Jul
2.24	Mark	Mandy	IRL	72	3 Jul
2.24	Patrick	Thavelin	SWE	70	15 Jul
2.24	Othmane	Belfaa	ALG	61	22 Jul
2.24	Cory	Siermachesky	CAN	69	1 Aug
2.23i	Valeriy	Apenkin	UKR	67	14 Feb
	(120)				
2.23i	Vladimir	Kostenko	UKR	70	14 Feb
2.23i	Stefan	Karlsson	SWE	58	21 Feb
2.23i	Aleksey	Makurin	RUS	72	28 Feb
2.23	Ed	Broxterman	USA	73	10 Apr
2.23	Konstantin	Matusevich	UKR	71	24 Apr
2.23	Darrin	Plab	USA	70	14 May
2.23	Abraham	Faust	USA		22 May
2.23	Stanislav	Mingazov	KGZ	67	19 Jun
2.23	Hossein	Shyan	IRN	71	24 Jun
2.23	Vyacheslav	Tyrtyshnik	UKR	71	3 Jul
	(130)				
2.23	Shigeki	Toyoshima	JPN	71	1 Aug
2.23	Steinar	Grini	NOR	69	1 Aug
2.23	Geoff	Parsons	GBR	64	8 Aug
2.23	Oleg	Palashevskiy	TJK	62	

Mark	Name		Nat	Born	Date
2.22i	Eric	Higgins	USA		26 Feb
2.22i	Ken	Hoffman	USA	73	12 Mar
2.22	Harrison	Carrington	USA		10 Apr
2.22	Billy	Green	USA	75	22 Apr
2.22	James	Shelton	USA	71	24 Apr
2.22	Khemraj	Naiko	MRI	72	8 May
	(140)				
2.22	Igor	Cavalleri	ITA	71	9 May
2.22	Mike	Williams	USA	71	16 May
2.22	Yoshiteru	Kaihoko	JPN	71	22 May
2.22	Petar	Malesev	YUG	72	26 May
2.22	Jamel	Green	USA	73	29 May
2.22	Frédéric	Derisbourg	FRA	67	29 May
2.22	Flippie	Van Vuuren	RSA	71	25 Jun
2.22	Kostas	Liapis	GRE	73	27 Jun
2.22	Hugo	Muñoz	PER	73	4 Jul
2.22	Dimitris	Tomaras	GRE	72	17 Jul
	(150)				
2.22	Marcus	Jahn	GER	72	2 Aug
2.22	Jan	Janku	TCH	71	22 Sep
2.21i	Bud	Hamilton	USA		15 Jan
2.21i	Herve	Ndi Ndi	FRA	72	30 Jan
2.21i	Howard	Williams	USA	71	30 Jan
2.21i	Kent	Deville	USA	69	30 Jan
2.21i	Leo	Zdráhal	TCH	67	7 Feb
2.21i	Clifford	Van Reed	USA	73	13 Feb
2.21i	Todd	Herman	USA		27 Feb
2.21	David	Anderson	AUS	65	27 Feb
	(160)				
2.21i	John	Thorp	USA	73	4 Mar
2.21i	Lee	Pool	USA	71	20 Mar
2.21	Mike	Greer	USA	71	5 May
2.21	Lou Cwee Peng		MAS	68	7 May
2.21	Travis	Clark	USA	73	15 May
2.21	Robert	Marchetti	USA		22 May
2.21	Konstadinos	Triadafilou	GRE	71	22 May
2.21	Christophe	Fontaney	FRA	64	23 May
2.21	Christian	Schenk	GER	65	19 Jun
2.21	Dimitar	Toychev	BUL	68	19 Jun
	(170)				

Mark	Name		Nat	Born		Mark	Name		Nat	Born	Date
2.21	Niclas	Grundner	AUT	74	27 Jun	2.21	Jordi	Rofes	ESP	76	8 Jul
2.21	Eric	Bishop	USA	76	Jun	2.21	Dillon	Phelps	USA	74	17 Jul
2.21	Attila	Zsivótzky	HUN	77	8 Jul	2.21	Charles	Lefrançois	CAN	72	19 Aug

Best outdoor marks for athletes with seasonal bests indoors

Mark	Name	Pos	Meet	Venue	Date	Mark	Name	Pos	Meet	Venue	Date
2.34	Grant	2=	WK	Zürich	4 Aug	2.26	Malchenko	1		Rostov na Donu	16 Jul
2.34	Sonn	4	WC	Stuttgart	22 Aug	2.25	Buglakov	4		Gomel	14 May
2.33	Beyer	1	NC	Duisburg	11 Jul	2.25	Thränhardt	3		Rehlingen	31 May
2.32	Sergiyenko	1		Nikopol	12 Jun	2.25	Noji	3	NC	Eugene	17 Jun
2.32	Sjöberg	6		Eberstadt	3 Jul	2.25	Margalit	1		Tel Aviv	11 Jul
2.31	Ortiz	7	WC	Stuttgart	22 Aug	2.25	Becker	2=		Barcelona	19 Jul
2.30	Matei	1	RomIC	Bucuresti	18 Jun	2.25	Isolehto	13Q	WC	Stuttgart	20 Aug
2.26	Papakostas	1	NC	Athinai	25 Jul						

Mark	Name	Date	Mark	Name	Date	Mark	Name	Date	Mark	Name	Date
2.24	Kokotis	5 Jun	2.23	Makurin	12 Jun	2.23	Viitala	19 Sep	2.22	Murrell	23 May
2.24	Bernhard	5 Jun	2.23	Kostenko	3 Jul	2.22	Lange	17 Apr	2.21	Pool	20 Mar
2.24	Klyugin	6 Nov	2.23	Avdeyenko	3 Jul	2.22	Jacoby	16 May	2.21	Higgins	24 Apr
									2.21	H Williams	22 May

Street exhibition

Mark	Name		Nat	Born	Pos	Meet	Venue	Date
2.25	Steinar	Grini	NOR	8.5.69	1		Bergen	22 May
2.24	Didier	Detchenique	CMR	4.10.72	2		Mantes la Ville	15 May
Extra trial	2.38	Topic			*	NC	Beograd	24 Jul

Ancillary marks

Mark	Name	Date	Mark	Name	Date	Mark	Name	Date
2.38	Sotomayor	27 Jul	2.37	Sotomayor	22 May	2.36	Conway	3 Jul
2.37i	Sjöberg	14 Mar	2.37	Sotomayor	23 Jul	2.35	Topic	1 Aug
2.37i	Sotomayor	14 Mar	2.37	Sotomayor	22 Aug			

POLE VAULT

Mark	Name		Nat	Born	Pos	Meet	Venue	Date
6.15i	Sergey	Bubka	UKR	4.12.63	1		Donyetsk	21 Feb
6.14i		Bubka			1		Liévin	13 Feb
6.05i		Bubka			1		Berlin	5 Mar
6.05		Bubka			1	GPF	London	10 Sep
6.01i		Bubka			1		Grenoble	7 Feb
6.00i	Rodion	Gataullin	RUS	23.11.65	1		Moskva	2 Feb
6.00i		Gataullin			2		Liévin	13 Feb
6.00		Bubka			1	Jen	San José	29 May
6.00		Gataullin			1	EP	Roma	27 Jun
6.00		Bubka			1	WC	Stuttgart	19 Aug
5.96i		Gataullin			1		Madrid	11 Feb
5.94		Bubka			1	Herc	Monaco	7 Oct
5.93		Bubka			1	Nik	Nice	21 Jul
5.93	Jean	Galfione	FRA	20.6.71	1	NC	Annecy	25 Jul
5.92		Galfione			1		Reims	30 Jun
5.91i		Bubka			1		San Sebastián	2 Mar
5.90i	Grigoriy	Yegorov	KZK	12.1.67	2		Moskva	2 Feb
5.90i	Igor	Trandenkov	RUS	17.8.66	1		Grenoble	7 Feb
5.90i	Maksim	Tarasov	RUS	12.12.70	2		Madrid	11 Feb
5.90i		Gataullin			1	WI	Toronto	13 Mar
5.90		Bubka			1	GGala	Roma	9 Jun
5.90		Tarasov			2	GGala	Roma	9 Jun
5.90	Denis	Petushinskiy	RUS	29.1.67	1	Znam	Moskva	13 Jun
5.90		Tarasov			1		Århus	1 Jul
5.90		Tarasov			1	Bisl	Oslo	10 Jul
5.90		Bubka			1	WK	Zürich	4 Aug
5.90		Yegorov			2	WC	Stuttgart	19 Aug
5.90		Tarasov			1	VD	Bruxelles	3 Sep
5.90		Yegorov			2	GPF	London	10 Sep
5.90		Gataullin			1		Oristano	12 Sep
	(30/7)							
5.85	Scott	Huffman	USA	30.11.64	1	McD	Sheffield	29 Aug
5.82	Jani	Lehtonen	FIN	11.8.68	1		Kuortane	26 Jun
5.81	Valeriy	Bukreyev	EST	15.6.64	1		Riga	29 May
	(10)							
5.80i	Werner	Holl	GER	28.1.70	1		Nordlingen	7 Mar
5.80	Pyotr	Bochkaryov	RUS	3.11.67	2		São Paulo	16 May
5.80	Greg	Duplantis	USA	22.1.62	2		Århus	1 Jul
5.80	Igor	Potapovich	KZK	6.9.67	2	Nik	Nice	21 Jul
5.75i	Philippe	D'Encausse	FRA	24.3.67	1	Mast	Grenoble	20 Mar

Mark	Name		Nat	Born	Pos	Meet	Venue	Date
5.75	Kory	Tarpenning	USA	27.2.62	3	Jen	San José	29 May
5.75	Pat	Manson	USA	29.11.67	4	Jen	San José	29 May
5.73	Tim	Bright	USA	28.7.60	3=	ASV	Köln	1 Aug
5.72	Simon	Arkell	AUS	1.7.66	1		Adelaide	14 Feb
5.72	Greg	West	USA	19.5.67	1	TexR	Austin	2 Apr
	(20)							
5.72	Andrey	Skvortsov	RUS	2.12.68	1		Schelklingen	10 Jun
5.71A	Okkert	Brits	RSA	22.8.73	1		Potchefstroom	8 May
5.71	Lawrence	Johnson	USA	7.5.74	1		Knoxville	12 Jun
5.71A	Paul	Benavides	MEX	5.11.64	1		El Paso	26 Jun
5.70i	Bill	Payne	USA	21.12.67	1		Reno	23 Jan
5.70i	Valeriy	Ishutin	UZB	5.9.65	4		Moskva	2 Feb
5.70i	Delko	Lesov	BUL	6.1.67	1		Sofia	6 Feb
5.70i	Yevgeniy	Bondarenko	RUS	8.10.66	1		Moskva	13 Feb
5.70i	Vasiliy	Bubka	UKR	26.11.60	4		Donyetsk	21 Feb
5.70i	Thierry	Vigneron	FRA	9.3.60	2	NC	Liévin	28 Feb
	(30)							
5.70	Aleksandr	Korchagin	KZK	25.1.72	2	Znam	Moskva	13 Jun
5.70	Dean	Starkey	USA	27.3.67	2	NC	Eugene	19 Jun
5.70	Jean-Marc	Tailhardat	FRA	12.4.66	3		Pau	26 Jun
5.70	Javier	Garcia	ESP	22.7.66	3	EP	Roma	27 Jun
5.70	Petri	Peltoniemi	FIN	6.3.70	2		Haapajärvi	13 Jul
5.70	István	Bagyula	HUN	2.1.69	1	WUG	Buffalo	16 Jul
5.70	Peter	Widén	SWE	2.7.67	1		Karlskrona	28 Jul
5.70	Brent	Burns	USA	2.5.69	1	USOF	San Antonio	30 Jul
5.65i	Konstantin	Semyonov	BLS	20.11.69	2		Minsk	18 Feb
5.65i	Andrea	Pegoraro	ITA	24.10.66	7	WI	Toronto	13 Mar
	(40)							
5.65	Scott	Krupilski	USA	19.1.64	1	S&W	Modesto	8 May
5.65	Mike	Holloway	USA	12.7.69	2	S&W	Modesto	8 May
5.65	Gérald	Baudouin	FRA	15.11.72	4		Pau	26 Jun
5.65	Yevgeniy	Krasnov	ISR	25.5.70	5		Pau	26 Jun
5.65	Andrey	Tivonchik	BLS	70	1		Stuttgart	31 Jul
5.65	Daniel	Marti	ESP	23.4.73	Q	WC	Stuttgart	17 Aug
5.65	Mårten	Ulvsbäck	SWE	5.6.66	Q	WC	Stuttgart	17 Aug
5.63	Heikki	Vääräniemi	FIN	21.12.69	2		Raahe	20 Jul
5.62	Patrik	Stenlund	SWE	11.10.68	3=		Karlskrona	28 Jul
5.62i	José Manuel	Arcos	ESP	19.1.73	1		Madrid	18 Dec
	(50)							
5.61i	Tim	McMichael	USA	22.2.67	2	NC	New York	26 Feb
5.61i	Brit	Pursley	USA	25.4.69	1		Lubbock	6 Mar
5.61	Jeff	Bray	USA	8.9.70	1		Gainesville	24 Apr
5.61	Martin	Eriksson	SWE	15.6.71	1		Landau	30 Jun
5.60i	Miroslaw	Chmara	POL	9.5.64	1		Bydgoszcz	16 Jan
5.60i	Gianni	Iapichino	ITA	2.3.69	1		Firenze	26 Jan
5.60i	Aleksandr	Chervonyi	UKR	26.3.70	1	NC	Kiev	13 Feb
5.60i	Sergey	Fomenko	UKR	7.6.67	2	NC	Kiev	13 Feb
5.60i	Aleksandr	Chernyayev	UKR	31.5.60	3		Minsk	18 Feb
5.60i	Igor	Yanchevskiy	RUS	11.3.68	4	NC	Moskva	27 Feb
	(60)							
5.60	Alberto	Ruiz	ESP	22.12.61	1		Barcelona	2 Jun
5.60	Mark	Buse	USA	30.11.72	1	NCAA	New Orleans	4 Jun
5.60	Adam	Smith	USA	4.10.71	2	NCAA	New Orleans	4 Jun
5.60	Martin	Amann	GER	23.11.70	2		Schelklingen	10 Jun
5.60	Alberto	Giacchetto ¶	ITA	21.2.73	2	WUG	Buffalo	16 Jul
5.60A	Angel	Garcia	CUB	5.1.67	1	CAC	Cali	1 Aug
5.57i	Nick	Hysong	USA	9.12.71	1		Flagstaff	20 Feb
5.55i	Aleksandr	Zhukov	MOL	25.1.65	2		Sofia	6 Feb
5.55	James	Miller	AUS	4.6.74	1		Perth	7 Feb
5.55i	Juan Gabriel	Concepción	ESP	7.8.72	1		Zaragosa	13 Feb
	(70)							
5.55	Jim	Drath	USA	19.9.68	2		Fresno	3 Apr
5.55	Alberto	Manzano	CUB	22.9.72	1	NC	Habana	14 May
5.55	Olivier	Lelong	FRA	2.4.70	1		Sotteville	23 May
5.55	Marc	Lugenbühl	GER	17.6.66	1		Hof	29 May
5.55	Doug	Fraley	USA	7.3.65	8	Jen	San José	29 May

Mark	Name		Nat	Born	Pos	Meet	Venue	Date
5.55	Tim	Lobinger	GER	3.9.72	3	OD	Jena	13 Jun
5.55	Stavros	Tsitouras	GRE	15.6.69	1	MedG	Narbonne	18 Jun
5.55	Asko	Peltoniemi	FIN	7.2.63	2=		Somero	11 Jul
5.55	Doug	Wood	CAN	30.1.66	1		North York	27 Jul
5.55	Yuriy	Yeliseyev	RUS	27.5.75	1		Liege	22 Sep
	(80)							
5.53	Dan	Burton	USA	11.3.67	1		Indianapolis	8 May
5.52	Kevin	Brown	USA	15.8.71	1		Chapel Hill	4 Apr
5.52	Rich	Fulford	USA	29.4.69	3	Gator	Knoxville	1 May
5.52	Mamadou	Johnson	USA	29.11.72	1		Providence	9 May
5.52	Mike	Edwards	GBR	19.10.68	1		Abilene	13 May
5.52	David	Cox	USA	7.8.72	1		El Paso	22 May
5.51i	Bill	Deering	USA	20.7.71	1		Syracuse	21 Feb
5.51	Marc	Osenberg	GER	15.3.69	1		Kevelaer	20 Jun
5.51	Zoltán	Farkas	HUN	7.3.70	1		Budapest	10 Jul
5.50i	Scotty	Miller	USA	8.8.69	1		Reno	16 Jan
	(90)							
5.50i	Carl-Johan	Alm	SWE	7.1.69	1		Malmö	6 Feb
5.50i	Sergey	Yesipchuk	UKR	1.10.67	3	NC	Kiev	13 Feb
5.50i	Ilian	Efremov	BUL	2.8.70	2	NC	Sofia	13 Feb
5.50i	Jeff	Buckingham	USA	14.6.60	1		Cleveland	13 Feb
5.50i	Frantisek	Jansa	TCH	12.9.62	1	NC	Praha	20 Feb
5.50	Miguel	Berrio	CUB	25.2.68	1		Habana	20 Feb
5.50i	David	Gracia	ESP	22.2.70	1	NC	San Sebastián	27 Feb
5.50i	Laurens	Looije	HOL	12.1.73	1	NC	Den Haag	27 Feb
5.50i	Bernhard	Zintl	GER	16.6.65	1	NC	Sindelfingen	27 Feb
5.50i	Justin	Daler	USA	12.4.71	3	NCAA	Indianapolis	13 Mar
	(100)							
5.50	Jon	Kelley	USA	19.12.69	1		Starkville	24 May
5.50	Pál	Rohánszky	HUN	28.9.70	4	Slovn	Bratislava	1 Jun
5.50	Scott	Hennig	USA	17.4.69	1		Houston	4 Jun
5.50	Ron	Johnson	USA	20.8.69	1		Seattle	8 Jun
5.50	Toshiyuki	Hashioka	JPN	19.1.64	1	NC	Tokyo	13 Jun
5.50	Garth	Willard	USA	7.6.69	8	NC	Eugene	18 Jun
5.50	Vitaliy	Stepanov	RUS	9.12.65	7	NC	Moskva	20 Jun
5.50	Florian	Wacker	GER	27.12.72	1		Oberhaugstett	4 Jul
5.50	Vyacheslav	Aristov	BLS	18.1.66	2		, POL	12 Jul
5.50	Martin	Voss	DEN	5.9.67	1		Århus	17 Jul
	(110)							
5.50	Marc	Vandevoir	FRA	17.6.71	1		Montgeron	18 Jul
5.50	Massimo	Allevi	ITA	23.11.69	1	NC	Bologna	3 Aug
5.50	Jean-Michel	Godard	FRA	19.1.71	1		Alicante	7 Aug
5.50	Gennadiy	Sidorov	BLS	13.3.67	1		Sopot	10 Aug

Mark	Name		Nat	Born	Date
5.46	Daren	McDonough	USA	74	17 Apr
5.45i	Helmar	Schmidt	GER	63	7 Mar
5.45	Simeon	Anastasiadis	GRE	68	23 May
5.45	Nicola	Salmaso	ITA	70	30 May
5.45	Fabrice	Le Monnier	FRA	73	26 Jun
5.45	Gennadiy	Voronin	RUS	71	10 Jul
	(120)				
5.45	Francisco	Mas	ESP	68	24 Jul
5.45	Juha	Rauhaniemi	FIN	68	30 Jul
5.45	Trond	Barthel	NOR	70	31 Jul
5.45	Raynald	Mury	SUI	68	1 Oct
5.42	Steve	Bridges	USA	70	14 May
5.42	Dmitriy	Markov	BLS	75	30 May
5.41	Brian	Adamick	USA	70	20 Mar
5.41	J.J	Miller	USA	73	7 May
5.41	Takumi	Takahashi	JPN	67	22 May
5.41	Kevin	McGuire	USA		26 May
	(130)				
5.41	Zdenek	Lubensky	TCH	62	30 Jun
5.41	Nick	Buckfield	GBR	73	9 Jul
5.41	Tim	Canfield	USA	63	22 Jul
5.40i	Gianfranco	Beda	ITA	68	18 Jan
5.40i	Aleksey	Gladkikh	RUS	71	26 Jan

Mark	Name		Nat	Born	Date
5.40i	Stefan	Dießler	GER	70	30 Jan
5.40A	Anthony	Curran	USA	59	1 Feb
5.40	Greg	Halliday	AUS	72	27 Feb
5.40i	Aleksey	Dubenskov	RUS	71	27 Feb
5.40i		Ge Yun	CHN	68	6 Mar
	(140)				
5.40i	Khalid	Lachheb	FRA	75	6 Mar
5.40i	Taoufik	Lacheeb	FRA	75	6 Mar
5.40i	Ignacio	Paradinas	ESP	66	6 Mar
5.40i	Edgardo	Diaz	PUR	68	12 Mar
5.40i	Zoltán	Bujtor	HUN	71	13 Mar
5.40i	Deszö	Szabó	HUN	67	14 Mar
5.40	Christian	Tamminga	HOL	74	9 May
5.40	Hideyuki	Takei	JPN	70	16 May
5.40	Giacomo	Befani	ITA	70	22 May
5.40	Michael	Kühnke	GER	73	28 May
	(150)				
5.40	Steve	Keating	USA	67	12 Jun
5.40	Hiroshi	Terada	JPN	71	13 Jun
5.40	Christos	Pallakis	GRE	71	23 Jun
5.40	Leonid	Murin	RUS	73	25 Jun
5.40	Teruyasu	Yonekura	JPN	71	27 Jun
5.40	Neil	Winter	GBR	74	2 Jul

Mark	Name		Nat	Born	Date
5.40	Jari	Holttinen	FIN	65	11 Jul
5.40	François	Thénault	FRA	72	18 Jul
5.40	Andrey	Isakov	KZK	70	23 Jul
5.40	F Nuno	Fernandes	POR	69	25 Jul
	(160)				
5.40	Martin	Tischler	AUT	71	8 Aug
5.40	Alain	Blondel	FRA	62	20 Aug
5.40	Marco	Andreini	ITA	61	5 Sep
5.40	Maurilio	Mariani	ITA	73	15 Sep
5.40i	Domitien	Mestre	BEL	73	19 Dec
5.36	Dan	McDowell	USA		6 Feb
5.35	Jeff	McGaugh	USA	69	16 Apr
5.35A	Riann	Botha	RSA	70	3 May
5.35	Tom	Jordan	USA		22 May
5.35	Todd	Pettyjohn	USA		23 May
	(170)				
5.35	Jeff	Hartwig	USA	67	26 May
5.35	Jon	Bazzoni	USA	70	26 May
5.35	John	Nelson	USA		29 May
5.35	Matthew	Belsham	GBR	71	26 Jun
5.35	Benoit	Lestrade	FRA	71	11 Jul
5.35	Viktor	Chistyakov	RUS	75	1 Aug
5.35	Gennadiy	Sukharev	BLS	65	17 Aug
5.35	Akifumi	Funatsu	JPN	74	10 Sep
5.35	Ichiro	Abe	JPN	70	18 Sep
5.34	Doug	Sharp	USA	69	1 May
	(180)				
5.32i	Erik	Noaksson	SWE	72	20 Feb
5.32	Dave	Christopher	USA		14 May
5.31	Eric	White	USA	64	10 Apr

Illegally weighted bar: 5.70 Mike Holloway USA 12.7.69 1 vGBR Edinburgh 2 Jul

Unconfirmed: 5.64 Bill Deering USA 20.7.71 1 Coral Gables 11 Feb

Exhibition - Market square event

Mark	Name		Nat	Born	Pos	Venue	Date
5.86	Valeriy	Bukreyev	EST	15.6.64	1	Chiari	5 Sep
5.80	Vasiliy	Bubka	UKR	26.11.60	1	Iglesias	9 Sep
5.73	Yevgeniy	Bondarenko	RUS	8.10.66	1	Recklinghausen	4 Jun
5.72	Andrea	Pegoraro	ITA	24.10.66	2	Iglesias	9 Sep
5.62	Gianni	Iapichino	ITA	2.3.69	2	Chiari	5 Sep
5.60	Marco	Andreini	ITA	8.10.61	3	Iglesias	9 Sep
5.60	Marc	Vandevoir	FRA	17.6.71	1	Vannes	28 Nov

Best outdoor marks for athletes with seasonal bests indoors

Mark	Name	Pos	Meet	Venue	Date
5.80	Trandenkov	3	NC	Moskva	20 Jun
5.75	D'Encausse	2		Pau	26 Jun
5.70	V.Bubka	2	Athl	Lausanne	7 Jul
5.65	Semyonov	1		Dreux	29 May
5.65	Bondarenko	1		Cottbus	23 Jun
5.65	Pegoraro	Q	WC	Stuttgart	17 Aug
5.60	Payne	5		São Paulo	16 May
5.60	Vigneron	1	ECP	Budapest	29 May
5.60	Fomenko	2	Slovn	Bratislava	1 Jun
5.60	Lesov	1		Sofia	19 Jun
5.60	Holl	1		Konstanz	22 Jun
5.60	Chernyayev	3		Århus	1 Jul
5.55	Arcos	1		Madrid	28 Jul
5.50	Buckingham	2		Lawrence	16 Apr
5.50	Yanchevskiy	2		Sochi	25 May
5.50	Hysong	1		Tucson	26 May
5.50	McMichael	1		Miaoli	30 May
5.50	Daler	4	NCAA	New Orleans	4 Jun
5.50	Pursley	6	NCAA	New Orleans	4 Jun
5.50	Concepción	1		Mataró	10 Jun
5.50	Deering	11	NC	Eugene	19 Jun

Mark	Name	Date
5.45	Zhukov	17 Aug
5.41	Miller	7 Apr
5.40	Chervoniy	15 May
5.40	Yesipchuk	15 May
5.40	Looije	16 May
5.40	Jansa	29 May
5.40	Efremov	1 Jun
5.40	Iapichino	12 Jun
5.40	Gladkikh	13 Jun
5.40	Ishutin	16 Jun
5.40	Schmidt	30 Jun
5.40	Zintl	30 Jun
5.40	Beda	30 Jun
5.40	Alm	18 Jul
5.40	K Lachheb	1 Oct
5.39	Bujtor	26 May
5.39	Diaz	12 Jun
5.35	T Lachheb	1 Oct

City square

Mark	Name	Pos	Meet	Venue	Date
5.60	Chervonyi	1		Praha	16 Jun
5.60	Ishutin	2		Sopot	3 Jul
5.53	Yanchevskiy	3	exh	Recklinghausen	4 Jun

Ancillary marks

Mark	Name	Date
6.05i	Bubka	3 Feb
5.90i	Gataullin	2 Feb
5.90i	Bubka	3 Feb
5.90i	Gataullin	23 Feb
5.90i	Bubka	21 Feb
5.90	Bubka	19 Aug
5.90	Bubka	10 Sep

LONG JUMP

Mark	Wind	Name		Nat	Born	Pos	Meet	Venue	Date
8.70	0.7	Mike	Powell	USA	10.11.63	1		Salamanca	27 Jul
8.59	0.4		Powell			1	WC	Stuttgart	20 Aug
8.54	0.3		Powell			1	GPF	London	10 Sep
8.53	0.9	Erick	Walder	USA	5.11.71	1	NCAA	New Orleans	3 Jun
8.51	0.4		Powell			1	Athl	Lausanne	7 Jul
8.50	0.9		Powell			1	BNP	Villeneuve d'Ascq	2 Jul
8.49	-0.6	Ivan	Pedroso	CUB	17.12.72	1	Barr	Habana	23 May
8.49	1.7		Powell			*	NC	Eugene	19 Jun
8.49	0.6		Powell			1	Indy	Indianapolis	25 Jun
8.48	0.5		Powell			1		Malmö	9 Aug
8.47	1.3		Pedroso			1	NC	Habana	12 May
8.47	-0.1		Powell			1	VD	Bruxelles	3 Sep
8.44i	-		Powell			1		Budapest	5 Feb
8.43	1.7		Powell			1	AusC	Brisbane	7 Mar

Mark	Wind	Name		Nat	Born	Pos	Meet	Venue	Date
8.43	0.8		Powell			1	Slovn	Bratislava	1 Jun
8.43	0.1		Powell			1	WK	Zürich	4 Oct
8.41i	-		Powell			1		Stockholm	9 Feb
8.41	1.3		Powell			*		Madrid	3 Jun
8.41	1.5	Craig	Hepburn	BAH	10.12.69	1	NC	Nassau	17 Jun
8.41	0.8		Powell			1		Rhede	6 Aug
8.39	0.8	Dion	Bentley	USA	26.8.71	2	NCAA	New Orleans	3 Jun
8.39	1.3		Powell			1	ASV	Köln	1 Oct
8.38	0.1	Roland	McGhee	USA	15.10.71	1	JO	Columbus	9 May
8.38	0.3		Powell			1	DNG	Stockholm	5 Jul
8.36i	-		Powell			1	vGBR	Glasgow	30 Jan
8.36A	0.6	Kareem	Streete-Thompson	USA	30.3.73	1		El Paso	10 Apr
8.34	1.1		Nai Hui-Fang	TPE	26.2.69	1	EAsiG	Shanghai	15 May
8.33i	-		Walder			1	NCAA	Indianapolis	12 Mar
8.33	0.9	Joe	Greene	USA	17.2.67	3	NC	Eugene	19 Jun
8.32	2.0		Pedroso			*		Madrid	3 Jun
		(30/9)							
8.30	0.0		Huang Geng	CHN	10.7.70	1	NG	Beijing	9 Sep
8.27	1.7	Ivaylo	Mladenov	BUL	6.10.73	1		Sofia	22 May
8.25	1.1	Anthuan	Maybank	USA	30.12.69	-	Drake R	Des Moines	24 Apr
8.25		Juan Felipe	Ortiz	CUB	13.8.64	1		Habana	25 Jun
8.24A	1.9	Larry	Myricks	USA	10.3.56	-		Sestriere	28 Jul
8.24	1.0	Stanislav	Tarasenko	RUS	23.7.66	1	CISM	Tours	30 Aug
8.21	-0.6	Vitaliy	Kirilenko	UKR	25.4.68	1		Oristano	12 Sep
8.18	2.0	Angel	Hernández	ESP	15.4.66	1	ECP	Budapest	29 May
8.18	0.3	Obinna	Eregbu	NGR	9.11.69	2	WUG	Buffalo	18 Jul
8.16	1.7	Mike	Conley	USA	5.10.62	3	BNP	Villeneuve d'Ascq	2 Jul
8.16	0.7	Tony	Walton	USA	3.6.69	1		Bad Cannstatt	4 Jul
		(20)							
8.15	1.6	Robert	Thomas	USA	7.8.73	1	MSR	Walnut	17 Apr
8.15	1.3	Nikolay	Antonov	BUL	17.8.68	2	NC	Sofia	1 Aug
8.14i	-	Allen	Johnson	USA	1.3.71	1		Johnson City	19 Feb
8.13		Mike	Francis	PUR	23.10.70	1		Raleigh	3 Apr
8.13	0.1	Yevgeniy	Semenyuk	UKR	11.12.68	1		Uzhgorod	8 May
8.13	0.7	Nobuharu	Asahara	JPN	21.6.72	1	AsiC	Manila	3 Dec
8.12	1.0	Tony	Barton	USA	17.10.69	3	GPF	London	10 Sep
8.11i	-	Milan	Gombala	TCH	29.1.68	1	NC	Praha	21 Feb
8.11		Percy	Knox	USA	14.10.69	1		Tucson	26 May
8.09i	-	Bogdan	Tudor	ROM	1.2.70	1	NC	Bucuresti	19 Feb
		(30)							
8.09		Juan Carlos	Garzón	CUB	16.2.74	1		Artemisa	23 Apr
8.09	0.3	Dietmar	Haaf	GER	6.3.67	1		Dillingen	4 Jun
8.09	0.0	Konstantin	Krause	GER	8.10.67	1		Bad Homburg	10 Jun
8.09	1.6	Francois	Fouche	RSA	5.6.63	2		Bad Cannstatt	4 Jul
8.09			Chao Chih-kuo	TPE	72	2	AsiC	Manila	3 Dec
8.08		Thorsten	Heide	GER	4.5.69	2		Bad Homburg	10 Jun
8.07i	-	Vladen	Kapustyanskiy	RUS	4.7.69	1		Sankt Peterburg	21 Feb
8.07		Mark	Mason	GUY	6.6.69	2		Raleigh	3 Apr
8.07A		Reggie	Jones	USA	8.5.71	2		El Paso	10 Apr
8.07		Dmitriy	Bagryanov	RUS	18.12.67	1		Moskva	24 May
		(40)							
8.07	0		Xu Bin	CHN	4.8.70	1	NC	Beijing	10 Jun
8.07	1.3	Alan	Turner	USA	19.3.69	*	NC	Eugene	19 Jun
8.07	1.6	Kader	Klouchi	FRA	1.6.69	*		Albi	27 Jun
8.06	0.4		Huang Baoting	CHN	.5.74	1		Beijing	3 May
8.06	1.1	Jaime	Jefferson	CUB	17.1.62	3	NC	Habana	12 May
8.06	0.4	Simone	Bianchi	ITA	27.1.73	1		Alicante	7 Aug
8.05	0.5	Aleksandr	Glovatskiy	BLS	2.5.70	Q		Gomel	25 Jun
8.05	0.2	Mattias	Sunneborn	SWE	27.9.70	1	vFIN	Stockholm	28 Aug
8.04	0.8	Galin	Georgiev	BUL	23.3.70	1		Pleven	17 Jul
8.04	0.6	Tibor	Ordina	HUN	31.10.71	1	NC	Budapest	5 Aug
		(50)							
8.04		Yuriy	Naumkin	RUS	68	1		Vladimir	15 Aug
8.03		Ayodele	Aladefa	NGR	29.12.70	1		Lagos	27 Feb
8.03		Nelson	Ferreira	BRA	1.1.73	1		Brasilia	1 May
8.03		Todd	Trimble	USA	2.6.71	2	JO	Columbus	9 May
8.03	-1.2	Joël	Plagnol	FRA	9.2.71	1		Heidelberg	6 Jun

Mark	Wind	Name		Nat	Born	Pos	Meet	Venue	Date
8.03	1.2	Viktor	Rudenik	BLS	30.3.64	1		Krakow	1 Jul
8.02	1.5		Jia Xinli	CHN	25.1.68	Q	NC	Beijing	10 Jun
8.02		Christian	Thomas	GER	31.3.65	3		Bad Homburg	10 Jun
8.02		Bernhard	Kelm	GER	23.12.67	4		Bad Homburg	10 Jun
8.02	0.6	Edrick	Floréal	CAN	5.10.66	2	Indy	Indianapolis	25 Jun
		(60)							
8.02	2.0	André	Müller	GER	15.11.70	4		Bad Cannstatt	4 Jul
8.02	-1.8	Aleksandr	Zharkov	RUS	16.4.71	1		Rostov na Donu	17 Jul
8.02	0.4	Georg	Ackermann	GER	13.7.72	1		Berlin	5 Sep
8.01i	-	Neil	Chance	USA	14.2.73	2		Johnson City	19 Feb
8.01Ai	-	Derek	Scurry	USA	1.10.73	1		Reno	27 Feb
8.01		Chris	Huffins	USA	15.4.70	D		Tucson	17 Mar
8.00i	-	Daniel	Ivanov ¶	BUL	4.11.65	1		Sofia	6 Feb
8.00i	-	Vasiliy	Sokov	RUS	7.4.68	2	NC	Moskva	28 Feb
7.99		Wendell	Williams	TRI	19.10.68	1		Port of Spain	12 Jun
7.99	0.5	Ivo	Krsek	TCH	21.3.67	2	GS	Ostrava	15 Jun
		(70)							
7.99	1.6	James	Sabulei	KEN	12.4.69	3	AfrC	Durban	27 Jun
7.99	1.1	Antonio	Corgos	ESP	10.3.60	2	NC	Gandia	3 Jul
7.99	0.7	Juha	Kivi	FIN	26.1.64	1	NC	Mikkeli	31 Jul
7.99	0.5	Spyros	Vasdekis	GRE	23.1.70	Q	WC	Stuttgart	19 Aug
7.99	0.4	Dan	O'Brien	USA	18.7.66	D	WC	Stuttgart	19 Aug
7.98Ai	-	Benjamin	Koech	KEN	23.6.69	1		Flagstaff	20 Feb
7.98i	-	Frans	Maas	HOL	13.7.64	1	NC	Den Haag	27 Feb
7.98	1.5	Marco	Delonge	GER	16.6.66	1		Berlin	20 May
7.96i	-	Sergey	Novozhilov	RUS	21.4.69	1		Chelyabinsk	23 Jan
7.96i	-	Fred	Salle	GBR	10.9.64	4		Glasgow	30 Jan
		(80)							
7.96	1.1	Marti	Dignó	CUB	28.8.62	1		Habana	19 Feb
7.96		Sergey	Zaozerskiy	RUS	27.1.64	1		Voronezh	24 Jul
7.96A		Elmer	Williams	PUR	8.10.64	1	CAC	Cali	30 Jul
7.96	1.4	Jarmo	Kärnä	FIN	4.8.58	2	NC	Mikkeli	31 Jul
7.95i	-		Zhou Ming	CHN	7.1.70	1		Yokohama	6 Mar
7.95		Danny	Johnson	USA	5.3.71	1	JUCO	Odessa	21 May
7.95	0.5	Gianni	Iapichino	ITA	2.3.69	2	NC	Bologna	3 Aug
7.94i	-	Roman	Orlik	TCH	29.5.72	2	NC	Praha	21 Feb
7.94	-0.2	Luis A	Bueno	CUB	22.5.69	1		Habana	25 Feb
7.94	1.2	Giovanni	Evangelisti	ITA	11.9.61	*	EP	Roma	26 Jun
		(90)							
7.94	0.1	Igor	Streltsov	UKR	1.5.65	2	NC	Kiev	3 Jul
7.94		Franck	Lestage	FRA	20.4.68	1		Tarbes	3 Jul
7.94		Andrey	Ignatov	RUS	3.2.68	2		Vladimir	15 Aug
7.93		Nat	Sowell	USA	73	1		Monroe	16 May
7.92i	-	Chris	Sanders	USA	8.5.72	1		Columbus	30 Jan
7.92	-0.1	Vladimir	Malyavin	TKM	4.3.73	1		Alma Ata	15 May
7.92		Robert	Emmiyan	ARM	16.2.65	2		São Paulo	16 May
7.92	1.8	Vyacheslav	Bordukov	RUS	1.1.59	4		Sochi	22 May
7.92	2.0	Teddy	Steinmayr	AUT	4.2.64	1		Ebensee	22 May
7.92	1.1	Vernon	George	USA	6.10.64	2	NYG	New York	22 May
		(100)							
7.92	-0.8	Alexander	Bub	GER	24.1.67	7		Bad Cannstatt	4 Jul
7.92	1.6	Mika	Kahma	FIN	25.9.66	1		Jyväskylä	10 Aug
7.92i		Franck	Zio	BKF	.71	1		Paris	9 Dec

7.91i	-	Vadim	Ivanov	RUS	68	23 Jan
7.91i	-	Viktor	Popko	UKR	68	13 Feb
7.91	-0.1	Georgois	Zambetakis	GRE	71	19 Jun
7.91		Paulo Sergio	De Oliveira	BRA	69	25 Jun
7.90		Yevgeniy	Pechyonkin	RUS	73	24 Apr
7.90		Jerome	Romain	DMN	71	21 May
7.90	1.9	Masaki	Morinaga	JPN	72	23 May
		(110)				
7.90	1.1	Kostas	Koukodimos	GRE	69	19 Aug
7.90	1.5		Lang Yong	CHN	73	9 Sep
7.89i	-	Sergey	Layevskiy	UKR	59	13 Feb
7.89i	-	Antonio	Davis	USA	72	5 Mar
7.89	0.8	Abdrey	Nikulin	BLS	68	6 Jul
7.89		Konstantin	Sarvatskiy	UZB		3 Dec
7.88		Milko	Campus	ITA	69	23 May
7.88	1.9	Gordon	Laine	USA	58	3 Jun
7.88	1.7	Cheikh Tidiane	Touré	SEN	70	25 Jul
7.88	2.0	Bruno	Frinolli	ITA	68	3 Sep
		(120)				
7.87		Leon	Gordon	JAM	74	2 Apr
7.87	1.9	Andrej	Benda	SVK	75	15 May
7.86		Jayson	Duff	USA	72	3 Apr
7.86	1.5	Ken	Nakajima	JPN	67	5 May
7.86		Yutaka	Fukazawa	JPN	66	23 May
7.86	1.6	Paul	Meier	GER	71	29 May
7.86	1.8	Yassin	Guellet	BEL	74	23 May
7.86	1.2	Andrey	Zirko	BLS	72	15 Jul
7.85		Helmuts	Rodke	LAT	67	4 Jun
7.85i		Emiel	Mellaard	HOL	66	27 Feb
		(130)				
7.85A		David	Lamai	KEN	64	12 Jun
7.85	0.9	Martin	Morkes	TCH	71	15 Jun

Mark	Wind	Name		Nat	Born	Date
7.85	0.8	Milan	Kovar	TCH	72	15 Jun
7.85		Erik	Nys	BEL	73	4 Jul
7.85	-1.8	Leonid	Voloshin	RUS	66	27 Oct
7.85	0.9	Hiroaki	Ishibe	JPN	73	26 Sep
7.85	1.6	Daisuke	Watanabe	JPN	75	26 Oct
7.84i	-	Ian	James	CAN	63	9 Jan
7.84i		Glenroy	Gilbert	CAN	68	27 Feb
7.84A	1.5	Danny	Beauchamp	SEY	69	8 May
		(140)				
7.84		Gordon	McKee	USA	66	16 May
7.84		LaMark	Carter	USA	70	3 Jun
7.84	0.9	Igor	Lysechko	UKR	70	3 Jul
7.84	0.8	Jai	Taurina	AUS	72	10 Dec
7.83i	-	Andrew	Owusu	GHA	72	27 Feb
7.83A	1.6	Stollie	Kotze	RSA	70	8 May
7.83		Csaba	Almási	HUN	66	19 May
7.83		Aleksandr	Savinov	RUS	74	26 May
7.82i	-	Ivan	Stoyanov	BUL	69	28 Jan
7.82		Diatori	Gildersleeve	USA	70	27 Mar
		(150)				
7.82		Nelson	Ferreira Rocha	BRA	69	16 May
7.82	1.3	Serge	Hélan	FRA	64	29 May
7.82	0.8	Roman	Golanowski	POL	69	29 May
7.82	-0.2	Boris	Ilin	UKR	72	7 Jun
7.82	1.3		Shao Lin	CHN	70	10 Jun
7.82A		Amos	Rutere	KEN	63	12 Jun
7.81A	0.9	Athian	Labuschagne	RSA	65	6 Feb
7.81i		Marvin	Forde	TRI	75	
7.81	0.9	David	Culbert	AUS	67	25 Feb
7.81i	-	Steve	Duren	USA	72	5 Mar
		(160)				
7.81		Victor	Agbebaku	NGR	70	17 Apr
7.81		Lotfi	Khaida	ALG	68	15 May
7.80i	-	Dany	Dhanéus	FRA	65	7 Feb
7.80A	1.4	Braam	Du Plooy	RSA	66	26 Feb
7.80	1.7	Cai Jun		CHN	68	10 Apr
7.80		Dennis	Harris	USA	68	8 May
7.80		Andris	Strikis	LAT	71	14 May
7.80	0.9	Tetsuya	Shida	JPN	71	26 Jun
7.80		Vitaliy	Kolpakov	UKR	72	10 Jul
7.80	2.0	Marc	van der Worp	HOL	70	24 Jul
		(170)				
7.80	0.1	Samir Marek Sidia		TUN	70	25 Jul
7.80	0.2	Zsolt	Szabó	HUN	64	5 Oct
7.80	-2.6	Ryan	Moore	AUS	74	4 Dec

Unconfirmed

Mark	Wind	Name		Nat	Born	Pos	Meet	Venue	Date
8.00		Konstantin	Sarvatskiy	UZB					
7.94		Konstandinos	Koukodimos	GRE	14.9.69				

Wind-assisted marks

Mark	Wind	Name		Nat	Born	Pos	Meet	Venue	Date
8.53	4.8		Powell			Q	NC	Eugene	18 Jun
8.53	2.2		Powell			1	NC	Eugene	19 Jun
8.50	2.3		Powell			1		Madrid	3 Jun
8.46	3.1		Walder			2	NC	Eugene	19 Jun
8.41	2.2		Pedroso			2		Madrid	3 Jun
8.40	2.1	Anthuan	Maybank	USA	30.12.69	1	DrakeR	Des Moines	24 Apr
8.38	3.3		Walder			1		Knoxville	15 May
8.37	3.6		Pedroso			1		Alcala	10 Jul
8.37A	3.8	Larry	Myricks	USA	10.3.56	1		Sestriere	28 Jul
8.35A	5.5	Reggie	Jones	USA	8.5.71	2		Sestriere	28 Jul
8.35A	2.8	Joe	Greene	USA	17.2.67	3		Sestriere	28 Jul
8.35	2.2	Ivaylo	Mladenov	BUL	6.10.73	1	NC	Sofia	1 Aug
8.32	3.6		Walder			Q	NC	Eugene	18 Jun
8.32	2.7	Obinna	Eregbu	NGR	9.11.69	1	AfrC	Durban	27 Jun
		(14 performances)							
8.30		Stacy	Brown	USA	26.2.72	1		Abilene	8 May
8.20		Neil	Chance	USA	14.2.73	1		Chapel Hill	16 Apr
8.17	6.0	Erki	Nool	EST	25.6.70	1		Riga	29 May
8.16A	4.5	Frans	Maas	HOL	13.7.64	4		Sestriere	28 Jul
8.15	3.3	Kader	Klouchi	FRA	1.6.69	1		Albi	27 Jun
8.11	3.4	Alan	Turner	USA	19.3.69	Q	NC	Eugene	18 Jun
8.09	3.1	Spyros	Vasdekis	GRE	23.1.70	1	NC	Athinai	23 Jul
8.05	2.3	Ayodele	Aladefa	NGR	29.12.70	2	AfrC	Durban	27 Jun
8.04	2.2	Giovanni	Evangelisti	ITA	11.9.61	1	EP	Roma	26 Jun
8.03		Benjamin	Koech	KEN	23.6.69	1		Las Vegas	10 Apr
8.02A		Gordon	McKee	USA	12.10.66	3		El Paso	10 Apr
8.02	6.4	Andris	Strikis	LAT	7.11.71	2		Riga	29 May
7.99	4.2	Chris	Sanders	USA	8.5.72	5	NCAA	New Orleans	3 Jun
7.99	2.5	Paulo Sergio	De Oliveira	BRA	9.5.69	1	SACh	Lima	3 Jul
7.98	3.3	Tetsuya	Shida	JPN	27.6.71	1	NC	Tokyo	12 Jun
7.95	3.0	Chris	Wright	BAH	8.8.71	2	NC	Nassau	17 Jun
7.95	2.2	Laurent	Broothaerts	BEL	1.3.66	1		Oordeghem	4 Jul
7.95	3.1	Paul	Meier	GER	27.7.71	D	EP/A	Oulu	10 Jul
7.94		Kevin	Wiley	USA	73	1		Lubbock	27 Mar
7.93		Nicola	Trentin	ITA	20.6.74	1		Selargius	29 Apr
7.93	2.4	Vyacheslav	Bordukov	RUS	1.1.59	1	Balt	Tallinn	3 Jul

Mark	Wind	Name		Nat	Born	Date
7.92	4.2	Helmuts	Rodke	LAT	67	29 May
7.91		LaMark	Carter	USA	70	16 May
7.91	2.3	Barrington	Williams	GBR	55	31 May
7.90		Hillary	Miller	USA	68	13 Mar
7.90		Nugent	Cotton	USA	68	8 May
7.90	2.2	Andreas	Steiner	AUT	64	22 May
7.90A	3.4	Lotfi	Khaida	ALG	68	28 Jul
7.89	3.0	Serge	Hélan	FRA	64	19 Jun
7.89	2.2	Daisuke	Watanabe	JPN	75	26 Oct
7.88	5.3	Micah	Otis	USA	72	8 May
7.88		Andrew	Owusu	GHA	72	15 May
7.88	3.9	Otto	Karki	FIN	71	29 May
7.88	4.5	Fausto	Frigerio	ITA	66	3 Sep
7.87		Kevin	Dilworth	USA	74	27 Mar

Mark	Wind	Name		Nat	Born	Date
7.87		Tyrell	Taitt	USA	71	16 Apr
7.87	2.1	Kerwin	Alcide	FRA	69	15 May
7.86A		Dennis	Harris	USA	68	10 Apr
7.86	3.2	Yoelvis	Quesada	CUB	73	12 May
7.85	4.8	Michael	Morgan	AUS	66	7 Mar
7.85		Diatori	Gildersleeve	USA	70	18 Jun
7.84		Brian	Thomas	CAN	70	15 May
7.84	3.3	Marc	van der Worp	HOL	70	26 Jun
7.84	4.6	Ryan	Moore	AUS	74	11 Dec
7.83		David	Bennett	USA		2 May
7.83?		Aleksandr	Savinok	UKR	67	26 May
7.81	2.2	Ian	Simpson	GBR	66	20 Jun

Best outdoor marks for athletes with seasonal bests indoors

Mark	Wind	Name	Pos	Meet	Venue	Date
8.09	1.0	Gombala	1	v2N	Praha	17 Jul
7.98	2.0	Kapustyanskiy	1	Balt	Tallinn	3 Jul
7.98	1.9	Koech	1		Koski	10 Jul
7.95	-1.0	Maas	1		Amsterdam	25 Jul
7.94		Scurry	1	SunA	Tempe	3 Apr
7.93	1.4	Tudor	4	WUG	Buffalo	18 Jul

Mark	Wind	Name	Date
7.91		A Johnson	16 Apr
7.89		C Sanders	26 May
7.89		Nikulin	7 Jul
7.86	1.3	Orlík	27 May
7.84	0.1	Zhou Ming	15 May
7.83	0.7	Sokov	12 Jun
7.83	1.4	James	31 Jul
7.82		Owusu	10 Apr
7.80		Duren	21 May

Wind assisted

Mark	Wind	Name	Pos	Venue	Date
7.98		Sokov	1	Cork	9 Jul
7.87	3.8	Salle			18 Sep
7.80	7.5	Mellaard			31 May

Low altitude best

Mark	Wind	Name	Pos	Meet	Venue	Date
8.31	1.2	Streete-Thompson	3	NCAA	New Orleans	3 Jun
8.05		Jones	2		Innsbruck	28 Aug
8.04	1.2	Myricks	2		Brussels	3 Sep
7.86	0.6	E.Williams	q	WC	Stuttgart	19 Aug

Wind assisted

Mark	Wind	Name	Pos	Meet	Venue	Date
8.17		Jones	2	SEC	Knoxville	15 May
7.94		McKee	1		San Marcos	23 Apr
7.84		Khaida	5	SEC	Knoxville	15 May

Exhibition - built up runway

Mark	Name		Nat	Born	Pos	Venue	Date
8.18	Mattias	Sunneborn	SWE	27.9.70	1	Iglesias	9 Sep
7.83	Nicola	Trentin	ITA	20.6.74	4	Iglesias	9 Sep

Questionable marks

Mark	Name		Nat	Born	Pos	Venue	Date
8.01A	Rogelio	Sainz	MEX	8.6.68	1	El Paso	Jun
8.00?	Konstantin	Sarvatskiy	UZB				.

Illegal mark: 8.07 Mark Mason GUY 6.6.69 2 Raleigh 3 Apr

Ancillary marks

Mark	Wind	Name	Date
8.48		Powell	25 Jun
8.46		Powell	7 Jul
8.46	0.3	Powell	27 Jul
8.46	0.4	Powell	27 Jul
8.45	0.5	Powell	27 Jul
8.43	-0.1	Powell	20 Aug
8.42		Powell	7 Jul
8.41	1.3	Powell	3 Jun
8.37	0.3	Powell	1 Jun
8.37	1.1	Powell	19 Jun
8.36	0.0	Powell	4 Aug
8.34	0.5	Powell	10 Sep
8.33	0.3	Powell	3 Jun
8.42w	2.4	Powell	19 Jun
8.35w	4.8	Powell	19 Jun
8.33Aw	5.4	Jones	28 Jul

TRIPLE JUMP

Mark	Wind	Name		Nat	Born	Pos	Meet	Venue	Date
17.86	0.3	Mike	Conley	USA	5.10.62	1	WC	Stuttgart	16 Aug
17.84	0.7		Conley			1		Bad Cannstatt	4 Jul
17.68	-0.5	Yoelvis	Quesada	CUB	4.8.73	1	Barr	Habana	23 May
17.65	0.0	Leonid	Voloshin	RUS	30.3.66	2	WC	Stuttgart	16 Aug
17.59i	-	Pierre	Camara	FRA	10.9.65	1	WI	Toronto	13 Mar
17.59	0.3	Vasiliy	Sokov	RUS	7.4.68	1	NC	Moskva	19 Jun
17.56	-0.4		Voloshin			2	NC	Moskva	19 Jun
17.54	0.5	Denis	Kapustin	RUS	5.10.70	2		Bad Cannstatt	4 Jul
17.44	0.1	Jonathan	Edwards	GBR	10.5.66	3	WC	Stuttgart	16 Aug
17.39	0.8		Conley			Q	WC	Stuttgart	15 Aug
17.37	1.1		Voloshin			3		Bad Cannstatt	4 Jul
17.36i	-	Maris	Bruziks	LAT	25.8.62	2	WI	Toronto	13 Mar
17.34	0.0		Voloshin			Q	WC	Stuttgart	15 Aug
17.34	0.1	Ralf	Jaros	GER	13.12.65	4	WC	Stuttgart	16 Aug
17.32	1.5	Anisio	Souza Silva (10)	BRA	18.6.69	1		Chaux-de-Fonds	8 Oct
17.31	1.1		Kapustin			1		Sotteville	3 Jul
17.30			Jaros			1	OD	Jena	13 Jun
17.30	0.5		Camara			1	NC	Annecy	24 Jul
17.29	-0.3		Souza Silva			1		Rio de Janeiro	26 Jun
17.28i	-	Oleg	Grokhovskiy	RUS	3.5.68	1		Moskva	27 Jan
17.28		Sergey	Arzamasov	KZK	9.4.71	1		Shymkent	29 Apr
17.28			Bruziks			1		Riga	20 May
17.28	0.5		Edwards			1	Pearl	Belfast	19 Jun
17.28	0.4	Vladimir	Melikhov	RUS	30.3.69	4		Bad Cannstatt	4 Jul
17.28	2.0		Camara			1		Limoges	10 Jul
17.28	0.5		Camara			5	WC	Stuttgart	16 Aug
17.27i	-	Brian	Wellman	BER	2.8.67	4	WI	Toronto	13 Mar
17.27		Aliacer	Urrutia	CUB	22.9.74	1		Artemisa	23 Apr
17.27	1.7		Bruziks			1		Riga	29 May
17.27	2.0	Kenny	Harrison	USA	13.2.65	2	NC	Eugene	17 Jun
17.27	-1.0		Edwards			2	EP	Roma	27 Jun

(31/16)

Mark	Wind	Name		Nat	Born	Pos	Meet	Venue	Date
17.26	1.1		Zou Sixin	CHN	8.5.67	1	NG	Beijing	12 Sep
17.25	1.8	Serge	Hélan	FRA	24.2.64	2		Limoges	10 Jul
17.23	1.2	Georges	Sainte-Rose	FRA	3.9.69	3		Limoges	10 Jul
17.22	0.9	Andrius	Raizgys	LIT	4.4.69	1		Kaunas	3 Jun
		(20)							
17.21	0.6	Tord	Henriksson	SWE	13.4.65	5		Bad Cannstatt	4 Jul
17.21	1.5	Tosi	Fasinro	GBR	28.3.72	1		Salamanca	27 Jul
17.17		Oleg	Sakirkin	KZK	23.1.66	2		Shymkent	29 Apr
17.16	-0.2	Edrick	Floréal	CAN	5.10.66	2	Herc	Monaco	7 Aug
17.14		Yuriy	Sotnikov	RUS	10.3.68	1		Sankt Peterburg	25 Jun
17.12i	-	Nikolay	Raev ¶	BUL	29.1.71	1		Sofia	28 Jan
17.06	1.8	Gennadiy	Markov	RUS	66	2		Sochi	23 May
17.03i	-	Oleg	Protsenko	RUS	11.8.63	1		Moskva	2 Feb
17.03	1.6	Toussaint	Rabenala	MAD	29.10.65	3		Sotteville	3 Jul
17.02		Daniel	Osorio	CUB	5.11.72	1		Habana	26 Feb
		(30)							
17.00	0.4	Osiris	Mora	CUB	3.10.73	1		Habana	20 Feb
17.00	1.9	Gregorio	Hernández	CUB	2.6.68	2	Barr	Habana	23 May
17.00		Yevgeniy	Timofeyev	RUS	22.2.74	1		Krasnodar	26 May
17.00	-0.1	Igor	Lapshin	BLS	8.8.63	1	Kuso	Kielce	16 Jun
17.00	1.5	Oleg	Denishchik	BLS	10.11.69	1	NC	Gomel	25 Jun
17.00		Armen	Martirosyan	ARM	69	1		Yerevan	10 Jul
16.98	0.0	Vladimir	Inozemtsev	UKR	25.5.64	1	NC	Kiev	4 Jul
16.98	0.1	Jerome	Romain	DMN	12.6.71	11	WC	Stuttgart	16 Aug
16.97i	-	Andrey	Kayukov	RUS	12.4.64	5	NC	Moskva	27 Feb
16.96		Reggie	Jones	USA	8.5.71	1	SEC	Knoxville	16 May
		(40)							
16.96	0.0		Duan Qifeng	CHN	20.1.73	2	NG	Beijing	12 Sep
16.95	1.3	Karsten	Richter	GER	25.7.72	6		Bad Cannstatt	4 Jul
16.94	1.3	Nikolay	Musiyenko	UKR	16.12.59	1		Kiev	16 May
16.94	-0.5		Xu Dongwen	CHN	23.12.68	3	NG	Beijing	12 Sep
16.92	-0.1	Lotfi	Khaida	ALG	20.12.68	5	Herc	Monaco	7 Aug
16.92		Dmitriy	Byzov	RUS	25.1.66	1		Rostov na Donu	19 Aug
16.90		Mike	Harris	USA	21.12.67	1		Seattle	15 May
16.89i	-	Sergey	Bykov	UKR	16.5.71	1	NC	Kiev	14 Feb
16.89	1.1	Milan	Mikulás	TCH	1.4.63	1	ECP	Budapest	30 May
16.89	1.1	Aleksey	Fatyanov	AZE	14.6.69	1	AsiC	Manila	4 Dec
		(50)							
16.88	1.6	Tyrone	Scott	USA	18.1.70	2	S&W	Modesto	8 May
16.88	0.3	Lázaro	Betancourt	CUB	18.3.63	3	Barr	Habana	23 May
16.88		Volker	Mai	GER	3.5.66	2	OD	Jena	13 Jun
16.87	1.4	Zsolt	Czingler	HUN	26.4.71	1		Budapest	7 Jul
16.87	1.1	Julian	Golley	GBR	12.9.71	*	WUG	Buffalo	15 Jul
16.87	1.9	Gyula	Pálóczi	HUN	13.9.62	1		Tata	31 Jul
16.86i	-	Erick	Walder	USA	5.11.71	1	NCAA	Indianapolis	13 Mar
16.86	1.4	Vasif	Asadov	AZE	27.8.65	5	NC	Moskva	19 Jun
16.86	0.5	Rogel	Nachum	ISR	21.5.67	Q	WC	Stuttgart	15 Aug
16.85	1.9	Juan M	López	CUB	7.4.67	5	Barr	Habana	23 May
		(60)							
16.83	1.8	Andrey	Zirko	BLS	1.7.72	1		Minsk	5 May
16.83	1.5	Aleksandr	Petrunin	RUS	29.1.67	4		Sochi	23 May
16.83	1.1	Redzinaldas	Stasaitis	LIT	5.4.67	1		Pärnu	31 Jul
16.82	1.1	Georgi	Dimitrov	BUL	12.2.71	1		Pleven	17 Jul
16.80i	-	Robert	Thomas	USA	7.8.73	1		Lincoln	6 Feb
16.80	-0.8	Aleksandr	Kovalenko	RUS	8.5.63	6	NC	Moskva	19 Jun
16.78	0.7	LaMark	Carter	USA	23.8.70	4	NCAA	New Orleans	5 Jun
16.77i	-	Joseph	Taiwo	NGR	24.8.59	1		Seattle	17 Jan
16.77	0.8	Jaroslav	Ivanov	BUL	19.8.73	1		Sofia	19 May
16.77		Michel	Martínez	CUB	6.11.74	2		Habana	18 Jun
		(70)							
16.75	1.5	Alex	Norca	FRA	18.1.69	*		Dijon	13 Jun
16.75	0.1	Jacek	Butkiewicz	POL	25.7.69	1		Slupsk	4 Aug
16.72i	-	Charlie	Simpkins	USA	19.10.63	4		Stuttgart	7 Feb
16.71	1.8	Ketill	Hantsveit	NOR	2.11.73	1		Bismo	17 Jul
16.69i	-	Gary	Johnson	USA	20.7.69	2	NC	New York	26 Feb
16.69			Park Min-soo	KOR	30.1.68	1		Seoul	16 Jun
16.69		Sergio	Saavedra	VEN	8.2.68	1	NC	Caracas	10 Oct

Mark	Wind	Name		Nat	Born	Pos	Meet	Venue	Date
16.67	-0.8		Zhou Qi	CHN	8.6.67	4	NG	Beijing	12 Sep
16.65i	-	Vladimir	Kravchenko	UKR	22.12.69	3	NC	Kiev	14 Feb
16.65i	-	Gennadiy	Glushchenko	UKR	26.5.70	1		Zaporozhe	20 Feb
		(80)							
16.64A	1.6	Wikus	Olivier	RSA	8.3.68	*		Potchefstroom	8 May
16.64		Keith	Holley	USA	8.11.69	1		Chapel Hill	15 May
16.63		Cátalin	Barbu	ROM	13.10.69	1	RomIC	Bucuresti	18 Jun
16.62i	-	Tyrell	Taitt	USA	19.4.71	2	NCAA	Indianapolis	13 Mar
16.62		Héctor	Marquetti	CUB	7.4.68	1		Santa Clara	8 May
16.62	1.0	Garfield	Anselm	FRA	7.6.66	2		La Chaux de Fonds	8 Aug
16.61i	-	Viktor	Popko	UKR	13.8.68	4	NC	Kiev	14 Feb
16.61	1.8		Zhang Jun	CHN	.1.74	1		Shijiazhuang	26 Apr
16.61		Antonio	Davis	USA	29.5.72	7	NCAA	New Orleans	5 Jun
16.60	0.7	Khristo	Markov	BUL	27.1.65	2		Stara Zagora	24 Jul
		(90)							
16.59i	-	Frank	Rutherford	BAH	23.11.64	2		Maebashi	14 Feb
16.58i	-	Kotzo	Kostov	BUL	9.1.68	2	NC	Sofia	13 Feb
16.58i	-	Parkev	Grigoryan	ARM	1.5.65	Q	WI	Toronto	12 Mar
16.58	2.0	Ray	Kimble	USA	19.4.53	4	vGBR	Edinburgh	2 Jul
16.58	1.0	Vyacheslav	Bordukov	RUS	1.1.59	2	Balt	Tallinn	4 Jul
16.57i	-	Theodoros	Tandanozis	GRE	29.9.64	1		Piraeus	15 Feb
16.56i	-	Aleksey	Dzhashitov	RUS	70	2		Volgograd	22 Jan
16.56i	-	Roland	McGhee	USA	15.10.71	1		Bloomington	6 Feb
16.55		Reggie	Jackson	USA	5.7.69	1		Fresno	3 Apr
16.54		César	Rizo	CUB	8.10.75	3		Artemisa	23 Apr
		(100)							
16.54	2.0	Pierre	Andersson	SWE	4.1.67	2	vFIN	Stockholm	29 Aug
16.54		Ionel	Eftimie	ROM	8.10.71	1	NC	Bucuresti	4 Sep

Mark	Wind	Name		Nat	Born	Date
16.53i	-	Yuriy	Osipenko	UKR	69	14 Feb
16.53	-1.1	Chen Yanping		CHN	66	12 Sep
16.52i		Cong Lizhi		CHN	73	16 Jan
16.52i	-	Arne	Holm	SWE	61	21 Feb
16.52		Marzouk	Al-Yoha	KUW	69	
16.52	1.9	Francis	Dodoo	GHA	60	10 Jul
16.52	1.1	Sergey	Kochkin	RUS	70	30 Aug
16.51		Robert	Cannon	USA	58	8 May
		(110)				
16.51		Lucian	Sfiea	ROM	63	18 Jun
16.50i	-	Andre	Ernst	GER	67	27 Feb
16.50	-0.3	Igor	Sautkin	RUS	72	24 Jul
16.49	1.0	Larry	Achike	GBR	75	12 Jun
16.49	1.2	John	Herbert	GBR	62	12 Jun
16.48i	-	Dan	Mitirica	ROM	69	19 Feb
16.48	1.4	M	Beyspekov	KZK		24 Jul
16.47		David	Nti-Berko	GHA	71	5 Jun
16.47		Avelino	De Souza	BRA	66	27 Jun
16.47A		Jacob	Katonon	KEN		3 Jul
16.47	1.6	Piotr	Weremczuk	POL	66	17 Jul
		(120)				
16.46	-0.2	Francis	Agyepong	GBR	65	15 Aug
16.45		Ricardo	Valiente	PER	68	2 Jul
16.45	2.0	Andrea	Matarazzo	ITA	69	2 Oct
16.44		Lucio	Hernández	CUB	69	8 May
16.44		Steve	Hanna	BAH	58	17 Jun
16.43i	-	Lars	Hedman	SWE	67	21 Feb
16.43	1.6	Kersten	Wolters	GER	65	4 Jul
16.43	1.6	Nikolay	Telushkin	RUS	74	30 Oct
16.42	1.9	Heikki	Herva	FIN	63	10 Jul
16.41		Dudson	Higgins	BAH	67	17 Jun
		(130)				
16.41	0.4	Paolo	Camossi	ITA	74	31 Jul
16.40i	-	Daniele	Buttiglione	ITA	66	13 Feb
16.40	0.3	Yevgeniy	Dergach	UKR	72	25 Apr
16.39	2.0	Ilya	Yashchuk	UKR	70	16 May
16.39	0.0	Lin Shenxing		CHN	69	10 Jun
16.39		Joel	Garcia	CUB	73	25 Jun
16.38	1.3	Julio	López	ESP	72	19 Jun
16.38	0.5	Dario	Badinelli	ITA	60	2 Oct
16.37i	-	Anzhel	Shikov	BUL	69	13 Feb
16.37		Helmuts	Rodke	LAT	67	13 May
		(140)				
16.37		Wolfgang	Knabe	GER	59	10 Jul
16.37	1.1	Damir	Tashpulatov	UZB	64	4 Dec
16.36	0.5	Hao Tong		CHN	70	26 Apr
16.36	-1.4	Gao Wuzhou		CHN	70	12 Sep
16.35	1.8	Cui Hongwei		CHN	72	26 Apr
16.35	-0.4	Rostislav	Dimitrov	BUL	74	31 Jul
16.34i	-	Aleksandr	Zayka	UKR	71	14 Feb
16.33	-1.2	Wang Baoying		CHN	72	10 Jun
16.33	0.7	Christos	Meletoglou	GRE	72	23 Jul
16.32i	-	Maurizio	Gifaldi	ITA	67	13 Feb
		(150)				
16.32	1.7	Clifton	Etheridge	USA	69	17 Jun
16.32		Messias José Baptista		BRA	68	27 Jun
16.32	0.9	Mohamed Karim Sassi		TUN	68	3 Jul
16.31A		Ben	Mugun	KEN	62	12 Jun
16.31	0.0	Andrew	Owusu	GHA	72	14 Jul
16.31	1.8	Luciano	Rigo	ITA	73	16 Jul
16.31		Csaba	Földessy	HUN	66	25 Sep
16.30i	-	Igor	Golov	RUS	68	22 Jan
16.30		Kendrick	Morgan	USA	73	17 Apr
16.30	-0.6	Andrey	Ledovskikh	UKR	72	16 May
		(160)				
16.30		Yevgeniy	Moskalenko	TKM		27 May

Best at low altitude

16.38 Valiente 25 Apr 16.35 -0.5 Olivier 24 Apr

Exhibition

Mark	Wind	Name		Nat	Born	Date
16.44		Jaroslav	Mrstík	TCH	67	11 Jul

Unconfirmed

Mark	Wind	Name		Nat	Born	Pos	Meet	Venue	Date
16.96		Damir	Tashpulatov	UZB	29.1.64				
16.86			Chen Hsin-yu	TPE		1		Taipeh	28 Apr

Disqualified for failing drugs test

Mark	Wind	Name		Nat	Born	Pos	Meet	Venue	Date
17.27i	-	Nikolay	Raev	BUL	29.1.71	-	WI	Toronto	13 Mar

Wind-assisted marks

Mark	Wind	Name		Nat	Born	Pos	Meet	Venue	Date
17.70	2.9	Jonathan	Edwards	GBR	10.5.66	1	v USA	Edinburgh	2 Jul
17.69	4.2		Conley			1	NC	Eugene	17 Jun

Mark	Wind	Name		Nat	Born	Pos	Meet	Venue	Date
17.60	2.1		Quesada			1	NC	Habana	14 May
17.55	3.5		Voloshin			1		Sevilla	5 Jun
17.46	2.4		Camara			1	EP	Roma	27 Jun
17.30	4.8	Tosi	Fasinro	GBR	28.3.72	1	NC	London	12 Jun
17.27	2.2		Edwards			1	McD	Sheffield	29 Aug
17.25	2.7	Zsolt	Czingler	HUN	26.4.71	1		Portsmouth	5 Jun
17.21	3.1	Toussaint	Rabenala	MAD	29.10.65	1		Victoria	27 Aug
17.10	4.2	Paul	Nioze	SEY	19.3.67	1		Belle Vue Mauricia	1 Aug
17.04	2.3	Reggie	Jones	USA	8.5.71	3	NC	Eugene	17 Jun
17.03	2.3	Andrey	Kayukov	RUS	12.4.64	3		Sochi	23 May
17.00	4.4	Francis	Agyepong	GBR	16.6.65	1		Enfield	3 Jul
16.97	2.9	Ray	Kimble	USA	19.4.53	4	NC	Eugene	17 Jun
16.94	3.9	Gyula	Pálóczi	HUN	13.9.62	1		Veszprém	22 Jul
16.91	3.0	Tyrell	Taitt	USA	19.4.71	1	NCAA	New Orleans	5 Jun
16.88	4.1	Julian	Golley	GBR	12.9.71	2	vUSA	Edinburgh	2 Jul
16.87	2.6	Erick	Walder	USA	5.11.71	3	NCAA	New Orleans	5 Jun
16.85	2.7	Alex	Norca	FRA	18.1.69	1		Bron	26 Jun
16.83		LaMark	Carter	USA	23.8.70	1		Monroe	17 May
16.80	2.3	Jaroslav	Ivanov	BUL	19.8.73	1		Sofia	15 May
16.77	2.1	Kotzo	Kostov	BUL	9.1.68	2		Sofia	15 May
16.76		Andrew	Owusu	GHA	8.7.72	1		Tuscaloosa	28 Mar
16.76	3.8	Arne	Holm	SWE	22.12.61	1		Mölndal	15 Jul
16.71A	2.4	Wikus	Olivier	RSA	8.3.68	1		Potchefstroom	8 May
16.71	2.2	Igor	Sautkin	RUS	72	1		Dzerzhinsk	30 Aug
16.68	4.4	Takashi	Komatsu	JPN	30.12.67	2	NC	Tokyo	13 Jun
16.67		Eric	Lancelin	USA	13.5.71	1		Natchitoches	24 Apr
16.67		David	Nti-Berko	GHA	71	5	NCAA	New Orleans	5 Jun
16.62	5.7	Vissen	Moonegan	MRI	3.7.71	2		Belle Vue Mauricia	1 Aug

Mark	Wind	Name		Nat	Born	Date
16.51	4.5	Charles	Friedek	GER	71	24 Jul
16.49		Hillary	Miller	USA	68	26 May
16.47A		Ivin	Haynes	BAR	68	28 Mar
16.46	2.6	Daniele	Buttiglione	ITA	66	12 Sep
16.45	4.2	Csaba	Földessy	HUN	66	6 Oct
16.41		Nat	Sowell	USA	73	17 May
16.41	2.7	Clifton	Etheridge	USA	69	16 Jun
16.40	3.8	Norifumi	Yamashita	JPN	62	13 Jun
16.38	2.3	Markku	Rokala	FIN	60	26 Jun
16.35		Danny	Johnson	USA	71	27 Mar
16.35	2.8	Johan	Meriluoto	FIN	74	29 May
16.35		Charles	Rogers	USA	71	17 Jun
16.34		Rich	Thompson	USA	69	28 Mar
16.33	4.5	Keniichi	Sumita	JPN	73	10 Sep

Best outdoor marks for athletes with seasonal bests indoors

Mark	Wind	Name	Pos	Meet	Venue	Date
17.14		Wellman	1	S&W	Modesto	8 May
17.01	1.0	Grokhovskiy	4		Sotteville	3 Jul
16.72		Kayukov	1		La Roche-sur-Yon	14 Jul
16.67		Walder	2	MSR	Walnut	17 Apr
16.63		Taiwo	4	S&W	Modesto	8 May
16.58	1.6	Protsenko	8	TSB	London	23 Jul

Mark	Wind	Name	Date
16.54	0.5	Grigoryan	13 Jun
16.51	0.3	Tantanozis	29 May
16.46		G Johnson	8 May
16.46		Kostov	31 Jul
16.46	-0.2	Rutherford	7 Oct
16.45		Mitirica	5 Sep
16.44	0.2	Osipenko	4 Jul
16.44	1.0	Cong Lizhi	12 Sep
16.43	0.5	Kravchenko	16 May
16.43		Thomas	26 May
16.38		Dzhasitov	23 May
16.34		Ernst	31 Jul
16.33		Shikov	15 May

Mark	Wind	Name	Pos	Meet	Venue	Date
16.71w	3.4	Simpkins	7	NC	Eugene	17 Jun
16.56w	2.7	Tantanozis	4	MedG	Narbonne	19 Jun

Ancillary marks

Mark	Wind	Name	Date
17.77	-0.3	Conley	16 Aug
17.76	1.1	Conley	4 Jul
17.70	-0.2	Conley	16 Aug
17.51	1.9	Quesada	22 May
17.48	-0.4	Voloshin	16 Aug
17.44		Sokov	19 Jun
17.35		Sokov	19 Jun
17.35		Voloshin	19 Jun
17.31		Voloshin	19 Jun
17.31	0.5	Edwards	16 Aug

Wind assisted

Mark	Wind	Name	Date
17.55	3.9	Voloshin	5 Jun
17.46	7.5	Voloshin	5 Jun
17.27	4.0	Conley	7 Jun

SHOT

Mark	Name		Nat	Born	Pos	Meet	Venue	Date
21.98	Werner	Gunthor	SUI	11.7.61	1	Gugl	Linz	25 Oct
21.97		Günthör			1	WC	Stuttgart	21 Aug
21.94		Günthör			1		Luzern	29 Jun
21.80	Randy	Barnes	USA	16.6.66	2	WC	Stuttgart	21 Aug
21.79		Barnes			1B		Rudlingen	24 Jul
21.77i	Mike	Stulce ¶	USA	21.7.69	1	v GBR	Birmingham	13 Feb
21.77		Günthör			1		Gisingen	3 Jul
21.72		Günthör			1	Athl	Lausanne	7 Jul
21.63		Günthör			1	EP/B	Bruxelles	12 Jun
21.56i	Jim	Doehring	USA	27.1.62	1	NC	Princeton	26 Feb
21.49		Günthör			1	WK	Zürich	4 Oct
21.48		Günthör			1		Bellinzona	26 Jun
21.47		Barnes			1	ISTAF	Berlin	27 Oct

Mark	Name		Nat	Born	Pos	Meet	Venue	Date
21.46		Barnes			2	Gugl	Linz	25 Oct
21.44i		Stulce			1	Sunk	Los Angeles	20 Feb
21.42		Günthör			1	Bisl	Oslo	10 Jul
21.38		Barnes			1	VD	Bruxelles	3 Sep
21.36i		Stulce			2	NC	Princeton	26 Feb
21.32i	Aleksandr	Bagach	UKR	21.11.66	1	NC	Kiev	13 Feb
21.29i		Doehring			1		Genova	17 Feb
21.29	Kevin	Toth	USA	29.12.67	1		Hechtel	31 Jul
21.28		Barnes			1	NC	Eugene	18 Jun
21.28		Günthör			1	NC	St Gallen	31 Jul
21.28		Günthör			1		Uttwil	11 Sep
21.27i		Stulce			1	WI	Toronto	12 Mar
21.26	Dragan	Peric	YUG	8.5.64	1	NC	Beograd	24 Jul
21.24		Günthör			1		Parma	15 Sep
21.23i		Toth			1		Boston	23 Jan
21.23		Günthör			1		Neufeld	19 Jun
21.21		Stulce			1		El Paso	10 Apr
21.21		Günthör			1	Alpen	Innsbruck	28 Oct
	(31/7)							
20.94i	Sergey	Smirnov	RUS	17.9.60	1	NC	Moskva	28 Feb
20.86	Yevgeniy	Palchikov	RUS	12.10.68	1		Abakan	30 May
20.84i	Aleksandr	Klimenko	UKR	27.3.70	2	NC	Kiev	13 Feb
	(10)							
20.82	C.J.	Hunter	USA	14.12.68	1	Pre	Eugene	5 Jun
20.65i	Paolo	Dal Soglio	ITA	29.7.70	1		Genova	10 Feb
20.55	Kalman	Konya	ex GER	27.10.61	2		Rüdlingen	25 Jul
20.53	Pétur	Gudmundsson	ISL	9.3.62	1		Helsingborg	25 Sep
20.48	Brent	Noon	USA	29.8.71	1		Athens	1 May
20.44i	Sergey	Nikolayev	RUS	12.11.66	1		Sankt Peterburg	23 Jan
20.40	Mikhail	Kostin	BLS	10.5.59	1		Grodno	15 Jul
20.31i	Vyacheslav	Lykho	RUS	16.1.67	2	NC	Moskva	28 Feb
20.31	Markus	Koistinen	FIN	1.5.70	1		Luumäki	13 Jun
20.27	Luciano	Zerbini ¶	ITA	16.2.60	1		Sestriere	28 Jul
	(20)							
20.21	Andrey	Nemchaninov	UKR	27.11.66	1	NC	Kiev	2 Jul
20.15	Sven	Buder	GER	23.6.66	1	NC	Duisburg	11 Jul
20.14	Klaus	Bodenmüller	AUT	6.9.62	4	Bisl	Oslo	10 Jul
20.08	Mika	Halvari	FIN	13.2.70	1		Kotka	4 Aug
20.07	Jonny	Reinhardt	GER	28.6.68	1		Dormagen	25 Jun
20.06i	Viktor	Bulat	BLS	1.4.71	1		Minsk	15 Jan
20.04	Gert	Weil	CHL	3.1.60	1		Runkel	31 Jul
20.03	John	Godina	USA	31.5.72	2	NCAA	New Orleans	5 Jun
20.03	Kent	Larsson	SWE	10.6.63	1	NC	Kvarnsveden	23 Jul
20.01i	Alessandro	Andrei	ITA	3.1.59	3		Genova	17 Feb
	(30)							
19.93i	Gregg	Tafralis	USA	9.4.58	4		Genova	17 Feb
19.92	Saulius	Kleiza	LIT	2.4.64	1		Kaunas	22 May
19.91	Aleksandr	Klimov	BLS	26.5.69	2		Mogilov	6 Jun
19.87	Vladimir	Yaryshkin	RUS	28.2.63	1		Rostov na Donu	15 Jul
19.84	Antero	Paljakka	FIN	1.8.69	1		Töysä	17 Jun
19.84	Paul	Edwards	GBR	16.2.59	1		Walton	8 Aug
19.81	Gheorge	Guset	ROM	28.5.68	1	RomIC	Bucuresti	18 Jun
19.77i	Kevin	Coleman	USA	5.5.69	1		Lincoln	13 Feb
19.72		Liu Hao	CHN	13.11.68	1	NG	Beijing	9 Sep
19.69		Ma Yongfeng	CHN	29.11.62	2	NG	Beijing	9 Sep
	(40)							
19.66	Christian	Nebl	AUT	21.4.64	1		Vöcklabruck	25 Jul
19.58i	Erik	de Bruin ¶	HOL	25.5.63	1	NC	Den Haag	28 Feb
19.57	Jenö	Kóczián	HUN	5.4.67	1		Budapest	10 Jul
19.57	Helmut	Krieger	POL	17.7.58	1		Suwalki	29 Aug
19.54	Chris	Volgenau	USA	30.3.69	3	WUG	Buffalo	17 Jul
19.53	Manuel	Martinez	ESP	7.12.74	Q	WC	Stuttgart	20 Aug
19.49	Carlos	Fandiño	CUB	10.6.69	1		Habana	8 Jul
19.48	Roman	Virastyuk	UKR	20.4.68	3		Odessa	21 May
19.44	Dimitrios	Koutsoukis ¶	GRE	8.12.62	1		Athinai	28 May
19.43	Sören	Tallhem	SWE	16.2.64	3	vFIN	Stockholm	28 Aug
	(50)							

Mark	Name		Nat	Born	Pos	Meet	Venue	Date
19.34i	Dirk	Urban	GER	14.1.69	2	NC	Sindelfingen	28 Feb
19.30	Courtney	Ireland	NZL	12.1.72	1	SWC	Austin	21 May
19.27	Giorgio	Venturi	ITA	23.6.66	1		Piacenza	11 Jul
19.23	John	Minns	AUS	31.5.67	1		Canberra	23 Feb
19.23	Merab	Kurashvili	GEO	30.1.71	1		Tbilisi	27 Jun
19.20	Vyacheslav	Spitsyn	RUS	11.2.65	1		Voronezh	24 Jul
19.19	Michael	Mertens	GER	27.12.65	2		Iffezheim	14 Jun
19.18	Vitalijus	Mitkus	LIT	9.6.65	2		Kaunas	22 May
19.13	Karel	Sula	SVK	30.6.59	1		Kosice	1 May
19.10	Corrado	Fantini	ITA	7.2.67	2		Bologna	29 May
	(60)							
19.08	Paul	Conlin	USA	16.7.70	1		Menomorice	8 May
19.06	Sergey	Rubtsov	KZK	4.9.65	1	NC	Almaty	23 Jul
19.04	Viktor	Kapustin	RUS	28.4.72	1		Bryansk	29 May
19.01	Dwight	Johnson	USA	5.11.69	1		Tucson	6 Feb
18.99i	Radoslav	Despotov	BUL	8.8.68	1		Sofia	28 Jan
18.99	Bilal Saad	Mubarak	QAT	18.12.72	2		Krefeld	4 Aug
18.97	Thomas	Hammersten	SWE	31.12.66	4	vFIN	Stockholm	28 Aug
18.95i	Matt	Simson	GBR	28.5.70	5	NCAA	Indianapolis	12 Mar
18.95	Tony	Harlin	USA	4.9.57	1		Holmdel	13 Jun
18.93	Rob	Carlson	USA	27.8.71	4	NCAA	New Orleans	5 Jun
	(70)							
18.92	Scott	Peterson	USA	9.11.72	4		El Paso	10 Apr
18.92	Igor	Avrunin	ISR	16.7.57	1		Tel Aviv	15 May
18.89	Steven	Albert	USA	1.4.64				24 Jul
18.89	Jan	Sandvik	FIN	17.5.69	1		Jalasjärvi	25 Jul
18.88i	Mark	Lacy	USA	24.4.70	1		Minneapolis	6 Feb
18.88	Jorge	Montenegro	CUB	21.9.68	1	CAG	Ponce	28 Nov
18.87i	Vladimir	Chernysh	UKR	14.2.68	1		Kharkov	26 Jan
18.86	Carel	le Roux	RSA	31.8.72	1		Potchefstroom	8 May
18.79	Piotr	Perzylo	POL	15.11.61	2		Lublin	4 Jun
18.77	Aleksey	Lukashenko	LAT	29.3.67	1		Riga	20 May
	(80)							
18.77	Claus-Dieter	Föhrenbach	GER	11.5.55	3		Iffezheim	14 Jun
18.75	Rick	Lyle	USA	26.2.71	2		Boulder	18 May
18.75	Elias	Louca	CYP	23.7.74	1		Limassol	14 Jul
18.72	Jan	Bártl	TCH	23.3.67	1		Praha	15 May
	19.06i dq				1	NC	Praha	20 Feb
18.72	Thorsten	Herbrand	GER	9.4.70			Essen	21 Aug
18.70	Anatoliy	Samolyuk	UKR	2.7.58	1		Odessa	21 Mar
18.70	Jordy	Reynolds	USA	10.5.69	2		Austin	8 May
18.66i	Joe	Bailey	USA	30.3.71	2		Reno	13 Feb
18.65	Luc	Viudès	FRA	31.1.56	4	MedG	Narbonne	17 Jun
18.64	Mikhail	Petrov	RUS	15.11.65	1		Moskva	25 Jul
	(90)							
18.64i	Kjell Ove	Hauge	NOR	20.2.69	1		Air Force Academy	27 Feb
18.63	Miroslav	Menc	TCH	16.3.71	1	v2N	Praha	17 Jun
18.62i	Costel	Grasu	ROM	5.7.67	2		Bucuresti	30 Jan
18.62	Oliver	Dück	GER	10.2.67	1		Hösbach	12 Jun
18.62	Dmitriy	Goncharuk	BLS	10.9.70	3	NC	Gomel	24 Jun
18.59		Cheng Shaobo	CHN	16.4.63	3	NG	Beijing	9 Sep
18.58	Tero	Lehtiö	FIN	24.8.63	1		Vihti	23 May
18.56	Chima	Ugwu	NGR	72	1		Lagos	22 May
18.55	José Luis	Martinez	ESP	25.8.70	1		Barcelona	22 May
18.50i	Chad	Goldstein	USA	28.3.71	4			26 Feb
	(100)							

Mark	Name		Nat	Born	Date
18.49	Dennis	Black	USA	73	3 Apr
18.46	Adewale	Olukoju	NGR	68	24 Apr
18.46	Ron	McKee	USA	59	22 May
18.45		Wu Hong	CHN	70	22 Mar
18.45	Martin	Bílek	TCH	73	5 Jun
18.44i	Andy	Meyer	USA	70	27 Feb
18.43	Burger	Lambrechts	RSA	73	24 Apr
18.42i	Phil	Caraher	USA	69	5 Feb
18.42	Xie Shengying		CHN	71	2 Apr
18.42	Pavel	Muzhikov	RUS	71	28 Aug
	(110)				
18.41	Henrik	Wennberg	SWE	66	26 Sep
18.40	Antti	Harju	FIN	74	1 Jul
18.39i	Yuriy	Belonog	UKR	74	30 Jan
18.39	Mark	Parlin	USA	73	8 May
18.38	Gary	Kirchhoff	USA	65	3 Apr
18.38		Li Wenkui	CHN	71	9 Sep
18.36	Ron	Willis	USA	71	1 May
18.33	Francisco	Ball	PUR	56	30 Jul
18.30	Albert	Schmider	GER	60	26 May
18.28i	J.D	Teach	USA	72	6 Mar
	(120)				

Mark	Name		Nat	Born	Date
18.27	Ekrem	Ay	TUR	64	4 Jul
18.24	Scott	Cappos	CAN	69	24 Jul
18.22	Shawn	Schleizer	USA		26 May
18.22	Marco	Dodoni	ITA	72	28 Jul
18.22	Sergey	Kot	UZB	60	20 Aug
18.21	Andy	Bloom	USA	73	15 May
18.21	Ralf	Kahles	GER	73	5 Sep
18.18i	Mike	Olson	USA		13 Mar
18.16	Jean-Louis	Lebon	FRA	67	23 May
18.15	Aleksey	Shidlovskiy	RUS	72	20 Jun
	(130)				
18.15	Anders	Axlid	SWE	66	23 Jul
18.15	John	McNamara	AUS	61	11 Dec
18.13i	Aaron	Gowell	USA	69	27 Feb
18.09i	Andrey	Golivets	UKR	72	13 Feb
18.07		Wen Jili	CHN	73	10 Apr
18.07	Adilson	Ramos De Souza	BRA	64	26 Jun
18.06	Stefan	Schröfel	GER	61	31 May
18.06	Mauri	Lindstedt	SWE	64	14 Jul
18.06	Lucio	Montenaro	ITA	68	9 Sep
18.05	Juha	Kemppainen	FIN	63	15 May
	(140)				
18.04i	Yuriy	Parkhomenko	UKR	73	13 Feb
18.04i	Greg	Hodel	USA	72	27 Feb
18.04i	John	Wirtz	USA	69	13 Mar
18.04	Ari	Uusitalo	FIN	68	7 Jul
18.03	Rod	Chronister	USA		8 May
18.03	Kristian	Pettersson	SWE	71	7 Oct
18.03	Giovanni	Tubini	ITA	64	8 Oct
18.02	Roar	Hoff	NOR	65	4 Jul
18.02	Arne	Pedersen	NOR	61	8 Oct
18.00i	Dave	Winkler	USA	71	30 Jan
	(150)				

Best outdoor marks for athletes with seasonal bests indoors

Mark	Name	Pos	Meet	Venue	Date
21.15	Doehring	2	ISTAF	Berlin	27 Aug
20.85	Bagach	1		Kiev	15 May
20.78	Klimenko	1		Odessa	21 May
20.43	Dal Soglio	1		Vicenza	3 Apr
19.87	Andrei	1	ECP	Budapest	29 May
19.77	Tafralis	1		Los Gatos	23 Jan
19.74	Nikolayev	2	NC	Moskva	20 Jun
19.66	Smirnov	3	NC	Moskva	20 Jun
19.28	Coleman	1		Boulder	18 May
19.16	de Bruin ¶	1	NC	Amsterdam	5 Jul
18.90	Simson	5	NCAA	New Orleans	5 Jun
18.84	Despotov	1		Sofia	19 May
18.72	Bartl	1		Praha	15 May
18.70	Chernysh	3	NC	Kiev	2 Jul
18.57	Bulat	4	NC	Gomel	23 Jul
18.56	Bailey	1		Los Angeles (Ww)	24 Apr

18.16 Urban 22 May | 18.09 Teach 17 Apr | 18.09 Gowell 15 May | 18.04 Meyer 18 May

Exhibition: 21.25 Peric Sremaka 15 Jun

Unconfirmed

Mark	Name		Nat	Born	Pos	Venue	Date
19.87	Sergey	Kot	UZB	60			
19.00	Khalid	Al Khalili	SAU	12.2.65	1	Riyadhl	5 Feb

Ancillary marks

Mark	Name	Date	Mark	Name	Date	Mark	Name	Date	Mark	Name	Date
21.83	Günthör	29 Jun	21.59	Günthör	21 Aug	21.46	Günthör	7 Jul	21.35i	Stulce	20 Feb
21.80	Barnes	21 Aug	21.55	Günthör	29 Jun	21.44	Günthör	26 Jun	21.33	Günthör	25 Aug
21.72	Günthör	3 Jul	21.55	Günthör	21 Aug	21.39	Günthör	3 Jul	21.33	Barnes	3 Sep
21.63	Günthör	29 Jun	21.50	Günthör	7 Jul	21.37	Günthör	25 Aug	21.30i	Stulce	20 Feb
21.62	Günthör	7 Jul	21.48	Günthör	29 Jun	21.36i	Stulce	20 Feb	21.29	Günthör	4 Aug

DISCUS

Mark	Name		Nat	Born	Pos	Meet	Venue	Date
68.42	Lars	Riedel	GER	28.6.67	1	OD	Jena	13 Jun
67.80		Riedel			1	GGala	Roma	9 Jun
67.76		Riedel			1	Lausit	Cottbus	23 Jun
67.72		Riedel			1	WC	Stuttgart	17 Aug
67.42		Riedel			1		Halle	15 May
67.12	Mike	Buncic	USA	25.7.62	1		Salinas	23 Jul
67.06	Erik	De Bruin	HOL	25.5.63	1	APM	Hengelo	20 Jun
67.02		Riedel			1	ISTAF	Berlin	27 Oct
66.90	Costel	Grasu	ROM	5.7.67	1		Snagov	22 May
66.90	Dmitriy	Shevchenko	RUS	13.5.68	2	WC	Stuttgart	17 Aug
66.86	Anthony	Washington	USA	16.1.66	1	ASV	Köln	1 Oct
66.82		Shevchenko			1		Sochi	23 May
66.78		Riedel			1		Betzdorf	1 Sep
66.76		Riedel			1		Lindau	8 Oct
66.66		Riedel			D		Schwerin	26 Sep
66.56		Riedel			2	ASV	Köln	1 Oct
66.48	Adewale	Olukoju	NGR	27.7.68	1	S&W	Modesto	8 May
66.30		Riedel			1	EP	Roma	26 Jun
66.18	Vasiliy	Kaptyukh	BLS	27.6.67	1	EP/C3	Rotterdam	13 Jun
66.12	Sergey	Lyakhov	RUS	1.3.68	1		Khimki	15 May
66.12	Jürgen	Schult (10)	GER	11.5.60	3	WC	Stuttgart	17 Aug
66.00		Riedel			1	WK	Zürich	4 Oct
65.96		De Bruin			1		Dublin	4 May
65.92	Romas	Ubartas ¶	LIT	26.5.60	Q	WC	Stuttgart	16 Aug
65.88		Riedel			Q	WC	Stuttgart	16 Aug
65.78		Riedel			2	APM	Hengelo	20 Jun
65.76		Grasu			2	Lausit	Cottbus	23 Jun

Mark	Name		Nat	Born	Pos	Meet	Venue	Date
65.74		De Bruin			3	ASV	Köln	1 Oct
65.66		De Bruin			2	EP/C3	Rotterdam	13 Jun
65.48		Riedel			1	NC	Duisburg	10 Jul
	(30/11)							
65.28	Vladimir	Zinchenko	UKR	25.7.59	1		Kiev	16 May
65.26	Vaclavas	Kidykas	LIT	17.10.61	1		Kaunas	23 May
64.52	Attila	Horváth	HUN	28.7.67	1		Szombathely	28 Apr
64.44	Juan	Martínez ¶	CUB	17.5.58	1		La Coruña	17 Jul
64.26	Andrey	Kokhanovskiy	UKR	11.1.68	2		Kiev	16 May
64.26	Luciano	Zerbini ¶	ITA	16.2.60	1	NC	Bologna	2 Aug
64.12	Randy	Heisler	USA	7.8.61	1		Bloomington	1 May
64.12	Alexis	Elizalde	CUB	19.9.67	1		Salamanca	3 Aug
64.08	Adam	Setliff	USA	15.12.69	1		Seattle	1 May
	(20)							
64.08	Roberto	Moya	CUB	11.2.65	1		Salamanca	27 Jul
63.70	Ramon	Jiménez-Gaona	PAR	10.4.69	4	Jen	San José	29 May
63.70	Dmitriy	Kovtsun	UKR	29.9.55	2	NC	Kiev	3 Jul
63.66	Luis M	Delis	CUB	6.12.57	2		Salamanca	3 Aug
63.52	Vésteinn	Hafsteinsson	ISL	12.12.60	1		Helsingborg	7 Jul
63.50	Carsten	Kufahl	GER	14.11.67	1		Dortmund	24 Apr
63.44	Mike	Gravelle	USA	13.4.65	2		Salinas	23 Jul
63.26	Nick	Sweeney	IRL	26.3.68	1		Helsingborg	19 Jun
63.26	Vladimir	Dubrovshchik	BLS	1.1.72	1	NC	Gomel	24 Jun
62.98	Werner	Reiterer	AUS	27.1.68	1		Brisbane	31 Jan
	(30)							
62.86	Vyacheslav	Demakov	RUS	3.6.68	2	NC	Moskva	19 Jun
62.84	Virgilijus	Alekna	LIT	13.2.72	1		Palanga	28 Aug
62.82	?Michael	Möllenbeck	GER	12.12.69	1		Sittard	24 Jul
	65.42?				1		Wesel	27 Jul
62.62	Viktor	Baraznovskiy	BLS	23.1.68	2	NC	Gomel	24 Jul
62.60	Marcel	Tîrle	ROM	19.10.66	2		Snagov	22 May
62.24	Valeriy	Yagovdik	BLS	16.9.63	1		Grodno	25 Jul
62.22	Ray	Lazdins	CAN	25.9.64	1		Winnipeg	11 Jun
62.06		Zhang Cunbiao	CHN	11.2.69	1		Shijiazhuang	2 Apr
62.00	Lars	Sundin	SWE	21.7.61	1		Karlstad	1 May
61.90	Andreas	Seelig	GER	6.7.70	6	OD	Jena	13 Jun
	(40)							
61.86	Christian	Erb	SUI	14.2.59	1		La Mesa	2 Jun
61.82	Sergey	Lukashok	ISR	20.6.58	1		Runkel	31 Jul
61.78		Yu Wenge ¶	CHN	18.2.66	1		Guangzhou	22 Mar
61.72	Imrich	Bugár	TCH	14.4.55	1		Praha	11 Sep
61.70	Marco	Martino	ITA	21.2.60	2		Tirrenia	22 Jun
61.60	Andy	Meyer	USA	9.11.70	1		Lincoln	26 May
61.44	Steve	Muse	USA	27.1.66	1	vGBR	Edinburgh	2 Jul
61.42	Yuriy	Vykpish	UKR	30.9.66	2		Budapest	15 Jun
61.38	Svein Inge	Valvik	NOR	20.9.56	1		Spikkestad	20 Sep
61.34		Li Shaojie	CHN	.12.75	1		Jinan	1 Apr
	(50)							
61.32	Brian	Milne	USA	7.1.73	1		Hot Springs	10 Apr
61.30	Robert	Weir	GBR	4.2.61	2	vUSA	Edinburgh	2 Jul
60.86	Bernd	Kneissler	GER	13.9.62	4	NC	Duisburg	10 Jul
60.80		Ma Wei	CHN	1.7.66	2		Guangzhou	22 Mar
60.78	Aleksandr	Borichevskiy	RUS	25.6.70	1		Sankt Peterburg	22 Jul
60.74	Dag	Solhaug	SWE	11.1.64	1		Helsinborg	2 Sep
60.70	Eggert	Bogason	ISL	19.7.60			Hafnarfjördur	15 May
60.62	Gabriel	Pedroso	CUB	12.1.68	2		Habana	5 Mar
60.56	John	Godina	USA	31.5.72	3	S&W	Modesto	8 May
60.54	Kamen	Dimitrov	BUL	18.1.62	1	NC	Sofia	31 Jul
	(60)							
60.48	John	Godina	USA	31.5.72	3	S&W	Modesto	8 May
60.48	Olaf	Többen	GER	19.12.62	5	NC	Duisburg	10 Jul
	62.86?				2		Wesel	27 Jul
60.46	Vitaliy	Sidorov	UKR	23.3.70	3		Kiev	15 May
60.42	Gregg	Hart	USA	21.8.70	1		Indianapolis	15 May
60.36	Gennadiy	Pronko	BLS	27.2.70	1		Stargard	12 Jun
60.32	Jean-Claude	Retel	FRA	11.2.68	1	NC	Annecy	24 Jul
60.26	Yuriy	Seskin	RUS	7.7.66	2	Znam	Moskva	12 Jun

Mark	Name		Nat	Born	Pos	Meet	Venue	Date
60.18	Lars Ola	Sundt	NOR	7.1.68	4	S&W	Modesto	8 May
60.16	Henrik	Wennberg	SWE	11.3.66	5	S&W	Modesto	8 May
60.02	Diego	Fortuna	ITA	14.2.68	1		Cesena	26 Sep
	(70)							
59.94	Mika	Muuka	FIN	13.11.66	1		Sipoo	24 May
59.92	Mickael	Conjungo	CAF	6.5.69	1	AfrC	Durban	25 Jun
59.86	Rick	Meyer	USA	21.10.61	5	NC	Eugene	18 Jun
59.82		Nu Erlang	CHN	25.2.62	3	NG	Beijing	13 Sep
59.80	Dragan	Peric	YUG	8.5.64	1		Nis	20 Jun
59.72	Lutz	Hager	GER	16.10.64			Medelby	7 Jul
59.64	Frédéric	Selle	FRA	15.3.57	1		Abbeville	15 May
59.54	Vyacheslav	Pachin	LIT	16.7.63	2		Kaunas	7 May
59.44		Li Webin	CHN	.1.67	1		Jinan	18 Mar
59.44		Han Jun	CHN	13.11.72	3	NC	Beijing	13 Jun
	(80)							
59.42	Håkan	Karlberg	SWE	18.2.67	1		San Marcos	23 Apr
59.38	Joachim	Tidow	GER	4.2.69	6	NC	Duisburg	10 Jul
59.34	Aleksandr	Yasinovchuk	UKR	4.8.66	5		Kiev	2 May
59.32	Gary	Kirchoff	USA	15.8.65	1		San Diego	1 May
59.30	Kevin	Fitzpatrick	USA	26.9.69	2	Indy	Indianapolis	25 Jun
59.24	Valeriy	Murasovas	LIT	9.5.64	3		Kaunas	7 May
59.22	Igor	Duginyets	RUS	20.5.56	3		Rostov na Donu	16 Jul
59.18	Jim	Seifert	USA	26.11.62	6	S&W	Modesto	8 May
59.12	Frits	Potgieter	RSA	13.3.74	1	AAA-j	Bedford	4 Jul
59.12	Marek	Stolarczyk	POL	10.6.64	1	NC	Kielce	25 Jul
	(90)							
59.02	John	Wirtz	USA	31.5.69	1		Berkeley	12 May
58.98	Manfred	Schmitz	GER	13.3.60			Krefeld	9 Jun
	59.52				1		Ludwigsburg	24 Apr
58.94		Liu Chengjiang	CHN	.2.69	3	NC	Beijing	10 Jun
58.86		Zhang Jinglong	CHN	22.11.61			Beijing	3 May
58.76	Kari	Pekola	FIN	27.9.65	1		Helsinki	12 Sep
58.72	Tero	Lehtiö	FIN	24.8.63	1		Vihti	23 May
58.72	Alwin	Wagner	GER	11.8.50			Gelnhausen	18 Jun
58.68	Rolf	Danneberg	GER	1.3.53	8	NC	Duisburg	10 Jul
58.66	Derrick	Farrell	USA	10.1.72	1	SEC	Knoxville	16 May
58.64	Lance	Davenport	USA	16.12.66	1		El Paso	27 Mar
58.62	Marek	Majkrzak	POL	12.10.65	1		Sopot	5 Augf
	(100)							

Mark	Name		Nat	Born	Date	Mark	Name		Nat	Born	Date
58.58	Jean	Pons	FRA	69	9 Oct	58.24	Johannes	Kerälä	FIN	72	14 Sep
58.56	Mansour	Ghourbani	IRN	62	8 Sep	58.18	Anton	Ellanskaya	UKR	71	2 May
58.50	József	Ficsor	HUN	65	31 May	58.18	Kjell Ove	Hauge	NOR	69	7 Dec
58.42	Peter	Gordon ¶	GBR	51	26 May		(110)				
58.40	Igor	Avrunin	ISR	57	11 Jul	58.10	Martti	Halmesmäki	FIN	66	29 Jun
58.32	Vasiliy	Petrov	UKR	66	3 Jul	58.00	Brent	Patera	USA	67	8 May
58.28	Frantz	Kruger	RSA	75	30 Oct	58.00	Jerzy	Strychalski	POL	62	13 Jun

Questionable marks

Mark	Name		Nat	Born	Pos	Venue	Date
65.84	Jim	Seifert	USA	26.11.62	1	East Stroudsburg	30 Jun
58.88	Sven	Buder	GER	23.6.66	D	Schwerin	26 Sep

Ancillary marks

Mark	Name	Date	Mark	Name	Date	Mark	Name	Date
68.32	Riedel	13 Jun	66.62	Riedel	27 Aug	66.08	Buncic	23 Jul
67.66	Riedel	13 Jun	66.26	Buncic	23 Jul	65.76	de Bruin #	20 Jun
67.34	Riedel	17 Aug	66.22	Riedel	13 Jun	65.54	de Bruin #	1 Aug
66.78	Riedel	13 Jun	66.14	Shevchenko	17 Aug	65.50	Washington	1 Aug

HAMMER

Mark	Name		Nat	Born	Pos	Meet	Venue	Date
82.78	Andrey	Abduvaliyev	TJK	30.6.66	1		Nitra	28 Aug
82.54	Sergey	Kirmasov	RUS	25.3.70	1		Sochi	22 May
82.28	Igor	Astapkovich	BLS	4.1.63	1		Sevilla	5 Jun
82.16	Sergey	Litvinov	RUS	23.1.58	1	Znam	Moskva	13 Jun
82.00		Litvinov			1	NC	Moskva	19 Jun
81.70	Aleksandr	Seleznyov	RUS	25.1.63	2		Sochi	22 May
81.70		Seleznyev			1		Rostov na Donu	17 Jul
81.64		Abduvaliyev			1	WC	Stuttgart	15 Aug
81.44	Sergey	Alay	BLS	11.6.65	1		Gomel	15 May
81.32	Vitaliy	Alisevich	BLS	15.6.67	1		Novopolotsk	6 Aug
81.20		Abduvaliyev			1		Rehlingen	31 May
81.14		Litvinov			1		Reims	30 Jun

Mark	Name		Nat	Born	Pos	Meet	Venue	Date
81.06		Kirmasov			1		Bryansk	29 May
81.00	Tibor	Gécsek	HUN	22.9.64	1		Budapest	6 Aug
80.88		Abduvaliyev			2		Sevilla	5 Jun
80.88		Astapkovich			1	NC	Gomel	24 Jul
80.80	Andrey	Skvaryuk	UKR	9.3.67	1		Kiev	3 May
80.80	Lance	Deal (10)	USA	21.8.61	1		Eugene	15 May
80.78		Litvinov			1	EP	Roma	27 Jun
80.68		Alay			1		Tallinn	13 Jul
80.52		Alay			3		Sevilla	5 Jun
80.36	Aleksey	Krykun	UKR	12.12.68	1		Donetsk	29 May
80.30		Alay			2	NC	Gomel	24 Jul
80.20		Astapkovich			1		Budapest	15 Jun
80.16		Abduvaliyev			1		Padova	29 Oct
80.08		Deal			1		Portland	22 May
80.04	Vasiliy	Sidorenko	RUS	1.5.61	2	NC	Moskva	19 Jun
79.98	Christophe	Epalle	FRA	23.1.69	1		Clermont-Ferrand	20 May
79.98		Astapkovich			2		Reims	30 Jun
79.98		Litvinov			1		Oristano	12 Sep
	(30/13)							
79.86	Aleksandr	Krasko	BLS	7.4.72	1		Gomel	15 Jul
79.80	Enrico	Sgrulletti	ITA	24.4.65	1		Tirrenia	22 Jun
79.64	Yuriy	Chernega	RUS	18.2.67	1		Stavropol	30 May
79.44	Vadim	Kolesnik	UKR	29.4.69	2		Donetsk	29 May
78.98	Igor	Nikulin	RUS	14.8.60	2		Rehlingen	31 May
78.72	Raphaël	Piolanti	FRA	14.11.67	1	NC	Annecy	23 Jul
78.62	Valeriy	Gubkin	BLS	3.9.67	2		Grodno	4 May
	(20)							
78.20	Konstantin	Astapkovich	BLS	23.10.70	2		Grodno	25 Jul
77.92	Andrey	Debelyi	UKR	8.1.71	3		Donetsk	29 May
77.68	Andrey	Budykin	RUS	14.4.71	2	Znam	Moskva	13 Jun
77.44	Ilya	Konovalov	RUS	7.12.71	3		Sochi	22 May
77.18	Gilles	Dupray	FRA	2.1.70	2		Sedan	30 May
77.18	Balázs	Kiss	HUN	21.3.72	1		Veszprém	22 Jul
76.94	Jüri	Tamm	EST	5.2.57	3		Rehlingen	31 May
76.92	Yuriy	Sedykh	RUS	11.6.55	1	ECP	Budapest	30 May
76.84	Norbert	Radefeld	GER	3.3.62	1		Rhede	6 Aug
76.50	Mikhail	Popel	BLS	25.5.66	3		Grodno	25 Jul
	(30)							
76.38	Pavel	Sedlácek	TCH	5.4.68	1		Praha	15 May
76.26	Benjaminas	Viluckis	LIT	20.3.61	1	EP/C2	København	13 Jun
76.24	Jaroslav	Chmyr	UKR	29.11.66	4		Kiev	15 May
76.14	Walter	Ciofani	FRA	17.2.62	3	NC	Annecy	23 Jul
76.12	Savas	Saritzoglou	GRE	19.7.71	1		Athinai	28 May
75.94	Frédéric	Kuhn	FRA	10.7.68	2		Sotteville	23 May
75.94	Karsten	Kobs	GER	16.9.71	2		Rhede	6 Aug
75.86	Alberto	Sánchez	CUB	3.2.73	1	NC	Habana	13 May
75.80	Iosif	Shaverdashvili	GEO	29.10.69	1		Tbilisi	27 May
75.76	Sergey	Gavrilov	RUS	22.5.70	6	Znam	Moskva	13 Jun
	(40)							
75.64	Andrey	Yevgenyev	RUS	9.7.73	1		Moskva	13 May
75.56.	Heinz	Weis	GER	14.7.63	1		Worms	25 Apr
75.36	Sean	Carlin	AUS	29.11.67	1		Auckland	30 Jan
75.18	Johann	Lindner	AUT	3.5.59	1		Hainfeld	23 Jun
74.76	Valeriy	Kocherga	UKR	12.9.63	5	NC	Kiev	3 Jul
74.74	Tore	Gustafsson	SWE	11.2.62	1		Helsingborg	4 Aug
74.62	Jörn	Hübner	GER	27.1.68	3		Rhede	6 Aug
74.60		Bi Zhong	CHN	5.9.68	1	EAsiG	Shanghai	15 May
74.52	Viktor	Baygush	UKR	16.12.63	4		Kiev	3 May
74.52	Andrey	Sukhanov	UKR	3.8.70	6	NC	Kiev	3 Jul
	(50)							
74.44	Mika	Laaksonen	FIN	21.3.68	1		Tucson	1 May
74.40	Lech	Kowalski	POL	17.1.61	1		Mielec	9 Jul
74.06	Emilio	Calabro'	ITA	4.2.69	1		Tirrenia	7 Mar
74.06	Dmitriy	Varich	UKR	28.2.72	2		Kiev	3 May
74.02	Hakim	Toumi	ALG	30.1.61	1		Alger	25 May
74.02	Donatas	Plunge	LIT	11.11.60	2	NC	Kaunas	20 Jun
73.98	Nicolas	Rougetet	FRA	27.7.70	2		Gueugnon	31 Jul

Mark	Name		Nat	Born	Pos	Meet	Venue	Date
73.78	József	Vida	HUN	9.1.63	3	NC	Budapest	6 Aug
73.52	Valeriy	Yevdokimov	RUS	73	2		Dzerzhinsk	29 Aug
73.50	Sergey	Vorobyov	RUS	29.1.64	1		Sankt Peterburg	21 Jul
	(60)							
73.44	Eladio	Hernández	CUB	18.2.63	1		Habana	13 Mar
73.44	Paul	Head	GBR	1.7.65	1		Corby	31 May
73.36	Per	Karlsson	SWE	21.4.67	2	MSR	Walnut	17 Apr
73.32	Jim	Driscoll	USA	15.8.65	Q	NC	Eugene	15 Jun
73.16	Andrés	Charadia	ARG	10.7.66	1		Santa Fé	19 Jun
73.16	Christos	Polichroniou	GRE	31.3.72	2		Iraklion	26 Jun
73.14	Vadim	Grabovoy	UKR	5.4.73	8		Kiev	3 May
73.10	Claus	Dethloff	GER	4.9.68	2		Halle	15 May
73.08	Lászlo	Rédei	HUN	17.7.70	1		Szombathely	26 May
72.92	Dmitriy	Marshin	BLS	24.2.72	2		Pinsk	6 Jul
	(70)							
72.80	Marko	Wahlman	FIN	6.4.69	1		Kangasala	5 Sep
72.72	Vadim	Khersontsev	RUS	8.7.74	3		Rostov na Donu	17 Jul
72.68	Sergey	Domrachov	UKR	27.3.68	9		Kiev	3 May
72.52	Jason	Byrne	GBR	9.9.70	1		London (Perivale)	19 Jun
72.42	Thomas	Neumann	GER	7.8.71	5		Rhede	6 Aug
72.38	Albert	Sinka	HUN	22.11.62	4	NC	Budapest	5 Aug
72.38	Kjell	Bystedt	SWE	24.5.60	3		Rimbo	21 Aug
72.36	Rumen	Koprivichin	BUL	2.10.62	1		Johannesburg	12 Jun
72.36	Giovanni	Sanguin	ITA	14.5.69	1		Padova	4 Jul
72.34	David	Chaussinand	FRA	19.4.73	2		Clermont-Ferrand	20 May
	(80)							
72.24	Nikolay	Lysenko	RUS	23.2.66	2		Stavropol	30 May
72.20	Nikolay	Davydov	RUS	70	2		Moskva	6 Aug
71.88	Marcel	Kunkel	GER	19.10.72	3		Halle	15 May
71.72	Taisto	Vierimaa	FIN	27.7.65	1		Alavieska	20 Jul
71.32	Sándor	Vörös	HUN	19.10.56	5	NC	Budapest	5 Aug
71.30	Stefan	Jönsson	SWE	14.2.64	1A		Rimbo	18 Aug
71.30	János	Verebes	HUN	25.2.69	4		Tapolca	21 Aug
71.26	Laurent	Bettolo	FRA	9.3.66	5		Reims	30 Jun
71.22	Vadim	Metla	RUS	73	3		Moskva	6 Aug
71.10	Vladimir	Bykov	RUS	70	1		Sochi	25 Apr
	(90)							
70.94	Samir	Haouam	ALG	68	2		Constantine	27 May
70.80	Sergey	Kochetkov	UKR	29.1.74	1		Yalta	23 Jan
70.78	Jean-Franc	Grégoire	FRA	10.3.68	3		Evreux	14 Jul
70.76	Nicola	Vizzoni	ITA	4.1.73	1		Alicante	7 Aug
70.74	Alexandros	Papadimitriou	GRE	18.6.73	1		El Paso	7 Dec
70.72	Jan	Bielecki	DEN	29.2.71	1		Athinai	1 Dec
70.70	Albert	Petukhov	UKR	5.3.74	2		Alushta	24 Apr
70.62	René	Diaz	CUB	13.1.67	1		Las Tunas	3 Apr
70.54	Stanislaw	Kapusta	POL	6.7.63	2	NC	Kielce	24 Jul
70.46	David	Smith	GBR	21.6.62	1		Hull	26 Jun
	(100)							

Mark	Name		Nat	Born	Date
70.44	Michael	Jones	GBR	63	21 May
70.34	Alex	Malachenko	BEL	67	19 Sep
70.28	Iannis	Milonas	GRE	71	28 May
70.22	Guillermo	Guzman	MEX	64	10 Jul
70.16	Vadim	Burakov	BLS	74	15 Jul
69.90	Yu Guangming		CHN	64	11 Apr
69.82	Paul	Carlin	AUS	70	18 Dec
69.80	Franck	Kuhn	FRA	65	15 May
69.76	Kevin	McMahon	USA	72	26 May
69.60	Bernard	Reibel	FRA	67	14 Jul
	(110)				
69.58	Kai	Maybach	GER	72	12 Jun
69.56		Li Jianhua	CHN	68	11 Apr
69.56	Vítor	Costa	POR	74	15 May
69.56	Jukka	Olkkonen	FIN	58	3 Jun
69.56	Loris	Paoluzzi	ITA	74	26 Oct
69.52	Arūnas	Medisauskas	LIT	70	3 Jun
69.46	Boris	Stoikos	CAN	69	2 Jun
69.40	Mario	Tschierschwitz	GER	62	26 Oct
69.38	Artyom	Rubanko	UKR	74	23 Jan
69.36	Raffaelle	Tomaino	ITA	62	11 Jul
	(120)				
69.26	Adrián	Annus	HUN	74	21 Oct
69.22	Alexander	Sporrer	GER	71	6 Jun
69.08	Holger	Klose	GER	72	3 Apr
69.02		Xu Weili	CHN	72	17 Apr
69.02	Achim	Strohschänk	GER	73	4 Sep
69.00	Scott	McGee	USA	68	15 May
69.00	Plamen	Minev	BUL	65	30 May

Unconfirmed: 71.84 ?Konstantin Vuychak UKR 72 2eB Odessa 21 May

Ancillary marks

Mark	Name	Date
80.92	Litvinov	13 Jun
80.84	Litvinov	13 Jun
80.56	Abduvaliyev	15 Aug
80.48	Litvinov	27 Jun
80.02	Astapkovich	5 Jun
79.98	Litvinov	27 Jun
79.88	Litvinov	27 Jun

JAVELIN

Mark	Name		Nat	Born	Pos	Meet	Venue	Date
95.66	Jan	Zelezny	TCH	16.6.66	1	McD	Sheffield	29 Aug
95.54		Zelezny			1		Pietersburg	6 Apr
91.40		Zelezny			1	BNP	Villeneuve d'Ascq	2 Jul
90.68		Zelezny			1	Nik	Nice	21 Jul
90.60		Zelezny			1		Stellenbosch	13 Apr
89.64		Zelezny			1	EP	Roma	27 Jun
88.90	Raymond	Hecht	GER	11.11.68	2	BNP	Villeneuve d'Ascq	2 Jul
88.36		Zelezny			1	Athl	Lausanne	7 Jul
88.28		Zelezny			1	GPF	London	10 Sep
88.26	Patrik	Bodén	SWE	30.6.67	1		Reykjavik	17 Jun
87.08		Zelezny			1	Slovn	Bratislava	1 Jun
86.94	Mike	Hill	GBR	22.10.64	1	NC	London	13 Jun
86.80		Zelezny			1	Toto	Fukuoka	18 Sep
86.78		Zelezny			1	TSB	London	23 Jul
86.48	Vladimir	Sasimovich	BLS	14.9.68	1		Kuortane	26 Jun
86.20	Andrey	Moruyev	RUS	8.5.70	1	CISM	Tours	28 Oct
86.16		Hecht			1		Hof	29 May
85.98		Zelezny			1	WC	Stuttgart	16 Aug
85.70	Andrey	Shevchuk	RUS	8.3.70	2	Slovn	Bratislava	1 Jun
85.70	Tom	Pukstys	USA	28.5.68	2		Kuortane	26 Jun
85.68	Seppo	Räty	FIN	27.4.62	1	NC	Mikkeli	1 Oct
85.66		Räty			1	Gold	Lahti	3 Jun
85.62		Hill			2	McD	Sheffield	29 Aug
85.32		Hecht			1		Luzern	29 Jun
85.10		Hill			1	v USA	Edinburgh	2 Jul
85.10	Steve	Backley (10)	GBR	12.2.69	2	TSB	London	23 Jul
84.96		Pukstys			3	TSB	London	23 Jul
84.84		Hecht			2	GPF	London	10 Sep
84.78	Kimmo	Kinnunen	FIN	31.3.68	2	WC	Stuttgart	16 Aug
84.74		Pukstys			1		København	25 Jul
	(30/11)							
84.58A	Tom	Petranoff	RSA	8.4.58	2		Pietersburg	6 Apr
84.58	Juha	Laukkanen	FIN	6.1.69	3		Kuortane	26 Jun
84.54	Gavin	Lovegrove	NZL	21.10.67	1		Wellington	20 Jan
84.36	Harri	Hakkarainen	FIN	16.10.69	1	v2N	Bondoufle	18 Sep
84.16	Peter	Borglund	SWE	29.1.64	1		Gävle	7 Jul
84.12	Boris	Henry	GER	14.12.73	1		Gengenbach	29 Aug
83.06	Ari	Pakarinen	FIN	14.5.69	Q	WC	Stuttgart	15 Aug
82.76		Zhang Lianbiao	CHN	25.1.69	Q	NC	Beijing	10 Jun
82.58	Dag	Wennlund	SWE	9.10.63	1		Karlskrona	28 Jul
	(20)							
82.38	Colin	Mackenzie	GBR	30.6.63	1		Edinburgh	7 Aug
82.20	Ivan	Mustapic	CRO	9.7.66	1		Zagreb	7 Jun
81.78	Marcis	Shtrobinders	LAT	12.6.66	1	NC	Riga	21 Jul
81.42	Vladimir	Ovchinnikov	RUS	2.8.70	3	Slovn	Bratislava	1 Jun
81.40	Yuriy	Rybin	RUS	5.6.63	1		Moskva	7 Aug
80.98	Terry	McHugh	IRL	22.8.63	1		Dublin	30 May
80.90	Phillip	Spies	RSA	21.5.70	1		Lindau	8 Aug
80.90	Donald	Sild	EST	3.10.68	1		Märjamaa	7 Sep
80.88	Dmitriy	Polyunin ¶	UZB	6.4.69	2		Caserta	6 Jun
80.76	Peter	Blank	GER	10.4.62	2		Halle	15 May
	(30)							
80.64	Vladimir	Parfyonov	UZB	17.6.70	1		Riga	29 May
	83.32	unconfirmed						
80.60	Sigurdur	Einarsson	ISL	28.9.62	1		Reykjavik	10 Aug
80.48	Andrew	Currey	AUS	7.2.71	6	TSB	London	23 Jul
80.46	Radoman	Scekic	YUG	1.10.67	1		Beograd	31 Jul
80.36	Ed	Kaminski	USA	26.3.68	2	vGBR	Edinburgh	2 Jul
80.32	Milos	Steigauf	TCH	5.2.69	1	v2N	Praha	17 Jun
80.30	Sami	Saksio	FIN	28.4.69	1		Karstula	11 Jun
80.18	Aleksey	Shchepin	RUS	3.4.72	3	NC	Moskva	19 Jun
80.08	Mika	Parviainen	FIN	19.12.70	4	Gold	Lahti	3 Jun
80.08	Marek	Kaleta	EST	17.12.61	2		Pärnu	31 Jul
	(40)							

Mark	Name		Nat	Born	Pos	Meet	Venue	Date
80.00	Vladimir	Ponomarenko	RUS	70	1		Stavropol	29 May
80.00	Alain	Storaci	FRA	5.6.67	6	Nik	Nice	21 Jul
80.00	Pascal	Lefèvre	FRA	25.1.65	1	NC	Annecy	24 Jul
79.64	Louis	Fouche	RSA	21.3.70	1	WUG	Buffalo	18 Jul
79.38	Andreas	Linden	GER	20.2.65	2		Mülheim-Kärlich	21 Aug
79.22	Stefan	König	GER	25.8.66	2		Kassel	26 May
79.20	Erik	Smith	USA	28.5.71	1	NCAA	New Orleans	4 Jun
79.06	Dainis	Küla	LAT	28.4.59	3		Pärnu	30 Jul
79.02	Fabio	De Gaspari	ITA	4.12.66	1	NC	Bologna	3 Aug
78.96	Mark	Roberson	GBR	13.3.67	2	AAA	Birmingham	17 Jul
	(50)							
78.88	Viktor	Zaitsev	UZB	6.6.66	6	BNP	Villeneuve d'Ascq	2 Jul
78.84	Jari	Hartikainen	FIN	28.4.67	2	CISM	Tours	28 Aug
78.60	Viktor	Yevsyukov	KZK	6.10.56	1	NC	Almaty	23 Jul
78.54A	Clinton	Lumsden	RSA	27.7.71	1		Boksburg	6 Feb
78.48	Vadim	Bavikin	ISR	4.10.70	4		Gengenbach	29 Aug
78.44	Konstantinos	Gatsioudis	GRE	17.12.73	1		Retinmo	22 May
78.34	Georgiy	Shapkin	RUS	30.8.66	2	Znam	Moskva	12 Jun
78.34	Ilkka	Kontinaho	FIN	16.9.64	2		Ruukki	15 Aug
78.26	Peter	Esenwein	GER	7.12.67	1		Konstanz	19 Jun
78.14	Rajmund	Kolko	POL	1.3.71	1	Kuso	Kielce	16 Jun
	(60)							
78.14	Mikko	Anttonen	FIN	5.7.63	1		Savonlinna	25 Jul
77.98	Milan	Stijepovic	SLO	8.3.68	1		Veszprém	22 Jul
77.74	Roald	Bradstock	GBR	24.4.62	1		Eagle Rock	8 May
77.70	Emil	Tsvetanov	BUL	14.3.63	1		Pleven	17 Jul
77.68	Brian	Keane	USA	5.4.70	3	DogwR	Knoxville	10 Apr
77.60	Tomasz	Damszel	POL	25.3.72	1	NC	Kielce	24 Jul
77.60	Miroslaw	Witek	POL	24.4.67	1		Bialogard	29 Sep
77.54	Mathias	Hold	GER	21.1.73	1		Moskva	24 Jul
77.54	Christian	Benninger	GER	15.3.71	5		Gengenbach	29 Aug
77.40	Vladimir	Novácek	TCH	23.8.68	2	v2N	Praha	17 Jun
	(70)							
77.38	Dariusz	Trafas	POL	5.6.72	1	SEC	Knoxville	15 May
77.30	Einar	Vilhjálmsson	ISL	1.6.60	8	TSB	London	23 Jul
77.22	Johan	van Lieshout	HOL	8.3.69	1		Diekirch	26 Jun
77.22	Ralf	Willinski	GER	20.9.67	4	NC	Duisburg	11 Jul
77.18	Constantin	Miclea	ROM	13.4.63	1		Bucuresti	29 May
77.18	Jens	Reimann	GER	21.3.69	1		Hamburg	4 Aug
76.88		Zhang Min	CHN	6.12.70	2	NC	Beijing	10 Jun
76.82	Juha	Karjailanen	FIN	5.7.62	1		Raahe	12 Aug
76.68A	Deon	Deetlefs	RSA	14.2.69	4		Pietersburg	6 Apr
76.66	Margus	Kübar	EST	31.1.71	2		Palafrugell	15 May
	(80)							
76.64	Julian	Sotelo	ESP	5.7.65	1		Getxo	8 May
76.60	Art	Skipper	USA	31.7.70	2	NC	Eugene	19 Jun
76.58	Kazuhiro	Mizoguchi	JPN	18.3.62	1		Toyonaka	25 Sep
76.50	Murray	Keen	AUS	17.5.65	1		Perth	7 Feb
76.46		Yang Hongtao ¶	CHN	.8.70	2	NG	Beijing	11 Sep
76.44	Jyrki	Blom	FIN	11.5.62	1		Kotka/Karhula	14 Jul
76.44	Marko	Hyytiäinen	FIN	27.11.66	1		Vantää	10 Aug
76.44		Tang Linhua	CHN	13.5.67	3	NG	Beijing	11 Sep
76.42		Guo Qiang	CHN	14.9.68	4	NG	Beijing	11 Sep
76.36	Andrey	Novikov	UKR	12.4.63	1	NC	Kiev	3 Jul
	(90)							
76.34		Li Rongxiang	CHN	.2.72	3	NC	Beijing	10 Jun
76.32		Sun Fei	CHN	24.1.68	5	NG	Beijing	11 Sep
76.24	Ari	Weckström	FIN	23.10.67	1		Saarijärvi	26 Jun
76.20	Rodrigo	Zelaya	CHI	12.6.68	1		Lubbock	16 Sep
76.10		Chen Junlin	CHN	31.5.67	6	NG	Beijing	11 Sep
76.08	Jarkko	Kinnunen	FIN	21.4.70	1eB		Pihtipudas	4 Jul
76.02	Joakim	Nilsson	SWE	30.3.71	4	NC	Kvarnsveden	24 Jul
75.92	Tero	Angeria	FIN	4.5.74	1		Pihtipudas	1 Jul
75.80	Tommi	Huotilainen	FIN	17.11.67	1		Hämeenlinna	8 Jul
75.80	Philippe	Lecurieux	FRA	22.5.58	2	NC	Annecy	24 Jul
	(100)							
75.80	Sulev	Lepik	EST	22.7.66	4		Pärnu	31 Jul

Mark	Name		Nat	Born	Date
75.78	Sergey	Makarov	RUS	73	12 Jun
75.76	Ville	Piippo	FIN	72	26 Sep
75.68	Nick	Batty	AUS	69	4 Sep
75.66	Oliver	Zschunke	GER	70	11 Jul
75.64	Mike	Barnett	USA	61	6 Jun
75.62	Hans	Schmidt	GER	69	15 May
75.60	Aleksandr	Fingert	ISR	65	10 Jul
75.58	Wang Wenzhong		CHN	67	15 Apr
75.58	Risto	Värttö	FIN	62	5 Jun
	(110)				
75.50	Tihomir	Mustapic	CRO	68	16 May
75.42	Kota	Suzuki	JPN	68	19 Sep
75.30	Garrett	Noel	USA	70	1 May
75.16	Andrzej	Antoniak	POL	72	16 Jun
75.12	John	Stapylton-Smith	NZL	61	7 Mar
75.12	Arndt	Pedersen	DEN	65	30 May
75.12	Jason	Bender	USA	60	30 Jul
75.06	Andrey	Maznichenko	UKR	66	3 Jul
75.02	Detlef	Michel	GER	55	21 Oct
74.92	Gary	Jensen	GBR	67	5 Jun
	(120)				
74.86	Ovidio	Trimino	CUB	69	12 May
74.82	Michel	Bertimon	FRA	57	24 Jul
74.72	Arne	Indrebø	NOR	69	1 Oct
74.72	Jean-Paul	Lakafia	FRA	61	9 Oct
74.58		Shi Dewu	CHN	75	2 May
74.58	Luis Carlos	Lucumi	COL	58	27 Nov
74.50	Nick	Nieland	GBR	72	3 May

Mark	Name		Nat	Born	Pos	Meet	Venue	Date
Indoors: 78.18	Aki	Parviainen	FIN	26.10.74	1		Kuopio	7 Mar
Extra trial: 80.06	Marko	Hyytiäinen	FIN	66	-		Helsinki (zoo)	2 Aug
Questionable marks								
79.22	Art	Skipper	USA	31.7.70	1		Eugene	16 Jul
74.78 ?	Ty	Sevin	USA		1		Houston	11 Jun
Disqualified for failing drugs test								
83.38dq	Dmitriy	Polyunin	UZB	6.4.69	-	WC	Stuttgart	16 Aug

Ancillary marks

Mark	Name	Date	Mark	Name	Date	Mark	Name	Date
95.34	Zelezny	29 Aug	87.58	Zelezny	10 Sep	86.08	Zelezny	10 Sep
89.88	Zelezny	21 Jul	87.06	Zelezny	29 Aug	85.90	Zelezny	1 Jun
89.74	Zelezny	27 Jun	86.94	Bodén	17 Jun	85.68	Zelezny	21 Jul
89.54	Zelezny	27 Jun	86.52	Zelezny	21 Jul	85.64	Zelezny	1 Jun
89.02	Zelezny	29 Aug	86.42	Zelezny	10 Sep	85.30	Zelezny	13 Apr
88.52	Zelezny	21 Jul	86.28	Zelezny	23 Jul	85.14	Zelezny	18 Sep
87.82	Zelezny	10 Sep	86.16	Zelezny	1 Jun	84.98	Zelezny	7 Jul

35 LB WEIGHT

Mark	Name		Nat	Born	Pos	Meet	Venue	Date
25.41	Lance	Deal	USA	21.8.61	1		Azusa	20 Feb
22.58i	Lou	Chisari	USA	10.10.68	1		Boston	16 Jan
21.84i	Marko	Wahlman	FIN	6.4.69	1	NCAA	Indianapolis	13 Mar
21.80i	Ron	Willis	USA	6.12.71	1		Lincoln	12 Feb
21.65i	Jim	Driscoll	USA	15.8.65	3		Cambridge	23 Jan
21.24i	Kevin	McMahon	USA	26.5.72	1		Ithaca	16 Jan
21.15i	Boris	Stoikos	CAN	9.10.69	3	NCAA	Indianapolis	13 Mar

PENTATHLON

Mark						Name		Nat	Born	Pos	Venue	Date
3921	7.30	60.18	22.45	44.52	4:36.97	Steve	Fritz	USA	1.11.67	1	Dallas	5 Apr
3848	7.07	56.94	22.58	47.44	4:39.55	Rob	Muzzio	USA	25.6.64	2	Dallas	5 Apr
3825	7.29	59.74	22.57	43.82	4:46.77	Sheldon	Blockburger	USA	19.9.64	3	Dallas	5 Apr
3763	7.03	58.30	22.58	44.32	4:44.68	Frank	Müller	GER	18.6.68	1	Zeven	12 Sep
3693	7.03	58.48	22.8w	40.80	4:37.8	Gerald	Bayer	GER	4.1.70	1	Treuchtlingen	26 Sep
3691	5.91	57.64	22.0	43.28	4:17.1	Roland	Clauss	GER	16.4.70	1	Obertshausen	8 May
3641	6.47	56.86	22.3	38.52	4:22.4	Alexander	Clauss	GER	16.4.70	2	Obertshausen	8 May
3638	6.73	61.50	23.25	38.52	4:32.10	Frank	Blasey	GER	.70	2	Zeven	12 Sep
3611	6.54	55.08	22.96	43.42	4:34.78	Kip	Janvrin	USA	8.7.65	4	Dallas	5 Apr
3598	6.64	52.54	22.4	39.10	4:25.1	Tapio	Linnemöller	GER	31.12.71	1	Herford	1 May
3548	7.13	52.42	22.40	42.88	5:08.31	Chris	Wilcox	USA	6.1.68	5	Dallas	5 Apr
3544	6.77	59.82	23.47	35.52	4:31.56	Jörg	Neblung	GER	.67	3	Zeven	12 Sep
3537	6.83	52.44	23.33	37.94	4:27.56	Thomas	Stewens	GER	10.9.66	1	Vaterstetten	28 Aug
3532	6.97	53.54	22.96	36.96	4:38.10	Mike	Maczey	GER	28.9.72	1	Wuppertal	20 Jul
3503	6.76	79.26	24.3	42.64	5:39.9	Boris	Henry	GER	14.12.73	1	Ludweiler	3 Oct
3489	6.52	56.84	23.64	46.76	4:58.64	Norbert	Demmel	GER	10.5.63	2	Vaterstetten	28 Aug

DECATHLON

Mark	Name		Nat	Born	Pos	Meet	Venue	Date
8817	Dan	O'Brien	USA	18.7.66	1	WC	Stuttgart	20 Aug
	10.57/0.9	7.99/0.4	15.41 2.03	47.46		14.08/0.0	47.92 5.20 62.56	4:40.08
8724	Eduard	Hämäläinen	BLS	21.1.69	2	WC	Stuttgart	20 Aug
	10.72/-0.9	7.05/0.0	15.49 2.09	47.64		13.57/0.0	49.26 5.30 61.88	4:39.34
8604		Hämäläinen			1		Götzis	30 May
	10.74/-0.3	7.67w/2.1	15.99 2.08	47.41		13.65/0.0	45.20 4.80 59.98	4:42.82
8548	Paul	Meier	GER	27.7.71	3	WC	Stuttgart	20 Aug
	10.57/0.9	7.57/1.1	15.45 2.15	47.73		14.63/0.0	45.72 4.60 61.22	4:32.05

Mark Name Nat Born Pos Meet Venue Date

8500 Christian Schenk GER 9.2.65 4 WC Stuttgart 20 Aug
11.22/-0.9 7.63/0.0 15.72 2.15 48.78 15.29/0.0 46.94 4.80 65.32 4:24.44
8460 Meier 2 Götzis 30 May
10.53/1.9 7.86/1.6 15.41 2.08 47.36 14.39/0.4 44.18 4.50 60.52 4:44.42
8444 Alain Blondel FRA 7.12.62 5 WC Stuttgart 20 Aug
10.94/-0.9 7.20/0.1 14.06 1.94 48.12 14.40/0.0 45.74 5.40 62.22 4:19.89
8398 Christian Plaziat FRA 28.10.63 6 WC Stuttgart 20 Aug
10.80/-0.9 7.50/0.6 14.47 2.09 47.91 14.36/0.0 41.74 5.00 56.96 4:26.31
8366 Meier 1 EP/A Oulu 11 Jul
10.96/ 7.95w/ 15.52 2.10 47.42 14.67/ 47.04 4.40 54.82 4:36.37
8362 Mike Smith CAN 16.9.67 3 Götzis 30 May
10.87/-0.3 7.76/1.7 15.30 2.05 48.25 14.72/0.0 46.80 4.60 66.44 4:52.38

8331 O'Brien 1 NC Eugene 17 Jun
10.72/ 7.54/ 15.81 2.09 48.62 14.01/ 43.84 5.05 57.98 5:09.41
8324 Steve Fritz USA 1.11.67 7 WC Stuttgart 20 Aug
10.83/0.9 7.52/0.8 13.87 2.03 48.40 13.99/0.0 41.62 4.90 57.68 4:23.56
8320 Gernot Kellermayr ¶ AUT 5.4.66 4 Götzis 30 May
10.47/1.9 7.66/1.3 14.83 1.96 47.56 14.12/0.4 42.50 5.00 58.24 4:54.78
8317 Fritz 1 Decast Talence 11 Sep
10.98/-0.6 7.57/0.5 13.68 2.06 49.69 14.21/-0.3 44.32 5.00 62.62 4:34.50
8297 Vitaliy Kolpakov (10) UKR 2.2.72 1 Kiev 6 Jun
10.97 7.40 15.19 2.12 47.83 14.33 46.16 4.40 57.68 4:32.20
8296 Sheldon Blockburger USA 19.9.64 1 Brescia 16 May
10.80/0.6 7.48/-0.0 14.98 2.12 49.12 14.34/1.1 42.74 4.70 60.90 4:40.08
8277 Plaziat 2 EP/A Oulu 11 Jul
11.09/ 7.52w/ 14.51 2.04 48.38 14.50/ 46.26 5.00 56.16 4:35.21
8237 Rob Muzzio USA 25.6.64 8 WC Stuttgart 20 Aug
11.11/-0.9 6.72/-0.2 16.99 1.94 49.82 14.51/0.0 47.90 5.00 64.50 4:34.43
8234 Plaziat 2 Decast Talence 11 Sep
11.06/-0.6 7.59/0.4 15.38 2.06 48.71 14.42/-0.3 40.64 4.90 56.36 4:33.58
8204 Blondel 3 EP/A Oulu 11 Jul
11.34/ 7.19/ 13.15 1.98 48.79 14.51/ 43.16 5.20 63.96 4:19.00

8188 Robert Zmelík TCH 18.4.69 5 Götzis 30 May
10.75/1.9 7.64w/3.2 14.00 1.99 48.94 13.98/0.4 42.48 4.90 58.72 4:49.17
8176w Fritz 2 NC Eugene 16 Jun
10.80/ 7.38/ 13.65 2.00 49.41 14.03W/5.1 43.00 4.85 61.28 4:37.89
8162 Kolpakov 3 Decast Talence 11 Sep
11.24/-0.6 7.41/-0.6 14.52 2.09 48.73 14.65/-0.3 46.88 4.80 59.36 4:45.74
8156 Lev Lobodin UKR 1.4.69 6 Götzis 30 May
10.82/-0.4 7.43w/2.2 14.74 1.99 48.63 14.05/0.4 43.04 4.90 54.32 4:42.85
8146 Mikhail Medved UKR 30.1.64 7 Götzis 30 May
11.16/-0.4 7.14w/4.0 16.21 2.20 49.94 14.38/1.4 50.82 4.90 55.66 4:52.33
8143 Blondel 4 Decast Talence 11 Sep
11.13/-0.6 7.43/-0.5 13.02 2.00 49.12 14.56/-0.3 40.70 5.10 59.68 4:20.21
8109 Schenk 1 NC Vaterstetten 20 Jun
11.29/0.9 7.19/-3.2 14.30 2.21 49.98 15.50/-0.2 47.54 4.60 61.88 4:33.35
8107 Plaziat 8 Götzis 30 May
10.85/1.9 7.30w/3.6 14.35 2.08 48.67 14.18/0.4 44.72 4.60 52.80 4:38.54
8101 Dezsö Szabó HUN 4.9.67 2 Brescia 16 May
11.10/0.6 7.07/ 13.82 2.00 48.54 14.66/1.1 40.16 5.20 59.02 4:25.20
8076 Petri Keskitalo FIN 10.3.67 4 Oulu 11 Jul
11.18/-2.3 7.65/1.3 14.83 1.95 49.76 14.59/-1.4 44.98 4.80 65.74 4:56.52
(30/17)
8075 Michael Kohnle GER 3.5.70 9 WC Stuttgart 20 Aug
11.16/-0.3 7.40/0.9 14.34 2.00 50.17 14.51/-0.1 44.70 5.00 62.10 4:47.95
8074 Torsten Voss GER 24.3.63 2 NC Vaterstetten 20 Jun
10.97/0.2 7.00/-2.1 15.92 1.94 49.59 14.38/-0.2 43.34 4.90 59.42 4:37.48
8061 Stefan Schmid GER 6.5.70 1 Aachen 8 Aug
10.97/ 7.24/ 13.25 1.94 48.70 15.19/ 40.74 4.90 69.98 4:30.66
(20)
8054 Tomás Dvorák TCH 11.5.72 1 CISM Tours 30 Aug
10.97/ 7.49/ 15.06 1.95 48.66 14.26/ 41.56 4.50 60.88 4:40.13
8052 Kip Janvrin USA 8.7.65 2 Aachen 8 Aug
11.31/ 6.78/ 14.22 1.91 48.90 14.79/ 45.70 5.00 61.54 4:16.00
8013w Aric Long USA 15.4.70 6 NC Eugene 16 Jun
11.23/ 7.10/ 14.78 2.12 50.23 14.52w/ 44.94 4.65 59.06 4:41.90

Mark	Name		Nat	Born	Pos	Meet	Venue	Date
8007	Chris	Huffins	USA	15.4.70	1	NCAA	New Orleans	5 Jun
	10.40w/	7.99w/	14.13 1.83	48.23		14.50/	46.26 4.10 57.66 4:51.20	
7995	Munehiro	Kaneko	JPN	6.6.68	1	EAsiG	Shanghai	14 May
	11.23/	7.27/	13.48 2.02	49.61		14.43/	45.80 4.90 60.24 4:47.90	
7986	Alex	Kruger	GBR	18.11.63	1		Alhama	2 May
	11.30/0.2	7.24/1.8	14.28 2.17	50.47		15.17/0.9	45.06 4.70 56.12 4:33.27	
7985	Thorsten	Dauth	GER	11.3.68	3	NC	Vaterstetten	20 Jun
	10.77/0.2	7.03/-4.4	15.80 2.06	48.89		14.63/-0.2	46.98 4.30 55.48 4:50.97	
7982w	Darrin	Steele	USA	20.3.69	1		Knoxville	24 May
7966	Indrek	Kaseorg	EST	16.12.67	1	NC	Pärnu	30 May
	11.24/-0.6	7.23/0.9	13.13 2.03	49.26		14.51/0.6	40.58 4.60 59.72 4:18.53	
7965	Henrik	Dågard	SWE	7.8.69	10		Götzis	30 May
	10.83/1.9	7.09w/2.5	14.25 1.84	48.08		14.69/0.6	43.34 4.80 68.08 4:54.42	
	(30)							
7944	Simon	Shirley	GBR	3.8.66	1		Azusa	10 Jun
	11.06w/	7.18w/3.4	12.38 2.09	49.90		15.12/	39.70 4.70 65.00 4:24.70	
7935w	Drew	Fucci	USA	26.5.67	7	NC	Eugene	16 Jun
	11.06	7.29	12.54 1.97	48.93				
7918w	Ronald	Blums	LAT	1.3.70	2	NCAA	New Orleans	5 Jun
	11.12w/	7.34w/	12.90 2.09	50.32		14.61/	41.28 4.80 57.22 4:32.89	
7912	Aleksandr	Zhdanovich	BLS	15.11.69	1		Minsk	5 Jun
	10.5/1.2	7.05/0.6	13.23 1.96	49.7		14.9/0.0	40.04 5.00 58.94 4:27.3	
7902	Yevgeniy	Dudakov	RUS	69	1		Krasnodar	19 May
	11.05/	7.41/	13.45 2.04	51.88		15.18/	46.76 5.10 50.80 4:39.68	
7889	Eugenio	Balanque	CUB	20.12.68	1	CAG	Ponce	24 Nov
	11.04/	7.16/	13.77 2.00	48.48		14.68/	43.28 4.64 57.90 4:44.46	
7886	Andrey	Kotsyubenko	RUS	3.1.70	1	NC	Moskva	19 Jun
	11.11/	7.18/	13.97 2.05	50.04		15.15/	43.76 4.60 58.10 4:31.97	
7883	Marcel	Dost	HOL	28.9.69	1		Helmond	12 Sep
	11.08/	7.12w/	13.30 2.00	49.43		14.67/	39.02 5.05 55.00 4:30.09	
7874	Sebastien	Levicq	FRA	25.6.71	1	WUG	Buffalo	18 Jul
	11.22/	6.99/	12.87 1.98	51.48		14.96/	41.14 5.10 63.46 4:23.74	
7871	Katsuhiko	Matsuda	JPN	10.5.65	2	NC	Tokyo	12 Jun
	10.87	7.40	12.59 1.96	48.80		14.46	38.06 4.80 57.06 4:35.71	
	(40)							
7871w/7839	Ubaldo	Ranzi	ITA	18.7.70	1	NC	Bologna	3 Aug
	10.96/	7.25W/5.5 (7.12)...13.01	2.00	48.87		14.94/	41.12 4.80 56.74 4:35.85	
7866	Sándor	Munkácsi	HUN	24.7.69	5		Brescia	16 May
	11.26/0.6	7.17/0.5	13.81 1.94	49.31		14.54/1.1	42.34 4.80 54.30 4:25.21	
7862w	Doug	Pirini	NZL	6.9.69	1		Auckland	10 Jan
	10.81w/3.1	7.49W/4.2	12.27 1.84	48.48		14.72w/2.7	43.50 4.80 53.52 4:29.68	
7831	Derek	Huff	USA	26.11.66	8	NC	Eugene	16 Jun
	11.03	7.15	15.25 2.00	50.84				
7829	William	Motti	FRA	25.7.64	13		Götzis	30 May
	11.56/1.4	7.00w/2.3	15.02 2.11	51.08		15.30/0.6	47.76 4.80 64.54 5:07.09	
7824		Cai Min	CHN	8.5.68	2	EAsiG	Shanghai	14 May
	10.68	7.79	14.28 1.93	49.32		14.36	41.10 4.80 51.98 4:55.22	
7821	Igor	Matsanov	BLS	13.4.70	1		Grodno	Jul
7813	Mirko	Spada	SUI	26.1.69	1	NC	Hochdorf	26 Jun
	11.48/0.5	6.91/1.9	14.53 1.92	50.22		14.32/1.6	43.68 4.70 58.78 4:28.48	
7809w	Ricky	Barker	USA	14.11.69	3		Austin	1 Apr
7800	Ruben	van Balen	HOL	27.1.71	1	NC	Emmen	6 Jun
	11.42/	7.00/	14.96 1.87	48.71		15.26/	45.38 4.50 58.64 4:22.01	
	(50)							
7787	Brian	Taylor	GBR	13.8.70	2		Emmelshausen	30 May
	10.35/1.4	7.37/-0.7	13.83 1.85	48.10		14.15/1.5	40.56 5.00 52.30 5:26.43	
7780		Guo Jin	CHN	29.7.70	1	NG	Beijing	10 Sep
	11.02/	7.43/	14.42 1.99	51.15		14.73/	44.16 4.20 58.24 4:40.05	
7767	Aleksandr	Bogdanov	UKR	29.4.70	2	NC	Kiev	6 Jun
	10.88/	7.23/	12.93 2.00	48.48		14.25/	39.32 4.20 54.99 4:32.23	
7764	Mikko	Valle	FIN	11.5.70	1	NC	Mikkeli	31 Jul
	11.08/1.1	7.02/1.0	12.88 1.93	49.14		15.26/0.2	38.46 5.05 66.90 4:48.37	
7749A	Raúl	Duany	CUB	4.1.75	1	CAC	Cali	31 Jul
	11.3	7.27	12.92 2.04	49.2		14.6	37.02 4.40 59.02 4:31.5	

Mark	Name		Nat	Born	Pos	Meet	Venue	Date
7748	Eric	Hollingsworth	GBR	6.12.62	2	vIT,TCH	Alzano	30 May
	11.02/1.1	7.01/ 13.98 1.92 49.58 15.26/-0.7 47.08 4.70 56.76 4:45.20						
7744	Andrey	Chernyavskiy	RUS	2.8.70	3		Krasnodar	19 May
	11.20/	7.15/ 13.50 1.97 49.67 14.66/ 39.80 5.00 48.04 4:28.91						
7744	Christian	Mandrou	FRA	24.6.65	14		Götzis	30 May
	11.16/-0.4	7.27/-0.2 12.95 1.96 48.59 14.76/0.0 39.26 4.30 62.32 4:33.08						
7742	Udo	Jacobasch	GER	30.8.70	3		Emmelshausen	30 May
	10.99/1.4	7.00/-0.3 14.05 1.97 50.25 14.67/1.5 43.24 4.80 55.00 4:49.37						
7738	Antonio	Peñalver	ESP	1.12.68	9	EP/A	Oulu	11 Jul
	11.34/	6.84/ 15.81 1.98 50.16 14.85/ 46.78 4.50 55.00 4:45.05						
	(60)							
7736w	Matt	Shelton	USA	3.6.69	3	NCAA	New Orleans	5 Jun
	10.67/	7.47W 12.18 2.04 47.78 14.40/ 38.14 4.10 51.42 4:38.37						
7734	Frank	Müller	GER	18.6.68	5	NC	Vaterstetten	20 Jun
	10.91/0.2	7.12/-2.1 13.99 2.00 48.94 15.17/-0.2 42.70 4.40 58.46 4:49.56						
7734	Ramil	Ganiyev	UZB	23.9.68	15=	WC	Stuttgart	20 Aug
	11.09/0.9	7.26/0.1 14.07 2.03 49.80 14.64/0.0 39.78 5.10 43.00 4:45.15						
7733	Rob	Pendergist	USA	12.7.70	1	FlaR	Gainesville	26 Mar
7719	Nikolay	Afanasyev	RUS	11.8.65	1		Voronezh	25 Jul
	11.64/	7.09/ 13.50 2.09 51.23 15.20/ 42.60 4.70 61.36 4:37.31						
7713	Jim	Stevenson	GBR	31.12.71	4	NCAA	New Orleans	5 Jun
	10.99w/	7.32/ 12.86 2.01 48.27 15.12/ 36.18 4.20 55.18 4:17.31						
7707	René	Schmidheiny	SUI	4.1.67	2	NC	Hochdorf	26 Jun
	11.48/0.5	7.17/0.5 15.90 1.92 52.52 15.00/1.6 47.22 4.40 66.50 4:55.20						
7704		Gong Guohua	CHN	2.1.64	2	NG	Beijing	10 Sep
	11.26/	7.50 14.73 1.93 52.80 15.40/ 46.48 4.80 62.18 5:03.01						
7702w	Tommy	Richards	USA	14.7.70	5	NCAA	New Orleans	5 Jun
7699	Rojs	Piziks	LAT	12.2.71	1		Priekuli	13 Jun
	11.2/	6.94/ 14.50 2.10 52.7 15.4/ 43.28 4.50 63.68 4:31.7						
	(70)							
7697	Helge	Günther	GER	10.4.69	7		Aachen	8 Aug
	11.22/	7.27/ 13.92 1.91 49.08 15.05/ 44.60 4.50 55.96 4:42.66						
7691	Viktor	Radchenko	UKR	11.5.68	15		Götzis	30 May
	11.77/1.4	6.99/2.0 14.81 1.99 51.93 14.72/1.4 42.98 5.00 63.50 4:57.78						
7686	Matt	Zuber	USA	30.9.66	1		Santa Barbara	17 May
7686	Grzegorz	Strominski	POL	19.5.70	1	NC	Kielce	13 Jun
	11.30	6.87 13.48 1.95 49.76 15.06 38.02 4.50 65.48 4:24.61						
7678		Lee Fu-an	TPE	4.6.64	3	EAsiG	Shanghai	14 May
	11.05	7.37 14.07 2.03 49.80 14.64 39.78 5.10 43.00 4:45.15						
7671	Enoch	Borozinski	USA	72	2		Santa Barbara	17 May
7667	Erwin	Reiterer	AUT	29.12.70	16		Götzis	30 May
	11.13w/2.1	7.35w/2.3 15.15 2.08 52.63 14.52/0.6 42.12 4.20 65.10 5:18.37						
7664	Enno	Tjepkema	HOL	5.6.65	3	NC	Emmen	6 Jun
	11.36/	6.99/ 14.04 1.96 50.51 15.04/ 38.18 4.40 68.08 4:34.13						
7659		Guo Zhengrong	CHN	20.4.72	1		Chengdu	17 Apr
	10.85/	7.20 13.51 1.94 50.00 15.14/ 43.24 4.70 57.14 4:59.39						
7650	Thomas	Görz	GER	10.3.72	1		Kreutzal	9 May
	11.09w/	7.63/ 14.40 1.84 49.60 15.99/ 43.82 4.70 49.70 4:34.52						
	(80)							
7647	David	Bigham	GBR	4.7.71	2		Alzano	30 May
	11.24/1.1	7.03/0.2 11.90 1.95 48.69 14.96/0.3 39.16 4.60 60.66 4:30.08						
7641		Zhao Bingchun	CHN	70	3	NG	Beijing	10 Sep
	11.11/	6.88 14.64 1.90 50.19 14.90/ 41.96 4.80 54.54 4:41.11						
7633	Miguel	Valle	CUB	29.9.68	3	Barr	Habana	23 May
	11.00/	7.01 13.86 1.85 50.37 14.75 38.54 4.70 60.62 4:38.93						
7630	Oleg	Urmakayev	RUS	14.1.65	4		Krasnodar	19 May
	11.73/	7.45/ 14.23 2.18 50.94 15.10/ 39.54 4.30 52.68 4:37.83						
7629	Dusán	Kovács	HUN	31.7.71	6	EP/B	Valladolid	11 Jul
	11.04/2.0	7.32/2.0 12.09 1.95 47.92 15.01/0.8 37.48 4.30 54.76 4:24.67						
7623	Peter	Neumaier	GER	30.6.67	7	NC	Vaterstetten	20 Jun
	10.90/0.9	6.86/-3.4 13.15 2.06 47.66 15.81/-0.2 36.20 4.40 56.52 4:23.52						
7621	Paul	Foxson	USA	16.4.71	2	FlaR	Gainesville	26 Mar

Mark	Name		Nat	Born	Pos	Meet	Venue	Date
7618	Pierre Alexandre	Vial	FRA	25.5.75	1		Versailles	27 Jun
	10.91 7.15 12.12 1.89 48.32 14.92 42.50 4.60 53.32 4:41.47							
7617w	Chris	Wilcox	USA	6.1.68	10	NC	Eugene	16 Jun
	10.75 6.98 14.53 2.00 49.32							
7614	Xavier	Brunet	ESP	5.2.71	1		Barcelona	31 Jul
	11.33/ 6.91/ 12.86 2.10 48.87 14.80/ 40.40 4.60 49.22 4:37.42							
	(90)							
7608	Sebastian	Chmara	POL	21.11.71	2	NC	Kielce	13 Jun
	11.36 7.38 14.26 1.98 50.54 14.88 36.86 4.70 51.46 4:35.64							
7607	Andrey	Nazarov	EST	9.1.65	3		Alhama	2 May
	11.14/-0.2 7.10/1.3 13.20 2.08 55.14 14.52/0.9 40.82 4.70 56.84 4:38.32							
7601	Oleg	Veretnikov	UZB	22.1.72	1	AsiC	Manila	4 Dec
	11.13/0.6 7.05/ 12.60 1.94 48.98 15.04/0.1 36.24 4.50 60.48 4:29.12							
7600	Peter	Winter	AUS	17.1.71	1	NC	Brisbane	9 Mar
	10.92/ 7.66/ 11.97 2.03 48.88 14.58/ 35.56 4.50 55.84 5:04.66							
7594	Dirk	Pajonk	GER	27.3.69	18		Götzis	30 May
	10.90/-0.3 7.13/0.8 13.77 1.93 48.68 14.90/1.4 37.80 4.40 50.72 4:33.15							
7588	Alvaro	Burrell	ESP	29.4.69	14	EP/A	Oulu	11 Jul
	11.18/ 6.57/ 13.81 1.95 47.68 14.83/ 44.12 4.30 47.56 4:24.65							
7585		Kim Tae-keun	KOR	71				
7576	Lawrence	Johnson	USA	7.5.74	1	SEC	Knoxville	14 May
	11.23 6.72 11.85 1.99 49.55 14.60 36.18 5.50 52.36 4:50.53							
7571	Rick	Schwieger	USA	17.6.69	1	MSR	Azusa	15 Apr
7570	Mário	Aníbal Ramos	POR	25.3.72	1		Lisboa	2 May
	11.34/ 6.75 14.50 2.07 50.33 14.94 41.88 4.31 52.94 4:35.93							
	(100)							

Mark	Name		Nat	Born	Date
7564	Mike	Bennett	USA	68	7 May
7553	Gerald	Bayer	GER	70	19 Sep
7541	Dmitriy	Sukhomazov	BLS	71	5 Jun
7535	Kim Tae-keun		KOR	71	14 May
7534	Christer	Holger	SWE	74	30 Jul
7531	Krasimir	Pethlichki	BUL	71	8 Aug
7527	Norbert	Demmel	GER	63	20 Jun
7527	Christian	Savoia	GER	72	8 Oct
7524	Anthony	Ott	HOL	69	6 Jun
7524	Wilfrid	Boulineau	FRA	70	27 Jun
	(110)				
7520	David	Cook	CAN	72	21 Apr
7519		Wei Wenhua	CHN	72	10 Sep
7517	Jarkko	Finni	FIN	72	13 Jun
7512	Mario	Sategna	USA	72	5 Jun
7512	Mike	Maczey	GER	72	20 Jun
7511	Matt	Dallow	NZL	72	15 Apr
7507	Kamil	Damasek	TCH	73	13 Jun
7501	Adonis	Keros	GRE	67	8 Oct
7500	Vitaliy	Nagubniy	RUS	73	19 May
7497	Terry	Simpson	USA	70	7 May
	(120)				
7494	Luciano	Asta	ITA	69	3 Aug
7493	Aleksandr	Dimov	RUS	73	19 Jun
7493	Beniamino	Poserina	ITA	70	3 Aug
7489	Takashi	Kiyokawa	JPN	69	14 May
7483w	Les	Kuorikoski	AUS	74	15 Aug
7482	Karl	Bertrandt	SWE	68	19 May
7477	Francisco J	Benet	ESP	68	6 Jun
7476	Jamel	Bourmada	FRA	71	27 Jun
7474	Nikolay	Sherin	RUS	69	19 May
7474	Shawn	Wilbourn	USA	67	31 Jul
	(130)				
7471w	Steve	Rowland	USA	69	24 May
7465	Bill	Schuffenhaur	USA	73	19 May
7465	Iwan	Brunner	SUI	69	6 Jun
7462	Savvas	Stafilidis	GRE	71	28 May
7459	Brendan	Tennant	AUS	72	9 Mar
7456w	Anthony	Brannen	GBR	68	2 May
7451	Robert	Wärff	SWE	70	13 Jun
7451	Cedric	Lopez	FRA	73	27 Jun
7440	Bobby	Tonker	USA	71	14 May
7439	Roland	Clauss	GER	70	29 Aug
	(140)				
7438	Jerome	Coyco	FRA	66	8 Aug
7435w	Todd	Lockwood	USA	72	20 May
7435	Pekka	Lahtinen	FIN	70	31 Jul
7433w	Paul	Jeffery	AUS	74	9 Mar
7432	Ivan	Babiy	UKR	63	6 Jun
7430	Zhang Hongxin		CHN	72	13 Jun
7428	Guido	Einbergs	LAT	71	9 Aug
7428	Thomas	Stewens	GER	66	20 May
7531	Krasimir	Petlichki	BUL	71	8 Aug
7425	Erkki	Nool	EST	70	2 May
	(150)				
7425	Maxwell	Seales	STL	70	19 May
7420	Jean-Bernard	Royer	FRA	62	16 May
7415	Glenn	Håkansson	SWE	66	5 Sep
7413	Yuriy	Baranovskiy	BLS	71	5 Jul
7412	José	Roman	PUR		17 Oct
7410		Zhao Feng	CHN	68	10 Sep
7410w	José A	Ureña	ESP	67	6 Jun
7405	Tarmo	Adamberg	EST	67	30 May
7400	Brad	Swanson	USA		25 Mar

Best low altitude

Mark	Name		Nat	Born	Pos	Meet	Venue	Date
7715		Duany			2	CAG	Ponce	24 Nov
	11.44/ 7.55/ 12.55 2.03 49.20 15.28/ 36.52 4.14 66.08 4:24.11							

Best marks without wind assistance

Mark	Name		Nat	Born	Pos	Meet	Venue	Date
7918		Fucci			4		Brescia	16 May
	11.12/0.6 7.40/0.5 12.82 2.03 49.48 14.40/1.1 39.34 5.00 59.44 4:47.46							
7839	*see above*	Ranzi			*	NC	Bologna	3 Aug

Mark	Name		Nat	Born	Pos	Meet	Venue	Date
7813		Pirini			*		Auckland	10 Jan
	10.81w/3.1 7.49W/4.2 12.27 1.84 48.48				14.72w/2.7 43.50 4.80 53.52 4:29.68			
7754	Aric	Long			6		Aachen	8 Aug
7734		Blums			16	WC	Stuttgart	20 Aug
	11.32/-0.3 7.15/0.4 12.96 1.97 50.55				14.67/-0.3 39.12 5.00 57.16 4:33.59			
7653		Steele			3	WUG	Buffalo	17 Jul
	10.88/ 7.21/ 13.57 1.89 48.98				14.46/ 41.62 4.40 56.98 4:54.09			

Best auto timed performance: 7507 Sukhomazov11 Jul
Uncoonfirmed: 7755u Oleg Veretlnikov UZB

One Hour Decathlon

Mark	Name		Nat	Born	Pos	Meet	Venue	Date
7652	Vitaliy	Kolpakov	UKR	2.2.72	1		Ostrava	24 Sep 93
	11.00/-0.7 7.42/+0.3 15.32 2.08 55.64				14.97/-1.7 42.06 4.70 60.02 5:07.95			
7634	William	Motti	FRA	25.7.64	2		Ostrava	24 Sep 93
	11.59/-0.7 7.18/+0.3 15.40 2.10 58.60				16.28/-1.7 50.40 4.70 71.46 5:13.35			
7591	Steve	Fritz	USA	1.11.67	3		Ostrava	24 Sep 93
	11.15/-1.7 7.12/+0.7 13.89 1.95 54.88				14.88/0.2 45.46 4.90 62.60 5:03.37			
7433	Kip	Janvrin	USA	8.7.65	4		Ostrava	24 Sep 93
	11.30/-1.9 6.78/-0.1 13.57 1.91 54.38				15.28/-1.2 41.50 4.70 62.36 4:33.23			
7187	Valter	Külvet	EST	19.2.64	1		Tallinn	5 Aug 93
	11.50 6.90 14.68 1.93 53.0415.66 48.60 4.00 56.24 5:02.87							

4 x 100 METRES RELAY

Mark	Team	Pos	Meet	Venue	Date
37.40	USA Drummond, Cason, D.Mitchell, L.Burrell	1s1	WC	Stuttgart	21 Aug
37.48	USA Drummond, Cason, D.Mitchell, L.Burrell	1	WC	Stuttgart	22 Aug
37.77	GBR C.Jackson, Jarrett, Regis, L.Christie	2	WC	Stuttgart	22 Aug
37.83	CAN Esmie, Gilbert, Surin, Mahorn	3	WC	Stuttgart	22 Aug
37.99	USA Drummond, Cason, C.Smith, Dees	1	WK	Zürich	4 Oct
37.99	CAN Esmie, Gilbert, Surin, Mahorn	2s1	WC	Stuttgart	21 Aug
38.00	Santa Monica TC (USA) Heard, Burrell, Marsh, C.Lewis	1	MSR	Walnut	17 Apr
38.05	GBR John, Jarrett, Braithwaite, L.Christie	3s1	WC	Stuttgart	21 Aug
38.12	USA Drummond, Cason, C.Smith, L.Burrell	1h3	WC	Stuttgart	21 Aug
38.19	Santa Monica TC (USA) Jefferson, Burrell, Marsh, C.Lewis	2	WK	Zürich	4 Oct
38.37	Commonwealth M.Adam/GBR, Jarret/GBR, Regis/GBR, R.Stewart/JAM	2	MSR	Walnut	17 Apr
38.39	CUB A.Simón, I.Garcia, Isasi, Aguilera	4	WC	Stuttgart	22 Aug
38.46	AUS Henderson, Marsh, Capobianco, Jackson	4s1	WC	Stuttgart	21 Aug
38.53	GBR John, Jarrett, Regis, L.Christie	1	EP	Roma	26 Jun
38.58	GER Blume, Kurnicki, Huke, Görmer	2s2	WC	Stuttgart	21 Aug
38.59	Santa Monica TC (USA) Marsh, Burrell, Heard, C.Lewis	1	Jer	Coquitlam	31 May
38.61	GHA Gariba, Boateng, Amegatcher, Tuffour	5s1	WC	Stuttgart	21 Aug
38.65	USA Bridgewater, Oaks, Miller, S Jefferson	1	WUG	Buffalo	18 Jul
38.66	CUB A.Simón, I.Garcia, Isasi, Aguilera	1h4	WC	Stuttgart	21 Aug
38.69	AUS Henderson, Marsh, Capobianco, Jackson	5	WC	Stuttgart	22 Aug
38.70	Louisiana State University (21performances by 7 nations)	1	NCAA	New Orleans	4 Jun
38.72	FRA Perrot, Sangouma, Trouabal, Marie-Rose	1	EP	Roma	26 Jun
38.77	CIV Lagazane, Zirignon, Waota, Meité	1h1	WC	Stuttgart	21 Aug
38.85	UKR Streltsov, Vanyaikin, Shlychkov, Dologodin (10)	1	EurR	Portsmouth	5 Jun
38.89	RUS Galkin, Ivanov, Fedoriv, Porkhomovskiy	3	EP	Roma	26 Jun
38.96	SWE Mårtensson, T.Eriksson, Hedner, Leandersson	3s2	WC	Stuttgart	21 Aug
38.97	JPN Inoue, Sugimoto, Miyata, Suzuki	2	WUG	Buffalo	18 Jul
39.00	GRE Genovelis, Panagiotopoulos, Nafpliotis, Terzian	6s1	WC	Stuttgart	21 Aug
39.04	NGR Eregbu, Imoh, Effiong, D.Ezinwa	4	WK	Zürich	4 Aug
39.16	Guandong (CHN)	1	NG	Beijing	12 Sep
39.17	ESP Trapero, Nolet, Mayoral, Talavera	5s2	WC	Stuttgart	21 Aug
39.29	ITA Amici, Madonia, Marras, Occhiena	1		Massa Marittima	6 Aug
39.32	LC Zürich (SUI) Burkart, Reimann, Semeraro, Dollé	1		Lausanne	23 May
39.32A	MEX López, Cardeñas, Adam, Miranda (20)	1		Ciudad México	21 Jun
39.33A	BAH Tynes, Young, Wells, Hepburn	1	CAC	Cali	31 Jul
39.46	HOL Perri, Franklin, Veurink, van der Vloot	1		Gisingen	3 Jul
39.52	HUN Sámi, Alexa, Rezák, A.Kovács	1	v2N	Praha	17 Jul
39.54	US Vöcklabruck (AUT) ¶ Ratzenberger, Renner, Berger, Kellermayr	1		Bad Homburg	10 Jun
39.61	THA	1	SEAG	Singapore	17 Jun

Mark		Name	Nat	Born	Pos	Meet	Venue	Date
39.67A	JAM	Shelton, Mair, Burrell, Dobson			2	CAC	Cali	31 Jul
39.75	Eletropaulo (BRA)	Souza, M Silva, A Silva, C Silva			1		Rio de Janeiro	27 Jun
39.77	NZL	Blythe, Keddell, Donaldson, Nketia			6h1	WC	Stuttgart	21 Aug
39.78	POL	Krzywanski, Mackowiak, Czajkowski, Kaniecki			7	EP	Roma	26 Jun
39.84	FIN	Haverinen, Länsivuori, Pakarinen, Haapasalo			1	vSWE	Stockholm	28 Aug
	(30)							

39.92A	BAR	31 Jul	40.09	KZK	20 Jun	40.25A	ECU	26 Apr	40.47	FIJ	16 Dec
39.93	INA	17 Jun	40.11	TPE	3 Dec	40.25	RSA	25 Jun	40.49	DEN	12 Jun
40.01	PUR	25 Nov	40.12	VEN	30 Apr	40.32	KOR	3 Dec	Hand timed		
40.04	BUL	12 Jun	40.16	BEL	12 Jun	40.35	SIN	17 Jun	40.1	Kecoso (KEN)	3 Jul
40.04A	COL	31 Jul	40.22	MAR	20 Jun	40.37	LAT	12 Jun	40.2A	CHI	3 Jul
40.07	TCH	5 Jun	40.24	TRI	21 Aug	40.38	BLS	12 Jun			

Best at low altitude

39.77	BAH	Wells, Young, Ferguson, Tynes	5 WUG	Buffalo	18 Jul
40.24	BAR	21 Aug			

4 x 200 METRES RELAY

Mark		Name	Pos	Meet	Venue	Date
1:20.80	Commonwealth	M.Adam/GBR, Jarrett/GBR, Regis/GBR, R.Stewart/JAM	1	SunA	Tempe	3 Apr
1:21.32	UKR	Vanyaykin, Tverdokhleb, Streltsov, Dolgodin	1	EurR	Portsmouth	5 Jun
1:21.54	GBR	John, Adam, Braithwaite, Regis	2	EurR	Portsmouth	5 Jun
1:21.63	RUS	Ivanov, Fedoriv, Fatun, Grigoryev	3	EurR	Portsmouth	5 Jun
1:21.79	Middle Tennessee (USA)		1	DogwR	Knoxville	10 Apr
1:22.23	ITA		4	EurR	Portsmouth	5 Jun

4 x 400 METRES RELAY

Mark		Name	Pos	Meet	Venue	Date
2:54.29	USA	Valmon 44.5, Watts 43.6, Reynolds 43.23, Johnson 42.94	1	WC	Stuttgart	22 Aug
2:58.72	USA	Valmon 45.1, Pettigrew 44.0, Mills 44.65, Johnson 44.96	1h2	WC	Stuttgart	21 Aug
2:59.82	KEN	Ochieng 46.2, Kemboi 45.3, Matiru 44.56, S.Kitur 43.75	2	WC	Stuttgart	22 Aug
2:59.99	GER	Lieder 45.5, Ka.Just 45.3, Hense 44.98, Schönlebe 44.21	3	WC	Stuttgart	22 Aug
3:00.09	FRA	Rapnouil 45.5, Hilaire 45.5, Farraudière 44.86, Diagana 44.19	4	WC	Stuttgart	22 Aug
3:00.25	GBR	Ladejo 45.8, Akabusi 45.2, Regis 44.7, Grindley 44.5	1	EP	Roma	27 Jun
3:00.44	RUS	Kliger 45.72, Kosov 45.09, Vdovin 44.73, Golovastov 44.90	5	WC	Stuttgart	22 Aug
3:00.46	CUB	Garcia 46.6, Herrera 45.5, Tellez 44.30, Hernández 44.12	6	WC	Stuttgart	22 Aug
3:00.75	RUS	Kliger, Kosov, Vdovin, Golovastov	2	EP	Roma	27 Jun
3:00.82	Ohio State Univ. (USA)	R.Jones, A.Payne, R.Smith, Nelloms	1	NCAA	New Orleans	5 Jun
3:00.82	KEN	Matiru 45.5, Kemboi 45.9, S.Kitur 44.49, Ochieng 44.94	1h3	WC	Stuttgart	21 Aug
3:00.94	FRA	Rapnouil, Hilaire, Jaffory, Diagana	3	EP	Roma	27 Jun
3:01.22	Baylor University (USA)	Fredericks, Minor, Miller, Green	2	NCAA	New Orleans	5 Jun
3:01.26	GER	Ka.Just 46.1, Lieder 45.0, Hense 45.39, Schönlebe 44.79	1h1	WC	Stuttgart	21 Aug
3:01.33	GER	Pfersich, Bittner, Lieder, Hense	4	EP	Roma	27 Jun
3:01.36	CUB	Martinez 46.9, Herrera 45.5, Tellez 44.69, Hernández 44.32	2h3	WC	Stuttgart	21 Aug
3:01.44	JAM	O'Connor 46.0, Blake 45.5, McFarlane 45.32, Haughton 44.55	7	WC	Stuttgart	22 Aug
3:01.51	RUS	Kliger 45.6, Kosov 45.4, Zharov 45.61, Golovastov 44.86	3h3	WC	Stuttgart	21 Aug
3:01.61	BUL	Georgiev 45.9, Stankulov 46.0, Raykov 45.07, Ivanov 44.66	2h1	WC	Stuttgart	21 Aug
3:01.70	JAM	O'Connor 46.5, Blake 45.1, McFarlane 45.83, Haughton 44.24	3h1	WC	Stuttgart	21 Aug
3:01.70	FRA	Farraudière 45.9, Hilaire 45.2, Noirot 45.37, Rapnouil 45.19	2h2	WC	Stuttgart	21 Aug
3:01.85	ITA	Nuti 46.4, Montanari 45.4, Aimar 44.78, Vaccari 45.31	4h3	WC	Stuttgart	21 Aug
	(22/10)					
3:02.43	JPN	Kan 46.9, Karube 45.1, Saito 45.23, Ono 45.12	3h2	WC	Stuttgart	21 Aug
3:02.64	NGR	Bosso 47.2, Okoli 45.9, Omagbemi 45.43, Bada 44.11	5h3	WC	Stuttgart	21 Aug
3:02.84	AUS	Coull, Clark, Kougellis, Ryan	1	NC	Brisbane	7 Mar
3:03.63	ALG	Hacini 45.8, Mariche 46.2, Talhaodi 46.51, Boumendil 45.08	4h2	WC	Stuttgart	21 Aug
3:04.27	HUN	Somfay, D.Kovács, G.Kiss, Arpási	3	WUG	Buffalo	18 Jul
3:04.35	CHN	Xie Hong, Yu Baoyi, Zhao Cunlin, Luo Xuming	1	EAsiG	Shanghai	16 May
3:04.79	MAR	Dahhan, Boukraa, Boukhari, Lahlou	2	MedG	Narbonne	20 Jun
3:05.84	NZL	Farrell, Cowan, Dale, Keddell	5h1	WC	Stuttgart	21 Aug
3:05.96	ESP	A.Sánchez, Cornet, M.Moreno, Heras	6	EP	Roma	27 Jun
3:06.38	SEN	Diumbia, Faye, H Mbaye, H Ndiaye	3	AfrC	Durban	27 Jun
	(20)					
3:06.39A	COL	Canizales, Rivas, Urrutia, Valencia	3	CAC	Cali	1 Aug
3:06.67	Funilense (BRA)	Sena, Araujo, Jenório, Chiamulera	1		Rio de Janeiro	27 Jun
3:06.83	CAN	Ogilvie, Amphlett, Gibbons, Goodwin	5	WUG	Buffalo	18 Jul
3:06.87	QAT	S Suleiman, M Khamis, F Ibrahim, I Ismail	1	CISM	Tours	30 Aug
3:06.96	TRI	Delice, Williams, Jules, de Silva	2	CAG	Ponce	28 Nov

Mark		Name	Pos	Meet	Venue	Date
3:07.18A	MEX	Escalante, Cardeñas, Miranda, Morales	4		Cali	1 Aug
3:07.30	THA	Kenchan, Tongtip, Poomipak, Tongiek	1	SEAG	Singapore	17 Jun
3:07.39	GRE	Papadopoulos, Linardatos, Panagiotopoulos, Kederis	1	EP/C1	Villach	13 Jun
3:07.82	FIN	Louramo, Pihlavisto, Hämeenniemi, Pakarinen	3	3-N	Bondoufle	19 Sep
3:08.00	BAH	Tigers			Miami	13 Jun

(30)

3:08.05	PUR	28 Nov	3:08.75	POL	17 Jul	3:09.5	CHI	4 Jul	3:09.88	NOR	13 Jun
3:08.08	SVK	13 Jun	3:08.83	SRI	25 Dec	3:09.54	INA	17 Jun	3:09.97	FIJ	16 Dec
3:08.22	AUT	13 Jun	3:08.91	IND	25 Dec	3:09.56	CZ Beograd		**Low altitude bests**		
3:08.31	SWE	13 Jun	3:09.07	MRI	28 Oct		((YUG)	20 Jun	3:08.37	MEX	21 Aug
3:08.33	SUI	13 Jun	3:09.1	BAR	8 May	3:09.65	UKR	27 Jun	3:08.96	COL	28 Nov
3:08.68	POR	13 Jun	3:09.30	BLS	13 Jun	3:09.88	LAT	13 Jun			

4 x 800 METRES RELAY

Mark	Team	Pos	Meet	Venue	Date
7:11.42	BLS Talonov, Ryabukhin, Borisov, Sereda	1	EurR	Portsmouth	5 Jun
7:11.96	RUS Melnikov, Samoylov, Loginov, Oleynikov	2	EurR	Portsmouth	5 Jun
7:12.66	GBR Heard, Sharpe, Yates, Robb	3	EurR	Portsmouth	5 Jun
7:14.34	Florida (USA) Jones, Lacy, Adderley, Peters	1	PennR	Philadelphia	24 Apr
7:15.85	George Mason (JAM) Bowen, Vernon-Watson, Cornwall, Morgan	2	PennR	Philadelphia	24 Apr
7:16.44	GER Janich, Kallweit, Otte, Reinert	4	EurR	Portsmouth	5 Jun
7:18.59	ESP	5	EurR	Portsmouth	5 Jun

4 x 1500 METRES RELAY

Mark	Team	Pos	Meet	Venue	Date
15:00.23	Villanova Nason, Going, Sumner, Quintana	1	PennR	Philadelphia	24 Apr
15:01.97	Wisconsin (USA) Dameworth, Bergstrom, Casiano, Schumacher	2	PennR	Philadelphia	24 Apr
15:02.63	Providence Univ Jackson, Carroll IRL, Burdis, Keith GBR	3	PennR	Philadelphia	24 Apr
15:06.08	Arkansas Univ. Mitchell, Morin, Schiefer, Bruton IRL	4	PennR	Philadelphia	24 Apr
15:08.24	TV Wattenscheid (GER) Janich, Schulze, Plätzer, Stenzel	1	NC	Dortmund	4 Jul
15:11.0	Jogging Iner Magignana (FRA)	1		Rennes	30 Jun

3000 METRES WALK

Mark	Name		Nat	Born	Pos	Meet	Venue	Date
11:13.8	Stefan	Johansson	SWE	11.4.67	1		Canberra	12 Jan
11:26.5	Tim	Berrett	CAN	23.1.65	2		Canberra	12 Jan
11:26.7	Jonathan	Matthews	USA	2.7.56	1		San Francisco	15 May
11:28.6	Allen	James	USA	14.4.64	2		San Francisco	15 May
11:31.3	Steve	Beercroft	AUS	14.3.71	1		Melbourne	2 Dec
11:35.8	Andrew	Jachno	AUS	13.4.62	4		Canberra	12 Jan
11:37.3	Riecus	Blignaut	RSA	12.11.68	1		Johannesburg	27 Feb
Indoors								
11:31.34+	Giovanni	De Benedictis	ITA	8.1.68	1+		Genova	10 Feb
11:37	Ján	Záhoncík	SVK	23.4.65	1		Hlohovec	3 Dec
11:38	Peter	Tichy	SVK	12.3.69	2		Hlohovec	3 Dec

5000 METRES WALK

Mark	Name		Nat	Born	Pos	Meet	Venue	Date
18:31.76	Frants	Kostyukevich	BLS	4.4.63	1	BNP	Villeneuve d'Ascq	2 Jul
18:35.87	Robert	Korzeniowski	POL	30.7.68	2	BNP	Villeneuve d'Ascq	2 Jul
18:36.84	Jozef	Pribilinec	SVK	6.7.60	3	BNP	Villeneuve d'Ascq	2 Jul
18:42.70		Korzeniowski			1		Reims	30 Jun
18:51.05	Stefan	Johansson	SWE	11.4.67	1		Stockholm	8 Jul
18:57.00	Jean-Claude	Corre	FRA	14.9.61	4	BNP	Villeneuve d'Ascq	2 Jul
18:57.20	Denis	Langlois	FRA	10.10.68	5	BNP	Villeneuve d'Ascq	2 Jul
18:57.54		Korzeniowski			1		Caserta	6 Jun
18:58.17	Mikhail	Shchennikov	RUS	24.12.67	2		Caserta	6 Jun
18:58.7	Nick	A'Hern	AUS	6.1.69	1	NC	Brisbane	6 Mar
	(10/8)							
19:01.27	Mikhail	Orlov	RUS	25.6.67	6	BNP	Villeneuve d'Ascq	2 Jul
19:02.77	Andrey	Makarov	RUS	2.6.71	7	BNP	Villeneuve d'Ascq	2 Jul
19:09.83	Sándor	Urbanik	HUN	15.12.64	2		Reims	30 Jun
19:09.88	Yevgeniy	Misyulya	BLS	13.3.64	8	BNP	Villeneuve d'Ascq	2 Jul
19:14.2	Igor	Kollár	SVK	25.6.65	1		Banská Bystrica	4 Sep
19:15.48	Jean-Oliver	Brosseau	FRA	23.6.67	9	BNP	Villeneuve d'Ascq	2 Jul
19:16.16	Oleg	Troshin	RUS	1.8.64	10	BNP	Villeneuve d'Ascq	2 Jul
19:18.51	Walter	Arena	ITA	30.5.64	3		Caserta	6 Jun
19:21.55	Arturo	Di Mezza	ITA	16.7.69	4		Caserta	6 Jun
19:26.6	Jan	Záhoncik	SVK	23.4.65	2		Banská Bystrica	4 Sep
19:37.2	Stefan	Malík	SVK	11.2.66	3		Banská Bystrica	4 Sep

Mark	Name		Nat	Born	Pos	Meet	Venue	Date
Indoors								
18:27.0	Frants	Kostyukevich	BLS	4.4.63	1		Minsk	23 Jan
18:28.50		Kostyukevich			1		Liévin	13 Feb
18:32.09	Robert	Korzeniowski	POL	30.7.68	1	NC	Spala	21 Feb
18:32.10	Mikhail	Shchennikov	RUS	24.12.67	1	WI	Toronto	14 Mar
18:35.91		Korzeniowski			2	WI	Toronto	14 Mar
18:36.98		Korzeniowski			2		Liévin	13 Feb
18:38.32		Korzeniowski			1	FraC	Liévin	27 Feb
18:40.83		Shchennikov			1	NC	Moskva	27 Feb
18:42.0	Yevgeniy	Misyulya	BLS	13.3.64	2		Minsk	23 Jan
18:43.48	Mikhail	Orlov	RUS	25.6.67	3	WI	Toronto	14 Mar
18:44.57		Orlov			2	NC	Moskva	27 Feb
18:46.45	Roman	Mrázek	SVK	21.2.62	1	TCH Ch	Praha	20 Feb
18:47.56	Tim	Berrett	CAN	23.1.65	1	NC	Winnipeg	20 Feb
18:51.15	Jean-Claude	Corre	FRA	14.9.61	2	NC	Liévin	28 Feb
18:51.21	Grigoriy	Kornyev	RUS	14.3.61	3	NC	Moskva	27 Feb
18:51.94		Misyulya			3		Liévin	13 Feb
18:52.3		Orlov			1		Moskva	28 Jan
18:53.02		Berrett			4	WI	Toronto	14 Mar
18:53.27	Andrey	Makarov	RUS	2.6.71	4	NC	Moskva	27 Feb
18:55.65		Shchennikov			1		Moskva	2 Feb
18:56.07		Korzeniowski			1h1	WI	Toronto	13 Mar
18:57.10		Corre			4		Liévin	13 Feb
18:57.38		Orlov			2		Moskva	2 Feb
	(23 performances)							
18:58.43	Miroslav	Bosko	SVK	26.9.68	2	TCH Ch	Praha	20 Feb
19:00.21	Ronald	Weigel	GER	8.8.59	1	NC	Sindelfingen	28 Feb
19:01.0	Igor	Plotnikov	RUS	12.7.64	2		Moskva	28 Jan
19:03.02	Sandor	Urbanik	HUN	15.12.64	1	NC	Budapest	5 Feb
19:03.1	Ilya	Markov	RUS	19.6.72	3		Moskva	28 Jan
19:05.5	Viktor	Osipov	RUS	4.5.65	4		Moskva	28 Jan
19:06.39	Pavol	Blazek	SVK	9.7.58	2		Budapest	5 Feb
19:08.30	Anatoliy	Kozlov	UKR	2.10.67	1	NC	Kiev	14 Feb
19:08.6	Oleg	Troshin	RUS	1.8.64	5		Moskva	28 Jan
19:12.36	Rudolf	Cogan	TCH	25.8.71	2		Wien	31 Jan
19:12.73	Costica	Balan	ROM	25.8.64	7	WI	Toronto	14 Mar
19:14.81	Sergey	Pyatachenko	UKR	7.8.65	2	NC	Kiev	14 Feb
19:14.98	Axel	Noack	GER	23.9.61	2	NC	Sindelfingen	28 Feb
19:15.10	Giovanni	De Benedictis	ITA	8.1.68	1		Genova	10 Feb
19:17.88	Giovanni	Perricelli	ITA	25.8.67	2		Genova	10 Feb
19:17.88	Bernd	Gummelt	GER	21.12.63	3	NC	Sindelfingen	28 Feb
19:19.05	Vladimir	Andreyev	RUS	7.9.66	6	NC	Moskva	27 Feb
19:22.20	Gyula	Dudás	HUN	10.8.66	3	NC	Budapest	5 Feb
19:24.12	José	Urbano	POR	1.3.66	1	NC	Braga	6 Mar
19:24.82	Jiri	Malysa	TCH	10.8.66	3	NC	Praha	20 Feb
19:27.68	Tomas	Kratochvíl	TCH	19.12.71	4	NC	Praha	20 Feb
19:28.55	Christophe	Cousin	FRA	22.5.65	4	NC	Liévin	28 Feb
19:28.87	Sergio	Vieira Galdino	BRA	7.5.69	5h1	WI	Toronto	13 Mar
19:29.28	Petér	Gábris	SVK	24.6.70	4		Budapest	5 Feb
19:34.4	Valeriy	Borisov	KZK	18.9.66	1		Karaganda	23 Jan
19:35.38	Michele	Didoni	ITA	7.3.74	1		Pesaro	20 Feb
19:37.21	Vladimir	Druchik	UKR	25.6.65	3	NC	Kiev	14 Feb
19:39.12	Sergey	Tyulenyev	RUS	14.3.71	4		Moskva	2 Feb
3 Miles Walk								
18:05.3i	Mikhail	Shchennikov	RUS	24.12.67	1		Moskva	31 Jan
18:06.5i	Andrey	Makarov	RUS	2.6.71	2		Moskva	31 Jan

10,000 METRES WALK

Mark	Name		Nat	Born	Pos	Meet	Venue	Date
39:28.20	Costica	Balan	ROM	25.8.64	1		Bucuresti	31 Jul
39:28.97	Jacek	Muller	POL	3.11.73	1		Sopot	20 Jun
39:30.95	Valentin	Kononen	FIN	7.3.69	1		Kangasniemi	6 Jun
39:50.73	Jefferson	Pérez	ECU	1.1.74	1	PAJ	Winnipeg	16 Jul
40:05.62	Michele	Didoni	ITA	7.3.74	1	EJ	San Sebastián	30 Jul

Mark	Name		Nat	Born	Pos	Meet	Venue	Date
40:21.98	Karol	Repasky	SVK	3.1.69	1		Kosice	1 May
40:25.83	Sergio	Spagnulo	ITA	7.10.62	1		Modena	22 May
40:26.08	Dmitriy	Yesipchuk	RUS	17.11.74	2	EJ	San Sebastián	30 Jul
40:27.29	Hirofumi	Sakai	JPN	10.2.65	1		Tokyo	21 May
40:35.54	Miroslav	Bosko	SVK	26.1.68	2		Kosice	1 May
	(10)							
40:36.21	Massimo	Fizialetti	ITA	7.2.65	1		Chieti	8 May
40:37.78	Heiko	Valentin	GER	31.5.74	3	EJ	San Sebastián	30 Jul

Mark	Name		Nat	Born	Date
40:43.18	Giovanni	Perricelli	ITA	67	8 May
40:47.5	Viktor	Mostovik	BLS	63	29 May
40:51.24	Giovanni	De Benedictis	ITA	68	29 Aug
40:52.94	Jani	Lehtinen	FIN	74	1 Jun
40:55.80	Salvatore	Cacia	ITA	67	8 May
40:55.83	Yevgeniy	Shmalyuk	RUS	76	30 Jul
40:57.03		Vainauskas	LIT		28 Oct
40:57.12	Michele	Lizio	ITA	71	8 May

Indoors

Mark	Name		Nat	Born	Pos	Meet	Venue	Date
39:46.72i	Mikhail	Orlov	RUS	25.6.67	1		Moskva	26 Jan
39:53.40i	Oleg	Troshin	RUS	1.8.64	2		Moskva	26 Jan
40:20.56i	Fanis	Shaikhudtinov	RUS	27.5.69	3		Moskva	26 Jan

20 KILOMETRES WALK

Mark	Name		Nat	Born	Pos	Meet	Venue	Date
1:18:33	Mikhail	Shchennikov	RUS	24.12.67	1	4-N	Livorno	10 Jul
1:19:08	Yuriy	Kuko	BLS	23.1.68	2	4-N	Livorno	10 Jul
1:19:39	Bernardo	Segura	MEX	11.2.70	1		Eschborn	12 Jun
1:19:41	Dmitriy	Dolnikov	RUS	19.11.72	1		Adler	14 Feb
1:19:42	Daniel	Garcia	MEX	28.10.71	2		Eschborn	12 Jun
1:19:43	Nikolay	Matyukhin	RUS	13.12.68	2		Adler	14 Feb
1:19:43	Vladimir	Andreyev	RUS	7.9.66	3		Adler	14 Feb
1:19:43		Chen Shaoguo	CHN	20.1.72	1	NG	Beijing	8 Sep
1:19:48+	Nick	A'Hern	AUS	6.1.69	1k		Hawkesbury	10 Jul
1:19:49		Bo Lingtang	CHN	12.8.70	2	NG	Beijing	8 Sep
	(10)							
1:19:52	Vyacheslav	Cherepanov	RUS	2.11.64	4		Adler	14 Feb
1:19:53	Yuriy	Gordeyev (10)	RUS	64	3	4-N	Livorno	10 Jul
1:19:56	Yevgeniy	Misyulya	BLS	9.3.64	1		Novopolotsk	8 May
1:19:56		Andreyev			4	4-N	Livorno	10 Jul
1:20:00		Li Mingcai	CHN	22.8.71	3	NG	Beijing	8 Sep
1:20:03	Frants	Kostyukevich	BLS	4.4.63	3		Eschborn	12 Jun
1:20:03	Viktor	Ginko	BLS	7.12.65	5	4-N	Livorno	10 Jul
1:20:09	Jacek	Muller	POL	3.11.73	4		Eschborn	12 Jun
1:20:12.3		A'Hern			1	SGP	Fana	8 May
1:20:19	Ilya	Markov	RUS	19.6.72	5		Adler	14 Feb
1:20:25	Mikhail	Khmelnitskiy	BLS	24.7.69	2		Novopolotsk	8 May
1:20:38	Artur	Shumak	BLS	19.10.63	6		Adler	14 Feb
1:20:38		Shumak			6	4-N	Livorno	10 Jul
1:20:41		Kuko			5		Eschborn	12 Jun
1:20:41		Tan Mingjun	CHN	17.7.70	4	NG	Beijing	8 Sep
1:20:42	Dmitriy	Golos	BLS	23.2.71	7		Adler	14 Feb
1:20:43		Shchennikov			8		Adler	14 Feb
1:20:44		Andreyev			1	NC	Cheboksary	6 Jun
1:20:49		Segura			1		Brandys nad Labem	23 May
1:20:50	Valentin	Massana	ESP	5.7.70	1		La Coruña	15 May
1:20:52	Viktor	Osipov	RUS	4.5.65	9		Adler	14 Feb
	(31/20)							
1:20:54		Mao Xinyuan	CHN	2.7.71	5	NG	Beijing	8 Sep
1:20:55	Robert	Korzeniowski	POL	30.7.68	2		La Coruña	15 May
1:20:55	Grigoriy	Kornev	RUS	14.3.61	2	NC	Cheboksary	6 Jun
1:20:59	Miguel	Rodriguez	MEX	15.5.62	3		La Coruña	15 May
1:21:10t	Igor	Kollár	SVK	25.6.65	1	NC	Banská Bystrica	3 Jul
1:21:11	Daniel	Plaza	ESP	3.7.66	4		La Coruña	15 May
1:21:12	Michele	Lizio	ITA	5.3.71	8	4-N	Livorno	10 Jul
1:21:16	Giovanni	de Benedictis	ITA	8.1.68	2		Sesto San Giovanni	1 May
1:21:22	Igor	Plotnikov	RUS	12.7.64	10		Adler	14 Feb
1:21:22		Zhou Yongshen	CHN	15.10.72	6	NG	Beijing	8 Sep
1:21:26	Robert	Ihly	GER	5.5.63	6		Eschborn	12 Jun
	(30)							
1:21:27	Massimo	Fizialetti	ITA	7.2.65	9	4-N	Livorno	10 Jul
1:21:31	Sergey	Tyulenev	RUS	14.3.71	12		Adler	14 Feb
1:21:33	Andrey	Makarov	RUS	2.1.71	3	NC	Cheboksary	6 Jun

Mark	Name		Nat	Born	Pos	Meet	Venue	Date
1:21:35	Jean-Olivier	Brosseau	FRA	23.6.67	7		Eschborn	12 Jun
1:21:39	Carlos	Mercenario	MEX	23.5.67	5		La Coruña	15 May
1:21:39	Pietro	Fiorini	ITA	11.3.67	10	4-N	Livorno	10 Jul
1:21:45		Shen Wenhui	CHN	25.5.73	7	NG	Beijing	8 Sep
1:21:50	Tomasz	Lipiec	POL	10.5.71	1		Mielec	16 Jun
1:21:51	Stefan	Johansson	SWE	11.4.67	8		Eschborn	12 Jun
1:21:54t	Pavol	Blazek	SVK	9.7.58	2	NC	Banská Bystrica	3 Jul
	(40)							
1:21:55		Sun Xiaoguang	CHN	15.1.65	3	NC	Shenzhen	18 Feb
1:21:59	Oleg	Plastun	RUS	20.11.63	15		Adler	14 Feb
1:22:01		Zhou Zhaowen	CHN	.5.69	5	NC	Shenzhen	18 Feb
1:22:13	Valeriy	Borisov	KZK	18.9.66	17		Adler	14 Feb
1:22:15.7t	Walter	Arena	ITA	30.5.64	2	SGP	Fana	8 May
1:22:16	Aleksey	Pershin	RUS	20.2.62	18		Adler	14 Feb
1:22:17	Oleg	Troshin	RUS	1.8.64	4	NC	Cheboksary	6 Jun
1:22:17	Magnus	Morenius	SWE	69	9		Eschborn	12 Jun
1:22:19		Hu Zhenrong	CHN	.2.71	7	NC	Shenzhen	18 Feb
1:22:22.6t	Valentin	Kononen	FIN	7.3.69	3	SGP	Fana	8 May
	(50)							
1:22:24	Gyula	Dudás	HUN	10.8.66	2	6-N	Békéscsaba	28 Mar
1:22:25.4t	Hirofumi	Sakai	JPN	10.2.65	1		Kanazawa	9 Jun
1:22:26	Sigitas	Vainauskas	LIT	12.12.66	19		Adler	14 Feb
1:22:30		Li Zewen	CHN	.10.73	8	NC	Shenzhen	18 Feb
1:22:38	Grzegorz	Muller	POL	3.11.73	10		Eschborn	12 Jun
1:22:40	José	Urbano	POR	1.3.66	1		Grândola	9 Jan
1:22:40.2	Tsutomu	Takushima	JPN	18.2.67	3	EAsiG	Shanghai	15 May
1:22:42		Zhao Yongsheng	CHN	.3.71	10	NC	Shenzhong	18 Feb
1:22:43	Sergey	Korepanov	KZK	9.5.64	20		Adler	14 Feb
1:22:43t	Ján	Záhoncík	SVK	23.4.65	3	NC	Banská Bystrica	3 Jul
	(60)							
1:22:47	Tim	Berrett	CAN	23.1.65	1		Washington DC	28 Mar
1:22:50	Konstantin	Nacharkin	RUS	71	21		Adler	14 Feb
1:22:50	Aleksey	Kronin	RUS	70	22		Adler	14 Feb
1:22:51	Arvidas	Vainauskas	LIT	12.12.66	23		Adler	14 Feb
1:22:51	Denis	Langlois	FRA	10.10.68	12		Eschborn	12 Jun
1:22:51	Thierry	Toutain	FRA	14.2.62	1		Yverdon	7 Aug
1:22:51		Wang Jun	CHN	27.12.72	10	NG	Beijing	8 Sep
1:22:52	Andrey	Popov	RUS	28.4.62	24		Adler	14 Feb
1:22:52.8	Viktoras	Meshauskas	LIT	4.11.70	1		Vilnius	19 Jun
1:22:55	Joel	Sánchez	MEX	6.8.64	13		Eschborn	12 Jun
	(70)							
1:23:01		Tian Niantang	CHN	.3.72	11	NC	Shenzhen	18 Feb
1:23:01	Mikhail	Orlov	RUS	25.6.67	5	NC	Cheboksary	6 Jun
1:23:02	Yuriy	Zubok	BLS	7.3.69	25		Adler	14 Feb
1:23:02	Jaime	Barroso	ESP	15.5.68	15		Eschborn	12 Jun
1:23:04		Wang Libin	CHN	.3.74	12	NC	Shenzhen	18 Feb
1:23:06	Arturo	Di Mezza	ITA	16.7.69	3		Termoli	16 May
1:23:08	Rytis	Arbaciauskas	LIT	15.1.71	26		Adler	14 Feb
1:23:09		Liu Xiaochun	CHN	7.8.72	13	NC	Shenzhen	18 Feb
1:23:09.1t	Sergio	Vieira Galdino	BRA	7.5.69	1		Rio de Janeiro	26 Jun
1:23:12		Zhai Wanbo	CHN	13.2.67	14	NC	Shenzhen	18 Feb
	(80)							
1:23:13	Aleksandr	Leskov	RUS	69	27		Adler	14 Feb
1:23:14	Giovanni	Perricelli	ITA	25.8.67	3		Sesto San Giovanni	1 May
1:23:21	Igor	Lyubomirov	RUS	9.11.61	6	NC	Cheboksary	6 Jun
1:23:21t	Karol	Repasky	SVK	3.1.69	3	NC	Banská Bystrica	3 Jul
1:23:23	Jan	Staef	SWE	11.1.62	17		Eschborn	12 Jun
1:23:27	Darrell	Stone	GBR	2.2.68	11	4-N	Livorno	10 Jul
1:23:28.0t	Petér	Gábris	SVK	24.6.70	5	SGP	Fana	8 May
1:23:29t	Miroslav	Bosko	SVK	26.9.68	5	NC	Banská Bystrica	3 Jul
1:23:30	Aleksey	Kuznetsov	RUS	21.11.70	28		Adler	14 Feb
1:23:31	Sándor	Urbanik	HUN	15.12.64	1	NC	Debrecen	15 May
	(90)							
1:23:31	Hartwig	Gauder	GER	10.11.54	2	NC	Duisburg	9 Jul
1:23:35	Aleksandr	Arkhipov	RUS	68	29		Adler	14 Feb
1:23:36	Ignacio	Zamudio Cruz	MEX	15.5.71	18		Eschborn	12 Jun
1:23:37	Aleksandar	Rakovic	YUG	13.4.68	4	6-N	Békécsaba	28 Mar

Mark	Name		Nat	Born	Pos	Meet	Venue	Date
1:23:37	Vladimir	Ostrovskiy	ISR	12.12.66	5	6-N	Békécsaba	28 Mar
1:23:40	Stefan	Malik	SVK	4.2.66				
1:23:44	Basilio	Labrador	ESP	29.3.67	20		Eschborn	12 Jun
1:23:45.7t	Costica	Balan	ROM	25.8.64	1		Ruse	10 Apr
1:23:46	Fernando	Vázquez	ESP	4.5.71	21		Eschborn	12 Jun
	(100)							

Mark	Name		Nat	Born	Date
1:23:47	Roman	Mrázek	SVK	62	28 Mar
1:23:51	Ronald	Weigel	GER	59	9 May
1:23:55	Mechislav	Vezhel	BLS	62	14 Feb
1:23:55	Zbigniew	Sadlej	POL	61	28 Mar
1:24:03	Jefferson	Pérez	ECU	74	4 Jul
1:24:19	Michele	Didoni	ITA	74	1 May
1:24:23	Robert	Valicek	SVK	69	
1:24:24	Satoshi	Yanagisawa	JPN	71	7 Nov
1:24:25	Janusz	Golawski	POL	66	28 Mar
1:24:26	Alberto	Cruz	MEX	72	23 May
	(110)				
1:24:29.17	Aleksey	Voyevodin	RUS	70	30 Aug
1:24:31A	Héctor	Moreno	COL	63	31 Jul
1:24:31.7t	Viktor	Mostovik	BLS	63	3 Jul
1:24:32	Simon	Baker	AUS	58	25 Jan
1:24:35	Long Guixiang		CHN	73	18 Feb
1:24:37.3t	Sverre	Jensen	NOR	66	1 Jul
1:24:40	Justus	Kavulanga	KEN		2 Jul
1:24:42	Aleksandr	Yakimchuk	RUS	72	14 Feb
1:24:42	Sergio	Spagnulo	ITA	62	18 May
1:24:43	Slawomir	Cielica	POL	70	16 May
	(120)				
1:24:44	Grzegorz	Rejewski	POL	70	1 Jul
1:24:45.7	Claudio Luiz	Bertolino	BRA	63	5 Jun
1:24:48.32	Yan	Leskov	RUS	72	30 Aug
1:24:49	Pavel	Vasilyev	RUS	70	6 Oct
1:24:50A	Querubin	Moreno	COL	59	4 Jul
1:24:50	Carlos	Ramones	VEN	64	9 Oct
1:24:51	Daisuke	Ikeshima	JPN	75	7 Nov
1:24:53	Hiromu	Sakai	JPN	70	4 Apr
1:24:56	Valeriy	Spitsyn	RUS	65	9 May
1:24:59	Stanislaw	Stosik	POL	72	28 Aug
	(130)				

Best 20,000m track performances if not shown above

Mark	Name	Born	Pos	Meet	Venue	Date
1:21:29.1	Chen Shaoguo		1	EAsiG	Shanghai	15 May
1:22:48	Johansson		1		Canberra	25 Jan
1:23:09.64	Markov	19.6.72	1		Dzerzhinsk	30 Aug
1:23:16.8	Pericelli		1		Roma	4 Apr
1:23:31.0	Dudás		1		Budapest	29 May
1:24:42.2	Spagnulo		3		Roma	4 Apr

30 KILOMETRESWALK

Mark	Name		Nat	Born	Pos	Venue	Date
2:04:00	Aleksandr	Potashov	BLS	12.3.62	1	Adler	14 Feb
2:05:36	Viktor	Ginko	BLS	7.12.65	2	Adler	14 Feb
2:05:53	Andrey	Plotnikov	RUS	12.8.67	3	Adler	14 Feb
2:06:27	Anatoliy	Grigoryev	RUS	60	4	Adler	14 Feb
2:07:26	Vyacheslav	Smirnov	RUS	4.5.57	5	Adler	14 Feb
2:07:58	Valentin	Massana	ESP	5.7.70	1	El Prat de Llobregat	28 Mar
2:09:20	Oleg	Troshin	RUS	1.8.64	6	Adler	14 Feb
2:09:35	Sergey	Katurayev	RUS	29.9.67	7	Adler	14 Feb
2:10:10	Mikhail	Shitikov	BLS	10.10.63	8	Adler	14 Feb
2:10:10	Nick	A'Hern	AUS	6.1.69	1	Melbourne	19 Dec
	(10)						
2:10:44	Stanislav	Vezhel	BLS	11.10.58	9	Adler	14 Feb
2:10:44.4	René	Piller	FRA	23.4.65	1	Vittel	21 Mar
2:11:05	Sergey	Pershin	RUS	4.6.68	10	Adler	14 Feb
2:11:14	German	Skurygin	RUS	23.12.63	11	Adler	14 Feb
2:12:12	Aleksey	Voyevodin	RUS	9.8.70	12	Adler	14 Feb
2:12:46	Jaime	Barroso	ESP	15.5.63	2	El Prat de Llobregat	28 Mar
2:12:57	Mikhail	Potashov	BLS	13.4.66	13	Adler	14 Feb
2:12:57	Yuriy	Andronov	RUS	71	14	Adler	14 Feb
2:13:04	Sergey	Syomin	RUS	71	15	Adler	14 Feb

Mark	Name		Nat	Born	Date
2:13:09	Jesús A	Garcia	ESP	69	28 Mar
2:13:14	Oleg	Bandurchenko	RUS	70	14 Feb
2:13:15	Pavel	Vasilyev	RUS	70	14 Feb
2:13:16	Fernando	Vázquez	ESP	71	28 Mar
2:13:18	José	Urbano	POR	66	
2:13:23	Rafael	Martin	ESP	70	28 Mar
2:13:30	Jean-Claude	Corre	FRA	61	4 Apr
2:13:38	Simon	Baker	AUS	58	19 Dec
2:13:43	Faustion	Ruiz	ESP	65	28 Mar
2:13:52	Dmitriy	Osipov	RUS	66	14 Feb

50 KILOMETRES WALK

Mark	Name		Nat	Born	Pos	Meet	Venue	Date
3:41:41	Jesús	Garcia	ESP	17.10.69	1	WC	Stuttgart	21 Aug
3:42:02	Valentin	Kononen	FIN	7.3.69	2	WC	Stuttgart	21 Aug
3:42:50	Valeriy	Spitsyn	RUS	5.12.65	3	WC	Stuttgart	21 Aug
3:43:50	Axel	Noack	GER	23.9.61	4	WC	Stuttgart	21 Aug
3:44:24	Robert	Korzeniowski	POL	30.7.68	1	NC	Zamosc	26 Sep
3:46:11	Valentin	Massana	ESP	5.7.70	1	NC	Reus	14 Feb
3:46:46	Basilio	Labrador	ESP	29.3.67	5	WC	Stuttgart	21 Aug
3:47:40	Thierry	Toutain	FRA	14.2.62	1	NC	Neuilly sur Marne	26 Sep
3:48:06		Garcia	ESP		2	NC	Reus	14 Feb

Mark	Name		Nat	Born	Pos	Meet	Venue	Date
3:48:57	René	Piller	FRA	23.4.65	6	WC	Stuttgart	21 Aug
3:49:17		Li Mingcai (10)	CHN	22.8.71	1	NG	Beijing	12 Sep
3:50:23	Tim	Berrett	CAN	23.1.65	7	WC	Stuttgart	21 Aug
3:50:28	Carlos	Mercenario	MEX	23.5.67	1	WP	Monterrey	25 Apr
3:50:53		Mercenario			8	WC	Stuttgart	21 Aug
3:51:44	Vitaliy	Popovich	UKR	22.10.62	1		Alushta	21 Feb
3:51:51	Jean-Claude	Corre	FRA	14.9.61	9	WC	Stuttgart	21 Aug
3:51:54	Giuseppe	De Gaetano	ITA	4.10.66	1	NC	Alife	21 Feb
3:52:33	Daniel	Plaza	ESP	3.7.66	3	NC	Reus	14 Feb
3:52:44		Labrador			4	NC	Reus	14 Feb
3:52:44		Garcia			2	WCp	Monterrey	25 Apr
3:52:44		Piller			2	NC	Neuilly-sur-Marne	26 Sep
3:52:46	Hartwig	Gauder	GER	10.11.54	1	NC	Kerpen-Horem	23 May
3:52:48	Andrés	Marin	ESP	18.7.61	5	NC	Reus	14 Feb
3:52:50	Sergey	Korepanov	KZK	9.5.64	10	WC	Stuttgart	21 Aug
3:52:55		Mercenario			1		Podebrady	5 Jun
3:53:23	Daniel	Garcia (20)	MEX	12.10.61	1		Cheboksary	5 Jun
3:53:41	Viktor	Ginko	BLS	7.12.65	11	WC	Stuttgart	21 Aug
3:54:07	German	Sánchez	MEX	15.9.66	12	WC	Stuttgart	21 Aug
3:54:15		Sánchez	MEX		3	WCp	Monterrey	25 Apr
3:54:22	Miguel	Rodriguez	MEX	15.5.62	4	WP	Monterrey	25 Apr
	(30/23)							
3:54:30	Giovanni	Perricelli	ITA	25.8.67	13	WC	Stuttgart	21 Aug
3:55:08		Jin Guohong	CHN	5.2.72	2	NG	Beijing	12 Sep
3:55:14	Massimo	Quiriconi	ITA	8.1.63	2	NC	Alife	21 Feb
3:55:21	Edel	Oliva	CUB	12.2.65	1	CAG	Ponce	27 Nov
3:55:44	Alain	Lemercier	FRA	11.1.57	3	NC	Neuilly sur Marne	26 Sep
3:55:57	Bruno	Pennocchio	ITA	7.11.62	3	NC	Alife	21 Feb
3:55:58	Vladimir	Soyka	UKR	29.10.65	2		Alushta	21 Feb
	(30)							
3:56:06	Volkmar	Scholz	GER	20.5.67	3	NC	Kerpen-Horem	23 May
3:56:17	Fumio	Imamura	JPN	5.11.66	1	NC	Wajima	4 Apr
3:56:18.8t	Denis	Terraz	FRA	5.2.58	1	SGP	Fana	8 May
3:56:19	German	Skurygin	RUS	23.12.63	3	NC	Cheboksary	5 Jun
3:56:49.6t	Zoltán	Czukor	HUN	18.12.62	1	SVK Ch	Banská Bystrica	4 Jul
3:57:11	Simon	Baker	AUS	6.2.58	14	WC	Stuttgart	21 Aug
3:57:20	Mike	Harvey	AUS	5.12.62	1	NC	Hawkesbury	10 Jul
3:57:29.5t	José	Urbano	POR	1.3.66	2	SGP	Fana	8 May
3:58:07		Zhou Yongsheng	CHN	15.10.72	3	NG	Beijing	12 Sep
3:58:20	Vyacheslav	Smirnov	RUS	14.5.57	16	WC	Stuttgart	21 Aug
	(40)							
3:59:05	Giacomo	Cimarrusti	ITA	9.6.65	4	NC	Alife	21 Feb
3:59:08	Oleg	Bandurchenko	UKR	16.9.70	3		Alushta	21 Feb
3:59:13	Tadahiro	Kosaka	JPN	10.2.60	2		Takahata	7 Nov
3:59:28	Yuriy	Andronov	RUS	71	1		Yaroslavl	6 Aug
3:59:36		Chen Shaoguo	CHN	20.1.71	1	NC	Shenzhong	21 Feb
3:59:48	Milos	Holusa	TCH	2.5.65	1	NC	Prerov	25 Apr
3:59:57	Antero	Lindman	FIN	25.12.64	1	NC	Kokemäki	5 Sep
3:59:59	Thomas	Wallstab	GER	29.1.68	4	NC	Kerpen-Horem	23 May
4:00:04	Paolo	Bianchi	ITA	7.10.70	5	NC	Alife	21 Feb
4:00:07		Xu Congxian	CHN	4.12.72	4	NG	Beijing	12 Sep
	(50)							
4:00:21	Jan	Holender	POL	12.3.64	2	NC	Zamosc	26 Sep
4:01:06	Joel	Sánchez	MEX	6.8.64	3		Podrebrady	6 Jun
4:01:18		Sun Xiaoguang	CHN	.1.65	5	NG	Beijing	12 Sep
4:01:28	Stefan	Malík	SVK	4.2.66	18	WC	Stuttgart	21 Aug
4:01:36	Jonathan	Matthews	USA	2.7.56	1		Palo Alto	14 Feb
4:01:37	Martin	Bermúdez	MEX	19.5.58	11	WP	Monterrey	25 Apr
4:01:46	Dariusz	Wojcik	AUS	29.9.59	2	NC	Hawkesbury	10 Jul
4:01:51		Zhai Wanbo	CHN	13.2.67	3	NC	Shenzhong	21 Feb
4:02:11	Pascal	Kieffer	FRA	6.5.61	4	NC	Neuilly sur Marne	26 Sep
4:02:13	José	Pinto	POR	19.6.56	1		Montijo	14 Feb
	(60)							
4:02:22		Mao Xinyuan	CHN	2.7.71	5	NC	Shenzhong	21 Feb
4:02:22	Sergey	Pershin	RUS	4.6.68	2		Yaroslavl	6 Aug
4:02:35		Jiao Baozhong	CHN	28.3.73	7	NC	Shenzhong	21 Feb

Mark	Name		Nat	Born	Pos	Meet	Venue	Date
4:02:41		Zhao Yongsheng	CHN	.3.71	6	NG	Beijing	12 Sep
4:03:09	Tomasz	Lipiec	POL	10.5.71	13	WP	Monterrey	25 Apr
4:03:14	Hirofumi	Sakai	JPN	10.2.65	3		Takahata	7 Nov
4:03:20	Aleksandr	Potashov	BLS	12.3.62	2	NC	Novopolotsk	8 May
4:03:21	Walter	Arena	ITA	30.5.64	6	NC	Alife	21 Feb
4:03:24	Julio César	Urias	GUA	11.1.72	3	CAG	Ponce	27 Nov
4:03:25	Valeriy	Yarets	BLS	27.3.56	3	POLCh	Zamosc	26 Sep
	(70)							
4:03:51		Ren Yan	CHN	10.2.69	8	NC	Shenzhong	21 Feb
4:03:55	Les	Morton	GBR	1.7.58	1	NC	Horsham	16 Oct
4:03:57	Nello	Corritore	ITA	11.4.71	7	NC	Alife	21 Feb
4:04:01	Ralf	Weise	GER	15.9.69	5	NC	Kerpen-Horem	23 May
4:04:06	Mechislav	Vezhel	BLS	25.1.62	4	POLCh	Zamosc	26 Sep
4:04:19	Pascal	Charrière	SUI	14.11.64	21	WC	Stuttgart	21 Aug
4:04:21	Rainer	Driesen	GER	20.8.61	6	NC	Kerpen-Horem	23 May
4:04:25	Yuriy	Kotlyar	UKR	27.3.65	4		Alushta	21 Feb
4:04:37	José	Marin	ESP	21.1.50	16	WP	Monterrey	25 Apr
4:04:44	Aleksandr	Voyevodin	RUS	1.3.70	6	NC	Cheboksary	6 Jun
	(80)							
4:04:50.2t	Peter	Malík	SVK	10.12.69	2	NC	Banská Bystrica	4 Jul
4:05:02	Sylvain	Caudron	FRA	10.9.69	5	NC	Neuilly sur Marne	26 Sep
4:05:10		Liu Xiaochun	CHN	7.8.72	9	NC	Shenzhong	21 Feb
4:05:15		Liu Gang	CHN	1.3.72	10	NC	Shenzhong	21 Feb
4:05:19	Massimo	Fizialetti	ITA	7.2.65	8	NC	Alife	21 Feb
4:05:20.7t	Modris	Liepins	LAT	3.8.66	3	SGP	Fana	8 May
4:05:29		Xu Wenquan	CHN	23.1.69	12	NC	Shenzhong	21 Feb
4:05:37	Faustino	Ruiz	ESP	20.9.65	7		Reus	14 Feb
4:05:44	Alessandro	Mistretta	ITA	6.3.71	9	NC	Alife	21 Feb
	4:02:52 unconfirmed				1		Monthey	18 Sep
4:05:50	Nikolay	Yamshchikov	UKR	19.5.61	5		Alushta	21 Feb
	(90)							
4:06:05	Thomas	Prophet	GER	22.5.72	7	NC	Kerpen-Horrem	23 May
4:06:28		Gui Zhixing	CHN	.7.72	13		Shenzhong	21 Feb
4:06:28	Jaime	Barroso	ESP	15.5.68	20	WCp	Monterrey	25 Apr
4:06:32	Orazio	Romanzi	ITA	16.9.70	10	NC	Alife	21 Feb
4:06:38	Fabio	Ruzzier	ITA	21.1.53	11	NC	Alife	21 Feb
4:07:11	Sergey	Katurayev	RUS	29.9.67	7	NC	Cheboksary	5 Jun
4:07:28	Vladimir	Strelchenko	UKR	14.12.70	6		Alushta	21 Feb
4:07:45	Nicola	Casini	ITA	17.4.73	12	NC	Alife	21 Feb
4:07:45	Miguel	Solis	MEX				Vera Cruz	28 Feb
4:07:56		Li Baojin	CHN	23.11.59	14	NC	Shenzhen	21 Feb
	(100)							

Mark	Name		Nat	Born	Date
4:07:57	Igor	Novitskiy	BLS	69	3 Oct
4:08:21		Han Wei	CHN	73	21 Feb
4:08:26	Gyula	Dudas	HUN	66	23 Oct
4:08:29	Hubert	Sonnek	TCH	62	25 Apr
4:08:57		Bo Lingtang	CHN	70	12 Sep
4:09:02		Zang Jiangbo	CHN	75	21 Feb
4:09:03	Adhemir	Domingues	BRA	59	30 Jan
4:09:03	Vincenzo	Genco	ITA	66	21 Feb
4:09:05	Christophe	Cousin	FRA	65	26 Sep
4:09:24	Yoshimi	Hara	JPN	68	4 Apr
	(110)				
4:09:34	Patrizio	Parcesepe	ITA	66	21 Feb
4:09:36	Ulf-Peter	Sjöholm	SWE	65	25 Apr
4:09:37	Johan	Moerdyk	RSA	67	30 Oct
4:09:39	Mikhail	Potashov	BLS	66	8 May
4:09:49	Herm	Nelson	USA	61	14 Feb
4:09:52	Nikolay	Fedorivskiy	UKR	67	21 Feb

WORLD JUNIOR MEN'S LISTS 1993

100 METRES

Mark	Wind		Name	Nat	Born	Pos	Meet	Venue	Date
10.26	2.0		Lin Wei	CHN	16.10.74	2	NG	Beijing	8 Sep
10.31	1.4	Tony	McCall	USA	16.6.74	1		Los Angeles (Ww)	12 Jun
10.32	1.3	Tim	Harden	USA	27.1.74	2h3	NCAA	New Orleans	3 Jun
10.32	0.6	Ibrahim	Meité	CIV	18.11.76	1s1	FraC	Annecy	24 Jul
10.37	1.0	Greg	Saddler	USA	29.6.74	2=		Tuscaloosa	28 Mar
10.37	1.9	Manuel	Cardeñas	MEX	4.9.74	2		México	8 May
10.38	-3.0	Jonathan	Burrell	USA	6.1.74	1	NC-j	Spokane	26 Jun
10.39		Jason	Shelton	JAM	19.3.74	1r2		Kingston	1 May
10.41	0.4	Charles	Mitchell	USA	29.1.75	1		Sacramento	12 Jun
10.43	1.6	Sébastien	Jamain	FRA	13.7.76	1B		Evry-Bondoufle	7 Jun
10.43	1.6	Bryan	Howard	USA	7.10.76	1		Norwalk	19 Jun
10.43	0.1	Maurice	Greene	USA	23.7.75	1		Knoxville	5 Aug
10.43	0.1	Soltane	Al-Sheib	QAT	.76	1		Doha	17 Nov
10.44	1.4	Hajime	Teramoto	JPN	1.1.77	1		Naruto	25 Oct
10.45	1.4	Atsuo	Narita	JPN	18.6.75	1		Aiomori	19 Jun
10.45	??-0.2	Eric	Frempong	CAN	1.10.75	1		Toronto	7 Aug
10.45	1.3	Masato	Ebisawa	JPN	13.11.75	3		Tokyo	17 Oct
10.46	1.4	Derrick	Steagall	USA	21.1.74	2		Los Angeles (Ww)	12 Jun
10.47	1.7	Nick	Rennie	AUS	23.11.74	6		Melbourne	25 Feb
10.47	-3.0	Jermaine	Stafford	USA	25.12.74	3	NC-j	Spokane	26 Jun
10.47	0.0	Danny	Joyce	GBR	9.9.74	1s3	EJ	San Sebastián	29 Jul

Wind assisted

Mark	Wind		Name	Nat	Born	Pos	Meet	Venue	Date
10.12		Héctor	Fuentes	CUB	27.7.74	1		Artemisa	22 Apr
10.24	3.4		Lin Wei	CHN	16.10.74	2	EAsiG	Shanghai	13 May
10.25	2.8	Greg	Saddler	USA	29.6.74	3h1		Knoxville	15 May
10.27	2.8	Ibrahim	Meité	CIV	18.11.76	1h1		Chaux-de-Fonds	8 Aug
10.30A	2.1	Obadele	Thompson	BAH	75	1	CAC	Cali	30 Jul
10.31		Alfredo	Garcia	CUB	5.2.74	2		Artemisa	22 Apr
10.34		Reyner	Padrón	CUB	12.2.75	3		Artemisa	22 Apr
10.34	2.8	Bryan	Howard	USA	7.10.76	1h3		Norwalk	4 Jun
10.34		Jason	Shelton	JAM	19.3.74	3		Kingston	20 Mar
10.35	6.7	Hosia	Abdallah	USA	1.5.74	2		Arlington	10 Apr
10.37		Gaspar	López	CUB	74	4		Artemisa	22 Apr
10.37	4.0	Brian	Lewis	USA	5.12.74	1		Sacramento	8 May
10.37	4.1	Atsuo	Narita	JPN	18.6.75	1		Aomori	29 May
10.37	2.6	Paulo	Neves	POR	12.11.74	1	NCU23	Lisboa	3 Jul
10.37	4.9	Allyn	Condon	GBR	24.8.74	1s2	NC-j	Bedford	3 Jul
10.38	4.9	Ejike	Wodu	GBR	15.12.74	2=s2	NC-j	Bedford	3 Jul
10.38	4.9	Kevin	Mark	GBR	19.10.76	2=s2	NC-j	Bedford	3 Jul
10.39A		Walter	Reed	USA	4.6.74	1		Boulder	4 Apr
10.40	5.7	Danny	Joyce	GBR	9.9.74	2		Blackpool	10 Jul
10.40		Jeff	Roberts	USA	.74	3		Athens, USA	17 Apr

Hand timing

Mark	Wind		Name	Nat	Born	Pos	Meet	Venue	Date
10.1		Tim	Harden	USA	27.1.74	2		Richmond	27 Mar
10.2	1.8	Hosia	Abdallah	USA	1.5.74	2		College Station	20 Mar
10.2		Jermaine	Sharp	USA	14.1.74	1		Monroe	26 Mar
10.2		Tony	Simmons	USA	8.12.74	1		Summit	18 May

Wind assisted

Mark	Wind		Name	Nat	Born	Pos	Meet	Venue	Date
10.0		Jermaine	Stafford	USA	25.12.74	1		Conondauga	1 May
10.1		Ben	Singleton	USA	26.5.75	1		Lynchburg	3 Apr
10.1		Andrew	Berry	USA	.74				16 Apr
10.2w		eight from USA							

200 METRES

Mark	Wind		Name	Nat	Born	Pos	Meet	Venue	Date
20.52	2.0	Charles	Mitchell	USA	29.1.75	1	GWest	Sacramento	12 Jun
20.57	2.0	Calvin	Harrison	USA	20.1.74	2	GWest	Sacramento	12 Jun
20.65		Edward	Hervey	USA	14.3.74	1		Walnut	1 May
20.70		Danny	McCray	USA	11.3.74	1		Waco	17 Apr
20.70	-3.0	Jermaine	Stafford	USA	25.12.74	1	NC-j	Spokane	27 Jun
20.72	1.5	Roshaan	Griffith	USA	21.2.74	3B		Austin	8 May
20.83	0.1	Tim	Harden	USA	27.1.74	2h3		Knoxville	15 May
20.84	1.0	Greg	Saddler	USA	29.6.74	4		Tuscaloosa	28 Mar
20.88		Jamil	Cherry	USA	76	1		Knoxville	7 Aug
20.90		Jonathan	Burrell	USA	6.1.74	1		Dayton	1 May

Mark		Name		Nat	Born	Pos	Meet	Venue	Date
20.93	-1.5	Michael	Barron	USA	74	2		Fayetteville	3 Apr
20.93		George	Page	USA	21.1.74	1		Tempe	10 Apr
20.93	0.0	Darius	Brewington	USA	20.2.75	1		Chapel Hill	22 May
20.95	-0.5	Mark	Keddell	NZL	13.2.75	1	NC	Wellington	6 Mar
20.95	1.0	Allyn	Condon	GBR	24.8.74	1	3N-j	Lübeck	26 Jun
20.98	0.0	Martin	Proulx	CAN	12.6.74	1	NC-j	Sherbrooke	11 Jul
20.99	0.0	Eric	Frempong	CAN	1.10.75	2	NC-j	Sherbrooke	11 Jul
21.00	-0.6	Todd	Blythe	NZL	8.1.75	1B	NC	Wellington	7 Mar
21.00		Maurice	Greene	USA	23.7.75	2		Knoxville	7 Aug
21.02	-1.0	Derrick	Steagall	USA	21.1.74	2		Elmhurst	19 Jun
Wind assisted									
20.55	2.6	Danny	McCray	USA	11.3.74	1A		College Station	10 Apr
20.74		Jeff	Roberts	USA	21.6.74	2		Abilene	8 May
20.84		Tony	Gaiter	USA	15.7.74	1			5 Mar
20.93		Andre	DeSaussure	USA	7.8.75	1		Van Nuys	27 May
20.95	3.5	Nick	Rennie	AUS	23.11.74	1	NC-j	Brisbane	6 Mar
20.99		Byron	Logan	USA	19.4.74	1		Bronx	30 May
21.06	2.1	Bryan	Howard	USA	7.10.76	1h3		Norwalk	4 Jun
21.08A	2.5	Carol	Hancke		31.10.74	1		Krugersdorp	1 Oct
Hand timed - Wind assisted									
20.6	2.9	Manuel	Cardeñas	MEX	4.9.74	1		Ciudad México	2 May
20.7		Andrew	Berry	USA	.74	1		Giddings	24 Apr
20.8		Jerod	Douglas	USA		1			20 Apr
20.8		Brandon	Crockett	USA		1			27 Apr

400 METRES

Mark	Name		Nat	Born	Pos	Meet	Venue	Date
45.07	Calvin	Harrison	USA	20.1.74	1	NC-j	Spokane	27 Jun
	45.10				1h1	NC-j	Spokane	26 Jun
	45.25				1		Norwalk	19 Jun
	45.47				1	GWest	Sacramento	12 Jun
	45.65				3	USOF	San Antonio	31 Jul
	45.79				1	PAJ	Winnipeg	15 Jul
	45.83				1h1		Norwalk	4 Jun
	45.92						San Jose	22 May
45.91	Raoul	Howard	USA	11.3.74	3		Abilene	13 May
	45.94							1 May
46.05	Ben	Beyers	USA	19.5.74	1h2		East Lansing	22 May
46.13	Guy	Bullock	GBR	15.10.75	1	EJ	San Sebastián	31 Jul
46.16	Danny	McCray	USA	11.3.74	3h2		Austin	20 May
46.20	Desmond	Johnson	USA	6.3.77	1		Baton Rouge	8 May
46.25	Alvin	Harrison	USA	20.1.74	2h1	NC-j	Spokane	26 Jun
46.35	Marlon	Ramsey	USA	.75	1		Austin	15 May
46.38	Mark	Keddell	NZL	13.2.75	1		North Shore	30 Jan
46.45	Tomonari	Ono	JPN	7.2.74	3		Naruto	28 Oct
46.46	Rene	Rodriguez	USA	6.4.74	1		Palo Alto	9 May
46.46	Kenji	Tabata	JPN	24.9.74	1		Fairfax	25 Jul
46.47	Hezron	Maina	KEN	16.4.74	1		Canberra	12 Dec
46.49	Robelis	Darroman	CUB	.74	1	NC	Habana	12 May
46.53	George	Page	USA	21.1.74	3		Berkeley	22 May
46.56A	Riaan	Dempers	RSA	4.3.77	1		Germiston	2 Apr
46.56	Davion	Clarke	JAM	30.4.76	1	Carif	Fort-de-France	10 Apr
46.58	Rikard	Rasmusson	SWE	20.5.74	1	v FIN	Stockholm	28 Aug
46.59	Marlon	Dechausay	CAN	31.1.75	1		Tokyo	27 Jun
46.61	Brian	Johnson	USA	.74	4	NC-j	Spokane	27 Jun
Hand timed								
45.4	Danny	McCray	USA	11.3.74	2		College Station	1 May
46.5A	Moses	Mabaso	RSA	28.5.77	1		Johannesburg	20 Nov

800 METRES

Mark	Name		Nat	Born	Pos	Meet	Venue	Date
1:45.46	Hezekiel	Sepeng	RSA	30.6.74	3s1	WC	Stuttgart	15 Aug
	1:45.64				5	WC	Stuttgart	17 Aug
	1:45.97A				1		Potchefstroom	26 Feb
	1:46.00				1	NC	Bellville	24 Apr
	1:46.05A				1		Pretoria	15 May
	1:46.26				1		Stellenbosch	13 Apr
	1:46.27				1h1	WC	Stuttgart	14 Aug

Mark	Name		Nat	Born	Pos	Meet	Venue	Date
1:46.00	Benson	Koech	KEN	10.11.74	4	APM	Hengelo	20 Jun
	1:46.24				1		Pau	26 Jun
1:46.06	Vincent	Malakwen	KEN	19.7.74	2B		Rieti	5 Sep
	1:46.1A						Eldoret	19 Jun?
1:46.38A	Marius	Van Heerden	RSA	8.9.74	2		Pretoria	3 May
1:46.42	Arthémon	Hatungimana	BUR	21.1.74	3	AfrC	Durban	27 Jun
1:46.79A	Johan	Botha	RSA	10.1.74	4		Pretoria	15 May
1:47.05	Alain	Miranda	CUB	19.10.75	1		Habana	26 Jun
1:47.24	Paul	Byrne	AUS	29.1.76	3		Canberra	11 Dec
1:47.28	Tomonari	Ono	JPN	7.2.74	1		Hiroshima	29 Apr
1:47.5A	Hailu	Zewde	ETH	74	2		Addis Ababa	27 May
1:47.78	Farah	Ibrahim Ali	QAT	15.5.74	1		Praha	23 Jun
1:47.97	Kevin	Sullivan	CAN	20.3.74	4		Lindau	8 Aug
1:48.06	Andrzej	Zahorski	POL	3.1.74	2		Bialystok	28 Aug
1:48.35	David	Matthews	IRL	9.4.74	5		Belfast	19 Jun
1:48.79	Igor	Tolokonnikov	RUS	9.2.74	4B	Znam	Moskva	13 Jun
1:48.79	Antonio	Franco	ESP	14.2.74	2		Alcorcón	24 Jun
1:48.8	Vladimir	Gorelyov	RUS	74	3		Voronezh	14 Aug
1:49.01	Massimo	Pegoretti	ITA	16.7.74	7		Rovereto	1 Sep
1:49.07A	Pieter	van Tonder	RSA	6.1.75	3		Germiston	2 Apr
1:49.12	Reyes	Estévez	ESP	2.8.76	4		Barcelona	19 Jul

1000 METRES

Mark	Name		Nat	Born	Pos	Meet	Venue	Date
2:18.37	Vincent	Malakwen	KEN	19.7.74	1	ISTAF	Berlin	27 Aug
2:18.46	Benson	Koech	KEN	10.11.74	4	Pre	Eugene	5 Jun
2:22.6	Glenn	Stojanovic	AUS	3.2.74	1		Sydney	23 Jan
2:23.4	Justin	Switf-Smith	GBR	28.8.74	1		Yate	3 May
2:23.9	Ali	Halimi	TUN	24.4.76	1		St Maur	8 Sep

1500 METRES

Mark	Name		Nat	Born	Pos	Meet	Venue	Date
3:36.47	Benson	Koech	KEN	10.11.74	4	Herc	Monte Carlo	7 Aug
	3:39.06				1	Slovn	Bratislava	1 Jun
3:39.43	Kevin	Sullivan	CAN	20.3.74	1h		North York	23 Jul
	3:40.18				1		Ottawa	3 Jul
	3:40.43				6h	WC	Stuttgart	19 Aug
3:41.61	Javier	Rodriguez	ESP	22.2.74	11		Barcelona	19 Jul
3:42.36	Reyes	Estévez	ESP	2.8.76	2r3		Toledo	19 Jun
3:42.89	Philip	Mosima	KEN	2.1.76	4		Kristiinankaupunki	13 Jul
3:43.08A	Hezekiel	Sepeng	RSA	30.6.74	2		Pretoria	3 May
3:43.53	Massimo	Pegoretti	ITA	16.7.74	6r2		Bologna	3 Sep
3:44.5	Ali	Halimi	TUN	24.4.76	2		St Maur	15 Sep
3:44.65	Mark	Taylor	AUS	14.11.74	3		Canberra	25 Jan
3:45.01		Song Mingyou	CHN	9.1.75	1h	NC	Beijing	10 Jun
3:45.4	Glenn	Stojanovic	AUS	3.2.74	4		Canberra	19 Jan
3:45.40	Justin	Switf-Smith	GBR	28.8.74	4rB		Loughborough	29 Jun
3:45.42	Sami	Ylihärsilä	FIN	14.6.75	8		Kristiinankaupunki	13 Jul
3:45.42	Igor	Murga	ESP	15.3.74	1		San Sebastián	27 Jul
3:45.95	Mikhail	Ulymov	RUS	74	1	NC-j	Vladimir	4 Jul
3:46.3	Terzin	Yunda	ZAM	77	1		Luanshya	13 Nov
3:46.38A	Arnoldus	Sepakwe	RSA	13.3.74	11		Pietersburg	6 Apr
3:46.73	Michael	Power	AUS	9.5.76	1		Melbourne	21 Nov
3:46.90	Giuseppe	Maffei	ITA	28.1.74	7		Bellinzona	26 Jun
3:47.04		Yang Guocai	CHN	.2.75			Guangzhou	22 Mar
3:47.04	Antonio	Franco	ESP	14.2.74	9h2	NC	Gandia	2 Jul

1 MILE

Mark	Name		Nat	Born	Pos	Meet	Venue	Date
3:59.29	Kevin	Sullivan	CAN	20.3.74	1		Waterloo	19 Jun
4:00.80	Glenn	Stojanovic	AUS	3.2.74	1		Melbourne	25 Feb
4:01.8	Massimo	Pegoretti	ITA	16.7.74	1		Trento	28 Sep
4:04.90	Mark	McKeown	NZL	27.5.74	1		Christchurch	15 Dec
4:04.9	Neil	Caddy	GBR	18.3.75	5		Exeter	21 Aug

2000 METRES

Mark	Name		Nat	Born	Pos	Meet	Venue	Date
5:04.4+	Ismael	Kirui	KEN	20.2.75	3	ISTAF	Berlin	27 Aug

3000 METRES

Mark	Name		Nat	Born	Pos	Meet	Venue	Date
7:39.82	Ismael	Kirui	KEN	20.2.75	3	ISTAF	Berlin	27 Aug
	7:42.99				11	Herc	Monaco	7 Aug
	7:45.62+				1m	WC	Stuttgart	16 Aug
	7:48+				m	WK	Zürich	4 Aug
8:00.34A	Christopher	Koskei	KEN	14.8.74	1		Pretoria	15 May
8:04.13	Phillip	Starr	NZL	27.9.74	2		Wellington	18 Dec
8:06.88	Marcel	Socha	POL	27.12.74	5		Sopot	23 May
8:10.22	Arnaud	Crépieux	FRA	18.5.74	6		Arras	26 Jun
8:10.52	Michael	Power	AUS	9.5.76	1		Melbourne	16 Dec
8:10.9	Benoît	Zwierzchiewski	FRA	19.8.76			Molle	8 Aug
8:11.33	Enoch	Skosana	RSA	20.2.74	8		Stellenbosch	15 Feb
8:11.6	Paul	Chemase	KEN	24.8.76	1		Canberra	13 Dec
8:12.6	António	Rebelo	POR	25.2.74	4		Lisboa	23 May
8:13.17+	Philip	Mosima	KEN	2.1.76			Turku	20 Jul
8:13.47	Stefano	Ciallella	ITA	22.4.74	8		Parma	15 Sep
8:14.1	Simone	Zanon	ITA	30.5.75	3		Roncade	11 Jun
8:14.6	Giuseppe	Maffei	ITA	28.1.74			S Donato Milanese	3 Jun
8:14.96	Darius	Burrows	GBR	8.8.75	11		Portsmouth	5 Jun

5000 METRES

Mark	Name		Nat	Born	Pos	Meet	Venue	Date
13:02.75	Ismael	Kirui	KEN	20.2.75	1	WC	Stuttgart	16 Aug
	13:06.50				5	WK	Zürich	4 Aug
	13:06.71				1	Athl	Lausanne	7 Jul
	13:11.82				1	VD	Bruxelles	3 Sep
	13:14.42				2		København	25 Jul
	13:21.67				6		Sevilla	5 Jun
	13:23.26				1	GPF	London	10 Sep
	13:27.50				2s2	WC	Stuttgart	14 Aug
13:41.49		Yang Guocai	CHN	.2.75	5	NG	Beijing	9 Sep
13:43.77	Philip	Mosima	KEN	2.1.76	9		Nurmijärvi	15 Jul
13:45.17	Kenji	Takao	JPN	23.3.75	2		Naruto	28 Oct
13:47.53	Masayuki	Kobayashi	JPN	4.4.74	3		Naruto	28 Oct
13:53.73	Vener	Kashayev	RUS	16.3.74	4		Moskva	13 Jun
13:54.18	Arnaud	Crépieux	FRA	18.5.74	3		Budapest	9 Jun
13:56.09	Meck	Mothuli	RSA	12.4.76	7	NC	Bellville	24 Apr
13:56.17	Michitane	Noda	JPN	25.3.75	4		Naruto	28 Oct
13:58.14	Nobuaki	Yonemitsu	JPN	25.6.74	3		Kumamoto	4 Apr
13:58.30	Daniel	Komen	KEN	17.5.76	1		Canberra	10 Dec
14:00.57		Sun Ripeng	CHN	25.1.74	15		Shizuoka	5 May
14:01.35	John	Maitai	KEN	22.4.76	1		Amagasaki	19 Sep
14:01.78	Daniel	Njenga	KEN	7.5.76	2		Amagasaki	19 Sep
14:02.07	Musyaki	Nguku	KEN	74	2		New Delhi	13 Sep
14:02.63	Kazuhiro	Matsuda	JPN	24.6.74	5		Naruto	28 Oct
14:03.1	Koichi	Kanazawa	JPN	6.3.74	3		Hachioji	20 Jun
14:03.59	Mark	McKeown	NZL	27.5.74	5		Auckland	23 Jan
14:04.86	Javier	Rodriguez	ESP	22.2.74	1		Palafrugell	15 May
14:06.5	Mounir	Khélil	FRA	24.7.74	5		Bourg-en-Bresse	18 Jun
14:07.5	Giuliano	Battocletti	ITA	1.8.75	2		Palermo	18 Jun
Possible junior								
13:40.7	Josephat	Machuka (b.73?)	KEN	12.12.75	3		Nairobi	29 Jul

10,000 METRES

Mark	Name		Nat	Born	Pos	Meet	Venue	Date
28:07.1A	Ismael	Kirui	KEN	20.2.75	1	NC	Nairobi	3 Jul
	28:14.2A				3	IS	Nairobi	11 Jun
	28:33.7A				1		Nairobi	29 Jul
28:34.0A	Musyaki	Nguku	KEN	74		2	Nairobi	29 Jul
28:41.72		Sun Ripeng	CHN	25.1.74	2	NG	Beijing	13 Sep
28:50.94	Meck	Mothuli	RSA	12.4.76	2		Port Elizabeth	17 May
28:55.85	Philip	Mosima	KEN	2.1.76	1		Tuusula	6 Jul
29:02.2	Kazuhiro	Matsuda	JPN	24.6.74	15		Hachioji	28 Nov
29:03.2	Michitane	Noda	JPN	25.3.75			Hachioji	5 Dec
29:04.39	Takaomi	Kawanami	JPN	18.1.74	5		Maebashi	2 May
29:19.3	Masanori	Takada	JPN	8.2.74			Hachioji	5 Dec
29:28.20	Koichi	Kanazawa	JPN	6.3.74	2		Tokyo	1 May

Mark		Name		Nat	Born	Pos	Meet	Venue	Date
29:29.5		Shigekatsu	Kondo	JPN	17.10.74			Hachioji	5 Dec
29:29.8		Kenji	Noguchi	JPN	23.2.75			Saitama	6 Oct
29:37.5		Hiroyuki	Kodama	JPN	20.4.74			Hachioji	5 Dec
29:37.75		Ricardo	Fernández	ESP	5.7.74	1	EJ	San Sebastián	31 Jul
29:39.1		Masayuki	Yoshida	JPN	6.12.74			Hachioji	5 Dec
29:39.72			Yang Guocai	CHN	.2.75	1		Beijing	4 May
29:39.9		Kenji	Takao	JPN	23.3.75	1		Miyazaki	17 Apr
29:40.00		Valeriy	Kuzmin	RUS	29.3.75	2	EJ	San Sebastián	31 Jul
29:41.5		Antonio	Andriani	ITA	4.1.74	4		Bologna	17 Jun
29:41.68		Aleksey	Sobolev	RUS	14.3.74	3	EJ	San Sebastián	31 Jul

Unconfirmed

29:29.8 Takashi Kanazawa JPN 29.8.74, 29:38.0 Kikuo Ozawa JPN 14.10.74, 29:40.5 Eiji Hinata JPN 10.1.74

Possible junior: 28:00.72 Josephat Machuka KEN 12.12.75 (73?) 4 AfrC Durban 25 Jun

MARATHON

Mark		Name		Nat	Born	Pos	Meet	Venue	Date
2:14:54		Luis Carlos	da Silva	BRA	.76	3		Blumenau	25 Jul
2:19:14		Kaesa	Tadesse	ETH	21.8.74	1		Livorno	14 Nov

2000 METRES STEEPLECHASE

Mark		Name		Nat	Born	Pos	Meet	Venue	Date
5:33.96		Samuel	Chepkok	KEN	76	1		Canberra	11 Dec
5:34.19		Paul	Chemase	KEN	24.8.76	2		Canberra	11 Dec
5:38.38		Adam	Dobrzynski	POL	19.12.74	1		Warszawa	18 Jul
5:40.10		Stefano	Ciallella	ITA	22.4.74	8		Caserta	6 Jun
5:42.22		Antonio	Alvárez	ESP	19.2.77	1		Valkenswaard	8 Jul
5:43.32		Johannes	Schmid	GER	17.4.74	1		Pliezhausen	9 May
5:45.34		Mariusz	Pulawski	POL	14.2.74	2		Warszawa	18 Jul
5:45.51		Domenico	D'Ambrosio	ITA	18.7.75			Caserta	6 Jun

3000 METRES STEEPLECHASE

Mark		Name		Nat	Born	Pos	Meet	Venue	Date
8:24.58		Christopher	Koskei	KEN	14.8.74	2	AfrC	Durban	25 Jun
		8:29.25				1		Port Elizabeth	17 May
		8:34.5A				3	IS	Nairobi	11 Jun
8:24.87			Sun Ripeng	CHN	25.1.74	1	NG	Beijing	11 Sep
8:41.15		Stefano	Ciallella	ITA	22.4.74	6		Arzignano	13 Jun
8:41.46		Daniel	Njenga	KEN	7.5.76	1		Utsunomiya	5 Aug
8:43.06		Adam	Dobrzynski	POL	19.12.74	4	Mal	Grudziadz	18 Jun
8:47.21		Javier	Rodriguez	ESP	22.2.74	2		Alicante	7 Aug
8:52.68		Pascal	Garin	FRA	19.12.74	3	EJ	San Sebastián	1 Aug
8:54.4		Mariano	Tarilo	ARG	74	1		Buenos Aires	7 Nov
8:55.25		Danielle	Banchini	ITA	21.4.74	17		Bologna	3 Aug
8:56.2		Domenico	D'Ambrosio	ITA	18.7.75	1		Roma	26 Sep
8:56.71		Marc	Ruiz	ESP	5.2.74	4	EJ	San Sebastián	1 Aug
8:56.75		Minoru	Arita	JPN	13.8.75	1h1		Naruto	25 Oct
8:57.11		José	Serrano	POR	75	5	EJ	San Sebastián	1 Aug
8:57.51		Jean-Nicolas	Duval	CAN	16.9.74	7		Montreal	2 Jul
8:57.99		Maximilian	Perrella	ITA	20.4.74	1		Pescara	9 May
8:58.24		Miroslaw	Bieniecki	POL	21.1.75	4		Zabrze	26 Jun
8:58.82		Giuseppe	Maffei	ITA	28.1.74	2		Milano	23 May
8:59.42		Clement	Hagima	ROM	18.5.74			Bucuresti	18 Jun
8:59.50		Mamoru	Kawagoe	JPN	7.10.75	2		Utsonimiya	5 Aug
8:59.70		Hasan	Yilmaz	TUR	74				

110 METRES HURDLES

Mark		Name		Nat	Born	Pos	Meet	Venue	Date
13.52	0.6	Ubeja	Anderson	USA	30.3.74	1		Knoxville	16 May
		13.53	0.1			1	FlaR	Gainesville	27 Mar
		13.62				1h1		Atlanta	22 May
		13.72	2.0			1h1	NCAA	New Orleans	3 Jun
		13.73				2		Atlanta	22 May
		13.57w	2.5			4h2	NC	Eugene	17 Jun
13.81	1.6	Jeff	Jackson	USA	14.3.74	1		San Marcos	27 Mar
13.81		Kevin	White	USA	16.8.74	1		Houston	30 Mar
13.85	0.9	Robin	Korving	HOL	29.7.74	1	EJ	San Sebastián	31 Jul
13.93	2.0	Curt	Young	USA	18.1.74	3		Abilene	13 May
13.94	-1.6	Willie	Hibler	USA	30.8.74	2		Fayetteville	3 Apr
13.95		Erick	Batle	CUB	10.12.74	1		Habana	18 Jun
13.99	-0.6	Prodomos	Katsantonis	CYP	20.10.75	1		Nicosia	15 May

Mark		Name		Nat	Born	Pos	Meet	Venue	Date
14.03	1.6	Wojciech	Sitek	POL	10.4.74	4h1	Kuso	Kielce	16 Jun
14.06	-2.5	Frank	Busemann	GER	26.2.75	1	3N-j	Lübeck	26 Jun
14.06	0.9	Tibor	Bédi	HUN	22.3.74	2	EJ	San Sebastián	31 Jul
14.12	1.9	Kehinde	Aladefa	NGR	19.12.74	3		Abilene	29 May
14.12	0.1	Tomasz	Krawczyk	POL	3.8.74	2h2	NC	Kielce	25 Jul
14.14		Emerson	Perin	BRA	17.3.75	4		Rio de Janeiro	27 Jun
14.15	1.4	Filip	Bickel	GER	12.2.75	1h1		Scheessel	30 May
14.20	0.0		Li Qiang	CHN	13.2.74			Guangzhou	22 Mar
14.20	-0.8	Dwayne	Riley	USA	9.12.74	2s2	PAJ	Winnipeg	16 Jul
14.20	0.6	Nobuto	Watanabe	JPN	20.10.76	1		Naruto	25 Oct
14.21	0.4	Laszlo	Sarucan	ROM	1.8.74	1s3	EJ	San Sebastián	30 Jul
14.23		Frank	Mensah	GHA	74	2		Athens, USA	1 May
14.23	0.0	Neil	Gardener	JAM	.74	1	NC-j	Kingston	3 Jul

Wind assisted

Mark		Name		Nat	Born	Pos	Meet	Venue	Date
13.75	4.3	Kevin	White	USA	16.8.74	1		Houston	20 Mar
13.77	3.1	Kehinde	Aladefa	NGR	19.12.74	1h1		Abilene	28 May
13.84	4.0	Tibor	Bédi	HUN	22.3.74	1		Veszprém	22 Jul
13.84A	2.7	Erick	Batle	CUB	10.12.74	1	CAC	Cali	1 Aug

Hand timed

Mark		Name		Nat	Born	Pos	Meet	Venue	Date
14.0		Mohamed	Abdel Saad	EGY	24.4.74	1		El Maadi	7 Jul
14.0		Filip	Bickel	GER	12.2.75				

400 METRES HURDLES

Mark	Name		Nat	Born	Pos	Meet	Venue	Date
50.00	Alejandro	Argudin	CUB	10.3.74	1	NC-j	Habana	14 May
50.23	Sammy	Biwott	KEN	23.7.74	3		Lisboa	19 Jun
50.27	Carlos	Silva	POR	8.6.74	1	EJ	San Sebastián	1 Aug
50.44	Eugene	van der Westhuizen	RSA	30.8.74	1		Cape Town	20 Mar
50.55	Kehinde	Aladefa	NGR	19.12.74	4		Abilene	29 May
50.79A	Jaco	Jonker	RSA	5.2.75	1		Germiston	2 Apr
50.93	Takahiro	Inoue	JPN	8.1.74	1h5		Tokyo	12 Sep
51.04	Francesco	Ricci	ITA	31.5.74	1s3	EJ	San Sebastián	31 Jul
51.10	Hideaki	Kawamura	JPN	15.9.74	1		Tsukuba	26 Sep
51.14	Inigo	Monreal	ESP	26.9.74	2s3	EJ	San Sebastián	31 Jul
51.15	Igor	Frolov	RUS	13.1.74	2h4	NC	Moskva	18 Jun
51.17	Noel	Levy	GBR	22.6.75	1	v2N	Lübeck	26 Jun
51.19	Chris	Carroll	AUS	9.5.74	1	NC-j	Brisbane	6 Mar
51.21	Jeff	Jackson	USA	14.3.74	1	Drake R	Des Moines	23 Apr
51.26	Mohamed	Al-Bishy	SAU	.75	1		Doha	19 Nov
51.30A	Wessel	Dippenaar	RSA	14.3.74	3		Bloemfontein	22 Feb
51.30A	Eugene	Massyn	RSA	11.9.74	3		Germiston	2 Apr
51.36	Nobuo	Narimatsu	JPN	4.2.74	1		Saeki	29 Sep
51.38	Tsuyoshi	Yasuda	JPN	10.12.74	1h		Tokyo	23 May

HIGH JUMP

Mark	Name		Nat	Born	Pos	Meet	Venue	Date
2.28		Bi Hongyong	CHN	16.11.74	2	NG	Beijing	11 Sep
2.26i	Sergey	Klyugin	RUS	24.3.74	1		Pescara	20 Feb
	2.24				1		Kineshma	6 Nov
2.25	Jagan	Hames	AUS	31.10.75	1		Adelaide	27 Nov
2.24	Aleksandr	Zhuravlyov	UKR	22.3.74	1=		Rovno	25 May
2.22	Billy	Green	USA	8.8.75	1		Ruston	22 Apr
2.21	Eric	Bishop	USA	7.6.76	1		Hampton	Jun
2.21	Niclas	Grundner	AUT	24.3.74	1		Südstadt	27 Jun
2.21	Attila	Zsivótzky	HUN	29.4.77	1		Valkenswaard	8 Jul
2.21	Jordi	Rofes	ESP	24.9.76	2		Valkenswaard	8 Jul
2.21	Dillon	Phelps	USA	1.12.74	1	PAJ	Winnipeg	17 Jul
2.20	Tomohiro	Nomura	JPN	11.10.75	1		Tokyo	1 May
2.20	Tomás	Janku	TCH	27.12.74	8	ECp	Roma	26 Jun
2.19	Jeff	Nadeau	USA	7.11.74	1		Van Nuys	13 May
2.19		Gao Yuanming	CHN	22.11.75	5	NG	Beijing	11 Sep
2.18	Charles	Ford	USA	.74	1		San Angelo	27 Mar
2.18	Derren	Hambrick	USA	.74			Florida	1 Apr
2.18	Ivan	Wagner	USA	17.12.76	2		San Antonio	10 Apr
2.18	Jeremy	Fischer	USA	16.2.76	1		Walnut	16 Apr
2.18	Kevin	Schleicher	USA	.74	1		Brooksville	30 Apr
2.18	Eugene	Grundy	USA	19.8.75	1		Fort Knox	22 May

Mark		Name		Nat	Born	Pos	Meet	Venue	Date
2.18		Michael	Caza	CAN	21.4.74	1		Windsor	28 May
2.18		Kristofer	Lamos	GER	1.1.74	1		Fulda	12 Jun
2.18		Luca	Zampieri	ITA	15.2.74	1		Bergamo	20 Jun
2.18		Vyacheslav	Voronin	RUS	.74	1	NC-j	Vladimir	3 Jul
2.18		Robert	Michniewski	POL	16.2.74	4	EJ	San Sebastián	1 Aug
2.18		Mika	Polku	FIN	19.7.75	1	NC-y	Kemi	8 Aug
2.18		Roland	Stark	GER	10.7.75	3		Berlin	5 Sep

POLE VAULT

Mark		Name		Nat	Born	Pos	Meet	Venue	Date
5.71		Lawrence	Johnson	USA	7.5.74	1		Knoxville	12 Jun
		5.61				1		Knoxville	1 May
		5.55				2	USOF	San Antonio	30 Jul
		5.52				2		Gainesville	24 Apr
		5.52				1		Chapel Hill	26 May
		5.51				1	NC-j	Spokane	26 Jun
5.55		James	Miller	AUS	4.6.74	1		Perth	7 Feb
5.55		Yuriy	Yeliseyev	RUS	27.5.75	1		Liége	22 Sep
5.46		Daren	McDonough	USA	29.5.74	1		Champaign	17 Apr
5.42		Dmitriy	Markov	BLS	14.3.75	1		Schwechat	30 May
5.40i		Khalid	Lachheb	FRA	16.1.75	3		La Roche-sur-Yon	6 Mar
		5.40				1	EJ	San Sebastián	1 Aug
5.40i		Taoufik	Lacheeb	FRA	16.1.75	4		La Roche-sur-Yon	6 Mar
		5.35				2	EJ	San Sebastián	1 Aug
5.40		Christian	Tamminga	HOL	30.4.74	1		Zierikzee	9 May
5.40		Neil	Winter	GBR	21.3.74	5	v USA	Edinburgh	2 Jul
5.35		Viktor	Chistyakov	RUS	9.2.75	3	EJ	San Sebastián	1 Aug
5.35		Akifumi	Funatsu	JPN	5.10.74	2		Tokyo	10 Sep
5.30		Aleksandr	Averbukh	RUS	1.10.74			Chelyabinsk	5 Jun
5.30		Martin	Kysela	TCH	25.3.74	4	EJ	San Sebastián	1 Aug
5.25		Manabu	Yokoyama	JPN	20.7.74	2		Tokyo	26 Jun
5.21		Tye	Harvey	USA	25.9.74	1		Modesto	19 May
5.20i		Michael	Stolle	GER	17.12.74	2		Minsk	27 Feb
5.20			Li Wei	CHN	.3.75	2		Beijing	4 May
5.20		Aleksandr	Danilovs	LAT	7.5.75	1		Riga	12 May
5.20		Alain	Andji	FRA	20.11.74	6		Dreux	29 May
5.20		Krzysztof	Kusiak	POL	13.5.74	1		Warszawa	12 Jun
5.20		Hideji	Suzuki	JPN	10.3.74	9	NC	Tokyo	13 Jun
5.20		Yevgeniy	Smiryagin	RUS	76	1		Yekaterinburg	19 Jun
5.20		Vadim	Desyaterik	UKR	8.3.76	1		Donetsk	22 Jun
5.20		Yevgeniy	Yefinochkin	UKR	25.4.75	2		Donetsk	22 Jun
5.20		Karel	Janko	TCH	2.4.74	1		Praha	23 Jun
5.20		Ariel	Mäki-Soini	FIN	23.7.75	7=		Somero	11 Jul
5.20		Yevgeniy	Smirnov	RUS	74	2		Rostov na Donu	15 Jul
5.20		Zdenek	Safár	TCH	28.2.75	1		Jablonec	17 Jul
5.20		Przemyslaw	Gurin	POL	17.2.75	1		Warszawa	18 Jul

LONG JUMP

Mark	Wind	Name		Nat	Born	Pos	Meet	Venue	Date
8.09		Juan Carlos	Garzón	CUB	16.2.74	1		Artemisa	23 Apr
		8.09	1.0			2	NC	Habana	12 May
		7.91A				2	CAC	Cali	30 Jul
8.06	0.4	Huang Baotin		CHN	.5.74	1		Beijing	3 May
7.87		Leon	Gordon	JAM	1.7.74	1		Kingston	2 Apr
7.87	1.9	Andrej	Benda	SVK	25.9.75	1		Bratislava	15 May
7.86	1.8	Yassin	Guellet	BEL	23.2.74	1		Merksem	23 May
7.85	1.6	Daisuke	Watanabe	JPN	29.5.75	*		Naruto	26 Oct
7.83		Aleksandr	Savinov	RUS	3.2.74	1		Krasnodar	26 May
7.81i		Marvin	Forde	TRI	30.7.75				
		7.65				4	USOF	San Antonio	31 Jul
7.80	-2.6	Ryan	Moore	AUS	18.10.74	*		Perth	4 Dec
7.78i		Matias	Ghansah	SWE	27.8.74	2		Stockholm	9 Feb
7.78		Michael	Hessek	GER	15.3.75	1	NC-j	Dortmund	4 Jul
7.76	0.7	Carl	Howard	GBR	27.1.74	1	EJ	San Sebastián	31 Jul
7.76	0.0	Takanori	Sugibayashi	JPN	14.3.76	3	Toto	Fukuoka	18 Sep
7.73		Christian	Walter	GER	17.11.76	1		Jena	5 Jun
7.72A	0.4	John	Oosthuizen	RSA	3.2.74	1		Germiston	2 Apr

Mark		Name		Nat	Born	Pos	Meet	Venue	Date
7.72	1.4	Vyacheslav	Korneychuk	UKR	24.2.74	1		Chernigov	26 Jun
7.72	0.7	Randy	Sedoc	HOL	8.9.75	3	NC	Amsterdam	24 Jul
7.71		Neil	Gardener	JAM	74	2		Kingston	2 Apr
7.71		Mikhail	Nesteruk	RUS	14.6.74	1	NC-j	Vladimir	4 Jul
Wind assisted									
7.93	3.0	Nicola	Trentin	ITA	20.6.64	1		Selargius	28 Apr
7.89	2.2	Daisuke	Watanabe	JPN	29.5.75	1		Naruto	26 Oct
7.87		Kevin	Dilworth	USA	14.2.74	1		Lubbock	27 Mar
7.84	4.6	Ryan	Moore	AUS	18.10.74	1		Perth	11 Dec
7.74	4.1	Shane	Hair	AUS	24.10.75	1		Canberra	11 Dec
7.73	2.1	Bogdan	Tarus	ROM	1.8.75	1	Balk-j	Thessaloniki	10 Jul

TRIPLE JUMP

Mark		Name		Nat	Born	Pos	Meet	Venue	Date
17.27		Aliecer	Urrutia	CUB	22.9.74	1		Artemisa	23 Apr
		16.56				3	NC	Habana	14 May
17.00		Yevgeniy	Timofeyev	RUS	22.2.74	1		Krasnodar	26 May
16.77		Michel	Martinez	CUB	6.11.74	2		Habana	18 Jun
16.61	1.8		Zhang Jun	CHN	.1.74	1		Shijiazhuang	26 Apr
16.54		César	Rizo	CUB	8.10.75	3		Artemisa	23 Apr
16.49	1.0	Larry	Achike	GBR	31.1.75	4	NC	London	12 Jun
16.43	1.6	Nikolay	Telushkin	RUS	24.7.74	3		Dzerzhinsk	30 Aug
16.41	0.4	Paolo	Camossi	ITA	6.1.74	1	EJ	San Sebastián	31 Jul
16.35	-0.4	Rostislav	Dimitrov	BUL	26.12.74	2	EJ	San Sebastián	31 Jul
16.24i	-	Viktor	Sotnikov	RUS	17.7.74	1		Volgograd	31 Jan
		16.17				1	NC-j	Vladimir	2 Jul
		16.54 unconfirmed							
16.23		Jorge	Baro	CUB	.74	4		Habana	2 Jul
16.12		Luis	Ferrer	CUB	75	7		Habana	14 May
16.07		Angel	Cabrera	CUB	75	4		Artemisa	23 Apr
16.04	1.3	Johan	Meriluoto	FIN	22.3.74	1		Vantaa	10 Aug
16.03i	-	Sergey	Perveyev	RUS	.74	2		Volgograd	31 Jan
15.96		Peter	Burge	AUS	3.4.74	1		Brisbane	19 Nov
15.92		Andre	Scott	USA	19.11.74	1		Jacksonville	20 Mar
15.87	0.0	Olivier	Borderan	FRA	20.2.76	1		Tarbes	17 Jul
15.86		Vyacheslav	Taranov	RUS	75	3		Krasnodar	26 May
15.86		Salvatore	Morello	ITA	.74			Napoli	12 Sep
Wind assisted									
16.35	2.8	Johan	Meriluoto	FIN	22.3.74	3		Riga	29 May
16.09	3.3	Olivier	Borderan	FRA	20.2.76	5	EJ	San Sebastián	31 Jul
15.97		Jonathan	Jordan	USA	26.11.74	1	NC-j	Spokane	27 Jun
15.91	2.1	D	Voskresenskiy	RUS	74	8		Sochi	23 May
15.78	9.2	Erik	Clinton	USA	29.1.74	2	NC-j	Spokane	27 Jun

SHOT

Mark	Name		Nat	Born	Pos	Meet	Venue	Date
19.53	Manuel	Martinez	ESP	7.12.74	Q	WC	Stuttgart	20 Aug
	19.17				1		Barcelona	24 Jul
	19.11				1	4N	Alicante	7 Aug
	19.03				12	WC	Stuttgart	21 Aug
	19.02				1	EJ	San Sebastián	1 Aug
18.75	Elias	Louca	CYP	23.7.74	1		Limassol	14 Jul
18.40	Arsi	Harju	FIN	18.3.74	3		Hämeenkyrä	1 Jul
18.39i	Yuriy	Belonog	UKR	9.3.74	1		Donetsk	30 Jan
17.97i	Jonathan	Ogden	USA	31.7.74				29 May
	17.55				1		Spokane	27 Jun
17.84i	Vladimir	Lukovkin	RUS	8.3.74	1		Volgograd	22 Jan
17.83	Avtar	Singh	IND	.74	1		Bombay	8 Nov
17.53	Christian	Schätze	GER	8.5.74	1		Gernsbach	24 Apr
17.38	Leif Dolonen	Larsen	NOR	3.4.75	2		Drammen	31 May
17.35	Ville	Tiisanoja	FIN	24.12.75	1		Tuusula	6 Jul
17.29	Kiril	Valchanov	BUL	1.3.74	1		Sofia	3 Jul
17.23	Detlef	Bock	GER	15.8.74	1		Osterode	8 Aug
17.19	Frits	Potgieter	RSA	13.3.74	1		Rustenburg	30 Oct
17.17	Friso	Hagman	HOL	14.3.74	1		Utrecht	20 May
16.90	Tinus	Pretorius	RSA	14.6.74	3		Rustenburg	30 Oct
16.78	Alexander	Holz	GER	5.9.74	4		Berlin	4 Sep

Mark	Name		Nat	Born	Pos	Meet	Venue	Date
16.77i	Ionel	Stefan	ROM	17.12.74	1		Bucuresti	6 Mar
16.70	Erdogan	Önder	TUR	.74			Ankara	15 May
16.68	Attila	Tóth	HUN	22.1.74	2		Veszprém	30 Jun
16.65	Carlos	Geronés	ESP	7.6.75	3		Villanova	13 Feb

DISCUS

Mark	Name		Nat	Born	Pos	Meet	Venue	Date
61.34		Li Shaojie	CHN	.12.75	1		Jinan	1 Apr
	60.86				1	NG	Beijing	13 Sep
	60.14				1		Shanghai	11 Apr
59.12	Frits	Potgieter	RSA	13.3.74	1	AAA-j	Bedford	4 Jul
58.28	Frantz	Kruger	RSA	22.5.75	1		Rustenburg	30 Oct
56.40	Mika	Loikkanen	FIN	20.2.74	1		Alavieska	1 Jul
55.74	Leonid	Cherevko	BLS	21.4.74				
	54.98				1	EJ	San Sebastián	30 Jul
55.56	Timo	Sinervo	FIN	5.8.75	2		Alavieska	4 Jul
55.42	Marco	Jakobs	GER	30.5.74	4		Recklinghausen	19 Jun
54.96		Gao Shan	CHN	.1.74	8		Shijiazhuang	26 Apr
54.84	Arkadiy	Tokayev	RUS	20.6.74				
	53.52				1	NC-j	Vladimir	4 Jul
53.96	José Luis	Valencia	ESP	23.7.74	1		Barcelona	26 Jun
53.88	Manuel	Pequeno	CUB	29.11.74	2		Habana	25 Jun
53.48	Róbert	Fazekas	HUN	18.8.75	2		Szombathely	6 Oct
53.02	Oleg	Ignatyev	RUS	74	3		Stavropol	30 May
53.00	Andrey	Kononchik	BLS	74	2	NC-j	Gomel	21 May
52.80	Andrey	Vitkovskiy	UKR	76	1		Odessa	20 Mar
52.52	Julio	Piñero	ARG	4.6.75	1	SAmJ	Barcelona, VEN	19 Jun
52.42	Alexander	Forst	GER	11.6.75	1		Dortmund	8 May
52.30	Marvin	Whylly	BAH	?	1	NC	Nassau	19 Jun
52.22	Ville	Tiisanoja	FIN	24.12.75	4		Nastola	17 Jun
52.14	Doug	Reynolds	USA	11.8.75	1	NC-j	Spokane	26 Jun
52.14	Robert	Russell	GBR	5.8.74	2	NC-j	Belford	4 Jul

HAMMER

Mark	Name		Nat	Born	Pos	Meet	Venue	Date
72.72	Vadim	Khersontsev	RUS	8.7.74	3		Rostov na Donu	17 Jul
70.80	Sergey	Kochetkov	UKR	29.1.74	1C		Yalta	23 Jan
70.70	Albert	Petukhov	UKR	5.3.74	2		Alushta	24 Apr
70.16	Vadim	Burakov	BLS	22.10.74	3		Gomel	15 Jul
69.56	Vítor	Costa	POR	28.5.74	1		Rennes	15 May
69.56	Loris	Paoluzzi	ITA	14.5.74	1		Gorizia	26 Oct
69.38	Artyom	Rubanko	UKR	21.3.74	3C		Yalta	23 Jan
69.26	Adrián	Annus	HUN	28.6.74	5		Tapolca	21 Aug
68.96	Eduard	Piskunov	UKR	7.6.76	3		Rovno	25 May
68.00	Koji	Murofushi	JPN	8.10.74	1		Sapporo	1 Aug
67.34	Szymon	Ziolkowski	POL	1.7.76	1		Bydgoszcz	4 Sep
67.06	Norbert	Horváth	HUN	13.3.75	2		Szombathely	26 May
67.02	Igor	Tugay	UKR	75	4	NC-j	Chernigov	26 Jun
66.92	Andrey	Mokrov	RUS	.74	3		Stavropol	30 May
66.36	Vasiliy	Shevchenko	UKR	76	4		Rovno	25 May
65.48	Sergey	Vasilyev	RUS	75	1	3N-j	Lübeck	26 Jun
65.34 ?	R	Cherkashin	UKR		7		Rovno	25 May
65.22	O	Sergeyev	RUS	77	1		Togliatti	15 Aug
64.76	Matthew	Dwight	AUS	2.7.74	1		Sydney	5 Jun
64.00	A	Baburkin	RUS	74	4		Rostov na Donu	17 Jul
63.60	Sergey	Lobzov	RUS	74	2	NC-j	Vladimir	2 Jul
	67.18 unconfirmed							

JAVELIN

Mark	Name		Nat	Born	Pos	Meet	Venue	Date
78.18i	Aki	Parviainen	FIN	26.10.74	1		Kuopio	7 Mar
	69.94				7		Lapinlahti	27 Jun
75.92	Tero	Angeria	FIN	4.5.74	1		Pihtipudas	1 Jul
74.58		Shi Dewu	CHN	20.4.75			Beijing	2 May
74.32	Markku	Liikala	FIN	8.8.74	1		Skien	22 Aug
73.54	Károly	Szabó	HUN	31.5.74	3	3-N	Praha	17 Jul
73.18	Matti	Närhi	FIN	17.8.75	1	NC-y	Kemi	7 Aug
73.00	Marius	Corbett	RSA	26.9.75	1		Cradock	19 Feb

Mark	Name		Nat	Born	Pos	Meet	Venue	Date
72.80	Dimitris	Polimerou	GRE	17.5.74	1	EJ	San Sebastián	1 Aug
72.46	Robert	Srovnal	TCH	13.6.75	1		Praha	2 Jun
72.36	Yoshiyuki	Yamamoto	JPN	14.12.74	1		Osaka	28 Aug
71.88	Delyle	Woods	USA	22.9.74	1	PAJ	Winnipeg	15 Jul
71.74	Teruhide	Takahashi	JPN	4.4.74	1		Hiratsuka	2 Oct
70.98	Dmitriy	Konstantinov	UKR	12.10.74	4		Donetsk	29 May
70.92		Xia Zhenghua	CHN	11.2.74	8	NC	Beijing	10 Jun
70.68	Tomoya	Ishigura	JPN	26.2.74	1		Tokyo	27 Jun
70.50	Isbel	Luaces	CUB	20.7.75	2	PAG-j	Winnipeg	15 Jul
70.34	Hannu	Virta	FIN	29.6.77	1		Tampere	12 Sep
70.24	Jörg	Tobisch	GER	29.12.75	3	EJ	San Sebastián	1 Aug
69.90	Andrey	Sokolov	RUS	.74	1	NC-j	Vladimir	3 Jul
Old model javelin								
74.40	Darby	Roberts	USA	28.1.75	1		Hill City	21 May

DECATHLON

Mark	Name		Nat	Born	Pos	Meet	Venue	Date
7749A	Raul	Duany	CUB	4.1.75	1	CAC	Cali	31 Jul
	11.3 7.27 12.92 2.04 49.2		14.6 37.02 4.40 59.02 4:31.5					
	7715				2	CAG	Ponce	24 Nov
	11.44 7.55 12.55 2.03 49.20		15.28 36.52 4.14 66.08 4:24.11					
7618	Pierre Alexandre	Vial	FRA	25.5.75	1		Versailles	27 Jun
	10.91 7.15 12.12 1.89 48.32		14.92 42.50 4.60 53.32 4:41.47					
7576	Lawrence	Johnson	USA	7.5.74	1		Knoxville	14 May
	11.23 6.72 11.85 1.99 49.55		14.60 36.18 5.50 52.36 4:50.53					
7534	Christer	Holger	SWE	16.1.74	1	EJ	San Sebastián	30 Jul
	11.43 7.22 12.12 1.94 49.80		15.11 39.82 4.50 53.98 4:20.36					
7483w	Les	Kuorikoski	AUS	16.3.74	1		Eskilstuna	15 Aug
	11.29 6.47W 13.44 1.88 50.93		15.52 4.32 4.60 63.74 4:35.62					
7433w	Paul	Jeffery	AUS	14.1.74	3	NC	Brisbane	9 Mar
	10.99 7.17W 11.75 1.82 48.93		15.73 37.92 4.60 59.70 4:35.71					
7417	Ryan	Theriault	USA	2.3.75	1		Tempe	30 May
	11.34 6.98 14.86 1.80 51.34		14.75 45.64 4.35 13.70 4:46.43					
7396	Jan	Podebradsky	TCH	1.3.74	2	EJ	San Sebastián	30 Jul
	11.17 6.61 12.66 1.88 48.49		14.85 36.70 4.30 50.76 4:13.94					
7351		Song Shulin	CHN	12.2.74	7	NG	Beijing	10 Sep
	11.42 6.73 13.03 1.87 50.53		15.63 40.80 4.90 53.96 4:36.44					
7339	Philipp	Huber	SUI	18.2.74	3		Landquart	6 Jun
	11.04w 6.97 13.52 1.89 49.48		15.58 32.64 4.50 49.98 4:23.00					
7338	Stefan	Vogt	GER	17.1.74	3	EJ	San Sebastián	30 Jul
	11.30 6.68 12.91 1.88 49.52		15.38 39.52 4.50 53.28 4:28.76					
7311	Benjamin	Jensen	NOR	13.4.75	4	EJ	San Sebastián	30 Jul
	11.41 6.93 11.02 2.03 50.22		15.05 33.58 4.70 52.20 4:30.30					
7262	Dirk	Schmidt	GER	20.2.74	1		Bernhausen	13 Jun
	11.06 7.34 12.61 2.03 50.25		15.64 37.16 4.30 45.60 4:47.38					
7238	Imants	Gailis	LAT	11.3.74	1		Murjani	9 May
	11.8 6.49 13.10 2.15 53.4		15.4 37.22 4.20 67.40 4:33.9					
7175	Jörg	Goedicke	GER	25.6.74	3		Bernhausen	13 Jun
	11.58 7.01 12.71 2.03 51.71		15.58 36.48 4.50 49.16 4:37.68					
7149	Sandijs	Ilgunas	LAT	13.1.74	2		Murjani	9 May
	11.0 6.80 12.74 1.85 50.4		15.3 36.60 4.20 56.42 4:33.0					
7148	Thibaut	Deschamps	FRA	10.4.74	1		Illzach	8 Aug
	10.99 6.99w 12.69 1.85 52.92		15.56 39.12 4.50 60.14 5:03.26					
7119	Klaus	Isekenmeier	GER	14.4.75	4		Bernhausen	13 Jun
	11.90 7.05 13.84 1.88 51.92		16.04 39.36 4.30 57.46 4:37.42					
7112	Gavin	Sunshine	GBR	19.2.74	7	EJ	San Sebastián	30 Jul
	11.09 7.11 10.63 1.94 49.43		15.41 32.52 4.60 46.12 4:39.95					
7104	Dalibor	Spoták	TCH	26.11.74	4		Wien	4 Jul
	11.46 6.73 13.10 2.08 50.49		15.24 37.24 3.80 52.50 4:47.73					
Best with legal wind:	7304	Kuorikoski			1		Brisbane	7 Nov

10,000 METRES WALK

Mark	Name		Nat	Born	Pos	Meet	Venue	Date
39:50.73	Jefferson	Pérez	ECU	1.1.74	1	PAJ	Winnipeg	15 Jul
40:05.62	Michele	Didoni	ITA	7.3.74	1	EJ	San Sebastián	30 Jul
40:26.08	Dmitriy	Yesipchuk	RUS	17.11.74	2	EJ	San Sebastián	30 Jul

Mark	Name		Nat	Born	Pos	Meet	Venue	Date
40:37.78	Heiko	Valentin	GER	31.5.74	3	EJ	San Sebastián	30 Jul
40:52.94	Jani	Lehtinen	FIN	23.2.74	1		Helsinki	1 Jun
40:55.83	Yevgeniy	Shmalyuk	RUS	14.1.76	4	EJ	San Sebastián	30 Jul
41:03.87	César	Rodriguez	ESP	7.10.76	5	EJ	San Sebastián	30 Jul
41:20.39	Mike	Trautmann	GER	13.3.74	6	EJ	San Sebastián	30 Jul
41:26.2	Lukasz	Szela	POL	10.2.75	2		Grodno	12 Sep
41:51.48	Kim	Lappalainen	FIN	6.4.74	2		Helsinki	1 Jun
41:55.0	Claus	Jorgensen	DEN	15.3.74	1		Veile	7 Aug
42:00.56	Sebastiano	Catania	ITA	13.4.75	7	EJ	San Sebastián	30 Jul
42:11.36	Daisuke	Ikeshima	JPN	30.1.75	2		Naruto	28 Sep
42:22.21	Tobias	Persson	SWE	26.7.75	8	EJ	San Sebastián	30 Jul
42:27.2	Yuriy	Onishchenko	UKR	30.7.74	1	NC-j	Chernigov	26 Jun
42:29.9	Aigars	Fadeyevs	LAT	27.12.75	1		Riga	14 Jul
42:33.1	Wojciech	Szela	POL	10.2.75	9		Zabrze	19 Jun
42:35.0	Dion	Russell	AUS	8.5.75	2		Mlebourne	19 Jun
42:40.82	Lars	Rolf	GER	23.7.74	1		Giessen	30 May
42:43.0	P	Andriyenko	UKR		2	NC-j	Chernigov	26 Jun

4 x 100 METRES RELAY

Mark	Team	Members	Pos	Meet	Venue	Date
39.72	USA	Broach, Harden, Stafford, Burrell	1	PAJ	Winnipeg	17 Jul
40.01	GBR	Condon, Joyce, Bolton, Wodu	1	EJ	San Sebastián	1 Aug
40.03	FRA	Pihery, Arnaud, Colombo, Guims	2	EJ	San Sebastián	1 Aug
40.21	UKR	Seniv, Kulbatskiy, Kabanov, Rurak	3	EJ	San Sebastián	1 Aug
40.26	CAN	Dos Santos, Proulx, Tomlin, Frempong	2	PAJ	Winnipeg	17 Jul
40.41	GER	Eisenbeis, Griszeki, Milde, Pannier	4	EJ	San Sebastián	1 Aug
40.48	ITA	Leonardi, Pignatti, Checcucci, Colombo	5	EJ	San Sebastián	1 Aug
40.52A	Transvaal (RSA)	Potgieter, Louw, Stroebel, Lindeque	1h1		Germiston	2 Apr
40.56	JAM	Shelton, Gordon, Reid, Burrell,	3	PAJ	Winnipeg	17 Jul
40.70	HUN	Németh, Maklary, Czebei, Bédi	4h1	EJ	San Sebastián	1 Aug
40.77	RUS	Rodchenko, Nikolayev, Konkov, Demin	5h1	EJ	San Sebastián	1 Aug
40.77	JPN	Takahashi, Narita, Hattori, Teramoto	1	EAsiJ	Hong Kong	14 Nov
	40.41 ??		1		Naruto	27 Oct
40.89	ESP	Sabater, D Diaz, A Gómez, Ugarte	3s2	EJ	San Sebastián	1 Aug
41.10	SUI	Ferraro, Demont, Harzenmoser, Rufener	1		Schwechat	10 Jul
41.18	HOL	Kruller, Sedoc, van Balkom, Korving	1		Tilburg	17 Jul
41.19	QAT		1		Doha	19 Nov
41.39	TPE		2	EAsiJ	Hong Kong	14 Nov
41.40	SAU		2		Doha	19 Nov
41.46	GUAD	Arron, Bilongue, Conchi, Ricard	1		Fort de France	11 Apr
41.48	NSW (AUS)		1		Canberra	12 Dec
41.2	BRA	Santos, Perin, Goulart, Moreira	1	SAmJ	Barcelona, Ven	20 Jun
41.4	VEN	Figueroa, Guzman, Cotty, Smith	2	SAmJ	Barcelona, Ven	20 Jun

4 x 400 METRES RELAY

Mark	Team	Members	Pos	Meet	Venue	Date
3:04.38	USA	Johnson, A Harrison, Beyers, C Harrison	1	PAJ	Winnipeg	17 Jul
3:07.39	GBR	Budden, Condon, Slythe, Bullock	1	EJ	San Sebastián	1 Aug
3:08.39	GER	Schnorrenberger, Weyhing, Dautzenberg, Seidler	2	EJ	San Sebastián	1 Aug
3:08.75	POL	Trelka, Sznurkowski, Mehlich, Rysiukiewicz	3	EJ	San Sebastián	1 Aug
3:09.00	CUB	Argudin, Lombillo, Miranda, Darroman	2	PAJ	Winnipeg	17 Jul
3:09.76	SWE		1		Skien	22 Aug
3:09.77	FIN	Pohjonen, Saarinen, Ikonen, Sainio	4	EJ	San Sebastián	1 Aug
3:09.83	CAN	Davis, Sullivan, Smith, Dechausay	3	PAJ	Winnipeg	17 Jul
3:10.08	JAM	M McDonald, Robinson, R McDonald, Watts	4	PAJ	Winnipeg	17 Jul
3:10.45	NZL	Sheddan, Cowan, Farrell, Keddell	1		Christchurch	15 Dec
3:10.78	JPN	Hattori, Yasui, Suzuki, Tsukada	1	EAsiJ	Hong Kong	13 Nov
3:11.55	ITA	Pizzoli, Groff, Juliano, Bertuzzi	2s1	EJ	San Sebastián	31 Jul
3:11.57	GRE	Tsimoulis, Gogos, Batsikas, Saris	3s1	EJ	San Sebastián	31 Jul
3:11.90	HUN	Bella, Szilagyi, Borszeki, Szell	3s2	EJ	San Sebastián	31 Jul
3:12.2	JAM		1		Philadelphia	1 Apr
3:12.49A	N.Transvaal (RSA)	Odendaal, Faure, White, van Zyl	1		Germiston	3 Apr
3:12.49	SAU		1		Doha	18 Nov
3:13.36	ESP	Martinez, Bayona, Bonilla, Andrés	4h1	EJ	San Sebastián	31 Jul

WORLD LIST TRENDS - 10th and 100th world list performance levels

Event	*1984*	*1985*	*1986*	*1987*	*1988*	*1989*	*1990*	*1991*	*1992*	*1993*
Men 10th Bests										
100m	10.14	10.11	10.10	10.09	**10.06**	10.11	10.10	10.07	10.07	**10.06**
200m	20.34	20.32	20.33	20.23	20.18	20.25	20.33	20.30	**20.15**	**20.15**
400m	44.83	44.91	44.72	44.72	44.61	44.89	44.91	44.88	**44.52**	44.62
800m	**1:43.93**	1:44.15	1:44.59	1:44.72	1:44.10	1:44.20	1:44.77	1:44.27	1:44.33	1:44.30
1500m	3:34.20	3:33.91	3:34.01	**3:33.66**	3:34.61	3:34.53	3:34.10	3:34.10	3:33.80	3:34.61
5000m	13:16.41	13:18.47	13:15.86	13:17.44	13:17.48	13:16.90	13:14.17	13:17.25	13:10.47	**13:08.03**
10000m	27:47.00	27:49.36	27:45.45	27:45.05	27:40.36	27:49.69	27:42.65	27:37.36	27:45.46	**27:30.17**
Marathon	2:10:05	2:09:05	2:09:57	2:10:34	**2:08:49**	2:09:40	2:10:10	2:10:08	2:09:30	2:10:06
3000mSt	8:17.27	8:18.02	8:16.59	8:16.46	8:16.04	8:17.64	8:15.95	8:14.41	**8:13.65**	8:15.33
110mh	13.45	13.46	13.40	13.39	13.36	13.37	13.28	13.37	13.33	**13.26**
400mh	48.74	49.03	48.71	48.56	48.65	48.79	48.61	48.92	48.60	48.73
HJ	2.33	2.35	2.34	2.34	**2.36**	2.34	2.35	2.34	2.34	2.35
PV	5.75	5.80	5.80	5.80	5.80	5.80	5.81	5.81	**5.85**	5.81
LJ	8.27	8.23	8.24	8.25	**8.31**	8.23	8.24	8.25	8.28	8.30
TJ	17.34	**17.48**	17.43	17.39	17.43	17.29	17.33	17.43	17.30	17.32
SP	**21.63**	21.32	21.49	21.22	21.16	21.02	20.86	20.43	20.93	20.84
DT	67.76	67.36	67.02	67.22	67.38	66.46	65.80	66.36	66.64	66.12
HT	80.50	80.20	80.68	80.74	81.88	79.38	80.90	80.56	80.46	80.80
JT (Old 84-5)	(90.94)	(91.56)	81.86	83.24	82.70	83.90	94.80	**86.32**	85.74	85.10
Decathlon	**8491**	8317	8302	8304	8387	8182	8275	8267	8237	8297

Other peak: DT: 68.20 (1982), note roughened tailed javelins were in use in 1991

Event	*1984*	*1985*	*1986*	*1987*	*1988*	*1989*	*1990*	*1991*	*1992*	*1993*
Men 100th Bests										
100m	10.36	10.35	10.36	10.34	10.34	10.36	10.34	10.33	**10.32**	**10.32**
200m	20.62	20.59	20.60	**20.54**	20.57	20.68	20.66	20.69	20.57	20.58
400m	46.03	45.99	46.01	46.00	45.99	46.22	46.31	46.13	**45.98**	45.99
800m	1:46.97	1:47.17	1:47.12	1:46.94	**1:46.91**	1:47.14	1:47.32	1:47.10	1:46.95	1:47.13
1500m	**3:37.10**	3:38.38	3:37.75	3:37.40	3:37.29	3:37.74	3:37.36	3:37.80	3:37.71	3:37.60
5000m	13:35.10	13:38.50	13:35.34	13:37.31	13:37.20	13:36.60	13:37.88	13:37.40	**13:31.44**	13:33.40
10000m	28:26.10	28:39.20	28:329.41	28:333.77	28:27.28	28:34.18	28:30.52	**28:24.70**	28:30.42	28:32.19
Marathon	2:13:20	2:13:39	2:13:38	2:13:34	2:13:08	2:13:37	2:13:30	2:13:13	2:13:22	**2:12:50**
3000mSt	8:35.35	8:35.95	8:35.65	8:37.20	8:35.24	8:36.95	8:35.93	8:35.40	**8:34.43**	8:36.57
110mh	13.91	13.94	13.90	13.86	13.83	13.93	13.85	13.86	**13.78**	13.85
400mh	50.53	50.65	50.41	50.54	50.52	50.55	50.45	50.68	50.50	50.45
HJ	**2.24**	**2.24**	2.23	**2.24**	**2.24**	**2.24**	2.23	2.23	**2.24**	**2.24**
PV	5.41	5.40	**5.50**	5.44	**5.50**	**5.50**	5.45	5.45	**5.50**	**5.50**
LJ	7.90	7.89	7.90	7.92	**7.93**	7.90	7.90	**7.93**	**7.93**	7.92
TJ	16.41	16.51	16.52	16.50	**16.60**	16.55	16.55	16.54	16.59	16.54
SP	**19.48**	19.34	19.33	19.09	19.17	18.94	18.79	18.57	18.79	18.50
DT	**60.96**	60.54	60.96	60.40	60.84	60.18	59.74	59.28	59.80	58.62
HT	**73.08**	72.96	72.36	72.00	72.34	71.50	71.26	70.20	70.70	70.46
JT	(81.52)	(81.40)	75.30	76.68	76.48	76.72	76.82	**77.14**	76.40	75.80
Decathlon	7630	7676	7686	7631	**7702**	7553	7594	7585	7567	7570

All-time peaks are shown in bold

WOMEN'S WORLD LISTS 1993

100 METRES

Mark	Wind	Name		Nat	Born	Pos	Meet	Venue	Date
10.82	1.5	Gail	Devers	USA	19.11.66	1	Athl	Lausanne	7 Jul
10.82	-0.3		Devers			1	WC	Stuttgart	16 Aug
10.82	-0.3	Merlene	Ottey	JAM	10.5.60	2	WC	Stuttgart	16 Aug
10.86	0.9	Gwen	Torrence	USA	12.6.65	1	VD	Bruxelles	3 Sep
10.87	-0.3		Ottey			1s1	WC	Stuttgart	16 Aug
10.87	-0.3		Torrence			2s1	WC	Stuttgart	16 Aug
10.89	-0.3		Torrence			3	WC	Stuttgart	16 Aug
10.90	-0.6		Ottey			1	Herc	Monaco	7 Aug
10.93	-0.9		Ottey			1A	WK	Zürich	4 Aug
10.94	1.2		Ottey			1	Bisl	Oslo	10 Jul
10.94	0.9	Irina	Privalova	RUS	22.11.68	2	VD	Bruxelles	3 Sep
10.96	1.4		Devers			1	BNP	Villeneuve d'Ascq	2 Jul
10.96	1.5		Ottey			2	Athl	Lausanne	7 Jul
10.96	-0.3		Privalova			4	WC	Stuttgart	16 Aug
10.97	1.5		Torrence			3	Athl	Lausanne	7 Jul
10.97	0.2	Mary	Onyali	NGR	3.2.68	1q2	WC	Stuttgart	15 Aug
10.98	1.2		Torrence			2	Bisl	Oslo	10 Jul
10.98	-0.9		Torrence			2A	WK	Zürich	4 Aug
11.00	1.1		Ottey			1	NC	Kingston	2 Jul
11.00	1.4		Privalova			2	BNP	Villeneuve d'Ascq	2 Jul
11.00	-0.9		Devers			3A	WK	Zürich	4 Aug
11.01	-0.5		Ottey			1	ISTAF	Berlin	27 Aug
11.02	0.0		Torrence			1q1	WC	Stuttgart	15 Aug
11.02	0.0		Liu Xiaomei	CHN	11.1.72	1	NG	Beijing	8 Sep
11.03	-0.6		Devers			1s2	WC	Stuttgart	16 Aug
11.03	-0.4		Torrence			1	GPF	London	10 Sep
11.04	0.5		Devers			1	DNG	Stockholm	5 Jul
11.04	-0.1		Torrence			1A	ASV	Köln	1 Aug
11.04	0.7		Devers			1q4	WC	Stuttgart	15 Aug
11.05	-0.3		Onyali			5	WC	Stuttgart	16 Aug
11.06	1.5		Privalova			4	Athl	Lausanne	7 Jul
11.06	-0.6		Privalova			2s2	WC	Stuttgart	16 Aug
11.06	-0.6		Onyali			3s2	WC	Stuttgart	16 Aug
		(33/6)							
11.08	0.1	Zhanna	Tarnopolskaya	UKR	6.7.72	1		Odessa	21 May
11.11	0.9	Inger	Miller	USA	12.12.72	1	MSR	Walnut	17 Apr
11.12	1.5	Holli	Hyche	USA	6.9.71	1		Indianapolis	26 May
11.12	1.1	Marie-José	Pérec	FRA	9.5.68	1	Nik	Nice	21 Jul
		(10)							
11.14	1.3	Petya	Pendareva	BUL	20.1.71	1		Sofia	15 May
11.16	1.6	Pauline	Davis	BAH	9.7.66	1	NC	Nassau	17 Jun
11.16	1.1	Michelle	Freeman	JAM	5.5.69	2	NC	Kingston	2 Jul
11.16	1.5	Michelle	Finn	USA	8.5.65	6	Athl	Lausanne	7 Jul
11.16	-0.1	Juliet	Cuthbert	JAM	9.4.64	2rA	ASV	Köln	1 Aug
11.17	-0.3	Natalya	Voronova	RUS	9.7.65	3s1	WC	Stuttgart	16 Aug
11.18	1.1	Nicole	Mitchell	JAM	5.6.74	3	NC	Kingston	2 Jul
11.19	-0.3	Liliana	Allen	CUB	24.6.70	4s1	WC	Stuttgart	16 Aug
11.20	1.5	Heather	Samuel	ANT	6.7.70	2		Indianapolis	26 May
11.20	1.7	Chandra	Sturrup	BAH	12.9.71	1		Abilene	29 May
		(20)							
11.20	1.6	Patricia	Girard	FRA	8.4.68	1		Limoges	10 Jul
11.22	1.1	Melinda	Gainsford	AUS	1.10.71	1	NEC	Melbourne	25 Feb
11.22	2.0	Beverly	McDonald	JAM	15.2.70	1h1		Austin	20 May
11.22	0.2	Louann	Williams	TRI	72	1	JUCO	Odessa	22 May
11.22	2.0	Dahlia	Duhaney	JAM	20.7.70	1s1	WUG	Buffalo	15 Jul
11.22	-0.3	Elinda	Vorster	RSA	8.12.65	6s1	WC	Stuttgart	16 Aug
11.23A	1.6	Cheryl	Taplin	USA	2.9.72	1		El Paso	10 Apr
11.23	-0.2	Melanie	Paschke	GER	29.6.70	1	NC	Duisburg	10 Jul
11.24	0.7	Merlene	Frazer	JAM	27.12.73	1s1	JUCO	Odessa	21 May
11.24	1.3		Tian Yumei	CHN	29.12.65	1h1	NG	Beijing	8 Sep
		(30)							

Mark	Wind	Name		Nat	Born	Pos	Meet	Venue	Date
11.25	1.0	Wenda	Vereen	USA	24.4.66	1	SunA	Tempe	3 Apr
11.25	1.9	Chryste	Gaines	USA	14.9.70	1		San Francisco	15 May
11.25	-0.4	Galina	Malchugina	RUS	17.12.62	1		Oristano	12 Sep
11.26	2.0	Beatrice	Utondu	NGR	23.11.69	3s1	WUG	Buffalo	15 Jul
11.27	-0.6	Faith	Idehen	NGR	5.2.73	1h4	NC	Lagos	16 Jun
11.27	1.2		Chen Yan	CHN	.11.73	1h3	NG	Beijing	8 Sep
11.28	1.4	Marion	Jones	USA	12.10.75	1h1		Norwalk	4 Jun
11.28	1.0	Sabine	Tröger	AUT	7.7.67	1		Lienz	6 Aug
11.28	0.0		Wang Ping	CHN	8.9.70	4	NG	Beijing	8 Sep
11.29	1.3	Tisha	Prather	USA	5.8.71	2	Gator	Knoxville	1 May
		(40)							
11.30	0.7	Dana	Collins	USA	23.7.73	2s1	JUCO	Odessa	21 May
11.31A	1.6	Sheila	Echols	USA	2.10.64	2		El Paso	10 Apr
11.31	1.4	Olga	Bogoslovskaya	RUS	20.5.64	5	BNP	Villeneuve d'Ascq	2 Jul
11.32	1.1	Michelle	Seymour	NZL	21.12.65	2	NEC	Melbourne	25 Feb
11.32	-0.2	Anelia	Nuneva	BUL	30.6.62	1		Granada	29 May
11.33	0.5		Wang Lei	CHN	4.3.71	1	NC	Jinan	3 Jun
11.33	1.6	Dedra	Davis	BAH	17.7.73	2	NC	Nassau	17 Jun
11.33	1.3		Chen Zhaojing	CHN	5.4.69	3h1	NG	Beijing	8 Sep
11.33	0.0		Qi Hong	CHN	.3.69	5	NG	Beijing	8 Sep
11.34	1.3		Huang Xiaoyan	CHN	3.12.69	4h1	NG	Beijing	8 Sep
		(50)							
11.35	1.1	Antonina	Slyusar	UKR	19.3.63	1h1		Kiev	15 May
11.35	0.3	Carlette	Guidry	USA	4.9.68	4	NYG	New York	22 May
11.35	1.2		Ou Yanlan	CHN	.1.74	2h3	NG	Beijing	8 Sep
11.36	1.3	Desislava	Dimitrova	BUL	19.6.72	2		Sofia	15 May
11.36	0.3	Heike	Drechsler	GER	16.12.64	2	Gugl	Linz	25 Aug
11.37	1.1	Viktoriya	Fomenko	UKR	2.10.71	2h1		Kiev	15 May
11.37	2.0	Bev	Kinch	GBR	14.1.64	1	NC	London	12 Jun
11.38	1.6		Wang Huei-chen	TPE	21.2.70	1	EAsiG	Shanghai	13 May
11.38	0.2	Irina	Slyusar	UKR	19.3.63	1h2		Kiev	15 May
11.38	1.8	Flirtisha	Harris	USA	21.2.72	1s1		Fairfax	15 May
		(60)							
11.38	1.7	Mary	Tombiri	NGR	23.7.72	2		Abilene	29 May
11.38	0.8	Christy	Opara	NGR	2.5.70	2q1		Buffalo	14 Jul
11.38	-1.1	Valérie	Jean-Charles	FRA	27.1.69	1	NC	Annecy	24 Jul
11.38	-1.1	Odiah	Sidibé	FRA	13.1.70	2	NC	Annecy	24 Jul
11.39		Alice	Brown	USA	20.9.60	1		Los Angeles	22 May
11.39	1.7	Hermin	Joseph	DMN	13.4.64	3		Abilene	29 May
11.39		Cleide	Amaral	BRA	17.7.67	1		Pres. Prudente	5 Jun
11.39	1.9	Sisko	Hanhijoki	FIN	25.4.62	1		Kuopio	5 Jun
11.39	1.5	Lucrécia	Jardim	POR	28.1.71	1	EP/C3	Rotterdam	12 Jun
11.39	0.8	Magalie	Simonieck	FRA	17.2.70	1	MedG	Narbonne	17 Jun
		(70)							
11.39	0.6		Wang Jing	CHN	16.1.75	3h2	NG	Beijing	8 Sep
11.39	1.2		Li Shuxiang	CHN	14.7.69	3h3	NG	Beijing	8 Sep
11.40	2.0	Ndèye Binta	Dia	SEN	8.4.73	1		Dakar	17 Apr
11.40	2.0	Stacey	Clack	USA	6.2.71	2h1		Austin	20 May
11.40	1.7	Twilet	Malcolm	JAM	5.2.69	3s1	NCAA	New Orleans	4 Jun
11.40	0.3	Zoya	Sokolova	RUS	3.4.70	1	Znam	Moskva	12 Jun
11.40	1.2	Marina	Trandenkova	RUS	7.1.67	1		Luxembourg	30 Jul
11.40	0.9	Teresa	Neighbors	USA	26.5.67	1A		Rhede	6 Aug
11.40	0.2	Sanna	Hernesniemi	FIN	9.3.71	5q2	WC	Stuttgart	15 Aug
11.41	-0.7	Silke	Knoll	GER	21.2.67	1		Dortmund	22 May
		(80)							
11.41	-0.2	Jacqueline	Poelman	HOL	5.10.73	1		Leiden	26 Jun
11.41	1.1	Gillian	Russell	JAM	28.9.73	6	NC	Kingston	2 Jul
11.41		Maya	Azarashvili	GEO	6.4.64	1		Ponzano Veneto	22 Jul
11.42		Dannette	Young	USA	6.10.64	1		Northridge	1 May
11.42	1.1	Lalao	Ravaonirina	MAD	8.11.63	3	FraC	Annecy	24 Jul
11.42	1.3		Pei Fang	CHN	1.2.71	5h1	NG	Beijing	8 Sep
11.43	0.1	Cathy	Freeman	AUS	16.2.73	1		Adelaide	14 Feb
11.43A	1.3	Melinda	Sergent	USA	72	1		El Paso	22 May
11.43	0.4	Yelena	Mizera	RUS	20.2.66	3	Slovn	Bratislava	1 Jun
11.43	-0.1	Miriam	Ferrer	CUB	18.6.63	5q3	WC	Stuttgart	15 Aug
		(90)							
11.44	0.2		You Yanyun	CHN	8.1.72			Guangzhou	20 Mar

Mark	Wind		Name	Nat	Born	Pos	Meet	Venue	Date
11.44	1.0		Yao Lin	CHN					13 May
11.44A	-0.4	Evette	De Klerk	RSA	21.8.65	2		Pretoria	15 May
11.44	0.4	Esther	Jones	USA	7.4.69	5	Indy	Indianapolis	25 Jun
11.45		Melissa	Morrison	USA	9.7.71	1		Boone	1 May
11.45	-0.4	Hana	Benesová	TCH	19.4.75	1	NC	Jablonec nad Nisou	3 Jul
11.45	0.8	Marcia	Richardson	GBR	10.2.72	3q1	WUG	Buffalo	14 Jul
11.45	1.3		Jiang Lan	CHN	.1.69	6h1	NG	Beijing	8 Sep
11.46A	-0.4	Yolanda	Steyn	RSA	22.8.72	3		Pretoria	15 May
11.46	1.1	Teresa	Foster	USA	11.4.72	2s2	JUCO	Odessa	20 May
		(100)							
11.46	-0.1	Irina	Pukha	UKR	10.1.73	h	NC	Kiev	2 Jul
11.46	0.6		Zhang Chunying	CHN	10.1.73	4h2	NG	Beijing	8 Sep

Mark	Wind		Name	Nat	Born	Date
11.47	1.9	Michelle	Collins	USA	71	20 May
11.47	0.5		Xiao Yehua	CHN	71	3 Jun
11.48	1.6	Eldece	Clarke	BAH	65	17 Jun
11.48	1.1	Maguy	Nestoret	FRA	69	24 Jul
11.49A		Eusebia	Riquelme	CUB	69	8 May
11.49	0.6	Benita	Kelley	USA	75	14 May
11.49	1.9	Crystal	Braddock	USA	70	20 May
11.49		Cleide	Amaral	BRA	67	30 May
		(110)				
11.50	1.3	Shantel	Twiggs	USA	72	23 Apr
11.50		Govindasamy	Shanti	MAS	67	7 May
11.50	1.5	Silke	Lichtenhagen	GER	73	4 Sep
11.50	0.6		Gao Han	CHN	71	8 Sep
11.51	1.1	Jane	Ovenden	AUS	72	25 Feb
11.51	-0.6	Evelyn	Ashford	USA	57	10 Jun
11.51		Bettina	Zipp	GER	72	19 Jun
11.51	-0.4	Erika	Suchovská	TCH	67	3 Jul
11.51	-0.2	Andrea	Philipp	GER	71	10 Jul
		(120)				
11.51	1.1	Georgette	Nkoma	CMR	65	14 Jul
11.52	1.5	Kay	Iheagwam	NGR		15 May
11.52A	0.5	Kwani	Stewart	USA	72	18 May
11.52			Ye Min	CHN	71	3 Jun
11.52	1.7	Nadezhda	Rashchupkina	RUS	63	12 Jun
11.52	1.1	Simmone	Jacobs	GBR	66	16 Jul
11.52	1.2		Tang Haiyun	CHN	73	8 Sep
11.52	0.7	Damarayathi	Darsha	SRI	75	1 Dec
11.53		Tamara	Cuffee	USA	71	1 May
11.53	0.9	Cheryl	Brantle	USA	69	16 May
		(130)				
11.53	1.1	Cheryl Ann	Phillips	JAM	70	2 Jul
11.53	1.6	Irina	Chernova	KZK	70	23 Jul
11.53	1.1	Violetta	Lapierre	FRA	63	24 Jul
11.54	2.0	Andrea	Anderson	USA	77	22 May
11.54		Lia	Murgu	ROM	69	29 May
11.54			Chen Chaoyi	CHN	73	2 Jun
11.54	2.0	Paula	Thomas	GBR	64	12 Jun

Best low altitude

11.26	1.3	Taplin	1	Gator	Knoxville	1 May
11.34	-0.8	Echols	4	Jen	San José	29 May

Mark	Wind		Name	Nat	Born	Date
11.54		Birgit	Rockmeier	GER	73	7 Aug
11.55		Sophia	Brown	JAM		10 Apr
11.55	1.0	Natasha	Reynolds	USA	72	15 May
		(140)				
11.55	1.6	Savatheda	Fynes	BAH	74	17 Jun
11.55	0.9	Yekaterina	Leshcheva	RUS	74	2 Jul
11.55	-0.2	Ulrike	Sarvari	GER	64	10 Jul
11.56		Jamie	Gray	USA		10 Apr
11.56	1.7	Yelena	Dubtsova	RUS	71	12 Jun
11.56	0.5	Yelena	Denishchik	BLS	68	23 Jul
11.56	-0.9	Jayne	Christian	GBR	63	28 Aug
11.57	1.7	Kim	Graham	USA	71	17 Apr
11.57	0.5	Lesa	Parker	USA	74	24 Apr
11.57	1.5	Pam	Lemons	USA		15 May
		(150)				
11.57			Guo Yinghua	CHN	68	2 Jun
11.57	0.4	Anzhelika	Shevchuk	UKR	69	2 Jul
11.57	1.3	Natalya	Anisimova	RUS	73	1 Aug
11.58	1.1	Petrina	Lacey	USA		20 May
11.58	0.2	LaReina	Woods	USA	72	22 May
11.58	1.9	Dainelkis	Pérez	CUB	76	22 May
11.58	1.7	Taiwo	Aladefa	NGR	71	29 May
11.58	0.4	Marina	Zhirova	RUS	63	1 Jun
11.58	2.0	Geraldine	McLeod	GBR	71	12 Jun
11.58	0.5	Katharine	Merry	GBR	74	30 Jul
		(160)				
11.58		Philomena	Mensah	GHA	75	7 Aug
11.58	0.7	Gabi	Rockmeier	GER	73	14 Aug
11.59	1.3	Zlatka	Georgieva	BUL	69	15 May
11.59		Sheryl	Covington	USA	71	22 May
11.59	1.5	Phynice	Kelley	USA		26 May
11.59	-0.6	Anzhela	Kravchenko	UKR	71	2 Jul
11.59		Aileen	McGillivary	GBR	70	21 Aug
11.59	-0.9	Christine	Bloomfield	GBR	68	28 Aug
11.60	-0.6	Lydia	De Vega	PHI	64	14 Jun
		(170)				
11.60	-0.2	Carla	Verniest	GER	73	10 Jul
11.60	-0.5	Olga	Voronova	RUS	68	6 Aug

11.52	1.9	Riquelme	22	May
11.58	1.0	de Klerk	6	Aug
11.60	0.3	Steyn	23	Jun

Irregular

Mark	Wind		Name	Nat	Born	Pos	Meet	Venue	Date
11.33		Patricia	Foufoué-Ziga	CIV	8.3.72	1		Yamoussousko	10 Apr
11.60		Hanitriniaina	Rakotondrabe	MAD	10	Apr			

Wind-assisted marks

Mark	Wind		Name	Nat	Born	Pos	Meet	Venue	Date
10.81	3.8	Irina	Privalova	RUS	12.11.68	1		Rieti	5 Sep
10.82	2.2		Devers			1	NC	Eugene	17 Jun
10.92	4.2		Devers			1h2	NC	Eugene	16 Jun
10.93	4.2	Holli	Hyche	USA	6.9.71	2h2	NC	Eugene	16 Jun
10.99	5.1		Onyali			1	S&W	Modesto	8 May
11.01		Beatrice	Utondu	NGR	23.11.69	1		Springfield	1 May
11.02	2.1	Nicole	Mitchell	JAM	5.6.74	1	Mutual	Kingston	1 May
11.03	2.2		Torrence			2	NC	Eugene	17 Jun
11.05	6.1	Beverly	McDonald	JAM	15.2.70	1		Arlington	10 Apr
11.05	2.3		Devers			1s2	NC	Eugene	16 Jun
11.06	2.6	Michelle	Finn	USA	8.5.65	1s1	NC	Eugene	16 Jun
11.07	5.1	Wenda	Vereen	USA	24.4.66	2	S&W	Modesto	8 May
11.08	3.2	Cheryl	Taplin	USA	2.9.72	1		Knoxville	16 May
11.13		Hermin	Joseph	DMN	13.4.64	1		Abilene	8 May

Mark	Wind	Name		Nat	Born	Pos	Meet	Venue	Date
11.14	2.2	Sheila	Echols	USA	2.10.64	5	NC	Eugene	17 Jun
11.15	4.4	Melinda	Gainsford	AUS	1.10.71	1h1		Sydney	20 Feb
11.15	2.5	Juliet	Campbell	JAM	17.3.70	1h2		Knoxville	15 May
11.16	3.2	Tisha	Prather	USA	5.8.71	3		Knoxville	16 May
11.16	3.8	Natalya	Voronova	RUS	9.7.65	2		Rieti	5 Sep
11.17		Twilet	Malcolm	JAM	5.2.69	1		New Orleans	15 May
11.17	3.8	Marina	Trandenkova	RUS	7.1.67	3		Rieti	5 Sep
11.19	2.6	Teresa	Neighbours	USA	26.5.67	3s1	NC	Eugene	16 Jun
11.21	2.8	Marion	Jones	USA	12.10.75	1h1		Mission Viejo	15 May
11.23	4.2	Yelena	Mizera	RUS	22.2.66	1		Cork	9 Jul
11.24	3.8	Carlette	Guidry	USA	4.9.68	4h3	NC	Eugene	16 Jun
11.27		Mary	Tombiri	NGR	23.7.72	2		Abilene	8 May
11.27	5.1	Christy	Opara Thompson	NGR	2.5.70	3	S&W	Modesto	8 May
11.31	2.3	Esther	Jones	USA	7.4.69	1h1	NC	Eugene	16 Jun
11.32		Shantel	Twiggs	USA	4.10.72	2		Terre Haute	16 May
11.33	2.8	Sanna	Hernesniemi	FIN	9.3.71	1		Punkalaidun	30 May
11.34	2.5	Crystal	Braddock	USA	13.12.70	2		Austin	21 May
11.36		Keisha	Owens	USA	7.4.73	2		New Orleans	15 May
11.37	2.7	Kim	Graham	USA	26.3.71	4		Austin	8 May
11.37	3.2	Andrea	Lloyd	JAM	10.8.71	5		Knoxville	16 May
11.37	4.2	Olga	Voronova	RUS	69	2		Cork	9 Jul
11.38		Casey	Custer	USA	11.11.74	1		Lubbock	2 May
11.39	3.3	Taiwo	Aladefa	NGR	19.12.71	1h1		Abilene	28 May
11.40	5.1	Katharine	Merry	GBR	21.9.74	1	NC-j	Bedford	3 Jul
11.41		Michelle	Collins	USA	12.2.71	1		Houston	17 Apr
11.42	4.2	Svetlana	Dolmatova	RUS	68	3		Cork	9 Jul
11.42A	2.3	Miriam	Ferrer	CUB	18.6.63	1	CAC	Cali	30 Jul
11.43		Cheryl Ann	Phillips	JAM	7.10.70	2		Athens	17 Apr
11.43	4.2	Simmone	Jacobs	GBR	5.9.66	4		Cork	9 Jul
11.43	3.9	Aileen	McGillivary	GBR	13.8.70	1	ScotC	Grangemouth	11 Jul
11.43	5.2	Dorota	Krawczak	POL	14.1.68	1	NC	Kielce	23 Jul
11.43	2.3	Violetta	Lapierre	FRA	15.10.63	1		Chaux-de-Fonds	8 Aug
11.44	4.3	Dyan	Webber	USA	9.4.66	1		Houston	20 Mar
11.44	6.1	Gwen	Clardy	USA	73	2		Arlington	10 Apr
11.44		Celena	Mondie-Milner	USA	6.8.68	1		San Marcos	23 Apr
11.46	4.2	Geraldine	McLeod	GBR	24.9.71	5		Cork	9 Jul

Mark	Wind	Name		Nat	Born	Date
11.47		Marlene	Garner	USA	71	24 Apr
11.47	2.4	Sheryl	Covington	USA	71	22 May
11.47	3.1	Marina	Filipovic	YUG	70	3 Jul
11.48		Tamara	Cuffee	USA	71	26 May
11.49	2.5	Ulrike	Sarvari	GER	64	9 Jul
11.49	2.5	Carla	Verniest	GER	73	9 Jul
11.50	2.2	Jane	Flemming	AUS	65	20 Feb
11.50	4.3	Jearl	Miles	USA	66	7 May
11.50		Tonja	Buford	USA	70	14 May
11.50	3.2	Jackie	Knox	USA	74	16 May
11.50	5.2	Anna	Leszczynska	POL	71	23 Jul
11.51	5.1	Charlotte	Vines	USA	71	8 May
11.51	4.6	Paula	Thomas	GBR	64	2 Jul
11.52		Buffy	James	USA	71	17 Apr
11.52		Yvette	Cole	USA		1 May
11.52	6.4	Cynthia	Jackson	USA	71	2 May
11.52	5.1	Karen	Clarke	CAN	71	8 May
11.52	3.6	Andrea	Anderson	USA	77	15 May
11.53		Tracie	Harris	USA		1 May
11.53	2.4	Stacey	Bowen	CAN	69	22 May
11.53	3.6	Lauren	Hewitt	AUS	78	11 Dec
11.54		Dasha	Patterson	USA		23 Apr
11.54A	4.1	Cathie	Guischard	TRI	70	24 Apr
11.55	3.5	Nanceen	Perry	USA	77	15 May
11.55	2.9	Michele	Duvigneau	FRA	69	13 Jun
11.55	2.2	Delphine	Combe	FRA	74	9 Jul
11.55	2.2	Marie-Joelle	Dogbo	FRA	75	9 Jul
11.56		Dawnette	Douglas	USA		16 Apr
11.56	5.1	Sophia	Smith	GBR	74	3 Jul
11.56	4.1	Kelly	Miller	NZL	77	10 Dec
11.57	6.1	DeMonica	Davis	USA	74	10 Apr
11.57A	2.7	LaReina	Woods	USA	72	8 May
11.57	5.6	Sandra	Castanheira	POR	73	3 Jul
11.58	3.0	Yelena	Sinyutina	RUS	64	27 Jun
11.58	2.3	Stefanie	Hütz	GER	70	28 Aug
11.59		Torvia	Bradley	USA		27 Mar
11.59	2.5	Sonja	Franklin	USA	70	21 May
11.59		Marisa	Masullo	ITA	59	22 May
11.59	3.0	Giada	Gallina	ITA	73	22 May
11.59	3.1	Aminah	Haddad	USA	78	4 Jun
11.59	4.0	Helen	Miles	GBR	67	22 Jul
11.59	2.3	Kerry Ann	Richards	JAM	76	30 Jul
11.60		Chantel	Rolle	BAH		24 Apr
11.60		Carmetia	Mackey	BAH	74	24 Apr
11.60	2.1	Nathalie	Fokoua	FRA	70	26 Jun
11.60	5.2	Izabela	Czajko	POL	71	23 Jul
11.60	2.6	Tara	Perry	CAN	74	16 Aug

Hand timed

Mark	Wind	Name		Nat	Born	Pos	Meet	Venue	Date
11.1	2.0	Hermin	Joseph	DMN	13.4.64	1		San Angelo	10 Apr
11.2	1.5	Marion	Jones	USA	12.10.75	1		Pomona	20 Mar
11.2	1.0	Margarita	Molchan	BLS	21.1.66	1		Gomel	4 May

Mark	Wind	Name		Nat	Born	Date
11.3		Yevgeniya	Sidorova	RUS	73	13 May
11.3	0.3	Monique	Hennagan	USA	76	14 May
11.3	0.5	Yelena	Fedorovich	RUS	71	29 May
11.3		Maya	Azarashvili	GEO	64	30 Jun
11.3		Natalya	Zhuk	BLS	68	6/7 Jul
11.3		Olga	Voronova	RUS	68	13 Aug
11.3	-1.7	Yekaterina	Leshcheva	RUS	74	29 Aug
11.4	1.5	Marliese	Steyn	RSA	73	13 Feb
11.4		Crystal	Braddock	USA	70	26 Mar
11.4		Tracie	Harris	USA		26 Mar

Mark	Wind	Name		Nat	Born	Pos	Meet	Venue	Date
11.4		Svetlana	Goncharenko	RUS	71				24 Apr
11.4	0.5	Oksana	Khreskina	RUS	72				29 May
11.4		Vera	Sychugova	RUS	63				29 May
11.4		Ionela	Tîrlea	ROM	76				7/8 Jun
11.4		Svetlana	Biktuna	UKR	65				17 Jun
11.4A	1.3	Miriam	Ferrer	CUB	63				30 Jul
11.4		Andrea	Philipp	GER	71				28 Aug
11.4	-1.7	Yelena	Dubtsova	RUS	71				29 Aug
Wind assisted									
10.9		Holli	Hyche	USA	6.9.71	1h		Terre Haute	15 May
11.0		Nicole	Mitchell	JAM	5.6.74	1		Kingston	26 Mar
11.0		Beverley	Langley	JAM	16.12.76	1		Kingston	26 Mar
11.4		others							

200 METRES

Mark	Wind	Name		Nat	Born	Pos	Meet	Venue	Date
21.77	1.0	Merlene	Ottey	JAM	10.5.60	1	Herc	Monaco	7 Aug
21.88	2.0	Irina	Privalova	RUS	22.11.68	1		Rieti	5 Sep
21.92	0.9	Gwen	Torrence	USA	12.6.65	1	VD	Bruxelles	3 Sep
21.98	0.0		Ottey			1	WC	Stuttgart	19 Aug
21.99	1.1	Marie-José	Pérec	FRA	9.5.68	1	BNP	Villeneuve d'Ascq	2 Jul
21.99	1.1		Privalova			2	BNP	Villeneuve d'Ascq	2 Jul
22.00	0.0		Torrence			2	WC	Stuttgart	19 Aug
22.08	0.9		Privalova			2	VD	Bruxelles	3 Sep
22.10	0.2		Torrence			1	Toto	Fukuoka	18 Sep
22.12	0.2		Ottey			1s2	WC	Stuttgart	19 Aug
22.13	0.0		Privalova			3	WC	Stuttgart	19 Aug
22.17	0.4		Privalova			1	Athl	Lausanne	7 Jul
22.20	0.0		Pérec			4	WC	Stuttgart	19 Aug
22.20	-0.5		Torrence			1s1	WC	Stuttgart	19 Aug
22.20	-0.5		Privalova			2s1	WC	Stuttgart	19 Aug
22.22	1.0		Privalova			2	Herc	Monaco	7 Aug
22.22	0.2	Galina	Malchugina	RUS	17.12.62	2s2	WC	Stuttgart	19 Aug
22.27	0.8		Ottey			1	Slovn	Bratislava	1 Jun
22.27	2.0		Malchugina			2		Rieti	5 Sep
22.29	1.0		Ottey			1	NC	Kingston	3 Jul
22.30	0.8		Privalova			1	EP	Roma	27 Jun
22.30	0.8		Pérec			2	EP	Roma	27 Jun
22.32	0.8		Malchugina			2	Slovn	Bratislava	1 Jun
22.32	1.0	Mary	Onyali	NGR	3.2.68	3	Herc	Monaco	7 Aug
22.32	0.0		Onyali			5	WC	Stuttgart	19 Aug
22.33	1.4	Inger	Miller	USA	12.12.72	1	MSR	Walnut	17 Apr
22.34	1.6	Holli	Hyche	USA	6.9.71	1	NCAA	New Orleans	5 Jun
22.35	-0.5	Natalya	Voronova	RUS	9.7.65	3s1	WC	Stuttgart	19 Aug
22.35	0.2		Onyali			3s2	WC	Stuttgart	19 Aug
22.37	2.0	Cathy	Freeman	AUS	16.2.73	3		Rieti	5 Sep
		(30/10)							
22.49	0.7	Melinda	Gainsford	AUS	1.10.71	1	NC	Brisbane	7 Mar
22.51	0.2	Dannette	Young	USA	6.10.64	4s2	WC	Stuttgart	19 Aug
22.56	-2.1		Chen Zhaojing	CHN	5.4.69	1	NG	Beijing	13 Sep
22.63	1.4	Wenda	Vereen	USA	24.4.66	3	MSR	Walnut	17 Apr
22.67	1.8	Beverly	McDonald	JAM	15.2.70	1h2	NCAA	New Orleans	2 Jun
22.70	-2.1		Liu Xiaomei	CHN	11.1.72	2	NG	Beijing	13 Sep
22.73	0.8	Yelena	Mizera	RUS	22.2.66	3	Slovn	Bratislava	1 Jun
22.75	-0.5	Silke-Beate	Knoll	GER	21.2.67	1		Dortmund	22 May
22.76	0.2	Evette	de Klerk	RSA	21.8.65	5s2	WC	Stuttgart	19 Aug
22.78	-1.3	Petya	Pendareva	BUL	20.1.71	1	NC	Sofia	1 Aug
		(20)							
22.79	1.6	Zhanna	Tarnopolskaya	UKR	6.7.72	1		Kiev	16 May
22.79	-2.1		Wang Ping	CHN	8.9.70	3	NG	Beijing	13 Sep
22.80	2.0	Juliet	Campbell	JAM	17.3.70	4		Rieti	5 Sep
22.81	1.6	Dahlia	Duhaney	JAM	20.7.70	1	Mutual	Kingston	1 May
22.81	1.6	Chryste	Gaines	USA	14.9.70	2s1	NC	Eugene	18 Jun
22.83	-0.5	Elinda	Vorster	RSA	8.12.65	6s1	WC	Stuttgart	19 Aug
22.85	2.0	Chandra	Sturrup	BAH	12.9.71	1		Abilene	29 May
22.87	0.9		Han Qing	CHN	4.3.70	2h1	NG	Beijing	12 Sep
22.87	0.9		Qi Hong	CHN	.3.69	3h1	NG	Beijing	12 Sep
22.88	1.8	Michelle	Collins	USA	12.2.71	2	SWC	Austin	21 May
		(30)							
22.89	1.6	Pauline	Davis	BAH	9.7.66	2	Mutual	Kingston	1 May
22.91	1.6	Merlene	Frazer	JAM	27.12.73	3	Mutual	Kingston	1 May
22.93	0.9	Juliet	Cuthbert	JAM	9.4.64	6	VD	Bruxelles	3 Sep

Mark	Wind	Name		Nat	Born	Pos	Meet	Venue	Date
22.95	1.5		Ma Yuqin	CHN	11.9.72	3h2	NG	Beijing	12 Sep
22.97	-0.4	Marina	Trandenkova	RUS	7.1.67	2		Dijon	13 Jun
22.98	-1.2	Carlette	Guidry	USA	4.9.68	3		Madrid	3 Jun
22.98	0.3	Kim	Graham	USA	26.3.71	1		Noisy-le-Grand	3 Jul
23.00	-0.3	Marion	Jones	USA	12.10.75	1		Norwalk	29 May
23.01	1.6	Michelle	Finn	USA	8.5.65	3s1	NC	Eugene	18 Jun
23.01	0.8	Sanna	Hernesniemi	FIN	9.3.71	5	EP	Roma	27 Jun
		(40)							
23.01	0.9		Pei Fang	CHN	1.2.71	4h1	NG	Beijing	12 Sep
23.02		Terri	Dendy	USA	8.5.65	1		Chapel Hill	26 May
23.02	1.2	Flirtisha	Harris	USA	21.2.72	3s1	NCAA	New Orleans	4 Jun
23.04A	0.4	Yolanda	Steyn	RSA	22.8.72	2		Pretoria	15 May
23.04	0.1	Cheryl	Taplin	USA	2.9.72	2h1	NCAA	New Orleans	2 Jun
23.05	0.2	Louann	Williams	TRI	72	1	JUCO	Odessa	22 May
23.06		Maya	Azarashvili	GEO	6.4.64	1		Maribor	23 Jun
23.08	1.8	Tisha	Prather	USA	5.8.71	1	Gator	Knoxville	1 May
23.08		Yelena	Ruzina	RUS	3.4.64	1		Voronezh	25 Jul
23.10	0.0	Svetla	Dimitrova	BUL	27.1.70	H	WC	Stuttgart	16 Aug
		(50)							
23.12	1.4	Liliana	Allen	CUB	24.6.70	1	NC	Habana	13 May
23.12	1.6	Esther	Jones	USA	7.4.69	4s1	NC	Eugene	18 Jun
23.12	0.4	Sabine	Tröger	AUT	7.7.67	1		Lienz	8 Aug
23.13	1		Wang Lei	CHN	4.3.71	2		Shijiazhuang	26 Apr
23.15	0.4	Yuliya	Sotnikova	RUS	70	1h6	NC	Moskva	20 Jun
23.16A	1.3	Heike	Drechsler	GER	16.12.64	1		Potchefstroom	8 May
23.16	1.6	Viktoriya	Fomenko	UKR	2.10.71	2		Kiev	16 May
23.16	1.6	Stacy	Bowen	CAN	17.12.69	5	NCAA	New Orleans	5 Jun
23.16	1.1	Tonja	Buford	USA	13.12.70	7	BNP	Villeneuve d'Ascq	2 Jul
23.16	0.4	Lucrécia	Jardim	POR	28.1.71	5q3	WC	Stuttgart	17 Aug
		(60)							
23.17	1.5		Du Xiujie	CHN	27.11.71	4h2	NG	Beijing	12 Sep
23.18	1.0	Anelia	Nuneva	BUL	30.6.62	2		Granada	29 May
23.19	0.0	Jackie	Joyner-Kersee	USA	3.3.62	H	WC	Stuttgart	16 Aug
23.20	1.2	Katharine	Merry	GBR	21.9.74	1	NC	London	13 Jun
23.22	-0.7	Marina	Zhirova	RUS	6.6.63	1		Sochi	23 May
23.23		Jana	Schönenberger	GER	28.1.71	1		Sindelfingen	29 May
23.25	-1.1	Nicole	Mitchell	JAM	5.6.74	1	Carif	Fort-de-France	11 Apr
23.25	0.8	Oksana	Dyachenko	RUS	26.11.74	5	Slovn	Bratislava	1 Jun
23.25	1.2	Anna	Koshelyeva	RUS	11.11.68	1		Sankt Peterburg	1 Aug
23.25	1.4	Yekaterina	Leshcheva	RUS	21.4.74	1		Jyväskylä	10 Aug
		(70)							
23.26	1.9	Anita	Mormand	FRA	20.2.71	1		Cayenne	26 Apr
23.26	0.9		Jiang Lan	CHN	.1.69	6h1	NG	Beijing	12 Sep
23.26	0.7	Idalmis	Bonne	CUB	2.2.71	1s1	CAG	Ponce	25 Nov
23.28	0.4	Sandra	Myers	ESP	9.1.61	1	EP/B	Bruxelles	13 Jun
23.29		Jearl	Miles	USA	4.9.66	1		Gainesville	17 Apr
23.29	1.1	Aileen	McGillivary	GBR	13.8.70	1	BelC	Bruxelles	25 Jul
23.29	-0.6	Damarayathi	Darsha	SRI	13.2.75	2	AsiC	Manila	4 Dec
23.30A	1.7	Kim	Mitchell	USA	11.1.71	1B		El Paso	10 Apr
23.30	1.2	Sally	Gunnell	GBR	29.7.66	2	NC	London	13 Jun
23.30	0.2		Wang Huei-Chen	TPE	21.2.70	1h7	WC	Stuttgart	17 Aug
		(80)							
23.31	1.4	Julia	Duporty	CUB	9.2.71	3	NC	Habana	13 May
23.31	1.8	Crystal	Braddock	USA	13.12.70	3s2	NCAA	New Orleans	4 Jun
23.32	1.1	Heather	Samuel	ANT	6.7.70	1		Indianapolis	26 May
23.32	0.4	Jane	Flemming	AUS	14.4.65	2H5		Götzis	29 May
23.33	1.5		Tang Haiyun	CHN	.9.73	5h2	NG	Beijing	12 Sep
23.34	1.5		Gao Jie	CHN	4.2.73	6h2	NG	Beijing	12 Sep
23.35	1.6	Antonina	Slyusar	UKR	19.3.63	3		Kiev	16 May
23.35	0.2	Zoya	Sokolova	RUS	3.4.70	1h3	NC	Moskva	19 Jun
23.35	1.1	Olga	Bogoslovskaya	RUS	20.5.64	8	BNP	Villeneuve d'Ascq	2 Jul
23.36A	0.4	Susan	Knox	RSA	28.12.71	4		Pretoria	15 May
		(90)							
23.36	0.5	Andrea	Lloyd	JAM	10.8.71	2h2		Knoxville	15 May
23.36	0.9		Sun Yanshi	CHN	8.9.71	7h1	NG	Beijing	12 Sep
23.37	0.5	Lydia	De Vega	PHI	26.12.64	1	SEAG	Singapore	16 Jun
23.38	1.5		Xiao Yehua	CHN	6.11.71	7h2	NG	Beijing	12 Sep
23.39	1.8	Sheryl	Covington	USA	3.3.71	4s2	NCAA	New Orleans	4 Jun

Mark	Wind	Name		Nat	Born	Pos	Meet	Venue	Date
23.39	1.2	Jacqueline	Poelman	HOL	5.10.73	1	WA	Sittard	6 Jun
23.39	0.3	LaVonna	Martin-Floreal	USA	18.11.66	2		Noisy-le-Grand	3 Jul
23.39	0.4	Marika	Johansson	SWE	27.10.70	1	NC	Kvarnsveden	25 Jul
23.40	2.0	Olga	Robinson	JAM		2	SWC	Abilene	29 May
23.40	1.8	Keisha	Owens	USA	7.4.73	3h2	NCAA	New Orleans	2 Jun
		(100)							
23.40	0.2	Svetlana	Goncharenko	RUS	28.5.71	3	Znam	Moskva	13 Jun

Mark	Wind	Name		Nat	Born	Date
23.42	-1.3	Maguy	Nestoret	FRA	69	18 Jun
23.42	?	Erika	Suchovská	TCH	67	23 Jun
23.43	1.6	Jennifer	Stoute	GBR	65	13 Jun
23.43	0.0	Irina	Slyusar	UKR	63	3 Jul
23.43	-0.7	Melanie	Paschke	GER	70	11 Jul
23.43A	1.0	Savatheda	Fynes	BAH	74	31 Jul
23.44	0.4	Sara	Wüest	SUI	69	7 Jul
23.44	1.2	Angelika	Haggenmüller	GER	69	11 Jul
23.45	-1.3	Valérie	Jean-Charles	FRA	69	18 Jun
		(110)				
23.45	1.3	Birgit	Rockmeier	GER	73	11 Jul
23.46	0.0	Steffanie	Smith	USA	71	1 May
23.46A	1.0	Patricia	Rodriguez	COL	70	31 Jul
23.46	-0.6	Govindasamy	Shanti	MAS	67	4 Dec
23.47	1.1	Ximena	Restrepo	COL	69	25 Nov
23.48	1.6	Omotayo	Akinremi	NGR	74	21 May
23.49	0.4	Kylie	Hanigan	AUS	71	23 Jan
23.49	1.5	Twilet	Malcolm	JAM	69	24 Apr
23.49	-0.8		Huang Mei	CHN	75	4 Jun
23.49		Ionela	Tîrlea	ROM	76	12 Jun
		(120)				
23.49	0.4	Zlatka	Georgieva	BUL	69	13 Jun
23.49	0.6	Andrea	Philipp	GER	71	11 Jul
23.49	1.9	Simmone	Jacobs	GBR	66	17 Jul
23.50	0.8	Stacey	Clack	USA	71	20 May
23.50	2.0	Mary	Tombiri	NGR	72	29 May
23.50A	1.0	Revolie	Campbell	JAM	72	31 Jul
23.51		Faith	Idehen	NGR	73	18 Jun
23.51		Gabi	Rockmeier	GER	73	11 Sep
23.52	0.2	Yelena	Dubtsova	RUS	71	13 Jun
23.52	-0.1	Natasha	Kaiser-Brown	USA	67	4 Aug
		(130)				
23.53	1.5	Dyan	Webber	USA	66	24 Apr
23.53A	-1.3	Shanelle	Porter	USA	72	18 May
23.53		Debbie Ann	Parris	JAM	73	26 May
23.53	1.3	Hana	Benesová	TCH	75	30 Jul
23.54	-0.2	Delphine	Combe	FRA	74	2 Jul
23.54	1.8	Yana	Burtasenkova	MOL	73	13 Jun
23.54	1.2	Stephanie	Douglas	GBR	69	13 Jun
23.55	1.2	Kendra	Mackey	USA	69	2 May
23.55A		Melinda	Sergent	USA	72	22 May
23.55		Kathleen	Van Hove	BEL	73	25 Jul
		(140)				
23.55		Svetlana	Moskalets	RUS	69	6 Aug
23.56	1.2	Tania	Van Heer	AUS	70	23 Jan
23.57	1.9	Nanceen	Perry	USA	77	15 May
23.57	1.2	Beverly	Kinch	GBR	64	13 Jun
23.57	0.9	Sophia	Smith	GBR	74	30 Jul
23.58	1.8	Heather	Van Norman	USA	70	1 May
23.58			Chen Chaoyi	CHN	73	13 Sep
23.59	0.4	Sølvi	Meinseth	NOR	67	13 Jun
23.59	1.2	Silke	Lichtenhagen	GER	73	11 Jul
23.60	0.3	Michelle	Seymour	NZL	65	25 Feb
		(150)				
23.60		Andrea	Anderson	USA	77	7 May
23.60		Layphane	Carnegie	JAM		21 May
23.60	1.7	Michelle	Lock	AUS	67	27 Nov
23.61	1.4	Patricia	Girard	FRA	68	28 May
23.61		Anja	Böhme	GER	71	29 May
23.61	-1.2	Michelle	Freeman	JAM	69	3 Jun
23.61	1.9	Rochelle	Stevens	USA	66	17 Jul
23.61	-0.7	Cathy	Rattray-Williams	JAM	63	21 Jul
23.61	1.3	Carmen	Bertmaring	GER	76	30 Jul
23.62	0.0	Monique	Hennagan	USA	76	14 May
		(160)				
23.63		Olga	Nazarova	RUS	62	10 Jun
23.63	1.4	Jennifer	Wilson	USA	76	17 Jul
23.63	-0.4	Nathalie	Fokoua	FRA	70	25 Jul
23.64	-0.1		Wang Jing	CHN	75	10 Apr
23.64	-1.9		Ye Shenglan	CHN	69	4 Jun
23.64	0.9	Izabela	Czajko	POL	71	25 Jul
23.64A	-0.3	Marcel	Winkler	RSA	70	30 Oct
23.65	-1.1	Astia	Walker	JAM	75	11 Apr
23.65	-0.4	Aline	André	FRA	73	25 Jul
23.66	0.0		Chen Yanchun	CHN	73	21 Mar
		(170)				
23.66	1.1	Shantel	Twiggs	USA	72	26 May
23.66		Karin	Janke	GER	63	30 May
23.66		Katia	de Jeus Santos	BRA	67	28 Jul
23.66		Georgette	Nkoma	CMR	65	17 Aug
23.67	0.8	Lalao	Ravaonirina	MAD	63	27 Jun
23.67		Youlanda	Warren	USA	72	20 Mar
23.67		Janis	Foster	USA	71	10 Apr
23.67		Aminah	Haddad	USA	78	7 May
23.67	1.9	Nadezhda	Rashchupkina	RUS	63	8 Jun
23.67	1.3	Marina	Filipovic	YUG	70	4 Jul
		(180)				
23.67	0.2	Philomena	Mensah	GHA	75	17 Aug
23.67		Evelyn	Ashford	USA	57	9 Oct
23.68	0.3	Renee	Poetschka	AUS	71	25 Feb
23.68	1.6	Celena	Mondie-Milner	USA	68	1 May
23.68	-1.9		Guo Lijuan	CHN	75	4 Jun
23.68	0.4	Maria	Staafgård	SWE	69	25 Jul
23.69	0.0	Svetlana	Buraga	BLS	65	16 Aug
23.70	2.0	Juan	Ball	USA		29 May
23.70	-0.3	Sisko	Hanhijoki	FIN	62	27 Jul
23.70	-0.7	Christine	Bloomfield	GBR	68	29 Aug
		(190)				

Best at low altitude

Mark	Wind	Name	Pos	Meet	Venue	Date
23.22	1.9	Y Steyn	2	AfrC	Durban	27 Jun
23.41		Knox				26 Jun
23.50	1.8	K Mitchell				2 Jun
23.60	0.0	Porter				10 Apr

Wind-assisted marks

Mark	Wind	Name		Nat	Born	Pos	Meet	Venue	Date
22.32	4.7	Dannette	Young	USA	6.10.64	1	vGBR	Edinburgh	2 Jul
22.56	3.2	Flirtisha	Harris	USA	21.2.72	1	WUG	Buffalo	17 Jul
22.64	2.1	Kim	Graham	USA	26.3.71	1		Austin	8 May
22.66	2.7	Juliet	Campbell	JAM	17.3.70	1h1		Knoxville	15 May
22.74	2.2	Silke-Beate	Knoll	GER	21.2.67	1	NC	Duisburg	11 Jul
22.76	3.5	Carlette	Guidry	USA	4.9.68	2s2	NC	Eugene	18 Jun
22.79	2.6	Marion	Jones	USA	12.10.75	1		Norwalk	22 May
22.79	3.2	Dahlia	Duhaney	JAM	20.7.70	2	WUG	Buffalo	17 Jul
22.80	3.2		Wang Huie-chen	TPE	21.2.70	3	WUG	Buffalo	17 Jul
22.81	2.4	Michelle	Finn	USA	8.5.65	3	NC	Eugene	19 Jun
22.86	2.7	Cheryl	Taplin	USA	2.9.72	2h1		Knoxville	15 May
22.87		Michelle	Collins	USA	12.2.71	1		Houston	2 May

Mark	Wind	Name		Nat	Born	Pos	Meet	Venue	Date
22.90	3.2	Liliana	Allen	CUB	24.6.70	5	WUG	Buffalo	17 Jul
22.97	2.2	Melanie	Paschke	GER	29.6.70	2	NC	Duisburg	11 Jul
22.98		Twilet	Malcolm	JAM	5.2.69	1		New Orleans	15 May
22.98	2.9	Sanna	Hernesniemi	FIN	9.3.71	1		Nastola	17 Jun
23.13	2.4	Yulia	Mukhetdinova	RUS	69	2h2	WUG	Buffalo	16 Jul
23.17	3.1	Teresa	Neighbors	USA	26.5.67	1B		Austin	8 May
23.19	3.1	Jearl	Miles	USA	4.9.66	2B		Austin	8 May
23.22A	6.2	Idalmis	Bonne	CUB	2.2.71	1	CAC	Cali	31 Jul
23.28	2.6	Georgette	Nkoma	CMR	16.6.65	3s2	WUG	Buffalo	17 Jul
23.32A	6.2	Debbie	Ferguson	BAH	16.1.76	2	CAC	Cali	31 Jul
23.33	2.2	Silke	Lichtenhagen	GER	20.11.73	3	NC	Duisburg	11 Jul
23.34		Hermin	Joseph	DMN	13.4.64	1		Abilene	8 May
23.36	5.3	Christy	Opara	NGR	2.5.70	1		Azusa	24 Apr
23.36		Dyan	Webber	USA	9.4.66	2		Houston	2 May
23.36	2.9	Sisko	Hanhijoki	FIN	25.4.62	2		Nastola	17 Jun
23.37		Keisha	Owens	USA	7.4.73	2		New Orleans	15 May
23.39		Yvette	Cole	USA		1		Houston	1 May
23.40		Sheila	Echols	USA	2.10.64	4		Houston	2 May

Mark	Wind	Name		Nat	Born	Date
23.43	3.1	Francine	Landre	FRA	70	8 Aug
23.45		Cheryl Ann	Phillips	JAM	70	17 Apr
23.46		Faith	Idehen	NGR	73	17 Apr
23.48	2.6	Aminah	Haddad	USA	78	22 May
23.51A	2.6	France	Gareau	CAN	67	26 May
23.51	2.2	Angelika	Haggenmüller	GER	69	11 Jul
23.54	2.3	Sølvi	Meinseth	NOR	67	31 Jul
23.55	4.3	Trevaia	Williams	USA	68	26 May
23.57		Alethea	Antoine	TRI		1 May
23.58	2.6	Andrea	Anderson	USA	77	22 May
23.60	2.4	Giada	Gallina	ITA	73	17 Jul
23.61		Carmetia	Mackey	BAH	74	24 Apr
23.61	2.8	Nelrae	Pasha	USA	70	1 May
23.62	3.4	Camille	Noel	CAN	74	11 Jul
23.63	2.4	Karin	Solbakken	NOR	67	4 Sep
23.64		Pam	Ashford	USA		14 May
23.64	4.7	Paula	Cohen	GBR	71	2 Jul
23.64	4.7	Tracy	Goddard	GBR	69	2 Jul
23.65	7.8	Gwen	Clardy	USA	73	10 Apr
23.66	2.4	De'Angelia	Johnson	USA	73	17 Apr
23.68	2.5	Cathie	Guischard	TRI	70	1 May

Hand timed

Mark	Wind	Name		Nat	Born	Pos	Meet	Venue	Date
22.3			Torrence			1		Port of Spain	8 May
22.7		Louann	Williams	TRI	72	2		Port-of-Spain	8 May
23.1		Hydieann	Harper	TRI		3		Port of Spain	8 May
23.2		Georgette	Nkoma	CMR	16.6.65	1		Garoua	8 Aug

Mark	Wind	Name		Nat	Born	Date
23.3	1.6	Nathalie	Fokoua	FRA	70	23 May
23.3		Yelena	Dubtsova	RUS	71	30 May
23.4		Kalawati	Saramma	IND	71	20 Jan
23.4		Alicia	Tyson	TRI		14 Mar
23.4	-0.1	Omotayo	Akinremi	NGR	74	22 May
23.4		Olga	Conte	ARG	66	23 May
23.4		Nina	Arnst	RUS	69	30 May
23.4		Cleide	Amaral	BRA	67	27 Jun
23.4	1.3	Aileen	McGillivary	GBR	70	1 Aug
23.4	1.3	Marcia	Richardson	GBR	72	1 Aug
23.4	1.3	Geraldine	McLeod	GBR	71	1 Aug
23.4	1.7	Margarita	Molchan	BLS	66	3 Aug

Wind assisted

Mark	Wind	Name		Nat	Born	Pos	Meet	Venue	Date
22.8	2.6	Michelle	Collins	USA	12.2.71	1		Los Angeles	10 Apr
22.9		Shantel	Twiggs	USA	4.10.72	1		Terre Haute	15 May
23.1		Andrea	Anderson	USA	17.9.77	1		Long Beach	Apr

Mark	Wind	Name		Nat	Born	Date
23.4	2.3	Brigitte	Mullen	AUS	66	20 Feb
23.5	3.9	Renee	Poetschka	AUS	71	9 Jan
23.5	2.5	Celena	Mondie-Milner	USA	68	10 Apr
23.5	2.2	Camara	Jones	USA	72	15 May

Indoors

Mark	Wind	Name		Nat	Born	Pos	Meet	Venue	Date
21.87			Ottey			1A		Liévin	13 Feb
22.15			Privalova			1	WI	Toronto	14 Mar
23.32	-	Sisko	Hanhijoki	FIN	25.4.62	1C		Liévin	13 Feb

Mark	Wind	Name		Nat	Born	Date
23.41	-	Karin	Janke	GER	63	7 Feb
23.42	-	Regula	Anliker-Aebi	SUI	65	21 Feb
23.51		Rochelle	Stevens	USA	66	26 Feb
23.66	-	Sandra	Seuser	GER	66	7 Feb
23.3		Zoya	Sokolova	RUS	70	14 Feb

300 METRES

Mark	Name		Nat	Born	Pos	Meet	Venue	Date
36.44	Sally	Gunnell	GBR	29.7.66	1	Vaux	Gateshead	30 Jul
36.50	Pauline	Davis	BAH	9.7.66	2	Vaux	Gateshead	30 Jul
36.87	Mariana	Florea	ROM	29.6.76	1		Southampton	6 Jun
37.02	Michelle	Collins	USA	12.12.71	3	Vaux	Gateshead	30 Jul
37.23	Irina	Radeyeva	RUS	15.9.68	2		Southampton	6 Jun
37.25	Rochelle	Stevens	USA	8.9.66	1		Bedford	24 Jul

Mark	Name		Nat	Born	Date
37.30	Cathy	Rattray-Williams	JAM	63	24 Jul
37.31	Kim	Graham	USA	71	30 Jul
37.48	Tracy	Goddard	GBR	69	6 Jun
37.71	Deon	Hemmings	JAM	68	24 Jul
37.76	Phylis	Smith	GBR	69	19 May
37.94	Terry	Dendy	USA	65	24 Jul

During 400m race - WC Stuttgart 17 Aug

36.10 Tatyana Alekseyeva RUS 7.10.63, 36.33 Jearl Miles USA 4.9.66, 36.47 Natasha Kaiser-Brown USA 14.5.67

Indoors

Mark	Name		Nat	Born	Pos	Meet	Venue	Date
35.45	Irina	Privalova	RUS	12.11.68	1		Moskva	17 Jan
36.87	Silke	Knoll	GER	21.2.67	1		Sindelfingen	14 Feb

Mark	Name		Nat	Born	Date
37.44	Tatyana	Alekseyeva	RUS	63	23 Jan
37.97	Svetlana	Bordukova	RUS	65	23 Jan

400 METRES

Mark	Name		Nat	Born	Pos	Meet	Venue	Date
49.81		Ma Yuqin	CHN	11.9.72	1	NG	Beijing	11 Sep
49.82	Jearl	Miles	USA	4.9.66	1	WC	Stuttgart	17 Aug
49.83	Gwen	Torrence	USA	12.6.65	1	Herc	Monaco	7 Aug
49.89	Irina	Privalova	RUS	12.11.68	1	Kuts	Moskva	30 Jul
50.11	Juliet	Campbell	JAM	17.3.70	1		Kingston	3 Jul
50.17	Natasha	Kaiser-Brown	USA	14.5.67	2	WC	Stuttgart	17 Aug
50.37		Torrence			1	Indy	Indianapolis	25 Jun
50.37	Ximena	Restrepo	COL	10.3.69	1		Salamanca	27 Jul
50.41		Kaiser-Brown			1s1	WC	Stuttgart	16 Aug
50.43		Miles			1	NC	Eugene	19 Jun
50.44	Sandie	Richards	JAM	6.11.68	3	WC	Stuttgart	17 Aug
50.45		Miles			1s2	WC	Stuttgart	16 Aug
50.46		Restrepo			2	Herc	Monaco	7 Aug
50.46		Miles			3	Herc	Monaco	7 Aug
50.49	Tatyana	Alekseyeva	RUS	7.10.63	2s1	WC	Stuttgart	16 Aug
50.52		Kaiser-Brown			2	Indy	Indianapolis	25 Jun
50.52		Alekseyeva			4	WC	Stuttgart	17 Aug
50.55		Miles			1A		Luzern	29 Jun
50.58		Campbell			1	NCAA	New Orleans	5 Jun
50.64		Richards			1	Mutual	Kingston	1 May
50.65		Richards			2s2	WC	Stuttgart	16 Aug
50.70		Miles			1		Pau	26 Jun
50.76		Richards			2		Salamanca	27 Jul
50.80		Kaiser-Brown			2A		Luzern	29 Jun
50.83	Sandra	Myers	ESP	9.1.61	3s2	WC	Stuttgart	16 Aug
50.83		Miles			1	Gugl	Linz	25 Aug
50.86		Ma Yuqin			1	NC	Jinan	3 Jun
50.87		Richards			3	Indy	Indianapolis	25 Jun
50.88		Alekseyeva			1h1	WC	Stuttgart	15 Aug
50.89		Campbell			1		Auburn	1 May
50.89		Campbell			3s1	WC	Stuttgart	16 Aug
50.89		Restrepo			4s2	WC	Stuttgart	16 Aug
	(32/10)							
51.00	Renee	Poetschka	AUS	1.5.71	1	NC	Brisbane	6 Mar
51.10	Maicel	Malone	USA	12.6.69	1		Padova	29 Aug
51.14	Yelena	Ruzina	RUS	3.4.64	5s2	WC	Stuttgart	16 Aug
51.17	Norfalia	Carabali	COL	21.1.67	4s1	WC	Stuttgart	16 Aug
51.21	Jillian	Richardson	CAN	10.3.65	3	Mutual	Kingston	1 May
51.25		Zhang Hengyun	CHN	25.10.74	2	NG	Beijing	11 Sep
51.29	Sally	Gunnell	GBR	29.7.66	1	vUSA	Edinburgh	2 Jul
51.30	Nelrae	Pasha	USA	28.10.70	1		Chapel Hill	8 May
51.34	Cathy	Freeman	AUS	16.2.73	2	TSB	London	23 Jul
51.44	Maria	Mutola	MOZ	27.10.72	1		Weinstadt	7 Aug
	(20)							
51.53		Liu Weiwei	CHN	11.5.71	3	NG	Beijing	11 Sep
51.55	Camara	Jones	USA	15.5.72	1	Pac-10	Berkeley	22 May
51.55	Aelita	Yurchenko	UKR	1.1.65	5s1	WC	Stuttgart	16 Aug
51.59	Dannette	Young	USA	6.10.64	1	SunA	Tempe	3 Apr
51.59	Michelle	Collins	USA	12.2.71	3s2	NC	Eugene	18 Jun
51.64	Inez	Turner	JAM	1.3.72	3	NC	Kingston	3 Jul
51.65	Cathy	Rattray-Williams	JAM	19.8.63	4	Mutual	Kingston	1 May
51.69		Ling Xueyan	CHN	14.2.72	5	NG	Beijing	11 Sep
51.70	Phylis	Smith	GBR	29.9.65	1	NC	London	13 Jun
51.72	Crystal	Irving	USA	26.5.70	2		Tempe	3 Apr
	(30)							
51.72	Lyudmila	Dzhigalova ¶	UKR	22.1.62	1		Kiev	15 May
51.73	Kendra	Mackey	USA	14.1.69	5	Indy	Indianapolis	25 Jun
51.75	Terri	Dendy	USA	8.5.65	1		Chapel Hill	15 May
51.77	Shanequa	Campbell	USA	1.9.72	2	Pac-10	Berkeley	22 May
51.77	Deon	Hemmings	JAM	9.10.68	4	NC	Kingston	3 Jul
51.81	Julia	Duporty	CUB	9.2.71	1	CAG	Ponce	25 Nov
51.82	Tina	Paulino	MOZ	7.7.73	1	AfrC	Durban	24 Jun
51.88	Camille	Noel	CAN	14.4.74	3	Pac-10	Berkeley	22 May

Mark	Name		Nat	Born	Pos	Meet	Venue	Date
51.88	Kim	Graham	USA	26.3.71	1		Atlanta	22 May
51.89	Yelena	Golesheva	RUS	12.7.66	3	NC	Moskva	20 Jun
	(40)							
51.90	Tatyana	Ledovskaya	BLS	21.5.66	1		Odessa	21 May
51.91	Anja	Rücker	GER	20.12.72	1		Lindau	8 Aug
51.92	Youlanda	Warren	USA	13.3.72	3	NCAA	New Orleans	5 Jun
51.92	Elsa	Devassoigne	FRA	17.10.69	2	EP	Roma	26 Jun
51.92	Francine	Landre	FRA	26.7.70	1	NC	Annecy	25 Jul
51.97	Michelle	Lock	AUS	29.3.67	1		Canberra	13 Mar
52.00		Guo Yue ¶	CHN	23.1.69	1h	NC	Jinan	2 Jun
52.01	Claudine	Williams	JAM	8.1.76	1	PAJ	Winnipeg	16 Jul
52.02	Beverley	Grant	JAM	17.10.74	5	NC	Kingston	3 Jul
52.04	Cynthia	Jackson	USA	12.9.71	1	SWC	Austin	21 May
	(50)							
52.05	Shanelle	Porter	USA	20.1.72	1h1	NCAA	New Orleans	3 Jun
52.07		Bai Xiaoyun	CHN	15.6.73	6	NG	Beijing	11 Sep
52.10	Mariana	Florea	ROM	29.8.76	1	RomIC	Bucuresti	18 Jun
52.14	Linda	Keough	GBR	26.12.63	3	EP	Roma	26 Jun
52.14	Marie-Louise	Bévis	FRA	12.10.72	1h1	NC	Annecy	24 Jul
52.15	Denise	Mitchell	USA	20.2.66	2		Chapel Hill	15 May
52.15	Nancy	McLeon	CUB	1.5.71	1	Barr	Habana	22 May
52.15	Maria	Figuereido	BRA	11.11.63	1		Rio de Janeiro	26 Jun
52.18A	Odalmis	Limonta	CUB	13.1.72	2	CAC	Cali	30 Jul
52.19	Regula	Zürcher/Scalabrin	SUI	5.1.69	1	NC	St Gallen	1 Aug
	(60)							
52.24	Omolade	Akinremi	NGR	13.9.74	3	MSR	Walnut	17 Apr
52.24	Magdalena	Nedelcu	ROM	12.5.74	1rB		Southampton	6 Jun
52.26	Kylie	Hanigan	AUS	18.11.71	1		Canberra	25 Jan
52.26	Emily	Odoemenam	NGR	24.10.70	2	AfrC	Durban	25 Jun
52.26	Evelyn	Elien	FRA	24.3.64	4	NC	Annecy	25 Jul
52.27	Vera	Sychugova	RUS	8.4.63	4	NC	Moskva	20 Jun
52.28	Irina	Radeyeva	RUS	15.9.68	5	NC	Moskva	20 Jun
52.28		Cao Chunying	CHN	.2.73	7	NG	Beijing	11 Sep
52.30	Steffanie	Smith	USA	23.2.71	1		Villanova	2 May
52.30	Monique	Hennagan	USA	26.5.76	1	NC-j	Spokane	27 Jun
	(70)							
52.32A	Evette	De Klerk	RSA	21.8.65	1		Pietersburg	6 Apr
52.33	Audrea	Sterling	JAM	1.7.68	1	NAIA	Abbotsford	22 May
52.35	Janeen	Jones	USA	19.8.72	2		Atlanta	3 Apr
52.36?	Luciana	Mendes	BRA	26.7.71	1		Pres. Prudente	5 Jun
	52.56				2		Rio de Janeiro	26 Jun
52.39	Rochelle	Stevens	USA	8.9.66	3	Vaux	Gateshead	30 Jul
52.40		Liang Yanping	CHN	.6.70	2h2	NG	Beijing	10 Sep
52.41	Joetta	Clark	USA	1.8.62	2		Tallahassee	26 May
52.43	Omotayo	Akinremi	NGR	13.9.74	3	SunA	Tempe	3 Apr
52.43	Nina	Arnst	RUS	21.3.69	7	NC	Moskva	20 Jun
52.43	Yelena	Nasonkina	UKR	11.8.62	1	NC	Kiev	3 Jul
	(80)							
52.44	Yvette	Cole	USA		1		Houston	14 May
52.47	Cynthia	Newsome	USA	5.4.76	2	NC-j	Spokane	27 Jun
52.48	Susan	Andrews	AUS	26.1.71	4	NC	Brisbane	6 Mar
52.52	Maree	Holland	AUS	25.7.63	5	NC	Brisbane	6 Mar
52.54	Olga	Robinson	JAM		1	SWC	Abilene	29 May
52.54		Li Xiumei	CHN	.1.68	3h2	NG	Beijing	10 Sep
52.55	Karin	Janke	GER	14.10.63	3	OD	Jena	13 Jun
52.55	Olga	Lysakova	UKR	24.11.71	2	NC	Kiev	3 Jul
52.56	Yelena	Shcherban	UKR	7.2.72	3	NC	Kiev	3 Jul
52.56	Linda	Kisabaka	GER	9.4.69	1B		Lindau	8 Aug
	(90)							
52.56	Rabia	Abdul Salam	MAS	5.11.73	2	AsiC	Manila	3 Dec
52.57	Zoila	Stewart	CRC	1.11.68	2	CAG	Ponce	25 Nov
52.58	Olga	Nazarova	RUS	28.2.62	2		Betzdorf	1 Sep
52.59	Fatima	Yusuf	NGR	1.4.71	4		København	25 Jul
52.59	Kathrin	Lüthi	SUI	7.10.69	2	NC	St Gallen	1 Aug
52.59	Aïssatou	Tandian	SEN	29.8.66	4h4	WC	Stuttgart	15 Aug
52.60	Noodang	Phimphoo	THA	15.10.68	1	SEAG	Singapore	14 Jun

Mark	Name		Nat	Born	Pos	Meet	Venue	Date
52.62	Tatyana	Chebykina	RUS	22.11.68	6	NC	Moskva	20 Jun
52.63	Tamyka	McCord	USA	23.6.71	1		Indianapolis	26 May
52.66	Heather	Van Norman	USA	22.4.70	2		Baton Rouge	17 Apr
	(100)							
52.66		Lu Xifang	CHN	16.12.73	h	NC	Jinan	2 Jun

Mark	Name		Nat	Born	Date
52.67	Jacqueline	Gayle	JAM	73	8 May
52.68		Du Xiujie	CHN	71	2 Jun
52.69	Nadezda	Kostovalová	TCH	71	15 Aug
52.73	Ester	Goossens	HOL	72	25 Jul
52.74	Sandra	Seuser	GER	66	9 Jul
52.75	Lillie	Leatherwood	USA	64	26 May
52.77	Kim	Mitchell	USA	71	16 May
52.77	Jana	Schönenberger	GER	71	8 Aug
52.78	Anna	Knoroz	RUS	70	13 Jun
	(110)				
52.79	Trevaia	Williams	USA	68	10 Apr
52.80	Rosey	Edeh	CAN	66	28 Aug
52.81	Marlene	Moreira Da Silva	BRA	68	26 Jun
52.83	Tanya	Dooley	USA	72	3 Jun
52.83		An Xiaohong	CHN	68	10 Sep
52.83	Kalawati	Saramma	IND	71	3 Dec
52.84	Debbie Ann	Parris	JAM	73	2 Jul
52.85	Pauline	Davis	BAH	66	24 Apr
52.86	Martha	Grossenbacher	SUI	59	29 Jun
52.86	Silke	Knoll	GER	67	1 Sep
	(120)				
52.88	Hana	Benesová	TCH	75	31 May
52.90	Lency	Montelier	CUB	71	2 Jul
52.92		Zhang Weimin	CHN	70	2 Jun
52.92	Jennifer	Stoute	GBR	65	2 Jul
52.92	Annett	Hesselbarth	GER	66	9 Jul
52.93	De'Angelia	Johnson	USA	73	21 May
52.93	Sølvi	Meinseth	NOR	67	12 Jun
52.93	Helen	Burkart	SUI	58	29 Jun
52.94	Ionela	Tîrlea	ROM	76	6 Jun
52.95	Revoli	Campbell	JAM	72	2 Jul
	(130)				
52.96	Doreen	Fahrendorff	GER	68	9 Jul
52.98	Idalmis	Bonne	CUB	71	12 May
52.98		Ye Shenglan	CHN	69	2 Jun
52.99	Stacy	Milligan	USA		21 May
52.99	Helga	Arendt	GER	64	9 Jul
52.99	Erika	Suchovská	TCH	67	4 Sep
53.01	Anita	Howard	USA	69	3 Apr
53.01	Surella	Morales	CUB	63	2 Jul
53.01 mx	Gretha	Tromp	HOL	64	18 Jul
	53.06				25 Jul
53.04	Ludmila	Formanová	TCH	74	4 Jul
	(140)				
53.06	Lyudmila	Kashchey	UKR	68	15 May
53.07	Grace	Birungi	UGA	73	23 Jun
53.10		Li Guilian	CHN	70	10 Sep
53.11	Ellen	Grant	JAM	74	3 Jul
53.12	Donna	Howard	USA	74	1 Aug
53.12	Yana	Burtasenkova	MOL	73	15 Aug
53.12	Mary	Onyali	NGR	68	18 Sep
53.14		Hu Yinmei	CHN	70	2 Jun
53.14	Elzbieta	Kilinska	POL	63	24 Jul
53.16	Lucie	Rangassamy	FRA	74	31 Jul
	(150)				
53.17	Tonja	Buford	USA	70	28 Mar
53.17	Sandra	Kuschmann	GER	74	31 Jul
53.19	Yuliana	Teneva	BUL	67	5 Jun
53.20	Jakki	Henderson	USA	70	29 May
53.20	Rita	Paulaviciene	LIT	69	24 Jun
53.21	Tamara	Kuprianovich	BLS	64	6 Jun
53.22	Olga	Moroz	UKR	70	15 May
53.22A	Tranquil	Wilson	USA		18 May
53.22	Valérie	Jaunatre	FRA	69	25 Jul
53.23	Francesca	Carbone	ITA	68	26 Jun
	(160)				
53.25	Celena	Mondie-Milner	USA	68	27 Mar
53.26	Mary	Awora	UGA		25 Jun
53.28	Barbara	Selkridge	USA	71	10 Apr
53.28	Anne	Renaud	FRA	70	9 May
53.28	Yolanda	Mackey	USA	67	18 Jun
53.28	Satu	Jääskeläinen	FIN	70	31 Jul
53.31A	Nicole	Green	USA	71	18 May
53.34	Julie	Jenkins	USA	64	10 Apr
53.34	Monika	Warnicka	POL	69	10 Jun
53.37	Rosangela	De Oliveira	BRA	67	5 Jun
	(170)				
53.37		Han Qing	CHN	70	14 Aug
53.38	Pam	Brooks	USA	72	14 May
53.38	Diane	Modahl	GBR	66	13 Jun
53.39		Chen Qin	CHN	71	2 Jun
53.42	Brigitte	Mullen	AUS	66	13 Feb
53.42	Bisi	Afolabi	NGR		18 Jun
53.44	Veronique	Poulain	FRA	67	3 Jul
53.44	Tatyana	Zakharova	RUS	69	15 Jul
53.46	Bettina	Kersten	GER	65	31 Jul
53.48		Liu Hongmin	CHN	71	4 May
53.49	Svetlana	Starkova	RUS	68	13 Jun
	(180)				
53.49	Silvia	Steimle	GER	73	9 Jul
53.50	Shelly Ann	Beckford	JAM		29 May
53.50	Sharlene	Milwood	USA	71	24 Jul

Indoors

Mark	Name		Nat	Born	Pos	Meet	Venue	Date
52.34	Karin	Janke	GER	14.10.63	1A	NC	Sindelfingen	28 Feb
52.37	Marina	Shmonina	RUS	9.2.65	1		Glasgow	30 Jan
52.48	Sandra	Seuser	GER	17.4.66	1		Berlin	17 Jan

Mark	Name		Nat	Born	Date
52.70	Kim	Batten	USA	69	14 Mar
52.73	Ester	Goossens	HOL	72	12 Mar
52.91	Silvia	Steimle	GER	73	7 Feb
52.94	Yelena	Andreyeva	RUS	69	28 Feb
53.09	Flirtisha	Harris	USA	72	12 Mar

Hand time

Mark	Name		Nat	Born	Pos	Meet	Venue	Date
51.5	Nancy	McLeon	CUB	1.5.71	1h		Habana	4 Nov
52.1	Natalya	Dukhnova	BLS	16.7.66	1		Gomel	14 May
52.3	Idalmis	Bonne	CUB	2.2.71	2h		Habana	4 Nov

Mark	Name		Nat	Born	Date
52.6	Tamara	Kuprianovich	BLS	64	14 May
52.7	Yelena	Goncharova	RUS	63	5 Jun
52.8	Yolanda	Mackey	USA	67	9 Apr
52.9	Meredith	Rainey	USA	68	15 Jul
53.1	Elzbieta	Kilinska	POL	63	17 Jul
53.1	Natalya	Chistyakova	RUS	70	13 Aug
53.3	Beverly	Pierre	TRI	73	7 May
53.3		Diaz	VEN		9 Oct
53.4	Lucrécia	Jardim	POR	71	22 May

Unconfirmed:

Mark	Name		Nat	Born	Pos	Meet	Venue	Date
52.2	Mary	Birungi	UGA				Kampala	15 May

Drugs ban:

Mark	Name		Nat	Born	Pos	Meet	Venue	Date
51.58		Guo Yue	CHN	23.1.69	4	NG	Beijing	11 Sep

Mark	Name		Nat	Born	Pos	Meet	Venue	Date

600 METRES

Mark	Name		Nat	Born	Pos	Meet	Venue	Date
1:25.96+	Maria	Mutola	MOZ	27.10.72	1k	WC	Stuttgart	17 Aug
1:26.0+e	Lyubov	Gurina	RUS	6.8.57	2k	WC	Stuttgart	17 Aug
1:26.2+e	Ella	Kovacs	ROM	11.12.64	3k	WC	Stuttgart	17 Aug
1:26.8 +	Diane	Modahl	GBR	17.6.66	+k	WC	Stuttgart	17 Aug
1:26.99	Sandra	Myers	ESP	9.1.61	1		Andújar	6 Sep
1:27.1 +	Kelly	Holmes	GBR	19.4.70	2k		Oslo	10 Jul
1:27.5i	Natalya	Dukhnova	BLS	16.7.66	1		Minsk	16 Jan
1:28.31	Linda	Keough	GBR	26.12.63	1		Birmingham	19 May
Indoors								
1:28.73	Zulfia	Filyova	RUS	65	1A		Moskva	2 Feb
1:28.97	Irina	Radeyeva	RUS	15.9.68	2A		Moskva	2 Feb

800 METRES

Mark	Name		Nat	Born	Pos	Meet	Venue	Date
1:55.43	Maria	Mutola	MOZ	27.10.72	1	WC	Stuttgart	17 Aug
1:55.54		Dong Liu	CHN	27.12.73	1	NG	Beijing	9 Sep
1:55.62		Mutola			1A	WK	Zürich	4 Aug
1:56.24		Qu Yunxia	CHN	25.12.72	2	NG	Beijing	9 Sep
1:56.25		Liu Dong			1h3	NG	Beijing	8 Sep
1:56.36		Mutola			1	AfrC	Durban	27 Jun
1:56.51		Mutola			1	Bisl	Oslo	10 Jul
1:56.56		Mutola			1	NYG	New York	22 May
1:56.58	Ella	Kovacs	ROM	11.12.64	1		Bucuresti	30 May
1:56.61		Kovacs			1	APM	Hengelo	20 Jun
1:56.62	Tina	Paulino	MOZ	7.7.73	2	NYG	New York	22 May
1:56.76	Svetlana	Masterkova	RUS	17.1.68	2rA		Zürich	4 Aug
1:56.96		Liu Li	CHN	12.3.71	1h2	NG	Beijing	8 Sep
1:57.00		Kovacs			3A	WK	Zürich	4 Aug
1:57.10	Lyubov	Gurina	RUS	6.8.57	2	WC	Stuttgart	17 Aug
1:57.18		Wang Yuan	CHN	8.4.76	2h2	NG	Beijing	8 Sep
1:57.18		Liu Li			3	NG	Beijing	9 Sep
1:57.31		Paulino			1s2	WC	Stuttgart	15 Aug
1:57.35		Mutola			1	GPF	London	10 Sep
1:57.38		Mutola			1	Banes	São Paulo	16 May
1:57.46		Kovacs			2s2	WC	Stuttgart	15 Aug
1:57.48		Kovacs			1	GGala	Roma	9 Jun
1:57.48		Paulino			1	Nik	Nice	21 Jul
1:57.5@		Kovacs			1	EP	Roma	26 Jun
1:57.56		Gurina			1	Athl	Lausanne	7 Jul
1:57.58		Masterkova			1		Odessa	21 May
1:57.58		Paulino			4A	WK	Zürich	4 Aug
1:57.63	Meredith	Rainey (10)	USA	15.10.68	3s2	WC	Stuttgart	15 Aug
1:57.75		Gurina			1		Padova	29 Aug
1:57.77		Lu Yi	CHN	10.4.74	4	NG	Beijing	9 Sep
1:57.82		Gurina			4s2	WC	Stuttgart	15 Aug
	(31/11)							
1:58.03	Natalya	Dukhnova	BLS	16.7.66	1	NC	Gomel	24 Jun
1:58.13	Lyudmila	Rogachova	RUS	10.10.66	2		Padova	29 Aug
1:58.17	Joetta	Clark	USA	1.8.62	3	NYG	New York	22 May
1:58.38	Oksana	Mernikova	BLS	21.11.67	2s	NC	Gomel	23 Jun
1:58.48		Chen Xuehui	CHN	.7.69	6	NG	Beijing	9 Sep
1:58.59		Zeng Yuying	CHN	.9.73	7	NG	Beijing	9 Sep
1:58.63		Zhang Yumei	CHN	25.11.71	8	NG	Beijing	9 Sep
1:58.64	Kelly	Holmes	GBR	19.4.70	5s2	WC	Stuttgart	15 Aug
1:58.88	Yelena	Afanasyeva	RUS	1.3.67	2	GGala	Roma	9 Jun
	(20)							
1:59.00	Diane	Modahl	GBR	17.6.66	6rA	WK	Zürich	4 Aug
1:59.03	Inna	Yevseyeva	UKR	14.8.64	3	GGala	Roma	9 Jun
1:59.13	Violeta	Beclea	ROM	26.3.65	2		Hengelo	20 Jun
1:59.17	Lilia	Nurutdinova ¶	RUS	15.12.63	4s1	WC	Stuttgart	15 Aug
1:59.23	Ellen	van Langen	HOL	9.2.66	4	VD	Bruxelles	3 Sep
1:59.42	Carla	Sacramento	POR	10.12.71	5	Nik	Nice	21 Jul
1:59.51	Maria	Figuereido	BRA	11.11.63	1		Lisboa	19 Jun
1:59.66	Birte	Bruhns	GER	4.11.70	6s2	WC	Stuttgart	15 Aug

Mark	Name		Nat	Born	Pos	Meet	Venue	Date
1:59.77	Julie	Jenkins	USA	12.8.64	6	NYG	New York	22 May
1:59.8e	Lyubov	Kremlyova	RUS	21.12.62	2	EP	Roma	26 Jun
	(30)							
1:59.86	Christine	Wachtel	GER	6.1.65	5s1	WC	Stuttgart	15 Aug
2:00.0A	Gladys	Wamuyu	KEN	23.12.72	1		Nairobi	29 Jul
2:00.03	Fabia	Trabaldo	ITA	5.3.72	6	GGala	Roma	9 Jun
2:00.04	Debbie	Marshall	USA	5.8.65	7	NYG	New York	22 May
2:00.07	Amy	Wickus	USA	25.6.72	2rB	WK	Zürich	4 Aug
2:00.1e	Yelena	Storchovaya	UKR	23.6.66	3	EP	Roma	26 Jun
2:00.20	Lyubov	Tsyoma	RUS	19.5.63	4h2	NC	Moskva	19 Jun
2:00.30	Letitia	Vriesde	SUR	5.10.64	3	APM	Hengelo	20 Jun
2:00.31	Alisa	Hill	USA	16.9.65	4	Banes	São Paulo	16 May
2:00.37	Luciana	Mendes	BRA	26.7.71	2		La Chaux-de-Fonds	8 Aug
	(40)							
2:00.41	Mitica	Constantin	ROM	18.8.62	1		Bucuresti	3 Jul
2:00.46	Rita	Paulaviciene	LIT	14.12.61	1		Port Alberni	2 Jun
2:00.49		Yan Wei	CHN	.10.71	h	NC	Jinan	5 Jun
2:00.63	Tamara	Kupriyanovich	BLS	26.9.64	2	Kuts	Moskva	30 Jul
2:00.72	Maria	Akraka	SWE	7.7.66	1	vFIN	Stockholm	28 Aug
2:00.75	Patricia	Djaté	FRA	3.1.71	3		Reims	30 Jun
2:00.75	Theresia	Kiesl	AUT	26.10.63	3rB	WK	Zürich	4 Aug
2:00.77	Sabine	Zwiener	GER	5.12.67	7s2	WC	Stuttgart	15 Aug
2:00.84	Liliana	Salagean	ROM	24.3.71	2		Bucuresti	3 Jul
2:00.92	Zulfiya	Filyova	RUS	65	2		St Maur	2 Jun
	(50)							
2:00.93	Sandra	Gasser	SUI	27.7.62	8	NYG	New York	22 May
2:01.14	Yelena	Zavadskaya	UKR	24.12.64	3		Odessa	21 May
2:01.20	Olga	Nelyubova	RUS	12.7.64	3	Kuts	Moskva	30 Jul
2:01.22	Tatyana	Grebenchuk	BLS	22.11.62	2	NC	Gomel	24 Jul
2:01.33	Larisa	Chzhao	RUS	4.2.72	5	Kuts	Moskva	30 Jul
2:01.36		Liu Wanjie	CHN	.11.75	h	NC	Jinan	2 Jun
2:01.39	Laura	Itcou	ROM	13.2.72	3		Bucuresti	3 Jul
2:01.40	Carmen	Stanciu	ROM	5.1.70	4		Bucuresti	3 Jul
2:01.41	Jasmin	Jones	USA	13.10.69	4		Reims	30 Jun
2:01.42	Dalia	Matuseviciené	LIT	12.11.62	1	IDag	Malmö	9 Aug
	(60)							
2:01.46		Wang Qingfen	CHN	27.3.73	5h2	NG	Beijing	8 Sep
2:01.47	Olga	Churbanova	RUS	16.7.65	1		Rostov na Donu	16 Jul
2:01.49		Liu Huirong	CHN	11.5.75	3h1	NG	Beijing	8 Sep
2:01.50	Irina	Podyalovskaya	RUS	19.10.59	2h1	NC	Moskva	19 Jun
2:01.5e	Malgorzata	Rydz	POL	18.1.67	7	EP	Roma	26 Jun
2:01.57 *	Tatyana	Dorovskikh ¶	UKR	12.8.61	4		Odessa	21 May
2:01.58	Stella	Jongmans	HOL	17.5.71	3	DNG	Stockholm	5 Jul
2:01.62	Olga	Kuznetsova	RUS	67	3h1	NC	Moskva	19 Jun
2:01.67	Anna	Brzezinska	POL	9.1.71	6h3	WC	Stuttgart	14 Aug
2:01.71	Yelena	Yaroshevich	BLS	12,12.66	3	NC	Gomel	24 Jun
	(70)							
2:01.73	Nadezhda	Loboyko	RUS	7.9.61	1		Madrid	3 Jun
2:01.77	Satu	Jääskeläinen	FIN	4.4.70	6	Nik	Nice	21 Jul
2:01.8	Yelena	Konchits	BLS	6.7.69	4		Gomel	15 May
2:01.82	Linda	Keough	GBR	26.12.63	8	ASV	Koln	1 Aug
2:01.82		Liu Jing	CHN	10.7.71	5h1	NG	Beijing	8 Sep
2:01.86		Xing Yuqin	CHN	.9.69	h	NC	Jinan	5 Jun
2:01.86	Monica	Westén	SWE	15.3.66	1		Gävle	7 Jul
2:01.96	Galina	Reznikova	RUS	25.4.61	4s1	NC	Moskva	19 Jun
2:02.01	Alla	Petukhova	RUS	20.10.70	6s2	NC	Moskva	19 Jun
2:02.03	Madele	Naudé	RSA	2.5.63	2		Pretoria	2 May
	(80)							
2:02.08	Ilse	Wicksell	RSA	10.8.59	9	ASV	Köln	1 Aug
2:02.20	Claudette	Groenendaal	USA	1.11.63	1	Vaux	Gateshead	30 Jul
2:02.23	Sandra	Dawson	AUS	2.11.70	1		Canberra	14 Mar
2:02.35	Alla	Kovpak	UKR	23.10.62	2	NC	Kiev	3 Jul
2:02.45	Simone	Weidner	GER	30.9.69	9	ISTAF	Berlin	27 Aug
2:02.48	Tatyana	Zemskova	RUS	19.3.65	1B	Znam	Moskva	12 Jun
2:02.54	Nicoletta	Tozzi	ITA	3.1.66	8	GGala	Roma	9 Jun
2:02.54	Irina	Stasenko	RUS	27.3.66	3		Lappeenranta	27 Jul

Mark	Name		Nat	Born	Pos	Meet	Venue	Date
2:02.55	Barbara	Gourdet	FRA	29.8.65	1	NC	Annecy	24 Jul
2:02.56	Svetlana	Miroshnik	UKR	3.6.68	3		Kiev	16 May
	(90)							
2:02.56	Shola	Lynch	USA	20.3.69	11	NYG	New York	22 May
2:02.64	Lyudmila	Borisova	RUS	8.3.66	1		Arras	26 Jun
2:02.65	Soraya	Vieira Telles	BRA	6.9.58	2		Rio de Janeiro	26 Jun
2:02.65	Sonia	Van Renterghem	BEL	15.6.65	9	VD	Bruxelles	3 Sep
2:02.70		Liang Shufang	CHN	2.8.72	6h1	NG	Beijing	8 Sep
2:02.7	Natalya	Tsyganova	UKR	7.2.71	1		Kharkov	18 Jun
2:02.76	Irina	Samorokova	RUS	66	2B	Znam	Moskva	12 Jun
2:02.77	Amaia	Andrés	ESP	26.6.66	3		Alcorcó	3 Jun
2:02.77	Olga	Burkanova	RUS	29.9.69	3		Pau	26 Jun
2:02.77	Regula	Zürcher/Scalabrin	SUI	5.1.69	6B	WK	Zürich	4 Aug
	(100)							

Mark	Name		Nat	Born	Date
2:02.78	Elsa	Amaral	POR	66	19 Jun
2:02.83	Daniela	Bran	ROM	68	30 May
2:02.83	Yelena	Mazovka	BLS	67	24 Jun
2:02.83		Liang Lihe	CHN	74	8 Sep
2:02.84	Yvonne	Murray	GBR	64	30 Jul
2:02.85	Viorica	Niga	ROM	68	31 Jul
2:02.85	Séverine	Foulon	FRA	73	24 Jul
2:02.87	Genesia	Eddins	USA	66	5 Jul
2:02.93	Anneke	Matthijs	BEL	69	3 Sep
	(110)				
2:02.96	Marjo	Piipponen	FIN	71	13 Jul
2:02.99	Kim	Sherman	USA		4 Jun
2:03.01	Viviane	Dorsile	FRA	67	24 Jul
2:03.06	Marlene	Moreira Da Silva	BRA	68	26 Jun
2:03.10	Munira	Gabbasova	RUS	67	12 Jun
2:03.22	Olga	Maryina	RUS	64	12 Jun
2:03.23	Kim	Toney	USA	72	4 Jun
2:03.23	Eduarda	Coelho	POR	68	19 Jun
2:03.25	Elizabeth	Onyambu	KEN	67	21 Jul
2:03.29	Margaret	Leaney	AUS	67	16 Dec
	(120)				
2:03.36	Marina	Yachmenyeva	RUS	61	16 Jul
2:03.4	Yelena	Bychovskaya	BLS	72	
2:03.44	Yelena	Goncharova	RUS	63	14 Jul
2:03.46	Nekita	Beasley	USA	69	1 Aug
2:03.49	Sarah	Renk	USA	70	19 Jun
2:03.5	Yelena	Kopytova	RUS	70	30 May
2:03.50	Melanie	Collins	AUS	67	14 Feb
2:03.52	Wendy	Old	AUS	60	25 Feb
2:03.52	Yelena	Martson	UKR	72	3 Jul
2:03.52	Adina	Valdez	TRI	61	5 Jul
	(130)				
2:03.52	Teresa	Zuñiga	ESP	64	27 Jul
2:03.53		Yu Taohua	CHN	71	8 Sep
2:03.55	Catherine	White	GBR	66	30 Jul
2:03.65	Jill	Stamison	USA	70	4 Jun
2:03.65	Joanne	Latimer	GBR	71	13 Jun
2:03.66	Lynn	Gibson	GBR	69	22 Aug
2:03.69	Aisling	Molloy	IRL	64	6 Jun
2:03.70	Ilinca	Mitrea	ROM	64	31 Jul
2:03.77	Aurelia	Scalabrin	SUI	67	31 May
2:03.78	Ludmila	Formanová	TCH	74	29 May
	(140)				
2:03.80	Simone	Meier	SUI	65	19 Jun
2:03.80	Petya	Strashilova	BUL	65	14 Jul
2:03.85	Daniela	Antipov	ROM	70	14 Jul
2:03.86	Hassiba	Boulmerka	ALG	68	18 Jun
2:03.89	Narelle	Parr	AUS	72	16 Dec
2:03.96	Svetlana	Opoleva	RUS	65	18 Jun
2:03.98	Yekaterina	Shukaylova	RUS	72	7 Aug
2:04.0 mx	Paula	Fryer	GBR	69	18 May
2:04.0	Selina	Kosgei	KEN	76	29 Jul
2:04.03		Tang Xueqing	CHN	74	3 May
	(150)				
2:04.05	Edna	Lankri	ISR	66	8 Aug
2:04.07	Ester	Goossens	HOL	72	12 Sep
2:04.08	Kati	Kovacs	GER	73	11 Jul
2:04.13	Nicole	Teter	USA	73	17 Jun
2:04.14	Vicky	Lynch	CAN	70	4 Jun
2:04.14	Inez	Turner	JAM	72	16 Jul
2:04.17	Teena	Colebrook	GBR	56	23 Jul
2:04.18	Olga	Secman	ROM	74	18 Jun
2:04.18	Natalya	Zaytseva	RUS	73	7 Aug
2:04.22	Larisa	Semenenko	UKR	66	2 Jul
	(160)				
2:04.23	Nicola	Knapp	CAN	67	1 Aug
2:04.33	Irina	Lopareva	RUS		18 Jun
2:04.4	Suzy	Hamilton	USA	68	22 Jul
2:04.43	Martina	Muck	GER	67	26 May
2:04.49	Anne	Bruns	GER	74	26 May
2:04.5	Alison	Wyeth	GBR	64	1 Aug

Indoors

Mark	Name		Nat	Born	Pos	Meet	Venue	Date
1:57.55		Mutola			1	WI	Toronto	14 Mar
2:02.51	Elsa	Amaral	POR	31.5.66	2A		Sindelfingen	14 Feb
2:02.53	Heike	Huneke	GER	16.10.66	3A		Sindelfingen	14 Feb

Mark	Name		Nat	Born	Date
2:03.61	Stefania	Savi	ITA	69	13 Feb
2:03.78	Jacqui	Parker	GBR	66	21 Feb
2:03.81	Laura	Bosman	HOL	67	27 Feb

drugs ban

Mark	Name		Nat	Born	Pos	Meet	Venue	Date
2:01.99	Minna	Lainio	FIN	22.8.68	1	NC	Mikkeli	1 Aug

1000 METRES

Mark	Name		Nat	Born	Pos	Meet	Venue	Date
2:32.40	Ella	Kovacs	ROM	11.12.64	1	BNP	Villeneuve d'Ascq	2 Jul
2:32.57	Maria	Mutola	MOZ	27.10.72	1	Pre	Eugene	5 Jun
2:32.97	Lyubov	Gurina	RUS	6.8.57	2	BNP	Villeneuve d'Ascq	2 Jul
2:33.55	Lyubov	Kremlyova	RUS	21.12.62	3	BNP	Villeneuve d'Ascq	2 Jul
2:33.96	Lyudmila	Rogachova	RUS	10.10.66	4	BNP	Villeneuve d'Ascq	2 Jul
2:34.66	Sonia	O'Sullivan	IRL	28.11.69	5	BNP	Villeneuve d'Ascq	2 Jul
2:35.03	Lilia	Nurutdinova ¶	RUS	15.12.63	6	BNP	Villeneuve d'Ascq	2 Jul
2:35.21	Ellen	van Langen	HOL	9.2.66	1	McD	Sheffield	29 Aug
2:35.49	Lyubov	Tsyoma	RUS	19.5.63	2	Pre	Eugene	5 Jun
2:35.86	Diane	Modahl	GBR	17.6.66	2	McD	Sheffield	29 Aug
	(10)							
2:35.92	Hassiba	Boulmerka	ALG	10.7.68	7	BNP	Villeneuve d'Ascq	2 Jul

Mark	Name		Nat	Born	Pos	Meet	Venue	Date
2:36.47	Oksana	Mernikova	BLS	21.11.67	1		Southampton	6 Jun
2:36.5		Gurina			1		Celle-St Cloud	5 Jul
2:36.56	Natalya	Dukhnova	BLS	16.7.66	2		Southampton	6 Jun
2:36.71	Fabia	Trabaldo	ITA	5.3.72	1	WK	Zürich	4 Aug
2:36.89	Liliana	Salageanu	ROM	24.3.71	3		Southampton	6 Jun
2:36.89		Dukhnova			3		Celle-St Cloud	5 Jul
2:36.96	Natalya	Betekhtina	RUS	8.9.61	4		Southampton	6 Jun
	(18/16)							
2:37.2	Yelena	Afanasyeva	RUS	27.5.65	2		Celle-St Cloud	5 Jul
2:37.27	Yekaterina	Podkopayeva	RUS	11.6.52	8	BNP	Villeneuve d'Ascq	2 Jul
2:37.29	Kelly	Holmes	GBR	19.4.70	4	McD	Sheffield	29 Aug
2:37.51	Joetta	Clark	USA	1.8.62	9	BNP	Villeneuve d'Ascq	2 Jul
	(20)							
2:37.76	Christine	Wachtel	GER	6.1.65	10	BNP	Villeneuve d'Ascq	2 Jul
2:37.89	Claudette	Groenendaal	USA	1.11.63	11	BNP	Villeneuve d'Ascq	2 Jul
2:38.00	Sarah	Howell	CAN	11.9.69	5	McD	Sheffield	29 Aug
2:38.27	Gladys	Wamuyu	KEN	23.12.72	6	McD	Sheffield	29 Aug
2:38.83	Lynn	Gibson	GBR	6.7.69	7	McD	Sheffield	29 Aug
2:39.0	Patricia	Djaté	FRA	3.1.71	4		La Celle/St-Cloud	5 Jul
2:39.2	Carla	Sacramento	POR	10.12.71	1		Lisboa	29 May
2:39.4 mx	Susie	Power	AUS	26.3.75	mx		Canberra	7 Jan
2:39.67	Ravilya	Agletdinova	BLS	10.2.60	5		Southampton	6 Jun
2:39.86	Ester	Goossens	HOL	21.2.72	3	WK	Zürich	4 Aug
	(30)							
Indoors								
2:35.46	Inna	Yevseyeva	UKR	14.8.64	2		Liévin	13 Feb
2:36.08	Yekaterina	Podkopayeva	RUS	11.6.52	3		Liévin	13 Feb
2:39.91	Nadezhda	Loboyko	RUS	7.9.61	2		Madrid	11 Feb

1500 METRES

Mark	Name		Nat	Born	Pos	Meet	Venue	Date
3:50.46		Qu Yunxia	CHN	25.12.72	1	NG	Beijing	11 Sep
3:51.92		Wang Junxia	CHN	9.1.73	2	NG	Beijing	11 Sep
3:57.46		Zhang Linli	CHN	6.3.73	3	NG	Beijing	11 Sep
3:58.00		Wang Junxia			1h	NC	Jinan	2 Jun
3:58.64		Wang Renmei	CHN	5.7.70	4	NG	Beijing	11 Sep
3:59.34		Liu Li	CHN	12.3.71	5	NG	Beijing	11 Sep
3:59.35	Violeta	Beclea	ROM	26.3.65	1	Herc	Monaco	7 Aug
3:59.38		Qu Yunxia			1h1	NG	Beijing	10 Sep
3:59.60	Sonia	O'Sullivan	IRL	28.11.69	2	Herc	Monaco	7 Aug
3:59.70		Zhang Lirong	CHN	3.3.73	6	NG	Beijing	11 Sep
3:59.81		Wang Yuan	CHN	8.4.76	7	NG	Beijing	11 Sep
4:00.05		Lu Yi (10)	CHN	10.4.74	8	NG	Beijing	11 Sep
4:00.50		Dong Liu	CHN	27.12.73	1	WC	Stuttgart	22 Aug
4:00.65		Zhang Lirong			2h1	NG	Beijing	10 Sep
4:00.96		Zhang Lirong			2h	NC	Jinan	2 Jun
4:01.45		Liu Li			1h2	NG	Beijing	10 Sep
4:01.49		Wang Qingfen	CHN	27.3.73	3h1	NG	Beijing	10 Sep
4:01.55		Wang Junxia			2h2	NG	Beijing	10 Sep
4:01.66		Zhang Linli			3h2	NG	Beijing	10 Sep
4:01.69		Yan Wei	CHN	12.10.71	4h1	NG	Beijing	10 Sep
4:01.71		Li Ying	CHN	24.6.75	4h2	NG	Beijing	10 Sep
4:01.72		O'Sullivan			1		Rieti	5 Sep
4:01.73		Liu Dong			5h2	NG	Beijing	10 Sep
4:01.79		Wang Yuan			5h1	NG	Beijing	10 Sep
4:01.82		Lu Yi			6h1	NG	Beijing	10 Sep
4:02.12		Li Ying			9	NG	Beijing	11 Sep
4:02.29	Malgorzata	Rydz	POL	18.1.67	3	Herc	Monaco	7 Aug
4:02.44		Wang Renmei			7h1	NG	Beijing	10 Sep
4:02.48	Yekaterina	Podkopayeva	RUS	11.6.52	4	Herc	Monaco	7 Aug
4:03.17	Alison	Wyeth	GBR	26.5.64	5	Herc	Monaco	7 Aug
	(30/17)							
4:03.32	Lyubov	Gurina	RUS	6.8.57	1		Hechtel	31 Jul
4:03.82	Fabia	Trabaldo	ITA	5.3.72	6	Herc	Monaco	7 Aug
4:04.29	Hassiba	Boulmerka	ALG	10.7.68	3	WC	Stuttgart	22 Aug
	(20)							

Mark	Name		Nat	Born	Pos	Meet	Venue	Date	
4:04.73	Gwen	Griffiths	RSA	30.8.67	7	Herc	Monaco	7	Aug
4:04.88	Lyubov	Kremlyova	RUS	21.12.62	2	Nik	Nice	21	Jul
4:04.97	Maria	Mutola	MOZ	27.10.72	3	Nik	Nice	21	Jul
4:05.10		Zhang Sanni	CHN	.12.70	6h2	NG	Beijing	10	Sep
4:05.61	Elena	Fidatov	ROM	24.7.60	8	Herc	Monaco	7	Aug
4:05.71	Oksana	Mernikova	BLS	21.11.67	1	NC	Gomel	25	Jun
4:05.77	Lyudmila	Rogachova	RUS	10.10.66	1	NC	Moskva	20	Jun
4:05.98	Vera	Chuvasheva	RUS	7.10.59	2	NC	Moskva	20	Jun
4:06.33	Carla	Sacramento	POR	10.12.71	2	EP/C3	Rotterdam	12	Jun
4:06.89	Theresia	Kiesl	AUT	26.10.63	3h1	WC	Stuttgart	20	Aug
	(30)								
4:07.03	Natalya	Betekhtina	RUS	8.9.61	5	NC	Moskva	20	Jun
4:07.15	Anna	Brzezinska	POL	9.1.71	4		Hechtel	31	Jul
4:07.17	Blandine	Bitzner	FRA	1.12.65	7	Nik	Nice	21	Jul
4:07.35	Helen	Chepngeno	KEN	2.8.67	9	Herc	Monaco	7	Aug
4:07.46	M Teresa	Zuñiga	ESP	28.12.64	4h1	WC	Stuttgart	20	Aug
4:07.86	Sandra	Gasser	SUI	27.7.62	1	Lausit	Cottbus	23	Jun
4:07.90	Elana	Meyer	RSA	10.10.66	1		Cape Town	20	Mar
4:07.95	Angela	Chalmers	CAN	6.9.63	5	WC	Stuttgart	22	Aug
4:08.17	Olga	Nelyubova	RUS	12.7.64	6	NC	Moskva	20	Jun
4:08.43		Tang Xueqing	CHN	16.10.74	8h1	NG	Beijing	10	Sep
	(40)								
4:08.60	Lilia	Nurutdinova ¶	RUS	15.12.63	2	Slovn	Bratislava	1	Jun
4:08.63	Yvonne	Murray	GBR	4.10.64	1	vUSA	Edinburgh	2	Jul
4:08.78		Wei Li	CHN	.1.72	h	NC	Jinan	2	Jun
4:08.87	Annette	Peters	USA	31.5.65	10	Herc	Monaco	7	Aug
4:08.92	Marina	Bastos	POR	7.7.71	1		Maia	21	Jul
4:08.95	Ravilya	Agledtinova	BLS	10.2.60	2	NC	Gomel	25	Jun
4:08.97	Leah	Pells	CAN	9.11.64	6h3	WC	Stuttgart	20	Aug
4:09.25	Daniela	Bran	ROM	13.4.68	2	NC	Bucuresti	5	Sep
4:09.30	Esther	Kiplagat	KEN	8.12.66	11	Herc	Monaco	7	Aug
4:09.36	Sarah	Howell	CAN	11.9.69	1		Montreal	5	Jul
	(50)								
4:09.45	Svetlana	Miroshnik	UKR	3.6.68	2	Znam	Moskva	12	Jun
4:09.46		Wang Chunmei	CHN	.4.76	7h2	NG	Beijing	10	Sep
4:09.67	Michelle	DiMuro	USA	15.5.67	2		Montreal	5	Jul
4:09.75	Bettina Romer	Andersen	DEN	18.2.65	6h1	WC	Stuttgart	20	Aug
4:09.85	Kristina	da Fonseca-Wollheim	GER	10.2.72	1		Berlin	14	Sep
4:09.98	Liliana	Salagean	ROM	24.3.71	1		Bucuresti	31	Jul
4:09.98		Liu Yan	CHN	.3.74	9h1	NG	Beijing	10	Sep
4:10.10	Roberta	Brunet	ITA	20.5.65	5		Rieti	5	Sep
4:10.21	Claudette	Groenendaal	USA	1.11.63	1		Eagle Rock	8	May
4:10.26	Simone	Weidner	GER	30.9.69	6		Rieti	5	Sep
	(60)								
4:10.28	Maria	Akraka	SWE	7.7.66	3	EP/C3	Rotterdam	13	Jun
4:10.32	Gabriela	Szabo	ROM	14.11.75	3	NC	Bucuresti	5	Sep
4:10.34		Liu Wanjie	CHN	.11.75	8h2	NG	Beijing	10	Sep
4:10.42	Luminita	Zaituc	ROM	9.10.68	1		Esch	28	Aug
4:10.69	Suzy	Hamilton	USA	8.8.68	2		Seattle	8	Jun
4:10.71	Olga	Churbanova	RUS	16.7.65	1		Rostov na Donu	15	Jul
4:10.72	Valentina	Tauceri	ITA	20.7.66	3		Bologna	3	Sep
4:10.94	Tatyana	Dorovskikh ¶	UKR	12.8.61	1		Dijon	13	Jun
4:11.03	Frédérique	Quentin	FRA	22.12.69	3	Slovn	Bratislava	1	Jun
4:11.19	Natalya	Dukhnova	BLS	16.7.66	2		Luzern	29	Jun
	(70)								
4:11.2	Yelena	Kopytova	RUS	14.3.70	2		Yekaterinburg	29	May
4:11.25	Iulia	Ionescu	ROM	3.7.65	1		Bucuresti	30	May
4:11.29	Alisa	Hill	USA	16.9.65	8h1	WC	Stuttgart	20	Aug
4:11.37	Viorica	Niga	ROM	22.11.68	1		Bucuresti	3	Jul
4:11.4	Yelena	Kaledina	RUS	3.10.68	3		Yekaterinburg	29	May
4:11.5	Linah	Chesire	KEN	1.3.73	1		Nairobi	28	Jul
4:11.6	Paula	Radcliffe	GBR	17.12.73	1		Loughborough	20	Jun
4:11.70	Simone	Meier	SUI	15.11.65	3		Luzern	29	Jun
4:11.76	Éva	Dóczi	HUN	24.9.70	5	Slovn	Bratislava	1	Jun
4:11.80	Soraya Vieira	Telles	BRA	6.9.58	1		Rio de Janeiro	27	Jun
	(80)								
4:11.89	Sonia	McGeorge	GBR	2.11.64	1	Vaux	Gateshead	30	Jul

Mark	Name		Nat	Born	Pos	Meet	Venue	Date
4:11.91	Andrea	Sollárová	SVK	1.2.71	6	Slovn	Bratislava	1 Jun
4:11.94	Katharina	Orthaber	SUI	9.9.63	2	Lausit	Cottbus	23 Jun
4:11.98	Antje	Beggerow	GER	10.12.73	3	Lausit	Cottbus	23 Jun
4:12.03	Lynne	Robinson	GBR	21.6.69	1	WUG	Buffalo	18 Jul
4:12.12	Lynn	Gibson	GBR	6.7.69	2	Vaux	Gateshead	30 Jul
4:12.18	Kathy	Franey	USA	25.12.67	4	v GBR	Edinburgh	2 Jul
4:12.19	Erika	König-Zenz	AUT	6.1.64	7	Slovn	Bratislava	1 Jun
4:12.20	Farida	Fates	FRA	2.2.62	2		Esch	28 Aug
4:12.23	Claudia	Lokar	GER	9.2.64	1		Menden	19 May
	(90)							
4:12.3	Susan	Parker	GBR	24.3.70	2		Loughborough	20 Jun
4:12.33	Marina	Yachmeneva	RUS	12.3.61	3		Rostov na Donu	15 Jul
4:12.4	Regina	Chistiakova	LIT	7.11.61	1	NC	Kaunas	20 Jun
	4:09.7	unconfirmed						
4:12.43	Julie	Speights	USA	70	2	WUG	Buffalo	18 Jul
4:12.5 mx	Sacha	Stephens	AUS	2.11.72	mx		Brisbane	20 Feb
4:12.51	Gina	Procaccio	USA	19.7.64	3	NC	Eugene	19 Jun
4:12.52	Jodie	Hebbard	AUS	14.7.66	1		Brisbane	8 Feb
4:12.54	Zoya	Kaznovskaya	UKR	22.9.66	1		Odessa	21 May
4:12.83	Klara	Kashapova	RUS	16.2.70	1		Parkano	13 Jun
4:12.93	Hilde	Stavik	NOR	6.9.62	1	NC	Tønsberg	1 Aug
	(100)							

Mark	Name		Nat	Born	Date
4:12.99		Xing Yuqin	CHN	69	2 Jun
4:13.0	Margaret	Ngotho	KEN	71	28 Jul
4:13.07	Marta	Kosmowska	POL	72	25 Jul
4:13.07	Ellen	van Langen	HOL	66	18 Sep
4:13.13	Elena	Cosoveanu	ROM	74	3 Jul
4:13.24		Han Feng	CHN		10 Sep
4:13.38	Margareta	Keszeg	ROM	65	18 Jun
4:13.57	Elisa	Rea	ITA	68	6 Aug
4:13.58	Katalin	Rácz	HUN	65	1 Jun
4:13.58	Ellen	Kiessling	GER	68	6 Aug
	(110)				
4:13.62	Jayne	Spark	GBR	70	30 Jul
4:13.65	Olga	Kuznyetsova	RUS	67	29 Jun
4:13.68	Getenesh	Urge	ETH	70	25 Jun
4:13.69	Laurence	Vivier	FRA	67	3 Jul
4:13.71		Yu Taohua	CHN	71	10 Sep
4:13.72	Jane	Ngotho	KEN	69	1 Sep
4:13.73	Fernanda	Ribeiro	POR	69	26 May
4:13.79	Anne	Hare	NZL	64	20 Jan
4:13.9	Robyn	Meagher	CAN	67	23 Jul
4:13.93	Tatyana	Pozdynakova	UKR	56	4 Jul
	(120)				
4:14.00	Jasmin	Jones	USA	69	29 May
4:14.01		Song Yuling	CHN		10 Sep
4:14.02	Nina	Christiansen	DEN	64	21 Jul
4:14.04	Darcy	Arreola	USA	68	19 Jun
4:14.04	M la Sallette	Mineiro	POR	68	21 Jul
4:14.18	Véronique	Pongérard	FRA	68	13 Jun
4:14.18	Edna	Lankri	ISR	66	5 Jul
4:14.2 mx	Angela	Raines-White	AUS	74	10 Jan
4:14.2	Robyn	Meagher	CAN	67	23 Jul
4:14.25	Katje	Hoffmann	GER	71	5 Jul
	(130)				
4:14.3	Joetta	Clark	USA	62	24 Apr
4:14.33	Debbie	Gunning	GBR	65	17 Jul
4:14.37	Elly	van Hulst	HOL	59	12 Jun
4:14.46	Susie	Power	AUS	75	25 Jan
4:14.48	Yelena	Gorodnicheva	UKR	70	4 Jul
4:14.55	Yelena	Mazovka	BLS	67	25 Jun
4:14.57	Margaret	Leaney	AUS	67	21 Nov
4:14.63		Liu Aicun	CHN		2 Jun
4:14.67	Vera	Norkina	RUS	68	20 Jun
4:14.68	Luminita	Alungulesei	ROM	66	30 May
	(140)				
4:14.69	Jennifer	Bravard	USA		8 Jun
4:14.69	Yoshiko	Ichikawa	JPN	76	18 Sep
4:14.72	Melanie	Choinière	CAN	72	18 Jul
4:14.73	Tamara	Koba	UKR	57	21 May
4:14.74		Ma Ningning	CHN	76	13 Nov
4:14.76		Choi Ok-son	PRK	70	13 May
4:14.76	Ivana	Kubesová	TCH	62	1 Jun
4:14.85	Olga	Kovpotina	RUS	68	15 Jul
4:14.95	Najat	Ouali	MAR	72	20 Jun

Unconfirmed

Mark	Name		Nat	Born
4:12.86	Anuta	Catuna	ROM	1.10.68

Drugs disqualification

Mark	Name		Nat	Born	Pos	Meet	Venue	Date
4:10.39	Minna	Lainio	FIN	22.8.68	1		Imatra	10 Jul

Indoors

Mark	Name		Nat	Born	Pos	Meet	Venue	Date
4:11.96	Elly	van Hulst	HOL	9.6.59	1	NC	Den Haag	27 Feb
4:11.97	Paula	Schnurr	CAN	15.1.64	3h1	WI	Toronto	13 Mar
4:12.43	Mitica	Constantin	ROM	18.8.62	3		Stuttgart	7 Feb

Mark	Name		Nat	Born	Date
4:13.20	Yvonne	van der Kolk	HOL	69	9 Feb
4:13.37	Katje	Hoffmann	GER	71	14 Feb
4:14.59	Diane	Modahl	GBR	66	9 Feb

1 MILE

Mark	Name		Nat	Born	Pos	Meet	Venue	Date
4:21.69	Violeta	Beclea	ROM	26.3.65	1	GGala	Roma	9 Jun
4:22.33	Lyudmila	Rogachova	RUS	10.10.66	2	GGala	Roma	9 Jun
4:22.46	Lyubov	Kremlyova	RUS	21.12.62	3	GGala	Roma	9 Jun
4:22.94	Sonia	O'Sullivan	IRL	28.11.69	4	GGala	Roma	9 Jun
4:23.08	Anna	Brzezinska	POL	9.1.71	5	GGala	Roma	9 Jun
4:23.78	Yekaterina	Podkopayeva	RUS	11.6.52	6	GGala	Roma	9 Jun
4:24.40		Kremlyova			1	GPF	London	10 Sep
4:24.97		O'Sullivan			2	GPF	London	10 Sep
4:27.0	Ceci	St.Geme	USA	13.4.63	1		Los Gatos	24 Jun
4:27.64		Beclea			3	GPF	London	10 Sep
	(10/7)							

Mark	Name		Nat	Born	Pos	Meet	Venue	Date
4:28.06	Hassiba	Boulmerka	ALG	10.7.68	5	GPF	London	10 Sep
4:30.03	Elisa	Rea	ITA	23.3.68	7	GGala	Roma	9 Jun
4:31.81	Alison	Wyeth	GBR	26.5.64	8	GPF	London	10 Sep
4:32.04	Maria	Akraka	SWE	7.7.66	9	GPF	London	10 Sep
4:35.28	Susie	Power	AUS	26.3.75	1		Hobart	17 Jan
Indoors								
4:30.23	Shelly	Steely	USA	23.10.62	1	NC	New York	26 Feb
4:30.43	Margareta	Keszeg	ROM	31.8.65	1		Fairfax	7 Feb
4:31.02	Alisa	Hill	USA	16.9.65	2	NC	New York	26 Feb
4:32.00	Yvonne	Murray	GBR	4.10.64	1	v USA	Birmingham	13 Feb
4:33.95	Paula	Schnurr	CAN	15.1.64	3		New York	5 Feb
4:34.44	Bev	Nicholson	GBR	10.6.67	2	v USA	Birmingham	13 Feb
4:35.16	Kathy	Franey	USA	25.12.67	1		Boston	16 Jan

2000 METRES

Mark	Name		Nat	Born	Pos	Meet	Venue	Date
5:29.41+		Wang Junxia	CHN	9.1.73	1h2	NG	Beijing	12 Sep
5:29.65		Wang Junxia			1+	NG	Beijing	13 Sep
5:35.16+		Zhang Linli	CHN	6.3.73	1h1	NG	Beijing	12 Sep
5:35.2+		Zhang Lirong	CHN	4.6.73	2h1	NG	Beijing	12 Sep
5:36.03	Yvonne	Murray	GBR	4.10.64	1	McD	Sheffield	29 Aug
5:38.50	Alison	Wyeth	GBR	26.5.64	2	McD	Sheffield	29 Aug
5:39.20	Paula	Radcliffe	GBR	17.12.73	3	McD	Sheffield	29 Aug
5:40.77+	Sonia	O'Sullivan	IRL	28.11.69	1	VD	Bruxelles	3 Sep
5:41.23		O'Sullivan	IRL	27.7.62	1+	WK	Zürich	4 Aug
5:41.5+	Elana	Meyer	RSA	10.10.66	2k	WK	Zürich	4 Aug
	(10/9)							
5:43.96	Sandra	Gasser	SUI	27.7.62	1		Arnsberg	9 Jun
5:44.59	Annette	Peters	USA	31.5.65	4	McD	Sheffield	29 Aug
5:44.77	Anna	Brzezinska	POL	9.1.71	5	McD	Sheffield	29 Aug
5:45.15	Debbie	Gunning	GBR	31.8.65	6	McD	Sheffield	29 Aug
5:45.23	Angela	Chalmers	CAN	6.9.63	7	McD	Sheffield	29 Aug
5:46.40	Sonia	McGeorge	GBR	2.11.64	8	McD	Sheffield	29 Aug
5:47.45	Margaret	Kagiri	KEN	64				29 Aug
5:50.21	Linah	Chesire	KEN	73				29 Aug
5:51.07	Yelena	Vyazova	UKR	160				9 Jun
5:52.03+	Lyudmila	Borisova	RUS	66				5 Jul
Indoors								
5:45.0	Bev	Nicholson	GBR	10.6.67	2		Birmingham	20 Feb
5:45.24	Christina	Mai	GER	3.9.61	1		Sindelfingen	14 Feb
5:47.86	Elly	van Hulst	HOL	59				14 Feb
5:49.10	Oksana	Mernikova	BLS	67				20 Feb

3000 METRES

Mark	Name		Nat	Born	Pos	Meet	Venue	Date
8:06.11		Wang Junxia	CHN	9.1.73	1	NG	Beijing	13 Sep
8:12.18		Qu Yunxia	CHN	25.12.72	2	NG	Beijing	13 Sep
8:12.19		Wang Junxia			1h2	NG	Beijing	12 Sep
8:12.27		Qu Yunxia			2h2	NG	Beijing	12 Sep
8:16.50		Zhang Linli	CHN	6.3.73	3	NG	Beijing	13 Sep
8:19.78		Ma Liyan	CHN	3.11.68	3h2	NG	Beijing	12 Sep
8:21.26		Ma Liyan			4	NG	Beijing	13 Sep
8:21.84		Zhang Lirong	CHN	3.3.73	5	NG	Beijing	13 Sep
8:22.06		Zhang Linli			1h1	NG	Beijing	12 Sep
8:22.44		Zhang Lirong			2h1	NG	Beijing	12 Sep
8:27.68		Wang Junxia			1	NC	Jinan	6 Jun
8:28.71		Qu Yunxia			1	WC	Stuttgart	16 Aug
8:28.74	Sonia	O'Sullivan	IRL	28.11.69	1	Bisl	Oslo	10 Jul
8:29.25		Zhang Linli			2	WC	Stuttgart	16 Aug
8:29.30		Qu Yunxia			2	NC	Jinan	6 Jun
8:30.12		O'Sullivan			1	WK	Zürich	4 Aug
8:30.30	Yvonne	Murray	GBR	4.10.64	2	Bisl	Oslo	10 Jul
8:30.86		O'Sullivan			1	VD	Bruxelles	3 Sep
8:31.95		Zhang Lirong			3	WC	Stuttgart	16 Aug
8:32.43		Murray			2	VD	Bruxelles	3 Sep
8:32.62		Murray			1	TSB	London	23 Jul
8:32.81	Elana	Meyer	RSA	10.10.66	3	Bisl	Oslo	10 Jul
8:33.38		O'Sullivan			4	WC	Stuttgart	16 Aug
8:33.40		O'Sullivan			1	APM	Hengelo	20 Jun
8:34.62		Meyer			2	WK	Zürich	4 Aug

Mark	Name		Nat	Born	Pos	Meet	Venue	Date
8:35.05		Zhang Lirong			3	NC	Jinan	6 Jun
8:35.48	Yelena	Romanova	RUS	20.3.63	2	APM	Hengelo	20 Jun
8:36.45		Ma Ningning	CHN	1.6.76	4	NC	Jinan	6 Jun
8:37.85		Meyer			2	TSB	London	23 Jul
8:38.12		O'Sullivan			1	GPF	London	10 Sep
	(30/10)							
8:38.42	Alison	Wyeth	GBR	26.5.64	5	WC	Stuttgart	16 Aug
8:39.74		Wei Li	CHN	.1.72	6	NG	Beijing	13 Sep
8:40.40	Paula	Radcliffe	GBR	17.12.73	7	WC	Stuttgart	16 Aug
8:40.78	Lyudmila	Borisova	RUS	8.3.66	8	WC	Stuttgart	16 Aug
8:40.99	Uta	Pippig	GER	7.9.65	3	WK	Zürich	4 Aug
8:41.67		Zhong Huandi	CHN	28.6.67	7	NG	Beijing	13 Sep
8:42.39		Li Ying	CHN	24.6.75	8	NG	Beijing	13 Sep
8:43.59	Annette	Peters	USA	31.5.65	4	WK	Zürich	4 Aug
8:43.76	Esther	Kiplagat	KEN	8.12.66	5	WK	Zürich	4 Aug
8:43.76	M Albertina	Dias	POR	26.4.65	6	WK	Zürich	4 Aug
	(20)							
8:44.04	Hellen	Chepngeno	KEN	2.8.67	7	WK	Zürich	4 Aug
8:44.93	Elena	Fidatov	ROM	24.7.60	2		Reims	30 Jun
8:45.86	Margareta	Keszeg	ROM	31.8.65	8	WK	Zürich	4 Aug
8:47.89		Wang Xiujie	CHN	20.11.73	4h1	NG	Beijing	12 Sep
8:47.92	Roberta	Brunet	ITA	20.5.65	4	APM	Hengelo	20 Jun
8:49.84		Wang Renmei	CHN	5.7.70	9	NG	Beijing	13 Sep
8:50.31	Olga	Bondarenko	RUS	2.6.60	3		Reims	30 Jun
8:50.39	Elly	van Hulst	HOL	9.6.59	5	APM	Hengelo	20 Jun
8:50.49	Yelena	Kopytova	RUS	14.3.70	11	WC	Stuttgart	16 Aug
8:50.97	Gabriela	Szabo	ROM	14.11.75	1	EJ	San Sebastián	1 Aug
	(30)							
8:51.17		Wang Xiuting	CHN	16.2.65	11	NG	Beijing	13 Sep
8:51.22	Annemari	Sandell	FIN	2.1.77	2	EJ	San Sebastián	1 Aug
8:51.33	Farida	Fates	FRA	2.2.62	4		Reims	30 Jun
8:51.35	Claudia	Lokar	GER	8.9.64	12	WC	Stuttgart	16 Aug
8:51.54	Luminita	Zaituc	ROM	9.10.68	2	RomIC	Bucuresti	18 Jun
8:51.91	Fernanda	Ribeiro	POR	23.6.69	1		Maia	10 Jul
8:52.16	Margareta	Maruseva	RUS	27.11.67	1		Århus	1 Jul
8:52.41		Wang Dongmei	CHN	3.12.73	7h1	NG	Beijing	12 Sep
8:52.46	Yelena	Vyazova	UKR	18.4.60	1		Lindau	8 Aug
8:52.55	Lynn	Jennings	USA	10.7.60	2		Lindau	8 Aug
	(40)							
8:52.61	Alina	Tecuta	ROM	10.11.71	3	RomIC	Bucuresti	18 Jun
8:52.71	Gwen	Griffiths	RSA	30.8.67	3	GGala	Roma	9 Jun
8:52.85	Zola	Pieterse	RSA	26.5.66	1		Bellville	7 May
8:52.99	Shelly	Steely	USA	23.10.62	2	NC	Eugene	17 Jun
8:53.36	Valentina	Tauceri	ITA	20.7.66	4	GGala	Roma	9 Jun
8:53.45	Kathrin	Wessel	GER	14.8.67	3		Lindau	8 Aug
8:53.50	Vera	Chuvasheva	RUS	7.10.59	2		Århus	1 Jul
8:53.63	Olga	Churbanova	RUS	16.7.65	2	Znam	Moskva	13 Jun
8:53.82	Päivi	Tikkanen	FIN	19.1.60	1		Nurmijärvi	15 Jul
8:53.93	Margaret	Kagiri	KEN	64	2		Dreux	29 May
	(50)							
8:54.17	Christine	Toonstra	HOL	22.6.66	6	GGala	Roma	9 Jun
8:54.45	Gina	Procaccio	USA	19.7.64	1		Chapel Hill	8 May
8:54.53	Daria	Nauer	SUI	21.5.66	5	Athl	Lausanne	7 Jul
8:55.01	M Conceição	Ferreira	POR	13.3.62	8	VD	Bruxelles	3 Sep
8:55.03	Sheila	Carrozza	USA	5.2.63	3	NC	Eugene	16 Jun
8:55.16	Iulia	Ionescu	ROM	3.7.65	3		Århus	1 Jul
8:55.27	Julia	Vaquero	ESP	18.9.70	1		Maia	28 Jul
8:55.4	Regina	Chistyakova	LIT	7.11.61	1		Vilnius	17 Jul
8:55.42	Yelena	Kaledina	RUS	3.10.68	1		Rostov na Donu	16 Jul
8:55.52	Anna	Brzezinska	POL	9.1.71	6	EP	Roma	26 Jun
	(60)							
8:55.56	Theresia	Kiesl	AUT	26.10.63	1		Rovereto	1 Sep
8:55.70	Annette	Sergent-Palluy	FRA	17.11.62	4		Dreux	29 May
8:55.98	Tatyana	Pentukova	RUS	23.6.65	2		Rostov na Donu	16 Jul
8:56.00	Katy	McCandless	USA	22.6.70	5	ASV	Köln	1 Aug
8:56.10	Svetlana	Miroshnik	UKR	3.6.68	2	Znam	Moskva	13 Jun
8:56.16	Hasiba	Boulmerka	ALG	10.7.68	9	VD	Bruxelles	3 Sep

Mark	Name		Nat	Born	Pos	Meet	Venue	Date
8:56.73	Katje	Hoffmann	GER	24.3.71	7	APM	Hengelo	20 Jun
8:56.75		Wang Yanfang	CHN	10.7.71	9	NC	Jinan	6 Jun
8:56.81	Estela	Estévez	ESP	24.2.65	8	Nik	Nice	21 Jul
8:56.92	Laurence	Vivier	FRA	21.11.67	5		Dreux	29 May
	(70)							
8:57.37	Mariko	Hara	JPN	27.12.70	1		Hiratsuka	26 Jun
8:57.69	Julia	Sakala	ZIM	12.7.69	8h1	WC	Stuttgart	14 Aug
8:57.75		Yan Wei	CHN	.10.71	10	NC	Jinan	6 Jun
8:58.01		Tang Hongwei	CHN	24.5.68	11	NC	Jinan	6 Jun
8:58.04	Catherina	McKiernan	IRL	30.11.69	9	Nik	Nice	21 Jul
8:58.09	Nina	Christiansen	DEN	7.6.64	2		København	25 Jul
8:58.20		Zhang Sanni	CHN	.12.70	6h2	NG	Beijing	12 Sep
8:58.26	Éva	Dóczi	HUN	24.9.70	3		Budapest	15 Jun
8:58.35	Maria	Guida	ITA	23.1.66	8	APM	Hengelo	20 Jun
8:58.50	Kathy	Franey	USA	25.12.67	2		Cork	9 Jul
	(80)							
8:58.52	Hilde	Stavik	NOR	6.9.62	3		København	25 Jul
8:58.52	Gitte	Karlshøj	DEN	14.5.59	4		København	25 Jul
8:58.6	Krishna	Stanton	AUS	18.5.66	1	NC	Brisbane	5 Mar
8:58.64	Malgorzata	Rydz	POL	18.1.67	4		Sevilla	5 Jun
8:58.36	Zoya	Kaznovskaya	UKR	22.9.66	1		Kiev	2 Jul
8:58.89	Elena	Murgoci	ROM	20.2.60			Bucurest	18 Jun
8:59.04	Andrea	Sollárová	SVK	1.2.71	9	APM	Hengelo	20 Jun
8:59.10	Junko	Kataoka	JPN	13.6.70	3	EAsiG	Shanghai	16 May
8:59.21	Ulla	Marquette	CAN	28.6.58	4		Lindau	8 Aug
8:59.70	Sally	Barsosio	KEN	21.3.78	1		Weinstadt	7 Aug
	(90)							
8:59.71	Susie	Power	AUS	26.3.75	1	NEC	Melbourne	25 Feb
8:59.86	Marta	Kosmowska	POL	4.4.72	1		Sopot	10 Aug
9:00.24	Christina	Mai	GER	3.9.61	8	EP	Roma	26 Jun
9:00.27	Denisa	Costescu	ROM	26.1.75			Bucuresti	18 Jun
9:00.31	Viktoria	Nenasheva	RUS	28.6.70	4	NC	Moskva	18 Jun
9:00.32	Silvia	Botticelli	ITA	14.3.68	12	GGala	Roma	9 Jun
9:00.34	Geraldine	Hendricken	IRL	19.4.70	3		Cork	9 Jul
9:00.55	Zahra	Ouaziz	MAR	20.12.69	2		Bron	26 Jun
9:00.62		Dong Li	CHN	9.12.73	8h2	NG	Beijing	12 Sep
9:00.65	Stela	Apetre	ROM	25.2.72			Bucuresti	18 Jun
	(100)							

Mark	Name		Nat	Born	Date
9:01.0	Grete	Koens	HOL	67	13 Aug
9:01.12	Colleen	de Reuck	RSA	64	24 Apr
9:01.14	Ravilya	Agletdinova	BLS	60	15 May
9:01.23	Angela	Chalmers	CAN	63	8 Jun
9:01.40	Renata	Sobiesiak	POL	70	10 Aug
9:01.61	Rosario	Murcia	FRA	64	3 Sep
9:01.62	Harumi	Hiroyama	JPN	68	13 Jun
9:01.65	Sonia	McGeorge	GBR	64	13 Jun
9:02.06	Blandine	Bitzner	FRA	65	29 May
9:02.50		Liu Shixiang	CHN	71	6 Jun
	(110)				
9:02.66	Gunhild	Halle	NOR	72	30 Jul
9:03.06	Clare	Eichner	USA	69	4 Jun
9:03.13	Leah	Pells	CAN	64	30 Jul
9:03.4	Natalya	Betekhtina	RUS	61	30 May
9:03.68	Frédérique	Capel	FRA	65	26 Jun
9:04.11	Tatyana	Byelovol	RUS	69	1 Jul
9:04.41	Libbie	Johnson	USA	65	17 Jun
9:04.66	Sarah	Howell	CAN	69	22 May
9:04.68	Orietta	Mancia	ITA	68	9 Jun
9:04.68	Dörte	Köster	GER	73	11 Jul
9:04.69	Rosalind	Taylor	USA	67	22 May
	(120)				
9:04.77	Susan	Hobson	AUS	58	25 Feb
9:04.91		Pan Xiurong	CHN	70	25 Apr
9:05.10	Camilla	Spires	RSA	69	17 May
9:05.47		Andronescu	ROM		30 May
9:05.65	Minori	Hayakari	JPN	72	28 Oct
9:05.80	Anne	Hare	NZL	64	23 Jan
9:05.84	Linden	Franks	NZL	61	2 Jan
9:06.03	Masako	Saito	JPN	74	28 Oct
9:06.09		Zheng Guixia	CHN	73	6 Jun
9:06.47	Liz	Wilson	USA	68	17 Jun
	(130)				
9:06.64	Cathy	Palacios	USA	68	21 May
9:06.7mx	Jayne	Spark	GBR	70	10 Aug
9:07.01	Zhan Jiangying		CHN	74	6 Jun
9:07.08	Azumi	Miyazaki	JPN	75	28 Oct
9:07.10	Milka	Mikhailova	BUL	72	17 Jul
9:07.3	Suzanne	Rigg	GBR	63	8 Jun
9:07.39	Fran	Ten Bensel	USA	69	4 Jun
9:07.53		Song Yuling	CHN		12 Sep
9:07.60	Anne Marie	Letko	USA	69	8 Aug
9:07.7	Nina	Byelikova	RUS	61	30 May
	(140)				
9:07.75	Marian	Freriks	HOL	61	29 May
9:07.93	Emma	Carney	AUS	71	25 Feb
9:07.99	Kaori	Takahashi	JPN	76	27 Oct
9:08.13	Marina	Rodchenkova	RUS	61	2 Oct
9:08.2	Laura	Mykytok	USA	68	7 May
9:08.52	Rosanna	Munerotto	ITA	62	5 Jun
9:08.56	Klara	Kashapova	RUS	70	22 Jun
9:08.61	Zahara	Hyde	GBR	63	13 Jun
9:08.89		Wang Fuli	CHN	71	12 Sep
9:08.93	Anja	Smolders	BEL	73	8 Aug
	(150)				
9:09.00	Bettina	Romer Andersen	DEN	65	1 Jul
9:09.02	Monika	Schäfer	GER	59	22 May
9:09.42	Simona	Staicu	ROM	71	9 Jun
9:09.46	Miwa	Sugawara	JPN	76	27 Oct
9:09.52	Michiko	Shimizu	JPN	70	2 Oct
9:09.58	Marzia	Gazzetta	ITA	67	1 Sep

Mark	Name		Nat	Born	Pos	Meet	Venue	Date
Drugs disqualification								
8:55.09	Tatyana	Dorovskikh	UKR	12.8.61	7	GGala	Roma	9 Jun
Indoors								
8:56.15	Olga	Kovpotina	RUS	10.1.68	1	NC	Moskva	27 Feb
8:59.94	Lyudmila	Rogachova	RUS	10.10.66	1		Paris	20 Feb

Mark	Name		Nat	Born	Date
9:01.84	Cristina	Misaros	ROM	69	2 Feb
9:03.81	Yelena	Samoshchenkova	RUS	68	27 Feb
9:03.89	Marina	Bastos	POR	71	28 Feb
9:06.05	Elaine	Van Blunk	USA	64	26 Feb
9:07.08	Letitia	Vriesde	SUR	64	31 Jan
9:07.6	Lauren	Gubicza	USA	71	20 Feb
9:09.46	Rodica	Moroianu	ROM	70	20 Feb
9:09.63	Natalia	Azpiazu	ESP	66	23 Jan

5000 METRES

Mark	Name		Nat	Born	Pos	Meet	Venue	Date
14:45.92	Sonia	O'Sullivan	IRL	28.11.69	1	ISTAF	Berlin	27 Aug
14:46.41	Elana	Meyer	RSA	10.10.66	1		Hechtel	31 Jul
14:50.29		Meyer	RSA		1	DNG	Stockholm	5 Jul
14:56.07	Annette	Peters	USA	31.5.65	2	ISTAF	Berlin	27 Aug
14:59.49		O'Sullivan	IRL		1	Toto	Fukuoka	18 Sep
15:05.12	M Albertina	Dias	POR	26.4.65	2		Hechtel	31 Jul
15:05.69+		Zhong Huandi	CHN	28.6.67	1	NG	Beijing	8 Sep
15:05.8e+		Wang Junxia	CHN	9.1.73	2	NG	Beijing	8 Sep
15:08.03	Tecla	Lorupe	KEN	5.5.71	3	ISTAF	Berlin	27 Aug
15:11.86		Peters	USA		2	DNG	Stockholm	5 Jul
15:13.10		Meyer	RSA		4	ISTAF	Berlin	27 Aug
15:15.04	Uta	Pippig	GER	7.9.65	5	ISTAF	Berlin	27 Aug
15:16.16	Claudia	Lokar	GER	8.9.64	6	ISTAF	Berlin	27 Aug
15:16.93	Roberta	Brunet	ITA	20.5.65	7	ISTAF	Berlin	27 Aug
15:17.76	Esther	Kiplagat	KEN	8.12.66	8	ISTAF	Berlin	27 Aug
15:18.00	Daria	Nauer (10)	SUI	21.5.66	9	ISTAF	Berlin	27 Aug
15:18.97		Meyer	RSA		1		Port Elizabeth	6 Mar
15:20.21		Kiplagat	KEN		3	DNG	Stockholm	5 Jul
15:20.32	Kathrin	Wessel	GER	14.8.67	10	ISTAF	Berlin	27 Aug
15:21.98	Hellen	Chepngeno	KEN	2.8.67	11	ISTAF	Berlin	27 Aug
	(20/12)							
15:22.01	Carmen	de Oliveira	BRA	17.8.65	3		Hechtel	31 Jul
15:22.95	Gitte	Karlshøj	DEN	14.5.59	12	ISTAF	Berlin	27 Aug
15:26.33	Annemari	Sandell	FIN	2.1.77	4	DNG	Stockholm	5 Jul
15:27.29	Elena	Murgoci	ROM	20.5.60	1		Bucuresti	31 Jul
15:27.39	Margaret	Kagiri	KEN	64	13	ISTAF	Berlin	27 Aug
15:27.76	Junko	Kataoka	JPN	13.6.70	1		Sapporo	1 Aug
15:28.47	Elly	van Hulst	HOL	9.6.59	14	ISTAF	Berlin	27 Aug
15:30.78	Harumi	Hiroyama	JPN	2.9.68	2	Toto	Fukuoka	18 Sep
	(20)							
15:31.01	Mahomi	Muranaka	JPN	31.10.66	3	Toto	Fukuoka	18 Sep
15:31.19	Valentina	Tauceri	ITA	20.7.66	1		Arzignano	13 Jun
15:31.81	Silvia	Botticelli	ITA	14.3.68	2		Arzignano	13 Jun
15:33.83	Claudia	Dreher	GER	2.5.71	2		Köln	7 May
15:34.0	Izumi	Maki	JPN	10.12.68	1		Amagasaki	9 Oct
15:34.93	Katy	McCandless	USA	22.6.70	15	ISTAF	Berlin	27 Aug
15:35.05	Kathy	Franey	USA	25.12.67	6	DNG	Stockholm	5 Jul
15:35.9	Yumi	Osaki	JPN	10.5.72	2		Amagasaki	9 Oct
15:36.62	Rosanna	Munerotto	ITA	3.12.62	3		Arzignano	13 Jun
15:36.78	Mariko	Hara	JPN	27.12.70	5	Toto	Fukuoka	18 Sep
	(30)							
15:36.94	Kayoko	Ogiwara	JPN	1.4.71	2		Tokyo	17 Oct
15:36.98	Maria	Guida	ITA	23.1.66	8	DNG	Stockholm	5 Jul
15:37.4	Megumi	Fujiwara	JPN	19.6.69	3		Amagasaki	9 Oct
15:38.83	Kumi	Araki	JPN	11.10.65	2		Shizuoka	5 May
15:39.1	Tsugumi	Fukuyama	JPN	10.4.68	4		Amagasaki	9 Oct
15:39.71	Michiko	Shimizu	JPN	22.9.70	6	Toto	Fukuoka	18 Sep
15:41.80	Eriko	Asai	JPN	20.10.59	3		Shizuoka	5 May
15:42.60	Alina	Tecuta	ROM	10.11.71	2		Bucuresti	31 Jul
15:42.93	Elaine	Van Blunk	USA	11.9.64	4		Hechtel	31 Jul
15:43.3	Marina	Rodchenkova	RUS	30.7.61	5		Amagasaki	9 Oct
	(40)							
15:43.53	Kayoko	Nishiyama	JPN	17.7.70	4		Tokyo	17 Oct
15:44.1+	Lynn	Jennings	USA	10.7.60	5k	WC	Stuttgart	21 Aug
15:44.18	Tatyana	Pentukova	RUS	23.6.65	1		Rostov na Donu	15 Jul

Mark	Name		Nat	Born	Date
15:44.27	Laura	Mykytok	USA	68	22 Apr
15:44.65	Linden	Franks	NZL	61	6 Feb
15:45.09	Maiko	Kawasaki	JPN	74	18 Sep
15:46.68	Yukiko	Kiyomiya	JPN	69	17 Oct
15:47.1	Kazuyo	Ibata	JPN	74	9 Oct
15:47.33	Helen	Moros	NZL	67	6 Feb
15:47.50	Zoya	Kaznovskaya	UKR	66	16 May
	(50)				
15:47.73	Christina	Mai	GER	61	7 May
15:47.86	Mineko	Yamanouchi	JPN	72	5 May
15:48.90	Chikako	Suzuki	JPN	69	17 Oct
15:49.43	Gina	Procaccio	USA	64	22 Apr
15:50.43	Julia	Vaquero	ESP	70	12 May
15:50.7	Kaori	Kumura	JPN	70	9 Oct
15:50.97		Chen Wenge	CHN		5 May
15:51.99	Tamara	Koba	UKR	57	16 May
15:52.02	Yuko	Kubota	JPN	74	5 May
15:52.4 mx	Lesley	Morton	NZL	63	21 Jul
	(60)				
15:53.46	Tomoe	Abe	JPN	71	5 May
15:54.3	Claudia	Metzner	GER	66	2 Jun
15:54.31	Anne Marie	Letko	USA	69	16 Jun
15:54.93	Trina	Painter	USA	66	1 Apr
15:55.83	Nela	Prescura	ROM	70	
15:56.0	Noriko	Wada	JPN	75	18 Dec
15:56.01	Yoko	Nomura	JPN	70	19 Sep
15:57.67	Suzanne	Rigg	GBR	63	7 Aug
15:58.18	Chris	McNamara	USA	66	5 May
15:58.78	Natsue	Koikawa	JPN	72	5 May
	(70)				
15:58.8	Teresa	Dyer	GBR	59	21 Jul
15:58.89	Madoka	Suzuki	JPN	75	17 Oct
15:59.0	Kerstin	Herzberg	GER	66	13 Aug
15:59.07	Naoki	Yamagashi	JPN	70	19 Sep
15:59.2		Zhu Ruixia	CHN	71	18 Dec
15:59.4	Mika	Adachi	JPN	76	18 Dec
15:59.8	Michiyo	Ando	JPN	72	27 Aug
Indoors					
15:49.52	Tracy	Dahl-Morris	USA	71	12 Mar
15:52.80	Deena	Drossin	USA	73	12 Mar
15:53.78	Carole	Zajac	USA	72	12 Mar

+ = time during 10000m race

10 000 METRES

Mark	Name		Nat	Born	Pos	Meet	Venue	Date
29:31.78		Wang Junxia	CHN	9.1.73	1	NG	Beijing	8 Sep
30:13.37		Zhong Huandi	CHN	28.6.67	2	NG	Beijing	8 Sep
30:49.30		Wang Junxia			1	WC	Stuttgart	21 Aug
31:08.42		Wang Junxia			1	NC	Jinan	2 Jun
31:09.25		Zhang Lirong	CHN	3.3.73	3	NG	Beijing	8 Sep
31:10.46		Ma Liyan	CHN	6.9.68	4	NG	Beijing	8 Sep
31:12.55		Zhong Huandi			2	WC	Stuttgart	21 Aug
31:15.38	Sally	Barsosio	KEN	21.3.78	3	WC	Stuttgart	21 Aug
31:16.28		Zhang Linli	CHN	6.3.73	5	NG	Beijing	8 Sep
31:21.20	Tecla	Lorupe	KEN	5.5.71	1		Warstein	6 Jul
31:23.92		Liu Jianying	CHN	19.11.71	6	NG	Beijing	8 Sep
31:28.83		Wei Li	CHN	.1.72	7	NG	Beijing	8 Sep
31:29.70	Uta	Pippig (10)	GER	7.9.65	1	APM	Hengelo	20 Jun
31:29.91		Lorupe			4	WC	Stuttgart	21 Aug
31:30.53	Lynn	Jennings	USA	10.7.60	5	WC	Stuttgart	21 Aug
31:30.60	M Conceição	Ferreira	POR	13.3.62	6	WC	Stuttgart	21 Aug
31:31.54		Wang Yongmei	CHN	3.10.68	8	NG	Beijing	8 Sep
31:32.15		Feng Wenhui	CHN	21.1.74	9	NG	Beijing	8 Sep
31:32.23		Wang Xiuting	CHN	16.2.65	10	NG	Beijing	8 Sep
31:32.50		Wang Yanfang	CHN	10.7.71	11	NG	Beijing	8 Sep
31:33.03	M Albertina	Dias	POR	26.4.65	7	WC	Stuttgart	21 Aug
31:34.82		Ferreira			1	EP/C3	Rotterdam	12 Jun
31:37.26	Anne Marie	Letko	USA	7.3.69	8	WC	Stuttgart	21 Aug
31:39.97		Pippig			9	WC	Stuttgart	21 Aug
31:40.51	Fernanda	Ribeiro	POR	23.6.69	10	WC	Stuttgart	21 Aug
31:44.57		Dias			1		Getxo	2 May
31:46.98		Ribeiro			2		Getxo	2 May
31:47.76	Carmen	de Oliveira	BRA	17.8.65	11	WC	Stuttgart	21 Aug
31:47.90		Ferreira			3		Getxo	2 May
31:50.39		Wang Dongmei	CHN	3.12.73	12	NG	Beijing	8 Sep
31:52.59		Dong Li	CHN	9.12.73	13	NG	Beijing	8 Sep
	(31/22)							
32:00.52	Kathrin	Wessel	GER	14.8.67	1	NC	Trier	15 May
32:02.44	Olga	Bondarenko	RUS	2.6.60	1	Znam	Moskva	12 Jun
32:05.33	Claudia	Lokar	GER	8.9.64	1		St Denis	11 Jun
32:07.19	Elaine	van Blunk	USA	11.9.64	3	NC	Eugene	16 Jun
32:08.60	Elena	Murgoci	ROM	20.5.60	1		Bucuresti	3 Jul
32:09.46	Nadezhda	Ilyina	RUS	2.4.64	2		Warstein	6 Jul
32:09.94		Ma Ningning	CHN	1.6.76	2	NC	Jinan	2 Jun
32:10.56	Kazumi	Kanbayashi	JPN	24.7.73	1		Kobe	25 Apr
	(30)							
32:11.21	Midori	Fumoto	JPN	18.12.71	2		Kobe	25 Apr
32:11.58	Iulia	Negura	ROM	26.1.67	2		St Denis	11 Jun
32:12.70	Maria	Guida	ITA	23.1.66	3		St Denis	11 Jun

Mark	Name		Nat	Born	Pos	Meet	Venue	Date
32:14.08	Yumi	Osaki	JPN	10.5.72	3		Kobe	25 Apr
32:14.74	Catherina	McKiernan	IRL	30.11.69	4	APM	Hengelo	20 Jun
32:15.43		Li Li	CHN	1.10.72	14	NG	Beijing	8 Sep
32:15.47	Junko	Kataoka	JPN	13.6.70	4		Kobe	25 Apr
32:15.69		Tang Hongwei	CHN	24.5.68	15	NG	Beijing	8 Sep
32:15.79	Izumi	Maki	JPN	10.12.68	1		Fukuoka	3 Oct
32:15.96	Alina	Tecuta	ROM	10.11.71	1		Bucuresti	29 May
	(40)							
32:18.40	Aura	Catuna	ROM	1.1.68	4		St Denis	11 Jun
32:19.79	Trina	Painter	USA	25.6.66	1	MSR	Walnut	16 Apr
32:19.85	Mahomi	Muranaka	JPN	31.10.66	5		Kobe	25 Apr
32:20.27	Kayoko	Nishiyama	JPN	17.7.70	6		Kobe	25 Apr
32:20.43	Kaori	Kumura	JPN	22.8.70	7		Kobe	25 Apr
32:22.18	Eriko	Asai	JPN	20.10.59	8		Kobe	25 Apr
32:25.6	M Manuela	Machado	POR	9.8.63	1		Braga	28 Jul
32:26.53		Wang Mingxia	CHN	6.6.71			Beijing	5 May
32:26.68	Suzana	Ciric	YUG	12.7.69	2	WUG	Buffalo	15 Jul
32:28.02	Elana	Meyer	RSA	10.10.66	6h2	WC	Stuttgart	19 Aug
	(50)							
32:28.50	Carolyn	Schuwalow	AUS	10.8.65	1	Zat	Melbourne	16 Dec
32:28.56		Tian Mei	CHN	27.11.71	16	NG	Beijing	8 Sep
32:28.66	Naomi	Yoshida	JPN	14.4.69	6h1	WC	Stuttgart	19 Aug
32:32.24	Helen	Moros	NZL	2.11.67	1	NC	Wellington	7 Mar
32:32.42	Vikki	McPherson	GBR	1.6.71	4	WUG	Buffalo	15 Jul
32:32.51	Olga	Appell	MEX	2.8.63	14	WC	Stuttgart	21 Aug
32:33.46	Viktoria	Nenasheva	RUS	28.6.70	1	EP	Roma	27 Jun
32:33.71		Liu Shixiang	CHN	.1.71	17	NG	Beijing	8 Sep
32:33.80		Wang Yili	CHN	.7.71	18	NG	Beijing	8 Sep
32:35.40	Michelle	Dillon	AUS	25.5.73	2	Zat	Melbourne	16 Dec
	(60)							
32:37.23	Inge	Schuurmans	USA	29.1.63	2	Jer	Coquitlam	30 May
32:39.50	Tamara	Koba	UKR	24.2.57	3	EP	Roma	27 Jun
32:39.70	Isabel	Juárez	MEX	10.9.66	3	Jer	Coquitlam	30 May
32:40.47	Lisa	Harvey	CAN	7.2.70	4	Jer	Coquitlam	30 May
32:41.29	Jennifer	Clague	GBR	6.8.73	5	APM	Hengelo	20 Jun
32:42.32	Irina	Petrova	BLS	13.2.62	3		Warstein	6 Jul
32:42.86	Anne	Hare	NZL	7.6.64	2	NC	Wellington	7 Mar
32:43.4	Hellen	Kimaiyo	KEN	8.9.68	2		Nairobi	29 Jul
32:43.46	Lyudmila	Matveyeva	RUS	1.2.57	2	Znam	Moskva	12 Jun
32:44.06	Suzanne	Rigg	GBR	29.11.63	4	EP	Roma	27 Jun
	(70)							
32:44.07		Zheng Guixia	CHN	24.6.73	7	NC	Jinan	2 Jun
32:44.21	Masami	Ishizaka	JPN	27.3.71	1		Naruto	15 May
32:47.20	Claudia	Dreher	GER	2.5.71	5	WUG	Buffalo	15 Jul
32:48.36	Rosanna	Munerotto	ITA	3.12.62	5	EP	Roma	27 Jun
32:48.52	Birhane	Adere	ETH	73	1	AfrC	Durban	23 Jun
32:50.30	Lorraine	Moller	NZL	1.6.55	1		Auckland	2 Jan
32:50.53	Geraldine	Hendricken	IRL	19.4.70	2	PennR	Philadelphia	22 Apr
32:50.75	Makiko	Okamoto	JPN	30.3.72	1		Tokyo	11 Sep
32:50.84	Chris	McNamara	USA	29.1.66	4	NC	Eugene	16 Jun
32:51.33	Monica	Pont	ESP	3.6.69	6	WUG	Buffalo	15 Jul
	(80)							
32:51.72	Rocio	Rios	ESP	13.3.69	4		Getxo	2 May
32:51.72	Päivi	Tikkanen	FIN	19.1.60	8h2	WC	Stuttgart	19 Aug
32:52.84	Fátima	Neves	POR	13.2.63	5		Getxo	2 May
32:53.73	Mericarmen	Diaz	MEX	15.7.70	3	MSR	Walnut	16 Apr
32:54.55	Lydia	Cheromei	KEN	11.5.77	2	AfrC	Durban	23 Jun
32:54.65	Rosario	Murcia	FRA	23.9.64	18	WC	Stuttgart	21 Aug
32:55.24	Laurie	Gomez-Henes	USA	16.4.70	5	NC	Eugene	16 Jun
32:55.32	Fatuma	Roba	ETH	72	3	AfrC	Durban	23 Jun
32:55.54	Kumi	Araki	JPN	11.10.65	3		Mito	9 May
32:55.78	Tomoe	Abe	JPN	13.8.71	2		Kumamoto	4 Apr
	(90)							
32:56.06	Ana Isabel	Alonso	ESP	16.8.63	6		Getxo	2 May
32:56.90	Yelena	Vyazova	UKR	18.4.60	1	NC	Kiev	3 Jul
32:57.06	Marcianne	Mukamurenzi	RWA	11.11.59	4	AfrC	Durban	23 Jun

Mark	Name		Nat	Born	Pos	Meet	Venue	Date
32:57.50		Chen Xiuying	CHN	13.1.73	20	NG	Beijing	8 Sep
32:57.54	Yuki	Tamura	JPN	21.4.67	1		Sendai	22 May
32:57.72	Maiko	Kawasaki	JPN	27.2.74	3		Kumamoto	4 Apr
32:59.03		Hong Duo	CHN		21	NG	Beijing	8 Sep
33:00.66	Chiaki	Shigaki	JPN	20.1.74	3		Fukuoka	3 Oct
33:00.88	Barbara	Moore	NZL	27.7.57	3	Zat	Melbourne	16 Dec
33:01.57	Nadia	Prasad/Bernard	FRA	6.10.67	2	NC	Annecy	23 Jul
	(100)							
33:01.57	Yukiko	Kiyomiya	JPN	4.3.69	4		Fukuoka	3 Oct

Mark	Name		Nat	Born	Date
33:01.81	Natsue	Koikawa	JPN	72	15 Jul
33:01.97	Noriko	Nasuhara	JPN	70	22 May
33:01.98	Rosa	Oliveira	POR	66	2 May
33:02.17	Chiharu	Sato	JPN	70	22 May
33:03.08	Marta	Kosmowska	POL	72	29 Aug
33:03.18	Claudia	Metzner	GER	66	27 Jun
33:05.13	Gitte	Karlshøj	DEN	59	19 Aug
33:05.30	Annick	Clouvel	FRA	63	11 Jun
33:05.52	Stefania	Statkuviene	LIT	63	8 Sep
	(110)				
33:05.60	Kerryn	McCann	AUS	67	16 Dec
33:05.89	Noriko	Kawaguchi	JPN	69	3 Oct
33:06.2	Gladys	Ondeyo	KEN	76	12 Jul
33:06.66	Marjan	Freriks	HOL	61	20 Jun
33:06.70	Yeshi Gebre Selassie		ETH	78	23 Jun
33:06.99	Kayoko	Ogiwara	JPN	71	22 May
33:08.4	Kerstin	Herzberg	GER	66	20 Aug
33:09.70	Vicki	Mitchell	USA	69	22 Apr
33:10.08	Margarita	Marusyeva	RUS	67	12 Jun
33:11.15	Chikako	Suzuki	JPN	69	9 May
	(120)				
33:11.34	Tatyana	Dzhabrailova	UKR	65	3 Jul
33:11.47	Michiyo	Ando	JPN	72	22 May
33:13.06		Wu Mei	CHN	73	8 Sep
33:13.62	Estela	Estévez	ESP	65	2 May
33:14.47	Nadezhda	Tatarenkova	RUS	68	12 Jun
33:14.80	Tanja	Kalinowski	GER	71	12 Aug
33:16.3	Carmen	Fuentes	ESP	65	1 Jun
33:17.05	Sara	Romé	SWE	61	29 Aug
33:17.9	Griselda	González	ARG	65	1 Jun
33:18.28	Miyoko	Asahina	JPN	69	4 Apr
	(130)				
33:20.16	Julia	Sakala	ZIM	69	19 Aug
33:20.38	Anna	Rybicka	POL	63	25 Jul
33:20.41	Ritva	Lemettinen	FIN	60	30 Jul
33:21.52	Masayo	Kitsuya	JPN	69	3 Oct
33:23.75	Laura	LaMena-Coll	USA	66	16 Apr
33:23.86	Kathy	Smith	USA	66	16 Apr
33:23.86	Sonia	Betancourt	MEX	71	16 Apr
33:23.94	Lucia	Rendon	MEX	70	16 Apr
33:25.05	Jacqueline	Mota	CAN	66	31 May
33:25.32	Mary	Donohue	IRL	62	12 Jun
	(140)				
33:25.99	Colleen	de Reuck	RSA	64	20 Jun
33:26.14	Nina	Christiansen	DEN	64	13 Jun
33:26.59	Renata	Sobiesiak	POL	70	29 Aug
33:27.20	Christine	Toonstra	HOL	66	23 Jul
33:27.52	Sonja	Krolik	GER	73	15 May
33:27.78	Véronique	Collard	BEL	63	24 Apr
33:28.10	M Albertina	Machado	POR	61	11 Jun
33:28.54	Mindy	Schmidt	USA	68	22 Apr
33:29.78	Aki	Yasaka	JPN	72	25 Apr
33:30.91	Mineko	Yamanouchi	JPN	72	21 May
	(150)				
33:31.7	Junko	Goto	JPN	71	25 Sep
33:32.0	Chizuko	Ishikawa	JPN	74	25 Sep
33:32.2	Tatyana	Pentukova	RUS	65	29 May
33:32.44	Sandra	Riemann	GER	73	15 May
33:32.77	Michelle	Byrne	USA		16 Apr
33:33.05	Danuta	Marczyk	POL	72	11 Jun
33:33.32	Michiko	Onuki	JPN	70	22 May
33:33.92	Helena	Barócsi	HUN	66	12 Jun
33:34.0	Natalya	Galushko	BLS	71	14 May
33:34.16	Kirsi	Rauta	FIN	62	29 Aug
	(160)				
33:34.45	Regina	Joyce	IRL	57	31 May
33:34.87	Lauren	Gubicza	USA	71	27 Mar
33:34.99	Carole	Zajac	USA	72	1 May
33:35.38	Teresa	Recio	ESP	63	2 May
33:35.38		Zhu Ruixia	CHN	71	8 Sep
33:35.22	Megumi	Fujiwara	JPN	69	13 Jun
33:35.56	Sue	Mahony	AUS	65	16 Dec
33:35.90	Hiroe	Tanikawa	JPN	68	3 Oct
33:36.34	Junko	Asari	JPN	69	9 May
33:38.22	Caryn	Landau	USA	73	27 Mar
	(170)				
33:38.44	Dörte	Köster	GER	73	15 May

ROAD RUNNING LISTS

10 KILOMETRES

Best performances

Mark	Name		Nat	Born	Pos	Meet	Venue	Date
31:52	Uta	Pippig	GER	7.9.65	1		Pittsburgh	26 Sep
31:53	Lisa	Ondieki	AUS	12.5.60	1	Revco	Cleveland	16 May
31:56	Judi	St Hilaire	USA	5.9.59	1	Cres C	New Orleans	20 Mar
31:57	Esther	Kiplagat	KEN	8.12.66	2	Revco	Cleveland	16 May
31:59	Anne Marie	Letko	USA	7.3.69	3	Revco	Cleveland	16 May
32:02	Lynn	Jennings	USA	10.7.60	1		Boston	11 Oct
32:05	Gladys	Ondeyo	KEN	76	1		Washington	18 Apr
32:06	Carmen	de Oliveira	BRA	17.8.65	2		Boston	11 Oct
	(8/8)							

Others with performances superior to track 10,000m bests

Mark	Name		Nat	Born	Pos	Meet	Venue	Date
32:07	Wilma	van Onna	HOL	13.6.65	1		Mobile	27 Mar
32:10	Derartu	Tulu	ETH	21.3.72	1	Hasan	Jakarta	24 Jan
32:10	Yelena	Vyazova	UKR	18.4.60	1		Paderborn	10 Apr
32:11	Claudia	Lokar	GER	9.2.64	2		Paderborn	10 Apr
32:17	Laurie	Gomez-Henes	USA	16.4.70	4		Boston	11 Oct
32:21	Tsugumi	Fukuyama	JPN	10.4.68	1		Nara	14 Mar
32:25	Hellen	Kimaiyo	KEN	8.9.68	1		Berlin	26 May
32:28	Lyudmila	Matveyeva	RUS	1.2.57	3		Berlin	26 May

Mark	Name		Nat	Born	Pos	Meet	Venue	Date
32:33	Katrin	Dörre	GER	6.10.61	4		Berlin	26 May
32:36	Angelina	Kanana	KEN	65	1		Michelstadt	30 May
32:38	Jody	Hawkins	USA		4	Revco	Cleveland	16 May
32:38	Mary	Slaney	USA	4.8.58	1		Phoenix	14 Nov
32:42	Diane	Bussa	USA	9.8.61	3		Mobile	27 Mar
32:47	Nadia	Prasad/Bernard	FRA	6.10.67	3		Chula Vista	17 Oct
32:48	Leah	Pells	CAN	9.11.64	1		Vancouver	18 Apr
32:50	Misti	Demko	USA		5	Revco	Cleveland	16 May
Downhill								
32:08	Joy	Smith	USA	5.1.62	1		Salt Lake City	24 Jul
32:15	Kellie	Archuletta	USA	24.11.61	2		Salt Lake City	24 Jul

15 KILOMETRES ROAD

Mark	Name		Nat	Born	Pos	Meet	Venue	Date
49:03	Carmen	de Oliveira	BRA	17.8.65	1	Gasp	Tampa	27 Feb
49:03	Lisa	Ondieki	AUS	12.5.60	2	Gasp	Tampa	27 Feb
49:11	Judi	St Hilaire	USA	5.9.59	3	Gasp	Tampa	27 Feb
49:16	Carolyn	Schuwalow	AUS	10.8.65	1	Casc	Portland	27 Jun
49:22	Manuela	Dias	POR	19.6.63	1		La Courneuve	30 May
49:42	Iulia	Negura	ROM	26.1.67	2		La Courneuve	30 May
49:47	Lynn	Jennings	USA	10.7.60	1		Tulsa	31 Oct
	(7/7)							
50:06	Jane	Omoro	KEN	.70	2	Casc	Portland	27 Jun
50:06	Tecla	Lorupe	KEN	5.5.71	1		Nijmegan	21 Nov
50:09	Ana Isabel	Alonso	ESP	16.8.63	1		Bilbao	28 Nov
	(10)							
50:12	Anne Marie	Letko	USA	7.3.69	3		Tulsa	31 Oct
50:21	Karen	Macleod	GBR	24.4.58	2		Nijmegan	21 Nov
50:22	Katrin	Dörre	GER	6.10.61	3		La Courneuve	30 May
50:26	Hellen	Kimaiyo	KEN	8.9.68	1		São Paulo	31 Dec
50:27	Karolina	Szabó	HUN	17.11.61	4	Gasp	Tampa	27 Feb
50:37	Helena	Barócsi	HUN	9.7.66	3		Nijmegan	21 Nov
50:37	Valentina	Yegorova	RUS	16.2.64	3	Casc	Portland	27 Jun
50:37	Yelena	Vyazova	UKR	18.4.60	4		La Courneuve	30 May
50:45	M Albertina	Dias	POR	26.4.65	3		São Paulo	31 Dec
50:48	Wilma	van Onna	HOL	13.6.65	5	Gasp	Tampa	27 Feb

10 MILES ROAD

Mark	Name		Nat	Born	Pos	Meet	Venue	Date
52:27	Judi	St Hilaire	USA	5.9.59	1		Washington	4 Apr
52:30	Pauline	Konga	KEN	10.4.70	2		Washington	4 Apr
52:53	Lynn	Jennings	USA	10.7.60	1		Flint	28 Aug
53:01	Iulia	Negura	ROM	26.1.67	1		Portsmouth	10 Oct
53:02	Anne Marie	Letko	USA	7.3.69	2		Flint	28 Aug
53:06	Karolina	Szabó	HUN	17.11.61	3		Washington	4 Apr
53:15	Elaine	Van Blunk	USA	11.9.64	1		Philadelphia	2 May
53:42	Suzanne	Rigg	GBR	29.11.63	2		Portsmouth	10 Oct
53:44	Andrea	Wallace	GBR	22.11.66	1		Plymouth	7 Mar
53:46	Wilma	van Onna	HOL	13.6.65	3		Flint	28 Aug

Downhill 400ft: Feb 14, Austin: 1. Jody Hawkins 51:54, 2. Trina Painter 52:07, 3. Diane Bussa 52:18
Downhill: Apr 11, Motherwell: 1. Karen Macleod GBR 53:42
Course not officially measured: Sep 19, Amsterdam: 1. Hellen Kimaiyo KEN 52:59, 2. Carla Beurskens 53:48

HALF MARATHON

Mark	Name		Nat	Born	Pos	Meet	Venue	Date
67:22	Elana	Meyer	RSA	10.10.66	1		Tokyo	24 Jan
68:34	Olga	Appell	MEX	2.8.63	2		Tokyo	24 Jan
69:22	Anuta	Catuna	ROM	1.10.68	1	NC	Bucuresti	21 Aug
69:35	Valentina	Yegorova	RUS	16.2.64	1		Sankt Peterburg	12 Jun
69:39	Andrea	Wallace	GBR	22.11.66	1		Bath	21 Mar
70:00	Angelina	Kanana	KEN	65	1		Remich	26 Sep
70:04	Katrin	Dörre	GER	6.10.61	3		Tokyo	24 Jan
70:04	Kaori	Kumura	JPN	22.8.70	1	AusC	Gold Coast	18 Jul
70:07	M Conceição	Ferreira	POR	13.3.62	1	WC	Bruxelles	3 Oct
70:09	Mari	Tanigawa	JPN	27.10.62	2	WC	Bruxelles	3 Oct
70:12	Tecla	Lorupe	KEN	9.5.71	3	WC	Bruxelles	3 Oct
70:13	Elena	Murgoci	ROM	20.5.60	2	NC	Bucuresti	21 Aug
70:15	Miyoko	Asahina	JPN	24.9.69	4	WC	Bruxelles	3 Oct

Mark	Name		Nat	Born	Pos	Meet	Venue	Date
70:17		Murgoci			5	WC	Bruxelles	3 Oct
70:26	Colleen	de Reuck	RSA	13.4.64	1		Philadelphia	19 Sep
70:27		Mikhailova	RUS		1		Niort	24 Oct
70:38	Naomi	Yoshida	JPN	14.4.69	1		Yamaguchi	20 Mar
70:38		Appell			1		Sapporo	18 Jul
70:39		Catuna			6	WC	Bruxelles	3 Oct
70:44		Kumura			2		Yamaguchi	20 Mar
70:50		de Reuck			1		Den Haag	3 Apr
70:59	Helena	Barócsi	HUN	9.7.66	2		Remich	26 Sep
71:00	Maiko	Kawasaki	JPN	27.2.74	2		Sapporo	18 Jul
71:02	Carolyn	Schuwalow	AUS	10.8.65	2		Philadelphia	19 Sep
71:03	Mariko	Hara	JPN	27.12.70	2	AusC	Gold Coast	18 Jul
	(25/20)							
71:07	Rosanna	Munerotto	ITA	3.12.62	1		Milano	3 Apr
71:07	Trina	Painter	USA	25.6.66	1		Orlando	11 Dec
71:09	Kayo	Sakai	JPN	13.10.71	3		Yamaguchi	20 Mar
71:13	Tatyana	Pentukova	RUS	23.6.65	2		Sankt Peterburg	12 Jun
71:19	Claudia	Metzner	GER	5.5.66	1		Roermond	18 Jul
71:21+	Uta	Pippig	GER	7.9.65	1M		New York	14 Nov
71:21	Fernanda	Ribeiro	POR	23.6.69	1		Maia	14 Nov
71:22	Fátima	Neves	POR	13.2.63	1		Esposende	18 Apr
71:22	Tatyana	Pozdnyakova	UKR	4.3.56	3		Sankt Peterburg	12 Jun
71:22	Yulia	Negura	ROM	26.1.67	7	WC	Bruxelles	3 Oct
	(30)							
71:23	Manuela	Dias	POR	19.6.63	1		Setúbal	4 Apr
71:33	Eriko	Asai	JPN	20.10.59	4		Tokyo	24 Jan
71:39	Albertina	Machado	POR	25.12.61	8	WC	Bruxelles	3 Oct
71:42	Marion	Sutton	GBR	7.10.63	1		Cambridge	11 Jul
71:43	Yuki	Tamura	JPN	21.4.67	4		Yamaguchi	20 Mar
71:44 dh	Lisa	Weidenbach	USA	13.12.61	1		Las Vegas (213m dh)	6 Feb
71:47	Reiko	Koizumi	JPN	20.12.69	5		Yamaguchi	20 Mar
71:49	Zola	Pieterse	RSA	26.5.66	1	NC	Durban	28 Aug
71:50	Yoshiko	Yamamoto	JPN	6.6.70	4		Sapporo	18 Jul
71:51	Yuri	Sakai	JPN	18.10.71	6		Yamaguchi	20 Mar
	(40)							
71:51	Alevtina	Naumova	RUS	16.1.61	4		Sankt Peterburg	12 Jun
71:52	Adriana	Barbu	ROM	17.10.61	9	WC	Bruxelles	3 Oct
71:53	Rosa	Oliveira	POR	25.7.66	2		Esposende	18 Apr
71:55	Zinaida	Semyonova	RUS	62	5		Sankt Peterburg	12 Jun
71:57	Tatyana	Dzhabrailova	UKR	14.3.65	5		Tokyo	24 Jan
71:58	Akari	Takemoto	JPN	29.12.71	10	WC	Bruxelles	3 Oct
71:59	Nadia	Prasad/Bernard	FRA	6.10.67	3		Philadelphia	19 Sep
72:04	Yelena	Vyazova	UKR	18.4.60	3		Remich	26 Sep
72:04	Maria Luisa	Muñoz	ESP	6.5.59	11	WC	Bruxelles	3 Oct
72:05	Natalya	Sorokivskaya	RUS	23.7.62	1		Egmond	10 Jan
(50)								
72:05	Makiko	Ito	JPN	18.1.73	5	AusC	Gold Coast	18 Jul
72:07	Stella	Castro	COL	62	1	CAC	Cali	1 Aug
72:07	Suzanne	Rigg	GBR	29.11.63	12	WC	Bruxelles	3 Oct
72:08	Natalya	Galushko	BLS	18.9.71	13	WC	Bruxelles	3 Oct
72:09	Michiko	Onuki	JPN	17.12.70	7		Yamaguchi	20 Mar
72:12	Annick	Clouvel	FRA	13.10.63	14	WC	Bruxelles	3 Oct
72:15	Hellen	Kimaiyo	KEN	8.9.68	1		Breda	3 Oct
72:17	Harumi	Suzuki	JPN	2.9.68	6		Tokyo	24 Jan
72:17	Fatuma	Roba	ETH	72	1		Addis Ababa	24 Apr
72:17	Alena	Peterková	TCH	13.11.60	1		Marseilles-Cassis	31 Oct
	(60)							
72:18	Ana	Nanu	ROM	24.6.73	4	NC	Bucuresti	21 Aug
72:18	Elaine	Van Blunk	USA	11.9.64	4		Philadelphia	19 Sep
72:21	Grette	Kirkeberg	NOR	3.9.64	1		Hokksund	3 Apr
72:22	Anna	Villani	ITA	21.6.66	1		Triggiano	26 Sep
72:22	Lidia	Camberg	POL	31.1.62	1		Gargnana	29 Sep
72:23	Ornella	Ferrara	ITA	17.4.68	2		Triggiano	26 Sep
72:24	Maiken	Sørum	NOR	12.1.68	1		Stavanger	16 Oct
72:28	Julia	Sakala	ZIM	12.7.69	16	WC	Bruxelles	3 Oct
72:30	Carla	Beurskens	HOL	10.2.52	2		Den Haag	3 Apr

Mark	Name		Nat	Born	Pos	Meet	Venue	Date
72:30	Päivi	Tikkanen	FIN	19.1.60	1		Berlin	4 Apr
	(70)							
72:30	Jane	Salumäe	EST	17.1.68	17	WC	Bruxelles	3 Oct

Mark	Name		Nat	Born	Date	Mark	Name		Nat	Born	Date
72:31	Megumi	Setoguchi	JPN	68	20 Mar	72:50	Farida	Sultanova	RUS	61	3 Apr
72:32	Olga	Bondarenko	RUS	60	26 Sep	72:50	Monica	O'Reilly	IRL	62	3 Oct
72:33	Martha	Ernstdóttir	ISL	64	3 Oct	72:51	Aura	Buia	ROM	70	21 Aug
72:38	Izumi	Maki	JPN	68	11 Jul	72:53	Monica	Pont	ESP	69	3 Oct
72:40	Susan	Hobson	AUS	58	21 Nov	72:54	Rosario	Murcia	FRA	64	12 Sep
72:43	Olga	Michurina	RUS	64	21 Aug	72:55	Lucília	Soares	POR	62	4 Apr
72:44	Nao	Otani	JPN	71	5 Dec	72:55	Nicole	Whiteford	RSA	65	3 Oct
72:45	Chikako	Suzuki	JPN	69	20 Mar	72:56	Chiharu	Sato	JPN	70	20 Mar
72:47	Chris	Boyd	USA	61	4 Oct		(90)				
	(80)					72:57	Yuko	Yoshino	JPN	72	20 Mar
72:49	Sachiyo	Soiyama	JPN	72	5 Dec	72:58	Ritva	Lemettinen	FIN	60	19 Jun

During Marathon

Mark	Name		Nat	Born	Pos	Meet	Venue	Date
71:41+	Olga	Markova	RUS	6.8.68	1M		Boston	19 Apr
72:27+	Liz	McColgan	GBR	24.5.64	2M		London	18 Apr

Short course - 97m - Lisboa 13 Mar

Mark	Name		Nat	Born	Pos	Mark	Name		Nat	Born	Pos
69:47	Nadezhda	Ilyina	RUS	2.4.64	1	70:59	Fátima	Neves	POR	13.2.63	6
70:02	Manuela	Dias	POR	19.6.63	2	72:27	M Manuela	Machado	POR	9.8.63	8
70:04	Tatyana	Pozdnyakova	UKR	4.3.56	3	72:40	Lucília	Soares	POR	10.1.62	9
70:06	Maria	Rebelo	FRA	29.1.56	4	72:44	Marzena	Helbik	POL	11.9.61	10
70:56	Bettina	Sabatini	ITA	21.3.66	5						

MARATHON

Mark	Name		Nat	Born	Pos	Meet	Venue	Date
2:24:07		Wang Junxia	CHN	9.1.73	1		Tianjin	4 Apr
2:24:32		Qu Yunxia	CHN	25.12.72	2		Tianjin	4 Apr
2:24:42		Zhang Linli	CHN	6.3.73	3		Tianjin	4 Apr
2:24:52		Zhang Lirong	CHN	3.3.73	4		Tianjin	4 Apr
2:25:27	Olga	Markova	RUS	6.8.68	1		Boston	19 Apr
2:25:36		Zhong Huandi	CHN	28.6.67	5		Tianjin	4 Apr
2:25:46		Ma Liyan	CHN	3.11.68	6		Tianjin	4 Apr
2:26:20	Renata	Kokowska	POL	4.12.58	1		Berlin	26 Sep
2:26:24	Uta	Pippig	GER	7.9.65	2		New York	14 Nov
2:26:26	Junko	Asari	JPN	22.9.69	1		Osaka	31 Jan
	(10)							
2:26:27	Tomoe	Abe	JPN	13.8.71	2		Osaka	31 Jan
2:26:36		Wang Yanfang	CHN	10.7.71	7		Tianjin	4 Apr
2:26:38		Xie Lihua	CHN	19.7.65	8		Tianjin	4 Apr
2:26:40	Valentina	Yegorova	RUS	16.2.64	1		Tokyo	21 Nov
2:26:49	M Albertina	Dias	POR	26.4.65	2		Berlin	26 Sep
2:27:09	Katrin	Dörre	GER	6.10.61	1		London	18 Apr
2:27:27	Lisa	Ondieki	AUS	12.5.60	2		London	18 Apr
2:27:38	Kamila	Gradus	POL	19.3.67	1		Nagoya	7 Mar
2:27:53	Akemi	Matsuno	JPN	27.4.68	2		Nagoya	7 Mar
2:28:03	Ramila	Burangulova	RUS	11.7.61	3		Nagoya	7 Mar
	(20)							
2:28:16		Wang Junxia			1	WCp	San Sebastián	31 Oct
2:28:22	Eriko	Asai	JPN	20.10.59	4		Nagoya	7 Mar
2:28:22	Mari	Tanigawa	JPN	27.10.62	2		Tokyo	21 Nov
2:28:52		Dörre			3		Tokyo	21 Nov
2:28:56	Olga	Appell	MEX	2.8.63	2		New York	14 Nov
2:29:05	Kristy	Johnston	USA	3.6.65	1		Houston	24 Jan
2:29:12	Yoshiko	Yamamoto	JPN	6.6.70	1		Amsterdam	26 Sep
2:29:16	Mitsuyo	Yoshida	JPN	29.10.66	1		Paris	25 Apr
2:29:21	Malgorzata	Sobanska	POL	25.4.69	3		Berlin	26 Sep
2:29:29		Asai			1	AusC	Gold Coast	18 Jul
2:29:29	Tatyana	Dzhabrailova	UKR	14.3.65	4		Berlin	26 Sep
2:29:37	Liz	McColgan	GBR	24.5.64	3		London	18 Apr
2:29:41		Yamamoto			3		Osaka	31 Jan
2:30:00	Kim	Jones	USA	2.5.58	2		Boston	19 Apr
	(34/30)							
2:30:02	Nobuko	Fujimura	JPN	18.12.65	4		Osaka	31 Jan
2:30:10	Carla	Beurskens	HOL	10.2.52	5		Nagoya	7 Mar
2:30:15		Gu Dongmei	CHN	5.1.74	9		Tianjin	4 Apr
2:30:16	Nadia	Prasad/Bernard	FRA	6.10.67	3		New York	14 Nov
2:30:31	Lorraine	Moller	NZL	1.6.55	5		Osaka	31 Jan

Mark	Name		Nat	Born	Pos	Meet	Venue	Date
2:30:34	Birgit	Jerschabek	GER	17.5.69	1	NC	Hannover	18 Apr
2:30:36	Maria	Rebelo	FRA	29.1.56	2		Paris	25 Apr
2:30:36		Li Yemei	CHN	1.2.71	1		Beijing	17 Oct
2:30:44	Nadezhda	Ilyina	RUS	2.4.64	3		Paris	25 Apr
2:30:54	M Manuela	Machado	POR	9.8.63	2	WC	Stuttgart	15 Aug
	(40)							
2:30:58	Miyoko	Asahina	JPN	24.9.69	6		Osaka	31 Jan
2:31:01	Maria Luisa	Muñoz	ESP	6.5.59	5	WCp	San Sebastián	31 Oct
2:31:03		Feng Wenhui	CHN	21.1.74	10		Tianjin	4 Apr
2:31:06		Wang Mingxia	CHN	6.6.71	11		Tianjin	4 Apr
2:31:15	Albina	Gallyamova	RUS	8.5.64	2		Houston	24 Jan
2:31:16	Laura	Fogli	ITA	5.10.59	5		Berlin	26 Sep
2:31:18	Carmen	de Oliveira	BRA	17.8.65	3		Boston	19 Apr
2:31:21	Monica	Pont	ESP	3.6.69	6	WCp	San Sebastián	31 Oct
2:31:27	Miyako	Iwai	JPN	15.2.68	7		Nagoya	7 Mar
2:31:32	Madina	Biktagirova	BLS	20.9.64	4		Tokyo	21 Nov
	(50)							
2:31:33	Rocio	Rios	ESP	13.3.69	7	WCp	San Sebastián	31 Oct
2:31:48	Aura	Buia	ROM	16.2.70	8		Nagoya	7 Mar
2:31:59	Emma	Scaunich	ITA	10.3.54	6		Berlin	26 Sep
2:32:00	Anna	Rybicka	POL	23.9.63	6		Tokyo	21 Nov
2:32:01	Frith	van der Merwe	RSA	26.5.64	4		Paris	25 Apr
2:32:03		Wang Xiuting	CHN	16.2.65	2		Beijing	17 Oct
2:32:07	Judit	Nagy-Földing	HUN	9.12.65	1		Reims	17 Oct
2:32:11	Farida	Sultanova	RUS	29.4.61	1		Kaliningrad	25 Apr
2:32:23	Marcia	Narloch	BRA	28.3.69	4		New York	14 Nov
	(60)							
2:32:33		Chon Gum-suk	PRK		9		Nagoya	7 Mar
2:32:37	Karolina	Szabó	HUN	17.11.61	3		Houston	24 Jan
2:32:40		Mun Gyong-ae	PRK	8.4.69	10		Nagoya	7 Mar
2:32:40		Wei Li	CHN	.1.72	13		Tianjin	4 Apr
2:32:42	Yvonne	Danson	GBR	22.5.59	3		Beijing	17 Oct
2:32:43	Teruko	Oe	JPN	16.6.69	11		Nagoya	7 Mar
2:32:52		Liu Yuying	CHN	.6.72	14		Tianjin	4 Apr
2:32:55		Chen Xiuying	CHN	13.1.73	15		Tianjin	4 Apr
2:33:02	Ikuyo	Goto	JPN	6.1.69	12		Nagoya	7 Mar
2:33:15		Tian Mei	CHN	27.11.71	17		Tianjin	4 Apr
	(70)							
2:33:18	Ritva	Lemettinen	FIN	9.9.60	1		Chicago	31 Oct
2:33:23		Han Yanping	CHN		18		Tianjin	4 Apr
2:33:26	Suzana	Ciric	YUG	12.7.69	4		Houston	24 Jan
2:33:38	Lisa	Weidenbach	USA	13.12.61	1		St Paul	3 Oct
2:33:43	Alena	Peterková	TCH	13.11.60	5		New York	14 Nov
2:33:46	Tatyana	Zuyeva	MOL	20.11.58	2		St Paul	3 Oct
2:33:49	Kirsi	Rauta	FIN	17.3.62	8		Berlin	26 Sep
2:33:52	Tatyana	Ivanova	RUS	22.6.70	6		Paris	25 Apr
2:34:03		Wang Hong	CHN	28.1.67	11		Osaka	31 Jan
2:34:03	Gordon	Bakoulis	USA	14.2.61	3		St Paul	3 Oct
	(80)							
2:34:04	Christel	Rogiers	BEL	9.3.63	1		Lyon	3 Oct
2:34:11	Linda	Somers	USA	7.5.61	1		Sacramento	5 Dec
2:34:12	Linda	Milo	BEL	9.7.60	2		Reims	17 Oct
2:34:15	Akiyo	Goto	JPN	13.7.70	13		Nagoya	7 Mar
2:34:15	Anne	van Schuppen	HOL	11.10.60	1		Rotterdam	18 Apr
2:34:28	Wilma	van Onna	HOL	13.6.65	2		Rotterdam	18 Apr
2:34:30	Karen	Macleod	GBR	24.4.58	1		Sevilla	21 Feb
2:34:31	Olga	Michurina	RUS	13.2.64	9	WCp	San Sebastián	31 Oct
2:34:33	Danuta	Bartoszek	CAN	19.8.61	5		Houston	24 Jan
2:34:33		Li Libin	CHN		19		Tianjin	4 Apr
	(90)							
2:34:35		Zhu Ruixia	CHN	71	20		Tianjin	4 Apr
2:34:36	Gabriela	Wolf	GER	28.10.60	1		Hamburg	23 May
2:34:38	Adriana	Barbu	ROM	17.1.61	1		Paris	14 Mar
2:34:44		Wang Yongmei	CHN	3.10.68	21		Tianjin	4 Apr
2:34:46	Lorraine	Hochella	USA	8.10.63	1		Duluth	19 Jun
2:34:47	Lyubov	Klochko	UKR	26.9.59	1		Cleveland	16 May

Mark	Name		Nat	Born	Pos	Meet	Venue	Date
2:34:47	Joy	Smith	USA	5.1.62	4		St Paul	3 Oct
2:34:58	Grazyna	Kowina	POL	6.5.62	6		Houston	24 Jan
2:34:59	Vera	Sukhova	RUS	9.7.63	2		Hamburg	23 May
2:35:04	Lynn	Harding	GBR	10.8.61	10	WCp	San Sebastián	31 Oct

Mark	Name		Nat	Born	Date
	(100)				
2:35:08	Ornella	Ferrara	ITA	68	31 Oct
2:35:15	Ann	Boyd	USA	63	19 Jun
2:35:16	Alina	Ivanova	RUS	69	21 Nov
2:35:19	Alevtina	Naumova	RUS	61	23 May
2:35:19	Ágota	Farkas	HUN	64	17 Oct
2:35:25	Olga	Loginova	RUS	69	17 Oct
2:35:39		Shang Jinjing	CHN	72	7 Mar
2:35:39	Lizanne	Bussières	CAN	61	3 May
2:35:43		Wu Mei	CHN	73	4 Apr
2:35:43	Joan	Samuelson	USA	57	19 Apr
	(110)				
2:35:45	Noriko	Kawaguchi	JPN	69	7 Mar
2:35:50	Tatyana	Pentukova	RUS	65	31 Oct
2:35:51	Chiyuki	Ona	JPN	70	7 Mar
2:35:56	Gail	Hall	USA	59	19 Jun
2:35:58	Fátima	Neves	POR	63	31 Oct
2:36:03		Li Jing	CHN	67	4 Apr
2:36:15	Isabelle	Guillot	FRA	61	31 Oct
2:36:16	Olga	Yudenkova	BLS	67	31 Oct
2:36:25	Josefa	Cruz	ESP	58	31 Oct
2:36:31	Natalya	Galushko	BLS	71	31 Oct
	(120)				
2:36:32	Cristina	Burca	ROM	73	26 Sep
2:36:41	Yumi	Kato	JPN	68	7 Mar
2:36:48	Maria	Curatolo	ITA	63	25 Apr
2:36:50	Sissel	Grottenberg	NOR	56	17 Oct
2:36:52	Isabela	Zatorska	POL	62	31 Jan
2:36:57	Lyutsia	Belyayeva	RUS	57	17 Oct
2:37:02	Anuta	Catuna	ROM	68	28 Nov
2:37:07	Irina	Petrova	RUS	62	3 Oct
2:37:08	Gillian	Horovitz	GBR	55	19 Jun
2:37:09	Akemi	Takayama	JPN	68	7 Mar
	(130)				
2:37:10	Janeth	Mayal	BRA	63	7 Mar
2:37:11	Andrea	Fleischer	GER	63	18 Apr
2:37:15	Zinaida	Semyonova	RUS	62	24 Oct
2:37:20	Yulia	Kovalyova	UKR	68	25 Apr
2:37:23	Maria Luisa	Irizar	ESP	64	7 Feb
2:37:24	Irina	Sklyarenko	UKR	64	25 Apr
2:37:25		Ren Hongmin	CHN		4 Apr
2:37:26	Danielle	Sanderson	GBR	62	31 Oct
2:37:27	Helena	Javornik	SLO	66	10 Oct
2:37:29	Yekaterina	Khramenkova	BLS	56	7 Mar
	(140)				
2:37:29	Naomi	Yoshizawa	JPN		21 Nov
2:37:32	Diane	Fitzpatrick	USA	58	5 Dec
2:37:33	Elisabeth	Krieg-Ruprecht	SUI	61	31 Oct
2:37:35A	Addis	Gezahegu	ETH	69	4 Jul
2:37:39		Liu Guicai	CHN	69	4 Apr
2:37:40	Tammy	Slusser	USA	65	31 Oct
2:37:41	Sigrid	Wulsch	GER	53	17 Oct
2:37:41	Elena	Murgoci	ROM	60	31 Oct
2:37:42	Yuka	Terunuma	JPN	68	31 Jan
2:37:42	Tatyana	Titova	RUS	65	19 Apr
	(150)				
2:37:47	Cristina	Pomacu	ROM	72	26 May
2:37:47	Jane	Welzel	USA	55	31 Oct
2:37:57	Silvana	Pereira	BRA	65	31 Oct
2:37:58	Grete	Kirkeberg	NOR	64	5 Jun
2:37:59	Nao	Otani	JPN	71	7 Mar
2:37:59	Sylviane	Lévesque-Geffray	FRA	53	25 Apr
2:38:01	Tomomi	Nishigai	JPN	70	7 Mar
2:38:02	Sonja	Krolik	GER	73	26 Sep
2:38:06	Marie-Hélène	Ohier	FRA	61	31 Oct
2:38:12	Tomomi	Akiyama	JPN	71	7 Mar
2:38:14	Cathy	Shum	IRL	61	25 Oct
	(160)				
2:38:18	Larisa	Zyusko	RUS	69	7 Mar
2:38:19	Mieke	Hombergen	HOL	57	17 Oct
2:38:20	Yelena	Razdrogina	RUS	69	7 Aug
2:38:20	Gabrielle	O'Rourke	NZL	67	24 Oct
2:38:21	Bente	Moe	NOR	60	18 Apr
2:38:25	Yelena	Sipatova	RUS	55	19 Apr
2:38:25	Rumyana	Panovska	BUL	66	26 May
2:38:27	Birgit	Schuckmann	GER	60	17 Oct
2:38:31	Aniela	Nikiel	POL	65	28 Nov
2:38:43	Maryse	Le Gallo	FRA	60	25 Apr
	(170)				
2:38:43	Franca	Fiacconi	ITA	65	14 Nov
2:38:47	Silvana	Cucchietti	ITA	57	31 Oct
2:38:59	Alina	Gubeyeva	RUS	61	7 Aug
2:39:00	Aurora	Pérez	ESP	57	31 Oct
2:39:03	Tamara	Karlyukova	RUS	71	10 Oct
2:39:12	Jenny	Dowie	AUS	59	7 Feb
2:39:13	Rika	Fujino	JPN	71	7 Mar
2:39:15	Irina	Bogachova	KGZ	61	16 May
2:39:16	Diane	Bussa	USA	61	3 May
2:39:17	Francoise	Maton	BEL	57	4 Sep
	(180)				
2:39:17	Jennifer	Martin	USA	61	24 Oct
2:39:23	Chikako	Suzuki	JPN	69	7 Mar
2:39:35	Marian	Freriks	HOL	61	24 Oct
2:39:36	Brenda	Walker	GBR	56	18 Apr
2:39:37	Mayumi	Kumagai	JPN	68	7 Mar
2:39:45	Marion	Sutton	GBR	63	15 Aug
2:39:45	Marzena	Helbik	POL	61	26 Sep
2:39:48	Maree	Turner	NZL	65	1 May
2:39:51		Pan Jinhong	CHN		4 Apr
2:39:53	Amy	Kattwinkel	USA	67	16 May
	(190)				
2:39:56	Marguerite	Buist	NZL	62	7 Mar

460m downhill

Mark	Name		Nat	Born	Pos	Meet	Venue	Date
2:31:47	Ana Isabel	Alonso	ESP	16.8.63	1		Sarra de Langrec	7 Nov

Boston (USA) has a net drop of 139 m between start (143 m) and finish (4 m)

100 KILOMETRES

Mark	Name		Nat	Born	Pos	Meet	Venue	Date
7:09:44	Ann	Trason	USA	30.8.60	1	IAU	Amiens	25 Sep
7:27:19	Carolyn	Hunter-Rowe	GBR	25.1.64	1	IAU WC	Torhout	8 Aug
7:27:39	Valentina	Shatyayeva	RUS	.63	2	IAU WC	Torhout	8 Aug
7:31:25	Valentina	Lyakhova	RUS	24.6.58	2	IAU	Amiens	25 Sep
7:34:54		Hunter-Rowe			1	IAU NC	Nottingham	23 May
7:38:01		Lyakhova			3	IAU WC	Torhout	8 Aug
7:40:55	Marta	Vass	HUN	6.7.62	1	IAU	Torhout	18 Jun
7:43:06		Vass			1	IAU EC	Winschoten	18 Sep
7:43:35		Shatyayeva			3	IAU	Amiens	25 Sep
7:44:29 *	Yelena	Maskina	RUS	.62	1	IAU	Moskva	8 Aug
7:44:30		Shatyayeva			2	IAU	Torhout	18 Jun
7:44:43		Lyakhova			1	IAU	Rodenbach	24 Apr

Mark	Name		Nat	Born	Pos	Meet	Venue	Date
7:46:44	Birgit	Lennartz	GER	22.11.65	1	IAU NC	Rheine-Elte	4 Sep
7:48:20		Maskina			4	IAU WC	Torhout	8 Aug
7:50:09	Hilary	Walker	GBR	9.11.53	2	IAU EC	Winschoten	18 Sep
7:50:40	Sybille	Möllensiep	GER	7.6.62	2	IAU	Rodenbach	24 Apr
7:50:57	Iris	Reuter	GER	27.6.61	2	IAU NC	Rheine-Elte	4 Sep
7:56:55	Jutta	Philippin	GER	14.4.60	3	IAU NC	Rheine-Elte	4 Sep
7:58:05	Huguette	Jouault	FRA	8.7.51	1		Chavagnes	22 May
7:58:11		Walker			5	IAU WC	Torhout	8 Aug
	(20/12)							
8:01:50	Kristine	Clark-Setnes	USA	28.12.59	6	IAU WC	Torhout	8 Aug
8:02:24	Eleanor	Robinson	GBR	20.11.47	3	IAU EC	Winschoten	18 Sep
8:02:50	Irina	Petrova	RUS	13.2.74	1	IAU	Faenza	29 May
8:03:50	Patricia	Lithgow	RSA	16.11.55	7	IAU WC	Torhout	8 Aug
8:09:10	Danielle	Geffroy	FRA	14.5.45	8	IAU WC	Torhout	8 Aug
8:12:05	Trudi	Thompson	GBR	18.1.59	9	IAU WC	Torhout	8 Aug
8:13:00	Sylvia	Watson	GBR	29.9.47	10	IAU WC	Torhout	8 Aug
8:14:58	Michelle	Jacquemin	FRA	10.6.49	2	IAU NC	Chavagnes	22 May
	(20)							
8:16:33	Ellen	McCurtin	USA	6.2.67	11	IAU WC	Torhout	8 Aug
8:17:02	Sue Ellen	Trapp	USA	4.3.46	12	IAU WC	Torhout	8 Aug
8:17:47	Susan	Detlefs	RSA	29.11.61	13	IAU WC	Torhout	8 Aug
8:18:00	Sigrid	Lomsky	GER	16.1.42	14	IAU WC	Torhout	8 Aug
8:20:09	Lorraine	Gersitz	USA	6.5.54	15	IAU WC	Torhout	8 Aug
8:20:29	Rösli	Brechbühl	SUI	14.3.52	1	IAU	Biel	4 Jun
8:21:02	Helga	Backhaus	GER	19.1.53	4	IAU NC	Rheine-Elte	4 Sep
8:22:09	Katharina	Janicke	GER	29.12.53	5	IAU NC	Rheine-Elte	4 Sep
8:22:14	Angelika	Böttcher	GER	16.10.49	6	IAU NC	Rheine-Elte	4 Sep
8:22:25	Eiko	Endo	JPN	15.1.50	1	IAU	Lake Saroma	27 Jun
	(30)							
8:26:03	Frances	Van Blerk	RSA	9.6.55	16	IAU WC	Torhout	8 Aug
8:27:19	Astrid	Benöhr	GER	8.10.57	1		Palamos	7 Mar
8:28:30	Doina	Nugent	IRL	8.3.61	1		Madrid	23 May
8:29:22	Susan	Ashley	GBR	10.10.52	17	IAU WC	Torhout	8 Aug
Track								
8:01:39	Hilary	Walker	GBR	9.11.53	1		Greenwich	4 Apr

** Moskva course was a small loop measured by steel tape*

24 HOURS

Mark	Name		Nat	Born	Pos	Meet	Venue	Date
Track races								
215.068km	Sandra	Brown	GBR	1.4.49	1		London (TB)	16/17 Oct
212.874	Marie-Therese	Debroise	FRA	.49	1	IAU	Arcueil	9/10 Oct
203.213	Wu Wing-Yee		HKG	31.8.62	1	IAU	Hong Kong	20.21 Feb
Road races								
243.657	Sigrid	Lomsky	GER	16.1.42	1	IAU EC	Basel	1/2 May
233.816	Sue Ellen	Trapp	USA	4.3.46	1	NC	Sylvania	18/19 Sep
226.330	Helga	Backhaus	GER	19.1.53	1	IAU	Apeldoorn	21/22 May
223.647		Backhaus			2	IAU EC	Basel	1/2 May
215.888	Anna	Dyck	GER	28.8.44	2	IAU	Apeldoorn	21/22 May
214.980		Dyck			3	IAU EC	Basel	1/2 May
212.981	Angelika	Böttcher	GER	16.10.49	3	IAU	Apeldoorn	21/22 May
210.598	Gisela	Fricke	GER	13.5.53	4	IAU	Apeldoorn	21/22 May
208.776	Pascale	Mahe	FRA	.32	1	NC	Fleurbaix	28/29 Aug
202.839	Hilary	Walker	GBR	9.11.53	1	NC	Feltham	28/29 May
202.718	Susen	Olsen	USA		2	NC	Sylvania	18/19 Sep

2000 METRES STEEPLECHASE

Mark	Name		Nat	Born	Pos	Meet	Venue	Date
6:17.42	Svetlana	Rogova	RUS	4.8.67	1	NC	Moskva	19 Jun
6:21.47		Rogova			1	Znam	Moskva	12 Jun
6:25.06	Lyudmila	Kuropatkina	RUS	66	2	NC	Moskva	19 Jun
6:29.07	Vera	Ragulina	UKR	19.4.68	1		Kiev	15 May
6:30.35		Ragulina			2	Znam	Moskva	12 Jun
6:32.81	Svetlana	Pospelova	RUS	70	3	Znam	Moskva	12 Jun
6:35.45	Yelena	Volobuyeva	RUS	.70	3	NC	Moskva	19 Jun
6:35.66	Svetlana	Vinogradova	RUS	.71	1		Dzerzhinsk	29 Aug
6:37.02	Yelena	Starikova	RUS	.71	4	NC	Moskva	19 Jun

100 METRES HURDLES

Mark	Wind	Name		Nat	Born	Pos	Meet	Venue	Date
12.46	0.2	Gail	Devers	USA	19.11.66	1	WC	Stuttgart	20 Aug
12.47	1.1	Marina	Azyabina	RUS	15.6.63	1s2	NC	Moskva	19 Jun
12.54	0.0		Azyabina			1A		Reims	30 Jun
12.57	-0.7		Devers			1A	WK	Zürich	4 Aug
12.58	0.5		Azyabina			1		Vénissieux	2 Jul
12.60	0.2		Azyabina			2	WC	Stuttgart	20 Aug
12.62	0.7		Azyabina			1		Moskva	6 Aug
12.63	0.3		Azyabina			1	EP	Roma	27 Jun
12.64	0.1		Zhang Yu	CHN	8.4.71	1	NG	Beijing	9 Sep
12.66	1.0		Azyabina			1h1	Znam	Moskva	13 Jun
12.66	1.5		Azyabina			1	Znam	Moskva	13 Jun
12.66	1.5		Azyabina			1	Gugl	Linz	25 Aug
12.67	-0.3		Devers			1s1	WC	Stuttgart	19 Aug
12.67	0.2	Lynda	Tolbert	USA	3.10.67	3	WC	Stuttgart	20 Aug
12.69	-0.9		Azyabina			1	NC	Moskva	19 Jun
12.69	-0.2		Azyabina			1h1		Moskva	6 Aug
12.70	0.3		Azyabina			1s2	WC	Stuttgart	19 Aug
12.71	-0.5	Svetla	Dimitrova	BUL	27.1.70	1		Sofia	31 Jul
12.73	0.2	Aliuska	López	CUB	29.8.69	4	WC	Stuttgart	20 Aug
12.74	-0.1		Devers			1h5	WC	Stuttgart	19 Aug
12.75	1.5	Eva	Sokolova	RUS	25.3.62	2	Gugl	Linz	25 Aug
12.75	0.1		Xie Liuying	CHN	1.67	2	NG	Beijing	9 Sep
12.76	-1.0		Azyabina			1A		Southampton	6 Jun
12.76	0.3		Devers			1	USOF	San Antonio	30 Jul
12.76	0.3		Tolbert			2s2	WC	Stuttgart	19 Aug
12.76	0.6		Sokolova			1s3	WC	Stuttgart	19 Aug
12.77	0.8	Michelle	Freeman	JAM	5.5.69	1	NC	Kingston	3 Jul
12.77	-0.3		Devers			1	Herc	Monaco	7 Aug
12.77	0.6		Freeman			2s3	WC	Stuttgart	19 Aug
12.78	0.7		Azyabina			1h2	NC	Moskva	18 Jun
12.78	1.6	LaVonna	Martin-Floreal	USA	18.11.66	1	Indy	Indianapolis	25 Jun
12.78	1.6		Tolbert	USA		2	Indy	Indianapolis	25 Jun
12.78	1.1		Azyabina	RUS		1	Nik	Nice	21 Jul
12.78	0.2		Sokolova	RUS		5	WC	Stuttgart	20 Aug
		(34/10)							
12.81	-0.3	Yordanka	Donkova	BUL	28.9.61	1		Granada	29 May
12.84	0.6	Dawn	Bowles	USA	12.11.68	3s3	WC	Stuttgart	19 Aug
12.85	-1.2	Yulia	Graudyn	RUS	13.11.70	1	OD	Jena	13 Jun
12.88	-0.3	Cécile	Cinélu	FRA	4.6.70	2s1	WC	Stuttgart	19 Aug
12.89	0.1	Nadezhda	Bodrova	UKR	13.7.61	1s	NC	Kiev	3 Jul
12.89	0.1	Jackie	Joyner-Kersee	USA	3.3.62	H	WC	Stuttgart	16 Aug
12.90	0.1		Zhou Hongyan	CHN	.4.70	3	NG	Beijing	9 Sep
12.91	1.2	Yelena	Sinyutina	RUS	12.5.64	1		Kuortane	26 Jun
12.91	1.9	Patricia	Girard	FRA	8.4.68	1	NC	Annecy	25 Jul
12.93	1.5	Yelena	Politika	UKR	24.8.64	1		Kiev	15 May
		(20)							
12.95	0.1	Svetlana	Buraga	BLS	4.9.65	H	WC	Stuttgart	16 Aug
12.98	1.8	Jane	Flemming	AUS	14.4.65	1	NC	Brisbane	6 Mar
12.98	-1.5	Kristin	Patzwahl	GER	16.7.65	1	NC	Duisburg	10 Jul
12.98	0.3	Brigita	Bukovec	SLO	21.5.70	3s2	WC	Stuttgart	19 Aug
12.99	0.6	Julie	Baumann	SUI	17.6.64	6s3	WC	Stuttgart	19 Aug
12.99	-1.1		Luo Bin	CHN	7.1.70	2h2	NG	Beijing	9 Sep
13.00	0.8	Gillian	Russell	JAM	28.9.73	2	NC	Kingston	3 Jul
13.00	-0.6	Tatyana	Reshetnikova	RUS	14.10.66	2rB	WK	Zürich	4 Aug
13.03	1.6	Dionne	Rose	JAM	7.11.69	3	Mutual	Kingston	1 May
13.03	-0.3	Jackie	Agyepong	GBR	5.1.69	4s1	WC	Stuttgart	19 Aug
		(30)							
13.05	0.2	Natalya	Kolovanova	UKR	1.8.64	1s	NC	Kiev	3 Jul
13.05	1.5		Zhu Yuqing	CHN	22.4.63	H	NG	Beijing	11 Sep
13.07	0.1		Feng Yinghua	CHN	25.11.66	3	NC	Jinan	3 Jun
13.08	1.8	Sally	Gunnell	GBR	29.7.66	1	AAA	Birmingham	16 Jul
13.08	-0.6	Marsha	Guialdo	USA	12.7.70	2	Vaux	Gateshead	30 Jul
13.10	0.2	Lyudmila	Khristosenko	UKR	14.10.66	2	NC	Kiev	3 Jul

Mark	Wind	Name		Nat	Born	Pos	Meet	Venue	Date
13.11	1.6	Cheryl	Dickey	USA	12.12.66	4	Mutual	Kingston	1 May
13.11	1.2	Nicole	Ramalalanirina	MAD	5.3.72	2		Beaupreau	29 May
13.11	0.1		Zhang Aimei	CHN	30.9.69	4	NC	Jinan	3 Jun
13.11		Liliane	Nastase	ROM	1.8.62	1	RomIC	Bucuresti	18 Jun
		(40)							
13.11	0.0	Natalya	Tochilova	RUS	21.5.64	3		Reims	30 Jun
13.11	1.9	Marie-Victoire	Preira	FRA	25.1.72	3	NC	Annecy	25 Jul
13.12	0.1		Pang Jiewen	CHN	23.11.67	4	NG	Beijing	9 Sep
13.13	0.9	Aleksandra	Paskhina	RUS	14.8.71	1h2	Znam	Moskva	13 Jun
13.13	1.1	Yelizaveta	Chernyshova	RUS	26.1.58	3s2	NC	Moskva	19 Jun
13.13	1.6	Anne	Piquereau	FRA	15.6.64	2		La Chaux de Fonds	8 Aug
13.14	0	Carla	Tuzzi	ITA	2.6.67	2		Caserta	6 Jun
13.14	-0.5	Natalya	Shekhodanova	RUS	29.12.71	1		Dzerzhinsk	29 Aug
13.15	0.1	Monifa	Taylor	USA	3.3.71	1		Knoxville	16 May
13.15	-1.1		Zhou JIng	CHN	.2.73	4h2	NG	Beijing	9 Sep
		(50)							
13.16	1.1	Allison	Williams	USA	1.6.71	1	PennR	Philadelphia	24 Apr
13.16	0.7	Yekaterina	Gorbatova	RUS	13.6.68	2		Moskva	6 Aug
13.17	1.1	Tonja	Buford	USA	13.12.70	2s1	NCAA	New Orleans	4 Jun
13.18	1.4	Doris	Williams	USA	30.6.68	1		Norwalk	30 May
13.20A	1.5	Donalda	Duprey	CAN	1.3.67	1r2		El Paso	10 Apr
13.20	1.9	Christine	Hurtlin	FRA	29.9.67	6	NC	Annecy	25 Jul
13.21	1.9	Nadège	Joseph	FRA	12.8.73	7	NC	Annecy	25 Jul
13.22	1.2	Joyce	Melendez	PUR	4.7.70	2		Kuortane	26 Jun
13.22	-1.1		Yu Rongxiu	CHN	.2.66	6h2	NG	Beijing	9 Sep
13.23	-0.8	Keturah	Anderson	CAN	9.1.68	2h2	WC	Stuttgart	19 Aug
		(60)							
13.24	0.1	Sabine	Braun	GER	19.1.65	3H5		Götzis	29 May
13.24	0.2	Melissa	Morrison	USA	9.7.71	1h1	NCAA	New Orleans	3 Jun
13.24	2.0	Keri	Maddox	GBR	4.7.72	2	NC	London	12 Jun
13.24	0.4	Ludmila	Olijare	LAT	5.2.58	2		Nurmijärvi	15 Jul
13.24	1.4	Maria José	Mardomingo	ESP	27.1.69	2		Salamanca	27 Jul
13.25	0.1	Maria	Kamrowska	POL	11.3.66	1	NC	Kielce	25 Jul
13.26	1.3	Monica	Grefstad	NOR	12.10.64	1	NC	Tønsberg	30 Jul
13.26A	1.7	Carolyn	Sterling	JAM	17.3.70	2	CAC	Cali	30 Jul
13.26	-0.5	Clova	Court	GBR	10.2.60	3h6	WC	Stuttgart	19 Aug
13.27	1.5	Yelena	Alistratyenko	UKR	15.1.71	3		Kiev	15 May
		(70)							
13.27	2.0	Chan	Sau-Ying	HKG	30.8.70	1h2	JapC	Tokyo	12 Jun
13.27	1.5		Liu Bo	CHN	12.3.72	H	NG	Beijing	11 Sep
13.27		Oraidis	Ramirez	CUB	11.11.73	2		Habana	29 Oct
13.28	1.8		Fu Ping	CHN	10.1.71	h		Shijiazhuang	25 Apr
13.28	1.4	Dorota	Krawczak	POL	14.1.68	1A	Kuso	Kielce	16 Jun
13.28	0.7	Ine	Langenhuizen	HOL	27.10.68	4	APM	Hengelo	20 Jun
13.28	-1.2	Angela	Thorp	GBR	7.12.72	2	v UKR	Kiev	29 Aug
13.28	0.1		Sun Xue	CHN	3.3.72	7	NG	Beijing	9 Sep
13.28	1.5		Ma Miaolan	CHN	18.1.70	H	NG	Beijing	11 Sep
13.29	2.0	Kim	Carson	USA	12.3.74	1h1		Knoxville	15 May
		(80)							
13.29	0.2	Olga	Shishigina	KZK	68	5	NC	Kiev	3 Jul
13.29	1.3	Sonia	Paquette	CAN	7.2.73	2h3	WUG	Buffalo	17 Jul
13.30	-1.5	Caren	Jung	GER	18.1.68	2	NC	Duisburg	10 Jul
13.31	1.1	Tamika	Higgins-Francis	USA	19.4.71	4	PennR	Philadelphia	24 Apr
13.32	0.7		Yu Qing	CHN	22.5.72	3		Shijiazhuang	25 Apr
13.32	0.6	Anna	Leszczynska	POL	15.2.71	1	3-N	Praha	17 Jul
13.32	-1.2	Samantha	Baker	GBR	14.4.72	3	v UKR	Kiev	29 Aug
13.32A	-0.6	Karen	van der Veen	RSA	7.1.66	1		Pretoria	6 Nov
13.34	1.8	Jayne	Moyes	AUS	25.1.66	2	NC	Brisbane	6 Mar
13.34		Kim	McKenzie	USA	21.3.61	2		Gainesville	30 Apr
		(90)							
13.34	-0.8	Sylvia	Dethier	BEL	20.5.65	1	EP/B	Bruxelles	13 Jun
13.34	-1.1		Song Guixian	CHN	9.6.71	7h2	NG	Beijing	9 Sep
13.36	0.5		Li Xiaoyan	CHN	26.6.72	4h1	NG	Beijing	9 Sep
13.37	1.6	Mary	Cobb	USA	15.1.68	6	Mutual	Kingston	1 May
13.37	0.1	Irina	Tyukhay	RUS	14.1.67	4H5		Götzis	29 May
13.37	1.3	Taiwo	Aladefa	NGR	19.12.71	3h3	WUG	Buffalo	17 Jul
13.37	2.0	Samantha	Farquharson	GBR	15.12.69	1		London	26 Jun

Mark	Wind	Name		Nat	Born	Pos	Meet	Venue	Date
13.38A	1.7	Damaris	Anderson	CUB	24.10.74	3	CAC	Cali	30 Jul
13.38	0.2	Gudrun	Lattner	GER	30.4.59	1		Stuttgart	31 Jul
13.38	0.4	Ayumi	Sasaki	JPN	24.7.67	1		Tokyo	17 Oct
		(100)							
13.38	0.4	Sriyani	Kulawansa	SRI	1.3.70	2	AsiC	Manila	2 Dec

Mark	Wind	Name		Nat	Yr	Date
13.39	2.0	Gudrún	Arnardóttir	ISL	71	15 May
13.39	1.4	Tiffany	Smith	USA	67	30 May
13.39	1.4	Urszula	Wlodarczyk	POL	65	16 Jun
13.39	-0.5	Svetlana	Laukhova	RUS	73	29 Aug
13.40	1.4	Cinnamon	Sheffield	USA	70	1 May
13.40	2.0	Tatyana	Blokhina	RUS	70	29 May
13.40	1.5	Lyubov	Prytkova	RUS	66	13 Jun
13.40		Svetlana	Moskalets	RUS	69	6 Aug
13.40		Taisia	Dobrovitskaya	BLS	67	28 Aug
		(110)				
13.41		Manuela	Marxer	LIE	65	28 Aug
13.42		Elisabeta	Anghel	ROM	67	29 May
13.42	0.5	Diane	Allahgreen	GBR	75	1 Aug
13.42	1.5		Wu Shuling	CHN	73	11 Sep
13.45A	-0.1	Annemarie	le Roux	RSA	63	2 May
13.45	1.3	Corinne	Bédard	FRA	63	15 May
13.46		Lenuta	Birzu	ROM	69	31 Jul
13.46	1.8	Jenny	Laurendet	AUS	62	6 Mar
13.46	0.1	Petra	Hassinger	GER	69	30 May
13.46	0.6	Naoko	Kobayashi	JPN	68	13 Jun
		(120)				
13.46	-0.1	Marina	Slushkina	RUS	60	18 Jun
13.46	-0.5	Svetla	Damova	BUL	73	31 Jul
13.46	1.5		Mou Lianjuan	CHN	73	11 Sep
13.47	0.0		Zhang Jing	CHN	71	22 Mar
13.47		Elsa	Jiménez	CUB	66	12 May
13.47	1.5	Nikki	Inglis	USA	72	16 May
13.48	1.6	Michelle	Campbell	GBR	69	24 Apr
13.49	2.0	Anjanette	Kirkland	USA	74	1 May
13.50	0.0	Rochelle	Frazier	USA	67	26 May

Best at low altitude

13.27 0.8 Sterling 4 NC Kingston 3 Jul

13.42 1.2 Duprey 6 Aug 13.54 -0.6 le Roux 23 Apr

Mark	Wind	Name		Nat	Yr	Date
13.50	0.5		Liu Huajin	CHN	60	9 Sep
		(130)				
13.51		Erica	Niculae	ROM	73	31 Jul
13.51	0.5	Debbie Ann	Parris	JAM	73	1 May
13.51	1.6	Rita	Schönenberger	SUI	62	26 Jun
13.51	0.6	Katrin	Blankenburg	GER	71	10 Jul
13.52	0.1	Kirsten	Bolm	GER	75	30 May
13.52	0.1	Vanessa	Koslowski	GER	75	30 May
13.52	-0.8	Lyudmila	Mikhaylova	RUS	69	19 Jun
13.53A	1.0	Seema	Kamal	CAN	69	26 May
13.53	1.2	Regina	Ahlke	GER	74	19 Jun
13.53		Kym	Carter	USA	64	28 Aug
13.54A	1.5	Tonya	Williams	USA	74	10 Apr
		(140)				
13.54		Mona	Steigauf	GER	70	9 May
13.54	1.5	Tatyana	Sableva	UKR	67	15 May
13.54		Birgit	Wolf	GER	69	20 Jun
13.55		Anu	Kaljurand	EST	69	31 Mar
13.55	1.5	Kwani	Stewart	USA	72	26 May
13.55	0.6	Claudia	Ruge	GER	75	10 Jul
13.55	0.5	Katja	Fust	GER	74	1 Aug
13.56		Felice	Lipscomb	USA	72	6 Mar
13.57	0.6	Giannina	Re ¶	ITA	71	29 Jun
13.58	1.2	Ana	Barrenechea	ESP	64	3 Jul
		(150)				
13.58	1.8	Kim	Wilson	AUS	67	6 Mar
13.58	1.5	Natasha	Reynolds	USA	72	16 May
13.58	1.1	Sheila	Burrell	USA	72	4 Jun
13.58	2.0	Naomi	Hashioka	JPN	68	26 Jun
13.58	1.6	Sophie	Marrot	FRA	75	17 Jul
13.59	0.7	Lena	Solli	NOR	69	24 Jul
13.60	1.2	Annette	Simon	FRA	71	29 May

Drugs disqualification

Mark	Wind	Name		Nat	Born	Pos	Meet	Venue	Date
13.11	-1.2	Ime	Akpan	NGR	27.4.72	1	WUG	Buffalo	18 Jul
13.54		Irina	Belova	RUS	27.3.68	H		Brescia	15 May

Wind-assisted marks

Mark	Wind	Name		Nat	Born	Pos	Meet	Venue	Date
12.62	2.1		Devers	USA		1	McD	Sheffield	29 Aug
12.63	2.8	Eva	Sokolova	RUS	25.3.62	1s1	NC	Moskva	19 Jun
12.70	2.1		Azyabina	RUS		2	McD	Sheffield	29 Aug
12.72	2.6		Tolbert	USA		1	NC	Eugene	18 Jun
12.73	3.2		Tolbert	USA		1s1	NC	Eugene	17 Jun
12.73	2.6		Devers	USA		2	NC	Eugene	18 Jun
12.73	4.0		Tolbert	USA		1	v GBR	Edinburgh	2 Jul
12.74	3.2	Dawn	Bowles	USA	12.11.68	2s1	NC	Eugene	17 Jun
12.74	4.0		Bowles	USA		2	v GBR	Edinburgh	2 Jul
12.75	4.6		Bowles	USA		1r2	S&W	Modesto	8 May
12.76	3.3		Bowles	USA		1h2	WUG	Buffalo	17 Jul
		(12 performances)							
12.89	4.1	Marsha	Guialdo	USA	12.7.70	1	SWC	Abilene	29 May
12.89	2.2	Brigita	Bukovec	SLO	21.5.70	1		Veszprém	17 Jul
12.91	4.6	Cheryl	Dickey	USA	12.12.66	2rA	S&W	Modesto	8 May
12.92	3.3	Nicole	Ramalalanirina	MAD	5.3.72	2h2	WUG	Buffalo	17 Jul
13.01	2.1	Jackie	Agyepong	GBR	5.1.69	4	McD	Sheffield	29 Aug
13.07	3.8	Monifa	Taylor	USA	3.3.71	3h1	NC	Eugene	17 Jun
13.07	2.3	Aleksandra	Paskhina	RUS	14.8.71	1		Moskva	24 Jul
13.09	2.8	Ime	Akpan ¶	NGR	27.4.72	1	Pac-10	Berkeley	22 May
13.12	2.5	Maria	Kamrowska	POL	11.3.66	1h1	NC	Kielce	25 Jul
13.13	2.1	Clova	Court	GBR	10.2.60	5	McD	Sheffield	29 Aug
13.14	2.6	Doris	Williams	USA	30.6.68	7	NC	Eugene	18 Jun
13.15	3.2	Tiffany	Smith	USA	18.8.67	4s1	NC	Eugene	17 Jun
13.19	4.1	Taiwo	Aladefa	NGR	19.12.71	2	SWC	Abilene	29 May
13.20A	2.1	Joyce	Melendez	PUR	4.7.70	1B		Provo	26 May
13.20	4.0	Keri	Maddox	GBR	4.7.72	4	v USA	Edinburgh	2 Jul

Mark	Wind	Name		Nat	Born	Pos	Meet	Venue	Date
13.22	3.1	Monica	Grefstad	NOR	12.10.64	1		Drammen	31 May
13.23	2.4	Tamika	Higgins-Francis	USA	19.4.71	4	NCAA	New Orleans	5 Jun
13.24	4.1	Sherlese	Taylor	USA		3	SWC	Abilene	29 May
13.25	3.0	Kwani	Stewart	USA	9.10.72	3s2	NCAA	New Orleans	4 Jun
13.28	3.2	Mary	Cobb	USA	15.1.68	2		Austin	8 May
13.33	3.2	Donna	Waller	USA	1.12.70	6s1	NC	Eugene	17 Jun
13.35	4.6	Angie	Taylor	USA	16.3.65	5r2	S&W	Modesto	8 May
13.35	2.2	Ayumi	Sasaki	JPN	24.7.67	1		Naruto	26 Oct
13.36		Kelli	Robinson	USA	18.2.71	2h1		Atlanta	22 May
13.36	4.0	Samantha	Farquharson	GBR	15.12.69	5	v USA	Edinburgh	2 Jul
13.39		Cinnamon	Sheffield	USA	70	2	May		

Mark	Wind	Name		Nat	Born	Date
13.42	2.5	Rita	Schönenberger	SUI	62	19 Jun
13.43	3.1	Lena	Solli	NOR	69	31 May
13.45	2.6	Ayo	Atterberry	USA	72	17 Apr
13.46		Latonya	Davenport	USA	71	1 May
13.46	4.6	Rochelle	Frazier	USA	67	8 May
13.47	4.1	Chelsa	Lancaster	USA		29 May
13.47	2.8	Anjanette	Kirkland	USA	74	3 Jun
13.48	4.1	Felicia	Harris	USA	68	29 May
13.48	2.8	Sheila	Burrell	USA	72	3 Jun
13.51		Kalleen	Madden	USA	71	19 May
13.55		Anu	Kaljurand	EST	69	3 Apr
13.56	2.5	Akiko	Morimoto	JPN	77	16 May
13.59	4.1	Robyn	Turner	USA		29 May
13.60	4.1	Arlesia	Harris	USA		29 May
13.60	2.5	Andrea	Hammel	SUI	66	19 Jun
13.60	3.3	Monica	Pellegrinelli	SUI	65	26 Jun

Hand timed

Mark	Wind	Name		Nat	Born	Pos	Meet	Venue	Date
12.3		Marina	Azyabina	RUS	15.6.63	1		Yekaterinburg	30 May
12.5			Azyabina			1h		Yekaterinburg	29 May
12.8	1.6	Taisia	Dobrovitskaya	BLS	8.12.67	1H		Minsk	5 Jun
12.9		Marina	Slushkina	RUS	2.8.60	1		Abakan	30 May
12.9		Liliane	Nastase	ROM	1.8.62	2		Trento	30 Jun
13.0		Oraidis	Ramirez	CUB	11.11.73	1		Habana	8 May
13.0		Elsa	Jiménez	CUB	13.4.66	2		Habana	8 May
13.0		Yekaterina	Gorbatova	RUS	13.6.68	1		Moskva	13 May
13.1	1.1	Tonja	Buford	USA	13.12.70	1		Champaign	17 Apr
13.1		Yelizaveta	Chernyshova	RUS	26.1.58	h		Yekaterinburg	29 May

Mark	Wind	Name		Nat	Born	Date
13.2	0.5	Mary	Cobb	USA	68	17 Apr
13.2		Irina	Burkhanova	RUS	69	29 May
13.3	0.5	Cinnamon	Sheffield	USA	70	17 Apr
13.3	0.5	Angie	Taylor	USA	65	17 Apr
13.3		Svetlana	Voloshina	RUS	69	29 May
13.3		Lyubov	Prytkova	RUS	66	15 Aug
13.4	0.0	Debbie Ann	Parris	JAM	73	17 Apr

Wind assisted

Mark	Wind	Name		Nat	Born	Pos	Meet	Venue	Date
13.1	3.0	Jayne	Moyes	AUS	25.1.66	1		Perth	18 Dec

Mark	Wind	Name		Nat	Born	Date
13.2	2.9	Melissa	Morrison	USA	71	3 Jul
13.2	2.5	Jenny	Laurendet	AUS	62	27 Nov
13.3	3.2	Samantha	Farquharson	GBR	69	9 Jul
13.4	2.3	Gillian	Ragus	AUS	76	20 Nov

Indoors

Mark	Wind	Name		Nat	Born	Pos	Meet	Venue	Date
12.9		Yelizaveta	Chernyshova	RUS	26.1.58	1rA		Moskva	28 Jan
12.9		Yelena	Sinyutina	RUS	12.5.64	2rA		Moskva	28 Jan
13.1		Aleksandra	Paskhina	RUS	71	3rA		Moskva	28 Jan

200 METRES HURDLES

Mark	Name		Nat	Born	Pos	Meet	Venue	Date
27.34	Virna	De Angeli	ITA	27.2.76	1		Brescia	12 Sep

400 METRES HURDLES

Mark	Name		Nat	Born	Pos	Meet	Venue	Date
52.74	Sally	Gunnell	GBR	29.7.66	1	WC	Stuttgart	19 Aug
52.79	Sandra	Farmer-Patrick	USA	18.8.62	2	WC	Stuttgart	19 Aug
53.48	Margarita	Ponomaryova	RUS	19.6.63	3	WC	Stuttgart	19 Aug
53.52		Gunnell			1	WK	Zürich	4 Aug
53.69		Farmer-Patrick			1	GPF	London	10 Sep
53.70		Farmer-Patrick			1	VD	Bruxelles	3 Sep
53.71		Ponomaryova			1s2	WC	Stuttgart	17 Aug
53.73		Gunnell			1	EP	Roma	26 Jun
53.82		Gunnell			2	GPF	London	10 Sep
53.84	Kim	Batten	USA	29.3.69	4	WC	Stuttgart	19 Aug
53.85		Gunnell			1	TSB	London	23 Jul
53.86		Gunnell			1	Athl	Lausanne	7 Jul
53.86		Batten			3	GPF	London	10 Sep
53.88		Farmer-Patrick			1s3	WC	Stuttgart	17 Aug
53.95		Gunnell			1s1	WC	Stuttgart	17 Aug
53.96		Farmer-Patrick			1	NC	Eugene	18 Jun
53.96		Han Qing	CHN	4.3.70	1	NG	Beijing	9 Sep
54.08		Gunnell			2	VD	Bruxelles	3 Sep
54.12	Deon	Hemmings	JAM	9.10.68	2s3	WC	Stuttgart	17 Aug
54.18		Batten			1	Bisl	Oslo	10 Jul

Mark	Name		Nat	Born	Pos	Meet	Venue	Date
54.20		Batten			2s2	WC	Stuttgart	17 Aug
54.24		Batten			1	Herc	Monaco	7 Aug
54.25		Gunnell			1	McD	Sheffield	29 Aug
54.29		Gunnell			1	Nik	Nice	21 Jul
54.32		Ponomaryova			2	WK	Zürich	4 Aug
54.37		Farmer-Patrick			1	ISTAF	Berlin	27 Aug
54.38	Tonja	Buford	USA	13.12.70	2s1	WC	Stuttgart	17 Aug
54.41		Batten			1		Rieti	5 Sep
54.42	Anna	Knoroz	RUS	30.7.70	2	EP	Roma	26 Jun
54.45		Ponomaryova			1	ASV	Köln	1 Aug
	(30/8)							
54.52		Ling Xueyan	CHN	14.2.72	3	NG	Beijing	9 Sep
54.53	Natalya	Torshina	KZK	4.10.68	3s2	WC	Stuttgart	17 Aug
	(10)							
54.53	Rosey	Edeh	CAN	13.8.66	4s2	WC	Stuttgart	17 Aug
54.60	Tatyana	Ledovskaya	BLS	21.5.66	3s3	WC	Stuttgart	17 Aug
54.64	Heike	Meissner	GER	29.1.70	3s1	WC	Stuttgart	17 Aug
54.90	Silvia	Rieger	GER	14.11.70	5s2	WC	Stuttgart	17 Aug
54.94	Nicoleta	Carutasu	ROM	14.2.64	3	EP	Roma	26 Jun
55.08	Olga	Nazarova	RUS	28.2.62	2	NC	Moskva	19 Jun
55.33	Vera	Ordina	RUS	4.6.68	1		Sevilla	5 Jun
55.51		Jiang Limei	CHN	.3.70	4	NG	Beijing	9 Sep
55.53	Monica	Westén	SWE	15.3.66	1	IDag	Malmö	9 Aug
55.59	Ann	Maenhout	BEL	8.2.69	2		Reims	30 Jun
	(20)							
55.64	Tatyana	Kurochkina	BLS	15.9.67	5s1	WC	Stuttgart	17 Aug
55.72		Zheng Liyuan	CHN	1.4.74	5	NG	Beijing	9 Sep
55.80	Donalda	Duprey	CAN	1.3.67	2	NC	Coquitlam	31 Jul
55.80	Debbie Ann	Parris	JAM	24.3.73	6s1	WC	Stuttgart	17 Aug
55.82	Monika	Warnicka	POL	26.4.69	5	EP	Roma	26 Jun
55.84	Gowry	Retchakan	GBR	21.6.60	6	Bisl	Oslo	10 Jul
55.84	LaTanya	Sheffield	USA	11.10.63	1	USOF	San Antonio	1 Aug
55.88		Guo Yue ¶	CHN	23.1.69	1	NC	Jinan	5 Jun
55.91	Birgit	Wolf	GER	11.9.69	1h		Konstanz	19 Jun
55.94	Alison	Poulin	USA	2.10.70	1		Fairfax	16 May
	(30)							
55.94	Trevaia	Williams	USA	7.9.68	4	NC	Eugene	18 Jun
56.03	Gesine	Schmidt	GER	26.6.71	5	ASV	Köln	1 Aug
56.09	Nezha	Bidouane	MAR	18.9.69	1	MedG	Narbonne	19 Jun
56.17	Linda	Kisabaka	GER	9.4.69	3	NC	Duisburg	11 Jul
56.18	Sylwia	Pachut	POL	21.7.70	1	NC	Kielce	25 Jul
56.21		Zhang Weimin	CHN	18.1.70	1	EAsiG	Shanghai	15 May
56.21	Janeene	Vickers	USA	3.10.68	2h2	NC	Eugene	17 Jun
56.23A	Lana	Uys	RSA	9.12.68	1		Pretoria	3 May
56.24		Chen Qin	CHN	.12.71	3h1	NG	Beijing	8 Sep
56.28	Kellie	Roberts	USA	16.6.69	5	NC	Eugene	18 Jun
	(40)							
56.38		Wang Lixia	CHN	.9.69	2	NC	Jinan	5 Jun
56.40	Svetlana	Starkova	RUS	68	2h4	NC	Moskva	18 Jun
56.43	Ionela	Tîrlea	ROM	9.2.76	1	EJ	San Sebastián	1 Aug
56.48	Ulrike	Heinz	GER	4.7.67	4	OD	Jena	13 Jun
56.48A	Tonya	Williams	USA	5.10.74	1		El Paso	10 Apr
56.48	Frida	Johansson	SWE	5.1.70	7s3	WC	Stuttgart	17 Aug
56.48		Fang Kunyao	CHN	.2.71	2h2	NG	Beijing	8 Sep
56.51		Li Xiumei	CHN	.1.68	2		Beijong	14 Aug
56.64		Rong Guiping	CHN	.3.72	1		Guangzhou	22 Mar
56.64	Carole	Nelson	FRA	27.1.71	2		Tarare	13 Jul
	(50)							
56.66		Zhu Mingming	CHN	.4.68	4h1	NG	Beijing	9 Sep
56.68	Jacqui	Parker	GBR	15.10.66	8s2	WC	Stuttgart	17 Aug
56.70	Jackie	Joyner-Kersee	USA	3.3.62	5	NYG	New York	22 May
56.76	Sandra	Cummings	USA	30.12.68	6	NYG	New York	22 May
56.76	Nadia	Zétouani	MAR	3.1.70	4		Reims	30 Jun
56.77A	Elena	Zamperioli	ITA	29.10.67	4		Sestriere	28 Jul
56.78	Elsa	Jiménez	CUB	13.4.66	1	NC	Habana	14 May
56.78A	Yelena	Goncharova	RUS	27.3.63	5		Sestriere	28 Jul

Mark	Name		Nat	Born	Pos	Meet	Venue	Date
56.86		Wu Hongjie	CHN	13.4.71			Shijiazhuang	25 Apr
56.86	Omotayo	Akinremi	NGR	13.9.74	1h2	NCAA	New Orleans	2 Jun
	(60)							
56.92	Yelena	Znamenskaya	RUS	2.6.66	1h2	NC	Moskva	18 Jun
56.96	Natasha	Reynolds	USA	72	2h1	NCAA	New Orleans	2 Jun
57.04	Renee	Poetschka	AUS	1.5.71	1	NC	Brisbane	7 Mar
57.04	Zuzana	Machotková	TCH	25.3.65	1h2	NC	Jablonec nad Nisou	3 Jul
57.05	Mirian	Knijn	HOL	12.8.66	1		Eagle Rock	8 May
57.05	Arnita	Green	USA	21.2.71	3h1	NCAA	New Orleans	2 Jun
57.06	Rebecca	Campbell	AUS	23.1.76	1	NC-j	Brisbane	6 Mar
57.09	Marta	Moreira	POR	29.11.66	1	WA	Sittard	6 Jun
57.11	Cecile	Clarinval	BEL	16.9.68	1h		La Louvière	4 Jul
57.12	Omolade	Akinremi	NGR	13.9.74	2	SunA	Tempe	3 Apr
	(70)							
57.13	Irena	Dominc	SLO	19.5.70	1A		Trento	30 Jun
57.15	Miriam	Alonso	ESP	6.6.70	1		Salamanca	27 Jun
57.17	Yulia	Tarasenko	RUS	28.3.68	1		Sankt Peterburg	22 Jul
57.23A	Karen	Swanepoel	RSA	2.10.65	2		Pretoria	3 May
57.34		Luan Chunmei	CHN	25.3.70	h	NC	Jinan	4 Jun
57.35	Anna	Ambraziene	LIT	14.4.55	5		Malmö	9 Aug
57.39	Pam	Brooks	USA	15.1.72	1	SWC	Austin	21 May
57.42	Anabella	Von Kesselstat	ARG	12.6.69	2	PorC	Lisboa	24 Jul
57.43	Marsha	Guialdo	USA	12.7.70	1h1		Abilene	27 May
57.43	Lency	Montelier	CUB	13.2.71	1h		Habana	2 Jul
	(80)							
57.43	Corinne	Pierre-Joseph	FRA	27.10.66	1		La Chaux-de-Fonds	8 Aug
57.51	Ester	Goossens	HOL	21.2.72	4	APM	Hengelo	20 Jun
57.55	Christine	Gray	USA	17.8.71	2	NAIA	Abbotsford	22 May
57.59	Jupira Maurina	das Graças	BRA	20.2.70	1	NC	Rio de Janeiro	25 Jun
57.68	Erin	Blunt	USA	74	1	Pac-10	Berkeley	22 May
57.69	Kathrin	Lüthi	SUI	7.10.69	2	WA	Sittard	6 Jun
57.69	Inna	Neplyuyeva	UKR	17.3.71	1h	NC	Kiev	2 Jul
57.69	Marie	Womplou	CIV	20.12.69	2		La Chaux-de-Fonds	8 Aug
57.70	Madelene	Gustafsson	SWE	24.12.69	5	IDag	Malmö	9 Aug
57.77	Gabriela	Fagaras	ROM	29.11.69	2	NC	Bucuresti	5 Sep
	(90)							
57.82	Åsa	Carlsson	SWE	19.12.72	3	NC	Kvarnsveden	25 Jul
57.85	Georgeta	Petrea	ROM	23.10.73			Bucuresti	3 Jul
57.87	Countess	Comadore	USA	27.1.67	6	Banes	São Paulo	16 May
57.88	Jane	Flemming	AUS	14.4.65	1		Sydney	21 Feb
57.90	Anita	Oppong	GER	12.7.74	2	EJ	San Sebastián	1 Aug
57.94	Clara	Torres	CUB	28.9.73	2h		Habana	2 Jul
57.99	Natalya	Ignatyuk	BLS	28.12.63	1	NC	Gomel	24 Jul
58.00	Karlene	Haughton	JAM	72	1		Austin	7 May
58.02	Tamika	Higgins-Francis	USA	19.4.71	2	SWC	Austin	21 May
58.02	Françoise	Dethier	BEL	20.5.65	1		Brussels	25 Jul
	(100)							

Mark	Name		Nat	Born	Date
58.04	Adrienne	Rainbird	AUS	70	7 Mar
58.04	Petra	Schellenbeck	GER	70	30 Jul
58.04	Virna	De Angeli	ITA	76	18 Sep
58.05	Carmen	Nistor	ROM	71	29 May
58.07		Xu Fuxia	CHN	72	5 Jun
58.07	Lana	Jekabsone	LAT	74	1 Aug
58.08	Vickie	Hudson	USA	71	26 May
58.09	Elzbieta	Zaborowska	POL	72	24 Jul
58.10	Gail	Luke	AUS	63	7 Feb
58.10	Alethea	Antoine	TRI		1 May
	(110)				
58.10	Michaela	Colluney	CAN	72	22 May
58.10	Tamara	Pavlova	UKR	69	3 Jul
58.20	Tatyana	Terechuk	UKR	69	2 Jul
58.23	Marjut	Töyli	FIN	67	1 Aug
58.25	Lyudmila	Khodasevich	UKR	59	2 Jul
58.26	Alla	Shilkina	UKR	68	3 Jul
58.29	Yulia	Bavilskaya	RUS	75	26 Jun
58.30	Brooke	Stanton	USA		1 May
58.31	Michelle	Morgan	JAM		9 Apr
58.31	Erica	Peterson	CAN	73	8 May
	(120)				
58.31	Susan	Smith	IRL	71	16 May
58.34	Lauren	Poetschka	AUS	74	6 Mar
58.34	Keisha	Marvin	USA	71	26 May
58.37	Daniela	Graiani	GER	70	30 Jul
58.38	Sandrine	Robin	FRA	71	6 Jun
58.38	Jennifer	Pearson	GBR	62	23 Jul
58.39	Helen	Carter	AUS	67	7 Mar
58.40	Leisa	Bruce	AUS	70	25 Jan
58.40	Mari	Bjone	NOR	70	31 Jul
58.43	Esther	Lahoz	ESP	63	6 Jun
	(130)				
58.44	Nicole	Schumann	SUI	71	1 Aug
58.49	Maria Luisa	Cilimbini	ITA	67	5 Jun
58.50	Tonya	Lee	USA	69	8 May
58.52	Vanessa	Jack	NZL	70	27 Feb
58.53	Céline	Jeannet	SUI	68	1 Aug
58.56	Lynn	Massey	NZL	62	27 Feb
58.58	Sylvina	Pais	IND		16 Nov
58.60	Ivana	Sekyrová	TCH	71	4 Jul
58.60A	Alejandra	Quintanar	MEX	67	31 Jul
58.62	Rosalyn	Mack	USA	71	9 May
	(140)				

Mark	First name	Name	Nat	Born	Date
58.63	Maja	Gorjup	SLO	73	5 Jun
58.64	Kylie	Robertson	AUS	74	25 Jan
58.65	Elma	Muros	PHI	67	16 Jun
58.65A	Maribelcy	Peña	COL	67	31 Jul
58.67	Galina	Kashcheyeva	UKR	63	15 May
58.70		Yang Xiaoming	CHN	70	4 Jun
58.71	Telisa	Young	USA	71	7 May
58.74	Winsome	Cole	JAM	74	17 Jul
58.75	Maria J	López	ESP	71	18 Jul
58.75	Kelly	Blair	USA	70	22 Apr
	(150)				
58.76	Kim	Blair	USA		16 May

Best at low altitude

Mark	Name	Pos	Meet	Venue	Date
56.55	Uys	5h1	WC	Stuttgart	16 Aug
57.12	Tonya Williams	4h1	NCAA	New Orleans	2 Jun
57.49	Goncharova	2		Limoges	10 Jul
57.59	Swanepoel	2	NC	Bellville	24 Apr
57.96	Zamperioli	1	NC	Bologna	3 Aug

Hand timed

Mark	First name	Name	Nat	Born	Pos	Meet	Venue	Date
57.2	Anabella	Von Kesselstat	ARG	12.6.69	1	SACh	Lima	3 Jul
57.3	Anna	Ambraziene	LIT	14.4.55	1	NC	Vilnius	20 Jun
57.4	Jupira Maurina	das Graças	BRA	20.2.70	2	SACh	Lima	3 Jul
57.5	Lauren	Poetschka	AUS	22.10.74	1		Perth	13 Nov
57.6	Michelle	Morgan	JAM		2		Knoxville	16 May
57.9	Tatyana	Terechuk	UKR	11.10.69	1		Dnepropetrovsk	2 Aug

Mark	First name	Name	Nat	Born	Date
58.1	Isabelle	Dherbecourt	FRA	73	4 Jul
58.2	Sylvina	Pais	IND		20 Jan
58.2	Marcela	Novotná	TCH	62	17 Jul
58.3	Celeste	Jenkins	USA		16 May
58.5	Ivana	Sekyrová	TCH	71	17 Jul
58.5	Daniela	Pistoia	ITA	65	12 Sep

Drugs disqualification

Mark	First name	Name	Nat	Born	Pos	Meet	Venue	Date
54.47		Guo Yue	CHN	23.1.69	2	NG	Beijing	9 Sep

HIGH JUMP

Mark	First name	Name	Nat	Born	Pos	Meet	Venue	Date
2.05	Stefka	Kostadinova	BUL	25.3.65	1	Toto	Fukuoka	18 Sep
2.04		Kostadinova			1		Worrstadt	29 May
2.02i		Kostadinova			1		München	12 Feb
2.02i		Kostadinova			1	WI	Toronto	13 Mar
2.02i	Heike	Henkel	GER	5.5.64	2	WI	Toronto	13 Mar
2.02		Kostadinova			1		Padova	29 Aug
2.01i		Henkel			1		Frankfurt am Main	10 Feb
2.01i	Ioamnet	Quintero	CUB	8.9.72	1		Berlin	5 Mar
2.01		Henkel			2		Worrstadt	29 May
2.01		Kostadinova			1	Athl	Lausanne	7 Jul
2.00i		Henkel			1		Arnstadt	23 Jan
2.00i		Kostadinova			1		Grenoble	7 Feb
2.00i		Henkel			1		Stuttgart	7 Feb
2.00i	Alina	Astafei	ROM	7.6.69	2		München	12 Feb
2.00i		Henkel			1		Sindelfingen	14 Feb
2.00i		Astafei			2		Sindelfingen	14 Feb
2.00i	Inga	Babakova	UKR	27.6.67	3	WI	Toronto	13 Mar
2.00	Tatyana	Shevchik	BLS	11.6.69	1		Gomel	14 May
2.00		Kostadinova			1		Sofia	22 May
2.00		Astafei			1	EP	Roma	27 Jun
2.00		Kostadinova			1	BNP	Villeneuve d'Ascq	2 Jul
2.00		Henkel			1	NC	Duisburg	10 Jul
2.00		Kostadinova			1		Stara Zagora	24 Jul
2.00		Kostadinova			1	WK	Zürich	4 Aug
2.00		Quintero			1	Herc	Monaco	7 Aug
2.00		Kostadinova			1	ISTAF	Berlin	27 Aug
2.00		Kostadinova			1	4-N	Salgotarjan	12 Sep
1.99i		Henkel			1		Wuppertal	5 Feb
1.99i		Astafei			2		Berlin	5 Mar
1.99i		Henkel			3		Berlin	5 Mar
1.99		Henkel			1		Rehlingen	31 May
1.99		Astafei			1	APM	Hengelo	20 Jun
1.99		Quintero			1	WC	Stuttgart	21 Aug
1.99	Yelena	Topchina	RUS	21.10.66	1		Rieti	5 Sep
1.99		Kostadinova			2		Rieti	5 Sep
	(35/7)							
1.98	Yelena	Rodina/Gulyayeva	RUS	14.8.67	1		Moskva	24 Jul
1.98	Silvia	Costa	CUB	4.5.64	3	WK	Zürich	4 Aug
1.97i	Yelena	Gribanova	RUS	2.3.72	3		München	12 Feb
	(10)							
1.97i	Britta	Bilac	SLO	4.12.68	3		Sindelfingen	14 Feb
1.97i	Alison	Inverarity	AUS	12.8.70	5	WI	Toronto	13 Mar

WOMEN 1993

Mark	Name		Nat	Born	Pos	Meet	Venue	Date
1.97	Sigrid	Kirchmann	AUT	29.3.66	3	WC	Stuttgart	21 Aug
1.97	Olga	Bolshova	MOL	16.6.68	3		Rieti	5 Sep
1.96i	Yelena	Panikarovskikh	RUS	4.12.59	1		Sankt Peterburg	9 Jan
1.95i	Sarka	Kaspárková	TCH	20.5.71	1		Banská Bystrica	27 Jan
1.95i	Yevgeniya	Zhdanova	RUS	21.7.66	1		Moskva	2 Feb
1.95i	Antonella	Bevilacqua	ITA	15.10.71	1	NC	Genova	13 Feb
1.95	Tatyana	Khramova	BLS	1.2.70	2		Gomel	14 May
1.95	Olga	Turchak	UKR	5.3.67	4		Wörrstadt	29 May
	(20)							
1.95	Heike	Balck	GER	19.8.70	6		Wörrstadt	29 May
1.95	Valentina	Gotovska	LAT	3.9.65	1	EP/C2	København	13 Jun
1.95	Niole	Zilinskiené	LIT	29.12.69	1	NC	Vilnius	19 Jun
1.95	Tanya	Hughes	USA	25.1.72	1	WUG	Buffalo	18 Jul
1.95	Larisa	Grigorenko	UKR	6.9.70	3	WUG	Buffalo	18 Jul
1.94i	Angie	Bradburn	USA	4.9.68	5		Frankfurt	10 Feb
1.94i	Marion	Hellmann	GER	6.4.67	9		München	12 Feb
1.94i	Jo	Jennings	GBR	20.9.69	9	WI	Toronto	13 Mar
1.94	Tisha	Waller	USA	1.12.70	1	NYG	New York	22 May
1.94	Yolanda	Henry	USA	2.12.64	2	Jen	San José	29 May
	(30)							
1.94	Svetlana	Zalevskaya	KZK	14.6.73	3	Znam	Moskva	13 Jun
1.94		Jln Ling	CHN	5.9.67	1	NG	Beijing	8 Sep
1.93i	Andrea	Baumert	GER	5.5.67	5		Berlin	5 Mar
1.93	Sabine	Braun	GER	19.1.65	1H		Götzis	29 May
1.93	Hanne	Haugland	NOR	14.12.67	Q	WC	Stuttgart	19 Aug
1.93	Amy	Acuff	USA	14.7.75	1	Alpen	Innsbruck	28 Aug
1.93	Sabrina	De Leeuw	BEL	19.8.74	1	McD	Sheffield	29 Aug
1.93	Yoko	Ota	JPN	14.1.75	4	Toto	Fukuoka	18 Sep
1.92i		Wang Wei	CHN	19.10.68	1		Yokohama	6 Mar
1.92i	Julieann	Broughton	USA	27.12.70	1	NCAA	Indianapolis	13 Mar
	(40)							
1.92	Sue	Rembao	USA	15.5.62	1		San Luis Obispo	20 Mar
1.92	Charmaine	Weavers	RSA	27.2.64	1		Pretoria	15 May
1.92	Larisa	Serebrinskaya	UKR	15.9.63	1		Kiev	15 May
1.92	Connie	Teaberry	USA	15.8.70	1		Indianapolis	26 May
1.92	Katarzyna	Majchrzak	POL	25.6.67	4	Slovn	Bratislava	1 Jun
1.92	Gwen	Wentland	USA	29.4.72	2	NCAA	New Orleans	5 Jun
1.92	Desislava	Alexandrova	BUL	21.10.75	1		Thessaloniki	10 Jul
1.92	Tatyana	Motkova	RUS	26.10.68	1		Rostov na Donu	16 Jul
1.92	Krisztina	Solti	HUN	28.4.68	1	NC	Budapest	5 Aug
1.92	Wanita	Dykstra	CAN	30.1.75	1		North York	8 Aug
	(50)							
1.92	Svetlana	Ruban	UZB	23.5.65	2	AsiC	Manila	4 Dec
1.91i	Oana	Musunoi	ROM	17.9.72	2		Banská Bystrica	27 Jan
1.91i	Sieglinde	Cadusch	SUI	28.8.67	1		Schwarzee	13 Feb
1.91	Sandrine	Fricot	FRA	4.6.68	1		Rennes	15 May
1.91	Judit	Kovács	HUN	7.6.69	1		Zalaegerszeg	31 May
1.91	Donata	Jancewicz	POL	17.6.69	1	Mal	Grudziadz	18 Jun
1.91	Inna	Gliznutsa	MOL	18.4.73	2	RomIC	Bucuresti	18 Jun
1.91	Yelena	Yelesina	RUS	5.4.70	5	NC	Moskva	19 Jun
1.91	Debbie	Marti	GBR	14.5.68	1		London	27 Jun
1.91	Sárka	Nováková	TCH	21.2.71	1	NC	Jablonec nad Nisou	3 Jul
	(60)							
1.91	Birgit	Kähler	GER	14.8.70	1		Luxembourg	30 Jul
1.91	Tatyana	Blokhina	RUS	12.3.70	H		Talence	4 Sep
1.90i	Manuela	Aigner	GER	26.3.73	6		Wuppertal	5 Feb
1.90	Galina	Isachenko	BLS	4.3.65	3		Gomel	14 May
	1.92 unconfirmed						in Poland	6 Jun
1.90	Nathalie	Lefébvre	FRA	2.9.71	1		Tours	23 May
1.90	Karol	Damon	USA	20.12.69	4	Jen	San José	29 May
1.90	Beata	Holub	POL	19.7.70	1	3-N	Praha	17 Jul
1.90	Niki	Bakogianni	GRE	9.6.68	1	NC	Athinai	25 Jul
1.90	Barbara	Mencik	FRA	22.12.70	2		Luxembourg	30 Jul
1.90	Roberta	Bugarini	ITA	19.9.69	2	NC	Bologna	2 Aug
	(70)							
1.90	Natalja	Jonckheere	BEL	21.10.70	1		Oordegem	4 Sep
1.89i	Yelena	Ivanova	RUS	23.1.71	2		Sankt Peterburg	23 Jan

Mark	Name		Nat	Born	Pos	Meet	Venue	Date
1.89i	Diana	Davies	GBR	7.5.61	2		Glasgow	30 Jan
1.89i	Alena	Varcholová	TCH	27.3.69	1		Jablonec nad Nisou	6 Feb
1.89i	Iwona	Kielan	POL	5.7.66	2		Jablonec nad Nisou	6 Feb
1.89i	Venelina	Veneva	BUL	13.6.74	1		Sofia	21 Feb
1.89	Andrea	Hughes	AUS	12.12.73	1		Melbourne	13 Mar
1.89		Guan Weihua	CHN	14.6.75	1		Shijiazhuang	25 Apr
1.89	Zuzana	Kováciková	TCH	16.4.73	7	Slovn	Bratislava	1 Jun
1.89	Eleonora	Milousheva	BUL	8.4.73	1		Sofia	19 Jun
	(80)							
1.89	Viktoria	Stepina	UKR	21.2.76	1	NC-j	Chernigov	26 Jun
1.89	Yelena	Razmyslovich	RUS	22.8.74	1		Vladimir	4 Jul
1.89	Orlane Maria	Lima Dos Santos	BRA	9.12.66	1		Sion	10 Aug
1.89		Ma Miaolan	CHN	18.1.70	H	NG	Beijing	11 Sep
1.89		Wang Fang	CHN	.4.72	H	NG	Beijing	11 Sep
1.89	Chinami	Sadahiro	JPN	17.8.72	3	AsiC	Manila	4 Dec
1.88i	Béatrice	Landès	FRA	4.8.67	1		Paris	16 Jan
1.88i	Holly	Kelly	USA	28.12.68	1		Johnson City	29 Jan
1.88i	Oksana	Gerashchenko	RUS	6.8.71	3		Moskva	2 Feb
1.88i	Caroline	Meinel	GER	28.4.73	1		München	12 Feb
	(90)							
1.88i	Tatyana	Gritsachuk	UKR	20.2.69	3	NC	Kiev	13 Feb
1.88i	Kym	Carter	USA	12.3.64	P	WI	Toronto	12 Mar
1.88		Zhen Xueping	CHN	.6.73	1		Guangzhou	20 Mar
1.88		Li Jun	CHN	.9.69	1		Beijing	5 May
1.88	Cécile	Carlier	FRA	28.10.68	1		Colombes	9 May
1.88	Yelena	Volf	RUS	2.3.69	H		Krasnodar	18 May
1.88		Ge Ping	CHN	11.1.61	1	NC	Jinan	6 Jun
1.88	Anna Maria	Ferraro	ITA	16.7.70	3		Caserta	6 Jun
1.88	Sharon	Foley	IRL	20.5.72	2	EP/C3	Rotterdam	13 Jun
1.88	Maryse	Maury	FRA	4.9.64	7	Nik	Nice	21 Jul
	(100)							
1.88	Svetlana	Bogomaz	UKR	16.7.74	1		Chernigov	4 Sep

Mark	Name		Nat	Yr	Date
1.87i	Erzsébet	Fazekas	HUN	71	5 Feb
1.87i	Gai	Kapernick	AUS	70	6 Feb
1.87i	Svetlana	Tkachova	RUS	70	6 Feb
1.87i	Monica	Iagar	ROM	73	19 Feb
1.87i	Thordis	Gisladóttir	ISL	61	21 Feb
1.87	Desiré	Du Plessis	RSA	65	29 Mar
1.87	Mary Beth	Labosky	USA	70	16 Apr
1.87	Denise	Gaztambide	USA	64	8 May
1.87		Fu Xiuhong	CHN	70	14 May
	(110)				
1.87	Claudia	Ellinger-Stiefel	SUI	69	20 May
1.87	Lisa	Coleman	USA	69	30 May
1.87	Clare	Look-Jaeger	USA	66	10 Jun
1.87	Kaisa	Lehtonen	FIN	66	20 Jul
1.87		Jing Xuejing	CHN	69	8 Aug
1.87	Megumi	Sato	JPN	66	18 Sep
1.87i	Christiane	Meyer	GER	72	17 Dec
1.86i	Stefania	Lovison	ITA	74	31 Jan
1.86i	Olga	Shirinskaya	RUS	71	31 Jan
1.86i	Klara	Kosenko	RUS	66	13 Feb
	(120)				
1.86i	Katja	Kilpi	FIN	74	13 Feb
1.86i	Wiebke	Schwart	GER	73	27 Feb
1.86	Carmel	Corbett	NZL	72	27 Mar
1.86	Irina	Mikhalchenko	UKR	72	15 May
1.86	Natalya	Shimon	UKR	75	25 May
1.86	Sherry	Gould	USA		5 Jun
1.86		Liu Bo	CHN	72	2 Jun
1.86	Constanza	Moroni	ITA	69	12 Jun
1.86	Lucienne	N'Da	CIV	65	27 Jun
1.86	Galina	Mikhailova	UKR	66	3 Jul
	(130)				
1.86	Svetlana	Ivanova	RUS	74	4 Jul
1.86	Kerstin	Schlawitz	GER	70	10 Jul
1.86	Zhanna	Dyatlovskaya	BLS	73	15 Jul
1.86	Irina	Vostrikova	RUS	70	24 Jul
1.86	Romy	Pleikies	GER	75	31 Jul
1.86	Olga	Kaliturina	RUS	76	10 Aug
1.86	Emelie	Färdigh	SWE	77	19 Sep
1.86	Tania	Murray	NZL	70	30 Oct
1.86	Jurgita	Voveryte	LIT74		
	(140)				
1.85i	Laura	Sharpe	IRL	69	17 Jan
1.85i	Corissa	Yasen	USA	73	26 Feb
1.85i	Yelena	Sadova	RUS	66	27 Feb
1.85i	Ingela	Sandqvist	SWE	67	7 Mar
1.85	Shelly	Nixon	USA	65	3 Apr
1.85	Jackie	Joyner-Kersee	USA	62	15 Jun
1.85	Nathalie	Teppe	FRA	72	18 Jun
1.85	Odile	Lesage	FRA	69	18 Jun
1.85	Svetlana	Lavrova	RUS	71	19 Jun
1.85	Kaisa	Gustafsson	FIN	69	27 Jun
1.85	Mónika	Csapo	HUN	71	17 Jul
	(150)				
1.85	Marika	Salminen	FIN	71	20 Jul
1.85	Helena	Klimek	GER	66	15 Aug
1.85		Tan Ruixia	CHN	69	23 Aug
1.85	Monika	Gollner	AUT	74	25 Sep
1.85i	Heike	Drechsler	GER	64	23 Dec

Best outdoor marks for athletes with indoor bests

Mark	Name	Pos	Meet	Venue	Date
1.96	Gribanova	1	Slovn	Bratislava	1 Jun
1.96	Babakova	2		Madrid	3 Jun
1.95	Inverarity	1		Hobart	17 Jan
1.94	Bradburn	1	Jen	San José	29 May
1.94	Zhdanova	1	Znam	Moskva	13 Jun
1.94	Bilac	3		Luzern	29 Jun
1.94	Bevilacqua	5	Herc	Monaco	7 Aug
1.92	Panikarovskikh	1		Sochi	22 May
1.92	Hellmann	9		Wörrstadt	29 May
1.92	Baumert	1		Schwerin	4 Jun
1.91	Wang Wei	2	NG	Beijing	8 Sep
1.90	Jennings	6	EP	Roma	27 Jun
1.88	Varcholová	1		Brno	8 May
1.88	Aigner	14		Wörrstadt	29 May
1.88	Ivanova	7	NC	Moskva	19 Jun

Mark		Name		Nat	Born	Pos	Meet	Venue	Date

1.87 Kapernick	1 May	1.86 Lovison	22 May	1.86 Broughton	5 Jun	1.85 Kelly	24 Apr
1.87 Musunoi	12 Sep	1.86 Schwart	1 Jun	1.86 Fazekas	14 Aug	1.85 Kielan	18 Jun
						1.85 Veneva	24 Jul

POLE VAULT

Mark			Name	Nat	Born	Pos	Meet	Venue	Date
4.11			Sun Caiyun	CHN	21.7.73	1		Guangzhou	21 Mar
4.07i			Sun Caiyun			1		Landau	31 Jan
4.06i			Sun Caiyun			1		Zweibrücken	29 Jan
3.95i			Shao Jingwen	CHN	8.3.71	2		Landau	31 Jan
3.93		Tanja	Cors	GER	22.4.71	1		Bad Gendersheim	23 May
3.90		Svetlana	Abramova	RUS	27.10.70	1		Schwechat	30 May
3.90			Sun Caiyun			1	NC	Jinan	5 Jun
3.85i			Shao Jingwen			2		Zweibrücken	29 Jan
3.85i			Cors			3		Zweibrücken	29 Jan
3.85			Cai Weiyan	CHN	25.10.73	2	NC	Jinan	5 Jun
3.85		Carmen	Haage	GER	10.9.71	1	NC	Duisburg	11 Jul
		(11/7)							
3.80		Nicole	Rieger	GER	5.2.72	1		Dillingen	4 Jun
3.80			Wu Weili	CHN	20.4.70	3	NC	Jinan	5 Jun
3.80		Galina	Yenvarenko	RUS	70	2	NC	Moskva	18 Jun
		(10)							
3.80		Christine	Adams	GER	28.2.74	1		Gladbeck	18 Jul
3.70		Veronika	Göbel	GER	9.6.75	1	NC-j	Dortmund	4 Jul
3.70		Gabriela	Mihalcea	ROM	27.1.64	1	NC	Bucuresti	5 Sep
3.60		Andrea	Müller	GER	29.6.74	2		Dillingen	4 Jun
3.60			Zhu Rong	CHN	5.4.72	4	NC	Jinan	5 Jun
3.60		Marion	Meyer	GER	9.7.75	1		Lübeck	26 Jun
3.60		Caroline	Ammel	FRA	22.11.73	3		Landau	30 Jun

3.56	Kate	Staples	GBR	65	11 Sep
3.55i	Jana	Kábová	TCH	74	29 Jan
3.50i	Janet	Zach	GER	75	17 Jan
	(20)				
3.50i	Daniela	Bártová	TCH	74	21 Feb
3.50	Marina	Andreyeva	RUS	73	8 May
3.50	Ariane	Knoll	GER	77	26 Jun
3.50	Nastja	Ryshich	GER	77	30 Jul
3.50		Du Juan	CHN	75	25 Oct
Outdoor best					
3.50		Zach			26 May
Exhibition					
3.57	Daniela	Bártová	TCH	74	10 Jul

LONG JUMP

Mark	Wind		Name	Nat	Born	Pos	Meet	Venue	Date
7.21	-0.4	Heike	Drechsler	GER	16.12.64	1	WK	Zürich	4 Aug
7.14	1.6		Drechsler			1	OD	Jena	13 Jun
7.13A	0.7		Drechsler			1		Pretoria	15 May
7.11	-0.3		Drechsler			1	WC	Stuttgart	15 Aug
7.10	-0.3		Drechsler			1	Bisl	Oslo	10 Jul
7.09	0.8		Drechsler			1	Toto	Fukuoka	18 Sep
7.08A	-0.4		Drechsler			1		Pretoria	2 May
7.08	0.3		Drechsler			1	Athl	Lausanne	7 Jul
7.08	-1.1	Jackie	Joyner-Kersee	USA	3.3.62	1	ISTAF	Berlin	27 Aug
7.07	1.1		Drechsler			2	ISTAF	Berlin	27 Aug
7.07	1.9		Drechsler			1	VD	Bruxelles	3 Sep
7.06	2.0	Ljudmila	Ninova	AUT	25.6.60	2		Sevilla	5 Jun
7.06			Drechsler			-	Lausit	Cottbus	23 Jun
7.06	0.0		Drechsler			1		Rhede	6 Aug
7.06			Drechsler			1		Rosenheim	11 Sep
7.05i	-		Drechsler			1	NC	Sindelfingen	27 Feb
7.05	1.9		Drechsler			-		Sevilla	5 Jun
7.04	1.4		Joyner-Kersee			H	WC	Stuttgart	17 Aug
7.02	2.0		Joyner-Kersee			1	NC	Eugene	19 Jun
7.02	-0.2		Drechsler			1	EP	Roma	27 Jun
7.02	2.0	Irina	Mushailova	RUS	6.1.67	2	Athl	Lausanne	7 Jul
7.02	0.4		Drechsler			1	Alpen	Innsbruck	28 Aug
7.01i	-		Drechsler			1		Sindelfingen	14 Feb
7.01	1.4		Yao Weili	CHN	6.5.68	1	NC	Jinan	3 Jun
7.01	0.3		Joyner-Kersee			2	Alpen	Innsbruck	28 Aug
6.99i	-	Mirela	Dulgheru	ROM	5.10.66	1		Bacau	23 Jan
6.99i	-		Drechsler			1		Karlsruhe	6 Mar
6.99	1.6	Larisa	Berezhnaya	UKR	28.2.61	5		Sevilla	5 Jun
6.98i	-		Berezhnaya			2		Sindelfingen	14 Feb
6.98	0.4		Berezhnaya			2	WC	Stuttgart	15 Aug
6.98	1.2		Berezhnaya			2		Rieti	5 Sep
		(31/7)							

Mark	Wind	Name		Nat	Born	Pos	Meet	Venue	Date
6.97	1.3		Ma Miaolan	CHN	18.1.70	*	NG	Beijing	10 Sep
6.94i	-	Marieta	Ilcu	ROM	16.10.62	1		Liévin	13 Feb
6.90i	-	Yolanda	Chen	RUS	26.7.61	2	NC	Moskva	27 Feb
		(10)							
6.87	2.0	Agata	Karczmarek	POL	29.11.63	1	NC	Kielce	24 Jul
6.86A	1.1	Fiona	May	GBR	12.12.69	3		Sestriere	28 Jul
6.85i	-	Estera	Szabo	ROM	11.10.67	3		Bacau	23 Jan
6.85		Susen	Tiedtke	GER	23.1.69	1		Berlin	8 Jun
6.85	-0.3	Yelena	Sinchukova	RUS	23.1.61	*	EP	Roma	27 Jun
6.84	0.0	Renata	Nielsen	DEN	18.5.66	3	Bisl	Oslo	10 Jul
6.83i	-	Inessa	Kravets #	UKR	5.10.66	2		Liévin	13 Feb
6.83	0.8	Lyudmila	Mikhailova	RUS	12.4.69	H		Krasnodar	18 May
6.83	0.5	Yelena	Khlopotnova	UKR	4.8.63	Q	WC	Stuttgart	14 Aug
6.79	1.7		Xiong Qiying	CHN	14.10.67	3	NG	Beijing	10 Sep
		(20)							
6.78i	-	Erica	Johansson	SWE	5.2.74	2	NC	Malmö	21 Feb
6.77	0.7	Daphne	Saunders	BAH	18.12.71	1	NCAA	New Orleans	2 Jun
6.77		Svetlana	Moskalets	RUS	1.11.69	1		Rostov na Donu	19 Aug
6.75	0.9	Lyudmila	Galkina	RUS	20.5.72	2	NC	Moskva	19 Jun
6.75A	0.8	Nicole	Boegman	AUS	5.3.67	*		Sestriere	28 Jul
6.74		Olga	Rubleva	RUS	28.10.74	1		Vladimir	3 Jul
6.73	1.0	Ana	Biryukova	RUS	27.9.67	3	NC	Moskva	19 Jun
6.73	-0.7	Olyinka	Idowu	GBR	25.2.72	1	U23v3	Alicante	7 Aug
6.72i	-	Antonella	Capriotti	ITA	4.2.62	1		Paris	20 Feb
6.72		Dedra	Davis	BAH	17.7.73	*	NC	Nassau	17 Jun
		(30)							
6.72	1.2	Anzhela	Atroshchenko	BLS	14.11.70	1	NC	Gomel	26 Jun
6.71i	-	Irina	Tyukhay	RUS	14.1.67	P		Sankt Peterburg	6 Feb
6.71	1.1		Yang Zhanxiang	CHN	.9.72	2		Shijiazhuang	25 Apr
6.71	1.5	Marion	Jones	USA	12.10.75	1		Norwalk	19 Jun
6.67i	-	Liliane	Nastase	ROM	1.8.62	1P		Bacau	10 Feb
6.68	0.3		Yang Juan	CHN	5.9.69	6	NG	Beijing	10 Sep
6.66i	-	Helga	Radtke	GER	16.5.62	1		Bad Segeberg	24 Jan
6.66i	-	Maria	Andrei	ROM	24.11.67	3		Bucuresti	30 Jan
6.64	0.5	Niurka	Montalvo	CUB	4.6.68	•	NC	Habana	14 May
6.63		Shana	Williams	USA	7.4.72	1		Villanova	2 May
		(40)							
6.63		Nina	Perevedentseva	RUS	64	1		Yekaterinburg	29 May
6.63	2.0	Ringa	Ropo	FIN	16.2.66	8		Sevilla	5 Jun
6.63		Dionne	Rose	JAM	7.11.69	1	NC	Kingston	2 Jul
6.62i	-	Yelena	Chicherova	RUS	9.8.58	1		Volgograd	22 Jan
6.62	1.7	Rita	Ináncsi	HUN	6.1.71	1	EP/B	Bruxelles	13 Jun
6.61	1.5	Andrea	Avila	ARG	4.4.70	1		Buenos Aires	23 May
6.61	-1.8	Sandrine	Hennart	BEL	12.12.72	1	NC	Bruxelles	24 Jul
6.61	0.8	Yelena	Stakhova	BLS	4.1.69	1		Grodno	25 Jul
6.61	0.9	Svetla	Dimitrova	BUL	27.1.70	H		Talence	11 Sep
6.60	1.0	Tatyana	Zhuravlyova	RUS	19.12.67	3H		Götzis	30 May
		(50)							
6.60	1.9		Wu Lingmei	CHN	1.2.71	Q	NC	Jinan	4 Jun
6.60		Camille	Jackson	USA	7.9.70	1		Austin	23 Jul
6.60	0.2	Valentina	Uccheddu	ITA	26.10.66	1		Arbus	24 Jul
6.59	2.0	Urszula	Wlodarczyk	POL	22.12.65	*	NC	Kielce	24 Jul
6.59	0.0		Wang Chunfang	CHN	5.3.70	3		Shijiazhuang	25 Apr
6.59	0.0		Liu Shuzhen	CHN	7.5.66	4		Shijiazhuang	25 Apr
6.58	0.0		Zhang Hongzhen	CHN	25.1.73	1		Guangzhou	20 Mar
6.58	1.7	Iva	Prandzheva	BUL	15.2.72	1		Sofia	15 May
6.58	0.9	Natalya	Popykina	RUS	11.12.70	H		Krasnodar	17 May
6.58		Marina	Slushkina	RUS	2.8.60	1		Abakan	29 May
		(60)							
6.58	-0.2	Svetlana	Buraga	BLS	4.9.65	H	WC	Stuttgart	17 Aug
6.57	1.0		Yu Hunxiu	CHN	9.10.73	1		Shanghai	11 Apr
6.57		Claudia	Gerhardt	GER	18.1.66	1		Wessel	15 Jun
6.57	-0.1	Christy	Opara Thompson	NGR	2.5.70	1		Durban	23 Jun
6.57		Viktoriya	Vershinina	UKR	11.6.71	1		Donetsk	29 Jun
6.56		Natalya	Novikova	RUS	.66	1		Voronezh	25 Jul
6.54i		Beatrice	Utondu	NGR	23.11.69	1		Montreal	17 Jan
6.54	0.9	Corinne	Hérigault	FRA	6.10.70	1		Heidelberg	5 Jun

Mark	Wind	Name		Nat	Born	Pos	Meet	Venue	Date
6.54	1.0	Sabine	Braun	GER	19.1.65	H	WC	Stuttgart	17 Aug
6.54	0.7	Vera	Olenchenko	RUS	21.3.59	2	CISM	Tours	30 Aug
		(70)							
6.53		Sheila	Hudson	USA	30.6.67	2	USOF	San Antonio	1 Aug
6.52		Jane	Flemming	AUS	14.4.65	2		Adelaide	14 Feb
6.52		Trinette	Johnson	USA	8.2.71	1		Tallahassee	10 Apr
6.52	0.5	Alla	Nechiporets	UKR	20.10.64	3	Kuso	Kielce	16 Jun
6.52	1.1	Kirsten	Bolm	GER	4.3.75	1		Berlin	4 Sep
6.51		Flora	Hyacinth	ISV	30.3.66	1		Baton Rouge	17 Apr
6.51	1.5	Larisa	Nikitina	RUS	29.4.65	H	EP/A	Oulu	10 Jul
6.51		Sharon	Couch	USA	13.9.69	-	USOF	San Antonio	1 Aug
6.50	1.2		Dong Yuping	CHN	1.3.63			Beijing	3 May
6.49	2.0	Ilona	Pazola	POL	22.3.69	1	Walas	Krakow	1 Jul
		(80)							
6.49	0.3	Yelina	Selina	KZK	64	2	AsiC	Manila	2 Dec
6.48i		Monyetta	Haynesworth	USA	23.6.73	1		Johnson City	6 Mar
6.48		Galina	Baranovskaya	BLS	18.6.66	1		Gomel	15 May
6.48		Joanne	Wise	GBR	15.3.71	1		Loughborough	23 Jun
6.48	1.3		Zhang Yinlan	CHN	14.2.70	*	NG	Beijing	10 Sep
6.48	0.4		Zeng Yujuan	CHN	23.3.71	8	NG	Beijing	10 Sep
6.47i		Diane	Guthrie	JAM	24.10.71	1		Johnson City	29 Jan
6.47		Natalya	Kayukova	RUS	10.12.66	2		Rostov na Donu	19 Aug
6.46		Sheila	Echols	USA	2.10.64	2		Baton Rouge	17 Apr
6.46	0.4	Iolanta	Khropach	UKR	22.9.74	1		Rovno	25 May
		(90)							
6.46	1.9	Nicole	Devonish	CAN	24.8.73	*		Ottawa	3 Jul
6.45		Virginia	Martinez	CUB	3.9.68	2		Habana	12 Mar
6.45		Jackie	Edwards	BAH	14.4.71	1		Los Gatos	12 Jun
6.45		Monica	Toth	ROM	7.3.70	2	NC	Bucuresti	4 Sep
6.44i	-	Irina	Belova ¶	RUS	17.2.68	2		Moskva	26 Jan
6.44i		Yana	Kuznyetsova	RUS	72	3	NC	Moskva	27 Feb
6.44		Elma	Muros	PHI	14.1.67	1	SEAG	Singapore	14 Jun
6.44	0.6	Tamara	Malesev	YUG	8.1.67	1		Nis	19 Jun
6.44	0.5	Nadine	Caster	FRA	15.10.65	5		Reims	30 Jun
6.44		Jelena	Blazevica	LAT	11.5.70	1	NC	Riga	21 Jul
		(100)							
6.44	0.1	Cristina	Nicolau	ROM	9.8.77	3	EJ	San Sebastián	30 Jul

Mark	Wind	Name		Nat	Born	Date
6.43i		Yelena	Volf	RUS	69	6 Feb
6.43		Katrin	Bartschat	GER	70	13 Jun
6.43	0.3	Elisa	Mosconi	ITA	66	2 Aug
6.43			Mou Lianjuan	CHN	73	12 Sep
6.42		Anna	Mironova	RUS	75	25 Jul
6.42	0.7	Antonella	Avigni	ITA	68	2 Aug
6.41		Cynthia	Tylor	USA	71	3 Apr
6.41		Yelena	Afanasyeva	RUS	66	7 Jun
6.41	0.4	Olga	Roslyakova	BLS	67	25 Jul
		(110)				
6.41	1.9	Virge	Naeris	EST	69	30 Jul
6.41		Stefanie	Hühn	GER	66	26 Aug
6.40		Irina	Vostrikova	RUS	70	25 Jul
6.40	1.0	Yelena	Lysak	RUS	75	30 Jul
6.40	0.4	Ayumi	Sasaki	JPN	67	3 Oct
6.39	2.0	Rita	Schönenberger	SUI	62	13 Jun
6.39		Ksenija	Predikaka	SLO	70	20 Jun
6.39	0.3	Tatyana	Kotova	UKR	70	1 Aug
6.39			Shi Guiqing	CHN	68	12 Sep
6.38		Aparecida	Barbosa de Souza	BRA	71	27 Feb
		(120)				
6.38	0.5	Mona	Steigauf	GER	70	30 May
6.38	0.7		Yu Jing	CHN	72	4 Jun
6.38	1.8	Marika	Salminen	FIN	71	30 Jul

Mark	Wind	Name		Nat	Born	Date
6.38	0.7		Miao Xiaojun	CHN	74	10 Sep
6.37i		Yelena	Semiraz	UKR	65	13 Feb
6.37		Chantal	Brunner	NZL	70	9 May
6.37		Twilet	Malcolm	JAM	69	15 May
6.37		Michaela	Frank	GER	69	15 Jun
6.37	0.1	Malgorzata	Sobczak	POL	70	10 Jul
6.36i	-	Sylvie	Borda	FRA	66	27 Feb
		(130)				
6.36	1.4		Xie Pingzhen	CHN		11 Apr
6.36	0.9		Xu Pin	CHN	70	5 May
6.36A		Anu	Kaljurand	EST	69	21 May
6.36		Tatyana	Dyatlova	BLS	75	22 May
6.36	1.2	Ermelinda	Shehu	ALB	74	11 Jul
6.36	0.1	Vanessa	Monar-Enweani	CAN	69	14 Jul
6.35i	-	Babett	Fuchs	GER	66	13 Feb
6.35i	-	Ingvild	Larsen	NOR	75	20 Feb
6.35i	-	Marcela	Podracká	SVK	70	20 Feb
6.35	1.5		Liu Qin	CHN	74	3 May
		(140)				
6.35		Regina	Frye	USA	72	8 May
6.35	-0.1	Hitomi	Takamatsu	JPN	74	23 May
6.35	2.0	Daniela	Kirsch	GER	68	6 Jun
6.35	1.5	Merethe	Myrvang	NOR	71	13 Jun
6.35	1.9		Lu Junhua	CHN	73	10 Sep

Subsequent to positive drugs test

Mark	Wind	Name		Nat	Born	Pos	Meet	Venue	Date
6.87	1.8	Inessa	Kravets	UKR	5.10.66	2	Bisl	Oslo	10 Jul
6.66	1.9	Irina	Belova	RUS	27.3.68	H		Brescia	16 May

Exhibition

Mark	Wind	Name		Nat	Born	Pos	Meet	Venue	Date
6.78		Liliana	Nastase	ROM	1.8.62	2	exh	Iglesias	9 Sep

Best outdoor marks for athletes with indoor seasonal bests

Mark	Wind	Name	Pos	Meet	Venue	Date
6.77		Dulgheru	3		Bucuresti	31 Jul
6.70A	0.6	Capriotti	7		Sestriere	28 Jul
6.70	0.7	Capriotti	1	NC	Bologna	2 Aug
6.66		Radtke	1		Rostock	28 May
6.65	0.0	Chen	2	Toto	Fukuoka	16 Sep
6.60	0.8	Tyukhay	1H		Götzis	30 May

Mark	Wind	Name		Nat	Born	Pos	Meet	Venue	Date

Mark	Wind	Name	Pos	Meet	Venue	Date
6.56	0.1	Johansson	1	EJ	San Sebastián	30 Jul
6.50		Ilcu	1	RomIC	Bucuresti	18 Jun
6.46	1.0	Nastase	3		Caorle	24 Jul
6.44	-0.3	Utondu	2	AfrC	Durban	23 Jun
6.39		Volf				19 May
6.38		Kuznyetsova				28 Aug

Wind-assisted marks

Mark	Wind	Name		Nat	Born	Pos	Meet	Venue	Date
7.19A	3.7	Susen	Tiedtke	GER	23.1.69	1		Sestriere	28 Jul
7.13	2.2		Drechsler			1	Lausit	Cottbus	23 Jun
7.12A	3.3		Drechsler			2		Sestriere	28 Jul
7.09	5.0	Jackie	Joyner-Kersee	USA	3.3.62	1	Jen	San José	29 May
7.08	2.6		Drechsler			1		Sevilla	5 Jun
7.07			Joyner-Kersee			H	NC	Eugene	16 Jun
7.06	3.4		Ma Miaolan	CHN	18.1.70	1	NG	Beijing	10 Sep
7.02	3.3	Inessa	Kravets #	UKR	5.10.66	3		Sevilla	5 Jun
7.01	3.4	Yelena	Khlopotnova	UKR	4.8.63	4		Sevilla	5 Jun
7.00	2.1		Drechsler			1		Rieti	5 Sep
		(10 performances)							
6.94	2.2	Yelena	Sinchukova	RUS	23.1.61	6		Sevilla	5 Jun
6.86		Daphne	Saunders	BAH	18.12.71	1		Knoxville	15 May
6.83A	3.2	Valentina	Uccheddu	ITA	26.10.66	4		Sestriere	28 Jul
6.81A	3.8	Nicole	Boegman	AUS	5.3.67	5		Sestriere	28 Jul
6.76	2.1	Dedra	Davis	BAH	17.7.73	1	NC	Nassau	17 Jun
6.75	2.6	Niurka	Montalvo	CUB	4.6.68	1	NC	Habana	14 May
6.75	3.2	Marion	Jones	USA	12.10.75	1		Norwalk	22 May
6.74	2.5		Zhang Yinlan	CHN	14.2.70	4	NG	Beijing	10 Sep
6.67	5.6	Urszula	Wlodarczyk	POL	22.12.65	2	NC	Kielce	24 Jul
6.66	2.3		Wang Chunfang	CHN	5.3.70	7	NG	Beijing	10 Sep
6.65	2.9	Sheila	Echols	USA	2.10.64	2	NC	Eugene	19 Jun
6.62	4.2	Sharon	Couch	USA	13.9.67	Q	NC	Eugene	18 Jun
6.60	2.7	Jackie	Edwards	BAH	14.4.71	3	NC	Nassau	17 Jun
6.59	3.2	Joanne	Wise	GBR	15.3.71	1	v USA	Edinburgh	2 Jul
6.58		Sheila	Hudson	USA	30.6.67	1	S&W	Modesto	8 May
6.58	3.2		Li Jing	CHN	21.10.69	2	NC	Jinan	3 Jun
6.57	3.2	Vanessa	Monar-Enweani	CAN	11.12.69	2	WUG	Buffalo	15 Jul
6.55		Trinette	Johnson	USA	8.2.71	1		Chapel Hill	16 Apr
6.55	2.4	Nicole	Devonish	CAN	24.8.73	1		Ottawa	3 Jul
6.54	2.3	Eloina	Echevarria	CUB	23.8.61	2	NC	Habana	14 May
6.53	2.4	Ingvild	Larsen	NOR	3.10.75	1		Florø	22 May
6.51	5.0	Ayumi	Sasaki	JPN	24.7.67	1		Ageo	18 Apr
6.51	3.4	Ksenija	Predikaka	SLO	11.3.70	2	MedG	Narbonne	20 Jun
6.48		Chandra	Sturrup	BAH	12.9.71	1		Williamsburg	3 Apr
6.46	3.6	Elisa	Mosconi	ITA	8.4.66	2		San Giovanni Vald	15 May
6.45	2.8	Silvija	Babic	CRO	12.12.68	3	MedG	Narbonne	20 Jun
6.44	3.2	Hitomi	Takamatsu	JPN	21.8.74	2	NC	Tokyo	13 Jun

Mark	Wind	Name		Nat	Born	Date
6.43	2.2	Svetlana	Akimova	RUS	69	16 Jul
6.42		Kim	Rowland	USA		8 May
6.41		Wendi	Simmons	USA	69	24 Apr
6.41	2.2	Ildikó	Fekete	HUN	66	6 Aug
6.40		Gwen	Loud	USA	61	8 May
6.37		Marieke	Veltman	USA	71	3 Jun
6.37	2.1	Ghada	Shouaa	SYR	73	19 Jun
6.36	2.3	Marvette	Collis	STV	74	22 May
6.36		Tamara	Cuffee	USA	71	26 May
6.36	2.9		Wang Yijing	CHN		10 Sep
6.35		Toshei	Woods	USA	72	26 May
6.35	3.7	Maria Jesús	Martin	ESP	65	10 Jul

Best low altitude marks

Mark	Wind	Name	Pos	Meet	Venue	Date
6.78	1.3	May	1		Oristano	12 Sep
6.77		Dulgheru	1		Bucuresti	31 Jul
6.72	1.7	Boegman	5	Bisl	Oslo	10 Jul
6.66		Radtke			Rostock	26 May
6.65	0.0	Chen	2	Toto	Fukuoka	18 Sep
6.85	Exh	May	1		Igelesias	9 Sep
6.85w	2.1	May	1		S Giovanni Valdano	15 May
6.70w	3.0	Uccheddu	4	EP	Roma	27 Jun

Best outdoor marks (wind assisted) for athletes with indoor seasonal bests

Mark	Wind	Name	Pos	Venue	Date
6.72	2.4	Ilcu	6	Sestriere	28 Jul
6.61	5.8	Radtke	1	Rostock	28 Aug

TRIPLE JUMP

Mark	Wind	Name		Nat	Born	Pos	Meet	Venue	Date
15.09	0.5	Ana	Biryukova	RUS	27.9.67	1	WC	Stuttgart	21 Aug
14.97	0.9	Yolanda	Chen	RUS	26.7.61	1	NC	Moskva	18 Jun
14.79	1.7	Irina	Mushailova	RUS	6.1.67	1	DNG	Stockholm	5 Jul
14.74	0.4		Biryukova			1	Gugl	Linz	25 Aug
14.71	1.6		Chen			1	BNP	Villeneuve d'Ascq	2 Jul
14.70	0.6	Inna	Lasovskaya	RUS	17.12.69	2	Slovn	Bratislava	1 Jun
14.70	0.1		Chen			2	WC	Stuttgart	21 Aug
14.68	1.0		Biryukova			*	Slovn	Bratislava	1 Jun
14.68	0.2		Lasovskaya			2	NC	Moskva	18 Jun
14.65	1.8		Chen			2	DNG	Stockholm	5 Jul

Mark	Wind	Name		Nat	Born	Pos	Meet	Venue	Date
14.64	-1.0		Lasovskaya			1	GGala	Roma	9 Jun
14.60	0.4		Biryukova			3	NC	Moskva	18 Jun
14.54	1.2		Chen			1	TSB	London	23 Jul
14.52	0.5		Lasovskaya			1		Luzern	29 Jun
14.52	-0.7		Lasovskaya			2	Athl	Lausanne	7 Jul
14.51	1.8	Niurka	Montalvo	CUB	4.6.68	1	Barr	Habana	22 May
14.50	-1.2		Mushailova			3	Athl	Lausanne	7 Jul
14.49	0.2	Inessa	Kravets #	UKR	5.10.66	3	DNG	Stockholm	5 Jul
14.47i			Kravets			1	WI	Toronto	14 Mar
14.46i			Chen			1	NC	Moskva	28 Feb
14.44	-0.8		Chen			2	GGala	Roma	9 Jun
14.44	1.0		Lasovskaya			2	Nik	Nice	21 Jul
14.40i			Lasovskaya			2	NC	Moskva	28 Feb
14.40	1.3	Galina	Chistyakova	RUS	26.7.62	2	TSB	London	23 Jul
14.39	1.3		Chen			1	GPF	London	10 Sep
14.38i			Kravets			1		Grenoble	7 Feb
14.38	1.7		Kravets			2	BNP	Villeneuve d'Ascq	2 Jul
14.36i			Chen			2	WI	Toronto	14 Mar
14.36	0.7		Chistyakova			3	BNP	Villeneuve d'Ascq	2 Jul
14.36	1.8		Biryukova			1		Padova	29 Aug
		(30/7)							
14.29	1.4		Ren Ruiping	CHN	1.1.75	1	NG	Beijing	13 Sep
14.28	0.9		Zhang Yan	CHN	.6.72	2	NG	Beijing	13 Sep
14.23	-0.2	Iva	Prandzheva	BUL	15.2.72	3	WC	Stuttgart	21 Aug
		(10)							
14.19	0.1	Helga	Radtke	GER	16.5.62	5	WC	Stuttgart	21 Aug
14.18	-0.1	Antonella	Capriotti	ITA	4.2.62	6	WC	Stuttgart	21 Aug
14.17	-0.5	Zhanna	Gureyeva	BLS	10.6.70	3	GGala	Roma	9 Jun
14.16	0.1	Sarka	Kaspárková	TCH	20.5.71	7	WC	Stuttgart	21 Aug
14.12	0.8		Ma Miaolan	CHN	18.1.70	3	NG	Beijing	13 Sep
14.05	1.9	Concepcion	Paredes	ESP	19.7.70	*		Madrid	29 May
14.03	0.8		Liu Jingming	CHN	1.2.72	5	NG	Beijing	13 Sep
14.00		Eloina	Echevarria	CUB	23.8.61	1		Habana	5 Mar
14.00	-1.8	Lyudmila	Dubkova	RUS	27.2.68	1		Rostov na Donu	17 Jul
13.99		Yelena	Semiraz	UKR	21.11.65	1		Dreux	29 May
		(20)							
13.98	1.0	Urszula	Wlodarczyk	POL	22.12.65	2	NC	Kielce	25 Jul
13.97	0.5	Natalya	Kayukova	RUS	10.12.66	4	NC	Moskva	18 Jun
13.93i	-	Iolanda	Oanta	ROM	11.10.65	1		Bacau	23 Jan
13.93		Monica	Toth	ROM	7.3.70	1		Bucuresti	29 May
13.92i	-	Yelena	Sinchukova	RUS	23.1.61	4		Grenoble	7 Feb
13.92i	-	Anja	Vokuhl	GER	17.8.73	2	NC	Sindelfingen	28 Feb
13.92	0.1		Zhang JIng	CHN	10.3.70	1		Guangzhou	21 Mar
13.91	0.1	Agnieszka	Stanczyk ¶	POL	20.1.71	1		Poznan	30 May
13.91A	1.3	Andrea	Avila	ARG	4.4.70	1	SAmC	Lima	4 Jul
13.88		Tanja	Bormann	GER	11.4.70	2		Bad Homburg	10 Jun
		(30)							
13.86		Sheila	Hudson	USA	30.6.67	1		Chico	1 May
13.86	1.8	Yelena	Lysak	RUS	19.10.75	1	EJ	San Sebastián	1 Aug
13.83	0.9	Tatyana	Matyashova	RUS	7.8.73	2	Znam	Moskva	12 Jun
13.81i	-	Tatyana	Fyodorova	RUS	67	5	NC	Moskva	28 Feb
13.80		Viktoriya	Vershinina	UKR	11.6.71	1		Donetsk	30 Jun
13.77		Petra	Laux-Schneider	GER	24.1.67	4		Bad Homburg	10 Jun
13.77		Laiza	Carrillo	CUB	27.11.68	1		Habana	25 Jun
13.75	1.8	Michelle	Griffith	GBR	6.10.71	4	WUG	Buffalo	18 Jul
13.74		Olga	Ukolova	RUS	72	2		Rostov na Donu	20 Aug
13.73	1.6		Wang Xiangrong	CHN	.2.76	*	NG	Beijing	13 Sep
		(40)							
13.71	0.5	Renata	Nielsen	DEN	18.5.66	1	EP/C2	København	12 Jun
13.71	1.9	Ildikó	Fekete	HUN	12.11.66	1	NC	Budapest	5 Aug
13.70i	-	Irina	Babakova	UKR	5.11.65	1	NC	Kiev	14 Feb
13.70		Ionela	Gogoase	ROM	4.2.70	1	NC	Bucuresti	5 Sep
13.68		Olga Lidia	Cepero	CUB	4.2.75	1		Habana	3 Jul
13.68		Cynthea	Rhodes	USA	30.9.68	1		Austin	23 Jul
13.66	-0.7	Sofia	Bozhanova	BUL	4.10.67	2	NC	Sofia	31 Jul
13.65	1.2	Caroline	Honoré	FRA	29.4.70	1	NC	Annecy	23 Jul
13.65	1.1	Natalya	Klimovets	BLS	11.4.74	2	EJ	San Sebastián	1 Aug

Mark	Wind	Name		Nat	Born	Pos	Meet	Venue	Date
13.63	2.0		Li Shuhua	CHN	10.7.68	8	NG	Beijing	13 Sep
		(50)							
13.62i	-	Sylvie	Borda	FRA	4.9.66	1	NC	Liévin	28 Feb
13.60	1.0	Rachel	Kirby	GBR	18.5.69	*	TSB	London	23 Jul
13.60	0.8	Lyudmila	Ninova	AUT	25.6.60	Q	WC	Stuttgart	20 Aug
13.57	0.9	Claudia	Haywood	USA	25.9.69	1	SWC	Austin	21 May
13.57	0.6	Vera	Olenchenko	RUS	21.3.59	2		Rostov na Donu	17 Jul
13.57	0.0	Yelena	Blazevica	LAT	11.5.70	10	WC	Stuttgart	21 Aug
13.56	2.0		Rong Hanmei	CHN	.12.69	*	NG	Beijing	13 Sep
13.55	-0.5	Olga	Kontsevaya	RUS	72	1		Bryansk	29 May
13.55	1.9	Ilona	Pazola	POL	22.3.69	*		Wroclaw	18 Sep
13.54	0.8	Lene	Espegren	NOR	8.5.71	1	NC	Tønsberg	31 Jul
		(60)							
13.53	1.5	Estrella	Roldán	ESP	4.6.62	2		Madrid	15 May
13.53	0.5	Irina	Melnikova	RUS	9.1.74	3	EJ	San Sebastián	1 Aug
13.52i	-	Flora	Hyacinth	ISV	10.3.66	Q	WI	Toronto	13 Mar
13.50	0.6	Olga	Skrebneva	BLS	7.11.74	2		Gomel	14 May
13.50		Angela	Barylla	GER	6.1.71	4	NC	Duisburg	11 Jul
13.48i	-	Ashia	Hansen	GBR	5.12.71	1	vUSA	Birmingham	13 Feb
13.48	0.0		Zhou Xiulian	CHN	.11.70	3	NC	Jinan	5 Jun
13.48		Lyudmila	Galkina	RUS	20.5.72	1		Arras	26 Jun
13.48		Olga	Boyko	UKR	6.7.75	1		Chernigov	4 Sep
13.47	0.0		Yu Yongping	CHN	28.11.73	1		Shijiazhuang	26 Apr
		(70)							
13.46		Loredana	Rossi	ITA	17.7.67	1		Cesena	30 May
13.44	0.4	Marika	Salminen	FIN	10.5.71	1	NC	Mikkeli	1 Aug
13.43	0.0		Zhang Hongzhen	CHN	25.1.73	3		Guangzhou	21 Mar
13.42i	-	Mary	Agyepong	GBR	31.10.65	1		Birmingham	20 Feb
13.42	0.5	Magalys	Pedroso	CUB	3.6.72	4	NC	Habana	13 May
13.42		Nicoleta	Filip	ROM	5.6.71			Bucuresti	18 Jun
13.41i		Tamara	Malesev	YUG	8.1.67	1		Beograd	3 Feb
13.41	1.8	Yelena	Stakhova	BLS	4.1.69	2		Gomel	26 Jun
13.41		Ksenija	Predikaka	SLO	11.3.70	4		Trento	30 Jun
13.41	1.6	Antonella	Avigni	ITA	19.1.68	3	NC	Bologna	3 Aug
		(80)							
13.40	0.3	Lisette	Cuza	CUB	26.2.75	5	NC	Habana	14 May
13.40		Yuliya	Baranova	UKR	12.8.72	2		Kiev	4 Sep
13.39i	-	Elena	Dumitrascu	ROM	14.5.74	2		Bucuresti	31 Jan
13.38	0.5	Barbara	Lah	ITA	24.3.72	1		Pesaro	15 May
13.38	1.4	Sandrine	Domain	FRA	6.9.71	3	NC	Annecy	23 Jul
13.37	2.0	Olga	Vasdeki	GRE	26.9.73	1		Athinai	29 May
13.36	1.4	Isabel	Aldecoa	CUB	21.6.71	4	Barr	Habana	22 May
13.36	1.9	Eva	Medovárszky	HUN	15.8.69	1		Veszprém	22 Jul
13.35	-0.3	Heike	Drechsler	GER	16.12.64	1		Miaoli	30 May
13.35	0.7	Roshandra	Glenn	USA	13.11.71	2	NCAA	New Orleans	4 Jun
		(90)							
13.34		Gundega	Sproge	LAT	12.12.72	1		Riga	11 May
13.33		Madalina	Coman	ROM	4.3.76	1		Bucuresti	12 Jun
13.32		Lenuta	Bîrzu	ROM	20.2.69			Bucuresti	13 Jul
13.29i	-	Ana I	Oliveira	POR	9.1.63	1		Braga	6 Mar
13.29	0.1	Tatyana	Olkhovaya	UKR	9.6.73	1		Alushta	25 Apr
13.28	0.6	Yaminoraydes	Martinez	CUB	16.7.73	6	NC	Habana	13 May
13.27	1.5	Nicole	Boegman	AUS	5.3.67	1	NC	Brisbane	6 Mar
13.27	-0.1		Yan Xueqin	CHN	.11.73	Q	NC	Jinan	2 Jun
13.27		Wendy	Brown	USA	28.1.66	2	USOF	San Antonio	31 Jul
13.26i	-	Oksana	Voloshina	RUS	74	1A		Volgograd	31 Jan
		(100)							
13.26A		Camille	Jackson	USA	7.9.70	2		El Paso	10 Apr

Mark	Wind	Name		Nat	Born	Date
13.25	0.4	Natalya	Telepnyeva	RUS	66	17 Jul
13.24	1.5	Malgorzata	Sobczak	POL	70	25 Jul
13.24	1.0		Zhao Tianyi	CHN	73	13 Sep
13.23	1.8	Naomi	Hashioka	JPN	68	1 Aug
13.22		Lisa	Austin	USA	73	16 May
13.22	-0.1	Larisa	Berezhnaya	UKR	61	5 Jul
13.22	0.6	Nkechi	Madubuko	GER	72	24 Jul
13.22	1.3		Li Huirong	CHN	65	13 Sep
13.21	1.0		Xu Pin	CHN	70	2 May
		(110)				
13.21		Luisa	Celesia	ITA	63	30 May
13.21		Dagmar	Urbánková	TCH	62	23 Jun
13.20	0.3		Li Jing	CHN	69	6 Jun
13.20		Maria	Andrei	ROM	67	18 Jun
13.20		Yelena	Chekovtsova	UKR	72	4 Sep
13.19i	-	Telisa	Young	USA	71	13 Mar
13.19		Inara	Curko	LAT	66	31 Jul
13.18	1.4	Sanni	Suhonen	FIN	69	10 Jul
13.17		Anna	Rodovich	UKR	76	22 Jun
13.16i	-	Alla	Petrunina	RUS	69	22 Jan
		(120)				
13.16i	-	Claudia	Gerhardt	GER	66	31 Jan

Mark	Wind	Name		Nat	Born	Date
13.16	0.3	Yannick	Gacon	FRA	56	23 Jul
13.15	1.2	Yoko	Morioka	JPN	68	3 Nov
13.14i	-	Yelena	Govorova	UKR	73	28 Feb
13.14	0.1	Valerie	Guiyoule	FRA	72	6 Jun
13.13i	-	Tatyana	Lebedyeva	RUS	76	31 Jan
13.13	0.0		Fu Xiaorong	CHN	68	26 Apr
13.13		Aparecida	Barbosa de Souza	BRA	71	1 May
13.13	0.9		Li Yong-ae	PRK	65	16 May
13.13		Ilaria	Marras	ITA	74	21 Jul
		(130)				
13.13		Serafina	Agafitei	ROM	72	31 Jul
13.12	-0.6	Nancy	Lanovaz	CAN	63	11 Jun
13.12		Irina	Melnikova II	RUS	75	4 Jul
13.12	0.2	Martha	Koulorizou	GRE	74	11 Jul
13.11	1.5	Christine	Gray	USA	71	4 Jun
13.10	-0.2	Chen Huoqiang		CHN		4 May
13.10		Mihaela	Gindila	ROM	74	16 May
13.09		Petra	Franke	GER	71	29 May
13.09		Leah	Kirklin	USA	70	4 Jun
13.08	0.0		Xiang Xiuli	CHN		31 Mar
		(140)				
13.08	0.8	Muriel	Glovil	FRA	68	4 Jul
13.07		Madelin	Martinez	CUB	76	22 Apr
13.07		Nathalie	Jacques-Gustave	FRA	76	6 Jun
13.06		Yana	Yesenova	RUS	76	30 May
13.06	0.7	Evette	Finikin	GBR	63	27 Jun
13.05i		Karen	Pittman	USA	70	9 Jan
13.05		Rene	Woodard	USA	71	8 May
13.05	1.5	Alexandra	Barlet	FRA	77	1 Aug
13.04		Suzette	Lee	JAM	75	19 Jun
13.03i	-	Yelena	Zagorovskaya	UKR	74	31 Jan
		(150)				
13.03		Jennifer	McDermott	USA	71	16 May
13.03		Annie	Moelo	FRA	62	29 May
13.03	1.0	Doris	Stelzmüller	SUI	63	1 Aug
13.02	0.0	Oksana	Rybakova	RUS	70	6 Jun
13.02	0.2	Svetlana	Churikova	RUS	68	18 Jun
13.01i		Daphne	Saunders	BAH	71	28 Feb
13.01i		Kelly	Dinsmore	CAN	71	10 Mar
13.01	0.6		Guo Qian	CHN	71	4 May
13.01	1.2	Karin	Grelsson	SWE	65	15 May
13.01		Felicia	Harris	USA	68	29 May
		(160)				
13.00	1.8	Jackie	Edwards	BAH	71	5 May
13.00	1.0	Maria	Sokova	RUS	70	12 Jun
13.00		Marina	Bondarenko	UKR	76	22 Jun
13.00	1.6	Anni	Paananen	FIN	71	22 Jun
13.00		Ramona	Molzan	GER	71	11 Jul

Previously disqualified for drugs use

Mark	Wind	Name		Nat	Born	Pos	Meet	Venue	Date
14.70	0.5	Inessa	Kravets			1	Nik	Nice	21 Jul
14.61	0.2		Kravets			1	Athl	Lausanne	7 Jul
14.05	0.3	Agnieszka	Stanczyk	POL	20.1.71	1	NC	Kielce	25 Jul

Wind-assisted

Mark	Wind	Name		Nat	Born	Pos	Meet	Venue	Date
14.74	2.7		Biryukova			1	Slovn	Bratislava	1 Jun
14.38	2.3		Lasovskaya			1		St Denis	11 Jun
14.32	4.9	Iva	Prandzheva	BUL	15.2.72	1		Sofia	3 Jul
14.16	3.2	Concepcion	Paredes	ESP	19.7.70	1		Madrid	29 May
14.07	2.8		Wang Xiangrong	CHN	.2.76	4	NG	Beijing	13 Sep
13.96	3.7	Monica	Toth	ROM	7.3.70	3	WUG	Buffalo	17 Jul
13.93	5.3	Michelle	Griffith	GBR	6.10.71	1	vUSA	Edinburgh	2 Jul
13.86	2.9	Claudia	Haywood	USA	25.9.69	1	NC	Eugene	17 Jun
13.85	3.5	Irina	Babakova	UKR	5.11.65	1		Kiev	16 May
13.80	4.5	Ana I	Oliveira	POR	9.1.63	1		Maia	11 Jul
13.77	2.7		Rong Hanmei	CHN	.12.69	7	NG	Beijing	13 Sep
13.64	2.1	Rachel	Kirby	GBR	18.5.69	5	TSB	London	23 Jul
13.64	2.8	Ilona	Pazola	POL	22.3.69	1		Wroclaw	18 Sep
13.59	4.0	Sandrine	Domain	FRA	6.9.71	1		Bron	26 Jun
13.56	3.4	Lene	Espegren	NOR	8.5.71	1		Lisleby	8 May
13.55	3.6	Ashia	Hansen	GBR	5.12.71	4	vUSA	Edinburgh	2 Jul
13.55	2.7		Zhao Tianyi	CHN	.3.73	9	NG	Beijing	13 Sep
13.53		Nkechi	Madubuko	GER	28.3.72	1		Basel	31 May
13.50	2.8	Barbara	Lah	ITA	24.3.72	Q	WUG	Buffalo	16 Jul
13.49	4.0	Camille	Jackson	USA	7.9.70	1		Knoxville	16 May
13.48	2.5	Eva	Medovárszky	HUN	15.8.69	2		Budapest	10 Jul
13.45	6.4	Wendy	Brown	USA	28.1.66	4	NC	Eugene	17 Jun
13.45	4.4	Annie	Moelo	FRA	10.11.62	3		Bron	26 Jun
13.44	2.5	Inara	Curko	LAT	11.11.66	2	NC	Riga	22 Jul
13.43		Ramona	Molzan	GER	1.8.71	1		Celle	31 Jul
13.33	2.2	Flora	Hyacinth	ISV	30.3.66	1		Pointe-a-Pitre	1 May
13.32	2.7	Leah	Kirklin	USA	28.11.70	3	NCAA	New Orleans	4 Jun
13.31	2.4	Evette	Finikin	GBR	25.9.63	3	NC	London	13 Jun
13.31		Natalya	Kuzina	RUS	70	1		Hyryla	6 Jul

Mark	Wind	Name		Nat	Born	Date
13.25	2.4		Li Yong-ae	PRK	65	16 May
13.24	2.2	Yoko	Morioka	JPN	68	5 May
13.22	3.0	Ilaria	Marras	ITA	74	3 Aug
13.21	2.7	Hanne	Haugland	NOR	67	7 Jul
13.20		Daphne	Saunders	BAH	71	16 May
13.19	3.6	Robyne	Johnson	USA	63	16 Jun
13.09	2.7	Anni	Paananen	FIN	71	10 Jul
13.06	3.5	Barbara	Ottaviani	ITA	68	25 Sep
13.05A	2.4	Kelly	Dinsmore	CAN	71	22 May
13.05	3.6	Nathalie	Prévôt	FRA	69	26 Jun
13.03		Connie	Henry	GBR	72	15 May
13.02		Althea	Moses	BIZ	70	8 May

Best outdoor marks for athletes with indoor seasonal bests

Mark	Wind	Name	Pos	Meet	Venue	Date
13.87		Vokuhl	3		Bad Homburg	10 Jun
13.83	-0.6	Sinchukova	6	GGala	Roma	9 Jun
13.57	0.3	Fyodorova	7	NC	Moskva	18 Jun
13.53	1.3	Babakova	6	Slovn	Bratislava	1 Jun
13.44	0.7	Borda	2	NC	Annecy	23 Jul
13.42		Oanta	2		Bucuresti	30 May
13.41	-0.2	Stakhova	1	NC	Gomel	25 Jul
13.31		Dumitrascu	1	Balk-j	Thessaloniki	11 Jul

Mark		Name	Nat	Born	Pos	Meet	Venue	Date

13.29 Oliveira 1 Lisboa 21 Jul | 13.09 1.0 Govorova 16 May | 13.00 0.9 Zagorovskaya 26 May
13.25 1.1 Hansen 27 Jun | 13.06 Hyacinth 17 Apr
13.14 Young 8 May | 13.04 1.8 Malesev 16 Jul

SHOT

Mark		Name	Nat	Born	Pos	Meet	Venue	Date
20.84	Svetlana	Krivelyova	RUS	13.6.69	1		Moskva	7 Aug
20.57		Huang Zhihong	CHN	7.5.65	1	WC	Stuttgart	15 Aug
20.45i		Krivelyova			1	NC	Moskva	27 Feb
20.32		Sui Xinmei	CHN	29.1.65	1		Beijing	31 Jul
20.24	Anna	Romanova	RUS	9.3.68	1		Bryansk	29 May
20.19		Romanova			1	NC	Moskva	19 Jun
20.18		Zhou Tianhua ¶	CHN	10.4.66	1		Beijing	3 Apr
20.16	Valentina	Fedyushina	UKR	18.2.65	1	NYG	New York	22 May
20.08i		Li Xiaoyun	CHN	10.7.71	1		Jinan	16 Jan
20.01i		Romanova		9.3.68	2	NC	Moskva	27 Feb
20.01		Krivelyova			1		Moskva	24 Jul
20.00	Svetla	Mitkova	BUL	17.6.64	1		Stara Zagora	24 Jul
19.97		Krivelyova			2	WC	Stuttgart	15 Aug
19.96		Krivelyova			Q	WC	Stuttgart	14 Aug
19.92	Astrid	Kumbernuss	GER	5.2.70	Q	WC	Stuttgart	14 Aug
19.90i	Larisa	Peleshenko (10)	RUS	29.2.64	1		Sankt Peterburg	23 Jan
19.90		Krivelyova			1		Moskva	25 Jul
19.90		Zhang Liuhong	CHN	16.1.69	2	NG	Beijing	8 Sep
19.89		Wang Yawen ¶	CHN	23.8.73			Shijiazhuang	2 Apr
19.88		Zhang Liuhong			1	EAsiG	Shanghai	16 May
19.83		Fedyushina			1		Sevilla	5 Jun
19.82i		Peleshenko			1		Paris	20 Feb
19.78	Kathrin	Neimke	GER	18.7.66	1		Halle	15 May
19.77		Zhang Zhiying	CHN	19.7.73	3	NG	Beijing	8 Sep
19.73	Lissette	Martinez	CUB	11.10.66	1		Habana	6 Mar
19.71i		Peleshenko			3	NC	Moskva	27 Feb
19.71	Stephanie	Storp	GER	28.11.68	1	TSB	London	23 Jul
19.71		Neimke			3	WC	Stuttgart	15 Aug
19.71		Huang Zhihong			1	VD	Bruxelles	3 Sep
19.70		Fedyushina			1	Banes	São Paulo	16 May
	(30/16)							
19.58		Cong Yuzhen	CHN	22.1.63	5	WC	Stuttgart	15 Aug
19.51	Mihaela	Oana	ROM	11.11.68	1		Bucuresti	30 May
19.33	Belsy	Laza	CUB	5.6.67	1		Habana	27 Feb
19.31i	Tatyana	Khorkulyova	BLS	1.1.64	1		Gomel	29 Jan
	(20)							
19.27		Wu Xianchun	CHN	.2.72	6	NG	Beijing	8 Sep
19.25	Connie	Price-Smith	USA	3.6.62	3	Jen	San José	29 May
19.22		Xie Hongxia	CHN	5.4.70	7	NG	Beijing	8 Sep
19.22	Viktoriya	Pavlysh	UKR	15.1.69	3	GPF	London	10 Sep
19.14	Danguolé	Urbikiene	LIT	10.12.62	1	NC	Vilnius	20 Jun
19.12i	Jana	Ciobanu	ROM	12.11.68	1		Bucuresti	30 Jan
19.11	Grit	Hammer	GER	4.6.66	2	OD	Jena	13 Jun
18.96	Ines	Wittich	GER	14.11.69	1		Essen	29 May
18.89	Irina	Khudorozhkina	RUS	13.10.68	1	CISM	Tours	29 Aug
18.77		Dong Bo	CHN	.2.71			Shijiazhuang	23 Apr
	(30)							
18.74		Wang Hong	CHN	.4.70	1		Chengdu	16 Apr
18.66		He Xiuqin	CHN	18.3.67	4	NC	Jinan	6 Jun
18.65		Wang Hui	CHN	6.7.73	8	NG	Beijing	8 Sep
18.60	Herminia	Fernández	CUB	4.11.67	1		Habana	9 Jul
18.55	Ramona	Pagel	USA	10.11.61	5	Banes	São Paulo	16 May
18.51		Tian Xiue	CHN	4.10.71	9	NG	Beijing	8 Sep
18.49		Zheng Hui	CHN	.12.73			Shijiazhuang	2 Apr
18.31	Krystyna	Danilczyk	POL	14.1.68	1	v2N	Praha	17 Jul
18.24		Zhou Shuqin	CHN	.1.68	8	NC	Jinan	6 Jun
18.13i	Marina	Antonyuk	RUS	12.5.62	1		Chelyabinsk	22 Jan
	(40)							
18.12	Corrie	de Bruin	HOL	26.10.76	1	APM	Hengelo	20 Jun

Mark	Name		Nat	Born	Pos	Meet	Venue	Date
18.10	Livia	Mehes	ROM	6.3.65	2	NC	Bucuresti	4 Sep
18.02	Danijela	Curovic	YUG	7.3.74	1	Balk-j	Thessaloniki	11 Jul
18.00		Cheng Xiaoyan	CHN	75	3		Beijing	27 Mar
17.93	Marika	Tuliniemi	FIN	19.7.74	1	EJ	San Sebastián	30 Jul
17.92i	Irina	Korzhanenko	RUS	16.5.74	1		Minsk	27 Feb
17.81i	Natalya	Gurskaya	BLS	15.1.72	2		Gomel	29 Jan
17.81		Liu Ying	CHN	21.1.74			Shijiazhuang	2 Apr
17.78i	Nadezhda	Lukyniv	UKR	14.5.68	3	NC	Kiev	13 Feb
17.77	Jacqueline	Goormachtigh	HOL	28.2.70	1		Vught	16 May
	(50)							
17.76	Deborah	Dunant	HOL	3.4.66	2	APM	Hengelo	20 Jun
17.76	Yekaterina	Shishchenko	UKR	24.12.71	1		Donetsk	29 Jun
17.73i	Agnese	Maffeis	ITA	9.3.65	1		Pesaro	24 Jan
17.70	Yumileisis	Cumba	CUB	4.2.75	2		Habana	3 Jul
17.68	Myrtle	Augee	GBR	4.2.65	1	v GBR	Edinburgh	2 Jul
17.65	Heike	Hopfer	GER	28.2.71	1		Berlin	8 Jun
17.56	Pam	Dukes	USA	15.5.64	1		San Luis Obispo	20 Mar
17.55i	Margarita	Ramos	ESP	26.6.66	4		Paris	20 Feb
17.54	Noelvis	Balanten	CUB	24.6.72	3		Habana	3 Jul
17.53	Natasa	Erjavec	SLO	15.5.68	1		Ljubljana	7 May
	(60)							
17.53		Yu Juan	CHN		1		Shanghai	10 Apr
17.51i	Lyudmila	Voyevudskaya	RUS	22.6.59	2		Moskva	13 Feb
17.51i	Agnes	Deselaers	GER	12.11.68	6	NC	Sindelfingen	28 Feb
17.40i	Mara	Rosolen	ITA	27.7.65	2		Genova	10 Feb
17.40	Rica	Brown	USA	3.4.69	2		San Luis Obispo	20 Mar
17.36	Dawn	Dumble	USA	25.2.72	1		Tucson	26 May
17.29	Virdzhinia	Tsurtsurika	RUS	20.11.68	1		Moskva	14 May
17.28	Yelena	Baltabayeva	KZK	5.11.62	4	Znam	Moskva	12 Jun
17.19	Stevanie	Wadsworth	USA	19.3.72	1		Austin	20 May
17.11	Elisangela	Adriano	BRA	27.7.72	1		Rio de Janeiro	27 Jun
	(70)							
17.10i	Anastasia	Pavlova	RUS	16.6.68	2		Sankt Peterburg	23 Jan
17.09i	Momika	Raizgiene	LIT	14.4.65	1		Panevezys	3 Feb
17.07i	Olga	Ilyina	RUS	7.1.73	1		Volgograd	22 Jan
17.07	Nadine	Kleinert	GER	20.10.75	2	EJ	San Sebastián	30 Jul
16.93i	Heike	Hartwig	GER	30.12.62	1		Berlin	17 Jan
16.91i	Danyel	Mitchell	USA	16.9.72	1	NCAA	Indianapolis	13 Mar
16.85i	Eileen	Vanisi	USA	28.3.72	2	NCAA	Indianapolis	13 Mar
16.76	Teresa	Machado	POR	22.7.69	1		São Jacinto	4 Apr
16.76	Karoliina	Lundahl	FIN	30.6.68	2		Limassol	5 Jun
16.76	Irina	Zhuk	UKR	15.1.66	1		Dnepropetrovsk	1 Aug
	(80)							
16.76	Elena	Hila	ROM	20.5.74	1	NC-j	Bucuresti	8 Aug
16.72	Kathrin	Koch	GER	23.4.68	1		Bloomington	1 May
16.72	Elena	Tapîrlan	ROM	4.2.74	2		Bucuresti	3 Jul
16.71	Valeyta	Althouse	USA	7.1.74	2		Berkeley	21 May
16.66	Claudia	Mues	GER	3.1.75	4	EJ	San Sebastián	30 Jul
16.65i	Maria	Tranchina	ITA	10.2.68	3		Genova	10 Feb
16.64i	Melisa	Weis	USA	22.5.71	4	NCAA	Indianapolis	13 Mar
16.62	Zdenka	Silhavá	TCH	15.6.54	1	PA	Praha	17 Jun
16.56	Asta	Ovaska	FIN	29.7.63	1	NC	Mikkeli	1 Aug
16.54	Peggy	Pollock	USA	1.5.60	6	NC	Eugene	19 Jun
	(90)							
16.53	Sona	Vasícková	TCH	14.3.62	1	NC	Jablonec nad Nisou	4 Jul
16.50	Renata	Katewicz	POL	2.5.65	2		Lublin	4 Jun
16.49	Beth	Bunge	USA	30.1.64	1		Columbia	20 Mar
16.46	Christy	Barrett	USA	24.8.69	1		Columbia	16 May
16.43	Manuela	Torazza	ITA	27.6.68	2		Pesaro	16 May
16.42	Sevgi	Sen	TUR	31.12.67				
16.40	Nadezhda	Frantseva	RUS	2.10.71	4		Rostov na Donu	15 Jul
16.34	Larisa	Lapa	UKR	9.4.72	1		Kiev	2 May
16.33	Alina	Pupo	CUB	9.3.75	2	PAJ	Winnipeg	17 Jul
16.30	Daniela	Costian	AUS	30.4.65	1	NC	Brisbane	6 Mar
	(100)							
16.30	JoAnn	Hacker	USA	23.9.70	1		Arlington	1 May

Mark		Name	Nat	Born	Date
16.28	Eha	Rünne	EST	63	22 Jun
16.27	Linda-Marie	Mårtensson	SWE	71	7 Jul
16.22	Aya	Suzuki	JPN	67	29 Apr
16.21	Jenni	Whelchel	USA	70	8 May
16.20i	Laverne	Eve	BAH	65	4 Mar
16.14	Kristen	Heaston	USA	75	19 Jun
16.13i	Maggie	Lynes	GBR	63	11 Dec
16.12	Fotini	Kyriakidou	GRE	71	16 May
16.10	Janet	Hill	USA	70	29 May
	(110)				
16.10	Nathalie	Bellotti	FRA	67	19 Jun
15.80	Sharon	Andrews	GBR	67	30 Jul
16.09i	Natalya	Shariy	UKR	62	13 Feb
16.09	Elli	Evangelidou	CYP	68	22 Apr
16.08		Lee Myung-sun	KOR	76	2 Dec
16.04	Edith	Krauss	GER	64	22 Jun
16.02	Paulette	Mitchell	USA	72	1 May
16.00	Chris	King	NZL	64	29 Dec
15.96	Mónika	Stefanovics	HUN	70	13 Jun
15.94	Alice	Matejková	TCH	69	22 May
15.93i	Fabienne	Locuty	FRA	68	28 Feb
	(120)				
15.93	Heike	Göppner	GER	69	1 May
15.92	Greet	Meulemeester	BEL	69	30 Jul

Best outdoor marks for athletes with indoor seasonal bests

Mark	Name	Pos	Meet	Venue	Date
19.23	Peleshenko	1	Znam	Moskva	12 Jun
18.81	Ciobanu	2		Bucuresti	30 May
18.17	Li Xiaoyun	2	EAsiG	Shanghai	16 May
18.07	Antonyuk	1		Yekaterinburg	29 May
17.70	Lukyniv	2	NC	Kiev	2 Jul
17.54	Ramos	1		Villanova	13 Feb
17.52	Maffeis	1		Lecco	1 May
17.40	Voyevudskaya	2		Rostov na Donu	15 Jul
17.08	Deselaers	2		Wipperfürth	15 May
17.02	Korzharenko	1		Lübeck	26 Jun
16.62	Tranchina	1		Pesaro	16 May
16.61	Weis	4	NC	Eugene	19 Jun
16.58	Rosolen	3		Limassol	5 Jun
16.56	Vanisi	3	USOF	San Antonio	1 Aug
16.49	Mitchell	1		Knoxville	16 May
16.41	Gurskaya	Q	NC	Gomel	23 Jul

16.15 Khorkhulyova 9 Jun | 16.10 Lynes 22 May | 16.02 Raizgiene 29 May | 15.90 Locuty 9 May

Drugs ban

Mark	Name	Pos	Meet	Venue	Date
20.00	Zhou Tianhua ¶	1	NG	Beijing	8 Sep

Note Chinese lists only to 17.51, so no doubt mnay more would be listed

DISCUS

Mark		Name	Nat	Born	Pos	Meet	Venue	Date
68.14	Larisa	Korotkevich	RUS	3.1.67	1		Vénissieux	2 Jul
67.52		Korotkevich			1	NC	Moskva	20 Jun
67.40	Olga	Burova	RUS	17.9.63	1	WC	Stuttgart	19 Aug
67.22		Korotkevich			1		Stavropol	30 May
66.62		Korotkevich			1		Krasnodar	8 May
66.32	Ellina	Zvereva	BLS	16.11.60	1		Bruxelles	12 Jun
66.08		Cao Qi	CHN	.1.74	1	NG	Beijing	12 Sep
66.02	Daniela	Costian	AUS	30.4.65	1		Brisbane	14 Feb
65.96	Maritza	Martén	CUB	16.8.63	1		Salamanca	27 Jul
65.94	Renata	Katewicz	POL	2.5.65	1		Lublin	4 Jun
65.64		Burova			1	ISTAF	Berlin	27 Aug
65.54		Zvereva			1		Bialystok	28 Aug
65.36		Costian			2	WC	Stuttgart	19 Aug
65.26		Zvereva			1	Walas	Krakow	1 Jul
65.26		Min Chunfeng	CHN	17.3.69	3	WC	Stuttgart	19 Aug
65.16	Nicoleta	Grasu	ROM	17.9.71	1		Snagov	22 May
65.14	Manuela	Tîrneci (10)	ROM	26.2.69	1		Bucuresti	29 May
65.12		Burova			1	Gugl	Linz	25 Aug
65.04		Zvereva			1	NC	Gomel	24 Jul
64.94		Korotkevich			1		Reims	30 Jun
64.94		Martén			1		Rhede	6 Aug
64.88		Costian			1	Lausit	Cottbus	23 Jun
64.70		Martén			1		Las Tunas	3 Apr
64.70		Martén			1	Barr	Habana	23 May
64.70		Costian			2	ISTAF	Berlin	27 Aug
64.68		Burova			2	NC	Moskva	20 Jun
64.62	Austrute	Mikelyte	LIT	5.5.69	1		Kaunas	22 May
64.62		Luan Zhili	CHN	6.1.73	Q	NC	Jinan	3 Jun
64.62		Martén			4	WC	Stuttgart	19 Aug
64.60		Martén			1		La Coruña	16 Jul
	(30/12)							
64.42		Zhao Yonghua	CHN	22.1.69	2	NG	Beijing	12 Sep
64.06	Ilke	Wyludda	GER	28.3.69	Q	WC	Stuttgart	17 Aug
64.00		Qiu Qiaoping	CHN	31.10.71	1		Beijing	3 May
63.92	Vladimíra	Malátová	TCH	15.5.67	1		Limassol	5 Jun
63.90	Larisa	Mikhalchenko	UKR	16.5.63	2		Reims	30 Jun
63.80		Zhang Hui	CHN	15.8.67			Beijing	31 Jul
63.70	Teresa	Machado	POR	22.7.69	1		São Jacinto	8 Aug
63.52	Connie	Price-Smith	USA	3.6.62	1	NC	Eugene	18 Jun
	(20)							

Mark	Name		Nat	Born	Pos	Meet	Venue	Date
63.24	Antonina	Patoka	RUS	12.1.64	2	Lausit	Cottbus	23 Jun
62.92	Anja	Gündler	GER	18.3.72	5	WC	Stuttgart	19 Aug
62.80	Jana	Lauren	GER	28.6.70	1		Berlin	11 May
62.64		Bao Dongying	CHN	13.4.73	4	NG	Beijing	12 Sep
62.62	Lyudmila	Filiminova	BLS	22.3.71	2		Grodno	4 May
62.60		Zhang Cuilan	CHN	.4.73	1		Shijiazhuang	26 Apr
62.54	Agnese	Maffeis	ITA	9.3.65	1		Tirrenia	22 Jun
62.52	Barbara	Hechavarría	CUB	6.8.66	6	WC	Stuttgart	19 Aug
62.32	Olga	Nikishina	UKR	29.4.66	1	NC	Kiev	3 Jul
62.06	Franka	Dietzsch	GER	22.1.68	8	WC	Stuttgart	19 Aug
	(30)							
61.98	Cristina	Boit	ROM	14.5.68	3		Bucuresti	29 May
61.94	Ursula	Weber	AUT	26.9.60	1		Amstetten	15 May
61.80	Mette	Bergmann	NOR	9.11.62	1		Holte	6 Jul
61.64	Valentina	Ivanova	RUS	1.5.63	1		Togliatti	16 Aug
61.50	Irina	Shabanova	RUS	4.3.64	1		Khimki	16 May
61.24		Chang Xinhong	CHN	.3.74	2	NC	Jinan	4 Jun
61.22	Ilona	Zakharchenko	UKR	16.6.67	2		Odessa	21 May
61.18	Svetla	Mitkova	BUL	17.6.64	Q	WC	Stuttgart	17 Aug
61.06	Zdenka	Silhavá	TCH	15.6.54	3		Nitra	28 Aug
60.80	Simone	Schmitt	GER	5.12.71	3		Halle	15 May
	(40)							
60.72	Jackie	McKernan	GBR	1.7.65	2	WUG	Buffalo	18 Jul
60.58		Wu Guihua	CHN	.10.70	2		Shijiazhuang	26 Apr
60.54	Irina	Grachova	RUS	11.1.63	2		Khimki	16 May
60.52	Alice	Matejková	TCH	11.1.69	4	v2N	Nitra	28 Aug
60.48	Marzena	Wysocka	POL	17.2.69	1	NC	Kielce	25 Jul
60.36	Jacqueline	Goormachtigh	HOL	28.2.70	1		Rotterdam	11 Jul
60.30		Wang Jinling	CHN	.10.65	4		Beijing	3 May
60.20	Ursula	Kreutel	GER	14.9.65	1		Crailsheim	17 Jul
60.16	Kristin	Kuehl	USA	30.7.70	2	NC	Eugene	18 Jun
59.98	Olga	Gómez	CUB	30.6.66	2		Habana	19 Feb
	(50)							
59.94		Qiu Ying	CHN	.5.71	6		Beijing	3 May
59.86		Cheng Xianhong	CHN	.10.68			Shijiazhuang	26 Apr
59.80		Jiang Qunhua	CHN	26.9.74	7		Beijing	3 May
59.80	Gabriele	Reinsch	GER	23.9.63	3	APM	Hengelo	20 Jun
59.80		Sun Hui	CHN				Beijing	14 Aug
59.78	Vilija	Zubaityté	LIT	8.11.63	2	NC	Vilnius	19 Jun
59.74		Xing Ailan	CHN	23.2.65	8		Beijing	3 May
59.70	Katerina	Vogoli	GRE	30.1.70	1		Khania	6 Jun
59.68	Atanaska	Angelova	BUL	21.9.72	1		Sofia	29 May
59.64	Astrid	Kumbernuss	GER	5.2.70	3	NC	Duisburg	10 Jul
	(60)							
59.50	Isabelle	Devaluez	FRA	17.3.66	1		Toulouse	19 May
59.30	Marie Paule	Geldhof	BEL	27.2.59	1		Eeklo	29 Aug
59.04	Kathrin	Koch	GER	23.4.68	1		Indianapolis	8 May
58.94	Carla	Garrett	USA	31.7.67	3	NC	Eugene	18 Jun
58.90		Li Qiumei	CHN	.9.74	1		Beijing	16 May
58.78	Agnès	Teppe	FRA	4.5.68	1		Salon-de-Provece	20 Feb
58.74	Irina	Yatchenko	BLS	30.10.65	Q	NC	Gomel	24 Jul
58.64	Dagmar	Galler	GER	20.12.61	4	APM	Hengelo	20 Jun
58.58	Katalin	Csöke	HUN	26.1.57	1		Budapest	10 Jul
58.52	Ramona	Pagel	USA	10.11.61	1		La Jolla	1 May
	(70)							
58.52		Wan Dong	CHN		1		Maebashi	2 May
58.48		Hu Honglian	CHN		1		Chengdu	17 Apr
58.40	Danijela	Curovic	YUG	7.3.74	1		Beograd	29 May
58.40	Theresa	Brick	CAN	4.5.65	1		Winnipeg	12 Jun
58.34	Yelena	Antonova	UKR	16.6.72	1		Donetsk	30 Jun
58.20	Viktoria	Boyko	UKR	20.1.74	1B		Yalta	24 Jan
58.14	Natalya	Sadova	RUS	7.2.72	1		Dzerzhinsk	28 Aug
58.00	Pam	Dukes	USA	15.5.64	2	MSR	Walnut	17 Apr
57.92	Marlen	Sánchez	CUB	12.1.71	2		Habana	5 Mar
57.82	Janet	Hill	USA	28.8.70	1		Walnut	18 May
	(80)							

Mark	Name		Nat	Born	Pos	Meet	Venue	Date
57.76	Lacy	Barnes	USA	23.12.64	3	S&W	Modesto	8 May
57.56		Li Shimei	CHN	68	8	NC	Jinan	4 Jun
57.56	Joanna	Wisniewska	POL	24.5.72	4		Bialystok	28 Aug
57.44	Anastasia	Kelesidou	GRE	28.11.72	1		Thessaloniki	18 Jul
57.42	Dawn	Dumble	USA	25.2.72	4	S&W	Modesto	8 May
57.24	Tatyana	Lugovskaya	UKR	17.4.69	4		Kiev	16 May
57.20	Natalya	Ampleyeva	BLS	25.9.72	1		Grodno	25 Jul
57.08	Sabine	Bieber	AUT	4.11.70	2		Wien	8 May
57.04	Danyel	Mitchell	USA	16.9.72	2		Knoxville	15 May
56.96	Angeles (90)	Barreiro	ESP	26.7.63	1		Getafe	25 May
56.92	Eha	Rünne	EST	25.5.63	2	EP/C2	København	12 Jun
56.86	Cathy	Griffin	CAN	18.9.69	2		Winnipeg	12 Jun
56.74	Ivana	Holubová	SVK	24.1.72	1		Nitra	23 May
56.66	Sonia	Godall	ESP	28.3.68	1		Barcelona	1 Aug
56.40		Zhang Yujin	CHN	.70	2		Jinan	1 Apr
56.28	Nanette	Van der Walt	RSA	22.2.59	1		Pietersburg	6 Apr
56.18	Corrie	de Bruin	HOL	23.10.76	1		Den Haag	23 May
55.90	Larisa	Zakorko	UKR	21.2.64	3		Odessa	21 May
55.74	Silke	Hachenberg	GER	2.10.68	2		Leverkusen	7 Jul
55.74	Amelia (100)	Moreira	BRA	30.7.65	1		Bad Köstritz	23 Sep

Mark	Name		Nat	Born	Date
55.56	Elju	Kubi	EST	51	4 Aug
55.48	Stella	Tsikouna	GRE	72	27 Mar
55.42	Mariya	Vavilova	RUS	73	25 Apr
55.38	Monia	Kari	TUN	71	17 Jun
55.32	Maricela	Bristel	CUB	71	23 May
55.26	Lizette	Etsebeth	RSA	63	26 Mar
55.22	Alison	Lever	AUS	72	27 Nov
55.20	Beatrice	Faumuina	NZL	74	23 Jan
55.18	Lynda	Lipson	USA	71	18 Jun
55.14	Sharon (110)	Andrews	GBR	67	6 Jun
55.14	Maria !sabel	Urrutia	COL	65	3 Jul
55.06	Suzy	Powell	USA	76	27 Jun
55.04	Zoubida	Laayouni	MAR	56	29 May
55.04	Liliana	Martinelli	ARG	70	25 Oct
54.90	Stacey	Schroeder	USA	74	3 Jun
54.74	Debbie	Callaway	GBR	64	22 Aug
54.68	Alice	Meyer	FRA	72	11 Jul
54.56	Heike	Hopfer	GER	71	11 May
54.50	Ikuko	Kitamori	JPN	63	5 Jun
54.50	Areti (120)	Abatzi	GRE	74	11 Jul
54.50		Yu Qingmei	CHN	J	13 Nov
54.40	Tracy	Axten	GBR	63	17 Jul
54.32	Kati	Siltovuori	FIN	71	26 Jun
54.24	Nicola	Talbot	GBR	72	15 May
54.20	Mara	Rosolen	ITA	65	22 Jun
54.18	Kirsi	Lindfors	FIN	75	23 Jun
54.16	Lyudmila	Starovoytova	BLS	74	20 Jun
54.14	Marina	Astafyeva	RUS	71	30 May
54.14	Maria	Marello	ITA	61	22 Jun
54.10	Oksana (130)	Andrusina	RUS	73	13 Jun
54.08	Kelly	Bodiford	USA		16 Apr

Note Chinese lists seen only to 56.40

HAMMER

Mark	Name		Nat	Born	Pos	Meet	Venue	Date
64.64	Olga	Kuzenkova	RUS	4.10.70	1		Krasnodar	20 Feb
64.12		Kuzenkova			1		Rostov na Donu	17 Jul
63.70	Svetlana	Sudak	BLS	17.11.71	1		Grodno	4 May
62.60		Kuzenkova			1		Cork	9 Jul
62.52	Mihaela	Melinte	ROM	27.3.75	1	NC-j	Bucuresti	8 Aug
62.34		Kuzenkova			1		Moskva	27 Jan
62.10		Kuzenkova			1	Znam	Moskva	12 Jun
61.48		Kuzenkova			1		Vladimir	14 Aug
60.90	Aya	Suzuki	JPN	18.11.67	1		Tokyo	23 Nov
60.34		Kuzenkova			1	NC	Moskva	19 Jun
59.80	Natalya	Vasilenko	UKR	15.8.74	1	NC-j	Chernigov	26 Jun
59.62	Lyudmila	Gubkina	BLS	28.5.72	1		Pinsk	6 Jul
59.50	Lyubov	Karpova	RUS	14.8.57	1		Moskva	6 Aug
59.06	Natalya	Panarina	RUS	6.5.75	1		Chelyabinsk	6 Jun
58.90	Debbie	Sosimenko	AUS	5.4.74	1		Hobart	17 Jan
58.60		Vasilenko			1		Kiev	15 May
58.44		Vasilenko			1		Yalta	23 Jan
58.36	Oksana	Zatsepilova (10)	RUS	20.4.74	2		Moskva	6 Aug
58.26		Sosimenko			1		Sydney	5 Jun
58.24	Marina (20/11)	Pirog	UKR	74	2	NC-j	Chernigov	26 Jun
58.16	Viktoriya	Polyanskaya	RUS	71	1		Krasnodar	25 Apr
58.10	Natalya	Ignatova	RUS	3.1.74	2		Chelyabinsk	6 Jun
58.10	Oksana	Silchenko	BLS	10.8.70	1		Grodno	25 Jul
57.96	Livia	Mehes	ROM	6.3.65	2	NC	Bucuresti	5 Sep

Mark	Name		Nat	Born	Pos	Meet	Venue	Date
56.76	Esther	Augee	GBR	1.1.64	1		Bromley	15 May
56.56	Lorraine	Shaw	GBR	2.4.68	1		Gloucester	26 Sep
56.44	Yelena	Grankina	UKR	30.6.74	2		Kiev	2 May
56.26	Theresa	Brick	CAN	4.5.65	1		Winnipeg	12 Jun
56.18	Sonja	Fitts	USA	4.10.70	1		Jamaica	16 Apr
	(20)							
56.00	Tatyana	Konstantinova	RUS	70	3		Krasnodar	20 Feb
55.42	Simone	Mathes	GER	13.3.75	1	3N-j	Lübeck	16 Jun
54.84	Olga	Malakhova	UKR	25.8.71	2		Kiev	15 May
54.80	Alice	Meyer	FRA	19.5.72	1		Montreuil	5 May
54.40	Bonnie	Edmondson	USA	17.4.64	1		Dedham	5 Jun
54.34	Tatyana	Demina	BLS	20.9.73	3		Grodno	4 May
54.32	Irina	Lungu	ROM	5.4.75			Bucuresti	6 Jun
54.02	Ann	Gardner	GBR	11.10.68	1		Loughborough	19 May
53.80	Yulia	Aleksandrovskaya	UKR	8.5.70	3		Kiev	15 May
53.64	Marion	Große/Rammelkamp	GER	27.12.68			Leverkusen	24 Jul
	(30)							
53.58	Liz	Legault	USA	4.5.70	2	NC	Eugene	15 Jun
53.20	Cécile	Lignot	FRA	19.11.71	1		Clermont-Ferrand	20 Jun
53.10	Tatyana	Lishchuk	UKR	18.1.73	1		Kiev	2 May

Mark	Name		Nat	Born	Date
52.90	Denise	Passmore	AUS	74	21 Feb
52.90	Irina	Kuznetsova	RUS	75	16 May
52.84	Fiona	Whitehead	GBR	70	29 Jun
52.76	Teresa	Game	NZL	73	25 Feb
52.62	Diana	Holden	GBR	75	3 Aug
52.60	Natalya	Kozhenyakina	BLS	75	20 Jun
	(40)				
52.16	Veronika	Ushakova	RUS	77	6 Jun
52.00	Alexandra	Earl-Given	USA	70	2 May

JAVELIN

Mark	Name		Nat	Born	Pos	Meet	Venue	Date
72.12	Trine	Hattestad	NOR	18.4.66	1	Bisl	Oslo	10 Jul
70.44		Hattestad			1	ISTAF	Berlin	27 Aug
69.96		Hattestad			1		Byrkjelo	8 Aug
69.18		Hattestad			1	WC	Stuttgart	22 Aug
68.96	Natalya	Shikolenko	BLS	1.8.64	1		Hamina	8 Jun
67.96		Hattestad			1	WK	Zürich	4 Aug
67.94	Karen	Forkel	GER	24.9.70	2	ISTAF	Berlin	27 Aug
67.92		Hattestad			1	VD	Bruxelles	3 Sep
67.46		N Shikolenko			3	ISTAF	Berlin	27 Aug
66.52		Hattestad			QA	WC	Stuttgart	21 Aug
66.36		N Shikolenko			1	ASV	Köln	1 Aug
66.34	Terese	Nekrosaite	LIT	19.10.61	1		Riga	29 May
66.24		Hattestad			2	ASV	Köln	1 Aug
66.20		Hattestad			1		Floro	22 May
66.16		N Shikolenko			2	VD	Bruxelles	3 Sep
65.98		Hattestad			1		Drammen	31 May
65.80		Forkel			2	WC	Stuttgart	22 Aug
65.80	Silke	Renk	GER	30.6.67	4	ISTAF	Berlin	27 Aug
65.68		N Shikolenko			1	OD	Jena	13 Jun
65.64		N Shikolenko			3	WC	Stuttgart	22 Aug
65.62	Felicia	Tilea	ROM	29.9.67	2	Bisl	Oslo	10 Jul
65.46		Renk			1	NC	Duisburg	10 Jul
65.44		Ha Xiaoyan	CHN	30.1.72	1	NG	Beijing	9 Sep
65.36		N Shikolenko			1		Krasnodar	20 Feb
65.36		Forkel			2	OD	Jena	13 Jun
65.36	Yekaterina	Ivakina	RUS	4.12.64	1	NC	Moskva	20 Jun
65.34		Ivakina			5	ISTAF	Berlin	27 Aug
65.26		Renk			1		Gladbeck	26 Jun
65.18	Tatyana	Shikolenko	BLS	10.5.68	4	WC	Stuttgart	22 Aug
65.12		Ivakina			5	WC	Stuttgart	22 Aug
65.02		N Shikolenko			3	Bisl	Oslo	10 Jul
65.00		Hattestad			1		Århus	1 Jul
	(32/10)							
64.98	Päivi	Alafrantti	FIN	8.5.64	1	vSWE	Stockholm	28 Aug
64.68		Han Jinli	CHN	.1.66			Shijiazhuang	25 Apr
64.54	Yelena	Medvedeva	RUS	9.7.65	2		Krasnodar	20 Feb
64.46	Martine	Bègue	FRA	22.12.69	1	NC	Annecy	23 Jul

Mark	Name		Nat	Born	Pos	Meet	Venue	Date
64.16		Zhao Yuhong	CHN	.6.72			Beijing	13 Mar
64.06		Zhang Li	CHN	26.6.61	2	NG	Beijing	9 Sep
63.96	Genowefa	Patla	POL	17.10.62	1		Dreux	30 May
63.92		Wang Lianyun	CHN	.10.69	1		Shanghai	11 Apr
63.88	Steffi	Nerius	GER	1.7.72	2	NC	Dortmund	10 Jul
63.74	Sueli	Pereira Santos	BRA	8.1.65	1		La Chaux de Fonds	8 Aug
	(20)							
63.68	Irina	Kostyuchenko	UKR	11.5.61	1		Kiev	16 May
63.46		Zhang Guihua	CHN	.3.70	1		Shijiazhuang	25 Apr
63.44	Dulce	Garcia ¶	CUB	2.7.65	1	NC	Habana	13 May
62.98	Donna	Mayhew	USA	20.6.60	1	NC	Eugene	19 Jun
62.30	Jette Ø	Jeppesen	DEN	14.3.64	1H		Randers	20 Jun
62.24		Luo Zhonghua	CHN	26.1.69	Q	NC	Jinan	2 Jun
62.18	Tatyana	Sudarikova	RUS	28.5.73	1		Dzerzhinsk	28 Aug
62.12		Song Ruiling	CHN	25.1.66			Shijiazhuang	25 Apr
62.10		Xu Demei	CHN	2.5.67	3	NG	Beijing	9 Sep
61.56	Dörthe	Barby	GER	21.6.73	2		Berlin	4 Sep
	(30)							
61.54	Claudia	Isaila	ROM	17.7.73	7	WC	Stuttgart	22 Aug
61.48	Isel	López	CUB	11.7.70	1	CAG	Ponce	25 Nov
61.44		Lee Young-sun	KOR	21.2.74	2	EAsiG	Shanghai	15 May
61.42	Carla	Muresan	ROM	17.2.67	1		Bucuresti	3 Jul
61.38	Ingrid	Thyssen	GER	9.1.56	1		Sittard	28 May
61.38	Heli	Rantanen	FIN	26.2.70	2		Hamina	8 Jun
61.38	Svetlana	Titova	RUS	69	2	NC	Moskva	20 Jun
61.30	Kinga	Zsigmond	HUN	19.4.64	6	Bisl	Oslo	10 Jul
61.28	Kirsten	Hellier	NZL	6.10.69	1		Auckland	23 Jan
61.26	Heli	Tolkkinen	FIN	3.8.73	1		Skien	22 Aug
	(40)							
61.12	Natalya	Yermolovich	BLS	29.4.64	1		Mogilev	6 Jun
61.06		Zhao Yingping	CHN	.2.73	Q	NC	Jinan	2 Jun
61.04	Renata	Strasek	SLO	8.4.72	1		Limassol	5 Jun
60.96	Tanja	Damaske	GER	16.11.71	1		Berlin	20 Jun
60.90	Nathalie	Teppe	FRA	22.5.72	1	MedG	Narbonne	20 Jun
60.86	Louise	McPaul	AUS	24.1.69	1		Adelaide	14 Feb
60.86	Antoaneta	Selenska	BUL	8.6.63	1		Stara Zagora	24 Jul
60.70	Nadine	Auzeil	FRA	19.8.64	1		Belfort	25 Jun
60.68		Ding Fenghua	CHN	27.6.64	Q	NC	Jinan	2 Jun
60.64	Anna	Verouli	GRE	13.11.56	1		Rethimno	22 May
	(50)							
60.10	Shelley	Holroyd	GBR	17.5.73	1	AAA	Birmingham	16 Jul
60.06	Silke	Gast	GER	30.4.72	3		Berlin	4 Sep
60.00	Sonya	Radicheva	BUL	8.6.68	2		Stara Zagora	24 Jul
59.86	Susanne	Riewe	GER	26.5.70	4	OD	Jena	13 Jun
59.84	Oksana	Yarygina	UZB	24.12.72	2	AsiC	Manila	3 Dec
59.70		Xin Xiaoli	CHN	22.9.66	3		Shijiazhuang	26 Apr
59.64		Xiang Zhengfeng	CHN				Beijing	2 May
59.64		Liu Cui	CHN	.8.71	3	NC	Jinan	3 Jun
59.62		Tang Lishuang	CHN	25.2.66	4		Shijiazhuang	26 Apr
59.60	Xiomara	Rivero	CUB	22.12.68	2		Habana	5 Mar
	(60)							
59.58	Sharon	Gibson	GBR	31.12.61	2	AAA	Birmingham	16 Jul
59.52	Sonia	Bicet	CUB	1.4.71	3		Habana	5 Mar
59.50		Ma Ling	CHN	.7.66	1		Beijing	3 May
59.50	Antje	Zöllkau	GER	23.6.63	1		Otigheim	31 May
59.42		Zhang Ru	CHN	28.2.71	2		Beijing	3 May
59.38		Liang Chunlian	CHN	27.1.75	5		Shijiazhuang	26 Apr
59.36	Kirsty	Morrison	GBR	28.10.75	1		Hoo	4 Sep
59.20	Emi	Matsui	JPN	20.2.63	1		Ageo	17 Apr
59.14		Wang Jiling	CHN	.10.65	11	NG	Beijing	9 Sep
58.84	Rita	Ramanauskaite	LIT	22.2.70	2		Kaunas	5 Feb
	(70)							
58.74		Ni Chunyan	CHN				Guangzhou	22 Mar
58.64	Juliane	Hoffmann	GER	13.12.73	3		Halle	15 May
58.54	Yvonne	Reichardt	GER	5.2.73	1		Obernai	11 Sep
58.42	Angeliki	Tsialakoudi	GRE	10.5.76	1		Athinai	29 May

Mark	Name		Nat	Born	Pos	Meet	Venue	Date
58.34	Jeanette	Völker	GER	10.5.72	2		Rosenheim	11 Sep
58.32	Yelena	Svezhentseva	UZB	21.12.68	2		Dijon	13 Jun
58.26	Mikaela	Ingberg	FIN	29.7.74	2	3N-j	Skien	21 Aug
58.16	Christine	Gast	GER	30.4.72	4		Berlin	4 Sep
58.12	Akiko	Miyajima	JPN	17.9.66	1		Gifu	16 May
57.92	Joanna	Stone	AUS	1.10.72	1		Brisbane	4 Dec
	(80)							
57.86	Irina	Solodkaya	UKR	24.6.69	2	NC	Kiev	3 Jul
57.80	Aysel	Tas	TUR	21.10.64	1		Izmir	1 May
57.80	Adigoni	Vourdoli	GRE	4.4.75	1	NC-j	Thessaloniki	2 Jul
57.68	Kate	Farrow	AUS	6.5.67	1		Perth	7 Feb
57.64	Manuela	Alizadeh	GER	29.1.63	1		Stuttgart	31 Jul
57.60	Doreen	Karasiewicz	GER	21.7.74	5		Berlin	4 Sep
57.48	Nikola	Tomecková	TCH	15.6.74	1	PA	Praha	17 Jun
57.44	Ashley	Selman	USA	21.4.70	1	NCAA	New Orleans	4 Jun
57.40	Kaye	Nordstrom	NZL	30.5.68	2	NC	Wellington	7 Mar
57.34	Paula	Huhtaniemi	FIN	17.2.73	1		Pihtipudas	1 Jul
	(90)							
57.22	Rose-May	Poilagi	FRA	9.2.72	4	NC	Annecy	23 Jul
57.10	Monica	Tîrle	ROM	18.1.69	3	RomIC	Bucuresti	18 Jun
57.02	Lada	Chernova	RUS	70	4	Znam	Moskva	12 Jun
57.00	Maria Caridad	Alvárez	CUB	30.8.75	1	PAJ	Winnipeg	16 Jul
56.92	Tamami	Fujii	JPN	27.10.71	2	NC	Tokyo	11 Jun
56.90	Laverne	Eve	BAH	16.6.65	1	NC	Nassau	17 Jun
56.66	Olga	Ivankova	UKR	7.1.73	1		Donetsk	29 Jun
56.64	Nadezhda	Kobrin	UKR	21.1.72	3	NC	Kiev	3 Jul
56.56	Valerie	Tulloch	CAN	13.7.72	2	NCAA	New Orleans	4 Jun
56.54	Cindy	Herceg	USA	10.5.70	1		Atlanta	22 May
	(100)							

Mark	Name		Nat	Born	Date
56.48	Amanda	Liverton	GBR	72	13 Jun
56.42	Lyudmila	Konon	RUS	69	22 May
56.24		Liu Jingqian	CHN	74	9 Sep
56.20	Alexandra	Mays	GER	74	22 May
56.18	Kristina	Jazbinbek	SLO	65	14 Aug
56.10	Cristina	Larrea	ESP	66	4 Jul
56.04	Sue	Howland	AUS	60	16 May
56.04	Ágnes	Preisinger	HUN	73	17 Jul
55.98	Diane	Royle	GBR	59	8 May
55.94	Erica	Wheeler	USA	67	15 May
	(110)				
55.88	Ewa	Rybak	POL	74	30 May
55.68	Valentina	Belajic	CRO		23 May
55.68	Heather	Berlin	USA	72	19 Jun
55.64	Herminia	Bouza	CUB	65	13 May
55.62	Meg	Foster	USA	65	26 May
55.50	Lena	Åström	SWE	64	18 Jul
55.38	Efi	Karatopouzi	GRE	68	16 May
55.34	Natalya	Cherniyenko	UKR	65	16 May
55.26	Clova	Court	GBR	60	20 Jun
55.24	Jaana	Paananen	FIN	66	31 Aug
	(120)				
55.22	Monika	Brodschneider	AUT	70	8 Aug
55.06	Kim	Hyatt	USA	68	22 May
55.04	Anikó	Koczka/Ladányi	HUN	70	31 May
55.02	Ingrid	Lammertsma	HOL	67	4 Jul
55.10	Chizuru	Mizuno	JPN	67	8 Nov
54.86	Mirelada	Manjani	ALB	76	22 Apr
54.72	Nicole	Carroll	USA	68	3 Apr
54.72	Jingli	Han	CHN		9 Sep
54.60	Tatyana	Bazorkina	KZK	73	23 Jul
54.58	Katalin	Szegvári	HUN	70	14 Aug
	(130)				
54.56	Vijitha	Amarasekera	SRI	61	8 May
54.44	Shinobu	Deguchi	JPN	75	14 Nov
54.40	Odeyme	Palma	CUB	71	13 Mar
54.20	Odalis	Palma	CUB	75	13 Mar
54.18	Joanna	Kapusta	POL	67	24 Jul
54.16	Maret	Kalviste	EST	55	4 Jul
54.12	Dimitra	Sargioti	GRE	75	13 Jun
54.04	Silvana	Koren	CRO	73	28 Aug
54.00	Veronica	Becuzzi	ITA	71	7 Mar
54.00	Karin	Colberg	SWE	67	25 Jul
	(140)				

HEPTATHLON

Mark	Name		Nat	Born	Pos	Meet	Venue	Date
6837	Jackie	Joyner-Kersee	USA	3.3.62	1	WC	Stuttgart	17 Aug
	12.89/0.1	1.81 14.38	23.19/		7.04/1.4		43.76 2:14.49	
6797	Sabine	Braun	GER	19.1.65	2	WC	Stuttgart	17 Aug
	13.25/0.1	1.90 14.62	24.12/		6.54/1.0		53.44 2:17.82	
6770		Joyner-Kersee			1	NC	Eugene	16 Jun
	13.01w/3.1	1.85 15.37	23.40/1.3		7.07w/		41.64 2:22.78	
6750		Ma Miaolan	CHN	18.1.70	1	NG	Beijing	12 Sep
	13.28/1.5	1.89 14.98	23.86/		6.64/ 45.82 2:15.33			
6703	Tatyana	Blokhina	RUS	12.3.70	1	Decast	Talence	11 Sep
	13.69/-0.6	1.91 14.94	23.95/-0.4		5.99/-0.3		52.16 2:09.65	
6635	Svetlana	Buraga	BLS	4.9.65	3	WC	Stuttgart	17 Aug
	12.95/0.1	1.84 14.55	23.69/		6.58/-0.2		41.04 2:13.65	
6605		Blokhina			1	NC	Moskva	20 Jun
	13.55/	1.86 13.77	24.02/		6.23/ 51.32 2:11.48			
6594	Svetla	Dimitrova	BUL	27.1.70	1		Götzis	30 May
	13.21/0.1	1.66 14.88	23.30/0.4		6.60/0.3		46.00 2:09.62	

Mark	Name		Nat	Born	Pos	Meet	Venue	Date
6569		Blokhina			2		Götzis	30 May
	13.40/2.0	1.87 13.30	23.77/0.4		6.21w/2.3		46.74 2:09.27	
6510	Svetlana	Moskalets	RUS	1.11.69	1		Moskva	7 Aug
	13.40/	1.82 13.54	23.55/		6.70/ 41.82 2:15.87			
6508		Dimitrova			4	WC	Stuttgart	17 Aug
	12.85/0.1	1.60 15.46	23.10/		6.32/1.0		47.02 2:13.60	
6500	Birgit	Clarius	GER	18.3.65	1	NC	Vaterstetten	20 Jun
	13.61/1.3	1.81 15.22	24.69w/2.1		6.08/-0.6		50.20 2:11.29	
6493		Clarius			3		Götzis	30 May
	13.67/2.0	1.81 14.90	24.72/-1.0		6.18/1.6		47.66 2:08.33	
6477		Buraga			1	EP/C1	Tallinn	11 Jul
	13.21/-1.8	1.84 14.00	23.88/		6.51/1.2		41.28 2:16.84	
6470		Dimitrova			1		Brescia	16 May
	13.07/-0.4	1.66 15.50	24.21/-0.0		6.28/0.1		48.18 2:12.21	
6415	Larisa	Nikitina	RUS	29.4.65	2	NC	Moskva	20 Jun
	13.80/	1.83 15.41	25.01/		6.25/ 50.94 2:20.77			
6415		Dimitrova			2	Decast	Talence	11 Sep
	13.03/-0.6	1.61 13.94	23.37/-0.4		6.61/0.9		45.02 2:13.87	
6406	Irina	Tyukhay (10)	RUS	14.1.67	4		Götzis	30 May
	13.37/0.1	1.81 14.18	24.31/-1.0		6.60/0.8		40.90 2:17.03	
6394	Urszula	Wlodarczyk	POL	22.12.65	5	WC	Stuttgart	17 Aug
	13.41/0.1	1.81 14.00	24.14/0.1		6.52/-0.2		42.64 2:18.28	
6394		Zhu Yuqing	CHN	22.4.63	2	NG	Beijing	12 Sep
	13.05/1.5	1.83 15.07	24.15/		6.06/ 45.50 2:22.65			
6369	Tatyana	Zhuravlyova	RUS	19.12.67	3	NC	Moskva	20 Jun
	14.16/	1.77 14.10	24.46/		6.55/ 44.80 2:10.92			
6357	Kym	Carter	USA	12.3.64	6	WC	Stuttgart	17 Aug
	13.62/-0.4	1.84 15.41	24.23/-0.2		6.08/-0.1		36.84 2:09.82	
6343	Jane	Flemming	AUS	14.4.65	7	WC	Stuttgart	17 Aug
	13.08/0.1	1.75 14.03	23.49/		6.21/1.3		42.12 2:16.93	
6341		Clarius			8	WC	Stuttgart	17 Aug
	13.74/0.2	1.81 15.46	25.14/0.1		5.64/-1.5		50.14 2:10.00	
6339	Anzhela	Atroshchenko	BLS	13.11.70	2	EP/C1	Tallinn	11 Jul
	13.82/-1.6	1.81 13.30	24.24/0.3		6.27/-0.6		43.52 2:09.64	
6337	Taisia	Dobrovitskaya	BLS	8.12.67	1		Minsk	6 Jun
	12.8/1.6	1.84 13.36	23.8		6.25/1.2		36.54 2:12.9	
6330		Zhuravlyova			1	EP/A	Oulu	11 Jul
	14.38/-1.0	1.81 14.30	24.35/-1.9		6.53/1.6		42.56 2:13.11	
6328		Zhuravlyova			5		Götzis	30 May
	14.11/2.0	1.78 13.92	24.42/-1.0		6.60/1.0		39.14 2:08.21	
6308	Lyudmila	Mikhailova	RUS	12.4.69	1A		Krasnodar	18 May
	13.74/	1.83 12.41	23.94/		6.83/0.8		35.54 2:14.05	
6290		Dobrovitskaya			9	WC	Stuttgart	17 Aug
	13.47/0.1	1.81 12.96	23.85/		6.08/1.3		43.52 2:13.42	
	(30/18)							
6263	Rita	Ináncsi	HUN	6.1.71	6		Götzis	30 May
	13.80/0.4	1.72 14.62	24.67/1.5		6.40/1.2		46.30 2:17.29	
6260	Liliane	Nastase	ROM	1.8.62	2		Brescia	16 May
	13.24/-0.4	1.72 13.36	24.05/-0.0		6.33/0.2		41.84 2:13.87	
	(20)							
6259	Ghada	Shouaa	SYR	9.10.73	1		Manila	2 Dec
	14.08/	1.77 14.17	24.67/		6.17 50.08 2:16.95			
6256	Nathalie	Teppe	FRA	22.5.72	1	MedG	Narbonne	19 Jun
	14.05/-5.0	1.85 12.53	25.84/-2.0		5.95/0.8		58.52 2:16.12	
6249		Wu Suzhen	CHN	27.8.73	3	NG	Beijing	12 Sep
	13.42/1.5	1.79 13.19	24.84/		5.98/ 46.42 2:09.62			
6214	Petra	Vaideanu	ROM	24.8.65	8		Götzis	30 May
	14.08/1.3	1.75 14.41	25.64/1.5		6.22w/3.5		49.66 2:13.86	
6207	Beatrice	Mau	GER	20.2.71	9		Götzis	30 May
	14.05/0.4	1.72 13.13	24.52/0.1		6.20/-0.3		49.34 2:12.31	
6205		Liu Bo	CHN	12.3.72	4	NG	Beijing	12 Sep
	13.27/1.5	1.83 12.75	24.74/		6.08/ 36.06 2:06.44			
6196	Mona	Steigauf	GER	17.1.70	10		Götzis	30 May
	13.61/0.1	1.84 11.36	24.26/-1.0		6.38/0.5		39.88 2:12.84	
6188		Shi Guiqing	CHN	19.4.68	5	NG	Beijing	12 Sep
	13.65/	1.80 13.10	24.37/		6.39/ 38.76 2:15.42			

Mark	Name		Nat	Born	Pos Meet	Venue	Date
6179	Yelena	Afanasyeva	RUS	23.2.66		Chelyabinsk	7 Jun
	13.4	1.73 13.42	24.0		6.41	37.54 2:15.4	
6154		Mu Lianjuan	CHN	28.6.73	6 NG	Beijing	12 Sep
	13.46/1.5	1.80 12.91	24.22/		6.43/ 34.06	2:14.50	
	(30)						
6131	Birgit	Gautzsch	GER	14.12.67	2 NC	Vaterstetten	20 Jun
	13.64/1.3	1.78 13.05	23.92w/2.1		5.92/-1.4	41.58 2:14.08	
6112		Dong Yuping	CHN	1.3.63	7 NG	Beijing	12 Sep
	13.97/	1.77 13.93	24.83/		6.19/ 42.04	2:15.72	
6106	Helle	Aro	FIN	9.12.60	1 NC	Mikkeli	1 Aug
	14.26/-0.1	1.74 13.37	25.49/0.9		6.12/1.9	49.52 2:12.48	
6094		Liu Qing	CHN	.4.70	8 NG	Beijing	12 Sep
	13.73/	1.71 12.72	24.24/		6.23/ 42.20	2:13.64	
6092		Zhang Xiaohui	CHN	23.3.71	9 NG	Beijing	12 Sep
	13.42/1.5	1.71 13.38	24.43/		6.16/ 40.06	2:14.28	
6083	Bettina	Braag	GER	15.11.65	3 NC	Vaterstetten	20 Jun
	13.78/1.3	1.81 12.87	23.91w/2.1		5.80/-1.2	39.88 2:13.08	
6073	Tatyana	Alisyevich	BLS	22.1.69	4 EP/C1	Tallinn	11 Jul
	14.22/-1.6	1.63 13.49	24.18/0.3		5.85/-0.1	52.74 2:13.42	
6067	Tina	Rättyä	FIN	12.11.68	13 WC	Stuttgart	17 Aug
	13.84/-0.3	1.72 12.84	24.61/0.4		6.06/1.0	43.96 2:11.96	
6066	Irina	Vostrikova	RUS	30.8.70	1	Voronezh	25 Jul
	14.35/	1.86 14.79	27.03/		6.40/ 44.44	2:21.81	
6058	Catherine	Bond-Mills	CAN	20.9.67	1 NC	Coquitlam	31 Jul
	13.93/0.7	1.79 13.21	24.64w/2.3		6.14/-2.4	41.68 2:18.10	
	(40)						
6038	Kelly	Blair	USA	24.11.70	1 NCAA	New Orleans	3 Jun
	13.78w/	1.76 12.09	24.15/		6.22w/	42.88 2:19.80	
6038	DeDe	Nathan	USA	20.4.68	3 NC	Eugene	16 Jun
	13.91/	1.76 13.49	24.85/		6.23w/	44.40 2:22.90	
6028	Yurka	Khristova	BUL	19.1.68	1 NC	Sofia	13 Jun
	13.91/	1.84 13.04	24.68/		6.24/ 37.94	2:20.97	
6019	Maria	Kamrowska	POL	11.3.66	6 EP/A	Oulu	11 Jul
	13.56/-1.4	1.66 14.61	24.90/-3.8		5.93/1.0	41.00 2:12.59	
6008	Natalya	Popykina	RUS	11.12.70	2A	Krasnodar	18 May
	14.05/	1.83 11.86	24.58/		6.58/ 34.88	2:18.70	
5993	Marina	Shcherbina	UKR	5.1.68	1 NC	Kiev	6 Jun
	13.95/	1.71 14.44	25.35/		5.76w/2.1	43.78 2:11.30	
5962	Giuliana	Spada	ITA	18.4.71	1 NC	Bologna	3 Aug
	13.91/-0.5	1.69 12.46	25.16/-0.4		6.22/-3.3	43.42 2:13.52	
5957	Clova	Court	GBR	10.2.60	1 AAA	Horsham	20 Jun
	13.48w/	1.54 13.68	24.04/		5.74/ 55.26	2:25.15	
5955	Ines	Krause	GER	10.7.65	5 NC	Vaterstetten	20 Jun
	14.03/1.3	1.75 13.28	25.16w/2.1		6.07/-1.1	39.30 2:12.96	
5936	Zhanna	Budilovskaya	UKR	6.4.72	2 NC	Kiev	6 Jun
	14.58/	1.74 12.47	25.10/		6.16/ 44.06	2:13.00	
	(50)						
5935		Wang Wenxiang	CHN	.3.73	1	Shijiazhuang	24 Apr
	14.46	1.77 14.66	25.84		5.90	42.66 2:14.91	
5903	Magalys	Garcia	CUB	23.10.71	1 CAG	Ponce	28 Nov
	13.90/	1.73 13.26	24.62/		5.71/ 47.52	2:23.42	
5902	Marcela	Podracká	SVK	13.3.70	15 WC	Stuttgart	17 Aug
	14.48/-0.3	1.78 12.57	25.52/0.3		5.92/0.7	48.50 2:18.65	
5896		Wang Fang	CHN	.4.72	10 NG	Beijing	12 Sep
	14.10/	1.89 10.20	25.03/		6.20/ 38.84	2:17.72	
5895	Barbara	Erni	SUI	7.3.72	2 EP/B	Valladolid	11 Jul
	14.10/0.8	1.72 12.18	24.66w/3.5		5.99/0.9	41.74 2:13.50	
5892	Sharon	Jaklofsky	AUS	30.9.68	2 NCAA	New Orleans	3 Jun
	13.63/	1.76 13.32	25.21/		6.19/ 40.76	2:27.42	
5888	Odile	Lesage	FRA	28.6.69	3 MedG	Narbonne	19 Jun
	14.13/-5.0	1.85 12.58	26.45/-2.0		6.15/0.4	40.50 2:17.61	
5882	Lyubov	Borisova	RUS	6.1.66	2	Voronezh	25 Jul
	14.55/	1.80 13.19	25.47/		6.21/ 35.18	2:12.53	
5878	Virge	Naeris	EST	12.12.69	1 NC	Pärnu	30 May
	13.89/-0.2	1.82 12.40	25.72/-0.3		6.05/0.2	43.66 2:24.15	
5854		Fu Xiuhong	CHN	6.5.70	1	Shanghai	10 Apr
	14.0	1.83 14.18	25.36		5.95 34.78	2:19.34	
	(60)						

Mark	Name		Nat	Born	Pos	Meet	Venue	Date
5840A	Regla	Cardeñas	CUB	21.1.75	2	CAC	Cali	31 Jul
	13.9/1.4	1.74 13.44	24.80w/2.1		6.29/ 37.58	2:23.5		
5838		Ding Ying	CHN	.10.76	11	NG	Beijing	12 Sep
	13.71/	1.80 12.58	25.25/		6.19/ 38.14	2:26.59		
5836	Manuela	Marxer	LIE	6.8.65	15		Götzis	30 May
	13.79/2.0	1.72 11.74	24.88/0.1		6.01/1.7		38.38 2:13.24	
5827	Yelena	Volf	RUS	2.3.69	4A		Krasnodar	18 May
	14.45/	1.77 14.20	25.75/		6.39/ 40.36	2:29.61		
5826	Anu	Kaljurand	EST	16.4.69	1	TexR	Austin	1 Apr
5776	Larisa	Tarasyuk	RUS	14.6.70	5A		Krasnodar	18 May
	14.92/	1.77 14.57	25.35/		5.82/ 39.42	2:18.40		
5774	Denise	Lewis	GBR	27.8.72	2	AAA	Horsham	20 Jun
	14.00w/	1.72 12.07	25.46/		6.01/ 45.54	2:23.30		
5773		Zhang Yi	CHN	10.11.73	7	NC	Jinan	3 Jun
	14.20/	1.74 14.76	25.25/		5.61/ 36.70	2:16.25		
5766	Ingrid	Didden	BEL	27.6.68	18		Götzis	30 May
	14.48/0.4	1.69 13.07	26.01w/3.1		5.93/-1.3		49.16 2:20.88	
	(70)							
5761		Hu Liping	CHN	29.2.68	8	NC	Jinan	3 Jun
	13.84/	1.65 12.46	24.95/		5.89/ 39.74	2:14.20		
5760w	Joanne	Henry	NZL	2.10.71	1		Christchurch	19 Dec
	14.68/1.6	1.70 13.10	25.48W/4.7		6.03/-0.7		42.64 2:16.86	
5759	Svetlana	Kazanina	KZK	71	1	NC	Almaty	24 Jul
	15.48	1.78 13.06	25.44		5.94		42.90 2:14.84	
5745		Zeng Yujuan	CHN	23.3.71	3		Shijiazhuang	24 Apr
	14.56	1.71 13.83	25.74		6.39 45.60	2:35.37		
5742		Zhang Jianwei	CHN	.4.71	9	NC	Jinan	3 Jun
	14.20/	1.68 13.35	24.14/		5.92/ 35.84	2:19.46		
5740		Zou Ying	CHN	.7.74	10	NC	Jinan	3 Jun
	14.19/	1.74 12.02	25.38/		5.89/ 39.52	2:14.67		
5738	Natalya	Pavlova	RUS	72	1B		Illzach	8 Aug
	14.12/	1.73 13.04	25.67/		5.93/ 38.82	2:17.59		
5735	Wendi	Simmons	USA	28.7.69	1	MSR	Azusa	15 Apr
	14.07/	1.70 11.31	24.65/		6.26/ 35.12	2:16.39		
5729	Irina	Matyusheva	UKR	5.9.65	3	NC	Kiev	6 Jun
	13.92/	1.77 12.72	26.19/		5.88/ 35.94	2:14.10		
5715	Anoeschka	Daans	HOL	10.3.65	1	NC	Emmen	6 Jun
	14.58/	1.72 12.34	25.02/		5.92/ 41.10	2:17.65		
	(80)							
5709	Louise	McPaul	AUS	24.1.69	1		Sydney	10 Jan
	14.95/	1.79 12.96	26.29/		5.66/ 53.16	2:27.07		
5692	Karin	Periginelli	ITA	5.2.70	2	NC	Bologna	3 Aug
	14.50/-0.5	1.72 11.38	25.52/-0.4		5.85/-1.7		42.50 2:12.71	
5688	Natalya	Toropchina	RUS	71	8	NC	Moskva	20 Jun
	14.23/	1.68 12.49	26.04/		5.76/ 42.64	2:12.43		
5685	Silke	Knut	GER	27.7.72	1	NC-j	Vaterstetten	20 Jun
	14.11/	1.69 12.04	25.35/		5.92/ 41.32	2:18.57		
5678	Kathleen	Gutjahr	GER	27.7.75	1		Bernhausen	13 Jun
	14.35/	1.80 11.83	25.85/		5.62/ 43.88	2:19.21		
5675	Larisa	Teteryuk	UKR	24.12.70	4	NC	Kiev	6 Jun
	15.03w/	1.74 13.91	25.92/		5.67/ 44.10	2:18.36		
5675	Yelena	Kovalyova	RUS	28.2.73	1		Dzerzhinsk	30 Aug
	14.54/	1.77 12.79	25.94/		5.77/ 44.52	2:23.06		
5674		Tang Yixiu	CHN	65	13	NC	Jinan	3 Jun
	14.59/	1.68 13.28	25.17/		6.03/ 39.20	2:20.35		
5670	Clare	Look-Jaeger	USA	17.6.66	1		Los Angeles	20 Mar
5668	Gesine	Schmidt	GER	26.6.71	2		Aichach	19 Sep
	14.26/	1.67 10.90	24.78/		5.97/ 37.18	2:10.41		
	(90)							
5664	Yelena	Bolkun	UKR	26.2.67	21		Götzis	30 May
	14.43/0.4	1.72 12.36	25.63/0.4		5.98/1.4		36.80 2:14.30	
5656	Doris	Stelzmüller	SUI	13.3.63	22		Götzis	30 May
	14.08/1.3	1.63 12.37	25.13/1.5		6.04/1.5		37.84 2:16.70	
5656	Marieke	Veltman	USA	18.9.71	3	NCAA	New Orleans	3 Jun
	14.08/	1.67 10.63	24.44/		6.37w/		37.10 2:22.92	

WOMEN 1993

Mark	Name		Nat	Born	Pos	Meet	Venue	Date
5647	Sabine	Smieja	GER	23.6.71	6	NC	Vaterstetten	20 Jun
	14.57/0.5	1.78 10.95	25.55/0.6		5.95/-2.1		41.12 2:18.54	
5644	Terry	Roy	USA	26.1.73	1	USOF	San Antonio	31 Jul
5642	Kalleen	Madden	USA	30.8.71	1		Austin	20 May
	13.51w/	1.79						
5641w	Shana	Williams	USA	7.4.72	5	NC	Eugene	16 Jun
	13.86/	1.76 9.46	25.02/		6.31W/		31.38 2:15.38	
5638	Marie	Collonville	FRA	23.11.73	3B		Illzach	8 Aug
	14.78/	1.82 10.21	25.46/		5.98/ 41.24		2:18.63	
5636		Ma Chun-Ping	TPE	3.8.71	3	EAsiG	Shanghai	16 May
	14.39/	1.82 12.36	25.26/		5.87/ 39.12		2:29.37	
5635	Elena	Milan	ITA	30.1.71	3	NC	Bologna	3 Aug
	14.15/-0.5	1.72 10.41	25.18/-0.4		5.83/-1.3		39.54 2:13.32	
	(100)							
5632	Diana	Koritskaya	RUS	22.275	1		Vladimir	3 Jul
	14.54/	1.69 11.79	24.95/		5.86/ 38.48		2:14.11	
5632	Emma	Beales	GBR	7.12.71	1		Wrexham	1 Aug
	14.50w/3.3	1.69 14.08	25.40w		5.96w/3.1		42.48 2:31.00	

Mark	First	Last	Nat	Born	Date
5628	Gertrud	Bacher	ITA	71	11 Jul
5628	Kim	Vanderhoek	CAN	70	31 Jul
5622	Jenny	Kelly	GBR	70	30 May
5613	Sabine	Schwarz	GER	67	20 Jun
5606	Nadezhda	Novikova	RUS	66	18 May
5601	Marjolijn	van Elk	HOL	69	6 Jun
5595	Guilaine	Belpérin	FRA	71	8 Aug
5592	Zita	Bálint	HUN	71	11 Jul
	(110)				
5591	Karin	Specht	GER	74	23 May
5578	a	Vlasova	KZK		24 Jul
5576	Lyudmila	Mashchenko	RUS	74	3 Jul
5562		Qiu Qin	CHN	73	3 Jun
5557	Patricia	Nadler	SUI	69	11 Jul
5548	Denise	Brungardt	USA		14 May
5547	Sharyn	Slachetka	USA	64	31 Jul
5546	Silke	Harms	GER	67	20 Jun
5540	Conceição	Geremias	BRA	56	27 Jun
5535	Svetlana	Bagayeva	RUS	66	16 Jul
	(120)				
5533	Birgit	Bauer	GER	70	20 Jun
5530	Astrid	Retzke	GER	73	20 Jun
5528	Emilie	Boulleret	FRA	73	8 Aug
5521	Marriet	van Aken	HOL	67	6 Jun
5516	Marina	Damceska	MKD	62	
5516	Angie	Taylor	USA	65	27 Jun
5513	Tila	Hautala	FIN	72	1 Aug
5508	Dagmar	Urbánková	TCH	62	13 Jun
5508	Ester	Goossens	HOL	72	12 Sep
5507	Elmira	Sokhovtinova	UKR	71	6 Jun
	(130)				
5502	Anke	Straschewski	GER	63	20 Jun
5502	Klarissa	Altdorfer	GER	75	18 Jul

45 Minute Heptathlon

Mark	Name		Nat	Born	Pos	Venue	Date
6214	Sabine	Braun	GER	19.6.65	1	Ingelheim	28 Aug
	13.43	1.83 14.44	24.82		6.43	44.96 2:32.35	
6154	Petra	Vaideanu'	ROM	24.8.65	2	Ingelheim	28 Aug
	13.62	1.77 14.56	25.71		5.92	47.90 2:15.73	
6043	Kym	Carter	USA	12.3.64	3	Ingelheim	28 Aug
	13.53	1.74 14.78	24.18		5.91	36.84 2:17.61	
6038	Urszula	Wlodarczyk	POL	22.12.65	4	Ingelheim	28 Aug
	13.55	1.80 14.52	26.27		6.34	34.60 2:21.26	
5886	Tatyana	Zhuravlyova	RUS	19.12.67	5	Ingelheim	28 Aug
		1.80 13.57	24.80		6.32	30.34 2:18.55	
5786	Birgit	Clarius	FRG	18.3.65	1	St.Moritz	17 Jul
5714	Manuela	Marxer	LIE	6.8.65	6	Ingelheim	28 Aug
5617	Beatrice	Mau	GER	20.2.71	7	Ingelheim	28 Aug

4 x 100 METRES RELAY

Mark	Team	Pos	Meet	Venue	Date
41.49	RUS Bogoslovskaya, Malchugina, Voronova, Privalova	1	WC	Stuttgart	22 Aug
41.49	USA Finn, Torrence, Vereen, Devers	2	WC	Stuttgart	22 Aug
41.94	JAM Freeman, Campbell, Mitchell, Ottey	3	WC	Stuttgart	22 Aug
42.34	USA Finn, Echols, Vereen, Devers	1h1	WC	Stuttgart	21 Aug
42.39	RUS Bogoslovskaya, Malchugina, Voronova, Trandenkova	1h2	WC	Stuttgart	21 Aug
42.40	JAM Freeman, Duhaney, Mitchell, Campbell	2h1	WC	Stuttgart	21 Aug
42.67	FRA Girard, Sidibé, Jean-Charles, Pérec	4	WC	Stuttgart	22 Aug
42.79	RUS Bogoslovskaya, Voronova, Trandenkova, Privalova	1	EP	Roma	26 Jun
42.79	GER Philipp, Zipp, Knoll, Paschke	5	WC	Stuttgart	22 Aug
42.81	GER Philipp, Zipp, Knoll, Paschke	3h1	WC	Stuttgart	21 Aug
42.89	CUB Ferrer, López, Duporty, Allen	6	WC	Stuttgart	22 Aug
42.92	GER Philipp, Zipp, Knoll, Paschke	1	ASV	Köln	1 Aug
42.93	USA Echols, Taplin,Gaines, Vereen	2	ASV	Köln	1 Aug
43.01	FRA Girard, Sidibé, Nestoret, Pérec	2	EP	Roma	26 Jun
43.16	Guangxi (CHN) Xiao Y, Tian Y, Huang M, Ou Y	1	NG	Beijing	11 Sep

Mark	Nat	Name	Pos	Meet	Venue	Date
43.31	FRA	Girard, Sidibé, Jean-Charles, Pérec	2h2	WC	Stuttgart	21 Aug
43.36	Sichuan (CHN)	Gao H, Jiang L, Lin X, Chen Y	2	NG	Beijing	12 Sep
43.37	USA	Braddock, Taplin, Harris, Gaines	1	WUG	Buffalo	18 Jul
43.37	FIN	Pirtimaa, Hanhijoki, Hernesniemi, Salmela	7	WC	Stuttgart	22 Aug
43.46	GER	Philipp, Zipp, Knoll, Paschke	3	EP	Roma	26 Jun
	(20/8 nations					
43.47	UKR	Shevchuk, Fomenko, A Slyussar, Tarnopolskaya	1		Kiev	16 May
43.49	NGR	Idehen, Utondu, Opara-Thompson, Onyali	1	AfrC	Durban	25 Jun
43.65	GBR	Richardson, Kinch, Jacobs, Thomas	4h2	WC	Stuttgart	21 Aug
43.67	HOL	Elissen, Poelman, de Lange,Bogaards	1	APM	Hengelo	20 Jun
44.28A	BAH	Ferguson, Fynes, Clarke, Sturrup	2	CAC	Cali	31 Jul
44.34	AUS	Ainsworth, Gainsford, Freeman, Van Heer	1		Canberra	25 Jan
44.36	CAN	Noel, Bowen, Paquette, Duprey	4h2	WC	Stuttgart	21 Aug
44.57	ITA	Sinico, Tarolo, Balzani, Gallina	3	v2N	Bondoufle	19 Sep
44.59	TPE	Kao Y-C, Chen S-C, Hsu P-C, Wang H-C	5h1	WC	Stuttgart	21 Aug
44.62	COL	Mera, Restrepo, Rodriguez, Carabali	2	CAG	Ponce	25 Nov
44.65	THA	Suajongprue, Dokduang, Sripet, Incharoen	1	SEAG	Singapore	17 Jun
44.73	POL	Czajko, Zakrzewska, Borejza, KKrawczak	7	EP	Roma	26 Jun
	(20)					
44.83	BUL		1	EP/B	Bruxelles	12 Jun
44.86	Funilense (BRA)	Jesus, Santos, Graças, Amaral	1		Rio de Janeiro	27 Jun
44.86	SUI	Schumann, Simasotchi, Wüest, Haug	1		Luzern	29 Jun
44.93	MAD	L Ramalalanirina, Rakotsudrake, N Ramalalanirina, Ravaonirina	2	AfrC	Durban	25 Jun
44.94	AUT	Hölbl, Tröger, Unger, Mayr	1	EP/C1	Villach	12 Jun
45.10	IND	Augustine, Saramma, Panda, Shyla	1		Dhaka	25 Dec
45.15	RSA	Styen, Vorster, Knox, de Klerk	3	AfrC	Durban	25 Jun
45.17	BLS		3	EP/B	Bruxelles	12 Jun
45.21	POR	Tavares, Castanheira, Regalo, Jardim	2	EP/C3	Rotterdam	12 Jun
45.21	TCH	Musinská, Canková, Spicková, Benesová	2	3-N	Praha	17 Jul
	(30)					

Mark	Nat	Date	Mark	Nat	Date	Mark	Nat	Date	Mark	Nat	Date
45.29	GHA	25 Jun	45.75	PUR	31 Jul	45.91	NOR	12 Jun	46.43	ISL	12 Jun
45.30	BEL	12 Jun	45.82	HUN	5 Jun	45.93	ESP	20 Jun	46.46	LAT	12 Jun
45.49	JPN	16 May	45.87	KZK	3 Dec	45.96	SRI	25 Dec	**Hand timed**		
45.49	SWE	12 Jun	45.89	GRE	12 Jun	46.04	Farul Constanta		45.1	GHA	28 May
45.50	PHI	17 Jun		(40)			(ROM)	5 Sep	46.5	CHI	4 Jul
45.70	MAS	17 Jun	45.9	ARG	4 Jul	46.22	DEN	12 Jun			

4 x 200 METRES RELAY

Mark	Nat	Name	Pos	Meet	Venue	Date
1:31.49	RUS	Sotnikova, Zhirova, Mizera, Sokolova	1	EurR	Portsmouth	5 Jun
1:31.98	UKR	A Slyussar, I Slyussar, Fomenko, Tarnopolskaya	2	EurR	Portsmouth	5 Jun
1:32.51	Alabama Un	Bowen CAN, Idehen NGR, Chapman, Lloyd JAM	1	DrakeR	Des Moines	23 Apr
1:34.00	GER	Knoll, Schönenberger, Janke, B Rockmeier	3	EurR	Portsmouth	5 Jun
1:34.00	GBR	Jacobs, Cohen, Douglas, Short	4	EurR	Portsmouth	5 Jun

4 x 400 METRES RELAY

Mark	Nat	Name	Pos	Meet	Venue	Date
3:16.71	USA	Torrence 49.0, Malone 49.4, Kaiser-Brown 49.48, Miles 48.78	1	WC	Stuttgart	22 Aug
3:18.38	RUS	Ruzina 50.8, Alekseyeva 49.3, Ponomaryova 49.78, Privalova 48.47	2	WC	Stuttgart	22 Aug
3:23.41	GBR	Keough 52.1, Smith 50.0, Goddard 51.44, Gunnell 49.90	3	WC	Stuttgart	22 Aug
3:23.82	JAM	Grant 51.6, Turner 50.6, Hemmings 50.61, Richards 51.01	1h1	WC	Stuttgart	21 Aug
3:23.83	JAM	Hemmings 51.1, Turner 51.1, Campbell 51.47, Richards 50.16	4	WC	Stuttgart	22 Aug
3:24.08	USA	Dendy 51.6, Collins 50.9, Malone 50.00, Kaiser-Brown 51.41	1h2	WC	Stuttgart	21 Aug
3:24.23	RUS	Golosheva, Ruzina, Sychugova, Alekseyeva	1	EP	Roma	27 Jun
3:24.28	Hebei (CHN)	An X, Bai X, Cao C, Ma Y	1	NG	Beijing	13 Sep
3:24.36	GBR	Smith, Goddard, Stoute, Gunnell	1	EurR	Portsmouth	5 Jun
3:24.62	RUS	Golseheva, Ruzina, Radeyeva, Alekseyeva	2	EurR	Portsmouth	5 Jun
3:24.67	RUS	Golosheva, Ruzina, Sychugova, Alekseyeva	2h1	WC	Stuttgart	21 Aug
3:25.49	GER	Meissner, Seuser, Rücker, Kisabaka	5	WC	Stuttgart	22 Aug
3:26.18	USA	Irving, Malone, Warren, Collins	1	WUG	Buffalo	18 Jul
3:27.04	GBR	Keough, Smith, Goddard, Gunnell	2h2	WC	Stuttgart	21 Aug
3:27.08	FRA	Devassoigne, Elien, Landre, Bévis	6	WC	Stuttgart	22 Aug
3:27.36A	JAM	Parris, Grant, Williams, Turner	1	CAC	Cali	1 Aug
3:27.37	UKR	Kashchey, Yurchenko, Nasonkina, Dzhigalova	2	EP	Roma	27 Jun
3:27.44	GER	Meissner, Seuser, Rücker, Kisabaka	3h2	WC	Stuttgart	21 Aug
3:27.78	AUS	Holland, Van Heer, Hanigan, Lock	1		Canberra	14 Mar

Mark		Name	Pos	Meet	Venue	Date
3:27.80	GER	Janke, Rücker, Schönenberger, Seuser	3	EP	Roma	27 Jun
3:27.94	TCH	Kostovalová, Dziurová, Benesová, Formanová	7	WC	Stuttgart	22 Aug
	(21/10)					
3:28.52	SUI	Burkart, Zürcher/Scalabrin, Brillante, Lüthi	8	WC	Stuttgart	22 Aug
3:28.95	CUB	McLeon, Limonta, Ramirez, Bonne	2	WUG	Buffalo	18 Jul
3:29.28	ROM	Tîrlea, Kovacs, Carutasu, Florea	6	EP	Roma	27 Jun
3:33.12	NGR	O'de Akinremi, O'yo Akinremi, Afolabi, Odoemenam	5h2	WC	Stuttgart	21 Aug
3:33.55	ESP	Reyes, Lahoz, Andrés, Myers	2	EP/B	Bruxelles	13 Jun
3:33.59	POL	Warnicka, Pachut, Grzywocz, Kilinska	7	EP	Roma	27 Jun
3:33.67	BLS		3	EP/B	Bruxelles	13 Jun
3:33.91	ITA	Carbone, Spuri, Perlino, Zamperioli	8	EP	Roma	27 Jun
3:34.16	BEL		5	EP/B	Bruxelles	13 Jun
3:34.29A	COL	Carabali, Gómez, Mora, Peña	3	CAC	Cali	1 Aug
	(20)					
3:34.76	POR	Mareira, Amaral, Regalo, Moura	6h2	WC	Stuttgart	21 Aug
3:34.9	Funilense (BRA)	Santos, Graças, Vera Cruz, Figueirado	1		Rio de Janeiro	27 Jun
3:35.83	MAS		1	SEAG	Singapore	17 Jun
3:36.06	IND	Pais, Saramma, Apsara, Wilson	2	AsiC	Manila	4 Dec
3:36.42	CAN	Bowen, Yakiwchuk, Gareau, Fraser	4	WUG	Buffalo	18 Jul
3:36.48	THA	Srimek, Chimrak, Sang-Ngeun, Phimphoo	2	SEAG	Singapore	17 Jun
3:36.93	Levski Sofia (BUL)		1		Limassol	5 Jun
3:37.08	SWE	Carlsson, Svantesson, C Johansson, Westén	2	EP/C3	Rotterdam	13 Jun
3:37.24	RSA	Gourie, de Jongh, Uys, de Klerk	2	AfrC	Durban	27 Jun
3:37.54	NOR		6	EP/B	Bruxelles	13 Jun
	(30)					

Mark	Nat	Date
3:37.76	FIN	29 Aug
3:38.71	HOL	13 Jun
3:38.95A	BAH	1 Aug
3:39.43A	PUR	1 Aug
3:39.66	GHA	27 Jun
3:39.80	HUN	13 Jun
3:39.86	UGA	27 Jun
3:39.87	KEN	27 Jun
3:40.0	TRI	8 May
3:40.67	SLO	13 Jun
	(40)	
3:40.85	JPN	16 May
3:40.9	PHI	17 May
3:40.98	GRE	13 Jun
3:41.66	MAS	3 Dec
3:42.05	MAD	27 Aug
3:42.14	Auckland (NZL)	7 Mar
3:42.64	LIT	13 Jun
3:43.40	ISR	11 Jul
3:43.42A	ARG	3 Jul
3:43.43A	CHI	3 Jul
3:43.59	AUT	13 Jun
3:43.72A	MEX	1 Aug
3:44.68	SVK	13 Jun
3:45.73	FIJ	16 Dec
3:45.75	DEN	13 Jun
3:45.97	IRL	13 Jun

4 x 800 METRES RELAY

Mark		Name	Pos	Meet	Venue	Date
7:57.08	RUS	Kuznetsova, Betekhtina, Burkanova, Masterkova	1	EurR	Portsmouth	5 Jun
7:57.21	ROM	Salageanu, Constantin, Beclea, Itcou	2	EurR	Portsmouth	5 Jun
8:03.85	BLS		3	EurR	Portsmouth	5 Jun
8:06.28	UKR	Kovpak, Stochevaya, Zavedskaya, Yevseyeva	4	EurR	Portsmouth	5 Jun
8:16.97	GER	Weidner, Bruhns, Muck, Wachtel	5	EurR	Portsmouth	5 Jun
8:20.73	GBR	Fryer, Gibson, Keopugh, Modahl	6	EurR	Portsmouth	5 Jun
8:21.39	ITA	Falvo, Tozzi, Rea, Trabaldo	7	EurR	Portsmouth	5 Jun

4 x 1500 METRES RELAY

Mark		Name	Pos	Meet	Venue	Date
17:55.51	Villanova (USA)	Spies, Zajac, Flowers, Goddard	1	PennR	Philadelphia	23 Apr

3000 METRES TRACK WALK

Mark		Name	Nat	Born	Pos	Meet	Venue	Date
11:48.24	Ileana	Salvador	ITA	16.1.62	1		Padova	29 Aug
11:52.01	Beate	Anders	GER	4.2.68	1		Lapinlahti	27 Jun
11:52.71	Kerry	Junna-Saxby	AUS	2.6.61	1	NEC	Melbourne	25 Feb
11:56.40	Elisabetta	Perrone	ITA	9.7.68	2		Padova	29 Aug
11:57.08		Junna-Saxby			1		Christchurch	16 Jan
11:59.60	Sari	Essayah	FIN	21.2.67	2		Lapinlahti	27 Jun
12:01.15		Anders			1		Keuruu	25 Jun
12:05.38		Essayah			2		Keuruu	25 Jun
12:06.15		Anders			3		Padova	29 Aug
12:06.82		Salvador			1		Caserta	6 Jun
12:07.98		Salvador			1		Bologna	3 Sep
12:11.53		Salvador			3		Lapinlahti	27 Jun
12:16.00	Katarzyna	Radtke	POL	31.8.69	1		Sopot	1 May
12:17.30		Salvador			3		Keuruu	25 Jun
12:18.91		Junna-Saxby			1		Brisbane	31 Jan
	(15/6)							
12:20.86	Yelena	Nikolayeva	RUS	1.2.66	2		Caserta	6 Jun
12:25.05	Madelein	Svensson	SWE	20.7.69	1		Stockholm	8 Jul
12:27.74	Jane	Saville	AUS	5.11.74	2	NEC	Melbourne	25 Feb

Mark	Name		Nat	Born	Pos	Meet	Venue	Date
12:28.0	Gabrielle	Blythe	AUS	9.3.69	3	SGP	Fana	9 May

Mark	Name		Nat	Born	Date
12:34.52	Anna Rita	Sidoti	ITA	69	6 Jun
12:44.65	Michaela	Hafner	ITA	73	3 Sep
12:47.9 mx	Anne	Manning	AUS	59	23 Oct
12:49.14	Jenny	Jones	AUS	67	25 Feb

Indoors

Mark	Name		Nat	Born	Pos	Meet	Venue	Date
11:49.73	Yelena	Nikolayeva	RUS	1.2.66	1	WI	Toronto	13 Mar
11:53.82		Junna-Saxby			3	WI	Toronto	13 Mar
11:55.35		Salvador			4	WI	Toronto	13 Mar
11:57.14		Anders			4	WI	Toronto	13 Mar
11:58.36		Salvador			1		Genova	13 Feb
12:01.22	Yelena	Arshintseva	RUS	5.4.71	5	WI	Toronto	13 Mar
12:03.36		Arshintseva			1	NC	Moskva	27 Feb
12:04.16	Anna Rita	Sidoti	ITA	25.7.69	6	WI	Toronto	13 Mar
12:04.41		Nikolayeva			2	NC	Moskva	27 Feb
12:06.10		Essayah			7	WI	Toronto	13 Mar
12:08.06	Yelena	Sayko	RUS	24.12.67	3	NC	Moskva	27 Feb
12:08.24		Sidoti			2		Genova	13 Feb
12:15.43		Nikolayeva			1h2	WI	Toronto	12 Mar
12:15.81	Tatyana	Ragozina	UKR	3.9.64	1	NC	Kiev	14 Feb
12:16.52		Anders			1		Berlin	14 Feb
12:16.90		Junna-Saxby			2h2	WI	Toronto	12 Mar
12:17.27		Anders			1	NC	Sindelfingen	28 Feb
12:17.33		Essayah			1	NC	Kuopio	20 Feb
12:18.10	Madelein	Svensson	SWE	20.7.69	8	WI	Toronto	13 Mar
12:18.95		Salvador			1		Genova	10 Feb
	(20 performances)							
12:18.96	Olimpiada	Ivanova	RUS	5.5.70	4	NC	Moskva	27 Feb
12:19.57	Yelena	Gruzinova	RUS	67	1		Moskva	2 Feb
12:20.79	Debbi	Lawrence	USA	15.10.61	3h1	WI	Toronto	12 Mar
12:20.86	Yulia	Korolyova	RUS	25.7.73	2		Moskva	2 Feb
12:23.06	Rimma	Makarova	RUS	18.7.63	5	NC	Moskva	27 Feb
12:23.7	Tamara	Kovalenko	RUS	5.6.64	1		Moskva	28 Jan
12:26.37	Yekaterina	Samoylenko	UKR	23.1.63	1		Budapest	5 Feb
12:29.74	Natalya	Serbinenko	UKR	27.1.59	2	NC	Kiev	14 Feb
12:29.98	Susana	Feitor	POR	28.1.75	1	NC	Braga	6 Mar

Mark	Name		Nat	Born	Date
12:30.56	Sada	Buksniene	LIT	67	12 Mar
12:32.24	Lidia	Fesenko	RUS	62	27 Feb
12:33.62	Alison	Baker	CAN	64	12 Mar
12:33.87	Norica	Cimpan	ROM	72	5 Feb
12:34.31	Zuzana	Zemková	SVK	67	5 Feb
12:35.90	Yevgenia	Guryeva	RUS	69	27 Feb
12:38.32	Simone	Thust	GER	71	14 Feb
12:39.45	Mária	Rosza	HUN	67	5 Feb
12:45.58	Kathrin	Born	GER	70	28 Feb
12:45.81	Ildikó	Ilyés	HUN	66	5 Feb
12:47.57	Janice	McCaffrey	CAN	59	23 Jan
12:49.50	Kamila	Holpuchová	TCH	73	5 Feb

5000 METRES WALK

TRACK

Mark	Name		Nat	Born	Pos	Meet	Venue	Date
20:30.0	Kerry	Junna-Saxby	AUS	2.6.61	1	NC	Brisbane	6 Mar
20:38.14		Junna-Saxby			1		Sydney	20 Feb
20:38.65	Sari	Essayah	FIN	21.2.67	1	NC	Mikkeli	31 Jul
20:48.55	Ileana	Salvador	ITA	16.1.62	1	NC	Bologna	2 Aug
20:51.2		Salvador			1		Piombino Dese	23 Jun
20:51.96	Katarzyna	Radtke	POL	31.8.69	1		Sopot	20 Jun
20:53.71	Elisabetta	Perrone	ITA	9.7.68	2	NC	Bologna	2 Aug
20:55.75	Beate	Anders	GER	4.2.68	1	NC	Duisburg	10 Jul
20:57.35		Salvador			1		Donnas	22 May
21:01.8	Susana	Feitor	POR	28.1.75	1	SGP	Fana	8 May

Mark	Name		Nat	Born	Date
22:40.47	Ildikó	Ilyés	HUN	66	30 May
22:40.82	Larisa	Ramazanova	RUS	71	24 Jul
22:40.83	Maria	Vasco	ESP	75	29 Jul
22:41.4	Yulia	Nifontova	RUS	74	
22:42.47	Tomoko	Uchida	JPN	72	19 Ded
22:44.20	Hilde	Gustavsen	NOR	68	30 Jul
22:46.5	Perry	Williams	IRL	66	28 May
22:49.0	Lisa	Paolini	IRL	62	6 Mar
	(50)				
22:51.8	Monica	Gunnarsson	SWE	65	22 Jul
22:53.47	Jantien	Saltet	AUS	72	20 Feb
22:56.30	Oksana	Obedkina	RUS	76	5 Jun
22:56.60	Cheryl	Webb	AUS	76	21 Feb

Indoors

Mark	Name		Nat	Born	Pos	Meet	Venue	Date
21:32.70	Rimma	Makarova	RUS	18.7.63	1		Moskva	26 Jan
21:33.59	Tamara	Kovalenko	RUS	5.6.64	2		Moskva	26 Jan
22:12.75	Yevgenia	Guryeva	RUS	2.12.69	3		Moskva	26 Jan
22:57.1	Hideko	Hirayama	JPN	6.4.65	1		Otsu	14 Mar

5 KILOMETRES ROAD WALK

Best performances and marks better than track bests

Mark	Name		Nat	Born	Pos	Meet	Venue	Date
21:10		Salvador			1		Arzignano	12 Jun
21:17	Yelena	Nikolayeva	RUS	1.2.66	1		L'Hospitalet	9 May

Mark	Name		Nat	Born	Pos	Meet	Venue	Date
21:36	Yelena	Arshintseva	RUS	5.4.71	2		L'Hospitalet	9 May
21:38	Encarnacion	Granados	ESP	30.1.72	3		L'Hospitalet	9 May
21:38		Junna-Saxby			1		Canberra	13 Jun
21:43	Yelena	Sayko	RUS	24.12.67	4		L'Hospitalet	9 May
22:03+	Marciela	Chavez	MEX	24.9.62	1m		Wajima	4 Apr
22:04+	Yuko	Sato	JPN	23.1.68	2m		Wajima	4 Apr
22:04+	Yuka	Kamioka	JPN	28.5.75	4m		Wajima	4 Apr
22:04+	Yuka	Mitsumori	JPN	8.1.72	5m		Wajima	4 Apr
22:15	Anna Rita	Sidoti	ITA	25.7.69	5		L'Hospitalet	9 May
22:16	Erika	Alfridi	ITA	22.2.68	4		Arzignano	12 Jun
22:17	Venera	Vasilyeva	RUS	17.3.76	2		Adler	14 Feb
22:21	Victoria	Herazo	USA	2.6.59	1		Kingsport	18 Sep
22:23	Tatyana	Gudkova	RUS	23.12.77	2		Moskva	25 Apr
22:24	Emi	Hayashi	JPN	9.7.72	1		Tokyo	1 Jan
22:26	Maribel	Rebollo	MEX	76	3		Eschborn	12 Jun
22:28+	Beata	Kaczmarska	POL	5.7.70			La Coruña	15 May
22:32	Maria	Vasco	ESP	26.12.75	4		Eschborn	12 Jun
22:34	Emilia	Cano	ESP	4.3.68	1		Viladecans	2 May
22:35	Yulia	Nifontova	RUS	14.5.74	5		Eschborn	12 Jun
22:37	Olga	Panferova	RUS	21.8.77	6		Eschborn	12 Jun

10 KILOMETRES WALK

Mark	Name		Nat	Born	Pos	Meet	Venue	Date
41:30	Ileana	Salvador	ITA	16.1.62	1		Livorno	10 Jul
41:48		Li Chunxiu	CHN	.8.69	1	NG	Beijing	8 Sep
41:56	Elisabeta	Perrone	ITA	9.7.68	2		Livorno	10 Jul
41:57		Gao Hongmiao	CHN	17.3.74	2	NG	Beijing	8 Sep
42:03	Yelena	Arshintseva	RUS	5.4.71	1		Adler	14 Feb
42:04	Yelena	Sayko	RUS	24.12.67	2		Adler	14 Feb
42:22.6t	Kerry	Junna-Saxby	AUS	2.6.61	1	SGP	Fana	8 May
42:23.7t		Salvador			2	SGP	Fana	8 May
42:24	Olympiada	Ivanova	RUS	5.5.70	3		Livorno	10 Jul
42:26		Wang Yan	CHN	3.5.71	1		Shenzhen	18 Feb
42:26.29t		Junna-Saxby			1		Sydney	10 Jan
42:32		Gao Hongmiao			2		Shenzhen	18 Feb
42:34	Yelena	Gruzinova (10)	RUS	67	3		Adler	14 Feb
42:37		Ivanova			4		Adler	14 Feb
42:37.0t	Sari	Essayah	FIN	21.2.67	3	SGP	Fana	8 May
42:41	Anna Rita	Sidoti	ITA	25.7.69	1		Eschborn	13 Jun
42:44		Long Yuwen	CHN	.8.75	3		Shenzhen	18 Feb
42:45	??	Li Yuxin	CHN	73	4		Shenzhen	18 Feb
42:46		Wang Yan			3	NG	Beijing	8 Sep
42:47		Liu Hongyu	CHN	1.2.76	5		Shenzhen	18 Feb
42:47	Larisa	Ramazanova	RUS	71	2		Eschborn	13 Jun
42:47.4t	Katarzyna	Radtke	POL	31.8.69	4	SGP	Fana	8 May
42:50		Gu Yan	CHN	17.3.74	4	NG	Beijing	8 Sep
42:52	Madeleine	Svensson	SWE	20.7.69	3		Eschborn	13 Jun
42:55		Radtke			4		Eschborn	12 Jun
42:57		Zhang Qinghua	CHN	6.2.73	6		Shenzhen	18 Feb
42:58.1t		Essayah			1		Brunflo	4 Jul
42:59		Essayah			1	WC	Stuttgart	14 Aug
43:01.0t		Wang Yan			1		Shenzhen	21 Feb
43:01		Liu Hongyu			5	NG	Beijing	8 Sep
43:03+		Junna-Saxby			1k		Hawkesbury	10 Jul
43:05.6t		Svensson			2		Brunflo	4 Jul
43:07		Song Lijuan	CHN	.2.76	6	NG	Beijing	8 Sep
	(33/21)							
43:09	Beate	Anders	GER	4.2.68	5		Eschborn	13 Jun
43:10		Fan Xiaoling	CHN	14.5.70	7	NG	Beijing	8 Sep
43:11	Yelena	Nikolayeva	RUS	1.2.66	1		La Coruña	15 May
43:15	Natalya	Misyulya	BLS	14.4.66	4		Livorno	10 Jul
43:21	Encarnacion	Granados	ESP	30.1.72	3	WC	Stuttgart	14 Aug
43:21	Mária	Rosza	HUN	12.2.67	1		Békéscsaba	28 Aug
43:28+	Gabrielle	Blythe	AUS	9.3.68	2k		Hawkesbury	10 Jul
43:28		Kong Yan	CHN	.4.71	8	NG	Beijing	8 Sep

Mark		Name	Nat	Born	Pos	Meet	Venue	Date
43:30		Sun Yan	CHN	.9.73	8		Shenzhen	18 Feb
	(30)							
43:34		Wei Linkun	CHN	.12.75	9	NG	Beijing	8 Sep
43:37	Yulia	Korolyova	RUS	25.7.73	5		Adler	14 Feb
43:44	Susana	Feitor	POR	28.1.75	1		Rio Maior	3 Apr
43:47		Tang Yinghua	CHN	18.5.73	9		Shenzhen	18 Feb
43:50		Cui Yingzi	CHN	26.1.71	10		Shenzhen	18 Feb
43:50	Valentina	Tsybulskaya	BLS	19.7.68	6		Livorno	10 Jul
43:51.4t		Zhu Xiaolan	CHN	1.7.72	4		Shenzhen	21 Feb
43:54	Rimma	Makarova	RUS	18.7.63	6		Eschborn	13 Jun
43:56	Lidiya	Fesenko	RUS	5.10.62	6		Adler	14 Feb
43:57		Jin Bingjie	CHN	3.6.71	11		Shenzhen	18 Feb
	(40)							
44:01		Xu Chunjuan	CHN	.10.72	13		Shenzhen	18 Feb
44:02	Leonarda	Yukhnevich	BLS	9.10.63	8		Eschborn	13 Jun
44:10	Maricela	Chavez	MEX	24.9.62	1		Brandys nad Labem	23 May
44:12	Yevgeniya	Guryeva	RUS	2.12.69	7		Adler	14 Feb
44:20	Kamila	Holpuchová	TCH	27.9.73	2		Brandys nad Labem	23 May
44:22	Irina	Tolstik	BLS	4.12.65	8		Adler	14 Feb
44:30		Mou Fangmei	CHN	.2.72	14		Shenzhen	18 Feb
44:38		Wang Na	CHN	.8.70	16		Shenzhen	18 Feb
44:42	Yulia	Odzilyayeva	RUS	70	1		Yaroslavl	6 Aug
44:43	Kathrin	Born	GER	4.12.70	11		Eschborn	13 Jun
	(50)							
44:44		Liu Caimei	CHN	.3.71	17		Shenzhong	18 Feb
44:46	Maribel	Rebollo	MEX	76	3		Brandys nad Labem	23 May
44:49	Tamara	Kovalenko	RUS	5.6.64	2		Yaroslavl	6 Aug
44:50	Vera	Makolova	RUS	17.2.66	12		Adler	14 Feb
44:53	Yuko	Sato	JPN	23.1.68	2		Wajima	4 Apr
44:53	Eva	Machuca	MEX	70	4		Brandys nad Labem	23 May
44:54	Marina	Kozneva	RUS	18.5.68	13		Adler	14 Feb
44:54	Lyudmila	Savinova	RUS	72	3		Yaroslavl	6 Aug
45:00	Maya	Sazonova	KZK	68	9	NC	Cheboksary	6 Jun
45:01.65t	Zinaida	Sviridenko	RUS	24.12.68	1		Rostov na Donu	16 Jul
	(60)							
45:04	Aniko	Szebenszky	HUN	12.8.65	1	6-N	Békéscsaba	28 Mar
45:05	Yuka	Mitsumori	JPN	8.1.72	1		Takahata	7 Nov
45:06	Ildikó	Ilyés	HUN	28.8.66	3	6-N	Békéscsaba	28 Mar
45:08	Svetlana	Nifontova	RUS	74	10	NC	Cheboksary	6 Jun
45:09	Andrea	Alföldi	HUN	22.9.64	4	6-N	Békéscsaba	28 Mar
45:11	Maria	Colin	MEX	7.3.66	3		Wajima	4 Apr
45:13	Lyudmila	Mayorova	RUS	6.11.68	14		Adler	14 Feb
45:13	Irina	Putintseva	RUS	69	15		Adler	14 Feb
45:13.35t	Irina	Savinova	RUS	72	2		Dzerzhinsk	29 Aug
45:15		He Yan	CHN		19		Shenzhen	18 Feb
	(70)							
45:16.2t	Natalya	Serbinenko	UKR	27.1.59	1		Donetsk	29 May
45:17	Cristiana	Pellino	ITA	21.9.70	11		Livorno	10 Jul
45:18	Vera	Kozhomina	MOL	70	16		Adler	14 Feb
45:18	Yuka	Kamioka	JPN	28.5.75	4		Wajima	4 Apr
45:19	Lyudmila	Lyubomirova	RUS	62	17		Adler	14 Feb
45:22	Anita	Liepina	LAT	67	1		Genève	27 Aug
45:23	Maria	Artynyuk	RUS	5.3.66	18		Adler	14 Feb
45:24	Tatyana	Ragozina	UKR	3.9.64	13	WC	Stuttgart	14 Aug
45:27	Teresa	Vaill	USA	20.11.62	1		Washington	28 Mar
45:28	Vicky	Lupton	GBR	17.4.72	12		Livorno	10 Jul
	(80)							
45:28.1t	Rossella	Giordano	ITA	1.12.72	1		Santhia	9 Sep
45:35	Beata	Kaczmarska	POL	5.7.70	16		Eschborn	12 Jun
45:41	Sada	Buksniene	LIT	22.6.67	1		Vilnius	19 Jun
45:42	Norica	Cimpan	ROM	22.3.72	6	6-N	Békéscsaba	28 Mar
45:43.86t	Olga	Leonenko	UKR	13.2.70	2	NC	Kiev	2 Jul
45:48	Rie	Mitsumori	JPN	26.10.74	2		Takahata	7 Nov
45:50	Sonata	Milusauskaite	LIT	31.8.73	2		Vilnius	19 Jun
45:53	Nato	Arakhelashvili	RUS	70	12	NC	Cheboksary	6 Jun
45:53	Zuzana	Zemková	SVK	17.7.67	18		Eschborn	12 Jun
45:53	Viera	Toporek	AUT	5.11.67	1		Jaslovske Bohunice	26 Jun
	(90)							

Mark	Name		Nat	Born	Pos	Meet	Venue	Date
45:55	Debbi	Lawrence	USA	15.10.61	1	NC	Eugene	17 Jun
45:59	Julie	Drake	GBR	21.5.69	7	6-N	Békéscsaba	28 Mar
46:02	Emi	Hayashi	JPN	9.7.72	6		Wajima	4 Apr
46:05	Emilia	Cano	ESP	4.3.68	19		Eschborn	12 Jun
46:06	Jenny	Jones	AUS	20.4.67	1		Canberra	28 Aug
46:10		Su Yuan	CHN		20		Shenzhen	18 Feb
46:11	Simone	Thust	GER	22.9.71	20		Eschborn	12 Jun
46:11.7t	Erika	Alfridi	ITA	22.2.68	4		Torino	4 Apr
46:12	Alfia	Galiullina	RUS	72	20		Adler	14 Feb
46:13	Miriam	Ramon	ECU	10.2.73	16	WC	Stuttgart	14 Aug
	(100)							

Mark	Name		Nat	Born	Date
46:14	Tomoko	Uchida	JPN	72	7 Nov
46:15.60t	Anne	Manning	AUS	59	10 Jan
46:16	Janice	McCaffrey	CAN	59	28 Mar
46:18.10t	Yelena	Kiselyova	RUS	73	29 Aug
46:24	Isilda	Gonçalves	POR	69	3 Apr
46:30	Beata	Betlej	POL	68	15 May
46:30	Maria Grazia	Orsani	ITA	69	12 Jun
46:31	Margarita	Smirnova	RUS	66	14 Feb
46:31	Beáta	Szászi	HUN	72	28 Mar
46:31	Lisa	Sheridan/Paolini	IRL	62	14 Aug
	(110)				
46:32	Rosario	Sánchez	MEX	71	12 Jun
46:34		Cong Yuwen	CHN		24 Apr
46:35	Yulia	Lisnik	MOL	66	6 Jun
46:39	Kazimiera	Mosio	POL	64	16 May
46:41		Fu Liqin	CHN	70	18 Feb
46:41	Teresa	Letherby	AUS	72	28 Aug
46:42	Sandy	Leddin	GER	70	12 Jun
46:46	Yelena	Antonovich	BLS	70	14 Feb
46:46.39t	Alison	Baker	CAN	64	31 Jul
46:48		Zhu Ping	CHN		18 Feb
	(120)				
46:48.03t	Galina	Mudrik	UKR	67	2 Jul
46:49	Linn	Murphy	NZL	60	18 Sep
46:50	Marta	Zukowska	POL	72	12 Jun
46:53	Raquel	del Caz	ESP	68	12 Jun
46:53	Lyudmila	Kazakova	BLS	69	14 Feb
46:53		Li Hongmei	CHN		18 Feb
46:53	Debbie	Van Orden	USA	59	26 Sep
46:54	Ginka	Radeva	BUL	73	16 Jun
46:58	Jane	Barbour	AUS	66	27 Jun
46:58.09t	Vera	Zozulya	UKR	70	2 Jul
	(130)				

Other track bests

Mark	Name	Pos	Meet	Venue	Date
43:33.7	Sidoti	2		Torino	4 Apr
43:39.4	Gao Hongmiao	2		Shenzhen	21 Feb
43:49.5	Liu Hongyu	3		Shenzhen	21 Feb
44:01.6	Perrone	3		Torino	4 Apr
44:09.1	Cui Yingzi	5		Shenzhen	21 Feb
44:11.7	Long Yuwen	6		Shenzhen	21 Feb
44:12.0	Blythe	5	SGP	Fana	8 May
44:13.1	Li Yuxin	7		Shenzhen	21 Feb
44:15.0	Sun Yan	8		Shenzhen	21 Feb
44:27.8	Jin Bingjie	9		Shenzhen	21 Feb
45:00.32	Li Chunxiu	1	EAsiG	Shanghai	14 May
45:00.7	Zhang Qinghua	10		Shenzhen	21 Feb
45:15.3	Xu Chunjuan	11		Shenzhen	21 Feb
45:26.73	Ivanova	2		Rostov na Donu	16 Jul
45:59.18	Granados	1	NC	Gandia	3 Jul
46:03.14	Cimpan				

Mark	Name	Date
46:18.58	Ramazanova	14 Jul
46:25.4	Jones	25 Jan
46:29.39	Sato	14 May
46:35.0	Gu Yan	21 Feb
46:38.13	Paolini	10 Jan
46:42.42	Kovalenko	16 Jul
46:42.8	Pellino	4 Apr
46:43.0	Wang Na	21 Feb

20 KILOMETRES WALK

Mark	Name		Nat	Born	Pos	Meet	Venue	Date
1:31:53	Ileana	Salvador	ITA	16.1.62	1	NC	Baia Domizia	25 Sep
1:33:03	Olympiada	Ivanova	RUS	5.5.70	1		Yaroslavl	6 Aug
1:33:37	Elisabetta	Perrone	ITA	9.7.68	2	NC	Baia Domizia	25 Sep
1:34:27	Anne	Manning	AUS	13.11.59	1	NC	Hawkesbury	10 Jul
1:36:16	Jenny	Jones-Billington	AUS	20.4.67	2	NC	Hawkesbury	10 Jul
1:37:04	Nadezhda	Ryashkina	RUS	22.1.67	2		Yaroslavl	6 Aug
1:38:13	Maria Grazia	Orsani	ITA	11.6.69	3	NC	Baia Domizia	25 Sep
1:39:02	Jane	Barbour	AUS	27.7.66	3	NC	Hawkesbury	10 Jul

WORLD LIST TRENDS - 10th and 100th world list performance levels

Event	*1984*	*1985*	*1986*	*1987*	*1988*	*1989*	*1990*	*1991*	*1992*	*1993*
Women 10th Bests										
100m	11.10	11.11	11.08	11.01	**10.92**	11.12	11.10	11.09	11.07	11.12
200m	22.36	22.55	22.39	22.40	**22.24**	22.53	22.42	22.58	22.44	22.37
400m	**49.74**	50.38	50.29	50.41	49.90	51.05	50.59	50.30	50.30	50.83
800m	1:57.20	1:57.42	1:58.11	1:57.46	**1:56.91**	1:58.84	1:57.82	1:58.67	1:57.93	1:57.63
1500m	4:00.18	4:02.05	4:02.92	4:01.20	4:01.02	4:04.98	4:04.56	4:05.04	4:01.23	4:00.05
3000m	8:37.36	8:42.19	8:39.25	8:42.16	8:37.70	8:45.04	8:46.86	8:42.02	8:42.09	**8:35.38**
10000m	32:30.91	32:25.62	31:56.59	31:46.61	31:42.02	32:14.65	31:55.80	31:45.95	**31:28.06**	31:29.70
Marathon	2:29:10	2:28:38	2:29:51	2:29:56	2:28:40	2:28:45	2:28:56	2:27:43	2:27:42	**2:26:26**
100mh	12.74	12.85	12.75	12.80	**12.73**	12.77	**12.73**	12.81	12.76	12.78
400mh	54.93	54.95	54.76	55.05	**54.49**	55.03	55.18	54.88	54.70	54.53
HJ	1.96	1.96	1.97	1.97	**1.98**	**1.98**	1.97	1.96	1.96	1.97
LJ	7.01	7.00	7.01	7.01	**7.07**	6.88	6.92	6.89	6.92	6.90
SP	20.55	20.39	20.60	**20.85**	20.81	20.02	20.12	19.74	19.78	19.90
DT	**68.56**	67.52	67.92	67.90	70.34	66.50	66.94	65.72	67.08	65.14
JT	66.56	68.20	67.80	67.64	**68.42**	65.54	66.10	65.32	65.02	65.18
Heptathlon	6424	6368	6403	6364	**6540**	6361	6359	6370	6460	6406
Other peak: 1500m 3:59.82 (1982)										
Women 100th Bests										
100m	11.51	11.44	11.51	11.48	**11.43**	11.53	11.54	11.53	11.45	11.46
200m	23.39	23.58	23.36	23.35	23.32	23.49	23.53	23.48	23.36	23.40
400m	52.63	52.89	52.50	52.64	**52.50**	52.81	53.00	53.03	52.60	52.66
800m	**2:01.50**	2:02.43	2:02.04	2:01.79	2:01.66	2:02.67	2:02.72	2:02.60	2:02.80	2:02.77
1500m	4:10.22	4:12.30	4:12.00	4:11.59	4:11.70	4:13.32	4:12.89	4:12.60	4:11.80	4:12.93
3000m	9:01.50	9:05.94	9:04.04	9:03.64	9:01.60	9:05.75	9:06.05	9:01.70	9:01.83	**9:00.65**
10000m	34:26.36	33:59.39	33:29.46	33:19.20	33:11.31	33:23.91	33:28.44	33:05.13	33:05.80	**33:01.57**
Marathon	2:37:29	2:38:17	2:37:58	2:37:06	2:35:29	2:37:04	2:36:48	2:35:40	2:36:14	**2:35:04**
100mh	13.48	13.48	13.47	13.45	13.39	13.47	13.42	13.41	**13.35**	13.38
400mh	58.07	58.00	57.89	57.87	57.50	57.79	57.88	57,72	**57.58**	58.02
HJ	1.87	1.87	**1.88**	**1.88**	**1.88**	1.87	1.87	1.87	**1.88**	**1.88**
LJ	6.48	6.48	6.48	6.46	**6.53**	6.45	6.42	6.44	6.45	6.44
SP	17.18	16.92	17.12	**17.19**	16.95	16.30	16.60	16.52	16.40	16.30+
DT	**58.50**	57.14	57.48	57.78	57.40	56.48	56.02	55.78	56.20	55.48
JT	57.74	57.44	57.20	57.82	**58.12**	56.80	56.48	56.08	56.36	56.56
Heptathlon	c5590	5566	5654	5701	**5741**	5696	5703	5671	5661	5635

All-time record levels indicated in bold

ADDITIONAL BIOGRAPHIES

Athletes who impressed with their form in early 1994

Jean-Charles GICQUEL (FRA) b.24 Feb 1967 Ploërmel 2.00m 81kg. ACR Locminé.
At HJ: WCh: '93- 11=; EC: '90- dnq 14; EI: '94- 2; ECp: '89- 8, '93- 2. French champion 1987, 1990.
Progression at HJ: 1981- 1.89, 1982- 1.97, 1983- 2.07, 1984- 2.09, 1985- 2.23, 1986- 2.21i/2.18, 1987- 2.27, 1988- 2.28, 1989- 2.27, 1990- 2.30, 1991- 2.25i/2.24, 1992- 2.23, 1993- 2.30, 1994- 2.35i.
French indoor records at 2.33 and 2.35 for European Indoor silver 1994.

Manuel MATIAS (POR) b.30 Mar 1962 Ferreira do Alentejo 1.72m 58kg. Maratona C.Portugal.
At Mar: WCh: '91- dnf; EC: '90- 8; WCp: '91- 2, '93- 36.
Progression at Mar: 1988- 2:10:19, 1989- 2:09.43, 1990- 2:14.27, 1991- 2:10:21, 1992- 2:08:38, 1993- 2:15:25, 1994- 2:08:33. pbs: 1500m 3:44.15 '87, 3000m 7:59.26 '89, 5000m 13:46.37 '90, 10000m 28:31.9 '88, 3000mSt 8:37.5 '86.
Has won three of his 14 marathons, his début at Paris 1988, Fukuoka 1989 and Gyeongju 1994. Second Berlin 1992. Fourth at Chicago 1988, London 1989.

Daniel SANGOUMA (FRA) b.7 Feb 1965 Saint Denis, Réunion 1.87m 84kg. CO Ulis. Marketing student.
At 200m (100m, 4 x100m relay): OG: '88- qf/3R, '92- (qf); WCh: '87- qf, '91- sf/2R, '93- (qf); WI: '85- 4; EI: '92- 2, '94- 1; EJ: '83- 8/4R; ECp: '85- 6, '89- 3/2R (2), '93- 4/2R (3). At 100m: EC: '90- 2/1R; WCp: '89- 3/3R; ECp: '91- 2/1R. Won French 100m 1990-1, 1993.
World 4x100m record 1990. French 100m record 1990.
Progression at 100m, 200m: 1981- 22.3w; 1982- 11.04/10.6, 21.88; 1983- 10.70/10.6/10.57w, 21.15; 1984- 10.62, 21.09; 1985- 10.1/10.45/

10.29w, 20.60; 1986- 10.59/10.42w, 21.04; 1987- 10.40, 20.73/20.67w; 1988- 10.52/10.44w, 20.46; 1989- 10.17, 20.20; 1990- 10.02; 1991- 10.18; 1992- 10.29, 20.52; 1993- 10.23/10.09dt, 20.63/20.60w. pbs: 60m 6.63i '92, 150m 15.23 '89, HJ 2.03 '90, LJ 7.91 '91.

Hezekiel SEPENG (RSA) b. 30 Jun 1974 1.78m 58kg.
At 800m: WCh: '93- 5; WJ: '92- 5. SA champion 1993.
Progression at 800m: 1992- 1:47.51, 1993- 1:45.46, 1994- 1:45.32. pbs: 400m 46.75 '93, 1500m 3:43.08 '93.

Women

Desislava ALEXANDROVA (BUL) b. 27 Oct 1975.
At HJ: EI: '94- 2; WJ: '92- 5=; EJ: '93- 2.
Progression at HJ: 1990- 1.75, 1991- 1.84, 1992- 1.91, 1993- 1.92, 1994- 1.96i.

Yelena ARSHINTSEVA (RUS) b.5 Apr 1971 Saransk 1.64m 54kg. Saransk Sp. Student
At 10kmW: WCh: '93- 12. At 3000mW: WI: '93- 5; EI: '94- 3. Won RUS 10kmW 1993.
Progression at 10kmW: 1990- 47:59, 1991- 43:52, 1992- 42:52, 1993- 42:03. pbs 11:57.48i '94, 5000mW 21:18.39 '92.

Sofia BOZHANOVA (BUL) b.4 Oct 1967 Purvomay 1.70m 58kg. Trakia Plovdiv. PE student.
At LJ: WCh: '87- 15; EC: '86- 10; EJ: '83- 6, '85- 1; ECp: '87- 3. At TJ: EI: '92- 2, '94- 3. Won Balkan TJ 1992, Bulgarian LJ 1990-1, TJ 1990.
Two Bulgarian triple jump records 1990-1.
Progression at LJ, TJ: 1981- 5.95, 1982- 6.26, 1983- 6.40, 1984- 6.45, 1985- 6.68, 1986- 6.71, 1987- 6.80, 1988- 6.70/6.72w, 1989- 6.20i, 1990- 6.51, 14.06; 1991- 6.47, 14.08; 1992- 6.20, 13.98i/13.73/13.77w; 1993- 5.99, 13.66; 1994- 14.52i.

Hellen CHEPNGENO (KEN) b.2 Aug 1967 Kericho District. Corporal in Prisons Service.
At 3000m: AfCh: '93- 3. World CC: '92- 15, '94- 1. Won Kenyan 1500m 1992.
Progression at 3000m: 1991- 9:47.5, 1992- 9:20.0, 1993- 8:44.04. pbs: 800m 2:06.6 '92, 1500m 4:07.35 '93, 5000m 15:21.98 '93.
Son born 1989. A high jumper and javelin thrower until injury made her turn to running.

Natalya DUKHNOVA (BLS) b.16 Jul 1966 1.76m 64kg.
At 800m: WCh: '93- h; EI: '94- 1. BLS champion 1992-3.
Progression at 800m: 1989- 2:02.1, 1990- 2:01.26, 1991- 2:01.87, 1992- 2:00.59, 1993- 1:58.01. pbs: 400m 52.1 '93, 1000m 2:36.56 '93, 1500m 4:11.19 '93.

Svetlana GONCHARENKO (RUS) b.28 May 1971 Rostov na Donu 1.76m 61kg. née Doronina. Novocherkassk TU. Student.
At 400m: EI: '94- 1. At 200m: EJ: '87- 5 (2 4x100mR).
Progression at 400m: 1988- 54.22, 1992- 53.69, 1993- 54.00, 1994- 51.62i. pbs: 100m 11.48 '92, 200m 23.40 '93, 300m 36.81i '94.

Anne PIQUEREAU (FRA) b.15 Jun 1964 Poitiers 1.71m 63kg. Stade Clermont-Ferrand. Studied Physiotherapy.
At 100mh: OG: '88- qf, '92- sf; WCh: '87- 5, '91- sf; EC: '86- sf, '90- sf; EJ: '81- 3; WSG: '85- 3; WCp: '92- 2; ECp: '87- 5. French champion 1988, 1992. At 60mh: WI: '91- 5; EI: '85- 3, '86- 2, '94- 3; WIG: '85- 3.
Progression at 100mh: 1980- 14.54/13.86w, 1981- 13.76/13.67w, 1982- 13.64/13.5w, 1983- 13.22/13.0, 1984- 13.39/13.30w, 1985- 12.89, 1986- 12.95, 1987- 12.82, 1988- 12.94/12.83w, 1989- 12.87, 1990- 12.82, 1991- 12.74, 1992- 12.85/12.70w, 1993- 13.13. pbs: 100m: 11.87/11.5 '87, 200m 24.1 '89, 50mh 6.83i '91, 60mh 7.88i '90, LJ 6.52 '91.

Fernanda RIBEIRO (POR) b,23 Jun 1969 Penafiel 1.61m 48kg. Maratona C.Maia,
At 10000m: WCh: '93- 11; EC: dnf. At 3000m: OG: '88- h, '92- h; WCh: '87- h; EC: '86- h, '90- dnf; WJ: '86- 4, '88- 2; EJ: '83- 11, '85- 4, '87- 1; EI: '94- 1. World CC: '94- 10. Won POR 1500m 1989-90, 3000m 1985, 1993; 10000m 1992.
Progression at 3000m, 10000m: 1982- 9:53.7, 1983- 9:21.71, 1984- 9:11.63, 1985- 9:14.19, 1986- 9:09.39, 1987- 8:56.53, 1988- 9:00.38, 1989- 9:04.33, 32:38.07; 1990- 9:03.35, 32:39.34; 1991- 8:57.64, 33:45.45; 1992- 8:56.10, 32:22.70; 1993- 8:51.91, 31:50.51. pbs: 800m 2:07.35 '91, 1500m 4:12.90 '91, Half Mar 71:11 '93.

Amendments to Biographies - KENYA
Simon CHEMOIYWO b.20 Apr 1968. Air Force technician.
Dominic KIRUI b.12 Apr 1965. Army corporal.
William SIGEI b.14 Oct 1969.

WORLD JUNIOR WOMEN'S LISTS 1993

100 METRES

Mark		Name		Nat	Born	Pos	Meet	Venue	Date
11.18	1.1	Nicole	Mitchell	JAM	5.6.74	3	NC	Kingston	2 Jul
		11.20	-0.3			7	WC	Stuttgart	16 Aug
		11.23	0.0			2q1	WC	Stuttgart	15 Aug
		11.26	-0.6			4s2	WC	Stuttgart	16 Aug
11.28	1.4	Marion	Jones	USA	12.10.75	1h1		Norwalk	4 Jun
		11.31	1.3			1		Norwalk	28 May
		11.31	1.4			1	GWest	Sacramento	12 Jun
		11.32	2.0			1		Norwalk	22 May
11.35	1.2		Ou Yanlan	CHN	.1.74	2h3	NG	Beijing	8 Sep
11.39	0.6		Wang Jing	CHN	16.1.75	3h2	NG	Beijing	8 Sep
11.45	-0.4	Hana	Benesová	TCH	19.4.75	1	NC	Jablonec nad Nisou	3 Jul
11.49	0.6	Benita	Kelley	USA	15.9.75	1		Columbia	14 May
11.52	0.7	Damarayathi	Darsha	SRI	13.2.75	1h4	AsiC	Manila	1 Dec
11.54	2.0	Andrea	Anderson	USA	17.9.77	2		Norwalk	22 May
11.55	1.6	Savatheda	Fynes	BAH	17.10.74	5	NC	Nassau	17 Jun
11.55	0.9	Yekaterina	Leshcheva	RUS	21.4.74	1	NC-j	Vladimir	2 Jul
11.57	0.5	Lesa	Parker	USA	8.1.74	4	PennR	Philadelphia	24 Apr
11.58	1.9	Dainelkis	Pérez	CUB	6.1.76	4	Barr	Habana	22 May
11.58	0.5	Katharine	Merry	GBR	21.9.74	2	EJ	San Sebastián	30 Jul
11.58		Philomina	Mensah	GHA	11.5.75	2		Weinstadt	7 Aug
11.62	1.6	Kanae	Ito	JPN	23.8.75	4	EAsiG	Shanghai	13 May
11.63	2.0	DeMonica	Davis	USA	24.1.74	1		San Marcos	27 Mar
11.63		Casey	Custer	USA	11.11.74	1		Arlington	17 Apr
11.64		Omotayo	Akinremi	NGR	13.9.74	1		Tempe	10 Apr
11.64	1.3	Ekaterina	Tosheva	BUL	1.2.74	4		Sofia	15 May
11.64	2.0	Delphine	Combe	FRA	6.12.74	1s	NC-j	Lens	9 Jul
Wind assisted									
11.02	2.1	Nicole	Mitchell	JAM	5.6.74	1	Mutual	Kingston	1 May
11.21	2.8	Marion	Jones	USA	12.10.75	1		Mission Viejo	15 May
11.38		Casey	Custer	USA	11.11.74	1		Lubbock	2 May
11.40	5.1	Katharine	Merry	GBR	21.9.74	1	NC-j	Bedford	3 Jul
11.50	3,2	Jackie	Knox	USA	.74	7		Knoxville	16 May
11.52	3.6	Andrea	Anderson	USA	17.9.77	1h5		Mission Viejo	15 May
11.53	3.6	Lauren	Hewitt	AUS	25.11.78	1		Canberra	11 Dec
11.55	3.5	Nanceen	Perry	USA	19.4.77	1		Austin	15 May
11.55	2.2	Delphine	Combe	FRA	6.12.74	1	NC-j	Lens	9 Jul
11.55	2.2	Marie-Joëlle	Dogbo	FRA	13.2.75	2	NC-j	Lens	9 Jul
11.56	5.1	Sophia	Smith	GBR	8.12.74	2	NC-j	Bedford	3 Jul
11.56	4.1	Kelly	Miller	NZL	5.6.77	1h2		Canberra	10 Dec
11.57	6.1	DeMonica	Davis	USA	24.1.74	3		Arlington	10 Apr
11.59	3.1	Aminah	Haddad	USA	13.9.78	1h3		Norwalk	4 Jun
11.59A	2.3	Kerry Ann	Richards	JAM	22.4.76	3	CAC	Cali	30 Jul
11.60		Carmetia	Mackey	BAH	74	3		Natchitoches	24 Apr
11.60	2.6	Tara	Perry	CAN	20.10.74	1		Kamloops	16 Aug
11.61		Amarachukwu	Eze	NGR	28.7.74				10 Apr
11.62	7.5	Tonya	Williams	USA	5.10.74	1		East Lansing	23 May
11.62		Kenya	Alex	USA	.74	3		San Marcos	23 Apr
Hand timed									
11.2	1.5	Marion	Jones	USA	12.10.75	1		Pomona	20 Mar
11.3	0.3	Monique	Hennagan	USA	26.5.76	1B		Columbia	14 May
11.3	-1.7	Yekaterina	Leshcheva	RUS	21.4.74	1		Dzerzhinsk	29 Aug
11.4		Ionela	Tîrlea	ROM	9.2.76	1		Bucuresti	7 Aug
Wind assisted									
11.0		Nicole	Mitchell	JAM	5.6.74	1s		Kingston	26 Mar
11.0		Beverley	Langley	JAM	16.12.76	1s		Kingston	26 Mar

200 METRES

Mark		Name		Nat	Born	Pos	Meet	Venue	Date
23.00	-0.3	Marion	Jones	USA	12.10.75	1		Norwalk	28 May
		23.01	1.7			1	GWest	Sacramento	12 Jun
		23.14	-2.1			1		Norwalk	19 Jun
23.20	1.2	Katharine	Merry	GBR	21.9.74	1	NC	London	13 Jun
		23.27	0.8			6	EP	Roma	27 Jun

Mark		Name		Nat	Born	Pos	Meet	Venue	Date
23.25	-1.1	Nicole	Mitchell	JAM	5.6.74	1	Carif	Fort-de-France	11 Apr
23.25	0.8	Oksana	Dyachenko	RUS	26.11.74	5	Slovn	Bratislava	1 Jun
23.25	1.4	Yekaterina	Leshcheva	RUS	21.4.74	1		Jyväskylä	10 Aug
23.29	-0.6	Damarayathi	Darsha	SRI	13.2.75	2	AsiC	Manila	4 Dec
23.43A	1.0	Savatheda	Fynes	BAH	17.10.74	2h2	CAC	Cali	31 Jul
23.48	1.6	Omotayo	Akinremi	NGR	13.9.74	1		Berkeley	21 May
23.49	-0.8		Huang Mei	CHN	.1.75	h	NC	Jinan	4 Jun
23.49		Ionela	Tîrlea	ROM	9.2.76	1		Bucuresti	12 Jun
23.53	1.3	Hana	Benesová	TCH	19.4.75	1h1	EJ	San Sebastián	30 Jul
23.54		Delphine	Combe	FRA	6.12.74	1		Vénissieux	2 Jul
23.57	1.9	Nanceen	Perry	USA	19.4.77	1		Austin	15 May
23.57	0.9	Sophia	Smith	GBR	8.12.74	1s2	EJ	San Sebastián	30 Jul
23.60		Andrea	Anderson	USA	17.9.77	1		Long Beach	7 May
23.61	1.3	Carmen	Bertmaring	GER	28.3.76	3h1	EJ	San Sebastián	30 Jul
23.62	0.0	Monique	Hennagan	USA	26.5.76	1		Columbia	14 May
23.63	1.4	Jennifer	Wilson	USA	27.6.76	1	PAJ	Winnipeg	17 Jul
23.64	-0.1		Wang Jing	CHN	16.1.75			Shanghai	10 Apr
23.65	-1.1	Astia	Walker	JAM	75	2	Carif	Fort-de-France	11 Apr
Wind assisted									
22.79	2.6	Marion	Jones	USA	12.10.75	1		Norwalk	22 May
		22.95	2.5			1		Mission Viejo	15 May
		23.12	2.5			1h1		Norwalk	4 Jun
23.32A	6.2	Debbie	Ferguson	BAH	16.1.76	2	CAC	Cali	31 Jul
23.48	2.6	Aminah	Haddad	USA	13.9.78	2		Norwalk	22 May
23.58	2.6	Andrea	Anderson	USA	17.9.77	3		Norwalk	22 May
23.61		Carmetia	Mackey	BAH	74	1		Natchitoches	24 Apr
23.62	3.4	Camille	Noel	CAN	14.4.74	1	NC-j	Sherbrooke	11 Jul
Hand timed									
23.4	-0.1	Omotayo	Akinremi	NGR	13.9.74	1		Berkeley	22 May
Wind assisted									
23.1		Andrea	Anderson	USA	17.9.77	1		Long Beach	Apr

400 METRES

Mark	Name		Nat	Born	Pos	Meet	Venue	Date
51.25		Zhang Hengyun	CHN	25.10.74	2	NG	Beijing	11 Sep
51.88	Camille	Noel	CAN	14.4.74	3	Pac-10	Berkeley	22 May
52.01	Claudine	Williams	JAM	8.1.76	1	PAJ	Winnipeg	16 Jul
52.02	Beverley	Grant	JAM	17.10.74	5	NC	Kingston	3 Jul
52.10	Mariana	Florea	ROM	29.8.76	1	RomIC	Bucuresti	18 Jun
	52.14				1		Bucuresti	29 May
	52.14				1	EJ	San Sebastián	31 Jul
	52.24				4	EP	Roma	26 Jun
52.24	Omolade	Akinremi	NGR	13.9.74	3	MSR	Walnut	17 Apr
52.24	Magdalena	Nedelcu	ROM	12.5.74	1B		Southampton	6 Jun
52.30	Monique	Hennagan	USA	26.5.76	1	NC-j	Spokane	27 Jun
52.43	Omotayo	Akinremi	NGR	13.9.74	3	SunA	Tempe	3 Apr
52.47	Cynthia	Newsome	USA	5.4.76	2	NC-j	Spokane	27 Jun
52.88	Hana	Benesová	TCH	19.4.75	1		Rehlingen	31 May
52.94	Ionela	Tirlea	ROM	9.2.76	1C		Southampton	6 Jun
52.99	Stacy	Milligan	USA	30.6.75	3		Austin	21 May
53.04	Ludmila	Formanová	TCH	2.1.74	2	NC	Jablonec nad Nisou	4 Jul
53.11	Ellen	Grant	JAM	17.10.74	1	NC-j	Kingston	3 Jul
53.12	Donna	Howard	USA	28.8.74	1		Baton Rouge	1 Aug
53.16	Lucie	Rangassamy	FRA	6.8.74	3	EJ	San Sebastián	31 Jul
53.17	Sandra	Kuschmann	GER	15.2.74	4	EJ	San Sebastián	31 Jul
53.57	Rebecca	Campbell	AUS	23.1.76	1	NC-j	Brisbane	7 Mar
53.60	Venda	Newhouse	USA	.74	5		Austin	21 May

800 METRES

Mark	Name		Nat	Born	Pos	Meet	Venue	Date
1:57.18		Wang Yuan	CHN	8.4.76	2h2	NG	Beijing	8 Sep
	1:58.16				5	NG	Beijing	9 Sep
1:57.77		Lu Yi	CHN	10.4.74	4	NG	Beijing	9 Sep
	1:59.39				2h3	NG	Beijing	8 Sep
	2:00.95				h	NC	Jinan	5 Jun
2:01.36		Liu Wanjie	CHN	1.11.75	h	NC	Jinan	2 Jun
	2:01.51				4h1	NG	Beijing	8 Sep

Mark	Name		Nat	Born	Pos	Meet	Venue	Date
2:01.49		Liu Huirong	CHN	11.5.75	3h1	NG	Beijing	8 Sep
2:02.83		Liang Lihe	CHN	.1.74	4h3	NG	Beijing	8 Sep
2:03.78	Ludmila	Formanová	TCH	2.1.74	3		Kerkrade	29 May
2:04.03		Tang Xueqing	CHN	16.10.74			Beijing	3 May
2:04.18	Olga	Secman	ROM	10.6.74			Bucuresti	18 Jun
2:04.4	Selina	Kosgei	KEN	17.6.76	2		Nairobi	29 Jul
2:04.49	Anne	Bruns	GER	3.7.74	5		Kassel	26 May
2:04.81	Elena	Cosoveanu	ROM	24.7.74	1	NC-j	Bucuresti	8 Aug
2:05.08	Nuria	Fernández	ESP	16.8.76	1		Toledo	19 Jun
2:05.35	Svetlana	Voronicheva	RUS	76	1		Valkenswaard	8 Jul
2:05.44	Alina	Cucerzan	ROM	28.7.74	2	NC-j	Bucuresti	8 Aug
2:05.55	Annet	Zierfuss	GER	21.10.74	9		Jena	13 Jun
2:05.6	Claudine	Williams	JAM	8.1.76	1		Kingston	26 Mar
2:05.65	Emilie	Neveu	FRA	11.12.76	2		Valkenswaard	8 Jul
2:06.18	Oksana	Kushnir	UKR	.75	2	NC-j	Chernigov	27 Jun
2:06.2	Sarah	Jamieson	AUS	24.3.75	1		Perth	23 Oct

1000 METRES

Mark	Name		Nat	Born	Pos	Meet	Venue	Date
2:39.4	Susie	Power	AUS	26.3.75	mx		Canberra	7 Jan

1500 METRES

Mark	Name		Nat	Born	Pos	Meet	Venue	Date
3:59.81		Wang Yuan	CHN	8.4.76	7	NG	Beijing	11 Sep
	4:01.79				5h1	NG	Beijing	10 Sep
	4:07.59				h	NC	Jinan	2 Jun
4:00.05		Lu Yi	CHN	10.4.74	8	NG	Beijing	11 Sep
	4:01.82				6h1	NG	Beijing	10 Sep
	4:04.24				h	NC	Jinan	2 Jun
	4:05.97				s	WC	Stuttgart	20 Aug
	4:06.06				4	WC	Stuttgart	22 Aug
4:01.71		Li Ying	CHN	24.6.75	4h2	NG	Beijing	10 Sep
	4:02.12				9	NG	Beijing	11 Sep
4:08.43		Tang Xueqing	CHN	16.10.74	8h1	NG	Beijing	10 Sep
4:09.46		Wang Chunmei	CHN	.4.76	7h2	NG	Beijing	10 Sep
4:09.98		Liu Yan	CHN	.3.74	9h1	NG	Beijing	10 Sep
4:10.32	Gabriela	Szabo	ROM	14.11.75	3	NC	Bucuresti	5 Sep
4:10.34		Liu Wanjie	CHN	.11.75	8h2	NG	Beijing	10 Sep
4:13.13	Elena	Cosoveanu	ROM	24.7.74	2		Bucuresti	3 Jul
4:14.2mx	Angela	Raines-White	AUS	22.3.74	mx		Brisbane	10 Jan
	4:20.04				1		Melbourne	21 Nov
4:14.46	Susie	Power	AUS	26.3.75	1		Canberra	25 Jan
4:14.69	Yoshiko	Ichikawa	JPN	18.4.76	3	Toto	Fukuoka	18 Sep
4:14.74		Ma Ningning	CHN	20.9.76	1	EAsiJ	Hong Kong	13 Nov
4:16.6	Mioara	Cosuleanu	ROM	31.1.76			Schwechat	30 May
4:16.96		Zhan Jianying	CHN	.6.74	h	NG	Beijing	10 Sep
4:17.04	Alina	Cucerzan	ROM	28.7.75		NC-j	Bucuresti	7 Aug
4:17.26	Marta	Dominguez	ESP	3.11.75	1	EJ	San Sebastián	1 Aug
4:17.31	Denica	Costescu	ROM	26.1.76			Bucuresti	29 May
4:17.49	Olga	Secman	ROM	10.6.74			Bucuresti	29 May
4:18.10	Annemari	Sandell	FIN	2.1.77	3	v SWE	Stockholm	29 Aug
4:18.57	Masako	Saito	JPN	24.11.74	4	Toto	Fukuoka	18 Sep

1 MILE

Mark	Name		Nat	Born	Pos	Meet	Venue	Date
4:35.28	Susie	Power	AUS	26.3.75	1		Hobart	17 Jan

3000 METRES

Mark	Name		Nat	Born	Pos	Meet	Venue	Date
8:36.45		Ma Ningning	CHN	20.9.76	4	NC	Jinan	6 Jun
8:42.39		Li Ying	CHN	24.6.75	8	NG	Beijing	13 Sep
	8:48.36				4h2	NG	Beijing	12 Sep
8:50.97	Gabriela	Szabo	ROM	14.11.75	1	EJ	San Sebastián	1 Aug
8:51.22	Annemari	Sandell	FIN	2.1.77	2	EJ	San Sebastián	1 Aug
	8:53.58				13	WC	Stuttgart	16 Aug
	8:54.75				5h2	WC	Stuttgart	14 Aug
8:59.70	Sally	Barsosio	KEN	21.3.78	1		Weinstadt	7 Aug
8:59.71	Susie	Power	AUS	26.3.75	1		Melbourne	25 Feb

Mark	Name		Nat	Born	Pos	Meet	Venue	Date
9:00.27	Denisa	Costescu	ROM	26.1.75			Bucuresti	18 Jun
9:06.03	Masako	Saito	JPN	24.11.74	2		Naruto	28 Oct
9:07.01		Zhan Jiangying	CHN	.6.74	20	NC	Jinan	6 Jun
9:07.08	Azumi	Miyazaki	JPN	3.3.75	3		Naruto	28 Oct
9:07.99	Kaori	Takahashi	JPN	29.1.76	1		Naruto	27 Oct
9:09.46	Miwa	Sugawara	JPN	5.9.76	2		Naruto	27 Oct
9:10.18	Miwako	Yamanaka	JPN	24.5.78	3		Naruto	27 Oct
9:11.16	Madoka	Suzuki	JPN	1.1.75	2		Tokyo	27 Jun
9:11.41	Esther	Wanjiru	KEN	27.3.77	1		Miyagi	30 May
9:12.27+	Gladys	Ondeyo	KEN	10.5.75	2k		Turku	20 Jul
9:12.52	Yuko	Kubota	JPN	5.10.74	3		Tokyo	27 Jun
9:13.46	Rose	Cheruiyot	KEN	21.7.76	1		Canberra	11 Dec
9:13.6	Kazuyo	Ibata	JPN	6.10.74			Amagasaki	11 Sep
9:14.47	Noriko	Wada	JPN	24.5.75	4		Tokyo	27 Jun
9:14.48	Merima	Denboba	ETH	21.8.74	2	AfrC	Durban	27 Jun

5000 METRES

Mark	Name		Nat	Born	Pos	Meet	Venue	Date
15:26.33	Annemari	Sandell	FIN	2.1.77	4	DNG	Stockholm	5 Jul
15:45.09	Maiko	Kawasaki	JPN	27.2.74	7	Toto	Fukuoka	18 Sep
15:47.1	Kazuyo	Ibata	JPN	6.10.74	6		Amagasaki	9 Oct
15:52.02	Yuko	Kubota	JPN	5.10.74	6		Shizuoka	5 May
15:56.0	Noriko	Wada	JPN	24.5.75	1		Kumamoto	18 Dec
15:58.89	Madoka	Suzuki	JPN	1.1.75	8		Tokyo	17 Oct
15:59.4	Mika	Adachi	JPN	14.1.76	4		Kumamoto	18 Dec
16:01.21	Yukiko	Okamoto	JPN		5		Amagasaki	19 Sep
16:05.9	Kaori	Hosokawa	JPN	21.9.75	1		Kyoto	28 Nov
16:06.6	Hiromi	Masuda	JPN	18.7.76			Osaka	26 Nov
16:06.6	Megumi	Tanaka	JPN	4.9.75	2		Kyoto	28 Nov
16:06.93	Azumi	Miyazaki	JPN	3.3.75	10	Toto	Fukuoka	18 Sep
16:11.30	Takako	Hise	JPN		10		Amagasaki	19 Sep
16:11.3	Rie	Ueno	JPN		5		Kumamoto	18 Dec
16:09.3	Tomoko	Morigaki	JPN	6.9.76	3		Kyoto	28 Nov
16:11.8	Atsuko	Morigaki	JPN		4		Kyoto	28 Nov
16:13.4	Yuka	Kawakami	JPN		6		Kumamoto	18 Dec

10,000 METRES

Mark	Name		Nat	Born	Pos	Meet	Venue	Date
31:15.38	Sally	Barsosio	KEN	21.3.78	3	WC	Stuttgart	21 Aug
	32:16.0A				1		Nairobi	29 Jul
	32:27.99				1h1	WC	Stuttgart	19 Aug
	32:43.4A				1	NC	Nairobi	3 Jul
31:32.15		Feng Wenhui	CHN	21.1.74	9	NG	Beijing	8 Sep
32:09.94		Ma Ningning	CHN	20.9.76	3	NC	Jinan	2 Jun
32:54.55	Lydia	Cheromei	KEN	11.5.77	2	AfrC	Durban	23 Jun
32:57.72	Maiko	Kawasaki	JPN	27.2.74	3		Kumamoto	4 Apr
33:00.66	Chiaki	Shigaki	JPN	20.1.74	3		Fukuoka	3 Oct
33:06.2	Gladys	Ondeyo	KEN	10.5.75	1		Alavus	12 Jul
33:06.70	Yeshi	Gebre Selassie	ETH	.78	5	AfrC	Durban	23 Jun
33:32.0	Chizuko	Ishikawa	JPN	14.2.74	3		Tokyo	25 Sep
33:44.80	Hiromi	Tsujimura	JPN	27.11.74	9		Kumamto	4 Apr
33:56.72	Hisako	Tanaka	JPN	6.4.75	1		Tokyo	26 Jun
34:04.0	Megumi	Shigaki	JPN	21.1.74	2		Saga	20 Aug
34:04.6	Nana	Nagakawa	JPN	27.8.74	2		Kurume	22 Oct
34:05.42	Miyako	Toba	JPN	22.2.75	2		Tokyo	26 Jun
34:05.76	Naoko	Kitai	JPN	23.3.76	3		Tokyo	26 Jun
34:09.25	Miyo	Koshinuma	JPN	8.10.74	5		Tokyo	11 Sep
34:09.75	Yukiko	Saito	JPN		4		Tokyo	26 Jun
34:10.88	Evi	Kato	JPN	25.8.75	5		Tokyo	26 Jun
34:11.35	Filiya	Shemeyeva	RUS	16.11.74	10	Znam	Moskva	12 Jun
34:13.48	Akiko	Nagai	JPN	18.3.74	4		Tokyo	21 May

MARATHON

Mark	Name		Nat	Born	Pos	Meet	Venue	Date
2:30:15		Gu Dongmei	CHN	5.1.74	9		Tianjin	4 Apr
2:31:03		Feng Wenhui	CHN	21.1.74	10		Tianjin	4 Apr

100 METRES HURDLES

Mark	Wind	Name		Nat	Born	Pos	Meet	Venue	Date
13.29	2.0	Kim	Carson	USA	12.3.74	1h1	SEC	Knoxville	15 May
13.38A	1.7	Damaris	Anderson	CUB	24.10.74	3	CAC	Cali	30 Jul
13.42	0.5	Diane	Allahgreen	GBR	21.2.75	1	EJ	San Sebastián	1 Aug
13.49	2.0	Anjanette	Kirkland	USA	24.2.74	2		College Station	1 May
13.52	0.1	Kirsten	Bolm	GER	4.3.75	3		Scheessel	30 May
13.52	0.1	Vanessa	Koslowski	GER	19.1.75	4		Scheessel	30 May
13.53	1.2	Regina	Ahlke	GER	3.1.74	1		Recklinghausen	19 Jun
13.54	1.5	Tonya	Williams	USA	5.10.74	5	El	Paso	10 Apr
13.55	0.6	Claudia	Ruge	GER	14.8.75	3s1	NC	Duisburg	10 Jul
13.55	0.5	Katja	Fust	GER	29.7.74	2	EJ	San Sebastián	1 Aug
13.58	1.6	Sophie	Marrot	FRA	13.2.75	1		Tarbes	17 Jul
13.61	1.4	Akiko	Morimoto	JPN	17.2.77	1		Utsunomiya	2 Aug
13.66	2.0	Edit	Vári	HUN	31.5.75	1		Zalaegerszeg	19 Jun
13.66	-0.5	Aya	Tanaka	JPN	16.9.75	1		Naruto	25 Oct
13.68	0.1	Aneta	Bednarczyk	POL	10.5.74	3	NC	Kielce	25 Jul
13.71			Ding Ying	CHN	.10.76	H	NG	Beijing	11 Sep
13.72	0.6	Marilia Leticia	Souza	BRA	74	1	SAmJ	Barcelona, VEN	19 Jun
13.72	0.6	Gilda	Massa	PER	76	2	SAmJ	Barcelona, VEN	19 Jun
13.75		Astia	Walker	JAM	.75	1		Fort de France	11 Apr
13.75A	-1.0	Domingue	Calloway	USA	19.7.78	3		Provo	26 May
Wind assisted									
13.47	2.8	Anjanette	Kirkland	USA	24.2.74	2h2	NCAA	New Orleans	3 Jun
13.56	2.5	Akiko	Morimoto	JPN	17.2.77	1		Ageo	16 May
13.61	2.7	Aya	Tanaka	JPN	16.9.75	1		Tokyo	27 Jun
13.61	2.3	Aneta	Bednarczyk	POL	10.5.74	2h1	EJ	San Sebastián	31 Jul
13.74A		Domingue	Calloway	USA	19.7.78	3		Provo	26 May
Hand timed									
13.4	2.3	Gillian	Ragus	AUS	5.4.76	2		Perth	20 Nov

400 METRES HURDLES

Mark	Name		Nat	Born	Pos	Meet	Venue	Date
55.72		Zheng Liyuan	CHN	1.4.74	5	NG	Beijing	9 Sep
	56.24				2h3	NG	Beijing	8 Sep
56.43	Ionela	Tîrlea	ROM	9.2.76	1	EJ	San Sebastián	1 Aug
	56.68				1	NC-j	Bucuresti	12 Jun
56.48A	Tonya	Williams	USA	5.10.74	1		El Paso	10 Apr
56.86	Omotayo	Akinremi	NGR	13.9.74	1h2	NCAA	New Orleans	2 Jun
57.06	Rebecca	Campbell	AUS	23.1.76	1	NC-j	Brisbane	6 Mar
57.12	Omolade	Akinremi	NGR	13.9.74	2	SunA	Tempe	3 Apr
57.68	Erin	Blunt	USA	74	1	Pac-10	Berkeley	22 May
57.90	Anita	Oppong	GER	12.7.74	2	EJ	San Sebastián	1 Aug
58.04	Virna	De Angeli	ITA	27.2.76	2	3-N	Bondouffle	18 Sep
58.07	Lana	Jekabsone	LAT	16.10.74	3	EJ	San Sebastián	1 Aug
58.29	Yulia	Bavilskaya	RUS	12.7.75	2	3N-j	Lübeck	26 Jun
58.34	Lauren	Poetschka	AUS	22.10.74	2	NC-j	Brisbane	6 Mar
58.64	Kylie	Robertson	AUS	26.2.74	3		Canberra	25 Jan
58.74	Winsome	Cole	JAM	30.5.74	3	PAJ	Winnipeg	17 Jul
58.83	Eusheka	Bartley	GUY	74	1		Auburn	1 May
58.88	Angela	Harris	USA	5.3.75	2h1	NC-j	Spokane	26 Jun
58.91	Ikiko	Yamagata	JPN	3.1.75	2		Tokyo	12 Sep
58.98	Anjanette	Kirkland	USA	24.2.74	1		College Station	1 May
59.04	Allison	Curbishley	GBR	3.6.76	3h2	EJ	San Sebastián	31 Jul
59.10	Yelena	Kardash	RUS	.74	1		Bryansk	17 Jul
59.10	Anastasia	Klimova	RUS	74	5	EJ	San Sebastián	1 Aug
Hand timed								
57.5	Lauren	Poetschka	AUS	22.10.74	1		Perth	13 Nov

HIGH JUMP

Mark	Name		Nat	Born	Pos	Meet	Venue	Date
1.93	Amy	Acuff	USA	14.7.75	1	Alpen	Innsbruck	28 Aug
1.93	Sabrina	De Leeuw	BEL	19.8.74	1	McD	Sheffield	29 Aug
	1.92				1		Nivelles	16 May
1.93	Yoko	Ota	JPN	14.1.75	4	Toto	Fukuoka	18 Sep
1.92	Desislava	Aleksandrova	BUL	27.10.75	1	Balk-J	Thessaloniki	10 Jul
1.92	Wanita	Dykstra	CAN	30.1.75	1		North York	8 Aug
1.89i	Venelina	Veneva	BUL	13.6.74	1		Sofia	20 Feb
	1.85				3		Stara Zagora	24 Jul

Mark		Name		Nat	Born	Pos	Meet	Venue	Date
1.89			Guan Weihua	CHN	14.6.75	1		Shijiazhuang	25 Apr
1.89		Viktoria	Stepina	UKR	21.2.76	1	NC-j	Chernigov	26 Jun
1.89		Yelena	Razmyslovich	RUS	22.8.74	1	NC-j	Vladimir	4 Jul
1.88		Svetlana	Bogomaz	UKR	16.7.74	1		Chernigov	4 Sep
1.86i		Stefania	Lovison	ITA	21.12.74	1		Verona	31 Jan
		1.86				1		San Bonifacio	22 May
1.86i		Katja	Kilpi	FIN	26.4.74	1	NC-j	Tampere	13 Feb
1.86		Natalya	Shimon	UKR	15.3.75	1		Rovno	25 May
1.86		Svetlana	Ivanova	RUS	8.2.74	2	NC-j	Vladimir	4 Jul
1.86		Romy	Pleikies	GER	5.2.75	4	EJ	San Sebastián	31 Jul
1.86		Olga	Kaliturina	RUS	9.3.76	1		Jyväskylä	10 Aug
1.86		Emelie	Färdigh	SWE	13.9.77	1		Västerås	19 Sep
1.86		Jurgita	Voveryte	LIT	.74				
1.85		Monika	Göllner	AUT	23.10.74	1		Bolzano	25 Sep
1.84			Liu Yan	CHN	.3.75	1			16 May
1.84		Mária	Melová	SVK	21.10.75	1		Banská Bystrica	6 Jun
1.84		Melinda	Boice	USA	29.12.74	1	GWest	Sacramento	12 Jun
1.84		Kajsa	Bergquist	SWE	12.10.76	1		Valkenswaard	7 Jul
1.84		Tanja	Leinonen	FIN	10.4.75	2	NC	Mikkeli	31 Jul

POLE VAULT

Mark		Name		Nat	Born	Pos	Meet	Venue	Date
3.80		Christine	Adams	GER	28.2.74	1		Gladbeck	18 Jul
3.70		Veronika	Göbel	GER	9.6.75	1	NC-j	Dortmund	4 Jul
3.60		Andrea	Müller	GER	29.6.74	2		Dillingen	4 Jun
3.60		Marion	Meyer	GER	9.7.75	1	3N-j	Lübeck	26 Jun
3.55i		Jana	Kabová	TCH	24.3.74	5		Zweibrücken	29 Jan
3.50i		Daniela	Bartová	TCH	74	1		Praha	21 Feb
		3.40				1		Praha	1 Jun
3.50i		Janet	Zach	GER	19.6.75	1		Berlin	17 Jan
		3.50						Cottbus	26 May
3.50		Ariane	Knoll	GER	1.7.77	4	3N-j	Lübeck	26 Jun
3.50		Nastja	Ryshich	GER	19.9.77	3		Stuttgart	30 Jul
3.50			Du Juan	CHN	.3.75	1		Beijing	25 Oct
3.45		Adriana	Fugaru	ROM	7.2.74	2		Bucuresti	30 May
3.40		Melina	Hamilton	NZL	15.6.76	1		Hamilton	3 Apr
3.40		Gianina	Rusu	ROM	7.12.74			Schwechat	30 May
Exhibition: 3.57		Daniela	Bartová	TCH	74	1		Rumburk	10 Jul

LONG JUMP

Mark		Name		Nat	Born	Pos	Meet	Venue	Date
6.78i	-	Erica	Johansson	SWE	5.2.74	2	NC	Malmö	21 Feb
		6.71i	-			6	WI	Toronto	12 Mar
		6.64i	-			6		Liévin	13 Feb
		6.61i	-			3	DNG	Stockholm	9 Feb
		6.61i	-			Q	WI	Toronto	12 Mar
		6.58i	-			5		Berlin	5 Feb
		6.56	0.1			1	EJ	San Sebastián	30 Jul
6.74		Olga	Rublyova	RUS	28.10.74	1	NC-j	Vladimir	3 Jul
6.71	1.5	Marion	Jones	USA	12.10.75	1		Norwalk	19 Jun
		6.58				1		Camarillo	30 Apr
6.52	1.1	Kirsten	Bolm	GER	4.3.75	1		Berlin	4 Sep
6.46	0.4	Iolanta	Khropach	UKR	22.9.74	1		Rovno	25 May
6.44	0.1	Cristina	Nicolau	ROM	9.8.77	3	EJ	San Sebastián	30 Jul
6.42		Anna	Mironova	RUS	15.10.75	2		Voronezh	25 Jul
6.40	1.0	Yelena	Lysak	RUS	19.10.75	4	EJ	San Sebastián	30 Jul
6.38	0.7		Miao Xiaojun	CHN	28.4.74	9	NG	Beijing	10 Sep
6.36		Tatyana	Dyatlova	BLS	12.1.75			Gomel	22 May
6.36	1.2	Ermelinda	Shehu	ALB	74	1	Balk-J	Thessaloniki	11 Jul
6.35i	-	Ingvild	Larsen	NOR	3.10.75	1	NC	Stange	20 Feb
6.35	1.5		Liu Qin	CHN	.74			Beijing	3 May
6.35	-0.1	Hitomi	Takamatsu	JPN	21.8.74	*		Tokyo	23 May
6.34		Lacene	Golding	JAM	24.3.75	1	NC-j	Kingston	3 Jul
6.33	1.7	Joanne	Dear	GBR	8.6.75	1		Birmingham	19 May
6.33		Lisette	Cusa	CUB	26.2.75	1		Habana	2 Jul
6.31		Icolyn	Kelly	JAM	1.7.74	1	JUCO	Odessa	22 May
6.31	0.7	Tatyana	Nikolayeva	UKR	26.2.76	2		Rovno	25 May

Mark		Name		Nat	Born	Pos	Meet	Venue	Date
6.31		Stephanie	Hort	GER	13.2.75	1	NC-j	Dortmund	3 Jul
6.30	1.0	Irina	Melnikova I	RUS	9.1.74	1	3N-j	Lübeck	26 Jun
Wind assisted									
6.75	2.7	Marion	Jones	USA	12.10.75	1		Norwalk	22 May
6.53	2.4	Ingvild	Larsen	NOR	3.10.75	1		Florø	22 May
6.44	3.2	Hitomi	Takamatsu	JPN	21.8.74	2	MpC	Tokyo	13 Jun
6.36		Marvette	Collis	STV	27.3.74	1		Redding	22 May

TRIPLE JUMP

Mark		Name		Nat	Born	Pos	Meet	Venue	Date
14.29	1.4		Ren Ruiping	CHN	1.1.75	1	NG	Beijing	13 Sep
		14.05				1	AsiC	Manila	4 Dec
		13.91	0.4			2	NC	Jinan	3 Jun
13.86	1.8	Yelena	Lysak	RUS	19.10.75	1	EJ	San Sebastián	1 Aug
		13.77				1	NC-j	Vladimir	4 Jul
		13.74	-0.3			1	NC-23	Dzerzhinsk	29 Aug
13.73	1.6		Wang Xiangrong	CHN	1.2.76	*	NG	Beijing	13 Sep
13.68		Olga Lidia	Cepero	CUB	4.5.75	1		Habana	3 Jul
13.65	1.1	Natalya	Klimovets	BLS	11.4.74	2	EJ	San Sebastián	1 Aug
13.53	0.5	Irina	Melnikova I	RUS	9.1.74	3	EJ	San Sebastián	1 Aug
13.50	0.6	Olga	Skrebneva	BLS	7.11.74	2		Gomel	14 May
13.48		Olga	Boyko	UKR	6.7.75	1		Chernigov	4 Sep
13.40	0.3	Lisette	Cusa	CUB	26.2.75	5	NC	Habana	13 May
13.39i	-	Elena	Dumitrascu	ROM	14.5.74	2		Bucuresti	31 Jan
		13.31	-0.1			1	Balk-j	Thessaloniki	11 Jul
13.33		Madalina	Coman	ROM	4.3.76	1		Bucuresti	12 Jun
13.26i		Oksana	Voloshina	RUS	74	1A		Volgograd	31 Jan
13.17		Anna	Rodovich	UKR	24.9.76	1		Donetsk	22 Jun
13.13i		Tatyana	Lebedyeva	RUS	21.7.76	1B		Volgograd	31 Jan
13.13		Ilaria	Marras	ITA	11.1.74	1		Pontedera	21 Jul
13.12		Irina	Melnikova II	RUS	14.5.75	3	NC-j	Vladimir	4 Jul
13.12	0.2	Martha	Koulorizou	GRE	11.5.74	2	Balk-J	Thessaloniki	11 Jul
13.10		Mihaela	Gindila	ROM	29.10.74			Bucuresti	16 May
13.07		Madelin	Martinez	CUB	10.2.76	1		Artemisa	22 Apr
13.07		Nathalie	Jacques-Gustave	FRA	12.5.76	1		Bondoufle	6 Jun
Wind assisted									
14.07	2.8		Wang Xiangrong	CHN	1.2.76	4	NG	Beijing	13 Sep
13.22	3.0	Ilaria	Marras	ITA	11.1.74	4	NC	Bologna	3 Aug

SHOT

Mark		Name		Nat	Born	Pos	Meet	Venue	Date
18.12		Corrie	de Bruin	HOL	26.10.76	1	APM	Hengelo	20 Jun
18.02		Danijela	Curovic	YUG	7.3.74	1	Balk-J	Thessaloniki	11 Jul
		17.94				1		Beograd	30 May
		17.89				2	NC	Beograd	25 Jul
		17.83				1		Beograd	1 Aug
18.00			Cheng Xiaoyan	CHN	75	3		Beijing	27 Mar
17.93		Marika	Tuliniemi	FIN	19.7.74	1	EJ	San Sebastián	30 Jul
17.92i		Irina	Korzhanenko	RUS	16.5.74	1		Minsk	27 Feb
		17.02				1	3N-j	Lübeck	26 Jun
17.81			Liu Ying	CHN	21.1.74			Shijiazhuang	2 Apr
17.70		Yumileisis	Cumba	CUB	4.2.75	2		Habana	3 Jul
17.07		Nadine	Kleinert	GER	20.10.75	2	EJ	San Sebastián	30 Jul
16.76		Elena	Hila	ROM	20.5.74	1	NC-j	Bucuresti	8 Aug
16.72		Elena	Tapirlan	ROM	4.2.74	2		Bucuresti	3 Jul
16.71		Valeyta	Althouse	USA	7.1.74	2		Berkeley	21 May
16.66		Claudia	Mues	GER	3.1.75	4	EJ	San Sebastián	30 Jul
16.33		Alina	Pupo	CUB	9.3.75	2	PAJ	Winnipeg	17 Jul
16.14		Kristen	Heaston	USA	23.11.75	1		Norwalk	19 Jun
16.08			Lee Myung-sun	KOR	12.2.76	2	AsiC	Manila	2 Dec
15.70		Yulia	Savchenko	UKR	15.4.74	1	NC-j	Chernigov	26 Jun
15.61		Olga	Ryabinkina	RUS	24.9.76	2		Rostov	15 May
15.60i		Melania	Racolta	ROM	29.10.74				
15.56i		Anja	Fuchs	GER	27.9.74	1		Düsseldorf	17 Jan
		15.43						Euskirchen	3 Jun
15.50		Teri	Steer	USA	3.10.75	1		York	25 Apr
15.50		Irina	Korotayeva	RUS	27.7.74	1	NC-j	Vladimir	2 Jul

Mark		Name	Nat	Born	Pos	Meet	Venue	Date

DISCUS

Mark		Name	Nat	Born	Pos	Meet	Venue	Date
66.08		Cao Qi	CHN	1.1.74	1	NG	Beijing	12 Sep
	61.58				1	AsiC	Manila	30 Nov
	60.80						Beijing	2 May
	60.32				4	NC	Jinan	4 Jun
	59.82				3		Shijiazhuang	26 Apr
61.24		Chang Xinhong	CHN	.3.74	2	NC	Jinan	4 Jun
	60.36				8	NG	Beijing	12 Sep
59.80		Jiang Qunhua	CHN	26.9.74	7		Beijing	3 May
58.90		Li Qiumei	CHN	.9.74	1			16 May
58.40	Danijela	Curovic	YUG	7.3.74	1		Beograd	29 May
58.20	Viktoria	Boyko	UKR	20.1.74	1B		Yalta	24 Jan
56.18	Corrie	de Bruin	HOL	26.10.76	1		Den Haag	23 May
55.20	Beatrice	Faumuina	NZL	23.10.74	1		Auckland	23 Jan
55.06	Suzy	Powell	USA	3.9.76	1	NC-j	Spokane	27 Jun
54.90	Stacey	Schroeder	USA	11.7.74	3	NCAA	New Orleans	3 Jun
54.50	Areti	Abatzi	GRE	14.5.74	2	Balk-j	Thessaloniki	11 Jul
54.50		Yu Qingmei	CHN	75	1	EAsiJ	Hong Kong	13 Nov
54.18	Kirsi	Lindfors	FIN	9.12.75	1		Pori	23 Jun
54.16	Lyudmila	Starovoytova	BLS	8.4.74	1		Grodno	20 Jun
53.60	Katalin	Divós	HUN	5.5.74	1		Szombathely	13 Oct
53.48	Sabine	Sievers	GER	3.3.75	1		Berlin	4 Sep
53.44	Christine	Adams	GER	28.2.74	2		Berlin	4 Sep
53.22	Husniye	Keskin	TUR	14.4.74	1		Ankara	9 Jun
53.14	Ulrike	Heidelmann	GER	10.1.74	1		Troisdorf	1 May
53.12	Martina	Greithanner	GER	21.10.74	1		Halle	15 May

HAMMER

Mark		Name	Nat	Born	Pos	Meet	Venue	Date
62.52	Mihaela	Melinte	ROM	27.3.75	1	NC-j	Bucuresti	7 Aug
	60.02				1	NC	Bucuresti	5 Sep
	58.44				1		Bucuresti	29 May
59.80	Natalya	Vasilenko	UKR	30.10.74	1	NC-j	Chernigov	27 Jun
	58.60				1		Kiev	15 May
	58.44				1		Yalta	23 Jan
59.06	Natalya	Panarina	RUS	6.5.75	1		Chelyabinsk	6 Jun
58.90	Debbie	Sosimenko	AUS	5.4.74	1		Hobart	17 Jan
	58.28				1		Sydney	5 Jun
58.36	Oksana	Zatsepilova	RUS	20.4.74	2		Moskva	6 Aug
58.24	Marina	Pirog	UKR	28.8.74	2	NC-j	Chernigov	27 Jun
58.10	Natalya	Ignatova	RUS	3.1.74	2		Chelyabinsk	6 Jun
56.44	Yelena	Grankina	UKR	30.6.74	2		Kiev	2 May
55.42	Simone	Mathes	GER	13.3.75	1	3N-j	Lübeck	16 Jun
54.32	Irina	Lungu	ROM	5.4.75			Bucuresti	6 Jun
52.90	Denise	Passmore	AUS	11.6.74	1		Melbourne	21 Feb
52.90	Irina	Kuznetsova	RUS	.75	1		Khimki	16 May
52.62	Diana	Holden	GBR	12.2.75	1		Haslemere	3 Aug
52.16	Veronika	Ushakova	RUS	8.11.77	3		Chelyabinsk	6 Jun

JAVELIN

Mark		Name	Nat	Born	Pos	Meet	Venue	Date
61.44		Lee Young-sun	KOR	21.2.74	2	EAsiG	Shanghai	15 May
	58.62				1	WSG	Buffalo	Jul
59.38		Liang Chunlian	CHN	27.1.75	5		Shijiazhuang	26 Apr
59.36	Kirsty	Morrison	GBR	28.10.75	1		Hoo	4 Sep
58.42	Angeliki	Tsiolakoudi	GRE	10.5.76	1		Athinai	29 May
58.26	Mikaela	Ingberg	FIN	29.7.74	2	3N-j	Skien	21 Aug
57.80	Adigoni	Vourdoli	GRE	4.4.75	1	NC-j	Thessaloniki	2 Jul
57.60	Doreen	Karasiewicz	GER	21.7.74	5		Berlin	4 Sep
57.48	Nikola	Tomecková	TCH	25.6.74	1	PA	Praha	17 Jun
57.00	Maria Caridad	Alvárez	CUB	30.8.75	1	PAJ	Winnipeg	16 Jul
56.24		Liu Jingqian	CHN	74	16	NG	Beijing	9 Sep
56.20	Alexandra	Mays	GER	16.8.74	1		Hamm	22 May
55.88	Ewa	Rybak	POL	22.12.74	1		Poznan	30 May
54.86	Mirelada	Manjani	ALB	76	1		Tirana	22 Apr
54.44	Shinobu	Deguchi	JPN	5.5.75	2	EAsiJ	Hong Kong	14 Nov

Mark	Name		Nat	Born	Pos	Meet	Venue	Date
54.20	Odalis	Palma	CUB	11.6.75	2		Santiago de Cuba	13 Mar
54.12	Dimitra	Sargioti	GRE	26.6.75	2		Thessaloniki	13 Jun
53.68	Korinna	Schulz	GER	13.9.78			Cottbus	12 May
53.52	Katalin	Antal	HUN	28.11.75	2		Szeged	2 Oct
53.48	Christina	Scherwin	DEN	11.7.76	6	EJ	San Sebastián	31 Jul
53.32	Nancy	Rahmsdorf	GER	11.10.75	1		Potsdam	13 Feb

HEPTATHLON

Mark	Name		Nat	Born	Pos	Meet	Venue	Date
5840A	Regla M	Cardeñas	CUB	21.1.75	2	CAC	Cali	31 Jul
		13.9 1.74 13.44 24.8w			6.29	37.58	2:23.5	
5838	Ding Ying		CHN	.10.76	11	NG	Beijing	12 Sep
		13.71 1.80 12.58 25.25			6.19	38.14	2:26.59	
5740		Zou Ying	CHN	.7.74	10	NC	Jinan	3 Jun
		14.19 1.74 12.02 25.38			5.89	39.52	2:14.67	
5678	Kathleen	Gutjahr	GER	27.7.75	1		Bernhausen	13 Jun
		14.35 1.80 11.83 25.85			5.62	43.88	2:19.21	
5632	Diana	Koritskaya	RUS	22.2.75	1	NC-j	Vladimir	3 Jul
		14.54 1.69 11.79 24.95			5.86	38.40	2:14.11	
5591	Karin	Specht	GER	23.6.74	1		Dresden	23 May
		13.90w 1.75 12.43 25.25			5.85	33.78	2:23.51	
5576	Lyudmila	Mashchenko	RUS	19.4.74	2	NC-j	Vladimir	3 Jul
		14.77 1.66 13.39 25.58			5.93	38.50	2:19.89	
5512	Viktoria	Postemskaya	UKR	13.1.74	1		Donetsk	30 Jun
		15.28 1.79 11.82 26.68			5.76	47.64	2:24.67	
5502	Klarissa	Altdörfer	GER	13.2.75	1		Balingen	18 Jul
		14.32 1.64 11.56 25.32			5.71	40.72	2:17.89	
5481	Helena	Vinarová	TCH	26.8.74	1	v2N-j	Alzano Lombardo	30 May
		14.22 1.78 10.49 25.46			6.15w	32.36	2:24.99	
5470	Deborah	Feltrin	ITA	10.3.76	2	v2N-j	Alzano Lombardo	30 May
		15.01 1.75 10.96 26.23			6.00w	43.06	2:24.05	
5462	Natalya	Kulikova	RUS	9.8.74	3	NC-j	Vladimir	3 Jul
		14.85 1.66 12.07 26.05			5.88	41.40	2:19.66	
5445	Jane	Jamieson	AUS	23.6.75	1	NC-y	Sydney	23 Mar
		15.05 1.67 13.06 25.11			5.78	40.24	2:27.16	
5413	Najuma	Fletcher	GUY	74			Fairfax	26 May
		14.36 1.77 10.02 24.97			6.22	26.08	2:21.56	
5411	Lyudmila	Kovalenko	UKR	18.3.75	2		Chernigov	27 Jun
		14.92 1.64 11.96 26.17			6.01	38.62	2:18.67	
5409	Ioana	Sirbu	ROM	29.8.76	1		Miaoli	30 May
5402	Deborah	den Boer	HOL	18.4.75	1	NC-j	Hoorn	29 May
		14.28w 1.68 11.11 25.14			5.76	39.60	2:27.88	
5402	Gabriela	Groth	GER	22.6.75	3		Lübeck	5 Sep
		14.87 1.68 11.41 25.87			5.88	44.20	2:27.81	
5391	Irina	Birina	RUS	.76	4	NC-j	Vladimir	3 Jul
		15.26 1.75 11.91 26.47			5.81	37.42	2:18.44	
5388	Katerina	Nekolná	TCH	23.6.75	3	j	Alzano Lombardo	30 May
	15.36 1.75 10.86 26.08		5.84 41.66 2:21.6					

5000 METRES WALK

Mark	Name		Nat	Born	Pos	Meet	Venue	Date
21:01.8	Susana	Feitor	POR	28.1.75	1	SGP	Fana	8 May
	21:21.80				1	EJ	San Sebastián	29 Jul
21:39.75	Natalya	Trofimova	RUS	17.1.75	2	EJ	San Sebastián	29 Jul
21:47.5	Jane	Saville	AUS	5.11.74	2	NC	Brisbane	6 Mar
21:49.65	Irina	Stankina	RUS	25.3.77	3	EJ	San Sebastián	29 Jul
22:33.02	Rie	Mitsumori	JPN	26.10.74	3		Otsu	19 Dec
22:35.8 mx	Simone	Wolowiec	AUS	12.2.74	mx		Melbourne	25 Nov
22:37.68	Olga	Panferova	RUS	21.8.77	3		Cheboksary	5 Jun
22:40.83	Maria	Vasco	ESP	26.12.75	4	EJ	San Sebastián	29 Jul
22:41.4	Yulia	Nifontova	RUS	14.5.74				
22:56.30	Oksana	Obedkina	RUS	3.9.76	4		Cheboksary	5 Jun
22:56.60	Cheryl	Webb	AUS	3.10.76	2		Sydney	21 Feb
23:02.98	Yvonne	Anders	GER	14.5.76	5	EJ	San Sebastián	29 Jul
23:03.4	Yuka	Ueoka	JPN	28.5.75	2		Otsu	14 Mar
23:05.13	Linda	Coffee	AUS	31.7.77	3		Sydney	21 Feb

Mark	Name		Nat	Born	Pos	Meet	Venue	Date
23:07.5	Bertha	Vera	ECU	31.12.74	1	SAmJ	Barcelona, VEN	20 Jun
23:10.69	Şofia	Avoila	POR	30.7.76	1		Rio Maior	3 Apr
23:23.46	Éva	Puskás	HUN	28.5.74	1		Schwechat	30 May
23:28.10	Eva	Pérez	ESP	18.7.75	7	EJ	San Sebastián	29 Jul
Road								
22:17	Venera	Vasilyeva	RUS	17.3.76	2		Adler	14 Feb
22:23	Tatyana	Gudkova	RUS	23.12.77	2		Moskva	25 Apr
22:26	Maria	Rebollo	MEX	76	3	11N	Eschborn	12 Jun
22:32	Maria	Vasco	ESP	26.12.75	4	11N	Eschborn	12 Jun
22:35	Yuliya	Nifontova	RUS	14.5.74	5	11N	Eschborn	12 Jun
22:37	Olga	Panferova	RUS	21.8.77	6	11N	Eschborn	12 Jun
23:10	Olga	Pastukhova	RUS	.74	3		Adler	14 Feb
23:16	Yelena	Alekseyeva	RUS	.77	2		Yaroslavl	6 Aug

10 KILOMETRES WALK

t = 10,000m track

Mark	Name		Nat	Born	Pos	Meet	Venue	Date
42:44	Long Yuwen		CHN	1.8.75	3		Shenzhen	18 Feb
	44:11.7t				6	NC	Shenzhen	21 Feb
42:47	Liu Hongyu		CHN	1.12.75	5	NC	Shenzhen	18 Feb
	43:49.5t				3		Shenzhen	21 Feb
42:50	Gu Yan		CHN	17.3.74	4	NG	Beijing	8 Sep
	43:58				12	NC	Shenzhen	18 Feb
	46:35.0t				12		Shenzhen	21 Feb
43:07	Song Lijuan		CHN	1.2.76	6	NG	Beijing	8 Sep
	43:11				7		Shenzhen	18 Feb
43:34	Wei Linkun		CHN	1.12.75	9	NG	Beijing	8 Sep
	44:37							15 Feb
43:44	Susana	Feitor	POR	28.1.75	1		Rio Maior	3 Apr
44:46	Maribel	Rebollo	MEX	76	3		Brandys nad Labem	23 May
45:08	Svetlana	Nifontova	RUS	14.5.74	10		Cheboksary	6 Jun
45:18	Yuka	Kamioka	JPN	28.5.75	4		Wajima	4 Apr
45:48	Rie	Mitsumori	JPN	26.10.74	2		Takahata	7 Nov
47:11	Maria	Vasco	ESP	26.12.75	3	El	Prat de Llobregat	28 Mar
47:18	Simone	Wolowiec	AUS	12.2.74	1		Melbourne	28 Nov
Born 1972 or 1973?:	41:57	Gao Hongmiao	CHN	17.3.74	2	NG	Beijing	8 Sep

4 x 100 METRES RELAY

Mark	Nat	Team	Pos	Meet	Venue	Date
44.31	GBR	Allahgreen, Merry, Smith, Mant	1	EJ	San Sebastián	1 Aug
44.38	FRA	Jalinier, Helbert, Combe, Félix	2	EJ	San Sebastián	1 Aug
44.60	GER	Roos, Brodbeck, Müller, Becker	3	EJ	San Sebastián	1 Aug
45.10	USA	Carson, Perry, Williams, Wilson	1	PAJ	Winnipeg	17 Jul
45.23	JAM	Dowdie, Langley, Mitchell, Robinson	1		Fort de France	11 Apr
45.50	SWE	Mårtensson, Vöcks, Holmqvist, Larsson	4	EJ	San Sebastián	1 Aug
45.53	BAH	Ferguson, Fynes, Williams, Rolle	2	Carif	Fort-de-France	11 Apr
45.59	ITA	Bettia, Cuccia, Da Boit, Farina	5	EJ	San Sebastián	1 Aug
45.75	CUB	Pérez, Hechevarría, Anderson, Nevra	2		Habana	22 May
45.85A		Transvaal U 19 (RSA) Bousema, Griesel, vd Merwe, O'Connor	1		Germiston	3 Apr

Mark	Team	Pos	Meet	Venue	Date
45.91	CAN	4	PAJ	Winnipeg	17 Jul
46.00	ESP	6	EJ	San Sebastián	1Aug
46.02	SUI	2		Luzern	29Jun
46.03	Saitama Sakae HS (JPN)	1		Tokyo	16Oct
46.11	RUS	1	NC-j	Vladimir	4 Jul
46.29	TPE	1	EAsiJ	Hong Kong	14Nov
46.33	FIN	2	vSWEj	Stockholm	28Aug

4 x 400 METRES RELAY

Mark	Nat	Team	Pos	Meet	Venue	Date
3:31.13	ROM	Tuta, Florea, Tîrlea, Nedelcu	1	EJ	San Sebastián	1 Aug
3:32.70	JAM	Cole, Jarrett, Grant, Williams	1	PAJ	Winnipeg	17 Jul
3:33.91	GER	Merkel, Bornscheuer, Oppong, Kuschmann	2	EJ	San Sebastián	1 Aug
3:37.64	USA	Weatherfoord, Newhouse, Newsome, Hennagan	2	PAJ	Winnipeg	17 Jul
3:39.32	BAH	Ferguson, Williams, Fynes, Rolle	2	Carif	Fort-de-France	11 Apr
3:39.76	RUS	Borisova, Strushkina, Leshcheva, Zvyagina	3	EJ	San Sebastián	1 Aug
3:41.53	FRA	Gagneur, Dufour, Lahouassa, Rangassamy	4	EJ	San Sebastián	1 Aug
3:41.68	ITA	Caddeo, Perin,Salvarini, de Angeli	5	EJ	San Sebastián	1 Aug
3:42.74	CAN	Bygrave, Rejouis, Twumasi, Watt	4	PAJ	Winnipeg	17 Jul
3:43.02	FIN	Niemalä, Engdal, Kemppainen, Suomi	1	vSWEj	Stockhom	29 Aug

Mark	Team	Pos	Meet	Venue	Date
3:43.24	PUR	5	PAJ	Winnipeg	17 Jul
3:43.47	HUN	6	EJ	San Sebastián	1Aug
3:43.58	Himejisha HS (JPN)	2		Tokyo	16Oct
3:43.65	TCH	1	4N-j	Schwechat	10 Jul
3:43.85	CHN	1	EAsiJ	Hong Kong	13Nov
3:45.04	GRE		Balk-j	Thessaloniki	11 Jul
3:45.04	TPE	3	EAsiJ	Hong Kong	13Nov
3:46.10	ESP	2	vFRAj	Tarbes	17 Jul

MEN'S INDEX 1993

This index includes men listed in the top 100 of all standard events and in shorter lists for world record distances such as 1000m and 3000m, but excludes other lists such as 300m, half marathon, pentathlon and 3000m walk.

** indicates athletes included in the biographies section.*

Name		Nat	Born	Ht/Wt	Event	1993 Mark	Pre-1993 Best
Abdellah	Abdelhak	MAR	13 Aug 68		1500	3:38.65	3:39.62 -91
Abdelmaksoud	El Hafani	EGY			400h	50.43	52.8 -91
* Abdenouz	Réda	ALG	25 Sep 68	170/63	800	1:45.40	1:44.98 -90
					1000	2:17.98	2:21.5 -90
					1500	3:38.94	3:47.15 -91
* Abduvaliyev	Andrey	TJK	30 Jun 66	186/112	HT	82.78	83.46 -90
Ackermann	Georg	GER	13 Jul 72	191/75	LJ	8.02	7.98 -92
Acres	Barry	AUS	19 Jul 65	180/72	800	1:46.95	1:45.70 -88
Adam	Alexander	GER	10 May 68	184/76	800	1:47.04	1:46.59 -90
Adams	Sean	USA	24 May 71	193/79	200	20.78, 20.61w, 20.4w	20.91w -92
Adán	José Carlos	ESP	22 Jul 67	166/57	5k	13:19.71	13:25.86 -91
					10k	27:59.49	27:59.76 -91
* Adeniken	Olapade	NGR	19 Aug 69	186/78	100	10.15, 10.00w	9.97 -92
					200	20.12	20.11, 20.00Aw -92
* Adkins	Derrick	USA	2 Jul 70	188/80	400h	48.39	48.60 -91
Afanasyev	Nikolay	RUS	11 Aug 65	187/80	Dec	7719	8090m -85
Aguilera	Jorge	CUB	16 Jan 66	172/64	100	10.22w	10.30 -86, 10.29Aw -90
Agyepong	Francis	GBR	16 Jun 65	178/71	TJ	17.00w	16.88, 17.00w -92
A'Hern	Nick	AUS	6 Jan 69	170/60	20kW	1:19:48, 1:20:12.3t	1:19:33, 1:20:18.5t -90
Aimar	Alessandro	ITA	5 Jun 67	178/68	400	45.76A	46.04 -91
Akabusi	Kriss	GBR	28 Nov 58	185/81	400h	48.73	47.82 -92
Akiyoshi	Shinichi	JPN	10 Feb 71	175/57	10k	28:31.93	
Akogyiram	Eric	GHA	25 Jun 69	170/68	100	10.29	10.23A, 10.24, 10.15w -90
Akonay	Boay	TAN	3 Jan 70	168/62	10k	28:18.97	27:50.27 -92
Aladefa	Ayodele	NGR	29 Dec 70	185/73	LJ	8.03, 8.05w	7.99 -90
Al-Asmari	Saad Shaddad	SAU	24 Jan 68	165/60	3kSt	8:24.80	9:08.86 -92
* Alay	Sergey	BLS	11 Jun 65	184/98	HT	81.44	82.00 -92
Albert	Stephen	USA	1 Apr 64	180/114	SP	18.89	19.11 -92
Alekna	Virgilijus	LIT	13 Feb 72	200/120	DT	62.84	60.86 -92
* Alisevich	Vitaliy	BLS	15 Jun 67	186/112	HT	81.32	82.16 -88
Allevi	Massimo	ITA	23 Nov 69	181/72	PV	5.50	5.50i -92
Alliegro	Raffaello	ITA	30 May 64		Mar	2:12:11	2:10:56sc -91
Alm	Carl-Johan	SWE	7 Jan 69	184/78	PV	5.50i	5.51 -92
Almeida	Vítor	POR	6 Mar 70	168/59	3kSt	8:29.04	8:36.34 -92
Alohan	Omokaro	NGR	18 Sep 71	180/70	400	45.80	46.56 -90
Al-Qahtani	Olayan Ali	SAU	23 Aug 71	168/60	5k	13:29.67	14:01.43 -92
Amagatcher	Solomon	GHA	20 Dec 70	180/70	400	45.42	45.42 -92
Amann	Martin	GER	23 Nov 70	188/77	PV	5.60	5.55 -92
Amer	Mohamed	UAE	23 Apr 67		3kSt	8:35.64	9:14.86 -92
Amos	Brian	USA	26 Dec 71	188/82	100	10.16w	10.57w -92
					110h	13.43, 13.42w	13.59 -91
Anderson	Chris	AUS	6 Apr 68		HJ	2.26	2.25 -92
Anderson	Tyler	USA	27 Apr 70	185/75	200	20.74Aw	20.93 -92
Anderson	Ubeja	USA	30 Mar 74	180/69	110h	13.52	-0-
Andersson	Pierre	SWE	4 Jan 67		TJ	16.54	16.20 -92
* Andrei	Alessandro	ITA	3 Jan 59	191/118	SP	20.01i, 19.87	22.91 -87
Andreini	Marco	ITA	8 Oct 61	182/81	PV	5.60ex	5.68 -89, 5.70ex -90
Andreyev	Vladimir	RUS	7 Sep 66		20kW	1:19:43	1:19:17 -91
Andronov	Yuriy	RUS	71		50kW	3:59:28	4:06:49 -91
Angeria	Tero	FIN	4 May 74	184/94	JT	75.92	72.92 -92
Anibal Ramos	Mário	POR	25 Mar 72	184/82	Dec	7570	7346 -92
Anselm	Garfield	FRA	7 Jun 66	174/63	TJ	16.62	16.49 -87
* Antibo	Salvatore	ITA	7 Feb 62	170/52	10k	28:27.48	27:16.50 -89
* Antón	Abel	ESP	24 Oct 62	179/63	3k	7:48.53	7:46.08 -87
					5k	13:17.48	13:20.67 -88
					10k	28:09.04	28:38.27 -91
* Antonov	Nikolay	BUL	17 Aug 68	194/86	LJ	8.15	7.59 -91
Anttonen	Mikko	FIN	5 Jul 63	181/83	JT	78.14	77.50 -87
* Aouita	Saïd	MAR	2 Nov 59	175/58	1500	3:37.60	3:29.46 -85
Arbiauskas	Rytis	LIT	15 Jan 71	172/62	20kW	1:23:08	1:24:17 -92
Arco	Pedro	ESP	7 Jul 64	175/61	10k	28:03.89	28:08.89 -92

Name		Nat	Born	Ht/Wt	Event	1993 Mark	Pre-1993 Best
Arconada	José	ESP	18 Jan 64	192/76	800	1:46.75	1:45.02 -90
Arcos	José Manuel	ESP	19 Jan 73	176/76	PV	5.62i, 5.55	5.32 -92
* Arena	Walter	ITA	30 May 64	173/67	20kW	1:22:15.7t	1:23:34 -92
					50kW	4:03:21	
Argudin	Alejandro	CUB	10 Mar 74	174/65	400h	50.00	51.25 -92
Arias	Hector	MEX	12 Oct 71	165/58	3kSt	8:34.55	8:36.2 -92
Aristov	Vyacheslav	UZB/BLS	18 Jan 66	174/65	PV	5.50	5.60i, 5.60 -91
Arkell	Simon	AUS	1 Jul 66	185/78	PV	5.72	5.70 -92
Arkhipov	Aleksandr	RUS	68		20kW	1:23:35	
Arzamasov	Sergey	KZK	9 Apr 71	189/77	TJ	17.28	17.11 -91
Asadov	Vasif	AZE	27 Aug 65	180/69	TJ	16.86	17.37i -88, 17.33 -90
Asahara	Nobuharu	JPN	21 Jun 72	179/69	100	10.19	10.3, 10.49 -92
					LJ	8.13	7.93 -92
Ashford	David	USA	24 Jan 64	188/83	110h	13.72	13.68, 13.65w -89
Asinga	Tommy	SUR	20 Nov 68	188/71	800	1:47.03	1:46.74 -92
* Astapkovich	Igor	BLS	4 Jan 63	191/118	HT	82.28	84.62 -92
Astapkovich	Konstantin	BLS	23 Oct 70	185/120	HT	78.20	74.24 -92
* Austin	Charles	USA	19 Dec 67	184/77	HJ	2.35i	2.40 -91
Avdeyenko	Gennadiy	BLS	4 Nov 63	202/84	HJ	2.30i	2.38i, 2.38 -87
Avrunin	Igor	ISR	16 Jul 57	195/119	SP	18.92	20.68 -83
					DT	58.40	67.14 -84
Azkueta	Jon	ESP	2 Jul 67	170/56	3kSt	8:35.10	8:27.91 -91
* Backley	Steve	GBR	12 Feb 69	196/95	JT	85.10	91.46 -92
* Bada	Sunday	NGR	22 Jun 69	188/79	400	44.63	44.99 -92
Baek Seung-do		KOR	16 Jun 68	172/56	Mar	2:12:34	2:10:07 -92
* Bagach	Aleksandr	UKR	21 Nov 66	194/125	SP	21.32i, 20.85	21.42 -89
* Bagryanov	Dmitriy	RUS	18 Dec 67	188/78	LJ	8.07	8.35 -92
* Bagyula	István	HUN	2 Jan 69	185/76	PV	5.70	5.92 -91
Bailey	Joe	USA	30 Mar 71	193/127	SP	18.66i, 18.56	18.12 -92
Baker	Derrick	USA	28 Dec 70	179/79	400	46.08	46.76 -92
* Baker	Simon	AUS	6 Feb 58	186/70	50kW	3:57:11	3:43:13 -89
Balan	Costica	ROM	25 Aug 64	171/60	20kW	1:23:45	1:24:33 -92
Balanque	Eugenio	CUB	20 Dec 68	188/75	Dec	7889	7908 -92
Baldini	Stefano	ITA	25 May 71	176/58	10k	28:25.98	28:50.16 -92
Baltus	Tonny	HOL	28 Dec 65	188/74	800	1:46.57	1:45.50 -89
Bandurchenko	Oleg	UKR	16 Sep 70	182/70	50kW	3:59:08	3:58:49 -90
Banks	Kenny	USA	12 Nov 66	178/75	HJ	2.24i	2.30 -86
Baraznovskiy	Viktor	BLS	23 Jan 68	200/123	DT	62.62	63.90 -90
* Barbosa	José Luiz	BRA	27 May 61	184/68	800	1:44.18	1:43.08 -91
					1000	2:17.60	2:17.36 -85
Barbu	Cátalin	ROM	13 Oct 69	189/78	TJ	16.63	16.41i -92
Barker	Ricky	USA	14 Nov 69	190/77	Dec	7803w	7931 -91
* Barkutwo	Philip	KEN	6 Oct 66	172/60	3k	7:47.78i	7:44.33 -92
					3kSt	8:23.44	8:05.37 -92
Barnes	Anthony	USA	23 Dec 65	170/66	100	10.25,10.21w	10.29 -91, 10.20Aw -88
Barnes	Matthew	GBR	12 Jan 68	167/60	1500	3:38.31	3:43.38 -92
* Barnes	Randy	USA	16 Jun 66	194/137	SP	21.80	23.12 -90
Barnett	Mike	USA	21 May 61	186/104	JT	75.64	82.06 -87
Barngetuny	Eliud	KEN	73		3k	7:49.80	7:49.74 -92
					3kSt	8:28.85	8:31.32 -92
* Barrios	Arturo	MEX	12 Dec 63	174/60	3k	7:43.51	7:35.71 -89
					5k	13:09.58	13:07.79 -89
					10k	27:34.27	27:08.23 -89
					Mar	2:12:21	2:14:09 -86
Barron	Michael	USA	21 Feb 73	183/84	100	10.25	10.58, 10.39w? -92
* Barroso	Jaime	ESP	15 May 68	165/55	20kW	1:23:02	1:23:37 -89
					50kW	4:06:28	3:48:08 -92
Bártl	Jan	TCH	23 Mar 67	195/122	SP	19.06i dq, 18.72	18.57i -90
* Barton	Tony	USA	17 Oct 69	190/74	HJ	2.31	2.32 -92
					LJ	8.12	7.53, 7.77w -90
Bartoszak	Michal	POL	21 Jun 70	180/68	1500	3:38.39	3:38.21 -91
					3k	7:47.68	7:50.42 -92
					5k	13:31.78	13:29.72 -92
Barzhagi	Luca	ITA	1 Jun 68		Mar	2:10:53	2:13:24 -92
Bassett	Donovan	USA	25 Oct 72	190/73	400h	50.35	52.49 -92
Bates	Michael	USA	19 Dec 69	180/86	200	20.58i	20.01 -92
Batle	Erick	CUB	10 Dec 74		110h	13.84Aw	14.51 -92
Baudouin	Gérald	FRA	15 Nov 72	183/75	PV	5.65	5.70 -92

Name		Nat	Born	Ht/Wt	Event	1993 Mark	Pre-1993 Best
Bauermeister	Kim-Lars	GER	20 Nov 70	170/56	3kSt	8:27.96	8:32.38 -92
* Baumann	Dieter	GER	9 Feb 65	178/62	2k	5:02.49i	4:59.88 -87
					3k	7:43.60i	7:33.91 -91
Bavikin	Vadim	ISR	4 Oct 70	186/90	JT	78.48	77.30 -92, 81.56R -91
* Bayissa	Fita	ETH	15 Dec 72	179/52	5k	13:05.40	13:13.03 -92
					10k	27:26.90	27:14.26 -92
Baygush	Viktor	UKR	16 Dec 63	182/110	HT	74.52	78.10 -88
Bazarov	Aleksey	ISR	14 Oct 63	184/75	400h	50.08	49.33 -88
Beblo	Leszek	POL	8 Jul 66	177/68	Mar	2:10:24	2:11:28 -92
Beck	Marty	USA	2 Mar 70	190/77	400h	49.77	49.59 -92
Becker	Gustavo	ESP	17 Jun 66	184/70	HJ	2.26i, 2.25	2.30 -92
Bedaso	Turbe	ETH	64		Mar	2:10:34	2:14:15 -91
Bedi	Tibor	HUN	22 Mar 74	181/68	110h	13.84w	14.02 -92
Beechum	Gabe	USA	28 Aug 71	182/66	HJ	2.25	2.27 -92
Béhar	Abdellah	FRA	5 Jul 63	170/55	3k	7:46.66	7:44.34 -92
					5k	13:28.39	13:25.62 -92
Béhar	Noureddine	MAR	8 Apr 66	170/56	1500	3:37.30	3:38.89 -92
* Belaout	Aïssa	ALG	12 Aug 68	170/63	3k	7:38.70	7:51.27 -92
					5k	13:08.03	13:23.11 -92
Belfaa	Othmane	ALG	18 Oct 61	192/76	HJ	2.24	2.28 -83
Belghazi	Ali	ALG	22 Sep 62	176/62	3kSt	8:32.98	8:31.67 -90
Belhadje	Mahiedine	ALG	20 Jan 63		10k	27:58.59	
Belikhov	Aleksandr	RUS	27 Dec 72	190/74	400h	50.27	49.47 -92
Belkessam	Ahmed	ALG	27 Mar 62	175/72	1000	2:18.25	2:19.23 -92
Bellino	Paolo	ITA	19 Aug 69	185/79	400h	49.77	49.33 -91
Bellmann	Uwe	GER	8 Jun 68	190/78	HJ	2.26	2.24 -90
Bello	Andrea	ITA	5 Nov 65		3kSt	8:34.01	8:39.92 -92
Bello	Jorge	ESP	28 Mar 63	187/70	3kSt	8:35.57	8:27.24 -86
Belokon	Vladimir	UKR	13 Feb 69	188/84	110h	13.48	13.58 -92, 13.4 -90
Benavides	Paul	MEX	5 Nov 64	188/78	PV	5.71	5.60 -86
Benfarès	Samir	FRA	6 Jun 68	183/63	1500	3:37.47	3:42.0 -92
Bennett	Mike	USA	22 Sep 68	190/86	Dec	7564	7636 -91
Bennici	Francesco	ITA	3 Oct 71	171/50	10k	28:32.26	27:56.74 -92
Benninger	Christian	GER	15 Mar 71	193/90	JT	77.54	76.62 -92
* Bentley	Dion	USA	26 Aug 71	193/86	LJ	8.39	8.16 -89
* Benvenuti	Andrea	ITA	13 Dec 69	185/75	800	1:44.55	1:43.92 -92
Benzine	Reda	ALG	71	180/63	5k	13:31.23	
Berger ¶	Andreas	AUT	9 Jun 61	174/78	100	10.15 *	10.15 -88, 10.08w -92
Bergstrom	Donovan	USA	3 Mar 70	180/67	3kSt	8:29.08	8:33.73 -92
Bermudez	Martin	MEX	19 May 58	175/70	50kW	4:01:37	3:43:36 -79
Bernaert	Luc	BEL	24 Jun 66	186/75	800	1:47.10	1:46.41 -87
					1500	3:37.00	3:37.91 -92
					Mile	3:56.89	4:05.3 -92
Bernardini	Severino	ITA	31 Mar 66		Mar	2:10:12	2:11:54 -90
Bernhard	Pierre	FRA	15 Feb 68	183/70	HJ	2.25i, 2.24	2.26 -91
* Berrett	Tim	CAN	23 Jan 65	178/65	20kW	1:22:47	1:22:39t -92
					50kW	3:50:23	3:50:55 -92
Berrio	Miguel	CUB	25 Feb 68	175/73	PV	5.50	5.40 -90
Bertocchi	Luigi	ITA	10 Jun 65	187/78	110h	13.84A	13.69 -92, 13.6 -84
Best	William	CAN	3 Sep 70		800	1:46.52	1:47.44 -92
Betancourt	Lázaro	CUB	18 Mar 63	190/83	TJ	16.88	17.78 -86
* Bettiol	Salvatore	ITA	28 Nov 61	178/57	Mar	2:11:44	2:10:08 -89
Bettolo	Laurent	FRA	9 Mar 66	180/97	HT	71.26	71.82 -90
Beukenkamp	Marco	HOL	15 May 63		400h	50.40	51.14 -86
* Beyer	Wolf-Hendrik	GER	14 Feb 72	199/85	HJ	2.36i, 2.33	2.32 -92
Beyers	Ben	USA	19 May 74	183/63	400	46.05	47.27 -91
Bi Hongyong		CHN	16 Nov 74		HJ	2.28	2.21 -92
Bi Zhong		CHN	5 Sep 68	188/110	HT	74.60	77.04 -89
Bianchi	Paolo	ITA	7 Oct 70		50kW	4:00:04	4:09:48 -92
Bianchi	Simone	ITA	27 Jan 73	183/74	LJ	8.06	7.75 -92
Bielecki	Jan	DEN	20 Feb 71	188/93	HT	70.72	
Bigham	David	GBR	4 Jul 71	175/74	Dec	7647	7904 -92
* Bile	Abdi	SOM	28 Dec 62	185/75	800	1:45.17	1:43.60 -89
					1000	2:18.07	2:14.50 -89
					1500	3:32.83	3:30.55 -89
					Mile	3:51.66	3:49.40 -88
* Birir	Jonah	KEN	12 Dec 71	168/52	1500	3:33.86	3:33.36 -92
					Mile	3:57.38	3:52.54 -92

Name		Nat	Born	Ht/Wt	Event	1993 Mark	Pre-1993 Best
* Birir	Matthew	KEN	5 Jul 72	172/62	3kSt	8:09.42	8:08.84 -92
Bisbas	Stelios	GRE	9 Nov 68	185/74	110h	13.66, 13.60w	13.78, 13.72w -89
Bitok	Ezekiel	KEN	15 Feb 66	173/55	5k	13:10.66	13:26.65 -91
* Bitok	Paul	KEN	26 Jun 70	173/57	2k	5:05.2+	5:05.6+ -92
					3k	7:34.98	7:33.28 -92
					5k	13:08.68	13:08.89 -92
Biwott	Gideon	KEN	26 Jun 66	176/68	400h	49.27, 49.2A	49.6A -91
Biwott	Sammy	KEN	23 Jul 74	183/65	400h	50.23	50.62 -92
Bjørkli	Frank	NOR	30 Jan 65		Mar	2:12:23	2:15:33 -92
Black	Chad	USA	3 Oct 72	183/74	110h	13.85	14.18 -92
Black	Kurt	USA	4 Oct 68	185/66	3kSt	8:23.52	8:38.8 -92
* Black	Roger	GBR	31 Mar 66	190/79	400	45.86	44.59 -86
Blake	Arthur	USA	19 Aug 66	180/68	110h	13.41	13.24 -88, 13.20w,13.2 -90
Blake	Dennis	JAM	6 Sep 70	186/70	400	45.72	45.77 -92
Blank	Peter	GER	10 Apr 62	194/93	JT	80.76	82.82R -90, 81.12 -92
* Blazek	Pavol	SVK	9 Jul 58	168/58	20kW	1:21:54t	1:18:13 -90
Blockburger	Sheldon	USA	19 Sep 64	188/84	Dec	8296	8301w -90, 8225 -92
Blom	Jyrki	FIN	11 May 62	183/88	JT	76.44	80.48 -86
* Blondel	Alain	FRA	7 Dec 62	186/78	Dec	8444	8387 -88
Blume	Marc	GER	28 Dec 73	180/68	100	10.30	10.37 -92
Blums	Ronald	LAT	1 Mar 70	190/86	Dec	7918w	7688 -92
Bo Lingtang		CHN	12 Aug 70	168/54	20kW	1:19:49	1:21:49.9t -91
Boateng	Nelson	GHA	14 May 68	176/68	100	10.24w	10.2 -89, 10.38 -91
					200	20.52	20.74, 20.46w -90, 20.4 -89
* Bochkaryov	Pyotr	RUS	3 Nov 67	186/76	PV	5.80	5.85i, 5.85 -92
* Bodén	Patrik	SWE	30 Jun 67	188/102	JT	88.26	89.10S -90
* Bodenmüller	Klaus	AUT	6 Sep 62	194/112	SP	20.14	21.03i -90, 20.79 -87
Bogason	Eggert	ISL	19 Jul 60		DT	60.70	
Bogdanov	Aleksandr	UKR	29 Apr 70	190/80	Dec	7767	7496 -92
Boldon	Ato	TRI	30 Dec 73	175/75	100	10.23	10.22 -92
					200	20.59	20.63 -92
Bolkun	Viktor	UKR	2 Jul 70	188/78	110h	13.70	13.74 -91
Bondarenko	Yevgeniy	RUS	8 Oct 66	190/82	PV	5.70i, 5.65, 5.73ex	5.70 -88
Bonfim	Joilto	BRA	11 Feb 65	181/78	110h	13.78	13.67 -92
Bordukov	Vyacheslav	RUS	1 Jan 59	184/72	LJ	7.92, 7.93w	8.21 -90
					TJ	16.58	17.37 -84, 17.39w -87
Borglund	Peter	SWE	29 Jan 64	183/85	JT	84.16	84.76S -89, 87.00R -91
Borichevskiy	Aleksandr	RUS	25 Jun 70		DT	60.78	59.12 -91
Borisov	Valeriy	KZK	18 Sep 66		20kW	1:22:13	1:20:58 -88
* Boroi	George	ROM	26 Aug 64	182/71	110h	13.34	13.53 -92
Borozinski	Enoch	USA	72		Dec	7671	7232 -92
Boru	Atoi	KEN	25 Oct 73	160/55	1500	3:34.61	3:36.4A -92
Bosko	Miroslav	SVK	26 Sep 68		20kW	1:23:29t	1:25:03 -91
Botha	Johan	RSA	10 Jan 74		800	1:46.79A	1:49.4A -92
Boumendil	Sadek	ALG	19 Aug 72	189/80	400	45.91	47.6, 47.92 -92
Bourgeois	Joel	CAN	25 Apr 71		3kSt	8:30.77	8:32.96 -92
* Boutayeb	Brahim	MAR	15 Aug 67	171/60	10k	28:24.61	27:21.46 -88
Bowen	Simon	JAM	23 Nov 70	185/68	800	1:46.38	1:49.56 -92
Box	Toby	GBR	9 Sep 72	190/80	100	10.25w, 10.4	10.70, 10.66w -92
Bradley	Aki	USA	7 Feb 71	175/66	100	10.30	10.41 -92
					200	20.69	20.74 -92
Bradstock	Roald	GBR	24 Apr 62	180/95	JT	77.74	83.84 -87
* Brahmi	Azzedine	ALG	13 Sep 66	178/72	3kSt	8:20.86	8:11.27 -92
* Brand	Steffen	GER	10 Mar 65	176/66	3kSt	8:15.33	8:16.60 -92
Brantly	Keith	USA	23 May 62	178/64	Mar	2:12:49	2:14:15 -92
Braunskill	Kevin	USA	31 Mar 69	170/70	100	10.11w	10.29 -90
					200	20.49	20.45,19.9 -90, 20.21w -91
Bray	Jeff	USA	8 Sep 70	183/68	PV	5.61	5.65 -92
* Bridgewater	Bryan	USA	7 Sep 70	178/75	100	10.08	10.15 -92
					200	20.11	20.15 -92
* Bright	Tim	USA	28 Jul 60	188/79	PV	5.73	5.82 -90
Brimacombe	Steve	AUS	7 May 71		100	10.32	10.57 -92
Brits	Okkert	RSA	22 Aug 73	198/82	PV	5.71	5.46 -91
Bronson	Bryan	USA	9 Sep 72	183/75	200	20.64	20.28 -92
					400	45.66	45.95 -92
					400h	49.07	51.19 -92
Brooks	Marcus	USA	21 Dec 70	186/75	400	45.77	46.84 -92

Name		Nat	Born	Ht/Wt	Event	1993 Mark	Pre-1993 Best
Broothaerts	Laurent	BEL	1 Mar 66		LJ	7.95w	7.90 -88
Brosseau	Jean-Olivier	FRA	23 Jun 67	172/61	20kW	1:21:35	1:24:25 -91
Brown	Brian	USA	9 Jan 67	190/73	HJ	2.25	2.34i -90, 2.32 -89
Brown	James	USA	72		200	20.78, 20.62w	
Brown	Jon	GBR	27 Feb 71	172/57	5k	13:19.78	13:24.84 -92
Brown	Kevin	USA	15 Aug 71	183/77	PV	5.52	5.52 -92
Brown	Stacy	USA	26 Feb 72	183/73	LJ	8.30w	7.69 -92
Brown	Von	USA	8 Jan 73	175/64	200	20.74w	
Brunet	Javier	ESP	5 Feb 71	178/74	Dec	7614	7621 -92
Brusseau	Thierry	FRA	22 Jul 64	182/63	3kSt	8:24.60	8:22.22 -91
Bruton	Niall	IRL	27 Oct 71	180/69	1500	3:37.16	3:41.04 -92
Bruwier	Jean-Paul	BEL	18 Feb 71	185/70	400h	49.83	50.48 -92
* Bruziks	Maris	LAT	25 Aug 62	185/70	TJ	17.36i, 17.28	17.56 -88
Bub	Alexander	GER	24 Jan 67	177/72	LJ	7.92	7.96 -92
* Bubka	Sergey	UKR	4 Dec 63	183/82	PV	6.15i, 6.05	6.13i, 6.13 -92
* Bubka	Vasiliy	UKR	26 Nov 60	184/79	PV	5.70i, 5.70, 5.80ex	5.86 -88
Buchleitner	Michael	AUT	14 Oct 69	190/71	3kSt	8:24.92	8:24.44 -92
Buckingham	Jeff	USA	14 Jun 60	170/72	PV	5.50i, 5.50	5.76 -83
Buckner	Tom	GBR	16 Apr 63	182/67	3kSt	8:27.26	8:25.50 -92
* Buder	Oliver-Sven	GER	23 Jun 66	200/125	SP	20.15	21.06 -90
Budovskiy	Valentin	UKR	6 Jan 70	201/74	HJ	2.24	2.20 -92
Budykin	Andrey	RUS	14 Apr 71	184/90	HT	77.68	77.34 -92
Bueno	Luis A	CUB	22 May 69	174/67	LJ	7.94	8.28 -88
Bugár	Imrich	TCH	14 Apr 55	196/120	DT	61.72	71.28 -83
Buglakov	Aleksandr	BLS	11 Aug 72		HJ	2.28i, 2.25	2.24i -92
* Bukreyev	Valeriy	EST	15 Jun 64	186/82	PV	5.81, 5.86ex	5.70 -92
Bulat	Viktor	BLS	1 Apr 71	192/105	SP	20.06i, 18.57	19.63 -92
Buldov	Dmitriy	RUS	2 Jul 68	191/79	110h	13.79	13.59 -91, 13.4 -90
* Bulkovskiy	Andrey	UKR	22 Jul 72	184/64	1500	3:37.51	3:44.57 -92
* Buncic	Mike	USA	25 Jul 62	193/113	DT	67.12	69.36 -91
Bundo	Pablo	ESP	13 Oct 70		3kSt	8:34.65	8:42.98 -92
Burakov	Vadim	BLS	22 Oct 74		HT	70.16	67.10 -92
Burke	Bill	USA	15 Oct 69	185/66	1500	3:35.74	3:38.82 -92
					Mile	3:56.83	3:58.70i -91
Burns	Brent	USA	2 May 69	193/88	PV	5.70	5.70 -92
Burrell	Alvaro	ESP	29 Apr 69	191/84	Dec	7588	8005 -92
* Burrell	Leroy	USA	21 Feb 67	183/82	100	10.02, 9.85w	9.88 -91
					200	20.35	20.12 -92, 19.61w -90
Burton	Dan	USA	11 Mar 67	185/75	PV	5.53	5.60i -91, 5.40 -90
Busch	Michael	GER	20 Nov 66	179/63	1500	3:36.30	3:36.64 -92
Buse	Mark	USA	30 Nov 72	191/77	PV	5.60	5.50 -92
Butkiewicz	Jacek	POL	25 Jul 69	187/78	TJ	16.75	16.05 -91, 16.41w -92
Buzza	Dave	GBR	6 Dec 62	183/64	Mar	2:11:06	2:12:37 -91
Bykov	Sergey	UKR	16 May 71	186/71	TJ	16.89i	16.98 -90
Bykov	Vladimir	RUS	70		HT	71.10	75.08 -92
Byrne	Jason	GBR	9 Sep 70	186/110	HT	72.52	73.80 -92
Bystedt	Kjell	SWE	24 May 60	189/120	HT	72.38	78.64 -88
Byzov	Dmitriy	TJK	25 Jan 66	183/75	TJ	16.92	16.88 -89
* Cacho	Fermin	ESP	16 Feb 69	175/63	800	1:45.46	1:45.37 -91
					1000	2:16.13	2:20.18i -92
					1500	3:32.01	3:32.03 -91
					Mile	3:53.68	3:50.74 -91
Cadogan	Gary	GBR	8 Oct 66	190/85	400h	49.25	-0-
Cadoni	Davide	ITA	4 May 73	183/81	800	1:46.63	1:46.93 -91
Cahill	Sean	IRL	26 Apr 67	184/82	110h	13.66A,13.70	14.26 -91, 14.06w -92
Cai Min		CHN	8 May 68	184/82	Dec	7824	7764 -92
Calabro'	Emilio	ITA	4 Feb 69	186/115	HT	74.06	72.68 -92
Caldwell	Chris	USA	29 Jan 71	185/75	800	1:47.05	1:47.23 -92
Calvaresi	Graziano	ITA	18 Oct 66		Mar	2:11:49	
* Camara	Pierre	FRA	10 Sep 65	181/74	TJ	17.59i, 17.30	17.34 -92
Campbell	Darren	GBR	12 Sep 73	186/75	100	10.29w	10.37, 10.28w -91
					200	20.55w	20.87, 20.68w -92
* Capobianco	Dean	AUS	11 May 70	180/79	100	10.25, 10.17w, 9.9w	10.36 -91
					200	20.18	20.39 -91
Caristan	Stéphane	FRA	31 May 64	187/75	400h	50.40	48.86 -92
Carlier	Jacky	FRA	8 Nov 61	182/66	3k	7:47.21	7:47.6 -90
					5k	13:28.27	13:39.53 -88

Name		Nat	Born	Ht/Wt	Event	1993 Mark	Pre-1993 Best
Carlin	Sean	AUS	29 Nov 67	198/110	HT	75.36	77.12 -92
Carlson	Rob	USA	27 Aug 71	196/114	SP	18.93	18.14 -92
Carnesolta	Angel	CUB	11 Sep 69	175/62	800	1:47.12	1:47.71 -91
Carosi	Angelo	ITA	20 Jan 64	182/66	3k	7:49.91	7:52.92 -91
					5k	13:25.38	13:34.65 -90
					3kSt	8:19.66	8:17.48 -90
Carroll	Mark	IRL	15 Jan 72		1500	3:39.67	3:43.36 -91
Carter	Jonathan	USA	5 May 72	178/73	100	10.30, 10.19w	10.51 -91
Carter	LaMark	USA	23 Aug 70	180/75	TJ	16.78, 16.83w	16.68 -92
Carter	Marcel	USA	26 Mar 71	170/66	100	10.29	10.29, 10.22w -92
					200	20.34	20.94 -91, 20.54w -92
Cascabelo	Marcelo	ARG	6 Feb 64	174/65	3kSt	8:34.38	8:25.63 -89
* Cason	Andre	USA	20 Jan 69	170/70	100	9.92, 9.79w	9.99 -91
Castillo	Gustavo	MEX	26 Apr 70	175/60	3kSt	8:28.91	8:34.63 -92
Castro	Artur de Freitas	BRA	12 Nov 67	172/52	Mar	2:10:06	2:12:52 -92
* Castro	Domingos	POR	22 Nov 63	167/56	3k	7:49.32	7:43.32 -89
					5k	13:14.65	13:14.41 -89
					10k	27:34.53	27:36.00 -89
Caudron	Sylvain	FRA	10 Sep 69		50kW	4:05:02	4:24:28 -92
Ceresoli	Ettori	ITA	11 Apr 70	192/70	HJ	2.25	2.24 -91
* Ceron	Dionicio	MEX	9 Oct 65	173/54	Mar	2:08:51	2:08:36 -92
Chance	Neil	USA	14 Feb 73	193/91	LJ	8.01i, 8.20w	7.89 -92
Chao Chih-kuo		TPE	72	178/70	LJ	8.09	7.68 -91
Charadia	Andres	ARG	10 Jul 66	192/100	HT	73.16	74.38 -92
Charrière	Pascal	SUI	14 Nov 64	184/68	50kW	4:04:19	4:04:03 -92
Chaston	Justin	GBR	4 Nov 68	178/64	3kSt	8:32.67	8:36.17 -92
Chaussinand	David	FRA	19 Apr 73	193/93	HT	72.34	73.42 -92
Chauvelier	Dominique	FRA	3 Aug 56	181/68	Mar	2:12:11	2:11:24 -89
Chékhémani	Abdelkadar	FRA	18 Jul 71	178/70	1500	3:39.51	3:41.81 -92
* Chelimo	Richard	KEN	21 Apr 72	163/54	3k	7:41.63	7:50.22 -91
					5k	13:05.14	13:10.46 -92
					10k	27:07.91	27:11.18 -91
* Chemoiywo	Simon	KEN	2 May 69	170/60	5k	13:09.68	13:18.95 -92
					10k	28:11.0A	28:45.4A -90
Chen Junlin		CHN	31 May 67	184/83	JT	76.10	77.82 -91
Chen Shaoguo		CHN	20 Jan 72	171/50	20kW	1:19:43	1:20:31.5t -92
					50kW	3:59:36	
Chen Wenzhong		CHN	29 Aug 70	178/65	100	10.25w	10.24 -92
Chen Yanhao		CHN	2 Jan 72		110h	13.59	13.87 -91
Cheng Shaobo		CHN	16 Apr 63	190/104	SP	18.59	19.32 -90
Cherepanov	Vyacheslav	RUS	2 Nov 64		20kW	1:19:52	1:20:34 -91
Chernega	Yuriy	RUS	18 Feb 67		HT	79.64	77.98 -89
Chernyavskiy	Andrey	RUS	25 Jun 70	183/78	Dec	7744	7721 -91
Chernyayev	Aleksandr	UKR	31 May 60	180/74	PV	5.60i, 5.60	5.71 -83
Chernysh	Vladimir	UKR	14 Feb 68	198/110	SP	18.87i, 18.70	19.24 -90
Chervonyi	Aleksandr	UKR	26 Mar 70	180/73	PV	5.60i, 5.60ex	5.50i, 5.45 -91
Chesang	Reuben	KEN	66	170/55	2k	5:02.43i	
					5k	13:31.80	
					3kSt	8:31.28	
Chesire	Joseph	KEN	12 Nov 57	167/57	1500	3:38.65	3:33.12 -92
* Chesire	Mike	KEN	1 Dec 69	170/52	3k	7:44.82	7:52.59 -91
					5k	13:16.15	13:29.13 -91
Chiamulera	Pedro	BRA	29 Jun 64	190/77	110h	13.79	13.87 -85
					400h	50.1A	49.34 -85
Chimusasa	Tendai	ZIM	28 Jan 71	180/60	5k	13:29.46	13:50.16 -92
					10k	27:57.84	29:17.26 -92
Chirchir	Gideon	KEN	66		5k	13:30.08	14:04.98 -90
					3kSt	8:19.34	8:31.77 -90
Chisley	Lamar	USA	15 Mar 72	170/64	200	20.62w	20.72 -92
Chmara	Miroslaw	POL	9 May 64	201/90	PV	5.60i	5,90 -88
Chmara	Sebastian	POL	21 Nov 71	188/76	Dec	7608	7424 -91
Chmyr	Jaroslav	UKR	29 Nov 66	190/105	HT	76.24	80.90 -90
Choumassi	M'amed	MAR	2 Dec 69	171/62	1500	3:38.08	3:40.3 -90
					3k	7:43.92	7:42.66 -91
					5k	13:27.83	13:22.44 -91
* Christie	Linford	GBR	2 Apr 60	189/82	100	9.87	9.92, 9.90w -91
					200	20.39, 20.19w	20.09 -88

Name		Nat	Born	Ht/Wt	Event	1993 Mark	Pre-1993 Best
Chumakov	Viktor	BLS	31 May 57	176/60	Mar	2:11:56	
Cimarrusti	Giacomo	ITA	9 Jun 65		50kW	3:59:05	
Ciofani	Walter	FRA	17 Feb 62	185/110	HT	76.14	78.50 -85
Cishahayo	Diomède	BUR	62	167/55	10k	28:25.70	30:31.40 -89
Clarico	Vincent	FRA	8 Jan 66	184/79	110h	13.68, 13.64w	13.68 -90
Clark	Cletus	USA	20 Jan 62	193/88	110h	13.73w	13.30 -88
Clark	Darren	AUS	6 Sep 65	178/77	400	45.53	44.38 -88
Clark	Ron	USA	1 Nov 69	185/75	100	10.15w	10.35 -91, 10.28w -90
					200	20.49	20.75, 20.69w -91, 20.3w -90
Clarke	Evon	JAM	2 Mar 65	182/76	100	10.31w	10.63w -92
					200	20.71	21.50 -90, 21.1 -91
					400	44.79	45.9, 46.05 -92
Clode	Phil	NZL	11 Mar 65	183/63	5k	13:32.70	13:30.64 -91
					10k	28:21.33	
Cojocaru	Daniel	ROM	27 May 69	188/76	100	10.24	10.31 -91
					200	20.79	20.80 -91
Coleman	Kevin	USA	5 May 69	188/118	SP	19.77i, 19.28	20.08 -92
Concepción	Jesús Gabriel	ESP	7 Aug 72	189/75	PV	5.55i, 5.50	5.45 -92
Conjungo	Mickael	CAF	6 May 68	194/94	DT	59.92	57.92 -92
* Conley	Mike	USA	5 Oct 62	185/77	LJ	8.16	8.43, 8.53w -85
					TJ	17.86	17.87 -87, 18.17w -92
Conlin	Paul	USA	16 Jul 70	188/123	SP	19.08	18.49 -92
* Conway	Hollis	USA	8 Jan 67	183/68	HJ	2.38	2.40i -91, 2.39 -89
Cooper	Obadiah	USA	8 Mar 70	173/75	200	20.70w	
Cordero	Domingo	PUR	17 Oct 65	188/73	400h	49.55	49.12 -91
Corgos	Antonio	ESP	10 Mar 60	183/78	LJ	7.99	8.23 -80
Corre	Jean-Claude	FRA	14 Sep 61	172/58	50kW	3:51:51	3:52:47.3 -92
Corritore	Nello	ITA	11 Apr 71		50kW	4:03:57	
Corstjens	Marc	BEL	31 Aug 65	175/65	1500	3:37.73	3:37.25 -90
					Mile	3:54.57	3:55.83 -91
Coull	Joshua	AUS	10 Nov 69		400	46.05	46.16 -92
Coutant	Bruno	FRA	27 Apr 63	182/70	3kSt	8:35.40	8:30.20 -87
Couto	Fernando	POR	4 Dec 59	165/59	5k	13:32.63	13:24.25 -89
					Mar	2:11:18	2:13:23 -92
Cox	David	USA	7 Aug 72	180/77	PV	5.52	5.42 -92
* Cram	Steve	GBR	14 Oct 60	186/69	1500	3:35.63	3:29.67 -85
					Mile	3:52.17	3:46.32 -85
Crampton	Peter	GBR	4 Jun 69	190/82	400h	50.34	-0-
* Crear	Mark	USA	2 Oct 68	186/79	110h	13.26, 13.22w, 12.9w	13.33, 13.2 -92
Creighton	Shaun	AUS	14 May 67	180/65	1500	3:38.59	3:40.70 -92
					3k	7:46.10	7:48.07 -90
					3kSt	8:16.22	8:20.37 -92
Crepaldi	Gianni	ITA	19 Oct 68	182/65	3kSt	8:27.35	8:28.31 -91
Crist	Kevin	USA	16 Jul 70	203/84	HJ	2.28	2.24 -92
Crisóstomo	Henrique	POR	10 Mar 62	176/54	10k	28:18.13	28:31.23 -89
Croghan	Mark	USA	8 Jan 68	175/60	3kSt	8:09.76	8:10.69 -91
Crook	Zeba	CAN	28 Dec 66		3kSt	8:34.89	8:31.2 -91
Cruz	Ignacio	MEX	15 May 71	172/61	20kW	1:23:36	1:24:33 -91
* Cruz	Joaquim	BRA	12 Mar 63	187/74	800	1:46.37	1:41.77 -84
Cui Hui		CHN	18 Jun 73		100	10.29	
Cummins	Kirk	BAR	8 Jan 72	173/77	100	10.28	10.59 -91
Cuñado	Teodoro	ESP	13 Feb 70	171/57	5k	13:31.17	13:35.70 -91
Currey	Andrew	AUS	7 Feb 71	193/95	JT	80.48	75.36 -92
Cushing-murray	Christian	USA	18 Oct 67	180/66	1500	3:37.94	3:37.94 -92
Czingler	Zsolt	HUN	26 Apr 71	186/76	TJ	16.87, 17.25w	16.49 -91
Czukor	Zoltán	HUN	18 Dec 62	187/68	50kW	3:56:50	3:55:15 -90
* da Silva	Robson	BRA	4 Sep 64	187/74	100	10.20, 10.19w	10.02 -86, 10.00A -88
					200	20.16	19.96, 19.7A -89
da Silva	André Domingos	BRA	26 Nov 72	190/69	100	10.19w	10.27 -92
					200	20.58	20.8, 21.20 -92
Dacha	Driss	MAR	29 Dec 62		Mar	2:11:43	2:13:03 -91
Dågard	Henrik	SWE	7 Aug 69	183/79	Dec	7965	8052 -90
Dahmen	Ralf	GER	9 Feb 68	188/74	3k	7:46.64	8:05.07 -92
Dailey	Mark	USA	11 Dec 68	186/73	800	1:46.65	1:46.14 -92
					1500	3:37.31	3:38.37 -92
					Mile	3:57.16	4:03.53i -92
* Dakov	Georgi	BUL	21 Oct 67	196/80	HJ	2.28	2.36 -90

Name		Nat	Born	Ht/Wt	Event	1993 Mark	Pre-1993 Best
Dakshevich	Gennadiy	UKR	15 Mar 66	178/75	110h	13.55	13.57 -91, 13.4 -87
* Dal Soglio	Paolo	ITA	29 Jul 70	189/110	SP	20.65i, 20.43	19.76 -92
Daler	Justin	USA	12 Apr 71	192/89	PV	5.50i, 5.50	5.60 -92
Damian	Mickaël	FRA	9 Nov 69	170/66	1500	3:38.6	3:41.0 -92
Damszel	Tomasz	POL	25 Mar 72	186/82	JT	77.60	76.92 -92
Daniel	Clarence	USA	11 Jun 61	183/79	400	46.05	44.75 -88
Danielson	Jonny	SWE	4 Sep 64	191/74	5k	13:29.47	13:20.29 -88
					10k	28:32.62	27:55.74 -89
Danneberg	Rolf	GER	1 Mar 53	198/125	DT	58.68	67.60 -87
Dasko	Mikhail	RUS	26 Jan 61	174/61	5k	13:27.07	13:16.73 -91
Dauth	Thorsten	GER	11 Mar 68	201/102	Dec	7985	8156 -91
Davenport	Lance	USA	16 Dec 66	193/105	DT	58.64	57.72 -89
David	Karel	TCH	8 Feb 64	180/65	Mar	2:11:57	2:11:13 -91
Davis	Antonio	USA	29 May 72	185/73	TJ	16.61	15.67 -92
Davis	Calvin	USA	2 Apr 72	183/79	400	45.04	45.85 -92
* Davis	Marc	USA	17 Dec 69	183/64	1500	3:37.12	3:48.14 -89
					3k	7:38.03	7:51.72i -92
					3kSt	8:14.26	8:33.93 -92
Davis	Terril	USA	21 Apr 68	183/64	800	1:46.24	1:44.44 -92
Davydov	Nikolay	RUS	70		HT	72.20	72.30 -91
* De Benedictis	Giovanni	ITA	8 Jan 68	180/58	20kW	1:21:16	1:20:29 -91
* de Bruin	Erik	HOL	25 May 63	186/110	SP	19.58i, 19.16 *	20.95 -86
					DT	67.06 *	68.12 -91
de Freitas	Matt	GBR	19 Sep 68		1500	3:39.66	3:40.84 -92
De Gaetano	Giuseppe	ITA	4 Oct 66		50kW	3:51:54	3:54:08 -91
De Gaspari	Fabio	ITA	4 Dec 66	183/82	JT	79.02	79.24 -92
de la Torre	Carlos	ESP	18 May 66	170/58	5k	13:33.48	13:29.85 -92
de la Torre	Elisardo	ESP	10 Oct 71	175/65	3kSt	8:32.67	8:40.0 -92
de Oliveira	Edgar	BRA	11 Nov 67	180/67	800	1:46.65	1:46.89 -91
					1500	3:38.45	3:34.80 -91
De Silva	Neil	TRI	15 Nov 69	175/75	400	45.40	45.81 -91, 45.8 -92
De Teresa	Tomás	ESP	5 Sep 68	179/66	800	1:46.23	1:44.99 -90
* Deal	Lance	USA	21 Aug 61	188/116	HT	80.80	81.08 -92
Dean-Neil	Andrew	USA	28 Jun 65	183/71	400h	50.40	50.30 -92
Debelyi	Andrey	UKR	8 Jan 71	184/105	HT	77.92	73.96 -90
Deering	Bill	USA	20 Jul 71	183/82	PV	5.64uc, 5.51i	5.60 -92
* Dees	Anthony	USA	6 Aug 63	193/95	110h	13.12	13.05 -91
Deetlefs	Deon	RSA	14 Feb 69		JT	76.68	76.98 -92
Delice	Patrick	TRI	12 Nov 67	184/77	100	10.22	10.33 -92
					200	20.32	20.81 -91, 20.74w -92
					400	44.58	45.06 -91
Delis	Luís M	CUB	6 Dec 57	185/96	DT	63.66	71.06 -83
DeLoach	Joe	USA	5 Jun 67	183/79	200	20.15	19.75 -88
Delonge	Marco	GER	16 Jun 66	194/81	LJ	7.98	8.27 -87
Demakov	Vyacheslav	RUS	8 Nov 68	191/100	DT	62.86	63.92 -92
D'Encausse	Philippe	FRA	24 Mar 67	184/77	PV	5.75i	5.72i -91, 5.70 -88
Denishchik	Oleg	BLS	10 Nov 69	190/80	TJ	17.00	17.53 -91
Denisov	Aleksey	RUS	30 Mar 67		HJ	2.28	2.24 -91
* Denmark	Robert	GBR	23 Nov 68	171/60	1500	3:39.62	3:38.34 -92
					3k	7:39.55	7:39.72 -92
					5k	13:16.48	13:10.24 -92
Desmangles	Gaetan	FRA	15 Dec 68	171/68	100	10.29rs	10.74 -90
Despotov	Radoslav	BUL	8 Aug 68	190/130	SP	18.99i, 18.84	20.13 -88
Detchenique	Didier	FRA	4 Oct 72	189/70	HJ	2.24 exh	2.24 -90
Dethloff	Claus	GER	4 Sep 68	187/97	HT	73.10	77.46 -92
Deutsch	Péter Tamás	HUN	10 Aug 68	203/89	HJ	2.24	2.27 -89
Di Lello	Luigi	ITA	31 May 68		Mar	2:12:08	
Di Mezza	Arturo	ITA	16 Jul 69	170/60	20kW	1:23:06	1:24:52.2t -92
* Di Napoli	Gennaro	ITA	5 Mar 68	185/61	1500	3:36.01	3:32.78 -90
					3k	7:42.68	7:45.85 -91
					5k	13:27.89	13:27.87 -90
Dia Bâ	Amadou	FRA	22 Sep 58	190/72	400h	49.74	47.23 -88
Diagana	Stéphane	FRA	23 Jul 69	184/75	400	45.26	45.18 -92
					400h	47.64	48.13 -92
Diaz	René	CUB	13 Jan 67	179/105	HT	70.62	69.96 -90
* Diemer	Brian	USA	10 Oct 61	176/64	3kSt	8:22.41	8:13.16 -84
Digno	Marti	CUB	28 Aug 62	179/75	LJ	7.96	8.17 -86

Name		Nat	Born	Ht/Wt	Event	1993 Mark	Pre-1993 Best
Dimitrov	Georgi	BUL	12 Feb 71	191/70	TJ	16.82	16.24 -92
Dimitrov	Kamen	BUL	18 Jan 62	194/112	DT	60.54	65.40 -86
Dinsamo	Belayneh	ETH	28 Jun 65	165/60	Mar	2:12:11	2:06:50 -88
Dirks	Tonnie	HOL	12 Feb 61	176/62	Mar	2:12:27	2:12:45 -92
Dixon	Malcolm	USA	11 Oct 59	188/89	110h	13.79	13.64 -86, 13.4 -81
						13.63w	13.54w-83
Dixon	Marcus	USA	6 Jul 70	193/77	110h	13.80, 13.65w	13.63 -91
do Carmo	Clodoaldo	BRA	27 Apr 68	172/60	3kSt	8:35.50	8:19.80 -92
do Prado Moura	Wender	BRA	22 Feb 69	181/62	3kSt	8:26.65	8:30.24 -92
Doakes	Ray	USA	12 Aug 73	203/82	HJ	2.28	2.24 -92
Dobson	Windell	JAM	5 Jan 70	183/75	200	20.67w	20.72 -91
* Doehring	Jim	USA	27 Jan 62	183/120	SP	21.56i, 21.15	21.60 -92
Doherty	John	IRL	22 Jul 61	175/60	5k	13:32.47	13:14.17 -90
Dolega	Karol	POL	19 Jul 63	184/71	Mar	2:12:59	2:13:18 -89
* Dollé	David	SUI	30 May 69	192/80	100	10.25	10.30 -92
					200	20.43	20.75 -92
Dollendorf	Marc	BEL	7 Feb 66	191/85	400h	49.82	49.94 -91
Dolnikov	Dmitriy	RUS	19 Nov 72	175/67	20kW	1:19:41	1:21:29 -92
Dologodin	Vladislav	UKR	23 Feb 72	188/83	100	10.32	10.59 -91, 10.3 -92
					200	20.38	21.43, 21.2 -91
Domingues	Adauto	BRA	20 May 61		3kSt	8:35.52	
Domrachov	Sergey	UKR	27 Mar 68		HT	72.56	75.18 -92
Donakowski	Gerard	USA	20 Feb 60	172/59	10k	28:23.96	27:58.41 -86
Döring	Mirko	GER	21 Jul 71	173/59	1500	3:38.83	3:40.51 -92
					2k	5:01.09i	
dos Santos	Diamantino	BRA	3 Feb 61	166/59	Mar	2:12:22	2:11:28 -91
dos Santos	Luiz Antonio	BRA	6 Apr 64		Mar	2:12:15	
dos Santos	Valdenor	BRA	21 Dec 69		Mar	2:10:20	
Dost	Marcel	HOL	28 Sep 69	195/82	Dec	7883	7686 -92
Dotson	Antonious	USA	24 Jul 70		400	46.00 unc	
Douglas	Atle	NOR	9 Jun 68	193/80	800	1:44.74	1:45.15 -92
Douglas	Troy	BER	30 Nov 62	173/71	200	20.69	20.70 -88, 20.3 -90
					400	45.57	45.37 -92
Doyi	Thomas	BUR			10k	28:26.63	
* Doyle	Simon	AUS	9 Nov 66	185/74	800	1:46.99	1:45.38 -91
					1500	3:33.39	3:31.96 -91
					Mile	3:52.56	3:49.91 -91
* Drake	Marino	CUB	13 Jun 67	193/73	HJ	2.25	2.34 -91
Drath	Jim	USA	19 Sep 68	180/80	PV	5.55	
Driesen	Rainer	GER	20 Aug 61	181/68	50kW	4:04:21	4:09:37 -88
Driscoll	Jim	USA	15 Aug 65	183/109	HT	73.32	74.58 -92
* Drummond	Jon	USA	9 Sep 68	175/72	100	10.03, 9.92w	10.10 -90, 10.03w -91
Du Yuechun		CHN	5 Jan 72	178/70	400h	50.08	50.54 -92
Duan Qifeng		CHN	20 Jan 73	172/60	TJ	16.96	16.07 -92
Duany	Raúl	CUB	4 Jan 75	179/79	Dec	7749	7403 -92
Dubrovchik	Vladimir	BLS	7 Jan 72	193/115	DT	63.26	61.80 -92
Dubus	Eric	FRA	28 Feb 66	182/70	1500	3:37.03	3:37.36 -90
					3k	7:48.98i	7:48.37 -91
Dudakov	Yevgeniy	RUS	69		Dec	7902	7315 -89
Dudás	Gyula	HUN	10 Aug 66	175/68	20kW	1:22:24	1:21:16 -91
Dudij	Karol	POL	24 Aug 70	182/72	1500	3:39.46	3:38.18 -92
Duffy	Pat	USA	4 May 65	190/83	110h	13.65, 13.51w	13.74, 13.70w -92
Dugdale	Paul	GBR	13 May 65	176/62	10k	28:22.48	28:55.43 -92
Duginyets	Igor	RUS	20 May 56	196/105	DT	59.22	68.52 -82
Duplantis	Greg	USA	22 Jan 62	168/66	PV	5.80	5.79 -88
Dupray	Gilles	FRA	2 Jan 70	186/97	HT	77.18	72.88 -92
Durbano	Walter	ITA	31 Mar 63		Mar	2:11:13	2:13:18 -90
* D'Urso	Giuseppe	ITA	15 Sep 69	178/56	800	1:44.83	1:45.31 -92
					1000	2:16.19	2:18.10 -92
Duval	Spencer	GBR	5 Jan 70	180/63	3kSt	8:32.77	8:41.13 -91
Dück	Oliver	GER	10 Feb 67	213/138	SP	18.62	18.93 -90
Dvorák	Tomás	TCH	11 May 72	186/83	Dec	8054	7748 -91
Dydalin	Andrey	RUS	7 Jun 66	190/90	110h	13.62	13.50 -92
Dymchenko	Sergey	UKR	23 Aug 67	202/82	HJ	2.25	2.37 -90
Dzashitov	Aleksey	RUS	70		TJ	16.56i	16.11i -92
Edel	Mikhail	RUS	7 Sep 69	185/79	110h	13.84	13.60 -92
Edler-Muhr	Werner	AUT	4 Feb 69	174/56	1500	3:39.38	3:41.56 -92

Name		Nat	Born	Ht/Wt	Event	1993 Mark	Pre-1993 Best
Edorh	Claude	GER	27 Feb 72	183/82	110h	13.73, 13.69w	13.82 -92
Edwards	Devon	USA	17 Feb 73		400	45.56	47.23 -92
* Edwards	Jonathan	GBR	10 May 66	180/74	TJ	17.44, 17.70w	17.43 -91
Edwards	Mike	GBR	19 Oct 68	189/81	PV	5.52	5.50 -91
Edwards	Paul	GBR	16 Feb 59	186/133	SP	19.84	20.33 -91
* Effiong	Daniel	NGR	17 Jun 72	187/79	100	9.98, 9.97w	10.11 -92
					200	20.15	20.45, 20.38w -92
Efremov	Ilian	BUL	2 Aug 70	189/74	PV	5.50i	5.55 -92
Eftimie	Ionel	ROM	8 Oct 71	190/80	TJ	16.54	
Eich	Carsten	GER	9 Jan 70	190/65	2k	5:04.15i	
					5k	13:30.97	13:32.25 -92
Einarsson	Sigurdur	ISL	28 Sep 62	188/100	JT	80.60	83.32 -92
* El Basir	Rachid	MAR	4 Oct 68	180/61	1500	3:35.51	3:34.40 -92
					Mile	3:55.25	3:54.84 -92
					2k	5:05.0+	
* El Khattabi	Larbi	MAR	16 May 67	174/68	3kSt	8:16.60	8:23.82 -92
El Maati	Chaham	MAR	15 Mar 66		Mar	2:11:55	
Elferink	Glen	RSA	21 May 73	178/74	200	20.66w	20.63A -92
Elizalde	Alexis	CUB	19 Sep 67	192/110	DT	64.12	62.52 -91
Emmiyan	Robert	ARM	16 Feb 65	178/69	LJ	7.92	8.86A -87, 8.61 -86
* Epalle	Christophe	FRA	23 Jan 69	194/110	HT	79.98	76.86 -92
Eplinius	Mark	GER	17 Sep 70	186/67	800	1:46.62i	1:45.32 -92
					1000	2:18.16i	2:20.39 -91
Erb	Christian	SUI	14 Feb 59	180/97	DT	61.86	64.04 -88
* Eregbu	Obinna	NGR	9 Nov 69	183/76	LJ	8.18, 8.32w	8.09, 8.18w -92
* Ereng	Paul	KEN	22 Aug 67	188/69	800	1:44.96	1:43.16 -89
Eriksson	Martin	SWE	15 Jun 71		PV	5.61	5.45 -92
Eriksson	Torbjörn	SWE	17 Apr 71	170/65	200	20.66	20.77 -92
Ermili	Saïd	MAR	63		Mar	2:12:29	2:11:56 -91
Esenwein	Peter	GER	7 Dec 67	188/85	JT	78.26	76.86 -92
Esmie	Robert	CAN	5 Jul 72	175/64	100	10.23	10.39 -92
* Espinosa	Andrés	MEX	4 Feb 63	16755	Mar	2:10:04	2:10:00 -91
Essaid	Mustapha	FRA	20 Jan 70	179/62	5k	13:23.94	13:42.25 -92
					10k	28:25.70	"29:23.00 -92
* Evangelisti	Giovanni	ITA	11 Sep 61	179/70	LJ	7.94, 8.04w	8.43 -87
Evans	Paul	GBR	13 Apr 61	183/66	10k	27:47.79	27:48.32 -92
Evans	Randall	USA	26 Oct 70	180/79	100	10.20, 10.19w	10.40 -91
					200	20.50	?
* Everett	Mark	USA	2 Sep 68	177/64	800	1:44.43	1:43.40 -92
Eyestone	Ed	USA	15 Jun 61	185/61	10k	28:30.60	27:41.05 -85
* Ezinwa	Davidson	NGR	22 Nov 71	184/82	100	10.14	9.96, 9.91dwr -92
Ezinwa	Osmond	NGR	22 Nov 71	182/79	100	10.12	10.09 -92, 9.8dt -90
Fairbrother	Simon	GBR	28 Mar 68	183/70	1500	3:38.66	3:38.64 -92
Falcon	Joe	USA	23 Jun 66	168/56	Mile	3:57.44i	
					3k	7:49.20i	7:46.57 -88
					10k	28:21.24	28:34.3 -87
Fandiño	Carlos	CUB	10 Jun 69	186/105	SP	19.49	19.13 -91
Fantini	Corrado	ITA	7 Feb 67	191/120	SP	19.10	18.72 -90
Fariña	Angel	ESP	21 May 67	180/67	1500	3:39.16	3:35.15 -90
Farkas	Zoltán	HUN	7 Mar 70	184/70	PV	5.51	5.50 -92
Farr	Alexander	GER	6 Jan 70		HJ	2.24i	2.22 -92
Farraudière	Jacques	FRA	27 Jan 66	188/81	400	46.01	46.14 -92
Farrell	Derrick	USA	10 Jan 72	196/119	DT	58.66	50.60 -92
Fasinro	Tosi	GBR	28 Mar 72	188/83	TJ	17.21, 17.30w	16.58, 16.81w -91
Fatun	Oleg	RUS	1 Nov 59	181/78	200	20.71	20.41A -87, 20.65 -89
Fatyanov	Aleksey	AZE	14 Jun 69	180/73	TJ	16.89	16.98 -91
Fedoriv	Andrey	RUS	11 Aug 63	177/80	100	10.23, 10.19w	10.21 -87
					200	20.54	20.53 -86
Fell	Graeme	CAN	19 Mar 59	190/75	3kSt	8:17.30	8:12.58 -85
Fenner	Mike	GER	24 Apr 71	186/80	110h	13.64	13.75 -92
Ferrari	Roberto	ITA	24 Mar 67	185/72	HJ	2.30	2.26 -91
Ferreira	Nelson	BRA	1 Jan 73	181/76	LJ	8.03	7.51 -92
Filho	Benevenuto	BRA	16 Jul 72		800	1:46.55	1:47.43 -92
Finch	Rodney	GBR	5 Aug 67		1500	3:37.97	3:43.1 -91
Fingert	Aleksandr	ISR	1 May 65	198/100	JT	75.60	80.18 -89
Fiorini	Pietro	ITA	11 Mar 67		20kW	1:21:39	1:26:02 -92
Fitzpatrick	Kevin	USA	26 Sep 69	193/105	DT	59.30	61.68 -92

Name		Nat	Born	Ht/Wt	Event	1993 Mark	Pre-1993 Best
Fíz	Martin	ESP	3 Mar 63	167/56	5k	13:33.05	13:20.01 -91
					10k	28:00.97	28:00.19 -91
					Mar	2:12:47	-0-
Fizialetti	Massimo	ITA	7 Feb 65		20kW	1:21:27	1:24:03 -90
					50kW	4:05:19	
Floréal	Edrick	CAN	5 Oct 66	190/82	LJ	8.02	8.20 -91, 8.39w -89
					TJ	17.16	17.23 -90, 17.29A -89
Flowers	Ross	USA	10 Aug 71	183/77	110h	13.84, 13.80w	14.23, 14.15w -92
Flowers	Shannon	USA	17 Sep 71		110h	13.73w	
Föhrenbach	Claus-Dieter	GER	11 May 55	187/110	SP	18.77	19.84 -85
Fomenko	Sergey	UKR	7 Jun 67	188/82	PV	5.60i, 5.60	5.70i -91, 5.65 -92
* Forsyth	Tim	AUS	17 Aug 73	196/73	HJ	2.35	2.34 -92
Fortuna	Diego	ITA	14 Feb 68		DT	60.02	56.46 -92
Foster	Greg	USA	4 Aug 58	190/88	110h	13.27	13.03 -81, 13.0 -79
Foster	Robert	JAM	12 Jul 70	190/88	110h	13.77A, 13.77,	13.89 -90
						13.65w	13.4, 13.65w -92
Fouche	François	RSA	5 Jun 63	191/80	LJ	8.09	8.21A -90, 8.03, 8.32Aw -89
Fouche	Louis	RSA	21 Mar 70		JT	79.64	79.28 -92
Fourie	Johan	RSA	2 Dec 59	180/70	1500	3:37.31	3:33.87 -87
Foxson	Paul	USA	16 Apr 71	193/93	Dec	7621	7878w/7817 -92
Fraga	Santiago	ESP	12 Dec 68	180/70	400h	50.42	50.20 -90
Fraley	Doug	USA	7 Mar 65	185/82	PV	5.55	5.80 -92
Francis	Mike	PUR	23 Oct 70	183/79	LJ	8.13	8.12i -92, 8.05 -91
Francis	Mitchell	JAM	13 Jun 72		400h	49.89	50.71 -92
* Franke	Stephane	GER	12 Feb 64	178/58	3k	7:40.11	7:58.19 -91
					5k	13:13.17	13:48.12 -92
					10k	27:57.98	28:04.41 -91
Frazier	Daryl	USA	23 Jan 71	190/79	200	20.61	21.34 -90
* Fredericks	Frank	NAM	2 Oct 67	180/73	100	10.03	9.95, 9.89w -91
					200	19.85	19.97 -92, 19.90w -91
* Freigang	Stephan	GER	27 Sep 67	177/64	10k	27:59.72	28:05.22 -90
					5k	13:30.40	13:35.33 -92
					Mar	2:11:53	2:14:00 -92
Frigerio	Fausto	ITA	13 Feb 66	182/76	110h	13.64A, 13.72	13.70 -90
Frinolli	Giorgio	ITA	12 Jul 70	183/72	400h	49.22	50.19 -92
* Fritz	Steve	USA	1 Nov 67	191/86	Dec	8324	8079 -91
Fucci	Drew	USA	26 May 67	188/84	Dec	7935w, 7918	8079 -91
Fuentes	Héctor	CUB	27 Jul 74	174/64	100	10.12w	10.80 -92
Fuhlbrügge	Hauke	GER	21 Mar 66	183/66	1500	3:36.03	3:34.15 -91
					2k	5:05.79i	
					3k	7:50.48	7:56.47 -91
					5k	13:33.49	14:01.81 -90
Fujishima	Koji	JPN	2 Jul 70	183/65	HJ	2.25	2.23 -90
Fukushima	Tadashi	JPN	29 Sep 64	171/53	10k	28:02.54	28:39.78 -92
Fukushima	Yuichiro	JPN	23 Apr 70	180/59	10k	28:16.27	28:47.64 -92
Fulford	Rich	USA	29 Apr 69	183/79	PV	5.52	5.60 -91
Fyodorkov	Grigoriy	RUS	9 Nov 64	198/82	HJ	2.26	2.31 -90
Gabris	Petér	SVK	24 Jun 70	175/68	20kW	1:23:28.0t	1:23:37 -92
Gajdus	Grzegorz	POL	16 Jan 67	181/70	Mar	2:11:07	2:12:36 -92
* Galfione	Jean	FRA	20 Jun 71	181/82	PV	5.93	5.90 -92
Galkin	Konstantin	RUS	25 Mar 65	189/71	HJ	2.28	2.26 -92
Galkin	Pavel	RUS	9 Oct 68	186/79	100	10.31	10.27 -90, 10.12w -92
Ganiyev	Ramil	UZB	23 Sep 68	186/80	Dec	7734	8160 -92
Gantt	Brandon	USA	28 Aug 72	185/79	110h	13.78	13.52 -92
Gao Shuhai		CHN	18 Oct 68	175/60	3kSt	8:33.60	8:34.32 -91
Gao Yonghong		CHN	4 May 70	182/72	400h	49.93	49.94 -92
García	Alfredo	CUB	75		100	10.31w	
García	Angel	CUB	5 Jan 67	174/67	PV	5.60	5.65 -92
* García	Daniel	MEX	28 Oct 71	164/55	20kW	1:19:42	1:22:16.1 t -92
					50kW	3:53:23	3:57:38 -92
García	Diego	ESP	12 Oct 61	172/62	Mar	2:10:58	2:10:30 -92
García	Ivan	CUB	29 Feb 72	178/70	100	10.1A	10.54 -92
					200	20.65, 20.53w	20.4, 20.95 -92
* García	Javier	ESP	22 Jul 66	177/71	PV	5.70	5.77i -92, 5.75 -90
* García	Jesus Angel	ESP	17 Oct 69	170/55	50kW	3:41:41	3:48:24 -92
Gariba	Salaam	GHA	23 Jan 69	172/71	100	10.29	10.27, 9.9 -91
Garzón	Juan Carlos	CUB	16 Feb 74	172/67	LJ	8.09	7.75 -92

Name		Nat	Born	Ht/Wt	Event	1993 Mark	Pre-1993 Best
Gaskin	Wendell	USA	7 Jan 73	183/75	100	10.21	10.45, 10.37w -91
Gaskins	Percell	USA	25 Apr 72	187/86	HJ	2.27i	2.18 -92
* Gataullin	Rodion	RUS	23 Nov 65	189/78	PV	6.00i, 6.00	6.02i, 6.00 -89
Gats	Carlos	ARG	11 Dec 69	181/72	200	20.5w	21.06 -90
Gatsioudis	Kostas	GRE	17 Dec 73	188/86	JT	78.44	80.30 -92
* Gauder	Hartwig	GER	10 Nov 54	186/70	20kW	1:23:31	1:20:51 -87
					50kW	3:52:46	3:39:45 -88
Gavela	Rodrigo	ESP	5 Jan 66	173/60	Mar	2:10:27	2:13:37 -90
Gavrilov	Sergey	RUS	22 May 70		HT	75.76	74.40 -92
Gayre	Christopher	USA	73		HJ	2.25	2.16 -92
* Gécsek	Tibor	HUN	22 Sep 64	184/100	HT	81.00	81.68 -88
Gemechu	Kebede	ETH	73		Mar	2:10:16	
George	Vernon	USA	6 Oct 64	190/81	LJ	7.92	8.24 -87, 8.46w -89
Georgiev	Galin	BUL	23 Mar 70	184/78	LJ	8.04	8.20 -92
Georgiev	Stanislav	BUL	6 Feb 71	181/65	200	20.67	
Giacchetto	Alberto	ITA	21 Feb 73	184/70	PV	5.60 *	5.20 -92
Gicquel	Jean-Charles	FRA	24 Feb 67	200/80	HJ	2.30	2.30 -90
Gilbert	Glenroy	CAN	31 Aug 68	183/79	100	10.16, 10.01w	10.27A, 10.29, 10.14w -92
					200	20.37	20.94 -92
Ginko	Viktor	BLS	7 Dec 65	186/76	20kW	1:20:03	1:23:33 -92
					50kW	3:53:41	3:48:42 -92
Gitonga	Charles	KEN	5 Oct 71	175/65	400	45.1A	45.7A -91
Giusto	Matt	USA	25 Oct 66	178/62	Mile	3:55.63	3:59.18 -91
					3k	7:41.60	7:49.96 -91, 7:48.74i -92
					5k	13:23.60	13:30.60 -92
Glinka	Waldemar	POL	9 Jan 68	179/70	1500	3:38.61	3:40.71 -91
Glovatskiy	Aleksandr	BLS	2 May 70	185/72	LJ	8.05	8.10 -90
Godard	Jean-Michel	FRA	19 Jan 71	194/85	PV	5.50	5.45 -91
Godina	John	USA	31 May 72	193/118	SP	20.03	19.68 -92
					DT	60.56	61.52 -92
Goldstein	Chad	USA	28 Mar 71		SP	18.50i	18.31i, 18.07 -92
Golley	Julian	GBR	12 Sep 71	183/76	TJ	16.87, 16.88w	16.95 -92
Golos	Dmitriy	BLS	23 Feb 71		20kW	1:20:42	1:24:09 -91
Golovastov	Dmitriy	RUS	14 Jul 71	191/72	400	45.65	45.85 -92
Golyas	Vladimir	RUS	25 Jan 71	182/63	3kSt	8:33.96	8:28.66 -92
Gombala	Milan	TCH	29 Jan 68	187/75	LJ	8.11i, 8.09	8.11, 8.42Aw, 8.18i.x -92
Gómez	Alejandro	ESP	11 Apr 67	178/60	10k	27:39.38	27:41.30 -90
Gommer	Henk	HOL	17 Nov 62	177/62	5k	13:30.25	13:37.99 -91
Goncharuk	Dmitriy	BLS	10 Sep 70		SP	18.62	19.25 -91
Gong Guohua		CHN	2 Jan 64	185/84	Dec	7704	7908 -90
González	Luis Javier	ESP	17 Jun 69	181/63	800	1:44.84	1:46.10 -91
Gordeyev	Yuriy	RUS	64		20kW	1:19:53	1:22:21 -92
Görmer	Steffen	GER	28 Jul 68	178/80	100	10.28	10.28 -89
Görz	Thomas	GER	10 Mar 72	187/83	Dec	7650	7630 -92
Gozzano	Marco	ITA	26 Sep 63	172/57	Mar	2:12:24	2:12:26 -91
Grabovoy	Vadim	UKR	5 Apr 73	191/98	HT	73.14	73.98 -92
Gracia	David	ESP	22 Feb 70	175/65	PV	5.50i	5.35 -92
* Graham	Winthrop	JAM	17 Nov 65	178/72	400	45.97	45.59 -88
					400h	47.60	47.62 -92
* Grant	Dalton	GBR	8 Apr 66	186/73	HJ	2.34i, 2.34	2.36 -91
* Grasu	Costel	ROM	5 Jul 67	191/105	SP	18.62i	19.42 -89
					DT	66.90	67.08 -92
Gravelle	Mike	USA	13 Apr 65	196/111	DT	63.44	65.24 -91
Gray	Bob	USA	31 Jan 70	181/77	400h	49.94	49.83 -92
* Gray	Johnny	USA	19 Jun 60	190/76	800	1:44.03	1:42.60 -85
Gray	Jordan	USA	9 Feb 71	185/75	400h	49.10	50.13 -92
Green	Andy	GBR	14 Dec 62		Mar	2:12:12	2:15:09 -92
Green	Ethridge	USA	10 Nov 69	188/70	200	20.78	20.78, 20.52w -92
* Green	Michael	JAM	7 Nov 70	176/73	100	10.09,10.01w	10.14 -92,10.02w -91
					200	20.73w	20.86 -91, 20.72i -92
* Greene	Joe	USA	17 Feb 67	183/68	LJ	8.33, 8.35Aw	8.38, 8.66Aw -92
Grégoire	Jean-Francois	FRA	10 Mar 68	182/98	HT	70.78	69.88 -92
Gregorek	John	USA	15 Apr 60	185/74	5k	13:27.2	13:17.44 -87
Griffith	Roshaan	USA	21 Feb 74	175/64	200	20.72	
Grigoryan	Parkev	ARM	1 May 65	186/74	TJ	16.58i, 16.54	17.01 -92
* Grindley	David	GBR	29 Oct 72	187/80	400	44.50	44.47 -92
Grini	Steinar	NOR	8 May 69		HJ	2.25 exh	2.23 -91

Name		Nat	Born	Ht/Wt	Event	1993 Mark	Pre-1993 Best
Grokhovskiy	Oleg	RUS	3 May 68	188/72	TJ	17.28i, 17.01	17.40 -91
* Grossard	Hubert	BEL	28 Mar 68	185/79	110h	13.47	13.56 -92
Grzegorzewski	Pawel	POL	4 Jul 66	186/77	110h	13.58, 13.4	13.80 -89
Guba	Vladislav	UKR	17 Dec 71	186/70	110h	13.71	14.01-91
Gubkin	Valeriy	BLS	3 Sep 67	190/93	HT	78.62	78.28 -92
Gudmundsson	Pétur	ISL	9 Mar 62	193/124	SP	20.53	21.26 -90
* Guebre Selassie	Haile	ETH	18 Apr 73	160/54	3k	7:47.8u+	
					5k	13:03.17	13:36.06 -92
					10k	27:30.17	28:03.99 -92
Guerra	Paulo	POR	21 Aug 70	174/64	10k	28:11.14	- 0 -
Gui Zhixing		CHN	Jul 72		50kW	4:06:28	4:09:07 -91
Guldberg	Mogens	DEN	2 Aug 63	184/65	3k	7:51.16i	7:43.78 -89
Günther	Helge	GER	10 Apr 69	192/87	Dec	7697	7719w -90, 7702 -91
Günthör	Werner	SUI	11 Jul 61	200/128	SP	21.98	22.75 -88
Guo Chaohui		CHN	Aug 73		400h	50.13	50.49 -91
Guo Jin		CHN	29 Jul 70		Dec	7780	7292 -91
Guo Qiang		CHN	14 Sep 68		JT	76.42	74.58 -91
Guo Zhenrong		CHN	20 Apr 72		Dec	7659	7506 -91
Gurny	Slawomir	POL	2 Sep 64	181/68	Mar	2:10:31	2:11:45 -91
Guset	Gheorge	ROM	28 May 68	185/110	SP	19.81	20.33 -91
Gustafsson	Tore	SWE	11 Feb 62	183/105	HT	74.74	80.14 -89
* Haaf	Dietmar	GER	6 Mar 67	173/67	LJ	8.09	8.25 -(i)89, 90, 8.30Aw -91
Haapakoski	Antti	FIN	6 Feb 71	187/74	110h	13.67	13.55 -92
Hacksteiner	Markus	SUI	18 Nov 64	186/72	3kSt	8:31.57	8:42.25 -84
Hafsteinsson	Vésteinn	ISL	12 Dec 60	190/113	DT	63.52	67.64 -89
Hager	Lutz	GER	16 Oct 64	200/105	DT	59.72	62.14 -90
Haïda	Mahjoub	MAR	1 Jul 70	180/75	800	1:44.97	1:46.24 -92
Hakkarainen	Harri	FIN	16 Oct 69	191/91	JT	84.36	83.46 -92
Hall	Darnell	USA	26 Sep 71	183/78	400	45.22	44.95 -92
Halvari	Mika	FIN	13 Feb 70	190/140	SP	20.08	18.71 -91
* Hämäläinen	Eduard	BLS	21 Jan 69	192/88	110h	13.57	14.26 -91
					Dec	8724	8483w -92, 8233 -91
Hamed	Zaïd Abou	SYR	22 Apr 70	182/75	400h	49.09	49.39 -92
Hames	Jagan	AUS	31 Oct 75		HJ	2.25	2.18 -92
Hammarsten	Thomas	SWE	31 Dec 66		SP	18.97	18.97 -92
Han Jun		CHN	13 Nov 72		DT	59.44	58.18 -91
Han Zongmin		CHN	1 Jan 70		5k	13:32.89	13:52.66 -91
Hanada	Katsuhiko	JPN	12 Jun 71	175/59	5k	13:28.73	13:58.13 -92
					10k	28:11.60	68.02 -92
* Hanlon	Tom	GBR	20 May 67	183/67	3kSt	8:19.99	8:12.58 -91
Hannah	Travis	USA	31 Jan 70	171/73	200	20.4w	21.3 -88
Hänninen	Harri	FIN	18 Oct 63	178/61	Mar	2:11:58	2:12:29 -92
Hanstveit	Ketill	NOR	2 Nov 73	176/65	TJ	16.71	15.98, 16.21w -92
Haouam	Samir	ALG	69		HT	70.94	
Haraguchi	Junji	JPN	22 Jun 67	175/56	10k	28:23.39	28:29.76 -92
Harden	Tim	USA	27 Jan 74	175/66	100	10.32	10.3, 10.2w -92
Hargraves	Peter	USA	30 Aug 72	180/75	100	10.26	10.64 -92
Harineki	Philemon	ZIM	12 May 71	170/59	1500	3:37.46	3:35.76 -91
(Hanneck)					Mile	3:57.06	3:53.13 -92
					3k	7:43.57	7:42.06 -92
					5k	13:14.76	
Harju	Antti	FIN	18 Mar 74	183/113	SP	18.40	17.60 -92
Harken	Brent	USA	1 Dec 61	194/77	HJ	2.26	2.35i -91, 2.31 -84
Harlin	Tony	USA	4 Sep 57	190/113	SP	18.95	20.57 -84
Harrington	Larry	USA	24 Nov 70	194/84	110h	13.62,	13.60, 13.4 -92
						13.49w, 13.3w	13.55w -92
Harris	Mike	USA	21 Dec 67	188/79	TJ	16.90	16.52, 16.82w -90
* Harrison	Calvin	USA	20 Jan 74	186/75	200	20.57	
					400	45.07	
* Harrison	Kenny	USA	13 Feb 65	178/75	TJ	17.27	17.93 -90
Hart	Gregg	USA	21 Aug 70	193/111	DT	60.42	59.56 -91
Hartikainen	Jari	FIN	28 Apr 67	183/81	JT	78.84	78.02 -92
Harvey	Mike	AUS	5 Dec 62	175/68	50kW	3:57:20	
Hashioka	Toshiyuki	JPN	19 Jan 64	181/71	PV	5.50	5.55 -86
Hassan	Ibrahim	GHA	71	182/72	200	20.61	21.0 -92
					400	45.60	46.8 -92
Hatungimana	Arthémon	BUR	21 Jan 74	178/63	800	1:46.42	-0-

Name		Nat	Born	Ht/Wt	Event	1993 Mark	Pre-1993 Best
Hauge	Kjell Ove	NOR	20 Feb 69	198/107	SP	18.64i	18.52 -92
* Haughton	Greg	JAM	10 Nov 73	185/79	400	44.78	46.88 -92
Hautala	Ville	FIN	19 Nov 68	174/59	3kSt	8:29.00	8:29.24 -92
* Hawkins	Courtney	USA	11 Jul 67	185/75	110h	13.25	13.28 -90
Hayata	Toshiaki	JPN	2 May 68	176/61	10k	28:18.58	28:17.63 -91
					Mar	2:11:04	
Head	Paul	GBR	1 Jul 65	193/115	HT	73.44	74.02 -90
* Heard	Floyd	USA	24 Mar 66	178/71	100	10.13w	10.10, 10.04w -91, 9.9w -90
					200	20.40	19.95 -87
* Hecht	Raymond	GER	11 Nov 68	190/90	JT	88.90	90.84R -91, 83.24 -90
Heffernan	Steve	USA	27 May 68	170/57	3kSt	8:36.20	8:43.12 -90
Heide	Thorsten	GER	4 May 69	189/79	LJ	8.08	7.87 -92
Heisler	Randy	USA	7 Aug 61	190/111	DT	64.12	67.62 -87
Heist	Michael	GER	2 May 65	185/70	3kSt	8:35.71	8:24.97 -90
* Hélan	Serge	FRA	24 Feb 64	176/70	TJ	17.25	17.45 -91
Helinurm	Marek	EST	6 May 63	182/82	400h	50.24	49.86 -85
Hellebuyck	Eddy	BEL	22 Jan 61		Mar	2:12:27	2:12:16 -89
Hemingway	Matt	USA	24 Oct 72	198/81	HJ	2.25	2.23 -92
Henderson	Kevin	USA	4 Feb 65	185/77	400h	49.21A, 49.30	48.68 -88
Henderson	Paul	AUS	13 Mar 71	184/81	100	10.28,10.27w,10.0w	10.58 -90, 10.36w -89
					200	20.63, 20.36w	21.03 -90
Henderson	Vincent	USA	20 Oct 72	175/66	100	10.11	10.32, 10.29w -92
Hendrix	Jason	USA	24 Oct 72	183/75	200	20.25	20.81 -91, 20.2w -92
Hennig	Scott	USA	17 Apr 69	186/81	PV	5.50	5.61 -91
Henriksson	Tord	SWE	13 Apr 65	189/83	TJ	17.21	17.26i, 17.15 -91
Henriques	Eduardo	POR	24 Mar 68	185/59	3k	7:51.00	7:55.84 - 90
					3kSt	8:34.12	8:28.38 -92
Henry	Boris	GER	14 Dec 73	193/98	JT	84.12	77.34 -92
* Hense	Olaf	GER	19 Nov 67	187/74	400	45.96	46.25 -92
					400h	48.48	49.01 -92
Hepburn	Craig	BAH	10 Dec 69	175/67	LJ	8.41	8.00A -92
Hepburn	Sylvanus	BAH	2 Mar 71	180/77	200	20.64, 20.59w	20.86 -92
Herbrand	Thorsten	GER	9 Apr 70	189/94	SP	18.72	18.84 -92
Hernández	Angel	ESP	15 Apr 66	179/73	LJ	8.18	8.18 -92
Hernández	Eladio	CUB	18 Feb 63	188/107	HT	73.44	72.64 -90
Hernández	Gregorio	CUB	2 Jun 68	190/76	TJ	17.00	16.99 -90
* Hernández	Roberto	CUB	6 Mar 67	179/67	400	46.01	44.14 -90
* Herold	Jens-Peter	GER	2 Jun 65	176/64	800	1:45.97	1:44.88 -90
					1000	2:16.52	2:16.78 -89
					1500	3:34.42	3:32.77 -92
					Mile	3:52.93	3:49.22 -88
					2k	4:56.23i	
Herrador	Antonio	ESP	29 Nov 66	178/62	1500	3:38.62	3:43.17 -92
Herrington	Terrance	USA	31 Jul 66	180/62	800	1:46.76	1:46.38 -88
					1500	3:36.21	3:35.77 -91
					Mile	3:56.75	3:54.13 -91
Hervey	Edward	USA	4 May 73	190/84	200	20.65	
Herwig	Torsten	GER	19 Oct 68	179/60	3kSt	8:28.01	8:30.06 -91
Hewlett	Godfrey	USA	25 Aug 72	188/80	100	10.27Aw	10.38 -91
Hilaire	Pierre-Marie	FRA	19 Nov 65	182/73	400	45.90	46.28 -92
* Hill	Mike	GBR	22 Oct 64	190/95	JT	86.94	86.32R -91, 85.32 -92
Hiratsuka	Jun	JPN	8 Jan 69	167/54	10k	27:59.91	28:11.09 -92
Hlabahlaba	David	RSA	9 Oct 61		800	1:46.78A	1:46.35 -89
Hodge	Neville	ISV	8 Dec 55	172/64	100	10.32	10.36 -90, 10.33w -89,10.1 -79?
Hoen	Steinar	NOR	8 Feb 71	193/77	HJ	2.32	2.30 -92
Hold	Mathias	GER	21 Jan 73	198/96	JT	77.54	75.16 -92
Holder	Monterio	USA	17 Oct 70	188/79	HJ	2.27	2.21 -92
Holender	Jan	POL	12 Mar 64	175/72	50kW	4:00:21	3:58:47 -91
Holl	Werner	GER	28 Jan 70	185/75	PV	5.80i, 5.60	5.60 -91
Holley	Keith	USA	8 Nov 69	175/72	TJ	16.64	16.77 -92
Hollingsworth	Eric	GBR	6 Dec 62		Dec	7748	7638 -92
Holloway	Mike	USA	12 Jul 69	196/86	PV	5.65, 5.70iwb	5.70 -92
Holman	Steve	USA	2 Mar 70	186/66	1500	3:35.29	3:34.95 -92
					Mile	3:52.73	3:53.31 -92
					3k	7:46.27i	7:59.45i -91
Holusa	Milos	TCH	2 May 65	174/62	50kW	3:59:48	3:54:13 -92
Hong	Bo	CHN	Oct 73		5k	13:32.46	13:53.58 -92

Name		Nat	Born	Ht/Wt	Event	1993 Mark	Pre-1993 Best
Honroth	Eric	USA	7 May 71		110h	13.6	
* Horváth	Attila	HUN	28 Jul 67	194/117	DT	64.52	67.06 -91
Howard	Raoul	USA	11 Mar 74	188/80	400	45.91	46.5 -92
Hu Gangjun		CHN	4 Dec 70		Mar	2:10:57	2:12:45 -92
Hu Zhenrong		CHN	Feb 71		20kW	1:22:19	1:25:49.4t -90
Huang Baoting		CHN	May 74		LJ	8.01	7.91 -92
* Huang Geng		CHN	10 Jul 70	179/72	LJ	8.30	8.22 -92
Hudec	Jirí	TCH	15 Aug 64	184/78	110h	13.71	13.48 -89, 13.46w -87
Huff	Derek	USA	26 Nov 66	185/86	Dec	7831	8181w -90, 8126m -92
Huffins	Chris	USA	15 Apr 70	188/84	LJ	8.01	7.96 -91
					Dec	8007	7854w -92
* Huffman	Scott	USA	30 Nov 64	175/75	PV	5.85	5.85 -92
Huke	Michael	GER	30 Mar 69	183/72	200	20.62	20.69 -91
Hunter	C.J.	USA	14 Dec 68	186/135	SP	20.82	20.62i, 20.34 -92
Huotilainen	Tommi	FIN	17 Nov 67	182/80	JT	75.80	76.46 -92
* Huruk	Jan	POL	27 Jan 60	178/65	Mar	2:11:57	2:10:07 -92
Hübner	Jörn	GER	27 Jan 68	188/113	HT	74.62	75.54 -89
Hyoung Jae-young		KOR	24 Feb 71		Mar	2:12:50	2:12:49 -92
Hysong	Nick	USA	9 Dec 71	183/77	PV	5.57i, 5.50	5.52 -92
Hyytiäinen	Marko	FIN	27 Nov 66	191/88	JT	76.44, 80.06xt	83.40 -90
Iapichino	Gianni	ITA	2 Mar 69	185/75	PV	5.60i, 5.62ex	5.60i, 5.60 -92
					LJ	7.95	7.85, 8.00w -92
Ibrahim Warsama Ahmed		QAT	66	180/60	1500	3:39.61	3:39.97 -92
					Mile	3:57.58	
Ignatov	Andrey	RUS	3 Feb 68	182/72	LJ	7.94	8.11 -90
* Ihly	Robert	GER	5 May 63	174/64	20kW	1:21:26	1:19:59 -92
Imamura	Fumio	JPN	5 Nov 66	178/63	50kW	3:56:17	3:59:18 -91
Imo	Chidi	NGR	27 Aug 63	188/77	100	10.20	10.00 -86, 9.92Aw -87
Impens	Christoph	BEL	9 Dec 69	184/69	1500	3:36.63	3:38.29 -90
					Mile	3:55.75	3:59.43 -90
Inoue	Satoru	JPN	21 Feb 71	168/65	100	10.21	10.20 -91
					200	20.72	21.03, 20.98w -89
* Inozemtsev	Vladimir	UKR	25 May 64	185/75	TJ	16.98	17.90 -90
Ionescu	Florin	ROM	3 Feb 71	179/66	3kSt	8:34.93	8:47.13 -92
Ireland	Courtney	NZL	12 Jan 72	193/110	SP	19.30	19.07 -92
Irvin	Brian	USA	30 Jul 70	180/68	200	20.51	21.33 -89
					400	45.63	45.28 -92
Isasi	Joel	CUB	31 Jul 67	167/69	100	10.28, 10.17w	10.18 -89, 9.9 -88
					200	20.72	20.96 -86
Isayev	Konstantin	RUS	7 Jul 73	188/73	HJ	2.26	2.23 -92
Ishutin	Valeriy	UZB	5 Sep 65	186/76	PV	5.70i	5.75i -89, 5.70 -87
* Ismail	Ibrahim	QAT	10 May 72	178/70	400	44.85	44.89 -92
Ismail Doka	Ali	QTR	73	174/65	400h	50.44	51.37 -92
Isolehto	Juha	FIN	6 Jun 68	191/74	HJ	2.27i, 2.25	2.29 -90
* Issangar	Mohamed	MAR	12 Dec 64	178/62	3k	7:39.30	7:39.40 -90
					5k	13:14.23	13:08.51 -90
Itsweire	Bernard	FRA	30 May 65	175/60	Mar	2:12:23	2:11:40 -89
Itt	Edgar	GER	8 Jun 67	186/75	400h	49.75	48.65 -88
Ivanov	Anton	BUL	18 Jul 71	177/69	400	45.61	46.20 -92
Ivanov	Daniel	BUL	4 Nov 65	194/86	LJ	8.00i *	8.03, 8.06w -92
Ivanov	Jaroslav	BUL	19 Aug 73	193/70	TJ	16.77, 16.80w	16.63 -92
* Jabbour	Brahim	MAR	1 Jan 70	178/56	3k	7:36.54	8:06.67 -92
					5k	13:08.86	13:36.44 -92
* Jackson	Colin	GBR	18 Feb 67	183/75	110h	12.91	13.04 -92, 12.95w-89
Jackson	Jeff	USA	14 Mar 74	183/73	110h	13.81	-0-
Jackson	Mark	CAN	15 May 69	190/85	400h	50.33	49.18 -92
Jackson	Reggie	USA	5 Jul 69	183/77	TJ	16.55	16.70, 16.92w -90
Jackson	Tim	AUS	4 Jul 69	185/80	100	10.26, 10.15w	10.31, 10.00w, 10.0 -89
Jacobasch	Udo	GER	30 Aug 70	196/92	Dec	7742	7627 -89
Jacoby	Jake	USA	24 Sep 61	198/84	HJ	2.24i	2.32i -90, 2.31 -87
Jallow	Dawda	GAM	22 Dec 69	180/70	400	45.48	45.76 -90
Janicki	Don	USA	23 Apr 60	175/61	Mar	2:11:39	2:11:16 -85
Jankowski	Henryk	POL	15 Oct 61	181/67	3kSt	8:34.64	8:22.33 -86
Jansa	Frantisek	TCH	12 Sep 62	180/76	PV	5.50i	5.62 -83
Janvrin	Kip	USA	8 Jul 65	183/84	Dec	8052	7994 -89, 8113w -90
* Jaros	Ralf	GER	13 Dec 65	193/85	TJ	17.34	17.66 -91
* Jarrett	Tony	GBR	13 Aug 68	188/82	110h	13.00	13.13 -91, 13.04w -92

Name		Nat	Born	Ht/Wt	Event	1993 Mark	Pre-1993 Best
Jean-Joseph	Jimmy	FRA	15 Oct 72		800	1:47.09	1:48.61 -92
Jeanmarie	Ivan	STL	28 Sep 72	183/77	400	45.83	46.54 - 91
* Jefferson	Jaime	CUB	17 Jan 62	189/78	LJ	8.06	8.53 -90
* Jefferson	Sam	USA	19 Apr 71	168/69	100	10.13, 10.05w	10.27 -92, 10.22w -91
					200	20.32	20.74w -92
Jenkins	Randy	USA	18 Sep 70	190/86	HJ	2.28	2.30 -91
Jesus	Luís	POR	19 Nov 68	170/65	5k	13:33.31	13:42.02 -90
					10k	28:06.70	- 0 -
Jett	James	USA	28 Dec 70	180/75	100	10.26	10.16, 10.10w -92
					200	20.75	20.33, 19.91w -92
Jett	Rod	USA	28 Oct 66	183/80	110h	13.54, 13.46w	13.43 -92
Jia Xinli		CHN	25 Jan 68		LJ	8.02	7.88 -91
Jiao Baozhong		CHN	28 Mar 73		50kW	4:02:35	4:08:49 -92
Jiménez	Anacleto	ESP	24 Feb 67	179/57	5k	13:33.60	13:26.33 -92
Jiménez-Gaona	Ramon	PAR	10 Apr 69	191/107	DT	63.70	64.30 -92
Jin Guohong		CHN	5 Feb 72		50kW	3:55:08	
Jin Suk-kuk		KOR	25 Oct 70	177/80	100	10.23w	10.42 -92
Johansson	Stefan	SWE	11 Apr 67	181/72	20kW	1:21:51	1:18:35.2 t -92
John	Jason	GBR	17 Oct 71	185/75	100	10.30, 10.12w	10.31 -92
					200	20.51w	20.89 -92
Johnson	Allen	USA	1 Mar 71	178/70	110h	13.47, 13.34w	13.63 -92
					LJ	8.14i	7.85 -91
Johnson	Charles	USA	3 Jan 72	183/86	400h	50.04A	51.83 -92
Johnson	Danny	USA	5 Mar 71		LJ	7.95	7.31 -92
Johnson	Dwight	USA	5 Nov 69	179/119	SP	19.01	20.10 -92
Johnson	Ferdana	USA	6 Oct 72		400	45.81	
Johnson	Forest	USA	19 Feb 72	183/73	400	45.68	45.87 -92
Johnson	Gary	USA	20 Jul 69	186/77	TJ	16.69i	16.42, 16.51i, 17.19w -92
Johnson	Lawrence	USA	7 May 74	183/83	PV	5.71	5.33 -92
					Dec	7576	
Johnson	Mamadou	USA	29 Nov 72	178/72	PV	5.52	5.02 -92
* Johnson	Michael	USA	13 Sep 67	185/78	100	10.12	10.21 -91, 10.13w -89
					200	20.06	19.79 -92
					400	43.65	43.98 -92
Johnson	Ron	USA	20 Aug 69	180/83	PV	5.50	5.45 -92
Johnston	Robbie	NZL	21 Aug 67		5k	13:30.36	13:25.11 -92
					10k	28:15.48	
Jones	Bryan	USA	13 Feb 72	186/86	400	45.80	46.73 -92
Jones	Chris	USA	8 Oct 73	181/79	400	45.23	46.47 -92
Jones	Darian	USA	15 Oct 69		110h	13.69w	
Jones	Reggie	USA	8 May 71	185/80	100	10.25	10.4 -91
					LJ	8.07A, 8.05, 8.35Aw	8.05A -92
					TJ	16.96, 17.04w	17.12 -92
Jönsson	Stefan	SWE	14 Feb 64	186/103	HT	71.30	75.30 -91
Jordaan	Naude	RSA	7 Jul 67		1500	3:38.99	3:40.31 -90
Joubert	Michael	AUS	11 May 70	168/59	400	45.88	46.03 -91
Jouÿs	Mathieu	FRA	13 Feb 72	180/73	110h	13.79, 13.67w	14.15 -92
Junqueira	João	POR	24 Jun 65	174/58	10k	28:15.94	28:28.57 -89
					3kSt	8:25.81	8:26.60 -92
Juzdado	Alberto	ESP	20 Aug 66	172/61	10k	28:26.87	29:02.52 -90
Kahan	Nathan	BEL	12 Feb 71	187/65	800	1:45.75	
Kahma	Mika	FIN	25 Sep 66	186/76	LJ	7.92	7.95 -91
Kaiser	Eric	GER	7 Mar 71	182/77	110h	13.48	13.72 -92
Kalboussi	Mahmoud	TUN	9 Feb 65	185/65	1500	3:38.63	3:35.73 -90
Káldy	Zoltán	HUN	7 Jan 69	176/59	5k	13:31.29	13:30.82 -92
Kaleta	Marek	EST	17 Dec 61	183/88	JT	80.08	83.80 -90
Kalogiannis	Athanassios	GRE	10 Sep 65	193/82	400h	49.93	48.80 -87
Kaminski	Ed	USA	26 Mar 68	190/97	JT	80.36	79.30 -92
Kan	Masayoshi	JPN	25 Feb 72	173/60	400	46.04	45.93 -92
Kaneko	Munehiro	JPN	6 Jun 68	182/79	Dec	7995	7916 -90
Kapkory	Josephat	KEN	2 Jan 67	175/57	10k	28:32.03	28:22.4 -92
* Kaptyukh	Vasiliy	BLS	26 Jun 67	197/117	DT	66.18	63.72 -90
Kapusta	Stanislaw	POL	6 Jul 63	186/103	HT	70.54	70.52 -90
* Kapustin	Denis	RUS	5 Oct 70	188/83	TJ	17.54	17.48 -92
Kapustin	Viktor	RUS	28 Apr 72		SP	19.04	18.90 -92
Kapustyanskiy	Vladen	RUS	4 Jul 69	176/72	LJ	8.07i, 7.98	8.01 -90
Karatayev	Andrey	UKR	6 Mar 66	188/71	110h	13.70	13.62 -88

Name		Nat	Born	Ht/Wt	Event	1993 Mark	Pre-1993 Best
Kariuki	Joseph	KEN	1 Jan 70		10k	28:18.02	
* Kariuki	Julius	KEN	12 Jun 61	181/62	3kSt	8:13.38	8:05.51 -88
Karjailanen	Juha	FIN	5 Jul 62	187/81	JT	76.82	78.62 -91
Karlberg	Håkan	SWE	18 Feb 67	196/108	DT	59.42	58.72 -92
Karlsson	Per	SWE	21 Apr 67	182/99	HT	73.36	69.92 -92
Kärnä	Jarmo	FIN	4 Aug 58	180/82	LJ	7.96	8.16, 8.34w -89
Karube	Shunji	JPN	8 May 69	183/70	400h	48.75	49.57 -91
Kaseorg	Indrek	EST	16 Dec 67	194/86	Dec	7966	7826 -92
Katsuki	Hidekazu	JPN	18 Apr 69	170/60	400h	49.21	49.64 -92
Kaul	Michael	GER	25 Jul 67	186/75	400h	50.17	49.76 -92
Kawashima	Shinji	JPN	4 Jun 66	166/53	Mar	2:10:41	2:14:22 -92
Kawauchi	Katsuhiro	JPN	9 Mar 73	168/54	5k	13:32.51	13:48.51 -92
Kayode	Oluyemi	NGR	7 Jul 68	180/75	100	10.28	10.17 -92
					200	20.35, 20.18Aw	20.22 -92
Kayukov	Andrey	RUS	12 Apr 64	187/75	TJ	16.97i, 16.72, 17.03w	17.23 -88
* Kazanov	Igor(s)	LAT	24 Sep 63	186/81	110h	13.26	13.34 -92, 13.1-88, 13.14w -86
Keachan	Chanond	THA	24 Jan 70	169/64	400h	50.46	50.60 -92
Keane	Brian	USA	5 Apr 70	196/89	JT	77.68	74.42 -92
Kearns	Thomas	IRL	2 Jun 66	190/82	110h	13.66A, 13.68, 13.62w	13.63 -92, 13.6 -90
Kederis	Konstadinos	GRE	11 Jun 73	180/72	200	20.76	21.05 -92
					400	45.70	46.85 -92
Keen	Murray	AUS	17 May 65	189/100	JT	76.50	79.30 -89
* Keino	Joseph	KEN	63	178/60	10k	27:55.9	27:35.77 -92
Keith	Andrew	GBR	25 Dec 71	185/63	1500	3:39.06	3:39.85 -92
					Mile	3:57.7i	3:58.79i -92
Kellermayr	Gernot	AUT	5 Apr 66	185/82	Dec	8320 *	8131 -92
Kelley	Jon	USA	19 Dec 69	180/73	PV	5.50	5.50 -92
Kelm	Bernhard	GER	23 Dec 67	173/62	LJ	8.02	7.97, 8.11w -92
* Kemboi	Simon	KEN	1 Mar 67	178/74	400	44.94, 44.7A	45.40, 44.8A -92
					800	1:45.87	
Kemei	David	KEN	70		3kSt	8:33.76	8:41.7A -91
* Kemei	William	KEN	22 Feb 69	183/64	1500	3:36.80	3:32.41 -92
* Kemp	Troy	BAH	18 Jun 66	187/69	HJ	2.37	2.35 -91
Kempainen	Bob	USA	18 Jun 66	183/70	10k	28:23.80	28:24.50 -91
					Mar	2:11:03	2:12:12 -91
* Kennedy	Bob	USA	18 Aug 70	183/66	Mile	3:56.71	3:58.11i, 3:59.03 -91
					3k	7:38.45	7:48.02 -91
					5k	13:14.91	13:22.17 -91
Kerälä	Johannes	FIN	1 Feb 72	187/95	DT	58.24	56.24 -92
* Kersh	George	USA	3 Jul 68	185/72	800	1:45.54	1:44.00 -92
					1000	2:17.20	2:19.80 -92
* Keskitalo	Petri	FIN	10 Mar 67	187/87	Dec	8076	8318 -91
* Keter	Erick	KEN	22 Jul 66	170/60	400h	48.24	48.28 -92
* Keter	Joseph	KEN	68		3kSt	8:21.04	8:21.74 -92
Khaida	Lotfi	ALG	20 Dec 68	180/75	TJ	16.92	16.85A-92, 16.89w -91
Khayatti	Fadhel	TUN	18 Jan 65	185/78	400h	49.87	49.83 -90
Khersontsev	Vadim	RUS	8 Jul 74		HT	72.72	68.58 -92
Khmelnitskiy	Mikhail	BLS	24 Jul 69	171/62	20kW	1:20:25	1:21:20 -90
* Kibet	David	KEN	24 Nov 63	189/68	1500	3:33.88	3:32.13 -92
					Mile	3:54.53	3:51.80 -91
					2k	5:04.09+	4:55.31 -92
* Kibet	Robert	KEN	4 May 64	173/64	800	1:44.26	1:43.70 -89
* Kidykas	Vaclavas	LIT	17 Oct 61	197/115	DT	65.26	68.44 -88
Kieffer	Pascal	FRA	6 May 61	171/66	50kW	4:02:11	4:06:42 -92
* Kim Jae-ryong		KOR	25 Apr 66	172/60	Mar	2:09:43	2:09:30 -92
Kim Soon-hyung		KOR	15 Jul 73	183/63	1500	3:38.60	3:40.26 -92
Kim Tae-keun		KOR	71		Dec	7585	7395 -91
* Kim Woan-ki		KOR	8 Jul 68		Mar	2:09:25	2:09:31 -92
Kimble	Ray	USA	19 Apr 53	183/77	TJ	16.58,16.97w	17.36 -87,17.53w -88
Kimino	Takahiro	JPN	19 Feb 73	176/62	HJ	2.32	2.29 -92
King	Larry	USA	27 Aug 68	170/64	100	10.28, 10.20w	10.34 -92
* Kingdom	Roger	USA	26 Aug 62	185/91	110h	13.40, 13.38w	12.92, 12.87w -89
Kinnunen	Jarkko	FIN	21 Apr 70	176/75	JT	76.08	79.70 -90
* Kinnunen	Kimmo	FIN	31 Mar 68	186/88	JT	84.78	90.82R -91, 83.42 -92
Kinuthia	Ibrahim	KEN	22 May 63	170/62	5k	13:17.65	13:09.76 -91
Kinyor	Barnabas	KEN	3 Aug 61	176/67	800	1:47.12	1:44.95 -91
					400h	49.06, 48,7A	48.90 -92

Name		Nat	Born	Ht/Wt	Event	1993 Mark	Pre-1993 Best
Kipkemboi	Simeon	KEN	15 Apr 60	190/74	400	45.5A	44.93 -90
Kipketer	Wilson	KEN	12 Dec 70	172/62	800	1:45.46	1:45.62 -92
					1000	2:18.57i	2:18.56i -92
Kipkoech	Johnstone	KEN	20 Dec 68	173/65	3kSt	8:23.48	8:18.59 -91
Kiplagat	Robert	KEN/DEN	12 Dec 72	185/66	1500	3:38.35	3:43.21 -91
* Kiprotich	Nixon	KEN	4 Dec 62	185/68	800	1:43.54	1:43.31 -92
					1000	2:18.63	2:16.45 -89
* Kiptanui	Moses	KEN	1 Oct 71	175/60	1500	3:35.44	3:34.0A -92
					2k	5:04.09+	4:52.53 -92
					3k	7:35.79	7:28.96 -92
					5k	13:14.62	13:00.93 -92
					3kSt	8:06.36	8:02.08 -92
Kirchoff	Gary	USA	15 Aug 65	193/125	DT	59.32	51.52 -91
* Kirilenko	Vitaliy	UKR	25 Apr 68	192/80	LJ	8.21	8.05 -92
* Kirmasov	Sergey	RUS	25 Mar 70		HT	82.54	81.14 -91
* Kirochi	Wilfred	KEN	12 Dec 66	167/62	1500	3:39.44	3:32.49 -92
* Kirui	Ismael	KEN	20 Feb 75	160/55	2k	5:04.4+	
					3k	7:39.82	7:56.04 -92
					5k	13:02.75	13:15.67 -92
					10k	28:07.1A	28:40.77 -90
Kiss	Balázs	HUN	21 Mar 72	188/109	HT	77.18	70.66 -91
* Kitur	Samson	KEN	25 Feb 66	186/77	400	44.34	44.18 -92
Kivi	Juha	FIN	26 Jan 64	189/75	LJ	7.99	8.02 -89
Klassen	Allen	CAN	17 Mar 68		1500	3:39.39	3:40.89 -92
					Mile	3:57.31	
Kleiza	Saulius	LIT	2 Apr 64	184/125	SP	19.92	20.91 -87
Klimas	Kestytis	LIT	26 Apr 69	180/75	100	9.9	10.33 -92
* Klimenko	Aleksandr	UKR	27 Mar 70	194/115	SP	20.84i, 20.78	20.84 -92
Klimov	Aleksandr	BLS	26 May 69	190/112	SP	19.91	19.11i, 18.90 -92
Klouchi	Kader	FRA	1 Jun 69		LJ	8.07, 8.15w	7.81, 7.96w -92
Klyugin	Sergey	RUS	24 Mar 74	184/77	HJ	2.26i, 2.24	2.27 -91
Kneissler	Bernd	GER	13 Sep 62	198/125	DT	60.86	61.86 -86
Knight	Anthony	JAM	17 Nov 70	181/77	110h	13.64	13.71 -92
Knight	David	USA	2 Apr 70	188/79	400	45.65A	46.10 -92
Knox	Percy	USA	14 Oct 69	172/75	LJ	8.11	8.02 -89
Kobayashi	Hideki	JPN	23 Jun 71	174/66	400h	50.37	51.87 -92
Kobs	Karsten	GER	16 Sep 71	196/109	HT	75.94	74.36 -92
Kocherga	Valeriy	UKR	12 Sep 63	192/120	HT	74.76	78.92 -86
Kochetkov	Sergey	UKR	29 Jan 74	180/90	HT	70.8	70.72 -92
Kocuvan	Miro	SLO	15 Jun 71	182/69	400h	49.71	50.38 -92
Kóczián	Jenö	HUN	5 Apr 67	176/102	SP	19.57	19.51 -92
Koech	Benjamin	KEN	23 Jun 69		LJ	7.98Ai, 7.98,	8.00A -92
						8.03w	8.08w -90
* Koech	Benson	KEN	10 Nov 74	176/65	800	1:46.00	1:44.77 -92
					1000	2:18.46	
					1500	3:36.47	3:42.7A -92
Koech	Jonah	KEN	2 Feb 68	172/59	5k	13:10.95	13:10.88 -92
					10k	28:28.67	28:08.50 -90
Koers	Marko	HOL	3 Nov 72	192/77	800	1:44.84	1:45.57 -92
					1500	3:38.05	3:43.99 -92
* Kohnle	Michael	GER	3 May 70	191/84	Dec	8075	8289 -90
Koistinen	Markus	FIN	1 May 70	198/130	SP	20.31	19.45 -92
Kokhanovskiy	Andrey	UKR	11 Jan 68	194/112	DT	64.26	65.66 -92
Kokotis	Dimitrios	GRE	12 Apr 72	190/70	HJ	2.25i, 2.24	2.23 -92
Kolesnichenko	Dmitriy	UKR	28 Feb 72	187/80	110h	13.66	14.08, 13.8 -92
Kolesnik	Sergey	UKR	31 May 69	199/73	HJ	2.25	2.22i -91
Kolesnik	Vadim	UKR	29 Apr 69	184/105	HT	79.44	78.14 -92
Kolko	Rajmund	POL	1 Mar 71	186/83	JT	78.14	75.68 -91
Kollár	Igor	SVK	25 Jun 65	175/62	20kW	1:21:10t	1:20:37 -90
Kolodziejczyk	Robert	POL	3 Aug 69	201/75	HJ	2.24	2.21 -92
* Kolpakov	Vitaliy	UKR	2 Feb 72	195/92	Dec	8297	7902 -92
Komar	Ivan	BLS	18 Mar 70	186/73	800	1:45.73	1:48.04 -91
Komatsu	Takashi	JPN	30 Dec 67	181/70	TJ	16.68w	16.76 -92
* Konchellah	Billy	KEN	20 Oct 61	188/74	800	1:44.22	1:43.06 -87
Konchellah	Patrick	KEN	63		800	1:45.71	1:46.6A -92
König	Stefan	GER	25 Aug 66	183/90	JT	79.22	80.40 -92
* Kononen	Valentin	FIN	7 Mar 69	181/69	20kW	1:22:22.6t	1:23:01 -91
					50kW	3:42:02	3:48:54 -91

Name		Nat	Born	Ht/Wt	Event	1993 Mark	Pre-1993 Best
Konovalov	Ilya	RUS	14 Mar 71	192/100	HT	77.44	77.04 -92
Kontinaho	Ilkka	FIN	16 Sep 64		JT	78.34	74.74 -92
Konya	Kalman	GER/HUN	27 Oct 61	192/115	SP	20.55	20.37 -89
Koprivichin	Rumen	BUL	2 Oct 62	190/110	HT	72.36	75.54 -89
Korchagin	Aleksandr	KZK	25 Jan 72	186/79	PV	5.70	5.60 -92
Korepanov	Sergey	KZK	9 May 64	170/61	20kW	1:22:43	
					50kW	3:52:50	3:55:47 -91
Korir	Julius	KEN	5 Dec 63	170/57	5k	13:33.24	13:22.07 -91
Kornev	Grigoriy	RUS	14 Mar 61	183/70	20kW	1:20:55	1:18:56 -90
* Kororia	Kibiego	KEN	25 Dec 71	180/64	3k	7:44.98	7:49.60 -92
					5k	13:11.89	13:29.91 -90
					10k	28:10.20	27:52.11 -92
Korving	Robin	HOL	29 Jul 74	188/81	110h	13.85	14.04 -92
* Korzeniowski	Robert	POL	30 Jul 68	168/60	20kW	1:20:55	1:19:14 -92
					50kW	3:44:24	3:46:42 -92
Kosaka	Tadahiro	JPN	10 Feb 60	178/65	50kW	3:59:13	3:58:39 -91
Kosgei	John	KEN	72		1500	3:39.55	3:43.98 -92
* Kosgei	Richard	KEN	29 Dec 70	170/55	3kSt	8:12.68	8:28.64 -92
Koskei	Christopher	KEN	14 Aug 74		3kSt	8:24.58	9:05.5 -91
Kosov	Dmitriy	RUS	28 Sep 68	187/80	400	45.80	45.97 -92
Kostin	Mikhail	BLS	10 May 59	194/125	SP	20.40	21.96 -86
Kostov	Kotzo	BUL	9 Jan 68	187/72	TJ	16.58i, 16.77w	16.43i -91, 16.40 -92
Kostyukevich	Frants	BLS	4 Apr 63	182/73	20kW	1:20:03	1:18:51 -90
* Koszewski	Dietmar	GER	26 Jul 67	193/89	110h	13.44	13.41, 13.39w -90
Kotewicz	Jaroslaw	POL	16 Mar 69	195/73	HJ	2.25	2.30 -91
Kotlarski	Piotr	POL	5 Apr 69	188/76	400h	50.24	50.56 -92
Kotlyar	Yuriy	UKR	27 Mar 65	182/67	50kW	4:04:25	
Kotov	Vladimir	BLS	21 Feb 58	168/57	Mar	2:12:50	2:10:58 -80
Kotsyubenko	Andrey	RUS	3 Jan 70		Dec	7886	7779 -92
Koutsoukis	Dimitrios	GRE	8 Dec 62	192/130	SP	19.44	20.74 -89
Kovác	Igor	SVK	12 May 69	183/70	110h	13.52	13.58 -92, 13.3w -91
Kovács	Attila	HUN	2 Sep 60	180/72	100	10.28	10.09 -87
Kovács	Dusan	HUN	31 Jul 71		400h	49.92	50.55 -92
					Dec	7629	7546 -91
Kovalenko	Aleksandr	RUS	8 May 63	178/80	TJ	16.80	17.77 -87
* Kovtsun	Dmitriy	UKR	29 Sep 55	191/120	DT	63.70	68.64 -84
Kowalski	Lech	POL	17 Jan 61	188/98	HT	74.40	75.98 -92
Krasko	Aleksandr	BLS	7 Apr 72		HT	79.86	76.10 -92
Krasnov	Yevgeniy	ISR	25 May 70	183/77	PV	5.65	5.60 -92
Krause	Konstantin	GER	8 Oct 67	189/79	LJ	8.09	8.04i, 8.03 -92
Kravchenko	Vladimir	UKR	22 Dec 69	186/74	TJ	16.65i	16.44 -92
Kreissig	Wolfgang	GER	29 Aug 70	193/73	HJ	2.25	2.24 -89
Krieger	Helmut	POL	17 Jul 58	195/135	SP	19.57	21.30 -86
Kroeker	Tim	CAN	25 May 71	186/87	110h	13.71A, 13.71, 13.51w	13.79 -92
Kronin	Aleksey	RUS	70		20kW	1:22:50	1:25:44 -91
Krsek	Ivo	TCH	21 Mar 67	184/78	LJ	7.99	8.03 -87, 8.04w -86
Kruger	Alex	GBR	18 Nov 63	193/86	Dec	7986	7804 -92
Krupilski	Scott	USA	19 Jan 64	185/82	PV	5.65	5.50 -89
Krykun	Aleksey	UKR	12 Mar 68	192/100	HT	80.36	75.12 -91
Kübar	Margus	EST	31 Jan 71	189/83	JT	76.66	80.48 -91
Kubista	Zdenek	TCH	21 Dec 66	193/79	HJ	2.24i	2.27i -90
Kucej	Jozef	SVK	23 Mar 65	181/72	400h	50.18	48.94 -89
Kufahl	Carsten	GER	14 Nov 67	203/125	DT	63.50	66.22 -90
Kuhn	Frédéric	FRA	10 Jul 68	180/105	HT	75.94	76.80 -92
Kuko	Yuriy	BLS	23 Jan 68	173/65	20kW	1:19:08	1:21:49 -92
Kula	Dainis	LAT	28 Apr 59	190/98	JT	79.06	81.72 -90
Kunkel	Marcel	GER	19 Oct 72	188/93	HT	71.88	72.42 -92
Kurach	Sergey	RUS	28 Mar 70	180/73	110h	13.75	13.47 -92
Kurashvili	Merab	GEO	30 Jan 71	191/126	SP	19.23	17.67 -91
Kurnicki	Robert	GER	27 Mar 65	189/75	200	20.46	20.68 -92
Kurochkin	Igor	BLS	2 May 66	198/88	400h	49.80	50.17 -92
Kuznetsov	Aleksey	RUS	21 Nov 70	180/62	20kW	1:23:30	1:22:49 -91
Kyllönen	Kai	FIN	30 Jan 65	185/75	110h	13.69, 13.64w	13.60 -91
Laaksonen	Mika	FIN	21 Mar 68	190/88	HT	74.44	72.36 -92
* Labrador	Basilio	ESP	29 Mar 67	165/62	20kW	1:23:44	1:27:53 -90
					50kW	3:46:46	3:54:45 -90
Lacan	Fabien	FRA	24 Sep 68	180/65	3kSt	8:28.96	8:27.8 -92

Name		Nat	Born	Ht/Wt	Event	1993 Mark	Pre-1993 Best
Lacy	Mark	USA	24 Apr 70	193/127	SP	18.88i	18.83 -92
Ladbrook	Mark	AUS	6 Feb 72		200	20.66w	21.10 -92
Ladejo	Du'aine	GBR	14 Feb 71	186/83	400	45.92A, 45.98, 45.2	45.25 -92
Lahlafi	Brahim	MAR	15 Apr 68	172/62	3k	7:50.01	
					5k	13:15.85	13:21.11 -90
Lahlali	Abdelhak	MAR	71	185/74	400h	50.04	51.6, 51.89 -92
Lahlou	Benyounès	MAR	3 Nov 64	180/78	400	45.54	45.03 -92
* Lambruschini	Alessandro	ITA	7 Jan 65	178/63	1500	3:38.24	3:35.27 -87
					3k	7:48.59	7:50.05i -92, 7:50.64 -91
					5k	13:30.96	13:54.24 -92
					3kSt	8:08.78	8:12.17 -88
Lancelin	Eric	USA	13 May 71	193/79	TJ	16.67w	15.77i -91
* Landsman	Johan	RSA	12 May 64	178/62	800	1:45.96	1:45.63 -91
					800	1:46.96A	1:45.63A -91
					1500	3:33.56	3:36.30 -91
					3k	7:49.57	7:48.75 -92
* Langat Kibet	Sammy	KEN	70	168/57	800	1:44.06	1:46.84 -92
Lange	Tom	USA	21 Feb 70	196/81	HJ	2.26i	2.30i -92, 2.28 -90
Langlois	Denis	FRA	10 Oct 68	173/60	20kW	1:22:51	1:22:27.9t -92
Langlois	Nate	USA	9 Jul 71	188/75	200	20.77	21.06 -92
Lapshin	Igor	BLS	8 Aug 63	189/74	TJ	17.00	17.69 -88
Laros	Marcel	HOL	10 Oct 71	182/64	1500	3:39.62	3:40.39 -92
					3kSt	8:34.66	8:37.06 -91
Larsson	Kent	SWE	10 Jun 63	180/102	SP	20.03	19.92 -91
* Laukkanen	Juha	FIN	6 Jan 69	186/86	JT	84.58	88.22 -92
Lautredoux	Jean-Pierre	FRA	5 May 66	184/62	3k	7:49.27	7:55.5 -92
					5k	13:27.12	13:39.04 -92
Laventure	Cyrille	FRA	29 Mar 64	187/62	2k	5:00.02	4:58.51 -90
					3k	7:47.55	7:43.82 -89
Lawson	Jerry	USA	2 Jul 66		Mar	2:10:29	2:14:33 -92
Lawson	John	RSA	24 Apr 66		200	20.76A	20.78A -92
Laynes	Jeff	USA	3 Oct 70	178/84	100	10.17	10.20, 10.08w -91
					200	20.76, 20.59w	20.59 -92
Lazdins	Ray	CAN	25 Sep 64	198/115	DT	62.22	65.72 -91
Le Roux	Carel	RSA	31 Aug 72		SP	18.86	18.53 -92
Leandersson	Thomas	SWE	8 Feb 66	188/83	100	10.29w	10.42 -91
Lecurieux	Philippe	FRA	22 May 58	187/90	JT	75.80	77.80 -89
Lee Bong-ju		KOR	69		Mar	2:10:27	
Lee Jin-il		KOR	2 Nov 73	183/68	800	1:47.13	1:46.34 -92
Lee Fu-an		TPE	4 Jun 64	184/74	Dec	7678	7739 -88
Lee Jin-taek		KOR	13 Apr 72	189/65	HJ	2.30	2.28 -92
Lefèvre	Pascal	FRA	25 Jan 65	190/92	JT	80.00	84.80 -90
Lehtiö	Tero	FIN	24 Aug 63	203/101	SP	18.58	17.16 -83
					DT	58.72	58.54 -83
* Lehtonen	Jani	FIN	11 Aug 68	179/72	PV	5.82	5.73 -91
* Lelei	Sammy	KEN	14 Aug 64	160/52	Mar	2:12:12	2:18:16 -92
Lelong	Olivier	FRA	2 Apr 70	185/77	PV	5.55	5.50i, 5.50 -92
Lemercier	Alain	FRA	11 Jan 57	174/66	50kW	3:55:44	3:50:00.2t -92
Lepik	Sulev	EST	22 Jul 66	192/95	JT	75.80	81.50 -92
Leskov	Aleksandr	RUS			20kW	1:23:13	
Lesov	Delko	BUL	6 Jan 67	181/69	PV	5.70i, 5.60	5.75i -92, 5.70 -91
Lestage	Franck	FRA	20 Apr 68	181/70	LJ	7.94	8.12, 8.22w -92
Levicq	Sebastien	FRA	25 Jun 71	186/81	Dec	7874	7867 -92
Lewin	Simon	AUS	3 Jan 72		800	1:47.06	1:47.06 -92
* Lewis	Carl	USA	1 Jul 61	188/80	100	10.02, 9.90w	9.86 -91, 9.78w -88
					200	19.99	19.75 -83
Lewis	Dave	GBR	15 Oct 61	179/64	10k	28:32.00	28:08.44 -88
Lewis	Rodney	USA	17 Jul 66	187/81	100	10.31w	10.23A -92
* Lewis	Steve	USA	16 May 69	188/84	400	44.54	43.87 -88
Li Mingcai		CHN	22 Aug 71	169/58	20kW	1:20:00	1:20:24.4t -92
					50kW	3:49:17	
Li Rongxian		CHN	Feb 72		JT	76.34	79.30 -91
Li Shaojie		CHN	Jan 75		DT	61.35	54.58 -92
Li Tao		CHN	15 Jan 68	176/68	100	10.24	10.26 -86
* Li Tong		CHN	6 May 67	190/84	110h	13.26, 13.0w	13.37, 13.31w -91
Li Webin		CHN	9 Dec 66		DT	59.44	60.66 -92
Li Zewen		CHN	Oct 73		20kW	1:22:30	1:23:36.9t -92

Name		Nat	Born	Ht/Wt	Event	1993 Mark	Pre-1993 Best
Lieder	Rico	GER	25 Mar 71	183/75	400	45.66	45.36 -91
Liepins	Modris	LAT	3 Aug 66	178/68	50kW	4:05:21	3:48:27 -90
Lill	Andrew	GBR	9 Aug 71	185/70	800	1:46.62	1:46.37 -92
Lin Wei		CHN	16 Oct 74	177/71	100	10.26, 10.24w	10.36 -92
Linden	Andreas	GER	20 Feb 65	185/90	JT	79.38	84.46 -91
Lindman	Antero	FIN	25 Dec 64		50kW	3:59:57	4:02:09 -92
Lindner	Johann	AUT	3 May 59	189/110	HT	75.18	79.70 -87
Lipiec	Tomasz	POL	10 May 71	185/72	20kW	1:21:50	
					50kW	4:03:09	4:01:13 -92
Little	Kevin	USA	3 Apr 68	183/70	100	10.24w	10.37, 10.11Aw -92
					200	20.56	20.33, 20.2w -92
* Litvinov	Sergey	RUS	23 Jan 58	180/100	HT	82.16	86.04 -86
Liu Gang		CHN	1 Mar 72		50kW	4:05:15	4:07:30 -91
Liu Hao		CHN	13 Nov 68		SP	19.72	19.04 -92
Liu Chenjiang		CHN	Feb 69		DT	58.94	
Liu Xiaochun		CHN	7 Aug 72		20kW	1:23:09	1:25:29.0t -92
					50kW	4:05:10	3:56:36 -92
Liverani	Andrea	ITA	9 Sep 64	184/66	HJ	2.24	2.23 -87
Lizio	Michele	ITA	5 Mar 71		20kW	1:21:12	
Lloyd	Andrew	AUS	14 Feb 59	174/56	10k	28:31.93	27:57.34 -87
Lobinger	Tim	GER	3 Sep 72	193/80	PV	5.55	5.50 -92
Lobodin	Lev	UKR	1 Apr 69	188/84	Dec	8156	8018 -91
Loginov	Andrey	RUS	27 Nov 72	183/63	1500	3:37.70	3:37.04 -92
Long	Aric	USA	15 Apr 70	190/92	Dec	8013w, 7754	8237 -92
Long	Tod	USA	18 Dec 70	183/75	400	45.45A	47.04 -92
Looije	Laurens	HOL	12 Jan 73	185/75	PV	5.50i	5.45 -92
Lopez	Danny	USA	25 Sep 68	175/63	3kSt	8:34.09	8:16.88 -92
López	Inocencio	ESP	30 Oct 66	183/64	3kSt	8:29.56	8:27.10 -90
López	Juan	CUB	7 Apr 67	189/81	TJ	16.85	17.28 -88
Löser	Dominique	GER	21 Jan 73	176/69	1500	3:39.62	3:41.47 -92
Louca	Elias	CYP	23 Jul 74		SP	18.75	17.84 -92
Loum	Oumar	SEN	31 Dec 73	184/79	200	20.58	21.06w -92
Love	Matthew	JAM	1 Aug 70		110h	13.83	
* Lovegrove	Gavin	NZL	21 Oct 67	187/95	JT	84.54	86.14 -92
Lugenbühl	Marc	GER	17 Jun 66	193/82	PV	5.55	5.55 -92
Lukashenko	Aleksey	LAT	29 Mar 67	185/100	SP	18.77	19.68 -92
Lukashok	Sergey	ISR	20 Jun 58	202/128	DT	61.82	66.64 -83
Luke	Gabriel	USA	26 Nov 69	184/78	400	45.70	45.22 -91
Lumsden	Clinton	RSA	27 Jul 71		JT	78.54	76.24 -92
* Lyakhov	Sergey	RUS	1 Mar 68	195/105	DT	66.12	66.64 -92
* Lykho	Vyacheslav	RUS	16 Jan 67	196/120	SP	20.31i	21.20 -87
Lyle	Rick	USA	26 Feb 71	198/125	SP	18.75	18.15i -91, 18.05 -92
Lyles	Kevin	USA	23 Jul 73	185/75	400	45.73	46.21 -92
Lynch	Lawrence	GBR	1 Nov 67	186/75	400h	50.49	50.19 -91
Lysenko	Nikolay	RUS	14 Jul 66	185/100	HT	72.24	80.32 -88
Lyubomirov	Igor	RUS	9 Nov 61		20kW	1:23:21	1:20:10 -88
Ma Wei		CHN	1 Jul 66	185/130	DT	60.80	59.94 -92
Ma Yongfeng		CHN	29 Nov 62	190/115	SP	19.69	19.78 -90
Maas	Frans	HOL	13 Jul 64	196/89	LJ	7.98i, 7.95,	8.07, 8.11i -89
						8.16Aw	8.27Aw -88
Mabry	Kendall	USA	71		110h	13.81w	13.82, 13.66w -92
Machuka	Josephat	KEN	12 Dec 73	160/55	10k	28:00.72	27:57.68 -92
Mackenzie	Colin	GBR	30 Jun 63	186/90	JT	82.38	82.60 -91
Madonia	Ezio	ITA	7 Aug 66	175/70	100	10.31, 10.22w	10.26 -90, 10.24w -91
Mafe	Ade	GBR	12 Nov 66	185/77	400	45.30	45.64 -92
Maher	Pete	CAN	30 Mar 60	195/79	Mar	2:12:50	2:11:46 -91
Mahorn	Atlee	CAN	27 Oct 65	187/80	100	10.20	10.16 -92, 10.01w -91
					200	20.42	20.17 -91
					400	45.79	45.62 -86
Mai	Volker	GER	3 May 66	194/75	TJ	16.88	17.50 -85
Mair	John	JAM	20 Nov 63	175/74	100	10.14w	10.18 -92, 10.16w -86
Majkrzak	Marek	POL	12 Oct 65	198/116	DT	58.62	61.54 -92
Makarevich	Anatoliy	BLS	19 May 70	185/71	800	1:46.75	1:44.84 -92
Makarov	Andrey	RUS	2 Jun 71	181/72	20kW	1:21:33	1:22:02 -92
Makoena	Johannes	RSA	25 Sep 69		800	1:46.31	1:47.41 -92
Makurin	Aleksey	RUS	21 Jul 72	188/79	HJ	2.24i	2.25 -92
Malachenko	Alex	BEL	5 Mar 67		HT	70.34	66.72 -91

Name		Nat	Born	Ht/Wt	Event	1993 Mark	Pre-1993 Best
Malakwen	Vincent	KEN	19 Jul 74	175/65	800	1:46.06	1:49.49 -92
					1000	2:18.37	
Malchenko	Sergey	RUS	2 Nov 63	190/74	HJ	2.28i, 2.26	2.38 -88
Malik	Peter	SVK	10 Dec 69		50kW	4:04:50.2t	
Malik	Stefan	SVK	4 Feb 66	183/69	50kW	4:01:28	3:59:10 -90
Malyavin	Vladimir	TKM	4 Mar 73	188/73	LJ	7.92	7.68, 7.89w -92
Mandrou	Christian	FRA	24 Jun 65	177/77	Dec	7744	7843 -92
Mandy	Mark	IRL	19 Nov 72	197/83	HJ	2.24	2.15 -92
Manson	Pat	USA	29 Nov 67	178/72	PV	5.75	5.71 -92
* Mansour	Talal	QAT	8 May 64	180/73	100	10.22, 10.20w	10.14, 9.9w -92
Manyisa	Kennedy	KEN	69		Mar	2:12:19	2:14:31 -91
Manzano	Alberto	CUB	22 Sep 72	185/75	PV	5.55	5.60 -92
Mao Xinyuan		CHN	2 Jul 71	170/61	20kW	1:20:54	1:20:35.4t -92
					50kW	4:02:22	3:53:36 -92
Maravilha	Alberto	POR	17 Dec 65	174/67	10k	28:17.69	28:25.8 -88
Margalit	Itai	ISR	25 Jan 70	190/72	HJ	2.26i, 2.25	2.23 -92
Marie-Rose	Bruno	FRA	20 May 65	193/87	100	10.31rs	10.16 -89
Marin	Andrés	ESP	18 Jul 61	162/50	50kW	3:52:48	3:52:16 -87
Marin	José	ESP	21 Jan 50	164/60	50kW	4:04:37	3:40:46 -83
Marinov	Robert	BUL	1 Feb 67	190/75	HJ	2.30	2.31 -92
Markin	Aleksandr	RUS	8 Sep 62	188/77	110h	13.81	13.20 -88
Markov	Gennadiy	RUS	66		TJ	17.06	16.71 -92
Markov	Ilya	RUS	19 Jun 72	173/66	20kW	1:20:19	1:23:27 -92
Markov	Khristo	BUL	27 Jan 65	185/76	TJ	16.60	17.92 -92
Marquetti	Héctor	CUB	7 Apr 68	175/70	TJ	16.62	16.91 -87
Marras	Giorgio	ITA	15 Oct 71	178/65	100	10.32	10.43, 10.38w -91
					200	20.66	20.82 -92
Marschner	Torsten	GER	17 Nov 68	194/75	HJ	2.26	2.30i -89, 2.28 -88
Marseille	Wagner	HAI	13 Sep 70		110h	13.84, 13.71w	13.80 -92
* Marsh	Damien	AUS	28 Mar 71	185/79	100	10.19	10.41, 10.37w -92
					200	20.49, 20.29w	20.70 -92, 20.6 -91
* Marsh	Michael	USA	4 Aug 67	178/68	100	10.20, 9.97w	9.93 -92
					200	20.04, 19.97w	19.73 -92
					400	45.53	46.21 -89
Marshin	Dmitriy	BLS	24 Feb 72		HT	72.92	63.24 -92
Marti	Daniel	ESP	23 Apr 73	184/74	PV	5.65	5.55 -92
* Martin	Eamonn	GBR	9 Oct 58	183/67	Mar	2:10:50	-0-
Martínez	José	ESP	25 Aug 70	182/115	SP	18.55	17.45 -91
Martínez	Manuel	ESP	7 Dec 74	185/117	SP	19.53	18.14 -92
Martínez	Michel	CUB	6 Nov 74		TJ	16.77	16.32 -92
Martínez	Juan	CUB	17 May 58	186/125	DT	64.44 *	70.00 -83
Martino	Marco	ITA	21 Feb 60	190/106	DT	61.70	67.62 -89
* Martins	Antonio	FRA	23 Aug 63	169/58	5k	13:21.23	13:14.47 -92
					10k	27:42.35	27:22.78 -92
Martirosyan	Armen	ARM	69		TJ	17.00	17.05 -92
Mason	Mark	GUY	6 Jun 69	178/70	LJ	8.07	8.05i -91, 7.86 -89
* Massana	Valentin	ESP	5 Jul 70	162/50	20kW	1:20:50	1:19:25 -92
					50kW	3:46:11	
Mateescu	Mugur	ROM	13 Jun 69	181/65	400h	50.08	49.98 -89
* Matei	Sorin	ROM	8 Jul 63	184/71	HJ	2.35i, 2.30	2.40 -90
* Matete	Samuel	ZAM	27 Jul 68	183/81	400	45.96	44.88 -91
					400h	47.60	47.10 -91
Matilu	Abedinego	KEN	21 Nov 68	175/73	400	45.59, 45.0A	45.3A, 46.10 -92
Matsanov	Igor	BLS	13 Apr 70	191/87	Dec	7821	7991 -92
Matsuda	Katsuhiko	JPN	10 May 65	182/78	Dec	7871	7619 -92
Matsue	Noriaki	JPN	17 Jul 71	174/68	400h	50.12	50.89 -92
Matthews	Jonathan	USA	2 Jul 56	185/75	50kW	4:01:36	4:12:28 -92
Matthias	Brendan	CAN	12 Aug 69		3k	7:50.90i	
Matyukhin	Nikolay	RUS	13 Dec 68		20kW	1:19:43	1:21:16 -91
Mayaka	Stephen	KEN	16 Nov 72		10k	28:18.29	28:49.5 -92
* Maybank	Anthuan	USA	30 Dec 69	185/75	200	20.79	20.70 -92
					400	44.99	45.04 -92
					LJ	8.25, 8.40w	7.83 -89
Maye	Sean	USA	24 Jun 69	190/72	400	45.98A	46.10 -91
Mayock	John	GBR	26 Oct 70	172/55	1500	3:36.45	3:37.76 -92
					Mile	3:57.30, 3:56.89i	3:56.90 -91
					3k	7:50.70	7:48.47i -92

Name		Nat	Born	Ht/Wt	Event	1993 Mark	Pre-1993 Best
Mbaye	Hamadou	SEN	21 Apr 60	183/75	400h	50.05	50.22 -88
McCall	Tony	USA	16 Jun 74	173/72	100	10.31	10.44 -92
McCants	Tom	USA	27 Nov 62	185/79	HJ	2.31i	2.37 -88
McCray	Danny	USA	11 Mar 74	183/84	200	20.70, 20.55w	21.24 -90
					400	45.4	45.74 -92
McCullough	Tony	USA			400h	50.36	50.92 -92
McFarlane	Danny	JAM	14 Feb 72	183/75	400	45.82	
McGhee	Roland	USA	15 Oct 71	180/70	LJ	8.38	8.06, 8.23w -92
					TJ	16.56i	
McGuirk	Matt	USA	15 Aug 64	185/75	3kSt	8:27.10	8:26.10 -92
McHugh	Terry	IRL	22 Aug 63	191/97	JT	80.98	84.54R -91, 78.08 -89
McKay	Kevin	GBR	9 Feb 69	178/62	1500	3:39.13	3:35.94 -92
					Mile	3:57.26	3:54.45 -92
* McKean	Tom	GBR	27 Oct 63	183/71	800	1:45.64	1:43.88 -89
McKee	Gordon	USA	12 Oct 66	183/80	LJ	8.02Aw	8.25 -91, 8.28A-92, 8.31w -90
McKennie	Tony	USA	26 Oct 67	178/73	400h	50.23	49.38 -92
McKenzie	David	GBR	3 Sep 70	186/84	400	45.75	46.21 -92
* McKoy	Mark	CAN	10 Dec 61	182/77	100	10.08	10.21 -86
					110h	13.08	13.11, 13.06w -92, 13.0 -85
McMichael	Tim	USA	22 Feb 67	173/65	PV	5.61i, 5.50	5.65 -89
Medved	Mikhail	UKR	30 Jan 64	199/89	Dec	8146	8330 -88
Meghoo	Greg	JAM	11 Aug 65	180/74	100	10.16w	10.35, 10.16w -86
Mehlich	Ronald	POL	26 Sep 69	189/85	110h	13.62	13.71 -92
* Meier	Paul	GER	27 Jul 71	194/86	LJ	7.95w	7.54 -92
					Dec	8548	8192 -92
Meité	Ibrahim	CIV	18 Nov 76	180/75	100	10.32, 10.27w	10.53 -92
Mekonnen	Abebe	ETH	9 Jan 64	158/59	Mar	2:12:00	2:07:35 -88
* Melikhov	Vladimir	RUS	30 Mar 69	186/76	TJ	17.28	17.13 -91
Menc	Miroslav	TCH	16 Mar 71	197/115	SP	18.63	18.04 -92
Meng Xianxin		CHN	4 Jan 69		3kSt	8:33.70	8:46.56 -92
Merande	Boniface	KEN	13 Feb 62	170/60	Mar	2:12:50	2:12:23 -92
* Mercenario	Carlos	MEX	23 May 67	175/63	20kW	1:21:39	1:19:24 -87
					50kW	3:50:28	3:42:03 -91
Mertens	Michael	GER	27 Dec 65	191/105	SP	19.19	19.47 -92
Meshauskas	Viktoras	LIT	4 Nov 70	170/60	20kW	1:22:53	1:21:44 -91
Metla	Vadim	RUS	73		HT	71.22	69.12 -92
Meyer	Andy	USA	9 Nov 70	193/120	DT	61.60	59.06 -92
Meyer	Rick	USA	21 Oct 61	196/118	DT	59.86	65.86 -86
Miclea	Constantin	ROM	13 Apr 63	185/87	JT	77.18	80.72 -88
Mikulás	Milan	TCH	1 Apr 63	193/84	TJ	16.89	17.53 -88
Miller	Cliffie	RSA	1 Feb 64		800	1:46.31	1:46.94 -92
Miller	James	AUS	4 Jun 74	188/79	PV	5.55	5.41 -92
Miller	Scotty	USA	8 Aug 69	178/80	PV	5.50i	5.60 -92
Miller	Tony	USA	15 Mar 69	181/77	100	10.32, 10.27w	10.18 -92
					200	20.55A	20.51, 20.5w -92
Miller -2	Tony	USA	12 Feb 71	193/85	400	45.74	45.48 -92
Mills	Derek	USA	9 Jul 72	175/68	400	44.62	44.86 -92
Mills	Keevan	USA	10 Jul 72	188/86	110h	13.72w	14.18 -92
Milne	Brian	USA	7 Jan 73	192/114	DT	61.32	63.22 -92
Milonas	Jannis	GRE	4 Jun 71	176/100	HT	70.28	66.26 -92
Minns	John	AUS	31 May 67	188/120	SP	19.23	19.64 -89
Minor	Deon	USA	22 Jan 73	193/82	400	45.74	44.75 -92
Miranda	Alain	CUB	19 Oct 75		800	1:47.05	1:50.50 -92
Miranda	Innocencio	MEX	23 Sep 61		Mar	2:12:52	2:13:14 -92
Mistretta	Alessandro	ITA	6 Mar 71		50kW	4:02:52	
* Misyulya	Yevgeniy	BLS	9 Mar 64	177/68	20kW	1:19:56	1:18:34 -89
Mitchell	Charles	USA	29 Jan 75		200	20.52	
* Mitchell	Dennis	USA	20 Feb 66	174/69	100	9.99, 9.85w	9.91 -91
					200	20.25	20.09A -89, 20.20 -92
Mitchell	Maurice	USA	14 May 71	196/86	400h	49.66A, 49.75	50.09 -92
Mitkus	Vitalijus	LIT	9 Jun 65	195/125	SP	19.18	20.36 -86
Mizoguchi	Kazuhiro	JPN	18 Mar 62	181/90	JT	76.58	87.60 -89
* Mladenov	Ivailo	BUL	6 Oct 73	184/73	LJ	8.27, 8.35w	7.94 -91
Modica	Vincenzo	ITA	2 Mar 71	168/53	10k	28:16.1	28:25.63 -91
Moen	Geir	NOR	26 Jun 69	189/85	100	10.30w	10.48 -92
					200	20.80	21.11 -91
* Mögenburg	Dietmar	GER	15 Sep 61	201/78	HJ	2.24i	2.39i -85, 2.36 -84

Name		Nat	Born	Ht/Wt	Event	1993 Mark	Pre-1993 Best
Mogotsi	Meshack	RSA	12 Dec 62		3kSt	8:36.55	
Mogotsi	Shadrack	RSA	12 Dec 62		3kSt	8:26.52	8:30.78 -90
Molina	Enrique	ESP	25 Feb 68	174/63	3k	7:42.38	7:57.87 -91
					5k	13:31.18	13:46.84 -91
Möllenbeck	Michael	GER	12 Dec 69	200/105	DT	62.82, 65.42dm	62.02 -92
* Moneghetti	Steve	AUS	26 Sep 62	176/60	10k	28:03.65	27:47.69 -92
					Mar	2:12:36	2:08:16 -90
Monteiro	Carlos	POR	14 Dec 65	178/64	3k	7:44.08	7:51.13 -91
					5k	13:22.79	13:22.70 -92
					10k	28:09.19	28:11.94 -90
Montenegro	Jorge	CUB	21 Sep 68	190/105	SP	18.88	19.55 -90
Moonegan	Vissen	MRI	3 Jul 71		TJ	16.62w	15.84 -92
Mora	Osiris	CUB	3 Oct 73	178/67	TJ	17.00	17.03 -92
Morán	Ramiro	ESP	17 May 69	173/60	3kSt	8:33.86	8:29.89 -92
* Morceli	Noureddine	ALG	28 Feb 70	172/62	800	1:45.71+	1:44.79 -91
					1000	2:13.73	2:15.26i -92
					1500	3:29.20	3:28.86 -92
					Mile	3:44.39	3:49.12 -91
					2k	5:00.09+	4:58.21 -92
					3k	7:29.24	7:37.34 -91
Morenius	Magnus	SWE	69		20kW	1:22:17	
Moreno	Fernando	ARG	2 Aug 67	186/76	HJ	2.24	2.22 -88
Morgan	Marco	USA	14 Apr 71	181/75	110h	13.85, 13.78w	13.76 -92
					400h	49.94	50.27 -92, 50.0 -91
Mori	Fabrizio	ITA	28 Jun 69	175/68	400h	49.23	48.92 -91
Morinière	Max	FRA	16 Feb 64	183/78	100	10.32, 10.29w	10.09 -87
* Morris	Ian	TRI	30 Nov 61	173/64	200	20.78	20.71 -88, 20.4, 20.45w -87
					400	44.89	44.21 -92
Morton	Les	GBR	1 Jul 58	170/64	50kW	4:03:55	3:57:48 -89
Moruyev	Andrey	RUS	8 May 70		JT	86.20	80.50 -91
Motchebon	Nico	GER	13 Nov 69	186/82	800	1:45.67	-0-
Motti	William	FRA	25 Jul 64	198/95	Dec	7829	8327w -87, 8306 -85
Mowatt	Dennis	JAM	28 Oct 69	180/75	100	10.29	10.37 -91, 10.13w -90
* Moya	Roberto	CUB	11 Feb 65	196/120	DT	64.08	65.68 -90
Mozgovoy	Viktor	BLS	6 Aug 61	178/65	Mar	2:12:41	2:13:16 -85
Mrázek	Roman	SVK	21 Jan 62	168/55	20kW	1:23:47	1:20:22, 1:20.47.8t -90
* Mtolo	Willie	RSA	5 May 64	178/62	Mar	2:12:33	2:08:15 -86
Mubarak	Bilal Saad	QAT	18 Dec 72	176/100	SP	18.99	18.01 -92
Müller	André	GER	15 Nov 70	188/78	LJ	8.02	8.11 -90
Müller	Frank	GER	18 Jun 68	193/80	Dec	7734	8256 -90
Muller	Grzegorz	POL	3 Nov 73	166/54	20kW	1:22:38	1:30:27 -92
Muller	Jacek	POL	3 Nov 73	164/53	20kW	1:20:09	1:28:33 -92
Munkácsi	Sándor	HUN	24 Jul 69	184/81	Dec	7866	8021 -92
Munuera	Francisco Jav.	ESP	7 Jul 72	180/64	3kSt	8:30.71	8:41.03 -90
Münzer	Oliver	AUT	16 Feb 70	182/66	800	1:46.87	1:46.97 -91
Murashov	Valeriy	LIT	9 May 64	196/115	DT	59.24	64.28 -88
Muravyov	Oleg	RUS	6 May 68		HJ	2.26i	2.23i, 2.20 -92
Murphy	Richard	USA	28 Apr 72	186/73	110h	13.71w	13.86, 13.73w -92
					400h	49.38	50.44 -92
Murrell	Chris	USA	20 Apr 71	193/79	HJ	2.24i	2.23 -92
Muse	Steve	USA	27 Jan 66	185/100	DT	61.44	60.40 -87
Musiyenko	Nikolay	UKR	16 Dec 59	183/76	TJ	16.94	17.78 -86
Mustapic	Ivan	CRO	9 Jul 66	196/106	JT	82.20	82.70 -92
Muuka	Mika	FIN	13 Nov 66	193/107	DT	59.94	61.92 -89
Muyaba	Fabian	ZIM	30 Sep 70	180/67	100	10.15	10.15, 10.14w -91
					200	20.75, 20.40w	20.78 -91
* Muzzio	Rob	USA	25 Jun 64	188/91	Dec	8237	8205 -84
Myles-Mills	John	GHA	19 Apr 66	180/68	200	20.69	20.83w-92, 20.85,20.6 -88
Myricks	Larry	USA	10 Mar 56	187/84	LJ	8.24A, 8.04, 8.37Aw	8.74 -88
Naaji	Atiq	FRA	21 Nov 66		1500	3:39.5	3:39.76 -92
Naali	Simon	TAN	9 Mar 66	168/57	Mar	2:11:44	2:10:38 -90
Naali	Thomas	TAN	69	168/60	Mar	2:11:38	2:10:08 -92
Nacharkin	Konstantin	RUS	71		20kW	1:22:50	1:25:49 -91
Nachum	Rogel	ISR	21 May 67	181/71	TJ	16.86	17.20 -92, 17.31w -91
Nai Hui-fang		TPE	26 Feb 69	178/75	LJ	8.34	8.07 -89
Nakamichi	Takayuki	JPN	17 Apr 69	173/70	100	10.19dt	10.35 -92, 10.31w -87
Nakamura	Akira	JPN	26 Jun 67	160/51	3kSt	8:33.66	8:28.98 -92

Name		Nat	Born	Ht/Wt	Event	1993 Mark	Pre-1993 Best
Nakashima	Shin	JPN	16 Dec 63		Mar	2:11:53	
Napier	Dino	USA	24 Nov 69	178/64	200	20.80	20.37A - 89, 20.61 -92
Naumkin	Yuriy	RUS	68		LJ	8.04	7.86 -91
Nazarov	Andrey	EST	9 Jan 65	190/80	Dec	7607	8322 -87
Nazhipov	Mukhamet	RUS	10 Sep 64	178/64	Mar	2:12:15	2:12:40 -92
N'Deti	Cosmas	KEN	24 Nov 71	168/57	Mar	2:09:33	2:14:28 -92
N'Diaye	Hachim	SEN	63		400	45.95	46.25 -92
Neal	Henry	USA	28 Oct 70	173/77	100	10.26	10.09, 10.07w -92, 10.0w -90
Nebl	Christian	AUT	21 Apr 64	180/112	SP	19.66	19.27 -91
Negere	Tena	ETH	72		Mar	2:12:53	2:09:04 -92
Nehemiah	Renaldo	USA	24 Mar 59	187/81	110h	13.73, 13.54w	12.93 -81, 12.91w, 12.8 -79
* Nelloms	Chris	USA	14 Aug 71	175/74	100	10.12w	10.33, 10.03w -92
					200	20.23, 20.17w	20.27, 19.94w -92
Nelson	Dan	USA	15 May 64	170/55	5k	13:28.41	13:35.72 -91
					10k	28:02.44	28:42.05 -91
					3kSt	8:34.0	8:22.90 -91
Nelson	David	GBR	11 Mar 67	188/78	110h	13.72	13.42 -91
Nemchaninov	Andrey	UKR	27 Nov 66	188/105	SP	20.21	20.95i -88, 20.60 -92
* Nerurkar	Richard	GBR	6 Jan 64	177/61	5k	13:30.06	13:23.36 -90
					10k	27:40.03	27:57.14 -91
					Mar	2:10:03	-0-
Neumaier	Peter	GER	30 Jun 67	187/77	Dec	7623	7948 -90
Neumann	Thomas	GER	7 Aug 71	189/93	HT	72.42	67.70 -92
Niang	Babacar	SEN	9 Sep 58	178/63	800	1:46.82	1:44.70 -86
Niaré	David	FRA	27 Sep 69	179/67	400h	50.14	50.51 -91
Nichols	Conrad	USA	23 Jun 73	188/72	800	1:46.69	1:48.08 -92
Nichols	Regan	USA	26 Jul 73	183/75	400h	50.17	50.60 -92
Nicolaisen	Anton	RSA	25 Jan 68		3kSt	8:28.93	8:22.48 -92
Niewoudt	Whaddon	RSA	6 Jan 70	178/62	1500	3:35.65	3:38.46 -92
					3kSt	8:26.31	8:19.00 -92
* Nikolayev	Sergey	RUS	12 Nov 66	189/122	SP	20.44i, 19.74	21.35 -89
* Nikulin	Igor	RUS	14 Aug 60	191/100	HT	78.98	84.48 -90
Nilsson	Joakim	SWE	30 Mar 71	178/79	JT	76.02	74.54 -92
Nioze	Paul	SEY	19 Mar 67		TJ	17.10w	16.80A -90, 16.74 -89
* Niyongabo	Vénuste	BUR	9 Dec 73	170/55	800	1:46.15	1:47.28 -92
					1500	3:36.30	3:38.59 -92
					Mile	3:54.71	-0-
					2k	4:58.15	
					3k	7:50.05	
* Nizigama	Aloÿs	BUR	66	168/55	3k	7:43.24	7:42.42 -92
					5k	13:12.14	13:29.08 -92
					10k	27:47.77	27:54.69 -92
Nkazamyampi	Charles	BUR	1 Nov 64	184/68	800	1:44.24	1:44.65 -92
					1000	2:17.05	2:19.41 -91
* Noack	Axel	GER	23 Sep 61	182/74	50kW	3:43:50	3:56:22 -85
Nogales	Benito	ESP	1 Aug 65	182/67	3kSt	8:36.20	8:23.52 -90
Nohilly	Tom	USA	27 Apr 66	183/65	3kSt	8:26.63	8:16.92 -92
Noji	Rick	USA	22 Oct 67	173/59	HJ	2.25i, 2.25	2.31 -92
Nonaka	Satoru	JPN	5 Sep 63	183/73	HJ	2.28	2.27 -85
Nool	Erki	EST	25 Jun 70	183/78	LJ	8.17w	7.77i -91
* Noon	Brent	USA	29 Aug 71	188/123	SP	20.48	20.26 -92
Norca	Alex	FRA	18 Jan 69	185/90	TJ	16.75,16.85w	16.82 -92,17.04w -91
Nordquist	Doug	USA	20 Dec 58	193/79	HJ	2.25	2.36 -90
Norris	Rory	USA	3 Mar 72	183/84	110h	13.80	13.62 -92
Novácek	Vladimir	TCH	23 Aug 68	186/92	JT	77.40	76.48 -92
Novikov	Andrey	UKR	12 Apr 63	184/97	JT	76.36	81.50 -90
Novozhilov	Sergey	RUS	21 Apr 69	185/69	LJ	7.96i	8.00 -88
N'senga	Jonathan	BEL	21 Apr 73	186/79	110h	13.76	14.14 -92
* Ntawulikura	Mathias	RWA	14 Jul 64	171/63	3k	7:43.79	7:41.64 -92
					5k	13:14.82	13:11.29 -92
					10k	27:47.59	27:49.32 -91
Nti-Berko	David	GHA	71	175/68	TJ	16.67w	16.15 -90
Nu Erlang		CHN	25 Feb 62		DT	59.82	61.82 -92
Nunes	Eronildo	BRA	31 Dec 70	183/75	400h	49.15	49.10 -92
Nuti	Andrea	ITA	4 Aug 67	185/74	400	45.35A, 45.56	45.50 -92
Nuttall	John	GBR	11 Jan 67	176/58	3k	7:51.58	7:51.81 -90
					5k	13:29.85	13:24.26 -92

Name		Nat	Born	Ht/Wt	Event	1993 Mark	Pre-1993 Best
Nyagin	Plamen	BUL	12 Mar 71	175/70	400h	50.34	50.68 -92
Nyberg	Claes	SWE	3 Mar 71	174/60	3k	7:50.36	7:56.62 -92
* Nylander	Sven	SWE	1 Jan 62	193/85	400h	49.21	48.37 -87
Oaks	David	USA	12 May 72	178/70	100	10.14A	?
					200	20.34	21.14 -90, 20.79w -91
					400	45.36	47.0 -92
* O'Brien	Dan	USA	18 Jul 66	188/84	LJ	7.99	8.08 -92, 8.11w -91
					Dec	8817	8891 -92
Occhiena	Carlo	ITA	24 Sep 72	180/69	100	10.29	10.57 -92
					200	20.60	21.05, 20.73Aw -92
* Ochieng	Kennedy	KEN	30 Dec 71	183/73	400	44.82, 44.5A	45.2A -92
Ødegård	Tor-Øyvind	NOR	28 Feb 69		800	1:46.67	1:47.98 -92
O'Donoghue	Peter	AUS	1 Oct 61	185/68	3k	7:45.57	7:46.86 -92
					5k	13:23.31	13:31.44 -92
Ogilvie	Peter	CAN	2 May 72	178/70	100	10.30w	10.40 -92
Okeke	Aham	NOR	19 Aug 69	176/70	100	10.27w	10.40 -87
					200	20.74w	20.96 -90
Okemwa	Samwel	KEN	68		Mar	2:11:47	2:14:12 -92
Ole Marai	Stephen	KEN	11 Nov 62	184/65	800	1:45.84	1:44.3A -89
Oleynikov	Aleksey	RUS	10 Aug 72	174/67	800	1:47.09	1:48.21 -91
Oliva	Edel	CUB	12 Feb 65	169/67	50kW	3:55:21	3:57:37 -92
Oliveira	Paulo S.	BRA	9 May 69		LJ	7.99Aw	7.89 -91
Olivier	Wikus	RSA	8 Mar 68		TJ	16.64A, 16.71Aw	16.56A -90
Olivo	Fabio	ITA	5 Feb 66	178/65	1500	3:39.17	3:38.63 -90
					3k	7:50.94	
* Olukoju	Adewale	NGR	27 Jul 68	193/115	DT	66.48	67.80 -91
Omagbemi	Victor	NGR	22 May 67	188/75	100	10.26w	10.27 -91
* O'Mara	Frank	IRL	17 Jul 60	176/61	3k	7:42.58	7:40.41 -89
					5k	13:17.72	13:13.02 -87
Omelyusik	Vasiliy	BLS	17 Mar 65		3kSt	8:34.4	8:39.43 -92
Omwoyo	Wilson	KEN	15 Apr 65	168/60	3k	7:47.16	7:48.31 -92
					5k	13:12.29	13:13.84 -92
Ondiek	Kennedy	KEN	12 Dec 66	175/66	100	9.9A	9.9A -91, 10.38, 10.30w -90
Ondieki	Julius	KEN			5k	13:32.15	
					10k	28:29.8A	28:37.9 -92
* Ondieki	Yobes	KEN	21 Feb 61	168/55	3k	7:39.43	7:34.18 -92
					5k	13:05.09	13:01.82 -91
					10k	26:58.38	28:25.44 -83
O'Neill	Francis	USA	25 Feb 70	180/64	3kSt	8:29.64	8:39.64 -91
Ongeri	Charles	KEN	62		10k	28:27.25	
Onohara	Hideki	JPN	16 Oct 68		100	10.28w	10.40 -92
Ordina	Tibor	HUN	31 Oct 71	191/78	LJ	8.04	7.86 -92
O'Reilly	Mike	GBR	23 Apr 58	168/53	Mar	2:10:39	2:11:05 -90
Orlík	Roman	TCH	29 May 72	182/71	LJ	7.94i	7.87 -92
Orlov	Mikhail	RUS	25 Jun 67	175/68	20kW	1:23:01	1:20:07 -90
* Ortiz	Arturo	ESP	18 Sep 66	194/70	HJ	2.31i, 2.31	2.34 -91
Ortiz	Juan	CUB	13 Aug 64	175/68	LJ	8.25	8.17A -90, 8.17 -92, 8.24w -87
* Osano	Thomas	KEN	4 Jun 70	164/53	5k	13:30.40	13:28.8+ -91
Osawa	Yoshuke	JPN	7 Sep 67	173/59	10k	28:32.31	28:09.06 -92
Osei	Kennedy	GHA	21 Oct 66	178/68	800	1:45.62	1:45.97 -92
Osenberg	Marc	GER	15 Mar 69	185/74	PV	5.51	5.30 -92
Osipov	Viktor	RUS	4 May 65	170/59	20kW	1:20:52	1:22:25 -91
Osman	Artur	POL	1 Mar 70	174/58	3kSt	8:36.57	8:31.02 -91
Osorio	Daniel	CUB	5 Nov 72	184/77	TJ	17.02	16.97 -92
* Osoro	Ondoro	KEN	3 Dec 67	168/63	3k	7:43.20	7:45.03 -91
					5k	13:15.21	13:11.77 -91
					10k	27:24.24	28:44.0A -92
Ostrovskiy	Vladimir	ISR	12 Dec 66	168/56	20kW	1:23:37	1:21:32 -90
* O'Sullivan	Marcus	IRL	22 Dec 61	176/61	1500	3:34.69	3:34.57 -92
					Mile	3:52.76	3:51.64 -89
Otieno	Samuel	KEN	10 Apr 73		10k	28:14.31	29:20.6A -92
Otte	Carsten	GER	29 Apr 71	193/78	800	1:47.07	1:48.75 -90
Ottoz	Laurent	ITA	10 Apr 70	180/64	110h	13.55A, 13.57	13.51 -92
					400h	50.35	50.28 -91
Otwori	Joseph	KEN	20 Jan 69	171/55	10k	28:22.68	28:18.91 -91
Ovchinnikov	Vladimir	RUS	2 Aug 70	190/90	JT	81.42	82.12 -90
Owens	John	USA	29 Oct 66	188/85	110h	13.79w	13.60 -92

Name		Nat	Born	Ht/Wt	Event	1993 Mark	Pre-1993 Best
Owusu	Andrew	GHA	8 Jul 72	180/75	TJ	16.76w	16.15, 16.27w -92
Pachin	Vyacheslav	LIT	16 Jul 63	188/100	DT	59.54	60.46 -92
Pajonk	Dirk-Achim	GER	27 Mar 69	190/80	Dec	7594	7942 -92
* Pakarinen	Ari	FIN	14 May 69	182/90	JT	83.06	84.00 -92
* Palchikov	Yevgeniy	RUS	12 Oct 68	198/110	SP	20.86	19.75 -92
Paljakka	Antero	FIN	1 Aug 69	201/117	SP	19.84	19.62 -92
Pálóczi	Gyula	HUN	13 Sep 62	185/67	TJ	16.87, 16.94w	16.70 -88
Pancorbo	Manuel	ESP	7 Jul 66	178/60	1500	3:36.20	3:34.37 -92
					Mile	3:52.96	3:59.58 -88
* Panetta	Francesco	ITA	10 Jan 63	175/64	3k	7:45.78	7:42.73 -87
					5k	13:06.76	13:17.71 -90
					10k	28:13.99	27:24.16 -89
					3kSt	8:22.95	8:08.57 -87
Pantel	Thierry	FRA	6 Jul 64	174/58	3k	7:43.4	7:53.73 -87
					5k	13:17.71	13:21.81 -90
					10k	28:02.71	27:31.16 -90
Papadimitriou	Alexandros	GRE	18 Jun 73	183/105	HT	70.16	69.48 -92
Papakostas	Lambros	GRE	20 Oct 69	193/78	HJ	2.29i, 2.26	2.36 -92
Parfyonov	Vladimir	UZB	17 Jun 70	198/105	JT	80.64	79.14 -92
Park Min-soo		KOR	30 Jan 68	181/73	TJ	16.69	16.40 -92
Parker	Andrew	JAM	11 Jan 65	190/77	110h	13.62	13.51 -87, 13.5 -86
Parker	Orlando	USA	7 Mar 72	183/77	100	10.22w, 9.7w-dt	10.4 -91
Parrilla	Jose	USA	31 Mar 72	172/65	400	46.09	45.84 -92
					800	1:45.13	1:43.97 -92
* Partyka	Artur	POL	25 Jul 69	192/71	HJ	2.37	2.37i -91, 2.34 -92
Parviainen	Aki	FIN	26 Oct 74	190/86	JT	78.18i	80.94 -92
Parviainen	Mika	FIN	19 Dec 70	195/105	JT	80.08	80.26 -92
Patera	Brent	USA	13 Apr 67	190/109	DT	58.00	60.30 -92
Patricio	Carlos	POR	9 Jan 64	176/59	Mar	2:11:00	2:13:29 -92
* Patrick	David	USA	12 Jun 60	183/72	400h	48.95	47.75 -88
Patrick	Paul	AUS	15 Sep 71		5k	13:33.21	13:42.8 -92
					10k	27:59.64	-0-
Patserin	Aleksey	UKR	16 May 67	178/66	3kSt	8:35.32	8:33.87 -89
Patterson	Tiberia	USA	26 Jan 71	185/74	110h	13.6	13.90, 13.82w -92
Paul	Lenny	GBR	25 May 58	186/82	100	10.32	10.40 -90, 10.25w -91
Payne	Aaron	USA	16 May 71	175/77	200	20.65w, 20.3	20.81, 20.65w -92
					400	45.45	45.43 -92
Payne	Bill	USA	21 Dec 67	188/77	PV	5.70i, 5.60	5.86 -91
Payne	Wade	BAR	3 Oct 71	172/70	400	45.93	46.5 -92
Pchelintsev	Vladimir	KZK	70		HJ	2.25i	2.20 -92
Pechyonkin	Yevgeniy	RUS	9 Oct 73	192/82	110h	13.60	13.77 -92
Peders	Guntis	LAT	15 Aug 73	193/76	110h	13.72w	14.08 -92
Pedroso	Gabriel	CUB	12 Jan 68		DT	60.62	63.26 -90
* Pedroso	Ivan	CUB	17 Dec 72	176/70	LJ	8.49	8.53, 8.79w -92
Pegoraro	Andrea	ITA	24 Oct 66	185/80	PV	5.65i, 5.65, 5.72ex	5.65, 5.70ex -92
Pekola	Kari	FIN	27 Sep 65	187/99	DT	58.76	58.66 -92
Peltoniemi	Asko	FIN	7 Feb 63	187/77	PV	5.55	5.72 -91
Peltoniemi	Petri	FIN	6 Mar 70	178/68	PV	5.70	5.60 -90
* Peñalver	Antonio	ESP	1 Dec 68	194/90	Dec	7738	8534w/8478 -92
Pendergist	Rob	USA	12 Jul 70	183/79	Dec	7733	7875 -92
Pennocchio	Bruno	ITA	7 Nov 62		50kW	3:55:57	4:03:36 -92
Pérez	José Andrés	ESP	27 Nov 69	175/65	10k	28:27.59	28:53.80 -92
Pérez	José	CUB	19 Mar 71	184/73	400h	49.28A, 49.34	50.96 -92
* Peric	Dragan	YUG	8 May 64	188/110	SP	21.26	20.91 -92
					DT	59.80	61.94 -91
* Perricelli	Giovanni	ITA	25 Aug 67	170/67	20kW	1:23:14	1:21:37 -91
					50kW	3:54:30	3:49:40 -91
Pershin	Aleksey	RUS	20 Feb 62	173/68	20kW	1:22:16	1:19:22.5t -88
Pershin	Sergey	RUS	4 Jun 68		50kW	4:02:22	3:56:53 -92
Perszke	Wieslaw	POL	18 Feb 60	172/61	Mar	2:11:15	2:12:00 -91
Perzylo	Piotr	POL	15 Nov 61	186/118	SP	18.79	20.23 -86
Peters	Scott	USA	14 Jul 71	193/74	800	1:46.35	1:46.40 -91
Peterson	Scott	USA	9 Nov 72	187/118	SP	18.92	18.21 -92
* Petranoff	Tom	RSA	8 Apr 58	186/105	JT	84.58	89.16S -91
Petrov	Mikhail	RUS	15 Nov 65		SP	18.64	19.36 -87
Petrov	Vasiliy	UKR	2 Jun 66	190/105	DT	58.32	60.46 -89
Petrunin	Aleksandr	RUS	29 Jan 67		TJ	16.83	16.70 -90, 16.77w -92

Name		Nat	Born	Ht/Wt	Event	1993 Mark	Pre-1993 Best
* Pettigrew	Antonio	USA	3 Nov 67	183/70	400	44.45	44.27 -89
Petukhov	Albert	UKR	5 Mar 74	184/107	HT	70.7	66.48 -92
* Petushinskiy	Denis	RUS	29 Jan 67	188/77	PV	5.90	5.72i, 5.70, 5.75ex -92
Peula	Antonio	ESP	21 Mar 66	171/67	3kSt	8:28.20	8:23.47 -90
Phélippeau	Herve	FRA	16 Sep 62	178/67	1500	3:38.49	3:33.54 -90
* Philibert	Dan	FRA	6 Aug 70	183/77	110h	13.42	13.33 -91
Phillips	Anthony	USA	5 Oct 70	190/95	100	10.21, 10.04w	10.53w -89
Phillips	Chris	USA	24 Jul 72	183/77	110h	13.58	13.81, 13.79w -91
Phiri	Bobang	RSA	5 May 68	179/72	400	45.86A	45.27 -92
* Pierce	Jack	USA	23 Sep 62	185/84	110h	13.06	13.06 -91
Pieterse	Ferrins	RSA	22 Mar 67		400h	49.86A, 50.36	49.48A -91
Pihlavisto	Vesa-Pekka	FIN	15 Apr 65	182/69	400h	50.19	50.12 -90
* Piller	René	FRA	23 Apr 65	168/56	50kW	3:48:57	3:51:17 -89
Piñera	Pedro	CUB	20 Dec 71	173/63	400h	50.04A, 50.12	49.97 -92
Pinheiro	Joaquim	POR	20 Dec 60	164/57	Mar	2:12:40	2:10:38 -91
Pinto	José	POR	19 Jun 56	181/69	50kW	4:02:13	3:52:43 -89
Piolanti	Raphael	FRA	14 Nov 67	184/95	HT	78.72	79.68 -92
Pirini	Douglas	NZL	6 Sep 69		Dec	7862	7550 -92
Pitayo	Martin	MEX	10 Nov 60	173/55	5k	13:26.46	13:27.16 -92
					Mar	2:12:54	2:09:41 -90
Pitillas	Oscar	ESP	16 Oct 71	185/62	400h	50.40	50.32 -92
Piziks	Rojs	HUN	12 Feb 71	195/90	Dec	7699	7402 -91
* Plaatjes	Mark	USA	1 Jun 61	173/64	Mar	2:12:39	2:08:58 -85
Plagnol	Joël	FRA	9 Feb 71	182/75	LJ	8.03	7.76 -87
Plasencia	Steve	USA	28 Oct 56	180/64	5k	13:26.03	13:19.37 -85
					10k	28:02.41	27:45.20 -90
Plastun	Oleg	RUS	20 Sep 63	182/64	20kW	1:21:59	1:21:11 -88
Plätzer	Stephan	GER	12 Sep 66	187/75	2k	5:05.18+	
* Plaza	Daniel	ESP	3 Jul 66	181/63	20kW	1:21:11	1:20:42 -92
					50kW	3:52:33	3:49:31 -92
* Plaziat	Christian	FRA	28 Oct 63	191/87	Dec	8398	8574 -90
Plotnikov	Igor	RUS	12 Jul 64		20kW	1:21:22	1:19:41 -91
Plunge	Donatas	LIT	11 Nov 60	195/118	HT	74.02	80.78 -889
Polichroniou	Christos	GRE	31 Mar 72	185/102	HT	73.16	67.74 -91
Polyunin	Dmitriy	UZB	6 Apr 69	186/85	JT	81.04, 83.38dq	85.74 -92
Ponomarenko	Vladimir	RUS	70		JT	80.00	74.76 -92
Popel	Mikhail	POL/BLS	25 May 66	192/100	HT	76.50	79.10 -87
Popescu	Eugen	ROM	12 Aug 62	194/78	HJ	2.28	2.31 -86
Popko	Viktor	UKR	13 Aug 68	188/75	TJ	16.61i	
Popov	Andrey	RUS	28 Apr 62		20kW	1:22:52	
* Popovich	Vitaliy	UKR	22 Oct 62	172/66	50kW	3:51:44	3:43:57 -89
Porkhomovskiy	Aleksandr	RUS	12 Aug 72	174/68	100	10.16	10.43, 10.27w -92
					200	20.80, 20.67w	21.60 -92
Porter	Pat	USA	31 May 59	183/63	10k	28:27.63	27:46.80 -88
Porter	William	USA	15 Apr 73	193/81	400h	50.45	50.81 -92
Portuondo	Omar	CUB	1 May 70	184/72	110h	13.75A	13.88 -89
Potapovich	Igor	KZK	6 Sep 67	185/75	PV	5.80	5.92 -92
* Potashov	Aleksandr	BLS	12 Mar 62	187/80	50kW	4:03:20	3:40:02 -90
Potgieter	Frits	RSA	13 Mar 74	195/110	DT	59.12	57.16 -92
Powell	Donovan	JAM	13 Jun 71	183/79	100	10.31, 10.21w	10.39 -90
* Powell	Mike	USA	10 Nov 63	188/77	LJ	8.70	8.95 -91
Prasad	Bahadur	IND	1 Sep 65	174/63	1500	3:38.95	3:41.33 -92
Prieto	Antonio	ESP	11 Jan 58	158/49	5k	13:31.42	13:18.53 -83
					10k	28:26.53	27:37.49 -90
Prijon	Miha	SLO	11 Mar 71	194/75	HJ	2.24	2.20 -88
Pronin	Vladimir	RUS	27 May 69	186/70	3kSt	8:32.03	8:34.94 -92
Pronko	Gennadiy	BLS	27 Feb 70		DT	60.36	60.66 -92
Prophet	Thomas	GER	22 May 72		50kW	4:06:05	-0-
* Protsenko	Oleg	RUS	11 Aug 63	190/82	TJ	17.03i, 16.58	17.75 -90
* Pukstys	Tom	USA	28 May 68	188/91	JT	85.70	83.30R -90, 83.20 -92
Pumalaynen	Leonid	RUS	13 Apr 70		HJ	2.25	2.25 -90
Pursley	Brit	USA	25 Apr 69	183/79	PV	5.61i, 5.50	5.50 -89
Qin Gang		CHN	10 Apr 70		3kSt	8:33.67	8:59.30 -92
* Quesada	Yoelvis	CUB	4 Aug 73	180/73	TJ	17.68	17.23 -92
Quintanilla	Armando	MEX	19 Apr 68	175/56	10k	27:51.41	27:49.24 -92
Quiriconi	Massimo	ITA	8 Jan 63	182/60	50kW	3:55:14	3:55:42 -92
Raatjes	Dan	USA	9 Feb 68		HJ	2.25	

Name		Nat	Born	Ht/Wt	Event	1993 Mark	Pre-1993 Best
Rabenala	Toussaint	MAD	29 Oct 65	178/71	TJ	17.03, 17.21w	17.05 -89
Radchenko	Viktor	UKR	11 May 68	190/89	Dec	7691	8148 -92
Radefeld	Norbert	GER	3 Mar 62	192/100	HT	76.84	78.28 -88
Radkiewicz	Przemyslaw	POL	25 Aug 70	194/75	HJ	2.28	2.21 -92
Raev	Nikolay	BUL	29 Jan 71	184/71	TJ	17.12i, 17.27idq	17.09 -92
Raizgys	Andrius	LIT	4 Apr 69	185/80	TJ	17.22	17.15 -92
Rakipov	Azat	BLS	29 Nov 68	174/56	1500	3:39.50, 3:38.97i	3:36.16 -92
Rakotombélontsoa	Hubert	MAD	8 Dec 68		400h	49.94	50.37 -92
Rakovic	Aleksandr	YUG	13 Apr 68		20kW	1:23:37	1:24:20 -92
Ramirez	Aaron	USA	29 Jul 64	178/64	3k	7:50.70	7:41.92 -91
Randich	Julius	KEN			10k	28:16.95	29:03.32 -92
Ranzi	Ubaldo	ITA	18 Jul 70	188/71	Dec	7875w, 7839	7449 -91
Rapnouil	Jean-Louis	FRA	24 Jan 66	174/69	400	45.55	46.05 -92
* Räty	Seppo	FIN	27 Apr 62	188/105	JT	85.68	96.96R -91, 90.60 -92
Reading	Robert	USA	9 Jun 67	193/82	110h	13.69,13.5	13.42A, 13.44, 13.19Aw -89
Rédei	Lászlo	HUN	17 Jul 70		HT	73.08	70.32 -92
Redwine	Stanley	USA	10 Apr 61	190/77	800	1:45.82	1:44.87 -84
Reese	Dan	USA	15 Oct 63	173/55	3kSt	8:28.69	8:25.72 -91
Regalo	José	POR	22 Nov 63	180/60	3k	7:51.44	7:43.00 -89
					5k	13:30.47	13:15.62 -88
					10k	28:06.91	28:02.4 -88
* Regis	John	GBR	13 Oct 66	181/94	100	10.15	10.20, 10.07w -90
					200	19.94	20.09 -92
					400	45.48	45.87 -92
Reilly	Brendan	GBR	23 Dec 72	195/77	HJ	2.25	2.31 -92
Reimann	Jens	GER	21 Mar 69	198/100	JT	77.18	79.78 -90
Reina	Reuben	USA	16 Nov 67	170/51	3k	7:49.84i, 7:50.63	7:43.02 -91
					5k	13:33.40	13:24.78 -91
Reinhardt	Jonny	GER	28 Jun 68	198/120	SP	20.07	19.00 -92
Reiterer	Erwin	AUT	29 Dec 70	186/79	Dec	7667	7430 -91
Reiterer	Werner	AUS	27 Jan 68	193/112	DT	62.98	65.62 -87
Ren Yan		CHN	10 Feb 69		50kW	4:03:51	3:57:17 -92
Renner ¶	Thomas	AUT	24 Dec 67	182/86	200	20.67	20.71 -91
Repasky	Karol	SVK	3 Jan 69		20kW	1:23:21t	1:26:18 -90
Retel	Jean-Claude	FRA	11 Feb 68	193/102	DT	60.32	58.78 -91
* Reynolds	Butch	USA	8 Jun 64	190/80	400	44.12	43.29 -88
Reynolds	Jordy	USA	10 May 69	190/118	SP	18.70	19.74 -92
Ribeiro	Juvenal	POR	9 Mar 64	174/60	10k	28:15.25	28:15.93 -91
Richards	Tommy	USA	14 Jul 70	188/79	Dec	7702w	7635 -91
Richardson	Mark	GBR	26 Jul 72	178/74	400	45.94i	45.09 -92
Richter	Bernhard	AUT	11 Dec 70	185/63	2k	5:04.89i	
Richter	Karsten	GER	25 Jul 72	194/80	TJ	16.95	16.35 -91
Rico	Isidro	MEX	15 May 61		Mar	2:10:45	2:09:28 -92
* Ridgeon	Jonathan	GBR	14 Feb 67	183/75	400h	50.42	48.73 -92
* Riedel	Lars	GER	28 Jun 67	198/110	DT	68.42	68.66 -92
Riepl	Anton	GER	28 Feb 69	176/63	HJ	2.26	2.23 -92
Ritter	Daniel	SUI	28 Dec 65	184/72	400h	50.38	50.35 -91
Rivas	Llimi	COL	9 Jun 68		400h	50.48	50.9 -92
Rizo	César	CUB	8 Oct 75		TJ	16.54	16.28 -92
* Robb	Curtis	GBR	7 Jun 72	186/72	800	1:44.92	1:45.16 -92
					1500	3:38.56	3:46.9 -90
Roberson	Mark	GBR	13 Mar 67	194/100	JT	78.96	80.92 -88
Roberts	Grant	RSA	22 May 71		400h	50.18A, 50.28	50.07A -92
Roberts	Jeff	USA	21 Jun 74	175/77	200	20.74w	20.8 -92
Robilliard	Xavier	FRA	13 Jun 67	191/72	HJ	2.28	2.27 -92
Robinson	Rohan	AUS	15 Nov 71	191/80	400h	49.36	49.35 -91
Rodal	Vebjørn	NOR	16 Sep 72	185/76	800	1:45.83	1:45.33 -92
Rodeghiero	Federico	ITA	11 Nov 71	186/69	HJ	2.24	2.24 -92
Rodrigues	António M	POR	14 Jun 63	177/61	Mar	2:11:18	-0-
Rodrigues	Pedro	POR	8 Jul 71	182/72	400h	50.07	49.46 -92
Rodriguez	Miguel	MEX	15 May 62	173/66	20kW	1:20:59	1:23:36 -89
					50kW	3:54:22	3:50:55 -92
Rohánszky	Pál	HUN	28 Sep 70		PV	5.50	5.21 -92
Rojas	Victor	ESP	9 Dec 68	165/58	1500	3:37.03	3:36.83 -90
Romain	Jerome	DMN	12 Jun 71	183/76	TJ	16.98	16.67 -92
Roney	Jerry	USA	5 Jan 70	183/80	110h	13.57, 13.5	13.52 -92
Rono	Peter	KEN	31 Jul 67	162/54	1500	3:39.08	3:34.54 -89

Name		Nat	Born	Ht/Wt	Event	1993 Mark	Pre-1993 Best
Rosen	Alex	USA	2 Jun 73	196/70	HJ	2.24	2.18i, 2.16 -91
Ross	Duane	USA	5 Dec 72	183/79	110h	13.74	13.97, 13.62w -92
Rossouw	Johan	RSA	20 Oct 65	176/73	200	20.55A,20.55	20.53 -87, 20.48A -88
Rosswess	Michael	GBR	11 Jun 65	186/73	100	10.23w	10.15 -91
Rota	Amos	ITA	16 Feb 70		800	1:46.87i	1:47.88 -91
Rothell	John	USA	29 Mar 72	183/73	400h	50.45	50.71 -92
Röttl	Herwig	AUT	30 Jan 68	184/81	110h	13.82	13.41 -92
Rougetet	Nicolas	FRA	27 Jul 70	196/120	HT	73.98	72.24 -91
Rouser	Jason	USA	22 Mar 70	198/80	400	45.36	44.82 -92
* Rousseau	Vincent	BEL	29 Jul 62	176/60	3k	7:48.13	7:39.41 -89
					5k	13:10.99	13:15.01 -86
					10k	27:23.18	27:50.17 -91
					Mar	2:09:13	-0-
Rubtsov	Sergey	KZK	4 Sep 65	190/140	SP	19.06	20.68 -88
Rudenik	Viktor	BLS	30 Mar 64	178/68	LJ	8.03	8.01 -90
Rudolph	Clyde	USA	15 Feb 72	170/70	100	10.29w	
					200	20.59	20.97w -92
Ruffini	Robert	SVK	26 Jan 67	185/70	HJ	2.28	2.34 -88
Ruiz	Alberto	ESP	22 Dec 61	178/76	PV	5.60	5.61 -86
Ruiz	Faustino	ESP	20 Sep 65	178/65	50kW	4:05:37	3:57:25 -91
Runge	Marco	GER	13 Dec 71		800	1:46.30	1:48.51 -92
Russell	Wesley	USA	3 Mar 71	183/73	400	45.22	45.52 -92
* Rutherford	Frank	BAH	23 Nov 64	185/82	TJ	16.59i	17.41 -92
* Ruto	Paul	KEN	3 Nov 60	184/68	800	1:43.92	1:44.33 -92
Rybin	Yuriy	RUS	5 Jun 63	186/85	JT	81.40	84.54S -91
Saavedra	Sergio	VEN	8 Feb 68		TJ	16.69	16.86A -89
Saber	Ashraf	ITA	2 Apr 73	184/70	400h	49.71	49.84 -92
Sabulei	James	KEN	12 Apr 69	172/65	LJ	7.99	8.00A -91
Saddler	Greg	USA	29 Jun 74		100	10.25w	10.51 -92
* Sahere	Abdelaziz	MAR	18 Sep 67	183/63	3kSt	8:15.25	8:12.21 -91
Saho	Nozomi	JPN	6 Mar 73	170/55	10k	27:58.47	29:14.9 -92
Sainah	Joseph	KEN	3 Jan 66		3kSt	8:32.07	
Sainte-Rose	Georges	FRA	3 Sep 69	184/66	TJ	17.23	17.24, 17.48w -91
* Saito	Yoshihiko	JPN	12 Feb 72	177/63	400h	48.68	49.01 -92
Sakai	Hirofumi	JPN	10 Feb 65	170/60	20kW	1:22:25.4t	1:23:05.4t -91
					50kW	4:03:14	4:03:28 -92
Sakhri	Sid-Ali	ALG	20 Dec 61	173/67	10k	28:30.01	29:03.59 -90
					Mar	2:11:09	2:13:29 -87
* Sakirkin	Oleg	KZK	23 Jan 66	182/72	TJ	17.17	17.58 -89
Saksio	Sami	FIN	28 Apr 69	190/95	JT	80.30	79.50 -92
Salah	Ahmed	DJI	31 Dec 56	180/60	Mar	2:12:40	2:07:07 -88
Salle	Fred	GBR	10 Sep 64	188/84	LJ	7.96i	7.97 -86
Salmi	Mohamed	ALG	11 Nov 63	168/61	Mar	2:12:47	2:13:13 -90
Samolyuk	Anatoliy	UKR	2 Jul 58	186/115	SP	18.70	19.94 -86
Sánchez	Alberto	CUB	3 Feb 73	180/92	HT	75.86	69.78 -92
* Sánchez	German	MEX	15 Sep 66	173/65	50kW	3:54:07	3:51:02 -92
Sánchez	Joel	MEX	6 Aug 64	175/53	20kW	1:22:55	1:21:07.8t -92
					50kW	4:01:06	
Sanders	Chris	USA	8 May 72	183/82	LJ	7.92i, 7.99w	8.17i, 8.05 -92
Sanders	Larry	USA	26 Apr 70	180/73	400h	49.24	
Sandvik	Jan	FIN	17 May 69	194/121	SP	18.89	19.06 -92
* Sang	Patrick	KEN	11 Apr 64	175/64	3kSt	8:07.53	8:06.03 -89
+ Sangouma	Daniel	FRA	7 Feb 65	187/84	100	10.23, 10.09rs	10.02 -90
					200	20.63, 20.60w	20.20 -89
Sanguin	Giovanni	ITA	14 May 69	179/92	HT	72.36	71.74 -90
Sankovich	Andrey	BLS	15 Jul 65		HJ	2.34	2.28i -90, 2.25 -92
Santos	Gilmar	BRA	16 Dec 70	185/78	800	1:45.88	1:46.18 -92
Saritzoglou	Savas	GRE	19 Jul 71	188/109	HT	76.12	75.30 -92
* Sasimovich	Vladimir	BLS	14 Sep 68	178/86	JT	86.48	87.08 -91
Sautkin	Igor	RUS	72		TJ	16.71w	16.14 -92
Savin	Vitaliy	KZK	23 Jan 66	180/86	100	10.18	10.08, 9.94w -92
Scekic	Radoman	YUG	1 Oct 67	187/102	JT	80.46	85.08R -91, 81.68 -89
* Schenk	Christian	GER	9 Feb 65	200/93	Dec	8500	8488 -88
Schmid	Stefan	GER	6 May 70	186/78	Dec	8061	8012 -92
Schmidheiny	René	SUI	4 Jan 67	189/90	Dec	7707	7864 -87
Schmidt	Hans-Günther	GER	19 Jan 69		JT	75.62	74.98 -90
Schmitz	Manfred	GER	13 Mar 60	195/118	DT	58.98	64.84 -90

Name		Nat	Born	Ht/Wt	Event	1993 Mark	Pre-1993 Best
Schoeman	Kobus	RSA	16 Nov 65	178/84	110h	13.64A, 13.74	13.65A-88, 13.73, 13.5 -87
Scholz	Volkmar	GER	20 May 67	187/72	50kW	3:56:06	3:55:19 -90
Schönlebe	Thomas	GER	6 Aug 65	185/76	400	45.99	44.33 -87
* Schult	Jürgen	GER	11 May 60	193/110	DT	66.12	74.08 -86
Schumacher	Jerry	USA	6 Aug 70	183/66	1500	3:39.46	3:40.28 -92
* Schwarthoff	Florian	GER	7 May 68	201/82	110h	13.27	13.13 -92
Schwieger	Rick	USA	17 Jun 69	196/84	Dec	7571	7877 -92
Scott	Otis	USA	19 Apr 71	188/73	400	45.91	46.12 -92
Scott	Robert	USA	1 Jan 72	183/75	100	10.0wdt	10.41, 10.24w -90
Scott	Tyrone	USA	18 Jan 70	186/77	TJ	16.88	17.03 -92
Scurry	Derek	USA	1 Oct 73	190/84	LJ	8.01Ai, 7.94	7.83 -92
Sdad	Mustapha	MAR	11 Apr 70	180/73	110h	13.79	14.10 -92
Sedlácek	Pavel	TCH	5 Apr 68	198/105	HT	76.38	76.46 -92
* Sedykh	Yuriy	RUS	11 Jun 55	185/106	HT	76.92	86.74 -86
Seelig	Andreas	GER	6 Jul 70	200/120	DT	61.90	60.82 -92
Segura	Bernardo	MEX	11 Feb 70	179/61	20kW	1:19:39	1:22:01 -91
Seid	Ibrahim	ETH			10k	28:25.43	
Seifert	Jim	USA	26 Nov 62	188/114	DT	59.18, 65.84qm	66.14 -92
* Seleznyov	Aleksandr	RUS	25 Jan 63	182/97	HT	81.70	80.62 -91
Selle	Frédéric	FRA	15 Mar 57	198/125	DT	59.64	62.96 -89
Semenyuk	Yevgeniy	UKR	11 Dec 68	175/65	LJ	8.13	8.05 -92
Semyonov	Konstantin	UZB/BLS	20 Nov 69	190/80	PV	5.65i, 5.65	5.70 -91
+ Sepeng	Ezekiel	RSA	30 Jun 74	178/58	800	1:45.46	1:47.51 -92
Serem	William	KEN	68		800	1:45.8A	1:49.0A -92
Sergiyenko	Yuriy	UKR	19 Mar 65	190/73	HJ	2.34i, 2.32	2.34i, 2.31 -85
Serrano	Antonio	ESP	8 Mar 65	179/65	5k	13:24.96	13:22.40 -91
					10k	27:47.33	27:59.21 -91
Seskin	Yuriy	RUS	7 Jul 66	196/100	DT	60.26	64.58 -88
Setliff	Adam	USA	15 Dec 69	193/122	DT	64.08	61.54 -92
Sgrulletti	Enrico	ITA	24 Apr 65	182/100	HT	79.80	77.78 -92
Shabunin	Vyacheslav	RUS	27 Sep 69		1500	3:36.59	3:40.49 -92
Shahanga	Alfredo	TAN	14 Apr 65	170/57	Mar	2:12:24	2:10:11 -89
Shapkin	Georgiy	RUS	30 Aug 66		JT	78.34	80.02 -89
* Sharpe	David	GBR	8 Jul 67	181/66	800	1:46.09	1:43.98 -92
Shaverdashvili	Iosif	GEO	29 Oct 69	182/90	HT	75.80	78.12 -91
* Shchennikov	Mikhail	RUS	24 Dec 67	182/70	20kW	1:18:33	1:19:07 -90
Shchepin	Aleksey	RUS	3 Apr 72	183/82	JT	80.18	78.62 -91
Shelton	Matt	USA	3 Jun 69	188/84	Dec	7736w	7870 -92
Shen Weihui		CHN	25 May 73		20kW	1:21:45	
Sherriff	Brian	ZIM	11 Nov 61	165/58	Mar	2:12:55	2:13:40 -87
Sherry	Peter	USA	22 Aug 68	185/68	5k	13:30.44	13:39.31 -91
* Shevchenko	Dmitriy	RUS	13 May 68	198/125	DT	66.90	67.30 -92
Shevchuk	Andrey	RUS	8 Mar 70		JT	85.70	81.76 -92
Shida	Tetsuya	JPN	27 Jun 71	181/70	LJ	7.98w	7.69 -92
Shirley	Simon	GBR	3 Aug 66	190/90	Dec	7944	8036 -88
* Shishkin	Vladimir	RUS	12 Jan 64	193/77	110h	13.54	13.21, 13.0 -88
Shtrobinders	Marcis	LAT	12 Jun 66	186/100	JT	81.78	80.32 -88
Shumak	Artur	BLS	19 Oct 63	179/70	20kW	1:20:38	1:20:10 -91
Siba	Lahoussine	MAR	67		1500	3:39.48	
* Sidorenko	Vasiliy	RUS	1 May 61	190/100	HT	80.04	82.54 -92
Sidorov	Gennadiy	BLS	13 Mar 67		PV	5.50	5.60 -92
Sidorov	Vitaliy	UKR	23 Mar 70	193/118	DT	60.46	59.60 -92
Siermachesky	Cory	CAN	20 Aug 69		HJ	2.24	2.25 -92
* Sigei	William	KEN	14 Oct 69	178/57	3k	7:37.73	7:39.51 -92
					5k	13:07.35	13:15.01 -92
					10k	27:16.81	28:35.0 -92
Sild	Donald-Aik	EST	3 Oct 68	198/103	JT	80.90	78.28 -89
Silio	Antonio	ARG	9 May 66	172/67	5k	13:31.26	13:19.64 -91
					10k	27:38.72	27:46.54 -91
Silva	Arnaldo	BRA	26 Mar 64	174/71	100	10.26	10.12A, 10.23 -88, 10.06w -85
Silva	Carlos	POR	8 Jun 74	174/64	400h	50.27	51.04 -92
* Silva	German	MEX	9 Jan 68	160/60	5k	13:26.11	13:40.30 -92
					10k	28:03.64	27:46.52 -92
Silva	Mário	POR	23 Jul 61	172/58	800	1:46.87	1:46.69 -91
					1500	3:39.95	3:35.76 -91
					2k	5:05.86	5:06.51 - 89
Simon	Andrés	CUB	15 Sep 61	160/67	100	10.31w	10.06 -87, 9.97w -85

Name		Nat	Born	Ht/Wt	Event	1993 Mark	Pre-1993 Best
Simpkins	Charlie	USA	19 Oct 63	186/76	TJ	16.72i	17.86 -85, 17.93w -88
Simretu	Alemayehu	ETH	66		3kSt	8:31.51	8:45.14 -92
Simson	Matt	GBR	28 May 70	197/125	SP	18.95i, 18.90	19.23 -91
Singoei Kiptoo	David	KEN	26 Jun 65	175/68	800	1:45.64	1:46.89 -91
Sinka	Albert	HUN	22 Nov 62	187/95	HT	72.38	81.18 -88
Sinnhuber	Björn	GER	1 Aug 68	178/70	200	20.68	21.04-87
Sinovas	Fernando	ESP	8 Jul 68	168/58	3kSt	8:31.29	8:30.23 -92
* Sjöberg	Patrik	SWE	5 Jan 65	200/82	HJ	2.39i, 2.32	2.42 -87
* Skah	Khalid	MAR	29 Jan 67	170/60	3k	7:40.0+, 7:39.67i	7:37.09 -90
					5k	13:04.67	13:09.10 -92
					10k	27:17.74	27:23.29 -91
Skipper	Art	USA	31 Jul 70	190/91	JT	76.60, 79.22qm	76.70 -92
Skurygin	German	RUS	23 Dec 63	169/65	50kW	3:56:19	3:50:25 -92
Skvaryuk	Andrey	UKR	9 Mar 67	187/100	HT	80.8	80.22 -92
Skvortsov	Andrey	RUS	2 Dec 68		PV	5.72	5.65 -91
* Smirnov	Sergey	RUS	17 Sep 60	192/126	SP	20.94i, 19.66	22.24 -86
Smirnov	Vyacheslav	RUS	4 May 57	177/65	50kW	3:58:20	3:46:08 -89
Smith	Adam	USA	4 Oct 71	185/76	PV	5.60	5.46 -92
Smith	Barry	USA	22 Feb 71		200	20.63	20.82-90
* Smith	Calvin	USA	8 Jan 61	178/69	100	10.06	9.93A, 9.97 -83, 9.87w -88
					200	20.50	19.99 -83
Smith	David	GBR	21 Jun 62	193/118	HT	70.46	77.30 -85
Smith	Erik	USA	28 May 71	193/100	JT	79.20	72.28 -92
Smith	Lamont	USA	11 Dec 72	188/73	400	45.30	46.05 -91
* Smith	Mike	CAN	16 Sep 67	196/96	Dec	8362	8549 -91
Smith	Robert	USA	4 Mar 72	186/89	400	45.95	45.73 -92
Smith	Steve	USA	11 Jan 71	190/66	HJ	2.25	2.27 -91
* Smith	Steve	GBR	29 Mar 73	185/70	HJ	2.37i, 2.37	2.37 -92
Smith	Van	USA	27 May 73	175/69	200	20.74w	
Söderman	Mikael	FIN	5 Nov 65	183/72	800	1:46.22	1:47.65 -92
Sokolov	Vladimir	RUS	5 Oct 63	196/75	HJ	2.30	2.26 -92
Smith	Van	USA	27 May 73	175/69	200	20.74w	
Sokov	Vasiliy	RUS	7 Apr 68	186/73	LJ	8.00i	8.18 -88
					TJ	17.59	17.52 -91, 17.73w -89
Solhaug	Dag	SWE	11 Jan 64	200/124	DT	60.74	59.64 -92
Solly	Jon	GBR	28 Jun 63	183/66	10k	28:32.19	27:51.76 -86
					Mar	2:12:30	2:12:07 -90
* Sonn	Ralf	GER	17 Jan 67	197/85	HJ	2.36i, 2.34	2.39i -91, 2.32 -89
Sotelo	Julian	ESP	5 Jul 65	195/100	JT	76.64	78.78 -92
Sotnikov	Yuriy	RUS	10 Mar 69	189/75	TJ	17.14	16.77 -91
* Sotomayor	Javier	CUB	13 Oct 67	195/82	HJ	2.45	2.44 -89
* Souza da Silva	Anisio	BRA	18 Jun 69	186/81	TJ	17.32	17.00 -90
Sowell	Nat	USA	73	183/77	LJ	7.93	7.19 -91
Soyka	Vladimir	UKR	29 Oct 65	172/62	50kW	3:55:58	3:51:24 -90
Spada	Mirko	SUI	26 Jan 69	192/86	Dec	7813	7718 -90
Spears	Derek	USA	73		110h	13.82	
					400h	50.49	53.95 -92
Spies	Phillip	RSA	21 May 70	188/87	JT	80.90	78.34 -92
* Spitsyn	Valeriy	RUS	5 Dec 65	178/67	50kW	3:42:50	3:48:38 -89
Spitsyn	Vyacheslav	RUS	11 Feb 65		SP	19.20	19.02 -89
* Spivey	Jim	USA	7 Mar 60	180/63	1500	3:34.67	3:31.01 -88
					Mile	3:52.37	3:49.80 -86
					3k	7:37.04	7:48.61 -88
					5k	13:25.92	13:19.24 -83
Staef	Jan	SWE	11 Jan 62	181/74	20kW	1:23:23	
Stafford	Jermaine	USA	25 Dec 74	183/81	200	20.70	21.23 -91
Staines	Gary	GBR	3 Jul 63	183/63	3k	7:48.97	7:41.79 -90
					5k	13:33.42	13:14.28 -90
					10k	28:02.24	27:48.73 -91
Stankulov	Tzvetoslav	BUL	1 Feb 69	182/73	200	20.80	21.31 -92
Stanton	Brian	USA	19 Feb 61	198/87	HJ	2.24	2.33 -88
Starkey	Dean	USA	27 Mar 67	188/77	PV	5.70	5.91 -92
Starodubtsev	Valeriy	RUS	14 Jan 62	185/70	800	1:46.95	1:45.32 -86
Stasaitis	Redzinaldas	LIT	5 Apr 67	183/71	TJ	16.83	16.47 -91
Steele	Darrin	USA	20 Mar 69	188/88	Dec	7982w	7699 -92
* Steele	Martin	GBR	20 Sep 62	170/66	800	1:43.84	1:46.32 -92
Steigauf	Milos	TCH	5 Feb 69	195/98	JT	80.32	79.08 -92

Name		Nat	Born	Ht/Wt	Event	1993 Mark	Pre-1993 Best
Steinmayr	Teddy	AUT	4 Feb 64	199/92	LJ	7.92	8.14 -89
Stenlund	Patrik	SWE	11 Oct 68	194/79	PV	5.62	5.50 -89
Stenzel	Rüdiger	GER	16 Apr 68	180/65	1500	3:36.08	3:36.41 -92
					Mile	3:56.89	3:56.02 -92
Stepanov	Vitaliy	RUS	9 Dec 65	186/76	PV	5.50	5.50 -90
Stephen	Hayden	TRI	9 Jan 72	188/77	400	45.70A	46.91, 46.3 -91
Stevens	Patrick	BEL	31 Jan 68	183/76	100	10.26w	10.32, 10.29A -90
					200	20.72	20.59, 20.41w -92
Stevenson	Jim	GBR	31 Dec 71	182/73	Dec	7713	7274 -90
* Stewart	Raymond	JAM	18 Mar 65	178/73	100	10.11	9.96 -91, 9.89w, 9.8w -87
					200	20.80	20.41 -88, 20.31w -87
Stipanov	Ruslan	UKR	19 Sep 71	192/76	HJ	2.27	2.25 -92
Stjepovic	Milan	SLO	8 Mar 68	180/83	JT	77.98	77.90 -92
Stolarczyk	Marek	POL	10 Jun 64		DT	59.12	57.06 -91
Stone	Darrell	GBR	2 Feb 68	175/60	20kW	1:23:27	1:25:05 -92
Storaci	Alain	FRA	5 Jun 67	194/88	JT	80.00	75.96 -90
Strang	David	GBR	13 Dec 68	175/70	1000	2:18.31i	
					Mile	3:56.86	3:59.40i -92
* Streete-Thompson	Kareem	CAY/USA	30 Mar 73	183/82	100	10.30, 10.19w	10.57, 10.46w -92
					LJ	8.36A, 8.31	8.12 -92, 8.46w -91
Strege	Martin	GER	21 Feb 66	178/63	3kSt	8:21.24	8:24.18 -92
Streltsov	Igor	UKR	1 May 65	184/74	LJ	7.94	8.31 -88
Strikis	Andris	LAT	7 Nov 71	193/90	LJ	8.02w	7.22 -91
Strizhakov	Oleg	RUS	18 Jul 63	179/61	5k	13:29.08	13:30.88 -84
					10k	28:24.59	28:16.15 -90
Strominski	Grzegorz	POL	19 May 70	186/82	Dec	7686	7025 -92
Strychalski	Jacek	POL	6 Mar 62	195/105	DT	58.00	62.54 -86, 62.66irr -87
Stulce	Mike	USA	21 Jul 69	191/123	SP	21.77i, 21.22	21.82 -90
Sudnik	Andrey	BLS	20 Aug 67	179/67	800	1:46.61	1:45.29 -88
Suhonen	Ari	FIN	19 Dec 65	185/65	800	1:45.85	1:44.10 -89
Sukhanov	Andrey	UKR	3 Aug 70		HT	74.52	74.24 -90
Sula	Karel	SVK	30 Jun 59	189/104	SP	19.13	20.71 -88
Sulcer	Mike	USA	14 Sep 71	180/73	100	10.29	10.42 -91
* Suleiman	Mohamed	QAT	23 Nov 69	170/60	1500	3:33.29	3:34.12 -92
					Mile	3:57.05i	
					3k	7:38.20	7:50.64 -92
Sullivan	Kevin	CAN	20 Mar 74	180/68	1500	3:39.43	3:39.11 -92
Sumawe	Julius	TAN	12 Sep 65		Mar	2:11:58	2:13:52 -92
Sumner	Brad	USA	4 Aug 70	185/75	800	1:46.33	1:46.77 -92
Sun Fei		CHN	24 Jan 68		JT	76.32	78.36 -91
Sun Ripeng		CHN	25 Jan 74	180/68	3kSt	8:24.87	8:41.23 -91
Sun Xiaoguang		CHN	15 Jan 65		20kW	1:21:55	1:21:35.3t -91
					50kW	4:01:18	3:46:41 -91
Sundin	Lars	SWE	21 Jul 61	193/107	DT	62.00	65.42 -87
Sundt	Lars Ola	NOR	7 Jan 68	196/102	DT	60.18	61.90 -92
Sunneborn	Mattias	SWE	27 Sep 70	187/82	LJ	8.05, 8.18ex	8.05i, 8.06w -92
* Surin	Bruny	CAN	12 Jul 67	180/81	100	10.02	10.05, 9.9 -92, 10.01w -91
					200	20.48	21.30 -89
Suzuki	Kenichi	JPN	6 Apr 67	175/63	Mar	2:11:56	
Svenøy	Jim	NOR	22 Apr 72	186/70	3kSt	8:28.51	8:42.67 -92
* Swartbooi	Lucketz	NAM	7 Feb 66		Mar	2:09:57	2:10:01 -92
Sweeney	Nick	IRL	26 Mar 68	195/121	DT	63.26	62.48 -92
Swift	Eugene	USA	14 Sep 64	180/75	110h	13.56, 13.52w	13.49 -91
* Szabó	Dezsö	HUN	4 Sep 67	184/82	Dec	8101	8436 -90
Szücs	Csaba	HUN	29 Jan 65	177/68	Mar	2:12:10	2:12:26 -90
Tadesse	Becho	ETH	68		Mar	2:10:27	2:15:37 -92
* Tafralis	Gregg	USA	9 Apr 58	183/129	SP	19.93i, 19.77	21.98 -92
Tailhardat	Jean-Marc	FRA	12 Apr 66	178/66	PV	5.70	5.70 -91
Taitt	Tyrell	USA	19 Apr 71	178/75	TJ	16.62i , 16.91w	16.34i -91
Taiwo	Joseph	NGR	24 Aug 59	183/74	TJ	16.77i, 16.63	17.22 -88, 17.47w -92
Takahashi	Koichi	JPN	7 Jun 62	176/59	Mar	2:10:55	2:11:47 -91
Takaoka	Toshinari	JPN	24 Sep 70	185/64	5k	13:23.98	13:20.43 -92
					10k	28:28.1	
Taki	Mohamed	MAR	71	172/61	1500	3:36.19	3:37.7 -92
Takushima	Tsutomu	JPN	18 Feb 67	173/62	20kW	1:22:40.2	1:25:58 -92
Talley	Keith	USA	28 Jan 64	191/88	110h	13.76A, 13.72w	13.31 -86
Tallhem	Sören	SWE	16 Feb 64	192/110	SP	19.43	20.91, 21.24i -85

Name		Nat	Born	Ht/Wt	Event	1993 Mark	Pre-1993 Best
* Tamm	Jüri	EST	5 Feb 57	193/120	HT	76.94	84.40 -84
Tan Mingjun		CHN	17 Jul 70		20kW	1:20:41	
Tandanozis	Theodoris	GRE	29 Sep 64	188/74	TJ	16.57i	16.65 -88, 16.71w -91
Tang Linhua		CHN	13 May 67	186/90	JT	76.44	79.80 -91
* Taniguchi	Hiromi	JPN	5 Apr 60	171/56	Mar	2:11:02	2:07:40 -88
* Tanui	Moses	KEN	20 Aug 65	165/55	3k	7:41.87	7:46.20 -89
					5k	13:22.82	13:17.80 -92
					10k	27:18.32	27:35.89 -91
* Tanui	William	KEN	22 Feb 64	183/70	800	1:44.30	1:43.30 -91
					1500	3:35.74	3:34.25 -90
					Mile	3:53.80	3:56.87 -92
Tao	Xu	CHN	Jan 72		HJ	2.25	2.20 -92
* Tarasenko	Stanislav	RUS	23 Jul 66	185/79	LJ	8.24	8.08 -92
Tarasov	Aleksey	RUS	26 Jan 69		Mar	2:12:56	
* Tarasov	Maksim	RUS	12 Dec 70	194/80	PV	5.90i, 5.90	5.90 -92
* Tarpenning	Kory	USA	27 Feb 62	180/76	PV	5.75, 5.75	5.89 -88
Tate	Tony	USA	31 Dec 73		200	20.80	
Tau	Jan	RSA	18 Nov 60		Mar	2:12:19	2:11:56 -92
Taylor	Brian	GBR	13 Aug 70	183/80	Dec	7787	7567 -90
Teape	Hugh	GBR	26 Dec 63	178/73	110h	13.69, 13.60w	13.44 -92
Telles	Sidnei	BRA	26 Jul 66	183/65	200	20.02	20.40 -92
					400	45.92	45.38 -92
Tellez	Norberto	CUB	23 Dec 72	180/73	400	45.51	45.70 -92
ten Kate	Marti	HOL	16 Dec 58	172/57	Mar	2:12:39	2:10:04 -89
Tengelei	Joseph	KEN	8 Dec 70	173/64	800	1:44.48	1:45.88 -92
* Tergat	Paul	KEN	17 Jun 69	183/61	5k	13:20.16	13:48.64 -92
					10k	27:18.43	29:46.8A -91
Terraz	Denis	FRA	5 Feb 58	183/74	50kW	3:56:19	3:54:12 -87
Terrelonge	Clive	JAM	30 Jun 69	189/72	800	1:45.61	1:45.96 -92
Terrier	Vincent	FRA	22 Dec 68	178/63	1500	3:38.85	3:44.00 -92
* Terry	Glenn	USA	10 Feb 71	193/82	110h	13.35, 13.24w	13.64, 13.4w -90
Terzian	Alexandros	GRE	24 Jun 68	180/74	100	10.20	10.61 -92
Tesfaye	Tafa	ETH	15 Nov 62		Mar	2:11:57	2:13:26 -91
Texada	David	USA	23 May 71	172/67	100	10.22dt	?
Thavelin	Patrick	SWE	29 Apr 70	193/82	HJ	2.24	2.26 -92
Thibault	Sebastien	FRA	25 Jul 70	183/74	110h	13.59	13.45, 13.44w -92
* Thiébaut	Pascal	FRA	6 Jun 59	175/60	1500	3:36.11	3:34.08 -92
Thigpen	Aaron	USA	18 Sep 64	170/71	100	10.31,10.18Aw	10.28 -91,10.02Aw -86
Thomas	Christian	GER	31 Mar 65	186/73	LJ	8.02	8.13 -89, 8.16w -90
Thomas	Eric	USA	7 Dec 73	180/75	400h	49.83	-0-
Thomas	Marlon	USA	5 Feb 71	180/75	100	10.29w, 9.8w-dt	10.39 -92
					200	20.70w	20.89 -92
Thomas	Robert	USA	7 Aug 73	185/78	LJ	8.15	7.98 -92
					TJ	16.80i	15.64 -91
Thompson	Derrick	USA	24 Feb 73	175/73	100	9.9w	10.4 -91
					200	20.59, 20.35w	
Thompson	Ian	BAH	8 Dec 68		HJ	2.25	2.28 -92
Thompson	Mark	JAM	2 Aug 67	185/82	400h	49.89	49.37 -92
Thompson	Obadele	BAR	75		100	10.30Aw	10.59w -92
Thompson	Rodney	USA	21 Nov 70	186/75	110h	13.74	13.77 -91, 13.71w -92
Thomson	Lochsley	AUS	20 Aug 73		HJ	2.25	2.31 -92
Thränhardt	Carlo	GER	5 Jul 57	199/85	HJ	2.26i, 2.25	2.42i -88, 2.37 -84
* Thys	Gert	RSA	12 Nov 71		Mar	2:09:31	2:17:16 -92
Tian Niantang		CHN	Mar 72		20kW	1:23:01	1:20:50.0t -92
Tidow	Joachim	GER	4 Feb 69	198/100	DT	59.38	62.26 -91
Tikhonov	Andrey	RUS	11 Dec 66	180/66	3k	7:48.94	7:44.54 -92
					5k	13:29.12	13:26.78 -92
Timofeyev	Yevgeniy	RUS	22 Feb 74		TJ	17.00	15.87i, 15.87 -92
Tirelli	Davide	ITA	12 Aug 66	178/65	1000	2:18.07	
					1500	3:35.42	3:34.61 -92
Tîrle	Marcel	ROM	19 Oct 66	195/109	DT	62.60	64.62 -91
Tivonchik	Andrey	BLS	70		PV	5.65	5.60 -92
Tjepkema	Enno	HOL	5 Jun 65	185/85	Dec	7664	7909 -85
Többen	Olaf	GER	19 Dec 62	196/124	DT	60.48, 62.86dm	65.50 -88
Tokunaga	Daisuke	JPN	28 Nov 65	162/50	Mar	2:11:09	2:12:13 -91
Tolbert	Rod	USA	11 Jun 67	185/75	200	20.67	20.38 -92
* Topic	Dragutin	YUG	12 Mar 71	197/77	HJ	2.38	2.37 -90

Name		Nat	Born	Ht/Wt	Event	1993 Mark	Pre-1993 Best
* Toth	Kevin	USA	29 Dec 67	193/127	SP	21.29	20.99 -92
Toumi	Hakim	ALG	30 Jan 61	180/105	HT	74.02	73.90 -92
* Toutain	Thierry	FRA	14 Feb 62	182/75	50kW	3:47:40	4:05:09 -92
Trafas	Dariusz	POL	5 Jun 72	188/87	JT	77.38	75.00 -92
* Trandenkov	Igor	RUS	17 Aug 66	191/80	PV	5.90i, 5.80	5.90 -92
Trapp	James	USA	28 Dec 70	181/80	100	10.30	10.14, 10.03w -92
					200	20.54	20.17 -92
Trentin	Nicola	ITA	20 Jun 74		LJ	7.93w	7.33 -92
Trimble	Todd	USA	2 Jun 71	178/77	LJ	8.03	8.05 -92
Troshin	Oleg	RUS	1 Aug 64		20kW	1:22:17	1:19:58 -88
* Trouabal	Jean-Charles	FRA	20 May 65	187/77	100	10.19	10.36, 10.25w -91
					200	20.20	20.30 -91
* Tsebe	David	RSA	9 Nov 66	172/56	Mar	2:12:07	2:08:07 -92
Tsitouras	Spiros	GRE	15 Jun 69	190/75	PV	5.55	5.40 -91
Tsvetanov	Emil	BUL	14 Mar 63	175/83	JT	77.70	80.12 -89
Tudor	Bogdan	ROM	1 Feb 70	174/66	LJ	8.09i, 7.93	8.08i, 8.06 -91
Tuffour	Emmanuel	GHA	2 Dec 66	180/70	100	10.23	10.12 -91
					200	20.44	20.50 -91
Tulloch	Andrew	GBR	1 Apr 67	183/75	110h	13.59	13.71 -91
Tura	Bizuneh Yai	ETH	15 Feb 70	176/60	3kSt	8:29.71	8:44.97 -92
Turbo	Tumo	ETH	70		Mar	2:10:31	2:14:55 -92
Turner	Alan	USA	19 Mar 69	180/76	LJ	8.07, 8.11w	8.06i -91, 8.21w -90
Turner	Scott	USA	26 Feb 72	183/84	200	20.77w	
					400	45.69	47.08 -90
* Tverdokhleb	Oleg	UKR	3 Nov 69	184/70	400h	48.62	48.63 -92
Tynes	Andrew	BAH	13 Feb 72	193/82	100	10.24Aw	10.39w -91
					200	20.22A, 20.48	20.7 -91, 20.49Aw -92
Tyulenev	Sergey	RUS	14 Mar 71	177/58	20kW	1:21:31	1:22:18 -92
Ubartas	Romas	LIT	26 May 60	202/123	DT	65.92 *	70.06 -88
Udelhoven	Jussi	GER/NOR	25 Feb 66	188/75	800	1:46.36	1:45.68 -92
Ugwu	Chima	NGR	72		SP	18.56	19.06 -92
Ulmala	Risto	FIN	7 May 63	184/63	5k	13:31.63	13:21.90 -91
					10k	28:18.21	27:53.00 -91
Ulvsbäck	Mårten	SWE	5 Jun 66	185/80	PV	5.65	5.41 -91
Uno	Masaki	JPN	13 Dec 72	180/63	HJ	2.28	2.25 -92
Urata	Haruo	JPN	9 Mar 62	171/57	10k	28:17.36	27:58.72 -91
Urban	Dirk	GER	14 Jan 69	188/101	SP	19.34i	18.56 -91
* Urbanik	Sándor	HUN	15 Dec 64	172/56	20kW	1:23:31	1:20:55 -92
Urbano	José	POR	22 Feb 66	174/56	20kW	1:22:40	1:21:41 -92
					50kW	3:57:29.5	3:59:33 -92
Urias	Julio César	GUA	11 Jan 72	170/52	50kW	4:03:24	
Urmakayev	Oleg	RUS	14 Jan 65	193/84	Dec	7630	7546 -89
Urrutia	Aliacer	CUB	22 Sep 74		TJ	17.27	16.59 -92
* Usov	Sergey	BLS	14 Jan 64	188/87	110h	13.55	13.27 -88
Vääräniemi	Heikki	FIN	21 Dec 69	187/74	PV	5.63	5.55 -92
Vaccari	Marco	ITA	17 Jul 66	180/69	400	45.98	45.47 -92
Vágó	Béla	HUN	3 Oct 63	176/63	3kSt	8:35.88	8:21.48 -88
Vainauskas	Arvidas	LIT	12 Dec 66	174/60	20kW	1:22:51	
Vainauskas	Sigitas	LIT	12 Dec 66	174/60	20kW	1:22:26	1:19:29 -89
* Valle	Emilio	CUB	21 Apr 67	182/70	110h	13.19	13.30, 13.21w -89
Valle	Miguel	CUB	29 Sep 68	181/81	Dec	7633	7798 -92
Valle	Mikko	FIN	11 May 70	181/73	Dec	7764	7504 -92
Vallin	Juan	MEX	7 Sep 69	185/72	400h	50.00A, 50.47	49.5 -90, 50.26 -92
* Valmon	Andrew	USA	1 Jan 65	186/78	400	44.28	44.35 -90
Valvik	Svein-Inge	NOR	20 Sep 56	190/112	DT	61.38	68.00 -82
van Balen	Ruben	HOL	27 Jan 71	200/97	Dec	7800	7447 -91
Van Calcar	Karl	USA	11 Jan 65	178/66	3kSt	8:27.60	8:23.95 -92
van der Westhuizen	Eugene	RSA	30 Aug 74		400h	50.44A	52.10 -92
* van Dijck	William	BEL	24 Jan 61	180/59	3kSt	8:24.03	8:10.01 -86
van Geyte	Gino	BEL	16 Mar 67		1500	3:38.08i	3:39.1 -92
van Heerden	Marius	RSA	8 Sep 74	179/67	800	1:46.38A	1:48.63 -92
van Lieshout	Johan	HOL	8 Mar 69	197/96	JT	77.72	79.16 -90
van Rensburg	François	RSA	2 Aug 70		1500	3:35.84	3:44.84 -91
Vandergrift	Paul	USA	16 May 69	186/70	1500	3:39.51	3:38.21 -92
* Vander-Kuyp	Kyle	AUS	30 May 71	192/76	110h	13.48	13.74 -92
Vandevoir	Marc	FRA	17 Jun 71	183/78	PV	5.50, 5.60ex	5.50 -91
Vanyaikin	Dmitriy	UKR	14 Jan 66	171/66	200	20.56	20.99 -89, 20.6 -86

Name		Nat	Born	Ht/Wt	Event	1993 Mark	Pre-1993 Best
Varich	Dmitriy	UKR	28 Feb 72	188/96	HT	74.06	66.54 -91
Vasdekis	Spyros	GRE	23 Jan 70	178/61	LJ	7.99, 8.09w	8.04 -91
Vázquez	Fernando	ESP	4 May 71	173/58	20kW	1:23:46	1:24:05 -91
Vdovin	Mikhail	RUS	15 Jan 67	182/73	400	45.89	47.23 -92
Venter	Johann	RSA	30 Dec 71		100	10.31A	10.64 -92
Venturi	Giorgio	ITA	23 Jun 66	187/102	SP	19.27	18.61 -91
Vera	Ricardo	URU	16 Sep 62	186/71	3kSt	8:23.65	8:23.02 -92
Vera	Rolando	ECU	27 Apr 65	155/47	10k	28:12.76	27:54.33 -88
Verebes	Janos	HUN	25 Feb 69		HT	71.30	69.60 -88
Verkys	Rolandas	LIT	17 Mar 67	193/77	HJ	2.27i	2.34 -91
Verster	Jean	RSA	23 Apr 65		3k	7:46.60	7:51.11 -92
Vesterinen	Pekka	FIN	13 Apr 66	189/84	110h	13.75	13.84 -92
Vetrov	Sergey	RUS	8 May 68	186/80	110h	13.85	13.66 -92
Vezhel	Mechislav	BLS	25 Jan 62	170/62	50kW	4:04:06	3:49:01 -91
Vial	Pierre Alexandre	FRA	25 May 75	180/70	Dec	7618	
Vialettes	Jean-Christophe	FRA	19 Dec 67	182/75	800	1:46.34	1:46.62 -91
Viali	Tonino	ITA	16 Sep 60	179/70	1500	3:37.94	3:42.25 -90
Viciosa	Isaac	ESP	26 Dec 69	175/68	1500	3:34.75	3:37.13 -91
Victor	Silvio	BRA	64		800	1:47.0	1:47.05 -92
Vida	József	HUN	9 Jan 63	192/115	HT	73.78	79.06 -84
Vieira Galdino	Sergio	BRA	7 May 69	165/57	20kW	1:23:09.1t	1:22:41.0t -91
Vierimaa	Taisto	FIN	27 Jul 65		HT	71.72	72.10 -92
Vigneron	Thierry	FRA	9 Mar 60	181/74	PV	5.70i, 5.60	5.91 -84
Vilhjálmsson	Einar	ISL	1 Jun 60	188/100	JT	77.30	86.80 -92
Viitala	Matti	FIN	26 Mar 66	190/78	HJ	2.24i	2.25 -90
Viluckis	Benjaminas	LIT	20 Mar 61	187/120	HT	76.26	82.24 -86
Vincent	Joël	FRA	19 Jan 69	192/79	HJ	2.26	2.29 -92
Virastyuk	Roman	UKR	20 Apr 68	190/120	SP	19.48	20.04i -91, 20.03 -90
Viudès	Luc	FRA	31 Jan 56	192/130	SP	18.65	19.84 -86
Vizzoni	Nicola	ITA	4 Nov 73	193/114	HT	70.76	69.32 -92
Volgenau	Chris	USA	30 Mar 69	188/111	SP	19.54	18.61i, 18.58 -92
Volkmann	Jens	GER	31 May 67	187/71	3kSt	8:23.56	8:22.85 -88
* Voloshin	Leonid	RUS	30 Mar 66	180/74	TJ	17.65	17.75 -91
Vorobey	Oleg	BLS	24 Nov 70		HJ	2.25	2.20 -92
Vorobyov	Sergey	RUS	29 Jan 64	184/91	HT	73.50	77.08 -90
Vörös	Sándor	HUN	19 Oct 56	196/115	HT	71.32	77.80 -88
Vorster	Dries	RSA	25 Oct 62	185/79	400h	49.52	48.49A -90, 48.59 -91
Voss	Martin	DEN	5 Sep 67	188/76	PV	5.50	5.45 -91
* Voss	Torsten	GER	24 Mar 63	186/88	Dec	8074	8680 -87
Voyevodin	Aleksandr	KZK	4 Mar 70	179/64	50kW	4:04:44	
Vuychak	Konstantin	UKR	72		HT	71.84?	
Vykpish	Yuriy	UKR	30 Sep 66	200/113	DT	61.42	63.24 -92
Wachenbrunner	Rainer	GER	11 Jan 62	184/62	5k	13:31.52	13:38.16 -85
					10k	28:24.50	28:16.20 -92
Wacker	Florian	GER	27 Dec 72	185/75	PV	5.50	5.20 -92
Wagner	Alwin	GER	11 Aug 50	196/122	DT	58.72	67.80 -87
Wahlman	Marko	FIN	6 Apr 69	194/104	HT	72.80	70.08 -90
* Walder	Erick	USA	5 Nov 71	186/77	LJ	8.53	8.47, 8.58w -92
					TJ	16.86i, 16.67, 16.87w	16.88i -92
Walem	Ruddy	BEL	30 Jun 67		3k	7:51.07	7:54.79 -90
Walker	Colin	GBR	29 Oct 62	173/61	3kSt	8:33.45	8:25.15 -92
* Wallenlind	Niklas	SWE	21 Nov 68	185/75	400h	49.45	48.35 -92
Wållgren	Fredrik	SWE	1 Oct 70		400h	50.45	50.67 -92
Wallstab	Thomas	GER	29 Jan 68	178/64	50kW	3:59:59	4:07:28 -91
Walton	Tony	USA	3 Jun 69	172/66	200	20.78A	
					LJ	8.16	8.08 -91
Wang Jun		CHN	27 Dec 72		20kW	1:22:51	1:23:39.5t -92
Wang Libin		CHN	Mar 74		20kW	1:23:04	1:21:21.3t -92
* Washington	Anthony	USA	16 Jan 66	186/109	DT	66.86	67.88 -92
Watanabe	Yasuyuki	JPN	8 Jun 73	175/58	10k	28:17.26	28:35.8 -91
Watson	Wayne	JAM	26 Mar 65	175/66	100	10.28, 10.24w	10.30 -90, 10.0w -89
* Watts	Quincy	USA	19 Jun 70	190/88	400	44.13A, 44.24	43.50 -92
Weckström	Ari	FIN	23 Oct 67	182/72	JT	76.24	71.04 -90
Weil	Gert	CHL	3 Jan 60	197/120	SP	20.04	20.90 -86
Weir	Robert	GBR	4 Feb 61	187/115	DT	61.30	62.50 -84
* Weis	Heinz	GER	14 Jul 63	193/110	HT	75.56.	82.84 -89
Weise	Ralf	GER	15 Sep 69	182/69	50kW	4:04:01	

Name		Nat	Born	Ht/Wt	Event	1993 Mark	Pre-1993 Best
* Wellman	Brian	BER	8 Sep 67	175/73	TJ	17.27i, 17.14	17.25 -92, 17.41w -91
Wennberg	Henrik	SWE	11 Mar 66	192/122	DT	60.16	58.88 -89
* Wennlund	Dag	SWE	9 Oct 63	188/97	JT	82.58	82.64S -87, 85.52R -91
West	Greg	USA	19 May 67	183/73	PV	5.72	5.65 -91
White	Kevin	USA	16 Aug 74	188/77	110h	13.81, 13.75w	-0-
Whiteley	Greg	USA	6 Jan 67	184/69	Mile	3:57.75	3:56.01 -91
					5k	13:24.55	13:37.53 -88
Widén	Peter	SWE	2 Jul 67	183/74	PV	5.70	5.75 -91
Widmer	Kevin	SUI	23 Sep 70		200	20.72	20.94 -92
Wilcox	Chris	USA	6 Jan 68	183/84	Dec	7617w	8032 -92
Wiley	Kevin	USA	73	175/77	LJ	7.94w	7.49 -92
Willard	Garth	USA	7 Jun 69	186/86	PV	5.50	5.45 -92
Williams	Elmer	PUR	8 Oct 64	180/68	LJ	7.96A	8.19A -89, 8.05 -92
Williams	Freddie	CAN	24 Feb 62	170/62	800	1:45.13	1:45.83 -91
Williams	Jeff	USA	31 Dec 64	183/68	100	10.23	10.21, 10.16w -91
					200	20.47	20.27, 20.25Aw -92
Williams	Tim	USA	27 May 63	186/79	200	20.41	20.30 -92
* Williams	Todd	USA	7 Mar 69	178/66	3k	7:47.69	7:54.47 -92
					5k	13:20.13	13:36.99 -92
					10k	27:40.37	28:05.9 -92
Williams	Wendell	TRI	19 Oct 68	170/75	LJ	7.99	7.89 -91
Willinski	Ralph	GER	20 Sep 67	187/98	JT	77.22	78.42 -92
Winston	Otis	USA	7 Nov 72	193/75	HJ	2.25	2.13 -92
Winston	Terry	USA	11 Jan 72	190/77	110h	13.78	13.82, 13.81w -92
Winter	Peter	AUS	17 Jan 71		Dec	7600	6553 -92
Wirtz	John	USA	31 May 69	190/111	DT	59.02	56.70 -91
Witek	Miroslaw	POL	24 Apr 67	183/91	JT	77.60	79.12 -88
Wojcik	Dariusz	AUS	29 Sep 59		50kW	4:01:46	3:58:30 -92
Wojcik	Piotr	POL	7 Feb 65	196/81	110h	13.64, 13.4	13.47 -91
Wolashe	Belaye	ETH	3 May 69		Mar	2:10:57	2:14:45 -92
Wood	Doug	CAN	30 Jan 66	182/78	PV	5.55	5.65i -92, 5.61 -91
Woodberry	Gerry	USA	23 Oct 69	168/68	100	10.15	10.24 -91
					200	20.69, 20.64w	21.03 -92
* Worku	Bikila	ETH	70	176/60	3k	7:47.6u+	7:55.2u -92
					5k	13:06.64	13:23.52 -92
Wright	Cameron	USA	7 Nov 72	193/77	HJ	2.27	2.20 -92
Wright	Chris	BAH	8 Aug 71		LJ	7.95w	
Wylie	Jeff	USA	28 Dec 68	193/75	HJ	2.26	2.24 -89
Xia Xianghai		CHN	17 Aug 71		100	10.26	10.36 -91
Xu Bin		CHN	4 Aug 70		LJ	8.07	8.19 -92
Xu Congxian		CHN	4 Dec 72		50kW	4:00:07	
Xu Dongwen		CHN	23 Dec 68		TJ	16.94	16.32 -92
Xu Wenquan		CHN	23 Jan 69		50kW	4:05:29	3:58:03 -92
Xu Xiaodong		CHN	12 Dec 73		HJ	2.26	2.23 -92
Yagovdik	Valeriy	BLS	16 Sep 63		DT	62.24	61.78 -92
Yamazaki	Kazuhiro	JPN	10 May 71	174/65	400h	49.08	49.74 -92
Yamshchikov	Nikolay	UKR	19 May 61	176/70	50kW	4:05:50	4:03:50 -89
Yanchevskiy	Igor	RUS	11 Mar 68	188/77	PV	5.60i, 5.50	5.70 -92
Yang Hongtao		CHN	Aug 70		JT	76.46 *	75.14 -91
Yang Xianjun		CHN	2 Nov 72		400h	49.59	51.20 -91
Yang Xu		CHN	27 Jun 70	188/62	HJ	2.31	2.30 -91
Yarets	Valeriy	BLS	27 Mar 56		50kW	4:03:25	3:46:28 -85
Yaryshkin	Vladimir	RUS	28 Feb 63		SP	19.87	20.80 -86
Yasinovchuk	Aleksandr	UKR	4 Aug 66	190/107	DT	59.34	
* Yates	Matthew	GBR	4 Feb 69	190/70	800	1:46.00	1:45.05 -92
					1500	3:35.04	3:34.00 -91
					Mile	3:52.75	3:57.33, 3:54.78i -92
					3k	7:50.82i	
Yawa	Xolile	RSA	29 Sep 62	169/50	10k	28:26.48	27:57.8 -89
					Mar	2:10:57	-0-
Ye Hu		CHN	15 Apr 73	174/62	100	10.29	10.45 -92
Yego	Gideon	KEN	6 May 60	178/65	400h	49.5A	48.7A -88, 49.09 -91
* Yegorov	Grigoriy	KZK	12 Jan 67	184/75	PV	5.90i, 5.90	5.90i, 5.87 -90
Yeliseyev	Yuriy	RUS	27 May 75		PV	5.55	5.20 -92
* Yemelin	Aleksey	RUS	16 Oct 68	203/90	HJ	2.30	2.34i, 2.34 -90
Yesipchuk	Sergey	UKR	1 Oct 67	191/78	PV	5.50i	5.55 -90
Yevdokimov	Valeriy	RUS	73		HT	73.52	72.00 -92

Name		Nat	Born	Ht/Wt	Event	1993 Mark	Pre-1993 Best
Yevgenyev	Andrey	RUS	17 Feb 73	182/100	HT	75.64	73.26 -92
Yevsyukov	Viktor	KZK	6 Oct 56	190/100	JT	78.60	85.16 -87
Yoshida	Takahisa	JPN	17 Feb 70	180/67	HJ	2.31	2.28 -90
Young	Bernard	BAH	29 Aug 66	185/82	100	10.28	
					200	20.72	
* Young	Kevin	USA	16 Sep 66	193/82	400	46.03	45.11 -92
					400h	47.18	46.78 -92
Yu Wenge ¶		CHN	18 Feb 66		DT	61.78	65.02 -92
Yudakov	Timur	RUS	12 Jul 66		110h	13.82, 13.5	13.68 -92
Zaboronok	Vladimir	BLS	11 Nov 68		HJ	2.28	2.25 -92
Zadoinov	Vadim	MOL	24 May 69	187/74	400h	49.54	48.61 -90
Záhoncík	Ján	SVK	23 Apr 65	174/63	20kW	1:22:43t	1:21:41 -92
Zaitsev	Viktor	UZB	6 Jun 66	198/92	JT	78.88	87.20 -92
Zalewski	Marek	POL	27 Jul 70	174/72	100	10.12w	10.36 -92
Zaliauskas	Alex	CAN	20 Apr 71	193/73	HJ	2.30	2.31 -91
Zaozerskiy	Sergey	RUS	27 Jan 64	185/73	LJ	7.96	8.22 -88
Zelaya	Rodrigo	CHI	12 Jun 68	183/82	JT	76.20	73.94 -91
* Zelezny	Jan	TCH	16 Jun 66	184/80	JT	95.66	94.74 -92
Zellner	Torrance	USA	6 Jan 70	187/75	400h	48.97	49.10 -92
Zemlyanskiy	Viktor	RUS	10 Feb 63	183/68	800	1:46.67	1:44.93 -85
Zerbini	Luciano	ITA	12 Feb 60	194/110	SP	20.27 *	20.54 -92
					DT	64.26 *	64.00 -84
Zhai Wanbo		CHN	13 Feb 67	172/63	20kW	1:23:12	1:22:37.5t -91
					50kW	4:01:51	3:47:23 -91
Zhang Cunbiao		CHN	11 Feb 69		DT	62.06	59.70 -92
Zhang Fukui		CHN	27 Jan 70	170/51	Mar	2:11:10	-0-
Zhang Jinglong		CHN	22 Nov 61		DT	58.86	61.72 -90
Zhang Jun		CHN	Jan 74		TJ	16.61	
Zhang Lianbiao		CHN	25 Jan 69	193/110	JT	82.76	82.60 -91
Zhang Min		CHN	6 Dec 79		JT	76,88	77.08 -91
Zhao Bingchun		CHN	70		Dec	7641	7332 -91
Zhao Cunlin		CHN	20 May 65	185/80	400	45.85	45.8 -89, 46.43 -87
Zhao Yongsheng		CHN	Mar 71		20kW	1:22:42	1:22:29.6t -91
					50kW	4:02:41	4:02:23 -92
Zharkov	Aleksandr	RUS	16 Apr 71	188/77	LJ	8.02	8.10 -92
Zharov	Innokentiy	RUS	23 Nov 68	180/73	400	45.88	?
Zhdanovich	Aleksandr	BLS	15 Nov 69	184/80	Dec	7912	8035 -92
Zhelonkin	Aleksey	RUS	1 Jan 66	170/53	Mar	2:10:44	2:15:08 -92
Zheng Jinsuo		CHN	30 Jun 70	188/84	110h	13.74	13.80 -92
Zhou Ming		CHN	7 Jan 70	180/65	LJ	7.95i	8.12 -92
Zhou Qi		CHN	8 Jun 67		TJ	16.67	16.24 -89
Zhou Yongsheng		CHN	15 Oct 72		20kW	1:21:22	1:20:50.0t -92
					50kW	3:58:07	
Zhou Zhaowen		CHN	16 May 67		20kW	1:22:01	1:22:40.2t -91
Zhou Zhongge		CHN	15 Feb 67	189/75	HJ	2.28	2.33 -90
Zhukov	Aleksandr	MOL	25 Jan 65	185/67	PV	5.55i	5.70 -87
Zhukovskiy	Oleg	BLS	15 Feb 70	196/76	HJ	2.31	2.23i -92
Zhuravlov	Aleksandr	UKR	22 Mar 74		HJ	2.24	2.15 -92
* Zinchenko	Vladimir	UKR	25 Jul 59	192/115	DT	65.28	68.88 -88
Zintl	Bernhard	GER	16 Jun 65	185/79	PV	5.50i	5.65 -89
Zirignon	Jean-Olivier	CIV	27 Apr 71	193/90	100	10.24	10.20 -91
Zirko	Andey	BLS	1 Jul 72		TJ	16.83	16.25 -92
Zisimides	Yiannis	CYP	17 Aug 67		100	10.14w	
* Zmelík	Robert	TCH	18 Apr 69	185/79	Dec	8188	8627 -92
Zoric	Stevan	YUG	25 May 71	199/75	HJ	2.30	2.31i 91, 2.28 -92
Zorko	Branko	CRO	1 Jul 67	180/73	1500	3:35.09	3:36.88 -92
					Mile	3:57.01	
* Zou Sixin		CHN	8 May 67	178/76	TJ	17.26	17.31 -90
Zschunke	Oliver	GER	29 Apr 70		JT	75.66	73.88 -92
Zuber	Matt	USA	30 Sep 66	185/86	Dec	7686	7553 -89
Zubok	Yuriy	BLS	7 Mar 69		20kW	1:23:02	1:24:42 -91

WOMEN'S INDEX 1993

** athletes so marked are included in the Biographies section.*

Name		Nat	Born	Ht/Wt	Event	1993 Mark	Pre-1993 Best
Abdul Salam	Rabia	MAS	5 Nov 73	162/48	400	52.56	54.27 -92
* Abe	Tomoe	JPN	13 Aug 71	150/38	10k	32:55.78	33:01.68 -92
					Mar	2:26:27	
Abramova	Svetlana	RUS	27 Oct 70		PV	3.90	3.50 -92
Acuff	Amy	USA	14 Jul 75	180/59	HJ	1.93	1.90 -92
Adams	Christine	GER	28 Feb 74		PV	3.80	3.70 -92
Adere	Birhane	ETH	73	175/49	10k	32:48.52	34:13.3 -92
Adriano	Elisangela	BRA	27 Jul 72	180/92	SP	17.11	17.36 -92
Afanasyeva	Yelena	RUS	11 Mar 67	164/51	800	1:58.88	1:57.77 -88
					1000	2:37.2	2:39.04 -91
Afanasyeva	Yelena	RUS	23 Feb 66	174/69	Hep	6179	6355 -92
Agletdinova	Ravilya	BLS	10 Feb 60	167/57	1500	4:08.95	3:58.48 -85
Agyepong	Jackie	GBR	5 Jan 69	172/63	100h	13.03,13.01w	13.17 -90,13.11w -92
Agyepong (Berkeley)	Mary	GBR	31 Oct 65	176/65	TJ	13.42i	13.56 -92
Aigner	Manuela	GER	26 Mar 73	183/63	HJ	1.90i, 1.88	1.93 -92
Akinremi	Omolade	NGR	13 Sep 74	158/60	400	52.24	52.76 -91
					400h	57.12	56.84 -92
Akinremi	Omotayo	NGR	13 Sep 74	158/60	400	52.43	52.53 -92
					400h	56.86	56.83, 56.4 -91
Akpan $	Ime	NGR	27 Apr 72	165/50	100h	13.11, 13.09w	13.03 -92,12.9w -90
Akraka	Maria	SWE	7 Jul 66	170/55	800	2:00.72	2:00.50 -91
					1500	4:10.28	4:08.92, 4:07.74i -92
					1M	4:32.04	
Aladefa	Taiwo	NGR	19 Dec 71	160/	100	11.39w	11.61 -92
					100h	13.37, 13.19w	13.34 -92
* Alafrantti	Päivi	FIN	8 May 64	178/82	JT	64.98	67.68 -90
Aldecoa	Isabel	CUB	21 Jun 71		100h	13.36	13.82 -92
* Alekseyeva	Tatyana	RUS	7 Oct 63	170/56	400	50.49	50.74 -89
+ Alexandrova	Desislava	BUL	27 Oct 75	176/55	HJ	1.92	1.91 -92
Alföldi	Andrea	HUN	22 Sep 64	164/63	5kW	22:15.48i	21:36.17 -92
					10kW	45:09	43:41 -92
Alfridi	Erika	ITA	22 Feb 68	168/51	5kW	22:16	24:40.61 -92
					10kW	46:11.7	44:34 -89
Alistratyenko	Yelena	UKR	15 Jan 71	167/58	100h	13.27	13.22 -92
Alisyevich	Tatyana	BLS	22 Jan 69		Hep	6073	
Alizadeh	Manuela	GER	29 Jan 63	172/78	JT	57.64	65.34 -88
* Allen	Liliana	CUB	24 May 70	170/62	100	11.19	11.10 -92
					200	23.12, 22.90w	22.98 -92
							22.97w -88, 22.7w -89
Alonso	Ana Isabel	ESP	16 Aug 63	154/44	10k	32:56.06	32:28.7 -88
					Mar	2:31:47dh	2:35:34 -92
Alonso	Miriam	ESP	6 Jun 70	164/54	400h	57.15	56.87 -92
Althouse	Valeyta	USA	7 Jan 74	175/102	SP	16.71	15.04 -92
Alvárez	Maria Caridad	CUB	30 Aug 75	165/62	JT	57.00	56.84 -92
Amaral	Cleide	BRA	17 Jul 67	165/68	100	11.39	11.59 -92
Amaral	Elsa	POR	31 May 66	168/59	800	2:02.51i	2:01.21 -90
Ambraziene	Anna	LIT	12 Apr 55	173/62	400h	57.35, 57.3	54.02 -83
Ampleyeva	Natalya	BLS	25 Sep 72		DT	57.20	57.40 -92
* Anders' - Gummelt	Beate	GER	4 Feb 68	169/54	5kW	20:55.75	20:07.52 -90
					10kW	43:09	42:11.5 -92
Andersen	Bettina Romer	DEN	18 Feb 65	167/52	1500	4:09.75	4:15.10 -92
Anderson	Andrea	USA	17 Sep 77		200	23.1w	
Anderson	Damaris	CUB	24 Oct 74		100h	13.38A	13.42 -92
Anderson	Keturah	CAN	9 Jan 68	163/62	100h	13.23	13.09 -92
Andrei' (Ionescu)	Maria	ROM	24 Nov 67	166/58	LJ	6.66i	6.58 -92
Andrés	Amaia	ESP	26 Jun 66	165/52	800	2:02.77	2:02.33 -92
Andrews	Susan	AUS	26 Jan 71	173/58	400	52.48	52.16 -92
Angelova	Atanaska	BUL	21 Sep 72	176/75	DT	59.68	55.08 -91
Antonova	Yelena	UKR	16 Jun 72	180/80	DT	58.34	61.94 -92
Antonyuk	Marina	RUS	12 May 62	182/91	SP	18.13i, 18.07	20.60 -86
Apetre	Stela	ROM	25 Feb 72		3k	9:00.65	9:10.40 -92

Name		Nat	Born	Ht/Wt	Event	1993 Mark	Pre-1993 Best
* Appell	Olga	MEX	2 Aug 63	173/59	10k	32:32.51	32:09.6 -92
					HMar	68:34	
					Mar	2:28:56	2:30:22 -92
Arakhelashvili	Nato	RUS	70		10kW	45:53	49:47 -91
Araki	Kumi	JPN	11 Oct 65	153/40	5k	15:38.83	15:37.72 -90
					10k	32:55.54	32:04.60 -92
Arnst	Nina	RUS	69		400	52.49	52.40 -92
Aro	Helle	FIN	9 Dec 60	175/66	Hep	6106	6030 -92
+ Arshintseva	Yelena	RUS	5 Apr 71	163/58	5kW	21:36	21:18.39 -92
					10kW	42:03	42:52 -92
Artynyuk	Maria	RUS	5 Mar 66	175/58	10kW	45:23	46:29 -92
Asahina	Miyoko	JPN	24 Sep 69	171/52	HMar	70:15	70:27 -92
					Mar	2:30:58	2:30:48 -92
Asai	Eriko	JPN	20 Oct 59	150/40	5k	15:41.80	15:45.77 -92
					10k	32:22.18	32:32.66 -92
					HMar	71:33	70:51 -92
					Mar	2:28:22	2:31:41 -92
* Asari	Junko	JPN	22 Sep 69	164/44	Mar	2:26:26	2:28:57 -92
* Astafei	Alina	ROM	7 Jun 69	181/60	HJ	2.00i, 2.00	2.00 -88
Atroshchenko	Anzhela	BLS	14 Oct 70	178/68	LJ	6.72	6.45i -92, 6.34 -90
					Hep	6339	6251 -92
Augee	Esther	GBR	1 Jan 64		HT	56.76	47.98 -92
Augee	Myrtle	GBR	4 Feb 65	173/86	SP	17.68	19.03 -90
Auzeil	Nadine	FRA	19 Aug 64	176/60	JT	60.70	63.30 -88
Avigni	Antonella	ITA	19 Jan 68	171/56	TJ	13.41	12.38 -90
Avila	Andrea	ARG	4 Apr 70	171/55	LJ	6.61	6.32 -92
					TJ	13.91A	13.12 -92
Azarashvili	Maya	GEO	6 Apr 64	170/60	100	11.41	11.08, 10.9 -88
					200	23.06	22.24 -88
* Azyabina	Marina	RUS	15 Jun 63	172/62	100h	12.47, 12.3	12.76 -92, 12.6 -90
* Babakova	Inga	UKR	27 Jun 67	180/57	HJ	2.00i, 1.96	2.02 -91
Babakova	Irina	UKR	14 Sep 65	172/60	TJ	13.70i, 13.53, 13.85w	13.92 -90
Babic	Silvija	CRO	12 Dec 68	171/52	LJ	6.45w	6.68 -90
Bai	Xiaoyun	CHN	15 Jun 73		400	52.07	53.33 -91
Baker	Alison	CAN	6 Aug 64	172/62	5kW	22:15.05	22:17.0 -92
Baker	Samantha	GBR	14 Apr 72	174/60	100h	13.32	13.47, 13.41w -91
Bakogianni	Niki	GRE	9 Jun 68	170/58	HJ	1.90	1.94 -92
Bakoulis' (Bloch)	Gordon	USA	14 Feb 61		Mar	2:34:03	2:33:01 -89
Balanten	Noelvis	CUB	24 Jun 72		SP	17.54	16.98 -92
* Balck	Heike	GER	19 Aug 70	178/57	HJ	1.95	2.01 -89
Baltabayeva' (Ortina)	Yelena	KZK	5 Nov 62		SP	17.28	19.26 -96
Bao	Dongying	CHN	13 Apr 73	178/85	DT	62.64	61.04 -92
Baranova	Yuliya	UKR	12 Aug 72	180/58	TJ	13.40	
Baranovskaya	Galina	BLS	18 Jun 66		LJ	6.48	6.90i, 6.62 -91
Barbu' (Andreescu)	Adriana	ROM	17 Jan 61	161/53	Mar	2:34:38	2:36:21 -87
Barby	Dörthe	GER	21 Jun 73	174/68	JT	61.56	56.70 -92
Barnes	Lacy	USA	23 Dec 64	168/75	DT	57.76	62.90 -89
Barócsi	Helena	HUN	9 Jul 66	162/48	HMar	70:59	70:01 -92
Barreiro	Angeles	ESP	26 Jul 63	170/75	DT	56.96	59.22 -92
Barrett	Christy	USA	24 Aug 69	173/80	SP	16.46	17.61 -92
* Barsosio	Sally	KEN	21 Mar 78	165/46	3k	8:59.70	9:17.13 -92
					10k	31:15.38	32:41.76 -92
Bartoszek	Danuta	CAN	19 Aug 61	168/52	Mar	2:34:33	2:34:41 -92
Barylla	Angela	GER	6 Jan 71	177/68	TJ	13.50	
Bastos	Marina	POR	7 Jul 71	165/50	1500	4:08.92	4:19.2 -90
* Batten	Kim	USA	29 Mar 69	170/57	400h	53.84	53.98 -91
* Baumann' (Rocheleau)	Julie	SUI	17 Jun 64	165/56	100h	12.99	12.76 -91
Baumert' (Arens)	Andrea	GER	5 May 67	182/66	HJ	1.93i, 1.92	1.98 -89
* Beclea	Violeta	ROM	26 Mar 65	166/50	800	1:59.13	1:58.7 -86
					1500	3:59.35	4:02.21 -91
					1M	4:21.69	4:27.29 -90
Beggerow	Antje	GER	10 Dec 73	169/54	1500	4:11.98	4:20.91 -92

Name		Nat	Born	Ht/Wt	Event	1993 Mark	Pre-1993 Best
Bègue	Martine	FRA	22 Dec 69	170/61	JT	64.46	57.78 -89
Belova	Irina ¶	RUS	27 Mar 68	175/62	LJ	6.66#, 6.44i	6.82 -92
Benesová	Hana	TCH	19 Apr 75	168/52	100	11.45	11.80 -92
* Berezhnaya	Larisa	UKR	28 Feb 61	178/66	LJ	6.99	7.24 -91
Bergmann	Mette	NOR	9 Nov 62	174/80	DT	61.80	63.12 -89
Betekhtina	Natalya	RUS	8 Sep 61		1000	2:36.96	
					1500	4:07.03	4:06.35 -88
Beurskens	Carla	HOL	10 Feb 52	165/46	Mar	2:30:10	2:26:34 -87
* Bevilacqua	Antonella	ITA	15 Oct 71	171/54	HJ	1.95i, 1.94	1.95 -92
Bévis	Marie-Louise	FRA	12 Oct 72	170/58	400	52.14	52.88 -92
Bicet	Sonia	CUB	1 Apr 71	171/69	JT	59.52	58.38 -92
Bidouane	Nezha	MAR	18 Sep 69	174/65	400h	56.09	55.08 -92
Bieber	Sabine	AUT	4 Nov 70	185/91	DT	57.08	54.60 -92
Biktagirova	Madina	BLS	20 Sep 64	158/50	Mar	2:31:32	2:26:23 -92
* Bilac	Britta	SLO	4 Dec 68	181/61	HJ	1.97i, 1.94	1.94i -90, 1.94 -92
* Biryukova'	Anna	RUS	27 Sep 67	174/60	LJ	6.73	6.89 -90
(Derevyankina)					TJ	15.09	13.30i -89
Bîrzu	Lenuta	ROM	20 Feb 69		TJ	13.32	13.16 -92
Bitzner	Blandine	FRA	1 Dec 65	165/50	1500	4:07.17	4:31.39 -92
Blair	Kelly	USA	24 Nov 70	181/62	Hep	6038	5485w -92
Blazhevica	Jelena	LAT	11 May 70	170/54	LJ	6.44	6.39 -90
					TJ	13.57	- 0 -
* Blokhina'	Tatyana	RUS	12 Mar 70	183/72	HJ	1.91	1.95 -92
(Sidorova)					Hep	6703	6484 -92
Blunt	Erin	USA	21 Apr 74	170/57	400h	57.68	
Blythe	Gabrielle	AUS	9 Mar 69	173/58	5kW	21:47.6mx,21:55.52	22:18.2 -92
					10kW	44:12.0, 43:28	44:21 -92
Bodrova	Nadezhda	UKR	13 Jul 61	170/58	100h	12.89	12.81 -91, 12.7 -90
* Boegman	Nicole	AUS	5 Mar 67	174/65	LJ	6.75A,6.72, 6.81Aw	6.87 -88
					TJ	13.27	
Bogoma	Svetlana	UKR	16 Jul 74	174/53	HJ	1.88	
Bogoslovskaya'	Olga	RUS	20 May 64	166/54	100	11.31	11.07 -92, 10.96w -89
(Naumkina)					200	23.35	
Boit	Cristina	ROM	14 May 68	170/80	DT	61.96	64.58 -88
(Sandru)							
Bolkun	Yelena	UKR	26 Feb 67	173/63	Hep	5664	6151 -91
Bolm	Kirsten	GER	4 Mar 75	181/69	LJ	6.52	6.13 -92
Bolshova	Olga	MOL	16 Jun 68	174/60	HJ	1.97	1.94 -92
Bond-Mills	Catherine	CAN	20 Sep 67	180/69	Hep	6058	5972 -92
Bondarenko	Olga	RUS	2 Jun 60	155/41	3k	8:50.31	8:33.99 -86
					10k	32:02.44	30:57.21 -86
Bonne	Idalmis	CUB	2 Feb 71	168/62	200	23.26, 23.22Aw	23.57 -92
					400	52.3	53.51 -92
Borda	Sylvie	FRA	4 Sep 66	172/63	TJ	13.62i, 13.44	13.33 -91, 13.63w -92
Borisova	Lyubov	RUS	6 Jan 66		Hep	5882	5654 -88
* Borisova	Lyudmila	RUS	8 Mar 66	172/57	800	2:02.64	2:01.30 -88
					3k	8:40.78	8:49.6 -91
Bormann	Tanja	GER	11 Apr 70	184/63	13.88	13.30 -92	
Born	Kathrin	GER	4 Dec 70	172/61	5kW	21:49.33	21:20.27 -91
					10kW	44:43	44:05 -90
Botticelli	Silvia	ITA	14 Mar 68	162/48	3k	9:00.32	9:25.73 -92
					5k	15:31.81	16:03.17 -92
* Boulmerka	Hassiba	ALG	10 Jul 68	158/49	1000	2:35.92	2:39.64 -90
					1500	4:04.29	3:55.30 -92
					1M	4:28.06	4:20.79 -91
					3k	8:56.16	
Bowen	Stacey	CAN	17 Dec 69	169/51	200	23.16	23.56 -92, 23.17w -91
* Bowles	Dawn	USA	12 Nov 68	168/52	100h	12.84, 12.74w	12.82, 12.70w -91
Boyko	Olga	UKR	6 Jul 75	168/55	TJ	13.48	12.65 -92
Boyko	Viktoria	UKR	20 Jan 74	180/80	DT	58.20	53.82 -92
Bozhanova	Sofia	BUL	4 Oct 67	172/52	TJ	13.66	14.08 -91
Braag	Bettina	GER	15 Nov 65	176/66	Hep	6083	5964 -90
Bradburn	Angie	USA	4 Sep 68	178/61	HJ	1.94i, 1.94	1.96i -92, 1.93 -91
Braddock	Crystal	USA	13 Dec 70	170/57	100	11.34w	11.52 -92
					200	23.31	23.83 -92
Bran	Daniela	ROM	13 Mar 68	170/52	1500	4:09.25	4:08.2 -90

Name		Nat	Born	Ht/Wt	Event	1993 Mark	Pre-1993 Best
* Braun	Sabine	GER	19 Jun 65	174/66	100h	13.24	13.02 -92
					HJ	1.93	1.94 -92
					LJ	6.54	6.73 -85
					Hep	6797	6985 -92
Brick	Theresa	CAN	4 May 65	165/72	DT	58.40	53.26 -92
Brooks	Pam	USA	15 Jan 72	175/59	400h	57.39	57.57 -91
Broughton	JulieAnne	USA	27 Dec 70	180/64	HJ	1.92	1.94 -90
Brown	Alice	USA	20 Sep 60	158/59	100	11.39	10.92 -88
Brown	Rica	USA	3 Apr 69	183/97	SP	17.40	16.51 -92
Brown	Wendy	USA	28 Jan 66	180/72	TJ	13.27, 13.45w	13.82 -88
* Bruhns	Birte	GER	4 Nov 70	171/60	800	1:59.66	1:59.17 -88
* Brunet	Roberta	ITA	20 May 65	168/55	1500	4:10.10	4:08.92 -88
					3k	8:47.92	8:42.64 -91
					5k	15:16.93	15:53.30 -92
Brzezinska	Anna	POL	9 Jan 71	171/58	800	2:01.67	2:02.53 -92
					1500	4:07.15	4:08.35 -92
					1M	4:23.08	- 0 -
					2k	5:44.77	
					3k	8:55.52	9:14.16 -92
Budilovskaya	Zhanna	UKR	6 Apr 72	175/59	Hep	5936	5885 -90
* Buford	Tonja	USA	13 Dec 70	176/62	200	23.16	23.42 -92
					100h	13.17, 13.1	13.07, 12.94w -92
					400h	54.38	54.75 -92
Bugarini	Roberta	ITA	19 Sep 69	178/60	HJ	1.90	1.86 -89
Buia	Aura	ROM	16 Feb 70	161/52	Mar	2:31:48	2:33:01 -92
Bukovec	Brigita	SLO	21 May 70	168/57	100h	12.98, 12.89w	13.12, 13.02w -92
Buksniene'	Sada	LIT	22 Jun 67	173/67	5kW	22:32	20.53 -89
(Eidikyte)					10kW	45:41	44:20 -87
Bunge	Beth	USA	30 Jan 64	178/81	SP	16.49	16.40i -92, 15.45 -90?
* Buraga	Svetlana	BLS	4 Sep 65	168/56	100h	12.95	12.86, 12.8 -88
					LJ	6.58	6.79i, 6.63 -87
					Hep	6635	6597 -88
* Burangulova	Ramilya	RUS	11 Jul 61	154/50	Mar	2:28:03	2:28:12 -92
Burkanova	Olga	RUS	29 Sep 69	177/61	800	2:02.77	2:00.28 -92
* Burova	Olga	RUS	17 Sep 63	184/85	DT	67.40	68.38 -92
Cadusch	Sieglinde	SUI	28 Aug 67	178/58	HJ	1.91i	1.90 -92
Cai	Weiyan	CHN	25 Oct 73		PV	3.85	4.00 -92
Caizalitin	Janeth	ECU	21 Apr 74	165/49	800	2:01.4	2:11.3 -92
* Campbell	Juliet	JAM	17 May 70	176/62	100	11.15w	11.49, 11.30w -90
					200	22.80, 22.66w	23.06 -92
					400	50.11	51.11 -92
Campbell	Rebecca	AUS	23 Jan 76		400h	57.06	59.93 -92
Campbell	Shanequa	USA	1 Sep 72	163/52	400	51.77	54.63 -90
Cano	Emilia	ESP	4 Mar 68	163/54	10kW	46:05	45:15 -92
Cao	Chunying	CHN	Feb 73		400	52.28	53.53 -91
* Cao	Qi	CHN	Jan 74		DT	66.08	61.56 -92
* Capriotti	Antonella	ITA	4 Feb 62	162/55	LJ	6.72i, 6.70	6.69 -89, 6.79w -92
					TJ	14.18	13.66 -92
Carabali	Norfalia	COL	21 Jan 67	163/51	400h	51.17	51.06 -92
Cardeñas	Regla	CUB	21 Jan 75	184/68	Hep	5840	5602 -92
Carlier	Cécile	FRA	28 Oct 68	175/58	HJ	1.88	1.86 -92
Carlsson	Åsa	SWE	19 Dec 72	169/62	400h	57.82	57.70 -92
Carrillo	Laiza	CUB	27 Nov 68	170/63	TJ	13.77	
Carrozza	Sheila	USA	5 Feb 63	163/46	TJ	8:55.03	9:14.47 -92
Carson	Kim	USA	12 Mar 74	170/56	100h	13.29	14.01 -92
* Carter	Kym	USA	12 Mar 64	188/77	HJ	1.88	1.89 -82
					Hep	6357	6256 -92
Carutasu	Nicoleta	ROM	14 Feb 64	173/64	400h	54.94	55.57 -92
Caster	Nadine	FRA	15 Oct 65	174/64	LJ	6.44	6.47 -92
Catuna	Anuta	ROM	1 Oct 68	152/48	1500	4:12.86u	
					10k	32:18.40	32:32.66 -92
					HMar	69:22	70:25 -92
Cepero	Olga	CUB	4 May 75		TJ	13.68	13.18, 13.51 -92
* Chalmers	Angela	CAN	6 Sep 63	172/56	1500	4:07.95	4:02.11 -92
Chan	Sau Ying	HKG	30 Aug 70	170/59	100h	13.27	13.82, 13.52w -91
Chang	Xinhong	CHN	Mar 74		DT	61.24	
Chavez	Maricela	MEX	24 Sep 62	162/50	5kW	22:03	22:28.7 -92
					10kW	44:10	45:03 -91

Name		Nat	Born	Ht/Wt	Event	1993 Mark	Pre-1993 Best
Chebykina	Tatyana	RUS	22 Nov 68		400	52.62	54.21 -92
Chen	Qin	CHN	Dec 71		400h	56.24	57.13 -91, 56.0 -92
Chen	Xiuying	CHN	13 Jan 73		10k	32:57.50	33:05.71 -92
					Mar	2:32:55	
Chen	Xuehui	CHN	Jul 69		800	1:58.48	2:05.9 -90
Chen	Yan	CHN	18 Apr 73		100	11.27	11.55 -91
* Chen	Yolanda	RUS	26 Jul 61	170/58	LJ	6.90i, 6.65	7.16 -88
					TJ	14.97	13.72 -92
Chen	Zhaojing	CHN	5 Apr 69	177/63	100	11.33	11.28 -92
					200	22.56	22.60 -92
Cheng	Xianhong	CHN	Oct 68		DT	59.86	62.32 -92
Cheng	Xiaoyan	CHN			SP	18.00	
+ Chepngeno	Helen	KEN	2 Aug 67	167/55	1500	4:07.35	4:16.3 -92
					3k	8:44.04	9:20.2 -92
					5k	15:21.98	
Chernova	Lada	RUS	70		JT	57.02	58.02 -91
Chernyshova	Yelizaveta	RUS	25 Jan 58	168/60	100h	13.13, 13.1,12.9i	12.68 -89
Cheromei	Lydia	KEN	11 May 77	162/47	10k	32:54.55	31:41.09 -92
Chesire	Linah	KEN	1 Mar 73	157/45	1500	4:11.5	4:16.2 -90
Chicherova	Yelena	RUS	9 Aug 58	172/58	LJ	6.62i	6.94 -84
Chistiakova	Regina	LIT	7 Nov 61	166/49	1500	4:09.7	4:05.96 -88
					3k	8:55.4	8:39.25 -86
* Chistyakova	Galina	RUS	26 Jul 62	169/53	TJ	14.40	14.62 -92
Chon	Gum-Suk	PRK	1 Jan 67	165/58	Mar	2:32:33	2:30:31 -89
Christiansen	Nina	DEN	7 Jun 64	159/45	3k	8:58.09	9:13.7 -92
Churbanova	Olga	RUS	16 Jul 64	169/51	800	2:01.47	
					1500	4:10.71	4:15.08 -91
					3k	8:53.63	8:58.03 -92
Chuvashova	Vera	RUS	7 Oct 59	164/58	1500	4:05.98	4:05.73 -90
					3k	8:53.50	8:58.8 -92
Chzhao	Larisa	RUS	4 Feb 72		800	2:01.33	
Cimpan	Norica	ROM	22 Mar 72	164/53	5kW	22:37.30	
					10kW	46:03.14, 45:42	46:05 -92
Cinélu	Cecile	FRA	4 Jun 70	165/53	100h	12.88	12.86, 12.82w -92
Ciobanu	Jana	ROM	12 Nov 68	176/102	SP	19.12i, 18.81	19.23 -88
Ciric	Suzana	YUG	12 Jul 69	164/47	10k	32:26.68	32:28.09 -91
					Mar	2:33:26	2:33:58 -92
Clack	Stacey	USA	6 Feb 71	175/65	100	11.40	11.60 -90, 11.48w -92
Clague	Jennifer	GBR	6 Aug 73		10k	32:41.29	- 0 -
Clardy	Gwen	USA	73	162/53	100	11.44w	
Clarinval	Cécile	BEL	16 Sep 68		400h	57.11	57.73 -92
* Clarius	Birgit	GER	18 Mar 65	176/65	Hep	6500	6.478 -92
* Clark	Joetta	USA	1 Aug 62	172/55	400	52.41	52.20 -92
					800	1:58.17	1:58.06 -92
					1000	2:37.51	2:37.9i -86, 2:39.13 -91
Cobb	Mary	USA	15 Jan 68	170/63	110h	13.37, 13.28w	13.05, 12.97w -91
Cole	Yvette	USA			200	23.39w	24.63 -89
					400	52.44	-
Colin	Maria	MEX	7 Mar 66	163/55	10kW	45:11	45:33 -86
Collins	Dana	USA	23 Jul 73	155/	100	11.30	11.73 -92
Collins	Michelle	USA	12 Feb 71	178/61	100	11.41w	11.36, 11.26w -92
					200	22.88, 22.87w,22.8w	22.80 -92
					400	51.59	-
Collonville	Marie	FRA	23 Nov 73	163/51	Hep	5638	5233w -92
Comadore	Countess	USA	27 Jan 67	165/56	400h	57.87	56.18 -92
Coman	Madalina	ROM	4 Mar 76	172/62	TJ	13.33	12.76 -92
* Cong	Yuzhen	CHN	22 Jan 63	175/90	SP	19.58	20.47 -88
Constantin	Mitica	ROM	18 Aug 62	174/56	800	2:00.41	1:57.87 -86
					1500	4:12.43i	4:03.04 -87
Cors	Tanja	GER	22 Apr 71		PV	3.93	3.83i, 3.72 -92
* Costa	Silvia	CUB	4 May 64	179/60	HJ	1.98	2.04 -89
Costescu	Denisa	ROM	26 Jan 75		3k	9:00.27	9:32.64 -92
* Costian	Daniela	AUS	30 Apr 65	181/87	SP	16.30	16.24 -91
					DT	66.02	73.84 -88
Couch	Sharon	USA	13 Sep 69	172/63	LJ	6.51, 6.62w	6.68 -92
Court	Clova	GBR	10 Feb 60	175/66	100h	13.26, 13.13w	13.28 -92
					Hep	5957	6022 -91

Name		Nat	Born	Ht/Wt	Event	1993 Mark	Pre-1993 Best
Covington	Sheryl	USA	3 Mar 71	170/58	200	23.39	23.49 -92
Csöke	Katalin	HUN	26 Jan 57	173/79	DT	58.58	63.20 -80
* Cui	Yingzi	CHN	26 Jan 71	159/51	10kW	44:09.1, 43:50	42:46.7 -92
Cumba	Yumileisis	CUB	4 Feb 75	185/85	SP	17.70	17.44 -92
Cummings	Sandra	USA	30 Dec 68	170/55	400h	56.76	55.77 -92
Curko	Inara	LAT	11 Nov 66	164/52	TJ	13.25, 13.44w	13.88 -89
Curovic	Danijela	YUG	7 Mar 74	183/90	SP	18.02	16.90 -92
					DT	58.40	55.52 -92
Custer	Casey	USA	11 Nov 74	160/47	100	11.38w	11.38 -92
* Cuthbert	Juliet	JAM	9 Apr 64	160/54	100	11.16	10.83 -92
					200	22.93	21.75 -92
Cuza	Lisette	CUB	26 Feb 75		TJ	13.40	11.59 -92
da Fonseca	Kristina	GER	10 Feb 72	169/52	1500	4:09.85	4:14.57 -92
Daans	Anoeschka	HOL	10 Mar 65		Hep	5715	5713 -89
Damaske	Tanja	GER	16 Nov 71	170/65	JT	60.96	61.06 -90
Damon	Karol	USA	20 Dec 69	178//59	HJ	1.90	1.90 -91
Danilczyk	Krystyna	POL	14 Jan 68	183/88	SP	18.31	19.42 -92
Danson	Yvonne	GBR	22 May 59	151/39	Mar	2:32:42	2:41:36 -92
Darsha	Darayathi	SRI	13 Feb 75		200	23.29	23.68 -92
das Gracas	Jupira Maur.	BRA	20 Feb 70	178/66	400h	57.59, 57.4	58.32, 57.6 -92
Davies	Diana	GBR	7 May 61	175/60	HJ	1.89i	1.95 -82
Davis	Dedra	BAH	17 Jul 73	168/62	100	11.33	
					LJ	6.72, 6.76w	6.35 -91, 6.56w -92
* Davis	Pauline	BAH	9 Jul 66	168/57	100	11.16	11.14, 10.9 -89
					200	22.89	22.44 -92, 22.1w -87
Dawson	Sandra	AUS	2 Nov 70		800	2:02.23	2:04.10 -92
de Bruin	Corrie	HOL	26 Oct 76	179/80	SP	18.12	16.60 -92
					DT	56.18	56.48 -92
de Klerk	Evette	RSA	21 Aug 65	170/51	100	11.44A	11.06, 10.94w -90
					200	22.76	22.06 -89
					400	52.32A	50.57 -86
de Leeuw	Sabrina	BEL	19 Aug 74	182/63	HJ	1.93	1.85 -92
de Oliveira	Carmen	BRA	17 Aug 65	160/46	5k	15:22.01	15:39.26 -90
					10k	31:47.76	32:35.04 -92
					Mar	2:31:18	
de Reuck	Colleen	RSA	13 Apr 64	164/47	HMar	70:26	68:38 -89
de Vega	Lydia	PHI	26 Dec 64	170/52	200	23.37	23.35 -86
Dendy	Terri	USA	8 May 65	168/55	200	23.02	23.20, 23.18w -88
					400	51.75	51.45 -88
Deselaers	Agnes	GER	12 Nov 68	178/84	SP	17.51i, 17.08	17.64i -92,17.55 -91
Dethier	Françoise	BEL	20 May 65		400h	58.02	58.60, 58.3 -92
Dethier	Sylvia	BEL	20 May 65	164/55	100h	13.34	12.98 -91
Devaluez	Isabelle	FRA	17 Mar 66	180/75	DT	59.50	59.00 -92
Devassoigne	Elsa	FRA	17 Oct 69	170/52	400	51.92	51.75 -92
* Devers	Gail	USA	19 Nov 66	163/52	100	10.82	10.82 -92
					100h	12.46	12.48 -91
Devonish	Nicole	CAN	24 Aug 73	179/68	LJ	6.46, 6.55w	6.43 -92
Dia	Ndèye Binta	SEN	8 Apr 73	160/55	100	11.40	11.64,11.54w -92
* Dias	M Albertina	POR	26 Apr 65	163/48	3k	8:43.76	8:43.08 -92
					5k	15:05.12	15.24.86 -90
					10k	31:33.03	31:42.70 -92
					Mar	2:26:49	- 0 -
Dias	Manuela	POR	19 Jun 63	160/45	HMar	71:23, 70:02 sh	
Diaz	Mericarmen	MEX	15 Jul 70	158/46	10k	32:53.73	32:42.6 -91
Dickey	Cheryl	USA	12 Dec 66	165/61	100h	13.11, 12.91w	12.97 -92, 12.8w -90
Didden	Ingrid	BEL	27 Jun 68	179/64	Hep	5766	6056 -91
* Dietzsch	Franka	GER	22 Jan 68	185/96	DT	62.06	68.26 -89
Dillon	Michelle	AUS	25 May 73		10k	32:35.40	
Dimitrova	Desislava	BUL	19 Jun 72	165/50	100	11.36	11.59 -92
* Dimitrova	Svetla	BUL	27 Jan 70	170/57	200	23.10	23.31 -88, 23.06w -92
					100h	12.71	13.22 -92, 12.9w -88
					LJ	6.61	6.64 -92
					Hep	6594	6.58 -92
DiMuro	Michelle	USA	15 May 67	158/50	1500	4:09.67	4:15.65 -92
Ding	Fenghua	CHN	27 Jun 64		JT	60.68	60.72 -87
Ding	Ying	CHN	Oct 76		Hep	5838	5211 -91
Djaté (- Taillard)	Patricia	FRA	3 Jan 71	173/58	800	2:00.75	2:03.25 -92

Name		Nat	Born	Ht/Wt	Event	1993 Mark	Pre-1993 Best
Dobrovitskaya	Taisia	BLS	8 Dec 67	179/62	100h	12.8	13.3 -92
					Hep	6337	6317 -92
Dóczi	Éva	HUN	24 Sep 70	167/55	1500	4:11.76	4:14.46 -90
					3k	8:58.26	9:01.68 -92
Dolmatova	Svetlana	RUS	68		100	11.42w	11.37 -91
Domain	Sandrine	FRA	6 Sep 71	176/63	TJ	13.38, 13.59w	13.42 -91
Dominc	Irena	SLO	19 May 70	166/55	400h	57.13	57.14 -92
Dong	Bo	CHN	Mar 71		SP	18.77	18.16 -89
Dong	Li	CHN	9 Dec 73		3k	9:00.62	
					10k	31:52.59	33:09.50 -92
Dong	Yuping	CHN	1 Mar 63	176/68	LJ	6.50	6.48 -88
					Hep	6112	6262 -90
* Donkova	Yordanka	BUL	28 Sep 61	175/67	100h	12.81	12.21 -88, 12.0w -86
Dorovskikh $	Tatyana	UKR	12 Aug 61	168/54	800	2:01.57	1:58.56 -85
					1500	4:10.94	3:57.92 -92
					3000	8:55.09 dq	8:26.53 -88
* Dörre - Heinig	Katrin	GER	6 Oct 61	170/57	HMar	70:04	
					Mar	2:27:09	2:25:24 -87
Drake	Julie	GBR	21 May 69	173/57	5kW	22:37.47	22:40 -91, 23:03.24 -90
					10kW	45:59	47:15 -90
* Drechsler	Heike	GER	16 Dec 64	181/70	100	11.36	10.91, 10.80w -86
					200	23.16A	21.71 -86
					LJ	7.21	7.48 -88, 7.63w -92
					TJ	13.35	
Dreher	Claudia	GER	2 May 71	169/52	5k	15:33.83	
					10k	32:47.20	32:44.41 -91
Du	Xiujie	CHN	27 Nov 71		5kW	23.17	23.38 -91
Dubkova	Lyudmila	RUS	27 Feb 68		TJ	14.00	13.81 -91
Duhaney	Dahlia	JAM	20 Jul 70	168/56	100	11.22	11.35 -91
					200	22.81, 22.79w	22.80 -92
Dukes	Pam	USA	15 May 64	183/85	SP	17.56	18.11 -97
					DT	58.00	61.14 -92
+ Dukhnova	Natalya	BLS	16 Jul 66	176/64	400	52.1	52.6 -89
					800	1:58.03	2:00.59 -92
					1000	2:36.56	
					1500	4:11.19	
* Dulgheru	Mirela	ROM	5 Oct 66	172/62	LJ	6.99i, 6.77	7.14 -92
Dumble	Dawn	USA	25 Feb 72	173/80	SP	17.36	17.36i -92, 17.26 -91
					DT	57.42	56.90 -92
Dumitrascu	Elena	ROM	14 May 74	176/68	TJ	13.39i, 13.31	13.32 -91
Dunant	Deborah	HOL	3 Apr 66	181/75	SP	17.76	17.92 -92
Duporty	Julia	CUB	9 Feb 71	171/63	200	23.31	23.46 -91
					400	51.81	53.27 -91
Duprey	Donalda	CAN	1 Mar 67	172/56	100h	13.20A	13.39 -92
					400h	55.80	56.29 -91
Dyachenko	Oksana	RUS	26 Nov 74	172/55	200	23.25	23.43 -92
Dykstra	Wanita	CAN	30 Jan 75		HJ	1.92	1.82 -92
Dzhabrailova	Tatyana	UKR	14 Mar 65	159/53	Mar	2:29:29	2:32:51 -91
Dzhigalova $	Lyudmila	UKR	22 Jan 62	178/64	400	51.72	50.33 -90, 49.9 -88
Echevarría	Eloina	CUB	23 Aug 61	168/63	LJ	6.54w	6.71 -92
					TJ	14.00	14.07 -92
Echols	Sheila	USA	2 Oct 64	165/52	100	11.31A, 11.14w	10.83 -88
					200	23.40w	22.90 -86
					LJ	6.46, 6.65w	6.94 -87
* Edeh	Rosey	CAN	16 Aug 66	173/54	400h	54.53	55.26 -92
Edwards	Jackie	BAH	14 Apr 71	172/64	LJ	6.45, 6.60w	6.69 -92
Elien	Evelyne	FRA	24 Mar 64	160/50	400	52.26	51.79 -88
Erjavec	Natasa	SLO	15 May 68	179/105	SP	17.53	17.21 -92
Erni	Barbara	SUI	7 Mar 72	180/62	Hep	5895	5292 -92
Espegren	Lene	NOR	8 May 71		TJ	13.54, 13.56w	12.75 -92
* Essayah	Sari	FIN	21 Feb 67	162/48	5kW	20:38.65	20:44.02 -91
					10kW	42:37.0	44:15.8 -92
						42:59	43:13 -91
Estévez	Estela	ESP	24 Feb 65	161/47	3k	8:56.81	8:55.58 -92
Eve	Laverne	BAH	16 Jun 65	179/77	JT	56.90	64.78 -89
Fagaras	Gabriela	ROM	29 Nov 69	174/60	400h	57.77	58.39 -92
Fan	Xiaoling	CHN	29 Mar 71		10kW	43:10	43:09.4 -92

Name		Nat	Born	Ht/Wt	Event	1993 Mark	Pre-1993 Best
Fang	Kunyao	CHN	Feb 71		400h	56.48	56.64 -92
* Farmer-Patrick	Sandra	USA	18 Aug 62	173/63	400	52.79	53.37 -89
Farquharson	Samantha	GBR	15 Dec 69	152/46	100h	13.37, 13.36w	13.28 -92
Farrow	Kate	AUS	6 May 67	176/70	JT	57.68	58.98 -90
Fates	Farida	FRA	2 Feb 62	166/49	1500	4:12.20	4:08.90 -90
					3k	8:51.33	9:01.64 -90
* Fedyushina	Valentina	UKR	18 Feb 65	190/90	SP	20.16	21.08 -88
Feitor	Susana	POR	28 Jan 75	159/52	5kW	21:01.8	21:30.91 -92
					10kW	43:44	45:24 -92
Fekete	Ildikó	HUN	12 Nov 66	166/53	TJ	13.71	13.60 -92
Feng	Wenhui	CHN	19 Jul 72	161/50	10k	31:32.15	33:41.8 -92
					Mar	2:31:03	2:37:44 -91
Feng	Yinghua	CHN	25 Nov 66	172/53	100h	13.07	13.08, 12.8 -92
Ferguson	Debbie	BAH	16 Jan 76		200	23.32w	24.2 -92
Fernández	Herminia	CUB	4 Nov 67	170/80	SP	18.60	17.91 -90
Ferraro	Anna Maria	ITA	16 Jul 70	172/57	HJ	1.88	1.82 -92
* Ferreira	M Conceição	POR	13 Mar 62	148/40	3k	8:55.01	8:53.27 -91
					10k	31:30.60	31:16.42 -92
					HMar	70:07	72:13 -92
Ferrer	Miriam	CUB	18 Jun 63	166/54	100	11.43, 11.42w	11.15 -92
Fesenko	Lidia	RUS	5 Oct 62		10kW	43:56	42:52 -91
* Fidatov	Elena	ROM	24 Jul 60	168/52	1500	4:05.61	4:04.55 -92
					3k	8:44.93	8:42.16 -87
* Figueiredo	Maria M.	BRA	11 Nov 63	170/60	400	52.15	50.62 -90
					800	1:59.51	1:59.53 -91
Filimonova	Lyudmila	BLS	22 Mar 71	184/76	DT	62.62	60.74 -91
Filip	Nicoleta	ROM	5 Jun 71	182/69	TJ	13.42	13.57i, 13.55 -92
Filyova	Zulfia	RUS	65		800	2:00.92	2:00.58 -92
Finikin	Evette	GBR	25 Sep 63		TJ	13.31w	13.46 -91
* Finn	Michelle	USA	8 May 65	165/52	100	11.16, 11.06w	11.05, 10.98w -90
					200	23.01, 22.81w	22.39 -92
* Flemming	Jane	AUS	14 Apr 65	168/56	200	23.32	23.59, 23.37w -88
					100h	12.98	13.17 -88, 13.04w -90
					400h	57.88	
					LJ	6.52	6.78 -90
					Hep	6343	6695 -90
Florea	Mariana	ROM	29 Aug 76	164/50	400	52.10	51.75 -92
Fogli	Laura	ITA	5 Oct 59	168/50	Mar	2:31:16	2:27:49 -88
Foley	Sharon	IRL	20 May 72	177/63	HJ	1.88	1.81 -92
Fomenko	Viktoriya	UKR	2 Oct 71	170/59	100	11.37	11.61 -91, 11.2 -92
					200	23.16	23.67, 23.4 -91
* Forkel	Karen	GER	24 Sep 70	172/64	JT	67.94	70.20 -91
Foufoué-Ziga	Patricia	CIV	8 Mar 72	164/58	100	11.33w	11.50 -92
Franey	Kathy	USA	25 Dec 67	163/54	1500	4:12.18	4:12.49 -90
					3k	8:58.50	9:12.39i -91, 9:14.46 -90
					5k	15:35.05	16:27.04 -90
Franks	Linden	NZL	11 May 61	164/49	5k	15:44.65	
Frantseva	Nadezhda	RUS	2 Oct 71		SP	16.40	18.04 -88
Frazer	Merlene	JAM	27 Dec 73	172/57	100	11.24	11.38 -92
					200	22.91	23.19 -92
* Freeman	Cathy	AUS	16 Feb 73	164/52	100	11.43	11.55 -92, 11.42w -89
					200	22.37	23.09 -92
					400	51.34	51.14 -92
* Freeman	Michelle	JAM	5 May 69	170/63	100	11.16	11.16, 11.13w -92
					100h	12.77	12.75 -92
Fricot	Sandrine	FRA	4 Jun 68	180/57	HJ	1.91	1.93 -92
Fu	Ping	CHN	10 Jan 71		100h	13.28	13.71 -91
Fu	Xiuhong	CHN	5 Jun 70	183/70	Hep	5854	6126 -91
Fujii	Tamami	JPN	27 Oct 71	165/65	JT	56.92	53.92 -89
Fujimura	Nobuko	JPN	18 Dec 65	163/48	Mar	2:30:02	
Fujiwara	Megumi	JPN	19 Jun 69	165/52	5k	15:37.4	15:38.32 -91
Fukuyama	Tsugumi	JPN	10 Apr 68	162/46	5k	15:39.1	15:43.2 -92
Fumoto	Midori	JPN	18 Dec 71	160/43	10k	32:11.21	32:04.40 -92
Fyodorova	Tatyana	RUS	67		TJ	13.81i, 13.57	13.74 -89
Gaines	Chryste	USA	14 Sep 70	170/57	100	11.25	11.16, 10.90w -92
					200	22.81	23.00 -92, 22.96w -91
* Gainsford	Melinda	AUS	1 Oct 71	175/63	100	11.22, 11.15w	11.38 -92
					200	22.49	22.68 -92

Name		Nat	Born	Ht/Wt	Event	1993 Mark	Pre-1993 Best
Galiullina	Alfia	RUS	72		10kW	46:12	46:12 -92
* Galkina	Lyudmila	RUS	20 May 72	174/56	LJ	6.75	6.63 -90
					TJ	13.48	13.67 -91
Galler	Dagmar	GER	20 Dec 61	176/80	DT	58.64	63.52 -90
Gallyamova	Albina	RUS	8 May 64		Mar	2:31:15	2:32:02 -92
* Gao	Hongmiao	CHN	17 Mar 74	162/51	10kW	41:57, 43:39.4	42:49.7 -92
Gao	Jie	CHN	4 Feb 73		5kW	23.34	23.42 -92
Garcia	Magalys	CUB	23 Oct 71	173/70	Hep	5903	5799 -90
Garcia $	Dulce	CUB	2 Jul 65	173/68	JT	63.44	67.90 -86
Garrett	Carla	USA	31 Jul 67	172/114	DT	58.94	60.54 -92
* Gasser	Sandra	SUI	27 Jul 62	169/52	800	2:00.93	1:58.90 -87
					1500	4:07.86	3:59.06 -87
					2k	5:43.96	
Gast	Christine	GER	30 Apr 72	179/66	JT	58.16	60.04 -91
Gast	Silke	GER	30 Apr 72	184/70	JT	60.06	59.90 -92
Gautzsch	Birgit	GER	14 Dec 67	180/68	Hep	6131	6425 -89
Ge	Ping	CHN	11 Jan 61	169/56	HJ	1.88	1.92 -83
Geldhof	Marie Paule	BEL	27 Feb 59	172/72	DT	59.30	60.30 -91
Gerashchenko	Oksana	RUS	6 Aug 71		HJ	1.88i	1.89 -91
Gerhardt	Claudia	GER	18 Jan 66	176/63	LJ	6.57	6.57i -91, 6.52 -90
Gibson	Lynn	GBR	6 Jul 69		1500	4:12.12	4:14.3 -92
Gibson	Sharon	GBR	31 Dec 61	168/77	JT	59.58	62.32 -87
Giordano	Rossella	ITA	1 Dec 72	172/52	5kW	21:45.52	22:47.62 -92
					10kW	45:28.1	46:35.6 -92
* Girard	Patricia	FRA	8 Apr 68	162/48	100	11.20	11.25 -89
					100h	12.91	12.91 -92
Glenn	Roshandra	USA	13 Nov 71	173/55	TJ	13.35	13.23 -92
Gliznutsa	Inna	MOL	18 Apr 73	184/63	HJ	1.91	1.89 -92
Godall	Sonia	ESP	28 Mar 68	172/65	HT	56.66	57.14 -92
Gogoase	Ionela	ROM	4 Feb 70	175/62	TJ	13.70	13.32 -91
Golesheva	Yelena	RUS	12 Jul 66	167/60	400	51.89	51.28 -89
Gómez	Olga	CUB	30 Jun 66	175/85	JT	59.98	62.56 -92
Gomez-Henes	Laurie	USA	16 Apr 70	168/50	10k	32:55.24	
Goncharenko	Svetlana	RUS	28 May 71	176/61	200	23.40	23.60 -92
Goncharova	Yelena	RUS	27 Mar 63	179/66	400h	56.78A	54.93 -86
Goormachtigh	Jacqueline	HOL	28 Feb 70	179/84	SP	17.77	16.98 -90
					DT	60.36	60.80 -92
Goossens	Ester	HOL	21 Feb 72	175/65	400h	57.51	57.73 -92
Gorbatova	Yekaterina	RUS	13 Jun 68		100h	13.16, 13.0	13.20 -91, 13.1 -88
Goto	Akiyo	JPN	13 Jul 70	159/40	Mar	2:34:15	
Goto	Ikuyo	JPN	6 Jan 69	160/47	Mar	2:33:02	
* Gotovska	Valentina	LAT	3 Sep 65	176/59	HJ	1.95	1.97 -90
Gourdet) (Le Gouillou)	Barbara	FRA	29 Aug 65	168/52	800	2:02.55	2:01.31 -88
Grachova	Irina	RUS	25 Jan 63		DT	60.54	58.38 -91
* Gradus	Kamila	POL	19 Mar 67	159/46	Mar	2:27:38	2:26:55 -91
Graham	Kim	USA	26 Mar 71	163/58	100	11.37w	11.42 -92
					200	22.98, 22.64w	23.03 -92
					400	51.88	53.03 -92
* Granados	Encarnacion	ESP	30 Jan 72	168/50	5kW	21:38	22:45.20 -91, 21:54 -92
					10kW	43:21,45:59.18	44:51,46:07.90 -92
Grankina	Yelena	UKR	30 Jun 74	174.85	HT	56.44	56.40 -92
Grant	Berenley	JAM	17 Oct74?		400	52.02	
* Grasu	Nicoleta	ROM	17 Sep 71	176/88	DT	65.16	65.66 -92
* Graudyn	Yulia	RUS	13 Nov 70	171/59	100h	12.85	12.82 -92
Gray	Christine	USA	17 Aug 71	173/61	400h	57.55	58.96 -89
Grebenchuk	Tatyana	BLS	22 Nov 62	168/58	800	2:01.22	1:57.35 -90
Green	Arnita	USA	21 Feb 71	170/55	400h	57.05	56.97 -92
Grefstad	Monica	NOR	12 Oct 64	173/61	100h	13.26, 13.22w	13,62, 13.35w -92
* Gribanova	Yelena	RUS	2 Mar 72	189/66	HJ	1.97i, 1.96	1.96 -92
Griffin	Cathy	CAN	18 Sep 69		DT	56.86	52.80 -92
Griffith	Michelle	GBR	6 Oct 71	173/64	TJ	13.75, 13.93w	13.50i -92, 13.34 -91
Griffiths	Gwen	RSA	30 Aug 67	174/50	1500	4:04.73	4:08.14 -92
					3k	8:52.71	8:49.48 -92
Grigorenko	Larisa	UKR	6 Sep 70	180/61	HJ	1.95	1.95 -92
Gritsachuk	Tatyana	UKR	20 Feb 69	173/55	HJ	1.88i	1.86 -92

Name		Nat	Born	Ht/Wt	Event	1993 Mark	Pre-1993 Best
Groenendaal	Claudette	USA	1 Nov 63	175/58	800	2:02.20	1:58.33 -85
					1000	2:37.89	2:38.17 -88
					1500	4:10.21	4:04.86 -86
Gruzinova	Yelena	RUS	67		10kW	42:34	44:18 -92
Gu	Dongmei	CHN	30 Sep 72	169/52	Mar	2:30:15	2:37:56 -92
Gu	Yan	CHN	17 Mar 74	174/60	10kW	42:50	43:15.1 -92
Guan	Weihua	CHN	14 Jun 75		HJ	1.89	
Gubkina	Lyudmila	BLS	28 May 72		HT	59.62	55.90 -92
Gudkova	Tatyana	RUS	23 Dec 77		5kW	22:23	23:01.35 -92
Guialdo	Marsha	USA	12 Jul 70	165/54	100h	13.08, 12.89w	13.23 -92
					400h	57.43	57.88 -92
Guida	Maria	ITA	23 Jan 66	160/49	3k	8:58.35	9:03.50 -89
					5k	15:36.98	15:41.69 -92
					10k	32:12.70	32:10.29 -92
* Guidry	Carlette	USA	4 Sep 68	168/50	100	11.35, 11.24w	10.94, 10.91w -91
					200	22.98, 22.76w	22.24 -92
* Gündler	Anja	GER	18 Mar 72	184/85	DT	62.92	60.66 -91
* Gunnell	Sally	GBR	29 Jul 66	167/58	200	23.30	23.69 -88, 23.38w -86
					400	51.29	51.11 -91
					100h	13.08	12.82, 12.80w -88
					400h	52.74	56.16 -91
Guo	Yue ¶	CHN	23 Jan 69	170/59	400	51.58dq, 52.00	53.18 -92
					400h	54.47dq, 55.88	56.66 -91
Gureyeva	Zhanna	BLS	10 Jun 70	178/54	TJ	14.17	13.90 -92
* Gurina	Lyubov	RUS	6 Aug 57	166/57	800	1:57.10	1:55.56 -87
					1000	2:32.97	2:33.08 -91
					1500	4:03.42	4:03.32 -92
Gurskaya	Natalya	BLS	15 Jan 72	175/74	SP	17.81i, 16.41	17.27i, 17.23 -92
Guryeva	Yevgenia	RUS	2 Dec 69	165/51	5kW	22:12.75	21:56 -92
					10kW	44:12	43:22 -92
Gustafsson	Madelene	SWE	24 Dec 69		400h	57.70	59.56 -91
Guthrie	Diane	JAM	24 Oct 71	174/66	LJ	6.47i	6.78 -92
Gutjahr	Kathleen	GER	27 Jul 75	176/65	Hep	5678	5668 -92
Ha	Xiaoyan	CHN	30 Jan 72	171/73		65.44	63.94 -92
Haage	Carmen	GER	10 Sep 71		PV	3.85	3.90 -92
Hachenberg	Silke	GER	2 Oct 68	177/77		55.74	55.94 -90
Hacker	JoAnn	USA	23 Sep 70	179/84	SP	16.30	16.33 -92
Hafner	Michaela	ITA	2 Aug 73		5kW	22:31.16	22:34.33 -92
Hamilton	Suzy	USA	8 Aug 68	160/48	1500	4:10.69	4:04.53 -92
Hammer	Grit	GER	4 Jun 66	180/93	SP	19.11	20.72 -87
Han	Jinli	CHN	Jan 66		JT	64.68	63.32 -88
* Han	Qing	CHN	4 Mar 70	170/54	200	22.87	22.79 -92
					400h	53.96	56.53 -90
Han	Yanping	CHN			Mar	2:33:23	2:41:37 -91
Hanhijoki	Sisko	FIN	25 Apr 62	165/53	100	11.39	11.24 -91
					200	23.32i, 23.36w	22.81 -92, 22.6w -92
Hanigan	Kylie	AUS	18 Nov 71	169/56	400	52.26	52.86 -92
Hansen	Ashia	GBR	5 Dec 71		TJ	13.48i, 13.25,13.55w	13.31 -92
Hara	Mariko	JPN	27 Dec 70	165/51	3k	8:57.37	8:59.52 -92
					5k	15:36.78	15:40.37 -92
					HMar	71:03	70:29 -92
Harding	Lynn	GBR	10 Aug 61	165/47	Mar	2:35:04	2:31:45 -89
Hare	Anne	NZL	7 Jun 64	167/55	10k	32:42.86	33:10.8 -92
Harper	Hydie Ann	TRI			200	23.1	23.6 -92
Harris	Flirtisha	USA	21 Dec 72	155/52	100	11.38	11.50 -92
					100	23.02, 22.56w	23.29 -92
Hartwig	Heike	GER	30 Dec 62	180/95	SP	16.93i	21.31 -88
Harvey	Lisa	CAN	7 Feb 70	173/54	10k	32:40.47	32:41.87 -91
* Hattestad	Trine	NOR	18 Apr 66	173/75	JT	72.12	71.44 -91
Haughton	Karlene	JAM	72		400h	58.00	58.69 -92
* Haugland	Hanne	NOR	14 Dec 67	178/60	HJ	1.93	1.96i, 1.94 -89
Hayashi	Emi	JPN	9 Jul 72	168/55	5kW	21:50.10	23:15.95 -91
					10kW	46:02	49:25 -92
Haynesworth	Monyetta	USA	23 Jun 73	162/55	LJ	6.48i	6.54 -92
Haywood	Claudia	USA	25 Sep 69	173/63	TJ	13.57, 13.86w	13.23i -92, 13.08 -91
							13.49w -92
He	Xiuqin	CHN	18 Mar 67		SP	18.66	18.23 -91

Name		Nat	Born	Ht/Wt	Event	1993 Mark	Pre-1993 Best
He	Yan	CHN			10kW	45:15	
Hebbard	Jodie	AUS	14 Jul 66	175/53	1500	4:12.52	4:09.99 -92
* Hechevarria	Barbara	CUB	6 Aug 66	174/94	DT	62.52	67.18 -89
Heinz	Ulrike	GER	4 Jul 67	174/66	400h	56.46	55.53 -89
Hellier (Smith)	Kirsten	NZL	6 Oct 69	174/73	JT	61.28	61.52 -92
Hellmann (Goldkamp)	Marion	GER	6 Apr 67	184/62	HJ	1.94i, 1.92	1.94 -92
* Hemmings	Deon	JAM	9 Oct 68	176/61	400	51.77	52.10 -92
					400H	54.12	54.70 -92
Hendricken	Geraldine	IRL	19 Apr 70	165/53	3K	9:00.34	9:02.00 -91
					10k	32:50.53	
* Henkel	Heike	GER	5 May 64	182/62	HJ	2.02i, 2.01	2.07 -92
Hennagan	Monique	USA	26 May 76		400	52.30	53.58 -92
Hennart	Sandrine	BEL	12 Dec 72	172/62	LJ	6.61	6.55 -90, 6.56w -91
Henry	Joanne	NZL	2 Oct 71	173/60	Hep	5760w	6278 -91
* Henry	Yolanda	USA	2 Dec 64	168/52	HJ	1.94	2.00 -90
Herazo	Victoria	USA	2 Jun 59	183/65	5kW	22:21	22:15.0 -92
Herceg	Cindy	USA	10 May 70	170/64	JT	56.54	53.02 -90
Hérigault	Corinne	FRA	6 Oct 70	165/53	LJ	6.54	6.45i, 6.28 -92
Hernesniemi	Sanna	FIN	9 Mar 71	169/52	100	11.40, 11.33w	11.47 -92
					200	23.01, 22.98w	23.29i -92
							23.47, 23.24w -91
Higgins-Francis	Tamika	USA	19 Apr 71	175/65	100h	13.31, 13.23w	13.82, 13.80w -91
					400h	58.02	62.88 -89
Hila	Elena	ROM	20 May 74	179/95	SP	16.76	15.60i -92
Hill	Alisa	USA	16 Sep 65	160/48	800	2:00.31	1:59.99 -91
					1500	4:11.29	4:08.32 -92
					1M	4:31.02i	4:30.72i -90, 4:33.64 -92
Hill	Janet	USA	28 Aug 70	176/82	DT	57.82	54.66 -88
Hiroyama' (Suzuki)	Harumi	JPN	2 Sep 68	160/50	5k	15:30.78	
Hochella	Lorraine	USA	8 Oct 63	152/43	Mar	2:34:46	2:37:08 -92
Hoffmann	Juliane	GER	13 Dec 73	175/65	JT	58.64	58.70 -92
Hoffmann	Katje	GER	24 Mar 71	170/54	3k	8:56.73	8:57.37 -92
Holland	Maree	AUS	25 Jul 63	172/55	400	52.52	50.24 -88
Holmes	Kelly	GBR	19 Apr 70	162/55	800	1:58.64	2:03.94 -92
					1000	2:37.29	
Holpuchová	Kamila	TCH	27 Sep 73	170/52	10kW	44:20	45:33 -92
Holroyd	Shelley	GBR	17 May 73	176/65	JT	60.10	57.82 -92
Holub	Beata	POL	19 Jul 70	185/60	HJ	1.90	1.96 -91
Holubová	Ivana	SVK	24 Jan 72		DT	56.74	55.54 -92
Hong	Duo	CHN			10k	32:59.03	
Honoré	Caroline	FRA	29 Apr 70	171/56	TJ	13.65	13.11, 13.37w -92
Hopfer	Heike	GER	28 Feb 71	179/87	SP	17.65	18.13 -91
Howell	Sarah	CAN	11 Sep 69	163/55	1500	4:09.36	4:11.74 -92
Hu	Honglian	CHN			DT	58.48	57.02 -92
Hu	Liping	CHN	29 Feb 68		Hep	5761	5632 -91
Huang	Xiaoyan	CHN	3 Dec 69	167/55	100	11.34	11.59 -91
* Huang	Zhihong	CHN	7 May 65	174/100	SP	20.57	21.52 -90
Hudson	Sheila	USA	30 Jun 67	160/58	LJ	6.53, 6.58w	6.73 -90
					TJ	13.86	14.23 -92
Hughes	Andrea	AUS	12 Dec 73	185/67	HJ	1.89	1.88 -91
* Hughes	Tanya	USA	25 Jan 72	185/59	HJ	1.95	1.97 -92
Huhtaniemi	Paula	FIN	17 Feb 73	167/60	JT	57.34	52.50 -92
Huneke	Heike	GER	16 Oct 66	167/54	800	2:02.53i	2:01.56 -92
Hurtlin	Christine	FRA	29 Sep 67	176/66	100h	13.20	12.83 -90
Hyacinth	Flora	ISV	30 Mar 66	172/62	LJ	6.51	6.71 -92
					TJ	13.52i, 13.33w	13.73 -87
Hyche	Holli	USA	6 Sep 71	165/52	100	11.12,10.93w,10.9w	11.45, 11.42w -92
					200	22.34	23.28 -92
Idehen	Faith	NGR	5 Feb 73	163	100	11.27	11.34 -89
Idowu	Oluyinka	GBR	25 Feb 72	178/65	LJ	6.73	6.69 -92, 6.71w -91
Ignatyuk	Natalya	BLS	28 Dec 63		400h	57.99	55.28 -91
* Ilcu	Marieta	ROM	16 Oct 62	173/65	LJ	6.94i, 6.72w, 6.50	7.08 -89
Ilyés	Ildikó	HUN	28 Aug 66	158/52	10kW	45:06	44:36 -92
Ilyina	Nadezhda	RUS	2 Apr 64	160/45	10k	32:09.46	32:11.66 -92
					Mar	2:30:44	

Name		Nat	Born	Ht/Wt	Event	1993 Mark	Pre-1993 Best
Ilyina	Olga	RUS	7 Jan 73	175/74	SP	17.07i	17.20 -92
Ináncsi	Rita	HUN	6 Jan 71	190/70	LJ	6.62	6.40 -91
					Hep	6263	6198 -91
Ingberg	Mikaela	FIN	29 Jul 74	173/64	JT	58.26	54.00 -92
* Inverarity	Alison	AUS	12 Aug 70	181/60	HJ	1.97i, 1.95	1.96 -92
Ionescu'	Iulia	ROM	3 Jul 65	171/52	1500	4:11.25	4:04.36 -88
(Besliu)					3k	8:55.16	8:41.54 -88
Irving	Crystal	USA	26 May 70	175/64	400	51.72	51.71 -92
Isachenko	Galina	BLS	4 Mar 65	176/60	HJ	1.90, 1.92u	1.96 -92
(Balgurina)							
Isaila	Claudia	ROM	17 Jul 73	167/62	JT	61.54	63.04 -92
Ishizaka	Masami	JPN	27 Mar 71	153/37	10k	32:44.71	32:16.24 -89
Itcou	Laura	ROM	13 Feb 72	171/54	800	2:01.39	2:01.42 -92
* Ivakina	Yekaterina	RUS	4 Dec 64	168/68	JT	65.36	64.24-
Ivankova	Olga	UKR	7 Jan 73	173/62	JT	56.66	55.04 -93
Ivanova	Olimpiada	RUS	5 May 70		5kW	21:39.3	
					10kW	42:24, 45:26.73	45:15 -87
Ivanova	Tatyana	RUS	22 Jun 70		Mar	2:33:52	2:43:31 -91
Ivanova	Valentina	RUS	1 May 63		DT	61.64	63.16 -89
Ivanova	Yelena	RUS	23 Jan 71	173/67	HJ	1.89i, 1.88	1.80i, 1.80 -92
Iwai	Miyako	JPN	15 Feb 68	157/45	Mar	2:31:27	2:34:42 -92
Jääskeläinen	Satu	FIN	4 Apr 70	165/52	800	2:01.77	2:11.30 -91
Jackson	Camille	USA	7 Sep 70	170/62	LJ	6.60	6.15 -90
					TJ	13.26A,13.49w	13.02 -90, 13.14w -92
Jackson	Cynthia	USA	12 Sep 71	170/59	400	52.04	55.69 -90
Jacobs	Simmone	GBR	5 Sep 66	163/53	100	11.43w	11.31 -88, 11.26w -84
Jaklofsky	Sharon	AUS	30 Sep 68	171/59	Hep	5892	6118w -89
Jancewicz	Donata	POL	17 Jun 69	189/68	HJ	1.91	1.93 -92
Janke	Karin	GER	14 Oct 63	178/63	400	52.55, 52.34i	50.64 -90
Jardim	Lucrécia	POR	28 Jan 71	159/49	100	11.39	11.42 -92
					200	23.16	23.09 -92
Jean-Charles	Valérie	FRA	27 Jan 69	169/56	100	11.38	11.36 -91
Jenkins	Julie	USA	12 Aug 64	168/57	800	1:59.77	1:57.82 -90
Jennings	Jo	GBR	20 Sep 69	174/60	HJ	1.94i, 1.90	1.90i -92, 1.90 -88
* Jennings	Lynn	USA	10 Jul 60	165/50	3k	8:52.55	8:44.60 -92, 8:40.45i -90
					5k	15:44.1	15:07.92 -90
					10k	31:30.53	31:19.89 -92
Jeppesen	Jette Ø	DEN	14 Mar 64	173/72	JT	62.30	59.32 -92
Jerschabek	Birgit	GER	17 May 69	163/47	Mar	2:30:34	2:31:42 -92
Jiang	Lan	CHN	Jan 69		100	11.45	11.62 -92
					200	23.26	
Jiang	Limei	CHN	Mar 70		400h	55.51	55.92 -92
Jiang	Qunhua	CHN	26 Sep 74		DT	59.80	59.27 -92
Jiménez	Elsa	CUB	13 Apr 66	165/57	100h	13.0	13.29 -89
					400h	56.78	56.56 -90
Jin	Bingjie	CHN	3 Jun 71	169/55	10kW	44:27.8, 43:57	43:16 -89
Jin	Ling	CHN	5 Sep 67	183/62	HJ	1.94	1.97 -89
* Johansson	Erica	SWE	5 Feb 74	176/69	LJ	6.78i, 6.56	6.72 -92
Johansson	Frida	SWE	5 Jan 70	167/57	400h	56.48	55.36 -91
Johansson	Marika	SWE	27 Oct 70	171/62	200	23.39	23.76 -91, 23.74w -92
Johnson	Trinette	USA	8 Feb 71	165/59	LJ	6.52, 6.55w	6.45 -92
Johnston	Kristy	USA	3 Jun 65	165/50	Mar	2:29:05	2:39:45 -91
Jonckheere	Natalja	BEL	21 Oct 70	185/60	HJ	1.90	1.88 -92
Jones	Camara	USA	15 May 72	171/61	400	51.55	52.07 -92
* Jones	Esther	USA	7 Apr 69	171/61	100	11.44, 11.31w	11.11, 10.99w -91
					200	23.12	22.47 -92, 22.37w -89
Jones	Janeen	USA	19 Aug 72	170/52	400	52.35	52.92 -92
Jones	Jasmin	USA	13 Oct 69	170/59	800	2:01.41	2:00.24 -90
Jones'	Jenny	AUS	20 Apr 67		5kw	22:08.5	22:25.81 -92
- Billington					10kW	46:06, 46:25.4	46:05.1 -92
* Jones	Kim	USA	2 May 58	170/53	Mar	2:30:00	2:26:40 -91
* Jones	Marion	USA	12 Oct 75	178/61	100	11.28, 11.21w, 11.2	11.14 -92, 11.12w-91
					200	23.00, 22.79w	22.58 -92
					LJ	6.71, 6.75w	
Jongmans	Stella	HOL	17 May 71	174/59	800	2:01.58	1:58.61 -92
Joseph	Hermin	DMN	13 Apr 64	155/52	100	11.39, 11.1, 11.13w	11.50 -92
					200	23.34w	24.28 -92

Name		Nat	Born	Ht/Wt	Event	1993 Mark	Pre-1993 Best
Joseph	Nadège	FRA	12 Aug 73	173/59	100h	13.21	13.77 -92
* Joyner-Kersee	Jackie	USA	3 Mar 62	178/70	200	23.19	22.30 -88
					100h	12.89	12.61 -92
					400h	56.70	55.05 -85
					LJ	7.08, 7.09w	7.45 -87
					Hep	6837	7291 -88
Juárez	Isabel	MEX	16 Sep 66	155/43	10k	32:39.70	34:14.0 -88
Jung	Caren	GER	18 Jan 68	169/55	100h	13.30	13.05 -92
* Junna-Saxby	Kerry	AUS	2 Jun 61	163/57	5kW	20:30.0	20:17.19 -90
					10kW	42:22.6	41:57.22 -90
Kaczmarska	Beata	POL	5 Jul 70	166/54	5kW	22:28	22:24 -92
					10kW	45:35	44:07 -92
Kagiri	Margaret	KEN	64		3k	8:53.93	9:13.81 -92
					5k	15:27.39	17:04.0 -91
Kähler	Birgit	GER	14 Aug 70	180/60	HJ	1.91	1.94 -91
* Kaiser-Brown	Natasha	USA	14 May 67	173/57	400	50.17	50.42 -92
Kaledina	Yelena	RUS	3 Oct 68		1500	4:11.4	4:13.13 -92
					3k	8:55.42	9:07.13 -92
Kaljurand	Anu	EST	16 Apr 69	174/64	Hep	5826	6142 -92
Kamioka	Yuka	JPN	28 May 75	154/47	5kW	22:04	
					10kW	45:18	
Kamrowska'	Maria	POL	11 Mar 66	176/68	100h	13.25, 13.12w	13.28, 13.16w -91
- Nowak					Hep	6019	6279w -91
Kanana	Angelina	KEN	65		HMar	70:00	76:33 -92
Kanbayashi	Kazumi	JPN	24 Jul 73	159/44	10k	32:10.56	
Karasiewicz	Doreen	GER	21 Jul 74	178/78		57.60	55.44 -91
Karczmarek	Agata	POL	29 Nov 63	172/62	LJ	6.87	6.97 -88
Karlshøj	Gitte	DEN	14 May 59	171/56	3k	8:58.52	8:44.35 -91
					5k	15:22.95	15:24.74 -90
Karpova	Lyubov	RUS	14 Aug 57	174/84	HT	59.50	61.80 -91
Kashapova	Klara	RUS	16 Feb 70		1500	4:12.83	4:17.02 -91
* Kaspárková	Sarka	TCH	20 May 71	185/68	HJ	1.95i	1.92 -92
					TJ	14.16	14.00 -92
Kataoka	Junko	JPN	13 Jun 70	158/45	3k	8:59.10	9:05.80 -92
					5k	15:27.76	
					10k	32:15.47	
* Katewicz	Renata	POL	2 May 65	180/95	SP	16.50	17.27 -87
					DT	65.94	66.18 -88
Kawasaki	Maiko	JPN	27 Feb 74	159/44	5k	15:45.09	
					10k	32:57.72	
					HMar	71:00	
Kayukova	Natalya	RUS	10 Dec 66	175/66	LJ	6.47	6.60 -92
					TJ	13.97	14.21i -92, 14.09 -91
Kazanina	Svetlana	KZK	71		Hep	5759	5711 -90
Kaznovskaya	Zoya	UKR	22 Sep 66	170/60	1500	4:12.54	4:08.8 -88
					3k	8:58.36	9:00.20 -90
Kelesidou	Anastasia	GRE	28 Nov 72	190/83	DT	57.44	54.34 -92
Kelly	Holly	USA	28 Dec 68	183/59	HJ	1.88i	1.86 -91
Keough	Linda	GBR	26 Dec 63	174/60	400	52.14	50.98 -91
					800	2:01.82	2:03.97 -91
* Keszeg	Margareta	ROM	31 Aug 65	165/51	1M	4:30.43i	4:24.02 -91
					3k	8:45.86	8:39.94 -92
* Khlopotnova	Yelena	UKR	4 Aug 63	172/64	LJ	6.83, 7.01w	7.31 -85
Khorkhulyova	Tatyana	BLS	15 Jul 64		SP	19.31i	19.59i, 19.28 -92
Khramova	Tatyana	BLS	1 Feb 70		HJ	1.95	1.85 -92
Khristosenko	Lyudmila	UKR	14 Oct 66	175/66	100h	13.10	12.94 -86, 12.8 -85
Khristova	Yurka	BUL	12 Jan 68	171/64	Hep	6028	5839 -87
Khropach	Iolanta	UKR	22 Sep 74	168/55	LJ	6.46	5.87 -92
Khudorozhkina	Irina	RUS	13 Oct 68	182/98	SP	18.89	19.16 -90
Kielan	Iwona	POL	5 Jul 66	184/58	HJ	1.89i	1.93 -91
* Kiesl	Theresia	AUT	26 Oct 63	172/60	800	2:00.75	2:01.06 -92
					1500	4:06.89	4:07.46 -92
					3k	8:55.56	
* Kimaiyo	Helen	KEN	8 Sep 68	163/50	10k	32:43.4	31:38.91 -92
Kinch	Beverly	GBR	14 Jan 64	162/58	100	11.37	11.29 -90, 11.13w -83
* Kiplagat	Esther	KEN	8 Dec 66	168/50	1500	4:09.30	4:10.38 -91
					3k	8:43.76	8:44.45 -92
					5k	15:17.76	15:07.87 -92

Name		Nat	Born	Ht/Wt	Event	1993 Mark	Pre-1993 Best
Kirby	Rachel	GBR	18 May 69	172/58	TJ	13.60, 13.64w	13.16 -91
* Kirchmann	Sigrid	AUT	29 Mar 66	181/63	HJ	1.97	1.95 -87
Kirklin	Leah	USA	28 Nov 70	178/64	TJ	13.32w	13.43 -92
Kisabaka	Linda	GER	9 Apr 69	165/50	400	52.56	52.01 -92
					400h	56.17	56.28 -92
Kiyomiya	Yukiko	JPN	4 Mar 69	153/43	5k	15:46.68	15:43.49 -92
					10k	33:01.57	33:06.25 -92
Kleinert	Nadine	GER	20 Oct 75	190/78	SP	17.07	17.07 -92
Klimovets	Natalya	BLS	11 Apr 74		TJ	13.65	13.25 -92
Klochko	Lyubov	UKR	26 Sep 59	167/55	Mar	2:34:47	2:28:47 -88
Knijn	Merian	HOL	12 Aug 66	178/61	400h	57.05	57.32 -88
* Knoll	Silke-Beate	GER	21 Feb 67	162/52	100	11.41	11.17 -92
					200	22.75, 22.74w	22.29 -92
* Knoroz' (Chuprina)	Anna	RUS	30 Jul 70	163/54	400h	54.42	55.12 -91
Knox	Susan	RSA	28 Dec 71		200	23.36	24.20 -91
Knut	Silke	GER	27 Jul 72	168/53	Hep	5685	5528 -92
Koba	Tamara	UKR	24 Feb 57	165/53	10k	32:39.50	32:34.95 -92
Kobrin	Nadezhda	UKR	21 Jan 72	166/63	JT	56.64	54.96 -92
Koch	Kathrin	GER	23 Apr 68	183/88	SP	16.72	17.53 -92
					DT	59.04	56.92 -92
* Kokowska	Renata	POL	4 Dec 58	170/57	Mar	2:26:20	2:27:36 -91
Kolovanova	Natalya	UKR	1 Aug 64	172/60	100h	13.05	12.81 -92
Konchits	Yelena	BLS	6 Jul 69		800	2:01.8	2:04.0 -92
Kong	Yan	CHN	Apr 71		10kW	43:28	44:30.4 -89
König-Zenz	Erika	AUT	6 Jan 64	169/55	1500	4:12.19	4:15.67i -92
Konstantinova	Tatyana	RUS	70		HT	56.00	57.42 -90
Kontsevaya	Olga	RUS	72		TJ	13.55	13.80 -90
Kopytova	Yelena	RUS	14 Mar 70	167/58	1500	4:11.2	4:13.75 -92
					3k	8:50.49	8:47.21 -92
Korolyova	Yulia	RUS	25 Jul 73	172/54	10kW	43:37	47:12 -92
* Korotkevich	Larisa	RUS	3 Jan 67	180/88	DT	68.14	71.30 -92
Korzhanyenko	Irina	RUS	10 May 74		SP	17.92i, 17.02	15.81 -92
Koshelyeva	Anna	RUS	11 Nov 68		200	23.25	
Kosmowska	Marta	POL	4 Apr 72	167/52	3k	8:59.86	9:26.62 - 91
* Kostadinova	Stefka	BUL	25 Mar 65	180/60	HJ	2.05	2.09 -87
* Kostyuchenkova	Irina	UKR	11 May 61	171/72	JT	63.68	67.00 -88
Kováciková	Zuzana	TCH	16 Apr 73	178/60	HJ	1.89	1.88 -92
* Kovacs	Ella	ROM	11 Dec 64	167/55	800	1:56.58	1:55.68 -85
					1000	2:32.40	2:35.86 -91
Kovács	Judit	HUN	7 Jun 69	166/53	HJ	1.91	1.94 -92
Kovalenko	Tamara	RUS	5 Jun 64		5kW	21:33.59i	21:04 -88
					10kW	44:49	42:46 -92
Kovalyova	Yelena	RUS	28 Feb 73	173/61	Hep	5675	5667 -92
Kovpak	Alla	UKR	23 Oct 62	172/56	800	2:02.35	2:00.96 -91
Kovpotina	Olga	RUS	10 Jan 68		3k	8:56.15i	9:09.65 -91
Kowina	Grazyna	POL	6 May 62	163/50	Mar	2:34:58	2:37:46 -91
Kozhomina	Vera	MOL	70		10kW	45:18	44:21 -91
Koznyeva	Marina	RUS	18 May 68		10kW	44:54	
Krause	Ines	GER	10 Jul 65	177/64	Hep	5955	6660 -88
* Kravets	Inessa	UKR	5 Oct 66	178/58	LJ	6.87dq, 6.83i, 7.02w	7.37 -92
					TJ	14.70dq, 14.49	14.95 -91
Krawczak	Dorota	POL	14 Jan 68	168/53	100	11.43w	11.78 -90
					100h	13.28	13.43 -92
* Kremlyova	Lyubov	RUS	21 Dec 62	166/52	800	1:59.8e	1:58.95 -94
					1000	2:33.55	2:34.84i -93
					1500	4:04.88	3:58.71 -92
					1M	4:22.46	4:24.50 -92
Kreutel	Ursula	GER	14 Sep 65	174/83	DT	60.20	65.32 -90
* Krivelyova	Svetlana	RUS	13 Jun 69	182/93	SP	20.84	21.06 -92
Kubi	Elju	EST	25 Mar 51	179/79	DT	55.56	65.00 -87
Kuehl	Kris	USA	30 Jul 70	183/86	DT	60.16	55.02 -92
* Kumbernuss	Astrid	GER	5 Feb 70	186/90	SP	19.92	20.77 -90
					DT	59.64	66.60 -88
Kumura	Kaori	JPN	22 Aug 70	157/40	10k	32:20.43	32:10.32 -92
					HMar	70:04	70:48 -92
Kuprianovich	Tamara	BLS	26 Sep 64	182/67	800	2:00.63	2:02.3 -92

Name		Nat	Born	Ht/Wt	Event	1993 Mark	Pre-1993 Best
Kurochkina	Tatyana	BLS	15 Sep 67	174/62	400h	55.64	54.39 -88
Kuzenkova	Olga	RUS	4 Oct 70		HT	64.64	65.40 -92
Kuzina	Natalya	RUS	70		100h	13.31w	13.12, 13.21w -92
Kuznyetsova	Olga	RUS	67		800	2:01.62	2:01.19 -92
Kuznyetsova	Yana	RUS	72		LJ	6.44i	6.36 -92
Lah	Barbara	ITA	24 Mar 72	180/60	TJ	13.38, 13.50w	12.91 -92
Lainio ¶	Minna	FIN	22 Aug 68	163/49	800	2:01.99 dq	2:07.97 -91
					1500	4:10.39 dq	4:15.95 -92
Landès	Béatrice	FRA	4 Aug 67	168/53	HJ	1.88i	1.90 -92
Landre	Francine	FRA	26 Jul 70	164/50	400	51.92	52.43 -92
Langenhuizen	Ine	HOL	27 Oct 68	176/72	100h	13.28	13.38 -88, 13.29w -91
Langley	Beverley	JAM	16 Dec 76	152/50	100	11.0w	11.81 -92
Lapa	Larisa	UKR	9 Apr 72	176/92	SP	16.34	
Lapierre	Violetta	FRA	15 Oct 63	164/53	100	11.43w, 11.53	11.55 -87
Larsen	Ingvild	NOR	3 Oct 75	179/65	LJ	6.53w	6.32 -92
* Lasovskaya	Inna	RUS	17 Dec 69	177/67	TJ	14.70	14.40i -89, 14.07 -92
Lauren	Jana	GER	28 Jun 70	182/82	DT	62.80	66.30 -89
Laux-Schneider	Petra	GER	24 Jan 67	180/67	TJ	13.77	13.50 -92
Lawrence	Debbie	USA	15 Oct 61	172/57	10kW	45:55	44:42 -92
* Laza	Belsy	CUB	5 Jun 67	174/96	SP	19.33	20.96 -92
Leddin	Sandy	GER	1 Nov 70	166/54	5kW	22:32.56	22:28.29 -91
* Ledovskaya	Tatyana	BLS	21 May 66	171/60	400	51.90	50.93, 50.4 -88
					400h	54.60	53.11 -91
Lee	Young-sun	KOR	21 Feb 74	163/63	JT	61.44	63.32 -92
Lefèbvre	Nathalie	FRA	2 Sep 71	183/61	HJ	1.90	1.87 -92
Lemettinen	Ritva	FIN	9 Sep 60	171/53	Mar	2:33:18	2:34:00 -89
Leonenko	Olga	UKR	13 Feb 70	169/51	5kW	22:20.0	21:30 -91, 21:38.86 -92
					10kW	45:43.86	44:18 -92
Lesage	Odile	FRA	28 Jun 69	178/65	Hep	5888	6141 -92
Leshcheva	Yekaterina	RUS	21 Apr 74		200	23.25	24.17 -92
Leszczynska	Anna	POL	15 Feb 71	176/63	100h	13.32	13.62 -89
* Letko	Anne Marie	USA	7 Mar 69	168/48	10k	31:37.26	32:26.65 -91
Lewis	Denise	GBR	27 Aug 72	173/64	Hep	5774	5812 -92
* Li	Chunxiu	CHN	13 Aug 69	171/63	10kW	45:00.32, 41:48	42:47.6 -92
Li	Jing	CHN	21 Oct 69		LJ	6.58w	6.77 -92
Li	Jun	CHN	Sep 69		HJ	1.88	1.88 -92
Li	Li	CHN	1 Oct 72		10k	32:15.43	
Li	Libin	CHN			Mar	2:34:33	
Li	Qiumei	CHN	Sep 74		DT	58.90	55.66 -91
Li	Shimei	CHN	68		DT	57.56	55.08 -91
Li	Shuhua	CHN	10 Jul 68		JT	13.63	13.69 -91
Li	Shuxiang	CHN	14 Jul 69	167/58	100	11.39	11.49 -91
Li	Xiaoyan	CHN	26 Jun 72		100h	13.36	13.58 -92
Li	Xiaoyun	CHN	10 Jul 71	179/87	SP	20.08i, 18.17	19.47 -91
Li	Xiumei	CHN	Jan 68		400	52.54	53.69 -92
					400h	56.80	56.46 -92
Li	Yemei	CHN	25 May 66		800	2:30:36	2:30:39 -92
Li	Ying	CHN	24 Jun 73	160/51	1500	4:01.71	4:09.04 -92
					3k	8:42.39	8:57.20 -92
Li	Yuxin	CHN	73		10kW	42:45, 44:13.1	44:19 -92
Liang	Chunlian	CHN	27 Jan 75		JT	59.38	
Liang	Shufang	CHN	2 Aug 72		800	2:02.70	2:05.77 -92
Liang	Yanping	CHN	Jun 70		400	52.40	53.53 -92
Lichtenhagen	Silke	GER	20 Nov 73	173/54	200	23.33w	23.54, 23.43w -92
Liepina	Anita	LAT	17 Nov 67	163/60	10kW	45:22	50:29.9 -88
Lima dos Santos	Orlane Maria	BRA	9 Dec 66	173/62	HJ	1.89	1.92 -89
Limonta	Odalmis	CUB	13 Jan 72	176/64	400	52.18A	52.75 -92
Ling	Xueyan	CHN	14 Feb 72		400	51.69	52.74 -92
					400h	54.52	56.40 -92
Liu	Bo	CHN	12 Mar 72		100h	13.27	14.09 -92
					Hep	6205	5706 -92
Liu	Caimei	CHN	Mar 71		10kW	44:44	45:19.6 -91
Liu	Cui	CHN	Aug 71		JT	59.64	60.45 -90
* Liu	Dong	CHN	27 Dec 73	173/55	800	1:55.54	2:02.4 -91
					1500	4:00.50	4:05.14 -92
Liu	Hongyu	CHN	1 Dec 75	158/54	5kW	21:55	
					10kW	42:47, 43:49.5	45:16 -91

Name		Nat	Born	Ht/Wt	Event	1993 Mark	Pre-1993 Best
Liu	Huirong	CHN	11 May 75		800	2:01.49	2:06.8 -92
Liu	Jianying	CHN	19 Nov 71		10k	31:23.92	33:06.95 -91
Liu	Jing	CHN	10 Jul 71		800	2:01.82	2:07.58 -90
Liu	Jingmin	CHN	1 Feb 72	169/48	TJ	14.03	13.84 -92
* Liu	Li	CHN	12 Mar 71	167/55	800	1:56.96	2:01.6 -91
					1500	3:59.34	4:00.20 -92
Liu	Qing	CHN	Apr 70		Hep	6094	5882 -91
Liu	Shixiang	CHN	Jan 71		10k	32:33.71	32:55.4 -90
Liu	Shufang	CHN	2 Aug 72		800	2:02.70	2:06.9 -92
Liu	Shuzhen	CHN	7 May 66	167/63	LJ	6.59	6.92 -90
Liu	Wanjie	CHN	Nov 75		800	2:01.36	2:03.8 -91
					1500	4:10.34	
Liu	Weiwei	CHN	11 May 71		400	51.53	53.45 -92
Liu	Xiaomei	CHN	11 Jan 72		100	11.02	11.60 -87
					200	22.70	23.88 -91
Liu	Yan	CHN	Mar 74		1500	4:09.98	
Liu	Ying	CHN	21 Jan 74		SP	17.81	17.59 -92
Liu	Yuying	CHN	Jun 72		Mar	2:32:52	
Lloyd	Andrea	JAM	10 Aug 71	170/	100	11.37w	11.59, 11.25w -90
					200	23.36	23.35 -91, 23.19w -90
Loboyko	Nadezhda	RUS	7 Sep 61	165/54	800	2:01.73	1:56.64 -90
Lock	Michelle	AUS	29 Mar 67		400	51.97	50.78 -92
Lokar'	Claudia	GER	9 Feb 64	160/47	1500	4:12.23	4:09.64 -87
(Borgschulze)					3k	8:51.35	8:54.13 -91
					5k	15:16.16	15:38.32 -91
					10k	32:05.33	32:43.64 -92
Long	Yuwen	CHN	Aug 75		10kW	42:44, 44:11.7	44:22.6 -91
Look-Jaeger	Clare	USA	17 Jun 66	174/64	Hep	5670	5644 -92
* López	Aliuska	CUB	29 Aug 69	169/53	100h	12.73	12.73 -90
* López	Isel	CUB	11 Jul 70	174/76	JT	61.48	66.18 -90
* Lorupe	Tecla	KEN	9 May 71	156/48	5k	15:08.03	
					10k	31:21.20	31:34.30 -92
					HMar	70:12	72:27 -92
Lu	Xifang	CHN	16 Dec 73		400	52.66	53.81, 53.6 -92
* Lu	Yi	CHN	10 Apr 74	160/56	800	1:57.77	2:02.91 -92
					1500	4:00.05	4:15.05 -92
Luan	Chunmei	CHN	25 Mar 70		400h	57.34	56.84 -92
Luan	Zhili	CHN	6 Jan 73		JT	64.62	60.28 -91
Lugovskaya	Tatyana	UKR	17 Apr 69	175/87	DT	57.24	60.06 -90
Lukyniv	Nadezhda	UKR	14 May 68	180/105	SP	17.78i, 17.70	18.01 -88
Lundahl	Karoliina	FIN	30 Jun 68	172/76	SP	16.76	16.55i -91, 16.48 -92
(Leppaluotto)							
Luo	Bin	CHN	7 Jan 70	166/49	100h	12.99	12.97 -90
Luo	Zhonghua	CHN	26 Jan 69	175/75	JT	62.24	64.52 -90
Lupton	Vicky	GBR	17 Apr 72	157/57	5kW	22:34.50	21:36, 22:12.21 -92
					10kW	45:28	46:28 -92
Lüthi	Kathrin	SUI	7 Oct 69	175/59	400	52.59	53.09 -92
					400h	57.69	58.74 -92
Lynch	Shola	USA	20 Mar 69	168/54	800	2:02.56	2:03.69 -92
Lysak	Yelena	RUS	19 Oct 75		TJ	13.86	13.43, 13.44w -92
Lysakova	Olga	UKR	24 Nov 71	180/67	400	52.55	
Lyubomirova	Lyudmila	RUS	62		10kW	45:19	44:57 -88
Ma	Chun-Ping	TPE	3 Aug 71	176/62	Hep	5636	5521 -91
Ma	Ling	CHN	Jul 66		JT	59.50	59.14 -91
* Ma	Liyan	CHN	3 Nov 68	156/50	3k	8:19.78	
					10k	31:10.46	
					Mar	2:25:46	
* Ma	Miaolan	CHN	18 Jan 70	176/63	100h	13.28	13.60 -90
					HJ	1.89	1.82 -90
					LJ	6.97, 7.06w	6.62 -90
					TJ	14.12	13.40 -91
					Hep	6750	6306 -90
Ma	Ningning	CHN	20 Sep 76	159/51	3k	8:36.45	
					10k	32:09.94	
* Ma	Yuqin	CHN	11 Sep 72		200	22.95	23.4 -92
					400	49.81	52.04 -91
* Machado	M Manuela	POR	9 Aug 63	161/52	10k	32:25.6	32:24.07 -91
					Mar	2:30:54	2:27:42 -92

Name		Nat	Born	Ht/Wt	Event	1993 Mark	Pre-1993 Best
Machado	Teresa	POR	22 Jul 69	170/80	SP	16.76	16.60 -92
					DT	63.70	63.48 -92
Machotkova	Zuzana	TCH	25 Mar 65	174/64	400h	57.04	56.50 -90
Machuca	Eva	MEX	14 Jan 70	154/45	10kW	44:53	46:44 -91
Mackey	Kendra	USA	14 Jan 69	178/55	400	51.73	50.46 -92
Macleod	Karen	GBR	24 Apr 58	168/50	Mar	2:34:30	2:37:54 -91
Madden	Kalleen	USA	30 Aug 71	176/59	Hep	5642	5408 -92
Maddox	Keri	GBR	4 Jul 72	170/62	100H	13.24, 13.20w	13.32 -91
Madubuko	Nkechi	GER	28 Mar 72	173/62		13.53w	
Maenhout	Ann	BEL	8 Feb 69	171/59	400h	55.59	56.21, 56.0 -92
Maffeis	Agnese	ITA	9 Mar 65	187/81	SP	17.73i, 17.52	17.70i -89, 17.56 -92
					DT	62.54	62.08 -92
Mai	Christina	GER	3 Sep 61	159/46	3k	9:00.24	8:54.16 -91
Majchrzak	Katarzyna	POL	25 Jun 67	186/67	HJ	1.92	1.92 -92
Makarova	Rimma	RUS	18 Jul 63	168/62	5kW	21:32.70i	21:46 -89, 22:02.1 -91
					10kW	43:54	45:14 -91
Maki	Izumi	JPN	10 Dec 68	161/43	5k	15:34.0	15:27.12 -91
					10k	32:15.79	31:40.30 -92
Makolova	Vera	RUS	17 Feb 66	160/46	10kW	44:50	43:04 -89
Malátová	Vladimira	TCH	15 May 67	178/79	DT	63.92	62.24 -92
* Malchugina	Galina	RUS	17 Dec 62	168/62	100	11.25	10.96 -92, 10.8 -88
					100	22.22	22.22 -92
Malcolm	Twilet	JAM	5 Feb 69		100	11.40, 11.17w	11.68 -89
- Williams					200	22.93w	23.89 -91, 23.76w -90
Malesev	Tamara	YUG	8 Jan 67	182/59	LJ	6.44	6.73 -91
					TJ	13.41i	13.51 -90
* Malone	Maicel	USA	12 Jun 69	176/63	400	51.10	50.33 -92
Manning	Anne	AUS	13 Nov 59		5kW	21:55.5	22:46.2 -92
					10kW	46:15.60	48:22 -92
Mardomingo	Maria José	ESP	27 Jan 69	165/56	100h	13.24	13.19 -91
* Markova	Olga	RUS	6 Aug 68	163/47	Mar	2:25:27	2:23:43 -92
Marquette	Ulla	CAN	28 Jun 58		3k	8:59.21	8:55.51 -92
Marshall	Debbie	USA	5 Aug 65	173/52	800	2:00.04	1:59.97 -88
* Martén	Maritza	CUB	17 Aug 63	177/93	DT	65.96	70.68 -92
Marti	Debbie	GBR	14 May 68	170/52	HJ	1.91	1.94i -91, 1.93 -92
* Martin-Floreal	LaVonna	USA	18 Nov 66	168/59	200	23.39	23.24 -87, 22.94w -85
					100h	12.78	12.69 -92
Martínez	Lisette	CUB	11 Oct 66	175/79	SP	19.73	18.90 -92
Martínez	Virginia	CUB	3 Sep 68	168/62	LJ	6.45	6.57 -91
Martínez	Yaminoraydes	CUB	16 Jul 73	173/63	100h	13.28	13.53 -92
Marusyeva	Margarita	RUS	18 Oct 67	170/60	3k	8:52.16	
Marxer	Manuela	LIE	6 Aug 65	172/60	Hep	5836	5924 -92
* Masterkova	Svetlana	RUS	17 Jan 68	170/57	800	1:56.76	1:57.23 -91
Matejková	Alice	TCH	11 Jan 69	181/74	DT	60.52	59.06 -91
Mathes	Simone	GER	13 Mar 75	171/75	HT	55.42	55.42 -92
Matsui	Emi	JPN	20 Feb 63	158/58	JT	59.20	60.52 -82
* Matsuno	Akemi	JPN	27 Apr 68	148/35	Mar	2:27:53	2:27:02 -92
Matuseviciené	Dalia	LIT	7 Jan 61	167/52	800	2:01.42	1:56.7 -88
Matveyeva	Lyudmila	RUS	1 Feb 57	155/49	10k	32:43.46	31:38.02 -88
Matyashova	Tatyana	RUS	2 Aug 73	182/62	TJ	13.83	13.85 -91
Matyusheva	Irina	UKR	5 Jun 65	176/61	Hep	5729	6424 -88
Mau	Beatrice	GER	20 Feb 71	174/66	Hep	6207	6267 -92
Maury	Maryse	FRA	4 Sep 64	178/61	HJ	1.88	1.96 -85
* May	Fiona (now ITA)	GBR	12 Dec 69	181/60	LJ	6.86A, 6.78	6.88 -90, 6.98w -89
Mayhew	Donna	USA	20 Jun 60	162/66	JT	62.98	63.66 -88
Mayorova	Lyudmila	RUS	6 Nov 68	168/62	10kW	45:13	45:15 -90
McCaffrey	Janice	CAN	20 Oct 59	163/47	10kW	46:16	45:06 -92
McCandless	Katy	USA	22 Jun 70	173/52	3k	8:56.00	9:19.45 -92
					5k	15:34.93	16:08.10 -92
* McColgan	Liz	GBR	24 May 64	168/45	Mar	2:29:37	2:27:32 -91
McCord	Tamyka	USA	23 Jun 71	176/59	400	52.63	53.41i -92, 53.98 -91
McDonald	Beverly	JAM	15 Feb 70	165/59	100	11.22, 11.05w	11.37 -91, 11.2 -87
					200	22.67	23.31 -92, 23.20w -90
McGeorge	Sonia	GBR	2 Nov 64	170/53	1500	4:11.89	4:10.75 -90
McGillivary	Aileen	GBR	13 Aug 70		100	11.43w	11.54 -92
					200	23.29	23.66, 23.4w -92
McKenzie	Kim	USA	21 Mar 61	165/58	100h	13.34	12.77 -92

Name		Nat	Born	Ht/Wt	Event	1993 Mark	Pre-1993 Best
McKernan	Jackie	GBR	1 Jul 65	178/73	DT	60.72	58.90 -91
* McKiernan	Catherina	IRL	30 Nov 69	165/48	3k	8:58.04	8:51.33 -92
					10k	32:14.74	
McLeon	Nancy	CUB	1 May 71	167/55	400	52.15, 51.5	52.53 -92
McNamara	Chris	USA	29 Jan 66	165/47	10k	32:50.84	33:14.95 -92
McPaul	Louise	AUS	24 Jan 69	173/64	JT	60.86	63.34 -91
					Hep	5709	5415 -91
McPherson	Vikki	GBR	1 Jun 71		10k	32:32.42	33:27.55 -92
Medovárszky	Éva	HUN	15 Aug 69	176/58	TJ	13.36, 13.48w	12.71 -92
Medvedyeva	Yelena	RUS	9 Jul 65	160/57	JT	64.54	65.68 -95
Mehes	Livia	ROM	6 Mar 65	174/90	SP	18.10	19.61 -86
					HT	57.96	56.46 -92
Meier	Simone	SUI	15 Nov 65	172/48	1500	4:11.70	4:09.97 -92
Meinel	Caroline	GER	28 Apr 73	175/57	HJ	1.88i	1.80 -91
* Meissner	Heike	GER	29 Jan 70	172/57	400h	54.64	54.77 -91
Melendez	Joyce	PUR	4 Jul 70	165/48	100h	13.22, 13.20w	13.36 -92
Melinte	Mihaela	ROM	27 Mar 75	170/78	HT	62.52	58.70 -92
Melnikova	Irina	RUS	9 Jan 74	170/57	HT	13.53	13.68 -90
Mencik	Barbara	FRA	22 Dec 70	174/57	HJ	1.90	1.90i -90, 1.88 -89
Mendes	Luciana	BRA	26 Jul 71	170/55	400	52.36	53.25 -92
					800	2:00.37	2:03.2 -91
Mernikova	Oksana	BLS	21 Nov 67	166/54	800	1:58.38	2:00.53 -91
					1000	2:36.47	
					1500	4:05.71	4:06.40 -91
Merry	Katharine	GBR	21 Sep 74	170/56	100	11.40w	11.52 -92, 11.47w -89
					200	23.20	23.50, 23.41w -91
Metzner	Claudia	GER	5 May 66	173/51	HMar	71:19	
* Meyer	Elana	RSA	10 Oct 66	159/45	1500	4:07.90	4:02.15 -92
					2k	5:41.5+	5:40.7 -92
					3k	8:32.81	8:32.00 -91
					5k	14:46.41	14:44.15 -92
					10k	32:28.02	31:11.75 -92
					HMar	67:22	67:59 -91
Michurina	Olga	RUS	13 Feb 64		Mar	2:34:31	2:41:36 -92
Mikelyte	Austra	LIT	5 May 69	185/92	DT	64.62	65.14 -91
Mikhailova	Lyudmila	RUS	12 Apr 69	174/61	LJ	6.83	6.37 -92
					Hep	6308	6112 -92
* Mikhalchenko	Larisa	UKR	16 May 63	181/93	DT	63.90	70.80 -88
Milan	Elena	ITA	30 Jan 71	169/57	Hep	5635	5408 -92
* Miles	Jearl	USA	4 Sep 66	170/60	200	23.29, 23.19w	23.34 -91
					400	49.82	50.19 -91
Miller	Inger	USA	12 Dec 72	164/56	100	11.11	11.16, 11.09w -92
					200	22.33	23.19, 22.43w -92
Milo	Linda	BEL	9 Jul 60		Mar	2:34:12	2:35:09 -90
Milousheva	Eleonora	BUL	8 Apr 73	180/54	HJ	1.89	1.91 -92
Milusauskaite	Sonate	LIT	31 Aug 73	163/51	10kW	45:50	
* Min	Chunfeng	CHN	17 Mar 69	175/82	DT	65.26	66.76 -91
Mineva	Nevena	BUL	14 Jun 72	165/52	5kW	22:33.00	22:27.15 -92
Miroshnik	Svetlana	UKR	3 Jun 68	162/52	800	2:02.56	2:03.63 -91
					1500	4:09.45	4:11.99 -92
					3k	8:56.10	9:02.84 -92
Misyulya	Natalya	BLS	12 Apr 66	157/47	10kW	43:15	44:39 -90
Mitchell	Danyel	USA	16 Sep 72	178/93	SP	16.91i, 16.49	16.40 -92
					DT	57.04	53.38 -92
Mitchell	Denise	USA	20 Feb 66	160/50	400	52.15	51.72 -87
Mitchell	Kim	USA	11 Jan 71	173/60	200	23.30A	23.74 -91, 23.31w -92
* Mitchell	Nicole	JAM	5 Jun 74	168/60	100	11.18, 11.02w	11.30, 11.26w -92
						11.0w	11.1 -92
					200	23.25	23.41 -91
* Mitkova	Svetla	BUL	17 Jun 64	178/97	SP	20.00	20.91 -87
					DT	61.18	69.42 -87
Mitsumori	Rie	JPN	26 Oct 74	158/45	5kW	22:33.02	24:04.77 -92
					10kW	45:48	48:51.6 -92
Mitsumori	Yuka	JPN	8 Jan 72	160/45	5kW	22:04, 22:29.68	22:49.3 -91
					10kW	45:05	46:26 -92
Miyajima	Akiko	JPN	17 Sep 66	162/59	JT	58.12	59.48 -91
Mizera	Yelena	RUS	20 Feb 66	162/56	100	11.43, 11.23w	11.32 -90
					200	22.73	22.49 -90

Name		Nat	Born	Ht/Wt	Event	1993 Mark	Pre-1993 Best
* Modahl	Diane	GBR	17 Jun 66	170/56	800	1:59.00	1:58.65 -90
					1000	2:35.46	2:37.06 -89
Moelo	Annie	FRA	10 Nov 62	167/57	TJ	13.45w, 13.02	13.02, 13.42w -91
Molchan	Margarita	BLS	21 Jan 66		100	11.2	11.4 -92
* Moller	Lorraine	NZL	1 Jun 55	174/58	10k	32:50.30	32:40.17 -88
					Mar	2:30:31	2:28:17 -86
Molzan	Ramona	GER	1 Aug 71	168/54	TJ	13.43w	13.19 -92
Monar-Enweani	Vannessa	CAN	11 Dec 69		LJ	6.57w	6.36 -92
Mondie-Milner	Celena	USA	6 Aug 68	169/57	100	11.44w	11.34 -90, 11.29w -88
* Montalvo	Niurka	CUB	4 Jun 68	170/53	LJ	6.64, 6.75w	6.88 -92
					TJ	14.51	13.92 -92
Montelier	Lency	CUB	13 Feb 71	163/55	400h	57.43	56.79 -92
Moore	Barbara	NZL	27 Jul 57		10k	33:00.88	32:12.78 -89
Moreira	Amelia	BRA	30 Jul 65	175/70	DT	55.74	48.88 -88
Moreira	Marta	POR	29 Nov 66	165/57	400h	57.09	57.11 -92
Morgan	Michelle	JAM			400h	57.6	58.13 -91
Mormand	Anita	FRA	20 Feb 71	172/60	200	23.26	23.32 -92
Moros	Helen	NZL	2 Nov 67	165/48	5k	15:47.33	
					10k	32:32.24	
Morrison	Kirsty	GBR	28 Oct 75	172.70	JT	59.36	53.22 -92
Morrison	Melissa	USA	9 Jul 71	165/49	100	11.45	
					100h	13.24, 13.2w	13.38 -92
Mosconi	Elisa	ITA	8 Apr 66	166/55	LJ	6.46w	
Moskalets'	Svetlana	RUS	1 Nov 69		LJ	6.77	6.29i, 6.25 -91
(Akimova)					Hep	6510	5792 -89
Motkova	Tatyana	RUS	26 Oct 68		HJ	1.92	1.89 -91
Mou	Fangmei	CHN	Feb 72		10kW	44:30	
Moyes	Jayne	AUS	25 Jan 66		100h	13.34, 13.1w	13.49 -91, 13.1w -92
Mu	Lianjuan	CHN	28 Jun 73	180/65	Hep	6154	5831 -92
Mues	Claudia	GER	3 Jan 75	192/77	SP	16.66	15.94 -92
Mukamurenzi	Marcianne	RWA	11 Nov 59	165/51	10k	32:57.06	32:27.90 -91
Mukhetdinova	Yulia	RUS	69		200	23.13w	23.48 -92
Mun	Gyong-ae	PRK	8 Apr 69	154/47	Mar	2:32:40	2:27:16 -89
Munerotto	Rosanna	ITA	3 Dec 62	169/53	5k	15:36.62	15:39.32 -92
					10k	32:48.36	32:05.75 -91
					HMar	71:07	69:38 -92
Muñoz	Maria Luisa	ESP	6 May 59	164/48	Mar	2:31:01	2:39:04 -91
Muranaka	Mahomi	JPN	31 Oct 66	162/45	5k	15:31.01	
					10k	32:19.85	
Murcia	Rosario	FRA	23 Sep 64	158/46	10k	32:54.65	31:42.83 -92
Muresan	Carla	ROM	17 Dec 67	172/62	DT	61.42	63.14 -92
(Dumitru)							
Murgoci	Elena	ROM	20 Feb 60	165/50	3k	8:58.89	8:58.28 -88
					5k	15:27.29	
					10k	32:08.60	32:20.7 -88
					HMar	70:13	
Muros	Elma	PHI	14 Jan 67	170/54	LJ	6.44	6.52 -89
* Murray	Yvonne	GBR	4 Oct 64	172/50	1500	4:08.63	4:01.20 -87
					1M	4:32.00i	4:23.06 -86
					2k	5:36.03	5:29.58 -86
					3k	8:30.30	8:29.02 -88
* Mushailova	Irina	RUS	6 Jan 67	164/56	LJ	7.02	6.89 -92
					TJ	14.79	13.81 -91
Musunoi	Oana	ROM	17 Sep 72	175/50	HJ	1.91i, 1.87	1.94 -92
* Mutola	Maria	MOZ	27 Oct 72	167/50	400	51.44	52.49 -92
					800	1:55.43	1:57.49 -92
					1000	2:32.57	- 0 -
					1500	4:04.97	4:02.60 -92
* Myers	Sandra	ESP	9 Jan 61	168/58	200	23.28	22.38 -90
					400	50.83	49.67 -91
Mykytok	Laura	USA	17 Sep 68	183/51	5k	15:44.27	
Naeris	Virge	EST	12 Dec 69	178/64	Hep	5878	5603 -92
Nagy-Földing	Judit	HUN	9 Sep 65	168/56	Mar	2:32:07	2:34:16 -90
Narloch	Marcia	BRA	28 Mar 69	151/39	Mar	2:32:23	2:32:42 -91
Nasonkina	Yelena	UKR	11 Aug 62	167/58	400	52.43	52.70 -92
* Nastase	Liliana	ROM	1 Aug 62	170/67	100h	13.11, 12.9	12.81 -91
					LJ	6.67i, 6.78 exh	6.78 -89
					Hep	6260	6619 -92

Name		Nat	Born	Ht/Wt	Event	1993 Mark	Pre-1993 Best
Nathan	DeDe	USA	20 Apr 68	180/74	Hep	6038	6162 -92
Naudé	Madele	RSA	2 May 63	174/52	800	2:02.03	2:01.28 -88
Nauer	Daria	SUI	21 May 66	172/48	3k	8:54.53	8:57.50 -91
					5k	15:18.00	15:28.55 -91
Nazarova	Olga	RUS	1 Jun 65	169/57	400	52.58	49.11 -88, 48.9 -88
Nazarova	Olga	RUS	28 Feb 62	177/63	400h	55.08	55.47 -88
Nechiporets	Alla	UKR	20 Oct 64	170/62	LJ	6.52	6.91 -90
Nedelcu	Magdalena	ROM	12 May 74	167/56	400	52.24	50.87 -92
* Negura	Iulia	ROM	26 Jan 67	166/56	10k	32:11.58	31:52.58 -91
					HMar	71:22	70:59 -92
Neighbors	Teresa	USA	26 May 67	162/54	100	11.40, 11.19w	11.28, 11.1 -92
					200	23.17w	23.45, 23.42w -92
* Neimke	Kathrin	GER	18 Jul 66	180/95	SP	19.78	21.21 -87
Nekrosaite	Terese	LIT	19 Oct 61	172/74	JT	66.34	67.64 -92
Nelson	Carole	FRA	27 Jan 71	162/51	400h	56.64	56.61 -92
Nelyubova	Olga	RUS	12 Jul 64	167/55	800	2:01.20	1:59.31 -88
					1500	4:08.17	4:06.41 -88
Nenasheva	Viktoria	RUS	16 Jun 70	160/50	3k	9:00.31	8:54.88 -92
					10k	32:33.46	32:40.33 -92
Neplyuyeva	Inna	UKR	17 Mar 71	178/63	400h	57.69	58.20 -92
Nerius	Steffi	GER	1 Jul 72	178/70	JT	63.88	60.02 -91
Neves	Fátima	POR	13 Feb 63	163/50	10k	32:52.84	33:40.55 -92
					HMar	71:22, 70:59 sh	
Newsome	Cynthia	USA	5 Apr 76		400	52.47	54.39 -92
Ni	Chunyan	CHN			JT	58.74	
Nicolau	Cristina	ROM	9 Aug 77	182/61	LJ	6.44	6.30 -92
* Nielsen	Renata	DEN	18 May 66	176/62	LJ	6.84	6.86 -91
					TJ	13.71	
Nifontova	Svetlana	RUS	74		10kW	45:08	
Nifontova	Yulia	RUS	14 May 74		5kW	22:35, 22:41.4	22:34.02 -92
Niga	Viorica	ROM	22 Nov 68	159/52	1500	4:11.37	4:09.00 -89
Nikishina	Olga	UKR	29 Apr 66	172/86	DT	62.32	63.54 -90
* Nikitina'	Larisa	RUS	29 Apr 65	177/70	LJ	6.51	6.75 -89
- Turchinskaya					Hep	6415	7007 -89
* Nikolayeva	Yelena	RUS	1 Feb 66	168/60	5kW	21:17	21:00.80 -91
					10kW	43:11	42:40 -92
* Ninova	Ljudmila	AUT	25 Jun 60	175/61	LJ	7.06	6.95 -91
					TJ	13.60	13.67i -92, 13.48 -91
Nishiyama	Kayoko	JPN	17 Jul 70	155/45	5k	15:43.53	
					10k	32:20.27	33:45.13 -91
Nkoma	Georgette	CMR	16 Jun 65	166/62	200	23.28w	23.85 -92
Noel	Camille	CAN	14 Apr 74	157/52	400	51.88	52.74 -92
Nordstrom	Kaye	NZL	30 May 68	163/74	JT	57.40	60.84 -92
Nováková	Sarka	TCH	21 Feb 71	185/62	HJ	1.91	1.95 -92
Novikova	Nadezhda	RUS	66		LJ	6.56	6.44 -92
* Nuneva	Anelia	BUL	30 Jun 62	167/57	100	11.32	10.85 -88
					200	23.18	22.01 -87
Nurutdinova $	Lilia	RUS	15 Dec 63	174/52	800	1:59.17	1:55.99 -92
					1k	2:35.03	2:33.84 -91
					1500	4:08.60	4:07.22 -92
* O'Sullivan	Sonia	IRL	28 Nov 69	173/53	1000	2:34.66	2:38.68 -90
					1500	3:59.60	4:01.23 -92
					1M	4:22.94	4:24.27 -92
					2k	5:40.77+	5:41.22 -91
					3000	8:28.74	8:37.92 -82
					5k	14:45.92	14:59.11 -92
Oana	Mihaela	ROM	11 Nov 68	176/86	SP	19.51	19.31 -92
Oanta	Iolanda	ROM	11 Oct 65	183/63	TJ	13.93i, 13.42	13.11i92
Odoemenam	Emily	NGR	24 Oct 70	170/61	400	52.26	53.05 -91
Odzilyayeva	Yulia	RUS	70		5kW	22:36.7	
					10kW	44:42	46:27 -92
Oe	Teruko	JPN	16 Jun 69	158/38	Mar	2:32:43	2:31:04 -92
Ogiwara	Kayoko	JPN	1 Apr 71	160/44	5k	15:36.98	
Okamoto	Makiko	JPN	30 Mar 72	168/49	10k	32:50.75	
Olenchenko	Vera	RUS	21 Mar 59		LJ	6.54	6.92 -85
					TJ	13.57	13.45 -90
Olijare	Ludmila	LAT	5 Feb 58	169/63	100h	13.24	12.90 -88, 12.89w -83, 12.6 -89

Name		Nat	Born	Ht/Wt	Event	1993 Mark	Pre-1993 Best
Oliveira	Ana Isabel	POR	9 Jan 63	172/60	TJ	13.29,13.80w	13.44i -90,12.95 -91
* Ondieki	Lisa	AUS	12 May 60	168/47	Mar	2:27:27	2:23:51 -88
* Onyali	Mary	NGR	3 Feb 68	168/54	100	10.97	11.04, 10.9 -91
					200	22.32	22.43 -88
Opara-Thompson	Christy	NGR	2 May 70	170/60	100	11.38, 11.27w	11.28 -92
					200	23.36w	23.53, 23.4 -82
					LJ	6.57	6.72 -92
Oppong	Anita	GER	12 Jul 74	180/65	400h	57.90	58.20 -92
* Ordina	Vera	RUS	4 Jun 68	172/56	400h	55.33	54.37 -92
Orsani	Maria Grazia	ITA	11 Jun 69	168/56	5kW	21:15.4	21:35.43 -92
Orthaber	Katharina	SUI	9 Sep 63	176/56	1500	4:11.94	4:10.63 -91
Osaki	Yumi	JPN	10 May 72	159/42	5k	15:35.9	15:52.4 -92
					10k	32:14.08	
Ota	Yoko	JPN	14 Jan 75	173/53	HJ	1.93	1.87 -92
* Ottey	Merlene	JAM	10 May 60	173/59	100	10.82	10.78 -90
					200	21.77	21.64 -91
Ou	Yanlan	CHN	Jan 74		100	11.35	11.71 -92
Ouaziz	Zahra	MAR	20 Dec 69	166/50	3k	9:00.55	9:10.7 -87
Ovaska	Asta	FIN	29 Jul 63	185/105	SP	16.56	18.57 -89
Owens	Keisha	USA	7 Apr 73		100	11.36w	11.60 -92
					200	23.40, 23.37w	24.63 -89
Pachut	Sylwia	POL	21 Jul 70	168/58	400h	56.18	58.10 -92
Pagel	Ramona	USA	10 Nov 61	183/86	SP	18.55	21.18 -88
					DT	58.52	61.92 -87
Painter	Trina	USA	25 Jun 66	165/50	10k	32:19.79	32:24.6 -92
					HMar	71:07	72:33 -92
Panarina	Natalya	RUS	6 May 75			59.06	55.12 -92
Panferova	Olga	RUS	21 Aug 77		5kW	22:37, 22:37.68	23:55.2 -92
Pang	Jiewen	CHN	23 Nov 67		100h	13.12	13.11 -90
Panikarovskikh	Yelena	RUS	4 Dec 59	172/64	HJ	1.96i, 1.92	1.98i -90, 1.95 -87
Paquette	Sonia	CAN	7 Feb 73	173/57	TJ	13.29	13.63 -92
Paredes	Concepcion	ESP	19 Jul 70	175/67	TJ	14.05, 14.16w	13.77, 14.03w -92
Parker	Jacqui	GBR	15 Oct 66	163/54	400h	56.68	56.15 -91
Parker	Susan	GBR	24 Mar 70		1500	4:12.43	4:17.91 -91
Parris	Debbie Ann	JAM	24 Mar 73	162/48	400h	55.80	57.34 -92
Paschke	Melanie	GER	29 Jun 70	168/54	100	11.23	11.56 -92
					200	22.97w	24.36 -92
Pasha	Nelrae	USA	28 Oct 70	170/60	400	51.30	51.35 -92
Paskhina	Aleksandra	RUS	14 Aug 71		100h	13.13, 13.1i,13.07w	13.63 -91
Patla	Genowefa	POL	17 Oct 62	175/73	JT	63.96	65.96 -91
Patoka	Antonina	RUS	12 Jan 64	182/95	DT	63.24	67.12 -89
Patzwahl	Kristin	GER	16 Jul 65	174/62	100h	12.98	12.80 -90
Paulaviciene	Rita	LIT	14 Dec 61	169/64	800	2:00.46	1:59.83 -92
* Paulino	Argentina	MOZ	7 Jul 73	166/59	400	51.82	52.34 -92
					800	1:56.62	2:03.81 -92
Pavlova	Anastasia	RUS	16 Jun 68	176/92	SP	17.10i	18.62i, 18.51 -92
Pavlova	Natalya	RUS	72		Hep	5738	5050 -92
* Pavlysh	Viktoria	UKR	15 Jan 69	174/80	SP	19.22	19.66 -92
Pazola	Ilona	POL	22 Mar 69	170/55	LJ	6.49	6.44 -92
					TJ	13.55, 13.64w	13.31 -92
Pedroso	Magalys	CUB	3 Jun 72		TJ	13.42	13.40 -92
Pei	Fang	CHN	1 Feb 71	163/53	100	11.42	11.44 -91
					200	23.01	23.27 -92
* Peleshenko	Larisa	RUS	29 Feb 64	187/95	SP	19.90i, 19.23	20.99 -87
Pellino	Cristiana	ITA	21 Sep 70	164/49	5kW	22:27.17	23:03.3 -91
					10kW	45:17	47:24 -91
Pells	Leah	CAN	9 Nov 64	170/55	1500	4:08.97	4:05.11 -89
Pendareva	Petya	BUL	20 Jan 71	162/50	100	11.14	11.33 -92
					200	22.78	23.11 -92
Pentukova	Tatyana	RUS	23 Jun 65		3k	8:55.98	9:03.29 -87
					5k	15:44.18	
					HMar	71:13	73:45 -92
* Pérec	Marie-José	FRA	9 May 68	180/60	100	11.12	10.96 -91
					200	21.99	22.20 -92
Pereira Santos	Sueli	BRA	8 Jan 65	165/63	JT	63.74	60.34 -88
Perevedentseva	Nina	RUS	64		LJ	6.63	6.66 -88
Periginelli	Karin	ITA	5 Feb 70	179/63	Hep	5692	5780 -92

Name		Nat	Born	Ht/Wt	Event	1993 Mark	Pre-1993 Best
* Perrone	Elisabetta	ITA	9 Jul 68	168/60	5kW	20:53.71	21:34.71 -92
					10kW	41:56, 44:01.6	44:19 -92
Peterková	Alena	TCH	13 Nov 60	167/53	Mar	2:33:43	2:30:36 -91
* Peters	Annette	USA	31 May 65	165/50	1500	4:08.97	4:09.7 -91
					2k	5:44.59	5:38.80 -92
					3k	8:43.59	8:42.09 -92
					5k	14:56.07	15:11.11 -92
Petrea	Georgeta	ROM	23 Oct 73	172/59	400h	57.85	57.13 -92
Petrova	Irina	BLS	13 Feb 62	167/54	10k	32:42.32	
Petukhova	Alla	RUS	20 Oct 70		800	2:02.01	2:04.61 -92
Phillips	Cheryl Ann	JAM	7 Oct 70	162/60	100	11.43w	11.41 -92, 11.33w -91
Phimphoo	Noodang	THA	15 Oct 68	162/50	400	52.60	53.70 -92
Pierre-Joseph	Corinne	FRA	27 Oct 66	166/57	400h	57.43	56.86 -89
* Pieterse	Zola	RSA	26 May 66	164/48	3k	8:52.85	8:28.83 -85
* Pippig	Uta	GER	7 Sep 65	167/55	3k	8:40.99	8:45.40 -91
					5k	15:15.04	15:04.87 -91
					10k	31:29.70	31:21.36 -92
					HMar	71:21	70:35 -91
					Mar	2:26:24	2:26:52 -91
+ Piquereau	Anne	FRA	15 Jun 64	171/65	100h	13.13	12.74 -91
Pirog	Marina	UKR	28 Aug 74	180/67	HT	58.24	53.10 -92
* Podkopayeva	Yekaterina	RUS	11 Jun 52	164/54	1000	2:37.27, 2:36.08i	2:36.08i -93
					1500	4:02.48	3:56.65 -84
					1M	4:23.78	4:29.36 -90
Podracka	Marcela	SVK	13 Mar 70	177/69	Hep	5902	6034 -89
Podyalovskaya	Irina	RUS	9 Oct 59	165/52	800	2:01.50	1:55.69 -84
Poelman	Jacqueline	HOL	5 Oct 73	171/65	100	11.41	11.44 -92
					200	23.39	23.28 -92
Poetschka	Lauren	AUS	22 Oct 74		400	57.5	60.3 -92
Poetschka	Renee	AUS	1 May 71	174/56	400	51.00	51.38 -91
					400h	57.04	
Poilagi	Rose-May	FRA	9 Feb 72	166/62	JT	57.22	51.52 -92
Politika	Yelena	UKR	24 Aug 64	172/70	100h	12.93	12.71 -86, 12.66w -88
Pollock	Peggy	USA	1 May 60	178/89	SP	16.54	17.79i -87, 17.58 -86
Polyanskaya	Viktoriya	RUS	71		HT	58.16	52.40 -92
* Ponomaryova	Margarita	RUS	19 Jun 63	176/63	400h	53.48	53.58 -84
Pont	Monica	ESP	3 Jun 69	161/48	10k	32:51.33	35:17.46 - 92
					Mar	2:31:21	- 0 -
Popykina	Natalya	RUS	11 Dec 70	174/66	LJ	6.58	
					Hep	6008	5773 -92
Porter	Shanelle	USA	20 Jan 72	178/67	400	52.05	51.93 -92
Poulin	Allison	USA	2 Oct 70	174/65	400h	55.94	57.06 -92
Power	Suzie	AUS	26 Mar 75	175/53	3k	8:59.71	9:04.30 -92
Pozdnyakova	Tatyana	UKR	4 Mar 56	164/59	HMar	71:22, 70:04 sh	
* Prandzheva	Iva	BUL	15 Feb 72	174/57	LJ	6.58	6.62 -92
					TJ	14.23, 14.32w	
Prasad	Nadia	FRA	6 Oct 67		10k	33:01.57	36:24.9 -89
(Bernard)					Mar	2:30:16	2:39:10 -91
Prather	Tisha	USA	5 Aug 71	166/55	100	11.29, 11.16w	11.47 -92
					200	23.08	23.64, 23.60w -92
Predikaka	Ksenija	SLO	11 Mar 70		LJ	6.51w	6.40 -92
					TJ	13.41	13.13 -92
Preira	Marie-Victoire	FRA	25 Jan 72	176/55	100h	13.11	14.24 - 90
Price-Smith	Connie	USA	3 Jun 62	192/93	SP	19.25	19.34 -91
					DT	63.52	64.82 -87
* Privalova	Irina	RUS	12 Nov 68	174/60	100	10.94, 10.81w	10.82, 10.81w -92
					200	21.88	21.93 -92
					400	49.89	-
Procaccio	Gina	USA	19 Jul 64	160/49	1500	4:12.51	4:06.6 -92
					3k	8:54.45	9:00.55 -92
Pupo	Alina	CUB	9 Mar 75		SP	16.33	15.26 -91
Putintseva	Irina	RUS	69		10kW	45:13	45:39 -92
Qi	Hong	CHN	Mar 69		100	11.33	11.43 -91
					200	22.87	23.09 -91
Qiu	Qiaoping	CHN	31 Oct 71	183/90	DT	64.00	66.08 -92
Qiu	Ying	CHN	May 71		DT	59.94	57.60 -91

Name		Nat	Born	Ht/Wt	Event	1993 Mark	Pre-1993 Best
* Qu	Yunxia	CHN	25 Dec 72	170/48	800	1:56.24	2:03.47 -89
					1500	3:50.46	3:57.08 -92
					3k	8:12.18	8:55.1 -91
					Mar	2:24:32	
Quentin	Fréderique	FRA	22 Dec 69	173/58	1500	4:11.03	4:10.45 -92
* Quintero	Ioamnet	CUB	8 Sep 72	178/62	HJ	2.01i, 2.00	1.98 -92
* Radcliffe	Paula	GBR	17 Dec 73	172/51	1500	4:11.6	4:16.82 -92
					2k	5:39.20	
					3k	8:40.40	8:51.78 -92
Radeyeva	Irina	RUS	15 Sep 68	166/57	400	52.28	52.49 -92
Radicheva	Sonya	BUL	8 Jun 68	170/65	JT	60.00	59.06 -92
* Radtke	Helga	GER	16 May 62	171/63	LJ	6.66i, 6.66	7.21 -84
					TJ	14.19	14.30, 14.44w -92
Radtke	Katarzyna	POL	31 Aug 69	161/45	5kW	20:51.96	21:00.28 -92
					10kW	42:47.4	43:34, 44:32.30 -92
Ragozina	Tatyana	UKR	3 Sep 64	162/51	5kW	21:22.6	21:34.34 -92
					10kW	45:24	44:13 -90
* Rainey	Meredith	USA	15 Oct 68	168/55	800	1:57.63	1:59.18 -92
Raizgiene' (Andris)	Monika	LIT	14 Apr 65		SP	17.09i	18.43 -89
Ramalalanirina	Nicole	MAD	5 Mar 72	164/57	100h	13.11, 12.92w	13.40 -92
Ramanuskaite	Rita	LIT	22 Feb 70		JT	58.84	58.48 -88
Ramazanova	Larisa	RUS	71		5kW	22:40.82	
					10kw	42:47, 46:18.58	44:06 -92
Ramirez	Oraidis	CUB	11 Nov 73	171/65	100h	13.27, 13.0	13.33 -92
Ramon	Miriam	ECU	10 Feb 73	158/50	10kW	46:13	46:16 -89
Ramos	Margarita	ESP	26 Jun 66	178/72	SP	17.55i, 17.54	17.71 -91
* Rantanen	Heli	FIN	26 Feb 70	174/72	JT	61.38	64.66 -91
Rattray-Williams	Cathy	JAM	19 Aug 63	160/48	400	51.65	50.82 -88
Rattyä	Tina	FIN	12 Nov 68	181/67	Hep	6067	6086 -91
Rauta	Kirsi	FIN	17 Mar 62	170/55	Mar	2:33:49	2:32:31 -92
Ravaonirina	Lalao	MAD	8 Nov 63	165/58	100	11.42	11.32 -91, 11.22w -88
Razmyslovich	Yelena	RUS	22 Aug 74		HJ	1.89	1.89 -91
Rea	Elisa	ITA	23 Mar 68	164/50	1M	4:30.03	
Rebelo	Maria	FRA	29 Jan 56	158/45	Mar	2:30:36	2:29:04 -91
Rebollo	Maribel	MEX	76		5kW	22:26	
					10kW	44:46	
Reichardt	Yvonne	GER	5 Feb 73	170/65	JT	58.54	61.74 -89
Reinsch	Gabriele	GER	23 Sep 63	185/88	DT	59.80	76.80 -88
Rembao	Sue	USA	15 May 62	177/59	HJ	1.92	1.96 -91
* Ren	Ruiping	CHN	Jan 75		TJ	14.29	13.10 -91
* Renk	Silke	GER	30 Jun 67	173/75	JT	65.80	71.00 -88
Reshetnikova	Tatyana	RUS	14 Oct 66	171/63	100h	13.00	12.73 -92
* Restrepo	Ximena	COL	10 Mar 69	175/58	400	50.37	49.64 -92
* Retchakan	Gowry	GBR	21 Jun 60	158/45	400h	55.84	54.63 -92
Reynolds	Natasha	USA	7 Jun 72	155/	400h	56.96	
Reznikova	Galina	RUS	17 Apr 61	157/49	800	2:01.96	1:58.4 -84
Rhodes	Cynthea	USA	30 Sep 68	168/57	TJ	13.68	13.33 -91
Ribeiro	Fernanda	POR	23 Jun 69	161/48	3k	8:51.91	8:56.10 -92
					10k	31:40.51	32:22.70 -92
					HMar	71:21	
* Richards	Sandie	JAM	6 Nov 68	170/61	400	50.44	50.19 -92
Richardson	Jillian	CAN	10 Mar 65	172/59	400	51.21	49.91 -88
Richardson	Marcia	GBR	10 Feb 72	173/67	100	11.45	11.53 -91
Rieger	Nicole	GER	5 Feb 72		PV	3.80	3.92 -92
* Rieger	Silvia	GER	14 Nov 70	175/55	400h	54.90	55.10 -92
Riewe	Susanne	GER	26 May 70	171/70	JT	59.86	63.46 -92
Rigg	Suzanne	GBR	29 Nov 63	168/52	10k	32:44.06	33:16.03 -92
Rios	Rocio	ESP	13 Mar 69	152/45	10k	32:51.72	33:27.14 -91
					Mar	2:31:33	2:31:46dh -82
Rivero	Xiomara	CUB	22 Dec 68	177/73	JT	59.60	64.56 -86
Roba	Fatuma	ETH	72	160/49	10k	32:55.32	34:26.87 -90
Roberts	Kellie	USA	16 Jun 69	168/60	400h	56.28	55.80 -92
Robinson	Kelli	USA	18 Feb 71	163/64	100h	13.36w	13.56 -92
Robinson	Lynne	GBR	21 Jun 69	158/46	1500	4:12.03	4:13.22 -92
Robinson	Olga	JAM			200	23.40	24.6 -92
					400h	52.54	54.6 -92

Name		Nat	Born	Ht/Wt	Event	1993 Mark	Pre-1993 Best
Rodchenkova	Marina	RUS	30 Jul 61	164/50	5k	15:43.3	15:19.26 -85
* Rodina-Gulyayeva	Yelena	RUS	14 Aug 67	181/62	HJ	1.98	1.99 -91
* Rogachova	Lyudmila	RUS	10 Oct 66	166/57	800	1:58.13	1:56.82 -88
					1000	2:33.96	2:37.09i -90
					1500	4:05.77	3:56.91 -92
					1M	4:22.33	4:21.30 -92
					3k	8:59.94i	
Rogiers	Christel	BEL	9 Mar 63		Mar	2:34:04	2:33:41 -91
Rogova	Svetlana	RUS	4 Aug 67		3kSt	6:17.42	6:14.52 -92
Roldán	Estrella	ESP	4 Jun 62	166/50	TJ	13.53	13.31 -92
* Romanova	Anna	RUS	9 Mar 68	180/87	SP	20.24	20.01i, 19.58 -92
* Romanova	Yelena	RUS	20 Mar 63	163/51	3k	8:35.48	8:30.45 -88
Rong	Guiping	CHN	Mar 72		400h	56.64	57.34 -92
Rong	Hanmei	CHN	Dec 69		TJ	13.56, 13.77w	13.37 -90
Ropars	Florence	FRA	25 Dec 70	156/47	100	11.44w	11.65 -92
* Ropo	Ringa	FIN	16 Feb 66	177/66	LJ	6.63	6.85 -90, 6.93w -92
Rose	Dionne	JAM	7 Nov 69	168/52	100h	13.03	13.03 -92
					LJ	6.63	6.58, 6.70w -92
Rosolen	Mara	ITA	27 Jul 65	175/80	SP	17.40i, 16.58	17.12 -92
Rossi	Loredana	ITA	17 Jul 67	163/50	TJ	13.46	13.45i, 13.28w -92?
Rosza	Mária	HUN	12 Feb 67	169/54	5kW	21:57.38i	21:24.76 -90
- Urbanik					10kW	43:21	43:53 -92
Roy	Terry	USA	26 Jan 73	173/65	Hep	5644	5524 -92
Ruban	Svetlana	UZB	23 May 65		HJ	1.92	1.94 -88
Rublyova	Olga	RUS	28 Oct 74	175/62	LJ	6.74	6.46 -92
Rücker	Anja	GER	20 Dec 72	174/56	400	51.91	51.33 -92
Rünne	Eha	EST	25 May 63	182/85	DT	56.92	63.18 -88
* Russell	Gillian	JAM	28 Sep 73	167/56	100	11.41	11.68 -90, 11.3w -89
					100h	13.00	13.07 -92
* Ruzina	Yelena	RUS	3 Apr 64	172/58	200	23.08	22.73 -88
					400	51.14	50.65 -90
Rybicka	Anna	POL	23 Sep 63	173/56	Mar	2:32:00	2:31:56 -82
* Rydz	Malgorzata	POL	18 Jan 67	165/52	800	2:01.5e	2:00.68 -91
					1500	4:02.29	4:01.91 -92
					3k	8:58.64	9:17.66 - 89
* Sacramento	Carla	POR	10 Dec 71	168/53	800	1:59.42	2:00.57 -92
					1500	4:06.33	4:04.10 -92
Sadahiro	Chinami	JPN	17 Aug 72	173/55	HJ	1.89	1.83 -92
Sadova	Natalya	RUS	7 Feb 72		DT	58.14	57.82 -92
Sakai	Kayo	JPN	13 Oct 71	156/41	HMar	71:09	71:15 -92
Sakala	Julia	ZIM	12 Jul 69	169/55	3k	8:57.69	9:47.51 -90
Salageanu	Liliana	ROM	24 Mar 71	171/55	800	2:00.84	1:59.17 -92
					1000	2:36.89	
					1500	4:09.98	
Salminen	Marika	FIN	10 May 71	173/52	TJ	13.44	13.18 -92
* Salvador	Ileana	ITA	16 Jan 62	163/52	5kW	20:48.55	20:28 -89, 20:42.31 -92
					10kW	41:30, 42:23.7	43:02.4, 42:07 -92
Samorokova	Irina	RUS	66		800	2:02.76	2:01.55 -91
Samuel	Heather	ANT	6 Jul 70	160/59	100	11.20	11.48 -92
					200	23.32	24.09, 23.5 -92
Sánchez	Marlen	CUB	12 Jan 71			57.92	56.68 -92
Sandell	Annemari	FIN	2 Jan 77	162/44	3k	8:51.22	8:56.02 -92
					5k	15:26.33	
Sasaki	Ayumi	JPN	24 Jul 67	163/51	100h	13.38, 13.35w	13.39 -92
					LJ	6.51w	6.36, 6.54w -91
Sato	Yuko	JPN	23 Jan 68	170/53	5kW	22:04,22:09.19	22:42.21 -92,22:16 -91
					10kW	44:53	46:02.5 -90
Saunders	Daphne	BAH	18 Dec 71	173/61	LJ	6.77, 6.86w	6.45 -92
Saville	Jane	AUS	5 Nov 74	164/53	5kW	21:47.5	21:58.64 -92
Savinova	Irina	RUS	72		10kW	45:13.35	45:43 -92
Savinova	Lyudmila	RUS	72		10kW	44:54	45:43 -92
* Sayko	Yelena	RUS	24 Dec 67	161/48	5kW	21:43	21:19.81 -92
					10kW	42:04	42:22 -91
Sazonova	Maya	KZK	68		10kW	45:00	46:00 -91
Scaunich	Emma	ITA	10 Mar 54	163/48	Mar	2:31:59	2:29:46 -88
Schmidt	Gesine	GER	26 Jun 71	184/65	400	56.03	56.54 -92
					Hep	5668	5666 -92

Name		Nat	Born	Ht/Wt	Event	1993 Mark	Pre-1993 Best
Schmitt	Simone	GER	5 Dec 71	182/85	DT	60.80	55.24 -92
Schnurr	Paula	CAN	15 Jan 64	160/54	1500	4:11.97i	4:04.80 -92
					1M	4:33.95i	4:31.75 -92
Schönenberger	Jana	GER	28 Jan 71	167/55	200	23.23	23.22 -91
Schuurmans	Inge	USA	29 Jan 63	170/49	10k	32:37.23	33:18.70 -92
Schuwalow	Carolyn	AUS	10 Aug 65	163/46	10k	32:28.50	31:54.95 -91
					HMar	71:02	
Selenska	Antoaneta	BUL	8 Jun 63	170/75	JT	60.86	71.88 -81
Selina	Yelena	KZK	64		LJ	6.49	6.54 -88
Selman	Ashley	USA	21 Apr 70	173/70	JT	57.44	57.24 -89
Semiraz	Yelena	UKR	21 Nov 65	168/57	TJ	13.99	14.35 -91
Sen	Sevgi	TUR	31 Dec 67		SP	16.42	16.96 -90
Serbinenko	Natalya	UKR	27 Jan 59	161/53	5kW	22:22.33	21:30 -89, 21:31.15 -92
					10kW	45:16.2	43:46 -89
Serebrinskaya	Larisa	UKR	15 Sep 63	183/58	HJ	1.92	1.91 -90
Sergent	Melinda	USA	72		100	11.43A	
Sergent-Palluy	Annette	FRA	17 Nov 62	156/46	3k	8:55.70	8:44.19 -88
Seuser	Sandra	GER	17 Apr 66	172/55	400	52.48i	52.76i, 53.72 -91
Seymour	Michelle	NZL	21 Dec 65	162/58	100	11.32	11.58, 11.46w -92
Shabanova	Irina	RUS	2 Aug 64		DT	61.50	67.34 -87
Shao	Jingwen	CHN	8 Mar 71		PV	3.95i	3.90 -91
Shaw	Lorraine	GBR	2 Apr 68		HT	56.56	45.24 -92
Shcherban	Yelena	UKR	7 Feb 72	168/58	400	52.56	53.73 -92
Shcherbina	Marina	UKR	5 Jan 68	180/67	Hep	5993	6192 -89
Sheffield	LaTanya	USA	11 Oct 63	165/57	400h	55.84	54.36 -88
Shekhodanova	Natalya	RUS	29 Dec 71	169/55	100h	13.14	13.23 -90, 13.0 -92
* Shevchik	Tatyana	BLS	11 Jun 69	178/59	HJ	2.00	1.96i, 1.96 -92
Shi	Guiqing	CHN	19 Apr 68		Hep	6188	6006 -89
Shigaki	Chiaki	JPN	20 Jan 74	153/47	10k	33:00.66	
* Shikolenko	Natalya	BLS	1 Aug 64	182/80	JT	68.96	70.36 -92
* Shikolenko	Tatyana	BLS	10 May 68	175/79	JT	65.18	64.98 -90
Shimizu	Michiko	JPN	22 Sep 70	163/46	5k	15:39.71	
Shishchenko	Yekaterina	UKR	24 Dec 71	180/90	SP	17.76	17.23 -91
Shishigina	Olga	KZK	68		100h	13.29	13.47 -91
Shmonina	Marina	RUS	9 Feb 65	164/51	400	52.37i	50.52 -90
Shouaa	Ghada	SYR	9 Oct 73	178/65	Hep	6259	5508 -92
Sidibé	Odiah	FRA	13 Jan 70	176/64	100	11.38	11.25A -89
* Sidoti	Anna Rita	ITA	25 Jul 69	150/40	5kW	22:06	21:30.5 -90
					10kW	42:41, 43:33.7	43:03 -92
Silhavá	Zdenka	TCH	15 Jun 54	178/84	SP	16.62	21.05 -83
					DT	61.06	74.56 -84
Simioneck	Magalie	FRA	17 Feb 70	171/57	100	11.39	11.45, 11.40w -91
Simmons	Wendi	USA	28 Jul 69	168/55	Hep	5735	5358 -92
* Sinchukova	Yelena	RUS	23 Jan 61	173/67	LJ	6.85, 6.94w	7.20 -91
					TJ	13.92i, 13.83	14.09 -92
Sinyutina	Yelena	RUS	12 May 64	169/56	100h	12.91, 12.9i	12.91 -87, 12.9 -90
Skrebnyeva	Olga	BLS	7 Nov 74		TJ	13.68	
Slushkina	Marina	RUS	2 Aug 60	169/61	100h	12.9	12.89 -90
					LJ	6.58	7.01 -85
Slyusar	Antonina	UKR	19 Mar 63	161/54	100	11.35	11.29 -90, 11.26w -89
					200	23.35	22.97 -90
Slyusar	Irina	UKR	19 Mar 63	160/56	100	11.38	11.05 -92
Smieja	Sabine	GER	23 Jun 71		Hep	5647	5236 -92
Smith	Joy	USA	5 Jan 62	165/46	Mar	2:34:47	2:34:20 -91
Smith	Phylis	GBR	29 Sep 65	168/52	400	51.70	50.40 -92
Smith	Steffanie	USA	23 Feb 71	165/55	400	52.30	52.50 -92
Smith	Tiffany	USA	18 Aug 67	169/57	100h	13.15w	
Sobanska	Malgorzata	POL	25 Apr 69	165/50	Mar	2:29:21	2:34:54 -92
* Sokolova	Eva	RUS	25 Mar 62	170/59	100h	12.75, 12.63w	12.70 -89
Sokolova	Zoya	RUS	3 Apr 70		100	11.40	11.44 -90
					200	23.35	23.30 -89
Sollárová	Andrea	SVK	1 Feb 71	168/50	1500	4:11.91	4:15.11 -91
					3k	8:59.04	8:59.23 -92
Solodkaya	Irina	UKR	24 Jun 69	178/76	JT	57.86	55.82 -92
Solti	Krisztina	HUN	28 Apr 68	171/53	HJ	1.92	1.88 -90
Somers	Linda	USA	7 May 61	163/46	Mar	2:34:11	2:33:37 -89
Song	Guixian	CHN	6 Sep 71		100h	13.34	13.73 -91

Name		Nat	Born	Ht/Wt	Event	1993 Mark	Pre-1993 Best
Song	Lijuan	CHN	Feb 76	166/54	10kW	43:07	
Song	Ruiling	CHN	25 Jan 66		JT	62.12	63.18 -92
Sosimenko	Debbie	AUS	5 Apr 74		HT	58.90	51.48 -92
Sotnikova	Yulia	RUS	70		200	23.15	23.03 -92
Spada	Giuliana	ITA	18 Apr 71	17q/63	Hep	5962	5.91w -92
Speights	Julie	USA	70		1500	4:12.43	4:20.53 -92
Sproge	Gundega	LAT	12 Feb 72	173/53	TJ	13.34	12.65 -92
St.Geme	Ceci	USA	13 Apr 63	165/49	1M	4:27.0	4:36.5 -82
Stakhova	Yelena	BLS	4 Jan 69		LJ	6.61	6.53 -91
					TJ	13.41i, 13.41	13.46 -91
Stanciu	Carmen	ROM	5 Jan 70	167/53	800	2:01.40	2:03.07 -92
Stanczyk ¶	Agnieszka	POL	20 Jan 71	168/55	TJ	14.05dq, 13.91	13.11 -91
Stankina	Irina	RUS	25 Mar 77		5kW	21:49.65	23:37.06 -92
Stanton	Krishna	AUS	18 May 66	171/56	3k	8:58.6	8:51.39 -92, 8:48.38i -87
Starkova	Svetlana	RUS	68		400h	56.40	58.49 -90
Stasenko	Irina	RUS	27 Mar 66	177/70	800	2:02.54	2:04.78 -92
Stavik	Hilde	NOR	6 Sep 62		1500	4:12.93	4:10.51 -92
					3k	8:58.52	8:59.05 -92
* Steely	Shelly	USA	23 Oct 62	168/52	1500	4:30.23i	4:25.49 -92
					3k	8:52.99	8:41.28 -92
Steigauf	Mona	GER	17 Jan 70	178/59	Hep	6196	6107 -92
Stelzmüller	Doris	SUI	13 Mar 63		Hep	5656	5745 -91
Stephens	Sacha	AUS	2 Nov 72		1500	4:12.5mx	4:14.46 -92
Stepina	Viktoria	UKR	21 Feb 76	175/55	HJ	1.89	1.83 -92
Sterling	Audrea	JAM	1 Jul 68	169/59	400	52.33	52.43 -92
Sterling	Carolin	JAM	17 Mar 70	172/59	100h	13.26A, 13.27	13.18 -92
* Stevens	Rochelle	USA	8 Sep 66	170/58	400	52.39	50.06 -92
Stewart	Kwani	USA	9 Oct 72	183/61	100h	13.25w	13.37, 13.35w -92
Stewart	Zoila	CRC	1 Nov 68	162/52	400	52.57	54.50 -92
Steyn	Yolanda	RSA	22 Aug 72	170/59	200	23.04A, 23.22	23.49 -92
Stone	Joanna	AUS	1 Oct 72		400h	57.92	54.02 -92
Storchevaya	Yelena	UKR	23 Jun 66	165/51	800	2:00.1e	1:59.09 -92
* Storp	Stephanie	GER	28 Nov 68	195/95	SP	19.71	20.34 -90
Strasek	Renata	SLO	8 Apr 72	165/63	JT	61.04	63.60 -92
Sturrup	Chandra	BAH	12 Sep 71	159/52	100	11.20	11.54 -92
					200	22.85	23.55 -92
					LJ	6.48w	6.22, 6.32w -92
Su	Yuan	CHN			10kW	46:10	43:42.8 -91
Sudak	Svetlana	BLS	17 Nov 71		HT	63.70	62.70 -92
Sudarikova	Tatyana	RUS	28 May 73	189/79	JT	62.18	58.48 -92
* Sui	Xinmei	CHN	29 Jan 65	172/90	SP	20.32	21.66 -90
Sukhova	Vera	RUS	9 Jul 63	164/53	Mar	2:34:59	2:30:09 -88
Sultanova	Firia	RUS	29 Apr 61	163/52	Mar	2:32:11	2:34:12 -92
Sun	Caijun	CHN	21 Jul 73		PV	4.11	4.05 -92
Sun	Hui	CHN			JT	59.80	
Sun	Xue	CHN	3 Mar 72		100h	13.28	13.53 -92
Sun	Yan	CHN	4 May 73	167/56	10kW	43:30, 44:15.0	44:24 -92
Sun	Yanshi	CHN	8 Sep 71		200	23.36	
Suzuki	Aya	JPN	18 Nov 67	168/75	HT	60.90	61.20 -89
* Svensson	Madelein	SWE	20 Jul 69	168/52	5kW	21:34.1	21:09.86 -92
					10kW	42:52	42:13.7 -92
Svezhentseva	Yelena	UZB	21 Dec 68	179/66	JT	58.32	61.76 -92
Sviridenko	Zinaida	RUS	24 Dec 68	161/48	5kW	21:42.5	22:19.3 -92, 22:02 -91
					10kW	45:01.65	44:51.8 -92
Swanepoel	Karen	RSA	2 Oct 65		400h	57.23A	57.58 -89
Sychugova	Vera	RUS	12 Jun 63	173/66	400	52.27	51.64 -88
Szabo	Estera	ROM	11 Oct 67	176/65	LJ	6.85i	6.67i -92, 6.68 -88
Szabo	Gabriela	ROM	14 Nov 75	158/42	1500	4:10.32	4:12.57 -92
					3k	8:50.97	8:48.28 -92
Szabó	Karolina	HUN	17 Nov 61	149/35	Mar	2:32:37	2:30:31 -86
Szebenszky	Anikó	HUN	12 Aug 65	169/58	10kW	45:04	44:54 -90
Takamatsu	Hitomi	JPN	21 Aug 74	163/51	LJ	6.44w	6.38 -92
Tamura	Yuki	JPN	21 Apr 67	154/43	10k	32:57.54	32:37.1 -91
Tandian	Aïssatou	SEN	29 Aug 66	172/68	400	52.59	51.92 -89
Tang	Haiyun	CHN	Sep 73		200	23.33	23.96 -92
Tang	Hongwei	CHN	24 May 68		3k	8:58.01	9:15.9 -91
					10k	32:15.69	

Name		Nat	Born	Ht/Wt	Event	1993 Mark	Pre-1993 Best
Tang	Lishuang	CHN	25 Feb 66		JT	59.62	59.62 -88
Tang	Xueqing	CHN	16 Oct 74		1500	4:08.43	4:17.1 -91
Tang	Yinghua	CHN	18 May 73		10kW	43:47	47:29 -90
Tang	Yixiu	CHN	1 Apr 65		Hep	5674	5832 -91
* Tanigawa	Mari	JPN	27 Oct 62	160/44	HMar	70:09	
					Mar	2:28:22	2:31:09 -92
Tapîrlan	Elena	ROM	4 Feb 74	174/92	SP	16.72	15.96 -92
Taplin	Cheryl	USA	2 Sep 72	165/56	100	11.23A,11.26,11.08w	11.3, 11.19w -92
					200	23.04	23.21 -92
Tarasenko	Yulia	RUS	28 Mar 68	182/62	400h	57.17	56.27 -92
Tarasyuk	Larisa	RUS	14 Jun 70	174/62	Hep	5776	5830 -91
* Tarnopolskaya	Zhanna	UKR	6 Jul 72	166/52	100	11.08	11.17 -92, 11.0 -91
					200	22.79	23.56 -91
Tas	Aysel	TUR	21 Oct 64		JT	57.80	60.82 -92
Tauceri	Valentina	ITA	20 Jul 66	172/54	1500	4:10.72	4:08.54 -92
					5k	15:31.19	
Taylor	Angie	USA	16 Mar 65	165/55	100h	13.35w	13.72 -91, 13.56w -90
Taylor	Monifa	USA	3 Mar 71	168/60	100h	13.15, 13.07w	12.80 -92
Taylor	Sherlese	USA			100h	13.24w	13.87, 13.64w -91
Teaberry	Connie	USA	15 Aug 70	179/66	HJ	1.92	1.89 -92
Tecuta	Alina	ROM	10 Nov 71	165/47	3k	8:52.61	
					5k	15:42.60	
					10k	32:15.96	33:14.78 -92
Teppe	Agnès	FRA	4 May 68	182/78	DT	59.18	60.14 -92
Teppe	Nathalie	FRA	22 May 72	183/61	JT	60.90	61.36 -89
					Hep	6256	6145 -92
Teteryuk	Larisa	UKR	24 Dec 70	179/67	Hep	5675	5725w -92
Thorp	Angela	GBR	7 Dec 72	171/60	110h	13.28	13.49 -91
Thust	Simone	GER	22 Sep 71	176/62	10kW	46:11	47:19 -92
Thyssen	Ingrid	GER	9 Jan 56	171/72	JT	61.38	69.68 -87
Tian	Mei	CHN	27 Nov 71		10k	32:28.56	33:06.60 -92
					Mar	2:33:15	2:36:33 -91
Tian	Xiue	CHN	4 Oct 71		SP	18.51	16.36 -91
Tian	Yumei	CHN	29 Dec 65	165/60	100	11.24	11.32, 11.2 -90
* Tiedtke-Greene	Susen	GER	23 Jan 69	175/56	LJ	6.85, 7.19wA	7.00 -91, 7.19w -92
Tikkanen	Päivi	FIN	19 Jan 60	164/50	3k	8:53.82	8:41.30 -91
					10k	32:51.72	31:45.02 -92
* Tilea	Felicia	ROM	29 Sep 67	167/74	JT	65.62	64.02 -90
Tîrle	Monica	ROM	18 Jan 69	169/69	JT	57.10	52.64 -91
Tîrlea	Ionela	ROM	9 Feb 76	165/48	400h	56.30	
Tirneci	Manuela	ROM	26 Feb 69	171/83	DT	65.14	66.16 -92
Titova	Svetlana	RUS	69		JT	61.38	61.04 -92
Tochilova	Natalya	RUS	21 May 64		100h	13.11	12.87 -88, 12.7 -90
* Tolbert (-Goode)	Lynda	USA	3 Oct 67	163/52	100h	12.67	12.71, 12.66w -92
Tolkkinen	Heli	FIN	3 Aug 73	166/56	JT	61.26	60.12 -92
Tolstik	Irina	BLS	4 Dec 65		10kW	44:22	43:52 -90
Tombiri	Mary	NGR	23 Jul 72	160/56	100	11.38, 11.27w	11.46 -91
Tomecková	Nikola	TCH	25 Jun 74	178/73	JT	57.48	59.78 -92
Toonstra	Christien	HOL	22 Jun 66	171/53	3k	8:54.17	8:45.96 -92
* Topchina	Yelena	RUS	28 Sep 66	178/59	HJ	1.99	1.96i, 1.95 -90
Toporek	Viera	AUT	5 Nov 67	165/49	10kW	45:53	45:41.3 -92
Torazza	Manuela	ITA	27 Jun 68	170/73	SP	16.43	15.98 -92
Toropchina	Natalya	RUS	25 Feb 71		Hep	5688	5588 -92
* Torrence	Gwen	USA	12 Jun 65	170/57	100	10.86	10.86 -92, 10.78w -88
					200	21.92	21.72 -92
					400	49.83	49.64 -92
Torres	Clara	CUB	28 Sep 73		400h	57.94	59.72 -91
* Torshina	Natalya	KZK	4 Oct 68	172/57	400h	54.53	55.43 -92
Toth	Monica	ROM	7 Mar 70	178/64	LJ	6.45	6.48 -92
					TJ	13.93, 13.96w	13.42 -92
Tozzi	Nicoletta	ITA	3 Jan 66	168/56	800	2:02.54	2:01.04 -90
Trabaldo	Fabia	ITA	5 Mar 72	168/53	800	2:00.03	1:59.51 -92
					1000	2:36.71	2:35.06 -92
					1500	4:03.82	4:06.05 -92
Tranchina	Maria	ITA	10 Feb 68	168/75	SP	16.65i, 16.62	16.27 -89
Trandenkova	Marina	RUS	7 Jan 67	170/58	100	11.40, 11.17w	11.08 -92
					200	22.97	22.50 -92

Name		Nat	Born	Ht/Wt	Event	1993 Mark	Pre-1993 Best
Trofimova	Natalya	RUS	17 Jan 75	164/55	5kW	21:39.75	21:58.91 -92
Tröger	Sabine	AUT	7 Jun 67	171/56	100	11.28	11.43 -92
					200	23.12	23.12 -92
Tsialakoudi	Angeliki	GRE	10 May 76	167/65	JT	58.42	47.80 -92
Tsikouna	Stella	GRE	19 Oct 72	171/75	DT	55.48	56.48 -92
Tsurtsurika	Virdzhinia	RUS	20 Nov 68		SP	17.29	16.42 -92
Tsybulskaya	Valentina	BLS	19 Jul 68		10kW	43:50	45:13 -92
Tsyoma	Lyubov	RUS	19 May 63	164/54	800	2:00.20	1:57.18 -86
					1000	2:35.49	
Tuliniemi	Marika	FIN	19 Jul 74	189/106	SP	17.93	16.92 -92
Tulloch	Valerie	CAN	13 Jul 72		JT	56.56	58.26 -92
* Turchak	Olga	UKR	5 Mar 67	188/58	HJ	1.95	2.01 -86
Turner	Inez	JAM	3 Dec 72	170/56	400	51.64	52.98 -92
Tuzzi	Carla	ITA	2 Jun 67	162/57	100h	13.14	13.08 -88
Twiggs	Shantel	USA	4 Oct 72	165/57	100	11.32w	11.62, 11.43w -92
					200	22.9w	
* Tyukhay	Irina	RUS	14 Jan 67	168/60	100h	13.37	13.32, 13.0 -88
					LJ	6.71i, 6.60	6.56 -89, 6.73w -92
					Hep	6406	6478 -92
Uccheddu	Valentina	ITA	26 Oct 66	166/45	LJ	6.60, 6.83wA, 6.70w	6.77 -91
Uchida	Tomoko	JPN	6 Aug 72	156/45	10kW	46:14	
Ukolova	Olga	RUS	72		TJ	13.74	13.36i -92, 13.09 -91
Urbikiene	Danguole	LIT	10 Dec 62	184/82	SP	19.14	20.27 -87
Utondu	Beatrice	NGR	23 Nov 69	162/59	100	11.26, 11.01w	11.08 -91, 10.9w -90
					LJ	6.54i, 6.44	6.61, 6.73w -91
Uys	Lana	RSA	9 Dec 68	172/62	400h	56.23A	56.25 -92
Vaideanu	Petra	ROM	24 Aug 65	170/66	Hep	6214	6343 -88
Vaill	Theresa	USA	20 Nov 62	163/54	5kW	21:28.17	22:26.00 -92, 22:24 -90
					10kW	45:27	45:16 -92
Van Blunk	Elaine	USA	11 Sep 64	162/48	5k	15:42.93	15:43.38 -91
					10k	32:07.19	32:37.55 -91
van der Merwe	Frith	RSA	26 May 64	170/51	Mar	2:32:01	2:27:36 -90
van der Veen	Karen	RSA	7 Jan 66		400h	58.00	55.99 -88
van der Walt	Nanette	RSA	22 Feb 59	178/78	DT	56.28	58.80 -96
van Hulst	Elly	HOL	9 Jun 59	177/56	1500	4:11.96i	4:03.63 -87
					3k	8:50.39	8:33.97 -88, 8:33.82i -89
					5k	15:28.47	15:17.08 -89
* van Langen	Ellen	HOL	9 Feb 66	172/54	800	1:59.23	1:55.54 -92
Van Norman	Heather	USA	22 Apr 70	170/61	400	52.66	53.05i -92, 53.59 -91
van Onna	Wilma	HOL	13 Jun 65	163/48	Mar	2:34:28	
Van Renterghem	Sonia	BEL	15 Jun 65		800	2:02.65	2:05.50 -92
van Schuppen	Anne	HOL	11 Oct 60	177/55	Mar	2:34:15	2:33:40 -92
Vanisi	Eileen	USA	28 Mar 72	178/82	SP	16.85i, 16.56	17.60 -91
Vaquero	Julia	ESP	18 Sep 70	160/47	3k	8:55.27	8:57.8 -92
Varcholová	Alena	TCH	27 Mar 69	179/53	HJ	1.89i, 1.88	1.93 -92
Vasco	Maria	ESP	26 Dec 75	158/47	5kW	22:32,22:40.83	22:34.26, 22;28 -92
Vasdeki	Olga	GRE	26 Sep 73	172/56	TJ	13.37	12.77 -92
Vasícková	Sona	TCH	14 Mar 62	174/78	SP	16.53	20.80 -88
Vasilenko	Natalya	UKR	30 Oct 74	167/71	HT	59.80	58.58 -92
Vasilyeva	Venera	RUS	17 Mar 76		5kW	22:17	22:14 -92
Veltman	Marieke	USA	18 Sep 71	170/59	Hep	5656	5366 -92
Veneva	Venelina	BUL	13 Jun 74	182/56	HJ	1.89i	1.93i -90, 1.91 -91
Vereen	Wenda	USA	24 Apr 66	160/54	100	11.25, 11.07w	11.17 -83
					200	22.63	22.93 -88, 22.75w -94
Verouli	Anna	GRE	13 Nov 56	164/74	JT	60.64	72.70 -84
Vershinina	Viktoria	UKR	11 Jun 71	177/58	LJ	6.57	6.62 -92
					TJ	13.80	
* Vickers	Janeene	USA	3 Oct 68	170/62	400h	56.21	53.47 -91
Vieira Telles	Soraya	BRA	6 Sep 58	168/54	800	2:02.65	1:59.92 -88
					1500	4:11.80	4:10.07 -88
Vivier	Laurence	FRA	21 Nov 67	167/52	3k	8:56.92	9:12.40 -92
Vogoli	Katerina	GRE	30 Jan 70	175/87	DT	59.70	57.86 -92
Vokuhl	Anja	GER	17 Aug 73	177/61	JT	13.92i, 13.87	13.47 -92
Volf	Yelena	RUS	2 Mar 69		HJ	1.88	
					Hep	5827	5975w -89
Völker	Jeanette	GER	10 May 72	178/74	JT	58.34	57.56 -92
Voloshina	Oksana	RUS	74		TJ	13.26i	12.91 -92

Name		Nat	Born	Ht/Wt	Event	1993 Mark	Pre-1993 Best
Von Kesselstat	Anabella	ARG	12 Jun 69	177/57	400h	57.42, 57.2	58.57 -92
* Voronova	Natalya	RUS	9 Jul 65	170/60	100	11.17, 11.16w	10.98 -88
					200	22.35	22.98 -92, 22.6 -85
Voronova	Olga	RUS	23 Feb 68	173/58	100	11.37w	11.36, 11.32w -88
Vorster	Elinda	RSA	8 Dec 65	167/54	100	11.22	11.22 -90
					200	22.83	22.58 -90
Vostrikova	Irina	RUS	30 Aug 70	177/64	Hep	6066	5892 -92
Vourdoli	Adigoni	GRE	4 Apr 75	170/66	JT	57.80	57.52 -92
Voyevudskaya	Lyudmila	RUS	22 Jun 59	175/90	SP	17.51i, 17.40	20.27 -87
* Vriesde	Letitia	SUR	5 Oct 64	159/50	800	2:00.30	1:57.96 -92
Vyazova	Yelena	UKR	18 Apr 60	163/51	3k	8:52.46	8:38.1 -87
					10k	32:56.90	31:09.40 -87
* Wachtel	Christine	GER	6 Jan 65	166/56	800	1:59.86	1:55.32 -87
					1000	2:37.76	2:30.67 -90
Wadsworth	Stevanie	USA	19 Mar 72	170/75	SP	17.19	16.19 -91, 16.14 -90
Wallace	Andrea	GBR	22 Nov 66	170/47	HMar	69:39	69:56 -91
Waller	Donna	USA	1 Dec 70	183/60	100h	13.33w	13.01, 12.94w -92
Waller	Tisha	USA	1 Dec 70	183/60	HJ	1.94	1.93i, 1.92 -91
Wamuyu	Gladys	KEN	23 Dec 72	167/63	800	2:00.0	2:01.5 -92
Wan	Dong	CHN			JT	58.52	
Wang	Chunfang	CHN	5 Mar 70	175/56	LJ	6.59, 6.66w	6.89 -91
Wang	Chunmei	CHN	5 Mar 70		1500	4:09.46	
Wang	Dongmei	CHN	3 Dec 73		3k	8:52.41	
					10k	31:50.39	33:08.44 -92
Wang	Fang	CHN	Apr 72		HJ	1.89	1.85 -91
					Hep	5896	5774 -92
Wang	Hong	CHN	28 Jan 67		Mar	2:34:03	2:36:30 -90
Wang	Hong	CHN	10 Apr 70	176/75	SP	18.74	17.33 -88
Wang	Hui	CHN	6 Jul 73		SP	18.65	19.00 -92
Wang	Huie-Chen	TPE	21 Feb 70	171/55	100	11.38	11.29, 11.2 -91
					200	23.30, 22.80w	22.56 -92
Wang	Jing	CHN	16 Jan 75		100	11.39	11.42 -92
Wang	Jinling	CHN	Oct 69		DT	60.30	62.02 -90
* Wang	Junxia	CHN	9 Jan 73	160/45	1500	3:51.92	4:17.18 -91
					2k	5:29.41+	
					3k	8:06.11	8:55.50 -92
					5k	15:05.8	
					10k	29:31.78	32:29.90 -92
					Mar	2:24:07	
Wang	Lei	CHN	4 Mar 71		100	11.33	11.44, 11.1 -92
					200	23.17	23.45 -92
Wang	Lianyun	CHN	Oct 69		JT	63.92	61.66 -92
Wang	Lixia	CHN	Sep 69		400h	56.38	56.09, 56.0 -92
Wang	Mingxia	CHN	6 Jun 71		10k	32:36.70	32:30.96 -92
					Mar	2:31:06	
Wang	Na	CHN	Aug 70		10kW	44:38	
Wang	Ping	CHN	8 Sep 70	161/57	100	11.28	11.43 -92
					200	22.79	23.04 -92
Wang	Qingfen	CHN	27 Mar 73		800	2:01.46	2:04.87 -89
					1500	4:01.49	4:09.42 -92
Wang	Renmei	CHN	5 Jul 70		1500	3:58.64	4:10.2 -91
					3k	8:49.86	8:59.62 -91
Wang	Wei	CHN	19 Oct 68	180/62	HJ	1.92i, 1.91	1.90 -92
Wang	Wenxiang	CHN	Mar 73		Hep	5935	5464 -91
Wang	Xiangrong	CHN	Feb 76		TJ	13.74, 14.07w	13.28 -91
Wang	Xiujie	CHN	20 Nov 73		3k	8:47.89	9:11.2 -92
* Wang	Xiuting	CHN	11 May 65	164/48	3k	8:51.17	8:50.68 -87
					10k	31:32.23	31:27.00 -87
					Mar	2:32:03	2:28:56 -92
* Wang	Yan	CHN	2 May 71	168/50	5kW	21:55	
					10kW	42:26, 43:01.0	42:50 -92
Wang	Yanfang	CHN	10 Jul 71		3k	8:56.75	9:04.34 -91
					10k	31:32.50	32:32.20 -91
					Mar	2:26:36	
Wang	Yawen ¶	CHN	23 Aug 73	187/87	SP	19.89	19.63 -92
Wang	Yili	CHN	4 Apr 71		10k	32:33.80	
Wang	Yongmei	CHN	3 Oct 68	162/51	10k	31:31.54	32:00.27 -91
					Mar	2:34:44	

Name		Nat	Born	Ht/Wt	Event	1993 Mark	Pre-1993 Best
* Wang	Yuan	CHN	8 Apr 76	165/53	800	1:57.18	2:05.6 -92
					1500	3:59.81	
Warnicka	Monika	POL	26 Apr 69	178/62	400h	55.82	56.25 -92
Warren	Youlanda	USA	13 Mar 72	163/52	400	51.92	51.55 -92
Weavers	Charmaine	RSA	27 Feb 64	178/65	HJ	1.92	2.00 -85
Webber	Dyan	USA	9 Apr 66	169/66	100	11.44w	11.31, 11.29w -92
					200	23.36w	22.88, 22.74w -92
Weber	Ursula	AUT	26 Sep 60	168/75	DT	61.94	63.28 -90
Wei	Li	CHN	Jan 72		1500	4:08.78	4:16.6 -92
					3k	8:39.74	
					10k	31:28.83	33:06.69 -91
					Mar	2:32:40	
Wei	Linkun	CHN	Dec 75		10kW	43:34	
Weidenbach	Lisa	USA	13 Dec 61	178/57	Mar	2:33:38	2:28:15 -89
Weidner	Simone	GER	30 Sep 69	173/55	800	2:02.45	2:03.90 -92
					1500	4:10.26	4:18.1 -91
Weis	Melisa	USA	22 May 71	176/80	SP	16.64i, 16.61	16.79 -92
Wentland	Gwen	USA	29 Apr 72	178/64	HJ	1.92	1.86i -92, 1.83 -90
* Wessel	Kathrin	GER	14 Aug 67	171/53	3k	8:53.45	8:44.81, 8:41.79i -88
					5k	15:20.32	14:58.71 -91
					10k	32:00.52	31:03.62 -91
* Westén	Monica	SWE	15 Mar 66	175/62	800	2:01.86	2:04.68 -92
					400h	55.53	54.69 -90
Wicksell' (de Kock)	Ilze	RSA	10 Aug 59	168/48	800	2:02.08	1:59.39 -83
Wickus	Amy	USA	25 Jun 72	163/57	800	2:00.07	2:03.56 -92
Williams	Allison	USA	1 Jul 71	160/55	100h	13.16	13.70, 13.44w -91
Williams	Claudine	JAM	8 Jan 76	175/62	400	52.01	51.66 -92
Williams	Doris	USA	30 Jun 68	171/64	100h	13.18, 13.14w	13.41 -89
Williams	Louann	TRI	72		100	11.22	11.72 -90
					200	23.05, 22.7	24.11 -90
Williams	Shana	USA	7 Apr 72	178/58	LJ	6.63	6.28 -92
					Hep	5641w	5414 -91
Williams	Tonya	USA	5 Oct 74		400h	56.48A	58.71 -92
Williams	Trevaia	USA	7 Sep 68	183/60	400h	55.94	55.94 -92
Wise	Joanne	GBR	15 Mar 71	164/50	LJ	6.48, 6.59w	6.57 -92, 6.69w -88
Wisniewska	Joanna	POL	24 May 72	178/82	DT	57.56	53.92 -91
Wittich	Ines	GER	14 Nov 69	188/90	SP	18.96	19.48 -87
* Wlodarczyk	Urszula	POL	22 Dec 65	180/67	LJ	6.59, 6.67w	6.40 -91
					TJ	13.98	13.58 -91
					Hep	6394	6425 -91
Wolf	Birgit	GER	11 Sep 69	175/58	400h	55.91	57.06 -92
Wolf	Gabriele	GER	28 Oct 60	165/53	Mar	2:34:36	2:31:45 -89
Wolowiec	Simone	AUS	12 Feb 74		5kW	22:35.8mx	24:30.60 -92
Womplou	Marie	CIV	20 Dec 69	161/46	400h	57.69	56.52 -92
Wu	Guihua	CHN	4 Oct 71		DT	60.58	58.68 -92
Wu	Hongjie	CHN	13 Apr 71		400h	56.86	57.42 -92
Wu	Lingmei	CHN	1 Feb 71		LJ	6.60	6.49 -91
Wu	Shuzhen	CHN	27 Aug 73		Hep	6249	5408 -91
Wu	Weili	CHN	20 Apr 70		PV	3.80	3.80 -90
Wu	Xianchun	CHN	Feb 72		SP	19.27	19.35 -92
* Wyeth	Alison	GBR	26 May 64	177/58	1500	4:03.17	4:05.52 -92
					1M	4:31:81	4:24.87 -91
					2k	5:38.50	5:42.08 -91
					3k	8:38.42	8:43.93 -92
* Wyludda	Ilke	GER	28 Mar 69	185/97	DT	64.06	74.56 -89
Wysocka	Marzena	POL	17 Feb 69	176/80	DT	60.48	56.56 -92
Xiang	Zhengfeng	CHN			JT	59.64	
Xiao	Yehua	CHN	6 Nov 71		200	23.38	23.48 -91
Xie	Hongxia	CHN	5 Apr 70		SP	19.22	19.00 -92
Xie	Lihua	CHN	19 Jul 65	162/50	Mar	2:26:38	2:28:53 -92
Xie	Liuying	CHN	Jan 67		100h	12.75	13.18 -92
Xin	Xiaoli	CHN	22 Sep 66	165/60	JT	59.70	64.32 -92
Xing	Ailan	CHN	23 Feb 65	175/86	DT	58.74	65.42 -88
Xing	Yuqin	CHN	Sep 69		800	2:01.86	2:03.03 -90
Xiong	Qiying	CHN	14 Oct 67	170/61	LJ	6.79	6.88 -88
Xu	Chunjuan	CHN	Oct 72		10kW	44:01, 45:15.3	45:00 -91

Name		Nat	Born	Ht/Wt	Event	1993 Mark	Pre-1993 Best
Xu	Demei	CHN	23 May 67	174/75	JT	62.10	68.78 -91
Yachmeneva	Marina	RUS	14 Aug 61	169/57	1500	4:12.33	4:02.84 -88
* Yamamoto	Yoshiko	JPN	6 Jun 70	159/44	Mar	2:29:12	2:26:26 -92
Yan	Wei	CHN	12 Oct 71	160/52	800	2:00.49	2:01.9 -91
					1500	4:01.69	4:07.69 -92
					3k	8:57.75	
Yan	Xueqin	CHN	Nov 73		TJ	13.27	13.03 -92
Yang	Juan	CHN	5 Sep 69	173/63	LJ	6.68	6.84 -92
Yang	Zhanxiang	CHN	Sep 72		LJ	6.71	6.40 -90
Yao	Lin	CHN			100	11.44	
Yao	Weili	CHN	6 May 68		LJ	7.01	6.64 -90
Yaroshevich	Irina	BLS	12 Dec 66		800	2:01.71	
Yarygina	Oksana	UZB	24 Dec 72	170/65	JT	59.84	59.90 -92
* Yatchenko	Irina	BLS	30 Oct 65	185/94	DT	58.74	68.94 -92
Ye	Shenglan	CHN	Jun 69		200	23.39	
* Yegorova	Valentina	RUS	16 Feb 64	156/52	HMar	69:35	
					Mar	2:26:40	2:28:18 -91
* Yelesina	Yelena	RUS	5 Apr 70	184/56	HJ	1.91	2.02 -90
Yenvarenko	Galina	RUS	70		PV	3.80	3.60 -92
Yermolovich	Natalya	BLS	29 Apr 64	175/80	JT	61.12	69.86 -85
* Yevseyeva	Inna	UKR	14 Aug 64	180/63	800	1:59.03	1:56.0 -88
					1000	2:35.46I	2:33.93I -92
Yoshida	Mitsuyo	JPN	29 Oct 66	172/50	Mar	2:29:16	2:30:25 -90
Yoshida	Naomi	JPN	14 Apr 69	160/44	10k	32:28.66	32:24.19 -92
					HMar	70:38	
You	Yanyun	CHN	8 Jan 72		100	11.44	11.49 -91
* Young	Dannette	USA	6 Oct 64	170/57	100	11.42	11.10 -88
					200	22.51, 22.32w	22.23 -88, 22.19w -90
					400	51.59	50.46 -92
Yu	Huaxiu	CHN	9 Oct 73		HJ	6.57	6.62 -92
Yu	Juan	CHN			SP	17.53	
Yu	Qing	CHN	22 May 72		100h	13.32	13.20 -91
Yu	Rongxiu	CHN	Feb 66		100h	13.22	12.99 -92
Yu	Yongping	CHN	28 Nov 73		TJ	13.47	12.76 -91
Yukhnevich	Leonarda	BLS	9 Oct 63		10kW	44:02	44:27 -90
Yurchenko	Aelita	UKR	1 Jan 65	167/56	400	51.55	49.47 -88
* Yusuf	Fatima	NGR	1 Apr 71	178/61	400	52.59	50.41 -91
Zaituc	Luminita	ROM	9 Oct 68	163/47	1500	4:10.42	4:10.58 -88
					3k	8:51.54	9:03.04 -89
Zakharchenko	Ilona	UKR	16 Jun 67	176/85	DT	61.22	64.80 -92
Zakorko	Larisa	UKR	21 Feb 64	178/96	DT	55.90	63.48 -90
Zalevskaya	Svetlana	KZK	14 Jun 73	184/63	HJ	1.94	1.89 -91
Zamperioli	Elena	ITA	29 Oct 67	170/53	400h	56.77A	56.59, 56.3 -92
Zatsepilova	Oksana	RUS	20 Apr 74		HT	58.36	53.02 -92
Zavadskaya	Yelena	UKR	24 Dec 64	171/60	800	2:01.14	1:59.36 -92
Zemková	Zuzana	SVK	17 Jul 67	170/60	5kW	22:26.8	21:17 -91, 22:37.9 -92
					10kW	45:53	44:54 -92
Zemskova	Tatyana	RUS	28 Mar 66	170/50	800	2:02.48	2:02.77 -91
Zeng	Yujuan	CHN	23 Mar 71		LJ	6.48	6.27 -92
					Hep	5745	
Zeng	Yuying	CHN	Sep 73		800	1:58.59	2:04.82 -92
Zetouani	Nadia	MAR	3 Jan 70	166/59	400h	56.76	57.31 -92
Zhang	Aimei	CHN	30 Sep 69		100h	13.11	13.05 -92
Zhang	Cuilan	CHN	Apr 73	174/78	DT	62.60	61.76 -92
Zhang	Guihua	CHN	Mar 70		JT	63.46	58.20 -91
Zhang	Hengyun	CHN	25 Oct 74	170/58	400	51.25	53.22 -92
Zhang	Hongzhen	CHN	25 Jan 73		TJ	13.43	13.10 -92
Zhang	Hui	CHN	15 Aug 67		DT	63.80	60.78 -90
Zhang	Jianwei	CHN	23 Mar 71		Hep	5742	5247 -92
Zhang	Jing	CHN	10 Mar 70	170/60	TJ	13.92	13.81 -92
* Zhang	Li	CHN	26 Jun 61	170/85	JT	64.06	70.42 -90
* Zhang	Linli	CHN	6 Mar 73	164/48	1500	3:57.46	4:15.96 -91
					2k	5:35.16	
					3k	8:16.50	8:46.86 -92
					10k	31:16.28	
					Mar	2:24:42	

Name		Nat	Born	Ht/Wt	Event	1993 Mark	Pre-1993 Best
* Zhang	Lirong	CHN	3 Mar 73	156/48	1500	3:59.70	4:19.17 -91
					2k	5:35.2	
					3k	8:21.84	8:48.45 -92
					10k	31:09.25	
					Mar	2:24:52	2:33:59 -91
* Zhang	Liuhong	CHN	16 Jan 69	181/86	SP	19.90	19.74 -91
Zhang	Qinghua	CHN	6 Feb 73		10kW	42:57, 45:00.7	43:10.4 -92
Zhang	Ru	CHN	28 Feb 71		JT	59.42	60.76 -92
Zhang	Sanni	CHN	Dec 70		1500	4:05.10	4:06.63 -92
					3k	8:58.20	9:04.85 -91
Zhang	Weimin	CHN	18 Jan 70		400h	56.21	55.21 -92
Zhang	Xiaohui	CHN	23 Mar 71		Hep	6092	5881 -92
Zhang	Yan	CHN	Jun 72		TJ	14.28	14.14 -92
Zhang	Yi	CHN	10 Nov 73		Hep	5773	5218 -92
Zhang	Yinlan	CHN	14 Feb 70		LJ	6.48, 6.74w	6.65 -92
* Zhang	Yu	CHN	8 Apr 71	180/64	100h	12.64	12.92 -92
Zhang	Yujin	CHN	70		DT	56.40	57.78 -91
Zhang	Yumei	CHN	25 Nov 71		800	1:58.63	2:01.53 -92
Zhang	Zhiying	CHN	19 Jul 73	174/80	SP	19.77	19.23 -92
Zhao	Tianyi	CHN	Feb 73		TJ	13.55w	
Zhao	Yinping	CHN	Feb 73		JT	61.06	53.62 -91
Zhao	Yonghua	CHN	22 Jan 69	181/84	DT	64.42	64.28 -91
Zhao	Yuhong	CHN	Feb 72	169/75	JT	64.16	62.52 -92
Zhdanova	Yevgenia	RUS	27 Jul 66	175/53	HJ	1.95i, 1.94	1.92i -90, 1.92 -91
Zhen	Xueping	CHN	Jun 73		HJ	1.88	1.91 -92
Zheng	Guixia	CHN	24 Jun 73		10k	32:44.07	32:35.75 -91
Zheng	Hui	CHN	Dec 73		SP	18.49	18.63 -92
Zheng	Liyuan	CHN	1 Apr 74		400h	55.72	58.78 -92
Zhirova	Marina	RUS	6 Jun 63	170/58	200	23.22	22.46 -85
Zhong	Hongzhen	CHN	25 Jan 73		LJ	6.58	
* Zhong	Huandi	CHN	28 Jun 67	155/43	3k	8:41.67	8:51.9 -91
					5k	15:05.69	15:30.15 -89
					10k	30:13.37	31:21.08 -92
					Mar	2:25:36	2:32:13 -87
Zhou	Hongyan	CHN	Apr 70		100h	12.90	13.38 -91
Zhou	Jing	CHN	Feb 73		100h	13.15	13.65 -91
Zhou	Shuqin	CHN	Jan 68		SP	18.24	19.40 -92
Zhou	Tianhua	CHN	10 Apr 66	172/94	SP	20.18	20.40 -91
Zhou	Xiulian	CHN	Nov 70		100h	13.48	13.91 -92
Zhu	Mingming	CHN	Apr 68		400h	56.66	57.50 -91
Zhu	Ruixia	CHN	71		Mar	2:34:35	
Zhu	Xiaolan	CHN	1 Jul 72		10kW	43:51.4	43:11.4 -92
* Zhu	Yuqing	CHN	22 Apr 63	180/68	100h	13.05	13.09 -92
					Hep	6394	6.84 -92
Zhuk	Irina	UKR	15 Jan 66	184/104	SP	16.76	17.94 -92
* Zhuravlyova	Tatyana	RUS	19 Dec 67	183/72	LJ	6.60	6.59 -90
					Hep	6369	6370 -91
Zilinskiené (Savickite)	Nele	LIT	29 Dec 69	177/61	HJ	1.95	1.94 -91
Znamenskaya	Yelena	RUS	2 Jun 66	180/66	400h	56.92	56.57 -92
Zöllkau	Antje	GER	23 Jun 63	172/70	JT	59.50	72.16 -84
Zou	Ying	CHN	Jul 74		Hep	5740	
Zsigmond	Kinga	HUN	19 Apr 64	172/68	JT	61.30	63.90 -92
Zubaityte	Vilia	LIT	8 Nov 63	180/90	DT	59.78	63.06 -88
* Zuñiga	M Teresa	ESP	28 Dec 64	167/56	1500	4:07.46	4:00.59 -92
Zürcher (Scalabrin)	Regula	SUI	5 Jan 69	165/55	400	52.19	52.69 -91
					800	2:02.77	2:03.10 -92
Zuyeva	Tatyana	MOL	20 Nov 58	154/49	Mar	2:33:46	2:31:00 -91
* Zveryova	Ellina	BLS	16 Nov 60	182/90	DT	66.32	71.58 -88
Zwiener	Sabine	GER	5 Dec 67	172/58	800	2:00.77	1:59.33 -88

WORLD All-TIME LISTS - INDOOR SPRINTS

50 METRES INDOORS

Mark	Wind	Name		Nat	Born	Pos	Meet	Venue	Date
5.55		Ben	Johnson ¶	CAN	30.12.61	1		Ottawa	31 Jan 87
5.61		Manfred	Kokot	GDR	3.1.48	1h		E.Berlin	4 Feb 73
5.61		James	Sanford	USA	27.12.57	1		San Diego	20 Feb 81
5.62		Emmit	King	USA	24.3.59	1		Kobe	5 Mar 86
5.62		Andre	Cason	USA	20.1.69	1		Los Angeles	15 Feb 92
5.63		Stanley	Floyd	USA	23.6.61	2		San Diego	20 Feb 81
5.64		Davidson	Ezinwa	NGR	22.11.71	2		Los Angeles	15 Feb 92
5.64		Aleksandr	Porkhomovskiy	RUS	12.8.72	1		Moskva	4 Feb 94
5.65		Marian	Woronin	POL	13.8.56	1	EI	Grenoble	21 Feb 81

60 METRES INDOORS

Mark	Wind	Name		Nat	Born	Pos	Meet	Venue	Date
6.41		Ben	Johnson ¶	CAN	30.12.61	1	WI	Indianapolis	7 Mar 87
6.41		Andre	Cason	USA	20.1.69	1		Madrid	14 Feb 92
6.45		Bruny	Surin	CAN	12.7.67	1		Liévin	13 Feb 93
6.48		Leroy	Burrell	USA	21.2.67	1		Madrid	13 Feb 91
6.48		Linford	Christie	GBR	2.4.60	1		Karlsruhe	1 Mar 94
6.49		Vitaliy	Savin	KZK	23.1.66	1		Moskva	23 Feb 91
6.49		Mark	McKoy	CAN	10.12.61	1		Karlsruhe	6 Mar 93
6.49		Colin	Jackson	GBR	18.2.67	1	EI	Paris	11 Mar 94
6.50		Lee	McRae	USA	23.1.66	2	WI	Indianapolis	7 Mar 87
6.51		Marian	Woronin	POL	13.8.56	1	EI	Liévin	21 Feb 87
		(10)							
6.51		Jason	Livingston ¶	GBR	17.3.71	1		Glasgow	8 Feb 92
6.51		Talal	Mansoor	QAT	8.5.64	2		Karlsruhe	6 Mar 93
6.51		Frank	Fredericks	NAM	2.10.67	2	WI	Toronto	12 Mar 93
6.51		Alexandros	Terzian	GRE	24.6.68	2	EI	Paris	11 Mar 94
6.52		Brian	Cooper	USA	21.8.65	2		Sherbrooke	24 Jan 88
6.52		Desai	Williams	CAN	12.6.59	2		Sindelfingen	5 Feb 88
6.52		Andrés	Simón	CUB	15.9.61	1	WI	Budapest	5 Mar 89
6.52		Chidi	Imoh	NIG	27.8.63	2		Piraeus	7 Mar 90
6.53		Sven	Matthes	GDR	23.8.69	1r1		Wien	13 Jan 88
6.53		Dennis	Mitchell	USA	20.2.66	4		Stuttgart	6 Feb 94
		(20)							
6.53		Michael	Green	JAM	7.11.70	1		Osaka	11 Feb 94
6.54		Houston	McTear	USA	12.2.67	1r1		Long Beach	7 Jan 78
6.54		Steffen	Bringmann	GDR	11.3.64	1s3	NC	Senftenberg	15 Feb 86
6.54		Mark	Witherspoon	USA	3.9.63	3	WI	Indianapolis	7 Mar 87
6.54		Jon	Drummond	USA	9.9.68	2		Liévin	13 Feb 93
6.54		Michael	Rosswess	GBR	11.6.65	3	EI	Paris	11 Mar 94
6.55		Christian	Haas	FRG	22.8.58	1s1	EI	Sindelfingen	1 Mar 80
6.55		Emmit	King	USA	24.3.59	1r2		Fairfax	14 Feb 88
6.55		James	Butler	USA	21.6.60	1		Zaragoza	26 Feb 88
6.55		Pierfrancesco	Pavoni	ITA	21.2.63	4		Piraeus	7 Mar 90
		(30)							
6.55		Joel	Isasi	CUB	31.7.67	3		Karlsruhe	6 Mar 93
6.55		Henry	Neal	USA	28.10.70	1	Mill	New York	4 Feb 94
6.56		Aleksandr	Aksinin	RUS	4.11.54	1s2	EI	Sindelfingen	1 Mar 80
6.56		Charles-Louis	Seck	SEN	11.5.65	1		Liévin	7 Feb 87
6.56		Bruno	Marie-Rose	FRA	20.5.65	2		Liévin	7 Feb 87
6.56		Ronald	Desruelles ¶	BEL	14.2.55	2h1		Sindelfingen	5 Feb 88
6.56		Andreas	Berger ¶	AUT	9.6.61	1	NC	Wien	27 Feb 88
6.56		Aaron	Thigpen	USA	18.9.64	2	NC	New York	28 Feb 92
6.56		Pavel	Galkin	RUS	9.10.68	1	NC	Lipetsk	27 Feb 94
6.57		Mel	Lattany	USA	10.8.59	1h2		Louisville	7 Feb 81
		(40)							
6.57		Frank	Emmelmann	GDR	15.9.61	2s3	NC	Senftenberg	15 Feb 86
6.57		Ricardo	Chacón	CUB	30.4.63	1		Oviedo	26 Feb 89
6.57		Sergey	Deminov	RUS	26.2.64	.s	NC	Chelyabinsk	3 Feb 90
6.57		Igor	Groshev	RUS	15.3.64	2	NC	Chelyabinsk	3 Feb 90
6.57		Ray	Stewart	JAM	18.3.65	5		Piraeus	7 Mar 90
6.57		Michael	Marsh	USA	4.8.67	3	NC	New York	28 Feb 92
6.57		Dmitriy	Bartenyev	RUS	8.3.69	1		Moskva	26 Jan 94

Mark	Wind	Name		Nat	Born	Pos	Meet	Venue	Date
6.57		Aleksandr	Slychkov	UKR	31.3.70	1	NC	Kiev	12 Feb 94
6.57		Robert	Esmie	CAN	5.7.72	1h1	USCh	Atlanta	4 Mar 94
		(49)							

50 METRES HURDLES INDOORS

Mark	Wind	Name		Nat	Born	Pos	Meet	Venue	Date
6.25		Mark	McKoy	CAN	10.12.61	1h1		Kobe	5 Mar 86
6.35		Greg	Foster	USA	4.8.58	1h3		Rosemont	27 Jan 85
6.36		Renaldo	Nehemiah	USA	24.3.59	1		Edmonton	3 Feb 79
6.41		Igor	Kovác	SVK	12.5.69	1		Praha	15 Feb 92
6.43		Tony	Dees	USA	6.8.63	1		Los Angeles	18 Jan 91
6.43		Mark	Crear	USA	2.10.68	2		Los Angeles	20 feb 93
6.45		Thomas	Munkelt	GDR	3.8.52	2		Ottawa	10 Feb 79
6.45		Tonie	Campbell	USA	14.6.60	1		Kobe	14 Mar 87
6.46		Frank	Siebeck	GDR	17.8.49	1r2		E.Berlin	3 Feb 74
6.46		Sam	Turner	USA	17.6.57	1		Kobe	9 Mar 85
6.47		Arto	Bryggare	FIN	26.5.58	1	EI	Grenoble	22 Feb 81
6.47		Roger	Kingdom	USA	26.8.62	1		Hamilton	13 Jan 89
6.47		Jirí	Hudec	TCH	15.8.64	2		Praha	15 Feb 92
6.47		Mike	Fenner	GER	24.4.71	1		Bad Segeberg	6 Mar 94
6.48		Javier	Moracho	SPA	18.8.57	2	EI	Grenoble	22 Feb 81
6.48		Igor	Kazanov	LAT	24.9.63	2		Budapest	12 Feb 92
6.48		Colin	Jackson	UK	18.2.67	1		Birmingham	14 Mar 92
6.49		Arthur	Blake	USA	19.8.66	1		Cleveland	17 Feb 90

60 METRES HURDLES INDOORS

Mark	Wind	Name		Nat	Born	Pos	Meet	Venue	Date
7.30		Colin	Jackson	UK	18.2.67	1		Sindelfingen	6 Mar 94
7.36r?		Greg	Foster	USA	4.8.58	1	Sunk	Los Angeles	6 Jan 87
		7.42				1		San Sebastián	15 Mar 91
7.37		Roger	Kingdom	USA	26.8.62	1		Piraeus	8 Mar 89
7.41r		Mark	McKoy	CAN	10.10.61	1	WI	Toronto	14 Mar 93
		7.44				1		Sindelfingen	3 Mar 91
7.42		Igor	Kazanov	LAT	24.9.63	1		Moskva	25 Feb 89
7.43		Tony	Dees	USA	6.8.63	3	WI	Toronto	14 Mar 93
7.47		Courtney	Hawkins	USA	11.7.67	1		Birmingham	22 Feb 92
7.48		Thomas	Munkelt	GDR	3.8.52	1	EI	Budapest	6 Mar 83
7.50		Stéphane	Caristan	FRA	31.3.64	1h1	NC	Liévin	8 Feb 87
7.50		Renaldo	Nehemiah	USA	24.3.59	1		Madrid	10 Mar 89
		(10)							
7.50		Anthony	Jarrett	UK	13.8.68	2	vUS,SU	Cosford	18 Mar 90
7.50		Georg	Boroi	ROM	26.8.64	1		Liévin	13 Feb 94
7.51		Tonie	Campbell	USA	14.6.60	1	WI	Indianapolis	8 Mar 87
7.51		Arthur	Blake	USA	19.8.66	1		Fairfax	4 Feb 90
7.52		Florian	Schwarthoff	FRG	7.5.68	1	NC	Sindelfingen	17 Feb 90
7.53		Liviu	Giurgian	ROM	26.7.62	1	NC	Bacau	13 Feb 88
7.53		Aleksandr	Markin	RUS	8.9.62	1		Moskva	22 Jan 89
7.54		Yuriy	Chervanyev	BLS	15.1.58	1	EI	Sindelfingen	2 Mar 80
7.54		Jack	Pierce	USA	23.9.62	2		Madrid	10 Mar 89
7.54		Tomasz	Nagórka	POL	2.10.67	3		Liévin	25 Jan 92
		(20)							
7.54		Mike	Fenner	GER	24.4.71	3		Sindelfingen	6 Mar 94
7.55		Dietmar	Koszewski	FRG	26.7.67	1		Sindelfingen	27 Feb 93
7.55		Vladimir	Belokon	UKR	13.2.69	1	NC	Kiev	13 Feb 94
7.56		Arto	Bryggare	FIN	26.5.58	1h1	EI	Budapest	6 Mar 83
7.56		Jon	Ridgeon	UK	14.2.67	1		Budapest	28 Feb 88
7.56		Ales	Höffer	CS	9.12.62	1	EI	Budapest	6 Mar 88
7.56		Philippe	Tourret	FRA	8.7.67	1	6N	Paris	23 Feb 91
7.56		Emilio	Valle	CUB	21.4.67	2		San Sebastián	3 Mar 94
7.57		Vladimir	Shishkin	RUS	16.6.64	1		Ghent	4 Feb 90
7.57		Mark	Crear	USA	2.10.68	3	NC	Atlanta	5 Mar 94
		(30)							
7.58		Sergey	Usov	BLS	14.1.64	1		Moskva	23 Feb 91
7.58		Dan	Philibert	FRA	6.8.70	3		Liévin	13 Feb 94
7.58		Allen	Johnson	USA	1.3.71	3		San Sebastián	3 Mar 94
7.59		Cletus	Clark	USA	20.1.62	2		Osaka	15 Jan 86
7.60		Javier	Moracho	SPA	18.8.57	1		San Sebastián	12 Feb 84
7.60		György	Bakos	HUN	6.7.60	1	EI	Piraeus	3 Mar 85

Mark	Wind	Name		Nat	Born	Pos	Meet	Venue	Date
7.60		Jirí	Hudec	CS	15.8.64	3		Karlsruhe	24 Feb 89
7.60		David	Nelson	UK	11.3.67	3	vUS,SU	Cosford	18 Mar 90
7.61		Andrey	Prokofyev	RUS	6.6.59	1	NC	Moskva	21 Feb 82
7.61		Rod	Woodson	USA	10.3.65	1		Indianapolis	7 Mar 87
		(40)							
7.61		Igor	Kovác	SVK	12.5.69	2r1		Stuttgart	2 Feb 92

WOMEN 50 METRES INDOORS

Mark	Name		Nat	Born	Pos	Meet	Venue	Date
6.00	Merlene	Ottey	JAM	10.5.60	1		Moskva	4 Feb 94
6.01	Irina	Privalova	RUS	12.11.68	1		Madrid	11 Feb 94
	5.99u+				1		Wien	6 Feb 94
	6.00 timing improperly aligned				1		Moskva	2 Feb 93
6.06	Angella	Issajenko' ¶	CAN	28.9.58	1		Ottawa	31 Jan 87
6.09	Zhanna	Tarnopolskaya	UKR	6.7.72	1h1		Moskva	2 Feb 93
6.11	Marita	Koch	GDR	18.2.57	1r2		Grenoble	2 Feb 80
6.12	Marlies	Göhr'	GDR	21.3.58	2r2		Grenoble	2 Feb 80
6.12	Silke	Möller'	GDR	20.6.64	1		Berlin	19 Feb 88
6.13	Jeanette	Bolden	USA	26.1.60	1		Edmonton	21 Feb 81
6.13	Michelle	Finn	USA	8.5.65	1		Los Angeles	15 Feb 92
6.13	Natalya	Merzlyakova	RUS	.65	2		Moskva	4 Feb 94
6.13	Yekaterina	Leshcheva	RUS	21.4.74	3		Moskva	4 Feb 94

WOMEN 60 METRES INDOORS

Mark	Name		Nat	Born	Pos	Meet	Venue	Date
6.92	Irina	Privalova	RUS	12.11.68	1		Madrid	11 Feb 93
6.95	Gail	Devers	USA	19.11.66	1	WI	Toronto	12 Mar 93
6.96	Merlene	Ottey	JAM	10.5.60	1		Madrid	14 Feb 92
7.00	Nelli	Cooman-Fiere	HOL	6.6.64	1	EI	Madrid	23 Feb 86
7.03	Anelia	Nuneva	BUL	30.6.62	2s1	EI	Liévin	22 Feb 87
7.04	Marita	Koch	GDR	18.2.57	1	NC	Senftenberg	16 Feb 85
7.04	Silke	Möller'	GDR	20.6.64	1s1	EI	Budapest	6 Mar 88
7.06	Katrin	Krabbe ¶	GER	22.11.69	1	NC	Dortmund	16 Feb 91
7.06	Olga	Bogoslovskaya'	RUS	20.5.64	1	NC	Lipetsk	26 Feb 94
7.07	Marlies	Göhr'	GDR	21.3.58	1	vFra	Liévin	1 Feb 86
	(10)							
7.07	Gwen	Torrence	USA	12.6.65	2	WI	Budapest	3 Mar 89
7.07	Michelle	Finn	USA	8.5.65	1	NC	New York	28 Feb 92
7.08	Angella	Issajenko' ¶	CAN	28.9.58	2	WI	Indianapolis	8 Mar 87
7.09	Juliet	Cuthbert	JAM	9.4.64	1		Sindelfingen	8 Mar 92
7.10	Ulrike	Sarvari	FRG	22.6.64	1	EI	Glasgow	3 Mar 90
7.11	Sofka	Popova	BUL	15.8.53	1s2	EI	Sindelfingen	2 Mar 80
7.11	Els	Vader	HOL	24.9.59	2s2	EI	Liévin	22 Feb 87
7.11	Alice	Brown	USA	20.9.60	1		Madrid	10 Mar 89
7.11	Yekaterina	Leshcheva	RUS	21.4.74	1h4		Moskva	26 Jan 94
7.12	Ingrid	Auerswald'	GDR	2.9.57	1	NC	Senftenberg	21 Jan 84
	(20)							
7.12	Angela	Bailey	CAN	28.2.62	4	WI	Indianapolis	8 Mar 87
7.12	Nadezhda	Rashchupkina	RUS	28.12.63	1		Moskva	20 Feb 88
7.12	Liliana	Allen	CUB	24.6.70	3	WI	Sevilla	8 Mar 91
7.12	Carlette	Guidry	USA	4.9.68	4		Madrid	11 Feb 93
7.13	Linda	Haglund ¶	SWE	15.6.56	2	EI	Milano	12 Mar 78
7.13	Beverly	Kinch	UK	14.1.64	2h2	EI	Madrid	23 Feb 86
7.13	Natalya	Kovtun	SU	27.5.64	h		Moskva	25 Feb 89
7.13	Laurence	Bily	FRA	5.5.63	2	EI	Glasgow	3 Mar 90
7.14	Natalya	German	UKR	12.11.63	1s2		Moskva	20 Feb 88
7.15	Marina	Markina	RUS	19.3.62	1		Moskva	25 Feb 89
	(30)							
7.15	Liliana	Allen	CUB	24.5.70	2s1	WI	Budapest	3 Mar 89
7.15	Evelyn	Ashford	USA	15.4.57	1		Osaka	12 Feb 90
7.15	Irina	Slyusar	UKR	19.3.63	1h	NC	Kiev	18 Jan 92
7.15	Teresa	Neighbors	USA	26.5.67	3	NC	New York	28 Feb 92
7.15	Michelle	Freeman	JAM	5.5.69	2		Fairfax	7 Feb 93
7.16	Renate	Stecher'	GDR	12.5.50	1	EI	Göteborg	10 Mar 74
7.16	Marina	Zhirova	RUS	6.6.63	1		Volgograd	30 Jan 87
7.16	Olga	Frolova	RUS	2.10.64	3		Moskva	20 Feb 88
7.16	Dawn	Sowell	USA	27.3.66	1	LAT	Inglewood	17 Feb 89
	(40)							

Mark	Wind	Name		Nat	Born	Pos	Meet	Venue	Date
7.16		Olga	Zolotaryova	RUS	1.11.61	4		Moskva	25 Feb 89
7.16		Galina	Malchugina	RUS	17.12.62	1h	NC	Chelyabinsk	3 Feb 90
7.16		Pauline	Davis	BAH	9.7.66	5	WI	Sevilla	8 Mar 91
7.16		Lyudmila	Antonova	UKR	4.8.70	s		Kiev	18 Jan 92
7.16		Patricia	Girard ¶	FRA	8.4.68	1s2	EI	Paris	12 Mar 94

WOMEN 50 METRES HURDLES INDOORS

Mark	Wind	Name		Nat	Born	Pos	Meet	Venue	Date
6.58		Cornelia	Oschkenat'	GDR	29.10.61	1s2		Berlin	20 Feb 88
6.65		Gloria	Siebert'	GDR	13.1.64	2		Berlin	20 Feb 88
6.65		Lyudmila	Narozhilenko ¶	RUS	21.4.64	1		Grenoble	7 Feb 93
6.73		Julie	Baumann ¶	SUI	17.6.64	2		Grenoble	7 Feb 93
6.74		Anneliese	Ehrhardt	GDR	18.6.50	1h		Berlin	4 Feb 73
6.74		Zofia	Bielczyk	POL	22.9.58	1	EI	Grenoble	21 Feb 81
6.75		Kerstin	Patzwahl	GDR	16.7.65	1		Berlin	5 Feb 89
6.76		Danuta	Perka	POL	22.6.56	1		Berlin	11 Feb 79
6.77		Grazyna	Rabsztyn	POL	20.9.52	2		Berlin	11 Feb 79
6.77		Yordanka	Donkova	BUL	28.9.61	3		Grenoble	7 Feb 93

WOMEN 60 METRES HURDLES INDOORS

Mark	Wind	Name		Nat	Born	Pos	Meet	Venue	Date
7.69		Lyudmila	Narozhilenko ¶	RUS	21.4.64	1	NC	Chelyabinsk	4 Feb 90
7.73		Cornelia	Oschkenat'	GDR	29.10.61	1		Wien	25 Feb 89
7.74		Yordanka	Donkova	BUL	28.9.61	1	NC	Sofia	14 Feb 87
7.75		Bettine	Jahn	GDR	3.8.58	1	EI	Budapest	5 Mar 83
7.76		Gloria	Siebert'	GDR	13.1.64	1		Sindelfingen	5 Feb 88
7.77		Zofia	Bielczyk	POL	22.9.58	1	EI	Sindelfingen	1 Mar 80
7.81		Jackie	Joyner-Kersee	USA	3.3.62	1		Fairfax	5 Feb 89
7.82		Yelizaveta	Chernyshova	RUS	26.1.58	1	WI	Budapest	5 Mar 89
7.82		Monique	Ewanje-Epée	FRA	11.7.67	1	6N	Paris	23 Feb
7.84		Grazyna	Rabsztyn	POL	20.9.52	1		Zabrze	17 Feb 80
		(10)							
7.85		Ginka	Zagorcheva	BUL	12.4.58	2		Sofia	7 Feb 87
7.85		Natalya	Grigoryeva	UKR	3.12.61	2	NC	Chelyabinsk	4 Feb 90
7.85		Gail	Devers	USA	19.11.66	1		Fairfax	6 Feb 94
7.86		Laurence	Elloy	FRA	3.12.59	1s2	EI	Madrid	22 Feb 86
7.86		Mihaela	Pogacian'	ROM	27.1.58	1s2	EI	Budapest	5 Mar 88
7.86		Lidiya	Yurkova '	BLS	15.1.67	3	NC	Chelyabinsk	4 Feb 90
7.87		Eva	Sokolova	RUS	25.3.61	1		Moskva	20 Feb 88
7.88		Anne	Piquereau	FRA	15.6.64	1	NC	Bordeaux	17 Feb 90
7.89		Kerstin	Knabe	GDR	7.7.59	2s2	EI	Madrid	22 Feb 86
7.89		Claudia	Zaczkiewicz'	FRG	4.7.62	1		Karlsruhe	7 Feb 88
		(20)							
7.89		Galina	Khaustova	RUS	4.7.65	2		Lipetsk	20 Jan 89
7.89		Marjan	Olyslager	HOL	8.3.62	2s1	WI	Budapest	5 Mar 89
7.90		Anneliese	Ehrhardt	GDR	18.6.50	1s1	EI	Göteborg	9 Mar 74
7.90		Lucyna	Kalek	POL	9.1.56	1		Warszawa	29 Jan 84
7.90		Michelle	Freeman	JAM	5.5.69	1	TAC	New York	26 Feb 93
7.91		Ulrike	Denk	FRG	10.5.64	4	EI	Madrid	22 Feb 86
7.91		Anne	Piquereau	FRA	15.6.64	3	EI	Paris	13 Mar 94
7.92		Nadezhda	Korshunova	UKR	19.4.61	1	SU Ch	Kishinyev	17 Feb 85
7.92		Kim	McKenzie	USA	21.3.61	2s2	WI	Budapest	5 Mar 89
7.93		Vera	Akimova'	RUS	5.6.59	1	SU Ch	Moskva	17 Feb 84
		(30)							
7.93		LaVonna	Martin	USA	18.11.66	2	NC	New Yprk	26 feb 93
7.93		Yulia	Graudyn	RUS	13.11.70	1		Moskva	27 Jan 94
7.93		Patricia	Girard ¶	FRA	8.4.68	1	NC	Bordeaux	26 Feb 94
7.94		Johanna	Klier'	GDR	13.9.52	1	EI	Milano	11 Mar 78
7.94		Sabine	Paetz/John'	GDR	16.10.57	2		Senftenberg	22 Jan 84
7.94		Svetlana	Laukhova	RUS	1.2.73	1	NC	Lipetsk	27 Feb 94
7.94		Brigita	Bukovec	SLO	21.5.70	4	EI	Paris	13 Mar 94
7.95		Danuta	Perka	POL	22.6.56	1	EI	Wien	24 Feb 79
7.95		Julie	Baumann ¶	SUI	17.6.64	1		Karlsruhe	31 Jan 92
7.96		Gabriele	Lippe/Roth	FRG	8.5.67	3	EI	Den Haag	19 Feb 89
		(40)							
7.96		Tatyana	Reshetnikova	RUS	14.10.66	2		Moskva	2 Feb 93
Drugs dq:	7.69	Lyudmila	Narozhilenko	SU	12.6.64	1		Liévin	13 Feb 93
Hand timed:	7.4	Lyudmila	Narozhilenko	SU	12.6.64	1		Kishinyev	25 Jan 90

1994 WORLD INDOOR LISTS

MEN

50 Metres

5.64	Aleks.Porkhomovskiy RUS	1	Moskva	4 Feb
5.67	Robert Esmie CAN	1	Los Angeles	19 Feb

55 Metres

6.09	Mark Witherspoon USA	1	Cedar Falls	18 Feb
6.11	Greg Saddler USA	1	Indianapolis	12 Mar
6.13	Tim Harden USA	2	Indianapolis	12 Mar

60 Metres

6.48	Linford Christie GBR	1	Karlsruhe	1 Mar
6.49	Colin Jackson GBR	1	Paris	11 Mar
6.50	Bruny Surin CAN	1	Madrid	11 Feb
6.51	Alexandros Terzian GRE	2	Paris	11 Mar
6.52	Leroy Burrell USA	3	Stuttgart	6 Feb
6.53	Dennis Mitchell USA	4	Stuttgart	6 Feb
6.53	Michael Green JAM	1	Osaka	11 Feb
6.54	Michael Rosswess GBR	3	Paris	11 Mar
6.55	Henry Neal USA	1	New York	4 Feb
6.56	Pavel Galkin RUS	1	Lipetsk	27 Feb
6.57	Dmitriy Bartenyev RUS	1	Moskva	26 Jan
6.57	Aleksandr Slychkov UKR	1	Kiev	12 Feb
6.57	Robert Esmie CAN	1h1	Atlanta	4 Mar
6.57	Mark McKoy CAN	2	Sindelfingen	6 Mar
6.58	Andre Cason USA	3	Madrid	11 Feb
6.58	Frank Fredericks NAM	2	Osaka	11 Feb
6.58	Ibrahim Meité CIV	3	Liévin	13 Feb
6.58	Andrey Grigoryev RUS	1s1	Lipetsk	26 Feb
6.59	Marc Blume GER	1	Dortmund	13 Jan
6.59	Joel Isasi CUB	4	Madrid	11 Feb
6.59	Jon Drummond USA	2	Maebashi	13 Feb
6.59	Aleks. Porkhomovskiy RUS	4	Paris	11 Mar
6.60	Oleg Kramarenko UKR	2	Kiev	13 Feb
6.60	Ray Stewart JAM	3	Karlsruhe	1 Mar
6.60	Greg Saddler USA	2	Atlanta	5 Mar

200 Metres

20.56	Linford Christie GBR	1	Ghent	9 Feb
20.57	Chris Nelloms USA	1	Atlanta	5 Mar
20.62	Frankie Fredericks NAM	1	Birmingham	26 Feb
20.68	Daniel Sangouma FRA	1h4	Paris	12 Mar
20.73	Clyde Rudolph USA	1h1	Atlanta	4 Mar
20.74	John Regis GBR	1	Glasgow	12 Feb
20.75	Kevin Braunskill USA	2	Atlanta	5 Mar
20.75	Geir Moen NOR	2h1	Paris	12 Mar
20.76	Vladislav Dologodin UKR	2	Paris	13 Mar
20.79	Robert Kurnicki GER	2	Sindelfingen	6 Mar
20.80	Rod Tolbert USA	2h1	Atlanta	4 Mar
20.80	Alvis Whitted USA	3h1	Atlanta	4 Mar
20.81	Michael Johnson USA	1	Maebashi	13 Feb
20.85	Aleks.Porkhomovskiy RUS	2	Liévin	13 Feb
20.85	Andrew Tynes BAH	2	Indianapolis	11 Mar
Oversized track				
20.76A	Andrew Tynes BAH	2	Air Academy	11 Mar

400 Metres

45.17	Michael Johnson USA	1	Birmingham	27 Feb
46.04	Antonio Pettigrew USA	1	Glasgow	12 Feb
46.08	Darnell Hall USA	1h2	Atlanta	4 Mar
46.11	Mark Richardson GBR	1	Glasgow	29 Jan
46.12	Steve Lewis USA	2	Fairfax	6 Feb
46.18	Calvin Davis USA	1r2	Indianapolis	12 Mar
46.26	Du'aine Ladejo GBR	1s1	Paris	12 Mar
46.37	Derrick Adkins USA	2	Atlanta	5 Mar
46.37	Chris Jones USA	1r1	Indianapolis	12 Mar
46.37	Milton Mallard USA	2r2	Indianapolis	12 Mar
46.40	Jason Rouser USA	3	Atlanta	5 Mar
46.41	Rico Lieder GER	2	Stuttgart	6 Feb
46.55	Roger Franklin USA	4	Atlanta	5 Mar
46.56	Mikhail Vdovin RUS	2	Paris	13 Mar
46.59	Andrea Nuti ITA	1	Genova	12 Feb
Oversized track				
46.35	Derek Mills USA	1	Lexington	29 Jan
46.48	Rich Jones USA	1	Ames	12 Feb

500 Metres

1:01.19	Mark Everett USA	1	New York	4 Feb

800 Metres

1:46.19	Paul Ereng KEN	1	Karlsruhe	1 Mar
1:46.35	Luis Javier Gonzalez ESP	1	Sevilla	3 Feb
1:46.38	Andrey Loginov RUS	1	Paris	13 Mar
1:46.66	Johnny Gray USA	1	Sindelfingen	6 Mar
1:46.76	Ivan Komar BLS	1B	Stuttgart	6 Feb
1:46.83	Nico Motchebon GER	2	Karlsruhe	1 Mar
1:46.90	Robert Kibet KEN	1	San Sebastián	3 Mar
1:46.91	Robin van Helden HOL	3	Karlsruhe	1 Mar
1:47.03	Michael Wildner AUT	4	Karlsruhe	1 Mar
1:47.05	David Kiptoo KEN	1	Atlanta	5 Mar
1:47.18	Ousmane Diarra FRA	3	Paris	13 Mar
1:47.24	Anatoliy Makarevich BLS	1	Budapest	5 Feb
1:47.31	Benson Koech KEN	2	San Sebastián	3 Mar
1:47.40	Torbjörn Johansson SWE	1	Malmö	30 Jan
1:47.45	Clive Terrelonge JAM	5	Karlsruhe	1 Mar
1:47.51	Valerit Starodubtsev RUS	2	Budapest	5 Feb
1:47.60	Tom McKean GBR	1	Glasgow	29 Jan
1:47.63	Gary Brown GBR	1	Glasgow	12 Feb

1500 Metres

3:38.46	Venuste Niyongabo BUR	1	Piraeus	28 Feb
3:39.57	Brank Zorko CRO	2	Piraeus	28 Feb
3:40.29	Benson Koech KEN	3	Piraeus	28 Feb
3:40.81	Mickael Damian FRA	1	Bordeaux	30 Jan
3:40.98	John Mayock GBR	1	Sevilla	4 Feb
3:41.0	Robin van Helden HOL	1	Dortmund	13 Feb
3:41.11	Rudi Vlasselaer BEL	1	Ghent	29 Jan
3:41.31	Manuel Pancorbo ESP	2	Sevilla	3 Feb
3:41.36	Stephan Kabat GER	1	Berlin	30 Jan
3:41.46	Jens-Peter Herold GER	1	Stuttgart	6 Feb
3:41.67	Bart Meganck BEL	2	Ghent	29 Jan
3:41.69	Mateo Canellas ESP	3	Sevilla	3 Feb
3:41.70	Abd. Checkhemani FRA	2	Bordeaux	27 Feb
3:41.76	Michael Buchleitner AUT	1	Vienna	6 Feb
3:41.79	Simon Vroemen HOL	1	Den Haag	30 Jan

1 Mile

3:53.74	Jens-Peter Herold GER	1	Karlsruhe	1 Mar
3:54.16	Eric Dubus FRA	2	Karlsruhe	1 Mar
3:54.28	Michael Buchleitner AUT	3	Karlsruhe	1 Mar
3:55.43	David Strang GBR	1	Boston	22 Jan
3:55.76	Mickael Damian FRA	4	Karlsruhe	1 Mar
3:56.29	Andy Keith GBR	2	Boston	22 Jan
3:56.44	Mark Carroll IRL	1	Boston	28 Jan
3:57.50	Mirco Döring GER	5	Karlsruhe	1 Mar
3:57.71	Moses Kiptanui KEN	2	Fairfax	6 Feb
3:57.88	Paul Vandergrift USA	3	Fairfax	6 Feb
3:58.00	Kevin Sullivan CAN	1	Notre Dame	5 Feb
3:58.15	Eamonn Coghlan IRL	1	Allston	20 Feb
3:58.39	Michal Bartoszak POL	4	Fairfax	6 Feb
3:58.46	Edgar de Oliveira BRA	5	Fairfax	6 Feb
3:58.67	Reuben Reina USA	1	Fayetteville	28 Jan
3:58.71	Niall Bruton IRL	1	New York	4 Feb
3:58.80	Marcus O'Sullivan IRL	2	New York	4 Feb

2000 Metres

5:03.88	Eric Dubus FRA	1	Grenoble	6 Feb
5:05.18	Sergey Melnikov RUS	2	Grenoble	6 Feb

3000 Metres

7:40.94	Moses Kiptanui KEN	1	Liévin	13 Feb
7:41.46	Isaac Viciosa ESP	1	Sevilla	3 Feb
7:41.90	Enrique Molina ESP	2	Liévin	13 Feb
7:42.54	Anacleto Jiménez ESP	1	Sevilla	27 Feb
7:46.02	Dieter Baumann GER	1	Dortmund	26 Feb
7:47.11	Stephane Franke GER	3	Liévin	13 Feb
7:47.90	Aïssa Belaout ALG	4	Sevilla	3 Feb
7:49.22	Venuste Niyongabo BUR	1	Ghent	9 Feb
7:49.83	Andy Keith GBR	1	Fairfax	6 Feb
7:49.85	Christophe Impens BEL	2	Ghent	9 Feb
7:49.91	Eric Dubus FRA	5	Liévin	13 Feb
7:50.16	Reuben Reina USA	1	New York	4 Feb
7:50.74	Brahim Boutayeb MAR	2	Sindelfingen	6 Mar
7:50.77	Khalid Kairouani MAR	1	Boston	22 Jan
7:50.85	Steffen Brand GER	1	Berlin	4 Feb
7:50.90	Josephat Kapkory KEN	1	Indianapolis	12 Mar
7:51.00	Brendan Mathias CAN	3	Fairfax	6 Feb
7:51.24	Jim Svenøy NOR	2	Indianapolis	12 Mar
7:51.35	Mark Carroll IRL	2	Boston	22 Jan
7:51.72	Danny Lopez USA	3	Ghent	9 Feb

5000 Metres

13:26.84	Mohamed Issangar MAR	1	Stockholm	8 Mar
13:31.02	Aïssa Belaout ALG	1	Stuttgart	6 Feb
13:32.90	Ismael Kirui KEN	2	Stockholm	8 Mar
13:33.51	Tendai Chimusasa ZIM	2	Stuttgart	6 Feb
13:36.16	Stephane Franke GER	3	Stuttgart	6 Feb

50 Metres Hurdles

6.47	Mike Fenner GER	1	Bad Segeberg	6 Mar
6.50	Li Tong CHN	1	Los Angeles	19 Feb
6.51	Dietmar Koszewski GER	1	Bad Segeberg	6 Mar
6.58	Mark Crtear USA	2	Los Angeles	19 Feb
6.59	Glenn Terry USA	3	Los Angeles	19 Feb

55 Metres Hurdles

7.03	Allen Johnson USA	1	Johnson City	22 Jan
7.11	Robert Foster JAM	1	Indianapolis	11 Mar

60 Metres Hurdles

7.30	Colin Jackson GBR	1	Sindelfingen	6 Mar
7.50	Georg Boroi ROM	1	Liévin	13 Feb
7.52	Mark McKoy CAN	1	Piraeus	28 Feb
7.54	Tony Dees USA	1	Atlanta	5 Mar
7.54	Mike Fenner GER	3	Sindelfingen	6 Mar
7.55	Vladimir Belokon UKR	1	Kiev	13 Feb
7.56	Emilio Valle CUB	2	San Sebastián	3 Mar
7.56	Greg Foster USA	2	Atlanta	5 Mar
7.57	Mark Crear USA	3	Atlanta	5 Mar
7.58	Tony Jarrett GBR	2	Glasgow	12 Feb
7.58	Dan Philibert FRA	3	Liévin	13 Feb
7.58	Allen Johnson USA	3	San Sebastiá	3 Mar
7.61	Igor Kovác SVK	1h	Karlsruhe	1 Mar
7.62	Jack Pierce USA	1	Osaka	11 Feb
7.62	Arthur Blake USA	3	Madrid	11 Feb
7.62	Igor Kazanov LAT	4	Liévin	13 Feb
7.63	Florian Schwarthoff GER	2	Berlin	4 Feb
7.63	Andrey Dydalin RUS	1	Lipetsk	27 Feb
7.65	Aleksandr Markin RUS	1	Moskva	27 Jan
7.65	Li Tong CHN	5	Madrid	11 Feb
7.65	Laurent Ottoz ITA	1	Genova	12 Feb

High Jump

2.40	Javier Sotomayor CUB	1	Wuppertal	4 Feb
2.38	Steve Smith GBR	2	Wuppertal	4 Feb
2.38	Hendrik Beyer GER	1	Weinheim	18 Mar
2.37	Dalton Grant GBR	1	Paris	13 Mar
2.36	Steinar Hoen NOR	1	Balingen	12 Feb
2.36	Troy Kemp BAH	2	Weinheim	18 Mar
2.35	Jean-Charles Gicquel FRA	2	Paris	13 Mar
2.34	Ralf Sonn GER	3	Balingen	12 Feb
2.32	Hollis Conway USA	2	Spala	27 Jan
2.32	Cristian Popescu ROM	1	Piraeus	20 Feb
2.32	Brendan Reilly GBR	4	Liverpool	24 Feb
2.32	Ray Doakes USA	1	Gainesville	27 Feb
2.31	Robert Ruffini SVK	2	Arnstadt	29 Jan
2.31	Grigoriy Fedorkov RUS	1	Lipetsk	26 Feb
2.31	Håkan Sarnblom NOR	3	Piraeus	28 Feb
2.31	Randy Jenkins USA	1	Indianapolis	11 Mar
2.31	Leonid Pumalaynen RUS	5	Paris	13 Mar
2.30	Ruslan Stipanov UKR	2	B. Bystrica	26 Jan
2.30	Artur Partyka POL	3	Spala	27 Jan
2.30	Lambros Papakostas GRE	2	Piraeus	4 Feb
2.30	Soran Zoric YUG	2	Piraeus	16 Feb

Pole Vault

6.05	Sergey Bubka UKR	1	Grenoble	6 Feb
5.90	Maksim Tarasov RUS	1	Madrid	11 Feb
5.90	Rodion Gataullin RUS	1	Liévin	13 Feb
5.90	Jean Galfione FRA	2	Liévin	13 Feb
5.90	Pyotr Bochkaryov RUS	1	Paris	12 Mar
5.83	Jani Lehtonen FIN	1	Stockholm	8 Mar
5.83	Lawrence Johnson USA	1	Indianapolis	12 Mar
5.80	Kory Tarpenning USA	2	Donetsk	20 Feb
5.80	Igor Trandenkov RUS	3	Donetsk	20 Feb
5.80	Denis Petushinskiy RUS	1	Piraeus	28 Feb
5.75	Vasiliy Bubka UKR	2	Cler.Ferrand	28 Jan
5.73	Igor Potapovich KZK	2	Stockholm	8 Mar
5.70A	Pat Manson USA	1	Reno	22 Jan
5.70	Bill Payne USA	1	Johnson City	22 Jan
5.70	Philippe D'Encausse FRA	3	Cler.Ferrand	28 Jan
5.70	Philippe Collet FRA	6	Cler.Ferrand	28 Jan
5.70	Aleksandr Korchagin	1	Moskva	1 Feb
5.70	Grigoriy Yegorov KZK	2	Moskva	1 Feb
5.70	Brent Burns USA	1	New York	4 Feb
5.70	Andrey Skvortsov RUS	1	Moskva	4 Feb
5.70	Scott Huffman USA	1	Ghent	9 Feb
5.70	István Bagyula HUN	4	Berlin	4 Mar

Long Jump

8.43	Stanislav Tarasenko RUS	1	Moskva	26 Jan
8.43	Erick Walder USA	1	Indianapolis	11 Mar
8.30	Ivailo Mladenov BUL	1	Piraeus	28 Feb
8.26	Ivan Pedroso CUB	2	Piraeus	28 Feb
8.23	Dmitriy Bagryanov RUS	1	Moskva	14 Jan
8.19	K.Streete-Thompson USA	1	Atlanta	5 Mar
8.16	Dietmar Haaf GER	1	Karlsruhe	6 Feb
8.11	Bogdan Tudor ROM	1	Bucuresti	27 Feb
8.10	Aleksandr Glovatskiy BLS	1	Gomel	15 Jan
8.09	Galin Georgiev BUL	1	Dobrich	5 Mar
8.09	Konst. Koukodimos GRE	2	Paris	13 Mar
8.06	Mike Powell USA	1	Budapest	5 Feb
8.06	Aston Morgan JAM	1	Lincoln	5 Mar
8.05	Angel Hernandez ESP	1	Madrid	11 Feb
8.01	Tony Walton USA	2	Atlanta	5 Mar
8.00	Chris Sanders USA	1	Ames	11 Feb
7.99	Milan Gombala TCH	1	Mannheim	11 Feb
7.99	Roland McGhee USA	1	Murfreesboro	26 Feb

Triple Jump

17.77	Leonid Voloshin RUS	1	Grenoble	6 Feb
17.47	Denis Kapustin RUS	1	Lipetsk	27 Feb
17.37	Vasiliy Sokov RUS	2	Lipetsk	27 Feb
17.35	Pierre Camara FRA	2	Grenoble	6 Feb
17.24	Erick Walder USA	1	Indianapolis	12 Mar
17.23	Serge Helan FRA	4	Paris	12 Mar
17.16	Maris Bruziks LAT	3	Grenoble	6 Feb
17.15	Yuriy Sotnikov RUS	3	Lipetsk	27 Feb
17.12	Aleksandr Glovatskiy BLS	1	Gomel	15 Jan
17.10	Ralf Jaros GER	1	Dortmund	25 Feb

17.05	Oleg Grokhovskiy RUS	4	Grenoble	6 Feb
17.02	Aleksandr Petrunin RUS	4	Lipetsk	27 Feb
16.98	Andrius Raizgys LIT	1	Moskva	4 Feb
16.96	Georges Sainte-Rose FRA	5	Paris	12 Mar
16.95	Brian Wellman BER	2	Fayetteville	28 Jan
16.95	Oleg Sakirkin KZK	5	Lipetsk	27 Feb
16.87	Vladimir Melikhov RUS	1	Birmingham	26 Feb
16.83	Jonathan Edwards GBR	2	Stuttgart	6 Feb
16.83	Yoelvis Quesada CUB	6	Grenoble	6 Feb
16.82	Jerome Domain DMN	1	Oklahoma C	12 Feb
16.81	Sergey ArzamazovKZK	3	Moskva	1 Feb
16.81	Lars Hedman SWE	1	Växjö	26 Feb

Shot

21.25	Kevin Toth USA	1	Atlanta	5 Mar
21.05	Aleksandr Bagach UKR	1	Kiev	1 Mar
20.86	C J Hunter USA	1	Air Academy	29 Jan
20.64	Dragan Peric YUG	1	S. Mitrovica	19 Mar
20.36	Yevgeniy Palchikov RUS	1	Glasgow	29 Jan
20.20	Randy Barnes USA	1	Los Angeles	19 Feb
20.07	Petur Gudmundsson ISL	1	Stockholm	8 Mar
20.03	John Godina USA	1	Indianapolis	11 Mar
20.02	Manuel Martinez ESP	1	Zaragoza	13 Jan
20.02	Paolo Dal Soglio ITA	1	Genova	5 Feb
19.93	Mika Halvari FIN	2	Stockholm	8 Mar
19.92	Viktor Bulat UKR	1	Gomel	15 Jan
19.73	Markus Koistinen FIN	2	Jyväskylä	27 Feb
19.73	Roman Virastyuk UKR	2	Kiev	12 Mar
19.72	Brent Noon USA	1	Gainesville	26 Feb
19.69	Sven Buder GER	1	Sassnitz	4 Feb
19.61	Sergey Nikolayev RUS	2	Lipetsk	27 Feb
19.60	Vyacheslav Lykho RUS	3	Lipetsk	27 Feb
19.56	Gheorghe Guset ROM	1	Bucuresti	6 Feb

35 Lb Weight

23.83	Lance Deal USA	1	Boston	22 Jan
22.71	Lou Chisari USA	1	Boston	20 Feb
22.20	Scott McGee USA	2	New York	4 Feb
21.98	Ron Willis USA	1	Columbia	29 Jan
21.86	Brian Murer USA	2	Indianapolis	12 Mar
21.83	Alex Papadimitrou GRE	3	Indianapolis	12 Mar

Heptathlon

6268	Christian Plaziat FRA	1	Paris	13 Mar
6119	Henrik Dagård SWE	2	Paris	13 Mar
6084	Alain Blondel FRA	3	Paris	13 Mar
6061	Tomás Dvorak TCH	4	Paris	13 Mar
5948	Igor Matsanov BLS	1	Zaporozhe	Feb
5945	Erki Nool EST	5	Paris	13 Mar
5944	Sándor Munkácsi HUN	6	Paris	13 Mar
5905	Frank Müller GER	2	Berlin	19 Feb
5888	Indrek Kaseorg EST	7	Paris	13 Mar
5859	Petri Keskitalo FIN	1	Kuopio	13 Feb
5839	Michael Kohnle GER	3	Berlin	19 Feb
5831	Valeriy Belousov RUS	1	Lipetsk	5 Feb
5816	Nikolay Afanasyev RUS	2	Lipetsk	5 Feb

5000 Metres Walk

18:32.0	Frants Kostyukevich BLS	1	Minsk	29 Jan
18:34.32	Mikhail Shchennikov RUS	1	Paris	13 Mar
18:40.0	Yevgeniy Misyula BLS	2	Minsk	30 Jan
18:40.32	Ronald Weigel GER	2	Paris	13 Mar
18:43.20	Denis Langlois FRA	3	Paris	13 Mar
18:48.13	Vladimir Andreyev RUS	2	Lipetsk	27 Feb
18:49.08	Grigoriy Kornev RUS	3	Lipetsk	27 Feb
18:50.48	Jean-Claude Corre FRA	1	Paris	30 Jan
18:54.72	Mikhail Orlov RUS	4	Lipetsk	27 Feb
18:56.05	Sandor Urbanik HUN	1	Budapest	5 Feb
19:01.03	Michele Didoni ITA	4	Paris	12 Mar
19:01.8	Jirí Malysa TCH	1	Ostrava	8 Jan
19:02.36	Igor Kollár SVK	1	Wien	29 Jan
19:05.1	Oleg Troshin RUS	2	Moskva	28 Jan
19:05.85	Axel Noack GER	2	Dortmund	26 Feb
19:06.81	Stefan Johansson SWE	2h1	Paris	12 Mar
19:07.5	Tomás Kratochvíl TCH	1	Praha	23 Jan
19:07.83	Giov. De Benedictis ITA	1	Genova	12 Feb
19:09.05	Pavol Blazek SVK	2	Wien	29 Jan
19:11.07	Anatoliy Kozlov UKR	1	Kiev	13 Feb

10,000 Metres Walk

39:42.50	Vladimir Andreyev RUS	1	Moskva	26 Jan
38:43.90	Mikhail Orlov RUS	2	Moskva	26 Jan

WOMEN

50 Metres

6.00	Merlene Ottey JAM	1	Moskva	4 Feb
6.01	Irina Privalova RUS	1	Madrid	11 Feb
	5.99u+	1	Wien	6 Feb
6.13	Natalya Merzlyakova RUS	2	Moskva	4 Feb
6.13	Yekat. Leshcheva RUS	3	Moskva	4 Feb
6.15	Olga Bogoslovskaya RUS	4	Moskva	4 Feb

55 Metres

6.67	Michelle Freeman JAM	1	JohnsonCity	22 Jan
6.70	Holli Hyche USA	1	Indianapolis	12 Mar
6.72	Cheryl Taplin USA	2	Indianapolis	12 Mar

60 Metres

6.93	Irina Privalova RUS	1	Liévin	13 Feb
6.99	Merlene Ottey JAM	1	Sindelfingen	6 Mar
7.00	Gail Devers USA	1	New York	4 Feb
7.06	Olga Bogoslovskaya RUS	1	Lipetsk	26 Feb
7.10	Gwen Torrence USA	1	Atlanta	5 Mar
7.10	Juliet Cuthbert JAM	2	Sindelfingen	6 Mar
7.11	Yekat. Leshcheva RUS	1h4	Moskva	26 Jan
7.15	Liliana Allen CUB	1	Piraeus	28 Feb
7.16	Patricia Girard FRA	1s2	Paris	12 Mar
7.17	Melanie Paschke GER	1	Dortmund	26 Feb
7.17	Natalya Anisimova RUS	2	Lipetsk	26 Geb
7.17	Natalya Merzlyakova RUS	3	Lipetsk	26 Feb
7.17	Nelli Cooman HOL	1	Paris	12 Mar
7.18	Natalya Voronova RUS	2	Moskva	26 Jan
7.18	Anzhela Kravchenko UKR	1	Kiev	13 Feb
7.18	Yelena Dubtsova RUS	4	Lipetsk	26 Feb
7.18	Petya Pendareva BUL	2s2	Paris	12 Mar
7.21	Michelle Freeman JAM	3	Fairfax	6 Feb
7.21	Galina Malchugina RUS	2	Piraeus	28 Feb
7.22	Éva Barati HUN	1	Budapest	26 Feb
7.22	Sheila Echols USA	1h3	Atlanta	5 Mar
Hand timed				
6.8	Yekat. Leshcheva RUS	1	Volgograd	22 Jan

200 Metres

22.16	Irina Privalova RUS	1	Liévin	13 Feb
22.41	Galina Malchugina RUS	1	Paris	13 Mar
22.74	Gwen Torrence USA	1	Atlanta	5 Mar
22.84	Natalya Voronova RUS	1B	Liévin	13 Feb
22.90	Holli Hyche USA	1	Indianapolis	12 Mar
22.91	Silke Knoll GER	1	Dortmund	26 Feb
22.92	Carlette Guidry USA	2	Atlanta	5 Mar
22.94	Merlene Ottey JAM	1	Budapest	5 Feb
22.95	Dannette Young USA	3	Atlanta	5 Mar
22.98	Michele Collins USA	4	Atlanta	5 Mar
23.00	Katharine Merry GBR	1	Glasgow	12 Feb
23.02	Melanie Paschke GER	2	Dortmund	26 Feb
23.11	Flirtisha Harris USA	2	Indianapolis	11 Mar
23.20	Yekat. Leshcheva RUS	1	Moskva	27 Jan
23.25	Dahlia Duhaney JAM	5	Atlanta	5 Mar
23.41	Jacqueline Poelman HOL	2s1	Paris	12 Mar
23.42	Wenda Vereen USA	1	Maebashi	13 Feb
23.44	Yulia Sotnikova RUS	1	Lipetsk	27 Feb

Hand timed

22.8	Natalya Voronova RUS	1h2	Moskva	27 Jan
23.0	Yekat. Leshcheva RUS	1h1	Moskva	27 Jan

300 Metres

36.81	Svetlana Goncharenko RUS	1	Moskva	4 Feb

400 Metres

51.62	Svetlana Goncharenko RUS	1	Paris	13 Mar
51.72	Maicel Malone USA	1	Atlanta	5 Mar
51.72	Sally Gunnell GBR	1	Sindelfingen	6 Mar
51.77	Tatyana Alekseyeva RUS	2	Paris	13 Mar
51.92	Viviane Dorsile FRA	3	Paris	13 Mar
51.99	Jearl Miles USA	2	Atlanta	5 Mar
52.11	Flirtisha Harris USA	1	Indianapolis	12 Mar
52.15	Nat. Kaiser-Brown USA	3	Atlanta	5 Mar
52.34A	Trevaia Williams USA	1	Reno	29 Jan
52.34	Magdalena Nedelcu ROM	1	Piraeus	28 Feb
52.59	Regula Zürcher SUI	1	Magglingen	24 Feb
52.61	Yelena Golesheva RUS	1	Moskva	11 Feb
52.66	Tatyana Zakharova RUS	1r3	Moskva	26 Jan
52.69	Juliet Campbell JAM	2	Fairfax	6 Feb
52.71	Janeen Jones USA	2	Indianapolis	12 Mar
52.77	Ionela Tîrlea ROM	2	Bucuresti	5 Feb
52.91	Melanie Neef GBR	1	Glasgow	29 Jan
52.92	Anja Rücker GER	2	Stuttgart	6 Feb

800 Metres

1:59.30	Violeta Beclea ROM	1	Grenoble	6 Feb
1:59.34	Natalya Dukhnova BLS	2	Grenoble	6 Feb
1:59.43	Ella Kovacs ROM	1	Bucuresti	6 Feb
1:59.5*	Maria Mutola MOZ	1	Los Angeles	19 Feb
	(2:00.21 - 880y)			
	2:00.14	1	Fairfax	6 Feb
2:00.57	Joetta Clark USA	2	Fairfax	6 Feb
2:01.12	Carla Sacramento POR	3	Paris	13 Mar
2:01.14	Mitica Constantin ROM	2	Karlsruhe	1 Mar
2:01.53	Letitia Vriesde SUR	2	Ghent	9 Feb
2:01.59	Yekat. Podkopayeva RUS	3	Grenoble	6 Feb
2:01.65	Amy Wickus USA	1	Champaign	12 Feb
2:01.82	Stella Jongmans HOL	4	Paris	13 Mar
2:02.18	Simone Weidner GER	1	Berlin	19 Feb
2:02.28	Malgorzata Rydz POL	3	Karlsruhe	1 Mar
2:02.38	Carmen Stanciu ROM	2	Bucuresti	6 Feb
2:02.39	Olga Kuznyetsova RUS	1	Stockholm	8 Mar

1000 Metres

2:36.84	Natalya Dukhnova BLS	1	Liévin	13 Feb
2:37.00	Yekat. Podkopayeva RUS	2	Liévin	13 Feb
2:37.26	Lyudmila Rogachova RUS	3	Liévin	13 Feb

1500 Metres

4:06.46	Yekat. Podkopayeva RUS	1	Paris	13 Mar
4:06.60	Lyudmila Rogachova RUS	2	Paris	13 Mar
4:06.98	Malgorzata Rydz POL	3	Paris	13 Mar
4:07.06	Violeta Beclea ROM	4	Paris	13 Mar
4:07.85	Tudorita Chidu ROM	1	Budapest	5 Feb
4:08.96	Liliana Salageanu ROM	2	Budapest	5 Feb
4:09.71	Carla Sacramento POR	1	Braga	19 Feb
4:10.30	Fernanda Ribeiro POR	2	Braga	19 Feb
4:10.68	Ellen Kiessling GER	5	Paris	13 Mar
4:10.92	Mitica Constantin ROM	1	Stuttgart	6 Feb
4:10.99	Teresa Zuñiga ESP	6	Paris	13 Mar
4:11.21	Anna Brzezinska POL	2	Stuttgart	6 Feb
4:11.80	Paula Schnurr CAN	1	Hamilton	14 Jan
4:12.44	Sarah Howell CAN	2	Hamilton	14 Jan
4:12.73	Sandra Gasser SUI	3	Stuttgart	6 Feb
4:12.87	Olga Kuznyetsova RUS	3	Lipetsk	27 Feb

1 Mile

4:28.64	Hassiba Boulmerka ALG	1	Fairfax	6 Feb
4:31.45	Kathy Franey USA	2	New York	4 Feb
4:32.08	Lyudmila Rogachova RU	3	Fairfax	6 Feb

3000 Metres

8:50.47	Fernanda Ribeiro POR	1	Paris	11 Mar
8:55.61	Margareta Keszeg ROM	2	Paris	11 Mar
8:56.90	Anna Brzezinska POL	3	Paris	11 Mar
8:57.18	Elly Van Hulst HOL	1	Den Haag	20 Feb
8:57.49	Christina Mai GER	4	Paris	11 Mar
8:58.85	Kay Gooch NZL	1	Indianapolis	12 Mar
8:59.95	Laurence Vivier FRA	5	Paris	11 Mar
9:02.5	Tudorita Chidu ROM	1	Budapest	23 Jan
9:04.35	Alison Wyeth GBR	6	Paris	11 Mar
9:04.6	Olga Bondarenko RUS	1	Volgograd	23 Jan
9:07.02	Laurence Duquenoy FRA	2	Bordeaux	26 Feb
9:07.5	Cheri Goddard USA	1	Boston	22 Jan
9:08.90	Sonia McGeorge GBR	1	Glasgow	12 Feb
9:09.09	Renata Sobesiak POL	7	Paris	11 Mar
9:09.7	Natalia Azpiazu ESP	2	Boston	22 Jan

50 Metres Hurdles

6.87	J. Joyner-Kersee USA	1	Los Angeles	19 Feb

55 Metres Hurdles

7.41	Michelle Freeman JAM	1	Johnson City	22 Jan
7.51	Gillian Russell JAM	1h1	Gainesville	13 Feb
7.56A	Lynda Tolbert-Goode USA	1h1	Reno	29 Jan
7.60	Diane Rose JAM	1	Indianapols	12 Mar

60 Metres Hurdles

7.83	Yordanka Donkova BUL	1	Liévin	13 Feb
7.85	Gail Devers USA	1	Fairfax	6 Feb
7.89	Eva Sokolova RUS	2	Paris	13 Mar
7.90	Michelle Freeman JAM	1	New York	4 Feb
7.91	Anne Piquereau FRA	3	Paris	13 Mar
7.93	Yulia Graudyn RUS	1	Moskva	27 Jan
7.93	Patricia Girard FRA	1	Bordeaux	26 Feb
7.94	Svetlana Laukhova RUS	1	Lipetsk	27 Feb
7.94	Brigita Bukovec SLO	4	Paris	13 Mar
7.97	Aleksandra Pashkina RUS	2	Moskva	27 Jan
7.97	J. Joyner-Kersee USA	2	New York	4 Feb
7.97	Yelena Sinyutina RUS	1s2	Lipetsk	27 Feb
7.97	Carla Tuzzi ITA	5	Paris	13 Mar
7.98	Svetla Dimitrova BUL	2	Sofia	5 Feb
7.98	Julie Baumann SUI	3	Madrid	11 Feb
8.02	Marina Azyabina RUS	2h1	Liévin	13 Feb
8.02	Aliuska López CUB	3	Liévin	13 Feb
8.02	Nadezhda Bodrova UKR	1	Kiev	13 Feb
8.03	Cécile Cinélu FRA	4s2	Paris	13 Mar
8.06	Tatyana Reshetnikova RUS	4	Moskva	4 Feb
8.06	Zhang Yu CHN	2	Osaka	11 Feb
8.06	Monica Grefstad NOR	3h1	Paris	13 Mar

High Jump

2.02	Alina Astafei ROM	1	Berlin	4 Mar
2.00	Yelena Gulyayeva RUS	1	Moskva	27 Jan
2.00	Britta Bilac SLO	1	Frankfurt	9 Feb
2.00	Stefka Kostadinova BUL	1	Stockholm	8 Mar
1.98	Antonella Bevilacqua ITA	1	Piraeus	28 Feb
1.98	Hanne Haugland NOR	2	Piraeus	28 Feb
1.98	Angie Bradburn USA	1	Atlanta	5 Mar
1.96	Larisa Mikhalchenko UKR	1	B. Bystrica	26 Jan
1.96	Tisha Waller USA	1	Fairfax	6 Feb
1.96	Desislava Alexandrova BUL	2	Paris	12 Mar
1.96	Sigrid Kirchmann AUT	3	Paris	12 Mar
1.96	Tatyana Shevchik BLS	4	Paris	12 Mar
1.94	Silvia Costa CUB	1	Spala	27 Jan
1.94	Sabrina Deleeuw BEL	1	Ghent	6 Feb
1.94	Marion Hellmann GER	3	Frankfurt	9 Feb
1.94	Svetlana Leseva BUL	4	Piraeus	16 Feb
1.94	Olga Bolshova MOL	5	Piraeus	28 Feb

1.93	Irina Gliznutsa MOL	1	Jablonec	29 Jan
1.92	Zuzana Kovácikovà TCH	1	Budapest	5 Feb
1.92	Sarka Novákovà TCH	2	Wien	6 Feb
1.92	Yelena Topchina RUS	2	Lipetsk	27 Feb

Pole Vault

4.08	Nicole Rieger GER	1	Karlsruhe	1 Mar
4.08	Sun Caiyun CHN	2	Karlsruhe	1 Mar
4.00	Andrea Müller GER	1	Sindelfingen	6 Mar
3.96	Gabriela Mihalcea ROM	1	Bucuresti	6 Feb
3.90	Svetlana Abramova RUS	1	Donetsk	20 Feb
3.90	Cai Weiyan CHN	4	Sindelfingen	6 Mar
3.80	Marina Andreyeva RUS	2	Lud'hafen	19 Feb
3.75	Daniela Bartová TCH	1	Praha	22 Feb
3.75	Carmen Haage GER	4	Zweibrücken	29 Jan
3.75	Tanja Cors GER	2	Dortmund	26 Feb

Long Jump

7.19	Heike Drechsler GER	1	Sindelfingen	6 Mar
7.13	J. Joyner-Kersee USA	1	Atlanta	5 Mar
6.89	Larisa Berezhnaya UKR	2	Sindelfingen	6 Mar
6.82	Daphne Saunders BAH	1	Gainesville	26 Feb
6.78	Ludmila Ninova AUT	1	Wien	6 Feb
6.72	Inessa Kravets UKR	3	Paris	11 Mar
6.71	Dedra Davis BAH	2	Indianapolis	11 Mar
6.69	Yelena Sinchukova RUS	1	Lipetsk	27 Feb
6.69	Ana Biryukova RUS	1	Stockholm	8 Mar
6.69	Valentina Uccheddu ITA	4	Paris	11 Mar
6.69	Mirela Dulgheru ROM	1	Bucuresti	6 Feb
6.68	Fiona May ITA (ex GBR)	1	Genova	12 Feb
6.67	Agata Karczmarek POL	2	Stuttgart	6 Feb
6.67	Lyudmila Galkina RUS	2	Lipetsk	26 Feb
6.65	Susen Tiedtke GER	2	Stockholm	8 Mar
6.61	Renata Nielsen DEN	3	Sindelfingen	6 Mar
6.60	Marieta Ilcu ROM	1	Bucuresti	23 Jan
6.60	Yelena Rupasova RUS	1	Perm	23 Jan
6.60	Svetlana Moskalets RUS	3	Lipetsk	26 Feb

Triple Jump

14.90	Inna Lasovskaya RUS	1	Liévin	13 Feb
14.72	Ana Biryukova RUS	2	Paris	13 Mar
14.52	Sofia Bozhanova BUL	3	Paris	13 Mar
14.46	Sarka Kaspárková TCH	4	Paris	13 Mar
14.44	Inessa Kravets UKR	2	Liévin	13 Feb
14.38	Iva Prandzheva BUL	5	Paris	13 Mar
14.21	Galina Chistyakova RUS	4	Grenoble	6 Feb
14.05	Helga Radtke GER	1	Dortmund	26 Feb
14.03	Tanja Bormann GER	2	Dortmund	26 Feb
13.96	Rodica Petrescu ROM	1	Bucuresti	29 Jan
13.91	Yelena Lysak RUS	1	Moskva	4 Feb
13.90	Yolanda Chen RUS	4	Liévin	13 Feb
13.88	Lyudmila Dubkova RUS	3	Moskva	27 Jan
13.86	Ashia Hansen GBR	1	London	29 Jan
13.85	Michelle Griffith GBR	1	Glasgow	12 Feb
13.82	Monica Toth ROM	1	Piraeus	20 Feb
13.80	Niurka Montalvo CUB	6	Grenoble	6 Feb
13.80	Sheila Hudson USA	1	Atlanta	5 Mar
13.78	Viktoriya Vershinina UKR	3	Budapest	5 Feb
13.78	Natalya Kuzina RUS	3	Lipetsk	27 Feb
13.77	Cynthia Rhodes USA	2	Atlanta	5 Mar
13.75	Tatyana Matyashova RUS	4	Lipetsk	27 Feb

Shot

20.82	Valentina Fedyushina UKR	1	Kiev	1 Mar
19.90	Mihaela Oana ROM	1	Bucuresti	6 Feb
19.56	Astrid Kumbernuss GER	1	Sassnitz	5 Feb
19.45	Larisa Peleshenko RUS	1	Lipetsk	27 Feb
19.44	Anna Romanova RUS	2	Lipetsk	27 Feb
19.36	Jana Ciobanu ROM	2	Bucuresti	6 Feb
19.18	Svetla Mitkova BUL	1	Sofia	5 Feb
19.14	Ines Wittich GER	1	Bad Segeberg	29 Jan
19.12	Huang Zhihong CHN	1	Maebashi	13 Feb
19.10	Stephanie Storp GER	1	Würselen93/	17 Dec
	19.02	2	Sassnitz	5 Feb
18.98	Grit Hammer GER	3	Sassnitz	5 Feb
18.57	Krystyna Danilczyk POL	6	Paris	13 Mar
18.50	Ramona Pagel USA	1	Atlanta	5 Mar
18.30	Zhukirina UKR	1	Kiev	12 Feb
18.28	Kathrin Neimke GER	2	Maebashi	13 Feb
18.03	Connie Price-Smith USA	1	Glasgow	12 Feb
18.03	Irina Khudorozhkina RUS	3	Lipetsk	26 Feb

Pentathlon

4801	Larisa Turchinskaya RUS	1	Paris	11 Mar
4775	Rita Ináncsi HUN	2	Paris	11 Mar
4668	Urszula Wlodarczyk POL	3	Paris	11 Mar
4620	Liliana Nastase ROM	4	Paris	11 Mar
4616	Lyudmila Mikhailova RUS	5	Paris	11 Mar
4565	Lyubov Borisova RUS	3	Lipetsk	4 Feb
4558	Kym Carter USA	2	Berlin	19 Feb
4517	Svetlana Buraga BLS	4	Berlin	19 Feb
4503	Ines Krause GER	6	Paris	11 Mar
4496	Maria Kamrowska POL	7	Paris	11 Mar
4489	Petra Vaideanu ROM	6	Berlin	19 Feb
4483	Birgit Clarius GER	7	Berlin	19 Feb
4478	Irina Tyukhay RUS	8	Berlin	19 Feb
4442	Nadezhda Novikova RUS	4	Lipetsk	4 Feb
4437	Tatyana Zhuravlyeva	11	Berlin	19 Feb
4421	Mona Steigauf GER	12	Berlin	19 Feb

3000 Metres Walk

11:54.32	Anna Rita Sidoti ITA	1	Paris	12 Mar
11:56.01	Beate Gummelt GER	2	Paris	12 Mar
11:57.48	Yelena Arshintseva RUS	3	Paris	12 Mar
11:57.49	Yelena Nikolayeva RUS	4	Paris	12 Mar
12:04.46	Leon. Yukhnevich BLS	5	Paris	12 Mar
12:11.07	Yelena Saiko RUS	2	Moskva	4 Feb
12:12.80	Sari Essayah FIN	6	Paris	12 Mar
12:15.48	Olga Leonenko UKR	1	Kiev	13 Feb
12:16.71	Elisabeta Perrone ITA	1	Genova	5 Feb
12:16.83	Olimpiada Ivanova RUS	3	Moskva	4 Feb
12:20.90	Tatyana Ragozina UKR	2	Kiev	13 Feb
12:21.07	Larisa Ramazanova RUS	4	Moskva	4 Feb
12:21.63	Kathrin Boyde GER	8	Paris	12 Mar
12:25.2	Irina Stankina RUS	1	Chelyabinsk	4 Feb
12:27.35	Susana Feitor POR			29 Jan

5000 Metres Walk

21:42.89	Olimpiada Ivanova RUS	1	Moskva	26 Jan
21:51.60	Nadezhda Ryashkina RUS	2	Moskva	26 Jan
21:54.31	Tamara Kovalenko RUS	3	Moskva	26 Jan
22:07.57	Zinaida Sviridenko RUS	4	Moskva	26 Jan

EUROPEAN INDOOR CHAMPIONSHIPS 1994

At Paris (Bercy) March 11-13

The world's two leading athletes of the 1994 indoor season produced the finest performances of the 23rd European Indoor Championships. Colin Jackson completed a unique 60m/60m hurdles double at these championships, his flat time of 6.49 being only a hundredth outside Linford Christie's recent European record, while Inna Lasovskaya fell just 2cm short of her pending world indoor record with 14.88 for victory in the greatest women's triple jump contest yet seen.

Yekaterina Podkopayeva, with the women's 1500m at the age of 41, became the oldest athlete ever to win a major international track championship. Nelli Cooman won a sixth title at 60m and there were fourth titles for Stefka Kostadinova, high jump, and Heike Drechsler, long jump.

Russian athletes won the most titles (9) and medals (19); Britain won five gold and two bronze medals, Germany 11 medals, four of them gold, and the French hosts 11 medals of which two were gold.

MEN

60 Metres
1 Colin Jackson GBR 6.49*
2 Alexandros Terzian GRE 6.51
3 Michael Rosswess GBR 6.54
4 Aleksandr Porkhomovskiy RUS 6.59
5 Daniel Sangouma FRA 6.65
6 Laurent Nevo FRA 6.75

200 Metres
1 Daniel Sangouma FRA 20.68
2 Vladislav Dologodin UKR 20.76
3 George Panagiotopoulos GRE 20.99
4 Evgenios Papadopoulos GRE 21.15
5 Darren Braithwaite GBR 21.30
6 Ioannis Nafpliotis GRE 21.61

400 Metres
1 Du'aine Ladejo GBR 46.53
2 Mikhail Vdovin RUS 46.56
3 Rico Lieder GER 46.82
4 Lutz Becker GER 47.74
5 Andrea Nuti ITA 50.05
dnf James Baulch GBR

800 Metres
1 Andrey Loginov RUS 1:46.38
2 Luis Javier González ESP 1:46.69
3 Ousmane Diarra FRA 1:47.18
4 Nico Motchebon GER 1:47.24
5 Torbjörn Johansson SWE 1:47.42
6 Bruno Konczlo FRA 2:00.33

1500 Metres
1 David Strang GBR 3:44.57
2 Branko Zorko CRO 3:44.64
3 A'lkader Chekhémani FRA 3:44.65
4 Manuel Pancorbo ESP 3:45.03
5 Vyacheslav Shabunin RUS 3:45.37
6 Mickael Damian FRA 3:45.54

3000 Metres
1 Kim Bauermeister GER 7:52.34
2 Ovidiu Olteanu ROM 7:52.37
3 Rod Finch GBR 7:53.99
4 Anacleto Jiménez ESP 7:55.78
5 Michael Buchleitner AUT 7:56.47
6 Andrés Martinez ESP 7:59.70

60 Metres Hurdles
1 Colin Jackson GBR 7.41 (7.39sf *)
2 Georg Boroi ROM 7.57
3 Mike Fenner GER 7.58
4 Dan Philibert FRA 7.60
5 Igor Kovác SVK 7.61
6 Jirí Hudec TCH 7.72

High Jump
1 Dalton Grant GBR 2.37
2 Jean-Charles Gicquel FRA 2.35
3 Hendrik Beyer GER 2.33
4 Steinar Hoen NOR 2.31
5 Leonid Pumalaynen RUS 2.31
6 Håkon Sarnblom NOR 2.29

Pole Vault
1 Pyotr Bochkaryov RUS 5.90*
2 Jean Galfione FRA 5.80
3 Igor Trandenkov RUS 5.75
4 Denis Petushinskiy RUS 5.75
5 István Bagyula HUN 5.70
6 Gianni Iapichino ITA 5.60

Long Jump
1 Dietmar Haaf GER 8.15
2 Kostas Koukodimos GRE 8.09
3 Bogdan Tudor ROM 8.07
4 Ivaylo Mladenov BUL 8.07
5 Stanislav Tarasenko RUS 8.02
6 Dmitriy Bagryanov RUS 8.01

Triple Jump
1 Leonid Voloshin RUS 17.44
2 Denis Kapustin RUS 17.35
3 Vasiliy Sokov RUS 17.31
4 Serge Hélan FRA 17.23
5 Georges Sainte-Rose FRA 16.96
6 Maris Bruziks LAT 16.83

Shot
1 Aleksandr Bagach UKR 20.66
2 Dragan Peric IEP (YUG) 20.55
3 Pétur Gudmundsson ISL 20.04
4 Manuel Martínez ESP 19.85
5 Oliver-Sven Buder GER 19.66
6 Paolo Dal Soglio ITA 19.62

5000 Metres Walk
1 Mikhail Shchennikov RUS 18:34.32
2 Ronald Weigel GER 18:40.32
3 Denis Langlois FRA 18:43.20
4 Michele Didoni ITA 19:01.03
5 Jean-Claude Corre FRA 19:10.24
6 Pavol Blazek SVK 19:14.00

Heptathlon
1 Christian Plaziat FRA 6268 (6.96, 7.74, 14.30, 2.10, 7.87, 5.00, 2:45.98)
2 Henrik Dågard SWE 6119
3 Alain Blondel FRA 6084
4 Tomás Dvorák TCH 6061
5 Erki Nool EST 5945
6 Sándor Munkácsi HUN 5944

WOMEN

60 Metres
1 Nelli Cooman HOL 7.17
2 Melanie Paschke GER 7.19
3 Patricia Girard FRA 7.19
4 Petya Pendareva BUL 7.24
5 Desislava Dimitrova BUL 7.25
6 Sabine Tröger AUT 7.31

200 Metres
1 Galina Malchugina RUS 22.41
2 Silke Knoll GER 22.96
3 Jacqueline Poelman HOL 23.43
4 Hana Benesová TCH 23.67
5 Giada Gallina ITA 23.79
6 Petya Pendareva BUL 23.89

400 Metres
1 Svetlana Goncharenko RUS 51.62
2 Tatyana Alekseyeva RUS 51.77
3 Viviane Dorsile FRA 51.92
4 Ionela Tîrlea ROM 53.13
5 Magdalena Nedelcu ROM 53.62
6 Kathrin Lüthi SUI 54.06

800 Metres
1 Natalya Dukhnova BLS 2:00.42
2 Ella Kovacs ROM 2:00.49
3 Carla Sacramento POR 2:01.12
4 Stella Jongmans HOL 2:01.82
5 Ester Goossens HOL 2:03.59
6 Yelena Storchovaya UKR 2:06.41

1500 Metres
1 Yekat. Podkopayeva RUS 4:06.46
2 Lyudmila Rogachova RUS 4:06.60
3 Malgorzata Rydz POL 4:06.98
4 Violeta Beclea ROM 4:07.06
5 Ellen Kiessling GER 4:10.68
6 Teresa Zuñiga ESP 4:10.99

3000 Metres
1 Fernanda Ribeiro POR 8:50.47
2 Margareta Keszeg ROM 8:55.61
3 Anna Brzezinska POL 8:56.90
4 Christina Mai GER 8:57.49
5 Laurence Vivier FRA 8:59.95
6 Alison Wyeth GBR 9:04.35

60 Metres Hurdles
1 Yordanka Donkova BUL 7.85
2 Eva Sokolova RUS 7.89
3 Anne Piquereau FRA 7.91
4 Brigita Bukovec SLO 7.94
5 Carla Tuzzi ITA 7.97
6 Patricia Girard FRA 7.98

High Jump

1 Stefka Kostadinova BUL 1.98
2 Desislava Alexandrova BUL 1.96
3 Sigrid Kirchmann AUT 1.96
4 Tatyana Shevchik BLS 1.96
5 Yelena Gulyayeva RUS 1.93
6 Hanne Haugland NOR 1.93

Long Jump

1 Heike Drechsler GER 7.06
2 Ljudmila Ninova AUT 6.78
3 Inessa Kravets UKR 6.72
4 Valentina Uccheddu ITA 6.69
5 Mirella Dulgheru ROM 6.61
6 Agata Karczmarek POL 6.60

Triple Jump

1 Inna Lasovskaya RUS 14.88*
2 Ana Biryukova RUS 14.72
3 Sofia Bozhanova BUL 14.52
4 Sarka Kaspárková TCH 14.46
5 Iva Prandzheva BUL 14.38
6 Inessa Kravets UKR 14.32

Shot

1 Astrid Kumbernuss GER 19.44
2 Larisa Peleshenko RUS 19.16
3 Svetla Mitkova BUL 19.09
4 Anna Romanova RUS 18.80
5 Grit Hammer GER 18.58
6 Krystyna Danilczyk POL 18.57

3000 Metres Walk

1 Annarita Sidoti ITA 11:54.32
2 Beate Gummelt GER 11:56.01
3 Yelena Arshintseva RUS 11:57.48
4 Yelena Nikolayeva RUS 11:57.49
5 Leonarda Yukhnevich BLS 12:04.46
6 Sari Essayah FIN 12:12.80

Pentathlon

1 Larisa Turchinskaya RUS 4801*
2 Rita Ináncsi HUN 4775
3 Urszula Wlodarczyk POL 4668
4 Liliana Nastase ROM 4620
5 Lyudmila Mikhailova RUS 4616
6 Ines Krause GER 4503

WORLD CROSS-COUNTRY CHAMPIONSHIPS 1994

At Budapest, Hungary March 26.

Senior Men (12,060m)

1 William Sigei KEN 34:29
2 Simon Chemoiywo KEN 34:30
3 Haile Guebre Silassie ETH 34:32
4 Paul Tergat KEN 34:36
5 Khalid Skah MAR 34:56
6 James Songok KEN 35:02
7 Addis Abebe ETH 35:11
8 Ayele Mezgebu ETH 35:14
9 Shem Kororia KEN 35:15
10 Mathias Ntawulikura RWA 35:19
11 Salah Hissou MAR 35:23
12 Dominic Kirui KEN 35:26
13 Paulo Guerra POR 35:27
14 Larbi Khattabi MAR 35:34
15 Khalid Boulami MAR 35:39
16 Mohamed Issangar MAR 35:40
17 Wilson Omwoyo KEN 35:41
18 Mustapha Essaid FRA 35:41
19 Pedro Arco ESP 35:42
20 Vincenzo Modica ITA 35:42
21 Martin Fíz ESP 35:43
22 Brahim Lahlafi MAR 35:43
23 José M Garcia ESP 35:44
24 Domingos Castro POR 35:48
25 Yahia Azaidj ALG 35:56
265 finishers

Teams

1	KEN	34	7	FRA	319
2	MAR	83	8	GBR	439
3	ETH	133	9	RUS	448
4	ESP	174	10	RSA	535
5	POR	210	11	BRA	540
6	ITA	312	12	USA	658

World Cross Challenge 1993/4

Final placings, after double points awarded at World Championships

Men

1 Guebre Silassie ETH 107
2 Willaam Sigei KEN 97
3 Ismael Kirui KEN 91
4 Paulo Guerra POR 85
5 Ezekiel Bitok KEN 77
6 Anthony Kiprono KEN 68

Junior Men (8,140m)

1 Philip Mosima KEN 24:15
2 Daniel Komen KEN 24:17
3 Abreham Tsige ETH 24:46
4 Philip Kemei KEN 24:49
5 Lemma Alemayehu ETH 25:00
6 Pablo Olmedo MEX 25:04
7 Tibebu Reta ETH 25:04
8 Reyes Estevez ESP 25:11
9 Melk Mothuli RSA 25:13
10 Salah Ghazi MAR 25:15
11 David Kiptum KEN 25:16
12 Tekalegne Shewaye ETH 25:20
13 Tolosa Gebre ETH 25:22
14 Benoit Zwierzchlewski FRA 25:25
15 Anwar Ali YEM 25:29
186 finishers

Teams

1	KEN	18	6	MEX	152
2	ETH	27	7	ESP	159
3	MAR	78	8	ITA	175
4	RSA	96	9	Yemen	194
5	JPN	118	10	RUS	195

Junior Women (4,300m)

1 Sally Barsosio KEN 14:04
2 Rose Cheruiyot KEN 14:05
3 Elizabeth Cheptanui KEN 14:15
4 Gabriela Szabo ROM 14:25
5 Ruth Biwott KEN 14:27
6 Naomi Mugo KEN 14:29
7 Pamela Chepchumba KEN 14:36
8 Azumi Miyazaki JPN 14:37
9 Shori Hotesa ETH 14:46
10 Berhane Dagne ETH 14:48
11 Nicola Slater GBR 14:49
12 Susie Power AUS 14:49
13 Abebe Tola ETH 14:50
14 Lelia Aman ETH 14:51
15 Miwa Sugawara JPN 14:55
138 finishers

Teams

1	KEN	11	6	RUS	158
2	ETH	46	7	ESP	200
3	JPN	60	8	RSA	212
4	ROM	83	9	AUS	217
5	GBR	119	10	GER	223

Senior Women (6,220m)

1 Helen Chepngeno KEN 20:45
2 Catherina McKiernan IRL 20:52
3 Conceição Ferreira POR 20:52
4 Merima Denboba ETH 20:57
5 Albertina Dias POR 20:59
6 Elana Meyer RSA 21:00
7 Zola Pieterse RSA 21:01
8 Farida Fates FRA 21:01
9 Olga Churbanova RUS 21:05
10 Fernanda Ribeiro POR 21:05
11 Margareta Keszeg ROM 21:06
12 Daria Nauer SUI 21:10
13 Silvia Sommaggio ITA 21:12
14 Getenesh Urge ETH 21:13
15 Claudia Stalder SUI 21:17
16 Julia Vaquero ESP 21:18
17 Simiyo Yamaguchi JPN 21:20
18 J Koech KEN 21:22
19 Gegi Asha ETH 21:24
20 Estela Estévez ESP 21:26
21 Carmen Fuentes ESP 21:27
22 Nina Belikova RUS 21:28
23 Nadezhda Galyamova RUS 21:30
24 Maria Guida ITA 21:32
25 Jane Omoro KEN 21:32
147 finishers

Teams

1	POR	55	7	ITA	127
2	ETH	65	8	JPN	134
3	KEN	75	9	FRA	138
4	RUS	84	10	USA	165
5	ESP	111	11	ROM	212
6	RSA	124	12	UKR	214

World Cross Challenge 1993/4

Final placings, after double points awarded at World Championships

Women

1 Catherina McKiernan IRL 141
2 Albertina Dias POR 123
3 Margareta Keszeg ROM 97
4 Farida Fates FRA 86
5= Olga Bondarenko RUS 74
5= Iulia Negura ROM 74